D1242377

OLD KENTUCKY ENTRIES AND DEEDS

BOOKS BY

Willard Rouse Jillson

GEOLOGY

Oil and Gas Resources of Kentucky, 1919-1920
Geology and Coals of Stinking Creek, 1919
Contributions to Kentucky Geology, 1920
Economic Papers on Kentucky Geology, 1921
Production of Eastern Kentucky Crude Oils, 1921
The Sixth Geological Survey, 1921
Oil Field Stratigraphy of Kentucky, 1922
Conservation of Natural Gas in Kentucky, 1922
Geological Research in Kentucky, 1923
The Coal Industry in Kentucky, 1922-1924
Kentucky State Parks, 1924
Mineral Resources of Kentucky, 1926
New Oil Pools of Kentucky, 1926
Mineral Resources of Louisville, 1926
Topography of Kentucky, 1927

HISTORY

The Big Sandy Valley, 1923
The Kentucky Land Grants, 1925
Old Kentucky Entries and Deeds, 1926

BIOGRAPHY

Edwin P Morrow—Kentuckian, 1922

VERSE

Songs and Satires, 1920

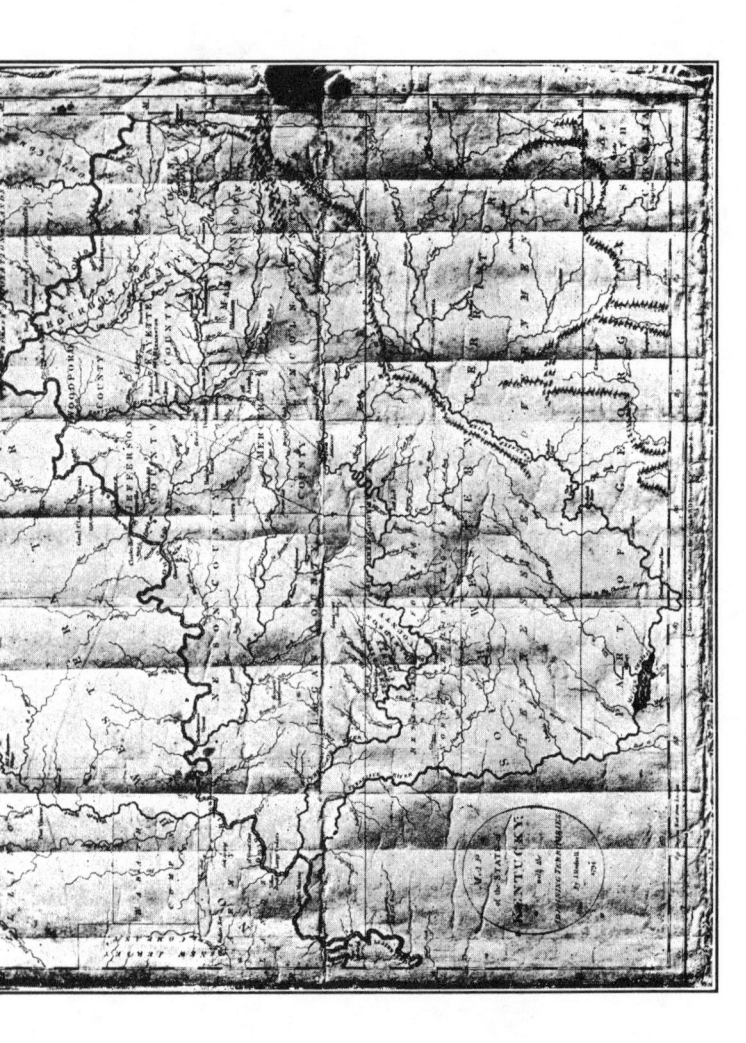

THE RUSSELL MAP OF KENTUCKY

This map, originally produced in 1794, was the first good map of Kentucky and the adjoining territories. It shows seven subdivisions of the three original Kentucky counties—Lincoln, Fayette and Jefferson. The Russell

FILSON CLUB PUBLICATIONS: NO. 34

OLD KENTUCKY ENTRIES AND DEEDS

A Complete Index to All of the Earliest Land Entries, Military Warrants, Deeds and Wills of the Commonwealth of Kentucky

BY

WILLARD ROUSE JILLSON, Sc.D.

State Geologist of Kentucky
and
Chairman of the Kentucky State Park Commission

Member of the American Historical Association, Mississippi Valley Historical Association, Kentucky State Historical Society, and The Filson Club

Illustrated

WITH A NEW PREFACE
by
WILLARD ROUSE JILLSON

Baltimore
GENEALOGICAL PUBLISHING CO., INC.
1987

Originally published as
Filson Club Publications: No. 34
Louisville, Kentucky, 1926
Reprinted with permission and with a new Preface
Genealogical Publishing Co., Inc.
Baltimore, 1969, 1972, 1978, 1987
Copyright © 1969
Genealogical Publishing Co., Inc.
Baltimore, Maryland
All Rights Reserved
Library of Congress Catalogue Card Number 73-86808
International Standard Book Number 0-8063-0193-7
Made in the United States of America

PREFACE

When, more than two score years ago, I labored long and almost without respite in the transcription of the land, military and associated legal records of a great body of Kentucky pioneers, filed with other early documents such as wills and contracts in the offices of the Secretary of State and the Clerk of the Court of Appeals in the Capitol at Frankfort, I came inadvertently to the feeling that perhaps I was preparing an index to a vast store of primary historical material of the utmost value, just at the time a new, widely-spread and aggressive trend of public interest in the earliest landowners and their families was asserting itself throughout the mid-western part of the United States. Today the volume in hand—*The Old Kentucky Entries and Deeds*—affords an unmeasurable treasure trove of more than 45,000 separate, legal records of authentic inscription and date for those whose interest centers on the earliest and most dependable functions and activities of the Commonwealth of Kentucky and its first citizens.

Since the first printing of this book, as arranged and sponsored by the farsighted Board of Trustees of the Filson Club of Louisville, Kentucky in 1926, the generous and continuous praise accorded it by learned historians, historical librarians and the public generally throughout our country and abroad, has served, since the first issue has been out of print and essentially unobtainable for more than 25 years, to validate the judgement of those gentlemen in Baltimore, Maryland, who, sensing the importance of perpetuating into the largely indeterminate future, the earliest recorded activities of the Kentucky pioneers, have set their hands, their hearts and their enterprise into the printing of this, the second printing of this foundation book of early Kentucky state and family history: *The Old Kentucky Entries and Deeds!*

WILLARD ROUSE JILLSON

Frankfort, Kentucky
May, 1969

FOREWORD

This work is logically a companion volume to the *Kentucky Land Grants* which was issued as Filson Club Publications No. 33 during the year 1925. While engaged in the research necessary to the preparation of the great body of documentary matter brought together in that book, it became evident that much important material having to do with the land of the Commonwealth of Kentucky remained without a complete index. These records consisted of two groups of manuscript documents: I. The early civil land entries, and military land warrants and entries in the State Land Office; and II. The first deeds, wills and powers of attorney relative to land lodged in the custody of the Clerk of the Court of Appeals at Frankfort.

Believing that these early land documents, issued under the laws of both the Commonwealths of Virginia and Kentucky during the latter part of the 18th and early part of the 19th century were not only of great historical importance, but also of inestimable genealogical and economic value, the writer undertook their compilation nearly a year ago. As here presented they are systematically arranged and follow a chronology similar to the *Kentucky Land Grants* This volume is thus a complete index to these old manuscript records and is designed as a source book for the use of historical workers generally, land title attorneys, abstract clerks, genealogists and others who may find interest in the first documents pertaining to the land in the Commonwealth of Kentucky.

Old State Capitol,
Frankfort, Kentucky,
February 1, 1926.

CONTENTS

ILLUSTRATIONS

OLD KENTUCKY ENTRIES AND DEEDS

CHAPTER I.

OLD KENTUCKY ENTRIES AND DEEDS

The boundaries of Kentucky were actually fixed, though rather indefinitely, in the Charter of Virginia which was written in 1609. This document after describing the distances along the Atlantic north and south of the mouth of Chesapeake Bay extended the lands "West and Northwest to the South Sea." Somewhat later the parallel of 36° 30' north was established as the southern boundary, while the Mississippi River was indicated as the limitation on the west and the Ohio River on the north. These early descriptions of Virginia's back country are clearly suggestive of the paucity of reliable information available concerning the land and its geography during the infancy of the Commonwealth. At this time Kentucky was entirely unknown to the English who were destined so shortly to settle and hold it in the face of active resistance on the part of the fortified French and their Indian allies.

The early government of the Colony of Virginia was somewhat communal in form. This was particularly true with respect to the land and its improvement. During the latter part of the first half-century of occupation, however, radical modifications were instituted and successfully maintained. Under Governor William Berkeley, in 1660, the government of Virginia became one essentially in which authority was vested in a privileged class of large land owners.[1] This concentration of power in the hands of a wealthy aristocratic minority, so similar to the established English social order, forced the less fortunate Colonists to the unfertile unprotected uplands back of the tidewater plantations which were early pre-empted and thoroughly settled in 1671.[2] Actually it brought about Bacon's Rebellion in 1676 and paved the way during the succeeding half-century for that notable migration which settled the great valley of Virginia almost immediately after the now famous expedition of Governor Alexander Spotswood across the Blue Ridge in 1716.

The early exploratory and pioneering movement into the rich intermountain limestone valley of Virginia had a deeper significance than was realized at the time. It was in fact the first Colonial expansion of importance beyond the original seaboard plantations. With it "the West" definitely took its place in American history. The great expanse of undulating limestone agricultural land developed an appeal which rapidly outgrew the bounds of the mother colony. Such records as exist for this early time show a great intermingling of Irish, English and Scotch from the Eastern tidewater, and Germans and other European nationals from Pennsylvania and the North. Hardy, restless, intrepid spirits, they were bound together by the strong bonds of common and all-surrounding dangers and hardships born of the wilderness. Within a few short years these men and women pushed the English colonial frontier boldly across the unmarked ridges of the Allegheny Mountains and brought about the discovery and settlement of Kentucky.

1C 1780
Teman   9th

Wm Montgomery Jr heir to Alexander Montgomery Enters
400 acres by virtue of a certificate &c lying on a branch of
Green River, about 2 Miles Northwardly from Archibald
McKinneys land to include his Improvement

George Adams Enters 400 acres by virtue of a Certificate &c
lying on the East fork of paint lick creek including 2
Improvements made by Wm McCormack & Thomas
Patton, adjoining the land of William Patton

Peter Wooley enters 400 acres by virtue of a Certificate &c
lying on the dividing Ridge of Dicks River & paint lick

Henry Boughman, heir to Jacob Boughman, enters 400
acres by virtue of a certificate &c lying on the North side
of Dicks River, about 2 miles above the mouth of Gilberts
Creek to include such settlement

William Cooper enters 400 acres by virtue of a
Certificate &c lying on the left hand fork of otter Creek
above the Clover Bottom including a spring

John Luttrell enters 400 acres by virtue of a certificate &c
lying on the Northwardly & Southwardly lines of the Bounds
of the land belonging to the Town of Boonsborough

John Farrow enters 400 acres by virtue of a certificate
&c lying on the South fork of the left hand fork of
otter Creek, near the head thereof known by the
name of Farrows land

Richard Henderson enters 400 acres by virtue of a
Certificate &c lying on both sides of otter Creek, above
Thomas Bartons land then up on both sides of the
Creek for quantity

John Cray enters 400 acres by virtue of a certificate &c lying on a small branch of the hanging fork
of Dicks River about 3/4 mile from said fork, on the
East side, & 2 miles from Logans to Include his
Improvement

As a prelude to this era of rapid Colonial expansion, there was, of course, much in the way of individual exploration. Hunters and traders acting upon individual initiative pressed into the uncharted West. Many failed to return, but the conquering spirit of the time could not be stayed. The period was an important one in accumulating general information with respect to the far western territory, but the actual permanent value of the earliest white explorations of the back country was relatively slight. Indeed so obscure were the earliest travels in Kentucky that records of some of them have only recently been disclosed and authenticated, while many probably will remain forever as vague and uncertain traditions. Gabriel Arthur,[3] a young Virginian, the first white man of record to see and traverse a considerable portion of Kentucky, entered this State, near where Catlettsburg now stands, in 1674. After being taken captive by the Shawnees he made his way across the maze of ridges composing the mountains of Eastern Kentucky to the old Cherokee village on the headwaters of the Tennessee River, sometime later returning to tidewater Virginia.

Shortly thereafter exploratory parties of Frenchmen traversed the waters of the Ohio, and a few years later, in 1750, Dr. Thomas Walker in the employment of the Loyal Land Company undertook his significant westward explorations across the Appalachians and through Cumberland Gap. In the following year Christopher Gist in similar capacity scouting for the Ohio Company came down from the North, and crossing the Ohio traversed Eastern Kentucky. These well known explorations were shortly followed by such men as John Finley,[4] James McBride[5] and others, concerning some of which there is neither record nor acceptable tradition. Then followed the great French and Indian war which for a period of almost exactly ten years from 1754 closed the western country to exploration. Finally in 1765 Colonel George Croghan came down the Ohio River, and in 1769 Daniel Boone following the trails blazed by the Long Hunters passed through Cumberland Gap into Kentucky. This immortal scout may fairly be accredited with having initiated the movement which culminated within a few years in the settlement of the rich agricultural limestone region of North Central Kentucky.

The movement of so large a body of adventuring immigrants into the new Kentucky country was not accomplished without friction. Ambitious schemes of land speculation furthered by wealthy non-resident purchasers constantly encountered the resolutely maintained claims of the poor squatter and homesteader, who depended neither infrequently nor unsuccessfully upon his actual occupation of the land backed by a rather free use of the rifle. Land disputes were of common occurrence, and bad feeling culminating in open fisticuffs and lonely homicides marked this dramatic period. Interest in the rich unappropriated land of Kentucky County was so intense as to overshadow the real dangers of the times, and General George Rogers Clark, as well as other commanders of lesser rank, frequently found great difficulty in enlisting sufficient troops to meet the imminent dangers of the rapid and bloody forays of the warring Indian tribes.

At last with the American Revolution in progress and her principal attentions directed to the winning of this conflict, Virginia, not unmindful of the chaotic land conditions which were developing within her western borders, sought a way out of the difficulty by legislative action. In 1772 Fincastle County, named for George, Lord Fincastle, son of Lord Dunmore, Governor of Virginia, was erected out of

West 1200 poles thence South 1066 poles thence East
1200 poles thence North 1066 poles to the Beginning

James Parberry asee of John Brown Enters 850 acres
of land on part of a Treasury Warrant No 7423 on
the waters of Licking Beginning at the South West
Corner of an Entry of 10000 acres made for Henry
[Banned] thence with his line Northwardly 400 poles
thence at right angles Westwardly for Quantity

James Breckinridge asee of William Breckenridge Enters
1000 Acres of land on part of a Treasury Warrant No 19203
on the waters of Elkhorn Beginning at three hoopwoods
Corner to Carter and William Phillips thence N45 E 400
poles crofsing the creek to two Sugartrees and two
buckeyes thence South 45 East 400 poles to a hoop
wood and honey Locust South 45 West 400 poles to a
buckeye and hopawood in Carters line thence with
the Same to the Beginning.

Also 2250 Acres of Same Warrant No 19203 On the North
fork of Elkhorn Beginning at three hoopwoods growing
from one Root Corner to Phillips and north his line
N45 W 500 poles to two elms near a draft N45 E
600 poles Crofsing a creek to a Sugartree S45 E 600 poles
to two Sugartrees thence South 45 West 500 poles to
the Beginning —

Also Enters 5000 Acres on part of the Same Warrant
No 19203 on the waters of Elkhorn to begin Elm buckeye
and ash Corner to Rupert Vandrigo and Blockley
and with Blockleys line South 20 West 400 poles to a
Sugartree and ash North 70 West 800 poles to a hoop
wood and buckeye North 20 East 400 poles to a
hoopwood Walnut and buckeye Corner to Christian
South 70 East 800 poles to the Beginning —

Botetourt County.[8] In 1777 the western portion of Fincastle County, including all of the lands west of the Tug Fork of the Big Sandy River, was set aside by the General Assembly of Virginia as Kentucky County.[8] During the short period from 1777 to 1780 Kentucky County included essentially the same territory now enclosed within this Commonwealth. In 1780 the "Mother Colony" divided Kentucky County into three parts, Jefferson, Lincoln and Fayette counties[9], and land in this territory, which had not already been taken up under laws previous to the celebrated general land laws of Virginia enacted in 1779, was entered upon, surveyed and granted according to the stipulations of this latter legislation.

The first surveys of importance in Kentucky were thus made while this territory was comprised within the limits of Fincastle County, Virginia. After 1777, the grants appear as in Kentucky County, Virginia. The earliest land grants during this period of rapid settlement were made in Colonial times under royal authority.[10] Many of them were taken up under the King's Proclamation of 1763.[11] All of these grants were governed by laws of an archaic nature, lax in specification and so general in application as actually to invite great confusion and no end of legal contests. Numerous enactments of the Virginia General Assembly had been approved by the King of England to prevent land frauds. Typical of these was an act[12] passed by Virginia in October, 1748, which stipulated the bounds of official procedure for county and other surveyors in entering upon unclaimed lands. Though bolstered up with a number of such minor enactments, the general land laws of the Old Dominion finally became so universally recognized as inadequate that special steps were taken during the latter days of the war for American Independence to prepare a new land code.

In May, 1779, Virginia finally passed a series of land laws which applied to all of the western country, including Kentucky. These new laws controlled the method by which most of the land was taken up in this State in the post-Colonial period. The first of these was an act concerning officers, sailors, and marines which declared that "at the end of the war every of the said soldiers, sailors, and marines, shall be entitled to a grant of 100 acres of any unappropriated land within this Commonwealth, and every of the officers commanding the said soldiers, sailors, or marines, shall be entitled to a grant of like quantity of lands as is allowed to the officers of the same rank in the Virginia regiments on continental establishment, which they shall locate according to the directions of the laws, for which no purchase shall be required on behalf of the Commonwealth".[13] This law further states that "every soldier who enlisted under Colonel George Rogers Clark, and continued therein till the taking the several posts in the Illinois country, shall at the end of the war be entitled to a grant of 200 acres of any unappropriated lands within this Commonwealth, on the terms herein before declared".[13]

Then followed an enactment to adjust and settle the titles of claimants to unpatented lands prior to the establishment of Virginia's land office.[14] The act provided that all surveys of waste and unappropriated land made upon any of the western waters before 1778, when executed by a commissioned surveyor in furtherance of large treasury warrant or military rights, were validated. To these were added those strictly military rights in the district set apart for officers and soldiers of Virginia in the Continental and State service. Many of these were surveyed under the direction of military officers, and location was adjudged upon

Nº 8

Surveyed

James M Marshall enters 1000 Acres Land part of a Military Warrant Nº 2380 Begining on Cumberland River at William Croghans upper Corner thence runing up Cumberland River 400 Poles on a straight line thence with Croghans line and with a line from the upper end of the straight line. so far as will include the Quantity

Nº 9

Surveyed

James Barron enters 2000 Acres Land part of a Military Warrant Nº 711. Begining at the upper corner of J M Marshalls entry of 1000 Acres. extending upp the Cumberland 800 poles when reduced to a straight line. thence Southwardly at right Angles for Quantity.

Nº 10 Thomas Marshall enters 1600 Acres Land part of a Military Warrant Nº 1349. Begining 200 poles Westerly of where the Kentucky Road leads to Cumberland Crosses the blue spring Creek. at the edge of the timbered land, runing at right angles with the general course of the timbered land North Eastwardly 250 poles thence up the Creek at right angles from the begining and the termination of the line 250 poles. so far as will include the Quantity

Nº 11 Richard Anderson Assee. enters 1110 ⅔ Acres Land part of a Military Warrant Nº 27 Begining at Joseph Carringtons lower Corner Nº 3 runing down the River Mississippi 1100 poles when reduced to a right line. thence at right angles for Quantity

Nº 12 Robert Todd enters 1000 Acres Land part of a Military Warrant Nº 2580 lying on mississippi River begining at the Mouth of Mayfield Creek on the lower side and runing up the said Creek with the meanders thereof 640 poles. when reduced to a straight line. then at right angles from the end of the said reduced line and upp the Mississippi River for Quantity. including Fort Jefferson and the Village

MILITARY ENTRIES IN KENTUCKY: 1784

basis of priority. Virginia also recognized and gave preferred rights covering certain quantities of land, usually 400 acres, to those settlers who prior to January 1, 1778, had made "a crop of corn or had resided in the country upon the western waters for at least one year." There were secured in the same manner pre-emption rights to not exceeding 400 acres per person. If prior to January 1, 1778, settlers "had marked out or chosen for themselves any waste or unappropriated lands, building a house or hut or made other improvements thereon", pre-emption rights were allowed covering any reasonable quantity of land including improvements but not to exceed 1,000 acres. Single pre-emptions, however, were not allowed for more than one such improvement.

Another class of rights of pre-emption to not more than 400 acres was also given. These were called "village rights" and were accorded to families who had settled in villages or stations but had raised a crop elsewhere. These rights were based upon priority. Pre-emption of 1,000 acres adjoining actual settlements was also allowed upon a basis of priority. Entries too were recognized upon military warrants, treasury warrants and pre-emption warrants where departure was made from the land to which the rights were attached, the basis of validation resting as previously upon priority of location with the county surveyor. County court orders in favor of poor persons were also recognized.[15] For the completion of details necessary to each of these land rights twelve months was generally allowed prior to forfeiture.

A further result of the general land law of May, 1779, was the division of the western territory of Virginia into four districts, the last or fourth of which comprised Kentucky County. For the Kentucky District, as for the others, the Governor was authorized with the advice of the Council to appoint four commissioners under the seal of the Commonwealth "to continue in office eight months for the purpose of collecting, adjusting and determining such claims, and four months thereafter for the purpose of adjusting the claims of settlers on lands surveyed for the aforesaid companies".[16]

At the same session an act was passed establishing a general land office. This law recited the terms and manner of granting waste and unappropriated lands.[17] It provided for a register, the issuance of land warrants by purchase through the Treasury, the appointment of county surveyors and deputies, and recording of land entries. Many minor but important details were included, particularly with respect to the entering of the land and preparation of the subsequent grants. Provision was introduced to prevent fraud in these land transactions, but unfortunately this portion of the law was quite frequently evaded and many unjust and indefensible claims were set up for choice land situated on the waters of Upper Salt River, Elkhorn, Stoner, Hinkston and other creeks in the much coveted Blue Grass country.

In the succeeding pages there are presented as completely as it was possible to get them the old land entries of this early Kentucky period. The Lincoln County entries, *Chapter II*, number 4,959, and extend from 1779 to 1787. They consist of two books. The Fayette County entries, *Chapter III*, number 7,008, date from 1782 to 1794 and are found in four books. The Jefferson County entries, *Chapter IV*, most numerous of all, total 11,518. They begin in 1779 and end in 1785. The Military Warrants, *Chapter V*, comprise a group of medium size totaling 4,744,

Land-Office Military Warrant, No. 135

To the principal SURVEYOR of the Land, let apart for the Officers and Soldiers of the Commonwealth of Virginia.

THIS shall be your WARRANT to survey and lay off in one or more Surveys, for George Washington

His Heirs or Assigns; the Quantity of four thousand, one

hundred, sixty six, 4166 two thirds   Washington

Acres of Land, due unto the said

in consideration of his Services for three years as a Lieutenant

in the Virginia Line

agreeably to a Certificate from the Governor and Council, which is received into the Land-Office GIVEN under my Hand, and the Seal of the said Office, this 20th Day of February in the Year One Thousand Seven Hundred and 83

GEORGE WASHINGTON MILITARY WARRANT: 1783

and extend from 1782 to 1793. The Military entries, *Chapter VI*, comprise the smallest group of all, with only 1,567 names extending in the period of record from 1784 to 1797. All of the above enumerated records are found in the Kentucky Land Office at Frankfort, Kentucky, except the Jefferson County entries, Chapter IV, which are found, as evident copies, in two old volumes lodged in the custody of the Jefferson County Court Clerk in Louisville.* There is reason to believe that because of their relatively small number the Lincoln entries may be incomplete, but if additional entry books for this old county still exist diligent search for them has failed to bring them to light.

The latter part of this volume is devoted to indexing the old manuscript records in the office of the Clerk of the Court of Appeals at Frankfort, Kentucky. During the early days of this Commonwealth the law provided for the recording of deeds and many other important legal instruments in Frankfort. *Chapter VII* presents the grantees 5,208, being recorded in these old deeds; *Chapter VIII* exhibits the grantors, who total 5,619. *Chapter IX* shows Court of Appeals, Deeds—Wills, and *Chapter X* presents a cross-indexed list of 1,909 grantors and grantees in power of attorney. Transcript of these latter records, Chapters VII to X, may be secured from the Clerk of the Court of Appeals at Frankfort, while for the former —Chapters II to VI—application should be made to the Register of the Land Office at Frankfort, except in the special case of the Jefferson County entries—Chapter IV— to the Clerk of Jefferson County, Louisville, Kentucky.

REFERENCES

[1] Howe, Henry.   *Historical Collections of Virginia.*   Charleston, S. C. 1849.

[2] Robinson, Morgan Poitiaux.   *Virginia Counties: Those Resulting from Virginia Legislation.*   Bulletin of the Virginia State Library. Vol. 9, pl. 8, p. 125. Richmond. 1916.

[3] Alford, Clarence W., and Bidgood, Lee.   *First Explorations of the Trans-Allegheny Region by the Virginians.* pp. 210, 226.   Cleveland.   1912.

[4] Cotterill, R. S.   *History of Pioneer Kentucky.*   p. 46. Cincinnati. 1917.

[5] Filson, John.   *The Discovery, Settlement and Present State of Kentucke.* p. 7. Wilmington, Delaware. 1784.

[6] Jillson, W. R.   *The Kentucky Land Grants.*   Filson Club Publications: No. 33, p. 5. Louisville. 1925.

[7] Campbell, Charles.   *History of the Colony and Ancient Dominion of Virginia.*   p. 572. Philadelphia. 1860.

[8] Robinson, Morgan Poitiaux.   *Virginia Counties: Those Resulting from Virginia Legislation.*   Bulletin of the Virginia State Library.   Vol. 9, pp. 140, 145, 146.   Richmond. 1916.

[9] Collins, Lewis.   *Historical Sketches of Kentucky.*   p. 24. Maysville. 1850.

[10] Wilson, Samuel M.   *First Land Court of Kentucky: 1779-1780.*   pp. 3, 4, 5.   Lexington.   1923.

[11] Henning, William Waller.   (Statutes at Large) *Laws of Virginia.* (May, 1779) Vol. 7, Proclamations.   pp. 663–669.   Richmond.   1822.

[12] General Assembly.   *Laws of Virginia,* Chapt. XIV. pp. 218, 221.   (Williamsburg, Va., October, 1748,) 1769.

[13] Henning, William Waller.   (Statutes at Large) *Laws of Virginia.* (May, 1779)   Vol. 10, Chapt. VI, pp. 23, 27.   Richmond.   1822.

[14] Henning, William Waller.   (Statutes at Large) *Laws of Virginia.*   (May, 1779)   Vol. 10, Chapt. XII, pp. 35–50.

[15] Littell, Wm. and Swigert, Jacob.   *Digest of the Statutes, Laws of Kentucky.* Vol. II, Chapt. CVII, pp. 712, 713.   Frankfort.   1822.

[16] Wilson, Samuel M.   *First Land Court of Kentucky: 1779-1780.*   p. 7.   Lexington.   1923.

[17] Henning, William Waller.   (Statutes at Large) *Laws of Virginia.*   (May, 1779)   Vol. 10, Chapt. XIII, pp. 50, 65.

*These volumes had been loaned to Col. Reuben T. Durrett, President of The Filson Club, and when his personal library was sold to the University of Chicago in May, 1913, they, through some error, were included in the shipment.   There they were located by Mr. R. C. Ballard Thruston, then Vice-President of the Club, and, upon his calling attention to the fact that they were official records of the state of Kentucky, the University returned them to the Jefferson County Court House.

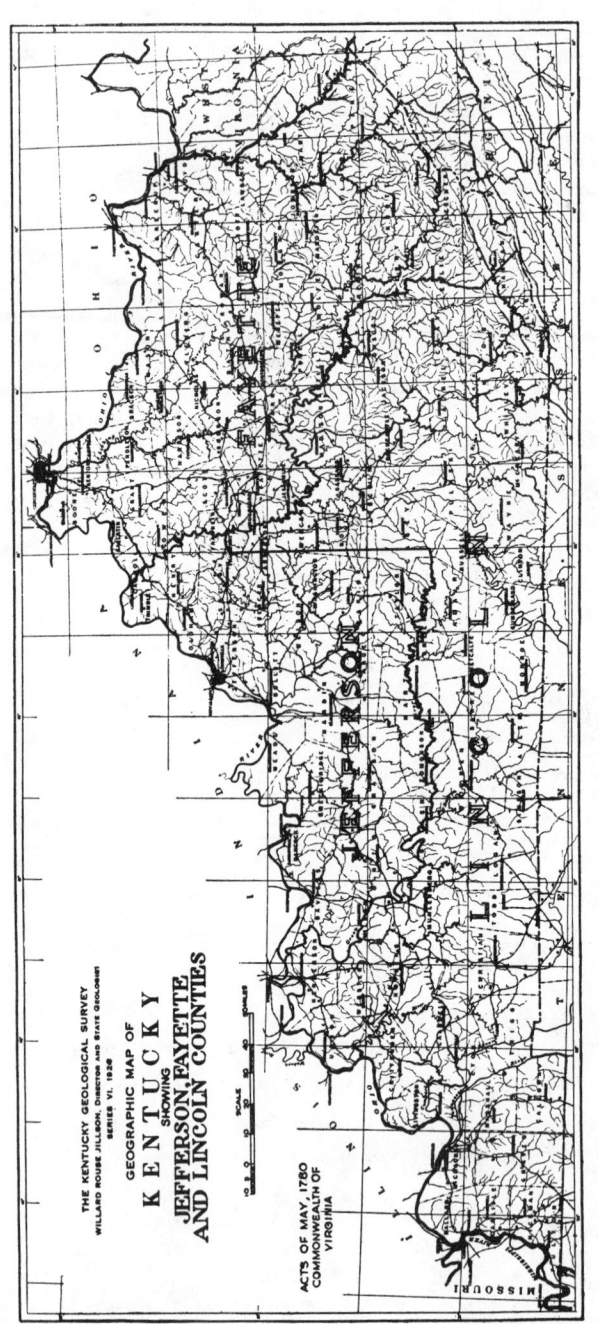

RECENT MAP OF KENTUCKY SHOWING THREE ORIGINAL COUNTIES: 1780

II

LINCOLN ENTRIES

(1779—1787)

Entree	Acres	Book	Page	Entry Date	Watercourse	Notes
Adams, W.	400	1	1	11- 4-1779	Salt R.	
Adams, Geo	400	1	10	2- 9-1780	E Fk Paint Lick Cr.	
Adams, Wm	600	1	23	4-26-1780	Salt R.	
Adams, Wm	400	1	23	4-26-1780	Salt R.	
Adams, Robt	500	1	65	6- 3-1780	Silver Cr.	
Adams, David	664	1	66	6- 3-1780	Salt R.	
Adams, Saml	1,000	1	80	6-26-1780	Salt R.	
Adams, Jno	200	1	162	10- 5-1781	Paint Lick	Withdrawn
Adams, Jas	50	1	188	12- 8-1781	E Fk Paint Lick	Withdrawn
Adams, David	195	1	265	5-24-1782	Salt R.	Withdrawn
Adams, Jas	281	1	314	12- 4-1782	Doctors Fk	
Adams & Crow	2,500	2	39	12-15-1783	3 Fks Ky R	
Adams & Crow	2,500	2	39	12-15-1783	M Fk Ky R	
Adams & Crow	2,500	2	39	12-15-1783	M Fk Ky R	
Adams & Crow	3,750	2	39	12-15-1783	M Fk Ky R	
Adams, Jno	200	2	46	1- 1-1784	None	
Adams, Jno	200	2	46	1- 1-1784	Br Silver Cr	
Adams, Wm	1,000	2	47	1- 3-1784	——— R.	
Adams, Richard	761½	2	90	4-16-1784	None	
Adams, Jos	50	2	209	4-23-1785	None	
Adams, Jos	50	2	209	4-23-1785	Silver Cr	
Adams, Jos	200	2	224	6- 9-1785	None	
Adams, David	195	2	256	12-30-1785	None	
Akins, Joseph	1,385¼	2	29	11- 3-1783	Hazel Cr	
Alder, Bartholomew	400	1	43	5-19-1780	Elk Lick	
Ale, Wm	80	1	360	2-11-1783	Gilberts Cr	
Allen, Wm	400	1	70	6-12-1780	None	Amended
Allen, Jno	500	1	80	6-30-1780	Drowning Cr	
Allen, Richard	500	1	80	6-30-1780	Otter Cr.	
Allen, Jos	500	1	161	10- 2-1781	Otter Cr.	
Allen, Wm	400	1	165	10-30-1781	None	
Allen, Thos	200	1	296	8-15-1782	Paint Lick	
Allen, Thos	150	1	298	9-21-1782	Lick Fk Paint Lick	
Allen, Thos	150	1	372	2-22-1783	None	
Allen, Thos	75	2	15	7- 2-1783	Paint Lick	
Allen, Thos	25	2	15	7- 2-1783	Hanging Fk	
Allen, Thos	12,000	2	156	10-28-1784	Rockcastle	
Allen, Thos..,	1,000	2	264	1-27-1785	Goose Cr	
Allen, Thos	1,000	2	266	1-27-1786	Goose Cr	
Allen, Thos	50	2	285	8- 8-1786	Drakes Camp Cr	
Allcock, Thos	300	1	28	4-29-1780	Ky R.	
Ammons, Thos	200	1	46	5-22-1780	None	
Ammons, Thos	400	1	46	5-22-1780	None	
Anderson, Jno	400	1	24	4-26-1780	Sugar Cr.	
Anderson, Jno	300	1	61	5-31-1780	N Fk Gilberts Cr	Withdrawn
Anderson, Jno	200	1	80	6-28-1780	S Fk Tates Cr	
Anderson, Jno	400	1	94	1-30-1781	Paint Lick & Silver Cr.	
Anderson, Jno	300	1	126	5-14-1781	N Fk Gilberts Cr	Withdrawn
Anderson, Jno	100	1	126	5-14-1781	M Fk Cedar Cr	Withdrawn
Anderson, Jno	100	1	168	11-10-1781	——— Cr	
Anderson, Jno	100	1	169	11-10-1781	M Fk Cedar Cr	
Anderson, Jno	200	1	169	11-10-1781	Paint Lick	
Anderson, Col Richard	1000	1	323	12-17-1782	Richland Cr	
Anderson, Jno	100	2	7	5-28-1783	Dix R.	
Anderson, David	8,000	2	87	4- 8-1784	Raccoon Cr	Withdrawn
Anderson, David	4,000	2	88	4- 8-1784	Linn Camp Cr	
Anderson, David	8,000	2	90	4-16-1784	Br Laurel R	
Anderson, David	4,000	2	273	3-20-1786	N Fk Ky R	
Anderson, Jno	100	2	318	5-14-1780	Cedar Cr	
Anthony, Joseph	200	1	27	4-29-1780	W Fk Tates Cr	
Anthony, Joseph	600	1	44	5-20-1780	Br Paint Lick	
Anthony, Jno	1,000	1	139	6-20-1781	Main Silver Cr	
Anthony, Jno	1,000	1	139	6-20-1781	Silver Cr	
Anthony, Jno	1,000	1	276	6-20-1782	Otter Cr	Withdrawn

Entree	Acres	Book	Page	Entry Date	Watercourse	Notes
Anthony, Jno	2,000	2	194	3-12-1785	Silver Cr	
Anthony, Jno	2,975½	2	194	3-12-1785	N Fk Rockcastle	
Anglin, Edwin	400	1	216	1-17-1781	Caseys Cr	
Arnold, Stephen	200	1	41	5-18-1780	Salt R	Withdrawn
Arnold, Stephen	300	1	41	5-18-1780	Harrods Landing	
Arnold, Stephen	250	1	47	5-23-1780	Ky R	
Arnold, Stephen	200	1	205	12-26-1781	Salt R	
Arnold, Stephen	200	1	205	12-26-1781	Ky R	
Arnold, Jno	1,000	1	231	2- 9-1782	———R	
Arnold, Jno	1,058⅔	1	347	1-27-1783	None	
Arnold, Jas	500	1	357	2- 8-1783	Ky R	
Arnold, Benj	200	1	367	2-17-1783	———Cr	
Arnold, Jos	200	1	367	2-17-1783	Ky R	
Arnold, Jos	64	2	13	6-20-1783	Ky R	
Arnold, Jos	64	2	13	6-20-1783	Ky R	
Arnold, Jos	268¾	2	27	10- 6-1783	Cave Spring Br	
Arnold, Jno	1,058⅔	2	122	6-28-1784	None	
Arnold, Benj	200	2	267	2- 6-1786	None	
Arnit, Wm	300	2	156	10-29-1784	Ky R	Withdrawn
Arnit, Wm	300	2	259	1-10-1786	Ky R	
Armstrong, Jno	300	1	80	7- 7-1780	l h Fk Dry Run	
Armstrong, Jno	100	1	81	7-18-1780	None	
Armstrong, Alexander	400	1	99	3- 6-1781	Salt R	Withdrawn
Armstrong, Wm	300	1	99	3- 6-1781	Ky R	
Armstrong, Wm	300	1	99	3- 6-1781	Ky R	
Armstrong, Jno	100	1	104	3-13-1781	None	
Armstrong, Jno	100	1	104	3-13-1781	None	
Armstrong, Alexander	400	1	115	4-12-1781	Salt R	
Armstrong, Alexander	400	1	115	4-12-1781	Salt R	
Armstrong, Saml	718	1	395	4-12-1783	Ky R	
Armstrong, Wm	637½	2	38	12-12-1783	S Fk Big Benson Cr	
Armstrong, Robt	515	2	45	12-24-1783	Big Benson Cr	Withdrawn
Armstrong, Robt	515	2	65	3- 4-1784	Big Benson Cr	
Armstrong, Robt	515	2	65	3- 4-1784	S Fk Big Benson Cr	
Armstrong, Robt	300	2	121	6-28-1784	S Fk Big Benson Cr.	
Armstrong, Wm	165½	2	127	7- 7-1784	W Fk S Fk Big Benson Cr	
Armstrong, Wm	165½	2	127	7- 7-1784	Ky R	
Armstrong, Robt	184	2	137	8- 4-1784	S Fk Benson Cr	
Armstrong, Robt	184	2	137	8- 4-1784	Hammons Cr	
Armstrong, Jno	250	2	162	12- 1-1784	Jacks Cr	
Archer, Jno & Edward	400	1	4	12- 7-1779	Dix R	
Alexander, Francis	1,763½	2	158	11-11-1784	Robinsons Cr	
Alexander, Jno	400	2	169	12-14-1784	Silver Cr	Withdrawn
Alexander, Jno	400	2	269	2-10-1786	Silver Cr	
Alexander, Neill	1,000	2	283	7-28-1786	Station Camp Cr	Surveyed
Astergus, Peter	400	2	116	6-15-1784	Hammons Cr	
Astergus, Peter	1,000	2	116	6-15-1784	E Fk Hammons Cr.	
Atkins, Saml	300	1	137	6-16-1781	None	
Austin, Jno	1,000	1	85	10-17-1780	Dix R	Withdrawn
Austin, Jno	1,000	1	160	9-22-1781	Dix R	
Austin, Jos	500	1	160	9-22-1781	Dix R	
Austin, Jno	500	2	55	2- 4-1784	Cumberland R	
Austin, Chapman	1,000	2	86	4- 5-1784	In Sinking Valley	
Austurgus, Jno	1,000	1	119	4-19-1781	Hammons Cr	
Austurgus, Jno	400	1	126	6-24-1780	Hammons Cr	
Ayers, Saml	683¾	2	276	5- 3-1786	Scaggs Cr	Surveyed
Baber, Ambrose	1,788	1	276	6-20-1782	N Fk Rockcastle	
Baber, Ambrose	1,788	2	162	12- 5-1784	Rockcastle	
Bacon, Lyddal	1,390	1	262	5-11-1782	E Fk Paint Lick	
Bacon, Lyddal	1,390	1	262	5-11-1782	Silver Cr	Amended
Bacon, Lyddal	2,782	1	284	7-13-1782	Paint Lick	Withdrawn
Bacon, Lyddal	1,390	2	139	8-12-1784	None	
Bacon, Lyddal	2,782	2	166	12-11-1784	Paint Lick & Sugar Crs	
Bacon, Lyddal	2,782	2	166	12-11-1784	N Fk Rockcastle	
Bacon, Lyddal	300	2	168	12-11-1784	Paint Lick	
Bacon, Lyddal	300	2	168	12-11-1784	None	
Bailey, Jno	600	1	334	1- 6-1783	Dix R	
Bailey, Jno	3,000	2	160	11-24-1784	Sturgeon Cr	
Bailey, Jno	100	2	309	3- 8-1790	Dix R	
Bailey, Jno	70	2	309	3- 8-1790	Dix R	
Bailey, Jno	2,162¾	2	311	8-11-1790	Cumberland R	
Bailey, Jane	25	2	312	1-26-1791	Dix R	
Baker, Isaac	100	1	55	5-27-1780	Calloway Cr	
Baker, Saml	1,000	1	76	6-22-1780	Salt R	Withdrawn
Baker, Martin	1,200	1	96	2-21-1780	——— R	
Baker, Saml	1,000	1	301	9-27-1782	Salt & Ky R	
Baker, Wm	2,000	2	282	7-13-1786	Green R	
Ball, Edward	300	1	42	5-18-1780	Fks Dix R	
Ball, Edward	322½	1	42	5-18-1780	Dix R	Withdrawn
Ball, Edward	322½	1	130	5-22-1781	Dix R	

Entree	Acres	Book	Page	Entry Date	Watercourse	Notes
Ball, Edward	322½	1	130	5-22-1781	Sugar Cr	
Ball, Edward	622½	1	134	5-18-1780	E Fk Elkhorn	Withdrawn
Ball, Edward	622½	1	301	9-27-1782	E Fk Elkhorn	
Banks, Henry	1,070	1	292	7-29-1782	——— Cr	
Banks & Barbour	50,000	2	159	11-11-1784	Cumberland R	
Banks, Henry	5,000	2	236	8-13-1785	N Fk Ky R	Withdrawn
Banks, Henry	5,000	2	237	8-13-1785	N Fk Ky R	Withdrawn
Banks, Henry	5,000	2	237	8-13-1785	N Fk Ky R	Withdrawn
Banks, Henry	5,000	2	237	8-13-1785	N Fk Ky R	Withdrawn
Banks, Henry	5,000	2	272	3-20-1786	N Fk Ky R	
Banks, Henry	5,000	2	273	3-20-1786	N Fk Ky R	
Banton, Wm	500	1	37	5-15-1780	None	Withdrawn
Banton, Wm	500	1	193	12-14-1781	None	Withdrawn
Banton, Wm	400	1	193	12-14-1781	None	Withdrawn
Banta, Abram	800	1	132	5-31-1781	Big Muddy Cr	
Barnett, Robt	400	1	62	6- 1-1781	Hanging Fk	
Barnett, Jas	50	1	113	4- 2-1781	Dix R	
Barnett, Jas	200	1	113	4- 2-1781	Hanging Fk	Withdrawn
Barnett, Jno	400	1	113	4- 2-1781	Hanging Fk	Withdrawn
Barnett, Robt	400	1	131	5-26-1781	Silver Cr	
Barnett, Jno	400	1	145	7-16-1781	Hanging Fk	
Barnett, Jas	200	1	145	7-16-1781	Hanging Fk	
Barnett, Jno	400	1	145	7-16-1781	None	
Barnett, Wm	50	1	145	7-16-1781	Silver Cr	
Barnett, Jas	200	1	146	7-16-1781	Green R	
Barnett, Jas	800	1	161	9-25-1781	Paint Lick	
Barnett, Robt	100	1	178	11-24-1781	Fks Dix R	
Barnett, Jno	600	1	182	12- 2-1781	Paint Lick & Silver Crs	
Barnett, Robt	300	1	188	12- 8-1781	Silver Cr	
Barnett, Jas	600	1	235	2-14-1782	S Fk Camp Cr	Withdrawn
Barnett, Jas	400	1	236	2-14-1782	Green R	Withdrawn
Barnett, Jas	500	1	237	2-14-1782	Green R	Withdrawn
Barnett, Jas	400	1	237	2-14-1782	Green R	
Barnett, Jas	200	1	237	2-14-1782	Green R	
Barnett, Jas	200	1	237	2-14-1782	Camp Cr	Withdrawn
Barnett, Jas	361	1	238	2-14-1782	Caseys Cr	Withdrawn
Barnett, Jas	400	1	242	2- 4-1782	Caseys Cr	Withdrawn
Barnett, Jas	500	1	242	3- 4-1782	None	Withdrawn
Barnett, Jas	300	1	242	3- 4-1782	Brushy Cr	Withdrawn
Barnett, Alexander	400	1	243	3- 4-1782	———R	
Barnett, Jos	400	1	243	3- 4-1782	None	
Barnett, Jos	600	1	338	1-11-1783	S Fk Caseys Cr	
Barnett, Jas	500	1	339	1-11-1783	Caseys Cr	
Barnett, Jas	200	1	339	1-11-1783	Caseys Cr	
Barnett, Jas	361	1	339	1-11-1783	——— Cr	
Barnett, Jas	400	1	339	1-11-1783	Caseys Cr	
Barnett, Jos	500	1	340	1-11-1783	None	
Barnett, Jos	800	2	46	1- 1-1784	E Fk Paint Lick	
Barnett, Alexander	188¾	2	61	2-24-1784	None	
Barnett, Jos	589	2	67	3- 8-1784	Benson Cr	
Barnett, Jno	1,158	2	115	6-12-1784	Green R	
Barnett, Joseph	500	2	115	6-12-1784	Green R	
Barnett, Jos	300	2	138	8- 9-1784	Brush Cr	
Barnett, Jos	500	2	139	8- 9-1784	Meadow Fk Paint Lick	
Barnett, Jos	500	2	139	8- 9-1784	None	Withdrawn
Barnett, Jos	500	2	169	12-14-1784	Co Line	
Barnett, Jos	500	2	169	12-14-1784	Walnut Meadow Fk	
Barnett, Wm	4,000	2	302	7- 4-1788	Yellow Cr	
Barnett, Alexander	400	2	304	2- 6-1789	Casey Cr & Green R	Surveyed
Barber, Jos	400	1	4	12-23-1779	Muddy Cr	
Barbour, Jas	50	1	26	4-28-1780	E Fk Skaggs Cr	Withdrawn
Barbour, Jas	50	1	26	4-28-1780	None	
Barbour, Jas	50	1	26	4-28-1780	Trace	Withdrawn
Barbour, Jos	1,000	1	38	5-16-1780	Otter Cr	
Barbour, Jas	2,000	1	38	5-16-1780	Skeggs Cr	
Barbour, Jas	1,000	1	56	5-29-1780	Dix R	
Barbour, Philip	3,000	1	287	7-18-1782	Tennessee R	Withdrawn
Barbour, Philip	3,000	1	287	7-18-1782	Tennessee R	Withdrawn
Barbour, Jas	285	1	287	7-19-1782	Ohio R	Withdrawn
Barbour, Ambrose	3,000	1	288	7-19-1782	Ohio R	Withdrawn
Barbour, Thos	5,000	1	288	7-19-1782	Cumberland R	Withdrawn
Barbour, Richard	3,000	1	288	7-19-1782	Tennessee R	Withdrawn
Barbour, Jos	50	1	310	11-24-1782	Scaggs Cr	
Barbour, Jos	50	1	310	11-24-1782	Dix R	
Barbour, Philip	3,000	1	310	11-24-1782	Tennessee R	
Barbour, Philip	3,000	1	310	11-24-1782	Tennessee R	
Barbour, Jos	2,850	1	310	11-24-1782	None	
Barbour, Ambrose	3,000	1	310	11-24-1782	None	
Barbour, Thos	5,000	1	311	11-24-1782	Cumberland R	
Barbour, Richard	3,000	1	311	11-24-1782	Tennessee R	

Entree	Acres	Book	Page	Entry Date	Watercourse	Notes
Barbour, Jos.	1,000	1	330	1- 1-1783	Br Muddy Cr	
Barbour, Richard	5,000	2	30	11- 4-1783	Cumberland R	
Barbour, Richard	5,000	2	30	11- 4-1783	Cumberland R	
Barbour, Jos.	10,000	2	102	5-14-1784	Cumberland R	
Barbour, Jos.	8,000	2	102	5-14-1784	Cumberland R	
Barbour & Banks	50,000	2	159	11-11-1784	Cumberland R	
Barbour, Richard	5,000	2	159	11-11-1784	Cumberland R	
Barbour, Richard	10,000	2	171	12-23-1784	Cumberland R	
Barbour, Thos.	10,000	2	171	12-23-1784	Cumberland R	
Barbour, Jos.	2,000	2	285	8-16-1786	Skeggs Cr	
Barbour, Jos.	5,000	2	305	5-27-1789	Laurel R	Surveyed
Bartlett, Wm.	1,000	2	16	7- 7-1783	Rockcastle	Withdrawn
Bartlett, Wm.	1,000	2	36	11-29-1783	Linn Camp Cr	
Bartlett, Wm.	1,000	2	36	11-29-1783	Crooked Cr	
Bartlett, Wm.	1,000	2	36	11-29-1783	Station Camp Cr	
Bartlett, Wm.	3,000	2	36	11-29-1783	Goose Cr	
Bartlett, Wm.	400	2	37	11-29-1783	None	Withdrawn
Bartlett, Wm.	400	2	41	12-17-1783	Rolling Fk	Withdrawn
Bartlett, Wm.	1,000	2	103	5-17-1784	N Fk Rolling Fk	Withdrawn
Bartlett, Wm.	400	2	150	10- 1-1784	None	
Bartlett, Wm.	400	2	150	10- 1-1784	Rolling Fk	
Bartlett, Wm.	1,000	2	151	10- 1-1784	Rolling Fk	
Bartlett, Wm.	800	2	151	10- 1-1784	None	Withdrawn
Bartlett, Wm.	1,000	2	151	10- 1-1784	Scaggs Cr	Withdrawn
Bartlett, Wm.	1,000	2	151	10- 1-1784	Br Dix R	Withdrawn
Bartlett, Wm.	800	2	185	2-21-1785	Scaggs Cr	
Bartlett, Wm.	800	2	185	2-21-1785	Dix & Rockcastle	Withdrawn
Bartlett, Wm.	1,000	2	248	11- 4-1785	Rockcastle	
Bartlett, Wm.	1,000	2	248	11- 4-1785	None	
Bartlett, Wm.	2,000	2	248	11- 4-1785	Richardson Cr	
Bartlett, Wm.	2,000	2	260	1-26-1786	Nigger Cr	
Bartlett, Wm.	2,000	2	260	1-26-1786	Goose Cr	
Bartlett, Wm.	2,000	2	260	1-26-1786	Richardson & Rockcastle	
Bartlett, Wm.	800	2	261	1-26-1786	Ky R	
Barbee, Thos.	350	1	180	11-28-1781	Beech Fk	Withdrawn
Barbee, Thos.	350	2	2	5-15-1783	Beech Fk	
Barbee, Jno.	390	2	41	12-18-1783	None	
Bard, Richard	1,000	2	77	3-27-1784	Benson Cr	
Bard, Richard	1,000	2	77	3-27-1784	Ky R	
Bard, Wm.	1,000	2	240	9-12-1785	S Fk M Fk 3 Fks .. Ky R	
Bard, Wm.	1,000	2	240	9-12-1785	——— Cr	
Barr & Donnell	100	2	146	9- 9-1784	Dix R	
Barr & Donnell	800	2	147	9- 9-1784	N Fk Dix R	
Barr & Donnell	325	2	274	4-10-1786	N Fk Dix R	
Bartman, Moses	61,958	2	111	6- 5-1784	Sexton Fk Goose Cr	
Bartman, Moses	4,000	2	229	7-14-1785	Cumberland R	
Barrat, Francis	1,000	2	205	4-13-1785	Dix R	
Barton, Thos.	400	1	2	11-11-1779	Otter Cr	
Barton, David	400	1	5	1-10-1780	Silver Cr	
Barton, Saml.	400	1	6	1-15-1780	Silver Cr	
Barton, Wm.	400	1	259	4-18-1782	None	
Barton, Thos.	800	2	116	6-15-1784	None	
Bass & Hutchings	300	1	335	1- 6-1783	None	
Batterton, Henry	500	1	37	5-15-1780	Dix R	
Bates, Thos F.	500	2	4	5-27-1783	Muddy Cr	
Baughtes, Daniel	400	1	72	6-16-1780	Rockcastle	
Beaversons, Jas.	400	1	65	6- 3-1780	Skeggs Cr	Amended
Beaversons, Jas.	400	1	268	5-28-1782	Rockcastle	
Beard, Wm.	50	2	245	10-12-1785	Ky R	
Beckner, Henry	300	1	112	4- 2-1781	S Fk Gilberts Cr	
Beckner, Henry	300	1	112	4- 2-1781	None	
Beddinger, Michael	400	1	28	4-29-1780	Middle Fk	
Bellesfelt, Peter	400	1	178	11-24-1781	Br Paint Lick	Withdrawn
Bellesfelt, Peter	400	1	212	1-11-1782	Camp Cr	
Bellesfelt, Peter	400	1	212	1-11-1782	Salt R	
Bellesfelt, Peter	450	2	191	3- 3-1785	Salt R	Withdrawn
Bellesfelt, Peter	50	2	191	3- 3-1785	Dix R	
Bellesfelt, Peter	450	2	293	7- 9-1787	Salt R	
Bell, Samuel	400	1	11	2- 9-1780	White Lick	
Bell, Samuel	1,000	1	39	5-17-1780	Salt R	
Bell, Jno.	250	1	49	5-23-1780	——— R	
Bell, Samuel	800	1	65	6- 3-1780	Silver Cr	
Bell, Samuel	300	1	139	6-20-1781	Silver Cr	Withdrawn
Bell, Samuel	300	1	144	7-16-1781	Silver Cr	
Bell, Samuel	300	1	144	7-16-1781	S Fk Silver Cr	
Bell, Samuel	150	1	144	7-16-1781	Paint Lick	
Bell, Samuel	250	1	144	7-16-1781	Br Paint Lick	
Bell, Thos.	600	1	182	12- 2-1781	S Fk Paint Lick	
Bell, Thos.	600	1	182	12- 2-1781	Paint Lick	

Entree	Acres	Book	Page	Entry Date	Watercourse	Notes
Bell, Samuel	300	1	182	12- 2-1781	E Fk Paint Lick	
Bell, Samuel	300	1	182	12- 2-1781	Silver Cr	Amended
Bell, Samuel	200	1	183	12- 2-1781	Silver Cr	
Bell, Thos	500	1	222	1-25-1782	E Fk Skaggs Cr	
Bell & McCracken	500	1	240	2-25-1782	Br Big Benson	
Bell, Saml	300	1	248	3-18-1782	Silver Cr	
Bell, Thos	500	1	250	3-20-1782	Fk Buck Cr	
Bell, Saml	350	1	366	2-17-1783	Paint Lick & Silver Cr	
Bell, Robt	621	2	180	2- 4-1785	None	
Bellenters, Florence	500	1	72	6-17-1780	Silver Cr	
Bennett, Wm	500	1	146	7-17-1781	Paint Lick	Withdrawn
Bennett, Wm	500	1	158	9- 6-1781	Paint Lick	
Bennett, Wm	500	1	158	9- 6-1781	Dix R	
Bennett, Wm	150	1	169	11-10-1781	Dix R	
Bennett, Wm	400	1	170	11-19-1781	Paint Lick	
Bennett, Benj	500	1	351	1-29-1783	Ky R	Withdrawn
Bennett, Benj	341	1	356	2- 7-1783	None	
Bennett, Benj	500	1	358	2- 8-1783	Ky R	
Bennett, Benj	750	1	358	2- 8-1783	None	
Benton, Jesse	400	1	12	2-19-1780	Silver Cr	
Benton, Jesse	1,000	1	60	5-30-1780	Silver Cr	
Bentley, Jno	400	1	227	2- 4-1782	Dix R	Withdrawn
Bentley, Jno	400	2	158	11-11-1784	None	
Berry, Richard	200	1	123	5- 2-1781	S Fk Doctors Fk	
Berry, Jno	400	1	223	1-26-1782	Robinson Cr	
Berry, Jno	400	1	315	12- 4-1782	Beech Fk	
Berry, Jno	600	1	315	12- 4-1782	Chaplins Fk	Amended
Berry, Jno	600	1	326	12-23-1782	Clay Lick	
Berry, Richard	400	1	359	2-10-1783	———Sp	
Berry, Richard	456½	2	53	2- 2-1784	None	
Best, Humphrey	400	1	14	2-21-1780	Paint Lick Cr	
Best, Humphrey	150	1	83	9-25-1780	——— Cr	
Best, Humphrey	250	1	83	9-25-1780	Fk Paint Lick	
Best, Humphrey	300	1	362	2-13-1783	Paint Lick	
Best, Sarah	562½	1	400	4-28-1783	Rockcastle	
Best, Humphrey	250	2	140	8-18-1784	Walnut Meadow Fk	
Best, Humphrey	100	2	179	1-25-1785	Paint Lick	Withdrawn
Best, Humphrey	300	2	239	8-29-1785	None	
Best, Humphrey	100	2	239	8-29-1785	None	
Best, Humphrey	300	2	239	8-29-1785	White Lick Fk	
Best, Humphrey	100	2	239	8-29-1785	Br Walnut Meadow	
Best, Sarah	562½	2	303	1-19-1789	Rockcastle	
Black, Thos	400	1	9	2- 9-1780	Hanging Fk Dix R	
Black, Edward	2,048	2	63	3- 1-1784	Cumberland R	
Black, Edward	2,048	2	64	3- 1-1784	None	
Black, Edward	———	2	64	3- 1-1784	None	Amended
Black, Edward	1,000	2	82	3-30-1784	None	
Blake, Thos	1,000	2	233	7-23-1785	None	
Blake, Edward	10,000	2	40	12-15-1783	None	
Blake, Edward	10,000	2	40	12-15-1783	None	
Blake, Edward	10,000	2	40	12-15-1783	None	
Blake, Edw	11,213	2	40	12-15-1783	None	
Blake, Edward	10,000	2	86	4- 5-1784	Laurel R	
Blancher & Jones	1,900	2	79	3-29-1784	Ky R	
Blankenbeker, Saml	400	1	362	2-13-1783	Paint Lick Cr	Withdrawn
Blankenbeker, Saml	500	1	362	2-13-1783	Ky R	
Blankenbeker, Saml	400	2	29	10-27-1783	Paint Lick	
Blankenbeker, Saml	500	2	29	10-27-1783	None	
Blankenbecker, Saml	900	2	29	10-27-1783	Drowning Cr	
Bledsoe, Anthony	400	1	13	2-21-1780	Tates Cr	
Bledsoe, Anthony	400	1	13	2-21-1780	Silver Cr	
Bledsoe, Anthony	1,000	1	27	4-29-1780	None	
Bledsoe, Anthony	1,000	1	27	4-29-1780	None	
Bledsoe, Joseph	1,000	1	194	12-17-1781	Sugar Cr	Withdrawn
Bledsoe, Joseph	2,000	1	209	1- 7-1782	Br Paint Lick	
Bledsoe, Joseph	500	1	231	2- 9-1782	Paint Lick	Withdrawn
Bledsoe, Joseph	500	1	231	2- 9-1782	None	
Bledsoe, Joseph	1,000	1	232	2-12-1782	Buck Cr	Withdrawn
Bledsoe, Joseph	2,000	1	233	2-13-1782	Sugar Cr	
Bledsoe, Moses	250	1	238	2-25-1782	Br Sugar Cr	
Bledsoe, Joseph	500	1	240	2-25-1782	None	
Bledsoe, Joseph	1,000	1	258	4-17-1782	E Fk Sugar Cr	
Bledsoe, Wm	1,000	1	278	6-22-1782	Sugar Cr	Amended
Bledsoe, Joseph	100	1	278	6-22-1782	Sugar Cr	
Bledsoe, Joseph	1,000	1	278	6-22-1782	Buck Cr	
Bledsoe, Joseph	2,000	1	279	6-27-1782	Silver & Paint Lick	1,000 acres withdrawn
Bledsoe, Wm M	250	1	290	7-22-1782	Long Fk Paint Lick	Withdrawn
Bledsoe, Joseph	500	1	299	9-24-1782	Paint Lick	
Bledsoe, Moses	250	1	299	9-24-1782	Sugar Cr	
Bledsoe, Joseph	500	1	299	9-24-1782	Silver & Tates Crs	

Entree	Acres	Book	Page	Entry Date	Watercourse	Notes
Bledsoe, Moses........	250	1	299	9–24–1782	None..............	
Bledsoe, Joseph......	250	1	332	1– 4–1783	Black Cr..........	Withdrawn
Bledsoe, Joseph......	1,367	1	358	2– 8–1783	Peter Cr...........	....
Bledsoe, Joseph......	1,367	1	358	2– 8–1783	Ky R & Silver Cr..	....
Bledsoe, Joseph......	200	1	374	2–25–1783	None..............	....
Bledsoe, Joseph......	700	1	374	2–25–1783	E Fk Otter Cr.....	....
Bledsoe, Joseph......	—	1	397	4–21–1783	Br Sugar Cr.......	....
Bledsoe, Joseph......	250	1	401	5– 7–1783	Paint Lick.........	....
Bledsoe, Joseph......	500	2	82	3–30–1784	Richland Cr.......	....
Bledsoe, Joseph......	1,000	2	109	6– 2–1784	None..............	....
Bledsoe, Joseph......	1,000	2	109	6– 3–1784	Br Stinking Cr.....	....
Bledsoe, Joseph......	600	2	109	6– 3–1784	Sugar Cr..........	....
Bledsoe, Joseph......	600	2	109	6– 3–1784	Stinking Cr.......	....
Bledsoe, Joseph......	291	2	110	6– 3–1784	Sugar Cr..........	....
Bledsoe, Wm........	1,000	2	160	11–18–1784	Sugar Cr..........	....
Bledsoe, Wm........	250	2	160	11–18–1784	Long Br Paint Lick.	....
Bledsoe, Wm M......	250	2	160	11–18–1784	Scotts Fk	....
Bledsoe, Moses.......	500	2	248	11– 4–1785	Ky R.............	....
Bockner, Henry.......	300	1	35	5–13–1780	S Fk Gilberts Cr...	Withdrawn
Bolling, Robt.........	5,000	1	285	7–18–1782	Laurel R..........	....
Boone, Squire........	400	1	4	12– 7–1779	Silver Cr..........	....
Boone, Squire........	500	1	30	5– 9–1780	Little Benson Cr...	....
Boone, Geo..........	500	1	37	5–15–1780	Calloway Cr.......	Withdrawn
Boone, Geo..........	462	1	80	6–28–1780	Ky R.............	....
Boone, Geo..........	500	1	124	5– 7–1781	Calloways Cr......	....
Boone, Geo..........	250	1	124	5– 7–1781	Tates Cr..........	....
Boone, Geo..........	200	1	124	5– 7–1781	Tates Cr..........	....
Boone, Geo..........	1,000	1	124	5– 7–1781	Tates Cr..........	....
Boone, Daniel........	1,000	1	132	5–31–1781	Silver Cr..........	....
Boone, Geo..........	325	1	162	10– 5–1781	Ky R.............	....
Boone, Geo..........	325	1	162	10– 5–1781	Farmers Lick......	....
Boone, Geo..........	621	1	358	2– 8–1783	Tates Cr..........	....
Boone, Saml.........	160	2	31	11–15–1783	Ky R.............	....
Boone, Joseph.......	1,000	2	161	11–24–1784	Sturgeon Cr.......	....
Boone, Geo..........	1,000	2	161	11–24–1784	None..............	....
Boone, Daniel........	100	2	232	7–23–1785	S Fk Ky R........	....
Boone, Geo..........	200	2	238	8–15–1785	Otter Cr..........	....
Booten, Lewis........	400	2	31	11–15–1783	Deep Cr..........	Withdrawn
Booten, Lewis........	400	2	31	11–15–1783	Br Chaplins Fk....	....
Booten, Lewis........	400	2	38	12– 8–1783	Deep Cr..........	....
Booten, Lewis........	1,000	2	38	12– 8–1783	Deep Cr..........	....
Boughman, Henry....	400	1	2	11–11–1779	Dix R............	....
Boughman, Henry....	400	1	10	2– 9–1780	Dix R............	....
Boughman, Jacob.....	50	1	25	4–27–1780	Big Fk Paint Lick	....
Boughman, Henry....	1,000	1	28	4–29–1780	Dix R............	....
Boughman, Jacob.....	50	1	114	4–11–1781	Big Fk Cr........	....
Boughman, Jacob.....	50	1	114	4–11–1781	None.............	....
Boulware, Wm.......	332	1	53	5–26–1780	1 h Fk Otter Cr...	Withdrawn
Bowman, Jno........	400	1	13	2–21–1780	Harrodsburg.......	....
Bowman, Joseph......	1,000	1	24	4–26–1780	Cane Run.........	....
Bowman, Jno........	1,000	1	24	4–26–1780	Cane Run.........	....
Bowman, Jno........	1,000	1	24	4–26–1780	None.............	....
Bowman, Abraham, Jno & Joseph.......	500	1	25	4–27–1780	Fk Dix R.........	....
Bowman, Jno, Abraham & Joseph.........	1,000	1	31	5–10–1780	Cane Run.........	....
Bowman, Jno, Abraham & Joseph.........	2,000	1	31	5–10–1780	Dix R............	....
Bowman, Jno, Abraham & Joseph.........	2,000	1	31	5–10–1780	Hanging Fk.......	....
Bowman, Jno, Abraham & Joseph.........	1,000	1	31	5–10–1780	Dix R............	....
Bowman, Jno, Abraham & Joseph.........	2,000	1	31	5–10–1780	Skeggs Cr...	....
Bowman, Jno, Abraham & Joseph.........	2,000	1	31	5–10–1780	Harrodsburg.......	....
Bowman, Jno, Abraham & Joseph.........	1,000	1	31	5–10–1780	Harrods Run......	Withdrawn
Bowman, Jno, Abraham & Joseph.........	1,000	1	31	5–10–1780	Hanging Fk.......	....
Bowman, Jno........	1,000	1	80	6–27–1780	Wilsons Run.......	....
Bowman, Jno & Co....	1,000	1	110	3–31–1781	Harrods Run......	....
Bowman, Jno........	50	2	25	9–20–1783	Dix R............	....
Bowman, Jno........	1,000	2	62	3– 1–1784	None.............	....
Bowman, Jno........	1,000	2	70	3–18–1784	Ky R.............	....
Bowls, Jno..........	400	1	106	3–23–1781	Drakes Camp Cr...	....
Bowls, Jno..........	6,757	1	401	5– 7–1783	Br Rockcastle.....	....
Boyd, Jno...........	372	1	91	10–31–1780	Br Salt R.........	....
Boyd & Myers........	1,993	2	296	3–10–1788	Cumberland R.....	....
Boyles, Barncy.......	200	1	61	5–31–1780	None.............	....
Boyles, Jno..........	1,000	1	342	1–23–1783	Little Muddy Cr...	....

Entree	Acres	Book	Page	Entry Date	Watercourse	Notes
Brasfield, Leonard.....	826½...	2	..258....	1- 5-1786....	None..............	....
Brasfield, Jacob.......	515½...	2	..258....	1- 5-1786....	None..............	....
Bradley, Jno..........	400....	1	..108....	3-26-1781....	Cedar Cr & Dix R .	....
Breckenridge & Filson .	1,000....	2	..299....	5-17-1788....	At Silver Mine.....	....
Briscoe, Parmener.....	400....	1	.. 17....	4-22-1780....	Br Salt R.........	....
Briscoe, Parmenor.....	400....	1	.. 75....	6-20-1780....	Salt R............	....
Briscoe, Parmenor.....	1,000....	1	.. 89....	10-27-1780....	None..............	....
Briscoe, Parmenor.....	600....	1	.. 99....	3- 6-1781....	None..............	....
Briscoe, Jno Jr......	400....	1	..121....	4-30-1781....	Dry Fk Salt R.....	....
Briscoe, Jno Jr......	1,000....	1	..122....	4-30-1781....	None..............	....
Briscoe, Jeremiah.....	400....	1	..254....	4- 4-1782....	———— R.........	....
Briscoe, Jeremiah.....	300....	1	..364....	2-14-1783....	N Fk Rowling Fk..	....
Briscoe, Jeremiah.....	200....	2	.. 47....	1- 5-1784....	Shawnee Run......	....
Briscoe, Jno Jr.......	1,000....	2	..240....	9- 8-1785....	Ky R.............	....
Briscoe, Garrard......	10,242...	2	..296....	3-15-1788....	Cumberland R.....	....
Bibb, Benj...........	487....	2	..161....	11-24-1784....	Sturgeon & Station Camp Crs.......	....
Bird, Col Abraham....	1,954¾...	2	.. 17....	7- 7-1783....	Ky R.............	....
Birt, Moses..........	50....	1	.. 49....	5-24-1780....	Otter Cr..........	....
Briggs, Samuel.......	400....	1	.. 9....	2- 9-1780....	Hanging Fk Dix R..........	....
Briggs, Samuel.......	1,000....	1	.. 53....	5-26-1780....	Hanging Fk.......	....
Briggs, Jos..........	1,000....	1	..132....	5-31-1781....	Muddy Cr.........	....
Bridges, James.......	400....	1	.. 6....	1-17-1780....	Muddy Cr.........	....
Brixdel, Jno.........	1,000....	1	..133....	5-31-1781....	Harrods Run.......	....
Brinton, Henry.......	338¾...	1	..303....	10- 2-1782....	N Fk Rowling Fk..	....
Brown, Jas..........	400....	1	.. 2....	11-11-1779....	Clarks Run........	....
Brown, Geo..........	1,000....	1	.. 35....	5-12-1780....	W Fk Gilberts Cr..	....
Brown, Wm..........	296....	1	.. 47....	5-23-1780....	Dix R............	....
Brown, Jas..........	1,000....	1	.. 63....	6- 1-1780....	Clarks Cr.........	....
Brown, Jas..........	500....	1	.. 76....	6-22-1780....	Ky R.............	Withdrawn
Brown, Thos.........	500....	1	.. 79....	6-26-1780....	None..............	....
Brown, Jos..........	200....	1	.. 82....	9-12-1780....	None..............	....
Brown, Absalom......	100....	1	..109....	3-30-1781....	Rockcastle.........	Withdrawn
Brown, Jas..........	250....	1	..134....	6-12-1781....	None..............	....
Brown, Jos..........	1,000....	1	..152....	8-14-1781....	None..............	....
Brown, Jas..........	50....	1	..168....	11-10-1781....	Hanging Fk.......	....
Brown, Jas..........	500....	1	..301....	9-27-1782....	None..............	....
Brown, Geo..........	1,000....	1	..319....	12- 9-1782....	W Fk Gilberts Cr..	....
Brown, Abraham......	125....	1	..320....	12-12-1782....	N Fk Dix R.......	....
Brown, Absalom......	60....	1	..320....	12-12-1782....	Br Dix R..........	....
Brown & Gamble......	1,746....	1	..367....	2-17-1783....	Shawnee Run......	....
Brown, Abraham......	359½...	2	.. 22....	8-12-1783....	N Fk Dix R.......	....
Brown, Abraham......	60....	2	.. 96....	4-24-1784....	None..............	....
Brown, Absalom......	100....	2	..186....	2-22-1785....	Rockcastle.........	....
Brown, Absalom......	100....	2	..186....	2-22-1785....	Dix R............	Withdrawn
Brown, Absalom......	100....	2	..293....	9-11-1787....	Dix R............	....
Brown, Sarah........	400....	2	..319....	9-11-1787....	Gilberts Cr........	....
Brooks, Samuel......	400....	1	.. 7....	2- 4-1780....	Silver Cr.........	....
Brooks, Jos..........	420....	1	..206....	1- 3-1782....	———— Cr........	Withdrawn
Brooks, Jos..........	420....	1	..206....	1- 3-1782....	Br Rowling Fk.....	Withdrawn
Brooks, Wm	400....	1	..221....	1-25-1782....	Green R..........	Withdrawn
Brooks, Jas..........	403....	1	..225....	1-29-1782....	McCormacks Br ...	....
Brooks, Geo.........	1,000....	1	..253....	3-29-1782....	Laurel R..........	....
Brooks, Wm.........	400....	1	..256....	4- 6-1782....	Green R..........	....
Brooks, Wm.........	400....	1	..256....	4- 6-1782....	———— R.........	....
Brook, Geo..........	2,000....	1	..286....	7-18-1782....	Yellow Cr.........	....
Brook, Geo..........	1,000....	1	..287....	7-18-1782....	S Fk Cumberland R	....
Brooks, Rev Ebenezer..	1,000....	1	..337....	1-10-1783....	Main Fk Station Camp.......	....
Brooks, Rev Ebenezer..	1,012½...	1	..348....	1-28-1783....	Main Fk Station Camp Cr.......	....
Brooks, Jos..........	183....	1	..366....	2-17-1783....	McCormacks Br....	....
Brooks, Jas..........	183....	1	..366....	2-17-1783....	Hanging Fk.......	....
Brooks, Jas..........	420....	1	..392....	4- 4-1783....	None..............	....
Brooks, Jos..........	420....	1	..393....	4- 4-1783....	Silver Cr.........	....
Brooks, Jos..........	420....	1	..393....	4- 4-1783....	N Fk Rowling Fk..	....
Brooks, Jos..........	420....	1	..393....	4- 4-1783....	Br Hanging Fk.....	....
Brooks, Jos..........	183....	1	..393....	4- 4-1783....	None..............	....
Brooks, Ebenezer.....	1,000....	2	..138....	8- 9-1784....	Paint Lick........	....
Brooks, Ebenezer.....	595¾...	2	..278....	6- 8-1786....	Paint Lick........	....
Broadhead, Daniel....	1,000....	2	..242....	9-29-1785....	Br Little Rockcastle	....
Broadhead, Daniel.....	10,000....	2	..242....	9-30-1785....	Cumberland R.....	....
Broadhead & Donne...	23,000....	2	..245....	10-18-1785....	N Fk Laurel R.....	Surveyed 13,000-a Withdrawn 10,000-a
Broadhead, Daniel.....	7,000....	2	..298....	4-24-1788....	Cumberland R.....	....
Broadhead, Daniel.....	7,855¾...	2	..302....	7- 4-1788....	Cumberland R.....	....
Broadhead, Daniel.....	9,718¾...	2	..302....	7-10-1788....	Cumberland R.....	....

Entree	Acres	Book	Page	Entry Date	Watercourse	Notes
Broomfield, Wm	200	1	125	5–11–1781	Doctors Fk	Withdrawn
Broomfield, Wm	200	1	141	6–22–1781	Doctors Fk	
Broomfield, Wm	200	1	141	6–22–1781	E Fk Doctors Fk	
Broyle, Adam	1,500	1	36	5–13–1780	Rockcastle	
Brumfield, Jos	275	1	174	11–20–1781	Hunters Trace	
Brumfield, Robt	50	1	177	11–23–1781	None	
Brumfield, Robt	20	1	325	12–23–1782	None	
Brumfield, John	300	1	359	2– 8–1783	Br Doctors Fk	
Brumfield, Wm	330	1	360	2–11–1783	None	Withdrawn
Brumfield, Wm	330	2	53	2– 2–1784	None	
Brumfield, Wm	130	2	53	2– 2–1784	None	
Bruce, Jno	1,000	1	23	4–26–1780	Paint Lick Cr	
Bruce, Jno	100	1	61	5–31–1780	Green R	
Bryan, Wm	300	1	30	5– 9–1790	Dix R	
Bryan, Jas	1,000	1	35	5–12–1780	Dix R	
Bryan, Wm	400	1	146	7–18–1781	Cane Run	
Bryan, Jno	500	1	209	1– 9–1782	Taylors Fk	
Bryant, Jno	200	1	71	6–12–1780	Hanging Fk	
Bryant, Jos. Jr	1,000	1	185	12– 4–1781	Main Fk & E Fk Sugar Cr	
Bryant, Jno	1,000	1	186	12– 4–1781	Sugar Cr	
Bryant, Jos Jr	1,000	1	207	1– 5–1782	Sugar Cr	
Bryant, Jos Jr	1,000	1	207	1– 5–1782	Hazel Patch	Withdrawn
Bryant, Jno	500	1	207	1– 5–1782	Dix R	Withdrawn
Bryant, Isaac	—	1	208	1– 5–1782	—— R	Withdrawn
Bryant, Jno	200	1	289	7–22–1782	Br Ky R	
Bryant, Jno	200	2	141	8–18–1784	Paint Lick	
Bryant, Jno	600	2	141	8–18–1784	Paint Lick	Withdrawn
Bryant, Jno	600	2	158	11– 9–1784	Paint Lick	
Bryant, Jno	500	2	163	12– 7–1784	McClures & Scotts Fk	Withdrawn
Bryant, Jno	990	2	168	12–11–1784	Muddy & Drowning Crs	
Bryant, Isaac	1,000	2	172	12–23–1784	Dix R	
Bryant, Jno	1,000	2	172	12–30–1784	Boones Mill Cr	
Bryant, Jno	500	2	173	1– 3–1785	Dix R	
Bryant, Jos Jr	1,000	2	174	1– 3–1785	Dix R	
Bryant, Jno	500	2	174	1– 3–1785	Dix R & Boones Mill Cr	Withdrawn
Bryant, Jos Jr	500	2	174	1– 3–1785	Dix R	Withdrawn
Bryant, Jos	500	2	181	2– 4–1785	Paint Lick	
Bryant, Jos	500	2	190	3– 2–1785	Paint Lick	
Bryant, Jos	500	2	190	3– 2–1785	Ky R	Withdrawn
Bryant, Jno	100	2	251	11–30–1785	Dix R & Scotts Br	Withdrawn
Bryant, Jno	25	2	256	12–31–1785	None	
Bryant, Jos	500	2	287	1–16–1787	Dix	
Bryant, Jos Jr	500	2	288	1–16–1787	Drakes Camp Cr	Amended & withdrawn
Bryant, Jos Jr	500	2	289	1–18–1787	None	Withdrawn
Bryant, Jos Jr	30	2	294	11–30–1787	Sugar Cr	
Bryant, Jno	1,000	2	302	12– 6–1788	Boones Mill Cr	
Bryant, Jno	150	2	316	4–19–1792	None	
Bryant, Jno	500	2	316	4–19–1792	Boones Mill Cr	
Bryant, Jno	500	2	316	4–19–1792	Dix R	
Bryant, Jos	500	2	317	4–19–1792	Ky R	
Bryant, Jos	500	2	317	4–19–1792	Sugar Cr	
Bryant, Jos Jr	60	2	317	4–19–1792	Sugar Cr	
Bryant, Jos Jr	500	2	317	4–19–1792	Drakes Camp Cr	
Buchannan, Geo	200	1	93	1–29–1781	Town Fk Salt R	
Buckannan, Arch	200	1	164	10–23–1781	Town Fk	
Buchannan, Jno	300	1	196	12–18–1781	Chaplins Fk	
Buchannan, Wm	200	1	348	1–27–1783	Hickory Nut Br	
Buchannan, Jos	215½	2	25	10– 2–1783	Ky R	
Buchannan, Alex	525	2	103	5–17–1784	1 h Fk Indian Cr	Withdrawn
Buchannan, Jno	131	2	104	5–24–1784	—— Cr	Amended
Buchannan, Alex	1,300	2	106	5–28–1784	—— Cr	
Buchannan, Alex	525	2	119	6–28–1784	1 h Fk Indian Cr	
Buchannan, Alex	525	2	119	6–28–1784	None	
Buchannan, Jno	131	2	137	8– 5–1784	None	
Buckner, Philip	100	1	18	4–22–1780	Br White Oak Cr	
Buckner, Philip	500	1	44	5–20–1780	Dix R	
Buckner, Philip	500	1	113	4– 2–1781	Gilberts Cr	
Buckner, Philip	1,000	1	249	3–20–1782	Stinking Cr	Surveyed
Buckner, Robt	1,000	1	309	11–24–1782	Br Cumberland R	
Buckner, Francis	1,000	1	309	11–24–1782	Richland Cr	
Buckner, Francis	2,000	1	309	11–24–1782	—— Cr	
Buckner, Robt	2,125	1	328	12–30–1782	Stinking Cr	
Buckner, Philip	100	1	387	3–19–1783	Br White Oak Cr	
Buckner, Philip	288	1	394	4– 7–1783	None	
Buckner, Philip	288	1	394	4– 7–1783	Stinking Cr	
Buckner, Wm	1,000	2	50	1–20–1784	—— Cr	
Buckner, Robt	10,000	2	55	2– 6–1784	None	
Buckner, Wm	390	2	205	4–13–1785	None	

Entree	Acres	Book Page	Entry Date	Watercourse	Notes
Buckner, Wm	390	2...258	1-10-1786	Ky R	
Buckner, Wm	30	2...276	5- 3-1786	Ky R	Surveyed
Buford, Abram	1,000	1...250	3-21-1782	Cumberland R	
Buford, Abram	130	1...265	5-23-1782	Elk Lick	
Buford, Abraham	1,000	1...244	3- 5-1782	Rolling Fk	
Buford, Abraham	1,000	1...260	5- 3-1782	Stinking Cr	
Buford, Abraham	1,000	1...260	5- 3-1782	Both Fks Stinking Cr	
Buford, Abraham	120	1...372	2-22-1783	Scotts Br	
Buford, Abraham	2,000	1...395	4-12-1733	None	Withdrawn
Buford, Abraham	1,000	1...395	4-12-1783	None	Withdrawn
Buford, Abraham	750	1...260	5- 3-1782	S Fk Stinking Cr	
Buford, Abraham	750	1...260	5- 3-1782	Stinking Cr	
Buford, Abraham	1,500	1...260	5- 3-1782	N Fk Sinking Cr	
Buford, Abraham	2,000	2... 1	5-15-1783	None	
Buford, Abraham	1,000	2... 1	5-15-1783	None	Withdrawn
Buford, Abraham	2,000	2... 1	5-15-1783	None	
Buford, Abraham	1,000	2... 2	5-15-1783	None	
Buford, Jas	276	2... 58	2-16-1784	None	
Buford, James	1,000	1... 16	3-17-1780	Dix R	
Buford, James	400	1... 16	3-17-1780	Scotts Cr	
Buford, James	400	1... 16	3-17-1780	White Oak	
Buford, Jos	76	1...270	6- 3-1782	Dix R	
Buford, Jos	276	1...270	6- 3-1782	Dix R	Withdrawn
Buford, Jos, Guardian	276	1...395	4-12-1783	None	
Buford, Jos, Guardian	276	1...395	4-12-1783	Dix R	Withdrawn
Buford, Jos, Guardian	376	2... 58	2-16-1784	W Fk Rowling Fk	
Bulger, Daniel	1,000	1... 60	5-30-1780	Bulgers Lick	
Bulger, Edward	400	1... 13	2-21-1780	Harrods Run	
Bulger, Edward	1,000	1... 32	5-10-1780	Harrods Run	
Bulger, Edward	1,000	1... 60	5-30-1780	None	
Bulger, Edward	400	1...117	4-19-1781	Hanging Fk	
Bulware, William	332	2... 28	10- 6-1783	l h Fk Otter Cr	
Bundron, Jno	800	1... 50	5-24-1780	Silver Cr	
Burks, Saml	400	1...244	3- 5-1782	Caney Cr	
Burns, Robt & Mary	6,000	2...182	2-14-1785	Rockcastle	
Burns & Myers	968½	2...299	4-24-1788	None	
Burnsides, Jos	313	2...298	4-22-1788	None	
Bunton, John	400	1... 3	11-11-1779	Cane Run	
Bunton, John	400	1... 63	6- 1-1780	Harrods Landing	
Bunton, Jno	500	2... 82	3-30-1784	Br N Fk Rolling Fk	Withdrawn
Bunton, Jno	500	2...306	8- 6-1789	N Fk Rowling Fk	
Burt, Charles	500	1... 79	6-26-1780	None	
Burton, Chas	3,339½	1...233	1- 4-1783	Rowling Fk	
Burton, Chas	3,000	1...333	1- 6-1783	Rowling Fk	
Burton, Chas	1,000	1...333	1- 6-1783	Co Line	Amended
Burton, Chas	1,000	1...334	1- 6-1783	Salt R	Withdrawn
Burton, Chas	1,000	1...334	1- 6-1783	Green R	
Burton, Chas	1,000	1...334	1- 6-1783	None	
Burton, Chas	1,000	1...334	1- 6-1783	None	
Burton, Chas	1,000	1...334	1- 6-1783	Scaggs Cr	Withdrawn
Burton, Chas	1,000	1...334	1- 6-1783	Rockcastle & Skeggs Cr	Withdrawn
Burton, Chas	1,000	2...184	2-19-1785	Rock Lick Fk Buck Cr	
Burton, Chas	1,000	2...184	2-19-1785	Rockcastle & Scaggs Cr	
Burton, Chas	1,000	2...184	2-19-1785	None	
Burton, Chas	2,000	2...261	1-27-1786	Rowling Fk	225 acres withdrawn
Burton, Chas	160	2...262	1-27-1786	None	Withdrawn
Burton, Chas	140	2...262	1-27-1786	None	
Burton, Chas	1,000	2...262	1-27-1786	None	
Burton, Chas	225	2...272	3- 8-1786	Chaplins Fk	
Burton, Chas	385	2...272	3- 8-1786	Chaplins Cr	374½ acres surveyed
Burton, Robert	1,000	1... 77	6-23-1780	Fk Otter Cr	
Burton, Wm	5,000	2...248	11- 2-1785	Rowling Fk	
Bush, Philip	400	1...399	4-26-1783	Silver Cr	
Bush, Philip	600	1...400	4-26-1783	Silver Cr	
Bush, Philip	1,039½	2...104	5-18-1784	Chaplins Fk	Withdrawn
Bush, Philip	500	2...163	12- 8-1784	Chaplins Fk	Withdrawn
Bush, Philip	1,039½	2...253	12- 6-1785	Chaplins Fk	
Bush, Wm	5,000	1...266	5-24-1782	Silver Cr	
Bush, Wm	3,000	1...266	5-24-1782	Browns Trace	
Bush, Wm	500	1...266	5-24-1782	Muddy Cr	
Bush, Wm	500	1...270	6- 5-1782	Taylors Fk Silver Cr	
Bush, Wm	1,250	1...270	6- 5-1782	Silver Cr	
Bush, Wm	1,250	1...270	6- 5-1782	Silver Cr	
Bush, Wm	812½	1...271	6- 5-1782	Station Camp Cr	
Bushong, Jno	400	2... 72	3-18-1784	Big Benson Cr	

Entree	Acres	Book	Page	Entry Date	Watercourse	Notes
Bustard, Claudius	500	1	228	2- 4-1782	Silver Cr	
Bustard, Claudius	500	1	228	2- 4-1782	Rockcastle	
Bustard, Claudius	500	1	264	5-17-1782	Rockcastle	
Bustard, Claudius	500	1	264	5-17-1782	Rockcastle	
Butler, Peter	400	2	206	4-18-1785	Br Salt R	
Butler, Peter	150	2	257	1- 3-1786	Ky R	
Button Jno	3,000	2	79	3-29-1784	Stinking Cr	
Caffery, Jno	540½	1	327	12-28-1782	Ky Line Cr	
Caldwell, Geo	500	1	49	5-24-1780	Salt R	Withdrawn
Caldwell, Geo	500	1	49	5-24-1780	None	Withdrawn
Caldwell, Geo	500	1	94	1-20-1781	Town Fk Salt R	Withdrawn
Caldwell, Geo	500	1	103	3-13-1781	Salt R	
Caldwell, Geo	500	1	103	3-13-1781	Sinking Spring	Withdrawn
Caldwell, Geo	200	1	103	3-13-1781	None	Withdrawn
Caldwell, Geo	200	1	105	3-19-1781	None	
Caldwell, Geo	200	1	105	3-19-1781	Town Fk	
Caldwell, Geo	500	1	114	4- 5-1781	Sinking Spring	
Caldwell, Geo	500	1	114	4- 5-1781	Salt R	
Caldwell, Geo	500	1	114	4-11-1781	Salt R	
Caldwell, Geo	1,000	1	117	4-19-1781	None	
Caldwell, Geo	400	1	117	4-19-1781	Salt R	
Caldwell, Geo	500	1	351	1-30-1783	Chaplins Fk	
Caldwell, Geo	500	1	351	1-30-1783	Chaplins Fk	
Caldwell, Jno	200	1	106	3-21-1781	l h Fk Dix R	
Caldwell, Jno	200	1	106	3-21-1781	None	
Caldwell, Jno	1,011	1	388	2-21-1783	Br Chaplins Fk	
Caldwell, Jno	200	2	271	3- 8-1786	None	
Caldwell, Jno	200	1	70	6-10-1790	Dix R	
Caldwell, John	200	1	70	6-10-1780	Dix R	Withdrawn
Caldwell, David	150	2	271	3- 8-1786	Chaplins Fk	
Calloway, Caleb	400	1	7	2- 4-1780	Calloway Cr	
Calloway, Caleb	200	2	24	9-20-1783	None	
Calloway, Flanders	400	1	6	1-18-1780	W Fk Otter Cr	
Calloway, Richard	400	1	7	2- 4-1780	M Fk Otter Cr	
Calloway, Richard	400	1	8	2- 5-1780	Silver Cr	
Calloway, Richard	625	1	34	5-11-1790	Otter Cr	
Calloway, Richard	1,000	1	59	5-30-1780	Drowning Cr	
Calloway, Richard	1,000	1	59	5-30-1780	None	
Calloway, Richard	500	1	138	6-20-1781	Silver Cr	
Calk, Wm	400	1	341	1-23-1783	Ky R	
Calk, Wm	100	2	3	5-23-1783	Ky R	
Calk, Wm	201½	2	57	2-16-1784	Ky R	
Calmer, Geo	1,000	1	78	6-24-1780	Silver Cr	
Campbell, Arthur	600	1	66	6- 3-1780	Buck Lick Cr	
Campbell, Arthur	600	1	92	6- 2-1780	Flatt Cr	
Campbell, Chas	400	1	358	2- 8-1783	None	
Campbell, Chas	1,000	1	186	12- 4-1781	None	
Campbell, Thos	400½	2	48	1-16-1784	S Fk Big Benson	
Campbell, Chas	600	2	152	7-14-1784	Gilbert Cr	
Campbell, Chas	1,000	2	152	10- 6-1784	Scaggs Cr	
Campbell, Geo	500	1	355	2- 6-1783	S Fk Big Benson	
Campbell, Geo	996	1	357	2- 8-1783	Big Benson Cr	Withdrawn
Campbell, Geo	500	1	357	2- 8-1783	None	
Campbell, Isaac	1,000	1	332	1- 4-1783	Salt R	
Campbell, Isaac	1,000	1	332	1- 4-1783	None	
Campbell, Isaac	400	2	22	9- 1-1783	None	
Campbell, Joseph	420	1	340	1-11-1783	Dix R	
Campbell, Jos	120	1	341	1-11-1783	Dix R	
Campbell, Jos	100	1	174	11-20-1781	S Fk Dix R	
Campbell, Jos	420	1	289	7-22-1782	Fks Dix R	Withdrawn
Campbell, Saml	250	1	342	1-23-1783	Ky R	
Campbell, Samuel	200	1	32	5-11-1780	Muddy Cr	
Campbell, Wm	875	1	278	6-22-1782	Sugar Cr	
Campbell, Wm	1,000	1	267	5-28-1782	Cumberland R	
Campbell, Wm	400	2	214	5-20-1785	None	
Campbell, Wm	400	1	214	5-20-1785	Dix R	
Campbell, Wm	200	2	214	5-20-1785	None	
Campbell, Geo	996	2	284	7-28-1786	S Fk Ky R	
Campbell, Wm	1,000	1	297	3-15-1788	Cumberland R	
Campbell & Downey	1,000	2	27	10- 6-1783	Dix & Ky R	
Campbell & Downey	400	1	269	6- 3-1782	M Fk Sugar Cr	
Campbell & Downey	2,000	1	269	6- 3-1782	Paint Lick & Silver Crs	
Campbell & Downey	1,000	1	269	6- 3-1782	Paint Lick & Sugar Cr	Withdrawn
Cameron, Chas	400	1	1	11- 8-1779	Dix R	
Cameron, Chas	1,000	1	30	4-29-1780	None	
Caperton, Hugh	200	1	354	2- 3-1783	Silver Cr	
Carlisle, Jas	50	1	140	6-21-1781	Ky R	
Carlisle, Jas	100	1	140	6-21-1781	Ky R	
Carlyle, Jno	200	2	29	10-29-1783	Millers Cr	

Entree	Acres	Book Page	Entry Date	Watercourse	Notes
Carmack, Aquillo & Jno	1,000	1...258	4-11-1782	Trace & Flat Lick	Withdrawn
Carmack, Aquilla & Jno	400	1...271	6- 8-1782	Sinking Fk Buck Cr	
Carmack, Aquilla & Jno	100	1...272	6- 8-1782	Cedar Cr	
Carmack, Aquilla & Jno	1,000	1...314	12- 3-1782	Flat Lick	
Carmichael, Partick	400	1...264	5-17-1782	——— Br	
Carpenter, Adam	200	2...183	2-16-1785	None	
Carpenter, C	400	1...326	12-23-1782	None	
Carpenter, Conrad	400	1... 8	2- 5-1780	Gordons Lick	
Carpenter, Conrad	1,000	1... 56	5-29-1780	Hanging Fk	
Carpenter, Geo	400	1...136	6-16-1781	Carpenters Cr	
Carpenter, Geo	200	1...136	6-16-1781	Br Carpenters Cr	
Carpenter, Geo	200	1...136	6-16-1781	Green R	Amended
Carpenter, George	400	1... 31	5- 9-1780	Carpenters Cr	Withdrawn
Carpenter, Jno	200	1... 43	5-19-1780	Rowling Fk Salt R	
Carpenter, Jno	200	1... 43	5-19-1780	Knob Lick	
Carpenter, Jno	1,000	1... 56	5-29-1780	None	
Carpenter, Jno	400	1...246	3-12-1782	Green R	
Carpenter, Jno	296	1...388	3-21-1873	Br Carpenters Cr	
Carpenter, Jno	300	2... 24	9-20-1783	r h Fk Otter Cr	
Carpenter, Jno	300	2... 80	3-19-1784	Br S Fk Rowling Fk	
Carpenter, Jno	100	2... 81	3-29-1784	None	
Carpenter, Jno	100	2... 81	3-29-1784	S Fk Rowling Fk	
Carpenter, Jno	400	1... 8	2- 5-1780	Gordons Lick	
Carpenters, Adam	270	1...326	12-23-1782	Cumberland Trace	
Carrington, Paul	1,000	1... 34	5-12-1780	Greers Lick Cr	
Carr, Jos	1,000	1... 85	10-17-1780	None	
Carter, Wm	1,000	1...209	1—9-1782	Sugar Cr	
Cartwright, Jesse	500	1...138	6-20-1781	Br Otter Cr	
Cartwright, Jesse	900	1...142	7-13-1781	Boones Fk	Withdrawn
Cartwright, Jesse	300	1...142	7-13-1781	Calloways Cr	
Cartwright, Jesse	200	1...142	7-13-1781	Jacks Cr	
Cartwright, Jesse	300	1...147	7-18-1781	Boones Fk	
Cartwright, Jesse	100	1...147	7-18-1781	Jacks Cr	
Cartwright, Jesse	300	1...148	7-30-1781	Calloways Cr	
Cartwright, Jesse	500	1...155	8-24-1781	Boones Fk	
Cartwright, Jesse	500	1...155	8-24-1781	Boones Fk	
Cartwright, Jesse	300	1...160	9-21-1781	Calloway Cr	Withdrawn
Cartwright, Jesse	356	1...226	1- 6-1783	None	
Cartwright, Jesse	1,400	1...345	1-24-1783	Ky R	
Cartwright, Jesse	356	1...368	2-19-1783	None	
Cartwright, Jesse	356	1...368	2-19-1783	None	Withdrawn
Cartwright, Jesse	600	1...369	2-19-1783	Ky R	
Cartwright, Jesse	600	1...370	2-19-1783	Boones Fk	Withdrawn
Cartwright, Jesse	600	1...382	3-18-1783	Silver Cr	
Cartwright, Jesse	172	1...382	3-18-1783	Silver Cr	
Cartwright, Jesse	330	1...382	3-18-1783	Boones Fk Silver Cr	
Cartwright, Jesse	558	1...383	3-18-1783	Silver Cr	
Cartwright, Jesse	330	2... 9	6- 4-1783	Dreanine Cr	
Cartwright, Jesse	330	2... 10	6- 4-1783	Boones Fk Silver Cr	
Cartwright, Jesse	600	2...164	12- 8-1784	None	
Cartwright, Jesse	200	2...164	12- 8-1784	Silver Cr	Withdrawn
Cartwright, Jesse	356	2...178	1-25-1785	None	
Cartwright, Jesse	170	2...178	1-25-1775	Drowning Cr	
Cartwright, Jesse	171	1...178	1-25-1785	Silver Cr	
Cartwright, Jesse	1,213	2...178	1-25-1785	Boones Fk Silver Cr	
Cartwright, Jesse	47	2...179	1-25-1785	Boones Fk	
Cartwright, Jesse	29	2...221	5-30-1785	Silver Cr	
Cartwright, Jesse	368¼	2...221	5-30-1785	Silver & Muddy Cr	
Cartwright, Thos	2,0000	2...190	3- 2-1785	Ky R	
Casey, Peter	400	1... 15	3- 2-1780	Shawnee Run	
Casey, Peter, Jr	1,000	1... 80	6-26-1780	Shawnee Run	
Casey, Wm	400	1... 81	7-25-1780	Cumberland Trace	
Cave, Wm	400	1...298	9-24-1782	None	
Cave, Richard	1,000	1...325	12-23-1782	Br Sugar Cr	
Cave, Richard	1,000	1...397	4-21-1783	None	
Chace & Wheeler	6,250	1...255	4- 6-1782	Mississippi R	Withdrawn
Chace & Wheeler	6,250	2...160	11-17-1784	Mississippi R	
Chapman, Wm	800	2... 83	4- 1-1784	Chaplins Fk	
Chapman, Wm	800	2...100	5- 6-1784	Chaplins Fk	
Chapman, Wm	800	1...100	5- 6-1784	Rockcastle & Laurel R	
Charlton, Henry	400	1... 75	6-19-1780	Scotts Cr	Withdrawn
Charlton, Robt	400	1... 75	6-19-1780	Sugar & Dix	Withdrawn
Charlton, Henry	400	1...305	10- 4-1782	Dix R	
Charlton, Robt	400	1...305	10- 4-1782	Sugar Cr & Dix R	
Charlton, Ramsey & Cox	150,177½	2...112	6- 5-1784	Green R	Withdrawn
Charlton, Ramsey & Cox	50,771½	2...126	7- 6-1785	None	Withdrawn

Entree	Acres	Book	Page	Entry Date	Watercourse	Notes
Chatten, Jno	1,000	1	50	5–24–1780	E Fk Little Muddy.	
Chinn, Chas	500	1	34	5–12–1780	Whitleys Cr	
Chinn, Chas	500	1	205	12–22–1781	Whitleys Cr	
Chinn, Chas	500	1	205	12–22–1781	Dix R	
Chrisholm, Walter	1,000	2	76	3–24–1784	Little N Fk Rowling Fk	
Chrisholm, Walter	320	2	259	1–10–1786	Little N Fk Rowling Fk	
Christian, Jno	9,406½	2	295	2–19–1788	Cumberland	2,000 acres withdrawn 7,406½ acres surveyed
Christian, Jno	2,000	2	298	4–24–1788	Cumberland R	
Clark & Hutchings	750	1	335	1– 6–1783	E Fk Barneys Br	
Clark, Christopher	1,000	1	37	5–15–1780	Shelby Cr	
Clark, Christopher	1,000	1	40	5–18–1780	Br Gilberts Cr	
Clark, Christopher	300	1	90	10–31–1780	Salt R	
Clark, Christopher	300	1	90	10–31–1780	Chaplins Fk	
Clark, Christopher	1,000	1	90	10–31–1780	Falls Trace	Withdrawn
Clark, Christopher	300	1	97	2–24–1781	Salt R	
Clark, Christopher	300	1	97	2–24–1781	Salt R	
Clark, Christopher	1,000	1	265	5–23–1782	Cedar & Buck Crs	
Clark, Christopher	806	1	265	5–23–1782	Cedar & Buck Crs	
Clark, Christopher	1,000	2	78	3–29–1784	Falls Trace	
Clark, Christopher	100	2	100	5– 7–1784	Chaplins Fk	
Clark, Col Geo R	74,962	1	88	10–26–1780	Tennessee R	
Clark, Francis	1,000	1	274	6–13–1782	S Fk Ky R	
Clark, Geo R	1,000	1	91	5–18–1780	Ohio R	
Clark, Geo R	1,000	1	91	5–18–1780	Ohio R	
Clark, Geo	1,000	1	91	5–18–1780	Ohio R	
Clark, Geo R	101,920	1	165	10–29–1781	Mississippi R	
Clark, Geo R	3,920	1	178	11–24–1781	Mississippi R	
Clark, Gen. Geo R	500	1	232	2–11–1782	Ohio R	Withdrawn
Clark, General	500	1	330	1– 1–1783	Mississippi R	
Clark, Jesse	750	1	208	1– 5–1782	Dix R	Withdrawn
Clark, Jesse	500	1	208	1– 5–1782	Dix R	
Clark, Jesse	750	2	200	3–26–1785	Dix R	
Clark, Jesse	750	2	200	3–26–1785	Dix R	
Clark, Robt Jr	3,000	1	277	6–20–1782	Fk Otter Cr	
Clark, Robt Jr	2,000	2	6	5–28–1783	—— R	
Clark, Robt	7,000	2	8	5–30–1783	Drowning Cr	
Clark, Robt	8,655	2	8	5–30–1783	Ky R	
Clark, Robt	4,687½	2	55	2– 6–1784	None	
Clark, Robt	5,000	2	100	5–10–1784	Salt R & Chaplins Fk	Withdrawn
Clark, Robt	759	2	189	3– 2–1785	M Fk Ky R	
Clark, Robt	5,000	2	265	1–27–1786	None	
Clark, Robt	5,000	2	267	1–27–1786	None	
Clark, Spencer	400	1	66	6– 3–1780	Skeggs Cr	
Clark, Wm	60	1	11	2–11–1780	Otter Cr	
Clary, Wm	50	1	114	4–11–1781	Cobians Cr	
Clarry, Wm	400	2	203	3–31–1785	None	
Clay, Green	1,000	1	166	11– 9–1781	Yellow Cr	Amended
Clay, Green	1,000	1	166	11– 9–1781	Cumberland R	Amended
Clay, Green	1,000	1	166	11– 9–1781	Tates Cr	Amended
Clay, Green	1,000	1	166	11– 9–1781	Br Paint Lick	Withdrawn
Clay, Green	100	1	166	11– 9–1781	Cumberland R	Amended
Clay, Green	100	1	166	11– 9–1781	Cumberland R	
Clay, Green	——	1	167	11– 9–1781	Cumberland R	Amended
Clay, Green	1,700	1	167	11– 9–1781	Tates Cr	Withdrawn
Clay, Green	1,700	1	171	11–19–1781	Tates Cr	
Clay, Green	1,700	1	171	11–19–1781	Tates Cr	
Clay, Green	5,000	1	171	11–19–1781	Tates & Jacks Crs	Amended
Clay, Green	400	1	172	11–19–1781	Sugar Cr	
Clay, Green	300	1	183	12– 3–1781	Br Cumberland R	
Clay, Green	1,000	1	186	12– 4–1781	Paint Lick & Sugar Cr	
Clay, Green	300	1	203	12–22–1781	Silver Cr	
Clay, Green	200	1	277	6–20–1782	Sugar Cr	
Clay, Green	1,700	1	277	6–20–1782	Tates Cr	
Clay, Green	300	1	289	7–22–1782	Silver Cr	
Clay, Green	5,000	1	289	7–22–1782	Tates & Jacks Crs	
Clay, Green	1,000	1	344	1–24–1783	Br Paint Lick	
Clay, Green	1,000	1	344	1–24–1783	Paint Lick	
Clay, Green	1,000	1	344	1–24–1783	Ky R	
Clay, Green	1,600	1	345	1–24–1783	Muddy & Drowning Cr	
Clay, Green	900	2	1	5– 8–1783	Muddy Cr	
Clay, Green	1,400	2	1	5–11–1783	None	
Clay, Green	57	2	12	6–20–1783	Muddy Cr	
Clay, Green	57	2	12	6–20–1783	None	

Entree	Acres	Book	Page	Entry Date	Watercourse	Notes
Clay, Green	1,518	2	12	6-20-1783	Tates Cr	
Clay, Green	1,400	2	14	6-20-1783	None	
Clay, Green	2,995¾	2	56	2- 6-1784	Silver	
Clay, Green	462	2	165	12-11-1784	Otter Cr	Withdrawn
Clay, Green	600	2	165	12-11-1784	None	
Clay, Green	47	2	166	12-11-1784	None	Withdrawn & amended
Clay, Green	860	2	167	12-11-1784	None	Withdrawn
Clay, Green	249	2	167	12-11-1784	Muddy & Drowning Crs	
Clay, Green	249	2	167	12-11-1784	Silver Cr	
Clay, Green	643	2	168	12-11-1784	Mulberry Lick	
Clay, Green	400	2	192	3-12-1785	None	
Clay, Green	400	2	192	3-12-1785	Tates & Otter Cr	
Clay, Green	460	2	192	3-12-1785	Silver Cr	
Clay, Green	290	2	192	3-12-1785	Otter Cr	
Clay, Green	900	2	195	3-12-1785	Tates Cr	
Clay, Green	172	2	216	5-26-1785	None	
Clay, Green	37	2	216	5-26-1785	None	
Clay, Green	47	2	216	5-26-1785	None	
Clay, Green	60	2	216	5-26-1785	Otter Cr	
Clay, Green	318	2	217	5-26-1785	Silver Cr	
Clay, Green	467	2	217	5-26-1785	Silver & Muddy Cr	
Clay, Green	3,418	2	218	5-28-1785	Tates Cr	
Clay, Green	1,000	2	219	5-28-1785	Yellow Cr	
Clay, Green	635	2	219	5-28-1785	—— R	
Clay, Green	100	2	219	5-28-1785	Cumberland R	
Clay, Green	100	2	219	5-28-1785	Cumberland R	
Clay, Green	100	2	220	5-28-1785	Cumberland R	
Clay, Green	300	2	220	5-28-1785	Cumberland Cane Brake	
Clay, Green	340	2	254	12-19-1785	Silver Cr	90 acres withdrawn
Clay, Green	90	2	283	7-13-1786	None	
Clay, Green	50	2	283	7-13-1786	Knob Lick	
Clay, Green	40	2	283	7-13-1786	Station Camp Cr	
Clay, Martin	2,231½	2	130	7-24-1784	Silver Cr	
Clay, Matthew	2,800	2	45	1- 1-1784	Silver	Withdrawn
Clay, Matthew	1,400	2	45	1- 1-1784	Station Camp Cr	
Clay, Matthew	2,800	2	46	1- 1-1784	Silver & Rockcastle	
Clay, Matthew	200	2	78	3-27-1784	Silver Cr	
Clay, Matthew	200	2	78	3-27-1784	Drowning Cr	
Clay, Matthew	200	2	93	4-22-1784	Rockcastle	
Clay, Matthew	100	2	93	4-22-1784	Cumberland Gap	
Clay, Matthew	100	2	93	4-22-1784	Silver Cr	
Clay, Matthew	1,700	2	207	4-23-1785	None	Amended
Clay, Matthew	600	2	208	4-23-1785	Silver Cr	
Clay, Matthew	600	2	208	4-23-1785	Boones Fk Silver Cr	
Clay, Matthew	1,700	2	217	5-26-1785	None	
Clay, Wm	400	1	20	4-26-1780	Cumberland Road	
Clay, Wm	400	1	21	4-26-1780	Small Run	
Cobbs, Jno	1,000	1	39	5-17-1780	Ky R	
Cobbs, Jno	2,000	1	185	12- 3-1781	N Fk Rockcastle	Withdrawn
Cobbs, Jno	2,000	1	186	12- 4-1781	N Fk Rockcastle	
Cobbs, Jno	1,000	1	189	12-10-1781	N Fk Rockcastle	
Cobbs, Jno	1,000	1	189	12-10-1781	N Fk Rockcastle	
Cobbs, Jno	3,000	1	275	6-18-1782	Hammons Cr	
Coby, Wm	200	1	328	12-28-1782	Chaplins Fk	
Cockerham, Wm	1,823	1	285	7-13-1782	Muddy Cr	
Cockerham, Wm	746	2	20	8- 4-1783	Muddy Cr	
Cockerham, Wm	746	2	20	8- 4-1783	None	
Coffer, Jesse	250	1	50	5-25-1780	Br Tates Cr	
Coffer, Jesse	250	1	51	5-25-1780	None	
Coffer, Jonas	724	1	380	3-15-1783	Tates Cr	
Coffee, Peter	250	1	100	3- 6-1781	None	
Coffee, Peter	250	1	100	3- 6-1781	Dix R	
Coffey, Chas	700	1	155	8-24-1781	Otter & Tates Crs	
Cohan, Jacob	2,000	1	291	7-27-1782	Cumberland R	
Coil, Andrew	400	1	14	2-21-1780	Dix R	
Cole, Elijah & Aquilla	400	2	5	5-28-1783	Hammonds Cr	
Colefoot, Jno	400	1	199	12-19-1781	Woods Fk	
Coleman, Daniel	100	1	26	4-28-1780	Sinking Br	
Coleman, Daniel	500	1	43	5-20-1780	Dix R	
Coleman, Jas	9,728	2	52	1-27-1784	Goose Cr	
Coleman, Julius	50	1	27	4-29-1780	Gilberts & Paint Lick	
Coleman, Robt	6,736	2	113	6- 8-1784	Rockcastle	
Coleman, Saml	6,000	2	113	6- 8-1784	E Fk Laurel R	Surveyed
Coleman, Thos	50	1	27	4-29-1780	Dix R	
Collier, Alexander	400	1	90	10-31-1780	M Fk Sugar Cr	
Collier, Alexander	200	1	169	11-10-1781	—— Cr	
Collier, Jno	100	1	169	11-10-1781	Fk Sugar Cr	

Entree	Acres	Book	Page	Entry Date	Watercourse	Notes
Collier, Jno	50	1	169	11–10–1781	None	
Collier, Jno	150	1	185	12– 4–1781	Elk Lick Br	
Collier, Jno	200	1	185	12– 4–1781	M Fk Sugar Cr	
Collier, Jno	30	1	191	12–14–1781	Br M Fk Sugar Cr	
Collier, Jno	30	1	191	12–14–1781	None	
Collier, Jno	100	1	279	6–22–1782	None	
Collier, Jno	100	1	279	6–22–1782	None	Withdrawn
Collier, Jno	100	1	313	12– 2–1782	None	
Collier, Jno	100	1	313	12– 2–1782	Sugar Cr	
Collins, Bartlett	100	2	129	7–21–1784	Paint Lick	Withdrawn
Collins, Bartlett	100	2	133	7–30–1784	Paint Lick	
Collins, Bartlett	250	2	134	7–30–1784	Back Cr	
Collins, Bartlett	300	2	134	8– 2–1784	Paint Lick	Amended
Collins, Bartlett	200	2	134	8– 2–1784	Paint Lick	Amended
Collins, Bartlett	200	2	138	8– 9–1784	None	
Collins, Bartlett	300	2	144	8–24–1784	None	
Collins, Bartlett	500	2	147	9–10–1784	Sugar Cr	
Collins, Bartlett	200	2	150	9–27–1784	Sugar Cr	
Collins, Bartlett	200	2	150	9–27–1784	Paint Lick	
Collins, Joseph	200	1	160	9–21–1781	Dix R	
Collins, Joseph Jr	200	1	84	10– 2–1780	Dix R	Withdrawn
Collins, Thos	400	1	23	4–26–1780	Paint Lick Cr	
Collins, Thos	400	1	39	5–17–1780	Hanging Fk	Withdrawn
Collins, Thos	400	1	129	5–21–1781	Hanging Fk	
Collins, Thos	167	1	130	5–21–1781	Dix R	
Collins, Thos	233	1	130	5–21–1781	1 h Trace	
Conner, Timothy	5,000	2	81	3–29–1784	N Br S Fk 3 Br Ky R	Amended
Conner, Timothy	5,000	2	204	4– 4–1785	Muddy Cr	
Consellia, Harman	400	1	3	11–15–1779	Salt R	
Constalles, Wm	150,771½	2	112	6– 5–1784	Green R	Withdrawn
Conway, Catlett	18,000	1	283	7– 6–1782	Dix R	
Conway, Henry	1,757	1	334	1– 6–1783	Glady Br	
Conway, Henry	1,962½	1	334	1– 6–1783	——— Br	
Cook, David	400	1	29	4–29–1780	Dix R	
Cook, David	200	1	180	12– 1–1781	None	Amended
Cook, David	100	1	180	12– 1–1781	Paint Lick	
Cook, David	200	1	180	12– 1–1781	Paint Lick	
Cook, David	300	1	191	12–14–1781	Ky R	
Cook, David	200	1	219	1–22–1782	Br Drakes Camp Cr	
Cook, David	350	1	388	3–21–1783	Paint Lick & Silver Crs	
Cook, David	200	1	399	4–31–1783	Drakes Camp Cr	
Cook, Jno	150	1	58	5–30–1780	Paint Lick	
Cook, Jno	250	1	219	1–22–1782	Paint Lick & Wooleys Cr	
Cook, Valentine	400	1	181	12– 1–1781	Br Rockcastle	Amended
Cook, Valentine	400	1	181	12– 1–1781	Br Rockcastle	Withdrawn
Cook, Valentine	500	1	200	12–19–1781	Spring Br	Withdrawn
Cook, Valentine	400	1	200	12–19–1781	Br Rockcastle	
Cook, Valentine	400	1	200	12–19–1781	None	
Cook, Valentine	400	1	218	1–22–1782	Br Rockcastle	
Cook, Valentine	400	1	218	1–22–1782	Small Br	
Cook, Valentine	400	1	218	1–22–1782	Br N Fk Rockcastle	
Cook, Valentine	400	1	218	1–22–1782	None	Withdrawn
Cook, Valentine	500	1	380	3– 8–1783	None	
Cook, Valentine	500	1	380	3– 8–1783	Paint Lick & Silver Crs	Amended
Cook, Valentine	500	2	88	4– 8–1784	None	
Cook, Valentine	100	2	172	1– 1–1785	Silver & Pairt Lick	
Cook, Valentine	100	2	172	1– 1–1785	Paint Lick	
Cook, Valentine	400	2	180	2– 4–1785	None	
Cook, Valentine	100	2	180	2– 4–1785	Dix R	
Cook, Valentine	400	2	314	2–22–1791	N Fk Rockcastle	
Cooper, Benj	100	1	170	11–16–1781	White Oak Cr	
Cooper, Benj	248	2	173	1– 2–1785	White Oak Cr	
Cooper, Benj	52	2	173	1– 3–1785	Ky R	
Cooper, Francis	400	1	176	11–23–1781	——— Cr	
Cooper, Wm	400	1	10	2– 9–1780	1 h Fk Otter Cr	
Cooper, Wm	1,000	1	29	4–29–1780	1 h Fk Otter Cr	Withdrawn
Cooper, Wm	100	1	140	6–21–1781	1 h Fk Otter Cr	
Cooper, Wm	1,000	1	140	6–21–1781	1 h Fk Otter Cr	
Copelin, Jacob	400	1	15	2–28–1780	Dix R	
Copelin, Jacob	1,000	1	57	5–29–1780	Dix R	
Cordnat, Michael	200	1	57	5–29–1780	Fk Camp Cr	
Cordnat, Michael	200	1	57	5–29–1780	Boones Mill Cr	
Corn & Swan	1,000	1	303	10– 2–1782	None	
Cosseart, Peter	600	1	83	9–25–1780	Br Muddy R	
Cossart, Peter	50	2	262	1–27–1786	Chaplins Fk	
Coughman, Jacob	1,000	1	78	6–23–1780	Harmons Cr	
Coughman, Jacob	400	2	57	2–12–1784	Br Hammons Cr	
Coursey, Wm	100	1	17	4–20–1780	Hanging Fk	

Entree	Acres	Book	Page	Entry Date	Watercourse	Notes
Coursey, Wm	250	2	99	5- 6-1784	Ky R	
Coventree, Wm	400	2	250	11-30-1785	Salt R	
Cowan, Andrew	1,000	1	87	10-23-1780	Boones Mill Cr	
Cowan, Andrew	1,000	1	87	10-23-1780	None	
Cowan, Daniel	400	1	14	2-22-1780	Chaplins Fk	
Cowan, David	300	2	212	3- 5-1791	Rockcastle	
Cowan, Jno	200	1	52	5-26-1780	Clarks Run	
Cowan, Jno	400	1	56	5-29-1780	N Fk Cane Rup	
Cowen, Robt	435	2	11	6-20-1783	Hammons Cr	
Cowen, Wm	300	1	370	2-19-1783	Cumberland Mt	
Craddock, Robt	7,789	2	286	10-18-1786	Rowling Fk	Withdrawn
Craddock, Robt	5,620	2	288	1-18-1787	Rowling Fk & Salt R	
Craddock, Robt	3,000	2	288	1-18-1787	Rowling Fk	Surveyed
Craddock, Robt	1,500	2	289	1-18-1787	Fks, Rowling Fk	Surveyed
Craig, Lewis	400	1	1	11- 5-1779	Silver Cr	
Craig, Jno	400	1	10	2- 9-1780	Dix R	
Craig, Jas	400	1	11	2- 9-1780	Hanging Fk Dix R	
Craig, Wm	400	1	11	2- 9-1780	Hanging Fk Dix R	
Craig, Samuel	337	1	17	4-21-1780	Hanging Fk	
Craig, Lewis	100	1	19	4-24-1780	Gilberts Cr	
Craig, Lewis	100	1	19	4-24-1780	Ky R	
Craig, Jno	50	1	20	4-25-1780	Ky R	
Craig, Lewis	1,000	1	23	4-16-1780	————	
Craig, Lewis	250	1	41	5-18-1780	Gilberts Cr	
Craig, Lewis	200	1	41	5-18-1780	Skeggs Cr	Withdrawn
Craig, Lewis	200	1	41	5-18-1780	Gilberts Cr	
Craig, Lewis	100	1	41	5-18-1780	Gilberts & Paint Lick	
Craig, Wm	1,000	1	63	6- 1-1780	Hanging Fk	
Craig, Jno	1,000	1	63	6- 1-1780	Hanging Fk	
Craig, Jos	1,000	1	63	6- 2-1780	Br Hanging Fk	
Craig, Jno Jr	1,000	1	63	6- 2-1780	Hanging Fk	
Craig, Jno	1,000	1	63	6- 2-1780	Hanging Fk	Withdrawn
Craig, Jno	1,000	1	63	6- 3-1780	Hanging Fk	
Craig, Robt	————	1	63	6- 2-1780	Hanging Fk	
Craig, Saml	1,000	1	63	6- 2-1780	Hanging Fk	
Craig, Jno	200	1	82	9-11-1780	Hanging Fk	Withdrawn
Craig, Lewis	200	1	101	3- 9-1781	Skeggs Cr	
Craig, Lewis	200	1	101	3- 9-1781	Gilberts Cr	Withdrawn
Craig, Jno	200	1	108	3-26-1781	Gilberts Cr	
Craig, Lewis	200	1	112	4- 2-1781	Gilberts Cr	
Craig, Lewis	200	1	112	4- 2-1781	None	
Craig, Jno	100	1	112	4- 2-1781	Gilberts Cr	
Craig, Robt	172	1	122	4-30-1781	Hanging Fk	
Craig, Robt	172	1	122	4-30-1781	Clarks Run	Withdrawn
Craig, Jno	200	1	130	5-22-1781	Hanging Fk	
Craig, Jno	1,000	1	130	5-22-1781	Hanging Fk	
Craig, Robt	172	1	135	6-12-1781	Clarks Run	
Craig, Jno	500	1	140	6-20-1781	Hanging Fk	
Craig, Jno	500	1	140	6-20-1781	Paint Lick & Silver	
Craig, Joseph	300	1	206	12-31-1781	None	
Craig, Joseph	200	1	209	1- 7-1782	Dix R	
Craig, Joseph	1,000	1	230	2- 9-1782	Paint Lick	Amended
Craig, Jno	1,200	1	257	4-11-1782	Paint Lick	
Craig, Benj	3,916	1	270	6- 5-1782	Station Camp Cr	
Craig, Benj	400	1	271	6- 8-1782	Salt R	
Craig, Benj	100	1	271	6- 8-1782	Salt R & Rowling Fk	
Craig, Joseph	3,000	1	278	6-22-1782	Silver Cr	
Craig, Joseph	500	1	280	6-27-1782	Tates & Silver Crs	
Craig, Jno	730	1	288	7-20-1782	None	Withdrawn
Craig, Jno	730	1	288	7-20-1782	Scaggs Cr	
Craig, Joseph	1,437	1	289	7-22-1782	Paint Cr	
Craig, Joseph	1,000	1	359	2- 8-1783	None	
Craig, Joseph	500	2	82	3-30-1784	Richland Cr	
Craig, Joseph	2,550	2	108	6- 2-1784	Paint Lick	
Craig, Joseph	2,550	2	108	6- 2-1784	Sturgeon Cr	
Craig, Jas	150,771½	2	112	6- 5-1785	Green R	Withdrawn
Craig, Jno	50	2	119	6-18-1784	Ky R	
Craig, James	8,000	2	221	6- 4-1785	None	Withdrawn
Craig, Jno	16,142½	2	222	6- 8-1785	None	
Craig, Jns	4,225	2	233	7-23-1785	S Fk Ky R	
Craig, Lewis	100	2	287	11-18-1786	Gilberts & Paint Lick	
Craig, Jno	4,000	2	309	6-16-1790	Cumberland R	
Crawford, Andrew	50	1	160	9-24-1781	Hanging Fk	
Crawford, Wm	1,000	1	241	2-25-1782	Mississippi	Withdrawn
Crawford, Jas	600	1	280	6-28-1782	Sugar Cr	
Crawford, Wm	1,000	1	349	1-29-1783	Mississipi R	
Crawford, Thos	50	2	153	10- 7-1784	Doctors Fk	
Crawford, Jno	1,000	2	287	10-24-1786	Hanging Fk	

Entree	Acres	Book	Page	Entry Date	Watercourse	Notes
Crew, David	1,000	1	88	10–26–1780	Br Muddy Cr	
Crews, David	100	1	135	6–16–1781	Tates Cr	
Crew, Wm	200	2	50	1–19–1784	Br Fall Lick Cr	
Crews, David	352	2	176	1–20–1785	Muddy Cr	
Crews, David	2	2	176	1–20–1875	Jacks Cr	
Crews, David	350	2	177	1–20–1785	Jacks Cr	
Creed, Matthew	350	1	171	11–19–1781	Woosleys Spring	
Crittenden, Wm	2,728	2	160	11–24–1784	Sturgeon Cr	
Crow, Wm	400	1	6	1–12–1780	Dix R	
Crow, Wm	1,000	1	86	10–17–1780	Doughertys Station	
Crow, Jno	1,000	1	86	10–19–1780	Dix R	
Crow, Jno	1,000	1	102	3–10–1781	Dix R	
Crow, Wm	360	1	138	6–19–1781	Dix R	
Crow & Wright	1,120	1	159	9–13–1781	Hammons Cr	
Crow, Jno	20	1	160	9–18–1781	Clarks Run	
Crow, Jas	300	1	161	9–26–1781	Ky R	
Crow, Jno	250	1	165	10–30–1781	S Fk Tates Cr	Withdrawn
Crow, Wm	100	1	180	11–27–1781	Dix R	
Crow, Wm	400	1	180	11–27–1781	Lick & Black Crs	
Crow, Jno	1,000	1	279	6–26–1782	Doctors & Chaplins Fks	
Crow & Stewart	3,000	1	281	6–28–1782	Big Benson Cr	
Crow & Stewart	1,700	1	281	6–28–1782	Ky Cr	
Crow & Srewart	1,628	1	281	6–28–1782	Hammons Cr	
Crow & McCracken	500	1	282	7– 2–1782	Hammons Cr	
Crow, Jno	500	1	283	7– 6–1782	Paint Lick & Silver	Withdrawn
Crow, Wm	100	1	296	8–15–1782	Dix R	
Crow, Wm	100	1	296	8–15–1782	Dix R	
Crow, Jno	100	1	308	10–22–1782	None	
Crow, Jno	100	1	309	10–22–1782	Dix R	
Crow, Jno	430	1	315	12– 6–1782	None	Withdrawn
Crow, Jno	400	1	330	1– 1–1783	Deep Cr	
Crow, Jno	500	1	331	1– 1–1783	Chaplins Fk	
Crow, Jno	200	1	331	1– 1–1783	Chaplins Fk	
Crow, Jno	200	1	331	1– 1–1783	None	
Crow, Jno	300	1	331	1– 1–1783	Dix R	
Crow, Jno	600	1	353	2– 1–1783	Chaplins Fk	
Crow, Jno	100	1	355	2– 4–1783	None	Withdrawn
Crow, Jno	142	1	365	1–14–1783	None	
Crow, Jno	464	1	371	2–20–1783	Chaplins Fk	
Crow, Jno	300	1	378	3– 1–1783	None	Withdrawn
Crow, Jno	1,400	1	379	3– 8–1783	Sugar Cr	Withdrawn
Crow, Jno	430	1	391	3–24–1783	None	
Crow, Jno	330	1	391	3–24–1783	Little Benson Cr	
Crow, Wm	200	2	27	10– 6–1783	Br Fall Lick Cr	Surveyed
Crow, Jno	300	2	32	11–17–1783	None	
Crow & Adams	2,500	2	39	12–15–1783	3 Fks Ky R	
Crow & Adams	2,500	2	39	12–15–1783	M Fk Ky R	
Crow & Adams	2,500	2	39	12–15–1783	M Fk Ky R	
Crow & Adams	3,750	2	39	12–15–1783	M Fk Ky R	
Crow & Griffin	2,500	2	39	12–15–1783	S Fk 3 Fks Ky R	
Crow & Griffin	2,500	2	39	12–15–1783	S Fk	
Crow & Griffin	2,335¾	2	40	12–15–1783	S Fk Ky R	
Crow, Jno	436	2	107	5–28–1784	Sugar Cr	
Crow & Ewing	6,406½	2	145	9– 1–1784	S Fk Ky R	
Crow & Lusk	1,000	2	146	9– 1–1784	S Fk Ky R	
Crow & Ewing	6,000	2	146	9– 1–1784	M Fk Ky R	Withdrawn
Crow, Wm	150	2	149	9–27–1784	Br Fall Lick	
Crow & Ewing	6,000	2	149	9–27–1784	M Fk Ky R	
Crow & Ewing	6,000	2	149	9–27–1784	M Fk Ky R	
Crow, Jno	400	2	195	3–14–1785	Deep Cr	
Crow, Jno	600	2	195	3–14–1785	Chaplin Fk	
Crow, Jno	964	2	204	4– 4–1785	Sugar Cr	
Crow, Jno	74	2	259	1–10–1786	Little Benson Cr	
Crow, Jno	174	2	259	1–10–1786	Dix R	
Crow, Wm & Jno	400	2	262	1–27–1786	Dix R	
Crow, Jno	500	2	285	7–31–1786	Ky R	
Crow, Jno	100	2	292	4– 2–1787	None	
Croghan, Wm	1,000	2	281	6–27–1786	Island Ohio R	
Croghan, Wm	200	2	281	6–27–1786	Island Ohio R	
Croghan, Wm	300	2	281	6–27–1786	Island Ohio R	
Croghan, Wm	50	2	281	6–27–1786	Island Ohio R	
Croghan, Wm	50	2	319	6–27–1786	Island Ohio R	
Crockett, Andrew	400	1	12	2–21–1780	Drakes Camp Cr	
Crockett, Andrew	1,000	1	60	5–30–1780	Stone Lick Cr	
Crockett, Jos	750	1	83	9–25–1780	Fk Paint Lick	
Crockett, Joseph	1,000	1	275	6–18–1782	Hammons Cr	
Culbertson, Jno	100	1	208	1– 5–1782	Bowles Fk	
Cummings, Chas	400	1	28	4–29–1780	None	
Cummins, Chas	250	1	55	5–26–1780	Br Green R	Withdrawn
Cummings, Chas	250	1	107	3–26–1781	None	
Cummings, Chas	250	1	107	3–26–1781	Clarks Run	

Entree	Acres	Book	Page	Entry Date	Watercourse	Notes
Cunningham, Jos......	292½	1	361	2-11-1783	Chaplins Fk	
Cunningham, Jos......	1,876½	2	106	5-28-1784	E Fk Robertson Cr.	Surveyed
Cunningham, Thos....	300	1	261	5- 8-1782	Chaplins Fk	
Cunningham, Thos....	522	1	161	5- 8-1782	—— Cr	
Cunningham, Thos....	300	1	261	5- 8-1782	—— Cr	
Curry, Jas..........	700	1	177	11-23-1781	None	
Curry, Jas..........	300	1	177	11-23-1781	None	
Curry, Jno..........	400	1	109	3-30-1781	Town Fk	
Curry, Jos..........	300	1	177	11-23-1781	None	
Curry, Wm..........	400	1	50	5-24-1780	Chaplins Fk	
Curry, Wm..........	400	1	161	9-25-1781	Salt R	
Curry, Wm..........	400	1	196	12-18-1781	Salt R	
Curry, Wm..........	279	2	65	3- 4-1784	Chaplins Fk	
Curd, Jno..........	1,000	1	32	5-11-1780	Rockcastle	Withdrawn
Curd, Jno..........	1,000	1	98	3- 6-1781	None	
Curd, Jno..........	1,000	1	98	3- 6-1781	Dix R	
Curd, Jno..........	1,000	1	312	11-27-1782	Rockcastle	
Crump, Goodrich......	1,000	1	227	2- 4-1782	S Fk Ky R	
Crump, Goodrich......	500	1	227	2- 4-1782	S Fk Ky R	
Crump, Goodrich......	500	1	227	2- 4-1782	S Fk Ky R	
Crump, Goodrich......	500	1	227	2- 4-1782	S Fk Ky R	
Crump, Goodrich......	500	1	228	2- 4-1782	S Fk Ky R	
Crump, Goodrich......	500	1	228	2- 4-1782	Rockcastle	
Crump, Goodrich......	500	1	228	2- 4-1782	Raccoon Cr	
Crump, Goodrich......	500	1	228	2- 4-1782	S Fk Ky R	
Crump, Goodrich......	500	1	228	2- 4-1782	Rockcastle	
Crump, Goodrich......	3,000	1	307	10- 6-1782	S Fk Ky R	
Crutcher, Henry......	3,000	1	335	1- 6-1783	Green R	
Crutcher, Jos........	150	2	139	8-12-1784	Ky R	
Crutchfield, Jno......	1,000	1	283	7-11-1782	Br Salt R	
Crutchfield, Jno......	1,000	1	290	7-22-1782	3 Fks Sugar Cr	
Crutchfield, Jno......	1,784	1	290	7-22-1782	Back Cr	
Crutchfield, Jno......	1,000	1	307	10- 6-1782	Drakes Cr	
Davis, Asel..........	400	1	12	1-19-1780	Dix R	
Davis, Azil..........	1,000	1	82	9- 2-1780	Br Dix R	
Davis, Edward........	300	1	40	5-18-1780	Dix R	
Davis, Edward........	200	1	40	5-18-1780	Br Sugar Cr	
Davis, Edward........	300	1	372	2-20-1783	Hanging Fk	
Davis, Edward........	150	1	372	2-20-1783	Sugar & Boones Mill Crs	
Davis, Edward........	150	1	372	2-20-1783	Sugar & Boones Mill Crs	
Davis, Edward........	150	2	7	5-28-1783	None	
Davis, Isaac.........	2,000	1	311	11-27-1782	Clear Fk	
Davis, Jas...........	400	1	23	4-26-1780	Whitley Station	
Davis, James.........	400	1	24	4-26-1780	None	
Davis, Jeffry........	400	1	44	5-20-1780	Br Paint Lick	
Davis, Joseph........	1,000	1	57	5-29-1780	E Fk Paint Lick	Amended
Davis, Joseph........	400	1	150	8- 1-1781	Paint Lick	
Davis, Joseph........	1,000	2	54	2- 2-1784	Walnut Meadow	
Davis, Jos...........	2,218½	1	311	11-27-1782	—— R	
Davis, Philma........	500	1	48	5-23-1780	None	
Davis, Philman.......	500	2	202	3-28-1785	None	
Davis, Robt..........	200	1	329	1- 1-1783	Fk Scrub Br	Withdrawn
Davis, Robt..........	400	1	329	1- 1-1783	Little S Fk	Withdrawn
Davis, Robt..........	200	2	253	12- 6-1785	Little S Fk	
Davis, Saml..........	50	1	66	6- 7-1780	Include Spring	Withdrawn
Davis, Sam...........	400	1	71	6-16-1780	Silver Cr	
Davis, Saml..........	400	1	244	3- 5-1782	Silver Cr	
Davis, Saml..........	300	1	244	3- 5-1782	None	
Davis, Saml..........	300	1	244	3- 5-1782	None	
Davis, Saml..........	50	1	258	4-11-1782	Br Cedar Cr	
Davis, Saml..........	50	1	258	4-11-1782	None	
Davis, Saml..........	250	1	324	12-19-1782	Gilmores Cr	
Davis, Samuel........	400	1	30	4-29-1780	Gilmors Lick	
Davis, Samuel........	50	1	121	4-24-1781	None	Withdrawn
Davis, Samuel........	50	1	121	4-24-1781	Br Cedar Cr	Withdrawn
Davis, Samuel........	5,000	1	354	2- 4-1783	Pittmans Cr	Withdrawn
Davis, Samuel........	1,000	1	392	3-31-1783	Br Silver Cr	
Davis, Samuel........	255½	2	23	9-18-1783	Silver Cr	
Davis, Samuel........	218	2	24	9-18-1783	Silver Cr	
Davis, Samuel........	5,000	2	88	4-12-1784	Pittman Cr	
Davis, Samuel........	100	2	89	4-12-1784	Silver Cr	
Davis, Samuel........	200	2	89	4-12-1784	None	
Davis, Samuel........	700	2	89	4-12-1784	None	
Davis, Samuel........	571	2	104	5-18-1784	White Lick Fk	
Davis, Samuel........	100	2	299	5- 3-1788	Crab Orchard Settlement	
Davis, Samuel........	1,000	2	187	2 23 1785	Silver Cr	
Davis, Walter C......	400	2	237	8 15-1785	Island Ohio R	
Davis, Walter C......	238	2	237	8-15-1785	Island Ohio R	

Entree	Acres	Book	Page	Entry Date	Watercourse	Notes
Davis, Wm	50	1	27	4-29-1780	Silver Cr	
Davis, Wm	400	1	85	10-17-1780	Dix R	
Darnaby, Edward	50	1	26	4-28-1780	Dix R	
Darnell & Barr	100	2	146	9- 9-1784	Dix R	
Darice, Joseph	50	1	350	1-29-1783	Little Benson Cr	
Dayer & Warrant	500	1	358	2- 8-1783	Rowling Fk	Withdrawn
Dannell & Barr	800	2	147	9- 9-1784	M Fk Dix R	
Dean, Robt	200	2	42	12-18-1783	Muddy Cr	
Deed, Jno, heirs	1,680	2	177	1-24-1785	Rockcastle	
Degroffenviedt, Isharmer	1,962½	1	284	7-13-1782	Ky R	Withdrawn
Degroffenveidt, Ischamer	1,962½	2	166	12-11-1784	N Fk Rockcastle	
Denton, Thos Sr	1,000	2	317	4-19-1792	None	Surveyed 93 acres
Dewitt, Wm	200	1	60	5-30-1780	Dix R	
Dewitt, Wm	200	1	87	10-23-1780	Boones Mill Cr	
Dewitt, Walter	100	1	165	10-23-1781	E Fk Sugar Cr	
Dewitt, Walter	100	1	165	10-23-1781	None	
Dewitt, Walter	550	2	145	8-24-1784	Ky R	
Dick, Alexander	12,000	2	156	10-28-1784	Rockcastle	
Dickens, Jno	400	1	38	5-16-1780	Doctors Fk	
Dickerson, Edward	500	1	254	3-30-1782	Paint Lick	Withdrawn
Dickerson, Edward	500	1	259	4-18-1782	Salt R	
Dickerson, Edward	500	1	267	5-28-1782	None	
Dickerson, Edward	250	1	267	5-28-1782	Salt R	
Dickerson, Edward	250	1	268	5-28-1782	———— Br	
Dickerson, Edward	500	2	252	12- 5-1785	Paint Lick	
Dickey, Jos	3,125	2	160	11-24-1784	Sturgeon Cr	
Dickey, Jno	1,250½	2	160	11-24-1784	Sturgeon Cr	
Dickson, Geo	115	1	46	5-22-1780	Br Dix R	
Dinwiddie, Alice	312½	1	352	2- 1-1783	Caney Cr	
Diver, Owen	1,000	1	28	4-29-1780	Hanging Fk	
Diver, Owen	400	1	79	6-24-1780	None	
Divine, Jno	400	2	73	3-20-1784	Salt R	
Dodd, Andrew	400	1	87	10-23-1780	Fk Givins Cr	
Dodd, Jno	3,571½	2	79	3-29-1784	Ky R	
Dougherty, Henry	125	1	84	10- 4-1780	Dix R	
Dougherty, Henry	200	1	85	10-17-1780	None	
Dougherty, Henry	200	1	104	3-13-1781	Dix R	
Dougherty, Henry	300	1	104	3-13-1781	M Fk Sugar Cr	
Dougherty, Henry	200	1	134	6-12-1781	Br Sugar Cr	
Dougherty, Henry	61	1	170	11-10-1781	Dix R	
Dougherty, Henry	61	1	170	11-10-1781	Dix R	
Dougherty, Henry	339	1	176	11-23-1781	Dix R	Amended
Dougherty, Henry	61	1	176	11-23-1781	Boones Mill Cr	
Dougherty, Henry	61	1	187	12- 8-1781	Dix R	
Dougherty, Henry	339	1	335	1- 6-1783	Dix R	
Dougherty, Jno	400	1	5	1-10-1780	Dix R	
Dougherty, Jno	600	1	28	4-29-1780	None	
Dougherty, Jno	20	1	128	5-18-1781	None	
Dougherty, Jno	20	1	128	5-18-1781	None	
Dougherty, Jno	80	2	310	7- 2-1790	Dix R	
Dougherty, Thos	1,000	1	344	1-24-1783	Calloways Cr	
Dougherty, Thos	1,504½	1	345	1-24-1783	Muddy Cr	
Dougherty, Thos	1,398½	1	395	4-12-1783	Ky R	
Dougherty, Wm	50	1	277	6-20-1782	Lost Fk Otter Cr	
Dougherty, Wm	200	1	277	6-20-1782	Silver Cr	Withdrawn
Dougherty, Wm	600	1	362	2-13-1783	Lost Fk	
Dougherty, Wm	50	1	389	3-24-1783	Hanging Fk	Amended
Dougherty, Wm	50	1	390	3-24-1783	None	
Dougherty, Wm	1,000	2	5	5-27-1783	None	
Dougherty, Wm	600	2	5	5-28-1783	Lost Fk Otter Cr	
Dougherty, Wm	200	2	10	6-17-1783	None	
Dougherty, Wm	200	2	10	6-17-1783	Taylors Fk	
Dougherty, Wm	50	2	11	6-17-1783	Hanging Fk	
Dougherty, Wm	600	2	18	7-14-1783	Lost Fk Otter Cr	
Dougherty, Wm	200	2	235	8- 7-1785	None	
Dougherty, Wm	200	2	235	8- 9-1785	Knob Lick	
Dougherty & Myers	2,562½	2	296	3-10-1788	Cumberland R	
Douglass, Alexander	400	1	86	10-21-1780	Crab Orchard Run	
Douglass, Alexander	50	1	247	3-15-1782	White Lick Br	
Douglass, Geo	200	1	175	11-23-1781	Scotts Cr	Withdrawn
Douglass, Geo	200	1	229	2- 6-1782	None	
Douglass, Geo	200	1	229	2- 6-1782	Sugar Cr	
Douglass, Nathaniel	896½	2	232	7-23-1785	Br S Fk Ky R	
Douglass, Samuel	200	1	295	8-13-1782	None	
Donelson, Jno	200	1	135	6-12-1781	Fk Cedar Cr	
Donalson, Jno	150	1	137	6-16-1781	Cedar Cr	
Donalson, Jno	125	1	137	6-16-1781	Cedar Cr	
Donelson, Jno	300	1	168	11-10-1781	Cedar Cr	Withdrawn
Donelson, Jno	225	1	204	12-22-1781	None	

Entree	Acres	Book	Page	Entry Date	Watercourse	Notes
Donalson, Jno	100	1	318	12- 9-1782	Bauld Hill Cr	
Donalson, Jno	300	1	319	12- 9-1782	Cedar Cr	
Donathan, Joseph	180	1	78	6-24-1780	Muddy Cr	
Done, Francis	200	1	73	6-17-1780	Drakes Camp Cr	
Donelson, Jno	100	1	364	2-14-1783	Cedar Cr	Withdrawn
Donelson, Jno	100	1	364	2-14-1783	None	
Donelson, Jno	100	1	364	2-14-1783	Cedar Cr	
Donelson, Jno	287¾	2	15	7- 1-1783	Fk Cedar Cr	
Donelson, Jno	300	2	119	6-18-1784	Cedar Cr	
Donelson & Moore	50,000	2	111	6- 5-1784	Sexton Fk Goose Cr	
Donnell & Barr	325	2	274	4-10-1786	N Fk Dix R	
Doran, Patrick	300	1	99	3- 6-1781	None	Withdrawn
Doran, Patrick	500	1	99	3- 6-1781	Town Fk	Withdrawn
Doran, Patrick	300	1	100	3- 6-1781	None	
Doran, Patrick	400	1	100	3- 6-1781	None	Withdrawn
Doran, Patrick	200	1	101	3- 9-1781	Chaplins Fk	Withdrawn
Doran, Patrick	200	1	101	3- 9-1781	None	
Doran, Patrick	500	1	122	4-30-1781	Town Fk Salt R	
Doran, Patrick	500	1	112	4-30-1781	Doctors Fk	
Doran, Patrick	200	1	123	5- 4-1781	—— Cr	
Doran, Patrick	400	1	124	5- 5-1781	Doctors Fk	
Doran, Patrick	400	1	127	5-18-1781	None	
Doran, Patrick	900	1	127	5-18-1781	Chaplins Fk	
Doran, Patrick	500	1	137	6-16-1781	Dry Fk & Chaplins	
Doran, Patrick	500	1	142	7-13-1781	Chaplins Fk	
Doran, Patrick	500	1	196	12-18-1781	Ky R	
Doran, Patrick	500	1	196	12-18-1781	None	Withdrawn
Doran, Patrick	500	1	197	12-18-1781	Br White Lick Fk	Amended
Doran, Patrick	237½	1	217	1-19-1782	Fk Falls Trace	
Doran, Patrick	500	2	41	12-15-1783	None	
Doran, Pat	634	1	255	4- 4-1782	None	
Doran, Pat	500	1	255	4- 4-1782	None	
Doran, Richard	500	1	124	5- 4-1781	—— Cr	
Downey, Jos	250	1	52	5-26-1780	Clear Cr	
Downey, Jno	300	1	52	5-26-1780	Middle Fk Sugar Cr	
Downey & Campbell	400	1	269	6- 3-1782	M Fk Sugar Cr	
Downey & Campbell	2,000	1	269	6- 3-1782	Paint Lick & Silver	
Downey & Campbell	1,000	1	269	6- 3-1782	Paint Lick Sugar Cr	Withdrawn
Downey & Campbell	1,000	2	27	10- 6-1783	Dix & Ky R	
Downey, Jno	1,000	1	280	6-28-1782	Paint Lick & Silver	
Downey, Jno	600	1	280	6-28-1782	Sugar Cr	
Downey, Jno	500	1	280	6-28-1782	M Fk Sugar Cr	
Downey & Maxwell	156	1	293	8- 2-1782	None	
Downey & Maxwell	50	1	294	8- 2-1782	None	
Downey, Wm	200	2	257	1- 5-1786	None	
Downing, Wm	200	2	92	4-22-1784	Dix R	Withdrawn
Donne & Broadhead	23,000	2	245	10-18-1785	N Fk Laurel R	13,000 acres surveyed 10,000 acres withdrawn
Dooley, Moses	50	1	20	4-26-1780	Clear Cr	Withdrawn
Dooley, Moses	500	1	52	5-26-1780	—— Cr	
Dooley, Moses	50	2	291	3-13-1787	Clear Cr	
Doone, Jno	10,000	2	301	7- 4-1788	N Fk Laurel R	
Dove, Francis	74	1	164	10-20-1781	Drakes Camp	
Dove, Frances	50	1	214	1-11-1782	Dove Spring Br	
Dove, Frances	200	1	214	1-22-1782	Hammons Lick	
Dolan, Pat	400	1	14	2-21-1780	Sinking Spring	
Dolan, Pat	400	1	75	6-21-1780	Ky R	
Dolan, Pat	166	1	83	9-20-1780	Clear Cr	
Dotey, Jno	200	1	305	10- 4-1782	Buck Cr	
Doty, Jno	300	2	141	8-18-1784	Br —— Cr	
Dorland, Garrett	1,200	2	249	11-17-1785	None	
Drake, Margaret	400	1	78	6-23-1780	Drowning Cr	
Drew, Jno	10,000	2	153	10-14-1784	Rockcastle	
Drew, Jno	27,500	2	153	10-14-1784	None	
Dryden, Wm	1,000	1	89	10-27-1780	Bull Lick	
Dryden, Wm	673	2	67	3-14-1784	Silver Cr	
Dryden, Wm	763	2	88	4- 8-1784	None	
Dryden, Wm	50	2	295	2-22-1788	Br Sugar Cr	Surveyed
Dryden & Edwards	312¾	2	235	8- 7-1785	Stone Lick	Withdrawn
Dryden & Edwards	262¾	2	297	3-15-1788	Stone Lick	
Dryden & Edwards	262¾	2	297	3-18-1788	Br Rowling Fk	Surveyed
Duncan, Geo	200	1	247	3-18-1782	—— Cr	Withdrawn
Duncan, Geo	200	2	92	4-22-1784	None	
Dunlap, Jos, heirs	1,000	1	79	6-26-1780	Robinson Cr	
Dunlap, Jos, heirs	1,000	1	79	6-26-1780	—— Cr	
Duberry & Hutchings	500	1	335	1- 6-1783	Br Green R	
Duberry & Hutchings	500	1	335	1- 6-1783	Br Scaggs Cr	
Dupey, Jno	1,000	1	219	1-22-1782	Paint Lick	
Dupey, Jno	200	1	219	1-22-1782	Dix R	
Dupey, Jos	500	1	219	1-22-1782	N Fk Rockcastle	Amended

Entree	Acres	Book	Page	Entry Date	Watercourse	Notes
Dupey, Jos.	1,500	1	219	1–22–1782	Dix R.	Withdrawn
Dupey, Jos.	1,500	2	186	2–22–1785	Dix R.	
Dupey, Jos.	1400	2	186	2–22–1785	Dix R.	
Dupey, Jos.	500	2	187	2–26–1785	Br N Fk Rockcastle	
Dupey, Jas.	100	2	191	3– 2–1785	Dix R.	
Durrell, Samuel	400	1	29	4–29–1780	Muddy Cr.	
Durrell, Samuel	600	1	69	6– 8–1780	Muddy Cr.	
Dyer & Warrant	500	1	395	4–12–1783	Rowling Fk.	
Eads, Wm, heirs	534	1	324	12–23–1782	Doctors Fk.	Withdrawn
Eads, Wm, heirs	534	2	92	4–19–1784	Doctors Fk.	
Eads, Wm, heirs	534	2	92	4–19–1784	Chaplins Fk.	
Early, Joseph	500	1	25	4–27–1780	Dix R.	Withdrawn
Early, Joseph	500	1	303	10– 2–1782	Dix R.	
Early, Jno.	5,000	1	333	1– 4–1783	Co Line	
Eaves, Mary	400	2	197	3–22–1785	Rowling Fk.	
Edgar, Thos.	400	1	11	2–19–1780	Cedar Cr.	
Edgar, Thos.	470	1	168	11–10–1781	Dix R.	
Edgar, Thos.	530	1	168	11–10–1781	None	
Edmiston, Wm	300	1	53	5–26–1780	Sugar Cr.	
Edmiston, Ann & Martha	600	2	170	12–18–1784	Dix & Green R.	Withdrawn
Edmiston, Mary	469½	2	170	12–18–1784	Green R.	Withdrawn
Edmiston, Martha & Margaret	1,085½	2	170	12–18–1784	Green R.	Withdrawn
Edmiston, Martha & Margaret	1,088½	2	204	4– 4–1785	None	
Edmiston, Martha & Margaret	1,088½	2	204	4– 4–1785	None	
Edmiston, Ann & Martha	600	2	204	4– 4–1785	None	
Edmiston, Mary	469½	2	204	4– 4–1785	None	
Edmiston, Martha & Margaret	1,088½	2	204	4– 4–1785	Casey Cr.	
Edmiston, Ann & Martha	600	2	204	4– 4–1785	None	
Edmiston, Mary	469½	2	204	4– 4–1785	None	
Edmiston, Wm	1,000	2	204	4– 4–1785	None	
Edmonson, Wm	948	2	115	6–12–1784	Green R.	Withdrawn
Edmonson, Wm	948	2	304	2– 6–1789	Green R.	Surveyed
Edmonson, Wm	405	2	304	2– 6–1789	Casey & Green R.	Surveyed
Edwards, Jno	1,000	1	59	5–30–1780	Tates Cr.	
Edwards, Jno	150	1	110	3–30–1781	——— Cr.	
Edwards, Jno	300	1	163	10–17–1781	None	
Edwards, Jno	500	1	194	12–16–1781	Fk Boone Mill Cr.	
Edwards, Jno	500	1	204	12–22–1781	Dix R.	
Edwards, Jno	300	1	205	12–28–1781	None	
Edwards, Jno	750	1	253	3–30–1782	Town Fk Salt R.	
Edwards, Jno	250	1	254	3–30–1782	Salt R.	
Edwards, Jno	862	1	267	5–27–1782	Salt R.	Withdrawn
Edwards, Jno	200	1	299	9–27–1782	Fk Otter Cr.	Withdrawn
Edwards, Jno	800	1	300	9–27–1782	E Fk Otter Cr.	
Edwards, Jno	600	1	300	9–27–1782	N Fk Dix R.	
Edwards, Jno	500	1	301	9–27–1782	S Fk Cedar Cr.	
Edwards, Jno	800	1	304	10– 4–1782	Inglish Cr.	
Edwards, Jno	2,000	1	375	2–25–1783	Salt R.	Withdrawn 1,157 acres
Edwards, Jno	1,845	1	375	2–25–1783	None	Withdrawn
Edwards, Jno	200	2	19	7–23–1783	Main Fk Otter Cr.	
Edwards, Jno	200	2	19	7–23–1783	Browns Cr.	
Edwards, Jno	400	2	30	11– 5–1783	None	
Edwards, Jno	400	2	31	11– 5–1783	r h Fk Fox Cr.	
Edwards, Jno	506	2	248	11–11–1785	Richardson Cr.	
Edwards, Jno	1,157	2	252	12– 5–1785	Salt R, Chaplins Fk.	
Edwards, Jno	1,845	2	265	1–27–1786	None	
Edwards, Jno	1,845	2	265	1–27–1786	None	
Edwards, Jno	1,845	2	267	1–27–1786	None	
Edwards, Jno	1,845	2	267	1–27–1786	None	
Edwards, Jno	862	2	285	7–28–1786	Salt R.	
Edward, Uriah	673¾	2	68	3–14–1784	None	
Edwards, Uriah	112¾	2	235	8– 3–1785	None	
Edwards & Dryden	313¾	2	235	8– 7–1785	Stone Lick	Withdrawn
Edwards & Dryden	262¾	2	297	3–15–1788	Stone Lick	
Edwards & Dryden	262¾	2	297	3–18–1788	Br Rowling Fk.	
Egbert, Lawrence	1,000	1	256	4– 9–1782	Hammons Lick	
Egbert, Lawrence	250	1	256	4– 9–1782	Boones Mill Cr.	Withdrawn
Egbert, Lawrence	250	1	295	8–13–1782	Sugar & Boones Mill Cr.	Withdrawn
Egbert, Lawrence	250	2	16	7– 7–1783	None	
Egbert, Lawrence	1,000	2	16	7– 7–1783	None	Withdrawn
Egbert, Lawrence	1,000	2	16	7– 7–1783	Linn Camp Cr.	Withdrawn
Egbert, Lawrence	1,000	2	16	7– 7–1783	Crooked Cr.	Withdrawn
Egbert, Lawrence	1,000	2	16	7– 7–1783	Station Camp Cr.	Withdrawn

Entree	Acres	Book	Page	Entry Date	Watercourse	Notes
Egbert, Lawrence	250	2	46	1- 1-1784	Sugar & Boones Crs	
Egbert, Lawrence	1,000	2	58	2-16-1784	None	
Elder, Andrew	68	2	4	5-27-1783	None	
Ellis, I	400	1	186	12- 5-1781	Cedar Cr	
Ellis, Richard	100,000	2	126	7- 5-1784	None	
Ellis, Richard	50,771½	2	222	6- 8-1785	Green R	
Ellis, Richard	8,000	3	222	6- 8-1785	None	
Ellis, Richard	42,629	2	222	6- 8-1785	Green R	
Ellis, Richard	6,000	2	224	6-14-1785	Green R	
Ellison, Jno	400	1	373	2-25-1783	Dix R	Withdrawn
Ellison, Jno	400	2	307	10-15-1789	Dix R	
Embree, Jno	591½	2	81	3-30-1784	——— Cr	
Estill, Ben	500	1	33	5-11-1780	Silver Cr	
Estill, Bond	200	1	33	5-11-1780	Otter Cr	
Estill, Bond	384	1	371	2-20-1783	Knob Lick	
Estill, James, heirs	1,000	2	9	6- 1-1783	None	
Estill, James	400	1	33	5-11-1780	Station Camp Cr	
Estill, James	500	1	33	5-11-1780	Mulberry Lick	
Estill, James	300	1	22	5-11-1780	Otter Cr	
Estill, James	200	1	128	5-18-1781	Tates Cr	
Estill, James	1,000	1	215	1-17-1782	Little & Big Muddy Cr	
Estill, Jas	400	1	33	5-11-1780	Otter Cr	
Estill, Jas	1,000	1	51	5-25-1780	Tates Cr	Amended
Estill, Jas	1,000	1	51	5-25-1780	Tates Cr	
Estill, Jas	400	1	128	5-18-1781	Otter Cr	
Estill, Joseph	1,000	1	198	12-19-1781	Main Station Camp Cr	
Estill, Jos	1,000	1	24	4-26-1780	Otter Cr	
Estill, Jos	400	1	33	5-11-1780	None	
Estill, Jos	400	1	51	5-25-1780	Ky R	
Estill, Jos	1,000	1	51	5-25-1780	Paint Lick Cr	
Estill, Jos	400	1	136	6-16-1781	Otter & Silver Crs	
Estill, Jos	200	1	136	6-16-1781	Otter Cr	
Estill, Jos	200	1	136	6-16-1781	Tates Cr	
Estill, Jos	1,000	1	167	11- 9-1781	Hays Fk	
Estill, Jos	400	1	167	11- 9-1781	Silver Cr	
Estill, Jos	600	1	167	11- 9-1781	Silver Cr	
Estill, Jos	200	1	167	11- 9-1781	Tates Cr	
Estill, Jos	1,000	1	198	12-19-1781	Otter Cr	
Estill, Jos	100	1	198	12-19-1781	Ky R	
Estill, Jos	300	1	199	12-19-1781	Vine Fk	
Estill, Jos	700	1	199	12-19-1781	Viney Fk	
Estill, Jos	400	1	199	12-19-1781	Br Silver Cr	
Estill, Jos	1,000	1	215	1-17-1782	None	
Estill, Jos	342	1	215	1-17-1782	Ky R	
Estill, Jno	200	1	371	2-20-1783	None	
Estill, Saml	400	1	52	5-25-1780	Muddy Cr	
Estill, Saml	762	2	36	11-29-1783	None	
Estill, Saml	238	2	36	11-29-1783	Tates Cr	
Estill, Saml	400	2	36	11-29-1783	Tates Cr	
Estill, Saml	200	2	38	12- 8-1783	Muddy Cr	
Estill, Saml	150	2	241	9-13-1785	Dix R	Withdrawn
Estill, Saml	150	2	243	10- 6-1785	Dix R	
Estill, Wallace	500	1	32	5-11-1780	Br Muddy Cr	
Estill, Wallace	500	1	32	5-11-1780	Mulberry Lick	
Estill, Wallace	400	1	33	5-11-1780	Muddy Cr	Withdrawn
Estill, Wallace	400	1	216	1-17-1782	Muddy Cr	
Estill, Wm & Saml	310½	2	268	2-10-1786	Ky R	
Evan, Nathaniel	1,000	1	105	3-13-1781	Hanging Fk	
Evan, Nathaniel	400	1	107	3-25-1781	None	
Evans, Nathaniel	100	1	194	12-17-1781	None	
Evans, Nathanial	136	1	194	12-17-1781	None	
Evans, Nathaniel	200	1	208	1- 5-1782	None	
Evans, Nathaniel	200	1	223	1-26-1782	None	
Ewing, Baker	400	1	85	10-10-1780	Silver Cr	
Ewing, Daniel	250	1	71	6-13-1780	Salt R	Withdrawn
Ewing, Daniel	250	1	329	1- 1-1783	Beech Fk	
Ewings, Daniel	250	1	159	9- 6-1781	Salt R	
Ewing, Daniel	250	1	159	9- 6-1781	Beech Fk	Withdrawn
Ewing, Wm	235	1	252	3-26-1782	Cranks Cr	
Ewing & Crow	6,406¼	2	145	9- 1-1784	S Fk Ky R	
Ewing & Crow	6,000	2	146	9- 1-1784	M Fk Ky R	Withdrawn
Ewing & Crow	6,000	2	149	9-27-1784	M Fk Ky R	
Ewing & Crow	6,000	2	149	9-27-1784	M Fk Ky R	
Ewing & Woods	1,000	2	87	4- 5-1784	S Fk Big Benson Cr	Withdrawn
Ewing & Woods	1,000	2	87	4- 5-1784	S Fk Big Benson Cr	Withdrawn
Ewing & Woods	812½	2	87	4- 5-1784	Br S Fk Big Benson	Withdrawn
Ewing & Woods	1,000	2	90	4-16-1784	None	
Ewing & Woods	1,000	2	90	4-16-1784	None	
Ewing & Woods	812½	2	91	4-16-1784	Br S Fk	
Farris, Isam	50	1	371	2-20-1783	None	

Entree	Acres	Book	Page	Entry Date	Watercourse	Notes
Farris, Isam	40	1	380	3- 8-1783	None	Withdrawn
Farris, Isam	100	1	389	3-24-1783	None	Withdrawn
Farris, Isam	100	1	396	4-18-1783	None	
Farris, Isam	50	1	397	4-19-1783	None	
Farris, Isam	150	1	397	4-19-1783	None	
Farris, Isham	50	2	18	7-14-1783	Spring Br	
Farris, Isham	200	2	146	9- 1-1784	None	
Farris, Nathan	50	1	332	1- 3-1783	————Br	
Farmer, Stephen	481¾	2	85	4- 3-1784	Laurel R	
Farrow, Jno	400	1	10	2- 9-1780	1 h Fk Otter Cr	
Fram, Thos	800	1	62	6- 1-1780	Dix R	
Frazor, Wm	3,000	2	117	6- 17-1784	Richland Cr	
Fenton, Bartholomew	250	1	207	1- 3-1783	None	Withdrawn
Fenton, Bartholomew	250	2	162	11-30-1784	None	
Ferguson, Chas	500	1	59	5-30-1780	Dix R	
Ferguson, Chas	400	1	76	6-22-1780	Doctors Fk	
Ferguson, Chas	100	1	124	5-11-1781	Doctors Fk	
Ferguson, Chas	500	2	25	9-20-1783	Dix R	
Ferguson, Jno	500	2	25	9-20-1783	W Fk Station Camp Cr	
Fields, Ezekiel	100	1	168	11-10-1781	Dix R	
Fields, Ezekiel	100	1	181	12- 1-1781	Wilsons Run	
Fields, Henry	400	1	78	6-23-1780	W Fk Otter Cr	
Fields, Wm	500	1	392	4- 4-1783	Estill Station	
Filson & Breckinridge	1,000	2	299	5-17-1788	At Silver Mine	
Finley, David	1,000	1	21	4-26-1780	Dix R	
Finley, David	300	1	52	5-26-1780	Silver Cr	
Finnie, Jas	805	1	44	5-20-1780	None	
Finnie, Jos	50	1	25	4-28-1780	S Fk Tates Cr	
Finnie, Jno	50	1	26	4-28-1780	S Fk Tates & Silver Cr	
Finnie, Jos	50	1	27	4-29-1780	Fks, Tates Cr	
Finnie, Jno	500	1	44	5-20-1780	S Fk Tates Cr	
Fishback, Jacob	1,000	1	82	9-12-1780	None	
Fishback, Jacob	1,000	1	116	4-16-1781	None	
Fishback, Jacob	200	2	233	7-29-1785	Dix R	
Fisher, Adam	400	1	9	2- 7-1780	Dix R	
Fisher, Adam	500	1	39	5-17-1780	Harrods Run	Withdrawn
Fisher, Adam	500	1	113	4- 5-1781	Dix R	
Fisher, Adam	500	1	114	4- 5-1781	Drakes Camp Cr	
Fisher, Adam	500	1	268	5-30-1782	Drakes Camp Cr	
Fisher, Barnett	400	1	8	2- 7-1780	Salt R	
Fisher, Barnett	500	1	244	3- 5-1782	None	
Fisher, Barnett	500	1	244	3- 5-1782	None	
Fisher, Jos	300	1	174	11-20-1781	M Fk Beech Fk	
Fisher, Stephen	1,000	2	35	11-27-1783	None	
Fisher, Stephen	698¾	2	76	3-24-1784	None	Withdrawn
Fisher, Stephen	698¾	2	264	1-27-1786	None	
Fisher, Stephen	698¾	2	266	1-27-1786	None	
Fisher, Stephen	1,000	1	43	5-19-1780	None	Withdrawn
Fisher, Stephen	1,000	1	93	1-29-1781	None	
Fleming, Robt	400	1	7	2- 3-1780	Muddy Cr	
Fleming, Robt	1,000	1	77	6-23-1780	Muddy Cr	
Fleming, Tarlton	4,000	1	285	7-18-1782	Laurel R	
Fleming, Thos	2,000	1	286	7-18-1782	Yellow Cr	
Fleming, Wm	10,000	2	40	12-15-1783	Green R	
Fleming, Wm	4,000	2	56	2- 6-1784	Green R	
Fleming, Wm	4,000	2	56	2- 6-1784	Dix R	
Fleming, Wm	2,054	2	63	3- 1-1784	Buck Cr	
Fleming, Wm	2,054	2	63	3- 1-1784	None	
Fleming, Wm	3,946	2	63	3- 1-1784	None	
Flinn, George	400	1	210	1- 9-1782	Green R	
Flood, Joseph	1,000	1	321	12-13-1782	Brushy Cr	
Flood, Joseph	1,000	1	321	12-13-1782	Caseys Cr	
Flood, Joseph	500	1	321	12-13-1782	None	
Flood, Joseph	500	1	321	12-13-1782	Green R	
Flournoy, Jno	1,450	1	197	12-18-1781	None	
Flournoy, Jno	500	1	201	12-19-1781	Sugar Cr	
Flournoy, Jno	1,000	1	201	12-19-1781	Boone Mill Cr	Withdrawn
Flournoy, Jno	1,000	1	201	12-19-1781	None	Amended
Flournoy, Jno	500	1	210	1- 9-1782	Ky R	
Flournoy, Jno	500	1	210	1- 9-1782	Ky R	
Flournoy, Jno	800	1	218	1-22-1782	None	
Flournoy, Jno	400	1	223	1-26-1782	Spring Br	
Flournoy, Jno	1,500	1	224	1-26-1782	Rowling & Beech Fk	
Flournoy, Jno	500	1	224	1-26-1782	None	Withdrawn
Flournoy, Jno	500	1	226	1-29-1782	Pine Lick	
Flournoy, Jno	500	1	231	2-14-1782	Ky R	
Flournoy, Jno	500	1	239	2-25-1782	None	
Flournoy, Jno	300	1	241	2-25-1782	Big Caney Cr	
Flournoy, Jno	2,000	1	245	3- 5-1782	Rowling Fk	
Flournoy, Jno	300	1	254	3-30-1782	None	Withdrawn

Entree	Acres	Book	Page	Entry Date	Watercourse	Notes
Flournoy, Jno	300	1	260	4-18-1782	None	
Flournoy, Jno	300	1	260	4-18-1782	Salt R	
Flournoy, Jno	477	1	349	1-29-1783	None	
Flournoy, Jno	477	1	349	1-29-1783	Beech Fk	
Flournoy, Jno	1,000	1	390	3-24-1783	Boones Mill Cr	
Flournoy, Jno	1,000	1	390	3-24-1783	Muddy Cr	
Flournoy, Jno	800	1	392	3-29-1783	None	
Flournoy, Jno	800	1	392	3-29-1783	Ky R	
Flournoy, Jno	1,400	2	7	5-30-1783	Rowling Fk	
Flournoy, Jno	1,400	2	7	5-30-1783	None	
Flournoy, Jno	200	2	51	1-20-1784	None	
Flournoy, Jno	400	2	295	12- 4-1787	None	
Flournoy, Lawrence	675	1	231	2-11-1782	Ky R	
Flournoy, Lawrence	500	1	232	2-11-1782	Big Benson Cr	
Flournoy, Lawrence	500	2	97	4-28-1784	Big Bensons Cr	
Folley, Richard	200	1	82	9- 2-1780	Dix R	
Folley, Richard	200	1	82	9- 2-1780	Allens Spring Br	Withdrawn
Folley, Richard	200	1	267	5-27-1782	Dix R	
Follis, Isaac	500	2	145	8-24-1784	Chaplins Fk	
Ford, Beag	400	1	67	6- 8-1780	Glovers Station	
Ford, Peter	400	2	31	11- 6-1783	Scaggs Cr	Withdrawn
Ford, Milton	10,000	2	272	3-20-1786	N Fk Ky R	
Ford, Peter	400	2	303	1-24-1789	Scaggs Cr	
Ford, Warner	400	1	360	2-11-1783	Cedar & Buck Crs	
Forbes, Wm	61,958	2	111	6- 5-1784	Sexton Fk Goose Cr	
Forman, Jacob	800	1	93	1-27-1781	Ky R	
Foster, Anthony	255½	1	367	2-17-1783	Ky R	
Foster, Anthony Jr	2,335	1	340	1-11-1783	Big Benson Cr	
Foster, Anthony Jr	575	2	171	12-18-1784	Bensons Cr	
Foster, Anthony Jr	575	2	171	12-18-1784	N Fk Rowling Fk	
Foster, Isaac	381½	1	348	1-28-1783	Hammons Cr	Withdrawn
Foster, Isaac	381½	2	11	6-20-1783	None	
Foster, Isaac	381½	2	11	6-20-1783	Hammons Cr	
Foush, Isaac, Jonathan, Geo., Daniel & Saml.	611½	2	189	3- 2-1785	None	
Fowler, Alexander	6,000	1	241	2-25-1782	Mississippi R	Withdrawn
Fowler, Alexander	4,000	1	241	2-25-1782	Mississippi R	Withdrawn
Fowler, Alexander	6,000	1	349	1-29-1783	Mississippi R	
Fowler, Alexander	4,000	1	349	1-29-1783	Mississippi R	
Fox, Jno	50	1	27	4-29-1780	Silver Cr	
Freeman, Elisha	262½	2	159	11-11-1784	Cumberland R	Surveyed
French, Henry	400	1	133	6- 4-1781	Hanging Fk	
French, Henry	400	1	137	6-19-1781	Hanging Fk	
French, Henry	200	1	138	6-19-1781	Hanging Fk	
French, Henry	200	1	138	6-19-1781	Hanging Fk	
French, Henry	200	1	336	1- 6-1783	Hanging Fk	
French, Jos	593¾	2	58	2-20-1784	Ky R	
French, Jos	——	2	94	4 23-1784	Ky R	
French, Jos	1,400	2	154	10-27-1784	Otter Cr	Withdrawn
French, Jos	1,400	2	154	10-27-1784	Silver Cr	
French, Jos	1,400	2	154	10-27-1784	Boonesboro	
French, Jos	1,300	2	155	10-27-1784	Silver Cr	
French, Jos	50	2	176	1-20-1785	Ky R	
French, Jos	50	2	176	1-20-1785	None	
French, Jos	5,500	2	177	1-22-1785	None	
French, Jos	25	2	260	1-25-1786	Howards Lower Cr	
French, Jos	548¾	2	270	2-25-1786	None	
Friend, Edward	1,500	1	192	12-14-1781	Big Fk Raccoon Cr	
Friend, Edward	1,500	1	193	12-14-1781	S Fk Ky R	
Froman, Jacob	600	1	94	1-30-1781	Ky R	
Froman, Jacob	400	1	94	1-30-1781	None	
Froman, Jacob	400	1	152	8-14-1781	Ky R	
Froman, Jacob	400	1	297	9- 2-1782	None	
Froman, Jacob	1,000	1	348	1-28-1783	None	
Froman, Jacob	400	1	383	3-18-1783	Ky R	
Fry, Jno	150	1	36	5-13-1780	Carpenters Cr	
Fry, Jno	100	1	36	5-13-1780	Carpenters Cr	
Fry, Jno	150	1	82	9-13-1780	Carpenters Cr	
Fry, Leah	150	2	31	11- 8-1783	Carpenters Cr	
Fugate, Townsend	400	1	176	11-23-1781	White Oak Cr	
Fugit, Townsend	359	2	172	12-31-1784	White Oak Cr	
Fugit, Townsend	70¼	2	172	12-31-1784	None	
Fulton, Jos	300	1	341	1-11-1783	Dix R	
Fulton, Jos	300	1	356	2- 8-1783	Dix R	
Fuqua, Joseph	400	1	67	6- 8-1780	Glovers Station	
Gaines, Daniel	800	1	350	1-29-1783	Big Benson Cr	
Gaines, Daniel	800	2	53	1-31-1784	Big Benson Cr	Withdrawn
Gaines, Daniel	800	2	77	3-27-1784	None	
Gaines, Daniel	2,000	2	119	6-26-1784	Fox Cr	
Gaines, Wm	200	1	38	5-16-1780	Cave Springs	
Gaines, Wm	200	1	38	5-16-1780	Dix R	
Gallaspie, Geo	163	2	164	12- 8-1784	None	Withdrawn

Entree	Acres	Book	Page	Entry Date	Watercourse	Notes
Gallaspie, Geo	163	2	178	1-25-1785	None	
Galloway, Jno	2,000	1	194	3-12-1785	N Fk Rockcastle	
Gamble & Brown	1,746	1	367	2-17-1783	Shawnee Run	
Gant, Thos; heirs	500	1	347	1-27-1783	Top Ridge	
Gant, Thos, heirs	500	1	347	1-27-1783	r h Fk Fox Cr	
Garland, Jno	20,313½	2	33	11-22-1783	Br Caseys Cr	Amended
Garland, Jno	12,500	2	34	11-22-1783	——— R	
Garland, Jno	17,187½	2	34	11-22-1783	——— R	
Garland, Jno	20,313½	2	47	1- 1-1784	Below Bryants Lick	
Garrard, Jos	500	1	264	5-23-1782	Goose Cr	
Garrard, Jos	500	1	264	5-23-1782	Fk Laurel R	
Garrard, Jos	500	1	282	6-28-1782	Paint Lick	
Garrett, Thos	500	1	43	5-20-1780	None	
Gass, Davis	400	1	184	12- 3-1781	None	
Gass, Jno	1,879½	2	286	10- 2-1786	Br Cumberland R	
Gass, Jno	2,321½	2	294	11- 3-1787	Clover Fk	
Gast, Thos	2,500	2	153	10-16-1784	None	
Gaston, Matthew	300	1	396	4-18-1783	Paint Lick	
Gatliff, Chas	80	2	49	1-19-1784	Dix R	Amended
Gatliff, Chas	13	2	94	4-23-1784	Dix R	
Gatliff, Chas	80	2	94	4-23-1784	None	Surveyed
Gates, Jas	400	1	7	2- 3-1780	Muddy Cr	
Ghone, Pat	1,000	1	74	6-19-1780	Doughertys Run	
Gibbs, Julius	800	1	44	5-20-1780	None	
Gilaspy, David	200	1	69	6- 9-1780	Br Ky R	
Gilaspy Jno	4,065	1	311	11-27-1782	Fk Linn Camp Cr	
Gilbert, Samuel	1,599	2	8	5-30-1783	None	
Giles, Jno	500	1	88	10-25-1780	Ky R	
Gilham, Wm	2,000	2	232	7-23-1785	Br S Fk Ky R	
Gillaspy, David	3,000	1	319	12- 9-1782	Sinking Br	Withdrawn
Gillaspy, David	2,000	1	319	12- 9-1782	Dix R & Brush Cr	Withdrawn
Gillaspy, David	1,000	1	319	12- 9-1782	Paint Lick	Withdrawn
Gillaspy, David	1,000	1	319	12- 9-1782	None	Amended
Gillaspy, David	500	1	319	12- 9-1782	None	Amended
Gillaspie, David	1,933	1	319	12- 9-1782	Stinking Cr	
Gillaspie, David	700	1	371	2-20-1783	Stinking Cr	
Gillaspie, David	100	1	371	2-20-1783	None	Withdrawn
Gillaspie, David	600	1	371	2-20-1783	None	
Gillaspie, David	100	1	388	3-21-1783	None	
Gillaspie, David	600	1	388	3-21-1783	None	
Gillaspie, David	700	1	388	3-21-1783	Paint Lick & Silver Crs	
Gillaspie, David	1,000	1	389	3-22-1783	None	
Gillaspie, David	600	1	389	3-22-1783	Br Ky R	
Gillaspie, David	400	1	389	3-22-1783	——— Cr	
Gillaspie, Wm	500	1	375	2-26-1783	Ky R	
Gillispie, David	1,000	1	398	4-21-1783	None	
Gillispie, David	500	1	398	4-21-1783	None	
Gillispie, David	3,000	2	393	6- 7-1787	Sinking Fk Buck Cr	
Gillispie, David	2,000	2	293	6- 7-1787	Dix R & Brush Cr	
Gilmore, James	400	1	11	2-11-1780	Hanging Fk Dix R	
Gilmore, Jno	50	1	25	4-26-1780	Harrods Cr	
Gilmore, Jos	500	1	71	6-16-1780	Hanging Fk	
Gilmore, Jos	1,000	1	101	3- 9-1781	Salt R	
Gilmore, Jos	300	1	120	4-24-1781	Chaplins Fk	
Gilmore, Jos	1,040	1	401	5- 7-1783	Hanging Fk	Amended
Gilmore, Jos	1,000	2	22	9- 6-1783	None	Amended
Gilmore, Jos	1,040	2	51	1-27-1784	None	
Gilmore, Jos	1,000	2	52	1-27-1784	None	
Gilmore, Jos	300	2	62	2-24-1784	Trough Lick Br	
Gilmore, Jos	300	2	62	2-27-1784	Br Station Camp Cr	
Gill, Wm	200	2	149	9-24-1784	None	
Gill, Wm	300	2	169	12-15-1784	Quirks Run	
Gill, Wm	100	2	170	12-15-1784	None	
Gillon & Marshall	500	2	276	5- 4-1786	S Fk Ky R	
Gist, Thos Jr	2,500	2	131	7-24-1784	Sycamore Cr	
Gist, Thos Jr	2,500	2	131	7-24-1784	None	Withdrawn
Gist, Thos Jr	5,000	2	131	7-24-1784	Laurel R	
Givens, Saml	400	1	13	2-21-1780	Blares Spring	
Givens, Saml	1,000	1	23	4-26-1780	Clarks Cr	
Givens, Geo	400	1	47	5-23-1780	Hanging Fk	
Given, Robt	200	2	264	1-27-1786	Cumberland R	
Given, Robt	100	2	264	1-27-1786	Cumberland R	
Given, Robt	200	2	266	1-27-1786	Cumberland R	
Given, Robt	100	2	266	1-27-1786	Cumberland R	
Glover, Jno	200	1	55	5-26-1780	Green R	
Goodnight, Michael	400	1	76	6-22-1780	Chaplins Fk	
Goodson, Frances	370	1	79	6-26-1780	Ky R	
Goodwin, Roswell	7,200	2	69	3-16-1784	S Fk Stinking Cr	
Goggins, Stephen	2,000	1	344	1-24-1783	Muddy Cr	
Goldman, Thos	1,600	1	20	4-25-1780	Gilberts Cr	
Gordon, Jas	400	1	2	11-11-1779	Shawnee Run	

Entree	Acres	Book	Page	Entry Date	Watercourse	Notes
Gordon, Geo	1,000	1	87	10-23-1780	Chaplins Fk	Withdrawn
Gordon, James	500	1	47	5-23-1780	Sinking Spring	
Gordon, Jas	50	1	17	4-18-1780	Sugar Cr	
Gordon, Jas	500	1	322	12-13-1782	None	
Gordon, Jas	100	2	74	3-22-1784	Ky R	Withdrawn
Gordon, Jas	100	2	148	9-23-1784	Ky R	
Gordon, Jas	200	2	149	9-23-1784	Shawnee Run	
Gordon, Jas	400	2	233	7-29-1785	——— Cr	
Gordon, Jno	1,000	1	28	4-29-1780	Shawnee Run	
Gordon, Jno	500	1	47	5-23-1780	Cedar Run	
Gordon, Saml	400	1	131	5-28-1781	Paint Lick	
Gordon, Wm	1,000	2	62	2-27-1784	Chaplins Fk	
Gotner, Frederick	270	2	274	4- 5-1786	Br Rowling Fk	
Grant & Scott	100	2	2	5-15-1783	Ky R	
Grant, Saml	150	2	3	5-27-1783	M Fk Sugar Cr	
Grant, Saml	200	2	29	10-27-1783	Ky R	
Grant, Saml	1,000	2	231	7-18-1785	Ky R	
Grant, Thos	1,250	1	363	2-14-1783	Otter Cr	
Grant, Wm	100	1	165	10-23-1781	Sugar Cr	
Grant, Wm	200	1	170	11-16-1781	None	
Grant, Wm	350	1	267	5-27-1782	Scotts Fk Dix R	
Grant, Wm	150	1	314	12- 3-1782	Dix R	
Graham, Francis	50	1	306	10- 6-1782	Dix R	
Graham, Francis	1,000	1	313	12- 2-1782	S Fk Big Benson Cr	
Graham, Francis	965½	1	313	12- 2-1782	None	
Graham, Francis	1,555	1	313	12- 2-1782	None	
Graham, Francis	1,000	1	313	12- 2-1782	None	
Graham, Francis	1,000	1	313	12- 2-1782	None	
Graves, Francis	600	2	143	8-19-1784	None	
Graves, Leonard	100	1	250	3-20-1782	N Fk Scaggs Cr	
Graves, Thos	703½	2	258	1- 5-1786	None	
Gray, Jos	1,000	1	263	5-16-1782	N Fk Stinking Cr	Surveyed
Gray, Jos	1,000	1	352	2- 1-1783	Richland Cr	
Gray, Jos	500	1	365	2-14-1783	S Fk Ky R	
Gray, Jos	500	1	365	2-14-1783	S Fk Ky R	
Gray, Jos	150	2	4	5-27-1783	Taylors Fk	
Gray, Jos	200	2	26	10- 4-1783	Mans Cr	
Gray, Jos	100	2	26	10- 4-1783	Sugar Cr	
Gray, Jos	400	2	163	12- 5-1784	Sugar Cr	Withdrawn
Gray, Jos	500	2	163	12- 5-1784	Br Sugar Cr	Withdrawn
Gray, Jos	400	2	269	2-10-1786	Sugar Cr	
Grayson, Jno	400	1	2	11-11-1779	Cane Run	
Grayson, Wm	400	1	12	2-19-1780	Chaplins Fk Salt R	
Grayble, Philip	4,000	1	255	4- 6-1782	Mississippi R	Withdrawn
Grayble, Philip	4,000	1	311	11-27-1782	Mississippi R	
Greenlee, Jno	200	1	85	10- 7-1780	Carpenters Cr	Withdrawn
Greenlee, Jno	200	1	120	4-24-1781	Carpenters Cr	
Greenlee, Jno	200	1	120	4-24-1781	Carpenters Cr	
Greenlee, Jno	260	2	27	10- 6-1783	——— R	
Greenlee, Mary	200	1	73	6-17-1780	Br Carpenters Cr	
Greenlee, Mary	200	1	73	6-17-1780	Green R	Withdrawn
Greenlee, Mary	60	1	143	7-13-1781	Br Carpenters Cr	
Greenlee, Mary	200	1	143	7-13-1781	Br Green R	
Greenlee, Mary	260	1	143	7-13-1781	Hanging Fk	Withdrawn
Greenlee, Mary	260	1	236	2-14-1782	Hanging Fk	
Greenup, Christopher	250	1	271	6- 5-1782	Big Br	
Greenup, Christopher	100	1	285	7-15-1782	S Fk N Fk Rockcastle	
Greenup, Christopher	150	1	285	7-15-1782	Dix R	
Greenup, Christopher	100	1	293	8- 2-1782	Dix R	
Greenup, Christopher	400	1	293	8- 2-1782	Falling Lick Cr	
Greenup, Christopher	100	1	292	8- 2-1782	Lick Cr	
Greenup, Christopher	400	1	293	8- 2-1782	Falling Lick Cr	
Greenup, Christopher	200	1	320	12-12-1782	Br Rockcastle	
Greenup, Christopher	100	1	399	4-25-1783	Hanging Fk	
Greenup, Christopher	30	1	399	4-25-1783	None	
Greenup, Christopher	50	2	304	3-12-1789	Big Br	
Gresham, Jno	1,666	2	72	3-18-1784	Sturgeon Cr	
Gresham, Thos	400	1	74	6-19-1780	Sugar & Dix	
Greenwood, Saml	500	1	81	8-18-1780	Fks Hunters Trace	Withdrawn
Greenwood, Saml	500	1	305	10- 4-1782	Fks Old Trace	
Griffin & Crow	2,500	2	39	12-15-1783	S Fk 3 Fks Ky R	
Griffin & Crow	2,500	2	39	12-15-1783	S Fk ———	
Griffin & Crow	2,335¾	2	40	12-15-1783	S Fk Ky R	
Grigsby, Nathaniel	2,000	2	73	3-19-1784	E Fk Rockcastle	
Grigsby, Nathaniel	5,187½	2	85	4- 3-1784	Cabbin Cr	Withdrawn
Grigsby, Nathaniel	5,000	2	85	4- 3-1784	Cumberland	Withdrawn
Grigsby, Nathaniel	5,187½	2	263	1-27-1786	Cabbin Cr	
Grigsby, Nathaniel	10,187½	2	264	1-27-1786	Goose Cr	
Grigsby, Nathaniel	5,187½	2	265	1-27-1786	Cumberland R	
Grigsby, Nathaniel	10,187½	2	266	1-27-1786	Goose & Laurel	Surveyed
Griffith, Rev David	2,976	1	241	2-25-1782	Mississippi	
Grisham, Saml	500	1	81	8-18-1780	E Fk Sugar Cr	

Entree	Acres	Book	Page	Entry Date	Watercourse	Notes
Grisham, Thomas	400	1	305	10- 4-1782	Sugar Cr	
Grubb, Haggason	100	1	97	2-28-1781	Tates Cr	
Grubb, Haggason	200	1	126	5-14-1781	Tates Cr	
Grubb, Higgerson	1,000	1	265	5-24-1782	None	
Grubb, Higgerson	1,000	1	266	5-24-1782	Otter Cr	Withdrawn
Grubb, Higgerson	200	1	273	6-12-1782	M Fk 3 Fks Otter Cr	Withdrawn
Grubb, Higgerson	200	1	383	3-18-1783	None	
Grubb, Higgerson	200	1	390	3-24-1783	None	
Grubb, Higgerson	860	2	165	12-11-1784	None	
Grubb, Higgerson	900	2	165	12-11-1784	Ky R	
Grubbs, Higgerson	50	1	337	1-10-1783	None	
Grubbs, Higgerson	1,000	1	337	1-10-1783	Otter Cr	
Grubbs, Higgerson	2,000	1	338	1-10-1783	Muddy Cr	
Grubbs, Higgerson	1,950	1	338	1-10-1783	None	
Grubbs, Higgerson	1,000	1	368	2-19-1783	Otter Cr	
Grubbs, Higgerson	1,000	1	368	2-19-1783	None	Withdrawn
Grubbs, Higgerson	1,000	1	382	3-18-1783	None	
Guerrant, Peter	1,000	1	183	12- 3-1781	Muddy Cr	
Guerrant, Jno	1,000	1	200	12-19-1781	Station Camp & Rockcastle	
Guerrant, Jno	1,000	1	200	12-19-1781	N Fk Rockcastle	Withdrawn
Gunnell, Thos	500	1	79	6-26-1780	Rockcastle	
Gurrant, Jno Jr	1,000	1	384	3-19-1783	Cabbin Cr	
Gurrant, Jno Jr	1,000	1	384	3-19-1783	Br M Fk Ky R	
Gurrant, Jno Jr	1,000	1	384	3-19-1783	M Fk Ky R	
Gurrant, Jno Jr	500	1	385	3-19-1783	M Fk Ky R	
Gurrant, Jno Jr	500	1	385	3-19-1783	M Fk Ky R	
Gurrant, Peter	1,000	2	93	4-22-1784	None	
Gurrent, Jno	1,000	1	207	1- 5-1782	N Fk Rockcastle	
Gurrent, Jno	1,000	1	207	1- 5-1782	N Fk Rockcastle	
Gurrent, Jno	1,000	1	207	1- 5-1782	N Fk Rockcastle	
Hadden, Saml	200	1	164	10-20-1781	Drakes Camp Cr	
Hadden, Saml	100	2	215	5-25-1785	Br Drakes Camp Cr	
Hadden, Saml	27½	2	215	5-25-1785	None	
Hadden, Saml	72½	2	224	6-14-1785	Dix R	
Hadon, Saml	100	1	214	1-11-1782	Drakes Camp Cr	Withdrawn
Halley, Jno	2,534	1	364	2-14-1783	Calloways Cr	
Halley, Jno	200	1	369	2-19-1783	None	
Halley, Jno	200	1	369	2-19-1783	Ky R	
Halley, Jno	400	1	369	2-19-1783	Otter Cr	
Halley, Jno	500	2	72	3-18-1784	Silver Cr	
Halley, Jno	1,056	2	72	3-18-1784	Ky R	
Halley, Jno	500	2	136	8- 3-1784	Ky R	Withdrawn
Halley, Jno	500	2	143	8-23-1784	Ky R	
Halley, Jno	400	2	144	8-24-1784	Otter Cr	
Hally, Jno	1,000	2	19	7-23-1783	Silver Cr	Withdrawn 500 acres
Hall, Jno	1,000	1	128	5-18-1781	Sugar Loaf Lick	
Hall, Jno	100	1	133	5-31-1781	Logans Cr	
Hall, Jno	100	1	17	7-14-1783	None	
Hall, Job	50	2	250	11-26-1785	Salt R	
Hall, Job	50	2	269	2-10-1786	None	Surveyed
Ham, Jas Wm	500	1	74	6-19-1780	Dix R	
Hamberger, Robt	1,000	1	62	6- 1-1780	Dix R	
Hammenly, Wm	350	1	127	5-17-1781	Dix R	Withdrawn
Hammenly, Wm	350	1	385	3-19-1783	None	
Hammenly, Wm	350	1	385	3-19-1783	M Fk Ky R	
Hampton, Andrew	1,000	1	239	2-25-1782	W Fk Sugar Cr	
Hampton, Andrew	1,000	2	42	12-18-1783	None	
Hampton, Andrew	828	2	110	6- 3-1784	Main W Fk Sugar Cr	
Hampton, Andrew	828	2	110	6- 3-1784	Stinking Cr	
Hamilton, Andrew	500	1	73	6-17-1780	Silver Cr	
Hamilton, Arch	350	1	42	5-19-1780	Br Ky R	
Hamilton, Jno	100	1	73	6-17-1780	Muddy Cr	
Hamilton, Wm	500	1	57	5-29-1780	Dix & Ky R	Withdrawn
Hamilton, Wm	500	1	156	8-30-1781	Clarks Run	
Hamilton, Wm	300	1	156	8-30-1781	Main Br Sugar Cr	
Hamilton, Wm	200	1	156	8-30-1781	—— Cr	
Hanna, Andrew	400	1	47	5-23-1780	None	Withdrawn
Hanna, Andrew	1,000	1	95	1-30-1781	Silver Cr	
Hansborough, Keziah	761	2	264	1-27-1786	E Fk N Fk Rockcastle	
Hansborough, Keziah	761½	2	266	1-27-1786	E Fk N Fk Rockcastle	
Hancock, Stephen	200	1	97	2-28-1781	None	
Hancock, Stephen	200	1	203	12-22-1781	Hammons Lick	
Hancock, Wm	250	1	50	5-25-1780	Br Tates Cr	
Hancock, Wm	200	1	95	2-10-1781	None	
Handcock, Stephen	400	1	7	2- 2-1780	Tates Cr	
Handcock, Stephen	50	1	81	8-23-1780	Silver Cr	
Hancock, Stephen	200	2	17	7-14-1783	Silver Cr	••
Handcock, Wm	400	1	6	1-18-1780	Otter & Tates Crs	

Entree	Acres	Book	Page	Entry Date	Watercourse	Notes
Harbeson, Anne	200	2	115	6-11-1784	None	
Harbeson, James	400	1	4	12-27-1779	Chaplins Fk	
Harbeson, Jas	1,000	1	79	6-26-1780	Dix & Ky R	
Harbeson, Jas	600	1	80	6-26-1780	Dix & Ky R	
Harbeson, Jno	1,000	1	179	11-26-1781	Chaplins Fk	
Harbeson, Jas	200	1	323	12-13-1782	None	
Harbeson, Jas	400	2	112	6- 5-1784	E Fk Raccoon Cr	
Hardwitch, Wm	1,000	2	41	12-17-1783	Rowling Fk	
Hardwitch, Wm	1,003¾	2	97	5- 1-1784	1st Br Rowling Fk	Withdrawn
Hardwitch, Wm	270	2	206	4-13-1785	Rowling Fk	
Hardwitch, Wm	1,003¾	2	244	10-11-1785	Br Rowling Fk	
Hardwitch, Wm	500	2	244	10-11-1785	Little S Fk Rowling Fk	
Hardwitch, Wm	100	2	244	10-11-1785	Rowling Fk	
Hariston, Geo	1,737½	2	254	12-19-1785	Rockcastle	
Harlan, Geo	200	2	189	3- 1-1785	None	
Harlan, Geo	200	2	189	3- 1-1785	Rowling Fk	Withdrawn
Harlan, Geo	200	2	249	11-11-1785	Rowling Fk	
Harlan, Geo	200	2	258	1- 9-1786	None	
Harlan, Jacob	400	1	364	2-14-1783	None	
Harlan, Silas	560	1	149	7-31-1781	N Fk Rowling Fk	
Harlan, Thos	1,920	2	307	2-13-1790	Clear Cr	
Hart, David	400	1	11	2-19-1780	Silver Cr	
Hart, David	1,000	1	28	4-29-1780	Silver Cr	
Hart, Jno	400	1	6	1-17-1780	Br Silver Cr	
Hart, Jno	1,000	1	132	5-31-1781	Little Fk Br	Amended
Hart, Jno	1,000	2	7	5-28-1783	Little Fk Br	
Hart, Malcolm	6,000	2	236	8-13-1785	Lick Cr 3 Fks Ky R	
Hart, Malcolm	7,000	2	236	8-13-1785	Lick Cr	
Hart, Malcolm	7,000	2	236	8-13-1785	Lick Cr	
Hart, Nathaniel	400	1	12	2-19-1780	Br Silver Cr	
Hart, Nathaniel	500	1	153	8-20-1781	Tates Bottom	Withdrawn
Hart, Nathaniel	200	1	153	8-20-1781	Ky R	
Hart, Nathaniel	300	1	153	8-20-1781	None	
Hart, Nathaniel	500	1	153	8-20-1781	Br Ky R	Withdrawn
Hart, Nathaniel	1,000	1	153	8-20-1781	——— Cr	Withdrawn
Hart, Nathaniel	2,000	1	153	8-20-1781	Br Ky R	
Hart, Nathaniel	500	1	153	8-20-1781	——— Cr	
Hart, Nathaniel	1,000	1	153	8-20 1781	M Fk Ky R	
Hart, Nathaniel	500	1	153	8-20-1781	Ky R	
Hart, Nathaniel	1,000	1	153	8-20-1781	N Fk Ky R	
Hart, Nathaniel	250	1	154	8-20-1781	Paint Lick	Withdrawn
Hart, Nathaniel	250	1	154	8-20-1781	Paint Lick	
Hart, Nathaniel	250	1	154	8-20-1781	Paint Lick	
Hart, Nathaniel	500	1	162	10-16-1781	Ky R	
Hart, Nathaniel	500	1	163	10-16-1781	Hinds Cr	
Hart, Nathaniel	500	1	163	10-16-1781	Sturgeon Cr	
Hart, Nathaniel	1,000	1	163	10-16-1781	Sturgeon Cr	
Hart, Nathaniel	1,500	1	163	10-16-1781	Calloways Cr	
Hart, Nathaniel	1,400	1	173	11-20-1781	Paint Lick	
Hart, Nathaniel	1,000	1	265	5-24-1784	Br Silver Cr	
Hart, Nathaniel	250	1	278	6-20-1782	None	
Hart, Nathaniel	1,000	1	292	7-30-1782	S Fk Otter Cr	
Hart, Nathaniel	400	1	293	7-30-1782	None	
Hart, Nathaniel	250	1	374	2-25-1783	None	
Hart, Nathaniel	250	1	374	2-25-1783	Silver Cr	
Hart, Thos	1,000	1	55	5-27-1780	Drowning Cr	
Harris, Edward	1,266½	1	377	3- 1-1783	Muddy Cr	
Harris, Edward	1,000	1	377	3- 1-1783	None	
Harris, Edward	400	1	377	3- 1-1783	Otter Cr	
Harris, Frederick	1,000	1	292	7-29-1782	Richland Cr	Surveyed
Harris, Hannah	1,000	1	38	5-17-1780	Br Ky R	
Harris, Jas	200	1	309	11-24-1782	Ky R	
Harris, Jos	200	1	310	11-24-1782	Main Fk Drakes Camp Cr	Withdrawn
Harris, Jas	400	2	23	9-18-1783	Silver Cr	
Harris, Jas	200	2	215	5-25-1785	Drake Camp Cr	
Harris, Joel	500	1	273	6-12-1782	Tates Cr	
Harris, Joel	500	1	274	6-12-1782	M Fk Otter Cr	
Harris, Joel	500	1	370	2-20-1783	Br Drowning Cr	
Harris, Jos	400	1	310	11-24-1782	Silver Cr	
Harris, Jno	5,000	1	328	12-30-1782	Raccoon Cr	
Harris, Jno	6,910	1	328	12-30-1782	Stinking Cr	
Harris, Jno	25,000	1	185	12- 4-1781	None	
Harris, Thos	1,000	1	121	4-28-1781	None	Withdrawn
Harris, Thos	200	1	273	6-12-1782	None	Withdrawn
Harris, Thos	200	1	383	3-18-1783	None	
Harris, Wm B	2,000	1	280	6-28-1782	Ky R	
Harris, Wm B	1,000	1	291	7-29-1782	N Fk Richland Cr	Surveyed
Harris & Minor	1,000	1	292	7-29-1782	Fk Raccoon Spr	
Harrison, Burt	400	1	3	11-11-1779	Sinking Sp	

Entree	Acres	Book	Page	Entry Date	Watercourse	Notes
Harrison, Cuthbert	1,000	2	140	8-12-1784	Falls Lick Cr	
Harrison, Cuthbert	200	2	188	2-28-1785	Silver Cr	
Harrison, Richard	1,000	2	38	11-29-1783	Ky R	
Harrison, Richard	1,000	1	77	6-23-1780	Ky R & Otter Cr	
Harrison, Thos	200	1	390	3-24-1783	Muddy Cr	
Harrison, Thos	1,000	1	155	8-25-1781	None	
Harrison, Thos	1,000	1	155	8-25-1781	Hanging Fk	
Harrison, Wm	300	1	237	2-14-1782	Caseys Cr	Withdrawn
Harrison, Wm	200	1	238	2-14-1782	Br Green R	Withdrawn
Harrison, Wm	200	1	238	2-14-1782	Caseys Cr	Withdrawn
Harrison, Wm	99	1	238	2-14-1782	Green R	Withdrawn
Harrison, Wm	799	1	339	1-11-1783	Caseys Cr	
Harrod, Edward	400	1	69	6-8-1780	Silver Cr	
Harrod, Jas	400	2	2	5-19-1783	Ky R	
Harrod, Jos	1,000	1	105	3-13-1781	None	
Harrod, Thos	400	1	2	11-11-1779	Sinking Br	
Harrods, Jas	1,000	1	45	5-20-1780	Knob Lick	Withdrawn
Harrods, James	1,000	1	104	3-13-1781	Knob Lick	
Harrods, Jos	400	1	109	3-28-1781	Salt R	
Hannon, Valentine	200	1	61	5-31-1780	Hanging Fk	
Hannon, Valentine	500	1	61	5-31-1780	Sugar Cr	
Harranden, Owen	200	1	342	1-23-1783	Drowning Cr	
Harvie, Jno	1,000	1	37	5-15-1780	Shelby Cr	
Harvie, Jno	750	1	306	10-6-1782	Turkey Cr	
Harvie, Jno	750	1	306	10-6-1782	Richland Cr	
Hawkins, Edmond	400	1	299	9-25-1782	Hanging Fk	
Hawkins, Edmund	200	1	38	5-15-1780	Shawnee Run	
Hawkins, Edmund	200	1	84	10-6-1780	N Fk Cedar Cr	Withdrawn
Hawkins & Terrell	1,000	1	119	4-19-1781	None	
Hawkins & Terrell	1,000	1	129	5-18-1781	None	
Hawkins & Terrell	400	1	134	6-12-1781	Gilberts Cr	
Hawkins, Jno	593	2	162	11-30-1784	Raccoon Cr	
Hawley, Jno	6,000	2	33	11-19-1783	Ky R	Withdrawn
Hawley, Jno	6,000	2	34	11-22-1783	Otter Cr	
Hays, Wm	400	1	7	2-3-1780	Silver Cr	
Hays, Wm	400	1	8	2-4-1780	Br Silver Cr	
Hays, Wm	400	1	132	5-31-1781	Otter Cr	
Hays, Wm	1,000	1	272	6-8-1782	Silver Cr	
Head, Jno Alfred	300	1	45	5-22-1780	None	
Headen, Saml	500	1	31	5-9-1780	Ky R	
Headon, Enoch	400	1	76	6-22-1780	Chaplins Fk	
Heard, Jno Jr	140	1	329	12-30-1782	—— R	Withdrawn
Heard, Jno Jr	140	1	350	1-29-1783	None	
Hedges, Josiah	400	2	128	7-16-1784	Rowling Fk	
Helm, Joseph	250	1	57	5-29-1780	Benson Cr	
Helm, Joseph	400	1	57	5-29-1780	S Fk Benson Cr	
Helm, Margiss	400	1	67	6-8-1780	Br Green R	
Helm, Margiss	1,000	1	67	6-8-1780	Br Green R	
Henderson, Alexander	——	1	86	10-17-1780	Paint Lick	Withdrawn
Henderson, Alexander	200	1	125	5-12-1781	Paint Lick	Withdrawn
Henderson, Alexander	200	1	125	5-12-1781	Br Paint Lick	
Henderson, Andrew	150	1	86	10-19-1780	Paint Lick	Withdrawn
Henderson, Andrew	100	1	86	10-19-1780	Paint Lick	Withdrawn
Henderson, Andrew	150	1	125	5-12-1781	Paint Lick	Withdrawn
Henderson, Andrew	100	1	125	5-12-1781	—— Cr	Withdrawn
Henderson, Andrew	250	1	125	5-12-1781	Paint Lick	Amended
Henderson, Jas	300	1	178	11-24-1781	Paint Lick	Withdrawn
Henderson, Jas	200	1	178	11-24-1781	None	Withdrawn
Henderson, Jno	1,000	1	77	6-23-1780	Silver Cr	
Henderson, Richard	400	1	10	2-9-1780	Otter Cr	
Henderson, Richard	400	1	13	2-21-1780	Otter Cr	
Henderson, Richard	1,000	1	77	6-23-1780	Otter Cr	
Henderson, Richard	1,000	1	77	6-23-1780	Otter Cr	
Henderson, Robt	200	1	178	11-24-1781	Paint Lick	
Henderson, Robt	200	1	216	1-19-1782	Paint Lick	Amended
Henderson, Robt	50	1	216	1-19-1782	Br Paint Lick	
Henderson, Robt	150	1	226	1-29-1782	Paint Lick	
Henderson, Robt	150	1	226	1-29-1782	Paint Lick	
Henderson, Robt	200	1	279	6-26-1782	Br Paint Lick	
Henderson, Robt	300	1	279	6-26-1782	Paint Lick	Withdrawn
Henderson, Robt	300	1	297	9-7-1782	Paint Lick	
Henderson, Robt	200	1	298	9-21-1782	Paint Lick	
Henderson, Robt	250	1	308	10-10-1782	Drowning Cr	Withdrawn
Henderson, Robt	250	1	373	2-25-1783	Drowning Cr	
Henderson, Robt	250	1	373	2-25-1783	Paint Lick	
Henderson, Robt	1,284½	1	373	2-25-1783	Paint Lick	Withdrawn
Henderson, Robt	400	1	373	2-25-1783	Paint Lick	
Henderson, Robt	250	1	86	10-19-1780	Paint Lick	
Henderson, Robt	125	1	125	5-11-1781	Paint Lick	Withdrawn
Henderson, Robt	125	1	125	5-12-1781	Paint Lick	
Henderson, Robt	123	1	131	5-22-1781	Paint Lick	
Henderson, Robt	125	1	131	5-23-1781	Paint Lick	

Entree	Acres	Book	Page	Entry Date	Watercourse	Notes
Henderson, Robt	250	1	155	8-20-1781	Paint Lick	
Henderson, Andrew	250	2	52	1-27-1784	None	
Henderson, Jos	300	2	144	8-23-1784	None	
Henderson, Jos	200	2	144	8-23-1784	None	
Henderson, Robt	600	1	374	2-25-1783	Silver Cr	
Henderson, Robt	100	2	2	5-15-1783	——— R	
Henderson, Robt	250	2	52	1-27-1784	Lick Cr	
Henderson, Robt	100	2	55	2- 4-1784	Paint Lick	
Henderson, Robt	100	2	55	2- 4-1784	——— Cr	
Henderson, Robt	300	2	66	3- 4-1784	None	
Henderson, Robt	200	2	66	3- 4-1784	Paint Lick	
Henderson, Robt	1,284½	2	107	6- 2-1784	M Paint Lick	
Henderson, Robt	300	2	107	6- 2-1784	Back Cr	
Henderson, Robt	250	2	107	6- 2-1784	Paint Lick Cr	
Henderson, Robt	450	2	108	6- 2-1784	Paint Lick	Amended
Henderson, Robt	100	2	108	6- 2-1784	Paint Lick	
Henderson, Robt	184½	2	108	6- 2-1784	Paint Lick	Withdrawn
Henderson, Robt	200	2	109	6- 2-1784	None	
Henderson, Robt	200	2	109	6- 2-1784	None	
Henderson, Robt	184½	2	128	7-14-1784	None	
Henderson, Robt	160	2	128	7-14-1784	Back Cr	Withdrawn
Henderson, Robt	400	2	130	7-24-1784	Paint Lick	
Henderson, Robt	40	2	133	7-30-1784	None	
Henderson, Robt	120	2	134	8- 2-1784	None	
Henderson, Robt	50	2	134	8- 2-1784	Lick Cr	
Henderson, Robt	1,000	2	134	8- 2-1784	None	
Henderson, Robt	370	2	135	8- 2-1784	Paint Lick	
Henderson, Robt	160	2	144	8-23-1784	Back Cr	
Henderson, Robt	130	2	144	8-23-1784	Paint Lick	
Henderson, Robt	450	2	144	8-24-1784	None	
Henderson, Robt	200	2	144	8-24-1784	Paint Lick	
Henderson, Robt	100	2	176	1-20-1785	E Fk Town Fk	
Henderson, Robt	150	2	198	3-25-1785	None	
Henderson, Robt	150	2	198	3-25-1785	Silver Cr	
Henderson, Robt	150	2	223	6- 9-1785	None	
Henderson, Robt	6,450	2	223	6- 9-1785	Copperas Lick	
Henderson, Robt	350	2	228	7-12-1785	None	
Henderson, Robt	200	2	228	7-14-1785	Paint Lick	
Henderson, Robt	150	2	229	7-14-1785	Paint Lick	
Henderson, Robt	30	2	279	6- 8-1786	Main Paint Lick	
Henderson & Jones	1,396½	2	155	10-27-1784	S Fk Sturgeon Cr	
Henry, Daniel	569½	1	351	1-30-1783	Chaplins Fk	
Henry, Saml	200	1	268	5-28-1782	Doctors Fk	
Henry, Saml	200	1	314	12- 4-1782	None	
Henry, Samuel	400	1	314	12- 4-1782	None	
Henry, Patrick	500	1	333	1- 4-1783	Cumberland Trace	
Henry, Patrick	500	1	333	1- 4-1783	Co Line	
Henry, Patrick	500	1	333	1- 4-1783	Co Line	
Henry, Wm	300	1	351	1-30-1783	None	
Henry, Wm	339	1	351	1-30-1783	Chaplins Fk	
Henry, Wm	200	1	325	12-23-1782	S Fk Doctors Fk	Withdrawn
Henry, Wm	300	1	328	12-28-1782	None	Withdrawn
Henry, Wm	200	2	96	4-24-1784	None	
Henry, Wm	200	2	96	4-27-1784	None	
Henry, Wm	8,000	2	97	4-29-1784	Laurel R	Withdrawn
Henry, Wm	8,000	2	175	1-14-1785	Laurel R	
Henry, Wm	3,000	2	262	1-27-1786	Green R	Surveyed
Herrold, Robt	300	1	235	2-14-1782	Green R	
Herrold, Robt	400	1	372	2-20-1783	Rowling Fk	
Hiatt, Jno	500	1	117	4-19-1781	Tates Cr	
Hicks, Wm	400	1	6	1-17-1780	Silver Cr	
Hicks, Wm	1,000	1	295	8-12-1782	Silver Cr	
Hickerson, Jno	400	1	238	2-19-1782	Green R	
Hickman, Wm	1,525½	2	93	4-22-1784	Ky R	
Higgins, Aaron	1,000	2	203	3-30-1785	Station Camp	
Higgins, Aaron	514	2	211	4-28-1785	Silver Cr	
Higgins, Henry	400	1	15	3- 2-1780	Harrods Landing	
Higgins, Henry	1,000	1	163	10-16-1781	Chaplins Fk	
Higgins, Peter	400	1	16	3- 2-1780	Harrodsburg Ldg	
Higgins, Peter	200	1	61	5-31-1780	Whitleys Cr	
Higgins, Peter	1,000	2	34	11-22-1783	None	Amended
Higgins, Peter	1,000	2	77	3-27-1784	None	
Higgins, Peter	668	2	78	3-27-1784	None	
Hill, Robt	383	2	221	6- 1-1785	Buck Cr	
Hill, Robt	200	2	221	6- 1-1785	Dix R	
Hinds, Jas	250	1	143	7-14-1781	Dix R	
Hinds, Jas	250	1	143	7-14-1781	None	Withdrawn
Hinds, Jas	250	1	291	7-29-1782	——— R	
Hinds, Jas	131	1	295	8-13-1782	Dix R	
Hinds, Jas	506	2	179	1-25-1785	Rockcastle	
Hinds, Jas	506	2	180	1-25-1785	None	
Hines, Andrew	25	1	26	4-28-1780	Benson Cr	

Entree	Acres	Book	Page	Entry Date	Watercourse	Notes
Hines, Jas	250	1	295	8-13-1782	None	
Hines, Jas	381	1	295	8-13-1782	Dix R	
Hite, Abraham	200	1	90	10-30-1780	Harrodsburg	
Hite, Abraham	500	1	90	10-31-1780	Salt R	Withdrawn
Hite, Abraham	500	1	155	8-24-1781	Salt R	
Hite, Abraham Sr	300	1	155	8-24 1781	Salt R	
Hite, Abraham Sr	300	2	157	11- 2-1784	Salt R	
Hite, Abraham	400	2	225	6-20-1785	Haydens Lick	
Hite, Abraham	600	1	191	12-14-1781	Salt R	
Hite, Isaac	400	1	12	2-21-1780	Harrodsburg	
Hite, Isaac	400	1	13	2-21-1780	Town Fk Salt R	
Hite, Isaac Sr	1,000	1	24	4-26-1780	None	
Hite, Isaac	500	1	25	4-27-1780	Fk Dix R	
Hite, Isaac	1,000	1	31	5-10-1780	Cane Run	
Hite, Isaac	2,000	1	31	5-10-1780	Dix R	
Hite, Isaac	2,000	1	31	5-10-1780	Hanging Fk	
Hite, Isaac	1,000	1	31	5-10-1780	Dix R	
Hite, Isaac	2,000	1	31	5-10-1780	Skeggs Cr	
Hite, Isaac	2,000	1	31	5-10-1780	Harrodsburg	
Hite, Isaac	1,000	1	31	5-10-1780	Harrods Run	Withdrawn
Hite, Isaac	1,000	1	31	5-10-1780	Hanging Fk	
Hite, Isaac	112	2	74	3-22-1784	Rockcastle	
Hite, Isaac	112	2	74	3-22-1784	Dix R	
Hite, Isaac	——	2	83	3-31-1784	Salt R	
Hodges, Daniel	938¼	2	161	11-24-1784	None	
Hodges, Jesse	112	1	70	6- 9-1780	Drowning Cr	
Hodges, Jesse	300	1	292	7-30-1782	Rocky Sp	
Hodges, Jesse	200	1	292	7-30-1782	None	
Hodges, Sarah & Mary	200	1	96	2-21-1781	Salt R	
Hogan, Jas	100	1	193	12-14-1781	Ky R	
Hogan, Jas	1,000	1	317	12- 9-1782	Ky R	Withdrawn
Hogan, Jos	100	1	318	12- 9-1782	White Oak Cr	
Hogan, Jos	1,000	2	3	5-21-1783	Rockcastle	
Hogan, Joseph	400	1	229	1- 6-1782	Br Dix R	Withdrawn
Hogan, Joseph	400	1	317	12- 7-1782	None	
Hogan, Wm	100	1	158	9- 5-1781	White Oak Cr	
Holder, Jno	1,000	1	337	1-10-1783	Silver Cr	
Holder, Jno	400	1	59	5-30-1780	Silver Cr	
Holliday, Wm	400	1	59	5-30-1780	None	
Hollingsworth, Jesse	2,000	2	159	11-17-1784	Mississippi R	
Hollingsworth, Jesse	2,000	1	226	1-29-1782	Carolina Line	Withdrawn
Holloway, Geo	200	2	33	11-19-1783	Cedar Cr	
Holtslaw, Jacob	400	1	9	2- 8-1780	Dix R	
Hoomes, Jno	10,000	1	294	8- 6-1782	Hammons Cr	
Hoomes, Jno	7,187	1	294	8- 6-1782	Salt R	
Hope, Richard & Adam	500	1	56	5-29-1780	Chaplins Cr	
Hord, Jas	325	1	133	6- 2-1781	Br Falls Trace	Withdrawn
Hord, Jas & Jno	1,443	1	312	12- 2-1782	Fk Dix R	Withdrawn
Hord, Jas & Jno	1,443	1	362	2-12-1783	Fk Dix R	
Hord, Jas	325	2	186	2-22-1785	Falls Trace	
Hord, Mordicai	8,593	2	254	12-19-1785	Rockcastle	
Hord, Mordeca	100	1	38	5-15-1780	Cumberland R	
Howe, Jno Wm	200	1	233	2-13-1782	Br M Fk Sugar Cr	
Howe, Jno Wm	100	1	233	2-13-1782	3 Fks Sugar Cr	Withdrawn
Howe, Jno Wm	100	1	244	3- 5-1782	M Fk Sugar Cr	Withdrawn
Howe, Jno Wm	300	1	269	6- 3-1782	Br Sugar Cr	Withdrawn
Howe, Jno Wm	200	2	10	6-17-1783	None	
Howe, Jno Wm	100	2	67	3-10-1784	M Fk Sugar Cr	Withdrawn
Howe, Jno Wm	300	2	185	2-19-1785	Br Sugar Cr	
Howe, Jno Wm	210	2	185	2-19-1785	None	
Howe, Jno Wm	30	2	185	2-19-1785	Boones Mill & Sugar Crs	
Howe, Jno Wm	100	2	286	10- 2-1786	Sugar Cr	
Hoye, Wm	1,000	1	69	6- 9-1780	Otter & Silver Cr	
Hoy, Wm	200	1	95	2-10-1781	Tates Cr	Withdrawn
Hoy, Wm	250	1	124	5- 7-1781	Tates Cr	
Hoy, Wm	200	1	124	5- 7-1781	Tates Cr	
Hoy, Wm	400	1	128	5-18-1781	Tates Cr	
Hoy, Wm	500	1	142	7-13-1781	Ky R	
Hoy, Wm	400	1	149	7-30-1781	Otter Cr	
Hoy, Wm	200	1	149	7-30-1781	Otter Cr	
Hoy, Wm	758	1	212	1- 9-1782	Muddy Cr	
Hoy, Wm	500	1	273	6- 8-1782	Otter Cr	
Hoy, Wm	400	1	303	10- 2-1782	M Fk Woods Fk	Withdrawn
Hoy, Wm	1,400	2	154	10-27-1784	Otter Cr	Withdrawn
Hoy, Wm	1,400	2	154	10-27-1784	Silver Cr	
Hoy, Wm	1,400	2	154	10-27-1784	Boonesboro	
Hoy, Wm	1,300	2	155	10-27-1784	Silver Cr	
Hoy, Wm	5,500	2	177	1-22-1785	None	
Hoy, Wm	400	2	236	8-10-1785	N Fk Woods Fk	
Hoy, Wm	100	2	270	2-25-1786	Otter Cr	
Hoy, Wm	50	2	270	2-25-1786	Tates Cr	

Entree	Acres	Book	Page	Entry Date	Watercourse	Notes
Hoy, Wm	100	2	270	2-25-1786	None	
Hoy, Wm	50	2	319	2-25-1786	Tates Cr	
Hudgens, Jas	600	1	67	6- 8-1780	Glovers Station	
Hudgens, Jno	200	1	67	6- 8-1780	Green R	
Hudson, Jno	656½	2	161	11-24-1784	None	
Hudson, Stevenson	400	1	53	5-26-1780	Carpenters Cr	Amended
Hudson, Wm	400	1	16	3- 7-1780	Paint Lick Cr	
Hudson, Wm	1,000	1	29	4-29-1780	Paint Lick Cr	
Hudson, Wm	500	1	49	5-23-1780	——— Cr	
Huffman, Philip	500	1	49	5-24-1780	——— Cr	
Huffman, Philip	500	1	62	6- 1-1780	Cane Run	
Huffman, Philip	500	1	62	6- 1-1780	Wilson Cr	
Hughes, Abraham	200	2	215	5-25-1785	Drakes Camp Cr	
Hughes, Jesse	400	1	317	12- 7-1782	Caseys Cr & Green R	
Hughes, Joseph	1,000	1	84	10- 7-1780	——— R	
Hughes, Joseph	1,000	1	115	4-13-1781	None	
Hughes, Jos	1,000	2	111	6- 3-1784	Sturgeon Cr	
Hughes, Thos	11,386¼	2	122	6-28-1784	Rockcastle	
Humphry, Thos	424	2	188	2-28-1785	Station Camp Cr	
Humphry, Abnor	5,437¼	2	188	2-28-1785	Silver Cr	
Hundley, Anthony	30,879	2	226	6-27-1785	Rockcastle	
Hurley, Thos	400	2	294	11-30-1787	Green R	Surveyed
Huston, Geo	923½	2	170	12-18-1784	Scaggs Cr	
Huston, Nathaniel	150	1	174	11-20-1781	Flat Lick Br	
Huston, Nathaniel	250	1	352	2- 1-1783	None	
Huston, Stephenson	400	1	53	5-26-1780	Green R	
Huston, Stevenson	400	2	13	6-20-1783	Carpenters Cr	
Huston, Stephen	200	1	299	9-24-1782	Carpenters Cr	Withdrawn
Huston, Stephenson	200	1	390	3-24-1783	Green R	
Huston, Stephenson	200	2	206	4-18-1785	Carpenters Cr	
Huston, Stephenson	200	2	206	4-18-1785	Rowling Fk	Surveyed
Hutching, Thos	200	1	195	12-17-1781	None	
Hutching, Thos	60	1	243	3- 4-1782	Whitleys Cr	
Hutching, Thos	100	1	333	1- 4-1783	Rock Lick	
Hutching & Pritchell	500	1	335	1- 6-1783	Mud Lick	Surveyed
Hutchings, Thos	300	1	195	12-17-1781	Logans Cr	
Hutchings, Thos	300	1	195	12-17-1781	Masons Cr	
Hutchings, Thos	100	1	333	1- 4-1783	None	
Hutchings, Thos	100	1	391	3-24-1783	Whitleys Cr	
Hutchings & Boss	300	1	335	1- 6-1783	None	
Hutchings & Clark	750	1	335	1- 6-1783	E Fk Barneys Br	
Hutchings & Duberry	500	1	335	1- 6-1783	Br Scaggs Cr	
Hutchings & Durley	500	1	335	1- 6-1783	Br Green R	
Hutton, Jos	325	2	15	7- 2-1783	None	
Hutton, Samuel	200	1	84	10- 4-1780	Ky R	
Inglish, Chas	400	1	66	6- 3-1780	Dix R	
Inglish, Chas	250	1	66	6- 3-1780	Rockcastle	
Inglish, Chas	250	1	66	6- 3-1780	Dix R	
Inglish, Chas	50	1	84	10- 4-1780	Bennet Meadow	Withdrawn
Inglish, Chas	84	1	104	3-13-1781	Dix R	
Inglish, Chas	84	1	104	3-13-1781	Rockcastle	
Inglish, Chas	84	1	127	5-18-1781	Rockcastle	
Inglish, Chas	84	1	127	5-18-1781	Rockcastle	
Inglish, Chas	50	1	127	5-18-1781	None	
Inglish, Chas	50	1	127	5-18-1781	Dix R	
Ingram, Saml	400	1	12	2-19-1780	M Fk Shawnee	
Irvin, Christopher	1,000	2	7	5-28-1783	Tates Cr	
Irvin, David	1,113¼	2	6	5-28-1783	Muddy Cr	
Irvin, David	1,000	2	6	5-28-1783	None	
Irvin, Magdolen	200	2	24	9-20-1783	Taylor Fk Silver Cr	
Irvin, Wm	400	2	232	7-23-1785	Drowning Cr	
Irwin, Abraham	500	1	32	5-11-1780	Harrods Run	Withdrawn
Irwin, Abraham	500	1	301	9-27-1782	Harrods Run	
Irwin, Christopher	1,000	1	64	6- 2-1780	Silver Cr	
Irwin, Christopher	500	1	64	6- 2-1780	None	
Irwin, Christopher Jr	400	1	7	2- 4-1780	Fk Tates Cr	
Irwin, Christopher Jr	1,000	1	59	5-30-1780	None	Amended
Irwin, Christopher Sr	1,000	1	59	5-30-1780	3 Fks Otter Cr	
Irwin, Christopher Sr	300	2	25	9-20-1783	None	
Irwin, Elizabeth	400	1	301	9-27-1782	Harrods Run	
Irwin, Elizabeth	400	1	37	5-15-1780	Haines Run	Withdrawn
Irwin, Margaret	150	1	98	2-28-1781	Town Fk	
Isaac, Jno	400	1	14	2-21-1780	Wilsons Run	
Isaac, Jno	1,000	1	204	12-22-1781	Wilsons Run	
Isaac, Jno	1,000	2	281	6-27-1786	None	
Isaacs, Jno	1,000	2	304	2- 6-1789	Knob Lick	
Jackman, Burwell	8,791	2	155	10-27-1784	Ky R	
Jackman, Richard	856	2	250	11-30-1785	Dix R	
Jackman, Jno	400	1	15	2-26-1780	Elkhorn Cr	
Jackman, Jno	270	1	275	6-13-1782	None	
Jackman, Jno	730	1	275	6-13-1782	None	

Entree	Acres	Book	Page	Entry Date	Watercourse	Notes
Jackman, Richard	400	1	15	2-26-1780	Dix R	
Jackman, Richard	600	1	70	6-10-1780	Hanging Fk	
Jackman, Richard	400	1	127	5-17-1781	Hanging Fk	
Jackman, Richard	400	1	131	5-22-1781	Hanging Fk	Withdrawn
Jackman, Richard	400	1	131	5-22-1781	None	Withdrawn
Jackman, Richard	400	1	158	9- 3-1781	None	
Jackman, Richard	400	1	158	9- 4-1781	None	
Jackman, Richard	150	1	169	11-10-1781	Dix R	Amended
Jackman, Richard	200	1	274	6-13-1782	Dix R	
Jackman, Richard	200	1	274	6-13-1782	Dix R	
Jackman, Richard	100	1	321	12-13-1782	Dix R	
Jackman, Richard	150	1	398	4-21-1783	——— R	
Jackman, Richard	150	2	162	11-25-1784	None	
Jackman, Richard	204¾	2	171	12-18-1784	Ky R	
Jackman, Richard	70	2	247	10-21-1785	Dix R	
Jackman, Richard	30	2	247	10-31-1785	Dix R	
Jackman, Wm.	400	1	135	5-18-1780	Elkhorn	
Jackson, Jno	150	1	98	2-28-1781	Main Silver Cr	
Jackson, Jno	45	1	289	7-22-1782	Silver Cr	
Jackson. Jno	55	2	1	5- 8-1783	Mulberry Lick	Withdrawn
Jackson, Jno	55	2	167	12-11-1784	Mulberry Lick	
Jackson, Jno	55	2	167	12-11-1784	None	
Jacobs, Jno	600	1	182	12- 2-1781	Paint Lick	
Jacobs, Jno	400	1	182	12- 2-1781	Paint Lick	
James, Abraham	400	1	13	2-21-1780	Hanging Fk	
James, Abraham	1,000	1	60	5-30-1780	None	
James, Geo	1,000	1	355	2- 4-1783	S Fk Cumberland R	
James, Geo	3,800	2	68	3-16-1784	Chaplins Fk	Amended
James, Geo	3,000	2	69	3-16-1784	None	Withdrawn
James, Geo	3,000	2	69	3-16-1784	None	1,500 acres withdrawn
James, Geo	1,000	2	69	3-16-1784	Chaplins Fk	
James, Geo	1,000	2	60	3-16-1784	Chaplins Fk	Withdrawn
James, Geo	1,200	2	69	3-16-1784	Chaplins Fk	974 acres withdrawn
James, Geo	1,300	2	90	4-16-1784	Glenns Cr	
James, Geo	3,800	2	106	5-28-1784	Chaplins Fk	
James, Geo	226	2	114	6- 9-1784	Powells Trace	
James, Geo	1,000	2	123	6-29-1784	Chaplins Fk	
James, Geo	974	2	123	6-29-1784	Powells Trace	
James, Geo	1,000	2	123	6-29-1784	Rowling Fk	
James, Geo	974	2	123	6-29-1784	None	
James, Geo	500	2	214	5-20-1785	Cumberland R	
James, Geo	200	2	230	7-14-1785	Chaplins Fk	
James, Geo	3,800	2	230	7-14-1785	Chaplins Fk	
James, Geo	20,000	2	234	8- 2-1785	Cumberland R	Withdrawn
James, Geo	80,000	2	234	8- 2-1785	Adj Benj Say	Amended & withdrawn
James, Geo	80,000	2	239	8-19-1785	Adj Benj Say	Withdrawn
James, Geo	1,000	2	243	10- 7-1785	Rowling Fk	
James, Geo	1,500	2	243	10- 7-1785	Chaplins Fk	
James, Geo	1,500	2	243	10- 7-1785	Rowling Fk	
James, Geo	80,000	2	244	10-11-1785	Adj Benj Say	
James, Geo	20,000	2	246	10-21-1785	Cumberland R	
James, Geo	14,000	2	246	10-21-1785	Rowling Fk	Surveyed
James, Geo	3,000	2	246	10-21-1785	None	Surveyed
James, Geo	3,000	2	247	10-21-1785	Rowling Fk	Surveyed
James, Geo	200	1	166	10-30-1781	None	
James, Joseph	1,000	1	60	5-30-1780	None	
James, Wm	542	1	156	8-30-1781	White Oak Cr	
James, Wm	542	1	157	8-30-1781	E Fk Sugar Cr	
Jameson, David	400	1	107	3-26-1781	W Fk Hammons Cr	Withdrawn
Jameson, David	400	1	108	3-26-1781	Salt R	
Jameson, David	400	1	163	10-17-1781	W Fk Hammons Cr	
Jameson, David	400	1	163	10-17-1781	Richland Cr	
Jenkins, Jas	12,000	2	142	8-19-1784	None	
Jenkins, Jas	38,000	2	143	8-19-1784	Ky R	
Johnson, Cave	1,000	2	163	12- 6-1784	Stone Lick Cr	
Johnson, Christopher	260	1	106	3-19-1781	None	
Johnson, Christopher	300	1	106	3-19-1781	M Fk Rowling Fk	Withdrawn
Johnson, Christopher	300	1	109	3-28-1781	M Fk Rowling Fk	
Johnson, Isaac	400	1	72	6-17-1780	Silver Cr	
Johnson, Jacob	200	1	123	5- 1-1781	Manns Cr	Withdrawn
Johnson, Jacob	200	2	263	1-27-1786	Manns Cr	
Johnson, Lewis	700	1	35	5-12-1780	Dix R	
Johnson, Thos	1,000	1	78	6-23-1780	Shawnee & Ky R	
Johnson, Zachariah	200	1	148	7-23-1781	Dix R	Withdrawn
Johnson, Zachariah	200	1	164	10-20-1781	Dix R	

Entree	Acres	Book	Page	Entry Date	Watercourse	Notes
Johnson, Christopher ..	500	1	181	12– 1–1781	None	
Johnson, Wm	1,000	2	269	2–10–1786	None	Withdrawn
Johnson, Wm	1,000	2	283	7–13–1786	None	
Johnson & Rhea	2,000	2	106	5–28–1784	Cane Cr	Surveyed
Jones, Foster	250	2	193	3–12–1785	S Fk Station Camp & Rockcastle	
Jones, Gus G	400	1	3	11–15–1779	Dix R	
Jones, Jno	100	1	171	11–19–1781	None	
Jones, Jno	100	1	171	11–19–1781	None	
Jones, Jno	———	2	23	9– 6–1783	None	
Jones, Jno	100	2	23	9– 6–1783	None	
Jones, Jno	16,000	2	79	3–29–1784	S Side Ky R	
Jones, Judith	819	2	64	3– 3–1784	None	
Jones, Robt	3,000	2	202	3–28–1785	Salt R	
Jones, Robt	2,000	2	212	5– 5–1785	None	Withdrawn
Jones, Robt	2,000	2	275	5– 3–1786	Scaggs Cr	Surveyed
Jones, Travis	500	1	45	5–22–1780	Br Hanging Fk	
Jones, Wilson	542	1	84	10– 2–1780	White Oak Cr	Withdrawn
Jones, Wm & Churchill .:	700	1	51	5–25–1780	Fk Salt R	
Jones, Wm & Churchill	300	1	51	5–25–1780	Fk Ky R	
Jones & Blancher	1,900	2	79	3–29–1784	Ky R	
Jones & Henderson	1,396½	2	155	10–27–1784	S Fk Sturgeon Cr	
Jordan, Wm	1,525	2	155	10–27–1784	Ky R	
Kavanaugh, Chas	400	1	318	12– 9–1782	Ky R	
Kavanaugh, Wm	150	1	191	12–14–1781	Dix R	
Kelbreath, Evan	1,000	1	113	4– 2–1781	Hanging Fk	
Kelley, David	407	1	88	10–25–1780	Falling Sp Br	
Kelley, Emanuel	1,000	1	277	6–20–1782	Otter Cr	
Kelley, Emanuel	1,000	1	328	12–30–1782	Silver Cr	Withdrawn
Kelley, Emanuel	1,000	1	328	12–30–1782	Trace	Withdrawn
Kelley, Emanuel	1,000	1	345	1–24–1783	Silver Cr	
Kelley, Emanuel	1,000	1	345	1–24–1783	Trace	
Kelley, Emanuel	1,000	2	274	4–10–1786	Otter Cr	
Kendricks, Solomon	400	1	78	6–24–1780	Silver Cr	
Kennady, Jno	50	1	17	4–19–1780	Silver Cr	
Kennady, Jno	1,000	1	21	4–26–1780	Kennadys Fk	
Kennady, Jno	100	1	21	4–26–1780	Kennadys Fk	Withdrawn
Kennady, Jno	1,000	1	21	4–26–1780	White Lick Fk	
Kennady, Jno	1,000	1	22	4–26–1780	Silver Cr	
Kennady, Jno	600	1	22	4–26–1780	Cedar Cr	
Kennady, Jno	1,000	1	22	4–26–1780	Dix R	
Kennady, Jno	50	1	48	5–23–1780	Harmons Lick	
Kennady, Jno	100	1	64	6– 2–1780	Paint Lick	
Kennady, Jno	200	1	64	6– 2–1780	Paint Lick	
Kennady, Jno	500	1	64	6– 2–1780	Drakes Camp Cr	
Kennady, Jno	500	1	65	6– 2–1780	Paint Lick	
Kennady, Jno	200	1	65	6– 3–1780	Br Paint Lick	
Kennady, Jno	200	1	65	6– 3–1780	Meadow Fk	
Kennady, Jno	50	1	65	6– 3–1780	Hammons Lick	
Kennady, Jno	200	1	65	6– 3–1780	Silver Cr	
Kennady, Jno	200	1	83	9–29–1780	Silver Cr	
Kennady, Jno	250	1	86	10–19–1780	Paint Lick	
Kennady, Jno	1,000	1	89	10–27–1780	None	
Kennady, Jno	250	1	90	10–31–1780	White Lick Fk	
Kennady, Jno	300	1	90	10–31–1780	Silver Cr	
Kennady, Jno Jr	———	1	5	1–10–1780	Kennadys Fk Paint Lick	
Kennady, Jno Jr	400	1	5	1–10–1780	Kennadys Fk Paint Lick	
Kennady, Jno Jr	400	1	6	1–15–1780	E Br Paint Lick Cr	
Kennady, Jno Sr	400	1	5	1–10–1780	Silver Cr	
Kennady, Jno Sr	500	1	22	4–26–1780	Silver Cr	
Kennady, Jno Sr	500	1	22	4–26–1780	Silver Cr	
Kennady, Joseph	400	1	3	11–25–1779	Silver Cr	
Kennady, Thos	350	2	158	11– 9–1784	Elk Garden	Withdrawn
Kennady, Thos	250	2	158	11– 9–1784	None	
Kennady, Thos	350	2	202	3–30–1785	Elk Garden	
Kennady, Thos	250	2	203	3–30–1785	None	
Kennady, Thos	500	2	203	3–30–1785	Paint Lick	100 acres withdrawn
Kennady, Thos	1,000	2	274	4–10–1786	Paint Lick	Surveyed
Kennady, Thos	100	2	277	5– 4–1786	Paint Lick	
Kennady, Wm	300	1	40	5–18–1780	Chaplins Fk	
Kennady, Wm	1,000	1	263	5–15–1782	Chaplins Fk	
Kennady & McJenny	1,884½	2	228	6–27–1785	Green R	
Kennady & McJenny	1,500	2	227	6–27–1785	Green R	
Kenton, Simon	200	1	83	9–19–1780	None	
Kenton, Simon	400	1	98	3– 3–1781	None	
Kenton, Simon	600	1	107	3–25–1781	None	
Kenton, Simon	300	1	109	3–30–1781	None	

Entree	Acres	Book	Page	Entry Date	Watercourse	Notes
Kenton, Simon	400	1	121	4-28-1781	Chaplins Fk	Withdrawn
Kenton, Simon	400	1	147	7-18-1781	Chaplins Fk	
Kenton, Simon	200	1	157	8-30-1781	None	
Kenton, Simon	500	1	177	11-24-1781	None	
Kenton, Simon	152½	1	394	4- 7-1783	None	
Kenton, Simon	152½	1	394	4- 7-1783	None	
Kenton, Simon	500	2	269	2-25-1786	——— Cr	
Keys, Geo	300	1	173	11-20-1781	Sugar Cr	
Kincannon, Andrew	1,000	1	139	6-20-1781	Silver Cr	
Kincannon, Andrew	400	1	139	6-20-1781	——— Cr	
Kincannon, Andrew	400	1	139	6-20-1781	Silver Cr	
Kinkead, Andrew	50	1	113	4- 2-1781	Dix R	
Kinkead, Andrew	150	1	46	5-22--1780	Br Dix R	
Kinkead, Andrew	100	1	58	5-30-1780	None	
Kinkead, Jno	1,000	1	49	5-24-1780	Knob Lick Road	Withdrawn
Kinkead, Jno	50	1	58	5-30-1780	Dix R	
Kinkead, Jno	400	1	83	9-23-1780	Silver Cr	
Kinkead, Jno	1,000	1	96	2-24-1781	Knob Lick Road	
Kinkead, Jno	300	1	96	2-24-1781	None	
Kinkead, Jno	300	1	97	2-24-1781	Salt R	
Kinkead, Jno	400	1	97	2-24-1781	Salt R	
Kinkead, Jno	50	1	113	4- 2-1781	Dix R	
Kinkead, Robt	100	1	46	5-22-1780	Br Paint Lick	
Kinkead, Robt	50	1	254	3-30-1782	Paint Lick Cr	
Kinkead, Thos	150	1	46	5-22-1780	Paint Lick Cr	
Kinkead, Wm	50	1	27	4-29-1780	Br Paint Lick	
Kinkead, Wm	250	1	46	5-22-1780	Paint Lick Cr	
Kinkead, Wm	100	1	46	5-22-1780	Br Dix R	
Kinkead, Wm	250	2	57	2-12-1784	Salt & Dix R	
Kirkham, Saml	400	1	83	9-19-1780	Quicks Cr	
Kirkham, Saml	200	1	157	8-30-1781	Dix R	Withdrawn
Kirkham, Saml	300	1	176	11-23-1781	None	
Kirkham, Saml	100	1	180	12- 1-1781	None	Withdrawn
Kirkham, Saml	100	1	230	2- 9-1782	None	
Kirkham, Saml	100	1	266	5-27-1782	None	
Kirkham, Saml	100	1	266	5-27-1782	Sugar Loaf Cr	
Kirkham, Saml	300	1	359	2-10-1783	Dix R	Withdrawn
Kirkham, Saml	400	1	360	2-10-1783	——— Br	Withdrawn
Kirkham, Saml	300	1	360	2-10-1783	Dix R	
Kirkham, Saml	200	1	360	2-10-1783	None	
Kirkham, Saml	300	2	65	3- 4-1784	Dix R	
Kirkham, Saml	400	2	65	3- 4-1784	Br Rock Castle	
Kirkham, Saml	650	2	65	3- 4-1784	Caseys & Brush Cr	
Kirkham, Saml	50	2	66	3- 4-1784	None	Surveyed
Kirkham, Saml	100	2	70	3-17-1784	Dix R	
Kirkham, Saml	100	2	70	3-17-1784	Balohill Cr	Surveyed
Kirkham, Saml	100	2	93	4-23-1784	Green R	Surveyed
Kirkham, Saml	100	2	181	2- 4-1785	None	
Kirkham, Saml	100	2	181	2- 4-1785	Dix R	
Kirkly, Francis	50	1	48	5-23-1780	Dix R	
Kirkly, Wm	400	1	1	11- 3-1779	Paint Lick Cr	
Kirkly, Wm	500	1	64	6- 2-1780	Paint Lick	
Kirkly, Wm	500	1	64	6- 2-1780	None	
Kirtley, Wm	1,786½	1	394	4- 7-1783	E Fk Stinking Cr	
Kitsmiller, Jno	4,000	1	255	4- 6-1782	Mississippi R	Withdrawn
Kitsmiller, Jno	4,000	1	311	11-27-1782	Mississippi R	
Knox, Geo	225	2	57	2-16-1784	——— R	
Knox, Geo	225	2	146	9- 9-1784	Dix R	
Knox, Jas	1,000	1	222	1-25-1782	Main Fk Skaggs Cr	
Knox, Jas	1,200	1	257	4-11-1782	Paint Lick	
Knox, Jas	825	2	249	11-15-1785	Scaggs Cr	Surveyed
Knox, Wm	8,000	2	182	2-14-1785	Cumberland R	
Knox, Wm	5,333	2	182	2-14-1785	Cumberland R	
Kyle, Wm	1,000	2	33	11-19-1783	Silver Cr	
Lackey, Robt	5,584¾	2	164	12-11-1784	Silver Cr	
Lair, Matthias	100	1	316	12- 6-1782	Dix R	Withdrawn
Laird, David	1,000	2	158	11-11-1784	None	
Lamb, Saml	600	1	262	5-15-1783	Dix R	
Lamb, Wm	510	1	52	5-26-1780	Dix R	
Lamb, Wm	300	1	52	5-26-1780	Dix R	Withdrawn
Lamb, Wm	300	1	304	10- 4-1782	Fks Dix R	
Lane, Jno	200	1	86	10-17-1780	——— Cr	
Lamme, Wm	100	1	308	10-10-1782	Dix R	
Langford, Stephen	300	2	315	3-15-1792	Main Rockcastle	
Lapsley, Jno	400	1	15	2-24-1780	N Fk Gillerts Cr	
Lapsley, Jno	500	5	56	5-27-1780	Fk Dry Run	
Lapsley, Jno	500	1	368	2-19-1783	None	
Lapsley, Jno	500	1	368	2-19-1783	Ky R	
LaRue, Jacob	5,000	1	381	3-18-1783	Big Benson Cr	
LaRue, Jacob	5,000	1	381	3-18-1783	Chopkins Fk	
LaRue, Jacob	6,921½	1	381	3-18-1783	Buffaloe Road	
LaRue, Jacob	100	1	382	3-18-1783	Dix R	

Entree	Acres	Book	Page	Entry Date	Watercourse	Notes
LaRue, Phebe	1,000	1	381	3-18-1783	——— Cr	
LaRue, Sarah	1,000	1	381	3-18-1783	Big Benson Cr	
Latham, Jno	1,000	1	251	3-26-1782	Cranks Cr	
Latham, Jno	500	1	251	3-26-1782	Cranks Gap	
Latham, Jno	2,000	1	251	3-26-1782	M Fk Cumberland R	
Latham, Jno	300	1	251	3-26-1782	Coxes Cr	
Latham, Jno	200	1	251	3-26-1782	Coxes Cr	
Latham, Jno	250	1	251	3-26-1782	Fks Coxes Cr	
Latham, Jno	250	1	252	3-26-1782	S Fk Cumberland R	
Latham, Jno	400	1	252	3-26-1782	Brownies Cr	
Latham, Jno	1,000	1	252	3-26-1782	N Fk Cumberland R	
Latham, Jno	600	1	252	3-26-1782	S Fk Cumberland R	
Latham, Jno	400	1	252	3-26-1782	Cranks Cr	
Latham, Jno	600	1	252	3-26-1782	Cumberland R	
Lawrence, Jos	200	2	276	5-29-1786	Ky R	Surveyed
Leach, Jno	1,000	2	188	2-28-1785	Br Silver Cr	
Leaper, Hugh	400	1	3	11-25-1779	S Fk Paint Lick Cr	
Ledgerwood, Jas	212½	1	214	1-11-1782	S Fk Little Hammons	Withdrawn
Ledgerwood, Jas	212½	1	230	2- 9-1782	S Fk Little Hammons	
Ledgerwood, Jas	212½	1	230	2- 9-1782	Little Benson Cr	
Ledgerwood, Wm	100	2	80	3-29-1784	Ky R	
Ledgerwood, Wm	300	2	256	12-30-1785	Ky R	
Lee, Chas	4,096	2	8	5-30-1783	Woods Fk	
Lee, Henry	4,000	2	296	3-10-1788	Cumberland	
Lee, Jacob	375	1	157	8-30-1781	Paint Lick	
Lee, Thos	500	1	100	3- 6-1781	Dix R	
Leitch, David	30,000	1	256	4- 6-1782	Mississippi R	
Leitch, David	5,000	1	297	8-15-1782	Mississippi R	
Leitch, David	5,000	1	297	8-15-1782	S Fk Rowling Fk	Withdrawn
Leitch, David	5,000	1	301	9-27-1782	Mississippi R	
Leitch, David	5,000	1	301	9-27-1782	Green	
Leitch, David	———	1	307	10- 6-1782	Mississippi R	
Leitch, David	500	1	307	10- 6-1782	N Fk Rowling Fk	
Lemair, Jas	1,000	1	45	5-22-1780	Knob Lick	
Lemme, Wm	1,000	1	29	4-29-1780	Whitleys Cr	
Lemme, Wm	100	1	85	10-17-1780	None	
Lewis, Andrew	11,386¼	2	122	6-28-1784	Rockcastle	
Lewis, Aaron	1,000	1	293	8- 2-1782	l h Fk Otter Cr	
Lewis, Aaron	1,000	1	303	10- 2-1782	Br Otter Cr	
Lewis, Betty	1,000	1	240	2-25-1782	Carolina Line	Withdrawn
Lewis, Betty	3,358	2	62	3- 1-1784	Carolina Line	
Lewis, Fielding	20,000	1	232	2-11-1782	Clarks R	Withdrawn
Lewis, Fielding	20,000	2	127	7- 7-1784	Clarks R	
Lewis, Ivison	500	1	74	6-19-1780	——— Cr	
Lewis, Jno	250	1	363	2-14-1783	Otter Cr	
Lewis, Jno	1,000	1	363	2-14-1783	Otter Cr	
Lewis, Jno	1,000	2	127	7- 7-1784	None	
Lewis, Jno	250	2	135	8- 2-1784	None	
Lewis, Jno	60,000	2	147	9-20-1784	Richland Cr	Withdrawn
Lewis, Jno	9,302	2	257	1- 5-1786	Linn Camp Cr	
Leveridge, Jno	300	1	162	10- 5-1781	Paint Lick	Withdrawn
Lillard, Christopher	300	1	330	1- 1-1783	——— Br	
Lillard, Christopher	400	1	377	2-27-1783	Deep Cr	
Lillard, Christopher	300	1	377	2-27-1783	Chopkins Fk	
Lillard, Christopher	300	2	243	10- 6-1785	None	
Lillard, Jno	200	1	327	12-28-1782	Br Chopkins Fk	
Lillard, Jno	300	1	330	1- 1-1783	Thompson Run	
Lillard, Jno	1,000	1	347	1-27-1783	None	
Lillard, Jno	1,000	1	347	1-27-1783	Buchannon Br	
Lillard, Joseph	1,000	1	380	3- 8-1783	Chopkins Fk	
Lillard, Thos	500	1	376	2-27-1783	Thompson Fk	Withdrawn
Lillard, Thos	200	1	377	2-27-1783	Chaplins Fk	Withdrawn
Lillard, Thos	300	2	13	6-20-1784	Chaplins Fk	
Lillard, Thos	2,373¾	2	95	4-24-1784	Chaplins Fk	Withdrawn
Lillard, Thos	200	2	123	6-29-1784	None	
Lillard, Thos	200	2	123	6-29-1784	Rowling Fk	
Lillard, Thos	2,373	2	124	7- 2-1784	Chopkins Fk	
Lillard, Thos	2,373	2	124	7- 2-1784	Chopkins Fk	
Lillard, Thos	270	2	184	2-19-1785	Chopkins Fk	
Lillard, Thos	270	2	184	2-19-1785	Salt R	
Lillard, Thos	230	2	241	9-23-1785	Thompson Fk	
Lillard, Thos	230	2	241	9-23-1785	Chopkins Fk	
Lindsey, Opie	1,835½	1	300	9-27-1782	Cedar & Buck Cr	
Linkhorn, Abram	800	1	325	12-23-1782	Green R	
Lipscomb, Wm	400	2	31	11-15-1783	Muddy Cr	
Little, Thos	551	2	114	6- 9-1784	Big Benson Cr	
Lord, Matthew	100	2	13	6-20-1783	Dix R	

Entree	Acres	Book	Page	Entry Date	Watercourse	Notes
Lockhart, Patrick	1,000	1	109	3-28-1781	None	
Lockhart, Levi	200	2	125	7- 3-1784	S Fk Ky R	
Lockhart, Levi	1,020	2	125	7- 3-1784	Sycamore Br	
Lockhart, Sarah	6,000	2	182	2- 4-1785	Rockcastle	
Logan, Ben	400	1	5	12-28-1779	Clarks Run	
Logan, Ben	400	1	5	12-28-1779	Dix R	
Logan, Ben	750	1	54	5-26-1780	Buffaloe Sp	
Logan, Ben	1,000	1	54	5-26-1780	None	
Logan, Ben	1,000	1	54	5-26-1780	None	
Logan, Ben	600	1	54	5-26-1780	None	
Logan, Ben	500	1	54	5-26-1780	Clarks Run	
Logan, Ben	600	1	54	5-26-1780	Hanging Fk	
Logan, Benj	500	1	107	3-26-1781	Clarks Run	
Logan, Benj	332½	1	147	7-18-1781	Downeys Cr	Withdrawn
Logan, Benj	437½	1	148	7-18-1781	None	
Logan, Benj	300	1	148	7-30-1781	None	
Logan, Benj	400	1	149	7-30-1781	Dix R	Withdrawn
Logan, Benj	200	1	149	7-30-1781	Hanging Fk	Withdrawn
Logan, Benj	200	1	149	7-30-1781	None	Withdrawn
Logan, Benj	332½	1	164	10-20-1781	Dix R	
Logan, Benj	119	1	164	10-20-1781	None	
Logan, Benj	213½	1	188	12- 8-1781	Paint Lick	
Logan, Benj	400	2	84	4- 2-1784	None	
Logan, Benj	200	2	84	4- 2-1784	None	
Logan, Benj	200	2	84	4- 2-1784	None	
Logan, Benj	800	2	84	4- 2-1784	Hanging Fk	Surveyed
Logan, Benj	300	2	314	10-10-1791	Hanging Fk	
Logan, Benj	300	2	314	10-10-1791	Hanging Fk	
Logan, Hugh	1,000	1	54	5-26-1780	Little Flat Lick	
Logan, Hugh	9,714¼	2	272	3-20-1786	——— R	
Logan, Hugh	150	2	313	7-20-1791	Green R	
Logan, Jas	50	1	16	4-18-1780	Br Hanging Fk	Withdrawn
Logan, Jas	50	1	17	4-18-1780	Br Oppo Fields Improvement	Withdrawn
Logan, Jas	400	1	29	4-29-1780	Br Hanging Fk	
Logan, Jas	400	1	29	4-29-1780	None	
Logan, Jas	50	1	119	4-24-1781	——— Cr	
Logan, Jas	50	1	120	4-24-1781	None	Withdrawn
Logan, Jas	50	1	121	4-30-1781	Br Hanging Fk	Withdrawn
Logan, Jas	50	1	152	8-20-1781	None	
Logan, Jas	50	1	152	8-20-1781	Hanging Fk	
Logan, Jas	750	1	389	3-22-1783	M Fk Ky R	
Logan, Jno	400	1	3	11-24-1779	St Asaphs Sp Br	
Logan, Jno	1,000	1	29	4-29-1780	Dry Run	
Logan, Jno	500	1	55	5-27-1780	Green R	
Logan, Jno	150	1	55	5-27-1780	Logans Fk	
Logan, Jno	500	1	71	6-13-1780	Green R	
Logan, Jno	1,000	1	71	6-15-1780	——— Cr	
Logan, Jno	1,000	1	71	6-15-1780	None	
Logan, Jno	400	1	141	6-29-1781	Green R	
Logan, Jno	400	1	141	6-29-1781	Paint Lick	
Logan, Jno	500	1	174	11-20-1781	——— Cr	
Logan, Jno	100	2	92	4-22-1784	Fks of ——— Cr	
Logan, Jno	1,400	2	154	10-27-1784	Otter Cr	Withdrawn
Logan, Jno	1,400	2	154	10-27-1784	Silver Cr	
Logan, Jno	1,400	2	154	10-27-1784	Boonesboro	
Logan, Jno	1,300	2	155	10-27-1784	Silver Cr	
Logan, Jno	5,500	2	177	1-22-1785	None	
Logan, Joseph	1,250	1	72	6-17-1780	Otter Cr	
Logan, Nathaniel	400	1	3	11-24-1779	St Asaphs Sp Br	
Logan, Nathaniel	1,000	1	71	6-15-1780	None	
Logan, Thos	200	1	174	11-20-1781	Br S Fk Dix R	
Logan, Wm	400	1	4	12-28-1779	Clarks Run	
Logan, Wm	400	1	53	5-26-1780	Clarks Run	
Logan, Wm	400	1	146	7-17-1781	None	
Logan, Wm	200	1	146	7-17-1781	None	
Logwood, Wm	1,000	1	224	1-26-1782	Big Bensons Cr	
Logwood, Wm	2,000	1	245	3- 5-1782	M Fk Rowling Fk	Withdrawn
Logwood, Wm	471	2	15	7- 3-1783	Rowling Fk	
Logwood, Wm	471	2	15	7- 3-1783	Ky R	
Long, Anderson	1,232½	2	268	2-10-1786	S Fk Ky R	
Long, Francis	200	1	324	12-19-1782	Station Camp Cr	
Long, Francis	100	1	52	5-25-1780	Silver Cr	
Long, Joseph	50	1	51	5-25-1780	Ky R	
Long, Joseph	500	1	72	6-17-1780	Silver Cr	
Long, Lawrence	1,600	1	284	7-13-1782	Silver Cr	
Long, Lawrence	2,500	1	284	7-13-1782	Silver Cr	Withdrawn
Long, Lawrence	2,500	2	220	5-28-1785	Silver Cr	
Long, Lawrence	2,500	2	220	5-28-1785	Ky R	
Longest, Caleb	450	1	75	6-19-1780	Br Ky R	
Longest, Caleb	50	1	75	6-19-1780	Ky R	

Entree	Acres	Book	Page	Entry Date	Watercourse	Notes
Longstrith, Jonathan	1,120	2	289	1-18-1787	None	Surveyed
Loval, Thos	400	1	107	3-25-1781	Hangings Fk	
Lovel, Thos	400	1	57	5-29-1780	Bulger Lick	Withdrawn
Loveridge, Jno	300	2	174	1- 3-1785	Paint Lick	
Loveridge, Jno	300	2	174	1- 3-1785	Paint Lick	
Lovingood, Harmon	539	2	106	5-28-1784	——— Cr	
Lusk, Saml	400	1	76	6-22-1780	Paint Lick	Withdrawn
Lusk, Saml	400	2	177	1-22-1785	None	
Lusk & Crow	1,000	2	146	9- 1-1784	S Fk Ky R	
Luttrell, Jno	400	1	10	2- 9-1780	Boonesboro	
Luttrell, Jno	400	1	12	2-19-1780	Boones Fk	
Luttrell, Jno	1,000	1	77	6-23-1780	None	
Luttrell, Jno, heirs	400	1	134	2-19-1780	Boones Fk	
Luttrell, Thos	1,000	1	78	6-23-1780	Silver Cr	
Lyddle, Thos	300½	2	131	7-27-1784	None	
Lyddle, Thos	200	2	319	7-27-1784	None	
Lyne, Jno	2,000	1	253	3-29-1782	Cumberland R	
Lyne, Jno	2,000	1	253	3-29-1782	Cumberland R	
Lyon, Jno	1,000	1	366	2-17-1783	Buck Cr	Withdrawn
Lyon, Jno	1,000	2	101	5-11-1784	Buck Cr	
Lyon, Saml	140	2	74	3-20-1784	Ky R	
McAfee, Geo	1,000	1	94	1-30-1781	Salt R	
McAfee, Geo	400	1	1	11-14-1779	Salt R	
McAfee, Geo	200	1	94	1-30-1781	None	Withdrawn
McAfee, Geo	200	1	115	4-12-1781	Salt R	
McAfee, Geo	124	1	152	8-13-1781	Salt R	
McAfee, Geo	200	1	380	3- 8-1783	Br Chaplins Fk	
McAfee, Geo	307	1	396	4-12-1783	Chaplins Fk	
McAfee, Jas	1,000	1	21	4-26-1780	Salt R	
MaAfee, Jas	500	1	217	1-19-1782	Salt R	
McAfee, Jas	1,000	1	217	1-19-1782	Hammons Cr	
McAfee, Jas	937½	1	347	1-27-1783	Salt R	
McAfee, Jas	500	2	48	1-12-1784	Salt R	
McAfee, Jas	103	2	137	8- 5-1784	Hammons Cr	
McAfee, Jas	103	2	138	8- 5-1784	None	
McAfee, Robt	500	1	211	1- 9-1782	Salt R	
McAfee, Robt	500	1	212	1- 9-1782	Salt R	
McAfee, Robt	300	1	212	1- 9-1782	Cedar Cr	
McAfee, Robt	200	1	212	1- 9-1782	N. Fk Cave Sp	
McAfee, Robt	300	1	212	1- 9-1782	Main Hammons Cr	
McAfee, Robt	200	1	212	1- 9-1782	1st Big Fork Hammons Cr	
McAfee, Robt	220	1	308	10-10-1782	Lick Br	
McAfee, Robt	200	2	104	5-24-1784	N Fk Cave Sp	
McAfee, Robt	200	2	104	5-24-1784	Hammons Cr	Withdrawn
McAfee, Robt	200	2	119	6-28-1784	Coughams Fk	
McAfee, Robt	200	2	119	6-28-1784	None	
McAfee, Robt	100	2	270	2-25-1786	Br Ky R	
McAfee, Saml	200	1	196	12-18-1781	Salt R	
McAfee, Wm	400	1	308	10-22-1782	None	
McAfee, Wm	400	1	308	10-22-1782	None	
McAfee, Wm	400	1	308	10-22-1782	None	
McAfee, Wm	1,000	2	64	3- 3-1784	Salt R	
McAnelly, Jno	400	1	187	12- 5-1781	S Fk Rowling Fk	
McAnelly, Jno	400	1	369	2-19-1783	Rowling Fk	Withdrawn
McAnelly, Jno	400	1	369	2-19-1783	None	Withdrawn
McAnelly, Jno	400	2	289	1-18-1787	Rowling Fk	
McAnelly, Jno	800	2	289	1-18-1787	Hanging Fk	
McAnelly, Jno	800	2	313	7-20-1791	Hanging Fk	
McBrayers, Jas	300	1	346	1-25-1783	Little Benson Cr	Withdrawn
McBrayers, Jas	101	1	350	1-29-1783	None	Withdrawn
McBrayers, Jas	300	1	376	2-26-1783	Little Benson Cr	
McBrayers, Jas	101	1	376	2-26-1783	None	
McBrayers, Jas	201	1	376	2-26-1783	1 h Fk Little Benson Cr	
McBrayers, Jas	200	1	376	2-26-1783	None	
McBrayers, Wm	124	1	121	4-30-1781	Clarks Run	Amended
McBrayers, Wm	400	1	129	5-18-1781	Chaplins Fk	
McBrayers, Wm	100	1	129	5-18-1781	None	
McBrayers, Wm	150	1	193	12-14-1781	Salt R	
McBrayers, Wm	370	1	355	2- 6-1783	S Fk Big Benson	
McBrayers, Wm	124	2	89	4-14-1784	None	
McBrayers, Wm	600	2	114	6- 9-1784	Falls Trace	
McBrayers, Wm	300	2	122	6-28-1784	Hammons Cr	
McBrayers, Wm	200	2	150	9-27-1784	None	
McBride, Wm	400	1	1	11- 6-1779	Harrods Run	
McBride, Wm	400	1	15	3- 2-1780	E Fk Paint Lick Cr	
McBride, Wm	1,000	1	24	4-26-1780	Harrods Run	
McBride, Wm	400	1	137	6-19-1781	None	
McBride, Wm	600	1	137	6-19-1781	Fk Paint Lick	
McBride, Wm	479	1	290	7-26-1782	Fk Cumberland R	
McCain, Robt	400	2	26	10- 4-1783	Masons Cr	

Entree	Acres	Book	Page	Entry Date	Watercourse	Notes
McCalister, Jno	400	2	43	12-20-1783	Benson Run	
McCalister, Jno	400	2	43	12-20-1783	Bensons Cr	
McCallister, Robt	1,000	1	175	11-23-1781	None	
McClure, Jno	200	2	215	5-25-1785	Drake Camp Cr	
McClure, Nathaniel	455	1	312	11-27-1782	Cane Run	Withdrawn
McClure, Nathaniel	455	1	322	12-13-1782	Chaplins Fk	
McClure, Nathaniel	200	1	322	12-13-1782	None	
McClure, Nathaniel	255	1	322	12-13-1782	McAfee Run	
McClure, Nathaniel	256	2	94	4-24-1784	None	
McCormack, Daniel	1,000	1	21	4-26-1780	Hanging Fk	
McCormack, Geo	1,000	1	156	8-30-1781	None	
McCormack, Geo	1,000	1	156	8-30-1781	Otter Cr	
McCormack, Jno	400	1	22	4-26-1780	Paint Lick Cr	
McCormack, Mary	400	2	26	10- 4-1783	None	
McCown, Jas Jr	50	1	93	1-22-1781	None	
McCown, Jas Jr	500	1	93	1-22-1781	None	
McCown, Jas Jr	456	1	326	12-23-1782	Salt R	
McCown, Jas Jr	100	1	391	3-24-1783	Ky R	
McCown, Jas Sr	400	1	326	12-23-1782	Ky R	
McCown, Jno	200	1	53	5-26-1780	Baileys Cr	
McCown, Jno	400	1	325	12-23-1782	Salt R	
McCown, Jno	103	1	325	12-23-1782	Little Hammons Cr	
McCoy, Alex	250	2	255	12-19-1785	Muddy Cr	
McCracken, Cyrus	200	1	177	11-24-1781	Salt R	
McCracken, Cyrus	200	1	177	11-24-1781	Salt R	
McCracken, Cyrus	1,500	1	378	3- 7-1783	None	
McCracken & Bell	500	1	240	2-25-1782	Br Big Benson	
McCracken & Crow	500	1	282	7- 2-1782	Hammons Cr	
McCraw, Edward	400	2	67	3-10-1784	Hanging Fk	
McCullock, Thos	500	1	93	1-17-1781	None	
McCullock, Thos	200	1	103	3-13-1781	Lick Br	
McCullock, Thos	200	2	313	8- 9-1791	Lick Br	
McDonald, Jas	400	1	1	11-11-1779	Dix R	
McDonald, Jas	400	1	2	11-11-1779	Gilberts Cr	
McDonald, Jas	1,000	5	56	5-29-1780	Dix R	
McDonald, Jas	1,000	1	88	10-27-1780	Gilberts Cr	
McDonald, Randolph	300	1	48	5-23-1780	Cedar Run	
McDonald, Randolph	300	1	322	12-13-1782	None	
McDonald, Randolph	300	1	322	12-13-1782	Caseys Cr	
McDowell, Col Saml	400	1	146	7-16-1781	Carpenters Cr	
McDowell, Col Saml	400	1	238	2-14-1782	Carpenters Cr	
McDowell, Col Saml	400	1	238	2-14-1782	Green R	
McDowell, Saml	250	2	256	12-31-1785	Dix R	
McElroy, James	100	1	123	5- 4-1781	Town Fk	
McElroy, Jas	650	1	135	6-15-1781	S Fk Doctors Fk	
McElroy, Saml	250	1	36	5-13-1780	Rowling Fk	
McElwee, Wm	1,000	2	124	7- 3-1784	Hanging Fk	Withdrawn
McElwee, Wm	1,000	2	290	1-22-1787	None	
McElwee, Wm	1,000	2	290	1-22-1787	Yellow Cr	Surveyed
McEndree, Richard	251½	2	258	1- 5-1786	None	
McFarland, Benj	2,267½	2	177	1-24-1785	Rockcastle	
McGarry, Hugh	400	1	13	2-21-1780	Br Silver Cr	
McGarry, Hugh	400	1	15	3- 1-1780	Ky R	
McGary, Hugh	825	1	116	4-16-1781	None	Withdrawn
McGary, Hugh	825	1	116	4-16-1781	None	
McGary, Hugh	825	1	116	4-16-1781	Ky R	
McGavock, Jas	243	1	258	4-17-1782	Ford Skaggs Cr	Surveyed
McGavock, Jas	1,511	1	287	7-18-1782	S Fk Cumberland R	Surveyed
McGehee, Saml	500	1	356	2- 8-1783	Salt R	
McGehee, Saml	500	1	357	2- 8-1783	—— Br	
McGuire, Jno	260	1	259	4-18-1782	Dix R	
McGuire, Jno	50	1	268	6- 1-1782	Dix R	
McGuire, Jno	260	1	269	6- 1-1782	Dix R	
McHann, Jas	500	1	305	10- 4-1782	Dix R	
McJenny & Kennady	1,500	2	227	6-27-1785	Green R	
McJenny & Kennady	1,884½	2	228	6-27-1785	Green R	
McKay, Alexander & Jane	200	2	53	2- 2-1784	Silver Cr	Withdrawn
McKay, Alexander & Jane	200	2	221	5-30-1785	Silver Cr	
McKay, Alexander & Jane	200	2	221	5-30-1785	Joes Lick Fk	
McKee, Robt	762½	1	387	3-21-1783	Harredsburg Sp	
McKee, Wm	500	1	41	5-18-1780	Hanging Fk	Withdrawn
McKee, Wm	300	1	41	5-18-1780	S Fk & Davis Cr	Withdrawn
McKee, Wm	200	1	41	5-18-1780	Davis Cr	Withdrawn
McKee, Wm	500	1	42	5-19-1780	E Fk Gilberts Cr	
McKee, Wm	300	1	43	5-19-1780	Clarks Run	Withdrawn
McKee, Wm	500	1	43	5-19-1780	Sugar & Paint Lick	
McKee, Wm	1,000	1	57	5-29-1780	Benson Cr	

Entree	Acres	Book	Page	Entry Date	Watercourse	Notes
McKee, Wm	500	1	316	12- 6-1782	Hanging & Doughertys	
McKee, Wm	300	1	316	12- 6-1782	Logan Cr	
McKee, Wm	300	1	316	12- 6-1782	Fks Clear Cr	
McKee, Wm	200	1	316	12- 6-1782	None	
McKenney, Archibald	400	1	9	2- 9-1780	Br Green R	
McKenney, Jas	400	1	29	4-29-1780	Hanging Fk	
McKenney, Jno	600	1	80	7- 4-1780	Rockcastle	
McKenzey, Jno	400	1	385	3-19-1783	Br Paint Lick	
McKenzie, Jno	200	1	181	12- 1-1781	E Fk Paint Lick	Withdrawn
McKenzie, Jno	200	2	256	12-26-1785	Paint Lick	Withdrawn
McKenzie, Jno	200	2	293	7-24-1787	Paint Lick	
McLardy & Watts	16,613¾	2	148	9-20-1784	Lynn Camp Cr	
McLawrence, Elizabeth	640	1	166	11- 9-1781	E Fk Richland Cr	Amended
McLawrence, Elizabeth	640	2	218	5-28-1785	Richland Cr	
McMurthry, Wm	25	1	260	4-18-1782	Dix R	
McMurtry, Jno	25	1	288	7-22-1782	None	
McMurtry, Joseph	74	1	288	7-22-1782	Cedar Cr	
McMurtry, Joseph	74	1	297	9- 2-1782	None	
McMurtry, Joseph	200	2	4	5-27-1783	Cedar Cr	Withdrawn
McMurtry, Joseph	200	2	18	7-22-1783	Cedar Cr	
McMurtry, Joseph	100	2	18	7-22-1783	Cedar Cr	
McMurtry, Joseph	200	2	102	5-17-1784	Ky R	
McMurtry, Wm	150,771½	2	112	6- 5-1784	Green R	Withdrawn
McNeely, Jas	100	1	145	7-16-1781	E Fk Paint Lick	
McNeely, Michael	250	1	64	6- 2-1780	Meadow Fk	
McNeely, Michael	150	1	64	6- 2-1780	Paint Lick	
McNeely, Michael	600	1	247	3-18-1782	Br N Fk Rowling Fk	
McNeely, Michael	100	2	255	12-23-1785	Little S Fk Rowling Fk	
McNeil, Peggie	1,000	1	78	6-23-1780	Clarks Run	
McNeil, Peggy	400	1	4	12-24-1779	Clarks Run	
McNight, Robt	200	1	367	2-17-1783	Walnut Meadow Fk	Withdrawn
McNight, Robt	200	2	270	3- 8-1786	Walnut Meadow Fk	
McNight, Wm	400	1	177	11-24-1781	Paint Lick & Silver Cr	
McNight, Wm	200	1	206	1- 3-1782	Br Rowling Fk	
McNight, Wm	200	1	207	1- 3-1782	S Fk Rowling Fk	
McRoberts, Alexander	400	1	73	6-17-1780	Robinsons Cr	
Machan, Thos	387	2	264	1-27-1786	Cumberland R	
Machan, Thos	387	2	266	1-27-1786	Cumberland R	
Madison, Gabriel	500	1	375	2-26-1783	Harrods Ldg	
Madison, Gabriel	400	1	375	2-26-1783	—— R	
Madison, Gabriel	500	2	99	5- 6-1784	Ky R	
Madison, Gabriel	500	2	99	5- 6-1784	Ky R	Withdrawn
Madison, Gabriel	500	2	205	4-13-1785	None	
Madison, Gabriel	610	2	205	4-13-1785	Dix R	Withdrawn
Madison, Gabriel	500	2	261	1-26-1786	Hammons Cr	
Madison, Gabriel	110	2	311	1- 8-1791	Dix R	
Madison, Geo	2,643½	2	105	5-28-1784	Hammons Cr	
Madison, Richard	1,875	2	117	6-17-1784	Richland Cr	
Madison, Rowland	150	1	147	7-18-1781	Br Hanging Fk	
Madison, Rowland	560	1	150	8- 3-1781	Dix R	Withdrawn
Madison, Rowland	8,000	1	306	10- 6-1782	Fraisers Cr	
Madison, Rowland	5,799½	1	306	10- 6-1782	—— Cr	
Madison, Rowland	1,000	2	50	1-20-1784	Robinsons Cr	
Madison, Rowland	560	2	50	1-20-1784	None	
Madison, Rowland	632	2	51	1-20-1784	Robinson Cr	
Madison, Thos	50	1	25	4-27-1780	None	Withdrawn
Madison, Thos	1,000	1	79	6-24-1780	Harrods Run	
Madison, Thos	76	1	150	8- 3-1781	None	Withdrawn
Madison, Thos	2,000	1	175	11-21-1781	Hammons Cr	
Madison, Thos	1,000	1	175	11-23-1781	None	
Madison, Thos	1,000	1	175	11-23-1781	None	
Madison, Thos	1,000	1	175	11-23-1781	None	
Madison, Thos	2,000	1	221	1-25-1782	Dix R	
Madison, Thos	1,000	1	275	6-18-1782	Hammons Cr	
Madison, Thos	50	2	136	8- 4-1784	Cedar Run	
Madison, Thos	4	2	237	8-15-1785	Dix R	
Madison, Thos	4	2	237	8-15-1785	None	
Madison, Wm, heirs	1,000	1	400	4-30-1783	Turkey Cr	
Madison, Wm, heirs	1,000	1	400	4-30-1783	Meadow Cr	
Magill, Jno	2,000	1	397	4-21-1783	Buck Cr	Withdrawn
Magill, Jno	416	1	398	4-21-1783	Paint Lick	
Magill, Jno	2,000	2	308	3- 8-1790	Buck Cr	
Magill, Jno	250	2	309	3- 8-1790	Green R	
Magill, Jno	250	2	311	8-27-1790	Green R	Surveyed
Mann, Wm	200	1	82	9-13-1780	Hickmans Cr	Withdrawn
Mann, Wm	200	1	114	4-11-1781	Br Ky R	
Mangor, Wm	300	1	136	6-16-1781	Green R	
Mangor, Wm	200	1	136	6-16-1781	Green R	

Entree	Acres	Book	Page	Entry Date	Watercourse	Notes
Margner, Jno	3,000	2	79	3-29-1784	Stinking Cr	
Marie, Jno	61,958	2	111	6- 5-1784	Sexton Fk Goose Cr	
Marrs, Wm	440	1	352	2- 1-1783	S Fk Big Benson Cr	
Marshall, Gilbert	400	1	126	5-17-1781	White Oak Cr	
Marshall, Humphry	1,000	1	296	8-13-1782	White Oak Cr	Surveyed
Marshall, Humphry	400	1	304	10- 4-1782	Rowling Fk	
Marshall, Humphry	100	1	304	10- 4-1782	Sulphur Lick	
Marshall, Markham	300	1	109	3-28-1781	M Fk Rowling Fk	
Marshall, Markham	200	1	181	12- 1-1781	None	
Marshall, Thos	2,150	1	77	6-22-1780	Gilberts Cr	
Marshall, Wm	200	1	209	1- 9-1782	None	
Marshall & Gillon	500	2	276	5- 4-1786	S Fk Ky R	
Martin, Joseph	400	1	24	4-26-1780	Br Hanging Fk	
Martin, Thos	910	2	158	11-11-1784	Trace to Holston	
Mason, Geo	500	1	356	2- 7-1783	None	
Mason, Geo	1,000	2	11	6-20-1783	S Fk Big Benson Cr	
Mason, Jas	400	1	3	11-11-1779	Dix R	
Mason, Jas	100	1	194	12-17-1781	Dix R	
Mason, Jas	400	1	194	12-17-1781	None	
Mason, Jas	57½	2	215	5-25-1785	Djx R	
Mason, Jno	1,000	1	239	2-25-1782	W Fk Sugar Cr	
Mason, Jno	1,000	1	298	9-24-1782	Ky R	
Mason, Jno	809	2	213	5- 9-1785	None	
Mason, Jno	500	2	213	5- 9-1785	E Fk Station Camp	
Mason, Jno	309	2	213	5- 9-1785	None	
Massie, Peter	30	1	273	6-12-1782	None	
Massie, Peter	970	1	273	6-12-1782	None	Withdrawn
Massie, Peter	1,000	1	274	6-12-1782	Calloway Cr	
Massie, Peter	970	1	368	2-19-1783	None	
Massie, Peter	1,000	2	216	5-26-1785	Ky R	
Massey, Nathaniel	7,000	2	190	3- 2-1785	Ky R	
Massey, Peter	400	1	337	1-10-1783	Otter Cr	
Massey, Peter	970	1	368	2-19-1783	None	
Masterson, Richard	500	1	369	2-19-1783	Muddy Cr	
Mathews, Jno	200	1	228	2- 6-1782	Scotts Cr	
Mathews, Jno	500	1	251	3-23-1782	Dix R	
Matthews, Jno	200	1	175	11-20-1781	Scotts Cr	Withdrawn
Matthews, Sampson	2,000	1	361	2-11-1783	Rockcastle & Skaggs Cr	
Maxwell, B	100	1	19	4-24-1780	Silver Cr	
Maxwell, B	100	1	19	4-24-1780	W Fk Silver Cr	
Maxwell, Bezeliel	1,000	1	280	6-28-1782	Paint Lick & Silver Cr	
Maxwell, Bezeliel	500	1	280	6-28-1782	M Fk Sugar Cr	
Maxwell, David	200	1	51	5-25-1780	Paint Lick Cr	
Maxwell, David	500	1	156	8-29-1781	Br Walnut Meadow Fk	
Maxwell, David	500	1	372	2-20-1783	Paint Lick	
Maxwell, David	300	1	372	2-20-1783	None	Withdrawn
Maxwell, David	620	2	60	2-23-1784	Paint Lick & Silver Cr	Amended
Maxwell, David	200	2	60	2-23-1784	McComacks Br	
Maxwell, David	620	2	101	5-12-1784	None	
Maxwell, David	300	2	175	1- 3-1785	None	
Maxwell, David	300	2	175	1- 3-1784	Paint Lick & Silver Cr	
Maxwell, Edley	200	2	290	1-22-1787	Drakes Camp Cr	
Maxwell, Jas	2,000	2	116	6-12-1784	Green R	
Maxwell, Jno	200	1	51	5-25-1780	Paint Lick Cr	
Maxwell, Jno	400	1	103	3-13-1781	None	
Maxwell, Jno	50	1	296	8-15-1782	None	
Maxwell & Downey	150	1	293	8- 2-1782	None	
Maxwell & Downey	50	1	294	8- 2-1782	None	
Maxey, Wm	500	1	44	5-20-1780	Drakes Cr	
Maxey, Wm	50	2	174	1- 3-1785	Scotts Fk	
May, Abner	700	2	318	5-31-1780	Rowling Fk	
May, Gabil	50	1	20	4-25-1780	Br Green R	
May, Geo	216	1	92	1-17-1781	Salt R	
May, Geo	216	1	101	3- 8-1781	Salt R	
May, Humphry	1,000	1	119	4-21-1781	Harrods Ldg	Withdrawn
May, Humphry	1,000	1	301	9-27-1782	Harrods Ldg	
May, Humphry	175	1	365	2-14-1783	None	
May, Wm	1,000	1	166	11- 9-1781	Fk Richland Cr	Amended
Mayo, Jno Jr	10,000	1	167	11- 9-1781	Fords Silver Cr	Amended
Mayo, Jno	3,000	1	172	11-19-1781	Sugar Cr	Amended
Mayo, Jno	10,000	1	186	1- 2-1781	Paint Lick & Silver Cr	
Mayo, Jno	3,000	1	383	3-18-1783	P int Lick	
Mayo, Jno Jr	7,000	1	173	11-20-1781	Tennessee R	
Mayo, Jno Jr	10,000	1	204	12-22-1781	Paint Lick	

Entree	Acres	Book	Page	Entry Date	Watercourse	Notes
Mayo, Jno Jr	10,000	1	184	12– 3–1781	None	....
Mayo, Jno Jr	2,800	2	225	6–20–1785	Silver & Paint Lick.	....
Mayo, Jno Jr	2,800	2	225	6–20–1785	Ky R	....
Mayo, Wm	500	1	173	11–20–1781	None	....
Mayo, Wm	8,000	1	186	12– 4–1781	Irvins Fk Tates Cr	....
Mayo, Wm	8,000	1	204	12–22–1781	Tate & Silver Crs	....
Mayo, Wm	7,177	1	284	7–13–1782	Silver & Paint Lick.	....
Mayo, Wm	8,000	2	16	7– 7–1783	Silver Cr	....
Mayo, Wm	2,277	2	167	12–11–1784	Silver Cr	....
Mayo, Wm	823	2	167	12–11–1784	None	....
Mayo, Wm	3,100	2	167	12–11–1784	N Fk Rockcastle	....
Mayo, Wm Jr	1,000	1	167	11– 9–1781	N Fk Rockcastle	....
Mayo, Wm Jr	1,000	1	168	11– 9–1781	N Fk Rockcastle	....
Mayo, Wm Jr	8,000	1	168	11– 9–1781	Tates & Silver Crs	....
Mayo, Wm Jr	2,000	1	172	11–19–1781	Otter Cr	....
Mayo, Wm Jr	1,000	1	172	11–19–1781	Otter Cr	Withdrawn
Mayo, Wm Jr	2,000	1	172	11–19–1781	Muddy Cr	....
Mayo, Wm Jr	2,000	1	172	11–20–1781	Silver Cr	....
Mayo, Wm Jr	11,000	1	178	11–24–1781	Tennessee R	....
Mayo, Wm Jr	4,000	1	202	12–21–1781	Station Camp Cr	....
Mayo, Wm Jr	1,000	1	203	12–21–1781	Muddy Cr	....
Mayo, Wm Jr	1,000	1	203	12–21–1781	Otter Cr	....
Mayo, Wm Jr	1,250	1	203	12–21–1781	Silver Cr	....
Mayo, Wm Jr	4,000	1	262	5–11–1782	Station Camp Cr	....
Mayo, Wm Jr	1,000	2	191	3–12–1785	N Fk Rockcastle	....
Mayo, Wm Jr	1,000	2	192	3–12–1785	N Fk Rockcastle	....
Mayo, Wm Sr	1,000	1	203	12–21–1781	——— Cr	Amended
Mayo, Wm Sr	1,000	2	218	5–28–1785	M Fk Richland Cr	....
Meares, Wm	340	2	137	8– 4–1784	S Fk Benson Cr	....
Meares, Wm	340	2	137	8– 4–1784	——— Br	....
Meeks, Jno	800	1	47	5–23–1780	Dix R	....
Menefee, Gerard	400	1	4	12–23–1779	Cedar Cr	....
Menefee, Jarrett	400	1	67	6– 8–1780	Cedar Cr	....
Menefee, Wm	200	1	67	6– 8–1780	Cedar Cr	....
Merewether, David	1,000	1	54	5–26–1780	Clarks Run	....
Merewether, Geo	1,000	1	159	9–18–1781	Boones Mill Cr	....
Merewether, Francis	200	1	205	12–31–1781	Shawnee Run	....
Merewether, Geo	1,000	1	29	4–29–1780	None	....
Merewether, Geo, heirs	250	2	117	6–18–1784	Boones Mill Cr	....
Merewether, Geo, heirs	250	2	118	6–18–1784	None	....
Merewether, Geo, heirs	250	2	118	6–18–1784	None	....
Merewether, Geo, heirs	250	2	118	6–18–1784	None	....
Mickie, Wm	500	1	311	11–27–1782	Clear Fk	....
Mickie, Wm	500	1	311	11–27–1782	Cumberland R	....
Miller, Abraham	1,000	1	87	10–24–1780	Br Hanging Fk	....
Miller, Alexander	300	1	235	1–14–1782	S Fk Careys Cr	Withdrawn
Miller, Alexander	300	1	236	2–14–1782	Green R	....
Miller, Alexander	300	1	339	1–11–1783	S Fk Camp Cr	....
Miller, Alexander	300	2	115	6–12–1784	——— R	....
Miller, Henry & Abraham	100	1	131	5–29–1781	None	....
Miller, Jacob	400	2	53	2– 2–1784	Drowning Cr	Withdrawn
Miller, Jacob	400	2	231	7–23–1785	Drowning Cr	....
Miller, Jacob	400	2	231	7–23–1785	Drowning Cr	....
Miller, Jno	150	1	340	1–11–1783	Cumberland Mt	....
Miller, Jno	150	1	346	1–25–1783	Cumberland Mt	....
Miller, Jno	500	2	79	3–29–1784	Ky R	....
Miller, Martha	400	1	250	3–20–1782	Cumberland R	....
Miller, Martha	170	2	186	2–23–1785	Cumberland R	....
Miller, Martha	170	2	187	2–23–1785	Cumberland R	....
Miller, Martha	170	2	278	5– 4–1786	Br Cumberland R	....
Miller, Thos	300	1	384	3–19–1783	M Fk Ky R	....
Miller, Wm	400	1	5	12–29–1779	Br Ky R	....
Miller, Wm	400	1	5	12–29–1779	Silver Cr	....
Miller, Wm	400	1	5	12–29–1779	Paint Lick Cr	....
Miller, Wm	1,000	1	22	4–26–1780	———	....
Miller, Wm	1,000	1	22	4–26–1780	——— Cr	....
Miller, Wm	1,000	1	22	4–26–1780	——— Cr	....
Miller, Wm	1,000	1	22	4–26–1780	——— Cr	....
Miller, Wm	500	1	162	10–12–1781	McCormack Cr	....
Miller, Wm	1,000	2	51	1–20–1784	E Fk Paint Lick	....
Minor, Alexander R	400	1	42	5–18–1780	Br Silver Cr	....
Mills, Jno	200	1	19	2–24–1780	Br Salt R	Withdrawn
Mills, Jno	200	2	38	11–29–1783	None	....
Minor, Jno S	400	1	59	5–30–1780	Deer Lick	....
Minor, Wm	2,000	2	205	4–13–1785	None	Amended
Minor, Wm	2,000	2	277	5– 4–1786	None	Surveyed
Minor & Harris	1,000	1	292	7–29–1782	Fk Raccoon Sp	....
Minor & Overton	500	1	291	7–27–1782	Ky R	....
Mitchell, Robt	2,000	1	291	7–27–1782	Fks Richland Cr	Surveyed
Mitchell, Robt	600	2	76	3–24–1784	Drowning Cr	....
Monroe, Hon Jas	20,000	2	156	10–28–1784	Rockcastle	....

Entree	Acres	Book	Page	Entry Date	Watercourse	Notes
Montague, Thos......	180....	2..	.276....	5- 4-1785..	..Hickman Cr.......	Surveyed
Montgomery, Alexander..........	150....	1..	. 54....	5-26-1780..	..Green R..........	....
Montgomery, Alexander..........	50....	1..	.235....	2-14-1782..	..——— R.........	Withdrawn
Montgomery, Alexander..........	500....	1..	.338....	1-11-1783..	..N Fk Caseys Cr...	....
Montgomery, Alexander..........	1,000....	2..	.157....	11- 2-1784..	..Green R & Sugar Loaf Cr........	....
Montgomery, Jno.....	160....	1..	.134....	6-12-1781..	..Hanging Fk.......	Withdrawn
Montgomery, Jno.....	200....	1..	.143....	7-13-1781..	..Carpenters Cr......	....
Montgomery, Jno.....	340....	1..	.143....	7-13-1781..	..Hanging Fk......	Withdrawn
Montgomery, Jno.....	340....	1..	.145....	7-16-1781..	..Hanging Fk.......	....
Montgomery, Jno.....	340....	1..	.145....	7-16-1781..	..Paint Lick........	....
Montgomery, Jno.....	160....	1..	.146....	7-18-1781..	..Hanging Fk.......	....
Montgomery, Jno.....	160....	1..	.146....	7-18-1781..	..E Fk Paint Lick...	....
Montgomery, Jno.....	200....	1..	.191....	12-14-1781..	..Rowling Fk.......	Withdrawn
Montgomery, Jno.....	300....	1..	.234....	2-14-1782..	..Paint Lick.......	....
Montgomery, Jno.....	200....	1..	.234....	2-14-1782..	..——— R........	....
Montgomery, Jno.....	200....	1..	.235....	2-14-1782..	..Rowling Fk.......	....
Montgomery, Jno.....	300....	1..	.236....	2-14-1782..	..Green R.........	Withdrawn
Montgomery, Jno.....	300....	1..	.236....	2-14-1782..	..Green R.........	Withdrawn
Montgomery, Jno.....	400....	2..	.318....	2- 9-1780..	..Flat Lick.........	....
Montgomery, Jno.....	200....	1..	. 53....	5-26-1780..	..Br Logan Cr.......	....
Montgomery, Jno Jr...	300....	1..	.339....	1-11-1783..	..None............	....
Montgomery, Jno Sr...	400....	1..	.235....	2-14-1782..	..S Fk Caseys Cr....	Withdrawn
Montgomery, Jno Sr...	300....	1..	.339....	1-11-1783..	..Bryants Lick......	....
Montgomery, Joseph...	500....	1..	.144....	7-16-1781..	..Silver Cr.........	....
Montgomery, Joseph...	200....	1..	.236....	2-14-1782..	..Green R.........	....
Montgomery, Joseph...	300....	1..	.236....	2-14-1782..	..Green R.........	....
Montgomery, Robt....	1,000....	1..	.373....	2-25-1783..	..Dix R...........	....
Montgomery, Saml....	996½....	2..	.241....	9-29-1785..	..Br Cumberland R..	....
Montgomery, Wm.....	400....	1..	. 9....	2- 9-1780..	..Green R.........	....
Montgomery, Wm.....	400....	1..	. 10....	2- 9-1780..	..Green R.........	....
Montgomery, Wm.....	200....	1..	. 37....	5-15-1780..	..Carpenters Cr.....	....
Montgomery, Wm.....	1,000....	1..	. 55....	5-26-1780..	..Br Green R.......	....
Montgomery, Wm.....	400....	1..	.134....	6-12-1781..	..Green R.........	....
Montgomery, Wm.....	100....	1..	.149....	7-30-1781..	..None............	....
Montgomery, Wm.....	50....	1..	.149....	7-30-1781..	..None............	....
Montgomery, Wm.....	400....	1..	.220....	1-25-1782..	..Green R.........	....
Montgomery, Wm.....	100....	1..	.221....	1-25-1782..	..Green R.........	....
Montgomery, Wm.....	600....	1..	.234....	2-14-1782..	..Green R.........	Withdrawn
Montgomery, Wm.....	500....	1..	.241....	3- 4-1782..	..Br Green R.......	Withdrawn
Montgomery, Wm.....	400....	1..	.242....	3- 4-1782..	..Bushy Cr........	Withdrawn
Montgomery, Wm.....	200....	1..	.242....	3- 4-1782..	..Green R.........	Withdrawn
Montgomery, Wm.....	200....	1..	.242....	3- 4-1782..	..Green R.........	....
Montgomery, Wm.....	300....	1..	.242....	3- 4-1782..	..Green R.........	Withdrawn
Montrgomery, Wm.....	200....	1..	.242....	3- 4-1782..	..Green R.........	Withdrawn
Montgomery, Wm.....	200....	1..	.242....	3- 4-1782..	..N Fk Caseys Cr...	Withdrawn
Montgomery, Wm.....	100....	1..	.243....	3- 4-1782..	..Green R.........	....
Montgomery, Wm.....	150....	1..	.243....	3- 4-1782..	..Dix R...........	....
Montgomery, Wm.....	425....	1..	.245....	3- 5-1782..	..N Fk Caseys Cr...	Withdrawn
Montgomery, Wm.....	500....	1..	.247....	3-15-1782..	..Carpenters Cr.....	....
Montgomery, Wm.....	700....	1..	.247....	3-15-1782..	..Carpenters Cr.....	....
Montgomery, Wm.....	100....	1..	.247....	3-15-1782..	..Br Green R.......	....
Montgomery, Wm.....	300....	1..	.265....	5-24-1782..	..Paint Lick.......	....
Montgomery, Wm.....	200....	1..	.272....	6- 8-1782..	..Carpenters Cr.....	....
Montgomery, Wm.....	400....	1..	.282....	7- 1-1782..	..Paint Lick........	....
Montgomery, Wm.....	425....	1..	.338....	1-11-1783..	..N Fk Caseys Cr....	....
Montgomery, Wm.....	400....	1..	.338....	1-11-1783..	..Green R.........	....
Montgomery, Wm.....	600....	1..	.338....	1-11-1783..	..Green R.........	....
Montgomery, Wm.....	500....	1..	.339....	1-11-1783..	..None...........	....
Montgomery, Wm.....	200....	1..	.339....	1-11-1783..	..None............	....
Montgomery, Wm.....	300....	1..	.339....	1-11-1783..	..None...........	....
Montgomery, Wm.....	200....	1..	.339....	1-11-1783..	..Caseys Cr........	....
Montgomery, Wm.....	200....	1..	.339....	1-11-1783..	..N Fk Caseys Cr....	....
Montgomery, Wm.....	400....	1..	.355....	2- 4-1783..	..Paint Lick.......	....
Montgomery, Wm.....	600....	1..	.366....	2-17-1783..	..Silver Cr........	....
Montgomery, Wm.....	200....	1..	.366....	2-17-1783..	..Hanging Fk.......	....
Montgomery, Wm.....	400....	1..	.366....	2-17-1783..	..Brush Cr........	....
Montgomery, Wm.....	200....	1..	.366....	2-17-1783..	..None...........	....
Montgomery, Wm.....	200....	1..	.373....	2-23-1783..	..None...........	....
Montgomery, Wm.....	200....	1..	.374....	2-25-1783..	..None...........	Withdrawn
Montgomery, Wm.....	200....	2..	. 48....	11-12-1748..	..None...........	....
Montgomery, Wm.....	400....	2..	. 61....	2-23-1784..	..None...........	....
Montgomery, Wm.....	200....	2..	. 61....	2-23-1784..	..Silver Cr........	....
Montgomery, Wm.....	200....	2..	. 61....	2-24-1784..	..Paint Lick........	....
Montgomery, Wm.....	200....	2..	.128....	7-15-1784..	..Silver Cr........	....
Montgomery, Wm.....	25....	2..	.189....	3- 1-1785..	..Clarks Run.......	....
Montgomery, Wm.....	220....	2..	.253....	12- 6-1785..	..Silver Cr........	....
Montgomery, Wm.....	400....	2..	.253....	12- 6-1785..	..Paint Lick........	....

Entree	Acres	Book	Page	Entry Date	Watercourse	Notes
Montgomery, Wm	100	2	290	3– 3–1787	Green R	Surveyed
Montgomery, Wm	100	2	290	3– 3–1787	Carpenters Cr	Surveyed
Montgomery, Wm	50	2	309	3– 8–1790	Silver Cr	
Montgomery, Wm	1,000	2	318	5–26–1780	Br Green R	
Montgomery, Wm Jr	300	1	237	2–14–1782	Caseys Cr	Withdrawn
Montgomery, Wm Jr	300	1	339	1–11–1783	Caseys Cr	
Moore, Henry	1,000	2	37	11–29–1783	Ky R	
Moore, Jas	300	1	160	9–21–1781	Mason Mill Cr	Withdrawn
Moore, Jas	300	2	22	9– 6–1783	None	
Moore, Jas	200	2	22	9– 6–1783	Dix R	
Moore, Jas Francis	2,000	1	241	2–25–1782	Mississippi R	Withdrawn
Moore, Jas F	12,000	1	350	1–29–1783	Mississippi R	
Moore, Jas F	2,000	1	350	1–29–1783	Mississippi R	
Moore, Jno	187½	1	323	12–18–1782	None	
Moore, Richard	1,000	1	254	4– 2–1782	E Fk Scaggs Cr	Withdrawn
Moore, Richard	2,000	2	37	11–29–1783	Goose Cr	
Moore, Richard	1,000	2	244	10–12–1785	Rockcastle	
Moore, Ricnard	1,000	2	244	10–12–1785	Little S Fk N Fk Rowling Fk	
Moore, Richard	1,000	2	293	6–25–1787	Fks Rowling Fk	Withdrawn
Moore, Robt	400	1	50	5–25–1780	Log Lick Trace	
Moore, Robt	550	2	54	2– 4–1784	Paint Lick	
Moore, Saml	3,900	2	54	2– 4–1784	None	
Moore, Wm	400	1	4	12–23–1779	Dix R	
Moore, Wm	50	1	20	4–25–1780	Town Fk	
Moore, Wm	50	1	20	4–25–1780	Buffaloe Lick	
Moore, Wm	50	1	20	4–25–1780	Big Cr	
Moore, Wm	400	1	176	11–23–1781	Green R	
Moore, Wm	400	1	179	11–26–1781	Green R	
Moore, Wm	400	1	179	11–26–1781	Green R	
Moore, Wm	217	1	302	9–30–1782	Craborchard Cr	
Moore, Wm	400	1	302	9–30–1782	None	
Moore & Rogers	12,000	1	251	3–21–1782	Mississippi R	Withdrawn
Moore & Donelson	50,000	2	111	6– 5–1784	Sextons & Goose Crs	
Morgan, Abraham	300	1	69	6– 8–1780	Tates Cr	
Morgan, Haynes	156	2	132	7–29–1784	Cedar Cr	
Morton, Jno	500	1	55	5–27–1780	Station Camp Cr	
Morton, Jno	200	1	359	2–10–1783	None	Withdrawn
Morton, Jno	150	1	361	2–11–1783	None	Withdrawn
Morton, Jno	300	2	30	11– 3–1783	Chaplins Fk	
Morton, Jno	200	2	30	11– 3–1783	None	
Morton, Jno	150	2	30	11– 3–1783	None	
Morton, Joseph	50	1	19	4–24–1780	Cumberland R	
Morton, Joseph	1,100	1	55	5–27–1780	None	
Morton, Richard	525	1	143	7–13–1781	Br Drakes Camp Cr	Withdrawn
Morton, Richard	10	2	284	7–28–1786	Drake Camp Cr	
Morris, Hugh	150	1	43	5–19–1780	Sugar Cr	
Morris, Hugh	50	2	318	4–19–1792	Ky R	
Morris, Wm	400	1	340	1–11–1783	2nd Fk Drakes Camp Cr	Withdrawn
Morris, Wm	890	2	101	5–14–1784	Cumberland R	
Morrison, Isaac	500	1	261	5– 7–1782	Mississippi & Ohio R	Withdrawn
Morrison, Isaac	500	1	161	5– 7–1782	None	Withdrawn
Morrison, Isaac	500	2	19	7–23–1783	Mississippi R	
Morrison, Isaac	500	2	19	7–23–1783	Dix R	
Morrison, Jas	400	1	83	9–25–1780	Br Paint Lick	
Morrison, Jas	50	1	102	3–10–1781	Br Silver Cr	
Morrison, Jas	00	1	102	3–10–1781	None	
Morrison, Jas	200	1	102	3–10–1781	Paint Lick Cr	
Morrison, Jas	400	1	253	3–29–1782	None	Withdrawn
Morrison, Jas	400	1	393	4– 4–1783	None	Withdrawn
Morrison, Thos	250	1	252	3–29–1782	Rowling Fk	
Morrison, Thos	411	1	252	3–29–1782	None	
Morrison, Wm	400	1	284	7–12–1782	Drakes Camp Cr	
Morrison, Wm	400	2	66	3– 4–1784	None	
Morrison, Wm	100	2	66	3– 4–1784	Paint Lick	
Morrison, Wm	400	2	98	5– 4–1784	None	
Morrison, Wm	100	2	135	8– 2–1784	Paint Lick	
Mosby, Jno	2,000	1	286	7–18–1782	Laurel R	
Mosby, Robt	1,000	1	283	7– 6–1782	Cumberland R	
Mosby, Robt	1,000	1	287	7–18–1782	S Fk Cumberland R	Surveyed
Mosby, Robt	128	2	105	5–25–1784	Salt R	Withdrawn
Mosby, Robt	174	2	228	6–27–1785	Salt R	
Mosby, Robt	174	2	249	11–17–1785	Salt R	
Mosby, Robt	128	2	298	4– 4–1788	Salt R	
Moseley, Robt	750	1	183	12– 3–1781	Viney Fk Muddy Cr	
Moseley, Robt	500	1	183	12– 3–1781	Drowning Cr	
Moseley, Thos	500	1	181	12– 1–1781	N Trace Skeggs Cr	
Moseley, Thos	1,100	1	183	12– 3–1781	Muddy Cr	
Motley, Joel	12,150	2	227	6–27–1785	None	
Mounce, Absalom	400	1	360	2–11–1783	None	
Mounce, Jno	400	1	87	10–23–1780	——— Cr	

Entree	Acres	Book	Page	Entry Date	Watercourse	Notes
Muldrough, Jno	50	1	122	4–30–1781	Clarks Run	
Muldrough, Jno	100	1	349	1–28–1783	None	Withdrawn
Muldrough, Jno	1,000	2	120	6–28–1784	None	
Murchie, Jno	3,487½	1	255	4– 6–1782	Mississippi R	
Murchie, Jno	500	1	301	9–27–1782	Mississippi R	
Murchie, Jno	500	1	302	9–27–1782	None	
Murchie, Jno	3,487½	1	307	10– 6–1782	Mississippi R	
Murchie, Jno	500	1	307	10– 6–1782	None	
Myers, Jacob	50	1	3	11–26–1779	Whitley Station	
Myers, Jacob	50	1	8	2– 7–1780	N Fk Dix R	
Myers, Jacob	50	1	9	2– 7–1780	N Fk Skeggs Cr	
Myers, Jacob	100	1	16	3– 7–1780	Dix R	
Myers, Jacob	490	1	35	5–12–1780	Dix R	
Myers, Jacob	400	1	35	5–13–1780	Dix R	Withdrawn
Myers, Jacob	200	1	35	5–13–1780	N E Fk Dix R	
Myers, Jacob	200	1	35	5–13–1780	Salt R	Withdrawn
Myers, Jacob	500	1	35	5–13–1780	S Fk Dix R	
Myers, Jacob	500	1	35	5–13–1780	S Fk Skeggs Cr	
Myers, Jacob	1,000	1	35	5–13–1780	Clarks Cr	Withdrawn
Myers, Jacob	400	1	94	1–30–1781	Boones Mill Br	
Myers, Jacob	400	1	94	1–30–1781	Hanging Fk	
Myers, Jacob	1,000	1	94	1–30–1781	Dix R	
Myers, Jacob	50	1	100	3– 6–1781	N Fk Dix R	
Myers, Jacob	50	1	100	3– 6–1781	Dix R	
Myers, Jacob	400	1	100	3– 6–1781	Hanging Fk	
Myers, Jacob	400	1	100	3– 6–1781	Hanging Fk	
Myers, Jacob	1,000	1	106	3–23–1781	Dix R	
Myers, Jacob	1,000	1	108	3–26–1781	Harrods Landing	
Myers, Jacob	1,000	1	108	3–26–1781	Silver Cr	
Myers, Jacob	1,000	1	108	3–26–1781	None	
Myers, Jacob	800	1	117	4–19–1781	Clarks Run	
Myers, Jacob	400	1	118	4–19–1781	Dix R	Withdrawn
Myers, Jacob	200	1	118	4–19–1781	Salt R	
Myers, Jacob	200	1	118	4–19–1781	Skeggs Cr	Withdrawn
Myers, Jacob	450	1	118	4–19–1781	Dix R	
Myers, Jacob	450	1	118	4–19–1781	Skeggs Cr	
Myers, Jacob	400	1	118	4–19–1781	Skeggs Cr	
Myers, Jacob	10,000	1	173	11–20–1781	Br Mississippi R	
Myers, Jacob	1,000	1	220	1–22–1782	Cumberland R	
Myers, Jacob	400	1	220	1–22–1782	Ky R	
Myers, Jacob	650	1	220	1–22–1782	Skeggs Cr	
Myers, Jacob	400	1	220	1–22–1782	Yellow Cr	
Myers, Jacob	343¾	1	220	1–22–1782	Richland Cr	
Myers, Jacob	5,000	1	223	1–26–1782	Mississippi R	Withdrawn
Myers, Jacob	200	1	223	1–26–1782	Dix R	
Myers, Jacob	5,000	1	226	1–29–1782	Br Mississippi R	Withdrawn
Myers, Jacob	313¼	1	246	3–15–1782	Dix R	Surveyed
Myers, Jacob	600	1	246	3–15–1782	Mississippi R	
Myers, Jacob	950	1	251	3–21–1782	Mississippi R	
Myers, Jacob	50	1	251	3–21–1782	Mouth Tennessee R	
Myers, Jacob	1,000	1	264	5–17–1782	Shawnee Run	
Myers, Jacob	400	2	19	7–23–1783	Dix R	
Myers, Jacob	100	2	19	7–23–1783	None	
Myers, Jacob	40	2	19	7–23–1783	Harrods Landing	
Myers, Jacob	260	2	19	7–23–1783	Harrods Landing	Withdrawn
Myers, Jacob	20	2	25	10– 2–1783	Harrods Landing	
Myers, Jacob	20	2	25	10– 2–1783	Dix R	
Myers, Jacob	500	2	48	1– 5–1784	None	
Myers, Jacob	5,000	2	84	4– 1–1784	Cumberland R	
Myers, Jacob	10,000	2	84	4– 1–1784	Ky R	
Myers, Jacob	240	2	84	4– 2–1784	None	
Myers, Jacob	240	2	84	4– 2–1784	None	Withdrawn
Myers, Jacob	1,000	2	132	7–29–1784	Island in Ohio R	
Myers, Jacob	5,000	2	140	8–12–1784	Mississippi R	
Myers, Jacob	5,000	2	147	9–10–1784	Mississippi R	
Myers, Jacob	418	2	255	12–24–1785	Laurel R	
Myers, Jacob	200	2	259	1–10–1786	Mississippi R	
Myers, Jacob	400	2	267	2– 6–1786	Mississippi R	
Myers, Jacob	100	2	268	2– 6–1786	Island Mississippi R	
Myers, Jacob	300	2	268	2– 6–1786	Mississippi R	Withdrawn
Myers, Jacob	100	2	273	3–22–1786	Dix R	
Myers, Jacob	300	2	282	7–11–1786	Mississippi R	
Myers, Jacob	180	2	282	7–11–1786	Clarks Cr	
Myers, Jacob	100	2	282	7–13–1786	Dix R	
Myers, Jacob	200	2	286	9–25–1786	Skeggs & Dix R	
Myers, Jacob	240	2	286	9–30–1786	None	
Myers, Jacob	201	2	291	3–28–1787	None	
Myers, Jacob	100	2	291	3–28–1787	Dix R	
Myers, Jacob	26	2	291	3–28–1787	Dix R	
Myers, Jacob	10,000	2	292	3–28–1787	Cumberland R	
Myers, Jacob	500	2	292	4– 2–1787	Scaggs Cr	
Myers, Jacob	3,000	2	300	6–23–1788	Cumberland R	

Entree	Acres	Book	Page	Entry Date	Watercourse	Notes
Myers, Jacob	1,000	2	300	6–26–1788	Cumberland R	
Myers, Jacob	400	2	300	6–26–1788	Cumberland R	
Myers, Jacob	600	2	301	6–26–1788	Stinking Cr	Withdrawn
Myers, Jacob	250	2	303	12–15–1788	Hanging Fk	
Myers, Jacob	173	2	303	12–15–1788	Boones Mill Cr	
Myers, Jacob	2,000	2	308	3– 6–1790	Clear Cr	1,000 acres withdrawn
Myers, Jacob	1,950	2	308	3– 6–1790	Clear Cr	Withdrawn
Myers, Jacob	1,000	2	310	7– 2–1790	Clear Cr	
Myers, Jacob	3,995	2	310	7– 2–1790	Cumberland R	Withdrawn
Myers, Jacob	2,000	2	310	7– 2–1790	Clear Cr	Withdrawn
Myers, Jacob	600	2	312	3–31–1791	Stinking Cr	
Myers, Jacob	46	2	312	3–31–1791	Dix R	
Myers, Jacob	458	2	313	3–31–1791	Cumberland R	
Myers, Jacob	3,995	2	314	12– 3–1791	Cumberland R	
Myers, Jacob	995	2	314	12– 3–1791	Yellow Cr	
Myers, Lewis	1,543½	2	299	4–24–1788	Cumberland R	Surveyed
Myers, Wm	500	1	147	7–18–1781	Paint Lick	
Myers, Wm	287	1	299	9–25–1782	Paint Lick	
Myers & Boyd	1,993	2	296	3–10–1788	Cumberland R	
Myers & Burns	968½	2	299	4–24–1788	None	
Myers & Doughtery	2,562½	2	296	3–10–1788	Cumberland R	
Myers & Overton	500	2	297	3–15–1788	Cumberland R	
Myers & Shannon	5,000	1	241	2–25–1782	Island Mississippi R	
Myers & Shields	1,315	2	296	3–10–1788	Cumberland R	
Myers & Shriver	2,000	1	311	11–24–1782	Mississippi R	
Myers & Shuber	2,000	1	250	3–21–1782	Mississippi R	Withdrawn
Nagle, Maurice	14,000	2	251	12– 5–1785	Ky R	
Nall, Martin Sr	400	1	191	12–14–1781	Br Salt R	
Nall, Wm	962	2	292	5–15–1787	Drakes Camp Cr	
Nevill, Jas	400	1	78	6–24–1780	Dix R	
Nevill, Jas	335	1	151	8–11–1781	Dix R	
Nevill, Jas	400	1	365	2–14–1783	None	
Nevill, Jas	1,000	1	400	4–28–1783	None	
Nevill, Jas	400	2	21	8– 4–1783	Hays Fk Silver Cr	Withdrawn
Nevill, Jas	400	2	98	5– 4–1784	Muddy Cr	
Nevill, Jas	400	2	98	5– 4–1784	None	
Nevill, Jas	400	2	98	5– 4–1784	Muddy Cr	
Newton, Joseph	100	1	76	6–22–1780	Br Hanging Fk	
Noel, Richard	6,000	2	110	6– 3–1784	S Fk 3 Fks Ky R	
Noel, Richard	3,000	2	110	6– 3–1784	Cranks Cr	
Noel, Richard	3,000	2	110	6– 3–1784	Cumberland R	
Noel, Richard Jr	6,000	2	103	5–17–1784	S Fk 3 Fks Ky R	Withdrawn
Noland, Jas	50	1	119	4–19–1781	Ky R	
North, Jno	3,000	1	306	10– 6–1782	Stinking Cr	
North, Jno	3,000	1	125	7– 5–1784	Stinking Cr	
North, Wm	3,206½	1	361	2–12–1783	Rockcastle	
North, Wm	10,000	1	361	2–12–1783	Buck Cr	
North, Wm	5,000	2	182	2–14–1785	N E Br Main Laurel R	
Nourse, Joseph	20,000	2	211	4–28–1785	None	Withdrawn
Nourse, Joseph	20,000	2	230	7–14–1785	None	
Nourse, Joseph	20,000	2	230	7–14–1785	Cumberland R	
Nourse, Joseph	20,000	2	238	8–19–1785	None	
Nourse, Joseph	200	2	238	8–19–1785	None	
Nourse, Joseph	200	2	238	8–19–1785	None	
Nowell, Oliver	50	1	49	5–23–1780	None	
Nunnery, Sherman	773	1	211	1– 9–1782	Ky R	
Nunnery, Sherman	773	1	302	9–30–1782	None	
Oaley, Wm	200	1	338	1–11–1783	Thompson Br	Amended
Oaley, Wm	200	2	162	11–25–1784	Thompsons Br	
Oldham, Mary Ann	500	1	154	8–20–1781	Paint Lick	
Oldham, Mary Ann	240	2	279	6– 8–1786	Br Silver Cr	
Oliver, Thos	200	1	105	3–15–1781	None	Withdrawn
Oliver, Thos	200	1	105	3–15–1781	Dix R	
Oliver, Thos	600	1	122	4–30–1781	Silver Cr	
Oliver, Thos	200	1	315	12– 4–1782	None	
Oliver, Thos	200	1	315	12– 4–1782	None	
O'Neil, Lodowick	4,000	2	143	8–23–1784	M Fk Ky R	
O'Neal, Robt	1,000	1	305	10– 4–1782	Back Cr	
Orchard, Jas	300	1	135	6–16–1781	None	Withdrawn
Orchard, Jas	300	1	142	7–13–1781	None	
Orchard, Jas	300	1	142	7–13–1781	None	
Overton, Clough	3½	1	262	5–11–1782	Sinking Cr	
Overton, Clough	6½	1	262	5–11–1782	None	
Overton, Clough	488	1	275	6–17–1782	Chaplins Fk	
Overton, Saml	10,000	2	142	8–19–1784	S Fk Ky R	
Overton & Minor	500	1	291	7–27–1782	Ky R	
Overton & Myers	500	2	297	3–15–1788	Cumberland R	
Overton & Walton	1,000	1	291	7–27–1782	Richland Cr	Surveyed
Owen, Brackett	1,000	2	247	11– 2–1785	None	Surveyed
Owen, Richard	200	2	132	7–29–1784	Island Ohio R	

Entree	Acres	Book	Page	Entry Date	Watercourse	Notes
Owens, Arthur	500	1	292	7–29–1782	Ky R	
Owens, Richard	50	2	132	7–29–1784	Cumberland R	
Owings, Jno Cocky	500	1	35	5–12–1780	Station Camp Cr	
Owings, Jno Cocky	400	1	255	4– 6–1782	Dix R	
Owings, Jno Cocky	400	1	276	6–20–1782	N Fk Rowling Fk	
Owings, Jno C	1,000	2	7	5–28–1783	Silver Cr	
Ownley, Jas	100	2	23	9–16–1783	Ky R	
Owsley, Thos	1,000	1	30	4–29–1780	None	
Owsley, Thos	700	1	30	4–29–1780	None	
Owsley, Thos	300	1	30	4–29–1780	None	
Owsley, Thos	1,000	1	30	5– 9–1780	Craborchard Run	Withdrawn
Owsley, Thos	100	1	30	5– 9–1780	Dix R	
Owsley, Thos	600	1	30	5– 9–1780	Dix R	
Owsley, Thos	500	1	30	5– 9–1780	None	Withdrawn
Owsley, Thos	1,000	1	105	3–16–1781	Craborchard Run	
Owsley, Thos	60	1	110	3–30–1781	Dix R	
Owsley, Thos	60	1	110	3–30–1781	Hammons Lick	
Owsley, Thos	485	2	117	6–18–1784	———	
Owsley, Thos	600	2	201	3–28–1785	None	
Owsley, Thos	200	1	379	3– 7–1783	None	
Owsley, Thos	800	2	91	4–19–1784	Dix R	600 acres withdrawn
Owsley, Thos	600	2	201	3–28–1785	Station Camp Cr	
Owsley, Wm	150	1	110	3–30–1781	Dix R	
Pally, James	400	1	24	4–26–1780	Dix R	
Parberry, Jas	3,000	1	272	6– 8–1782	Buck Cr	
Parberry, Jas	500	1	272	6– 8–1782	Buck Cr	Surveyed
Parberry, Jas	500	1	272	6– 8–1782	Br Buck Cr	
Pattein, Roger	312	1	143	7–14–1781	Paint Lick	
Patterson, Jno	1,000	1	56	5–27–1780	Hanging Fk	
Patterson, Zekiel	200	1	98	2–28–1781	Hanging Fk	Withdrawn
Patterson, Zekiel	200	1	161	9–25–1781	Hanging Fk	Withdrawn
Pattie, Jno	250	1	189	12–10–1781	Boones Trace	Withdrawn
Pattie, Jno	1,000	1	194	12–17–1781	Sugar Cr	
Pattie, Jno	700	1	195	12–17–1781	2 Fks Buck Cr	
Pattie, Jno	200	1	195	12–17–1781	——— Cr	
Pattie, Jno	100	1	195	12–17–1781	None	
Pattie, Jno	1,000	1	307	10 –6–1782	Sugar Cr	
Pattie, Jno	250	1	401	5– 7–1783	Boones Trace	
Pattillo, Jas	495	1	378	3– 1–1783	Rowling Fk	Withdrawn
Pattillo, Jas	495	2	107	6– 2–1784	Br S Fk Rowling Fk	
Pattillo, Jas	495	2	108	6– 2–1784	Hunters Trace	
Patton, Rodger	400	1	393	4– 4–1783	Rowling Fk	
Patton, Rodger	312	2	17	7–14–1783	None	
Patton, Wm	400	1	38	5–15–1780	Hanging Fk	Withdrawn
Patton, Wm	400	1	96	2–17–1781	W Fk Hanging Fk	
Patton, Wm	400	1	102	3–10–1781	Hanging Fk	
Patton, Wm	200	1	102	3–10–1781	E Fk Paint Lick	
Patton, Wm	200	1	102	3–10–1781	Hanging Fk	
Patton, Wm	4,472	1	145	7–16–1781	Walnut Meadow Fk	
Patton, Alexander	200	1	145	7–16–1781	Hanging Fk	
Patton, Wm	300	1	245	3– 5–1782	Paint Lick	Withdrawn
Patton, Wm	300	2	270	3– 8–1786	None	
Pauling, Henry	400	1	1	11– 3–1779	Boones Mill Cr	
Pawerbecker, Peter	500	1	42	5–18–1780	Tates Cr	
Paxton, Thos	1,000	1	210	1– 9–1782	Little Benson Cr	
Paxton, Thos	1,000	1	211	1– 9–1782	Little Benson Cr	
Paxton, Thos	1,000	1	211	1– 9–1782	Fk Big Benson Cr	
Paxton, Thos	500	1	211	1– 9–1782	Fk Big Benson Cr	
Paxton, Thos	500	1	230	2– 9–1782	R H Fk Little Hammons Cr	
Payne, Francis	3,000	2	79	3–29–1784	Stinking Cr	
Payne, Jno	1,000	1	18	4–24–1780	Hammons Cr	
Paye, Jno	1,200	1	45	5–22–1780	Silver Cr	
Payne, Wm	1,000	2	49	1–19–1784	Fall Lick Cr	
Payne, Wm	500	2	49	1–19–1784	None	
Payne, Wm	500	2	49	1–19–1784	None	
Payne, Wm	500	2	49	1–19–1784	None	
Payne, Wm	1,000	2	50	1–19–1784	None	
Payne, Wm	500	2	50	1–19–1784	Dix R	
Payne, Wm	500	2	59	2–21–1784	Rockcastle	
Payne, Wm	1,000	2	59	2–21–1784	Br Rockcastle	
Payne, Wm	500	2	59	2–21–1784	Silver Cr	
Payne, Wm	500	2	60	2–21–1784	Station Camp Cr	
Payne, Wm	500	2	60	2–21–1784	Rockcastle	
Payne, Wm	1,000	2	91	4–19–1784	Hammons Lick	
Payne, Wm	1,000	2	121	6–28–1784	None	
Payne, Wm	1,000	2	140	8–12–1784	Paint Lick	
Payne, Wm	500	2	183	2–18–1785	Rockcastle	
Payne, Wm	367	2	183	2–18–1785	Dix R	

Entree	Acres	Book	Page	Entry Date	Watercourse	Notes
Payne, Wm	367	2	184	2–18–1785	Rockcastle	
Payne, Wm	500	2	188	2–28–1785	Silver Cr	
Payne, Wm	880	2	201	3–28–1785	None	
Payne, Wm	880	2	201	3–28–1785	Dix R & Paint Lick	
Payton, Ephram	300	1	246	3–12–1782	N Fk Rowling Fk	
Pearey, Jno	400	2	44	12–24–1783	Big Benson Cr	
Pearey, Jno	285	2	45	12–24–1783	S Fk Big Benson Cr	
Pearle, Wm	200	1	55	5–27–1780	Dix R	Withdrawn
Pearle, Wm	400	1	70	6– 9–1780	Dix R	
Pearle, Wm	200	1	70	6–12–1780	Mud Lick	
Pearle, Wm	350	1	274	6–12–1782	Browns Mill Cr	Surveyed
Pearle, Wm	100	2	306	8– 6–1789	Cedar Cr	Surveyed
Pearle, Wm	45	2	306	8– 7–1789	Gilberts Cr	
Pearle, Wm	200	2	316	4–19–1792	Rockcastle	Surveyed
Pearle, Wm	200	2	316	4–19–1792	Rockcastle	Surveyed
Pearle, Wm	200	2	316	4–19–1792	Rockcastle	Surveyed
Pendland, Alexander	200	1	66	6– 7–1780	Fk Paint Lick	Withdrawn
Pendland, Alexander	200	1	116	4–16–1781	Paint Lick	
Pendleton, Henry	3,666	2	172	12–23–1784	Cumberland R	
Pennick, Jno	400	1	16	3– 3–1780	Dix R	
Perkins, Abraham	200	2	90	4–16–1784	Sinking Valley	
Perkins, Nicholas	1,875	1	327	12–28–1782	Green R	
Perkins, Peter	3,000	1	327	12–28–1782	Caseys Cr	
Perkins, Thos	1,000	2	206	4–22–1785	M Fk Upper 3 Fks	Amended
Perkins, Thos	2,000	2	207	4–22–1785	—— Cr	Amended
Perkins, Thos	6,000	2	207	4–22–1785	—— Cr	Amended
Perkins, Thos	6,892¾	2	207	4–22–1785	—— Cr	Amended
Perkins, Thos	1,000	2	279	6– 8–1786	M Fk Ky R	
Perkins, Thos	6,892¾	2	279	6– 8–1786	M Fk Ky R	
Perkins, Thos	2,000	2	280	6– 8–1786	M Fk Ky R	
Perkins, Thos	6,000	2	280	6– 8–1786	M Fk Ky R	
Perren, Joseph	700	2	269	2–10–1786	Caseys Cr	
Perren, Joseph	723½	2	269	2–10–1786	Canoe Cr	
Perren, Josephus	700	1	317	12– 6–1782	Caseys Cr	Withdrawn
Perren, Josephus	723½	1	317	12– 7–1782	Canoe Cr	
Perry, Richard	400	1	246	3–12–1782	N Fk Casey Cr	
Peters, Edward	50	2	64	3– 3–1784	None	
Peters, Edward	50	2	64	3– 3–1784	None	
Peters, Jno	80	2	92	4–22–1784	Green R	
Peters, Jno	20	2	92	4–22–1784	—— R	
Peters, Jno	80	2	213	5–16–1785	—— R	
Petit, Benj	400	1	15	2–23–1780	Hanging Fk	
Petit, Benj	500	1	23	4–26–1780	Br Kingston Fk	
Pettenger, Richard	430	1	352	2– 1–1783	S Fk Big Benson Cr	
Petit, Benj	400	1	179	11–26–1781	—— Cr	
Petit, Benj	200	1	272	6– 8–1782	Green R	
Peyton, Craven	100	1	49	5–24–1780	Ky R	
Peyton, Elijah	200	2	263	1–27–1786	Mans Cr	
Peyton, Elverton	400	1	62	5–31–1780	Silver Cr	
Peyton, Ephram	200	1	213	1–11–1782	Green R	
Peyton, Jno	20,000	2	185	2–22–1785	Hammons Cr	
Peyton, Robt T	1,000	2	275	5– 3–1786	Rockcastle	
Phillips, Chas	500	1	205	12–26–1781	Rowling Fk & Buck Cr	
Phillips, Chas	296	2	120	6–28–1784	Rowling & Buck Fk	
Phillips, Chas	296	2	120	6–28–1784	Rowling Fk	
Phillips, Joseph	400	1	6	1–14–1780	W Fk 3 Fks Otter Cr	
Phillips, Joseph	1,000	1	58	5–30–1780	—— Cr	
Phillips, Joseph	400	2	5	5–27–1783	None	
Phillips, Thos	400	1	6	1–14–1780	W Fk Otter Cr	
Phillips, Wm	50	1	27	4–29–1780	Red R	
Pigg, Hezakiah	1,943¾	2	30	11– 3–1783	—— Cr	
Pitman, Jno	750	1	101	3– 9–1781	Quicks Run	
Pitman, Thos	500	2	95	4–24–1784	Cumberland R	
Poage, Jas	500	2	263	1–27–1786	Laurel R	
Poage, Jas	500	2	264	1–27–1786	Goose Cr	
Poage, Jas	500	2	266	1–27–1786	Goose Cr	
Poage, Robt	250	1	81	7–22–1780	Ky R	
Poage & Ray	900	2	263	1–27–1786	Laurel R	
Poage & Ray	900	2	265	1–27–1786	None	
Pollock, Berkly Wm	150	2	74	3–20–1784	Shawnee Run	
Popman, Jno	400	1	6	1–15–1780	Drakes Camp Cr	
Popham, Jno	1,000	1	113	4– 5–1781	Drakes Camp Cr	
Powell, Lewis	1,000	1	95	2–17–1781	None	
Poynter, Jno	100	1	298	9–21–1782	Br Drakes Camp Cr	
Poynter, Thos	400	1	298	9–21–1782	Drakes Camp Cr	
Prather, Thos	1,000	1	85	10– 7–1780	None	

Entree	Acres	Book	Page	Entry Date	Watercourse	Notes
Prentis, Wm	10,000	2	34	11–22–1783	———— R	
Prentis, Wm	8,600	2	40	12–15–1783	Green R	
Prentis, Wm	16,000	2	143	8–19–1784	None	
Prewitt, Isham	691½	2	85	4– 3–1784	Laurel R	
Prewitt, Jos	100	2	56	2–11–1784	None	
Prewitt, Jos	937½	2	196	3–19–1785	Br N Fk Rockcastle	
Prewitt, Jos	100	2	196	3–19–1785	None	
Prewitt, Jos	1,000	2	196	3–19–1785	None	
Price, Jno	200	1	282	6–29–1782	Green R	Withdrawn
Price, Jno	600	1	282	6–29–1782	Green R	
Price, Jno	200	1	304	10– 4–1782	Logan Cr & Green R	
Price, Jno	200	2	12	6–20–1783	Green R	
Price, Wm	1,318	2	12	6–20–1783	Tates Cr	
Price, Wm	2,000	1	289	7–22–1782	Tates Cr	
Pringle, Jno	15,0771½	2	112	6– 5–1784	Green R	Withdrawn
Pringle, Jno	50,771½	2	126	7– 6–1784	None	Withdrawn
Pritchell & Hutching	500	1	335	1– 6–1783	Mud Lick	Surveyed
Proctor, Hezakial	1,200	2	43	12–18–1783	Stinking Cr	
Proctor, Jno	1,000	2	42	12–18–1783	None	Withdrawn
Proctor, Keziah	1,200	2	315	3–15–1792	Stinking Cr	
Proctor, Littlepage	400	1	215	1–17–1782	Drowning Cr	
Proctor, Nicholas	400	1	69	6– 9–1780	Silver Cr	
Proctor, Reubin	400	1	225	1–26–1782	Drowning Cr	
Proctor, Reubin	1,100	2	1	5– 8–1783	Estills Station	
Pullen, Loftus	50	1	58	5–30–1780	Paint Lick Cr	
Quetimous, Jos	500	1	116	4–17–1781	Ky R	
Quinn, Benj	1,000	1	34	5–12–1780	S Fk Tates Cr	
Quinn, Jos	50	1	26	4–28–1780	r h Fk S Fk Tates Cr	
Quinn, Jas	1,027	1	44	5–20–1780	None	
Quinn, Thos	1,028	1	44	5–20–1780	None	
Quirk, Edmond	416¾	1	92	1–17–1781	White Oak Spring	
Quirk, Edmond	600	1	93	1–17–1781	Br Dix R	Withdrawn
Quirk, Edmond	416¾	1	148	7–20–1781	None	
Quirk, Edmond	600	1	148	7–20–1781	Br Dix Br	
Quirk, Edward	400	1	62	6– 1–1780	Quirks Cr	
Quirk, Edward	400	1	127	5–17–1781	Quirks Cr	
Quirk, Thos	300	1	133	5–31–1781	Mud Lick	Surveyed
Ragain, Robt	11,386½	2	122	6–28–1784	Rockcastle	
Rains, Jno	200	1	125	5–12–1781	Fks Carpenters Cr	Amended
Rains, Jno	200	2	43	12–20–1783	None	
Randfro, Jos	400	1	98	2–28–1781	Rockcastle	
Rantfro, Jas	100	1	116	4–17–1781	Br Rockcastle	
Rantfro, Jos	200	1	117	4–17–1781	Chaplins Fk	
Ray, Joseph	200	1	275	6–20–1782	Paint Lick	
Ray & Poage	900	2	263	1–27–1786	Laurel R	
Ray & Poage	900	2	265	1–27–1786	None	
Raynolds, Geo	400	1	79	6–24–1780	Dix R	
Raynolds, Jos	61,958	2	111	6– 5–1784	Sexton Fk Goose Cr	
Read, Alexander	250	1	152	8–14–1781	Knob Lick	
Read, Alexander	250	1	152	8–14–1781	E Fk Sugar Cr	
Read, Andrew	200	1	339	1–11–1783	None	
Read, Ann	200	1	236	2–14–1782	Green R	
Read, Jno	1,000	1	69	6– 8–1780	None	
Read, Jno	400	1	135	11–11–1779	Knob Lick	
Read, Jno	4,287½	2	56	2– 6–1784	None	
Read, Jno	500	2	100	5–10–1784	White Oak Cr	
Read, Jno	1,000	1	53	5–26–1780	Br Green R	
Read, Jos	500	1	73	6–17–1780	Drowning Cr	
Read, Saml	250	1	163	10–16–1781	Sugar Cr	
Read, Saml	250	1	42	5–18–1780	S Fk Knob Lick	Withdrawn
Read, Samuel	250	1	163	10–16–1781	S Fk Knob Lick	
Read, Wm	400	1	60	5–31–1780	Logan Cr	
Read, Wm	300	1	60	5–31–1780	Paint Lick Cr	
Read, Wm	300	1	61	5–31–1780	Hickmans Cr	
Read, Wm	400	1	123	5– 2–1781	Logans Cr	
Read, Wm	400	1	123	5– 1–1781	S Fk Clarks Run	Withdrawn
Read, Wm	400	1	140	6–21–1781	Clarks Run	
Read, Wm	400	1	141	6–21–1781	Logans Cr	Withdrawn
Read, Wm	400	2	183	2–14–1785	S Fk Ky R	
Read & Ridgely	4,000	2	273	3–20–1786	N Fk Ky R	
Read & Ridgely	8,000	2	273	3–20–1786	N Fk Ky R	
Reading, Geo	200	1	196	12–17–1781	Dix R	Withdrawn
Reading, Geo	300	1	197	12–18–1781	Ky R	Withdrawn
Reading, Geo	280	1	392	3–29–1783	S Fk Rowling Fk	
Reading, Geo	300	2	27	10– 6–1783	Silver Cr	
Reading, Geo	200	2	28	10– 6–1783	Silver Cr	
Reading, Geo	200	2	28	10– 6–1783	Silver Cr	
Reading, Geo	200	2	28	10– 6–1783	Silver Cr	
Reading, Geo	200	2	28	10– 6–1783	None	
Reading, Geo	400	2	32	11–17–1783	Salt R	

Entree	Acres	Book	Page	Entry Date	Watercourse	Notes
Reading, Geo	783	2	32	11–17–1783	Salt R	
Reading, Geo	300	2	51	1–20–1784	Ky R	
Reading, Geo	300	2	83	3–31–1784	Ky R	
Reading, Geo	300	2	132	7–29–1784	N Fk Rowling Fk	Withdrawn
Reading, Geo	300	2	196	3–19–1785	None	
Reading, Geo	150	2	196	3–19–1785	Ky R	
Reading, Geo	200	2	197	3–19–1785	Dix R	
Reading, Geo	200	2	197	3–19–1785	Dix R	
Reading, Geo	400	2	240	8–29–1785	None	
Reading, Jno & Geo	823½	2	86	4– 5–1784	Big Benson Cr	Withdrawn
Reading, Jno M & Geo Jr	823½	2	121	6–28–1784	None	
Reading, Jno M & Geo Jr	250	2	122	6–29–1784	N Fk Rowling Fk	
Reed, Jonathan	300	1	225	1–29–1783	Lick Fk	
Reed, Joseph	200	1	375	2–26–1783	Dix R	
Reed, Robt	300	2	105	5–28–1784	None	Amended
Reed, Robt	3,000	2	114	6– 8–1784	None	
Reed, Robt	1,000	2	117	6–17–1784	Ky R	
Reed, Robt	1,975	2	139	8–12–1784	None	
Reed, Samuel	300	1	226	1–29–1782	None	
Rees, Azor	1,000	1	204	12–22–1781	Cane Run	
Reid, Alexander	250	1	42	5–18–1780	Br Knob Lick Cr	Withdrawn
Reid, Alexander	200	1	208	1– 5–1782	Br Drowning Cr	
Reid, Alexander	945	2	180	2– 4–1785	Green R	Surveyed
Reid, Alexander	400	1	230	2– 8–1782	Ky R	
Reid, Alexander Jr	600	1	249	3–20–1782	Stinking Cr	Surveyed
Reid, Alexander Jr	1,000	2	105	5–28–1784	Br Silver Cr	
Reid, Jas	250	1	42	5–18–1780	S Fk Silver Cr	
Reid, Jas	200	1	72	6–17–1780	Ky R	
Reid, Jas	300	1	72	6–17–1780	Station Camp Cr	
Reid, Saml	300	2	232	7–23–1785	None	
Reid, Saml	107	2	232	7–23–1785	Paint Lick	
Reid & Stewart	200	1	146	7–16–1781	Green R	
Rentfro, Jos	200	1	190	12–11–1781	W Fk Drakes Camp Cr	
Rentfro, Jos	400	1	190	12–11–1781	Hammans Lick	
Rentfro, Jos	200	1	190	12–11–1781	Rockcastle	
Rentfro, Jos	400	1	190	12–11–1781	Rockcastle	Withdrawn
Rentfro, Jos	400	1	190	12–11–1781	Boones Trace	
Rentfro, Jos	350	1	201	12–21–1781	None	Amended
Rentfro, Jos	250	1	225	1–26–1782	None	
Rentfro, Jos	100	1	285	7–15–1782	Drake Camp Cr	
Rentfro, Jos	300	1	302	9–30–1782	Hammans Lick	
Rentfro, Jos	200	1	302	9–30–1782	Rockcastle	
Rentfro, Jos	200	1	302	9–30–1782	Drakes Camp Cr	
Rentfro, Jos	250	1	321	12–13–1782	Hammans Lick	
Rentfro, Jos	250	1	322	12–13–1782	None	Withdrawn
Rentfro, Jos	500	1	399	4–26–1783	Drakes Camp Cr	
Rentfro, Jos	350	2	40	12–15–1783	Drakes Cr	
Rentfro, Jos	300	2	41	12–15–1783	None	
Rentfro, Jos	17	2	151	10– 1–1784	None	
Rentfro, Jos	250	2	151	10– 1–1784	None	
Rentfro, Jos	125	2	151	10– 1–1784	None	
Rentfro, Jos	67	2	152	10– 1–1784	None	Surveyed
Rentfro, Jos	125	2	152	10– 1–1784	Hammans Lick Cr	
Rentfro, Joshua	500	2	72	3–18–1784	Paint Lick	
Rentfro, Joshua	700	2	126	7– 5–1784	Silver Cr	
Rentfro, Joshua	400	2	129	7–21–1784	Silver Cr	Withdrawn
Rentfro, Joshua	589½	2	175	1–19–1785	Ky. R	Withdrawn
Rentfro, Joshua	700	2	200	3–26–1785	Silver Cr	
Rentfro, Joshua	400	2	200	3–26–1785	Silver Cr	
Rentfro, Joshua	1,100	2	200	3–26–1785	N Fk Rockcastle	
Rentfro, Joshua	589½	2	275	4–10–1786	None	Surveyed
Reynolds, Geo	1,000	1	132	5–31–1781	Dix R	
Reynolds, Jno	600	2	311	9– 4–1790	Rowling Fk	
Rhea & Johnston	2,000	2	106	5–28–1784	Cane Cr	Surveyed
Rhodes, David	500	2	193	3–12–1785	S Fk Station Camp & Rockcastle	
Rhodes, Jno	20	1	19	4–25–1780	Tates Cr	
Rhodes, Jno	400	1	50	5–24–1780	l h Fk Otter Cr	
Rhodes, Jno	400	1	50	5–25–1780	Tates Cr	
Rice, David	500	2	157	11– 2–1784	Lick on Chaplins Fk	
Rice, David	500	2	157	11– 2–1784	Glens Lick	
Rice, Fisher	1,000	1	313	12– 2–1782	S Fk Ky R	
Rice, Fisher	1,075½	1	336	1– 9–1783	Fk Station Camp	
Rice, Fisher	400	1	341	1–22–1783	Ky R	
Rice, Fisher	4,200	1	341	1–22–1783	—— R	
Rice, Fisher	1,000	1	367	2–19–1783	Drowning Cr	
Rice, Fisher	1,000	1	368	2–19–1783	Drowning Cr	

Entree	Acres	Book	Page	Entry Date	Watercourse	Notes
Rice, Fisher	1,000	1	370	2–19–1783	Drowning Cr	
Rice, Fisher	1,400	1	377	3– 1–1783	Chaplins Fk	
Rice, Fisher	1,070½	2	100	5– 6–1784	Chaplins Fk	
Rice, Jno	500	1	43	5–20–1780	Tates Cr	
Rice, Saml	250	2	44	12–20–1783	None	
Rice, Saml	250	2	140	8–18–1784	Silver Cr	
Rice, Saml	250	2	140	8–18–1784	Paint Lick	
Rice, Saml	1,300	2	141	8–18–1784	Silver Cr	
Rice, Saml	1,300	2	141	8–18–1784	Paint Lick	
Rice, Saml	199½	2	141	8–18–1784	——— Cr	
Rice, Saml	1,971	2	166	12–11–1784	Silver Cr	Withdrawn
Rice, Saml	200	2	203	3–30–1785	None	
Rice, Saml	200	2	203	3–30–1785	Station Camp	
Rice, Saml	330	2	213	5– 9–1785	None	
Rice, Saml	330	2	213	5– 9–1785	E Fk Station Camp	
Rice & Walker	6,800	2	78	3–29–1784	Ky R	
Richards, Humphrey	10,000	2	254	12–19–1785	Goose Cr	
Richardson, Jesse	25	1	110	3–30–1781	Dix R	
Richardson, Jesse	50	1	173	11–20–1781	Burnt Meadow Cr	
Richardson, Jesse	100	2	164	12–10–1784	None	
Richardson, Wm	300	1	110	3–30–1781	N Fk Dix R	
Richerson, Jonathan	1,000	1	263	5–16–1782	Richland Cr	Withdrawn
Richerson, Jonathan	1,000	1	263	5–16–1782	Robinsons Cr	Withdrawn
Richerson, Jonathan	940	1	263	5–16–1782	Silver Cr	Withdrawn
Richerson, Jonathan	1,000	2	32	11–15–1783	Richland Cr	
Richerson, Jonathan	1,000	2	32	11–15–1783	Robinsons Cr	
Richerson, Jonathan	940	2	32	11–15–1783	Silver Cr	
Ridgely & Read	4,000	2	273	3–20–1786	N Fk Ky R	
Ridgely & Read	8,000	2	273	3–20–1786	N Fk Ky R	
Rife, Christopher	500	2	129	7–16–1784	Martins Cr	
Riney, Jacob	29,000	2	73	3–19–1784	Raccoon Cr	
Ritchey, Jos	400	1	357	2– 8–1783	1 st Big Cr to ——— R	
Ritchey, Jos	400	1	357	2– 8–1783	Ky R	
Ritchie, Jos	50	1	25	4–27–1780	Salt R	
Ritchie, Jos	400	1	117	4–17–1781	Ky R	Withdrawn
Robards, Joseph	448	2	305	5–11–1789	Craborchard Cr	Surveyed
Robards, Joseph	866½	2	305	5–11–1789	None	
Roberts, Benj	400	1	225	1–29–1782	Lick Br	
Roberts, Geo	500	1	53	5–26–1780	Doctors Fk	
Roberts, Hezakiah	100	1	204	12–22–1781	Dix R & Falling Lick Cr	
Roberts, Jno	1,000	1	208	1– 5–1782	None	
Roberts, Joseph	500	1	248	3–18–1782	Rowling Fk	
Robertson, Alexander	600	1	138	6–20–1781	Robinson Cr	
Robertson, Alexander	400	1	307	10– 6–1782	None	
Robertson, Alex	400	2	136	8– 4–1784	None	
Robertson, Alex	400	2	137	8– 4–1784	Hanging Fk	
Robertson, Geo	50	1	240	2–25–1782	Doctors Fk	
Roberson, Jos	475	1	229	2– 6–1782	None	
Robertson, Jno	3,837	2	8	5–30–1783	Drowning Cr	
Robins, Jos	400	1	67	6– 8–1780	Knob Lick Road	
Robinson, Alexander	300	1	75	6–20–1780	Dix R	Withdrawn
Robinson, Alexander	300	2	11	6–17–1783	Dix R	
Robinson, Alexander	1,300	2	11	6–20–1783	Fk Bensons Cr	
Robinson, Geo	200	1	48	5–23–1780	Cumberland Trace	
Robinson, Geo	200	2	202	3–28–1785	Rowling Fk	
Robinson, Jos	400	1	64	6– 2–1780	——— Cr	
Robinson, Jos	200	1	320	12–12–1782	Ky R	Withdrawn
Robinson, Jos	200	1	346	1–25–1783	Ky R	
Robinson, Jos	200	1	346	1–25–1783	Little Hammons Cr	
Robinson, Jos	382	1	346	1–25–1783	Hammons Cr	
Robinson, Jos	200	1	356	2–7– 1783	None	
Robinson, Jos	382	1	356	2– 7–1783	None	
Robinson, Jno	400	1	302	9–30–1782	None	
Robinson, Jno	200	1	323	12–18–1782	Muddy Cr	
Robinson, Jno	1,000	2	181	2– 4–1785	None	
Robinson, Jno	1,000	2	181	2– 4–1785	Paint Lick	Withdrawn
Robinson, Jno	1,000	2	199	3–26–1785	None	
Robinson, Jno	1,000	2	199	3–26–1785	E Fk Rockcastle	
Robinson, Wm	1,025	1	72	6–17–1780	Silver Cr	
Robinson, Wm	400	1	100	3– 8–1781	White Oak Cr	
Rodes, Robt	500	2	114	6– 9–1784	Silver Cr	
Rodgers, Jno	12,000	1	350	1–29–1783	Mississippi R	
Rogers, Anthony	250	1	103	3–13–1781	——— Cr	
Rogers, Byso	600	1	92	5–18–1780	None	
Rogers, Geo	600	1	92	5–18–1780	None	
Rogers, Jno	500	1	92	5–18–1780	None	
Roges & Moore	12,000	1	251	3–21–1782	Mississippi R	Withdrawn
Romine, Isaac	400	1	195	12–17–1781	Salt R	
Ronald, Geo	50	1	133	6– 4–1781	Harrodsburg	Withdrawn

Entree	Acres	Book	Page	Entry Date	Watercourse	Notes
Ronald, Geo	250	1	133	6– 4–1781	None	
Ronalds, Geo	250	1	135	6–15–1781	None	
Ronalds, Geo	50	1	147	7–18–1781	None	
Ronalds, Geo	50	1	148	7–18–1781	None	
Ronald, Wm	10,000	1	183	12– 3–1781	Mississippi R	
Ross, Ambrose	300	1	164	10–20–1781	Paint Lick	
Ross, Ambrose	150	2	47	1– 5–1784	Paint Lick	
Ross, Ambrose	350	2	59	2–20–1784	W Fk Silver Cr	
Ross, Ambrose	300	2	59	2–20–1783	Br Silver Cr	
Ross, Ambrose	1,519	2	228	6–27–1785	——— R	
Ross, Elizabeth	200	1	304	10– 4–1782	Trace	Withdrawn
Ross, Elizabeth	200	1	304	10– 4–1782	Drakes Cr	
Ross, Elizabeth	200	2	215	5–25–1785	Trace	
Ross, Elizabeth	200	2	215	5–25–1785	Drake Camp Cr	
Ross, Hugh	250	1	309	11–24–1782	Drakes Camp Cr	Withdrawn
Ross, Hugh	150	1	323	12–18–1782	None	
Ross, Hugh	4,000	1	353	2– 1–1783	Silver Cr	Withdrawn
Ross, Hugh	1,000	1	353	2– 1–1783	Silver Cr	Withdrawn
Ross, Hugh	2,000	1	354	2– 4–1783	Silver & Paint Lick	
Ross, Hugh	200	1	354	2– 4–1783	Silver Cr	
Ross, Hugh	2,000	1	379	3– 7–1783	Paint Lick & Silver Cr	Withdrawn
Ross, Hugh	1,000	1	379	3– 7–1783	Silver Cr	Withdrawn
Ross, Hugh	150	2	23	9–18–1783	Drakes Camp Cr	
Ross, Hugh	4,000	2	24	9–18–1783	Silver Cr	
Ross, Hugh	100	2	47	1– 5–1784	Hammons Lick	
Ross, Hugh	100	2	48	1– 5–1784	None	
Ross, Hugh	250	2	99	5– 5–1784	Small Br	
Ross, Hugh	238½	2	99	5– 5–1784	Silver Cr	
Ross, Hugh	1,000	2	265	1–27–1786	Silver Cr	
Ross, Hugh	1,000	2	267	1–27–1786	Silver Cr	
Ross, Hugh	2,083	2	307	2–12–1790	Clear Cr	
Ross, Hugh	400	2	318	5–30–1780	Silver Cr	
Rowenters, Banister	200	1	18	4–24–1780	Flat Caney Land	
Rowin, Wm	400	1	162	10–12–1781	Dix R	
Rowin, Wm	140	2	152	10– 7–1784	——— R	
Rowlings, Sealy	5,000	2	111	6– 5–1784	Stimpson Cr	
Runnels, Chas	400	1	206	1– 3–1782	N Fk Rowling Fk	
Runnels, Chas	250	1	207	1– 3–1782	None	
Runnels, Chas	1,150	2	46	1– 1–1784	Hanging Fk	
Runnels, Chas	100	2	63	3– 1–1784	Br Hanging Fk	
Russell, Edward	1,000	1	381	3–15–1783	Muddy Cr	
Russell, Joseph	250	1	53	5–26–1780	Small Deer Lick	Withdrawn
Russell, Joseph	250	1	120	4–24–1781	Deer Lick	
Russell, Joseph	250	1	121	4–24–1781	Br Dix R	
Rutherford, Jno	400	1	174	11–20–1781	Br Dix R	
Rutherford, Jno	400	1	175	11–20–1781	None	
Rutherford, Jno	400	1	190	12–14–1781	Br Hanging Fk	
Rutherford, Jno	500	2	116	6–15–1784	Hanging Fk	
Rutherford, Jno	500	2	308	3– 8–1790	None	Surveyed
Rutherford, Jno Jr	400	1	190	12–14–1781	None	
Rutherford, Joseph	200	1	169	11–10–1781	Br Dix R	
Rutherford, Joseph	100	1	170	11–10–1781	Cooks Br	
Rutherford, Joseph	200	1	209	1– 5–1782	Boughmans Trace	
Rutherford, Joseph	200	1	320	12–12–1782	——— Cr	
Rutherford, Joseph	500	1	321	12–12–1782	Canoe Cr	Withdrawn
Rutherford, Joseph	500	1	321	12–13–1782	Canoe Cr	100 acres withdrawn
Rutherford, Joseph	200	1	321	12–13–1782	——— R	
Rutherford, Joseph	100	2	60	2–21–1784	Canoe Cr	
Rutherford, Joseph	100	2	60	2–21–1784	Dix R	
Rutherford, Robt	6,437½	2	113	6– 8–1784	Rockcastle	
Rutherford, Robt	8,000	2	191	3– 4–1785	Rockcastle	
Rutherford, Robt	3,000	2	225	6–15–1785	Rockcastle	
Rutherford, Robt	3,000	2	270	2–28–1786	None	Surveyed
Rutherford, Robt	2,000	2	275	5– 3–1786	None	Surveyed
Sale, Robt	3,500	2	306	10–15–1789	Cumberland R	
Salley, Abram	500	1	383	3–19–1783	S Fk Ky R	
Salley, Abram	500	1	383	3–19–1783	M Fk Ky R	
Salley, Abram	500	1	383	3–19–1783	M Fk Ky R	
Salley, Abram	500	1	384	3–19–1783	M Fk Ky R	
Samuel, Jno	600	1	48	5–23–1780	——— Cr	
Samuel, Jno	600	2	202	3–28–1785	None	
Sanders, Peter	100	2	294	12– 4–1787	None	Withdrawn
Sanders, Peter	300	2	295	12– 8–1787	Hanging Fk	Withdrawn
Saunders, Jno	2,502	1	307	10– 6–1782	Robinsons Cr	Withdrawn
Saunders, Jno	200	1	359	2–10–1783	Gilberts Cr	
Saunders, Jno	2,702	2	83	3–31–1784	Robersons Cr	
Saunders, Jno	270	2	169	12–11–1784	Ky R	
Saunders, Joseph	500	1	87	10–23–1780	Pond Cr	Withdrawn
Saunders, Joseph	500	1	171	11–19–1781	Clarks Run	

Entree	Acres	Book	Page	Entry Date	Watercourse	Notes
Saunders, Joseph	500	1	171	11–19–1781	S Fk Tates Cr	
Saunders, Joseph	500	1	187	12– 6–1781	S Fk N Fk Otter Cr	
Saunders, Peter	400	2	311	9– 4–1790	Hanging Fk	
Saunders, Robt	300	1	349	1–28–1783	Tates Cr	
Say, Benj	62,869	2	209	4–28–1785	Cumberland R	Amended
Say, Benj	27,131	2	229	7–14–1785	Fks ——— Cr	Amended
Say, Benj	90,000	2	238	8–19–1785	Fks ——— Cr	
Say, Dr Benj	61,958	2	111	6– 5–1784	Sexton Fk Goose Cr	
Scott, Geo	200	1	52	5–26–1780	Dix R	Withdrawn
Scott, Geo	200	1	149	8– 1–1781	Dix R	
Scott, Geo	200	1	150	8– 1–1781	Dix R	
Scott, Geo	200	1	150	8– 8–1781	Ky R	
Scott, Geo	225	2	26	10– 6–1783	Dix R	
Scott, Geo	150	2	27	10– 6–1783	None	Withdrawn
Scott, Geo	100	2	48	1–12–1784	Ky R....	
Scott, Geo	229	2	153	10–16–1784	None	Withdrawn
Scott, Geo	150	2	173	1– 3–1785	None	
Scott, Geo	150	2	173	1– 3–1785	None	
Scott, Geo	79	2	225	6–20–1785	Smiths Old Stations	
Scott, Geo	79	2	225	6–20–1785	Smiths Cr	
Scott, Joseph	1,000	1	102	3–10–1781	Paint Lick Cr	Amended
Scott, Joseph	250	1	151	8– 8–1781	Silver Cr	
Scott, Joseph	250	1	151	8– 8–1781	Paint Lick	
Scott, Joseph	1,000	2	24	9–18–1783	None	
Scott, Robt	200	1	16	4–18–1780	Dix R	
Scott, Samuel	400	1	11	2– 9–1780	Dix R	
Scott & Grant	100	2	2	5–15–1783	Ky R	
See, Jacob	515½	1	379	3– 8–1783	Sugar Cr	
Shannon, Thos	200	1	115	4– 5–1781	Clarks Run	
Shannon & Myers	5,000	1	241	2–25–1782	Island Mississippi R	
Sharp, Abraham	400	2	149	9–27–1784	Salt R	Amended
Sharp, Abraham	400	2	153	10–20–1784	None	
Sharp, Abraham	725	2	175	1–19–1785	Cave Spring Br	
Sharp, Adam	1,050	2	133	7–30–1784	None	
Sharp, Jas	563	2	214	5–20–1785	——— Cr	
Sharp, Jno	2,230	2	133	7–30–1784	Ky R	
Shaver, David	650	2	303	12–15–1788	Cumberland R	
Shelby, David	400	1	45	5–22–1780	Paint Lick	
Shelby, Evan	100	1	18	4–24–1780	Cumberland R	
Shelby, Isaac	100	1	45	5–20–1780	Knob Lick Br	
Shelby, Jno	1,000	1	4	——1780	Chaplins Fk	
Shelp, Jno	60	1	84	10– 5–1780	Salt Cr	
Shelton, David	150	1	19	4–24–1780	Jacks Cr	
Shelton, David	50	1	19	4–24–1780	Cumberland R	
Shelton, Saml	50	1	336	1– 6–1783	Dix R	
Shelton, Thos	1,000	2	135	8– 3–1784	Rockcastle	
Shelton, Thos	700	2	136	8– 3–1784	Rockcastle	
Shelton, Wm	1,778¼	1	274	6–12–1782	Drowning Cr	
Shelton, Wm	1,778	1	274	6–12–1782	Drowning Cr	
Shepherd, Peter	1,000	1	40	5–18–1780	Chaplins Fk	
Shepherd, Peter	1,000	1	40	5–18–1780	Benson Cr	
Shepherd, Peter	400	1	40	5–18–1780	Br Ky R	
Shepherd, Peter	800	1	173	11–20–1781	Mississippi R	
Shepherd, Peter	300	1	296	8–15–1782	Dix R	Withdrawn
Shepherd, Peter	400	1	297	8–15–1782	——— R	
Shepherd, Peter	300	1	305	10– 4–1782	Dix R	
Shepherd, Peter	400	1	305	10– 4–1782	None	
Shepherd, Peter	1,000	2	71	3–18–1784	Rowling Fk	
Shepherd, Peter	500	2	71	3–18–1784	Rowling Fk	
Shepherd, Peter	280	2	71	3–18–1784	Chaplins Fk	
Shepherd, Peter	480	2	71	3–18–1784	Glenns Cr	
Shepherd, Wm	250	1	181	12– 1–1781	Nalls Br	
Shepherd, Wm	250	1	314	12– 4–1782	None	Amended
Shepherd, Wm	250	2	98	5– 1–1784	None	
Shields, Hugh	5,000	1	375	2–25–1783	Otter Cr	
Shields & Myers	1,315	2	296	3–10–1788	Cumberland R	
Shirley, Michael	203	1	161	10– 2–1781	——— Cr	Withdrawn
Shirley, Michael	158	1	200	12–19–1781	Main Silver Cr	
Shirley, Michael	400	1	342	1–23–1783	Ky R	
Shirley, Michael	300	1	343	1–23–1783	Station Camp Cr	
Shirley, Michael	569	1	343	1–23–1783	Br Muddy Cr	
Shirley, Michael	250	2	14	6–20–1783	Buck Cr	
Shirley, Michael	203	2	21	8–12–1783	Silver Cr	
Shirley, Michael	100	2	21	8–12–1783	Ky R	
Shirley, Michael	300	2	21	8–12–1783	None	
Shirley, Michael	569	2	116	6–15–1784	None	
Shirley, Michael	103	2	129	7–23–1784	Muddy Cr	
Shiver, David	4,000	1	255	4– 6–1782	Mississippi R	Withdrawn
Shiver, David	1,000	2	77	3–27–1784	Bensons Cr	
Shore, Thos	2,000	1	78	6–24–1780	E Fk Muddy Cr	
Shore, Thos	1,500	1	110	3–30–1781	Station Camp Cr	

Entree	Acres	Book	Page	Entry Date	Watercourse	Notes
Shore, Thos.	560	1	110	3–30–1781	Silver Cr.	
Shriver & Myers	2,000	1	311	11–24–1782	Mississippi R.	
Shriver, David	4,000	1	311	11–27–1782	Mississippi R.	
Shuber & Myers	2,000	1	250	3–21–1782	Mississippi R.	Withdrawn
Sinclair, Alexander	1,000	1	39	5–17–1780	Dix R.	
Sinclair, Alexander	1,000	1	48	5–23–1780	Br Ky R.	
Sinclair, Alexander	1,000	1	48	5–23–1780	Gilberts Cr.	
Sinclair, Alexander	1,000	1	48	5–23–1780	None.	
Simpson, David	200	1	253	3–29–1782	None.	
Simpson, David	200	1	282	7– 1–1782	None.	
Simpson, David	200	1	282	7– 1–1782	None.	
Simpson, Keziah	500	1	154	8–20–1781	——— R.	
Simpson, Keziah	500	1	154	8–20–1781	Paint Lick.	Withdrawn
Simpson, Keziah	500	2	152	10– 7–1784	None.	
Simpson, Keziah	500	2	152	10– 7–1784	Paint Lick.	Withdrawn
Simpson, Keziah	500	2	223	6– 9–1785	Paint Lick.	
Simpson, Keziah	500	2	223	6– 9–1785	None.	
Simpson, Richard Jr	500	1	154	8–20–1781	Paint Lick.	
Simpson, Richard Jr	500	2	66	3– 4–1784	Paint Lick.	
Simpson, Wm.	300	1	139	6–20–1781	Silver Cr.	
Singleton, Daniel	281	2	258	1– 5–1786	None.	
Singleton, Edward	10,607⅔	2	206	4–13–1785	None.	Withdrawn
Singleton, Edward	10,607⅔	2	208	4–23–1785	Raccoon Cr.	
Singleton, Edward	10,607⅔	2	209	4–23–1785	Laurel R.	Withdrawn
Singleton, Edward	1,882½	2	231	7–18–1785	Fk Benson Cr.	Withdrawn
Singleton, Edmond	500	1	348	1–27–1783	Br Salt R.	
Singleton, Edmond	500	1	348	1–27–1783	Chaplins Fk.	
Singleton, Edmond	400	1	352	1–30–1783	Hammons Cr.	
Singleton, Edmond	250	1	352	1–30–1783	l h Fk Hammons Cr	
Singleton, Edmond	19,607⅔	2	293	9–25–1787	Laurel R.	
Singleton, Edmond	1,882½	2	319	9–11–1787	Fks Benson Cr.	
Sissme, Wm, W	400	1	8	2– 7–1780	Whitleys Cr.	
Sinnett, Richard	400	1	263	5–17–1782	Chaplins Fk.	
Skillem, Geo.	500	1	43	5–19–1780	E Fk Givens Run.	
Skillem, Geo.	300	1	43	5–19–1780	E Fk Doughterys Cr.	
Skillem, Geo.	250	1	43	5–19–1780	Dix R.	Surveyed
Skillem, Geo.	250	1	43	5–19–1780	Br Big Fk Dix R.	
Skillem, Wm.	200	2	318	4–27–1780	Doughterys Cr.	
Slaughter, Geo.	400	1	12	2–19–1780	Bensons Cr.	
Slaughter, Geo.	4,660½	1	316	12– 6–1782	Salt R.	
Slaughter, Geo.	1,400	1	318	12– 9–1782	Salt R.	
Slaughter, Geo.	1,200	1	318	12– 9–1782	Ky R.	
Slaughter, Geo.	1,200	2	64	3– 4–1784	S Fk Bensons Cr.	
Slaughter, Geo.	10,000	2	101	5–10–1784	Rowling Fk.	
Slaughter, Geo.	1,000	2	212	4–28–1785	l Br Benson Cr.	
Slaughter, Geo.	4,660½	2	226	6–20–1785	None.	
Slaughter, Geo.	5,619	2	274	4–10–1786	S Fk Ky R.	Amended &
Slaughter, Geo.	5,619	2	290	1–22–1787	None.	Surveyed
Slaughter, Robt.	400	1	2	11–11–1779	Shawnee Run.	
Slaughter, Robt.	1,000	1	268	5–30–1782	None.	
Slaughter, Robt.	1,000	2	211	4–28–1785	l h Fk Benson Cr.	
Slaughter, Robt Jr	400	1	12	2–19–1780	Bensons Cr.	
Slaughter, Robt Jr	1,000	1	23	4–26–1780	Shawnee Run.	
Slaughter, Thos.	500	2	227	6–27–1785	Stinking Cr.	
Slone, Jno.	500	1	107	3–26–1781	None.	
Slone, Jno.	327	1	151	8– 8–1781	None.	
Slone, Jno.	327	1	151	8– 8–1781	Harrisons Fk.	
Slone, Pat.	400	1	14	2–21–1780	Hanging Fk.	
Sleet, Jas.	100	2	300	6–26–1788	Hanging Fk.	
Smease, Lewis	400	1	36	5–13–1780	Doctors Fk.	Withdrawn
Smease, Lewis	600	1	36	5–13–1780	Knobs.	Withdrawn
Smith, Jos.	400	1	74	6–19–1780	Dix R.	
Smith, Jos.	200	1	192	12–14–1781	Gilberts Cr.	
Smith, Jos.	1,250	1	192	12–14–1781	Br Rockcastle.	
Smith, Jos.	400	1	194	12–14–1781	Sugar Cr.	
Smith, Jos.	1,000	1	194	12–16–1781	Boones Mill Cr.	
Smith, Jos.	500	1	194	12–16–1781	Boones Mill Cr.	Amended
Smith, Jos.	500	1	243	3– 5–1782	None.	
Smith, Jos.	400	1	243	3– 5–1782	Boones Mill Cr.	Withdrawn
Smith, Jos.	250	1	243	3– 5–1782	White Oak Crs.	Withdrawn
Smith, Jos.	400	1	306	10– 4–1782	None.	
Smith, Jos.	400	1	306	10– 4–1782	Boones Mill Cr.	
Smith, Jos.	250	1	306	10– 4–1782	White Oak Cr.	
Smith, Jos.	149	2	81	3–29–1784	None.	
Smith, Jos.	149	2	81	3–29–1784	Dix R.	Withdrawn
Smith, Jos.	300	2	81	3–29–1784	Boones Mill Cr.	Withdrawn
Smith, Jos.	100	2	83	4– 1–1784	Dix R.	Withdrawn
Smith, Jos.	149	2	234	8– 3–1785	Dix R.	
Smith, Jos.	300	2	234	8– 3–1785	None.	
Smith, Jos.	149	2	234	8– 3–1785	Dix R.	
Smith, Jos.	100	2	234	8– 3–1785	Dix R.	

Entree	Acres	Book	Page	Entry Date	Watercourse	Notes
Smith, Jos	200	2	235	8– 3–1785	Dix R	
Smith, Jos	100	2	301	6–28–1788	Dix R	
Smith, Ballard	20,000	2	205	4–13–1785	Rockcastle	Withdrawn
Smith, Ballard	20,000	2	206	4–13–1785	Rockcastle	Withdrawn
Smith, Ballard	20,000	2	209	4–23–1785	Rockcastle	
Smith, Ballard	40,000	2	209	4–23–1785	Rockcastle	
Smith, Daniel	1,000	1	311	11–27–1782	Clear Fk	
Smith, Geo	1,100	1	37	5–15–1780	Taylor Fk Silver Cr	
Smith, Geo	10,018	1	185	12– 4–1781	None	
Smith, Geo	600	1	192	12–14–1781	Br Rockcastle	
Smith, Geo	600	1	192	12–14–1781	Rockcastle	
Smith, Geo	1,200	1	192	12–14–1781	——— Cr	
Smith, Geo	1,000	1	219	1–22–1782	Long Trace	
Smith, Geo	1,735	1	318	12– 9–1782	Ky R	
Smith, Geo	1,800	1	323	12–13–1782	Little S Fk N Fk Rowling	
Smith, Geo	1,000	1	326	12–27–1782	——— Cr	
Smith, Geo	1,735	1	355	2– 4–1783	None	
Smith, Geo	100	1	397	4–21–1783	Long Br	
Smith, Geo	1,000	2	14	6–20–1783	S Fk N Fk Rowling Fk	
Smith, Geo	1,000	2	14	6–20–1783	Drowning Cr	
Smith, Geo	100	2	34	11–22–1784	Dix R	
Smith, Geo	438	2	181	2– 4–1785	None	
Smith, Geo	438	2	182	2– 4–1785	None	
Smith, Geo S	500	1	37	5–15–1780	W Fk Gilberts Cr	Withdrawn
Smith, Geo S	1,000	1	181	12– 1–1781	Paint Lick	Withdrawn
Smith, Geo S	500	1	193	12–14–1781	N Fk Gilberts Cr	
Smith, Geo S	1,000	2	207	4–22–1785	None	
Smith, Jno	200	1	155	8–24–1781	Otter & Tates Crs	
Smith, Jno	300	1	286	7–18–1782	Yellow Cr	Withdrawn
Smith, Jno	300	1	315	12– 4–1782	Yellow Cr	
Smith, Reubin	2,000	2	171	12–18–1784	Ky R	
Smith, Scarlett	200	1	227	1–29–1782	Dix R	
Smith, Thos	1,000	1	192	12–14–1781	Boones Old Trace	
Smith, Thos	1,253	1	327	12–27–1782	None	Withdrawn
Smith, Thos	1,253	1	354	2– 4–1783	S Fk Big Benson	
Smith, Thos	1,253	1	354	2– 4–1783	Ky R	
Smith, Thos	1,253	2	96	4–28–1784	None	Withdrawn
Smith, Thos	1,253	2	120	6–28–1784	Ky R	
Smith, Thos	1,253	2	120	6–28–1784	Ky R	
Smith, Wm	200	1	74	6–19–1780	Ky R	Withdrawn
Smith, Wm	200	1	108	3–27–1781	Paint Lick	
Smith, Wm	200	1	108	3–27–1781	None	
Smith, Wm	200	2	21	8–12–1783	Ky R	
Smith, Wm	100	2	21	8–12–1783	Ky R	
Smith, Wm	1,000	2	162	11–24–1784	None	
Smith, Zachariah	400	1	9	2– 7–1780	Harrods Run	
Smith, Zachariah	1,000	1	56	5–29–1780	Harrods Run	
Smith, Zachariah	520	1	148	7–20–1781	Dix R	Withdrawn
Smith, Zachariah	520	1	150	8– 1–1781	Dix R	
Smith, Zachariah	520	1	150	8– 1–1781	Ky R	
Snoddy, Jno	1,000	1	300	9–27–1782	Mulberry Lick	
South, Jno	1,000	1	293	8– 2–1782	1 h Fk Otter Cr	
South, Jno	400	1	370	2–19–1783	Otter Cr	
South, Jno	1,000	2	35	11–27–1783	Ky R	
South, Jno	1,000	2	35	11–27–1783	S Fk Ky R	
South, Jno	200	2	35	11–27–1783	Ky R	
South, Jno	800	2	35	11–27–1783	Ky R	
South, Jno	932½	2	133	7–30–1784	Otter Cr	
South, Jno	1,400	2	154	10–27–1784	Otter Cr	Withdrawn
South, Jno	1,400	2	154	10–27–1784	Silver Cr	
South, Jno	1,400	2	154	10–27–1784	Boonesboro	
South, Jno	1,300	2	155	10–27–1784	Silver Cr	
South, Jno	400	2	174	1– 3–1785	S Fk Otter Cr	
South, Jno	5,500	2	177	1–22–1785	None	
Southall, Jos	9,786¼	2	298	1–27–1788	Cumberland R	
Sparks, Benj	500	2	180	1–25–1785	None	
Spears, Geo	400	1	9	2– 8–1780	Gordons Lick	
Spears, Geo	400	1	34	5–12–1780	Hanging Fk	Withdrawn
Spears, Geo	400	1	151	8– 7–1781	Hanging Fk	
Spears, Geo	200	1	151	8– 7–1781	Carpenters Cr	
Spears, Geo	200	1	151	8– 7–1781	Carpenters Cr	
Spears, Geo	1,000	1	377	6– 1–1780	Gordons Lick	
Spears, Geo	100	2	305	5–27–1789	Hanging Fk	Surveyed
Speed, Jos	50	1	26	4–28–1780	Rowling Fk	
Speed, Jos	1,000	1	96	2–24–1781	None	
Speed, Jos	200	1	105	3–16–1781	None	
Speed, Jos	200	1	310	11–24–1782	None	
Speed, Jos	3,000	1	310	11–24–1782	Cumberland Trace	Amended
Speed, Jos	800	1	338	1–11–1783	Chaplins Fk	

Entree	Acres	Book	Page	Entry Date	Watercourse	Notes
Speed, Jos	3,000	1	396	4–12–1783	———— Cr	
Speed, Jos	207½	1	401	5– 1–1783	None	Withdrawn
Speed, Jos	207½	2	34	11–22–1783	None	
Speed, Jos	396	2	34	11–22–1783	None	
Speed, Jos	603½	2	34	11–22–1783	Station Camp Cr	
Spencer, Edward	600	1	81	8–18–1780	Sugar Cr	
Spiller, Philip	250	1	34	5–11–1780	Knob Lick Br	
Stafford, Wm	100	2	20	7–31–1783	Cedar Cr	
Stanson, Edward	863	2	180	2– 4–1785	Caseys Cr	
Starns, Isaac	500	1	303	10– 2–1782	Ky R	
Starns, Jacob	400	1	49	5–23–1780	Otter Cr	
Starns, Jacob	1,000	1	303	10– 2–1782	None	
Starke, Jos	500	1	95	2–10–1781	N Fk Tates Cr	
Steel, Robt	500	1	152	8–13–1781	Salt R	
Steel, Robt	597	2	312	3– 5–1791	Rockcastle	
Stephens, Abraham	400	1	176	11–23–1781	None	Withdrawn
Stephens, Abram	400	1	179	11–26–1781	None	
Stephens, Geo Wm	1,000	1	112	3–31–1781	Ky R	
Stephens, Geo Wm	1,000	2	27	10– 6–1783	Dix R	
Stephens, Geo Wm	1,000	2	27	10– 6–1783	Mulberry Lick	
Stephens, Geo Wm	500	2	189	3– 2–1785	S Fk Ky R	
Sterne, Peyton	6,072¾	2	106	5–28–1784	Br Laurel R	
Sterns, Jacob	400	1	7	2– 2–1780	Ky R	
Stevens, Geo	650	1	51	5–25–1780	Ky R	
Stevenson, Thos	1,000	1	71	6–15–1780	E Fk ———— Cr	
Stewart, Jno	1,000	1	335	1– 6–1783	Mud Lick	Surveyed
Stewart, Thos	1,600	1	249	3–20–1782	Br Cumberland R	Surveyed
Stewart, Thos	1,600	2	187	2–23–1785	Fighting Cr	
Stewart, Thos	720	2	187	2–23–1785	Fighting Cr	Withdrawn
Stewart, Thos	720	2	278	5– 4–1786	Fighting Cr	
Stewart, Thos	120	2	278	5– 4–1786	None	
Stewart, Wm	400	1	5	12–29–1779	Chaplins Fk	
Stewart, Wm	50	1	28	4–29–1780	Doctors Fk	
Stewart, Wm	400	1	29	4–29–1780	Clarks Run	
Stewart, Wm	500	1	36	5–13–1780	Chaplins Fk	
Stewart, Wm	600	1	89	10–30–1780	Clarks Run	Withdrawn
Stewart, Wm	800	1	89	10–30–1780	Doctors Fk	
Stewart, Wm	560	1	89	10–30–1780	Doctors Fk	
Stewart, Wm	400	1	99	3– 6–1781	Town Fk	Withdrawn
Stewart, Wm	1,000	1	99	3– 6–1781	Chaplins Fk	
Stewart, Wm	500	1	101	3– 8–1781	Chaplins Fk	Withdrawn
Stewart, Wm	400	1	105	3–19–1781	Town Fk	
Stewart, Wm	400	1	106	3–19–1781	None	
Stewart, Wm	200	1	123	5– 2–1781	Doctors Fk	
Stewart, Wm	300	1	126	5–17–1781	Clarks Run	
Stewart, Wm	300	1	126	5–17–1781	Doctors Fk	
Stewart, Wm	500	1	137	6–16–1781	Chaplins Fk	
Stewart, Wm	300	1	158	9– 5–1781	Clarks Run	
Stewart, Wm	200	1	158	9– 5–1781	Chaplins Fk	
Stewart, Wm	220	1	159	9–11–1781	Clear Cr	
Stewart, Wm	100	1	159	9–11–1781	Bone	
Stewart, Wm	1,000	1	281	6–28–1782	None	
Stewart, Wm, heirs	10,000	2	71	3–18–1784	E Fk Laurel R	Surveyed
Stewart, Wm, heirs	10,000	2	71	3–18–1784	Chaplins Fk	
Stewart & Crow	3,000	1	281	6–28–1782	Big Benson Cr	
Stewart & Crow	1,628	1	281	6–28–1782	Hammons Cr	
Stewart & Crow	1,700	1	281	6–28–1782	Ky R	
Stewart & Reid	200	1	146	7–16–1781	Green R	
Street, Wm	1,691¼	1	276	6–20–1782	Dix R	Withdrawn
Street, Wm	1,691¼	2	162	12– 5–1784	Dix R	
Steel, Robt	500	1	100	3– 8–1781	Salt R	Withdrawn
Strother, Benj	500	2	105	5–28–1784	M Fk Richland Cr	
Stull, Martin	400	1	14	2–22–1780	Town Fk Salt R	
Sublett, Benj	2,000	1	276	6–20–1782	Skaggs Cr	Amended
Sublett, Benj	1,178⅔	1	276	6–20–1782	Stinking Cr	
Sublett, Benj	2,000	2	200	3–26–1785	Skaggs Cr	
Summer, Jno	1,000	2	59	2–20–1784	W Fk Silver Cr	
Summers, Jno	40	2	155	10–27–1784	Drake Camp Cr	Withdrawn
Summers, Jno	10	2	156	10–28–1784	Drake Camp Cr	Withdrawn
Summers, Jno	600	2	175	1–17–1785	Fk Round Stone Lick	Amended
Summers, Jno	600	2	208	4–23–1785	None	
Summers, Jno	40	2	227	6–27–1785	Drake Camp Cr	
Summers, Jno	10	2	227	6–27–1785	None	
Summers, Jno	15	2	225	6–27–1785	Drakes Camp Cr	
Swan, Jno	1,000	1	162	10–13–1781	White Oak Sp	
Swann, Jno	3,000	1	167	11– 9–1781	Br Paint Lick	
Swan & Corn	1,000	1	303	10– 2–1782	None	
Swann, Jno	1,300	2	13	6–20–1783	Paint Lick	
Swann, Jno	1,300	2	13	6–20–1783	Station Camp	
Swearingen, Benoni	400	1	28	4–29–1780	None	

Entree	Acres	Book	Page	Entry Date	Watercourse	Notes
Swearingen, Thos	400	1	28	4–29–1780	M Fk Muddy Cr	
Swearingen, Thos	1,000	1	59	5–30–1780	Salt R	
Swearingen, Thos	1,000	1	389	3–24–1783	Chaplins Settlement	
Swope, Benedict	1,000	1	106	3–23–1781	None	
Swope, Benedict	300	1	119	4–22–1781	Dix R	
Swope, Benedict	1,000	1	223	1–26–1782	Dix R	
Swope, Benedict	4,000	1	255	4– 6–1782	Mississippi R	Withdrawn
Swope, Benedict	4,000	1	311	11–27–1782	Mississippi R	
Swope, Jacob	200	2	291	3–13–1787	None	
Swope, Jacob	200	2	291	3–13–1787	None	
Talbot, Jno	2,500	1	264	5–23–1782	N Fk Laurel R	
Talbot, Jno	2,500	2	142	8–18–1784	Salt R	
Talbot, Jno	2,500	2	273	3–21–1786	Salt R	
Taliaferro, Peter	400	1	70	6–12–1780	Green R	
Tanner, David	300	1	161	10– 3–1781	Br S Fk Tates Cr	
Tanner, David	300	1	273	6– 8–1782	None	
Tanner, David	1,000	1	277	6–20–1782	Otter Cr	
Tarvin, Jno	250	1	195	12–17–1781	None	
Tarvin, Jno	250	1	195	12–17–1781	Drakes Camp Cr	
Tate, Caleb	1,750	2	249	11–15–1785	None	
Tate, Jno	400	1	65	6– 3–1780	Hammons & White Lick	
Tate, Robt	400	1	8	2– 4–1780	Br Silver Cr	
Tate, Robt	561½	2	161	11–24–1784	Sturgeon & Station Camp Crs	
Taylor, Chas	1,000	1	382	3–18–1783	Little Benson Cr	
Taylor, Francis	1,000	1	249	3–20–1782	Stinking Cr	Surveyed
Taylor, Geo	250	1	33	5–11–1780	Cedar Cr	
Taylor, Hubbard	400	1	112	4– 2–1781	Gilberts Cr	
Taylor, Hubbard	1,200	1	257	4–11–1782	Paint Lick	
Taylor, Hubbard	200	1	257	4–11–1782	Fk Skaggs Cr	
Taylor, Hubbard	1,000	1	257	4–11–1782	Paint Lick	
Taylor, Hubbard	50	1	315	12– 4–1782	Cedar Run	
Taylor, Hubbard	100	1	332	1– 3–1783	Br Dix R	Surveyed
Taylor, Isaac	1,000	1	393	4– 7–1783	Salt R	
Taylor, James	250	1	222	1–25–1782	Main Fk Skaggs Cr	
Taylor, Jas	500	1	257	4–11–1782	None	
Taylor, Jas	500	1	394	4– 7–1783	—— Cr	
Taylor, Capt Jesse	1,750	1	62	6– 1–1780	Chaplins Fk	
Taylor, Jno	1,000	1	92	5–18–1780	None	
Taylor, Peter	800	1	33	5–11–1780	None	
Taylor, Peter	1,000	1	50	5–24–1780	E Fk Otter Cr	
Taylor, Peter	1,000	1	50	5–24–1780	E Fk Muddy Cr	
Taylor, Peter	250	2	44	12–20–1783	Otter Cr	Withdrawn
Taylor, Peter	250	2	254	12–19–1785	Otter Cr	
Taylor, Philip	400	1	119	4–19–1781	Hammons Cr	
Taylor, Richard	400	1	8	2– 4–1780	r h Fk Otter Cr	
Taylor, Saml	300	1	184	12– 3–1781	Rockcastle	
Taylor, Saml	1,000	1	184	12– 3–1781	Hazel Patch	
Taylor, Sam	1,000	1	189	12–10–1781	N Fk Rockcastle	
Taylor, Sam	1,000	1	189	12–10–1781	N Fk Rockcastle	
Taylor, Saml	950	2	57	2–16–1784	None	Withdrawn
Taylor, Saml	950	2	201	3–28–1785	None	
Taylor, Saml	950	2	201	3–28–1785	Shawnee Run	
Teator, Geo	400	1	21	4–26–1780	Dix R	
Teator, Geo	300	1	97	2–27–1781	Salt R	
Teator, Geo	200	1	115	4–13–1781	Dix R	
Teator, Geo	100	1	115	4–13–1781	Br Salt R	
Teator, Geo	200	1	134	6–12–1781	Sugar Cr	
Teators, Geo	100	2	286	10– 2–1786	None	
Teators, Saml	600	2	185	2–19–1785	None	
Telford, Jeremiah	200	1	129	10–31–1780	Ky R	
Telford, Jeremiah	200	1	129	8–11–1780	Ky R	
Telford, Wm	1,128½	2	44	12–20–1783	Big Benson Cr	Withdrawn
Telford, Wm	1,128½	2	75	3–24–1784	Big Benson Cr	
Terrell, Edmond	150	1	280	6–26–1782	Paint Lick	Withdrawn
Terrell, Edmond	150	1	294	8– 5–1782	Paint Lick	Withdrawn
Terrell, Edward	500	2	223	6– 9–1785	None	
Terrell, Edward	150	2	224	6– 9–1785	None	
Terrell, Edward	150	2	224	6– 9–1785	None	
Terrell, Edward	300	2	224	6– 9–1785	None	
Terrell, Jno	450	1	50	5–24–1780	Muddy Cr	
Terrell, Robt	100	1	102	3–13–1781	Rockcastle	
Terrell, Robt	100	1	103	3–13–1781	Sinking Spring	
Terrell, Robt	100	1	346	1–27–1783	Boones Road	
Terrell, Robt	100	1	346	1–27–1783	Sinking Spring	
Terrell & Hawkins	1,000	1	119	4–19–1781	None	
Terrell & Hawkins	1,000	1	129	5–18–1781	None	
Terrell & Hawkins	400	1	134	6–12–1781	Gilberts Cr	
Terry, Jno	200	1	159	9– 7–1781	Main Fk Sugar Cr	
Terry, Jno	100	1	172	11–19–1781	Sugar Cr	

Entree	Acres	Book	Page	Entry Date	Watercourse	Notes
Thomas, Jos	300	1	48	5–23–1780	Ky R	
Thomas, Mark	325	1	241	2–25–1782	None	
Thomas, Michael	400	1	76	6–21–1780	Dix R	
Thomas, Robt	2,373¾	2	95	4–24–1784	Chaplins Fk	Withdrawn
Thomas, Robt	2,373	2	124	7– 2–1784	Chaplins Fk	
Thomas, Robt	2,373	2	124	7– 2–1784	Chaplins Fk	
Thomas, Wm	100	2	58	2–20–1784	Ky R	
Thomas, Wm	50	2	58	2–20–1784	Stone Lick Cr	
Thomas, Wm	6	2	102	5–14–1784	None	
Thomas, Wm	106	2	236	8–10–1785	Ky R	
Thompson, Geo	400	1	11	2–11–1780	Dix R	
Thompson, Geo	400	1	71	6–16–1780	Dix R	Withdrawn
Thompson, Geo	380	1	116	4–16–1781	None	
Thompson, Geo	620	1	116	4–16–1781	None	
Thompson, Geo	1,000	1	180	11–28–1781	Dix R	
Thompson, Geo	6,600	2	136	8– 3–1784	Stinking Cr	
Thompson, Geo	19,250	2	136	8– 3–1784	Rockcastle	
Thompson, Jas	1,000	1	387	3–19–1783	Pitmans Cr	Withdrawn
Thompson, Jos	1,000	1	387	3–19–1783	Pitmans Cr	Withdrawn
Thompson, Jos	266	1	387	3–19–1783	Br Pitmans Cr	Withdrawn
Thomspon, Jos	500	1	387	3–19–1783	Br Buck Cr	Withdrawn
Thompson, Jos	1,000	2	54	2– 4–1784	Pitman Cr	
Thompson, Jos	1,000	2	54	2– 4–1784	Pitmans Cr	
Thompson, Jos	266	2	54	2– 4–1784	Br Pitman Cr	
Thompson, Jos	500	2	54	2– 4–1784	Brush Cr	
Thompson, Jos	4,266	2	54	2– 4–1784	None	
Thompson, Joseph	698	2	10	6–17–1783	None	
Thompson, Saml	500	1	239	2–25–1782	Green R	
Thompson, Saml	500	1	239	2–25–1782	Caseys Cr	
Thompson, Wm	1,000	1	64	6– 2–1780	Ky R	Withdrawn
Thompson, Wm	100	1	294	8– 3–1782	Clarks Run	Withdrawn
Thompson, Wm	200	1	324	12–19–1782	Dix R	
Thompson, Wm	100	1	331	1– 1–1783	Clarks Run	
Thompson, Wm	200	1	331	1– 1–1783	Clarks Run	Withdrawn
Thompson, Wm	371	1	396	4–12–1783	None	Withdrawn
Thompson, Wm	200	2	68	3–16–1784	Clarks Run	
Thompson, Wm	371	2	68	3–16–1784	None	
Thompson, Wm	300	2	68	3–16–1784	Goose Cr	
Thompson, Wm	231	2	68	3–16–1784	——— Br	
Thompson, Wm	40	2	68	3–16–1784	None	Withdrawn
Thompson, Wm	1,000	2	115	6– 9–1784	Harrods Landing & Shawnee Run	
Thompson, Wm	40	2	125	7– 5–1784	None	
Thompson, Wm	40	2	125	7– 5–1784	Clarks Run	
Thurman, Jno	350	1	142	7–13–1781	Muddy Cr	
Thurman, Jno	350	1	142	7–13–1781	None	
Thurmond, Jno	1,750	1	88	10–25–1780	Muddy & Drowning Cr	
Todd, Robt	100	1	44	5–20–1780	Main Fk Richland Cr	
Todd, Robt	880	1	323	12–17–1782	Hazel Patch	
Todd, Saml	50	1	17	4–20–1780	Dix R	
Todd, Saml	50	1	17	4–20–1780	Dix R	
Todd, Samuel	400	1	157	8–31–1781	Hammons Cr	
Tomkins, Humphry	300	1	261	5–11–1782	Br Paint Lick	
Tomkins, Humphry	379	1	261	5–11–1782	Long Fk S Fk Paint Lick	
Tompkins, Humphry	1,000	1	312	11–27–1782	Cane Cr	
Tompkins, Humphry	300	2	169	12–11–1784	Paint Lick	
Tompkins, Humphry	700	2	169	12–11–1784	None	
Tompkins, Terah	1,000	2	3	5–21–1783	Hazel Patch Cr	Surveyed
Tomkins, Wm	3,482	2	154	10–27–1784	Ky R	
Tomlinson, Geo	200	2	230	7–14–1785	Otter Cr	Withdrawn
Tomlinson, Geo	200	2	238	8–15–1785	Otter Cr	
Townsend, Jas	459¼	2	103	5–18–1784	Otter Cr	
Trabue, Jas	800	1	69	6– 8–1780	Dix R	
Trabue, Jas	790	1	391	3–24–1783	Br Dix R	
Trabue, Jas	410	1	391	3–24–1783	M Fk Ky R	
Trabue, Daniel	1,000	1	128	5–18–1781	Green R	Withdrawn
Trabue, Daniel	500	1	128	5–18–1781	Green R	Withdrawn
Trabue, Daniel	1,000	1	386	3–19–1783	Green R	
Trabue, Daniel	500	1	386	3–19–1783	None	
Trabue, Daniel	500	1	386	3–19–1783	M Fk Ky R	
Trabue, Daniel	500	1	386	3–19–1783	M Fk Ky R	
Trabue, Daniel	500	1	386	3–19–1783	M Fk Ky R	
Trabue, Jno	200	1	82	9– 5–1780	Dix R	
Trabue, Jno	1,000	1	128	5–18–1781	Green R	Withdrawn
Trabue, Jno	1,000	1	386	3–19–1783	Green R	
Trabue, Jno	500	1	386	3–19–1783	M Fk Ky R	
Trabue, Jno	500	1	387	3–19–1783	M Fk Ky R	
Trap, Martin	50	1	378	3– 6–1783	N Fk Old Lick	

Entree	Acres	Book	Page	Entry Date	Watercourse	Notes
Trent, Jno B	1,000	1	30	4-29-1780	Tates & Otter Cr	
Tredway, Moses	10,000	1	253	3-29-1782	Laurel R	
Treadway, Wm	400	1	335	1- 6-1783	Glady Fk	
Trigg, Stephen	360	1	39	5-17-1780	Shawnee Run	
Trigg, Stephen	900	1	39	5-17-1780	Hammonds Cr	
Trigg, Stephen	400	1	61	5-31-1780	Skeggs Cr	Withdrawn
Trigg, Stephen	400	1	61	5-31-1780	N Fk Skeggs Cr	
Trigg, Stephen	1,000	1	88	10-27-1780	Dix R	
Trigg, Stephen	240	1	89	10-27-1780	None	Withdrawn
Trigg, Stephen	591	1	89	10-27-1780	——— R	
Trigg, Stephen	400	1	118	4-19-1781	Skeggs Cr	
Trigg, Stephen	240	1	118	4-19-1781	None	
Trigg, Stephen	600	1	118	4-19-1781	Gilberts Cr	Withdrawn
Trigg, Stephen	200	1	120	4-24-1781	Green R	Withdrawn
Trigg, Stephen	150	1	131	5-23-1781	Br Paint Lick	Withdrawn
Trigg, Stephen	140	1	140	6-21-1781	Dix R	
Trigg, Stephen	200	1	143	7-14-1781	Green R	
Trigg, Stephen	150	1	144	7-14-1781	Br Paint Lick	
Trigg, Stephen	300	1	144	7-14-1781	Main Paint Lick	
Trigg, Stephen	100	1	179	11-27-1781	Br Paint Lick	
Trigg, Stephen	600	1	248	3-20-1782	Gilberts Cr	
Trigg, Stephen	529	1	248	3-20-1782	S Fk N Fk Rock-castle	
Trigg, Stephen	71	1	248	3-20-1782	S Fk N Fk Rock-castle	Surveyed
Triplett, Simon	150	2	28	10- 6-1783	Raccoon Spring	
Triplett, Simon	250	2	28	10- 6-1783	Laurel R	
Triplett, Simon	300	2	29	10- 6-1783	Yellow Cr	
Triplett, Simon	325	1	29	10- 6-1783	Br Cumberland R	
Troutman, Michael	400	1	61	5-31-1780	Paint Lick Cr	
True, Jas	350	1	38	5-17-1780	Dix R	Withdrawn
True, Jas	350	1	258	4-11-1782	Dix R	
True, Jas	350	1	258	4-11-1782	Green R	
Turpin, Henry	600	1	210	1- 9-1782	Br Ky R	
Turpin, Wm	100	1	187	12- 6-1781	Stone Fk	
Turpin, Wm	100	1	187	12- 6-1781	Tates Cr	Withdrawn
Turpin, Wm	50	1	187	12- 6-1781	Tates Cr	Withdrawn
Turpin, Wm	25	2	9	6- 1-1783	Stoners Fk	
Turpin, Wm	100	2	9	6- 1-1783	Tates Cr	
Turpin, Wm	50	2	9	6- 1-1783	Tates Cr	
Turpin, Wm	175	2	9	6- 4-1783	Silver Cr	
Underwood, Francis	100	1	231	2-11-1782	Dix R	
Underwood, Francis	675	1	401	5- 7-1783	Dix R	
Underwood, Francis	100	2	9	6- 4-1783	Dix R	
Underwood, Gideon	943½	2	86	4- 3-1784	None	
Vance, Joseph	1,000	1	98	2-28-1781	Br Hanging Fk	
Vancliff, Wm	720	1	157	9- 3-1781	Paint Lick	
Vancleave, Wm	280	1	401	4-30-1783	Paint Lick	
Vanmatre, Isaac	—	2	313	7-27-1791	Hanging Fk	
Vanmeter, Jacob	400	1	276	6-20-1782	N Fk Rowling Fk	
Vardeman, Peter	100	1	170	11-16-1781	Dix R	
Vardeman, Peter	100	1	170	11-16-1781	Dix R	
Vichris, Nicholas	400	1	117	4-19-1781	Tates Cr	
Walker, Benj	551	2	70	3-17-1784	S Br Ky R	
Walker, Henry	1,000	2	95	4-24-1784	Cumberland R	
Walker, Joel	400	1	7	2- 3-1780	Big Bend Muddy Cr	
Walker, Joel	500	1	60	5-30-1780	Muddy Cr	
Walker, Joel	500	1	60	5-30-1780	Muddy Cr	
Walker, Joel	500	2	37	11-29-1783	Muddy Cr	
Walker, Joel	500	2	38	11-29-1783	Muddy Cr	
Walker, Merry	500	2	80	3-29-1784	Little Benson Cr	
Walker, Merry	500	2	85	4- 3-1784	Dix R	
Walker, Merry	533	2	86	4- 3-1784	Ky R	
Walker, Wm	400	1	7	2- 3-1780	Ky R	
Walker, Wm	1,000	1	62	6- 1-1780	Ky R	
Walker & Rice	6,800	2	78	3-29-1784	Ky R	
Walkins, Jno	800	1	35	5-12-1780	Dix R	
Walkins, Jno	200	1	35	5-12-1780	None	
Wallace, Adam	400	1	15	2-25-1780	Gilberts Cr & Dix R	
Wallace, Caleb	500	1	31	5-10-1780	Cane Run	
Wallace, Caleb	500	1	31	5-10-1780	Cane Run	
Wallace, Caleb	100	1	316	12- 6-1782	Cane Run	Withdrawn
Wallace, Caleb	100	1	329	12-30-1782	Cane Run	
Wallace, Caleb	100	1	394	4- 7-1783	N Fk Rockcastle	
Wallace, Jno	217½	2	65	3- 4-1784	Muddy Cr	
Wallace, Samuel	500	1	47	5-23-1780	Br Boone Mill Cr	Withdrawn
Wallace, Saml	500	1	329	12-30-1782	Boones Mill Cr	
Walton, Matthew	1,000	2	106	5-28-1784	Chaplins Fk	
Walton, Matthew	10,000	2	241	9-23-1785	None	Amended

Entree	Acres	Book	Page	Entry Date	Watercourse	Notes
Walton, Matthew	5,000	2	245	10–18–1785	Drowning & Station Camp	
Walton, Matthew	3,000	2	246	10–18–1785	Station Camp Cr	
Walton, Matthew	10,000	2	246	10–21–1785	None	
Walton, Matthew	10,000	2	247	11– 2–1785	None	6000 acres withdrawn
Walton, Matthew	6,000	2	288	1–18–1787	None	
Walton, Matthew	6,000	2	288	1–18–1787	S Fk Rowling Fk	
Walton, Robt	1,000	1	32	5–11–1780	Otter & Silver Cr	
Walton & Overton	1,000	1	291	7–27–1782	Richland Cr	Surveyed
Ward, Jno	400	1	288	7–19–1782	S Fk Little Hammons Cr	
Ward, Jno	200	1	329	12–30–1782	Gilberts Cr	Withdrawn
Ward, Jno	200	1	350	1–29–1783	Gilberts Cr	
Ward, Jno	200	1	350	1–29–1783	Br Ky R	
Ware, Isaac	200	1	26	4–28–1780	Ky R	
Ware, Isaac	1,767	2	257	1– 5–1786	Richland & Laurel	
Ware, Jas	500	1	74	6–17–1780	Large Cane Cr	
Ware, Markham	100	1	320	12–12–1782	Dix R	
Ware, Robt	100	1	18	4–22–1780	N Fk White Oak Cr	Withdrawn
Ware, Robt	100	1	257	4–11–1782	White Oak Cr	
Ware, Robt	1,000	1	222	1–25–1782	Skeggs Cr	Amended
Ware, Robt	100	1	257	4–11–1782	Paint Lick	Withdrawn
Ware, Robt	100	1	387	3–19–1783	Paint Lick	
Ware, Robt	1,000	2	277	5– 4–1786	None	
Ware, Wm	500	1	312	11–27–1782	Salt R	Withdrawn
Ware, Wm	500	1	340	1–11–1783	N Fk Rowling Fk	
Ware, Wm	3,020½	2	75	3–22–1784	None	
Warton, Jas	1,000	1	300	9–27–1782	Fk Muddy Cr	
Warrant, Jas	200	1	129	5–18–1781	Br Dix R	
Warrant, Thos	500	1	52	5–25–1780	Otter Cr	
Warrant, Wm	1,000	1	69	6– 8–1780	Clarks Run	
Warrant, Wm	200	1	129	5–21–1781	None	Withdrawn
Warrant, Wm	200	1	148	7–19–1781	None	
Warrant, Wm	111½	1	395	4–12–1783	None	
Warrant & Dayer	500	1	358	2– 8–1783	Rowling Fk	Withdrawn
Warrant & Dayer	500	1	395	4–12–1783	Rowling Fk	
Warren, Jas	200	1	27	4–29–1780	Dix R	Withdrawn
Watkins, Jno	500	1	95	2–10–1781	Hammons Fk	Withdrawn
Watkins, Jno	1,000	1	95	2–10–1781	Dix R	
Watkins, Jno	500	1	126	5–16–1781	Sugar Cr	
Watkins, Jno	1,000	1	193	12–14–1781	Big Fk Goose Cr	
Watkins, Jno	1,500	1	343	1–23–1783	Browns Mill Cr	Amended
Watkins, Jno	500	2	28	10– 6–1783	Hammons Cr	
Watkins, Jno	1,500	2	96	4–24–1784	None	
Watkins, Jno	500	2	188	2–26–1785	Dix R	
Watkins, Wm	400	1	81	8–18–1780	None	Withdrawn
Watkins, Wm	300	1	81	8–18–1780	Dix R	Withdrawn
Watkins, Wm	400	1	81	8–18–1780	2nd Fk Sugar Cr	
Watkins, Wm	400	2	49	1– 6–1784	None	
Watkins, Wm	300	2	49	1–16–1784	None	
Watson, Patrick	350	2	240	9–12–1785	N Fk M Fk 3 Fks Ky R	
Watson, Wm	975	1	334	1– 6–1783	Dix R	
Watts, Jno	16,000	2	148	9–20–1784	None	
Watts & McLardy	16,613¾	2	148	9–20–1784	Lynn Camp Cr	
Webb, Foster Jr	2,000	1	253	3–29–1782	Br Laurel R	
Webb, Foster Jr	2,000	1	253	3–29–1782	Fk Laurel R	
Webb, Foster Jr	2,000	1	253	3–29–1782	None	
Webb, Foster Jr	7,000	1	253	3–29–1782	None	
Webb, Jno	5,000	2	128	7–16–1784	16 Mile Tree	
Webb, Jno	2,000	2	128	7–16–1784	Green R	
Welch, Nicholas	1,000	1	189	12–10–1781	None	
Welch, Nicholas	1,000	1	201	12–21–1781	None	
Wells, Carty	356½	1	308	10–21–1782	Dix R	Surveyed
West, Edward	1,313½	2	110	6– 3–1784	Cumberland R	
West, Edward	415½	2	110	6– 3–1784	——— R	
Westerville, Jas	400	1	75	6–21–1780	Silver Cr	
Wheeler, Moses	50	1	27	4–29–1780	Ky R	
Wheeler & Chace	6,250	1	255	4– 6–1782	Mississippi R	Withdrawn
Wheeler & Chace	6,250	2	160	11– 7–1784	Mississippi R	
White, Aquila	400	2	10	6–17–1783	Br Muddy Cr	
White, Elisha	2,000	1	336	1– 6–1783	Cumberland R	
White, Jno	3,000	1	182	12– 2–1781	Silver Cr	
White, Jno	3,000	1	393	4– 4–1783	Silver Cr	Withdrawn
White, Katherine	400	2	159	11–11–1784	Lovells Cr	
Whithers, Geo	500	1	34	5–11–1780	Sinking Cr	
Whitlock, Chapman	400	2	73	3–20–1784	None	
Whitlock, Chapman	400	2	55	2– 6–1784	None	
Whitley, Wm	400	1	3	11–11–1779	Cedar Cr	
Whitley, Wm	1,000	1	24	4–26–1780	None	

Entree	Acres	Book	Page	Entry Date	Watercourse	Notes
Whitley, Wm	400	1	119	4–21–1781	Dix R	
Whitley, Wm	100	1	141	6–29–1781	Br Cedar Cr	Withdrawn
Whitley, Wm	100	2	23	9–18–1783	None	Withdrawn
Whitley, Wm	100	2	69	3–16–1784	Cedar Cr	
Whitley, Wm	200	2	69	3–16–1784	None	
Whitley, Wm	100	2	319	3–16–1784	None	
Whitted, Wm	250	1	133	6– 4–1781	Quicks Run	Withdrawn
Whitted, Wm	230	1	139	6–20–1781	Quicks Run	
Whittle, Jno	502½	2	57	2–16–1784	Rockcastle	
Wilkinson, Jas	12,000	2	156	10–28–1784	Rockcastle	
Wilkinson, Jno	400	1	23	4–26–1780	Br Dix R	
Wilkinson, Jno	400	2	42	12–18–1783	Dix R	
Williams, Alfred	250	2	138	8– 9–1784	Silver Cr	
Williams, Alfred	250	2	142	8–18–1784	Paint Lick	Withdrawn
Williams, Alfred	70	2	197	3–22–1785	None	
Williams, Alfred	250	2	197	3–22–1785	——— R	
Williams, Alfred	150	2	198	3–22–1785	Silver Cr	Surveyed
Williams, Alfred	170	2	198	3–22–1785	Paint Lick & Silver Crs	
Williams, Alfred	84	2	250	11–23–1785	Silver Cr	
Williams, Alfred	84	2	250	11–23–1785	Silver Cr	
Williams, David	560	1	89	10–30–1780	Salt R	Withdrwan
Williams, David	560	2	44	12–20–1783	Salt R	
Williams, Thos	250	1	32	5–11–1780	Craborchard Run	
Williams, Thos	250	1	32	5–11–1780	Dix R	Withdrawn
Williams, Thos	250	1	104	3–13–1781	Dix R	
Williams, Thos	250	1	104	3–13–1781	Br Drakes Camp Cr	
Willis, Edward	2,373¾	2	95	4–24–1784	Chaplins Fk	Withdrawn
Willis, Edward	2,373	2	124	7– 2–1784	Chaplins Fk	
Willis, Edward	2,373	2	124	7– 2–1784	Chaplins Fk	
Willis, Edward	200	2	272	3– 8–1786	Chaplins Fk	
Willis, Edward	100	2	272	3– 8–1786	Chaplins Fk	
Willis, Edward	200	2	272	3– 8–1786	Salt R	
Willis, Edward	437	2	282	7–13–1786	Chaplins Fk	
Willis, Edward	2,000	2	283	7–13–1786	Green R	
Willis, Edward	460	2	283	7–28–1786	Salt R	
Willis, Edward	550	2	284	7–28–1786	Drake Camp Cr	
Willis, Joseph	200	1	190	12–10–1781	Chaplins Fk	
Willis, Joseph	300	1	221	1–25–1782	Trace to Salt Works	
Willis, Joseph	200	1	327	12–28–1782	Deep Cr	
Willis, Joseph Jr	400	1	36	5–13–1780	Chaplins Fk	
Willis, Joseph Jr	100	1	66	6– 3–1780	Chaplins Fk	
Willis, Joseph Sr	300	2	243	10– 7–1785	Chaplins Fk	
Willis, Joseph Sr	200	2	243	10– 7–1785	None	
Willis, Joseph Sr	200	1	187	12– 8–1781	Br Chaplins Fk	
Willis, Joseph Sr	300	1	330	1– 1–1783	Chaplins Fk	
Willis, Joseph Sr	300	1	353	2– 1–1783	Chaplins Fk	Withdrawn
Willis, Joseph Sr	288	2	243	10– 7–1785	Salt R	
Willis, Wm	400	1	18	4–24–1780	Dix R	
Willis, Wm	400	1	18	4–24–1780	Dix R	Withdrawn
Willis, Wm	100	1	18	4–24–1780	Dix R	
Willis, Wm	1,117	2	161	11–24–1784	None	
Willis, Wm	400	2	280	6–26–1786	None	Surveyed
Wilson, Geo	9,925	2	260	1–26–1786	Goose Cr	
Wilson, Geo	200	2	268	2– 6–1786	Goose Cr	
Wilson, Geo	100	2	271	3– 8–1786	None	
Wilson, Henry	400	2	95	4–24–1784	Richland Cr	
Wilson, Henry	400	2	268	2– 6–1786	Cumberland R	
Wilson, Isaac	461	2	183	2–14–1785	None	
Wilson, Isaac	300	2	183	2–14–1785	None	Withdrawn
Wilson, Isaac	300	2	199	3–26–1785	None	
Wilson, Isaac	300	2	199	3–26–1785	Rockcastle	
Wilson, Jno	50	1	18	4–22–1780	———	
Wilson, Jno	250	1	39	5–17–1780	Smiths Cr	
Wilson, Jno	400	1	400	4–29–1783	Ky & Dix R	
Wilson, Robt	1,000	1	157	9– 3–1781	Crooked Cr	Withdrawn
Wilson, Robt	400	1	400	4–30–1783	Green	Withdrawn
Wilson, Robt	1,000	2	3	5–23–1783	Crooked Cr	
Wilson, Thos	400	1	14	2–22–1780	Wilsons Run	
Winston, Isaac	1,600	1	286	7–18–1782	S Fk Cumberland R	Surveyed
Winston, Isaac	1,600	1	286	7–18–1782	M Fk Cumberland R	Surveyed
Winston, Isaac	1,800	1	286	7–18–1782	N Fk Cumberland R	Surveyed
Withers, Geo	500	1	99	3– 6–1781	Sinking Cr	
Withers, Jas	500	1	45	5–22–1780	Station & Muddy Cr	
Withers, Jno	500	1	45	5–22–1780	Station Camp Cr	
Withers, Thos	804	1	36	5–15–1780	Ky R	Surveyed
Wood, Andrew	50	1	56	5–27–1780	Dix R	
Wood, Arch	200	1	179	11–24–1781	None	
Wood, David	1,000	1	86	10–23–1780	None	
Wood, Jno	400	1	32	5–11–1780	Br Muddy Cr	
Wood, Jno	700	1	34	5–11–1780	Dry Br	

Entree	Acres	Book	Page	Entry Date	Watercourse	Notes
Wood, Michael	600	2	272	3–17–1786	Salt Lick	
Woodfin, Saml	1,500	1	188	12– 8–1781	Ky R	
Woodfin, Saml	1,000	1	188	12– 8–1781	——— R	
Woodfin, Saml	1,000	1	188	12– 8–1781	Paint Lick	Withdrawn
Woodfin, Saml	2,000	1	189	12– 8–1781	Sugar Cr	
Woodfin, Saml	1,000	1	213	1–11–1782	Paint Lick	
Woodfin, Saml	1,700	1	213	1–11–1782	Paint Lick & Sugar Crs	
Woodfin, Saml	300	1	213	1–11–1782	None	Withdrawn
Woodfin, Saml	200	1	214	1–11–1782	None	Withdrawn
Woodfin, Saml	200	1	214	1–11–1782	None	Withdrawn
Woodfin, Saml	500	1	217	1–19–1782	None	Withdrawn
Woodfin, Saml	300	1	246	3–12–1782	——— Cr	
Woodfin, Saml	200	1	315	12– 6–1782	None	
Woodfin, Saml	200	1	315	12– 6–1782	None	
Woodfin, Saml	200	1	316	12– 6–1782	None	
Woodfin, Saml	500	1	324	12–19–1782	Doctors Fk	
Woodfin, Saml	1,500	2	179	1–25–1785	Paint Lick & Sugar Crs	
Woodfin, Saml	700	2	179	1–25–1785	Rockcastle	
Woods, Adam	300	1	198	12–19–1781	Little Muddy Cr	
Woods, Adam	300	1	216	1–17–1782	Silver Cr	
Woods, Adam	300	1	216	1–17–1782	None	
Woods, Andrew, heirs	300	2	94	4–24–1784	Cumberland R	
Woods, Andrew	500	1	23	4–26–1780	Hawkins Br	
Woods, Andrew	500	1	23	4–26–1780	Br Dix R	
Woods, Arch	200	1	179	11–24–1781	Paint Lick	
Woods, Arch	500	1	198	12–19–1781	Muddy Cr	
Woods, Arch	500	1	215	1–17–1782	None	
Woods, Arch	400	1	222	1–25–1782	Chaplins Fk	
Woods, Arch	1,000	1	344	1–24–1783	Muddy Cr	
Woods, Arch	1,000	2	6	5–28–1783	Tates Cr	
Woods, Arch	1,000	2	6	5–28–1783	Otter Cr	
Woods, Arch	1,378	2	7	5–28–1783	Br Muddy Cr	
Woods, Arch	1,400	2	35	11–29–1783	Dix R	
Woods, Archibald	400	1	176	11–23–1781	White Oak Cr	
Woods, David	300	1	240	2–25–1782	Hammons Cr	
Woods, David	100	1	217	1–19–1782	Salt R	
Woods, David	400	1	227	2– 4–1782	None	
Woods, David	200	1	240	2–25–1782	——— Cr	
Woods, Jas	200	1	44	5–20–1780	Salt R	
Woods, Jas	200	1	44	5–20–1780	Salt R	
Woods, Jno	1,000	1	197	12–19–1781	Muddy Cr	
Woods, Jno	500	1	197	12–19–1781	Silver Cr	
Woods, Jno	500	1	198	12–19–1781	Muddy Cr	
Woods, Jno	400	1	198	12–19–1781	None	
Woods, Jno	200	1	199	12–19–1781	Br Drowning Cr	
Woods, Jno	500	1	199	12–19–1781	Station Camp	
Woods, Jno	300	1	199	12–19–1781	Station Camp	
Woods, Jno	400	1	215	1–17–1782	None	
Woods, Jno	400	1	215	1–17–1782	Muddy Cr	
Woods, Jno	200	1	229	2– 8–1782	Br Ky R	
Woods, Jno	2,000	1	336	1– 9–1783	Main Fk Station Camp	
Woods, Jno	2,000	1	367	2–19–1783	Drowning Cr	
Woods, Jno	500	2	20	8– 4–1783	Silver Cr	
Woods, Jno	400	2	116	6–12–1784	Estills Station	
Woods, Martha	600	1	202	12–21–1781	None	
Woods, Martha	139	2	193	3–12–1785	Station Camp Cr	
Woods, Martha	600	2	193	3–12–1785	None	
Woods, Martha	139	2	194	3–12–1785	——— R	
Woods, Mary	600	1	202	12–21–1781	Station Camp Cr	
Woods, Mary	410	2	193	3–12–1785	Station Camp Cr	
Woods, Mary	600	2	193	3–12–1785	None	
Woods, Mary	410	2	194	3–12–1785	Rockcastle	
Woods, Michael	400	1	177	11–23–1781	Ky R	
Woods, Michael	600	1	353	2– 1–1783	Silver Cr	
Woods, Michael	1,000	1	370	2–20–1783	None	
Woods, Michael	100	2	75	3–22–1784	None	
Woods, Michael	200	2	75	3–22–1784	Kennady Settlement	
Woods, Michael	250	2	75	3–23–1784	None	
Woods, Michael	100	2	88	4–12–1784	Paint Lick	
Woods, Michael	696½	2	96	4–24–1784	Dix R	
Woods, Michael	413	2	148	9–22–1784	Quirks Run	
Woods, Michael	700	2	148	9–22–1784	Quirks Run	
Woods, Michael	450	2	173	1– 3–1784	Mans Cr	
Woods, Michael	1,000	2	242	10– 4–1785	Lick	600 acres withdrawn
Woods, Michael	1,689½	2	312	3– 5–1791	Rockcastle	
Woods, Richard	400	1	182	12– 2–1781	E Br Paint Lick	
Woods, Richard	400	1	182	12– 2–1781	S Fk Paint Lick	

Entree	Acres	Book	Page	Entry Date	Watercourse	Notes
Woods, Samuel	3,765	1	313	12- 2-1782	Bensons Cr	
Woods, Saml	1,168	1	357	2- 8-1783	Salt R	
Woods, Saml	700	2	91	4-16-1784	S Fk Big Benson Cr	
Woods, Saml	575	2	91	4-16-1784	S Fk Big Benson Cr	
Woods, Wm	400	1	247	3-18-1782	S Fk Rowling Fk	
Woods, Wm	1,800	2	101	5-12-1784	Cumberland R	
Woods & Ewing	1,000	2	87	4- 5-1784	S Fk Big Benson Cr	Withdrawn
Woods & Ewing	1,000	2	87	4- 5-1784	S Fk Big Benson Cr	Withdrawn
Woods & Ewing	812½	2	87	4- 5-1784	Br S Fk Big Benson Cr	Withdrawn
Woods & Ewing	1,000	2	90	4-16-1784	None	
Woods & Ewing	1,000	2	90	4-16-1784	None	
Woods & Ewing	812½	2	91	4-16-1784	Br S Fk	
Woodson, Drury	2,351¼	2	208	4-23-1785	Ky R	
Woodson, Drury	1,882½	2	231	7-18-1785	Benson, Hammons & Indian	Withdrawn
Woodson, Drury	1,882½	2	293	9-11-1787	Fks Benson Cr	Withdrawn
Woodson, Jno Sr	1,200	1	208	1- 5-1782	Dix R	
Woodson, Jno Sr	1,200	2	199	3-26-1785	Dix R	
Woodson, Jno Sr	1,200	2	199	3-26-1785	Rockcastle	
Woodson, Matthew	3,936½	2	231	7-18-1785	None	
Wooley, Henry	200	1	58	5-30-1780	Paint Lick	
Wooley, Henry	300	1	58	5-30-1780	Wooleys Br	
Wooley, Wm	400	1	58	5-30-1780	Solomons Br	
Wooley, Jno	1,000	1	62	6- 1-1780	Paint Lick	
Wooley, Peter	400	1	10	2- 9-1780	Dix R	
Woolfalk, Jno	5,702½	2	301	7- 4-1788	Rockcastle	3,000 acres withdrawn
Woolfalk, Sowyell	600	2	212	5- 5-1785	None	
Woolfalk, Sowyell	500	2	212	5- 5-1785	Station Camp Cr	
Woolridge, Edmond	500	1	128	5-18-1781	None	Withdrawn
Woolridge, Edmond	1,000	1	184	12- 3-1781	None	
Woolridge, Edmond	12,000	1	184	12- 3-1781	None	
Woolridge, Edmond	1,000	1	233	2-13-1782	N Fk E Fk Buck Cr	Withdrawn
Woolridge, Edmond	1,000	1	233	2-13-1782	Sinking Cr	Withdrawn
Woolridge, Edmond	1,000	1	234	2-13-1782	Scaggs Cr	
Woolridge, Edmond	500	1	234	2-13-1782	Rockcastle	
Woolridge, Edmond	1,000	1	234	2-13-1782	Main Fk Buck Cr	
Woolridge, Edmond	1,000	1	259	4-17-1782	E Fk Buck Cr	
Woolridge, Edmond	1,000	1	259	4-18-1782	W Fk Sugar Cr	Withdrawn
Woolridge, Edmond	1,000	1	290	7-26-1782	Sinking Cr	
Woolridge, Edmond	1,000	1	290	7-26-1782	Silver Cr	
Woolridge, Edmond	2,000	1	343	1-23-1783	Sugar Cr	Withdrawn
Woolridge, Edmond	1,000	1	343	1-23-1783	Sugar Cr	Withdrawn
Woolridge, Edmond	500	1	385	3-19-1783	Green R	
Woolridge, Edmund	500	1	385	3-19-1783	M Fk Ky R	
Woolridge, Edmund	1,000	1	399	4-25-1783	Sugar Cr	
Woolridge, Edmond	2,000	2	130	7-23-1784	Sugar Cr	
Woolridge, Edmond	1,000	2	130	7-23-1784	Sugar Cr	
Woolridge, Edmond	3,000	2	130	7-23-1784	N Fk S Fk 3 Fks Ky. R	
Woolridge, Edward	1,400	1	202	12-21-1781	W Fk Station Camp Cr	
Woolridge, Edward	600	1	202	12-21-1781	Main Fk Station Camp	
Worthington, Edward	400	1	2	11-11-1779	Salt R	
Wran, Wm	1,618½	2	214	5-25-1785	Rockcastle	
Wray, James	400	1	1	11- 3-1779	Salt R	
Wright, Jas	100	1	161	9-26-1781	Salt Lick	
Wright, Jno	50	1	88	10-25-1780	None	
Wright, Jno	633¾	2	258	1- 5-1785	None	
Wright, Margaret	600	2	76	3-24-1784	Drowning Cr	
Wright, Saml	600	2	76	3-24-1784	None	
Wright, Wm	1,182	2	145	8-24-1784	Sturgeon Cr	
Wright & Crow	1,120	1	159	9-13-1781	Hammons Cr	
Wrice, Saml	250	1	295	8-13-1782	Paint Lick	Withdrawn
Wrice, Saml	250	1	296	8-13-1782	Paint Lick	
Wrice, Saml	250	2	44	12-20-1783	Silver Cr	Withdrawn
Wyatt, Wm	500	1	122	5- 1-1781	Hanging Fk	
Wyatt, Wm	300	2	131	7-27-1784	Hanging Fk	
Wyatt, Wm	300	2	131	7-27-1784	None	
Yager, Adam	400	1	36	5-15-1780	Rockcastle	
Yager, Cornelius	—	1	9	2- 9-1780	Hanging Fk Dix R	
Yager, Jno	400	1	37	5-15-1780	—— Cr	
Yoakum, Mathias	1,000	1	23	4-26-1780	Chaplins Fk	
Young, Jno	500	1	240	2-25-1782	Chaplins Fk	
Young, Wm	400	1	28	4-29-1780	E Fk Gilberts Cr	
Young, Wm	400	2	306	8- 7-1789	M Br Gilberts Cr	
Young, Jas & Joseph	200	1	25	4-27-1780	Dix R	Surveyed

III

FAYETTE ENTRIES

(1782—1794)

Entree	Acres	Book	Page	Entry Date	Watercourse	Notes
Abercrombie, Jos	16,000	3	111	12–27–1783	None	Surveyed
Abercrombie, Jas	14,000	3	113	12–27–1783	None	Surveyed
Abner, John	500	2	85	1–18–1783	None	Surveyed
Abner, John	200	2	265	4– 7–1783	Ky R	Surveyed
Abner, John	1,800	2	292	5–23–1783	Br M Licking	Withdrawn
Acnat, James	975	2	277	4–23–1783	Howards Upper Cr	Withdrawn
Adams, George	1,344	1	388	1– 7–1783	N Fk Licking	Amended
Adams, George	——	2	258	3–27–1783	None	....
Adams, John	200	1	42	12– 4–1782	—— Cr	....
Adams, Jno	2,003	3	22	10–31–1783	Br Licking	....
Adams, Josiah	3,208	3	131	1– 1–1784	None	Surveyed
Adams, Josiah	3,208	3	189	2–28–1784	None	Surveyed
Adams, Littleton & Thos	15,979½	3	136	1– 2–1784	None	Surveyed
Adams, Richard	2,000	1	250	12–24–1782	Br M Fk Licking	....
Adams, Richard	2,000	2	254	3–24–1783	Junction Ohio & Ky R	....
Adams, Richard	20,000	3	302	4–26–1784	None	....
Adams, Richard	5,000	3	337	5–19–1784	None	Withdrawn
Adams, Richard	1,895	3	337	5–19–1784	None	Withdrawn
Adams, Richard	3,105	3	337	5–19–1784	None	Withdrawn
Adams, Richard	5,000	3	338	5–19–1784	None	Withdrawn
Adams, Richard	10,000	3	340	5–19–1784	None	Withdrawn
Adams, Richard	2,950	3	341	5–20–1784	None	Withdrawn
Adams, Richard	3,000	3	342	5–20–1784	None	Withdrawn
Adams, Richard	4,050	3	342	5–20–1784	None	Withdrawn
Adams, Richard	10,000	3	343	5–20–1784	Sandy	....
Adams, Richard	3,000	3	343	5–20–1784	None	Withdrawn
Adams, Richard	2,000	3	343	5–20–1784	None	Withdrawn
Adams, Richard	5,000	3	350	5–29–1784	Licking	Surveyed
Adams, Richard	5,937½	3	363	6–14–1784	Licking	Surveyed
Adams, Richard	26,895	4	56	10–17–1784	None	....
Adams, Richard	20,000	4	56	10–17–1784	None	....
Adams, Richard	7,046	4	56	10–17–1784	None	Withdrawn
Adams, Richard	2,954	4	57	10–17–1784	None	Withdrawn
Adams, Richard	20,000	4	141	3–31–1785	None	.....
Adams, Richard	7,046	4	143	4– 5–1785	None	....
Adams, Richard	2,954	4	143	4– 5–1785	None	......
Adams, Richard	10,000	4	143	4– 5–1785	Ohio R	....
Adams, Richard Jr	5,000	4	211	7–27–1785	None	....
Adams & Crow	4,000	3	89	12–15–1783	Goose Cr	Surveyed
Adams & Crow	3,000	3	89	12–15–1783	M Fk Ky R	Surveyed
Adams & Crow	3,000	3	89	12–15–1783	N Fk 3 Fks Ky R	Surveyed
Adams & Crow	2,500	3	90	12–15–1783	N Fk 3 Fks Ky R	....
Adams & Crow	2,500	3	90	12–15–1783	R	Surveyed
Adams & Crow	2,500	3	90	12–15–1783	M Fk Ky R	Surveyed
Adams & Crow	2,500	3	90	12–15–1783	—— Cr	Surveyed
Adcock, Edward	500	3	152	1–16–1784	None	....
Adcock, Jno	500	3	151	1–16–1784	N Fk —— Cr	....
Adkins, William	200	1	115	12–12–1782	N Fk Elkhorn	....
Adkins & Young	1,000	4	29	9– 7–1784	Glens Cr	....
Agan, William	500	2	301	5–30–1783	Greers Cr	Withdrawn
Agan, Wm	1,500	4	284	3–23–1786	N Fk Ky R	....
Akins, Samuel	1,000	2	291	5–23–1783	Clear Cr	....
Akins, Wm	3,300	4	191	6– 1–1785	None	....
Alcock, Robert	2,500	1	40	12– 4–1782	Licking	....
Alcock, Thomas	2,000	2	119	1–24–1783	Blue Lick Fk	Surveyed
Alexander, Andrew	775	4	69	11–19–1784	None	....
Alexander, Jno	526	4	165	4–29–1785	None	....
Alexander, William	3,000	1	148	12–16–1782	N Fk Licking	Surveyed
Alexander, Wm	6,549	4	143	4– 5–1785	None	....
Alexander, Wm	21,000	4	169	4–30–1785	Main Fk Sandy R	Withdrawn
Alexander, Wm	21,000	4	170	5– 3–1785	Main Fk Sandy R	....
Allen, Grant & Wm	1,575	3	105	12–20–1783	S Fk Licking	Surveyed
Allen, Grant & Wm	1,575	3	231	3–20–1784	Licking	Surveyed
Allen, James	400	1	23	12–17–1782	Licking	....

Entree	Acres	Book	Page	Entry Date	Watercourse	Notes
Allen, Jno	4,980½	3	135	1–2–1784	None	
Allen, Jno	282¾	3	176	2–9–1784	None	
Allen, M	1,000	3	105	12–20–1783	S Fk Licking	
Allen, M	2,995½	3	272	4–6–1784	Licking	
Allen, M	2,095½	4	131	3–12–1785	S Fk Blue Lick	
Allen, M	80	4	269	2–6–1786	N Fk Elkhorn	
Allen, Thomas	5,000	1	315	12–30–1782	None	
Allen, Thos	412½	4	62	10–29–1784	S Fk Licking	
Allen, Wm Jr	1,000	4	261	1–18–1786	S Fk Sandy	
Allen, Wm Jr	1,000	4	261	1–18–1786	——— Cr	
Allen, Wm Jr	3,681¾	4	272	2–15–1786	Sandy	Amended
Allen & Fowler	3,681¾	4	294	4–29–1786	None	
Allegree, John	750	1	303	12–27–1782	None	Surveyed
Allison, Halbert	400	2	191	2–13–1783	None	Surveyed
Anderson, Doctor	2,000	2	59	1–14–1783	None	Withdrawn
Anderson, Doctor	2,000	4	232	11–7–1785	Ohio R	
Anderson, Jacob	1,629	2	75	1–16–1783	Mill Cr	
Anderson, James	2,440	2	34	1–10–1783	Ohio R	Surveyed
Anderson, Joseph	4,980½	3	135	1–2–1784	None	
Anderson, Nelson	1,000	2	236	3–12–1783	None	Surveyed
Anderson, Nelson Jr	2,000	2	170	2–7–1783	Hinkstons Mill Creek	
Anderson, Richard C	1,000	1	272	12–25–1782	Paint Lick Cr	
Anderson, Richard C	1,000	1	272	12–25–1782	Paint Lick Cr	
Anderson, Richard C	1,000	1	273	12–25–1782	Paint Cr	
Anderson, Richard C	1,000	1	273	12–25–1782	Paint Lick Cr	
Anderson, Thomas	1,267½	2	59	1–14–1783	None	Surveyed
Andrews, Robert Rev	1,000	2	299	5–29–1783	None	Surveyed
Anthony, Joseph	1,000	3	144	1–13–1784	Little Sandy	
Arbuckle, John	600	2	242	3–13–1783	None	
Archer, Stephen	1,000	1	92	12–10–1782	N Fk Elkhorn	Surveyed
Archer, Stephen	1,343	2	27	1–10–1783	None	Surveyed
Armstrong, Andrew	1,000	3	381	6–23–1784	——— Cr	
Armstrong, James	3,381	3	260	3–31–1784	N E Fk Licking	
Armstrong, James	2,000	3	261	3–31–1784	N Fk Licking	
Armstrong, Jas	3,381	3	330	5–13–1784	None	
Armstrong, Jas & Archibald	7,736	3	330	5–13–1784	Licking	562½ acres withdrawn
Armstrong, Robt	1,000	3	261	3–31–1784	——— Cr	Surveyed
Armstrong, Robt	1,000	4	65	11–5–1784	N E Fk Licking	Surveyed
Armstrong, Robt	1,000	4	88	1–8–1785	Licking	Surveyed
Armstrong, Robt	3,267	4	127	3–5–1785	None	Surveyed
Arnal, James	300	2	35	1–11–1783	None	
Arnold, James	700	1	124	12–12–1782	None	
Arnold, James	1,093	2	4	1–8–1783	None	Surveyed
Arnold, Jas	1,093	3	293	4–16–1784	None	
Arnold, Jas	1,000	4	310	1–29–1787	None	
Arnold, Jno	1,015	3	163	1–22–1784	Clear Cr	Withdrawn
Arnold, Jno	150	4	144	4–9–1785	Clear Cr	
Arnold, Thos	1,015	3	232	3–18–1784	None	Surveyed
Arnold, Wm	6,710¾	3	408	7–14–1784	Eagle Cr	Withdrawn
Arnold & Campbell	800	3	255	3–30–1784	Bank Lick Cr	Surveyed
Arnold & Young	500	3	232	3–18–1784	——— R	Surveyed
Arnold & Young	198	3	367	6–14–1784	Clear Cr	
Asberry, Daniel	400	3	419	7–30–1784	None	
Asberry, Daniel	———	4	72	11–27–1784	None	
Ash, Francis	600	1	113	12–12–1782	None	Surveyed
Ash, Francis	1,500	4	25	8–31–1784	Clear Cr	Withdrawn
Ash, Francis	1,500	4	27	9–2–1784	Clear Cr	
Ash, Francis	600	4	46	10–5–1784	Ky R	Withdrawn
Ash, Francis	500	4	49	9–12–1784	Ky R	Withdrawn
Ash, Francis	400	4	49	9–12–1784	Ky R	Withdrawn
Ash, Francis	600	4	66	11–10–1784	None	
Ash, Francis	1,500	4	66	11–10–1784	None	Surveyed
Ash, Francis & Uriah	15,979½	3	136	1–2–1784	None	Surveyed
Ash & Marshall Jr	2,750	3	418	7–30–1784	Licking	Withdrawn
Ash & Marshall Jr	2,750	4	25	8–31–1784	None	
Ashby, Benjamin	1,000	1	131	12–13–1782	N Fk Elkhorn	
Ashby, Benjamin	1,000	1	132	12–13–1782	N Br M Fk Hingstons	
Ashby, Benjamin	1,500	1	387	1–7–1783	N Fk Licking	Withdrawn
Ashby, Benjamin	1,500	2	7	1–9–1793	None	
Ashby, Benjamin	500	2	8	1–9–1783	Sinking Cr	Surveyed
Ashby, Benjamin	1,000	2	9	1–9–1783	Stoners Fk	Surveyed
Ashby, Benjamin	50	2	23	1–9–1783	Hingston Fk	
Ashby, Benj	403	2	214	2–28–1783	None	
Ashby, John	200	2	216	2–28–1783	None	Surveyed
Ashby, Jno	207	3	352	6–2–1784	None	Withdrawn
Ashby, John Jr	207	1	3	1–13–1783	None	
Ashby, John Jr	1,693	1	387	1–7–1783	S & M Fk Licking	Withdrawn

Entree	Acres	Book	Page	Entry Date	Watercourse	Notes
Ashby, John Jr	1,000	2	210	2–26–1783	None	Surveyed
Ashby, John Jr	1,693	2	213	2–28–1783	None	Surveyed
Ashby, John Jr	1,450½	3	160	1–21–1784	Licking	Surveyed
Ashby, Jno Jr	207	4	49	9–12–1784	Ky R	Withdrawn
Ashby, Jno Jr	207	4	91	1–15–1785	None	....
Ashby, Jno Jr	207	4	91	1–15–1785	None	....
Ashby, Robert	234¾	2	10	1– 9–1783	None	Surveyed
Ashby, Robert	234¾	2	213	2–28–1783	Cedar Cr	Surveyed
Ashby, Jr & Marshall Jr	207	3	418	7–29–1784	None	Withdrawn
Ashby, Jr & Marshall Jr	207	4	49	9–12–1784	None	....
Ashby & Cowls	2,000	3	126	1– 1–1784	Howards Upper Cr	Withdrawn
Ashby & Cowls	1,000	3	126	1– 1–1784	Lulbergrud Cr	....
Ashby & Cowls	1,000	3	427	1– 1–1784	Sandy R	....
Atkinson, Isaiah	3,000	4	93	1–17–1785	None	....
Atkinson, Jos	1,587¼	4	147	4–10–1785	Little Sandy	....
Atual, James	950	3	92	12–16–1783	Howards Upper Cr	Surveyed
Austin, Chapman	400	3	149	1–15–1784	Ky R	Surveyed
Austin, John	1,005	2	195	2–14–1783	Saven Cr	Withdrawn
Austin, John	2,000	2	236	3–12–1783	None	Surveyed
Austin, John	1,005	2	376	10–13–1783	Br Eagle Cr	Surveyed
Austin, Stephen	10,000	3	118	12–29–1783	N Fk Big Sandy	Surveyed
Austin, Thos	1,000	3	148	1–15–1784	Ky R	Surveyed
Back, Joseph	791	2	111	1–23–1783	Sycamore Fk Hinkstons	Surveyed
Back, Joseph	791	2	166	2– 6–1783	Br Licking	Surveyed
Backley, Jno	400	3	150	1–15–1784	Ky R	....
Badget, Edmund	968	2	116	1– 2–1783	None	Surveyed
Bagby, Jno	6,800¾	4	273	2–15–1786	Sandy	....
Bagby, Jno	6,800	4	295	4–29–1786	None	....
Bagby, Wm	400	3	287	4–14–1784	Summerset Cr	....
Bailey, Jeremiah G	2,212½	2	199	2–17–1783	None	....
Bailey, Jno	375	3	26	10–31–1783	None	....
Bain, Isaac	57,499¼	4	50	9–13–1784	Ky R	Withdrawn
Baker, Samuel	1,000	1	96	12–10–1782	Lulbergrud	....
Baker, Thos	1,575	4	257	1–16–1786	Salt Rock Fk	....
Ball, Edward	622½	1	4	11–29–1783	Eagle Creek	....
Ballard, Wm	1,000	4	304	8–12–1786	S Fk Elkhorn	....
Ballinger, Richard	1,000	4	196	6– 9–1785	Ky R	....
Ballinger, Richard	334¾	4	197	6– 9–1785	S Fk Elkhorn	....
Ballinger, Richard	400	4	197	6– 9–1785	Stamping Br	....
Ballinger, Richard	250	4	197	6–10–1785	None	....
Ballinger, Richard	250	4	198	6–10–1785	Lulbergrud Cr	....
Ballinger, Richard	1,000	4	338	9–10–1794	None	....
Ballinger, Richard	1,234½	4	338	9–10–1794	None	....
Bank, Adam	3,140	1	215	12–21–1782	Ohio R	Surveyed
Banks & Orr	12,500	4	121	2–16–1785	Elkhorn	Withdrawn
Banks & Orr	9,500	4	125	3– 5–1785	Ky R	Amended & withdrawn
Bantons, William	500	1	4	1–13–1783	Br Hingstons Fk	....
Barbour, Ambrose	3,000	1	203	12–20–1782	Licking	Amended
Barbour, Ambrose	3,000	1	203	12–20–1782	Hingston Fk	....
Barbour, Ambrose	—	3	351	5–31–1784	Br Cabbin Cr	Surveyed
Barbour, Richard	1,000	1	127	12–13–1782	Mill Cr	....
Barbour, Richard	1,000	1	131	12–13–1782	Lees Cr	Surveyed
Barbour, Thomas	6,000	1	130	12–13–1782	None	Surveyed
Barbour, Thos	—	3	256	3–30–1784	None	Surveyed
Barbour & Maury	10,000	3	55	11–21–1783	Ohio R	Surveyed
Barby, Andrew	286	4	31	9– 9–1784	S Licking	Surveyed
Barby, Thos	4,037	4	31	9– 9–1784	None	Withdrawn
Barby, Thos	4,037	4	63	11– 2–1784	None	....
Bard, James	1,000	2	69	1–15–1783	Licking	Surveyed
Barker, John	3,000	1	265	12–24–1782	Stoners Fk	....
Barker & Morgan	656¼	3	132	1– 2–1784	None	....
Barker & Ewing	11,000	3	345	5–24–1784	None	Amended
Barksdale, Lelborne	1,387½	2	61	1–14–1783	None	Surveyed
Barksdale, Peter	750	4	134	3–19–1785	None	....
Barksdale, Wm	2,000	2	207	2–22–1783	S W Br Licking	Withdrawn
Barksdale, Wm	2,000	4	128	3– 7–1785	None	....
Barksdale, Wm	2,000	4	128	3– 7–1785	Br Green R	....
Barksdale, Wm	1,039½	4	128	3– 7–1785	Cr & R	....
Barnett, Alexander	500	2	65	1–15–1783	Ky R	....
Barnett, Alexander	1,000	4	160	4–29–1785	None	....
Barnett, Jas	1,336	4	160	4–29–1785	None	....
Barnett, James Jr	500	2	185	2–13–1783	Br Sandy	....
Barnett, John	1,200	1	153	12–17–1782	N Fk Licking	....
Barnett, John	1,937¾	2	130	1–27–1783	None	....
Barnett, George	1,000	1	349	1– 2–1783	None	....
Barnett, George	1,800	2	137	1–27–1783	Hickmans Cr	Withdrawn
Barnett, George	1,800	2	204	2–19–1783	None	....
Barnett, George	5,000	2	204	2–19–1783	Br Ohio R	....

Entree	Acres	Book	Page	Entry Date	Watercourse	Notes
Barnett, Thomas	1,155	2	186	2–13–1783	None	
Barnett, William	1,200	2	131	1–27–1783	None	
Barnett, William	1,675½	2	193	2–14–1783	Br Red R	
Barrett, Wm	1,000	4	160	4–29–1785	None	
Barr, Isaac	7,000	4	62	10–29–1784	Main Licking	
Barr, Isaac	57,499¼	4	57	10–23–1784	Eagle Cr	Surveyed
Barr, Isaac	1,000	4	210	7–22–1785	None	
Barr, Isaac	1,000	4	280	3–23–1786	None	
Barr, Capt Isaac	10,000	4	53	10–16–1784	Locust Cr	
Barr, Isaac & Archibald	1,000	4	55	10–16–1784	None	
Barr, Isaac & Archibald	1,000	4	54	10–16–1784	None	
Barr, James	456⅔	3	366	6–14–1784	Br Big Bone Lick	
Barr, Jas	500	3	366	6–14–1784	Ohio R	Surveyed
Barr, James	377⅔	3	367	6–14–1784	Stoners Fk	
Barr, John	4,463	2	237	3–12–1783	None	
Barr, Robt	2,000	4	118	2–12–1785	Br Licking	
Barr, Robt, Isaac & Richard	12,225	4	70	11–25–1784	Slate Cr	
Barr Archibald & Robt Jas & Jno & Isaac	16,961	4	210	7–22–1785	Br Ky R	Withdrawn
Barr, A & Robt, & Jas & Isaac	16,961	4	280	3–23–1786	None	
Barr & Donnell	14,000	4	53	10–16–1784	None	
Barr & Donnell	2,000	4	282	3–23–1786	S Fk Sandy	
Barr & Donnell	2,961	4	282	3–23–1786	Main Licking	
Barr & Stewart	5,000	4	53	10–16–1784	Locust Cr	
Barr & Stewart	12,000	4	209	7–22–1785	None	
Barr, Stewart & Donnell	57,499½	4	57	10–23–1784	None	
Barrall & Mercer	600	3	265	4– 1–1784	None	
Barthot, David	126,140	3	298	4–22–1784	1 h Fk 3 Fks Ky R	Surveyed & amended
Bartlett, Harry	1,000	2	43	1–11–1783	E Fk Hustons Fk	Withdrawn
Bartlett, Harry	1,000	2	87	1–18–1783	None	
Bartlett, Henry	2,000	3	232	3–18–1784	Clear Cr	Surveyed
Barton, Daniel	2,146	1	372	1– 6–1783	Lees Lick Cr	
Bates, Thomas F	8,255	2	231	3–11–1783	Br Red R	Surveyed
Bath, Jas	400	3	68	12– 1–1783	Br Salt Rock Lick	Surveyed
Bathe, Sarah	500	1	142	12–14–1782	Br Gests Cr	
Batia, David	1,245½	2	318	7– 7–1783	Clear & Jessamine Cr	
Battalle, Hays	4,000	2	114	1–23–1783	Licking	
Baty, Jno	200	4	234	11–19–1785	None	Withdrawn
Beale, Charles	350	1	60	12– 6–1782	Little Benson Cr	Surveyed
Beale, Charles	150	1	61	12– 6–1782	Green Cr	Withdrawn
Beale, Richard	650	1	298	12–27–1782	Ky R	Surveyed
Beale, Richard Eustace	1,743	2	327	7–19–1783	S Fk Elkhorn	Withdrawn
Beale, Richard Eustace	743	2	327	7–19–1783	S Fk Elkhorn	Withdrawn
Beale, Richard E	1,743	2	325	7–18–1783	M Fk Elkhorn	Withdrawn
Beale, Richard E	1,468	3	14	10–25–1783	Lower Twin Cr	Withdrawn
Beale, Richard E	743	3	17	10–29–1783	Twin Cr	
Beale, Richard E	150	4	301	6–20–1786	Elkhorn	
Beale, Samuel	1,000	1	158	12–17–1782	Elkhorn	
Beall, Charles	150	1	146	12–14–1782	Main Elkhorn	
Beall, Richard E	743	3	162	1–22–1784	Lower Twin Cr	150 acres withdrawn
Beall, Richard E	650	3	327	5– 7–1784	Elkhorn	Surveyed
Beall, Richard E	650	3	329	5–12–1784	Ky R	Surveyed
Beall, Thos	1,000	4	310	1–29–1787	None	
Beard, Henry	1,092½	3	152	1–16–1784	Ky R	
Beasly, Charles	1,200	1	279	12–26–1782	Glenns Cr	Surveyed
Beasly, John	1,000	1	220	12–21–1782	None	
Beasly, John	1,000	1	222	12–21–1782	None	
Beason, Mercer	1,000	2	304	5–31–1783	12 miles of Upper Blue Lick —— R	Surveyed
Beast, Maideman	1,273	3	152	1–16–1784	—— R	
Beaty, John	2,498	2	277	4–23–1783	Severns Cr	Surveyed
Beaty, Jno	200	4	323	5– 9–1788	None	
Beaucamp, Jesse	40	4	340	9–13–1802	Town Fk Elkhorn	
Beckly, Chas	300	4	93	1–17–1785	None	
Bedinger, Adam	281	2	203	2–19–1783	Salt Sp Fk, Licking	Surveyed
Bedinger, Peter	1,200	2	68	1–15–1783	None	Withdrawn
Bedinger, Peter	1,200	3	385	6–24–1784	None	
Bedford, Thomas	3,000	2	100	1–21–1783	None	Surveyed
Beeson, Edward	820	4	192	6– 1–1785	Ohio R	Withdrawn
Beeson, Edward	820	4	196	6– 9–1785	Ohio R	
Bell, Charles	1,000	1	59	12– 5–1782		Surveyed
Bell, Charles	1,000	1	59	12– 5–1782	N F Clear Cr & Green Cr	
Bell, Chas	1,000	1	60	12– 6–1782	Dry Run	Surveyed
Bella, Geo	1,000	3	16	10–25–1783	Flat Cr	Surveyed

Entree	Acres	Book	Page	Entry Date	Watercourse	Notes
Bell, Henry	3,000	1	148	12–16–1782	Raven Cr	Surveyed
Bell, Henry	2,000	3	149	1–15–1784	Ky R	Surveyed
Bell, James	14,237	3	80	12–10–1783	Licking	Surveyed
Bell, James	1,937	2	187	2–13–1783	None	
Bell, John	436	2	76	1–16–1783	Mill Cr	
Bell, Jno	7,736	3	330	5–13–1784	Licking	562½ acres withdrawn
Bell, Jno	4,000	4	223	9–30–1785	Little Sandy	
Bell, Joseph	3,000	2	205	2–21–1783	None	Withdrawn
Bell, Joseph	250	2	275	4– 9–1783	Hickman Cr	Surveyed
Bell, Joseph	1,000	2	302	5–30–1783	Huskins Run	Withdrawn
Bell, Joseph	3,000	2	307	6– 6–1783	South Elkhorn	Surveyed
Bell, Joseph	1,000	3	241	3–26–1784	None	
Bell, Joseph	1,000	3	322	5– 3–1784	None	
Bell, Joseph	3,000	3	334	5–16–1784	None	
Bell, Samuel	750	2	190	2–13–1783	None	Surveyed
Bell, Thomas	2,000	1	226	12–21–1782	Red R	
Bell, Thomas	2,000	1	226	12–21–1782	Licking	
Bell, Thomas	4,000	1	258	12–24–1782	E Fk Eagle Cr	
Bell, Thomas	4,000	1	258	12–24–1782	M Elkhorn	Withdrawn
Bell, Thomas	4,000	1	258	12–24–1782	Turkey Foot Fk, S Fk Eagle Cr	Surveyed
Bell, Thomas	1,015	2	4	1– 8–1783	None	Surveyed
Bell, Thomas	2,000	2	85	1–18–1783	Main Fk Eagle Cr.	Surveyed
Bell, Thomas	2,000	2	180	2–11–1783	Br Ohio R	Surveyed
Bell, Thomas	1,900	2	186	2–13–1783	None	
Bell, Thomas	1,900	2	186	2–13–1783	None	
Bell, Thomas	1,000	2	319	7– 7–1783	Ky R	
Bell, Wm	12,000	3	108	12–27–1783	Sandy R	Withdrawn
Bell, Wm	8,000	3	109	12–27–1783	Sandy R	Withdrawn
Bell, Wm	2,000	3	109	12–27–1783	Alexander Cr	
Bell, Wm	5,000	3	110	12–27–1783	Main Fk Sandy R	Withdrawn
Bell, Wm	15,000	3	110	12–27–1783	Main Fk Sandy R	Surveyed
Bell, Wm	12,000	3	111	12–27–1783	S Fk Sandy R	Withdrawn
Bell, Wm	8,000	3	111	12–27–1783	N Fk Sandy R	
Bell, Wm	20,000	3	113	12–27–1783	E Fk Licking	Surveyed
Bell, Wm	3,000	3	114	12–27–1783	Ohio R	
Bell, Wm	6,000	3	114	12–27–1783	Ohio R	Withdrawn
Bell, Wm	2,000	3	114	12–27–1783	E Fk Limestone Cr.	Withdrawn
Bell, Wm	10,000	3	117	12–29–1783	Br Lees Cr	Withdrawn
Bell, Wm	10,000	3	117	12–29–1783	Limestone Cr	Surveyed
Bell, Wm	3,000	3	121	12–29–1783	S Fk Sandy R	Withdrawn
Bell, Wm	3,000	3	121	12–29–1783	Main Fk	Withdrawn
Bell, Wm	12,000	3	220	3–11–1784	Sandy	Surveyed
Bell, Wm	8,000	3	221	3–11–1784	Sandy R	2,000 acres surveyed
Bell, Wm	4,000	3	221	3–11–1784	None	Withdrawn
Bell, Wm	15,000	3	221	3–11–1784	None	14,950 acres surveyed
Bell, Wm	12,000	3	222	3–11–1784	E Fk Licking	Surveyed
Bell, Wm	10,000	3	222	3–11–1784	Ohio R	
Bell, Wm	5,000	3	223	3–11–1784	Ohio R	Amended
Bell, Wm	6,000	3	223	3–11–1784	Ohio R	Withdrawn
Bell, Wm	——	3	223	3–11–1784	Main Fk Sandy	
Bell, Wm	5,000	3	263	4– 1–1784	None	
Bell, Wm	11,000	3	264	4– 1–1784	Ohio R	
Bell, Wm	7,400	3	264	4– 1–1784	Licking	Surveyed
Bell, Wm	3,630	3	264	4– 1–1784	None	Surveyed
Bell, Wm	7,000	3	309	4–29–1784	Limestone Cr	
Bell, Wm	2,000	4	141	4– 1–1785	Sandy R	
Bell & Gaines	4,000	3	334	5–16–1784	Ohio R	
Bell, Jas & Hannah	1,875	3	158	1–21–1784	Licking	
Bell & McDougall	8,708	3	162	1–22–1784	Licking	
Belt, Thomas	2,000	2	251	3–21–1783	Lulbegruds Cr	Surveyed
Bemfort, Abraham	15,000	1	215	12–21–1782	Big Bone Cr	Surveyed
Bennepecker, Peter	3,103½	2	339	8– 2–1783	—— Cr	
Bennett, Daniel	1,000	1	290	12–27–1782	E Br Stowers Fk	
Bennett, Joshua	500	2	335	7–30–1783	None	Surveyed
Bennett, Joshua	2,000	3	399	7–10–1784	Br Licking	930 acres surveyed
Bennett, Lewanah	400	1	52	12– 5–1782	Hunting Cr	Surveyed
Bennett, William	1,000	1	186	12–19–1782	S Fk Elkhorn	Surveyed
Bennett, William	500	2	67	1–15–1783	Stowers Fk	Withdrawn
Bennett, Wm	1,000	4	50	9–13–1784	None	
Berry, Francis	400	2	240	3–13–1783	M Fk Coopers Run.	Withdrawn
Berry, Francis	100	2	241	3–13–1783	None	Withdrawn
Berry, Joseph	1,256	2	216	2–28–1783	Ky R	Surveyed
Berry, Joseph	8,000	4	299	5–22–1786	None	
Berry, Joseph	8,000	4	299	5–24–1786	Br Boones Cr	4,050 acres surveyed

Entree	Acres	Book	Page	Entry Date	Watercourse	Notes
Berry, Joseph	8,000	4	301	7–11–1786	Raven Cr	Surveyed
Berry, Samuel	500	1	11	11–30–1782	Hingstons Fk	....
Berry, Thomas	525	2	243	3–13–1783	None	....
Berry, William	818	2	241	3–13–1783	None	....
Berry & Calk	2,000	3	98	12–19–1783	None	Surveyed
Berry & Calk	1,000	3	98	12–19–1783	Howard Upper Cr	Surveyed
Berry & Calk	1,000	3	99	12–19–1783	None	Surveyed
Berry & Calk	1,000	3	127	1– 1–1784	None	Surveyed
Berry, Hazlerigg & Lewis	8,000	4	233	11– 9–1785	Ky R	Withdrawn
Berry & Fishback	2,205	3	23	10–31–1783	None	....
Bilbo, Wm	500	4	278	2–27–1786	None	....
Binns, Charles	1,000	2	48	1–13–1783	Ky R & Clear Cr	Surveyed
Binns, Charles	500	2	216	2–28–1783	Ky R & Clear Cr	Surveyed
Binns, Charles	1,000	2	229	3–10–1783	Hickmans Cr	Surveyed
Binns, John Alex	500	2	229	3–10–1783	Hickmans Cr	Surveyed
Binns, Charles, Jr	800	2	237	3–12–1783	Licking	Surveyed
Binns, John A & Chas Jr	2,000	2	340	8– 5–1783	Indian Creek	....
Binns, Charles	1,000	2	340	8– 5–1783	Shelleys Sp Br	Surveyed
Binns, Jno Alex	3,200	3	142	1–13–1784	Elkhorn & Ky R	Withdrawn
Binns, Chas	1,000	3	166	1–26–1784	Hickman Cr	....
Binns, Chas	2,000	3	314	4–30–1784	Ky R	Withdrawn
Binns, Chas	315	3	361	6–12–1784	None	....
Binns, Chas	315	3	362	6–12–1784	Hickman Cr	....
Binns, Chas	1,500	4	18	8–20–1784	Ky R	....
Binns, Chas	2,000	4	28	9– 4–1784	Clear Cr & Ky R	700 acres surveyed
Binns, Chas & Jno A	10,437½	3	248	3–29–1784	Slate Cr	....
Binns, John Alexander	32,000	4	141	4– 1–1785	Main Licking	....
Bird, William	4,849	2	32	1–10–1783	Tigerts Cr	....
Black, Saml	1,500	4	68	11–18–1784	Br Ohio R	....
Black, William	2,000	1	164	12–18–1782	S Fk Eagle Cr	....
Black, Wm	600	4	238	12–13–1785	Salt Rock Fk	....
Black, Wm	765	4	239	12–13–1785	——— Cr	....
Blackburn, Benjamin	1,000	2	280	4–28–1783	Shannons Run	....
Blackburn & Morgan	1,559	3	133	1– 2–1784	None	....
Blackwell, Jas	1,000	4	184	5–28–1785	Cedar Cr	Surveyed
Blackwell, Joseph	19,062½	3	266	4– 3–1784	Br Hinkston Fk	Withdrawn
Blackwell, Joseph	19,062½	3	418	7–30–1784	Slate Cr	....
Blaine, Ephram	8,000	3	117	12–29–1783	N Fk Licking	Withdrawn
Blaine, Ephram	5,000	3	118	12–29–1783	Ohio R	....
Blaine, Ephram	5,000	3	222	3–11–1784	——— R	....
Blaine, Ephram	1,000	3	358	6–12–1784	Ohio R	....
Blaine, Ephram	3,000	3	359	6–12–1784	Ohio R	....
Blaine, Ephram	8,000	3	359	6–12–1784	Ohio R	....
Blaine, Ephram	6,000	3	359	6–12–1784	Ohio R	....
Blaine, Ephram	2,000	3	359	6–12–1784	Little Sandy R	....
Blaine, Ephram	8,000	4	34	9–13–1784	Little Sandy R	....
Blaine, Ephram	1,000	4	34	9–13–1784	Cabbin Cr	Surveyed
Blaine, Ephram	3,000	4	35	9–15–1784	Ohio R	....
Blair, Wm	1,471	4	161	4–29–1785	None	....
Blake, Joseph Jr	1,000	3	192	3– 1–1784	Ky R	....
Blake & Mitchell	1,000	3	216	3–10–1784	Hustons Fk	Withdrawn
Blake & Mitchell	1,000	3	216	3–10–1784	Hinkston Fk	Withdrawn
Blake & Mitchell	1,000	3	216	3–10–1784	Hinkston Fk	Withdrawn
Blake & Mitchell	1,400	3	217	3–10–1784	N Fk Elkhorn	Withdrawn
Blake & Mitchell	3,000	3	217	3–10–1784	None	....
Blake & Mitchell	1,400	3	217	3–10–1784	Elkhorn & Licking	Withdrawn
Blake & Mitchell	403	3	217	3–10–1784	Hustons Fk	Withdrawn
Blake & Mitchell	400½	3	217	3–10–1784	Hustons Fk	Withdrawn
Blake & Mitchell	407	3	218	3–10–1784	W Fk Hickman Cr	Withdrawn
Blake & Mitchell	1,400	3	231	3–20–1784	None	....
Blancett, Rhodam	500	2	292	5–23–1783	Hingston Fk	Surveyed
Blancett, Rhodam	1,057	2	292	5–23–1783	Hinkston Fk	....
Blanchard, David	100	2	309	6– 7–1783	None	Surveyed
Blanchard, David	938½	2	313	6– 9–1783	Little Sandy	....
Blanchard, David	20,000	2	336	7–31–1783	McConnells Fk Licking	Surveyed
Blanchard, David	3,000	4	173	5– 9–1785	None	....
Blanchard, David	3,000	4	173	5– 9–1785	None	....
Blankenbicker, Samuel	517½	4	343	4–10–1785	None	....
Bledsoe, Aaron	500	1	33	11–16–1784	——— Cr	....
Bledsoe, Aaron	750	1	319	12–30–1782	Br S Fk Licking	....
Bledsoe, Aaron	683	2	2	1– 8–1783	Bank Lick Cr	Surveyed
Bledsoe, Aaron	1,083	2	37	1–11–1783	Sandy	....
Bledsoe, John	910¾	2	35	1–10–1783	Lick of Tygerts Cr	....
Bledsoe, John	1,610	2	35	1–10–1783	Clay Lick on Tygerts Cr	....
Bledsoe, Joseph	2,000	1	160	12–17–1782	Road to Sweet Lick	....

Entree	Acres	Book	Page	Entry Date	Watercourse	Notes
Bledsoe, Joseph	500	1	306	12–28–1782	None	Surveyed
Bledsoe, Joseph	1,000	1	318	12–30–1782	Licking & Ky	Surveyed
Bledsoe, Joseph	500	1	318	12–30–1782	None	Surveyed
Bledsoe, Moses	250	2	92	1–20–1783	Hickman Cr	Withdrawn
Bledsoe, Moses	250	2	206	2–21–1783	None	....
Bledsoe, Moses	689½	3	398	7– 9–1784	N Fk Elkhorn	....
Bledsoe, William	300	1	1	11–28–1782	Elkhorn	Surveyed
Bledsoe, William	500	1	196	12–20–1782	Licking	....
Bledsoe, William	250	1	318	12–30–1782	None	Surveyed
Boesakzodale, Daniel	2,000	1	14	11–30–1782	None	....
Boggs, Robert	500	1	164	12–18–1782	Stoners Fk	Withdrawn
Boggs, Robert	500	1	203	12–20–1782	Hickmans Cr & Ky	Surveyed
Boggs, Robert	1,000	2	103	1–21–1783	Stoners Fk	Surveyed
Boggs, Robt	200	3	393	7– 2–1784	None	76 acres surveyed
Boggs, Robt	200	4	38	9–18–1784	None	Surveyed
Bolling, Robt Jr	5,000	4	247	12–23–1785	None	....
Bolling, Robt	5,000	4	309	11–21–1786	None	....
Boon, David	1,000	1	54	12– 5–1782	Licking	Surveyed
Boon, George	500	1	292	12–27–1782	Ky R	....
Boone, Daniel	1,000	1	103	12–11–1782	None	Surveyed
Boone, Daniel	125	1	287	12–26–1782	Hickmans Cr	....
Boone, Daniel	375	1	287	12–26–1782	None	....
Boone, Daniel	10,000	1	288	12–26–1782	None	....
Boone, Daniel	1,000	1	292	12–27–1782	None	Surveyed
Boon, Daniel	500	1	292	12–27–1782	Ky R	Surveyed
Boon, Daniel	1,000	1	293	12–27–1782	Red River	....
Boone, Daniel	500	1	293	12–27–1782	Jessamine & Ky R	....
Boone, Daniel	500	1	294	12–27–1782	Red R	....
Boone, Daniel	500	2	138	1–28–1783	Hickman Cr	....
Boon, Daniel	750	2	208	2–24–1783	E Fk Hickmans Cr	Surveyed
Boone, Daniel	500	2	234	3–12–1783	Hickmans Cr	....
Boone, Daniel	3,000	2	234	3–12–1783	Ky R	Withdrawn
Boone, Daniel	300	2	235	3–12–1783	Ky R	Withdrawn
Boone, Daniel	200	2	235	3–12–1783	Hickman Cr	....
Boone, Daniel	300	2	271	4– 7–1783	Boones Cr	Surveyed
Boone, Daniel	200	2	271	4– 8–1783	Boones Cr	Surveyed
Boone, Daniel	1,000	2	282	5– 2–1783	None	Surveyed
Boone, Daniel	500	4	16	8–16–1784	None	....
Boone, Daniel	2,500	4	16	8–16–1784	Ky R	....
Boone, Daniel	300	4	17	8–16–1784	Paint Lick	....
Boone, Daniel	300	4	17	8–17–1784	Main Licking	Surveyed
Boone, Daniel Jr	2,000	1	294	12–27–1782	Hingston Fk & Blue Lick	Surveyed
Boone, Daniel Jr	1,000	4	61	10–28–1784	None	....
Boone, Daniel Jr	1,000	4	67	11–12–1784	None	....
Boone, Daniel Jr	1,000	4	67	11–12–1784	None	Surveyed
Boone, Daniel Sr	500	3	189	2–28–1784	None	....
Boone, Daniel Sr	1,000	3	189	2–28–1784	4 Mile Cr	Surveyed
Boone, Hugh	1,000	2	247	3–15–1783	None	....
Boone, Isaac	1,000	2	247	3–15–1783	None	Surveyed
Boone, Israel	1,000	1	103	12–15–1782	None	Surveyed
Boone, Jacob	500	2	248	3–15–1783	None	Surveyed
Boone, Jonathan	1,000	2	247	3–15–1783	None	Surveyed
Boone, Levi	500	1	295	12–27–1782	Upper Blue Lick	Surveyed
Boone, Ovid	500	2	248	3–15–1783	None	Surveyed
Boone, Saml	1,200	3	412	7–17–1784	N Fk Licking	....
Boone, Samuel	500	2	248	3–15–1783	None	....
Boone, Samuel	340	2	285	5–12–1783	Big Fk Elkhorn	Surveyed
Boone, Saml Jr	500	3	412	7–17–1784	N Fk Licking	....
Boone, Saml Jr	500	3	412	7–17–1784	None	....
Boone, Samuel Sr	500	1	295	12–27–1782	None	Surveyed
Boone, Squire	500	3	412	7–17–1784	None	....
Boone, Thomas	500	2	248	3–15–1783	None	....
Boon, Thomas	1,000	1	103	12–11–1782	None	Surveyed
Boone, Thomas, heirs	800	1	260	12–24–1782	Br Licking	Surveyed
Boone & Winston	11,875	3	189	2–28–1784	Ky R	....
Booker, Jno	40,000	3	404	7–14–1784	Fk Licking	....
Booth, William	16,000	1	91	12–10–1782	Slate Cr	Surveyed
Booth, William	1,000	1	250	12–24–1782	Br M Fk Licking	....
Booth, Bartholomew	20,000	2	261	3–31–1783	Severns Cr	Surveyed
Booth, Bartholomew	10,000	2	261	3–31–1783	Ky R	Surveyed
Bostick, John	1,487	2	112	1–23–1783	Raven Cr	Surveyed
Bosworth, Obediah	1,000	4	77	12–16–1784	Buffaloe Lick	....
Botts, Joseph	1,000	1	64	12– 6–1782	E Br Licking Cr	....
Bowdain, Presan	5,923	3	40	11–12–1783	None	....
Bowdain & Young	5,000	3	178	2–10–1784	None	....
Bowman, Andrew	1,000	3	161	1–21–1784	Hinkston Fk	....
Bowman, Jno	3,000	2	337	8– 1–1783	Elkhorn & Hickman Cr	Surveyed
Bowman, John	3,000	2	349	8–14–1783	————	Surveyed

Entree	Acres	Book	Page	Entry Date	Watercourse	Notes
Bowman, John	3,000	2	350	8–14–1783	None	
Bowman, John	1,000	2	368	10– 1–1783	Jessamine Cr	
Bowman, Jno	3,000	3	8	10–15–1783	Harrods Salt Lick Cr	
Bowman, Cox & Morgan	850	4	51	10–13–1784	Eagle Cr	
Bourn, Adam	1,200	3	382	6–23–1784	—— Cr	
Bourn, Daniel, Robt & Jno	225,000	3	353	6– 4–1784	Ky R	Amended
Boyd, Jno	493½	4	165	4–29–1785	None	
Boyd, Jno	493½	4	165	4–29–1785	None	
Boyd & Morgan	1,000	3	130	1– 1–1784	Ohio R	
Bradford, Benj	150	3	387	6–28–1784	Near Lexington Race Path	
Bradford, Henry	3,791¾	1	246	12–23–1782	Br Licking	
Bradford, Harry	2,877	2	72	1–16–1783	None	Surveyed
Bradford, Jos	65	4	342	1–20–1817	None	
Bradford, Jno	3,146	3	128	1– 1–1784	Eagle Cr	Withdrawn
Bradford, Jno	4,541	3	133	1– 2–1784	Ohio & Licking	
Bradford, Jno	1,468	3	162	1–22–1784	Stoners Fk	
Bradford, Jno	2,500	3	187	2–21–1784	Elkhorn	Withdrawn
Bradford, Jno	2,500	3	386	6–28–1784	Elkhorn	Surveyed
Bradford, Jno	1,400	4	301	6–19–1786	None	
Bradford & Fox	50	3	322	5– 3–1784	None	
Brading, Nathaniel	3,000	4	71	11–26–1784	Slate Cr	Surveyed
Brading, Nathaniel	2,000	4	71	11–26–1784	Slate Cr	
Bradley, Edmund	1,000	1	321	12–30–1782	Jessamine Cr	Surveyed
Bradley, Leonard	110	4	33	9–11–1784	None	
Bradley, Leonard	220	4	33	9–11–1784	None	
Bradley, Leonard K	350	3	352	6– 2–1784	None	Withdrawn
Bradley, Leonard K	350	4	335	4– 6–1792	4 Mile Cr	Surveyed
Bradley & Payne	345	4	40	9–22–1784	None	Surveyed
Bradley & Taylor	2,500	4	287	3–28–1786	None	Amended
Bradley & Taylor	2,000	4	287	3–28–1786	None	Amended
Bradley & Taylor	2,500	4	289	4– 8–1786	None	
Bradley & Taylor	2,000	4	289	4– 8–1786	None	
Bradshaw, William	1,668½	2	232	3–12–1783	None	
Brame, Walter	20,000	4	155	4–20–1785	Sandy	6,873 acres withdrawn
Brame & Marshall	3,000	3	337	5–19–1784	None	Withdrawn
Brame & Marshall	3,000	4	56	10–17–1784	None	
Brame & Marshall	3,000	4	58	10–23–1784	None	Surveyed
Brame & Marshall	3,000	4	155	4–20–1785	None	Withdrawn
Bramblett, James	916½	2	303	5–31–1783	None	
Bramlett, Jas	200	4	188	6– 1–1785	None	
Bramlett, Jas	240½	4	188	6– 1–1785	—— Br	
Bramblett, William	400	1	5&6	11–29–1784	Stoners Fk Lciking Cr	
Bramlet, William	400	1	42	12– 4–1782	—— Cr	
Branard, Jno	1,996	3	277	4– 7–1784	Millers Cr	
Branch, Thos	5,000	3	115	12–27–1783	None	
Branham, Thos	5,000	4	270	2– 7–1786	Main Licking	
Brazer, Thomas	1,000	2	226	3–10–1783	None	
Breckinridge, Jas	1,000	4	262	1–21–1786	Elkhorn	
Breckinridge, Jas	2,250	4	262	1–21–1786	N Fk Elkhorn	Withdrawn
Breckinridge, Jas	2,000	4	262	1–21–1786	Elkhorn	Withdrawn
Breckinridge, Jas	1,000	4	263	1–21–1786	None	Withdrawn
Breckinridge, Jas	1,000	4	263	1–21–1786	Elkhorn	Withdrawn
Breckinridge, Jas	1,000	4	338	12– 9–1794	None	
Breckinridge, Jas	6,250	4	338	12– 9–1794	None	
Breckinridge, Jno	1,400	4	189	6– 1–1785	Hustons Fk	Withdrawn
Breckinridge, Jno	400	4	189	6– 1–1785	Stoners Fk	Withdrawn
Breckinridge, Jno	400	4	189	6– 1–1785	Fk Licking	Withdrawn
Breckinridge, Jno	1,400	4	192	6– 1–1785	None	
Breckinridge, Jno	5,000	4	192	6– 1–1785	Ohio R	Withdrawn
Breckinridge, Jno	5,000	4	196	6– 9–1785	Ohio R	
Breckenridge & Meredith	72	4	342	9– 9–1816	None	
Brent, Chas	1,125	3	14	10–17–1783	Br Licking	
Brent, Jno	1,000	3	380	6–21–1784	Licking	
Brent, William	1,000	1	151	12–16–1782	W Fk Licking Cr	
Brewer, Barrett	1,636½	2	99	1–21–1783	None	
Brewer, John	1,181	2	100	1–20–1783	None	Surveyed
Brewer, Sackville	1,636½	2	99	1–21–1783	Ohio R	Surveyed
Bright & Albertus	273	4	217	8– 7–1785	None	
Brink, Samuel	1,000	1	317	12–30–1782	Boggs Fk	Surveyed
Brink, Saml	500	3	411	7–17–1784	Licking	
Briscoe, John	1,000	1	157	12–17–1782	Glenns Cr	Surveyed
Briscoe, John	400	2	135	1–27–1783	Glens Cr	
Briscoe, Jno	1,000	3	17	10–29–1783	None	Surveyed
Briscoe, John, Sr	1,000	1	157	12–17–1782	None	Surveyed
Briscoe, Parmenas	10,000	4	171	5– 6–1785	Ohio R	Withdrawn
Briscoe, Parminas	10,000	4	172	5– 6–1785	Ohio R	Withdrawn

Entree	Acres	Book	Page	Entry Date	Watercourse	Notes
Briscoe, Parminas	10,000	4	139	3–25–1785	M Fk Licking	Withdrawn
Briscoe, Parminos	10,000	4	173	5– 9–1785	None	
Briscoe, Parminos	657	4	187	6– 1–1785	Eagle Cr	
Briscoe, Parminos	2,000	4	188	6– 1–1785	S Fk Licking	
Briscoe, Parminos	1,000	4	188	6– 1–1785	Ky R	
Briscoe, Parminos	2,750	4	188	6– 1–1785	S Fk Elkhorn	
Briscoe, Parmanos	1,657	4	269	2– 7–1786	Stoners & Hinkston	Surveyed
Briscoe, Parmanos	657	4	270	2– 7–1786	Eagle Cr	Surveyed
Broadhead, Daniel	20,000	2	370	10– 4–1783	Mill Cr	
Broadhead, Daniel	7,500	3	11	10–16–1783	Br Hinkston Cr	
Brockman, Jno	2,162¾	3	46	11–15–1783	Clear & Jessamine	Surevyed 500 Withdrawn 500
Brockman, Jno	2,162⅔	3	62	11–27–1783	None	
Brooke, John	1,000	1	142	12–14–1782	Br Licking	Withdrawn
Brooke, Ebenezer	1,000	2	23	1– 9–1783	Fk Licking	
Brooke, Thomas	7,000	2	114	1–23–1783	Stoners Fk	
Brooks, Abenezer	1,500	2	276	4–22–1783	Br Ohio R	Surveyed
Brooks, Ebenezer	5,317½	2	231	3–12–1783	Br Ohio R	
Brooks, Ebenezer	1,000	4	217	8– 6–1785	None	Withdrawn
Brooks, Ebenezer	1,000	4	261	1–20–1786	None	
Brooks, Ebenezer	1,000	4	261	1–20–1786	None	Withdrawn
Brooks, Ebenezer	1,000	4	270	2– 7–1786	Sandy	
Brooks, Geo	7,000	4	248	12–23–1785	None	
Brooks, James	9,314½	2	129	1–27–1783	None	
Brooks, John	1,000	1	204	12–20–1782	Licking	Surveyed
Brooks, Thomas	3,231	1	297	12–27–1782	Hingston & M Licking	
Brooks, Thomas	1,500	2	232	3–12–1783	Hingston & Licking	
Brooks, William	1,000	1	54	12– 4–1782	Ky R & Marble Cr	
Brooks & Clay	3,942¼	4	157	4–27–1785	Bank Lick	
Brough, Thos	500	4	83	1– 7–1785	None	Withdrawn
Brough, Thos	500	4	83	1– 8–1785	rh Fk Clear Ck	Withdrawn
Brough, Thos	500	4	85	1– 8–1785	None	Withdrawn
Brough, Thos	500	4	92	1–15–1785	None	
Brough, Thos	500	4	92	1–15–1785	None	
Brough & Morrow	3,018	4	80	12–30–1784	S Fk Elkhorn	Withdrawn
Brough & Morrow	3,018	4	83	1– 8–1785	None	
Brough & Morrow	1,400	4	83	1– 8–1785	Hustons Fk	Withdrawn
Brough & Morrow	1,000	4	84	1– 8–1785	Flat Cr	Withdrawn
Brough & Morrow	1,000	4	92	1–17–1785	None	
Brough & Morrow	3,518	4	92	1–17–1785	Main Licking	
Brown, Abraham	2,473½	3	321	5– 3–1784	None	
Brown, Absalom	1,311½	2	14	11– 9–1783	None	
Brown, Alexander	16,000	3	21	10–30–1783	Ohio R	Surveyed
Brown, Andrew	500	4	243	12–15–1785	Big Bone & Licking	
Brown, Casper	400	2	304	5–31–1783	Woods Fk Licking	
Brown, Edward	100	1	38	12– 4–1782	Shoemakers Cr	Surveyed
Brown, Elijah	10,000	3	115	12–27–1783	N Fk Big Sandy R	Surveyed
Brown, Evan	4,000	1	376	1– 6–1783	Flat Cr	Surveyed
Brown, Jacob	1,000	2	71	1–16–1783	Ky R	Surveyed
Brown, Jacob	1,000	2	72	1–16–1783	Ky R	Surveyed
Brown, James	500	1	87	12– 9–1782	Stoners Fk	
Brown, John	1,000	2	2	1– 8–1783	None	Surveyed
Brown, Jno	2,685	3	27	10–31–1783	Ohio R	
Brown, Jno	400	3	419	7–30–1784	Licking	
Brown, Jno	1,000	4	72	11–27–1784	None	
Brown, Jno	2,469½	4	176	5– 9–1785	None	
Brown, Robt	8,000	3	81	12–10–1783	N Fk Licking	Withdrawn
Brown, Robt	10,101	3	81	12–10–1783	N Fk Licking	Withdrawn
Brown, Robt	8,000	3	325	5– 6–1784	None	
Brown, Robt	10,101	3	325	5– 6–1784	None	
Brown, Robt	18,101	3	325	5– 6–1784	Br Licking	Surveyed
Brown, Thomas	300	2	91	1–20–1783	Sulphur Lick	
Brown, Thomas	1,000	2	108	1–23–1783	Sycamore Fk Hinkston	Surveyed
Brown, Thos	38,000	3	58	11–25–1783	N Fk Big Bone Lick	Amended
Brown, Thos	8,968	3	178	2–10–1784	None	Withdrawn
Brown, Thos	1,370	3	253	3–30–1784	None	Surveyed
Brown, Thos	8,968	3	326	5– 6–1784	None	
Brown, Thos	4,968	3	326	5– 6–1784	None	3700 acres withdrawn
Brown, Thos	2,000	3	326	5– 6–1784	Ohio R	Surveyed
Brown, Thos	1,000	3	326	5– 6–1784	Ohio R	Surveyed
Brown, Thos	5,000	4	250	12–27–1785	S Fk Sandy	
Brown, Thos	5,000	4	251	12–27–1785	None	
Brown, Thos	3,700	4	274	2–17–1786	None	
Brown & Dunlap	2,469½	4	177	5– 9–1785	None	
Brown & Morgan	38,000	3	177	2–10–1784	None	
Brown & Morgan	18,000	4	337	11–13–1793	Ohio R	

Entree	Acres	Book	Page	Entry Date	Watercourse	Notes
Brown & Sharp	1,200	4	274	2–17–1786	Eagle Cr	
Brown & Sharp	1,500	4	275	2–17–1786	Big Bone Lick	
Brownlow, John	1,000	1	3	1–13–1783	Ohio	
Bruce, Alexander	6,000	3	107	12–26–1783	Lulbergreed Cr	
Bruce, Alexander	3,500	3	107	12–26–1783	Lulbergreed Cr	
Bruce, Alexander	2,000	3	108	12–26–1783	Lulbergreed Cr	Surveyed
Bruce, Alexander	1,000	3	108	12–26–1783	Howards Cr	Withdrawn
Bruce, Alexander	1,000	3	161	1–21–1784	None	
Bruce, John	1,610	2	2	1– 8–1783	Hickmans Cr	Withdrawn
Bruce, John	1,610	2	106	1–22–1783	None	
Brumley, John	3,000	1	386	1– 7–1783	N Fk Licking	Surveyed
Brunsfield, Jas	1,387½	4	134	3–19–1785	None	
Brunt, Jno	600	3	57	11–24–1783	Hinkston Cr	
Bryan, David	1,000	2	300	5–30–1783	Br Elkhorn	Surveyed
Bryan, Enoch O	3,561½	3	24	10–31–1783	None	
Bryan, John	1,000	2	185	2–13–1783	None	
Bryan, John	500	2	207	2–24–1783	Licking	
Bryan, Thomas, heirs	1,000	2	225	3– 8–1783	None	Surveyed
Bryant, Guy	500	1	24	12–17–1782	——— Cr	Surveyed
Bryant, Jno	600	4	75	12– 4–1784	None	
Buchannan, James	500	1	41	12– 4–1782	Howards Cr	Withdrawn
Buchannan, James	1,000	1	41	3–15–1783	Br Licking	Withdrawn
Buchannan, James	500	1	41	12– 4–1782	Howards Upper Cr	Withdrawn
Buchannan, James	1,000	1	41	12– 4–1782	——— Cr	
Buchannan, James	50	1	42	12– 4–1782	Two Mile Cr	
Buchannan, James	1,000	1	42	12– 4–1782	None	
Buchannan, James	1,700	1	90	12– 9–1782	Harrods Cr	Surveyed
Buchanan, James	1,000	2	249	3–15–1783	Br Licking	
Buckhannon, James	400	2	307	6– 6–1783	Strodes Fk Licking	
Buchannan, Jas	1,000	4	24	8–30–1784	None	
Buchannan, Jas	500	4	24	8–30–1784	None	
Buchannan, Jno	525	4	161	4–29–1785	None	
Buchannan, Robert	500	2	17	1– 9–1783	None	
Buchannan, Robt	446	4	162	4–29–1785	None	
Buchannan & Tanner	1,488	4	24	8–30–1784	M Br Licking	
Buckner, Francis	15,000	1	370	1– 6–1783	Slate Cr	
Buckner, Jane	709½	2	243	3–14–1783	Elkhorn	Surveyed
Bucker, Philip	7,000	1	355	1– 2–1783	Locust Cr	Surveyed
Buckner, Robt	4,000	3	234	3–22–1784	Buckner	Withdrawn
Buckner, Robt	4,000	3	234	3–22–1784	Rock House Cr	
Buckner, Robt	5,000	3	235	3–22–1784	Ky R	
Buckner, William	500	2	112	1–23–1783	Lulbegreeds	
Buckner, Wm Jr	2,000	3	53	11–21–1783	Br Red R	Surveyed
Buckner & Sanders	5,038¾	3	17	10–30–1783	Ohio R	
Buford, Abraham	10,000	1	222	12–21–1782	S Licking	
Buford, William	1,978½	2	78	1–17–1783	S Fk Eagle Cr	Surveyed
Bullitt, Alexander	3,000	4	69	11–23–1784	None	
Bullitt, Alexander	100	4	253	1– 9–1786	None	
Bullitt, Alexander S	1,920	3	385	6–24–1784	Main Elkhorn	Surveyed
Bullitt, Alexander S	3,000	3	387	6–28–1784	Fk Elkhorn	Withdrawn
Bullitt, Alexander S	2,253	3	387	6–28–1784	Ky R & Cedar Cr	
Bullitt, Alexander S	3,000	3	387	6–28–1784	Ohio R	
Bullitt, Alexander S	5,000	3	396	7– 7–1784	Main Licking	Surveyed
Bullitt, Alexander S	2,570	3	407	7–14–1784	Hinkston Fk	Surveyed
Bullitt, Alexander S	1,000	3	407	7–14–1784	Main Licking	
Bullitt, Cuthbert	6,046¾	2	214	2–28–1783	Licking	
Bullitt, Cuthbert	5,000	4	63	11– 2–1784	None	Withdrawn
Bullitt, Cuthbert	2,000	4	225	10– 7–1785	None	
Bullitt, Cuthbert	3,000	4	285	3–26–1786	None	Withdrawn
Bullett, Cuthbert	8,000	4	285	3–26–1786	Ohio R	
Bullitt & Triplett	20,000	3	406	7–14–1784	Large Cr	
Bullitt & Triplett	7,187	4	55	10–16–1784	Main Licking	
Bullard, Jno	300,306⅔	3	190	2–28–1784	3 Fks Ky R	
Bullock, Nathanial	1,000	2	96	1–20–1783	None	Surveyed
Bullock, Nathaniel	200	2	96	1–20–1783	None	
Bullock, William	10,000	1	49	12– 5–1782	——— Cr	
Burcitt, Frederick	1,550	3	41	11–12–1783	None	
Burge, Drury	3,784	4	266	1–30–1786	——— R	Withdrawn
Burge, Drury	2,096½	4	291	4–22–1786	None	
Burks, Thos	2,617½	4	107	2– 5–1785	——— Cr	
Burks, Thos	2,617½	4	242	12–14–1785	None	
Burney, Simon	1,000	2	226	3–10–1783	Stoney Cr	Surveyed
Burnly & Smith	1,000	3	389	6–30–1784	None	
Burnly & Smith	1,000	3	391	6–30–1784	S Fk Elkhorn	
Burnnett, Wm	1,000	4	209	7–20–1785	Glenns Cr	Surveyed
Burrall & Mercier	7,000	3	114	12–27–1783	E Fk Licking	Withdrawn
Burrall & Mercier	6,000	3	118	12–29–1783	Buffaloe Rd	
Burton, Chas	3,000	4	134	3–19–1785	None	Withdrawn
Burton, Chas	3,000	4	149	4–10–1785	None	
Burton, Robert	4,000	1	287	12–26–1782	None	Surveyed

Entree	Acres	Book	Page	Entry Date	Watercourse	Notes
Burwell, Jonathan	10,000	3	263	4– 1–1784	None	
Bush, William	1,000	2	74	1–16–1783	None	Surveyed
Bush, Jno	1,000	3	150	1–15–1784	None	
Busine, John	800	2	135	1–27–1783	Ky R	
Butland, Jas	126,140	3	298	4–22–1784	1 h Fk 3 Fks Ky R	Surveyed, amended
Butler, Percival	21,000	4	169	4–30–1785	None	Surveyed
Butler, Peter	100	4	221	9– 8–1785	Ky R	
Butler, Peter	100	4	221	9– 8–1785	None	
Butler, Peter	100	4	252	12–31–1785	None	
Butler, W C	50,000	3	374	6–19–1784	None	Surveyed
Butler, Jno	1,000	3	164	1–22–1784	Bank Lick Cr	Withdrawn
Button, Jno	1,000	3	243	3–26–1784	None	
Byrum & Walker	461½	4	63	11– 2–1784	None	
Cabell, Joseph	3,405½	4	322	4–27–1788	Sovern Cr	
Caldwell, Daniel	1,275	2	188	2–13–1783	None	Surveyed
Caldwell, David	5,000	3	111	12–27–1783	Main N Fk Sandy	Surveyed
Caldwell, David	3,165½	3	241	3–26–1784	Johnsons Fk	
Caldwell, George	3,000	1	85	12– 9–1782	Elkhorn	Withdrawn
Caldwell, George	500	1	133	12–13–1782	Gests Cr	Withdrawn
Caldwell, George	300	1	154	12–17–1782	N Fk Licking	
Caldwell, George	3,000	1	155	12–17–1782	Licking Cr	Surveyed
Caldwell, Geroge	2,000	2	126	1–27–1783	Crewes Cr	Withdrawn
Caldwell, Geo	1,000	4	79	12–29–1784	None	
Caldwell, Geo	500	4	136	3–19–1785	None	
Caldwell, John	500	1	109	12–11–1782	Elkhorn	
Caldwell, Jno	563	4	43	9–24–1784	Fleming Cr	
Caldwell, Robert	1,931	2	60	1–14–1783	S E Riddles Station	Surveyed
Caldwell, Matthew	400	2	93	1–20–1780	Buffaloe Rd	Surveyed
Calhoon, Jno	4,000	3	107	12–22–1783	W Fk Licking	Surveyed
Calk, William	1,000	1	63	12– 6–1782	———	Surveyed
Calk, William	400	1	63	12– 6–1782	Licking Cr	
Calk, William	700	1	63	12– 6–1782	——— Cr	
Calk, Wm	3,000	2	227	3–10–1783	Br Licking	Surveyed
Calk, William	2,457½	2	228	3–10–1783	Licking Cr	
Calk, William	2,235	2	228	3–10–1783	Licking Cr	Surveyed
Calk, Wm	1,784	2	270	4– 7–1783	Licking	
Calk, Wm	653½	2	270	4– 7–1783	None	
Calk, Wm	2,000	2	376	10–13–1783	Small Mt Cr	
Calk, Wm	10,937½	2	376	10–13–1783	Licking	
Calk, Wm	1,000	3	99	12–19–1783	None	
Calk & Berry	2,000	3	98	12–19–1783	None	
Calk & Berry	1,000	3	99	12–19–1783	None	Surveyed
Calk & Berry	1,000	3	98	12–19–1783	Howards Upper Cr	Surveyed
Calk & Berry	1,000	3	127	1– 1–1784	None	Surveyed
Calk & Kay	1,288½	3	127	1– 1–1784	Br Red R	
Call & Parker	5,000	3	100	12–19–1783	None	Surveyed
Callis, Garland	4,000	3	23	10–31–1783	Ohio R	
Calloway, Caleb	3,602	1	391	1– 7–1783	Spencers Cr & Hinkstons Fk	Surveyed
Calloway, Caleb	2,000	3	75	12– 9–1783	Red R	
Calloway, Flanders	900	1	137	1–28–1783	Hickman Cr	Surveyed
Calloway, Flanders	1,100	2	283	5– 2–1783	——— Br	Withdrawn
Calloway, Flanders	1,000	4	327	2–18–1789	Elkhorn & Licking	
Calloway, Jas	2,592½	4	145	4–10–1785	None	
Calmes, Marquis Sr & Jr	343	3	103	12– 20–1783	Red R	Withdrawn
Calmes, Marquis Sr & Jr	343	3	142	1–13–1784	Sulbergreed & Howards Cr	
Campbell, Charles	2,000	1	148	12–16–1782	Johnsons Fk	
Campbell, David	1,000	2	185	2–14–1783	None	
Campbell, Jas	2,000	4	191	6– 1–1785	Ohio R	Withdrawn
Campbell, Jas	2,000	4	195	6– 9–1785	Ohio R	
Campbell, John	1,000	1	181	12–18–1782	Licomptisn Br	Surveyed
Campbell, John	1,000	1	230	12–23–1782	Pettis Cr	
Campbell, John	100	1	230	12–23–1782	McConnells Cr	
Campbell, Jno	800	3	393	7– 1–1784	None	Withdrawn
Campbell, Jno	600	4	22	8–27–1784	None	
Campbell, Jno	172	4	22	8–27–1784	Jessamine Cr	Amended & withdrawn
Campbell, Jno	628	4	23	8–27–1784	None	Surveyed
Campbell, Jno	172	4	29	9– 6–1784	None	
Campbell, Jno	172	4	125	3– 4–1785	None	
Campbell, Patrick	1,262	3	153	1–16–1784	Fk Lick Cr	Withdrawn
Campbell, Patrick	1,262	4	158	4–29–1785	None	
Campbell, Patrick	1,262	4	159	4–29–1785	None	
Campbell, Robert	1,000	1	198	12–20–1782	Big Bone Lick	Surveyed
Campbell, Robert	1,500	1	296	12–27–1782	None	Surveyed
Campbell, Wm	3,000	3	153	1–16–1784	Br Lick Cr	Withdrawn

Entree	Acres	Book	Page	Entry Date	Watercourse	Notes
Campbell, Wm	2,568¾	3	158	1–21–1784	Main Licking	Surveyed
Campbell, Wm	473¾	3	235	3–22–1784	Rockhouse Cr	Withdrawn
Campbell, Wm	3,000	4	157	4–29–1785	None	
Campbell, Wm	5,000	4	159	4–29–1785	None	
Campbell, Wm	3,726½	4	160	4–29–1785	None	
Campbell & Arnold	800	3	255	3–30–1784	Bank Lick Cr	Surveyed
Campbell & Willis	1,000	3	255	3–30–1784	Bank Lick Cr	Surveyed
Cannon, Luke	9,000	4	254	1–12–1786	Red R	
Cannon & Crittenden	9,000	4	130	3– 7–1785	Red R	Surveyed
Cantsman, Benj	1,000	4	116	2–12–1785	None	
Caperton, Hugh	200	2	233	3–12–1783	Paint Lick Cr	
Caperton, Hugh	1,600	2	233	3–12–1783	Paint Lick Cr	
Carnahan, Jos	1,000	4	215	8– 5–1785	N Fk Licking	
Carrnegg & Paul	300,306⅔	3	190	2–28–1784	3 Fks Ky R	
Carman, Jno	1,000	3	192	3– 1–1784	Ky R	
Carman, Jno	300,306⅔	3	190	2–28–1784	3 Fks Ky R	
Carney, John	1,000	2	258	3–27–1783	Main Fk Licking Cr	
Carneal, Thomas	1,600	1	31	12–18–1782	Dry Cr	Surveyed
Carneal, Thomas	1,200	2	19	1– 9–1783	None	Surveyed
Carneale, Thomas	2,003	2	18	1– 9–1783	Elkhorn	
Carneale, Thomas	260	2	140	1–29–1783	Elkhorn	
Carneale, Thos	2,003	4	340	1– 9–1800	None	
Carman & Thompson	19,531¼	3	358	6–10–1784	Adjoin P D Roberts & Co	
Carr & Young	1,387¾	4	228	10–23–1785	Sandy	
Carrington, George Jr	3,353¾	2	221	3– 3–1783	6 Miles Ohio R	
Carrington, Timothy	300	2	268	4– 7–1783	Howards Upper Cr & Licking	Surveyed
Carrington, William	300	2	252	3–21–1783	Pastime Cr	Surveyed
Carruthers, James	1,000	2	304	5–31–1783	S Fk Elkhorn	Surveyed
Carter, Chas	769	4	203	6–28–1785	Cabbin Cr	
Carter, Jno	29,936	3	424	8–11–1784	Cumberland Mt	
Carthright, Jesse	1,038½	2	64	1–14–1783	E Br Stoners Fk	Withdrawn
Cartwright, Jessey	750	2	309	6– 7–1783	None	
Cartwright, John	4,000	2	273	4– 8–1783	S Fk Sulbergreed	
Cartwright, Thos	10,000	4	282	3–23–1786	N Fk Ky R	
Cartwright, Wm	10,000	3	220	3–11–1784	——— Cr	Surveyed
Cary, Wm	500	3	102	12–19–1783	——— R	Surveyed
Cary, Wm	500	3	102	12–19–1783	Stephens Cr	Surveyed
Cary, Wm	250	3	154	1–17–1784	Ky R	Withdrawn
Cary, Wm	250	3	154	1–17–1784	Ky R	Withdrawn
Cary, Wm	500	3	167	1–26–1784	Hickman Cr	Surveyed
Cary, Wm	250	3	214	3–10–1784	Elkhorn	
Cary, Wm	250	3	215	3–10–1784	Ky R	
Cary, Wm	500	4	216	8– 5–1785	None	Surveyed
Cary, Wm	500	4	216	8– 5–1785	None	
Cary, Richard M	676½	2	191	2–13–1783	None	Surveyed
Cason, Wm	2,100	3	97	12–18–1783	None	
Cassady, Benjamin, heirs	1,000	2	211	2–27–1783	M Fk Stoners	Surveyed
Cassady, Michael	1,105	2	17	1– 9–1783	Br N Fk Licking	Surveyed
Castnell, Jno	200	4	133	3–15–1785	N E Fk Licking	
Cather, Edward	400	1	59	12– 5–1782	Sinking Spring	Surveyed
Cathers, Edward	250	4	322	3–21–1788	None	
Catlett, Robert	666	2	214	2–28–1783	N Fk Licking	
Cave, Thos	5,000	3	161	1–21–1784	Howards Cr	Withdrawn
Cave, William	1,000	1	284	12–26–1782	Clear Cr	Surveyed
Caves, Thos	5,000	3	207	3– 9–1784	Cedar Cr	Surveyed
Cavin, Thos	2,000	3	200	3– 3–1784	Ohio R	
Cavin & Craig	7,416	3	165	1–23–1784	Eagle Cr	
Cecil, Wm	1,000	4	185	5–30–1785	Lower S Fk Big Bone Lick	Surveyed
Cellers, James	5,000	4	427	12–27–1783	Sandy R	
Chadox, Chas	4,537½	3	23	10–31–1783	None	
Chambers, David	500	4	96	1–21–1785	None	
Champ, Thos	5,926⅔	3	204	3– 5–1784	Eagle Cr	
Charlton, Thos	1,000	3	75	12– 8–1783	N Fk Elkhorn	Surveyed
Cherry, Moses	1,000	1	46	12– 4–1782	N Fk Elkhorn	Surveyed
Chiles, Henry	2,500	4	240	12–13–1785	Salt Rock Fk	
Chiles, Jno	5,662	4	103	2– 2–1785	Main Licking	Surveyed
Chiles, Jno Jr	1,584	4	239	12–13–1785	Salt Rock Fk	
Chiles, Walter	500	1	24	12–17–1782	——— Cr	
Chiles, William	850	1	12	11–30–1782	Hingston Fk	
Chilton, David	300	1	53	12– 5–1782	Ky R	
Chinch, Robert	2,497	2	279	4–25–1783	Elkhorn	Surveyed
Chinn, Charles	1,000	2	241	3–13–1783	None	
Chinn, Thos	2,000	3	165	1–23–1784	Eagle Cr	
Chinoweth, Richard	8,000	4	294	4–29–1786	Licking	
Christian, Israel	200	1	9	12–29–1782	Hingstons & Stoners Fk	Surveyed
Christian, Israel	1,000	1	48	12– 4–1782	Bullitts Fk	

Entree	Acres	Book	Page	Entry Date	Watercourse	Notes
Christian, Isarel	2,000	1	53	12– 5–1782	——— Cr	Surveyed
Christian, Isarael	350	1	54	12– 5–1782	Br Licking Cr	Surveyed
Christian, Israel	500	1	209	12–20–1782	Sandy Cr	Amended
Christian, Israel	500	1	209	12–20–1782	Sandy Cr	Amended
Christian, Israel	2,000	1	262	12–24–1782	None	Surveyed
Christian, Israel	1,000	1	348	1– 2–1783	Salt Lick	....
Christian, Israel	1,000	1	348	1– 2–1783	Sandy R	....
Christian, Israel	1,000	1	349	1– 2–1783	Sandy R	....
Christian, Israel	2,000	1	349	1– 2–1783	Sandy	Withdrawn
Christian, Israel	1,000	2	223	3– 7–1783	Br Sandy R	Withdrawn
Christian, Israel	1,000	2	223	3– 7–1783	Sandy R	Withdrawn
Christian; Israel	1,000	2	224	3– 7–1783	Big Sandy	Withdrawn
Christian, Israel	2,000	3	26	10–31–1783	None	....
Christian, Israel	500	3	146	1–14–1784	Sandy R	....
Christian, Israel	1,000	3	188	2–25–1784	Salt Lick	....
Christian, Israel	1,000	3	188	2–25–1784	Sandy R	....
Christian, Israel	1,000	3	188	2–25–1784	Sandy R	....
Christie, Thos.	400	3	244	3–26–1784	Hinkston Mill Cr	....
Churchill, Anne	207	1	113	12–12–1782	None	Surveyed
Churchwell, Armstead	24,000	3	119	12–29–1783	Ohio R	....
Churchwell, Armstead	8,000	3	119	12–29–1783	Elkhorn	Withdrawn
Churchwell, Armstead	8,000	3	153	1–17–1784	Main Elkhorn	Surveyed
Churchwell & Morgan	7,834	3	134	1– 2–1784	Ohio & Licking	....
Clark, Christopher	412½	2	319	7–10–1783	Ohio R	....
Clark, George R	8,000	2	255	3–24–1783	Ohio R	....
Clark, George R	10,000	2	256	3–24–1783	Severns Cr	....
Clark, George R	12,000	2	256	3–24–1783	Ohio R	....
Clark, James	60,500	2	316	6–12–1783	None	Surveyed
Clark, James	6,000	2	316	6–12–1783	Fks Licking	....
Clark, James	30,000	2	346	8–13–1783	Ohio R	....
Clark, James	5,000	2	351	8–14–1783	Indian Cr	Surveyed
Clark, James	4,000	2	351	8–14–1783	Ky R	Withdrawn
Clark, James	12,000	2	356	8–18–1783	Ohio R	Surveyed
Clark, James	3,000	2	357	8–18–1783	Ky R	Withdrawn
Clark, James	2,000	2	359	8–25–1783	Sandy Cr	....
Clark, James	3,000	2	365	9–22–1783	Ohio R	Withdrawn
Clark, James	6,000	2	365	9–22–1783	Ohio R	Withdrawn
Clark, James	6,000	2	370	10– 4–1783	None	Withdrawn
Clark, James	3,000	2	370	10– 4–1783	Crooked Cr	....
Clark, Jas	1,000	3	6	10–15–1783	None	....
Clark, Jas	4,000	3	7	10–15–1783	Harrods Lick Cr	....
Clark, Jas	3,000	3	12	10–17–1783	Ky R	1,025 acres surveyed
Clark, Jas	3,000	3	12	10–17–1783	Indian Cr	Withdrawn
Clark, Jas	30,000	3	45	11–14–1783	None	....
Clarks, Jas	6,000	4	152	4–12–1785	None	Withdrawn
Clark, Jas	——	4	153	4–20–1785	None	....
Clark, Jas	5,500	4	156	4–21–1785	Ohio R	Withdrawn
Clark, Jas	8,500	4	248	12–23–1785	Ohio R	....
Clark, James	40,185½	4	252	12–30–1785	None	....
Clark, John	1,000	2	139	1–29–1783	Ohio R	Surveyed
Clark, John	3,000	2	257	3–27–1783	Severn Cr	Surveyed
Clark, Jno	20,000	2	336	7–31–1783	McConnells Fk Licking	Surveyed
Clark, Jno	6,445	3	377	6–19–1784	Br Ohio R	Surveyed
Clark, Jno & Co	34,705¾	4	249	12–27–1785	——— R	....
Clark, Obediah	40,000	3	404	7–14–1784	Fks Licking	....
Clark, Robt	2,000	3	233	3–22–1784	Lick Cr	....
Clark, Robt Jr	2,000	4	123	2–21–1785	Ohio R	....
Clark, Robt Jr	10,000	4	123	2–21–1785	Upper Blue Lick	Amended
Clark, Robt Jr	2,500	4	147	4–10–1785	None	....
Clark, Robt Jr	10,000	4	226	10–13–1785	Upper Blue Lick	....
Clark, Thos	25	4	318	12–22–1787	Ky R	....
Clark, Thos	25	4	318	12–22–1787	Ky R	....
Clark & McBride	5,000	3	351	6– 1–1784	N Fk Licking	Surveyed
Clarkson, Joseph	3,892½	4	54	10–16–1784	None	....
Clarkson, Wm	100	4	327	2– 7–1789	Jones Fk Elkhorn	....
Clay, Francis Wainright	1,000	2	182	2–12–1783	Clear Cr	Surveyed
Clay, Green	200	1	33	12–16–1782	Ky R	Surveyed
Clay, Green	200	1	33	12– 3–1782	Ky R	Withdrawn
Clay, Green	200	1	34	12– 3–1782	below mouth Tates Cr	Surveyed
Clay, Green	400	1	37	12– 4–1782	Bank Lick Cr	Surveyed
Clay, Green	200	1	55	12– 5–1782	Ky R	....
Clay, Green	600	1	55	12– 5–1782	Lick Cr	Surveyed
Clay, Green	800	2	83	1–17–1783	None	Surveyed
Clay, Green	1,400	2	83	1–17–1783	Green Cr	....
Clay, Green	1,267½	2	84	1–18–1783	None	Surveyed
Clay, Green	200	2	286	5–14–1783	Tates Cr	....
Clay, Green	800	2	320	7–14–1783	None	Surveyed

Entree	Acres	Book	Page	Entry Date	Watercourse	Notes
Clay, Green	200	2	321	7–14–1783	Tates Cr	
Clay, Green	170	4	235	11–30–1785	Stoners Fk	
Clay, Green	240	4	235	11–30–1785	Stoners Fk	
Clay, Green	340	4	236	11–30–1785	Ky R	
Clay, Henry	626	3	277	4– 7–1784	Millers Cr	
Clay, Marton	10,000	3	97	12–18–1783	Little Sandy	
Clay & Brooks	3,942½	4	157	4–27–1785	Bank Lick	
Clayton, John	868½	2	62	1–14–1783	None	Surveyed
Clayton, Samuel	1,000	1	343	1– 1–1783	Gists Cr	
Clements, Roger	1,500	2	273	4– 9–1783	Sycamore Fk	Surveyed
Cleveland, Alexander	558½	1	149	12–16–1782	Adjoining Settlement Russells Sp.	
Cleveland, Alexander	458½	1	149	12–16–1782	None	
Cleveland, Alexander	907	4	305	10– 9–1786	Boggs Fk Boone Cr	
Cleveland, Eli	442	1	305	12–28–1782	Ky R & Boones Cr.	Surveyed
Cleveland, Eli	1,000	2	373	10– 7–1783	None	
Clevaland, Eli	3,000	4	183	5–24–1785	Boones Cr	Withdrawn
Cleveland, Eli	3,000	4	222	9–21–1785	None	
Cleveland, Eli	3,000	4	222	9–21–1785	Gests Cr	
Cleveland, Eli	300	4	223	9–30–1785	None	
Cleveland, Eli	3,000	4	311	1–29–1787	Br Boones Cr	
Cleveland, Eli	3,000	4	322	3–12–1788	None	
Cleveland, Eli	200	4	333	1– 5–1791	Raven Cr	
Cleveland, Eli	200	4	333	4– 1–1791	None	
Cleveland, Eli	1,483	4	333	4– 1–1791	Br Red R	
Cleveland, Eli	150	4	341	1– 8–1816	None	
Cleveland, Eli	500	4	341	1–11–1816	None	Surveyed
Cleveland, Eli	312	4	342	4– 3–1816	None	
Cleveland, Eli	285	4	342	4–19–1816	None	Surveyed
Cleveland, Eli	430	4	342	5– 1–1816	None	Surveyed
Cleveland, Oliver & Eli	2,731	1	304	12–28–1782	Raven Cr	Withdrawn
Cleveland, Oliver & Eli	1,000	2	180	2–11–1783	Licking	Withdrawn
Cleveland, Oliver & Eli	2,731	3	278	4– 7–1784	Licking	
Cleveland & Shortridge	2,000	4	222	9–21–1785	Boggs Fk Boones Cr.	Withdrawn
Cleveland & Shortridge	9,922	4	222	9–21–1785	Gests Cr	
Cleveland & Shortridge	2,000	4	223	9–30–1785	Boggs Fk Boone Cr	
Cleveland & Shortridge	9,622	4	223	9–30–1785	None	
Cleveland & Shortridge	2,000	4	322	3–12–1788	None	
Clinkingbard, William	500	2	177	2– 8–1783	Hingston Fk	Withdrawn
Clinkenbeard, William	300	1	52	12– 5–1782	Br Brushy Cr	Surveyed
Clinkinbeard, William	600	1	53	12– 5–1782	R h Fk Brushy Cr	Surveyed
Clinkenbeard, William	500	1	53	12– 5–1782	Hingston Fk	Withdrawn
Clinkingbeard, William	250	2	309	6– 7–1783	Turkey Cr	
Clinkenbeard, Wiiliam	500	2	332	7–28–1783	Ohio R	Surveyed
Clinkenberg, Wm	750	3	53	11–21–1783	Br Red R	
Clinkenberg, Wm	500	3	68	12– 1–1783	Sandy	Surveyed
Clough, Geo	600	4	306	10–23–1786	Ky R	
Cloyd, Jas	2,148	4	167	4–29–1785	None	
Clubb, Wm	18	4	340	1– 1–1802	None	
Clymer, George	10,000	1	9	11–30–1782	None	Surveyed
Clymer, George	2,000	1	312	11–30–1782	Fk Bank Lick Cr	Surveyed
Clymer, George	2,000	1	15	11–30–1782	Big Bone Lick	Surveyed
Clymer, George	2,000	1	15	12– 2–1782	Big Bone Lick	Surveyed
Coalter & McWhites	1,657	4	164	4–29–1785	None	
Coalter, & McWhites	1,637	4	165	4–29–1785	None	
Cobbs, James	1,000	2	72	1–16–1783	None	
Cobbs, John	2,500	1	185	12–19–1782	Eagle Cr	
Cobbs, John	1,000	1	84	12– 9–1782	Eagle Cr	
Cobbs, John Assee	1,000	1	84	12– 9–1782	Eagle Cr	
Cobbs, John Assee	500	1	84	12– 9–1782	Eagle Cr	Surveyed
Cockburn, Robert	1,000	1	378	1– 6–1783	Br Hingston	
Cocke, William	500	1	6	1–14–1783	Sinking Cr	Withdrawn
Cocke, William	1,500	1	6	12–13–1782	S Fk Licking Cr	Withdrawn
Cocke, William	500	2	8	1– 9–1783	None	
Cocke, William	2,000	2	8	1– 9–1783	N Fk Licking	
Cocke, Wm	2,943½	2	14	1– 9–1783	Br Licking	
Cocke, William	662½	2	274	4– 9–1783	N Fk Licking	
Cofer, Josiah	750	1	242	12–23–1782	Ky R	Surveyed
Cofer, Josiah	1,250	1	243	12–23–1782	Stoners Fk	
Coffer & Gunnell	1,000	4	81	12–31–1784	None	
Coffer & Gunnell	844	4	82	12–31–1784	Gray Lick	Withdrawn
Coffer & Gunnell	800	4	116	2–11–1785	Boones Cr	
Coffer & Gunnel¹	844	4	184	5–24–1785	None	
Coffer & Gunnell	1,000	4	184	5–24–1785	None	
Coffer & Gunnell	800	4	184	5–24–1785	None	
Coger, Michael	762	3	72	12– 5–1783	Ohio R	Withdrawn
Coger, Michael	762	4	316	11– 5–1787	None	
Cogran, Robt	1,000	4	14	8–14–1784	Sandy Cr	Surveyed
Cogran, Robt	1,000	4	14	8–14–1784	None	Surveyed
Cogran, Robt	1,000	4	14	8–14–1784	None	Surveyed
Cogran, Robt	1,000	4	14	8–14–1784	None	Surveyed

Entree	Acres	Book	Page	Entry Date	Watercourse	Notes
Cogran, Robt	1,000	4	14	8–14–1784	None	Surveyed
Cogran, Robt	1,000	4	15	8–14–1784	None	Surveyed
Cogran, Robt	1,000	4	15	8–14–1784	None	Surveyed
Cogran, Robt	1,000	4	15	8–14–1784	None	Surveyed
Cogran, Robt	1,000	4	15	8–14–1784	None	Surveyed
Cogran, Robt	1,000	4	15	8–14–1784	None	Surveyed
Cogran, Robt	1,000	4	15	8–14–1784	None	Surveyed
Cogran, Robt	1,100	4	15	8–14–1784	None	Surveyed
Cogswell, Dr Joseph	300	4	266	1–30–1786	——— R	Withdrawn
Cogswell, Dr Joseph	300	4	291	4–22–1786	None	....
Cogswell & Weakly	9,666½	4	292	4–22–1786	Ky R	....
Cohan, Jacob	5,000	1	285	12–26–1782	Main Fk Licking	Surveyed
Cohan, Jacob	2,000	4	215	8– 2–1785	None	....
Cohan, Jacob	5,000	4	296	4–29–1786	None	....
Cole, Joseph	1,822	2	131	1–27–1783	None	....
Cole, Richard	100	4	280	3–21–1786	S Fk Elkhorn	....
Coleman, Daniel	40,000½	1	350	1– 2–1783	M Licking	....
Coleman, Daniel	13,501½	1	371	1– 6–1783	Slate Cr	....
Coleman, James	1,000	2	351	8–14–1783	Ky R	....
Coleman, Jas	3,000	3	95	12–17–1783	Hinkston Fk	....
Coleman, Jas	3,000	4	89	1–14–1785	Slate Cr	....
Collers, Jas	8,000	3	109	12–27–1783	——— Cr	Surveyed
Collers, Jas	8,000	3	109	12–27–1783	——— Cr	Surveyed
Collier, John	1,355	2	25	1–10–1783	Eagle Cr	Surveyed
Colliers, Dillard	375	3	357	6–10–1784	Glens Cr	Surveyed
Collins, Dillard	1,000	3	357	6–10–1784	None	Withdrawn
Collins, Dillard	1,000	4	29	9– 7–1784	Clear Cr	....
Collins, Elisha	400	1	32	12– 3–1782	N Br Red R	Surveyed
Collins, Joel	400	1	33	12– 3–1782	Red R	Surveyed
Collins, Joseph	400	1	358	1– 4–1783	Red R	....
Collins, Joseph	3,428	2	193	2–14–1783	Ky R	....
Collins, Joseph	1,451	3	1	10–13–1783	None	....
Collins, Joseph	250	3	371	6–17–1784	Ky R	....
Collins, Jonah	1,000	3	185	2–14–1784	None	....
Collens, Josiah	400	2	116	1–24–1783	None	Surveyed
Collins, Stephen	400	1	32	12– 3–1782	——— Cr	....
Collins, Stephen	500	1	32	12– 3–1782	Red R	....
Collins, Stephen	200	1	33	12– 3–1782	Red R	Surveyed
Collins, Stephen	500	1	357	1– 3–1783	Red R	Surveyed
Colwell, Jas	2,000	3	121	12–29–1783	S Fk Sandy	....
Colwell & Moylan	7,000	3	264	4– 1–1784	None	Surveyed
Combs, Cuthbert	1,011¾	3	34	11– 8–1783	Sulbergreed	Withdrawn
Combs, Cuthbert	200	3	104	12–20–1783	Sulbergreed Cr	Surveyed
Combs, Cuthbert	208½	3	143	1–13–1784	None	Surveyed
Combs, Cuthbert	360	3	143	1–13–1784	Howards Upper Cr	....
Combs, Edward	500	2	47	1–13–1783	Br Beaver Dam Cr	....
Combs, Joseph	4,200	2	263	4– 1–1783	Eagle Cr	Surveyed
Combs, Jno	805½	3	104	12–23–1783	Sulbergreed Cr	Surveyed
Combs & Ashby	1,000	3	427	1– 1–1784	Sand R	....
Combs & Ashby	1,000	3	126	1– 1–1784	Sulbergreed Cr	....
Combs & Ashby	2,000	3	126	1– 1–1784	Howards Upper Cr	Withdrawn
Conellys, William	300	2	92	1–20–1783	None	Withdrawn
Conelly, William	300	2	206	2–21–1783	Jessamine Cr	Surveyed
Coughran, Robert	562	3	53	1–21–1783	Br Licking	Withdrawn
Coughran, Robert	562	3	425	8–13–1784	Br Licking	....
Conn, Thomas	2,196	1	369	1– 4–1783	Elkhorn & Licking	....
Connelly, Arthur	1,003	3	95	12–17–1783	Big Bone Lick	Withdrawn
Connelly, Arthur	1,003	3	136	1– 5–1784	Big Bone Lick	Withdrawn
Connelly, Arthur	2,111½	3	365	6–14–1784	None	Withdrawn
Connelly, Arthur	1,003	4	286	3–27–1786	None	....
Connelly, Arthur	1,456	4	316	11– 3–1787	None	....
Connelly, Thos	1,688	3	94	12–17–1783	None	Surveyed
Connelly & Nickell	769½	3	364	6–14–1784	None	....
Conner & Headon	4,345½	4	166	4–29–1785	None	Withdrawn
Conner & Hayden	4,345½	4	175	5– 9–1785	None	....
Conner & Headen	4,343½	4	176	5– 9–1785	None	....
Connelly & Hooker	2,003	4	286	3–27–1786	Eagle Cr	Surveyed
Constable, Mr	30,000	4	136	3–21–1785	None	Withdrawn
Constable, Mr	90,000	4	189	6– 1–1785	None	....
Constant, Jno	1,300½	1	340	1– 1–1783	Br Strand Fk	Surveyed
Constant, John	500	1	340	12–31–1782	Br Hingston Fk	Surveyed
Constant, John	500	1	340	12–31–1782	Br Stoners Fk	Surveyed
Constant, John	1,000	1	341	12–31–1782	None	....
Constant, John	500	1	369	1– 4–1783	None	Withdrawn
Constant, Jno	500	2	11	1– 9–1783	Elkhorn	Surveyed
Constant, Jno	500	3	54	11–21–1783	Red R	....
Constant, Jno	711	3	410	7–16–1784	Licking	....
Constant, Jno	500	3	410	7–16–1784	Licking	....
Contsman, Benedict	176½	3	120	12–29–1783	None	....
Conway, Miles W	637½	2	217	2–28–1783	Ky R	Surveyed
Cook, Benjamin	843½	2	100	1–20–1783	None	Surveyed
Cook, Jno	500	4	144	4– 5–1785	None	....

Entree	Acres	Book	Page	Entry Date	Watercourse	Notes
Cook, John	959¾	2	62	1–14–1783	None	Surveyed
Cook, Valentine	400	1	55	12– 5–1782	Glens Cr	
Cook, Valentine	400	1	395	1– 7–1783	Coyds Fk	
Cook, Valentine	497	2	233	3–12–1783	Paint Cr	
Cook, Valentine	50	3	355	6– 8–1784	Green Cr	
Cooke, Nathaniel	3,000	1	274	12–25–1782	S Fk Licking	
Cooke, Valentine	400	1	54	12– 5–1782	Clear Cr	Surveyed
Cooke, William	250	1	132	1– 9–1782	Gists Cr	Withdrawn
Coolidge, Judge	8,000	3	21	10–30–1783	Ohio R	
Cooper, Benjamin	400	1	226	12–21–1782	S Fk Caspers Run	
Cooper & Johnson	1,000	3	257	3–30–1784	None	Surveyed
Copage, Isaac	500	4	259	1–16–1786	Sandy	
Com, Solomon	1,000	1	108	12–11–1782	S Fk Elkhorn & Locust	Surveyed
Couchman, Benjamin	1,000	1	363	1– 4–1783	Hinkstons Fk	
Couchman, Benjamin	1,000	1	363	1– 4–1783	None	Surveyed
Couchman, Benjamin	1,000	1	364	1– 4–1783	None	
Couchman, Benjamin	1,333	1	364	1– 4–1783	None	
Couchman, Benjamin	2,000	1	364	1– 4–1783	Br Hingston Fk	Withdrawn
Couchman, Benj	209	4	253	1– 9–1786	Red R	
Couchman, Benj	9,000	4	254	1–12–1786	Red R	
Couchman & McIntire	1,000	3	67	12– 1–1783	Sandy	Surveyed
Couchman, Benedict	1,200	1	342	1– 1–1783	Hingston Fk	Withdrawn
Couchman, Benedict	1,200	1	363	1– 4–1783	None	
Couchman, Benedict	1,200	1	364	1– 4–1783	Hinkstons Fk	Withdrawn
Couchman, Benedict	1,200	3	67	12– 1–1783	Sandy	Surveyed
Couchman, Benedict	1,200	3	77	12– 9–1783	N Br Cr	
Coudriman, Benedict	1,200	1	335	12–31–1782	Br Howards Cr	Withdrawn
Cougham, Robert	562	2	203	2–19–1783	Salt Sp Fk Licking	Withdrawn
Coulter, Joseph	45,987¾	3	281	4–10–1784	Main Fk Licking	Surveyed
Coulter, Michael	1,637½	2	205	2–21–1783	South Elkhorn	Withdrawn
Courtney, Carmack	328	2	201	2–17–1783	None	
Cousins, Francis	1,000	3	239	3–25–1784	Licking Cr	
Courtsman, Benedict	400	4	117	2–12–1785	None	
Coutzmans, Benedict	1,200	2	231	3–11–1783	Hinkstons Fk	Withdrawn
Cowan, John	1,200	2	210	2–27–1783	Br Licking	Surveyed
Cowan, John	2,000¾	2	250	3–17–1783	Br Ohio R	
Cowin, Jno	1,000	4	135	3–19–1785	None	
Cox, Henry	1,500	1	237	12–33–1782	Br Licking	Surveyed
Cox, Henry	1,500	1	237	12–23–1782	Br Licking	
Cox, Henry	1,000	1	238	12–23–1782	Hingstons Fk	Surveyed
Cox, Henry	1,000	1	238	12–23–1782	E Br Hingston Fk	Surveyed
Cox, John	1,000	2	369	10– 4–1783	S Fk Licking	
Cox, Bowman & Morgan	850	4	51	10–13–1784	Eagle Cr	
Crabb, John	2,000	2	199	2–17–1783	None	
Crabtray, James	1,250	1	307	12–28–1782	Calk & Hingston Fk	
Crabtrey, James	1,250	2	81	1–17–1783	None	
Craddock, Charles	3,000	1	275	12–25–1782	Hingston & Stoners Fk	Surveyed
Craddock, Richard	3,000	1	276	12–25–1782	Flat Lick Fk	Withdrawn
Craddock, Richard	3,000	2	108	1–23–1783	Sycamore Fk Hingston	Surveyed
Craddock & Morgan	3,000	3	356	6– 9–1784	None	
Craig, Adam	14,000	1	262	12–24–1782	N Fk Licking	Surveyed
Craig, Alexander	1,300	4	259	1–16–1786	Br S Fk Sandy	
Craig, Andrew	5,000	4	308	11–21–1786	None	
Craig, Benjamin	300	1	39	12– 4–1782	Canoe Cr	Surveyed
Craig, Benjamin	2,263	2	19	1– 9–1783	N Fk Elkhorn	Withdrawn
Craig, Benjamin	2,265	2	123	1–25–1783	None	Withdrawn
Craig, Benjamin	1,865	2	123	1–25–1783	None	Surveyed
Craig, Benjamin	400	2	144	1–31–1783	None	Surveyed
Craig, Benjamin	600	2	153	2– 1–1783	N Elkhorn	
Craig, David	400	4	162	4–29–1785	None	
Craig, Elijah	250	4	201	6–17–1785	None	
Craig, Elijah	80	4	289	4– 8–1786	Bryans Station	
Craig, Elijah	240	4	303	7–31–1786	S Fk Elkhorn	
Craig, Elijah	39	4	308	11–20–1786	Hickman Cr	
Craig, Jas	30,000	4	136	3–21–1785	None	Withdrawn
Craig, Jas	90,000	4	308	6– 1–1785	None	
Craig, Jeremiah	400	1	123	12–12–1782	Little Hickman	
Craig, John	500	1	3	1–13–1783	Elkhorn	Surveyed
Craig, John	500	1	5	11–29–1783	Elkhorn	Withdrawn
Craig, John	400	1	20	1–14–1783	None	Surveyed
Craig, John	1,000	1	44	12– 4–1782	W Fk Clear Cr	Surveyed
Craig, John	1,000	1	66	1–20–1783	Big Dry Run	Amended
Craig, John	1,000	1	67	12– 6–1782	Dry Br	Surveyed
Craig, John	1,000	1	68	12– 6–1782	Dry Run Cr	Surveyed
Craig, John	1,000	1	68	12– 6–1782	Hingston Fk	Surveyed
Craig, John	1,000	1	69	12– 6–1782	Hingston Fk	Surveyed

Entree	Acres	Book	Page	Entry Date	Watercourse	Notes
Craig, John	1,000	1	69	12– 9–1782	Green C & Main Licking	Surveyed
Craig, John	1,000	1	70	12– 9–1782	———	Surveyed
Craig, John	1,000	1	70	12– 9–1782	——— Cr	Surveyed
Craig, John	1,000	1	70	12– 9–1782	Br Licking	Surveyed
Craig, John	1,000	1	70	12– 9–1782	N Fk Elkhorn	Surveyed
Craig, John	400	1	71	12– 9–1782	N Fk Elkhorn	Surveyed
Craig, John	1,000	1	71	12– 9–1782	M Lawrence Cr	Amended
Craig, John	1,000	1	71	12– 9–1782	———	Surveyed
Craig, John	1,000	1	71	12– 9–1782	Timber Ridge Run	Surveyed
Craig, John	1,000	1	71	12– 9–1782	Lees Cr	....
Craig, John	1,000	1	72	12– 9–1782	N E Br Licking	Surveyed
Craig, John	1,000	1	72	12– 9–1782	——— Cr	Surveyed
Craig, John	1,000	1	73	12– 9–1782	——— Cr	Surveyed
Craig, John	1,000	1	73	12– 9–1782	N E Br Licking	Surveyed
Craig, John	———	1	73	12– 9–1782	Br Licking	Surveyed
Craig, John	1,000	1	74	12– 9–1782	N F Br Licking	Surveyed
Craig, John	1,000	1	74	12– 9–1782	E Fk Copper Run	Surveyed
Craig, John	1,000	1	75	12– 9–1782	Br Clear Creek	Surveyed
Craig, John	1,000	1	75	12– 9–1782	Clear Creek	Surveyed
Craig, John	1,000	1	75	12– 9–1782	Clear Cr	Withdrawn
Craig, John	1,000	1	76	12– 9–1782	N Fk Clear Cr	Surveyed
Craig, John	1,000	1	76	12– 9–1782	———	Surveyed
Craig, John	1,000	1	76	12– 9–1782	Greens Cr	Surveyed
Craig, John	1,000	1	77	12– 9–1782	Lees Cr	Surveyed
Craig, John	1,000	1	77	12– 9–1782	Hingstons Fork	Surveyed
Craig, John	1,000	1	77	12– 9–1782	M Br Clear Cr	Surveyed
Craig, John	1,000	1	77	12– 9–1782	N Fk Elkhorn	Surveyed
Craig, John	1,000	1	78	12– 9–1782	——— Cr	Surveyed
Craig, John	1,000	1	78	12– 9–1782	N Fk Licking	Surveyed
Craig, John	1,000	1	78	12– 9–1782	W Fk Licking	Surveyed
Craig, John	1,000	1	79	12– 9–1782	N Fk Buck Lick	Surveyed
Craig, John	1,000	1	79	12– 9–1782	——— Cr	Surveyed
Craig, John	1,000	1	79	12– 9–1782	——— Cr	Surveyed
Craig, John	1,000	1	79	12– 9–1782	——— Cr	Surveyed
Craig, John	1,000	1	79	12– 9–1782	——— Cr	Surveyed
Craig, John	1,000	1	79	12– 9–1782	Mill Cr	Surveyed
Craig, John	1,000	1	80	12– 9–1782	N Fk McConnells Run	Surveyed
Craig, John	1,000	1	80	12– 9–1782	Hingston Fk	Surveyed
Craig, John	1,000	1	80	12– 9–1782	Clear Cr	Surveyed
Craig, John	1,000	1	81	1–13–1783	None	Surveyed
Craig, John	1,000	1	81	1–13–1783	Hingston Fk	Surveyed
Craig, John	1,000	1	81	1–13–1783	Stoners Fk	Surveyed
Craig, John	1,000	1	81	1–13–1783	N F Hingstons Fork	Surveyed
Craig, John	1,000	1	81	1–13–1783	Elkhorn	Surveyed
Craig, John	1,000	1	82	12– 9–1782	N Fk Elkhorn	Surveyed
Craig, John	1,000	1	82	12– 9–1782	Stoners Fk	Surveyed
Craig, John	1,000	1	82	12– 9–1782	———	Surveyed
Craig, John	1,000	1	105	12–11–1782	Jones Fk Elkhorn	Surveyed
Craig, John	2,000	1	105	12–11–1782	None	Withdrawn
Craig, John	1,000	1	106	12–11–1782	Jessamine Cr	Withdrawn
Craig, John	1,000	1	106	12–11–1782	None	Withdrawn
Craig, John	200	1	106	12–11–1782	Ohio R	Surveyed
Craig, John	500	1	107	12–11–1782	Ohio R	Withdrawn
Craig, John	200	1	107	12–11–1782	Ohio R	Withdrawn
Craig, John	500	1	107	12–11–1782	None	Surveyed
Craig, John	1,000	1	112	12–11–1782	Elkhorn	Surveyed
Craig, John	1,000	1	112	12–11–1782	None	Surveyed
Craig, John	1,000	1	117	12–12–1782	Br Hickman Cr	Withdrawn
Craig, Jno	400	1	118	12–12–1782	Hickmans Creek	Surveyed
Craig, John Hawkins	2,000	1	119	12–12–1782	S Fk Elkhorn	Surveyed
Craig, John Hawkins	1,000	1	120	12–12–1782	Ohio	....
Craig, John	500	1	121	12–12–1782	Elkhorn	Withdrawn
Craig, John	1,000	1	122	12–12–1782	N Fk Licking	Surveyed
Craig, John	500	1	123	12–30–1782	Todds Station	Withdrawn
Craig, John	1,000	1	125	12–13–1782	Trace Fk Dix R	Surveyed
Craig, John	1,000	1	127	12–13–1782	None	Surveyed
Craig, John	200	1	135	12–13–1782	Cane Run	....
Craig, John	500	1	161	12–17–1782	Clear Cr	Surveyed
Craig, John	200	1	204	12–20–1782	Elkhorn	Amended
Craig, John	2,450	2	28	1–10–1783	N Fk Licking	
Craig, John	600	2	28	1–10–1783	Br Ohio R	Surveyed
Craig, John	500	2	52	1–13–1783	None	Surveyed
Craig, John	1,000	2	52	1–13–1783	Millers	Surveyed
Craig, John	200	2	54	1–13–1783	None	Surveyed
Craig, John	400	2	64	1–14–1783	None	Surveyed
Craig, John	500	2	74	1–16–1783	None	Surveyed
Craig, John	1,000	2	154	2– 1–1783	None	Withdrawn
Craig, John	1,000	2	207	2–22–1783	None	Withdrawn
Craig, John	2,000¾	2	250	3–17–1783	Br Ohio R	....

Entree	Acres	Book	Page	Entry Date	Watercourse	Notes
Craig, John	1,000	2	283	5–11–1783	Clear Cr	Withdrawn
Craig, John	1,000	2	284	5–11–1783	Clear Cr	Withdrawn
Craig, John	1,000	2	289	5–21–1783	None	Surveyed
Craig, John	1,000	2	289	5–21–1783	None	....
Craig, John	——	2	294	5–26–1783	None	Surveyed
Craig, John	1,000	2	303	5–31–1783	None	....
Craig, John	1,000	2	312	6– 9–1783	None	Surveyed
Craig, Jno	500	3	50	11–17–1783	Clear Cr	Withdrawn
Craig, Jno	1,000	3	56	11–24–1783	None	Surveyed
Craig, Jno	500	3	175	2– 5–1784	Glenns Cr	Surveyed
Craig, Jno	2,000	3	225	3–11–1784	None	....
Craig, Jno	2,000	3	225	3–12–1784	Boones Cr	....
Craig, Jno	1,000	3	228	3–16–1784	Elkhorn	Surveyed
Craig, Jno	200	3	249	3–29–1784	None	....
Craig, Jno	3,000	3	250	3–30–1784	Licking	Withdrawn
Craig, Jno	2,000	3	295	4–21–1784	None	Surveyed
Craig, Jno	1,000	3	299	4–23–1784	None	....
Craig, Jno	500	3	320	5– 1–1784	Boones Cr	....
Craig, Jno	250	3	321	5– 3–1784	Glenns Cr	Surveyed
Craig, Jno	2,000	3	372	6–18–1784	N Fk Elkhorn	....
Craig, Jno	2,000	3	373	6–18–1784	None	Withdrawn
Craig, Jno	2,000	3	373	6–18–1784	None	Withdrawn
Craig, Jno	2,000	3	373	6–18–1784	None	Withdrawn
Craig, Jno	2,000	3	373	6–18–1784	S Fk Elkhorn	Withdrawn
Craig, Jno	2,000	3	373	6–18–1784	S Fk Elkhorn	Withdrawn
Craig, Jno	2,000	3	374	6–18–1784	S Fk Elkhorn	Withdrawn
Craig, Jno	2,000	3	374	6–18–1784	S Fk Elkhorn	Withdrawn
Craig, Jno	2,000	3	374	6–18–1784	S Fk Elkhorn	Withdrawn
Craig, Jno	2,000	3	374	6–18–1784	S Fk Elkhorn	1,200 acres withdrawn
Craig, Jno	6,000	3	374	6–18–1784	Gerts Cr	Withdrawn
Craig, Jno	2,000	3	375	6–18–1784	Gerts Cr	Withdrawn
Craig, Jno	2,000	3	375	6–18–1784	S Fk Elkhorn	Withdrawn
Craig, Jno	1,000	3	375	6–18–1784	S Fk Elkhorn	....
Craig, Jno	2,000	3	375	6–18–1784	N Fk Elkhorn	Withdrawn
Craig, Jno	1,000	3	375	6–18–1784	Clear Cr	Withdrawn
Craig, Jno	2,000	3	375	6–18–1784	N Fk Elkhorn	....
Craig, Jno	2,000	3	376	6–18–1784	Ohio R	Withdrawn
Craig, Jno	1,000	3	376	6–18–1784	Ohio R	Withdrawn
Craig, Jno	500	3	390	6–30–1784	None	....
Craig, Jno	500	3	390	6–30–1784	None	....
Craig, Jno	2,000	3	413	7–17–1784	N Fk Elkhorn	Withdrawn
Craig, Jno	2,000	3	413	7–21–1784	N Fk Elkhorn	....
Craig, Jno	400	3	414	7–21–1784	None	Withdrawn
Craig, Jno	1,200	3	414	7–21–1784	None	Withdrawn
Craig, Jno	18,518	3	414	7–23–1784	None	....
Craig, Jno	40,518	3	415	7–23–1784	None	....
Craig, Jno	3,800	4	65	11– 5–1784	None	....
Craig, Jno	2,000	4	67	11–16–1784	Wolfpen Cr	Surveyed
Craig, Jno	1,000	4	67	11–16–1784	S Fk Elkhorn	Withdrawn
Craig, Jno	500	4	68	11–16–1784	None	Surveyed
Craig, Jno	400	4	83	1– 7–1785	Boones Cr	Withdrawn
Craig, Jno	200	4	83	1– 7–1785	Boones Cr	Withdrawn
Craig, Jno	——	4	95	1–19–1785	Mud Lick Cr	....
Craig, Jno	500	4	95	1–19–1785	None	....
Craig, Jno	400	4	101	1–28–1785	None	....
Craig, Jno	3,000	4	118	2–14–1785	Cabbin Cr	....
Craig, Jno	1,500	4	119	2–14–1785	—— R	....
Craig, Jno	5,000	4	154	4–20–1785	None	....
Craig, Jno	20,000	4	155	4–20–1785	Sandy	6,873 acres withdrawn
Craig, Jno	400	4	201	6–17–1785	None	....
Craig, Jno	200	4	201	6–17–1785	Boones Cr	....
Craig, Jno	3,000	4	222	9–23–1785	None	....
Craig, Jno	1,282	4	222	9–23–1785	Big Bone Lick	800 acres withdrawn
Craig, Jno	800	4	234	11–22–1785	None	....
Craig, Jno	20,000	4	246	12–21–1785	None	....
Craig, Jno	5,000	4	246	12–21–1785	None	....
Craig, Jno	25,000	4	246	12–21–1785	Ohio R	Withdrawn
Craig, Jno	20,000	4	255	1–14–1786	Ohio R	....
Craig, Jno	1,000	4	299	5–12–1786	S Fk Elkhorn	....
Craig, Jno	400	4	308	11–21–1786	Glenns Cr	....
Craig, Jno	1,000	4	309	11–21–1786	Glenns Cr	....
Craig, Jno	2,000	4	336	6– 3–1792	None	....
Craig, Jno	13,000	4	339	11–12–1797	None	....
Craig, Jno & Jno	1,715	4	95	1–19–1785	Mud Lick Cr	....
Craig, Jno & Jno	1,715½	4	95	1–18–1785	None	....
Craig, John & John Jr	1,715½	2	284	5–11–1783	Turkey Foot Cr	Withdrawn
Craig, John Sr	3,770	2	182	2–12–1783	Clear Cr	....

Entree	Acres	Book	Page	Entry Date	Watercourse	Notes
Craig, John Hawkins...	1,000....	1...	120...	12–12–1782....	nr Mud Lick.......	
Craig, John Hawkins ..	1,000....	1...	161...	12–17–1782....	Clear Cr.........	Withdrawn
Craig, John H........	500....	1...	217...	12–21–1782....	Glenns Cr........	Surveyed
Craig, John Hawkins ..	1,000....	1...	377...	1– 7–1783....	None............	Withdrawn
Craig, John Hawkins ..	1,000....	2...	182...	2–12–1783....	None............	Surveyed
Craig, John Hawkins..	3,770....	2...	182...	2–12–1783....	Clear Cr.........	
Craig, Jno H.,.......	1,000....	3...	57...	11–24–1783....	Glenns Cr........	Withdrawn
Craig, Jno H........	1,000....	3...	91...	12–16–1783....	N Fk Glenns Cr....	Withdrawn
Craig, Jno H........	1,000....	3...	285...	4–12–1784....	None............	
Craig, Jno Sr........	1,000....	3...	285...	4–12–1784....	Clear Cr.........	Withdrawn
Craig, Jno H........	9,783....	4...	147...	4–10–1785....	None............	
Craig, Jno H........	9,783....	4...	181...	5–19–1785....	None............	....
Craig, Jno H........	500....	4...	303...	7–31–1786....	None............	Withdrawn
Craig, Jno H........	370....	4...	320...	2–19–1788....	None............	
Craig, Jno H........	100....	4...	324...	6– 9–1788....	Glenns Cr........	
Craig, Joseph........	1,000....	1...	192...	12–19–1782....	Clear Cr.........	Withdrawn
Craig, Joseph........	300....	4...	60...	10–26–1784....	Jessamine Cr.....	
Craig, Lewis........	400....	1...	1...	11–28–1782....	Hickman Cr.......	Surveyed
Craig, Lewis........	500....	1...	1...	11–28–1782....	————	Withdrawn
Craig, Lewis........	100....	1...	2...	11–28–1782....	Hickman Cr.......	Withdrawn
Craig, Lewis........	400....	1...	2...	11–28–1782....	————.	Surveyed....
Craig, Lewis........	400....	1...	6...	12–13–1782....	Hickman Cr.......	Surveyed
Craig, Lewis........	500....	1...	6...	12–13–1782....	None............	Surveyed
Craig, Lewis........	1,000....	1...	17...	12– 4–1782....	None............	Surveyed
Craig, Lewis........	1,000....	1...	36...	12– 4–1782....	trace to Dick R....	Surveyed
Craig, Lewis........	1,000....	1...	39...	12– 4–1782....	bet Green & Glen Cr	Withdrawn
Craig, Lewis........	1,000....	1...	98...	12–10–1782....	Clear Cr.........	Surveyed
Craig, Lewis........	1,000....	1...	98...	12–10–1782....	Clear Cr.........	Surveyed
Craig, Lewis........	400....	1...	101...	12–10–1782....	Elkhorn & Clear Cr	Surveyed
Craig, Lewis........	3,500....	1...	101...	12–10–1782....	Locust & Salt Lick Cr.........	
Craig, Lewis........	2,000....	1...	125...	12–12–1782....	Twin Creeks......	Surveyed
Craig, Lewis........	1,000....	1...	125...	12–13–1782....	5 Miles Ky R.....	
Craig, Lewis........	500....	1...	126...	12–12–1782....	5 Miles Sandy R....	....
Craig, Lewis........	500....	1...	126...	12–13–1782....	Sandy R.........	
Craig, Lewis........	1,000....	2...	12...	1– 9–1783....	Hustons Fk.......	Surveyed
Craig, Lewis........	1,000....	2...	42...	1–11–1783....	Green Cr........	Withdrawn
Craig, Lewis........	250....	2...	42...	1–11–1783....	None............	Surveyed
Craig, Lewis........	1,000....	2...	43...	1–11–1783....	Shawnees Trace....	Withdrawn
Craig, Lewis........	500....	2...	85...	1–18–1783....	None............	Withdrawn
Craig, Lewis........	1,000....	2...	123...	1–23–1783....	None............	Withdrawn
Craig, Lewis........	200....	2...	145...	1–31–1783....	None............	Withdrawn
Craig, Lewis........	1,000....	2...	147...	1–31–1783....	Grears Cr........	Surveyed
Craig, Lewis........	500....	2...	147...	1–31–1783....	Grears Cr........	Withdrawn
Craig, Lewis........	500....	2...	147...	1–31–1783....	N Fk Elkhorn.....	....
Craig, Lewis........	500....	2...	147...	1–31–1783....	N Fk Elkhorn.....	....
Craig, Lewis........	200....	2...	147...	1–31–1783....	None............	....
Craig, Lewis........	1,000....	2...	156...	2–12–1783....	S Elkhorn........	Withdrawn
Craig, Lewis........	2,500....	3...	32...	11– 4–1783....	None............	Withdrawn
Craig, Lewis........	2,000....	3...	32...	11– 4–1783....	Jessamine & Clear Cr	Withdrawn
Craig, Lewis........	2,500....	4...	47...	11–15–1785....	None............	Withdrawn
Craig, Lewis........	2,000....	3...	61...	11–25–1783....	Hickman Cr.......	Withdrawn
Craig, Lewis........	2,000....	3...	62...	11–27–1783....	None............	....
Craig, Lewis........	1,000....	3...	172...	2– 2–1784....	None............	....
Craig, Lewis........	500....	3...	172...	2– 2–1784....	None............	....
Craig, Lewis	3,500....	3...	206...	3– 9–1784....	Locust Cr........	
Craig, Lewis	1,000....	3...	265...	4– 1–1784....	Sandy R.........	Withdrawn
Craig, Lewis	200....	3...	283...	4–10–1784....	Hickman & Jessamine.......	Withdrawn
Craig, Lewis........	200....	3...322...		5– 3–1784....	None............	....
Craig, Lewis........	400....	3...389...		6–30–1784....	None............	....
Craig, Lewis........	400....	3...389...		6–30–1784....	Clear Cr.........	Withdrawn
Craig, Lewis........	630....	3...391...		6–30–1784....	S Elkhorn........	Withdrawn
Craig, Lewis........	300....	3...419...		8– 2–1784....	Jessamine Cr	52 acres surveyed
Craig, Lewis........	400....	3...419...		7–30–1784....	Clear Cr........	....
Craig, Lewis........	630....	4...201...		6–17–1785....	S Fk Elkhorn.....	....
Craig, Lewis........	1,500....	4...237...		12– 7–1785....	S Fk Elkhorn.....	
Craig, Lewis........	1,000....	4...237...		12– 7–1785....	Ohio R..........	Withdrawn
Craig, Lewis........	1,500....	4...298...		5–11–1786....	None............	
Craig, Lewis........	150....	4...307...		10–30–1786....	Main Fk Elkhorn ..	
Craig, Lewis........	1,000....	4...310...		1–29–1787....	None............	....
Craig, Lewis........	1,500....	4...311...		3– 6–1787....	W Fk Hickman Cr.	Surveyed
Craig, Lewis........	2,000....	4...312...		3– 6–1787....	S Fk Elkhorn.....	
Craig, Lewis........	200....	4...317...		12–10–1787....	Ky R...........	Surveyed
Craig, Lewis........	125....	4...317...		12–10–1787....	Ky R...........	
Craig, Lewis........	100....	4...325...		12–17–1788....	Jones Fk Elkhorn..	75 acres surveyed
Craig, Lewis........	245....	4...328...		4– 1–1789....	None............	....
Craig, Lewis........	400....	4...328...		4– 1–1789....	None............	....
Craig, Lewis.........	520....	4...328...		4– 1–1789....	None............	....

Entree	Acres	Book	Page	Entry Date	Watercourse	Notes
Craig, Lewis	120	4	329	4– 1–1789	None	
Craig, Lewis	500	4	331	6–22–1790	None	
Craig, Lewis	200	4	332	6–22–1790	None	
Craig, Lewis	100	1	10	11–29–1782	Hickmans Cr	
Craig, Toliver Jr	500	3	389	6–30–1784	None	
Craig, Toliver Jr	500	3	389	6–30–1784	S Fk Elkhorn	
Craig & Cavin	7,416	3	165	1–23–1784	Eagle Cr	
Craig & Fox	2,000	3	207	3– 9–1784	Hickman Cr	1,000 acres withdrawn
Craig & Fox	1,000	3	208	3– 9–1784	None	Withdrawn
Craig & Fox	1,000	3	252	3–30–1784	Licking	
Craig & Fox	200	3	253	3–30–1784	None	Surveyed
Craig & Headon	3,916	4	157	4–27–1785	None	
Craig & Headon	3,916	3	250	3–30–1784	Buffalo Rd	Withdrawn
Craig & Johnson	50,000	3	249	3–29–1784	Licking	Surveyed
Craig & Johnson	2,000	3	325	5– 6–1784	None	
Craig & Johnson	2,892	3	330	5–13–1784	None	
Craig & Smith	600	3	390	6–30–1784	Bryans Station	
Craig & Smith	600	3	390	6–30–1784	None	
Craig & Smith	600	3	391	6–30–1784	None	
Craig & Smith	600	3	391	6–30–1784	N Fk Elkhorn	
Craig & Smith	639	3	391	6–30–1784	N Fk Elkhorn	
Craig & Smith Sr	1,250	3	389	6–30–1784	None	
Craig & Taylor	500	4	119	2–15–1785	Ohio R	
Craig & Taylor	500	4	120	2–15–1785	Ohio R	
Crancane, Geo	3,566⅔	3	45	11–14–1783	Ohio R	
Crawford, James	1,000	2	16	1– 9–1783	Ohio R	
Crawford, Jas	6,136¼	3	66	12– 1–1783	None	
Crawford, Joseph	1,000	3	187	2–21–1784	N Fk Elkhorn	
Crawford, Joseph	1,000	3	188	2–24–1784	None	
Crawford, Wm	1,218	3	406	7–14–1784	Main Fk Licking	
Crawford, William Jr	500	1	28	12– 3–1782	S Br Licking	
Crigler, Christopher	1,800	1	120	12–12–1782	Lees Lick	
Crigler, Christopher	29,936	3	424	8–11–1784	Cumberland Mt	
Crighton, Robert	1,200	2	18	1– 9–1783	None	Surveyed
Crimm, Jno	1,000	1	290	12–27–1782	E Br Stoners Fk	
Crimm, Joseph	4,980½	3	135	1– 2–1784	None	
Crittenden, John	998	1	98	12–10–1782	S Fk Elkhorn	Amended
Crittenden, John	476	1	330	12–31–1782	None	
Crittenden, John	10,000	2	20	1– 9–1783	Licking Cr	
Crittenden, John	4,767	2	175	2– 8–1783	None	
Crittenden, John	998	2	177	2– 8–1783	None	
Crittenden, Jno	8,000	2	255	3–24–1783	Ohio R	
Crittenden, Jno	10,000	2	256	3–24–1783	Severns Cr	
Crittenden, Jno	12,000	2	256	3–24–1783	Ohio R	
Crittenden, Jno	60,000	3	237	3–24–1784	N Fk Elkhorn	30,000 acres withdrawn
Crittenden, Jno	30,000	4	82	1– 5–1785	Slate Cr	11,00 acres withdrawn
Crittenden, Jno	9,000	4	130	3– 7–1785	None	
Crittenden, & Cannon	9,000	4	130	3– 7–1785	Red R	Surveyed
Crittenden, Jno	9,000	4	254	1–12–1786	Red R	
Crockett, Andrew	1,000	3	184	2–14–1784	Wells Cr	Surveyed
Crockett, Andrew	400	3	283	4–12–1784	Howards Cr	
Crockett, James	1,000	1	331	12–31–1782	Br Howards Cr	Surveyed
Crocus, Jno	805¼	4	135	3–19–1785	None	
Croutcher, Henry	400	3	51	11–18–1783	Eagle & Severn Cr	Surveyed
Croutcher, Henry	10,000	4	218	8–20–1785	None	Withdrawn
Croutcher, Jas	100	4	326	1–23–1789	Elkhorn Cr	
Croutcher & Maury	10,000	4	218	8–20–1785	None	
Croutcher & Parker	2,375	3	123	12–30–1783	None	Surveyed
Crow, James	405	1	350	1– 2–1783	Green R	
Crow, James	1,000	2	1	1– 8–1783	N Fk Elkhorn	
Crow, James	500	2	91	1–20–1783	None	
Crow, Jas	567½	4	264	1–29–1786	N Fk Eagle Cr	
Crow, Jacob	400	2	301	5–30–1783	Greers Cr	
Crow, Wm	1,100½	2	302	5–30–1783	None	
Crow & Adams	4,000	3	89	12–15–1783	Goose Cr	Surveyed
Crow & Adams	3,000	3	89	12–15–1783	M Fk Ky R	Surveyed
Crow & Adams	3,000	3	89	12–15–1783	N Fk 3 Fks Ky R	Surveyed
Crow & Adams	2,500	3	90	12–15–1783	N Fk 3 Fks Ky R	
Crow & Adams	2,500	3	90	12–15–1783	—— R	Surveyed
Crow & Adams	2,500	3	90	12–15–1783	M Fk Ky R	Surveyed
Crow & Adams	2,500	3	90	12–15–1783	—— Cr	Surveyed
Cruchfield, Stapleton	1,650	1	21	12– 2–1782	Howards Upper Cr	Withdrawn
Crump, Abner	5,859½	3	319	5– 1–1784	Small Mt Cr	
Crump, Goodrich	5,000	1	367	1– 4–1783	Licking Cr	
Crutcher, Henry	10,000	2	376	10–13–1783	Ohio R	Withdrawn
Crutcher, Henry	11,000	3	69	12– 3–1783	Fks —— Cr	Surveyed
Crutcher, Henry	10,000	4	242	12–14–1785	Salt Rock Fk	
Crutcher, Henry	3,000	4	275	2–18–1787	Br S Fk Sandy	

Entree	Acres	Book	Page	Entry Date	Watercourse	Notes
Crutcher, Henry	4,000	4	275	2–18–1786	S Fk Sandy	
Crutcher, Hugh, Jno & Jas	10,000	3	77	12– 9–1783	N Fk Licking	Surveyed
Crutcher & Tebbs	3,000	3	35	11– 8–1783	Buffaloe Rd	
Crutcher & Tibbs	10,000	3	13	10–17–1783	Blue Lick	Surveyed
Crutchfield, John	9,000	1	231	12–23–1782	Licking	
Crutchfield, John	2,678	1	316	12–30–1782	None	
Crutchfield, Jno	1,000	4	242	12–14–1785	Salt Rock Fk	
Crutchfield, Stapleton	1,250	3	88	12–15–1783	Licking	
Culberson, Samuel	500	1	358	1– 4–1783	None	
Culberson, Thomas	500	1	358	1– 4–1783	Ky R	
Cullwill, George	1,000	1	27	12– 3–1782	S Fk Licking	
Cummings, Chas Rev	200	4	232	11– 7–1785	Ohio R	
Cunningham, Ann	1,092	2	58	1–13–1783	Ky R	
Cunningham, Thomas	1,000	2	226	3–10–1783	Ohio R	Surveyed
Curd, Chas	1,000	3	152	1–16–1784	None	
Curd, Edward	2,000	3	151	1–16–1784	Ky R	
Curd, John	700	1	109	12–11–1782	Br Licking	Withdrawn
Curd, John	5,000	2	210	2–27–1783	Hickmans Cr	Withdrawn
Curd, John	5,000	2	210	2–27–1783	Hickman Cr	Withdrawn
Curd, John	5,000	2	232	3–12–1783	Hickmans Cr	Surveyed
Curd, Jno	700	4	267	2– 6–1786	None	
Curd, Jno	16	4	268	2– 6–1786	Ky R	
Curd, Joseph	7,146	3	151	1–15–1784	N Fk Ky R	
Curd, Joseph	5,075	3	151	1–16–1784	―――― R	
Curd, Joseph	500	3	151	1–16–1784	―――― Cr	
Curry & Ross	10,000	4	107	2– 5–1785	Buckhorn Fk	
Curry & Ross	10,000	4	283	3–23–1786	―――― R	
Curry & Ross	10,000	4	283	3–23–1786	―――― R	Surveyed
Curry & Ross	10,000	4	283	3–23–1786	――――	
Curry & Ross	10,000	4	283	3–23–1786	―――― R	Surveyed
Curry & Ross	10,000	4	283	3–23–1786	None	Surveyed
Curry & Ross	11,062½	4	284	3–23–1786	Quick Sand Cr	Surveyed
Curry & Ross	126.843	4	314	3–21–1787	Br Big Bone Lick	
Curry & Ross	136.843	4	315	3–21–1787	None	
Custer, Arnold	1,000	3	233	3–18–1784	N Fk Elkhorn	Surveyed
Dabney, Chas	2,259½	3	327	5– 7–1784	Paint Lick	
Dale, Geo	1,000	4	212	7–28–1785	None	
Dalziel, Thos	223½	2	9	1– 9–1783	None	
Dandrige, Bartholomew	50	1	39	12– 4–1782	Elkhorn Cr	
Dandrige, Bartholomew	1,000	1	61	12– 6–1782	Elkhorn Waters	
Dandrige, Bartholomew	15,656	4	144	4–10–1785	Little Sandy	
Daniel, Daniel	4,000	2	350	8–14–1783	Jessamine Cr	
Daniel, Robt	1,205	3	18	10–30–1783	None	
Daniel, Robt	2,070	4	167	4–29–1785	None	
Daniel, Thomas	1,000	1	4	11–13–1783	Main Licking	
Daniel, Thomas	200	1	4	11–29–1783	Br Ky R	Surveyed
Daniel, Walker	50	1	14	11–30–1782	Millers Cr	Withdrawn
Daniel, Walker	43	1	33	11–16–1784	Head of Raven Cr	
Daniel, Walker	5,789	1	336	12–31–1782	S Fk Licking	Surveyed
Daniel, Walker	23,692	1	372	1– 6–1783	S Fk Licking	Surveyed
Daniel, Walker	2,600	2	10	1– 9–1783	Holdus Cr	Withdrawn
Daniel, Walker	2,000	2	315	6–12–1783	Br Ohio R	
Daniel, Walker	2,000	2	316	6–12–1783	Indian Cr	
Daniel, Walker	4,250	2	316	6–12–1783	Ky R	
Daniel, Walker	2,000	2	371	10– 4–1783	None	
Daniel, Walker	2,000	3	7	10–15–1783	Ohio R	
Daniel, Walker	2,500	3	41	11–12–1783	Br Licking	
Daniel, Walker	300	3	42	11–12–1783	Ky R	Surveyed
Daniel, Walker	2,000	3	182	2–12–1784	Hickman Cr	
Daniel, Walker	1,700	3	183	2–12–1784	Licking	Withdrawn
Daniel, Walker	15,375	3	331	5–13–1784	Ohio R	
Daniel, Walker	6,000	3	331	5–13–1784	―――― Cr	
Daniel, Walker	3,922	3	332	5–13–1784	S Fk Licking	1,000 acres withdrawn
Daniel, Walker	1,000	3	333	5–14–1784	S Fk Licking	
Daniel, Walker	334	3	386	6–28–1784	Ky R	Withdrawn
Daniel, Walker	334	4	43	9–24–1784	None	
Daniel & Barr	14,000	4	53	10–16–1784	None	
Daniel & Harrison	6,923½	3	268	4– 6–1784	None	
Daniel & Marshall	4,000	3	44	11–14–1783	Ohio R	Withdrawn
Daniel & Marshall	4,000	3	44	11–14–1783	Ohio R	Withdrawn
Daniel & Marshall	2,000	3	45	11–14–1783	None	Withdrawn
Daniel & Marshall	3,000	3	183	2–12–1784	None	Withdrawn
Daniels, Joshua	300	2	104	1–21–1783	N Fk Elkhorn	Withdrawn
Darby, Daniel	30,000	3	113	12–27–1783	E Fk Licking	Surveyed
Darnaby, Edward	8,959¾	3	333	5–14–1784	None	4,479¾ acres withdrawn
Darnell, Jeremiah	5,312½	3	124	12–31–1783	Eagle Cr	
Davis, David	1,000	2	247	3–15–1783	None	Surveyed
Davis, Evans	1,000	4	126	3– 5–1785	N E Fk Licking	Surveyed

Entree	Acres	Book	Page	Entry Date	Watercourse	Notes
Davis, Evans	1,000	4	127	3– 5–1785	N E Fk Licking	Surveyed
Davis, Evans	1,000	4	127	3– 5–1785	E Fk Licking	Surveyed
Davis, Evans	1,060	4	127	3– 5–1785	N E Fk Licking	Surveyed
Davis, Evans	1,408¾	4	127	3– 5–1785	N E Fk Licking	....
Davids, Geo	306½	4	203	6–28–1785	Cabbin Cr	....
Davis, Isaac Jr	1,000	3	39	11–12–1783	Licking	Surveyed
Davis, Isaac	1,000	3	275	4– 7–1784	None	....
Davis, Isaac	800	3	275	4– 7–1784	Small Mt Cr	Surveyed
Davis, James	581	2	225	3– 8–1783	Br Ky R	Surveyed
Davis, James	400	2	277	4–23–1783	Br Licking	....
Davis, John	719	2	200	2–17–1783	None	....
Davis, Jonathan	1,398½	2	170	2– 7–1783	Hinkstons Mill Cr	....
Davis, Joseph	1,562	2	204	2–19–1783	None	....
Davis, Samuel	4,000	2	187	2–13–1783	N E Upper Blue Lick	....
Davis, Samuel	2,000	3	93	12–16–1783	Br Licking	....
Davis, Samuel	1,475	3	93	12–16–1783	Salt Lick Cr War Road	....
Davis, Thomas	775	2	360	8–25–1783	Stoners Fk	....
Davis, Thos	350	4	241	12–14–1785	Eagle Cr	....
Davis, William	10,000	1	221	12–21–1782	S Licking	....
Daw, Phillip	1,493¾	2	215	2–28–1783	Licking	....
Dawsing, Wm	1,000	4	339	1– 5–1795	None	....
Dawson, Jno	543	3	170	1–29–1784	Blue Lick Fk	....
Deal, Thos	1,000	3	320	5– 1–1784	N Fk Licking	....
Dean, Adam	1,000	4	159	4–29–1785	None	....
Dean, Wm	1,000	4	159	4–29–1785	None	....
Dean & Dean	300 306⅔	3	190	2–28–1784	3 Fks Ky R	....
Delaney, Joseph	3,617½	2	235	3–12–1783	None	....
Denham & Turner	470	3	412	7–17–1784	None	....
Denwiddie, Jas	1,314	3	54	11–21–1783	Red R	Surveyed
Denwiddie, Jas	2,500	4	76	12–16–1784	Big Mud Lick	....
Denwiddie, Jas	449	4	309	1– 5–1787	Hickman Cr	....
Deyerl, Peter	2,179	2	118	1–24–1783	Hinkston & Stoners Fk	Surveyed
Dick & McBride	4,000	3	339	5–19–1784	None	Surveyed
Dickason, Archer	750	1	29	12–17–1782	1st large Cr below Cedar Cr	Surveyed
Dickerson, John	800	2	72	1–17–1783	None	....
Dickerson, Jno	500	3	399	7– 9–1784	None	....
Dickerson, Jno	2,000	4	332	11– 9–1790	Hickman Cr	....
Dickerson, Martin	400	1	251	12–24–1782	None	....
Dickerson, Martin	1,000	2	72	1–16–1783	None	....
Dickerson, Martin	2,000	4	332	11– 9–1790	Hickman Cr	....
Dickerson, Valentine	800	1	156	12–17–1782	N Fk Elkhorn	Surveyed
Dickerson, William	800	1	156	12–14–1782	N Fk Elkhorn	Surveyed
Dickey, James	1,500	1	295	12–27–1782	Main & Fk Licking	Surveyed
Dickey, Jas	1,500	1	295	12–27–1782	Main & N Fk Licking	....
Dickey, Jos	1,000	3	74	12– 8–1783	Hinkston Fk	....
Dickey, Jos	881¼	3	244	3–26–1784	None	Surveyed
Dickey, Jos	93¾	4	185	5–31–1785	N Fk Red R	....
Dickey, Jos	1,000	4	310	1–25–1787	None	....
Dickey, Jas	300	4	310	1–25–1787	Glens & Elkhorn	....
Dickey, Jno	384	4	163	4–29–1785	None	....
Dickey, Michael	56	4	311	3– 1–1787	Br N Elkhorn	....
Dierly, Peter	1,000	1	268	12–25–1782	None	Withdrawn
Dierly, Peter	700	2	246	3–15–1783	S Fk Elkhorn & Clear Cr	....
Dillen, Andrew	5,119	2	31	1–10–1783	Clay Lick	Surveyed
Doakes, Robt	1,033	4	116	2–11–1785	None	Surveyed
Dobbins, Edward	2,000	2	376	10–13–1783	Small Mt Cr	....
Dobbin, John	1,000	1	103	12–11–1782	None	Surveyed
Dobbs, William	800	2	149	2– 1–1783	Ohio R	Surveyed
Dodd, Jno	3,571¼	3	165	1–23–1784	Bank Lick Cr	....
Dodd, Jno	3,571½	3	243	3–26–1784	None	....
Doggett, George	1,000	2	314	6– 9–1783	Br Licking	Withdrawn
Doggett & Morgan	1,840	4	287	3–28–1786	None	....
Doherty, James	506¼	1	344	1– 1–1783	Gasts Cr	....
Donald, Jno	12,225	4	70	11–25–1784	Slate Cr	....
Donalson, Wm	500	3	12	10–17–1783	None	....
Donnell, Jno	57,499¼	4	50	9–13–1784	Ky R	Withdrawn
Donnell, Jno	57,499¼	4	57	10–23–1784	Eagle Cr	Surveyed
Donnell, Jno	2,100	4	66	11–11–1784	Licking Cr	....
Donnell, Jno	2,000	4	118	2–12–1785	Br Licking	....
Donnell, Jno	16,961	4	210	7–22–1785	Br Ky R	Withdrawn
Donnell, Jno	1,000	4	210	7–22–1785	None	....
Donnell, Jno	16,961	4	280	3–23–1786	None	....
Donnell, Jno	1,000	4	280	3–23–1786	None	....
Donnell, Jno	2,160	4	280	3–23–1786	None	Surveyed
Donnell, Jno	2,644¾	4	281	3–23–1786	S Fk Sandy	Surveyed

Entree	Acres	Book	Page	Entry Date	Watercourse	Notes
Donnell, Jno	300	4	281	3–23–1786	Salt Rock Fk	
Donnell, Jno	700	4	281	3–23–1786	——— Cr	
Donnell, Jno	4,000	4	281	3–23–1786	Tripletts Cr	
Donnell, Jno	1,000	4	281	3–23–1786	Little Indian Trace	
Donnell & Barr	2,000	4	282	3–23–1786	S Fk Sandy	
Donnell & Barr	2,961	4	282	3–23–1786	Main Licking	
Donnell & Morgan	4,332½	3	180	2–11–1784	Eagle Cr	Surveyed
Donnell & Morgan	12,000	4	209	7–22–1785	None	
Donnell, Stewart & Barr	57,499½	4	57	10–23–1784	None	
Dooley, Geo	12,613	3	226	3–14–1784	Licking	Withdrawn
Dooley, Geo	12,613	3	241	3–26–1784	Locust Cr	Withdrawn
Dooley, Geo	3,165½	3	241	3–26–1784	Johnsons Fk	
Dooley, Geo	12,613	4	265	1–30–1786	N Fk Ky R	Withdrawn
Dooley, Geo	12,613	4	291	4–22–1786	None	
Doran, Patrick	534	1	158	12–17–1782	Clear Cr	Surveyed
Dorr, Alexander	5,000	4	297	4–29–1786	Ohio R	
Doughtery, Geo	6,136¼	3	66	12– 1–1783	None	
Douglass, David	3,072	3	148	1–15–1784	Red R	Surveyed
Douglass, John, heirs	400	1	117	12–12–1782	Little Mt Cr	
Dowden, Jno Ashfore	100	4	212	7–28–1785	None	
Dowden, Thos	225	4	212	7–28–1785	None	
Dowse, Edward	15,000	4	39	9–21–1784	Br Licking	Surveyed
Dowse, Edward	2,000	4	64	11– 5–1784	Main Licking	
Dowdwell, Jos	1,000	4	272	2–15–1786	Slate Cr	
Dowling, Edmund	1,000	1	24	12–17–1782	Hingston Fk	Surveyed
Downing, Jno	400	4	85	1– 8–1785	Ky R	Withdrawn
Downing, Jno	750	4	85	1– 8–1785	N Fk Elkhorn	Withdrawn
Downing, Jno	400	4	85	1– 8–1785	S Fk Elkhorn	Withdrawn
Downing, Jno	200	4	85	1– 8–1785	Ky R	Withdrawn
Downing, Jno	1,000	4	86	1– 8–1785	None	Withdrawn
Downing, Jno	3,250	4	181	5–19–1785	None	
Dowsing, William	1,000	1	256	12–24–1782	Town Fk	Withdrawn
Dowsing, William	4,000	1	255	12–24–1782	N Fk Eagle Cr	
Dowing & Turpin	4,250	4	181	5–19–1785	None	
Dozer, Zack	10,000	3	281	4–10–1784	Eagle Cr	Withdrawn
Dozer, Zack	10,000	4	130	3–10–1785	None	
Drake, Ephraim	1,000	1	331	12–31–1782	None	Surveyed
Drake, Ephriam	500	2	77	1–17–1783	Howards Cr	
Drake, Samuel	1,000	2	76	1–17–1783	Ky R	Surveyed
Drake, Samuel	477	3	85	12–13–1783	Hinkston Fk	Withdrawn
Drake, Samuel	477	3	231	3–20–1784	Hinkston Fk	
Dramagoale, Alexander	1,222½	3	318	5– 1–1784	None	
Draydon, William	1,000	2	5	1– 8–1783	W Fk Howards Cr.	Surveyed
Dryden, Wm	200	3	167	1–26–1784	None	Surveyed
Dryden, Wm	300	3	168	1–26–1784	None	Withdrawn
Drayden, Wm	200	3	168	1–26–1784	None	Withdrawn
Dryden, Wm	100	4	205	7– 4–1785	None	
Dryden, Wm	250	4	205	7– 4–1785	Lower Howards Cr.	
Dryden, Wm	50	4	206	7– 4–1785	None	
Dryden, Wm	300	4	207	7– 4–1785	Howards lower Cr.	
Dryden, Wm	100	4	207	7– 4–1785	None	
Dye, Wm	6,000	4	221	9–12–1785	None	
Dudgeon, Alex	4,348½	2	117	1–24–1783	None	Surveyed
Dudgeon, John	885	2	117	1–24–1783	None	Surveyed
Dudgeon, Ralph	400	1	154	12–17–1782	N Fk Licking	
Duff, Timothy	2,034	4	115	2–10–1785	None	
Duglas, John	250	1	51	12– 5–1782	Br Hingston	Surveyed
Duncan, Andrew	375	4	163	4–29–1785	None	
Duncan, James	1,000	1	46	12– 4–1782	Br Cain Run	Surveyed
Duncan, Jos	440	3	52	11–21–1783	Br Licking	Surveyed
Dunken, James	500	2	18	1– 9–1783	None	Withdrawn
Duncan, Nimrod	325	1	8	11–29–1782	Blue Lick	Surveyed
Dunn, Thos	400	4	291	4–18–1786	Hinkston Fk	
Duncan & Wilson	500	3	406	7–14–1784	Br Licking	
Dunlap, Alexander	350	1	60	12– 6–1782	———	Withdrawn
Dunlap, Alexander	2,469¼	4	167	4–29–1785	None	Withdrawn
Dunlap, Alexander	1,000	4	168	4–30–1785	None	Withdrawn
Dunlap, Alexander	2,469¼	4	176	5– 9–1785	None	
Dunlap, Alexander	1,000	4	176	5– 9–1785	None	
Dunlap, Alexander	1,000	4	177	5– 9–1785	None	
Dunlap, Alexander	400	4	294	4–29–1786	Br Licking	
Dunlap, James	1,200	1	40	12– 4–1782	——— Cr	Surveyed
Dunlap, Wm	831½	3	243	3–26–1784	S Fk Licking	
Dunlap, Wm	4,666¼	4	167	4–29–1785	None	2,000 acres withdrawn
Dunlap, Wm	2,000	4	176	5– 9–1785	None	
Dunlap, Wm	2,000	4	177	5– 9–1785	None	
Dunlap & Brown	2,469½	4	177	5– 9–1785	None	
Dunlap & McBride	400	3	228	3–16–1784	N Fk Licking	Surveyed
Dupee, James	1,000	1	175	12–18–1782	Br Stoner Fk	Surveyed

Entree	Acres	Book	Page	Entry Date	Watercourse	Notes
Dupee, James	1,000	1	176	12–18–1782	Br Stoners Fk	
Duprey, John	667	2	314	6–10–1783	None	
Dupey, James	4,500	2	238	3–13–1783	None	Surveyed
Dupey, John	6,000	2	238	3–12–1783	Br Salt Spring Fk	Surveyed
Dupey, Jno	5,054½	2	238	3–13–1783	Hingston & M Fk Licking	Surveyed
Durby, Peter	1,000	4	202	6–23–1785	Elkhorn	
Durham, John	2,035	2	127	1–27–1783	Upper Salt Sp	Surveyed
Durham, John	2,035	2	127	1–27–1783	Upper Salt Sp	
Duvall & Marshall	20,000	3	295	4–21–1784	None	
Eagins, William	1,000	2	301	5–30–1783	N Fk Greer Cr	Surveyed
Eagle, George	500	2	248	3–15–1783	None	
Eagleston, Edward	4,743	3	122	12–29–1783	None	
Eales, John	300	2	275	4– 9–1783	None	
Early, Joel	12,338	1	119	12–12–1782	Hickman Cr	Withdrawn
Easley, Joel	1,250	3	331	5–13–1784	None	
Early, Joel	29,936	3	424	8–11–1784	Cumberland Mt	
Early, Joseph	500	1	9	11–29–1782	N Fk Elkhorn	Surveyed
Early, Joseph	2,000	1	243	12–23–1782	Elkhorn & Coopers Run	Surveyed
Early, Joseph	1,000	1	243	12–23–1782	Kingston Fk	Surveyed
Early, Joseph	1,000	1	244	12–23–1782	Ky R	Surveyed
Early, Joseph, heirs	2,000	3	144	1–13–1784	Big Bone Lick	
Early, Samuel	450	4	137	3–22–1785	Licking	
Eastin, Achilles	600	1	390	1– 7–1783	Coopers Run	Amended
Eastin, Achilles	600	2	171	2– 7–1783	None	
Eastin, Achilles	290	2	193	2–14–1783	None	
Eastin, Achilles	310	2	193	2–14–1783	None	Surveyed
Eastin, Achilles	930	2	257	3–27–1783	N Fk Elkhorn	Surveyed
Eastin, Augustine	1,000	3	269	4– 6–1784	None	
Eastin, Augustine	2,000	3	269	4– 6–1784	Stoners Fk	
Eastin, Augustine	7,000	3	297	4–22–1784	Locust Cr	Withdrawn
Eastin, Augustine	7,000	4	299	5–24–1786	None	Surveyed
Eastin, Augustus	10	2	194	2–14–1783	Coopers Run	Surveyed
Eastin, Elizabeth	1,344½	2	86	1–18–1783	None	
Eastin, Griffin A	1,550	3	251	3–30–1784	Lees Cr	Withdrawn
Easley, Joseph	2,000	2	13	1– 9–1783	Ky R	Surveyed
Edleman, Catherine	55	2	241	3–13–1783	S Fk Licking	
Edmiston, Elizabeth	286	1	345	1– 1–1783	N Licking	
Edmiston, Jno	2,073½	4	161	4–29–1785	None	
Edmiston, Jno	500	4	163	4–29–1785	None	
Edmiston, John	855½	1	334	12–31–1782	Indian Cr	Surveyed
Edmiston, Martha Margaret	1,059	4	162	4–29–1785	None	
Edmiston, Morlose Jr	489	4	163	4–29–1785	None	
Edmiston, Samuel	615	4	163	4–29–1785	None	
Edmiston, Samuel	615	4	339	10–15–1796	None	
Edmiston, Samuel	675	4	162	4–29–1785	None	
Edmiston, Wm	1,445	4	161	4–29–1785	None	
Edmiston & Huntsman	1,445	4	106	2– 5–1785	Rockhouse Fk	
Edmiston & Huntsman	1,445	4	107	2– 5–1785	Rockhouse Fk	
Edmiston & Huntsman	1,445	3	307	4–29–1785	Licking	Withdrawn
Edmonson, Jno	5,500¼	3	238	3–25–1784	None	
Edmunson, John	1,000	2	242	3–13–1783	None	
Edwards, John	1,000	1	35	12–14–1782	Coopers Run	
Edwards, John	200	1	88	12– 9–1782	Lulbergreed Cr	
Edwards, John	7,000	1	92	12–10–1782	Licking	Surveyed
Edwards, John	5,000	1	104	12–11–1782	Spencers Cr	Surveyed
Edwards, John	1,000	1	108	12–11–1782	N Fk Elkhorn & Locust Cr	Surveyed
Edwards, John	1,000	1	242	12–23–1782	Br Hingston Fk	Surveyed
Edwards, John	2,000	1	242	12–23–1782	Spencers Cr	
Edwards, John	600	1	393	1– 8–1783	Lulbergreed Cr	
Edwards, Sandford	1,000	1	104	12–11–1782	None	
Egbert, Lawrence	500	2	145	1–31–1783	None	Surveyed
Elliott, Robt	750¼	1	135	3–19–1785	None	
Elliott, Wm	4,000	3	86	12–13–1783	Ohio	
Elliott, Wm	1,222½	3	86	12–13–1783	Licking	
Elliott, Wm	1,000	3	86	12–13–1783	None	
Elliott, Wm	600	3	87	12–13–1783	None	
Ellis, John	200	1	114	12–12–1782	N Fk Elkhorn	
Ellis, Joseph	2,067½	4	148	4–10–1785	None	
Ellis, Richard	722	3	404	7–13–1784	None	
Ellis, Richard	4,000	4	42	9–22–1784	None	
Ellis, Richard	92,000	4	189	6– 1–1785	Main Licking	Withdrawn
Ellis, Richard	92,000	4	207	7–13–1785	None	
Ellis, Richard	92,000	4	20	7–13–1785	Licking	
Ellis, William	1,000	2	16	1– 9–1783	None	
Ellis, Wm	1,000	3	379	6–19–1784	Licking	Withdrawn
Ellis, Wm	500	4	336	3——1793	None	

Entree	Acres	Book	Page	Entry Date	Watercourse	Notes
Ellis, Wm	1,000	4	336	3–10–1793	None	
Ellis & Marshall	781	3	403	7–13–1784	None	Withdrawn
Ellis & Marshall	781	3	404	7–13–1784	None	
Ellis & Marshall	1,400	3	408	7–14–1784	Slate Cr	
Ellis & Marshall	878	3	409	7–14–1784	Coal Bank	
Elzey, Wm	6,000	3	356	6– 9–1784	Brs Fk Sandy	
Embree, Eff & Lawrence	225,000	3	353	6– 4–1784	Ky R	Amended
Emerick, Ballis	300,306⅔	3	190	2–28–1784	3 Fks Ky R	
Emerson, Ash	1,000	1	337	12–31–1782	Dry Run	Surveyed
Emerson, Ash	1,000	1	93	12–10–1782	Dry Run	Withdrawn
Emerson, Hugh	1,000	1	92	12–10–1782	N Fk Elkhorn	Surveyed
Emerson, Tilley	750	1	25	12–17–1782	——— Cr	
Ervin, Elizabeth	400	1	17	12– 2–1782	Gists Cr	
Erwin, William	400	1	30	12– 3–1782	——— Cr	
Erwine, Abraham	500	1	16	12– 2–1782	Gists Cr	Surveyed
Eustace, William	1,000	2	287	5–16–1783	Gesses Cr	Surveyed
Eustace, William	——	2	295	5–28–1783	None	Surveyed
Eubank, Kellis	738	4	321	3–10–1788	4 Mile Cr	Surveyed
Evans, Geo	18,000	3	95	12–17–1783	Ohio R	Surveyed
Evans, Jno	1,500	4	103	2– 2–1785	Main Licking	
Evans, Nathaniel	1,000	1	93	12–15–1782	S Fk Elkhorn	Surveyed
Evans, Nathaniel	400	1	94	12–10–1782	Jesses Cr	
Evans, Nathaniel	1,000	1	94	12–19–1782	None	Surveyed
Evans, Nathaniel	1,000	1	94	12–10–1782	None	Surveyed
Evans, Nathaniel	1,000	1	94	12–10–1782	Sinking Cr	
Evans, Nathaniel	600	1	95	12–23–1782	Cedar Cr	Withdrawn
Evans, Nathaniel	400	1	95	12–23–1782	Cedar Cr	Withdrawn
Evans, Nathaniel	400	1	95	12– 4–1782	Ky R	Withdrawn
Evans, Nathaniel	500	1	145	12–14–1782	S Fk Elkhorn	
Evans, Nathaniel	400	1	146	12–16–1782	Ky R	
Evans, Nathaniel	560	1	316	12–30–1782	None	Withdrawn
Evans, Nathaniel	200	1	380	1– 6–1783	E Fk Jessamine	
Evans, Nathaniel	600	1	380	1– 6–1783	Br Jessamine Cr	Withdrawn
Evans, Nathaniel	400	1	389	1– 7–1783	E Fk Jessamine	Withdrawn
Evans, Nathaniel	627	1	389	1– 7–1783	None	Withdrawn
Evans, Nathaniel	768½	2	55	1–13–1783	None	
Evans, Nathaniel	279	2	157	2– 1–1783	N Elkhorn	Surveyed
Evans, Nathaniel	600	3	119	12–29–1783	None	
Evans, Nathaniel	1,000	3	314	4–30–1784	Clear Cr	Surveyed
Evans, Nathaniel	76	4	63	11– 2–1784	None	
Evans, Nathaniel	400	4	225	10– 4–1785	None	
Evans, Nathaniel	1,000	1	44	12– 4–1782	Cane Run	Surveyed
Evans, Nathaniel	700	2	16	1– 9–1783	S Fk Licking	
Evers, Thomas	890½	2	132	1–27–1783	None	
Every, George	1,000	2	227	3–10–1783	Stoney Cr	
Ewell, Jesse	35,987¼	3	83	12–12–1783	Ohio R	Withdrawn
Ewell, Jesse	35,987¼	3	299	4–24–1784	Ohio R	Amended
Ewell, Jesse	35,987¼	4	175	5– 9–1785	Ohio R	Surveyed
Ewing, John	500	1	39	12– 4–1782	Mouth Prettys Run	
Ewing, John	500	1	39	12– 4–1782	Pretty Run	
Ewing & Barker	11,000	3	345	5–24–1784	None	Amended
Ewing & Parker	11,000	4	120	2–15–1785	None	
Fagan, Daniel	11,000	3	335	5–17–1784	Ohio R	Surveyed
Fallis, Isaac	1,342½	4	173	5– 7–1785	None	
Fallis, Thomas	500	1	157	12–17–1782	Cedar Cr	
Farrow, George	4,578⅔	1	386	1– 7–1783	S & Middle Fk Licking	Withdrawn
Farrow, George	2,518⅔	2	12	1– 9–1783	N Fk Licking	Surveyed
Farrow, George	2,000	2	213	2–28–1783	N Fk Licking	
Farrow, Jno	3,571¾	3	2	10–14–1783	Licking	Surveyed
Farrow, Jno	300	3	202	3– 4–1784	Grassy Lick & M Fk Licking	Surveyed
Farrow, Joseph	1,000	2	262	4– 1–1783	N Fk Licking	Surveyed
Farrow, Joseph	5,926¾	3	204	3– 5–1784	Eagle Cr	
Farrow, Thornton	1,000	2	263	4– 1–1783	Buck Lick Cr	Surveyed
Farrow, William	1,000	2	263	4– 1–1783	Buck Lick Cr	Surveyed
Farrow, William	453	2	274	4– 9–1783	N Fk Licking	
Faulkner, John	1,000	2	86	1–18–1783	Ky R	
Fenley, Thomas	1,100½	2	302	5–30–1785	None	
Feglin, Thomas	200	2	74	1–16–1783	None	
Ferguson, Jno	15	4	342	6–15–1817	None	
Ficklin, John	2,097	2	339	8– 2–1783	——— Cr	
Field, Benj	400	2	217	3– 1–1783	None	Withdrawn
Fields, Benj	3,000	2	217	3– 1–1783	Licking	Withdrawn
Fields, Benj	400	4	30	9– 9–1784	None	
Fields, Benj	3,000	4	30	9– 9–1784	None	
Fields, Benj	4,813	4	30	9– 9–1784	None	Withdrawn
Fields, Benj	488	4	31	9– 9–1784	Licking	Surveyed
Fields, Benj	4,813	4	82	1– 5–1785	None	
Field, Ezekial	750	1	5	11–29–1783	E Br Licking	Withdrawn

Entree	Acres	Book	Page	Entry Date	Watercourse	Notes
Field, Ezekiel	1,000	1	112	12–11–1782	N Br Licking	Surveyed
Field, Henry	4,140	1	247	12–24–1782	Buffalo Rd	....
Field, Henry	22,000	3	267	4– 5–1784	Licking	Surveyed
Fields, Henry	22,000	4	63	11– 2–1784	None	Surveyed
Field, Henry	400	4	291	4–18–1786	Hinkston Fk	....
Filson, Jno	5,600	3	101	12–19–1783	Big Bone Lick	....
Filson, Jno	4,922½	3	102	12–19–1783	None	Surveyed
Filson, Jno	2,446½	3	106	12–20–1783	Ohio R	....
Fink, Andrew	1,000	1	306	12–28–1782	Bank Lick Cr	Surveyed
Fink, Mark	1,500	2	73	1–16–1783	Main Fk Licking	...
Fink, Mark	645½	2	90	1–20–1783	None	Surveyed
Finley, Jno	1,000	3	43	11–14–1783	Licking	....
Finley, Geo	1,000	4	158	4–29–1785	Fk Licking	....
Finney, Benj	2,129½	3	160	1–21–1784	Licking	Surveyed
Finnie, James	5,740	3	80	12–10–1783	Main Licking	Surveyed
Firn, Edwin	1,000	1	280	12–26–1782	N Fk Licking	....
Fishback, Jacob	624	2	111	1–23–1783	Sycamore Fk Hinkston	Surveyed
Fishback, Jacob	624	2	166	2– 6–1783	Br Licking	Surveyed
Fishback & Berry	2,205	3	23	10–31–1783	None	....
Fishback & McShane	3,138	3	135	1– 2–1784	None	Surveyed
Fishback & Morgan	40,000	3	58	11–25–1783	Br N Fk Big Bone Lick	Withdrawn
Fishback & Morgan	40,000	3	127	1– 1–1784	Big Bone Lick	....
Fishback & Morgan	4,430	4	327	1–28–1789	Ohio R	....
Fisher, Adam	500	1	18	12– 4–1782	S Fk Licking	Surveyed
Fisher, Adam	231½	1	382	1– 6–1783	None	Withdrawn
Fisher, Adam	500	1	394	1– 7–1783	Logans Lick S Fk Licking	Surveyed
Fisher, Adam	231½	4	31	9– 9–1784	Licking	Surveyed
Fisher, Barnett	967½	2	90	1–20–1783	S Fk Licking	....
Fitzhugh, William	60,000	2	253	3–24–1783	Carr Fk Ky R	Surveyed
Fitzhugh, Wm	12,000	3	19	10–30–1783	Ohio R	Surveyed
Flack, Wm	1,000	4	164	4–29–1785	None	....
Flanagan, Dominick	1,000	1	136	12–13–1782	Licking	....
Flanagan, Dominick	1,000	1	353	1– 2–1783	Cain Run	Surveyed
Flanagan, Dominick	766½	1	353	1– 2–1783	Cabin Cr	....
Flanagan, Dominick	500	1	361	1– 4–1783	S Fk Licking	....
Flanagan, Dominick	500	1	361	1– 4–1783	None	....
Flanagan, Dominick	1,000	1	365	1– 4–1783	Turkey Foot Cr	....
Flanagan, Dominick	700	2	16	1– 9–1783	S Fk Licking	....
Flanagan, Dominick	768½	2	55	1–13–1783	None	....
Flaranay, Matthew	1,000	1	158	12–17–1782	Clear Cr	Surveyed
Fleming, Chas	3,750	4	71	11–26–1784	M Fk Ky R	Withdrawn
Fleming, Chas	2,375	4	74	12– 2–1784	N Fk Licking	Withdrawn
Fleming, Chas	3,000	4	79	12–29–1784	None	Withdrawn
Fleming, Chas	1,500	4	80	12–29–1784	None	Withdrawn
Fleming, Chas	2,000	4	91	1–15–1785	None	Withdrawn
Fleming, Chas	40,000	4	104	2– 2–1785	None	....
Fleming, Chas	18,000	4	104	2– 2–1785	Ohio R	....
Fleming, Chas	22,000	4	104	2– 2–1785	None	....
Fleming, Chas	2,000	4	120	2–15–1785	Ky R	....
Fleming, Chas	800	4	120	2–15–1785	Ky R	....
Fleming, Chas	20,000	4	143	4– 5–1785	None	....
Fleming, Chas	650	4	154	4–20–1785	None	....
Fleming, Chas	20,000	4	155	4–20–1785	Sandy	6,873 acres withdrawn
Fleming, Chas	4,373	4	157	4–28–1785	None	....
Fleming, Chas	22,000	4	157	4–28–1785	None	....
Fleming, Chas	26,373	4	157	4–28–1785	None	....
Fleming, Chas	3,750	4	337	6– 2–1794	None	....
Fleming, Chas	10,184	4	337	6– 2–1794	None	....
Fletcher, James	4,125	2	135	1–27–1783	Br Ohio R	....
Fleming, John	1,000	1	143	12–14–1782	Br Hingston	Surveyed
Fleming, John	1,000	1	143	12–14–1782	Br Hingston Fk	Surveyed
Fleming, John	1,000	1	143	12–14–1782	Br Hingston Fk	Surveyed
Fleming, John	1,000	1	144	12–14–1782	Hingston & Licking	Surveyed
Fleming, John	1,000	1	144	12–14–1782	None	Surveyed
Fleming, John	1,000	1	239	12–23–1782	Br Stoners Fk	Withdrawn
Fleming, John	1,000	1	239	12–23–1782	Br Hingston Fk	....
Fleming, John	1,000	1	326	12–30–1782	Hingstons Fk	....
Fleming, John	1,000	1	327	12–30–1782	Hingstons Fk	Withdrawn
Fleming, John	1,000	1	327	12–30–1782	Hingstons Fk	Withdrawn
Fleming, John	1,000	1	327	12–30–1782	Hingstons Fk	Withdrawn
Fleming, John	1,000	1	328	12–30–1782	Hingstons Fk	Withdrawn
Fleming, John	1,000	1	328	12–30–1782	Hingstons Fk	....
Fleming, John	1,000	1	363	1– 4–1783	Br Hingston Fk	Surveyed
Fleming, John	1,000	1	368	1– 4–1783	Br Hingston Fk	....
Fleming, John	1,000	1	368	1– 4–1783	Hinkstons Fk	....
Fleming, John	1,500	1	368	1– 4–1783	Hinkstons Fk	....

Entree	Acres	Book	Page	Entry Date	Watercourse	Notes
Fleming, John	1,500	1	369	1– 4–1783	—— Cr	Surveyed
Fleming, John	468½	2	71	1–16–1783	N Br Hingston Fk	Surveyed
Fleming, John	1,000	2	103	1–21–1783	Hinkstons Fk	Surveyed
Fleming, John	1,000	2	178	2– 8–1783	Johnsons Fk Licking	Surveyed
Fleming, John	165	2	321	7–14–1783	Howards Cr	Surveyed
Fleming, John	165	2	348	8–13–1783	None	Surveyed
Fleming, Jno	10,687	3	64	12– 1–1783	S Fk Big Sandy	Surveyed
Fleming, Jno	914	3	148	1–15–1784	Hinkston Fk	....
Fleming, Jno	193	3	181	2–12–1784	Hinkston	Withdrawn
Fleming, Jno	1,000	3	288	4–14–1784	Hinkston Fk	Surveyed
Fleming, Jno	241	4	77	12–16–1784	Hingston	Surveyed
Fleming, Jno	48¾	4	193	6– 1–1785	None	....
Fleming, Lucy	468½	2	71	1–16–1783	N Br Hingston Fk	Surveyed
Fleming, Tarlton	7,000	3	333	5–13–1784	—— R ——Cr	....
Fleming, Thos.	5,000	4	247	12–23–1785	None	....
Fleming, Thos M	7,000	3	332	5–13–1784	Ohio R	....
Fleming, William	1,220	2	9	1– 9–1783	None	Surveyed
Fleming, Wm	193	3	180	2–11–1784	Hinkston & Licking	....
Fleming, Wm	400	4	72	12– 1–1784	Huston Fk	....
Fleming, Wm	7,000	4	247	12–23–1785	None	Surveyed
Fleming, Wm B	7,000	3	332	5–13–1784	S Fk Licking	....
Fletcher, William	200	1	3	1–13–1783	None	....
Fletcher, Wm	219	4	140	3–28–1785	Lulbergreed Cr	Surveyed
Floyd, John	600	1	3	11–28–1782	Boones Cr	Surveyed
Floyd, John	1,000	1	116	12–12–1782	N Fk Elkhorn	....
Floyd, John, heirs	1,000	2	305	5–31–1783	None	Surveyed
Flournoy, Matthew	2,000	2	134	1–28–1783	Eagle Cr	Surveyed
Flournoy, Matthew	1,000	2	134	1–27–1783	None	....
Flournoy, Matthew	1,000	2	134	1–28–1783	Eagle Cr	....
Flournoy, Matthew	1,000	2	135	1–28–1783	Ky R	....
Flucker, Wm	219	2	16	1– 9–1787	Lulbergreed & Little Mt Cr	Withdrawn
Foley, James	103¾	2	295	5–26–1783	Lulbergreed Cr	....
Forbes, Hugh	——	2	281	4–29–1783	——	Surveyed
Forbes, Hugh	500	2	339	8– 2–1783	None	Withdrawn
Forbes, Hugh	2,000	3	96	12–17–1783	None	Withdrawn
Forbes, Hugh	500	3	162	1–22–1784	Br Licking	Withdrawn
Forbes, Hugh	1,000	4	42	9–22–1784	Main Fk Licking	....
Forbes, Hugh	500	4	52	10–13–1784	Br Licking	....
Forbes, Hugh	2,000	4	300	5–24–1786	None	....
Forbes, Hugh	50	4	305	9–17–1786	Boones Cr	....
Forbes, Hugh	100	4	334	6–23–1791	Boone Cr	....
Forbes, James	1,000	1	113	12–12–1782	Jones Fk Elkhorn	Surveyed
Forbes, John	1,000	2	56	1–13–1783	None	Surveyed
Forbes, William	1,000	1	113	12–12–1782	Wolf Cr	Surveyed
Forbes, Wm	1,000	1	295	12–27–1782	None	Surveyed
Ford, Lewis Christopher & Samuel	40,000	3	404	7–14–1784	Fk Licking	....
Ford & Morgan	2,887½	3	132	1– 2–1784	None	....
Foskner, John	750	2	122	1–25–1783	Greers Cr	Surveyed
Forsythe, Benjamin	2,000	2	374	10–13–1783	Lower Town Cr	....
Forsythe, Benjamin	1,223	2	374	10–13–1783	None	....
Forrester, Geo P	1,000	4	17	8–19–1784	Ky R	....
Foster, Jeremiah	6,093¾	3	159	1–21–1784	Licking	Surveyed
Foster, Thomas	400	2	51	1–13–1783	Stoners Fk	Surveyed
Foster, Thos & David	2,884	3	79	12–10–1783	Sandy	Surveyed
Foster & Fowler	3,375	4	295	4–29–1786	None	....
Fountain, Moses	1,014½	2	113	1–23–1783	Raven Cr	Surveyed
Fowler, Jno	2,500	3	204	3– 5–1784	Main Elkhorn	....
Fowler, Jno	3,380	3	205	3– 5–1784	None	Surveyed
Fowler, Jno	5,000	3	205	3– 8–1784	None	Surveyed
Fowler, Jno	1,060	3	207	3– 9–1784	Main Elkhorn	Surveyed
Fowler, Jno	400	3	211	3– 9–1784	Hustons Fk	Withdrawn
Fowler, Jno	600	3	214	3–10–1784	None	....
Fowler, Jno	500	3	259	3–30–1784	Strodes Fk	Withdrawn
Fowler, Jno	1,120	3	288	4–14–1784	Hinkston Fk	....
Fowler, Jno	8,000	3	294	4–19–1784	None	Withdrawn
Fowler, Jno	1,000	3	300	4–24–1784	None	Withdrawn
Fowler, Jno	8,000	3	303	4–26–1784	None	....
Fowler, Jno	400	3	315	4–30–1784	None	....
Fowler, Jno	1,000	3	383	6–23–1784	Main Licking	....
Fowler, Jno	1,077½	3	383	6–23–1784	None	....
Fowler, Jno	1,000	3	383	6–23–1784	Br Main Licking	....
Fowler, Jno	2,000	3	383	6–23–1784	Main Licking	....
Fowler, Jno	1,000	3	384	6–23–1784	—— Cr	....
Fowler, Jno	1,000	3	384	6–23–1784	—— Cr	....
Fowler, Jno	1,293	3	385	6–24–1784	Cedar Cr	Surveyed
Fowler, Jno	1,000	3	399	7–10–1784	Br Flemings Cr	Surveyed
Fowler, Jno	304½	3	402	7–13–1784	Slate Cr	....
Fowler, Jno	1,000	4	58	10–25–1784	None	....

Entree	Acres	Book	Page	Entry Date	Watercourse	Notes
Fowler, Jno	5,000	4	70	11-25-1784	None	
Fowler, Jno	6,000	4	70	11-25-1784	Slate Cr	
Fowler, Jno	1,000	4	261	1-18-1786	S Fk Licking	
Fowler, Jno	1,000	4	261	1-18-1786	——— Cr	
Fowler, Jno	30,000	4	266	1-30-1786	Ohio R	Withdrawn
Fowler, Jno	30,000	4	272	2-15-1786	None	
Fowler, Jno	6,800¾	4	273	2-15-1786	Sandy	
Fowler, Jno	6,800	4	295	4-29-1786	None	
Fowler, Jno Jr	5,000	3	206	3- 8-1784	None	Surveyed
Fowler, Jno Jr	5,000	3	206	3- 8-1784	None	Withdrawn
Fowler, Jno Jr	3,440	3	206	3- 9-1784	Main Elkhorn	Surveyed
Fowler, Jno Jr	1,000	3	208	3- 9-1784	N Fk Elkhorn	Withdrawn
Fowler, Jno Jr	400	3	208	3- 9-1784	N Fk Elkhorn	Withdrawn
Fowler, Jno Jr	1,000	3	209	3- 9-1784	Flat Cr	Withdrawn
Fowler, Jno Jr	600	3	209	3- 9-1784	Hickman Cr	Withdrawn
Fowler, Jno Jr	500	3	210	3- 9-1784	Br Licking	
Fowler, Jno Jr	1,000	3	210	3- 9-1784	Hinkton Fk	
Fowler, Jno Jr	1,000	3	210	3- 9-1784	Hinkston Fk	Withdrawn
Fowler, Jno Jr	400	3	210	3- 9-1784	E Fk Hickman Cr	Withdrawn
Fowler, Jno Jr	1,400	3	211	3- 9-1784	E Fk Hustons Fk	Withdrawn
Fowler, Jno Jr	1,000	3	211	3- 9-1784	Hustons Fk	Withdrawn
Fowler, Jno Jr	1,000	3	212	3- 9-1784	Hustons Fk	Withdrawn
Fowler, Jno Jr	400	3	212	3- 9-1784	W Fk Hickman Cr	Withdrawn
Fowler, Jno Jr	2,000	3	213	3- 9-1784	Hinkston Fk	Withdrawn
Fowler, Jno Jr	1,000	3	213	3- 9-1784	Greens Cr	Withdrawn
Fowler, Jno Jr	1,000	3	214	3-10-1784	Glenns Cr	Withdrawn
Fowler, Jno Jr	250	3	214	3-10-1784	Licking	Withdrawn
Fowler, Jno Jr	10,717½	3	259	3-30-1784	None	Withdrawn
Fowler, Jno Jr	200	3	259	3-30-1784	Marble Cr	Withdrawn
Fowler, Jno Jr	400	3	259	3-30-1784	None	Withdrawn
Fowler, Jno Jr	1,000	3	260	3-30-1784	None	Withdrawn
Fowler, Jno Jr	1,000	3	260	3-30-1784	None	Withdrawn
Fowler, Jno Jr	500	3	268	4- 6-1784	Strodes Fk	
Fowler, Jno Jr	27,405	3	293	4-16-1784	Licking	Withdrawn
Fowler, Jno Jr	1,000	3	303	4-26-1784	None	Withdrawn
Fowler, Jno Jr	10,771½	3	305	4-28-1784	None	
Fowler, Jno Jr	27,405	3	307	4-29-1784	None	
Fowler, Jno Jr	1,000	3	315	4-30-1784	None	
Fowler, Jno Jr	1,000	3	315	4-30-1784	Hinkston Fk	
Fowler, Jno Jr	400	3	315	4-30-1784	None	
Fowler, Jno Jr	1,400	3	315	4-30-1784	None	
Fowler, Jno Jr	1,000	3	315	4-30-1784	None	
Fowler, Jno Jr	1,000	3	315	4-30-1784	None	
Fowler, Jno Jr	400	3	315	4-30-1784	None	
Fowler, Jno Jr	2,000	3	315	4-30-1784	None	
Fowler, Jno Jr	1,000	3	315	4-30-1784	None	
Fowler, Jno Jr	1,000	3	315	4-30-1784	None	
Fowler, Jno Jr	1,850	3	316	4-30-1784	None	
Fowler, Jno Jr	15,352	3	318	5- 1-1784	Small Mt Cr	Surveyed
Fowler, Jno Jr	11,292	3	319	5- 1-1784	None	
Fowler, Jno Jr	15,352	3	323	5- 4-1784	None	
Fowler, Jno Jr	1,000	3	354	6- 4-1784	Cedar Cr	
Fowler, Jno Jr	365	3	401	7-13-1784	Big Slate Cr	Surveyed
Fowler, Jno Jr	2,113½	3	402	7-13-1784	Big Slate Cr	
Fowler & Allen	3,681¼	4	294	4-29-1786	None	
Fowler Jr & Campbell Jr	4,000	3	255	3-30-1784	N Fk Licking	Withdrawn
Fowler & Foster	3,375	4	295	4-29-1786	None	
Fowler Jr & Leitch	30,771½	3	306	4-28-1784	None	
Fowler Jr & Marshall Jr.	4,000	3	256	3-30-1784	N Fk Licking	Withdrawn
Fowler Jr & Marshall Jr.	3,800	3	256	3-30-1784	None	Withdrawn
Fowler Jr & Marshall Jr.	3,000	3	258	3-30-1784	None	Withdrawn
Fowler Jr & Marshall Jr.	3,000	3	258	3-30-1784	N Fk Licking	Withdrawn
Fowler Jr & Marshall Jr.	20,698	3	279	4- 8-1784	None	
Fowler & Marshall	2,000	3	324	5- 4-1784	Flat Cr	Surveyed
Fowler & Marshall	20,698	4	125	3- 1-1785	None	Surveyed
Fowler & Marshall	640	3	305	4-28-1784	Ky R	Surveyed
Fowler & Massie	50	4	304	9- 1-1786	Ohio R	
Fowler & Massie	100	4	326	12-30-1788	None	
Fowler & Massie Jr	372½	4	266	1-30-1786	Elkhorn	Withdrawn
Fowler & Massie Jr	1,000	4	279	3- 3-1786	Hingston Fk	
Fowler & Orr	1,193¾	4	276	2-19-1786	Ohio R	
Fowler & Overton	3,000	4	294	4-29-1786	Sandy	
Fowler & Pettis	1,162⅔	4	273	2-15-1786	None	Amended
Fowler & Pettis	462¾	4	295	4-29-1786	Sandy	
Fowler & Searcy	400	4	302	7-28-1786	Ky R	
Fowler & Trotter	3,375	4	273	2-15-1786	Sandy	Amended
Fowler & Trotter	19,756	4	274	2-15-1786	Sandy	Amended
Fox, Arthur	100	2	219	3- 1-1783	Shannons Br	Surveyed
Fox, Arthur	400	2	220	3- 3-1783	Greers Cr	Withdrawn

Entree	Acres	Book	Page	Entry Date	Watercourse	Notes
Fox, Arthur	80	2	220	3– 3–1783	Shannon Run & Sinking Cr	Surveyed
Fox, Arthur	200	2	220	3– 3–1783	Ky R	Withdrawn
Fox, Arthur	707	2	222	3– 5–1783	None	
Fox, Arthur	5,831¾	3	91	12–16–1783	S Fk Glenn Cr	Withdrawn
Fox, Arthur	5,831¾	3	286	4–12–1784	None	1,700 acres withdrawn
Fox, Arthur	200	3	322	5– 3–1784	Ky R	Withdrawn
Fox, Arthur	1,480	3	328	5– 7–1784	None	Surveyed
Fox, Arthur	60	3	346	5–25–1784	None	
Fox, Arthur	60	3	346	5–25–1784	None	
Fox, Arthur	300	3	354	6– 4–1784	Green Cr	Withdrawn
Fox, Arthur	600	3	369	6–16–1784	Ky R	Surveyed
Fox, Arthur	1,100	3	369	6–16–1784	Ky R	Withdrawn
Fox, Andrew	50	4	16	8–16–1784	Greers Cr	Surveyed
Fox, Arthur	1,231¾	4	27	9– 2–1784	None	
Fox, Arthur	200	4	74	12– 2–1784	None	Withdrawn
Fox, Arthur	400	4	74	12– 2–1784	——— Br	Withdrawn
Fox, Arthur	200	4	97	1–22–1785	None	
Fox, Arthur	1,000	4	159	4–29–1785	N Fk Licking	250 acres withdrawn
Fox, Arthur	1,025	4	204	6–28–1785	Locust Cr	
Fox, Arthur	1,250	4	204	6–28–1785	None	
Fox, Arthur	800	4	204	6–28–1785	None	
Fox, Arthur	400	4	204	6–28–1785	None	
Fox, Arthur	707	4	204	6–24–1785	Ohio R	
Fox, Arthur	250	4	206	7– 4–1785	Ohio R	
Fox, Arthur	2,496	4	206	7– 4–1785	Ohio R	
Fox, Arthur	1,000	4	206	7– 4–1785	Br N Fk Licking	
Fox, Arthur	250	4	208	7–14–1785	Ky R	Withdrawn
Fox, Arthur	250	4	210	7–23–1785	None	
Fox, Arthur	800	4	210	7–23–1785	Ohio R	
Fox, James	500	2	6	1– 8–1783	Lulbergreed Cr	Withdrawn
Fox, James	500	2	278	4–23–1783	Howards Upper Cr	Withdrawn
Fox, James	995	3	198	3– 2–1784	Slate Cr	Surveyed
Fox, Richard	800	4	234	11–22–1785	Locust Cr	
Fox & Bradford	50	3	322	5– 3–1784	None	
Fox & Craig	2,000	3	207	3– 9–1784	Hickman Cr	1,000 acres withdrawn
Fox & Craig	1,000	3	208	3– 9–1784	None	Withdrawn
Fox & Craig	1,000	3	252	3–30–1784	Licking	
Fox & Craig	200	3	253	3–30–1784	None	Surveyed
Frame, Wm	1,495¼	4	258	1–16–1786	——— Cr	
Franklin, Thos	4,000	3	220	3–11–1784	Ohio R	
Franklin, Thos	225,000	3	357	6–10–1784	Ky R	
Franklin, Thos	225,000	3	413	7–17–1784	M Fk Ky R	
Franklin, Thos	108,344	3	415	7–26–1784	N & M Fk Ky R	
Franklin, Thos	108,344	3	415	7–26–1784	Ky R	Surveyed
Franklin, Thos	8,000	3	115	12–27–1783	N Fk Big Sandy R	Surveyed
Franklin, Thos & Moria B	225,000	3	353	6– 4–1784	Ky R	Amended
Franklin, Edward	4,319	2	35	1–11–1783	Sandy Cr	
Franks, Robert	2,000	2	3	1– 8–1783	None	Surveyed
Frazer, Joseph	338¼	4	264	1–29–1786	N Fk Eagle Cr	
Frazer, Joseph	787	4	265	1–29–1786	None	
French, James	700	1	86	12– 9–1782	Stoners Fk	
French, James	15,913	1	281	12–26–1782	Ohio R	Surveyed
French, James	9,000	2	121	1–25–1783	Salt Sp Fk	Surveyed
French, Jas	110	4	33	9–11–1784	None	
French, Jas	220	4	33	9–11–1784	None	
French, Jas	4,000	4	329	2– 5–1790	Ky R	Withdrawn
French, Jas	4,000	4	330	2– 5–1790	None	
French, Jas	200	4	330	5–17–1790	4 Mile Cr	
French, Jas	200	4	331	5–17–1790	4 Mile Cr	
French, Jas	700	4	331	5–17–1790	4 Mile Cr	Withdrawn
French, Jas	800	4	331	6– 9–1790	None	
French, Jas	2,800	4	331	6– 9–1790	4 Mile Cr	
French, Jas	200	4	334	7–11–1790	4 Mile Cr	
Freeman, Jas	540	4	23	8–30–1784	Ky R	Withdrawn
Freeman, Jas	578	4	84	1– 8–1785	None	
French, Henry	970½	2	159	2– 3–1783	Elkhorn	Surveyed
French, Henry	1,900	2	322	7–14–1783	Ky R	
French, Henry	294	3	90	12–15–1783	Elkhorn	Surveyed
French, Henry	10,000	4	104	2– 2–1785	Main Licking	
French, Stephen	1,000	1	25	12–17–1782	——— Cr	Surveyed
French, Stephen	2,000	2	121	1–25–1783	Br Salt Sp Fk	Withdrawn
French, Stephen	2,205	3	2	10–14–1783	Licking	
French, Stephen	2,000	3	274	4– 6–1784	Hinkston Fk	Surveyed
French & Haggans	1,787½	3	173	2– 4–1784	Ky R	Surveyed
Freeman & Orr	988	4	122	2–18–1785	None	
Freeman & Orr	548	4	84	1– 8–1785	Hingston Fk	Withdrawn

Entree	Acres	Book	Page	Entry Date	Watercourse	Notes
French & Tribble	15,410	3	173	2– 4–1784	Ky R	
Fryer, Robt	500	3	279	4– 8–1784	Small Mt Cr	Surveyed
Fryer, Robt	46½	3	347	5–27–1784	Boones Cr	
Fulkison, Abram	200	4	334	4–29–1791	——— R	Surveyed
Fullerton, William	3,000	2	368	10– 1–1783	S Fk Hinkston	
Fullerton, Wm	3,000	4	339	8–18–1795	None	
Fulton, Jno	850	4	165	4–29–1785	None	
Fulton, Jno	973	3	309	4–29–1784	None	
Fulton & Swearengen	1,000	4	8	8–14–1784	Sandy Cr	Surveyed
Gahagan, Anthony	3,566⅔	3	45	11–14–1783	Ohio R	
Gains, Daniel	2,800	1	192	12–19–1782	———	Surveyed
Gaines, Daniel	1,000	2	101	1–21–1783	Br N Fk Elkhorn	
Gaines, Daniel	1,000	2	101	1–21–1783	N Fk Elkhorn	Surveyed
Gaines, Daniel	1,000	2	106	1–22–1783	N Fk Elkhorn	Withdrawn
Gaines, Daniel	9,300	2	117	1–24–1783	Scott Sp Fk & Hinkstons	Amended
Gaines, Daniel	9,300	2	167	2– 6–1783	None	
Gaines, Daniel	1,000	2	223	3– 7–1783	None	
Gaines, Daniel	45,987¾	3	281	4–10–1784	Main Fk Licking	Surveyed
Gaines, Daniel	1,000	3	334	5–16–1784	None	
Gaines, James	586½	2	190	2–13–1783	None	Surveyed
Gaines, Richard	9,106½	3	55	11–21–1783	Ohio R	Surveyed
Gaines, Richard	9,106½	3	63	11–27–1783	None	Surveyed
Gaines, Wm	732½	3	252	3–30–1784	None	
Gaines & Bell	4,000	3	334	5–16–1784	Ohio R	
Gaither, Ephraim	2,049	2	184	2–13–1783	Salt Lick Trace	
Gale, Matthew	1,000	1	314	12–30–1782	Glenns Cr	Surveyed
Gale, Matthew	1,000	1	314	12–30–1782	Glenns Cr	Withdrawn
Gale, Matthew	1,000	3	413	7–17–1784	None	Surveyed
Gale, John	500	1	112	12–11–1782	5th Big Fk Elkhorn	
Galloway, George	700	2	332	7–28–1783	None	Surveyed
Galloway, George	500	2	360	9– 9–1783	Harrods Salt Lick Cr	
Galloway, George	700	3	366	6–14–1784	None	Surveyed
Galloway, James	500	2	360	9– 9–1783	——— Cr	
Galloway, John	10,662½	2	338	8– 1–1783	Ohio R	
Galloway, Joseph	1,500	2	362	9–10–1783	Salt Lick Cr	
Galloway, Samuel	1,500	2	362	9–10–1783	Salt Lick Cr	
Galloway, William	800	2	332	7–28–1783	None	Surveyed
Gamble, Robert	1,000	1	200	12–20–1782	Big Bone Lick	Surveyed
Gamble, Jno & Agness	500	3	364	6–14–1784	None	
Ganhan, Thos	500	3	197	3– 2–1784	Grassy Lick	Surveyed
Garnet, Reuben	1,492	2	19	1– 9–1783	Lulbergreed Cr	Amended
Garnet, Reuben	1,492	2	209	2–26–1783	None	
Garrant, John	1,000	2	240	3–13–1783	None	
Garnett, Jas	625	3	412	7–17–1784	N Fk Licking	
Garnett, Robt	1,833	3	150	1–15–1784	None	
Garrard, James	1,000	1	93	5–24–1782	Stoners Fk	
Garrard, James	4,000	1	241	12–23–1782	Lulbegrud Cr	Surveyed
Garrard, James	800	2	91	1–20–1783	Stoners Fk	Withdrawn
Garrard, James	500	2	113	1–23–1783	None	
Garrard, James	700	2	227	3–10–1783	None	Withdrawn
Garrard, Jas	5,000	3	162	1–22–1784	Licking	Surveyed
Garrard, Jas	700	4	115	2– 9–1785	None	
Garrard, Jas	300	4	152	4–12–1785	Stoners Fk	
Garrard, Col James	1,000	1	91	12–13–1782	S Fk Licking Cr	Surveyed
Garrard, Wm	4,000	3	173	2– 4–1784	4 Mile Cr	Withdrawn
Garrard, Wm	4,000	4	219	8–20–1785	None	
Garrard, Wm	4,000	4	219	8–31–1785	N Fk Licking	
Gass, John	1,000	2	300	5–30–1783	Johnsons Fk Licking	Surveyed
Gates, Ephraim	5,643	2	17	1– 9–1783	Br Main Licking	Surveyed
Gates, Matthew	1,000	4	253	1– 9–1786	None	
Gates, Wm	603	4	136	3–19–1785	None	
Gatewood, Henry	1,000	1	220	12–21–1782	Elkhorn	
Gatewood, Wm	300	4	341	11–21–1814	S Fk Elkhorn	
Gatliff, Charles	1,000	2	296	5–28–1783	Ohio R	
Gaur, Michael	597½	2	89	1–20–1783	S Fk Licking	Surveyed
Gay, John	6,380	2	94	1–20–1783	N Fk Eagle Cr	
Gay, John	1,000	2	204	2–19–1783	Laurences Cr	Surveyed
Gay, John	1,000	2	319	7–11–1783	S Fk Elkhorn	
Gentry & McCullock	893	4	212	7–28–1785	None	
George, Nicholas	400	1	160	12–17–1782	Licking	Surveyed
George, Nicholas	1,400	3	1	10–14–1783	Br Red R	
George, Jesse	3,311¾	4	213	7–30–1785	None	
Gibbons, Jas	10,000	4	170	5– 3–1785	None	Surveyed
Gibson, Geo	3,535½	4	199	6–17–1785	N Fk Ky R	
Gibson, John	657	1	37	12– 4–1782	Turkey Foot Fk	Surveyed
Gibson, Jno	4,525½	4	97	1–24–1785	Main Licking	
Gibson, Jno	10,000	4	99	1–24–1785	Slate Cr	
Gibson, Jno	400	4	200	6–17–1785	N Fk Ky R	

Entree	Acres	Book	Page	Entry Date	Watercourse	Notes
Gibson, Jno	400	4	200	6–17–1785	N Fk Ky R	
Gibson, Wm	2,236½	4	183	5–24–1785	None	
Gibson, Wm	500	4	184	5–28–1785	Red R	
Gilasspie, David	1,500	2	232	3–12–1783	Hingston & Licking	
Gill, John	400	2	7	1– 8–1783	M Fk Licking	
Gill, Wm	12,613	3	226	3–14–1784	Licking	Withdrawn
Gill, Wm	12,613	3	241	3–26–1784	Locust Cr	Withdrawn
Gill, Wm	2,700	4	240	12–13–1785	Salt Rock Fk	
Gill, Wm	12,613	4	265	1–30–1786	N Fk Ky R	Withdrawn
Gill, Wm	12,613	4	291	4–22–1786	None	
Gill & Rice	12,613	4	292	4–22–1786	Ky R	
Gillaspl, William	1,000	2	65	1–14–1783	Ky R	
Gillaspie, David	7,000	2	114	1–23–1783	Stoners Fk	
Gillispie, David	400	1	30	12– 3–1782	Licking & Eagle Cr	
Gillispie, William	300	1	30	12– 3–1782	——— Cr	
Gilmore, James	500	3	394	7– 5–1784	Hingston Fk	
Gilpin, Israel	300	3	175	2– 9–1784	None	
Gilpin, Israel	790	3	175	2– 9–1784	——— Cr	
Gist, Mordica	5,000	3	126	1– 1–1784	Lick Cr	Surveyed
Gist, Thos	10,000	3	137	1– 7–1784	None	Surveyed
Gist, Thos	6,000	3	137	1– 7–1784	None	Surveyed
Gist, Thos Jr	10,000	3	108	12–27–1783	Ohio R	
Gist, Thos Jr	2,500	4	57	10–20–1784	Lick Cr	Surveyed
Givin, David	2,000	2	187	2–13–1783	None	
Givins, George	800	1	149	12–16–1782	Johnson Fk	
Givens, George	601	2	190	2–13–1783	Johnsons Fk	
Givens, Samuel	850	1	151	12–16–1782	S Fk Elkhorn	Surveyed
Gleaves, William	562	2	242	3–13–1783	None	
Glover, Jno	1,743¾	3	361	6–12–1784	W Fk Licking	Withdrawn
Glover, Wm	1,000	4	161	4–29–1785	Licking	
Goare, Henry	9,500	2	113	1–23–1783	Barren Cr	Surveyed
Goddard & Dery	300,306⅔	3	190	2–28–1784	3 Fks Ky R	
Goldson, Anthony	200	2	57	1–13–1783	None	
Gooch, James	500	1	97	12–10–1782	———	
Goode, Mark	2,091½	4	134	3–19–1785	None	Withdrawn
Goode, Mack	2,091¼	4	149	4–10–1785	None	
Goode, Wm	45,987¾	3	281	4–10–1784	Main Fk Licking	Surveyed
Goode, Wm	600	4	88	1–11–1785	None	
Goode, Wm	2,400	4	121	2–16–1785	Ohio R	
Goodloe, Henry	5,000	2	30	1–10–1783	S Br Licking	
Goodloe, Henry	2,000	2	30	1–10–1783	Main Fk Licking	Surveyed
Goodloe, Henry	3,250	2	31	1–10–1783	Licking	
Goodwin, Peter	2,000	1	31	12–18–1782	Licking	
Goodwin, Peter	1,000	1	38	12– 4–1782	S Br Stoners Fk	
Gordon, James	500	2	58	1–13–1783	Glens Cr	
Gordon, Wm	8,959¾	3	333	5–14–1784	None	4,479¾ acres
Grafford, Thomas	1,000	1	86	12– 9–1782	Stoners Fk	
Graham, Christopher	500	4	192	6– 1–1785	Strodes Fk	Withdrawn
Graham, Christopher	3,355¼	4	215	8– 2–1785	Ohio R	
Graham, Christopher	500	4	333	4– 7–1791	None	
Graham, Edward	20,000	4	45	9–30–1784	Ohio R	Withdrawn
Graham, Francis	300	3	308	4–29–1784	None	
Graham, George	2,000	2	215	2–28–1783	Licking	
Graham, George	1,150	2	257	3–27–1783	Severn Cr	Surveyed
Graham, Geo	4,857½	3	24	10–31–1783	None	
Graham, James	1,187	2	203	2–19–1783	Salt Sp Fk Licking	Withdrawn
Graham, Jas	1,187	3	53	11–21–1783	Br Licking	
Graham, Jno	1,000	4	50	9–13–1784	Br Red R	
Graham, Richard	1,500	2	215	2–28–1783	Licking	
Graham, Richard	60,000	2	253	3–24–1783	Cow Fk Ky R	Surveyed
Graham, Richard	33,815	2	361	9–10–1783	Harvards Upper Cr	Surveyed
Graham, Richard	80,406¼	3	18	10–30–1783	Ohio R	Surveyed
Graham, Richard	138,320	3	19	10–30–1783	Ohio R	Surveyed
Graham, Richard	1,174	3	26	10–31–1783	None	
Graham, Richard	27,000	3	370	6–16–1784	Tygrets Cr	
Graham & James	20,500	3	38	11–12–1783	Br Licking	Surveyed
Graham & James	20,500	3	386	6–28–1784	——— Cr	Surveyed
Grant, Peter	33,668¾	3	21	10–30–1783	Ohio R	10,610 acres surveyed 6,958 acres withdrawn
Grant, Peter	6,958	4	279	3– 3–1786	None	
Grant, Peter	17,100¾	4	296	4–29–1786	Sandy	Withdrawn
Grant, Samuel	400	3	227	3–14–1784	N Fk Elkhorn	Surveyed
Grant, Samuel	1,550	3	251	3–30–1784	Lees Cr	Withdrawn
Grant, Samuel	400	3	269	4– 6–1784	None	Withdrawn
Grant, Samuel	1,749	3	269	4– 6–1784	Stoners Fk	
Grant, Samuel	1,000	3	269	4– 6–1784	None	
Grant, Samuel	2,000	3	269	4– 6–1784	Stoners Fk	
Grant, Samuel	7,000	3	297	4–22–1784	Locust Cr	Withdrawn
Grant, Samuel	7,000	4	299	5–24–1786	None	Surveyed

Entree	Acres	Book	Page	Entry Date	Watercourse	Notes
Grant, Samuel	1,749	4	302	7–28–1786	Hickman Cr	
Grant, Samuel	1,049	4	303	7–28–1786	S Fk Elkhorn	
Grant, Samuel	400	4	303	7–31–1886	S Fk Elkhorn	
Grant, Thos	75	4	130	3–12–1785	Huskins Run	
Grant, Thos	80	4	131	3–12–1785	Hingston Fk	Surveyed
Grant & Griffin	3,000	3	144	1–13–1784	None	
Grant & Griffin	5,000	3	145	1–13–1784	E Fk Coopers Run	
Grant & Griffin	2,000	3	145	1–13–1784	Hinkston Fk	Surveyed
Grantland, Gideon	1,000	1	56	12– 5–1782	Ohio R	
Grantland, Gideon	1,000	1	57	12– 5–1782	——— R	
Grantland, Gideon	1,000	1	57	12– 5–1782	——— R	
Grasson, William	200	1	113	12–12–1782	5th Big Fk Elkhorn	
Gratz, Benard & Michael	1,000	3	425	8–14–1784	——— Cr	Surveyed
Gratz, Benard & Michael	1,000	3	426	8–14–1784	Sandy	Surveyed
Gratz, Benard & Michael	4,000	3	426	8–14–1784	Sandy	Surveyed
Gratz, Benard & Michael	1,000	4	5	8–14–1784	Sandy Cr	Surveyed
Gratan, John	1,100	1	53	12– 5–1782	———Cr	
Graves, Jno	1,000	3	7	10–15–1783	Deer Lick	
Graves & Robinson	1,480	3	178	2–10–1784	None	
Gray, Drakeford	416	3	199	3– 2–1784	Slate Cr	Surveyed
Gray, James	1,500	2	181	2–12–1783	Main Licking	
Gray, John	1,000	1	201	12–20–1782	Licking	
Gray, Richard	300	3	200	3– 2–1784	Small Mt Cr	Surveyed
Grayhill, Jacob	3,000	4	103	2– 2–1785	None	Surveyed
Grayson, Benj	2,000	3	160	1–21–1784	Licking	Surveyed
Grayson, Benj	500	3	230	3–17–1784	Strouds Fk	Withdrawn
Grayson, Benj	664¼	3	230	3–17–1784	Br Eagle Cr	Withdrawn
Grayson, Benj	1,000	3	306	4–28–1784	Strouds Fk	Withdrawn
Grayson, Benj	500	3	312	4–29–1784	None	
Grayson, Benj	1,000	3	312	4–29–1784	None	
Grayson, Benj	1,000	3	312	4–30–1784	Hancock Fk	
Grayson, Benj	500	3	312	4–30–1784	Strodes Fk	
Grayson, Benj	1,000	3	335	5–18–1784	Clear Cr	Withdrawn
Grayson, Benj	1,000	3	335	5–18–1784	Manchester Sprg Br	Withdrawn
Grayson, Benj	1,000	3	362	6–14–1784	Hingston Fk	
Grayson, Benj	1,000	3	363	6–14–1784	M Fk Licking	
Grayson, Benj	1,000	3	372	6–17–1784	Hustons Fk	
Grayson, Benj	1,000	3	372	6–17–1784	Hustons Fk	
Grayson, Benj	1,400	3	392	7– 1–1784	N Fk Elkhorn	Withdrawn
Grayson, Benj	1,000	3	395	7– 6–1784	None	
Grayson, Benj	700	3	395	7– 6–1784	N Fk Elkhorn	Withdrawn
Grayson, Benj	300	3	395	7– 6–1784	M Fk Licking	
Grayson, Benj	802	4	28	9– 3–1784	Hickmans Cr	Surveyed
Grayson, Benj	200	4	77	12–16–1784	None	
Grayson, Benj	1,700	4	78	12–16–1784	None	
Grayson, Benj	1,000	4	83	1– 7–1785	Grassy Lick	Withdrawn
Grayson, Benj	1,000	4	86	1– 8–1785	None	
Grayson, Benj	905	4	86	1– 8–1785	Br N Fk Elkhorn	Withdrawn
Grayson, Benj	905	4	121	2–18–1785	None	
Grayson, Benj	37,256	4	142	4– 5–1785	None	28,245 acres withdrawn
Grayson, Spencer	12,500	4	172	5– 6–1785	None	
Grayson, Spencer	12,500	4	172	5– 6–1785	Ohio R	
Grayson, Rev Spence	12,500	3	179	2–11–1784	Ohio	
Grayson, William	15,455	2	257	3–25–1783	Ohio R	
Grayson, Wm	70,000	3	18	10–30–1783	Ohio R	
Grayson, Wm	4,000	3	28	11– 3–1783	Br S Fk Eagle Cr	
Grayson, Wm	12,000	3	30	11– 3–1783	Upper Blue Lick	Surveyed
Grayson, Wm	1,000	3	35	11– 8–1783	None	
Grayson, Wm	10,000	3	37	11–12–1783	Br Licking	Surveyed
Grayson, Wm	12,500	3	115	12–27–1783	Licking & Ohio R	Withdrawn
Grayson, Wm	5,000	4	247	12–21–1785	Ohio R	
Grayson, Wm	4,000	4	277	2–27–1786	Ohio R	Withdrawn
Grayson, Wm	5,000	4	294	4–29–1786	None	
Grayson, Wm	5,000	4	297	4–29–1786	Ohio R	
Grayson, Col Wm	10,000	3	146	1–13–1784	12 Mile Cr	Withdrawn
Grayson, Col Wm	10,000	4	244	12–17–1785	Ohio R	
Grayson & Hedgman	25,000	3	157	1–19–1784	S Fk Licking	Withdrawn
Grayson & Hedgman	25,000	3	245	3–26–1784	N Fk Licking	Withdrawn
Grayson & Hedgman	54	4	85	1– 8–1785	Ky R	
Grayson & Hedgman	25,000	4	179	5–12–1785	Licking	Withdrawn
Grayson & Hedgman	25,000	4	247	12–21–1785	Ohio R	
Grayson & Marshall	300	3	215	3–10–1784	M Fk Licking	Withdrawn
Grayson & Marshall	250	3	215	3–10–1784	Hustons Fk	Withdrawn
Grayson & Marshall	342	4	78	12–20–1784	Strodes Fk Licking	
Grayson & Marshall	48¾	4	193	6– 1–1785	None	
Grayson & Marshall	342	4	201	6–17–1785	None	

Entree	Acres	Book	Page	Entry Date	Watercourse	Notes
Grayson & Marshall Jr	300	3	307	4–28–1784	None	
Grayton, Jno	400	3	150	1–15–1784	None	
Green, Harry	292	1	116	12–12–1782	S Fk Elkhorn	Surveyed
Green, Henry	50	2	218	3– 1–1783	None	Withdrawn
Green, John	1,000	1	225	12–21–1782	Sandy	
Green, John	1,000	1	225	12–21–1782	Sandy	
Green, John	2,311	1	225	12–21–1782	Sandy	Withdrawn
Green, John Jr	6,000	1	65	12– 6–1782	Elkhorn	Surveyed
Green, John Jr	1,000	1	177	12–18–1782	Ohio R	
Green, Willis	6,000	1	301	12–27–1782	M Fk Elkhorn	Amended
Green; Willis	4,000	1	302	12–27–1782	Lees Cr	Surveyed
Green, Willis	3,000	1	302	12–27–1782	None	Amended
Green, Willis	6,000	2	163	2– 4–1783	None	
Green, Willis	6,000	4	28	9– 2–1784	None	
Green's, Entry of	4,000	1	302	12–27–1782	Lick Cr	Surveyed
Green & Steele	1,000	3	62	11–27–1783	None	Withdrawn
Greenlee, Jno	2,000	4	158	4–29–1785	None	
Greenlee, Mary	2,600	4	158	4–29–1785	None	
Greenup, Christopher	1,200	1	370	1– 4–1783	None	Surveyed
Greenup, Christopher	400	1	381	1– 6–1783	None	Surveyed
Greenup, Christopher	1,000	2	69	1–16–1783	Mill Cr	
Greenup, Christopher	51	2	81	1–17–1783	Ky R	Withdrawn
Greenup, Christopher	50	2	98	1–20–1783	Ky R	Withdrawn
Greenup, Christopher	50	2	103	1–21–1783	None	Withdrawn
Greenup, Christopher	51	2	104	1–21–1783	None	
Greenup, Christopher	300	2	104	1–21–1783	N Fk Elkhorn	Withdrawn
Greenup, Christopher	331	2	107	1–22–1783	None	Surveyed
Greenup, Christopher	2,000	2	120	1–24–1783	Cane Run	Withdrawn
Greenup, Christopher	625	2	132	1–27–1783	None	
Greenup, Christopher	50	2	133	1–27–1783	None	Surveyed
Greenup, Christopher	1,000	2	155	2– 1–1783	Glens Cr	Withdrawn
Greenup, Christ	150	2	178	2–10–1783	Ky R	
Greenup, Christ	100	2	178	2–10–1783	None	Withdrawn
Greenup, Christopher	100	2	179	2–10–1783	None	Withdrawn
Greenup, Christopher	150	2	236	3–12–1783	None	
Greenup, Christopher	300	2	333	7–28–1783	Ky R	
Greenup, Christ	800	2	371	10– 6–1783	Jessamine Cr	Surveyed
Greenup, Christ	1,983	2	373	10– 8–1783	None	
Greenup, Christopher	2,000	3	45	11–15–1783	Savern Cr	
Greenup, Christopher	550	3	174	2– 5–1784	Ky R	Surveyed
Greenup, Christopher	300	4	44	9–24–1784	None	Surveyed
Greenup, Christopher	550	4	101	1–28–1785	None	Surveyed
Greenup, Christopher	100	4	112	2– 7–1785	None	
Greenup, Samuel	703	2	53	1–13–1783	Clear Cr	Withdrawn
Greenup, Samuel	703	2	192	2–13–1783	N Fk Elkhorn	Surveyed
Greenup & Queally	1,000	4	306	10–14–1785	Ohio R	
Griffin, Jno	1,071¼	4	148	4–10–1785	None	
Griffin, Jno T	1,000	3	269	4– 6–1784	None	
Griffin, Jno T	2,000	3	269	4– 6–1784	Stoners Fk	
Griffin, Jno T	7,000	3	297	4–22–1784	Locust Cr	Withdrawn
Griffin, Jno T	7,000	4	299	5–24–1786	None	Surveyed
Griffin & Grant	3,000	3	144	1–13–1784	None	
Griffin & Grant	5,000	3	145	1–13–1784	E Fk Coopers Run	
Griffin & Grant	2,000	3	145	1–13–1784	Hinkston Fk	Surveyed
Griffith, Abel	300	3	156	1–19–1784	Hinkston Fk	Surveyed
Griffith, Abel	300	3	193	3– 1–1784	None	Surveyed
Griffith, Evan	2,051¼	3	23	10–31–1783	Ohio R	
Griffith, William	50	1	50	12– 5–1782	Stoners Fk	
Griffith, William	1,612½	1	343	1– 1–1783	None	Withdrawn
Griffith, William	1,612½	2	60	1–14–1783	None	Surveyed
Grimes, James	1,000	3	394	7– 5–1784	None	
Grimes, Jno	2,205½	3	71	12– 5–1783	None	Amended
Grismon, Daniel	2,000	2	13	1– 9–1783	Ohio R	
Gunnell, Robt	3,655	3	312	4–30–1784	Small Mt	Surveyed
Gunnell, Thos	1,500	3	94	12–17–1783	Big Bone Lick	Surveyed
Gunnell & Coffer	1,000	4	81	12–31–1784	None	
Gunnell & Coffer	844	4	82	12–31–1784	Grassy Lick	Withdrawn
Gunnell & Coffer	800	4	116	2–11–1785	Boones Cr	
Gunnell & Coffer	844	4	184	5–24–1785	None	
Gunnell & Coffer	1,000	4	184	5–24–1785	None	
Gunnell & Coffer	800	4	184	5–24–1785	None	
Gunnell, Henry Robt & Wm	12,311	3	194	3– 2–1784	Fks Hinkston	
Gunnell, Jno & Wm	5,000	4	183	5–24–1785	None	
Gunnell, Jno & Wm	5,000	4	81	12–31–1784	Boones Cr	Withdrawn
Hacker, Nathaniel	1,086½	3	141	1–12–1784	None	
Hadden, Wm	100	4	316	11–15–1786	Jessamine Cr	
Haggins, Jno	300	3	104	12–20–1783	——— Cr	Surveyed
Haggins, Jno	150	3	104	12–20–1783	S Fk Licking	Surveyed
Haggins & French	1,787½	3	173	2– 4–1784	Ky R	Surveyed
Haines, Thomas	400	1	10	11–29–1782	Glenns Cr	Surveyed

Entree	Acres	Book	Page	Entry Date	Watercourse	Notes
Halbert, Isaac.........	300....	1...	293....	12–27–1782....	Jessamine & Ky....	Surveyed
Halbert, Isaac.........	12,311....	3...	194....	3– 2–1784....	Fk Hinkston.......	Surveyed
Halbert, Richard......	300....	1...	21....	12– 2–1782....	——— Cr.......	....
Hall, Caleb...........	1,308....	2...	212....	2–27–1783....	None............	Withdrawn
Hall, Caleb...........	1,308....	2...	279....	4–26–1783....	N Fk Licking......	Withdrawn
Hall, Caleb...........	1,308....	3...	229....	3–17–1784....	N Fk Licking......	Withdrawn
Hall, Edward & Moses.	1,880¼....	3...	364....	6–15–1784....	None............	Surveyed
Hall, John...........	1,000....	1...	219....	12–21–1782....	None............	Surveyed
Hall, Moses..........	440¾....	3...	364....	6–14–1784....	None............	....
Hally & Richards......	11,931½....	3...	129....	1– 1–1784....	Ohio R...........	....
Hamilton, Andrew....	2,000....	2...	75....	1–16–1783....	Eagle Cr..........	Surveyed
Hamilton, Andrew....	977....	2...	76....	1–16–1783....	Licking..........	Surveyed
Hamilton, John.......	1,000....	2...	322....	7–14–1783....	Cedar Cr.........	Surveyed
Hamilton, John.......	1,000....	2...	322....	7–14–1783....	Leestown & Elkhorn.........	Surveyed
Hammon, Philip.......	1,600....	2...	233....	3–12–1783....	Paint Lick Cr.....	....
Hammon, Philip.......	200....	2...	233....	3–12–1783....	Paint Lick Cr.....	....
Hampton, Andrew.....	1,000....	1...	124....	12–12–1782....	Clear Cr..........	Surveyed
Hampton, Richard.....	1,000....	4...	169....	4–30–1785....	S Fk Big Sandy R..	Surveyed
Hancock, Stephen.....	1,400....	2...	118....	1–23–1783....	Licking..........	....
Hancok, William......	400....	1...	57....	12– 5–1782....	———————	Surveyed
Hancock, William.....	1,400....	2...	118....	1–24–1783....	Licking..........	....
Handley, William.....	2,000....	2...	221....	3– 3–1783....	6 Miles S Ohio R...	Surveyed
Haney & Smith.......	5,000....	3...	92....	12–16–1783....	Lulbergreed Cr.....	Surveyed
Hanna, Joseph........	200½....	4...	290....	4–17–1786....	Eagle Cr..........	....
Hanshaw, Wm........	5,000....	4...	190....	6– 1–1785....	Ohio R...........	....
Haptanstall, Abraham.	1,000....	2...	374....	10–13–1783....	Lower Twin Cr....	Withdrawn
Haptanstall, Abram....	——....	3...	28....	11– 3–1783....	S Fk Elkhorn.....	Surveyed
Harbeson, George.....	50....	1...	389....	1– 7–1783....	None............	....
Harbeson, George.....	400....	1...	389....	1– 7–1783....	M Fk Clear Cr.....	Surveyed
Harbeson, Jas........	591....	4...	112....	2– 5–1785....	Ky R............	....
Hardage, James.......	300....	2...	278....	4–23–1783....	Elkhorn..........	Withdrawn
Harden, James........	1,000....	2...	211....	2–27–1783....	M Fk Stoners Fk...	....
Hardin, Wm..........	569¼....	4...	227....	10–13–1785....	Ky R............	....
Hardway, Charles.....	400....	2...	63....	1–14–1783....	None............	Surveyed
Hardwick, Jno.......	50....	4...	335....	12–23–1791....	2 Mile Cr........	....
Hardy, Samuel.......	61,534½....	2...	26....	1–10–1783....	M Br Licking......	....
Hardy, Saml.........	61,534½....	2...	26....	1–10–1783....	M Br Licking......	....
Hargrave, Jno........	2,000....	3...	381....	6–23–1784....	Br Licking........	....
Harl, John..........	828½....	2...	359....	8–23–1783....	Main Elkhorn......	Surveyed
Harls, John..........	1,000....	2...	359....	8–23–1783....	S Fk Eagle Cr.....	....
Harris, Benjamin.....	1,500....	1...	232....	12–23–1782....	N Fk Licking......	Surveyed
Harris, Benjamin.....	1,500....	1...	232....	12–23–1782....	Licking..........	Surveyed
Harris, Benjamin.....	1,000....	1...	232....	12–23–1782....	Hingstons Fk......	....
Harris, Benjamin.....	1,000....	1...	233....	12–23–1782....	Stoner Fk........	Surveyed
Harris, Benjamin.....	1,500....	1...	240....	12–23–1782....	Br Licking........	Surveyed
Harris, Benjamin.....	1,000....	1...	240....	12–23–1782....	Br Hingston Fk ...	Surveyed
Harriss, Edward.......	1,000....	2...	52....	1–13–1783....	Hustons Fk.......	Surveyed
Harris, Edward.......	100....	2...	229....	3–10–1783....	N Fk Elkhorn.. ..	....
Harris, Francis Eppes.	1,000....	1...	233....	12–23–1782....	Hingstons Fk......	Surveyed
Harris, Francis Eppes.	1,000....	1...	234....	12–23–1782....	Hingstons Fk......	....
Harris, Fredrick......	500....	3...	125....	12–31–1783....	Rose Run.........	Withdrawn
Harris, Fredrick......	500....	3...	125....	12–31–1783....	Big Mud Lick......	....
Harris, Joel.........	1,000....	1...	257....	12–24–1782....	4 Mile Cr........	Withdrawn
Harris, Joel.........	1,000....	1...	259....	12–24–1782....	Br Licking........	....
Harriss, Joel.........	500....	1...	259....	12–24–1782....	Br Stoners Fk......	Withdrawn
Harriss, Joel.........	500....	1...	259....	12–24–1782....	None............	....
Harriss, Joel.........	500....	1...	259....	12–24–1782....	Wolf Cr..........	Withdrawn
Harriss, Joel.........	500....	1...	369....	1– 4–1783....	None............	......•••
Harris, John.........	30,000....	1...	186....	12–19–1782....	Trace Licking......	Surveyed
Harris, John.........	4,000....	1...	186....	12–19–1782....	Brs Ohio R........	....
Harris, John.........	4,000....	1...	187....	12–19–1782....	Tuttle Cr.........	....
Harris, John.........	4,000....	1...	187....	12–19–1782....	———————	....
Harris, John.........	4,000....	1...	187....	12–19–1782....	None............	....
Harris, John.........	4,000....	1...	187....	12–19–1782....	None............	....
Harris, John.........	5,000....	1...	188....	12–19–1782....	Fks Licking Cr.....	Surveyed
Harris, John.........	5,000....	1...	188....	12–19–1782....	Licking Cr........	Surveyed
Harris, John.........	5,000....	1...	189....	12–19–1782....	Licking Cr........	Surveyed
Harris, John.........	5,000....	1...	189....	12–19–1782....	Licking..........	Surveyed
Harris, John.........	5,000....	1...	189....	12–19–1782....	Licking..........	Surveyed
Harris, John.........	5,000....	1...	189....	12–19–1782....	Licking..........	Surveyed
Harris, John.........	5,000....	1...	190....	12–19–1782....	Licking Cr........	Withdrawn
Harris, John.........	5,000....	1...	190....	12–19–1782....	Licking Cr........	Withdrawn
Harriss, John........	26,597½....	1...	269....	12–25–1782....	Licking..........	Surveyed
Harris, Jno..........	5,000....	3...	281....	4–10–1784....	Licking..........	Withdrawn
Harris, Jno..........	10,000....	4...	71....	11–25–1784....	None............	....
Harris, Joseph.......	1,500....	1...	234....	12–23–1782....	E Br Grassy Lick..	Surveyed
Harris, Joseph.......	1,000....	1...	234....	12–23–1782....	Hingstons Fk......	....
Harris, Joseph.......	500....	1...	235....	12–23–1782....	None............	....
Harris, Michael......	243¾....	2...	56....	1–13–1783....	Licking..........	Surveyed
Harris, Randolph......	970¼....	3...	184....	2–13–1784....	Severn Cr.........	Surveyed

Entree	Acres	Book	Page	Entry Date	Watercourse	Notes
Harris, Thos.	10,000	3	84	12–12–1783	Ohio R.	Withdrawn
Harris, Thos.	2,000	3	137	1– 5–1784	None.	....
Harris, Thos.	4,618	3	291	4–15–1784	N Elkhorn.	....
Harris, Thos.	10,000	3	325	5– 6–1784	Licking.	Surveyed
Harris, Wm.	584	3	235	3–22–1784	Main Br Ky.	Withdrawn
Harris, Wm.	2,883½	4	160	4–29–1785	None.	....
Harris, Wm B.	1,000	3	125	12–31–1783	Mud Lick.	....
Harris, Jno & Jordan	44,109¼	3	237	3–25–1784	None.	Surveyed
Harris, Jno & Jordan	44,109¼	3	349	5–29–1784	Licking.	Surveyed
Harris & Spilman	17,372	3	194	3– 2–1784	Hinkston Fk.	Surveyed
Harrison, Benj.	500	3	186	2–17–1784	Licking.	....
Harrison, Cuthbert	4,550	3	339	5–19–1784	None.	Surveyed
Harrison, Cuthbert & Geo.	4,000	4	99	1–24–1785	Slate Cr.	....
Harrison, Hiram	500	4	303	8– 2–1786	S Fk Boones Cr.	Surveyed
Harrison, Jeremiah	500	2	201	2–17–1783	None.	....
Harrison, Samuel	562	1	375	1– 6–1783	S Fk Elkhorn.	Surveyed
Harrison, Sam	1,200	1	378	1– 6–1783	Hinkstons Fk.	Surveyed
Harrison, Wm.	15,500	3	262	3–31–1784	Licking.	....
Harrison, Benj & Lawrence	1,097½	3	171	1–29–1784	None.	....
Harrison & Daniel	6,923½	3	268	4– 6–1784	None.	....
Harrison & Mason	2,000	3	345	5–25–1784	Lower Blue Lick.	....
Hart, David	2,000	1	97	12–10–1782	Small Mountain Cr.	....
Hart, Jno.	1,000	3	52	11–21–1783	Br Licking.	Surveyed
Hart, Nathaniel	400	1	83	12– 9–1782	Ky R.	Withdrawn
Hart, Nathaniel	400	1	92	12–10–1782	Ky R.	....
Hart, Nathaniel	400	4	36	9–15–1784	None.	....
Hart, Nathaniel	400	4	36	9–17–1784	Strouds Cr.	....
Hart, Nathaniel, heirs	500	1	96	12–10–1782	Ky R.	....
Hart, Nathaniel, heirs	500	1	97	12–10–1782	Lulbergrud.	....
Hart, Nathaniel, heirs	1,000	1	110	12–11–1782	Lulbergrud.	....
Hart, Robt.	1,000	3	140	1–12–1784	None.	Surveyed
Hart, Thomas	500	1	89	12– 9–1782	Stoners Fk & Howards Cr.	....
Hart, Thomas	1,500	1	95	12–10–1782	Stoners & Howards Crs.	....
Hart, Thomas	500	1	97	12–10–1782	Lulbergrud.	....
Hartley, Thomas	1,000	1	366	1– 4–1783	Br Hingston Fk.	....
Hartley, Thos.	1,000	1	366	1– 4–1783	Licking.	....
Harvie, Jno Wm.	50	4	313	3–21–1787	—— R.	....
Harvie, William	648¼	1	221	12–21–1782	Rows Run.	Amended
Harvie, William	900	2	81	1–17–1783	Licking Cr.	Surveyed
Harvie, William	648¼	2	145	1–31–1783	None.	....
Haskins, Wm.	——	4	278	2–27–1787	Hinkson Mill Cr.	Surveyed
Hathaway, Jno.	200	3	26	10–31–1783	None.	....
Hathaway, Jno.	2,000	3	25	10–31–1783	None.	....
Hathway, Jas.	2,448	3	273	4– 6–1784	Small Mt Cr.	Surveyed
Hawkins, John	200	1	39	12– 4–1782	Hickmans Cr.	Withdrawn
Hawkins, John	200	1	110	12–11–1782	Hickman Cr.	....
Hawkins, John	4,000	1	122	12–12–1782	N Fk Licking.	....
Hawkins, John	500	1	129	12–13–1782	Mouth Big Mianinai	Surveyed
Hawkins, John	1,000	2	280	4–29–1783	None.	....
Hawkins, John	1,000	2	299	5–29–1783	None.	Surveyed
Hawkins, Jno.	1,200	3	52	11–21–1783	Br Licking.	Surveyed
Hawkins, John Jr.	50	1	130	12–13–1782	Eagle Cr.	Surveyed
Hawkins, Martin	400	1	309	12–28–1782	E Fk Hickmans Cr.	Surveyed
Hawkins, Philaman	700	1	126	12–13–1782	Fks Licking & Ohio	....
Hawkins, & Stewart	62,306	4	223	9–30–1785	None.	....
Hawkins & Terrell	1,000	2	297	5–29–1783	N Fk Licking.	Surveyed
Hawkins & Terrell	1,000	2	298	5–29–1783	Br Licking.	....
Hawkins & Terrell	1,000	2	298	5–29–1783	Bensons Cr.	Withdrawn
Hawkins & Terrell	1,000	2	298	5–29–1783	Fks Elkhorn.	Surveyed
Hawkins & Terrell	1,000	2	298	5–29–1783	None.	....
Hawkins & Terrell	1,000	2	298	5–29–1783	Licking.	Surveyed
Hawkins & Terrell	1,000	2	298	5–29–1783	Dry Run.	Surveyed
Hawkins & Terrell	1,000	2	299	5–29–1783	Fks Elkhorn.	Surveyed
Hawkins & Terrell	1,000	2	299	5–29–1783	None.	Surveyed
Hawse, Samuel	3,700	1	11	11–30–1782	None.	....
Hawse, Samuel	5,000	1	30	12–18–1782	—— Cr.	Surveyed
Hawse, Samuel	1,500	1	30	12–18–1782	—— Cr.	Surveyed
Hawse, Samuel	1,000	1	31	12–18–1782	Cabbin Cr.	....
Hay, Wm.	400	1	2	11–28–1782	Licking.	....
Hay, William	400	1	87	12– 9–1782	Hickmans Cr & Ky R.	Surveyed
Hay, William	400	1	87	12– 9–1782	Lulbergrud Cr.	....
Hay, William	400	1	88	12– 9–1782	None.	....
Hay, William	3,000	1	105	12–11–1782	Lulbergrud.	....
Hay, William	300	1	109	12–11–1782	None.	....
Hay, William	1,000	1	133	12–13–1782	Stoners Fk.	....
Hay, William	1,000	1	241	12–23–1782	Stoners Fk.	Surveyed

Entree	Acres	Book	Page	Entry Date	Watercourse	Notes
Hay, William	2,000	1	269	12–25–1782	Hingstons Fk	Surveyed
Hay, William	1,000	1	392	1– 7–1783	Ky R	....
Hay, William	821½	1	392	1– 7–1783	S E Fk Lulbergrud	....
Hay, William	2,700	1	393	1– 8–1783	Br Hingstons Fk	Surveyed
Hay, William	200	1	395	1– 9–1783	Seven Mile Cr	....
Hay, Wm	500	4	329	5–12–1789	None	....
Hay, Wm	1,000	4	335	2–14–1792	None	....
Hay, Wm	2,650	4	335	2–14–1792	None	....
Hay, William	400	1	2	11–28–1782	Licking	....
Hayes, William	1,000	2	194	2–14–1783	Hickman Cr	Withdrawn
Hayes, William	1,000	2	207	2– 4–1783	Hickman Cr	Withdrawn
Hayes, William	500	2	229	3–10–1783	None	Withdrawn
Hayes, William	1,000	2	233	3–12–1783	None	Withdrawn
Hayes, William	500	2	282	4–29–1783	Hickmans Cr	Withdrawn
Hayes, William	1,000	2	282	5– 2–1783	None	Surveyed
Hayes, William	1,000	2	303	5–31–1783	Ky R	Withdrawn
Hayes, William	1,000	2	334	7–29–1783	Br Licking	....
Hayes, William	1,000	2	334	7–29–1783	Licking	....
Hayes, William	1,500	2	334	7–29–1783	Licking	....
Hayes, William	1,800	2	335	7–29–1783	Licking	....
Hays, Wm	1,000	1	43	12– 4–1782	——— Cr	Surveyed
Hays, William	1,000	1	43	12– 4–1782	——— Cr	Surveyed
Hays, William	1,000	1	43	12– 4–1782	——— Cr	Surveyed
Hays, William	50	1	87	12– 9–1782	7 Mile Cr	....
Hays, William	200	1	88	12– 9–1782	Lulbergrud Cr	....
Hayes, William	1,000	1	111	12–11–1782	None	Surveyed
Hayes, William	1,000	1	292	12–27–1782	None	Withdrawn
Hays, William	1,500	3	152	1–16–1784	Br Licking	....
Hays, Wm	1,200	3	169	1–26–1784	Boones Cr	Withdrawn
Hays, Wm	500	3	152	1–16–1784	——— Br	....
Hays, Wm	1,200	4	222	9–23–1785	Boones Cr	....
Hays, Wm	500	4	329	4– 1–1789	None	....
Hays, Wm	2,650	4	329	5–12–1789	Ky R	....
Hays, Christopher	1,000	3	187	2–24–1784	None	....
Hayden, Ezekiel	4,946	2	31	1–10–1783	Flat Cr	....
Hayden, John	1,000	1	284	12–26–1782	Clear Cr	Surveyed
Hayden, John	9,712½	2	26	1–10–1783	Licking	Surveyed
Hayden, William	500	1	357	1– 3–1783	Ky R	Surveyed
Hayden, William	200	2	175	2– 8–1783	Ky R	....
Hayden, William	——	2	322	7–14–1783	None	Surveyed
Hayden, William	258	2	323	7–15–1783	None	....
Hayden & Conner	4,345½	4	175	5– 9–1785	None	Surveyed
Haydon, Ezekiel	263½	2	125	1–25–1783	None	Withdrawn
Haydon, William	500	2	77	1–17–1783	N Fk Elkhorn	....
Haydon, William	500	2	79	1–17–1783	None	....
Haydon, William	500	2	104	1–21–1783	None	....
Haydon, William	500	2	148	1–31–1783	None	Surveyed
Haydon, William	500	2	202	2–18–1783	None	Surveyed
Hayden, Wm	200	4	113	2– 7–1785	Ky R	Amended
Haydock, Jno	225,000	3	353	6– 4–1784	Ky R	Withdrawn
Hazlerigg, Jas	6,000	4	229	10–28–1785	Boones Cr	Withdrawn
Hazlerigg, Jas	8,000	4	299	5–22–1786	None	....
Hazlerigg, Jas	8,000	4	301	7–11–1786	Raven Cr	....
Hazlerigg, Jas	8,000	4	299	5–24–1786	Br Boones Cr	4,058 acres surveyed
Hazlerigg, Berry & Lewis	8,000	4	233	11– 9–1785	Ky R	Withdrawn
Hazlerig, Charles	4,900	2	246	3–15–1783	None	....
Head, Hadly	4,004¼	3	160	1–21–1784	Licking	Surveyed
Headon, James	1,000	1	44	12– 4–1782	——— Cr	....
Headon & Conner	2,000	4	166	4–29–1785	None	Withdrawn
Headon & Conner	4,343½	4	176	5– 9–1785	None	....
Headon & Craig	3,916	3	250	3–30–1784	Buffaloe Rd	Withdrawn
Headon & Craig	3,916	4	157	4–27–1785	None	....
Hearndon, David	400	2	28	1–10–1783	Licking	Surveyed
Hearndon, Sam	400	2	28	1–10–1783	Licking	Surveyed
Hedgeman, Jno	8,500	3	419	8– 3–1784	Br Licking	2,500 acres withdrawn
Hedgman, Jno	2,000	4	78	12–16–1784	Big Sandy R	Withdrawn
Hedgman, Jno	2,000	4	84	1– 8–1785	None	....
Hedgman, Jno	1,000	4	84	1– 8–1785	Flat Cr	....
Hedgman, Jno	1,000	4	84	1– 8–1785	N Fk Elkhorn	....
Hedgman, Jno	657	4	84	1– 8–1785	Turkeyfoot Fk	....
Hedgman, Jno	1,000	4	86	1– 8–1785	None	....
Hedgman, Jno	1,000	4	86	1– 8–1785	Grassy Lick	Withdrawn
Hedgman, Jno	1,000	4	121	2–18–1785	None	....
Hedgman, Jno	1,000	4	122	2–18–1785	None	....
Hedgman, Jno	1,500	4	172	5– 6–1785	None	....
Hedgeman & Grayson	25,000	3	157	1–19–1784	S Fk Licking	Withdrawn
Hedgman & Grayson	25,000	3	245	3–26–1784	N Fk Licking	Withdrawn
Hedgman & Grayson	54	4	85	1– 8–1784	Ky R	....
Hedgman & Grayson	25,000	4	179	5–12–1785	Licking	Withdrawn

Entree	Acres	Book	Page	Entry Date	Watercourse	Notes
Hedgman & Grayson..	25,000	4	247	12–21–1785	Ohio R	
Heiatt, Stephen	500	1	128	12–13–1782	None	Surveyed
Height, Thomas	600	1	153	12–17–1782	N Fk Licking	
Helm, Meridith	918	3	293	4–18–1784	S Fk Licking	
Henderson, David	1,000	1	274	12–25–1782	Big Bone Lick & Big Miami	Withdrawn
Henderson, David	801	2	174	2– 8–1783	S Fk Elkhorn	Amended
Henderson, David	801	2	295	5–27–1783	None	Withdrawn
Henderson, David	1,908	3	139	1– 8–1784	None	
Henderson, David	801	3	414	7–22–1784	None	
Henderson, David	801	4	67	11–15–1784	Main Licking	Surveyed
Henderson, David & Jas	2,417¾	3	160	1–21–1784	None	Amended
Henderson, James	1,000	1	334	12–31–1782	None	
Henderson, James	1,000	2	65	1–14–1783	Red R	
Henderson, James	200	2	65	1–15–1783	Ky R	
Henderson, Jas	500	3	156	1–19–1784	None	
Henderson, James	3,708	3	163	1–22–1784	Licking	
Henderson, Jas	1,908	4	337	5–17–1794	None	
Henderson, Jas	1,800	4	337	5–17–1794	None	
Henderson, Robt	2,000	3	158	1–21–1784	Main Licking	Surveyed
Henderson, Robt	500	4	24	8–30–1784	Ohio R	
Henderson, Thos	1,000	3	215	3–10–1784	None	
Henderson, William	11,351½	1	356	1– 3–1783	Ky R	Surveyed
Henderson, Wm	11,351½	4	338	10– 8–1794	None	
Hendricks, George	1,000	1	360	1– 4–1783	E Br Hustons Fk	Surveyed
Henry, Daniel	500	2	191	2–13–1783	None	Surveyed
Henry, Daniel	2,328½	4	169	4–30–1785	Sandy R	Surveyed
Henry, Patrick	1,000	2	272	12–25–1782	N Fk Sandy	
Henry, Peter	1,200	2	68	1–15–1783	Br Hingston Fk	
Henry, Peter	2,400	2	184	2–13–1783	None	
Henry, Samuel	2,000	1	148	12–16–1782	N Fk Licking	Surveyed
Henry, William	1,000	2	297	5–29–1783	Licking	Surveyed
Henry, Wm	1,080	4	100	1–27–1785	None	Surveyed
Henry, Wm	6,920	4	100	1–27–1785	N Fk Licking	
Henton, Joseph	5,316	1	377	1– 6–1783	Main Br Jessamine	Withdrawn
Henton, Joseph	1,000	2	301	5–30–1783	N Fk Glenns Cr	
Herndon, David	1,000	4	310	1–29–1787	None	
Herndon, Joseph	937½	2	48	1–13–1783	None	
Herndon, Thomas	200	1	20	1–14–1783	Elkhorn	
Herndon, Thos	3,694	4	323	5– 9–1788	Cedar Cr	
Hice, George	900	1	306	12–28–1782	Br 4 Mile Cr	
Hice, Jacob	1,179	1	307	12–28–1782	Hingstons Fk	
Hickman, Wm	10,000	4	223	9–30–1785	Little Sandy	
Higgins, Aaron	3,093½	2	3	1– 8–1783	Bank Lick Cr	Surveyed
Higgins, Aaron	1,000	2	80	1–17–1783	Bank Lick Cr	Surveyed
Higs, Wm T	2,000	4	15	8–14–1784	None	Surveyed
Higs, Wm T	500	4	16	8–14–1784	None	Surveyed
Hill, Ephraim	800	2	73	1–16–1783	None	
Hill, Joel	400	2	51	1–13–1783	None	Surveyed
Hill, Wm	12,613	3	226	3–14–1784	Licking	Withdrawn
Hill, Wm	12,613	3	241	3–26–1784	Locust Cr	Withdrawn
Hill, Wm	12,613	4	265	1–30–1786	N Fk Ky R	Withdrawn
Hill, Wm	12,613	4	291	4–22–1786	None	
Hinch, John	1,000	1	308	12–28–1782	N Fk Greens Cr	Surveyed
Hinch, Samuel	1,000	1	308	12–28–1782	N Fk Greens Cr	Surveyed
Hind, James	926	2	339	8– 2–1783	——— Cr	
Hinkston, John	1,000	1	57	12– 5–1782	Mill Cr	Surveyed
Hinkston, John	1,000	1	193	12–20–1782	S Br Licking	Surveyed
Hinkston, John	600	2	148	1–31–1783	Hinkstons Fk	Surveyed
Hinkston, Jno	2,000	3	57	11–24–1783	S Fk Licking	Surveyed
Hinkston, Jno	60	3	106	12–20–1783	S Fk Licking	
Hite, Abraham	600	3	5	10–15–1783	None	Surveyed
Hite, Isaac	4,000	2	336	8– 1–1783	Br Ky R	Withdrawn
Hite, Isaac	4,000	2	349	8–14–1783	None	
Hite, Isaac	4,000	2	350	8–14–1783	Jessamine Cr	
Hite, Isaac	4,000	3	8	10–15–1783	Harrods Lick Cr	
Hite, Isaac	11,580	4	147	4–10–1785	Little Sandy	
Hite, Peter	1,000	3	40	11–12–1783	None	
Hix, Harris	937½	3	184	2–13–1784	Severn Cr	Surveyed
Hix, Wm	1,628	3	184	2–13–1784	Severn Cr	Surveyed
Hizer, Christopher	1,000	4	152	4–12–1785	Fk Licking	Surveyed
Hoard, Jas	1,500	4	227	10–20–1785	None	
Hoard, James	1,500	4	68	11–16–1784	Big Bone Lick	
Hoard, Thos	1,000	3	270	4– 6–1784	Licking	
Hoard, Thos	130	3	397	7– 8–1784	None	
Hoard, Thos	75	3	397	7– 8–1784	None	
Hoard, Thos	3,000	4	150	4–10–1785	None	
Hoard, Thos	1,000	3	229	3–17–1784	S Fk Licking	Withdrawn
Hobbs & Read	3,000	3	234	3–22–1784	Rock House Cr	Withdrawn
Hodge, Elenor	672½	2	143	1–30–1783	N Fk Elkhorn	Surveyed

Entree	Acres	Book	Page	Entry Date	Watercourse	Notes
Hodge, Eleaner & Jno..	295½	4	164	4–29–1785	None	
Hodge, John	300	2	323	7–14–1783	Elkhorn	Withdrawn
Hodge, John	672½	2	342	8– 7–1783	Hingston Fk	Withdrawn
Hodge, Jno	672½	4	164	4–29–1785	None	
Hodge, Jno	672½	4	164	4–29–1785	Licking	
Hodges, Jesse	2,000	4	237	12– 9–1785	None	
Hodgson, Robt	300,306⅔	3	190	2–28–1784	3 Fks Ky R	
Hogan, James	1,000	2	122	1–25–1783	Little Hickman	Surveyed
Hogan, Jas	200	4	313	3–12–1787	Canoe Cr	Surveyed
Hogan, James	50	1	43	12– 4–1782	Hickman Cr	
Hogan, James & Assee.	50	1	34	12– 4–1782	Ky R	Surveyed
Hogan, John	400	1	10	11–29–1782	N Fk Elkhorn	
Hogshead, David	1,000	2	70	1–16–1783	Mill Cr	Surveyed
Hogshead, David	772	2	70	1–16–1783	Br Mill Cr	Surveyed
Hogshead, James	328	2	84	1–18–1783	S Br Eagle Cr	Surveyed
Hogshead, James	861½	2	85	1–18–1783	M Fk Eagle Cr	Surveyed
Holder, John	200	1	10	11–29–1782	Howards Cr	
Holder, John	380	1	12	11–30–1782	None	
Holder, John	1,000	1	32	12– 3–1782	——— Cr	Surveyed
Holder, John	200	1	158	12–17–1782	Ky R	Amended
Holder, John	100	1	158	12–17–1782	Ky R	Amended
Holder, John	200	1	159	12–17–1782	Boones Cr	
Holder, John	200	1	159	12–17–1782	Jouetts Cr	
Holder, John	500	1	159	12–17–1782	Ky R	
Holder, John	2,000	1	160	12–17–1782	Hickman	Surveyed
Holder, John	2,186	1	160	12–17–1782	Licking	Surveyed
Holder, John	1,000	1	160	12–17–1782	Stones Fk	Surveyed
Holder, John	100	1	175	12–18–1782	Howards Lower Cr	Withdrawn
Holder, John	2,000	1	176	12–18–1782	None	
Holder, John	600	1	176	12–18–1782	Hingstons Fk	
Holder, John	2,000	1	176	12–18–1782	Rocky Ford and Stoners Fk	Surveyed
Holder, John	1,000	1	223	12–21–1782	Licking Cr	Surveyed
Holder, John	2,000	1	224	12–21–1782	Ohio R	Surveyed
Holder, John	1,000	1	224	12–21–1782	Br Licking	
Holder, John	1,000	1	319	12–30–1782	None	
Holder, John	800	1	319	12–30–1782	None	
Holder, John	1,000	2	79	1–17–1783	None	
Holder, John	100	2	203	2–19–1783	Ky R	
Holder, John	1,000	2	258	3–27–1783	None	Surveyed
Holder, John	200	2	317	6–14–1783	Howards Cr	
Holder, Jno	10,687	3	64	12– 1–1783	S Fk Big Sandy	Surveyed
Holder, Jno	50,612½	4	88	1–12–1785	Ky R	Surveyed
Holder, Jno	6,212	4	121	2–16–1785	Red R	Surveyed
Holder, Jno	380	4	183	5–24–1785	None	
Holder, Jno	200	4	226	10–13–1785	Silver Cr	
Holder & Taylor	49,665½	3	416	7–26–1784	Ky R	Surveyed
Holder & Walton	200	4	224	10– 3–1785	None	
Holladay, William	1,000	2	225	3– 8–1783	Ohio R	Surveyed
Holladay, Benjamin	3,000	1	13	11–30–1782	Br Licking	
Holladay, James	800	1	13	11–30–1782	None	
Holland, Jno	460	3	196	3– 2–1784	Bank Lick Cr	Withdrawn
Holland, Jno	460	4	221	9–17–1785	Fk Lick R	
Hollingsworth, Levi	1,000	3	425	8–14–1784	——— Cr	Surveyed
Hollingsworth, Levi	1,000	3	426	8–14–1784	Sandy	Surveyed
Hollingsworth, Levi	4,000	3	426	8–14–1784	Sandy	Surveyed
Hollingsworth, Levi	1,000	4	5	8–14–1784	Sandy Cr	Surveyed
Holly, John	400	2	273	4– 9–1783	S Fk Elkhorn & Ky R	
Holmes, Basil	15,135½	1	244	12–23–1782	Upper Blue Lick	
Holmes, John	4,819	2	114	1–23–1783	Main Fk Licking	
Holmes, Joseph	4,000	3	294	4–16–1784	——— Cr	746 acres surveyed
Holmes, Joseph	406	3	294	4–16–1784	Fk Clear Cr	Surveyed
Holt, Joseph	5,399½	2	99	1–21–1783	Ohio R	Surveyed
Holt, Joseph	5,399½	2	112	1–23–1783	None	Surveyed
Holt, Thomas	5,000	1	218	12–21–1782	Salt Sp Fk	
Holt, Thomas	2,000	1	218	12–21–1782	M Fk Licking	
Holt, Thomas	2,000	1	218	12–21–1782	Main Fk Licking	
Holt, Thomas	1,000	1	219	12–21–1782	Licking	
Holt, Thomas	5,000	1	221	12–21–1782	S Fk of Mill Cr	
Holt, Thos	3,431	4	124	2–23–1785	Slate Cr	
Hooker & Connelly	2,003	4	286	3–27–1786	Eagle Cr	Surveyed
Hopkins, Garrard	2,000	1	310	12–28–1782	Hustons Fk	Surveyed
Hopkins, Jas	1,201½	4	320	2–17–1788	Ky R	
Horine, Jacob	500	2	318	7– 7–1783	Slate Cr	Surveyed
Horine, Michael	97½	2	297	5–29–1783	Ohio R	
Housley & States	4,176	3	60	11–25–1783	Ohio R	
Houston, John	5,619½	1	345	1– 1–1783	Br Licking	
Houston, Jno	93	1	372	1– 6–1783	Lees Lick Cr	
Howard, Benj	1,000	4	61	10–28–1784	None	

Entree	Acres	Book	Page	Entry Date	Watercourse	Notes
Howard, Charles	1,000	2	227	3–10–1783	Ohio R	Surveyed
Howard, James	900	1	275	12–25–1782	Hingston & Stoners Fk	Surveyed
Howard, John	1,000	2	232	3–12–1783	Howards Cr	Surveyed
Howard, Jno	750	4	335	5–25–1792	N Fk Elkhorn	
Howard, John	1,000	2	317	6–14–1783	Ky R	Surveyed
Howard, Wm	500	3	16	10–29–1783	——— R	
Howard, Wm	600	3	423	8– 6–1784	N Fk Licking	
Howard & Leitch	15,000	4	8	8–14–1784	Twins Cr & Ky R	
Howard & Morgan	900	3	356	6– 9–1784	None	Surveyed
Howard & Overton	2,000	3	262	3–31–1784	None	
Howard & Overton	800	3	262	3–31–1784	None	
Howard & Robertson	407¾	4	198	6–11–1785	None	
Howe, John William	1,000	2	195	2–14–1783	Saven Cr	Withdrawn
Howe, John W	700	2	315	6–11–1783	Salt Lick	
Howe, John W	700	2	315	6–11–1783	Bitter Lick	
Howe, Jno W	798	2	315	6–11–1783	———	
Howe, John William	1,000	2	375	10–13–1783	Eagle Cr	
Hoy, William	4,000	2	272	4– 8–1783	S Fk Lulbegrud	
Hoy, William	1,000	2	272	4– 8–1783	S Fk Lulbegrud	
Huber, Geo	4,398	3	370	6–16–1784	None	
Hudson, Jacob	563½	3	272	4– 6–1784	Licking	Withdrawn
Hudson, Jacob	563½	4	151	4–10–1785	None	
Hudson, Jacob	563½	4	151	4–10–1785	None	
Huffman & Mackin	2,000	4	128	3– 6–1785	Johnson Fk	
Hughes, Jas	500	4	135	3–19–1785	None	Withdrawn
Hughes, Neel	1,000	3	95	12–11–1783	Big Bone Lick	Surveyed
Hughes, Wm	1,000	3	149	1–15–1784	None	Surveyed
Hull, John	1,000	1	7	12–13–1782	Elkhorn	Surveyed
Humble, Michael	500	2	266	4– 7–1783	None	
Humphrey, Josua	834½	4	167	4–29–1785	None	Withdrawn
Humphrey, Josua	834½	4	177	5– 9–1785	None	
Humphrey, J	834½	4	176	5– 9–1785	None	
Humphrey, Uriah	1,000	4	146	4–10–1785	Little Sandy	
Humphreys, Joshua	4,769	2	288	5–20–1783	S F Licking	
Humphries, Joshua	500	2	352	8–15–1783	Main Br Eagle Cr	
Humston, Edward	12,734¼	3	134	1– 2–1784	N Fk Big Bone Cr	
Hunt, Richard	500	4	163	4–29–1785	None	
Hunter, Henry	300	3	393	7– 3–1784	Hickmans Cr	
Hunter, Henry	200	4	81	12–31–1784	Hickmans Cr	
Hunter, Jacob	800	1	152	12–17–1782	Ky R	Surveyed
Hunter, Jacob	200	1	373	1– 6–1783	Marble Cr	Surveyed
Hunter, Moses	1,000	1	366	1– 4–1783	N Fk Licking	
Hunter, Moses	1,171	2	185	2–13–1783	Hinkstons Fk	
Hunter, Moses	1,000	2	215	2–28–1783	Licking	
Hunter, Moses	2,000	2	313	6– 9–1783	Br Red R	Surveyed
Hunter, Moses	5,500	4	190	6– 1–1785	Ohio R	
Hunter, Titus	2,000	4	148	4–10–1785	None	
Hunter, Wm	21,791	3	191	3– 1–1784	Licking	
Hunter & Morgan	1,000	3	133	1– 2–1784	None	
Huntsman & Edmeston	1,445	3	307	4–29–1784	Licking	Withdrawn
Huntsman & Edmeston	1,445	4	106	2– 5–1785	Rockhouse Fk	
Huntsman & Edmeston	1,445	4	107	2– 5–1785	Rockhouse Fk	
Huskins, Wm	400	3	227	3–16–1784	None	
Huston, Daniel	3,000	2	368	10– 1–1783	S Fk Hingston	
Huston, David	3,000	4	339	8–18–1795	None	
Huston, Geo	1,400	4	161	4–29–1785	None	
Huston, John	500	1	31	12–18–1782	Four Mile Cr	
Huston, Samuel	400	1	29	12– 3–1782	Hingston Fk	Surveyed
Hutchison, David	10,000	1	372	1– 6–1783	Raven Cr	
Hutchison, Joseph	1,200	2	263	4– 1–1783	Eagle Cr	Surveyed
Hutchison, Joseph	5,926¾	3	204	3– 5–1784	Eagle Cr	
Hutchison, Peter	2,000	3	368	6–15–1784	None	Surveyed
Hyatt, John	500	2	145	1–31–1783	None	Surveyed
Imlay, Gilbert	1,400	3	36	11–11–1783	Br Licking	Surveyed
Imlay, Gilbert	1,000	3	36	11–11–1783	Licking	Surveyed
Imlay, Gilbert	1,000	3	37	11–11–1783	Fk Licking	Surveyed
Imlay, Gilbert	13,976	3	37	11–11–1783	Br Licking	Surveyed
Ingaedozer, Jas	4,463	2	237	3–12–1783	None	
Irvin, Andrew	625	2	61	1– 4–1783	None	Surveyed
Irvine, David	4,000	2	118	1–24–1783	None	Amended
Irvine, David	3,812	2	364	9–22–1783	Ky Run	
Isaacs, Isaiah	5,000	1	285	12–26–1782	Main Fk Licking	Surveyed
Isaacs, Isaiah	5,000	4	215	8– 2–1785	Ohio R	
Jack, Samuel	500	2	208	2–25–1783	S Fk Licking	
Jackman, Adam	1,000	2	11	1– 9–1783	M Br Licking	
Jackman, Joseph	1,125	1	278	12–25–1782	Stoners Fk	
Jackman, Richard	400	1	28	12– 3–1782	Eagle Cr	
Jackman, Richard	1,000	1	241	12–23–1782	Br Licking	Surveyed
Jackman, Richard	400	2	265	4– 3–1783	N Fk Licking	
Jackman, Richard	100	2	297	5–28–1783	N Fk Licking	Withdrawn

Entree	Acres	Book	Page	Entry Date	Watercourse	Notes
Jackman, Richard	1,132	3	54	11–21–1783	Ky R	
Jackman, Richard	1,000	3	189	2–28–1784	Licking	
Jackman, Thos	398½	3	411	7–17–1784	None	
Jackson, Jarvis	300	2	337	8– 1–1783	Ky R	
Jackson, John	400	1	123	12–13–1782	Hingstons Fk	
Jackson, John	400	1	123	12–12–1782	Hingstons Fk	
Jackson, John	1,000	2	251	3–21–1783	Hinkstons Fk	Surveyed
Jacob, Robert Clark	10,079	1	261	12–24–1782	Hingston & M Licking	Surveyed
Jacob, Robert Clark	10,000	1	260	12–24–1782	None	Surveyed
Jacoby, Francis	3,800	4	218	8–10–1785	Eagle Cr	
James, Geo	5,000	3	65	12– 1–1783	None	Surveyed
James, Geo	5,000	3	65	12– 1–1783	Salt Rock Cr	Surveyed
James, Geo	10,000	3	65	12– 1–1783	None	Surveyed
James, Geo	10,000	3	65	12– 1–1783	None	Surveyed
James, Geo	10,000	3	66	12– 1–1783	Salt Rock	Surveyed
James, Philip	1,708	3	39	11–12–1783	Slate Cr	
James & Graham	20,500	3	38	11–12–1783	Br Licking	Surveyed
James & Graham	20,500	3	386	6–28–1784	——— Cr	Surveyed
Jamison, David	500	1	7	12–13–1782	Marble & Hickman	Surveyed
Jamison, David	5,000	1	279	12–26–1782	Ind Cros Licking Cr.	Surveyed
Jamison, David	10,000	3	238	3–25–1784	None	
Jamison, Geo	843¾	4	165	4–29–1785	None	
Jamison, Geo	4,000	4	183	5–24–1785	Eagle Cr	Surveyed
Jamison, Geo	5,062½	4	184	5–28–1785	Main Licking	
Jamison, John	983	1	307	12–28–1782	F Br Stoners Fk	
January, Ephraim	1,500	1	377	1– 6–1783	Br Eagle Cr	
January, Ephraim	1,500	1	377	1– 7–1783	Shoemakers Cr	
January, Ephraim	1,000	2	50	1–11–1783	Clear Cr	Surveyed
January, James	750	1	134	12–13–1782	Evans Mill Cr	Withdrawn
January, James	5,000	1	298	12–27–1782	Fvans Mill Cr	
January, James	2,000	1	299	12–27–1782	M Fk Shoemakers Cr	Surveyed
January, James	409	1	300	12–27–1782	S Fk Elkhorn	
January, James	750	1	300	12–27–1782	Evans Mill Cr	
January, James	2,303	1	376	1– 6–1783	M Fk Clear Cr	Surveyed
January, Jas	1,787	3	153	1–17–1784	None	Withdrawn
January, Jas	1,787	4	236	12– 2–1785	None	
Jarbad, Joseph	885	2	184	2–13–1783	None	
Jarrell, Thos	5,364½	4	94	1–17–1785	N Fk Licking	Surveyed
Jenkins, Jas	40,000	3	404	7–14–1784	Fk Licking	
Jenkins, Jas	3,037½	3	276	4– 7–1784	Millers Cr	
Jenkins, Wm	500	3	288	4–14–1784	S Fk Big Sandy	
Jenkins & Overton	20,000	3	404	7–13–1784	Main Licking	
Jett, Stephen	791	2	111	1–23–1783	Sycamore Fk Hinkston	Surveyed
Jett, Stephen	791	2	166	2– 6–1783	Br Licking	Surveyed
Johns, John	2,000	2	36	1–11–1783	Sandy	
Johnson, Benjamin	10,000	1	118	12–12–1782	Hickman & Jessa-mine Cr	Surveyed
Johnson, Benjamin	5,000	1	131	12–13–1782	N Fk Elkhorn	Surveyed
Johnson, Cave	300	1	127	12–13–1782	Ohio R	
Johnson, Cave	3,000	1	317	12–30–1782	Licking	Withdrawn
Johnson, Cave	500	2	31	1–10–1783	Hinkstons Fk	Surveyed
Johnson, Cave	500	2	167	2– 6–1783	Hinkstons Fk	Surveyed
Johnson, Cave	2,000	3	27	11– 1–1783	Main Licking	Surveyed
Johnson, Cave	400	3	254	3–30–1784	Stoners Fk	Withdrawn
Johnson, Cave	3,000	3	295	4–21–1784	None	
Johnson, Cave	625	3	299	4–23–1784	Glenns Cr	Surveyed
Johnson, Cave	345	3	327	5– 6–1784	None	Withdrawn
Johnson, Cave	400	3	351	6– 1–1784	Licking	Surveyed
Johnson, Cave	50	3	376	6–18–1784	——— R	Withdrawn
Johnson, Cave	200	3	388	6–28–1784	Licking	Surveyed
Johnson, Cave	230	3	398	7– 9–1784	Hingston & Stoners Fks	Surveyed
Johnson, Cave	1,570	3	399	7– 9–1784	Main Fk Licking	
Johnson, Cave	345	4	229	10–28–1785	N Fk Elkhorn	Surveyed
Johnson, Cave	50	4	300	6– 6–1786	None	
Johnson, Cave & Ben	4,500	3	295	4–21–1784	None	Surveyed
Johnson, Cave & Benj	5,571	3	327	5– 6–1784	None	
Johnson, Cave & Robt	2,000	3	326	5– 6–1784	None	Surveyed
Johnson, Jonah	501	3	252	3–30–1784	None	
Johnson, John	515	2	41	1–11–1783	N Br Elkhorn	Surveyed
Johnson, John	500	2	41	1–11–1783	Glens Cr	Withdrawn
Johnson, John	2,300	2	41	1–11–1783	Drennons Lick Cr	Surveyed
Johnson, Jno	540	4	75	12– 4–1784	Br Ohio R	
Johnson, Jno	500	4	303	7–31–1786	None	
Johnson, Lancelot	500	1	98	12–10–1782	Small Mountain Cr.	
Johnson, Rinaldo	60,000	2	253	3–24–1783	Cow Fk Ky R	Surveyed
Johnson, Robert	2,000	1	19	12– 4–1782	Dry Cr	Surveyed
Johnson, Robert	1,000	1	68	12– 6–1782	Dry Run Cr	Surveyed
Johnson, Robert	1,000	1	68	12– 6–1782	Hingston Fk	Surveyed

Entree	Acres	Book	Page	Entry Date	Watercourse	Notes
Johnson, Robert	1,000	1	69	12– 6–1782	Hingston Fk	Surveyed
Johnson, Robert	1,000	1	69	12– 9–1782	Green Cr & Main Licking	Surveyed
Johnson, Robert	1,000	1	70	12– 9–1782	———— Cr	Surveyed
Johnson, Robert	1,000	1	70	12– 9–1782	———— Cr	Surveyed
Johnson, Robert	1,000	1	70	12– 9–1782	Br Licking	Surveyed
Johnson, Robert	1,000	1	70	12– 9–1782	N Fk Elkhorn	Surveyed
Johnson, Robert	400	1	71	12– 9–1782	Br N Fk Elkhorn	Surveyed
Johnson, Robert	1,000	1	71	12– 9–1782	M Br Lawrence Cr	Amended
Johnson, Robert	1,000	1	71	12– 9–1782	————	Surveyed
Johnson, Robert	1,000	1	71	12– 9–1782	Timber Ridge Run	Surveyed
Johnson, Robert	1,000	1	71	12– 9–1782	Lees Cr	....
Johnson, Robert	1,000	1	72	12– 9–1782	N E Br Licking	Surveyed
Johnson, Robert	1,000	1	72	12– 9–1782	———— Cr	Surveyed
Johnson, Robert	1,000	1	73	12– 9–1782	———— Cr	Surveyed
Johnson, Robert	1,000	1	73	12– 9–1782	N E Br Licking	Surveyed
Johnson, Robert	————	1	73	12– 9–1782	Br Licking	Surveyed
Johnson, Robert	1,000	1	74	12– 9–1782	Br N Fk Licking	Surveyed
Johnson, Robert	1,000	1	74	12– 9–1782	Br E Fk Coper Run	Surveyed
Johnson, Robert	1,000	1	75	12– 9–1782	Br Clear Cr	Surveyed
Johnson, Robert	1,000	1	76	12– 9–1782	N Fk Clear Cr	Surveyed
Johnson, Robert	1,000	1	76	12– 9–1782	————	Surveyed
Johnson, Robert	1,000	1	76	12– 9–1782	Greens Cr	Surveyed
Johnson, Robert	1,000	1	77	12– 9–1782	Lees Cr	Surveyed
Johnson, Robert	1,000	1	77	12– 9–1782	Hingston Fk	Surveyed
Johnson, Robert	1,000	1	77	12– 9–1782	M Br Clear Cr	Surveyed
Johnson, Robert	1,000	1	77	12– 9–1782	N Fk Elkhorn	Surveyed
Johnson, Robert	1,000	1	78	12– 9–1782	———— Cr	Surveyed
Johnson, Robert	1,000	1	78	12– 9–1782	N Fk Licking	Surveyed
Johnson, Robert	1,000	1	78	12– 9–1782	W Fk Licking	Surveyed
Johnson, Robert	1,000	1	79	12– 9–1782	N Fk Buck Lick	Surveyed
Johnson, Robert	1,000	1	79	12– 9–1782	———— Cr	Surveyed
Johnson, Robert	1,000	1	79	12– 9–1782	———— Cr	Surveyed
Johnson, Robert	1,000	1	79	12– 9–1782	———— Cr	Surveyed
Johnson, Robert	1,000	1	79	12– 9–1782	Mill Cr	Surveyed
Johnson, Robert	1,000	1	80	12– 9–1782	N Fk McConnells Run	Surveyed
Johnson, Robert	1,000	1	80	12– 9–1782	Hingston Fk	Surveyed
Johnson, Robert	1,000	1	80	12– 9–1782	Clear Cr	Surveyed
Johnson, Robert	1,000	1	81	1–13–1783	None	Surveyed
Johnson, Robert	1,000	1	81	1–13–1783	Hingston Fk	Surveyed
Johnson, Robert	1,000	1	81	1–13–1783	Stoners Fk	Surveyed
Johnson, Robert	1,000	1	81	1–13–1783	N Fk Hingstons Fk	Surveyed
Johnson, Robert	1,000	1	81	1–13–1783	Elkhorn	Surveyed
Johnson, Robert	1,000	1	82	12– 9–1782	N Fk Elkhorn	Surveyed
Johnson, Robert	1,000	1	82	12– 9–1782	Stoners Fk	Surveyed
Johnson, Robert	1,000	1	82	12– 9–1782	————	Surveyed
Johnson, Robert	200	1	87	12– 9–1782	Cave Run	Surveyed
Johnson, Robert	1,000	1	108	12–11–1782	None	Surveyed
Johnson, Robert	731	1	116	12–12–1782	N Fk Elkhorn	Surveyed
Johnson, Robert	1,000	1	117	12–12–1782	Br Jessamine Cr	Surveyed
Johnson, Robert	500	1	128	12–13–1782	N Fk Elkhorn	Surveyed
Johnson, Robert	500	1	196	12–20–1782	Licking	....
Johnson, Robert	500	1	196	12–20–1782	Licking	....
Johnson, Robert	1,200	1	306	12–28–1782	None	Surveyed
Johnson, Robert	500	1	306	12–28–1782	None	Surveyed
Johnson, Robert	2,000	2	3	1– 8–1783	None	Surveyed
Johnson, Robert	2,000	2	3	1– 8–1783	None	Surveyed
Johnson, Robert	2,000	2	4	1– 8–1783	None	Surveyed
Johnson, Robert	400	2	27	1–10–1783	N Fk Elkhorn	Withdrawn
Johnson, Robert	400	2	28	1–10–1783	Millers Cr	Surveyed
Johnson, Robert	2,000	2	29	1–10–1783	None	Surveyed
Johnson, Robert	1,000	2	29	1–10–1783	Buckhorn Cr	Surveyed
Johnson, Robert	910½	2	35	1–10–1783	Lick of Tygerts Cr	....
Johnson, Robert	1,610	2	35	1–10–1783	Clay Lick on Tygerts Cr	....
Johnson, Robert	2,100	2	36	1–11–1783	Sandy	....
Johnson, Robert	2,000	2	36	1–11–1783	Sandy	....
Johnson, Robert	1,046	2	37	1–11–1783	Sandy	....
Johnson, Robert	1,000	2	52	1–13–1783	Millers Cr	Surveyed
Johnson, Robert	2,000	2	170	2– 7–1783	Hinkstons Mill Cr	....
Johnson, Robert	1,266	2	170	2– 7–1783	None	....
Johnson, Robert	400	2	172	2– 7–1783	Cane Run & N Fk Elkhorn	Surveyed
Johnson, Robert	100	2	173	2– 7–1783	N Fk Elkhorn	....
Johnson, Robert	300	2	173	2– 7–1783	N Fk Elkhorn	Withdrawn
Johnson, Robert	200	2	173	2– 7–1783	N Fk Elkhorn	Surveyed
Johnson, Robert	100	2	213	2–28–1783	None	Surveyed
Johnson, Robert	781	2	243	3–14–1783	Elkhorn	Surveyed
Johnson, Robert	709½	2	243	3–14–1783	Elkhorn	Surveyed

Entree	Acres	Book	Page	Entry Date	Watercourse	Notes
Johnson, Robt.., ...	1,000	2	289	5–21–1783	None	Surveyed
Johnson, Robt	1,000	2	289	5–21–1783	None	
Johnson, Robert	200	2	290	5–21–1783	Elkhorn	
Johnson, Robert	200	2	290	5–21–1783	Elkhorn	
Johnson, Robert	400	2	290	5–21–1783	Elkhorn	
Johnson, Robert	80	2	291	5–21–1783	N Fk Elkhorn	Surveyed
Johnson, Robert	80	2	291	5–21–1783	N Fk Elkhorn	
Johnson, Robert	300	2	291	5–21–1783	Shannons Run	
Johnson, Robt	——	2	294	5–26–1783	None	Surveyed
Johnson, Robt	1,000	2	303	5–31–1783	None	
Johnson, Robt	10,662½	2	338	8– 1–1783	Ohio R	
Johnson, Robt	500	2	360	9– 9–1783	Harrods Salt Lick Cr	
Johnson, Robt	500	2	360	9– 9–1783	—— Cr	
Johnson, Robt	1,500	2	362	9–10–1783	Salt Lick Cr	
Johnson, Robt	1,500	2	362	9–10–1783	Salt Lick Cr	
Johnson, Robt	400	3	14	10–25–1783	None	Withdrawn
Johnson, Robt	1,000	3	74	12– 8–1783	S Fk Elkhorn	Surveyed
Johnson, Robt	1,093	3	171	1–31–1784	None	Surveyed
Johnson, Robt	1,000	3	171	1–31–1784	None	Surveyed
Johnson, Robt	1,000	3	171	1–31–1784	None	Surveyed
Johnson, Robt	——	3	180	2–11–1784	None	Surveyed
Johnson, Robt	50	3	181	2–12–1784	N Fk Elkhorn	
Johnson, Robt	775	3	192	3– 1–1784	Elkhorn	Surveyed
Johnson, Robt	9,115	3	251	3–30–1784	Licking	
Johnson, Robt	100	3	253	3–30–1784	N Fk Elkhorn	
Johnson, Robt	1,000	3	291	4–16–1784	Bank Lick Cr	Surveyed
Johnson, Robt	224	3	291	4–16–1784	None	Surveyed
Johnson, Robt	92	3	292	4–16–1784	N Fk Elkhorn	Surveyed
Johnson, Robt	400	3	292	4–16–1784	None	Surveyed
Johnson, Robt	150	3	292	4–16–1784	None	
Johnson, Robt	180	3	292	4–16–1784	N Fk Elkhorn	Surveyed
Johnson, Robt	430	3	294	4–19–1784	None	
Johnson, Robt	7,537	3	303	4–26–1784	None	
Johnson, Robt	390	3	376	6–18–1784	N Fk Elkhorn	Surveyed
Johnson, Robt	200	3	414	7–21–1784	Cane Run	Surveyed
Johnson, Robt	416	4	47	10– 9–1784	N Fk Elkhorn	Surveyed
Johnson, Robt	434	4	47	10– 9–1784	N Fk Elkhorn	Withdrawn
Johnson, Robt	1,000	4	200	6–17–1785	None	
Johnson, Robt	281	4	253	1– 9–1786	N Fk Elkhorn	
Johnson, Robt	300	4	316	10–30–1787	N Fk Elkhorn	
Johnson, Samuel	100	2	53	1–13–1783	Small Sinking Spring	Withdrawn
Johnson, Samuel	100	2	281	4–29–1783	None	
Johnson, Samuel	214	3	85	12–12–1783	None	Withdrawn
Johnson, Samuel	1,000	3	180	2–11–1784	War Road	Surveyed
Johnson, Samuel	700	4	94	1–18–1785	Jessamine Cr	Surveyed
Johnson, Samuel	214	4	94	1–18–1785	Ky R	
Johnson, Samuel	575	4	343	1–18–1785	Jessamine Cr	Surveyed
Johnson, Thomas	950	1	356	1– 3–1783	S Fk Clear Cr	Surveyed
Johnson & Cooper	1,000	3	257	3–30–1784	None	Surveyed
Johnson & Craig	50,000	3	249	3–29–1784	Licking	Surveyed
Johnson & Craig	2,000	3	325	5– 6–1784	None	
Johnson & Craig	2,892	3	330	5–13–1784	None	
Johnson & Walker	4,987½	3	76	12– 9–1783	Salt Lick Cr	Withdrawn
Johnson & Walker	4,987½	3	303	4–26–1784	None	Withdrawn
Johnston, Cave	400	1	49	12– 5–1782	Bank of Ohio	Surveyed
Johnston, James	100	1	48	12– 4–1782	Ky R	
Johnston, Peter, heirs	1,000	2	301	5–30–1783	Licking	
Johnston, Robert	2,000	1	22	12– 3–1782	Elkhorn	
Johnston, Robert	1,000	1	31	12–18–1782	Ohio	Surveyed
Johnston, Robert	1,000	1	41	12– 4–1782	—— Cr	Surveyed
Johnston, Robert	1,000	1	46	12– 4–1782	—— Cr	Surveyed
Johnston, Robert	300	1	47	12– 4–1782	Clifts of River	Withdrawn
Johnston, Robert	1,000	1	65	12– 6–1782	Licking	Surveyed
Johnston, Robert	1,000	1	65	12– 6–1782	—— Cr	
Johnston, Robert	1,000	1	66	1–20–1783	Big Dry Run	Amended
Johnston, Robert	1,000	1	67	12– 6–1782	Dry Branch	Surveyed
Johnston, Robert	1,000	1	75	12– 9–1782	Clear Cr	
Johnston, Wm	714	3	136	1– 5–1784	None	
Joice, Daniel & Edward	50,000	3	377	6–19–1784	None	Surveyed
Jolley, James	1,000	2	295	5–26–1783	None	
Jones, David	1,603½	1	344	1– 1–1783	None	
Jones, Gabriel, heirs	1,000	4	305	10– 9–1786	None	
Jones, Henry	6,066	3	164	1–22–1784	Bank Lick Cr	Withdrawn
Jones, Henry	6,066	3	243	3–26–1784	None	
Jones, Henry	6,066	4	321	2–19–1788	None	
Jones, John	500	1	18	12– 4–1782	None	Surveyed
Jones, John	700	1	212	12–21–1782	None	Surveyed
Jones, Jno	10,000	3	164	1–22–1784	Bank Lick Cr	
Jones, Jno	8,000	3	164	1–22–1784	Bank Lick Cr	
Jones, Jno	400	3	233	3–22–1784	r h Fk Stamping Ground Cr	

Entree	Acres	Book	Page	Entry Date	Watercourse	Notes
Jones, Jno	18,000	3	243	3-26-1784	None	
Jones, Thomas	250	2	101	1-21-1783	None	
Jones, William	4,000	1	360	1- 4-1783	S Fk Bank Lick Cr.	Surveyed
Jones, William	500	1	360	1- 4-1783	Fk Salt Lick	
Jones, William	4,000	1	376	1- 6-1783	Flat Cr	Surveyed
Jones, William	3,925	2	47	1-13-1783	Red R	
Jones, William	2,000	2	69	1-15-1783	N Fk Licking	Surveyed
Jones, William	500	2	124	1-25-1783	Raven Cr	
Jones, Wm	2,700	3	134	1- 2-1784	None	Surveyed
Jouitt, Jno	1,000	4	307	10-30-1786	Ky R	
Judy, Jacob	5,662	3	406	7-14-1784	Licking	
Julian, James	10,000	3	324	5- 4-1784	Br S Fk Sandy	Surveyed
Julian, James	11,202½	3	324	5- 4-1784	Br Licking	Surveyed
Kavenaugh, Charles	1,000	1	247	12-23-1782	McConnells Run	Surveyed
Kay, John	10,937½	2	376	10-13-1783	Licking	
Kay & Calk	1,288½	3	127	1- 1-1784	Br Red R	
Kee, James	1,000	3	150	1-15-1784	None	
Keevers, Duval	4,600	2	184	2-13-1783	None	
Keith, Alexander	70	4	209	7-20-1785	None	
Keith, John	993½	1	303	12-27-1782	Licking & Elkhorn	
Keith, Thos	33,668¾	3	20	10-30-1783	Ohio R	20,626 acres surveyed 1,342 acres withdrawn
Keith, Thos	13,042	4	279	3- 3-1786	None	
Keith, Thos	13,042	4	279	3- 3-1786	Br S Fk Sandy	
Keith & Morgan	1,000	3	131	1- 2-1784	None	
Kelgore, George	800	2	267	4- 7-1783	W Fk Howards Upper Cr	Surveyed
Kelley, Edmund	3,000	1	320	12-30-1782	Robert Taylors Cr.	Withdrawn
Kelley, John	390	1	36	12- 4-1782	Between Ohio & Licking	
Kelley, Samuel	50	1	52	12- 5-1782	Hickman Cr	Withdrawn
Kelley, Samuel	1,000	2	305	6- 2-1783	None	Surveyed
Kelly, Samuel	250	3	91	12-15-1783	None	Surveyed
Kelley, Emanuel	2,270	3	192	3- 1-1784	Licking	
Kelley, Joseph	5,926¾	3	204	3- 5-1784	Eagle Cr	
Kelley, Samuel	50	4	69	11-19-1784	None	Withdrawn
Kelly, Emanuel	1,556	1	367	1- 4-1783	Br Hinkstons Fk	Withdrawn
Kelly, Emanuel	500	1	367	1- 4-1783	Licking	Withdrawn
Kelly, Emanuel	1,038½	2	64	1-14-1783	E Br Stoners Fk	Withdrawn
Kelly, Emanuel	4,774½	2	120	1-24-1783	Sycamore Fk Hinkston	Surveyed
Kelly, Emanuel	4,130	2	161	2- 4-1783	Sycamore Fk	Withdrawn
Kelly, Emanuel	1,556	2	319	7-10-1783	None	Withdrawn
Kelly, Joseph	3,000	2	373	10- 6-1783	Br Ohio R	Surveyed
Kelly, Samuel	731	2	212	2-27-1783	S Fk Elkhorn	Surveyed
Kelly, Samuel	765	4	165	4-29-1785	None	
Kelly, Samuel	765	4	164	4-29-1785	None	
Kelney, Peter	325	1	7	12-13-1782	Hinkstons Fk	
Kelpatrick, Jas	2,543	3	96	12-17-1783	Licking	
Kembrough, Robt	6,800¼	4	273	2-15-1786	Sandy	
Kembrough, Robt	6,800	4	295	4-29-1786	None	
Kenedy, Thomas	328	2	285	5-12-1783	Hingston Fk	Withdrawn
Kenedy, William	1,000	2	33	1-10-1783	Ohio R	Withdrawn
Kenedy, William	1,000	2	33	1-10-1783	Wells Cr	Withdrawn
Kenkaid, John	5,000	2	237	3-13-1783	Br Ohio R	
Kenkead, Jno	300	3	308	4-29-1784	Ohio R	
Kenkead, Jno	300	3	308	4-29-1784	None	
Kennady, Thos	288	3	416	7-27-1784	Strodes Fk	Surveyed
Kennady, Thos	9,288	4	50	9-13-1784	None	Surveyed
Kennady, Wm	850	4	52	10-14-1784	Ohio R	
Kennady, Wm	9,951	4	149	4-10-1785	None	
Kennady, Wm	22,496	4	149	4-10-1785	None	
Kennady, Wm	12,545	3	262	3-31-1784	None	Withdrawn
Kennady, Wm	9,951	3	268	4- 6-1784	None	Withdrawn
Kennady, Wm	5,150	4	216	8- 5-1785	Licking & Ohio R	
Kennedy, John	930½	2	132	1-27-1783	None	
Kennedy, Joseph	1,000	1	202	12-20-1782	None	Surveyed
Kennedy, Robert	1,559½	2	131	1-27-1783	None	
Kennedy, William	50	1	50	12- 5-1782	Stoners Fk	
Kennedy, William	200	1	210	12-20-1782	Hickmans Cr	Surveyed
Kennedy, William	400	1	210	12-20-1782	Hickman Cr	Surveyed
Kennedy, William	1,000	1	211	12-20-1782	None	
Kennedy, William	400	1	211	12-20-1782	None	Surveyed
Kennedy, William	400	1	211	12-20-1782	Ohio R	Surveyed
Kennedy, William	1,000	1	212	12-20-1782	Stoners Fk	
Kennedy, William	400	1	213	12-20-1782	Ohio R	Surveyed
Kennedy, William	600	1	213	12-20-1782	Ohio R	Surveyed
Kennedy, William	400	1	236	12-23-1782	Buffalo Road	

Entree	Acres	Book	Page	Entry Date	Watercourse	Notes
Kennedy, William	300	1	237	12–23–1782	None	
Kennedy, William	400	2	32	1–10–1783	Ohio R	Surveyed
Kennedy, William	400	2	32	1–10–1783	Ohio R	
Kennedy, William	2,625	2	129	1–27–1783	None	
Kennedy, William	1,400	2	138	1–29–1783	Ohio R	Surveyed
Kennedy, William	1,500	2	149	2– 1–1783	Ohio R	Surveyed
Kennedy, William	1,000	2	150	2– 1–1783	Ohio R	Surveyed
Kennedy, William	1,400	2	151	2– 1–1783	Wells Cr	Surveyed
Kennedy, William	800	2	152	2– 1–1783	Ohio R	Surveyed
Kennedy, William	1,025	2	152	2- 1–1783	Ohio R	
Kennedy, William	1,000	2	153	2– 1–1783	Gists Cr	
Kennedy, William	1,000	2	156	2– 1–1783	Lees Cr	Surveyed
Kennedy, William	400	2	202	2–18–1783	Stoners Fk	
Kennerly, Jno	1,000	3	411	7–17–1784	None	
Kenney, Matthew	500	1	164	12–18–1782	Br Marble Cr	Withdrawn
Kenny, Joseph	1,000	1	383	1– 6–1783	Coopers Run	
Kenny, Matthew	500	2	103	1–21–1783	None	
Kenney, James	409¾	3	388	6–29–1784	Stoners Fk	
Kennon, Luke	60,000	3	237	3–24–1784	N Fk Elkhorn	30,000 acres withdrawn
Kennon, Luke	30,000	4	82	1– 5–1785	Slate Cr	11,000 acres withdrawn
Kennon, Luke	9,000	4	130	3– 7–1785	None	
Kenton, John	5,000	1	345	1– 1–1783	House Cr	Surveyed
Kenton, Mark	4,750	3	245	3–26–1784	Johnsons Fk	Amended
Kenton, Mark	4,750	3	335	5–17–1784	None	
Kenton, Philip C & Thos	2,000	3	335	5–17–1784	——— Cr	
Kenton, Simon	2,000	1	346	1– 2–1783	Wells Cr	Surveyed
Kenton, Simon	5,119	2	31	1–10–1783	Clay Lick	Surveyed
Kenton, Simon	5,496	2	32	1–10–1783	Tagarts Cr	
Kenton, Simon	200	2	41	1–11–1783	None	
Kenton, Simon	4,045	3	156	1–19–1784	Licking	Surveyed
Kenton, Simon	1,000	3	244	3–26–1784	Cane Run	
Kenton, Simon	15,000	4	211	7–28–1785	Tygerts Cr	
Kerchevall, Jno	200	4	298	4–29–1786	None	
Kercheval, Jno	5,500	4	298	4–29–1786	None	
Kerns, Thos	2,000	4	193	6– 6–1785	N Fk Ky R	
Kimbro, Robt	400	3	42	11–13–1783	3 Fks R	
Kimbro, Robt	400	3	42	11–13–1783	Howards Big Cr	
King, Henry	1,000	3	364	6–14–1784	None	
King, John	2,943½	2	14	1– 9–1783	Br Licking	
King, John E	2,457½	2	228	3–10–1783	Licking Cr	
King, John E	500	2	274	4– 9–1783	N Fk Licking	
Kincaid, Andrew	2,026	2	19	1– 9–1783	Br Eagle Cr	Surveyed
Kincaid, Wm	1,000	3	147	1–15–1784	Big Bone Lick Cr	
Kinkead, John	664½	2	84	1–18–1783	Br Eagle Cr	Surveyed
Kinkead, William	2,026	2	19	1– 9–1783	Br Eagle Cr	Surveyed
Kinkead, Samuel	712	2	189	2–13–1783	None	
Kinney, Daniel	285	3	170	1–29–1784	Lower Blue Lick	
Kinney, Joseph	400	4	140	3–25–1785	Caperos Fk Licking	
Kircheval, Jno	2,000	3	392	7– 1–1784	S Fk Licking	
Kircheval, Jno	200	3	392	7– 1–1784	None	Withdrawn
Kirchwell, Jno	10,083¼	4	133	3–16–1785	Caperos Lick	Withdrawn
Kircheval, Wm	413⅔	3	252	3–30–1784	Buffaloe Road	
Kirkwell, Jno	10,083¾	4	229	10–28–1785	None	
Kizer, Christopher	1,000	3	202	3– 4–1784	None	Withdrawn
Kokintaffer, Christopher	1,000	3	74	12– 8–1783	Hinkston Fk	
Kurtz, Nicholas	846¼	4	336	10– 6–1792	None	
Kurtz, Nicholas	846¼	4	336	10– 6–1792	S Fk Elkhorn & Jessamine	
Lackie, Samuel	1,200	2	131	1–27–1783	None	
Laele, George	49	2	241	3–13–1783	None	
Lair, Andrew	346½	2	240	8– 5–1783	Indian Cr	
Lamb, Wm	400	1	32	12– 3–1782	None	
Lamb, William	400	2	219	3– 1–1783	None	Surveyed
Lambert, Daniel	550	1	21	12– 2–1782	——— Cr	
Lambert, David	1,000	2	310	6– 7–1783	None	
Lambert, David	1,000	2	310	6– 7–1783	None	
Lambert, David	1,000	2	311	6– 7–1783	None	
Lambert, David	9,000	2	311	6– 9–1783	Gap Sciota Mt	
Lancaster, Ralph	10,000	4	133	3–13–1785	Licking	
Lancaster, Ralph	10,000	4	171	5– 6–1785	None	
Lang, John	400	1	124	12–12–1782	Clear Cr	
Lang, Joseph	600	2	66	1–15–1783	Ky R	Surveyed
Langham, Elias	6,666⅔	3	34	11– 8–1783	Clear Cr	Surveyed
Langham, Elias	3,566⅔	3	45	11–14–1783	Ohio R	
Langham, Elias	2,500	3	48	11–17–1783	Slate Cr	
Langham, Elias	2,600	3	49	11–17–1783	Slate Cr	
Langham, Elias	450	3	64	12– 1–1783	Jessamine Cr	
Langham, Elias	1,400	3	69	12– 4–1783	S Fk Sandy	

Entree	Acres	Book	Page	Entry Date	Watercourse	Notes
Langham, Elias	1,250	3	70	12–14–1783	—— Cr	
Langham, Elias	1,166⅔	3	358	6–12–1784	Big Sandy	
Lapsley, James	3,672	2	24	1–10–1783	None	
Lapsley, Jas	3,672	4	336	11–13–1793	None	
Lapsley, Joseph	675	2	24	1–10–1783	None	
Lapsley, Joseph	675	1	24	11–13–1793	None	
Lapsley, Samuel	1,000	1	199	12–20–1782	Big Bone Lick	Surveyed
Lawrence, Jno	225,000	3	353	6– 4–1784	Ky R	Amended
Lawrence, Joseph	459½	4	146	4–10–1785	None	
Lawrence, Saml	3,000	4	145	4–10–1785	Little Sandy	
Lay, Francis W	400	4	196	6– 9–1785	None	
Lay, Winright	2,000	1	121	12–12–1782	N Fk Clear Cr	Surveyed
Layne, Hordage	1,000	3	273	4– 6–1784	Small Mt Cr	Surveyed
Layne, James H	300	3	198	3– 2–1784	Hinkston Fk	Surveyed
Leathers, John	1,000	1	219	12–21–1782	None	
Leathers, Joshua	1,250	2	4	1– 8–1783	None	Surveyed
LeCompte, Charles	400	2	102	1–21–1783	N Fk Elkhorn	Surveyed
LeCompte, Charles	1,000	2	102	1–21–1783	Br N Fk Elkhorn	Surveyed
Ledgerwood, Wm	500	4	17	8–17–1784	—— R	Surveyed
Lee, Arthur	9,937½	1	384	1– 6–1783	Blue Lick	
Lee, Chas	1,705	4	289	4–13–1786	None	
Lee, Chas	1,705	3	186	2–18–1784	Ohio R	
Lee, Edmund	6,000	2	198	2–17–1783	M Licking	Surveyed
Lee, Henry	1,000	2	158	2– 1–1783	Licking	Surveyed
Lee, Henry	200	3	140	1–10–1784	None	
Lee, Henry	400	3	307	4–29–1784	Hinkston Fk	
Lee, Henry	1,000	3	312	4–30–1784	Glenns Cr	
Lee, Henry	250	3	313	4–30–1784	Licking	
Lee, Henry	400	3	313	4–30–1784	Hickman Cr	
Lee, Henry	1,000	3	313	4–30–1784	Hinkston & Spencer Crs	
Lee, Henry	419½	3	313	4–30–1784	Br Licking	
Lee, Henry	200	3	313	4–30–1784	Marble Cr	
Lee, Henry	400	3	314	4–30–1784	S Fk Elkhorn	
Lee, Henry	400	3	315	4–30–1784	Hinkston Fk	
Lee, Henry	1,000	3	316	4–30–1784	N Fk Elkhorn	
Lee, Henry	400	3	316	4–30–1784	N Fk Elkhorn	
Lee, Henry	1,000	3	316	4–30–1784	Hustons Fk	
Lee, Henry	1,000	3	317	4–30–1784	Huston Fk	
Lee, Henry	2,000	3	317	4–30–1784	Hinkston Fk	
Lee, Henry	1,000	3	348	5–28–1784	Clear Cr	
Lee, Henry	4,933	4	69	11–23–1784	Cedar Cr	
Lee, Henry	8,862½	4	156	4–21–1785	None	
Lee, Henry	9,862½	4	157	4–26–1785	None	Withdrawn
Lee, Henry	9,862½	4	246	12–21–1785	Ohio R	
Lee, Henry	400	4	290	4–13–1786	Lawrence Cr	
Lee, Henry	400	4	290	4–13–1786	Lawrence Cr	
Lee, Jno	1,000	3	400	7–10–1784	N Fk Licking	Surveyed
Lee, Jno	1,000	4	101	1–28–1785	Main Fk Elkhorn	Surveyed
Lee, Richard	10,000	2	128	1–27–1783	Main Fk Licking	Surveyed
Lee, Richard	1,000	2	158	2– 1–1783	Licking Cr	Surveyed
Lee, Richard	4,806	2	197	2–17–1783	None	Surveyed
Lee, Richard Bland	6,000	2	198	2–17–1783	M Licking	
Lee, Thomas	1,400	2	17	1– 9–1783	Graves Cr	Surveyed
Lee, Thos	2,296	4	263	1–21–1786	None	Withdrawn
Lee, Thos	2,296	4	270	2– 7–1786	Sandy	
Lee, William	1,000	2	51	1–13–1783	None	Surveyed.
Leeper, John	224	2	243	3–13–1783	None	
Leforce, Benne	1,000	4	210	7–22–1785	None	
Leforce, Randolph	200	3	69	12– 3–1783	None	
Lehee, Abijah	425	4	220	9– 3–1785	Step Stone Cr	
Lehee, Abijah	75	4	220	9– 3–1785	—— Cr	
Leitch, David	15,000	1	224	12–21–1782	N Fk M Licking	Surveyed
Leitch, David	300	3	225	3–11–1784	Howards Cr	Withdrawn
Leitch, David	50,000	3	289	3–25–1784	Br Hinkston Fk	Withdrawn
Leitch, David	20,000	3	305	4–28–1784	None	
Leitch, David	50,000	3	349	5–29–1784	Licking	Surveyed
Leitch, David	52,000	3	396	7– 7–1784	Licking	6,000 acres withdrawn
Leitch, David	5,000	3	402	7–13–1784	None	
Leitch, David	450	3	402	7–13–1784	Big Slate Cr	
Leitch, David	2,000	3	402	7–13–1784	Small Mt & Licking	
Leitch, David	2,000	3	403	7–13–1784	Main Licking	
Leitch, David	550	3	403	7–13–1784	Licking	
Leitch, David	8,000	3	417	7–28–1784	None	
Leitch, David	3,000	3	417	7–28–1784	None	2,750 acres surveyed
Leitch, David	8,000	3	417	7–28–1784	None	2,750 acres surveyed
Leitch, David	27,000	3	418	7–30–1784	None	

Entree	Acres	Book	Page	Entry Date	Watercourse	Notes
Leitch, David	250	3	418	7–30–1784	None	
Leitch, David	30,250	3	418	7–30–1784	None	Withdrawn
Leitch, David	9,000	3	421	8– 5–1784	None	
Leitch, David	9,000	3	422	8– 5–1784	Licking	
Leitch, David	7,000	4	5	8–14–1784	None	
Leitch, David	30,250	4	13	8–14–1784	None	
Leitch, David	20,000	4	58	10–25–1784	None	
Leitch, David	300	4	58	10–25–1784	None	
Leitch, David	10,550	4	58	10–25–1784	None	Withdrawn
Leitch, David	18,550	4	69	11–23–1784	None	
Leitch, David	15,000	4	70	11–25–1784	Slate Cr	
Leitch, David	52,000	3	246	3–26–1784	Hinston Fk	Withdrawn
Leitch, David	3,550	4	70	11–25–1784	Slate Cr	
Leitch & Fowler Jr	30,771½	3	306	4–28–1784	None	
Leitch & Howard	15,000	4	8	8–14–1784	Twins Cr & Ky R	
Lenwright, John	1,600	1	43	12– 4–1782	Salt Sp Trace	
Leslie, George	500	2	150	2– 1–1783	Ohio R	
Letherman, Christian	2,000	4	112	2– 5–1785	—— Cr	
Letherman, Christian	1,000	4	112	2– 5–1785	—— Cr	
Lewis, Aaron	200	1	42	12– 4–1782	—— Cr	
Lewis, Aaron	500	1	248	12–24–1782	None	
Lewis, Aaron	1,000	1	248	12–24–1782	Red River	
Lewis, Aaron	10,000	1	249	12–23–1782	Licking	Surveyed
Lewis, Aaron	1,000	1	305	12–28–1782	Licking	
Lewis, Aaron	1,000	1	391	1– 7–1783	None	
Lewis, Aaron	8,000	4	299	5–22–1786	None	
Lewis, Aaron	8,000	4	299	5–24–1786	Br Boones Cr	4,058 acres surveyed
Lewis, Aaron	8,000	4	301	7–11–1786	Raven Cr	Surveyed
Lewis, Fielding	40,518	3	415	7–23–1784	None	
Lewis, Howell	1,250	1	45	12– 4–1782	Grassey & Bank Lick Crs	Surveyed
Lewis, Howell	1,250	1	45	12– 4–1782	Licking	Surveyed
Lewis, Howell	1,000	1	46	12– 4–1782	Fks of Licking	
Lewis, Howell Sr	3,500	1	45	12– 4–1782	Grassey & M Fk Bank Cr	Surveyed
Lewis, John	1,000	2	25	1–10–1783	Br Ky R	Surveyed
Lewis, John	600	2	224	3– 7–1783	Sycamore Fk	
Lewis, John	1,000	2	226	3–10–1783	Ohio R	Surveyed
Lewis, Jno	3,000	3	155	1–17–1784	Elkhorn	Withdrawn
Lewis, Jno	4,466	3	276	4– 7–1784	M Fk Millers Cr	
Lewis, Jno	3,000	3	371	6–16–1784	None	
Lewis, Jno	8,347½	3	371	6–16–1784	Elkhorn	6,847½ acres surveyed
Lewis, Jno	1,000	4	100	1–27–1785	None	
Lewis, Jno	1,000	4	101	1–27–1785	None	
Lewis, Jno	100	4	300	6– 5–1786	Jessamine Cr	
Lewis, Lewis	1,000	1	347	1– 2–1783	Br Sandy	
Lewis, Robert	2,000	2	29	1–10–1783	None	Surveyed
Lewis, Thomas	2,000	2	269	4– 7–1783	Stoners Fk	Surveyed
Lewis, Thos	5,000	3	8	10–15–1783	Ohio R	
Lewis, Thos	6,000	4	231	11– 4–1785	Town Fk Elkhorn	Surveyed
Lewis, William	1,000	1	348	1– 2–1783	Br Sandy	
Lewis, William	1,000	1	348	1– 2–1783	Br Sandy	
Lewis, William	1,000	1	348	1– 2–1783	Br Sandy	
Lewis, Berry & Hazlerigg	8,000	4	233	11– 9–1785	Ky R	Withdrawn
Lewis & Marshall	5,000	3	9	10–15–1783	None	
Lewis & Morgan	4,661	3	129	1– 1–1784	Ohio R	
Lewis & Morgan	3,000	3	195	3– 2–1784	Clements Fk	
Lewis & Waller	5,000	4	151	4–10–1785	Cabbin Cr	
Lewis & Wilkinson	20,000	4	155	4–20–1785	None	
Lightfoot, William	4,569	1	286	12–26–1782	None	Surveyed
Lightle, William	622½	1	351	1– 2–1783	N Fk Elkhorn	Surveyed
Lincoln, Hannaniah	8,972½	2	77	1–17–1783	Ky R	Surveyed
Lincoln, Hanniah	1,000	2	247	3–15–1783	None	
Lincoln, Hanniah	200	3	169	1–26–1784	Ky R & Hickman Cr	
Lindsey, Arthur	400	1	104	12–11–1782	S Fk Elkhorn	Surveyed
Lindsey, James	1,000	1	44	12– 4–1782	E Fk S Elkhorn	Surveyed
Lindsey, James	1,000	2	209	2–26–1783	None	Surveyed
Lindsey, Joseph, heirs	400	2	78	1–17–1783	M Fk Elkhorn	Surveyed
Lindsey, Joseph, heirs	1,000	2	79	1–17–1783	Town Fk Elkhorn	
Lindsey, Joseph, heirs	313	4	300	6– 3–1786	Ky R	
Lindsey, William	1,000	1	45	12– 4–1782	E Fk S Elkhorn	Surveyed
Lindsey, William	293	2	92	1–20–1783	None	Surveyed
Lindsey, William	1,000	2	209	2–26–1783	None	Surveyed
Lines & Payne	500	3	410	7–16–1784	Jessamine Cr	
Linkhorn, Abraham	500	1	111	12–11–1782	—— R	
Linn, Nathan	400	2	300	5–30–1783	Hingston Fk	
Lipscomb, Joel	1,000	1	12	11–30–1782	Hingstons Fk	

Entree	Acres	Book	Page	Entry Date	Watercourse	Notes
Lipscomb, Thomas	1,400	1	13	11–30–1782	Licking	
Lipscomb, Wm	1,538	3	149	1–15–1784	None	Surveyed
Lipscomb, Wm	400	3	43	11–14–1783	Above Three Fks R	
Little, Edward	1,000½	1	382	1– 6–1783	Licking	Surveyed
Little, Hon Robert	1,000	4	191	6– 1–1785	Ohio R	Withdrawn
Little, William	1,000	1	390	1– 7–1783	None	
Little, William	1,200	2	72	1–16–1783	Licking	Surveyed
Little, William	1,000	2	119	1–24–1783	M Fk Elkhorn	
Littlepage, John Carter	20,000	2	128	1–27–1783	Br M Fk Licking	Surveyed
Litton, Solomon	400	2	51	1–13–1783	M Fk Coopers Run	
Lockhart, Jacob	1,200	1	107	12–11–1782	———	Surveyed
Lockhart, Jacob	13,225	4	211	7–28–1785	None	
Lodge, Jas	225,000	3	353	6– 4–1784	Ky R	Amended
Logan, Benjamin	1,161	1	161	12–17–1782	Ohio R	
Logan, David	300	3	377	6–19–1784	None	
Logan, Hugh	1,156½	4	111	2– 5–1785	Lick Cr	
Logan, Hugh	525	4	112	2– 5–1785	——— Cr	
Logan, Hugh	1,695	4	112	2– 5–1785	Ky R	
Logan, Hugh	1,000	4	112	2– 5–1785	Ky R	
Logan, James	1,042	2	67	1–15–1783	E Br Stoners Fk	Withdrawn
Logan, James	1,043	2	117	1–24–1783	E Br Stoners Fk	Surveyed
Logan, Jno	2,000	4	161	4–29–1785	None	
Logan, John	500	2	76	1–17–1783	Elkhorn & Licking	
Logan, Robt	3,165½	3	241	3–26–1784	Johnsons Fk	
Logewood, William	500	2	272	4– 8–1783	Howards Ck	Surveyed
Logwood, Edmond	500	1	145	12–14–1782	Licking	
Logwood, Edmund	10,000	2	244	3–14–1783	Br Ohio R	Surveyed
Logwood, Thomas	14,667	1	281	12–25–1782	Licking Cr	
Logwood, Thomas	5,000	1	296	12–27–1782	Main & N Fk Licking	
Logwood, Thos	2,000	3	148	1–15–1784	Br Licking	Surveyed
Lohira, Peter	15,000	4	212	7–28–1785	None	
Long, David	3,708	2	254	3–24———	——— R	
Long, James	1,286	1	380	1– 6–1783	Red R	
Long, Joseph	330	2	66	1–15–1783	——— Cr	
Long, Joseph	300	2	66	1–15–1783	——— Cr	
Long, Lawrence	15,000	1	216	12–21–1782	N & S Fk Licking	Surveyed
Long, Laurence	4,999½	1	217	12–21–1782	Eagle Cr	Surveyed
Long, Laurence	6,000	1	247	12–24–1782	Licking	Withdrawn
Long, Laurence	4,000	1	248	12–23–1782	Licking	Withdrawn
Long, Laurence	400	2	58	1–13–1783	Br Ky R	Surveyed
Long, Laurence	4,000	4	72	11–27–1784	None	
Long, Lawrence	4,000	4	72	11–27–1784	Licking	
Long, Lawrence	6,000	4	95	1–19–1785	Mud Lick	
Long, Samul	1,286	1	380	1– 6–1783	Red R	
Looney, Benjamin	500	1	21	12– 2–1782	Indian Cr	
Louise, Francis	2,000	1	35	12–18–1782	Hickman & Jessamine Crs	Surveyed
Love, Joseph	937½	4	21	8–22–1784	Upper Twin Cr	
Lovely, Capt Wm	70,000	4	199	6–15–1785	Br Salt Lick Cr	
Lowery, Jas	591	3	78	12– 9–1783	Shawnee Ford Ky R	Surveyed
Lowry, John	500	2	157	2– 1–1783	None	Surveyed
Lowry, John	1,000	2	171	2– 7–1783	McConnells Run	Surveyed
Lunsden, Geo	6,800¾	4	273	2–15–1786	Sandy	
Lunsden, Geo	6,800	4	295	4–29–1786	None	
Lunsford, Lewis	1,000	2	6	1– 8–1783	Stoners Fk	
Lunsford, Lewis	2,802¾	4	323	5 –9–1788	None	
Lyle, Elizabeth	2,000	2	168	2– 6–1783	Slate Cr	
Lyle, James	500	1	201	12–20–1782	Big Bone Lick	Surveyed
Lyle, James	500	2	139	1–29–1783	Ohio R	Surveyed
Lyle, James	1,000	2	188	2–13–1783	None	
Lyle, Jane	2,000	2	168	2– 6–1783	Slate Cr	
Lyle, Jno	5,310½	4	190	6– 1–1785	Ohio R	
Lyle, Samuel	3,000	2	167	2– 6–1783	Slate Cr	
Lynch, Charles	5,000	1	223	12–21–1782	None	
Lynch, William	7,000	1	284	12–26–1782	None	
Lynn, Andrew	1,000	2	7	1– 9–1783	Crooked Cr	Surveyed
Lyon, Jno	1,025½	2	279	4–26–1783	Eagle Cr	Surveyed
Lyon, Jno	3,311¾	4	213	7–30–1785	None	
Lyon, Philip	5,217½	3	118	12–29–1783	N Fk Sandy	Surveyed
Lyon, Saml	100	4	227	10–20–1785	None	
Lyon, Thos	15,000	3	119	12–29–1783	Big Sandy R	Surveyed
McAlexander, Alexander	400	1	22	12– 3–1782	None	Surveyed
McAlexander, James	1,200	1	21	12– 3–1782	Upper Blue Lick	
McAlexander, John	1,200	1	21	12– 3–1782	Upper Blue Lick	
McAlexander, Samuel	1,200	1	21	12– 3–1782	Upper Blue Lick	
McBride, James	1,000	2	88	1–18–1783	Sinking Cr	Surveyed
McBride, James	400	2	311	6– 9–1783	S Fk Elkhorn	Withdrawn
McBride, James	160	2	311	6– 9–1783	None	Surveyed
McBride, Jas	397	3	228	3–16–1784	M Fk Licking	

Entree	Acres	Book	Page	Entry Date	Watercourse	Notes
McBride, Jas	400	3	228	3–16–1784	None	Withdrawn
McBride, Jas	100	3	298	4–22–1784	S Fk Elkhorn	Withdrawn
McBride, Jas	10,000	3	338	5–19–1784	Br N Fk Licking & Ohio R	Surveyed
McBride, Jas	60	3	341	5–20–1784	None	Surveyed
McBride, Jas	400	4	124	3– 1–1785	Licking & Elkhorn	Withdrawn
McBride, Jas	500	4	278	3– 1–1786	None	
McBride, Wm	400	4	166	4–29–1785	None	
McBride & Clark	5,000	3	351	6– 1–1784	N Fk Licking	Surveyed
McBride & Dick	4,000	3	339	5–19–1784	None	Surveyed
McBride &Dunlap	400	3	228	3–16–1784	N Fk Licking	Surveyed
McBride Primon	1,000	3	339	5–19–1784	None	Surveyed
McCall, Wm &	500	4	119	2–15–1785	Slate Cr	
McCallister, James	450	1	23	12–17–1782	——— Cr	Surveyed
McCallister, James	711	3	409	7–16–1784	None	
McCallister, Robert	3,900	2	340	8– 5–1783	Indian Cr	
McCampbell, Solomon	250	4	225	10– 4–1785	S Fk Licking	
McCann, Joseph	1,338½	2	183	2–12–1783	Br Big Sandy	
McCann, Joseph	735½	4	236	12– 4–1785	Ky R	
McCann, Neal	1,338½	2	184	12–13–1783	Big Sandy & Tuttles Cr	
McCannico, Christopher	14,137	1	280	12–26–1782	Licking	Surveyed
McCary, Richard	2,012½	1	181	12–18–1782	N Fk Licking	
McClain, Daniel	500	1	380	1– 6–1783	Beaver Fk	
McClain, Daniel	1,000	3	378	6–19–1784	None	Withdrawn
McClain, Daniel	1,000	4	22	8–22–1784	None	Withdrawn
McClaidy, Alexander	3,694¼	4	68	11–18–1784	Haw Cr	Withdrawn
McClanahan, James	500	1	35	12–18–1782	——— Cr	Withdrawn
McClanahan, James	500	1	35	12–18–1782	None	Withdrawn
McClanahan, James	1,000	1	162	12–18–1782	Elkhorn	Surveyed
McClanahan, Thomas	1,000	1	24	12–17–1782	Howards Upper Cr	Surveyed
McClanahan, Thos	2,230	1	206	12–20–1782	Elkhorn & Licking	
McClanahan, Thomas Jr	197⅓	2	82	1–17–1783	Elkhorn & Licking	Surveyed
McClanahan, William	641	1	23	12–17–1782	——— Cr	
McClanahan, William	500	1	30	12–18–1782	——— Cr	Withdrawn
McClanahan, William	500	1	162	12–18–1782	Elkhorn	Surveyed
McClanahan, William	500	2	179	2–10–1783	None	Surveyed
McClardy, Alexander	3,694¼	4	292	4–22–1786	None	
McClelland, Alexander	400	2	305	5–31–1783	None	
McClelland, Alexander	400	4	155	4–21–1785	None	
McClung, James	1,000	2	93	1–20–1783	Eagle Cr	
McClung, James	1,000	2	94	1–20–1783	S Br Eagle Cr	
McClung, John	1,000	2	93	1–20–1783	Eagle Cr	
McClung, John	276	2	169	2– 6–1783	Slate Cr	
McClung, William	1,625	2	94	1–20–1783	Main Br Eagle Cr	
McClure, James	1,000	2	223	3– 7–1783	None	Surveyed
McClure, John	1,236	2	223	3– 7–1783	None	Surveyed
McClure, Jno	1,000	3	380	6–22–1784	Jessamine Cr	
McClure, Jno	500	4	69	11–19–1784	None	
McClure, Jno	1,000	4	336	6– 3–1792	None	
McClure, Samuel	800	2	122	1–25–1783	Licking	Surveyed
McClure, Thos	375	4	163	4–29–1785	None	
McClure & Stephenson	841¼	3	381	6–23–1784	——— Cr	
McClurg, Samuel	2,250	3	261	3–31–1784	N E Fk Licking	Withdrawn
McColla, Daniel	1,000	2	331	7–23–1783	Ky R	
McConal, Thos	4,000	4	89	1–14–1785	Great Mud Lick Cr	
McConatt, Thomas	5,500	2	245	3–15–1783	Trace Ky R	
McConnall, Francis	2,200	1	320	12–30–1782	Lawrence Cr	
McConnall, Francis	300	1	321	12–30–1782	Ky R	Withdrawn
McConnell, Andrew	1,000	1	62	12– 6–1782	Main Fk Elkhorn	
McConnell, Francis	2,974¾	2	95	1–20–1783	E Fk Eagle Cr	
McConnell, Francis	500	2	150	2– 1–1783	N Fk Elkhorn	Withdrawn
McConnell, Francis	339	2	150	2– 1–1783	None	
McConnell, Francis	300	2	205	2–19–1783	Lawrences Cr	
McConnell, Francis	1,560	2	347	8–13–1783	Ky & Cedar Cr	
McConnell, Francis	560	2	354	8–16–1783	None	
McConnell, Francis	500	2	355	8–16–1783	Eagle Cr	Surveyed
McConnell, James	922	2	93	1–20–1783	Fks N Fk Eagle Cr	
McConnell, William	1,000	1	62	12– 1–1782	S Fk of Elkhorn	Surveyed
McConnell, William	765	2	48	1–13–1783	Clear Cr	Withdrawn
McConnell, William	500	2	305	5–31–1783	Main Fk Elkhorn	
McConnell, William	300	2	318	7– 7–1783	S Fk Elkhorn	
McConnell, William	500	2	368	9–25–1783	Fks Elkhorn	
McConnell, Wm	765	3	265	4– 2–1784	Clear Cr	
McConnell, Wm	3,500	4	166	4–29–1785	None	Withdrawn
McConnell, Wm	3,500	4	175	5– 9–1785	None	
McConnell, Wm	3,500	4	176	5– 9–1785	None	
McCormick, William	1,000	1	141	12–14–1782	Ky R	Surveyed
McCown, Alexander	1,019½	2	187	2–13–1783	None	Surveyed

Entree	Acres	Book	Page	Entry Date	Watercourse	Notes
McCoy, Robert	1,000	2	302	5–30–1783	Br Glens Cr	Surveyed
McCrackin, Cyrus	1,000	1	60	12– 6–1782	Dry Run	Surveyed
McCrackin, Cyrus	1,500	1	335	12–31–1782	None	
McCrackin, Cyrus	1,000	2	7	1– 9–1783	Glenns Cr	Surveyed
McCrackin, Cyrus	500	2	7	1– 9–1783	None	Withdrawn
McCrackin, Cyrus	50	2	8	1– 9–1783	1st bottom below Leestown	Surveyed
McCrackin, Cyrus	400	2	8	1– 9–1783	None	Surveyed
McCrackin, Cyrus	1,000	2	12	1– 9–1783	None	
McCrackin, Cyrus	1,000	2	66	1–15–1783	None	Withdrawn
McCrackin, Cyrus	500	2	67	1–15–1783	None	Withdrawn
McCrackin, Cyrus	1,000	2	88	1–18–1783	None	
McCrackin, Cyrus	1,000	2	155	2– 1–1783	None	
McCrackin, Cyrus	500	2	177	2– 8–1783	N Fk Elkhorn	Surveyed
McCrackin, Cyrus	1,500	2	196	2–17–1783	N Elkhorn	Surveyed
McCrackin, Cyrus	500	3	30	11– 4–1783	N Fk Elkhorn	
McCrackin, Cyrus	500	3	250	3–30–1784	Fks Elkhorn	Withdrawn
McCrackin, Cyrus	500	3	362	6–12–1784	None	
McCrackin, Cyrus	500	3	362	6–12–1784	None	
McCrackin, Cyrus	1,000	3	362	6–12–1784	N Fk Elkhorn	
McCrackin, Cyrus	150	4	18	8–20–1784	None	
McCrackin, Cyrus	1,000	1	59	12– 5–1782	————	Surveyed
McCrackin, Cyrus	1,000	1	59	12– 5–1782	N Fk Clear Cr & Green Cr	
McCrackin, Isaac	1,000	1	113	12–12–1782	Jones Fk Elkhorn	Surveyed
McCrackin, Isaac	1,000	1	113	12–12–1782	Wolf Cr	Surveyed
McCrackin, Isaac	1,000	1	295	12–27–1782	None	Surveyed
McCracken, John	1,000	2	197	2–17–1783	None	Surveyed
McCrackin, Ovid	1,000	2	7	1– 9–1783	Main Fks Elkhorn	Surveyed
McCrackin, Rachel	1,000	2	205	2–21–1783	None	Surveyed
McCrackin, Sylvester	1,000	1	55	12– 5–1782	Glenns Cr	
McCrackin, William	1,000	2	7	1– 8–1783	N Fk Elkhorn	Surveyed
McCrackin & Williams	250	3	31	11– 4–1783	N Fk Elkhorn	Surveyed
McCray, Jas	8,000	4	134	3–19–1785	r h Fk Tygerts Cr	Withdrawn
McCray, Jas	8,000	4	148	4–10–1785	None	
McCrosty, James	1,631½	2	190	2–13–1783	None	Surveyed
McCullock & Gentry	893	4	212	7–28–1785	None	
McCune, William	400	1	26	12–17–1782	Mill Cr	
McCune, William	400	1	26	2–18–1785	———— Cr	Withdrawn
McCune, William	400	1	26	2–18–1785	———— Cr	Surveyed
McCune, William	400	1	26	2–18–1785	Mill Cr	Surveyed
McCune, William	400	1	26	12– 3–1782	Licking & Elkhorn	Surveyed
McCune, Wm	400	1	26	12– 3–1782	Elkhorn & Licking	Surveyed
McCune, William	900	1	57	12– 5–1782	——————	Surveyed
McCune, Wm	400	4	121	2–18–1785	None	
McCullock, Jno	1,000	3	201	3– 4–1784	Cedar Cr	
McCulley, Geo	10,000	3	109	12–27–1783	Big Sandy R	Surveyed
McCulley, Geo	20,200	4	169	4–30–1785	N Fk Sandy R	Surveyed
McCulley, Geo	28,000	4	171	5– 3–1785	Sandy R	Surveyed
McCulley, Geo	4,000	4	171	5– 3–1785	Main Fk Licking	
McDaniel, James	252	3	143	1–13–1784	None	
McDaniel, Francis	140	3	357	6–10–1784	None	Withdrawn
McDaniel, Francis	860	3	360	6–12–1784	Haw Cr	Withdrawn
McDermid, Francis	1,000	1	349	1– 2–1783	Stone Lick	Surveyed
McDermid, Francis	140	3	379	6–19–1784	Haw Cr	Surveyed
McDonald, Eneas	1,000	3	334	5–14–1784	None	Surveyed
McDonald, E	1,000	4	80	12–30–1784	Townsends Cr	
McDonald, James	200	1	141	12–14–1782	Licking	
McDonnall, John	800½	2	249	3–15–1783	Jessamine Cr	
McDonnall, Hugh	250	3	51	11–21–1783	N Fk Elkhorn	
McDougale, John	2,138	2	88	1–18–1783	Licking	Surveyed
McDougall & Bell	8,708	3	162	1–22–1784	Licking	
McDowell, Alexander	1,218½	2	92	1–20–1783	Fk N Fk Eagle Cr	
McDowell, James	1,000	1	64	12– 6–1782	E Br Licking Cr	
McDowell, John	1,000	1	199	12–20–1782	Big Bone Lick	Surveyed
McDowell, Joseph	500	4	20	8–22–1784	Flemings Cr	
McDowell, Joseph	500	3	405	7–14–1784	Main Fk Licking	Surveyed
McDowell, Joseph	500	3	407	7–14–1784	Br Main Licking	Withdrawn
McDowell, Joseph	400	3	425	8–13–1784	Main Licking	
McDowell, Joseph	600	4	20	8–22–1784	M Fk Flemings Cr	
McDowell, Joseph	500	4	20	8–22–1784	None	
McDowell, Samuel	400	1	62	12– 6–1782	S Fk Elkhorn	Surveyed
McDowell, Samuel	600	1	64	12– 6–1782	———— Cr	
McDowell, Samuel	600	1	85	12– 9–1782	Fk Licking Cr	
MacDowell, Samuel	2,000	1	196	12–20–1782	9 or 10 miles from Big Bone Lick	Surveyed
McDowell, Samuel	1,000	1	197	12–20–1782	Big Bone Lick	Surveyed
McDowell, Samuel	1,000	1	200	12–20–1782	Big Bone Lick	Surveyed
McDowell, Samuel	800	1	201	12–20–1782	S Fk Elkhorn	
McDowell, Samuel	2,006	2	168	2– 6–1783	None	
McDowell, Samuel	590	2	169	2– 6–1783	Slate Cr	

Entree	Acres	Book	Page	Entry Date	Watercourse	Notes
McDowell, William....	1,000....	1...	64....	12– 6–1782....	E Br Licking......	....
McEleny, Saml	5,364½....	4....	94....	1–17–1785....	N E Fk Licking....	Surveyed
McElheny, John......	1,000....	1...200....		12–20–1782....	Big Bone Lick.....	Surveyed
McFall, John.........	175....	2...217....		3– 1–1783....	None.............	....
McFall, Jno.........	108....	2...240....		3–13–1783....	Mill Cr...........	Surveyed
McFates, Jno........	400....	4...	62....	10–29–1784....	None.............	....
McFeeters, Jno.......	500....	4...	38....	9–18–1784....	None.............	....
McFeeters, Jno.......	400....	3...393....		7– 2–1784....	Hickmans Cr......	Withdrawn
McFetters, Jno.......	400....	4...233....		11– 9–1785....	None.............	....
McFetters, Jno.......	97....	4...234....		11–21–1785....	None.............	....
McGee & Robinson...	15,246....	3...178....		2–10–1784....	Sandy............	....
McGehee, Samuel.....	500....	3...	13....	10–17–1783....	Elkhorn..........	....
McGuire, Jno.........	6,212½....	3...420....		8– 4–1784....	4 Mile Cr........	Withdrawn
McGuire, Jno.........	6,212....	4...120....		2–16–1785....	None.............	....
McIlroy, James	750....	1...154....		12–17–1782....	N Fk Licking.....	....
McIntire, Jno........	400....	1...141....		12–14–1782....	Br Licking.......	....
McIntire, John.......	1,000....	1...246....		12–23–1782....	Br Licking.......	Surveyed
McIntire, John.......	500....	1...336....		12–31–1782....	Br Licking.......	....
McIntire, John.......	500....	1...337....		12–31–1782....	Br Stoners Fk.....	Surveyed
McIntire, John.......	3,000....	1...342....		1– 1–1783....	Br Hingston Fk....	Withdrawn
McIntire, John.......	1,000....	2...324....		7–17–1783....	Br Red R.........	....
McIntire, John.......	1,500....	2...343....		8– 8–1783....	Br Licking........	....
McIntire, John.......	1,000....	2...348....		8–14–1783....	——— Cr.......	Withdrawn
McIntire, Nicholas....	———....	1...	83....	12– 9–1782....	Strouds Sp........	Surveyed
McIntire, Nicholas....	1,000....	1...139....		12–14–1782....	Licking...........	Surveyed
McIntire & Couchman.	1,000....	3...	67....	12– 1–1783....	Sandy............	Surveyed
McJenkins, William....	3,000....	2...338....		8– 1–1783....	None.............	....
McKay, Robt.........	———....	3...169....		1–26–1784....	None.............	Surveyed
McKee, Jno..........	2,000....	4...	39....	9–22–1784....	N Fk Eagle Cr....	....
McKee, William......	1,072½....	2...169....		2– 6–1783....	Slate Cr..........	Withdrawn
McKeeters, William...	1,637....	2...205....		2–21–1783....	So Elkhorn........	Withdrawn
McKenney, Alexander .	500....	2...160....		2– 4–1783....	N Fk Elkhorn.....	Surveyed
McKenney, David	1,000....	2...182....		2–12–1783....	Clay Lick........	Withdrawn
McKenney, David....	200....	2...196....		2–14–1783....	N Fk Elkhorn.....	Surveyed
McKenney, David	1,000....	2...342....		8– 8–1783....	Licking Water....	Withdrawn
McKenney, David....	1,000....	3...	73....	12– 8–1783....	Br Ky R..........	....
McKenney, David....	1,000....	3...	73....	12– 8–1783....	Licking...........	Surveyed
McKenney, David....	750....	3...247....		3–27–1784....	E Fk Licking......	Surveyed
McKenney, David....	1,000....	4...	97....	1–24–1785....	None.............	....
McKenney, John......	1,500....	2...160....		2– 4–1783....	N Fk Elkhorn.....	Withdrawn
McKenney, John......	500....	2...197....		2–17–1783....	None.............	....
McKenney, Jno.......	15,000....	3...243....		3–26–1784....	S Fk Licking.....	....
McKenney, Jno.......	500....	3...365....		6–14–1784....	None.............	....
McKenney, Jno.......	5,000....	4...	98....	1–24–1785....	None.............	....
McKenney, John & Alex	1,090....	2...163....		2– 4–1783....	Lees Cr..........	Surveyed
McKenney, John & Alex	547....	2...179....		2–10–1783....	S Fk Eagle Cr.....	....
McKenney, John & David.............	1,211....	2...196....		2–14–1783....	N Fk Elkhorn.....	Surveyed
McKenney, Robert....	537....	4...	97....	1–24–1785....	None.............	....
McKernen, Michael....	2,000....	4...190....		6– 1–1785....	Ohio R...........	....
McKettrick, Anthony..	11,517½....	1...384....		1– 6–1783....	Willow Cr........	....
McLelland, Alexander .	1,000....	1...	38....	12– 4–1782....	Big Bone Cr......	Surveyed
McLelland, Alexander .	1,000....	1...	43....	12– 4–1782....	——— Cr.......	Surveyed
McLelland, John Jr .	1,000....	1...	62....	12– 6–1782....	....	....
McLelland, Jno Sr	1,000....	1...	62....	12– 6–1782....	N Fk Licking......	Surveyed
McLelland, Wm......	1,000....	1...317....		12–30–1782....	S Fk Licking......	Surveyed
McLenaenn & Morrin.	4,708....	3...	60....	11–25–1783....	Locust Cr........	....
McMahan, Jno.......	4,935....	3...120....		12–29–1783....	None.............	Withdrawn
McMahan, Jno.......	2,625....	4...	22....	8–22–1784....	None.............	Withdrawn
McMillian, Jas.......	4,000....	2...272....		4– 8–1783....	S Fk Lulbegrud....	....
McMillian, Jas	1,000....	2...272....		4– 8–1783....	S Fk Lulbegrud....	....
McMillian, James.....	600....	1...	98....	12–10–1782....	None.............	Surveyed
McMillian, James.....	4,000....	2...241....		12–23–1782....	Lulbegrud Cr.....	Surveyed
McMillion, James.....	365....	2...271....		4– 7–1783....	Howards Cr.......	Surveyed
McMillion, James.....	316....	2...271....		4– 7–1783....	S Fk Lulbegrud....	Surveyed
McMillion, James.....	1,000....	1...	83....	12– 9–1782....	Hingston & Spencer Cr......	Surveyed
McMillion, Robert.....	500....	2...272....		4– 8–1783....	Howards Cr.......	Surveyed
McMillion, Robert.....	1,000....	2...278....		4–25–1783....	Stoners Fk........	Surveyed
McMillian, Samuel ...	2,062½....	2...	75....	1–16–1783....	Licking...........	Surveyed
McMillian, Samuel	1,500....	3...202....		3– 4–1784....	Br S Fk Licking....	Withdrawn
McMillian, Samuel....	8,000....	3...236....		3–23–1784....	S Fk Licking......	....
McMillin, William....	596....	2...241....		3–13–1783....	None.............	....
McMillian & Massie ..	8,000....	3...169....		1–26–1784....	S Fk Licking......	Withdrawn
McMillian & Patterson	2,000....	3...	72....	12– 8–1783....	S Fk Mill Cr......	....
McMillian & Patterson	1,453¾....	3...	73....	12– 8–1783....	Hinkston Fk......	Surveyed
McMillian & Patterson	3,000....	3...	74....	12– 8–1783....	Hinkston Fk......	....
McMillian & Patterson	6,000....	4...153....		4–19–1785....	Fks Licking.......	....
McMullen, Joseph.....	5,000....	1...163....		12–18–1782....	Gists Cr..........	....
McMullen, Joseph.....	3,729....	1...205....		12–20–1782....	Ohio R...........	....
McMullen, Samuel....	5,000....	1...221....		12–21–1782....	S Fk Will Cr......	....

Entree	Acres	Book	Page	Entry Date	Watercourse	Notes
McMullin, Samuel	8,700	1	303	12-27-1782	N Fk Elkhorn	Surveyed
McMurty, Joseph	100	1	101	12-10-1782	Jessamine Cr	
McMurty, Joseph	700	1	301	12-27-1782	Ky R	Surveyed
McMurty, Joseph	300	1	301	12-27-1782	Jessamine Cr	Withdrawn
McMurty, Joseph	300	4	25	8-31-1784	Jessamine Cr	Surveyed
McMurty, Joseph	138	4	37	9-18-1784	Jessamine Cr	
McMurty, William	50	1	102	12-10-1782	Ky R	
McMurty, Wm	30,000	4	136	3-21-1785	None	Withdrawn
McMurty, Wm	90,000	4	189	6- 1-1785	None	
McNair, David	2,750	3	15	10-25-1783	Big Bone Cr	
McNutt, James	400	1	46	12- 4-1782	Sinking Br	Surveyed
McPherson, Wm	20,200	4	170	5- 3-1785	None	Surveyed
McWilliams, Wm	2,000	4	191	6- 1-1785	Ohio R	Withdrawn
McWilliams, Wm	2,000	4	195	6- 9-1785	Ohio R	
McWhites & Coalter	1,657	4	164	4-29-1785	None	
McWhites & Coalter	1,637	4	165	4-29-1785	None	
Machan, John	1,000	2	296	5-28-1783	None	Surveyed
Machan, Thomas	400	2	296	5-28-1783	Coopers Run	
Macher, John	2,999	1	268	12-25-1782	Stoners Fk	
Macher, Jno	2,000	3	76	12- 9-1783	Hinkston Fk	
Macher, Jno	2,000	3	77	12- 9-1783	Br Licking	Surveyed
Macher, Jno	2,000	3	142	1-13-1784	Cedar Cr	Withdrawn
Macher, Jno	2,000	3	243	3-26-1784	S Fk Licking	
Mackin & Huffman	2,000	4	128	3- 6-1785	Johnson Fk	
Maddison, James	2,000	2	80	1-17-1783	None	Surveyed
Maddison, Thomas	4,000	1	175	12-18-1782	Br Ohio R	Surveyed
Maddox, Thos	1,000	4	65	11-10-1784	None	
Maddox & Morgan	1,000	3	300	4-24-1784	Elkhorn & Licking	Withdrawn
Maddox & Morgan	1,000	4	65	11- 5-1784	None	
Madison, Ambrose	1,000	1	255	12-24-1782	None	Surveyed
Madison, Ambrose	6,029½	3	37	11-12-1783	Sandy Cr	
Madison, Gabriel	3,000	2	21	1- 9-1783	Savern Cr	Surveyed
Madison, James	2,000	1	255	12-24-1782	Main Elkhorn	Amended
Madison, Thos	200	4	37	9-18-1784	None	
Major, Wm	1,811½	4	243	12-17-1785	——— Cr	
Major, Wm & Lewis	1,000	4	257	1-16-1786	S Fk Sandy	
Malaci, Jno	5,000	3	118	12-29-1783	None	
Mallory, Uriah	1,000	1	17	12- 4-1782	None	Surveyed
Mallory, Uriah	500	1	161	12-17-1782	None	
Mallory, Urriel	2,320¾	2	3	1- 8-1783	None	Surveyed
Maney, Elizabeth	200	4	239	12-13-1785	Salt Rock Fk	
Marble, Abner	400	3	176	2- 9-1784	None	
Marble, Abner	800	3	96	12-17-1783	None	Surveyed
March, Jno	465	3	199	3- 2-1784	Slate Cr	Surveyed
Marks, Elisha & Abel	16,790½	3	301	4-26-1784	Elkhorn & Licking	
Marks, Jno	2,600	3	277	4- 7-1784	Millers Cr	
Marshall, Chas	1,500	3	266	4- 3-1784	None	Withdrawn
Marshall, Chas	1,000	3	271	4- 6-1784	Licking	Withdrawn
Marshall, Chas	4,437	3	338	5-19-1784	None	Withdrawn
Marshall, Chas	2,218¾	3	378	6-19-1784	None	Withdrawn
Marshall, Chas	1,000	3	384	6-23-1784	Cabbin Cr	Surveyed
Marshall, Chas	1,000	3	388	6-30-1784	None	Surveyed
Marshall, Chas	440	4	16	8-16-1784	Greers Cr	Surveyed
Marshall, Chas	1,168	4	23	8-27-1784	Clear Cr	Surveyed
Marshall, Chas	104	4	44	9-24-1784	S Fk Elkhorn	
Marshall, Chas	1,500	4	53	10-14-1784	None	
Marshall, Chas	332	4	53	10-14-1784	Ohio R	
Marshall, Chas	2,218¾	4	56	10-17-1784	None	
Marshall, Chas	1,532	4	59	10-25-1784	None	Surveyed
Marshall, Chas	200	4	60	10-27-1784	N Fk Licking	Withdrawn
Marshall, Chas	60	4	60	10-27-1784	Greers Cr	Withdrawn
Marshall, Chas	10	4	61	10-27-1784	None	Withdrawn
Marshall, Chas	100	4	61	10-28-1784	None	Surveyed
Marshall, Chas	15	4	61	10-28-1784	None	Withdrawn
Marshall, Chas	55	4	66	11-12-1784	Br Lawrences Cr	Withdrawn
Marshall, Chas	200	4	72	11-27-1784	Lees Lick	
Marshall, Chas	500	4	118	2-14-1785	None	Withdrawn
Marshall, Chas	1,000	4	150	4-10-1785	None	
Marshall, Chas	20,000	4	155	4-20-1785	Sandy	6,873 acres withdrawn
Marshall, Chas	500	4	155	4-20-1785	None	
Marshall, Chas	350	4	209	7-20-1785	Ky R	Surveyed
Marshall, Chas	5,000	4	211	7-27-1785	None	
Marshall, Chas	210	4	217	8- 7-1785	None	
Marshall, Chas	130	4	218	8-13-1785	Clear Cr	
Marshall, Chas	100	4	321	3- 3-1788	Ky R	
Marshall, Chas & Wm	2,750	4	214	8- 2-1785	None	
Marshall, Chas & Wm	570	4	214	8- 2-1785	Strodes Fk	
Marshall, Chas & Wm Jr	1,508½	4	218	8-13-1785	None	Withdrawn

Entree	Acres	Book	Page	Entry Date	Watercourse	Notes
Marshall, Chas & Wm Jr.	500	4	220	9– 3–1785	None	
Marshall, Chas & Wm.	1,878	4	219	8–31–1785	None	Surveyed
Marshall, Chas & Wm.	110	4	33	9–11–1784	None	
Marshall, Chas & Wm.	220	4	33	9–11–1784	None	
Marshall, David	300	3	172	2– 2–1784	S Fk Licking	Surveyed
Marshall, David	2,000	3	240	3–25–1784	Hinkston Fk	
Marshall, Humphrey	1,000	1	207	12–20–1782	Salt Lick Cr	Withdrawn
Marshall, Humphrey	1,000	1	207	12–20–1782	Ky R	Amended
Marshall, Humphrey	1,000	1	207	12–20–1782	Big Sandy R	Withdrawn
Marshall, Humphrey	800	1	208	12–20–1782	Big Sandy	Withdrawn
Marshall, Humphrey	860	1	208	12–20–1782	E Fk Licking	Withdrawn
Marshall, Humphrey	3,500	1	222	12–21–1782	M Fk S Fk Licking	
Marshall, Humphrey	3,000	2	139	1–29–1783	Ohio R	Surveyed
Marshall, Humphrey	3,000	2	162	2– 4–1783	None	Surveyed
Marshall, Humphrey	1,875	2	210	2–27–1783	None	Surveyed
Marshall, Humphrey	50	2	218	3– 1–1783	None	
Marshall, Humphrey	860	2	222	3– 7–1783	Waters Hickmans Cr	Surveyed
Marshall, Humphrey	120	2	273	4– 9–1783	None	Surveyed
Marshall, Humphrey	80	2	291	5–21–1783	N Fk Elkhorn	
Marshall, Humphrey	200	2	326	7–19–1783	Mouth Big Paint Lick	Surveyed
Marshall, Humphrey	100	2	326	7–19–1783	Mouth Big Paint Lick	Surveyed
Marshall, Humphrey	800	2	328	7–19–1783	Big Paint Lick	Withdrawn
Marshall, Humphreys	500	2	331	7–23–1783	Ky R	Surveyed
Marshall, Humphreys	500	2	347	8–13–1783	None	Withdrawn
Marshall, Humphry	560	2	353	8–15–1783	None	Surveyed
Marshall, Humphreys	1,000	2	357	8–19–1783	Elkhorn	Surveyed
Marshall, Humphreys	500	2	360	9–10–1783	Hingston & Stoners	Surveyed
Marshall, Humphry	351	3	27	11– 1–1783	Ky R	Withdrawn
Marshall, Humphry	125	3	38	11–12–1783	None	Withdrawn
Marshall, Humphry	318	3	85	12–12–1783	Elkhorn	
Marshall, Humphry	800	3	122	12–30–1783	None	Surveyed
Marshall, Humphry	800	3	247	3–29–1784	None	Surveyed
Marshall, Humphry	1,360	3	309	4–29–1784	None	900 acres withdrawn
Marshall, Humphry	351	4	238	12–10–1785	None	
Marshall, Humphry	900	4	245	12–20–1785	Ky R	
Marshall, Humphry	580	4	245	12–20–1785	Ky R	
Marshall, Humphry	1,086½	4	313	3– 6–1787	Ky R	
Marshall, Humphry	250	4	317	11–15–1787	Fk S Elkhorn	Surveyed
Marshall, Humphry Jr.	400	3	341	5–20–1784	Ky R	Surveyed
Marshall, Humphry & Wm Jr.	4,000	3	230	3–17–1784	N Fk Licking	Withdrawn
Marshall, Humphry & Wm Jr.	2,000	3	231	3–18–1784	N Fk Licking	
Marshall, Humphry & Wm Jr.	2,000	3	301	4–24–1784	None	
Marshall, Humphry & Wm Jr.	4,000	3	305	4–28–1784	None	
Marshall, Jas	600	4	96	1–20–1785	Elkhorn	
Marshall, John	200	1	136	12–14–1782	Ohio R	Surveyed
Marshall, Jno	40,000	3	19	10–30–1783	Salt Lick Cr	Withdrawn
Marshall, Jno	1,000	3	103	12–19–1783	None	Withdrawn
Marshall, Jno	10,000	3	131	1– 2–1784	None	Withdrawn
Marshall, Jno	60,000	3	237	3–24–1784	N Fk Elkhorn	30,000 acres withdrawn
Marshall, Jno	30,000	4	82	1– 5–1785	Slate Cr	11,000 acres withdrawn
Marshall, Jno	9,000	4	130	3– 7–1785	None	
Marshall, Jno	500	4	248	12–23–1785	Buck Pond	
Marshall, Jno	100	4	285	3–25–1785	None	
Marshall, John Jr	1,000	1	7	12–13–1782	Dry Cr	Withdrawn
Marshall, John Jr	1,000	1	15	12– 2–1782	Dry Cr	
Marshall, John Jr	1,500	1	15	12– 2–1782	None	Withdrawn
Marshall, John Jr	500	1	16	12– 2–1782	Sinking Cr	Surveyed
Marshall, John Jr	1,300	1	338	12–31–1782	None	Withdrawn
Marshall, John Jr	6,052	1	356	1– 3–1783	None	Surveyed
Marshall, Jno Jr	1,300	2	10	1– 9–1783	None	Surveyed
Marshall, John Jr	10,659½	2	39	1–11–1783	N Fk Licking	Surveyed
Marshall, John Jr	2,000	2	40	1–11–1783	N Fk Licking	Surveyed
Marshall, John Jr	4,002	2	43	1–11–1783	Lawrence Cr	
Marshall, John Jr	4,816½	2	44	1–11–1783	N Fk Licking	Surveyed
Marshall, John Jr	8,304½	2	44	1–11–1783	N Fk Licking	Surveyed
Marshall, John Jr	4,000	2	45	1–11–1783	N Fk Licking	Surveyed
Marshall, John Jr	6,000	2	46	1–11–1783	Lees Cr	Withdrawn
Marshall, John Jr	14,150	2	47	1–11–1783	Ohio R	
Marshall, John Jr	500	2	49	1–13–1783	1st Fk Cedar Cr	
Marshall, John Jr	500	2	49	1–13–1783	Ky R	Surveyed
Marshall, John Jr	3,816½	2	49	1–13–1783	None	
Marshall, Jno Jr	15,121	3	110	12–27–1783	N Fk Licking	Withdrawn

Entree	Acres	Book	Page	Entry Date	Watercourse	Notes
Marshall, Jno Jr	1,086½	3	213	3–10–1784	N Fk Licking	Withdrawn
Marshall, Jno Jr	6,700	3	265	4– 2–1784	Licking	Withdrawn
Marshall, Jno Jr	1,000	3	271	4– 6–1784	Licking	Withdrawn
Marshall, Jno Jr	1,086½	3	328	5– 7–1784	Ohio R	Withdrawn
Marshall, Jno Jr	200	3	341	5–20–1784	Clear Cr	
Marshall, Jno Jr	1,000	3	357	6–10–1784	None	
Marshall, Jno Jr	1,000	3	371	6–16–1784	None	
Marshall, Jno Jr	30,000	4	130	3– 7–1785	None	
Marshall, Jno Jr	1,000	4	150	4–10–1785	None	
Marshall, Jno Jr	1,000	4	151	4–10–1785	None	
Marshall, Jno Jr	60,000	4	153	4–20–1785	None	
Marshall, Jno Jr	5,000	4	153	4–20–1785	Main Licking	Withdrawn
Marshall, Jno Jr	5,000	4	213	7–30–1785	Cabbin Cr	500 acres withdrawn
Marshall, Jno Jr	2,000	4	214	8– 2–1785	None	
Marshall, Jno Jr	1,000	4	216	8– 5–1785	None	
Marshall, Jno Jr	1,400	4	225	10– 7–1785	Tygerts Cr	
Marshall, Jno Jr	600	4	225	10– 7–1785	N Fk Licking	Surveyed
Marshall, Jno Jr	5,000	4	233	11– 8–1785	N Fk Licking	
Marshall, Jno Jr	1,000	4	242	12–14–1785	Sandy	Withdrawn
Marshall, Jno Jr	8,000	4	261	1–20–1786	Br S Fk Sandy	Surveyed
Marshall, Jno Jr	1,000	4	264	1–29–1786	None	
Marshall, Jno Jr	500	4	264	1–29–1786	None	
Marshall, Jno Jr	1,500	4	264	1–29–1786	Salt Rock Fk	Withdrawn
Marshall, Jno Jr	1,500	4	268	1– 6–1786	None	
Marshall, Jno Jr	1,500	4	268	2– 6–1786	None	Withdrawn
Marshall, Jno Jr	1,500	4	276	2–19–1786	——— Cr	Withdrawn
Marshall, Jno Jr	100	4	285	3–25–1785	3 Islands	
Marshall, Jno Jr	1,500	4	287	3–28–1786	——— Cr	
Marshall, Jno Jr	150	4	293	4–22–1786	None	
Marshall, Lewis & Geo.	70,000	3	369	6–16–1784	I h Fks Ky R	Surveyed
Marshall, Mathew	1,000	3	311	4–29–1784	M Fk Licking	
Marshall, Robt	1,708	4	193	6– 6–1785	N Fk Ky R	
Marshall, Thomas Jr	11,065	2	45	1–11–1783	None	
Marshall, William	340	1	209	12–20–1782	None	Surveyed
Marshall, William	2,000	1	349	1– 2–1783	None	Surveyed
Marshall, Wm	500	3	242	3–26–1784	Licking	
Marshall, Wm	1,000	3	271	4– 6–1784	Licking	Withdrawn
Marshall, Wm	1,000	3	296	4–21–1784	Licking	Withdrawn
Marshall, Wm	2,000	3	336	5–19–1784	None	Withdrawn
Marshall, Wm	1,388	4	55	10–17–1784	None	
Marshall, Wm	1,382½	4	58	10–23–1784	None	Surveyed
Marshall, Wm	1,000	4	150	4–10–1785	None	
Marshall, Wm	1,000	4	151	4–10–1785	None	
Marshall, Wm & Chas.	106	4	218	8–13–1785	None	Surveyed
Marshall, Wm & Chas.	553	4	32	9–10–1784	Glenns Cr	Withdrawn
Marshall, Wm & Chas.	553	4	37	9–18–1784	None	
Marshall, Wm Jr	1,000	3	230	3–17–1784	N Fk Licking	Withdrawn
Marshall, Wm Jr	4,923	3	254	3–30–1784	N Fk Licking	Withdrawn
Marshall, Wm Jr	50	3	258	3–30–1784	2 Mile Cr	Withdrawn
Marshall, Wm Jr	50	3	282	4–13–1784	None	
Marshall, Wm Jr	50	3	287	4–14–1784	Huston Fk	Withdrawn
Marshall, Wm Jr	1,800	3	302	4–26–1784	Licking & Elkhorn	Withdrawn
Marshall, Wm Jr	1,000	3	304	4–26–1784	Elkhorn & Licking	Withdrawn
Marshall, Wm Jr	650	3	327	5– 7–1784	Elkhorn	Surveyed
Marshall, Wm Jr	650	3	329	5–12–1784	Ky R	Surveyed
Marshall, Wm Jr	155½	3	341	5–20–1784	Ky R & Elkhorn	Withdrawn
Marshall, Wm Jr	1,000	3	342	5–20–1784	None	
Marshall, Wm Jr	3,000	3	355	6– 7–1784	Ohio R	
Marshall, Wm Jr	127	3	356	6– 8–1784	None	
Marshall, Wm Jr	1,000	3	361	6–12–1784	Clear Cr	Withdrawn
Marshall, Wm Jr	4,923	3	363	6–14–1784	None	
Marshall, Wm Jr	1,000	3	387	6–28–1784	None	
Marshall, Wm Jr	600	3	400	7–10–1784	Br Fleming Cr	Withdrawn
Marshall, Wm Jr	1,000	3	400	7–10–1784	None	Withdrawn
Marshall, Wm Jr	425	3	403	7–13–1784	Main Licking	Amended
Marshall, Wm Jr	600	3	409	7–14–1784	None	
Marshall, Wm Jr	1,200	3	409	7–16–1784	None	Surveyed
Marshall, Wm Jr	663	3	412	7–17–1784	None	Withdrawn
Marshall, Wm Jr	663	3	422	8– 5–1784	None	
Marshall, Wm Jr	665	3	422	8– 5–1784	Fleming Cr	Surveyed
Marshall, Wm Jr	245	3	423	8–11–1784	Boones Cr	Withdrawn
Marshall, Wm Jr	245	3	425	8–13–1784	None	Withdrawn
Marshall, Wm Jr	93	4	23	8–30–1784	None	
Marshall, Wm Jr	450	4	23	8–30–1784	None	
Marshall, Wm Jr	1,321	4	23	8–30–1784	None	586 acres surveyed 735 acres withdrawn
Marshall, Wm Jr	1,250	4	26	9– 1–1784	Main Elkhorn	Surveyed
Marshall, Wm Jr	735	4	36	9–18–1784	None	Withdrawn

Entree	Acres	Book	Page	Entry Date	Watercourse	Notes
Marshall, Wm Jr.....	245	4	36	9-18-1784	Ky R	....
Marshall, Wm Jr.....	617	4	37	9-18-1784	Ky R	
Marshall, Wm Jr.....	425	4	43	9-24-1784	None	
Marshall, Wm Jr.....	130	4	43	9-24-1784	None	Withdrawn
Marshall, Wm Jr.....	120	4	45	9-30-1784	None	Withdrawn
Marshall, Wm Jr.....	500	4	49	9-12-1784	Clear Cr	
Marshall, Wm Jr.....	50	4	49	9-12-1784	Hickmans Cr	Withdrawn
Marshall, Wm Jr.....	300	4	52	10-14-1784	Ky R	Withdrawn
Marshall, Wm Jr.....	300	4	52	10-14-1784	Ky R	Withdrawn
Marshall, Wm Jr.....	1,500	4	59	10-25-1784	None	Withdrawn
Marshall, Wm Jr.....	300	4	68	11-16-1784	None	Withdrawn
Marshall, Wm Jr.....	300	4	69	11-20-1784	Ky R	Withdrawn
Marshall, Wm Jr.....	1,500	4	76	12- 6-1784	None	....
Marshall, Wm Jr.....	389	4	76	12- 6-1784	Ky R	
Marshall, Wm Jr.....	155½	4	91	1-15-1785	None	
Marshall, Wm Jr.....	153	4	91	1-15-1785	Ky R	
Marshall, Wm Jr.....	300	4	92	1-15-1785	Elkhorn & Ky R	
Marshall, Wm Jr.....	142	4	92	1-15-1785	None	
Marshall, Wm Jr.....	2,000	4	124	2-23-1785	S Fk Elkhorn	Withdrawn
Marshall, Wm Jr.....	300	4	126	3- 5-1785	None	
Marshall, Wm Jr.....	2,450	4	141	4- 1-1785	None	
Marshall, Wm Jr.....	37,256	4	142	4- 5-1785	None	28,245 acres withdrawn
Marshall, Wm Jr.....	28,000	4	194	6- 7-1785	Ohio R	....
Marshall, Wm Jr.....	26,500	4	195	6- 7-1785	Ohio R	Surveyed
Marshall, Wm Jr.....	245	4	208	7-14-1785	None	
Marshall, Wm Jr.....	245	4	209	7-14-1785	Main Elkhorn	Surveyed
Marshall, Wm Jr.....	130	4	211	7-25-1785	Clear Cr	
Marshall, Wm Jr.....	365	4	213	8- 2-1785	N Fk Licking	
Marshall, Wm Jr.....	1,400	4	269	2- 6-1786	None	Withdrawn
Marshall, Wm Jr.....	400	4	319	2- 9-1788	None	....
Marshall, Wm Jr.....	50	4	328	3-10-1789	None	Withdrawn
Marshall, Wm Jr.....	——	4	268	2- 6-1786	None	Withdrawn
Marshall, Wm Sr.....	6,413½	4	265	1-29-1786	Sandy	Withdrawn
Marshall, Wm Sr.....	5,000	4	268	2- 6-1786	Sandy	
Marshall, Wm Sr.....	1,413¼	4	269	2- 6-1786	None	Withdrawn
Marshall, Wm Sr.....	1,400	4	276	2-19-1786	None	
Marshall, Wm Sr.....	7,813	4	276	2-19-1786	Sandy	Withdrawn
Marshall Jr & Ash...	2,750	3	418	7-30-1784	Licking	Withdrawn
Marshall Jr & Ash...	2,750	4	25	8-31-1784	None	
Marshall & Ashby Jr...	207	3	418	7-29-1784	None	
Marshall Jr & Ashby Jr	207	4	49	9-12-1784	None	
Marshall Jr & Fowler Jr	4,000	3	255	3-30-1784	N Fk Licking	Withdrawn
Marshall Jr & Fowler Jr.	4,000	3	256	3-30-1784	N Fk Licking	Withdrawn
Marshall Jr & Fowler Jr.	3,800	3	256	3-30-1784	None	Withdrawn
Marshall Jr & Fowler Jr.	3,000	3	258	3-30-1784	None	Withdrawn
Marshall Jr & Fowler Jr.	3,000	3	258	3-30-1784	N Fk Licking	Withdrawn
Marshall Jr & Fowler Jr.	20,698	3	279	4- 8-1784	None	....
Marshall & Fowler Jr...	2,000	3	324	5- 4-1784	Flat Cr	Surveyed
Marshall Jr & Grayson.	300	3	307	4-28-1784	None	....
Marshall Jr & Massie..	50	3	414	7-22-1784	None	Surveyed
Marshall & Braun.....	3,000	4	58	10-23-1784	None	Withdrawn
Marshall & Brame.....	3,000	3	337	5-19-1784	None	Withdrawn
Marshall & Braun.....	3,000	4	155	4-20-1785	None	Withdrawn
Marshall & Daniel....	4,000	3	44	11-14-1783	Ohio R	Withdrawn
Marshall & Daniel....	4,000	3	44	11-14-1783	Ohio R	Withdrawn
Marshall & Daniel....	2,000	3	45	11-14-1783	None	Withdrawn
Marshall & Daniel....	3,000	3	183	2-12-1784	None	Withdrawn
Marshall & Duvall....	20,000	3	295	4-21-1784	None	....
Marshall & Ellis......	781	3	403	7-13-1784	None	Withdrawn
Marshall & Ellis......	781	3	404	7-13-1784	None	....
Marshall & Ellis......	1,400	3	408	7-14-1784	Slate Cr	....
Marshall & Ellis......	878	3	409	7-14-1784	Coal Bank	....
Marshall & Fowler.....	640	3	305	4-28-1784	Ky R	Surveyed
Marshall & Fowler.....	20,698	4	125	3- 1-1785	None	Surveyed
Marshall & Grayson....	300	3	215	3-10-1784	M Fk Licking	Withdrawn
Marshall & Grayson....	250	3	215	3-10-1784	Hustons Fk	....
Marshall & Grayson...	342	4	78	12-20-1784	Strodes Fk Licking.	....
Marshall & Grayson..	48¾	4	193	6- 1-1785	None	....
Marshall & Grayson...	342	4	201	6-17-1785	None	....
Marshall & Lewis....	5,000	3	9	10-15-1783	Bank Lick Cr	Withdrawn
Marshall & Smith.....	10,000	3	171	1-31-1784	Bank Lick Cr	Withdrawn
Marshall & Smith.....	4,437	3	378	6-19-1784	None	....
Marshall & Smith.....	1,000	4	19	8-21-1784	Clear Cr	....
Marshall & Smith.....	1,000	4	19	8-21-1784	Clear Cr	....
Marshall & Smith.....	1,000	4	19	8-21-1784	Clear Cr	Withdrawn
Marshall & Smith.....	1,420	4	19	8-21-1784	Clear Cr	Withdrawn
Marshall & Smith.....	580	4	19	8-21-1784	Clear Cr	Withdrawn
Marshall & Smith.....	1,000	4	18	8-20-1784	Clear Cr	....
Marshall & Smith.....	1,420	4	23	8-30-1784	None	
Marshall & Smith....	580	4	30	9- 7-1784	Clear Cr	Amended

Entree	Acres	Book	Page	Entry Date	Watercourse	Notes
Marshall & Smith	580	4	41	9–22–1784	Glens Cr	
Marshall & Smith	1,000	4	55	10–17–1784	None	
Marshall & Smith	1,000	4	57	10–23–1784	None	Surveyed
Marshall & Smith	400	4	59	10–25–1784	Hickman Cr	Withdrawn
Marshall & Smith	600	4	59	10–25–1784	—— Cr	Withdrawn
Marshall & Wilkinson	2,000	4	124	2–23–1784	None	
Marshall & Waller	450	4	155	4–20–1875	Great Miami	Surveyed
Markham Barnard	13,122	3	100	12–19–1783	Eagle Cr	
Marlett, Abraham	1,000	2	69	1–15–1783	Br Hingston Fk	
Marney, Wm	5,113	3	416	7–26–1784	Ky R	
Marques, Jno	8,000	3	164	1–22–1784	Bank Lick Cr	
Martin, Arch	1,000	2	52	1–13–1783	None	
Martin, John	1,000	1	36	12–4–1782	S Fk Licking	Surveyed
Martin, John	2,000	1	178	12–18–1782	None	
Martin, John	1,000	1	178	12–18–1782	S Fk Licking	Surveyed
Martin, John	2,000	1	179	12–18–1782	S Fk Licking	Withdrawn
Martin, John	2,000	1	179	12–18–1782	S Fk Licking	Surveyed
Martin, John	3,000	1	180	12–18–1782	None	Amended
Martin, John	1,000	1	183	12–19–1782	None	Withdrawn
Martin, John	3,000	2	73	1–16–1783	Hickmans Cr	Surveyed
Martin, John	2,000	2	73	1–16–1783	Br Silver Cr	Surveyed
Martin, John	2,000	2	73	1–16–1783	None	
Martin, John	1,000	2	74	1–16–1783	None	
Martin, John	500	2	89	1–20–1783	S Fk Licking	
Martin, John	1,000	2	89	1–20–1783	S Fk Licking	Surveyed
Martin, Jno	804	4	197	6–10–1785	Howards Upper Cr	
Martin, Jno	400	4	197	6–10–1785	Hustons Fk	
Martin, Jno	400	4	197	6–10–1785	Hustons Fk	Surveyed
Martin, Henry	325	1	114	12–12–1782	N & N E Cr	
Martin, Hugh	400	2	377	10–13–1784	Ky R	
Martin, Samuel	1,000	2	211	2–27–1783	Jessamine Cr	Withdrawn
Martin, Samuel	1,000	2	222	3–7–1783	None	Surveyed
Martin, Samuel	1,500	2	284	5–11–1783	Hickman Cr	Withdrawn
Martin, Samuel	200	4	48	10–12–1784	Hingston	
Martin, Samuel	1,300	4	99	1–24–1785	None	
Mason, George	5,496	2	32	1–10–1783	Tagerts Cr	
Mason, John	5,000	2	15	1–9–1783	Br Ohio R	
Mason, John	7,589	2	15	1–9–1783	Little Sandy	
Mason, John	5,000	2	42	1–1–1783	None	
Mason, John	1,192	2	64	1–14–1783	Hickman Cr	
Mason, Micajah	1,000	2	194	2–14–1783	Severn Cr	Surveyed
Mason, Peter	1,000	2	15	1–9–1783	Gregers Cr	Withdrawn
Mason, Peter	1,000	2	148	1–31–1783	Greers Cr	
Mason, Peter	1,209	3	200	3–3–1784	Main Fk Licking	
Mason, Richard	27,000	3	111	12–27–1783	S Fk Big Sandy R	
Mason, Stephen T	10,000	4	25	8–31–1784	Sandy Cr	
Mason, Stephen T	500	4	30	9–7–1784	Glens Cr	
Mason & Harrison	2,000	3	345	5–25–1784	Lower Blue Lick	
Massey, Nathaniel	8,000	3	236	3–23–1784	S Fk Licking	
Massey, Thomas	1,000	1	381	1–6–1783	Licking	
Massey, Thomas	5,000	2	343	8–8–1783	None	Withdrawn
Massey, Thos	500	3	191	3–1–1784	Hinkston & Stoners Fk	
Massie, Nathaniel	2,000	3	70	12–4–1783	S Fk Sandy	Withdrawn
Massie, Nathaniel	2,000	3	139	1–7–1784	Buffaloe Road	
Massie, Nathaniel	372½	4	79	12–20–1784	Stoners Cr	
Massie, Nathaniel	2,000	4	181	5–19–1785	Stoners Fk	
Massie, Nathaniel	1,000	4	181	5–19–1785	Hingston Fk	
Massie, Thos	1,002	3	407	7–14–1784	None	
Massie Jr & Fowler	372½	4	266	1–30–1786	Elkhorn	Withdrawn
Massie Jr & Fowler	1,000	4	279	3–3–1786	Hingston Fk	
Massie & Fowler	50	4	304	9–1–1786	Ohio R	
Massie & Fowler	100	4	326	12–20–1788	None	
Massie & McMillan	8,000	3	169	1–26–1784	S Fk Licking	Withdrawn
Massie & Marshall Jr	50	3	414	7–22–1784	None	
Massie & Marshall Jr	125	3	352	6–3–1784	Hingston Fk	
Masterson, James	1,121½	1	389	1–7–1784	Hinkstons Fk	
Masterson, Richard	325	1	8	11–29–1782	N Fk Licking	
Masterson, Richard	1,000	2	133	1–27–1783	None	
Masterson, Richard	1,000	2	138	1–28–1783	Mastersons Cr	Surveyed
Masterson, Richard	2,000	2	161	2–4–1783	Hustons Fk	
Masterson, Richard	500	2	192	2–13–1783	N Fk Elkhorn	Surveyed
Masterson, Richard	1,500	2	230	3–11–1783	Eagle Cr	Surveyed
Masterson, Richard	1,270	2	263	4–1–1783	N Fk Licking	
Masterson, Richard	10,000	2	266	4–17–1783	Ohio R	Surveyed
Masterson, Richard	1,025½	2	279	4–26–1783	Eagle Cr	Surveyed
Masterson, Richard	1,193½	3	78	12–10–1783	Grassy Lick Cr	
Masterson, Richard	22,277½	3	154	1–17–1784	Hunters Trace	
Masterson, Richard	1,193½	4	276	2–19–1786	None	
Masterson, & Taylor	1,000	3	46	11–15–1783	Ohio R	
Mathews, Gregory	785	3	151	1–16–1784	—— Cr	

Entree	Acres	Book	Page	Entry Date	Watercourse	Notes
Matson, James	68	2	71	1–16–1783	Hingston Fk	Amended
Matson, James	1,000	2	71	1–16–1783	Hingston Fk	Withdrawn
Matson, James	2,143	2	172	2– 7–1783	None	....
Matson, James	662	2	172	2– 7–1783	None	....
Matson, James	1,000	2	174	2– 8–1783	Hinkstons Fk	....
Matthews, Joseph	500	1	200	12–20–1782	Big Bone Lick	Surveyed
Matthews, Newman	750	1	35	12–14–1782	Clear & Jessamine Cr	....
Maurice, Jno	30,000	3	113	12–27–1783	E Fk Licking	Surveyed
Mauroney, Sylvester	1,381	4	217	8– 7–1785	None	....
Maury, Abraham	5,500	1	228	12–21–1782	None	Surveyed
Maury, Abraham	2,000	1	228	12–21–1782	None	....
Maury, Abraham	10,000	2	376	10–13–1783	Ohio R	Withdrawn
Maury, Abraham Jr	2,500	2	341	8– 7–1783	None	Surveyed
Maury, Abraham & Perkins	25	2	358	8–20–1783	Ky R	....
Maury, Enoch	3,529½	4	54	10–16–1784	None	....
Maury, Jas	15,000	4	199	6–15–1785	S Fk Licking	....
Maury, Jas	14,000	4	199	6–15–1785	None	....
Maury, Matthew & Fontaine	4,000	1	228	12–21–1782	N Fk Eagle Cr	....
Maury, Matthew & Fontaine	1,000	1	256	12–24–1782	Lindseys Run	....
Maury, Reubin	3,000	4	54	10–16–1784	None	....
Maury & Barbour	10,000	3	55	11–21–1783	Ohio R	Surveyed
Maury & Croutcher	10,000	4	218	8–20–1785	None	....
Maxwell, Alexander	444	2	377	10–13–1783	N Fk Elkhorn	Surveyed
Maxwell, Alexander	281	3	16	10–29–1783	N Fk Elkhorn	....
Maxwell, Thos	2,035	3	38	11–12–1783	Slate Cr	....
Maxwell, Wm	5,451	3	66	12– 1–1783	Salt Rock Cr	....
May, Banister & Co	10,000	2	254	3–24–1783	Ohio R	....
May, Banister & Co	40,000	2	259	3–29–1783	Ohio R	Surveyed
May, Banister & Co	20,000	2	259	3–29–1783	Br Ohio R	Surveyed
May, Banister & Co	10,000	2	259	3–29–1783	Br Ohio R	Withdrawn
May, Banister & Co	10,000	2	260	3–29–1783	Br Ohio R	Surveyed
May, Banister & Co	40,000	2	270	4– 8–1783	E Fk Eagle Cr	Surveyed
May, Banister & Co	5,000	3	365	6–14–1784	Small Lick	Withdrawn
May, Banister & Co	3,000	4	96	1–22–1785	None	Surveyed
May, Banister & Co	1,000	4	97	1–22–1785	None	....
May, Banister & Co	6,000	4	98	1–24–1785	None	Surveyed
May, Banister & Co	5,000	4	98	1–24–1785	Ohio R	....
May, Banister & Co	5,000	4	98	1–24–1785	None	....
May, Gabriel	500	1	153	12–17–1782	N Fk Licking	....
May, George	100	1	1	11–28–1782	Hingstons Fk	....
May, George	60	1	2	11–28–1782	Main Fk Licking Cr	....
May, George	40	1	2	11–28–1782	Sandy Cr	....
May, George	100	1	3	11–28–1782	Licking Cr	....
May, George	600	2	25	1–10–1783	Holders Cr	....
May, George	400	2	25	1–10–1783	None	....
May, John	200	1	359	1– 4–1783	Lick Cr	Surveyed
May, John	500	2	217	3– 1–1783	None	....
May, John	433½	2	218	3– 1–1783	Sulphur Salt Lick	....
May, Jno	5,000	4	309	1– 5–1787	Ky R	....
May, Richard	400	2	171	2– 7–1783	None	Surveyed
May, Stephen	1,000	1	90	12– 9–1782	Elkhorn & Licking	Withdrawn
May, William	1,000	2	4	1– 8–1783	Licking	Surveyed
May & Ross	60,000	4	78	12–20–1784	Br Ohio R	Surveyed
Mayo, John	10,000	2	255	3–24–1783	Br Ohio R	....
Mayo, John	30,000	1	358	1– 4–1783	Licking Cr	....
Mehan, Jno	450	3	98	12–18–1783	Mill Cr	Surveyed
Melton, John	1,000	1	193	12–19–1782	So Fk Licking	Surveyed
Melton, Jno	1,000	1	193	12–20–1782	S Fk Licking	Surveyed
Melton, John	1,000	1	194	12–20–1782	W Fk Coopers Run	....
Melton, John	1,000	1	194	12–20–1782	Elkhorn & Licking	Surveyed
Melton, John	1,000	1	194	12–20–1782	None	Surveyed
Melton, John	500	1	194	12–20–1782	Indian Cr	Surveyed
Melton, John	500	1	194	12–20–1782	None	Surveyed
Melton, John	1,000	1	195	12–20–1782	S Fk Licking	Surveyed
Melton, John	1,000	1	195	12–20–1782	S Fk Licking	Surveyed
Mennis, Robert	50	2	198	2–17–1783	Main Fk Licking	....
Meny, Prettyman	3,000	1	132	12–13–1782	Buffalo Road	Surveyed
Mercer, Jno D	10,000	3	263	4– 1–1784	None	....
Mercier & Burrall	7,000	3	114	12–27–1783	E Fk Licking	Withdrawn
Mercier & Burrall	6,000	3	118	12–29–1783	Buffaloe Road	....
Mercier & Barral	600	3	265	4– 1–1784	None	....
Meredith, Samuel	1,000	1	6	12–13–1782	Br Licking R	....
Meredith, Samuel	1,000	1	7	12–13–1782	Main Fk Licking	Surveyed
Meredith, Samuel	200	1	7	12–13–1782	Ky R	....
Meredith, Samuel	1,000	1	9	11–30–1782	None	Surveyed
Meredith, Samuel	2,000	1	9	11–30–1782	Fk Bank Lick Cr	Surveyed
Meredith, Samuel	20,000	1	11	11–30–1782	Slate Cr	....

Entree	Acres	Book	Page	Entry Date	Watercourse	Notes
Meredith, Samuel	400	1	14	11–30–1782	Licking	
Meredith, Samuel	2,000	1	15	12– 2–1782	Big Bone Lick	Surveyed
Meredith, Samuel	2,000	1	15	11–30–1782	Big Bone Lick	Surveyed
Meredith, Samuel	400	1	14	11–30–1782	Hingstons Fk	
Meredith, William	500	2	10	1– 9–1783	Ohio R	
Meredith & Breckenridge	72	4	342	9– 9–1816	None	
Meriweather, James	500	1	28	12– 3–1782	S Fk Elkhorn	Surveyed
Merham & Fishback	3,138	3	135	1– 2–1784	None	Surveyed
Metcalfe, Chas	950	3	25	10–31–1783	Ohio R	
Metcalfe, Jno	2,972	3	157	1–19–1784	Licking	Surveyed
Metcalfe, Jno	1,520	3	227	3–14–1784	Licking	Surveyed
Metcalfe, Jno	3,800	4	218	8–10–1785	Eagle Cr	
Michael, John Frederick	133	1	202	12–20–1782	Hingstons Fk	Surveyed
Michael, Jno Frederick	200	1	202	12–20–1782	Hingstons Fk	Surveyed
Michan, Jno	450	3	358	6–10–1784	None	Surveyed
Middleton, John	1,000	1	72	12– 9–1782	Elkhorn	
Middleton, Jno	400	4	327	3– 2–1789	Little N Fk Elkhorn	
Middleton & Shortridge	708½	4	81	12–31–1784	None	
Miles, John	2,200	2	239	3–13–1783	None	
Miller, Chas	126,140	3	298	4–22–1784	1 h Fk 3 Fks Ky R.	Surveyed and amended
Miller, Ebeneezer	7,231	2	338	8– 2–1783	Indian Cr	
Miller, George	500	2	233	3–12–1783	Bank Lick Cr	
Miller, Geo	8,000	4	285	3–26–1786	Ohio R	
Miller, Henry	1,687	1	102	12–10–1782	None	
Miller, Henry	4,000	1	283	12–26–1782	Buffalo Road	Surveyed
Miller, John	1,000	1	40	12– 4–1782	Hingston Fk	Surveyed
Miller, Jno & Thos	2,850	3	50	11–17–1783	Ohio R	Withdrawn
Miller, Jno & Thos	4,000	3	49	11–17–1783	Ohio R	Withdrawn
Miller, Jno &Thos	2,851½	3	56	11–21–1783	Ohio R	Amended withdrawn
Miller, Jno & Thos	1,000	3	56	11–21–1783	——— R	Surveyed
Miller, Jno & Thos	1,051	3	56	11–21–1783	Ohio R	Withdrawn
Miller, Jno & Thos	2,851½	3	328	5– 7–1784	None	Withdrawn
Miller, Jno & Thos	2,851½	4	144	4– 9–1785	None	
Miller, Jno & Thos	5,701½	4	144	4–10–1785	Ohio R	Withdrawn
Miller, Jno & Thos	400	4	319	1– 9–1788	None	
Miller, Thomas	2,000	2	239	2–13–1783	None	
Miller, Thomas	2,000	2	240	3–13–1783	None	
Miller, Wm	1,000	1	395	1– 7–1783	Br S Fk Licking	Surveyed
Miller, Wm	2,000	3	50	11–17–1783	None	Withdrawn
Miller & Patterson	10,000	4	174	5– 9–1785	None	
Miller & Patterson	5,000	4	175	5– 9–1785	None	Withdrawn
Miller & Patterson	5,000	4	175	5– 9–1785	None	
Miller & Patterson	5,000	4	285	3–26–1786	None	
Mills, Edward	2,000	2	310	6– 7–1783	Br Ohio R	
Mills, Isham	1,000	2	108	1–23–1783	Sycamore Fk Hingston	Surveyed
Mills, Isham	1,000	2	108	1–23–1783	Sycamore Fk Hingston	Surveyed
Mills, Isham	700	2	163	2– 4–1783	Sycamore Fk	Surveyed
Mills, Isham	1,000	2	165	2– 5–1783	Br Licking	Surveyed
Mills, Thomas	678½	2	312	6– 9–1783	Ohio R	
Minton, John	500	1	28	12– 3–1782	Mill Cr	
Mitchell, Daniel	4,904½	2	115	1–23–1783	Ohio R	Surveyed
Mitchel, David	1,000	1	55	12– 5–1782	Br Cane Run	Surveyed
Mitchell, David	1,000	1	55	12– 5–1782	Br Clear Cr	Surveyed
Mitchell, David	200	2	89	1–20–1783	Green Cr	Surveyed
Mitchell, David	1,000	2	119	1–24–1783	None	Surveyed
Mitchell, David	100	2	221	3– 3–1783	None	
Mitchell, Edward	500	3	271	4– 6–1784	Licking	Withdrawn
Mitchell, Edward	137	4	113	2– 7–1785	None	
Mitchell, Edward	363	4	150	4–10–1785	None	
Mitchell, Ignatius	7,375	3	147	1–15–1784	Ohio R	Surveyed
Mitchell, Ignatius	1,000	3	192	3– 1–1784	Ky R	
Mitchell, Ignatius	1,000	4	77	12–16–1784	Ohio R	Surveyed
Mitchell, James	2,133	4	54	10–16–1784	None	
Mitchell, John	500	1	344	1– 1–1783	Gists Cr	
Mitchell, Jno	1,510½	3	175	2– 5–1784	Hickman Cr	Withdrawn
Mitchell, Jno	50,000	3	377	6–19–1784	None	Surveyed
Mitchell, Jno	1,510½	4	204	6–29–1785	None	
Mitchell, Jno	1,510½	4	205	6–30–1785	Hickman Cr	
Mitchell, Jno Sr & Jno Jr	1,000	4	310	1–29–1787	None	
Mitchell, Robert	3,475	1	322	12–30–1782	None	Withdrawn
Mitchell, Robert	1,653	1	342	1– 1–1783	None	Withdrawn
Mitchell, Robert	500	1	345	1– 1–1783	Gasts Cr	
Mitchell, Robert	3,944½	2	116	1–24–1783	None	Surveyed

Entree	Acres	Book	Page	Entry Date	Watercourse	Notes
Mitchell, Robt	3,125	3	344	5–24–1784	Big Bone Lick	Withdrawn
Mitchell, Robt	3,125	3	377	6–18–1784	None	
Mitchell, Robt	6,445	3	377	6–19–1784	Br Ohio R	
Mitchell, Robt	1,653	4	148	4–10–1785	None	
Mitchell, Robt	3,475	4	149	4–10–1785	None	
Mitchell, Robt	5,128	4	149	4–10–1785	Little Sandy	
Mitchell, Robt	1,000	4	215	8– 2–1785	Ohio R	
Mitchell, Rosannah	150	2	174	2– 7–1783	N Fk Elkhorn	Amended
Mitchell, Rossanah	150	2	212	2–28–1783	None	
Mitchell, William	1,168	1	359	1– 4–1783	None	
Mitchell, Wm	300	1	375	1– 6–1783	S Fk Elkhorn	Surveyed
Mitchell, William	200	2	353	8–16–1783	S Fk Licking	
Mitchell & Blake	1,000	3	216	3–10–1784	Huston Fk	Withdrawn
Mitchell & Blake	1,000	3	216	3–10–1784	Hinkston Fk	Withdrawn
Mitchell & Blake	1,000	3	216	3–10–1784	Hinkston Fk	Withdrawn
Mitchell & Blake	1,400	3	217	3–10–1784	N Fk Elkhorn	Withdrawn
Mitchell & Blake	3,000	3	217	3–10–1784	None	
Mitchell & Blake	1,400	3	217	3–10–1784	Elkhorn & Licking	Withdrawn
Mitchell & Blake	400½	3	217	3–10–1784	Hustons Fk	Withdrawn
Mitchell & Blake	403	3	217	3–10–1784	Hustons Fk	Withdrawn
Mitchell & Blake	407	3	218	3–10–1784	W Fk Hickman Cr.	Withdrawn
Mitchell & Blake	1,400	3	231	3–20–1784	None	
Mitchell & Blake Jr	1,400	3	317	4–30–1784	N Fk Elkhorn	
Mitchell & Blake Jr	1,500	3	317	4–30–1784	Licking & Elkhorn	
Mitchell & Blake Jr	400½	3	317	4–30–1784	Hustons Fk	
Mitchell & Blake Jr	407	3	317	4–30–1784	W Fk Hickman	
Mitchell & Blake Jr	403	3	317	4–30–1784	Hustons Fk	
Mitchell & Steele	1,000	4	306	10–14–1786	Ohio R	
Moffitt, George	500	1	51	12– 5–1782	E Br Licking	
Moffitt, John	500	1	51	12– 5–1782	Dry Run	
Moffitt, Thomas	500	1	51	12– 5–1782	Dry Run	
Monroe, James	4,242½	1	385	1– 7–1783	None	
Monroe, James	5,000	2	312	6– 9–1783	None	Withdrawn
Monroe, James	10,000	2	329	7–19–1783	Ohio R	Surveyed
Monroe, James	10,000	2	330	7–22–1783	——— R	
Monroe, James	10,000	2	341	8– 5–1783	None	Surveyed
Monroe, James	15,625	2	342	8– 7–1783	None	Surveyed
Monroe, James	42,656¼	3	238	3–25–1784	N Fk Elkhorn	Withdrawn
Monroe, Jas	42,656½	4	228	10–23–1785	None	
Monroe, James, heirs	5,000	2	297	5–29–1783	Salt Sp Fk	Withdrawn
Monroe, Jno	2,000	4	189	6– 1–1785	Ohio R	
Montague, Thomas	1,000	1	10	11–29–1782	Hingstons Fk	
Montague, Thos	5,000	3	159	1–21–1784	Fk Sandy R	
Montigue, Thos	20,073	3	79	12–10–1783	Licking	
Montgomery, Alexander	1,000	2	189	2–13–1783	None	
Montgomery, James	8,965½	3	333	5–14–1784	Eagle Cr	
Montgomery, Jas	8,959¾	3	333	5–14–1784	None	4,479¾ acres withdrawn
Montgomery, Jane	525	2	127	1–27–1783	Haw Cr	
Montgomery, John	500	2	17	1– 9–1783	Br N Fk Licking	Surveyed
Montgomery, John	1,000	2	188	2–13–1783	None	
Montgomery, John	500	2	189	2–13–1783	None	
Montgomery, John	437½	2	261	3–31–1783	S Fk Elkhorn	
Montgomery, Jno	29,936	3	424	8–11–1784	Cumberland Mt	
Montgomery, Margaret	750	4	161	4–29–1785	None	
Montgomery, Thomas	2,331	2	126	1–27–1783	S Fk Licking	
Montgomery, William	463½	2	189	2–13–1783	None	
Montgomery, Wm	815	4	162	4–29–1785	None	
Moody, James	31,111½	3	116	12–27–1783	Main Fk Licking	Withdrawn
Moody, Jas	10,111½	4	151	4–10–1785	None	
Moody, Jas	24,000	3	116	12–27–1783	Lawrence Cr	Withdrawn
Moody, James	24,000	3	166	1–24–1784	Br S Fk Licking	10,000 acres withdrawn 14,000 acres surveyed
Moody, Jas	31,000	3	235	3–22–1784	S Fk Licking	Surveyed
Moore, Andrew	1,000	1	379	1– 6–1783	None	Withdrawn
Moore, Andrew	1,000	2	48	1–13–1783	Ky R & Clear Cr	
Moore, Andrew	3,943½	2	130	1–27–1783	None	
Moore, Andrew	1,000	4	316	10–30–1787	None	
Moore, Archibald	545	2	63	1–14–1783	None	Surveyed
Moore, Clean	9,922	3	96	12–17–1783	None	
Moore, George	1,000	1	283	12–25–1782	Licking	Surveyed
Moore, Hugh	480	4	182	5–21–1785	Br N Fk Elkhorn	
Moore, Joseph	4,000	1	261	12–24–1782	War Road & Licking	Surveyed
Moore, Jeremiah	3,000	1	394	1– 8–1783	Harrods Upper Cr	Surveyed
Moore, Jeremiah	3,000	2	1	1– 8–1783	Howards Upper Cr.	Surveyed
Moore, Jeremiah	3,000	2	1	1– 8–1783	Stoners Fk	Surveyed
Moore, Jeremiah	5,000	2	2	1– 8–1783	Small Mt & M Fk Hingston	3,000 acres withdrawn

Entree	Acres	Book	Page	Entry Date	Watercourse	Notes
Moore, Jeremiah	5,600	2	5	1– 8–1783	Upper Howards Cr.	
Moore, Jeremiah	914½	2	5	1– 8–1783	Br Licking	Withdrawn
Moore, Jeremiah	3,000	2	13	1– 9–1783	Stoners Fk	Withdrawn
Moore, Jeremiah	2,800	2	14	1– 9–1783	Br Licking	Withdrawn
Moore, Jeremiah	914½	2	253	3–21–1783	Stoners Fk	Withdrawn
Moore, Jeremiah	3,812½	3	1	10–14–1783	Licking	Surveyed
Moore, Jeremiah	3,000	3	270	4– 6–1784	None	Surveyed
Moore, Jeremiah	3,000	3	270	4– 6–1784	None	
Moore, Jeremiah	914½	3	270	4– 6–1784	Hinkston Fk & Licking	
Moore, Jeremiah	2,800	3	270	4– 6–1784	None	
Moore, Jeremiah	1,000	3	270	4– 6–1784	Hinkston Fk & Licking	Surveyed
Moore, Jeremiah	1,500	3	273	4– 6–1784	Licking	
Moore, Moses	1,000	1	58	12– 5–1782	————	Surveyed
Moore, Peter	2,106½	2	170	2– 7–1783	Coopers Run	Withdrawn
Moore, Peter	2,106¼	2	200	2–17–1783	Coopers Run	Surveyed
Moore, Peter	1,000	2	200	2–17–1783	None	Surveyed
Moore, Samuel	400	3	199	3– 2–1784	Small Mt Cr	Withdrawn
Moore, Samuel	400	3	276	4– 7–1784	Small Mt Cr	Surveyed
Moore, Thomas	685	1	299	12–27–1782	Elkhorn	
Moore, William	1,000	2	219	3– 1–1783	N Fk Elkhorn	Surveyed
Moore, William	800½	2	249	3–15–1783	Jessamine Cr	
Moore, Wm	200	4	166	4–29–1785	None	
Moore & Shannon	2,000	3	11	10–16–1783	Ohio R	
Moorin, Jno	2,160¼	4	55	10–16–1784	None	
Moorsin & McLenanen	4,708	3	60	11–25–1783	Locust Cr	
Mordico, Joseph	200	4	271	2–13–1786	Big Sandy	
Morgan, Charles	3,000	1	275	12–25–1782	Hingston & Stoners Fk	Surveyed
Morgan, Charles	3,000	1	276	12–25–1782	Flat Lick Fk	Withdrawn
Morgan, Charles	975	1	277	12–25–1782	Flat Lick Fk	Withdrawn
Morgan, Charles	1,000	1	289	12–27–1782	E Br Stoners Fk	Withdrawn
Morgan, Charles	1,000	1	290	12–27–1782	E Br Stoners Fk	
Morgan, Charles	500	1	291	12–27–1782	Timber Fk Stoners	Withdrawn
Morgan, Charles	500	1	324	12–30–1782	Fallen Timber Fk	Surveyed
Morgan, Charles	933	1	361	1– 4–1783	E Br Stoners Fk	
Morgan, Charles	2,375	1	375	1– 6–1783	Clemenes Fk & Hinkstons	Amended
Morgan, Charles	1,000	2	67	1–15–1783	E Br Stoners Fk	Withdrawn
Morgan, Charles	975	2	107	1–22–1783	Flat Lick Fk	Surveyed
Morgan, Chas	482	2	163	2– 4–1783	Howards Cr	Surveyed
Morgan, Chas	1,000	2	165	2– 5–1783	Br Licking	Surveyed
Morgan, Charles	6,000	2	165	2– 5–1783	Br Licking	
Morgan, Charles	1,000	2	313	6– 9–1783	Br Licking	Withdrawn
Morgan, Charles	4,000	2	314	6– 9–1783	None	Withdrawn
Morgan, Chas	4,980½	3	135	1– 2–1784	None	
Morgan, Chas	2,445	3	179	2–11–1784	W Fk Howards Cr.	2,000 acres withdrawn 445 surveyed
Morgan, Chas	1,000	3	193	3– 2–1784	Br Stoners Fk	
Morgan, Chas	12,311	3	194	3– 2–1784	Fks Hinkston	
Morgan, Chas	8,959¾	3	333	5–14–1784	None	4,479¾ acres withdrawn
Morgan, Chas	222	3	407	7–14–1784	lower Howards Cr.	Withdrawn
Morgan, Chas	6,710¾	3	408	7–14–1784	Eagle Cr	Withdrawn
Morgan, Chas	2,000	3	423	8–11–1784	Boones Cr	Withdrawn
Morgan, Chas	687½	3	423	8–11–1784	Boones Cr	
Morgan, Chas	500	3	424	8–11–1784	lower Howards Cr.	
Morgan, Chas	812½	3	424	8–11–1784	Stoners Fk	
Morgan, Chas	4,479¾	4	32	9–10–1784	Eagle Cr	
Morgan, Chas	3,335¼	4	32	9–10–1784	Eagle Cr	Withdrawn
Morgan, Chas	687½	4	51	10–13–1784	Boone Cr	
Morgan, Chas	57,499¼	4	57	10–23–1784	Eagle Cr	Surveyed
Morgan, Chas	500	4	76	12–16–1784	Eagle Cr	
Morgan, Chas	5,934	4	115	2–10–1785	None	
Morgan, Chas	3,800	4	218	8–10–1785	Eagle Cr	
Morgan, Chas	100	4	227	10–18–1785	Boones Cr	
Morgan, Chas	1,360	4	286	3–27–1786	None	
Morgan, Chas	1,360	4	286	3–27–1786	Boones Cr	Surveyed
Morgan, Chas	4,000	4	287	3–28–1786	None	
Morgan, Chas	260	4	315	10–19–1787	None	
Morgan, Chas	260	4	315	10–19–1787	Ky R	
Morgan, Chas	60	4	325	12–17–1788	Boones & Jouitts Co.	
Morgan, Chas	1,900	4	325	12–17–1788	Boones & Howards Cr	
Morgan, Charles & Assee	250	1	5	11–29–1783	Main Br Stoners Fk	Withdrawn
Morgan, David Brig Genl	2,000	1	388	1– 7–1783	Licking Cr	
Morgan, Daniel	4,000	1	114	12–12–1782	None	Surveyed
Morgan, Daniel	2,000	1	388	1– 7–1783	None	Surveyed

Entree	Acres	Book	Page	Entry Date	Watercourse	Notes
Morgan, Daniel	468	2	216	2–28–1783	None	
Morgan, Ralph	903½	2	344	8– 9–1783	Br Licking	Withdrawn
Morgan, Ralph	1,556	2	354	8–16–1783	Br Hingston Fk	Surveyed
Morgan, Ralph	903¾	3	68	12– 1–1783	Br S Fk Sandy	
Morgan, Ralph	1,000	3	68	12– 1–1783	Br Hinkston Fk	Withdrawn
Morgan, Ralph	500	3	162	1–22–1784	Upper Blue Lick	
Morgan, Ralph	500	3	162	1–22–1784	Mud Lick Cr	
Morgan, Ralph	1,000	3	162	1–22–1784	Fks ——— Br	
Morgan, Ralph	1,000	3	323	5– 4–1784	Big Slate Cr	Withdrawn
Morgan, Ralph	1,000	3	401	7–10–1784	None	
Morgan, Ralph	1,000	3	401	7–10–1784	None	
Morgan, Ralph	1,000	3	401	7–10–1784	Big Slate Cr	Surveyed
Morgan, Ralph	766½	3	408	7–14–1784	Slate Cr	
Morgan, Ralph	50	4	42	9–24–1784	Rocky Fk	
Morgan, Ralph	288	4	43	9–24–1784	Rocky Fk	
Morgan, Ralph	7,000	4	62	10–29–1784	Main Licking	
Morgan, Ralph	12,225	4	70	11–25–1784	Slate Cr	
Morgan, Ralph	2,000	4	118	2–12–1785	Br Licking	
Morgan, Ralph	400	4	239	12–13–1785	Salt Rock Fk	
Morgan, Ralph	1,500	4	243	12–17–1785	Licking	
Morgan, Simon	375	3	25	10–31–1783	None	
Morgan, Simon	2,750	4	214	8– 2–1785	None	
Morgan, Simon	1,508½	4	218	8–13–1785	None	Withdrawn
Morgan, Simon	1,878	4	219	8–31–1785	None	Surveyed
Morgan, Wm	17,604	3	58	11–25–1783	N Fk Big Bone Lick	Amended
Morgan, Wm	17,604	3	177	2–10–1784	N Fk Big Bone Lick	
Morgan, Wm & Chas	15,979½	3	136	1– 2–1784	None	Surveyed
Morgan & Barker	656¼	3	132	1– 2–1784	None	
Morgan & Blackburn	1,559	3	133	1– 2–1784	None	
Morgan & Boyd	1,000	3	130	1– 1–1784	Ohio R	
Morgan & Brown	38,000	3	177	2–10–1784	None	
Morgan & Brown	18,000	4	337	11–13–1793	Ohio R	
Morgan, Cox & Bowman	850	4	51	10–13–1784	Eagle Cr	
Morgan & Churchill	7,834	3	134	1– 2–1784	Ohio & Licking	
Morgan & Craddock	3,000	3	356	6– 9–1784	None	
Morgan & Doggett	1,840	4	287	3–28–1786	None	
Morgan & Donnell	4,332½	3	180	2–11–1784	Eagle Cr	Surveyed
Morgan & Donnell	12,000	4	209	7–22–1785	None	
Morgan & Fishback	40,000	3	58	11–25–1783	Br N Fk Big Bone Lick	Withdrawn
Morgan & Fishback	40,000	3	127	1– 1–1784	Big Bone Lick	
Morgan & Fishback	4,430	4	327	1–28–1789	Ohio R	
Morgan & Ford	2,887½	3	132	1– 2–1784	None	
Morgan & Howard	900	3	356	6– 9–1784	None	Surveyed
Morgan & Hunter	1,000	3	133	1– 2–1784	None	
Morgan & Keith	1,000	3	131	1– 2–1784	None	
Morgan & Lewis	3,000	3	195	3– 2–1784	Clements Fk	
Morgan & Lewis	4,661	3	129	1– 1–1784	Ohio R	
Morgan & Maddox	1,000	3	300	4–24–1784	Elkhorn & Licking	Withdrawn
Morgan & Maddox	1,000	4	65	11– 5–1784	None	
Morgan & Parker	806¼	3	132	1– 2–1784	None	
Morgan & Payne	5,000	3	128	1– 1–1783	Ohio R	
Morgan & Payne	3,000	3	128	1– 1–1784	Ohio R	
Morgan & Piper	1,541	3	130	1– 1–1784	N Fk Big Bone Cr	Surveyed
Morgan & Piper	7,093	3	127	1– 1–1784	N Fk Big Bone Lick	
Morgan & Piper	7,093	3	59	11–25–1783	N Fk Big Bone Lick	Surveyed
Morgan & Rogers	3,375	3	135	1– 2–1784	None	Surveyed
Morgan & Spilman	7,812	4	287	3–28–1786	None	
Morgan & Walton	1,478½	3	356	6– 9–1784	Eagle Cr	
Morris, James	500	2	230	3–11–1783	Eagle Cr	Surveyed
Morris, Richard	1,000	2	299	5–29–1783	None	Surveyed
Morrison, Isaac	400	3	94	12–16–1783	Lius Mud Lick	
Morrison, James	2,474	2	130	1–27–1783	None	
Morrison, Jas	1,000	4	215	8– 5–1785	N Fk Licking	
Morrison, John	400	1	37	12– 4–1782	Fk Lick Cr	Surveyed
Morrison, Thomas	2,474	2	130	1–27–1783	None	
Morrison, Wm	1,000	3	379	6–19–1784	Licking	
Morrow & Brough	3,018	4	80	12–30–1784	S Fk Elkhorn	Withdrawn
Morrow & Brough	3,018	4	83	1– 8–1785	None	
Morrow & Brough	1,400	4	83	1– 8–1785	Hunters Fk	Withdrawn
Morrow & Brough	1,000	4	84	1– 8–1785	Flat Cr	Withdrawn
Morrow & Brough	1,000	4	92	1–17–1785	None	
Morrow & Brough	3,518	4	92	1–17–1785	Main Licking	
Morton, John	3,000	1	23	12– 3–1782	S Fk Licking	Surveyed
Morton, John	1,000	1	27	12– 3–1782	S Fk Licking	
Morton, John	1,000	1	28	12– 3–1782	S Fk Licking	Surveyed
Morton, Jno	1,000	4	46	10– 5–1784	N Fk Hingston	Withdrawn
Morton, Jno	1,000	4	46	10– 5–1784	N Fk Hingston	Surveyed
Morton, Benjamin	2,975½	2	193	2–14–1783	Big Sandy	

Entree	Acres	Book	Page	Entry Date	Watercourse	Notes
Morton, Wm	400	3	360	6–12–1784	None	
Morton & Venible	4,507	3	123	12–30–1783	None	Surveyed
Morton & Venible	4,000	3	123	12–30–1783	Big Bone Cr	
Mosby, John	30,000	1	135	12–13–1782	N E from Upper Blue Lick	Surveyed
Mosby, John	20,000	1	137	12–14–1782	S Fk Elkhorn	Surveyed
Mosby, John	30,000	1	138	12–14–1782	Br Main Fk Licking	Withdrawn
Mosby, John	5,100	1	138	12–14–1782	Ohio R	Surveyed
Mosby, John	3,000	1	140	12–14–1782	None	Surveyed
Mosby, John	1,000	1	140	12–14–1782	Big Sandy	
Mosby, John	500	1	140	12–14–1782	Salt Spring	
Mosby, John	500	1	140	12–14–1782	Big Sandy R	
Mosby, Jno	30,000	1	146	12–16–1782	Br M Licking	
Mosby, John	5,000	1	147	12–16–1782	Ohio R	
Mosby, John	10,000	1	147	12–14–1782	Johnsons Fk Licking	Surveyed
Mosby, John	3,000	1	150	12–16–1782	Ohio R	
Mosby, John	10,000	1	152	12–17–1782	Br Main Licking	Surveyed
Mosby, John	1,000	1	178	12–18–1782	None	Surveyed
Mosby, John	5,737	1	367	1– 4–1783	None	
Mosby, John	3,000	2	1	1– 1–1783	Elkhorn & Licking	Withdrawn
Mosby, Jno	2,448	3	105	12–20–1783	Indian Cr	
Mosby, Jno	250	3	106	12–20–1783	Indian Cr	
Mosby, Joseph	400	1	32	12– 3–1782	None	
Mosby, Joseph	1,000	2	209	2–26–1783	Woods Run	Surveyed
Mosby, Joseph	1,000	4	107	2– 5–1785	—— Cr	
Mosby, Nicholas	6,805	2	123	1–25–1783	None	Surveyed
Mosby, Robert	1,000	2	206	2–21–1783	Townsend Cr	Surveyed
Mosby, Robt	3,000	3	83	12–12–1783	Licking	
Mosby, Robt	3,000	3	84	12–12–1783	Licking	
Mosby, Robt	3,000	3	184	2–13–1784	Lower Twin Cr	Surveyed
Mosby, Thomas	1,650	1	339	12–31–1782	Hingston Fk	
Moseby, Nicholas	3,487½	4	251	12–30–1785	Ohio R	
Moseby, Nicholas	3,487½	4	277	2–19–1786	None	
Moseley, Thomas Assn	500	1	55	12– 5–1782	Licking	
Mosly, Caleb	400	4	239	12–13–1785	—— Cr	
Moss, Fredrick	1,500	4	239	12–13–1785	Ky R	
Moss, Johns	1,000	2	2	1– 8–1783	Jessamine	Surveyed
Moss, John	2,900	2	39	1–11–1783	None	Surveyed
Moss, Jno	——	2	106	1–22–1783	None	Surveyed
Moss, Jno	3,063½	3	24	10–31–1783	None	
Mountjoy, Edmond	1,000	4	267	2– 3–1786	None	
Moylan & Colwell	7,000	3	264	4– 1–1784	None	Surveyed
Mullens, Peter	600	2	200	2–17–1783	None	
Munday, Jno	3,041½	4	146	4–10–1785	Little Sandy	
Munday, Jno	1,000	4	146	4–10–1785	None	
Murehead, Charles	203	2	268	4– 7–1783	Stoners Fk	Withdrawn
Murehead, Chas	203	3	197	3– 2–1784	Small Mt Cr	Surveyed
Murry, Jas	20,000	4	179	5–12–1785	None	Surveyed
Muse, Phebe	400	2	267	4– 7–1783	W Br Howards Upper Cr	
Muse, Richard	1,000	1	369	1– 4–1783	None	Withdrawn
Muse, Richard	1,000	2	157	2– 1–1783	None	Surveyed
Myans, William	2,375	1	375	1– 6–1783	Clemenes Fk Hinkstons	Amended
Myers, Jacob	1,000	1	383	1– 6–1783	Shannons Run	Surveyed
Myers, Jacob	10,000	2	55	1–13–1783	Ky R	Surveyed
Myers, Jacob	801	2	55	1–13–1783	Licking	Surveyed
Myers, Jacob	1,000	2	55	1–13–1783	Licking	Surveyed
Myers, Jacob	1,000	2	56	1–13–1783	Licking	
Myers, Jacob	5,195	2	57	1–13–1783	Ky R	Surveyed
Myers, Jacob	2,437½	2	57	1–13–1783	Br Ohio R	Surveyed
Myers, Jacob	1,674	2	142	1–30–1783	Slate Cr	Surveyed
Myers, Jacob	1,000	2	142	1–30–1783	Slate Cr	
Myers, Jacob	1,000	2	146	1–31–1783	Br Slate Cr	Withdrawn
Myers, Jacob	1,000	2	146	1–31–1783	S Fk Licking	Surveyed
Myers, Jacob	1,000	2	146	1–31–1783	None	Surveyed
Myers, Jacob	1,000	2	146	1–31–1783	Fk Elkhorn	Surveyed
Myers, Jacob	1,000	2	147	1–31–1783	Br Hustons Fk	Surveyed
Myers, Jacob	1,000	2	149	2– 1–1783	M Elkhorn & W Fk Cane Run	Surveyed
Myers, Jacob	1,000	2	297	5–28–1783	Buffaloe Road	
Myers, Jacob	500	2	317	6–14–1783	Licking	Surveyed
Myers, Jacob	1,000	2	318	7– 7–1783	Big Slate Cr	Withdrawn
Myers, Jacob	1,000	2	318	7– 7–1783	Slate Cr	
Myers, Jacob	2,000	3	39	11–12–1783	None	
Myers, Jacob	1,041½	3	48	11–17–1783	Slate Cr	Surveyed
Myers, Jacob	6,000	3	48	11–17–1783	Slate Cr	Withdrawn

Entree	Acres	Book	Page	Entry Date	Watercourse	Notes
Myers, Jacob	6,000	3	226	3-14-1784	Prickly Ash Cr	4,800 acres withdrawn 1,200 acres surveyed
Myers, Jacob	800	3	226	3-14-1784	None	
Myers, Jacob	2,000	3	283	4-12-1784	None	Surveyed
Myers, Jacob	1,000	3	284	4-12-1784	Slate Cr	
Myers, Jacob	500	3	284	4-12-1784	Mud Lick Cr	Surveyed
Myers, Jacob	500	3	284	4-12-1784	Mud Lick	
Myers, Jacob	2,314	3	284	4-12-1784	None	
Myers, Jacob	4,800	3	285	4-12-1784	None	4,500 acres surveyed
Myers, Jacob	5,000	4	36	9-18-1784	Sandy Cr	
Myers, Jacob	5,000	4	42	9-24-1784	None	
Myers, Jacob	6,000	4	89	1-14-1785	Slate Cr	Surveyed
Myers, Jacob	1,000	4	90	1-15-1785	Licking	400 acres withdrawn
Myers, Jacob	1,000	4	91	1-15-1785	Licking	
Myers, Jacob	3,000	4	174	5- 9-1785	Slate Cr	Withdrawn
Myers, Jacob	6,000	4	174	5- 9-1785	Slate Cr	Withdrawn
Myers, Jacob	6,000	4	187	6- 1-1785	Slate Cr	
Myers, Jacob	3,000	4	230	11- 4-1785	Slate Cr	1,600 acres withdrawn
Myers, Jacob	2,000	4	230	11- 4-1785	Licking	
Myers, Jacob	5,000	4	230	11- 4-1785	Main Licking	
Myers, Jacob	1,000	4	231	11- 4-1785	None	
Myers, Jacob	1,000	4	231	11- 4-1785	None	
Myers, Jacob	2,000	4	234	11-19-1785	None	
Myers, Jacob	5,000	4	234	11-20-1785	None	
Myers, Jacob	1,000	4	236	12- 2-1785	Ky R	Surveyed
Myers, Jacob	3,000	4	254	1-14-1786	Main Licking	
Myers, Jacob	3,000	4	254	1-14-1786	Main Licking	
Myers, Jacob	3,000	4	255	1-14-1786	Main Licking	
Myers, Jacob	1,000	4	255	1-14-1786	Slate Cr	
Myers, Jacob	2,000	4	255	1-14-1786	Br Licking	
Myers, Jacob	846	4	256	1-14-1786	Slate Cr	
Myers, Jacob	600	4	260	1-16-1786	Slate Cr	
Myers, Jacob	300	4	260	1-18-1786	Slate Cr	
Myers, Jacob	1,500	4	301	7-15-1786	——— R	
Myers, Jacob	1,400	4	302	7-15-1786	None	
Myers, Jacob	12,000	4	339	1-17-1795	None	
Myers, Joseph	1,000	2	57	1-13-1783	Br Ohio R	Surveyed
Myers, Lewis	1,000	2	53	1-13-1783	Ky R	Surveyed
Nabb, Samuel M	729½	2	242	3-13-1783	None	
Nall, Martin	1,000	2	231	3-11-1783	None	Surveyed
Nall, William	1,000	1	61	12- 6-1782	Fk Green Cr	
Nall, Wm	2,112	3	72	12- 5-1783	——— Cr	Withdrawn
Nall, Wm	2,112	4	315	3-21-1787	None	
Neblack, Jno	100	4	335	3- 5-1792	Boggs Fk	
Neel, Barnard	500	1	19	12- 4-1782	Licking	
Neel, Benjamin	1,000	1	303	12-27-1782	Paint Lick	
Neel, Benjamin	2,000	1	304	12-28-1782	Br M Fk Licking	
Neel, Bernard	500	1	19	12- 4-1782	Licking	
Neel, Lott	250	1	19	12- 4-1782	Licking	
Neel, Samuel	2,416½	4	193	6- 6-1785	N Fk Ky R	
Neel, Thomas	500	1	19	12- 4-1782	None	
Nelson, James	995	4	265	1-29-1786	Br Eagle Cr	
Nesbit, Samuel	1,000	1	40	12- 4-1782	Middle Fk Licking	Surveyed
Nesbit, William	1,000	1	40	1- 4-1783	S Fk Licking	Surveyed
Neth, Lewis	20,000	4	155	4-20-1785	Sandy	6,873 acres withdrawn
Neth & Williams	7,000	4	56	10-17-1784	None	Withdrawn
Neth & Williams	7,000	4	56	10-17-1784	N Fk Licking	Withdrawn
Neth & Williams	700	4	73	12- 2-1784	None	
Neth & Williams	8,000	4	73	12- 2-1784	None	Wthdrawn
Neth & Williams	5,312	4	117	2-12-1785	None	
Neth & Williams	4,000	4	143	4- 5-1785	None	Withdrawn
Neth & Williams	4,940	4	143	4- 5-1785	None	
Neth & Williams	8,000	4	153	4-20-1785	None	
Neth & Williams	2,683	4	154	4-20-1785	Main Licking	Withdrawn
Neth & Williams	640	4	154	4-20-1785	None	
Neth & Williams	400	4	154	4-20-1785	None	
Neth & Williams	2,060	4	154	4-20-1785	None	
Neth & Williams	4,940	4	154	4-20-1785	None	
Netherland, Benjamin	192	1	4	11-29-1783	Salt Lick Cr	
Netherland, Benjamin	———	1	20	1-14-1783	Fowlers Lick	
Netherland, Benjamin	———	1	34	12- 3-1782	——— Cr	
Netherland, John	1,000	1	129	12-13-1782	N Br N Elkhorn	Surveyed
Netherland, Benjamin	1,000	1	129	12-13-1782	E Fk Eagle Cr	
Netherland, John	1,000	1	129	12-13-1782	E Fk Eagle Cr	
Netherland, John Sr	2,000	1	130	12-13-1782	Licking	Surveyed

Entree	Acres	Book	Page	Entry Date	Watercourse	Notes
Netherland, Benjamin.	1,000	1	134	12–13–1782	Br Licking	Surveyed
Netherland, Benjamin..	2,000	1	134	12–13–1782	Br Big Bone Lick..	Surveyed
Netherland, Benjamin..	500	1	142	12–14–1782	E Fk Eagle Cr	....
Netherland, Benjamin.	500	1	144	12–14–1782	Big Bone Lick	....
Netherland, Benjamin..	1,000	1	150	12–16–1782	S Fk Elkhorn	Surveyed
Netherland, Benjamin.	500	1	150	12–16–1782	None	Withdrawn
Netherland, Benjamin.	500	1	151	12–16–1782	N Fk Elkhorn	Surveyed
Netherland, Benjamin.	1,000	1	297	12–27–1782	Mill Cr	Withdrawn
Netherland, Benjamin.	2,000	1	313	12–30–1782	Hickman Cr	....
Netherland, Levi.....	6,000	1	313	12–30–1782	Clover Bottom	Surveyed
Netherland, Benjamin.	2,000	1	314	12–30–1782	Jessamine Cr	....
Netherland, Benjamin.	500	1	323	12–30–1782	Br N Fk Elkhorn	....
Netherland, Benjamin.	2,400½	1	346	1– 2–1783	K T R	Surveyed
Netherland, Benjamin.	2,000	1	365	1̅ 4–1783	Hickmans Cr	Surveyed
Netherland, Benjamin.	500	1	364	1̅ 4–1783	Hickmans Cr	....
Netherland, Benjamin.	2,316½	1	365	1– 4–1783	Jessamine & Ky R..	Surveyed
Netherland, Benjamin.	5,316	1	377	1– 6–1783	Main Br Jessamine.	Withdrawn
Netherland, Benjamin.	5,316	1	381	1– 6–1783	Main Fk Jessamine.	Withdrawn
Netherland, Benjamin.	1,610	2	2	1– 8–1783	Hickmans Cr	Withdrawn
Netherland, Benjamin.	1,303	2	25	1–10–1783	Eagle Cr	Surveyed
Netherland, Benjamin.	1,355	2	25	1–10–1783	Eagle Cr	Surveyed
Netherland, Benjamin.	937½	2	48	1–13–1783	None	....
Netherland, Benjamin.	423	2	75	1–16–1783	N & S Fk Elkhorn..	Surveyed
Netherland, Benjamin.	2,500	2	101	1–21–1783	None	....
Netherland, Benjamin.	960	2	106	1–22–1783	None	Surveyed
Netherland, Benjamin.	1,610	2	106	1–22–1783	None	....
Netherland, Benjamin.	1,000	2	124	1–23–1783	None	....
Netherland, Benjamin.	500	2	141	1–29–1783	Ky R	....
Netherland, Benjamin.	1,000	2	224	3– 8–1783	Mill Cr	....
Netherland, Benjamin.	65	2	266	4– 7–1783	Ky R	Surveyed
Netherland, Benjamin.	1,000	2	323	7–14–1783	Hinkstons Fk	Surveyed
Netherland, Benjamin.	2,400½	2	332	7–28–1783	Ky R	Surveyed
Nett & Williams......	400	4	27	9– 2–1784	None	Withdrawn
Nett & Williams......	2,000	4	27	9– 2–1784	None	Withdrawn
Nett & Williams......	1,960	4	27	9– 2–1784	None	Withdrawn
Neth & Williams.....	2,000	4	38	9–20–1784	None	....
Neth & Williams.....	2,640	4	38	9–20–1784	Br Licking	Withdrawn
Neth & Williams.....	640	4	39	9–20–1784	None	....
Nevill, James.........	250	1	27	12– 3–1782	Ky R	Surveyed
Nevill, James.........	1,000	1	103	12–11–1782	None	Surveyed
Nevill, James.........	1,000	2	3	1– 8–1783	None	Surveyed
Nevill, James.........	250	1	27	12– 3–1782	Boones Cr	Surveyed
Nevill, John..........	1,000	2	177	2– 8–1783	Stoners Fk	....
Newman, George......	500	1	196	12–20–1782	Licking	....
Newman, George.....	500	1	196	12–20–1782	Licking	....
Niblick, John.........	1,000	2	308	6– 6–1783	None	Surveyed
Niblie, John	222	2	286	5–14–1783	None	Surveyed
Nickell & Connelly....	769½	3	364	6–14–1784	None	....
Noble, Anthony......	1,000	2	185	2–13–1783	None	Surveyed
Noble, Anthony......	1,000	2	215	2–28–1783	Licking	Surveyed
Norris, Ezekiel.......	262½	1	334	12–31–1782	Coopers Run	....
Norris, Ezekiel.......	839	1	334	12–31–1782	Coopers Run	....
Nourse, Joseph........	2,000	3	114	12–27–1783	E Fk Licking	Withdrawn
Nourse, Joseph........	1,000	3	121	12–29–1783	S Fk Licking	....
Nourse, Joseph........	10,000	3	263	4– 1–1784	None	....
O'Bannon, Jno	4,980½	3	135	1– 2–1784	None	....
O'Daniel, John........	2,701	2	235	3–12–1783	N E Fk Licking....	Surveyed
Oldfield, Catherine.....	500	1	293	12–27–1782	Jessamine & Ky....	.........·..
Oliver, James........	500	1	296	12–27–1782	None	Surveyed
Oliver, Jno..........	500	3	196	3– 2–1784	Bank Lick Cr	Withdrawn
Oliver, Jno..........	500	4	221	9–17–1785	None	....
Oliver, Thomas.......	1,000	2	133	1–28–1783	Cedar Cr	....
Oliver, Thos.........	1,232½	4	55	10–16–1784	None	....
O'Neal, Robt........	1,000	1	192	12–19–1782	Clear Cr	Surveyed
O'Neal, Robert........	500	2	29	1–10–1783	N Fk Licking	....
O'Rear, Wm..........	726½	4	220	9– 3–1785	Ky R	Surveyed
Orr, Alexander........	7,000	3	128	1– 1–1784	Ohio R	Withdrawn
Orr, Alexander.......	10,000	3	130	1– 1–1784	Ohio R	Surveyed
Orr, Alexander.......	11,000	3	146	1–13–1784	None	....
Orr, Alexander.......	15,625	3	159	1–21–1784	Licking	Surveyed
Orr, Alexander D.....	1,000	4	132	3–13–1785	Ky R	Withdrawn
Orr, Alexander D.....	37,256	4	142	4– 5–1785	None	28,245 acres withdrawn
Orr, Alexander D.....	28,000	4	194	6– 7–1785	Ohio R	....
Orr, Alexander D.....	3,430	4	195	6– 7–1785	Ohio R	Withdrawn
Orr, Alexander D.....	26,500	4	195	6– 7–1785	Ohio R	Surveyed
Orr, Alexander D.....	1,000	4	244	12–20–1785	None	....
Orr, Alexander D.....	7,000	4	244	12–20–1785	None	....

Entree	Acres	Book	Page	Entry Date	Watercourse	Notes
Orr, Jno	50,000	3	157	1–19–1784	Raven Cr	37,000 acres Surveyed 13,000 acres withdrawn
Orr, Jno	400	3	216	3–10–1784	Hustons Fk	Withdrawn
Orr, Jno	400	3	307	4–28–1784	M Fk Licking	Withdrawn
Orr, Jno	9,500	4	131	3–12–1785	Ky R	
Orr, Jno	3,000	4	180	5–12–1785	None	
Orr, Jno	2,000	4	182	5–20–1785	None	
Orr, Jno	9,500	4	244	12–20–1785	None	
Orr, Jno	3,000	4	244	12–20–1785	None	
Orr, Jno & Alexander	20,500	4	244	12–20–1785	Ohio R	Surveyed
Orr & Banks	12,500	4	121	2–16–1785	Elkhorn	Withdrawn
Orr & Banks	9,500	4	125	3– 5–1785	Ky R	Amended & withdrawn
Orr & Fowler	1,193¾	4	276	2–19–1786	Ohio R	
Orr & Freeman	548	4	84	1– 8–1785	Hingston Fk	Withdrawn
Orr & Freeman	988	4	122	2–18–1785	None	
Orr & Wilkinson	3,277	4	200	6–17–1785	Ohio R	Surveyed
Orrick, Nicholas	2,000	4	191	6– 1–1785	Ohio R	Withdrawn
Orrick, Nicholas	2,000	4	196	6– 9–1785	Ohio R	
Osborne, Reps	1,603	4	134	3–19–1785	None	Withdrawn
Osborne, Reps	1,603	4	149	4–10–1785	None	
Outten, Abraham	2,000	3	150	1–15–1784	None	
Overton, Clough	1,000	3	305	4–27–1784	E Fk Licking	
Overton, Jos	500	4	141	4– 1–1785	None	
Overton, Jos	1,541	4	141	4– 1–1785	Ky R	
Overton, Jos Sr	3,000	4	272	2–15–1786	Big Sandy	
Overton, Samuel	40,000	3	404	7–14–1784	Fks Licking	
Overton, Waller	1,000	2	287	5–17–1783	None	Surveyed
Overton, Wallis	——	3	43	11–14–1783	E Fk Hickman Cr	
Overton & Fowler	3,000	2	294	4–29–1786	Sandy	
Overton & Howard	2,000	3	262	3–31–1784	None	
Overton & Howard	800	3	262	3–31–1784	None	
Overton & Jenkins	20,000	3	404	7–13–1784	Main Licking	
Overton & Pettice	800	3	56	11–22–1784	None	Surveyed
Overton & Walton	1,500	4	259	1–16–1786	Br S Fk Sandy	
Owens, Wm	4,375	4	146	4–10–1785	None	
Owing, John Cockey	1,000	1	103	12–11–1782	None	Surveyed
Owing, Jno C	400	2	300	5–30–1783	Hingston Fk	
Owing, Jno C	1,000	2	300	5–30–1783	Johnson Fk Licking	Surveyed
Owing, Jno C	1,000	2	300	5–30–1783	Br Elkhorn	Surveyed
Owing, Jno C	1,000	2	300	5–30–1783	Licking	
Owing, Jno Cockey	10,000	3	224	3–11–1784	Slate Cr	Withdrawn amended
Owing, Jno Cockey	2,000	3	224	3–11–1784	Slate Cr	Surveyed
Owing, Jno C	8,000	4	91	1–15–1785	None	
Owings, Jno Cockey	1,000	2	56	1–13–1783	None	
Owings, John C	1,000	2	88	1–18–1783	Sinking Cr	Surveyed
Owings, Jno Cockey	1,000	2	299	5–30–1783	S E Deals Lick	Surveyed
Owings, John C	1,000	2	299	5–30–1783	S Elkhorn	Surveyed
Owings, John C	1,000	2	300	5–30–1783	Fk Licking	Surveyed
Owings, Jno C	400	2	300	5–30–1783	Licking Cr	Surveyed
Owings, John C	1,000	2	300	5–30–1783	4 Mile Cr	Surveyed
Owings, John C	1,000	2	300	5–30–1783	Jessamine Cr	Surveyed
Owings, John C	1,000	2	307	6– 6–1783	W Fk Sandy	
Owings, Jno C	2,000	3	285	4–12–1784	None	
Owings, Jno C	8,000	3	285	4–12–1784	None	Amended
Owings, Jno Cockey	1,000	3	323	5– 4–1784	Slate Cr	
Owings, Jno C	2,000	3	323	5– 4–1784	Slate Cr	
Owings, Jno C	500	3	371	6–17–1784	None	
Owings & Read	2,000	3	234	3–22–1784	None	
Owsley, Thomas	3,462	1	195	12–20–1782	N Fk Licking	
Page, Mathew	6,250	2	244	3–14–1783	Br Ohio R	
Page, William	1,046	2	37	1–11–1783	Sandy	
Pannell, William	1,000	2	30	1–10–1783	N Br Clear Cr	Surveyed
Pannell, William	400	2	30	1–10–1783	Hingston Br Licking Cr	
Pannel, Wm	——	3	249	3–29–1784	None	Surveyed
Parberry, James	1,000	1	59	12– 5–1782	Hingston	Surveyed
Parberry, James	1,000	1	381	1– 6–1783	N Fk Elkhorn	Surveyed
Parberry, James	300	2	125	1–27–1783	N Fk Elkhorn	Surveyed
Parberry, James	933¾	2	225	3– 8–1783	Hingston Fk	
Parberry, Jas	1,000	4	51	10–13–1784	None	Surveyed
Parberry, Jas	850	4	262	1–20–1786	Licking	
Parish, Russell, Trustees for	2,718¾	4	145	4–10–1785	Little Sandy	
Parke, Arthur, heirs	325	2	133	1–27–1783	None	
Park, Arthur, heirs	325	2	353	8–16–1783	—— Cr	Surveyed
Parker, Alexander	2,000	3	107	12–22–1783	S Fk Bank Lick Cr	Withdrawn
Parker, Alexander	2,000	3	107	12–22–1783	None	Withdrawn

Entree	Acres	Book	Page	Entry Date	Watercourse	Notes
Parker, Alexander	5,500	3	137	1– 6–1784	Br N Fk Big Bone Lick Cr	Withdrawn
Parker, Alexander	2,000	3	139	1–10–1784	Big Bone Lick	Surveyed
Parker, Alexander	2,000	4	93	1–17–1785	None	
Parker, Alexander	5,500	4	93	1–17–1785	Ohio R	Withdrawn
Parker, Jas	4,000	3	99	12–19–1783	None	Surveyed
Parker, Jas	1,400	4	93	1–17–1785	Hustons Fk	625 acres withdrawn
Parker, Jas	1,000	4	93	1–17–1785	Hingston Fk	
Parker, Jas	380	4	94	1–18–1785	E Fk Stoners Fk	
Parker, Jas	5,000	4	102	1–28–1785	Slate Cr	
Parker, Jas	295	4	103	2– 2–1785	Hingston Fk	
Parker, Jas	208¼	4	103	2– 2–1785	None	
Parker, Jas	5,000	4	122	2–18–1785	None	
Parker, Jas	657	4	122	2–18–1785	Eagle Cr	
Parker, Jas	1,000	4	122	2–18–1785	N Fk Elkhorn	
Parker, Jas	400	4	122	2–18–1785	McConnells Run	
Parker, Jas	300	4	123	2–18–1785	Howards Upper Cr	
Parker, Jas	1,000	4	123	2–19–1785	Grassy Lick	
Parker, Jas	625	4	153	4–15–1785	Ohio R	Surveyed
Parker, John	1,000	2	8	1– 9–1783	Ravens Cr	Withdrawn
Parker, Jno	1,000	2	87	1–18–1783	None	Withdrawn
Parker, John	1,000	2	158	2– 1–1783	None	Surveyed
Parker, John	2,000	2	288	5–20–1783	S Fk Licking	Surveyed
Parker, John	1,906	2	364	9–22–1783	Ohio R	Surveyed
Parker, Jno	440	3	51	11–20–1783	Eagle Cr	Surveyed
Parker, Jno	1,000	4	90	1–15–1785	None	
Parker, Jno	1,000	4	90	1–15–1785	Hingston Fk	
Parker, Jno	1,000	4	90	1–15–1785	Hingston Fk	Withdrawn
Parker, Jno	750	4	90	1–15–1785	N Fk Elkhorn	
Parker, John & Robt	1,000	2	63	1–14–1783	Raven Cr	Amended
Parker, John & Robt	2,343	2	155	2– 1–1783	Hickmans Cr	Surveyed
Parker, John & Robert	200	2	265	4– 7–1783	Ky R	Surveyed
Parker, John & Robert	1,000	2	308	6– 7–1783	Ky R	Withdrawn
Parker, John & Robert	300	2	333	7–28–1783	below Leestown	
Parker, John & Robert	1,000	2	354	8–16–1783	Cedar Cr	
Parker, Jno & Robt	4,500	3	99	12–19–1783	None	Surveyed
Parker, Jno & Robt	1,000	4	140	3–25–1785	Big Bone Lick Cr	
Parker, Richard	800	1	22	12– 3–1782	None	Surveyed
Parker, Robert	1,000	2	8	1– 9–1783	Raven Cr	Withdrawn
Parker, Rob	1,000	2	87	1–18–1783	None	Withdrawn
Parker, Robert	1,000	2	158	2– 1–1783	None	Surveyed
Parker, Robert	125	2	164	2– 5–1783	Hickmans Cr	Withdrawn
Parker, Robert	125	2	304	5–31–1783	Marble Cr	Withdrawn
Parker, Robert	600	2	308	6– 7–1783	Tates Cr	
Parker, Robert	100	2	325	7–19–1783	Ky R	Surveyed
Parker, Robert	904	2	326	7–19–1783	Ky R	
Parker, Robert	200	2	329	7–21–1783	Ky R	Surveyed
Parker, Robt	1,000	2	331	7–24–1783	Hickmans Cr	Surveyed
Parker, Robt	1,560	2	347	8–13–1783	Ky & Cedar Cr	
Parker, Robert	560	2	354	8–16–1783	None	
Parker, Robert	560	2	355	8–16–1783	Eagle Cr & Ky R	Surveyed
Parker, Robt	1,000	2	355	8–16–1783	None	Surveyed
Parker, Robt	500	4	138	3–25–1785	Hickmans Cr	
Parker, Robt	67	4	182	5–19–1785	None	
Parker, Robt	300	4	182	5–19–1785	None	
Parker, Robt	750	4	182	5–20–1785	None	
Parker, Robt	967	4	339	1–17–1795	None	
Parker & Ewing	11,000	4	120	2–15–1785	None	
Parker & Call	5,000	3	100	12–19–1783	None	Surveyed
Parker & Croutcher	2,375	3	123	12–30–1783	None	Surveyed
Parker & Morgan	806½	3	132	1– 2–1784	None	
Parker & Todd	1,000	3	21	10–30–1783	Ky R	
Parker & Todd	500	3	33	11– 7–1783	Ky R	
Parker & Todd	500	3	33	11– 7–1783	Ky R	
Parker & Todd	500	3	36	11– 8–1783	Ky R	
Parker & Venible	2,788	3	122	12–30–1783	Big Bone Cr	Surveyed
Parks, Ezekiel	783	4	243	12–17–1785	None	
Parks, Ezekiel	400	4	243	12–17–1785	S Fk Sandy	
Parks, Ezekiel	200	4	244	12–17–1785	––––– Cr	
Parsons, George	4,000	1	382	1– 7–1783	E Br Grassy Lick	
Parsons, George	1,318½	1	382	1– 6–1783	Hinktons Fk	Amended
Paskins, Joseph	400	1	89	12– 9–1782	Br Ohio R	
Patrick, Chas	2,750	3	15	10–25–1783	Big Bone Cr	
Patrick, Jno	45,987¼	3	281	4–10–1784	Main Fk Licking	Surveyed
Patty, Jno	29,936	3	424	8–11–1784	Cumberland Mt	
Patterson, Charles	5,625	2	246	3–15–1783	None	Surveyed
Patterson, Chas	8,000	4	285	3–26–1786	Ohio R	
Patterson, Daniel	15,000	2	21	1– 9–1783	N Fk Licking Cr	
Patterson, David	15,000	3	177	2– 9–1784	Big Bone Lick	Surveyed
Patterson, Francis	1,000	1	47	12– 4–1782	S Br N Elkhorn	Surveyed

Entree	Acres	Book	Page	Entry Date	Watercourse	Notes
Patterson, Joseph	1,000	1	273	12–25–1782	Hingston Fk	
Patterson, Joseph	2,165¼	3	242	3–26–1784	Br Licking	
Patterson, Matthew	534	1	288	12–27–1782	N Fk Elkhorn	Surveyed
Patterson, Nelson	5,859½	3	319	5– 1–1784	Small Mt Cr	
Patterson, Robert	160	1	359	1– 4–1783	None	Withdrawn
Patterson, Robert	40	1	359	1– 4–1783	None	Withdrawn
Patterson, Robert	1,000	1	378	1– 6–1783	None	
Patterson, Robert	400	1	379	1– 6–1783	None	Withdrawn
Patterson, Robert	400	1	379	1– 6–1783	None	Withdrawn
Patterson, Robert	500	2	124	1–27–1783	N Fk Elkhorn	Surveyed
Patterson, Robert	645	2	169	2– 6–1783	Stamping Ground Br	Withdrawn
Patterson, Robert	200	2	218	3– 1–1783	None	Withdrawn
Patterson, Robert	200	2	260	3–29–1783	None	Surveyed
Patterson, Robert	400	2	320	7–11–1783	None	Surveyed
Patterson, Robt	300	3	93	12–16–1783	None	Withdrawn
Patterson, Robt	245	3	365	6–14–1784	None	
Patterson, Robt	300	3	365	6–14–1784	None	
Patterson, Robt	631	3	366	6–14–1784	Ohio R	Surveyed
Patterson, Robt	100	4	41	9–22–1784	None	
Patterson, Samuel	12,500	1	260	12–24–1782	Licking	Surveyed
Patterson, Thos	1,000	4	261	1–18–1786	S Fk Sandy	
Patterson, Thos	1,000	4	261	1–18–1786	——— Cr	
Patterson, William	1,000	2	29	1–10–1783	Licking	
Patterson & McMillian	2,000	3	72	12– 8–1783	S Fk Mill Cr	
Patterson & McMillian	1,453¾	3	73	12– 8–1783	Hinkston Fk	Surveyed
Patterson & McMillian	3,000	3	74	12– 8–1783	Hinkston Fk	
Patterson & McMillian	6,000	4	153	4–19–1785	Fk Licking	
Patterson & Miller	10,000	4	174	5– 9–1785	None	
Patterson & Miller	5,000	4	175	5– 9–1785	None	Withdrawn
Patterson & Miller	5,000	4	175	5– 9–1785	None	
Patterson & Miller	5,000	4	285	3–26–1786	None	
Paul, James	1,571	1	378	1– 6–1783	Camp Run	
Paul, James	664	1	383	1– 6–1783	Evans Mill Cr	
Paulin, Henry	1,000	4	240	12–13–1785	Mud Lick Cr	
Paulin, Henry	1,000	4	241	12–13–1785	——— Cr	
Paulin, Henry	531	4	241	12–13–1785	Main Fk Slate Cr	
Paulin, Henry	1,000	4	241	12–13–1785	——— Cr	
Paulin, Henry T	681	4	241	12–13–1785	S Fk Sandy	
Payne, Edward	1,000	2	181	2–11–1783	Sulbergreed	Surveyed
Payne, Edward	3,000	2	227	3–10–1783	Br Licking	Surveyed
Payne, Edward	2,235	2	228	3–10–1783	Licking Cr	Surveyed
Payne, Edward	1,000	2	269	4– 7–1783	Stoners Fk & Stoners Station	Surveyed
Payne, Edward	3,000	3	15	10–25–1783	None	Withdrawn
Payne, Edward	400	3	15	10–25–1783	Sulbergreed & Hinkston	276 acres Surveyed 174 acres withdrawn
Payne, Edward	515½	3	31	11– 4–1783	Hinkston Fk	33 acres surveyed 185 acres withdrawn
Payne, Edward	1,000	3	203	3– 4–1784	Slate Cr	Surveyed
Payne, Edward	124	4	64	11– 5–1784	None	
Payne, Edward	185½	4	64	11– 5–1784	None	
Payne, Francis	8,000	3	164	1–22–1784	Bank Lick Cr	
Payne, Henry	1,400	3	67	12– 1–1783	Jessamine Cr	
Payne, Henry	5,000	3	78	12–10–1783	N Fk Licking	4,400 acres surveyed 600 acres withdrawn
Payne, Henry	500	3	193	3– 1–1784	Hingston Fk	Surveyed
Payne, Henry	2,000	3	290	4–14–1784	Hingston Fk	Surveyed
Payne, Henry	500	4	104	2– 3–1785	None	Surveyed
Payne, Henry	600	4	226	10–13–1785	Town Fk Elkhorn	266 acres surveyed 200 acres withdrawn
Payne, Henry	200	4	229	10–28–1785	None	
Payne, Jno	1,458	3	179	2–10–1784	Sulbergreed	Surveyed
Payne, Jno	1,270	3	347	5–27–1784	None	
Payne, Jno	336	3	348	5–27–1784	None	
Payne, Jno	75	4	21	8–22–1784	None	Surveyed
Payne, Jno	300	4	21	8–22–1784	Grassy Lick	Withdrawn
Payne, Jno	110	4	33	9–11–1784	None	
Payne, Jno	220	4	33	9–11–1784	None	
Payne, Jno	61	4	64	11– 5–1784	None	
Payne, Jno	300	4	73	12– 2–1784	Grassy Lick	Surveyed
Payne, Jno	127	4	74	12– 2–1784	None	

Entree	Acres	Book	Page	Entry Date	Watercourse	Notes
Payne, Jno	523	4	74	12– 2–1784	None	Amended, surveyed
Payne, Jno	1,194	4	89	1–14–1785	None	
Payne, Jno	61	4	174	5– 9–1785	None	
Payne, Jno	1,270	4	174	5– 9–1785	None	Surveyed
Payne, Jno & Edward	523	4	169	4–30–1785	None	427 acres surveyed
Payne, Sanford	400	3	203	3– 4–1784	Slate Cr	Surveyed
Payne, William	500	2	268	4– 7–1783	Howards Upper Cr & Licking	Surveyed
Payne, Wm	1,406½	3	23	10–31–1783	None	
Payne, Wm & Jno	2,000	4	114	2– 9–1785	Slate Cr	Surveyed
Payne, Wm & Jno	1,315	4	168	4–29–1785	None	
Payne, Wm & Jno	1,315	4	178	5–12–1785	None	
Payne, Wm & Jno	3,000	4	178	5–12–1785	Slate Cr	
Payne & Bradley	345	4	40	9–22–1784	None	Surveyed
Payne & Lines	500	3	410	7–16–1784	Jessamine Cr	
Payne & Morgan	5,000	3	128	1– 1–1784	Ohio R	
Payne & Morgan	3,000	3	128	1– 1–1784	Ohio R	
Peak, Jesse	50	4	88	1–14–1785	——— R	Surveyed
Peake, James	400	2	67	1–15–1783	Hickman Cr	
Pearle, Samuel	3,311¾	4	213	7–30–1785	None	
Pearman, Samuel	3,473½	2	307	6– 4–1783	Ohio R	Withdrawn
Pears, Isaac	500	3	405	7–14–1784	Main Fk Licking	
Pears, Isaac	500	3	422	8– 6–1784	None	
Pears, Isaac	516	3	422	8– 6–1784	Main Fk Licking	Surveyed
Pearsal, Mary	225,000	3	353	6– 4–1784	Ky R	Amended
Peebles, Jno	465	4	104	2– 3–1785	Licking	
Pelham, Chas	1,000	1	386	1– 7–1783	S Fk Elkhorn	Surveyed
Pelham, Charles	15,000	2	19	1– 9–1783	N Fk Licking	Surveyed
Pelham, Charles	13,000	2	20	1– 9–1783	N Fk Licking	
Pendergrass, Jesse	1,000	3	229	3–17–1784	Ky R	Surveyed
Pendleton, Philip	1,000	4	253	1– 9–1786	N Fk Licking	Surveyed
Peniman, Benonia	2,000	4	103	2– 2–1785	None	
Penland, Alexander	400	1	177	12–18–1782	Raven Cr	Surveyed
Penland, Alexander	1,600	1	279	12–26–1782	W Br Licking	Surveyed
Penland, Alexander	400	4	17	8–16–1784	———	Surveyed
Penlang, Alex	5,000	2	66	1–15–1783	E Br Stoners Fk	
Pennabaker, Peter	500	2	317	7– 7–1783	Slate Cr	Surveyed
Pennebaker, Peter	2,000	2	340	8– 5–1783	Indian Cr	
Penticost, Dorsey	1,000	3	425	8–14–1784	——— Cr	Surveyed
Penticost, Dorsey	1,000	3	426	8–14–1784	Sandy	Surveyed
Penticost, Dorsey	4,000	3	426	8–14–1784	Sandy	Surveyed
Penticost, Dorsey	1,000	4	5	8–14–1784	Sandy Cr	Surveyed
Perkins, Benjamin	4,000	2	349	8–14–1783	None	
Perkins, Benj	2,750	2	349	8–14–1783	None	
Perkins, Constant	4,000	2	358	8–20–1783	Ky R & Elkhorn	Surveyed
Perkins, Constant	3,200	2	364	9–22–1783	Big Bone Lick Cr	
Perkins, Constant	500	3	246	3–26–1784	Br N Fk Elkhorn	
Perkins, Joseph	400	2	125	1–27–1783	Fks Licking	Surveyed
Perkins, Thos	12,953	4	88	1–14–1785	Main Br Licking	
Perkins, William	6,714	1	391	1– 7–1783	Spencers Cr & Hingstons	
Perkins, Wm	3,000	3	185	2–16–1784	Fks Licking	
Peroin, Josephus	1,000	1	22	12– 3–1782	——— Cr	Surveyed
Peroin, Joseph	346½	4	135	3–19–1785	None	
Perry, David	1,200	1	42	12– 4–1782	Little Mianus	Surveyed
Perry, David	1,000	1	93	12–10–1782	None	Surveyed
Perry, Jno & Jas	1,000	3	138	1– 7–1784	Upper Blue Lick	
Perry, Jno & Jas	1,000	3	138	1– 7–1784	Upper Blue Lick	
Perry, Samuel	1,000	3	397	7– 8–1784	Ohio R	Surveyed
Pettis & Fowler	1,162⅔	4	273	2–15–1786	None	Amended
Pettis & Fowler	462¾	4	295	4–29–1786	Sandy	
Pettis & Overton	800	3	56	11–22–1783	None	Surveyed
Peyton, Francis	1,000	3	22	10–30–1783	Ky R & Clear Cr	Surveyed
Peyton, Francis	2,288	4	213	7–30–1785	None	
Phillips, Jno	126.140	3	298	4–22–1784	l h Fk 3 Fks Ky R	Surveyed amended
Phillips, Jno	30,000	4	169	4–30–1785	S Fk Sandy R	Surveyed
Phillips, Moses	5,556	3	368	6–15–1784	Licking	908, acres Surveyed 4,547¾ acres withdrawn
Phillips, Moses	4,547¾	4	324	7– 9–1788	None	
Phillips, William	1,000	2	226	3–10–1783	Ohio R	Surveyed
Phillips & Young	100,000	3	167	1–26–1784	N E Fk Eagle Crs	
Phillips & Young	100,000	3	185	2–17–1784	Eagle Cr	
Pickett, Geo	70,000	3	369	6–16–1784	l h Fk 3 Fks Ky R	Surveyed
Pickett, Martin	5,000	1	265	12–25–1782	Stoners Fk	Withdrawn
Pickett, Martin	5,600	2	23	1– 9–1783	W Fk Hingston Fk	Surveyed
Pickett, Martin	100,192	3	116	12–29–1783	Eagle Cr	Surveyed

Entree	Acres	Book	Page	Entry Date	Watercourse	Notes
Pickett, Martin	100,192	3	297	4-22-1784	Br Elkhorn	
Pickett & Weaver	23,875	3	350	5-29-1784	Eagle Cr	Surveyed
Pierce, Isaac	984	4	20	8-22-1784	M Fk Flemings Cr	
Pinkerton, Henry	1,000	2	304	5-31-1783	S Fk Elkhorn	Surveyed
Piper & Morgan	7,093	3	59	11-25-1783	N Fk Big Bone Lick	Surveyed
Piper & Morgan	7,093	3	127	1- 1-1784	N Fk Big Bone Lick	
Piper & Morgan	1,541	3	130	1- 1-1784	N Fk Big Bone Cr.	Surveyed
Piper & Morgan	7,093	3	177	2-10-1784	None	Surveyed
Plankenbaker, Henry	1,317½	2	90	1-20-1783	S Fk Licking	
Platt, E S	300,306⅔	3	190	2-28-1784	3 Fks Ky R	
Poage, Elijah	45,987¾	3	281	4-10-1784	Main Fk Licking	Surveyed
Poage, James	1,000	1	198	12-20-1782	Big Bone Lick	Surveyed
Poage, Thos	1,000	4	48	10-12-1784	M Licking	
Poe, James	1,200	1	357	1- 3-1783	S Fk Licking	Surveyed
Poindexter, John	250	1	48	12- 4-1782	——— Cr	
Poindexter, Thomas	10,000	2	309	6- 7-1783	None	
Poindexter, Thomas	2,000	2	312	6- 9-1783	———— Br	
Pollard, Jno	2,499¾	4	267	2- 3-1786	None	
Pollock, Alexander	1,000	2	51	1-13-1783	None	Surveyed
Pollock, William	2,000	2	3	1- 8-1783	None	Surveyed
Pomdry, George	400	2	26	1-10-1783	Licking	
Pope, Geo	6,136¼	3	66	12- 1-1783	None	
Pope, William	2,578	2	360	9- 9-1783	Br Bank Lick Cr	
Porter, Joseph	1,500	2	166	2- 6-1783	Br Licking	Surveyed
Porter, Philip	2,578	3	94	12-17-1783	None	Surveyed
Porter, Samuel	2,956	3	177	2-10-1784	None	Surveyed
Porter, Samuel	1,076⅔	3	411	7-17-1784	N Fk Licking	
Porter, Wm	50	4	334	4-14-1791	N Fk Elkhorn	
Porter, Benjamin & Abner	2,000	2	86	1-18-1783	Ky R	
Powell, Levin	1,000	1	58	12- 5-1782	Mill Cr	Surveyed
Powell, Levin	1,000	1	59	12- 5-1782	N Fk Licking	Surveyed
Powell, Levin	1,000	4	147	4-10-1785	Ky R	
Powell, Levin	1,500	4	147	4-10-1785	Limestone Cr	
Power, James	1,000	2	265	4- 7-1783	Buckhorn Run	Surveyed
Power, Jas	700	3	172	2- 2-1784	Hingston Fk	Surveyed
Power, James	3,496¼	3	240	3-25-1784	Hingston Fk	
Power, Jermiah	224	4	42	9-22-1784	Br Licking	
Power, Jermiah	315	3	320	5- 1-1784	None	Surveyed
Power & Weeden	14,166¼	3	301	4-26-1784	Licking	Withdrawn
Power & Weeden	14,166¼	4	275	2-28-1786	None	
Power & Weeden	14,166¼	4	275	2-18-1786	Sandy	
Powers, James	1,000	1	57	12- 5-1782	————	Surveyed
Powers, James	1,000	2	266	4- 7-1783	S Fk Licking	Surveyed
Powers, Jas	700	3	236	3-23-1784	None	
Preston, James Patton	200	1	209	12-20-1782	Licking Cr	
Preston, James Patton	200	2	83	1-17-1783	Upper Blue Lick	
Preston, Robert	1,000	2	249	3-15-1783	Hickmans Cr	
Preston, William	200	2	83	1-17-1783	Upper Blue Lick	
Preston, William Jr	200	1	209	12-20-1782	Licking Cr	
Prewitt, Isham	1,000	1	344	1- 1-1783	Gists Cr	Withdrawn
Prewitt, Isham	1,200	2	136	1-27-1783	Wells Cr	
Prewitt, Isham	800	2	136	1-27-1782	Wells Cr	Surveyed
Prewitt, Isham	1,000	2	137	1-28-1783	Wells Cr	Surveyed
Price, Charles	1,000	1	90	12- 9-1782	Elkhorn & Licking	Withdrawn
Price, James	906¼	2	125	1-27-1783	Stoners Fk	
Price, John	2,000	2	339	8- 2-1783	——— Cr	
Price, Jno	7,953½	3	368	6-15-1784	E Fk Licking	
Price, Jno	8,000	3	422	8- 5-1784	Large S Fk Sandy	
Price, Jno	1,200	4	67	11-12-1784	Drenning Lick Cr	Surveyed
Price, Jno	50	4	328	3-28-1789	E Fk Hickman	
Price, Robt	4,476¾	2	125	1-27-1783	Licking	
Price, Robert	——	2	144	1-30-1783	None	
Price, William	2,000	2	182	2-12-1783	Br Ohio R	
Primon, Jas	1,000	4	267	2- 3-1786	None	
Primon & McBraide	1,000	3	339	5-19-1784	None	Surveyed
Prince, Jeremiah	200	1	8	11-29-1782	Eagle Cr	
Pringle, Jno	10,000	4	137	3-21-1785	None	Withdrawn
Pringle, Jno	10,000	4	189	6- 1-1785	None	
Printer, Wm	4,334½	3	115	12-27-1783	Lees Cr	
Proctor, Joseph	2,100	1	366	1- 4-1783	E Fk Brushy Cr	
Proctor, Joseph	2,000	1	375	1- 6-1783	Clemens Fk Hingstons	
Proctor, Joseph	1,500	2	110	1-23-1783	Sycamore Fk Hingstons	Surveyed
Proctor, Nicholas	1,000	1	321	12-30-1782	Licking	Surveyed
Proctor, Nicholas, Sr	500	2	111	1-23-1783	S Fk Hingstons	Surveyed
Proctor, Nicholas, Sr	500	2	166	2- 6-1783	Br Licking	Surveyed
Proctor, Reuben	500	1	339	12-31-1782	None	
Proctor, Reuben	1,000	1	274	12-25-1782	Hingston & Stoners Fk	Surveyed

Entree	Acres	Book	Page	Entry Date	Watercourse	Notes
Pryor, John	6,000	2	50	1–13–1783	None	Surveyed
Purkins, Thos	1,000	4	299	5–12–1786	r h Fk Ky R	
Quirk, Edmund	1,000	2	242	3–13–1783	None	
Quirk, Thomas	500	2	179	2–10–1783	None	
Quirk, Thomas	500	2	283	5– 2–1783	S Fk Elkhorn	Surveyed
Quirk, Thomas	1,000	2	374	10– 8–1783	Ky R	Withdrawn
Quirk, Thos	40	4	263	1–21–1786	None	
Queally & Greenup	1,000	4	306	10–14–1786	Ohio R	
Ragnit, C B	50,000	3	377	6–19–1784	None	Surveyed
Raidkins, Lawrence	500	2	248	3–15–1783	None	
Randell, Chilton	500	1	49	12– 5–1783	Stoners Fk Licking	
Randolph, James	1,500	3	272	4– 6–1784	Main Fk Licking	
Randolph, Nathaniel	1,000	2	301	5–30–1783	Ky R	
Ransdell, Thomas	1,000	1	113	12–12–1782	None	Surveyed
Raperton, Frederick	50	1	39	12– 4–1782	Fk Boones Cr	
Raperton, Frederick	400	1	181	12–19–1782	3rd Fk Boones Cr	
Raperton, Frederick	400	1	289	12–27–1782	Stoners Fk	Surveyed
Rash, Nicholas	300.306⅔	3	190	2–28–1784	3 Fks Ky R	
Ratcliff, Richard	12,311	3	194	3– 2–1784	Fks Hingston	Surveyed
Rawlins, Wm	3,165½	3	241	3–26–1784	Johnsons Fk	
Rayburn, Robert	1,000	1	49	12– 5–1782	S Fk Elkhorn	
Rayland, Samuel	2,066¼	3	410	7–17–1784	Ohio R	
Read, Nathaniel	1,000	4	45	10– 2–1784	Marble Cr	Surveyed
Read, Wm	1,791½	3	138	1– 7–1784	None	Surveyed
Read & Hobbs	3,000	3	234	3–22–1784	Rockhouse Cr	Withdrawn
Read & Owings	2,000	3	234	3–22–1784	None	
Read & Simms	3,000	4	110	2– 5–1785	None	
Reading, George	400	2	191	2–13–1783	None	
Reading, Geo	300	3	176	2– 9–1784	S Fk Licking	
Reading, Geo	500	3	185	2–17–1784	Coopers Fk	Withdrawn
Reading, Geo	300	3	377	6–18–1784	None	
Reding, George	945½	1	360	1– 4–1783	Coopers Cr	Withdrawn
Reding, Geo	444	3	98	12–18–1783	S Fk Licking	Surveyed
Reed, Andrew	1,000	1	199	12–20–1782	Big Bone Lick	Surveyed
Reed, Andrew	1,929½	2	187	2–13–1783	None	
Reed, Alexander	1,200	2	186	2–13–1783	——— Cr	
Reed, Alex Jr	1,000	1	357	1– 3–1783	S Fk Licking	
Reed, James	2,473½	3	321	5– 3–1784	None	
Reed, Jno	1,500	4	110	2– 5–1785	Lick Cr	
Reed, Jno	1,500	4	110	2– 5–1785	Ky R	
Reed, Jno	1,500	4	111	2– 5–1785	Lick Cr	
Reed, Jno	1,500	4	111	2– 5–1785	Lick Cr	
Reed, Thomas	2,000	1	357	1– 3–1783	S Fk Licking	
Reed, Wm	500	3	83	12–12–1783	None	
Reed & Ridgely	8,000	4	284	3–23–1786	N Fk Ky R	
Reed & Ridgely	2,000	4	285	3–23–1786	Round Bottom	
Reed & Ridgely	4,000	4	285	3–23–1786	N Fk Ky R	
Renfro, James	500	3	363	6–14–1784	Elkhorn	
Renfro, James	681	3	363	6–14–1784	None	Surveyed
Renfro, James	681	3	363	6–14–1784	Elkhorn	
Renon, Lewis	400	2	79	1–17–1783	Br Licking	
Revis, Thos	1,000	3	224	3–11–1784	Sinking Cr	Surveyed
Reynolds, Thos	6,445	3	377	6–19–1784	Br Ohio R	
Reynolds, Thos	1,000	4	69	11–25–1784	None	Surveyed
Reynolds, Thos	400	4	180	5–17–1785	M Fk Elkhorn	
Reynolds, Thos	400	4	317	11–20–1787	Main Elkhorn	Surveyed
Rice, Aman B	4,351½	1	382	1– 6–1783	Ohio R	
Rice, David	1,508	2	62	1–14–1783	None	Surveyed
Rice, Fisher	2,000	2	95	1–20–1783	N Fk of Ky R	
Rice, Fisher	2,000	2	96	1–20–1783	Br N Fk Ky R	
Rice, Fisher	663	2	95	1–20–1783	N Fk Ky R	
Rice, Geo	2,000	4	180	5–12–1785	None	Withdrawn
Rice, Geo	10,531	4	180	5–12–1785	None	Surveyed
Rice, John	1,000	2	272	4– 8–1783	W Fk Licking	
Rice, Samuel	2,700	1	343	1– 1–1783	Gists Cr	
Rice, Thomas	1,000	1	17	1–21–1783	M Hickman Cr	Surveyed
Rice, Thomas	5,000	1	219	12–21–1782	None	Amended
Rice, Thomas	1,000	2	102	1–21–1783	Br Jessamine Cr	Surveyed
Rice, William	600	2	201	2–17–1783	None	
Rice, Wm	12,613	3	226	3–14–1784	Licking	Withdrawn
Rice, Wm	12,613	3	241	3–26–1784	Locust Cr	Withdrawn
Rice, Wm	12,613	4	265	1–30–1786	N Fk Ky R	Withdrawn
Rice, Wm	12,613	4	291	4–22–1786	None	
Rice & Gill	12,613	4	292	4–22–1786	Ky R	
Richards, Elijah	200	4	64	11– 5–1784	——— Cr	Surveyed
Richards, Isaac	1,000	1	309	12–28–1782	Clear Cr	Surveyed
Richard, Jas	500	3	246	3–26–1784	E Fk Licking	Surveyed
Richards, Lewis	325	1	8	11–29–1782	Br Licking Cr	
Richards & Hally	11,931½	3	129	1– 1–1784	Ohio R	

Entree	Acres	Book	Page	Entry Date	Watercourse	Notes
Richards & Young	1,546¾	3	179	2–10–1784	None	
Richardson, John	318	2	202	2–18–1783	None	
Richardson, Jno	442	4	135	3–19–1785	None	
Richardson, Sandie	3,123	3	61	11–27–1783	Hickman & Jassamine	Surveyed
Richardson, Wm	944	3	62	11–27–1783	Hickman & Jassamine	Amended
Richardson, Wm	——	3	421	8– 5–1783	None	582 acres surveyed
Richie, John	1,900	1	387	1– 7–1783	Little Miami	
Richie, John	147½	1	388	1– 7–1783	None	
Richie, Wm	600	3	202	3– 4–1784	None	
Riddle, Thos	1,800	2	292	5–23–1783	Br M Licking	Withdrawn
Ridgely, Richard	8,000	4	258	1–16–1786	S Fk Sandy	
Ridgely, Richard	4,000	4	259	1–16–1786	S Fk Sandy	
Ridgely, Richard	4,000	4	258	1–16–1786	S Fk Sandy	
Ridgely & Ship	6,000	4	326	1–17–1789	Cedar Cr	
Ridgely, Richard	4,000	4	259	1–16–1786	S Fk Sandy	
Ridgely & Reed	8,000	4	284	3–23–1786	N Fk Ky R	
Ridgely & Reed	2,000	4	285	3–23–1786	Round Bottom	
Ridgely & Reed	4,000	4	285	3–23–1786	N Fk Ky R	
Ridgely & Ship	12,268¾	4	257	1–16–1786	Licking	
Ridley, William	2,000	1	45	12– 4–1782	Grassy Cr	Surveyed
Ringo, Peter	1,000	4	289	4–13–1786	Little Mt Cr	
Rixey, Richard	1,000	1	288	12–27–1782	E Br Stoners Fk	Surveyed
Rixey, Richard	1,000	3	17	10–29–1783	Twin Cr	Surveyed
Rixey, Richard	5,800	3	39	11–12–1783	Br Licking	
Roberts, Benjamin	500	1	20	1–14–1783	Howards Cr	Amended
Roberts, Benjamin	500	2	294	5–24–1783	None	Surveyed
Roberts, Joseph	500	2	186	2–13–1783	—— Cr	
Roberts, P D	300,306⅔	3	190	2–28–1784	3 Fks Ky R	
Robertson, Alexander	4,396	1	351	1– 2–1783	Main & N Fk Licking	Surveyed
Robertson, Alexander	300	3	163	1–22–1784	Lower Twin Cr	Surveyed
Robertson, Wm	618	4	228	10–23–1785	Big Sandy	
Robertson & Howard	407¾	4	198	6–11–1785	None	
Robinson, Benjamin	1,000	1	5	11–29–1783	None	Surveyed
Robinson, John	1,200	1	306	12–28–1782	None	Surveyed
Robinson & Graves	1,480	3	178	2–10–1784	None	
Robinson & McGee	15,246	3	178	2–10–1784	Sandy	
Robinson & Young	16,000	3	177	2–10–1784	Sandy	
Roborson, Mathew	20,000	4	35	9–15–1784	Red R	
Rodes, John	1,406	2	87	1–18–1783	Licking	Surveyed
Rodgers, John	400	2	161	2– 4–1783	Millers Cr	
Roe, Edmund	500	2	197	2–17–1783	None	Surveyed
Roe, Henry	1,000	3	200	3– 3–1784	S Fk Licking	
Rogers, Joseph	575	4	47	10– 8–1784	N Fk Elkhorn	
Rogers, Andrew	949½	2	60	1–14–1783	None	Surveyed
Rogers, John	500	1	25	12–27–1782	—— Cr	Surveyed
Rogers, John	1,000	1	109	12–11–1782	Elkhorn	Surveyed
Rogers, John	5,000	1	342	1– 1–1783	Gists Cr	Withdrawn
Rogers, Jno	2,100	1	366	1– 4–1783	E Fk Brushy Cr	
Rogers, Jno	9,500	3	329	5–12–1784	Sandy	
Rogers, Jno	5,000	4	148	4–10–1785	None	
Rogers, Jno	5,000	4	149	4–10–1785	Little Sandy	
Rogers, Joseph	500	1	267	12–25–1782	N Fk Elkhorn	Surveyed
Rogers, Joseph	2,000	1	85	12– 9–1782	Elkhorn	Surveyed
Rogers, Joseph	1,000	1	268	12–25–1782	Br S Fk Licking	
Rogers, Joseph	2,000	2	4	1– 8–1783	None	Surveyed
Rogers, Thomas	600	1	110	12–11–1782	Elkhorn	
Rogers, William	3,585	2	27	1–10–1783	Clear Cr	
Rogers & Morgan	3,375	3	135	1– 2–1784	None	Surveyed
Rose, Daniel	500	4	300	5–24–1786	None	
Rose, David	500	4	79	12–28–1784	Slate Cr	Withdrawn
Rose, Hugh	600	2	306	6– 4–1783	Strodes Fk Licking	
Rose, John	6,875	2	126	1–27–1783	Crewes Cr	Withdrawn
Rose, Jno	4,000	4	79	12–29–1784	None	
Rose, Jno	2,000	4	79	12–29–1784	N Fk Licking	
Rose, Jno	2,000	4	80	12–29–1784	Tigerts Cr	
Rose, Rose	400	2	307	6– 4–1783	Strodes Fk Licking	
Ross, David	4,000	4	105	2– 5–1785	Buck Cr	
Ross, David	4,000	4	105	2– 5–1785	Rockhouse Fk	
Ross, David	4,000	4	105	2– 5–1785	Rockhouse Fk	
Ross, David	5,000	4	105	2– 5–1785	Rockhouse Fk	
Ross, David	5,000	4	106	2– 5–1785	Rockhouse Fk	
Ross, David	5,781	4	106	2– 5–1785	Rockhouse Fk	Withdrawn
Ross, David	5,000	4	106	2– 5–1785	Rockhouse Fk	
Ross, David	5,000	4	106	2– 5–1785	Rockhouse Fk	
Ross, David	10,000	4	106	2– 5–1785	Rockhouse Fk	Withdrawn
Ross, David	5,000	4	283	3–23–1786	N Fk Ky R	Surveyed
Ross, David	8,000	4	314	3–21–1787	Ky R	Withdrawn

Entree	Acres	Book	Page	Entry Date	Watercourse	Notes
Ross, David	8,000	4	315	3–21–1787	None	
Ross, Hugh	1,000	2	66	1–15–1783	E Fk Stoners	
Ross & Curry	10,000	4	107	2– 5–1785	Buckhorn Fk	
Ross & Curry	10,000	4	108	2– 5–1785	Buckhorn Fk	
Ross & Curry	10,000	4	108	2– 5–1785	Buckhorn Fk	Withdrawn
Ross & Curry	10,000	4	108	2– 5–1785	Buckhorn Fk	
Ross & Curry	10,000	4	108	2– 5–1785	Buckhorn Fk	
Ross & Curry	10,000	4	108	2– 5–1785	Buckhorn Fk	Withdrawn
Ross & Curry	10,000	4	109	2– 5–1785	Buck Cr	Withdrawn
Ross & Curry	6,000	4	109	2– 5–1785	Buck Cr	Withdrawn
Ross & Curry	6,000	4	109	2– 5–1785	Buck Cr	
Ross & Curry	4,000	4	109	2– 5–1785	Buck Cr	Withdrawn
Ross & Curry	4,000	4	109	2– 5–1785	Buck Cr	
Ross & Curry	6,062½	4	109	2– 5–1785	Buck Cr	Withdrawn
Ross & Curry	5,000	4	110	2– 5–1785	None	Withdrawn
Ross & Curry	6,000	4	110	2– 5–1785	Br Rockhouse Cr	
Ross & Curry	10,000	4	283	3–23–1786	—— R	
Ross & Curry	10,000	4	283	3–23–1786	—— R	Surveyed
Ross & Curry	10,000	4	283	3–23–1786	—— R	
Ross & Curry	10,000	4	283	3–23–1786	—— R	Surveyed
Ross & Curry	10,000	4	283	3–23–1786	None	Surveyed
Ross & Curry	11,062½	4	284	3–23–1786	Quick Sand Cr	Surveyed
Ross & Curry	126,843	4	314	3–21–1787	Br Big Bone Lick	Withdrawn
Ross & Curry	136,843	4	315	3–21–1787	None	
Ross & May	60,000	4	78	12–20–1784	Br Ohio R	Surveyed
Rough, Adam	1,000	4	306	10–18–1786	Glenns Cr	
Rout, Ann	393½	4	23	8–30–1784	Ky R	Surveyed
Row, Edmond	781	2	243	3–14–1782	Elkhorn	Surveyed
Row, George, Jr	750	1	50	12– 5–1782	Kingstons Fk	Surveyed
Row, William	1,000	2	157	2– 1–1783	Greers Ck	Withdrawn
Rowland, David	628½	2	284	5–11–1783	Greers Ck	Surveyed
Rowland, David	1,462	3	297	4–22–1784	Locust Cr	
Rubsaman, Jacob	50,000	1	229	12–21–1782	Ohio & Licking	20,000 acres withdrawn
Rubsaman, Jacob	20,000	2	37	1–11–1783	Ohio & Licking	
Rucker, Ambrose	40,000	2	23	1– 9–1783	Kingstons Fk & Salt Spring Fk Licking	Surveyed
Rucker, Anthony	1,000	4	327	3– 2–1789	4 Mile Cr	
Rucker, Jno	333½	4	137	3–22–1785	None	
Ruddle, Cornelius	1,697	2	35	1–11–1783	Sandy	
Rumsey, Jno	5,267½	3	282	4–10–1784	None	Surveyed
Runner, Michael	169	2	57	1–13–1783	None	
Russell, Jas	1,856	3	52	11–21–1783	Br Licking	Surveyed
Russell, Albert	1,856	4	76	12–16–1784	Salt Spring Fk	
Rust, Jno	8,259½	4	36	9–18–1784	Main Licking	
Russell, Joseph	306	4	100	1–27–1785	Licking	
Russell, William	500	1	270	12–25–1782	S Fk Sandy	
Russell, William	500	1	270	12–25–1782	S Fk Sandy	
Russell, William	1,000	1	271	12–25–1782	Great Paint Lick	
Russell, William	1,000	1	270	12–25–1782	S Fk Sandy	
Russell, William	200	1	271	12–25–1782	Boones Cr	
Russell, William	2,000	1	347	1– 2–1783	Paint Lick Cr	
Russell, William	2,000	1	346	1– 2–1783	Paint Lick Cr	
Rutherford, Robt	2,000	4	190	6– 1–1785	Ohio R	
Ryan, Michael	2,000	4	238	12–13–1785	None	
Ryan, Thomas	1,000	2	111	2–27–1783	Br Ohio R	
Sadler, Thomas	1,363	2	61	1–14–1783	None	Surveyed
Said, William	254	2	251	3–21–1783	Hingston Fk	Surveyed
Said, Wm	2,458	3	129	1– 1–1784	Ohio R	
Sale, Robt	5,627½	3	69	12– 3–1783	Hingston Fk	Amended
Sale, Robt	5,627½	3	203	3– 4–1784	Main Licking	
Sally, Abraham	300	1	264	12–25–1782	Ky R	
Sally, Abraham	300	1	264	12–25–1782	Howards Upper Cr	
Sally, Abraham	500	2	238	3–13–1783	None	
Sally, Abraham	500	4	178	5–12–1785	Greys Run	
Samwalt, George	400	2	304	5–31–1783	Greers Lick	
Sanders, John	500	1	35	12– 4–1782	Fks Licking & Ohio	
Sanders, John	1,000	1	121	12–12–1782	Clear Cr	
Sanders, Jno	100	4	298	5–11–1786	None	Withdrawn
Sanders, Jno	585	4	315	3–21–1787	Hickman Cr	
Sanders, Peter	2,473½	3	321	5– 3–1784	None	
Sanders, Robert	300	1	1	12–20–1782	Boone Cr	Surveyed
Sanders, Robert	4,000	1	197	12–20–1782	M Elkhorn	Surveyed
Sanders, Robert	500	1	197	12–20–1782	None	Withdrawn
Sanders, Robert	1,000	1	198	12–20–1782	W Fk McConnells Run	
Sanders, Robert	812	1	198	12–20–1782	None	
Sanders, Robert	300	1	198	12–20–1782	None	Surveyed
Sanders, Robert	4,119	1	217	12–21–1782	Ky R	

Entree	Acres	Book	Page	Entry Date	Watercourse	Notes
Sanders, Robert	500	1	363	1–4–1783	Hickmans Cr	Surveyed
Sanders, Robert	500	2	6	1–8–1873	Stoners Fk	
Sanders, Robert	200	2	65	1–14–1783	Hickmans Cr	Surveyed
Sanders, Robert	3,000	2	244	3–14–1783	Br Stamping Ground Cr	Surveyed
Saunders, Robert	1,616	1	128	12–13–1782	Licking	Surveyed
Sanders & Buckner	5,038¾	3	17	10–30–1783	Ohio R	
Sandige, Austin	500	1	13	11–30–1782	Br Licking	
Sandige, Joseph	600	1	13	11–30–1782	Br Licking	
Sandridge, David	3,000	1	24	12–17–1782	——— Cr	
Sandridge, David	1,000	1	25	12–17–1782	Indian Cr	Surveyed
Saunders, Jno	100	4	310	1–29–1787	S Fk Elkhorn	Surveyed
Savage, James	1,679	3	80	12–10–1783	Licking	
Sawden, Wm	3,165½	3	241	3–26–1784	Johnsons Fk	
Sawyers, William	2,000	1	61	12–6–1782	———	
Say, Jno C & Philip C	15,979½	3	136	1–2–1784	None	Surveyed
Scaggs, Theophiles	5,749½	4	40	9–22–1784	N Fk Eagle Cr	
Scott, Chas Genl	1,421½	4	251	12–30–1785	Ohio R	Withdrawn
Scott, Chas Genl	1,100	4	256	1–14–1786	S Fk Sandy	
Scott, Chas Genl	20,000	4	267	1–30–1786	Little Sandy	Withdrawn
Scott, Chas Genl	6,421½	4	277	2–19–1786	None	
Scott, Chas Genl	9,909	4	277	2–23–1786	Ohio R	
Scott, Chas Genl	150	4	277	2–27–1786	Ohio R	
Scott, Gen	20,000	4	272	2–15–1786	None	
Scott, Brig General	1,637½	2	123	1–23–1783	Jessamine Cr	Surveyed
Scott, Gabriel	100	4	133	3–16–1785	Jessamine Cr	
Scott, Jno	398½	3	411	7–17–1784	None	
Scott, Jno	29,936	3	424	8–11–1784	Cumberland Mt	
Scott, Thos	500	3	344	5–24–1784	None	Surveyed
Scott, William	300	1	380	1–6–1783	Ky R	Withdrawn
Scott, Wm	1,000	3	223	3–11–1784	Clear Cr	Surveyed
Scott, Wm	2,235½	3	343	5–24–1784	None	Surveyed
Scott, Wm	440	3	354	6–7–1784	Clear Cr	Withdrawn
Scott, Wm	640	3	355	6–7–1784	Clear Cr	Surveyed
Scott, Wm	300	4	213	8–2–1785	None	
Scott, Wm	300	4	214	8–2–1785	Clear Cr	Withdrawn
Scott, Wm	300	4	316	10–19–1787	Ky R	
Scott, Wm	400	4	316	10–30–1787	Clear Cr	
Scott, Wm	300	4	316	10–30–1787	Clear Cr	
Scott, William	500	1	25	12–17–1782	Hingston Fk	
Scott & Tale	1,550½	4	126	3–5–1785	N E Fk Licking	
Scrags, Allen	400	1	6	11–29–1783	None	
Searcy, Bartlett	400	1	152	12–17–1782	None	Surveyed
Searcy, Bartlett	400	3	191	3–1–1784	Hinkston Fk	
Searcy, Bartlett	400	4	298	5–5–1786	Ky R	Surveyed
Searcy, Reuben	1,000	2	51	1–13–1783	None	Surveyed
Searcy, Reuben	500	1	142	12–14–1782	Gists Cr	Withdrawn
Searcy, Reuben	500	2	345	8–9–1783	——— Cr	
Searcy, Reuben	1,000	3	14	10–25–1783	None	
Searcy & Fowler	400	4	302	7–28–1786	Ky R	
Sebree, Milly, heirs	575	4	47	10–8–1784	None	
Sebree, Richard	2,000	1	119	12–12–1782	Licking	Surveyed
Self, John	200	1	114	12–12–1782	None	
Sellus, John	1,000	1	57	12–5–1782	———	Surveyed
Settle, Edward	2,800	3	131	1–1–1784	None	Surveyed
Settle, Robt Hon	1,000	4	195	6–9–1785	Ohio R	
Settle, Robt Hon	1,000	4	195	6–9–1785	Ohio R	
Settle, Thos	4,958	3	130	1–1–1784	None	Surveyed
Shackelford, Zachariah	862½	3	46	11–15–1783	Little Sandy	
Shannon, John	1,000	2	282	4–29–1783	Shannons Run	
Shannon, William	400	2	78	1–17–1783	Slate Cr	
Shannon, Wm	1,000	3	12	10–16–1783	Ky R	
Shannon & Moore	2,000	3	11	10–16–1783	Ohio R	
Sharp, John	2,000	1	384	1–6–1783	S Br S Fk Eagle Cr	Withdrawn
Sharp, Jno	20,000	2	336	7–31–1783	McConnells Fk Licking	Surveyed
Sharp, Thos	1,900	3	150	1–15–1784	None	
Sharp, Thos	1,281¼	4	280	3–21–1786	Eagle Cr	
Sharp, William	1,000	1	41	12–4–1782	——— Cr	Surveyed
Sharp & Brown	1,200	4	274	2–17–1786	Eagle Cr	
Sharp & Brown	1,500	4	275	2–17–1786	Big Bone Lick	
Sharpe, John	251	1	339	12–31–1782	Glens Cr	Surveyed
Sharpe, John	2,000	1	384	1–6–1783	Eagle Cr	Withdrawn
Sharpe, John	2,000	2	335	7–31–1783	Eagle Cr	
Shaw, Joseph	2,000	3	339	5–19–1784	None	
Shaw, Jno	500	3	340	5–19–1784	None	Surveyed
Shearley, Michael	700	1	392	1–7–1783	Br Ky R	
Shearley, Michael	300	1	392	1–7–1783	Ky R	
Sheets, Jno & Jacob	2,481¾	4	185	5–28–1785	Eagle Cr	Surveyed
Shelby, Isaac	1,875	2	262	4–1–1783	Hickman Cr	Surveyed

Entree	Acres	Book	Page	Entry Date	Watercourse	Notes
Shelton & Southerland .	6,307	4	212	7–30–1785	None	
Shepherd, Adam	1,000	1	17	12– 4–1782	None	Surveyed
Shepherd, Adam	500	2	317	7– 7–1783	Slate Cr	Surveyed
Shepherd, Adam	7,231	2	338	8– 2–1783	Indian Cr	
Shepherd, Adam	2,097	2	339	8– 2–1783	——— Cr	
Shepherd, Adam	2,000	2	339	8– 2–1783	——— Cr	
Shepherd, Abraham	1,000	1	373	1– 6–1783	Hingston Fk	
Shepherd, Abraham	1,000	1	374	1– 6–1783	Hingstons Fk	
Shepherd, Abraham	1,000	1	374	1– 6–1783	Hingstons Fk	
Shepherd, Abraham	531	1	374	1– 6–1783	None	
Shepherd, Abraham	1,000	1	374	1– 4–1783	Br Hingston Fk	
Shepherd, Abraham	1,000	1	374	1– 6–1783	Hingston Fk	Surveyed
Shepherd, Abraham	1,000	1	375	1– 6–1783	None	Surveyed
Shepherd, Barliss	3,295	3	234	3–22–1784	Bush Cr	
Shelton, John	1,000	2	331	7–24–1783	Hickmans Cr	Surveyed
Shelton, John	1,000	2	355	8–16–1783	None	Surveyed
Shepherd, Peter	4,000	1	162	12–18–1782	Buffalo Road	
Shepherd, Peter	1,000	1	163	12–18–1782	None	Surveyed
Shepherd, Peter	1,000	1	163	12–18–1782	Upper Blue Lick	Surveyed
Shepherd, Wm	7,270½	3	195	3– 2–1784	Hinkston Fk	Surveyed
Shepherd, Wm	714½	3	289	4–14–1784	S Fk Big Sandy	
Shepherd, Wm	700	3	289	4–14–1784	S Fk Big Sandy	
Shepherd, Wm	2,387½	4	55	10–16–1784	None	
Shepherd & Allen	1,000	3	310	4–29–1784	S Fk Licking	
Shenan, Henry	2,000	4	191	6– 1–1785	None	Withdrawn
Ship, Colby	300	4	310	1–24–1787	None	Surveyed
Ship, Colby	200	4	313	3–21–1787	N Fk Elkhorn	
Ship, Colby	3,694	4	323	5– 9–1788	Cedar Cr	
Ship, Colby	12	4	325	11–27–1788	N Fk Elkhorn	
Ship, Laban	1,000	4	257	1–16–1786	Licking	
Ship, Laban	2,802½	4	323	5– 9–1788	None	
Ship & Ridgeley	12,268½	4	257	1–16–1786	Licking	
Ship & Ridgely	6,000	4	326	1–17–1789	Cedar Cr	
Ship & Todd	3,603½	3	120	12–29–1783	None	Surveyed
Shipp, Richard W & Cally	29,936	3	424	8–11–1784	Cumberland Mt	
Shirley, Michael	——	1	392	1– 7–1783	Red R	
Shirley, Michael	250	2	143	1–30–1783	Ky R	
Shirley, Michael	250	2	143	1–30–1782	Ky R	
Shore, Thomas	10,000	1	262	12–24–1782	N Fk Licking	Surveyed
Shore, Thomas	936	2	230	3–11–1783	None	Surveyed
Shore, Thos	16,500	3	301	4–26–1784	None	
Shortridge, Geo	1,000	4	81	12–31–1784	Hingston Fk	Surveyed
Shortridge, Samuel	100	1	151	12–16–1782	Br Ky R	Withdrawn
Shortridge, Samuel	100	4	76	12–16–1784	None	
Shortridge, Samuel	100	4	138	3–25–1785	Ky R	
Shortridge & Cleveland	2,000	4	222	9–21–1785	Boggs Fk Boones Cr	Withdrawn
Shortridge & Cleveland	9,922	4	222	9–21–1785	Gests Cr	
Shortridge & Cleveland	2,000	4	223	9–30–1785	Boggs Fk Boones Cr	
Shortridge & Cleveland	9,622	4	223	9–30–1785	None	
Shortridge & Cleveland	2,000	4	322	3–12–1788	None	
Shortridge & Middleton	708½	4	81	12–31–1784	None	
Shriver, Andrew	800	2	56	1–13–1783	Eagle Cr	
Shriver, Jacob	2,000	2	55	1–13–1783	Ohio R	
Shull, Joseph	1,000	1	284	12–26–1782	Br Licking	Surveyed
Shull, William	200	1	239	12–23–1782	Br Hingston Fk	Surveyed
Sicks, John	1,000	2	300	5–30–1783	Licking	
Simmens, Wm	1,500	4	110	2– 5–1785	Ky R	
Simmens, Wm	1,500	4	111	2– 5–1785	Lick Cr	
Simmens, Wm	1,500	4	111	2– 5–1785	Lick Cr	
Simmens, & Read	3,000	4	110	2– 5–1785	None	
Simins, Charles	2,000	2	335	7–31–1783	S Fk Eagle Cr	Surveyed
Simpson, Richard Jr	500	3	379	6–19–1784	Licking	
Sims, Wm	1,500	4	111	2– 5–1785	Ky R	
Singleton, Christopher	653½	2	270	4– 7–1783	None	
Singleton, Edward	650	1	42	12– 4–1782	Licking	
Singleton, Edward	3,000	1	351	1– 2–1783	S Fk Licking	Surveyed
Singleton, Edmond	2,000	1	352	1– 2–1783	S Licking	
Singleton, Edmond	1,000	1	352	1– 2–1783	Blue Lick	
Singleton, Edward	1,000	1	362	1– 4–1783	3 Miles up Will Cr	
Singleton, Edward	1,000	1	362	1– 4–1783	S Licking	
Singleton, Edward	281½	2	39	1–11–1783	None	
Singleton, Edmund	1,000	1	362	1– 4–1783	None	
Singleton, Edmund	6,000	2	27	1–10–1783	Main Br Licking	
Singleton, Robert	1,784	2	270	4– 7–1783	Licking	
Sinclair, Robert	1,978	1	277	12–25–1782	Br Hingston Fk	Surveyed
Sisvey, Bartlett	400	1	23	12–17–1782	———	Surveyed
Skinner, Cornelius	2,466½	4	238	12–13–1785	Br Fk Sandy	
Skillem. Wm	2,000	4	261	1–18–1786	Salt Rock Fk	
Slaughter, Geo	650	3	150	1–15–1784	Ky R	
Slaughter, Lawrence	3,750	2	235	3–12–1783	None	

Entree	Acres	Book	Page	Entry Date	Watercourse	Notes
Slaughter, Robert	3,225	2	236	3–12–1783	None	
Sleet, James	1,000	1	196	12–20–1782	Br Cabin Cr	
Smith, Adam	1,000	1	47	12– 4–1782	N Fk Eagle Cr	
Smith, Adam Rev	400	2	58	1–14–1783	W Br Hickmans Cr.	Surveyed
Smith, Alexander	393	2	252	3–21–1783	Pastime Lick Cr	Surveyed
Smith, Alexander	600	3	279	4– 8–1784	Small Mt Cr & M Fk Hinkston	
Smith, Caleb	2,802¾	4	323	5– 9–1788	None	
Smith, Charles	648	1	278	12–25–1782	Br Hingston Fk	Withdrawn
Smith, Charles	648	2	111	1–23–1783	Spencers Cr & Hinkstons	Amended
Smith, Charles	648	2	166	2– 6–1783	Br Licking	
Smith, Charles	2,000	2	237	3–12–1783	None	
Smith, Chas	450	3	96	12–17–1783	Licking	
Smith, Chas	1,000	4	128	3– 7–1785	None	
Smith, Clayton	1,708	3	25	10–31–1783	None	
Smith, Edmund	581	3	411	7–17–1784	None	
Smith, Enoch	500	1	393	1– 8–1783	Hingston & Licking	Withdrawn
Smith, Enoch	1,500	1	394	1– 8–1783	Howards & S Fk Licking	Withdrawn
Smith, Enoch	1,500	1	394	1– 8–1783	Hingston Fk	Surveyed
Smith, Enoch	1,000	2	180	2–11–1783	Licking & Stoners Fk	Surveyed
Smith, Enoch	500	2	250	3–21–1783	Howards Upper Cr.	Surveyed
Smith, Enoch	500	3	193	3– 1–1784	Stoners Fk	Surveyed
Smith, Enoch	1,000	3	197	3– 2–1784	Small Mt Cr	Surveyed
Smith, Enoch	300	4	81	12–31–1784	Elkhorn	
Smith, Enoch	300	4	184	5–24–1785	None	
Smith, Francis	8,000	1	355	1– 3–1783	Locust Cr	Surveyed
Smith, George	500	1	3	1–13–1783	Ky R	
Smith, George	1,344½	2	86	1–18–1786	None	
Smith, George	1,000	2	154	2– 1–1783	None	Surveyed
Smith, Geo	3,000	4	105	2– 5–1785	Licking	Surveyed
Smith, James	1,000	1	51	12– 5–1782	Br Licking	Surveyed
Smith, James	900	1	156	12–17–1782	Br Licking	Withdrawn
Smith, James	750	1	241	12–23–1762	Br Licking	Withdrawn
Smith, James	7,171	2	245	3–15–1783	Kentucky R	
Smith, Jas	1,000	3	5	10–15–1783*	——— Cr	
Smith, Jas	183	3	5	10–15–1783	——— Cr	
Smith, James	4,437	3	338	5–19–1784	None	Withdrawn
Smith, Jas	2,218¾	3	378	6–19–1784	None	Withdrawn
Smith, James	750	3	421	8– 5–1784	None	
Smith, James	900	3	421	8– 5–1784	None	
Smith, James	1,650	3	421	8– 5–1784	Br N Fk Licking	Surveyed
Smith, Jas	1,000	4	28	9– 4–1784	Ky R	Withdrawn
Smith, Jas	1,000	4	29	9– 4–1784	Ky R	Withdrawn
Smith, Jas	1,000	4	41	9–22–1784	Ky R	
Smith, Jas	2,218¾	4	56	10–17–1784	None	
Smith, James	1,600	4	59	10–25–1784	Br Licking	Surveyed
Smith, Jas	450	4	60	10–25–1784	None	Withdrawn
Smith, Jas	450	4	60	10–27–1784	None	
Smith, Jas	1,500	4	219	8–31–1785	None	Surveyed
Smith, John	1,000	2	141	1–29–1783	Br Hickman Cr	Surveyed
Smith, John	400	2	144	1–30–1783	N Fk Hickman Cr	Surveyed
Smith, John	480	2	207	2–22–1783	None	
Smith, Jno	111	2	241	3–13–1783	None	Surveyed
Smith, Jno	1,575	3	105	12–20–1783	S Fk Licking	Surveyed
Smith, Jno	1,575	3	231	3–20–1784	Licking	Surveyed
Smith, Jno	45,987¾	3	281	4–10–1784	Main Fk Licking	Surveyed
Smith, Jno	1,000	4	319	1– 9–1788	N Fk Elkhorn	910 acres surveyed
Smith, Joseph	2,750	3	15	10–25–1783	Big Bone Cr	
Smith, Joseph	3,000	4	201	6–21–1785	Ohio & Licking	
Smith, Joseph	1,000	4	202	6–21–1785	Step Stone Cr	
Smith, Mereweather	20,000	2	255	3–24–1783	Ohio & Ky R.	
Smith, Nathaniel	1,003	3	204	3– 5–1784	Eagle Cr	
Smith, Obediah	62,278¼	3	237	3–25–1784	Licking	Surveyed
Smith, Obediah	62,781¼	3	349	5–29–1784	Licking	Surveyed
Smith, Robert	2,175½	2	86	1–18–1783	Ky R	Surveyed
Smith, Robt	4,374	3	277	4– 7–1784	Millers Cr	
Smith, Saml	500	1	37	12– 4–1782	Bet Clear & Jessamine Cr	Surveyed
Smith, Samuel	400	2	21	1– 9–1783	S Fk Elkhorn	Amended
Smith, Samuel	400	2	213	2–28–1783	None	
Smith, Saml	500	3	97	12–18–1783	None	
Smith, Scarlet	500	1	117	12–12–1782	Eagle Cr	
Smith, Temple	1,000	2	156	2– 1–1783	Grassy Lick Cr	Surveyed
Smith, Thos	1,000	3	336	5–19–1784	None	Withdrawn
Smith, Thos	1,200	4	26	8–31–1784	Ky R	Withdrawn
Smith, Thos	350	4	46	10– 8–1784	Jessamine Cr	Amended
Smith, Thos	100	4	47	10– 9–1784	Jessamine Cr	Withdrawn
Smith, Thos	350	4	49	9–12–1784	None	

Entree	Acres	Book	Page	Entry Date	Watercourse	Notes
Smith, Thos	1,000	4	62	10–29–1784	None	
Smith, Thos	1,000	4	62	10–29–1784	Main Elkhorn	Withdrawn
Smith, Thos	450	4	66	11–10–1784	None	Surveyed
Smith, Thos	1,200	4	179	5–12–1787	None	
Smith, Thos	200	4	207	7–13–1785	None	
Smith, Thos	7,062½	3	126	1– 1–1784	None	
Smith, Valentine	400	1	198	12–20–1783	N Fk Elkhorn	
Smith, William	361	1	34	12– 3–1782	——— Cr	Surveyed
Smith, William	1,000	1	47	12– 4–1782	7 Miles below mouth Licking	Surveyed
Smith, William	900	2	148	1–31–1782	Hinkstons Fk	
Smith, William	1,000	2	154	2– 1–1783	Stoner Fk	Withdrawn
Smith, William	361	2	212	2–28–1785	None	Surveyed
Smith, William	12,301	2	245	1–15–1783	Stamping Ground Cr	
Smith, William	361	2	321	7–14–1783	None	
Smith, Wm	300	3	104	12–20–1783	Indian Cr	Withdrawn
Smith, Wm	1,000	3	196	3– 2–1784	Stoners Fk	Surveyed
Smith, Wm	2,812½	3	275	4– 7–1784	Hinkston Fk	Surveyed
Smith, Wm	109¼	4	101	1–28–1785	Fk Licking	
Smith, Wm	300	4	101	1–28–1785	Hingston Fk	Withdrawn
Smith, Wm	63	4	113	2– 7–1785	None	
Smith, Wm	12,301	4	129	3– 7–1785	None	Amended
Smith, Wm	2,000	4	138	3–24–1785	None	
Smith, Wm	109¾	4	150	4–10–1785	None	
Smith, Wm	190¼	4	150	4–10–1785	None	
Smith, Wm	700	4	150	4–10–1785	None	
Smith, Withers	1,500	4	308	11–21–1786	None	
Smith, Withers	1,000	2	252	3–21–1783	Stoners Fk	Withdrawn
Smith, Withers	1,081	2	253	3–21–1783	Br Stoners Fk	
Smith, Wither	1,000	3	347	5–27–1784	Licking	
Smither, William	1,406½	2	87	1–18–1783	Ky R	
Smith & Burnly	1,000	3	391	6–30–1784	S Fk Elkhorn	
Smith & Burnly	1,000	3	389	6–30–1784	None	
Smith Sr & Craig	1,250	3	389	6–30–1784	None	
Smith & Craig	600	3	391	6–30–1784	None	
Smith & Craig	600	3	390	6–30–1784	None	
Smith & Craig	600	3	390	6–30–1784	Bryans Station	
Smith & Craig	600	3	391	6–30–1784	N Fk Elkhorn	
Smith & Craig	639	3	391	6–30–1784	N Fk Elkhorn	
Smith & Haney	5,000	3	92	12–16–1783	Lulbergrud Cr	Surveyed
Smith & Marshall	10,000	3	171	1–31–1784	Bank Lick Cr	Withdrawn
Smith & Marshall	4,437	3	378	6–19–1784	None	
Smith & Marshall	1,000	4	18	8–20–1784	Clear Cr	Withdrawn
Smith & Marshall	1,000	4	19	8–21–1784	Clear Cr	Withdrawn
Smith & Marshall	1,000	4	19	8–21–1784	Clear Cr	
Smith & Marshall	1,000	4	19	8–21–1784	Clear Cr	
Smith & Marshall	1,420	4	19	8–21–1784	Clear Cr	Withdrawn
Smith & Marshall	580	4	19	8–21–1784	Clear Cr	Withdrawn
Smith & Marshall	1,420	4	23	8–30–1784	None	
Smith & Marshall	580	4	30	9– 7–1784	Clear Cr	Amended
Smith & Marshall	580	4	41	9–22–1784	Glens Cr	
Smith & Marshall	1,000	4	55	10–17–1784	None	
Smith & Marshall	1,000	4	57	10–23–1784	None	Surveyed
Smith & Marshall	400	4	59	10–25–1784	Hickmans Cr	Withdrawn
Smith & Marshall	600	4	59	10–25–1784	——— Cr	Withdrawn
Smith & Wilkinson	12,550	3	92	12–16–1783	Br Licking	Withdrawn
Smith & Wilkerson	12,550	3	274	4– 6–1784	None	
Smith & Wilkinson	8,500	4	309	12–23–1786	None	
Somers, John	100	1	180	12–18–1782	Jessamine Cr	
Somevalt, Stuffel	400	2	305	6– 2–1783	Greers Cr	Surveyed
Somevalt, Stuffel	669½	2	306	6– 2–1783	Licking	
South, John	75	1	19	12– 4–1782	Lulbergrud Cr	
South, John	1,000	2	80	1–17–1783	Br Ky R	
South, John	500	2	80	1–17–1783	4 Mile Cr	Surveyed
South, John	1,000	2	81	1–17–1783	E Br Stoners Fk	Withdrawn
South, Jno	10,000	3	75	12– 9–1783	Br Licking	
South, Jno	1,000	3	360	6–12–1784	Howard Upper Cr	Surveyed
South, Jno	1,000	4	133	3–16–1785	Red R	
South, Jno	5,618	4	168	4–30–1785	None	Withdrawn
South, Jno	898	4	168	4–30–1785	None	Withdrawn
South, Jno	5,618	4	175	5– 9–1785	None	
South, Jno	898	4	175	5– 9–1785	None	
South, Jno	6,516	4	176	5– 9–1785	None	
South, Jno Jr	1,600	3	360	6–12–1784	Main Licking	
South & Taylor	5,000	3	173	2– 4–1784	4 Mile Cr	
South & Taylor	10,000	3	244	3–26–1784	Ky R	Surveyed
South & Taylor	5,000	3	360	6–12–1784	W Fk Licking	
Southerland, John	500	1	54	12– 5–1782	Ky R	Amended
Southerland, John	500	2	282	5– 2–1783	None	
Southerland & Shelton	6,307	4	212	7–30–1785	None	

Entree	Acres	Book	Page	Entry Date	Watercourse	Notes
Spalding, John	1,500	1	216	12–21–1782	Big Bone Cr	
Sparr, Mathias	500	3	385	6–24–1784	Main Licking	
Spaw, Mathias	400	1	215	12–21–1782	Green Cr	Surveyed
Spaw, Mathias	400	2	104	1–21–1783	Green Cr	Surveyed
Spears, Edward	1,000	4	305	10–11–1786	S Fk Elkhorn	
Speed, James	14,000	1	245	12–23–1782	Gists Cr	Surveyed
Speed, James	6,156	1	251	12–24–1782	Stoners Fk	
Speed, James	8,000	1	286	12–26–1782	Ohio R	Surveyed
Speer, Joseph	1,000	4	208	7–13–1785	Ohio R	Withdrawn
Speer, Richard	845	2	6	1– 8–1783	4 Mile Cr	Withdrawn
Speer, Richard	845	2	267	4– 7–1783	4 Mile & Licking	Surveyed
Speer, Richard	300	3	273	4– 6–1784	Howard Upper Cr	Surveyed
Spencer, Joseph	1,266	2	170	2– 7–1783	None	
Spilman, Jas	842	3	268	4– 6–1784	Licking	Surveyed
Spilman & Harris	17,372	3	194	3– 2–1784	Hinkston Fk	Surveyed
Spilman & Morgan	7,812	4	287	3–28–1786	None	
Sprigg, Edward	1,000	2	275	4–22–1783	W Fk Licking	Amended
Stafford, William	960	2	145	1–31–1783	None	
Stafford, William	500	2	195	2–14–1783	Cane Run	Surveyed
Stafford, Wm	8,304	3	183	2–12–1784	Eagle Cr	
Stafford, Wm	1,000	4	219	8–20–1785	None	
Stafford, Wm	1,000	4	219	8–20–1785	None	
Stafford, Wm	50	4	311	3– 2–1787	Ky R	
Stafford, Wm	200	4	320	2–15–1788	——— R	Surveyed
Stafford, Wm	184	4	335	12–23–1791	Marble Cr	
Stamp, Jno Molly & Wm	3,800	4	218	8–10–1785	Eagle Cr	
Standard, Geo	1,000	4	275	2–17–1786	Eagle Cr	
Stanley, Wm	8,959½	3	333	5–14–1784	None	4,479¾ acrse withdrawn
Starke, Jeremiah	600	1	1	11–28–1782	Licking	Surveyed
Starke, Jeremiah	400	2	153	2– 1–1783	E Fk Howards Upper Cr	Surveyed
Starns, Adam	1,000	1	307	12–28–1782	W Fk Stoners Fk	
Starns, Adam	500	1	308	12–28–1782	Fk Howards Cr	Surveyed
Starns, Frederick	1,000	1	307	12–28–1782	W Fk Stoners Fk	
Starns, Frederick	500	1	308	12–28–1782	Fk Howards Cr	Surveyed
Starns, Jacob	1,000	1	308	12–28–1782	Strodes Fk Licking	
Starns, Jo	1,000	1	307	12–28–1782	W Fk Stoners Fk	
Starns, Joseph	500	1	308	12–28–1782	Fk Howards Cr	Surveyed
Starns, Samuel	1,000	1	307	12–28–1782	W Fk Stoners Fk	
Starns, Samuel	500	1	308	12–28–1782	Fk Howards Cr	Surveyed
Steele, Andrew	200	1	37	12– 4–1782	Stickes Run	Surveyed
Steele, Andrew	1,000	1	99	12–10–1782	N & S Fks Elkhorn	Surveyed
Steele, Andrew	619½	2	70	1–16–1783	S Fk Elkhorn	Withdrawn
Steele, Andrew	1,000	2	120	1–24–1783	None	
Steele, Andrew	1,619½	2	140	1–29–1783	None	Withdrawn
Steele, Andrew	619½	2	159	2– 3–1783	Steeles Run	Surveyed
Steel, Andrew	500	2	179	2–10–1783	None	
Steele, Andrew	1,000	3	152	1–16–1784	Fk Lick Cr	Withdrawn
Steele, Andrew	1,000	3	248	3–29–1784	Licking	
Steele, Andrew	45,987¾	3	281	4–10–1784	Main Fk Licking	Surveyed
Steele, Andrew	550	3	388	6–29–1784	Steeles Run	Surveyed
Steele, Andrew	200	4	65	11– 5–1784	None	
Steele, Andrew	200	4	65	11– 5–1784	Br S Fk Elkhorn	Surveyed
Steele, Andrew	1,000	4	204	6–30–1785	Jessamine Cr	
Steele, Andrew	1,000	4	263	1–28–1786	Br S Fk Elkhorn	
Steele, Andrew	1,000	4	297	4–29–1786	None	
Steele, Andrew	1,000	4	297	4–29–1786	Ohio R	
Steele, David	1,000	1	236	12–23–1782	Small Cr	Surveyed
Steele, David	685½	2	115	1–24–1783	None	
Steele, Hugh	9,922	4	173	5– 9–1785	Ohio R	
Steele, James	1,000	1	236	12–23–1782	Small Cr	Surveyed
Steele, Jean	1,000	1	235	12–23–1782	Main Elkhorn	Withdrawn
Steel, John	4,000	1	182	12–19–1782	W Br Grassy Cr	Surveyed
Steel, John	2,000	1	182	12–18–1782	Fk Lick Cr	Surveyed
Steele, John	800	1	246	12–23–1782	Elkhorn	Withdrawn
Steele, Jno	386	3	304	4–26–1784	Clear Cr	
Steele, Jno	400	4	162	4–29–1785	None	
Steele, Jno	129	4	269	2– 7–1786	None	
Steele, Jno & Wm	300	3	248	3–29–1784	Fk Lick Cr	Withdrawn
Steele, Jno & Wm	800	4	158	4–29–1785	None	
Steele, Jno & Wm	249	4	269	2– 7–1786	Hickman Cr	Withdrawn
Steele, Jno & Wm	249	4	318	12–29–1787	None	
Steele, Jno & Wm	———	4	318	12–29–1787	Ky R	
Steele, Kitty	1,000	1	235	12–23–1782	Main Elkhorn	Withdrawn
Steele, Kitty, Polly Jean & Sally	1,000	3	227	3–16–1784	Ky R	
Steele, Nathaniel	553	2	119	1–24–1783	Red R	Withdrawn
Steele, Nathaniel	553	4	297	4–29–1786	None	
Steele, Nathaniel	553	4	297	4–29–1786	Ohio R	

Entree	Acres	Book	Page	Entry Date	Watercourse	Notes
Steele, Polly	1,000	1	235	12–23–1782	Main Elkhorn	Withdrawn
Steele, Richard	900	1	46	12– 4–1782	Big Bone Cr	
Steele, Richard	1,000	1	46	12– 4–1782	N Fk Elkhorn	Surveyed
Steele, Robert	1,000	1	236	12–23–1782	Small Cr	Surveyed
Steele, Sally	1,000	1	235	ʼ12–23–1782	Main Elkhorn	Withdrawn
Steele, Samuel	1,000	1	236	12–23–1782	Small Cr	Surveyed
Steele, Saml	800	4	159	4–29–1785	None	
Steele, William	1,000	1	40	12– 4–1782	Sturgeons Fk	Surveyed
Steele, William	500	1	182	12–18–1782	S Fk Lick Cr	
Steele, William	500	1	182	12–18–1782	Br Ky R	Surveyed
Steele, Wm	890½	3	63	11–29–1783	None	
Steele, Wm	1,000	3	166	1–24–1784	None	
Steele, Wm	400	4	162	4–29–1785	None	
Steele, Wm	120	4	269	2– 7–1786	None	
Steele, Wm	1,000	4	318	12–31–1787	N Fk Elkhorn	
Steele, Wm	54	4	341	9– 4–1810	Elkhorn	
Steele & Green	1,000	3	62	11–27–1783	None	Withdrawn
Steele & Mitchell	1,000	4	306	10–14–1786	Ohio R	
Stephens, Benj	500	1	127	12–13–1782	Greers Cr	
Stephenson, Jas	273½	4	166	4–29–1785	None	
Stephenson, James	500	1	28	12– 3–1782	Mill Cr	
Stephenson, Wm	350	3	371	6–16–1784	Elkhorn	
Stephenson & McClure	841½	3	381	6–23–1784	—— Cr	
Sterrett, Cairus	1,000	3	340	5–20–1784	N Fk Licking	Surveyed
Sterrett, Cairus	1,000	3	382	6–23–1784	—— Br	
Sterrett, Cairus	1,000	3	382	6–23–1784	Br Licking	
Stevens, John	1,000	1	182	12–19–1782	Ohio & Licking	
Stevens, John	1,000	1	183	12–18–1782	None	
Stevens, Jacob	300	3	361	6–12–1784	Licking	Surveyed
Stevenson, Jas	1,858	3	382	6–23–1784	Br Main Licking	
Stevenson, John	50	2	198	2–17–1783	Main Fk Licking	Surveyed
Stevenson & Samuel	1,385½	2	249	3–15–1783	None	Surveyed
Stevenson, William	780	2	303	5–31–1783	S Fk Elkhorn	Withdrawn
Stevenson, Will	780	4	294	4–29–1786	None	
Stevenson, Will	350	4	294	4–29–1786	None	
Stewart, David	2,500	2	336	7–31–1783	S Br S Fk Eagle Cr	Withdrawn
Stewart, Hugh	14,906½	2	306	6– 2–1783	M Licking	Withdrawn
Stewart, Hugh	15,000	3	101	12–19–1783	Eagle Cr	Surveyed
Stewart, Hugh	15,000	3	101	12–19–1783	Eagle Cr	Surveyed
Stewart, Hugh	15,000	3	205	3– 8–1784	None	Withdrawn
Stewart, Hugh	15,000	4	132	3–13–1785	None	
Stewart, Hugh	7,023½	4	172	5– 6–1785	None	Surveyed
Stewart, Hugh	14,906½	4	178	5–12–1785	Licking	Withdrawn
Stewart, Hugh	6,335	4	245	12–20–1785	None	Surveyed
Stewart, Hugh	14,906½	4	245	12–21–1785	Ohio R	
Stewart, Isaac	12,225	4	70	11–25–1784	Slate Cr	
Stewart, Jas	57,499½	4	50	9–13–1784	Ky R	Withdrawn
Stewart, Jas	57,499½	4	57	10–23–1784	Eagle Cr	Surveyed
Stewart, Jas	16,961	4	210	7–22–1785	Br Ky R	Withdrawn
Stewart, Jas	16,961	4	280	3–23–1786	None	
Stewart, William	1,000	2	297	5–28–1783	Greers Cr	
Stewart & Barr	5,000	4	53	10–16–1784	Locust Cr	
Stewart & Barr	12,000	4	209	7–22–1785	None	
Stewart, Barr & Donnell	57,499½	4	57	10–23–1784	None	
Stewart & Hawkins	62,306	4	224	9–30–1785	None	
Stewart & Young	3,121¾	3	179	2–10–1784	None	
Stoane, Bryant	1,700	2	375	10–13–1783	Br Eagle Cr	
Stockdon, George	1,000	2	321	7–14–1783	Br Licking	
Stockdon, Robt	2,473½	3	321	5– 3–1784	None	Surveyed
Stockdon, Geo	1,708	3	420	8– 5–1784	Licking	
Stoker, Basil	1,000	2	287	5–16–1783	Hinkstons Fk & Licking	Surveyed
Stockton, George	500	1	29	12–17–1782	Hingston Fk of Licking	Surveyed
Stockton, George	1,000	1	365	1– 4–1783	None	Surveyed
Stockton, Geo	200	3	400	7–10–1784	Hinkston Fk	
Stotes & Hornby	4,176	3	60	11–25–1783	Ohio R	
Strode, James	1,003	1	373	1– 6–1783	Br Licking	
Strode, James	2,000	2	246	3–15–1783	None	Surveyed
Strode, Rachael	1,000	1	373	1– 6–1783	Licking	Surveyed
Strode, Samuel	347½	2	348	8–13–1783	None	Surveyed
Stripling, Sigesmund	1,000	4	301	6–14–1786	Ky R	Surveyed
Strother, Joseph	1,106	1	345	1– 1–1783	2 & 4 Mile Cr	
Strother, Joseph	4,000	2	243	3–13–1783	None	
Strother, Joseph	3,221½	2	250	3–15–1783	Ky R	
Strother, Joseph	5,480	3	129	3– 7–1784	Ohio	Withdrawn
Strother, Joseph	5,480	4	249	12–23–1785	None	
Strother, William Jr	1,108	2	352	8–15–1783	None	Withdrawn
Stuart, David	9,003	3	191	3– 1–1784	Licking	
Stuart, Hugh	14,906½	2	287	5–20–1783	Main Licking	Withdrawn

Entree	Acres	Book	Page	Entry Date	Watercourse	Notes
Stuart, Hugh	15,000	3	112	12–27–1783	None	Withdrawn
Stuart, Hugh	6,335	3	112	12–27–1783	Eagle Cr	Withdrawn
Stuart, Hugh	3,278½	4	233	11–12–1785	None	
Stuart, William	400	2	280	4–29–1783	None	Surveyed
Stuart, William	600	2	281	4–29–1783	None	Surveyed
Stuart, William	1,000	2	281	4–29–1786	Blockfords Fk Glenns Cr	Surveyed
Stuart, William	1,000	2	296	5–26–1783	M Fk Licking	Surveyed
Stuart, Wm	1,000	2	296	5–28–1783	r h Fk Lawrences Cr.	Surveyed
Stucker, Jacob	153	1	202	12–20–1782	Hingstons Fk	Surveyed
Sturges, Daniel	2,000	1	52	12– 5–1782	Cr Hingston	Surveyed
Sundath, John	1,001	1	361	1– 4–1783	E Br Stoners Fk	
Suggatt, James	500	1	133	12–13–1782	None	
Suggett, Jas	3,400	1	133	12–13–1782	1st Cr Big Buffaloe Cr	Amended
Suggett, John	3,400	1	133	12–13–1782	1st Cr Big Buffaloe Cr	Amended
Summit, Christian	328	2	208	2–24–1783	Hinkstons Fk	
Sumvalt, Andrew	471½	3	88	12–13–1783	Br Hinkston Fk	Surveyed
Sutton, James	1,000	1	38	12– 4–1782	Licking	
Sutton, James	100	1	38	12– 4–1782	Shoemakers Cr	
Sutton, James	500	1	38	12– 4–1782	Fk Licking	
Sutton, John	500	2	6	1– 8–1783	4 Mile W Br S Fk Licking	Surveyed
Sutton, Robert	1,168½	2	102	1–21–1783	Ohio R	Surveyed
Swan, Charles	1,200	1	98	12–10–1782	Clear Cr	Surveyed
Swan, Elizabeth	1,000	2	77	1–17–1783	Br Licking	
Swan, John	1,000	2	167	2– 6–1783	N Fk Elkhorn	
Swann, Jno, heirs	1,000	2	83	1–17–1783	N Fk Elkhorn	Surveyed
Swann, Justinian	1,000	1	157	12–17–1782	Lecompts Cr	Surveyed
Swearingin, Benoni	300	2	323	7–17–1783	N Fk Red R	
Swearingin, Benoni	700	2	324	7–17–1783	Red R	
Swearingin, Hezekiah	500	1	52	12– 5–1782	——— Cr	Surveyed
Swearingin, Thomas	500	1	29	12– 3–1782	Head Spg Red R	
Swearingin, Thomas	500	1	82	12– 9–1782	N Br Licking	
Swearingen, Thomas	1,000	1	214	12–20–1782	Hingston Fk	Surveyed
Swearingen, Thomas	1,000	1	214	12–20–1782	None	
Swearingen, Thomas	1,000	1	238	12–23–1782	Br Hingston Fk	Surveyed
Swearingen, Thomas	1,000	1	324	12–30–1782	Hingston Fk	
Swearingen, Thomas	1,000	1	325	12–30–1782	Hingstons Fk	
Swearingen, Thomas	1,000	1	325	12–30–1782	Hingston Fk	
Swearingen, Thomas	1,000	1	325	12–30–1782	Hingston Fk	
Swearingen, Thomas	1,000	1	326	12–30–1782	Hingstons Fk	Surveyed
Swearingen, Thomas	2,000	1	329	12–30–1782	Hingstons Fk	
Swearingen, Thomas	1,000	1	329	12–30–1782	Br Hingston Fk	Surveyed
Swearingen, Thomas	1,000	1	329	12–30–1782	Br Hingston Fk	
Swearingen, Thomas	2,000	1	332	12–31–1782	Hingston Fk	Surveyed
Swearingen, Thomas	2,000	1	332	12–31–1782	Stoners Fk Licking	
Swearingen, Thomas	1,000	1	333	12–31–1782	Stoners Sp	Surveyed
Swearingen, Thomas	1,000	1	333	12–31–1782	Stoners Fk Licking	Withdrawn
Swearingen, Thos	1,000	1	333	12–31–1782	Stoners & Hingstons	Withdrawn
Swearingen, Thomas	400	1	335	12–31–1782	Hingston Fk	
Swearingen, Thomas	1,000	1	336	12–31–1782	None	Withdrawn
Swearingen, Thomas	1,000	1	341	12–31–1782	Br Stoners Fk	Withdrawn
Swearingen, Thomas	1,000	1	341	12–31–1782	Stoners Fk	Withdrawn
Swearingen, Thomas	1,000	1	341	12–31–1782	Br Hingston Fk	Withdrawn
Swearingin, Thomas	1,000	1	342	1– 1–1783	Br N Fk Licking	Withdrawn
Swearingen, Thomas	1,000	1	362	1– 4–1783	Br Hingston Fk	Surveyed
Swearingen, Thomas	500	1	367	1– 4–1783	Strodes Fk	Withdrawn
Swearingen, Thomas	1,000	1	368	1– 4–1783	None	Surveyed
Swearingen, Thomas	1,000	2	11	1– 9–1783	None	Withdrawn
Swearingen, Thomas	750	2	11	1– 9–1783	Hingston Fk	
Swearingin, Thomas	500	2	18	1– 9–1783	Stoners Fk	Withdrawn
Swearingen, Thomas	1,000	2	105	1–22–1783	Hingstons & Stoners Fk	Withdrawn
Swearingen, Thomas	500	2	105	1–22–1783	Hingston Fk	
Swearingen, Thomas	1,000	2	285	5–13–1783	Johnsons Fk Licking	Surveyed
Swearingen, Thomas	40	2	293	5–23–1783	Strodes Fk Licking	
Swearingin, Thomas	2,000	2	313	6– 9–1783	Br N Fk	Surveyed
Swearingen, Thomas	500	2	361	8–10–1783	Howards lower Cr	Surveyed
Swearingen, Thomas	1,500	2	361	8–10–1783	Ohio R	Withdrawn
Swearingin, Thos	500	3	2	10–15–1783	None	Surveyed
Swearingin, Thos	1,000	3	3	10–15–1783	Br Salt Sp	
Swearingin, Thos	500	3	3	10–15–1783	——— Cr	
Swearingin, Thos	1,000	3	4	10–15–1783	——— Cr	
Swearingin, Thos	1,000	3	6	10–15–1783	——— Cr	
Swearingin, Thos	1,000	3	54	11–21–1783	Br Red R	
Swearingin, Thos	500	3	55	11–21–1783	Ky R	
Swearingin, Thos	10,687	3	64	12– 1–1783	S Fk Big Sandy	
Swearingin, Thos	———	3	76	12– 9–1783	None	Surveyed
Swearingin, Thos	340	3	148	1–15–1784	Big Slate Cr	

Entree	Acres	Book	Page	Entry Date	Watercourse	Notes
Swearingin, Thos.	1,000	4	7	8–14–1784	Sandy Cr	Surveyed
Swearingin, Thos.	1,000	4	7	8–14–1784	Sandy	Surveyed
Sweringin, Van	1,000	1	52	12– 5–1782	Johnstons Fk Licking	Surveyed
Swearingin, Van	1,000	1	83	12– 9–1782	Licking	
Swearingin, Van	1,000	1	98	12–10–1782	Clear Cr	Surveyed
Swearingen, & Fulton	1,000	4	8	8–14–1784	Sandy Cr	Surveyed
Sykes, Wm	126,140	3	298	4–22–1784	1 h Fk 3 Fks Ky R.	Surveyed amended
Symes, Wm	30,000	4	255	1–14–1786	Licking	
Tabb, John	10,000	1	252	12–24–1782	Stoners & Hingstons	Surveyed
Tabb, John	5,000	1	253	12–24–1782	None	Surveyed
Tabb, John	5,000	1	253	12–24–1782	None	Surveyed
Tabb, John	18,000	1	253	12–24–1782	Lees Cr	Surveyed
Tabb, John	4,532	1	254	12–24–1782	Ohio R	Surveyed
Talbot, Jeremiah	1,000	4	305	10–11–1786	Fk Elkhorn	
Talbott, James	5,218	2	364	4– 3–1783	Ohio & Licking	Surveyed
Talbott, Isham	1,000	2	1	1– 8–1783	Cypress Cr	
Talbott, Isham	3,400	2	1	1– 8–1783	Red R	
Talbott, Isham	2,200	2	143	1–30–1783	E Br Hustons Fk	
Talbot, Isham	6,016½	2	264	4– 3–1783	Bank Lick Cr	Surveyed
Talbot, Isham	2,500	3	183	2–12–1784	Br Cedar Cr	
Talbot, Isham	3,600	4	117	2–12–1785	Blue Lick	
Talbott, Isham Jr	2,200	1	358	1– 4–1783	Red R	Withdrawn
Talbot, Jno	552	4	117	2–12–1785	Main Licking	
Tandy, Wm	500	4	333	3–21–1791	N Fk Elkhorn	
Tanner & Buchannan	1,488	4	24	8–30–1784	M Br Licking	
Tapp, Vincent	4,600	2	366	9–23–1783	Ohio R	Surveyed
Tapp, Vincent	4,600	2	367	9–23–1783	Ohio R	Surveyed
Tapp, Vincent	2,320	2	367	9–23–1783	Ohio R	Withdrawn
Tapp, Vincent	6,710½	3	408	7–14–1784	Eagle Cr	Withdrawn
Tapp, Vincent	2,320	4	323	5–27–1788	None	
Tarrison, Bartholomew	20,000	3	110	12–27–1783	S Fk Big Sandy R.	
Tarrison, Bartholomew	10,000	3	110	12–27–1783	S Fk Sandy R	Surveyed
Tarrison & Bros	300,306⅔	3	190	2–28–1784	3 Fks Ky R	
Tate, Cobb	1,000	4	148	4–10–1785	None	
Tate, Chas	400	3	3	10–15–1783	None	Surveyed
Tate, Jno	500	3	41	11–12–1783	Ky R	Surveyed
Tate, Jno	500	3	41	11–12–1783	Ky R	Surveyed
Tate & Scott	1,550½	4	126	3– 5–1785	N E Fk Licking	
Taylor, Benjamin	17,500	1	354	1– 2–1783	Locust Cr	Surveyed
Taylor, Charles	5,984	1	271	1– 6–1783	Slate Cr	
Taylor, Caroline M.	2,000	4	90	1–14–1785	Slate Cr	
Taylor, Edmond	1,000	4	119	2–15–1785	S Fk Elkhorn	Surveyed
Taylor, Edmund	10,000	3	233	3–22–1784	Buck Cr	Withdrawn
Taylor, Francis	3,000	2	38	1–11–1783	Slate Cr	
Taylor, George	5,937½	2	372	10– 6–1783	Ky R	Surveyed
Taylor, Geo	14,666½	3	59	11–25–1783	N Fk Licking	
Taylor, Geo	5,791½	3	62	11–27–1783	Cabbin Cr	Surveyed
Taylor, Geo	1,008	3	203	3– 5–1784	Eagle Cr	
Taylor, James	12,000	1	370	1– 4–1783	Slate Cr	
Taylor, Jesse	2,400	4	231	11– 5–1785	Elkhorn	
Taylor, John	1,000	1	321	12–30–1782	Millers Cr	
Taylor, John	4,000	1	337	12–31–1782	3rd Fk Stoners Fk	
Taylor, John	3,000	1	338	12–31–1782	Stoners & Hingston	Surveyed
Taylor, John	500	1	339	12–31–1782	Howards Lick	
Taylor, John	24,449	1	352	1– 2–1783	Main Licking	
Taylor, John	9,600	1	371	1– 6–1783	Slate Cr	
Taylor, John	1,000	1	379	1– 6–1783	Elkhorn	
Taylor, John	2,000	2	21	1– 9–1783	Br Hingston Fk	Surveyed
Taylor, John	2,000	2	22	1– 9–1783	Stoners Fk Licking	
Taylor, John	2,000	2	22	1– 9–1783	Br Hingston Fk	
Taylor, John	1,000	2	22	1– 9–1783	Hinkstons Fk	
Taylor, John	6,000	2	109	1–23–1783	Hinkstons Fk	Amended
Taylor, John	1,000	2	122	1–25–1783	4 Mile Cr	
Taylor, John	6,000	2	165	2– 5–1783	Br Licking	
Taylor, Jno	5,000	3	32	11– 6–1783	Licking	Withdrawn
Taylor, Jno	574	3	36	11–11–1783	Buck Lick Cr	
Taylor, Jno	5,000	3	75	12– 9–1783	None	Withdrawn
Taylor, Jno	5,000	3	75	12– 9–1783	None	Withdrawn
Taylor, Jno	4,000	3	195	3– 2–1784	Bramletts Lick	Surveyed
Taylor, Jno	5,000	3	205	3– 8–1784	None	Surveyed
Taylor, Jno	1,550	3	251	3–30–1,84	Lees Cr	Withdrawn
Taylor, Jno	2,000	3	409	7–14–1784	Main Licking	
Taylor, Jno	4,500	4	51	10–13–1784	Licking	
Taylor, Jno	1,500	4	51	10–13–1784	None	Surveyed
Taylor, Jno	1,500	4	238	12–10–1785	None	Surveyed
Taylor, Jno	50	4	300	6– 6–1786	Greers Cr	Surveyed
Taylor, Jonathan	2,220	3	171	1–31–1784	None	Withdrawn
Taylor, Jonathan	2,220	3	277	4– 7–1784	Millers Cr	
Taylor, Reuben	11,250	1	355	1– 3–1783	Fk Licking	Surveyed

Entree	Acres	Book	Page	Entry Date	Watercourse	Notes
Taylor, Thornton	3,165½	3	241	3–26–1784	Johnsons Fk	....
Taylor, William	20,000	1	352	1– 2–1783	Locust Cr	Surveyed
Taylor & Bradley	2,500	4	287	3–28–1786	None	Amended
Taylor & Bradley	2,000	4	287	3–28–1786	None	Amended
Taylor & Bradley	2,500	4	289	4– 8–1786	None	....
Taylor & Bradly	2,000	4	289	4– 8–1786	None	....
Taylor & Craig	500	4	119	2–15–1785	Ohio R	....
Taylor & Craig	500	4	120	2–15–1785	Ohio R	....
Taylor & Holder	49,665½	3	416	7–26–1784	Ky R	Surveyed
Taylor & Masterson	1,000	3	46	11–15–1783	Ohio R	....
Taylor & South	5,000	3	173	2– 4–1784	4 Mile Cr	....
Taylor & South	10,000	3	244	3–26–1784	Ky R	Surveyed
Taylor & South	5,000	3	360	6–12–1784	W Fk Licking	....
Tebbs, Daniel	500	1	8	11–29–1782	Steeles Run	Surveyed
Tebbs, Daniel	500	1	8	11–29–1782	Licking Cr	....
Tebbs, John	500	2	292	5–23–1783	Stepstone Cr	Withdrawn
Tebbs, Jno	500	2	294	5–24–1783	Stepstone Cr	Withdrawn
Tebbs & Crutcher	3,000	3	35	11– 8–1783	Buffaloe Rd	....
Templin, Terah	2,063½	3	311	4–29–1784	S Fk Licking	....
Templin, Terrah	2,063½	3	58	11–24–1783	Hinkston Fk	Withdrawn
Terrell, Edmond	1,050	3	159	1–21–1784	Licking	Surveyed
Terrpin, Horatia	1,000	4	85	1– 8–1785	Hingston Fk	Withdrawn
Terrell, Robt	1,000	3	411	7–17–1784	Licking	....
Terrell, Robt	400	4	217	8– 9–1785	Salt Sp	Surveyed
Terrell, Robt	400	4	220	9– 1–1785	None	Surveyed
Terrells & Hawkins	1,000	1	100	12–10–1782	S Fk Elkhorn	Surveyed
Terrells & Hawkins	1,000	2	297	5–29–1783	N Fk Licking	Surveyed
Terrells & Hawkins	1,000	2	298	5–29–1783	Br Licking	....
Terrells & Hawkins	1,000	2	298	5–29–1783	Bensons Cr	Withdrawn
Terrills & Hawkins	1,000	2	298	5–29–1783	Fks Elkhorn	Surveyed
Terrells & Hawkins	1,000	2	298	5–29–1783	None	....
Terrells & Hawkins	1,000	2	298	5–29–1783	Licking	Surveyed
Terrells & Hawkins	1,000	2	298	5–29–1783	Dry Run	Surveyed
Terrills & Hawkins	1,000	2	299	5–29–1783	Fks Elkhorn	Surveyed
Terrells & Hawkins	1,000	2	299	5–29–1783	None	Surveyed
Terry, Joseph	2,000	1	43	12– 4–1782	Br Hicksman	Surveyed
Testo, Elexie	300,306⅔	3	190	2–28–1784	S Fks Ky R	....
Thomas, Catherine	1,000	1	136	12–13–1782	Jessamine Cr	Surveyed
Thomas, Charles Moragn	4,000	1	376	1– 6–1783	Flat Cr	Surveyed
Thomas, Jas	4,504¼	4	40	9–22–1784	None	Withdrawn
Thomas, Jas	4,504¼	4	96	1–21–1785	None	....
Thomas, Jas	4,504¼	4	340	11–11–1800	None	....
Thomas, Moses	1,000	1	393	1– 8–1783	S Fk Licking Cr	Surveyed
Thomas, Moses	1,000	2	277	4–23–1783	Stoners and Rockyford Fk	Surveyed
Thomas, Moses	1,000	4	150	4–10–1785	Slate Cr	Surveyed
Thomas, Philman	1,500	4	237	12– 7–1785	None	Surveyed
Thomas, Philmore	370	4	320	2–19–1788	None	....
Thomas, Phileman	1,200	4	332	6–22–1790	Marble Cr	....
Thomas, Rowland	2,238	1	121	12–12–1782	Licking	....
Thomas, Wm	600	4	202	6–23–1785	Eagle Cr	....
Thompson, Anthony	500	1	33	12– 3–1782	Mud Lick	....
Thompson, Anthony	400	1	47	12– 4–1782	—— Cr	Surveyed
Thompson, Anthony	500	1	47	12– 4–1782	Dry Cr	Surveyed
Thompson, Anthony	1,550	1	61	12– 6–1782	Br Big Bone Cr	....
Thornton, Anthony	33,750	1	357	1– 2–1783	Lower Blue Lick & N Fk Licking	....
Thornton, John	1,286	1	385	1– 7–1783	None	....
Thornton, Francis	2,434	3	282	4–10–1784	Eagle Cr	....
Thornton, Rev Thos	1,462½	4	221	9–17–1785	None	....
Thornberry, Samuel	3,950	1	355	1– 3–1783	None	Surveyed
Throckmorton, Thos	4,000	3	345	5–25–1784	Blue Lick Fk	....
Throckmorton, Thos	2,000	3	345	5–25–1784	—— Cr	....
Thompson, Andrew	3,000	4	203	6–28–1785	Cabbin Cr	....
Thompson, Andrew	1,500	4	230	11– 3–1785	None	....
Thompson, Eley	642½	2	109	1–23–1783	Fk Hinkstons	Surveyed
Thompson, Ephram & Richard	300,306⅔	3	190	2–28–1784	3 Fks Ky R	....
Thompson, George	1,000	1	76	12– 9–1782	Clear Cr	Amended
Thompson, George	1,000	1	126	12–13–1782	None	Withdrawn
Thompson, George	1,000	2	291	5–22–1783	None	Withdrawn
Thompson, George	1,000	2	296	5–28–1783	r h Fk of Lawrence Cr	Surveyed
Thompson, Geo	1,000	3	290	4–15–1784	Clear Cr	Surveyed
Thompson, Geo	3,000	3	309	4–29–1784	S Fk Licking	Withdrawn
Thompson, Geo	3,000	3	311	4–29–1784	Licking	Withdrawn
Thompson, Geo	3,000	4	322	4–28–1788	None	....
Thompson, Geo	3,000	4	323	4–28–1788	None	....
Thompson, Henry	1,000	1	317	12–30–1782	N Fk S Br Licking	Surveyed
Thompson, Hugh	400	1	104	12–11–1782	Town Fk	....

Entree	Acres	Book	Page	Entry Date	Watercourse	Notes
Thompson, Hugh	400	2	330	7–22–1783	Town Fk	
Thompson, Jas	1,000	3	2	10–15–1783	Shelby Fk Hickman Cr	
Thompson, Jas	506	3	40	11–12–1783	None	
Thompson, Jas	200	3	64	11–29–1783	Hickman Cr	
Thompson, Jno	1,170	4	167	4–29–1785	None	Withdrawn
Thompson, Jno	1,170	4	176	5– 9–1785	None	
Thompson, Jno	1,170	4	177	5– 9–1785	None	
Thompson, Jesse	642½	2	109	1–23–1783	Sycamore Fk Hinkston	Surveyed
Thompson, Jonah	750	2	14	1– 9–1783	Br Licking	Withdrawn
Thompson, Jonah	750	3	275	4– 7–1784	Small Mt Cr	
Thompson, Joseph	1,000	2	254	3–24–1783	None	
Thompson, Joseph	200	4	163	4–29–1785	None	
Thompson, Joseph	366	4	208	7–14–1785	Red R	
Thompson, Lawrence	50	1	5	11–29–1783	Seven Mile Cr	
Thompson, Lawrence	200	1	34	12– 4–1782	Seven Mile Cr	
Thompson, Lawrence	2,500	1	95	12–10–1782	Lulbergreed	Surveyed
Thompson, Lawrence	1,000	1	83	12– 9–1782	Hingston & Spencer Cr	Surveyed
Thompson, Lawrence	500	1	96	12–10–1782	Licking	
Thompson, Lawrence	4,000	1	96	12–10–1782	Licking	
Thompson, Lawrence	4,000	1	96	12–10–1782	Licking	
Thompson, Lawrence	4,000	2	272	4– 8–1783	S Fk Lulbergreed	
Thompson, Lawrence	1,000	2	272	4– 8–1783	S Fk Lulbergreed	
Thompson, Martha	1,000	1	227	12–21–1782	Ohio R	Withdrawn
Thompson, Martha, Rebeca & Sarah	1,000	3	283	4–10–1784	M Fk Licking	Surveyed
Thompson, Rebekah	1,000	1	227	12–21–1782	Ohio R	Withdrawn
Thompson, Robert	1,000	1	104	12–11–1782	Town Fk	Surveyed
Thompson, Robt	686	3	147	1–15–1784	Big Bone Lick	
Thompson, Sarah	1,000	1	227	12–21–1782	Ohio R	Withdrawn
Thompson, Thomas	1,000	1	383	1– 6–1783	N Fk Elkhorn	Withdrawn
Thompson, Thomas	1,000	2	19	1– 9–1783	None	Surveyed
Thompson, Thos	1,000	4	307	10–23–1786	N Fk Elkhorn	
Thompson, Wm	1,000	4	111	2– 5–1785	Lick Cr	
Thompson & Caman	19,531¼	3	358	6–10–1784	Adjoin P D Roberts & Co	
Tibbs, Jno	1,000	2	323	7–14–1783	Hingston Fk	Surveyed
Tibbs, John	20,000	2	336	7–31–1783	McConnells Fk Licking	Surveyed
Tibbs, Jno	1,000	3	28	11– 3–1783	Limestone Cr	Surveyed
Tibbs, Jno		3	28	11– 3–1783	Limestone Cr	Surveyed
Tibbs, Moses	5,000	3	100	12–19–1783	Eagle Cr	
Tibbs, Thos, heirs	1,000	3	27	11– 3–1783	N Fk Licking	Surveyed
Tibbs, Wm	5,000	3	29	11– 3–1783	None	
Tibbs, Wm	15,625	3	29	11– 3–1783	Licking & Salt Lick	
Tibbs, Wm	11,639	3	30	11– 3–1783	Salt Lick Cr	
Tibbs, & Crutcher	10,000	3	13	10–17–1783	Blue Lick	Surveyed
Tibbs & Masterson	3,000	3	155	1–19–1784	Limestone Cr	Surveyed
Tibbs & Young	15,000	3	56	11–22–1783	W Fk Bank Lick	Surveyed
Tigrett, John	1,000	1	79	12– 9–1782	N Fk Buck Lick	Surveyed
Tilford, Robt	2,124	4	167	4–29–1785	Licking	
Tilford, Wm	1,128½	4	165	4–29–1785	None	
Tilman, Daniel	200	1	60	12– 6–1782	N Fk Licking	
Tilson, Jno	5,000	4	323	5–31–1788	None	
Todd, Ann	560	4	332	1–24–1790	Marble Cr	
Todd, David	400	1	310	12–28–1782	M Fk Cane Run	Surveyed
Todd, James	400	1	65	12– 6–1782		Surveyed
Todd, Jane	500	1	136	12–13–1782	Main Br Eagle Cr	
Todd, Jane	2,000	1	56	12– 5–1782	N E Fk Eagle Cr	
Todd, Jane	1,000	1	227	12–21–1782	None	Withdrawn
Todd, Jane	1,000	2	362	9–13–1783	Hickman Cr	
Todd, Jane	900	2	362	9–13–1783	Hickman Cr	Withdrawn
Todd, Jane	1,700	2	375	10–13–1783	W Fk Eagle Cr	
Todd, Jane	400	4	75	12– 4–1784	None	Withdrawn
Todd, Jane	1,000	1	56	12– 5–1782	Jessamine	Surveyed
Todd, John	25	1	36	12– 4–1782	Shawnee Run	Surveyed
Todd, John	25	1	36	12– 4–1782	Cedar Run	Surveyed
Todd, John	3,000	2	73	1–16–1783	Hickman Cr	Surveyed
Todd, John	2,000	2	73	1–16–1783	Br Silver Cr	Surveyed
Todd, John	2,000	2	73	1–16–1783	None	
Todd, John	1,000	2	74	1–16–1783	None	
Todd, John	3,000	2	96	1–20–1783	S Fk Licking	
Todd, Jno	500	3	423	8– 7–1784	Big Bone Lick	
Todd, Jno	500	4	34	9–13–1784	None	Amended
Todd, Jno	725	4	125	3– 4–1785	Indian Cr	Surveyed
Todd, Jno	500	4	198	6–11–1785	None	Surveyed
Todd, John, heirs	1,000	1	311	12–28–1782	None	Surveyed
Todd, John Sr	1,000	1	310	12–28–1782	W Fk Hickmans Cr	Surveyed
Todd, John Senr	904	2	326	7–19–1783	Ky R	

Entree	Acres	Book	Page	Entry Date	Watercourse	Notes
Todd, Rev John	2,000	1	66	12– 6–1782	Main Br Eagle Cr	
Todd, Rev John	1,000	1	66	12– 6–1782	——— Cr	
Todd, Rev Jno	1,000	1	84	12– 9–1782	None	Amended
Todd, Rev John	3,000	1	263	12–24–1782	Lick Br	
Todd, Rev John	2,000	1	263	12–24–1782	Ohio & Lawrence Cr	Withdrawn
Todd, Rev John	1,666⅔	1	263	12–24–1782	Licking & Ohio R	Withdrawn
Todd, Rev John	———	3	15	10–25–1783	Ky R	Surveyed
Todd, Rev Jno & Robt.	2,000	3	201	3– 4–1784	Buffaloe Road	
Todd, Jno & Robt	1,000	2	97	1–20–1783	M Fk Eagle Cr	
Todd, Jno & Robt	1,000	2	97	1–20–1783	M Fk Eagle Cr	
Todd, Jno & Robt	1,200	2	97	1–20–1783	M Fk Eagle Cr	
Todd, Jno & Robt	1,000	2	98	1–20–1783	M Fk Eagle Cr	
Todd, John & Robt	500	2	294	5–24–1783	Br ——— R	
Todd, John & Robert.	6,666⅔	2	306	6– 2–1783	Bank Lick Cr	Surveyed
Todd, Jno & Robt	276⅔	4	339	1–17–1795	None	
Todd, Levi	300	1	88	12– 9–1782	S Fk Elkhorn	Surveyed
Todd, Levi	———	1	266	12–25–1782	Hawkins Spg	Surveyed
Todd, Levi	1,000	1	266	12–25–1782	Hickmans Cr	Surveyed
Todd, Levi	200	1	267	12–25–1782	None	Surveyed
Todd, Levi	2,000	1	313	12–30–1782	Hickman Cr	Surveyed
Todd, Levi	6,000	1	313	12–30–1782	Clover Bottom	Surveyed
Todd, Levi	2,000	1	314	12–30–1782	Jessamine Cr	
Todd, Levi	25¼	1	347	1– 1–1783	None	Surveyed
Todd, Levi	50	2	54	1–13–1783	Elkhorn	
Todd, Levi	200	2	54	1–13–1783	W Fk Hickman Cr.	Surveyed
Todd, Levi	800	2	82	1–17–1783	W Br Hickman & N Fk Elkhorn	Surveyed
Todd, Levi	200	2	141	1–29–1783	None	Surveyed
Todd, Levi	300	3	82	12–11–1783	W Fk Hickman Cr.	Withdrawn
Todd, Levi	300	3	84	12–12–1783	W Fk Hickman Fk.	Withdrawn
Todd, Levi for Edward Hawkins	400	1	34	12– 4–1782	Clear Cr	Surveyed
Todd, Owen	400	3	49	11–17–1783	Br Lecomptos Run.	Surveyed
Todd, Owen	400	3	94	12–17–1783	None	Surveyed
Todd, Robert	25	1	36	12– 4–1782	Shawnee Run	Surveyed
Todd, Robert	25	1	36	12– 4–1782	Cedar Run	Surveyed
Todd, Robert	2,000	1	66	12– 6–1782	Main Br Eagle Cr	
Todd, Robert	1,000	1	66	12– 6–1782	——— Cr	
Todd, Robert	3,000	1	263	12–24–1782	Lick Br	
Todd, Robert	15	2	58	1–14–1783	Adjoins Lexington	Withdrawn
Todd, Robert	600	2	59	1–14–1783	W Br Hickmans Cr.	
Todd, Robert	200	2	88	1–18–1783	None	Withdrawn
Todd, Robert	3,000	2	96	1–20–1783	S Fk Licking	
Todd, Robert	13	2	107	1–22–1783	None	Withdrawn
Todd, Robert	180	2	289	5–20–1783	W Fk Hickman Cr.	
Todd, Robert	560	2	323	7–15–1783	Main Elkhorn	Withdrawn
Todd, Robert	560	2	325	7–19–1783	Buffaloe Road	Surveyed
Todd, Robert	560	2	329	7–19–1783	Ky R	Withdrawn
Todd, Robert	28	2	338	8– 1–1783	None	Surveyed
Todd, Robert	1,560	2	347	8–13–1783	Ky & Cedar Cr	
Todd, Robert	200	2	348	8–14–1783	Island M Elkhorn	Withdrawn
Todd, Robert	3,000	2	352	8–14–1783	None	Withdrawn
Todd, Robert	2,619	2	352	8–15–1783	None	Withdrawn
Todd, Robert	505	2	353	8–15–1783	S Br Eagle Cr	Surveyed
Todd, Robert	560	2	354	8–16–1783	None	
Todd, Robert	60	2	357	8–20–1783	Ky R	Surveyed
Todd, Robert	200	2	358	8–20–1783	Eagle Cr	
Todd, Robert	1,000	2	363	9–16–1783	Licking	
Todd, Robert	1,000	2	363	9–16–1783	N E Br Licking	
Todd, Robert	600	2	363	9–17–1783	Br Hickman Cr	Surveyed
Todd, Robert	2,000	2	366	9–23–1783	Ohio Run	Surveyed
Todd, Robt	60	3	43	11–14–1783	Hickman Cr	
Todd, Robt	160	3	51	11–18–1783	Br Hickman Cr	Surveyed
Todd, Robt	474	3	63	11–29–1783	None	Surveyed
Todd, Robt	1,000	3	94	12–17–1783	None	Surveyed
Todd, Robt	4,743	3	122	12–29–1783	None	
Todd, Robt	6,000	3	140	1–10–1784	Br Big Bone Lick	Withdrawn
Todd, Robt	1,200	3	155	1–17–1784	None	Withdrawn
Todd, Robt	160	3	163	1–22–1784	E Fk Hickman Cr.	Surveyed
Todd, Robt	2,417¼	3	167	1–26–1784	Ohio R	
Todd, Robt	2,000	3	169	1–27–1784	S Fk Licking	Withdrawn
Todd, Robt	3,000	3	170	1–27–1784	Licking	Withdrawn
Todd, Robt	300	3	182	2–12–1784	Turkey Foot Fk Eagle Cr	
Todd, Robt	5,619	3	182	2–12–1784	Licking & Ohio	Withdrawn
Todd, Robt	3,000	3	201	3– 4–1784	Main Elkhorn	Withdrawn
Todd, Robt	1,100	3	278	4– 8–1784	Hickman Cr	
Todd, Robt	1,000	3	304	4–26–1784	Clear Cr	Surveyed
Todd, Robt	1,200	3	344	5–24–1784	Hickman Cr	
Todd, Robt	640	3	344	5–24–1784	Silver Cr	Withdrawn
Todd, Robt	5,916	4	38	9–18–1784	None	

Entree	Acres	Book	Page	Entry Date	Watercourse	Notes
Todd, Robt	14	4	75	12– 4–1784	Indian Cr	
Todd, Robt	3,000	4	125	3– 4–1785	None	
Todd, Robt	2,550	4	181	5–19–1785	Big Bone Cr	Withdrawn
Todd, Robt	635	4	201	6–17–1785	None	Withdrawn
Todd, Robt	500	4	243	12–15–1785	None	
Todd, Robt & Jno	6,666¾	4	153	4–19–1785	Licking	Surveyed
Todd, Robt Jr	13,275	4	338	1– 2–1795	None	
Todd, Robt R S	640	4	140	3–25–1785	None	
Todd & Parker	1,000	3	21	10–30–1783	Ky R	
Todd & Parker	500	3	33	11– 7–1783	Ky R	
Todd & Parker	500	3	33	11– 7–1783	Ky R	
Todd & Parker	500	3	36	11– 8–1783	Ky R	
Todd & Ship	3,603¾	3	120	12–29–1783	None	
Todd & Venible	5,859	3	122	12–30–1783	None	Surveyed
Toll, Stephen	2,000	3	175	2– 5–1784	None	Surveyed
Toll, Stephen	2,000	4	293	4–22–1786	Eagle Cr	Withdrawn
Tomkins, Humphrey	1,012	1	195	12–20–1782	Br Ohio R	
Tomkins, Humphrey	1,321	1	391	1– 7–1798	Hinkstons Fk Licking	
Tomlin, William	1,410½	1	364	1– 4–1783	Lies Cr	
Tomlinson, George	2,593½	2	310	6– 7–1783	None	
Tomlinson, Nicholas	100	4	326	12–30–1788	None	
Tompkins, Humphrey	2,000	2	47	1–13–1783	Red R	
Tompkins, Humphrey	1,000	2	192	2–13–1783	S Fk Big Sandy	
Tompkins, Humphrey	3,441	3	79	12–10–1783	S Fk Sandy	
Tompkins, Humphrey	441	4	235	11–29–1785	None	Withdrawn
Tompkins, Jno	7,991½	3	66	12– 1–1783	S Fk Sandy	Surveyed
Tompkins, Jno	7,991½	4	256	1–16–1786	None	Surveyed
Tompkins, William	2,000	1	375	1– 6–1783	Clemmes Fk Hingstons	
Torrence, Jno	200	4	309	11–21–1786	None	
Torrence, John	400	1	61	12– 6–1782	Rows Cr	Withdrawn
Trabue, James	5,165½	2	239	3–13–1783	Hinkstons Fk	Withdrawn
Trabue, Jas	2,400	3	287	4–13–1784	————	Surveyed
Trabue, Jas	400	3	287	4–13–1784	Mill Cr	
Trabue, Jno	700	3	286	4–13–1784	None	Surveyed
Train, Silas	400	4	293	4–22–1786	Hinkston Mill Cr	
Train, Silas, heirs	400	4	182	5–23–1785	None	Withdrawn
Travis, Champion	2,400	2	38	1–11–1783	Slate Cr	
Travis, Champion	1,200	2	344	8– 9–1783	Br Licking	Surveyed
Travis, Champion	1,200	2	344	8– 9–1783	None	Surveyed
Travis, Champion	1,200	2	344	8– 9–1783	None	Surveyed
Travis, Champion	————	2	345	8–10–1783	Upper Blue Licks	Surveyed
Treadway, John	140	1	185	12–19–1782	None	Withdrawn
Treadway, Jno	150	4	231	11– 7–1785	Hickman Cr	Surveyed
Treadway, Jno	100	4	333	11– 9–1790	N Fk Elkhorn	
Treadway & Waters	200	4	235	11–30–1785	None	Surveyed
Treageng, Daniel	2,000	3	25	10–31–1783	None	
Treasury, Rev John	1,000	1	66	12– 6–1782	Salt Lick Fk	Withdrawn
Tree, Jack	955	1	383	1– 6–1783	None	Surveyed
Tribble & French	15,410	3	173	2– 4–1784	Ky R	
Trimble, James	6,000	1	227	12–21–1782	Big Miami	Surveyed
Trimble, William	1,000	1	108	12–11–1782	None	Withdrawn
Trimble, William	1,000	1	110	12–11–1782	Howards Cr	Surveyed
Trimble, William	750	1	111	12–11–1782	Hingstons Fk	
Trimble, William	1,000	2	271	4– 8–1783	S Fk Lulbegrud	
Triplet, Francis	1,600	2	330	7–21–1783	Ohio R	
Triplett, Francis	1,410	2	343	8– 8–1783	Br Licking	Withdrawn
Triplett, Francis	410	3	77	12– 9–1783	Flat Lick Cr	Withdrawn
Triplett, Francis	410	3	194	3– 2–1784	Hinkston Fk	
Triplett, Francis	500	4	20	8–21–1784	Stoners & Lingston Fks	
Triplett, Francis	5,000	4	63	11– 2–1784	None	Withdrawn
Triplett, Francis	2,000	4	225	10– 7–1785	None	
Triplett, Francis	3,000	4	285	3–26–1786	None	Withdrawn
Triplett, Francis	8,000	4	285	3–26–1786	Ohio R	
Triplett, Francis, heirs	3,010	4	339	8–18–1795	None	
Triplett, Simon	500	3	9	10–15–1783	Ohio R	
Triplett, Simon	1,000	3	10	10–15–1783	Ohio R	
Triplett, Simon	1,637½	3	13	10–17–1783	Indian Cr	
Triplet, William	1,000	1	58	12– 5–1782	E Fk Licking	Surveyed
Triplett, William	1,000	2	280	4–28–1783	N Fk Licking	Surveyed
Triplett, Wm	————	3	120	12–29–1783	None	Surveyed
Triplett, Wm	2,000	4	19	8–21–1784	Ky R	Surveyed
Triplett & Bullitt	20,000	3	406	7–14–1784	Large Cr	
Triplett & Bullitt	7,187	4	55	10–16–1784	Main Licking	
Trotter, David	3,378	4	87	1– 8–1785	Licking	Surveyed
Trotter, Jas	1,828	4	87	1– 8–1785	Licking	Surveyed
Trotter, Jas	1,740	4	87	1– 8–1785	None	Surveyed
Trotter, Joseph	5,958	4	87	1– 8–1785	Licking	Surveyed

Entree	Acres	Book	Page	Entry Date	Watercourse	Notes
Trotter & Fowler	3,375	4	273	2–15–1786	Sandy	Amended
Trotter & Fowler	19,756	4	274	2–15–1786	Sandy	Amended
Truman, Edward	1,500	4	151	4–12–1785	Fks Licking	Surveyed
Tulley, Mathew	3,694	4	323	5– 9–1788	Cedar Cr	
Turner, Lewis E	333	3	290	4–15–1784	Licking	
Turner & Denham	470	3	412	7–17–1784	None	
Turnhull, Wm	10,000	4	271	2–13–1786	Main Licking	Surveyed
Turnwalt, Adam	300	2	343	8– 8–1783	Hingston Fk	Surveyed
Turpin, Horatia	10,000	3	350	5–29–1784	None	Withdrawn
Turpin, Horatia	10,000	3	379	6–19–1784	Licking	Withdrawn
Turpin, Horatia	10,000	3	380	6–22–1784	None	Withdrawn
Turpin, Horatia	10,000	3	417	7–27–1784	Licking	
Turpin, Horatia	1,400	4	102	2– 2–1785	Howards Upper Cr	Withdrawn
Turpin, Horatio	500	4	103	2– 2–1785	None	Withdrawn
Turpin, Horatio	1,400	4	120	2–16–1785	None	
Turpin, Horatio	30,000	4	186	6– 1–1785	Logans Trace	
Turpin, Horatio	2,659½	4	186	6– 1–1785	None	
Turpin, Horatio	5,000	4	186	6– 1–1785	Licking	
Turpin, Horatio	5,000	4	186	6– 1–1785	Licking	
Turpin, Horatio	5,000	4	186	6– 1–1785	Licking	
Turpin, Horatio	5,000	4	187	6– 1–1785	Licking	
Turpin, Horatio	5,000	4	187	6– 1–1785	Licking	
Turpin, Horatio	5,000	4	187	6– 1–1785	Licking	
Turpin, Thomas	1,200	1	353	1– 2–1783	Green Cr	Withdrawn
Turpin, Thomas	1,500	1	354	1– 2–1783	Green Cr	Withdrawn
Turpin, Thomas	1,300	1	354	1– 2–1783	Licking & Elkhorn	Surveyed
Turpin, Thomas	7,000	1	367	1– 4–1783	Licking Cr	
Turpin, Thos	10,000	2	15	1– 9–1783	Siota	Surveyed
Turpin, Thomas	7,500	2	26	1–10–1783	None	Surveyed
Turpin, Thomas	10,000	2	42	1–11–1783	Br Ky R	
Turpin, Thos	7,500	2	124	1–25–1783	None	Surveyed
Turpin, Thomas	1,200	2	264	4– 3–1784	Bank Lick Cr	Surveyed
Turpin, Thos & Horatio	7,294½	3	239	3–25–1784	None	Withdrawn
Turpin, Thos & Horatia	7,294½	3	349	5–29–1784	None	
Turpin, Thos & Horatia	7,294½	2	71	11–26–1784	Main Licking	
Turpin & Downing	4,250	4	181	5–19–1785	None	
Tuts, Thomas	400	2	183	2–13–1783	Br Ky R	Surveyed
Tuts, Thos	1,000	4	317	12–14–1787	Br Ky R	
Twyman, James	400	2	38	1–11–1783	Millers Cr	Withdrawn
Twyman, James	200	2	345	8–12–1783	Licking	
Twyman, Jas	400	3	351	6– 1–1784	None	
Twyman, Reubin	7,537	3	303	4–26–1784	None	
Tyler, Chas	25,000	3	81	12–10–1783	None	Surveyed
Tyler, Chas	25,000	3	82	12–11–1783	Ohio & Salt Lick Cr	Surveyed
Tyler, Chas	30,640	3	106	12–22–1783	Br Ohio R	
Underwood, Geo	5,000	3	155	1–17–1784	Eagle Cr	
Underwood, Geo	7,500	3	242	3–26–1784	S Fk Licking	Surveyed
Underwood, Geo	1,300	4	340	11– 4–1799	N Fk Elkhorn	
Underwood, Francis	10,000	3	159	1–21–1784	Licking	Surveyed
Underwood, Francis	759	3	267	4– 3–1784	Licking	Withdrawn
Underwood, Francis	759	3	307	4–28–1784	Licking	
Underwood, Thomas	2,000	1	56	12– 5–1782	Br Ohio R	Surveyed
Underwood, Thomas	1,000	1	58	12– 5–1782	Br Ky R	Amended
Underwood, Thomas	1,000	1	86	12– 9–1782	———	
Underwood, Thomas	1,000	2	159	2– 3–1783	Elkhorn	
Underwood, Thos	5,000	4	296	4–29–1785	Sandy	
Upshaw, Jno	3,000	3	239	3–25–1784	None	
Upshaw, Jno	3,000	3	349	5–29–1784	Licking	
Vainordall, Jno	500	4	22	8–22–1784	Upper Twin Br	
Vance, David	400	2	320	7–11–1783	None	Surveyed
Vance, David	400	3	93	12–16–1783	None	Surveyed
Vance, David	186	3	365	6–14–1784	None	
Vaughan, James	1,000	1	5	11–29–1783	None	Surveyed
Vaughan, Jas	799½	4	35	9–15–1784	None	
Vaughn, Edmund	10,000	1	139	12–14–1782	Ohio R	Amended
Vaughn, Edmund	9,700	1	139	12–14–1782	Woof Pen Cr	Surveyed
Venible, Abraham	1,000	3	247	3–29–1784	Raven Cr	Surveyed
Venible & Parker	2,788	3	122	12–30–1783	Big Bone Cr	Surveyed
Venible & Morton	4,000	3	123	12–30–1783	Big Bone Cr	
Venible & Morton	4,507	3	123	12–30–1783	None	Surveyed
Venible & Todd	5,859	3	122	12–30–1783	None	Surveyed
Vigier, William	1,775	2	183	2–12–1783	Licking	
Wade, Richard	500	3	425	8–13–1784	None	Amended
Wade, Richard	500	4	41	9–22–1784	None	Surveyed
Wade, Richard	500	4	242	12–14–1785	None	
Wade, Richard	500	4	304	8– 3–1786	None	Surveyed
Walfork, Archillis	4,125	3	87	12–13–1783	Licking	
Walfork, Francis	1,000	3	10	10–16–1783	Blue Lick	
Walfork, Francis	1,000	3	10	10–16–1783	——— Cr	
Walfork, Francis	500	3	85	12–13–1783	——— Cr	
Walfork, Francis	1,000	3	86	12–13–1783	Ohio R	

Entree	Acres	Book	Page	Entry Date	Watercourse	Notes
Walfork, Francis	500	4	86	12–13–1783	None	
Walfork, Francis	4,000	3	87	12–13–1783	Licking	
Walfork, Francis	1,000	3	88	12–13–1783	Flat Cr	
Walfork, Francis	1,000	3	88	12–13–1783	N Fk Licking	
Walker, David	150	4	324	8– 4–1788	Hickman Cr	
Walker, Joseph	1,000	3	242	3–26–1784	None	
Walker, John	1,000	2	126	1–27–1783	S Fk Licking	
Walker, Jno	7,537	3	303	4–26–1784	None	
Walker, Jno	625	4	48	10–12–1784	M Licking	
Walker, Mathew	1,000	3	35	11– 8–1783	Licking	
Walker, Mathew	1,000	4	260	1–18–1786	S Fk Sandy	
Walker, Merry	17,600	1	192	12–19–1782	Big Miami	Surveyed
Walker, Merry	2,562½	1	99	12–10–1782	Lees Lick	Surveyed
Walker, Merry	103,518	3	141	1–12–1784	Sandy R	Withdrawn
Walker, Merry	26,000	3	181	2–12–1784	Br Ohio R	
Walker, Merry	62,000	3	249	3–29–1784	None	
Walker, Merry	40,518	3	372	6–18–1784	None	
Walker, William	21,400	1	191	12–19–1782	Raven Cr	Surveyed
Walker, William	2,500	1	281	12–26–1782	E Fk Eagle Cr	
Walker, William	1,000	1	390	1– 7–1783	Raven Cr	Surveyed
Walker & Johnson	4,987½	3	76	12– 9–1783	Salt Lick Cr	Withdrawn
Walker & Johnson	4,987½	3	303	4–26–1784	None	
Wall, Robt	731	3	406	7–14–1784	Licking	
Wallace, Caleb	1,000	2	256	3–25–1783	N Fk Licking	
Wallace, Caleb	1,000	3	336	5–19–1784	None	Withdrawn
Wallace, Caleb	1,000	4	58	10–23–1784	None	Surveyed
Wallace, Robert	1,500	1	111	12–11–1782	None	
Wallace, Robert	400	1	294	12–27–1782	Hingston & Blue Lick	
Waller, Jno	1,500	3	394	7– 6–1784	None	1,380 Acres.. surveyed
Waller, Jno	1,500	3	394	7– 6–1784	Lees Cr	
Waller, Jno	5,000	4	63	11– 2–1784	None	Withdrawn
Waller, Jno	900	4	203	6–28–1785	Cabbin Cr	
Waller, Jno	400	4	267	2– 3–1786	r h Fk Little Sandy	
Waller, Jno	8,000	4	285	3–26–1786	Ohio R	
Waller & Byrum	461½	4	63	11– 2–1784	None	
Waller & Lewis	5,000	4	151	4–10–1785	Cabbin Cr	
Waller & Marshall	450	4	155	4–20–1785	Great Miami	Surveyed
Walls, Jno	400	4	324	9– 7–1788	None	
Walls, George	500	1	158	12–17–1782	None	Surveyed
Walls, George	1,000	1	185	12–19–1782	Clear Cr	Surveyed
Walls, George	4,445	2	214	2–28–1783	S Fk Elkhorn	Surveyed
Walls, Thomas	400	1	186	12–19–1782	Licking	
Walton, John	2,000	1	224	12–21–1782	S Fk Elkhorn	Surveyed
Walton John	1,000	1	224	12–21–1782	Ohio R	Surveyed
Walton, Jno	2,000	4	225	10– 7–1785	Br Licking	
Walton, Jno	3,000	4	285	3–26–1786	None	Withdrawn.
Walton, Matthew	1,000	1	32	12– 3–1782	——— Cr	Surveyed
Walton, Matthew	2,186	1	160	12–17–1782	Licking	Surveyed
Walton, Matthew	1,000	1	160	12–17–1782	Stones Fk	
Walton, Matthew	1,000	1	160	12–17–1782	Stoners Fk	Surveyed
Walton, Matthew	600	1	176	12–18–1782	Hingstons Fk	
Walton, Matthew	2,000	1	176	12–18–1782	Rocky Ford & Stoners Fk	Surveyed
Walton, Matthew	2,000	1	223	12–21–1782	Ohio R	Withdrawn
Walton, Matthew	1,000	1	223	12–21–1782	Licking Cr	Surveyed
Walton, Matthew	1,000	1	319	12–30–1782	None	
Walton, Matthew	800	1	319	12–30–1782	None	
Walton, Matthew	2,812½	1	360	1– 4–1783	E Br Brushy Fk	
Walton, Matthew	2,000	3	61	11–25–1783	Br Ky R	
Walton, Matthew	8,000	3	61	11–25–1783	None	Withdrawn
Walton, Matthew	1,000	3	185	2–17–1784	Licking	
Walton, Matthew	9,000	4	35	9–15–1784	Red R	
Walton, Matthew	2,000	4	198	6–15–1785	None	
Walton, Matthew	8,000	4	198	6–15–1785	None	
Walton, Matthew	10,000	4	199	6–15–1785	Ky R	2,000 acres withdrawn
Walton, Matthew	200	4	224	10– 3–1785	None	
Walton, Matthew	1,400	4	224	10– 3–1785	Johnson Fk	
Walton, Wm	1,000	4	21	8–22–1784	None	
Walton, Wm	2,388½	4	21	8–22–1784	None	
Walton & Holder	200	4	224	10– 3–1785	None	
Walton, & Morgan	1,478½	3	356	6– 9–1784	Eagle Cr	
Walton & Overton	1,500	4	259	1–16–1786	Br S Fk Sandy	
Ward, Joseph	45,987½	3	281	4–10–1784	Main Fk Licking	Surveyed
Ward, Markham	500	4	264	1–29–1786	Salt Rock Fk	Withdrawn
Ward, Wm	639	3	139	1– 8–1784	Br Limestone Cr	
Ward, Wm	1,000	3	147	1–14–1784	Br N Fk Licking	Surveyed
Ward, Wm	2,000	3	257	3–30–1784	N Fk Licking	Surveyed
Ward, Wm	4,000	3	257	3–30–1784	——— Cr	Surveyed

Entree	Acres	Book	Page	Entry Date	Watercourse	Notes
Ward, Wm	3,771½	3	260	3-31-1784	N E Fk Licking	Withdrawn
Ward, Wm	3,531	3	261	3-31-1784	Br N E Fk Licking	Withdrawn
Ward, Wm	2,000	3	280	4-10-1784	M Fk Licking	Surveyed
Ward, Wm	3,531	3	282	4-10-1784	None	....
Ward, Wm	5,267½	3	282	4-10-1784	None	Surveyed
Ward, Wm	7,736	3	330	5-13-1784	Licking	562½ acres withdrawn
Ward, Wm	562½	4	113	2- 9-1785	None	....
Ward, Wm	3,771½	4	114	2- 9-1785	None	....
Ward, Wm	4,333½	4	114	2- 9-1785	None	....
Ward, Wm	1,000	4	114	2- 9-1785	None	Surveyed
Ward, Wm	791½	4	114	2- 9-1785	N E Fk Licking	....
Ward, Wm	680	4	132	3-15-1785	Boones Cr	....
Ward, Wm	20	4	132	3-15-1785	E Fk Hickmans Cr	....
Ward, Wm	20	4	133	3-15-1785	None	....
Ward, Wm	700	4	252	1- 7-1786	None	....
Ward, Wm	300	4	252	1- 7-1786	None	....
Ward, Wm	440	4	288	4- 8-1786	Boones Cr	....
Ward, Wm	150	4	288	4- 8-1786	E Fk Hickman Cr	....
Wardlow, James	7,291	3	308	4-29-1784	None	....
Ware, Isaac	1,767	3	61	11-25-1783	Hickman Cr	Withdrawn
Ware, Isaac	861½	3	144	1-13-1784	Little Sandy	....
Ware, Isaac	1,767	4	225	10- 5-1785	None	....
Ware, James	1,500	1	114	12-12-1782	None	Surveyed
Ware, Jas	840	4	64	11- 5-1784	Br E Fk Licking	Surveyed
Ware, Markham	500	4	271	2- 9-1786	Sandy	....
Warford, Jno	1,000	3	125	12-31-1783	Licking	Surveyed
Warren, James	500	2	275	4-22-1783	Hickmans and Jessamine Cr	Withdrawn
Warren, James	311½	2	276	4-22-1783	None	Withdrawn
Warren, James	500	3	247	3-29-1784	N Fk Licking	Withdrawn
Warren, James	811½	3	328	5- 7-1784	Ohio R	Withdrawn
Warren, Jas	811½	4	152	4-12-1785	Main Licking	....
Warren, Wm	1,452½	4	89	1-14-1784	Slate Cr	....
Warren, Wm	1,452½	4	174	5- 9-1785	None	Amended
Warren, Wm	1,452½	4	260	1-16-1786	None	Surveyed
Washington, Henry	2,583	4	55	10-16-1784	None	....
Wasson, James	200	2	328	7-19-1783	Ky R	....
Wasson, James	300	2	348	8-14-1783	Ky R	Surveyed
Waters, John	1,250	1	184	12-19-1782	N Fk Elkhorn	Surveyed
Waters, Jno	100	4	333	11- 9-1790	None	....
Waters, Thos	45,987¾	3	281	4-10-1784	Main Fk Licking	Surveyed
Waters & Treadevoy	200	4	235	11-30-1785	None	Surveyed
Watkins, Benjamin	1,000	2	13	1- 9-1783	Greers Cr	....
Watkins, Edward	2,000	1	354	1- 2-1783	None	....
Watkins, Henry	1,687	2	239	3-13-1783	Br Boones Fk Licking	....
Watkins, Jas	1,570	3	226	3-12-1784	None	....
Watkins, James	1,570	3	427	1-27-1784	Licking	Withdrawn
Watkins, Jas	1,000	4	1	8-14-1784	None	Surveyed
Watkins, Jas	1,000	4	1	8-14-1784	None	Surveyed
Watkins, Jas	5,000	4	1	8-14-1784	Sandy Cr	Surveyed
Watkins, Jas	1,000	4	1	8-14-1784	Sandy Cr	Surveyed
Watkins, Jas	1,000	4	1	8-14-1784	None	Surveyed
Watkins, Jas	1,000	4	1	8-14-1784	Sandy Cr	Surveyed
Watkins, Jas	1,000	4	1	8-14-1784	None	Surveyed
Watkins, Jas	1,000	4	2	8-14-1784	Sandy Cr	Surveyed
Watkins, Jas	1,000	4	2	8-14-1784	Sandy Cr	Surveyed
Watkins, Jas	4,000	4	2	8-14-1784	Sandy Cr	Surveyed
Watkins, Jas	1,000	4	2	8-14-1784	Sandy Cr	Surveyed
Watkins, Jas	1,000	4	2	8-14-1784	Sandy Cr	Surveyed
Watkins, Jas	5,000	4	3	8-14-1784	Sandy Cr	Surveyed
Watkins, Jas	1,000	4	3	8-14-1784	Sandy Cr	Surveyed
Watkins, Jas	1,000	4	3	8-14-1784	Sandy Cr	Surveyed
Watkins, Jas	1,000	4	3	8-14-1784	Sandy Cr	Surveyed
Watkins, Jas	3,000	4	3	8-14-1784	Sandy Cr	Surveyed
Watkins, Jas	1,000	4	4	8-14-1784	Sandy Cr	Notes
Watkins, Jas	1,000	4	4	8-14-1784	Sandy Cr	Surveyed
Watkins, Jas	4,000	4	4	8-14-1784	Sandy Cr	Surveyed
Watkins, Jas	1,000	4	4	8-14-1784	Sandy Cr	Surveyed
Watkins, Jas	1,000	4	4	8-14-1784	Sandy Cr	Surveyed
Watkins, Jas	1,000	4	4	8-14-1784	Sandy Cr	Surveyed
Watkins, Jas	3,000	4	5	8-14-1784	Sandy Cr	Surveyed
Watkins, Jas G	1,401	3	157	1-19-1784	None	....
Watkins, Joel	903½	2	61	1-14-1783	S E of Riddles Station	Surveyed
Watkins, John	2,000	1	19	12- 4-1782	Dry Cr	Surveyed
Watkins, Joseph	600	3	297	4-22-1784	Locust Cr	....
Watkins, Nicholas	4,000	2	309	6- 7-1783	None	....

Entree	Acres	Book	Page	Entry Date	Watercourse	Notes
Watkins, Nicholson....	4,500	2	311	6– 9–1783	None	
Watkins, Robert.......	3,500	2	309	6– 7–1783	None	
Watkins, Robert.......	4,000	2	312	6– 9–1783	None	
Watkins, Thomas......	1,000	2	171	2– 7–1783	Coopers Run	
Watkins, Thomas......	50	2	171	2– 7–1783	Coopers Run	Surveyed
Watson, Jno..........	2,000	3	11	10–16–1783	Hinkston Fk.	Surveyed
Watson, Josiah........	5,000	1	41	12–14–1782	Br of Licking	Surveyed
Watson, Josiah........	4,000	1	184	12–19–1782	N F Elkhorn	Surveyed
Watson, Josiah........	4,450	1	184	12–19–1782	N Fk Mill Cr	Surveyed
Watson, Josiah........	6,000	1	249	12–24–1782	Licking	Surveyed
Watson, Josiah........	4,000	1	249	12–24–1782	Mill Cr	Withdrawn
Watson, Josiah........	5,000	1	249	12–24–1782	Br Licking	
Watson, Josiah........	4,000	5	75	1–16–1783	Licking	Surveyed
Watson, Wm..........	1,126	3	150	1–15–1784	Ky R.	
Watts, Robert........	500	1	161	12–17–1782	Dry Cr	Surveyed
Watts, Robt..........	2,593½	2	310	6– 7–1783	None	
Weadon & Power......	14,166½	3	301	4–26–1784	Licking	Withdrawn
Weakly & Cogswell..	9,666½	4	292	4–22–1786	Ky R	
Weakly, Robt, Robt & Saml.............	3,576	4	291	4–22–1786	None	
Weakly, Robt, Wm & Saml.............	3,576	4	68	11–18–1784	None	Withdrawn
Weaver, Jacob.......	126,140	3	298	4–22–1784	1 h Fk 3 Fks Ky R..	Surveyed amended
Weaver, Jacob & others.............	126,140	3	395	7– 7–1784	None	Surveyed
Weaver, Jno.........	3,343½	3	124	12–31–1783	None	Surveyed
Weaver, Tilman......	4,750	3	124	12–31–1783	None	Withdrawn
Weaver, Tilman......	8,000	3	187	2–19–1784	Eagle Cr	
Weaver, Tilman......	4,750	3	397	7– 8–1784	None	
Weaver, Tilman......	800	4	337	6– 3–1794	None	
Weaver & Pickett.....	23,875	3	350	5–29–1784	Eagle Cr	Surveyed
Weaver & Wright.....	749	3	397	7– 8–1784	Licking	Surveyed
Webb, Augustine.....	29,936	3	424	8–11–1784	Cumberland Mt	
Webb, Jno Jr........	20,000	3	310	4–29–1784	Licking	Withdrawn
Webb, Jno Jr........	20,000	4	322	4–28–1788	None	
Webb, Richard C.....	4,000	2	31	1–10–1783	Flat Cr	
Webb, William C.....	1,876	2	36	1–11–1783	None	
Webber, Philip.......	1,000	1	65	12– 6–1782	—— Cr	
Weber, William......	1,000	1	65	12– 6–1782	Licking	Surveyed
Webster, Samuel.....	1,000	2	240	3–13–1783	None	
Weeden & Power.....	14,166½	4	275	2–18–1786	None	
Weeden & Power.....	14,166½	4	275	2–18–1786	Sandy	
Wegglesworth, Jas....	3,928	3	97	12–18–1783	None	
Wegglesworth & Young.	16,000	3	177	2–10–1784	None	
Welch, John..........	3,530	2	29	1–10–1783	Cabbin & Harbor Cr	
West, Edward........	2,100	2	36	1–11–1783	Sandy	
Westcat, Sennings G..	300,306⅔	3	190	2–28–1784	3 Fks Ky R	
Whaley, James.......	983	2	278	4–23–1783	W Br Howards Upper Cr	Withdrawn
Whaley, James.......	983	3	198	3– 2–1784	W Fk Howards Upper Cr	Surveyed
Whaley, Wm.........	295	3	156	1–19–1784	Hinkston Fk	Surveyed
Wheat, Bardale......	1,000	1	369	1– 4–1783	None	Surveyed
White, Anthony Walton.............	20,000	1	228	12–21–1782	Ohio R & Licking	Surveyed
White, Jno..........	500	1	13	11–30–1782	Br Licking	
White, Moses........	250	1	48	12– 4–1782	—— Cr	
Whitesides, Peter.....	50,000	3	377	6–19–1784	None	Surveyed
Whitehouse, James...	200	1	156	12–17–1782	Ohio R	
Whitledge, John......	1,000	1	63	12– 6–1782	Stoners Fk	Surveyed
Whitledge, Robert....	1,000	2	24	1–10–1783	Coopers Run	Surveyed
Whitledge, Thomas...	1,000	2	24	1–10–1783	M Fk Coopers Run.	Surveyed
Whitledge, Thos......	75	3	47	11–15–1783	Licking	
Whitledge, Thos......	250	3	47	11–15–1783	None	Amended
Whitledge, Thos......	250	4	27	9– 1–1784	None	
Whitledge, Thos......	175	4	27	9– 1–1784	None	
Whitted, William.....	750	2	18	1– 9–1783	None	
Wigginton, Henry....	7,270½	3	195	3– 2–1784	Hinkston Fk	Surveyed
Wigginton, John......	1,000	1	24	12–17–1782	Howards Upper Cr.	Surveyed
Wilcox, Daniel.......	500	1	124	12–13–1782	Br Elkhorn	Surveyed
Wilhoit, Aaron.......	851½	2	90	1–20–1783	None	Surveyed
Wilhoit, John........	920	2	90	1–20–1783	None	Surveyed
Wilhoit, Nichoclos....	1,143½	2	90	1–20–1783	None	Surveyed
Wilkerson, James......	10,000	3	183	2–12–1784	Ohio	Withdrawn
Wilkinson, Jas........	2,000	3	186	2–18–1784	Ohio R	Withdrawn
Wilkinson, Jas........	40,518	3	415	7–23–1784	None	
Wilkinson, Jas........	10,000	4	137	3–22–1785	None	
Wilkinson, Jas........	40,518	4	137	3–22–1785	None	Withdrawn
Wilkinson, Jas........	32,000	4	137	3–22–1785	Ohio R	Surveyed

Entree	Acres	Book	Page	Entry Date	Watercourse	Notes
Wilkinson, Jas.	37,256	4	142	4– 5–1785	None	28,245 acres withdrawn
Wilkinson, Jas.	28,000	4	194	6– 7–1785	Ohio R	
Wilkinson, Jas.	26,500	4	195	6– 7–1785	Ohio R	Surveyed
Wilkerson, Jno.	3,050	3	274	4– 6–1784	Hinkston Fk	Surveyed
Wilkerson, Jno.	1,000	3	275	4– 7–1784	None	Surveyed
Wilkerson, Moses	7,270½	3	195	3– 2–1784	Hinkston Fk	Surveyed
Wilkinson & Lewis	20,000	4	155	4–20–1785	None	
Wilkinson & Marshall	2,000	4	124	2–23–1785	None	
Wilkinson & Orr	3,277	4	200	6–17–1785	Ohio R	Surveyed
Wilkinson & Smith	12,550	3	92	12–16–1783	Br Licking	Withdrawn
Wilkinson & Smith	8,500	4	309	12–23–1786	None	
Wilkinson & Smith	12,550	3	274	4– 6–1784	None	
Will, Wm	300,306⅔	3	190	2–28–1784	3 Fks Ky R	
Willes, Lewis	1,500	3	87	12–13–1783	Br Licking	
Willes, Wm	1,000	3	5	10–15–1783	Clear Cr	
Willes & Campbell	1,000	3	255	3–30–1784	Bank Lick Cr	Surveyed
Willey, Jane	560	1	20	12– 2–1782	Lawrence Cr	Surveyed
Williams, Alfred	10,000	3	144	1–13–1784	None	
Williams, David	3,770½	3	143	1–13–1784	S Fk Eagle Cr	
Williams, David	200	3	218	3–10–1784	Elkhorn	Withdrawn
Williams, David	272	3	218	3–10–1784	Jessamine & Ky R	Withdrawn
Williams, David	800	3	219	3–10–1784	Greers Cr	Withdrawn
Williams, David	1,000	3	219	3–10–1784	Br Shands Fk R	Withdrawn
Williams, David	200	3	219	3–10–1784	Stoners Fk	Withdrawn
Williams, David	1,400	3	219	3–10–1784	Hancock Fk	Withdrawn
Williams, David	15,500	3	240	3–25–1784	Br Hinkston Fk	Withdrawn
Williams, David	10,000	3	296	4–22–1784	Eagle Cr	Amended
Williams, David	10,000	3	299	4–23–1784	None	
Williams, David	200	3	300	4–24–1784	None	
Williams, David	272	3	300	4–24–1784	None	
Williams, David	800	3	300	4–24–1784	None	
Williams, David	1,000	3	300	4–24–1784	None	
Williams, David	200	3	300	4–24–1784	None	
Williams, David	1,400	3	300	4–24–1784	None	
Williams, David	15,500	4	82	1– 5–1785	Slate Cr	
Williams, David	10,000	4	180	5–12–1785	None	Surveyed
Williams, Edward	287	1	391	1– 7–1783	Br M Fk Lulbegrud	
Williams, Jas.	12,500	4	73	12– 2–1784	Ohio R	Withdrawn
Williams, Jas.	12,500	4	73	12– 2–1784	None	Withdrawn
Williams, Jas.	12,500	4	129	3– 7–1785	Ky R	Withdrawn
Williams, Jas.	12,500	4	178	5–11–1785	Twinn Cr	Surveyed
Williams, Jas.	1,060½	4	183	5–24–1785	Clear Cr	Withdrawn
Williams, Jas.	1,060½	4	319	2–14–1788	None	
Williams, Jas.	11,751	4	319	2–14–1788	Ky R	582 acres surveyed Amended
Williams, Jas.	16,751	4	326	12–30–1788	Ky R	
Williams, John	1,000	1	309	12–28–1782	S Fk Elkhorn	Surveyed
Williams, John	1,000	2	9	1– 9–1783	None	Surveyed
Williams, John	4,000	2	78	1–17–1783	E Fk Licking	
Williams, John	1,000	2	289	5–21–1783	Licking	
Williams, Jno.	495	3	198	3– 2–1784	Slate Cr	Surveyed
Williams, Jno.	100	4	39	9–20–1784	None	
Williams, Jno.	11	4	73	12– 2–1784	None	
Williams, Jno.	139	4	75	12– 4–1784	None	
Williams, Jno.	400	4	136	3–19–1785	M Fk Licking	
Williams, Jno.	283½	4	252	1– 2–1786	S Fk Elkhorn	
Williams, Jno.	60	4	278	3– 1–1786	S Fk Elkhorn	
Williams, Jno.	200	4	279	3– 2–1786	Town Fk Elkhorn	
Williams, Joseph	20,000	4	155	4–20–1785	Sandy	6,873 acres withdrawn
Williams, Peggy	110	3	376	6–18–1784	None	Surveyed
Williams, Thomas	250	2	275	4– 9–1783	Eagle Cr	
Williams, William	1,000	2	227	3–10–1783	Ohio R	Surveyed
William & McCracken	250	3	31	11– 4–1783	N Fk Elkhorn	Surveyed
Williams & Neth	7,000	3	401	7–10–1784	None	Withdrawn
Williams & Neth	400	4	27	9– 2–1784	None	Withdrawn
Williams & Neth	2,000	4	27	9– 2–1784	None	Withdrawn
Williams & Neth	1,960	4	27	9– 2–1784	None	Withdrawn
Williams & Neth	2,000	4	38	9–20–1784	None	
Williams & Neth	2,640	4	38	9–20–1784	Br Licking	Withdrawn
Williams & Neth	640	4	39	9–20–1784	None	
Williams & Neth	7,000	4	56	10–17–1784	None	Withdrawn
Williams & Neth	7,000	4	56	10–17–1784	N Fk Licking	Withdrawn
Williams & Nith	700	4	73	12– 2–1784	None	
Williams & Nith	8,000	4	73	12– 2–1784	None	Withdrawn
Williams & Neth	5,312	4	117	2–12–1785	None	
Williams & Neth	4,000	4	143	4– 5–1785	None	Withdrawn
Williams & Neth	4,940	4	143	4– 5–1785	None	
Williams & Neth	8,000	4	153	4–20–1785	None	

Entree	Acres	Book	Page	Entry Date	Watercourse	Notes
Williams & Neth	2,683.	4	154	4–20–1785	Main Licking	Withdrawn
Williams & Neth	640	4	154	4–20–1785	None	....
Williams & Neth	400	4	154	4–20–1785	None	....
Williams & Neth	2,060	4	154	4–20–1785	None	Withdrawn
Williams & Neth	4,940	4	154	4–20–1785	None	....
Williams & Neth	7,000	4	171	5– 5–1785	None	Withdrawn
Williams & Neth	7,000	4	172	5– 6–1785	————	Withdrawn
Williams & Neth	2,688	4	212	7–30–1785	Cabbin Cr	....
Williams & Neth	7,000	4	256	1–14–1786	None	....
Willing, Chas	22,000	3	112	12–27–1783	Lower Blue Lick	Surveyed
Willing, Chas	22,000	3	221	3–11–1784	None	Surveyed
Willing, Chas	22,000	3	254	3–30–1784	None	Surveyed
Willing, Chas	1,000	3	425	8–14–1784	———— Cr	Surveyed
Willins, Chas	1,000	3	426	8–14–1784	Sandy	Surveyed
Willing, Chas	4,000	3	426	8–14–1784	Sandy	Surveyed
Willing, Chas	1,000	4	5	8–14–1784	Sandy Cr	Surveyed
Willson, William	600	2	185	2–13–1783	Plum Lick & Grassy Cr	Withdrawn
Wilson, Edward	500	2	18	1– 9–1783	None	Withdrawn
Wilson, Edward	600	2	68	1–15–1783	None	....
Wilson, Edward	1,000	3	381	6–23–1784	Br Main Licking	....
Wilson, Edward	1,000	4	205	6–30–1785	Licking	....
Wilson, Geo	1,000	3	247	3–27–1784	Hinkston Mill Cr	....
Wilson, Geo	9,925	3	346	5–26–1784	Otter Cr	....
Wilson, Geo	9,925	4	242	12–14–1785	None	....
Wilson, Jas	1,000	3	425	8–14–1784	———— Cr	Surveyed
Wilson, Jas	1,000	3	426	8–14–1784	Sandy	Surveyed
Wilson, Jas	4,000	3	426	8–14–1784	Sandy	Surveyed
Wilson, Jas	1,000	4	5	8–14–1784	Sandy Cr	Surveyed
Wilson, Jas & Co	1,000	4	5	8–14–1784	Sandy Cr	Surveyed
Wilson, Jas & Co	3,000	4	5	8–14–1784	Sandy Cr	Surveyed
Wilson, Jas & Co	1,000	4	6	8–14–1784	Sandy Cr	Surveyed
Wilson, Jas & Co	1,000	4	6	8–14–1784	Sandy Cr	Surveyed
Wilson, Jas & Co	6,000	4	6	8–14–1784	Sandy Cr	Surveyed
Wilson, Jas & Co	1,000	4	6	8–14–1784	Sandy Cr	Surveyed
Wilson, Jas & Co	1,000	4	6	8–14–1784	Sandy Cr	Surveyed
Wilson, Jas & Co	1,000	4	6	8–14–1784	Sandy Cr	Surveyed
Wilson, Jas & Co	1,000	4	7	8–14–1784	Sandy Cr	Surveyed
Wilson, Jas & Co	1,000	4	7	8–14–1784	Sandy Cr	Surveyed
Wilson, Jas & Co	1,000	4	7	8–14–1784	Sandy Cr	Surveyed
Wilson, Jas & Co	1,000	4	8	8–14–1784	Sandy Cr	Surveyed
Wilson, Jas & Co	1,000	4	8	8–14–1784	Sandy Cr	Surveyed
Wilson, Jas & Co	1,000	4	9	8–14–1784	Sandy Cr	Surveyed
Wilson, Jas & Co	1,000	4	9	8–14–1784	Sandy Cr	Surveyed
Wilson, Jas & Co	1,000	4	9	8–14–1784	Sandy Cr	Surveyed
Wilson, Jas & Co	1,000	4	9	8–14–1784	Sandy Cr	Surveyed
Wilson, Jas & Co	1,000	4	10	8–14–1784	Sandy Cr	Surveyed
Wilson, Jas & Co	1,000	4	10	8–14–1784	Sandy Cr	Surveyed
Wilson, Jas & Co	1,000	4	10	8–14–1784	Sandy Cr	Surveyed
Wilson, Jas & Co	1,000	4	10	8–14–1784	Sandy Cr	Surveyed
Wilson, Jas & Co	1,000	4	10	8–14–1784	Sandy Cr	Surveyed
Wilson, Jas & Co	1,000	4	11	8–14–1784	Sandy Cr	Surveyed
Wilson, Jas & Co	1,000	4	11	8–14–1784	Sandy Cr	Surveyed
Wilson, Jas & Co	1,000	4	11	8–14–1784	Sandy Cr	Surveyed
Wilson, Jas & Co	1,000	4	11	8–14–1784	Sandy Cr	Surveyed
Wilson, Jas & Co	1,000	4	11	8–14–1784	Sandy Cr	Surveyed
Wilson, Jas & Co	1,000	4	12	8–14–1784	Sandy Cr	Surveyed
Wilson, Jas & Co	1,000	4	12	8–14–1784	Sandy Cr	Surveyed
Wilson, Jas & Co	3,000	4	12	8–14–1784	Sandy Cr	Surveyed
Wilson, Jas & Co	1,000	4	12	8–14–1784	Sandy Cr	Surveyed
Wilson, Jas & Co	1,000	4	13	8–14–1784	Sandy Cr	Surveyed
Wilson, Jas & Co	1,000	4	13	8–14–1784	Sandy Cr	Surveyed
Wilson, Jas & Co	1,000	4	13	8–14–1784	Sandy Cr	Surveyed
Wilson, Jas & Co	1,000	4	13	8–14–1784	Sandy Cr	Surveyed
Wilson, Jas & Co	1,000	4	13	8–14–1784	Sandy Cr	Surveyed
Wilson, Jas & Co	1,000	4	14	8–14–1784	Sandy Cr	Surveyed
Wilson, Jno	5,267½	4	282	4–10–1784	None	Surveyed
Wilson, Jno	225,000	3	353	6– 4–1784	Ky R	Amended
Wilson, Jno, heirs	200	4	22	8–22–1784	Baileys Run	....
Wilson, Joseph	1,000	1	101	12–10–1782	Mill Cr	....
Wilson. Joseph	1,000	1	102	12–10–1782	Mill Cr	Surveyed
Wilson, Martha	999	4	163	4–29–1785	None	....
Wilson, Matthew	803	4	87	1– 8–1785	Licking	Surveyed
Wilson, Robert	800	2	351	8–14–1783	Indian Cr	....
Wilson, Samuel	1,000	2	51	1–13–1783	None	Surveyed
Wilson, Thos	1,000	4	208	10–27–1780	Clear Cr	....
Wilson, Wm	200	3	420	8– 5–1784	None	Surveyed

Entree	Acres	Book	Page	Entry Date	Watercourse	Notes
Wilson, Wm	600	3	384	6–24–1784	Main Licking	
Wilson, Wm	200	3	417	7–27–1784	Br Licking	
Wilson, Wm	920½	4	48	10–12–1784	M Licking	
Wilson, Wm	5,364¼	4	94	1–17–1785	N E Fk Licking	Surveyed
Wilson, Wm	4,250	4	160	4–29–1785	None	
Wilson, Wm	800	4	205	6–30–1785	None	
Wilson & Duncan	500	3	406	7–14–1784	Br Licking	
Wiman, John	168¾	2	24	1–10–1783	Hinkstons	
Winecup, Cornelius	1,000	2	11	1– 9–1783	Hingston Fk	Withdrawn
Winecup, Cornelius	1,000	2	324	7–17–1783	N Fk Red R	
Winecup, Cornelius	1,000	3	67	12– 1–1783	Sandy	Surveyed
Wingfield, Chas	400	4	165	4–29–1785	None	
Winn, Jas	34,240	3	20	10–30–1783	Ohio R	
Winn, John	2,632	1	385	1– 7–1783	None	
Winn, Minor	2,632	1	385	1– 7–1783	None	
Winn, Minor	7,926	3	24	10–31–1783	Ohio R	
Winslow, Benjamin	1,100	1	9	11–29–1782	Red R	
Winslow, Beverly	3,187½	1	283	12–26–1782	Br Eagle Cr	
Winston, Beverly	5,000	2	41	1–11–1783	Licking	
Winston, Goddis	5,000	1	262	12–24–1782	Buffaloe Rd & Cedar Cr	Surveyed
Winston & Boone	11,875	3	189	2–28–1784	Ky R	
Winters, William	1,500	2	247	3–15–1783	Licking	Surveyed
Wiseman, Christian	1,000	3	354	6– 7–1784	Big Bone Lick	
Withers, Abijah	373½	4	258	1–16–1786	———— Cr	
Withers, Jas	795½	4	193	6– 6–1785	N Fk Ky R	
Withers, Jas	500	4	194	6– 6–1785	None	
Withers, Margaret	1,554	4	267	2– 3–1786	None	
Womack, Allen	5,000	2	345	8–12–1783	Br Ohio R	
Woner, Peter	500	2	318	7– 7–1783	None	Surveyed
Wood, Archibald	1,500	1	393	1– 8–1783	Lulbegrud	
Wood, Wm	2,000	4	227	10–13–1785	Johnson Fk	
Woodruff, John	360	1	50	12– 5–1782	Stoners Fk	
Woods, Andrew	400	4	105	2– 5–1785	Buck Horn	Withdrawn
Woods, Andrew	400	4	107	2– 5–1785	Buckhorn Fk	
Woods, Andrew	400	4	107	2– 5–1785	None	
Woods, Patrick	1,528½	4	165	4–29–1785	Licking	
Woods, Richard	6,121	2	129	1–27–1783	None	
Woodson, Tucker M & Samuel	500	4	18	8–19–1784	None	
Woodson, Tucker M & Samuel	598	4	18	8–20–1784	Twins Cr	
Woodward, Chesley	848½	2	119	1–24–1783	Red R	
Woody, Jno	1,198	4	173	5– 7–1785	Ohio R	
Wooldridge, Edmond	5,000	1	145	12–14–1782	Licking	
Wooldridge, Edmond	5,000	1	146	12–14–1782	None	
Wooldridge, Edmund	3,863	2	43	1–11–1783	None	
Wooldridge, Edmund	5,985⅓	2	314	6–10–1783	Licking	
Woolford, Francis	2,500	3	161	1–21–1784	———— Cr	
Woolford, Francis	1,000	3	4	10–15–1783	Main Licking	
Woolfork, Francis	1,000	3	4	10–15–1783	———— Cr	
Wright, David	1,483½	2	159	2– 4–1783	Br Ky R	
Wright, David	1,400	2	276	4–22–1783	N Fk Elkhorn	
Wright, Dennis	500	1	12	11–30–1782	Hingston Fk	
Wright, Joseph	562½	1	346	1– 2–1783	Br 4 Mile Cr	Surveyed
Wright, Capt Patrick	4,000	4	283	3–23–1786	Sandy Cr	
Wright & Weaver	749	3	397	7– 8–1784	Licking	Surveyed
Wyatt, John	1,000	2	226	3–10–1783	Ohio R	Surveyed
Wyatt, Thomas	200	1	114	12–12–1782	None	
Yyatt, Wm	400	3	124	12–30–1783	None	Surveyed
Yagers, John Sr	820	1	118	12–12–1782	Stoners Fk	Withdrawn
Yagers, Jno Sr	820	3	421	8– 5–1784	Hingston Fk	Withdrawn
Yagers, Jno Sr	820	4	77	12–16–1784	Hingston	
Yancy, Charles	1,000	1	89	12– 9–1782	N Fk Licking	Surveyed
Yancey, Charles	400	1	111	12–11–1782	Main Fk Licking	Surveyed
Yancey, Charles	2,828	2	36	1–11–1783	Sandy	
Yancy, Chas	800	3	42	11–13–1783	None	
Yancy, Chas	3,025	3	149	1–15–1784	Ky R	Surveyed
Yancy, Chas	1,000	3	412	7–17–1784	N Fk Licking	
Yandes, Jacob	300	1	18	12– 4–1782	Riddles Station	Surveyed
Yates, Michael	1,820	1	11	11–30–1782	Clear Cr	
York, Edward	2,000	3	405	7–14–1784	None	Withdrawn
York, Edward	2,000	4	137	3–22–1785	None	
Young, Francis	4,562	3	347	5–27–1784	Haw Cr	
Young, Henry	20,000	1	205	12–20–1782	Main Fk Licking	Surveyed
Young, John	1,744	2	63	1–14–1783	None	Surveyed
Young, John	200	2	199	2–17–1783	Main Licking	Surveyed
Young, John	50	2	199	2–17–1783	Main Fk Licking	
Young, Jno	2,231	3	1	10–13–1783	Ohio R	
Young, Jno	9,375	3	112	12–27–1783	None	Amended

Entree	Acres	Book	Page	Entry Date	Watercourse	Notes
Young, Jno	22,943¾	3	113	12–27–1783	E Fk Licking	Withdrawn
Young, Jno	9,375	3	221	3–11–1784	None	
Young, Jno	22,943¾	3	263	3–31–1784	Main Fk Licking	Surveyed
Young, John Jr	1,769	2	378	10–13–1783	S Side Ohio R	
Young, John Jr	3,000	2	378	10–13–1783	Ohio R	
Young, Jno & Chas	126,140	3	298	4–22–1784	1 h Fk 3 Fks Ky R	Surveyed amended
Young, Peter	1,209	1	343	1– 1–1783	None	Withdrawn
Young, Peter	1,209	2	34	1–10–1783	Ohio R	Surveyed
Young, Richard	1,000	1	119	12–12–1782	Br Ohio R	
Young, Richard	1,000	1	119	12–12–1782	Sinking Cr	Surveyed
Young, Richard	16,219¾	1	282	12–26–1782	None	Surveyed
Young, Richard	6,300	2	27	1–10–1783	—— Cr	
Young, Richard	3,770	2	182	2–12–1783	Clear Cr	
Young, Richard	590	3	321	5– 3–1784	Glens Cr	Surveyed
Young, Richard	1,156¾	3	330	5–13–1784	Glens Cr	Withdrawn
Young, Richard	1,156¾	3	351	5–31–1784		292 acres withdrawn 250 acres surveyed
Young, Richard	198	3	367	6–14–1784	None	Withdrawn
Young, Richard	292	3	367	6–14–1784	None	Withdrawn
Young, Richard	614	4	29	9– 7–1784	Glens Cr	280 acres withdrawn 155 acres surveyed
Young, Richard	292	4	33	9–10–1784	Clear Cr	
Young, Richard	250	4	203	6–27–1785	Clear Cr	125 acres withdrawn
Young, Richard	30	4	288	4– 5–1786	None	
Young, Richard	250	4	288	4– 5–1786	Clear Cr	
Young, Richard	179	4	289	4–13–1786	—— R	Withdrawn
Young, Richard	129	4	312	3– 6–1787	Ky R	
Young, Richard	500	4	212	3– 6–1787	Ky R	
Young, Richard	125	4	324	6–12–1788	Clear Cr	Surveyed
Young, Robt	25,000	3	70	12– 4–1783	N Fk Licking	Surveyed
Young, Robt	5,000	3	71	12– 4–1783	None	
Young, Robt	1,000	4	251	12–30–1785	Ohio R	
Young, Saml	300,306¾	3	190	2–28–1784	3 Fks Ky R	
Young, Thos	1,000	4	207	7–13–1785	N Fk Licking	
Young, Thos & Robt	5,000	3	50	11–18–1783	None	Surveyed
Young & Adkins	1,000	4	29	9– 7–1784	Glens Cr	
Young & Arnold	500	3	232	3–18–1784	—— R	Surveyed
Young & Arnold	198	3	367	6–14–1784	Clear Cr	
Young & Carr	1,387¾	4	228	10–23–1785	Sandy	
Young & Bowdain	5,000	3	178	2–10–1784	None	
Young & Phillips	100,000	3	167	1–26–1784	N E Fk Eagle Cr	
Young & Phillips	100,000	3	185	2–17–1784	Eagle Cr	
Young & Richards	1,546¾	3	179	2–10–1784	None	
Young & Robinson	16,000	3	177	2–10–1784	Sandy	
Young & Stewart	3,121¾	3	179	2–10–1784	None	
Young & Tibbs	15,000	3	56	11–22–1783	W Fk Bank Lick	Surveyed
Young & Wegglesworth	16,000	3	177	2–10–1784	None	
Zunwalt, Adam	500	3	82	12–10–1783	None	Surveyed

IV.

JEFFERSON ENTRIES

(1779-1785)

Entree	Acres	Book	Page	Entry Date	Watercourse	Notes
Abbott, James	400	A	290	9-10-1783	Bush Cr	
Abeehard, Martin	500	A	71	5-18-1780	Kentucky R	
Abell, Peter	1,000	A	283	7-25-1783	Blackfords Cr	
Abell, Peter	1,006	A	283	7-25-1783	Big Tarr Sp	Withdrawn
Abell, Peter	1,000	A	288	9- 1-1783	Otter Cr	Surveyed
Abell, Peter	500	A	298	10-23-1783	Pottengers Cr	Surveyed
Abell, Peter	100	A	341	2-26-1784	Beech Fk	
Abercrombie, Charles	600	A	114	5-30-1780	Jessamine Cr	
Abercrombie, Charles	1,200	A	114	5-30-1780	Kentucky R	
Abercrombie, Charles	200	A	122	6- 2-1780	Licking	
Abercrombie, Charles	400	A	122	6- 2-1780	Licking	
Abercrombie, Charles	600	A	181	10-23-1780	Hickmans Cr	
Abney, John	1,500	A	230	12-17-1782	Sinking Cr	Withdrawn
Abney, John	1,500	A	230	12-17-1782	Green R	Surveyed
Abney, John	1,500	A	259	1-31-1783	Sinking Cr	Surveyed
Abney, John	1,500	A	259	1-31-1783	Pittmans Cr	
Adams, David	400	A	2	11- 3-1779	Salt R	Surveyed
Adams, David	1,000	A	26	4-26-1780	Salt R	Surveyed
Adams, David	664	A	123	6- 2-1780	Salt R	
Adams, Francis	400	A	243	12-26-1782	Pond Cr	
Adams, Geo	400	A	13	2- 9-1780	Paint Lick Cr	
Adams, Gowan	400	A	101	5-26-1780	N Fk Licking	
Adams, James	1,000	A	83	5-23-1780	N Fk Elkhorn	
Adams, James	500	A	255	1-20-1783	Rough Cr	
Adams, James	1,000	A	255	1-20-1783	Mill Cr	Surveyed
Adams, James	100	A	275	4- 9-1783	Limestone Cr	
Adams, James	200	A	275	4- 9-1783	Sinking Cr	
Adams, James	200	A	275	4- 9-1783	Sinking	
Adams, James	716	A	291	9-13-1783	N Fk Rough Cr	
Adams, James	395	B	6	9-13-1784	Cumberland Fk	
Adams, James	500	B	10	10-11-1784	————	
Adams, Richard	4,000	A	81	5-22-1780	Green R	Withdrawn
Adams, Richard	2,000	A	81	5-22-1780	Green R	
Adams, Richard	4,000	A	130	6-12-1780	Green R	Surveyed
Adams, Richard	2,000	A	249	1- 8-1783	Path Fk Gesses Cr	1,000 acres withdrawn
Adams, Robert	500	A	121	6- 2-1780	Silver Cr	
Adams, Samuel	1,000	A	36	4-29-1780	Salt R	Withdrawn
Adams, Samuel	1,000	A	152	6-26-1780	Salt R	
Adams, Samuel	187	A	237	12-21-1782	Wm Hightower	Withdrawn
Adams, Samuel	187	A	257	1-24-1783	Wm Hightower	Withdrawn
Adams, Samuel	187	A	257	1-24-1783	Salt R	
Adams, Samuel M	400	A	236	12-20-1782	Pottingers Cr	
Adams, Thomas	1,000	A	268	3-28-1783	Sinking Cr	
Adams, Wm	400	A	2	11- 3-1779	Salt R	
Adams, Wm	1,000	A	26	4-26-1780	Salt R	
Adkins, John	350	A	114	5-30-1780	Howards Cr	50 miles
Alcock, Thomas	2,000	A	167	8-17-1780	Green R	Withdrawn
Alcock, Thomas	1,000	A	190	3-15-1781	Gess Fk	Surveyed
Alcock, Thomas	560	A	228	12-16-1782	Gests Fk	Surveyed
Alcock, Thomas	1,000	A	234	12-19-1782	Blackford Cr	Surveyed
Alcock, Thomas	1,000	B	25	12-10-1784	————	Surveyed
Alder, Barthol	400	A	76	5-19-1780	Rolling Fk	
Alexander, Francis	1,763½	A	348	3-22-1784	Green R	Withdrawn
Alexander, Francis	1,763½	A	374	7-27-1784	————	Withdrawn
Alexander, John	1,231½	A	374	7-27-1784	Green R	
Alexander, Wm	50	A	186	3-14-1781	Long Lick	Withdrawn
Alexander, Wm	1,000	A	186	3-14-1781	Coxes Cr	Surveyed
Alexander, Wm	700	A	186	3-14-1781	Fromans Cr	Withdrawn
Alexander, Wm	1,000	A	199	3-23-1781	Tumbling Cr	
Alexander, Wm	700	A	200	3-26-1781	Fromans Cr	
Alexander, Wm	650	A	211	6- 9-1781	W Fk Cedar Cr	
Alexander, Wm	200	A	217	8- 2-1781	Salt R	
Alexander, Wm	1,000	A	222	12-11-1782	Hardens Cr	300 acres withdrawn
Alexander, Wm	50	A	254	1-15-1783	Long Lick Cr	
Alexander, Wm	300	A	277	4-14-1783	Salt R	

Entree	Acres	Book	Page	Entry Date	Watercourse	Notes
Alexander, Wm	300	A	277	4-14-1783	Phillips Station	
Alexander, Wm	1,900	A	346	3-12-1784	——	
Allan, Benj	322	A	354	4-16-1784	Rolling Fk	
Allan, Elizabeth	400	A	171	9-13-1780	Green R	
Allan, James	500	A	87	5-23-1780	Clear Cr	
Allan, James	300	A	87	5-23-1780	Brashears Cr	
Allan, James	500	A	87	5-23-1780	Brashears Cr	
Allan, James	1,000	A	294	10-11-1783	Pattons Cr	
Allan, James	750	A	352	4-15-1784	Beech Fk	
Allan, James	2,000	A	352	4-15-1784	Tarr Sp Fk	
Allen, James et al	1,000	A	279	6- 7-1783	Beaver Dam Fk	
Allan, Jas et al	2,000	A	295	10-11-1783	Panther Cr	
Allan, Jas et al	2,000	A	295	10-11-1783	Rough Cr	Withdrawn
Allan, Jas et al	2,000	A	297	10-15-1783	Rough Cr	Withdrawn
Allan, James et al	2,894	A	364	6- 4-1784	Barbour & Bank	
Allan, James et al	2,000	A	364	6- 4-1784	Rough Cr	
Allan, James et al	894	A	364	6- 4-1784	——	Withdrawn
Allan, James et al	6,894	B	43	4-14-1785	——	
Allan, John	500	A	156	6-30-1780	Drowning Cr	
Allan, Joseph	300	A	158	7- 3-1780	4 Mile Cr	
Allan, Joseph	1,000	A	352	4-15-1784	——	
Allan, Joseph	1,000	A	352	4-15-1784	Limestone Cr	
Allan, Joseph et al	5,000	A	284	7-27-1783	Pattons Cr	Surveyed
Allan, Thomas	500	A	98	5-25-1780	Hammons Cr	
Allan, Thomas	1,000	A	225	12-13-1782	Blackfords Cr	
Allan, Ukanah	650	A	256	1-24-1783	Panthers Cr	
Allan, Wm	400	A	77	5-20-1780	Hardings Cr	Withdrawn
Allan, Wm	400	A	130	6-12-1780	Green R	
Allan, Wm	400	A	141	6-21-1780	Ohio R	Withdrawn
Allan, Wm	200	A	191	3-15-1781	Salt R	
Allan, Wm	600	A	198	3-19-1781	Cedar Cr	Surveyed 300 acres withdrawn
Allan, Wm	300	A	215	7-18-1781	Cedar Cr	Surveyed
Allan, Wm	250	A	305	11-17-1783	Limestone Cr	Withdrawn
Allan, Wm	250	A	305	11-17-1783	Limestone Cr	Withdrawn
Allan, Wm	200	A	334	1-24-1784	Hardins Cr	
Allan, Wm	300	A	334	1-24-1784	Beech Fk	
Allan, Wm	250	A	334	1-24-1784	Limestone Cr	
Allan, Wm	250	A	334	1-24-1784	Limestone Cr	
Allan, Wm	500	A	337	2-10-1784	Sinking Cr	
Allan, Wm	400	A	342	3- 2-1784	Beech Fk	
Allan, Wm	400	A	342	3- 2-1784	Ohio R	Withdrawn
Allan, Wm	200	A	346	3-16-1784	Myers Premption	Surveyed
Allan, Wm	800	B	34	1-22-1785	——	
Allcock, Thomas	300	A	35	4-29-1780	Paint Lick	Mil
Allcock, Thomas	2,000	A	190	3-15-1781	Panther Cr	
Allcock, Thomas	1,000	A	191	3-15-1781	Floyds Fk	
Allcock, Thomas	645	A	302	11-10-1783	Floyds Fk	
Alleger, Giles	500	A	213	7- 2-1781	Peytons Cr	
Allison, Charles	200	A	175	10- 6-1780	Beech Fk	Mil Surveyed
Allison, Charles	200	A	179	10-19-1780	Cedar Cr	
Allison, John	500	A	313	12- 5-1783	Beech Fk	
Alnat, James	975	A	53	5-15-1780	——	
Alsop, Samuel	500	A	183	10-27-1780	Green R	Surveyed
Alvey, John	200	A	254	1-18-1783	Willsons Cr	
Alvey, John	215	A	254	1-18-1783	Beech Fk	Withdrawn
Alvey, John	400	A	254	1-18-1783	Willsons Cr	
Alvey, John	200	A	273	4- 7-1783	Buffaloe Run	
Alvey, John	200	A	327	1- 5-1784	Buffaloe Cr	
Alvey, John	415	A	341	2-25-1784	Youngers Cr	
Alvey, John	200	A	341	2-25-1784	Buffaloe Cr	Withdrawn
Alvey, John	215	A	341	2-25-1784	Beech Fk	
Amerson, Jane	400	A	236	12-20-1782	Soverins Run	
Ammons, Thomas	400	A	85	5-22-1780	Elkhorn	
Ammons, Thomas	1,000	A	85	5-22-1780	Bulger Cr	
Anderson, George	800	A	254	1-17-1783	Green R	
Anderson, James	1,000	A	369	7- 1-1784	Beargrass Cr	
Anderson, John	400	A	27	4-26-1780	N Fk Gilbert Cr	
Anderson, John	300	A	116	5-31-1780	N Fk Gilbert Cr	
Anderson, John	100	A	207	4-17-1781	Rowling Fk	
Anderson, John et al	200	A	154	6-28-1780	S Fk Tates Cr	
Anderson, Joseph	400	A	337	2-11-1784	Sulphur Lick Run	
Anderson, Michael et al	17,175	A	132	6-15-1780	Green R	
Anderson, Nicholas	387	A	91	5-24-1780	Little Mt Cr	
Anderson, Nicholas	400	A	95	5-24-1780	Little Mt Cr	
Anderson, Col R C	1,068	B	12	11- 9-1784	Panther Cr	
Anderson, Wm	1,000	A	79	5-20-1780	Hickmans Cr	
Anderson, Wm	400	A	120	6- 1-1780	Hickmans Cr	
Anderson, Wm	2,000	A	178	10-10-1780	S Fk Licking	
Andrew, Robert	1,000	A	261	2- 4-1783	Salt R	415 acres withdrawn

Entree	Acres	Book	Page	Entry Date	Watercourse	Notes
Andrew, Robert	1,000	A	261	2- 4-1783	Salt R	628 acres surveyed
Andrew, Robert	415	A	267	2-28-1783	Salt R	Surveyed
Andrew, Robert	372	A	272	3-31-1783	Brashears Cr	
Andrews, Robert	2,000	A	233	12-19-1782	Green R	Withdrawn
Andrews, Robert	2,000	A	261	2- 4-1783	Green R	Withdrawn
Andrews, Robert	415	A	267	2-28-1783	Salt R	Warrant returned
Andrews, Rev Rob	200	A	154	6-28-1780	Brashears Cr	
Andrews, Rev Rob	2,000	A	278	4-14-1783	————	1,143 acres surveyed
Anthony, Joseph	200	A	34	4-29-1780	Tates Cr	Mil
Anthony, Joseph	600	A	80	5-20-1780	Paint Lick Cr	
Applegate, Hezekiah	400	A	17	2-29-1780	Plumb Cr	Surveyed
Arbuckle, Thomas	400	A	27	4-26-1780	Salt R	Surveyed
Archer, Abraham	2,000	A	137	6-19-1780	Johnstons Fk	
Archer, Edward	5,000	A	235	12-20-1782	Beaver Dam Cr	
Archer, John	400	A	5	12- 7-1779	Dicks R	
Archer, Zach et al	1,000	A	209	5-23-1781	Little Ky R	Surveyed
Armstrong, Alex	428	A	251	1- 9-1783	Chaplin Fk	Surveyed
Armstrong, Alex	1,100	A	251	1- 9-1783	Brashears Cr	
Armstrong, Alex	1,100	A	377	8-12-1784	————	
Armstrong, Benoni	9,093¾	A	356	4-24-1784	Green R	
Armstrong, James	10,000	A	357	4-28-1784	Rolling Fk	
Armstrong, John	300	A	160	7- 7-1780	Salt R	
Armstrong, John	100	A	160	7- 7-1780	Salt R	
Armstrong, Martin	1,000	A	181	10-24-1780	Ohio R	Surveyed
Arnatt, Wm	360	A	260	2- 3-1783	Still Cr	
Arnold, Humphrey	500	A	125	6- 5-1780	Tuckahoe Cr	
Arnold, Mark	600	A	98	5-25-1780	Ohio R	
Arnold, Mark	600	A	122	6- 2-1780	Little Miami	
Arnold, Mark	400	A	123	6- 3-1780	Ohio R	
Arnold, Mark	1,200	A	258	1-27-1783	Hardens Cr	
Arnold, Stephen	300	A	70	5-18-1780	Salt R	
Arnold, Stephen	200	A	70	5-18-1780	Salt R	
Arnold, Stephen	250	A	87	5-23-1780	Kentucky R	
Arnold, Wm	800	A	85	5-22-1780	Licking Cr	
Ash, Francis	600	A	150	6-26-1780	Mid Fk Licking	
Ashby, Benjamin	500	A	155	6-29-1780	Bennetts Pond	
Ashby, Benjamin	500	A	158	7- 3-1780	S Fk Licking	
Ashby, Bladen	500	A	241	12-25-1782	Beech Fk	Surveyed
Ashby, Bladen	500	A	290	9-10-1783	Doeritts Cr	
Ashby, Hankerson	500	A	242	12-25-1782	Shot Pouch Cr	
Ashby, Hankerson	500	A	242	12-25-1782	Shot Pouch Cr	Surveyed
Ashby, Hankerson	500	A	311	11-29-1783	Shot Pouch Cr	
Ashby, Hankerson	1,000	B	44	5-10-1785	————	500 acres surveyed
Ashby, Nath	600	A	129	6- 9-1780	Guess Cr	
Ashby, Stephen	1,000	A	211	6-11-1781	Simpsons Cr	Surveyed
Ashcraft, Elizabeth	1,800	B	31	1- 3-1785	————	276 acres surveyed returned
Ashcraft, Jediah	400	A	217	8- 8-1781	Nolin Cr	Withdrawn
Ashcraft, Jediah	200	A	282	7- 1-1783	Linn Camp Cr	Withdrawn
Ashcraft, Jediah	200	A	282	7- 1-1783	Middle Cr	Surveyed
Ashcraft, Jediah	400	A	282	7- 1-1783	Nolin Cr	Withdrawn
Ashcraft, Jediah	200	A	293	10- 6-1783	Middle Cr	Withdrawn
Ashcraft, Jediah	200	A	293	10- 6-1783	Linn Camp Cr	Withdrawn
Ashcraft, Jediah	200	A	294	10- 7-1783	Middle Cr	Withdrawn
Ashercraft, Elizabeth	400	B	27	12-18-1784	Bear Cr	Surveyed
Ashercraft, Jediah	200	A	294	10- 7-1783	Lynn Camp Cr	
Ashercraft, Jediah	400	A	370	7- 6-1784	————	200 acres surveyed
Ashercraft, Jediah	1,276	B	27	12-18——	Bear Cr	
Ashley, John	1,000	A	150	6-26-1780	Mid Fk Licking	
Ashley, Lewis	300	A	40	5- 9-1780	Fk Licking	
Askin, John, heirs	1,000	A	201	4- 2-1781	Hardens Cr	
Askin, John	1,000	A	201	4- 2-1781	Cartright Cr	
Askins, Edward	600	A	126	6- 7-1780	Beargrass	Surveyed
Askins, Wm	400	A	102	5-27-1780	Salt R	
Atherton, Aaron	200	A	338	2-13-1784	Prices Cr	
Atherton, Aaron	100	A	338	2-13-1784	Prices Cr	
Atherton, Aaron	200	A	338	2-13-1784	Knobb Cr	
Atherton, Aaron	400	A	338	2-13-1784	Beech Fk	
Atherton, Aaron	1,088¾	A	372	7-21-1784	————	400 acres surveyed
Atherton, Aaron	400	A	372	7-21-1784	Brush Cr	
Atkins, John	1,678	A	271	3-28-1783	Brush Cr	
Atkinson, Joseph	500	A	48	5-12-1780	Hardins Cr	Surveyed
Augustus, John	400	A	149	6-24-1780	Hammons Cr	
Austin, Chapman	2,000	A	151	6-26-1780	Jessamine Cr	
Austin, Chapman	4,000	A	151	6-26-1780	S Fk Licking	

Entree	Acres	Book	Page	Entry Date	Watercourse	Notes
Austin, Chapman	4,000	A	151	6–26–1780	Red R	
Austin, Chapman	1,000	A	163	7–22–1780	Rowling Fk	Withdrawn
Austin, Chapman	1,000	A	348	3–27–1780	Rolling Fk	
Austin, John	1,000	A	151	6–26–1780	Kentucky R	
Austin, John	1,000	A	151	6–26–1780	Red R	
Austin, John	1,000	A	151	6–26–1780	Red R	
Austin, John	2,000	A	151	6–26–1780	N Fk Elkhorn	
Austin, John	1,250	A	179	10–17–1780	Salt R	
Austin, John	1,000	A	179	10–17–1780	Dicks R	
Austin, Thomas	1,000	A	151	6–26–1780	Lulbergrud Cr	
Austin, Thomas	4,000	A	151	6–26–1780	Wm Moore	
Austin, Thomas	1,000	A	182	10–25–1780	Br Salt R	
Austin, Thomas	1,000	A	182	10–25–1780	Robinsons Cr	
Austin, Thomas	1,000	A	182	10–25–1780	Robert Todd	240 acres surveyed withdrawn
Austin, Thomas	1,000	A	182	10–25–1780	Elk Lick	
Austin, Thomas	1,000	A	182	10–25–1780	Robinsons Cr	Surveyed
Austin, Thomas	240	A	345	3– 9–1784	Robinsons Cr	Surveyed
Austin, Thomas	240	A	345	3– 9–1784	Robinsons Cr	230 acres surveyed
Baffman, Christian	400	A	9	1–18–1780	Baffmans Fk	
Bagley, Wm	400	A	83	5–22–1780	Buck Lick Cr	
Bailey, John et al	1,000	A	298	10–25–1783	Floyds Fk	Surveyed
Bailey, Pierce	500	A	55	5–15–1780	Simpsons Cr	
Baird, Robert	100	B	8	9–23–1784	Stewart Cr	
Baird, Robert	300	B	8	9–23–1784	Stewart Cr	
Baker, Isaac	900	A	103	5–27–1780	Harrods Cr	
Baker, Isaac	100	A	103	5–27–1780	Ky R	
Baker, Isaac	1,000	A	103	5–27–1780	Salt R	
Baker, John	800	A	88	5–23–1780	Cartwright Cr	Surveyed
Baker, John	400	A	103	5–27–1780	Harrods Cr	
Baker, John	400	A	103	5–27–1780	Harrods Cr	
Baker, John	1,000	A	108	5–29–1780	Mid Fk Licking	
Baker, John	500	A	162	7–18–1780	Falls Green R	
Baker, John	400	A	209	5–10–1781	Cedar Cr	Surveyed
Baker, John	1,000	A	244	12–26–1782	Buffaloe Run	
Baker, John	1,000	A	244	12–26–1782	Coxes Cr	Surveyed
Baker, John	400	A	244	12–26–1782	Pottengers Cr	
Baker, John et al	400	A	259	2– 3–1783	Floyds Fk	
Baker, Martin	1,200	A	150	6–24–1780	Hardins Cr	Withdrawn
Baker, Martin	1,200	A	165	8–11–1780	Hardins Cr	Withdrawn
Baker, Martin	1,200	A	186	10–31–1780	Salt R	Withdrawn
Baker, Michael	375½	A	377	8– 9–1784	Ohio R	
Baker, Samuel	1,000	A	142	6–22–1780	Salt R	
Baker, Walter	200	A	176	10– 9–1780	Beech Fk	Surveyed
Baker, Walter	460	A	176	10– 9–1780	Salt R	
Baker, Walter	340	A	176	10– 9–1780	Town Fk	
Baker, Walter	1,200	A	253	1–15–1783	Hardens Cr	Surveyed
Baker, Walter	1,000	A	362	5–28–1784	Ohio R	200 acres surveyed
Baker, Wm	1,000	A	140	6–21–1780	Ky R	Surveyed
Baley, John	400	A	5	12– 7–1779	Brashears Cr	Surveyed
Ball, Edward	300	A	70	5–17–1780	Fk Dicks R	
Ball, Edward	622½	A	70	5–18–1780	Dick R	
Ball, Edward	322½	A	70	5–18–1780	Dicks R	
Ball, Thomas	500	A	219	8–22–1781	Pitmans Cr	
Ballanger, Jeremiah	300	A	101	5–26–1780	N Fk Licking	
Ballanger, John	150	A	210	6– 1–1781	Beech Fk	
Ballanger, Richard	1,598¾	B	41	3– 4–1785	———	Surveyed
Ballanger, Richard	1,598¾	A	296	10–15–1783	Robinson Cr	1,000 acres withdrawn
Ballanger, Richard	1,000	A	342	2–27–1784	Robinsons Cr	Withdrawn
Ballanger, Richard	1,000	A	342	2–27–1784	Robinsons Cr	Surveyed
Ballard, Bland Jr	100	A	291	9–13–1783	Beargrass Cr	Withdrawn
Ballard, Bland Jr	325	A	344	3– 3–1784	Harrods Cr	Surveyed
Ballard, Bland Jr	100	A	344	3– 3–1784	Beargrass Cr	Withdrawn
Ballard, Bland Wm	325	A	198	3–17–1781	Pond Cr	Surveyed
Ballard, Bland Wm	325	A	196	3–17–1781	———	Withdrawn
Ballard, James	325	A	345	3– 5–1784	Harrods Cr	Surveyed
Ballard, Proctor	325	A	163	7–29–1780	Round Stone Cr	
Ballard, Smith	806	A	234	12–19–1782	Floyds Fk	Surveyed
Baltis, Leonard	400	A	188	3–15–1781	Middle Cr	Withdrawn
Baltis, Leonard	600	A	188	3–15–1781	Middle Cr	Withdrawn
Baltis, Leonard	500	A	188	3–15–1781	Fromans Cr	
Baltis, Leonard	1,000	A	299	10–27–1783	Rough Cr	Surveyed
Baltis, Leonard	400	A	299	10–27–1783	Middle Cr	Withdrawn
Baltis, Leonard	600	A	299	10–27–1783	Middle Cr	
Baltis, Leonard	1,500	A	363	6– 4–1784	———	500 acres surveyed
Bank, Leonard	437½	A	296	10–14–1783	Robinsons Cr	
Banks, Adam	1,000	A	58	5–15–1780	Licking	

Entree	Acres	Book	Page	Entry Date	Watercourse	Notes
Banks, Henry	2,000	A	227	12-14-1782	Bullskin Cr	Surveyed
Banks, Henry	1,500	A	300	11- 1-1783	Mid Fk Sinking Cr	
Banks, Henry	654½	A	301	11- 1-1783	Plum Cr	Withdrawn
Bank, Henry	10,000	A	301	11- 1-1783	Brashears Cr	1,000 acres withdrawn
Banks, Henry	20,000	A	302	11- 7-1783	Ohio R	17,100 acres surveyed
Bank, Henry	80,000	A	304	11-14-1783	Salt R	50,000 acres surveyed
Banks, Henry	5,000	A	304	11-14-1783	Green R	Surveyed
Banks, Henry	5,000	A	306	11-19-1783	Brashears Cr	
Banks, Henry	5,000	A	306	11-19-1783	Brashears Cr	Withdrawn
Banks, Henry	5,000	A	307	11-21-1783	Chaplins Fk	Surveyed
Banks, Henry	5,000	A	307	11-21-1783	Plumb Cr	Withdrawn
Banks, Henry	5,000	A	307	11-20-1783	Rolling Fk	
Banks, Henry	2,000	A	309	11-25-1783	Kelleys Cabin	Withdrawn
Banks, Henry	5,000	A	309	11-25-1783	Elk Cr	Withdrawn
Banks, Henry	3,000	A	309	11-25-1783	Salt R	Withdrawn
Banks, Henry	5,000	A	315	12-15-1783	Ky R	Surveyed
Banks, Henry	5,000	A	315	12-15-1783	Ky R	Surveyed
Banks, Henry	3,000	A	316	12-15-1783	————	Withdrawn
Banks, Henry	2,000	A	316	12-15-1783	————	Withdrawn
Banks, Henry	6,541½	A	316	12-15-1783	Plumb Cr	
Banks, Henry	168¾	A	317	12-15-1783	Ohio R	Surveyed
Banks, Henry	3,500	A	317	12-15-1783	Salt R	
Banks, Henry	10,000	A	317	12-15-1783	Rough Cr	Withdrawn
Banks, Henry	12,541½	A	317	12-15-1783	Clifty Cr	12,500 acres surveyed
Banks, Henry	3,331¼	A	318	12-16-1783	Ohio R	1,831 acres withdrawn
Banks, Henry	5,000	A	321	12-22-1783	Brashears Cr	Withdrawn
Banks, Henry	400	A	321	12-20-1783	Nolinn Cr	
Banks, Henry	8,000	A	327	1- 5-1784	Rough Cr	
Banks, Henry	6,000	A	327	1- 5-1784	Jones Cr	Withdrawn
Banks, Henry	1,000	A	327	1- 5-1784	Salt R	Withdrawn
Banks, Henry	1,000	A	327	1- 5-1784	Kelleys Cabbin	Withdrawn
Banks, Henry	2,000	A	330	1-15-1784	Little Ky R	
Banks, Henry	2,000	A	330	1-14-1784	Elk Cr	
Banks, Henry	50,000	A	335	1-27-1784	Bacon Cr	Amended
Banks, Henry	5,000	A	336	2- 2-1784	Cedar Cr	Surveyed
Banks, Henry	5,000	A	336	2- 2-1784	Plumb Cr	
Banks, Henry	10,000	A	349	3-30-1784	Ohio R	Surveyed
Banks, Henry	6,000	A	354	4-19-1784	Patton & Pope	Withdrawn
Banks, Henry	2,375	A	355	4-19-1784	Beech Fk	Surveyed
Banks, Henry	2,375	A	355	4-19-1784	Beech Fk	Withdrawn
Banks, Henry	5,000	A	355	4-19-1784	Long Lick Cr	
Banks, Henry	5,000	A	355	4-19-1784	Nolinn Cr	Withdrawn
Banks, Henry	6,000	A	355	4-19-1784	Salt R	3,110 acres surveyed
Banks, Henry	782	A	366	6-18-1784	Rolling Fk	Surveyed
Banks, Henry	782	A	366	6-18-1784	Middle Cr	
Banks, Henry	50,000	A	369	7- 1-1784	————	4,218 acres surveyed
Banks, Henry	50,000	A	369	7- 1-1784	————	5,000 acres surveyed
Banks, Henry	10,000	A	375	7-29-1784	Rough Cr	Withdrawn
Banks, Henry	40,557	B	10	10- 7-1784	————	3,225 acres surveyed
Banks, Henry	8,041½	B	10	10- 7-1784	————	6,500 acres surveyed
Banks, Henry	10,000	B	10	10- 7-1784	————	168 acres surveyed
Banks, Henry	4,731½	B	22	12- 1-1784	Mill Cr	Withdrawn
Banks, Henry	1,831¼	B	22	12- 1-1784	Ohio R	Withdrawn
Banks, Henry	2,900	B	22	12- 1-1784	Ohio R	Withdrawn
Banks, Linn	2,000	A	315	12-13-1783	Mil	Mil withdrawn
Banks, Linn	200	A	352	4-13-1784	Green R	
Banks, Linn	200	A	352	4-13-1784	Wm Patton	Withdrawn
Banton, Wm	500	A	59	5-16-1780	McDonalds Settlement	
Barbee, John	400	A	67	5-17-1780	Lees Cr	
Barbee, John	500	A	67	5-17-1780	Elkhorn	
Barbee, Joshua	1,500	A	309	11-25-1783	————	
Barbee, Thomas	350	A	288	8-25-1783	Pottengers Cr	
Barnee, Thomas	6,000	A	309	11-25-1783	Pottengers Cr	Surveyed
Barbee, Thomas	2,000	A	309	11-25-1783	Thomas Hord	
Barbee, Thomas	2,100	A	309	11-25-1783	Ohio R	
Barbee, Thomas	2,399	B	48	6-20-1785	————	
Barber, Thomas	5,000	A	42	5-10-1780	Panther Cr	Surveyed
Barber, Thomas	5,000	A	42	5-10-1780	Panther Cr	Surveyed
Barbour, Ambrose	3,000	A	231	12-17-1782	Panther Cr	
Barbour, James	400	A	6	12-23-1779	Muddy Cr	

Entree	Acres	Book	Page	Entry Date	Watercourse	Notes
Barbour, James	150	A	31	4–28–1780	E Fk Skeggs Cr	Mil
Barbour, James	2,000	A	60	5–16–1780	Panther Cr	Surveyed
Barbour, James	2,000	A	60	5–16–1780	Panther Cr	Surveyed
Barbour, James	2,000	A	60	5–16–1780	Panther Cr	Surveyed
Barbour, James	3,000	A	60	5–16–1780	Panther Cr	Surveyed
Barbour, James	1,000	A	62	5–16–1780	Otter Cr	....
Barbour, James	2,000	A	62	5–15–1780	Skeggs Cr	....
Barbour, James	1,000	A	108	5–29–1780	Dicks R	....
Barbour, James	300	A	167	8–17–1780	Panther Cr	....
Barbour, James	200	A	167	8–17–1780	Panther Cr	....
Barbour, James	50	A	222	12–11–1782	Ohio R	Mil
Barbour, James	50	A	223	12–12–1782	Ohio R	....
Barbour, James	1,000	A	224	12–13–1782	Ohio R	Surveyed
Barbour, James	2,850	A	238	12–21–1782	Panther Cr	Surveyed
Barbour, James	10,000	A	313	12– 8–1782	Panther Cr	....
Barbour, James	1,858½	A	362	5–29–1782	Barbour & Banks	....
Barbour, Mordicai	20,718¾	A	301	11– 3–1783	14 miles from OhioR	Withdrawn
Barbour, Mordicai	19,500	A	354	4–16–1784	—— R	Withdrawn
Barbour, Mordicai	19,500	A	358	5– 3–1784	Barbour & Banks	
Barbour, Mordicai	19,500	A	358	5– 3–1784	———	Withdrawn
Barbour, Mordicai	20,718¾	A	359	5– 7–1784	Elliott & Co	
Barbour, Mordicai	20,718¾	A	359	5– 7–1784	———.	Withdrawn
Barbour, Phillip	3,000	A	233	12–19–1782	Panther Cr	Mil
Barbour, Phillip	3,000	A	233	12–19–1782	Ohio R	Mil surveyed
Barbour, Phillip	4,000	A	246	1– 6–1783	18 Mile Cr	Surveyed
Barbour, Phillip	2,756	A	246	1– 6–1783	Otter Cr	
Barbour, Phillip	1,000	A	246	1– 6–1782	Otter Cr	Surveyed
Barbour, Phillip	4,000	A	267	3–28–1783	Ohio R	Surveyed
Barbour, Phillip	5,000	A	318	12–16–1833	Otter Cr	3,000 acres surveyed
Barbour, Phillip	3,708	A	368	6–22–1784	———.	Surveyed
Barbour, Phillip et al	50,000	A	301	11– 3–1783	Otter Cr	Surveyed
Barbour, Phillip et al	20,000	A	301	11– 3–1783	14 miles from Ohio R	Surveyed
Barbour, Phillip et al	100,000	A	301	11– 3–1783	14 miles from Ohio R	42,400 acres surveyed
Barbour, Phillip et al	60,000	A	301	11– 3–1783	14 miles from Ohio R	Surveyed
Barbour, Phillip et al	121,782	A	301	11– 3–1783	14 miles from Ohio R	Surveyed
Barbour, Phillip et al	50,000	B	11	11– 6–1784	———	Withdrawn
Barbour, Phillip et al	7,600	B	46	5–23–1785	———.	
Barbour, Richard	1,200	A	70	5–18–1780	Beach Fk	Surveyed
Barbour, Richard	1,000	A	70	5–18–1780	Br Licking	....
Barbour, Richard	500	A	166	8–16–1780	In the Barrens	Surveyed
Barbour, Richard	300	A	166	6–16–1780	In the Barrens	Surveyed
Barbour, Richard	200	A	166	8–16–1780	In the Barrens	Surveyed
Barbour, Richard	5,000	A	166	8–16–1780	Green R	3,000 acres surveyed
Barbour, Richard	1,000	A	167	8–17–1780	Panther Cr	....
Barbour, Richard	800	A	222	12–11–1782	Salt R	....
Barbour, Richard	3,000	A	227	12–14–1782	Ohio R	Surveyed
Barbour, Richard	5,000	A	301	11– 3–1783	18 Mile Island	Surveyed
Barbour, Richard	5,000	A	301	11– 3–1783	18 Mile Island	Withdrawn
Barbour, Richard	5,000	A	310	11–28–1783	Panther Cr	....
Barbour, Richard	5,000	A	310	11–28–1783	Ohio R	Withdrawn
Barbour, Richard	10,000	A	310	11–28–1783	Panther Cr	....
Barbour, Richard	20,000	A	310	11–28–1783	Ohio R	10,000 acres withdrawn
Barbour, Richard	5,000	A	323	12–26–1783	Nollin Cr	....
Barbour, Richard	1,400	A	354	4–16–1784	Pattons Cr	Surveyed
Barbour, Richard	5,000	B	11	11– 6–1784	———.	Withdrawn
Barbour, Richard	10,000	B	22	12– 3–1784	———	Withdrawn
Barbour, Richard	800	B	44	4–25–1785	Salt R	....
Barbour, Thomas	2,500	A	227	12–14–1782	Ohio R	Surveyed
Barbour, Thomas	5,000	A	227	13–12–1782	Panther Cr	....
Barbour, Thomas	2,000	A	227	12–14–1782	In the Barrens	Surveyed
Barbour, Thomas	500	A	234	12–19–1782	Ohio R	Surveyed
Barbour, Thomas	925	A	310	11–28–1783	Panther Cr	....
Barbour, Thomas	10,000	A	354	4–16–1784	Barbour & Bank	Withdrawn
Barbour, Thomas	10,000	B	22	12– 3–1784	———	Withdrawn
Barcley, Hugh	1,336	A	257	1–25–1783	Ohio R	....
Bard, David	1,000	A	203	4– 3–1781	Beech Fk	Surveyed
Bard, Richard	560	A	331	1–16–1784	Big Cr	....
Bard, Richard	1,000	A	347	3–17–1784	———	500 acres returned
Barker, John	500	A	98	5–25–1780	N Fk Licking	....
Barkley, Matthew	400	A	236	12–20–1782	Rolling Fk	Withdrawn
Barkley, Matthew	400	B	36	1–27–1785	Rolling Fk	Withdrawn
Barksdale, Daniel	500	A	88	5–13–1780	Floyds Fk	Surveyed
Barksdale, John	100	A	88	5–23–1780	Floyds Fk	Mil surveyed
Barnes, Henry	948½	A	271	3–28–1783	Brush Cr	....
Barnett, Alex	1,000	A	253	1–14–1783	Green R	....
Barnett, Alex	1,000	B	43	4–18–1785	———	Withdrawn
Barnett, Ambrose	1,486	A	147	6–24–1780	———	....

Entree	Acres	Book	Page	Entry Date	Watercourse	Notes
Barnett, Ambrose	500	A	150	6–26–1780	M Fk Ky R	
Barnett, Ambrose	986	A	150	6–26–1780	M Fk Ky R	
Barnett, Ambrose	1,075	A	161	7–17–1780	Eagle Cr	
Barnett, James	1,000	A	147	6–24–1780	Goose Cr	
Barnett, James	300	A	156	6–30–1780	Robinson Cr	Withdrawn
Barnett, James	1,000	A	161	7–17–1780	Eagle Cr	
Barnett, James	987	A	162	7–17–1780	Eagle Cr	
Barnett, James	300	A	221	11– 9–1782	———	Withdrawn
Barnett, James	300	A	224	12–13–1782	Green R	
Barnett, James	1,336	A	252	1–14–1783	Sinking Cr	Withdrawn
Barnett, James	461	A	253	1–14–1783	Caseys Cr	
Barnett, James	600	A	253	1–14–1783	Casey Cr	
Barnett, James	600	A	253	1–14–1783	Casey Cr	
Barnett, James	1,278	A	262	2–12–1783	Rowling Fk	
Barnett, James	1,278	A	262	2–13–1783	Rowling Fk	
Barnett, James	375	A	287	8–12–1783	Rough Cr	
Barnett, James	200	A	370	7– 8–1784	Sinking Cr	
Barnett, James	1,661	B	40	2–19–1785	———	
Barnett, James	1,336	B	43	4–18–1785	Sinking Cr	
Barnett, Jas & John	2,500	A	319	12–17–1783	Long Falls Co	
Barnett, Joseph	100	A	205	4– 7–1781	James Rogers Premption	
Barnett, Joseph	325	A	225	12–13–1782	Rowling Fk	
Barnett, Joseph	150	A	225	12–13–1782	N Fk Prices Cr	
Barnett, Joseph	500	A	227	12–14–1782	Little Cain Cr	
Barnett, Joseph	1,000	A	230	12–17–1782	Boiling Spring Cr	Withdrawn
Barnett, Joseph	500	A	234	12–19–1782	Two Island Cr	Withdrawn
Barnett, Joseph	500	A	234	12–19–1782	Two Island Cr	Withdrawn
Barnett, Joseph	781	A	234	12–19–1782		Withdrawn
Barnett, Joseph	500	A	234	12–19–1782	Two Island Cr	Withdrawn
Barnett, Joseph	1,000	A	234	12–19–1782	Two Island Cr	Withdrawn
Barnett, Joseph	1,000	A	234	12–19–1782	Ohio R	Withdrawn
Barnett, Joseph	500	A	235	12–19–1782	Rolling Fk	
Barnett, Joseph	600	A	235	12–19–1782	M Fk Brush Cr	Surveyed
Barnett, Joseph	200	A	235	12–19–1782	Rowling Fk	
Barnett, Joseph	200	A	235	12–19–1782	Prices Cr	
Barnett, Joseph	500	A	235	12–19–1782		
Barnett, Joseph	500	A	235	12–19–1782	Two Island Cr	Withdrawn
Barnett, Joseph	200	A	239	12–23–1782	Rolling Fk	
Barnett, Joseph	200	A	239	12–23–1782	Pottengers Cr	Withdrawn
Barnett, Joseph	618	A	249	1– 8–1783	Rowling Fk	Withdrawn
Barnett, Joseph	1,000	A	249	1– 8–1783	Rowling Fk	Withdrawn
Barnett, Joseph	1,000	A	249	1– 8–1783	Ohio R	Withdrawn
Barnett, Joseph	643½	A	249	1– 8–1783	Rough Cr	
Barnett, Joseph	500	A	249	1– 8–1783	Rock Cr	
Barnett, Joseph	2,082	A	249	1– 8–1783	Boiling Spring Cr	Withdrawn
Barnett, Joseph	400	A	250	1– 8–1783	Rolling Fk	
Barnett, Joseph	300	A	255	1–20–1783	Rowling Fk	
Barnett, Joseph	200	A	255	1–20–1783	Cedar Cr	
Barnett, Joseph	400	A	262	2–12–1783	Little Barren	
Barnett, Joseph	1,000	A	262	2–12–1783	Rowling Fk	
Barnett, Joseph	1,000	A	262	2–12–1783	Pottengers Cr	
Barnett, Joseph	37,000	A	280	6–20–1783	Rough Cr	
Barnett, Joseph	3,000	A	280	6–20–1783	Rough Cr	
Barnett, Joseph	1,618	A	281	6–20–1783	Rolling Fk	Withdrawn
Barnett, Joseph	1,618	A	281	6–20–1783	Rolling Fk	Withdrawn
Barnett, Joseph	500	A	285	8– 7–1783	Two Island Cr	Withdrawn
Barnett, Joseph	1,000	A	285	8– 7–1783	Hardens Cr	
Barnett, Joseph	1,000	A	286	8–12–1783	Indian Camp Cr	
Barnett, Joseph	1,500	A	286	8–12–1783	Indian Camp Cr	Withdrawn
Barnett, Joseph	2,281	A	286	8–12–1783	Rough Cr	
Barnett, Joseph	3,082	A	286	8–12–1783	Rough Cr	
Barnett, Joseph	3,700	A	286	8–12–1783	Rough Cr	
Barnett, Joseph	6,382	A	286	8–12–1783	Two Island Cr	Withdrawn
Barnett, Joseph	1,000	A	286	8–12–1783	Boiling Spring Cr	Withdrawn
Barnett, Joseph	559½	A	292	10– 3–1783	Green R	
Barnett, Joseph	750	A	292	10– 3–1783	Rolling Fk	
Barnett, Joseph	500	A	292	10– 3–1783	Mill Cr	
Barnett, Joseph	500	A	307	11–20–1783		
Barnett, Joseph	1,500	A	320	12–17–1783	Indian Camp Cr	Surveyed
Barnett, Joseph	100	A	320	12–17–1783	Rolling Fk	
Barnett, Joseph	100	A	320	12–17–1783	Rolling Fk	
Barnett, Joseph	1,000	A	329	1–14–1784	Long Falls Cr	
Barnett, Joseph	1,500	A	329	1–13–1784	Rough Cr	
Barnett, Joseph	500	A	330	1–15–1784	Cedar Cr	
Barnett, Joseph	2,082	A	339	2–14–1784	———	
Barnett, Joseph	7,000	A	343	3– 3–1784	———	
Barnett, Joseph	1,500	A	362	5–26–1784	———	
Barnett, Joseph	1,800	A	365	6–12–1784	———	Withdrawn
Barnett, Joseph	1,000	A	365	6–12–1784	———	
Barnett, Joseph	1,000	A	365	6–12–1784	Lewis Cr	
Barnett, Joseph	1,000	A	365	6–12–1784	Green R	Withdrawn

Entree	Acres	Book	Page	Entry Date	Watercourse	Notes
Barnett, Joseph	1,000	A	365	6–12–1784	Green R	Withdrawn
Barnett, Joseph	1,000	A	365	6–12–1784	Matthew Waltons	....
Barnett, Joseph	400	A	374	7–28–1784	Panthers Fk	Withdrawn
Barnett, Joseph	2,600	A	374	7–28–1784	Panther&Hardens Cr	Withdrawn
Barnett, Joseph	3,000	A	374	7–28–1784	Rough Cr	Withdrawn
Barnett, Joseph	5,800	B	5	9–11–1784	——	....
Barnett, Joseph	1,000	B	6	9–13–1784	——	....
Barnett, Joseph	3,600	B	6	9–13–1784	Rough Cr	....
Barnett, Joseph	170	B	6	9–13–1784	Rolling Fk	....
Barnett, Joseph	300	B	6	9–13–1784	Prices Cr	....
Barnett, Joseph	200	B	6	9–13–1784	Rolling Fk	....
Barnett, Joseph	230	B	6	9–13–1784	J Rogers Premption	....
Barnett, Joseph	100	B	6	9–13–1784	——	....
Barnett, Joseph	1,800	B	7	9–22–1784	Rough Cr	....
Barnett, Joseph	6,000	B	7	9–22–1784	Rough Cr	....
Barnett, Joseph	400	B	7	9–22–1784	Ash Spring	Withdrawn
Barnett, Joseph	2,600	B	7	9–22–1784	Prathers & Hardens Cr	Withdrawn
Barnett, Joseph	1,800	B	7	9–22–1784	——	Withdrawn
Barnett, Joseph	1,000	B	36	1–27–1785	——	Withdrawn
Barnett, Joseph	6,000	B	36	1–27–1785	Muddy Fk	....
Barnett,¦Joseph	3,000	B	36	1–27–1785	Rough Cr	....
Barnett, Joseph	1,500	B	36	1–27–1785	Muddy Cr	....
Barnett, Joseph	1,500	B	36	1–27–1785	Muddy Cr	....
Barnett, Wm	1,000	A	252	1–14–1783	Green R	Withdrawn
Barnett, Wm	1,000	B	43	4–18–1785	Green R	....
Barnett, Wm	500	B	49	6–17–1785	——	....
Barr, John	3,500	A	251	1– 9–1783	Pittmans Cr	....
Barr, John	1,174	A	352	4–13–1784	Big & Little Barren Rs	....
Barrackman, Jacob	400	A	190	3–15–1781	Coxes Cr & Salt R	....
Barrackman, John	300	A	126	6– 7–1780	S Fk Salt R	Withdrawn
Barrackman, John	400	A	190	3–15–1781	Salt R	....
Barrackman, John	200	A	219	8–24–1781	Watkins Run	Surveyed
Barrackman, John	200	A	219	8–24–1781	Watkins Run	Surveyed
Barrackman, John	400	A	307	11–20–1783	——	....
Barret, Robert	400	A	119	6– 1–1780	Hanging Fk	....
Barrett, Alex	1,000	A	252	1–14–1783	Sinking Cr	Withdrawn
Barrett, Chas	200	A	20	4–18–1780	Clear Cr	Mil
Barrett, John et al	1,000	A	96	5–24–1780	——	Surveyed
Barrett, Fisher	400	A	12	2– 7–1780	Salt R	....
Barrett, Lemuel	500	A	362	6– 1–1784	Ohio R	....
Barrett, Lemuel	500	A	363	6– 2–1784	Ohio R	....
Barrett, Wm	500	A	135	6–17–1780	Nolin Cr	....
Bartlett, Anthony	2,000	B	12	11–10–1784	Beargrass Cr	Surveyed
Bartlett, Anthony	500	B	13	11–10–1784	Glenns Cr	....
Bartlett, Anthony	1,000	B	13	11–10–1784	Brashears Cr	....
Bartlett, Anthony	1,500	B	46	5–23–1785	——	....
Bartlett, Wm	750	A	75	5–19–1780	Floyds Fk	Mil surveyed
Bartley, Elisha	400	A	3	11–15–1779	Elkhorn	....
Barton, David	400	A	7	1–10–1780	Licking Cr	....
Barton, David	400	A	7	1–10–1780	Silver Cr	....
Barton, Josh	490	A	7	1–10–1780	Four Mile Run	....
Barton, Roger	928	A	282	7– 1–1783	Nole Linn Cr	....
Barton, Roger	700	A	285	8– 7–1783	Caney Cr	Withdrawn
Barton, Roger	800	A	285	8– 7–1783	Caney Cr	Withdrawn
Barton, Roger	800	A	288	9– 8–1783	Rough Cr	Withdrawn
Barton, Roger	700	A	292	10– 3–1783	Nole Linn Cr	Surveyed
Barton, Roger	700	A	292	10– 3–1783	Nolin Cr	Withdrawn
Barton, Roger	428	A	307	11–20–1783	——	....
Barton, Roger	700	A	307	11–20–1783	——	....
Barton, Roger	1,500	A	343	3– 3–1784	Green R	Withdrawn
Barton, Roger	1,500	B	27	12–18–1784	——	Withdrawn
Barton, Saml	400	A	8	1–15–1780	Silver Cr	....
Barton, Thomas	400	A	3	11–11–1779	Otter Cr	....
Barton, Thomas	800	A	154	6–28–1780	Otter Cr	....
Barton, Thomas	510	A	360	5–14–1784	——	Entered in Lincoln
Battale, Hay	3,000	A	346	3–12–1784	Ashes Cr	Amended
Batterton, Henry	500	A	57	5–15–1781	Dicks R	....
Baughman, Henry	1,000	A	36	4–29–1780	Dicks R	....
Bayles, Barney	200	A	116	5–31–1780	Whitleys Cr	....
Beal, Samuel	7,000	A	46	5–11–1780	Ohio R	1,000 withdrawn
Beal, Samuel	3,500	A	46	5–11–1780	Ohio & Wabash	2,500 withdrawn
Beal, Samuel	19,346	A	46	5–11–1780	Limestone Cr	Withdrawn
Beal, Samuel	5,000	A	131	6–13–1780	Ohio R	Withdrawn
Beal, Samuel	2,000	A	131	6–13–1780	Ohio R	Withdrawn
Beal, Samuel	2,000	A	164	8–11–1780	Ohio R	Withdrawn
Beal, Samuel	20	A	187	3–15–1781	Sullivans Trace	Withdrawn
Beal, Samuel	6,000	A	187	3–15–1781	S Fk Beargrass Cr	....

Entree	Acres	Book	Page	Entry Date	Watercourse	Notes
Beal, Samuel	8,000	A	187	3-15-1781	Green R	
Beal, Samuel	6,000	A	187	3-15-1781	Green R	Withdrawn
Beal, Samuel	2,000	A	188	3-15-1781	Ohio R	
Beal, Samuel	5,000	A	226	12-14-1782	Kentucky R	Surveyed
Beal, Samuel	346	A	259	1-31-1783	Hardens Cr	
Beal, Samuel	10,000	A	272	4- 3-1783	Barrens Green R	
Beal, Samuel	1,000	A	277	4-14-1783	Ohio R	
Beal, Samuel	1,000	B	40	2- 8-1785	————	100 Surveyed
Beall, Brooke	2,600	A	48	5-12-1780	Sinking Cr	Surveyed
Beall, Brooke	400	A	48	5-12-1780	Floyds Fk	
Beall, Brooke	200	A	48	5-12-1780	Floyds Fk	Surveyed
Beall, Brooke	800	A	48	5-12-1780	Green R	Surveyed
Beall, Charles	500	A	49	5-12-1780	Glens Road	
Beall, Charles	500	A	49	5-12-1780	Elkhorn	
Beall, Charles	150	A	51	5-13-1780	Elkhorn	
Beall, Charles	250	A	51	5-13-1780	Elkhorn	
Beall, Nathan	500	A	213	6-30-1781	Rowling Fk	Surveyed
Beall, Samuel	2,000	A	19	4-13-1780	Brashears Cr	Mil surveyed
Beall, Samuel	2,450	A	23	4-24-1780	Ohio R	
Beall, Samuel et al	1,400	B	29	12-30-1784	Clear Cr	
Beall, Samuel	2,000	A	32	4-29-1780	Ohio R	Withdrawn
Beall, Samuel	4,000	A	32	4-29-1780	Ohio R	Withdrawn
Beall, Samuel	4,000	A	32	4-29-1780	Ohio R	Withdrawn
Beall, Samuel	6,000	A	32	4-28-1780	Bullitts Lick	Mil Withdrawn
Beall, Samuel	2,000	A	32	4-28-1780	Ohio R	Mil withdrawn
Beall, Samuel	1,000	A	32	4-29-1780	Boone Lick Cr	
Beall, Samuel	400	A	32	4-29-1780	Kentucky R	Mil
Beall, Samuel	600	A	32	4-28-1780	Drenning Lick	
Beall, Samuel	1,000	A	32	4-29-1780	Ohio R	Mil
Beall, Samuel	19,346	A	48	5-12-1780	Limestone Cr	Withdrawn
Beall, Samuel	10,000	A	60	5-16-1780	Bet Green & Ohio	
Beall, Samuel	1,000	A	62	5-16-1780	Wm Byrds	Surveyed
Beall, Samuel	7,000	A	64	5-17-1780	Green R	Withdrawn
Beall, Samuel	2,000	A	64	5-17-1780	Little Ky R	Surveyed
Beall, Samuel	800	A	121	6- 2-1780	Silver Cr	
Beall, Samuel	2,000	A	165	8-11-1780	Green R	Mil withdrawn
Beall, Samuel	4,000	A	187	3-15-1781	Goose Cr	Surveyed
Beall, Samuel	19,000	A	188	3-15-1781	Hardens Cr	
Beall, Samuel	1,000	A	189	3-15-1781	Floyds Fk & Bullskin	Surveyed
Beall, Samuel	1,000	A	189	3-15-1781	18 Mile Cr	Surveyed
Beall, Samuel	2,000	A	189	3-15-1781	Bullskin Cr	
Beall, Samuel	500	A	189	3-15-1781	Ashleys	Withdrawn
Beall, Samuel	200	A	189	3-15-1781	Floyds Fk	
Beall, Samuel	300	A	189	3-15-1781	Floyds Fk	
Beall, Samuel	500	A	189	3-15-1781	Floyds Fk	
Beall, Samuel	2,000	A	189	3-15-1781	Bullskin Cr	Surveyed
Beall, Samuel	2,000	A	189	3-15-1781	Bullskin Cr	
Beall, Samuel	2,000	A	189	3-15-1781	Floyds & Bullskin	
Beall, Samuel	2,000	A	189	3-15-1781	Floyds & Bullskin	Surveyed
Beall, Samuel	2,000	A	189	3-15-1781	Floyds & Bullskin	Surveyed
Beall, Samuel	500	A	189	3-15-1781	Bullskin	
Beall, Samuel	3,000	A	189	3-15-1781	Ohio R	1,100 acres surveyed
Beall, Samuel	2,000	A	202	4- 2-1781	Green R	
Beall, Samuel	5,000	A	206	4-12-1781	Ohio R	
Beall, Samuel	3,000	A	206	4-12-1781	Ohio R	
Beall, Samuel	3,000	A	206	4-12-1781	Ohio R	
Beall, Samuel	3,000	A	206	4-12-1781	Green R	Withdrawn
Beall, Samuel	2,000	A	206	4-12-1781	Winstons	Withdrawn
Beall, Samuel	2,000	A	206	4-12-1781	Winstons	Withdrawn
Beall, Samuel	2,000	A	206	4-12-1781	Yellow Banks	Withdrawn
Beall, Samuel	5,000	A	206	4-12-1781	Ohio R	
Beall, Samuel	6,000	A	206	4-12-1781	Salt R	
Beall, Samuel	2,000	A	206	4-12-1781	Yellow Banks	
Beall, Samuel	4,000	A	206	4-12-1781	Ohio R	Withdrawn
Beall, Samuel	450	A	206	4-12-1781	Ohio R	
Beall, Samuel	2,000	A	206	4-12-1781	Ohio & Green Rs	
Beall, Samuel	1,500	A	206	4-12-1781	Wobache Island	
Beall, Samuel	500	A	206	4-12-1781	Ashbys Survey	
Beall, Samuel	500	A	207	4-14-1781	————	
Beall, Samuel	2,000	A	221	11- 9-1782	Yellow Cr	
Beall, Samuel	3,000	A	221	11- 9-1782	Green R	Withdrawn
Beall, Samuel	2,000	A	224	12-13-1782	Kentucky R	Surveyed
Beall, Samuel	2,000	A	224	12-13-1782	Kentucky R	
Beall, Samuel	5,000	A	224	12-13-1782	Kentucky R	Surveyed
Beall, Samuel	2,000	A	262	2-14-1783	Fish Pool	Withdrawn
Beall, Samuel	6,000	A	262	2-14-1783	Beargrass Cr	

Entree	Acres	Book	Page	Entry Date	Watercourse	Notes
Beall, Samuel	2,000	A	274	4- 9-1783	Goose Cr	Withdrawn
Beall, Samuel	2,000	A	274	4- 9-1783	Fishpool & Fern Cr.	....
Beall, Samuel	188	A	278	4-14-1783	————	....
Beall, Samuel	1,346	B	40	2- 8-1785	————	1,000 acres surveyed
Beall, Walter	1,000	A	48	5-12-1780	Green R	Surveyed
Beall, Walter	1,000	A	48	5-12-1780	Green R	Surveyed
Beall, Walter	2,000	A	106	5-27-1780	Green R	Surveyed
Beall, Walter	1,000	A	106	5-27-1780	Green R	Surveyed
Beall, Walter	2,000	A	106	5-27-1780	Green R	Surveyed
Beall, Walter	1,000	A	119	6- 1-1780	Pottengers Cr	....
Beall, Walter	10,000	A	195	3-16-1781	Panther Cr	Surveyed
Bealla, Brook	400	A	334	1-21-1784	————	....
Bealle, Brooke	200	B	2	8-26-1784	————	Surveyed
Beard, James	300	A	190	3-15-1781	Stewarts Cr	....
Beard, Richard	325	A	136	6-19-1780	Stewart Cr	Surveyed
Beard, Richard	50	A	136	6-19-1780	Buffaloe Cr	Surveyed
Beard, Richard	200	A	136	6-19-1780	Buffaloe Cr	Surveyed
Beard, Richard	2,000	A	136	6-19-1780	Kentucky R	1,000 acres withdrawn
Beard, Richard	500	A	203	4- 3-1781	Buffaloe Cr	....
Beard, Richard	500	A	203	4- 3-1781	W Fk Withers Run.	....
Beard, Richard	1,000	A	212	6-23-1781	Drennons Cr	Warrant sent Lincoln
Beard, Richard	1,000	A	212	6-23-1781	Ky R	Warrant sent Lincoln
Beard, Richard	25	B	30	12-27-1784	Buffaloe Cr	....
Beard, Wm	200	A	136	6-19-1780	Salt R	....
Beard, Wm	1,000	A	212	6-23-1781	Buffaloe Cr	....
Bearonrs, James	400	A	121	6- 2-1780	Sceggs Cr	....
Beasley, John	400	A	8	1-17-1780	Coopers Cr	....
Beasley, Major	400	A	7	1-10-1780	Stewarts Sp	....
Beasley, Major	1,000	A	224	12-22-1782	Falls Ohio R	....
Beason, John	400	A	42	5-10-1780	Long Lick Run	....
Beatty, James	2,000	A	94	5-24-1780	Stoners Fk	....
Beaty, James	400	A	152	6-26-1780	Clear Cr	....
Beckley, Wm	400	A	10	2- 3-1780	Sinking Fk	....
Bedenger, Mich	200	A	134	6-15-1780	Ky R	....
Bedford, Thomas	1,223½	A	308	11-22-1783	Beech Fk	....
Bedinger, Michael	400	A	36	4-29-1780	Muddy Cr	....
Bell, Charles	1,000	A	83	5-22-1780	S Fk Elkhorn	....
Bell, Charles	2,000	A	132	6-15-1780	N Fk Licking	....
Bell, Charles	2,000	A	132	6-15-1780	N Fk Licking	....
Bell, David	400	A	4	11-15-1797	Hickmans Cr	....
Bell, David	1,000	A	38	4-29-1780	Hickmans Cr	....
Bell, Florence	500	A	135	6-17-1780	Silver Cr	....
Bell, James	50	A	205	4- 6-1781	Beech Fk	....
Bell, James	1,037	A	237	12-21-1782	Ashes Cr	....
Bell, John	250	A	92	5-24-1780	Ky R	....
Bell, John	400	A	138	6-20-1780	Plumb Cr	Withdrawn
Bell, John	400	A	138	6-20-1780	Salt R	Withdrawn
Bell, John	800	A	194	3-16-1781	Coxes Cr & Trace	Surveyed
Bell, John	800	A	194	3-16-1781	Plumb Cr	....
Bell, John	1,015½	A	258	1-27-1783	Beech Fk	Withdrawn
Bell, John	1,015½	A	348	3-27-1784	Salt R	....
Bell, John	1,015½	A	348	3-27-1784	Beech Fk	Withdrawn
Bell, Joseph	500	A	125	6- 5-1780	Ky R	....
Bell, Joseph	500	A	125	6- 5-1780	Hickman Cr	....
Bell, Joseph	1,000	A	162	7-18-1780	Clay Lick	....
Bell, Joseph	1,000	A	162	7-18-1780	Tucahoe Cr	....
Bell, Joseph	1,000	A	162	7-18-1780	Tucahoe Cr	....
Bell, Joseph	973	A	258	1-27-1783	Mid Fk Beech Fk	....
Bell, Samuel	400	A	13	2- 9-1780	Kennedys Run	Surveyed
Bell, Samuel	613	B	29	12-20-1784	Clear Cr	Surveyed
Bell, Samuel	187	B	29	12-20-1784	Mid Fk Beech Fk	....
Bell, Samuel	1,000	A	67	5-17-1780	Salt R	....
Bell, Samuel	1,000	A	132	6-15-1780	Pittmans Cr	....
Bell, Samuel	993½	A	258	1-27-1783	Mid Fk Beech Fk	....
Bell, Samuel	260½	A	326	12-31-1783	Brashears Cr	200 acres withdrawn
Bell, Samuel	1,000	A	326	12-31-1783	Brashears Cr	Surveyed
Bell, Samuel	1,260½	A	338	2-12-1784	————	....
Bell, Samuel	500	A	348	3-27-1784	Salt R	....
Bell, Samuel	600	B	46	5-23-1785	Battle Cr	Surveyed
Bell, Samuel et al	3,000	B	51	11- 9-1785	————	1,240 acres surveyed
Bell, Thomas	800	A	190	3-15-1781	W Fk Coxes Cr	....
Bell, Thomas	3,000	A	278	4-14-1783	Floyds Fk	....
Bell, Thomas	800	A	356	4-28-1784	Cox Cr	Amended
Bell, Wm	75,000	A	314	12- 9-1783	Barbour & Banks	Surveyed
Bell, Wm	5,000	B	10	10- 7-1784	————	1,567 acres surveyed

Entree	Acres	Book	Page	Entry Date	Watercourse	Notes
Bellan, Robert	400	A	15	2-22-1780	Ky R	
Belmain, Alex	1,000	A	91	5-24-1780	Brashears Cr	Surveyed
Belt, Thomas	1,000	A	43	5-11-1780	Stoners Fk	
Bennett, John	600	A	241	12-25-1782	W Fk Caney Cr	Surveyed
Bennett, John	150	A	287	8-18-1783	Nolinn Cr	Withdrawn
Bennett, Wm	700	A	287	8-12-1783	Rough Cr	
Bennet, Joseph	300	A	87	5-23-1780	Hunting	
Bennett, Fisher	50	A	30	4-28-1780	Ky R	Mil
Bennett, Fisher	400	A	117	5-31-1780	Licking	
Bennett, Fisher	500	A	122	6- 2-1780	Ohio R	
Bennett, Wm	400	A	87	5-23-1780	Hunting Cr	
Bennett, Wm	400	A	139	6-21-1780	S Fk Elkhorn	
Bennitt, John	150	A	249	1- 8-1783	Nole Linn Cr	Surveyed
Bennitt, John	400	B	40	2-10-1785	Coxes Cr	
Benton, Jesse	400	A	14	2-19-1780	Silver Cr	
Benton, Jessy	1,000	A	115	5-30-1780	Silver Cr	
Berdine, Jacob	400	A	161	7- 8-1780	Licking	
Berkley, Wm	300	A	38	4-29-1780	Lawrence Cr	
Berry, Aaron	131½	A	336	2- 3-1784	Beech Fk	
Berry, Benj	400	A	130	6-12-1780	Beech Fk	
Berry, Benj	1,000	A	145	6-23-1780	Lulbergrud Cr	
Berry, Charles	1,000	A	93	5-24-1780	Simpsons Cr	
Berry, James	400	A	115	5-30-1780	Stoners Fk	
Berry, Richard	600	A	89	5-23-1780	Beech Fk	Surveyed
Berry, Thomas	750	A	154	6-28-1780	S & N Fk Licking	
Best, Humphrey	400	A	15	2-21-1780	Paint Lick Cr	
Best, Humphrey	150	A	173	9-23-1780	Paint Lick Cr	
Best, Humphrey	250	A	173	9-23-1780	Paint Lick Cr	
Bethell, Wm	400	A	173	9-23-1780	Beech Fk	Withdrawn
Bethell, Wm	400	A	205	4- 7-1781	Cedar Cr	
Bethell, Wm	400	A	207	4-14-1781	Rowling Fk	
Bibbs, Ben	1,150	A	157	7- 3-1780	Red R	
Biggs, John	300	A	266	2-25-1783	Brashears Cr	
Billie, Peter	400	A	126	6- 7-1780	Pond Cr	Surveyed
Billie, Peter	400	A	126	6- 7-1780	Brashears Cr	Surveyed
Bird, Abraham	1,993	A	376	8- 9-1784	Ohio R	
Birt, Moses	850	A	95	5-24-1780	Col Henderson	
Black, James	1,000	A	27	4-26-1780	Licking	Mil
Black, James	300	A	179	10-17-1780	Brush Cr	Surveyed
Black, James	300	A	235	12-20-1782	Little Barren	Withdrawn
Black, James	300	A	262	2-12-1783	Joseph Black	Withdrawn
Black, James	300	A	262	2-12-1783	Green R	
Black, Joseph	600	A	225	12-13-1782	Green R	
Black, Samuel	900	A	93	5-24-1780	Pleasant Run	Withdrawn
Black, Thos	400	A	13	2- 9-1780	Hanging Fk	
Black, Wm	1,000	A	118	6- 1-1781	Town Fk	
Black, Wm	50	A	142	6-22-1780	Rowling Fk	Mil
Blackford, Joseph	400	A	16	2-24-1780	N Fk Clear Cr	
Blackford, Joseph	400	A	148	6-24-1780	Ky R	
Blackford, Joseph	400	A	148	6-24-1780	N Fk Glenns Cr	
Blades, Wm et al	1,255	A	364	6- 7-1784	Rolling Fk	
Blain, Alex	1,000	A	342	2-27-1784	Robinsons Cr	
Blair, Alex	1,000	A	314	12-12-1783	Caseys Cr	
Blair, Alex	5,291	A	364	6- 7-1784	Green R	
Blair, Alex	3,000	A	374	7-28-1784	Caseys Cr	
Bland, John	1,500	A	128	6- 8-1780	Beards Cr	450 acres surveyed
Bland, John	550	A	210	5-29-1781	Simpsons Cr	Surveyed
Bland, John	1,500	A	373	7-24-1784	———	450 acres surveyed
Bland, Thos Jr	6,050	A	10	2- 2-1780	Ohio Yellow Banks	Mil 1,763
Bland, Thos Jr	400	A	13	2-19-1780	Ohio below falls	
Blaire, Alex	400	A	54	5-15-1780	Mid Fk Licking	
Blane, Alex	1,200	A	55	5-15-1780	Mid Fk Licking	
Blane, James	2,000	A	55	5-15-1780	Fk Licking	
Blankenbecker, Jacob	1,876	A	240	12-24-1782	Panther Cr	
Blankenbecker, Jacob	900	A	240	12-23-1782	Pleasant Run	
Blanton, Joshua	457½	A	303	11-11-1783	Floyds Fk	
Blanton, Thomas	300	A	85	5-22-1780	Glens Cr	Mil
Blaydes, Wm et al	1,255	B	3	8-26-1784	Rolling Fk	Amended
Bledsoe, Aaron	300	A	114	5-30-1780	Howards Cr	
Bledsoe, Anthony	400	A	15	2-21-1780	N Fk Elkhorn	
Bledsoe, Anthony	400	A	15	2-21-1780	Silver Cr	Surveyed
Bledsoe, Anthony	400	A	15	2-21-1780	S Br Tates Cr	Surveyed
Bledsoe, Anthony	2,000	A	33	4-29-1780	Bledsoe settlement	Surveyed
Bledsoe, Anthony	1,000	A	43	5-11-1780	Blue Licks	
Bledsoe, Anthony	1,000	A	46	5-11-1780	Ky R	
Bledsoe, John	500	A	84	5-22-1780	N Fk Licking	
Bledsoe, John	250	A	247	1- 7-1782	Green R	
Bledsoe, John	1,000	A	247	1- 7-1783	Green R	
Bledsoe, Joseph	1,300	A	223	12-12-1782	Green R	
Bledsoe, Wm M	4,000	A	320	12-17-1783	Blackford Cr	Surveyed

Entree	Acres	Book	Page	Entry Date	Watercourse	Notes
Bloxom, Richard	1,000	A	156	6–30–1780	Thomas Logwood	
Blunt, Francis	500	A	184	10–30–1780	Nolin Cr	
Boffman, Christinah	1,000	A	99	5–25–1780	Boons Cr	
Boggs, James	400	A	129	6– 9–1780	Stoners Fk	100 acres withdrawn
Boggs, James	100	A	182	10–26–1780	Boggs Fk	
Boggs, Robert	400	A	24	4–25–1780	Boones Cr	Surveyed
Boggs, Robert	100	A	24	4–25–1780	Br Ky R	
Bohannon, George	500	A	121	6– 2–1780	Salt R	300 acres surveyed
Bohannon, Wm	400	A	121	6– 2–1780	Paint Lick Cr	Surveyed
Boldock, Levi	783½	A	352	4–13–1784	Green R	
Boldock, Levi	250	A	352	4–13–1784	Caseys Cr	
Bollin, Garet	1,000	A	108	5–29–1780	N Fk Licking	
Bolling, Garrett	1,000	A	147	6–24–1780	Green R	
Bolling, Garret	1,200	A	147	6–24–1780	Yellow Cr	
Bolling, Henry	1,000	A	147	6–24–1780	Yellow Cr	
Bolling, Wm	400	A	160	7– 6–1780	Yellow Cr	
Bougher, Daniel	400	A	134	6–16–1780	Rockcastle	
Boutain, Jacob	600	A	147	6–24–1780	N Fk Licking	
Bouter, Abraham	400	A	128	6– 8–1780	Hingstons Fk	
Bonter, Henry	400	A	128	6– 8–1780	Licking Cr	
Bonter, Samuel	400	A	128	6– 8–1780	Hingstons Fk	
Boone, Charles	50	A	202	4– 2–1781	Rowling Fk	
Boone, Charles	500	A	208	4–30–1781	Salt R	456 acres surveyed
Boone, Charles	268	A	208	4–19–1781	————	Withdrawn
Boone, Charles	268	A	208	4–19–1781	Floyds Fk	Withdrawn
Boone, Charles	749	A	211	6– 9–1780	Cedar Cr	
Boone, Charles	1,050	A	225	12–13–1782	Cartrights Cr	
Boone, Daniel	400	A	8	1–17–1780	Licking Cr	
Boone, Daniel	1,000	A	39	5– 9–1780	N Fk Elkhorn	
Boone, Daniel	500	A	174	10– 4–1780	Boons Cr	Mil
Boone, Daniel et al	500	A	158	7– 3–1780	Jouetts Cr	Mil
Boone, Enoch M	1,000	A	240	12–24–1782	Ky R	
Boone, George	500	A	57	5–15–1780	Calloway Cr	
Boone, George	462	A	154	6–28–1780	Ky R	
Boone, Hezekial	1,200	A	259	2– 3–1783	Drennons Lick	
Boone, Isaiah	1,000	A	240	12 24–1782	Jephthas Cr	
Boone, Israel	400	A	8	1–17–1780	Boones Cr	
Boone, Israel	200	A	108	5–29–1780	Salt R	
Boone, Moses	1,000	A	240	12–24–1782	Ky R	
Boone, Sarah	250	A	108	5–29–1780	Porters Premption	
Boone, Sarah	1,000	A	240	12–24–1782	Salt R	
Boone, Sarah	50	A	302	11– 7–1783	Clear Cr & Fox Run	
Boone, Sarah	50	B	27	12–16–1784	————	
Boone, Squire	400	A	5	12– 7–1779	Brashear Cr	
Boone, Squire	400	A	5	12– 7–1779	Silver Cr	
Boone, Squire	200	A	38	5– 9–1780	Gists Fk	
Boone, Squire	500	A	38	5– 9–1780	Little Benson Cr	
Boone, Squire	400	A	107	5–29–1780	Ohio R	
Boone, Squire	78	A	213	7– 2–1781	Gess Cr	
Boone, Squire	200	A	213	7– 2–1781	Beargrass Cr	Surveyed
Boone, Squire	122	A	213	7– 2–1781	Clear Cr	Surveyed
Boone, Squire	12,335	A	240	12–24–1782	Drennons Lick Cr	5,945 acres surveyed
Boone, Squire	308	A	248	1– 7–1783	Gesses Cr	
Boone, Squire	46	A	248	1– 7–1783	Nicholas Meriwether	Surveyed
Boone, Squire	446	A	248	1– 7–1783	Bensons Cr	
Boone, Squire	12,335	A	251	1–10–1783	Drennons Lick Cr	
Boone, Squire	2,000	A	260	2– 4–1783	Drennons Lick	Surveyed
Boone, Squire	1,000	A	260	2– 3–1783	Drennons Lick	Withdrawn
Boone, Squire	1,000	A	260	2– 3–1783	Salt R	
Boone, Squire	2,000	A	260	2– 3–1783	Coxes Cr	
Boone, Squire	450	A	302	11– 7–1783	Clear Cr	Surveyed
Boone, Squire	1,000	B	326	12–16–1784	————	400 acres surveyed
Boone, Squire	1,000	B	27	12–17–1784	Drennins Lick	Surveyed
Boone, Squire	20,000	B	30	12–29–1784		2,000 acres surveyed
Boone, Squire	1,000	B	44	5–14–1785	————	Withdrawn
Boone, Squire	1,000	B	45	5–14–1785	Salt R	
Boone, Thos	400	A	8	1–17–1780	Licking Cr	
Borden, Joseph	2,000	A	156	6–30–1780	Green R	
Bottaile, Hay	3,000	A	235	12–19–1782	Salt R	
Bottaile, Hay	1,500	A	235	12–19–1782	Ashes Cr	
Bottom, John	750	A	225	12–13–1782	Muddy Cr	
Boughman, Henry	400	A	3	11–11–1779	Dicks R	
Boughman, Henry	400	A	13	2– 9–1780	Dicks R	Entered before
Boughman, Jacob	50	A	29	4–27–1780	Paint Lick	Mil
Boulie, Ritchie	465	A	84	5–22–1780	S Fk Licking	

Entree	Acres	Book	Page	Entry Date	Watercourse	Notes
Boulware, Wm.	332	A	101	5-26-1780	Otter Cr	
Bowder, James	200	A	23	4-24-1780	Glens Cr	Mil
Bowder, James	50	A	31	4-28-1780	Elkhorn	Mil
Bowdry, James	500	A	66	5-17-1780	Greens Cr	
Bowlare, Wm.	333	A	297	10-20-1783	Panther & Green	
Bowler, Ben	950	A	28	4-27-1780	Elkhorn Cr	Mil
Bowler, Wm	518½	A	374	7-27-1784	Green R	
Bowles, John	750	A	53	5-15-1783	———	
Bowles, John	800	B	29	12-20-1784	Rolling Fk	
Bowles, John	800	B	31	1- 3-1785	———	
Bowling, Alex	200	A	151	6-26-1780	Nolins Cr	Surveyed
Bowling, Alex	400	A	151	6-26-1780	Nolins Cr	Surveyed
Bowls, Ben	100	A	34	4-29-1780	Licking	Mil
Bowman, Abraham	400	A	15	2-21-1780	Goose Cr	Surveyed
Bowman, Abraham	1,000	A	27	4-26-1780	Goose Cr	
Bowman, Abraham	———	A	322	12-25-1783	Goose Cr	Amended
Bowman, Ben	600	A	52	5-13-1780	Fk Licking	
Bowman, Ben	900	A	102	5-27-1780	S Fk Licking	
Bowman, Isaac	400	A	17	2-28-1780	Delaware Cr	
Bowman, Isaac	1,000	A	27	4-26-1780	Cane Run	
Bowman, John	400	A	15	2-21-1780	Harrods Run	
Bowman, John	400	A	15	2-21-1780	Dicks R	Surveyed
Bowman, John	400	A	17	2-28-1780	Jessamine Cr	
Bowman, John	400	A	18	3- 2-1780	Fox Run	
Bowman, John	1,000	A	27	4-26-1780	Jessamine Cr	
Bowman, John	1,000	A	27	4-26-1780	Brashears Cr	
Bowman, John	1,000	A	27	4-26-1780	Cane Run	
Bowman, John	1,000	A	27	4-26-1780	Cane Run	
Bowman, John	1,000	A	153	6-27-1780	Bullitts Lick	
Bowman, John	1,000	A	153	6-27-1780	Willsons Run	
Bowman, John	1,000	A	153	6-27-1780	Hammons Run	
Bowman, John	400	A	304	11-13-1783	Panther Cr	Surveyed
Bowman, John	5,000	A	368	6-26-1784	———	400 acres surveyed
Bowman, John & Co.	5,000	A	53	5-13-1780	Salt Spring Cr	Surveyed, withdrawn
Bowman, John & Co.	2,000	A	53	5-13-1780	Dicks R	Withdrawn
Bowman, Joseph	400	A	15	2-21-1780	Cane Run	Surveyed
Bowman, Joseph	1,000	A	27	4-26-1780	Cane Run	
Bowyer, Michal	3,293	A	270	3-28-1783	Brush Cr	
Boyd, James	400	A	254	1-16-1783	Bensons Cr	
Boyd, John	400	A	168	8-22-1780	S Fk Cedar Cr	
Boyd, John	372	A	186	10-31-1780	Salt R	
Boyd, Samuel	1,500	A	361	5-25-1784	Pittmans Cr	Withdrawn
Boyd, Samuel	1,500	A	361	5-25-1784	Rolling Fk	Surveyed
Boyd, Samuel	1,500	B	1	8-12-1784	Gideon Smith	
Boyd, James	1,000	B	31	1- 8-1785	Rolling Fk	
Boyd, Samuel	1,500	B	9	9-27-1784	———	1399 acres, surveyed
Boyle, Stephen	400	A	134	6-16-1780	Howard & Licking	
Bozoth, John	224	A	363	6- 2-1784	Clay Lick Cr	Surveyed
Bozoth, John	223½	B	31	1- 3-1785	———	
Brabstone, Nich	400	A	37	4-29-1780	S Fk Elkhorn	
Bradford, Daniel	455	A	66	5-17-1780	Elkhorn	
Bradford, John	1,000	A	119	6- 1-1780	Hogans Sett	
Bradford, John	1,000	A	119	6- 1-1780	Fk Elkhorn	
Bradford, John	1,000	A	119	6- 1-1780	Elkhorn	Surveyed
Bradford, John	450	A	171	9-12-1780	N Fk Elkhorn	
Bradford, John	440	A	178	10-16-1780	Lexington	
Bradford, John & Wm.	1,000	A	119	6- 1-1780	Hogans Sett	
Brading, Nathaniel	1,406½	A	352	4-14-1784	Ohio R	
Bradley, Edwin	400	A	12	2- 5-1780	Jessamine	
Bradley, John	303	A	39	5- 9-1780	Licking	
Bradley, John	400	A	254	1-17-1783	Green R	
Bradley, John	1,000	A	269	3-28-1783	Rolling Fk	
Bradley, John	639½	A	319	12-17-1783	Green R	
Bradley, Jonas	1,000	A	131	6-12-1780	Kentucky R	
Bradley, Jonas	1,000	A	131	6-12-1780	Kentucky R	
Bradley, Jonas	1,000	A	254	1-17-1783	Green R	
Bradley, Wm.	2,718	A	250	1- 9-1783	Brashears Cr	
Brady, Morris	400	A	136	6-19-1780	Salt R	Withdrawn
Brady, Morris	300	A	136	6-19-1780	Pottengers Cr	Withdrawn
Brady, Morris	300	A	136	6-19-1780	Pottengers Cr	
Brady, Morris	350	A	169	9- 4-1780	Beech Fk	Withdrawn
Brady, Morris	500	A	169	9- 4-1780	Cedar Cr	
Brady, Morris	250	A	169	9- 4-1780	Cedar Cr	Withdrawn
Brady, Morris	300	A	173	9-23-1780	Pottengers Cr	Surveyed
Brady, Morris	400	A	199	3-26-1781	Salt R	
Brady, Morris	300	A	200	3-26-1781	Cedar Cr	
Brady, Morris	600	A	207	4-18-1781	Pottengers Cr	
Brady, Morris	200	A	207	4-14-1781	Beech Fk	

Entree	Acres	Book	Page	Entry Date	Watercourse	Notes
Brady, Morris	200	A	207	4-14-1781	Beech Fk	
Brady, Morris	250	A	217	8- 7-1781	Cedar Cr	
Bragg, Thomas	500	A	95	5-24-1780	Salt R	Mil
Bramham, Richard	200	A	29	4-27-1780	N Fk Elkhorn	Mil
Brand, John	400	B	45	5-16-1785	Drenning Lick	Surveyed
Branham, Danl	550	A	143	6-22-1780	Marble Cr	
Branham, Danl	550	A	165	8-11-1780	Kentucky R	
Branham, David	550	A	86	5-22-1780	Marble Cr	Withdrawn
Brannon, Thomas	500	A	183	10-27-1780	Green R	Surveyed
Bransan, Linar	400	A	102	5-27-1780	Duncans Premption	
Brash, Richard	400	A	5	12- 8-1779	Brashire Cr	Surveyed
Brashear, Marsham	400	A	5	12- 8-1779	Salt R	Surveyed
Brashears, Marsham	1,000	A	36	4-29-1780	Salt R	
Brashears, Marsham	1,000	A	133	6-15-1780	Salt R	Surveyed
Brashear, Marsham	1,000	A	347	3-17-1784	———	600 acres returned
Brashears, Richard	1,000	A	131	6-12-1780	Brashears Cr	500 acres surveyed
Brashears, Wm	400	A	6	12-23-1779	Floyds Fk	
Brashears, Wm	400	A	45	5-11-1780	Floyds Fk	Surveyed
Brashears, Wm	1,000	A	115	5-30-1780	Salt R	Surveyed
Brayle, Adam	1,500	A	56	5-15-1780	Rockcastle R	
Brayle, Adam	1,500	A	56	5-15-1780	Licking	
Brayle, Jacob	400	A	56	5-15-1780	Licking	
Brayle, Mathias	500	A	56	5-15-1780	Licking	
Brayle, Michal	400	A	56	5-15-1780	Licking	
Brayle, Moses	800	A	56	5-15-1780	Green R	
Brayle, Nicholas	1,400	A	56	5-15-1780	Green R	
Breacanridge, Alex	2,125	A	194	3-16-1781	Floyds Fk & Bullskin	
Breacanridge, Alex	100	A	318	12-16-1783	Harrods Cr	Surveyed
Brecanridge, Alex	1,396	A	318	12-16-1783	Ohio R	Surveyed
Breckenridge, Alex	3,000	A	207	4-14-1781	Bullskin	Surveyed
Breckenridge, Alex	841	A	276	4-12-1783	Floyds Fk	Surveyed
Breckenridge, Alex	490	A	276	4-12-1783	Little Bullskin Cr	Surveyed
Breckenridge, Alex	3,000	A	276	4-12-1783	Floyds Fk	Surveyed
Breckenridge, Alex	1,331	A	278	4-14-1783	———	490 acres surveyed
Breckenridge, Alex	841	A	360	5-14-1784	———	
Breckenridge, Alex	704	A	368	6-22-1784	Harrods Cr	Surveyed
Breckenridge, Alex	2,100	A	372	7-21-1784	———	Surveyed
Breckenridge, Alex	96	A	372	7-21-1784	Ohio R	
Breckenridge, Alex	1,514	B	40	2- 9-1785	Floyds Fk	
Breckenridge, Alex	632	B	41	2-28-1785	Muddy Fk	
Breckenridge, Alex	1,519	B	47	5-30-1785	———	
Breckenridge, Elizabeth	250	B	50	10-14-1785	Cane Run	Surveyed
Breckenridge, Elizabeth	250	B	50	10-14-1785	Sturgis Run	Surveyed
Breckenridge, James	6,108¾	B	43	4-18-1785	Floyds Fk	Withdrawn
Breckenridge, James	500	B	50	11- 1-1785	Salt R	
Breckenridge, James	19,473¾	B	51	11- 4-1785	Ohio R	
Breckenridge, John	1,000	A	74	5-19-1780	Beargrass Cr	Surveyed
Breckenridge, John	2,000	A	341	2-26-1784	Floyds Fk	
Breckenridge, John	2,000	A	341	2-26-1784	Floyds Fk	
Breckenridge, John	2,000	A	265	2-21-1783	Floyds Fk	Surveyed
Breckenridge, Lettice	1,000	A	74	5-19-1780	S Fk Licking	
Breckenridge, Lettice	1,000	A	74	5-19-1780	S Fk Licking	
Breckenridge, Lettice	500	A	75	5-19-1780	Harrods Cr	Surveyed
Breckenridge, Lettice	1,200	A	130	6-10-1780	S Fk Licking	
Breckenridge, Lettice	4,458	A	357	5- 1-1784	Floyds Fk	
Breckenridge, Robert	2,500	A	276	4-12-1783	Floyds Fk	Surveyed
Breckenridge, Wm	24,688	A	349	4- 5-1784	Ohio R	Withdrawn
Brend, James	1,000	A	123	6- 3-1780	Salt R	Surveyed
Brend, James	1,000	A	199	3-24-1781	Salt R	Surveyed
Brent, Charles	500	A	151	6-26-1780	Rockcastle	
Brent, George	500	A	53	5-15-1780	———	Surveyed
Brent, George	500	A	98	5-25-1780	N Fk Licking	
Brent, John	1,000	A	125	6- 5-1780	Rolling Fk	
Brent, John	1,000	A	125	6- 5-1780	Rolling Fk	
Brent, Wm	1,125	A	39	5- 9-1780	Licking Cr	
Brent, Wm	1,125	A	166	8-16-1780	Sinking Cr	
Bridges, James	400	A	9	1-17-1780	Muddy Cr	
Briggs, Saml	400	A	13	2- 9-1780	Hanging Fk	
Briggs, Saml	1,000	A	101	5-26-1780	Hanging Fk	
Briggs, Wm	500	A	283	7- 4-1783	Salt R	
Briggs, Wm	400	A	341	2-25-1784	Salt R	Surveyed
Briggs, Wm	400	A	375	7-29-1784	———	Surveyed
Briggs, Wm	500	B	2	8-18-1784	———	
Brisco, Gerrard	200	A	63	5-16-1780	Doe Run	
Brisco, Gerrard	1,000	A	63	5-16-1780	Barrens & Doe Run	
Brisco, Gerrard	2,000	A	63	5-16-1780	Coxes Cr	158 acres surveyed
Brisco, Gerrard	1,000	A	63	5-16-1780	S Fk Coxes Cr	

Entree	Acres	Book	Page	Entry Date	Watercourse	Notes
Brisco, Gerrard	1,000	A	63	5-16-1780	Salt R	Surveyed
Brisco, Gerrard	1,000	A	63	5-16-1780	Limestone Cr	....
Brisco, Gerrard	600	A	63	5-16-1780	Salt R	....
Brisco, Gerrard	400	A	63	5-16-1780	Town Fk	Withdrawn
Brisco, Gerrard	500	A	63	5-16-1780	Floyds Fk	Surveyed
Brisco, Gerrard	200	A	63	5-16-1780	Salt R	....
Brisco, Gerrard	500	A	63	5-16-1780	M Fk Coxes Cr	....
Brisco, Gerrard	200	A	63	5-15-1783	Lick Cr	....
Brisco, Gerrard	400	A	63	5-16-1780	Salt R	Withdrawn
Brisco, Gerrard	1,000	A	63	5-16-1780	N Fk Coxes Cr	....
Brisco, Gerrard	400	A	63	5-16-1780	Little Ky R	....
Brisco, Gerrard	400	A	74	5-19-1780	Clear Cr	....
Brisco, Gerrard	1,700	A	74	5-19-1780	18 Mile Cr	....
Brisco, John	500	A	20	4-14-1780	Simpson Cr	Mil
Brisco, John	500	A	20	4-14-1780	Simpson Run	Withdrawn
Brisco, John	500	A	20	4-14-1780	Simpson Cr	Withdrawn
Brisco, John	500	A	20	4-14-1780	Cares Cr	....
Brisco, John	500	A	20	4-14-1780	Simpson	Mil surveyed
Brisco, John	1,000	A	36	4-29-1780	Salt R	Surveyed
Brisco, John	500	A	40	5- 9-1780	Salt R	....
Brisco, John	1,500	A	40	5- 9-1780	S Fk Beech Fk	Surveyed
Brisco, John Sr	400	A	22	4-22-1780	Kentucky R	....
Brisco, Walter	1,000	A	141	6-21-1780	Eagle Cr	....
Briscoe, Gerrard	1,500	A	74	5-19-1780	S Fk Big Cr	....
Briscoe, Gerrard	400	A	209	5-28-1781	Salt R	....
Briscoe, Gerrard	842	A	220	8-24-1781	E Fk Cartrights Cr	....
Briscoe, Gerrard	1,000	A	220	8-24-1781	Hardens Cr	....
Briscoe, Garrard	1,842	A	220	8-24-1781	Combs	Withdrawn
Briscoe, John	———	A	35	4-29-1780	Simpson Run	Withdrawn
Briscoe, John	400	A	139	6-21-1780	Ky R	....
Briscoe, John	1,000	A	140	6-21-1780	Ky R	....
Briscoe, John	1,000	A	362	5-28-1784	———	500 acres surveyed
Briscoe, Pasimen	400	A	22	4-22-1780	Boiling Springs	....
Briscoe, Parmenus	400	A	45	5-11-1780	Long Lick Cr	Surveyed
Briscoe, Parmenus	500	A	45	5-11-1780	Long Lick Cr	....
Briscoe, Parmenus	400	A	138	6-21-1780	Salt R	....
Briscoe, Parmenus	1,000	A	183	10-27-1780	His Sett	....
Briscoe, Parmenus	400	B	46	5-19-1785	....	....
Bristoe, James	1,000	A	53	5-13-1780	Cedar Cr	....
Broadhead, Daniel	500	A	210	5-30-1781	Beech Fk	....
Broadhead, Daniel	500	A	210	5-30-1781	Beech Fk	....
Broadhead, Daniel	255	A	287	8-16-1783	Caney Cr	....
Broadhead, Daniel	330	A	287	8-16-1783	S Fk Caney Cr	....
Broadhead, Daniel	600	A	288	9- 8-1783	Nolin Cr	Surveyed
Broadhead, Daniel	1,000	A	288	9- 8-1783	S Fk Nolin Cr	Surveyed
Broadhead, Daniel	1,000	A	290	9-10-1783	Rock Lick	Surveyed
Broadhead, Daniel	600	A	298	10-25-1783	Salt R	....
Broadhead, Daniel	1,000	A	299	10-28-1783	Little Ky R	....
Broadhead, Daniel	3,000	A	299	10-28-1783	Beech Cr	Surveyed
Broadhead, Daniel	1,400	A	299	10-28-1783	Beech Fk	Mil surveyed
Broadhead, Daniel	590	A	306	11-19-1783	Brashears Cr	Surveyed
Broadhead, Daniel	85	A	307	11-20-1783	———	Surveyed returned
Broadhead, Daniel	1,000	A	313	12- 5-1783	Brashear Cr	....
Broadhead, Daniel	1,300	A	323	12-25-1783	Floyds Fk	....
Broadhead, Daniel	3,300	A	323	12-25-1783	Little Ky R	....
Broadhead, Daniel	500	A	336	2- 2-1784	Salt R	....
Broadhead, Daniel	4,737½	A	357	4-29-1784	Otter Cr	....
Broadhead, Daniel	590	B	19	11-26-1784	———	500 acres surveyed
Broadhead, Daniel Jr	1,000	A	301	11- 1-1783	Plum Cr	Withdrawn
Broadhead, Daniel Jr	2,000	A	301	11- 1-1783	Plum Cr	....
Broadhead, Daniel Jr	5,000	A	301	11- 1-1783	....	Withdrawn
Broadhead, Daniel Jr	8,000	A	316	12-15-1783	Plum Cr	....
Broadwater, Charles	1,000	A	73	5-19-1780	Cartrights Cr	....
Brock, John	3,795	A	271	3-28-1783	Brush Cr	....
Brockman, John	800	A	217	8- 2-1781	Long Lick Cr	....
Brockman, Samuel	1,500	A	157	7- 3-1780	Licking	....
Brockman, Samuel	500	A	243	12-25-1782	Coxes Cr	....
Brooks, James	420	A	255	1-20-1783	Rolling Fk	Withdrawn
Brooks, James	420	A	296	10-15-1783	Robinsons Cr	Withdrawn
Brooks, James	420	A	352	4-13-1784	Robertsons Cr	Withdrawn
Brooks, James	420	A	352	4-13-1784	Joseph Roberts	Withdrawn
Brooks, James et al	1,500	A	263	2-15-1783	Rolling Fk	Surveyed
Brooks, James et al	1,500	A	263	2-15-1783	Rolling Cr	Surveyed
Brooks, Joseph	600	A	237	12-21-1782	Mays Grove	Surveyed
Brooks, Joseph	200	A	237	12-21-1782	Soverins Valley	....
Brooks, Joseph	1,000	A	254	1-16-1783	Tick Cr	Surveyed
Brooks, Joseph	600	A	255	1-20-1783	Rock Lick Cr	Surveyed
Brooks, Joseph	500	A	255	1-20-1783	Rock Lick Cr	Surveyed
Brooks, Joseph	400	A	255	1-20-1783	Rock Lick Cr	Surveyed

Entree	Acres	Book	Page	Entry Date	Watercourse	Notes
Brooks, Joseph........	400	A	321	12–18–1783	Salt R.............	....
Brooks, Joseph........	400	A	346	3–16–1784	Blue Lick Cr.......	150 acres withdrawn
Brooks, Joseph........	400	A	346	3–16–1784	Blue Lick Run.....	....
Brooks, Joseph........	200	B	10	10–11–1784	————	....
Brooks, Saml.........	400	A	11	2–4–1780	Silver Cr.........	....
Brooks, Wm..........	400	A	11	2–4–1784	Marble Cr.........	....
Broughton, Charles....	250	A	45	5–11–1780	Long Lick Cr......	....
Broughton, Charles....	500	A	191	3–15–1781	————	....
Brown, Ben..........	2,400	A	137	6–19–1780	Green R...........	....
Brown, Coleman......	562½	A	245	12–28–1782	Hardens Cr........	480 acres surveyed
Brown, Coleman......	362½	B	39	2–4–1785	————	....
Brown, Daniel........	400	A	3	11–11–1779	Cartright Cr.......	Surveyed
Brown, Daniel........	300	A	106	5–27–1780	His Settlement.....	Surveyed
Brown, Daniel........	700	A	106	5–27–1780	His Settlement.....	Surveyed
Brown, Dudley........	800	A	82	5–22–1780	Beech Fk..........	Surveyed
Brown, James.........	400	A	3	11–11–1779	Clarks Run........	....
Brown, James.........	325	A	135	6–17–1780	Ohio R...........	....
Brown, James.........	967	A	142	6–22–1780	Beech Fk..........	....
Brown, James.........	500	A	142	6–22–1780	Ky R.............	....
Brown, James.........	467	A	149	6–24–1780	M Fk Licking......	....
Brown, James.........	400	A	176	10–9–1780	Fromans Cr........	....
Brown, James, heirs...	1,000	A	120	6–1–1780	Clarks Cr.........	....
Brown, James, heirs...	1,000	A	151	6–26–1780	Robinsons Cr......	....
Brown, James, heirs...	1,000	A	151	6–26–1780	Robinsons Cr......	....
Brown, James et al....	200	A	170	9–12–1780	Salt R...........	....
Brown, John..........	400	A	172	9–19–1780	Cooper Run.......	....
Brown, John..........	1,000	A	307	11–20–1783	Big Clifty Cr......	....
Brown, Joseph........	1,000	A	198	3–19–1781	Clear Cr..........	Withdrawn
Brown, Pat..........	400	A	151	6–26–1780	Rowling Cr........	....
Brown, Robert........	300	A	199	3–20–1781	Beech Fk..........	Surveyed
Brown, Thomas.......	800	A	68	5–17–1780	Locust Cr Ohio R..	....
Brown, Thomas.......	500	A	151	6–26–1780	Rockcastle.........	....
Brown, Thomas.......	1,000	A	209	5–23–1781	Pond Cr..........	Withdrawn
Brown, Thomas.......	400	A	249	1–8–1783	Nole Linn Cr......	Surveyed
Brown, Thomas.......	400	A	286	8–9–1787	Severens Valley....	....
Brown, Wm..........	296	A	88	5–23–1780	Dicks R...........	....
Brown, Wm..........	200	A	151	6–26–1780	Nolins Cr.........	Withdrawn
Brown, Wm..........	600	A	151	6–26–1780	Nolins Cr.........	Withdrawn
Brown, Wm..........	800	A	154	6–27–1780	Nolin Cr..........	Surveyed
Brown, Wm..........	800	B	15	11–12–1784	Nole Linn Cr......	Amended
Brownfield, Edw......	400	B	7	9–18–1784	Jediah Ashercraft ..	Withdrawn
Brownfield, Edw......	400	B	29	12–20–1784	Nole Linn Cr......	Surveyed
Brownfield, Edw......	400	B	29	12–20–1784	————	Withdrawn
Brownfield, Edw......	400	B	31	1–3–1785	————	Surveyed
Brownlee, Wm........	1,000	A	268	3–28–1783	Green R...........	....
Brownlee, Wm........	1,000	A	268	3–28–1783	Samuel Bell.......	....
Brownlee, Wm........	500	A	268	3–28–1783	Sinking Cr........	....
Brownlee, Wm........	500	A	268	3–28–1783	Brush Cr.........	....
Brownlee, Wm........	500	A	268	3–28–1783	Brush Cr.........	....
Brownlee, Wm........	500	A	268	3–28–1783	Brush Cr.........	....
Broyle, Stephen.......	200	A	134	6–16–1780	Hingstons Fk......	....
Broyle, Stephen.......	200	A	134	6–16–1780	Coffees Premption..	....
Bruce, Charles,......	1,000	A	237	12–21–1782	Stewarts Cr........	....
Bruce, Jno..........	400	A	2	11–3–1779	Paint Lick........	Surveyed
Bruce, John..........	1,000	A	26	4–26–1780	Paint Lick Cr.....	....
Bruce, John..........	100	A	116	5–31–1770	Hanging Fk.......	....
Bruce, John..........	800	A	116	5–31–1780	Clays Sett........	....
Bruce, John..........	1,000	A	129	6–9–1780	N Fk Licking.....	....
Brush, Wm..........	2,000	A	271	3–28–1783	Green R...........	....
Brusterby, Henry et al.	150	A	334	1–24–1784	————	....
Bruster, Henry	1,000	A	120	6–1–1780	Bowling Fk........	Surveyed
Bryan, Alex..........	400	A	213	7–4–1781	Otter Cr..........	....
Bryan, David........	1,000	A	48	5–12–1780	Salt R...........	....
Bryan, Geo..........	400	A	8	1–17–1780	Cane Run.........	....
Bryan, Geo..........	936	A	28	4–27–1780	Cane Run.........	....
Bryan, Guy..........	9,000	A	332	1–20–1784	Long Lick Cr......	Surveyed
Bryan, James.........	400	A	8	1–17–1780	Cane Run.........	....
Bryan, James.........	1,000	A	50	5–12–1780	Dicks R & Sugar Cr	....
Bryan, James.........	100	A	256	1–24–1783	Fromans Cr........	....
Bryan, James.........	200	A	256	1–24–1783	Fromans Cr........	....
Bryan, James Jr......	970	A	28	4–27–1780	Cane Run.........	....
Bryan, John..........	500	A	58	5–15–1780	Taylors Fk........	....
Bryan, Jno Sr........	400	A	14	2–19–1780	Hustons Fk........	Surveyed
Bryan, Joseph........	400	A	8	1–17–1780	N Fk Elkhorn.....	....
Bryan, Joseph Sr.....	925	A	28	4–27–1780	N Fk Elkhorn.....	....
Bryan, Morgan.......	400	A	8	1–17–1780	N Fk Elkhorn.....	....
Bryan, Morgan Jr....	400	A	28	4–27–1780	Boons Cr.........	....
Bryan, Morgan Sr....	975	A	28	4–27–1780	N Fk Elkhorn.....	....
Bryan, McDonald.....	400	A	10	2–2–1780	Harrards Cr.......	....
Bryan, Saml..........	400	A	8	1–17–1780	N Fk Elkhorn.....	....

Entree	Acres	Book	Page	Entry Date	Watercourse	Notes
Bryan, Saml	400	A	9	1–17–1780	N Fk Elkhorn	
Bryan, Samuel	1,000	A	28	4–27–1780	N Fk Elkhorn	Surveyed
Bryan, Sarah	400	A	8	1–17–1780	N Fk Elkhorn	
Bryan, Wm	400	A	8	1–17–1780	N Fk Elkhorn	
Bryan, Wm	400	A	14	2–19–1780	Elkhorn	
Bryan, Wm	400	A	17	2–28–1780	Hingston	
Bryan, Wm	1,000	A	28	4–27–1780	Bryan Settlement	
Bryan, Wm	1,000	A	28	4–27–1780	Bryan Settlement	
Bryan, Wm	400	A	36	4–29–1780	Cane Run	Surveyed
Bryan, Wm	1,000	A	36	4–29–1780	Bowmans Cr	
Bryan, Wm	1,000	A	38	5– 9–1780	N Fk Elkhorn	Withdrawn
Bryan, Wm	300	A	38	5– 9–1780	Dicks R	
Bryan, Wm	1,000	A	38	5– 9–1780	Dicks R	
Bryan, Wm	500	A	38	5– 9–1780	Black Oak Ridge	
Bryan, Wm	500	A	38	5– 9–1780	Painted Stone tract	Surveyed
Bryan, Wm	1,000	A	48	5–12–1780	Salt R	
Bryan, Wm	500	A	372	7–17–1784	—	337 acres surveyed returned
Bryan, Wm	932	A	285	8– 5–1783	Floyds Fk	
Bryan, Wm	1,000	A	285	8– 5–1783	Floyds Fk	Withdrawn
Bryan, Wm	1,932	A	285	8– 5–1783	Floyds Fk	Surveyed
Bryan, Wm	1,000	B	27	12–17–1784	—	500 acres surveyed
Bryant, John	200	A	131	6–12–1780	Dicks R	
Bryant, Joseph	200	A	226	12–13–1782	Green R	
Bryant, Thomas	1,200	A	291	9–13–1783	N Fk Rough Cr	
Bryant, Wm	1,000	A	77	5–20–1780	Pond Cr Ohio R	Surveyed
Bryant, Wm	500	A	77	5–20–1780	Pond Cr Ohio R	337 acres surveyed
Bryant, Wm	932	A	77	5–20–1780	Pond Cr Ohio R	Withdrawn
Bryant, Wm	200	A	120	6– 1–1780	—	Withdrawn
Buchanan, James	500	A	132	6–15–1780	Robinsons Cr	
Buchanan, James	1,000	A	132	6–15–1780	Robinsons Cr	
Buchanan, James	1,000	A	338	2–12–1784	Brashears Cr	Surveyed
Buchannan, James	1,000	B	51	11– 9–1785	—	
Buchanan, Jas, heirs	500	A	267	3–28–1783	Samuel Beal	
Buchanan, Jas et al	240	A	325	12–31–1783	Gists Cr	Surveyed
Buchanan, Jas et al	1,000	A	325	12–31–1783	Gess Cr	Surveyed
Buchanan, Wm	500	A	177	10–10–1780	S Fk Elkhorn	
Buckeyes, John	400	A	102	5–27–1780	Floyds Fk	
Buckner, Anthony	400	A	7	1–11–1780	S Fk Licking	
Buckner, Anthony	1,000	A	33	4–29–1780	Buckner Settlement	
Buckner, George	7,183	A	328	1– 9–1784	Robinson Cr	7,042 acres surveyed
Buckner, George	41	B	48	6–20–1785	—	
Buckner, Henry	300	A	51	5–13–1780	S Fk Gilberts Cr	
Buckner, Philip	100	A	22	4–22–1780	Br White Oak Cr	Mil
Buckner, Phillip	500	A	79	5–20–1780	Dicks R	
Buckner, Phillip	1,000	A	228	12–16–1782	Gests Cr	Surveyed
Buckner, Phillip	100	A	267	3–28–1783	Sinking Cr	Mil
Buckner, Robert	2,000	A	268	3–28–1783	Panther Cr	Surveyed
Buckner, Wm	500	A	227	11–14–1782	Stone Cr	Withdrawn
Buckner, Wm	500	A	228	12–16–1782	Licking Cr	Surveyed
Buckner, Wm	1,000	A	229	12–16–1782	Fk Sinking Cr	Surveyed
Buckner, Wm	500	A	230	12–17–1782	Ky R	Surveyed
Buckner, Wm	244	A	243	12–16–1782	Rough Cr	Surveyed
Buckner, Wm	1,544½	A	270	3–28–1783	Rough Cr	Surveyed
Buckner, Wm	500	A	275	4– 9–1783	Meeting Cr	
Buckner, Wm	500	A	275	4– 9–1783	Roundstone Cr	
Buckner, Wm	690	A	276	4–10–1783	Sinking Cr	Surveyed
Buckner, Wm	810	A	370	7– 8–1784	Sinking Fk	Surveyed
Buckner, Wm Sr	2,000	A	268	3–28–1783	Robinsons Cr	Surveyed
Buckner, Wm Jr	1,000	B	25	12–10–1784	—	203 acres surveyed
Buford, Abram	1,000	A	232	12–18–1782	Rock Lick Cr	
Buford, Abraham	10,000	A	232	12–12–1782	Green R	
Buford, Abram	2,000	A	232	12–18–1782	Rough Cr	
Buford, Abram	1,000	A	232	12–18–1782	Caney Cr	
Buford, Abram	1,000	A	232	12–18–1782	Caney Cr	
Buford, Abram	1,000	A	232	12–18–1782	Mountain Cr	
Buford, Abraham	1,000	A	232	12–18–1782	Mountain Cr	
Buford, Abraham	300	A	247	1– 7–1782	Long Lick Cr	
Buford, Abraham	1,000	A	247	1– 7–1783		
Buford, Abraham	1,500	A	247	1– 7–1783	Beech Fk	
Buford, Abraham	1,000	A	247	1– 7–1783	Rolling Fk	
Buford, Abraham	3,000	A	247	1– 7–1783	Sulphur Cr	
Buford, Abraham	500	A	247	1– 7–1782	Camp Cr	
Buford, Abraham	700	A	247	1– 7–1782	Beech Cr	
Buford, Abraham	500	A	247	1– 7–1783	Sulphur Cr	
Buford, Abram	2,000	A	248	1– 7–1788	Benson Cr	
Buford, Abram	1,000	A	248	1– 7–1783	Drennons Fk	

Entree	Acres	Book	Page	Entry Date	Watercourse	Notes
Buford, Abraham	1,000	A	290	9–10–1783	Rock Lick	Amendment
Buford, Abraham	3,000	A	307	11–20–1783	———	
Buford, James	1,000	A	20	4–17–1780	Dicks R	Mil
Buford, James	400	A	20	4–17–1780	Sugar Cr	
Buford, James	400	A	20	4–17–1780	White Oak Cr	
Buford, John	6,400	A	23	4–24–1780	Ohio R	Mil
Bulger, Daniel	1,000	A	115	5–30–1780	Bulgers Lick	
Bulger, Edward	400	A	15	2–21–1780	Harrods Run	
Bulger, Edward	1,000	A	41	5–10–1780	Harrods Run	Surveyed
Bulger, Edward	1,000	A	115	5–30–1780	His sett	Surveyed
Bull, Thomas	400	A	160	7– 6–1780	Clear Cr	Surveyed
Bull, Thomas	188¾	A	372	7–17–1784	Brush Cr	Withdrawn
Bull, Thomas	300	A	372	7–21–1784	———	Withdrawn
Bull, Thomas	188¾	A	372	7–21–1784	———	
Bull, Thomas	330	A	372	7–17–1784	Pittmans Cr	
Bullard, Richard	1,050	A	84	5–22–1780	Licking	
Bullitt, Cuthbert	1,000	A	22	4–21–1780	Green R	Mil Surveyed
Bullitt, Cuthbert	1,000	A	32	4–28–1780	———	Mil
Bullitt, Cuthbert	4,300	A	56	5–15–1780	Beech Fk	Surveyed
Bullitt, Cuthbert	8,000	A	62	5–16–1780	N Fk Licking	
Bullitt, Cuthbert	1,000	A	104	5–27–1780	Ohio R	Withdrawn
Bullitt, Cuthbert	1,000	A	104	5–27–1780	Ohio R	Withdrawn
Bullitt, Cuthbert	400	A	141	6–21–1780	Ohio R	Surveyed
Bullitt, Cuthbert	400	A	141	6–21–1780	Ohio R	Surveyed
Bullitt, Cuthbert	1,000	A	195	3–17–1781	Ohio R	Surveyed
Bullitt, Cuthbert	1,000	A	195	3–17–1781	Ohio R	
Bullitt, Cuthbert	2,000	A	285	8– 5–1783	Floyds Fk	1,589 acres surveyed 411 acres withdrawn
Bullitt, Cuthbert	411	A	311	12– 1–1783	Floyds Fk	
Bullitt, Cuthbert	1,000	A	366	6–21–1784	———	
Bullitt, Cuthbert	2,000	B	48	6–20–1785	———	1,000 acres surveyed
Bullitt, Cuth et al	7,187	A	366	6–21–1784	Robertsons Cr	
Bullitt, Cuth et al	10,000	A	366	6–21–1784	Robertson Cr	
Bullitt, Cuth et al	10,000	A	366	6–21–1784	Robertson Cr	
Bullitt, Cuth et al	800	A	366	6–21–1784	———	Withdrawn
Bullitt, Cuth et al	800	B	44	4–25–1785	———	Amended
Bullock, Edward	2,000	A	91	5–24–1780	Cartrights Cr	Surveyed
Bullock, Edward	1,200	A	91	5–24–1780	Salt R	Withdrawn
Bullock, Edward	1,200	A	207	4–16–1781	Simpson Cr	
Bullock, James	2,000	A	20	4–18–1780	Clear Cr	Mil
Bullock, John	400	A	8	1–17–1780	Licking Cr	
Bullock, John	800	A	156	6–30–1780	Elkhorn	
Bullock, Nath	400	A	8	1–17–1780	S Fk Licking	
Bundron, John	800	A	95	5–24–1780	Silver Cr	
Bunton, John	400	A	120	6– 1–1780	Harrods Landings	
Bunton, John	500	A	208	5– 2–1781	Bensons Cr	
Burdill, Frederick	300	A	67	5–17–1780	Elkhorn	
Burford, Abraham	2,708½	A	267	3–28–1783	Long Lick Cr	Surveyed
Burford, Abraham	7,700	B	2	8–19–1784	———	
Burger, John	400	A	118	6– 1–1781	Licking	
Burk, John	400	A	282	7– 2–1783	Green R	
Burk, John	400	A	334	1–21–1784	———	
Burk, Richard	300	A	94	5–24–1780	Green Cr	
Burk, Richard	1,000	A	224	12–13–1782	Cartrights Cr	Surveyed
Burk, Samuel	400	A	284	7–30–1783	Goose Cr	
Burk, Thomas	200	A	97	5–25–1780	Beech Fk	Surveyed
Burk, Thomas	800	A	97	5–25–1780	Beech Fk	Surveyed 322 acres withdrawn
Burk, Thomas	532	A	160	7– 7–1780	Eagle Cr	
Burk, Thomas	322	A	277	4–12–1783	Hardens Cr	
Burk, Thomas	322	A	277	4–12–1783	———	Withdrawn
Burk, Thomas	522	A	317	12–16–1783	———	
Burk, Wm	400	A	11	2– 4–1780	Harrods Lower Cr	
Burley, Zack et al	50	A	18	4–13–1780	Ohio R	Mil
Burley, Zack et al	50	A	18	4–13–1780	Island Ohio R	
Burley, Zack et al	100	A	19	4–13–1780	Ohio R	Mil
Burley, Zack et al	100	A	19	4–13–1780	Ohio R	Mil
Burley, Zack et al	100	A	19	4–13–1780	Ohio R	Mil
Burley, Zack et al	100	A	19	4–13–1780	Ohio R	Mil
Burner, Peter	500	A	226	12–14–1782	Rowling Fk	
Burner, Peter	500	A	226	12–14–1782	Rowling Fk	
Burner, Peter	1,000	A	226	12–14–1782	Rowling Fk	500 acres withdrawn
Burnett, John	100	A	200	3–26–1781	Cedar Run	
Burnett, John	400	A	207	4–18–1781	———	
Burnett, John	400	A	284	7–30–1783	———	
Burnett, John	450	B	34	1–25–1785	Cedar Run	
Burnett, John	400	B	46	5–26–1785	———	

Entree	Acres	Book	Page	Entry Date	Watercourse	Notes
Burnett, Joseph	4,000	A	329	1-13-1784	——	
Burney, David	400	A	10	2- 3-1780	Licking	
Burnley, Zack	5,919	A	264	2-15-1783	Green R	Surveyed
Burras, Charles	2,000	A	241	12-25-1782	Salt R	Surveyed
Burras, Charles	2,284	A	241	12-25-1782	Plumb Cr	
Burras, Wm	400	A	255	1-20-1783	Cartright Cr	
Burrose, Thomas	1,000	A	114	5-30-1780	2 Mile Cr	
Burrose, Thomas	1,000	A	114	5-30-1780	2 Mile Cr	
Burrows, Wm	100	A	372	7-19-1784	Salt R	
Burton, James	1,000	A	88	5-23-1780	Floyds Fk	Surveyed
Burton, James, heirs	400	A	16	2-25-1780	Jessimine Cr	
Burton, James, heirs	1,000	A	36	4-29-1780	Clear Cr	
Burton, John	400	A	3	11-11-1779	Cane Run	
Burton, May	1,262½	A	310	11-25-1783	Pittmans Cr	
Burton, Robert	1,000	A	143	6-23-1780	Howards Cr	
Burton, Robert	1,000	A	144	6-23-1780	Otter Cr	
Burton, Robert	1,000	A	144	6-23-1780	Rockhouse Br	
Bush, Christopher	100	A	219	8-14-1781	Dorrett Cr	Surveyed
Bush, Christopher	100	A	219	8-14-1781	Hardens Cr	Surveyed
Bush, Christopher	200	A	219	8-14-1781	Hardens Cr	Surveyed
Bush, Christopher	200	A	244	12-27-1782	——	195¾ acres surveyed
Bush, Christopher	400	A	257	1-25-1783	Hargises Cr	Withdrawn
Bush, Christopher	100	A	311	11-29-1783	Clover Lick Cr	Surveyed amended
Bush, Christopher	400	A	311	11-29-1783	Hardens Cr	
Bush, Christopher	400	A	311	11-29-1783	Harges Cr	Withdrawn
Bush, Christopher	498	A	351	4-12-1784	Tuels Cr	Surveyed
Bush, Christopher	206	B	10	10- 7-1784	Tuels Cr	Withdrawn
Bush, Christopher	206	B	49	6-17-1785	——	
Bush, Francis	500	A	271	3-28-1783	Sinking Cr	
Bush, Philip	2,000	A	35	4-29-1780	Willports Cr	Mil
Bush, Wm	200	A	40	5- 9-1780	Buffaloe Road	
Bush, Wm	600	A	40	5- 9-1780	Kentucky R	
Bush, Wm	200	A	40	5- 9-1780	Howards Cr	
Bush, Wm	1,000	A	114	5-30-1780	Howards Cr	
Bush, Wm	250	A	114	5-30-1780	Howards Cr	
Bush, Wm	1,000	A	114	5-30-1780	2 Mile Cr	
Bush, Wm	1,000	A	114	5-30-1780	Howards Cr	
Bush, Wm	1,000	A	114	5-30-1780	Howards Cr	
Bush, Wm	1,000	A	114	5-30-1780	Howards Cr	
Bush, Wm	1,000	A	114	5-30-1780	2 Mile Cr	
Bush, Wm	1,000	A	114	5-30-1780	Howards Cr	
Bush, Wm	500	A	271	3-28-1783	Sinking Cr	
Bush, Wm	1,000	A	271	3-28-1783	Green R	
Bush, Wm	680	A	271	3-28-1783	Green R	
Butler, Joseph	583	A	103	5-27-1780	Floyds Fk	
Butler, Joseph	1,000	A	113	5-30-1780	Green R	
Butler, Joseph	383	A	345	3-12-1784		
Butler, Peter	400	A	139	6-21-1780	Salt R	
Butt, Thomas	688¾	B	39	2- 7-1785	Panther Cr	
Butt, Thomas	300	B	39	2- 7-1785	——	
Buzau, Jesse	1,000	A	337	2-12-1784	Big Cr	Withdrawn
Buzan, Phillip	1,000	A	337	2-12-1784	Fox Run	
Buzan, Phillip	500	B	27	12-16-1784	——	
Buzan, Wm	1,000	A	337	2-12-1784	Clear Cr	
Byne, Edmund	1,000	A	82	5-22-1780	Soverence Cr	
Byne, Edmund	1,000	A	103	5-27-1780	N Fk Licking	
Byne, Edmund	1,000	A	103	5-27-1780	Limestone Cr	
Byne, Edmund	1,000	A	149	6-24-1780	Licking	
Byrd, Robert	1,000	A	160	7- 8-1780	Buffaloe Road	
Byrds, Mrs	6,000	A	131	6-13-1780		
Byres, Daniel	400	A	236	12-20-1782	Rolling Fk	
Byrn, Samuel	1,000	A	146	6-24-1780	Cabbin Cr	
Calaway, Richard	625	A	45	5-11-1780	Otter Cr	
Calaway, Richard	1,800	A	45	5-11-1780	Howards Cr	
Calaway, Richard	1,000	A	113	5-30-1780	Dreanings Cr	
Calaway, Zach	1,000	A	179	10-17-1780	Salt R	
Caldwell, David	400	A	93	5-24-1780	Beech Fk	
Caldwell, Geo	400	A	3	11- 8-1779	Salt R	Surveyed
Caldwell, Geo	400	A	4	11-25-1779	Cartright Cr	Surveyed
Caldwell, Geo	1,000	A	26	4-26-1780	Salt R	Surveyed
Caldwell, Geo	1,000	A	26	4-26-1780	Cartrights Cr	Surveyed
Caldwell, Geo	1,000	A	59	5-16-1780	Gass Cr	
Caldwell, Geo	1,000	A	60	5-16-1780	Gass Cr	
Caldwell, Geo	500	A	93	5-24-1780	Salt R	
Caldwell, Geo	500	A	93	5-24-1780	Salt R	
Caldwell, Geo	5,087	A	240	12-24-1782	Rough Cr	Surveyed
Caldwell, Geo	636	A	270	3-28-1783	Beech Fk	
Caldwell, Geo	5,587	A	355	4-21-1784	——	
Caldwell, John	200	A	130	6-10-1780	Dicks R	
Caldwell, John	200	A	130	6-10-1780	Dicks R	

Entree	Acres	Book	Page	Entry Date	Watercourse	Notes
Caldwell, Robert	400	A	15	2–22–1780	Cartwright Cr	
Caldwell, Robert	500	A	56	5–15–1780	Beech Fk	Surveyed
Caldwell, Robert	500	A	93	5–24–1780	Indian & Clay Lick	
Caldwell, Robert	1,000	A	201	4– 2–1781	Cartright Cr	Surveyed
Calhoon, George	115	A	303	11–11–1783	Gilkers Run	
Calhoun, George	194	A	375	7–31–1784	Short Cr	Withdrawn
Calhoun, George	80	B	27	12–18–1784	Simpsons Cr	
Calhoun, George	300	B	27	12–18–1784	Beech Fk	
Calhoun, George	194	B	33	1–21–1785	Short Cr	Withdrawn
Calhoun, George	300	B	34	1–21–1785	Beech Fk	
Calhoun, George	314	B	34	1–21–1785	Gilkeys Run	
Calhoun, George	600	A	311	12– 1–1783	Gilkies Run	
Calhoun, George	959	A	264	2–15–1785	Rolling Fk	Withdrawn
Calines, Marquis	50	A	39	5– 9–1780	Lulbulgued Cr	Withdrawn
Calk, Wm	400	A	100	5–26–1780	S Fk Licking	
Calk, Wm	200	A	100	5–26–1780	S Fk Licking	
Callaway, Caleb	400	A	11	2– 4–1780	Otter Cr	
Callaway, Caleb	1,000	A	113	5–30–1780	His Sett	
Callaway, Flanders	400	A	9	1–18–1780	Otter Cr	
Callaway, Jas	400	A	9	1–18–1780	Hustons Fk	
Callaway, John	400	A	11	2– 4–1780	M Fk Licking	
Callaway, Miajah	400	A	9	1–18–1784	Husston Fk	
Callaway, Richd	400	A	11	2– 4–1780	M Fk Otter	
Callaway, Richd	400	A	12	2– 5–1780	Silver Cr	
Callimes, Marquis	400	A	10	2– 3–1780	Lulbrilgrud Cr	
Calmes, George	1,000	A	147	6–24–1780	Muddy Cr	
Calmes, George	667½	A	155	6–29–1780	Glens Cr	
Calmes, Marquis	1,000	A	145	6–23–1780	Lulbulgrude Cr	
Calmes, Marquis	750	A	162	7–18–1780	Lulbrelgrud	500 acres withdrawn
Calmes, Marquess	250	A	195	3–16–1781	Mays Cr	
Calmes, Marquess Jr	250	A	195	3–16–1781	Mays Cr	
Calmes, Marquis Sr	1,000	A	145	6–23–1780	Lulbelgrunde Cr	
Calmer, Martin	560	A	172	9–20–1780	Rowling Fk	Withdrawn
Calman, Martin	280	A	216	7–31–1781	Cartrights Cr	
Calman, Martin	560	A	216	7–31–1781	Coperas Lick	
Calmes, Miriam	250	A	155	6–29–1780	Bennetts Pond	
Calvin, Chas & Dan	800	A	209	5–23–1781	Pond Cr	Withdrawn
Cameron, Angus	400	A	17	2–28–1780	N Fk Licking	
Cameron, Angus	100	A	184	10–30–1780	Pottengers Cr	
Cameron, Angus	100	A	184	10–30–1780	Fk Landing Run	
Cameron, Angus	200	A	196	3–17–1781	Pottingers Cr	
Cameron, John	1,000	A	118	6– 1–1780	Floyds Fk	
Cameron, Chas	400	A	2	11– 8–1779	Dicks R	
Camp, Edward	400	A	327	1– 3–1784	Falls Ohio R	Surveyed
Camp, Reuben	800	A	130	6–12–1780	Beech Fk	774 acres surveyed
Camp Reuben	200	B	15	11–12–1784	Rough Cr	
Camp Reuben	26	B	44	5–10–1785	———	
Campbell, Arch	591	A	58	5–15–1780	Licking	
Campbell, Arthur	400	A	122	6– 2–1780	Ohio R	
Campbell, Arthur	400	A	122	6– 2–1780	Green R	
Campbell, Arthur	600	A	122	6– 2–1780	Flat Cr	
Campbell, Arthur	600	A	122	6– 2–1780	Buck Lick Cr	
Campbell, Joel	2,003¾	A	348	3–26–1784	Wolf Cr	
Campbell, John	1,000	A	92	5–24–1780	N Fk Elkhorn	
Campbell, John	500	A	94	5–24–1780	Tick Cr	Surveyed
Campbell, John	1,000	A	299	10–25–1783	Fox Run	
Campbell, John	1,400	A	366	6–22–1784	Brashears Cr	Surveyed
Campbell, John	400	A	366	6–22–1784	Pond Cr	
Campbell, John	1,458	A	367	6–22–1784	Drennings Lick	Surveyed
Campbell, John	2,398	A	367	6–22–1784	Gesses Cr	Surveyed
Campbell, John	1,114	A	367	6–22–1784	Gesses Cr	Surveyed
Campbell, John	1,400	A	367	6–22–1784	Gesses Cr	Surveyed
Campbell, John	800	A	367	6–22–1784	Gesses Cr	Surveyed
Campbell, John	1,400	A	367	6–22–1784	Gesses Cr	Surveyed
Campbell, John	1,400	A	367	6–22–1784	Gesses Cr	Surveyed
Campbell, John	1,400	A	367	6–22–1784	Gesses Cr	Surveyed
Campbell, John	1,400	A	367	6–22–1784	Gesses Cr	Surveyed
Campbell, John	1,400	A	367	6–22–1784	Gesses Cr	Surveyed
Campbell, John	1,400	A	367	6–22–1784	Gesses Cr	Notes
Campbell, John	1,400	A	367	6–22–1784	Gesses Cr	Surveyed
Campbell, John	1,400	A	367	6–22–1784	Gesses Cr	Surveyed
Campbell, John	1,400	A	367	6–22–1784	Brashers Cr	Surveyed
Campbell, John	1,400	A	367	6–22–1784	Brashears Cr	Surveyed
Campbell, John	1,400	A	367	6–22–1784	Brashears Cr	Surveyed
Campbell, John	1,400	A	367	6–22–1784	Brashears Cr	Surveyed
Campbell, John	1,400	A	367	6–22–1784	Brashears Cr	Surveyed
Campbell, John	1,400	A	367	6–22–1784	Brashears Cr	Surveyed
Campbell, John	508	B	2	8–24–1784	———	Surveyed amended

Entree	Acres	Book	Page	Entry Date	Watercourse	Notes
Campbell, Samuel.....	1,094	B	2	8–19–1784	Valley Cr	....
Campbell, John.......	5,000	B	11	11– 6–1784	———	1,890 acres surveyed
Campbell, John.......	2,000	B	11	11– 6–1784	———	1,000 acres surveyed
Campbell, John.......	1,500	B	11	11– 8–1784	Guests Cr	....
Campbell, John.......	3,920	B	41	2–28–1785	Bensons Cr	Surveyed
Campbell, John.......	5,000	B	48	6–20–1785	———	3,920 acres surveyed
Campbell, Samuel.....	200	A	44	5–11–1780	Muddy Cr	....
Campbell, Samuel.....	400	A	131	6–12–1780	Clear Cr	....
Campbell, Samuel.....	1,000	A	131	6–12–1780	Clear Cr	Withdrawn
Campbell, Samuel.....	1,000	A	238	12–23–1782	Clear Cr	....
Campbell, Samuel.....	1,000	A	349	3–29–1784	Spring Cr	Withdrawn
Campbell, Samuel.....	374	B	2	8–19–1784	Harden Cr	....
Campbell, Thomas.....	500	A	349	3–29–1784	Hardens Cr	....
Camron, John.........	400	A	139	6–21–1780	S Fk Licking	....
Camron, Luke........	400	A	139	6–21–1780	S Fk Licking	....
Canby, Samuel.......	1,000	A	232	12–18–1782	Pottengers Cr	690 acres surveyed 250 acres withdrawn
Canby, Samuel.......	500	A	233	12–18–1782	Buck Cr	519 acres surveyed
Canby, Samuel.......	500	A	233	12–18–1782	Buck Cr	....
Canby, Samuel.......	1,000	A	233	12–18–1782	Hardens Cr	....
Canby, Samuel.......	425	A	278	4–14–1783	Brashears Cr	....
Canby, Samuel.......	250	A	312	12– 4–1783	Rolling Fk	Surveyed
Canby, Samuel.......	1,000	A	362	5–31–1784	———	940 acres surveyed
Caneron, Charles.....	1,000	A	38	4–29–1780	———	
Cannady, Easher.....	1,167	A	374	7–27–1784	Green R	....
Caney, Jas..........	400	A	11	2– 4–1780	Stoners Fk	....
Canney, Wm........	100	A	21	4–20–1780	Hanging Fk	Mil
Cannon, Francis......	400	A	178	10–10–1780	S Fk Licking	....
Cannon, John........	1,000	A	177	10– 9–1780	S Fk Licking	....
Cannon, John........	1,645	A	375	7–29–1784	Harrods Cr	....
Cannon, Luke........	1,000	A	177	10–10–1780	His Sett	....
Canton, Simon.......	400	A	10	2– 3–1780	Elkhorn	....
Canton, Simon.......	1,000	A	26	4–26–1780	Lawrence Cr	....
Canton, Simon.......	1,000	A	82	5–22–1780	N Fk Licking	....
Canton, Simon.......	300	A	105	5–27–1780	Severence Cr	....
Canton, Simon.......	800	A	179	10–17–1780	Lawrence Cr	....
Cantsman, Benedick...	1,000	A	27	4–26–1780	Howards Cr	....
Capelin, Jacob.......	400	A	17	2–28–1780	Dicks R	....
Cardnot, Micheal.....	200	A	109	5–29–1780	Boones Mill Cr	....
Cardnot, Micheal.....	200	A	109	5–29–1780	Fk Camp Cr	....
Cardnot, Micheal.....	400	A	147	6–24–1780	Pennsylvania Run	....
Carey, Edward.......	1,000	A	87	5–23–1780	Little Ky R	Surveyed
Carland, Thomas.....	400	A	80	5–20–1780	Brashears Cr	....
Carlane, Thos........	400	A	14	2–19–1780	M Fk Salt R	....
Carlane, Thomas.....	400	A	65	5–17–1780	S Fk Clear Cr	....
Carlane, Thomas.....	400	A	65	5–17–1780	Brashears Cr	....
Carlem, Thomas......	1,000	A	118	6– 1–1781	His Sett	....
Carline, Thomas.....	1,000	A	349	3–30–1784	Brashears Cr	....
Carlton, Robert.......	400	A	137	6–19–1780	Sugar Cr	....
Carnal, Thomas......	500	A	65	5–17–1780	Licking	....
Carman, Joseph......	1,000	A	260	2– 3–1783	Nole Linn Cr	....
Carman, Joseph......	1,000	A	260	2– 3–1783	Big Benson Cr	....
Carman, Joseph......	1,000	A	260	2– 3–1783	Benson Cr	....
Carpenter, Adam.....	400	A	135	6–17–1780	Silver Cr	....
Carpenter, Conrad....	400	A	12	2– 5–1780	Gordons Lick	....
Carpenter, Conrad....	1,000	A	107	5–29–1780	Dicks R	....
Carpenter, George....	400	A	39	5– 9–1780	Carpenter Cr	....
Carpenter, John......	400	A	12	2– 5–1780	Gordons Lick	....
Carpenter, John......	200	A	76	5–19–1780	Knob Lick	....
Carpenter, John......	200	A	76	5–19–1780	Rowling Fk	....
Carpenter, John......	1,000	A	107	5–29–1780	His Sett	....
Carr, Gideon.........	400	A	58	5–15–1780	Licking	....
Carr, James..........	1,000	A	178	10–17–1780	John Cowan	....
Carr, John...........	325	A	191	3–15–1781	Salt R	....
Carr, John...........	325	A	191	3–15–1781	Salt R	....
Carr, John...........	500	A	191	3–15–1781	Grove Timber	....
Carr, John...........	587¾	A	285	8– 7–1783	Rolling Fk	....
Carr, John...........	587¾	A	285	8– 7–1783	Crooked Cr	....
Carr, John...........	587¾	A	285	8– 7–1785	Mill Cr	....
Carr, John...........	200	A	285	8– 7–1783	Cane Run	....
Carr, John...........	387¾	A	285	8– 7–1783	Cedar Cr	....
Carr, John...........	150	B	25	12–13–1784	Willsons Cr	....
Carr, John...........	150	B	25	12–13–1784	Willsons Cr	....
Carr, John...........	200	B	25	12–13–1784	Cane Run	....
Carr, John...........	200	B	25	12–13–1784	Willsons Cr	....

Entree	Acres	Book	Page	Entry Date	Watercourse	Notes
Carr, John	300	B	25	12-13-1784	Crooked Cr	
Carr, John	1,500	B	25	12-13-1784	Crooked Cr	
Carr, John	200	B	25	12-13-1784	————	
Carr, John	1,500	B	25	12-13-1784	Cane Run	
Carr, John	500	B	25	12-13-1784	Lick Cr	
Carr, Micajale	600	A	57	5-15-1780	Licking	
Carr, Walter	150	A	29	4-27-1780	M Fk Licking	Mil
Carr, Walter	1,000	A	39	5- 9-1780	Licking	
Carr, Walter	1,200	A	123	6- 3-1780	Salt R	
Carrington, Ed	18,875	B	42	3- 4-1785	————	920 acres surveyed
Carrington, Ed	2,000	A	369	7- 3-1784	Otter Cr	
Carrington, Ed	16,875	A	369	7- 3-1784	Rough Cr	9,120 acres surveyed
Carrington, Paul	1,000	A	49	5-12-1780	Rolling Fk	
Carrington, Paul	1,000	A	49	5-12-1780	Chaplins Cr	
Carrington, Tim	300	A	76	5-19-1780	Stoners Fk	
Carrington, Tim	198	A	65	5-17-1790	Stoners Fk	
Carrington, Wm	300	A	76	5-19-1780	Pasture Lick	
Carter, Abednegoe	330½	A	349	4- 5-1784	————	
Carter, Abednegoe	1,100	A	349	4- 5-1784	Pottengers Cr	
Carter, Abednegoe	400	A	370	7- 6-1784	————	
Carter, Bednego	300	A	207	4-17-1781	Pottengers Cr	
Carter, Bednego	100	A	207	4-17-1781	Knobb Cr	Withdrawn
Carter, Bednego	100	A	217	8- 2-1781	N Fk Knobb Cr	Surveyed
Carter, Bednego	100	A	217	8- 2-1781	Knobb Cr	
Carter, Mesheek	200	A	174	9-29-1780	James Rogers	
Carter, Mesheek	400	A	174	9-29-1780	Rowling Fk	Surveyed
Carter, Mesheek	200	A	174	9-29-1780	Beards Run	
Carter, Mesheck	200	A	210	6- 5-1781	Rowling Fk	
Carter, Mesheck	1,000	A	281	6-30-1783	————	400 acres surveyed
Carter, Shadrack	560	A	136	6-19-1780	Pottengers Cr	Withdrawn
Carter, Shadrack	560	A	170	9-12-1780	Beech & Rolling Fk	
Carter, Shadrack	232½	A	334	1-24-1784	Beech Fk	
Carter, Shadrack	400	A	376	8- 5-1784	Pottengers Cr	
Carter, Shadrack	400	B	6	9-13-1784	————	
Carter, Thomas	200	A	217	8- 2-1781	Pottengers Cr	Surveyed
Carter, Wm	1,000	A	80	5-20-1780	Sugar Cr	
Carter, Wm	500	A	84	5-22-1780	Buck Lick Cr	
Carter, Wm	1,000	A	84	5-22-1780	Buck Lick Cr	
Cartright, Joseph	200	A	322	12-22-1783	Rolling Fk	
Cartright, Joseph	500	A	375	7-29-1784	————	400 acres surveyed
Cartright, Joseph	200	A	375	7-29-1784	————	
Cartright, Sam, heirs	400	A	17	2-28-1780	Cartright Cr	
Cartright, Sam, heirs	1,000	A	204	4- 4-1781	Cartright Cr	Surveyed
Carts, Conrad	300	A	176	10- 9-1780	Bullskin Cr	
Carty, Wells	400	A	70	5-18-1780	Falls Ohio Bullits Lick	Surveyed
Cary, Edward	500	A	48	5-12-1780	Floyds Fk	
Case, Lydia	400	A	262	2-12-1783	Rolling Fk	
Case, Reuben	400	A	304	11-14-1783	Salt R	Surveyed
Case, Susanna	400	A	236	12-20-1782	Caney Cr	
Casey, Peter	400	A	18	3- 2-1780	Shawnee Run	
Casey, Peter	2,000	A	40	5- 9-1780	Gists Cr	
Casey, Peter	1,000	A	40	5- 9-1780	N Fk Hingston	
Casey, Peter	1,000	A	152	6-26-1780	Shawney Run	
Casey, Peter	600	A	326	1- 1-1783	Salt R	
Casey, Peter	1,400	A	326	1- 1-1784	Salt R	
Casey, Wm	800	A	109	5-29-1780	Ohio R	
Casey, Wm	400	A	163	7-25-1780	Ridge Knobs	
Cashwiler, Joseph	400	A	143	6-22-1780	Beech Fk Cedar Cr	
Cassel, Henry	600	A	71	5-18-1780	Pottengers Cr	Surveyed
Casselman, Wm Jr	1,000	A	210	6- 1-1781	Brashears Cr	
Casselman, Wm Jr	————	A	345	3-11-1784	Beargrass Cr	Amended
Castleman, Jacob	400	A	254	1-17-1783	Salt R	
Castleman, Wm	400	A	251	1-10-1783	Brashears Cr	
Cathers, Edward	200	A	102	5-26-1780	Jessamine Cr	
Cathers, Edward	200	A	102	5-26-1780	Jessamine Cr	
Catlett, Alex	1,000	A	77	5-20-1780	Fern Cr	
Catlett, Charles	1,065	A	310	11-26-1783	Floyds Fk	
Catlett, Charles	2,000	A	310	11-26-1783	Floyds Fk	
Catlett, James	1,000	A	48	5-12-1780	Floyds Fk	Surveyed
Catlett, John	981	A	310	11-26-1783	Floyds Fk	
Catlett, Peter	4,468½	A	359	5- 7-1784	Cedar Cr	
Catlett, Peter	3,000	A	361	5-19-1784	Rough Cr	
Catlett, Peter	3,000	A	376	8- 2-1784	————	
Caughman, Jacob	400	A	10	2- 3-1780	Hammonds Cr	
Cave, Richard	1,000	A	26	4-26-1780	Shawnee Run	Surveyed
Cave, Richard	200	A	34	4-29-1780	————	Mil
Cave, Richard	100	A	39	5- 9-1780	Licking	

Entree	Acres	Book	Page	Entry Date	Watercourse	Notes
Cave, Thomas	3,000	A	353	4-15-1784	Long Lick Cr	
Cave, Wm	50	A	30	4-28-1780		Mil
Cave, Wm	1,700	A	52	5-13-1780	Bowman Cr	Mil
Chambers, Thomas	500	A	46	5-12-1780	Bowmans Cr	Mil
Chambers, Thomas	50	A	222	12-12-1782	Coxes Cr	
Chaplin, Abraham	400	A	3	11-11-1779	Shawnee Run	
Chaplin, Abraham, heir	1,000	A	276	4-10-1783	Bullskin Cr	Surveyed
Chapman, Phillip	1,000	A	165	8-11-1780	Pond Cr	
Charton, Henry	400	A	137	6-19-1780	Dicks R	
Charlton, Henry	400	A	328	1-12-1784	Robert Chartons	
Charlton, Robert	400	A	328	1-12-1784	Beech Fk	
Chase, Samuel	3,125	B	20	11-26-1784	Salt R	
Chatten, John	1,000	A	96	5-24-1780	Little Muddy Cr	Surveyed
Chelton, Charles	1,250	A	165	8-11-1780	Green R	Surveyed
Chelton, Charles	1,250	A	165	8-11-1780	Green R	Surveyed
Chenwith, Wm	600	A	216	7-30-1781	Rock Cr	Surveyed
Cherry, Wm	500	A	249	1- 8-1783	Floyds Fk	Surveyed
Cherry, Wm	713½	A	249	1- 8-1783	Salt R	Surveyed
Chew, Joseph	2,000	A	23	4-24-1780	Mid Fk	Mil
Childs, Walter	500	A	39	5- 9-1780	Licking	
Childs, Wm	500	A	39	5- 9-1780	Licking	
Chiles, John	1,000	A	29	4-27-1780	Stoners Fk	Mil
Chiles, John	5,106	A	263	2-15-1783	Sinking Cr	Withdrawn
Chiles, John Jr	1,584	A	263	2-15-1783	Sinking Cr	Withdrawn
Chiles, John Jr	5,106	A	347	3-17-1784	Sinking Cr	Withdrawn
Chiles, John Jr	1,584	A	347	3-17-1784	Sinking Cr	Withdrawn
Chiles, Walter	150	A	29	4-27-1780	M Fk Licking	Mil
Chinn, Ben	1,000	A	55	5-15-1780	Hingstons Fk	
Chinn, Charles	500	A	47	5-12-1780	Whitleys Cr	
Chinn, Charles	500	A	47	5-12-1780	Chaplins Ck	Surveyed
Chinn, Charles	1,000	A	47	5-12-1780	Salt R	Surveyed
Chinn, Elijah		A	361	5-22-1784	Ky R	
Chinn, Rawleigh	500	A	41	5-10-1780	E Fk Licking	
Chinn, Thomas	1,000	A	101	5-26-1780	Holders Cr	
Chenwith, Richard	2,000	B	50	10-14-1785	Floyds Fk	Surveyed
Christian, Israel	100	A	33	4-29-1780	Salt R	Mil
Christian, Israel	1,500	A	192	3-16-1781	Nole Lynn Cr	Surveyed
Christian, Israel	500	A	192	3-16-1781	Rowling Fk	Surveyed
Christian, Israel	1,000	A	192	3-16-1781	Rowling Fk	Surveyed
Christian, Israel	500	A	192	3-16-1781	Knobb Cr	Surveyed
Christain, Israel	2,000	A	376	8- 2-1784		1,500 acres surveyed
Christain, Israel	1,500	B	17	11-15-1784		500 acres surveyed
Christmass, Wm	2,000	A	230	12-17-1784	Bullitts Lick	Surveyed
Churchill, Anne	1,000	A	145	6-23-1780	Licking	
Cimmins, Chas	207	A	150	6-26-1780		
Clark, Christopher	400	A	36	4-29-1780	James Harrod	
Clark, Christopher	400	A	9	1-18-1780	E Fk Licking	
Clark, Christopher	1,000	A	69	5-18-1780	Gilberts Cr	
Clark, Christopher	1,000	A	153	6-26-1780	Parberry	
Clark, Chris, et al	1,000	A	153	6-26-1780	E Fk Licking	
Clark, Chris Jr	1,000	A	64	5-17-1780	Chaplins Fk	
Clark, Daniel	1,000	A	228	12-14-1782	Green R	
Clark, Daniel	4,000	B	7	9-20-1784	Glasscock	Withdrawn
Clark, Geo	30,000	B	10	10- 7-1784	Elk Lick	
Clark, Geo Rogers	400	A	8	1-12-1780	Dicks R	
Clark, Geo Rogers	400	A	6	12-23-1779	Drenings Lick	
Clark, Geo Rogers	200	A	31	4-28-1780	Floyds Fk	Mil
Clark, Geo Rogers	1,000	A	69	5-18-1780	Ohio R	
Clark, Geo Rogers	1,000	A	69	5-18-1780	Ohio R	
Clark, Geo Rogers	1,000	A	69	5-18-1780	Ohio R	
Clark, John	750	A	61	5-16-1780	Town Fk	
Clark, John	1,000	A	61	5-16-1780	Beech Fk	
Clark, James	400	A	99	5-25-1780	Ohio R	
Clark, James	400	A	99	5-25-1780	Ohio R	
Clark, Jonathan	7,000	B	4	9- 2-1784	Rowling Fk	200 acres withdrawn
Clark, Mcicajah	834	A	337	2-11-1784	Little Barren R	
Clark, Mcicajah, et al	500	A	337	2-11-1784	Green R	
Clark, Robert	1,523	A	241	12-25-1782	Salt R	Surveyed
Clark, Spencer	400	A	121	6- 2-1780	Scaggs Cr	
Clark, Thomas	1,000	A	51	5-13-1780	Fk Licking	
Clark, Wm	120	A	13	2-11-1780	Otter Cr	Mil 1763
Clark, Wm	60	A	13	2-11-1780	Otter Cr	Mil 1763
Clark, Wm	400	A	13	2-11-1780	Licking Cr	
Clark, Wm	400	A	98	5-25-1780	Ohio R	
Clarke, Christopher	1,000	A	146	6-24-1780	E Fk Licking	
Clarke, Christopher	1,000	A	186	10-31-1780	Kentucky R	
Clarke, Christopher	1,000	A	186	10-31-1780	Kentucky R	
Clarke, Christopher	300	A	186	10-31-1780	Chaplins Fk	
Clarke, Christopher	300	A	186	10-31-1780	Salt R	

Entree	Acres	Book	Page	Entry Date	Watercourse	Notes
Clarke, Christopher....	400	A	227	12–14–1781	Ohio R.	Surveyed
Clarke, Christopher....	312	A	238	12–21–1782	Chaplins Fk.	....
Clarke, Daniel........	6,000	A	358	5– 3–1784	Rowling Fk.	....
Clarke, Daniel........	4,000	A	358	5– 3–1784	Rowling Fk.	Withdrawn
Clarke, Francis........	750	A	225	12–12–1782	Green R.	....
Clarke, George........	1,000	A	179	10–17–1780	His Sett.	....
Clarke, Geo Rogers....	74,962	A	182	10–26–1780	Ohio & Tenn Rs....	Amendment offered
Clarke, John..........	1,000	A	331	1–16–1784	Clear Cr.	Surveyed
Clarke, Robert........	50	A	223	12–12–1782	Ohio R.	Surveyed
Clarke, Wm...........	1,040½	A	328	1– 9–1784	Robinson Cr.	Surveyed
Clarkson, Minoah.....	800	A	114	5–30–1780	Licking.	....
Clay, Henry..........	400	A	2	11– 3–1779	Stoners Fk.	....
Clay, Henry..........	1,000	A	26	4–26–1780	Clay Settlement....	....
Clay, Wm............	400	A	25	4–26–1780	Sugar Loaf Lick....	....
Clay, Wm............	400	A	25	4–26–1780	Sugar Loaf Lick....	....
Clayton, John........	500	A	201	4– 2–1781	Mid Fk Licking Cr.	....
Clear, Geo...........	400	A	14	2–19–1780	Huston Fk.	Surveyed
Clear, George........	500	A	137	6–19–1780	Floyds Fk.	....
Clear, George........	500	A	137	6–19–1780	Floyds Fk.	Surveyed
Cleaver, Benj........	100	B	33	1–13–1785	Horse Run.	....
Cleaver, Benj........	100	B	33	1–13–1785	————	Withdrawn
Cleaver, Benj........	100	B	10	10– 6–1784	Beech Fk.	Withdrawn
Cleaver, Wm.........	400	A	334	1–23–1784	Cedar Cr.	....
Cleaver, Wm.........	600	A	346	3–16–1784	Beech Fk.	....
Cleaver, Wm.........	1,000	A	346	3–16–1784	Hardens Cr.	....
Cleaver, Wm.........	400	B	9	10– 6–1784	Hardens Cr.	....
Cleaver, Wm.........	200	B	9	10– 6–1784	Lin Run.	Withdrawn
Cleaver, Wm.........	100	B	9	10– 6–1784	Beech Fk.	Withdrawn
Cleaver, Wm.........	300	B	33	1–13–1784	Benj Linn Run....	....
Cleaver, Wm.........	100	B	33	1–13–1785	Beech Fk.	....
Clefton, Charles......	488	A	209	5–23–1781	Pond Cr.	Withdrawn
Cleland, Phillip......	1,000	A	285	8– 5–1783	Lick Cr.	Surveyed
Clemmond, John......	500	A	225	12–13–1782	Green R.	....
Clenkinbeard, Isaac....	500	A	134	6–16–1780	Licking.	....
Clerk, Jas Scott......	2,950	A	6	12–23–1779	S Fk Licking.	Withdrawn
Cleveland, Alex.......	1,000	A	36	4–29–1780	Boones Cr.	....
Cleveland, Alex.......	1,000	A	156	6–30–1780	His Sett.	....
Cleveland, Eli........	575	A	107	5–29–1780	Tick Cr.	....
Cleveland, Eli........	1,000	A	107	5–29–1780	Salt R.	....
Cleveland, James......	1,000	A	70	5–17–1780	S Fk Licking.	....
Clifton, Baldwin......	1,000	A	320	12–18–1783	————	....
Clifton, Burdett.......	200	B	23	12– 7–1784	Hardens Cr.	....
Clifton, Burdett.......	1,181	A	263	2–15–1783	Hardens Cr.	Surveyed
Climor, George........	11,000	A	222	12–12–1782	Harrods Cr.	Surveyed
Cline, John..........	563	A	248	1– 7–1783	Gesses Cr.	Withdrawn
Cline, John..........	563	A	369	7– 3–1784	Gesses Cr.	Withdrawn
Cline, Peter..........	500	A	94	5–24–1780	Tick Cr.	....
Cline, Peter..........	200	A	213	7– 2–1781	Tick Cr.	130 acres surveyed
Clodes, Wm..........	1,181	A	241	12–25–1782	Rough Cr.	....
Cloyd, James........	1,000	A	86	5–23–1780	Rowling Fk.	Surveyed
Clyne, John..........	563	A	369	7– 3–1784	Gesses Cr.	Withdrawn
Cobbs, James........	1,000	A	100	5–26–1780	Holders Cr.	....
Cobbs, John..........	1,000	A	67	5–17–1780	Kentucky R.	....
Cobbs, John..........	1,000	A	67	5–17–1780	Floyds Fk.	Surveyed
Cobbs, John..........	1,000	A	67	5–17–1780	Ohio R.	....
Cobbs, John..........	2,000	A	81	5–22–1780	Green R.	....
Cobbs, Robert........	6,032½	A	260	2– 3–1783	Ohio R.	....
Cobourn, John........	15,000	A	330	1–14–1784	Bear Cr.	12,000 acres surveyed
Coburn, Jas..........	400	A	3	11–11–1779	Salt R.	....
Coburn, James, heir...	1,000	A	349	3–30–1784	Mulberry Cr.	....
Cock, John...........	500	A	30	4–28–1780	N Fk Goose Cr.	Mil
Cocks, Enoch........	486	A	293	10– 3–1783	Pottengers Cr.	Surveyed
Cocke, Nathanel.....	12,560	A	238	12–21–1782	Green R.	....
Cocke, Nathaniel.....	12,560	A	258	1–27–1783	Green R.	....
Cockran, Hugh.......	402	A	193	3–16–1781	Floyds Fk.	....
Coffer, Jesse........	500	A	96	5–25–1780	Licking.	....
Coffer, Jesse........	250	A	96	5–25–1780	Tates Cr.	....
Coffer, Jesse........	250	A	96	5–25–1780	Tates Cr.	....
Coffer, Jesse........	1,000	A	113	5–30–1780	His Sett.	....
Coger, Michal........	2,500	A	109	5–29–1780	Simpsons Cr.	....
Coghill, Thomas......	1,500	A	101	5–26–1780	N Licking.	....
Coil, Andrew.........	400	A	15	2–21–1780	Dicks R.	....
Colbert, George......	986	A	285	8– 5–1783	Salt R.	....
Coleman, Daniel.....	100	A	31	4–28–1780	Dicks R.	Mil
Coleman, Daniel.....	500	A	78	5–20–1780	Dicks R.	Mil
Coleman, Daniel.....	1,000	A	183	10–27–1780	Green R.	Surveyed
Coleman, Daniel, et al.	5,113¾	A	309	11–25–1783	Blackford Cr.	....
Coleman, James.......	500	A	58	5–15–1780	Licking.	....
Coleman, James.......	2,000	A	158	7– 3–1780	4 Mile Cr.	....

Entree	Acres	Book	Page	Entry Date	Watercourse	Notes
Coleman, John	1,000	A	65	5-17-1780	Licking	
Coleman, John D	400	A	315	12-13-1783	S Fk Rolling Fk	
Coleman, Julian	50	A	34	4-29-1780	————	Mil
Coleman, Julius	1,000	A	183	10-27-1780	Green R	Surveyed
Coleman, Peter	600	A	282	7- 1-1783	Little Kentucky R.	
Coleman, Peter	500	A	282	7- 1-1783	Goose Cr	260 acres surveyed
Coleman, Peter	1,400	A	284	7-30-1783	Little Kentucky R.	Surveyed
Coleman, Peter	600	A	284	7-30-1783	Little Kentucky R.	
Coleman, Peter	500	A	303	11-10-1783	Floyds Fk	Withdrawn
Coleman, Peter	1,219	A	303	11-10-1783	Floyds Fk	Withdrawn
Coleman, Peter	1,310	A	344	3- 3-1784	Floyds Fk	Surveyed
Coleman, Peter	500	A	344	3- 3-1784	Robert Akin	
Coleman, Peter	1,219	A	344	3- 3-1784	Robert Akin	Withdrawn
Coleman, Robert	10,000	A	325	12-31-1783	Middle Cr	Withdrawn
Coleman, Robert	12,231	A	338	2-14-1784	————	Withdrawn
Coleman, Robert	12,231	A	338	2-14-1784	Green Knobb	Withdrawn
Coleman, Robert	12,231	A	338	2-12-1784	Green R	Withdrawn
Coleman, Robert	10,000	A	352	4-15-1784	Salt R	Surveyed
Coleman, Robert	12,231	A	352	4-15-1784	Pond Cr	Surveyed
Coleman, Robert	12,231	A	352	4-15-1784	Thomas Middleton	Withdrawn
Coleman, Robert	10,000	A	352	4-15-1784	Middle Cr	Withdrawn
Coleman, Shelby	400	A	157	6-30-1780	Licking	
Coleman, Thomas	50	A	35	4-28-1780	Dicks R	
Coleman, Thomas	1,000	A	183	10-27-1780	Green R	
Coleman, Wm	400	A	157	6-30-1780	Licking	Surveyed
Collett, Dan & Eliz	4,000	A	316	12-15-1783	Drinnens Lick Cr	Surveyed
Collett, Dan & Eliz	4,000	B	24	12-10-1784	————	Surveyed
Collett, John	10,000	A	315	12-15-1783	Pond Cr	Withdrawn
Collett, John	10,000	A	367	6-22-1784	Drennings Lick	Surveyed
Collett, John	10,000	A	367	6-22-1784	Pond Cr	Withdrawn
Collins, Alex	400	A	186	10-31-1780	Mid Fk Sugar Cr	
Collins, Edmund	200	A	85	5-22-1780	N Fk Licking	
Collins, Francis	1,864½	A	310	11-25-1783	Pittmans Cr	
Collins, Joseph	400	A	154	6-28-1780	Lick Bank Cr	
Collins, Joseph Jr	200	A	174	9-29-1780	Dicks R	
Collins, Josiah	400	A	123	6- 3-1780	Elkhorn Cr	
Collins, Josiah	400	A	154	6-28-1780	Kentucky R	
Collins, Lebudon	250	A	189	3-15-1781	Beech Fk	Withdrawn
Collins, Lebudon	250	A	189	3-15-1781	Coxes Cr	Withdrawn
Collins, Robert	400	A	82	5-22-1780	Sugar Cr	Withdrawn
Collins, Spencer	560	A	80	5-22-1780	Floyds Fk	Withdrawn
Collins, Spencer	560	A	155	6-29-1780	Floyds Fk	300 acres withdrawn
Collins, Spencer	400	A	238	12-23-1782	Cartright Cr	
Collins, Samuel	560	A	356	4-27-1784	————	
Collins, Thomas	400	A	26	4-26-1780	Paint Lick Cr	
Collins, Thomas	400	A	65	5-17-1780	Hanging Fk	
Collins, Thomas	400	A	126	6- 7-1780	Crooked Cr	Surveyed
Collins, Thomas	400	A	242	12-25-1782	Willsons Cr	Surveyed
Collins, Wm E	325	A	189	3-15-1781	Beech Fk	Withdrawn
Collins, Wm E	325	A	207	4-14-1781	Coxes Cr	Surveyed
Collins, Zebulon	500	A	198	3-19-1781	S Fk Coxes Cr	Withdrawn
Collins, Zebulon	250	A	198	3-19-1781	Coxes Cr	
Collins, Zebulon	500	A	204	4- 5-1781	Fromans Cr	Surveyed
Collins, Zebulon	280	A	258	1-27-1783	Wm E Collins	262 acres withdrawn
Collins, Zebulon	500	A	330	1-14-1784	————	
Colston, Rawley	25,000	A	77	5-20-1780	Eagles Cr	Withdrawn
Colston, Rawley	25,000	A	81	5-22-1780	Eagle Cr	Withdrawn
Colvert, George	1,000	A	310	11-27-1783	————	Surveyed
Combs, Ben	600	A	162	7-17-1780	Eagle Cr	
Combs, Cuthbert	400	A	1	11- 3-1779	Howards Cr	
Combs, Cuthbert	1,000	A	37	4-29-1780	Combs Sett	
Combs, Edward	400	A	306	11-19-1783	Rolling Fk	
Combs, Edward	400	A	306	11-19-1783	Lead Cr	
Combs, Fielding	500	A	90	5-23-1780	Howards Cr	
Combs, Jacob	500	B	31	12-29-1784	————	
Combs, Jaques	6,000	A	332	1-20-1784	Long Lick Cr	Withdrawn
Combs, Jaques	6,000	A	358	5- 4-1784	Rolling Fk	
Combs, Jaques	6,000	A	358	5- 4-1784	————	Withdrawn
Combs, John	200	A	164	8-11-1780	Goose Cr	Withdrawn
Combs, John	200	B	14	11-12-1784	Goose Cr	Withdrawn
Combs, John	200	B	14	11-12-1784	Rough Cr	
Combs, Joseph	1,000	A	37	4-29-1780	Howards Cr	
Combs, Joseph	1,000	A	63	5-16-1780	Floyds Fk	Surveyed
Combs, Joseph	500	A	104	5-27-1780	Floyds & Town Fk	
Combs, Joseph	1,000	A	105	5-27-1780	Simpson Cr	Surveyed
Combs, Joseph	1,000	A	263	2-14-1783	Simpsons Cr	
Combs, Wm	400	A	4	11-15-1797	Beach Fk Salt R	Surveyed
Combs, Wm	1,000	A	37	4-29-1780	Stewarts Cr	Surveyed
Combs, Wm	1,000	A	52	5-13-1780	Combs Sett	

Entree	Acres	Book	Page	Entry Date	Watercourse	Notes
Connally, John	1,000	B	11	11– 6–1784		
Connell, Ann	500	A	224	12–12–1782	Cartrights Cr	
Connell, Ann	500	A	224	12–12–1782	Salt R	
Conner, Francis	400	A	254	1–16–1783	Coxes Cr	
Conner, Francis	400	A	254	1–15–1783	Otter Cr	Withdrawn
Conner, George	800	A	254	1–16–1783	Coxes Cr	
Conner, Lewis	750	A	78	5–20–1780	Bowmans Cr	50 Mil
Conner, Richard	300	A	160	7– 7–1780	Coxes Cr	
Conner, Richard	260	A	200	3–26–1781	Simpsons Cr	
Connor, Francis	400	A	159	7– 4–1780	Otter Cr	Withdrawn
Connor, George	400	A	159	7– 4–1780	Otter Cr	Withdrawn
Connor, George	400	A	159	7– 4–1780	Otter Cr	Withdrawn
Connor, George	400	A	254	1–15–1783	Otter Cr	Withdrawn
Connor, Lewis	50	A	30	4–28–1780	Bowman Cr	Mil
Connor, Lewis	500	A	52	5–13–1780	Bowmans Cr	
Connor, Richard	260	A	160	7– 7–1780	Coxes Cr	Withdrawn
Conrod, Nicholas	1,000	A	251	1– 9–1783	Pittmans Cr	
Consellea, Herman	400	A	4	11–15–1779	East Fk Salt R	
Constant, John	400	A	36	4–29–1780	Strodes Fk	
Constant, John	1,000	A	36	4–29–1780	Elkhorn	
Conway, John Jr	1,000	A	37	4–29–1780	Conway Sett	
Conway, John	400	A	252	1–13–1783	Beech Fk	
Conway, John	400	A	333	1–20–1784	Pottengers Cr	
Condor, James	325	A	189	3–15–1781	Floyds Fk	
Coocke, Benj	1,000	A	260	2– 4–1783	Beaver Dam Fk	
Cook, John	150	A	112	5–30–1780	Paint Lick Cr	
Cook, David	400	A	36	4–29–1780	Dicks R	
Cooke, Edward	1,500	A	236	12–20–1782	Beaver Dam	Surveyed
Cooke, James	400	A	237	12–21–1782	Rowling Fk	Surveyed
Cooke, John	500	A	224	12–13–1782	W Fk Coxes Cr	
Coombs, Ben	1,000	A	145	6–23–1780	Lulbelgube Cr	
Coombs, Cuthbert	1,000	A	56	5–15–1780	Simpson Cr	
Cooper, Wm	400	A	13	2– 9–1780	Otter Cr	
Cooper, Wm	1,000	A	37	4–29–1780	Otter Cr	
Cooper, Wm	1,000	A	157	6–30–1780	His Sett	
Copelin, Jacob	1,000	A	111	5–29–1780	Dick R	
Copelin, Jacob	400	A	111	5–29–1780	Dicks R	
Copelin, Jacob	400	A	111	5–29–1780	Rowling Fk	
Copper, Jesse	400	A	11	2– 4–1780	Stoners Fk	
Corbley, John	200	B	47	6– 8–1785		
Corbley, John	146	B	48	6–17–1785	Chinowith Run	
Corey, Edward	200	A	35	4–29–1780	Ky R	
Cory, Edward	50	A	21	4–20–1780	Green R	Withdrawn
Cory, Edward	50	A	21	4–20–1780	Green R	Mil withdrawn
Cory, Edward	50	A	21	4–20–1780	Green R	Mil withdrawn
Cory, Edward	50	A	21	4–20–1780	Falls Green R	Mil withdrawn
Cory, Edward	50	A	21	4–20–1780	Green R	Withdrawn
Cory, Edward	50	A	21	4–20–1780	Cabbin Cr	Mil withdrawn
Cory, Edward	50	A	21	4–20–1780	Cabbin Cr	Mil withdrawn
Cory, Edward	50	A	21	4–20–1780	Cabbin Cr	Mil withdrawn
Cory, Edward	200	A	35	4–29–1780	2 mile Cr	Mil
Cossart, Peter	600	A	173	9–23–1780	Muddy Cr	
Cotton, Nath	350	A	175	10– 6–1780	Hardens Cr	
Cotton, Nath	350	A	175	10– 6–1780	Beech Fk	
Couchman, Ben	500	A	134	6–16–1780	Mid Fk Licking	
Couchman, Ben	500	A	134	6–16–1780	His premption	
Coughman, Jacob	1,000	A	146	6–24–1780	Harmons Cr	
Coughman, Jacob	250	A	205	4– 9–1781	Cedar Cr	Surveyed
Coughman, Stopkel	250	A	209	5– 7–1781	W Fk Coxes Cr	Surveyed
Cowan, Andrew	1,000	A	181	10–23–1780	Boons Mill Cr	
Cowan, David	400	A	16	2–22–1780	Chaplin Cr	
Cowan, David	1,000	A	293	10– 4–1783	Rolling Fk	
Cowan, David	1,000	A	293	10– 4–1783	Rolling Fk	Withdrawn
Cowan, David	1,000	A	295	10–13–1783	Rolling Fk	Withdrawn
Cowan, David	1,000	B	4	9– 3–1784	Rolling Fk	Withdrawn
Cowan, David	900	B	4	9– 3–1784	Popes Cr	Surveyed
Cowan, David	900	B	4	9– 3–1784		Surveyed
Cowan, Jarrard	933	A	361	5–25–1784	Cloyds Cr	Withdrawn
Cowan, Jarrard	1,000	B	4	9– 3–1784		
Cowan, Jarrard	1,000	B	4	9– 3–1784	Popes Cr	Surveyed
Cowan, Jarrard	933	B	4	9– 3–1784		
Cowan, John	400	A	2	11– 3–1779	Harrods Cr	Surveyed
Cowan, John	400	A	11	2– 3–1780	Buffalo Rd	
Cowan, John	1,000	A	27	4–26–1780	Harrods Cr	
Cowan, John	1,000	A	27	4–26–1780	Harrods Cr	Surveyed

Entree	Acres	Book	Page	Entry Date	Watercourse	Notes
Cowan, John	1,000	A	99	5–26–1780	Hawkins Lick	....
Cowan, John	50	A	100	5–26–1780	Harrods Cr	....
Cowan, John	200	A	100	5–26–1780	Clarks Run	....
Cowan, John	400	A	107	5–29–1780	N Fk Cane Run	....
Cowan, John	———	A	311	12– 1–1783	Ohio R	Amended
Cowan, John	240	A	314	12–11–1783	Ohio R	Surveyed
Cowan, John	1,500	A	361	5–25–1784	Pittmans Cr	Withdrawn
Cowan, John	675	A	361	5–25–1784	Cloyds Cr	....
Cowan, John	240	B	4	9– 3–1784	———	....
Cowan, John	1,500	B	4	9– 3–1784	Pittmans Cr	....
Cowan, John	1,175	B	31	1– 8–1785	Rolling Fk	....
Cowan, John	675	B	31	1– 8–1785	———	....
Cowan, Wm	400	A	10	2– 3–1784	Stoners Cr	Withdrawn
Cowan, Wm	1,000	A	38	4–29–1780	Cowans Settl	....
Cowdon, James	2,000	A	270	3–28–1783	Green R	Mil
Cowell, David	5,000	B	43	4–11–1785	———	1,270 acres surveyed
Cowell, Dr David	12,000	A	332	1–20–1784	———	Withdrawn
Cowell, Dr David	3,700	A	358	5– 4–1784	Rowling Fk	
Cowell, Dr David	8,270	A	358	5– 3–1784	Salt R	Surveyed
Cowherd, James	1,160	A	264	2–15–1783	Brashears Cr	Withdrawn
Cowheard, James	1,160	A	335	1–27–1784	Beargrass Cr	Withdrawn
Cowherd, Jonathan	1,500	A	99	5–26–1780	Clear Cr	Surveyed
Cowherd, Jonathan	1,000	A	99	5–26–1780	Green R	721 acres surveyed
Cowherd, Jonathan	2,000	A	99	5–26–1780	Green R	1,577 acres surveyed
Cowherd, Jonathan	800	A	264	2–15–1783	Brashears Cr	Withdrawn
Cowherd, Jonathan	800	A	335	1–27–1784	Beargrass Cr	
Cox, David	312	A	197	3–17–1781	———	Withdrawn
Cox, David	1,000	A	197	3–17–1781	Coxes Cr	Surveyed
Cox, David	312	A	203	4– 3–1781	Fromans Cr	Surveyed
Cox, David	297	A	254	1–16–1783	Coxs Cr	....
Cox, David	132	A	254	1–16–1783	Rodgers Fk	Surveyed
Cox, David	429	A	267	2–28–1783	Not surveyed	Warrant returned
Cox, David	1,000	A	355	4–23–1784	Coxes Cr	Surveyed
Cox, Gabriel	400	A	314	12–12–1783	Salt R	Withdrawn
Cox, Gabriel	600	A	326	1– 1–1784	Brashears Cr	Withdrawn
Cox, Gabriel	600	A	332	1–19–1784	Salt R	....
Cox, Gabriel	400	A	332	1–19–1784	Salt R	....
Cox, Gabriel	642	A	347	3–22–1784	Salt R	Surveyed
Cox, Gabriel	148	A	356	4–28–1784	Salt R	Surveyed
Cox, Gabriel	1,242	A	375	7–29–1784	———	642 acres surveyed
Cox, Gabriel	2,625	A	375	7–29–1784	———	148 acres surveyed
Cox, Isaac	500	A	144	6–23–1780	Coxes Cr	Withdrawn
Cox, Isaac	300	A	161	7–10–1780	Coxes Cr	Withdrawn
Cox, Isaac	500	A	176	10– 9–1780	S Fk Coxes Cr	Withdrawn
Cox, Isaac	300	A	197	3–17–1781	Coxes Cr	Withdrawn
Cox, Isaac	400	A	197	3–17–1781	His Premption	Surveyed
Cox, Isaac	1,000	A	197	3–17–1781	———	Surveyed
Cox, Isaac	250	A	211	6–11–1781	Stewarts Cr	Withdrawn
Cox, Isaac	1,000	A	261	2– 4–1783	Salt R	Withdrawn
Cox, Isaac	258	A	267	2–28–1783	250 acres surveyed	Warrant returned
Cox, Isaac	400	A	267	3–28–1783	Beech Fk	Withdrawn
Cox, Isaac	456	A	272	3–31–1783	Salt R	Surveyed
Cox, Isaac	300	A	278	4–14–1783	Nolin Cr	Surveyed
Cox, Isaac	500	A	280	6–18–1783	Fromans Fk	Withdrawn
Cox, Isaac	500	A	283	7– 4–1783	Salt R	Withdrawn
Cox, Isaac	1,000	A	283	7– 4–1783	Salt R	Withdrawn
Cox, Isaac	500	A	288	8–29–1783	Coxes Cr	Withdrawn
Cox, Isaac	500	A	288	8–29–1783	Coxes Cr	Withdrawn
Cox, Isaac	500	A	290	9–10–1783	Coxes Cr	Withdrawn
Cox, Isaac	500	A	291	9–13–1783	Mill Cr	Surveyed
Cox, Isaac	1,000	A	299	10–28–1783	Nolelinn Cr	Surveyed
Cox, Isaac	1,000	A	299	10–28–1783	Youngers Cr	....
Cox, Isaac	5,000	A	299	10–28–1783	Rudes Cr	Surveyed
Cox, Isaac	1,000	A	331	1–16–1784	———	Returned
Cox, Isaac	2,700	A	332	1–19–1784	N & S Fk Harrods	....
Cox, Isaac	400	A	332	1–19–1784	Beech Fk	....
Cox, Isaac	300	A	332	1–19–1784	John Whitledges	....
Cox, Isaac	500	A	332	1–19–1784	———	....
Cox, Isaac	500	A	332	1–19–1784	Coxes Cr	Withdrawn
Cox, Isaac	300	A	333	1–21–1784	———	Amended
Cox, Isaac	2,700	A	333	1–21–1784	Hards Cr	200 acres surveyed
Cox, Isaac	500	A	355	4–23–1784	Coxes Cr	Withdrawn
Cox, Isaac	190	A	355	4–23–1784	Coxes Cr	

Entree	Acres	Book	Page	Entry Date	Watercourse	Notes
Cox, Isaac	1,200	A	355	4–19–1784	Clear Cr	
Cox, Isaac	62	A	356	4–28–1784	Plumb Cr	Withdrawn
Cox, Isaac	220	A	363	6– 4–1784	Stewarts Cr	Surveyed
Cox, Isaac	250	A	363	6– 4–1784	Salt R	Surveyed
Cox, Isaac	190	A	371	7–16–1784	————	
Cox, Isaac	300	B	6	9–13–1784	Coxes Cr	Surveyed
Cox, Isaac	944	B	6	9–13–1784	————	Withdrawn
Cox, Isaac	152	B	13	11–11–1784	Coxes Cr	
Cox, Isaac	110	B	24	12–10–1784	Fromans Cr	Surveyed
Cox, Isaac	62	B	24	12–10–1784	————	Withdrawn
Cox, Isaac	644	B	32	1–12–1785	Coxes Cr	
Cox, Isaac	75	B	34	1–25–1785	Cedar Cr	
Cox, Isaac	600	B	39	2– 4–1785	Salt R	
Cox, Isaac	600	B	39	2– 4–1785	————	Withdrawn
Cox, Isaac	75	B	46	5–26–1785	————	
Cox, Isaac et al	1,922	B	48	6–14–1785	Salt R	
Cox, James	2,700	A	335	1–31–1784	Harrods Cr	Amended
Cox, James	190	A	371	7–16–1784	Buffaloe Cr	
Cox, James	952	A	375	7–29–1784	————	
Cox, John	1,000	A	242	12–25–1782	Drennons Lick Cr	Surveyed
Cox, Susannah	315	A	362	6– 1–1784	————	
Cox, Susannah	315	A	362	6– 1–1784	Salt R	
Craddick, Wm	1,500	A	307	11–20–1783	————	
Craddick, Wm	1,500	A	234	12–19–1782	Rough Cr	
Craig, Ben	400	A	26	4–26–1780	N Fk Elkhorn	
Craig, Ben	500	A	27	4–26–1780	Licking	Mil
Craig, Ben	100	A	27	4–26–1780	Ky R	Mil
Craig, Ben	250	A	30	4–27–1780	Boggs Fk	Mil
Craig, Ben	500	A	70	5–18–1780	W Br Licking Cr	
Craig, Ben	1,000	A	163	7–21–1780	N Fk Green Cr	
Craig, Benj	3,916	A	246	1– 6–1783	Green R	
Craig, Ben	1,000	A	247	1– 7–1783	Green R	
Craig, Benj	250	A	247	1– 7–1783	Green R	
Craig, Benj	250	A	247	1– 7–1783	Green R	
Craig, Elijah	400	A	2	11– 5–1779	Salt R	Surveyed
Craig, Elijah	400	A	2	11– 5–1779	Elkhorn	
Craig, Elijah	500	A	27	4–26–1780	Licking Cr	Mil
Craig, Elijah	500	A	29	4–27–1780	Gestes Cr	Mil
Craig, Elijah	200	A	29	4–27–1780	Cane Run	Mil
Craig, Elijah	463	A	34	4–29–1780	————	Mil
Craig, Elijah	700	A	39	5– 9–1780	Ohio R	
Craig, Elijah	500	A	58	5–15–1780	Elkhorn	
Craig, Elijah	1,000	A	62	5–16–1780	18 Mile Cr	Surveyed
Craig, Elijah	800	A	66	5–17–1780	Ohio R	
Craig, Elijah	300	A	84	5–22–1780	18 Mile Cr	
Craig, Elijah	1,000	A	115	5–30–1780	Salt R	
Craig, James	400	A	13	2– 9–1780	Hanging Fk	
Craig, James	1,000	A	120	6– 1–1780	Hanging Fk	
Craig, James	2,000	A	148	6–24–1780	Indian Cr	
Craig, John	400	A	13	2–29–1780	Hanging Fk	
Craig, John	400	A	17	2– 8–1780	Glens Cr	
Craig, John	200	A	25	4–25–1780	Carters Line	Mil surveyed
Craig, John	200	A	25	4–25–1780	Ky R	Mil
Craig, John	200	A	27	4–26–1780	Glens Cr	Mil
Craig, John	150	A	30	4–28–1780	Ky R	Mil
Craig, John	350	A	34	4–29–1780	Ohio R	Surveyed
Craig, John	1,000	A	65	5–17–1780	N Fk Licking	
Craig, John	1,000	A	65	5–17–1780	Elkhorn	Surveyed
Craig, John	1,000	A	66	5–17–1780	Ohio R	
Craig, John	1,000	A	66	5–17–1780	Ohio R	
Craig, John	600	A	75	5–19–1780	Clear Cr	
Craig, John	400	A	75	5–19–1780	N Fk Elkhorn	Surveyed
Craig, John	2,000	A	75	5–19–1780	Little Ky R	Surveyed
Craig, John	100	A	80	5–22–1780	Glens Cr	
Craig, John	800	A	85	5–22–1780	Kitchams Cabbin	
Craig, John	1,000	A	85	5–22–1780	Ohio R	
Craig, John	1,000	A	120	6– 1–1780	Hanging Fk	
Craig, John	1,000	A	120	6– 1–1780	Hanking Fk	
Craig, John	1,000	A	120	6– 1–1780	Hanging Fk	
Craig, John	1,000	A	120	6– 1–1780	Hanging Fk	
Craig, John	200	A	170	9–11–1780	Hanging Fk	
Craige, John	1,820	A	341	2–21–1784	Reedy Cr	
Craig, John	3,180	A	341	2–21–1784	Reedy Cr	1,300 acres surveyed
Craig, John	1,000	A	361	5–25–1784	Pittmans Cr	
Craig, John	743	A	361	5–25–1784	Pittmans Cr	
Craig, John	500	A	373	7–26–1784	Pittmans Cr	
Craig, John	3,700	B	40	2–19–1785	————	
Craig, John Jr	500	A	65	5–17–1780	N Fk Licking	
Craig, Jeremiah	50	A	24	4–25–1780	N Fk Glens Cr	Mil
Craig, Jeremiah	500	A	54	5–15–1780	M Fk Licking	

Entree	Acres	Book	Page	Entry Date	Watercourse	Notes
Craig, Jeremiah	500	A	54	5–15–1780	M Fk Licking	
Craig, Jeremiah	500	A	54	5–15–1780	Glens Cr	
Craig, Joseph	300	A	29	4–27–1780	Jessamine	
Craig, Joseph	50	A	31	4–28–1780	————	Mil
Craig, Joseph	1,000	A	65	5–17–1780	N Fk Licking	
Craig, Joseph	1,000	A	85	5–22–1780	Ohio R	
Craig, Lewis	25	A	2	11– 6–1779	Russell Springs	Withdrawn
Craig, Lewis	400	A	2	11– 5–1779	Silver Cr	
Craig, Lewis	400	A	17	2–28–1780	S Fk Elkhorn	
Craig, Lewis	50	A	23	4–24–1780	Glens Cr	Mil
Craig, Lewis	50	A	23	4–24–1780	Glens Cr	Mil
Craig, Lewis	600	A	23	4–24–1780	N Fk Elkhorn	Mil
Craig, Lewis	200	A	24	4–25–1780	Rockhouse Br	Mil
Craig, Lewis	100	A	24	4–25–1780	Ky R	
Craig, Lewis	100	A	24	4–25–1780	Gilbert & Paint Lick	Mil
Craig, Lewis	200	A	25	4–25–1780	Upper Harrods Cr	
Craig, Lewis	1,000	A	26	4–26–1780	N Fk Elkhorn	
Craig, Lewis	1,000	A	26	4–26–1780	N Fk Elkhorn	
Craig, Lewis	1,000	A	27	4–26–1780	Licking	Mil
Craig, Lewis	250	A	30	4–28–1780	M Fk Elkhorn	Mil
Craig, Lewis	25	A	32	4–29–1780	Rock Spring	
Craig, Lewis	100	A	34	4–29–1780	Gilberts Cr	
Craig, Lewis	4,000	A	34	4–29–1780	Elkhorn	Mil
Craig, Lewis	2,000	A	34	4–29–1780	Salt Spring	Mil
Craig, Lewis	500	A	34	4–29–1780	N Fk Elkhorn	
Craig, Lewis	1,000	A	34	4–29–1780	Cabbin Cr	Mil
Craig, Lewis	400	A	34	4–29–1780	————	
Craig, Lewis	150	A	35	4–29–1780	Ky R	Mil
Craig, Lewis	300	A	39	5– 9–1780	N Fk Elkhorn	
Craig, Lewis	300	A	39	5– 9–1780	S Fk Elkhorn	
Craig, Lewis	400	A	39	5– 9–1780	————	
Craig, Lewis	700	A	47	5–12–1780	N Fk Elkhorn	Withdrawn
Craig, Lewis	700	A	53	5–13–1780	Elkhorn	400 acres withdrawn
Craig, Lewis	600	A	59	5–16–1780	N Elkhorn	
Craig, Lewis	1,000	A	59	5–16–1780	Clear Cr	
Craig, Lewis	1,000	A	59	5–16–1780	Clear Cr	
Craig, Lewis	1,000	A	62	5–16–1780	N Fk Elkhorn	
Craig, Lewis	50	A	66	5–17–1780	Island Ohio R	
Craig, Lewis	800	A	66	5–17–1780	Ohio R	
Craig, Lewis	800	A	66	5–17–1780	Ohio R	
Craig, Lewis	100	A	69	5–18–1780	Gilberts Cr	
Craig, Lewis	200	A	69	5–18–1780	Gilberts Cr	
Craig, Lewis	200	A	69	5–18–1780	Dicks R	
Craig, Lewis	250	A	69	5–18–1780	Gilbert Cr	
Craig, Lewis	1,000	A	85	5–22–1780	Elkhorn Fk	
Craige, Lewis	2,800	A	249	1– 8–1783	Reed Cr	Surveyed
Craig, Lewis	2,231	A	302	11– 7–1783	Mulberry Cr	
Craig, Lewis	2,000	B	31	1– 3–1785	————	
Craig, Lewis	231	B	31	1– 3–1785	————	
Craig, Lewis et al	400	A	2	11– 6–1779	Gilberts Cr	Surveyed
Craig, Lewis et al	400	A	2	11– 5–1779	Hanging Fk Dix R	Surveyed
Craig, Lewis et al	1,000	A	26	4–26–1780	N Fk Elkhorn	
Craige, Lewis et al	1,000	A	80	5–20–1780	Their Premption	Surveyed
Craig, Robert	400	A	120	6– 1–1780	Hanging Fk	
Craig, Samuel	337	A	22	4–21–1780	Br Hanging Fk	Mil
Craige, Samuel	1,000	A	120	6– 1–1780	Hanging Fk	
Craig, Toliver	500	A	54	5–15–1780	M Fk Licking	
Craig, Toliver Jr	500	A	63	5–16–1780	N Fk Elkhorn	
Craig, Wm	400	A	13	2– 9–1780	Hanging Fk	
Craig, Wm	1,000	A	120	6– 1–1780	Hanging Fk	
Crain, James	2,000	A	281	6–30–1783	Tick Cr	Surveyed
Crane, James	250	A	75	5–19–1780	Floyds Cr	Mil surveyed
Crane, James	1,000	A	109	5–29–1780	Eatons Cr	
Crawford, Ben	500	A	115	5–31–1780	Licking	
Crawford, David	1,000	A	87	5–23–1780	Clear Cr	Surveyed
Crawford, David	1,000	A	246	1– 6–1783	Harrods Cr	Surveyed
Crawford, George	1,250	A	254	1–15–1783	Hardens Cr	
Crawford, George	1,268	A	254	1–15–1783	Rolling Fk	
Crawford, John	1,500	A	246	1– 6–1783	Geses Cr	Surveyed
Crawford, John	500	A	246	1– 6–1783	E Fk Clear Cr	
Crawford, John	350	A	246	1– 6–1783	Coxes Cr	
Crawford, John	350	A	246	1– 6–1783	Coxes Cr	
Crawford, John	1,000	A	247	1– 7–1783	Nolin Cr	
Crawford, John	1,095	A	255	1–20–1783	Rolling Fk	Withdrawn
Crawford, John	1,095	A	296	10–15–1783	Robinsons Cr	
Crawford, Nathan	1,427½	A	315	12–13–1783	Robinsons Cr	
Crawford, Nelson	1,145	A	360	5–13–1784	————	
Crawford, Peter	400	A	203	4– 3–1781	Little Ky R	
Crawford, Val, heirs	1,000	A	148	6–24–1780	Indian Cr	Mil

Entree	Acres	Book	Page	Entry Date	Watercourse	Notes
Crawford, Wm.	500	A	124	6– 3–1780	Licking	
Crawford, Wm.	400	A	124	6– 3–1780	Licking	
Crawford, Wm.	200	A	150	6–26–1780	N Fk Licking	
Crawford, Wm.	1,000	A	324	12–26–1783	Little Ky R	Mil
Crettenden, John	400	A	155	6–29–1780	Sinking Spring	
Crettenden, John	300	A	155	6–29–1780	S Fk Elkhorn	Withdrawn
Crettenden, John	998	A	160	7– 7–1780	Eagle Cr	
Crenshaw, Thomas	1,456½	A	242	12–25–1782	Plumb Cr	Surveyed
Criss, George	220	A	258	1–27–1783	Paul Froman	300 acres surveyed
Crittenden, John	400	A	7	1–11–1780	Licking Cr	Surveyed
Crittenden, John	1,000	A	33	4–29–1780	Sinking Cr	Surveyed
Crittenden, John	493	A	158	7– 3–1780	Ohio R	
Crockett, Andrew	400	A	15	2–21–1780	Drakes Camp Cr	
Crockett, Andrew	1,000	A	115	5–30–1780	Stone Lick Cr	
Crockett, Andrew	1,000	A	146	6–24–1780	N Fk Licking	
Crockett, James	1,000	A	146	6–24–1780	Newells Land	
Crockett, James	750	A	173	9–23–1780	Paint Lick Cr	
Crockett, John	1,500	A	318	12–16–1783	18 Mile Cr	Surveyed
Crockett, Walter	1,000	A	265	2–21–1783	Floyds Fk	Surveyed
Crow, John	400	A	139	6–21–1780	S W Stephen F Garrison	
Crow, John	1,000	A	179	10–19–1780	Dicks R	
Crow, John	300	A	235	12–20–1782	Sinking Run	Surveyed
Crow, John	200	A	235	12–20–1782	S Fk Nole Linn Cr	Surveyed
Crow, John	500	A	235	12–19–1782	Caney Cr	202 acres surveyed
Crow, John	1,500	A	236	12–20–1782	Green R	Surveyed
Crow, John	1,458	A	237	12–21–1782	Read Cr	Surveyed
Crow, John	4,000	A	249	1– 8–1783	Reed Cr	Surveyed
Crow, John	1,031	A	302	11– 7–1783	Green R	640 acres surveyed
Crow, John	250	A	302	11– 7–1783	Green R	
Crow, John	1,157	A	302	11–10–1783	Bear Cr	Surveyed
Crow, John	843	A	302	11–10–1783	S Fk Nolelinn Cr	Surveyed
Crow, John	6,000	A	320	12–17–1783	Blackfords Cr	
Crow, John	1,000	A	344	3– 3–1784	Reedy Cr	Surveyed
Crow, John	1,919	A	345	3– 9–1784	———	Surveyed returned
Crow, John	1,458½	B	10	10–11–1784	———	Surveyed
Crow, John	1,000	B	31	1– 3–1785	———	
Crow, John	3,000	B	31	1– 3–1785	———	1,500 acres surveyed returned
Crow, John	3,000	B	31	1– 3–1785	———	1,500 acres surveyed
Crow, John	298	B	49	6–17–1785	Simpson Cr	
Crow, Thomas	4,787	A	236	12–20–1782	Beaver Dam	Surveyed
Crow, Walter	500	A	302	11–10–1783	Bear Cr	Surveyed
Crow, Wm.	1,000	A	179	10–17–1780	His Sett	
Crow, Wm.	800	A	226	12–13–1782	Floyds Fk	
Crow, Wm.	759½	A	266	2–25–1783		
Crow, Wm.	800	A	266	2–25–1783	Indian Lick	
Crow, Wm.	1,000	A	266	2–25–1783	Indian Licks	
Crow, Wm.	650	A	311	12– 1–1783	Bear Cr	
Crowder, John	891	A	311	11–29–1783	Chaplins Fk	
Crowder, Wm.	687	A	234	12–19–1782	Rough Cr	
Crowder, Wm.	687	A	307	11–20–1783		
Crowder, Wm.	1,375	A	326	1– 1–1784	Big Cr	
Crume, Daniel	500	A	106	5–17–1780	Beech Fk	Surveyed
Crume, Phillip	1,000	A	105	5–27–1780	Beech Fk	Surveyed
Crume, Phillip	201	A	317	12–16–1783	Beech Fk	
Crump, Goodrich	2,000	A	304	1–113–1783	Panther Cr	
Crump, Goodrich	600	A	304	11–13–1783	Panther Cr	
Crump, Twiner	400	A	47	5–12–1780	Hingston Fk	
Cruse, David	1,000	A	182	10–26–1780	Muddy Cr	
Cruse, David	400	A	182	10–26–1780	Licking	
Cruse, David	200	A	182	10–25–1780	Ky R	Mil
Cruse, David	1,000	A	182	10–25–1780	Muddy Cr	Withdrawn
Crutcher, Henry	5,000	A	341	2–23–1784	Brashears Cr	Surveyed
Crutcher, James	3,000	A	270	3–28–1783	Panther Cr	Withdrawn
Crutcher, James	3,000	A	309	11–25–1783	Green R	Withdrawn
Crutcher, James	3,000	A	309	11–25–1783	Panther Cr	Withdrawn
Crutcher, James	500	A	328	1– 9–1784	Rolling Fk	
Crutcher, James	500	A	338	2–12–1784	Floyds Fk	Withdrawn
Crutcher, James	1,000	B	8	9–27–1784	Robinsons Cr	
Crutcher, James	3,000	B	12	11–11–1784	———	Withdrawn
Crutcher, James	3,000	B	17	11–17–1784	Drennens Lick	Withdrawn
Crutcher, James	500	B	18	11–17–1784	Drennens Lick Cr	Withdrawn
Crutcher, James	500	B	18	11–17–1784	———	Withdrawn
Crutcher, James	3,000	B	43	4–15–1785	Drennens Lick	

Entree	Acres	Book	Page	Entry Date	Watercourse	Notes
Crutchfield, John......	50	A	35	4–29–1780	Chaplins Fk......	Mil
Crutchfield, John......	5,000	A	244	12–26–1782	Fromans Cr......	....
Cryble, Joseph........	400	A	102	5–27–1780	Floyd Fk......	....
Culbertson, Samuel....	500	A	275	4– 9–1783	Caney Cr......	Withdrawn
Culbertson, Samuel....	1,000	A	330	1–15–1784	Little Clifty Cr.....	Surveyed
Culbertson, Samuel....	1,031	A	285	8– 7–1783	Caney Cr......	Withdrawn
Culbertson, Samuel....	515	A	285	8– 5–1783	Cartright Cr......	Withdrawn
Culbertson, Samuel....	500	A	288	9– 1–1783	Floyds Fk......	....
Culbertson, Samuel....	500	A	289	9– 8–1783	Rough Cr......	....
Culbertson, Samuel....	500	A	289	9– 8–1783	Nolelin Cr......	....
Culbertson, Samuel....	515	A	290	9–10–1783	Cartright Cr......	Withdrawn
Culbertson, Samuel....	500	A	331	1–16–1784	Caney Fk......	Withdrawn
Culbertson, Samuel....	515	A	341	2–26–1784	Harrods Cr......	Withdrawn
Culbertson, Samuel....	515	A	346	3–12–1784	Harrods Cr......	Withdrawn
Culbertson, Samuel....	515	A	346	3–12–1784	————	Withdrawn
Culbertson, Samuel....	1,031	A	353	4–16–1784	Simpsons Cr......	Withdrawn
Culbertson, Samuel....	1,031	A	353	4–16–1784	Nole Linn Cr......	....
Culbertson, Samuel....	170	B	30	12–23–1784	....	Withdrawn
Culbertson, Samuel....	170	B	30	12–23–1784	....	Surveyed
Culbertson, Samuel....	82	B	49	6–17–1785	....	Withdrawn
Culbertson, Sam W....	2,000	A	257	1–25–1783	Big & Little Clifty Cr......	1,000 acres surveyed 1,000 acres withdrawn
Culbertson, Sam W....	500	A	257	1–25–1783	Caney Cr.........	Surveyed
Cullum, George.......	300	A	155	6–29–1780	Salt R.........	......
Cullum, George.......	700	A	155	6–29–1780	Salt R.........	Surveyed
Cullum, George.......	1,000	B	34	1–22–1785	————	700 acres surveyed
Cummings, Wm......	400	A	294	10–11–1783	Pattons Cr......	....
Cummins, Charles.....	250	A	102	5–26–1780	Cummins premption	Surveyed
Cundiff, John.........	1,000	A	146	6–24–1780	Cabbin Cr......	....
Cunningham, James...	400	A	125	6– 5–1780	Hingston Fk......	....
Cunningham, James...	100	A	125	6– 5–1780	Hingston Fk......	....
Cunningham, Thomas..	335	A	246	1– 1–1783	Stewarts Cr......	Withdrawn
Cunningham, Thomas..	400	A	246	1– 1–1783	Stewart Cr......	Withdrawn
Cunningham, Thomas..	353	A	252	1–13–1783	Mill Cr.........	Withdrawn
Cunningham, Thomas..	400	A	252	1–13–1783	George Hart......	....
Cunningham, Thomas..	1,135	A	252	1–13–1783	Beech Fk.........	600 acres surveyed 535 acres withdrawn
Cunningham, Thomas..	1,200	A	252	1–13–1783	Mill Cr.........	700 acres surveyed 500 acres withdrawn
Cunningham, Thomas..	100	A	253	1–15–1783	Beech Fk......	....
Cunningham, Thomas..	535	A	253	1–15–1783	Beech Fk......	....
Cunningham, Thos....	135	A	254	1–18–1783	Beech Fk......	....
Cunningham, Thos....	200	A	254	1–17–1783	Beech Fk......	....
Cunningham, Thos....	100	A	254	1–17–1783	Beech Fk......	....
Cunningham, Thos....	300	A	254	1–17–1783	Pottengers Cr......	....
Cunningham, Thomas..	500	A	255	1–18–1783	Skeggs Cr......	Surveyed
Cunningham, Thomas..	700	A	255	1–18–1783	Mill Cr......	....
Cunningham, Thomas..	500	A	255	1–18–1783	Mill Cr......	Surveyed
Cunningham, Thomas..	1,000	A	264	2–15–1783	Cartright Cr......	....
Cunningham, Thomas..	400	A	275	4– 9–1783	S Fk Nole Linn Cr..	Surveyed
Cunningham, Thomas..	400	A	291	9–13–1783	Mill Cr......	Withdrawn
Cunningham, Thomas..	688	A	291	9–13–1783	Stewarts Cr......	Withdrawn
Cunningham, Thomas..	353	A	291	9–13–1783	Mill Cr......	Withdrawn
Cunningham, Thomas..	335	A	291	9–13–1783	George Harts......	Withdrawn
Cunningham, Thos....	709	A	306	11–19–1783	Bear Cr......	Surveyed
Cunningham, Thomas..	400	A	314	12–10–1783	Simpsons Cr......	....
Cunningham, Thomas..	688	A	336	2– 5–1784	Mill Cr......	Surveyed
Cunningham, Thomas..	500	A	345	3–11–1784	Beech Fk......	Withdrawn
Cunningham, Thomas..	10,000	A	351	4–12–1784	Sulphur Lick Cr....	....
Cunningham, Thomas..	10,000	A	351	4–12–1784	Brush Cr....	....
Cunningham, Thomas..	500	A	355	4–19–1784	Beech Fk......	Withdrawn
Cunringham, Thomas..	3,112½	A	364	6– 4–1784	————	600 acres surveyed
Cunningham, Thomas..	353	A	377	8–11–1784	————	....
Cunningham, Thomas..	100	B	4	8–31–1784	Beech Fk......	....
Cunningham, Thomas..	100	B	4	8–31–1784	Coxes Cr......	Withdrawn
Cunningham, Thomas..	709½	B	41	3– 2–1785	————	Surveyed
Cunningham, Thos et al.	688	A	336	2– 7–1784	Rough Cr......	....
Cunningham, Thos et al.	400	A	254	1–18–1783	Rolling Fk......	....
Cunningham, Walter..	1,000	A	30	4–28–1780	S Fk Beargrass......	Mil
Cunningham, Walter...	1,000	A	263	2–15–1783	5 miles from Falls..	Mil
Cuple, Christain.......	1,100	A	354	4–16–1784	Pattons Cr........	Surveyed

Entree	Acres	Book	Page	Entry Date	Watercourse	Notes
Curd, Benj et al	1,500	B	10	10–11–1784	———	
Curd, Charles	50	A	35	4–29–1780	Howards Cr	Mil
Curd, Charles	800	A	63	5–16–1780	Ohio R	
Curd, Edmund	4,625	A	328	1–12–1784	Falls Ohio R	
Curd, Edward	1,002	A	53	5–13–1780	Kentucky R	
Curd, John	1,000	A	43	5–11–1780	Kentucky R	
Curd, John	1,000	A	43	5–11–1780	Licking	
Curd, John	1,000	A	43	5–11–1780	Green R	
Curd, John	1,000	A	43	5–11–1780	Rockcastle	
Curd, John	2,000	A	43	5–11–1780	Ohio R	Withdrawn
Curd, John	1,000	A	43	5–11–1780	Coxes Cr	Withdrawn
Curd, John	1,000	A	43	5–11–1780	Bullitts Lick	Withdrawn
Curd, John	1,000	A	43	5–11–1780	1 lumb Cr	Withdrawn
Curd, John	1,000	A	222	12–9–1782	Coxes Cr	
Curd, John	1,000	A	222	12–9–1782	Little Kentucky R	Withdrawn
Curd, John	1,000	A	222	12–9–1782	Col Christain	Withdrawn
Curd, John	1,000	A	272	3–31–1783	Salt R	
Curd, John	1,000	A	272	3–31–1783	Ohio R	Withdrawn
Curd, John	1,000	A	347	3–17–1784	Brashears Cr	
Curd, John	1,000	A	347	3–17–1784	Ohio R	Withdrawn
Curd, John	1,829	B	10	10–11–1784	———	
Curd, John et al	1,500	A	287	8–16–1783	Beech Fk	
Curd, Joseph	400	A	74	5–19–1780	N Fk Elkhorn	
Curd, Joseph	300	A	74	5–19–1780	N Fk Elkhorn	
Curd, Wm	1,000	A	53	5–13–1780	Kentucky R	
Curry, James	400	A	3	11–11–1779	Salt R	Surveyed
Curry, James	300	A	159	7–5–1780	His Sett	
Curry, James	700	A	159	7–5–1780	His Sett	
Curry, James	9,376	A	343	3–3–1784	Bear & Reedy Cr	Withdrawn
Curry, James	9,376	B	37	1–28–1785	Nole Linn Cr	
Curry, James	9,376	B	37	1–27–1785	Bear Cr	Withdrawn
Curry, John	400	A	96	5–24–1780	Chaplins Fk	
Curry, John	1,039¾	A	259	1–30–1783	Glen Cr	Surveyed
Curry, Thomas	500	A	190	3–15–1781	N Fk Floyds Fk	Surveyed
Curry, Wm	400	A	96	5–24–1780	Chaplins Fk	
Dabney, Charles	1,000	A	147	6–24–1780	Yellow Cr	
Dabney, G	1,000	A	147	6–24–1780	Yellow Cr	
Dagerly, Thos	400	A	5	12–7–1779	Brashear Cr	
Dalton, David	600	A	327	1–7–1784	Salt R	
Dalton, David	600	A	322	12–22–1783	Salt R	Withdrawn
Dalton, David	296	A	341	2–26–1784	———	
Daniel, Thos	400	A	11	2–4–1780	Stoners Fk	
Daniel, Thos	2,000	A	156	6–30–1780	Green R	
Daniel, Vivion	500	A	301	11–1–1783	Rock Lick Cr	
Daniels, Vivion	500	B	49	6–17–1785	———	
Daniel, Walker	960	A	78	5–20–1780	Holders Cr	
Daniel, Walker	960	A	97	5–25–1780	Holders Cr	
Daniel, Walker	400	A	230	12–17–1782	Coxes Cr	Withdrawn
Daniel, Walker	2,000	A	230	12–17–1782	Rough Cr	
Daniel, Walker	500	A	231	12–17–1782	Robinsons Cr	
Daniel, Walker	2,000	A	231	12–17–1782	Green R	1,000 acres withdrawn
Daniels, Walker	1,000	A	231	12–17–1782	Kentucky R	
Daniel, Walker	1,000	A	231	12–17–1782	Green R	
Daniel, Walker	700	A	234	12–19–1782	Salt R	505 acres surveyed withdrawn
Daniel, Walker	1,000	A	235	12–20–1782	Ohio R	Surveyed
Daniel, Walker	1,000	A	235	12–20–1782	Green R	
Daniel, Walker	8,017	A	238	12–21–1782	Indian Camp Cr	Surveyed
Daniel, Walker	8,843	A	238	12–21–1782	Floyds Fk	Surveyed
Daniel, Walker	4,000	A	243	12–25–1782	Green R	Surveyed
Daniel, Walker	4,843	A	244	12–27–1782	Indian Camp Cr	6,000 acres surveyed
Daniel, Walker	800	A	250	1–8–1783	N Fk Caney Cr	Withdrawn
Daniel, Walker	600	A	263	2–15–1783	Rolling Fk	Withdrawn
Daniel, Walker	1,500	A	263	2–15–1783	Rowling Fk	600 acres surveyed; 900 acres withdrawn
Daniel, Walker	400	A	263	2–14–1783	Coxes Cr	Withdrawn
Daniel, Walker	1,000	A	272	3–31–1783	Camp Run	
Daniel, Walker	2,000	A	276	4–10–1783	Nole Linn Cr	Surveyed
Daniel, Walker	1,000	A	276	4–10–1783	Nole Linn Cr	Surveyed
Daniel, Walker	1,102	A	283	7–12–1783	Rough Cr	
Daniel, Walker	900	A	284	8–4–1783	Rolling Fk	Withdrawn
Daniel, Walker	600	A	284	8–4–1783	Rowling Fk	
Daniel, Walker	1,694	A	285	8–7–1783	Rowling Fk	
Daniel, Walker	500	A	285	8–5–1783	Indian Camp Cr	
Daniel, Walker	2,000	A	302	11–7–1783	Bear Cr	Surveyed
Daniel, Walker	8,843	A	310	11–26–1783	———	Surveyed

Entree	Acres	Book	Page	Entry Date	Watercourse	Notes
Daniel, Walker	400	A	322	12–25–1783	Coxes Cr	Surveyed
Daniel, Walker	700	A	322	12–25–1783	Salt R	Amended
Daniel, Walker	1,000	A	323	12–26–1783	Salt R	
Daniel, Walker	1,000	A	323	12–26–1783	Salt R	
Daniel, Walker	3,000	A	323	12–26–1783	near Kentucky R	
Daniel, Walker	800	A	339	2–14–1784	N Fk Caney Cr	Surveyed
Daniel, Walker	2,000	A	340	2–18–1784	Ohio R	
Daniel, Walker	372	A	345	3–12–1784	Beech Fk	
Daniels, Walker	20,000	A	345	3–12–1784	Green R	
Daniel, Walker	8,000	A	354	4–16–1784	Floyds Fk	
Daniel, Walker	2,500	A	355	4–24–1784	Hardins Cr	
Daniel, Walker	1,000	A	355	4–24–1784	Big Spring	
Daniel, Walker	8,000	A	369	7– 1–1784		
Daniel, Walker	1,500	A	372	7–21–1784	————	600 acres surveyed
Daniel, Walker	3,000	A	372	7–21–1784	————	428 acres surveyed
Daniel, Walker	5,954	A	372	7–21–1784	————	3,000 acres surveyed
Daniel, Walker	500	A	372	7–21–1784	————	400 acres surveyed
Daniel, Walker	8,843	B	47	5–26–1785	————	
Daniel, Walker	206	B	49	6–17–1785	————	
Daniel, Wm M	500	A	63	5–16–1780	N Fk Elkhorn	
Danton, Thomas	400	A	36	4–29–1780	Sinking Cr	Surveyed
Darnaby, Edward	50	A	31	4–28–1780	Dicks R	Mil
Darnel, John	844	A	65	5–17–1780	Pastures Lick Cr	
Dart, Joseph	500	A	87	5–23–1780	Hunting Cr	
Dandridge, Wm et al	3,750	A	237	12–21–1782	Kentucky E	Surveyed
Daugherty, John	600	A	36	4–29–1780	Gilmers Sett	
Davey, Brewer	1,000	A	315	12–13–1783	Salt R	
Davey, Brewer W	3,000	A	314	12–12–1783	Mill Cr	Surveyed
Davey, Brewer W	2,000	A	315	12–13–1783	Little Kentucky R	
Davidson, John	1,000	A	226	12–14–1783	Indian Kick Cr	
Davie, Alex W	559½	A	323	12–26–1783	Rowling Fk	
Davie, Alex W	2,000	A	323	12–26–1783	Salt R	
Davie, Alex W	2,233	A	323	12–26–1783	Kentucky R	Withdrawn
Davie, Alex W	2,000	A	323	12–26–1783	Kentucky R	Withdrawn
Davie, Alex W	2,128½	A	323	12–26–1783	Kentucky R	Surveyed
Davey, Alex W	4,233	A	349	4– 2–1784	Kentucky R	Surveyed
Davie, Alex Wm	2,233	A	349	4– 2–1784	Big Benson Cr	
Davie, Alex W	2,000	A	349	4– 2–1784	Big Benson Cr	Withdrawn
Davie, Alex et al	1,000	A	358	5– 3–1784	Kentucky R	Surveyed
Davis, Allen	500	A	126	6– 7–1780	Pond Cr	Surveyed
Davis, Asil	400	A	14	2–19–1780	Clear Cr	
Davis, Asil	1,000	A	168	9– 2–1780	Clear Cr	
Davis, Azariah	400	A	1	11– 3–1779	Salt R	Surveyed
Davis, Azariah	1,000	A	36	4–29–1780	Harrodsburg Run	Surveyed
Davis, Cornelius	300	A	125	6– 5–1780	Beech Fk	
Davis, Cornelius	300	A	132	6–14–1780	Simpson Cr	Surveyed
Davis, Cornelius	300	A	132	6–14–1780	Chaplins Fk	Withdrawn
Davis, Cornelius	300	A	210	5–30–1781	Beech Fk	
Davis, Edward	300	A	69	5–18–1780	Ohio R	
Davis, Edward	200	A	69	5–18–1780	Dicks R	
Davis, Henry	400	A	245	12–30–1782	Willsons Cr	
Davis, Henry	400	B	7	9–20–1784	Elk Cr	
Davis, Henry	400	B	7	9–20–1784	————	Withdrawn
Davis, Hugh	473¾	A	300	10–29–1783	Beech Fk	
Davis, Isaac	800	A	100	5–26–1780	Licking	
Davis, Isaac	800	A	100	5–26–1780	Licking	
Davis, Isaac	1,002	A	100	5–26–1780	Licking	
Davis, Isaac	1,000	A	100	5–26–1780	Small Mt Cr	
Davis, Isaac	560	A	223	12–12–1782	Wolf Cr	Surveyed
Davis, Isaac	500	A	227	12–14–1782	Mill Cr	Surveyed
Davis, Isaac	300	A	300	10–29–1783	Beech Fk	
Davis, Isaac	300	A	328	1–12–1784	Beech Fk	
Davis, Isaac	600	A	373	7–24–1784	————	
Davis, Isaac Jr	1,000	A	173	9–22–1780	Chaplins Fk	
Davis, James	400	A	26	4–26–1780	Whitley Station	
Davis, James	400	A	27	4–26–1780	Whitley Station	
Davis, James	250	A	64	5–17–1780	Beech Fk	
Davis, James	250	A	65	5–17–1780	Beech Fk	Withdrawn
Davis, James	1,000	A	138	6–20–1780	Flat Cr	
Davis, James	400	A	143	6–22–1780	Beech Fk	
Davis, James	500	A	163	7–29–1780	Green R	
Davis, James	800	A	334	1–24–1784	Mid Fk Sinking Cr	
Davis, James	400	A	334	1–24–1784	Green R	
Davis, Jesse	1,000	A	128	6– 8–1780	Beech Fk	
Davis, Jesse	1,650	A	128	6– 8–1780	Beech Fk	1,250 acres withdrawn

Entree	Acres	Book	Page	Entry Date	Watercourse	Notes
Davis, Jesse	600	A	129	6- 9-1780	Simpson Cr	Surveyed
Davis, Jesse	1,250	A	221	11- 9-1782	Beech Fk	Withdrawn
Davis, Jesse	1,250	A	223	12-12-1782	Brashears Cr	Surveyed
Davis, Jesse	500	A	300	10-29-1783	Beech Fk	....
Davis, Jesse	700	A	300	10-29-1783	Chaplins Fk	....
Davis, Jesse	400	A	304	11-14-1783	Sunfish Run	Surveyed
Davis, Jesse	1,000	A	364	6-11-1784	———	Amended
Davis, Jesse	1,300	A	373	7-24-1784	———	Returned
Davis, Jesse	3,000	A	373	7-24-1784	———	400 acres surveyed
Davis, Jeffery	400	A	80	5-20-1780	Br Paint Lick	....
Davis, John	245	A	53	5-15-1780	———	....
Davis, John	400	A	74	5-19-1780	Licking	....
Davis, John	400	A	95	5-24-1780	Stoners Fk	....
Davis, John	500	A	136	6-19-1780	Pottengers Cr	Withdrawn
Davis, John	500	A	174	9-29-1780	Pottengers Cr	Surveyed
Davis, John	1,000	A	181	10-24-1780	Pleasant Run	Surveyed
Davis, John	1,000	A	196	3-17-1781	Simpsons Cr	....
Davis, John	6,000	A	233	12-18-1782	Rough Cr	....
Davis, John R	2,000	A	233	12-18-1782	Mulberry Run	....
Davis, Joseph	600	A	67	5-17-1780	Licking	....
Davis, Joseph	1,000	A	84	5-22-1780	Licking	....
Davis, Joseph	1,000	A	109	5-29-1780	Paint Lick Cr	....
Davis, Joseph	400	A	281	6-20-1783	Chaplins Fk	Surveyed
Davis, Lewis	1,000	A	182	10-25-1780	Rowling Fk	Surveyed
Davis, Nathan	1,000	A	100	5-26-1780	Coxes Cr	....
Davis, Nathan	1,000	A	100	5-26-1780	Coxes Cr	....
Davis, Owen	1,000	A	36	4-29-1780	Dicks R	....
Davis, Philemon	500	A	90	5-23-1780	Rowling Fk	....
Davis, Phillip	1,000	A	178	10-10-1780	Panther Cr	....
Davis, Robert	400	A	38	4-29-1780	Dicks R	....
Davis, Robert	100	A	43	5-11-1780	Salt R	Surveyed
Davis, Robert	800	A	43	5-11-1780	Salt R	Surveyed
Davis, Samuel	400	A	38	4-29-1780	Gilmans Lick	....
Davis, Samuel	50	A	127	6- 8-1780	Hugh McGary Setl.	Mil
Davis, Samuel	400	A	134	6-16-1780	Silver Cr	....
Davis, Samuel	400	A	149	6-24-1780	Silver Cr	....
Davis, Samuel	3,500	A	233	12-18-1782	Yellow Cr	....
Davis, Wm	50	A	33	4-29-1780	Sugar Cr	Mil
Davis, Wm	400	A	37	4-29-1780	Clear Cr	....
Davis, Wm	1,000	A	125	6- 5-1780	Beards Cr	Withdrawn
Davis, Wm	1,000	A	125	6- 5-1780	Beech Fk	....
Davis, Wm	750	A	132	6-14-1780	Simpsons Cr	....
Davis, Wm	1,000	A	173	9-22-1780	Beech Fk	Surveyed
Davis, Wm	1,000	A	173	9-20-1780	Salt R	Withdrawn
Davis, Wm	400	A	179	10-17-1780	Dicks R	....
Davis, Wm	1,000	A	210	5-29-1781	Beards Cr	Withdrawn
Davis, Wm	400	A	304	11-14-1783	Sunfish Run	....
Davis, Wm	1,000	A	304	11-14-1783	Beech Fk	Withdrawn
Davis, Wm	2,000	A	364	6-11-1784	———	1,000 acres surveyed
Davis, Wm	350	A	371	7-12-1784	Salt R	....
Davis, Wm	250	A	371	7-12-1784	Mill Cr	....
Davis, Wm	750	B	37	1-27-1785	Clear Fk	....
Davis, Wm	750	B	37	1-27-1785	Simpsons Cr	Withdrawn
Day, Peter	200	A	154	6-27-1780	Elkhorn	....
Day, Sam	1,000	A	91	5-24-1780	Clear Cr	Surveyed
Day, Wm	400	A	58	5-15-1780	Simpsons Cr	....
Day, Wm	400	A	254	1-18-1783	Cartright Cr	Surveyed
Deacon, James	200	A	179	10-17-1780	Rowling Fk	....
Deacon, James	200	A	179	10-17-1780	Beech Fk	....
Deal, George	500	A	191	3-15-1781	Coxes Cr	Surveyed
Dean, Charles	1,399	A	66	5-17-1780	Rolling Fk	....
Defarges, Peter	100	B	44	5-10-1785	———	....
Defuges, Peter	500	A	183	10-27-1780	Green R	Surveyed
De La Porte, Joseph	5,000	A	44	5-11-1780	Ohio R	....
Demeree, John	400	A	249	1- 8-1783	Floyds Fk	....
Demerie, Peter	700	A	259	2- 3-1783	Clear Cr	323 acres surveyed
Deneal, James	50	A	47	5-12-1780	Beach Fk	Surveyed
Deneal, James	500	A	212	6-21-1781	Pleasant Run	Surveyed
Deneal, Wm	1,000	A	47	5-12-1780	Beach Fk	Surveyed
Dennis, Samuel	600	A	64	5-17-1780	Beech Fk	....
Dennis, Samuel	400	A	73	5-19-1780	Beech Fk	Surveyed
Dennis, Samuel	400	A	152	6-26-1780	Licking Cr	....
Dennis, Samuel	600	A	201	4- 2-1781	Beech Fk	....
Dennis, Samuel	600	B	2	8-24-1784	———	....
Denton, Arthur	1,000	A	181	10-24-1780	Ohio R	Surveyed
Denton, Dianna	400	A	6	17-24-1779	Shawnee Run	Surveyed
Denton, Dianna	1,000	A	181	10-24-1780	His Sett	Surveyed
Denton, John	400	A	107	5-29-1780	Licking	....

Entree	Acres	Book	Page	Entry Date	Watercourse	Notes
Denton, Thos........	400	A	1	11– 3–1779	Salt R...........	Surveyed
Denton, Thos........	400	A	14	2–19–1780	Salt R...........	Surveyed
Denton, Thos........	400	A	16	2–25–1780	Green R..........	Surveyed
Denton, Thos........	1,000	A	181	10–24–1780	His Sett..........	Surveyed
Denton, Thos........	264	A	319	12–17–1783	Rolling Fk........	....
Denton, Thos........	300	A	319	12–17–1783	Green R..........	....
Depue, James.......	1,000	A	42	5–10–1780	S Fk Licking.....	....
Depue, John........	1,000	A	42	5–10–1780	Mid Fk Licking....	....
Depue, John........	1,000	A	42	5–10–1780	S Fk Licking.....	....
Dewitt, Wm.........	200	A	115	5–30–1780	Sugar Cr.........	Withdrawn
Dewitt, Wm.........	200	A	115	5–30–1780	E Fk Sugar Cr....	....
Dewitt, Wm.........	200	A	181	10–23–1780	Boons Mill Cr.....	....
Deyerle, Peter......	2,179	A	239	12–23–1782	Little Ky R.......	Surveyed
Dick, Alexander.....	5,000	A	313	12– 5–1783	....	Withdrawn
Dick, Alexander.....	5,000	A	313	12– 5–1783	Ohio R...........	Withdrawn
Dick, Alexander.....	5,000	A	325	12–27–1783	Ohio R...........	Withdrawn
Dick, Alexander.....	5,000	B	23	12– 4–1784	Ohio R...........	Withdrawn
Dick, Alexander.....	5,000	B	23	12– 4–1784	Ohio R...........	Withdrawn
Dick, Alexander.....	5,000	B	38	1–29–1785	———......	
Dick, Alexander.....	5,000	B	38	1–29–1785	———......	Withdrawn
Dickens, John.......	400	A	64	5–16–1780	Doctors Fk Chaplin	
Dickens, Richard....	600	A	263	2–15–1783	Ashes Cr.........	Surveyed
Dickenson, John.....	800	A	100	5–26–1780	Holders Cr........	....
Dickerson, Martin...	1,000	A	100	5–26–1780	Holders Cr........	....
Dickerson, Robert....	400	A	83	5–22–1780	Buck Lick Cr......	....
Dickey, James & John.	200	A	147	6–24–1780	James Henderson...	
Dickson, George......	115	A	86	5–22–1780	Dicks R..........	....
Dickson, Turner.....	8,000	A	232	12–18–1782	Panther Cr.......	Surveyed
Dickson, Turner.....	6,000	A	232	12–18–1782	Panther Cr.......	Surveyed
Dierly, Peter........	400	A	281	6–30–1783	Brush Cr.........	Surveyed
Dierly, Peter........	500	B	6	9–13–1784	Brush Cr.........	
Diggs, Edwards......	1,000	A	222	12–12–1782	Brashears Cr......	
Dine, Andrew........	500	A	227	12–14–1782	Drennings Lick Cr..	....
Dinwiddie, James.....	400	A	216	7–21–1781	Bacon Cr.........	Withdrawn
Dinwiddie, James.....	400	A	216	7–21–1781	Pleasant Run.....	....
Dinwiddie, James.....	400	A	335	1–31–1784	Harrods Cr.......	....
Dinwiddie, James.....	400	A	335	1–31–1784	Bacon Cr.........	....
Dinwiddy, Sam......	400	A	55	5–15–1780	Mid Fk Licking....	....
Ditto, Henry........	975	A	315	12–15–1783	Lick Cr..........	812 acres surveyed
Ditto, Henry........	5,000	B	24	12–10–1784	———.......	875 acres surveyed
Dobbs, Wm..........	800	A	90	5–23–1780	Ohio R..........	....
Dochester, James.....	400	A	15	2–21–1780	Hingstons Cr......	....
Dochester, James.....	1,000	A	27	4–26–1780	Hingston Fk......	....
Dodd, Andrew.......	400	A	181	10–23–1780	Givins Cr.........	....
Dodge, Israel........	2,000	A	372	7–16–1784	Beargrass Cr......	Withdrawn
Dodge, Israel........	1,000	A	372	7–16–1784	Beargrass Cr......	Withdrawn
Dodge, Israel........	1,000	A	372	7–16–1784	Falls Ohio R......	Withdrawn
Dodge, Israel........	1,000	A	372	7–16–1784	Beargrass Cr......	Withdrawn
Dodge, Israel........	1,000	A	372	7–16–1784	Beargrass Cr......	Withdrawn
Doelin, John........	1,000	A	169	9– 9–1780	Licking...........	....
Dolan, Pat..........	400	A	15	2–21–1780	Shawnee Run.....	....
Dolan, Pat..........	1,000	A	44	5–11–1780	Adam Roughs Cr...	....
Dolan, Pat..........	400	A	140	6–21–1780	Clear Cr.........	....
Dolan, Pat..........	166	A	173	9–20–1780	Ky R............	....
Donaldson, John.....	1,050	A	34	4–29–1780	Licking...........	....
Donaldson, John.....	1,000	A	46	5–11–1780	Pittmans.........	Withdrawn
Donathan, Joseph....	180	A	146	6–24–1780	Muddy Cr........	....
Donelson, John......	1,000	A	142	6–22–1780	Green R..........	....
Donelson, Pat.......	1,000	A	120	6– 1–1780	S Fk Licking......	Surveyed
Donnalson, Pat.......	992	A	147	6–24–1780	Stoners Fk.......	....
Donnell, John et al...	1,000	B	8	9–25–1784	Gesses Cr........	Surveyed
Dooley, Moses.......	50	A	25	4–26–1780	Clear Cr.........	Mil
Dooley, Moses.......	500	A	99	5–26–1780	Mid Fk Sugar Cr...	....
Dooley, Thomas......	495	A	54	5–15–1780	....	....
Doom, Jacob........	400	A	173	9–20–1780	Rowling Fk.......	Withdrawn
Doom, Jacob........	400	A	216	7–31–1781	Indian Cr........	Surveyed
Doom, Jacob........	400	A	216	7–31–1781	Coperas Lick......	
Dorrett, John........	150	A	212	6–26–1781	Hardens Cr.......	Surveyed
Dorrett, John........	300	A	233	12–18–1782	Fk Harden Cr.....	Surveyed
Dorritt, John........	500	A	159	7– 6–1780	Clover Lick.......	Surveyed
Dorritt, John........	500	A	159	7– 6–1780	Hardens Cr.......	
Dorsey, Thomas.....	3,125	A	235	12–19–1782	Salt R...........	Surveyed
Dorsey, Thomas.....	3,125	A	235	12–19–1782	Salt R...........	Surveyed
Dotson, Wm........	400	A	106	5–27–1780	Beach Fk........	Surveyed
Doudall, James.......	500	A	106	5–29–1780	Floyds Fk........	....
Doudall, James.......	500	A	106	5–29–1780	Floyds Fk........	....
Doudall, James.......	500	A	106	5–29–1780	N Fk Drenens Lick Cr.......	....
Doughterty, Henry.....	125	A	174	10– 4–1780	Dicks R..........	....

Entree	Acres	Book	Page	Entry Date	Watercourse	Notes
Dougherty, Henry	200	A	178	10–17–1780	Dicks R	
Dougherty, James	500	A	56	5–15–1780	Beech Fk	Surveyed
Dougherty, James	500	A	93	5–24–1780	Beach Fk	Withdrawn
Dougherty, James	500	B	20	11–26–1784	Beech Fk	Withdrawn
Dougherty, James	500	B	34	1–24–1785	Rolli g Fk	
Dougherty, Jno	400	A	7	1–10–1780	Dicks R	
Dougherty, Joseph	1,000	A	181	10–23–1780	Hatrods Cr	Surveyed
Douglas, James	400	A	4	12–7–1779	Hingston Fk	
Douglas, James	400	A	15	2–21–1780	Jessamine Cr	
Douglas, James	400	A	16	2–24–1780	Ohio R	
Douglas, James	312	B	10	10–11–1784	————	
Douglas, James	510	A	372	7–17–1784		
Douglass, James	1,000	A	54	5–15–1780	Yellow Banks	
Douglass, James	1,000	A	60	5–16–1780	Ohio R	
Douglass, James	500	A	82	5–22–1780	Big Bone Lick	
Douglas, James	1,000	A	92	5–24–1780	Jessamine Cr	
Douglass, James	1,000	A	117	5–31–1780	Soverins Premption	
Douglass, James	1,000	A	122	6–2–1780	Little Meame	
Douglass, John	400	A	134	6–16–1780	Hingstons Fk	
Douglass, Alexander	400	A	180	10–19–1780	Dicks R	
Dove, Francis	200	A	135	6–17–1780	Drakes Camp Cr	
Dowdall, James	600	A	106	5–29–1780	Great Prairie	
Dowdall, James	3,016	A	259	2–3–1783	Floyds Fk	Surveyed
Dowdall, John	500	A	73	5–19–1780	Town Fk	
Dowdall, John	500	A	100	5–26–1780	Salt R	
Dowdall, Thomas	500	A	100	5–26–1780	Town Fk	
Downey, James	250	A	99	5–26–1780	Clear Cr	
Downey, John	300	A	99	5–26–1780	Mid Fk Sugar Cr	
Doyle, Edward	1,200	A	311	11–29–1783	Floyds Fk	
Doyle, Edward	996	A	337	2–12–1784	Brashears Cr	Surveyed
Dozier, James	500	A	210	5–30–1781	Stuarts Cr	300 acres withdrawn
Dozier, James	3,500	A	251	1–9–1783	Pittmans Cr	Withdrawn
Dozier, James	1,000	A	310	11–26–1783	Hardens Cr	
Dozier, James	1,000	A	310	11–26–1783	Pittmans Cr	Withdrawn
Dozier, John, et al	522	A	311	12–1–1783	————	
Dozier, John, et al	500	A	311	12–1–1783	Mill Cr	
Dozier, Zachariah	300	A	213	7–2–1781	Hardens Cr	100 acres withdrawn
Dozier, Zachariah	100	A	217	8–8–1791	Hardens Cr	
Dozier, Zachariah	100	A	218	8–8–1782	Stewarts Cr	
Dozier, Zachariah	1,000	A	234	12–19–1782	Saunders	Surveyed
Dozier, Zachariah	300	A	307	11–20–1783	————	
Dozier, Zachariah	2,209½	A	319	12–17–1783	Rough Cr	2,000 acres surveyed
Dozier, Zachariah	951	A	366	6–19–1784	————	360 acres surveyed
Dozier, Zachariah	1,278½	A	366	6–19–1784	————	639 acres surveyed
Dozier, Zachariah	1,209½	A	366	6–19–1784	————	1,000 acres surveyed
Dozier, Zachariah	308	A	373	7–26–1784	————	
Dozier, Zachariah	308	B	5	9–7–1784	————	
Dozier, Zach et al	414¾	A	319	12–17–1783	Green R	Surveyed
Dozier, Zach et al	1,000	A	319	12–17–1783	Rough Cr	Surveyed
Dozier, Zach et al	1,000	A	319	12–17–1783	Rough Cr	Surveyed
Drake, Ephriam	400	A	11	2–3–1780	Hingston Fk	
Drake, John	400	A	145	6–23–1780	Battle Cr	Surveyed
Drake, Margaret	400	A	145	6–23–1780	Drowning Cr	
Drake, Philip	1,500	A	40	5–9–1780	Mid Fk Licking	
Drew, John	37,500	B	31	1–3–1785	Entered in Lincoln	
Dryden, Wm	1,000	A	182	10–27–1780	Silver Cr	
Dudley, Ambrose	250	A	86	5–22–1780	Elkhorn	
Dulaney, Joseph	425½	A	309	11–25–1783	Pittmans Cr	
Dulin, Edward	500	A	163	7–22–1780	Sinking Cr	Withdrawn
Dulin, Edward	500	A	169	9–9–1780	Licking	
Dulin, John	200	A	147	6–24–1780	Little Barren R	
Dulin, John	300	A	147	6–24–1780	Licking	
Dulin, John	200	A	147	6–24–1780	Sinking Cr	Withdrawn
Dulin, John	500	A	163	7–22–1780	Sinking Cr	Withdrawn
Dulin, John Sr	500	A	163	7–22–1780	Yellow Cr	Withdrawn
Duling, Thadius	988	A	54	5–15–1780	————	
Dumpard, Danl	400	A	8	1–17–1778	Huston Fk	
Dunbarr, James	400	A	243	12–26–1782	Ohio R	
Duncan, Charles	310	A	223	12–12–1782	Pond Cr	
Duncan, Charles	250	A	223	12–12–1782	Floyds Fk	Withdrawn
Duncan, Charles	560	A	256	1–21–1783	Beech Fk	332 acres surveyed, 218 acres withdrawn
Duncan, Charles	468	A	327	1–9–1784	————	Surveyed

Entree	Acres	Book	Page	Entry Date	Watercourse	Notes
Duncan, Charles	218	A	327	1– 9–1784	Beech Fk	
Duncan, Charles	250	A	327	1– 9–1784	Floyds Fk	
Duncan, Charles	250	A	370	7– 8–1784	———	
Duncan, George	200	A	358	5– 7–1784	Robertson Cr	
Duncan, James	400	A	10	2– 3–1780	S Fk Elkhorn	
Duncan, James	800	A	79	5–20–1780	Strodes Fk	
Duncan, James	500	A	134	6–16–1780	Stoners Fk	
Duncan, James	500	A	134	6–16–1780	Stoners Fk	
Duncan, John	400	A	132	6–15–1780	Hingstons Fk	
Duncan, Joseph	554	A	52	5–13–1780	Licking	
Duncan, Samuel	400	A	336	2– 7–1784	Bear Cr	
Duncan, Chas et al	560	A	364	6– 7–1784	Rolling Fk	308 acres withdrawn
Dunn, John	400	A	18	3– 1–1780	Licking Cr	
Dunwiddie, James	450	A	104	5–27–1780	Licking	
Dunwoodie, James	400	A	185	10–30–1780	Pleasant Run	Withdrawn
Duprey, Bartholmew	2,000	A	72	5–18–1780	Stoners Cr	
Duprey, Bartholmew	950	A	72	5–18–1780	Stoners Fk	
Durce, Saml	400	A	36	4–29–1780	Muddy Cr	
Duree, Samuel	650	A	128	6– 8–1780	Muddy Cr	50 Mil
Durham, John	1,000	A	225	12–13–1782	Blackfords Cr	
Duvall, John P	1,000	A	136	6–17–1780	N Fk Licking	
Duvall, John P	1,000	A	140	6–21–1780	Clover Lick Br	
Duvall, John P	1,000	A	140	6–21–1780	Hardens Cr	Surveyed
Duvall, John P	2,000	A	207	4–14–1781	Clover Lick Run	1,000 acres withdrawn
Duvall, John P	1,000	A	207	4–14–1781	Tuels Run	Surveyed
Duvall, John P	1,000	A	207	4–14–1781	Limestone Cr	Surveyed
Duvall, John P	1,000	A	207	4–14–1781	Clover Lick	Surveyed
Duvall, John P	1,000	A	278	6– 7–1783	Clover Lick Cr	
Duvall, John P	1,000	A	278	6– 7–1783	Clover Lick Cr	Withdrawn
Duvall, John P	700	A	279	6– 7–1783	Hardens Cr	
Duvall, John P	300	A	279	6– 7–1783	Hardens Cr	
Duvall, John P	1,000	A	279	6– 7–1783	Hardens Cr	
Duvall, John P	400	A	351	4–10–1784	———	200 acres surveyed, returned
Dyall, John	1,000	B	5	9– 9–1784	Coxes Cr	
Dye, Isaac	1,000	A	313	12– 8–1783	Cave Cr	
Dye, Isaac	700	A	293	10– 4–1783	N Fk Caney Cr	Withdrawn
Dye, Isaac	700	A	293	10– 4–1783	Fk Clear Cr	
Dye, Isaac	700	A	292	10– 3–1783	N Fk Caney Cr	Withdrawn
Dye, Isaac	500	A	223	12–12–1782	N Fk Cain Cr	Surveyed
Dye, Isaac	500	A	223	12–12–1782	Big Clifty Cr	Surveyed
Dye, Isaac	300	A	221	11– 9–1782	———	Withdrawn
Dye, Isaac	300	A	221	11– 9–1782	Hines & McCarty	
Dye, Isaac	200	A	215	7–13–1781	Soverins Valley	
Dye, Isaac	200	A	215	7–13–1781	E Fk Soverins Val	
Dye, Isaac	400	A	185	10–30–1780	Valley Cr	Withdrawn
Dye, Isaac	300	A	184	10–30–1780	Freemans Cr	Withdrawn
Dye, Isaac	300	A	170	9– 9–1780	Green R	Withdrawn
Dye, James	400	A	111	5–29–1780	Benson Cr	Surveyed
Dysart, James	200	A	156	6–30–1780	Buffaloe Cr	Surveyed
Eades, Charles	300	A	262	2–12–1783	Prices Cr	
Eakin, Robert	360	A	183	10–27–1780	Mid Fk Floyds	Surveyed
Eares, Mary	400	A	108	5–29–1780	Rowling Cr	
Eares, Mary	400	B	4	9– 2–1784	In Lincoln	
Early, Joseph	400	A	1	11– 3–1779	Bastons Fk	Surveyed
Early, Joseph	500	A	28	4–27–1780	Dicks R	
Early, Joseph	1,000	A	28	4–27–1780	Big Bone Lick	Mil
Early, Joseph	1,500	A	58	5–15–1780	Stoners Fk	
Early, Joseph	1,000	A	58	5–15–1780	Fk of Licking	
Early, Joseph	772	A	72	5–19–1780	Licking	
Early, Joseph	1,000	A	72	5–19–1780	Licking Cr	
Early, Joseph	1,000	A	72	5–19–1780	Licking Cr	
Early, Joseph	1,000	A	72	5–19–1780	Licking Cr	
Early, Joseph	400	A	82	5–22–1780	S Fk Licking	
Early, Joseph	1,000	A	115	5–30–1780	Salt R	
Eastin, Augustine	200	A	28	4–27–1780	Cooper Run	Mil
Eastin, Augustine	500	A	45	5–11–1780	Shawnee Trace	
Eastin, Augustine	500	A	46	5–11–1780	Coopers R	
Eastland, Wm	1,750	A	225	12–13–1782	Muddy Cr	
Easton, Austin	1,000	A	146	6–24–1780	Boons Cr	
Easton, Elisabeth	3,000	A	167	8–17–1780	Panther Cr	
Eastwood, John	500	A	94	5–24–1780	Gists Cr	Surveyed
Eastwood, John	400	A	94	5–24–1780	Tick Cr	Surveyed
Eastwood, John	200	A	266	2–26–1783	Cane Cr	
Eastwood, John	200	A	334	1–21–1784	———	
Easty, Wm	500	A	104	5–27–1780	Chaplins Fk	
Eddes, Charles	2,671½	A	280	6–20–1783	Rough Cr	
Eddes, Charles	5,448	A	280	6–20–1783	Rough Cr	

Entree	Acres	Book	Page	Entry Date	Watercourse	Notes
Edgar, Thomas	400	A	14	2–19–1780	Cedar Cr	
Edgar, Thomas	3,700	A	228	12–16–1782	N Fk Licking Cr	Surveyed
Edgar, Thomas	4,000	A	280	6– 9–1783	———	
Edlimond, Cathrine	345	A	127	6– 8–1780	S Fk Licking	
Edminson, Martha & Mary	1,088½	B	20	11–26–1784	Green R	Withdrawn
Edminston, Ann	498	B	20	11–26–1784	———	Withdrawn
Edminston, Ann	498	A	252	1–14–1783	Green R	Withdrawn
Edminston, John	1,218	B	43	4–18–1785	———	Withdrawn
Edminston, John	1,218	A	253	1–14–1783	Sinking Cr	Withdrawn
Edminston, John	300	A	122	6– 2–1780	Beech Fk	
Edminston, John	300	A	122	6– 2–1780	Licking Cr	
Edminston, Martha	102	B	20	11–26–1784	———	Withdrawn
Edminston, Martha & Marg	1,088½	A	252	1–14–1783	Green R	Withdrawn
Edminston, Mary	469½	B	20	11–26–1784	———	Withdrawn
Edminston, Mary	102	A	252	1–14–1783	Green R	Withdrawn
Edminston, Mary	469½	A	252	1–14–1783	Green R	Withdrawn
Edminston, Samuel	400	A	122	6– 2–1780	Beech Fk	
Edminston, Wm	1,445	B	43	4–18–1785	Green R	
Edminston, Wm	1,445	A	252	1–14–1783	Green R	Withdrawn
Edminston, John	500	B	44	4–19–1785	Sinking Cr	Withdrawn
Edminston, John	300	A	!01	5–26–1780	Sugar Loaf Lick	
Edmonds, Wm	996½	A	375	7–29–1784	Harrods Cr	
Edmonson, John	100	A	31	4–28–1780	Bush Fk	Mil
Edmonson, John	100	A	31	4–28–1780	W Fk Sinking Cr	
Edmund, Wm	2,000	A	157	7– 3–1780	Licking	
Edwards, Ben	500	A	55	5–15–1780	Salt R	
Edwards, Ben	1,000	A	55	5–15–1780	Salt R	
Edwards Ben	2,140	A	195	3–17–1781	Ohio R	
Edwards, Harden	1,000	A	285	8– 5–1783	Floyds Fk	
Edwards, Harden	800	A	285	8– 5–1783	Phillips Premption	
Edwards, Harry	50	A	29	4–27–1780	Elkhorn	Mil
Edwards, Headen	1,800	A	285	8– 5–1783	———	Surveyed
Edwards, John	1,500	A	59	5–16–1780	Floyds Fk	
Edwards, John	500	A	64	5–17–1780	Kentucky R	Withdrawn
Edwards, John	1,000	A	112	5–30–1780	Tates Cr	
Edwards, John	1,000	A	156	6–30–1780	Green R	
Edwards, John	1,000	A	210	6– 1–1781	Salt R	Withdrawn
Edwards, John	5,000	A	246	1– 6–1783	Ohio R	Surveyed
Edwards, John	2,000	A	247	1– 6–1783	Drennons Lick	
Edwards, John	3,000	A	247	1– 6–1783	Fishpoole Cr	
Edwards, John	1,000	A	262	2–12–1783	Salt R	Surveyed
Edwards, John	1,000	A	262	2–12–1783	———	Withdrawn
Edwards, John	1,000	A	262	2–12–1783	———	Withdrawn
Edwards, John	2,000	A	267	2- 28–1783	500 acres survey	Warrant returned
Edwards, John	500	A	327	1– 5–1784	Brashears Cr	Surveyed
Edwards, John	500	A	327	1– 5–1784	Brashears Cr	Withdrawn
Edwards, Molly	400	A	62	5–16–1780	Ohio R	
Edwards, Robert	15,000	A	361	5–25–1784		
Edwards, Sandford	400	A	141	6–21–1780	Clear Cr	
Egbert, Lawrence	500	A	63	5–16–1780	Green R	
Eggleston, Edmund	1,600	A	82	5–22–1780	Harden Cr	
Ellott, Thomas	2,000	A	25	4–25–1780	S Fk Licking	Mil
Ellott, Wm	1,000	A	37	4–29–1780	Shannons Run	
Elliott, James	400	A	4	12– 7–1779	Cedar Cr	
Elliott, Robt	1,000	A	162	7–18–1780	Brashears Cr	Surveyed
Elliott, Wm	1,000	A	166	8–11–1780	Green R	
Elliotte, Robt	400	A	5	12– 8–1779	Brashear Cr	Surveyed
Ellis, Charles	701	A	246	1– 6–1783	Green R	Withdrawn
Ellis, Charles	701	A	352	4–13–1784	Green R	Withdrawn
Ellis, Charles	701	A	352	4–13–1784	Robertson Cr	
Ellis, John	400	A	9	1–17–1780	N Fk Elkhorn	
Ellis, John	1,308	A	241	12–25–1782	Salt R	
Ellis, Josiah	984	A	246	1– 6–1783	Robinsons Cr	
Ellis, Wm	500	A	29	4–27–1780	M Fk Licking	Mil
Ellis, Wm	500	A	29	4–27–1780	Gestes Cr	Mil
Ellis, Wm	1,000	A	39	5– 9–1780	Licking	
Ellison, Chalres	200	A	177	10– 9–1780	P Run	Withdrawn
Embre, John	261½	A	271	3–28–1783	Brush Cr	
Embre, Richard	261	A	271	3–28–1783	Brush Cr	
Embry, John	500	A	114	5–30–1780	———	
Embry, John	400	A	114	5–30–1780	Boones Sett	
Embry, Richard	400	A	113	5–30–1780	Licking	
Emmerson, Tilly	500	A	39	5– 9–1780	Licking	
English, Charles	50	A	175	10– 4–1780	Burnt Meadow	
Epperson, Rich	400	A	11	2– 4–1780	Wolf Fk Licking	
Epperson, Wm	1,000	A	113	5–30–1780	His Sett	
Eppes, Francis	3,000	A	170	9– 9–1780	Ohio R	
Erichson, Severin	6,000	A	332	1–20–1784	Long Lick Cr	Surveyed

Entree	Acres	Book	Page	Entry Date	Watercourse	Notes
Erwin, John	400	B	5	9–11–1784	Willsons Cr	Withdrawn
Erwin, John	400	B	25	12–13–1784	Willson Cr	
Erwin, John	400	B	25	12–10–1784	Willson Cr	Withdrawn
Essery, John	325	A	191	3–15–1781	Doe Run	Withdrawn
Essery, John	325	A	214	7– 4–1781	Beech Fk	
Essery, John	200	A	217	8– 2–1781	Doe Run	
Essery, John	200	A	217	7–31–1781	———	Withdrawn
Esteer, Christain	200	A	243	12–26–1782	Salt R	
Estill, Ben	500	A	44	5–11–1780	Silver Cr	
Estill, Boud	200	A	44	5–11–1780	Otter Cr	
Estill, James	1,000	A	27	4–26–1780	Otter Cr	
Estill, James	400	A	44	5–11–1780	OtterCr	
Estill, James	400	A	44	5–11–1780		
Estill, James	300	A	44	5–11–1780	Otter Cr	
Estill, James	100	A	44	5–11–1780	Ohio R	
Estill, James	500	A	44	5–11–1780	Muddy Cr	
Estill, James	400	A	44	5–11–1780	Ky R	
Estill, James	1,000	A	98	5–25–1780	Lees Br	
Estill, James	400	A	98	5–25–1780	Ky R	
Estill, James	400	A	98	5–25–1780	Ky R	
Estill, James	400	A	98	5–25–1780	Licking	
Estill, James	400	A	98	5–25–1780	Licking	
Estill, James	1,000	A	99	5–25–1780	Tates Cr	
Estill, James	1,000	A	99	5–25–1780	Stoners Fk	
Estill, James	1,000	A	99	5–25–1780	Paint Lick	
Estill, James	400	A	99	5–25–1780	Ky R	
Estill, James	1,000	A	99	5–25–1780	Tates Cr	
Estill, James	400	A	99	5–25–1780	Ky R	
Estill, James	400	A	135	6–17–1780	Licking	
Estill, Samuel	400	A	99	5–25–1780	Glens Cr	
Estill, Samuel	400	A	99	5–25–1780	Muddy Cr	
Estill, Wallace	400	A	44	5–11–1780	Muddy Cr	
Estill, Wallace	500	A	44	5–11–1780	Muddy Cr	
Estill, Wallace	500	A	44	5–11–1780	Muddy Cr	
Estis, Thomas	600	B	43	4–11–1785	———	
Etherton, Aaron	200	A	247	1– 7–1783	Prices Cr	
Euastace, John	4,000	A	34	4–29–1780	Elkhorn R	Mil
Euen, Samuel	250	A	319	12–17–1783	Green R	
Evans, David	400	A	264	2–15–1783	Salt R	Surveyed
Evans, Nathaniel	400	A	12	2– 9–1780	N Fk Cane Run	
Evans, Nathaniel	1,000	A	205	4– 5–1782	Floyds Fk	
Evans, Nathaniel	500	A	211	6–11–1781	Hardens Cr	
Evans, Nathaniel	400	A	211	6–11–1781	Hardens Cr	
Evans, Nathaniel	500	A	211	6–11–1781	Hardins Cr	
Evans, Thomas	800	A	255	1–20–1783	Joining Brown	
Eversol, Christain	400	A	193	3–16–1781	Rowling Fk	Surveyed
Evins, Evan	400	A	8	1–15–1778	Mill Cr	
Ewing, Baker	400	A	177	10 9–1780	Silver Cr	
Ewing, Baker	2,000	A	234	12–19–1782	Rough Cr	
Ewing, Baker	413	A	244	12–7–1782	Little Clifty Cr	Withdrawn
Ewing, Baker	400	A	262	2–12–1783	Ashes Cr	Surveyed
Ewing, Baker	588½	A	273	4– 8–1783	Big Clifty Cr	Surveyed
Ewing, Baker	413	A	273	4– 8–1783	———	Withdrawn
Ewing, Baker	800	A	274	4– 8–1783	Caney & Rough Cr	Surveyed
Ewing, Baker	2,413	A	307	11–20–1783	———	
Ewing, Baker	500	A	332	1–17–1784	———	400 acres surveyed
Ewing, Daniel	250	A	131	6–13–1780	Salt R	
Ewing, John	200	A	136	6–19–1780	Coxes Cr	Withdrawn
Ewing, John	500	A	136	6–19–1780	Coxes Cr	Withdrawn
Ewing, John	200	A	262	2–12–1783	Joining Norse	Withdrawn
Ewing, John	500	A	262	2–11–1783	Joining Norse	
Ewing, John	2,812	A	356	4–24–1784	Green R	
Ewing, Reuben	200	A	244	12–26–1782	Rough Cr	Surveyed
Ewing, Reuben	200	A	331	1–17–1784	———	
Ewing, Urban	400	A	244	12–27–1782	Little Clifty Cr	297 acres surveyed 103 acres withdrawn
Ewing, Urban	103	A	273	4– 8–1783	———	Withdrawn
Ewing, Urban	103	A	274	4– 8–1783	Rough Cr	Surveyed
Ewing, Young	400	A	244	12–27–1782	Little Clifty Cr	Surveyed
Fagans, Daniel	500	A	104	5–27–1780	Indian Licks	
Fagans, Daniel	500	A	104	5–27–1780	Indian Licks	
Faith, Elisabeth	400	A	250	1– 9–1783	Ohio R	
Fall, Aurther T	950	A	76	5–19–1780	Stoners Fk	
Fallie, Richard	200	A	169	9– 2–1780	Dicks R	
Fallie, Richard	200	A	169	9– 2–1780	Dicks R	
Fallis, Isaac	500	A	60	5–16–1780	Chaplins Fk	

Entree	Acres	Book	Page	Entry Date	Watercourse	Notes
Fallis, Isaac	500	A	365	6–15–1785	——	
Fallis, Isaac	1,342½	A	365	6–15–1784	——	1,000 acres surveyed
Fallis, Isaac	342½	A	365	6–15–1784	——	
Fallis, Isaac	342½	B	4	9– 2–1784	——	
Fallis, Isaac	1,000	A	258	1–27–1783	Brush Cr	
Fallis, Thomas	1,000	A	258	1–27–1783	Pleasant Run	
Fallis, Thomas	2,500	A	258	1–27–1783	Beech Cr	Surveyed
Fallis, Thomas	1,000	A	258	1–27–1783	Rolling Fk	
Faner, Joseph	500	A	98	5–25–1780	N Fk Licking	
Farmer, Wm	300	A	155	5–29–1780	Salt R	Withdrawn
Farmer, Wm	700	A	155	6–29–1780	Salt R	Surveyed
Farmer, Wm	300	A	191	3–15–1781	Floyds Fk	
Farr, John	500	A	198	3–19–1781	Coxes Cr	Surveyed
Farris, George	1,000	A	39	5– 9–1780	——	Withdrawn
Farrow, John	400	A	13	2– 9–1780	S Fk Otter Cr	
Farrow, John	300	A	43	5–11–1780	Stoners Fk	
Fauquier, Robert et al.	900	A	209	5–23–1781	Little Ky R	Surveyed
Favour, Caleb et al	1,000	B	34	1–25–1785	Beech Fk	
Feagan, Daniel	1,000	A	242	12–25–1782	Cartright Cr	
Feagan, Daniel	2,000	A	320	12–17–1783	Little Ky R	Surveyed
Fearn, Thomas	800	A	119	6– 1–1780	Dicks R	
Fears, Wm	266¾	A	54	5–15–1780	Yellow Banks	
Feilding, John et al	1,155½	A	310	11–26–1783	Eagle Cr	
Fennall, James	1,000	A	113	5–30–1780	Beech Fk	Surveyed
Fennil, James	100	A	333	1–20–1784	Richeys Cr	
Ferguson, Charles	500	A	114	5–30–1780	Dicks R	
Ferguson, Josh	700	A	44	5–11–1780	Beech Fk	Surveyed
Ferrell, Wm	826	A	311	11–29–1783	Chaplins Fk	
Fichlin, Thomas	450	A	222	12–11–1782	Green R	Withdrawn
Field, Benj	325	A	181	10–24–1780	Flatt Lick	
Field, Benj	325	B	12	11– 9–1784	Panther Cr	
Field, Ezekiel	2,000	A	12	2– 7–1780	Elkhorn	Mil 1763
Field, Ezekiel	2,000	A	12	2– 7–1780	Elkhorn	Mil 1763
Field, Ezekiel	1,000	A	12	2– 7–1780	Elkhorn	Mil 1763
Field, Henry	400	A	2	11– 5–1779	Licking	
Field, Henry	400	A	2	11– 5–1779	Deals Run LickingR	
Field, Henry	1,000	A	150	6–26–1780	Glens & Clear Cr	
Field, Henry Jr	2,000	A	42	5–10–1780	Hingston Fk	
Field, John	1,000	A	150	6–26–1780	S Fk Licking	
Field, Thomas	400	A	209	5–23–1781	Pond Cr	Withdrawn
Field, Wm	400	A	17	2–28–1780	Wilsons Run	Surveyed
Fields, Benj	400	A	309	11–25–1783	Ohio R	Withdrawn
Fields, Benj	400	B	11	11– 8–1784	Panther Cr	
Fields, Benj	400	B	11	11– 8–1784	——	Withdrawn
Fields, Daniel et al	——	A	166	8–11–1780	Pond Cr	Withdrawn
Fields, Henry	400	A	145	6–23–1780	W Fk Otter Cr	
Fields, Henry	1,000	A	145	6–23–1780	Licking	
Fields, Henry	1,000	A	145	6–23–1780	Licking	
Fields, Wm	400	A	140	6–21–1780	Wilsons Cr	Surveyed
Fields, Wm	1,000	A	179	10–17–1780	His Sett	Surveyed
Fiet, Henry	500	A	51	5–13–1780	Ky R	
Fiet, Peter	500	A	51	5–13–1780	Ky R	
Findley, David	300	A	99	5–26–1780	Silver Cr	
Finley, David	1,000	A	25	4–26–1780	Dicks R	
Finley, George	400	A	170	9–12–1780	Glens Cr	
Finley, George	250	A	229	12–16–1782	N Fk Pottengers Cr	
Finley, Isaac	400	A	78	5–20–1780	Cartright Cr	Surveyed
Finley, James et al	3,185½	A	311	12– 1–1783	Green R	
Finley, John	500	A	308	11–24–1783	Mulberry Cr	
Finley, John	250	A	363	6– 2–1784	Brush Cr	
Finley, Joseph	400	A	78	5–20–1780	Beargrass Cr	Surveyed
Finley, Joseph	400	A	372	7–17–1784	——	273 acres surveyed
Finley, Wm et al	2,828	A	311	12– 1–1783	Bear Cr	Surveyed
Finley, Wm et al	1,000	B	33	1–14–1785	——	
Finn, James	400	A	15	2–21–1780	Wilsons Cr	
Finnell, John	1,015	A	232	12–18–1782	Green R	
Finnie, James	50	A	30	4–28–1780	S Fk Tates Cr	Mil
Finnie, James	50	A	34	4–29–1780	Tates Cr	
Finnie, James	805	A	79	5–20–1780	Tates Cr	
Finnie, John	50	A	30	4–28–1780	Tates & Silver Cr	Mil
Finnie, John	500	A	79	5–20–1780	Tates Cr	
Fishback, Jacob	1,000	A	171	9–12–1780	Holtelau Sett	
Fishback, Jacob	1,000	A	248	1– 8–1783	Sinking Cr	
Fishback, Jacob	——	A	247	3–17–1784	Licking Cr	Amended
Fishback, Jacob	——	B	11	11– 8–1784	Sinking Cr	Amended
Fisher, Adam	400	A	12	2– 7–1780	Dicks R	
Fisher, Adam	500	A	66	5–17–1780	Pleasant Run	Withdrawn
Fisher, Adam	500	A	66	5–17–1780	Harrods Run	
Fisher, Adam	500	A	221	11–26–1781	Pleasant Run	

Entree	Acres	Book	Page	Entry Date	Watercourse	Notes
Fisher, Barnett........	500	A	73	5–19–1780	Pleasant Run......	Withdrawn
Fisher, Barnett........	500	A	82	5–22–1780	S Fk Rowling Fk...	Surveyed
Fisher, Barnett........	436	A	259	1–29–1783	Rolling Fk.........	....
Fisher, Barnett........	250	A	261	2– 6–1783	Beech Fk.........	....
Fisher, Barnett........	200	A	265	2–25–1783	Beech Fk.........	....
Fisher, Ben............	500	A	138	6–20–1780	Flatt Cr..........	....
Fisher, Paul...........	400	A	127	6– 8–1780	Mid Fk Licking....	
Fisher, Stephen........	400	A	17	2–28–1780	Jones Settlement...	Surveyed
Fisher, Stephen........	1,000	A	73	5–19–1780	Beech Fk.........	Surveyed
Fisher, Stephen........	1,000	A	73	5–19–1780	Barnett Fishers Sett	
Fisher, Stephen........	50	A	131	6–14–1780	Beech Fk.........	....
Fisher, Stephen........	1,000	A	220	8–24–1781	Green R..........	Mil
Fisher, Stephen........	436	A	259	1–29–1783	Bowling Fk.......	
Fisher, Stephen........	400	A	263	2–15–1783	Ashes Cr.........	Surveyed
Fisher, Stephen........	500	A	363	6– 2–1784	Rough Cr.........	....
Fitch, John...........	800	A	119	6– 1–1780	Simpson Cr.......	Withdrawn
Fitch, John...........	800	A	119	6– 1–1780	Coxes Cr.........	....
Fitch, John...........	400	A	133	6–15–1780	Coxes Cr.........	....
Fitch, John...........	800	A	133	6–15–1780	Coxes Cr.........	300 acres withdrawn
Fitch, John...........	400	A	133	6–15–1780	Coxes Cr.........	....
Fitch, John...........	300	A	170	9–12–1780	Simpsons Cr.......	Surveyed
Fitch, John...........	200	A	171	9–13–1780	Coxes Cr.........	Surveyed
Fitch, John...........	400	A	199	3–19–1781	Coxes Cr.........	Surveyed
Fitsgerald, Wm.......	500	A	98	5–25–1780	N Fk Licking......	....
Fitzgerald, John......	1,000	A	146	6–24–1780	N Fk Licking......	....
Fitzhugh, Wm.......	2,000	A	351	4–10–1784	Green R..........	Withdrawn
Fitzhugh, Wm.......	3,156	A	351	4–12–1784	Rock Lick Cr......	3,150 acres surveyed
Fitzhugh, Wm.......	3,000	A	351	4–12–1784	Rough Cr.........	Surveyed
Fitzhugh, Wm.......	3,156	A	352	4–15–1784	Daniel Brodhead...	Amended
Fitzhugh, Wm.......	15,000	A	352	4–15–1784	Lost Run.........	Withdrawn
Fitshugh, Wm.......	6,000	A	354	4–19–1784	Salt R...........	....
Fitzhugh, Wm.......	2,000	A	354	4–16–1784	Salt R...........	910 acres surveyed
Fitzhugh, Wm.......	2,000	A	354	4–16–1784	John Lewis.......	Withdrawn
Fitzhugh, Wm.......	310	A	356	4–28–1784	Salt R...........	....
Fitzhugh, Wm.......	15,000	A	360	5–18–1784	Rough Cr.........	....
Fitzhugh, Wm.......	882½	B	42	3–24–1785	———	....
Fitzhugh, Wm.......	2,006	B	46	5–26–1785	———	....
Flanagen, Domenick...	400	A	18	3– 3–1780	Cane Run........	....
Flannagan, Dominic...	525	A	262	2–12–1783	Mill Cr..........	....
Fleming, John.........	50	A	138	6–20–1780	Licking..........	....
Fleming, Joseph.......	400	A	259	1–29–1783	Pond Cr..........	....
Fleming, Robt........	400	A	11	2– 3–1780	Muddy Cr........	....
Fleming, Robert.......	1,000	A	144	6–23–1780	Muddy Cr........	....
Fleming, Wm.........	500	A	32	4–29–1780	Pilmans Cr........	Surveyed withdrawn
Fleming, Wm.........	500	A	32	4–29–1780	Panther Cr........	Surveyed
Fleming, Wm.........	500	A	32	4–29–1780	Pitmans Cr........	Mil
Fleming, Wm.........	200	A	32	4–29–1780	Panther Cr........	Mil Surveyed
Fleming, Wm.........	1,000	A	32	4–28–1780	Panther Cr........	Mil
Fleming, Wm.........	1,000	A	36	4–29–1780	Goose Cr.........	Surveyed
Fleming, Wm.........	1,000	A	37	4–29–1780	Harrods Cr.......	Surveyed
Fleming, Wm.........	1,000	A	40	5– 9–1780	S Fk Licking......	....
Fleming, Wm.........	1,000	A	40	5– 9–1780	Goose Cr.........	Surveyed
Fleming, Wm.........	1,000	A	40	5– 9–1780	Br Hustons Fk....	....
Fleming, Wm.........	1,000	A	117	5–31–1780	Rowling Fk.......	....
Fleming, Wm.........	963	A	117	5–31–1780	Beech Fk.........	Withdrawn
Fleming, Wm.......10,000	10,000	A	233	12–19–1782	Floyds Fk........	Withdrawn
Fleming, Wm.......16,000	16,000	A	233	12–19–1782	Cedar Cr.........	Surveyed
Fleming, Wm.........	1,000	A	243	12–25–1782	Indian Camp Cr...	....
Fleming, Wm.........	400	A	253	1–15–1783	Mill Cr..........	Surveyed
Fleming, Wm.........	400	A	253	1–15–1783	Mill Cr..........	Surveyed
Fleming, Wm.........	963	A	337	2–11–1784	Cartright Cr......	....
Fleming, Wm.........	963	A	337	2–11–1784	Beech Fk.........	....
Fletcher, James......	1,865½	A	270	3–28–1783	Panther Cr........	Withdrawn
Fletcher, James......	1,865½	A	295	10–13–1783	Green R..........	....
Flin, Peter..........	400	A	18	3– 6–1780	Brashears Cr......	....
Flipper, Joseph........	400	A	215	7–18–1781	Cedar Cr.........	....
Floyd, David..........	50	A	34	4–29–1780	Salt R...........	Mil
Floyd, David..........	900	A	105	5–27–1780	Beech Fk.........	....
Floyd, Henry.........	700	A	214	7– 3–1781	Rowling Fk.......	200 acres withdrawn
Floyd, Henry.........	400	A	214	7– 8–1781	Brush Fk........	Surveyed
Floyd, Henry.........	200	A	215	7–17–1781	Rowling Fk	Surveyed
Floyd, Henry.........	850	B	46	5–23–1785	———	....
Floyd, James..........	1,000	A	373	7–27–1784	———	500 acres surveyed
Floyd, Jenny..........	400	A	297	10–23–1783	Beargrass Cr......	Surveyed

Entree	Acres	Book	Page	Entry Date	Watercourse	Notes
Floyd, Jenny	500	B	41	2–28–1785	———	400 acres surveyed
Floyd, John	400	A	1	11– 3–1779	4 Mile Cr	
Floyd, John	1,000	A	32	4–28–1780	4 Mile Cr	Mil
Floyd, John	400	A	35	4–29–1780	N Fk Elkhorn	Mil
Floyd, John	1,600	A	35	4–29–1780	Boones Cr	Mil
Floyd, John	400	A	43	5–11–1780	Ohio R	Surveyed
Floyd, John	600	A	43	5–11–1780	Ohio R	
Floyd, John	500	A	44	5–11–1780	Ohio R	
Floyd, John	2,900	A	130	6–12–1780	Floyds Fk	Surveyed
Floyd, John	500	A	169	9– 9–1780	Beargrass Cr	Withdrawn
Floyd, John	500	A	194	3–16–1781	Beargrass Cr	Withdrawn
Floyd, John	500	A	194	3–16–1781	Beargrass Cr	
Floyd, John	500	A	207	4–14–1781	———	Surveyed
Floyd, John	500	A	207	4–14–1781	———	Withdrawn
Floyd, John	400	A	218	8– 8–1781	Beargrass Cr	Surveyed
Floyd, John	500	A	373	7–27–1784	———	300 acres surveyed
Floyd, John	500	A	373	7–27–1784	———	100 acres surveyed
Floyd, Robert	500	A	277	4–13–1783	The Knobbs	
Floyd, Wm Preston	1,000	A	230	12–17–1782	Ohio R	Surveyed
Flournoy, Wm	492	A	42	5–10–1780	Hingston Fk	
Folher, Fulkerson	300	A	226	12–14–1781	Rolling Fk	
Folks, John	300	A	219	8–20–1781	Bullskin Cr	Surveyed
Folks, John	200	B	31	12–29–1784		
Follis, Isaac	1,000	A	245	12–30–1782	Beech Fk	Surveyed
Forbbs, David	1,000	A	175	10– 6–1780	S Fk Licking	
Forbis, Hugh	1,000	A	175	10– 6–1780	His settlement	
Forbis, Jas	400	A	8	1–17–1780	Elkhorn Cr	
Forbis, John	400	A	8	1–17–1780	Philips Survey	
Forbis, Wm	400	A	8	1–17–1780	Wolf Cr	
Forbs, Hugh	1,000	A	175	10– 6–1780	S Fk Licking	
Ford, Boaz	400	A	127	6– 8–1780	Green R	
Ford, Jonathan	500	A	226	12–14–1782	Rowling Fk	
Ford, Jonathan	500	A	227	12–14–1782	Drennings Lick Cr	
Fore, Peter	400	A	181	10–23–1780	N Fk Licking	
Forker, James et al	1,000	A	209	5–23–1781	Drinnons Lick Cr	Surveyed
Forkner, John	750	A	67	5–17–1780	N Fk Elkhorn	
Forsythe, Ben	800	A	80	5–20–1780	Fk Licking	
Forsythe, Robert	500	A	103	5–27–1780	Salt R	Surveyed
Foster, Anthony	60	A	363	6– 4–1784	Beech Fk	Withdrawn
Foster, Anthony	500	A	363	6– 4–1784	Beech Fk	
Foster, Anthony	600	A	363	6– 4–1784	Beech Fk	
Foster, Anthony	540	A	368	6–26–1784	Snake Cr	Withdrawn
Foster, Anthony	800	A	368	6–26–1784	Fromans Cr	
Foster, Anthony	540	B	8	9–27–1784	Snake Cr	Withdrawn
Foster, Anthony	60	B	8	9–27–1784	Beech Fk	Withdrawn
Foster, Anthony	300	B	9	9–27–1784	Buffaloe Cr	Withdrawn
Foster, Anthony	300	B	9	9–27–1784	Beech Fk	
Foster, Anthony	600	B	35	1–26–1785	Beech Fk	Amended
Foster, Anthony	300	B	35	1–25–1785	Beech Fk	
Foster, Anthony	300	B	35	1–25–1785	Buffaloe Run	
Foster, Wm	50	A	21	4–20–1780	Cabbin Cr	Mil withdrawn
Foster, Wm	50	A	32	4–29–1780	Green R	
Foster, Wm	500	A	340	2–18–1784	Ohio R	
Foushee, Francis	1,000	A	60	5–16–1780	Licking	Withdrawn
Fowler, Alex	5,000	A	324	12–26–1783	Millers Run	
Fowler, Alex	5,000	A	324	12–26–1783	Little Ky R	
Fowler, Berry M	500	B	6	9–13–1784		
Fowler, John	352	A	371	7–12–1784	Pittmans Cr	
Fowler, John	1,148	A	371	7–12–1784	Mid Fk Brush Cr	
Fox, James	495	A	43	5–11–1780	Hingston Fk	
Fox, John	800	A	20	4–17–1780	Blue Licks	Mil
Fox, John	50	A	33	4–29–1780	Silver Cr	Mil
Fox, Joseph	1,000	A	199	3–20–1781	Ky R	Mil
Fox, Joseph	1,000	A	250	1– 9–1783	James Patton	Surveyed
Franciscus, Geo	1,000	A	280	6–19–1783	Green R	
Francis, James	200	A	38	5– 9–1780	Panther Cr	
Francis, Thomas	500	A	76	5–19–1780	Stoners Fk	
Franklin, John	628	A	255	1–20–1783	Caney Cr	
Fraiser, Joseph	1,000	A	86	5–23–1780	S Fk Elkhorn	
Frasier, Wm	1,000	A	86	5–23–1780	Frasier Sett	
Frazer, Joseph	400	A	7	1–10–1780	Lawrence Cr	
Frazer, Wm	400	A	7	1–10–1780	N Fk Elkhorn	
Freeman, Elisha	400	A	236	12–20–1782	Nole Linn Cr	
Freeman, Elisha Jr	400	A	236	12–20–1782	Nole Linn Cr	
Freeman, Wm	560	A	223	12–12–1782	Mill Cr	
French, Henry	250	A	171	9–15–1780	Nolin Cr	
French, Henry	250	A	192	3–16–1781	Nolin Cr	

Entree	Acres	Book	Page	Entry Date	Watercourse	Notes
French, Henry	400	A	205	4– 9–1781	Brashears Cr	Surveyed
French, Henry	750	A	214	7– 4–1781	Otter Cr	....
French, Jacob	300	A	171	9–15–1780	Fk Nolin Cr	....
French, Jacob	50	A	192	3–16–1781	Valley Cr	....
French, Jacob	100	A	216	7–21–1781	Valley Cr	Surveyed
French, Jacob	100	A	290	9–10–1783	Nole Lynn Cr	Surveyed
French, James	400	A	7	1–11–1780	S Fk Sinking Cr	....
French, James	1,000	A	33	4–29–1780	French Sett	....
French, James	600	A	91	5–24–1780	Licking	....
French, James	800	A	94	5–24–1780	Licking	....
French, Wm.	1,000	A	100	5–26–1780	Licking	....
Frickland, Thomas	450	A	222	12–11–1781	Beach Fk	....
Frigg, John	250	A	211	6– 9–1781	Coxes Cr	Surveyed
Frigg, John	200	A	217	8– 7–1781	Long Lick Cr	Surveyed
Friggs, John Sr	500	A	368	6–29–1784	Brush Cr	....
Fristoe, John	200	A	55	5–15–1780	Cedar Cr	....
Fristoe, John	1,000	A	90	5–23–1780	Howards Cr	....
Fristoe, John	500	A	90	5–23–1780	Simpson Cr	Surveyed
Fristoe, John	1,000	A	92	5–24–1780	Simpson Cr	Surveyed
Fristoe, Wm	500	A	70	5–18–1780	Floyds Fk	....
Fristoe, Wm	500	A	102	5–27–1780	Floyds Fk	....
Froman, Jacob	1,000	A	171	9–13–1780	Salt R	Surveyed
Froman, Jacob	500	A	172	9–19–1780	Mill Cr	Surveyed
Froman, Jacob	500	A	172	9–18–1780	Salt & Ohio R	Withdrawn
Froman, Jacob	450	A	172	9–18–1780	Falls Salt R	Withdrawn
Froman, Jacob	50	A	172	9–18–1780	Ohio R	Withdrawn
Froman, Jacob	500	A	172	9–18–1780	Coxes Cr	Withdrawn
Froman, Jacob	500	A	176	10– 9–1780	Salt R	....
Froman, Jacob	400	A	176	10– 9–1780	Fromans Cr	Surveyed
Froman, Jacob	500	A	200	3–26–1781	Rowling Fk	....
Froman, Jacob	450	A	200	3–26–1781	Falls Salt R	....
Froman, Jacob	150	A	216	7–21–1781	Coxes Cr	Surveyed
Froman, Jacob	300	A	216	7–21–1781	Cox Cr	Surveyed
Froman, Jacob	44	A	274	4– 8–1783	Beech Fk	....
Froman, Jacob	44	A	331	1–16–1784		....
Froman, Jacob	700	A	331	1–16–1784	Bullitts Lick	670 acres surveyed
Froman, Paul	400	A	102	5–27–1780	Froman Cr	....
Froman, Paul	400	A	102	5–27–1780	Froman Cr	....
Froman, Paul	400	A	102	5–27–1780	Froman Cr	....
Froman, Paul	1,000	A	172	9–18–1780	Coxes Cr	Surveyed
Froman, Paul	1,000	A	172	9–18–1780	Simpsons Cr	Surveyed
Froman, Paul	600	A	176	10– 9–1780	Rowling Fk	....
Froman, Paul	50	A	184	10–30–1780	Rowling Fk	....
Froman, Paul	500	A	184	10–30–1780	Simpson Cr	....
Froman, Paul	400	A	199	3–24–1781	Coxes Cr	Withdrawn
Froman, Paul	400	A	199	3–24–1781	Mill Cr	....
Froman, Paul	400	A	205	4– 5–1781	Coxes Cr	Surveyed
Froman, Paul	200	A	205	4– 5–1781	Coxes Cr	....
Froman, Paul	1,500	A	334	1–23–1784	Salt R	136 acres withdrawn
Froman, Paul	106	A	334	1–23–1784	Beech Fk	Withdrawn
Froman, Paul	4,602	A	359	5–10–1784		670 acres surveyed
Froman, Paul	802	A	359	5–10–1784	Long Lick Cr	....
Froman, Paul	136	B	18	11–18–1784	Long Lick Cr	....
Froman, Paul	136	B	18	11– 8–1784		Withdrawn
Froman, Robert	500	A	228	12–14–1782	Short Cr	....
Froman, Robert	500	B	10	10–11–1784		....
Fronay, Lazurus D	3,000	A	81	5–22–1780	Green R	....
Fronchee, Francis	1,000	A	84	5–22–1780	N Fk Licking	Withdrawn
Froney, Lazurus D	3,000	A	81	5–22–1780	Green R	....
Froney, Lazurus D	4,000	A	81	5–22–1780	Green R	....
Frost, Ebenezer	1,000	A	156	6–30–1780	Boons Cr	....
Frowman, Jacob	50	A	331	1–17–1784		....
Frowman, Paul	560	A	244	12–26–1782	Coxes Cr	454 acres surveyed 106 acres withdrawn
Frowman, Paul	106	A	331	1–17–1784		....
Fry, Abram	500	A	176	10– 9–1780	Mill Cr	....
Fry, Abram	550	A	176	10– 9–1780	Coxes Cr	Withdrawn
Fry, Abraham	500	A	199	3–24–1781	Coxes Cr	Withdrawn
Fry, Abraham	500	A	204	4– 5–1781	Coxes Cr	....
Fry, Benjamin	1,000	A	106	5–29–1780	Long Lick Run	....
Fry, Benjamin	100	A	111	5–29–1780	Rowling Fk	....
Fry, John	100	A	55	5–15–1780	Carpenters Cr	....
Fry, John	150	A	55	5–15–1780	Hanging Fk	Withdrawn
Fry, John	150	A	55	5–15–1780	Carpenters Cr	Withdrawn
Fry, John	150	A	171	9–13–1780	Carpenters Cr	....
Fry, Samuel	2,000	A	24	4–25–1780	N Br Panther Cr	Mil

Entree	Acres	Book	Page	Entry Date	Watercourse	Notes
Fry, Susanna	560	A	169	9-11-1780	N Fk Licking	
Fry, Wm	953	A	302	11- 7-1783	Bear Cr	Surveyed
Fryar, Robert	500	A	93	5-24-1780	Stoners Fk	
Frye, Ben	400	A	153	6-26-1780	Salt R	
Fryer, Robert	500	A	53	5-15-1780	Stoners Fk	
Fryer, Robert	500	A	75	5-19-1780	Stoners Fk	
Funck, Henry Jr	600	A	192	3-16-1781	Middle Cr	Surveyed
Funck, Jacob	1,500	A	192	3-16-1781	Shaws Cr	200 acres surveyed 800 acres withdrawn
Funck, Jacob	250	A	193	3-16-1781	Middle Cr	Surveyed
Funck, Jacob	250	A	193	3-16-1781	Middle Cr	Surveyed
Funck, Jacob	600	A	193	3-16-1781	Soverins Valley	Surveyed
Funck, Jacob	400	A	193	3-16-1781	Soverins Valley	294 acres surveyed, 106 acres withdrawn
Funck, Jacob	400	A	214	7- 3-1781	Rudes Sta & Mt Cr	Withdrawn
Funck, Jacob	75	A	219	8-20-1781	Billys Cr	Surveyed
Funck, Jacob	50	A	219	8-20-1781	Soverns Valley Cr	Surveyed
Funck, Jacob	250	A	219	8-20-1781	Nole Linn Cr	
Funk, Henry	50	A	171	9-15-1780	Clay Lick	
Funk, Henry	500	A	193	3-16-1781	Soverins Valley	Surveyed
Funk, Henry	1,000	A	193	3-16-1781	Rough Cr	
Funk, Henry	500	A	194	3-16-1781	Nolin Cr	Surveyed
Funk, Jacob	2,400	A	102	5-26-1780	Green R	800 acres withdrawn, surveyed
Funk, Jacob	2,000	A	102	5-27-1780	Ohio R	800 acres, withdrawn
Funk, Jacob	1,000	A	102	5-27-1780	Middle Cr	Surveyed
Funk, Jacob	2,500	A	168	9- 2-1780	Soverins Valley	1900 acres withdrawn
Funk, Jacob	100	A	169	9- 2-1780	Soverins Cr	27 acres surveyed 73 acres withdrawn
Funk, Jacob	75	A	169	9- 2-1780	Billys Cr	
Funk, Jacob	100	A	169	9- 2-1780	Rowling Fk	Surveyed, withdrawn
Funk, Jacob	200	A	169	9- 2-1780	Middle Cr	Surveyed
Funk, Jacob	400	A	169	9- 2-1780	Middle Cr	Surveyed
Funk, Jacob	300	A	169	9- 2-1780	Soverins Valley	250 acres withdrawn
Funk, Jacob	50	A	171	9-14-1780	Otter Cr	Withdrawn
Funk, Jacob	100	A	296	10-13-1783	————	Surveyed
Funk, Jacob	600	A	296	10-13-1783	Soverins Valley	Surveyed
Funk, Jacob	800	A	296	10-13-1783	Harges Run	Withdrawn
Funk, Jacob	4,309	A	299	10-28-1783	Valley Cr	Surveyed
Funk, Jacob	300	A	299	10-27-1783	Billys Cr	Surveyed
Funk, Jacob	600	A	299	10-27-1783	Noelinn Cr	Surveyed
Funk, Jacob	116	A	299	10-27-1783	East Cr	Withdrawn
Funk, Jacob	73	A	299	10-27-1783	Mill Seat Grove	Withdrawn
Funk, Jacob	600	A	299	10-27-1783	Middle Cr	Surveyed
Funk, Jacob	50	A	300	11- 1-1783	Shaws Cr	Surveyed, withdrawn
Funk, Jacob	100	A	300	11- 1-1783	Shaws Cr	Surveyed
Funk, Jacob	100	A	300	11- 1-1783	Soverins Valley	Withdrawn
Funk, Jacob	150	A	300	11- 1-1783	Valley Cr	Surveyed
Funk, Jacob	150	A	300	11- 1-1783	Rudes Cr	Surveyed
Funk, Jacob	88	A	300	11- 1-1783	Rolling Fk	Surveyed
Funk, Jacob	262	A	300	11- 1-1783	Middle Cr	Surveyed
Funk, Jacob	500	A	300	11- 1-1783	Hardens Cr	Surveyed
Funk, Jacob	100	A	314	12- 8-1783	————	
Funk, Jacob	500	A	314	12- 8-1783	————	Withdrawn
Funk, Jacob	300	A	314	12- 8-1783	Rough Cr	Surveyed
Funk, Jacob	200	A	314	12- 8-1783	Rough Cr	Surveyed
Funk, Jacob	142	A	363	6- 4-1784	————	
Funk, Jacob	400	A	363	6- 4-1784	————	58 acres surveyed
Fulkerson, Phillip	250	A	229	12-16-1782	Harrods Cr	
Fulkerson, Phillip	250	A	229	12-16-1782	Pottengers Cr	
Fullerton, Wm	1,000	A	290	9-11-1783	Long Lick Cr	Surveyed
Fullerton, Wm	1,000	A	290	9-11-1783	Rock Lick Cr	Surveyed
Fullerton, Wm	2,000	A	290	9-11-1783	Rough Cr	Surveyed
Fullerton, Wm	2,000	A	291	9-11-1783	Cartright Cr	560 acres withdrawn
Fullerton, Wm	1,000	A	291	9-11-1783	Rock Lick Cr	Surveyed
Fullerton, Wm	1,000	A	291	9-11-1783	Rock Lick Cr	Surveyed
Fullerton, Wm	2,700½	A	361	5-25-1784	Green R	Withdrawn

Entree	Acres	Book	Page	Entry Date	Watercourse	Notes
Fullerton, Wm	2,700	A	377	8-12-1784	————	
Fullerton, Wm	10,000	B	1	8-12-1784	Rough Cr	
Fullerton, Wm	560	B	1	8-12-1784	Cartright Cr	Withdrawn
Fullerton, Wm	1,440	B	2	8-26-1784	————	
Fulwither, Henry	1,000	A	220	8-24-1781	Beargrass Cr	Surveyed
Fuqua, Joseph	400	A	127	6-8-1780	Green R	
Furgeson, Charles	400	A	142	6-22-1780	Doctors Fk	
Furguson, John	500	A	146	6-24-1780	Cabbin Cr	
Furr, Edward	800	A	98	5-25-1780	N Fk Elkhorn	
Gain, Richard	3,200	A	307	11-20-1783	Big Clifty Cr	
Gaines, Daniel	800	A	352	4-13-1784	Brush Cr	
Gaines, Richard	500	A	93	5-24-1780	Beech Fk	
Gaines, Richard	2,203	A	241	12-25-1782	Wolf Run	
Gaines, Thomas	1,107½	B	23	12-4-1784	————	554 acres surveyed
Gaines, Wm	200	A	63	5-16-1780	Cave Spring	
Gaines, Wm	200	A	64	5-16-1780	Cave Spring	
Gaines, Daniel	1,000	A	255	1-20-1783	In Barrens	
Gaines, Daniel	1,000	A	255	1-20-1783	Brush Cr	
Gains, Daniel	1,000	A	255	1-20-1783	Brush Fk	
Gains, Daniel	100	A	255	1-20-1783	Brush Cr	
Gains, Daniel	353½	A	256	1-23-1783	Green R	
Gains, Richard	400	A	89	5-23-1780	Beech Fk	
Gains, Richard Jr	400	A	67	5-17-1780	Beech Fk	
Gains, Thomas	1,107½	A	307	11-20-1783	Big Clifty Cr	554 acres surveyed
Gains, Thomas	500	A	361	5-25-1784	Cloyds Cr	
Gainhart, Mich	400	A	147	6-24-1780	Pennsylvania Run	
Gainheart, Mich	400	A	109	5-29-1780	Floyds Fk	
Gaither, John	500	A	92	5-24-1780	Floyds Fk	
Galloway, John	400	A	294	10-10-1783	Floyds Fk	Surveyed
Galt, Wm	1,060	A	342	2-27-1784	Robinson Cr	Withdrawn
Galt, Wm	1,060	A	351	4-13-1784	Robinsons Cr	Withdrawn
Galt, Wm	1,060	A	351	4-13-1784	Green R	
Gant, Jeremiah	100	A	81	5-22-1780	Beech Fk	
Gardner, Josiah	500	A	157	7-3-1780	Licking	
Gardenner, Joseph	500	A	43	5-11-1780	Stoners Fk	
Garner, Wm	325	A	209	5-18-1781	Pond Cr	Withdrawn
Garnett, John	500	A	129	6-9-1780	E Fk Jessamine Cr	
Garnett, John	500	A	219	8-24-1781	Pleasant Run	
Garnett, John	500	A	308	11-24-1783	Pleasant Run	Withdrawn
Garnett, John	500	A	308	11-24-1783	Beech Fk	
Garnett, Joshua	366¾	A	40	5-9-1780	Elkhorn	
Garnitt, John	500	A	78	5-20-1780	Jessamine Cr	
Garr, Adam	800	A	73	5-19-1780	Pleasant Run	Surveyed
Garr, Lewis	375	A	73	5-19-1780	Beech Fk	Surveyed
Garrard, James	400	A	41	5-10-1780	Salt R	
Garrard, James	1,000	A	93	5-24-1780	Stoners Fk	
Garrard, James	22	A	267	2-28-1783	————	Not surveyed warrant returned
Garrard, James	2,018	A	250	1-9-1783	Bulgers Lick	
Garrard, James et al	400	A	262	2-12-1783	Harrods Cr	
Garrald, Thomas	500	A	167	8-17-1780	Robinsons Cr	Surveyed
Garrard, Wm	2,000	A	250	1-9-1783	Bulgers Lick	
Garrett, Edmund	428	A	40	5-9-1780	Big Fk Elkhorn	
Garrett, Henry	400	A	7	1-10-1780	Brashears Cr	Surveyed
Garrett, Henry	1,000	A	145	6-24-1780	Fox Run	Surveyed
Garrett, Henry	1,000	A	157	6-30-1780	James Minor	
Garrett, James	900	A	158	7-3-1780	Hingston Fk	
Garrett, Rueben	1,164¾	A	40	5-9-1780	Elkhorn	
Gass, David	400	A	10	2-3-1780	S Fk Elkhorn	
Gass, David	400	A	60	5-16-1780	Stoners Fk	
Gass, David	1,500	A	103	5-27-1780	Lee Cr	
Gass, David	550	A	114	5-30-1780	Stoners Fk	
Gates, James	400	A	11	2-3-1780	Muddy Cr	
Gatliff, Charles	400	A	124	6-3-1780	John Machans	
Gavat, James	1,000	A	268	3-28-1783	Rolling Fk	
Gay, Thomas	400	A	55	5-15-1780	M Fk Licking	
Gayle, John	50	A	23	4-24-1780	Dicks R	Mil
Gayle, John	500	A	52	5-13-1780	N Fk Elkhorn	
Gayle, John	600	A	84	5-22-1780	N Fk Licking	
Gayle, John	100	A	169	9-5-1780	Ky R	Mil
Gayle, Matthew	500	A	42	5-10-1780	Johnstons Fk	
Gayle, Matthew	100	A	34	4-29-1780	Beech Fk	Mil
Gayle, Matthew	450	A	58	5-15-1780	Licking	
Gayle, Wm	750	A	52	5-13-1780	N Fk Elkhorn	
Geddins, Francis	400	A	191	3-15-1781	Coxes Cr	
Gellespy, David	400	A	277	4-14-1783	Otter Cr	
George, Wm	500	B	47	5-26-1785	————	
Gerat, James	1,414	A	236	12-20-1782	Clover Lick Cr	Surveyed

Entree	Acres	Book	Page	Entry Date	Watercourse	Notes
Gerrard, Eli	400	A	15	2–21–1780	Rolling Fk	Surveyed
Gerrard, Eli, heirs	1,000	A	146	6–24–1780	Rowling Fk	Surveyed
Gess, David	1,000	A	247	1– 7–1783	Green R	....
Gibbs, Julian	800	A	79	5–20–1780	Tates Cr	....
Gibson, George	3,000	A	310	11–27–1783	Rough Cr	Withdrawn
Gibson, George	3,000	B	47	6–15–1785	Rough Cr	Withdrawn
Gibson, John	400	A	310	11–27–1783	Rough Cr	Withdrawn
Gibson, John	400	A	310	11–27–1783	Rough Cr	Withdrawn
Gibson, John	400	B	47	6–15–1785	————	Withdrawn
Gibson, John	400	B	47	6–15–1785	Rough Cr	Withdrawn
Gibson, Wm	250	A	63	5–16–1780	Greens Cr	....
Gibson, Wm	400	A	127	6– 8–1780	Sinking Cr	....
Gilaspy, Davis	200	A	129	6– 9–1780	Ky R	....
Gilaspy, Wm	400	A	3	11–11–1779	Boones Cr	Surveyed
Gilbert, Robert	1,000	A	109	5–29–1780	Ohio R	....
Gilbert, Robert	300	A	122	6– 2–1780	Brashears Cr	....
Gilbert, Robert	1,000	A	125	6– 5–1780	Ohio R	Surveyed
Giles, John	500	A	182	10–25–1780	Ky R	....
Gilkey, John	50	A	163	7–29–1780	S Fk Beech Cr	Mil
Gilkey, John	100	A	261	2– 6–1783	Beech Fk	....
Gilkey, John	330	A	282	7– 2–1783	Gilkeys Run	....
Gilkey, John	100	A	203	4– 3–1781	Beech Fk	....
Gilkey, John	100	A	272	4– 3–1783	————	Warrant returned
Gilkey, John	1,000	A	337	2–10–1784	Beech Fk	....
Gill, John	1,190	A	265	2–19–1783	Hardens Cr	....
Gill, John	1,273	A	270	3–28–1783	Beech Fk	Surveyed
Gill, Samuel	1,000	A	303	11–10–1783	Nolelin Cr	Surveyed
Gill, Samuel et al	1,327½	A	357	5– 1–1784	Floyds Fk	....
Gill, Thomas	1,000	A	303	11–10–1783	Valley Cr	Surveyed
Gillaspy, David	2,985	A	256	1–21–1783	Benson Cr	....
Gillaspie, David	777½	A	364	6– 4–1784	————	....
Gillaspie, David	254	A	377	8–11–1784	————	....
Gillaspy, Wm	1,000	A	131	6–12–1780	Boons Cr	Surveyed
Gillaspy, Wm	1,618	A	256	1–21–1783	Ky R	....
Gillaspie, Wm	1,618	B	48	6–20–1785	————	....
Gillespy, James et al	1,000	A	311	12– 1–1783	Bear Cr	....
Gillis, Wm	200	A	186	3–14–1781	Salt R	....
Gillison, John	1,000	A	97	5–25–1780	Beach Fk	Surveyed
Gillison, John	1,000	A	245	12–28–1782	Beech Fk	....
Gilmore, James	400	A	13	2–11–1780	Hanging Fk	....
Gilmore, James	500	A	133	6–15–1780	Dicks R	Mil
Gilmore, James	1,000	A	230	12–17–1782	Battle Cr	Surveyed
Gilmore, James	150	A	237	12–21–1782	Ohio R	....
Gilmore, John	100	A	27	4–26–1780	Harrods Cr	Mil
Gilmore, John	50	A	122	6– 2–1780	Ohio R	Mil
Gilmore, George	1,000	A	209	5–19–1781	Rowling Fk	....
Gilmore, George	1,000	A	210	6– 5–1781	Hardens Cr	Surveyed
Gilmore, George	400	A	211	6– 5–1781	Hardins Cr	Surveyed
Gilmore, George	625	A	288	9– 1–1783	Floyds Fk	Surveyed
Gimblin, Andrew	400	A	12	2– 5–1780	Dicks R	Surveyed
Gimblen, Andrew	400	A	152	6–25–1780	Dicks R	....
Gimblen, Andrew	600	A	152	6–26–1780	Dicks R	....
Giroux, Honere	6,000	A	330	1–14–1784	Little Ky R	4,860 acres surveyed
Gist, Joshua et al	2,925	A	188	3–15–1781	Ohio R	....
Givans, Samuel	300	A	115	5–31–1780	Town Fk	....
Givans, Samuel	700	A	116	5–30–1780	N Fk Sinking Cr	....
Givans, Samuel	885½	A	258	1–27–1783	Beech Fk	Withdrawn
Givans, Samuel	885½	A	258	1–27–1783	Brush Cr	....
Givans, Geo & Sam	1,000	A	124	6– 3–1780	Indian Cr	....
Givans, Geo & Sam	1,000	A	124	6– 3–1780	Indian Cr	....
Givens, Samuel	1,000	A	26	4–26–1780	Clarks Cr	....
Givins, Samuel	400	A	15	2–21–1780	Clarks Run	....
Givins, Geo & Sam	1,000	A	124	6– 3–1780	Licking	....
Givins, Geo & Sam	1,000	A	124	6– 3–1780	Licking	....
Glen, David	400	A	16	2–25–1780	Glen Cr	....
Glenn, Joseph	400	A	306	11–19–1783	Salt Lick Cr	....
Glover, John	200	A	102	5–26–1780	Green R	....
Glass, David	500	A	46	5–11–1780	Stoners Fk	....
Glass, John	400	A	10	2– 3–1780	Johnstons Fk	....
Glass, Robert	1,000	A	118	6– 1–1780	Beech Fk	....
Glasscock, George	1,000	A	70	5–18–1780	S Fk Bank Lick	....
Glasscock, George	4,687½	A	348	3–29–1784	Rolling Fk	....
Goggins, Richard et al	322¾	A	283	7–12–1783	Knoxes Cr	....
Googins, Richard et al	966¾	A	284	8– 2–1783	Hardens Cr	....
Goldman, Thomas	1,600	A	24	4–25–1780	Gilberts Cr	Mil
Goldson, John	750	A	57	5–15–1780	Licking	....
Golson, Anthony	992	A	64	5–17–1780	Bayleys Trace	....
Goode, Robert	400	A	154	6–28–1780	Nolin Cr	Withdrawn
Goode, Robert	500	A	169	9– 9–1780	Yellow Cr	....
Goode, Robert	1,000	A	169	9– 9–1780	Yellow Cr	....

Entree	Acres	Book	Page	Entry Date	Watercourse	Notes
Goode, Robert........	100	A	219	8-22-1781	Buffaloe Cr........	Surveyed
Goode, Robert........	400	A	343	3- 3-1784	Green R...........	....
Goode, Robert........	400	A	343	3- 3-1784	Nolelinn Cr.......	....
Goode, Robert........	1,000	A	362	5-26-1784	——...........	100 acres surveyed
Goode, Wm..........	1,125	A	351	4-13-1784	Robertsons Cr.....	....
Goode, Wm..........	4,000	A	351	4-13-1784	Green R...........	....
Goode, Wm..........	4,125	B	24	12-10-1784	—— ——	....
Goodman, Danl.......	400	A	11	2- 3-1780	S Fk Brashears.....	....
Goodman, Daniel, heirs	1,000	A	144	6-23-1780	Beargrass Cr.......	....
Goodman, Samuel....	1,000	A	207	4-14-1781	Bullskin Cr........	Surveyed
Goodnight, David....	390	A	129	6- 8-1780	Johnsons Fk.......	....
Goodnight, John.....	392	A	127	6- 8-1780	S Fk Licking......	....
Goodnight, Mich.....	400	A	142	6-22-1780	Chaplins Fk.......	....
Goodnight, Mich.....	200	A	176	10¹ 9-1780	Poplar Neck.......	....
Goodson, Francis.....	370	A	150	6-26-1780	Ky R.............	....
Goodwin, Isaac......	648	A	371	7-12-1784	Green R...........	....
Goodwin, Peter.......	3,000	A	224	12-12-1782	Read Cr..........	....
Goodwin, Samuel.....	400	A	174	9 29-1780	Beech Fk.........	Withdrawn
Goodwin, Samuel.....	500	A	210	6- 5-1781	Rowling Fk & Hardens Cr......	Surveyed
Goodwin, Samuel.....	150	A	357	4-28-1784	Beech Fk.........	....
Goodwin, Samuel.....	400	A	357	4-28-1784	Beech Fk.........	....
Goodwin, Samuel.....	250	A	358	5- 4-1784	Beech Fk.........	Withdrawn
Goodwin, Samuel.....	200	B	34	1-25-1785	Beech Fk.........	....
Goodwin, Samuel.....	50	B	34	1-25-1785	Beech Fk.........	....
Goore, Wm..........	400	A	332	1-19-1784	Rolling Fk........	....
Goore, Wm..........	400	A	332	1-19-1784	Rolling Fk........	....
Goore, Wm..........	2,000	A	332	1-19-1784	Sinking Cr........	....
Gorcham, Thomas....	500	A	54	5-15-1780	——........	....
Gordon, James.......	50	A	21	4-18-1780	Sugar Cr..........	Mil
Gordons, James......	2,000	A	58	5-16-1780	Licking...........	....
Gordon, James.......	500	A	89	5-23-1780	Graysons Settlement	....
Gordon, James.......	100	A	89	5-23-1780	Ky R.............	....
Gordon, James.......	400	A	89	5-23-1780	Sugar Cr..........	....
Gordon, John........	400	A	3	11-11-1779	Shawnee Run......	....
Gordon, John........	1,000	A	36	4-29-1780	Shawnee Run......	....
Gordon, John........	500	A	89	5-23-1780	Clear Run.........	....
Gordon, John Jr......	325	A	167	8-17-1780	Robinsons Cr......	....
Gordon, Wm........	1,000	A	180	10-23-1780	Chaplins Fk.......	....
Gore, Geo & Abraham.	1,000	A	71	5-18-1780	Licking...........	....
Gore, John..........	1,000	A	38	5- 9-1780	Licking...........	....
Govat. James........	414	A	363	6- 2-1784	Brush & Rolling Fk	....
Grabel, Phillip.......	1,000	A	230	12-17-1782	Ky R.............	....
Grace, Joseph.......	200	A	210	6- 1-1781	Beech Fk.........	Withdrawn
Grace, Joseph.......	200	A	348	3-23-1784	Simpsons Cr.......	....
Grace, Joseph.......	200	A	348	3-23-1784	Beech Fk.........	Withdrawn
Grady, Wm.:......	1,000	A	98	5-25-1780	Benson Cr........	....
Graham, Christopher ..	1,000	A	73	5-19-1780	Salt R...........	....
Graham, Chris et al...	1,500	A	72	5-18-1780	Kentucky.........	....
Graham, Francis......	450	A	259	1-29-1783	Cartright Cr......	Mil
Graham, George......	1,000	A	177	10-10-1780	S Fk Licking......	....
Graham, John........	300	A	227	12-14-1782	Green R...........	....
Graham, Richard.....	2,000	A	58	5-16-1780	Licking...........	....
Graham, Richard.....	750	A	68	5-18-1780	E Fk Cabbin Cr....	....
Graham, Richard.....	750	A	68	5-18-1780	E Fk Cabbin Cr....	....
Graham, Richard.....	600	A	68	5-18-1780	E Fk Cabbin Cr....	....
Graham, Richard.....	2,200	A	68	5-18-1780	E Fk Cabbin Cr....	....
Graham, Richard.....	400	A	139	6-21-1780	Ohio R...........	Surveyed
Graham, Richard.....	1,000	A	177	10-10-1780	S Fk Elkhorn......	....
Graham, Richard.....	1,000	A	177	10-10-1780	Ohio R...........	....
Graham, Richard.....	4,000	A	177	10-10-1780	S Fk Licking......	....
Graham, Richard.....	1,500	A	177	10-10-1780	Cabbins Cr........	....
Graham, Richard.....	1,000	A	267	3-28-1783	Ohio R...........	Surveyed
Graham, Thomas.....	400	A	137	6-19-1780	Sugar Cr..........	....
Graig, Lewis et al....	1,000	A	26	4-26-1780	Gilberts Cr.......	Surveyed
Grant, Isreal.........	400	A	9	1-17-1780	Mid Fk Licking....	....
Grant, Jane..........	400	A	273	4- 7-1783	S Fk Reedy Cr.....	Withdrawn
Grant, Jane..........	306	A	306	11-19-1783	Bear Cr..........	....
Grant, Jno..........	400	A	7	1-10-1780	Deals Run.........	Surveyed
Grant, John.........	600	A	28	4-27-1780	Grants Station.....	Surveyed
Grant, John.........	200	A	28	4-27-1780	Steals Run........	....
Grant, John.........	300	A	28	4-27-1780	Grants Station.....	Mil
Grant, John.........	210	A	171	9-12-1780	His Premption.....	....
Grant, John.........	400	A	171	9-12-1780	Licking...........	....
Grant, Wm..........	200	A	28	4-27-1780	Steals Run........	Mil
Grant, Wm..........	500	A	28	4-27-1780	N Fk Elkhorn......	....
Grant, Wm..........	300	A	28	4-27-1780	Steals Run........	....
Grant, Wm..........	1,000	A	28	4-27-1780	Mid Fk Licking....	....
Grant, Wm Jr.......	400	A	9	1-17-1780	N Fk Elkhorn......	....
Grant, Wm Sr.......	1,000	A	28	4-27-1780	Grant Settlement...	....
Grant, Wm Sr.......	400	A	28	4-27-1780	Elkhorn..........	....

Entree	Acres	Book	Page	Entry Date	Watercourse	Notes
Gratton, John	500	A	220	8–29–1781	Hardens Cr	Surveyed
Gratton, John	500	A	220	8–29–1781	Rowling Fk	Surveyed
Gratton, John et al	957½	B	6	9–14–1784	Pond Cr	....
Graves, Thomas	200	A	123	6– 2–1780	Ohio R	....
Gray, Drakeford	461	A	54	5–15–1780		....
Gray, Richard	300	A	43	5–11–1780	Stoners Fk	....
Graybill, Jacob	950	B	16	11–12–1784	Bear Cr	Surveyed
Graybill, Jacob	1,050	B	16	11–12–1784	Reedy & Bear Cr	Surveyed
Grayson, John	400	A	3	11–11–1779	Cane Run	....
Grayson, Wm	400	A	14	2–19–1780	Beech Fk	Surveyed
Grayson, Wm	400	A	14	2–19–1780	Chaplins Fk	....
Green, John	1,002	A	166	8–11–1780	Green R	....
Green, John Jr	1,000	A	57	5–15–1780	Ohio R	....
Green, John Jr	1,000	A	57	5–15–1781	Beech Fk	....
Green, Joseph	325	A	176	10– 9–1780	Beech Fk	Withdrawn
Green, Wm	400	A	42	5–10–1780	Licking	....
Green, Wm	1,000	A	42	5–10–1780	Licking	....
Green, Wm	60,000	A	324	12–26–1783	Nolin Cr	Surveyed
Green, Willis	1,000	A	165	8–11–1780	Green R	Withdrawn
Green, Willis	1,000	A	194	3–16–1781	Panther Cr	Withdrawn
Green, Willis	1,000	A	208	4–18–1781	Harrods Cr & Ohio	Withdrawn
Green, Willis	1,000	A	221	11– 9–1782	18 Mile Cr	....
Green, Willis	1,000	A	224	12–13–1782	Simpsons Cr	Surveyed
Green, Willis	500	A	237	12–21–1782	Beech & Chaplins Fk	Withdrawn
Green, Willis	200	A	241	12–25–1782	Rolling Fk	....
Green, Willis	1,000	A	241	12–25–1782	Beech Fk	Surveyed
Green, Willis	500	A	248	1– 7–1783	Bear Cr	Surveyed
Green, Willis	500	A	248	1– 7–1783	Bear Cr	Surveyed
Green, Willis	500	A	248	1– 7–1783	Bear Cr	Surveyed
Green, Willis	500	A	248	1– 7–1783	Bear Cr	Surveyed
Green. Willis	500	A	248	1– 7–1783	Bear Cr	Surveyed
Green, Willis	500	A	248	1– 7–1783	Bear Cr	Surveyed
Green, Willis	2,000	A	251	1–10–1783	Simpson & Coxes Cr	55 acres withdrawn
Green, Willis	2,000	A	252	1–10–1783	Coxes Cr	Withdrawn
Green, Willis	1,000	A	255	1–20–1783	Coxes Cr	Withdrawn
Green, Willis	1,500	A	257	1–25–1783	Cartrights Cr	Surveyed
Green, Willis	325	A	261	2– 5–1783	Murrays Run	145 acres
Green, Willis	325	A	261	2– 5–1783	Lick Cr	....
Green, Willis	500	A	262	2–11–1783	Rolling Fk	Withdrawn
Green, Willis	200	A	262	2–11–1783	Beech Fk	Withdrawn
Green, Willis	1,000	A	262	2–11–1783	Coxes Cr	....
Green, Willis	2,000	A	264	2–18–1783	Coxes Cr	1,506 acres surveyed
Green, Willis	1,000	A	264	2–15–1783	Coxes Cr	Withdrawn
Green, Willis	200	A	264	2–15–1783	Beech Fk	....
Green, Willis	1,000	A	265	2–25–1783	Ash Crofts Cr	Surveyed
Green, Willis	1,345	A	266	2–26–1783	Big Clifty Cr	Surveyed
Green, Willis	2,000	A	266	2–26–1783	Coxes Cr	....
Green, Willis	1,000	A	266	2–26–1783	Beaver Dam Fk	Surveyed
Green, Willis	1,000	A	266	2–26–1783	Beaver Dam Fk	Withdrawn
Green, Willis	500	A	266	2–25–1783	Beech & Chaplins Fk	Surveyed
Green, Willis	970	A	266	2–25–1783	Ash Croft Cr	....
Green, Willis	710	A	267	2–28–1783	N Fk Caney Cr	Surveyed
Green, Willis	500	A	273	4– 7–1783	Bear Cr	Surveyed
Green, Willis	500	A	273	4– 7–1783	Bear Cr	Surveyed
Green, Willis	500	A	273	4– 7–1783	Bear Cr	Surveyed
Green, Willis	6,290	A	307	11–20–1783	————	....
Green, Willis	3,473½	B	8	9–22–1784	Rough Cr	....
Greenlee, John	200	A	176	10– 6–1780	Carpenters Cr	....
Greenlee, John	1,000	A	176	10– 6–1780	Bensons Cr	....
Greenlee, John	2,000	A	252	1–14–1783	Robinsons Cr	....
Greenlee, John	2,000	B	43	4–18–1785	————	Withdrawn
Greenlee, Mary	200	A	135	6–17–1780	Green R	....
Greenlee, Mary	200	A	135	6–17–1780	Carpenters Cr	....
Greenlee, May	2,600	A	252	1–14–1783	Sinking Cr	Withdrawn
Greenlee, Mary	2,600	B	43	4–18–1785	Licking Cr	Withdrawn
Greenough, Wm	60,000	A	347	3–17–1784	Nole Linn Cr	Surveyed amended
Greenup, Christopher	1,500	A	132	6–15–1780	S Fk Licking	....
Greenup, Christopher	150	A	345	3– 9–1784	Ky R	....
Greenup, Christopher	100	A	345	3– 9–1784	Barrens Big Cr	....
Greenrough, Wm	60,000	A	335	1–27–1784	Nole Linn	Surveyed amended
Greenwall, Joseph	325	A	266	2–26–1783	Nolelin Cr	Withdrawn
Greenwall, Joseph	325	A	266	2–26–1783	Nolelin Cr	Surveyed
Greenwall, Joseph	325	A	243	12–26–1782	Nolelin Cr	Withdrawn
Greenwall, Joseph	325	A	243	12–26–1782	James Davis	....
Greenwood, Samuel	500	A	168	8–17–1780	Old Hunters Trace	....
Gregsby, Nathaniel	6,521	A	331	1–16–1784	Salt R	....
Gresham, George	1,000	A	290	9–10–1783	Salt R	....
Gresham, Geo et al	500	A	281	6–27–1783	Salt R	....

Entree	Acres	Book	Page	Entry Date	Watercourse	Notes
Gresham, Geo et al....	518	A	281	6-27-1783	Salt R	
Gresham, Geo et al....	650	A	304	11-14-1783	Ashes Cr	Surveyed
Gresham, Geo et al....	518	B	47	5-26-1785		....
Gresham, Samuel......	500	A	168	8-17-1783	E Fk Sugar Cr	
Gresham, Thomas.....	400	A	328	1-12-1784	Beech Fk	
Griffith, Abel........	300	A	43	5-11-1780	Hingston Fk	....
Griffith, David.......	500	A	22	4-22-1780	Green R	Mil surveyed
Griffith, David.......	500	A	22	4-21-1780	Ohio R	Withdrawn
Griffith, David.......	500	A	22	4-21-1780	Ohio R	Withdrawn
Griffith, David.......	1,000	A	22	4-21-1780	Green R	Mil surveyed
Griffith, David.......	500	A	31	4-28-1780	Town Fk	Mil
Griffith, David.......	1,000	A	35	4-29-1780	Stony Cr	
Griffith, David.......	7,000	A	72	5-18-1780	Ky R	840 acres withdrawn
Griffith, David.......	1,000	A	242	12-25-1782	Drennons Lick Cr..	Surveyed
Griffith, David.......	3,000	A	366	6-16-1784	——	1,500 acres surveyed
Grigsby, Nathaniel...	333½	A	46	5-11-1780	Salt R	
Grigsby, Nathaniel...	333	A	148	6-24-1780	Fk Yellow Cr	
Grigsby, Nathaniel...	1,000	A	315	12-15-1783	Beech Fk	Surveyed
Grigsby, Nathaniel...	300	A	315	12-15-1783	Chaplins Fk	Surveyed
Grigsby, Nathaniel...	500	A	315	12-15-1783	Chaplins Fk	425 acres surveyed
Grigsby, Nathaniel...	500	A	317	12-16-1783	Chaplins Fk	Surveyed
Grigsby, Nathaniel...	500	A	317	12-16-1783	Chaplins Fk	
Grigsby, Nathaniel...	500	A	317	12-16-1783	Long Cr	Surveyed
Grigsby, Nathanal....	1,000	A	317	12-16-1783	Beech Fk	Surveyed
Grigsby, Nathaniel...	333	A	357	5- 1-1784	——	
Griner, David........	1,600	A	270	3-28-1783	Robinsons Cr	Surveyed
Groom, John.........	500	A	122	6- 2-1780	Ohio R	....
Grubs, Hickerson.....	400	A	115	5-30-1780	Licking	....
Grubs, Hickerson.....	400	A	115	3-30-1780	Licking	....
Grubs, Hickerson.....	400	A	115	5-30-1780	Licking	....
Grundie, George.....	150	A	245	12-28-1782		
Grundwood, Samuel...	500	A	328	1-12-1784	John & James Woods	
Grundy, George......	150	A	223	12-12-1782	Beech Fk	Withdrawn
Grundy, George......	150	A	245	12-30-1782	John Grundy	
Grundy, George......	150	A	245	12-28-1782	——	Withdrawn
Grundy, George......	150	A	342	3- 2-1784	——	
Grundy, John........	110	A	223	12-12-1782	Cartright Cr	Withdrawn
Grundy, John........	150	A	223	12-12-1782	——	
Grundy, John........	150	A	223	12-12-1782	Cartright Cr	Withdrawn
Grundy, John..:.....	500	A	223	12-12-1782	Cartright Cr	377 acres surveyed
Grundy, John........	825	A	238	12-23-1782	Beech Fk	Surveyed
Grundy, John........	50	A	246	1- 6-1783	Beech Fk	
Grundy, John........	150	A	249	1- 8-1783	Beech Fk	Surveyed
Grundy, John........	150	A	249	1- 8-1783	Cartrights Cr	
Grundy, John........	150	A	265	2-19-1783	Beech Fk	Surveyed
Grundy, John........	150	A	265	2-19-1783	Cartright Cr	Withdrawn
Grundy, John........	200	A	334	1-21-1784	——	....
Grundy, John........	300	A	342	3- 2-1784	——	....
Grymes, Philip.......	1,500	A	88	5-23-1780	Stoners Cr	
Grymes, Philip.......	1,600	A	88	5-23-1780	Stoners Cr	
Gullatt, John........	405	A	126	6- 7-1780	Pond Cr	Surveyed
Gum, Jacob Jr.......	975	B	27	12-18-1784	Indian Camp Cr...	Surveyed
Gum, Jacob Jr.......	875	A	343	3- 3-1784	Green R	Surveyed
Gum, Shepherd......	300	A	288	9- 8-1783	S Fk Nolin Cr	Surveyed
Gunnall, Allen.......	500	A	78	5-20-1780	Coxes Cr	Surveyed
Gunnell, Allen.......	500	A	73	5-19-1780	Buffaloe Cr	Surveyed
Gunnell, Henry......	600	A	73	5-19-1780	Buffaloe Cr	Surveyed
Gunnell, John.......	500	A	78	5-20-1780	Coxes Cr	Surveyed....
Gunnell, Thomas.....	500	A	151	6-26-1780	Rockcastle	
Gunnell, Wm........	500	A	73	5-19-1783	Buffaloe Cr	Surveyed
Gunnell, Wm........	250	A	78	5-20-1780	Coxes Cr	Surveyed
Guthrie, Alex.......	500	A	168	8-29-1780	Wolf Cr	....
Guthrie, James......	200	A	262	2-12-1783	Rolling Fk	....
Guthrie, James......	400	B	46	5-23-1785	Floyds Fk	Surveyed
Guthrie, Rueben.....	400	A	17	2-26-1780	Buntons Lick	....
Haddon, Nehemiah....	1,000	A	302	11- 7-1783	Bear Cr	....
Haggan, James.......	902	A	28	4-27-1780	N Fk Elkhorn	....
Haggin, Jas.........	400	A	12	2- 5-1780	S Fk Sinking	....
Haggin, John........	400	A	12	2- 5-1780	Coopers Run	....
Haggin, John........	1,000	A	146	6-24-1780	Coopers Run	....
Haggin, John........	500	A	172	9-19-1780	Coopers Run	....
Haggin, Wm........	400	A	14	2-19-1780	Panther Cr	....
Haile, Nicholas......	500	A	46	5-12-1780	Floyds Fk	....
Haile, Nicholas......	500	A	66	5-17-1780	Brashears Cr	....
Hale, Martin........	200	A	22	4-22-1780	Cartright Cr	Mil
Hale, Martin........	133	A	22	4-22-1780	Beech Fk	Surveyed
Hale, Martin........	667	A	22	4-22-1780	Beech Fk	Surveyed
Hale, Martin........	500	A	22	4-22-1780	Hardins Cr	Surveyed

Entree	Acres	Book	Page	Entry Date	Watercourse	Notes
Hale, Martin	500	A	22	4-22-1780	Beech Fk	Mil surveyed
Hales, Peter	4,000	A	303	11-11-1783	Little Ky R	
Hall, David	50	A	32	4-29-1780	Green R	
Hall, Eliz & Sarah	200	A	32	4-28-1780	Sinking	
Hall, John	400	A	11	2- 4-1780	Rocky Ford Fk	
Hall, John	500	A	40	5- 9-1780	Large Fk Licking	
Hall, Leonard	400	A	13	2- 9-1780	Elkhorn	
Hall, Leonard	400	A	13	2- 9-1780	Licking Cr	
Hall, Leonard	1,000	A	153	6-27-1780	Elkhorn	
Hall, Leonard	1,000	A	153	6-27-1780	Licking	
Hall, Leonard	400	A	210	5-30-1780	Green R	
Hall, Richard	50	A	33	4-29-1780	Hickman Cr	Mil
Hall, Sarah	200	A	210	6- 5-1781	Fromans Cr	
Hall, Wm	400	A	314	12- 9-1783	Beech Fk	
Hall, Wm	1,000	A	343	3- 3-1784	Green R	Withdrawn
Hall, Wm	1,000	B	8	9-22-1784	Clear Fk	
Hall, Wm	1,000	B	8	9-22-1784	———	Withdrawn
Halleday, John	400	A	18	3- 2-1780	Sinking Cr	Surveyed
Halleday, Wm	400	A	114	5-30-1780	Asil Davis	
Halles, John	400	A	28	4-27-1780	Near Dobbins	
Halley, John	500	A	41	5-10-1780	S Licking	
Halley, John	500	A	80	5-20-1780	S Fk Licking	
Halley, Richard	400	A	41	5-10-1780	S Licking	
Halley, Wm	1,000	A	43	5-11-1780	Stoners Fk	
Halley, Wm	750	A	80	5-20-1780	N Br Soverins Cr	
Halliard, Wm	50	A	35	4-29-1780	Soverins Cr	Mil
Hamburger, Robert	1,000	A	119	6- 1-1780	Dicks R	
Hamilton, Andrew	500	A	135	6-17-1780	Brookses Sett	
Hamilton, Andrew	500	A	135	6-17-1780	Silver Cr	
Hamilton, Arch	350	A	72	5-19-1780	Ky R	
Hamilton, Arch	500	A	181	10-23-1780	E Fk Bensons Cr	
Hamilton, Arch	500	A	181	10-23-1780	Bensons Big Cr	
Hamilton, James	300	B	25	12-13-1784	Wilsons Cr	
Hamilton, John	100	A	135	6-17-1780	Ky R	
Hamilton, John	100	A	135	6-17-1780	Muddy Cr	
Hamilton, John	400	A	317	12-16-1783	Falls Ohio R	Surveyed
Hamilton, John A	90,000	A	332	1-20-1784	McWilliams	98,000 acres withdrawn
Hamilton, J A	40,000	A	340	2-20-1784	Salt R	Surveyed Withdrawn
Hamilton, Wm	500	A	34	4-29-1780	———	
Hamilton, Wm	500	A	97	5-25-1780	Licking	
Hamilton, Wm	500	A	97	5-25-1780	Dick & Ky R	Withdrawn
Hamilton, Wm	500	A	109	5-29-1780	Clarks Run	
Hamilton, Wm	500	A	132	6-15-1780	Robinsons Cr	
Hamlin, John A	90,000	A	340	2-18-1784	Barbour & Banks	Amended
Hamlin, John A	15,000	A	341	2-23-1784	Beech Fk	
Hamlin, John A	30,000	A	341	2-23-1784	Beech Fk	
Hamlin, John A	45,000	A	341	2-23-1784	The Barrens	Withdrawn
Hamlin, John A	5,000	A	342	3- 1-1784	Plumb Cr	Withdrawn
Hamlin, John A	5,000	A	342	3- 1-1784	———+	Withdrawn
Hamlin, John A	15,000	A	357	4-30-1784	Green R	Withdrawn
Hamlin, John A	15,000	A	357	4-30-1784	Salt R	Withdrawn
Hamlin, John A	5,000	B	47	5-26-1785	Plumb Cr	
Hammond, Martin	400	A	14	2-18-1780	Br Licking Cr	
Hammonds, Martin	1,000	A	144	6-23-1780	Flatt Cr	
Hammer, Andrew	200	A	216	7-21-1781	Valley Cr	
Hampton, Andrew	500	A	66	5-17-1780	Elkhorn	
Hampton, David	1,000	A	28	4-27-1780	Two Mile Cr	
Hampton, John	100	A	154	6-27-1780	Station Camp Cr	
Hanbrough, Morias	1,000	A	213	7- 2-1781	Bullskin Cr	Surveyed
Hanbrough, Morias	1,000	A	213	7- 2-1781	Fox Run	
Hanbrough, Morias	325	A	213	7- 2-1781	Floyds Fk	
Hanburry, Mozias	500	A	70	5-18-1780	Tick Cr	Surveyed
Hancock, Stephen	50	A	168	8-23-1780	Silver Cr	Mil
Hancock, Wm	400	A	9	1-18-1780	Tates Cr	
Hancock, Wm	250	A	96	5-25-1780	Tates Cr	
Handcock, Lee	400	A	12	2- 5-1780	N Fk Licking	
Handcock, Stephen	400	A	10	2- 2-1780	Tates Cr	
Handley, John	1,000	A	69	5-18-1780	Licking	
Handley, John	1,000	A	227	12-14-1782	Clear Cr	
Handley, John	200	A	279	6- 7-1783	Hines Prempt	
Handley, John	200	A	279	6- 7-1783	Mays Cr	
Handley, John	200	A	290	9-10-1783	Short Cr	
Handley, John	200	A	297	10-15-1783	Mountain Cr	
Handley, John	200	A	297	10-15-1783	Long Lick Cr	Surveyed
Handley, John	330	A	297	10-15-1783	Long Lick Cr	
Handley, John	8,000	A	331	1-16-1784	Green R	7,500 acres surveyed
Handley, John	4,000	A	351	4-10-1784	Panther Cr	
Handley, John	200	B	10	10-11-1784	———	Amended
Handley, John	4,000	B	33	1-12-1785	Panther Cr	
Handley, John	200	B	35	7-26-1785	———	

Entree	Acres	Book	Page	Entry Date	Watercourse	Notes
Handley, John	500	B	49	6–17–1785		
Hane, Christopher	200	A	230	12–17–1782	Salt R	Withdrawn
Hane, Christopher	200	A	245	12–20–1782	Salt R	Surveyed
Hane, Christopher	200	B	46	5–19–1785		Surveyed
Hanley, John	1,000	A	226	12–13–1782	Floyds Fk	Surveyed
Hanley, John	500	A	228	12–14–1782	Sinking Cr	300 acres surveyed 200 acres withdrawn
Hanley, John	200	A	243	12–26–1782	Short Cr	Withdrawn
Hanley, John	300	A	244	12–26–1782	Rock Lick Cr	Surveyed
Hanley, John	300	A	244	12–26–1782	Rock Lick Cr	Surveyed
Hanley, John	200	A	244	12–26–1782	Otter Cr	
Hanley, John	450	A	257	1–25–1783	Sinking Cr	200 acres withdrawn
Hann, John	1,000	A	28	4–27–1780	Bryan Sett	
Hanna, Andrew	400	A	87	5–23–1780	Boons Mile Cr	
Hannah, James	1,000	A	215	7–20–1781	Drennons Lick Cr	Surveyed
Hansberry, Morias	500	A	221	9– 7–1781		Returned
Hansborough, Morias	1,691½	A	249	1– 8–1783	Floyds Fk	Surveyed
Hansburry, James	1,200	A	70	5–18–1780	Br Beargrass Cr	
Hansburry, Mozias	500	A	70	5–18–1780	Floyds Fk	
Harbeson, John	400	A	152	6–26–1780	S Fk Licking	
Harbeson, Arthur	400	A	6	12–27–1779	Chaplins Fk	Surveyed
Harbeson, Arthur	1,000	A	152	6–26–1780	His Sett	
Harbeson, James	400	A	6	12–27–1779	Chaplins Fk	
Harbeson, James	1,000	A	152	6–26–1780	His Sett	
Harbeson, James, heir	737	A	328	1–12–1784	Joseph Trotter	
Hardage, James	1,000	A	40	5– 9–1780	N Fk Elkhorn	
Harden, Ben	800	A	77	5–20–1780	Cartright Cr	Surveyed
Harden, Ben	400	A	139	6–21–1780	S Fk Hardens Cr	
Harden, Ben	400	A	221	9– 7–1781		Returned
Harden, Ben	500	A	350	4– 9–1784	Hardens Cr	
Harden, Ben	1,000	B	11	11– 8–1784	Tuels Cr	
Harden, Daniel	400	A	202	4– 2–1781	Beech Fk	Surveyed
Harden, George	500	A	60	5–16–1780	Bullitts Lick	Withdrawn
Harden, George	500	A	264	2–15–1783		Withdrawn
Harden, George	531	A	310	11–26–1783	Hardens Cr	
Harden, John	400	A	56	5–15–1780	Green R	Withdrawn
Harden, John	500	A	76	5–19–1780	Pleasant Run	Surveyed
Harden, John	1,500	A	76	5–19–1780	Pleasant Run	Surveyed
Harden, John	1,000	A	175	10– 6–1780	Beech Fk Salt R	
Harden, John	400	A	202	4– 2–1781	Tuels Run	Surveyed
Harden, John	200	A	202	4– 2–1781	Clover Lick Cr	Surveyed
Harden, John	400	A	202	4– 2–1781	Clover Lick Cr	Withdrawn
Harden, John	1,000	A	202	4– 2–1781	Ohio R	Surveyed
Harden, John	400	A	202	4– 2–1781	Clover Lick Cr	Surveyed
Harden, John	400	A	202	4– 2–1781	Last Run on Barrens	
Harden, John	400	A	202	4– 2–1781	Terils Cr	
Harden, John	200	A	209	5–29–1781	Green R	Withdrawn
Harden, John	400	A	212	6–26–1781	Clover Lick	Surveyed
Harden, John	200	A	220	8–29–1781	Otter Cr	
Harden, John	200	A	220	8–29–1781		Withdrawn
Harden, John	500	A	351	4–10–1784	Panther Cr	
Harden, John Jr	200	B	11	11– 8–1784	Tuels Cr	
Harden, Joseph	1,000	A	103	5–27–1780	Clear Cr	
Harden, Katey	200	A	77	5–20–1780	Cartrights Cr	
Harden, Lydia	200	A	77	5–20–1780	Cartrights Cr	Surveyed
Harden, Mark	400	A	79	5–20–1780	Cartright Cr	
Harden, Mark	500	A	140	5–21–1780	Green R	
Harden, Mark	1,500	A	140	6–21–1780	Green R	
Harden, Mark	1,000	A	175	10– 6–1780	Hardens Cr	
Harden, Mark	1,500	A	221	9– 7–1781	Green R	Returned
Harden, Marten	1,000	A	76	5–19–1780	Hardens Cr	
Harden, Martin	1,000	A	76	5–19–1780	Pleasant Run	
Harden, Marten	1,000	A	221	9– 7–1781	Green R	Returned
Hardin, Vangelist	400	A	18	3– 8–1780	Fern Cr	Surveyed
Harden, Wm	800	A	56	5–15–1780	Hardins Cr	
Harden, Wm	1,200	A	56	5–15–1780	Green R	Surveyed
Harden, Wm	400	A	56	5–15–1780	Cedar Cr	Withdrawn
Harden, Wm	400	A	140	6–21–1780	Falls Harden Cr	300 acres surveyed 100 acres withdrawn
Harden, Wm	400	A	140	6–21–1780	S Fk Hardens Cr	Surveyed
Harden, Wm	100	A	202	4– 2–1781	Tuels Run	Surveyed
Harden, Wm	100	A	202	4– 2–1781	Tuels Run	Surveyed
Harden, Wm	297	A	312	12– 3–1783	Limestone Cr	Surveyed
Harden, Wm	1,000	A	336	2– 5–1784	Blackford Cr	
Harden, Wm	1,000	A	336	2– 4–1784	Hardens Sett	Surveyed

Entree	Acres	Book	Page	Entry Date	Watercourse	Notes
Harden, Wm	400	A	350	4- 9-1784	Salt R	Withdrawn
Harden, Wm	100	A	360	5-14-1784	———	
Harden, Wm	100	B	40	2-10-1785	———.	Withdrawn
Harden, Wm	50	B	40	2-10-1785		
Harding, John S	250	A	66	5-17-1780	Floyds Fk	
Harding, Mark	1,500	A	76	5-19-1780	Hardens Cr	Withdrawn
Harding, Mark	500	A	76	5-19-1780	Hardens Cr	
Harding, Thomas	400	A	39	5- 9-1780	Buffaloe Road	Surveyed
Hardy, John	295	A	53	5-15-1780	———.	
Hargan, Michal	778	A	377	8- 9-1784	Rolling Fk	
Hargan, Michal	400	B	1	8-14-1784	Rowling Fk	Withdrawn
Harges, Thomas	415	A	340	2-17-1784	Long Lick Cr	Surveyed
Harges, Thomas	500	A	362	5-31-1784	—— —	415 acres surveyed
Hargess, Thomas	500	A	257	1-25-1783	Long Lick Cr	Surveyed
Hargies, Thomas	400	A	224	12-13-1782	Long Lick Cr	Surveyed
Hargin, Michal	400	A	377	8- 9-1784	Rolling Fk	Withdrawn
Hargin, Michal	400	B	1	8-14-1784	Rowling Fk	Withdrawn
Hargin, Michael	1,400	B	2	8-13-1784	Rowling Fk	
Hargin, Michael	400	B	9	9-29-1784	———.	Withdrawn
Hargin, Michael	1,100	B	9	9-29-1784	James Patton	
Hargin, Michael	400	B	9	9-27-1784	Rolling Fk	Surveyed
Hargin, Michael	1,600	B	9	9-27-1784	Rolling Fk	
Hargrass, Thomas	400	A	102	5-27-1780	Hargrass Cr	
Harlen, Silas	400	A	2	11- 8-1779	Boiling Sp	Surveyed
Harlen, Silas	1,000	A	42	5-10-1780	Salt R	Surveyed
Harlen, Silas	1,000	A	142	6-22-1780	Salt R	
Harlen, Silas	560	A	199	3-21-1781	Coxes Cr & Salt R.	
Harlen, Silas	560	A	199	3-21-1781	Coxes Cr & Salt R..	
Harlen, Silas	750	A	205	4- 5-1781	Green R	
Harlen, Silas	750	A	205	4- 5-1781	Nolin Cr	Withdrawn
Harlen, Silas	350	A	215	7-18-1781	Rowling Fk	Surveyed
Harlen, Silas	350	A	215	7-18-1781	Green R	
Harlen, Silas	750	A	215	7-18-1781	Beech Fk	
Harlin, Jacob	400	A	108	5-29-1780	Rowling Fk	Surveyed
Harlin, James	400	A	107	5-29-1780	N Fk Cane Run	
Haris, James	3,000	A	238	12-21-1782	Green R	Surveyed
Harison, John F	1,000	A	224	12-13-1782	Simpsons Cr	663 acres withdrawn
Harling, Silas	1,100	B	44	5-10-1785	——	
Harmon, Jacob	1,000	A	92	5-24-1780	Floyds Fk	Surveyed
Harndy, Joseph	400	A	210	6- 5-1781	Pottengers Cr	Surveyed
Harned, Edward	400	A	254	1-16-1783	Fromans Cr	
Harned, Jonathan	400	A	241	12-15-1782	Beach Fk	
Harned, Wm	400	A	241	12-25-1782	Beech Fk	
Harnie, John	5,000	A	51	5-13-1780	Green R	Surveyed
Harold, Wm	1,500	A	49	5-12-1780	Beech Fk	Surveyed
Harper, Edwards	400	A	95	5-24-1780	Licking Cr	
Harper, John	400	A	95	5-24-1780	Lulbergreed	
Harper, Mark	392	A	28	4-27-1780	Elkhorn	
Harrell, James	400	A	106	5-27-1780	Beech Fk	Surveyed
Harrell, Moses	1,000	A	106	5-27-1780	Beech Fk	Surveyed
Harrell, Wm	1,000	A	105	5-27-1780	Beech Fk	Surveyed
Harries, James	8,000	A	237	12-20-1782	Sinking Cr	Surveyed
Harries, James	2,000	A	237	12-20-1782	Robinsons Cr	Surveyed
Harries, James	2,000	A	237	12-20-1782	Robinsons Cr	Surveyed
Harris, Christopher	1,200	A	66	5-17-1780	N Fk Licking	
Harris, Elias	1,000	A	157	7- 3-1780	Licking	
Harris, Frederick	600	A	96	5-24-1780	Mulberry Cr	
Harris, Fredersick	3,422	A	312	12- 4-1783	Kentucky R	
Harris, Frederick	1,000	A	336	2- 5-1784	Ohio R	
Harris, Hannah	1,000	A	64	5-17-1780	Kentucky R	
Harris, James	150	A	250	1- 8-1783	Bear Cr	Surveyed
Harris, James	560½	A	257	1-25-1783	Rough Cr	Withdrawn
Harris, James	8,000	A	280	6-14-1783	——	
Harris, James	400	A	299	10-28-1783	Cedar Cr	
Harris, James	150	B	41	3- 4-1785	——	
Harris, Nellson	1,000	A	90	5-24-1780	Brashears Cr	
Harris, Ran & Nath	1,300	A	56	5-15-1780	N Fk Elkhorn	
Harris, Samuel	100	A	219	8-23-1781	Mountain Cr	
Harris, Wm	400	A	253	1-14-1783	Casey Cr	
Harris, Wm	300	A	373	7-24-1784	——	
Harrison, Ben	500	A	148	6-24-1780	S Fk Licking	
Harrison, Benj, et al	2,000	A	328	1-12-1784	Falls Ohio R	
Harrison, Burr	400	A	3	11-11-1779	Sinking Sp	
Harrison, Burr	2,000	A	219	8-24-1781	Floyds Fk	Mil
Harrison, Cuthbert	1,000	A	47	5-12-1780	Floyds Fk	Surveyed
Harrison, Cuthbert	1,000	A	47	5-12-1780	Chaplins Fk	Surveyed
Harrison, Cuthbert	5,000	A	105	5-27-1780	Rowling Fk	Surveyed
Harrison, George	1,000	A	104	5-27-1780	Rowling Fk	Withdrawn
Harrison, George,	1,000	A	104	5-27-1780	Floyds Fk	Surveyed
Harrison, George	2,000	A	104	5-27-1780	Drennens Lick	Surveyed

Entree	Acres	Book	Page	Entry Date	Watercourse	Notes
Harrison, George	1,000	A	257	1-25-1783	Rowling Fk	Surveyed
Harrison, George	1,000	A	257	1-25-1783	Rowling Fk	
Harrison, Jesse	815	A	332	1-19-1784	Harrods Cr	Surveyed
Harrison, John	1,000	A	247	1- 7-1783	Ohio R	Surveyed
Harrison, John	12,825¾	A	313	12- 8-1783	——	Surveyed
Harrison, John P.	1,000	A	61	5-16-1780	Floyds Fk	Surveyed
Harrison, John P.	1,000	A	61	5-16-1780	Simpson Cr	Surveyed
Harrison, John P.	1,000	A	104	5-27-1780	Simpsons Cr	Withdrawn
Harrison, John P.	1,000	A	221	11- 9-1782	Simpsons Cr	Withdrawn
Harrison, John P.	633	A	356	4-27-1784	Salt R	Withdrawn
Harrison, John P.	633	A	356	4-27-1784	Simpson Cr	
Harrison, John P.	633	B	26	12-13-1784	Drennings Lick Cr	
Harrison, John P.	633	B	26	12-13-1784	Plumb Cr	Withdrawn
Harrison, Matt & Cuth.	1,000	A	56	5-15-1780	Simpson Cr	Surveyed
Harrison, Peter	1,000	A	82	5-22-1780	Ohio R	
Harrison, Richard	560	A	78	5-20-1780	Licking R	
Harrison, Richard	1,000	A	144	6-23-1780	Muddy Cr	
Harrison, Richard	560	A	178	10-17-1785	Nolin Cr	
Harrison, Thomas	200	A	46	5-11-1780	Salt R	
Harrison, Valentine	1,000	A	104	5-27-1780	Simpson Cr	Withdrawn
Harrison, Valentine	500	A	116	5-31-1780	White Oak Cr	
Harrison, Valentine	200	A	116	5-31-1780	Hanging Fk	
Harrison, Valentine	1,750	A	262	2-11-1783	Rolling Fk	Withdrawn
Harrison, Valentine	1,000	A	263	2-15-1783	Simpson Cr	Withdrawn
Harrison, Valentine	1,000	A	266	2-26-1783	Simpsons Cr	
Harrison, Valentine	1,750	A	312	12- 4-1783	Beargrass Cr	Surveyed & withdrawn
Harrison, Valentine	750	A	312	12- 4-1783	Beech Fk	Surveyed
Harrison, Valentine	2,000	A	320	12-17-1783	Drennons Lick Cr	Surveyed
Harrison, Valentine	1,500	A	320	11-17-1783	Chaplins Fk	
Harrison, Valentine	1,500	A	320	12-17-1783	Beech Fk	Surveyed
Harrison, Valentine	500	A	325	12-29-1783	Chaplins Fk	
Harrison, Valentine	750	A	325	12-29-1783	Chaplins Fk	
Harrison, Valentine	6,250	A	362	5-31-1784	——	2,000 acres surveyed
Harrison, Valentine	1,750	A	362	5-31-1784	——	1,743 acres surveyed
Harrison, Wm	500	A	124	6- 3-1780	Clay Lick	
Harrison, Wm	500	A	124	6- 3-1780	Clay Lick	
Harrison, Wm	1,000	A	124	6- 3-1780	W Fk Licking	
Harrison, Wm	2,000	A	147	6-24-1780	S Fk Licking	
Harrison, Wm clerk	2,000	A	170	9- 9-1780	Ohio R	Surveyed
Harrison, Wm	30	A	304	11-14-1783	Simpsons Cr	
Harrison, Wm	3,000	B	32	1- 8-1785		1,000 acres surveyed
Harrod, Edward	400	A	128	6- 8-1780	Silver Cr	
Harrod, Jas	400	A	3	11-11-1779	Harrods Run	Surveyed
Harrod, James	1,000	A	36	4-29-1780	Prather Settlement	Surveyed
Harrod, James	1,000	A	80	5-20-1780	Nob Lick	
Harrod, James	1,000	A	156	6-30-1780	His Settlement	
Harrod, James	1,000	A	259	1-30-1783	Brashears Cr	Surveyed
Harrod, James	1,000	A	306	11-19-1783	Green R	Surveyed
Harrod, James	2,175	A	376	8- 2-1784	——	715 acres surveyed
Harrod, James	1,000	A	376	8- 2-1784		
Harrod, Thos	400	A	3	11-11-1779	Sinking Spg	Surveyed
Harrold, Wm	1,000	A	56	5-15-1780	Beech Fk	Surveyed
Hart, David	400	A	14	2-19-1780	Silver Cr	
Hart, David	1,000	A	36	4-29-1780	Silver Cr	
Hart, David	1,000	A	157	7- 3-1780	Licking	
Hart, George	1,000	A	118	6- 1-1781	Chaplin Fk	Surveyed
Hart, George	400	A	139	6-21-1781	Chaplins Fk	Surveyed
Hart, George	200	A	240	12-24-1782	Beach Fk	Withdrawn
Hart, George	320	A	246	1- 1-1783	Beards Premption	Withdrawn
Hart, George	320	A	246	1- 1-1783	Stewarts Cr	
Hart, George	500	A	287	8-18-1783	Geo Hart Sr Settl	Withdrawn
Hart, George	500	A	287	8-18-1783	Geo Hart Sr Settl	Withdrawn
Hart, George	520	A	291	9-13-1783	Simpson Cr	Withdrawn
Hart, George	500	A	318	12-17-1783	——	Withdrawn
Hart, George	500	A	318	12-17-1783	——	Withdrawn
Hart, George	300	A	320	12-18-1783	Beech Fk & Cox Cr	Withdrawn
Hart, George	200	A	349	3-29-1784	Beech Fk	Withdrawn
Hart, George	400	A	375	7-29-1785	In Lincoln	
Hart, George	787	B	5	9-11-1784	——	
Hart, George	452½	B	5	9-11-1784	——	
Hart, John	325	A	209	5-23-1781	Mountain Cr	Withdrawn
Hart, John	125	A	210	6- 5-1781	Green R	Surveyed
Hart, John	325	A	210	6- 5-1781	Green R	Surveyed
Hart, John	50	A	257	1-25-1783	——	
Hart, John	50	A	257	1-25-1783	Mountain Cr	
Hart, Joseph	320	A	291	9-13-1783	Beards Premption	Withdrawn
Hart, Joseph	200	A	291	9-13-1783	Beech Fk	Withdrawn

Entree	Acres	Book	Page	Entry Date	Watercourse	Notes
Hart, Leonard	400	A	128	6- 8-1780	Beards Cr	
Hart, Miles	500	A	232	12-18-1782	Pleasant Cr	Surveyed
Hart, Miles	400	A	287	8-13-1783	————	Surveyed
Hart, Nath	400	A	14	2-19-1780	Silver Cr	
Hart, Nath	400	A	14	2-19-1780	Rock Durida, Ohio	
Hart, Nath	3,000	A	153	6-27-1780	Fk Licking	
Hart, Thomas	800	A	74	5-19-1780	Constant Fk	
Hart, Thomas	1,000	A	103	5-27-1780	Drowning Cr	
Hart, Thomas	3,500	A	157	7- 3-1780	Licking	
Hart, Y & C	10,000	A	324	12-26-1783	Nolelinn Cr	Withdrawn
Hart, Y & C	20,000	A	324	12-26-1783	Nolelinn Cr	Withdrawn
Hart, Y & C	30,000	A	347	3-17-1784	Nolin & Green R	Surveyed
Hart, Y & C	10,000	A	347	3-17-1784	Wm Pollard	Withdrawn
Hart, Y & C	20,000	A	347	3-17-1784	Wm Pollards	Withdrawn
Hart, Y & C	30,000	A	353	4-15-1784	Green R	Surveyed amended
Hartley, James	1,000	A	341	2-26-1784	Plumb Cr	
Hartley, Thomas	6,000	A	314	12-10-1783	Linn Camp Cr	Withdrawn
Hartley, Thomas	10,000	A	321	12-20-1783	Green R	Withdrawn
Hartley, Thomas	6,000	A	326	1- 2-1784	Green R	
Hartley, Thomas	6,000	A	334	1-23-1784	Brashears Cr	Surveyed
Hartley, Thomas	3,655	A	334	1-23-1784	Green R	
Hartley, Thomas	5,345	A	341	2-26-1784	Brashears Cr	
Hartley, Thomas	6,345	A	341	2-26-1784	Green R	Withdrawn
Harvie, James	560¾	B	16	11-12-1784	Cave Cr	
Harvie, James	560¾	B	16	11-12-1784	————	Withdrawn
Harvie, John	50	A	33	4-29-1780	Hickman Cr	Mil
Harvie, John	2,000	A	51	5-13-1780	Ohio R	
Harvie, John	1,000	A	81	5-22-1780	Hickman & Boons Crs	
Harvie, John	400	A	204	4- 4-1781	Green R	Surveyed
Harvie, John	6,000	A	227	12-14-1782	Green R	Surveyed
Harvie, John	18,000	A	232	12-18-1782	Green R	Surveyed
Harvie, John	500	A	241	12-15-1782	Green R	Surveyed
Harvie, John	400	A	344	3- 3-1784	Nole Linn Cr	
Harvie, John et al	2,000	A	57	5-15-1780	Salt R	
Harvie, John et al	1,000	A	57	5-15-1780	Hammonds Cr	
Harvie, John et al	1,000	A	57	5-15-1780	Chaplins Fk	
Harvie, John et al	1,000	A	60	5-16-1780	Licking	
Harvie, John et al	2,000	A	60	5-16-1780	Green R	Surveyed
Harvie, John et al	1,000	A	60	5-16-1780	Ohio R	
Harvie, John et al	1,000	A	60	5-16-1780	Ohio R	
Harvie, John et al	2,000	A	60	5-16-1780	Sinking Cr	
Harvie, John et al	10,000	A	72	5-18-1780	Ohio R	
Harvie, Robert	5,000	A	308	11-22-1783	Bear Cr	Withdrawn
Harvie, Robert	5,000	A	308	11-22-1783	Bear Cr	Withdrawn
Harvie, Robert	3,000	A	343	3- 3-1784	Green R	Surveyed
Harvie, Robert	5,000	A	343	3- 3-1784	Bear Cr	
Harvie, Robert	5,000	A	343	3- 3-1784	Bear Cr	
Harvie, Robert	400	A	344	3- 3-1784	Bear Cr	Withdrawn
Harvie, Robert	1,400	A	344	3- 3-1784	Green R	Surveyed
Harvie, Robert	1,400	A	344	3- 3-1784	Green R	Surveyed
Harvie, Robert	1,400	A	344	3- 3-1784	Indian Camp Cr	Surveyed
Harvie, Robert	2,000	A	344	3- 3-1784	Ashcraft Cr	
Harvie, Robert	500	B	16	11-12-1784	Long Lick Cr	
Harvie, Robert	400	B	16	11-12-1784	Bear Cr	Withdrawn
Harvie, Robert	3,000	B	16	11-12-1784	————	Surveyed
Harvie, Robert	1,000	B	49	6-17-1785	————	
Hastressters, John	400	A	9	1-17-1780	Silver Cr	
Hatcher, Ben	600	A	42	5-10-1780	S Fk Licking	
Hathaway, James	2,448	A	64	5-17-1780	Small Mt. Cr	
Hattclaw, Jacob	400	A	12	2- 8-1780	Dicks R	
Hawes, Samuel	1,200	A	223	12-12-1782	Green R	
Hawes, Samuel	2,500	A	223	12-12-1782	Green R	
Hawes, Samuel	7,500	A	224	12-12-1782	Ohio R	Withdrawn
Hawkins, Edmund	200	A	61	5-16-1780	Kentucky R	
Hawkins, Edmund	400	A	61	5-16-1780	S Fk Elkhorn	
Hawkins, Edmund	200	A	61	5-16-1780	Bank Lick Cr	
Hawkins, Edmund	1,000	A	61	5-16-1780	Jessamine Cr	
Hawkins, Edmund	600	A	61	5-16-1780	Clear Cr	
Hawkins, Edmund	200	A	61	5-16-1780	Kentucky R	Withdrawn
Hawkins, Edmund	200	A	168	8-23-1780	N Fk Cedar Cr	
Hawkins, Edmund	200	A	168	8-23-1780	Elkhorn	
Hawkins, Edmund	200	A	175	10- 6-1780	N Fk Cedar Cr	
Hawkins, John	400	A	3	11-11-1779	Salt R	Surveyed
Hawkins, John	1,000	A	26	4-26-1780	Hickman Cr	
Hawkins, John	100	A	37	4-29-1780	Hickmans Cr	
Hawkins, John	400	A	139	6-21-1780	Ohio R	
Hawkins, John	28,000	A	314	12- 9-1783	Barbour & Barth	Surveyed
Hawkins, John et al	1,000	A	115	5-30-1780	Licking	
Hawkins, Joseph	50	A	39	5- 9-1780	Clear Cr	
Hawkins, Joseph	500	A	99	5-26-1780	Clear Cr	Surveyed

Entree	Acres	Book	Page	Entry Date	Watercourse	Notes
Hawkins, Martin	200	A	31	4-28-1780	Kentucky R	Mil
Hawkins, Martin	1,000	A	210	5-30-1781	Town Fk Salt R	Surveyed
Hawkins, Martin	1,000	A	210	5-30-1781	Simpsons Cr	Surveyed
Hawkins, Matthew	700	A	319	12-17-1783	Green R	....
Hawkins, Thos	400	A	2	11- 3-1779	Hickmans Cr	....
Haws, Samuel	7,500	A	302	11-10-1783	Ohio R	Withdrawn
Haydon, Enoch	200	A	83	5-22-1780	Elkhorn	....
Haydon, Enoch	400	A	142	6-22-1780	Chaplins Fk	....
Haydon, Enoch	500	A	271	3-28-1783	Brush Cr	....
Haydon, John	1,000	A	65	5-17-1780	Licking	....
Haydon, John	400	A	85	5-22-1780	Ohio R	....
Hayden, Jessa	250	A	85	5-22-1780	N Fk Licking	....
Hayes, Wm	400	A	10	2- 3-1780	Silver Cr	....
Hayes, Wm	400	A	10	2- 3-1780	M Fk Licking	....
Hayes, Wm	400	A	11	2- 4-1780	Head of Otter Cr	....
Hayes, Wm	400	A	11	2- 4-1780	Licking Cr	....
Hayes, Wm	400	A	11	2- 3-1780	M Fk Licking	....
Haynes, Andrew	200	A	257	1-25-1783	Youngers Cr	....
Haynes, Andrew	200	A	257	1-25-1783	Youngers Cr	Surveyed
Haynes, Andrew	400	A	257	1-25-1783	Youngers Cr	Surveyed
Haynes, John	700	A	67	5-17-1780	Cane Run	....
Haynes, Joseph	2,000	A	243	12-25-1782	George Merrill	....
Haynes, Michal	1,000	A	71	5-18-1780	N Fk Licking	....
Hays, Gabriel	2,000	A	359	5- 7-1784	Brashears Cr	....
Hays, Gabriel	100	B	9	10- 5-1784	Valley Cr	....
Hays, Hugh	2,000	A	252	1-14-1783	Robinsons Cr	....
Hays, John	50	A	33	4-29-1780	Elkhorn	Mil
Hazelrigg, Wm	750	A	154	6-27-1780	Kentucky R	....
Hazelrigg, James	350	A	154	6-27-1780	Kentucky R	....
Hazelrigg, John	300	A	154	6-27-1780	Kentucky R	....
Head, John Alfred	500	A	83	5-22-1780	Hanging Fk	....
Head, James	500	A	309	11-25-1783	Green R	....
Headen, Ben	400	A	37	4-29-1780	Lees Ground	....
Headon, Edwards	800	A	62	5-16-1780	Bullitt Lick Trace	Withdrawn
Headon, Edwards	1,000	A	62	5-16-1780	Bullitt Lick Trace	Withdrawn
Headon, James	100	A	29	4-27-1780	nr Leesburg	Mil
Headon, John	50	A	29	4-27-1780	nr Leesburg	Mil
Headon, Samuel	1,000	A	39	5- 9-1780	Kentucky R	....
Headon, Wm	1,000	A	37	4-29-1780	Elkhorn Cr	....
Heath, James	393	A	28	4-27-1780	Coopers Run	....
Heath, Wm	5,625	B	4	9- 2-1784	Rowling Fk	....
Hedger, John	1,000	A	178	10-10-1780	Ohio R	....
Hedgers, John	2,000	A	177	10-10-1780	S Fk Licking	Mil
Hedges, James	200	A	93	5-24-1780	Licking	....
Helius, Marquis	1,000	A	127	6- 8-1780	Elk Garden	....
Helius, Marquis	400	A	127	6- 8-1780	Green R	....
Helm, John	500	A	248	1- 7-1783	Sinking Cr	100 acres surveyed 400 acres withdrawn
Helm, John	100	A	265	2-20-1783	Indian Camp Cr	....
Helms, John	400	A	286	8- 9-1783	E Fk Mill Cr	Surveyed
Helm, John	200	A	360	5-18-1784	Tuels Cr	Withdrawn
Helm, John	200	A	360	5-18-1784	Floyds Fk	Withdrawn
Helm, John	84	A	361	5-19-1784	Clover Cr	....
Helm, John	416	A	361	5-19-1784	Clover Cr	Surveyed
Helm, John	380	A	361	5-19-1784	Clover Cr	Surveyed
Helm, John	400	A	376	8- 2-1784	————	726 acres surveyed
Helm, John	200	B	3	8-27-1784	Tarr Spring Fk	Withdrawn
Helm, John	204	B	12	11- 9-1784	Tarr Spring Fk	....
Helm, John	200	B	32	1- 8-1785	Tarr Spring Fk	....
Helm, John	200	B	32	1- 8-1785	Tarr Spring Fk	Withdrawn
Helm, Joseph	1,000	A	106	5-29-1780	Doe Run	....
Helm, Joseph	200	A	108	5-29-1780	Kentucky R	....
Helm, Joseph	400	A	108	5-29-1780	Benson Cr	....
Helm, Joseph	250	A	108	5-29-1780	Bensons Big Cr	Surveyed
Helm, Joseph	800	A	116	5-30-1780	Floyds Fk	Surveyed
Helm, Joseph	400	A	180	10-21-1780	Bullskin Cr	Surveyed
Helm, Joseph	2,000	A	259	2- 3-1783	Drennons Lick Cr	....
Helm, Joseph	420	A	259	2- 3-1783	Brashears Cr	....
Helm, Joseph	80	A	259	2- 3-1783	Clear Cr	Withdrawn
Helm, Joseph	1,500	A	259	2- 3-1783	Clear Cr	....
Helm, Joseph	6,045	A	259	2- 3-1783	Drennons Lick Cr	....
Helm, Joseph	1,000	A	372	7-19-1784	————	250 acres surveyed
Helm, Joseph	80	A	376	8- 5-1784	Clear Cr	....
Helm, Joseph	1,317	A	376	8- 5-1784	Clear Cr	Mil
Helm, Joseph	600	B	5	9-11-1784	————	....
Helm, Leonard	400	A	5	12- 8-1779	Jessamine Cr	....
Helm, Leonard	1,000	A	162	7-18-1780	His Sett	....
Helm, Lynah	2,500	A	236	12-20-1782	Coxes Cr	....

Entree	Acres	Book	Page	Entry Date	Watercourse	Notes
Helm, Lynah	300	A	292	10- 1-1783	Floyds Fk	
Helm, Lynah	1,200	A	298	10-25-1783	Salt R	200 acres withdrawn
Helm, Lynah	1,000	A	298	10-25-1783	Salt R	
Helm, Lynah	200	A	314	12- 9-1783	Salt R	
Helm, Meredith	375	A	111	5-29-1780	Tick Cr	Surveyed
Helm, Meredith	1,000	A	111	5-29-1780	Tick Cr	352 acres surveyed
Helm, Meredith	1,000	A	227	12-14-1782	Brashears Cr.,	Surveyed
Helm, Meredith	1,000	A	236	12-20-1782	Brashears Cr	Surveyed
Helm, Meredith	1,000	A	372	7-19-1784	———	352 acres surveyed
Helm, Meredith Sr	1,100	A	154	6-28-1780	N & S Fk Licking	
Helm, Thomas	500	A	62	5-16-1780	Soverins Valley	Surveyed
Helm, Thomas	325	A	172	9-18-1780	Flint Cr	Withdrawn
Helm, Thomas	325	A	172	9-18-1780	Harden Cr	Withdrawn
Helm, Thomas	500	A	172	9-18-1780	Clover Lick Run	Withdrawn
Helm, Thomas	500	A	172	9-18-1780	Ohio R	Withdrawn
Helm, Thomas	1,000	A	172	9-18-1780	Green R	Withdrawn
Helm, Thomas	400	A	192	3-16-1781	Freemans Cr	Surveyed
Helm, Thomas	500	A	192	3-16-1781	Pond Cr	
Helm, Thomas	2,000	A	93	3-16-1781	Fremans Cr	Surveyed
Helm, Thomas	560	A	217	8- 2-1781	Bear Cr	Withdrawn
Helm, Thomas	250	A	221	11- 9-1782	Bear Cr	
Helm, Thomas	400	A	221	11- 9-1782	Rock Cr	
Helm, Thomas	600	A	221	11- 9-1782	Rock Cr	
Helm, Thomas	400	A	221	11- 9-1782	Rock Cr	
Helm, Thomas	560	A	223	12-12-1782	Bear Cr	Surveyed
Helm, Thomas	100	A	306	11-19-1783	Green R	Surveyed
Helm, Thomas	515	A	306	11-19-1783	Bear Cr	Surveyed
Helm, Thomas	200	A	306	11-19-1783	Green R	Surveyed
Helm, Thomas	500	A	312	12- 3-1783	Bear Cr	Surveyed
Helm, Thomas	1,820	B	23	12- 4-1784	Reedy Cr	
Helm, Thomas	2,800	B	23	12- 4-1784	Reedy Cr	
Helm, Thomas	4,000	B	23	12- 4-1784	Green R	
Helm, Wm	1,000	A	88	5-23-1780	Beargrass Cr	
Helm, Wm	637	A	88	5-23-1780	Brashears Cr	Withdrawn
Helm, Wm	1,300	A	88	5-23-1780	Meadow Run	1,000 acres surveyed
Helm, Wm	2,000	A	162	7-17-1780	Eagle Cr	
Helm, Wm	1,000	A	263	2-15-1783	Hardens Cr	Surveyed
Helm, Wm	637	A	376	8- 5-1784	S Boons Premptions	Withdrawn
Helms, John	200	A	248	1- 7-1783	Floyds Fk	Withdrawn
Helms, John	100	A	248	1- 7-1783	Grove	Withdrawn
Helms, John	200	B	3	8-27-1784	Tuels Cr	
Helms, Thomas	250	A	215	7-17-1781	Bear Cr	Withdrawn
Helms, Thomas	600	A	215	7-17-1781	Rock Cr	Withdrawn
Helms, Thomas	400	A	215	7-17-1781	N Fk Rock Cr	Withdrawn
Helms, Thomas	400	A	215	7-17-1781	Rock Cr	Withdrawn
Helms, Thomas	560	A	221	11- 9-1782	———	Withdrawn
Helms, Thomas	650	A	223	12-12-1782	Bear Cr	Surveyed
Helms, Thomas	200	A	224	12-12-1782	Bear Cr	Surveyed
Helmes, Thomas	400	A	224	12-12-1782	Bear Cr	Surveyed
Helmes, Thomas	400	A	224	12-12-1782	Bear Cr	Surveyed
Helms, Wm	300	A	221	11- 9-1782	Meadow Run	Withdrawn
Helms, Wm	300	A	224	12-12-1782	Meadow Run	
Henderson, Alex	200	A	167	8-17-1780	Phanter Cr	
Henderson, Alex	200	A	179	10-19-1780	Paint Lick Cr	
Henderson, Andrew	150	A	180	10-17-1780	Paint Lick Cr	
Henderson, Andrew	150	A	180	10-17-1780	Paint Lick Cr	
Henderson, Bennett	2,000	A	51	5-13-1780	Ohio R	
Henderson, Bennett	2,351	A	241	12-25-1782	Plumb Cr	Surveyed
Henderson, Bennett	732½	B	29	12-20-1784	Robertson Cr	
Henderson, David	400	A	147	6-24-1780	Coopers Run	
Henderson, James	200	A	28	4-27-1780	Stoners Fk	Mil
Henderson, John	1,000	A	144	6-23-1780	Silver Cr	
Henderson, Nath	400	A	14	2-19-1780	Hingston Fk	
Henderson, Nath	1,000	A	143	6-22-1780	M Fk Hingston	
Henderson, Richard	400	A	13	2- 9-1780	Otter Cr	
Henderson, Richard	400	A	15	2-21-1780	Otter Cr	
Henderson, Richard	1,000	A	143	6-23-1780	Otter Cr	
Henderson, Richard	1,000	A	143	6-23-1780	Otter Cr	
Henderson, Robert	250	A	179	10-19-1780	Paint Lick Cr	
Henderson, Samuel	400	A	11	2- 3-1780	Harrods Lick	
Henderson, Samuel	400	A	11	2- 3-1784	Licking	
Henderson, Samuel	400	A	87	5-23-1780	Brashears Cr	
Henderson, Samuel	1,000	A	143	6-23-1780	Licking Cr	
Henderson, Samuel	1,000	A	143	6-23-1780	His Sett	
Henderson, Wm	400	A	14	2-19-1780	Br Licking Cr	
Henderson, Wm	1,000	A	144	6-23-1780	His Sett	
Henderson, Wm	400	A	147	6-24-1780	Coopers Run	
Hendrik, Geo	400	A	12	2- 5-1780	Hustons Fk	

Entree	Acres	Book	Page	Entry Date	Watercourse	Notes
Henley, Leonard	4,878	A	323	12-25-1783	Nolelin Cr	
Henning, David et al	470	A	329	1-13-1784	Rock Lick Cr	
Henry, Patrick	3,000	A	237	12-21-1782	Ky R	Surveyed
Henery, Samuel	500	A	64	5-17-1780	Whitebear Cr	
Henry, Samuel	500	A	89	5-23-1780	Rowling Fk	
Henry, Wm	300	A	298	10-25-1783	Green R	
Henry, Wm	500	A	300	11- 1-1783	Rolling Fk	
Henry, Wm	3,788	A	300	11- 1-1783	M Fk Sinking Cr	1,000 acres withdrawn
Henry, Wm	1,000	A	308	11-22-1783	M Fk Sinking Cr	
Henry, Wm	1,000	A	308	11-22-1783	M Fk Sinking Cr	Withdrawn
Herendon, Edward	1,500	A	75	5-19-1780	Little Ky R	
Herndon, Edward	500	A	227	12-14-1782	Rough Cr	
Herndon, Edward	7,023	A	239	12-23-1782	Brashears Cr	Surveyed
Herndon, Jacob	2,145	A	332	1-19-1784	Sinking Cr	
Herndon, Edward	1,000	A	85	5-22-1780	12 Mile Cr	
Herring, Wm	325	A	199	3-22-1781	Pond Cr	Withdrawn
Hervell, Joseph	50	A	24	4-25-1780	Green R	Mil
Heslop, Wm	1,000	A	33	4-29-1780	Brashears	Mil surveyed
Heslop, Wm	2,000	B	23	12- 4-1784	————	Mil surveyed
Hester, Conrad	278	A	278	4-14-1783	————	
Hiatt, Stephen	50	A	29	4-27-1780	N Fk Elkhorn	Mil
Hickman, Charles	800	B	15	11-12-1784	Rough Cr	
Hickman, Charles et al	1,000	B	15	11-12-1784	Rough Cr	
Hickman, James	2,000	A	19	4-13-1780	Huricane & Ohio R	Mil
Hickman, James, heir	2,000	A	126	6- 5-1780	Licking	Mil
Hickman, John	200	A	25	4-25-1780	Drennings Lick Cr	Surveyed
Hickman, Wm	10,000	A	359	5- 7-1784	Buffaloe Run	
Hicks, Wm	400	A	8	1-17-1780	Silver Cr	
Higat, John	500	A	63	5-16-1780	Greens Cr	
Higginbothom, Jacob	492¾	A	342	2-27-1784	Caseys Cr	
Higginbothom, Jos	847¾	A	296	10-15-1783	Robinsons Cr	
Higgins, Aaron	1,106	A	83	5-22-1780	Buck Lick Cr	
Higgins, Aaron	400	A	139	6-21-1780	Buck Lick Cr	
Higgins, Henry	400	A	18	3- 2-1780	Harrodsburg Path	
Higgins, James	400	A	139	6-21-1780	Buck Lick Cr	
Higgins, Peter	400	A	18	3- 2-1780	Harrodsburg Path	
Higgins, Peter	200	A	116	5-31-1780	Whitleys Cr	
Higgon, Wm	400	A	83	5-22-1780	Buck Lick Cr	
Hightower, Wm	200	A	35	4-29-1780	Salt R	Mil withdrawn
Hightower, Wm	200	A	176	10- 9-1780	Salt R	Surveyed
Hightower, Wm	200	A	272	4- 3-1783	Beech Fk	
Hightower, Wm	200	A	217	8- 2-1781	Salt R	Withdrawn
Hightower, Wm	200	A	256	1-21-1782	Salt R	
Hightower, Wm	200	A	256	1-21-1783	Salt R	Mil
Hightower, Wm	200	A	272	3-31-1783	Ashes Cr	Withdrawn
Hightower, Wm	200	A	278	4-14-1783	————	Treas warrant
Hill, Atkinson	325	A	174	9-29-1780	Beech Fk & Coxs Cr	Withdrawn
Hill, Atkinson	325	A	174	9-29-1780	Cedar Cr	Surveyed
Hill, Atkinson	325	A	188	3-15-1781	Coxes Cr & Beech Fk	
Hill, Atkinson	410	A	342	3- 2-1784	————	
Hill, Atkinson	100	A	342	3- 2-1784	————	
Hill, Ephraim	800	A	101	5-26-1780	Holders Cr	
Hill, Peter	500	A	150	6-26-1780	Stoners Fk	
Hill, Thomas	400	A	121	6- 2-1780	Salt R	200 acres surveyed
Himley, Ulreck	250	B	47	5-14-1785	————	
Hinch, George	210	B	29	12-20-1784	Bear Cr	
Hinch, George	210	B	31	1- 3-1785	————	Surveyed
Hinch, Wm	200	A	214	7- 4-1781	S Fk Nolins Cr	Withdrawn
Hinch, Wm	200	A	215	7-18-1781	Nolin Cr	Withdrawn
Hinch, Wm	400	A	219	8-22-1781	Nolin Cr	Withdrawn
Hinch, Wm	200	A	219	8-22-1781	S Fk Nolin Cr	Withdrawn
Hinch, Wm	400	A	243	12-26-1782	Nolelin Cr	
Hinch, Wm	400	A	243	12-26-1782	Nolelin Cr	
Hinds, Andrew	200	A	233	12-18-1782	Soverins Valley	Surveyed
Hinds, Thomas	600	A	340	2-17-1784	Ashcraft Cr	Surveyed
Hines, Andrew	25	A	31	4-28-1780	Benson Cr	Mil
Hines, Andrew	25	A	30	4-28-1780	Bush Fk	Mil
Hines, Andrew	200	A	133	6-15-1780	Fern Cr	Surveyed
Hines, Andrew	100	A	133	6-15-1780	Beech Fk	
Hines, Andrew	400	A	133	6-15-1780	Green R	
Hines, Andrew	400	A	133	6-15-1780	Green R	
Hines, Andrew	100	A	219	8-23-1781	————	Withdrawn
Hines, Andrew	250	A	241	12-25-1782	Sinking Cr	Withdrawn
Hines, Andrew	500	A	243	12-26-1782	Millseat Grove	Surveyed
Hines, Andrew	300	A	243	12-26-1782	Youngers & Sulpher Lick	
Hines, Andrew	337	A	249	1- 8-1783	Nole Linn	Withdrawn
Hines, Andrew	250	A	251	1- 9-1783	Bear Cr	
Hines, Andrew	250	A	251	1- 9-1783	Sinking Cr	

Entree	Acres	Book	Page	Entry Date	Watercourse	Notes
Hines, Andrew	337	A	265	2-25-1783	Nole Linn Cr	Withdrawn
Hines, Andrew	200	A	266	2-26-1783	———	Surveyed
Hines, Andrew	200	A	266	2-26-1783	Youngers Cr	
Hines, Andrew	400	A	266	2-26-1783	Youngers Cr	
Hines, Andrew	500	A	266	2-25-1783	Bear Cr	Surveyed
Hines, Andrew	500	A	273	4- 7-1783	Fk Bear Cr	Withdrawn
Hines, Andrew	500	A	273	4- 7-1783	Bear Cr	Withdrawn
Hines, Andrew	165	A	288	9- 8-1783	Bacon Cr	Surveyed
Hines, Andrew	215	A	288	9- 8-1783	Bacon Cr	Surveyed
Hines, Andrew	72	A	296	10-14-1783	Mill Cr	Surveyed
Hines, Andrew	1,205	A	322	12-24-1783	Fremans Cr	Surveyed
Hines, Andrew et al	100	A	266	2-25-1783	Fk Little Clefty Cr	
Hines, Andrew et al	150	A	288	9- 8-1783	Nolin Cr	Surveyed
Hines, Andrew et al	100	A	344	3- 3-1784	Nole Linn Cr	Surveyed
Hines, James	500	A	313	12- 8-1783	Cave Cr	Surveyed
Hingston, John	400	A	124	6- 3-1780	His settlement	
Hingston, John	400	A	124	6- 3-1780	His settlement	
Hingston, John	400	A	124	6- 3-1780	His settlement	
Hingston, John	400	A	149	6-24-1780	S Fk Licking	
Hinton, Evan	400	A	10	2- 3-1780	Brashears Cr	Surveyed
Hinton, Evan	1,000	A	36	4-29-1780	Fox Run	
Hite, Abraham	50	A	31	4-28-1780	Rowling Fk	Mil
Hite, Abraham	50	A	31	4-28-1780	Cocks Cr	Withdrawn
Hite, Abraham	100	A	30	4-28-1780	Ky R	Mil
Hite, Abraham	200	A	30	4-28-1780	Fern Cr	Mil
Hite, Abrahem	1,000	A	30	4-28-1780	N Fk Goose Cr	Mil surveyed
Hite, Abraham	1,000	A	30	4-28-1780	S Fk Goose Cr	Mil
Hite, Abraham	50	A	35	4-29-1780	Goose Cr	Mil withdrawn
Hite, Abraham	1,000	A	152	6-26-1780	Fern Cr	Withdrawn
Hite, Abraham	1,000	A	152	6-26-1780	His settlement	
Hite, Abraham	1,000	A	152	6-26-1780	His settlement	Surveyed
Hite, Abraham	1,000	A	153	6-26-1780	Fern Cr	Surveyed
Hite, Abraham	500	A	185	10-31-1780	Salt R	Surveyed
Hite, Abraham	200	A	185	10-30-1780	Town Harrodsburg	Mil
Hite, Abraham	400	A	185	10-30-1780	———	100 acres Mil
Hite, Abraham	900	A	185	10-30-1780	Ky R	
Hite, Abraham	600	A	185	10-30-1780	Jessamine Cr	
Hite, Abraham	600	A	185	10-30-1780	Hickmans Cr	Mil
Hite, Abraham	2,000	A	220	8-24-1781	Green R	Withdrawn
Hite, Abraham	100	A	222	12-11-1782	Rowling Fk	Surveyed
Hite, Abraham	50	A	222	12- 9-1782	Coxes Cr	
Hite, Abraham	2,000	A	346	3-12-1784	Sinking Cr	Withdrawn
Hite, Abraham Jr	1,000	A	152	6-26-1780	Goose Cr	Surveyed
Hite, Abraham Jr	2,694	A	253	1-15-1783	Little Ky R	Surveyed
Hite, Abraham Jr	1,400	B	23	12- 8-1784	———	Withdrawn
Hite, Abraham Sr	400	A	15	2-21-1780	Goose Cr	Surveyed
Hite, Abraham Sr	400	A	15	2-17-1780	N Fk Goose Cr	Surveyed
Hite, George	50	A	30	4- 28-1780	N Fk Goose Cr	Mil
Hite, Isaac	400	A	15	2-21-1780	Town Fk	
Hite, Isaac	1,000	A	27	4-26-1780	Harrodsburg	
Hite, Isaac	1,000	A	152	6-26-1780	Town Fk	
Hite, Isaac	1,000	A	152	6-26-1780	Town Fk	
Hite, Isaac	600	A	196	3-17-1781	Rowling Fk	
Hite, Isaac	500	A	224	12-13-1782	Ashes Cr	Withdrawn
Hite, Isaac	500	A	232	12-18-1782	Chesnutt Flatt	
Hite, Isaac	500	A	232	12-18-1782	Clover Lick Cr	Surveyed
Hite, Isaac	500	A	232	12-18-1782	Limestone Cr	Surveyed
Hite, Isaac	500	A	232	12-18-1782	Hardens Settl	Surveyed
Hite, Isaac	1,000	A	232	12-18-1782	Hardens Cr	Surveyed
Hite, Isaac	1,000	A	233	12-18-1782	Rock Lick Cr	
Hite, Isaac	3,087½	A	240	12-24-1782	Drennons Lick	Surveyed
Hite, Isaac	318	A	240	12-24-1782	Rolling Fk	Surveyed
Hite, Isaac	2,694	A	253	1-15-1783	Little Ky R	Surveyed
Hite, Isaac	1,618	A	258	1-25-1783	Cartright Cr	1,003 acres 615 acres withdrawn
Hite, Isaac	800	A	290	9-10-1783	Coxes Cr	
Hite, Isaac	800	A	290	9-10-1783	———	615 acres surveyed 203 withdrawn
Hite, Isaac	600	A	291	9-15-1783	———	
Hite, Isaac	505	A	308	11-24-1783	Beech Fk	Withdrawn
Hite, Isaac	1,000	A	308	11-22-1783	Ky R	Withdrawn
Hite, Isaac	1,000	A	335	1-31-1784	Simpsons Cr	Surveyed
Hite, Isaac	1,000	A	336	1-31-1784	S Fk Simpsons Cr	Surveyed
Hite, Isaac	500	A	346	3-12-1784	Ashes Cr	
Hite, Isaac	500	A	346	3-12-1784	Ashes Cr	Withdrawn
Hite, Isaac	505	A	346	3-12-1784	Beech Fk	
Hite, Isaac	755	B	44	5-10-1785	———	

Entree	Acres	Book	Page	Entry Date	Watercourse	Notes
Hite, Isaac	28	B	44	4–25–1785	Ohio R	
Hite, Isaac	203	B	44	4–25–1785	Cartright Cr	
Hite, Isaac	1,003	B	48	6–20–1785	———	
Hite, Isaac	2,000	B	51	11– 4–1785	Ohio R	
Hite, Isaac	1,000	B	51	11– 4–1785	Ohio R	Withdrawn
Hite, Isaac	1,000	B	51	11– 3–1785	Ky R	Withdrawn
Hite, Isaac et al	500	A	28	4–27–1780	Wilsons Run	Mil
Hite, Isaac et al	500	A	28	4–27–1780	Dicks R	Mil
Hite, Isaac et al	1,000	A	28	4–27–1780	Bowman Settl	Mil surveyed
Hite, Isaac et al	1,000	A	41	5–10–1780	Limestone Cr	
Hite, Isaac et al	1,800	A	41	5–10–1780	Green R	
Hite, Isaac et al	5,000	A	41	5–10–1780	Little Ky	Withdrawn
Hite, Isaac et al	1,000	A	41	5–10–1780	Brashears Cr	
Hite, Isaac et al	1,000	A	41	5–10–1780	Salt R	
Hite, Isaac et al	1,000	A	41	5–10–1780	Ohio R	
Hite, Isaac et al	1,000	A	41	5–10–1780	Hanging Fk	
Hite, Isaac et al	5,000	A	41	5–10–1780	Delaware Cr	
Hite, Isaac et al	2,000	A	41	5–10–1780	Fern Cr	
Hite, Isaac et al	1,000	A	41	5–10–1780	Beargrass	Surveyed
Hite, Isaac et al	1,000	A	41	5–10–1780	Harrods Cr	Surveyed
Hite, Isaac et al	1,000	A	41	5–10–1780	Floyds Fk	Surveyed
Hite, Isaac et al	2,000	A	41	5–10–1780	Cane Run	Withdrawn
Hite, Isaac et al	1,000	A	41	5–10–1780	Harrods Run	
Hite, Isaac et al	2,000	A	41	5–10–1780	Rockcastle R	
Hite, Isaac et al	1,000	A	41	5–10–1780	Kentucky	
Hite, Isaac et al	2,000	A	41	5–9–1780	Hanging Fk	
Hite, Isaac et al	2,000	A	41	5–9–1780	Cane Run	964 acres surveyed
Hite, Isaac et al	3,000	A	41	5–9–1780	Cane Run	
Hite, Isaac et al	2,000	A	326	1–1–1784	Fern Cr	Withdrawn
Hite, Isaac Jr	5,000	A	89	5–23–1780	Salt R	Surveyed
Hite, Isaac Sr	400	A	15	2–21–1780	Sinking Spg	
Hite, Isaac Sr	2,586½	A	242	12–25–1782	Drennons Lick Cr	Surveyed
Hite, Isaac Sr	2,586½	A	251	1–9–1783	Drennons Lick	
Hite, Isaac Sr	3,000	A	354	4–16–1784	Rolling Fk	2,519 acres surveyed
Hite, Jacob	500	A	70	5–18–1780	Harrods Cr	Withdrawn
Hite, Jacob	5,000	A	340	2–21–1784	Harrods Cr	
Hite, Joseph	400	A	15	2–21–1780	Harrods Cr	Surveyed
Hite, Joseph	1,000	A	152	6–26–1780	Harrods Cr	Surveyed
Hite, Joseph	1,400	A	326	1–1–1784	———	Withdrawn
Hite, Joseph	———	A	334	1–21–1784	Harrods Cr	Surveyed & amended
Hoagland, Cornelius	1,000	A	160	7–7–1780	Rowling Fk	
Hoagland, Cornelius	1,000	A	187	3–15–1781	Ohio R	
Hoagland, Christopher	600	A	226	12–14–1782	Rowling Fk	
Hoak, Samuel	2,000	A	367	6–22–1784	Harrods Cr	
Hoard, Thomas	975	A	270	3–28–1783	Green R	Surveyed
Hodgen, Robert	1,000	A	180	10–19–1780	Drinnens Lick	Surveyed
Hodgen, Robert	300	A	180	10–19–1780	Ky R	Withdrawn
Hodgen, Robert	700	A	213	7–2–1781	Peytons Cr	
Hodges, Joseph	400	A	9	1–18–1780	Woolf Cr	
Hodges, Joseph	400	A	118	6–1–1781	Rowling Fk	
Hodges, Jesse	112	A	129	6–9–1780	Kentucky R	
Hodgins, Robert	10,000	A	260	2–3–1783	Nole Linn Cr	
Hodgins, Robert	300	B	44	5–14–1785	Ky R	Withdrawn
Hodgins, Robert	1,800	B	45	5–14–1785	———	
Hoff, Charles	1,000	A	187	3–15–1781	Ohio R	
Hogan, James Jr	400	A	12	2–7–1780	N Fk Elkhorn	
Hogan, Jas Sr	400	A	12	2–7–1780	N Fk Elkhorn	
Hogan, Richard	400	A	1	11–3–1779	Cane Run	Surveyed
Hogan, Wm	400	A	12	2–7–1780	N Fk Elkhorn	
Hogg, Peter	400	A	15	2–21–1780	Ky R	
Hogg, Peter	1,000	A	32	4–28–1780	Falls Ohio R	Surveyed
Hogg, Peter	1,000	A	211	6–12–1781	Drennings Lick	Surveyed
Hogg, Richard	15,000	A	314	12–12–1783	Little Ky R	
Hold, Wm	400	A	252	1–13–1783	Beech Fk	
Holder, John	400	A	113	5–30–1780	Silver Cr	
Holder, John	1,000	A	145	6–24–1780	Hustons Fk	
Holder, John	1,000	A	145	6–24–1780	Hustons Fk	
Holeman, Edward	400	A	5	12–7–1779	Buck Run	
Holeman, Edward	1,000	A	126	6–7–1780	His settlement	
Holeman, Edward	900	A	376	8–5–1784	Drinning Cr	Surveyed
Holeman, George	400	A	4	12–7–1779	Brashears Cr	Surveyed
Holeman, George	1,000	A	227	12–14–1782	Clear Cr	Surveyed
Holeman, Henry	1,000	A	144	6–23–1780	Clear Cr	
Holesclaw, James	300	A	140	6–21–1780	S Fk Hardens Cr	
Holesclaw, James	300	A	140	6–21–1780	S Fk Hardens Lick	
Holland, Francis	1,000	A	230	12–17–1782	Salt R	Surveyed
Holliday, Benjamin	1,000	A	232	12–18–1782	Battle Cr	Surveyed
Holliday, Joseph et al	262½	A	364	6–7–1784	Rolling Fk	
Holliday, Joseph et al	262½	B	3	8–26–1784	Rolling Fk	

Entree	Acres	Book	Page	Entry Date	Watercourse	Note
Hollihay, Joseph et al..	262½	B	49	8–26–1784	————	Amended
Holliday, Wm.	1,000	A	75	5–19–1780	Floyds Fk	Mil surveyed
Hollingsworth, Jesse.	2,000	B	24	12–10–1784	Green R	....
Hollingsworth, Levi	9,000	B	45	5–16–1785	Salt R	Surveyed
Hollingsworth, Levi	26	B	49	6–17–1785	....	....
Hollingworth, Levi et al	16,406¼	B	45	5–16–1785	Salt R	Surveyed
Holmes, Benjamin	580	A	125	6– 5–1780	W Fk Licking	....
Holmes, James	500	A	107	5–29–1780	Salt R	....
Holmes, James	400	A	243	12–26–1782	Ohio R	....
Holser, John	400	A	7	1–10–1780	Boons Cr	....
Holt, Abraham	400	A	213	7– 2–1781	Bullskin Cr	....
Holt, John	4,000	A	233	12–18–1782	Muddy Run	....
Holt, John H	10,250	A	345	3–11–1784	Barbour & Banks	....
Holt, Thomas	5,000	A	233	12–18–1782	Rough Cr	....
Honey, James	1,000	A	123	6– 3–1780	Salt R	....
Honey, James	1,000	A	199	3–24–1781	Salt R	Surveyed
Honeyman, Robert	2,000	A	91	5–24–1780	Beech Fk	Surveyed
Honeyman, Robert	1,000	A	91	5–24–1780	Buffaloe Cr	Surveyed
Hoomes, John	3,250	A	167	8–17–1780	Green R	Withdrawn
Hoomes, John	3,250	A	190	3–15–1781	Green R	Surveyed
Hoomes, John	3,250	A	90	3–15–1781	Panther Cr	....
Hoomes, John	13,412	A	303	11–12–1783	Green R	....
Hoopwood, Moses	300	A	66	5–17–1780	George Willson	....
Hope, Rich & Adam	500	A	106	5–29–1780	Chaplin Fk	....
Hopkins, Garrard	2,000	A	58	5–16–1780	Licking	....
Hopkins, John	800	A	196	3–17–1781	Fern Cr	Surveyed
Hopkins, John	500	A	250	1– 9–1783	Pattons Line	253 acres surveyed
Hoptonstall, Abraham	1,000	A	166	8–16–1780	Panther Cr	Surveyed
Hopwood, Moses	300	A	257	1–25–1783	Floyds Fk	....
Hord, Aggy	800	A	84	5–22–1780	N Fk Licking	....
Hord, James	1,000	A	61	5–16–1780	Ohio R	Withdrawn
Hord, James	1,000	A	66	5–17–1780	N Fk Licking	....
Hord, James	5,000	A	270	3–28–1783	Panther Cr	Withdrawn
Hord, James	5,000	A	295	10–13–1783	Green R	....
Hord, James	1,443	A	295	10–13–1783	Panther Cr	....
Hord, James	1,443	A	295	10–13–1783	Panther Cr	Withdrawn
Hord, James & John	1,443	A	270	3–28–1783	Panther Cr	Withdrawn
Hord, James & John	1,000	A	369	6–30–1784	————	....
Hord, Jesse	750	A	101	5–26–1780	N Fk Liking	Mil
Hord, John	200	A	34	4–29–1780	Hinston Cr	....
Hord, John	500	A	87	5–23–1780	N Fk Licking Cr	....
Horine, Michael	260	A	159	7– 5–1780	Licking	....
Horine, Michael	200	A	244	12–26–1781	Ohio R	....
Horine, Michael	500	A	321	12–18–1783	Knob Cr	Surveyed
Horine, Michael	1,000	A	321	12–18–1783	Salt R	600 acres surveyed
Horine, Michael	745	A	321	12–18–1783	Knobb Cr	....
Horine, Michael	560	A	366	6–17–1784	Fayette Cr	260 acres surveyed
Horine, Michael	500	A	377	8–10–1784	Ohio R	240 acres surveyed
Hord, Mordecai	100	A	61	5–16–1780	Cumberland R	....
Hord, Mordecai	300	A	61	5–16–1780	Ohio R	Withdrawn
Hord, Mordecai	300	A	66	5–17–1780	Mid Fk Licking	....
Hord, Mordecai	2,000	A	74	5–19–1780	S Fk Licking	....
Hord, Mordecai	600	A	354	4–16–1784	Kentucky R	Withdrawn
Hord, Mordecai	600	A	354	4–16–1784	Salt R	Withdrawn
Hord, Mordicai	200	B	4	9– 2–1784	....	....
Hord, Mordicai	600	B	25	12–13–1784	Drennings Lick Cr	....
Hord, Mordicai	600	B	25	12–13–1784	Kentucky R	Withdrawn
Hord, Richard	761	A	270	3–28–1783	Green R	Surveyed
Hord, Thomas	6,009	A	309	11–25–1783	Panther Cr	....
Hord, Thomas	8,000	A	309	11–25–1783	Green R	....
Hord, Thomas	6,000	A	309	11–25–1783	Panther Cr	....
Horndon, Zach	1,000	A	156	6–30–1780	Elkhorn	....
Hornsby, Joseph	1,200	A	203	4– 3–1781	Salt R	Surveyed
Hornsby, Joseph	1,200	A	203	4– 2–1781	Salt R	Surveyed
Hornsby, Joseph	400	A	262	2–12–1783	Prathers Cr	....
Hornsby, Joseph	400	A	291	9–13–1783	....	....
Hornsby, Joseph	400	A	294	10–10–1783	Floyds Fk	....
Hornsby, Joseph	400	A	299	10–27–1783	....	Surveyed
Hornsby, Joseph	400	A	316	12–15–1783	Big Kentucky R	....
Hornsby, Joseph	400	A	355	4–19–1784	Ohio R	....
Horton, A	400	A	250	1– 9–1783	Ohio R	....
Hotder, John et al	400	A	8	1–17–1780	Huston R	....
Hourine, Jacob	500	A	321	12–18–1783	Knob Cr	Surveyed
Honsault, Fred	400	A	277	4–12–1783	Hardens Cr	....
House, Andrew	1,000	A	346	3–16–1784	Drinnins Lick Cr	Withdrawn
House, Andrew	————	A	347	3–17–1784	Drinnins Lick Cr	....
Howard, Edward	300	B	49	6–17–1785	....	....
Howard, Euastace	50	A	35	4–29–1780	Salt R	Mil

Entree	Acres	Book	Page	Entry Date	Watercourse	Notes
Howard, John	4,000	A	194	3–16–1781	Harrods Cr	
Howard, John	7,945½	A	242	12–25–1782	Ohio R	Surveyed
Howard, Mordicai	600	A	52	5–13–1780	Kentucky R	Surveyed
Howard, Mordicai	600	A	53	5–13–1780	Salt R	Withdrawn
Howard, Wm	300	A	319	12–17–1783	Green R	
Howlett, Austin	300	A	125	6– 5–1780	W Fk Licking	
Hoy, Wm	1,000	A	129	6– 9–1780	Otter & Silver Cr	
Hoye, Wm	1,000	A	129	6– 9–1780	Licking	
Hudson, David	500	A	78	5–20–1780	Shawnee Run	
Hudson, James	500	A	78	5–20–1780	Shawnee Run	
Hudson, Nath	1,000	A	37	4–29–1780	Hingston Fk	
Hudson, Wm, heir	1,000	A	37	4–29–1780	Paint Lick Cr	
Hudson, Wm, heirs	400	A	18	3– 7–1780	Paint Lick Cr	
Hudson, Zach	100	A	33	4–29–1780	Kentucky R	Mil
Hudgen, Robert	200	A	149	6–24–1780	Hingstons Fk	
Hudgens, James	600	A	127	6– 8–1780	Green R	
Hudgens, John	200	A	127	6– 8–1780	Green R	
Hueston, John	1,500	A	293	10– 4–1783	Rolling Fk	1,260 acres surveyed
Hueston, John	240	B	1	8–12–1784	David Cowan	Withdrawn
Huff, Charles	1,000	A	160	7– 7–1780	Rowling Fk	
Huffman, Phillip	500	A	92	5–24–1780	E Fk Coxes Cr	Surveyed
Huffman, Philip	500	A	92	5–24–1780	Willsons Cr	
Huffman, Phillip	500	A	356	4–27–1784	Coxes Cr	
Huffman, Phillip	500	A	356	4–27–1784	Rolling Fk	
Hughes, Ben	500	A	180	10–21–1780	Floyds Fk	Surveyed
Hughes, David	400	A	75	5–19–1780	Hunting Cr	
Hughes, James	500	A	300	10–29–1783	Panthers Cr	
Hughes, James	500	A	300	10–29–1783	Panther Cr	
Hughes, John	400	A	244	12–27–1782	Ashes Cr	Surveyed
Hughes, John	100	A	265	2–19–1783	Coxes Cr	Surveyed
Hughes, John	100	A	331	1–16–1784	————	Surveyed
Hughes, Joseph	1,000	A	175	10– 6–1780	Salt R	
Hughes, Joseph	1,000	A	212	6–21–1781	Pleasant Run	
Hughes, Thomas	50	A	33	4–29–1780	Ohio R	Mil
Hughes, Thomas	1,000	A	91	5–24–1780	Brashears Cr	Surveyed
Hughes, Thomas	1,000	A	91	5–24–1780	Brashears Cr	Surveyed
Hughes, Thomas	2,000	B	25	12–10–1784	————	1,000 acres surveyed
Hughs, Wm	200	A	32	4–29–1780	Licking	Mil
Hughs, Wm	2,000	A	32	4–29–1780	Licking	Mil
Huils, Henry	500	A	307	11–20–1783	Nole Linn Cr	
Huls, Henry	500	A	336	2– 4–1784	Salt R	
Humber, John	800	A	374	7–27–1784	Caseys Cr	
Humble, Conrad	500	A	140	6–21–1780	Clear Cr	
Humble, Conrad	1,285	A	376	8– 9–1784	Ohio R	
Humble, Michael	750	A	376	8– 9–1784	Ohio R	
Hume, John	1,000	A	209	5–18–1781	Salt R	Surveyed
Hume, John	1,000	B	1	8–14–1784	Salt R	Amended
Humphreys, John	600	A	44	5–11–1780	Beech Fk	Surveyed
Humphreys, John	1,078⅔	A	281	6–20–1783	Nolin Cr	
Humphries, Uriah	50	A	141	6–22–1780	Rowling Fk	Mil
Humphries, Wm	400	A	66	5–17–1780	Plum Cr Salt R	
Humphries, Wm Sr	400	A	66	5–17–1780	Plum Cr Salt R	
Humphrey, Richard	200	A	33	4–29–1780	Ky R	Mil
Hundley, Anthony	1,000	A	311	11–29–1783	E Fk Valley Cr	Surveyed
Hundley, Anthony	63,000	A	312	12– 4–1783	Chaplins Fk	28,229 scres withdrawn
Hundley, Anthony	40,000	A	359	5–10–1784		
Hundley, Anthony	2,124	A	359	5– 7–1784	Hinckes Run	Surveyed
Hundley, Anthony	2,400	B	35	1–26–1785	Knobb Cr	
Hundon, Zach	1,000	A	158	7– 3–1780	Hingston Fk	
Hundson, Wm	500	A	92	5–24–1780	Ky R	
Hunley, Anthony	28,229	B	44	4–25–1785	————	Withdrawn
Hunley, Thomas et al	1,000	A	337	2– 7–1784	Rough Cr	
Hunt, Jonathan	1,000	A	29	4–27–1780	Bryan settlement	
Hunt, Jonathan	50	A	178	10–16–1780	Geo Skillerns	
Hunt, Nathaniel	2,500	A	333	1–20–1784	Harrods Cr	Withdrawn
Hunt, Nathaniel	2,500	A	347	3–16–1784	Harrods Cr	Surveyed
Hunt, Nathaniel	4,000	A	358	5– 4–1784	Salt R	Surveyed
Hunt, Samuel	3,000	A	333	1–20–1784	————	Surveyed
Hunt, Samuel	3,000	A	358	5– 3–1784	Salt R	Surveyed amended
Hunter, James	1,000	A	64	5–17–1780	Jessamine Cr	
Hunter, John	1,000	A	57	5–15–1780	Rolling Fk	
Hunter, John	1,000	A	73	5–19–1780	Cartrights Cr	
Hunter, John	50	A	204	4– 4–1781	Beech Fk	
Hunter, John	50	A	221	11–26–1781	————	
Hunter, John	50	A	335	1–27–1784	Beech Fk	
Hunter, Miles	2,000	A	227	12–14–1782	Bullskin Cr	Surveyed
Huntsman, Josiah	200	A	130	6–10–1780	Mid Fk Licking	
Hurst, James	1,000	A	73	5–19–1780	Buffaloe Cr	Surveyed

Entree	Acres	Book	Page	Entry Date	Watercourse	Notes
Hurst, John	1,000	A	57	5-15-1780	Rolling Fk	
Hurst, John	1,000	A	106	5-27-1780	Cartright Cr	Surveyed
Huse, Benj	500	A	111	5-29-1780	S Jeptha Mt	Surveyed
Huse, Morgan	500	A	111	5-29-1780	S Jeptha Mt	Surveyed
Huse, Morgan	500	A	180	10-21-1780	Jepthas Mt	Surveyed
Huskins, Wm	400	A	149	6-24-1780	Huskins Run	
Huston, George	693½	A	266	2-26-1783	Brashears Cr	
Huston, George	600	A	266	2-25-1783	N Fk Robinsons Cr	
Huston, John	1,000	A	291	9-11-1783	Rocky Run	148 acres withdrawn
Huston, John	500	A	291	9-11-1783	Rock Lick Cr	Withdrawn
Huston, John	1,500	A	361	5-25-1784	Pittmans Cr	Withdrawn
Huston, John	1,500	A	377	8-12-1784	Sulphur Lick	Withdrawn
Huston, John	648	B	2	8-25-1784	Rock Lick	
Huston, John	148	B	2	8-25-1784	Rocky Run	
Huston, John	500	B	2	8-25-1784	Rock Lick	Withdrawn
Huston, Stephen	400	A	101	5-26-1780	Carpenters Cr	
Huston, Stephen	400	A	101	5-26-1780	Carpenters Cr	
Hutcheson, John	1,000	A	65	5-17-1780	Licking	
Hutcheson, Joseph	1,000	A	40	5- 9-1780	Salt R	
Hutcheson, Joseph	1,000	A	259	2- 3-1783	Drennons Lick Cr	
Hutcheson, Peter	400	A	41	5-10-1780	Floyds Fk	
Hutchion, Ben	500	A	69	5-18-1780	Chaplin & Town Fk	Surveyed
Hutchison, Jeremiah	500	A	100	5-26-1780	Stoners Cr	
Hutchison, Wm	800	A	117	5-31-1780	Town Fk	
Hutten, Samuel	200	A	174	10- 4-1780	Ky R	
Hyndes, Andrew	417	B	30	12-24-1784	Youngers Cr	
Hyndes, Andrew	300	B	30	12-23-1784	Rough Cr	
Hynds, Andrew	700	B	15	11-12-1784	Rough Cr	
Hynds, Andrew	500	B	16	11-13-1784	Short Cr	Amended
Hynds, Andrew	2,287	B	31	1- 3-1785	——	700 acres surveyed
Hynds, Andrew	12,900	B	35	1-26-1785	Green R	
Hynds, Hannah	400	B	14	11-12-1784	Rough Cr	
Hynds, Andrew et al	953	B	14	11-12-1784	Indian Camp Cr	Withdrawn
Hynds, Andrew et al	953	B	15	11-12-1784	——	Withdrawn
Hynds, Andrew et al	1,300	B	15	11-12-1784	Indian Camp Cr	Surveyed
Hynes, Andrew	1,000	B	30	12-23-1784	Rolling Fk	Surveyed
Hynes, Andrew	2,000	B	32	1- 8-1785	——	500 acres surveyed
Hynes, Andrew	500	B	30	12-23-1784	Cave Cr	
Hynes, Andrew	500	B	15	11-12-1784	Short Cr	
Hynes, Andrew	400	B	5	9-11-1784	——	
Hynes, Andrew	3,000	A	375	7-29-1784	Green R	
Hynes, Andrew	35,000	A	375	7-29-1784	Green R	Surveyed
Hynes, Andrew	400	A	366	6-18-1784	Valley Cr	
Hynes, Andrew	400	A	363	6- 4-1784	——	100 acres surveyed
Hynes, Andrew	1,205	A	362	5-31-1784	——	310 acres surveyed
Hynes, Andrew	200	A	335	1-27-1784	Short Cr	
Hynes, Andrew	1,000	A	313	12- 8-1783	Cave Cr	
Hynes, Andrew	150	A	307	11-20-1783	——	
Hynes, Andrew	128	A	300	11- 1-1783	Shaws Cr	Surveyed
Hynes, Andrew	400	A	296	10-14-1783	Buffaloe Cr	
Hynes, Andrew	200	A	296	10-14-1783	Valley Cr	Surveyed
Hynes, Andrew	200	A	296	10-14-1783	Buffaloe Cr	Surveyed
Hynes, Andrew	100	A	257	1-25-1783	In Barrens	Surveyed
Hynes, Andrew	500	A	257	1-25-1783	Bear Cr	Withdrawn
Hynes, Andrew	300	A	241	12-25-1782	Mill Cr	280 acres surveyed
Hynes, Andrew	280	A	241	12-25-1782	Mill Cr	Surveyed
Hynes, Andrew et al	5,000	B	31	1- 3-1785	——	1,300 acres surveyed
Hynes, Andrew et al	3,100	A	360	5-18-1784	——	100 acres surveyed
Hynes, Andrew et al	2,000	A	331	1-16-1784	Short Cr	
Hynes, Andrew et al	1,000	A	330	1-16-1784	Short Cr	
Hynes, Andrew et al	537	A	307	11-20-1783	——	
Hynes, Andrew et al	150	A	307	11-20-1783	——	
Hynes, Thomas	1,081	A	353	4-15-1784	Green R	
Iarms, George	150	A	371	7-12-1784	Cartright Cr	
Iarms, George	150	A	371	7-12-1784	Rolling Fk	
Iarms, George	150	A	371	7-12-1784	Rolling Fk	
Iarms, George	70	A	371	7-12-1784	Pottengers Cr	
Iarmes, George	30	A	371	7-12-1784	Pottengers Cr	
Immuel, George M	6,000	A	358	5- 4-1784	Rolling Fk	
Immuel, George M	6,000	A	358	5- 4-1784	——	Withdrawn
Inglish, Charles	400	A	123	6- 3-1780	Dicks R	
Inglish, Charles	250	A	123	6- 3-1780	Rockcastle	
Inglish, Charles	250	A	123	6- 3-1780	Dicks R	50 acres withdrawn

Entree	Acres	Book	Page	Entry Date	Watercourse	Notes
Ingram, Jonathan....	400	A	14	2–19–1780	Rolling Fk	Surveyed
Ingram, Saml	400	A	14	2–19–1780	Shawnee Run	
Ingram, Wm	500	A	158	7– 3–1780	Licking	....
Innis, James	2,000	A	237	12–21–1782	Little Kentucky R.	
Innis, James	2,000	A	237	12–21–1782	Little Kentucky R.	Surveyed
Innis, James	3,750	A	237	12–21–1782	Little Kentucky R.	Surveyed
Innis, Harry	4,500	B	47	6– 4–1785	Ohio R	Surveyed
Innis, Hugh	1,000	A	37	4–29–1780	L Blue Lick	
Innis, Hugh	200	A	67	5–17–1780	Sinking Cr	
Innis, Hugh	1,000	A	121	6– 2–1780	Licking	....
Irwin, Abraham	500	A	44	5–11–1780	Harrods Cr	
Irwine, Abraham	500	A	46	5–12–1780	Cartrights Cr	
Irwin, Christopher	400	A	11	2– 4–1780	Tates Cr	
Irwin, Christopher	400	A	113	5–30–1780	M Fk Licking	
Irvin, Christopher	500	A	120	6– 1–1780	His Sett	
Irwin, Christopher	1,000	A	120	6– 1–1780	Silver Cr	....
Irwin, Christopher	300	A	245	12–28–1782	Trace Fk Pittmans Cr	....
Irwin, Christopher	796½	A	245	12–28–1782	N Fk Pittmans Cr	
Irvin, James	3,625	A	331	1–16–1784	Salt R	
Irwin, John	400	A	93	5–24–1780	Beech Fk	
Irwin, Robert	50	A	123	6– 3–1780	Green R	Mil
Irwin, Robert	500	A	123	6– 3–1780	Green R	....
Irvine, Christopher	1,000	A	113	5–30–1780	3 Fks Otter Cr	
Irvine, Christopher	1,000	A	113	5–30–1780	His Sett	....
Irvine, Christopher	1,178	A	253	1–15–1783	Cartright Cr	Surveyed
Irvine, Christopher	1,400	A	253	1–15–1783	Cartright Cr	Surveyed
Irvine, Christopher	1,000	A	362	5–31–1784	————	....
Irvine, Elizabeth	400	A	60	5–16–1780	Harris Run	
Irvine, Wm Jr	2,578	A	269	3–28–1783	Beech Fk	
Irvine, Richard	6,180	A	241	12–25–1782	Rough Cr	
Isaacs, John	400	A	15	2–21–1780	Wilsons Run	
Jackman, Adam	1,000	A	70	5–18–1780	Licking	Withdrawn
Jackman, Adam	1,000	A	167	8–11–1780	Mastersons Premption	....
Jackman, John	400	A	16	2–26–1780	Elkhorn Cr	
Jackman, Richard	400	A	16	2–26–1780	Dicks Cr	
Jackman, Wm	400	A	70	5–18–1780	Elkhorn	
Jackson, Congrave	200	A	173	9–22–1780	Licking	
Jackson, Jeremiah	3,000	A	318	12–16–1783	Floyds Fk	
Jackson, Joel	333¾	A	54	5–15–1780	Yellow Banks	
Jackson, John	1,000	A	47	5–12–1780	Hingston Fk	
Jackson, John	400	A	173	9–22–1780	S Fk Licking	
Jackson, John	400	A	173	9–22–1780	Licking	
Jackson, Joseph	500	A	47	5–12–1780	Salt R	Surveyed
Jackson, Joseph	500	A	98	5–25–1780	N Licking	
Jackman, Richard	600	A	130	6–10–1780	Dicks R	
Jackson, Samuel	500	A	97	5–25–1780	Holders Cr	....
Jackson, Wm	400	A	246	1– 6–1783	Cartrights Cr	Surveyed
James, Abraham	400	A	15	2–21–1780	Hanging Fk	
James, Abraham	1,000	A	115	5–30–1780	His Sett	
James, George	7,963	A	264	2–15–1783	Rolling Fk	S u r v e y e d 3,963 acres withdrawn
James, George	450	A	264	2–15–1783	Rolling Fk	400 acres withdrawn
James, George	50	A	264	2–15–1783	Pottengers Cr	
James, George	788	A	264	2–15–1783	Rolling Fk	Withdrawn
James, George	250	A	264	2–15–1783	Rowling Fk	
James, George	200	A	268	3–28–1783	Elk Grove	Surveyed
James, George	200	A	268	3–28–1783	Nolelinn Cr	Surveyed
James, George	400	A	268	3–28–1783	Pottengers Meat Camp	Withdrawn
James, George	3,000	A	275	4–10–1783	Rowling Fk	Surveyed
James, George	3,000	A	275	4–10–1783	————	Withdrawn
James, George	963	A	280	6– 9–1783	————	Surveyed
James, George	788	A	281	6–30–1783	Rolling Fk	Surveyed
James, George	1,500	A	282	7– 3–1783	Rough Cr	Surveyed
James, George	1,000	A	282	7– 1–1783	Nole Linn Cr	Surveyed
James, George	400	A	283	7–25–1783	Sinking Cr	....
James, George	150	A	283	7– 4–1783	Hardens Cr	Surveyed
James, George	350	A	283	7– 4–1783	Cartright Cr	Withdrawn
James, George	2,000	A	283	7– 3–1783	Mill Cr	Surveyed
James, George	1,500	A	283	7– 3–1783	Mays Grove Fk	Surveyed
James, George	3,000	A	283	7– 3–1783	Mays Grove Fk	Surveyed
James, George	2,000	A	283	7– 3–1783	Fk Rough Cr	Surveyed
James, George	50	A	284	8– 4–1783	Rowling Fk	Withdrawn
James, George	100	A	287	8–25–1783	Otter Cr	Surveyed
James, George	500	A	287	8–18–1783	Cartright Cr	
James, George	3,000	A	287	8–16–1783	Linn Camp Cr	1,850 acres withdrawn

Entree	Acres	Book	Page	Entry Date	Watercourse	Notes
James, George........	963	A	288	8–25–1783	Rolling Fk.........	Surveyed
James, George........	400	A	288	8–25–1783	Knobbs Cr........	Withdrawn
James, George........	400	A	292	10– 3–1783	Otter Cr.........	Surveyed
James, George........	2,000	A	298	10–23–1783	Cartright Cr..:....	Withdrawn
James, George........	3,000	A	302	11– 7–1783	Cartright Cr.......	Surveyed
James, George........	300	A	321	12–22–1783	Sulphur Lick Cr....	Surveyed
James, George........	5,000	A	342	3– 3–1784	Green R.........	Surveyed
James, George........	5,000	A	342	3– 3–1784	Rolling Cr........	Surveyed
James, George........	2,000	A	342	3– 3–1784	Pottengers Cr.....	Surveyed
James, George........	3,000	A	342	3– 3–1784	Pottengers Cr.....	Surveyed
James, George........	5,000	A	344	3– 3–1784	Clear Cr.........	Surveyed
James, George........	1,500	A	344	3– 3–1784	Caney Cr........	Surveyed
James, George........	10,000	A	344	3– 3–1784	Middle Cr........	Withdrawn
James, George........	2,000	A	344	3– 3–1784	Nole Linn Cr......	Withdrawn
James, George........	2,000	A	350	4–10–1784	Hardens Cr.......	Withdrawn
James, George........	2,000	A	350	4–10–1784	Cartright Cr.......	Withdrawn
James, George........	2,496	A	359	5– 7–1784	Caney Cr........	Surveyed
James, George........	5,688	A	359	5– 7–1784	Clear Cr.........	Surveyed
James, George........	1,684	A	359	5– 7–1784	Chas Minn Thruston........	Withdrawn
James, George........	2,000	A	364	6– 7–1784	Hardens Cr.......	....
James, George........	2,000	A	364	6– 7–1784	Hardens Cr.......	Withdrawn
James, George........	50	A	365	6–16–1784	Rolling Fk........	Withdrawn
James, George........	350	A	365	6–16–1784	Cartright Cr.......	Surveyed
James, George........	1,000	A	365	6–16–1784	Green R.........	Withdrawn
James, George........	1,000	A	365	6–16–1784	Pottengers Cr.....	....
James, George........	5,000	A	365	6–16–1784	Green R.........	400 acres
James, George........	5,000	A	365	6–16–1784	Green R.........	withdrawn
James, George........	400	A	366	6–16–1784	Hardens Cr.......	....
James, George........	400	A	366	6–16–1784	Prather Cr.......	Withdrawn
James, George........	800	A	366	6–16–1784	Prathers Cr.......	Surveyed
James, George........	400	A	366	6–16–1784	Knobb Cr........	....
James, George........	300	A	370	7– 9–1784	Otter Cr.........	....
James, George........	200	A	370	7– 9–1784	Sulphur Lick Cr....	....
James, George........	950	A	374	7–28–1784	Rolling Fk........	....
James, George........	2,000	A	374	7–28–1784	Cedar Cr.........	....
James, George........	1,000	A	374	7–28–1784	Pottengers Cr.....	500 acres withdrawn
James, George........	1,850	A	374	7–28–1784	Rough Cr.........	....
James, George........	1,850	A	374	7–28–1784	Linn Camp Cr.....	....
James, George........	500	A	375	7–29–1784	———.........	300 acres surveyed
James, George........	500	A	375	7–29–1784	———.........	450 acres surveyed
James, George........	200	B	3	8–26–1784	Rolling Fk........	....
James, George........	300	B	3	8–26–1784	Pottengers Cr.....	Withdrawn
James, George........	500	B	3	8–26–1784	Pottengers Cr.....	Withdrawn
James, George et al....	500	A	264	2–15–1783	Rolling Fk........	Surveyed
James, George et al....	500	A	277	4–14–1783	Rowling Fk........	....
James, George et al....	500	A	277	4–14–1783	———.........	Withdrawn
James, George et al....	443	A	282	7– 1–1783	Pond Cr.........	Surveyed
James, George et al....	1,000	A	329	1–13–1784	Rough Cr.........	....
James, George et al....	500	A	370	7– 9–1784	Rolling Fk........	Surveyed amended
James, John..........	500	A	151	6–26–1780	Stoner...........	....
James, John..........	1,477½	A	227	8–16–1783	Pottengers Cr.....	Withdrawn
James, John..........	1,477½	A	292	10– 3–1783	Rough Cr.........	Withdrawn
James, John..........	1,477½	A	292	10– 3–1783	Pottengers Cr.....	Withdrawn
James, John..........	1,477½	B	37	1–28–1785	Rough Cr.........	....
James, John..........	1,472½	B	37	1–28–1785	Rough Cr.........	Withdrawn
James, Joseph........	1,000	A	115	5–30–1780	Nob Lick.........	....
James, Joseph........	500	A	264	2–15–1783	Rolling Fk........	Withdrawn
James, Joseph........	500	A	321	12–22–1783	Rolling Fk........	Withdrawn
Jameson, Andrew.....	50	A	35	4–29–1780	Bank Lick Cr......	Mil
Jameson, David......	500	A	39	5– 9–1780	Licking..........	....
Jameson, David......	3,000	A	39	5– 9–1780	Br Licking........	....
Jameson, David......	400	A	222	12–12–1782	Brashears Cr......	400 acres withdrawn
Jameson, David......	400	A	357	5– 1–1784	———.........	Withdrawn
Jameson, David......	400	A	357	5– 1–1784	———.........	Withdrawn
Jameson, John.......	200	A	252	1–10–1783	Coxes Cr.........	....
Jameson, Thomas....	2,500	A	39	5– 9–1780	Br Licking........	....
Jamison, David......	400	A	223	12–12–1782	Wolf Run.........	....
Jamison, John.......	1,000	A	38	4–29–1780	Clear Cr.........	....
Jamison, John.......	400	A	38	4–29–1780	S Fk Elkhorn......	....
Jamison, John.......	1,000	A	58	5–15–1780	N Fk Licking......	....
Jamison, John.......	1,000	A	178	10–16–1780	Clear Cr.........	....
Jamison, John.......	400	A	178	10–16–1780	Fk Elkhorn.......	Entered before
Jarboe, Stephen......	400	A	200	3–29–1781	Cartrights Cr......	....
Jarboe, Stephen......	635	A	208	5– 1–1781	Beech Fk.........	....

Entree	Acres	Book	Page	Entry Date	Watercourse	Notes
Jenkins, James	1,143¾	A	249	1– 8–1783	Brush Cr	
Jenkins, Wm	295	A	53	5–15–1780	——	
Johnson, Arwalker	200	A	24	4–25–1780	Br Ky R	
Johnson, Arwalker	500	A	24	4–25–1780	Br Hickman Cr	
Johnson, Cave	50	A	32	4–28–1780	——	Mil
Johnson, Cave	400	A	39	5– 9–1780	Licking	
Johnson, Cave	400	A	39	5– 9–1780	Elkhorn	
Johnson, David	1,000	A	35	4–29–1780	Panther Cr	
Johnson, Edward et al	1,000	A	204	4– 5–1781	Harrods Cr	
Johnson, Gedediah	200	A	84	5–22–1780	Buck Lick Cr	
Johnson, James	500	A	274	4– 8–1783	Sinking Run	Surveyed
Johnson, Richard	1,000	A	33	4–29–1780	Blue Lick	
Johnson, Richard	2,000	A	303	11–12–1783	Floyds Fk	
Johnson, Robert	700	A	39	5– 9–1780	S Fk Elkhorn	
Johnson, Robert	2,500	A	39	5– 9–1780	N Fk Elkhorn	
Johnson, Robert	200	A	217	8– 7–1781	Coxes Cr	Withdrawn
Johnson, Robert	200	A	217	8– 7–1781	Caney Fk	
Johnson, Robert	200	A	218	8– 8–1781	Sprigg & Fitch	
Johnson, Robert	3,000	A	247	1– 6–1783	Ky R	Surveyed
Johnson, Robert	350	A	282	7– 2–1783	Bensons Cr	Withdrawn
Johnson, Thos	400	A	6	12–27–1779	Rolling Fk	
Johnson, Thos et al	400	A	6	12–23–1779	S Fk Licking	
Johnson, Thos et al	400	A	6	12–23–1779	S Fk Licking	
Johnson, Wm	200	A	128	6– 8–1780	Beech Fk	Withdrawn
Johnston, Arwalker	500	A	20	4–17–1780	Glens Cr	Mil withdrawn
Johnston, Ben	200	A	23	4–24–1780	Mid Fk Licking	Mil
Johnston, Ben	1,000	A	23	4–24–1780	E Fk Sinking Cr	
Johnston, Ben	1,000	A	23	4–24–1780	E Fk Sinking Cr	Withdrawn
Johnston, Ben	1,000	A	23	4–24–1780	Sinking Cr	
Johnston, Ben	1,000	A	23	4–24–1780	Ohio R	Mil surveyed
Johnston, Ben	1,000	A	33	4–29–1780	Licking	Withdrawn
Johnston, Ben	1,000	A	35	4–29–1780	Licking	
Johnston, Benj	400	A	236	12–20–1782	Short Cr	
Johnston, Benj	1,000	B	26	12–14–1784	Clear Cr	
Johnston, Benj	600	B	26	12–14–1784	Nolin Cr	
Johnston, Benj	1,000	B	26	12–14–1784	S Fk Nole Linn Cr	
Johnston, David	400	A	14	2–19–1780	Panther Cr	
Johnston, David	750	A	373	7–23–1784	——	
Johnston, Isaac	400	A	135	6–17–1780	Silver Cr	
Johnston, James	500	A	302	11– 7–1783	Bear Cr	
Johnston, John	1,137½	A	260	2– 3–1783	Beech Fk	
Johnston, John	1,000	A	270	3–28–1783	Pittmans Cave	
Johnston, John	2,000	A	270	3–28–1783	Green R	
Johnston, Joseph	30,000	A	361	5–25–1784	——	3,000 acres surveyed
Johnston, Lewis	700	A	50	5–12–1780	Dicks R	
Johnston, Noel	15,000	A	348	3–26–1784	Wolf Cr	
Johnston, Peter	400	A	15	2–21–1780	Blue Licks	
Johnston, Richard	1,000	A	33	4–29–1780	Licking	Mil
Johnston, Richard	200	A	315	12–13–1783	Long Lick Cr	Withdrawn
Johnston, Richard	500	A	315	12–13–1783	Cedar Cr	
Johnston, Richard	200	A	321	12–18–1783	Cedar Cr	
Johnston, Richard	200	A	321	12–18–1783	Long Lick Run	
Johnston, Richard	200	A	333	1–20–1784	Bullitts Lick	
Johnston, Richard	200	A	333	1–20–1784	Cedar Cr	Withdrawn
Johnston, Robert	400	A	141	6–21–1780	Cane Run	
Johnston, Robert	350	A	197	3–17–1781	Coxes Cr	350 acres withdrawn
Johnston, Robert	150	A	212	6–21–1781	Coxes Cr	Withdrawn
Johnston, Robert	500	A	246	1– 6–1783	Coxes Cr	
Johnston, Robert	4,000	A	247	1– 6–1783	Little Ky R	Surveyed
Johnston, Robert	3,000	A	247	1– 6–1783	Ky R	Surveyed
Johnston, Samuel	400	A	86	5–23–1780	Elkhorn	
Johnston, Tandy	500	A	342	2–27–1784	Robinsons Cr	
Johnston, Thos	400	A	12	2– 5–1780	Floyds Fk	Surveyed
Johnston, Thomas	1,000	A	145	6–24–1780	S Fk Licking	
Johnston, Thomas	1,000	A	145	6–24–1780	S Fk Licking	Surveyed
Johnston, Thomas	1,000	A	145	6–24–1780	Elkhorn	
Johnston, Thomas	1,000	A	145	6–24–1780	Rowling	
Johnston, Thomas	1,000	A	145	6–24–1780	Shawnee Run	
Johnston, Thomas	1,000	A	146	6–24–1780	S Fk Licking	
Johnston, Wm	200	A	174	9–29–1780	Poplar Neck	
Johnston, Wm	200	A	174	9–29–1780	Beech Fk	Surveyed
Johnston, Wm	1,000	A	243	12–36–1782	Clay Lick	
Johnston, Wm	400	A	304	11–14–1783	Floyds Fk	Withdrawn
Johnston, Wm	600	A	313	12– 8–1783	Little Bullskin Cr	Withdrawn
Johnston, Wm	50,000	A	316	12–15–1783	Bacon Cr	Surveyed
Johnston, Wm	862	A	354	4–19–1784	Plumb Cr	Surveyed
Johnston, Wm	400	A	354	4–19–1784	Floyds Fk	Withdrawn
Johnston, Wm	600	A	354	4–19–1784	Little Bullskin Cr	Withdrawn

Entree	Acres	Book	Page	Entry Date	Watercourse	Notes
Johnston, Wm	50,000	A	368	6–22–1784	————	37,216 acres surveyed
Johnston, Wm	12,784	B	4	8–27–1784	Rough Cr	Surveyed
Johnston, Wm	12,784	B	4	8–27–1784	—————	Withdrawn
Johnston, Wm	1,000	B	19	11–26–1784	—————	
Jones, Benjamin	400	A	94	5–24–1780	Mill Cr	
Jones, Christopher	400	A	240	12–24–1782	Soverins Run	
Jones, David	400	A	8	1–17–1780	Cane Run	
Jones, Gabriel	2,500	A	67	5–17–1780	Knobb Salt R	Surveyed
Jones, John	500	A	94	5–24–1780	Licking	
Jones, John	6,000	A	237	12–21–1782	Drennons Lick Cr	
Jones, John G	400	A	3	11–15–1779	Dicks R	
Jones, Joseph	3,000	A	34	4–29–1780	Floyds Fk	Mil surveyed
Jones, Joseph	1,250	A	48	5–12–1780	Floyds Fk	Surveyed
Jones, Kennon	1,000	A	77	5–20–1780	Eagle Cr	Withdrawn
Jones, Kennon	1,000	A	77	5–20–1780	Salt R	Withdrawn
Jones, Kennon	1,000	A	186	10–31–1780	Eagle Cr	
Jones, Kennon	1,000	A	191	3–15–1781	Floyds Fk	
Jones, Kennon	1,000	A	217	8– 2–1781	Doe Run	Withdrawn
Jones, Kennon	1,000	A	217	8– 7–1781	Salt R	
Jones, Kennon	100	A	259	2– 1–1783	Salt R	Surveyed
Jones, Kennon	900	A	259	2– 1–1783	Salt R	Surveyed
Jones, Kennon	1,000	A	259	2– 1–1783	Ohio R	
Jones, Kennon	1,000	B	39	2– 8–1785	—————	
Jones, Ralph	600	A	192	3–16–1781	Rowling Fk	Surveyed
Jones, Rawleigh et al	550	A	98	5–25–1780	Town Fk	2nd book begins
Jones, Robt	400	A	14	2–19–1780	Eagle Cr	
Jones, Samuel	40,000	A	349	4– 2–1784	Ohio R	Withdrawn
Jones, Samuel	40,000	A	349	4– 2–1784	Ohio R	Withdrawn
Jones, Taverner	500	A	83	5–22–1780	Hanging Fk	
Jones, Wm	542	A	174	9–29–1780	Whiteoak Fk	
Jones, Wm & Churchill	300	A	98	5–25–1780	Kentucky R	
Jones, Wm & Churchill	700	A	98	5–25–1780	Salt R	
Jourdan, John	1,500	A	377	8–12–1784	John Huston	
Jourdon, John	1,500	A	293	10– 4–1783	Rolling Fk	Withdrawn
Karchwell, Wm	110½	A	213	6–30–1781	Pottingers Cr	Surveyed
Kasner, Casper	400	A	124	6– 3–1780	N Fk Elkhorn	
Keene, John	644	A	243	12–25–1782	Salt R	
Keith, Alex	200	A	200	3–26–1781	Fromans Cr	
Keith, Alex	200	A	348	3–23–1784	Fromans Cr	
Keith, John	1,000	A	123	6– 3–1780	Green R	
Keith, John	200	A	137	6–19–1780	Willsons Cr	Withdrawn
Keith, John	200	A	137	6–19–1780	Coxes Cr	Surveyed
Keith, John	400	A	145	6–23–1780	Licking & Elkhorn	
Keith, John	200	A	173	9–22–1780	Beech Fk	
Keith, John	200	A	200	3–26–1781	Fromans Cr	
Keith, John	200	A	200	3–26–1781	Willsons Cr	
Keith, Wm	250	A	199	3–26–1781	Fromans Cr	Surveyed
Keith, Wm	50	A	200	3–26–1781	Fromans Cr	Withdrawn
Keith, Wm	50	A	254	1–16–1783	Fromans Cr	
Keith, Wm	50	A	254	1–16–1783	Harned Improvment	Withdrawn
Keith, Wm	5,000	B	18	11–18–1784	—————	
Keith, Wm	1,000	B	31	1– 3–1785	—————	
Keith, Wm	300	B	46	5–26–1785	—————	
Keller, Abraham	1,000	A	38	4–29–1780	Bowmans Cr	
Keller, Abraham	400	A	82	5–22–1780	Elkhorn	
Keller, Isaac	500	A	27	4–26–1780	Elkhorn Cr	
Keller, Isaac	1,500	A	248	1– 8–1783	Floyds Fk	Surveyed
Keller, Jacob	500	A	27	4–26–1780	Elkhorn Cr	
Keller, Jacob	400	A	82	5–22–1780	Coopers Run	
Keller, John	400	A	82	5–22–1780	Elkhorn	
Kelley, David	407	A	182	10–25–1780	Ky R	
Kelley, James	182	A	344	3– 3–1784	Green R	
Kelley, Mordecai	500	A	91	5–24–1780	Licking	
Kemp, Edward	300	A	125	6– 5–1780	Salt R	
Kemp, Edward	100	A	126	6– 5–1780	Salt R	
Kemp, James	2,500	A	194	3–16–1781	Bullskin & Floyds Fk	
Kemp, James	9,750	A	234	12–19–1782	Floyds Fk	Surveyed
Kemp, John	1,500	A	164	8–11–1780	Knobs Salt R	1,113 acres surveyed
Kemp, John	1,000	B	43	3–25–1785	—————	
Kemp, Reubin	400	A	126	6– 5–1780	Beech Fk	Surveyed
Kenady, John	1,000	A	183	10–27–1780	—————	Surveyed
Kencheloe, Wm	500	A	224	12–13–1782	Brashears Cr	
Kendall, Wm	200	A	108	5–29–1780	Beech Fk	Surveyed
Kendall, Wm	200	A	108	5–29–1780	Beech Fk	Withdrawn
Kendall, Wm	100	A	200	3–26–1781	—————	
Kendall, Wm	200	A	224	12–13–1782	Beech Fk	Withdrawn
Kendall, Wm	200	A	246	1– 6–1783	Beach Fk	
Kendall, Wm	200	A	249	1– 8–1783	Beech Fk	

Entree	Acres	Book	Page	Entry Date	Watercourse	Notes
Kendall, Wm	100	A	326	1- 3-1784	Beech Fk	Surveyed
Kendall, Wm	200	A	326	1- 3-1784	Buffaloe Cr	Surveyed
Kendall, Wm	224	A	341	2-26-1784	Beech Fk	
Kendall, Wm	150	A	342	3- 2-1784	————	
Kendall, Wm	500	A	349	4- 9-1784	Fromans Cr	Withdrawn
Kendall, Wm	305	A	360	5-17-1784	Beech Fk	Surveyed withdrawn
Kendall, Wm	50	A	360	5-14-1784	Fromans Cr	Withdrawn
Kendall, Wm	135	A	368	6-26-1784	Fromans Cr	50 acres withdrawn
Kendall, Wm	135	A	368	6-26-1784	Beech Fk	Withdrawn
Kendall, Wm	355	A	376	8- 5-1784	Beech Fk	
Kendall, Wm	260	B	1	8-14-1784	Buffaloe Cr	
Kendall, Wm	50	B	9	9+27-1784	Beech Fk	
Kendall, Wm	50	B	9	9-27-1784	Fromans Cr	Withdrawn
Kendall, Wm	452	B	9	9-27-1784	Beech Fk	
Kendall, Wm	200	B	9	9-27-1784	Beech Fk	Withdrawn
Kendall, Wm	252	B	9	9-27-1784	Beech Fk	Withdrawn
Kendrick, Christopher	500	A	193	3-16-1781	Rowling Fk	Withdrawn
Kendrick, Christain	500	A	214	7- 3-1781	Sulphur Lick	Surveyed
Kendrick, Solomon	400	A	148	6-24-1780	Silver Cr	
Kenedy, Wm	1,000	A	232	12-18-1781	Ohio R	
Kennady, James	1,000	A	27	4-26-1780	Licking	
Kennady, John	400	A	10	2- 3-1780	Stoners Fk	
Kennady, John	50	A	21	4-19-1780	Silver Cr	Mil
Kennady, John	1,000	A	25	4-26-1780	Paint Lick	
Kennady, John	1,000	A	25	4-25-1780	Paint Lick	
Kennady, John	1,000	A	25	4-26-1780	Paint Lick Cr	Surveyed
Kennady, John	1,000	A	26	4-26-1780	Dicks R	Surveyed
Kennady, John	500	A	26	4-26-1780	Silver Cr	Surveyed
Kennady, John	500	A	26	4-26-1780	Silver Cr	
Kennady, John	600	A	26	4-26-1780	Cedar Cr	
Kennady, John	1,000	A	26	4-26-1780	Silver Cr	Surveyed
Kennady, John	50	A	90	5-23-1780	Hammonds Lick	Surveyed
Kennady, John	300	A	121	6- 2-1780	Silver Cr	Withdrawn
Kennady, John	200	A	121	6- 2-1780	Silver Cr	
Kennady, John	200	A	121	6- 2-1780	Hammons Cr	Surveyed
Kennady, John	200	A	121	6- 2-1780	Paint Lick Cr	
Kennady, John	200	A	121	6- 2-1780	Paint Lick Cr	
Kennady, John	1,000	A	128	6- 8-1780	Stoners Fk	
Kennady, John	2,750	A	156	6-30-1780	Elkhorn	
Kennady, John	200	A	174	9-29-1780	Silver Cr	
Kennady, John	250	A	179	10-19-1780	Paint Lick	
Kennady, John	300	A	185	10-31-1780	Silver Cr	
Kennady, John	250	A	185	10-31-1780	Whitlick Fk	
Kennady, John	460	A	306	11-19-1783	Rolling Fk	Surveyed
Kennady, Joseph	1,000	A	128	6- 8-1780	Stoner Fk	
Kennady, Thomas	1,000	A	27	4-26-1780	Licking	
Kennady, Thos	400	A	10	2- 3-1780	Strodes Fk	
Kennady, Wm	400	A	18	3- 3-1780	Ohio R	
Kennady, Wm	400	A	63	5-16-1780	Ohio R	
Kennady, Wm	1,000	A	69	5-18-1780	Ohio R	
Kennady, Wm	300	A	69	5-18-1780	Chaplins Fk	
Kennady, Wm	600	A	89	5-23-1780	Ohio R	
Kennady, Wm	400	A	98	5-25-1780	Licking	
Kennady, Wm	200	A	124	6- 3-1780	Ohio R	
Kennady, Wm	400	A	124	6- 3-1780	Hickmans Cr	
Kennady, Wm	600	A	124	6- 3-1780	Ohio R	
Kennady, Wm	6,000	A	344	3- 3-1784	Long Lick Cr	
Kennedy, John	460	A	376	8- 2-1784	————	Surveyed
Kennedy, John	400	A	7	12-10-1780	Paint Lick	Surveyed
Kennedy, John	400	A	7	1-10-1780	Paint Lick	Surveyed
Kennedy, Jno Jr	400	A	8	1-15-1780	Paint Lick Cr	Surveyed
Kennedy, John Sr	400	A	7	1-10-1780	Silver Cr	
Kennedy, Joseph	400	A	4	11-25-1779	Silver Cr	Surveyed
Kenny, James	1,000	A	137	6-19-1780	S Fk Licking	
Kenny, John	500	A	144	6-23-1780	Rowling Fk	
Kenny, John	1,062	A	160	7- 7-1780	Rowling Fk	
Kenny, John	900	A	227	12-14-1782	Drennings Lick Cr	
Kenny, John	900	A	227	12-14-1782	Drennings Lick Cr	
Kenny, Joseph	400	A	141	6-21-1780	Coopers Run	
Kenny, Thomas	1,000	A	225	12-13-1782	Cr of Green R	Withdrawn
Kenny, Thomas	1,000	A	225	12-13-1782	Green R	Withdrawn
Kenny, Thomas	2,000	A	314	12-10-1783	Cartright Cr	700 acres
Kenny, Thomas	1,000	A	340	2-18-1784	Beech Fk	
Kenny, Thomas	700	A	340	2-18-1784	Cartright Cr	
Kenny, Thomas	700	A	340	2-18-1784	Cartright Cr	
Kenton, Simon	2,200	A	138	6-20-1780	N Fk Licking	
Kenton, Simon	200	A	172	9-19-1780	Quirks Cr	
Kerchwall, John	1,000	A	161	7-17-1780	Eagle Cr	
Kester, George	500	A	140	6-21-1780	Clear Cr	
Kester, Isaac	500	A	140	6-21-1780	Clear Cr	Withdrawn

Entree	Acres	Book	Page	Entry Date	Watercourse	Notes
Kester, Isaac..........	500	A	221	11- 9-1782	Clear Cr..........	....
Kester, Konrod........	278	A	275	4- 9-1783	———...........	....
Ketcham, Jonathan....	1,000	A	162	7-18-1780	Salt R..........	....
Ketcham, Jonathan...	400	A	5	12- 7-1779	Town Fk Salt R....	....
Key, James..........	400	A	149	6-24-1780	Stoners Fk........	....
Key, Moses...........	2,531	A	257	1-25-1783	Guesses Cr........	Surveyed
Keykendall, Moses.....	400	A	279	6- 7-1783	Hardens Cr........	Surveyed
Keykendall, Moses.....	1,000	A	308	11-22-1783	Ky R.............	Withdrawn
Keykendall, Moses.....	210	A	312	12- 3-1783	Limestone Cr......	
Keykendall, Moses.....	1,000	A	360	5-18-1784	Rough Cr.........	Withdrawn
Keykendall, Moses.....	1,000	A	360	5-18-1784	Beech Fk.........	Withdrawn
Keykendall, Moses.....	210	A	360	5-18-1784	Clover Cr.........	Withdrawn
Keykendall, Moses.....	210	A	360	5-18-1784	Limestone Cr.....	Withdrawn
Keykendall, Moses.....	500	A	361	5-18-1784	———..........	400 acres surveyed Retd
Keykendall, Moses.....	1,000	A	361	5-18-1784	———..........	590 acres surveyed Retd
Keykendall, Moses.....	210	B	12	11- 9-1784	Tewels Cr.........	Surveyed
Keykendall, Moses.....	210	B	12	11- 9-1784	———..........	Withdrawn
Keykendall, Moses.....	1,000	B	32	1- 8-1785	Tarr Spg Fk......	....
Keykendall, Moses.....	1,000	B	32	1- 8-1785	N Fk Rough Cr....	....
Kidd, Daniel..........	427	A	270	3-28-1783	Robinsons Cr......	....
Keith, Isaiah..........	1,600	A	55	5-15-1780	Salt R...........	....
Kilbreath, Evan.......	100	A	142	6-22-1780	Rowling Fk........	....
Kilgore, George.......	800	A	76	5-19-1780	Stoners Fk........	....
Kilpatrick, Joseph.....	400	A	226	12-13-1782	Little Clifty Cr.....	Surveyed
Kilpatrick, Moses.....	1,706	B	35	1-26-1785	Hardens Cr........	Withdrawn
Kimberlen, John......	882	B	6	9-13-1784	Rough Cr.........	
Kincheloe, Wm.......	1,000	A	259	2- 1-1783	Chaplins Fk.......	Surveyed
Kinchler, Thomas.....	700	A	368	6-29-1784	Hardens Cr........	
Kinchler, Thomas.....	200	A	368	6-29-1784	Beech Fk.........	
Kinchloe, Wm........	400	A	209	5-29-1781	Chaplins Fk.......	Surveyed
Kinchloe, Wm........	700	A	254	1-17-1783	Brashears Cr......	Surveyed
Kincheloe, Wm.......	506	A	283	7- 4-1783	Chaplins Fk.......	....
Kinchloe, Wm........	6,606	A	328	1-12-1784	———..........	....
Kindall, Wm..........	200	B	6	9-13-1784	Beech Fk.........	Withdrawn
Kindall, Wm..........	252	B	6	9-13-1784	Beech Fk.........	Withdrawn
Kindall, Wm..........	452	B	6	9-13-1784	———..........	
Kindall, Wm..........	400	B	6	9-13-1784	———..........	100 acres surveyed
King, John...........	10,000	A	55	5-15-1780	Ohio R...........	Surveyed
King, John...........	500	A	62	5-16-1780	Poplar Flat.......	Surveyed
King, John...........	1,000	A	250	1- 9-1783	Bulgers Cr........	....
King, John...........	2,201	A	303	11-10-1783	Little Ky R.......	....
King, John E.........	1,875	A	263	2-15-1783	Hardens Cr.......	800 acres withdrawn
King, John E.........	7,181	A	263	2-15-1783	Hardens Cr.......	....
King, John E.........	200	A	264	2-15-1783	Long Lick Run.....	
King, John E.........	200	A	283	7- 4-1783	Beech Fk.........	Withdrawn
King, John E.........	200	A	305	11-15-1783	Beech Fk.........	Withdrawn
King, Nimrod.........	200	A	45	5-11-1780	Floyds Fk........	Surveyed
King, Peter..........	127½	A	355	4-21-1784	Sovernins settlement	....
King, Smith..........	500	A	43	5-11-1780	Hingston Fk.......	
King, Valentine.......	500	A	62	5-16-1780	Poplar Flat.......	Surveyed
King, Wm...........	1,000	A	62	5-16-1780	Poplar Flat.......	Surveyed
King, Withers........	600	A	55	5-15-1780	Long Lick........	Surveyed
Kinkaid, Wm.........	50	A	34	4-29-1780	Paint Lick	Mil
Kinkead, Andrew......	150	A	86	5-22-1780	Dicks R..........	
Kinkead, Andrew......	100	A	112	5-30-1780	Wm Kinkead......	....
Kinkead, John........	1,000	A	94	5-24-1780	Knob Lick Rd.....	....
Kinkead, John........	50	A	112	5-30-1780	Dicks R..........	....
Kinkead, John........	50	A	112	5-30-1780	Dicks R..........	....
Kinkead, John........	400	A	173	9-23-1780	Silver Cr.........	....
Kinkead, Robert......	100	A	86	5-22-1780	Paint Lick Cr.....	....
Kinkead, Thomas.....	150	A	86	5-22-1780	Paint Lick Cr.....	....
Kinkead, Wm........	250	A	86	5-22-1780	Dicks R..........	....
Kinkead, Wm........	1,000	A	86	5-22-1780	Paint Lick.......	....
Kirby, Samuel........	1,285	A	250	1- 9-1783	Pattons Cr........	384 acres surveyed
Kirkendall, Moses.....	1,000	A	80	5-20-1780	Licking Cr........	....
Kirkendall, Moses.....	1,000	A	217	8- 2-1781	Salt R...........	....
Kirkham, Samuel.....	400	A	172	9-19-1780	Salt R...........	....
Kirkley, Elijah........	250	A	29	4-27-1780	Beech Fk.........	Mil
Kirkley, Elijah........	250	A	29	4-27-1780	Beech Fk.........	Mil
Kirkley, Elijah........	1,000	A	94	5-24-1780	Beech Fk.........	....
Kirkley, Francis.......	1,200	A	91	5-24-1780	Clear Cr.........	....
Kirkley, Francis.......	1,000	A	91	5-24-1780	Clear Cr.........	....
Kirkley, Francis.......	300	A	92	5-24-1780	Clear Cr.........	....
Kirkley, Francis.......	50	A	92	5-24-1780	Dicks R..........	Mil
Kirkley, Jeremiah.....	500	A	94	5-24-1780	Rowling Fk.......	....
Kirkley, Jeremiah.....	500	A	94	5-24-1780	Beech Fk.........	....
Kirkley, Wm..........	400	A	1	11- 3-1779	Paint Lick Cr......	....

Entree	Acres	Book	Page	Entry Date	Watercourse	Notes
Kirkley, Wm	500	A	120	6- 1-1780	His settlement	
Kirkley, Wm	500	A	120	6- 1-1780	Paint Lick Cr	
Kirkpatrick, Joseph	462	A	298	10-24-1783	Nolin Cr	Surveyed
Kirkpatrick, Joseph	300	A	298	10-24-1783	Nolin Cr	
Kirkpatrick, Joseph	500	A	325	12-29-1783	Little Clifty Cr	
Kirkpatrick, Joseph	500	A	325	12-29-1783	Little Clifty Cr	
Kirkpatrick, Joseph	1,000	A	325	12-29-1783	Little Clifty Cr	
Kirkpatrick, Joseph	600	A	325	12-29-1783	Rough Cr	Surveyed
Kirkpatrick, Joseph	100	A	339	2-14-1784	Rough Cr	Surveyed
Kirkpatrick, Joseph	762	A	345	3- 9-1784		
Kirkpatrick, Joseph	630	A	360	5-14-1784	——	
Kirkpatrick, Joseph	2,600	A	362	5-26-1784	——	
Kirkpatrick, Joseph	500	A	370	7- 6-1784	——	100 acres surveyed
Kirkpatrick, Joseph	150	A	373	7-26-1784	Linn Camp Cr	
Kirkpatrick, Moses	1,706	A	373	7-24-1784	Harrods Cr	Withdrawn
Kirkpatrick, Moses	1,000	A	373	7-24-1784	Harrods Cr	Surveyed
Knight, John	1,350	A	239	12-23-1782	Floyds Fk	Surveyed
Knox, James	400	A	155	6-30-1780	Green R	
Knox, James	400	A	156	6-30-1780	Buffaloe Cr	Withdrawn
Knox, James	500	A	225	12-13-1782	Sinking Cr	Withdrawn
Knox, James	500	A	225	12-13-1782	Green R	Surveyed
Knox, James	1,000	A	226	12-13-1782	Sinking Cr	Surveyed
Knox, James	400	A	254	1-16-1783	Green R	Surveyed
Knox, James	500	A	276	4-10-1783	John McClenackan	
Knox, James	500	A	276	4-10-1783	Sinking Cr	
Knox, James	1,000	A	280	6- 9-1783	——	800 acres surveyed
Knox, James	3,000	A	338	2-12-1784	Bullskin Cr	
Knox, James	1,000	A	338	2-12-1784	Ohio R	
Knox, James	800	A	338	2-12-1784	Little Bullskin Cr	
Knox, James	200	A	338	2-12-1784	Bullskin Cr	Surveyed
Knox, James	4,800	B	43	4-11-1785	——	
Koufman, Jacob	1,000	B	47	6-14-1785	——	
Koy, John	400	A	236	12-20-1782	Rolling Fk	
Kune, Francis	1,000	A	54	5-15-1780	——	
Kutkendall, Moses	300	A	248	1- 7-1783	Nole Linn Cr	
Kuykendall, Moses	300	A	248	1- 7-1783	Rock Cr	
Kuykendall, Moses	400	A	248	1- 7-1783	Bear Cr	Surveyed
Kuykendall, Moses	500	A	248	1- 7-1783	Bear Cr	Surveyed
Kuykendall, Moses	500	A	248	1- 7-1783	Bear Cr	Surveyed
Kuykendall, Moses	2,765	A	265	2-21-1783	Ky R	Surveyed
Kuykendall, Moses	200	A	265	2-21-1783	Green R	
Kuykendall, Moses	1,000	A	265	2-20-1783	Beech Fk	Withdrawn
Kuykendall, Moses	400	A	265	2-20-1783	Bear Run	Withdrawn
Kuykendall, Moses	400	A	265	2-20-1783	Hardens Cr	190 acres surveyed 210 acres withdrawn
Kuykendall, Moses	1,000	B	51	11- 3-1785	Ky R	Withdrawn
Lacey, John	1,000	A	37	4-29-1780	S Fk Licking	
Lackey, Samuel	509	A	351	4-13-1784	Green R	
Laell, George	351	A	127	6- 8-1780	Mid Fk Licking	
Lafferty, Thomas	500	A	134	6-16-1780	Stoners Fk	
Lair, Andrew	300	A	105	5-27-1780	Ky R	
Lair, Andrew	192	A	105	5-27-1780	Elkhorn	Withdrawn
Lair, Andrew	192	A	138	6-20-1780	Ky R	
Lair, John	400	A	105	5-27-1780	Johnstons Fk	
Lair, Wm	400	A	105	5-27-1780	Johnstons Fk	
Laird, David	636½	A	258	1-27-1783	Cedar Lick Cr	Surveyed
Laird, David	1,000	A	348	3-22-1784	Green R	Withdrawn
Laird, David	1,000	A	374	7-27-1784	——	Withdrawn
Laird, James	1,294	A	361	5-25-1784	Pittmans Cr	
Lamb, Samuel	1,000	A	123	6- 3-1780	Licking	
Lamb, Wm	400	A	99	5-26-1780	Ky R	
Lamb, Wm	100	A	99	5-26-1780	Samuel Scotts Premption	Withdrawn
Lamb, Wm	300	A	99	5-26-1780	Fk Dicks R	
Lamb, Wm	510	A	99	5-26-1780	Fk Dicks R	
Lamme, Samuel	4,016	A	254	1-15-1783	Rowling Fk	
Lamme, Wm	1,000	A	36	4-29-1780	Whitley Cr	
Landage, David	998	A	269	3-28-1783	Rowling Fk	
Lane, Wm	600	A	26	4-26-1780	N Fk Elkhorn	
Lane, Wm	1,000	A	251	1- 9-1783	Coxes Cr	Withdrawn
Lane, Wm	1,000	A	251	1- 9-1783	Simpson Cr	Withdrawn
Lane, Wm	2,000	A	251	1- 9-1783	Simpson Cr	
Lane, Wm	2,000	A	354	4-16-1784	Ky R	
Lane, Wm	1,000	A	354	4-16-1784	Cox & Simpsons Cr	Withdrawn
Lapsley, John	400	A	16	2-24-1780	Gilberts Cr	
Lapsley, John	250	A	97	5-25-1780	Big Bottom	Withdrawn
Lapsley, John	250	A	97	5-25-1780	Big Bottom	Withdrawn
Lapsley, John	500	A	105	5-27-1780	Fk Dry Run	

Entree	Acres	Book	Page	Entry Date	Watercourse	Notes
Lapsley, John	250	A	106	5–27–1780	Salt R	
Lapsley, John	250	A	106	5–27–1780	Town Fk	
Larue, Isaac	1,000	A	108	5–29–1780	Ky R	
Larue, Isaac	300	A	180	10–21–1780	Big Cr	
Larue, Isaac	300	A	180	10–21–1780	Bullskin Cr	Surveyed
Larue, Isaac	400	A	180	10–21–1780	Meadow Run	Surveyed
Larue, Isaac	1,000	A	376	8– 5–1784	Gesses Cr	
Larue, Isaac	18,000	B	2	8–24–1784	———	
Larue, Isaac	1,000	B	15	11–12–1784	Knobb Cr	
Larue, Jabez	500	A	180	10–21–1780	Little Bullskin	Surveyed
Larue, Jabez	7,000	A	321	12–20–1783	Sandy Cr	3,000 acres
Larue, Jabez	3,000	A	354	4–19–1784	Coxes Cr	
Larue, Jabez	3,000	A	354	4–19–1784	Nole Linn Cr	Withdrawn
Larue, Jabez	8,000	B	40	2– 8–1785	———	
Laren, Jacob	400	A	57	5–15–1780	Clear Cr	
Larue, Jacob	1,800	B	31	12–29–1784	———	
Larue, James	700	A	180	10–19–1780	Drinnens Lick	
Larue, James	8,000	A	321	12–20–1783	Sandy Cr	
Larue, James	8,000	A	321	12–20–1783	Sandy Cr	Withdrawn
Larue, James	15,000	B	43	3–25–1785	———	
Larue, John	1,000	A	118	6– 1–1781	Fk Brashears Cr	Surveyed
Larue, John	200	A	179	10–17–1780	Fountain Blue	
Larue, John	1,000	A	179	10–17–1780	Valley Cr	Surveyed
Larue, John	2,000	A	180	10–21–1780	Clear & Floyds Fk	
Larue, John	1,000	B	27	12–17–1784	Brashears Cr	
Larue, John	1,000	B	27	12–17–1784	Ohio R	Withdrawn
Larue, John	23,000	B	43	3–25–1785	———	6,000 acres surveyed
Latham, Richard	963½	A	336	2– 3–1784	Green R	500 acres withdrawn
Latham, Richard	500	A	337	4–28–1784	Beech Fk	
Latham, Richard	500	A	357	4–28–1784	Green R	Withdrawn
Latham, Robert	1,079½	A	265	2–21–1783	Beech Fk	Withdrawn
Latham, Robert	1,079½	A	368	6–22–1784	Beach Fk	
Latham, Robert	1,079½	B	12	11– 9–1784	Panther Cr	
Lavering, Abraham	400	A	83	5–22–1780	Elkhorn	
Lawrence, David	1,000	A	181	10–24–1780	Rowling Fk	
Lawrence, John	1,000	A	182	10–24–1780	Rowling Fk	Surveyed
Lawrence, John	1,000	A	311	12– 1–1783	Bear Cr	
Lawrence, Samuel	1,000	A	181	10–24–1780	Rowling Fk	
Lawrence, Solomon	1,000	A	182	10–24–1780	Rowling Fk	Surveyed
Lawson, John	1,000	A	96	5–24–1780	Harrods Cr	Surveyed
Layne, Wm	2,000	A	242	12–25–1782	Simpsons Cr	Withdrawn
Leaper, Hugh	400	A	4	11–25–1779	Paint Lick Cr	Surveyed
Lear, Andrew	400	A	261	2– 6–1783	Mill Cr	Surveyed
Ledgerwood, Wm	800	A	77	5–20–1780	Howards Cr	Withdrawn
Ledgerwood, Wm	1,000	A	77	5–20–1780	Harrods Lick	
Ledgerwood, Wm	800	A	156	6–30–1780	Elkhorn	
Lee, Handcock	400	A	12	2– 8–1780	Elkhorn Cr	
Lee, Handcock	1,500	A	47	5–12–1780	S Fk Elkhorn	
Lee, Hancock	500	A	47	5–12–1780	Leestown	
Lee, Hancock, heirs	1,000	A	185	10–30–1780	Main Fk Elkhorn	
Lee, Henry	400	A	12	2– 8–1780	N Fk Licking	
Lee, Henry	1,000	A	55	5–15–1780	———	
Lee, Henry	4,000	A	55	5–15–1780	N Fk Licking	
Lee, Henry	3,000	A	162	7–18–1780	Green R	
Lee, Jacob	500	A	239	12–23–1782	Muddy Run	
Lee, Jacob	1,000	A	215	7–17–1781	Hardens Cr	
Lee, John	1,000	A	47	5–12–1780	Panther Cr	Surveyed
Lee, John	1,000	A	185	10–30–1780	Main Fk Elkhorn	
Lee, Joseph	300	A	245	12–31–1782	Rowling Fk	200 acres surveyed 100 acres withdrawn
Lee, Josiah	100	A	319	12–17–1783	Rolling Fk	
Lee, Josiah	100	A	319	12–17–1783	Rolling Fk	Withdrawn
Lee, Mark	500	A	109	5–29–1780	Long Lick	Withdrawn
Lee, Richard	400	A	12	2– 8–1780	N Fk Licking	
Lee, Richard	100	A	197	3–17–1781	Rowling Fk	
Lee, Richard	100	A	209	5–10–1781	Rowling Fk	Withdrawn
Lee, Richard	100	A	323	12–26–1783	Rowling Fk	
Lee, Richard	100	A	323	12–26–1783	Rowling Fk	
Lee, Samuel	400	A	374	7–28–1784	Rolling Cr	
Lee, Wm	400	A	14	2–19–1780	Hustons Fk	
Lee, Wm	400	A	236	12–20–1782	Rowling Fk	
Lee, Wm & Henry	750	A	93	5–24–1780	N Fk Licking	
Lee, Wm & Henry	750	A	94	5–24–1780	N Fk Licking Cr	
Leitch, David	14,000	A	233	12–19–1782	Salt R	Surveyed
Leitch, David	6,000	A	233	12–18–1782	Rough Cr	
Leitch, David	15,000	A	233	12–18–1782	N Fk Caney Cr	1,300 acres withdrawn
Leitch, David	13,000	A	233	12–18–1782	Rough Cr	Surveyed

Entree	Acres	Book	Page	Entry Date	Watercourse	Notes
Leitch, David	5,000	A	233	12–18–1782	Green R.	
Leitch, David	9,100	A	306	11–20–1783	Rough Cr.	
Leitch, David	400	A	306	11–20–1783	Rough Cr.	
Leitch, David	600	A	206	11–20–1783	Mountain Cr.	
Leitch, David	2,000	A	206	11–20–1783	Nolelinn Cr.	
Leitch, David	4,000	A	306	11–20–1783	Rough Cr.	
Leitch, David	1,000	A	306	11–20–1783	Nolelinn Cr.	Surveyed
Leitch, David	3,900	A	307	11–21–1783	Bacon Cr.	Surveyed
Leitch, David	5,000	A	338	2–12–1784	————	
Leitch, David	1,300	A	339	2–17–1784	————	Surveyed withdrawn
Leitch, David	15,000	A	339	2–16–1784	Rough Cr.	Surveyed amended
Leitch, David	11,214½	A	345	3–11–1784	Barbour & Banks	
Leitch, David	10,000	A	345	3–11–1784	Barbour & Banks	Withdrawn
Leitch, David	3,311	A	357	4–29–1784	Rolling Fk.	Withdrawn
Leitch, David	10,000	A	358	5– 3–1784	Barbour & Banks	
Leitch, David	10,000	A	358	5– 3–1784	————	Withdrawn
Leitch, David	10,000	A	361	5–18–1784	————	
Leitch, David	1,000	A	364	6– 4–1784	Middle Cr.	Amended
Leitch, David	3,311	A	370	7–12–1784	Prathers Cr.	
Leitch, David	3,311	A	370	7–12–1784	Prathers Cr.	Withdrawn
Leitch, David	3,311	A	370	7–12–1784	————	Withdrawn
Leitch, David	7,800	A	370	7– 9–1784	————	2,000 acres surveyed
Leitch, David	3,311	B	7	9–20–1784	————	Amended
Lemair, James	1,000	A	153	6–26–1780	Beech Fk.	
Lemair, John	400	A	113	5–30–1780	Rowling Fk.	Withdrawn
Lemair, John	400	A	174	9–29–1780	Beech Fk.	Surveyed
Lemaster, Jemima	400	A	359	5–10–1784	Beech Fk.	
Lemme, Wm.	1,000	A	178	10–17–1780	Sam Scotts	
Lenham, Dennis	12,000	A	333	1–21–1784	Salt R.	
Lent, Wm.	300	A	173	9–22–1780	Simpsons Cr.	Withdrawn
Lent, Wm.	300	A	175	10–14–1780	Simpsons Cr.	
Lent, Wm.	350	A	300	10–29–1783	————	Surveyed
Lerew, Jabas	400	A	111	5–29–1780	Benson Cr.	Surveyed
Lerew, James	400	A	111	5–29–1780	Benson Cr.	
Lerew, Phoebe	1,000	A	149	6–24–1780	Kentucky R.	
Lerue, Jabez	5,000	A	260	2– 3–1783	Coxes Cr.	Withdrawn
Lerue, Isaac	5,000	A	260	2– 3–1783	Jepthas Mt.	
Lerue, Jabez	3,000	A	260	2– 3–1783	Coxes Cr.	Withdrawn
Lerue, Jabez	2,000	A	260	2– 3–1783	Nole Linn Cr.	
Lerue, Jabez	1,000	A	315	12–15–1783	Nolelinn Cr.	
Lerue, Jabez	3,000	A	315	12–15–1783	Coxes Cr.	
Lerue, Jabez	5,000	A	315	12–15–1783	Coxes Cr.	
Lerue, Isaac	5,000	A	260	2– 3–1783	Otter Cr.	
Lerue, Isaac	5,000	A	260	2– 3–1783	Coxes Cr.	
Lerue, Isaac, Sr	3,835½	A	260	2– 3–1783	Grove in Barren	
Lerue, Isaac, Sr	6,250	A	261	2– 4–1783	Rolling Fk.	
Lerue, Jacob	18,000	A	260	2– 3–1783	Floyds Fk.	Surveyed
Lerue, Jacob	8,000	A	260	2– 3–1783	Salt R.	Withdrawn
Lerue, James	5,000	A	260	2– 3–1783	Salt R.	
Lerue, James	5,000	A	260	2– 3–1783	Barren Spring Run.	
Lerue, James	5,000	A	260	2– 3–1783	nr Drennons Lick	Surveyed
Lerue, James	5,000	A	260	2– 3–1783	Salt R.	Surveyed
Lerue, James	5,000	A	261	2– 4–1783	Bensons Cr.	
Lerue, John	21,000	A	260	2– 3–1783	Floyds Fk.	Surveyed
Lerue, John	5,000	A	260	2– 3–1783	Kentucky R.	
Lerue, John	8,000	A	260	2– 3–1783	Ohio R.	1,000 acres withdrawn
Lerue, John	6,000	A	260	2– 3–1783	Nole Linn Cr.	Surveyed
Lerue, John	6,000	A	260	2– 3–1783	Floyds Fk.	
Lesley, Alexander	350	A	197	3–17–1781	Coxes Cr.	
Lettemore, George	1,000	A	212	6–23–1781	His Improvement	Surveyed
Lewis, Aaron	200	A	197	3–17–1781	Pottingers Cr.	Withdrawn
Lewis, Aaron	200	A	209	5–10–1781	Prathers Cr.	
Lewis, Aaron	200	A	212	6–21–1781	Pottengers Cr.	
Lewis, Charles	1,000	A	123	6– 3–1780	Green R.	
Lewis, Daniel	500	A	220	8–24–1781	Beech Fk.	
Lewis, David	6,000	A	339	2–17–1784	Reedy Cr.	Surveyed, amended
Lewis, Feilding	5,000	A	57	5–15–1780	Panther Cr.	Withdrawn
Lewis, Feilding	5,000	A	57	5–15–1780	Panther Cr.	Withdrawn
Lewis, Fielding	1,000	A	74	5–19–1780	Fish Pool	Surveyed
Lewis, Feilding	10,000	A	194	3–16–1781	Panther Cr.	
Lewis, Feilding	10,000	A	195	3–16–1781	Panther Cr.	Surveyed
Lewis, James	1,811¾	A	161	7– 8–1780	Licking	Withdrawn
Lewis, James	500	A	223	12–12–1782	Beech Fk.	
Lewis, James	400	A	275	4– 9–1783	Caney & Reed Cr.	
Lewis, James	2,000	B	40	2– 8–1785	————	1,750 acres surveyed
Lewis, James	8,000	B	39	2– 8–1785	————	

Entree	Acres	Book	Page	Entry Date	Watercourse	Notes
Lewis, James	500	B	39	2- 8-1785	————	200 acres surveyed
Lewis, Jerjon	500	A	137	6-19-1780	Sugar Cr	
Lewis, John	400	A	2	11- 8-1779	Salt R	
Lewis, John	2,000	A	5	12-11-1779	Mill Cr	500 acres withdrawn
Lewis, John	100	A	18	4-13-1780	Ohio R	Withdrawn
Lewis, John	100	A	18	4-13-1780	Ohio R	Withdrawn
Lewis, John	100	A	18	4-13-1780	Ohio R	Withdrawn
Lewis, John	100	A	18	4-13-1780	Ohio R	Withdrawn
Lewis, John	100	A	18	4-13-1780	Ohio R	Withdrawn
Lewis, John	500	A	33	4-29-1780	Limestone	
Lewis, John	1,500	A	33	4-29-1780	Limestone	
Lewis, John	600	A	51	5-13-1780	Simpsons Cr	Withdrawn
Lewis, John	1,000	A	161	7- 8-1780	Mill Cr	
Lewis, John	400	A	217	7-31-1781	Pleasant Run	
Lewis, John	22,000	A	233	12-18-1782	Floyds Fk	Surveyed
Lewis, John	10,000	A	234	12-19-1782	Floyds Fk	Surveyed
Lewis, John	50,000	A	234	12-19-1782	Green R	
Lewis, John	400	A	263	2-15-1783	Beech Fk	Surveyed
Lewis, John	600	A	266	2-26-1783	Simpsons Cr	
Lewis, John	83,262	A	356	4-27-1784	Ohio R	Withdrawn
Lewis, John, et al	1,000	A	214	7- 7-1781	Hardens Cr	Surveyed
Lewis, John	1,811¼	B	23	12- 4-1784	————	Surveyed
Lewis, John	1,000	B	9	9-27-1784	Ohio R	Withdrawn
Lewis, John	1,000	B	9	9-27-1784	Beargrass Cr	
Lewis, John	60,000	A	373	7-24-1784	————	Withdrawn
Lewis, John	400	A	366	6-18-1784	Pottengers Cr	
Lewis, Joseph	200	A	303	11-12-1783	Pleasant Cr	
Lewis, Joseph	200	A	303	11-12-1783	Long Lick Cr	
Lewis, Joseph	1,000	A	303	11-12-1783	Rock Lick Cr	
Lewis, Joseph	6,000	A	304	11-14-1783	Big Reedy Cr	Surveyed
Lewis, Joseph	600	A	305	11-14-1783	Bear Cr	Withdrawn
Lewis, Joseph	10,704	A	306	11-19-1783	Nole Linn Cr	Withdrawn
Lewis, Joseph	3,000	A	306	11-19-1783	Bear Cr	Surveyed
Lewis, Joseph	3,420	A	310	11-27-1783	Beargrass Cr	Withdrawn
Lewis, Joseph	1,500	A	312	12- 3-1783	Little Yellow Banks Cr	Surveyed
Lewis, Joseph	3,000	A	312	12- 3-1783	Rudy & Bear Cr	Withdrawn
Lewis, Joseph	500	A	313	12- 8-1783	Cave Cr	
Lewis, Joseph	1,000	A	313	12- 8-1783	Cave Cr	
Lewis, Joseph	11,227	A	319	12-17-1783	Lewis Cr	
Lewis, Joseph	1,070	A	319	12-17-1783	Nole Linn	
Lewis, Joseph	315	A	321	12-20-1783	Little Yellow Banks Cr	160 acres surveyed
Lewis, Joseph	8,229	A	329	1-13-1784	Lewis Cr	
Lewis, Joseph	3,420	A	329	1-13-1784	Brashears Cr	Withdrawn
Lewis, Joseph	2,000	A	364	6- 7-1784	Pottengers Cr	Withdrawn
Lewis, Joseph et al	10,000	A	297	10-20-1783	Panther & Green	Withdrawn
Lewis, Joseph et al	6,000	A	364	6-12-1784	Robertsons Cr	1,500 acres withdrawn
Lewis, Joseph et al	10,000	A	364	6-12-1784	Panther Cr	
Lewis, Joseph	2,000	A	376	8- 5-1784	————	Withdrawn
Lewis, Joseph	16,000	A	376	8- 5-1784	Green R	9,200 acres surveyed
Lewis, Joseph	4,000	A	376	8- 5-1784	Green R	Withdrawn
Lewis, Joseph	4,000	A	376	8- 5-1784	————	Withdrawn
Lewis, Joseph	2,000	A	376	8- 5-1784	Indian Camp	Withdrawn
Lewis, Joseph	2,100	A	375	8- 2-1784	Bear Cr	Withdrawn
Lewis, Joseph	3,000	A	375	8- 2-1784	Reedy & Bear Cr	Withdrawn amended
Lewis, Joseph	200	A	374	7-28-1784	Indian Lick Cr	Surveyed
Lewis, Joseph	2,000	A	373	7-24-1784	————	Withdrawn
Lewis, Joseph	2,000	A	373	7-26-1784	————	Withdrawn
Lewis, Joseph	2,000	A	373	7-26-1784	Pottengers Cr	Withdrawn
Lewis, Joseph	2,000	A	373	7-26-1784	————	Withdrawn amended
Lewis, Joseph	5,000	A	373	7-27-1784	Rough Cr	
Lewis, Joseph	190	A	371	7-16-1784	Buffaloe Cr	
Lewis, Joseph	2,000	A	370	7- 8-1784	————	Withdrawn
Lewis, Joseph	2,000	A	370	7- 8-1784	Cedar Cr	
Lewis, Joseph	6,000	A	369	7- 1-1784	Mid Fk Robinsons Cr	Withdrawn
Lewis, Joseph	850	A	369	7- 1-1784	Coxes Cr	Withdrawn
Lewis, Joseph	1,000	A	368	6-26-1784	————	Withdrawn
Lewis, Joseph	500	A	366	6-19-1784	————	160 acres surveyed
Lewis, Joseph, et al	2,000	B	36	1-27-1785	Rolling Fk	Withdrawn
Lewis, Joseph, et al	10,000	B	35	1-26-1785	————	
Lewis, Joseph, et al	5,000	B	35	1-26-1785	Beech Fk	
Lewis, Joseph, et al	4,000	B	34	1-21-1785	Indian Lick	
Lewis, Joseph, et al	4,000	B	2	8-26-1784	Rolling Fk	

Entree	Acres	Book	Page	Entry Date	Watercourse	Notes
Lewis, Joseph, et al	2,000	B	2	8–26–1784	Rolling Fk	....
Lewis, Joseph, et al	5,000	A	376	8– 5–1784	————	
Lewis, Joseph, et al	10,000	A	376	8– 5–1784	Indian Camp	Withdrawn
Lewis, Joseph, et al	600	A	376	8– 5–1784	18 Mile Cr	
Lewis, Joseph, et al	600	A	373	7–24–1784	18 Mile Cr	Withdrawn
Lewis, Joseph, et al	1,000	A	368	6–29–1784	Robertsons Cr	Withdrawn
Lewis, Joseph, et al	1,000	A	368	6–29–1784	Pittmans Cr	Withdrawn
Lewis, Joseph	4,000	B	49	6–17–1785	————	....
Lewis, Joseph	2,000	B	48	6–17–1785	Salt R	....
Lewis, Joseph	400	B	47	6– 6–1785	Salt R	....
Lewis, Joseph	700	B	44	4–20–1785	Mill Cr	Withdrawn
Lewis, Joseph	250	B	44	4–25–1785	Salt R	....
Lewis, Joseph	4,000	B	40	2– 8–1785	————	....
Lewis, Joseph	31,604	B	40	2-1 8–1785	————	9,600 acres surveyed
Lewis, Joseph	773¾	B	40	2– 8–1785	————	....
Lewis, Joseph	375	B	39	2– 7–1785	Green R	....
Lewis, Joseph	2,100	B	38	1–29–1785	————	Withdrawn
Lewis, Joseph	500,	B	38	1–29–1785	————	Withdrawn
Lewis, Joseph	1,500	B	38	1–29–1785	————	Withdrawn
Lewis, Joseph	3,039	B	38	1–31–1785	Bear Cr	
Lewis, Joseph	1,000	B	35	1–26–1785	————	Withdrawn
Lewis, Joseph	1,000	B	35	1–26–1785	Beech Fk	
Lewis, Joseph	3,125	B	34	1–25–1785	Bacon Cr	Surveyed
Lewis, Joseph	600	B	33	1–12–1785	Rough Cr	....
Lewis, Joseph	3,000	B	33	1–13–1785	Beech Fk	
Lewis, Joseph	700	B	32	1– 8–1785	Mill Cr	Withdrawn
Lewis, Joseph	3,000	B	32	1– 8–1785	Tarr Spring Fk	
Lewis, Joseph	200	B	32	1–12–1785	Clover Cr	
Lewis, Joseph	15,508	B	31	1– 3–1785	————	Surveyed
Lewis, Joseph	2,000	B	31	1– 3–1785	————	
Lewis, Joseph	3,000	B	31	1– 3–1785	————	
Lewis, Joseph	3,000	B	30	12–23–1784	Bacon Cr	Surveyed
Lewis, Joseph	643	B	28	12–18–1784	S Fk Caney Cr	Surveyed
Lewis, Joseph	1,000	B	28	12–20–1784	Rolling Fk	
Lewis, Joseph	4,800	B	17	11–14–1784	Muddy Cr	Withdrawn
Lewis, Joseph	3,000	B	17	11–14–1784	Rough Cr	....
Lewis, Joseph	600	B	17	11–14–1784	Beech Fk	
Lewis, Joseph	500	B	17	11–14–1784	Long Lick Cr	Withdrawn
Lewis, Joseph	9,200	B	17	11–14–1784	Little Reedy Cr	Amended
Lewis, Joseph	4,000	B	17	11–14–1784	Beech Fk	Withdrawn
Lewis, Joseph	1,950	B	16	11–12–1784	Indian Camp Cr	Surveyed
Lewis, Joseph	6,800	B	14	11–11–1784	————	Withdrawn
Lewis, Joseph	4,000	B	14	11–11–1784	————	Withdrawn
Lewis, Joseph	6,800	B	14	11–11–1784	Caney Cr	
Lewis, Joseph	6,365	B	14	11–11–1784	Caney Cr	Surveyed
Lewis, Joseph	4,800	B	14	11–12–1784	Muddy Cr	Withdrawn
Lewis, Joseph	2,000	B	14	11–12–1784	————	Withdrawn
Lewis, Joseph	1,500	B	14	11–12–1784	Cave Cr	Surveyed
Lewis, Joseph	6,000	B	13	11–11–1784	Big Reedy Cr	Surveyed amended
Lewis, Joseph	9,000	B	5	9–11–1784	————	200 acres surveyed
Lewis, Joseph	2,000	B	3	8–26–1784	Pottengers Cr	Withdrawn
Lewis, Joseph	2,000	B	3	8–26–1784	Pottengers Cr	
Lewis, Nicholas	600	A	207	4–14–1781	Rowling	Surveyed
Lewis, Nicholas	1,000	A	209	5–19–1781	Pottengers Cr	....
Lewis, Nicholas	800	A	222	12–11–1782	Green R	
Lewis, Nicholas	800	A	222	12–11–1782	Green R	....
Lewis, Nicholas	1,000	A	277	4–14–1783	Salt R	Surveyed
Lewis, Nicholas	1,000	A	277	4–14–1783	Salt R	Surveyed
Lewis, Nicholas	500	A	288	9– 8–1783	Nolins Cr	Surveyed
Lewis, Nicholas	500	A	288	8–25–1783	Pottengers Cr	Surveyed
Lewis, Nicholas	2,000	A	289	9– 8–1783	Nolelin Cr	1307 acres surveyed
Lewis, Nicholos	700	A	298	9– 8–1783	Nolen Cr	Surveyed
Lewis, Nicholas	600	A	289	9– 8–1783	Nolelin Cr	Surveyed
Lewis, Nicholas	200	A	289	9– 8–1783	Bacon Cr	Surveyed
Lewis, Nicholas	300	A	289	9– 7–1783	Noelin Cr	
Lewis, Nicholas	200	A	289	9– 8–1783	Noelinn Cr	Surveyed
Lewis, Nicholas	500	A	289	9– 8–1783	Barrens	Surveyed
Lewis, Nicholas	320	A	289	9– 8–1783	Bacon Cr	Surveyed
Lewis, Nicholas	721	A	291	9–11–1783	Sandy Cr	Surveyed
Lewis, Nicholas	563	A	291	9–11–1783	Sandy Cr	Surveyed
Lewis, Nicholas	300	A	295	10–11–1783	Sinking Cr	....
Lewis, Nicholas	200	A	295	10–11–1783	Clover Cr	....
Lewis, Nicholas	500	A	295	10–11–1783	Shottpouch Cr	Surveyed
Lewis, Nicholas	10,000	A	309	11–25–1783	————	Withdrawn
Lewis, Nicholas	2,000	A	362	5–31–1784	————	1,000 acres surveyed
Lewis, Nicholas et al	770	A	288	9– 8–1783	N Fk Caney Cr	Surveyed
Lewis, Nicholas	200	B	40	2– 8–1785	————	....

Entree	Acres	Book	Page	Entry Date	Watercourse	Notes
Lewis, Nicholas	4,000	B	40	2– 8–1785	———	
Lewis, Nicholas	300	B	40	2– 8–1785	———	
Lewis, Nicholas	500	B	17	11–15–1784	———	307 acres surveyed returned
Lewis, Nicholas	500	A	370	7– 6–1784	———	270 acres surveyed
Lewis, Nicholas	500	A	370	7– 6–1784	———	270 acres surveyed
Lewis, Thomas	2,000	A	62	5–16–1780	Stoners Fk	
Lewis, Thomas	500	A	88	5–23–1780	Stoners Fk	
Lewis, Thomas	1,000	A	141	6–21–1780	Simpsons Cr	Withdrawn
Lewis, Thomas	1,000	A	221	11– 9–1782	Simpsons Cr	Withdrawn
Lewis, Thomas	500	A	223	12–12–1782	Cartrights Cr	Surveyed
Lewis, Thomas	1,000	B	32	1– 8–1785	———	500 acres, surveyed
Lewis, Wm	100	A	33	4–29–1780	Boones Cr	Mil
Lewis, Wm	100	A	33	4–29–1780	Boones Cr	Mil
Lewis, Wm	2,000	A	66	5–17–1780	N Fk Elkhorn	
Lewis, Wm	1,000	A	123	6– 3–1780	Green R	
Lewis, Wm	1,000	A	141	6–21–1780	Benson Cr	
Lewis, Wm	2,100	A	309	11–25–1783	Green R	Withdrawn
Lewis, Wm	2,100	A	321	12–22–1783	Green R	
Lewis, Wm	800	B	12	11– 9–1784	Panther Cr	
Lewis, Zachariah	2,000	A	32	4–29–1780	Hickmans Cr	Mil
Lietch, David	500	A	305	11–17–1783	Bear Cr	
Lietch, David	1,000	A	305	11–17–1783	Bear Cr	
Lietch, David	2,000	A	305	11–17–1783	Noellinn Cr	Surveyed
Lietch, David	500	A	305	11–17–1783	Noellinn Cr	
Lietch, David	1,000	A	305	11–17–1783	Noellinn Cr	Surveyed
Lietch, David	1,000	A	305	11–17–1783	Nolelinn Cr	
Lietch, David	2,000	A	305	11–17–1783	Salt R	
Lightfoot, Mildred	9,431	A	309	11–25–1783	18 Mile Cr	
Lightfoot, Phillip	1,581	A	298	10–23–1783	Rolling Fk	
Lillard, Ephraim	1,000	A	269	3–28–1783	Rowling Fk	
Lillard, James	656	A	269	3–28–1783	Rowling Fk	
Lilley, Thomas	440	A	175	10– 6–1780	S Fk Licking	
Lillard, Thomas	250	A	301	11– 7–1783	Chaplins Fk	
Lillard, Thomas	750	A	301	11– 7–1783	Glens Cr	Surveyed
Lillard, Thomas	2,809½	B	41	3– 4–1785	———	
Limine, Wm	400	A	12	2– 5–1780	Whitleys Cr	
Lincoln, Hannaniah	890	A	291	9–13–1783	Cartright Cr	
Lincoln, Hannaniah	1,000	A	314	12– 9–1783	Beech Fk	
Linder, Jacob	500	A	239	12–23–1782	E Fk Short Cr	Withdrawn
Linder, Jacob	500	A	239	12–23–1782	Short Cr	Withdrawn
Linder, Jacob	500	A	239	12–23–1782	Short Cr	Withdrawn
Linder, Jacob	1,000	A	240	12–24–1782	Short Cr	Surveyed
Linder, Jacob	1,000	A	240	12–24–1782	Short Cr	Surveyed
Linder, Jacob	737	A	273	4– 7–1783	Clifty Cr	Surveyed
Linder, Jacob	500	A	287	8–12–1783	Short Cr	Surveyed
Linder, Jacob	200	A	290	9–10–1783	Nolin Cr	Surveyed
Linder, Jacob	500	A	291	9–30–1783	Nole Linn Cr	Surveyed
Linder, Jacob	4,000	A	341	2–21–1784		
Lindsay, Fulton	1,000	A	37	4–29–1780	Elkhorn Cr	
Lindsey, Arthur	400	A	178	10–17–1780	Fulton Lindsey	
Lindsey, John	300	A	363	6– 4–1784	Pottengers Cr	Mil
Lindsey, John	300	A	363	6– 4–1784	———	Withdrawn
Lindsey, John	500	A	362	6– 1–1784	Ohio R	300 acres withdrawn
Line, Edward	1,400	A	309	11–17–1783	Ohio R	Amended
Line, Edmund	160	A	327	1– 5–1784	———	Surveyed returned
Line, Edmund	400	A	328	1– 9–1784	———	Surveyed
Line, Edmund	400	A	345	3–12–1784	———	
Linkhorn, Abraham	800	A	126	6– 7–1780	Green R Lick	
Linn, Ben et al	400	A	18	3– 8–1780	S Fk Beargrass	Surveyed
Linn, Benjamin	100	A	196	3–17–1781	Beech Cr	
Linn, Wm et al	1,000	A	142	6–22–1780	Blue Lick	
Lithgrow, Alexander	1,000	A	177	10–10–1780	W Fk Licking	
Little, Mich	500	A	51	5–13–1780	Otter Cr	
Littlepage, John D	500	A	32	4–29–1780	Drennens Lick Cr	Mil surveyed
Lockhart, Jacob	50	A	24	4–25–1780	Br Kentucky R	Mil
Lockhart, Jacob	1,200	A	23	4–24–1780	Sinking Cr	Mil
Lockhart, Joseph	500	A	21	4–20–1780	Harr Cf	Mil
Lockhead, David	900	A	267	3–28–1783	Kentucky R	Surveyed
Logan, Benj	400	A	6	12–28–1779	Clarks Run	
Logan, Benj	400	A	6	12–28–1779	Boones Cr	
Logan, Benj	400	A	4	12– 7–1779	Beargrass	Surveyed
Logan, Benj	400	A	7	12–28–1779	Dicks R	
Logan, Benj	600	A	101	5–26–1780	Hanging Fk	
Logan, Benj	500	A	101	5–26–1780	Clarkask Run	
Logan, Benj	600	A	101	5–26–1780	Big Flat Lick	

Entree	Acres	Book	Page	Entry Date	Watercourse	Notes
Logan, Benj	1,000	A	101	5-26-1780	Montgomries Sett	
Logan, Benj	1,000	A	101	5-26-1780	Logans Cr	
Logan, Benjamin	750	A	101	5-26-1780	Logans Cr	
Logan, Benj et al	3,500	A	272	4- 3-1783	Mill Cr	
Logan, Benj et al	3,500	A	360	5-18-1784	———	
Logan, Hugh	1,000	A	101	5-26-1780	Little Flat Lick	
Logan, Hugh	6,000	A	376	8- 5-1784	Robertson Cr	
Logan, Hugh	6,108	A	377	8- 9-1784	———	
Logan, James	50	A	21	4-18-1780	Hanging Fk	Mil
Logan, James	100	A	21	4-18-1780	Hanging Fk	Mil
Logan, James	400	A	36	4-29-1780	Givens Run	
Logan, James	400	A	36	4-29-1780	Hanging Fk	
Logan, James	1,000	A	219	8-22-1781	Rowling Fk	Surveyed
Logan, John	1,000	A	37	4-29-1780	Chaplins Fk	
Logan, John	500	A	102	5-27-1780	Green R	
Logan, John	150	A	102	5-27-1780		
Logan, John	500	A	131	6-12-1780	Green R	
Logan, John	1,000	A	132	6-15-1780	Yeagers Sett	
Logan, John	1,000	A	132	6-15-1780	His Sett	
Logan, John	400	A	142	6-22-1780	Green R	
Logan, John	400	A	142	6-22-1780	Green R	
Logan, John	400	A	142	6-22-1780	Green R	
Logan, John	1,000	A	179	10-17-1780	Licking	
Logan, Nath	400	A	4	11-24-1779	St. Asaphs Spring	
Logan, Nath	400	A	4	11-24-1779	St. Asaphs Spring	
Logan, Nath	1,000	A	132	6-15-1780	His Sett	
Logwood, Thomas	1,000	A	156	6-30-1780	John Kennady	
Logan, Wm	400	A	6	12-28-1779	Clarks Run	
Logan, Wm	400	A	101	5-26-1780	Clarks Run	
Logston, Thomas	325	A	325	12-29-1783	Little Clifty Cr	
Lomax, Thomas	400	A	20	4-15-1780	Knob Lick Road	Mil withdrawn
Lomax, Thomas	400	A	20	4-15-1780	Silver Cr	Withdrawn
Lomax, Thomas	1,200	A	21	4-19-1780	Little Kentucky	Mil surveyed
Lomax, Thomas	2,000	A	23	4-24-1780	Br Cabbin Cr	
Lomax, Thomas	800	A	23	4-24-1780	Knob Lick & Silver Cr	Withdrawn
Lomax, Thomas	800	A	25	4-25-1780	Little Kentucky	Surveyed
Loney, Amos	1,400	A	229	12-16-1782	Salt R	
Long, Francis	100	A	99	5-25-1780	Silver Cr	Mil
Long, Joseph	250	A	134	6-17-1780	Kentucky R	
Long, Joseph	500	A	134	6-17-1780	Otter Cr	
Long, Joseph	500	A	134	6-17-1780	Silver Cr	
Long, Joseph	250	A	135	6-17-1780	Kentucky R	
Long, Joseph	250	A	135	6-17-1780	Kentucky R	
Long, Joseph	250	A	135	6-17-1780	Kentucky R	
Long, Josiah	50	A	96	5-25-1780	Kentucky R	Mil
Long, Wm	325	A	191	3-15-1781	Pond Cr	
Longest, Caleb	50	A	137	6-19-1780	Kentucky R	Mil
Longest, Caleb	450	A	137	6-19-1780	Kentucky R	
Longest, Richard	250	A	98	5-25-1780	Chaplins Fk	
Longest, Thimothy	150	A	31	4-28-1780	N Fk Elkhorn	Mil
Longest, Wm	400	A	255	1-20-1783	N Fk Rough Cr	
Longhorn, John	3,000	A	126	6- 7-17—	Wolf Cr	
Longhorn, Morris	3,000	A	126	6- 7-1780	Wolf Cr	
Longston, Thomas	325	A	362	5-26-1784	———	
Lout, Daniel	400	A	277	4-12-1783	Hardens Cr	
Lovel, Thomas	400	A	108	5-29-1780	Bulgers Lick	
Loveless, John	400	A	38	4-29-1780	Coopers Run	
Loving, Joha	1,000	A	328	1- 9-1784	Robinsons Cr	Surveyed
Loving, Wm	1,000	A	266	2-25-1783	Brush Cr	
Loving, Wm	1,000	A	368	6-22-1784	Mid Fk Brush Cr	
Loving, Wm	500	A	368	6-22-1784	Mid Fk Brush Cr	
Loving, Wm	500	B	29	12-20-1784	S Fk Brush Cr	
Loving, Wm	2,000	B	29	12-20-1784	Mid Fk Sinking Cr	
Low, Nicholas	30,000	A	325	12-31-1783	Clear Cr	Surveyed
Loyd, Dr. Thomas	200	A	32	4-29-1780	Elkhorn	Mil
Loyon, Samuel	1,000	A	179	10-17-1780	Hingston Fk	
Lowry, John	400	A	141	6-21-1780	N Fk Elkhorn	
Lugget, John	500	A	39	5- 9-1780	S Fk Elkhorn	
Lusk, Samuel	400	A	142	6-22-1780	Paint Lick Cr	
Luttrell, John	400	A	13	2- 9-1780	Kentucky R	
Luttrell, John	400	A	14	2-19-1780	Silver Cr	
Luttrell, John	1,000	A	144	6-23 1780	Boonsborough	
Luttrill, John, heir	1,000	A	145	6-23-1780	Boons Fk Silver Cr	
Lutts, Phillip	1,000	A	220	8-24-1781	Bullskin Cr	Surveyed
Lyle, James	500	A	89	5-23-1780	Ohio R	
Lyle, John	5,000	A	330	1-15-1784	Ohio R	
Lynder, Jacob	200	A	241	12-25-1782	Cave Cr	Surveyed
Lynder, Jacob	200	A	241	12-25-1782	Cave Cr	Surveyed
Lynder, Jacob	300	A	241	12-25-1782	Cave Cr	Surveyed

Entree	Acres	Book	Page	Entry Date	Watercourse	Notes
Lynder, Jacob	200	A	291	9–30–1783	E Fk Short Cr	Withdrawn
Lynder, Jacob	300	A	291	9–30–1783	Short Cr	Withdrawn
Lynder, Jacob	300	A	299	10–25–1783	Nolelin Cr	Surveyed
Lyne, Edmund	400	A	11	2– 3–1780	M Fk Licking	
Lyne, Edmund	400	A	37	4–29–1780	Kentucky R	Surveyed
Lyne, Edmund	1,000	A	52	5–13–1780	Salt R	Withdrawn
Lyne, Edmund	1,400	A	52	5–13–1780	Harrods Cr	940 acres surveyed
Lyne, Edmund	1,000	A	221	11– 9–1782	Coxes Cr	Withdrawn
Lyne, Edmund	400	A	222	12–11–1782	Rowling Fk	Surveyed
Lyne, Edmund	200	A	222	12–11–1782	Rough Cr	
Lyne, Edmund	200	A	222	12–11–1782	Rowling Fk	Surveyed
Lyne, Edmund	200	A	222	12–11–1782	Hardens Cr	Surveyed
Lyne, Edmund	400	A	281	6–26–1783		Surveyed
Lyne, Edmund	140	A	327	1– 3–1784	Harrods Cr	Surveyed
Lyne, George	1,000	A	52	5–13–1780	Ohio R	Surveyed
Lyne, Henry	500	A	52	5–13–1780	Ohio R	Surveyed
Lyne, John	2,000	A	260	2– 3–1783	Drennons Cr	
Lynn, Wm	400	A	185	10–31–1780	Harrods Cr	
Lynn, Wm	400	A	185	10–31–1780	Harrods Cr	
Lynn, Wm	400	A	185	10–31–1780	Dry Run	Surveyed
Lyon, Samuel	400	A	139	6–21–1780	Hingstons Fk	
Lyon & Lempreize	15,000	A	324	12–27–1783	Nolelin Cr	Withdrawn
Lyons & Simpreize	15,000	A	350	4–10–1784	Nole Linn Cr	Surveyed
Lytch, Samuel	400	A	180	10–21–1780	Bullskin & Clear Cr	M Book
Lytch, Samuel	600	A	180	10–21–1780	Gess Cr	
McAdams, Samuel	509	A	176	10– 9–1780	Beech Fk	Withdrawn
McAdams, Samuel	209	A	212	6–25–1781	Mid Fk Pottengers Cr	Surveyed
McAdams, Samuel	509	A	212	6–25–1781	Beech Fk	Withdrawn
McAdams, Samuel	300	A	221	11– 9–1782	Beech Fk	Withdrawn
McAdams, Samuel	300	A	222	12–11–1782	Pottengers Cr	Withdrawn
McAdams, Samuel	300	A	276	4–12–1783	Pottengers Cr	Surveyed
McAdams, Samuel	300	A	276	4–12–1783	Pottengers Cr	Withdrawn
McAdams, Samuel	1,000	A	292	10– 3–1783	Pottengers Cr	Surveyed
McAdams, Samuel	100	B	17	11–17–1784	Pottengers Cr	
McAdams, Samuel	100	B	31	1– 3–1785	————	
McAfee, Geo	400	A	2	11– 3–1779	Salt R	
McAfee, James	400	A	2	11– 3–1779	Salt R	Surveyed
McAfee, James	1,000	A	25	4–26–1780	Salt R	
McAfee, James	1,000	A	26	4–26–1780	Salt R	Surveyed
McAfee, Robert	400	A	1	11– 3–1779	Salt R	Surveyed
McAfee, Robert	400	A	79	5–20–1780	Salt R	Withdrawn
McAfee, Robert	600	A	79	5–20–1780	Salt R	Surveyed
McAfee, Robert	100	A	136	6–19–1780	————	Surveyed
McAfee, Samuel	400	A	2	11– 3–1779	Salt R	Surveyed
McAfee, Samuel	1,000	A	27	4–26–1780	McAfee settlement	Surveyed
McAfee, Samuel	1,000	A	271	3–31–1783	Beech Fk	Withdrawn
McAfee, Samuel	1,000	A	368	6–22–1784	Beech Fk	
McAfee, Wm	400	A	2	11– 3–1779	Salt R	Surveyed
McAfee, Wm	1,000	A	27	4–26–1780	McAfee settlement	Surveyed
McAlexander, Alex	700	A	239	12–23–1782	Casey Cr	
McAlexander, Alex	3,312⅔	A	253	1–14–1783	Robinsons Cr	
McAlexander, Alex	600	A	253	1–14–1783	Caseys Cr	
McBrayer, Wm	400	A	2	11– 3–1779	Chaplins Fk	
McBrayers, Wm	1,000	A	87	5–23–1780	Chaplins Fk	Surveyed
McBride, Francis	200	A	113	5–30–1780	Beech Fk	Surveyed
McBride, Isaac	400	A	37	4–29–1780	S Fk Elkhorn	
McBride, James	500	A	81	5–22–1780	Elkhorn & Licking	
McBride, James	400	A	170	9– 9–1780	Ky R	
McBriar, James	200	A	373	7–27–1784	————	
McBride, Wm	400	A	18	3– 2–1780	Paint Lick Cr	
McBride, Wm	1,000	A	27	4–26–1780	Harrods Run	
McBride, Wm	200	A	42	5–10–1780	Beech Fk	
McBord, Wm	400	A	2	11– 6–1779	Harrods Run	
McCallister, James	1,000	A	27	4–26–1780	Licking	
McCallister, James	1,000	A	27	4–26–1780	Licking	Mil
McCallister, James		A	375	7–29–1784	In Fayette	
McCallister, Robert	6,000	A	255	1–20–1783	Salt R	Surveyed
McCallister, Robert	250	A	349	4– 2–1784	Kentucky R	Surveyed
McCallister, Robert	250	B	40	2– 8–1785		
McCallister, Robt et al	750	A	223	12–12–1782	Green R	
McCann, Jas	400	A	3	11–11–1779	Salt R	Surveyed
McCarty, Thomas	400	A	212	6–25–1781	Fromans Cr	Surveyed
McCarty, Thomas	400	A	212	6–25–1781	Floyds Fk	Surveyed
McCarty, Thomas	400	A	212	6–25–1781	Floyds Fk	Surveyed
McCarty, Thomas	1,248	A	282	7– 2–1783	Little Ky R	
McCarty, Thomas	400	A	341	2–26–1784	Fremans Cr	
McCarty, Thomas	400	A	342	2–26–1784	Floyds Fk	
McCarty, Thomas	30	A	342	2–26–1784	Floyds Fk	
McCarty, Thomas	2,000	A	367	6–22–1784	————	
McCarty, Thomas	1,115	A	368	6–29–1784	Beargrass Cr	Surveyed
McCarty, Thomas	855	A	369	7– 3–1784	Beargrass Cr	

Entree	Acres	Book	Page	Entry Date	Watercourse	Notes
McCarty, Thomas.....	200	A	375	7–29–1784	———.	
McCarty, Thomas.....	4,000	B	48	6–17–1785	———.	1,115 acres
McCastline, John......	400	A	244	12–27–1782	Ben Pope et al.....	surveyed
McCawley, James.....	400	A	7	1–10–1780	Fish Pool Cr.....	
McCawley, James.....	560	A	155	6–29–1780	near Fish Pool Cr...	
McCawley, James.....	560	B	19	11–25–1784		Amended
McCayenters, James...	1,500	A	105	5–27–1780	Beech Fk..........	Withdrawn
McClanahan, Robert..	1,000	A	33	4–29–1780	Brashears..........	Mil surveyed
McClanachan, Thos ...	400	A	10	2– 3–1780	Big Fk Elkhorn....	
McClanachan, Thos...	400	A	10	2– 3–1780	Big Fk Elkhorn....	
McClanachan, Thos....	1,000	A	26	4–26–1780	Elkhorn Cr........	
McClanachan, Thos...	400	A	26	4–26–1780	Haggin Trace......	
McClanachan, Thomas.	300	A	29	4+27–1780	Elkhorn...........	Mil
McClanachan, Wm...	300	A	336	2– 3–1784	Buffaloe Cr.......	
McClellan, Abraham...	400	A	10	2– 3–1784	N Fk Elkhorn.....	
McClellan, Benjamin..	400	A	141	6–21–1780	Buckhorn Run.....	
McClellan, John.......	328½	A	343	3– 3–1784	Caney Run........	
McClellan, Wm.......	400	A	149	6–24–1780	S Fk Licking......,	
McClenachan, Alex....	1,327½	A	357	5– 1–1784	Floyds Fk.........	
McClenachan, John....	1,000	A	223	12–12–1782	Clover Lick Cr.....	
McClenachan, John....	385	A	336	2– 3–1784	Green R..........	
McClenchan, Jno, heirs	2,000	A	155	6–30–1780	Green R..........	Surveyed
McClenchan, Jno, heirs	2,000	A	155	6–30–1780	Green R..........	Surveyed
McClenchan, Jno, heirs	2,000	A	155	6–30–1780	Green R..........	Mil surveyed
McClenchan, Jno. heirs.	1,000	A	363	6– 2–1784	Brush Cr..........	
McClenchan, Thomas..	500	A	98	5–25–1780	Clear Cr..........	
McClenchan, Thomas..	500	A	98	5–25–1780	Clear Cr..........	
McClenchan, Wm.....	300	A	319	12–17–1783	Buffaloe Cr.......	Withdrawn
McClenchan, Wm.....	200	A	333	1–21–1784	Cedar Cr..........	
McCleroy, Hugh.......	500	A	46	5–12–1780	Beech Fk.........	
McClure, George......	400	A	18	3– 3–1780	Bullskin Cr........	
McClure, George......	1,000	A	184	10–30–1780	Bullskin Cr........	
McClure, John........	1,000	A	38	4–29–1780	Mid Fk Licking.....	
McCollister, James....	1,000	A	134	6–16–1780	Thomas Kennadies.	
McConnall, Andrew...	400	A	149	6–24–1790	Fk Elkhorn........	
McConnall, Francis...	400	A	10	2– 3–1780	S Fk Elkhorn......	
McConnall, Francis...	1,000	A	37	4–29–1780	Elkhorn...........	
McConnall, Francis...	500	A	59	5–16–1780	Licking...........	
McConnall, Francis...	500	A	59	5–16–1780	Lawrence Cr.......	
McConnall, Francis...	500	A	59	5–16–1780	Lawrence Cr.......	
McConnall, Francis...	500	A	59	5–16–1780	E Fk Licking......	
McConnaıl, Francis...	500	A	59	5–16–1780	Elkhorn...........	
McConnall, Francis...	500	A	59	5–16–1780	Fk Elkhorn........	
McConnall, Francis...	500	A	59	5–16–1780	Ky R.............	
McConnall, Wm......	400	A	10	2– 3–1780	S Fk Elkhorn......	
McConnall, Wm......	400	A	10	2– 3–1780	Sinking Spring.....	
McConnall, Wm......	1,000	A	37	4–29–1780	Fk Elkhorn........	
McConnall, Wm......	800	A	71	5–18–1780	Lawrence Cr.......	
McConnall, Wm......	800	A	71	5–18–1780	E Fk Licking......	
McConnall, Wm......	400	A	72	5–18–1780	E Fk Licking......	
McConnall, Wm......	600	A	72	5–18–1780	S Fk Licking......	
McConnall, Wm......	200	A	72	5–18–1780	S Fk Elkhorn......	
McConnall, Wm......	800	A	72	5–18–1780	Licking...........	
McConnall, Wm......	800	A	72	5–18–1780	Lawrence Cr.......	
McConnall, Wm......	1,000	A	72	5–18–1780	Lawrence Cr.......	
McConnall, Wm......	400	A	72	5–18–1780	Shannons Run.....	
McConnall, Wm......	400	A	72	5–18–1780	S Fk Clear Cr.....	
McConnall, Wm......	600	A	78	5–20–1780	E Fk Licking......	
McConnall, Wm......	400	A	149	6–24–1780	Hingstons Cr......	
McConnalı, Wm......	1,000	A	175	10– 6–1780	S Fk Elkhorn.....	
McConnelı, Alex......	400	A	10	2– 3–1780	S Fk Elkhorn.....	
McConnell, Alex......	400	A	37	4–29–1780	S Fk Elkhorn.....	
McConnell, Alex......	1,000	A	37	4–29–1780	McConnell sett.....	
McCorkall, James.....	1,000	A	112	5–30–1780	N Fk Elkhorn.....	
McCorkall, James.....	1,000	A	268	3–28–1783	Sinkings Cr.......	Surveyed
McCormack, Daniel...	1,000	A	25	4–26–1780	Hanging Fk.......	
McCormack, John.....	400	A	26	4–26–1780	Paint Lick Cr......	
McCoun, James.......	1,000	A	26	4–26–1780	Salt R...........	Surveyed
McCoun, James.......	720	A	251	1– 9–1783	Chaplins Fk......	Withdrawn
McCoun, James.......	380	A	251	1– 9–1783	Salt R...........	Surveyed
McCoun, James.......	400	A	251	1– 9–1783	Salt R...........	Surveyed
McCoun, James.......	720	A	292	10– 3–1783	Chaplins Fk......	Withdrawn
McCoun, James Jr....	1,000	A	26	4–26–1780	Salt R...........	Surveyed
McCoun, James Jr....	400	A	97	5–25–1780	Town Fk..........	Surveyed
McCoun, John........	200	A	100	5–26–1780	Bealeys Fk........	
McCoun, John........	360	A	292	10– 3–1783	Brashears Cr.......	Surveyed
McCoun, James.......	1,500	A	377	8–12–1784	———.	
McCowan, Jas........	400	A	2	11– 3–1779	Salt R...........	Surveyed
McCowan, John.......	400	A	10	2– 3–1780	Salt R...........	Surveyed
McCoy, James........	1,500	A	245	12–28–1782	Beech Fk..........	

Entree	Acres	Book	Page	Entry Date	Watercourse	Notes
McCoy, James	1,500	A	245	12-28-1782	Beech Fk	Surveyed
McCoyle, Michael	200	A	122	6- 2-1780	Greens Cr	
McCracken, Cyrus	400	A	9	1-18-1780	Glens Cr	
McCracken, Cyrus	50	A	38	4-29-1780	Ky R	
McCracken, Cyrus	50	A	122	6- 2-1780	Ohio R	Mil
McCracken, Cyrus	150	A	153	6-26-1780	Elkhorn	Withdrawn
McCracken, Cyrus	500	A	161	7-10-1780	N Fk Elkhorn	
McCracken, Cyrus	150	A	161	7-10-1780	Elkhorn	
McCracken, Isaac	1,000	A	242	12-25-1782	Drennons Lick Cr	Surveyed
McCracken, James	400	A	38	4-29-1780	Elkhorn	
McCracken, John	400	A	9	1-18-1780	S Fk Elkhorn	
McCracken, John	500	A	37	4-29-1780	S Fk Elkhorn	
McCracken, Seneca et al	1,000	A	215	7-18-1781	Rowling Fk	
McCracken, Wm	400	A	7	12-28-1779	Stoners Fk	
McCracken, Wm	400	A	12	2- 5-1780	Ky R	
McCracken, Wm	1,000	A	161	7-10-1780	Ky R	
McCracken, Wm	1,000	A	161	7-10-1780	Ky R	
McCracken, Wm	1,000	A	61	7-10-1780	Stoners Cr	
McCracking, Isaac	500	A	227	12-14-1782	Near Drenning Lick	
McCracking, Isaac	500	A	227	12-14-1782	Elkhorn Cr	
McCraw, Sam et al	1,000	B	26	12-14-1784	Rock Lick Cr	
McDonald, Clement	300	A	45	5-11-1780	Rolling Fk	
McDonald, Jas	400	A	3	11-11-1779	Gilberts Cr	
McDonald, Jas	400	A	3	11-11-1779	Gilberts Cr	
McDonald, Jas	1,000	A	108	5-29-1780	Dicks R	
McDonald, Jas, heirs	1,000	A	182	10-27-1780	Gilberts Cr	
McDonald, Wm	500	A	195	3-17-1781	Beech Fk	
McDonald, James	1,000	A	197	3-17-1781	Coxes Cr	Surveyed
McDonnald, Randolph	300	A	90	5-23-1780	Cedar Run	
McDonnall, Catherine	1,200	A	234	12-19-1782	N Fk Coxes Cr	Withdrawn
McDonnall, Nancy etal	1,200	A	360	5-18-1784	Cox Cr	Withdrawn
McDonnall, Nancy etal	1,200	A	360	5-18-1784	Rough Cr	
McDurrid, Francis	400	A	16	2-23-1780	Upper Blue Lick	
McDougal, Robert	300	A	73	5-19-1780	Buffaloe Cr	
McDowell, Joseph	1,940	A	308	11-22-1783	E Fk Bear Cr	
McDowell, Joseph	1,500	A	332	1-20-1784	Harden Cr	
McDowell, Joseph	1,500	A	332	1-20-1784	Beech Fk	
McDowell, Joseph	300	A	332	1-20-1784	Beech Fk	
McDowell, Joseph	500	A	332	1-20-1784	Hardens Cr	
McDowell, Joseph	200	A	333	1-20-1784	Hardens Cr	
McDowell, Samuel	900	A	226	12-13-1782	Brush Cr	Surveyed
McDowell, Samuel	100	A	227	12-14-1782	Robinsons Cr	Surveyed
McElhose, John	500	A	210	6- 5-1781	Rowling Fk	
McElhose, John	500	B	13	11-11-1784	————	
McElroy, Hugh	1,000	A	93	5-24-1780	Rowling Fk	
McElroy, Samuel	250	A	55	5-15-1780	Rolling Fk	
McElroy, Samuel	1,001½	B	24	12-10-1784	Green R	
McFall, John	892	A	28	4-27-1780	Licking	Mil
McFarland, John	1,000	A	343	3- 3-1784	————	Surveyed
McFarland, John	1,000	A	363	6- 2-1784	Muddy Cr	
McGaery, Hugh	400	A	18	3- 1-1780	Shawnee Run	Surveyed
McGaery, Hugh	400	A	18	3- 1-1780	Kentucky R	
McGaery, Hugh	400	A	1	11- 3-1779	Shawnee Spring	Surveyed
McGarry, Hugh	400	A	15	2-21-1780	Silver Cr	
McGarry, Hugh	1,000	A	27	4-26-1780	Shawnee Run	Surveyed
McGarry, Hugh	400	A	40	5- 9-1780	Rolling Fk	
McGee, David	400	A	10	2- 2-1780	Dewits Cr	
McGee, David	100	A	171	9-13-1780	Howards Cr	
McGee, David	1,000	A	171	9-13-1780	His Sett	Surveyed
McGee, Jacob	500	A	200	3-26-1781	Rowling Fk	
McGee, John	1,000	A	25	4-26-1780	Salt R	Surveyed
McGee, John	500	A	172	9-19-1780	Coxes Cr	
McGee, John	360	A	292	10- 3-1783	Salt R	Surveyed
McGee, John	1,600	A	327	1- 7-1784	Beargrass Cr	Withdrawn
McGee, John	800	A	376	8- 2-1784	Soverins Run	
McGee, John	1,000	A	376	8- 2-1784	Brashears Cr	Withdrawn
McGee, John	360	A	377	8-12-1784	————	
McGee, John	1,327⅓	B	8	9-22-1784	————	327½ acres surveyed
McGee, John	600	B	39	2- 4-1785	————	Withdrawn
McGee, Patrick	400	A	216	7-21-1781	Simpsons Cr	Surveyed
McGee, Patrick	250	A	218	8- 9-1781	Coxes Cr	
McGee, Patrick	250	A	218	8- 9-1781	Plumb Cr	
McGee, Patrick	500	A	303	11-12-1783	Salt R	
McGee, Thomas	450	A	53	5-13-1780	Salt R	Surveyed
McGee, Thomas	500	A	93	5-24-1780	Simpsons Cr	Withdrawn
McGee, Thomas	560	A	93	5-24-1780	Salt R	Surveyed
McGee, Thomas	1,500	A	154	6-28-1780	Willsons Cr	
McGee, Thomas	500	A	155	6-28-1780	Salt R	450 acres surveyed 50 acres withdrawn

Entree	Acres	Book	Page	Entry Date	Watercourse	Notes
McGee, Thomas	600	A	199	3–17–1781	Salt R	Surveyed
McGee, Thomas	200	A	200	3–26–1781	Coxes Cr	Surveyed
McGee, Thomas	200	A	211	6– 9–1781	Coxes Cr	Surveyed
McGee, Thomas	500	A	211	6– 9–1781	Coxes Cr	Surveyed
McGee, Thomas	500	A	211	6– 9–1781	6 Mile Simpson Cr.	Withdrawn
McGee, Thomas	50	A	218	8– 8–1781	Barren Run	
McGee, Thomas	1,000	A	244	12–26–1782	Willsons Cr	Surveyed
McGee, Thomas	500	A	245	12–28–1782	Coxes Cr	Surveyed
McGee, Thomas	400	A	247	1– 7–1783	Willsons Cr	
McGee, Thomas	1,000	A	252	1–10–1783	Gesses Cr	
McGee, Thomas	184	A	256	1–21–1783	Beech Fk	
McGee, Thomas	200	A	288	8–25–1783	Coxes Cr	Surveyed
McGee, Thomas	200	A	297	10–15–1783	Willsons Cr	Withdrawn
McGee, Thomas	410	A	329	1–14–1784	———	
McGee, Thomas	60	A	329	1–14–1784	———	
McGee, Thomas	500	A	329	1–14–1784	———	
McGee, Thomas	560	A	331	1–16–1784	———	
McGee, Thomas	700	A	331	1–16–1784	———	
McGee, Thomas	1,000	B	8	9–25–1784	Gesses Cr	Surveyed
McGee, Thomas	1,000	B	8	9–25–1784	Gesses Cr	Withdrawn
McGee, Thomas	400	B	43	4–11–1785	———	200 acres surveyed
McGee, Wm	400	A	10	2– 2–1780	Coopers Run	
McGee, Wm	500	A	171	9–13–1780	Rail Camp	
McGee, Wm	1,000	A	171	9–13–1780	Coopers Run	
McGee, Wm	50	A	205	4– 6–1781	Hardens Cr	Mil
McGehie, Samuel	400	A	181	10–23–1781	S Fk Licking	
McGehie, Wm	500	A	205	4– 6–1781	Hardens Cr	Mil
McGehie, Wm	300	A	97	5–25–1780	Robinsons Cr	
McGiffin, Nathan	550	A	291	9–30–1783	Middle Cr	
McGill, Wm	375	A	353	4–15–1784	Pitmans Cr	
McGinsay, John	500	A	129	6– 9–1780	Beech Fk	
McGruder, Alex	1,000	A	44	5–11–1780	Sunfish Run	Surveyed
McHann, James	500	A	137	6–19–1780	Dicks R	
McHann, James	500	A	328	1–12–1784	John & James Wood	
McHenny, John	400	A	102	5–27–1780	S Fk Licking	
McIntire, John	1,000	A	132	6–14–1780	S Fk Rowling	
McIntire, Nicholas	1,000	A	75	5–19–1780	Licking	
McIntire, Nicholas	1,000	A	75	5–19–1780	Licking	
McIntire, Richard	100	A	85	5–22–1780	Jessamine	
McJemcy, John	1,000	A	252	1–14–1783	Green R	
McKee, James	200	A	222	12–11–1782	Coxes Cr	Withdrawn
McKee, James	200	A	235	12–20–1782	Coxes Cr	Withdrawn
McKee, James	200	A	251	1–10–1783	Cartright Cr	
McKee, James	200	A	251	1–10–1783	Coxes Cr	
McKee, James	400	A	251	1–10–1783	Cartright Cr	
McKee, James	200	A	261	2– 4–1783	Cartright Cr	
McKee, James	200	A	261	2– 4–1783	Coxes Cr	
McKee, James	600	A	264	2–15–1783	Cartright Cr	400 acres withdrawn
McKee, James	400	A	290	9–10–1783	Cartright Cr	Withdrawn
McKee, John	327⅔	A	251	1– 9–1783	Salt R	Surveyed
McKee, John	600	A	251	1– 9–1783	Drennons Lick	
McKee, John	400	A	251	1– 9–1783	Drennons Lick	
McKee, Thomas	200	A	200	3–26–1781	Coxes Cr	Withdrawn
McKee, Thomas	500	A	217	8– 2–1781	Coxes Cr	Surveyed
McKee, Wm	200	A	70	5–18–1780	S Dicks R	
McKee, Wm	300	A	70	5–18–1780	E Fk Logan Run	
McKee, Wm	500	A	70	5–18–1780	Hanging Fk & Docherty	
McKee, Wm	500	A	72	5–19–1780	Sugar Cr	
McKee, Wm	300	A	72	5–19–1780	Dicks R	
McKee, Wm	500	A	72	5–18–1780	E Fk Gilberts Cr	
McKee, Wm	800	A	97	5–25–1780	Clear Cr	
McKee, Wm	800	A	97	5–25–1780	S Fk Clear Cr	Withdrawn
McKee, Wm	1,000	A	108	5–29–1780	Bensons Cr	
McKee, Wm	500	A	115	5–30–1780	Rail Camp	Withdrawn
McKee, Wm	400	A	181	10–23–1780	Licking Cr	
McKegg, James	400	A	341	2–26–1784	Plumb Run	
McKendric, John	200	A	35	4–29–1790	Rolling Fk	Mil
McKenny, Arch	400	A	13	2– 9–1780	Branch Green R	
McKenney, Arch	400	A	17	2–28–1780	Stoner Fk	
McKenzie, Mary	400	A	248	1– 7–1783	N Fk Floyds Fk	
McKey, Wm	1,000	A	222	12–11–1782	Ohio R	
McKey, Wm	300	A	223	12–12–1782	Ohio R	
McKinney, Archibald	1,000	A	100	5–26–1780	Stoners Fk	
McKinney, James	400	A	36	4–29–1780	Hanging Fk	
McKinnie, John	600	A	158	7– 3–1780	Rockcastle	
McKinzie, John	400	A	36	4–29–1780	Salt R	Withdrawn
McKinzie, Mordock	560	A	156	6–30–1780	Licking Cr	
McMahon, Rich	1,000	A	244	12–27–1782	Pond Cr	Surveyed
McMahon, Rich et al	1,000	A	244	12–27–1782	Flatt Lick	Surveyed

Entree	Acres	Book	Page	Entry Date	Watercourse	Notes
McManness, John.....	400	A	162	7–18–1780	His Improvement..	Surveyed
McManus, George.....	400	A	284	8– 4–1788	Little Kentucky R..	....
McManus, John........	400	A	284	8– 4–1783	....	....
McMullin, James......	400	A	11	2– 4–1780	Fk Hourards Cr...	....
McMullin, Robt.......	400	A	11	2– 4–1780	S Fk Hourards Cr..	....
McMullin, Robt.......	1,000	A	180	10–19–1780	Howards Cr........	....
McMullin, Sam.......	400	A	9	1–18–1780	S Fk Licking......	....
McMullin, Sam.......	1,000	A	37	4–29–1780	Hingston Fk.......	....
McMullin, Wm.......	400	A	11	2– 4–1780	Sinking Cr........	....
McMurtry, Joseph.....	100	A	35	4–29–1780	Dicks R...........	Withdrawn
McMurtry, Joseph.....	100	A	138	6–20–1780	Dicks R...........	....
McMurtry, Wm......	250	A	160	7– 6–1780	Jessamine Cr......	....
McMurry, John.......	1,000	A	144	6–23–1780	Rowling Fk........	....
McNeel, Peggy.......	1,000	A	146	6–24–1780	Clarks Run........	....
McNeeley, Michael....	250	A	121	6– 2–1780	Paint Lick Cr.....	....
McNeeley, Michael....	150	A	121	6– 2–1780	Paint Lick Cr.....	....
McNeil, Arch.........	500	A	59	5–16–1780	Kentucky R........	....
McNeil, Mary A......	400	A	162	7–18–1780	Rowling Fk........	....
McNeill, Peggy.......	400	A	6	12–24–1779	Clarks Run........	....
McQuarts, Henry......	500	A	180	10–21–1780	Clear Cr..........	Surveyed
McRoberts, Alex......	400	A	96	5–25–1780	————————	Withdrawn
McRoberts, Alex......	400	A	135	6–17–1780	Robinson Cr.......	....
McWilliams, Wm......	98,000	A	314	12– 9–1783	Barbour & Bank...	Surveyed
Machan, John........	400	A	12	2– 5–1780	Hingston Cr.......	....
Macker, John........	500	A	335	1–31–1784	Cane Run..........	Surveyed
Macher, John........	332	A	308	11–22–1783	Coxes Cr..........	Surveyed
Macher, John........	1,651	A	308	11–22–1783	Cane Cr...........	....
Mackie, John........	500	A	92	5–24–1780	Cain Run..........	Surveyed
Mackie, John........	500	A	92	5–24–1780	Coxes Cr..........	Surveyed
Mackie, John........	500	A	92	5–24–1780	Bullitts Lick......	Surveyed
Mackie, John........	500	A	92	5–24–1780	Willsons Cr.......	....
Machis, John........	500	A	356	4–27–1784	Coxes Cr..........	....
Machis, John........	500	A	356	4–27–1784	Wilsons Cr........	....
Madden, George......	400	A	37	4–29–1780	Licking...........	....
Maddox, David......	1,448¾	A	248	1– 7–1783	Sinking Cr........	Surveyed
Maddox, David......	602	A	248	1– 7–1783	Mid Fk Sinking Cr.	Surveyed
Maddox, David......	806½	A	248	1– 7–1783	Maple Swamp Cr...	....
Madison, Ambrose....	1,000	A	166	8–16–1780	Panther Cr........	Surveyed
Madison, Ambrose....	1,000	A	166	8–16–1780	Panther Cr........	Surveyed
Madison, Gabriel.....	2,000	B	39	2– 8–1785	————————	....
Madison, Gabriel.....	5,000	B	32	1– 8–1785	————————	2,400 acres surveyed
Madison, Gabriel.....	2,000	B	13	11–11–1784	————————	Withdrawn
Madison, Gabriel.....	400	B	13	11–11–1784	————————	Withdrawn
Madison, Gabriel.....	2,400	B	13	11–11–1784	Indian Camp Cr...	Surveyed
Madison, Gabriel.....	2,000	A	344	3– 3–1784	Green R...........	Withdrawn
Madison, Gabriel.....	2,000	A	35	4–29–1780	Ohio R............	Mil Surveyed
Madison, Gabriel.....	1,000	A	35	4–29–1780	Simpson Run......	Mil
Madison, Gabriel.....	4,000	A	229	12–16–1782	Rough Cr..........	....
Madison, Gabriel.....	2,000	A	240	12–24–1782	Muddy Run.......	....
Madison, Gabriel.....	2,000	A	305	11–19–1783	Green R...........	Withdrawn
Madison, Gabriel.....	2,000	A	305	11–19–1783	Green R...........	Withdrawn
Madison, Gabriel.....	2,000	A	308	11–24–1783	Bear Cr...........	....
Madison, Gabriel.....	500	A	311	12– 1–1783	Ohio R............	Withdrawn
Madison, Gabriel.....	1,000	A	313	12– 8–1783	————————	400 acres surveyed
Madison, Gabriel.....	2,000	A	332	1–20–1784	Harrods Cr........	....
Madison, Gabriel.....	500	A	332	1–20–1784	Ohio R............	....
Madison, Gabriel.....	2,000	A	344	3– 3–1784	————————	Withdrawn
Madison, James.....	8,000	A	40	5– 9–1780	Masons Tract......	Surveyed
Madison, James.....	2,000	A	40	5– 9–1780	Panther Cr........	Surveyed
Madison, James.....	1,250	A	43	5–11–1780	Salt R............	Withdrawn
Madison, James......	50	A	167	8–17–1780	Hargass Fk........	Mil
Madison, James......	50	A	167	8–17–1780	Hargass Fk........	Mil
Madison, James......	50	A	167	8–17–1780	Hargass Fk........	Mil
Madison, James......	200	A	167	8–11–1780	Hargass Fk........	Surveyed
Madison, James......	500	A	167	8–17–1780	Hargass Fk........	Surveyed
Madison, James......	200	A	167	8–17–1780	Hargass Fk........	Mil surveyed
Madison, James......	2,000	A	192	3–15–1781	Panther Cr........	....
Madison, James......	2,000	A	192	3–15–1781	Panther Cr........	Withdrawn
Madison, Rev James..	1,250	A	183	10–27–1780	Salt R...........	Surveyed
Madison, John.......	3,000	A	194	3–16–1781	Bullskin..........	Mil surveyed
Madison, Thomas....	200	A	29	4–27–1780	Cedar Run........	....
Madison, Thomas....	1,000	A	149	6–24–1780	Dicks R...........	....
Madison, Wm.......	1,000	A	112	5–30–1780	Fish Pool.........	Surveyed
Madison, Wm.......	2,000	A	194	3–16–1781	Bullskin..........	Surveyed
Madison, Wm.......	1,000	A	201	4– 2–1781	Ohio R............	Surveyed
Major, John.........	100	A	28	4–27–1780	Elkhorn...........	Mil
Major, John.........	1,000	A	49	5–12–1780	Elkhorn...........	....
Malcalf, Wm........	500	A	98	5–25–1780	N Fk Licking......	....
Mallary, Uriel.......	2,000	A	47	5–12–1780	Elkhorn...........	....
Mallary, Uriel........	3,000	A	40	5– 9–1780	Elkhorn...........	....

Entree	Acres	Book	Page	Entry Date	Watercourse	Notes
Mallory, Uriel	900	A	60	5-16-1780	Elkhorn	
Mallory, Roger	500	A	157	6-30-1780	Lulbrelgrud	
Man, Alexander	358	A	311	11-28-1783	Panther Cr	
Man, John	1,000	A	151	6-26-1780	Mid Fk Ky R	
Mann, Wm	200	A	171	9-13-1780	Kentucky R	
Manefee, Wm	400	A	4	11-25-1779	Dix R Cedar Cr	Surveyed
Maning, J H	500	A	340	2-21-1784	Harrods Cr	
Manning, Nath	500	A	52	5-13-1780	Harrods Cr	
Manion, James	984¾	A	352	4-13-1784	Green R	
Manson, Peter	1,500	A	41	5-10-1780	Hingston Fk	
Manson, Peter	1,089	A	186	10-31-1780	Hickmans Run	
Manson, Peter	1,000	A	214	7- 7-1781	Rowling Fk	Surveyed
March, John	465	A	43	5-11-1780	Stoners Fk	
Marks, Jas & B C	22,000	A	58	5-15-1780	Licking	
Marr, Alexander	1,000	A	167	8-17-1780	Panther Cr	
Marshall, Humphrey	1,000	A	235	12-20-1782	Coxes Cr	Surveyed
Marshall, Humphrey	500	A	235	12-20-1782	David Cox	Withdrawn
Marshall, Humphry	500	A	238	12-23-1782	Coxes Cr	Surveyed
Marshall, Humphrey	1,000	A	244	12-26-1782	Simpsons Cr	Surveyed
Marshall, Humphrey	1,000	A	244	12-26-1782	Salt R	Surveyed
Marshall, Humphry	500	A	254	1-16-1783	Coxes Cr	Withdrawn
Marshall, Humphry	500	A	254	1-16-1783	David Cox	
Marshall, Humphrey	1,000	A	256	1-21-1783	Plumb Cr	Surveyed
Marshall, Humphrey	1,000	A	256	1-21-1783	Coxes Cr	
Marshall, Humphrey	2,000	A	280	6-19-1783	Ky R	
Marshall, Humphry	3,000	A	280	6-19-1783	Ky R	
Marshall, Humphry	145	A	327	1- 8-1784	Salt R	Surveyed
Marshall, Humphry	355	A	327	1- 7-1784	Camp Run	Surveyed
Marshall, Humphry	180	A	363	6- 4-1784	Simpson Cr	
Marshall, Humphry	220	B	2	8-19-1784		220 acres surveyed
Marshall, John	15,000	A	133	6-15-1780	Upper Salt Lick	
Marshall, John	1,477	A	133	6-15-1780	N Fk Licking	
Marshall, John	500	A	250	1- 9-1783	Pattons	Surveyed
Marshall, John	280½	A	341	2-26-1784	Beech Fk	Withdrawn
Marshall, John	1,868	A	361	5-25-1784	Fittmans Cr	
Marshall, John	280½	B	4	9- 7-1784	Beech Fk	
Marshall, John	280½	B	4	9- 7-1784		Withdrawn
Marshall, John Jr	5,000	A	150	6-24-1780	N Fk Elkhorn	
Marshall, Thomas	1,000	A	132	6-14-1780	Floyds Fk	Withdrawn
Marshall, Thomas	1,000	A	132	6-14-1780	near Bullitts Lick	
Marshall, Thomas	10,500	A	133	6-15-1780	N Fk Licking	
Marshall, Thomas	2,400	A	141	6-21-1780	Hardens Cr	
Marshall, Thomas	2,150	A	143	6-22-1780	Gilberts Cr	
Marshall, Thomas	1,400	A	165	8-11-1780	Hardens Cr	Withdrawn
Marshall, Thomas	1,400	A	172	9-18-1780	Ohio R	Withdrawn
Marshall, Thomas	600	A	186	10-31-1780	Ohio R	
Marshall, Thomas	1,400	A	211	6- 5-1781	Ohio R	
Marshall, Thomas	1,000	A	221	10- 6-1781	Bullitts Lick	
Marshall, Thomas	1,000	A	221	10- 6-1781	Floyds Fk	Withdrawn
Marshall, Thomas	200	A	284	7- 4-1783		
Marshall, Thomas	1,205	A	317	12-16-1783	Hardens Cr	
Marshall, Wm	400	A	107	5-29-1780	Hingston Millseat Cr	
Marshall, Wm	1,000	A	250	1- 9-1783	Capt Patton	Surveyed
Marston, Joseph	500	A	239	12-23-1782	Cartrights Cr	
Marston, Thomas	500	A	239	12-23-1782	Beech Cr	
Martin, Alex	200	A	95	5-24-1780	James Estill	
Martin, Arch	1,000	A	37	4-29-1780	S Fk Licking	
Martin, Bruce	500	A	90	5-23-1780	Licking	Surveyed
Martin, Hudson	900	A	211	6- 5-1781	Nicholas Lewis	Surveyed
Martin, Hudson	100	A	211	5- 6-1781	Rowling Fk	156 acres withdrawn
Martin, Hudson	100	A	277	4-12-1783	Hardens Cr	Surveyed
Martin, Hudson	100	A	277	4-12-1783	Rowling Fk	
Martin, John	400	A	5	12- 8-1779	S Fk Licking Cr	
Martin, John	1,000	A	36	4-29-1780	Martin Settl	
Martin, John	1,418	A	54	5-15-1780	S Fk Licking	
Martin, John	333	A	54	5-15-1780		
Martin, John	666	A	54	5-15-1780		
Martin, John	583	A	54	5-15-1780	Licking	
Martin, John	100	A	87	5-23-1780	Ohio R	Withdrawn
Martin, John	1,000	A	103	5-27-1780	S Fk Licking	
Martin, John	20	A	116	5-31-1780	Green R	
Martin, John	1,333½	A	129	6-10-1780	Hustons Cr	Withdrawn
Martin, John	1,333½	A	160	7- 6-1780	Hustons Fk	
Martin, John	4,000	A	242	12-25-1782	Green R	
Martin, John	500	A	242	12-25-1782	Brashears Cr	
Martin, John	2,000	A	242	12-25-1782	Breashears Cr	
Martin, John	1,000	A	242	12-25-1782	Plumb Cr	Surveyed
Martin, John	500	A	244	12-27-1782	Green R	
Martin, John	792½	A	356	4-24-1784	Green R	Withdrawn
Martin, John	192½	A	365	6-16-1784	Green R	

Entree	Acres	Book	Page	Entry Date	Watercourse	Notes
Martin, John	3,000	A	365	6–16–1784	Green R	
Martin, John	3,000	A	365	6–16–1784	Green R	
Martin, John	7,921½	A	365	6–16–1784		
Martin, John et al	400	A	87	5–22–1780	S Fk Beargrass	Withdrawn
Martin, John et al	400	A	247	1– 6–1783	Ky R	Surveyed
Martin, John et al	400	A	246	1– 6–1783	Ky R	Surveyed
Martin, Jonathan	400	A	5	12– 7–1779	4 Mile Cr	Surveyed
Martin, Jonathan	400	A	96	5–24–1780	Floyds Fk	Surveyed
Martin, Jonathan	1,000	A	120	6– 1–1780	Boons Cr	
Martin, Joseph	1,000	A	27	4–26–1780	Hanging Fk	
Martin, Mary	400	A	333	1–20–1780	Cartrights Cr	
Martin, Rawleigh	400	A	151	6–26–1780	Nolin Cr	
Martin, Samuel	334	A	173	9–20–1780	Beech Fk	
Martin, Thomas	500	A	96	5–24–1780	Floyds Fk	
Martin, Thomas	354½	A	244	12–27–1782	Coxes Cr	
Martin, Thomas	910	A	348	3–22–1784	Green R	Withdrawn
Martin, Thomas	910	A	374	7–27–1784	Green R	Withdrawn
Martin, Thomas et al		A	374	7–27–1784		
Mason, George	2,200	A	6	12–23–1779	Licking Cr	Withdrawn
Mason, George	2,200	A	6	12–22–1779	Licking Cr	Withdrawn
Mason, George	2,000	A	6	12–22–1779	Licking Cr	Withdrawn
Mason, George	4,500	A	6	12–22–1779	Licking Cr	Withdrawn
Mason, George	8,100	A	6	12–22–1779	Licking Cr	Withdrawn
Mason, George	8,200	A	6	12–22–1779	Licking Cr	Wirhdrawn
Mason, George	8,300	A	6	12–22–1779	Licking Cr	Withdrawn
Mason, George	8,400	A	6	12–22–1779	Licking Cr	Withdrawn
Mason, George	8,000	A	6	12–22–1779	Licking Cr	Withdrawn
Mason, George	4,000	A	5	12–22–1779	Licking Cr	Withdrawn
Mason, George	37,000	A	34	4–29–1780	Panther & Green	10 entries surveyed
Mason, George	400	A	84	5–22–1780	Buck Lick Cr	
Mason, George	8,200	A	183	10–27–1780	Panther Cr	Surveyed
Mason, George	8,400	A	183	10–27–1780	Panther Cr	Surveyed
Mason, George	2,000	A	230	12–17–1782	Green R	
Mason, Jas	400	A	3	11–11–1779	Dicks R	
Mason, John	400	A	84	5–22–1780	Buck Lick Cr	
Mason, Micajale	400	A	84	5–22–1780	Buck Lick Cr	
Mason, Richard	45,456½	A	330	1–14–1784	Ky R	Withdrawn
Mason, Richard	45,456	B	46	5–19–1785	Ky R	Withdrawn
Mason, Thomas	800	A	185	10–31–1780	Beech Fk	Surveyed
Massie, Nath	1,000	A	59	5–16–1780	Ky R	Mil
Massey, Nath	200	A	157	7– 3–1780	Indian Cr	Mil
Massey, Reuben	200	A	92	5–24–1780	Licking	
Masterson, Richard	200	A	278	4–14–1783	Pittmans Cr	
Masterson, Thomas	1,000	A	140	6–21–1780	Clover Lick Run	Withdrawn
Masterson, Thomas	400	A	347	3–17–1784	Beech Fk	
Mathews, Archer	5,000	A	228	12–14–1782	Sinking Cr	Surveyed
Mathews, Sampson	3,000	A	226	12–13–1782	Rough Cr	Surveyed
Mathews, Sampson	2,000	A	226	12–13–1782	Clear Cr	Surveyed
Matthew, Archer	1,000	A	228	12–16–1782	Green R	
Matthew, Sampson	3,000	A	328	1– 9–1784	Simpson Cr	
Matthew, Sampson	1,600	B	41	3– 4–1785	Floyds Fk	
Matthew, Sampson	1,600	B	41	3– 4–1785		Withdrawn
Matthew, Sampson	3,083	B	42	3– 4–1785		1,483 acres surveyed
Matthew, Sarah	750	A	268	3–28–1783	Robinsons Cr	Surveyed
Matthew, Wm	1,128	A	315	12–13–1783	John Harvie	
Matthews, Anne	750	A	267	3–28–1783	Robinsons Cr	
Matthews, Sampson	7,770½	A	242	12–25–1782	Caney Cr	6,170 acres surveyed 1,600 acres withdrawn
Matson, James	1,200	A	58	5–16–1780	Licking	
Manlin, Jacob	1,029	A	367	6–22–1784	Rough Cr	
Maulin, Jacob	1,000	A	368	6–22–1784		
Maury, Abraham et al	1,400	A	287	8–13–1783	Floyds Fk	
Maury, George	1,000	A	227	12–14–1782	Ohio R	
Maxey, Wm	500	A	80	5–20–1780	Drakes Camp Cr	
Mazwell, Bazaleal	100	A	24	4–25–1780	Silver Cr	Mil
Maxwell, Bazaleal	100	A	24	4–25–1780	Silver Cr	
Maxwell, Bazaleal	200	A	97	5–25–1780	Elkhorn	
Maxwell, David	200	A	97	5–25–1780	Paint Lick	
Maxwell, John	200	A	97	5–25–1780	Paint Lick Cr	
May, Abner	350	A	28	4–27–1780	Rolling Fk	Mil
May, Abner	700	A	116	5–30–1780	Rowling Fk	
May, David	500	A	76	5–20–1780	Clear Cr	Withdrawn
May, David	500	A	76	5–20–1780	Salt R	Withdrawn
May, David	500	A	186	10–31–1780	Salt R	
May, David	500	A	192	3–15–1781	Floyds Fk	Withdrawn
May, David	500	A	217	8– 2–1781	Simpsons Cr	Surveyed
May, David	500	A	217	8– 2–1781	Brashears Cr	

Entree	Acres	Book	Page	Entry Date	Watercourse	Notes
May, David	500	A	245	12–28–1782	Salt R	450 acres withdrawn
May, David	450	A	259	2– 1–1783	Simpsons Cr	Withdrawn
May, David	450	A	259	2– 1–1783	Simpson Cr	
May, David	450	A	266	2–26–1783	——	
May, David	500	A	278	4–14–1783	Simpsons Cr	Surveyed
May, Gabriel	350	A	25	4–25–1780	Pine Lick Cr	
May, Gabriel	350	A	28	4–27–1780	Rolling Fk	Mil
May, Gabriel	900	A	129	6– 9–1780	Licking	
May, George	600	A	221	9– 7–1781	——	Returned
May, George	15,331	B	37	1–28–1785	Otter Cr	
May, George	15,331	B	37	1–28–1785	Rough Cr	Withdrawn
May, George	1,000	B	37	1–28–1785	Green R	
May, George	300	B	39	2– 8–1785	——	
May, George	10,000	B	39	2– 8–1785	——	7,000 acres surveyed returned
May, Humphry	1,000	A	269	3–28–1783	Beech Fk	
May, James	400	A	121	6– 2–1780	Lexington	
May, James	534	A	252	1–10–1782	Rolling Fk	Surveyed
May, John	50	A	6	12–28–1779	Hunting Path	Withdrawn
May, John	1,950	A	9	2– 2–1780	Ohio Yellowbanks	Mil 1,763
May, John	15	A	11	2– 3–1780	Otter Cr	Withdrawn
May, John	400	A	16	2–23–1780	Falls Ohio R	Withdrawn
May, John	5	A	17	2–28–1780	Ohio R	
May, John	1,000	A	19	4–13–1780	Green R	Mil withdrawn
May, John	2,000	A	19	4–13–1780	Green R	Mil withdrawn
May, John	4,000	A	19	4–13–1780	Green R	Mil withdrawn
May, John	1,000	A	19	4–13–1780	Green R	Mil withdrawn
May, John	1,000	A	19	4–13–1780	Green R	Mil withdrawn
May, John	1,000	A	19	4–13–1780	Indian Camp Cr	Withdrawn
May, John	1,000	A	19	4–13–1780	Fish Pools	
May, John	1,000	A	19	4–13–1780	Ohio R	Mil withdrawn
May, John	2,000	A	19	4–13–1780	Brashears Cr	Mil surveyed
May, John	500	A	19	4–13–1780	Limestone Run	Mil
May, John	800	A	19	4–13–1780	Limestone Run	
May, John	750	A	20	4–14–1780	Fern Cr	Surveyed
May, John	2,000	A	20	4–14–1780	Green R	Withdrawn
May, John	4,500	A	20	4–13–1780	Ohio R	Mil
May, John	200	A	21	4–20–1780	Cumberland Ford	Withdrawn
May, John	200	A	21	4–18–1780	Dicks R	Withdrawn
May, John	200	A	22	4–24–1780	Cumberland R	Withdrawn
May, John	2,000	A	23	4–24–1780	Ohio R	Withdrawn
May, John	5,000	A	23	4–24–1780	Cabbin Cr	Withdrawn
May, John	3,000	A	23	4–24–1780	Ohio R	Withdrawn
May, John	3,000	A	23	4–24–1780	Ohio R	Withdrawn
May, John	3,000	A	23	4–24–1780	Ohio R	Withdrawn
May, John	3,000	A	23	4–24–1780	Ohio R	Mil
May, John	350	A	24	4–25–1780	Harrods Cr	Surveyed
May, John	200	A	24	4–25–1780	Harrods Cr	Withdrawn
May, John	400	A	24	4–25–1780	Harrods Cr	Mil withdrawn
May, John	5,000	A	25	4–25–1780	Ohio R	Withdrawn
May, John	1,000	A	25	4–25–1780	Ohio R	
May, John	100	A	25	4–25–1780	Otter Cr	Mil
May, John	100	A	29	4–27–1780	Flat Lick	Mil surveyed
May, John	2,000	A	30	4–28–1780	French Cr	
May, John	100	A	30	4–28–1780	Harrods Cr	Withdrawn
May, John	2,000	A	32	4–28–1780	Ohio R	Withdrawn
May, John	50	A	32	4–29–1780	Buffaloe Lick	
May, John	200	A	32	4–28–1780	Ohio	Withdrawn
May, John	245	A	38	4–29–1780	Ohio	
May, John	5	A	38	4–29–1780	Hunters Path	
May, John	200	A	38	4–29–1780	Ohio R	
May, John	50	A	38	4–29–1780	Ohio R	Mil
May, John	300	A	41	5–10–1780	Ohio R	
May, John	60	A	41	5–10–1780	Diamond Island	
May, John	500	A	41	5–10–1780	Ohio & Wabash R	
May, John	500	A	41	5–10–1780	Ohio & Cumb R	Withdrawn
May, John	500	A	41	5–10–1780	Ohio & Wabash R	
May, John	640	A	42	5–10–1780	Fern Cr	
May, John	1,500	A	42	5–10–1780	Ohio R	
May, John	3,000	A	42	5–10–1780	Ohio R	
May, John	3,000	A	42	5–10–1780	Otter Cr	

Entree	Acres	Book	Page	Entry Date	Watercourse	Notes
May, John	100	A	49	5–12–1780	Ohio R	Withdrawn
May, John	2,000	A	52	5–13–1780	Salt R	....
May, John	2,000	A	52	5–13–1780	Salt R	Withdrawn
May, John	2,000	A	52	5–13–1780	Drenings Lick	....
May, John	2,000	A	52	5–13–1780	Salt R	Surveyed
May, John	2,000	A	52	5–13–1780	Fern Cr	....
May, John	5,000	A	58	5–15–1780	French Cr	....
May, John	5,000	A	58	5–15–1780	Otter Cr	....
May, John	2,000	A	58	5–15–1780	Salt R	Withdrawn
May, John	10,000	A	61	5–16–1780	bet Green & Ohio R	....
May, John	8,000	A	68	5–17–1780	Ohio R	....
May, John	2,500	A	77	5–20–1780	Eagle Cr	....
May, John	500	A	80	5–20–1780	Ky R	....
May, John	400	A	81	5–22–1780	N Fk Beargrass	Withdrawn
May, John	4	A	87	5–23–1780	Ky R	Withdrawn
May, John	7	A	87	5–23–1780	Ky R	....
May, John	4	A	87	5–23–1780	Station Camp Cr	Withdrawn
May, John	800	A	103	5–27–1780	Salt R	Withdrawn
May, John	100	A	113	5–30–1780	Beech Fk Salt R	....
May, John	200	A	116	5–31–1780	Salt Spring Cr	....
May, John	1,000	A	116	5–31–1780	Green R	....
May, John	1,000	A	117	5–31–1780	Sinking Cr	Withdrawn
May, John	3,000	A	119	6– 1–1780	Ohio R	....
May, John	2,000	A	119	6– 1–1780	Ohio R	Withdrawn
May, John	2,000	A	124	6– 3–1780	Ohio R	Withdrawn
May, John	1,000	A	124	6– 3–1780	Ohio R	Mil withdrawn
May, John	100	A	125	6– 5–1780	Ky R	Mil
May, John	50	A	125	6– 3–1780	Beargrass Cr	....
May, John	2,000	A	125	6– 3–1780	Ohio R	Mil
May, John	360	A	128	6– 8–1780	Salt R	Mil withdrawn
May, John	200	A	129	6– 9–1780	Rowling Fk	Withdrawn
May, John	200	A	129	6– 9–1780	Ky R	Withdrawn
May, John	2,000	A	131	6–13–1780	Ohio R	Withdrawn
May, John	3,000	A	131	6–13–1780	Ohio R	Withdrawn
May, John	200	A	131	6–12–1780	Salt R	Withdrawn
May, John	200	A	131	6–12–1780	Ohio R	Withdrawn
May, John	1,000	A	143	6–23–1780	Fishpool Cr	Withdrawn
May, John	400	A	148	6–24–1780	Elkhorn	....
May, John	400	A	148	6–24–1780	Clear Cr	....
May, John	400	A	148	6–24–1780	Dry Run	....
May, John	400	A	148	6–24–1780	N Fk Elkhorn	....
May, John	100	A	156	6–30–1780	Pond Cr	Withdrawn
May, John	400	A	161	7–14–1780	Harrods Cr	....
May, John	1,000	A	161	7–14–1780	Harrods Cr	....
May, John	200	A	162	7–18–1780	Ohio R	Withdrawn
May, John	200	A	162	7–18–1780	Ohio R	Withdrawn
May, John	200	A	163	7–22–1780	Ohio R	Withdrawn
May, John	2,000	A	164	8–11–1780	Mrs Byrd	....
May, John	5,000	A	164	8–11–1780	Ohio R	Withdrawn
May, John	5,000	A	164	8–11–1780	Cabbin Cr	Withdrawn
May, John	3,000	A	164	8–11–1780	Ohio R	....
May, John	1,000	A	164	8–11–1780	Green R	Withdrawn
May, John	2,000	A	164	8–11–1780	Green R	....
May, John	2,000	A	164	8–11–1780	Ohio R	Withdrawn
May, John	5,000	A	164	8–11–1780	Beach Fk	Surveyed
May, John	450	A	164	8–11–1780	Ohio R	Withdrawn
May, John	50	A	164	8–11–1780	3rd Island Ohio	....
May, John	500	A	164	8–11–1780	Falls Bullitts Lick	....
May, John	12,000	A	165	8–11–1780	Pond Cr	Withdrawn
May, John	400	A	165	8–11–1780	Ky R	....
May, John	800	A	165	8–29–1780	Bullitts Lick	Withdrawn
May, John	100	A	165	8–11–1780	Ohio R	....
May, John	100	A	165	8–11–1780	Ohio R	Withdrawn
May, John	5,000	A	165	8–11–1780	Green R	....
May, John	3,000	A	166	8–11–1780	Green R	2,000 acres surveyed
May, John	400	A	168	8–29–1780	Ky R	Withdrawn
May, John	400	A	168	8–22–1780	S Fk Cedar Cr	....
May, John	100	A	168	8–22–1780	Ohio R	Mil
May, John	100	A	171	9–14–1780	Otter Cr	....
May, John	50	A	173	9–22–1780	Beech Fk	Withdrawn
May, John	200	A	173	9–21–1780	Shawney Run	Mil
May, John	200	A	176	10– 9–1780	Shawnee Run	....
May, John	1,000	A	177	10– 9–1780	Hingston Fk	....
May, John	500	A	177	10– 9–1780	Beech Fk	Twice entered
May, John	2,000	A	177	10– 9–1780	Otter Cr	Surveyed
May, John	7,000	A	177	10– 9–1780	Otter Cr	Withdrawn
May, John	1,000	A	178	10–10–1780	Fish Pool Cr	....
May, John	200	A	179	10–19–1780	Harrods Cr	....
May, John	600	A	179	10–19–1780	Beargrass Cr	Withdrawn

Entree	Acres	Book	Page	Entry Date	Watercourse	Notes
May, John	400	A	186	10–31–1780	Ky R.	
May, John	5,000	A	187	3–15–1781	Floyds Fk.	Surveyed
May, John	5,000	A	187	3–15–1781	Jacob Myers	
May, John	100	A	187	3–15–1781	Salt Lick	Withdrawn
May, John	200	A	188	3–15–1781	Otter Cr.	
May, John	400	A	188	3–15–1781	Salt R.	
May, John	150	A	188	3–15–1781	Pond Cr.	
May, John	400	A	188	3–15–1781	Flat Lick	
May, John	500	A	188	3–15–1781	Floyds Fk.	
May, John	2,000	A	188	3–15–1781	Ohio R.	
May, John	50	A	188	3–15–1781	Otter Cr.	
May, John	200	A	191	3–15–1781	Floyds Fk.	
May, John	500	A	191	3–15–1781	Ohio R.	
May, John	450	A	191	3–15–1781	Ohio R.	
May, John	500	A	191	3–15–1781	Floyds Fk.	
May, John	200	A	200	3–26–1781	Salt R.	Withdrawn
May, John	500	A	200	3–29–1781	Rowling Fk.	
May, John	1,000	A	201	4– 2–1781	Stewart Cr.	
May, John	300	A	201	4– 2–1781	Ohio R.	
May, John	6,000	A	202	4– 2–1781	Ohio R.	
May, John	3,000	A	202	4– 2–1781	Ohio R.	
May, John	3,000	A	202	4– 2–1781	Fern Cr.	
May, John	50	A	202	4– 2–1781	Fern Cr.	
May, John	12,000	A	202	4– 2–1781	Ohio R.	
May, John	1,000	A	202	4– 2–1781	1st Cr Yellow Banks	
May, John	300	A	205	4– 6–1781	Drennons Lick	Withdrawn
May, John	200	A	205	4– 6–1781	Ky R.	Withdrawn
May, John	10,000	A	207	4–16–1781	Samuel Beall	
May, John	300	A	208	5– 1–1781	Bear Cr.	
May, John	200	A	211	6– 5–1781	Coxes Cr.	
May, John	500	A	212	6–21–1781	Rowling Fk.	
May, John	160	A	212	6–15–1781	Floyds Fk.	
May, John	308	A	212	6–15–1781	Ohio R.	
May, John	160	A	212	6–15–1781	Salt R.	Withdrawn
May, John	100	A	214	7–12–1781	Long Lick Cr.	Surveyed
May, John	200	A	215	7–19–1781	Long Lick Cr.	
May, John	200	A	215	7–19–1781	Drennons Cr.	
May, John	200	A	215	7–12–1781	Beech Fk.	
May, John	300	A	215	7–12–1781	Otter Cr.	Withdrawn
May, John	200	A	217	8– 2–1781	Beech Fk.	
May, John	400	A	218	8– 8–1781	Ohio R.	Surveyed
May, John	400	A	218	8– 8–1781	Sinking Sp.	
May, John	300	A	220	8–29–1781	Long Lick Cr.	Surveyed
May, John	200	A	220	8–29–1781	Long Lick Cr.	
May, John	300	A	220	8–24–1781	Otter Cr.	
May, John	300	A	220	8–24–1781	Beech Fk.	
May, John	1,000	A	221	9– 7–1781	Fox Run	Surveyed
May, John	1,000	A	221	9– 7–1781	Brashears Cr.	
May, John	1,000	A	221	9– 7–1781	Brashears Cr.	
May, John	1,000	A	221	9– 7–1781	Floyds Fk.	
May, John	400	A	221	9– 7–1781	Beargrass Cr.	Surveyed
May, John	1,000	A	221	9– 7–1781	Hardens Cr.	Surveyed
May, John	3,500	A	222	12–11–1781	Harrods Cr.	Surveyed
May, John	2,200	A	222	12–11–1782	Brashears Cr.	Surveyed
May, John	100	A	230	12–17–1782	Salt R.	
May, John	300	A	230	12–17–1782	Brashears Cr.	Surveyed
May, John	450	A	230	12–17–1782	Ohio R.	Surveyed
May, John	300	A	230	12–17–1782	Long Lick Cr.	
May, John	200	A	230	12–17–1782	Salt R.	
May, John	1,000	A	230	12–17–1782	Otter Cr.	
May, John	400	A	231	12–17–1782	2nd Falls Rough Cr	
May, John	500	A	231	12–17–1782	Rough Cr.	
May, John	100	A	231	12–17–1782	Rough Cr.	Surveyed
May, John	4,000	A	233	12–18–1782	Ohio R.	
May, John	3,000	A	233	12–18–1782	Ohio R.	400 acres surveyed
May, John	3,129	A	234	12–19–1782	Ohio R.	Surveyed 200 acres withdrawn
May, John	5,533	A	234	12–19–1782	Ohio R.	Surveyed
May, John	11,533	A	234	12–19–1782	Ohio R.	
May, John	200	A	235	12–20–1782	Ohio R.	
May, John	500	A	237	12–21–1782	Drennons Lick	
May, John	3,000	A	237	12–21–1782	Ky R.	Surveyed
May, John	1,000	A	238	12–23–1782	Rolling Fk.	
May, John	1,000	A	238	12–23–1782	Rowling Fk.	
May, John	400	A	243	12–25–1782	Rowling Fk.	
May, John	500	A	243	12–25–1782	Beach Fk.	Withdrawn
May, John	2,500	A	243	12–25–1782	Green R.	
May, John	100	A	244	12–27–1782	Salt R.	Withdrawn
May, John	100	A	245	12–28–1782	Beech Fk.	Withdrawn
May, John	1,000	A	247	1– 6–1783	McCawley Sett.	

Entree	Acres	Book	Page	Entry Date	Watercourse	Notes
May, John	1,000	A	251	1- 9-1783	Pleasant R	
May, John	200	A	252	1-10-1782	Stewarts Cr	
May, John	2,000	A	253	1-15-1783	Goose Cr	Withdrawn
May, John	4,000	A	253	1-15-1783	Goose Cr	Withdrawn
May, John	206	A	253	1-15-1783	Otter Cr	
May, John	2,000	A	253	1-15-1783	Goose Cr	Withdrawn
May, John	4,000	A	253	1-15-1783	Goose Cr	Withdrawn
May, John	206	A	253	1-15-1783	Otter Cr	
May, John	500	A	254	1-15-1783	Ky R	Surveyed
May, John	500	A	255	1-20-1783	Cox Cr	Withdrawn
May, John	1,000	A	255	1-20-1783	Rolling Fk	
May, John	1,109½	A	258	1-27-1783	Beech Fk	890 acres surveyed
May, John	400	A	258	1-27-1783	Coxes Cr	
May, John	400	A	258	1-27-1783	Coxes Cr	
May, John	500	A	258	1-27-1783	Cedar Cr	Surveyed
May, John	600	A	258	1-27-1783	Coxes Cr	
May, John	600	A	258	1-27-1783	Beech Fk	
May, John	500	A	261	2-10-1783	Coxes Cr	
May, John	700	A	261	2- 4-1783	Salt R	Surveyed
May, John	300	A	261	2- 4-1783	Salt R	Surveyed
May, John	1,000	A	261	2- 4-1783	Rolling Fk	
May, John	1,000	A	261	2- 4-1783	Ohio R	Surveyed
May, John	1,000	A	261	2- 4-1783	Simpsons Cr	Withdrawn
May, John	5,000	A	261	2- 4-1783	Little Ky R	Surveyed
May, John	2,000	A	262	2-14-1783	Goose Cr	
May, John	4,000	A	262	2-14-1783	Goose Cr	Withdrawn
May, John	1,000	A	264	2-15-1783	Clear Cr	Withdrawn
May, John	400	A	264	2-15-1783	Rolling Fk	
May, John	2,000	A	264	2-15-1783	Cane Run	
May, John	1,081	A	264	2-15-1783	Ohio R	
May, John	500	A	264	2-15-1783	Rolling Fk	
May, John	200	A	264	2-15-1783	Beech Fk	
May, John	738½	A	265	2-19-1783	Coxes Cr	
May, John	500	A	266	2-26-1783	Caney Run	
May, John	500	A	266	2-26-1783	Youngers Cr	
May, John	1,000	A	266	2-26-1783	Gesses Cr	Withdrawn
May, John	6,000	A	270	3-28-1783	Beech Cr	
May, John	5,000	A	274	4- 8-1783	French Cr	
May, John	4,041	A	276	4-10-1783	————	
May, John	10,000	A	276	4-10-1783	Drennons Lick Cr	Withdrawn
May, John	5,000	A	277	4-14-1783	Green R	
May, John	5,000	A	277	4-14-1783	Salt R	
May, John	1,000	A	277	4-14-1783	Ohio R	
May, John	300	A	277	4-14-1783	Ohio R	Withdrawn
May, John	400	A	277	4-13-1783	Mouth Wabash R	Withdrawn
May, John	500	A	277	4-13-1783	Cumberland R	Withdrawn
May, John	450	A	278	4-14-1783	————	Surveyed
May, John	5,000	A	278	4-14-1783	————	500 acres surveyed
May, John	2,020	A	285	8- 7-1783	Cartright Cr	
May, John	2,020	A	291	9-11-1783	Cartright Cr	Amendment
May, John	1,235	A	297	10-18-1783	Beech Fk	
May, John	450	A	323	12-26-1783	Ohio R	Amended
May, John	2,000	A	325	12-29-1783	Caney Cr	
May, John	1,990	A	339	2-16-1784	Caney Cr	Surveyed
May, John	14,200	A	340	2-17-1784	Reedy Cr	Surveyed amended
May, John	1,000	A	361	5-25-1784	————	
May, John	1,990	A	362	5-31-1784	————	Surveyed
May, John	1,000	B	19	11-25-1784	Bullitts Lick	Amended
May, John	100	B	27	12-17-1784	————	
May, John	1,000	B	39	2- 8-1785	————	
May, John	2,534	B	39	2- 8-1785	————	534 acres surveyed returned
May, John	1,000	B	40	2- 8-1785	————	Surveyed
May, John	200	B	46	5-19-1785	————	
May, John et al	50	A	2	11- 6-1779	Licking Cr	Withdrawn
May, John et al	50	A	2	11- 6-1779	Licking Cr	Withdrawn
May, John et al	10	A	13	2-12-1780	Limestone Run	
May, John et al, heirs	400	A	148	6-24-1780	Buck Lick Cr	
May, John et al	1,000	A	221	9- 7-1781	Coxes Cr	Surveyed
May, John et al	1,000	A	221	9- 7-1781	Coxes Cr	No warrant
May, John et al	1,000	A	221	9- 7-1781	Hardens Cr	Surveyed
May, John et al	1,000	A	221	9- 7-1781	Rowling Fk	
May, John et al	1,500	A	222	12-11-1782	Ashes Cr	Surveyed
May, John et al	400	A	238	12-23-1782	Rolling Fk	Surveyed
May, John et al	1,000	A	238	12-23-1782	Pottinger Cr	
May, John et al	160,000	A	267	3-28-1783	Green and Ohio R	41,178 acres withdrawn
May, John et al	3,000	A	267	3-28-1783	Ohio R	Withdrawn

Entree	Acres	Book	Page	Entry Date	Watercourse	Notes
May, John et al	10,000	A	267	3-28-1783	Clover Lick Cr	Surveyed
May, John et al	5,000	A	267	3-28-1783	Ohio R	Withdrawn
May, John et al	5,000	A	267	3-28-1783	Ohio R	
May, John et al	40,000	A	267	3-28-1783	Green R	
May, John et al	500	A	272	4- 7-1783	Reedy Cr	Withdrawn
May, John et al	500	A	272	4- 7-1783	Caney & Little Reedy Cr	
May, John et al	2,000	A	272	4- 7-1783	Caney & Little Reedy Cr	Surveyed
May, John et al	2,000	A	272	4- 7-1783	Caney & Little Reedy Cr	Surveyed
May, John et al	6,000	A	272	4- 7-1783	Green R	Surveyed
May, John et al	3,567	A	273	4- 7-1783	Bear Cr	Surveyed
May, John et al	6,000	A	273	4- 7-1783	Green R	Surveyed
May, John et al	500	A	273	4- 7-1783	Reedy Cr	Withdrawn
May, John et al	1,000	A	273	4- 7-1783	Caney Cr	Surveyed
May, John et al	600	A	273	4- 7-1783	Reedy Cr	Withdrawn
May, John et al	1,000	A	273	4- 7-1783	Reedy Cr	Withdrawn
May, John et al	500	A	273	4- 7-1783	Reedy Cr	Withdrawn
May, John et al	15,000	A	274	4- 9-1783	Little Ky R	Surveyed
May, John et al	5,000	A	274	4- 9-1783	Ohio R	Withdrawn
May, John et al	3,000	A	274	4- 8-1783	Ohio R	
May, John et al	2,933	A	274	4- 8-1783	Rough Cr	
May, John et al	2,000	A	274	4- 8-1783	Bennitts Cr	Withdrawn
May, John et al	1,000	A	275	4-10-1783	Little Clifty Cr	Surveyed
May, John et al	2,000	A	275	4- 9-1783	In Barrens	Surveyed
May, John et al	4,000	A	275	4- 9-1783	Ohio R	
May, John et al	2,000	A	276	4-10-1783	Otter Cr	
May, John et al	40,000	A	276	4-10-1783	Little Ky R	Surveyed
May, John et al	10,000	A	277	4-14-1783	Salt R	Surveyed
May, John et al	60,000	A	277	4-14-1783	Green & Ohio R	Amendment
May, John et al	10,000	A	278	4-14-1783	Wolf Cr	
May, John et al	400	A	278	4-14-1783	Nolin Cr	
May, John et al	1,000	A	278	4-14-1783	Nolin Cr	
May, John et al	1,000	A	278	4-14-1783	Nolin Cr	
May, John et al	5,000	A	278	4-14-1783	Ohio R	
May, John et al	8,000	A	278	4-14-1783	Salt R	
May, John et al	2,600	A	278	4-14-1783	Wolf Cr	
May, John et al	4,800	A	279	6- 7-1783	Green & Ohio R	18,396 acres
May, John et al	500	A	281	7- 1-1783	Nolin Cr	Surveyed
May, John et al	500	A	281	7- 1-1783	Nolin Cr	Surveyed
May, John et al	1,000	A	281	7- 1-1783	Nolin Cr	Surveyed
May, John et al	10,000	A	281	7- 1-1783	Dunnings Cr	
May, John et al	2,000	A	282	7- 2-1783	Rock Cr	
May, John et al	700	A	282	7- 1-1783	Nolin Cr	
May, John et al	800	A	282	7- 1-1783	Nolin & Barren	Surveyed
May, John et al	2,000	A	282	7- 1-1783	Nolin & Barren	Surveyed
May, John et al	2,500	A	282	7- 1-1783	Nolin & Barren	Surveyed
May, John et al	500	A	286	8- 9-1783	Caney Cr	Surveyed
May, John et al	500	A	286	8- 9-1783	Caney Cr	Surveyed
May, John et al	9,000	A	286	8- 9-1783	Caney Cr	Surveyed
May, John et al	1,000	A	286	8- 9-1783	Caney Cr	Surveyed
May, John et al	12,000	A	286	8- 9-1783	Ohio R	Withdrawn
May, John et al	500	A	303	11-11-1783	Nole Linn Cr	
May, John et al	300	A	303	11-11-1783	—	
May, John et al	300	A	303	11-11-1783	Rowling Fk	
May, John et al	1,000	A	303	11-11-1783	Nole Linn Cr	
May, John et al	1,000	A	303	11-11-1783	Belleys Cr	Surveyed
May, John et al	1,000	A	303	11-11-1783	Nole Linn Cr	
May, John et al	1,500	A	303	11-11-1783	Rough Cr	
May, John et al	14,200	A	304	11-14-1783	Big Reedy Cr	Surveyed
May, John et al	1,000	A	305	11-17-1783	Reedy Run	Amended
May, John et al	2,000	A	325	12-31-1783	Clear Fk	Withdrawn
May, John et al	8,000	A	325	12-29-1783	Beaver Dam Fk	4,000 acres withdrawn
May, John et al	1,000	A	328	1-12-1784	Falls Ohio R	
May, John et al	7,000	A	329	1-13-1784	Green R	Withdrawn
May, John et al	4,000	A	329	1-13-1784	Joseph Burnett	
May, John et al	11,658	A	329	1-13-1784	Green R	Surveyed
May, John et al	1,460	A	329	1-13-1784	Green R	Withdrawn
May, John et al	1,460	A	329	1-13-1784	Green R	Withdrawn
May, John et al	1,100	A	329	1-13-1784	Green R	Withdrawn
May, John et al	300	A	330	1-15-1784	Little Clifty Cr	750 acres withdrawn
May, John et al	2,400	A	330	1-15-1784	Green R	Surveyed
May, John et al	2,000	A	337	2-12-1784	Big Cr	Surveyed
May, John et al	1,500	A	337	2-11-1784	Cartright Cr	
May, John et al	778	A	339	2-16-1784	Caney & Rough Cr	Surveyed
May, John et al	2,450	A	339	2-16-1784	Caney Cr	Surveyed
May, John et al	1,178	A	339	2-16-1784	Green R	Withdrawn
May, John et al	1,272	A	339	2-16-1784	Caney Cr	
May, John et al	1,000	A	339	2-16-1784	Caney Cr	Surveyed

Entree	Acres	Book	Page	Entry Date	Watercourse	Notes
May, John et al.	1,000	A	340	2-17-1784	Nole Linn Cr	
May, John et al.	3,022	A	344	3- 3-1784	Green R	Withdrawn
May, John et al.	7,200	A	350	4-10-1784	Panther Cr	
May, John et al.	7,200	A	350	4-10-1784	Panther Cr	Withdrawn
May, John et al.	4,000	A	353	4-16-1784	Green R	
May, John et al.	8,000	A	353	4-16-1784	Big Clifty Cr	
May, John et al.	21,041	A	360	5-18-1 84	——	1,000 acres surveyed
May, John et al.	15,000	A	360	5-18-1784	——	5,170 acres surveyed
May, John et al.	300	A	369	7- 3-1784	Mays Grove	Amended
May, John et al.	20,000	A	369	7- 1-1784	——	1,178 acres surveyed
May, John et al.	20,000	A	369	7- 1-1784	——	10,000 acres surveyed
May, John et al.	15,000	A	369	7- 1-1784	——	1,000 acres surveyed
May, John et al.	20,000	B	2	8-19-1784	——	4,056 acres surveyed
May, John et al.	10,500	B	13	11-11-1784	Green R	
May, John et al.	14,200	B	13	11-11-1784	——	Surveyed amended
May, John et al.	1,100	B	31	1- 3-1785	——	Surveyed
May, John et al.	11,560	B	36	1-27-1785	Rough Cr	
May, John et al.	2,000	B	36	1-27-1785	Clear Fk	
May, John et al.	7,000	B	36	1-27-1785	Green R	Withdrawn
May, John et al.	1,460	B	36	1-27-1785	Green R	Withdrawn
May, John et al.	1,100	B	36	1-27-1785	Green R	Withdrawn
May, John et al.	1,000	B	37	1-27-1785	Big Clifty Cr	
May, John et al.	3,022	B	37	1-27-1785	——	Withdrawn
May, John et al.	4,800	B	39	2- 8-1785	——	
May, John et al.	1,000	B	39	2- 2-1785	Bear Cr	
May, John et al.	500	B	39	2- 2-1785	Green R	Withdrawn
May, John et al.	500	B	39	2- 2-1785	Green R	Withdrawn
May, John et al.	2,000	B	40	2- 8-1785	——	Surveyed
May, John et al.	20,000	B	40	2- 8-1785	——	
May, John et al.	2,560	B	43	4-15-1785	——	
May, Richard	250	A	114	5-30-1780	Pond Cr	
May, Wm.	400	A	7	1-10-1780	Licking Cr	
May, Wm.	6,000	A	23	4-24-1780	Salt R	
May, Wm.	2,500	A	49	5-12-1780	Ohio R	Withdrawn
May, Wm.	2,000	A	49	5-12-1780	Ohio R	Withdrawn
May, Wm.	400	A	49	5-12-1780	Island Ohio R	Withdrawn
May, Wm.	200	A	161	7-10-1780	Otter Cr	Surveyed
May, Wm.	300	A	161	7-10-1780	Soverins Valley	Surveyed
May, Wm.	804	A	245	12-30-1782	Coxes Cr	Withdrawn
May, Wm.	2,000	A	245	12-30-1782	Coxes Cr	Surveyed 500 acres withdrawn
May, Wm.	500	A	252	1-10-1783	Bensons Cr	Surveyed
May, Wm.	500	A	252	1-10-1783	Coxes Cr	
May, Wm.	400	A	259	1-30-1783	——	1,500 acres surveyed
May, Wm.	404	A	259	1-30-1783	Coxes Cr	Surveyed
May, Wm.	804	A	259	1-30-1783	Coxes Cr	
May, Wm.	2,000	A	271	3-31-1783	Yellow Bank Cr	Surveyed
May, Wm.	2,000	A	271	3-31-1783	Tuels Run	Surveyed
May, Wm.	10,000	A	271	3-31-1783	Hardens Cr	Surveyed
May, Wm.	3,000	A	271	3-31-1783	Tuels Cr	2,000 acres withdrawn
May, Wm.	5,000½	A	271	3-31-1783	Rough Cr	Surveyed
May, Wm.	20,000	A	271	3-31-1783	Hardens Cr	Surveyed 2,000 acres withdrawn
May, Wm.	500	A	271	3-28-1783	Coxes Cr	
May, Wm.	2,304	A	271	3-28-1783	Coxes Cr	Surveyed
May, Wm.	2,000	A	271	3-28-1783	Ohio R	Withdrawn
May, Wm.	4,000	A	271	3-28-1783	Deer Cr	
May, Wm.	1,000	A	271	3-28-1783	Hardens Cr	326 acres surveyed 674 acres withdrawn
May, Wm.	2,000	A	271	3-28-1783	Rough Cr	
May, Wm.	2,000	A	271	3-28-1783	Tuels Run	
May, Wm.	3,000	A	271	3-28-1783	Clover Lick Cr	2,000 acres surveyed
May, Wm.	10,000	A	271	3-28-1783	Rough Cr	983 acres surveyed
May, Wm.	5,000	A	271	3-28-1783	Hardins Cr	Surveyed
May, Wm.	500	A	272	3-31-1783	Ky R	
May, Wm.	5,000	A	272	3-31-1783	Long Lick Cr	
May, Wm.	3,000	A	273	4- 7-1783	Bear Cr	Surveyed

Entree	Acres	Book	Page	Entry Date	Watercourse	Notes
May, Wm	6,000	A	274	4– 8–1783	Caney Cr	
May, Wm	4,000	A	274	4– 8–1783	Caney Cr	
May, Wm	419	A	274	4– 8–1783	Little Caney Cr	Surveyed
May, Wm	2,180	A	274	4– 8–1783	Big Clifty Cr	Surveyed
May, Wm	400	A	275	4–10–1785	Middle Cr	
May, Wm	1,500	A	275	4–10–1783	Hardens Cr	1,000 acres withdrawn
May, Wm	1,500	A	275	4–10–1783	Limestone Cr	1,126 acres surveyed 374 acres withdrawn
May, Wm	300	A	275	4– 9–1783	Sinking Cr	
May, Wm	200	A	275	4– 9–1783	Nole Linn Cr	Surveyed
May, Wm	500	A	275	4– 9–1783	Clover Lick Cr	
May, Wm	1,900	A	275	4– 9–1783	Clover Lick Cr	1,190 acres surveyed
May, Wm	800	A	276	4–10–1783	Bartons Fk	Surveyed
May, Wm	1,000	A	276	4–10–1783	Mill Cr	Surveyed 200 acres withdrawn
May, Wm	1,000	A	276	4–10–1783	Mill Cr	Surveyed 200 acres withdrawn
May, Wm	401	A	277	4–14–1783	Salt R	Surveyed
May, Wm	2,000	A	277	4–14–1783	Panther Cr	Withdrawn
May, Wm	20,000	A	278	4–14–1783	———	Treasurers warrant
May, Wm	500	A	284	8– 4–1783	———	
May, Wm	1,000	A	284	8– 4–1783	Hardins Cr	Withdrawn
May, Wm	500	A	284	7–27–1783	Nolelin Cr	Withdrawn
May, Wm	500	A	284	7–27–1783	Rolling Fk	Withdrawn
May, Wm	600	A	285	8– 7–1783	Hardens Cr	Surveyed
May, Wm	400	A	285	8– 7–1783	Tuels Run	
May, Wm	2,000	A	285	8– 9–1783	Harden Cr	Surveyed
May, Wm	5,000	A	286	8– 9–1783	Caney Cr	
May, Wm	400	A	286	8– 9–1783	Clover Cr	
May, Wm	150	A	287	8–18–1783	Rowling Fk	Withdrawn
May, Wm	400	A	289	9– 8–1783	Hardens Cr	
May, Wm	400	A	289	9– 8–1783	Mill Cr	Withdrawn
May, Wm	2,000	A	291	9–30–1783	Nole Linn Cr	
May, Wm	500	A	291	9–13–1783	———	Surveyed
May, Wm	5,000	A	292	10– 3–1783	Rough Cr	
May, Wm	10,000	A	292	10– 3–1783	Sinking Fk Brush Cr	2,535 acres surveyed
May, Wm	800	A	292	9–30–1783	Rough Cr	250 acres surveyed
May, Wm	400	A	292	9–30–1783	Meeting Cr	
May, Wm	500	A	293	10– 6–1783	Caney Cr	
May, Wm	500	A	293	10– 6–1783	Nolelin Cr	Surveyed
May, Wm	6,000	A	293	10– 6–1783	Mill Cr	3,000 acres withdrawn
May, Wm	1,000	A	293	10– 6–1783	Barren Run	Surveyed
May, Wm	500	A	293	10– 4–1783	Nolelin Cr	Surveyed
May, Wm	500	A	293	10– 4–1783	Nolelin Cr	
May, Wm	2,000	A	294	10–11–1783	Clover Lick Cr	Surveyed
May, Wm	674	A	294	10–11–1783	Shottpouch Cr	Surveyed
May, Wm	1,000	A	294	10–11–1783	Sinking Cr	
May, Wm	500	A	294	10– 7–1783	Barren Run	Surveyed
May, Wm	400	A	294	10– 7–1783	Middle Cr	Surveyed
May, Wm	500	A	294	10– 8–1783	Middle Cr	Surveyed
May, Wm	850	A	294	10– 7–1783	Cox Cr	Withdrawn
May, Wm	350	A	294	10– 7–1783	Rolling Fk	Withdrawn
May, Wm	1,420	A	294	10– 7–1783	N Fk Caney Cr	Surveyed
May, Wm	1,000	A	295	10–11–1783	Nolin Cr	
May, Wm	200	A	295	10–11–1783	Clover Lick Cr	
May, Wm	1,000	A	295	10–11–1783	Clover Lick Cr	Surveyed
May, Wm	500	A	295	10–11–1783	Tuels Cr	
May, Wm	500	A	295	10–11–1783	Beech Fk	
May, Wm	1,000	A	295	10–11–1783	Clover Lick Cr	Surveyed
May, Wm	600	A	296	10–14–1783	Nolin Cr	Surveyed
May, Wm	4,000	A	296	10–14–1783	Mill Cr	
May, Wm	200	A	296	10–14–1783	Valley Cr	Surveyed
May, Wm	500	A	296	10–14–1783	Rough Cr	Surveyed
May, Wm	10,000	A	296	10–14–1783	Rough Cr	Surveyed
May, Wm	4,000	A	297	10–23–1783	Floyds Fk	Withdrawn
May, Wm	300	A	297	10–18–1783	Rock Cr	
May, Wm	300	A	297	10–18–1783	Long Cr	
May, Wm	1,000	A	297	10–15–1783	Rock Lick Cr	
May, Wm	1,000	A	297	10–15–1783	Sinking Run	
May, Wm	550	A	297	10–15–1783	Rock Lick Cr	Surveyed
May, Wm	552	A	297	10–15–1783	Rough Cr	Withdrawn
May, Wm	5,000	A	298	10–25–1783	Salt R	

Entree	Acres	Book	Page	Entry Date	Watercourse	Notes
May, Wm	2,500	A	298	10–24–1783	Reedy Cr	
May, Wm	3,000	A	298	10–24–1783	Reedy Cr	Surveyed
May, Wm	1,500	A	298	10–24–1783	Floyds Fk	Withdrawn
May, Wm	800	A	298	10–24–1783	Caney Cr	Surveyed
May, Wm	1,000	A	298	10–24–1783	Floyds Fk	Surveyed
May, Wm	600	A	299	10–28–1783	Nolelinn & Sinking Cr	
May, Wm	1,000	A	299	10–27–1783	Johns Pauls	Surveyed
May, Wm	1,000	A	301	11– 7–1783	Clear Cr	
May, Wm	1,000	A	301	11– 7–1783	——	
May, Wm	470	A	301	11– 7–1783	Fox Run	
May, Wm	1,000	A	301	11– 7–1783	Fox Run	Surveyed
May, Wm	600	A	302	11– 7–1783	Floyds Fk	
May, Wm	298	A	302	11– 7–1783	——	Surveyed
May, Wm	200	A	302	11– 7–1783	Soverins Valley Cr	
May, Wm	2,000	A	303	11–10–1783	Floyds Fk	Withdrawn
May, Wm	1,300	A	303	11–10–1783	Little Ky R	Withdrawn
May, Wm	2,000	A	303	11–10–1783	Little Ky R	Withdrawn
May, Wm	500	A	304	11–14–1783	Bear Cr	
May, Wm	3,000	A	304	11–14–1783	Bear Cr	Surveyed
May, Wm	2,100	A	305	11–19–1783	Green R	Surveyed
May, Wm	21,000	A	305	11–19–1783	Green R	Withdrawn
May, Wm	2,000	A	305	11–17–1783	Bear Cr	Withdrawn
May, Wm	1,000	A	305	11–17–1783	Bear Cr	Withdrawn
May, Wm	3,000	A	305	11–17–1783	Bear Cr	
May, Wm	1,000	A	305	11–14–1783	Rudy Run	
May, Wm	700	A	305	11–14–1783	Middle Cr	Surveyed
May, Wm	24,000	A	305	11–14–1783	Bear Cr	
May, Wm	2,000	A	305	11–14–1783	Bear Cr	Withdrawn
May, Wm	3,000	A	306	11–19–1783	Beech Fk	Surveyed
May, Wm	374	A	312	12– 3–1783	Limestone Cr	Surveyed
May, Wm	500	A	312	12– 3–1783	Tarr Spring Fk	444 acres surveyed
May, Wm	1,500	A	312	12– 3–1783	Sugar Tree Cr	Surveyed
May, Wm	1,000	A	312	12– 3–1783	Little Yellow Bank Cr	
May, Wm	10,000	A	320	12–17–1783	Green R	1,990 acres withdrawn
May, Wm	1,500	A	322	12–24–1783	Bear Cr	Withdrawn
May, Wm	711	A	325	12–29–1783	Ashes Cr	
May, Wm	1,000	A	325	12–29–1783	Floyds Fk	Surveyed
May, Wm	335	A	327	1– 7–1784	Fern Cr	
May, Wm	1,135	A	327	1– 7–1784	Sinking Cr	Withdrawn
May, Wm	1,990	A	339	2–16–1784	Green R	Withdrawn
May, Wm	410	A	339	2–14–1784	N Fk Caney Cr	Surveyed
May, Wm	550	A	344	3– 3–1784	Rough Cr	
May, Wm	1,400	A	348	3–22–1784	Bullskin Cr	Withdrawn
May, Wm	10,000	A	350	4–10–1784	Rough Cr	6,740 acres surveyed
May, Wm	5,000	A	350	4–10–1784	Rough Cr	Surveyed
May, Wm	2,000	A	350	4–10–1784	Green R	Withdrawn
May, Wm	3,000	A	350	4–10–1784	Clover Cr	Surveyed
May, Wm	2,000	A	350	4–10–1784	Clover Cr	Surveyed
May, Wm	3,000	A	350	4–10–1784	Hardens Cr	
May, Wm	1,282	A	351	4–12–1784	Tarr Spring Fk	
May, Wm	1,000	A	351	4–12–1784	——	270 acres surveyed
May, Wm	5,000	A	351	4–10–1784	Green R	
May, Wm	5,000	A	351	4–12–1784	Rough Cr	
May, Wm	10,000	A	351	4–12–1784	Rough Cr	
May, Wm	2,000	A	352	4–14–1784	Big Benson Cr	Surveyed
May, Wm	10,000	A	353	4–16–1784	Green R	6,870 acres surveyed
May, Wm	10,000	A	353	4–16–1784	Green R	
May, Wm	15,331	A	353	4–16–1784	Rough Cr	Withdrawn
May, Wm	2,000	A	353	4–16–1784	Rock Cr	
May, Wm	2,000	A	353	4–15–1784	——	
May, Wm	500	A	353	4–15–1784	Dog Cr	
May, Wm	1,000	A	353	4–15–1784	Nolelinn Cr	
May, Wm	2,000	A	354	4–16–1784	Rowling Fk	
May, Wm	10,000	A	355	4–21–1784	Ohio R	Surveyed
May, Wm	3,000	A	355	4–19–1784	Nolelin Fk	Withdrawn
May, Wm	2,000	A	355	4–19–1784	Salt R	
May, Wm	1,000	A	355	4–19–1784	Rowling Fk	
May, Wm	1,373	A	355	4–19–1784	Salt R	
May, Wm	5,000	A	356	4–28–1784	Ohio R	Withdrawn
May, Wm	850	A	356	4–28–1784	Cox Cr	Withdrawn
May, Wm	3,000	A	356	4–28–1784	Cox Cr	
May, Wm	300	A	356	4–24–1784	Salt R	
May, Wm	5,000	A	356	4–24–1784	Rough Cr	
May, Wm	5,000	A	356	4–24–1784	Indian Camp Cr	Surveyed
May, Wm	200	A	356	4–24–1784	Bacon Cr	Withdrawn
May, Wm	422	A	357	4–30–1784	Coxes Cr	

Entree	Acres	Book	Page	Entry Date	Watercourse	Notes
May, Wm	963	A	357	4–30–1784	Green R	500 acres withdrawn
May, Wm	978	A	357	4–30–1784	Panther Cr	
May, Wm	10,800	A	357	4–30–1784	Green R	Withdrawn
May, Wm	2,000	A	357	4–29–1784	Salt R	Withdrawn
May, Wm	1,300	A	357	4–29–1784	Little Ky R	
May, Wm	2,000	A	357	4–29–1784	Little Ky R	Withdrawn
May, Wm	1,500	A	357	4–29–1784	Floyds Fk	Withdrawn
May, Wm	4,000	A	357	4–29–1784	Floyds Fk	
May, Wm	40,000	A	357	4–28–1784	Ohio R, Panther Cr.	
May, Wm	45	A	358	5– 4–1784	Green R 4th Island	
May, Wm	20	A	358	5– 4–1784	Green R 3rd Island	
May, Wm	20	A	358	5– 4–1784	Green R 2nd Island	
May, Wm	15	A	358	5– 4–1784	Ohio R 1st Island	
May, Wm	6,800	A	360	5–18–1784	Rough Cr	Withdrawn
May, Wm	6,835	A	360	5–18–1784	Green R	Withdrawn
May, Wm	3,422	A	360	5–18–1784	Ohio R	
May, Wm	20,000	A	360	5–18–1784	———	
May, Wm	422	A	360	5–13–1784	Coxes Cr	Withdrawn
May, Wm	3,000	A	360	5–13–1784	Coxes Cr	Withdrawn
May, Wm	9,760	A	362	5–31–1784	———	Surveyed
May, Wm	500	A	362	5–27–1784	Nole Linn Cr	Surveyed
May, Wm	1,461	A	362	5–26–1784	———	375 acres surveyed
May, Wm	500	A	366	6–17–1784	———	200 acres surveyed
May, Wm	162	A	366	6–16–1783	Clover Cr	surveyed
May, Wm	1,300	A	368	6–26–1784	Green R	
May, Wm	623	A	369	7– 3–1784	Rough Cr	Surveyed
May, Wm	38	A	369	7– 3–1784	———	Withdrawn
May, Wm	311	A	369	7– 3–1784	Coxes Cr	Surveyed
May, Wm	500	A	369	7– 1–1784	Coxes Cr	Withdrawn
May, Wm	20,000	A	370	7– 6–1784	———	18,000 acres surveyed
May, Wm	6000	A	375	8– 2–1784	Tarr Spring Fk	Withdrawn
May, Wm	4,000	A	375	8– 2–1784	———	Withdrawn
May, Wm	5,170	B	2	8–19–1784	———	200 acres surveyed
May, Wm	2,304	B	2	8–19–1784	———	
May, Wm	51,500	B	5	9–13–1784	Nole Linn Cr	Surveyed
May, Wm	40,000	B	5	9–11–1784	Ohio R	Withdrawn
May, Wm	10,000	B	7	9–14–1784	Green R	Surveyed
May, Wm	7,500	B	7	9–14–1784	Sinking Cr	
May, Wm	800	B	31	1– 3–1785	———	
May, Wm	3,000	B	39	2– 8–1785	———	
May, Wm	3,130	B	40	2– 8–1785	———	
May, Wm	2,000	B	43	4–15–1785	———	
May, Wm et al	3,034	A	312	12– 4–1783	Floyds Fk	Surveyed
Mayby, Wm	19,205	A	362	5–31–1784	———	
Mayhall, Humphrey	1,000	A	251	1–10–1783	Coxes & Simpson Cr	Withdrawn
Mead, Samuel	400	A	92	5–24–1780	Salt R	
Melton, Elijah	500	A	173	9–22–1780	Simpsons Cr	
Melton, Rich	500	A	173	9–22–1780	Simpsons Cr	
Melton, Wm	500	A	76	5–19–1780	N Fk Licking	
Menefee, Gerrard	400	A	6	12–23–1779	Cedar Cr	
Menefee, Jarrett	400	A	127	6– 8–1780	Cedar Cr	
Menefee, Wm	200	A	127	6– 8–1780	Cedar Cr	
Mercer, Isabella	1,612	A	330	1–15–1784	Floyds Fk	
Meredeth, Samuel	200	A	129	6– 9–1780	Ohio R	
Meredeth, Samuel	2,050	A	192	3–15–1784	Floyds Fk	Mil withdrawn
Meredeth, Samuel	1,050	A	217	8– 2–1781	Beech Fk	Withdrawn
Meredeth, Samuel	953	A	217	8– 2–1782	Simpsons Cr	Withdrawn
Meredeth, Samuel	2,003	A	241	12–25–1782	Rowling Fk	———
Meredeth, Samuel	1,050	A	241	12–25–1782	Salt R	Withdrawn
Meredeth, Samuel	953	A	241	12–25–1782	Simpsons Cr	Withdrawn
Meredeth, Samuel	119¾	A	356	4–27–1784	Simpson Cr	
Merewether, David W.	1,000	A	101	5–26–1780	Clarks Run	
Merewether, James	1,200	B	10	10–11–1784	———	883 acres surveyed
Merewether, James	2,943½	B	50	10–26–1785	Goose Cr	
Merewether, James	888	A	54	5–15–1780	Yellow Banks	Surveyed
Merewether, James	2,000	A	204	4– 4–1781	Floyds Fk	Surveyed
Merewether, Nich	400	A	2	11– 3–1779	Beargrass	
Merewether, James	3,000	A	204	4– 4–1781	S Fk Goose Cr	Surveyed
Merewether, Nich	666	A	22	4–21–1780	Beargrass	Mil surveyed
Merewether, Nich	60	A	30	4–28–1780	Sandy Island Ohio	
Merewether, Nich	40	A	30	4–28–1780	Rocky Island	Mil
Merewether, Nich	1,000	A	36	4–29–1780	Beargrass Cr	
Merewether, Nich	1,000	A	36	4–29–1780	Boone settlement	
Merewether, Nich	2,972	A	54	5–15–1780	Yellow Banks	Surveyed

Entree	Acres	Book	Page	Entry Date	Watercourse	Notes
Merewether, Nich	1,000	A	292	10- 3-1783	Salt R	Surveyed
Merewether, Nich	666	A	360	5-10-1784	———	
Merewether, Nich	4,000	A	372	7-17-1784	———	2,972 acres surveyed
Merewether, Wm	100	A	242	12-25-1782	Fromans Cr	Withdrawn
Merewether, Wm	200	A	242	12-25-1782	Paul Froman	Withdrawn
Merewether, Wm	280	A	242	12-25-1782	Wm E Collins	Withdrawn
Merewether, Wm	1,000	A	242	12-25-1782	Simpsons Cr	Surveyed
Merewether, Wm	1,000	A	242	12-25-1782	Salt R	Surveyed
Merewether, Wm	100	A	243	12-26-1782	Coxes Cr	Surveyed
Merewether, Wm	100	A	243	12-26-1782	P Fromans	....
Merewether, Wm	1,420	A	243	12-26-1782	Cartright Cr	....
Merewether, Wm	3,000	A	243	12-26-1782	Floyds Fk	....
Merewether, Wm	1,125	A	243	12-26-1782	Harrods Cr	....
Merewether, Wm	10,000	A	236	1-23-1783	Hardens Cr	....
Merewether, Wm	280	A	258	1-27-1783	Wm E Collins	....
Merewether, Wm	200	A	258	1-27-1783	Paul Fromans	Withdrawn
Merewether, Wm	200	A	307	11-20-1783	———	....
Merewether, Wm	3,900	A	329	1-12-1784	———	....
Merewether, Wm	375	A	341	2-23-1784	———	....
Merewether, Wm	613	A	341	2-23-1784	———	....
Merewether, Wm	613	A	341	2-21-1784	Clover Lick Cr	....
Merewether, Wm	164	A	341	2-21-1784	Rock Lick Cr	....
Meridith, Samuel	2,050	A	212	6-21-1781	Floyds Fk	1,000 acres surveyed 1,050 acres withdrawn
Meriweather, James	1,000	A	207	4-14-1781	Goose Cr	....
Meriweather, James	1,000	A	207	4-14-1781	Floyds Fk	....
Meriweather, Nich	2,000	A	294	10- 7-1783	Buffaloe Cr	Surveyed
Meriweather, Nich	600	A	297	10-18-1783	Muddy Cr	Withdrawn
Meriweather, Nich	2,000	A	369	7- 1-1784	Beargrass Cr	Withdrawn
Meriweather, Nich et al	600	A	288	8-29-1783	Rough Cr	500 acres withdrawn
Meriweather, Wm	700	A	213	7-18-1781	———	Withdrawn
Meriweather, Wm	500	A	2f9	8-24-1781	———	Surveyed
Meriweather, Wm	2,000	A	220	8-29-1781	Green R	....
Meriweather, Wm	375	A	294	10-10-1783	Clover Lick	Surveyed
Meriweather, Wm	625	A	294	10-10-1783	Long Lick Cr	Surveyed
Meriweather, Wm	2,600	A	294	10-10-1783	Rock Lick	....
Meriweather, Wm	480	B	7	9-20-1784	Elk Cr	Surveyed
Meriweather, Geo	1,000	A	37	4-29-1780	Stock Field	1,490 acres surveyed
Meriweather, Geo	1,490	A	54	5-15-1783	Yellow Banks	
Meriweather, Geo	2,000	A	372	7-17-1784	———	
Meriwether, Martha	400	A	289	9- 8-1783	Valley Cr	....
Meriwether, Nich et al	2,000	A	289	9- 8-1783	Nolelin Cr	Surveyed
Meriwether, Nich et al	1,000	A	289	9- 8-1783	Nole Linn Cr	....
Meriwether, Nich et al	600	B	39	2- 1-1785	Rolling Fk	Mil
Merry, Prettyman	50	A	31	4-28-1780	———	....
Marry, Prettyman	2,000	A	39	5- 9-1780	Ohio R	....
Merryman, Moses	600	A	44	5-11-1780	Floyds Fk	....
Merton, Richard	1,517	A	348	3-23-1784	Green R	....
Metlock, Isom et al	1,337½	A	251	1-10-1783	Green R	Surveyed
Meyers, Jacob	400	A	17	2-28-1780	Salt R	Surveyed
Meyers, Jacob	50	A	21	4-20-1780	Floyds Fk	Surveyed
Meyers, Jacob	50	A	21	4-20-1780	Ohio R	....
Meyers, Jacob	150	A	24	4-25-1780	N Fk Beargrass	Surveyed
Meyers, Jacob	4,355	A	365	6-12-1784	———	....
Micham, Dudley	500	A	63	5-16-1780	Glens Cr	....
Mick, Isaac	400	A	80	5-20-1780	Pleasant Run	Surveyed
Middleton, John	1,000	A	241	12-25-1782	Rough Cr	....
Middleton, John	1,000	A	248	1- 7-1783	Swamp Cr	....
Middleton, Thomas	10,000	A	325	12-31-1783	Knobb Cr	Surveyed
Milcher, Isaac	10,000	A	43	5-11-1780	Big Bone Cr	....
Miller, Abraham	1,000	A	181	10-24-1780	Hanging Fk	....
Miller, Abraham	581	A	308	11-24-1783	Green R	....
Miller, Alex	425	A	121	6- 2-1780	Bullitts Lick	....
Miller, Andrew	400	A	148	6-24-1780	Dowlans Run	....
Miller, Andrew	1,000	A	180	10-19-1780	Glens Cr	....
Miller, Andrew	———	A	184	10-30-1780	Glens Cr	....
Miller, Charles	1,000	A	357	5- 1-1784	Beech Fk	Amended
Miller, Earnest	500	A	323	12-26-1783	Thomas Denton	....
Miller, Ebenezer	260	A	297	10-20-1783	Rolling Fk	....
Miller, Ebenezer	300	A	297	10-18-1783	Rolling Fk	....
Miller, Ebenezer	200	A	337	2-11-1784	———	....
Miller, Hans	280	A	218	8- 8-1781	Cartright Cr	....
Miller, Henry	1,000	A	180	10-19-1780	Clear Cr	....
Miller, Henry	500	A	361	5-22-1784	Floyds Fk	....
Miller, Henry	500	A	361	5-22-1784	Floyds Fk	....
Miller, Joseph	1,018½	A	253	1-14-1783	Sinking Cr	Withdrawn
Miller, John	400	A	17	2-29-1780	Licking Cr	....

Entree	Acres	Book	Page	Entry Date	Watercourse	Notes
Miller, John	400	A	181	10-23-1780	S Fk Clear Cr	
Miller, John	1,000	A	186	3-14-1781	Fox Run	Surveyed
Miller, John	402	A	193	3-16-1781	Floyds Fk	
Miller, John K	1,000	A	229	12-16-1782	Brashears Cr	
Miller, Michael	400	B	16	11-12-1784	Clay Lick Cr	Surveyed
Miller, Pat	150	A	142	6-22-1780	S Fk Rowling Fk	
Miller, Wm	400	A	7	12-29-1779	Paint Lick Cr	
Miller, Wm	400	A	7	12-29-1779	Silver Cr	
Miller, Wm	400	A	7	12-29-1779	Br of Ky R	
Miller, Wm	400	A	17	2-29-1780	Licking Cr	
Miller, Wm	1,000	A	26	4-26-1780	Paint Lick Cr	
Miller, Wm	1,000	A	26	4-26-1780	Paint Lick Cr	
Miller, Wm	1,000	A	26	4-26-1780	Townsends Run	
Miller, Wm	1,000	A	26	4-26-1780	Locust Bend	
Miller, Wm	1,000	A	26	4-26-1780	————	
Million, Robert	500	A	70	5-18-1780	————	
Millner, John	867	A	223	12-12-1782	Rough Cr	
Millner, John	200	A	224	12-12-1782	————	
Mills, John	200	A	23	4-24-1780	Harrods Cr	
Mimms, David	550	A	59	5-16-1780	Licking	
Minor, Dabney	3,000	A	331	1-16-1784	Rough Cr	
Minor, Garrett et al	5,000	A	312	12- 4-1783	Ohio R	
Minor, Garrett et al	2,000	A	329	1-12-1784	Neatherland & Harrison	Surveyed
Minor, Garrett et al	500	A	370	7- 6-1784	————	
Minor, Garrett et al	500	A	370	7- 6-1784	Drennons Lick Cr	
Minor, Garrett et al	2,000	B	41	2-28-1785	————	
Minor, James	2,000	A	157	6-30-1780	Lulbergrud	
Minor, John	1,000	A	56	5-15-1780	Floyds Fk	Surveyed
Minor, John	2,000	A	56	5-15-1780	Simpson Cr	Withdrawn
Minor, John	2,000	A	211	6-11-1781	Simpsons Cr	Surveyed
Minor, John S	400	A	112	5-30-1780	Otter Cr	
Minter, John	500	A	224	12-12-1782	Lick Run	Surveyed
Mires, Jacob	1,000	A	197	3-17-1781	James Wallace	
Mires, Michael	550	A	195	3-16-1781	Otter Cr	
Mitchel, David	400	A	52	5-13-1780	Beech Fk	Surveyed
Mitchel, David	1,000	A	52	5-13-1780	Hingstons Cr	
Mitchel, David	500	A	52	5-13-1780	Floyds Fk	Surveyed
Mitchel, David	500	A	52	5-13-1780	Floyds Fk	Surveyed
Mitchel, David	1,000	A	52	5-13-1780	Floyds Fk	Surveyed
Mitchell, David et al	1,600	A	52	5-13-1780	Cockes Cr	Surveyed
Mitchell, David et al	2,906	A	313	12- 5-1783	Ohio R	Withdrawn
Mitchell, David	250	A	39	5- 9-1780	Ky R	100 acres withdrawn
Mitchell, David	150	A	39	5- 9-1780	S Fk Elkhorn	
Mitchell, David	100	A	153	6-26-1780	Ky R	
Mitchell, David	200	A	170	9- 9-1780	Ky R	
Mitchell, David	3,000	A	249	1- 8-1783	Ohio R	Withdrawn
Mitchell, David	547	A	249	1- 8-1783	Coxes Cr	Surveyed
Mitchell, David	2,906	A	365	6-12-1784	————	Withdrawn
Mitchell, David	3,000	A	365	6-12-1784	Salt R	Withdrawn
Mitchell, David et al	5,906	A	365	6-12-1784	Otter Cr	Surveyed
Mitchell, Richard	100	A	29	4-27-1780	Ky R	Mil
Mitchell, Robert	719½	A	375	7-29-1784	————	
Mitchell, Wm	1,000	A	75	5-19-1780	Coxes Cr	Surveyed
Monday, Edward	600	A	90	5-23-1780	Rowling Fk	
Monnee, John	400	A	181	10-23-1780	Silver Cr	
Monroany, Wm	500	A	284	8- 4-1783	Chaplins Fk	
Montague, Thomas	500	A	27	4-26-1780	Licking	Mil
Mantague, Thomas	500	A	30	4-28-1780	S Fk Elhorn	Mil
Montague, Thomas	500	A	30	4-28-1780	Grants Station	Mil
Montague, Thomas	200	A	30	4-28-1780	Hinston Fk	Mil
Montgomery, Alex	50	A	253	1-14-1783	Green R	Mil
Montgomery, James	300	A	171	9-13-1780	Howards Cr	
Montgomery, James	500	A	171	9-13-1780	Coopers Run	
Montgomery, James	200	A	182	10-26-1780	Beech Fk	
Montgomery, James	500	A	182	10-26-1780	Beech Fk	
Montgomery, James	200	A	202	4- 2-1781	Green R	
Montgomery, James	100	A	251	1-10-1783	Robinsons Cr	
Montgomery, John	400	A	13	2- 9-1780	Flat Lick	
Montgomery, John	400	A	253	1-14-1783	Green R	
Montgomery, John	600	A	253	1-14-1783	Green R	
Montgomery, Wm	400	A	13	2- 9-1780	Pine Lick Green R.	
Montgomery, Wm	200	A	61	5-16-1780	Carpenters Cr	
Montgomery, Wm	1,000	A	102	5-26-1780	Green R	
Montgomery, Wm	2,000	A	113	5-30-1780	Nolelin Cr	
Montgomery, Wm	1,000	A	113	5-30-1780	Nolelin Cr	
Montgomery, Wm	500	A	201	4- 2-1781	Chaplins Fk	
Montgomery, Wm	800	A	238	12-23-1782	Green R	Withdrawn
Montgomery, Wm	600	A	238	12-23-1782	Green R	585 acres surveyed
Montgomery, Wm	1,460	A	239	12-23-1782	Caseys Cr	

Entree	Acres	Book	Page	Entry Date	Watercourse	Notes
Montgomery, Wm.....	300	A	253	1–14–1783	Green R	....
Montgomery, Wm.....	600	A	253	1–14–1783	Green R	....
Montgomery, Wm Jr..	400	A	13	2– 9–1780	Green R	....
Montgomery, Wm Jr..	1,000	A	102	5–26–1780	Green R	....
Montgomrie, Alex.....	150	A	101	5–26–1780	Green R	....
Montgomorie, John....	200	A	101	5–26–1780	Logan Cr	....
Moody, Benj..........	1,000	A	234	12–19–1782	Saunders	Surveyed
Moody, Benj..........	1,000	A	234	12–19–1782	Saunders	Surveyed
Moody, Benj..........	1,200	A	291	9–13–1783	Samuel Oldham	....
Moody, Benj..........	1,800	A	307	11–21–1783	Beech Fk	....
Moody, Benj..........	3,000	A	307	11–21–1783	Beech Fk	Surveyed
Moody, Benj..........	1,000	A	319	12–17–1783	Green R	....
Mooney, Adam........	500	A	134	6–16–1780	Stoners Fk	....
Moore, Harbin.......	1,000	A	239	12–23–1782	Hardens Cr	Surveyed
Moore, James........	1,000	A	43	5–11–1780	Stoners Fk	....
Moore, James........	1,000	A	372	7–16–1784	Fish Pool Cr	....
Moore, James........	300	A	22	4–21–1780	S Fk Beargrass Cr..	Mil
Moore, James F......	400	A	22	4–21–1780	S Fk Bear Cr	Mil
Moore, James F......	300	A	23	4–24–1780	Ohio R	Mil withdrawn
Moore, James F......	400	A	141	6–21–1780	S Fk Beargrass	....
Moore, James F......	400	A	168	8–29–1780	Salt R	Surveyed
Moore, James F......	150	A	317	12–16–1783	Beargrass Cr	....
Moore, James F......	300	A	317	12–16–1783	Ohio R	....
Moore, James F......	1,300	B	19	11–26–1784	Brashears Cr	Withdrawn
Moore, James F......	2,000	B	19	11–22–1784	Floyds Fk	Mil
Moore, James F et al.	10,000	A	274	4– 8–1783	Ohio R	Withdrawn
Moore, James F et al.	10,000	A	274	4– 8–1783	Ky R	Withdrawn
Moore, James F et al	20,000	A	274	4– 8–1783	Little Ky R	1,000 acres withdrawn
Moore, James F et al.	20,000	A	274	4– 8–1783	Limestone Cr	19,200 acres withdrawn
Moore, James F et al.	3,775	A	315	12–15–1783	Drinning Lick Cr...	....
Moore, James F et al.	438	A	316	12–15–1783	Bullskin Cr	....
Moore, James F et al.	2,000	A	316	12–15–1783	Bullskin Cr	....
Moore, James F et al.	1,000	A	316	12–15–1785	Bullskin Cr	....
Moore, James F et al.	2,000	A	316	12–15–1783	Bullskin Cr	....
Moore, James F et al.	2,000	A	316	12–15–1783	Bullskin Cr	....
Moore, James F et al.	1,562	A	316	12–15–1783	Drinnens Lick	Surveyed
Moore, James F et al.	900	A	316	12–15–1783	Drinnons Lick Cr..	866 acres surveyed
Moore, James F et al.	655	A	316	12–15–1783	Drinnens Lick Cr...	....
Moore, James F et al.	5,670	A	316	12–15–1783	Drennons Lick	....
Moore, James F et al.	3,871	A	317	12–16–1783	Bullskin Cr	....
Moore, James F et al.	2,000	A	317	12–16–1783	Bullskin Cr	....
Moore, James F et al.	4,000	A	317	12–16–1783	Bullskin Cr	....
Moore, James et al...	1,000	A	318	12–16–1783	Drinnens Lick Cr...	Surveyed
Moore, James F et al..	1,000	A	318	12–16–1783	————	Withdrawn
Moore, James F et al..	10,000	A	318	12–16–1783	Ohio R	Amended
Moore, James F et al..	129	A	318	12–16–1783	Drinnens Lick Cr...	Surveyed
Moore, James F et al..	3,000	A	324	12–26–1783	Little Ky R	Surveyed
Moore, James F et al..	1,000	A	324	12–26–1783	Little Ky R	....
Moore, James F et al..	2,000	A	324	12–26–1783	Little Ky R	Withdrawn
Moore, James F et al..	3,000	A	324	12–26–1783	Little Ky R	....
Moore, James F et al..	3,000	A	324	12–26–1783	Little Ky R	....
Moore, James F et al..	2,000	A	324	12–26–1783	Little Ky R	....
Moore, James F et al..	5,000	A	324	12–26–1783	Millers Run	....
Moore, James F et al..	2,000	A	334	2–14–1784	Little Ky R	Surveyed
Moore, James F et al..	2,800	A	365	6–14–1784	Bullskin Cr	Surveyed
Moore, James F et al..	2,800	A	365	6–14–1784	Ohio R	....
Moore, James F et al..	400	B	10	10– 7–1784	Ohio R	Withdrawn
Moore, James F et al..	20,000	B	12	11– 9–1784	————	995 acres surveyed
Moore, James F et al..	400	B	18	11–17–1784	Bullskin Cr	145 acres withdrawn
Moore, James F et al..	400	B	18	11–17–1784	————	Withdrawn
Moore, James F et al..	917½	B	18	11–17–1784	Drennons Lick Cr..	Withdrawn
Moore, James F et al..	3,882½	B	18	11–17–1784	Big Cr	Withdrawn
Moore, James F et al..	2,000	B	18	11–17–1784	Clear Cr	Withdrawn
Moore, James F et al..	6,800	B	18	11–17–1784	Limestone Cr	....
Moore, James F et al..	20,000	B	19	11–26–1784	————	6,000 acres surveyed returned
Moore, James F et al..	145	B	22	12– 3–1784	Clear Cr	....
Moore, James F et al..	145	B	22	12– 4–1784	————	Withdrawn
Moore, Jeremiah.....	1,000	A	62	5–16–1780	Stoners Fk	....
Moore, Jeremiah.....	1,000	A	76	5–19–1780	Stoners Fk	....
Moore, Jeremiah.....	200	A	80	5–20–1780	Billys Cr	Surveyed
Moore, Jeremiah.....	200	A	80	5–20–1780	Soverins Cr	Surveyed
Moore, Jeremiah.....	1,000	A	93	5–24–1780	Stoners Fk	....
Moore, John..........	1,000	A	158	7– 3–1780	Drennons Lick Cr..	....

Entree	Acres	Book	Page	Entry Date	Watercourse	Notes
Moore, John	800	A	191	3–15–1781	Floyds Fk	Surveyed
Moore, Joseph	1,000	A	374	7–27–1784	Green R	....
Moore, Moses	400	A	148	6–24–1780	S Fk Licking	....
Moore, Moses	1,100	A	191	3–15–1781	Floyds Fk	....
Moore, Richard	400	A	158	7– 3–1780	Davis Hart	....
Moore, Robert	400	A	96	5–25–1780	Log Lick Trace	....
Moore, Rob & Gooch	1,000	A	58	5–15–1780	Licking	....
Moore, Samuel	400	A	43	5–11–1780	Stoners Fk	....
Moore, Samuel	400	A	148	6–24–1780	Knob Lick	....
Moore, Samuel	400	A	150	6–24–1780	Knobb Lick	....
Moore, Samuel	700	A	153	6–26–1780	Licking	....
Moore, Samuel	1,000	A	162	7–18–1780	His Sett	....
Moore, Simon	1,000	A	36	4–29–1780	Shawnee Run	....
Moore, Thomas	400	A	89	5–23–1780	Cartright Cr	....
Moore, Thomas	1,261	A	270	3–28–1783	Beech Fk	....
Moore, Thomas	1,430	A	270	3–28–1783	Beech Fk	....
Moore, Thomas, et al	2,000	A	148	6–24–1780	Mill Cr	....
Moore, Wm	400	A	6	12–23–1779	Crab Orchard	Surveyed
Moore, Wm	400	A	9	1–17–1780	Licking Cr	....
Moore, Wm	50	A	25	4–25–1780	Salt R	Mil surveyed
Moore, Wm	50	A	25	4–25–1780	Town Fk Salt R	Mil surveyed
Moore, Wm	100	A	25	4–25–1780	Town Fk Salt R	Mil surveyed
Moore, Wm	1,000	A	35	4–29–1780	Moores Sett	....
Moore, Wm	7,000	A	39	5– 9–1780	————	Surveyed
Moore, Wm	3,000	A	39	5– 9–1780	Panther Cr	Surveyed
Moore, Wm	2,858	A	158	7– 3–1780	Richard Moore	....
More, John	500	A	257	1–25–1783	His Sett	....
More, John	500	A	257	1–25–1783	Rowling Fk	....
More, John	400	A	17	2–28–1780	Rolling Fk	....
Morgan, Abraham	300	A	128	6– 8–1780	Tates Cr	....
Morgan, Charles	467	A	124	6– 3–1780	Lawrence Cr	....
Morgan, Charles	150	A	341	2–21–1784	Cedar Run	Withdrawn
Morgan, Charles	150	A	347	3–22–1784	Cedar Cr	Withdrawn
Morgan, Charles, heir	1,000	A	119	6– 1–1780	Stoners Fk	....
Morgan, Daniel	1,000	A	150	6–24–1780	M Fk Licking	....
Morgan, Daniel	2,000	A	150	6–24–1780	M Fk Licking	....
Morgan, Ralph	400	A	128	6– 8–1780	Wolf Cr	....
Morgan, Ralph	400	A	128	6– 8–1780	Strouds Fk	....
Morgan, Ralph	1,000	A	128	6– 8–1780	Wolfs Cr	....
Morgan, Sarah	400	A	236	12–20–1782	Rolling Fk	....
Morgan, Wm	400	A	128	6– 8–1780	Glens Cr	....
Moris, Wm	1,000	A	249	1– 8–1783	Benson Cr	Surveyed
Moris, Wm	1,000	A	249	1– 8–1783	Benson Cr	....
Moris, Wm	1,000	A	249	1– 8–1783	Benson Cr	....
Moris, Wm	2,000	A	249	1– 8–1783	Benson Cr	1,800 acres surveyed
Morony, Wm	325	A	191	3–15–1781	Pond Cr	Withdrawn
Morris, Ezekiel	400	A	144	6–23–1780	Hardens Cr	Surveyed
Morris, Hugh	50	A	30	4–28–1780	Sugar Cr	Mil
Morris, Hugh	150	A	75	5–19–1780	Sugar Cr	....
Morris, James	400	A	173	9–23–1780	Paint Lick Cr	....
Morris, James et al	4,000	A	331	1–16–1784	Green R	....
Morris, Robert	2,000	A	187	3–15–1781	Ohio R	....
Morris, Robert	2,000	A	187	3–15–1781	Below Yellow Banks	....
Morris, Thomas	750½	A	328	1–12–1784	————	....
Morris, Thomas	750½	A	371	7–12–1784	Beech Fk	....
Morris, Thomas	750½	A	371	7–12–1784	————	Withdrawn
Morrison, Isaac	500	A	225	12–13–1782	Mill Cr	Withdrawn
Morrison, Isaac	500	A	225	12–13–1782	Rowling Fk	Withdrawn
Morrison, Isaac	1,000	A	225	12–13–1782	Rowling Fk	Withdrawn
Morrison, Isaac	300	A	225	12–13–1782	Rowling Fk	....
Morrison, Isaac	400	A	225	12–13–1782	Rowling Fk	Withdrawn
Morrison, Isaac	300	A	225	12–13–1781	Fromans Cr	Withdrawn
Morrison, Isaac	200	A	225	12–13–1782	Sinking Cr	100 acres withdrawn
Morrison, Isaac	300	A	225	12–13–1782	Simpsons Cr	Withdrawn
Morrison, Isaac	400	A	256	1–23–1783	Pottengers Cr	Withdrawn
Morrison, Isaac	400	A	256	1–23–1783	Rolling Fk	Withdrawn
Morrison, Isaac	300	A	275	4– 9–1783	Beech Fk	Withdrawn
Morrison, Isaac	300	A	275	4– 9–1783	Fromans Road	....
Morrison, Isaac	500	A	285	8– 7–1783	Caney Cr	Withdrawn
Morrison, Isaac	400	A	285	8– 7–1783	Caney Cr	....
Morrison, Isaac	400	A	285	8– 7–1783	Pottengers Cr	Withdrawn
Morrison, Isaac	50	A	287	8–18–1783	Otter Cr	....
Morrison, Isaac	400	A	287	8–18–1783	Caney Cr	Withdrawn
Morrison, Isaac	600	A	290	9–10–1783	Floyds Fk	....
Morrison, Isaac	1,437	A	314	12–10–1783	Pottengers Cr	Withdrawn
Morrison, Isaac	4,587	A	318	12–17–1783	Green R	....
Morrison, Isaac	1,437	A	318	12–17–1783	James McAdams	Withdrawn
Morrison, Isaac	300	A	318	12–17–1783	Simpsons Cr	....
Morrison, Isaac	300	A	318	12–17–1783	Beech Fk	....

Entree	Acres	Book	Page	Entry Date	Watercourse	Notes
Morrison, Isaac	500	A	318	12-17-1783	Rolling Fk	
Morrison, Isaac	1,000	A	320	12-18-1783	Pottengers Cr	
Morrison, Isaac	400	A	326	1- 2-1784	Salt Lick Cr	
Morrison, Isaac	400	A	326	1- 2-1784	Salt Lick Cr	Withdrawn
Morrison, Isaac	400	A	333	1-20-1784	Cartright Cr	
Morrison, Isaac	300	A	334	1-24-1784	Simpsons Cr	Surveyed
Morrison, Isaac	1,000	A	334	1-24-1784	Blackford Cr	
Morrison, Isaac	500	A	334	1-24-1784	Mill Cr	
Morrison, Isaac	500	A	343	3- 3-1784	Caney Cr	Surveyed
Morrison, Isaac	1,000	A	346	3-16-1784	Ashes Cr	Withdrawn
Morrison, Isaac		A	347	3-17-1784	Ashes Cr	Withdrawn
Morrison, Isaac	100	A	360	5-12-1784	Beech Fk	
Morrison, Isaac	100	A	360	5-12-1784	Sinking Cr	Withdrawn
Morrison, Isaac	500	B	31	1- 3-1785	————	Surveyed
Morrison, Isaac	400	B	33	1-14-1785	Hardens Cr	
Morrison, Isaac	400	B	33	1-14-1785	—————	Withdrawn
Morrison, Isaac	200	B	35	1-26-1785	—————	
Morrison, Isaac	1,300	B	46	5-19-1785	—————	
Morrison, James	9,800	A	341	2-26-1784	Brashears Cr	Surveyed
Morrison, James et al	20,109¼	A	331	1-16-1784	Green R	
Morrison, Thomas	500	A	255	1-20-1783	Rolling Fk	
Morriss, Austin	2,000	A	185	10-31-1780	Kentucky R	
Morriss, Robert	200	A	68	5-18-1780	Yellow Banks	Withdrawn
Morriss, Wm	1,000	A	31	4-28-1780	Mulberry Cr	Mil surveyed
Morriss, Wm	400	A	37	4-29-1780	S Fk Licking	
Morriss, Wm	1,000	A	31	4-28-1780	Mulberry Cr	Surveyed
Morriss, Wm	1,200	B	46	5-23-1785		
Morrow, James	400	A	171	9-13-1780	Floyds Fk	
Mortimer, John	4,125	A	246	1- 6-1783	18 Mile Cr	Surveyed
Morton, John	500	A	103	5-27-1780	Station Camp Cr	
Morton, John	200	A	103	5-27-1780	Kentucky R	
Morton, John	300	A	103	5-27-1780	Kentucky R	
Morton, John	700	A	157	6-30-1780	Licking	
Morton, John	1,000	A	260	2- 4-1783	Rudes Cr	
Morton, John	845	A	265	2-21-1783	Robinsons Cr	
Morton, John	783½	A	301	11- 7-1783	—————	Surveyed
Morton, Joseph	50	A	24	4-24-1780	Cumberland R	Mil
Morton, Joseph	1,100	A	103	5-27-1780	Drowning Cr	
Morton, Joseph	500	A	111	5-29-1780	Barren Springs	
Morton, Joseph	900	A	111	5-29-1780	Rights Premption	
Morton, Joseph	900	A	111	5-29-1780	Floyds Fk	Surveyed
Morton, Richard	500	A	95	5-24-1780	Crooked Run	
Morton, Richard	250	A	95	5-24-1780	Salt R	
Morton, Richard	255	A	95	5-24-1785	N Fk Coxes Cr	Withdrawn
Morton, Richard	300	A	136	6-19-1780	Coxes Cr	272 acres surveyed
Morton, Richard	300	A	137	6-19-1780	Rowling Fk	188 acres surveyed
Morton, Richard	412	A	334	1-21-1784	—————	
Morton, Richard	255	A	360	5-14-1784	Coxes Cr	
Morton, Richard	350	B	5	9- 7-1784	Bear Cr	Surveyed
Morton, Samuel	400	A	264	2-15-1783	Rolling Fk	
Morgan, Simon	500	A	32	5- 9-1780	—————	Withdrawn
Morgan, Simon	862	A	38	5- 9-1780	Big Old Trace	Withdrawn
Morgan, Simon	500	A	38	5- 9-1780	—————	Withdrawn
Morgan, Simon	445	A	38	5- 9-1780	S Fk Limestone	Withdrawn
Morton, Thomas	400	A	264	2-15-1783	Rolling Fk	
Morton, Wm J	916½	A	54	5-15-1780	Hawkins Run	
Mosely, Robert	1,000	A	45	5-11-1780	Elkhorn	
Mosely, Robert	200	A	246	1- 6-1783	Willsons Cr	
Mosely, Robert	300	A	246	1- 6-1783	Willsons Cr	
Mosely, Robert	305	A	254	1-17-1783	Willsons Cr	
Moses, Thos	400	A	9	1-17-1780	Stoners Fk	
Moss, Frederick	400	A	101	5-26-1780	Holders Cr	
Moss, Thomas	1,148	A	371	7-12-1784	Brush Cr	
Motleys, Joel	12,150	A	312	12- 4-1783	Chaplins Fk	
Mountgomrie, Thomas	400	A	102	5-26-1780	Carpenters Cr	
Mountgomery, John	800	A	100	5-26-1780	Townsends Sett	
Muirhead, Charles	205	A	65	5-17-1780	Pasture Lick Cr	
Mukes, John	800	A	88	5-23-1780	Dicks R	
Mukes, John	400	A	88	5-23-1780	Kentucky R	
Muldrow, John	1,000	A	86	5-23-1780	Rowling Fk	Surveyed
Muldrough, Hugh	1,000	A	118	6- 1-1781	Town Fk	
Mumford, Thos B	3,000	A	144	6-23-1780	Green R	Withdrawn
Mumford, Thos B	3,000	A	144	6-23-1780	Sulphur Lick Cr	Withdrawn
Munday, Ben	500	A	84	5-22-1780	N Fk Licking	
Munday, Ben	50	A	34	4-29-1780	Beech Fk	Mil
Munday, James	50	A	20	4-17-1780	Sugar Run	Mil withdrawn
Munday, James	750	A	89	5-23-1780	Rowling Fk	
Munday, James	50	A	167	8-17-1780	Sugar Run	

Entree	Acres	Book	Page	Entry Date	Watercourse	Notes
Mundhall, John	400	A	341	2-26-1784	Floyds Fk	....
Munford, Thos B	6,000	A	220	8-29-1781	Green R	Surveyed
Munford, Thomas B	600	A	220	8-29-1781	Green R	....
Munroney, Sylvester	325	A	200	3-16-1781	Pond Cr	200 acres withdrawn
Murchie, John	500	A	234	12-19-1782	Green R	....
Murchie, John	2,987	A	235	12-19-1782	Salt R	Surveyed
Murphy, Arch	500	A	158	7- 3-1780	Goose Cr	....
Murray, Edward	400	A	6	12-23-1779	Murrays Run	....
Murray, John	335	A	40	5- 9-1780	Buck Fk	Withdrawn
Murray, Wm	400	A	66	5-17-1780	Pleasant Run	....
Murrill, George	1,500	A	242	12-52-1782	Green R	....
Murrill, George	3,281	A	242	12-25-1782	Green R	....
Murry, Anthony	500	A	95	5-24-1780	Salt Spring Trace	....
Murry, Elizabeth	2,000	A	33	4-29-1780	Brasher Cr	Mil surveyed
Murry, Wm	2,000	A	299	10-27-1783	John Pauls	Mil surveyed
Muschett, James	1,000	A	165	8-11-1780	Green R	Withdrawn
Muschett, James	500	A	208	4-18-1781	Harrods Cr & Ohio R	Withdrawn
Muschett, James	500	A	221	11- 9-1782	18 Mile Cr	....
Muschett, James	1,000	A	339	2-16-1784	Panther Cr	....
Muse, Battaile	1,000	A	56	5-15-1780	Simpson Cr	Surveyed
Muse, Battaile	1,000	A	263	2-14-1783	Simpsons Cr	Surveyed
Muse, George	1,000	A	20	4-14-1780	Ohio R	Mil
Muse, George	950	A	22	4-22-1780	White Oak Cr	Mil withdrawn
Muse, George	1,300	A	87	5-23-1780	Little Ky R	Surveyed
Muse, Phoebe	400	A	75	5-19-1780	Stoners Fk	....
Muter, George	2,000	A	137	6-19-1780	Licking	....
Myers, Jacob	50	A	5	12- 9-1779	Skeggs Cr	Withdrawn Mil
Myers, Jacob	50	A	5	12- 9-1779	Dicks R	Withdrawn Mil
Myers, Jacob	40	A	4	11-26-1779	Rolling Fk	Surveyed Mil
Myers, Jacob	50	A	4	11-26-1779	Shawnee R	Withdrawn Mil
Myers, Jacob	15	A	4	11-26-1779	Island, Falls Ohio	Surveyed Mil
Myers, Jacob	50	A	4	11-26-1779	Rockcastle R	Mil
Myers, Jacob	50	A	12	2- 7-1780	Skeggs Cr	Mil 7163
Myers, Jacob	50	A	12	2- 7-1780	N Fk Dicks	Mil 1763
Myers, Jacob	25	A	13	2-11-1780	Yellow Banks	....
Myers, Jacob	400	A	14	2-19-1780	Green R Falls	....
Myers, Jacob	100	A	16	2-25-1780	Green R	....
Myers, Jacob	50	A	16	2-25-1780	N Fk Elkhorn	....
Myers, Jacob	50	A	16	2-25-1780	S Fk Elkhorn	....
Myers, Jacob	50	A	16	2-25-1780	Fk Elkhorn	....
Myers, Jacob	50	A	16	2-25-1780	Mill Cr	....
Myers, Jacob	100	A	16	2-25-1780	Bear Grass Cr	Mil withdrawn
Myers, Jacob	100	A	18	3- 7-1780	N Fk Elkhorn	....
Myers, Jacob	100	A	18	3- 7-1780	Boones Cr	....
Myers, Jacob	400	A	18	3- 3-1780	Beach Fk	....
Myers, Jacob	100	A	21	4-20-1780	Ohio R	Surveyed
Myers, Jacob	200	A	21	4-20-1780	Beargrass	Withdrawn
Myers, Jacob	150	A	24	4-25-1780	N Fk Beargrass	Surveyed
Myers, Jacob	150	A	32	4-29-1780	Skeggs Cr	Surveyed
Myers, Jacob	400	A	50	5-13-1780	Ohio R	Surveyed
Myers, Jacob	490	A	50	5-13-1780	Dicks R	Surveyed
Myers, Jacob	1,000	A	50	5-12-1780	Elkhorn	....
Myers, Jacob	1,000	A	50	5-12-1780	Fk Elkhorn	....
Myers, Jacob	500	A	50	5-12-1780	Licking	....
Myers, Jacob	500	A	50	5-12-1780	Licking	....
Myers, Jacob	2,000	A	50	5-12-1780	Licking	....
Myers, Jacob	5,000	A	50	5-12-1780	Licking	....
Myers, Jacob	5,000	A	50	5-12-1780	Licking	....
Myers, Jacob	2,000	A	50	5-12-1780	Licking	....
Myers, Jacob	16,200	A	50	5-12-1780	Green R	8,200 acres withdrawn
Myers, Jacob	860	A	51	5-13-1780	Jessamine Cr	....
Myers, Jacob	500	A	51	5-13-1780	Licking	....
Myers, Jacob	1,000	A	51	5-13-1780	Clarks Run	....
Myers, Jacob	400	A	51	5-13-1780	Salt R	Surveyed
Myers, Jacob	200	A	51	5-13-1780	Greers Cr	....
Myers, Jacob	400	A	51	5-13-1780	Otter Cr	Surveyed
Myers, Jacob	500	A	51	5-13-1780	S Fk Skeggs Cr	....
Myers, Jacob	500	A	51	5-13-1780	S Fk Dicks R	....
Myers, Jacob	200	A	51	5-13-1780	Salt R	....
Myers, Jacob	600	A	51	5-13-1780	Beech Fk	Withdrawn ..
Myers, Jacob	600	A	51	5-13-1780	Cartright Cr	Surveyed
Myers, Jacob	1,000	A	51	5-13-1780	Fk Indian Cr	....
Myers, Jacob	200	A	51	5-13-1780	Licking	....

Entree	Acres	Book	Page	Entry Date	Watercourse	Notes
Myers, Jacob	200	A	51	5–13–1780	N Fk Dicks R	Surveyed
Myers, Jacob	200	A	51	5–13–1780	Green R	Surveyed
Myers, Jacob	700	A	51	5–13–1780	Pottenger Cr	Surveyed
Myers, Jacob	400	A	51	5–13–1780	Hanging Fk	....
Myers, Jacob	800	A	51	5–13–1780	Pottinger Cr	Surveyed
Myers, Jacob	100	A	51	5–13–1780	Blue Clay Lick	....
Myers, Jacob	100	A	51	5–13–1780	Salt R	....
Myers, Jacob	100	A	51	5–13–1780	N Fk Johnstons Fk	....
Myers, Jacob	1,000	A	51	5–31–1780	Cartright Cr	Surveyed
Myers, Jacob	200	A	51	5–13–1780	Panther Cr	....
Myers, Jacob	300	A	158	7– 3–1780	Wolf Cr	....
Myers, Jacob	400	A	163	7–22–1780	Green R	Surveyed
Myers, Jacob	300	A	165	8–11–1780	Ohio R	....
Myers, Jacob	100	A	172	9–19–1780	Diamond Island	....
Myers, Jacob	400	A	186	3–14–1781	Salt R	....
Myers, Jacob	1,000	A	187	3–14–1781	Simpsons Cr	Surveyed
Myers, Jacob	3,000	A	189	3–15–1781	Green R	Surveyed
Myers, Jacob	200	A	189	3–15–1781	Salt R	Withdrawn
Myers, Jacob	1,000	A	189	3–15–1781	Salt R	Surveyed
Myers, Jacob	1,000	A	189	3–15–1781	Ohio R	Surveyed
Myers, Jacob	7,200	A	189	3–15–1781	Green R	Surveyed
Myers, Jacob	520	A	191	3–15–1781	Clears Station	....
Myers, Jacob	1,000	A	203	4– 3–1781	Fk Sinking Cr	Surveyed
Myers, Jacob	1,000	A	203	4– 3–1781	Green R	Surveyed
Myers, Jacob	1,000	A	203	4– 3–1781	Sinking Cr	Surveyed
Myers, Jacob	1,000	A	203	4– 3–1781	Buffaloe Cr	Surveyed
Myers, Jacob	23	A	280	6–19–1781	Diamond Island	....
Myers, Jacob	1,000	A	289	9– 8–1783	Pond Cr	Surveyed
Myers, Jacob	500	A	294	10–11–1789	Kentucky R	Surveyed
Myers, Jacob	500	A	294	10–11–1783	Kentucky R	Surveyed
Myers, Jacob	1,000	A	299	10–27–1783	Diamond Island	Surveyed
Myers, Jacob	1,500	A	322	12–24–1783	Mill Cr	....
Myers, Jacob	500	A	326	1– 3–1784	Rolling Fk	....
Myers, Jacob	200	A	326	1– 3–1784	Rolling Fk	....
Myers, Jacob	701	A	327	1– 5–1784	———	....
Myers, Jacob	5,604½	A	359	5–10–1784	Salt R	....
Myers, Jacob	4,000	A	362	5–25–1784	———	....
Myers, Jacob	400	A	366	6–18–1784	Salt R	....
Myers, Jacob	200	A	373	7–22–1784	Ohio R	....
Myers, Jacob	200	A	373	7–22–1784	Ohio R	....
Myers, Jacob	500	A	373	7–21–1784	———	....
Myers, Jacob	100	A	377	8–10–1784	Falls Ohio R	Withdrawn
Myers, Jacob	158	A	377	8–10–1784	Rolling Fk	....
Myers, Jacob	200	A	377	8–10–1784	Ohio R	....
Myers, Jacob	200	A	377	8–10–1784	Ohio R	....
Myers, Jacob	558	A	377	8–10–1784	———	Withdrawn
Myers, Jacob	2,000	A	377	8–10–1784	Ohio R	Withdrawn
Myers, Jacob	500	A	377	8–10–1784	Beech Fk	....
Myers, Jacob	400	A	378	3–14–1781	Salt R	Error
Myers, Jacob	3,000	B	19	11–26–1784	Green R	....
Myers, Jacob	1,000	B	19	11–26–1784	Fox Run	Surveyed
Myers, Jacob	1,200	B	20	11–26–1784	Salt R	Surveyed
Myers, Jacob	200	B	20	11–26–1784	Salt R	Withdrawn
Myers, Jacob	2,000	B	20	11–26–1784	Ohio R	Withdrawn
Myers, Jacob	2,000	B	20	11–26–1784	Ohio R	Withdrawn
Myers, Jacob	100	B	20	11–26–1784	Falls Ohio R	....
Myers, Jacob	100	B	20	11–26–1784	———	Withdrawn
Myers, Jacob	30,000	B	20	11–26–1784	Falls Green R	....
Myers, Jacob	3,000	B	20	11–26–1784	Green R	....
Myers, Jacob	2,000	B	20	11–26–1784	Green R	....
Myers, Jacob	1,000	B	22	12– 3–1784	Drenning Lick Cr	Withdrawn
Myers, Jacob	1,000	B	22	12– 3–1784	Big Cr	Withdrawn
Myers, Jacob	1,000	B	22	12– 1–1784	Big Cr	Withdrawn
Myers, Jacob	3,000	B	24	12–10–1784	———	1,000 acres surveyed
Myers, Jacob	1,396½	B	24	12– 9–1784	Salt R	Surveyed
Myers, Jacob	1,000	B	24	12– 9–1784	Gess Cr	Withdrawn
Myers, Jacob	800	B	24	12– 9–1784	Ohio R	Withdrawn
Myers, Jacob	1,325	B	24	12– 9–1784	Ohio R	Withdrawn
Myers, Jacob	1,600	B	24	12– 9–1784	Ohio R	Withdrawn
Myers, Jacob	1,113	B	24	12– 9–1784	Knobbs Salt R	Withdrawn
Myers, Jacob	1,000	B	37	1–27–1785	———	123½ acres surveyed
Myers, Jacob	2,600	B	42	3–24–1785	———	900 acres surveyed
Myers, Jacob	500	B	42	3–24–1785	———	250 acres surveyed
Myers, Jacob	1,000	B	42	3–24–1785	Drennings Lick	Withdrawn
Myers, Jacob	1,000	B	42	3–24–1785	Big Cr	Withdrawn
Myers, Jacob	1,000	B	42	3–24–1785	Big Cr	Withdrawn
Myers, Jacob	800	B	42	3–24–1785	Dry Run	Withdrawn

Entree	Acres	Book	Page	Entry Date	Watercourse	Notes
Myers, Jacob	1,600	B	42	3–24–1785	————	Withdrawn
Myers, Jacob	1,000	B	42	3–24–1785	Gesses Cr	Withdrawn
Myers, Jacob	1,325	B	42	3–24–1785	————	Withdrawn
Myers, Jacob	1,113	B	42	3–24–1785	Falls Ohio R	....
Myers, James	2,000	A	190	3–15–1781	Green R	Surveyed
Myers, Wm	400	A	15	2–21–1780	Wilsons Run	Surveyed
Myers, Wm	1,000	A	27	4–26–1780	Wilson Run	Surveyed
Myres, Jacob	500	A	198	3–17–1781	Salt R	Withdrawn
Myres, Jacob	400	A	198	3–17–1781	Otter Cr	• Withdrawn
Myres, Jacob	100	A	198	3–17–1781	Green R	Withdrawn
Myres, Jacob	400	A	203	4– 3–1781	Otter Cr	....
Myres, Jacob	1,000	A	203	4– 3–1781	Pleasant Run	....
Myres, Jacob	1,000	A	203	4– 3–1781	Willsons Cr	Surveyed
Myres, Jacob	400	A	203	4– 3–1781	Green R	....
Myres, Jacob	1,000	A	203	4– 3–1781	Salt R	....
Myres, Jacob	1,000	A	203	4– 3–1781	Coxes Cr	Surveyed
Myres, Jacob	300	A	204	4– 5–1781	Wolf Cr	....
Myres, Jacob	300	A	204	4– 5–1781	Wolf Cr	....
Myres, Jacob	500	A	204	4– 5–1781	Salt R	Surveyed
Myres, Jacob	400	A	204	4– 4–1781	Mill Cr	Surveyed
Myres, Jacob	400	A	204	4– 4–1781	Beech Fk	Surveyed
Myres, Jacob	400	A	205	4– 5–1781	Rowling Fk	Surveyed
Myres, Jacob	200	A	205	4– 5–1781	Salt R	....
Myres, Jacob	2,000	A	206	4–10–1781	Coxes Cr	1,000 acres surveyed
Myres, Jacob	100	A	206	4–11–1781	Bullgers Lick	....
Myres, Jacob	400	A	206	4–11–1781	Rowling Fk	Surveyed
Myres, Jacob	200	A	209	5–18–1781	Cartrights Cr	....
Myres, Jacob	1,000	A	221	11– 9–1781	Falls Green R	Withdrawn
Myres, Jacob	1,000	A	221	9– 7–1781	————	Returned
Myres, Jacob	1,000	A	222	12–12–1782	Simpsons Cr	577 acres surveyed
Myres, Jacob	1,000	A	229	12–16–1782	Coxes Cr	777 acres surveyed
Myres, Jacob	500	A	232	12–18–1782	Otter Cr	....
Myres, Jacob	500	A	232	12–18–1782	Ohio R	....
Myres, Jacob	500	A	232	12–18–1782	Rolling Fk	....
Myres, Jacob	825	A	238	12–23–1782	Floyds Fk	Withdrawn
Myres, Jacob	2,583¾	A	238	12–23–1782	Coxes Cr	1,025 acres surveyed 1,558 acres withdrawn
Myres, Jacob	800	A	240	12–24–1782	Coxes Cr	777 acres surveyed
Myres, Jacob	500	A	240	12–24–1782	Beach Fk	Withdrawn
Myres, Jacob	500	A	240	12–24–1782	Rolling Fk	....
Myres, Jacob	2,000	A	240	12–24–1782	Salt R	Surveyed
Myres, Jacob	100	A	240	12–24–1782	Coxes Cr	....
Myres, Jacob	301½	A	240	12–24–1782	Cartright Cr	....
Myres, Jacob	300	A	240	12–24–1782	Panther Cr	....
Myres, Jacob	100	A	240	12–24–1782	Beech Fk	....
Myres, Jacob	500	A	240	12–24–1782	Ohio R	Surveyed
Myres, Jacob	800	A	240	12–24–1782	Cartright Cr	Surveyed
Myres, Jacob	600	A	240	12–24–1782	Cartright Cr	Surveyed
Myres, Jacob	1,000	A	244	12–27–1782	Coxes Cr	666 acres surveyed
Myres, Jacob	1,000	A	244	12–27–1782	Coxes Cr	....
Myres, Jacob	100	A	250	1– 9–1783	Salt R	Withdrawn
Myres, Jacob	300	A	250	1– 8–1783	————	Withdrawn
Myres, Jacob	800	A	250	1– 8–1783	Bacon Cr	Surveyed
Myres, Jacob	700	A	250	1– 8–1783	Coxes Cr	Withdrawn
Myres, Jacob	1,500	A	250	1– 8–1783	Salt R	Surveyed
Myres, Jacob	400	A	250	1– 8–1783	Cartright Cr	....
Myres, Jacob	600	A	250	1– 8–1783	Cartright Cr	....
Myres, Jacob	400	A	256	1–21–1783	Salt R	....
Myres, Jacob	400	A	256	1–21–1783	Salt R	Withdrawn
Myres, Jacob	250	A	259	2– 1–1783	Simpsons Cr	....
Myres, Jacob	250	A	259	2– 1–1783	Salt R	Surveyed
Myres, Jacob	200	A	259	1–30–1783	Salt R	Withdrawn
Myres, Jacob	300	A	259	1–30–1783	Salt R	....
Myres, Jacob	500	A	259	1–30–1783	Simpson Cr	Withdrawn
Myres, Jacob	9,000	A	265	2–25–1783	Coxes Cr	Surveyed
Myres, Jacob	200	A	265	2–24–1783	Bullskin Cr	....
Myres, Jacob	957¾	A	265	2–24–1783	————	....
Myres, Jacob	1,000	A	265	2–21–1783	Long Falls Green R	....
Myres, Jacob	4,000	A	265	2–21–1783	Green R	....
Myres, Jacob	716	A	265	2–21–1783	Simpsons Cr	....
Myres, Jacob	1,000	A	265	2–21–1783	Salt R	Withdrawn
Myres, Jacob	500	A	265	2–21–1783	Simpsons Cr	Surveyed
Myres, Jacob	3,408	A	278	4–14–1783	————	825 acres surveyed

Entree	Acres	Book	Page	Entry Date	Watercourse	Notes
Myres, Jacob	1,000	A	359	5-10-1784	Bulgers Lick	Surveyed
Myres, Jacob	2,000	A	359	5-10-1784	Bulgers Lick	Surveyed
Myres, Jacob	300	A	366	6-17-1784	———	....
Myres, Jacob	476½	A	372	7-16-1784	Salt R	Surveyed
Myres, Jacob	123½	A	372	7-16-1784	Diamond Island	Surveyed
Myres, Jacob et al	1,000	A	203	4- 3-1781	Falls Green R	....
Myres, Jacob et al	400	A	204	4- 4-1781	Fromans Cr	Surveyed
Myres, Jacob et al	1,000	A	204	4- 4-1781	Cartrights Cr	Surveyed
Myres, Joseph.	1,000	A	203	4- 3-1781	Fox Run	Surveyed
Myres, Jost	1,000	A	230	12-17-1782	Drining Lick	Surveyed
Myres, Jost	400	A	230	12-17-1782	Fox Run	Surveyed
Nall, Barnard	250	A	30	4-28-1780	Hustons Fk	Mil
Nall, James	500	A	97	5-25-1780	Beach Fk	Surveyed
Nall, Martin	1,000	A	65	5-17-1780	Rolling Fk	....
Nall, Martin.	1,000	A	65	5-17-1780	Rolling Fk	....
Nall, Martin	50	A	122	6- 2-1780	Ohio R	Mil
Nall, Martin	400	A	139	6-21-1780	Salt R	....
Nall, Martin	400	A	139	6-21-1780	Ohio R	....
Nall, Martin	1,000	A	199	3-20-1781	Salt R	Mil surveyed
Nall, Martin	2,000	A	317	12-16-1783	———	Surveyed
Nall, Richard	307	A	97	5-25-1780	Beech Fk	Surveyed
Nall, Richard	133	A	97	5-25-1780	Beech Fk	....
Nall, Wm	500	A	122	6- 2-1780	Ohio R	....
Nall, Wm	750	A	123	6- 2-1780	Green R	....
Nalle, Francis	500	A	97	5-25-1780	Beech Fk Salt R	Surveyed
Nalle, Francis	892½	A	245	12-28-1782	Beech Fk	133 surveyed returned
Nalle, Richard	440	A	352	4-15-1784	———	....
Nash, Francis	701	A	248	1- 7-1783	18 Mile Cr	....
Nash, James	500	A	61	5-16-1780	Cartright Cr	....
Nash, James	500	A	97	5-25-1780	Cartrights Cr	....
Nash, Travers	586	A	241	12-25-1782	Mill Cr	....
Neal, Ben.	1,000	A	62	5-16-1780	Salt R	....
Neal, George	175	A	241	12-25-1782	Sulphur Lick Cr	Surveyed
Neal, George	285	B	30	12-23-1784	Clear Cr	Surveyed
Neal, George	110	B	31	1- 3-1785	———	....
Neall, George	325	B	41	3- 4-1785	———	175 acres surveyed
Neal, Joseph	1,000	A	62	5-16-1780	Salt R	Withdrawn
Neatherland, Benj	400	A	263	2-15-1783	Simpsons Cr	Withdrawn
Neatherland, Benj	600	A	263	2-15-1783	Simpson Cr	Surveyed
Neatherland, Benj	1,500	A	283	7- 4-1783	Salt R	....
Neatherland, Benj	1,500	A	284	7-30-1783	Little Ky R	....
Neatherland, Benj	500	A	284	7-30-1783	Little Ky R	Surveyed
Neatherland, Benj	1,000	A	284	7-30-1783	Little Ky R	Surveyed
Neatherland, Benj	2,000	A	284	7-30-1783	Little Ky R	Surveyed
Neatherland, Benj	500	A	295	10-11-1783	Floyds Fk	....
Neatherland, Benj	100	A	297	10-23-1783	Beargrass Cr	....
Neatherland, Benj	1,000	A	298	10-24-1783	Ohio R	Amended
Neatherland, Benj	400	A	298	10-23-1783	Floyds Fk	....
Neatherland, Benj	1,000	A	312	12- 4-1783	Green R	....
Neatherland, Benj	1,000	A	312	12- 4-1783	Green R	....
Neatherland, Benj	4,322½	A	321	12-20-1783	Nole Linn Cr	Surveyed
Neatherland, Benj	162	A	334	1-21-1784	Salt R	1,662 acres surveyed
Neatherland, Benj	4,991	B	10	10-11-1784	———	....
Neatherland, Benj	2,000	B	32	1- 8-1785	———	....
Neatherland, Benj	100	B	41	2-28-1785	———	....
Neatherland, Benj et al	1,000	A	259	2- 1-1783	Salt R	Withdrawn
Neatherland, Benj et al	1,000	A	263	2-15-1783	Salt R	....
Neatherland, Benj et al	2,000	A	272	3-31-1783	Camp Run	Surveyed
Neatherland, Benj et al	5,000	A	286	8-12-1783	Rough Cr	Withdrawn
Neatherland, Benj et al	6,000	A	295	10-11-1783	Floyds Fk	....
Neatherland, Benj et al.	10,035	A	295	10-11-1783	Floyds Fk	Surveyed
Neatherland, Benj et al	2,000	A	297	10-23-1783	Floyds Fk	Withdrawn
Neatherland, Benj et al	400	A	298	10-25-1783	Simpson Cr	Surveyed
Neatherland, Benj et al	400	A	298	10-25-1783	Plumb Run	Withdrawn
Neatherland, Benj et al	600	A	298	10-25-1783	Simpsons Cr	Surveyed
Neatherland, Benj et al	3,000	A	301	11- 1-1783	Floyds Fk	....
Neatherland, Benj et al	1,002	A	303	11-10-1783	Floyds Fk	Surveyed
Neatherland, Benj et al	800	A	303	11-10-1783	Floyds Fk	Withdrawn
Neatherland, Benj et al	5,000	A	310	11-26-1783	Rough Cr	....
Neatherland, Benj et al.	2,000	A	329	1-12-1784	Bear Cr	Surveyed
Neelson, Robert	1,000	B	16	11-12-1784	———	....
Neely, John	937½	A	308	11-22-1783	N Fk Bear Cr	....
Neil, Benj	1,000	A	107	5-29-1780	Drinnons Lick	Surveyed
Neil, Joseph	500	A	107	5-29-1780	Floyds Fk	Surveyed
Neil, Joseph	500	A	107	5-29-1780	Floyds Fk	....
Nelson, Abraham	3,000	B	16	11-12-1784	Green R	....
Nelson, Abraham	3,000	B	31	1- 3-1785	———	....

Entree	Acres	Book	Page	Entry Date	Watercourse	Notes
Nelson, Anderson	2,000	A	151	6–26–1780	Goose Cr	
Nelson, Edward	400	A	9	1–18–1780	Sinking Cr	
Nellson, John	1,000	A	288	8–26–1783	Knobb Cr	Surveyed
Nelson, Robert	380	B	45	5–16–1785	Kentucky R	Surveyed
Nelson, Robert	520	B	45	5–16–1785	Kentucky R	Surveyed
Nelson, Robert	962	B	45	5–16–1785		Surveyed
Nelson, Wm	1,500	A	84	5–22–1780	Johnstons Fk	
Netherland, Benj	2,000	A	255	1–18–1783	Simpsons Cr	
Netherland, Benj	1,000	A	289	9– 8–1783	Ohio R	
Netherland, Benj	6,600	A	371	7–16–1784	——	
Netherland, Benj et al.	2,000	A	254	1–17–1783	Brashears Cr	Surveyed
Netherland, Benj et al.	5,000	A	282	7– 2–1783	Rough Cr	Withdrawn
Nevill, James	400	A	148	6–24–1780	Dicks R	
Nevill, John	1,000	A	281	6–30–1783	Kentucky R	Surveyed
Newall, James	1,000	A	269	3–28–1783	Beech Fk	
Newell, John	400	A	38	4–29–1780	E Fk Licking	
Newell, James	1,000	A	267	3–28–1783	Ohio R..*	
Newell, Theodorick	421	A	40	5– 9–1780	N Fk Elkhorn	
Newland, Jacob	400	A	80	5–20–1780	Drennens Lick	Surveyed
Newland, Jacob	1,000	A	176	10– 6–1780	Pleasant Run	Surveyed
Newland, Jacob	600	A	183	10–30–1780	Beech Fk	
Newland, Jacob	400	A	184	10–30–1780	Pleasant Run	
Newman, John P	400	A	373	7–24–1784	——	
Newman, John P	400	A	374	7–28–1784	Beech Fk	
Netton, Joseph	100	A	141	6–22–1780	Hanging Fk	Withdrawn
Nisbel, Sam	400	A	18	3– 1–1780	Licking Cr	
Nisbel, Wm	400	A	18	3– 1–1780	Licking Cr	
Nitner, Henry	400	A	53	5–13–1780	Licking	
Nixon, Thomas	30,000	A	332	1–20–1784	McWilliams	98,000 acres withdrawn
Nixon, Thomas	20,000	A	345	3– 4–1784	Green R	Surveyed
Nixon, Thomas	10,000	A	345	3– 4–1784	Little Barren R	5,000 acres withdrawn
Nixon, Thomas	5,000	A	348	3–22–1784	Little Barren R	Withdrawn
Noel, Taylor	50	A	31	4–28–1780	Elkhorn	Mil
Nourse, James	2,500	A	31	4–28–1780	S Fk Harrods Cr	Surveyed
North, John	14,638	A	349	4– 5–1784	Ohio R	
North, Wm	5,000	A	228	12–16–1782	Beech Fk	
Norton, John W	6,000	A	81	5–22–1780	Ohio R	
Nourse, Charles	1,000	A	73	5–19–1780	Harrods Cr	
Nourse, Jacob	1,000	B	26	12–13–1784	Ky R	
Nourse, James	1,000	A	30	4–28–1780	Hingston Fk	Surveyed
Nourse, James	1,000	A	30	4–28–1780	Goose Cr	Surveyed
Nours, James	1,750	A	32	4–29–1780	Limestone	Surveyed
Nourse, James	2,000	A	32	4–29–1780	Little Yellow Bank	Withdrawn
Nourse, James	750	A	33	4–27–1780	Floyds Fk	Withdrawn
Nourse, James	1,000	A	33	4–29–1780	Licking	
Nourse, James	1,000	A	33	4–27–1780	Salt R	
Nourse, James	1,000	A	33	4–29–1780	Salt R	Surveyed
Nourse, James	2,500	A	375	7–29–1784	——	Mil 1,000acres surveyed
Nourse, James	750	B	23	12– 8–1784	Harrods Cr	
Nourse, James	750	B	23	12– 8–1784	Beargrass Cr	Withdrawn
Nourse, James	3,000	B	23	12– 8–1784	1,000 in Fayette	Surveyed
Nourse, Joseph	1,000	A	354	5–13–1780	Harrods Cr	Withdrawn
Nourse, Joseph	400	A	53	5–13–1780	Nolin Cr	Surveyed
Nourse, Joseph	600	A	53	5–13–1780	Green R	Surveyed
Nourse, Joseph	2,000	A	315	12–15–1783	——	1,000 acres surveyed
Nourse, Joseph	1,000	A	354	4–16–1784	Harrods Cr	Withdrawn
Nourse, Joseph	1,000	B	54	4–16–1784	Harrods Cr	Withdrawn
Nourse, Joseph	1,000	A	53	5–13–1780	Harrods Cr	Withdrawn
Nourse, Joseph	1,000	A	53	5–13–1780	Green R	Surveyed
Nourse, Joseph	1,000	B	26	12–13–1784	Kentucky R	
Nowil, Olive	50	A	92	5–24–1780	Kentucky R	
Noxon, Thomas	30,000	A	34	3– 5–1784	Ramsey & Cox	Withdrawn
Nutter, Christain	250	A	212	6–25–1781	N Fk Floyds Fk	
O'Banion, John	1,000	A	54	5–15–1780	Lawrence Cr	
Obannan, Wm	1,046	A	326	1– 1–1784	Salt R	Withdrawn
Obannion, Wm	1,046	A	23	12– 8–1784	Salt R	Withdrawn
Oglesby, Jacob	981¼	A	296	10–14–1783	Pittmans Cr	
Oglesby, Thomas	256¾	A	296	10–14–1783	Rolling Fk	
Oldham, Conway	1,000	A	109	5–29–1780	Eatons Cr	
Oldham, George	500	A	161	7– 8–1780	Licking	
Oldham, Samuel	4,000	A	109	5–29–1780	Rowling Fk	3,222 acres surveyed 778 acres withdrawn
Oldham, Samuel	5,000	A	247	1– 7–1783	Ohio R	1,751 acres surveyed
Oldham, Samuel	500	A	248	1– 8–1783	Noelin Cr	

Entree	Acres	Book	Page	Entry Date	Watercourse	Notes
Oldham, Samuel	500	A	248	1- 7-1783	Noelin Cr	100 acres surveyed
Oldham, Samuel	2,000	A	248	1- 8-1783	Bear Cr	Surveyed
Oldham, Samuel	4,000	A	255	1-20-1783	Ohio R	
Oldham, Samuel	500	A	255	1-20-1783	Rock Lick Cr	475 acres surveyed
Oldham, Samuel	500	A	255	1-20-1783	Rough Cr	Surveyed
Oldham, Samuel	2,000	A	255	1-20-1783	Rough Cr	Surveyed
Oldham, Samuel	3,000	A	255	1-20-1783	Rough Cr	Surveyed
Oldham, Samuel	2,000	A	255	1-20-1783	Panther Cr	Surveyed
Oldham, Samuel	134	A	261	2-11-1783	Salt R	
Oldham, Samuel	575	A	262	2-11-1783	Pond Cr	
Oldham, Samuel	177	A	262	2-11-1783	9 Mile Falls Ohio R	
Oldham, Samuel	1,000	A	262	2-11-1783	11 Mile Falls Ohio R	593 acres surveyed
Oldham, Samuel	500	A	262	2-11-1783	Salt R	
Oldham, Samuel	614	A	262	2-11-1783	Salt R	
Oldham, Samuel	6,000	A	295	10-11-1783	Kentucky R	Surveyed
Oldham, Samuel	778	A	326	1- 2-1783	Pottengers Cr	
Oldham, Samuel	400	A	370	7-10-1784	Beargrass Cr	
Oldham, Samuel	20,000	A	371	7-16-1784	——	12,851 acres surveyed
Oldham, Samuel	1,000	A	371	7-16-1784	——	222 acres surveyed
Oldham, Samuel	200	A	371	7-16-1784	Beargrass Cr	
Oldham, Samuel	500	B	13	11-11-1784	Ohio R	Surveyed
Oldham, Samuel	276	B	13	11-11-1784	——	Surveyed
Oldham, Samuel	250	B	13	11-11-1784	Ohio R	Surveyed
Oldham, Wm	560	A	109	5-29-1780	——	Surveyed
Oldham, Wm	400	A	119	6- 1-1780	Floyds Fk	Surveyed
Oldham, Wm	200	A	238	12-23-1782	Pottengers Cr	
Oldham, Wm	1,000	A	247	1- 7-1783	Hardens Cr	Withdrawn
Oldham, Wm	500	A	247	1- 7-1783	Mill Cr	Withdrawn
Oldham, Wm	500	A	247	1- 7-1783	Bullskins	Surveyed
Oldham, Wm	500	A	247	1- 7-1783	Pond Cr	Surveyed
Oldham, Wm	500	A	247	1- 7-1783	Ohio R	
Oldham, Wm	500	A	247	1- 7-1783	Ohio R	
Oldham, Wm	500	A	247	1- 7-1783	Ohio R	Surveyed
Oldham, Wm	5,825	A	258	1-27-1783	Tewels Cr	5,225 acres surveyed
Oldham, Wm	3,800	A	258	1-27-1783	Yellow Bank Cr	Surveyed
Oldham, Wm	500	A	298	10-25-1783	Clear Cr	277 acres surveyed
Oldham, Wm	400	A	326	1- 2-1784	Pottengers Cr	
Oldham, Wm	400	A	326	1- 2-1784	Pottengers Cr	
Oldham, Wm	9,325	A	327	1- 5-1784	——	6,725 acres surveyed
Oldham, Wm	104	B	50	9-24-1785	Ohio R	
Oldham, Wm	1,000	A	238	12-23-1782	Pottengers Cr	
Oliver, Benj	50	A	35	4-29-1780	Salt R	Mil
Oliver, John	200	A	243	12-26-1782	18 Mile Cr	
Oliver, Thomas	1,000	A	207	4-13-1781	Gess Cr	Surveyed
Oliver, Thomas et al	1,000	A	249	1- 8-1783	Buffaloe Cr	
Oliver, Thomas et al	2,000	A	249	1- 8-1783	Geses Cr	Surveyed
Oliver, Turner	400	A	244	12-26-1782	Coxes Cr	
Oliver, Wm	400	A	159	7- 4-1780	Coxes Cr	
O'Neal, Bryant	400	A	71	5-18-1780	Beech Fk	
O'Neil, Thomas	370¼	A	282	7- 2-1783	Gilkeys Run	
Orondorff, Conrod	300	A	71	5-18-1780	Pottengers Cr	Withdrawn
Orondorff, Conrod	300	A	201	4- 2-1781	Pottengers Cr	
Orr, Alexander et al	5,000	A	324	12-26-1783	Kentucky R	
Osborne, Wm	400	A	74	5-19-1780	Pleasant Run	
Osburn, Ebenezer	250	A	209	5-23-1781	Fromans Cr	Surveyed
Osburn, Ebenezer	1,000	B	13	11-11-1784	——	250 acres surveyed
Ousley, Thomas	1,000	A	39	5- 9-1780	Simpsons Cr	
Ousley, Thomas	500	A	39	5- 9-1780	Cedar Cr	
Ousley, Thomas	700	A	39	5- 9-1780	Dick R	
Ousley, Thomas	1,000	A	39	5- 9-1780	Crab Orchard Run	
Overton, Clough	1,000	A	26	4-26-1780	Salt R	Surveyed
Overton, Clough	400	A	26	4-26-1780	Salt R	Surveyed
Overton, C & W	600	A	46	5-11-1780	Salt R	
Overton, C & W	117	A	138	6-20-1780	Salt R	Surveyed
Overton, C & W	50	A	138	6-20-1780	Clear Cr	
Overton, C & W	50	A	357	5- 1-1784	Clear Cr	
Overton, James	1,000	A	87	5-23-1780	W Fk Pleasant Run	
Overton, James	100	A	185	10-31-1780	Fromans Cr	Surveyed
Overton, James Jr	100	A	35	4-29-1780	Eagle Cr	Mil withdrawn
Overton, James Jr	800	A	91	5-24-1780	Fromans Cr	Surveyed
Overton, James Jr	100	A	159	7- 5-1780	Kentucky R	Withdrawn

Entree	Acres	Book	Page	Entry Date	Watercourse	Notes
Overton, John	4,000	A	207	4-14-1781	Bullskin	Surveyed
Overall, John	250	A	227	12-14-1782	Long Lick Cr	Surveyed
Overall, John	276	A	353	4-15-1784	Long Lick Cr	Surveyed
Overall, John	276	B	49	6-17-1785	————	
Overton, Waller	1,150	A	75	5-19-1780	Floyds Fk	Surveyed
Owen, John C	500	A	50	5-12-1780	Hingston Fk	
Owen, John C	500	A	50	5-12-1780	Licking Cr	
Owen, John C	500	A	50	5-12-1780	Mill Cr	
Owen, John C	1,400	A	343	3- 3-1784	Caney Run	Withdrawn
Owen, John C	1,160	B	28	12-18-1784	Ramers Cr	Withdrawn
Owen, John C	1,100	B	28	12-18-1784	Big Caney Cr	Withdrawn
Owens, Brackett	1,000	A	295	10-13-1783	Beargrass Cr	Withdrawn
Owens, John C	1,000	A	50	5-12-1780	Wolf Cr	
Owens, John C	600	A	50	5-12-1780	N Fk Elkhorn	
Owens, John C	400	A	50	5-12-1780	S Fk Elkhorn	
Owens, John C	500	A	50	5-12-1780	Floyds Fk	
Owens, John C	500	A	50	5-12-1780	Station Camp Cr	
Owens, John C	500	A	50	5-12-1780	Mid N Fk Elkhorn	
Owens, John C	1,000	A	343	3- 3-1784	Caney Run	Withdrawn
Owens, John C	1,000	A	343	3- 3-1784	Caney Run	Withdrawn
Owens, John C	1,200	A	343	3- 3-1784	Caney Run	Withdrawn
Owens, John C	1,400	A	343	3- 3-1784	Caney Run	Withdrawn
Owens, John C	1,200	A	343	3- 3-1784	Caney Run	Withdrawn
Owens, John C	1,400	A	343	3- 3-1784	Caney Run	Withdrawn
Owens, John C	1,000	A	352	4-14-1784	Big Benson Cr	Surveyed
Owens, John C	4,000	A	352	4-14-1784	Big Benson Cr	Surveyed
Owens, John C	10,000	B	27	12-18-1784	————	Withdrawn
Owens, John C	1,730	B	28	12-18-1784	Caney Cr	
Owens, John C	1,150	B	28	12-18-1784	Caney Cr	
Owens, John C	1,400	B	28	12-18-1784	Caney Cr	
Owens, John C	1,325	B	28	12-18-1784	Ramers Cr	
Owens, John C	1,350	B	28	12-18-1784	Big Caney Cr	Withdrawn
Owens, John C	785	B	28	12-18-1784	Big Caney Cr	
Owens, John C et al	2,000	A	50	5-12-1780	Fk Licking	
Owens, Owen	1,000	A	229	12-16-1782	Sinking Cr	Surveyed
Owens, Owen	1,000	A	268	3-28-1783	W Fk Brush Cr	
Owens, Wm	400	A	72	5-18-1780	Poplar Flat	
Owens, Wm	1,000	B	6	9-13-1784		
Owing, John C	400	A	204	4- 5-1781	Wolf Cr	
Owing, Edward et al	1,000	A	50	5-13-1780		
Owing, Edward et al	1,000	A	50	5-12-1780	N Fk Licking	
Owins, John C	400	A	21	2-21-1780	Jessamine Cr	
Owings, J C	500	A	46	5-11-1780	J Glass Sett	
Owings, J C	1,000	A	337	2-12-1784	Cedar Cr	
Owings, J C	1,000	A	337	2-12-1784	Cedar Cr	
Owins, John C	1,750	A	347	3-17-1784	Wolf Cr	Withdrawn
Owings, John C	1,750	A	377	8-10-1784		Withdrawn
Ownby, James	1,400	A	243	12-26-1782	Drennons Lick Cr	
Owsley, Henry	455	A	180	10-19-1780	Salt Lick	
Owsley, Thomas	1,000	A	38	4-29-1780	Moores Sett	
Owsley, Thomas	1,000	A	38	4-29-1780	Owsley Sett	
Owsley, Thomas	738	A	108	5-29-1780	N Floyds Fk	Surveyed
Owsley, Wm	500	A	109	5-29-1780	Green R	
Paddock, Sarah	400	A	250	1- 9-1783	Ohio R	Surveyed
Page, Robert	500	A	266	2-25-1783	Gesses Cr	
Page, Wm	240¾	A	351	4-13-1784	Robinsons Cr	
Paltz, John	400	A	108	5-29-1780	Pensilvania Run	
Panebaker, Wm	500	A	292	10- 1-1783	Rolling Fk	Withdrawn
Panibaker, Wm	500	A	297	10-20-1783	Rolling Fk	
Pannell, David	2,000	A	109	5-29-1780	Ohio R	
Pannell, Wm	150	A	30	4-28-1780	Hingston Fk	Mil
Pannell, Wm	500	A	52	5-13-1780	Soverins Cr	
Pannell, Wm	500	A	78	5-20-1780	Jessamine Cr	
Pannell, Wm	500	A	78	5-20-1780	Jessamine Cr	
Pannell, Wm	1,000	A	146	6-24-1780	Hingstons Fk	
Parberry, James	400	A	9	1-17-1780	Green Cr	
Parberry, James	400	A	9	1-18-1780	Green Cr	
Parberry, James	50	A	13	2-19-1780	Blue Licks	Mil 1,763
Parberry, James	400	A	15	2-21-1780	Lower Blue Licks	
Parberry, James	50	A	34	4-29-1780	Licking Cr	
Parberry, James	400	A	37	4-29-1780	L Blue Licks	
Parberry, James	250	A	75	5-19-1780	Huston Buffaloe Rd	
Parberry, James	300	A	80	5-20-1780	Green & Licking R	
Parberry, James	400	A	80	5-20-1780	Green Cr	
Parberry, James	1,000	A	118	6- 1-1781	His settlement	
Parberry, James	1,000	A	120	6- 1-1780	Elkhorn	
Parberry, James	400	A	121	6- 2-1780	Licking	
Park, Arthur	400	A	244	12-27-1782	Clear Cr	Withdrawn
Park, Arthur	400	A	338	2-12-1784	Bullskin Cr	Surveyed

Entree	Acres	Book	Page	Entry Date	Watercourse	Notes
Park, Arthur	400	A	338	2-12-1784	———	
Park, Joseph	400	A	244	12-27-1782	Clear Cr	Withdrawn
Park, Joseph	400	A	338	2-12-1784	Bullskin Cr	Surveyed
Park, Joseph	400	A	338	2-12-1784	Clear Cr	
Parker, Nathaniel	1,401	B	36	1-27-1785	Rough Cr	
Parker, Richard	50	A	20	4-14-1780	Beech Fk	Mil withdrawn
Parker, Richard	200	A	20	4-14-1780	Cartright Cr	Mil surveyed
Parker, Richard	200	A	20	4-14-1780	Cartright Cr	Mil surveyed
Parker, Richard	250	A	199	3-20-1781	Cartright Cr	Surveyed
Parker, Richard	50	A	277	4-12-1783	Beech Fk	
Parker, Richard	50	A	277	4-12-1783	———	Withdrawn
Parker, Richard	93½	A	317	12-16-1783	Beech Fk	
Parker, Richard	750	A	331	1-16-1784	Cartright Cr	
Parkers, James	1,000	A	162	7-18-1780	Falls Green R	
Parks, Thomas	446	A	268	3-28-1783	Rowling Fk	Withdrawn
Parks, Thomas	1,200	A	268	3-28-1783	Rowling Fk	
Parks, Thomas	446	A	287	8-18-1783	Rolling Fk	Withdrawn
Parks, Thomas	446	A	364	6- 7-1784	Otter Cr	
Parks, Thomas	446	A	364	6- 7-1784	Rolling Fk	Withdrawn
Pate, Anthony	5,728	A	270	3-28-1783	Green R	
Patterson, John	1,000	A	106	5-27-1780	Dick R	
Patterson, John	1,000	B	50	10-31-1785	Floyds Fk	
Patterson, John	1,000	B	50	10-31-1785	Floyds Fk	
Patterson, Matthew	400	A	157	7- 3-1780	Red R	
Patterson, Robt	400	A	9	1-18-1780	S Fk Elkhorn	
Patterson, Samuel	2,474	A	319	12-17-1783	Muddy Cr	
Patter, Wm	500	A	96	5-25-1780	Stoners Cr	
Pattie, James	800	A	86	5-22-1780	Joining Thompson	
Patton, Benj	516½	A	256	1-23-1783	Coxes Cr	
Patton, Benj	150	A	256	1-21-1783	Coxes Cr	
Patton, James	400	A	174	9-29-1780	Town Fk	Surveyed
Patton, James	50	A	174	9-29-1780	Brashears Cr	Mil surveyed
Patton, James	125	A	243	12-26-1782	18 Mile Cr	Surveyed
Patton, James	400	A	243	12-26-1782	18 Mile Cr	Surveyed
Patton, James	8,400	A	243	12-26-1782	18 Mile Cr	
Patton, James	2,718	A	250	1- 9-1783	Brashears Cr	
Patton, James et al	30,000	A	250	1- 9-1783	Brashears Cr	Surveyed
Patton, James et al	853	A	283	7- 4-1783	Ohio R	
Patton, Matthew	1,000	A	170	9-11-1780	Fern Cr	Withdrawn
Patton, Matthew	550	A	195	3-16-1781	Nolin Cr	Surveyed
Patton, Matthew	550	A	215	7-20-1781	Nole Linn Cr	Surveyed
Patton, Matthew	750	A	281	6-26-1783	Cartright Cr	50 acres withdrawn
Patton, Matthew	550	A	283	7- 4-1783	Fern Cr	Surveyed
Patton, Matthew	350	A	285	8- 5-1783	Pleasant Run	Surveyed
Patton, Matthew	50	A	285	8- 5-1783	Pleasant Run	
Patton, Matthew	300	A	308	11-24-1783	Beech Fk	
Patton, Matthew	1,350	A	326	1- 1-1784	Big Cr	Withdrawn
Patton, Matthew	1,350½	A	360	5-14-1784	———	350 acres surveyed
Patton, Matthew	700	A	368	6-29-1784	Harrods Cr	
Patton, Matthew	700	A	368	6-29-1784	———	Withdrawn
Patton, Matthew	12,000	A	370	7- 8-1784	———	Withdrawn
Patton, Matthew	500	A	370	7- 8-1784	Big Cr	
Patton, Roger	963¾	A	326	1- 1-1784	———	
Patton, Roger	477¾	A	334	1-21-1784	Isaac Hite Jr	
Patton, Thomas	229½	A	255	1-20-1783	Harrods Cr	
Patton, Wm	400	A	61	5-16-1780	Hanging Fk	
Patton, Wm	2,500	A	250	1- 9-1783	Brashears Cr	Withdrawn
Patton, Wm	1,500	A	256	1-23-1783	Green R	Surveyed
Patton, Wm	1,500	A	315	12-13-1783	Sinking Cr	Withdrawn
Patton, Wm	1,500	A	315	12-13-1783	Green R	
Patty, John	500	A	58	5-15-1780	Ky R	
Patty, George	477	A	58	5-15-1780	Licking	
Patzell, John	400	A	109	5-29-1780	Floyds Fk	Surveyed
Paul, John	1,000	A	178	10-16-1780	Bullskin Cr	
Paul, John	50	A	218	8- 8-1781	Nole Linn Cr	
Paul, John	150	A	218	8- 8-1781	Nolin Cr	Surveyed
Paul, John	1,000	A	245	12-28-1782	Fox Run	
Paul, John	400	A	245	12-28-1782	Drennons Lick Cr	Surveyed
Paul, John	3,000	A	258	1- 27-1783	Fox Run	Surveyed
Paul, Peter	50	A	178	10-16-1780	Bullskin Cr	Surveyed
Paul, Peter	400	A	245	12-28-1782	Guess Cr	Surveyed
Paul, Peter	300	A	245	12-28-1782	Bullskin Cr	Withdrawn
Paul, Peter	250	A	291	9-30-1783	Middle Cr	Withdrawn
Paul, Peter	250	A	293	10- 4-1783	Middle Cr	
Paul, Peter	250	A	293	10- 4-1783	Middle Cr	Withdrawn
Paul, Peter	300	A	339	2-14-1784	Bullskin Cr	
Paulin, Henry	400	A	1	11- 3-1779	Boons Mill Cr	

Entree	Acres	Book	Page	Entry Date	Watercourse	Notes
Paulin, Henry	800	A	41	5- 9-1780	Smiths settlement	
Paullin, Henry	400	A	141	6-21-1780	Buck Lick Cr	
Paulin, Henry	1,000	A	226	12-13-1782	Beech Fk	Surveyed
Paxton, Thomas	1,231½	A	340	2-18-1784	Ohio R	
Payne, Adam	400	A	195	3-16-1781	Bull Cr	
Payne, Archer	667	A	129	6-10-1780	Licking	
Payton, Craven	1,000	A	38	5- 9-1780	Fk Licking	
Payton, Craven	500	A	38	5- 9-1780	———	
Payne, Edward	400	A	3	11-11-1779	Lulbiel Cr	
Payne, Edward	1,000	A	37	4-29-1780	Hingston Fk	
Payne, Edward	2,000	A	62	5-16-1780	Stoners Fk	
Payne, George	1,333¾	A	54	5-15-1780	Hawkins Run	
Payne, Henry	500	A	62	5-16-1780	Stoners Fk	
Payne, John	1,000	A	22	4-24-1780	Hamonds Cr	Mil
Payne, John	2,000	A	32	4-29-1780	Licking	Mil
Payne, John	1,200	A	81	5-22-1780	Silver Cr	
Payne, John	1,000	A	100	5-26-1780	Chaplins Fk	Withdrawn
Payne, John	1,000	A	100	5-26-1780	Ky R	
Payne, John	1,166¼	A	129	6- 9-1780	S Fk Licking	
Payne, John	1,000	A	133	6-15-1780	Dry Fk	
Payne, John	2,146	A	312	12- 3-1783	Yellow Banks Cr	
Payne, John Jr	1,166⅔	A	54	5-15-1780	S Fk Licking	
Payne, Samuel	350	A	243	12-26-1782	18 Mile Cr	
Payne, Samuel	1,144½	A	364	6- 4-1784	Barbour & Banks	
Payne, Sandford	400	A	62	5-16-1780	Stoners Fk	
Payton, Wm	750	A	38	5- 9-1780	Salt R	
Payne, Wm	500	A	62	5-16-1780	Stoners Fk	Withdrawn
Payne, Wm	500	A	80	5-20-1780	Stoners Fk	Withdrawn
Payne, Wm	500	A	90	5-23-1780	Licking	
Payne, Wm	1,000	A	213	7- 2-1781	Floyds Fk	
Payne, Wm	350	A	243	12-26-1782	18 Mile Cr	
Peachey, Wm	5,000	A	34	4-29-1780	Ohio R	Mil
Peachey, Wm	5,000	A	35	4-29-1780	Dry Cr	Mil
Peake, Jesse	300	A	91	5-24-1780	Licking	
Peake, Jesse	400	A	184	10-30-1781	Small Mt Cr	
Peake, Wm	400	A	91	5-24-1780	Licking	
Peakenters, James	400	A	9	1-17-1780	Licking Cr	
Pearce, Thomas	196½	A	252	1-10-1781	Pleasant Run	Surveyed
Pearle, Samuel	500	A	98	5-25-1780	Joseph Farror Premption	
Pearle, Samuel	500	A	104	5-27-1780	Chaplin Fk	
Pearle, Wm	400	A	129	6- 9-1780	Dicks R	
Pearle, Wm	200	A	130	6-12-1780	Dicks R	
Pearle, Wm	2,000	A	104	5-27-1780	Dicks R	Withdrawn
Pearman, Samuel, heirs	1,000	A	348	3-27-1784	Salt R	
Pearman, Samuel, heirs	1,000	A	348	3-27-1784	Willsons Cr	Surveyed
Pearman, Samuel, heirs	1,000	A	348	3-27-1784	Fromans Cr	Surveyed
Peekings, Samuel	200	A	73	5-19-1780	Beech Fk	
Peekings, Samuel	800	A	73	5-19-1780	Buffaloe Cr	Surveyed
Pemberton, Bennett	300	A	84	5-22-1780	Licking	
Pemberton, John	500	A	290	9-10-1783	Salt R	
Pemberton, John	500	A	304	11-14-1783	Ashes Cr	Amended
Pendergrass, Jesse	400	A	4	12- 7-1779	near mouth Ky R	
Pendergrass, Margret	600	A	119	6- 1-1780	His settlement	Surveyed
Pendergrass, Margret	400	A	5	12- 7-1779	Brashears Cr	
Pendleton, Henry	3,666	A	354	4-19-1784	Mordecai Barbour	Withdrawn
Pendleton, Henry	3,666	B	22	12- 3-1784	———	Withdrawn
Pendleton, Phillip	2,000	A	31	4-28-1780	S Fk Licking	Mil
Pendleton, Phillip	2,000	A	31	4-28-1780	Br Ohio R	Mil
Pendleton, Wm	1,000	A	117	5-31-1780	His settlement	
Penn, Gabriel	1,586	A	303	11-11-1783	Indian Camp Cr	Withdrawn
Penn, Gabriel	1,000	A	305	11-15-1783	Big Clifty Cr	Surveyed
Penn, Gabriel	972½	A	307	11-22-1783	Big Clifty Cr	Surveyed
Penn, Gabriel	972½	A	340	2-17-1784	Big Clifty Cr	Amended
Penn, Gabriel	1,586	B	19	11-20-1786	———	Withdrawn
Penn, Gabriel	1,586	B	19	11-20-1784	———	
Penn, John	500	A	38	5- 9-1780	Buffaloe Rd	
Penn, John	1,000	A	38	5- 9-1780	Ohio R	
Penn, John	1,000	A	38	5- 9-1780	Ohio R	
Penn, John	500	A	38	5- 9-1780	Painted Stone Tract	Surveyed
Penn, John	2,000	A	52	5-13-1780	Chaplin & Beach Fk	Surveyed
Penn, John	1,000	B	27	12-17-1784	———	Surveyed
Pennerbecker, Peter	500	A	71	5-18-1780	Tates Cr	
Pennerbecker, Peter	500	A	71	5-18-1780	S Fk Rowling Fk	Withdrawn
Pennerbeker, Peter	1,000	A	71	5-18-1780	S Fk Rowling Fk	Withdrawn
Pennerbecker, Peter	1,000	A	175	10- 6-1780	S Fk Licking	
Pennerbecker, Peter	1,000	A	175	10- 6-1780	S Fk Rowling Fk	
Penney, John	500	A	84	5-22-1780	N Fk Licking	
Perkins, Benj	596	A	53	5-13-1780	Cedar Cr	
Perry, Davis	400	A	149	6-24-1780	S Fk Elkhorn	
Perry, Joseph	1,000	A	93	5-24-1780	Rowling Fk	

Entree	Acres	Book	Page	Entry Date	Watercourse	Notes
Perry, Joseph	1,000	A	93	5-24-1780	Rowling Fk	
Peters, James	400	A	70	5-18-1780	Floyds Fk	
Peters, John	400	A	18	3- 1-1780	Buffalo Rd	
Peters, Richard	3,500	A	43	5-11-1780	Big Bone Cr	
Peterson, Henry	147	A	293	10- 3-1783	Pottengers Cr	Withdrawn
Peterson, Henry	147	B	3	8-27-1784	Pottengers Cr	
Peterson, Henry	147	B	3	8-26-1784	Pottengers Cr	Withdrawn
Petitt, Benj	400	A	16	2-23-1780	Hanging Fk	
Petton, Benj	200	A	252	1-10-1783	Pottengers Cr	
Petton, Benj	300	A	252	1-10-1783	Pottengers Cr	
Pew, Jonathan	1,000	A	100	5-26-1780	S Fk Coxes Cr	
Peyton, Craven	800	A	95	5-24-1780	Fk Licking	
Peyton, Craven	100	A	95	5-24-1780	Ky R	
Peyton, Craven	100	A	95	5-24-1780	Ky R	
Peyton, Elverton	400	A	117	5-31-1780	Silver Cr	
Peyton, Francis	1,000	A	94	5-24-1780	S Fk Licking	
Peyton, Francis	1,000	A	95	5-24-1780	N Fk Licking	
Peyton, Francis	1,000	A	95	5-24-1780	Licking	
Peyton, Francis	1,000	A	95	5-24-1780	Licking	
Peyton, Harrison	500	A	73	5-19-1780	Coxes Cr	
Peyton, Henry	1,000	A	58	5-16-1780	Licking	
Peyton, James	400	A	159	7- 5-1780	Slate Cr	
Peyton, James	2,000	A	319	12-17-1783	Rough Cr	
Peyton, Thomas	3,000	A	170	9- 9-1780	Ohio R	Surveyed
Peyton, Timothy	1,000	A	177	10- 9-1780	S Fk Licking	
Peyton, Wm	1,000	A	206	4-13-1781	Small Br Salt R	Surveyed
Peyton, Wm	500	A	206	4-13-1781	Mulberry Cr	
Peyton, Wm	1,500	A	206	4-13-1781	Floyds Fk	Surveyed
Peyton, Wm	1,000	A	206	4-13-1781	Clear Cr	Surveyed
Peyton, Wm	500	A	207	4-13-1781	S Fk Clear Cr	Surveyed
Peyton, Wm	300	A	213	7- 2-1781	Fox Run	
Peyton, Wm, heirs	1,000	A	206	4-13-1781	Plumb Cr	Surveyed
Peyton, Wm, heirs	1,000	A	206	4-13-1781	Clear Cr	Surveyed
Phalhamus, Jacob et al	3,000	A	349	3-30-1784	Salt R	
Phalon, Thomas	2,000	A	238	12-23-1782	Battle Cr	
Phelps, George	400	A	112	5-30-1780	Brashears Cr	Surveyed
Phelps, John	100	A	310	11-26-1783	Floyds Fk	
Phelps, John	800	A	310	11-26-1783	Floyds Fk	
Phelps, John	1,000	A	310	11-26-1783	Floyds Fk	
Phelps, Joseph	400	A	8	1-14-1780	Otter Cr	
Phelps, Josiah	1,000	A	112	5-30-1780	His settlement	
Phelps, Julian	400	A	240	12-24-1782	Rough Cr	
Phelps, Thos	400	A	8	1-14-1780	Otter Cr	
Phillips, Aaron	5,000	A	272	4- 3-1783	——	Warrant returned
Phillips, Colonel	50	A	119	6- 1-1780	4 Mile Cr	Mil
Phillips, George	400	A	230	12-17-1782	Floyds Fk	
Phillips, Jenkins	1,000	A	71	5-18-1780	S Fk Beargrass Cr	
Phillips, Jenkins	1,000	A	71	5-18-1780	Buck Lick Cr	
Phillips, Jenkins	350	A	71	5-18-1780	Green R	
Phillips, Jenkins	1,350	A	363	6- 2-1784	——	1,000 acres surveyed
Phillips, John	200	A	144	6-23-1780	Rowling Fk	Mil
Phillips, John	500	A	144	6-23-1780	Salt R	
Phillips, John	500	A	144	6-23-1780	Salt R	
Phillips, John	500	A	144	6-23-1780	Rowling Fk	
Phillips, John	500	A	144	6-23-1780	S Fk Rowling Fk	
Phillips, John	1,000	A	144	6-23-1780	Shawnee Lick Br	Surveyed
Phillips, John	43,726	A	330	1-14-1784	Green R	39,376 acres surveyed
Phillips, John	10,726	B	46	5-19-1785	——	10,379 acres surveyed
Phillips, Jonas	800	A	227	12-14-1782	Drennings Lick Cr	
Phillips, Joseph	9,000	A	333	1-20-1784	County Line	
Phillips, Joseph	2,320	A	358	5- 4-1784	Long Lick Cr	
Phillips, Phillip	3,000	A	358	5- 3-1784	Salt R	
Phillips, Joseph	6,680	A	358	5- 3-1784	Chaplins Fk	Surveyed
Phillips, Joseph	5,000	B	43	4-11-1785	——	
Phillips, Mary	475½	A	366	6-19-1784	——	
Phillips, May	475½	A	319	12-17-1783	Green R	
Phillips, Moses	1,000	A	60	5-16-1780	N Fk Licking	
Phillips, Peter	1,000	A	152	6-26-1780	Town Fk	Surveyed
Phillips, Peter	400	A	335	1-31-1784	Town Fk	Surveyed
Phillips, Phillip	300	A	219	8-24-1781	Nole Linn Cr	Surveyed
Phillips, Phillip	200	A	219	8-24-1781	Nolin Cr	Surveyed
Phillips, Phillip	500	A	226	12-13-1782	Little Clifty Cr	Surveyed
Phillips, Phillip	560	A	230	12-17-1782	Rough Cr	
Phillips, Phillip	187	A	235	12-19-1782	Nole Linn Cr	Surveyed
Phillips, Phillip	337	A	238	12-21-1782	Nole Linn Cr	Withdrawn
Phillips, Phillip	400	A	239	12-23-1782	Linn Camp Cr	Withdrawn
Phillips, Phillip	200	A	239	12-23-1782	Linn Camp Cr	Withdrawn

Entree	Acres	Book	Page	Entry Date	Watercourse	Notes
Phillips, Phillip	300	A	239	12-23-1782	Nole Linn Cr	Surveyed
Phillips, Phillip	100	A	239	12-23-1782	Nole Linn Cr	Surveyed
Phillips, Phillip	200	A	239	12-23-1782	Nole Linn Cr	Surveyed
Phillips, Phillip	300	A	239	12-23-1782	Nole Linn Cr	Surveyed
Phillips, Phillip	300	A	240	12-23-1782	Linn Camp Cr	....
Phillips, Phillip	100	A	247	1- 7-1783	Nole Linn Cr	Surveyed
Phillips, Phillip	400	A	247	1- 7-1783	Nolin Cr	Surveyed
Phillips, Phillip	764	A	247	1- 7-1783	Nole Linn Cr	
Phillips, Phillip	512	A	248	1- 7-1783	Nole Linn Cr	Withdrawn
Phillips, Phillip	300	A	248	1- 7-1783	Nolin Cr	Surveyed
Phillips, Phillip	337	A	249	1- 8-1783	Nole Linn	Withdrawn
Phillips, Phillip	512	A	275	4-10-1783	Rough Cr	Withdrawn
Phillips, Phillip	512	A	275	4-10-1783		Withdrawn
Phillips, Phillip	600	A	275	4- 9-1783	Lynn Camp Cr	....
Phillips, Phillip	736	A	275	4- 9-1783	Beaver Dam Fk	Surveyed
Phillips, Phillip	200	A	282	7- 2-1783	Nolelin Cr	Surveyed
Phillips, Phillip	400	A	282	7- 2-1783	Rough Cr	Withdrawn
Phillips, Phillip	245	A	282	7- 1-1783	Nolin Fk	Surveyed
Phillips, Phillip	327	A	282	7- 1-1783	Kennadys Run	Surveyed
Phillips, Phillip	200	A	286	8- 9-1783	Watkins Run	Surveyed
Phillips, Phillip	312	A	286	8- 9-1783	Bacon Cr	....
Phillips, Phillip	200	A	288	9- 8-1783	Nolin Cr	Surveyed
Phillips, Phillip	233	A	288	9- 8-1783	Bacon Cr	Surveyed
Phillips, Phillip	415	A	289	9- 8-1783	Knob Cr	....
Phillips, Phillip	400	A	293	10- 6-1783	Nole Linn	
Phillips, Phillip	400	A	293	10- 6-1783	Rough Cr	Withdrawn
Phillips, Phillip	350	A	306	11-19-1783	Bear Cr	Withdrawn
Phillips, Phillip	650	A	306	11-19-1783	Bear Cr	
Phillips, Phillip	764	A	307	11-20-1783	————	....
Phillips, Phillip	500	A	307	11-20-1783	————	
Phillips, Phillip	187	A	307	11-20-1783	————	Returned
Phillips, Phillip	710	A	307	11-20-1783	————	Returned
Phillips, Phillip	428	A	307	11-20-1783	————	....
Phillips, Phillip	2,637	A	207	11-20-1783	————	....
Phillips, Phillip	200	A	307	11-20-1783	————	....
Phillips, Phillip	415	A	307	11-20-1783	————	....
Phillips, Phillip	500	A	307	11-20-1783	————	Warrant returned
Phillips, Phillip	3,000	A	333	1-20-1784	————	Surveyed
Phillips, Phillip	150	A	358	5- 7-1784	Nole Linn Cr	....
Phillips, Phillip	15,000	A	333	1-20-1784		Withdrawn
Phillips, Phillip	630	A	339	2-16-1784	Rough Cr	Surveyed
Phillips, Phillip	300	A	359	5- 7-1784	Nole Linn Cr	....
Phillips, Phillip	630	A	360	5-14-1784		....
Phillips, Phillip	300	A	362	5-26-1784		....
Phillips, Phillip	2,500	A	363	6- 2-1784	Green R	Withdrawn
Phillips, Phillip	500	A	368	6-26-1784	Green R	
Phillips, Phillip	1,500	B	7	9-18-1784	Little Reedy Cr	Withdrawn
Phillips, Phillip	1,000	B	7	9-14-1784	Indian Camp Cr	Surveyed
Phillips, Phillip	1,000	B	7	9-14-1784	Little Reedy	Withdrawn
Phillips, Phillip	350	B	15	11-12-1784	————	Withdrawn
Phillips, Phillip	385	B	16	11-12-1784	Bear Cr	Surveyed
Phillips, Phillip	624	B	28	12-20-1784	Beech Fk	....
Phillips, Phillip	624	B	31	1- 3-1785	————	....
Phillips, Phillip	66½	B	31	1- 3-1785	————	....
Phillips, Phillip	10,000	B	42	3-24-1785	Falls Ohio R	Withdrawn
Phillips, Phillip	10,000	B	44	5-10-1785	————	Withdrawn
Phillips, Phillip	4,000	B	49	6-17-17—	————	....
Phillips, Phillip et al	537	A	288	9- 8-1783	Jacobs Knobb	....
Phillips, Phillip et al	100	B	17	11-15-1784	————	....
Phillips, Phillip et al	872	B	17	11-14-1784	Green R	Surveyed
Phillips, Phillip et al	9,000	B	35	1-26-1785	Green R	....
Phillips, Ralph	15,000	A	353	4-16-1784	Rowling Fk	....
Phillips, Ralph	15,000	A	353	4-16-1784	Samuel Hunt	Withdrawn
Phillips, Richard	2,050	A	35	4-29-1780	Upper Salt Springs	Mil
Phillips, Thomas	375	A	112	5-30-1780	Salt R	Withdrawn
Phillips, Thomas	400	A	119	6- 1-1780	Beargrass	....
Phillips, Thomas	395	A	190	3-15-1781	Long Lick	
Phillips, Thomas	300	A	192	3-16-1781	Willsons Cr	Withdrawn
Phillips, Thomas	75	A	192	3-16-1781	Long Lick Cr	....
Phillips, Thomas	300	A	216	7-21-1781	Jacob Fromans	Surveyed
Philps, Thomas	500	A	263	2-15 1783	Harden Cr	
Phillips, Thomas	500	B	46	5-26-1785	————	
Phillips, Wm:	50	A	34	4-29-1780	Ky R	Mil
Phillips, Wm	1,000	A	154	6-27-1780	Elkhorn	
Pickens, Samuel	1,000	B	42	3- 4-1785	....	800 acres surveyed
Pickett, Martin	3,075	A	49	5-12-1780	Licking	
Pickett, Martin	525	A	219	8-24-1781	Middle Cr	Withdrawn
Pickett, Martin	600	A	219	8-24-1781	Buffaloe Cr	Withdrawn
Pickett, Martin	1,125	B	28	12-20-1784	Big Caney Cr	Surveyed

Entree	Acres	Book	Page	Entry Date	Watercourse	Notes
Pickett, Martin	525	B	28	12–20–1784	Middle Cr	
Pickett, Martin	600	B	28	12–20–1784	Buffaloe Cr	Withdrawn
Pickett, Martin	875	B	48	6–20–1785	———	
Pigman, Jesse	1,000	A	175	10- 6–1780	Clear Cr	
Pigman, Jesse	4,000	A	363	6- 2–1784	———	
Pile, Wm	350	A	305	11–15–1783	Beech Fk	Withdrawn
Pile, Wm	350	A	327	1- 7–1784	Beech Fk	
Pile, Wm	250	A	370	7- 6–1784	John Wrens	
Pindland, Alex	200	A	126	6- 7–1784	Paint Lick Cr	
Pinix, James	400	A	130	6–12–1780	S Fk Hardens Cr	
Piper, Wm	3,663	A	320	12–18–1783	Beech Fk	
Pirkins, Benj	600	A	45	5–11–1780	Steels Cr	
Pitman, John	400	A	245	12–28–1782	Green R	Surveyed
Pitman, Hepkins	50	A	23	4–24–1780	Elkhorn & Sinking	Mil
Pitman, Wm	500	A	143	6–22–1780	Pittmans Cr	Surveyed
Pitmans, Hipkins	200	A	86	5–22–1780	Grants Station	
Pittman, John	1,555	B	10	10–11–1784	———	400 acres surveyed
Pitts, Younger	1,500	A	52	5–13–1780	N Fk Elkhorn	
Platt, Ebenezer	6,000	A	333	1–20–1784	Coxes Cr	Surveyed
Pleasant, Robert Jr	2,540	A	237	12- 21–1784	Drennons Lick Cr	Surveyed
Poage, Anne	400	A	36	4–29–1780	Ky R	Surveyed
Poage, Anne	400	A	125	6- 5–1780	McGareys Sp	Surveyed
Poage, Robert	400	A	15	2–21–1780	Floyds Fk	
Poage, Robert	400	A	18	3- 3–1780	E Fk Licking	
Poage, Robert	600	A	137	6–19–1780	His settlement	
Poage, Robert	250	A	163	7–22–1780	Ky R	
Poage, Robert	1,510	A	246	1- 6–1783	Mid Fk Robinsons Cr	
Poage, Thos	400	A	1	11- 3–1779	Hickmans Cr	
Poage, Thomas	1,000	A	26	4–26–1780	Hickmans Cr	
Poage, Thomas	1,200	B	8	9–27–1784	Green R	
Poindexter, John	50	A	31	4–28–1780	Drenning Lick	Withdrawn
Poindexter, John	2,000	A	59	5–16–1780	Lulbrelgrud Cr	
Poindexter, John	400	A	157	7- 3–1780	Lulbrelgrud	
Poindexter, John	50	A	221	10- 1–1781	Drennons Lick Cr	Withdrawn
Polhemus, Jacob	3,000	A	354	4–16–1784	Salt R	Surveyed
Polhamus, Jacob et al	3,000	A	333	1–20–1784	———	Withdrawn
Polhamus, Jacob et al	3,000	A	349	3–30–1784	———	Surveyed
Polick, Alex	400	A	17	2–29–1780	Licking Cr	
Pollard, Wm	50,000	A	324	12–26–1783	Nolelin Cr	Surveyed
Pollard, Wm	50,000	A	347	3–17–1784	Green R	Surveyed amended
Polly, James	400	A	27	4–26–1780	Ky R	
Pomeroy, George	400	A	373	7–23–1784	Beargrass Cr	
Ponsonby, Richard	10,000	A	195	3–16–1781	Panther Cr	
Pope, Benj	400	A	101	5–26–1780	Brashears Cr	Surveyed
Pope, Benj	1,200	A	236	1–23–1783	Cartright Cr	
Pope, Benj	500	A	320	12–18–1783	Beech Fk	
Pope, Benj	400	A	321	12–20–1783	Hardins Cr	Withdrawn
Pope, Benj	400	A	346	3–16–1784	Clear Cr	
Pope, Benj	400	B	34	1–22–1785	Coxes Cr	
Pope, Benj	1,400	B	46	5–26–1785	———	Surveyed
Pope, Benj	1,000	B	48	6–17–1785	Floyds Fk	Surveyed
Pope, Benj et al	1,400	A	238	12- 23–1782	Floyds Fk	
Pope, Benj et al	2,275	A	243	12–26–1782	18 Mile Cr	
Pope, Benj et al	5,000	A	243	12–26–1782	18 Mile Cr	
Pope, Benj et al	5,000	A	244	12–27–1782	joining 4,000 entry	
Pope, George	1,000	A	208	4–30–1781	Mill Cr	Surveyed
Pope, George	400	A	265	2–21–1783	Mill Cr	Surveyed
Pope, George	1,000	A	377	8- 9–1784	Mill Cr	
Pope, Henry	300	A	197	3–17–1781	Rowling Fk	Surveyed
Popham, John	400	A	8	1–15–1780	Drakes Camp Cr	
Popham, John	500	A	65	5–17–1780	Rolling Fk	
Pope, John	300	B	44	4–20–1785	Salt R	Surveyed
Pope, John	300	B	46	5–26–1785	———	
Pope, Nathaniel	50	A	32	4–29–1780	Licking Cr	Mil
Pope, Nathaniel	750	A	156	6–30–1780	Elkhorn	Surveyed
Pope, Wm	100	A	35	4–29–1780	Fern Cr	Surveyed
Pope, Wm	50	A	35	4–29–1780	Fern Cr	Mil surveyed
Pope, Wm	500	A	77	5–20–1780	Pond Cr	Withdrawn
Pope, Wm	400	A	77	5–20–1780	Brushy Pond Cr	Withdrawn
Pope, Wm	1,000	A	77	5–20–1780	Brushy Pond Cr	Surveyed
Pope, Wm	1,000	A	77	5–20–1780	Brushy Pond Cr	Surveyed
Pope, Wm	400	A	126	6- 7–1780	Brushy Pond	Surveyed
Pope, Wm	400	A	126	6- 7–1780	Brushy Pond	Surveyed
Pope, Wm	400	A	126	6- 7–1780	Brushy Pond	Withdrawn
Pope, Wm	400	A	126	6- 7–1780	Brushy Pond	Surveyed
Pope, Wm	1,100	A	199	3–20–1782	Brushy Pond Cr	Surveyed
Pope, Wm	400	A	204	4- 4–1781	Fern Cr	
Pope, Wm	400	A	204	4- 4–1781	Fern Cr	
Pope, Wm	400	A	204	4- 4–1781	Fern Cr	Surveyed

Entree	Acres	Book	Page	Entry Date	Watercourse	Notes
Pope, Wm	400	A	207	4-13-1781	Allans Line	Surveyed
Pope, Wm	2,343½	A	246	1- 6-1783	Falls Ohio R	629 acres surveyed 1,714½ withdrawn
Pope, Wm	400	A	250	1- 9-1783	Brushy Pond Cr	Surveyed
Pope, Wm	400	A	250	1- 9-1783	Brushy Pond Cr	....
Pope, Wm	1,400	A	311	12- 1-1783	Falls Ohio R	Withdrawn
Pope, Wm	314½	A	327	1- 5-1784	Falls Ohio R	Withdrawn
Pope, Wm	500	A	327	1- 5-1784	Brashears Cr	Surveyed
Pope, Wm	2,345½	A	372	7-17-1784	————	629 acres surveyed
Pope, Wm et al	900	B	50	10-13-1785	Floyds Fk	
Pope, Wm et al	400	A	336	2- 4-1784	Salt R	Surveyed
Porter, Abner	500	A	78	5-20-1780	Jessamine Cr	....
Porter, John	400	A	4	12-7-1779	Brashears Cr	....
Porter, John	500	B	2	8-25-1784	————	————
Porter, John	500	B	2	8-25-1784	Brashears Cr	————
Porter, Samuel	400	A	100	5-26-1780	Millers Cr	....
Porter, Thomas	1,076⅔	A	58	5-15-1780	Howards Cr	....
Porter, Wm	1,500	A	157	7- 3-1780	Licking	....
Pottenger, Samuel	400	A	17	2-28-1780	Pottingers Cr	Surveyed
Pottenger, Samuel	400	A	192	3-16-1781	Pottengers Cr	Surveyed
Pottenger, Samuel	400	A	203	4- 3-1781	N Fk Pottengers Cr	Surveyed 240 acres withdrawn
Pottenger, Samuel	400	A	245	12-20-1782	His settlement	Surveyed
Pottenger, Samuel	200	A	245	12-30-1782	His settlement	Surveyed
Pottenger, Samuel	1,000	A	291	9-15-1783	————	160 acres surveyed
Pottengers, Samuel	240	A	291	9-15-1783	Cedar Lick	Withdrawn
Potter, Samuel	1,000	A	212	6-23-1781	Drennons Lick	Surveyed
Potts, John	500	A	153	6-26-1780	Cedar Run	....
Potts, John	100	A	197	3-17-1781	Simpsons Cr	....
Potts, John	100	A	197	3-17-1781	E Fk Coxes Cr	....
Potts, John	100	B	49	6-17-1785	————	Surveyed
Powell, Edmund	11,139½	A	239	12-23-1782	Floyds Fk	Surveyed
Powell, Edmund	11,139½	A	240	12-24-1782	Floyds Fk	Surveyed
Powell, Edmund	2,398	A	242	12-25-1782	————	Surveyed
Powell, Edmund	657	A	243	12-25-1782	Floyds Fk	Surveyed
Powell, Leven	1,000	A	41	5- 9-1780	Bullskin Cr	Surveyed
Powell, Leven	2,000	A	41	5- 9-1780	Falls Ohio R	....
Powell, Leven	500	A	45	5-11-1780	Floyds Fk	....
Powell, Levin	500	A	46	5-12-1780	Clear Cr	....
Powell, Leven	1,000	A	46	5-12-1780	Floyds Fk	Withdrawn
Powell, Leven	1,500	A	46	5-12-1780	Ohio R	....
Powell, Leven	1,000	A	47	5-12-1780	Hingston Cr	....
Powell, Leven	2,000	A	47	5-12-1780	Simpson Cr	Surveyed
Powell, Leven	1,500	A	61	5-16-1780	Limestone	....
Powell, Leven	1,000	A	100	5-26-1780	Salt R	....
Powell, Leven	1,000	A	104	5-27-1780	Licking Cr	....
Powell, Leven	1,000	A	104	5-27-1780	Mill Cr	Withdrawn
Powell, Leven	500	A	104	5-27-1780	Salt R	300 acres surveyed 200 acres withdrawn
Powell, Leven	500	A	104	5-27-1780	Salt R	....
Powell, Leven	2,000	A	104	5-27-1780	Ohio R	....
Powell, Leven	1,000	A	104	5-27-1780	Ky R	....
Powell, Leven	500	A	104	5-27-1780	Salt R	Withdrawn
Powell, Leven	500	A	104	5-27-1780	Salt R	Withdrawn
Powell, Leven	1,000	A	104	5-27-1780	Salt R	Withdrawn
Powell, Leven	1,000	A	105	5-27-1780	Fern Cr	Withdrawn
Powell, Leven	2,000	A	170	9- 9-1780	Harrods Salt Lick Cr	....
Powell, Leven	1,000	A	197	3-17-1781	Ohio R	Surveyed
Powell, Leven	500	A	197	3-17-1781	Floyds Fk	....
Powell, Leven	500	A	197	3-17-1781	Salt R	....
Powell, Leven	250	A	204	4- 4-1781	Town Fk Salt R	Withdrawn
Powell, Leven	1,200	A	204	4- 3-1781	Salt R	Surveyed
Powell, Leven	500	A	221	11-26-1781	————	....
Powell, Leven	500	A	336	1-31-1784	Salt R	Amended
Powell, Leven	100	A	336	1-31-1784	Harrods Cr	....
Powell, Leven	150	A	336	1-31-1784	Harrods Cr	Surveyed
Powell, Leven	250	A	336	1-31-1784	Town Fk	....
Powell, Leven	1,000	A	346	3-12-1784	Harrods Cr	58 acres surveyed
Powell, Leven	1,000	A	346	3-12-1784	Floyds Fk	Withdrawn
Powell, Leven	200	A	354	4-16-1784	Beargrass Cr	60 acres surveyed
Powell, Leven	200	A	354	4-16-1784	Salt R	....
Powell, Leven	1,000	B	26	12-16-1784	————	300 acres surveyed

Entree	Acres	Book	Page	Entry Date	Watercourse	Notes
Powell, Leven	942	B	48	6-20-1785	————	
Powell, Nicholas	1,000	A	93	5-24-1780	Simpsons Cr	
Powell, Rice	500	A	66	5-17-1780	Elkhorn	
Powell, Thomas	200	A	335	1-30-1784	Floyds Fk	
Powell, Wm	1,000	A	329	1-14-1784	Long Falls Cr	
Power, Alex	9,943	A	330	1-14-1784	Ky R	3,088 acres surveyed
Power, James	400	A	148	6-24-1780	Mid Fk Licking	
Power, James	200	A	214	7- 4-1781	S Fk Noll Linn Cr	
Power, James	200	A	214	7- 4-1781	S Fk Nolins Cr	Withdrawn
Power, James	600	A	215	7-18-1781	Nolins Cr	Withdrawn
Power, James	302	A	219	8-20-1781	Nolin Cr	Withdrawn
Powers, James	600	A	221	11- 9-1782	Nolin Cr	
Powers, James	312	A	221	11- 9-1782	Nolyn Cr	
Powers, James	200	A	221	11- 9-1782	Wm Hinks	
Powers, James	1,112	A	226	12-13-1782	Little Clifty Cr	Surveyed
Powers, James	50	A	235	12-19-1782	Barren Run	Mil
Powers, James	200	A	272	4- 3-1783	Hardens Cr	Surveyed
Powers, James	1,312	A	370	7- 6-1784		1,112 acres surveyed
Praile, Wm	800	A	79	5-20-1780	Chaplins Fk	Surveyed
Prather, Basil	700	A	79	5-20-1780	Ohio R	
Prather, Basil	800	A	79	5-20-1780	Clear Cr	
Prather, Basil	500	A	79	5-20-1780	Jessamine Cr	Withdrawn
Prather, Basil	500	A	174	10- 4-1780	Jessamine Cr	Surveyed
Prather, Basil	1,000	A	176	10- 6-1780	Pleasant Run	
Prather, Henry	400	A	5	12- 9-1779	Shawnee Run	Surveyed
Prather, Henry	1,000	A	42	5-10-1780	Shawnee Run	Surveyed
Prather, Henry	400	A	79	5-20-1780	Clear Cr	
Prather, James	400	A	79	5-20-1780	Ohio R	
Prather, John S	600	A	183	10-27-1780	Simpsons Cr	Surveyed
Prather, Thomas	2,000	A	79	5-20-1780	Hardings Cr	
Prather, Thomas	1,000	A	176	10- 6-1780	James Harrod	
Prather, Thomas	241	A	237	12-21-1782	Hardins Cr	
Pratt, Thomas	495½	A	371	7-12-1784	Green R	
Preston, Francis	500	A	318	12-16-1783	Floyds Fk	Withdrawn
Preston, Rob & Walter	1,000	A	112	5-30-1780	Salt R	Surveyed
Preston, Thos L	1,000	A	230	12-17-1782	Ohio R	Surveyed
Preston, Wm	400	A	17	2-28-1780	Hurricane Cr	Surveyed
Preston, Wm	100	A	32	4-29-1780	Beargrass	Mil surveyed
Preston, Wm	300	A	35	4-29-1780	Ky R	Mil surveyed
Preston, Wm	500	A	74	5-19-1780	Beargrass Cr	Surveyed
Preston, Wm	500	A	74	5-19-1780	Elkhorn	
Preston, Wm	1,000	A	74	5-19-1780	Spring Cr	
Preston, Wm	1,000	A	91	5-24-1780	Ohio R	Surveyed
Preston, Wm	1,031	A	194	3-16-1781	Floyds Fk	
Preston, Wm	500	A	201	4- 2-1781	Ohio R	Mil
Preston, Wm	1,000	A	201	4- 2-1781	Ohio R	Surveyed
Prewitt, Isham	800	A	89	5-23-1780	Ohio R	
Prewitt, Isham	400	A	269	3-28-1783	Beech Fk	
Price, Ben	400	A	203	4- 3-1781	Rowling Fk	
Price, Charles	1,000	A	127	6- 8-1780	Hickmans Cr	
Price, Daniel	500	A	372	7-16-1784	————	Entered in Lincoln
Price, Henry	1,000	A	354	4-19-1784	Little Ky	Surveyed
Price, John	200	A	29	4-27-1780	near Leesburg	Mil
Price, John	500	A	66	5-17-1780	Ky R	
Prihe, John	400	A	85	5-22-1780	Ohio R	
Price, John	500	A	93	5-24-1780	Stoners Cr	
Price, John	500	B	47	5-26-1785	————	
Price, Meredith	400	A	250	1- 9-1783	Pattons Line	
Price, Meredith	2,941	A	250	1- 9-1783	Pattons Cr	Surveyed
Price, Meredith	2,000	A	355	4-21-1784	————	Surveyed
Price, Meredith	325	B	46	5-26-1785	————	108 acres surveyed
Price, Meredith	1,000	B	46	5-26-1785	————	333 acres surveyed
Prichart, Isaac	1,000	A	96	5-24-1780	S Fk Clear Cr	
Pringle, Jacob	400	A	172	9-18-1780	Green R	
Pringle, Jacob	400	A	176	10- 9-1780	Fromans Cr	
Pringle, John	299¾	A	239	12-23-1782	Beech Fk	Withdrawn
Pringle, John	299¾	A	323	12-25-1783	Beech Fk	
Proctor, Charles	500	A	277	4-14-1783	Pottingers Cr	
Proctor, Ebbin	325	A	163	7-29-1780	Round Stone Cr	
Proctor, Nicholas	400	A	129	6- 9-1780	Silver Cr	
Proctor, Col Thos	12,000	A	333	1-20-1784	Joseph Phillips	Withdrawn
Proctor, Col Thos	12,000	A	349	4- 2-1784	————	Withdrawn
Proctor, Col Thos	12,000	B	45	5-16-1785	Manns Lick	Amended
Province, John Wm	500	A	155	6-29-1780	Ohio R	Withdrawn
Province, John Wm	560	A	155	6-29-1780	Ohio R	Withdrawn
Province, John Wm	360	A	162	7-18-1780	Hargass Fk	

Entree	Acres	Book	Page	Entry Date	Watercourse	Notes
Province, John Wm....	1,060	A	190	3–15–1781	Horgases Fk	....
Puckett, John........	500	A	225	12–13–1782	Green R	....
Puckett, S A..........	500	A	225	12–13–1782	Green R	....
Pullen, Loftus........	50	A	112	5–30–1780	Paint Lick Cr	Mil
Pulliam, Benj.........	1,000	A	268	3–28–1783	Rowling Fk	Withdrawn
Pulliam, Benj.........	1,000	A	287	8–18–1783	Cartright Cr	Withdrawn
Pulliam, Benj.........	1,000	A	350	4–10–1784	Hardens Cr	....
Pulliam, Benj.........	1,000	A	350	4–10–1784	Cartright Cr	Withdrawn
Pulliam, Joseph......	400	A	92	5–24–1780	Licking	....
Purcell, George......	1,000	A	66	5–17–1780	N Fk Elkhorn	....
Purcell, George......	1,000	A	76	5–19–1780	N Fk Licking	....
Purcell, Thomas.....	200	B	33	1–13–1785	————	....
Purdie, Peachy.......	1,000	A	125	6–3–1780	Ohio R	Withdrawn
Purdie, Peachy.......	3,000	A	194	3–16–1781	Brashears Cr	....
Purdie, Peachy.......	1,000	A	194	3–16–1781	Ohio R	Withdrawn
Purele, Lawrence.....	1,000	A	334	1–21–1784	Salt R	....
Pyatt, Jacob.........	400	A	226	12–13–1782	Floyds Fk	Surveyed
Quater, James........	370	A	192	3–16–1781	Bullskin	....
Quattarmus, James...	400	A	190	3–15–1781	Floyds Fk	Surveyed
Quartermus, James...	375	A	288	9–1–1783	Flat Lick	Withdrawn
Quatremus, James....	375	A	294	10–10–1783	Beargrass Cr	Withdrawn
Quartermus, James...	6,875	A	365	6–12–1784	————	400 acres surveyed
Quinn, Ben..........	1,000	A	48	5–12–1780	Tates Cr	....
Quinn, James........	50	A	30	4–28–1780	S Fk Tates Cr	Mil
Quinn, James........	1,027	A	79	5–20–1780	Tates Cr	....
Quinn, Thomas.......	1,028	A	79	5–20–1780	Tates Cr	....
Quirk, Edward.......	400	A	171	9–15–1780	Bank Lick Cr	....
Quirk, Edward.......	400	A	119	6–1–1780	Quirks Cr	....
Quirk, Thomas.......	4,000	A	264	2–15–1783	Ohio R	Surveyed
Quirk, Thomas.......	500	A	246	1–6–1783	Harrods Cr	....
Quirk, Thomas.......	2,000	A	246	1–6–1782	N Fk Floyds Cr	....
Quirk, Thomas.......	100	A	246	1–6–1783	18 Mile Cr	70 acres surveyed
Quirk, Thomas.......	500	A	246	1–6–1783	18 Mile Cr	....
Quirk, Thomas.......	500	A	246	1–6–1783	18 Mile Cr	....
Quirk, Thomas.......	2,000	A	246	1–6–1783	Floyds Fk	1,322 acres surveyed
Quirk, Thomas.......	178	B	47	5–30–1785	————	....
Raburne, John........	600	B	35	1–26–1785	Chaplin Fk	Mil withdrawn
Raburne, John........	600	A	259	2–3–1783	Chaplins Fk	Mil withdrawn
Ragnet, C P..........	30,000	A	323	12–26–1783	Green R	Surveyed
Ragnet, C P..........	15,000	A	350	4–10–1784	Middle Cr	Withdrawn
Ragnet, C P..........	23,300	A	353	4–16–1784	Nolin Cr	Surveyed
Ragnet, C P..........	15,000	A	353	4–16–1784	Rolling Fk	Withdrawn
Ragnet, P C..........	15,000	A	349	4–2–1784	Salt R	....
Ragnet, P C..........	15,000	A	350	4–10–1784	Rolling Fk	Withdrawn
Ragnet, P D..........	8,300	A	353	4–16–1784	Valley & Middle Cr	Surveyed
Ramey, Sanford......	1,000	A	94	5–24–1780	Mill Cr	....
Ramsey, Larkin......	465	A	85	5–22–1780	Licking Cr	....
Ramsey, Nathaniel...	6,000	A	353	4–15–1784	Rough Cr	....
Ramsey & Cox.......	21,000	A	332	1–20–1784	McWilliams	98,000 acres withdrawn
Ramsey & Cox.......	21,000	A	342	2–28–1784	J A Hamlins	Withdrawn
Ramsey & Cox.......	21,000	A	346	3–16–1784	Chaplins Fk	Surveyed
Ramsey & Cox.......	21,000	A	357	4–30–1784	Chaplins Fk	Surveyed
Randolph, Edmund...	9,000	A	46	5–11–1780	Ohio R	Withdrawn
Randolph, Edmund...	9,000	A	49	5–12–1780	Ohio R	Withdrawn
Randolph, Edmond...	9,000	A	187	3–15–1781	Goose & Harrods Cr	....
Randolph, Edmond...	9,000	A	187	3–15–1781	Ohio R	....
Randolph, Michal....	500	A	308	11–22–1783	Beech Fk	....
Randolph, Nath......	400	A	5	12–7–1779	Blue Lick	....
Randolph, Nath......	1,000	A	36	4–29–1780	Blue Lick settlement	....
Randolph, Thos M et al	3,000	A	10	2–7–1780	Ohio Yellow Bks	Mil 1,763
Rankin, James.......	150	A	246	1–6–1783	Beach Fk	....
Rankin, James.......	50	A	246	1–6–1783	Gilkeys Run	....
Rankin, James.......	100	A	246	1–6–1783	Pottengers Cr	....
Rankins, Wm.........	1,000	A	258	1–27–1783	Rowling Fk	....
Ransdall, Thomas....	1,000	A	153	6–26–1780	Licking	....
Raphael, Southy......	200	A	149	6–24–1780	Cabbin Cr	....
Raquet, P C..........	15,000	A	332	1–20–1784	Long Lick Cr	Withdrawn
Raquet, C P..........	15,000	A	335	1–27–1784	Green R	Withdrawn
Raquet, C P..........	15,000	A	335	1–27–1784	Middle Cr	Surveyed amended
Ratcliff, Richard.....	1,000	A	160	7–6–1780	Ky R	....
Rawson, Joseph......	1,000	A	235	12–20–1782	Ky R	....
Ray, Abraham........	400	A	238	12–23–1782	S Fk Caney Cr	Surveyed

Entree	Acres	Book	Page	Entry Date	Watercourse	Notes
Ray, Absalom	400	A	83	5–22–1780	Beech Fk	
Ray, Anne	400	A	216	7–30–1781	Bear Cr	Surveyed
Ray, Benjamin	400	A	83	5–22–1780	Beech Fk	
Ray, Elizabeth	400	A	216	7–30–1781	Clay Lick	Surveyed
Ray, John	400	A	82	5–22–1780	Beech Fk	
Ray, John	800	A	82	5–22–1780	Beech Fk	112 acres withdrawn surveyed
Ray, John	1,344	A	211	6–11–1781	Clear Cr	Withdrawn
Ray, John	3,400	A	211	6–11–1781	Rowling Fk	Surveyed
Ray, John	1,200	A	212	6–15–1781	Salt R	
Ray, John	400	A	214	7– 7–1781	Town Fk Salt R	
Ray, John	400	A	214	7– 7–1781	Lick Cr	
Ray, John	400	A	214	7– 7–1781	Willsons Cr	
Ray, John	400	A	214	7– 7–1781	Rowling Fk	
Ray, John	400	A	256	1–21–1783	Bear Cr	
Ray, John	500	A	236	1–21–1783	Buffaloe Cr	
Ray, John	300	A	256	1–21–1783	Buffaloe Cr	Withdrawn
Ray, John	1,344	A	276	4–12–1783	Rowling Fk	
Ray, John	1,344	A	276	4– 2–1783	Poplar Level	Withdrawn
Ray, John	1,000	A	298	10–23–1783	Cedar Cr	Withdrawn
Ray, John	1,000	A	298	10–23–1783	Lick Cr	845 acres withdrawn
Ray, John	1,000	A	302	11– 7–1783	Beech Fk	
Ray, John	800	A	327	1– 3–1784	Fromans Cr	688 acres withdrawn
Ray, John	300	A	327	1– 3–1784	Buffaloe Cr	
Ray, John	688	A	333	1–20–1784	Buffaloe Cr	Surveyed
Ray, John	688	A	333	1–20–1784	Fromans Cr	
Ray, John	112	A	342	2–28–1784	———	
Ray, John	400	A	345	3–11–1784	N Fk Lick Cr	Withdrawn
Ray, John	445	A	349	3–29–1784	Lick Cr	
Ray, John	4,744	A	351	4–12–1784	———	
Ray, John	500	A	363	6– 4–1784	Fromans Cr	
Ray, John Jr	112	B	23	12– 7–1784	Beech Fk	
Ray, John Jr	112	B	23	12– 7–1784	———	Withdrawn
Ray, Joseph	400	A	216	7–30–1781	Bear Cr	Surveyed withdrawn
Ray, Joseph	400	A	256	1–21–1783	Bear Cr	Withdrawn
Ray, Joseph	400	A	375	8– 2–1784	Bear Cr	Amended
Ray, Margret	400	A	216	7–30–1781	Bear Cr	Surveyed
Ray, Nicholas	1,000	A	153	6–26–1780	Salt R	
Ray, Nicholas	1,000	A	153	6–26–1780	Beech Fk	
Ray, Nicholas	400	A	153	6–26–1780	Salt R	
Ray, Phillip	400	A	216	7–30–1781	Clay Lick	
Ray, Rachel	400	A	216	7–30–1781	Bear Cr	Surveyed
Ray, Richard	400	A	83	5–22–1780	Beech Fk	
Ray, Samuel	400	A	238	12–20–1782	Ritchies Run	
Ray, Sarah	400	A	216	7–30–1781	Clay Lick	Surveyed
Rayburn, Matthew	856	B	51	11– 9–1785	18 Mile Cr	
Read, John	400	A	3	11–11–1779	Dicks R	Surveyed
Read, John	1,000	A	272	3–31–1783	Sinking Cr	
Read, John	500	A	308	11–24–1783	Mulberry Cr	
Read, John	268½	A	308	11–24–1783	Bear Cr	Surveyed
Read, John	1,000	A	308	11–24–1783	Bear Cr	
Read, John	1,000	A	308	11–24–1783	Bear Cr & Green R	
Read, John	1,000	A	337	2–11–1784	Little Barren R	
Read, John	1,000	A	337	2–11–1784	Little Barren R	
Read, John	500	B	8	9–27–1784	Cedar Cr	
Read, John	1,800	B	8	9–27–1784	Mulberry Cr	Withdrawn
Read, John	2,268½	B	17	11–13–1784	———.	240 acres surveyed
Read, Joseph	400	A	128	6– 8–1780	Cartright Cr	Surveyed
Read, Joseph	1,000	A	154	6–28–1780	S Fk Rowling	
Read, Wm	300	A	115	5 31–1780	White Oak Run	
Read, Wm	300	A	115	5–31–1780	Fk Paint Lick Cr	
Read, Wm	400	A	115	5–31–1780	Logans Cr	
Rector, Henry	1,000	A	58	5–16–1780	Stepstone Cr	
Rector, Henry	1,000	A	58	5–16–1780	N Fk Elkhorn	
Rector, John	593¾	A	375	7–29–1784		
Redd, John	577	A	341	2–26–1784	Breashears Cr	
Redd, Mordecai	1,000	A	57	5–15–1780	Floyds Fk	
Redd, Mordicai	1,500	A	155	6–29–1780	S Fk Elkhorn	
Redd, Mordica	2,137	A	302	11– 7–1783	Floyds Fk	
Reddett, Josiah	3,000	A	157	6–30–1780	Licking	
Reds, John	500	A	90	5–23–1780	McBride	
Reece, Joel	200	A	219	8–14–1781	Ohio R	Withdrawn
Reed, Alex	300	A	375	7–29–1784	———	
Reed, Alex, et al	4,620	A	328	1– 9–1784	Robinsons Cr	Surveyed
Reed, Andrew	325	A	188	3–15–1781	Freemans Run	
Reed, Andrew	1,500	A	371	7–12–1784	Rough Cr	

Entree	Acres	Book	Page	Entry Date	Watercourse	Notes
Reed, Andrew	225	B	49	6–17–1785	———	
Reed, James	500	A	135	6–17–1780	Drowning Cr	Mil
Reed, James	400	A	154	6–27–1780	Ky R	
Reed, James	2,000	A	232	12–18–1782	Sinking Cr	
Reed, James	800	B	12	11– 9–1784	———	Surveyed
Reed, John	400	A	268	3–28–1783	Green R	
Reed, John	349⅔	A	283	7– 4–1783	Green R	
Reed, John	349	A	284	8– 2–1783	Chaplins & Beech Fk	
Reed, John	1,800	A	302	11– 7–1783	Mulberry Cr	Withdrawn
Reed, Joseph	400	A	128	6– 8–1780	Hardins Cr	
Reed, Joseph	200	A	337	2–11–1784	———	
Reed & Ford	10,000	A	313	12– 5–1783	Ohio R	
Reeis, Aazon	1,000	A	179	10–19–1780	Cane Run	
Reese, Joel	400	A	175	10– 6–1780	Hickman Cr	Surveyed
Reese, Joel	400	A	184	10–27–1780	Rowling Fk	Surveyed
Reeves, Brewer et al	1,000	A	314	12–12–1783	Mill Cr	Surveyed
Reeves, James	1,720	B	45	5–16–1785	Ky R	Surveyed
Reeves, Thomas	400	A	314	12–12–1783	Mill Cr	Surveyed
Reeves, Thomas	100	A	349	4– 2–1784	Mill Cr	Surveyed
Reeves, Thomas	1,146½	A	349	4– 2–1784	Mill Cr	Surveyed
Reeves, Thomas	2,000	A	349	4– 2–1784	Ky R	
Reeves, Thomas	3,250	A	349	4– 2–1784	Ky R	Surveyed
Reid, Alexander	400	A	71	5–18–1780	S Br Silver Cr	
Reid, Alexander	250	A	71	5–18–1780	Knob Lick Cr	
Reid, Alexander	200	A	207	4–14–1781	Overton & Reed	Mil
Reid, Alexander	3,556½	A	232	12–18–1782	Sinking Cr	Surveyed
Reid, Alexander	100	A	335	1–30–1784	Beech Fk	
Reid, Andrew	3,005½	A	252	1–14–1783	Sinking Cr	
Reid, Andrew	200	A	253	1–14–1783	Green R	
Reid, James	250	A	71	5–18–1780	S Br Silver Cr	
Reid, James	300	A	135	6–17–1780	Station Camp Cr	
Reid, James	200	A	135	6–17–1780	Ky R	Mil
Reid, James	1,000	A	232	12–18–1782	Robinsons Cr	Surveyed
Reid, James	2,152	A	328	1– 9–1783	Robinsons Cr	
Reid, John	1,000	A	100	5–26–1780	Green R	
Reid, John	1,000	A	128	6– 8–1780	His settlement	
Reid, John	349	A	280	6–14–1783	Chaplins Fk	Withdrawn
Reid, Samuel	250	A	71	5–18–1780	Knob Lick Cr	
Reinecker, Geo	1,000	A	280	6–19–1783	Green R	
Remey, Jacob	666⅔	A	46	5–11–1780	Salt R	
Ren, Richard	400	A	4	12– 7–1779	Drinnings Cr	
Rench, Andrew	400	A	198	3–17–1781	Salt R	Surveyed
Rennicks, John	400	A	18	3– 3–1780	Dicks R	Surveyed
Reynolds, George	400	A	150	6–24–1780	Dicks R	
Reynols, James	500	A	58	5–15–1780	Licking	
Rhea, John	291	A	370	7– 8–1784	Sinking Cr	
Rhoads, John	400	A	59	5–16–1780	Mill Cr	
Rhoads, John	2,000	A	59	5–16–1780	Mill Cr	
Rhoads, John	400	A	90	5–23–1780	S Fk Licking	
Rhoads, Clifton	800	A	59	5–16–1780	Floyds Fk	Surveyed
Rhoades, Henry	300	A	164	7–29–1780	Coxes Cr	Surveyed
Rhoades, John	400	A	96	5–25–1780	Tates Cr	
Rhodes, John	400	A	96	5–24–1780	Otter Cr	
Ribinson, James	200	A	121	6– 2–1780	Paint Lick Cr	
Rice, Benajah	1,000	A	177	10–10–1780	Timothy Payton	
Rice, Benjamin	500	A	94	5–24–1780	Gists Cr	
Rice, David	500	A	93	5–24–1780	Indian Cr	
Rice, David	500	A	127	6– 7–1780	Chaplins Fk	
Rice, Fisher	3,000	A	250	1– 8–1783	Little Caney Cr	
Rice, Fisher	6,000	A	262	2–12–1783	Nolin Cr	3,000 acres withdrawn
Rice, Fisher	1,000	A	262	2–12–1783	Otter Cr	
Rice, Fisher	3,000	A	280	6–20–1783	Rough Cr	
Rice, Fisher	3,000	A	280	6–20–1783	Nolin Cr	Withdrawn
Rice, Fisher et al	4,311	A	329	1–13–1784	Rough Cr	
Rice, Fisher et al	12,000	A	329	1–13–1784	Pitmans Cr	6,000 acres surveyed
Rice, Fisher et al	12,000	B	3	8–26–1784	Pittmans Cr	Amended
Rice, Fisher et al	10,311	B	44	5–10–1785	Pittmans Cr	
Rice, George	800	A	373	7–27–1784	Beech Fk	
Rice, John	500	A	79	5–20–1780	Tates Cr	
Rice, Joseph	1,000	A	373	7–27–1784	Beech Fk	
Rice, Richard	1,000	A	126	6– 7–1780	His settlement	Surveyed
Rich, Samuel	1,000	A	105	5–27–1780	Ky R	Surveyed
Richard, Samuel	300	A	197	3–17–1781	Nolin Cr	
Richard, Samuel	200	A	197	3–17–1781	Grove in Barrens	
Richard, Samuel	200	A	197	3–17–1781	Nolin Cr	
Richards, John	300	B	48	6–20–1785	———	
Richardson, Daniel	1,000	A	120	6– 1–1780	Licking	
Richardson, Holt	1,000	A	24	4–25–1780	Fk Licking	
Richardson, John	4,000	A	358	5– 7–1784	Beech Fk	Mil surveyed

Entree	Acres	Book	Page	Entry Date	Watercourse	Notes
Richardson, John C....	667	A	160	7– 7–1780	Eagles Cr	
Richardson, Marquis...	475	A	161	7–10–1780	Coxes Cr	338 acres surveyed
Richardson, Marquis...	475	B	49	6–17–1785	————	388 acres surveyed
Richardson, Samuel....	200	A	160	7– 7–1780	Eagle Cr	
Richardson, Samuel....	400	A	161	7–10–1780	Coxes Cr	Withdrawn
Richardson, Sandy.....	300	A	157	7– 3–1780	Red R	
Richardson, Turner....	400	A	81	5–22–1780	Green	
Richardson, Turner....	250	A	205	4– 6–1781	Beech Fk	Mil
Richerson, Holt......	1,000	A	23	4–24–1780	Sinking	Mil
Richerson, Joseph.....	10,000	A	236	12–20–1782	Green R	
Riches, John......	3,500	A	256	1–23–1783	Green R	Withdrawn
Richeson, John........	3,500	A	297	10–14–1783	Brush Cr	
Richey, John.........	100	A	250	1– 8–1783	Beech Fk	
Richey, John.........	400	B	46	5–23–1785	————	
Richie, John........	400	A	330	1–14–1784	Beech Fk	
Richie, Wm.........	400	A	217	8– 2–1781	Chaplins Fk	Withdrawn
Riddle, Cornelius......	400	A	106	5–29–1780	Licking	
Riddle, George.......	400	A	14	2–19–1780	Licking Cr	
Riddle, George.......	1,000	A	106	5–29–1780	Fk Licking	
Riddle, Isaac..........	400	A	13	2–19–1780	Licking Cr	
Riddle, Isaac..........	500	A	106	5–29–1780	His settlement	
Riddle, Isaac..........	1,000	A	107	5–29–1780	His settlement	
Riddle, Isaac et al.....	1,000	A	102	5–27–1780	N Fk Elkhorn	
Riddle, Isaac et al.....	2,000	A	127	6– 8–1780	Fk Liking	
Riddle, John.........	500	A	107	5–29–1780	Licking	
Riddle, Samuel.......	250	A	176	10– 6–1780	Rowling Fk	
Ridgley, Charles......	1,000	A	203	4– 3–1781	Bullskin Cr	Surveyed
Ridgley, Matthew.....	1,500	A	196	3–17–1780	Nolin Cr	Mil
Ridgley, Matthew.....	500	A	196	3–17–1781	Mill Cr	
Ridley, Matthew.....	200	A	196	3–17–1781	Mill Cr	
Ridley, Matthew.....	200	A	197	3–17–1781	Cane Run	
Ridley, Matthew....c.	600	A	197	3–17–1781	Ohio R	
Ridley, Matthew.....	1,000	A	197	3–17–1781	Nolin Cr	
Ridley, Matthew.....	400	A	197	3–17–1781	Salt R	
Ried, Alex...........	400	A	43	5–11–1780	Fern Cr	Surveyed
Ried, Alex...........	200	A	335	1–30–1784	Beech Fk	
Ried, John K........	666⅔	A	54	5–15–1780	————	
Right, Walter........	325	A	191	3–15–1781	Pond Cr	Withdrawn
Riley, John..........	1,031½	A	315	12–15–1783	Salt R	
Rims, Giles..........	200	A	24	4–25–1780	Fk Licking	Mil
Ringoe, Peter........	400	A	8	1–11–1780	S Br Elkhorn	
Ritcheson, John......	4,000	A	255	1–20–1783	Beech Fk	
Ritchey, James.......	50	A	28	4–27–1780	Salt R	
Ritchey, John........	250	A	176	10– 6–1780	Clay Lick & Beech.	
Ritchey, John........	300	A	185	10–31–1780	Beech Fk	
Ritchey, John........	300	A	237	12–21–1782	Beech Fk	
Ritchey, John........	250	A	198	3–17–1781	Beech Fk	
Ritchie, John........	100	A	226	12–14–1782	Beech Fk	Withdrawn
Ritchie, John........	50	A	226	12–14–1782	Beech Fk	
Ritchie, John........	68	A	238	12–23–1782	Beech Fk	
Ritchie, Wm........	400	A	297	10–15–1783	Chaplins Fk	Withdrawn
Rite, John..........	1,384	B	46	5–26–1785	————	
Roase, Duncan.......	8,000	A	237	12–21–1782	Floyds Fk	Surveyed
Roberson, Isaac......	400	A	11	2– 3–1780	Hinstons Fk	
Robert, Ben.........	400	A	139	6–21–1780	Near Falls Ohio R..	
Robert, George......	1,000	A	293	10– 4–1783	Pittmans Cr	Surveyed
Robert, Joseph......	1,000	A	77	5–20–1780	Brushy Pond Cr	
Robert, Joseph......	1,000	A	94	5–24–1780	Licking	
Robert, Joseph......	500	A	255	1–20–1783	N Fk Rowling Fk..	
Robert, Wm.........	650	A	218	8– 8–1781	Rock Cr	
Robert, Wm.........	4,809	A	313	12– 5–1783	Brashears Cr	Withdrawn
Robert, Wm.........	3,000	B	40	2– 8–1785	————	
Roberts, Benj.......	1,000	A	63	5–16–1780	Br Licking	
Roberts, Benj.......	400	A	82	5–22–1780	Licking	
Roberts, Benj.......	1,000	A	129	6– 9–1780	Licking	
Roberts, Benj.......	100	A	166	8–11–1780	Otter Cr	
Roberts, Benj.......	850½	A	246	1– 6–1783	Beech Fk	
Roberts, Benj.......	10,000	A	250	1– 9–1783	Thomas Spencer....	Surveyed
Roberts, Benj.......	400	A	254	1–18–1783	Cartright Cr	
Roberts, Benj.......	1,000	A	289	9–10–1783	Clover Lick Cr....	Withdrawn
Roberts, Benj.......	400	A	289	9–10–1783	Douitts Cr	
Roberts, Benj.......	500	A	289	9–10–1783	Chestnut Flat	
Roberts, Benj.......	1,400	A	289	9–10–1783	Scottpouch Cr	Withdrawn
Roberts, Benj.......	500	A	289	9–10–1783	Hardens Cr	
Roberts, Benj.......	1,000	A	289	9–10–1783	Hardens Cr	
Roberts, Benj.......	1,000	A	289	9–10–1783	Hardens Cr	
Roberts, Benj.......	200	A	290	9–10–1783	Hardens settlement.	
Roberts, Benj.......	600	A	294	10–11–1783	Hardens Cr	Amended
Roberts, Benj........	300	A	294	10–11–1783	Hardens Cr	

Entree	Acres	Book	Page	Entry Date	Watercourse	Notes
Roberts, Benj	16,250	A	295	10–13–1783	Green & Panther	Surveyed
Roberts, Benj	500	B	32	1–12–1785	Beech Fk	
Roberts, Benj	500	B	32	1–12–1785	——	Withdrawn
Roberts, Benj et al	400	A	210	5–30–1781	Goose Cr	
Roberts, Benj et al	20,000	A	250	1– 9–1784	Brashears Cr	Surveyed
Roberts, Ben Sr	1,000	A	83	5–22–1780	Licking	
Roberts, Betty	377	A	238	12–21–1782	Beach Fk	
Roberts, George	500	A	100	5–26–1780	Doctors Fk	Withdrawn
Roberts, George	500	A	125	6– 5–1780	Tuckahoe Cr	Withdrawn
Roberts, George	500	A	293	10– 4–1783	Tuckahoe Cr	Withdrawn
Roberts, George	500	A	293	10– 4–1783	Doctors Fk	Withdrawn
Roberts, James	800	A	63	5–16–1780	Ohio R	
Roberts, John	10,000	A	243	12–26–1782	18 mile Cr	Surveyed
Roberts, Joseph	800	A	90	5–23–1780	Brashears Cr	
Roberts, Joseph	1,000	A	107	5–29–1780	S Jephthas Mt	
Roberts, Joseph	1,000	A	107	5–29–1780	Great Prairie	Surveyed
Roberts, Joseph	1,000	A	107	5–29–1780	Brashears Cr	Surveyed
Roberts, Joseph	1,000	A	213	7– 2–1781	Gess Cr	
Roberts, Joseph	506¼	A	296	10–15–1783	Robinsons Cr	Withdrawn
Roberts, Joseph	374	A	296	10–14–1783	Rolling Fk	
Roberts, Joseph	506¼	A	341	2–27–1784	Robinsons Cr	
Roberts, Joseph	506¼	A	342	2–27–1784	——	
Roberts, Joseph	2,904	B	11	11– 8–1784	Panther Cr	
Roberts, Joseph	1,000	B	27	12–17–1784	——	
Roberts, Thomas	88	A	238	12–21–1782	Beach Fk	
Roberts, Wm	1,500	A	63	5–16–1780	N Fk Elkhorn	
Roberts, Wm	800	A	63	5–16–1780	Ohio R	
Roberts, Wm	675	A	218	8– 8–1781	Nolin Cr	
Roberts, Wm	3,000	A	283	7–27–1783	Pattons Cr	Surveyed
Roberts, Wm	1,000	A	283	7– 4–1783	N Fk Harrods Cr	Withdrawn
Roberts, Wm	1,000	A	283	7– 4–1783	N Fk Harrods Cr	800 acres withdrawn
Roberts, Wm	4,809	A	329	1–13–1784	Brashears Cr	Withdrawn
Robertson, Alex	400	A	14	2–19–1780	Shawnee Run	Surveyed
Robertson, Alex	1,000	A	36	4–29–1780	Beech Fk	Surveyed
Robertson, Alex	300	A	138	6–20–1780	Ky R	
Robertson, Alex	300	A	138	6–20–1780	Beech Fk	
Robertson, David	1,000	A	13	2–16–1780	Brashears Cr	Mils 1,763 withdrawn
Robertson, George	10,000	A	235	12–20–1782	Beaver Dam Cr	
Robertson, James	2,200	A	194	3–16–1781	Floyds Fk & Bullskin	Surveyed
Robertson, John	400	A	245	12–30–1782	Cartright Cr	Withdrawn
Robertson, John	1,284	A	245	12–28–1782	Cartright Cr	Surveyed
Robertson, John	300	A	251	1–10–1783	Pottengers Cr	284 acres surveyed
Robertson, John	984	A	251	1–10–1783	Pottengers Cr	Surveyed
Robertson, John	400	A	251	1–10–1783	Cartright Cr	Surveyed
Robertson, John	16	A	322	12–22–1783	Pottengers Cr	Surveyed
Robertson, Robert	400	A	11	2–13–1780	——	
Robertson, Thomas	953½	A	328	1– 9–1784	Robinsons Cr	Surveyed
Robinson, Alex	1,000	A	138	6–20–1780	Cedar Run	Surveyed
Robinson, David	400	A	3	11–11–1779	Boones Cr	Surveyed
Robinson, David	400	A	16	2–23–1780	Brashears Cr	
Robinson, David	1,000	A	37	4–29–1780	Boones Cr	Surveyed
Robinson, David	1,000	A	149	6–24–1780	Boons Cr	
Robinson, James	500	A	121	6– 2–1780	Paint Lick	
Robinson, James	250	A	121	6– 2–1780	Paint Lick	Withdrawn
Robinson, James	250	A	121	6– 2–1780	Paint Lick Cr	Withdrawn
Robinson, James	500	A	121	6– 2–1780	Drakes Camp Cr	
Robinsons, James	400	A	121	6– 2–1780	Carpenters Cr	
Robinsons, James	400	A	127	6– 8–1780	Knob Licks	
Robinsons, James	1,970½	A	291	9–13–1783	N Fk Rough Cr	
Robinson, George	200	A	90	5–23–1780	Rowling Fk	
Robinson, John	200	A	29	4–27–1780	Hogan settlement	Mil
Robinson, Wm	1,000	A	97	5–25–1780	Cartright Cr	Surveyed
Robinson, Wm	300	A	114	5–30–1780	Big Sandy Cr	
Robinson, Wm	1,025	A	135	6–17–1780	Silver Cr	
Robinson, Wm	1,000	A	149	6–24–1780	Boons Cr	Surveyed
Rochester, Nath	700	A	158	7– 3–1780	Millers Cr	
Rodes, David	437	A	296	10–15–1783	Robinsons Cr	
Rodes, David	766½	A	296	10–14–1783	Robinsons Cr	
Rodes, John	10	A	24	4–25–1780	Boones Cr	
Rodes, John	20	A	24	4–25–1780	Boones Cr	
Rodes, John	20	A	24	4–25–1780	Tates Cr	
Rodgers, Andrew	500	A	45	5–11–1780	S Fk Licking	
Rodgers, James	1,000	A	199	3–26–1781	Cedar Cr	
Rodgers, Jonathan	400	A	200	3–26–1781	Coxes Cr	
Rodgers, Jonathan	400	A	211	6– 5–1781	Rowling Fk	
Rodgers, Joseph	2,000	A	45	5–11–1780	N Fk Elkhorn	
Rodgers, Joseph	1,000	A	146	6–24–1780	Beargrass Cr	
Rodgers, Joseph	400	A	272	4– 3–1783	Bear Run	

Entree	Acres	Book	Page	Entry Date	Watercourse	Notes
Rodgers, Joseph	400	A	272	4- 3-1783	Bear Run	
Rodgers, Byrd	600	A	69	5-18-1780	Ohio R	
Rogers, George	200	A	31	4-28-1780	Eagle Cr	Mil
Rogers, George	1,241	A	46	5-12-1780	Island Ohio R	
Rogers, George	600	A	69	5-18-1780	Ohio R	
Rogers, George	1,000	A	162	7-18-1780	Fox Run	Surveyed
Rogers, George	1,000	A	166	8-11-1780	Green R	Withdrawn
Rogers, George	500	A	339	2-16-1784	Bear Cr	Surveyed
Rogers, George	1,000	A	334	2-16-1784	Panther Cr	Withdrawn
Rogers, George	1,000	B	8	9-23-1784	————	500 acres surveyed
Rogers, John	500	A	69	5-28-1780	Ohio R	
Rogers, John	5,000	A	318	12-16-1783	Ohio R	
Rogers, John	68,728½	A	318	12-16-1783	Nole Linn Cr	Surveyed
Rogers, John	50,000	A	318	12-16-1783	Ohio R	Surveyed
Rogers, John	5,000	A	353	4-16-1784	————	
Rogers, John et al	3,000	A	316	12-15-1783	Big Cr	
Rogers, John et al	6,000	A	316	12-15-1783	Big Ky R	
Rogers, John et al	3,000	A	316	12-15-1783	Big Ky R	
Rogers, Jonathan	700	A	200	3-26-1781	Fromans Cr	
Rogers, Jonathan	438	A	334	1-21-1784	————	
Rogers, Jonathan	400	A	365	6-12-1784	————	
Rogers, Matthew	100	A	256	1-23-1783	Cedar Cr	Surveyed
Rogers, Matthew	500	A	334	1-21-1784	————	Returned
Rolling, Stephen	400	A	279	6- 7-1783	Valley Cr	Surveyed
Rollins, Sam et al	2,802	A	280	6-19-1783	Green R	
Rooker, John	400	A	12	2- 5-1780	4 Mile Cr	
Rose, Martin	400	A	245	12-30-1782	Drennons Lick	Surveyed
Rose, Martin	400	A	245	12-30-1782	Ky R	Surveyed
Rosey, Wm	500	A	49	5-12-1780	Elkhorn	
Ross, Francis	300	A	73	5-19-1780	Buffaloe Cr	Surveyed
Ross, Hugh	400	A	115	5-30-1780	Silver Cr	
Ross, James	400	A	16	2-24-1780	Br Ohio R	
Ross, Joseph	400	A	259	1-29-1783	————	
Ross, Phillip	2,000	A	30	4-28-1780	Harrods Cr	Mil surveyed
Ross, Phillip	1,000	A	334	1-21-1784	Harrods Cr	Amended
Ross, Wm	800	A	78	5-20-1780	Holders Cr	
Rosson, Wm	230	A	298	10-23-1783	Rolling Fk	
Rough, Adam	400	A	22	4-22-1780	Roughs Run	
Rough, Adam	400	A	139	6-21-1780	Ky R	
Rough, Adam, heir	400	A	139	6-21-1780	Ky R	
Roundtree, Wm	400	A	94	5-24-1780	Mill Cr	
Routt, John	400	A	69	5-18-1780	Beech Fk	
Routt, John	120	A	138	6-20-1780	Ky R	
Routt, John	242	A	138	6-20-1780	Dick R	
Rowe, George	750	A	221	10- 4-1781	Beech Fk	
Rowe, George Jr	750	A	205	4- 6-1781	Beech Fk	Withdrawn
Rowland, Thomas	400	A	17	2-26-1780	Hickmans Cr	
Rowland, Thomas	500	A	24	4-25-1780	Licking Cr	
Rowland, Thomas	500	A	24	4-25-1780	Licking	Mil
Rowland, Thomas	400	A	25	4-26-1780	Ky R	Surveyed
Rowland, Thomas	1,000	A	25	4-26-1780	Hickmans Cr	
Rowland, Thomas	400	A	28	4-27-1780	Ky R	Surveyed
Rowland, Thomas	350	A	35	4-29-1780	Licking	Mil
Rowland, Thomas	450	A	73	5-19-1780	Brashears Cr	Surveyed
Rowland, Thomas	840	A	73	5-19-1780	Coxes Cr	Surveyed
Rowland, Thomas	50	A	106	5-27-1780	Ky R	
Rowland, Thomas	80	A	106	5-27-1780	Ky R	
Rowland, Thomas	30	A	106	5-27-1780	Ky R	
Rowland, Thomas	840	A	198	3-19-1781	Coxes Cr	
Rowland, Thomas	100	A	205	4- 6-1780	Beech Fk	Surveyed withdrawn
Rowland, Thomas	200	A	230	12-17-1782	Brashears Cr	
Rowland, Thomas	145	A	297	10-15-1783	Beargrass Cr	Surveyed
Rowland, Thomas	200	A	355	4-24-1784	————	
Rowland, Thomas	10	A	362	6- 1-1784	————	
Rowland, Thomas	640	A	362	6- 1-1784	————	145 acres surveyed
Rowland, Thomas	200	B	46	5-19-1785	————	
Rowlings, Stephen	50	A	214	7- 3-1781	E Fk Valley Cr	Surveyed
Rowlings, Stephen	400	B	46	5-23-1785	Floyds Fk	Surveyed
Rowly, Bannester	200	A	22	4-24-1780	Br Hanging Fk	
Ruddle, James	500	A	103	5-27-1780	Licking	
Ruddle, John	400	A	103	5-27-1780	S Fk Licking	
Ruddle, John	500	A	103	5-27-1780	Licking	
Rude, Jesse	400	A	205	4- 5-1781	Long Lick Cr	Surveyed
Runner, Michal	200	A	243	12-26-1782	————	Withdrawn
Runner, Michal	200	A	279	6- 7-1783	Mays Cr	Surveyed
Ruse, Joel	1,000	A	67	5-17-1780	Yellow Banks	Withdrawn
Russell, Joseph	250	A	101	5-26-1780	Montgomrie settle	
Russell, Robert	1,000	A	309	11-25-1783	Green R	Withdrawn

Entree	Acres	Book	Page	Entry Date	Watercourse	Notes
Russell, Robert	1,000	A	321	12-22-1783	Green R	Withdrawn
Russell, Robert S	500	B	12	11- 9-1784	Panther Cr	
Russell, Wm	3,000	A	38	4-29-1780	Cedar Lick	Withdrawn
Russell, Wm	3,000	A	119	6- 1-1780	Pittmans Cr	Surveyed
Russell, Wm	100	A	184	10-30-1780	N Fk Pottingers Cr	
Russell, Wm	2,000	A	196	3-17-1781	Rough Cr	
Russell, Wm	3,000	A	196	3-17-1781	Nolin Cr	Mil
Russell, Wm	300	A	204	4- 4-1781	Pottengers Cr	
Russell, Wm	851	A	238	12-21-1782	Green R	Surveyed
Russell, Wm	1,000	A	309	11-25-1783	Green R	
Russell, Wm	1,000	A	309	11-25-1783	Green R	
Russell, Wm	1,041	B	12	11- 9-1784	Panther Cr	
Rust, John	10,000	A	326	1- 2-1784	Green R	
Rust, John	4,043¾	B	12	11- 9-1784	Rolling Fk	
Ryan, Joseph	400	A	345	3- 9-1784	Cartright Cr	
Ryan, Michael	10,000	A	232	12-18-1782	Green R	
Ryan, Michael	4,000	A	313	12- 5-1783	Salt R	Withdrawn
Ryan, Michael	48,000	A	313	12- 5-1783	Salt R	Surveyed
Ryan, Michael	20,000	A	325	12-31-1783	Green R	Surveyed
Ryan, Michael	4,000	B	38	1-29-1785	Willson Cr	
Ryan, Michael	4,000	B	38	1-29-1785	——————	Withdrawn
Ryan, Michael	4,000	B	38	1-29-1785	Willsons Cr	Withdrawn
Ryan, Michael	4,000	B	38	1-28-1785	——————	Withdrawn
Ryley, Barney	50	A	30	4-28-1780	Salt R	Surveyed
Ryon, Michal	4,000	A	313	12- 5-1783	Ky R	
Ryon, Michal	20,000	A	313	12- 5-1783	Ky R	
Ryon, Michael	4,000	A	313	12- 5-1783	Ky R	
Said, Wm	246	A	54	5-15-1780	——————	
Said, Wm	254	A	76	5-19-1780	Stoners Fk	
St. Clair, Alex	1,000	A	67	5-17-1780	4 Mile Cr	
St. Clair, Alex	1,000	A	67	5-17-1780	Slate Cr	
St. Clair, Alex	1,000	A	67	5-17-1780	Slate Cr	
St. Clair, Alex	1,000	A	67	5-17-1780	Slate Cr	
St. Clair, Alex	1,000	A	67	5-17-1780	Dicks R	
St. Clair, Alex	1,029	A	227	12-14-1782	Brashears Cr	
St. Clair, Alex	1,000	A	227	12-14-1782	Brashears Cr	
St. Clair, Alex	1,000	A	227	12-14-1782	Brashears Cr	
St. Clair, Alex	2,000	A	227	12-14-1782	Bullskin Cr	Surveyed
St. Clair, Alex	2,000	A	229	12-16-1782	Brashears Cr	Surveyed
St. Clair, Alex	1,986½	A	328	1- 9-1784	Brush Cr	
Salsbury, John et al	6,000	A	340	2-18-1784	Rough Cr	
Sally, John	400	A	159	7- 4-1780	Knob Lick Br	
Sally, George	400	A	158	7- 4-1780	Willsons Cr	
Sally, Phillip	400	A	159	7- 4-1780	Willson Cr	
Sally, Wm Jr	400	A	159	7- 4-1780	Knob Lick Cr	
Sammons, Richard	300	A	192	3-16-1781	Pottengers Cr	Surveyed
Sampson, Matthew	1,350	A	35	4-29-1780	Fern Cr	Mil surveyed
Samuel, G M	6,000	A	332	1-20-1784	——————	Withdrawn
Samuel, James	950	A	90	5-23-1780	Rowling Fk	
Samuel, James	280	A	214	7- 7-1781	Willsons Cr	
Samuel, James	400	B	38	1-29-1785	Cane Cr	
Samuel, John	600	A	90	5-23-1780	Rowling Fk	
Samuel, Peter	366⅔	A	40	5- 9-1780	Elkhorn	
Samuel, Reuben	500	A	183	10-27-1780	Floyds Fk	Surveyed
Samuels, James	47	A	74	5-19-1780	Willsons Cr	
Samuels, James	300	A	74	5-19-1780	Willsons Cr	Withdrawn
Samuels, James	280	A	118	6- 1-1780	Long Lick Cr	
Samuels, James	100	B	38	1-29-1785	Willsons Cr	
Samuels, James	100	B	38	1-29-1785	Willsons Cr	
Sance, Jacob	400	A	8	1-17-1780	Cane Run	
Sanders, John	300	A	29	4-27-1780	Elkhorn	Mil
Sanders, Joseph	200	A	145	6-23-1780	S Fk Cedar Cr	
Sanders, Robert	400	A	39	5- 9-1780	Licking	
Sandford, Robert	3,000	A	285	8- 5-1783	Floyds Fk	Surveyed
Sandford, Wm P	1,000	A	277	4-14-1783	Salt R	Surveyed
Sandford, Wm P	1,000	A	277	4-14-1783	Cartright Cr	
Sandiford, David	3,000	A	354	4-19-1784	Little Bullskin Cr	Withdrawn
Saunders, John	700	A	67	5-17-1780	Locust Cr Ohio R	
Saunders, John	200	A	199	3-20-1781	Beech Fk	Surveyed
Saunders, John	4,000	A	231	12-17-1782	Rough Cr	
Saunders, John	1,000	A	231	12-17-1782	Rough Cr	Surveyed
Saunders, John	1,000	A	231	12-17-1782	Rough Cr	Surveyed
Saunders, John	2,000	A	231	12-17-1782	Rough Cr	Surveyed
Saunders, John	3,000	A	231	12-17-1782	Falls Rough Cr	
Saunders, John	3,000	A	231	12-17-1782	Rough Cr	Surveyed
Saunders, John	1,000	A	232	12-18-1782	Battle Cr	Surveyed
Saunders, John	2,000	A	339	2-16-1784	Falls Rough Cr	Surveyed amended
Saunders, John	1,000	A	339	2-16-1784	Rough Cr	Surveyed amended
Saunders, Joseph	500	A	181	10-23-1780	Pond Cr	

Entree	Acres	Book	Page	Entry Date	Watercourse	Notes
Saunders, Joseph	50	A	198	3-17-1781	Rolling Fk	
Saunders, Nath	500	A	86	5-22-1780	Ohio R	
Saunders, Nath	6,000	A	246	1- 6-1782	Floyds Fk	
Saunders, Paul	200	A	183	10-27-1780	Green R	Mil
Saunders, Peter	1,000	A	67	5-17-1780	S Fk Licking	
Saunders, Reuben	2,001	A	271	3-28-1783	Brush Cr	
Saunder, Robert	250	A	42	5-10-1780	Licking	
Saunders, Robert	1,000	A	58	5-15-1780	Licking	
Saunders, Samuel	400	A	244	12-27-1782	Pittmans Cr	
Saunders, Thomas	1,000	A	156	6-30-1780	Licking	
Saunders, Thomas	500	A	198	3-17-1781	Floyds Fk	Surveyed
Saunders, Thomas	500	A	198	3-17-1781	Pond Cr	
Saunderson, Thomas	500	A	158	7- 4-1780	Willsons Cr	
Sayers, Robert	2,000	A	32	4-29-1780	Elkhorn	Mil
Sayne, Hardage	1,000	A	71	5-18-1780	Licking	
Sayne, Wm	1,000	A	70	5-18-1780	N Fk Elkhorn	
Scayers, Wm B	500	A	75	5-19-1780	Small Mt Cr	
Scayers, Wm B	1,000	A	75	5-19-1780	Coxes Cr	Surveyed
Scidmore, Deborah et al	400	A	265	2-19-1783	Beech Fk	
Sconce, Robert	625	A	266	2-26-1783	Brashears Cr	
Scott, George	200	A	99	5-26-1780	Dicks R	
Scott, George	411¾	A	217	7-31-1781	Cartright Cr	
Scott, George	1,000	A	232	12-18-1782	Clifty Cr	Surveyed
Scott, James	2,950	A	6	12-23-1779	S Fk Licking	Withdrawn
Scott, James	2,950	A	34	4-29-1780	Panther Cr	Withdrawn
Scott, James	532	A	73	5-19-1780	Limestone Run	
Scott, James	1,200	A	100	5-26-1780	Licking	
Scott, James	250	A	111	5-29-1780	Floyds Fk	Surveyed
Scott, James	1,000	A	127	6- 7-1780	Salt Spring Cr	
Scott, James	2,950	A	194	3-16-1781	Panther Cr	
Scott, James	2,950	A	195	3-16-1781	Panther Cr	
Scott, James	1,375	A	232	12-18-1782	Clifty Cr	Surveyed
Scott, Robert	200	A	20	4-18-1780	Dicks R	Mil surveyed
Scott, Roger	500	A	130	6-10-1780	Hingston Fk	
Scott, Saml	400	A	13	2- 9-1780	Dicks R	
Scott, Sam	1,000	A	36	4-29-1780	Scott settlement	Surveyed
Scott, Thomas	637	A	232	12-18-1782	Panther Cr	Surveyed
Scott, Thomas	15,000	A	324	12-27-1783	Nolelin Cr	Withdrawn
Scott, Thomas	15,000	A	350	4-10-1784	Rolling Fk	Surveyed
Scott, Thomas	15,000	A	350	4-10-1784	Nole Linn Cr	Withdrawn
Scott, Wm	700	A	44	5-11-1780	Beech Fk	Surveyed
Scott, Wm	400	A	108	5-29-1780	Licking Cr	
Scott, Wm et al	200	A	257	1-25-1783	Long Lick Cr	Surveyed
Scott, Wm et al	200	A	257	1-25-1783	Long Lick Cr	Surveyed
Scott, Wm et al	250	A	257	1-25-1783	Long Lick Cr	Surveyed
Scott, Wm et al	400	A	257	1-25-1783	Long Lick Cr	Surveyed
Scruggs, Isham	500	A	104	5-27-1780	Chaplins Fk	
Seaman, Charles	1,000	A	79	5-20-1780	Drennens Lick	Surveyed
Seaman, Jonah	500	A	97	5-25-1780	Drennens Lick Cr	
Seaman, Jonah et al	400	A	139	6-21-1780	Fox Run	Surveyed
Searcy, Bartett	400	A	8	1-17-1780	Rockhouse Br	
Searcy, Reuben	400	A	8	1-17-1780	Licking Cr	
Searcy, Richard	400	A	9	1-17-1780	Howards Cr	
Sears, Wm B	1,000	A	64	5-17-1780	Stevens Fk	
Seberry, John	1,000	A	45	5-11-1780	N Fk Elkhorn	
See, James	400	A	5	12- 7-1779	Brashears Cr	
Sellars, John	400	A	149	6-24-1780	S Fk Licking	
Selley, Wm	250	A	144	6-23-1780	Licking	
Seman, James	1,000	A	81	5-22-1780	Beech&Chaplins Fk	
Seman, James	1,000	A	82	5-22-1780	Knob Lick	
Session, George	400	A	224	12-13-1782	W Fk Coxes Cr	
Severns, John	200	A	213	6-30-1781	Gilkeys Run	
Severns, John	300	A	213	6-30-1781	Beech Fk	
Severns, John	700	A	260	2- 4-1783	Rolling Fk	
Sevin, John	500	A	55	5-15-1780	Hardens Cr	
Shackleford, Samuel	492	A	248	1- 7-1783	Drennons Lick Cr	Surveyed
Shackleford, Samuel	400	A	248	1- 7-1783	Gests Cr	
Shanklin, Robert	400	A	15	2-21-1780	Floyds Fk	Surveyed
Shanklin, Robert	1,000	A	146	6-24-1780	Floyds Fk	
Shannon, Hugh	400	A	10	2- 3-1780	Lower Blue Lick	
Shannon, Hugh	1,000	A	126	6- 7-1780	Licking	
Shannon, John Jr	800	A	288	9- 1-1783	Floyds Fk	Surveyed
Shannon, John Jr	2,474½	B	12	11- 9-1784	———	800 acres surveyed
Shannon, Sarah	304	A	293	10- 4-1783	S Fk Beargrass Cr	Withdrawn
Shannon, Sarah	196	A	293	10- 4-1783	Beargrass & Bear Cr	Withdrawn
Shannon, Sarah	500	A	318	12-16-1783	Brashears Cr	Withdrawn
Shannon, Sarah	304	A	318	12-16-1783	S Fk Beargrass Cr	Withdrawn
Shannon, Sarah	196	A	318	12-16-1783	Beargrass Cr	
Shannon, Sarah	500	A	354	4-19-1784	Floyds Fk	Surveyed
Shannon, Sarah	500	A	354	4-19-1784	Brashears Cr	Withdrawn

Entree	Acres	Book	Page	Entry Date	Watercourse	Notes
Shannon, Thomas....	708½	A	256	1–21–1783	Pitmans Cr	....
Shannon, Thomas....	400	A	268	3–28–1783	Robinsons Cr	....
Shannon, Thomas....	874½	B	12	11– 9–1784	———	....
Shannon, Thos et al...	1,674	A	288	9– 1–1783	Pond Cr	Withdrawn
Shannon, Thos et al..	1,500	A	318	12–16–1783	Beargrass Cr	Withdrawn
Shannon, Thos et al..	174½	A	320	12–18–1783	Pond Cr	....
Shannon, Thos et al..	500	B	18	11–17–1784	Gess & Clear Cr	Withdrawn
Shannon, Thos et al..	1,000	B	18	11–17–1784	Drennons Lick Cr..	Withdrawn
Shannon, Thos et al..	1,500	B	18	11–17–1784	Brashears Cr	....
Shannon, Wm	2,000	A	74	5–19–1780	Stoners Fk	....
Shannon, Wm	1,680	A	74	5–19–1780	Licking	....
Shannon, Wm	2,000	A	75	5–19–1780	Hunting Cr	....
Shannon, Wm	2,000	A	75	5–19–1780	Stoners Fk	....
Shannon, Wm	2,140	A	75	5–19–1780	Hunting Cr	....
Shannon, Wm	200	A	75	5–19–1780	Licking	....
Shannon, Wm	560	A	77	5–20–1780	Brashears Cr	Surveyed
Shannon, Wm	560	A	77	5–20–1780	Ky R	Withdrawn
Shannon, Wm	560	A	107	5–29–1780	Blue Lick Fk	....
Shannon, Wm	560	A	107	5–29–1780	Elkhorn	....
Shannon, Wm	560	A	107	5–29–1780	Elkhorn Cr	....
Shannon, Wm	360	A	107	5–29–1780	Fk Cane Run	....
Shannon, Wm	500	A	108	5–29–1780	Salt R	Surveyed
Shannon, Wm	560	A	108	5–29–1780	Coxes Cr	Surveyed
Shannon, Wm	560	A	108	5–29–1780	Chaplins Fk	....
Shannon, Wm	560	A	108	5–29–1780	Licking	....
Shannon, Wm	560	A	109	5–29–1780	Brashears Cr	Surveyed
Shannon, Wm	560	A	109	5–29–1780	Bullskin Cr	Surveyed
Shannon, Wm	560	A	111	5–29–1780	Hardens Cr	Surveyed
Shannon, Wm	560	A	111	5–29–1780	Hardens Cr	....
Shannon, Wm	560	A	111	5–29–1780	Hardens Cr	Surveyed
Shannon, Wm	560	A	112	5–30–1780	Gists Cr	....
Shannon, Wm	560	A	112	5–30–1780	Licking	....
Shannon, Wm	560	A	112	5–30–1780	Big Dry Run	....
Shannon, Wm	1,000	A	126	6– 7–1780	S Fk Cane Run	....
Shannon, Wm	560	A	147	6–24–1780	Ky R	....
Shannon, Wm	1,233½	A	248	1– 7–1783	Flatt Lick	Surveyed
Shannon, Wm	560	B	12	11– 9–1784	———	522 acres surveyed
Shannon, Wm	54½	B	22	12– 3–1784	Guess Cr	Withdrawn
Shannon, Wm	400	B	22	12– 1–1784	Clear Cr	Withdrawn
Shannon, Wm	685	B	22	12– 1–1784		Withdrawn
Shannon, Wm	55	B	23	12– 4–1784	Clear Cr	Withdrawn
Shannon, Wm	55	B	42	3–24–1785	Brashears Cr	Withdrawn
Shannon, Wm	400	B	42	3–24–1785	Brashears Cr	....
Shannon, Wm	5,432	B	42	3–24–1785	Drennings Lick	....
Sharp, Abraham	1,125	A	377	8–12–1784	Brashears Cr	....
Sharp, James B	1,000	A	229	12–16–1783	Simpsons Cr	....
Sharp, James B	1,000	A	373	7–27–1784	———	620 acres surveyed
Sharp, Thomas	492	A	65	5–17–1780	Elkhorn	....
Sharpe, Andrew	1,125	A	250	1– 9–1783	Brashears Cr	Withdrawn
Shastern, Renny	600	A	86	5–22–1780	Joining Thompson	....
Shath, John	200	A	84	5–22–1780	Licking	....
Shaw, Benham	200	A	363	6– 4–1784	———	....
Shelby, David	400	A	81	5–22–1780	Paint Lick	....
Shelby, Evan	1,000	A	19	4–13–1780	Panther Cr	Mil
Shelby, Evan	500	A	19	4–13–1780	Pleasant Run	Mil surveyed
Shelby, Evan	200	A	19	4–13–1780	Mud Fk Beargrass..	Mil surveyed
Shelby, Evan	500	A	20	4–14–1780	Chaplins Fk	Mil withdrawn
Shelby, Evan	200	A	22	4–24–1780	Cumberland R	....
Shebly, Evan	400	A	22	4–24–1780	N Fk Elkhorn	....
Shelby, Evan	500	A	22	4–24–1780	Ky R	....
Shelby, Evan	300	A	33	4–29–1780	Hickmans Cr	....
Shelby, Evan	500	A	42	5–11–1780	Salt R	Withdrawn
Shelby, Evan	500	A	42	5–11–1780	Pittmans Cr	Withdrawn
Shelby, Evan	500	A	42	5–11–1780	Hickmans Cr	Withdrawn
Shelby, Evan	500	A	42	5–11–1780	Harrods Run	....
Shelby, Evan	500	A	130	6–12–1780	Sinking Cr	....
Shelby, Isaac	400	A	4	11–24–1797	Knob Lick	Surveyed
Shelby, Isaac	100	A	20	4–14–1780	Hanging Fk	Mil withdrawn
Shelby, Isaac	500	A	20	4–14–1780	Green R	Mil withdrawn
Shelby, Isaac	500	A	20	4–17–1780	Lexington track	Mil withdrawn
Shelby, Isaac	200	A	20	4–17–1780	Knob Lick	....
Shelby, Isaac	200	A	20	4–17–1780	Knob Lick	....
Shelby, Isaac	500	A	22	4–24–1780	Elkhorn Cr	Mil surveyed
Shalby, Isaac	1,000	A	33	4–29–1780	Shelby settlement..	Surveyed
Shelby, Isaac	100	A	80	5–20–1780	Knob Lick Cr	....

Entree	Acres	Book	Page	Entry Date	Watercourse	Notes
Shelby, Isaac..........	1,500	A	142	6–22–1780	Hickmans Cr......	....
Shelby, Isaac.........	800	A	143	6–23–1780	Hickmans Cr......	Withdrawn
Shelby, Isaac.........	800	A	145	6–24–1780	Holders Cr.........	200 acres withdrawn
Shelby, Isaac.........	1,000	A	145	6–23–1780	Douglass Survey...	....
Shelby, Isaac.........	800	A	145	6–23–1780	Licking...........	....
Shelby, James........	400	A	6	12–28–1779	Hickmans Cr......	....
Shelby, James........	1,000	A	33	4–29–1780	Shelby settlement...	....
Shelby, John........	1,000	A	20	4–17–1780	Chaplins Fk......	Mil
Shelby, John........	500	A	22	4–24–1780	N Fk Elkhorn......	Withdrawn
Shelby, John........	500	A	35	4–29–1780	N Fk Elkhorn......	Mil withdrawn
Shelby, John Jr......	500	A	42	5–11–1780	N Fk Elkhorn......	....
Shelby, John Sr......	300	A	142	6–22–1780	N Fk Licking......	....
Shelby, Wm........	50	A	33	4–29–1780	Hickmans Cr......	Mil
Shelp, John..........	400	A	7	1–10–1779	Licking Cr.........	....
Shelp, John..........	50	A	30	4–28–1780	Goose Cr..........	Mil
Shelp, John..........	1,000	A	37	4–29–1780	Licking...........	....
Shelp, John..........	400	A	102	5–27–1780	Mid Fk Licking....	....
Shelp, John..........	60	A	173	9–20–1780	Salt R............	Withdrawn
Shelp, John..........	150	A	175	10– 4–1780	Salt R............	....
Shelp, John..........	175	A	175	10– 4–1780	Goose Cr..........	....
Shelton, David.......	50	A	24	4–24–1780	Cumberland R.....	....
Shelton, David.......	150	A	24	4–24–1780	Jacks Cr..........	Mil
Shelton, David.......	1,658	A	130	6–12–1780	Woolf Cr..........	....
Shelton, David.......	1,000	A	144	6–23–1780	His entry 165 acres.	....
Shelton, John.......	666⅔	A	54	5–15–1780	——————	....
Shelton, Peter.......	986	A	136	6–19–1780	Salt R............	....
Shelton, Wm.......	1,600	A	92	5–24–1780	Drennons Lick Cr..	....
Shepherd, Adam......	67	A	21	4–20–1780	Mouth Salt R.....	....
Shepherd, Adam......	300	A	24	4–25–1780	N Fk Clear Cr.....	....
Shepherd, Adams.....	200	A	24	4–25–1780	Bullits Lick.......	....
Shepherd, Adams.....	100	A	24	4–25–1780	Salt R............	Withdrawn
Shepherd, Adam......	100	A	184	10–30–1780	Salt R............	....
Shepherd, Adam......	800	A	229	12–16–1782	Wolf Cr..........	Surveyed
Shepherd, Adam......	200	A	229	12–16–1782	Rolling F	Surveyed
Shepherd, Adam......	1,000	A	233	12–18–1782	Rowling F	....
Shepherd, Adam......	1,000	A	238	12–21–1782	Rolling F	....
Shepperd, Adam......	600	A	278	4–14–1783	Rowling F	Surveyed
Shepperd, Adam......	1,000	A	278	4–14–1783	Rowling F	Withdrawn
Shepherd, Adam......	150	A	280	6–19–1783	Rolling F	Surveyed
Shepherd, Adam......	400	A	280	6–19–1783	Rolling Fk........	....
Shepherd, Adam......	165	A	280	6–19–1783	Rolling F	Surveyed
Shepherd, Adam......	170	A	280	6–19–1783	Rolling F	Surveyed
Shepherd, Adam......	1,000	A	280	6–19–1783	Rowling F	....
Shepherd, Adam......	1,000	A	280	6–19–1783	Rolling F	Surveyed
Shepherd, Adam......	500	A	28.?	7– 4–1783	Tarr Cr..........	....
Shepherd, Adam......	900	A	297	10–18–1783	Rolling Fk........	....
Shepherd, Adam......	400	A	297	10–18–1783	Salt R............	....
Shepherd, Adams.....	1,000	A	299	10–29–1783	Rowling Fk........	Withdrawn
Shepherd, Adam......	500	A	300	10–29–1783	Knobbs...........	....
Shepherd, Adam......	300	A	304	11–14–1783	Rolling Fk........	....
Shepherd, Adam......	400	A	304	11–14–1783	Brush Cr..........	....
Shepherd, Adam......	400	A	304	11–14–1783	Fern Cr...........	....
Shepherd, Adam......	300	A	304	11–14–1783	Knobb Cr.........	....
Shepherd, Adam......	1,000	A	304	11–14–1783	Rolling Fk........	....
Shepherd, Adam......	1,000	A	320	12–17–1783	Green R..........	Surveyed
Shepherd, Adam......	415	A	325	12–27–1783	Rolling Fk........	....
Shepherd, Adam......	400	A	325	12–27–1783	Knobb Cr.........	....
Shepherd, Adam......	7,928	A	325	12–27–1783	——————	1,000 acres surveyed
Shepherd, Adam......	300	B	50	10– 5–1785	Drennons Lick Cr..	....
Shepherd, Adam et al..	1,000	B	45	5–16–1785	Ky R.............	....
Shepherd, Peter......	1,000	A	68	5–18–1780	Rolling Fk........	Withdrawn
Shepherd, Peter......	1,000	A	68	5–18–1780	Rolling Fk........	....
Shepherd, Peter......	700	A	68	5–18–1780	Dicks R...........	....
Shepherd, Peter......	300	A	68	5–18–1780	N Fk Licking......	....
Shepherd, Peter......	400	A	68	5–18–1780	Bensons Cr........	....
Shepherd, Peter......	1,000	A	68	5–18–1780	Beech Fk..........	Withdrawn
Shepherd, Peter......	1,000	A	68	5–18–1780	Bensons Cr........	....
Shepherd, Peter......	1,000	A	68	5–18–1780	Beech Fk..........	Withdrawn
Shepherd, Peter......	500	A	68	5–18–1780	Beech Fk..........	....
Shepherd, Peter......	1,000	A	68	5–18–1780	Chaplins Fk.......	....
Shepherd, Peter......	200	A	68	5–18–1780	Mill Cr Ky R......	Surveyed
Shepherd, Peter......	1,000	A	68	5–18–1780	Floyds Fk.........	Surveyed
Shepherd, Peter......	900	A	68	5–18–1780	Falls Salt R.......	....
Shepherd, Peter......	600	A	68	5–18–1780	Rolling Fk........	Surveyed
Shepherd, Peter......	300	A	68	5–18–1780	Salt R............	Withdrawn
Shepherd, Peter......	700	A	68	5–18–1780	Clear Cr..........	....
Shepherd, Peter......	500	A	68	5–18–1780	Severins Valley.....	....
Shepherd, Peter......	500	A	68	5–18–1780	Rolling Fk........	Surveyed

Entree	Acres	Book	Page	Entry Date	Watercourse	Notes
Shepherd, Peter	400	A	68	5–18–1780	Shawnee Run	Withdrawn
Shepherd, Peter	1,000	A	68	5–18–1780	Mill Cr Salt R	100 acres withdrawn
Shepherd, Peter	2,000	A	68	5–18–1780	Floyds Fk	100 acres surveyed
Shepherd, Peter	1,000	A	68	5–18–1780	Rolling Fk	Surveyed
Shepherd, Peter	500	A	69	5–18–1780	Floyds Fk	Surveyed
Shepherd, Peter	1,000	A	69	5–18–1780	Cartright Cr	Surveyed
Shepherd, Peter	1,000	A	69	5–18–1780	Cartrights Cr	Withdrawn
Shepherd, Peter	1,000	A	69	5–18–1780	Rolling Fk	....
Shepherd, Peter	400	A	168	8–29–1780	Shawnee Run	....
Shepherd, Peter	300	A	184	10–30–1780	Salt R	....
Shepherd, Peter	100	A	197	3–17–1781	Rolling Fk	Surveyed
Shepherd, Peter	300	A	208	4–30–1781	Beech Fk	....
Shepherd, Peter	700	A	216	7–31–1781	N Fk Licking	....
Shepherd, Peter	800	A	216	7–31–1781	N Fk Rowling	Withdrawn
Shepherd, Peter	500	A	216	7–31–1781	N Fk Rowling	....
Shepherd, Peter	1,000	A	216	7–31–1781	N Fk Rowling	....
Shepherd, Peter	1,000	A	221	10– 4–1781	Beech Fk	....
Shepherd, Peter	2,000	A	221	9– 7–1781		Returned
Shepherd, Peter	50	A	222	12– 9–1781	Tarr Spring Cr	....
Shepherd, Peter	50	A	222	12– 9–1781	Tarr Spring Cr	....
Shepherd, Peter	100	A	222	12– 9–1782	Mill Cr	Withdrawn
Shepherd, Peter	500	A	225	12–13–1782	Wolf Cr	Surveyed
Shepherd, Peter	400	A	226	12–13–1782	Rowling Fk	Withdrawn
Shepherd, Peter	500	A	229	12–16–1782	Ky R	....
Shepherd, Peter	500	A	229	12–16–1782	Green R	Withdrawn
Shepherd, Peter	1,248⅞	A	229	12–16–1782	Brashears Cr	....
Shepherd, Peter	500	A	229	12–16–1782	Ky R	....
Shepherd, Peter	1,000	A	229	12–16–1782	Brashears Cr	Surveyed
Shepherd, Peter	1,000	A	229	12–16–1782	Brashears Cr	Surveyed
Shepherd, Peter	5,000	A	241	12–25–1782	Brashears Cr	....
Shepherd, Peter	500	A	262	2–11–1783	Rolling Fk	....
Shepherd, Peter	500	A	262	2–11–1783	Sinking Cr	....
Shepherd, Peter	1,000	A	280	6–19–1783	———	....
Shepherd, Peter	1,896	A	280	6–19–1783	———	Surveyed
Shepherd, Peter	1,600	A	280	6–19–1783	———	Surveyed
Shepherd, Peter	1,000	A	315	12–13–1783	Beech & Chaplins Fk	....
Shepherd, Peter	400	A	323	12–26–1783	Rowling Fk	....
Shepherd, Peter	400	A	323	12–26–1783	Rowling Fk	....
Shepherd, Peter	1,000	A	323	12–26–1783	Salt R	....
Shepherd, Peter	1,000	A	323	12–26–1783	Floyds Fk	....
Shepherd, Peter	2,013	A	325	12–27–1783	———	....
Shepherd, Peter	200	A	342	2–28–1784	Rolling Fk	Withdrawn
Shepherd, Peter	2,000	A	342	2–27–1784		....
Shepherd, Wm	100	A	348	3–29–1784	Long Lick Cr	....
Shepherd, Wm	250	A	259	1–29–1783	Cartright Cr	Withdrawn
Shepherd, Wm	250	A	276	4–10–1783	Coxes Cr	....
Shepherd, Wm	250	A	276	4–10–1783	Cartright Cr	....
Shervin, Samuel	1,000	A	126	6– 7–1780	Salt Spring Cr	Mil
Shervin, Samuel	400	A	127	6– 7–1780	Boone Lick Cr	....
Shervin, Samuel	1,000	A	127	6– 7–1780	Wolf Cr	Mil
Sherwin, Samuel	1,600	A	170	9– 9–1780	Ohio R	....
Shields, Pat	300	A	122	6– 2–1780	N Fk Green Cr	....
Shields, Pat	260	A	122	6– 2–1780	Ky R	....
Shields, Pat	2,000	A	314	12–12–1783	Mill Cr	....
Shirley, James	1,161½	A	368	6–26–1784	Green R	Surveyed
Shiveley, Jacob	361	A	133	6–16–1780	Rowling Fk	....
Shively, Christ	1,000	A	102	5–27–1780	Mans Lick	....
Shone, Patrick	400	A	15	2–21–1780	Hanging Fk	....
Shone, Patrick	1,000	A	136	6–19–1780	Doughertys Run	....
Shore, Bennam	1,000	A	113	5–30–1780	Soverins Valley	....
Shore, Thomas	1,000	A	146	6–24–1780	Goose Cr	....
Shore, Thomas	2,000	A	147	6–24–1780	Muddy Cr	....
Shriver, David	1,000	A	204	4– 3–1781	Bensons Cr	Warrant sent to Lincoln
Shriver, David	1,000	A	229	12–16–1782	Ky R	....
Shriver, David	1,000	A	229	12–16–1782	Big Benson Cr	Surveyed
Shriver, David	1,000	B	24	12–10–1784	Green R	....
Silvia, Abraham	300	A	76	5–19–1780	George Brent	....
Simes, James	1,318	A	241	12–25–1782	Salt R	Surveyed
Simmerman, George	1,000	A	37	4–29–1780	Licking	....
Simmon, Richard	400	A	276	4–12–1783	Pottengers Cr	Surveyed
Simms, Charles	500	A	22	4–21–1780	Ohio R	Withdrawn
Simms, Charles	500	A	22	4–21–1780	Ohio R	Withdrawn
Simms, Charles	500	A	22	4–21–1780	Walpers Cr	Withdrawn
Simms, Charles	711	A	22	4–21–1780	Br Town Fk	....
Simms, Charles	750	A	22	4–21–1780	Br Town Fk	Surveyed
Simms, Charles	———	A	35	4–29–1780	Big Miami	Withdrawn
Simms, Charles	500	A	35	4–29–1780	Big Miami R	....

Entree	Acres	Book	Page	Entry Date	Watercourse	Notes
Simms, Edward......	300	A	105	5-27-1780	Beech Fk	88 acres surveyed withdrawn
Simms, Edward......	88	A	277	4-12-1783	Beech Fk	....
Simms, Edward......	88	A	277	4-12-1783	Beech Fk	Withdrawn
Simpson, Thomas.....	500	A	79	5-20-1780	Simpson Cr	Surveyed
Simpson, John........	1,000	A	86	5-23-1780	Rowling Fk	Surveyed
Simpson, Thomas.....	1,000	A	118	6- 1-1781	Town Fk	....
Simpson, Thomas.....	1,308	A	279	6- 7-1783	Barrens	....
Simpson, Thomas.....	1,293	A	280	6-14-1783	Hardens Cr	....
Sinclair, Alex........	1,000	A	33	4-29-1780	Green R	Surveyed
Sinclair, Alex........	1,000	A	91	5-24-1780	Gilberts Cr	....
Sinclair, Alex........	1,000	A	91	5-24-1780	Gilberts Cr	....
Sinclair, Alex........	1,000	A	91	5-24-1780	Ky R	....
Sinclair, Alex........	2,000	A	155	6-30-1780	Green R	Surveyed
Sinclair, Alex........	6,190	A	270	3-28-1783	Brush Cr	....
Sinclair, Alex........	50	A	338	2-12-1784	Bullskin Cr	Mil
Sinclair, Alex........	300	A	363	6- 2-1784	Brush Cr	....
Singleton, Andrew....	708	B	5	9- 7-1784	———	Mil
Singleton, Christ.....	800	A	35	4-29-1780	Rolling Fk	....
Singleton, Christ.....	500	A	105	5-27-1780	Beech Fk	....
Singleton, Christ.....	2,000	A	105	5-27-1780	Beech Fk	....
Singleton, Edmund....	500	A	84	5-22-1780	Buck Lick Cr	....
Singleton, John.......	500	A	345	3-11-1784	Beech Fk	....
Singleton, John.......	708	A	364	6- 7-1784	Rolling Fk	....
Singleton, John.......	308	B	3	8-26-1784	Rolling Fk	Amended
Singleton, John.......	708	B	3	8-26-1784	———	Withdrawn
Singleton, John.......	308	B	3	8-26-1784	———	....
Singleton, Minoah....	1,000	A	67	5-17-1780	S Licking	Mil
Singleton, Robt......	50	A	35	4-29-1780	Salt R	Surveyed
Sinkhorn, Abraham....	400	A	107	5-29-1780	Floyds Fk	....
Sinkler, John........	400	A	147	6-24-1780	Licking	....
Skeggs, Henry........	400	A	15	2-21-1780	Green R	Surveyed
Skeggs, James........	150	A	179	10-17-1780	Green R	Surveyed
Skeggs, James........	150	A	179	10-17-1780	Brush Cr	....
Skeggs, James........	150	A	179	10-17-1780	Green R	Surveyed
Skeggs, James........	1,000	A	368	6-29-1784	Brush Cr	....
Skeggs, James........	150	A	377	8- 9-1784	———	....
Skillern, George......	100	A	20	4-14-1780	Elkhorn	Withdrawn
Skillern, George......	1,000	A	72	5-19-1780	Elkhorn	Withdrawn
Skillern, George......	250	A	72	5-19-1780	Big Fk Dicks R	....
Skillern, George......	230	A	72	5-19-1780	S Dicks R	....
Skillern, George......	300	A	72	5-19-1780	E Fk Doughterys	....
Skillern, George......	500	A	72	5-19-1780	Sugar Cr	....
Skillern, George......	1,200	A	88	5-23-1780	Elkhorn Cr	....
Skillern, Wm........	200	A	28	4-27-1780	Doughtery Cr	Mil
Skillern, Wm P.......	500	A	88	5-23-1780	Harrods Cr	....
Skinner, Alex........	1,500	B	47	6-15-1785	Harrods Cr	....
Skinner, Alex........	1,500	B	5	9-10-1784	Harrods Cr	Withdrawn
Slaughter, Cadwalder..	500	A	105	5-27-1780	Beech Fk	....
Slaughter, Cadwalder..	800	A	105	5-27-1780	Beech Fk	....
Slaughter, George.....	400	A	14	2-19-1780	Bensons Cr	Mil
Slaughter, George.....	50	A	136	6-19-1780	Island at Falls	....
Slaughter, George.....	1,000	A	146	6-24-1780	Bensons Cr	....
Slaughter, George.....	325	A	161	7-14-1780	Pond Cr	....
Slaughter, George.....	325	A	161	7-14-1780	Pond Cr	....
Slaughter, George.....	2,925	A	166	8-11-1780	Pond Cr	Withdrawn
Slaughter, George.....	325	A	178	10-10-1780	Falls Salt R	....
Slaughter, George.....	700	A	195	3-17-1781	Brashears Cr	Withdrawn
Slaughter, George.....	1,040	A	196	3-17-1781	Pond Cr	Surveyed
Slaughter, George.....	560	A	196	3-17-1781	Bullits Lick	Withdrawn
Slaughter, George.....	500	A	196	3-17-1781	Falls Ohio R	Withdrawn
Slaughter, George.....	400	A	196	3-17-1781	Pond Cr	Withdrawn
Slaughter, George.....	1,500	A	196	3-17-1781	Floyds Fk	Withdrawn
Slaughter, George.....	500	A	196	3-17-1781	Pond Cr	Withdrawn
Slaughter, George.....	400	A	196	3-17-1780	Brashears Cr	Withdrawn
Slaughter, George.....	400	A	198	3-19-1781	Pond Cr	Withdrawn
Slaughter, George.....	965	A	198	3-17-1781	Pond Cr	Surveyed
Slaughter, George.....	960	A	198	3-17-1781	Pond Cr	Surveyed
Slaughter, George.....	1,000	A	198	3-17-1781	Fishpool Cr	....
Slaughter, George.....	2,925	A	198	3-17-1781	Pond Cr	....
Slaughter, George.....	400	A	218	8- 8-1781	Floyds Fk	....
Slaughter, George.....	940	A	218	8- 8-1781	Pond Cr	....
Slaughter, George.....	560	A	218	8- 8-1781	Bullitts Lick	....
Slaughter, George.....	500	A	218	8- 8-1781	Falls Ohio R	....
Slaughter, George.....	1,500	A	218	8- 8-1781	Floyds Fk	....
Slaughter, George.....	500	A	218	8- 8-1781	Flatt Lick	....
Slaughter, George.....	400	A	218	8- 8-1781	Beargrass Cr	Surveyed
Slaughter, George.....	700	A	218	8- 8-1781	Brashears Cr	Surveyed
Slaughter, George.....	400	A	218	8- 8-1781	Clear Station	....
Slaughter, George.....	500	A	251	1- 9-1783	Drennons Lick	....

Entree	Acres	Book	Page	Entry Date	Watercourse	Notes
Slaughter, George	1,311	A	272	3-31-1783	Sinking Cr	
Slaughter, George	325	A	325	12-29-1783	———	Surveyed
Slaughter, George	850	A	351	4-12-1784	———	Returned
Slaughter, George	1,550½	A	352	4-15-1784	Blackford Cr	
Slaughter, George	30,000	A	352	4-15-1784	———	Withdrawn
Slaughter, George	7,260½	A	355	4-21-1784	———	
Slaughter, George	550	B	10	10-11-1784	———	140 acres surveyed
Slaughter, Geo Jr, heirs	400	A	16	2-26-1780	18 Mile Cr	Surveyed
Slaughter, James	1,300	A	143	6-22-1780	Coxes Cr	Surveyed
Slaughter, Lawrence	400	A	14	2-19-1780	Elkhorn	
Slaughter, Lawrence	1,000	A	49	5-12-1780	Licking	
Slaughter, Lawrence	50	A	143	6-22-1780	Simpsons Cr	
Slaughter, Lawrence	1,000	A	146	6-24-1780	Elkhorn	
Slaughter, Lawrence	2,500	A	250	1- 9-1783	Ohio R	
Slaughter, Robt	400	A	14	2-19-1780	Elkhorn	
Slaughter, Robt	1,000	A	146	6-24-1780	Cain Run	
Slaughter, Robt Jr	400	A	14	2-19-1780	Bensons Cr	
Slaughter, Robt Jr	400	A	3	11-11-1779	Shawnee Run	
Slaughter, Robt Jr	1,000	A	26	4-26-1780	Shawnee	
Slaughter, Robt Sr	1,000	A	164	6-24-1780	Cane Run	
Slaughter, Wm Jr	400	A	14	2-19-1780	Eagle Cr	
Slate, James	500	A	155	6-29-1780	Tuckahoe Cr	
Smiley, Edwards	88	A	317	12-16-1783	———	
Smiley, Wm	150	A	218	8- 8-1781	Coxes Cr	Surveyed
Smiley, Wm	200	A	218	8- 8-1781	Coxes Run	
Smiley, Wm	180	A	252	1-13-1783	Cox Cr	Surveyed
Smiley, Wm	100	A	264	2-18-1783	Coxes Cr	Withdrawn
Smiley, Wm	280	A	281	6-27-1783	———	180 acres surveyed
Smiley, Wm	350	A	281	6-27-1783	———	
Smith, Adam	400	A	141	6-21-1780	Cane Run	Surveyed.
Smith, Rev Adam	1,000	A	82	5-22-1780	Ohio R	Mil
Smith, Rev Adam	2,500	A	230	12-17-1782	Harts Cr	
Smith, Alex	393	A	53	5-15-1780	Pasture Lick Cr	
Smith, Alex	600	A	93	5-24-1780	Stoners Fk	
Smith, Anne	200	A	97	5-25-1780	Cartrights Cr	Surveyed
Smith, Ballard et al	7,500	A	366	6-21-1784	———	Surveyed
Smith, Charles	500	A	163	7-21-1780	near Drennons Lick	Surveyed
Smith, Charles	550	A	170	9-12-1780	Licking	
Smith, Charles	500	A	170	9-12-1780	Ky R	
Smith, Charles	500	A	170	9-12-1780	Ky R	
Smith, Charles et al	400	A	74	5-19-1780	Johnstons Cr	
Smith, Charles et al	1,000	A	74	5-19-1780	S Fk Licking	
Smith, Charles et al	1,000	A	74	5-19-1780	Stoners Fk	
Smith, Charles et al	3,500	A	132	6-15-1780	Licking	
Smith, Enoch	1,000	A	37	4-29-1780	Small Mt Cr	
Smith, Enoch	1,000	A	53	5-15-1780	Pasture Lick Cr	
Smith, Enoch	400	A	3	11-11-1779	Hingston Fk	
Smith, Ezekiel	9,000	A	333	1-20-1784	———	Surveyed
Smith, Ezekiel	9,000	A	358	5- 3-1784	Ramsey & Cox	Surveyed
Smith, Francis	2,050	A	194	3-16-1781	Bullskin	Surveyed
Smith, Francis	200	A	276	4-12-1783	Floyds Fk	Surveyed
Smith, Gedion	1,000	A	361	5-25-1784	Pittmans Cr	
Smith, George	400	A	7	12-29-1779	Harrods Run	
Smith, George	1,100	A	57	5-15-1780	Silver Cr	
Smith, George	1,000	A	64	5-17-1780	Stoners Fk	
Smith, George	1,500	A	157	6-30-1780	Lulbergrud	
Smith, George S	600	A	175	10- 6-1780	Harrods Run	Surveyed
Smith, Granville	500	A	59	5-16-1780	Gilberts Cr	
Smith, Granville	5,500	A	194	3-16-1781	Harrods Cr	Surveyed
Smith, Granville	6,750	A	234	12-19-1782	Floyds Fk	Surveyed
Smith, Granville	500	B	5	9-11-1784	———	4 acres surveyed
Smith, Granville	500	B	42	3-22-1785	Floyds Fk	
Smith, Granville et al	1,000	B	42	3-23-1785	Floyds Fk	Surveyed
Smith, Isaac	1,000	A	112	5-30-1780	Fern Cr	
Smith, James	400	A	137	6-19-1780	Dicks R	
Smith, James	2,000	A	187	3-15-1781	Ohio R	Surveyed
Smith, John	400	A	2	11- 3-1779	Sinking Spring	Surveyed
Smith, John	400	A	14	2-19-1780	Hickmans Cr	
Smith, John	3,000	A	19	4-13-1780	Green R	Mil withdrawn
Smith, John	5,000	A	19	4-13-1780	Panther Cr	Mil
Smith, John	6,000	A	19	4-13-1780	Panther Cr	Mil
Smith, John	4,000	A	19	4-13-1780	Indian Camp Cr	Mil withdrawn
Smith, John	500	A	25	4-25-1780	Upper Ohio R	
Smith, John	500	A	25	4-25-1780	Brashears Cr	Mil withdrawn
Smith, John	500	A	35	4-29-1780	Fallen Timber Cr	

Entree	Acres	Book	Page	Entry Date	Watercourse	Notes
Smith, John	250	A	41	5-10-1780	Fishpool	Mil
Smith, John	500	A	56	5-15-1780	S Fk Licking	....
Smith, John	400	A	89	5-23-1780	Green R	....
Smith, John	500	A	92	5-24-1780	Grays Run	....
Smith, John	1,000	A	92	5-24-1780	Indian Cr	....
Smith, John	500	A	92	5-24-1780	Jessamine	....
Smith, John	1,000	A	92	5-24-1780	Jessamine	....
Smith, John	1,000	A	92	5-24-1780	Licking	....
Smith. John	289	A	127	6- 8-1780	Broad Run	....
Smith, John	400	A	127	6- 8-1780	Mid Fk Licking	....
Smith, John	200	A	162	7-17-1780	Cane Run	....
Smith, John	300	A	162	7-17-1780	Cane Run	....
Smith, John	500	A	162	7-17-1780	Cane Run	Surveyed
Smith, John	4,000	A	164	8-11-1780	Indian Camp Cr	....
Smith, John	7,000	A	165	8-11-1780	Green R	Withdrawn
Smith, John	1,000	A	181	10-24-1780	His settlement	Surveyed
Smith, John	500	A	183	10-27-1780	Green R	Surveyed
Smith, John	7,000	A	202	4- 2-1781	Ohio R	....
Smith, John	300	A	227	12-14-1782	Green R	....
Smith, John	1,000	A	307	11-20-1783	Big Clifty Cr	Surveyed
Smith, John	600	A	345	3-11-1784	Brashears Cr	....
Smith, John	2,000	B	8	9-22-1784	Panther	Mil returned
Smith, John et al	2,000	A	361	5-25-1784	Rolling Fk	....
Smith, Jonathan et al	1,334	A	22	4-21-1780	Brashears Cr	Surveyed
Smith, Joseph	200	A	19	4-13-1780	Bullittsburg	Mil
Smith, Joseph	50	A	30	4-28-1780	Mid Fk Licking	Mil
Smith, Joseph	1,000	A	109	5-29-1780	S Fk Simpsons Cr	....
Smith, Joseph	4,000	A	109	5-29-1780	Rowling Fk	....
Smith, Lawrence	400	A	244	12-27-1782	Brush Cr	....
Smith, Nancy	1,000	A	247	1- 7-1783	Clifty Cr	....
Smith, Richard E	1,314½	B	1	8-14-1784	Casey Cr	....
Smith, Robert	500	A	86	5-22-1780	S Fk Salt Lick Cr	....
Smith, Robert	20,000	A	324	12-26-1783	Nolelinn Cr	Withdrawn
Smith, Robert	20,000	A	347	3-17-1784	Knob Cr	Surveyed
Smith, Robert	20,000	A	347	3-17-1784	Nolelin Cr	....
Smith, Robert	5,200	A	353	4-16-1784	Nole Linn & Green R	Surveyed
Smith, Robert	14,800	A	353	4-16-1784	Otter&Brush Cr	Surveyed amended
Smith, Robert	10,000	A	364	6-12-1784	———	4,000 acres surveyed
Smith, Samuel	200	A	217	8- 2-1782	Tumbling Cr	....
Smith, Samuel	600	A	230	12-17-1782	Willsons Cr	....
Smith, Samuel	300	A	230	12-17-1782	Willsons Cr	....
Smith, Samuel	200	A	230	12-17-1782	Willsons Cr	....
Smith, Samuel	400	A	230	12-17-1782	Willsons Cr	Surveyed
Smith, Samuel	500	A	230	12-17-1782	Willsons Cr	....
Smith, Samuel	500	A	230	12-17-1782	Willson Cr	....
Smith, Samuel	1,500	A	230	12-17-1782	Willsons Cr	Withdrawn
Smith, Samuel	1,000	A	230	12-17-1782	Coxes Cr	....
Smith, Samuel	500	A	297	10-15-1783	Salt R	....
Smith, Samuel	500	A	300	10-29-1783	Coxes Cr	....
Smith, Samuel	400	B	38	1-29-1785	Cane Run	....
Smith, Samuel	500	B	38	1-29-1785	Cane Cr	....
Smith, Thomas	1,013½	A	276	4-12-1783	Floyds Fk	Surveyed
Smith, Wm	200	A	137	6-19-1780	Paint Lick Cr	....
Smith, Wm	977	A	150	6-24-1780	Flatt Cr	....
Smith, Wm	1,000	A	154	6-27-1780	Elkhorn	....
Smith, Wm	1,000	A	157	6-30-1780	Wm Cooper	....
Smith, Wm	1,000	A	241	12-25-1782	Drinnens Lick Cr	Surveyed
Smith, Wm	1,618	A	242	12-25-1782	Drennings Lick Cr	Surveyed
Smith, Wm	1,000	A	308	11-22-1783	Ky R	Withdrawn
Smith, Wm	1,000	B	51	11- 3-1785	Ky R	Withdrawn
Smith, Wm et al	808½	A	364	6- 7-1784	Rolling Fk	....
Smith, Wm et al	808½	B	3	8-26-1784	———	Amended
Smith, Wm B	400	A	14	2-19-1780	Green R Panther Cr	....
Smith, Wm B	1,000	A	143	6-23-1780	Panther Cr	....
Smith, Withers	1,000	A	64	5-17-1780	Stoners Fk	....
Smith, Zachariah	400	A	12	2- 7-1780	Harrods Run	....
Smith, Zachariah	1,000	A	108	5-29-1780	Harrods Cr	....
Smock, Henry	1,080	A	272	3-31-1783		....
Smock, Henry	500	A	272	3-31-1783	John Holladys	Withdrawn
Smock, Henry	367	A	293	10- 3-1783	Beech Fk	Withdrawn
Smock, Henry	500	A	309	11-25-1783	Pittmans Cr	....
Smock, Henry	500	A	309	11-25-1783	Hollidays settlement	Withdrawn
Smock, Henry	859	A	348	3-27-1784	Pottengers Cr	....
Smock, Henry	367	A	364	6- 7-1784	Otter Cr	....
Smock, Henry	367	A	364	6- 7-1784	———	....
Smyth, John	1,000	A	223	12-12-1782	Rowling F	....
Smythe, John	1,000	A	223	12-12-1782	S Fk Hardens Cr	....
Smyth, Samuel	400	A	118	6- 1-1780	Mill Cr	....
Smyth, Samuel	400	A	185	10-31-1780	Willsons Cr	....

Entree	Acres	Book	Page	Entry Date	Watercourse	Notes
Smyth, Samuel	1,000	A	229	12-16-1782	Harrods Cr	Surveyed
Smyth, Samuel	2,100	A	377	8- 9-1784		
Snack, Henery	325	A	163	7-29-1780	Round Stone Cr	
Snyder, Adam	390	A	232	12-18-1782	Ky R	
Snyder, John	562	A	232	12-18-1782	Ky R	
Sodawskie, Jacob	400	A	12	2- 9-1780	Clear Cr	Withdrawn
Sodoski, James	1,000	A	36	4-29-1780	Licking Cr	
Sodowjki, Jacob	400	A	373	7-27-1784	————	
Sodowski, Jacob	400	A	17	2-29-1780	Shannon Run	
Sodowski, Jonathan	400	A	7	1-10-1780	Jassemine Cr	
Sodowsky, James	200	A	219	8-20-1781	Cartrights Cr	Surveyed
South, John	1,000	A	120	6- 1-1780	Johnsons Fk	
South, John	450	A	154	6-27-1780	Boone Cr	
South, John, heir	1,000	A	112	5-30-1780	Stoners Fk	
South, John Jr	400	A	7	1-10-1780	Licking Cr	
South, John Sr	400	A	10	2- 2-1780	Licking Cr	
South, John Sr	400	A	112	5-30-1780	Licking	
South, John Sr	1,000	A	112	5-30-1780	His settlement	
Southall, James	400	A	64	5-17,1780	Rolling F	
Southall, James	1,000	A	70	5-18-1780	Chaplins Fk	
Southall, James	1,000	A	109	5-29-1780	Ohio R	
Southall, James	1,000	A	109	5-29-1780	Rowling Fk	
Southall, James	1,000	A	109	5-29-1780	Rowling Fk	
Souther, Jacob	581	A	337	2- 7-1784	Bear Cr	
Souther, Jacob	400	A	337	2- 7-1784	Nole Linn Cr	
Southerland, John	200	A	253	1-15-1783	Beech Fk	Surveyed
Southerland, John	400	A	253	1-15-1783	Rolling F	Surveyed
Southerland, John	400	A	253	1-15-1783	Pottengers Cr	Surveyed
Soverins, Gawer	400	A	15	2-21-1780	Beech Fk	Surveyed
Soverins, Gower	1,000	A	146	6-24-1780	Beech Fk	Surveyed
Soverins, John	100	A	31	4-28-1780	Soverin Cr	Surveyed
Soverins, John	100	A	31	4-28-1780	Hines settlement	Mil surveyed
Soverins, John	300	A	113	5-30-1780	Soverins Valley	Surveyed
Soverins, John	300	A	113	5-30-1780	Soverins Valley	Surveyed
Soverins, John	200	A	221	9- 7-1781		Returned
Soverins, John	200	A	213	6-30-1781	Gilkeys Run	
Spangler, Wm	885	A	201	4- 2-1781	18 Mile Cr	
Spangler, Wm	1,000	A	201	4- 2-1781	Goose Cr	
Sparr, Matthew	500	A	168	8-29-1780	Stoner Fk	
Spaw, Jacob	400	A	123	6- 2-1780	Green R	Surveyed
Spead, James	400	A	91	5-24-1780	Ohio R	Surveyed
Spead, James	400	A	91	5-24-1780	Ohio R	Surveyed
Spead, James	600	A	116	5-31-1780	Green R	
Spead, James	800	A	116	5-31-1780	N Fk Green R	
Spead, James	800	A	205	4- 6-1781	Above Pittmans Sta	
Speak, Henry	500	A	100	5-26-1780	Floyds Fk	
Spear, Christopher	20	A	127	6- 8-1780	Hingstons Fk	
Spear, Christopher	400	A	127	6- 8-1780	Hingstons Cr	
Spear, George	400	A	12	2- 8-1780	Hanging Fk	
Spear, George	600	A	47	5-12-1780	Fern Cr	
Spear, George	1,000	A	47	5-12-1780	Drinnens Cr	
Spear, George	400	A	48	5-12-1780	Hanging Fr	
Spear, George	600	A	48	5-12-1780	Cartrights Cr	
Spear, George	1,000	A	118	6- 1-1781	Hanging Fk	
Spear, Henry	400	A	40	5- 9-1780	Mill Cr	
Spear, Henry	400	A	40	5- 9-1780	Mill Cr	
Spear, Henry	800	A	73	5-19-1780	Floyds Fk	
Spear, Henry	800	A	73	5-19-1780	Rolling Fk	Surveyed
Spears, Jacob	400	A	243	12-26-1782	Fern Cr	Surveyed
Speard, Mathias	500	A	134	6-16-1780	Licking	
Spears, Theodisus	400	A	134	6-16-1780	Licking	
Spears, Theodisus	400	A	134	6-16-1780	Howards Cr	
Speed, James	50	A	31	4-28-1780	Rowling Fk	Mil
Speed, James	800	A	88	5-23-1780	Green R	Withdrawn
Speed, James	1,000	A	88	5-23-1780	Beargrass	375 acres surveyed
Speed, James	600	A	88	5-23-1780	Mannslick	
Speed, James	400	A	90	5-23-1780	Ohio R	Withdrawn
Speed, James	3,200	A	90	5-23-1780	Ohio R	200 acres withdrawn
Speed, James	400	A	143	6-22-1780	Green R	
Speed, James	100	A	258	1-27-1783	Green R	
Speed, James	700	A	258	1-27-1783	Green R	
Speed, James	700	A	258	1-27-1783		
Speed, James	1,510	A	270	3-28-1783	Beech Fk	
Speed, James	500	A	356	4-24-1784	Beargrass Cr	
Speers, Phillip	400	A	159	7- 4-1780	Cedar Cr	
Speers, Valentine	400	A	159	7- 4-1780	Cedar Cr	
Spencer, Edward	600	A	168	8-17-1780	Cane & Sugar Cr	
Spencer, Thomas	400	A	250	1- 9-1783	Samuel Kirby	Surveyed
Spiers, Jacob	400	A	111	5-29-1780	Rowling Fk	

Entree	Acres	Book	Page	Entry Date	Watercourse	Notes
Spiers, Jacob	800	A	111	5–29–1780	Rowling Fk	
Spiers, Wm	400	A	159	7– 4–1780	Cedar Cr	
Spiller, Phillip	250	A	45	5–11–1780	Salt R	
Spiller, Phillip	231	A	238	12–21–1782	Floyds Fk	
Spiller, Phillip	257	B	30	12–24–1784	Clear Cr	
Spilman, Charles	800	A	67	5–17–1780	Cane Run	
Spilman, Henry et al	400	A	218	8– 9–1781	Long Lick Cr	Surveyed
Spindel, John	50	A	31	4–28–1780	Elkhorn	Mil
Spindel, John	1,000	A	40	5– 9–1780	Elkhorn	
Spindel, John	1,000	A	40	5– 9–1780	N Fk Elkhorn	
Spindel, John	623	A	40	5– 9–1780	Big Fk Elkhorn	
Sprigg, Osburn	400	A	195	3–17–1781	Chinoiths Run	Surveyed
Sprigg, Osburn	400	A	195	3–16–1781	Brashears Cr	
Sprigg, Osburn	50	A	206	4–12–1781	Beech Fk	
Spriggs, Joseph	793	B	34	1–24–1785	Murrys Run	
Spriggs, Joseph	400	B	34	1–24–1785	Murrys Run	
Spriggs, Joseph	419	A	261	2–11–1783	10 mile Falls Ohio	247 acres surveyed
Spriggs, Joseph	3,000	A	281	6–30–1783	Ky R	Surveyed
Spriggs, Leven	200	B	8	9–27–1784	Beech Fk	
Spriggs, Osburn	500	A	133	6–15–1780	Mid Fk Soverins	
Spriggs, Osburn	100	A	141	6–21–1780	Mill Cr	Withdrawn
Spriggs, Osburn	100	A	141	6–21–1780	Soverins Valley	Surveyed
Spriggs, Osburn	2,000	A	193	3–16–1781	Brashears Cr	Surveyed
Spriggs, Osborn	990	A	195	3–16–1781	Mays Cr	
Spriggs, Osburn	400	A	195	3–16–1781	Chenwith Cr	
Spriggs, Osburn	1,000	A	195	3–16–1781	Fox Run	Surveyed
Spriggs, Osburn	400	A	195	3–16–1781	Floyds Fk	Surveyed
Spriggs, Osburn	400	A	195	3–16–1781	Salt R	Surveyed
Spriggs, Osburn	1,000	A	198	3–17–1781	Edward settlement	Surveyed
Spriggs, Osborne	1,800	A	233	12–18–1782	Green R	1,100 acres surveyed
Springler, Daniel	250	A	241	12–25–1782	Mill Cr	
Springer, Dennis	655	B	10	10– 7–1784	Shotpouch Cr	
Springer, Isaac	1,000	A	307	11–20–1783	Big Clifty Cr	Surveyed
Spurr, Richard	500	A	43	5–10–1780	Hingston Fk	
Spurr, Richard	300	A	75	5–19–1780	Hingstons Fk	
Squires, Samuel	300	A	226	12–14–1782	Sinking Cr	
Squires, Samuel	200	A	226	12–14–1782	Brush Cr	Withdrawn
Squires, Samuel	500	A	227	12–14–1782	Drennings Lick Cr	
Squires, Samuel	150	A	240	12–24–1782	S Fk Brush Cr	
Squires, Samuel	200	A	240	12–24–1782	Sand Lick	
Stafford, Wm	400	A	13	2–11–1780	Marble Cr	
Stafford, Wm	1,000	A	181	10–23–1780	His settlement	
Stafford, Wm	1,000	A	181	10–23–1780	Brashears Cr	Surveyed
Stagg, Wm	1,000	A	346	3–16–1784	Panther Cr	
Stapleton, John	400	A	118	6– 1–1781	Chaplins Fk	
Stapleton, John	400	A	206	4–13–1781	Gesses Cr	
Staples, Joseph	1,000	A	266	2–26–1783	Brush Cr	
Standford, Robert	986	A	285	8– 5–1783	Salt R	
Standford, Robert	2,000	A	285	8– 5–1783	Salt R	
Standiford, David	300	A	165	8–11–1780	Beargrass Cr	Withdrawn
Standiford, David	1,000	A	304	11–14–1783	Floyds Fk	Withdrawn
Standiford, David	500	A	353	4–15–1784	Floyds Fk	Surveyed
Standiford, David	1,000	A	353	4–15–1784	Floyds Fk	
Standiford, David	1,000	A	354	4–19–1784	Little Ky R	
Standiford, David	2,000	A	354	4–19–1784	Ky R	
Standiford, David	300	B	19	11–26–1784	Beargrass Cr	Withdrawn
Standiford, David	5,000	B	19	11–26–1784	——	500 acres surveyed
Standley, John	85	A	362	5–31–1784	——	
Standley, Wm	200	A	35	4–29–1780	Rolling Fk	Mil
Standley, Wm	348	A	268	3–28–1783	Robinsons C	
Stansberry, Thos	800	A	109	5–29–1780	Floyds Fk	Surveyed
Stansberry, Thos	400	A	60	5–16–1780	Willsons Cr	
Stansberry, Thos	400	A	60	5–16–1780	Floyds Fk	
Starke, Bolling	5,000	A	72	5–18–1780	Little Yellow Banks	
Starns, Jacob	500	A	81	5–22–1780	Howard Cr	
Starns, Jacob	500	A	81	5–22–1780	Br Licking Cr	
Statam, Charles	975	A	28	4–27–1780	Cane Run	
Statam, Charles	800	A	154	6–27–1780	Elkhorn	
Steal, Andrew	400	A	186	10–31–1780	S Fk Elkhorn	
Steal, Wm	400	A	17	2–29–1780	Licking Cr	
Steal, Wm	400	A	18	3– 3–1780	N Fk Elkhorn	
Steel, Martin	400	A	15	2–22–1780	Town Cr	
Steele, Andrew	1,106	A	253	1–15–1783	Ky R	
Steele, Andrew	1,106	A	253	1–15–1783	Ky R	
Steele, Richard	500	A	223	12–12–1782	Ohio R	Surveyed
Steele, Richard	100	A	224	12–12–1782	Little Ky R	
Steele, Richard	225	A	224	12–12–1782	——	Surveyed

Entree	Acres	Book	Page	Entry Date	Watercourse	Notes
Steele, Richard	325	B	31	1- 3-1785	———	225 acres surveyed
Stephen, George	645	A	336	1-31-1784	Pleasant Run	Withdrawn
Stephen, Hancock	200	A	96	5-25-1780	Silver Cr	
Stephens, Benj	1,000	A	65	5-17-1780	W Fk Licking	
Stephens, Benj	2,000	A	340	2-18-1784	Rough Cr	
Stephens, Benj	6,000	A	346	3-15-1784	Rough Cr	
Stephens, George	1,000	A	281	6-26-1783	Beech Fk	645 acres withdrawn
Stephens, George	1,000	A	336	1-31-1784	Harrods Cr	
Stephens, Jacob	966	A	279	6- 7-1783	Clover Cr	Surveyed
Stephens, Samuel	100	A	292	10- 3-1783	Pottengers Cr	
Stephenson, David	———	A	363	6- 3-1784	———	
Stephenson, David	5,317½	A	363	6- 2-1784	Brush Cr	Brush Cr
Stephenson, David	5,317½	A	378	6- 2-1784	Brush Cr	Error
Stephenson, James	500	A	224	12-12-1782	Cartrights Cr	
Stephenson, James	400	A	246	1- 6-1783	Floyds Fk	Surveyed
Sterns, Valentine	1,000	A	112	5-30-1780	Licking	
Stevens, Benj	786¼	A	347	3-22-1784	Salt R	766 acres surveyed
Stevens, Benj	5,000	A	348	3-22-1784	Plumb Cr	Surveyed
Stevens, Benj	1,000	A	344	3- 3-1784	Nole Linn Cr	Surveyed
Stevens, Benj	2,304	B	2	8-19-1784	———	Surveyed
Stevens, Benj	7,786½	B	43	4-11-1785	———	
Stevens, Benj	50	A	84	5-22-1780	S Fk Licking	Mil
Stevens, Edward	1,000	A	61	5-16-1780	S Fk Harrods Cr	Surveyed
Stevens, Edward	2,000	A	61	5-16-1780	Ohio R	
Stevens, Edward	1,000	A	71	5-18-1780	Harrods Cr	
Stevens, Edward	2,000	A	71	5-18-1780	Cartrights Cr	Surveyed
Stevens, Edward	1,000	A	83	5-22-1780	Licking	
Stevens, Edward	3,000	A	366	6-16-1784	———	2,000 acres surveyed
Stevens, George	650	A	98	5-25-1780	Ky R	
Stevens, Geo W	2,877	A	361	5-25-1784	Pittmans Cr	
Stevens, James	2,276½	A	271	3-28-1783	Brush Cr	
Stevens, John	2,250	A	114	5-30-1780	Licking	
Stevens, Mary	400	A	236	12-20-1782	Rolling Fk	
Stevens, Richard	500	A	46	5-11-1780	Chaplins Fk	Surveyed
Stevens, Richard	300	A	91	5-24-1780	Floyds Fk	
Stevens, Richard	500	A	104	5-27-1780	Salt R	Surveyed
Stevens, Richard	1,000	B	23	12- 4-1784	———	
Stevens, Richard, heirs	2,000	A	33	4-29-1780	Beargrass	Mil surveyed
Stevens, Richard, heirs	1,500	A	33	4-29-1780	Beargrass	Mil
Stevens, Richard, heirs	500	A	33	4-29-1780	Glens Cr	Mil
Stevens, Samuel	1,000	A	37	4-29-1780	Shannons Run	
Stevens, Samuel	100	A	375	7-29-1784	———	
Stevens, Samuel	530	A	375	7-29-1784	———	250 acres surveyed
Stevenson, Edward	863	A	252	1-14-1783	Green R	
Stevenson, Edward	863	B	20	11-26-1784	Green R	Withdrawn
Stevenson, Hugh	1,000	A	148	6-24-1780	Indian Cr	Mil
Stevenson, James	971¼	A	332	1-19-1784	Harrods Fk	Surveyed
Stevenson, Thomas	1,000	A	132	6-15-1780	John Logans settlement	
Stevins, Thomas et al	600	A	98	5-25-1780	Town Fk	
Steward, John	1,000	B	33	1-20-1785	———	
Steward, Wm	1,000	A	55	5-15-1780	Cartright Cr	
Stewart, Charles	1,000	A	197	3-17-1781	Mill Cr	
Stewart, James	400	A	160	7- 6-1780	Beach Fk	
Stewart, John	1,000	A	23	4-24-1780	Prestons Cave Cr	Withdrawn
Stewart, John	1,000	A	21	4-19-1780	Elkhorn	Mil withdrawn
Stewart, John	1,000	A	21	4-19-1780	Little Ky	Surveyed
Stewart, John	1,000	A	216	7-21-1781	Hardens Cr	Surveyed
Stewart, John	1,000	A	220	8-29-1781	E Fk Beargrass Cr	
Stewart, John	200	A	247	1- 7-1783	Panther Cr	
Stewart, Rob & Thos	6,908½	A	377	8-11-1784	Rolling Fk	
Stewart, Thomas	200	A	25	4-25-1780	Little Ky	Mil surveyed
Stewart, Thomas	1,000	A	223	12-12-1782	Sinking Cr	Mil
Stewart, Wm	400	A	7	12-29-1779	Chaplins Fk	
Stewart, Wm	400	A	18	3- 1-1780	Mill Cr	
Stewart, Wm	300	A	35	4-29-1780	Mill Cr	Mil
Stewart, Wm	250	A	35	4-29-1780	Doctors Fk	
Stewart, Will	1,000	A	37	4-29-1780	Licking Cr	
Stewart, Will	400	A	37	4-29-1780	Clarks Run	
Stewart, Wm	500	A	55	5-15-1780	Chaplins Fk	
Stewart, Wm	500	A	55	5-15-1780	Beech Fk	
Stewart, Wm	1,000	A	55	5-15-1780	Jessamine Cr	
Stewart, Wm	1,000	A	55	5-15-1780	Jessamine Cr	
Stewart, Wm	550	A	64	5-17-1780	Beech Fk	
Stewart, Wm	4,000	A	141	6-21-1780	Lawrence Cr	

Entree	Acres	Book	Page	Entry Date	Watercourse	Notes
Stewart, Wm	560	A	184	10–30–1780	Chaplins Fk	
Stewart, Wm	800	A	184	10–30–1780	Doctors Fk	
Stewart, Wm	600	A	184	10–30–1780	Clarks Run	
Stewart, Wm	600	A	184	10–30–1780	Mill Cr	Surveyed
Stewart, Wm	600	A	184	10–30–1780	Mill Cr	Surveyed
Stewart, Wm	600	A	184	10–30–1780	S Fk Harlins Cr	Surveyed
Stewart, Wm	——	A	197	3–17–1781	Rowling Fk	
Stewart, Wm	1,000	A	201	4– 2–1781	Pleasant Run	
Stewart, Wm	600	A	201	4– 2–1781	Pleasant Run	
Stewart, Wm	400	A	201	4– 2–1781	Rowling Fk	Surveyed
Stewart, Wm	500	A	201	4– 2–1781	Rowling Fk	Surveyed
Stewart, Wm	400	A	201	4– 2–1781	Rowling Fk	Surveyed
Stewart, Wm	500	A	201	4– 2–1781	Buffaloe Cr	200 acres withdrawn
Stewart, Wm	500	A	201	4– 2–1781	Stewarts Cr	Surveyed
Stewart, Wm	500	A	215	7–18–1781	Mill Cr	Surveyed
Stewart, Wm	100	A	219	8–20–1781	Lick Cr	
Stewart, Wm	300	A	219	8–20–1781	Cartrights Cr	
Stewart, Wm	700	A	219	8–20–1781	Sun Fish Cr	
Stewart, Wm	100	A	220	8–29–1781	Rowling Fk	Surveyed
Stewart, Wm	200	A	220	8–29–1781	Hardens Cr	
Stewart, Wm	6,100	A	220	8–24–1781	Jefferson Cr	Not surveyed
Stewart, Wm	500	A	220	8–24–1781	Stewarts Cr	Surveyed
Stewart, Wm	200	A	221	9– 7–1781	Mill Cr	
Stewart, Wm	3,640	A	230	12–17–1782	Green R	
Stewart, Wm	1,000	A	230	12–17–1782	Ky R	
Stewart, Wm	4,259	A	240	12–24–1782	Panther Cr	
Stewarts, John	1,000	A	212	6–25–1781	Beargrass Cr	
Stigler, Samuel	2,750	A	238	12–21–1782	Green R	
Stille, John	9,895	A	330	1–14–1784	Ky R	
Stocksell, Edmund H	500	A	299	10–27–1783	Knob Cr Salt R	
Stocksell, Edmund H	1,000	A	299	10–27–1783	Salt R	
Stole, Wm	205	A	290	9–10–1783	Cartright Cr	
Stone, John	500	A	38	5– 9–1780	Drennens Lick	
Stone, Uriah	400	A	13	2–11–1780	Brashears Cr	
Stone, Val	500	A	90	5–23–1780	Howards Cr	
Stone, Wm Jr	500	A	43	5–11–1780	Stoner Fk	
Stone, Wm Jr	500	A	43	5–11–1780	Stoners Fk	
Stoner, Jacob	400	A	9	2– 2–1780	Hines Bend Ky R	
Storey & Willis	21,000	A	333	1–20–1784	County Line	Surveyed
Storey & Willis	——	A	357	5– 1–1784	Hammons Cr	Surveyed
Storey & Willis	1,300	A	358	5– 3–1784	Long Lick Cr	1,060 acres surveyed
Storey & Willis	7,000	A	358	5– 3–1784	Salt R	Surveyed
Storey & Willis	10,000	B	43	4–11–1785	——	
Storms, Jacob	150	A	92	5–24–1780	Ky R	Mil
Storms, Jacob	400	A	92	5–24–1780	Otter Cr	
Storms, Jacob	1,000	A	111	5–29–1780	Licking	
Storms, Jacob	1,000	A	111	5–29–1780	Settlement	
Storms, John	1,000	A	111	5–29–1780	Strodes Fk	
Stover, John	500	A	193	3–16–1781	Soverins Valley	Surveyed
Stover, John	300	A	295	10–13–1783	Soverins Valley	Surveyed
Stover, Joseph	300	A	193	3–16–1781	N Fk Buffaloe Cr	Withdrawn
Stover, Joseph	200	A	193	3–16–1781	Shaws Cr	Surveyed
Stover, Joseph	300	A	193	3–16–1781	Billys Cr	Withdrawn
Stover, Joseph	300	A	299	10–27–1783	Billys Cr	Surveyed withdrawn
Streep, Jacob	1,000	A	284	8– 4–1783	Little Ky R	
Strode, James	1,000	A	27	4–26–1780	Licking Cr	
Strode, John	1,000	A	27	4–26–1780	Licking Cr	
Strode, John	400	A	74	5–19–1780	Stoners Fk	
Strode, Samuel	500	A	57	5–15–1780	Licking	
Strode, Samuel	500	A	57	5–15–1780	Licking	
Strother, French	500	A	49	5–12–1780	Licking	
Strother, French	500	A	57	5–15–1781	S Fk Licking	
Strother, French	500	A	70	5–18–1780	Licking	
Strother, French	2,433	A	242	12–25–1782	Drennons Lick Cr	Surveyed
Sturgus, James	400	A	120	6– 1–1780	Floyds Fk	Surveyed
Sturgus, Peter	400	A	15	2–21–1780	Hammonds	Surveyed
Sturgus, Peter	1,000	A	120	6– 1–1780	Hammonds Cr	
Sturman, Richard	500	A	89	5–23–1780	Rowling Fk	
Sublett, Lewis	405	A	42	5–10–1780	S Fk Licking	
Sudden, John	1,000	A	57	5–15–1780	Simpson Cr	
Sudden, Thomas	1,000	A	57	5–15–1780	near Kinch Sta	
Sudwill, Hugh	1,000	A	138	6–20–1780	Licking	
Sullivan, Daniel	400	A	126	6– 7–1780	Rowling Fk	Surveyed
Sullivan, Daniel	2,000	A	244	12–27–1782	Falls Ohio	Surveyed withdrawn
Sullivan, Daniel	400	A	248	1– 7–1783	Pond Cr	Surveyed
Sullivan, Daniel	660	A	293	10– 4–1783	Floyds Fk	Surveyed
Sullivan, Daniel	140	A	293	10– 4–1783	Beargrass Cr	Surveyed

Entree	Acres	Book	Page	Entry Date	Watercourse	Notes
Sullivan, Daniel	600	A	299	10-27-1783	Fox Run	Surveyed
Sullivan, Daniel	400	A	302	11- 7-1783	Ky R	Surveyed
Sullivan, Daniel	1,000	A	302	11- 7-1783	Clear Cr	440 acres surveyed
Sullivan, Daniel	1,400	A	302	11- 7-1783	———	420 acres surveyed
Sullivan, Daniel	310	A	330	1-14-1784	Fox Run	Surveyed
Sullivan, Daniel	100	A	338	2-12-1784	Slurgus Run	Surveyed
Sullivan, Daniel	234	B	7	9-14-1784	Pond Cr	
Sullivan, David	1,000	B	12	11- 9-1784		315 acres surveyed
Sullivan, Daniel	1,734	B	33	1-13-1785	———	
Sullivan, Daniel	2,000	B	41	2-28-1785		420 acres surveyed
Sullivan, James	1,000	A	27	4-26-1780	Rolling Fk	Surveyed
Sullivan, James	400	A	202	4- 3-1781	Col Broadhead	Surveyed
Sullivan, James	400	A	282	7- 1-1782	Pond Cr	Surveyed
Sullivan, James	1,000	A	371	7-16-1784	Beargrass Cr	
Summers, George	1,000	A	124	6- 3-1780	Lawrence Cr	
Summers, George	1,000	A	124	6- 3-1780	Lawrence Cr	
Summers, John	400	A	78	5-20-1780	Coxes Cr	
Summers, John Jr	1,000	A	61	5-16-1780	Rolling Fk	
Summers, Paul	5,000	A	314	12- 9-1783	Barbour & Banks	Surveyed
Summers, Simon	1,000	A	73	5-19-1780	Coxes Cr	586 acres withdrawn
Summers, Simon	500	A	74	5-19-1780	Rolling Fk	Surveyed
Summers, Simon		A	290	9-10-1783	Isaac Cox	
Summers, Simon	580	A	290	9-10-1783	Coxes Cr	Withdrawn
Summitt, John	630	A	258	1-27-1783	Beech Fk	
Surean, Lewis	600	A	55	5-15-1780		Withdrawn
Surean, Lewis	400	A	55	5-15-1780	Doctors Fk	Withdrawn
Surean, Lewis	1,000	A	184	10-30-1780	Green R	
Sutherland, John	470	B	30	12-29-1784	Cedar Lick Cr	
Sutherland, John	60	B	30	12-29-1784	Beech Fk	
Sutherland, John	70	B	30	12-29-1784	Beech Fk	
Sutton, James	500	A	175	10- 6-1780	S Fk Elkhorn	
Sutton, John	1,200	A	274	4- 8-1783	Ky R	Surveyed
Swan, John	1,100	A	96	5-24-1780	N Fk Elkhorn	
Swan, John	100	A	196	3-17-1781	Nolin Cr	
Swan, John	500	A	196	3-17-1781	Mill Cr	Mil
Swan, John	400	A	256	1-21-1783	Pottengers Cr	Surveyed
Swan, Richard	1,000	A	176	10- 6-1780	Pleasant Run	
Swan, Samuel, heir	1,000	B	12	11- 8-1784	Rowling Fk	
Swann, John	1,000	A	195	3-16-1781	Mays Cr	
Swank, John	400	A	168	8-21-1780	N Fk Buffaloe Cr	Surveyed 200 acres withdrawn
Swank, John	200	A	205	4- 9-1781	N Fk Buffaloe Cr	Withdrawn
Swank, John	200	A	205	4- 9-1781	N Fk Buffaloe Cr	
Swank, John	200	A	218	8- 8-1781	Soverins Valley	Surveyed
Swarengen, Thomas	1,000	A	113	5-30-1780	Salt R	
Swearengan, Thos	500	A	27	4-26-1780	Stoners Fk	Mil
Swearengan, Thos	1,000	A	27	4-26-1780	Stoners Spring	Mil
Swearengan, Thos	3,000	A	88	5-23-1780	Licking	2,000 acres withdrawn
Swearengen, Benony	400	A	36	4-29-1780	Muddy Cr	
Swearengen, Dan	400	A	9	1-18-1780	Licking Cr	
Swearengen, Thos	400	A	36	4-29-1780	Muddy Cr	
Swearengen, Thos	400	A	112	5-30-1780	Fk Licking	
Swearengen, Thos	400	A	119	6- 1-1780	Licking	
Swerengen, Thos	50	A	124	6- 3-1780	Lead Mine	
Swerengen, Thos	50	A	124	6- 3-1780	Lead Mine	Mil
Swearengen, Thos	2,000	A	130	6-10-1780	Licking	
Swearengen, Van	1,000	A	75	5-19-1780	Johnston Cr	
Swearing, Thomas	100	A	16	2-25-1780	Br Ohio R	Mil withdrawn
Swearinger, Thos	700	A	31	4-28-1780	N Br Licking	Mil
Swearingin, Thos	1,000	A	74	5-19-1780	Licking	
Swope, Benedick	500	A	71	5-18-1780	Licking	
Swope, Benedick	500	A	71	5-18-1780	Salt R	
Swope, Benedick	500	A	71	5-18-1780	Rowling Fk	
Swope, Benedick	500	A	71	5-18-1780	Green R	Surveyed
Swope, Benedick	500	A	71	5-18-1780	Rowling Fk	
Swope, Benedick	500	A	72	5-18-1780	Rowling Fk	
Swoope, Benedict	250	A	229	12-16-1782	Brashears Cr	
Swope, Benedict	1,000	B	19	11-22-1784	———	500 acres surveyed
Synder, Jacob	1,000	A	257	1-25-1783	Rough Cr	300 acres withdrawn
Tagert, John	560	A	130	6-12-1780	Beach Fk	
Talbot, Isham	2,941	A	342	2-28-1784	Salt R	

Entree	Acres	Book	Page	Entry Date	Watercourse	Notes
Talbot, John	50	A	268	3-28-1783	Sinking Cr	
Talbot, John	50	A	205	4- 6-1781	Rowling Fk	
Talbot, John	1,000	A	348	3-24-1784	Salt R	Withdrawn
Talbot, John	1,100	A	348	3-24-1784	Salt R	Withdrawn
Talbot, John	1,400	A	348	3-24-1784	Salt R	Withdrawn
Talbot, John	1,000	A	377	8-12-1784	Salt R	
Talbot, John	1,100	A	377	8-12-1784	Salt R	Withdrawn
Talbot, John	1,400	A	377	8-12-1784	Salt Run	
Talbot, Thomas	750	A	190	3-15-1781	Cane Run	
Talbot, Thomas	325	A	209	5-18-1781	Beargrass Cr	
Talbot, Thomas	750	A	365	6-12-1784	————	
Talbot, Wm	600	A	66	5-17-1780	Flat & Pond Cr	Surveyed
Talbot, Wm	600	A	263	2-15-1783	Salt Lick	
Talliafaro, Richard	1,781½	A	348	3-26-1784	Wolf Cr	
Tandy, Smith	500	A	225	12-13-1782	Knoxes Lick	Withdrawn
Tandy, Smith	1,000	A	225	12-13-1782	Sinking Cr	Surveyed
Tandy, Smyth	500	A	270	3-28-1783	Brush Cr	
Tandy, Smith	500	A	270	3-28-1783	Knoxes Lick	
Tankersley, George	1,000	A	228	12-16-1782	Brush Cr	Surveyed
Tanner, John	500	A	42	5-11-1780	Licking	
Tanner, John	500	A	145	6-23-1780	4 Mile Cr	
Tanner, John	1,000	A	157	7- 3-1780	Licking	
Tanner, John Jr	2,000	A	157	7- 3-1780	Licking	
Tate, Francis	1,000	A	88	5-23-1780	Floyds Fk	Surveyed
Tate, Francis	2,000	A	87	5-23-1780	Little Ky R	
Tate, John	400	A	121	6- 2-1780	Paint Lick	Surveyed
Tate, Robert	400	A	11	2- 4-1780	Silver Cr	
Tatum, Absalom	2,358	A	158	7- 3-1780	4 Mile Cr	
Tatum, Nathan	250	A	125	6- 5-1780	Douglass	
Tavers, John	400	A	284	8- 4-1783	Lick Run	
Tawson, Ezekiel	500	A	59	5-16-1780	Beargrass Cr	
Taylor, Benj	325	A	188	3-15-1781	Pond Cr	
Taylor, Edmund	1,000	A	34	4-29-1780	S Fk Elkhorn	Mil
Taylor, Edmund	1,250	A	48	5-12-1780	Beargrass	Surveyed
Taylor, Edmund	250	A	48	5-12-1780	Beargrass	
Taylor, Edmund	200	A	77	5-20-1780	Beargrass Cr	
Taylor, Edmund	1,000	A	78	5-20-1780	Ohio R	
Taylor, Edmund	3,000	A	87	5-23-1780	Little Ky R	Surveyed
Taylor, Edmund	1,000	A	91	5-24-1780	Ohio R	
Taylor, Edmund	500	A	142	6-22-1780	Beargrass Cr	Withdrawn
Taylor, Edmund	3,000	A	167	8-11-1780	Green R	Surveyed
Taylor, Edmund	2,000	A	168	8-17-1780	Elkhorn	
Taylor, Edmund	1,000	A	218	8- 8-1781	Ohio R	Mil surveyed
Taylor, Edmund	1,000	A	302	11- 7-1783	Floyds Fk	Surveyed
Taylor, Edmund	1,000	A	302	11- 7-1783	Beargrass Cr	Withdrawn
Taylor, Edmund	500	A	308	11-22-1783	Sinking Fk	Withdrawn
Taylor, Edmund	1,000	A	308	11-22-1783	Beargrass Cr	Withdrawn
Taylor, Edmund	500	A	308	11-22-1783	Beargrass Cr	Withdrawn
Taylor, Edmund	1,500	A	317	12-15-1783	Beargrass Cr	Surveyed
Taylor, Edmund	500	A	317	12-15-1783	Beargrass Cr	Surveyed
Taylor, Edmund	4,151¼	A	330	1-15-1784	John Kings	
Taylor, Edmund	400	A	330	1-15-1784	Floyds Fk	
Taylor, Edmund	50	A	330	1-15-1784	Salt R	
Taylor, Edmund	799	A	331	1-16-1784	————	
Taylor, Edmund	8,201	A	331	1-16-1784	————	
Taylor, Edmund	2,000	B	47	6- 2-1785	Beargrass Cr	
Taylor, Francis	1,000	A	85	5-22-1780	Ohio	
Taylor, Francis	1,000	A	88	5-23-1780	Floyds Fk	Surveyed
Taylor, Francis	3,000	A	166	8-16-1780	Panther Cr	Withdrawn
Taylor, Francis	3,000	A	222	12- 9-1782	Panther Cr	Withdrawn
Taylor, Francis	3,000	A	224	12-13-1782	Ohio R	Surveyed
Taylor, Francis	1,000	A	228	12-16-1782	Bullskin Cr	Surveyed
Taylor, Francis	3,000	A	229	12-16-1782	Blackford Cr	
Taylor, Francis	2,531¼	A	310	11-26-1783	————	
Taylor, George	250	A	44	5-11-1780	Cedar Cr	
Taylor, George	570¾	A	330	1-15-1784	Floyds Fk	
Taylor, Hubbard	1,000	A	242	12-25-1782	Sinking Cr	Surveyed
Taylor, Hubbard	7,522	A	251	1- 9-1783	Ohio R	Surveyed
Taylor, Hubbard	2,000	A	280	6- 7-1783	————	
Taylor, Hubbard	1,000	A	302	11- 7-1783	Ohio R	Withdrawn
Taylor, Hubbard	500	A	309	11-26-1783	Green R	
Taylor, James	500	A	20	4-14-1780	Ohio R	Mil
Taylor, James	500	A	20	4-14-1780	Licking & Ohio R	Mil
Taylor, James	500	A	20	4-14-1780	Licking Cr	Mil
Taylor, James	300	A	22	4-22-1780	Dicks R	Mil surveyed
Taylor, James	300	A	31	4-28-1780	Dicks R	
Taylor, James	1,500	A	48	5-12-1780	Floyds Fk	Surveyed
Taylor, James	1,000	A	88	5-23-1780	Floyds Fk	Surveyed
Taylor, James	2,000	A	88	5-23-1780	Floyds Fk	Surveyed
Taylor, James	1,000	A	183	10-27-1780	Floyds Fk	
Taylor, James	1,000	A	183	10-27-1780	Floyds Fk	

Entree	Acres	Book	Page	Entry Date	Watercourse	Notes
Taylor, James	1,000	A	218	8- 8-1781	Ohio R	Mil surveyed
Taylor, James	250	A	228	12-16-1782	Hardens Cr	
Taylor, James	2,906	A	228	12-16-1782	Sinking Cr	Surveyed 406 acres withdrawn
Taylor, James	500	A	232	12-18-1782	Sinking Cr	Surveyed
Taylor, James	2,875	A	237	12-21-1782	Patrick Henrys	Surveyed
Taylor, James	406	A	267	3-28-1783	Green R	
Taylor, James	406	A	267	3-28-1783	Sinking Cr	Withdrawn
Taylor, James	1,000	A	302	11- 7-1783	Bullskin Cr	
Taylor, James	1,000	A	305	11-19-1783	Green R	Withdrawn
Taylor, James	1,000	A	308	11-24-1783	Green R	Withdrawn
Taylor, James	1,000	A	309	11-25-1783	Blackford Cr	
Taylor, James	500	A	318	12-16-1783	Ohio R	
Taylor, James	1,000	A	344	3- 3-1784	Big Reedy	
Taylor, Jesse	6,000	A	117	6- 1-1780	Green R	
Taylor, Jesse	3,000	A	117	5-31-1780	Rowling Fk	
Taylor, Jesse	6,000	A	118	6- 1-1780	———	
Taylor, Jesse	1,750	A	118	6- 1-1780	Chaplins Fk	
Taylor, Jesse	6,000	A	118	6- 1-1780	Ohio R	
Taylor, Jesse	9,000	A	118	6- 1-1780	Drennens Lick	Surveyed
Taylor, Jesse	2,000	A	118	5-31-1780	Ohio R	
Taylor, Jesse	6,000	A	128	6- 8-1780	Sinking Cr	
Taylor, Jesse	3,000	A	129	6- 9-1780	———	
Taylor, John	1,000	A	36	4-29-1780	Strodes Fk	
Taylor, John	1,000	A	69	5-18-1780	Ohio R	
Taylor, John	1,000	A	75	5-19-1780	Floyds Fk	Surveyed
Taylor, John	3,000	A	84	5-22-1780	Johnstons Fk	
Taylor, John	1,000	A	85	5-22-1780	Ohio R	
Taylor, John	1,000	A	87	5-23-1780	Little Ky R	Surveyed
Taylor, John	500	A	151	6-26-1780	Stoners	
Taylor, John	6,000	A	270	3-28-1783	Beech Cr	1,230 acres surveyed 4,770 acres withdrawn
Taylor, John	4,770	A	362	5-26-1784	Rolling Fk	
Taylor, John	4,770	A	362	5-26-1784	Beech Fk	Withdrawn
Taylor, John	6,000	B	42	3-22-1785	———	1,230 acres surveyed
Taylor, Muse	350	A	86	5-22-1780	Green R	
Taylor, Peter	800	A	44	5-11-1780	Otter Cr	
Taylor, Peter	1,000	A	96	5-26-1780	Muddy Fk	
Taylor, Peter	1,000	A	96	5-24-1780	E Fk Otter Cr	
Taylor, Peter	1,000	A	130	6-12-1780	Stoners Fk	
Taylor, Phillip	1,000	A	268	3-28-1783	Panther Cr	Surveyed
Taylor, Phillip	2,000	A	369	6-30-1784	———	1,000 acres surveyed
Taylor, Richard	400	A	11	2- 4-1780	Otter Cr	
Taylor, Richard	1,100	A	35	4-29-1780	Ohio R	Mil withdrawn
Taylor, Richard	500	A	48	5-12-1780	Floyds Fk	Surveyed
Taylor, Richard	500	A	75	5-19-1780	Floyds Fk	
Taylor, Richard	1,000	A	85	5-22-1780	Ohio R	
Taylor, Richard	1,000	A	132	6-15-1780	May & Thompson	
Taylor, Richard	1,000	A	298	10-25-1783	Floyds Fk	
Taylor, Samuel	600	A	154	6-27-1780	Red R	
Taylor, Thornton	1,000	A	228	12-16-1782	Panther Cr	Surveyed
Taylor, Wm	1,000	A	48	5-12-1780	Floyds Fk	Surveyed
Taylor, Wm	300	A	86	5-22-1780	Cabbin Cr	
Taylor, Wm	500	A	281	6-20-1783	Rock Cr	
Taylor, Wm	1,000	A	321	12-20-1783	Clover Cr	Withdrawn
Taylor, Wm	1,000	A	365	6-14-1784	Pittmans Cr	Surveyed
Taylor, Wm	1,000	A	365	6-14-1784	Clover Cr	
Taylor, Wm	1,000	A	268	6-26-1784	Buffaloe Run	
Taylor, Wm	500	B	2	8-19-1784	———	
Taylor, Wm	1,000	B	5	9-11-1784	———	
Taylor, Wm	10	B	44	5-10-1785	Goose Cr	
Taylor, Zachariah	3,098	A	266	2-25-1783	Robertsons Cr	
Teas, Mary	400	A	207	4-14-1781	Bullskin Cr	Surveyed
Teator, George	400	A	25	4-26-1780	Dicks R	
Teator, George	200	A	30	4-28-1780	N Fk Beargrass	Withdrawn
Teeters, George	2,000	A	256	1-24-1783	Brush Cr	Mil
Telford, David	500	A	81	5-22-1780	Lees Br	
Telford, Jeremiah	400	A	128	6- 8-1780	Clear Cr	Withdrawn
Telford, Jeremiah	400	A	81	5-20-1780	S Fk Clear Cr	Withdrawn
Telford, Jeremiah	200	A	166	8-11-1780	Chaplin R	
Telford, Jeremiah	200	A	186	10-31-1780	Chaplins Fk	
Telford, Jeremiah	600	A	230	12-17-1782	Cedar Cr	
Telford, Jeremiah	400	A	230	12-17-1782	Salt R	
Telford, Jeremiah	448½	A	242	12-25-1782	Salt R	
Telford, Wm	500	A	81	5-20-1780	N Fk Licking	
Temple, Ben	2,000	A	183	10-27-1780	Floyds Fk	

Entree	Acres	Book	Page	Entry Date	Watercourse	Notes
Temple, Smith	1,000	A	64	5–17–1780	Stoners Fk	
Templin, Moses	400	A	265	2–19–1783	Rolling Fk	
Templin, Tirah	400	A	128	6– 8–1780	near Riddle Sta.	
Templin, Tirah	400	A	128	6– 8–1780	near Riddle Sta.	
Templing, Terah	600	A	246	1– 6–1783	Athens Fk	
Tennant, John	4,000	A	167	8–17–1780	Green R	Withdrawn
Tennant, John	4,000	A	190	3–15–1781	Green R	Surveyed
Tennant, John	4,000	A	190	3–15–1781	Panther Cr	
Tennant, John	2,563	A	242	12–25–1782	Panther Cr	Surveyed
Terrel, John	450	A	95	5–24–1780	Muddy Fk	
Terrel, Robert	544½	A	95	5–24–1780	Licking	
Terrel, Robert	400	A	95	5–24–1780	Muddy Cr	
Terrel, Richard	525	A	79	5–20–1780	Mulberry Cr	
Terrell, Richard	3,000	A	337	2–10–1784	Salt R	Surveyed
Terrell, Richard	3,000	B	41	2–28–1785	——	100, acres surveyed
Terrell, Richard	403½	B	41	2–28–1785	Sinking Fk	
Terrell, Samuel	600	A	79	5–20–1780	Mulberry Cr	
Terrell & Hawkins	1,000	A	200	4– 2–1781	Town&RowlingFk	Surveyed
Terrell & Hawkins	1,000	A	200	3–26–1781	Nest Cr	Surveyed
Terrell & Hawkins	1,000	A	201	4– 2–1781	Town Fk	Surveyed
Terrell & Hawkins	1,000	A	201	4– 2–1781	Salt R	Surveyed
Terrell & Hawkins	1,000	A	201	4– 2–1781	Rowling Fk	
Terrell & Hawkins	1,000	A	201	4– 2–1781	Rowling Fk	
Terrell & Hawkins	1,000	A	201	4– 2–1781	Green R	Surveyed
Terrell & Hawkins	1,000	A	201	4– 2–1781	Green R	Surveyed
Terrell & Hawkins	1,000	A	210	5–30–1781	Mill Cr	Surveyed
Terrell & Hawkins	400	A	216	7–21–1781	Salt R	Surveyed
Terrell & Hawkins	1,000	A	345	3– 9–1784	Bensons Cr	
Terry, John	325	A	163	7–29–1780	Round Stone Cr	
Teters, George	200	A	256	1–24–1783	Beargrass Cr	Withdrawn
Teters, George	250	A	341	2–26–1784	Floyds Fk	
Tharp, James	1,780	A	270	3–28–1783	Beech Fk	
Tharp, Othey	1,000	A	270	3–28–1783	Beech Fk	
Tharp, Wm	1,000	A	270	3–28–1783	Beech Fk	
Thixton, Wm	400	A	252	1–13–1783	Beech Fk	
Thomas, Edmund	325	A	345	3– 5–1784	Harrods Cr	
Thomson, George	1,000	A	341	2–21–1784	Fox Run	Surveyed
Thomas, James	300	A	92	5–24–1780	Ky R	
Thomas, John	295	A	53	5–15–1780	——	
Thomas, John	3,000	B	31	1– 3–1785	———	1,000 acres surveyed
Thomas, Lewis	1,000	A	309	11–24–1783	Hardens Cr	Surveyed
Thomas, Mark	1,075	A	243	12–26–1782	Harrods Cr	
Thomas, Michael	400	A	141	6–25–1780	Dicks R	
Thomas, Moses	1,000	A	43	5–11–1780	Hingston Fk	
Thomas, Moses	250	A	93	5–24–1780	Fk Licking	
Thomas, Moses	1,000	A	93	5–24–1780	Stoners&RockyFk	
Thomas, Richard	400	A	4	9–15–1779	S Fk Elkhorn	Withdrawn
Thomas, Richard	400	A	139	6–21–1780	Brashesrs Cr	
Thomas, Richard	1,000	A	179	10–19–1780	Mulberry Cr	
Thomas, Robert	500	A	301	11– 7–1783	Chaplins Fk	
Thomas, Robert	1,500	A	301	11– 7–1783	Glens Cr	Surveyed
Thomas, Robert	3,119¼	A	342	3– 3–1784	Pottengers Cr	
Thomas, Robert	3,059½	B	41	3– 4–1785	——	
Thomas, Robert	6,119¼	B	41	3– 4–1785	———	
Thomas, Robert et al	30,000	A	301	11– 7–1783	Glens Cr	Surveyed
Thomas, Robert et al	2,000	A	342	3– 2–1784	Rolling Fk	
Thompson, Anthony	50	A	21	4–20–1780	Crooked Cr	Withdrawn
Thompson, Anthony	50	A	21	4–20–1780	Green R	Withdrawn
Thompson, Anthony	50	A	21	4–20–1780	Buckhorn Cr	Mil withdrawn
Thompson, Anthony	50	A	21	4–20–1780	Buckhorn Cr	Mil withdrawn
Thompson, Anthony	50	A	21	4–20–1780	Buckhorn Cr	Withdrawn
Thompson, Anthony	200	A	21	4–20–1780	Green R	Mil withdrawn
Thompson, Anthony	400	A	32	4–29–1780	Licking Cr	
Thompson, Anthony	1,000	A	255	1–20–1783	Rolling Fk	
Thompson, Anthony	3,000	A	297	10–18–1783	Rough Cr	
Thompson, Charles	50	A	33	4–29–1780	Selby settlement	Mil
Thompson, David	900	A	122	6– 2–1780	Ohio R	Mil
Thompson, George	400	A	13	2–11–1780	Dicks R	
Thompson, George	400	A	17	2–29–1780	Fox Run	Surveyed
Thompson, George	2,000	A	23	4–24–1780	Ohio R	
Thompson, George	5,000	A	84	5–22–1780	Licking	
Thompson, George	400	A	133	6– 1–1780	Dicks R	Withdrawn
Thompson, George	400	A	149	6–24–1780	Dicks R	
Thompson, Hugh	400	A	178	10–17–1780	Town Fk	
Thompson, Israel	3,000	A	62	5–16–1780	Mill Cr	Surveyed
Thompson, Israel	500	A	105	5–27–1780	Ky R	
Thompson, Israel	2,000	A	220	8–24–1781	Lick Cr	Withdrawn

Entree	Acres	Book	Page	Entry Date	Watercourse	Notes
Thompson, Israel	2,000	A	221	11- 9-1782	———	Withdrawn
Thompson, Israel	2,000	A	226	12-14-1782	Caney Fk	Surveyed
Thompson, Israel	1,000	A	226	12-14-1782	Caney Fk	Surveyed
Thompson, Israel	1,000	A	226	12-14-1782	Caney Fk	Surveyed
Thompson, Israel	1,461	A	370	7- 9-1784	Ky R	
Thompson, Israel	1,461	B	26	12-13-1784	Drennons Lick Cr	Withdrawn
Thompson, Israel Sr	1,000	A	348	3-23-1784		119 acres returned
Thompson, James	500	A	155	6-29-1780	S Fk Elkhorn	
Thompson, James	1,000	A	237	12-21-1782	Read Cr	Surveyed
Thompson, James	2,458½	B	10	10-11-1784	———	100 acres surveyed
Thompson, John	667	A	250	1- 9-1783	Pattons Line	Surveyed
Thompson, John	400	A	258	1-27-1783	Coxes Cr	
Thompson, Jonah	4,000	A	105	5-27-1780	Ohio R	
Thompson, Jonah	1,000	A	310	11-27-1783	Beargrass Cr	
Thompson, Jonah	1,000	A	355	4-19-1784	Ohio R	
Thompson, Nancy	1,000	A	105	5-27-1780	Ky R	Surveyed
Thompson, Rhoads	900	A	157	7- 3-1780	Red R	
Thompson, Robert	50	A	122	6- 2-1780	Ohio R	Mil
Thompson, Robert	1,000	A	178	10-17-1780	Town Fk	
Thompson, Robert	1,200	A	231	12-18-1782	Salt R	Surveyed
Thompson, Robert	782	A	296	10-14-1783	Robinsons Cr	
Thompson, Robert	1,200	A	315	12-13-1783	Wm Bush	
Thompson, Roger	1,000	A	81	5-22-1780	Green R	
Thompson, Samuel	1,000	A	105	5-27-1780	Ky R	Surveyed
Thompson, Thos	400	A	8	1-17-1780	Boiling Spring	
Thompson, Uriah	232	B	15	11-12-1784	Big Clifty Cr	
Thompson, Uriah	223	B	31	1- 3-1785	———	
Thompson, Wm	1,000	A	83	5-22-1780	———	Withdrawn
Thompson, Wm	1,000	A	96	5-24-1780	Wm Stewart	Surveyed
Thompson, Wm	1,000	A	98	5-25-1780	Ohio R	
Thompson, Wm	1,000	A	115	5-30-1780	Chaplins Fk	Surveyed
Thompson, Wm	1,000	A	120	6- 1-1780	Ky R	
Thompson, Wm	500	A	191	3-15-1781	Coxes Cr	
Thompson, Wm	1,000	A	298	10-25-1783	Salt R	Surveyed
Thornberry, John	1,861	A	260	2- 3-1783	Beech Fk	Withdrawn
Thornberry, John	1,861	A	298	10-25-1783	Floyds Fk	
Thornton, George	1,000	A	167	8-17-1780	Robinsons Cr	
Thornton, John	500	A	147	6-24-1780	Yellow Cr	
Thornton, John	500	A	147	6-24-1780	Yellow Cr	
Thruston, Charles M	400	A	2	11- 3-1779	N S Green R	Surveyed
Thruston, Charles M	400	A	2	11- 3-1779	Mill Cr	
Thruston, Charles M	1,450	A	34	4-29-1780	Harrods Cr	Mil
Thruston, Charles M	1,000	A	36	4-29-1780	Mill Cr	
Thruston, Charles M	6,000	A	47	5-12-1780	Thruston settlement	
Thruston, Charles M	600	A	57	5-15-1780	Nolin Cr	
Thruston, Charles M	1,400	A	57	5-15-1780	Nolin Cr	Surveyed
Thruston, Charles M	2,000	A	57	5-15-1780	Nolin Cr	Surveyed
Thruston, Chas M	400	A	60	5-16-1780	Little Ky	Surveyed
Thruston, Charles M	8,000	A	85	5-22-1780	Walpers Cr	
Thruston, Charles M	4,000	A	85	5-22-1780	Floyds Fk	Surveyed
Thruston, Charles M	2,000	A	85	5-22-1780	Ohio R	
Thruston, Charles M	750	A	91	5-24-1780	Floyds Fk	
Thruston, Charles Minn	15,000	A	167	5-11-1780	Green R	Surveyed
Thruston, Charles Minn	400	A	218	8- 8-1781	Drinnens Cr	Surveyed
Thruston, John	500	A	75	5-19-1780	Floyds Fk	Surveyed
Thruston, John	1,000	A	75	5-19-1780	Floyds Fk	Surveyed
Thruston, Robert	1,000	A	48	5-12-1780	Floyds Fk	Surveyed
Thruston, Robert	1,000	A	88	5-23-1780	Little Ky	Surveyed
Thurmond, John	1,750	A	182	10-25-1780	Muddy & Drowning Cr	
Thurmond, Phillip	797	A	315	12-13-1783	Green R	
Tilles, Griffin	400	A	263	2-15-1783	Hardens Cr	
Timberlake, John	400	A	200	3-29-1781	Cane Run	Surveyed
Timberlake, Richard	2,000	A	85	5-22-1780	S Fk Licking	
Timberlaque, John	400	A	176	10- 9-1780	Cedar Cr	
Tinney, Wm	10,000	A	346	3-12-1784	Long Lick Cr	Surveyed amended
Tinney, Wm	10,000	A	332	1-20-1784	Long Lick Cr	Surveyed
Tinney, James	412½	A	95	5-24-1780	Licking Cr	
Tipton, Ben	1,000	A	136	6-17-1780	N Fk Licking	
Tipton, John	750	A	136	6-17-1780	N Blue Lick	
Tith, John	500	A	319	12-17-1783	Rough Cr	
Titus, Ebenezer	1,000	A	132	6-15-1780	Pittmans Cr	
Tobin, Joseph	400	A	159	7- 6-1780	Clover Cr	
Tobin, Joseph	500	A	160	7- 6-1780	Clover Lick Run	Surveyed
Tobin, Joseph	500	A	160	7- 6-1780	Clover Lick Run	Surveyed
Tobin, Thomas	500	A	223	12-12-1782	Clover Cr	Surveyed
Tobin, Thomas	500	A	251	1-25-1783	Long Lick Cr	Surveyed
Tobin, Thomas	400	A	271	3-31-1783	Hardins Cr	

Entree	Acres	Book	Page	Entry Date	Watercourse	Notes
Tobin, Thomas	400	A	284	8- 4-1783	Tarr Spring Fk	Surveyed
Tobin, Thomas	400	A	290	9-11-1783	Hardins Cr	Amendment
Tobin, Thomas	223	B	3	8-27-1784	Ohio R	....
Todd, Charles	2,000	A	242	12-25-1782	Blackford Cr	Surveyed
Todd, Charles	1,486¼	A	242	12-25-1782	Rough Cr	Surveyed
Todd, John	50	A	21	4-20-1780	Ky R	Mil
Todd, John	400	A	21	4-19-1780	S Fk Elkhorn	....
Todd, John	200	A	21	4-19-1780	Manslick	Surveyed
Todd, John	200	A	21	4-19-1780	Harrods Cr	Mil
Todd, John	400	A	22	4-22-1780	S Fk Elkhorn	Entered before
Todd, John	1,000	A	37	4-29-1780	Hickmans Cr	....
Todd, John	400	A	42	5-10-1780	Clear Cr	....
Todd, John	400	A	42	5-10-1780	Ky R	....
Todd, John	400	A	60	5-16-1780	Gists Cr	....
Todd, John	1,000	A	60	5-16-1780	Gists Cr	Surveyed
Todd, John Jr	400	A	3	11-15-1779	Hickmans Cr	....
Todd, John Jr	1,000	A	119	6- 1-1780	Hickory Fk	....
Todd, John Sr	400	A	18	3- 3-1780	Hickmans Cr	....
Todd, Levi	400	A	37	4-29-1780	S Fk Elkhorn	....
Todd, Levi	200	A	61	5-16-1780	S Fk Elkhorn	....
Todd, Levi	400	A	61	5-16-1780	Ky R	....
Todd, Levi	800	A	62	5-16-1780	Elkhorn	500 acres withdrawn
Todd, Levi	400	A	149	6-24-1780	Mill Cr	....
Todd, Levi	500	A	158	7- 3-1780	Elkhorn	....
Todd, Samuel	50	A	21	4-20-1780	Ky R	Mil
Todd, Samuel	50	A	21	4-20-1780	Ky R	Mil
Todd, Samuel	400	A	65	5-17-1780	Hammonds Cr	....
Todd, Samuel	400	A	65	5-17-1780	Stoners Fk	....
Todd, Samuel	400	A	96	5-24-1780	Bullskin Cr	Surveyed
Todd, Robert	100	A	79	5-20-1780	Richland Cr	....
Todd, Robert	400	A	79	5-20-1780	Brashears Cr	Surveyed
Todd, Robert	500	A	135	6-17-1780	Robinsons Cr	....
Todd, Robert	400	A	135	6-17-1780	Green R	Withdrawn
Todd, Robert	400	A	135	6-17-1780	Green R	Withdrawn
Todd, Robert	200	A	150	6-26-1780	Nolin Cr	Surveyed
Todd, Robert	300	A	150	6-26-1780	Nolin Cr	Surveyed
Todd, Robert	400	A	150	6-26-1780	Nolin Cr	....
Todd, Robert	200	A	151	6-26-1780	Azariah Davis	Surveyed
Todd, Robert	300	B	49	6-17-1785	————	....
Toleafero, Peter	400	A	130	6-12-1780	Green R	....
Tom, Jacob	825	A	229	12-16-1782	Beech Fk	200 acres withdrawn
Tomlin, Wm	400	A	120	6- 1-1780	Cane Run	....
Tomlinson, Jesse	1,000	A	107	5-29-1780	N Fk Elkhorn	....
Tomlinson, Joseph	1,000	A	138	6-20-1780	Blue Lick Fk	....
Tompkins, John	500	A	93	5-24-1780	Licking	....
Toom, Jacob	625	A	280	6-20-1783	Cartright Cr	Surveyed
Tooms, Jacob	200	A	333	1-20-1784	Beech Fk	....
Topp, Roger	400	A	17	2-29-1780	Brashears Cr	....
Topp, Roger	1,000	A	101	5-26-1780	Brashears Cr	....
Towns, Oswell	400	A	8	1-17-1780	Hingston Fk	....
Towns, Oswell	1,000	A	28	4-27-1780	Hingston Fk	....
Townsend, John	400	A	10	2- 3-1780	Townsends Fk	....
Trabue, Daniel	400	A	119	6- 1-1780	Salt R	Surveyed
Trabue, James	600	A	96	5-25-1780	S Fk Licking	....
Trabue, James	500	A	97	5-25-1780	Fk Licking	....
Trabue, James	500	A	97	5-25-1780	Hingstons Fk	....
Trabue, James	1,000	A	97	5-25-1780	Fk Licking	....
Trabue, James	1,450	A	128	6- 8-1780	Mill Cr	....
Trabue, James	800	A	128	6- 8-1780	Dicks R	....
Trabue, John	1,000	A	127	6- 8-1780	Hickmans Cr	....
Trabue, John	2,000	A	128	6- 8-1780	near Riddle Sta	....
Trabue, John	200	A	169	9-15-1780	Dicks R	....
Trabue, John	200	A	171	9-15-1780	Licking Cr	....
Trabue, John Jr	400	A	127	6- 8-1780	Hickmans Cr	....
Trabue, Wm	1,000	A	128	6- 8-1780	S Fk Licking	....
Trabue, Wm	3,000	A	128	6- 8-1780	Mill Cr	....
Trassy, Samuel	500	A	263	2-15-1783	Rolling Fk	Surveyed
Travis, Edward	500	A	67	5-17-1780	Ohio R	....
Travis, Edward	1,000	A	67	5-17-1780	Brashears Cr	Surveyed
Travis, Edward	1,500	B	41	3- 4-1785	————	500 acres surveyed
Travis, Robert	500	A	212	6-21-1781	Pleasant Run	Surveyed
Travis, Robert	500	A	220	8-24-1781	Pleasant Run	Surveyed
Travis, Robert	500	A	225	12-13-1782	Ashes Cr	Withdrawn
Travis, Robert	1,000	A	281	6-27-1783	————	....
Travis, Robert	500	A	346	3-12-1784	Ashes Cr	....
Travis, Robert	500	A	346	3-12-1784	Ashes Cr	Withdrawn
Trener, James	1,000	A	269	3-28-1781	Beech Fk	....
Tribble, Andrew	500	A	114	5-30-1780	Howards Cr	....
Trigg, Stephen	400	A	14	2-19-1780	Harrods Cr	Surveyed

Entree	Acres	Book	Page	Entry Date	Watercourse	Notes
Trigg, Stephen	200	A	21	4–20–1780	Licking & Ohio R	Mil
Trigg, Stephen	1,000	A	64	5–17–1780	N Fk Elkhorn	....
Trigg, Stephen	2,000	A	64	5–17–1780	Elkhorn	....
Trigg, Stephen	400	A	65	5–17–1780	Brashears Cr	....
Trigg, Stephen	900	A	65	5–17–1780	Hammonds Cr	Surveyed
Trigg, Stephen	1,000	A	65	5–17–1780	Dicks R	Withdrawn
Trigg, Stephen	1,000	A	65	5–17–1780	Dicks R	Withdrawn
Trigg, Stephen	360	A	65	5–17–1780	Shawnee Run	
Trigg, Stephen	400	A	117	5–31–1780	N Fk Skeggs Cr	
Trigg, Stephen	400	A	117	5–31–1780	Skeggs Cr	....
Trigg, Stephen	1,000	A	117	5–31–1780	Harrods Cr	....
Trigg, Stephan	400	A	139	6–21–1780	Shawney Run	Surveyed
Trigg, Stephen	1,000	A	182	10–27–1780	Brashears Cr	....
Trigg, Stephen	591	A	182	10–27–1780	Dicks R	Surveyed
Trigg, Stephen	240	A	182	10–27–1780	Dicks R	
Trigg, Stephen	2,000	A	182	10–27–1780	Dicks R	....
Trigg, Stephan et al	200	A	33	4–29–1780	Pond Cr	Surveyed
Trigg, Stephen et al	400	A	7	1–10–1780	S Fk Elkhorn	
Triggs, John	250	A	198	3–19–1781	Coxes Cr	Withdrawn
Trimble, Wm	750	A	114	5–30–1780	Fk Howards Cr	
Triplett, Francis	1,000	A	103	5–27–1780	Rowling Fk	
Triplett, Francis	300	A	104	5–27–1780	Rowling Fk	
Triplett, Peter H	325	A	163	7–29–1780	Round Stone Cr	
Triplett, Reuben	1,000	A	103	5–27–1780	Rowling Fk	
Triplett, Reuben	1,000	A	112	5–30–1780	Green R	
Triplett, Simon	1,000	A	66	5–17–1780	N Fk Licking	
Triplett, Simon	500	A	66	5–17–1780	Beech Fk	Surveyed
Triplett, Simon	750	A	103	5–27–1780	Beech Fk	Surveyed
Triplett, Simon	292	A	103	5–27–1780	Beech Fk	Surveyed
Triplett, Simon	1,000	A	103	5–27–1780	Floyds Fk	Surveyed
Triplett, Simon	1,000	A	103	5–27–1780	Floyds Fk	Surveyed
Triplett, Simon	1,000	A	113	5–30–1780	Green R	....
Triplett, Simon	875	A	345	3–12–1784	———	....
Trotter, Joseph	1,254	A	245	12–28–1782	Beech Fk	
Trotter, Joseph	2,000	A	245	12–28–1782	Beech Fk	Surveyed
Trotter, Joseph	1,000	A	245	12–28–1782	Beech Fk	Surveyed
Trotter, Joseph	2,000	A	245	12–28–1782	Ohio R	
Trotter, Joseph	2,000	A	322	12–25–1783	Beech Fk	Amended
Trotter, Joseph	1,000	A	322	12–25–1783	Beech Fk	Amended
Trotter, Joseph	6,254	A	372	7–16–1784	———	300 acres surveyed
Troutman, John	400	A	138	6–20–1780	Plumb Cr	....
Troutman, John	1,948½	A	349	4–2–1784	Salt R	....
Troutman, Michael	560	A	102	5–27–1780	Ohio R	....
Troutman, Michal	400	A	111	5–29–1780	Ky R	....
Troutman, Michal	400	A	111	5–29–1780	Brashears Cr	Surveyed
Troutman, Michal	400	A	116	5–30–1780	Paint Lick Cr	
Troutman, Michal	400	A	125	6–5–1780	Floyds Fk	....
Troutman, Michael	200	A	126	6–7–1780	S Fk Clear Cr	
Troutman, Michael	500	A	126	6–7–1780	Beech Fk	Surveyed
Troutman, Michael	100	A	221	9–7–1781	———	Returned
True, Jacob	955	A	28	4–27–1780	Cane Run	....
True, James	350	A	64	5–17–1780	Dicks R	....
Truman, Edw	1,500	A	135	6–17–1780	Licking	....
Tucker, Travis	1,000	A	81	5–22–1780	Green R	....
Tucker, Drewery	1,051½	A	296	10–15–1783	Caseys Cr	....
Tumbles, Ben	500	A	137	6–20–1780	Coxes Cr	....
Tumbles, Ben	500	A	138	6–19–1780	Licking	....
Tune, Argillian	1,000	A	225	12–13–1782	Muddy Cr	....
Turner, George	2,000	A	228	12–14–1782	Green R	Surveyed
Turner, James	1,000	A	261	2–6–1783	Green R	
Turner, James	1,000	A	261	2–6–1783	Pittmans Cr	
Turner, James	1,000	A	261	2–6–1783	Green R	
Turner, James	1,000	A	261	2–6–1783	S Fk Rolling Fk	Withdrawn
Turner, James	1,000	A	261	2–6–1783	Rolling Fk	Withdrawn
Turner, James	1,000	A	261	2–6–1783	Green R	....
Turner, James	3,665	A	296	10–15–1783	Robinsons Cr	Withdrawn
Turner, James	1,000	A	317	12–15–1783	Rolling Fk	....
Turner, James	3,615	A	345	3–9–1784	Green R	....
Turner, James	1,115½	A	345	3–9–1784	Robinsons Cr	....
Turner, James	2,550	A	345	3–9–1784	Robinsons Cr	....
Turner, James	1,000	A	374	7–28–1784	Caseys Cr	....
Turner, James	1,000	A	374	7–28–1784	Rolling Fk	Withdrawn
Turner, Lewis E	500	A	62	5–16–1780	Stoners Fk	Withdrawn
Turner, Lewis E	500	A	80	5–20–1780	Stoners Fk	
Turner, Thomas	1,000	A	28	4–27–1780	Elkhorn	....
Turpin, Henry	600	A	59	5–16–1780	Ky R	....
Tutt, Wm	50	A	122	6–2–1780	Ohio	Mil
Tuttle, Chatwell	300	A	226	12–14–1782	Beach Fk	....
Tuttle, Moses	500	A	170	9–9–1780	Ky R	....
Tuttle, Moses	100	A	190	3–15–1781	Mill Cr	....
Tuttle, Moses	400	A	190	3–15–1781	Rowling Fk	Withdrawn

Entree	Acres	Book	Page	Entry Date	Watercourse	Notes
Tuttle, Moses	1,000	A	190	3–15–1781	Ky R	
Tuttle, Moses	2,000	A	208	5– 5–1781	Harrods Cr	
Tuttle, Moses	3,000	A	208	5– 5–1781	Harrods Cr	
Tuttle, Moses	400	A	208	5– 5–1781	Rowling Fk	
Tuttle, Moses	400	A	224	12–13–1782	Meatpen Cr	Withdrawn
Tuttle, Moses	900	A	225	12–13–1782	Meatpen Cr	Withdrawn
Tuttle, Moses	1,100	A	314	12–10–1783	Hardens Cr	Withdrawn
Tuttle, Moses	900	A	318	12–17–1783	————	Withdrawn
Tuttle, Moses	400	A	318	12–17–1783	Meat Pen Cr	
Tuttle, Moses	600	A	333	1–20–1784	Hardens Cr	
Tuttle, Moses	6,000	A	340	2–18–1784	Hardens Cr	
Tuttle, Moses	600	A	340	2–18–1784	Hardens Cr	Withdrawn
Tuttle, Moses	1,300	A	319	12–17–1783	Green R	
Twiman, George	400	A	282	7– 2–1783	Floyds Fk	Surveyed
Twiman, Reuben	500	A	78	5–20–1780	Jessamine Cr	
Twiman, Samuel	150	A	54	5–15–1780	Chaplins Fk	
Twiman, Wm	600	A	78	5–20–1780	Clear Cr	
Tyler, Charles	1,000	A	113	5–30–1780	Little Benson Cr	
Tyler, Edward	500	A	240	12–24–1782	Salt R	Surveyed
Tyler, Edward	503½	A	283	7–12–1783	Cinwith Run	Surveyed
Tyler, Edward	1,003½	A	370	7– 9–1784	————	500 acres surveyed
Tyler, Edmund et al	10,000	A	330	1–15–1784	Ohio R	
Tyler, James	1,000	A	111	5–29–1780	Ky R	Surveyed
Tyler, John	500	A	53	5–13–1780	Simpsons Cr	
Tyler, Robert	500	A	94	5–24–1780	Tick Cr	Surveyed
Tyler, Robert	400	A	213	7– 2–1781	Tick Cr	
Tyler, Robert	500	A	240	12–24–1782	Tick Cr	Withdrawn
Tyler, Robert	2,000	A	240	12–24–1782	Drennons Lick Cr	Surveyed
Tyler, Robert	200	A	248	1– 7–1782	Tick Cr	Surveyed
Tyler, Robert	300	A	248	1– 7–1783	Gesses Cr	767 acres surveyed
Tyler, Robert	200	A	284	8– 4–1783	Tick Cr	Withdrawn
Tyler, Robert	556	A	284	8– 4–1783	Clear Cr	Withdrawn
Tyler, Robert	500	A	284	8– 4–1783	Clear Cr	Withdrawn
Tyler, Robert	500	A	284	8– 4–1783	Clear Cr	Withdrawn
Tyler, Robert	1,556	A	367	6–22–1784	Harrods Cr	
Tyler, Robert	550	A	367	6–22–1784	Clear Cr	
Tyler, Robert	500	A	367	6–22–1784	Clear Cr	
Tyler, Robert	500	A	367	6–22–1784	Clear Cr	
Tyler, Robert	953	A	367	6–22–1784	Tick Cr	Withdrawn
Tyler, Robert	200	A	367	6–22–1784	Tick Cr	Withdrawn
Tyler, Robert	500	A	367	6–22–1784	Tick Cr	200 acres surveyed
Tyler, Robert	3,453	A	368	6–22–1784	————	2,200 acres surveyed
Tyler, Robert	953	A	369	7– 3–1784	Harrods Cr	
Tyler, Robert	953	A	369	7– 3–1784	Tick Cr	Withdrawn
Tyler, Robert	1,000	A	369	7– 3–1784	Beargrass Cr	Withdrawn
Tyler, Robert	7,000	A	369	7– 3–1784	Harrods Cr	
Tylor, Wm et al	3,000	A	284	7–27–1783	Pattons Cr	Surveyed
Underwood, George	2,000	A	45	5–11–1780	N Fk Elkhorn	
Underwood, George	1,000	A	252	1–13–1783	Rowling Fk	
Underwood, George	1,000	A	252	1–13–1783	Rowling Fk	Surveyed
Underwood, George	1,000	A	277	4–14–1783	Elliott settlement	
Underwood, Francis	1,000	A	45	5–11–1780	N Fk Elkhorn	
Underwood, John	1,000	A	179	10–17–1780	Sun Fish Cr	Surveyed
Underwood, Thomas	6,587½	A	239	12–23–1782	Floyds Fk	
Upshaw, Thomas	575	A	86	5–22–1780	Dry Cr	
Urquart, Walter	5,684	A	281	6–30–1783	Brush Cr	
Vansarsdalle, Lucas	7,409¼	A	259	2– 3–1783	Floyds Cr	Surveyed
Vance, David	1,000	A	37	4–29–1780	S Fk Elkhorn	
Vance. John	1,000	A	37	4–29–1780	S Fk Elkhorn	
Vance, John	1,000	A	120	6– 1–1780	Licking Cr	
Vanse, Wm	982½	A	251	1– 9–1783	Pleasant R	Surveyed
Vancleave, Benj	400	A	5	12– 7–1779	Brashears Cr	
Vancleave, Benj	1,000	A	36	4–29–1780	Clear Cr	Surveyed
Vanceleave, John	300	A	213	7– 2–1781	Bullskin Cr	
Vanmeter, Abraham	800	A	94	5–24–1780	Gists Cr	
Vanmeter, Abraham et al	500	A	180	10–21–1780	Drinnins Lick Cr	
Vanmeter, James	300	A	280	6–14–1783	Simpsons Cr	Surveyed
Vanmeter, Jacob	100	A	214	7– 3–1781	Billeys Cr	Surveyed
Vanmeter, Jacob	400	A	215	7–17–1781	Rock Cr	Withdrawn
Vanmeter, Jacob	400	A	215	7–17–1781	Rock Cr	Surveyed
Vanmeter, Jacob	400	A	226	12–13–1782	Green R	Withdrawn
Vanmeter, Jacob	1,000	A	233	12–19–1782	Cedar Cr	564 acres surveyed 400 acres withdrawn
Vanmeter, Jacob	400	A	235	12–20–1782	Green R	
Vanmeter, Jacob	400	A	235	12–20–1782	Green R	
Vanmeter, Jacob	238	A	244	12–27–1782	Cox Cr	Surveyed

Entree	Acres	Book	Page	Entry Date	Watercourse	Notes
Vanmeter, Jacob	1,000	A	253	1-14-1783	Salt R	Withdrawn
Vanmeter, Jacob	1,000	A	256	1-21-1728	Simpsons Cr	Withdrawn
Vanmeter, Jacob	400	A	257	1-25-1783	Panther Cr	Withdrawn
Vanmeter, Jacob	400	A	257	1-25-1783	Rock Cr	Withdrawn
Vanmeter, Jacob	1,000	A	263	2-15-1783	Simpsons Cr	Withdrawn
Vanmeter, Jacob	295	A	264	2-18-1783	Coxes Cr	
Vanmeter, Jacob	400	A	265	2-25-1783	N Fk Caney Cr	Surveyed
Vanmeter, Jacob	337	A	265	2-25-1783	Little Clifty Cr	Surveyed
Vanmeter, Jacob	400	A	265	2-25-1783	Panther Cr	Withdrawn
Vanmeter, Jacob	400	A	266	2-25-1783	N Fk Caney Cr	Surveyed
Vanmeter, Jacob	400	A	303	11-10-1783	Rolling Fk	
Vanmeter, Jacob	66	A	347	3-17-1784	Coxes Cr	Withdrawn
Vanmeter, Jacob	300	A	350	4-10-1784	Billys Cr	Surveyed
Vanmeter, Jacob	3,000	A	350	4-10-1784	Nolin Cr	Surveyed
Vanmeter, Jacob	2,675	A	351	4-10-1784	Panther Cr	
Vanmeter, Jacob	1,238	A	368	6-2-1784	———	600 acres surveyed
Vanmeter, Jacob	500	B	10	10-7-1784	Donitts Cr	
Vanmeter, Jacob	700	B	10	10-7-1784	Simpsons Cr	Withdrawn
Vanmeter, Jacob	500	B	17	11-15-1784	———	400 acres surveyed returned
Vanmeter, Jacob	3,275½	B	17	11-15-1784	———	600 acres surveyed
Vanmeter, Jacob	2,675	B	33	1-12-1785	———	Amended
Vanmeter, Jacob et al	400	A	265	2-19-1783	Bushes Cr	
Vanmeter, Solomon	500	A	52	5-13-1780	Doe Run	
Vanmeter, Solomon	1,000	A	52	5-13-1780	Harrods Cr	Withdrawn
Vanmeter, Solomon	500	A	52	5-13-1780	Harrods Cr	Surveyed
Vanmeter, Solomon	1,000	A	53	5-13-1780	Brashears Cr	
Vanmeter, Solomon	500	A	334	1-21-1784	Harrods Cr	Surveyed
Vanmeter, Solomon	1,000	A	346	3-12-1784	Ky R	Withdrawn
Vanmeter, Solomon	1,000	A	346	3-12-1784	Harrods Cr	Withdrawn
Vanmeter, Solomon	2,500	A	366	6-16-1784	———	500 acres surveyed
Vanmeter, Sllomon	1,000	B	26	12-13-1784	Drenning Lick Cr	Surveyed
Vanmeter, Solomon	1,000	B	26	12-13-1784	Ky R	
Vaughn, Andrew	200	A	254	1-16-1783	Coxes Cr	Surveyed
Vaughan, Andrew	300	A	263	2-15-1783	Ashes Cr	Surveyed
Vaughn, Andrew	600	A	321	12-18-1783	Salt R	Surveyed
Vaughn, Andrew	620½	A	327	1-5-1783	Salt R	
Vaughn, Andrew	100	A	332	1-19-1784	Rolling Cr	
Vaughn, Andrew	400	A	335	1-27-1784	Salt R	Surveyed
Vaughn, Andrew	200	A	334	1-21-1784	———	Returned
Vaughn, Andrew	1,416	B	5	9-7-1784	———	400 acres surveyed
Vaughn, James	1,500	A	234	12-19-1782	Rough Cr	
Vaughn, John	853	A	283	7-4-1783	Ohio R	
Vaughn, Robert	2,500	A	234	12-19-1782	Green R	Surveyed
Vaughn, Robert	5,000	A	261	2-8-1783	Hardens Cr	
Vaughn, Robert	5,000	A	360	5-14-1784	———	600 acres surveyed
Vaughan, Shad	1,333⅓	A	54	5-15-1780		
Veal, Thomas	400	A	126	6-5-1780	Hunters Trace	
Veech, John	1,000	A	373	7-23-1784	Beargrass Cr	Withdrawn
Veech, John et al	1,800	A	284	7-30-1783	Little Ky R	Surveyed
Veneble, Abraham B	1,000	A	303	11-11-1783	Little Ky R	
Vertrees, John	400	A	170	9-9-1780	Buffaloe Cr	Surveyed 77 acres withdrawn
Vertrees, John	200	A	202	4-2-1781	Green R	Withdrawn
Vertrees, John	600	A	202	4-2-1781	Green R	Surveyed 145 acres withdrawn
Vertrees, John	400	A	208	5-7-1781	Rowling Fk	Surveyed
Vertrees, John	100	A	218	8-8-1781	Mountain Cr	Withdrawn
Vertrees, John	322	A	218	8-8-1781	Mountain Cr	Withdrawn
Vertrees, John	422	A	241	12-25-1782	Short Cave Cr	400 acres surveyed
Vertrees, John	100	A	241	12-25-1782	Mountain Cr	
Vertrees, John	322	A	241	12-25-1782	Mountain Cr	
Vivion, John	1,550	A	114	5-30-1780	4 Mile Cr	
Virtreese, John	1,000	A	109	5-29-1780	Green R	Withdrawn
Virtreese, John	345	A	214	7-3-1781	Mountain Cr	Withdrawn
Voss, Edward	10,000	A	294	10-11-1783	Pattons Cr	Surveyed
Voss, Edward	5,000	A	294	10-11-1783	Pattons Cr	Surveyed
Voss, Edward	5,000	A	364	6-4-1784	Mill Cr	
Wadger, Thomas	400	A	200	3-26-1781	Simpsons Cr	
Wafford, John	200	A	90	5-23-1780	Nolin Cr	Surveyed
Wafford, John	600	A	90	5-23-1780	Simpsons Cr	Surveyed
Waford, John	400	A	149	6-24-1780	Brashears Cr	Surveyed
Waford, John	300	A	194	3-16-1781	Ohio R	Withdrawn

Entree	Acres	Book	Page	Entry Date	Watercourse	Notes
Waggoner, James	500	A	78	5–20–1780	Hickmans Cr	
Waide, Richard	400	A	9	1–18–1780	Lee's Cr	
Waits, Reuben, heirs	1,000	A	131	6–12–1780	———	
Wakeland, Wm C	800	A	89	5–23–1780	Ohio R	
Wakeland, Wm C	400	A	124	6– 3–1780	Fern Cr	
Walden, Ambrose	50	A	34	4–29–1780	Beech Fk	Mil
Walden, Ambrose	1,333	A	82	5–22–1780	Johnstons Fk	
Waldron, John	1,666¾	A	82	5–22–1780	Johnstons Cr	
Walker, Anthony et al	614	A	235	12–19–1782	Rough Cr	
Walker, Anthony et al	4,218¾	A	235	12–19–1782	Beaver Dam Cr	
Walker, Daniel	400	A	231	12–17–1782	Shawney Lick Cr	Surveyed
Walker, Daniel	1,000	A	231	12–17–1782	Simpsons Cr	Surveyed
Walker, Daniel	800	A	272	4– 3–1783	Not surveyed	Warrant returned
Walker, Daniel	1,495	A	276	4–10–1783	Falls Rough Cr	
Walker, Daniel	1,500	A	276	4–10–1783	Little Clifty Cr	
Walker, Daniel	1,000	A	278	4–14–1783	Ashes Cr	
Walker, Daniel	1,000	A	278	4–14–1783	Wolf Cr	
Walker, Daniel	1,000	A	278	4–14–1783	Wolf Cr	
Walker, Joel	400	A	11	2– 3–1780	Muddy Cr	
Walker, Joel	500	A	115	5–30–1780	Muddy Cr	
Walker, Joel	500	A	115	5–30–1780	Muddy Cr	
Walker, John	977	A	48	5–12–1780	Cartright Cr	Surveyed
Walker, John	600	A	79	5–20–1780	Hardins Cr	Wthdrawn
Walker, John	600	A	140	6–21–1780	Ohio R	Surveyed
Walker, John	2,000	A	307	11–20–1783	Big Clifty Cr	Surveyed
Walker, Merry	2,000	A	157	6–30–1780	Licking	
Walker, Wm	400	A	11	2– 3–1780	Mouth Red R	
Walker, Wm	4,000	A	157	6–30–1780	Licking	
Walker, Wm	2,307½	A	331	1–17–1784	Bear Cr	
Walker, Wm, heirs	1,000	A	118	6– 1–1781	Ky R	
Wall, Thomas	150	A	343	3– 3–1784	Floyds Fk	
Wallace, Adam	400	A	16	2–25–1780	Gilberts Cr	
Wallace, Caleb	1,000	A	40	5– 9–1780	Cave Run	
Wallace, Caleb	500	A	269	3–28–1783	Beech Fk	100 acres surveyed 400 acres withdrawn
Wallace, Caleb	500	A	269	3–28–1783	Beech Fk	Surveyed
Wallace, Caleb	1,000	A	269	3–28–1783	Beech Fk	
Wallace, Caleb	4,000	A	307	11–22–1783	Bear Cr	Withdrawn
Wallace, Caleb	2,000	A	307	11–22–1783	Bear Cr	Withdrawn
Wallace, Caleb	750	A	307	11–22–1783	Bear Cr	
Wallace, Caleb	400	A	331	1–17–1784	Ohio R	Surveyed
Wallace, Caleb	400	A	331	1–17–1784	Goose Cr	Withdrawn
Wallace, Caleb	400	A	337	2–11–1784	Ohio R	Withdrawn
Wallace, Caleb	400	A	359	5– 8–1784	Hardens Cr	
Wallace, Caleb	500	A	359	5– 7–1784	Beech Fk	Withdrawn
Wallace, Caleb	6,000	B	35	1–26–1785	———	Withdrawn
Wallace, Caleb	1,000	B	41	3– 4–1785		
Wallace, Samuel	500	A	87	5–23–1780	Boons Mile Cr	
Wallace, Samuel	30	A	238	12–21–1782	Naked Barrens	
Wallace, Samuel	567	A	238	12–21–1782	Hardens Cr	Surveyed
Wallace, Samuel	500	A	249	1– 8–1783	Harlens Cr	Surveyed
Wallace, Samuel	765	A	336	2– 4–1784	Salt R	
Wallace, Samuel	2,106	A	336	2– 4–1784	Salt R	
Wallace, Samuel	30	B	43	4–15–1785		
Waller, John	1,000	B	20	11–26–1784	Cartright Cr	
Waller, Joseph	400	A	7	1–10–1780	Sinking Cr.s	
Waller, Wm Ed	200	A	84	5–22–1780	Buck Lick Cr	
Wallis, James	400	A	18	3– 1–1780	Hardins Cr	
Walls, George	400	A	261	2–11–1783	12MilesOhioFalls.	Surveyed
Walls, George	2,000	A	315	12–15–1783	Salt R	
Walls, George	2,000	A	367	6–22–1784	Big Ky R	
Walters, Francis	1,035½	A	315	12–13–1783	Green R	
Walton, Edward	1,000	A	27	4–26–1780	Huston Fk	
Walton, Edward	1,000	A	27	4–26–1780	Huston Fk	
Walton, Edward	1,000	A	44	5–11–1780	Hustons Fk	
Walton, George	1,818	A	249	1– 8–1783	Green R	Surveyed
Walton, George	2,382	A	249	1– 8–1783	Green R	Surveyed
Walton, George	2,382¾	A	339	2–14–1784	———	
Walton, John	1,500	A	234	12–19–1782	Rough Cr	
Walton, John	1,279	A	369	7– 1–1784	Harrods Cr	
Walton, Josiah	700	B	4	9– 7–1784	———	Withdrawn
Walton, Josiah	500	B	4	9– 7–1784	———	Withdrawn
Walton, Josiah	1,200	B	5	9– 7–1784	Green R	
Walton, Matthew	3,000	A	230	12–17–1782	Lynn Camp Cr	Withdrawn
Walton, Matthew	1,000	A	230	12–17–1782	Boiling Springs Cr	Withdrawn
Walton, Matthew	150	A	239	12–23–1782	Bacon Run	Surveyed
Walton, Matthew	150	A	239	12–23–1782	Bacon Cr	Surveyed

Entree	Acres	Book	Page	Entry Date	Watercourse	Notes
Walton, Matthew.....	300	A	239	12–23–1782	Nole Linn Cr.......	Surveyed 45 acres withdrawn
Walton, Matthew.....	400	A	239	12–23–1782	Nole Linn Cr.....	Surveyed
Walton, Matthew.....	200	A	239	12–23–1782	Cane Run..........	Surveyed
Walton, Matthew.....	400	A	239	12–23–1782	Cane Run..........	Surveyed
Walton, Matthew....	1,200	A	239	12–23–1782	Little Clifty Cr.....	Surveyed
Walton, Matthew....	6,500	A	239	12–23–1782	Drennons Lick Cr..	....
Walton, Matthew.....	700	A	257	1–25–1783	Rough Cr..........	Surveyed
Walton, Matthew.....	5,028	A	261	2– 8–1783	Hardens Cr........	Surveyed
Walton, Matthew.....	1,000	A	269	3–28–1783	Cartrights Cr......	Surveyed
Walton, Matthew.....	14	A	269	3–28–1783	Bacon Cr..........	Surveyed
Walton, Matthew.....	63	A	269	3–28–1783	Bacon Cr..........	....
Walton, Matthew.....	45	A	269	3–28–1783	————	Withdrawn
Walton, Matthew.....	200	A	269	3–28–1783	Little Caney Cr....	Surveyed
Walton, Matthew.....	421	A	269	3–28–1783	Bacon Cr..........	Surveyed
Walton, Matthew.....	300	A	269	3–28–1783	Little Caney Cr....	Surveyed
Walton, Matthew.....	200	A	269	3–28–1783	S Fk Beacon Cr....	Surveyed
Walton, Matthew.....	425	A	269	3–28–1783	Linn Camp Cr.....	404 acres surveyed
Walton, Matthew.....	730	A	269	3–28–1783	Linn Camp Cr.....	Surveyed
Walton, Matthew.....	704	A	269	3–28–1783	N Fk Caney Cr....	Surveyed
Walton, Matthew.....	1,400	A	269	3–28–1783	Bear Cr..........	....
Walton, Matthew.....	1,000	A	270	3–28–1783	Pleasant Run.....	Surveyed
Walton, Matthew.....	1,000	A	271	3–28–1783	Cartright Cr.......	....
Walton, Matthew.....	5,000	A	272	4– 3–1783	————	Warrant returned
Walton, Matthew.....	3,562	A	272	4– 3–1783	118 acres surveyed..	Warrant returned
Walton, Matthew.....	2,000	A	278	4–14–1783	————	Treas warrant
Walton, Matthew....	9,415	A	286	8–12–1783	Rough Cr..........	....
Walton, Matthew....	3,000	A	286	8–12–1783	Green R..........	Withdrawn
Walton, Matthew....	1,000	A	286	8–12–1786	Boiling Springs.....	Withdrawn
Walton, Matthew....	2,000	A	287	8–12–1783	Rough Cr..........	....
Walton, Matthew....	2,000	A	311	12– 1–1783	Beech Fk..........	Surveyed
Walton, Matthew....	2,00	A	320	12–18–1783	Beech Fk..........	Surveyed
Walton, Matthew....	2,000	A	320	12–18–1783	Beech Fk..........	Surveyed
Walton, Matthew....	1,000	A	320	12–18–1783	Beech Fk..........	Surveyed
Walton, Matthew....	11,300	A	320	12–17–1783	Clear Fk..........	....
Walton, Matthew....	500	A	327	1– 5–1784	Beech Fk..........	....
Walton, Matthew....	500	A	327	1– 3–1784	Beech Fk..........	....
Walton, Matthew....	2,000	A	327	1– 3–1784	Beech Fk..........	....
Walton, Matthew....	1,500	A	328	1– 9–1784	Cartright Cr.......	Surveyed
Walton, Matthew....	20,000	A	333	1–21–1784	Salt R.............	....
Walton, Matthew....	155	A	334	1–27–1784	Cartright Cr.......	....
Walton, Matthew....	1,000	A	334	1–23–1784	Hardens Cr........	....
Walton, Matthew....	2,000	A	334	1–23–1784	Salt R.............	Surveyed
Walton, Matthew....	757	A	335	1–27–1784	Rock Lick Cr......	Surveyed
Walton, Matthew....	500	A	337	2–11–1784	Beech Fk..........	....
Walton, Matthew....	115	A	337	2–11–1784	Beech Fk..........	....
Walton, Matthew....	250	A	337	2–11–1784	Cartright Cr.......	....
Walton, Matthew....	300	A	337	2–11–1784	Hardens Cr........	....
Walton, Matthew....	1,000	A	342	2–27–1784	Cartright Cr.......	....
Walton, Matthew....	600	A	345	3– 9–1784	Beech Fk..........	....
Walton, Matthew....	170	A	347	3–22–1784	Blackford Cr.......	Surveyed
Walton, Matthew....	1,000	A	347	3–22–1784	Salt R.............	Amended
Walton, Matthew....	1,940	A	358	5– 7–1784	Rolling Fk........	Surveyed
Walton, Matthew....	200	A	359	5– 8–1784	Beech Fk..........	....
Walton, Matthew....	1,500	A	359	5– 8–1784	Hardens Cr........	....
Walton, Matthew....	1,000	A	359	5– 8–1784	Hardens Cr........	....
Walton, Matthew....	5,028	A	360	5–14–1784	————	Surveyed
Walton, Matthew....	1,000	A	360	5–14–1784	————	Amended
Walton, Matthew....	2,000	A	361	5–25–1784	Pittmans Cr.......	Surveyed
Walton, Matthew....	7,000	A	361	5–22–1784	Cumberland Trace.	....
Walton, Matthew....	6,760	A	362	5–26–1784	————	....
Walton, Matthew....	9,000	A	362	5–26–1784	————	1,940 acres surveyed
Walton, Matthew....	18,357	A	362	5–26–1784	————	....
Walton, Matthew....	30,000	A	362	5–26–1784	————	5,757 acres surveyed
Walton, Matthew....	4,000	A	362	5–26–1784	————	2,000 acres surveyed
Walton, Matthew....	500	A	362	5–26–1784	————	....
Walton, Matthew....	625	A	375	7–29–1784	————	Amended
Walton, Matthew et al	400	A	254	1–17–1783	Cane Run.........	Withdrawn
Walton, Matthew et al	300	A	259	1–29–1783	Beech Fk.........	Withdrawn
Walton, Matthew et al	4,023	A	261	2– 6–1783	Beech Fk.........	Surveyed
Walton, Matthew et al	2,000	A	261	2– 8–1783	Beech Fk.........	Surveyed
Walton, Matthew et al	1,400	A	261	2– 8–1783	Beech Fk..........	150 acres withdrawn
Walton, Matthew et al	600	A	267	2–28–1783	Beech Fk..........	Withdrawn

Entree	Acres	Book	Page	Entry Date	Watercourse	Notes
Walton, Matthew et al	150	A	269	3-28-1783	Beech Fk	
Walton, Matthew et al	600	A	269	3-28-1783	Mill Cr	Withdrawn
Walton, Matthew et al	300	A	269	3-28-1783	Stewart Cr	Withdrawn
Walton, Matthew et al	400	A	269	3-28-1783	Cane Run	
Walton, Matthew et al	6,000	A	272	4- 3-1783	———	832 acres surveyed warrant returned
Walton, Matthew et al	12,000	A	312	12- 4-1783	Chaplins Fk	2,650 acres withdrawn
Walton, Matthew et al	2,650	B	44	4-25-1785	———	Withdrawn
Walton, Robert	1,000	A	44	5-11-1780	Otter Cr	
Walton, Thomas	1,000	A	44	5-11-1780	Calaway settlement	
Wanant, Thomas	500	A	99	5-25-1780	Otter Cr	
Ward, Lewis	325	A	164	7-29-1780	Round Stone Cr	
Ward, Wm	100	A	20	4-17-1780	S Fk Elkhorn	Mil
Ward, Wm	2,000	A	21	4-20-1780	Wells Br	Mil
Ware, Edward	482	A	167	8-17-1780	Robinsons Cr	
Ware, Edward	482	A	167	8-17-1780	Robinsons Cr	
Ware, Isaac	250	A	30	4-28-1780	Ky R	Mil
Ware, Isaac	50	A	122	6- 2-1780	Ohio R	Mil
Ware, James	1,000	A	133	6-15-1780	Licking Cr	
Ware, James	500	A	136	6-17-1780	Dicks R	
Ware, James	1,500	A	149	6-24-1780	Mid Fk Licking	
Ware, Robert	100	A	22	4-22-1780	N Fk White Oak Cr	Mil
Ware, Robert	1,000	A	183	10-27-1780	Green R	Surveyed
Ware, Robert	100	A	267	3-28-1783	Sinking Cr	Surveyed
Ware, Robert	479½	A	270	3-28-1783	Green R	Surveyed
Ware, Wm	500	A	255	1-20-1783	N Fk Rowling Fk	Surveyed
Warford, John	800	A	164	8-11-1780	Rowling Fk	200 acres withdrawn
Warford, John	400	A	164	8-11-1780	Green R	Surveyed
Warford, John	300	A	205	4- 5-1781	Limestone	Withdrawn
Warford, John	100	A	210	6- 5-1781	Green R	Withdrawn
Warford, John	200	A	218	8- 8-1781	Rowling Fk	Surveyed
Warford, John	100	A	221	11- 9-1782	Nole Lynn	
Warford, John	300	A	221	11- 9-1782	Nole Lynn	Withdrawn
Warford, John	400	A	225	12-13-1782	Short Cr	Surveyed
Warford, John	600	A	334	1-21-1784	———	
Warford, John	1,000	A	348	3-23-1784	———	400 acres returned
Warford, Moses	———	A	370	7- 6-1784	Brashears Cr	240 acres surveyed
Warrant, Wm	1,000	A	128	6- 8-1780	Clark Run	
Warren, James	200	A	33	4-29-1780	Dicks R	Mil
Warren, James	4,000	A	276	4-12-1783	Floyd Fk	Surveyed
Warren, Wm	592	A	321	12-18-1783	Youngers Cr	Surveyed
Warren, Wm	850	A	335	1-27-1784	Nole Linn	Withdrawn
Warren, Wm	500	A	335	1-27-1784	Green R	Withdrawn
Warren, Wm	1,087	A	350	4-10-1784	Nolelinn Cr	Surveyed
Warren, Wm	1,087	A	350	4-10-1784	Nolelinn Cr	Surveyed
Warren, Wm	300	A	362	5-27-1784	Youngers Cr	Surveyed
Warren, Wm	370	A	362	5-27-1784	Younger Cr	250 acres surveyed
Warren, Wm	680	A	362	5-27-1784	Nole Linn Cr	Surveyed
Warren, Wm	850	A	362	5-27-1784	Nole Linn Cr	Withdrawn
Warren, Wm	500	A	362	5-27-1784	Green R	Withdrawn
Washington, Warner	1,000	A	330	1-15-1784	Floyds Fk	
Waters, Phillemon	325	A	219	8-14-1781	Cartrights Cr	Withdrawn
Waters, Phillemon	325	A	220	8-29-1781	Cartrights Cr	
Waters, Phillemon	175	A	224	12-12-1782	Soverins Run	
Waters, Phillemon	150	A	224	12-12-1782	Cartright Cr	
Waters, Phillemon	425	A	351	4-10-1784	Cartright Cr	
Waters, Phillemon	400	A	372	7-21-1784	Beech Fk	
Waters, Phillemon	300	A	372	7-21-1784	Soverins Valley	
Watkins, Edward	600	A	97	5-25-1780	Licking	
Watkins, George	1,000	A	169	9- 9-1780	Yellow Cr	
Watkins, Henry	1,500	A	154	6-27-1780	Elkhorn	
Watkins, Isham	400	A	159	7- 5-1780	Elkhorn	Withdrawn
Watkins, Isham	400	A	185	10-31-1780	Hardens Cr	Surveyed
Watkins, John	800	A	49	5-12-1780	Dicks R	
Watkins, John	600	A	249	1- 8-1783	Hardens Cr	
Watkins, John	3,500	A	263	2-15-1783	———	
Watkins, John	500	A	297	10-20-1783	Panther & Green	
Watkins, John	3,400	A	320	12-18-1783	Parker & Phillips sta	
Watkins, Joseph	1,750	A	28	4-27-1780	Elkhorn	Mil
Watkins, Joseph	600	A	34	4-29-1780	Licking	Mil
Watkins, Joseph	400	A	97	5-25-1780	S Fk Licking	
Watkins, Samuel	400	A	236	12-20-1782	Cane Run	Surveyed
Watkins, Thomas	100	A	33	4-29-1780	———	
Watkins, Thomas	200	A	34	4-29-1780	Licking	Mil
Watkins, Wm	400	A	168	8-17-1780	Sugar Cr	

Entree	Acres	Book	Page	Entry Date	Watercourse	Notes
Watkins, Wm	300	A	168	8-17-1780	Dicks R	
Watkins, Wm	400	A	168	8-17-1780	Scotts Premption	
Watkins, Wm	410	A	339	2-14-1784	North&BennettsFk	Surveyed
Watkins, Wm	190	A	342	3- 3-1784	Caney Fk	Surveyed
Watkins, Wm	1,000	A	343	3- 3-1784		
Watson, David	930¾	A	322	12-22-1783	Rolling Fk	
Watson, Henry	400	A	287	8-16-1783	Camp Run	
Watson, Josiah	300	A	228	12-16-1782	Mill Cr	
Watson, Josiah	850	A	228	12-16-1782	Simpsons Cr	Surveyed
Watson, Josiah	600	A	228	12-16-1782	Simpsons Cr	Surveyed
Watson, Josiah	500	A	228	12-16-1782		Withdrawn
Watson, Josiah	400	A	228	12-16-1782	Cartright Cr	
Watson, Josiah	1,000	A	228	12-16-1782	Cartright Cr	
Watson, Josiah	400	A	228	12-16-1782	Cartrights Cr	Surveyed
Watson, Josiah	500	A	228	12-16-1782	Cartright Cr	Surveyed
Watson, Josiah	700	A	228	12-14-1782	Beech Fk	Withdrawn
Watson, Josiah	400	A	229	12-16-1782	Harrods Cr	
Watson, Josiah	400	A	229	12-16-1782	Meatpen Cr	
Watson, Josiah	1,000	A	229	12-16-1782	Harrods Cr	
Watson, Josiah	1,600	A	229	12-16-1782	Drennons Lick Cr	Withdrawn
Watson, Josiah	650	A	229	12-16-1782	Breashear Cr	
Watson, Josiah	1,200	A	229	12-16-1782	Brashears Cr	Withdrawn
Watson, Josiah	1,200	A	229	12-16-1782	Brashears Cr	Withdrawn
Watson, Josiah	550	A	229	12-16-1782	18 Mile Cr	Surveyed
Watson, Josiah	550	A	229	12-16-1782	18 Mile Cr	Surveyed
Watson, Josiah	500	A	229	12-16-1782	18 Mile Cr	Surveyed
Watson, Josiah	4,000	A	322	12-22-1783	Pottengers Cr	
Watson, Josiah	1,600	A	322	12-22-1783		Withdrawn
Watson, Josiah	1,200	A	322	12-22-1783	Brashears Cr	Withdrawn
Watson, Josiah	1,200	A	322	12-22-1783	Brashears Cr	Withdrawn
Watson, Wm	400	A	57	5-15-1780	Ky R	
Watson, Wm	955	A	57	5-15-1780	Ky R	
Wawmack, Mass	1,236	A	303	11-11-1783	Little Ky R	
Weathers, James	200	A	118	6- 1-1780	Ky R	
Weathers, James	600	A	118	6- 1-1780	Ky R	
Weathers, Wm	2,000	A	375	7-29-1784	Harrods Cr	
Webb, Augustine	2,000	A	227	12-14-1782	Drennns Lick	Surveyed
Webb, C R	1,000	A	117	5-31-1780	Mid Fk Licking	
Webb, C W	600	A	117	5-31-1780	Cabbin Cr	
Webb, Forest	500	A	39	5- 9-1780	Upper Blue Lick	
Webb, George	6,000	A	81	5-22-1780	Green R	
Webb, John Vivan	1,000	A	227	12-14-1782	Clifty Cr	Surveyed
Webb, John Vivan	1,000	A	227	12-14-1782	Sinking Cr	Surveyed
Webb, R C	1,430	A	117	5-31-1780	Licking Cr	
Webb, R C	1,025	A	117	5-31-1780	Cabbin Cr	
Webb, R C	1,250	A	122	6- 2-1780	Ohio R	
Webb, Wm	950	A	116	5-31-1780	Licking	
Webb, Wm	2,000	A	116	5-31-1780	Stoners Fk	
Webb, Wm	1,000	A	116	5-31-1780	Middle Fk	
Webb, Wm	1,250	A	117	5-31-1780	Cabbins Cr	
Webb, Wm	1,000	A	117	5-31-1780	Blue Lick	
Webb, Wm	1,450	A	138	6-20-1780	Flatt Cr	
Webb, Wm	3,000	A	232	12-18-1783	Drennons Lick	Surveyed
Webb, Wm C	1,715	A	247	1- 7-1783	Barren Cr	Surveyed
Weeble, Wm	325	A	199	3-22-1781	Coxes Cr	Surveyed
Weeden, Charles	4,000	A	85	5-22-1780	Ohio R	
Weeden, Gen George	1,000	A	153	6-26-1780	Salt R	
Weedon, Gen George	2,000	A	153	6-26-1780	Beech Fk	
Weedon, Gen George	244½	A	330	1-15-1784	Floyds Fk	
Weible, John	250	A	184	10-30-1780	Cartrights Cr	
Weiseger, Joseph	1,890	A	357	4-29-1784	Salt R	Withdrawn
Weisegar, Joseph	1,890	A	371	7-12-1784	Rolling Fk	
Weisegar, Joseph	1,890	A	371	7-12-1784		Withdrawn
Weiseger, Joseph	1,890	B	7	9-20-1784		Amended
Weiseger, Joseph	1,890	B	43	4-11-1785		
Weist, Henry	800	A	125	6- 5-1780	Knob Lick	Surveyed
Weist, Henry	400	A	125	6- 5-1780	Licks from Falls	
Weist, Henry	400	A	125	6- 5-1780	Hammonds Cr	
Welch, James	1,000	A	83	5-22-1780	Licking	Surveyed
Welch, Jane	500	A	259	2- 1-1783	Panther Cr	
Welch, John	300	A	106	5-27-1780	Slate Cr	
Welch, John	300	A	106	5-27-1780	Salt R	Surveyed
Welch, John	300	A	106	5-27-1780	Floyds Fk	Surveyed
Welch, John	300	A	106	5-27-1780	Floyds Fk	Withdrawn
Welch, John	300	A	208	4-19-1781	Floyds Fk	Surveyed
Welch, John	300	A	208	4-19-1781	Floyds Fk	
Welch, John	1,200	A	369	7- 1-1784		300 acres surveyed
Welch, Wm	1,000	A	273	4- 7-1783	Caney Cr	Surveyed
Welford, Robert	1,000	A	224	12-12-1782	Fishpool Cr	
Welford, Robert	2,091	A	242	12-25-1782	N E Fk Panther Cr	Surveyed
Welford, Robert	1,000	A	242	12-25-1782	N E Fk Panther Cr	Surveyed

Entree	Acres	Book	Page	Entry Date	Watercourse	Notes
Well, Samuel	500	A	178	10-10-1780	Licking	
Well, Samuel	500	A	178	10-10-1780	Sulphur Cr	Surveyed
Well, Samuel	500	A	178	10-10-1780	Sulphur Cr	
Well, Samuel	500	A	178	10-10-1780	Beargrass Cr	Withdrawn
Wellford, Robert	5,000	A	167	8-17-1780	Green R	Withdrawn
Wellford, Robert	1,000	A	190	3-15-1781	Green R	Surveyed
Wellford, Robert	3,000	A	190	3-15-1781	N E Fk Panther Cr	Surveyed
Wellford, Robert	5,000	A	190	3-15-1781	Panther Cr	
Wells, Samuel	500	A	178	10-10-1780	S Fk Beargrass Cr	
Wells, Samuel	200	A	190	3-15-1781	Grove in Barrens	
Wells, Samuel	210	A	190	3-15-1781	Salt R	
Wells, Samuel	600	A	190	3-15-1781	Salt R	
Wells, Samuel	150	A	191	3-15-1781	Grove Timber	
Wells, Samuel	300	A	264	2-15-1783	Rolling Fk	
Wells, Samuel	1,853	A	264	2-15-1783	Floyds Cr	Surveyed
Wells, Samuel	500	A	247	1- 6-1783	Beargrass Cr	
Wells, Samuel	500	A	248	1- 7-1783	Beargrass Cr	
Wells, Samuel	500	A	371	7-12-1783	Clear Cr	Surveyed
Wells, Samuel	2,500	B	45	5-26-1785	————	500 acres surveyed
Wells, Samuel	600	A	365	6-12-1784	————	
Welten, John	400	A	152	6-26-1780	Rowling Fk	
Werble, John	250	B	47	6-14-1785	————	
West, Charles	400	A	49	5-12-1780	Floyds Fk	
West, Charles	1,000	A	49	5-12-1780	Salt R	
West, Charles	600	A	49	5-12-1780	Salt R	
West, Charles	2,000	A	104	5-27-1780	Long Lick Cr	
West, Edward	200	A	166	8-11-1780	Green R	Withdrawn
West, Edward	200	A	208	4-18-1781	Panther Cr	
West, John	217	B	47	5-26-1785	————	
West, John	217	A	250	1- 9-1783	Pattons Line	90 acres surveyed
Westcoat, George	10,000	A	352	4-15-1784	Salt R	Surveyed
Wescot, George	10,000	A	352	4-15-1784	Thomas Middleton	Withdrawn
Wescott, George	10,000	A	325	12-31-1783	Knobb Cr	Withdrawn
Westerville, James	400	A	140	6-21-1780	Silver Cr	
Whaley, James	983	A	53	5-15-1780	————	
Whaley, James	1,500	A	76	5-19-1780	N Fk Licking	
Whalley, Wm	295	A	43	5-11-1780	Hingston Fk	
Wheeler, Luke	3,125	B	20	11-26-1784	Salt R	Surveyed
Wheeler, Moses	50	A	32	4-28-1780	Drowning Cr	
Whitacre, Aquilla	200	A	183	10-30-1780	Cedar Cr	178 acres surveyed 22 acres withdrawn
Whitacre, Aquilla	600	A	183	10-30-1780	Brashears Cr	460 acres surveyed
Whitacre, Aquilla	1,000	A	183	10-30-1780	Brashears Cr	Surveyed
Whitaker, Aquilla et al	1,000	A	183	10-30-1780	Fox Run	Surveyed
Whitaker, Isaac	400	A	77	5-20-1780	Ky R	Withdrawn
Whitaker, Isaac	400	A	148	6-24-1780	Brashears Cr	Withdrawn
Whitaker, Isaac	400	A	208	4-30-1781	Brashears Cr	
Whitaker, John	200	A	188	3-15-1781	Cedar Cr	Surveyed
Whitaker, John	300	A	188	3-15-1781	Clear Cr	
Whitaker, John	200	A	208	4-30-1781	Cedar Cr	
Whitaker, John	250	A	211	6- 5-1781	Cedar Cr	Withdrawn
Whitaker, John	150	A	218	8- 9-1781	Coxes Cr	Surveyed
Whitaker, John	60	A	256	1-24-1783	His 300 acres	Surveyed
Whitaker, John	20	A	256	1-24-1783	His 300 acres	Withdrawn
Whitaker, John	250	A	256	1-24-1783	————	Withdrawn
Whitaker, John	22	A	265	2-21-1783	Cedar Cr	
Whitaker, John	22	A	265	2-24-1783	Joining Knobbs	Withdrawn
Whitaker, John	250	A	334	1-26-1784	————	
Whitaker, John	340	A	335	1-27-1784	————	
Whitaker, John	300	A	335	1-27-1784	Cedar Cr	150 acres surveyed
Whitaker, John	300	A	335	1-27-1784	Cedar Cr	
Whitaker, John	600	A	375	7-29-1784	————	
Whitaker, John	100	B	11	11- 8-1784	Cedar Cr	
Whitaker, John	50	B	11	11- 8-1784	Cedar Cr	
Whitaker, John	150	B	11	11- 8-1784	Cedar Cr	Withdrawn
White, Anthony W	10,000	A	234	12-19-1782	Bear Cr	Surveyed
White, Anthony W	15,000	A	235	12-19-1782	Caney Cr	Surveyed
White, Anthony W	5,000	A	235	12-19-1782	Rough Cr	
White, Anthony W	10,000	A	325	12-29-1783	Bear Cr	Surveyed
White, David	412	A	373	7-26-1784	Pittmans Cr	
White, Elias	200	A	29	4-27-1780	————	
White, John	50	A	29	4-27-1780	Stoner Fk	Mil
White, John	808	A	311	11-28-1783	Panther Cr	
White, Moses	200	A	31	4-28-1780	Ky R	Withdrawn
White, Moses	50	A	31	4-28-1780	Ky R	Mil
White, Moses	100	A	221	10- 1-1781	Ky R	

Entree	Acres	Book	Page	Entry Date	Watercourse	Notes
White, Moses	100	A	221	10- 1-1781	Ky R	Withdrawn
White, Moses	500	A	303	11-12-1783	Bullitts Lick	....
White, Moses	500	A	321	12-18-1783	In Barrens	....
White, Moses	500	A	321	12-18-1783	Doe Run	....
White, Wm	400	A	16	2-24-1780	Harrods Cr	....
White, Wm	1,000	A	157	6-30-1780	Lulbergrud	....
Whitehead, John	665½	A	293	10- 3-1783	Hardens Cr	....
Whiteledge, Thomas	600	A	311	11-29-1783	Floyds Fk	400 acres withdrawn
Whiteledge, Thomas	1,260	A	346	3-12-1784	———	....
Whiteledge, Thomas	1,000	A	353	4-15-1784	Coxes Cr	....
Whiteledge, Thomas	100	A	375	7-29-1784	Coxes Cr	....
Whiteledge, Thomas	300	B	11	11- 8-1784	Brashears Cr	....
Whiteledge, Thomas	3,400	B	49	6-17-1785	———	....
Whiteledge, John	500	A	198	3-19-1781	Coxes Cr	Surveyed
Whitledge, John	1,000	A	260	2- 3-1783	Beech Fk	....
Whitledge, Robt	400	A	12	2- 5-1780	Coopers Run	....
Whitledge, Thomas	400	A	12	2- 5-1780	Coopers Run	....
Whitledge, Thomas	250	A	236	12-20-1782		....
Whitledge, Thomas	400	A	236	12-20-1782	W Fk Coxes Cr	Surveyed
Whitledge, Thomas	300	A	258	1-27-1783	Cartright Cr	....
Whitledge, Thomas	310	A	277	4-14-1783	Hardens Cr	Surveyed
Whitledge, Thomas	1,000	A	298	10-25-1783	Salt R	....
Whitledge, Thomas	500	A	304	11-14-1783	Coxes Cr	....
Whitledge, Thomas	400	A	375	7-29-1784	Floyds Fk	....
Whitley, Wm	400	A	3	11-11-1779	Cedar Cr	....
Whitley, Wm	400	A	13	2- 9-1780	Dicks R	Surveyed
Whitley, Wm	500	A	26	4-26-1780	Whitley Sta	....
Whitley, Wm	400	A	27	4-26-1780	Whitley Sta	....
Whitley, Wm	500	A	27	4-26-1780	Whitley Sta	....
Whittaker, Aquilla	800	A	77	5-20-1780	Brashears Cr	Withdrawn
Whittaker, Aquilla	2,070	A	321	12-18-1783	Cedar Cr	....
Whittaker, Elisha	400	A	77	5-20-1780	Ky R	....
Whittaker, Jesse	480	A	77	5-20-1780	Ky R	....
Whittaker, John	150	A	211	6- 5-1781	Cedar Cr	Surveyed
Whittaker, John	22	A	321	12-18-1783	———	....
Whittaker, John	22	A	321	12-18-1783	Cedar Cr	Withdrawn
Whittaker, John	220	A	372	7-17-1784		273 acres surveyed
Wickliff, Aaronton	200	A	76	5-19-1780	Beech Fk	....
Wickliff, Aranton	500	A	209	5-29-1781	Simpsons Cr	Surveyed
Wickliff, Aaronton	2,000	A	373	7-24-1784	———	500 acres surveyed
Wickliff, Charles	400	A	76	5-19-1780	Cartrights Cr	....
Wickliff, Martin	400	A	76	5-19-1780	Cartright Cr	....
Wickliff, Martin	400	A	209	5-29-1781	Cartrights Cr	Withdrawn
Wickliff, Martin	400	A	216	7-26-1781	Robert Wickliff	....
Wickliff, Martin	400	A	216	7-26-1781	Cartrights Cr	Withdrawn
Wickliff, Martin	1,000	A	226	12-14-1782	Drennings Lick Cr	....
Wickliff, Robert	400	A	76	5-19-1780	Cartrights Cr	....
Wickliff, Robert	400	A	209	5-29-1781	Cartright Cr	....
Wickliff, Robert	400	A	216	7-26-1781	Charles Wickliff	....
Wickliff, Robert Sr	400	A	76	5-19-1780	Cartright Cr	....
Wickliff, Robert Sr	400	A	216	7-26-1781	Cartrights Cr	....
Wickerham, Adam	400	A	140	6-21-1780	Brashears Cr	Surveyed
Wickerham, Adam	1,000	A	206	4-13-1781	Clear Cr	....
Wickerham, Jacob	200	A	113	5-30-1780	Ky R	....
Wickerham, Jacob	300	A	113	5-30-1780	Ky R	....
Wickerham, Peter	200	A	113	5-30-1780	Ky R	Withdrawn
Wickerham, Peter	200	A	213	7- 3-1781	Ky R	Withdrawn
Wickerham, Peter	300	A	214	7- 3-1781	Ky R	....
Wildrick, R	54,000	A	351	4-12-1784	Green R	Withdrawn
Wildrick, R	55,000	A	353	4-16-1784	Nole Linn & Bear Cr	Withdrawn
Wildrick, R	34,000	A	353	4-16-1784	———	Withdrawn
Wildrick, R	55,000	A	375	8- 2-1784	Nole Linn Cr	Withdrawn amended
Wilkerson, James	2,000	B	44	4-25-1785	Ohio R	Withdrawn
Wilkerson, James	5,979¾	A	324	12-26-1783	Mid Fk Clear Cr	....
Wilkerson, James	2,000	A	323	12-26-1783	Ohio R	Withdrawn
Wilkerson, James et al	3,000	A	323	12-26-1783	Ohio R	....
Wilkerson, John	500	A	80	5-20-1780	Licking	....
Wilkerson, John	400	A	27	4-26-1780	Hingston Mill Cr	....
Wilkerson, John	400	A	26	4-26-1780	Dicks R	....
Willcocks, Henry	30,000	A	364	6-11-1784	Rolling Fk	Amended
Willcocks, John	30,000	A	324	12-27-1783	Nolelinn Cr	Withdrawn
Willcocks, John	30,000	A	335	1-27-1784	Nole Linn Cr	Withdrawn
Willcocks, John	30,000	A	350	4-10-1784	Rolling Fk	Surveyed
Willcocks, John	30,000	A	350	4-10-1784		Withdrawn
Willett, Griffin	400	A	192	3-16-1781	Pottengers Cr	Surveyed
Willett, Samuel	100	A	192	3-16-1781	Pottengers Cr	Withdrawn
Willett, Samuel	100	A	192	3-16-1781	Pottengers settlement	Withdrawn
Willett, Samuel	200	A	192	3-16-1781	Pottengers Cr	Surveyed

Entree	Acres	Book	Page	Entry Date	Watercourse	Notes
Willett, Samuel	200	A	276	4–12–1783	Pottengers Cr	
Willett, Samuel	100	A	276	4–12–1783	Pottengers settlement	Withdrawn
Willett, Samuel	200	A	290	9–10–1783	————	Surveyed
Williams, Alfred	50	A	31	4–28–1780	N Fk Elkhorn	Mil surveyed
Williams, Charles	1,000	A	42	5–10–1780	Blue Licks	
Williams, David	400	A	18	3– 2–1780	Harrods Cr	Surveyed
Williams, David	322	A	80	5–20–1780	Ky R	
Williams, David	560	A	184	10–30–1780	Salt R	
Williams, David	1,000	A	251	1– 9–1783	Harrods Cr	Surveyed
Williams, David	1,000	A	326	1– 1–1784	Salt R	
Williams, Edward	400	A	18	3– 2–1780	Floyds Fk	Surveyed
Williams, Edward	200	A	91	5–24–1780	Lulbergrud Cr	
Williams, Edwards	400	A	95	5–24–1780	Lulbergrud Cr	
Williams, Edward	1,000	A	146	6–24–1780	Floyds Fk	Surveyed
Williams, Evan	600	A	169	9– 4–1780	Cedar Cr	
Williams, Evan	400	A	169	9– 4–1780	Beech Fk	Surveyed withdrawn
Williams, Evan	400	A	169	9– 4–1780	Cane Cr	
Williams, Evan	400	A	326	1– 3–1784	Beech Fk	
Williams, George	1,000	A	47	5–12–1780	Hingston Fk	
Williams, George	500	A	163	7–22–1780	Yellow Cr	Withdrawn
Williams, George	500	A	163	7–22–1780	Yellow Cr	Withdrawn
Williams, George	1,000	A	169	9– 9–1780	Licking	
Williams, George	1,450½	A	263	2–15–1783	Hardens Cr	
Williams, George Jr	500	A	76	5–19–1780	Pasture Lick Cr	
Williams, John	400	A	9	1–18–1780	Sinking Cr	
Williams, John	400	A	15	2–21–1780	E Fk Licking	
Williams, John	400	A	15	2–21–1780	Hawkins R	
Williams, John	1,000	A	44	5–11–1780	Lees Cr	
Williams, John	495	A	65	5–17–1780	Licking	
Williams, John	400	A	70	5–18–1780	S Fk Goose Cr	
Williams, John	500	A	108	5–29–1780	Gists Cr	
Williams, John	150	A	115	5–31–1780	Blue Lick Fk	
Williams, John	400	A	151	6–26–1780	Jessamine Cr	
Williams, John	985	A	180	10–19–1780	N Fk Licking	
Williams, John	984½	A	334	1–27–1784	Beech Fk	
Williams, John Jr	1,000	A	83	5–22–1780	Lees Cr	
Williams, John Jr	400	A	83	5–22–1780	E Fk Licking	
Williams, John Jr	400	A	83	5–22–1780	Licking	
Williams, John Jr	1,000	A	89	5–23–1780	Beargrass Cr	Surveyed
Williams, John Jr	1,000	A	152	6–26–1780	Jessamine Cr	
Williams, John Jr	1,000	A	152	6–26–1780	N Fk Elkhorn	
Williams, John Jr	1,000	A	152	6–26–1780	Hoskins Run	
Williams, John Jr	1,000	A	152	6–26–1780	E Fk Licking	
Williams, John P	1,000	A	60	5–16–1780	Floyds Fk	
Williams, Thomas	400	A	16	2–22–1780	Fk Lawrences Cr	
Williams, Thomas	250	A	43	5– 1–1780	Dicks R	
Williams, Thomas	250	A	43	5–11–1780	Crab Orchard Run	
Willimas, Thomas	221½	A	212	6–30–1781	Pottengers Cr	Surveyed
Williams, Vincent	3,000	A	239	12–23–1782	Drennons Lick	Surveyed
Willis, Edward	250	A	301	11– 7–1783	Chaplins Fk	
Willis, Edward	750	A	301	11– 7–1783	Glens Cr	Surveyed
Willis, Edward	250	B	41	3– 4–1785	————	
Willis, Joseph Jr	400	A	56	5–15–1780	Chaplins Fk	
Willis, Joseph Jr	100	A	125	6– 5–1780	Chaplins Fk	
Willis, Wm	100	A	23	4–24–1780	Dicks R	
Willis, Wm	400	A	23	4–24–1780	Dicks R	
Willis, Wm	400	A	23	4–24–1780	Dicks R	Mil
Willis, Wm	1,000	A	78	5–20–1780	Jessamine Cr	
Willis, Wm	500	A	129	6– 9–1780	Harrods Cr	
Willson, Bernard	350	A	86	5–22–1780	Salt Lick Cr	
Willson, Edward	1,000	A	83	5–22–1780	Licking	
Willson, Edward	500	A	134	6–16–1780	Stoners Fk	
Willson, Edward	1,000	A	161	7–14–1780	Howards Cr	
Willson, George	400	A	282	7– 1–1783	Falls Ohio R	Withdrawn
Willson, George	208½	A	294	10–10–1783	Fern Cr	Amended
Willson, George	5,000	A	301	11– 3–1783	Clear Cr	Withdrawn
Willson, George	452	A	301	11– 3–1783	Clear Cr	Withdrawn
Willson, George	800	A	322	12–25–1783	Beech Fk	
Willson, George	400	A	323	12–25–1783	Beech Fk	
Willson, George	400	A	330	1–14–1784	Harrods Fk	Surveyed
Willson, George	40,926	A	350	4– 9–1784	Panther Cr	Surveyed
Willson, George	1,004	B	4	8–27–1784		
Willson, George	100	B	12	11– 9–1784	Falls Ohio R	Surveyed
Willson, George	600	B	22	12– 3–1784	Clear Cr	
Willson, George	8,620	B	23	12– 4–1784	Panther Cr	Withdrawn
Willson, George	800	B	24	12–10–1784	Beech Fk	
Willson, George	800	B	24	12–10–1784	————.	Withdrawn
Willson, George	800	B	32	1– 8–1785	————	Amended
Willson, George	5,000	B	37	1–28–1785	Rolling Fk	
Willson, George	5,000	B	37	1–28–1785	Brashear Cr	Withdrawn
Willson, George et al	400	A	200	3–29–1781	Coxes Cr	Surveyed

Entree	Acres	Book	Page	Entry Date	Watercourse	Notes
Willson, George et al...	400	A	282	7- 2-1783	Willsons Cr	Surveyed
Willson, George et al...	1,082½	B	22	12- 1-1784	Drening Lick Cr	452 acres withdrawn
Willson, Henry	300	A	74	5-19-1780	Shawnee Run	
Willson, Henry	400	A	117	5-31-1780	Coxes Cr	300 acres withdrawn
Willson, Henry	400	A	123	6- 3-1780	Fromans Cr	Withdrawn
Willson, Henry	400	A	125	6- 5-1780	Ky R	Withdrawn
Willson, Henry	400	A	177	10- 9-1780	Salt R	Surveyed
Willson, Henry	300	A	219	8-14-1781	Askins Fk	
Willson, Henry	500	A	221	11- 9-1782	Beech Fk	Withdrawn
Willson, Henry	400	A	341	2-21-1784	Fromans Cr	
Willson, Henry Sr	100	A	117	5-31-1780	Coxes Cr	
Willson, John	250	A	66	5-17-1780	Smith Cr, Dix R	Surveyed
Willson, John	400	A	90	5-23-1780	Floyds Fk	
Willson, John	500	A	159	7- 5-1780	Jouetts Cr	
Willson, John	400	A	215	7-18-1781	Fromans Cr	Surveyed
Willson, Robert	1,000	A	120	6- 1-1780	Coxes Cr	
Willson, Robert	1,000	A	341	2-23-1784	Crooked Cr	
Willson, Robert	400	A	341	2-23-1784	Crooked Cr	
Willson, Samuel	500	A	121	6- 2-1780	N Fk Cartright	Withdrawn
Willson, Samuel	500	A	162	7-18-1780	W Fk Cartright Cr	
Willson, Thomas	1,000	A	182	10-27-1780	Clear Cr	
Willson, Thomas Jr	500	A	183	10-27-1780	His settlement	
Willson, Wm	1,000	A	83	5-22-1780	Licking	
Willson, Wm	839	A	341	2-26-1784	——	Withdrawn
Willson, Wm	839	B	48	6-17-1785	——	Withdrawn
Willson, Wm	839	B	48	6-20-1785	Salt R	
Wilson, Edward	1,000	A	23	4-24-1780	Howards Cr	Mil
Wilson, Henry	1,000	A	26	4-26-1780	Salt R	Surveyed
Wilson, Henry	400	A	128	6- 8-1780	Beech Fk	Withdrawn
Wilson, Francis	400	A	17	2-28-1780	Rolling Fk	
Wilson, James	400	A	37	4-29-1780	N Fk Elkhorn	
Wilson, John	50	A	22	4-22-1780	Smiths Br	Mil surveyed
Wilson, Robt	400	A	5	12- 7-1779	Town Fk Salt R	Surveyed
Wilson, Samuel	400	A	18	2-29-1780	Licking Cr	
Wilson, Thomas	400	A	16	2-22-1780	Wilsons Run	
Windor, Isaac	600	A	358	5- 1-1784	——	
Winfrey, Reuben	500	A	97	5-25-1780	S Fk Licking	
Wingfield, John	1,000	A	185	10-31-1780	Twinns 2 Cr	
Winn, George	1,000	A	74	5-19-1780	S Fk Licking	
Winn, Owen	500	A	74	5-19-1780	S Fk Licking	Withdrawn
Winn, Owen	500	A	88	5-23-1780	Licking	
Winn, Thomas	400	A	41	5-10-1780	S Licking	
Winston, Isaac	1,600	A	82	5-22-1780	Ky R	Surveyed
Winston, Isaac	5,400	A	82	5-22-1780	Yellow Cr	Surveyed
Winston, Wm	1,875	A	263	2-15-1783	Harden Cr	
Wise, Peter	1,000	A	160	7- 6-1780	Yellow Cr	
Witherley, Wm	2,524¾	A	323	12-25-1783	Nolelin Cr	
Withers, George	500	A	45	5-11-1780	Sinking Cr	
Withers, James	1,000	A	77	5-20-1780	Beargrass	Surveyed
Withers, James	500	A	84	5-22-1780	Station & Muddy Cr	
Withers, John	500	A	84	5-22-1780	Station Camp Cr	
Withers, John et al	1,000	A	112	5-30-1780	Clear Cr	
Withers, Thomas	804	A	56	5-15-1780	Ky R	
Withers, Thomas	804	A	56	5-15-1780	Hammonds	Withdrawn
Withers, Thomas	804	A	193	3-16-1781	Ky R	
Withers, Wm	325	A	72	5-18-1780	Floyds Fk	
Withers, Wm	1,000	A	150	6-26-1780	Beech Fk	
Withers, Wm	500	A	285	8- 5-1783	——	Surveyed
Withers, Wm	1,062½	A	291	9-13-1783	Rough Cr	
Withers, Wm Jr	500	A	45	5-11-1780	Salt R	
Withers, Wm Jr	1,000	A	45	5-11-1780	Salt R	
Withers, Wm Sr	500	A	45	5-11-1780	Green R	
Withers, Wm Sr	500	A	45	5-11-1780	Green R	
Withrow, Samuel et al	1,000	A	204	4- 4-1781	Beech Fk	Surveyed
Womack, Wm	750	A	154	6-28-1780	S & N Fk Licking	
Wood, Alijah	400	A	9	1-17-1780	Boones Cr	
Wood, Andrew	50	A	106	5-29-1780	Dicks R	Mil
Wood, Charles	875	A	314	12-12-1783	Mill Cr	Surveyed
Wood, Henry	264	A	256	1-21-1783	Cartright Cr	
Wood, James	400	A	73	5-19-1780	Floyds Fk	
Wood, James	200	A	80	5-20-1780	Salt R	
Wood, James	200	A	80	5-20-1780	Salt R	
Wood, James	1,500	A	287	8-12-1783	Rough Cr	
Wood, John	400	A	44	5-11-1780	Muddy Cr	
Wood, John	700	A	45	5-11-1780	Salt R	Surveyed
Wood, John & Jas	2,000	A	328	1-12-1784	Beech Fk	
Wood, Joseph Jr	1,000	A	161	7- 8-1780	Cabbin Cr	
Wood, Joseph Jr	1,000	A	161	7- 8-1780	Limestone	
Wood, Thomas	1,000	A	266	2-25-1783	Beaver Dam Fk	Surveyed
Wodd, Thomas	1,000	A	266	2-25-1783	Bear Cr	Withdrawn

Entree	Acres	Book	Page	Entry Date	Watercourse	Notes
Wood, Thomas	1,000	A	232	12–18–1782	Bear Cr	Withdrawn
Woodard, Wm	400	A	17	2–29–1780	Brashears Cr	Twice entered
Woodard, Wm	1,000	A	261	2– 5–1783	Clear Cr	
Woodfolk, Towel	1,298	A	271	3–28–1783	Brush Cr	
Woodger, John	400	A	191	3–15–1781	Coxes Cr	Surveyed
Woodger, Thomas	400	A	191	3–15–1781	Simpsons Cr	Withdrawn
Woodger, Thomas	1,000	A	296	10–15–1783	Indian Camp Cr	
Woodger, Thomas	900	A	351	4–12–1784	Rough Cr	
Wooding, Robert	1,256	A	355	4–24–1784	Rolling Fk	
Woodroff, John	400	A	36	4–29–1780	Strodes Fk	
Woodroff, John	400	A	186	10–31–1780	Strouds Fk	Twice entered
Woodrow, Andrew	2,000	A	152	6–26–1780	Salt R	Mil withdrawn
Woodrow, Andrew	500	A	196	3–17–1781	Brashears Cr	Withdrawn
Woodrow, Andrew	500	A	196	3–17–1781	Brashears Cr	Withdrawn
Woodrow, Andrew	2,000	A	196	3–17–1781	Brashears Cr	Withdrawn
Woodrow, Andrew	2,000	A	221	11– 9–1782	Brashears Cr	Withdrawn
Woodrow, Andrew	900	A	222	12– 9–1782	Rough Cr	Surveyed
Woodrow, Andrew	300	A	222	12– 9–1782	Falls Rough Cr	
Woodroe, Andrew	300	A	222	12– 9–1782	Rough Cr	
Woodrow, Andrew	500	A	222	12– 9–1782	Sinking Cr	Mil surveyed
Woodrow, Andrew	1,500	B	32	1– 8–1785	———	900 acres surveyed
Woods, Andrew	1,000	A	26	4–26–1780	Hawkins Br	
Woods, Andrew	800	A	99	5–25–1780	Ohio R	
Woods, Andrew	604	A	118	6– 1–1781	Lees Cr	
Woods, David	1,000	A	180	10–23–1780	Hagans settlement	
Woods, David et al	2,179	A	292	10– 3–1783	Town Fk	
Woods, James	1,500	B	37	1–28–1785	Rough Cr	Withdrawn
Woods, James	1,500	B	38	1–28–1785	Clear Cr	
Woods, John	2,000	A	328	1–12–1784	Beech Fk	
Woods, Richard	512½	A	258	1–27–1783	Rolling Fk	
Woods, Samuel	800	A	254	1–16–1783	Benson Cr	
Woods, Wm	1,000	A	49	5–12–1780	S Fk Elkhorn	
Woods, Wm	1,000	A	49	5–12–1780	Harrods Lick	
Woodsides, Wm	500	A	38	5– 9–1780	Clear Cr	Surveyed
Woodson, Samuel	666⅔	A	54	5–15–1780	———	
Woodward, Chesley	400	A	115	5–30–1780	Licking	
Woodward, Wm	400	A	4	12– 7–1779	Brashears Cr	Surveyed
Wooldridge, Edmund	1,000	A	156	6–30–1780	Floyds Fk	
Wooldridge, Edmund	1,000	A	128	6– 8–1780	S Fk Licking	
Wooley, Henry	300	A	112	5–30–1780	Paint Lick Cr	
Wooley, Henry	200	A	112	5–30–1780	Paint Lick Cr	
Wooley, John	1,000	A	118	6– 1–1781	Paint Lick	
Wooley, Peter	400	A	13	2– 9–1780	Paint Lick Cr	
Wooley, Wm	400	A	112	5–30–1780	Paint Lick Cr	
Woolfolk, John	1,000	A	301	11– 1–1783	Floyds Fk	240 acres surveyed
Woolfolk, John	12,613½	A	330	1–15–1784	Ohio R	10,075 acres withdrawn
Woolfolk, John	1,500	A	338	2–12–1784	Ohio R	
Woolfolk, John	1,500	A	338	2–12–1784	Ohio R	
Woolfolk, John	4,000	B	5	9–11–1784	Pond Cr	
Woolfolk, John	100	B	5	9–11–1784	Pond Cr	
Woolfolk, John	1,000	B	5	9–11–1784	———	
Woolfolk, John	7,100	B	5	9–11–1784	———	Withdrawn
Woolfolk, John	1,000	B	29	12–20–1784	Mill Cr	
Woolfolk, John	1,000	B	29	12–20–1784	———	Withdrawn
Woolfolk, John	375	B	46	5–23–1785	Floyds Fk	
Woolfolk, John	375	B	46	5–23–1785	Ohio R	Withdrawn
Woolfolk, John	1,000	B	47	6–15–1785	———	Withdrawn
Woolfolk, John	100	B	48	6–14–1785	Floyds Fk	
Woolfolk, Richard et al	400	B	29	12–20–1784	Salt R	
Woolfolk, Robert	4,895½	A	313	12– 5–1783	Lick Cr	
Woolsey, Wm	1,000	A	71	5–18–1780	Bull Skin Cr	
Woolsey, Wm	1,000	A	71	5–18–1780	Ky R	
Wren, John	500	A	73	5–19–1780	Buffaloe Cr	Surveyed
Wren, John	500	A	183	10–27–1780	Simpsons Cr	Surveyed
Wren, Wm	500	A	73	5–19–1780	Buffaloe Cr	Surveyed
Wren, Wm	500	A	224	12–13–1782	Simpsons Cr	Surveyed
Wren, Wm	500	A	263	2–14–1783	———	Surveyed
Wrey, James	400	A	1	11– 3–1779	Salt R	
Wright, Dennis	200	A	39	5– 9–1780	Licking	
Wright, James	225	A	223	12–12–1782	Green R	Withdrawn
Wright, James	225	A	224	12–12–1782	———	Withdrawn
Wright, John	50	A	182	10–25–1780	Ky R	Mil
Wright, Joshua	400	A	148	6–24–1780	Floyds Fk	
Wright, Pat	1,000	A	137	6–19–1780	Johnsons Fk	
Wright, Thomas	1,093	A	232	12–18–1782	Salt R	Surveyed
Wright, Wm	325	A	181	10–24–1780	Pond Cr	
Wroe, Benjamin	2,296	A	260	2– 3–1783	Beech Fk	
Wustenhunt, Jacob	400	A	10	2– 2–1780	Hickmans Cr	

Entree	Acres	Book	Page	Entry Date	Watercourse	Notes
Work, Henry	2,000	A	302	11- 7-1783	Mulberry Cr	
Work, Wm	2,000	A	374	7-29-1784	Beargrass Cr	
Worthing, Edward	560	A	83	5-22-1780	Pottengers Cr	Surveyed
Worthington, Edward	400	A	3	11-11-1779	Shawnee Run	
Worthington, Edward	1,000	A	75	5-19-1780	Brashears Cr	
Worthington, Edward	560	A	83	5-22-1780	Simpsons Cr	
Yager, Adam	400	A	56	5-15-1780	Lk Fk Rockcastle	
Yager, Cornelius	400	A	12	2- 9-1780	Hanging Fk	
Yager, Cornelius	400	A	73	5-19-1783	Pleasant Run	
Yager, John	400	A	56	5-15-1780	Lk Fk Rockcastle	
Yager, Nicholas	1,000	A	73	5-19-1780	Chaplins Fk	Surveyed
Yancy, Archelaus	500	A	156	6-30-1780	John Yancey	
Yancy, Charles	800	A	156	6-30-1780	Elkhorn	
Yancy, Charles	800	A	156	6-30-1780	Thomas Logwood	
Yancy, Charles	1,000	A	156	6-30-1780	Thomas Logwood	
Yancy, John	500	A	156	6-30-1780	Nathaniel Popes	
Yates, Michael	50	A	23	4-24-1780	Mid Fk Licking	Mil
Yates, Michael	1,820	A	223	12-12-1782	Read Cr	
Yates, Wm	1,000	A	340	2-17-1784	Rough Cr	Withdrawn
Yates, Wm	1,000	B	14	11-12-1784	Rough Cr	Withdrawn
Yates, Wm	1,000	B	14	11-12-1784	Indian Camp Cr	Withdrawn
Yates, Wm	1,000	B	15	11-12-1784	———	Withdrawn
Yates, W m	600	B	15	11-12-1784	Bear Cr	Surveyed
Yates, Wm	400	B	15	11-12-1784	Bear Cr	
Yates, Wm	400	B	15	11-12-1784	Bear Cr	
Yeagar, Absalom	250	B	27	12-17-1784	Salt R	
Yokam, Mathias	1,000	A	26	4-26-1780	Chaplins Cr	
Young, Bryan	400	A	209	5-29-1781	Salt R	Surveyed
Young, Bryant	325	A	223	12-11-1782	Beech Fk	
Young, Charles	60,028¼	A	332	1-20-1784	McWilliams	98,000 acres withdrawn
Young, Charles	1,242	A	341	2-21-1784	The Barrens	
Young, Charles	51,000	A	343	3- 3-1784	Green R	
Young, Charles	60,028½	A	343	3- 3-1784	Ramsey & Cox	Withdrawn
Young, James	1,000	A	123	6- 3-1780	Green R	
Young, James	1,000	A	338	2-14-1784	———	
Young, Jas & Jos	200	A	29	4-27-1780	Dicks R	Mil
Young, John	1,000	A	64	5-17-1780	Baleys Trace	
Young, John	325	A	163	7-29-1780	Round Stone Cr	
Young, John	325	A	208	5- 7-1781	Pond Cr	Surveyed
Young, Leonard	200	A	83	5-22-1780	Buck Lick Cr	
Young, Richard	500	A	27	4-26-1780	Glens Cr	Mil
Young, Richard	1,000	A	65	5-17-1780	Big Lick	
Young, Richard	300	A	75	5-19-1780	Glens Cr	
Young, Ruebin	100	A	29	4-27-1780	Lees Br	Mil
Young, Rueben	500	A	65	5-17-1780	Elkhorn	
Young, Reuben	500	A	75	5-19-1780	Lees Branch	
Young, Samuel	8,000	A	338	2-14-1784	———	Withdrawn
Young, Samuel	8,800	A	352	4-15-1784	———	Withdrawn
Young, Samuel	4,000	A	352	4-14-1784	Salt R	Surveyed
Young, Samuel	4,000	A	352	4-14-1784	Salt R	Surveyed
Young, Wm	400	A	36	4-29-1780	Gilberts Cr	
Young, Wm	400	A	36	4-29-1780	Gilberts Cr	
Young, Wm	1,000	A	169	9- 9-1780	Ohio R	
Young, Wm	1,500	A	373	7-24-1784	———	
Yourm, Mathias	400	A	14	2-19-1780	near Harrodsburg	Surveyed
Zegler, James	250	A	264	2-15-1783	Rowling Fk	Surveyed
Zigler, James	250	A	375	7-29-1784	———	
Zimmerman, Geo	400	A	8	1-12-1780	Licking Cr	

V.
MILITARY WARRANTS
(1782–1793)

Name	Acres	Warrant	Service	Date
Aaron, William	100	1179	3 years soldier Virginia line	6–25–1783
Abbott, Reuben	200	1129	During war soldier Virginia line	6–24–1783
Abbott, Robert	200	801	3 years sergeant Virginia line	6–13–1783
Abner, Simon	200	4419	During war soldier Virginia line	7–17–1788
Absalom, Edmond	200	1509	During war soldier Virginia line	8– 6–1783
Acre, Ambrose	100	3685	3 years soldier Virginia line	1–11–1785
Adams, James	400	1039	3 years corporal Virginia line	6–24–1783
Adams, Jacob	200	1153	During war soldier Virginia line	6–24–1783
Adams, John	200	4009	During war soldier Virginia line	11–25–1785
Adams, Mallory	100	4362	3 years soldier Virginia line	1–11–1788
Adams, Thomas	100	2007	3 years soldier Virginia line	12– 2–1783
Aiken, George	200	3714	3 years sergeant Virginia line	1–20–1785
Ailstock, William	100	2736	3 years soldier Virginia line	3– 8–1784
Akin, Joel	100	2975	3 years soldier Virginia line	4–20–1784
Aldin, James	100	4488	3 years soldier Virginia line	2–23–1790
Aldin, Samuel	100	4489	3 years soldier Virginia line	2–23–1790
Aldridge, James	100	2191	3 years soldier Virginia line	12–22–1783
Aldridge, John	100	4274	3 years soldier Virginia line	4– 7–1787
Aldridge, Richard	100	2457	3 years soldier Virginia line	2–11–1784
Alexander, Ellis	200	363	During war soldier state line	4–18–1783
Alexander, George Dent	6,000	3142	3 years surgeon Virginia line	6–10–1784
Alexander, James	100	3441	3 years soldier Virginia line	9–15–1784
Alexander, James	200	4159	3 years corporal Virginia line	5–24–1786
Alexander, William	100	649	3 years private Virginia line	5–27–1783
Alford, Jacob	100	2238	3 years soldier Virginia line	1–12–1784
Alford, John	200	3447	During war soldier Virginia line	9–21–1784
Allen, Daniel	200	3589	During war soldier Virginia line	12–20–1784
Allen, David	2,000	1347	3 years lieutenant Virginia line	7–10–1783
Allen, David	666⅔	1348	3 years lieutenant Virginia line	7–10–1783
Allen, David	200	3115	3 years corporal Virginia line	5–30–1784
Allen, Edward	2,666⅔	1938	3 years lieutenant Virginia line	11–22–1783
Allen, Francis	200	2389	3 years corporal Virginia line	2– 3–1784
Allen, John	100	2803	3 years soldier Virginia line	3–22–1784
Allen, John	100	3310	3 years soldier Virginia line	7– 2–1784
Allen, John	1,000	3597	3 years captain Virginia line	12–21–1784
Allen, John	2,500	3598	3 years captain Virginia line	12–21–1784
Allen, Joseph	100	848	3 years soldier Virginia line	6–17–1783
Allen, Mason	200	1361	During war soldier Virginia line	7–12–1783
Allen, Reuben	466⅔	1398	7 years sergeant Virginia line	7–19–1783
Allen, Thomas	100	1464	3 years soldier Virginia line	8– 1–1783
Allen, Thomas	200	2431	3 years boatswain Virginia navy	2– 9–1784
Allen, Thomas	200	3977	3 years sergeant Virginia line	10– 3–1785
Alligroe, William	200	4444	During war sailor Virginia navy	12–15–1788
Allison, John	6,000	122	3 years lieutenant state line	2–11–1783
Almond, John	100	2168	3 years sailor Virginia navy	12–20–1783
Alman, William	200	1939	3 years gunner Virginia navy	11–22–1783
Altop, Thomas	200	1681	During war soldier Virginia line	8–27–1783
Alva, Robert	100	2193	3 years soldier Virginia line	12–22–1783
Amanda, Ambrose	2,666⅔	4424	3 years gunner Virginia navy	7–17–1788
Amberson, James	200	1145	During war soldier Virginia line	6–24–1783
Ammond, Peter	233⅓	3732	7 years soldier Virginia line	2– 7–1785
Amonite, Daniel	100	3027	3 years soldier Virginia line	4–27–1784
Anderson, Charles	200	555	3 years sergeant Virginia Cont. line	5– 7–1783
Anderson, Daniel	200	965	3 years sergeant Virginia line	6–20–1783
Anderson, Henry	200	2327	3 years drum major Virginia line	1–31–1784
Anderson, Henry	100	1021	3 years soldier Virginia line	6–23–1783
Anderson, Isaac	100	178	3 years soldier Virginia state line	3–13–1783
Anderson, Isaac	200	558	During war soldier state line	5– 8–1783
Anderson, James	200	897	During war soldier Virginia line	6–20–1783
Anderson, James	100	898	3 years soldier Virginia line	6–20–1783
Anderson, James	200	2551	During war soldier Virginia line	2–20–1784
Anderson, John	100	970	3 years soldier Virginia line	6–20–1783
Anderson, John	200	1862	3 years sergeant Virginia line	11– 6–1783
Anderson, John	4,666⅔	2367	7 years captain Virginia line	2– 2–1784
Anderson, Matthew	100	580	3 years soldier Virginia line	5–14–1783
Anderson, Nathanial	2,666⅔	2235	3 years lieutenant Virginia line	1–12–1784
Anderson, Richard	100	4496	3 years soldier Virginia line	5–28–1790
Anderson, Richard C	6000	35	3 years lieutenant-col. Va. Cont. line	12– 9–1782
Anderson, Robert	100	646	3 years soldier Virginia line	5–28–1783
Anderson, William	100	2337	3 years soldier Virginia line	1–31–1784
Anderson, William	200	2846	During war soldier Virginia line	3–30–1784
Anderson, William	100	2852	3 years soldier Virginia line	4– 1–1784

Name	Acres	Warrant	Service	Date
Anderton, John	100	1712	3 years soldier Virginia line	9- 2-1783
Anderton, Isaac	100	1713	3 years soldier Virginia line	9- 2-1783
Anderton, Ralph	100	2335	3 years soldier Virginia line	1-31-1784
Andrews, Adam	100	2557	3 years soldier Virginia line	2-20-1784
Andrews, Banjamin	200	1685	3 years sergeant Virginia line	8-29-1783
Andrews, Claiborn	100	901	3 years soldier Virginia line	6-20-1783
Andrews, Henry	100	2984	3 years soldier Virginia line	4-21-1784
Andrews, Jesse	200	1547	3 years sergeant Virginia line	8-11-1783
Andrews, Moses	200	4171	During war soldier Virginia line	6-14-1786
Andrews, William	200	2237	3 years sergeant Virginia line	1-12-1784
Angel, Baker	100	2020	3 years sailor Virginia navy	12- 6-1783
Angel, William	100	1561	3 years soldier Virginia line	8-12-1783
Angell, William	100	1748	3 years sailor Virginia navy	9-11-1783
Anglin, Isaac	100	1876	3 years soldier Virginia line	11- 7-1783
Angle, James	100	1423	3 years drummer Virginia line	7-24-1783
Angle, John	200	529	During war soldier state line	5- 2-1783
Angle, Robert	100	645	3 years soldier Virginia line	5-28-1783
Anthony, James	200	3056	During war soldier Virginia line	5- 7-1784
Antill, Jacob	100	4238	3 years soldier Virginia line	12-13-1786
Appleby, Samuel	200	4577	During war soldier Virginia line	
Archer, Benjamin	100	4271	3 years soldier Virginia line	4- 7-1787
Archer, Isaac	200	871	During war soldier Virginia line	6-19-1783
Archer, Jeremiah	100	4279	3 years soldier Virginia line	4- 7-1787
Archer, Joseph	2,666⅔	49	3 years lieutenant Virginia Cont. line	12-14-1782
Archer, Leroy	100	3449	3 years soldier Virginia line	9-23-1784
Archer, Peter Field	2,666⅔	50	3 years lieutenant Virginia line	12-14-1783
Archer, Richard	2,666⅔	2607	During war subaltern Virginia line	2-24-1784
Archer, Robert	100	3061	3 years soldier Virginia line	5- 8-1784
Armistead, Adam	100	3420	3 years soldier Virginia line	8-28-1784
Armond, John	100	1863	3 years soldier Virginia line	11- 6-1784
Armistead, Robert	100	2696	3 years soldier Virginia line	3- 3-1784
Armstead, Thomas	4,000	78	3 years captain infantry Virginia state	12-28-1782
Armstead, William	100	1952	3 years soldier Virginia line	11-22-1783
Armistead, William	4,000	2375	3 years captain Virginia line	2- 3-1784
Armstrong, Abel	100	3028	3 years soldier Virginia line	4-27-1784
Armstrong, Adam	100	2336	3 years soldier Virginia line	1-31-1784
Armstrong, Adam	200	3483	During war soldier Virginia line	10-26-1784
Armstrong, Ambrose	100	3010	3 years soldier Virginia line	4-23-1784
Armstrong, James	100	3789	3 years soldier Virginia line	3-26-1785
Armstrong, James	200	3790	During war soldier Virginia line	3-26-1785
Armstrong, James	400	4143	During war sergeant Virginia line	4-12-1786
Armstrong, Jesse	200	3086	During war soldier Virginia line	5-21-1784
Armstrong, John	100	1780	3 years soldier Virginia line	9-20-1783
Armstrong, Tobias	200	1649	During war soldier Virginia line	8-23-1783
Arnold, Elijah	100	3560	3 years soldier Virginia line	12- 8-1784
Arnold, James	100	1976	3 years soldier Virginia line	11-26-1783
Arnold, John	200	1615	3 years sergeant Virginia line	8-21-1783
Arnold, Lewis	100	1979	3 years soldier Virginia line	11-27-1783
Arnold, Lindsay	200	2953	During war soldier Virginia line	4-17-1784
Arnold, Samuel	200	2583	3 years sergeant Virginia line	2-21-1784
Arnold, William	100	3346	3 years soldier Virginia line	7-20-1784
Arnold, William	200	2441	3 years corporal Virginia line	2- 9-1784
Arrell, David	400	3800	3 years captain Virginia line	4-12-1785
Arrington, William	200	1207	During war soldier Virginia line	6-26-1783
Ashby, Benjamin	2,666⅔	2197	3 years lieutenant Virginia line	12-22-1783
Ashby, John	200	2644	7 years corporal Virginia line	2-26-1784
Ashburn, Luke	100	1993	3 years seaman Virginia navy	11-28-1783
Ashby, Stephen	4,000	3591	Services as captain Virginia line	12-21-1784
Ashby, Thomas	100	959	3 years soldier Virginia line	6-20-1783
Ashlock, Richard	100	2283	3 years soldier Virginia line	1-26-1784
Askew, James	100	1	3 years Virginia infantry	8- 8-1782
Aspenwal, John	100	1819	3 years soldier Virginia line	10- 3-1783
Aspinwale, John	200	2348	During war soldier Virginia line	1-31-1784
Asselin, Thomas	200	678	3 years sergeant Virginia line	5-29-1783
Atcheson, David	233⅓	3249	During war soldier Virginia line	6-29-1784
Athey, Benjamin	100	3245	3 years soldier Virginia line	6-29-1784
Athey, Thomas	100	3247	3 years soldier Virginia line	6-25-1784
Atkins, Lewis	200	1172	7 years sergeant Virginia line	4-22-1783
Atkinson, John	100	381	3 years soldier Virginia line	6- 5-1783
Atkinson, Major	100	748	3 years soldier Virginia line	5-30-1783
Atkinson, Reuben	100	689	3 years soldier Virginia line	4-28-1783
Atkinson, Thomas	400	461	During war corporal Virginia line	9-15-1783
Atkinson, William	200	1766	During war soldier Virginia line	8- 1-1783
Aubany, Thomas	200	1471	During war soldier Virginia line	8-30-1783
Auber, Peter	100	1697	3 years soldier Virginia line	
Aubrey, Alias Avery, Samuel	100	3821	3 years soldier Virginia line	4-22-1785
Austin, John Wilson	400	432	During war sergeant-major state line	4-26-1783
Austin, John W	200	277	3 years sergeant Virginia line	4- 3-1783
Averheart, Andrew	200	3841	During war soldier Virginia line	4-29-1785
Baptiste, Jean	200	2322	During war soldier Virginia line	1-30-1784

Name	Acres	Warrant	Service	Date
Bacon, Burwell	200	576	3 years corporal Virginia line	5-14-1783
Bacon, Ludwell	100	2982	3 years soldier Virginia line	4-21-1784
Bacon, Robert	200	1111	During war soldier Virginia line	6-24-1783
Bagnall, Lou	200	4517	During war soldier Virginia line	2- 3-1791
Bailey, Auselin	100	2013	3 years soldier Virginia line	12- 5-1783
Bailey, James	100	2784	3 years soldier Virginia line	3-18-1784
Bailey, James	100	3518	3 years soldier Virginia line	11-11-1784
Bailey, James	400	3715	During war corporal Virginia line	1-20-1785
Bailey, Jesse	100	3400	3 years sailor Virginia navy	8-17-1784
Bailey, John	4,000	2688	3 years captain Virginia line	3- 3-1784
Bailey, Edward	200	1682	3 years sergeant Virginia line	8-28-1783
Bailey, Michael	200	494	During war soldier state line	4-30-1783
Bailey, Pierce	200	3973	During war soldier Virginia line	9-13-1785
Bailey, Southy	200	2298	During war soldier Virginia line	1-26-1784
Bailey, Thomas	100	2113	3 years soldier Virginia line	12-13-1783
Bailey, William	200	1520	During war soldier Virginia line	8- 7-1783
Bailey, William	100	2447	3 years soldier Virginia line	2-10-1784
Bailey, William	100	3021	3 years soldier Virginia line	4-26-1784
Bailey, Zaddock	200	3510	During war soldier Virginia line	11- 8-1784
Baker, James	200	476	During war drummer state line	4-30-1783
Baker, Thomas	100	1309	3 years soldier Virginia line	6-30-1783
Baker, Richard	200	3809	During war soldier Virginia line	4-18-1785
Baldwin, Cornelius	6,000	289	3 years surgeon Virginia Cont. line	4- 4-1783
Baldwin, John	100	2149	3 years soldier Virginia line	12-17-1783
Baley, Simon	100	2156	3 years soldier Virginia line	12-19-1783
Ball, Aaron	100	1583	3 years soldier Virginia line	8-19-1783
Ball, Burgess	7,777	905	7 years lieutenant Virginia line	6-20-1783
Ball, Daniel	2,666⅔	2669	3 years lieutenant Virginia line	3- 2-1784
Ball, James	100	3925	3 years soldier Virginia line	6-21-1785
Ball, William	200	3680	During war soldier Virginia line	1-11-1785
Balls, Nathanial	200	2194	3 years sergeant Virginia line	12-22-1783
Ballance, Henry	200	1899	3 years sergeant Virginia line	10-21-1783
Ballance, Willis	200	1898	3 years corporal Virginia line	10-21-1783
Ballard, Dudley	100	4358	3 years soldier Virginia line	1- 4-1788
Ballard, William	2,666⅔	160	3 years lieutenant artillery	3- 7-1783
Ballard, William	2,666⅔	1960	3 years pilot Virginia navy	11-24-1783
Ballenger, John	100	1190	3 years soldier Virginia line	6-26-1783
Ballinger, William	200	4443	3 years sergeant Virginia line	12-13-1788
Ballow, Charles	200	1429	3 years sergeant Virginia line	7-27-1783
Balmain, Rev Alexander	6,666⅔	286	3 years chaplain	7- 1-1784
Baltard, Robert	6,000	3295	3 years lieutenant-colonel Virginia line	8- 5-1783
Banks, James	2,666⅔	1504	3 years sailing master Virginia navy	8- 5-1783
Banks, William	100	1505	3 years sailor Virginia navy	6-21-1784
Barbee, Daniel	200	3181	3 years sergeant Virginia line	2-11-1784
Barbee, Elijah	200	2453	During war soldier Virginia line	6-26-1783
Barbee, Francis	200	1210	3 years corporal Virginia line	6-26-1783
Barbee, John	200	1209	3 years corporal Virginia line	6-21-1784
Barbee, John	200	3178	3 years sergeant Virginia line	6-21-1784
Barbee, Joshua	200	3179	3 years sergeant Virginia line	4- 1-1783
Barbee, Thomas	4,000	241	3 years captain Virginia Cont. line	6-21-1784
Barbee, William	100	3180	3 years soldier Virginia line	6-25-1783
Barbour, James	2,666⅔	1173	3 years lieutenant Virginia line	8-26-1783
Barbour, Phillip	2,666⅔	1670	3 years lieutenant Virginia line	11- 6-1783
Barham, Moody	100	1861	3 years soldier Virginia line	4-20-1784
Barker, Charles	100	2968	3 years soldier Virginia line	4-22-1784
Barker, Edward	100	3002	3 years soldier Virginia line	6-26-1784
Barker, John	100	3212	3 years soldier Virginia line	1- 5-1786
Barksdale, Daniel	100	4065	3 years soldier Virginia line	6-25-1784
Barksdale, John	2,666⅔	3211	3 years lieutenant Virginia line	11-22-1783
Barlow, Thomas	100	1926	3 years soldier Virginia line	4-29-1785
Barnes, Andrew	200	3835	During war soldier Virginia line	12-19-1783
Barnes, James	200	2153	During war soldier Virginia line	6-19-1783
Barnes, John	100	872	3 years soldier Virginia line	1-25-1785
Barnes, John	100	3720	3 years soldier Virginia line	3- 1-1785
Barnes, John	200	3766	During war soldier Virginia line	4-14-1783
Barnes, William	100	327	3 years soldier Virginia Cont. line	5- 3-1786
Barnes, William	100	4151	3 years soldier Virginia line	8-21-1783
Barnett, Ambrose	100	1610	3 years soldier Virginia line	6-24-1783
Barnett, John	200	1100	During war soldier Virginia line	4-12-1784
Barnett, Michael	100	2918	3 years soldier Virginia line	3-31-1784
Barns, Robert	100	211	3 years soldier Virginia Cont. line	8-12-1785
Barnwell, James	100	3951	3 years soldier Virginia line	6-24-1783
Barr, William	200	1049	During war soldier Virginia line	1-21-1784
Barrett, Criswell	4,000	2257	3 years captain Virginia line	1-21-1784
Barrett, William	4,000	2256	3 years captain Virginia line	6- 2-1783
Barren, James Esqr	7,777¾	711	7 years commodore Virginia navy	6-26-1783
Barron, Fielding	100	1218	3 years soldier Virginia line	2- 2-1785
Barron, Fielding	400	3729	During war sergeant Virginia line	6- 3-1783
Barron, Richard	5,333¾	722	3 years captain Virginia navy	12-10-1785
Barry, Simon	100	4031	3 years private Virginia line	4-12-1783
Bartlett, John	200	321	During war soldier cavalry	

Name	Acres	Warrant	Service	Date
Bartlett, John	400	1324	During war sergeant Virginia cavalry	7- 4-1783
Bartley, Alexander	100	3405	3 years soldier Virginia line	8-20-1784
Bartley, Joshua	200	3128	3 years corporal Virginia line	6- 5-1784
Bartley, Ralph	100	3282	3 years sailor Virginia navy	7- 1-1784
Bartley, William	100	1585	3 years soldier Virginia line	8-19-1783
Barton, James	100	2445	3 years soldier Virginia line	2-10-1784
Barton, Henry	100	4505	3 years soldier Virginia line	11-25-1790
Baskerville, Samuel	1,500	631	7 years lieutenant line	5-23-1783
Baskerville, Samuel	1,610⅔	632	7 years lieutenant Virginia line	5-23-1783
Basey, William	400	4257	During war sergeant Virginia line	2-16-1787
Basey, William	100	4258	3 years soldier Virginia line	2-16-1787
Batchelor, Peter	200	3287	During war sergeant Virginia line	7- 1-1784
Bates, John	200	1788	During war soldier Virginia line	9-24-1783
Bates, John	200	4197	During war soldier Virginia line	8-23-1786
Batson, Thomas	100	3271	3 years sailor Virginia navy	7- 1-1784
Batterton, Samuel	100	3225	3 years soldier Virginia line	6-28-1784
Baughan, Aris	100	208	3 years soldier Virginia state line	3-28-1783
Baughan, William	100	2357	3 years soldier Virginia line	1-31-1784
Baumgartner, Henry	200	4610	During war private Virginia line	4-15-1793
Bay, William	100	17	3 years soldier Virginia Cont. line	11-21-1782
Bayles, Jesse	100	4333	3 years soldier Virginia line	11-12-1787
Bayles, William	100	1556	3 years soldier Virginia line	8-12-1783
Bayley, James	200	2620	3 years sergeant Virginia line	2-24-1784
Bayley, Noah	100	1824	3 years soldier Virginia line	10- 6-1783
Baylie, Peter	100	2021	3 years sailor Virginia navy	12- 6-1783
Bayling, Matthew	200	1674	3 years drummer Virginia line	8-27-1783
Baylis, Henry	2,666⅔	3549	3 years lieutenant Virginia line	11-30-1784
Baylop, Thomas	4,000	3099	3 years captain Virginia line	5-25-1784
Baylor, George	6,666⅔	101	3 years colonel light dragoons	1-30-1783
Baylor, George	2,222	2317	7 years colonel Virginia line	1-29-1784
Baylor, Walker Capt	2,000	628	3 years captain Virginia line	5-23-1783
Baylor, Walker Capt	2,000	629	3 years captain Virginia line	5-23-1783
Baynham, John	2,666⅔	2790	3 years lieutenant Virginia line	3-19-1784
Baytop, James	400	1564	3 years captain Virginia line	8-13-1783
Baytop, John	2,666⅔	1565	3 years lieutenant Virginia line	8-13-1783
Beal, William	400	1877	During war sergeant Virginia line	11- 7-1783
Beale, Robert	4,666⅔	198	7 years captain Virginia Cont. line	3-26-1783
Beasley, Larkin	100	4394	3 years soldier Virginia line	3-25-1788
Beasley, Richard	100	773	3 years soldier Virginia line	6- 9-1783
Beatte, Robert	4,000	853	3 years captain Virginia line	6-17-1783
Beatley, William	100	3270	3 years sailor Virginia navy	7- 1-1784
Beaver, Samuel	200	740	3 years corporal Virginia line	6- 4-1783
Beaver, William	100	1698	3 years drummer Virginia line	8-30-1783
Beavers, Benjamin	200	1700	3 years sergeant Virginia line	9- 1-1783
Bebby, Edward	100	3508	3 years sailor Virginia navy	11- 8-1784
Becam, Robert	200	863	During war soldier Virginia line	6-18-1783
Beck, John	2,666⅔	852	3 years lieutenant Virginia line	6-17-1783
Beckham, William	100	3292	3 years soldier Virginia line	7- 1-1784
Bedford, James	400	2705	During war sergeant Virginia line	3- 4-1784
Bedenger, Henry	4,000	291	3 years captain Virginia Cont. line	4- 5-1783
Bedinger, Daniel	100	292	3 years soldier Virginia Cont. line	4- 5-1783
Bedinger, Daniel	2,666⅔	2211	3 years lieutenant Virginia line	12-23-1783
Bedinger, Henry	666⅔	2856	7 years captain Virginia line	4- 1-1784
Bedinger, Henry	1,333⅓	4627	8 years captain Virginia line	10-29-1793
Bedworth, William	200	1881	During war soldier Virginia line	10-15-1783
Beekham, James	100	3846	3 years soldier Virginia line	5- 2-1785
Beeks, Christopher	100	924	3 years soldier Virginia line	6-20-1783
Beelor, Maxmillion	100	2995	3 years soldier Virginia line	4-21-1784
Been, John	100	2172	3 years sailor Virginia navy	12-20-1783
Beers, James	200	2033	During war soldier Virginia line	12- 6-1783
Beham, James	200	1121	During war soldier Virginia line	6-24-1783
Belcher, George	100	2606	3 years soldier Virginia line	2-24-1784
Belcher, Robert	100	1857	3 years soldier Virginia line	11- 5-1783
Belfield, John	533⅓	1849	3 years major Virginia line	11- 1-1783
Bell, Henry	2,666⅔	2261	3 years lieutenant Virginia line	1-21-1784
Bell, James	200	1769	3 years sergeant Virginia	9-16-1783
Bell, John	1,666⅔	4107	——————	2- 7-1784
Bell, John	1,000	4108		2- 7-1786
Bell, John	100	927	3 years soldier Virginia line	6-20-1783
Bell, Ning	100	1420	3 years soldier Virginia line	7-22-1783
Bell, Thomas	100	3377	3 years soldier Virginia line	8- 4-1784
Bell, William	100	2855	3 years soldier Virginia line	4- 1-1784
Bell, William	100	3434	3 years soldier Virginia line	9- 7-1784
Belom, William	400	471	During war sergeant state line	4-29-1783
Belvin, George	100	1930	3 years soldier Virginia line	10-29-1783
Belvin, Lewis	100	1931	3 years soldier Virginia line	10-29-1783
Belvin, Robert	200	2180	3 years matross Virginia line	5-11-1790
Bennet, William	100	4492	3 years soldier Virginia line	12-20-1783
Bennett, Artaxs	2,666⅔	4437	3 years gunman Virginia navy	10-22-1788
Bennett, Arton	100	2989	3 years soldier Virginia line	4-21-1784

Name	Acres	Warrant	Service	Date
Benningfield, Henry	100	2712	Artificer Virginia line	3- 5-1784
Benson, William	100	2619	3 years sergeant Virginia line	2-24-1784
Bentley, Jeremiah	100	1904	3 years soldier Virginia line	10-23-1783
Bentley, William	4,000	48	3 years captain 5th Virginia Cont. line	12-14-1782
Bentley, William	6,666⅔	784	7 years military service Virginia line	6-10-1783
Beny, John	100	3638	3 years soldier Virginia line	12-30-1784
Beny, Thomas	100	3641	3 years soldier Virginia line	12-30-1784
Berkley, William	100	968	3 years soldier Virginia line	6-20-1783
Bernard, Thomas	200	2227	3 years corporal Virginia line	1-10-1784
Bernard, William	2,666⅔	785	3 years lieutenant Virginia line	6-10-1783
Berry, David	100	3523	3 years soldier Virginia line	11-15-1784
Berry, James	100	2772	3 years soldier Virginia line	3-18-1784
Berry, John	200	1110	During war soldier Virginia line	6-24-1783
Berry, George	4,000	1840	3 years captain Virginia line	10-31-1783
Berry, Nathaniel	100	2304	3 years captain Virginia line	1-28-1784
Berwick, James	2,666⅔	4036	1st Lieutenant Virginia line	12-15-1785
Bethel, Calentine	100	4296	3 years soldier Virginia line	6-14-1787
Bidgood, Philip	200	2738	During war soldier Virginia line	3- 8-1784
Bierly, Jacob	100	3870	3 year soldier Virginia line	5-10-1785
Bigbie, William	200	1601	During war soldier Virginia line	8-20-1783
Biggs, Benjamin	2,000	224	3 years captain Virginia Cont. line	4- 1-1783
Biggs, Benjamin	2,000	225	3 years captain Virginia Cont. line	4- 1-1783
Biggs, John	200	1629	During war soldier Virginia line	8-22-1783
Bingley, Lewis	100	270	3 years soldier state line	4- 3-1783
Bird, Joshua	100	3593	3 years soldier Virginia line	12-21-1784
Bird, Thomas	100	2061	3 years soldier Virginia line	12- 9-1783
Bird, Thomas	400	3741	During war sergeant Virginia line	2- 7-1785
Bird, Reuben	200	2255	During war soldier Virginia line	1-21-1784
Bird, Richard	100	3803	3 years soldier Virginia line	4-12-1785
Biscoe, James	200	1953	3 years boatswain Virginia navy	11-22-1783
Bishaw, John	100	1767	3 years soldier Virginia line	9-16-1783
Bishop, Joseph	100	1800	3 years soldier Virginia line	9-30-1783
Biswell, John	400	1858	During war corporal Virginia line	11- 6-1783
Black, George	100	946	3 years soldier Virginia line	6-20-1783
Black, Matthew	100	4381	3 years soldier Virginia line	1-29-1788
Blackmore, George	2,666⅔	1834	3 years lieutenant Virginia line	10- 7-1783
Blackmore, Thomas	200	3969	3 years soldier Virginia line	9- 6-1785
Blackburn, Julius	200	4064	3 years sergeant Virginia line	1- 3-1786
Blackson, Pridax	200	1832	During war soldier Virginia line	10- 7-1783
Blackwell, John Capt	4,666⅔	587	7 years captain Virginia line	5-16-1783
Blackwell, Joseph	4,000	329	3 years captain Virginia Cont. line	4-14-1783
Blackwell, Samuel	4,000	1871	3 years captain Virginia line	10-15-1783
Blackwell, Thomas	400	1811	3 years captain Virginia line	9-30-1783
Blair, Daniel	200	1379	During war soldier Virginia line	7-15-1783
Blair, John Capt, Lieut	4,000	43	3 years captain lieutenant Virginia Cont. line	12-12-1782
Blair, Robert	100	962	3 years soldier Virginia line	6-20-1783
Blair, Samuel	100	3873	3 years soldier Virginia line	5-10-1785
Blake, Charles	100	813	3 years soldier Virginia line	6-13-1783
Blakey, John	100	563	3 years state Cont. line	5- 8-1783
Blakey, John	200	585	3 years corporal state line	5-15-1783
Blalock, Zackariah	100	1340	3 years soldier Virginia line	7- 9-1783
Bland, James	100	281	3 years soldier Virginia line	4- 3-1783
Bland, James	200	3149	During war soldier Virginia line	6-11-1784
Bland, John	100	2937	3 years soldier Virginia line	4-16-1784
Bland, Theaderick	6,666⅔	209	3 years colonel Cont. cavalry	3-28-1783
Blankenship, Daniel	200	3516	During war soldier Virginia line	11-10-1784
Blankenship, Womack	200	571	— years corporal Virginia Cont. line	5-12-1783
Bledsoe, Miller	100	3403	3 years soldier Virginia line	8-18-1784
Bloxam, Arthur	200	4061	During war soldier Virginia line	12-31-1785
Bluford, William	100	3136	3 years soldier Virginia line	6- 8-1784
Blundel, Samuel	100	3277	3 years soldier Virginia line	7- 1-1784
Blunden, Seth	2,666⅔	2095	3 years midshipman Virginia navy	12-10-1783
Blunden, Swann	100	2071	3 years sailor Virginia navy	12-10-1783
Blunder, William	100	2070	3 years sailor Virginia navy	12-10-1783
Blys, William	100	2400	3 years soldier Virginia line	2- 3-1784
Boan, Joseph	100	3260	3 years soldier Virginia line	6-30-1784
Bodins, John	200	2853	3 years sergeant Virginia line	4- 1-1784
Bohanan, Ambrose	4,666⅔	285	7 years captain & lieutenant artillery	4- 3-1784
Bohannon, Henry	100	1390	3 years soldier Virginia line	7-18-1783
Boils, David	200	1595	During war soldier Virginia line	8-20-1783
Boley, Preston	400	3948	During war corporal Virginia line	8-10-1785
Bolling, John	100	2230	3 years soldier Virginia line	1-12-1784
Bolling, Joseph	100	3093	3 years soldier Virginia line	5-22-1784
Bollington, John	100	2905	3 years soldier Virginia line	4- 7-1784
Bolmare, Obadiah	100	457	3 years soldier state line	4-28-1783
Bolter, Bolling	200	2053	3 years sergeant Virginia line	12- 9-1783
Bomer, Richard	200	1705	3 years sergeant Virginia line	9- 2-1783
Bond, George	100	2051	3 years soldier Virginia line	12- 9-1783
Bond, John	100	4263	3 years soldier Virginia line	3-25-1787
Booker, Lewis	4,000	2331	7 years captain Virginia line	1-31-1784

Name	Acres	Warrant	Service	Date
Booker, Lewis............	666⅔	..2332	....7 years captain Virginia line.........	1-31-1784
Booker, Richeson.........	200	...1169	....3 years sergeant Virginia line........	6-24-1783
Booker, Samuel..........	4,000	 71	...3 years captain Virginia Cont. line....	12-24-1782
Booth, James............	200	... 536	....During war soldier state line.........	5- 2-1783
Booth, George...........	200	..4523	...3 years corporal Virginia line.........	5- 5-1791
Booth, William..........	200	..3284	...3 years master & pilot Virginia line..	7- 1-1784
Bose, alias Booze, John ...	200	..4353	...During war soldier Virginia line......	12-19-1787
Boston, Adam............	200	.. 318	....During war soldier cavalry	4-12-1783
Boswell, Machon.........	4,000	 93	...3 years captain Virginia line..........	1-11-1783
Botkins, Charles.........	100	..2832	...3 years soldier Virginia line..........	3-27-1784
Bott, Thomas............	4,000	... 305	...3 years captain Virginia Cont. line....	4- 8-1783
Botts, Archibald.........	200	... 947	...3 years sergeant Virginia line.........	6-20-1783
Botts, Leonard...........	400	..3578	...During war corporal Virginia line....	12-15-1784
Boulware, Samuel........	100	..4280	...3 years soldier Virginia line..........	4- 9-1787
Bourne, John............	100	..4312	...3 years soldier Virginia line..........	10-15-1787
Boush, Charles...........	2,666⅔	..3023	...3 years lieutenant Virginia navy......	4-27-1784
Boush, Dennis...........	100	... 966	...3 years soldier Virginia line..........	6-20-1783
Boush, Goodrich.........	5,333⅓	..4519	...During war captain Virginia navy......	3- 1-1791
Boush, Robert...........	1,666⅔	..3411	...3 years subaltern Virginia line........	8-25-1784
Boush, Robert...........	700	..3412	...3 years subaltern Virginia line........	8-25-1784
Boush, Robert...........	300	..3413	...3 years subaltern Virginia line........	6-30-1784
Bowdire, Lewis..........	100	..3250	...3 years soldier Virginia line..........	6-23-1783
Bowen, Henry...........	200	..1031	...3 years sergeant Virginia line.........	4-21-1784
Bowen, James...........	100	..2983	...3 years soldier Virginia line..........	6- 5-1783
Bowen, John............	2,666⅔	.. 741	...3 years lieutenant Virginia line.......	12-20-1783
Bowen, John............	200	..2163	...3 years sergeant Virginia line.........	6- 9-1783
Bowen, Francis..........	100	.. 774	...3 years drummer Virginia line.........	12-20-1782
Bowen, Thomas..........	4,000	 64	...3 years captain Virginia Cont. line....	4-17-1784
Bower, Robert...........	200	..2952	...3 years sergeant Virginia line.........	10-22-1789
Bowers, George..........	100	..4471	...3 years soldier Virginia line..........	2-11-1784
Bowers, Jacob...........	200	..2462	...3 years soldier Virginia line..........	12- 5-1785
Bowers, Morris..........	100	..4021	...During war soldier Virginia line......	8-11-1783
Bowers, Philip..........	100	..1545	...3 years soldier Virginia line..........	9-10-1783
Bowling, Thornberry.....	100	..1739	...3 years soldier Virginia line..........	2-20-1784
Bowles, Thomas..........	200	..2546	...3 years sergeant Virginia line.........	2-18-1784
Bowles, Zackariah........	100	..2514	...3 years soldier Virginia line..........	1-31-1783
Bowman, James..........	200	..2325	_____	
Bowman, John...........	100	..2749	...3 years soldier Virginia line..........	3-10-1784
Bowman, Mackness.......	100	..2730	...3 years soldier Virginia line..........	3- 6-1784
Bowyer, Michael.........	4,000	..3224	...Services captain Virginia line.........	6-28-1784
Bowyer, Thomas.........	4,000	... 659	...3 years captain Virginia line..........	5-27-1783
Bowry, Giles............	100	..3972	...3 years soldier Virginia line..........	9-12-1785
Bowry, Henry...........	2,666⅔	..1652	...3 years lieutenant Virginia line.......	8-23-1783
Boy, Henry.............	100	..4206	...3 years soldier Virginia line..........	8-31-1786
Boyce, William..........	2,666⅔	..3671	...Service lieutenant Virginia line.......	1- 5-1785
Boyd, James............	100	..2229	...3 years soldier Virginia line..........	1-12-1784
Boyd, John.............	100	..2881	...3 years soldier Virginia line..........	4- 5-1784
Boyd, Francis...........	100	..1838	...3 years soldier Virginia line..........	10- 9-1783
Boyle, Charles...........	100	..1355	...3 years soldier Virginia line..........	7-12-1783
Boyle, Walter...........	100	..3669	...3 years sailor Virginia navy..........	1- 4-1785
Boyles, William.........	2,666⅔	..3167	...3 years lieutenant Virginia line.......	6-17-1784
Bozwell, Robert.........	200	... 486	...During war soldier state line.........	4-30-1783
Bozwell, Robert.........	100	..2060	...3 years soldier Virginia line..........	12- 9-1783
Bozzell, George.........	200	..4614	...During war private Virginia line......	5-27-1793
Brabston, William.......	200	..2039	...During war soldier Virginia line......	12- 9-1783
Brackenridge, Capt Alexander...........	4,000	... 617	...3 years captain Virginia line..........	5-22-1783
Brackenridge, Robert.....	3,666⅔	..1653	...7 years lieutenant Virginia line.......	8-23-1783
Bradford, Charles........	2,666⅔	..4467	...3 years lieutenant Virginia line.......	10- 5-1789
Bradford, Henry........	200	..2155	...3 years sergeant Virginia line.........	12-19-1783
Bradford, Samuel K.....	4,000	... 350	...3 years captain & lieutenant artillery.	4-17-1783
Bradley, James..........	4,000	..2665	...3 years captain Virginia line..........	3- 2-1784
Bradley, John...........	400	..1666	...During war sergeant Virginia line.....	8-25-1783
Bradley, William........	200	..1893	...3 years sergeant Virginia line.........	11-12-1783
Bradshaw, Robert........	200	..2482	...3 years corporal Virginia line........	2-13-1784
Brady, Christopher.......	2,666⅔	..3477	...3 years subaltern Virginia line........	10-19-1784
Brady, Joseph...........	200	..4265	...3 years corporal Virginia line........	3-28-1787
Brady, Luke............	200	..1620	...During war soldier Virginia line......	8-22-1783
Brady, Michael..........	400	..1831	...8 years corporal Virginia line........	10- 7-1783
Brain, William..........	200	..4330	...During war soldier Virginia line......	11- 6-1787
Bragg, Benjamin.........	200	..3485	...During war soldier Virginia line......	10-26-1784
Bragg, Joel.............	100	..2702	...3 years soldier Virginia line..........	3- 4-1784
Bragg, William..........	200	..2575	...3 years corporal Virginia line........	2-21-1784
Branam, John...........	200	..1599	...During war soldier Virginia line......	8-20-1783
Branan, Thomas.........	466⅔	..1563	...During war sergeant Virginia line.....	8-12-1783
Brandom, Lewis.........	200	..2436	...3 years sergeant Virginia line.........	2- 9-1784
Brandon, Peter..........	200	..1093	...During war soldier Virginia line......	6-24-1783
Branham, Eben..........	200	... 671	...3 years sergeant Virginia line.........	5-29-1783
Branham, John..........	400	..3049	...During war corporal Virginia line....	5- 6-1784
Branham, William.......	200	..3418	...During war soldier Virginia line......	8-27-1784
Brann, Andrew..........	200	..2003	...During war soldier Virginia line......	12- 1-1783

Name	Acres	Warrant	Service	Date
Brann, Joseph	200	4305	During war soldier Virginia line	8-18-1787
Bransford, William	200	1594	During war soldier Virginia line	8-20-1783
Bransom, Benjamin	200	2649	3 years sergeant Virginia line	2-28-1784
Branson, John	200	4581	During war fifer Virginia line	6-16-1792
Brasheer, Richard	4,000	2687	3 years captain Virginia line	3- 3-1784
Braughton, William	400	2550	During war sergeant Virginia line	2-20-1784
Brawner, John	200	3048	During war soldier Virginia line	5- 6-1784
Bray, James	100	4260	3 years soldier Virginia line	3- 8-1787
Bray, John	100	3556	3 years soldier Virginia line	12- 6-1784
Brayson, Robert	200	1393	During war soldier Virginia line	7-18-1783
Brayson, Robert	33⅓	2697	7 years soldier Virginia line	3- 3-1784
Brazen, William	200	1130	During war soldier Virginia line	6-24-1783
Breadlove, Wm B	200	480	During war soldier state line	4-30-1783
Bready, John	200	1092	During war soldier Virginia line	6-24-1783
Brean, John	200	1137	During war soldier Virginia line	6-24-1783
Brent, John	100	889	3 years soldier Virginia line	6-20-1783
Brent, John	200	1765	During war soldier Virginia line	9-15-1783
Brent, John	200	4531	During war soldier Virginia line	8- 3-1791
Brent, William	6,666⅔	698	3 years colonel Virginia line	5-31-1783
Brewer, Henry	100	626	3 years drummer Virginia line	5-23-1783
Briant, James	100	3343	3 years soldier Virginia line	7-19-1784
Bridges, John	200	4485	During war dragoon Virginia line	12-19-1789
Bridgewater, Levi	100	3770	3 years soldier Virginia line	3- 5-1785
Bridgman, Boswell	200	3034	During war soldier Virginia line	5- 1-1784
Bridgman, Franklin	100	1534	3 years soldier Virginia line	8- 9-1783
Bridgman, Hezekiah	100	1823	3 years soldier Virginia line	10- 6-1783
Bridgman, Joseph	200	1236	3 years drummer Virginia line	6-27-1783
Bridgman, Thomas	200	1584	During war soldier Virginia line	8-19-1783
Brimer, Isaac	100	359	3 years soldier state line	4-18-1783
Briscoe, John	100	1914	3 years colonel Virginia line	11-20-1783
Britain, John	2,666⅔	1487	3 years sailing master Virginia navy	8- 4-1783
Britt, John	100	1220	3 years soldier Virginia line	6-26-1783
Brittain, Samuel	200	4460	During war soldier Virginia line	6- 4-1789
Brittan, John	200	2914	3 years sergeant Virginia line	4-12-1784
Brittle, Thomas	200	4027	During war soldier Virginia line	12- 9-1785
Britton, John	200	1050	During war soldier Virginia line	6-24-1783
Broaddus, William	1,666⅔	2538	3 years subaltern Virginia line	2-19-1784
Broadfield, Charles	100	3162	3 years soldier Virginia line	6-16-1784
Broadus, Edward	100	3676	3 years Virginia soldier line	1- 5-1785
Broadus, James	2,666⅔	2518	3 years ensign Virginia line	2-19-1784
Broadus, Richard	100	3683	3 years soldier Virginia line	1-11-1785
Broadus, Robert	100	553	During war soldier state line	5- 7-1783
Broadus, William	1,000	2537	3 years subaltern Virginia line	2-19-1784
Brock, Elias	100	2167	3 years soldier Virginia line	12-20-1783
Brodie, Lodowick	6,000	106	3 years surgeon state line	2- 1-1783
Bromfield, William	100	4079	3 years soldier Virginia line	1-14-1786
Bromley, John	1,000	4240	3 years surgeon mate Virginia line	12-13-1786
Bromley, John	500	4241	3 years surgeon mate Virginia line	12-13-1786
Bromley, John	1,166⅔	4242	3 years surgeon mate Virginia line	12-13-1786
Brook, Walter Esqr	6,666⅔	991	3 years commander Virginia navy	6-21-1783
Brooke, Francis	2,666⅔	2265	End war lieutenant Virginia line	1-21-1784
Brooke, John	2,666⅔	2267	End war lieutenant Virginia line	1-21-1784
Brookes, John	200	3352	During war soldier Virginia line	7-22-1784
Brooking, Samuel	200	2535	3 years corporal Virginia line	2-19-1784
Brooks, Benjamin	200	1089	During war soldier Virginia line	6-24-1783
Brooks, Charles	200	1072	During war soldier Virginia line	6-24-1783
Brooks, George	100	650	3 years soldier Virginia line	5-27-1783
Brooks, James	100	2536	3 years soldier Virginia line	2-19-1784
Brook, James	200	4116	During war soldier Virginia line	3- 7-1786
Brooks, John	200	504	During war soldier state line	5- 1-1783
Brooks, Edmund	2,666⅔	2541	During war lieutenant Virginia line	2-19-1784
Brooks, Nathaniel	100	182	3 years soldier Virginia line	3-17-1783
Brooks, Thomas	100	2054	3 years soldier Virginia Cont. line	12- 9-1783
Broom, John	200	1694	3 years sergeant Virginia line	8-30-1783
Brough, William	100	1034	3 years sailor Virginia navy	6-24-1783
Browder, Harrison, Frederick & Samuel	300	4173	3 years soldiers Virginia line	6-15-1786
Browder, Isham	100	4165	3 years soldier Virginia line	6- 3-1786
Brown, Absalom	100	931	3 years soldier Virginia line	6-20-1783
Brown, Aries	200	3084	3 years corporal Virginia line	5-20-1784
Brown, Benjamin	100	764	3 years sailor Virginia navy	6- 7-1783
Brown, Duncan	100	2779	3 years soldier Virginia line	3-18-1784
Brown, George	100	1918	3 years soldier Virginia line	10-25-1783
Brown, George	200	4020	3 years sergeant Virginia line	12- 3-1785
Brown, Henry	200	672	3 years sergeant Virginia line	5-29-1783
Brown, Henry	100	2599	3 years soldier Virginia line	2-23-1784
Brown, Isaac	100	945	3 years soldier Virginia line	6-20-1783
Brown, Jacob	3,110⅔	630	7 years lieutenant Virginia line	5-23-1783
Brown, James	100	1915	3 years soldier Virginia line	10-25-1783
Brown, James	100	2573	3 years soldier Virginia line	2-21-1784
Brown, John	200	406	During war soldier Virginia line	4-25-1783

Name	Acres	Warrant	Service	Date
Brown, John	200	1618	During war soldier Virginia line	8-21-1783
Brown, John	100	1992	3 years seaman Virginia navy	11-28-1783
Brown, John	200	2542	During war soldier Virginia line	2-19-1784
Brown, John	100	2552	3 years soldier Virginia line	2-20-1784
Brown, John	200	2294	3 years sergeant Virginia line	1-26-1784
Brown, John	100	3198	3 years soldier Virginia line	6-23-1784
Brown, John	200	4285	3 years sergeant Virginia line	5-24-1787
Brown, John Lee	200	322	3 years corporal cavalry	4-12-1783
Brown, Jonathan	100	1846	3 years soldier Virginia line	10-31-1783
Brown, Robert	100	1533	3 years trumpeter Virginia line	8- 9-1783
Brown, Robert	100	1874	3 years soldier Virginia line	10-15-1783
Brown, Robert	100	2296	3 years soldier Virginia line	1-26-1784
Brown, Robert	2,666⅔	2996	3 years lieutenant Virginia line	1- 2-1785
Brown, Robert	100	3665	3 years soldier Virginia line	9-24-1783
Brown, Samuel	200	1785	During war soldier Virginia line	6-20-1783
Brown, Thomas	400	879	3 years drum major Virginia line	6-28-1784
Brown, Thomas	100	3227	3 years soldier Virginia line	5-30-1783
Brown, William	100	694	3 years soldier Virginia line	6- 2-1783
Brown, William	6,000	712	3 years reg. surgeon Virginia line	3-25-1783
Brown, Windsor	4,666⅔	195	7 years captain Virginia state line	11-21-1787
Browning, William	100	4337	3 years soldier Virginia line	4- 5-1784
Brownlee, Thomas	100	2883	3 years soldier Virginia line	5-30-1783
Brownlee, William	4,000	681	3 years captain Virginia line	5-21-1783
Browser, James	200	606	During war private Virginia line	2- 3-1784
Bruce, George	200	2378	3 years corporal Virginia line	6-23-1783
Bruce, John	200	1029	3 years sergeant Virginia line	4-20-1784
Bruce, William	200	2969	3 years sergeant Virginia line	12-20-1783
Bruin, Peter Bryan	5,333⅓	2183	3 years major Virginia line	6-24-1783
Brumingham, William	200	1133	During war soldier Virginia line	6-26-1783
Brumley, Robert	100	1208	3 years soldier Virginia line	5- 6-1785
Brunagem, Patrick	200	3849	During war soldier Virginia line	6-21-1785
Brusely, Charles	200	3918	During war soldier Virginia line	10-16-1782
Brush, James	200	11	3 years sergeant Virginia Cont. line	6-24-1783
Brute, Thomas	200	1103	During war soldier Virginia line	8-10-1785
Bryant, Thomas	100	3950	3 years soldier Virginia line	2- 3-1784
Bryant, William	200	2394	End of war soldier Virginia line	4-19-1784
Bryant, William	100	2964	3 years soldier Virginia line	2-21-1784
Bryant, William	100	2571	3 years soldier Virginia line	12-16-1783
Bryent, John	100	2139	3 years lieutenant Virginia line	3-29-1787
Buchanan, John	2,666⅔	4267	3 years soldier Virginia line	8-21-1783
Buck, John	100	1612	3 years seaman Virginia navy	11-22-1783
Buck, John Smith	100	1955	During war soldier Virginia line	6-20-1783
Buckley, Abraham	100	929	During war soldier Virginia line	6-27-1783
Buckley, Joshua	200	909	7 years soldier Virginia line	1-23-1784
Buckley, Michael	233⅓	1255	7 years captain Virginia line	4-21-1784
Buckner, Thomas	4,666⅔	2273	During war soldier Virginia line	5-29-1783
Buffington, David	200	2991	3 years colonel Virginia line	6-21-1785
Buford, Abraham	6,666⅔	673	During war soldier Virginia line	1-17-1786
Buford, John	200	3905	3 years soldier Virginia line	1-17-1786
Buknall, James	100	4081	3 years soldier Virginia line	9-12-1783
Buknall, Thomas	100	4082	During war corporal Virginia line	8- 5-1783
Bullen, Luke	400	1755	3 years seaman Virginia navy	12-20-1783
Bulley, John	100	1502	3 years boatswain Virginia navy	11-22-1783
Bully, Edward	200	2181	3 years sailor Virginia navy	6-19-1784
Bully, Thomas	100	1957	3 years subaltern Virginia line	6-19-1784
Bullock, Rice	200	3171	3 years subaltern Virginia line	4- 8-1785
Bullock, Rice	666⅔	3172	During war soldier Virginia line	11-19-1785
Bumback, Peter	200	3799	3 years soldier Virginia line	2- 2-1784
Bunch, Winslow	100	3998	3 years soldier Virginia Cont. line	1-12-1784
Bunch, Winston	100	110	During war soldier Virginia line	8-23-1783
Bundy, Francis	200	2243	During war soldier state line	5- 5-1783
Bunn, Daniel	200	1644	3 years soldier Virginia line	1- 5-1784
Bunnett, Wm	200	544	3 years soldier Virginia line	5- 7-1785
Buns, John	100	2221	3 years soldier Virginia line	6-27-1783
Bunting, Sacker	100	3859	During war soldier Virginia line	4- 2-1784
Burch, Samuel	100	1259	3 years lieutenant Virginia line	7-17-1783
Burdorn, John	200	2861	3 years soldier Virginia line	8- 4-1784
Burfoot, Thomas	2,666⅔	1384	During war sergeant Virginia line	7-17-1788
Burfott, William	100	3378	3 years sergeant Virginia line	2-24-1784
Burge, William	400	4416	3 years soldier Virginia line	6-20-1783
Burgess, Dawson	200	2618	3 years gunner Virginia navy	11-22-1783
Burgett, Cornelius	100	948	During war fifer Virginia line	8-23-1783
Burk, James	100	1958	3 years soldier Virginia line	6-21-1785
Burk, John	200	1651	3 years soldier Virginia line	7-19-1784
Burk, Mathew	100	3909	3 years sergeant Virginia line	6-30-1784
Burk, Nicholas	100	3341	3 years soldier Virginia line	9- 4-1783
Burk, Samuel	200	3265	3 years soldier Virginia line	8-20-1783
Burk, Thomas	100	1727	During war soldier Virginia line	5-24-1784
Burk, William	200	1607	During war soldier Virginia line	3- 5-1784
Burke, William	200	3097	3 years soldier Virginia line	3- 5-1784
Burks, John	100	2708	3 years soldier Virginia line	

Name	Acres	Warrant	Service	Date
Burnes, Jeremiah	200	611	During war soldier Virginia line	5-21-1783
Burnett, John	200	1843	During war soldier Virginia line	10-31-1783
Burnett, Millington	200	4414	3 years corporal Virginia line	7-17-1788
Burns, Frederick	100	258	3 years soldier state line	4- 3-1783
Burns, John	100	2822	3 years soldier Virginia line	3-26-1784
Burns, Thomas	200	3771	During war soldier Virginia line	3- 8-1785
Burns, William	200	2099	During war soldier Virginia line	12-11-1783
Burrago, Charles	100	2929	3 years soldier Virginia line	4-13-1784
Burton, Archibald	100	3063	3 years soldier Virginia line	5-10-1784
Burton, Hutchins	2,666⅔	1273	3 years lieutenant Virginia line	6-28-1783
Burton, James	100	650	3 years soldier Virginia line	5-28-1783
Burton, William	100	2355	3 years soldier Virginia line	1-31-1784
Burwell, Nathaniel	4,666⅔	2133	7 years captain Virginia line	12-15-1783
Bushop, Solomon	100	976	3 years soldier Virginia line	6-20-1783
Bushop, Thomas	100	2794	3 years soldier Virginia line	3-19-1784
Busley, James	100	4155	3 years soldier Virginia line	5- 9-1786
Busley, John	100	4156	3 years soldier Virginia line	5- 9-1786
Bustor, Saunders	100	1385	3 years soldier Virginia line	7-17-1783
Butler, Edward	200	2175	During war sailor Virginia navy	12-20-1783
Butler, John	400	464	During war sergeant artillery	4-28-1783
Butler, Joseph	200	532	During war soldier state line	5- 2-1783
Butler, Lawrence	4,000	199	3 years captain Virginia line	3-26-1783
Butler, Samuel	2,666⅔	2379	During war lieutenant Virginia line	2- 3-1784
Butler, William	100	3458	3 years soldier Virginia line	10- 7-1784
Butler, William	100	4377	3 years soldier Virginia line	1-23-1788
Butt, Zachariah	100	2985	3 years soldier Virginia line	4-21-1784
Button, Harmon	100	1194	3 years soldier Virginia line	6-26-1783
Bynes, Thomas	100	3642	3 years soldier Virginia line	12-30-1784
Byrd, John	100	2289	3 years soldier Virginia line	1-26-1784
Byrd, Otway	6,000	3367	Services as lieutenant Virginia line	7-30-1784
Cabbell, Samuel J	1,000	1177	7 years lieutenant colonel Virginia line	6-25-1783
Cabell, Colonel Samuel I	6,000	9	3 years lieut col Virginia Infantry	9-30-1782
Cain, Mathias	200	4413	During war soldier Virginia line	7-17-1788
Calbert, John	200	723	3 years soldier Virginia line	6- 3-1783
Calfrey, Charles	100	1341	3 years soldier Virginia line	7- 9-1783
Call, Richard	5,333⅓	2260	3 years major Virginia line	1-21-1784
Callaham, Major	100	2588	3 years soldier Virginia line	2-23-1784
Callender, Eliazer	5,333⅓	103	3 years captain in state navy	1-30-1783
Calmes, Marquis	4,000	345	3 years captain Virginia Cont. line	4-12-1783
Calvert, Joseph	2,666⅔	2679	3 years lieutenant Virginia line	3- 3-1784
Campbell, William	4,000	10	3 years captain Virginia regiment	10-15-1782
Camble, Dennis	200	1622	During war soldier Virginia line	8-22-1783
Camburn, John	200	410	During war soldier Virginia line	4-25-1783
Camp, James	100	2563	3 years soldier Virginia line	2-20-1784
Camp, James	100	4104	3 years soldier Virginia line	2- 6-1786
Camp, Marshall	200	4127	During war soldier Virginia line	3-14-1786
Camp, Thomas	400	2799	During war corporal Virginia line	3-20-1784
Campbell, Archibald	200	895	During war soldier Virginia line	6-20-1783
Campbell, Archibald	2,666⅔	2014	3 years lieutenant Virginia line	12- 5-1783
Campbell, David	200	3979	3 years sergeant Virginia line	10-15-1785
Campbell, Dennis	200	2999	During war soldier Virginia line	4-21-1784
Campbell, John	100	4341	3 years soldier Virginia line	11-28-1787
Campbell, John	100	4520	3 years soldier Virginia line	4-19-1791
Campbell, Richard	6,000	3001	3 years lieutenant Virginia line	4-22-1784
Campbell, Samuel	2,666⅔	16	3 years lieutenant Virginia Cont. line	11-13-1782
Campbell, Thomas	100	4216	3 years soldier Virginia line	10- 4-1786
Campbell, William	100	2833	3 years soldier Virginia line	3-27-1784
Campbell, William	5,000	2200	————	12-23-1783
Camron, Hugh	100	3079	3 years soldier Virginia line	5-17-1784
Canafax, Edward	100	1550	3 years soldier Virginia line	8-11-1783
Canary, William	100	2105	3 years soldier Virginia line	12-12-1783
Cannon, Luke	2,666⅔	701	3 years lieutenant Virginia line	5-31-1783
Canore, Andrew	200	3334	During war soldier Virginia line	7-19-1784
Cansey, James	100	2069	3 years seaman Virginia navy	12-10-1783
Capts, Obadiah	100	3599	3 years soldier Virginia line	12-21-1784
Carbine, Henry	100	2902	3 years soldier Virginia line	4- 7-1784
Cardiff, Miles	100	3962	3 years soldier Virginia line	8-13-1785
Cardwell, John	100	2421	3 years soldier Virginia line	2- 6-1784
Cardwell, William	100	4405	3 years soldier Virginia line	6-12-1788
Carey, Benjamin	4,000	745	3 years captain Virginia line	6- 5-1783
Carey, James	100	564	3 years soldier Cont. line	5- 9-1783
Carey, James	200	3322	3 years sergeant Virginia line	7-13-1784
Carey, Samuel	2,666⅔	990	3 years lieutenant Virginia line	6-21-1783
Carilton, Lewis	100	3229	3 years soldier Virginia line	6-29-1784
Carlton, William	100	3051	3 years soldier Virginia line	5- 6-1784
Carnahan, John	100	2093	3 years soldier Virginia line	12-10-1783
Carnal, William	200	1447	During war soldier Virginia line	7-31-1783
Carnes, Joshua	200	3781	During war soldier Virginia line	3-17-1785
Carnes, Patrick	4,000	2223	3 years captain Virginia line	1- 7-1784
Carnes, Daniel	200	549	During war soldier state line	5- 6-1783
Carney, Martin	2,666⅔	838	3 years lieutenant Virginia line	6-16-1783

Name	Acres	Warrant	Service	Date
Carney, Patrick	200	1660	During war soldier Virginia line	8–25–1783
Carnick, Patrick	100	257	3 years soldier state line	4– 3–1783
Carny, Anthony	400	3456	During war sergeant Virginia line	10– 7–1784
Caroine, Jeremiah	200	4129	During war soldier Virginia line	3–18–1786
Carpenter, Christopher	200	1076	During war soldier Virginia line	6–24–1783
Carpenter, George	100	3156	3 years soldier Virginia line	6–14–1784
Carpenter, John	200	1428	3 years sergeant Virginia line	7–26–1783
Carpenter, John	200	4294	During war soldier Virginia line	6–14–1787
Carr, Joseph	400	3459	During war sergeant Virginia line	10–12–1784
Carr, Samuel	4,666⅔	4511	During war captain Virginia navy	12– 9–1790
Carr, William	100	1214	3 years soldier Virginia line	6–26–1783
Carr, William	200	2249	During war soldier Virginia line	1–16–1784
Carr, William	100	4342	3 years soldier Virginia line	11–28–1787
Carrell, John	200	1840	3 years sergeant Virginia line	10– 9–1783
Carrell, Joseph	100	1216	3 years soldier Virginia line	6–26–1783
Carrick, James	100	2785	3 years soldier Virginia line	3–18–1784
Carrick, Patrick	200	1181	During war soldier Virginia line	6–25–1783
Carrington, Clement	2,666⅔	2239	End war ensign Virginia line	1–12–1784
Carrington, Edward	7,000	1792	7 years lieutenant colonel Virginia line	9–25–1783
Carrington, George	2,666⅔	1935	3 years lieutenant Virginia line	10–31–1783
Carrington, Mayo	4,000	24	3 years captain Virginia Cont. line	11–29–1782
Carrington, Mayo	6,666⅔	568	7 years captain Virginia Cont. line	5–10–1783
Carrol, Berry	100	1728	3 years soldier Virginia line	9– 8–1783
Carroll, Edward	400	353	During war sergeant Virginia line	4–17–1783
Carroll, John	200	434	During war soldier state line	4–26–1783
Carroll, Joseph	100	1492	3 years soldier Virginia line	8– 4–1783
Carroll, Thomas	200	1796	During war soldier Virginia line	9–26–1783
Carter, Armstad	100	1881	3 years soldier Virginia line	11–10–1783
Carter, Charles	100	775	3 years soldier Virginia line	6– 9–1783
Carter, Dale	100	3582	3 years soldier Virginia line	12–16–1784
Carter, George	100	3575	3 years soldier Virginia line	12–15–1784
Carter, Henry	100	1193	3 years soldier Virginia line	6–26–1783
Carter, James	200	498	During war soldier state line	5– 1–1783
Carter, John	100	691	3 years soldier Virginia line	5–30–1783
Carter, John	100	1683	3 years sailor Virginia navy	8–29–1783
Carter, John	200	2836	3 years sergeant Virginia line	3–27–1784
Carter, John	200	3497	3 years sergeant Virginia line	11– 4–1784
Carter, John C	4,000	306	7 years captain Virginia Cont. line	4– 8–1783
Carter, Joseph	100	579	3 years soldier Virginia line	5–14–1783
Carter, Nicholas	200	1065	During war soldier Virginia line	6–24–1783
Carter, Obediah	200	3384	3 years sergeant Virginia line	8– 6–1784
Carter, Richard	200	1056	During war soldier Virginia line	6–24–1783
Carter, Robert	200	1882	3 years sergeant Virginia line	11–10–1783
Carter, Robert	200	2419	During war soldier Virginia line	2– 6–1784
Carter, Thomas	6,000	1506	3 years doctor Virginia navy	8– 6–1783
Carter, Thomas	100	3266	3 years soldier Virginia line	7– 1–1784
Carter, William	100	1317	3 years soldier Virginia line	7– 1–1783
Carter, William	100	3055	3 years soldier Virginia line	5– 7–1784
Carter, William Sr	6,000	4569	3 years surgeon Virginia hospital	2– 7–1792
Cartwright, Jesse	100	2901	3 years soldier Virginia line	4– 7–1784
Cartwright, Justiman	466⅔	1909	During war sergeant Virginia line	11–19–1783
Cartwright, Peter	100	3876	3 years soldier Virginia line	5–10–1785
Carver, Lawrence	200	515	During war soldier state line	5– 1–1783
Case, William	100	1919	3 years soldier Virginia line	10–25–1783
Case, William	200	2038	During war soldier Virginia line	12– 9–1783
Casell, William	100	932	3 years soldier Virginia line	6–20–1783
Casey, Archibald	200	729	3 years soldier Virginia line	6– 3–1783
Casey, James	100	3971	3 years soldier Virginia line	9–12–1785
Casey, John	200	3484	During war soldier Virginia line	10–26–1784
Casey, Robert	100	994	3 years soldier Virginia line	6–21–1783
Cash, Warren	100	140	3 years soldier Virginia line	2–21–1783
Cason, James	100	1807	3 years soldier Virginia line	9–30–1783
Cason, John	200	1805	3 years sergeant Virginia line	9–30–1783
Cason, William	100	1806	3 years soldier Virginia line	9–30–1783
Cassady, James	466⅔	3731	7 years sergeant Virginia line	2– 7–1785
Casse, William	100	951	3 years soldier Virginia line	6–20–1783
Cassidy, Michael	100	2091	3 years soldier Virginia line	12–10–1783
Caswell, Michael	100	4316	3 years soldier Virginia line	10–23–1787
Casy, John	200	3513	During war soldier Virginia line	11– 9–1784
Catlett, Thomas	4,000	1198	3 years captain Virginia line	6–26–1783
Cave, James	100	2031	3 years soldier Virginia line	12– 6–1783
Cavender, James	200	538	During war soldier state line	5– 2–1783
Cavender, Joseph	400	1733	During war sergeant Virginia line	9– 8–1783
Cavenear, Garret	200	1046	During war soldier Virginia line	6–24–1783
Cawthorn, William	100	2513	3 years soldier Virginia line	2–18–1784
Cayner, Matthew	100	1711	3 years soldier Virginia line	9– 2–1783
Chaffin, John	200	1469	During war soldier Virginia line	8– 1–1783
Chamberlain, George	4,000	751	3 years lieutenant Virginia line	6– 5–1783
Chambers, Alexander	100	868	3 years soldier Virginia line	6–19–1783
Chambers, David	100	1239	3 years soldier Virginia line	6–27–1783
Chambers, James	100	3926	3 years soldier Virginia line	6–21–1785

Name	Acres	Warrant	Service	Date
Chambers, James........	200	4249	During war soldier Virginia line......	1- 6-1787
Chambers, Robert.......	200	3201	3 years sergeant Virginia line........	6-24-1784
Chandler, Jesse..........	200	4482	During war soldier Virginia line.....	12- 2-1789
Chandler, Thomas.......	1,666⅔	3763	3 years lieutenant Virginia navy.....	2-28-1785
Chandler, Thomas.......	1,200	3764	3 years lieutenant Virginia navy.....	2-28-1785
Chaners, John..........	100	193	3 years soldier Virginia Cont. line....	3-24-1783
Chapen, Benjamin.......	6,000	4565	During war surgeon Virginia navy	1-21-1792
Chapin, John............	100	1302	3 years soldier Virginia line.........	6-30-1783
Chapin, Solomon........	100	3852	3 years soldier Virginia line.........	5- 6-1785
Chaplin, Abraham.......	2,666⅔	2683	3 years lieutenant Virginia line.......	3- 3-1784
Chapman, John..........	4,000	789	3 years captain state line............	6-12-1783
Chapman, John..........	200	2124	3 years sergeant Virginia line.......	12-15-1783
Chapman, Thomas.......	100	926	3 years soldier Virginia line.........	6-20-1783
Charity, Charles.........	200	2789	During war soldier Virginia line	3-18-1784
Charles, Samuel.........	200	1860	3 years sergeant Virginia line	11- 6-1783
Charles, William.........	100	1850	3 years soldier Virginia line.........	10-11-1783
Charles, William.........	100	1850	3 years soldier Virginia line.........	10-11-1783
Chatham, John..........	200	2904	During war soldier Virginia line	4- 7-1784
Chavers, James..........	100	3717	3 years soldier Virginia line.........	1-22-1785
Chavers, Robert W	100	3503	3 years soldier Virginia line.........	11- 4-1784
Chavers, Samuel........	100	4003	3 years soldier Virginia line.........	11-19-1785
Chavious, James.........	100	3999	3 years soldier Virginia line.........	11-19-1785
Chelton, John...........	4,000	1249	3 years captain Virginia line.........	6-27-1783
Chenault, John..........	100	3775	3 years soldier Virginia line.........	3-12-1785
Cheserounds, John.......	100	2724	3 years soldier Virginia line.........	3- 6-1784
Cherry, William.........	1,000	1982	3 years captain Virginia line........	11-28-1783
Cherry, William.........	3,000	1983	3 years captain Virginia line........	11-28-1783
Chevalier, Anthony......	100	1691	3 years soldier Virginia line.........	8-30-1783
Childress, Alexander	100	3713	3 years soldier Virginia line.........	1-20-1785
Childress, Henry........	100	2196	3 years soldier Virginia line.........	12-22-1783
Childress, Meredith......	100	2809	3 years soldier Virginia line.........	3-23-1784
Childress, Meredith......	100	4373	3 years soldier Virginia line.........	1-23-1788
Childress, Mosby........	100	1744	3 years soldier Virginia line.........	9-11-1783
Chilton, Newman........	200	1373	3 years corporal Virginia line........	7-15-1783
Chinworth, John........	100	1027	3 years soldier Virginia line.........	6-23-1783
Chisam, James..........	100	2574	During war soldier Virginia line	2-21-1784
Chizham, James.........	100	4004	3 years soldier Virginia line.........	11-23-1785
Chowning, Christopher....	100	4344	3 years soldier Virginia line.........	11-28-1787
Chowning, Thomas.......	100	2395	3 years soldier Virginia line.........	2- 3-1784
Christee, James.........	200	309	During war soldier Virginia line	4- 9-1783
Christian, James........	400	3442	During war corporal Virginia line	9-15-1784
Christian, Nicholas......	200	2966	3 years steward Virginia line........	4-19-1783
Christie, Thomas........	7,000	1912	7 years surgeon Virginia line........	10-25-1783
Chunn, Sylvester........	100	3189	3 years soldier Virginia line.........	6-23-1784
Church, John............	200	1478	During war soldier Virginia line	8- 2-1783
Chusholin, George.......	233½	1248	During war soldier Virginia Cont. line	6-27-1783
Claiborne, Richard......	2,666⅔	2347	During war lieutenant Virginia line ..	1-31-1784
Clark, David............	200	1143	During war soldier Virginia line	6-24-1783
Clark, Edmond..........	200	3237	3 years sergeant Virginia line	6-29-1784
Clark, George Rogers....	10,000	2292	3 years brigadier general Virginia line.	1-26-1784
Clark, James............	200	692	3 years sergeant Virginia line	5-30-1783
Clark, John.............	4,000	307	3 years captain Virginia Cont. line...	4- 8-1783
Clark, John.............	100	3138	3 years soldier Virginia line.........	6- 9-1784
Clark, Moses............	200	1857	During war soldier Virginia line	10-13-1783
Clark, Thomas..........	200	2286	During war soldier Virginia line	1-26-1784
Clark, William..........	100	1536	3 years soldier Virginia line.........	8- 9-1783
Clarke, Edward.........	100	328	3 years soldier Virginia artillery.....	4-14-1783
Clarke, Edmund.........	2,666⅔	2359	3 years lieutenant Virginia line.......	2- 2-1784
Clarke, Henry..........	200	3161	3 years soldier Virginia line........	6-16-1784
Clarke, James..........	100	2782	3 years soldier Virginia line........	3-18-1784
Clarke, John...........	100	3758	3 years soldier Virginia line.........	2-19-1785
Clarke, Jonathan........	7,000	172	7 years lieutenant Virginia Cont. line .	3-10-1783
Clarke, Robert..........	100	3621	3 years soldier Virginia line........	12-23-1784
Clarke, Robert..........	200	3940	During war soldier Virginia line	8- 2-1785
Clarke, William.........	100	2259	3 years soldier Virginia line.........	1-21-1784
Clarke, William.........	2,666⅔	2681	3 years lieutenant Virginia line.......	3- 3-1784
Clarks, Richard.........	2,666⅔	2684	3 years lieutenant Virginia line.......	3- 3-1784
Clavenger, Edward......	100	915	3 years soldier Virginia line.........	6-20-1783
Claverins, James........	4,000	2410	3 years captain Virginia line.........	2- 5-1784
Clay, Mathew..........	2,666⅔	52	3 years lieutenant Virginia line........	12-14-1782
Clay, Thomas..........	4,000	2278	3 years captain Virginia line.........	1-23-1784
Clayton, Henry.........	100	3165	3 years soldier Virginia line.........	6-16-1785
Clayton, Joseph........	200	1337	During war soldier Virginia line	7- 8-1783
Clayton, Phillip........	2,666⅔	794	3 years lieutenant Virginia line.......	6-12-1783
Clement, Edward W	100	4145	3 years soldier Virginia line.........	4-19-1786
Clements, Maco..........	7,000	738	7 years surgeon Virginia Cont. line...	6- 4-1783
Clemons, John..........	200	3050	During war soldier Virginia line	5- 6-1784
Clendeny, George........	100	4431	3 years sailor Virginia navy.........	8- 4-1788
Clerk, Hezekiah.........	100	3691	3 years soldier Virginia line.........	1-20-1785
Cleveland, John..........	100	2970	3 years soldier Virginia line.........	4-20-1784
Cliffton, Joshua.........	233½	1252	7 years soldier Virginia line.........	6-27-1783

Name	Acres	Warrant	Service	Date
Clift, William	200	1614	3 years soldier Virginia line	8–21–1783
Climen, James	400	1438	3 years sergeant Virginia line	7–28–1783
Clod, Robert	200	663	3 years soldier Virginia line	5–28–1783
Clough, John	400	3200	During war sergeant Virginia line	6–24–1784
Cloyd, William	200	1119	During war soldier Virginia line	6–24–1783
Coats, George	100	2737	3 years soldier Virginia line	3– 8–1784
Coats, Samuel	100	4230	3 years sailor Virginia navy	11–16–1786
Cochran, William	200	1998	3 years sergeant Virginia line	11–29–1783
Cock, Benjamin	100	4176	3 years soldier Virginia line	6–20–1786
Cocke, Colin	4,666⅔	2323	7 years captain Virginia line	1–30–1784
Cocke, Michael	100	2084	3 years soldier Virginia line	12–10–1783
Cockran, Samuel	200	2372	3 years sergeant Virginia line	2– 3–1784
Cockrell, Littleton	100	3272	3 years sailor Virginia navy	7– 1–1784
Cofer, George	200	589	3 years corporal Virginia line	5–17–1783
Coffin, John	100	4579	3 years soldier Virginia line	6–16–1792
Coffin, Samuel	100	4580	3 years soldier Virginia line	6–16–1792
Cogay, John	100	2511	3 years soldier Virginia line	2–18–1784
Coggin, Herbert	200	478	During war state line	4–30–1783
Cogwill, Frederick	100	1924	3 years soldier Virginia line	10–27–1784
Colbert, Elisha	100	3185	3 years soldier Virginia line	6–22–1784
Colbert, John	100	3305	3 years soldier Virginia line	7– 2–1784
Colden, James	100	265	3 years soldier state line	4– 3–1783
Colder, James	200	450	During war soldier state line	4–28–1783
Coldwater, John	200	3336	During war soldier Virginia line	7–19–1784
Cole, Hamlin	200	697	3 years sergeant Virginia line	5–31–1783
Cole, John	200	2792	3 years sergeant Virginia line	3–19–1784
Cole, Thomas	100	533	During war soldier state line	5– 2–1783
Cole, William	200	319	During war soldier cavalry	4–12–1783
Cole, William	100	4239	3 years soldier Virginia line	12–13–1786
Coleman, Jacob	1,000	226	3 years lieutenant Virginia Cont. line	4– 1–1783
Coleman, Jacob	1,000	227	3 years lieutenant Virginia Cont. line	4– 1–1783
Coleman, James	100	3843	3 years soldier Virginia line	4–30–1785
Coleman, John	2,666⅔	2141	3 years ensign Virginia line	12–16–1783
Coleman, Joseph	200	2719	3 years sergeant Virginia line	3– 6–1784
Coleman, Richard	100	2909	3 years soldier Virginia line	4– 8–1784
Coleman, Richard	4,000	2240	3 years captain Virginia line	1–12–1784
Coleman, Samuel	2,666⅔	156	3 years lieutenant artillery Virginia line	3– 4–1783
Coleman, Samuel	100	4550	3 years soldier Virginia line	11–22–1791
Coleman, Thomas	200	2693	3 years sergeant Virginia line	3– 3–1784
Coleman, Thomas	100	2797	3 years Virginia line	3–19–1784
Coleman, Whitehead	400	1186	3 years captain Virginia line	6–26–1783
Coleman, Wyatt	3,110½	2435	7 years lieutenant Virginia line	2– 9–1784
Colgin, William	100	4332	3 years soldier Virginia line	10–12–1787
Coller, James	100	3426	3 years soldier Virginia line	8–28–1784
Collingsworth, John	100	144	3 years soldier state line	2–22–1783
Collins, Adam	100	3083	3 years soldier Virginia line	5–20–1784
Collins, George	100	1223	3 years soldier Virginia line	6–26–1783
Collins, John	200	841	3 years sergeant Virginia line	6–16–1783
Collins, John	200	3042	3 years soldier Virginia line	5– 4–1784
Collins, Mason	100	816	3 years Virginia soldier in artillery	6–14–1783
Collins, Peter	200	1882	During war soldier Virginia line	10–15–1783
Collins, Richard	100	3205	3 years soldier Virginia line	6–24–1784
Collins, Thomas	200	3774	3 years sergeant Virginia line	3–11–1785
Collins, Thomas	200	4255	During war soldier Virginia line	1–31–1787
Collinsworth, Edward	100	143	3 years soldier state line	2–22–1783
Colquhon, James	100	836	3 years soldier Virginia line	6–16–1783
Colvin, James	100	2884	3 years soldier Virginia line	4– 5–1784
Colvin, Jeremiah	200	1978	3 years sergeant Virginia line	11–27–1783
Compton, Augustive	100	1970	3 years soldier Virginia line	11–26–1783
Conant, John	200	2011	During war soldier Virginia line	12– 4–1783
Conard, James	100	3927	3 years soldier Virginia line	6–21–1785
Coney, Drury	100	4276	3 years soldier Virginia line	4– 7–1787
Conley, Asa	200	1264	During war soldier Virginia line	6–27–1783
Conley, Timothy	200	3351	During war soldier Virginia line	7–22–1784
Connally, William	200	1132	During war soldier Virginia line	6–24–1783
Connelly, Philip	100	3872	3 years soldier Virginia line	5–10–1785
Conner, Edward	2,666⅔	3788	3 years cornet Virginia line	3–25–1785
Conner, James	200	3246	3 years sergeant Virginia line	6–29–1784
Conner, John	200	53	3 years sergeant Virginia regiment	12–14–1782
Conner, John	400	557	During war sergeant state line	5– 7–1783
Conner, John	100	2978	3 years soldier Virginia line	4–20–1784
Connor, Philip	200	382	3 years sergeant Virginia Cont. line	4–23–1783
Connor, Terrence	200	3968	3 years soldier Virginia line	9– 6–1785
Conrod, Jacob	200	1064	During war soldier Virginia line	6–24–1783
Consolver, Charles	100	3391	3 years soldier Virginia line	8–13–1784
Consolver, John	200	32	During war soldier Virginia Cont. line	12– 2–1782
Conway, Joseph	3,110⅔	1627	7 years lieutenant Virginia line	8–22–1783
Conway, Samuel	200	2543	3 years corporal Virginia line	2–19–1784
Cook, Joseph	200	2184	During war soldier Virginia line	12–20–1783

Name	Acres	Warrant	Service	Date
Cook, William	200	1783	3 years sergeant Virginia line	9–23–1783
Cook, William	100	3609	3 years soldier Virginia line	12–22–1784
Cook, William	2,666⅔	4329	3 years gunner Virginia navy	11– 3–1787
Cook, Zackariah	100	4144	3 years soldier Virginia line	4–13–1786
Cooke, Pleasant	4,000	3223	3 years captain Virginia line	6–28–1784
Cooke, William	400	2821	During war sergeant Virginia line	3–26–1784
Cooley, Isaac	100	820	3 years soldier Virginia line	6–14–1783
Coombes, Francis	200	31	Soldier Virginia Cont. line	12– 2–1782
Coon, Anthony	100	2888	3 years soldier Virginia line	4– 5–1784
Coons, Frederick	100	1197	3 years soldier Virginia line	6–26–1783
Cooper, Apoles	2,666⅔	4338	3 years lieutenant Virginia line	11–23–1787
Cooper, Charles	100	3754	3 years soldier Virginia line	2–14–1785
Cooper, Ephram	400	1498	During war sergeant Virginia line	8– 5–1783
Cooper, Leonard	1,000	3472	7 years captain Virginia line	10–18–1784
Cooper, Leonard	1,000	3473	7 years captain Virginia line	10–18–1784
Cooper, Leonard	1,000	3474	7 years captain Virginia line	10–18–1784
Cooper, Leonard	1,000	3475	7 years captain Virginia line	10–18–1784
Cooper, Leonard	666⅔	3476	7 years captain Virginia line	10–18–1784
Cooper, Reuben	200	3795	3 years sergeant Virginia line	4– 5–1785
Cooper, Spencer	400	1543	3 years corporal Virginia line	8– 9–1783
Cooper, Thomas	100	4283	3 years soldier Virginia line	4–16–1787
Cooper, William	200	1308	During war soldier Virginia line	6–30–1783
Cope, Thomas	100	3670	3 years soldier Virginia line	1– 4–1785
Copland, William	200	1696	3 years corporal Virginia line	8–30–1783
Coppinger, Higgins	200	1523	During war soldier Virginia line	8– 7–1783
Coram, William	233⅓	1445	During war soldier in Virginia line	7–31–1783
Corbell, Peter	200	1746	3 years corporal Virginia line	9–11–1783
Corbett, John	200	1880	During war soldier Virginia line	10–15–1783
Corder, James	400	527	During war corporal state line	5– 2–1783
Cordones, John	200	1128	During war soldier Virginia line	6–24–1783
Cornelius, Josiah	100	2129	3 years soldier Virginia line	12–15–1783
Cornelius, William	200	2432	3 years gunner Virginia navy	2– 9–1784
Cornelius, William	100	4224	3 years sailor Virginia navy	11– 1–1786
Cosby, Thomas	100	3505	3 years soldier Virginia line	11– 5–1784
Cosby, Snyder	400	3077	During war sergeant Virginia line	5–14–1784
Cosby, William	400	4351	During war sergeant Virginia line	12– 6–1787
Cottle, William	200	4533	During war soldier Virginia line	10–18–1791
Cottorel, William	2,666⅔	1577	3 years midshipman Virginia navy	8–18–1783
Cougall, John	100	2559	3 years soldier Virginia line	2–20–1784
Courtney, Samuel	233⅓	1297	During war soldier Virginia line	6–30–1783
Courtney, Thomas	200	482	During war soldier state line	4–30–1783
Coverley, Thomas	2,000	1413	7 years lieutenant Virginia line	7–22–1783
Coverley, Thomas	1,110⅔	1414	7 years lieutenant Virginia line	7–22–1783
Cowherd, Francis	4,000	173	3 years captain Virginia Cont. line	3–11–1783
Cowherd, Francis	100	2642	7 years captain Virginia line	2–26–1784
Cowherd, James	200	1518	3 years sergeant Virginia line	8– 7–1783
Cowne, Augustine	2,666⅔	159	3 years lieutenant state line	3– 7–1783
Cowne, Robert	4,000	158	3 years captain artillery	3– 7–1783
Cowper, Richard	233⅓	1392	During war soldier Virginia line	7–18–1783
Cowthon, Christopher	200	562	3 years sergeant Cont. line	5– 8–1783
Cox, Presley	100	1855	3 years soldier Virginia line	11– 4–1783
Cox, Radford	200	641	3 years corporal Virginia line	5–26–1783
Cox, Samuel	100	2616	3 years soldier Virginia line	2–24–1784
Cox, William	200	1356	3 years sergeant Virginia line	7–12–1783
Cox, William	200	1661	During war soldier Virginia line	8–25–1783
Coxor, William	200	1042	During war fifer Virginia line	6–24–1783
Craddock, Henry	200	189	3 years sergeant Virginia Cont. line	3–20–1783
Craddock, Robert	2,666⅔	187	3 years lieutenant Virginia Cont. line	3–20–1783
Crafford, Charles	200	1154	During war soldier Virginia line	6–24–1783
Craig, James	4,000	2024	3 years captain Virginia line	12– 6–1783
Craig, John	100	3493	3 years soldier Virginia line	11– 2–1784
Craig, Thomas	200	1069	During war soldier Virginia line	6–24–1783
Craig, William	200	1088	During war soldier Virginia line	6–24–1783
Craker, William	200	542	3 years drum major state line	5– 3–1783
Crale, John	2,666⅔	188	3 years lieutenant Virginia Cont. line	3–20–1783
Cralle, Redham K	100	3845	3 years soldier Virginia line	5– 2–1785
Crame, James	4,000	2089	3 years captain Virginia line	12–10–1783
Cratton, William	200	750	3 years soldier Virginia line	6– 5–1783
Crawford, David	100	1244	3 years soldier Virginia line	6–27–1783
Crawford, John	2,666⅔	308	3 years lieutenant Virginia Cont. line	4– 9–1783
Crawford, John	200	953	3 years soldier Virginia line	6–20–1783
Crawford, John	100	1024	3 years soldier Virginia line	6–23–1783
Crawford, Robert	200	1044	During war soldier Virginia line	6–24–1783
Crawford, John	444	2562	7 years lieutenant Virginia line	2–20–1784
Crawford, Nehemiah	100	4611	3 years private Virginia line	5–27–1793
Crawford, William	6,666⅔	851	– years colonel Virginia Cont. line	6–17–1783
Crawley, James	100	1493	3 years soldier Virginia line	8– 4–1783
Craze, Redman	10	2101	3 years soldier Virginia line	12–11–1783
Creamer, William	100	2592	3 years soldier Virginia line	2–23–1784
Creed, Thomas	466⅔	4532	7 years sergeant Virginia line	9–19–1791
Creekman, William	100	261	3 years soldier state line	4– 3–1783

Name	Acres	Warrant	Service	Date
Crews, Edward	100	3251	3 years soldier Virginia line	6–30–1784
Crews, Joseph	200	3989	3 years soldier Virginia line	10–29–1785
Crittenden, John	2,666⅔	1007	3 years lieutenant Virginia line	6–23–1783
Crittendon, William	100	2284	3 years soldier Virginia line	1–26–1784
Crocket, Presley	100	2382	3 years soldier Virginia line	2– 3–1784
Crockett, Joseph	6,666⅔	168	3 years lieutenant & colonel Cont. line	3– 9–1783
Croghan, William	5,333⅔	25	3 years major Virginia Cont. line	11–29–1782
Croglian, William	888⅔	1922	7 years major Virginia line	11–21–1783
Croglian, William	6,400	1923		11–21–1783
Cronclur, Charles	200	453	During war soldier state line	4–28–1783
Crook, Joseph	200	3857	3 years sergeant Virginia line	5– 6–1785
Crosby, William	100	3637	3 years soldier Virginia line	12–30–1784
Cropper, James	200	3862	During war soldier Virginia line	5– 7–1785
Cropper, John	6,666⅔	995	Lieutenant colonel Virginia line	6–21–1783
Cross, John	200	3602	During war soldier Virginia line	12–21–1784
Cross, Samuel	200	653	3 years sergeant Virginia line	5–27–1783
Cross, Richard	100	4451	3 years soldier Virginia line	2–26–1789
Crossen, Gustavus	100	4357	3 years soldier Virginia line	12–28–1787
Crosslick, Edward	100	2660	3 years soldier Virginia line	3– 1–1784
Croxton, John	100	3417	3 years soldier Virginia line	8–27–1784
Croxton, Richard	100	3376	3 years soldier Virginia line	8– 4–1784
Crowder, Robert	100	1989	3 years seaman Virginia navy	11–28–1783
Crowley, David	100	845	3 years soldier Virginia line	6–16–1783
Crowson, John Hanson	100	3826	3 years soldier Virginia line	4–26–1785
Crump, Capt Abner	4,000	505	3 years captain state line	5– 1–1783
Crump, Thomas	100	1537	3 years soldier Virginia line	8– 9–1783
Crump, Jesse	200	645	3 years sergeant Virginia line	5–26–1783
Crumpt, Benjamin	400	516	During war sergeant state line	5– 1–1783
Cruswell, Samuel	200	1147	During war soldier Virginia line	6–24–1783
Crutchfield, Stapleton	100	797	3 years soldier Virginia line	6–12–1783
Culbertson, James	4,000	1868	3 years captain Virginia line	11– 6–1783
Cullickan, John	200	3921	During war soldier Virginia line	6–21–1795
Culls, Shadrack	200	484	During war soldier state line	4–30–1783
Culls, William	200	483	During war soldier state line	4–30–1783
Cumberford, Isaac	100	4010	3 years soldier Virginia line	12– 2–1785
Cumbs, Daniel	100	902	3 years soldier Virginia line	6–20–1783
Cummins, George	100	3748	3 years soldier Virginia line	2– 9–1785
Cunningham, James	200	1083	During war soldier Virginia line	6–24–1783
Cunningham, Nathaniel	200	1549	3 years sergeant Virginia line	8–11–1783
Cunningham, William	5,333	783	3 years major Virginia line	6–10–1783
Curl, Richard	200	1631	During war soldier Virginia line	8–22–1783
Currel, Jacob	100	4223	3 years sailor Virginia navy	11– 1–1786
Currell, James	1,333⅓	4473	3 years midshipman Virginia navy	10–29–1789
Currell, James	1,333⅓	4474	3 years midshipman Virginia navy	10–29–1789
Curry, James	4,000	348	3 years captain Virginia Cont. line	4–16–1783
Curtice, Henry	100	3278	3 years sailor Virginia navy	7– 1–1784
Curtis, James	100	2946	3 years soldier Virginia line	4–17–1784
Curtis, John	200	4535	During war soldier Virginia line	11–10–1791
Custard, George	100	3692	3 years soldier Virginia line	1–20–1785
Custard, John	100	3701	3 years soldier Virginia line	1–20–1785
Cuthburt, William	200	2652	3 years corporal Virginia line	2–28–1784
Cypress, Andrew	233⅓	1232	7 years soldier Virginia line	6–27–1783
Cyrus, Bartholomew	200	1467	3 years soldier Virginia line	8– 1–1783
Dabney, Charles	6,666⅔	28	3 years lieutenant Colonel Virginia state line	11–30–1782
Dade, Francis	4,000	2312	3 years captain Virginia line	1–29–1784
Dagnell, Stephen	200	713	3 years private Virginia line	6– 2–1783
Dailey, James	200	1530	3 years soldier Virginia line	8– 8–1783
Dailey, John	200	3910	During war soldier Virginia line	6–21–1785
Daingerfield, William	400	3615	During war sergeant Virginia line	12–23–1784
Dallis, Robert	100	3891	3 years soldier Virginia line	6–15–1785
Dally, George	200	3684	During war soldier Virginia line	1–11–1785
Danby, Jonathan	100	2495	3 years soldier Virginia line	2–14–1784
Dandridge, Alexander Spotwoods	1,000	1224	3 years captain Virginia line	6–26–1783
Dandridge, Alexander Spotswood	1,000	1226	3 years captain Virginia line	6–26–1783
Dandridge, Alexander Spotswood	1,000	1225	3 years captain Virginia line	6–26–1783
Dandridge, Alexander Spotswood	1,000	1227	3 years captain Virginia line	6–26–1783
Dandridge, John	4,000	77	3 years captain artillery Cont. line	12–28–1782
Dandridge, Robert	2,666⅔	727	3 years lieutenant Virginia line	6– 3–1783
Daniel, Christopher	100	4493	3 years soldier Virginia line	5–12–1790
Daniel, George	100	3190	3 years sailor Virginia navy	6–23–1784
Daniel, John	200	1228	3 years captain Virginia line	6–26–1783
Daniel, W	100	3157	3 years soldier Virginia line	6–14–1784
Daniel, Thomas	100	3191	3 years sailor Virginia navy	6–23–1784
Danley, John	100	866	3 years soldier Virginia line	6–19–1783
Dapsley, Samuel	4,000	387	3 years captain Virginia line	4–23–1783
Darby, Darmon	100	3160	3 years pilot Virginia navy	6–15–1784

Name	Acres	Warrant	Service	Date
Darby, Nathaniel.........	3,110⅜	...1299	....7 years lieutenant Virginia line.......	6–30–1783
Daring, Henry...........	3,110⅜	...4507	....During war ensign Virginia line.....	11–27–1790
Dark, William..........	1,111⅓	...4490	....7 years lieutenant colonel Virginia line............................	3– 5–1790
Darke, William..........	6,666⅔	... 812	....Lieutenant colonel Virginia line.....	6–13–1783
Darnold, Aaron.........	100	...1809	....3 years drummer Virginia line.......	9–30–1783
Darvill, William.........	2,666⅔	...4376	....3 years lieutenant Virginia line.....	1–23–1788
Daugherty, Patrick.....	200	... 880	....3 years soldier Virginia line.........	6–20–1783
Daulton, Moses.........	200	...1762	....3 years sergeant Virginia line.......	9–13–1783
Davenport, Claiborn.......	100	...1814	....3 years soldier Virginia line.........	10– 2–1783
Davenport, Joel.........	100	...2391	....3 years soldier Virginia line.........	2– 3–1784
Davenport, Moses.......	100	...4497	....3 years soldier Virginia line.........	6–24–1790
Davenport, Moses.......	100	...4499	....3 years soldier Virginia line.........	6–24–1790
Davenport, Opie........	2,666⅔	...2415	....End war lieutenant Virginia line.....	2– 5–1784
Davenport, William......	4,000	...4019	....3 years captain Virginia line.........	12– 3–1785
Davice, Richard.........	200	... 682	....3 years sergeant Virginia line.......	5–30–1783
Davidson, Joseph.......	100	...2661	....3 years soldier Virginia line.........	3– 1–1784
Davies, William........	200	... 843	....During war soldier Virginia line.....	6–16–1783
Davies, William........	7,777⅔	...2452	....7 years colonel Virginia line.......	2–11–1784
Davis, Acquilla.........	200	...3603	....During war soldier Virginia line.....	12–21–1784
Davis, Arthur..........	200	...4075	....During war soldier Virginia line.....	1–13–1786
Davis, James..........	100	...1372	....3 years soldier Virginia line.........	7–14–1783
Davis, James..........	100	...2171	....3 years soldier Virginia line.........	12–20–1783
Davis, James..........	100	...2955	....3 years soldier Virginia line.........	4–17–1784
Davis, Jeduthin........	100	...4231	....3 years sailor Virginia navy.........	11–16–1786
Davis, John...........	200	... 121	....3 years sergeant Virginia line.......	2–10–1783
Davis, John...........	200	... 330	....During war soldier cavalry........	4–14–1783
Davis, John...........	100	...1313	....3 years soldier Virginia line.........	6–30–1783
Davis, John...........	100	...1586	....3 years soldier Virginia line.........	8–20–1783
Davis, John...........	200	...3374	....3 years sergeant Virginia line.......	8– 3–1784
Davis, John...........	200	...3423	....During war soldier Virginia line.....	8–28–1784
Davis, John...........	100	...3640	....3 years seaman Virginia navy.....	12–30–1784
Davis, Joseph..........	200	... 426	....During war soldier Virginia line.....	4–26–1783
Davis, Joseph..........	200	...3122	....3 years soldier Virginia line.........	6– 5–1784
Davis, Henry..........	100	...4319	....3 years soldier Virginia line.........	10–23–1787
Davis, Lewis C........	100	... 417	....3 years soldier Virginia line.........	4–26–1783
Davis, Nicholas........	100	...3293	....3 years soldier Virginia line.........	7– 1–1784
Davis, Samuel.........	100	...1866	....3 years soldier Virginia line.........	10–14–1783
Davis, Samuel.........	200	...3111	....During war soldier Virginia line.....	5–29–1784
Davis, Spillsby.........	400	...1446	....During war sergeant Virginia line....	7–31–1783
Davis, Thomas.........	400	...3915	....During war corporal Virginia line.....	6–21–1785
Davis, Thompson.......	200	...4135	....During war soldier Virginia line.....	3–23–1786
Davis, William.........	200	... 444	....During war soldier state line.......	4–26–1783
Davis, William.........	200	...1482	....3 years sergeant Virginia line........	8– 2–1783
Davis, William.........	200	...2342	....During war soldier Virginia line.....	1–31–1784
Davis, William.........	400	...3981	....During war corporal Virginia line....	10–18–1785
Davis, William.........	100	...4363	....3 years soldier Virginia line.........	12–14–1788
Davison, Ambrose.......	100	...3088	....3 years soldier Virginia line.........	5–22–1784
Davison, David.........	200	...3274	....During war soldier Virginia line.....	7– 1–1784
Davison, John.........	200	...3089	....During war soldier Virginia line.....	5–22–1784
Davison, Josiah.........	100	...2416	....3 years soldier Virginia line.........	2– 6–1784
Dawes, Joseph.........	6,000	... 83	....3 years sergeant Virginia Cont. line..	12–31–1782
Dawson, Francis........	400	...1965	....3 years sergeant Virginia line.......	11–25–1783
Dawson, Henry.........	1,300	... 232	....3 years lieutenant Virginia Cont. line.	4– 1–1783
Dawson, Henry.........	1,366⅔	... 233	....3 years lieutenant Virginia Cont. line.	4– 1–1783
Dawson, James.........	200	...3444	....During war soldier Virginia line.....	9–20–1784
Dawson, Thomas.......	100	...1335	....3 years soldier Virginia line.........	7– 5–1783
Day, George...........	100	...2097	....3 years sailor Virginia navy.........	12–10–1783
Day, John............	200	...2458	....During war soldier Virginia line.....	2–11–1784
Day, Thomas..........	100	...3802	....3 years soldier Virginia line.........	4–12–1785
Day, Westbrook........	100	...4243	....3 years soldier Virginia line.........	12–21–1786
Day, William..........	100	...3544	....3 years soldier Virginia line.........	11–29–1784
Deaman, Robert........	200	...3567	....3 years soldier Virginia line.........	12– 9–1784
Dean, John...........	200	... 357	....During war soldier state line.......	4–17–1783
Dean, John...........	200	...1246	....3 years sergeant Virginia line........	6–27–1783
Dean, Joseph.........	100	... 912	....3 years soldier Virginia line.........	6–20–1783
Dean, Joshua..........	100	...1380	....3 years soldier Virginia line.........	7–16–1783
Dean, Michael.........	100	... 911	....3 years soldier Virginia line.........	6–20–1783
Dear, Benjamin........	100	...3231	....3 years soldier Virginia line.........	0–29–1784
Death, William.........	200	... 910	....3 years sergeant Virginia line.......	6–20–1783
Decker, Nicholas........	100	...3709	....3 years soldier Virginia line.........	1–20–1785
Decker, Samuel........	100	...3092	....3 years soldier Virginia line.........	5–22–1784
Dedman, Samuel........	200	...3383	....3 years sergeant Virginia line........	8– 5–1784
Deklauman, Christian Charles...............	1,000	...3117	....3 years major Virginia line..........	6– 4–1784
Deklauman, Christian Charles...............	1,000	...3118	....3 years major Virginia line..........	6– 4–1784
Deklauman, Christian Charles...............	1,000	...3119	....3 years major Virginia line..........	6– 4–1784
Deklauman, Christian Charles...............	2,333⅓	...3120	....3 years major Virginia line..........	6– 4–1784

Name	Acres	Warrant	Service	Date
Delany, Anthony	200	3126	3 years corporal Virginia line	6- 5-1784
Delaplane, James	2,666⅔	1332	3 years lieutenant Virginia line	7- 5-1783
Delozer, Aza	00	2118	During war soldier Virginia line	12-13-1783
Delozier, Richard D	200	4138	3 years soldier Virginia line	3-31-1786
Demer, Jacob	200	1667	3 years drum major Virginia line	8-26-1783
Demon, Timothy	2,666⅔	4559	During war lieutenant Virginia line	12-13-1791
Demonile, Samuel	100	3219	3 years seaman Virginia navy	6-26-1784
Demsey, John	100	960	3 years soldier Virginia line	6-20-1783
Dener, Jacob	400	1657	During war sergeant Virginia line	8-23-1783
Denholm, Archibald	4,000	635	3 years captain Virginia line	5-24-1783
Dennis, Henry	233⅓	1688	During war soldier Virginia line	8-30-1783
Dennis, William	200	4060	During war soldier Virginia line	12-31-1785
Denross, John	200	2874	During war soldier Virginia line	4- 5-1784
Dent, John	2,000	3943	3 years lieutenant Virginia line	8- 9-1785
Dent, John	666⅔	3944	3 years lieutenant Virginia line	8- 9-1785
Denton, John	100	1931	3 years soldier Virginia line	11-22-1783
Denton, Thomas	400	4508	During war sergeant Virginia line	11-27-1790
Denny, Henry	466⅔	2044	During war sergeant Virginia line	12- 9-1783
Depriest, Robert	100	1560	3 years drummer Virginia line	8-12-1783
Deressett, Samuel	200	4434	During war soldier Virginia line	9-13-1788
Deshazo, William	100	4597	3 years private Virginia line	12- 8-1792
Deshper, John	100	4504	3 years soldier Virginia line	11-13-1790
Devere, Isaac	200	1160	During war soldier Virginia line	6-24-1783
Devier, John	100	1916	3 years soldier Virginia line	11-20-1783
DeWit, Henry	100	2826	3 years soldier Virginia line	3-26-1784
Dewitt, Peter	100	3555	3 years soldier Virginia line	12- 6-1784
Dewney, John	200	1399	3 years sergeant Virginia line	7-21-1783
Dick, Alexander	5,333⅓	2302	3 years major Virginia line	1-27-1784
Dickerson, Edmund	5,333⅓	207	3 years major Virginia line	3-27-1784
Dickey, Alexander	233⅓	1904	7 years soldier Virginia line	11-18-1783
Dickie, William	100	787	3 years soldier Virginia line	6-11-1783
Dicks, George	200	4073	During war soldier Virginia line	1-13-1786
Dickson, James	200	1686	During war soldier Virginia line	8-29-1783
Didlake, James	200	4575	3 years sergeant Virginia line	5- 7-1792
Diggs, Dudley	2,666⅔	130	3 years lieutenant of cavalry	2-18-1783
Dihense, Edward	200	618	During war private Virginia line	5-22-1783
Dikes, Henry	100	4455	3 years sailor Virginia navy	12-24-1788
Dillard, Edward	100	2703	3 years soldier Virginia line	3- 4-1784
Dillon, Jesse	200	94	- years corporal Virginia Cont. line	1-14-1783
Dishman, James	200	2268	End war soldier Virginia line	1-21-1784
Diskin, Daniel	100	4284	3 years soldier Virginia line	4-16-1787
Dix, Thomas	4,000	152	3 years captain of artillery	2-27-1783
Dixon, Anthony F	1,000	2137	3 years regular surgeon Virginia line	12-16-1783
Dixon, Anthony T	5,000	2138	3 years regular surgeon Virginia line	12-16-1783
Dixon, Edward	100	3776	3 years soldier Virginia line	3-12-1785
Dixon, James	100	2065	3 years soldier Virginia line	12- 9-1783
Dixon, Joseph	200	3847	During war soldier Virginia line	5- 2-1785
Dobbins, Charles	200	1568	During war soldier Virginia line	8-14-1783
Dobson, Robert	2,666⅔	1486	3 years sailing master Virginia navy	8- 4-1783
Dockerty, John	200	1113	3 years soldier Virginia line	6-24-1783
Dodd, William	100	993	3 years soldier Virginia line	6-21-1783
Doe, John	200	1587	During war soldier Virginia line	8-20-1783
Doe, John	100	3192	3 years sailor Virginia line	6-23-1784
Dogan, Henry	100	2187	3 years soldier Virginia line	12-22-1783
Dogget, Clement	100	3279	3 years sailor Virginia navy	7- 1-1784
Doil, Robert	200	2010	During war soldier Virginia line	12- 2-1783
Doland, John	200	3743	During war soldier Virginia line	2- 7-1785
Dolby, William	200	4521	3 years sergeant Virginia line	4-21-1791
Doll, Joseph	100	2386	3 years soldier Virginia line	2- 3-1784
Dollens, William	200	1290	During war soldier Virginia line	6-28-1783
Doller, William	100	955	3 years soldier Virginia line	6-20-1783
Donnakin, Daniel	100	2146	3 years soldier Virginia line	12-18-1783
Doren, James	200	4617	3 years corporal Virginia line	6-29-1793
Doren, Terence	100	2948	3 years soldier Virginia line	4-17-1784
Dowdy, Claiborne	100	3380	3 years soldier Virginia line	8- 5-1784
Dowell, William	100	857	3 years soldier Virginia line	
Dowell, William	100	1921	3 years soldier Virginia line	10-27-1783
Downs, John	100	5	3 years soldier Virginia Cont. line	8-29-1782
Downton, George	100	3572	3 years soldier Virginia line	12-15-1784
Downton, William	200	2819	3 years gunner mate Virginia line	3-25-1784
Downey, Michael	100	2516	3 years soldier Virginia line	2-18-1784
Doyle, John	200	2584	During war soldier Virginia line	2-23-1784
Doyle, Robert	200	1641	During war soldier Virginia line	8-23-1783
Drake, Andrew	100	967	3 years soldier Virginia line	6-20-1783
Drake, Michael	200	1888	During war soldier Virginia line	10-17-1783
Drake, Thomas	2,666⅔	4327	3 years lieutenant Virginia line	11- 3-1787
Draper, George	2,000	1156	Regimental surgeon Virginia line	6-24-1783
Draper, George	2,000	1157	3 years regimental surgeon Virginia line	6-24-1783
Draper, George	2,000	1158	3 years regimental surgeon Virginia line	6-24-1783
Draper, Robert	100	3726	3 years soldier Virginia line	1-31-1785
Drew, John	1,000	2201	End war lieutenant Virginia line	12-23-1783

Name	Acres	Warrant	Service	Date
Drew, John.............	1,666⅔	..2212	End war lieutenant Virginia line.....	12–23–1783
Drew, Thomas Haynes....	4,000...	23	3 years captain Virginia Cont. line ...	11–29–1782
Drew, Thomas H.........	4,000...	47	3 years captain Garrison regiment....	12–14–1782
Driskill, Dennis.........	100....	2654	3 years soldier Virginia line	3– 1–1784
Driver, Edward..........	200....	1310	3 years sergeant Virginia line	6–30–1783
Driver, Francis...........	200....	142	3 years sergeant Virginia line	2–22–1783
Drummond, Alexander....	200....	3739	During war soldier Virginia line......	2– 7–1785
Drummond, John.........	466⅔...	1484	7 years sergeant Virginia line........	8– 2–1783
Drummond, Joshua.......	100....	2624	3 years soldier Virginia line	2–24–1784
Drury, Benjamin.........	200....	472	During war soldier state line	4–29–1783
Drury, Henry............	466⅔...	2044	7 years private Virginia line	12– 9–1783
Drury, Samuel..........	100....	1215	3 years soldier Virginia line	6–26–1783
Dudley, Henry..........	4,000...	27	3 years captain Virginia state line ...	11–30–1782
Dudley, Robert.........	2,666⅔...	1168	3 years lieutenant Virginia line	6–24–1783
Dudley, Robert.........	100....	4593	3 years private Virginia line	11–15–1792
Duel, Henry............	200....	346	During war soldier cavalry	4–16–1783
Duff, Adam..............	200....	3633	3 years sergeant Virginia line	12–29–1784
Duff, Edward............	6,000...	586	3 years as surgeon Virginia line	5–16–1783
Duffey, James...........	100....	591	3 years soldier Virginia line	5–17–1783
Duffey, James...........	200....	1070	During war soldier Virginia line.....	6–24–1783
Dugar, Robert..........	200....	157	3 years sergeant Virginia Cont. line ...	3– 6–1783
Dugmore, John..........	100....	1768	3 years soldier Virginia line	9–16–1783
Dulany, Thomas.........	100....	1212	3 years soldier Virginia line	6–26–1783
Dunbar, Hamilton........	200....	3749	3 years sergeant Virginia line	2– 9–1785
Dunbarr, James..........	200....	1014	3 years sergeant Virginia line	6–23–1783
Duncan, Charles..........	100....	1473	3 years soldier Virginia line	8– 1–1783
Duncan, John...........	100....	4441	3 years soldier Virginia line	11– 1–1788
Duneth, John...........	200....	1320	During war soldier Virginia line......	7– 2–1783
Dungie, James...........	100....	2285	3 years soldier Virginia line	1–26–1784
Dunlop, John...........	200....	3550	During war soldier Virginia line......	12– 2–1784
Dunn, James...........	200....	1779	During war soldier Virginia line......	9–20–1783
Dunn, James...........	100....	3471	3 years soldier Virginia line	10–19–1784
Dunn, John.............	200....	507	During war soldier state line	5– 1–1783
Dunn, John.............	100....	1532	3 years soldier Virginia line	8– 8–1783
Dunn, Joshua...........	100....	1836	3 years soldier Virginia line	10– 7–1783
Dunn, Patrick..........	100....	3881	3 years soldier Virginia line	5–23–1785
Dunn, Richard..........	100....	273	3 years soldier state line...........	4– 3–1783
Dunnavent, Abraham....	100....	3062	3 years soldier Virginia line	5–10–1784
Dunston, Alman.........	100....	3065	3 years soldier Virginia line	5–10–1784
Dunstan, Warner........	100....	2848	3 years soldier Virginia line	3–30–1784
Dunton, Stephen........	200....	391	During war soldier Virginia line......	4–24–1783
Dupee, William.........	200....	2218	During war soldier Virginia line......	1– 5–1784
Dupriest, John..........	200....	730	3 years sergeant Virginia line	6– 3–1783
Durham, James..........	100....	1846	3 years soldier Virginia line	10–10–1783
Duval, Daniel...........	4,000...	2483	3 years captain Virginia line	2–13–1784
Dwen, Robert...........	100....	4433	3 years soldier Virginia line	9– 5–1788
Dwen, William..........	200....	4432	3 years sergeant Virginia line	9– 5–1788
Dye, Jonathan..........	2,666⅔...	1968	3 years lieutenant Virginia line	11–26–1783
Dyer, Francis...........	100....	4486	3 years soldier Virginia line	12–29–1789
Dyer, Samuel...........	100....	1213	3 years soldier Virginia line	6–26–1783
Dykes, Robert..........	100....	1719	3 years seaman Virginia navy	9– 2–1783
Dyles, John............	100....	2591	3 years sailor Virginia navy	2–23–1784
Dyllard, John..........	200....	1521	During war soldier Virginia line......	8– 7–1783
Eagle, William..........	100....	4282	3 years soldier Virginia line	4–11–1787
Eakin, Samuel..........	200....	2092	3 years sergeant Virginia line	12–10–1783
Earlywine, Daniel.......	200....	1081	During war soldier Virginia line	6–24–1783
Easten, Richard.........	2,666⅔...	294	3 years lieutenant Virginia Cont. line .	4– 5–1783
Easten, William.........	200....	1269	3 years lieutenant Virginia line	6–28–1783
Eastin, Philip..........	3,110⅔...	302	7 years lieutenant Virginia Cont. line.	4– 8–1783
Eastwood, Demsey.......	100....	1303	3 years soldier Virginia line.........	6–30–1783
Eaton, Joseph..........	100....	1864	3 years soldier Virginia line	10–14–1783
Eaton, Michaga.........	100....	2949	3 years soldier Virginia line	4–17–1784
Eaton, William..........	100....	3679	3 years soldier Virginia line	1– 8–1785
Ebb, William...........	100....	3895	3 years soldier Virginia line	6–16–1785
Ebbs, John.............	200....	3988	During war soldier Virginia line	10–28–1785
Eddens, Samuel.........	4,000...	206	3 years captain of artillery..........	3–27–1783
Edge, John.............	100....	2293	3 years soldier Virginia line	1–26–1784
Edmonds, Daniel........	200....	2847	During war soldier Virginia line......	3–30–1784
Edmonds, Elias.........	6,000...	166	3 years lieutenant & colonel artillery..	3– 9–1783
Edmonds, Leroy........	6,666⅔...	3158	7 years captain Virginia line	6–14–1784
Edmondson, William.....	200....	1030	3 years sergeant Virginia line	6–23–1783
Edmundson, Benjamin...	2,666⅔...	2723	3 years lieutenant Virginia line	3– 6–1784
Edmundson, Richard....	200....	1962	3 years sergeant Virginia line	11–24–1783
Edmunds, Thomas.......	4,000...	40	3 years captain service U. S..........	12–11–1782
Edwards, Benjamin......	200....	518	During war soldier state line........	5– 1–1783
Edwards, Edmund.......	200....	2130	During war soldier Virginia line......	12–15–1783
Edwards, Enoch........	100....	1940	3 years seaman Virginia navy.......	11–22–1783
Edwards, Ellis..........	100....	3280	3 years sailor Virginia navy.........	7– 1–1784
Edwards, George........	100....	4398	3 years soldier Virginia navy........	4–16–1788
Edwards, James.........	100....	2798	3 years soldier Virginia line.........	3–20–1784
Edwards, John..........	200....	1339	During war soldier Virginia line......	7– 9–1783

Name	Acres	Warrant	Service	Date
Edwards, John	100	1573	3 years soldier Virginia line	8-15-1783
Edwards, Leroy	4,000	1476	3 years captain Virginia line	8- 2-1783
Edwards, Richard	100	721	3 years soldier Virginia line	6- 3-1783
Edwards, Rodham	100	2096	3 years sailor Virginia navy	12-10-1783
Edwards, Spencer	100	3723	3 years soldier Virginia line	1-28-1785
Edwards, Thomas	100	648	3 years soldier Virginia line	5-27-1783
Edwards, William	100	2022	3 years sailor Virginia navy	12- 6-1783
Eggleston, Joseph	5,333⅓	1386	3 years major Virginia line	7-17-1783
Eggleston, William	2,666⅔	2366	3 years lieutenant Virginia line	2- 2-1784
Elam, Loderick	100	1818	3 years soldier Virginia line	10- 3-1783
Elder, Ephram	200	1578	During war soldier Virginia line	8-18-1783
Eldridge, Christopher	100	3933	3 years soldier Virginia line	8- 1-1785
Elliott, Alexander	2,666⅔	4402	3 years midshipman Virginia navy	6- 1-1788
Elliott, George	4,000	4403	3 years captain Virginia navy	1- 6-1788
Elliott, James	200	2585	End war soldier Virginia line	2-23-1784
Elliott, Jeremiah	200	534	During war soldier state line	5- 2-1783
Elliott, Jidethan	100	2924	3 years carpenter Virginia navy	4-13-1784
Elliott, William	200	1929	3 years corporal Virginia line	11-22-1783
Elliott, Wyatt	200	781	3 years sergeant Virginia line	6-10-1783
Ellis, James	100	2420	3 years drummer Virginia line	2- 6-1784
Ellis, John	200	2561	3 years sergeant Virginia line	2-20-1784
Ellis, Mathew	100	4396	3 years soldier Virginia line	4- 3-1788
Elllis, William	100	2566	3 years soldier Virginia line	2-20-1784
Ellmore, Daniel	100	554	During war soldier Virginia state line	5- 7-1783
Ellmore, William	400	570	3 years soldier Virginia line	5-12-1783
Elmore, John	200	2673	3 years sergeant Virginia line	2-11-1784
Elmore, George	100	1407	3 years soldier Virginia line	7-21-1783
Elms, James	100	3344	3 years soldier Virginia line	7-19-1784
Elms, James	100	4539	3 years soldier Virginia line	11-10-1791
Elms, William	200	4540	3 years sergeant Virginia line	11-10-1791
Elwell, Thomas	400	4122	During war corporal Virginia line	3- 7-1786
Elzey, Edward	100	575	3 years private Virginia line	5-14-1783
Elzy, Edward	200	703	During war soldier Virginia line	5-31-1783
Emanuel, Henry	200	1675	During war soldier Virginia line	8-27-1783
Emerson, Henry	200	2406	3 years sergeant Virginia line	2- 4-1784
Emmins, William	200	718	3 years sergeant Virginia line	6- 3-1783
Emmons, John	200	3762	During war soldier Virginia line	2-28-1785
Emry, Thomas	200	339	During war soldier state line	4-15-1783
Engel, Windel	200	4475	During war soldier Virginia line	11- 3-1789
English, Charles	100	253	3 years soldier state line	4- 3-1783
English, Charles	200	1292	During war soldier Virginia line	6-28-1783
English, John	200	1106	During war soldier Virginia line	6-24-1783
Epperson, Samuel	200	3887	During war soldier Virginia line	6- 6-1785
Eppes, Richard	200	1860	3 years sergeant Virginia line	10-14-1783
Eppes, William	4,000	1475	3 years captain lieutenant Virginia line	8- 1-1783
Eppes, Wyatt	100	2706	3 years soldier Virginia line	3- 4-1784
Epps, William	4,000	674	3 years captain Virginia line	5-29-1783
Ermin, Thomas	100	4126	3 years soldier Virginia line	3-11-1786
Erskine, Charles	200	2505	3 years subaltern Virginia line	2-17-1784
Eskridge, Edwin	2,666⅔	4072	3 years midshipman Virginia navy	1-13-1786
Eskridge, George	200	3491	3 years sergeant Virginia line	10-29-1784
Eskridge, Samuel	2,666⅔	4266	3 years lieutenant Virginia navy	3-28-1787
Eskridge, William	1,000	295	3 years lieutenant Virginia Cont. line	4- 5-1783
Eskridge, William	2,666⅔	296	7 years lieutenant Virginia Cont. line	4- 5-1783
Estes, Elisha	200	837	3 years sergeant Virginia line	6-16-1783
Estis, George	100	4105	3 years soldier Virginia line	2- 7-1786
Estis, Rowland	100	4106	3 years soldier Virginia line	2- 7-1786
Ethel, Benjamin	100	3822	3 years soldier Virginia line	4-22-1785
Etherington, John	100	3986	3 years soldier Virginia line	10-21-1785
Etter, John	200	4083	During war soldier Virginia line	1-18-1786
Eubank, John	200	3812	3 years corporal Virginia line	4-20-1785
Euban, Royal	100	875	3 years Virginia cavalry	6-19-1783
Eustace, John	4,000	2157	3 years captain Virginia line	12-19-1783
Eustace, John	2,666⅔	2637	During war lieutenant Virginia line	2-26-1784
Evans, Charles	100	747	3 years soldier Virginia line	6- 5-1783
Evans, George	6,000	2450	3 years surgeon Virginia line	2-10-1784
Evans, Henry	100	2493	3 years soldier Virginia line	2-14-1784
Evans, John	200	2198	During war soldier Virginia line	12-23-1783
Evans, Joseph	200	4512	3 years sergeant Virginia line	12- 9-1790
Evans, Philip	100	1406	3 years soldier Virginia line	7-21-1783
Evans, Philip	2,666⅔	4331	3 years carpenter Virginia navy	11- 9-1787
Evans, Stephen	400	4043	During war corporal Virginia line	12-17-1785
Evans, Thomas	200	412	During war soldier Virginia line	4-25-1783
Evans, Thomas	100	3399	3 years soldier Virginia line	8-17-1784
Evans, William	1,000	247	3 years lieutenant Virginia Cont. line	4- 2-1783
Evans, William	1,666⅔	248	3 years lieutenant Virginia Cont. line	4- 2-1783
Evans, William	100	1481	3 years soldier Virginia line	8- 2-1783
Evans, William	200	3941	During war soldier Virginia line	8- 3-1785
Everhart, Lawrence	200	3501	3 years sergeant Virginia line	11- 4-1784
Ewell, Capt Charles	4,000	583	3 years captain state line	5-15-1783
Ewell, Thomas	400	1329	3 years captain Virginia line	7- 5-1783

Name	Acres	Warrant	Service	Date
Ewing, Alexander	2,666¾	6	3 years lieutenant Virginia Cont. line	9- 3-1782
Ewing, Edward	100	4069	During war soldier Virginia line	1- 6-1786
Faintleroy, Henry	4,000	1967	3 years captain Virginia line	11-26-1783
Fair, James	200	546	3 years sergeant state line	5- 5-1783
Fall, Henry	100	1442	3 years soldier Virginia line	7-30-1783
Falvey, Patrick	200	485	During war soldier state line	4-30-1783
Farguson, William	100	3395	3 years soldier Virginia line	8-16-1784
Farenholtz, David	100	1731	3 years soldier Virginia line	9- 8-1783
Faris, William	100	1861	3 years soldier Virginia line	10-14-1783
Farmer, Jesse	100	2232	3 years soldier Virginia line	1-12-1784
Farmer, John	200	3652	During war soldier Virginia line	12-31-1784
Farmer, Lodswick	100	2817	3 years soldier Virginia line	3-25-1784
Farrell, John	200	885	3 years drummer Virginia line	6-20-1783
Farrell, John	100	886	3 years drummer Virginia line	6-20-1783
Farrow, Robert	200	510	During war soldier state line	5- 1-1783
Fathorn, Edward	200	2295	During war soldier Virginia line	1-26-1784
Fauntleroy, Griffin	4,000	3221	3 years captain Virginia line	6-26-1784
Fauntleroy, Moore	6,222	4494	During war major Virginia line	5-25-1790
Fautz, Valentine	100	1001	3 years soldier Virginia line	6-21-1783
Fay, Joseph	100	2699	3 years soldier Virginia line	3- 3-1784
Feagle, Michael	100	3727	3 years soldier Virginia line	1-31-1785
Feagon, John	200	468	During war soldier state line	4-29-1783
Feant, George	100	3742	3 years soldier Virginia line	2- 7-1785
Feant, Philip	200	3740	During war soldier Virginia line	2- 7-1785
Fear, Edmund	100	4222	3 years soldier Virginia line	10-28-1786
Fear, Jacob	200	2048	During war soldier Virginia line	12- 9-1783
Fears, Thomas	200	520	During war soldier state line	5- 1-1783
Febiger, Christian	7,777⅓	2279	7 years colonel Virginia line	1-24-1784
Feely, Timothy	2,666⅔	4427	3 years lieutenant Virginia line	7-29-1788
Feggins, James	200	2049	During war soldier Virginia line	12- 9-1783
Fenn, Thomas	4,000	125	3 years captain of artillery	2-13-1783
Fennell, Reuben	100	1910	3 years soldier Virginia line	11-19-1783
Fenol, John	100	3113	3 years soldier Virginia line	5-29-1784
Ferguson, John	100	2733	3 years soldier Virginia line	3- 6-1784
Ferguson, John	100	3025	3 years fifer Virginia line	4-27-1784
Ferguson, Robert	2,666⅔	3404	3 years surgeon Virginia navy	8-20-1784
Ferguson, Robert	200	4503	During war soldier Virginia line	11-10-1790
Ficklin, Charles	100	3879	3 years soldier Virginia line	5-20-1785
Field, Reuben	4,000	244	3 years captain Virginia Cont. line	4- 1-1783
Field, William	100	1305	3 years soldier Virginia line	6-30-1783
Fielder, George	100	4463	3 years soldier Virginia line	9-18-1789
Figg, Thomas	100	3465	3 years soldier Virginia line	10-15-1784
Filbuy, George	200	3863	During war soldier Virginia line	5- 7-1785
Finch, James	200	465	During war soldier state line	4-28-1783
Finley, Archibald	100	982	3 years soldier Virginia Cont. line	6-20-1783
Finley, Samuel	6,222	1450	During war major Virginia line	7-31-1783
Finn, Philip	100	3710	3 years soldier Virginia line	1-20-1785
Finnegan, Patrick	200	1047	During war soldier Virginia line	6-24-1783
Finney, John	200	1077	During war soldier Virginia line	6-24-1783
Finney, Reuben	200	4017	During war soldier Virginia line	12- 3-1785
Finnie, William	2,000	3526	3 years colonel Virginia line	11-20-1784
Finnie, William	2,000	3527	3 years colonel Virginia line	11-20-1784
Finnie, William	2,000	3528	3 years colonel Virginia line	11-20-1784
Finnie, William	666⅔	3529	3 years colonel Virginia line	11-20-1784
Fishback, Jacob	200	4534	During war soldier Virginia line	10-26-1791
Fisher, John	100	655	3 years soldier Virginia line	5-27-1783
Fisher, Thomas	200	1596	During war soldier Virginia line	8-20-1783
Fisher, William	200	3900	During war soldier Virginia line	6-21-1785
Fitzgerald, James	100	1358	3 years soldier Virginia line	7-12-1783
Fitzgerald, James	200	1935	During war soldier Virginia line	11-22-1783
Fitzgerald, John	4,666⅔	2309	7 years captain Virginia line	1-29-1784
Fitzgerald, John	5,333⅓	2868	3 years major Virginia line	4- 2-1784
Fitzhugh, Perregaine	2,666⅔	3455	3 years lieutenant Virginia line	10- 6-1784
Fitzhugh, Peregrine	1,333⅓	4008	3 years captain Virginia line	11-25-1785
Fitzhugh, William	2,666⅔	2547	During war lieutenant Virginia line	2-20-1784
Fitzhugh, Wm Beverly	1,000	3712	3 years soldier Virginia line	1-20-1785
Fitzpatrick, James	200	3545	During war soldier Virginia line	11-29-1784
Fitzpatrick, Solomon	400	2558	During war sergeant Virginia line	2-20-1784
Fitzsimmons, Nicholas	100	1829	3 years soldier Virginia line	10- 7-1783
Flass, Isaac	200	883	During war soldier Virginia line	6-20-1783
Flatford, Robert	100	870	3 years soldier Virginia line	6-19-1783
Flatford, Robert	400	1701	During war sergeant Virginia line	9- 1-1783
Flaugherty, James	200	918	3 years sergeant Virginia line	6-20-1783
Flay, John	200	550	During war soldier state line	5- 6-1783
Fleet, Henry	2,666⅔	1988	3 years midshipman Virginia navy	11-28-1783
Fleet, John	2,666⅔	469	3 years lieutenant state line	4-29-1783
Fleetwood, Isaac	100	2430	3 years seaman Virginia navy	2- 9-1784
Fleming, Charles	6,000	1880	3 years lieutenant colonel Virginia line	11- 8-1783
Fleming, John	200	1758	3 years sergeant Virginia line	9-12-1783
Fleming, John	5,333⅓	2764	3 years major Virginia line	3-16-1784
Fleming, John	200	3543	During war soldier Virginia line	11-27-1784

Name	Acres	Warrant	Service	Date
Fleming, Ludwell Carter ..	100	3066	3 years soldier Virginia line	5-10-1784
Fleming, Thomas	6,666⅔	2763	3 years colonel Virginia line	3-16-1784
Fleming, William	400	1650	During war captain Virginia line	8-23-1783
Flemming, Bernard	100	3012	3 years soldier Virginia line	4-24-1784
Flemister, Lewis	233⅓	1582	During war soldier Virginia line	8-18-1783
Fletcher, Stephen	200	1605	During war soldier Virginia line	8-20-1783
Fletcher, Thomas	200	373	During war soldier state line	4-19-1783
Flin, Thomas	100	2354	3 years soldier Virginia line	1-31-1784
Fling, Edward	200	4410	During war soldier Virginia line	7-11-1788
Fling, Philip	100	383	3 years soldier Virginia line	4-23-1783
Flinn, Esburn	400	3735	During war sergeant Virginia line	2- 7-1785
Flint, John	100	2067	3 years carpenter Virginia line	12-10-1783
Flippin, Robert	100	1488	3 years soldier Virginia line	8- 4-1783
Flournoy, Jacob	100	696	3 years soldier Virginia line	5-31-1783
Flournoy, Samuel	200	1574	3 years sergeant Virginia line	8-15-1783
Flowers, John	200	2602	3 years sergeant Virginia line	2-24-1784
Floyd, Thomas	100	867	3 years soldier Virginia line	6-19-1783
Floyd, William	200	2046	During war soldier Virginia line	12- 9-1783
Foley, Enock	100	4037	3 years private Virginia line	12-15-1785
Forchand, Darby	100	3885	3 years soldier Virginia line	6- 1-1785
Forrest, George	100	537	3 years soldier Cont. line	5- 2-1783
Forrest, Zackarel	200	2437	3 years sergeant Virginia line	2- 9-1784
Fortune, Gardner	100	284	3 years soldier Virginia line	4- 3-1783
Fortune, Nathan	200	1659	During war soldier Virginia line	8-25-1783
Fossie, Christopher	200	4078	During war soldier Virginia line	1-14-1786
Foster, Cosby	200	2767	During war soldier Virginia line	3-17-1784
Foster, Edmond	200	3757	3 years corporal Virginia line	2-19-1785
Foster, George	200	1870	During war soldier Virginia line	10-15-1783
Foster, James	4,000	2633	3 years captain Virginia line	2-25-1784
Foster, John	200	1377	3 years sergeant Virginia line	7-15-1783
Foster, John	100	1912	3 years soldier Virginia line	11-20-1783
Foster, John	2,666⅔	2610	During war subaltern Virginia line	2-24-1784
Foster, John	100	2931	3 years soldier Virginia line	4-15-1784
Foster, Peter	200	1440	3 years sergeant Virginia line	7-28-1783
Foster, Peter	100	2210	3 years sailor Virginia navy	12-23-1783
Foster, Robert	2,666⅔	624	3 years lieutenant Virginia line	5-23-1783
Foster, Thomas	100	4086	3 years soldier Virginia line	1-21-1786
Foster, William	200	1863	During war soldier Virginia line	10-14-1783
Foster, William	200	1994	During war soldier Virginia line	11-29-1783
Foster, William	100	2851	3 years soldier Virginia line	4- 1-1784
Fouchand, John	100	3038	3 years soldier Virginia line	5- 3-1784
Fowler, Anderson	100	2397	3 years soldier Virginia line	2- 3-1784
Fowler, Jo	100	4112	3 years soldier Virginia line	3- 2-1786
Fowler, John	100	3974	3 years soldier Virginia line	9-13-1785
Fowler, Joseph	200	1112	During war soldier Virginia line	6-24-1783
Fowler, Robert Martin	100	4498	3 years soldier Virginia line	6-24-1790
Fowler, William	4,000	145	3 years captain Virginia line	2-24-1783
Fox, John	100	4152	3 years soldier Virginia line	5- 6-1786
Fox, Lewis	100	686	3 years soldier Virginia line	5-30-1783
Fox, Nathaniel	4,000	707	3 years captain Virginia line	5-31-1783
Fox, Nathanial	666⅔	2545	7 years captain Virginia line	2-19-1784
Foy, Capt Thomas	4,000	599	3 years captain Virginia line	5-20-1783
Frails, Charles	100	4554	3 years soldier Virginia line	11-29-1791
Frainam, David	100	3060	3 years soldier Virginia line	5- 8-1784
Francis, Christopher	100	3468	3 years soldier Virginia line	10-18-1784
Franklin, Henry	100	3090	3 years soldier Virginia line	5-22-1784
Franklin, James	100	335	3 years soldier Virginia line	4-14-1783
Franklin, John	200	3901	During war soldier Virginia line	6-21-1785
Franklin, Joseph	200	2009	3 years corporal Virginia line	12- 3-1783
France, Lewis	100	980	3 years soldier Virginia line	6-20-1783
France, Peter	100	944	3 years soldier Virginia line	6-20-1783
Fraser, Roderick	200	2645	3 years sergeant Virginia line	2-26-1784
Frazer, Alexander	400	1096	Sergeant during war Virginia line	6-24-1783
Frazer, Falvey	2,666⅔	2839	3 years lieutenant Virginia line	6-10-1784
Frazer, James	400	3144	During war sergeant Virginia line	6-10-1784
Freeland, Isaac	100	3514	3 years soldier Virginia line	11- 9-1784
Freeman, Anderson	200	2831	3 years sergeant Virginia line	3-26-1784
Freeman, Coldrop	200	4076	During war soldier Virginia line	1-14-1786
Freeman, Hezehiah	100	2492	3 years soldier Virginia line	2-14-1784
Freeman, John	200	4371	During war soldier Virginia line	1-23-1788
Frend, James	100	4308	3 years soldier Virginia line	9-22-1787
French, Richard	100	2253	3 years soldier Virginia line	1-21-1784
French, Thomas	200	881	3 years soldier Virginia line	6-20-1783
Friskett, George	200	4193	During war soldier Virginia line	8- 8-1786
Fritts, George	100	4172	3 years soldier Virginia line	6-14-1786
Frogett, William	200	493	During war soldier state line	4-30-1783
Fromaget, Daniel	200	1257	During war soldier Virginia line	6-27-1783
Frowman, Elijah	100	2288	3 years soldier Virginia line	1-26-1784
Fryer, Richard	100	3531	3 years soldier Virginia line	11-22-1784
Fukeway, Joseph	100	2713	3 years soldier Virginia line	3- 5-1784
Fullin, William	100	4080	3 years soldier Virginia line	1-16-1786

Name	Acres	Warrant	Service	Date
Furbush, William	200	1966	3 years sergeant Virginia line	11–25–1783
Furguson, Larkin	100	2840	3 years soldier Virginia line	3–29–1784
Furley, James	100	4235	3 years soldier Virginia line	12–11–1786
Gagney, Lewis	200	3331	During war soldier Virginia line	7–19–1784
Gaibon, Benjamin	100	4233	3 years sailor Virginia navy	11–16–1786
Gains, John	100	1872	3 years private Virginia navy	11– 7–1783
Gaines, Thomas	200	2530	3 years sergeant Virginia line	2–19–1784
Gains, Wm Henning	4,000	456	— years Capt. Lieut. Virginia Art	4–28–1783
Galbreath, Robert	200	1702	3 years sergeant Virginia line	9– 1–1783
Galders, Jesse	100	4384	3 years soldier Virginia line	2– 2–1788
Galaspy, Thomas	100	3202	3 years soldier Virginia line	6–24–1784
Gallady, Joseph	400	4121	During war corporal Virginia line	3– 7–1786
Gallahue, Charles	4,000	4087	3 years captain Virginia line	1–21–1786
Gallaspy, George	100	3494	3 years soldier Virginia line	11– 3–1784
Galleway, Terry	100	2226	3 years soldier Virginia line	1–10–1784
Galley, William	200	3214	During war soldier Virginia line	6–26–1784
Galt, John Minston	6,000	3432	Services surgeon Virginia line	9– 2–1784
Galt, Patrick	6,000	194	Services as surgeon Virginia Reg	3–24–1783
Gamble, Robert	4,000	1494	3 years captain Virginia line	8– 4–1783
Gammells, Nathan	200	708	3 years sergeant Virginia line	5–31–1783
Gardner, Caswell	200	4315	3 years sergeant Virginia line	10–23–1787
Gardner, George	400	501	During war corporal state line	5– 1–1783
Gardner, John	200	1764	3 years sergeant Virginia line	9–13–1783
Gardner, Thomas	200	3587	3 years sergeant Virginia line	12–18–1784
Garland, Capt Peter	4,000	560	3 years captain Cont. line	5– 8–1783
Garner, John	200	1773	During war soldier Virginia line	9–18–1783
Garner, John	100	2646	3 years soldier Virginia line	2–26–1784
Garner, Presly	100	1794	3 years seaman Virginia navy	9–26–1783
Garner, William	200	1772	During war soldier Virginia line	9–18–1783
Garner, Willlam	100	3574	3 years soldier Virginia line	12–15–1784
Garnett, Anthony	100	3562	3 years soldier Virginia line	12– 8–1784
Garrett, John	100	3924	3 years soldier Virginia line	6–21–1785
Garrett, Mark	200	475	3 years sergeant state line	4–29–1783
Garvin, Benjamin	100	4346	3 years soldier Virginia line	11–30–1787
Gary, John	200	85	3 years sergeanr artillery	12–31–1782
Gary, John	200	1590	3 years sergeant Virginia line	8–20–1783
Gaskins, Thomas	6,000	765	3 years lieutenant colonel Virginia line	6– 7–1783
Gaskins, Thomas	1,000	2641	7 years lieutenant colonel Virginia line	2–26–1784
Gassaway, James	100	913	3 years soldier Virginia line	6–20–1783
Gassaway, John	100	957	3 years soldier Virginia line	6–20–1783
Gasky, Richard	200	400	During war soldier Virginia line	4–25–1783
Gates, Horatio	2,000	802	7 years major general Virginia line	6–13–1783
Gates, Horatio	2,000	803	7 years major general Virginia line	6–13–1783
Gates, Horatio	2,000	804	7 years major general Virginia line	6–13–1783
Gates, Horatio	2,000	805	7 years major general Virginia line	6–13–1783
Gates, Horatio	2,000	806	7 years major general Virginia line	6–13–1783
Gates, Horatio	2,000	807	7 years major general Virginia line	6–13–1783
Gates, Horatio	2,500	808	7 years major general Virginia line	6–13–1783
Gates, Horatio	1,000	809	7 years major general Virginia line	6–13–1783
Gates, Horatio	2,500	810	7 years major general Virginia line	6–13–1783
Gates, John	100	613	3 years soldier Virginia line	5–21–1783
Gehagan, John	200	4095	During war soldier Virginia line	1–25–1786
Gellen, Casper	200	503	During war soldier state line	5– 1–1783
Gennison, Joseph	200	1148	During war soldier Virginia line	6–24–1783
Gentry, James	200	561	3 years captain Virginia Cont. line	5– 8–1783
Gentry, William	100	1771	3 years soldier Virginia line	9–17–1783
George, Benjamin	100	4469	3 years sailor Virginia navy	10–22–1789
George, Francis	200	1263	During war soldier Virginia line	6–27–1784
George, James Mayo	100	1267	3 years soldier Virginia line	6–28–1783
George, John	100	3853	3 years soldier Virginia line	5– 6–1785
George, Robert	4,000	3032	3 years captain Virginia line	4–29–1784
George, William	4,000	1984	3 years captain Virginia line	11–28–1783
Geran, Henry	200	3408	During war soldier Virginia line	8–23–1784
Geraull, John	4,000	2678	3 years captain Virginia line	3– 3–1784
Gesnor, John	200	3747	During war soldier Virginia line	2– 8–1785
Gester, John	100	3860	3 years private in Virginia navy	5– 7–1785
Gibbs, Churchill	2,666⅔	3103	3 years lieutenant Virginia line	5–26–1784
Gibbs, Joseph	200	3832	During war soldier Virginia line	4–29–1785
Gibbs, William	100	985	3 years soldier Virginia line	6–20–1783
Gibson, Aaron	200	2715	3 years sergeant Virginia line	3– 5–1784
Gibson, Jacob	100	2626	3 years soldier Virginia line	2–24–1784
Gibson, John	1,000	218	3 years colonel Virginia Cont. line	4– 1–1783
Gibson, John	1,000	219	3 years colonel Virginia Cont. line	4– 1–1783
Gibson, John	1,000	220	3 years colonel Virginia Cont. line	4– 1–1783
Gibson, John	3,666⅔	221	3 years colonel Virginia Cont. line	4– 1–1783
Gibson, John Jr	2,666⅔	724	3 years sailing master Virginia navy	6– 3–1783
Gibson, George	6,666⅔	4115	3 years ensign Virginia line	10–31–1783
Gibson, Robert	200	778	3 years colonel Virginia line	3– 4–1786
Gilbert, Joseph	200	1433	3 years captain Virginia line	6–10–1783
Gilchrist, Geo	5,333⅓	791	During war soldier Virginia line	7–27–1783
			3 years major Virginia line	6–12–1783

Name	Acres	Warrant	Service	Date
Giles, James............	100....	987....	3 years soldier Virginia line.........	6–20–1783
Giles, John.............	2,666⅔...	67....	– years ensign Virginia Cont. line.....	12–21–1782
Gill, Erasmus...........	4,666⅔...	1325....	7 years captain Virginia line........	7– 4–1783
Gill, Samuel............	4,000....	3033....	3 years captain Virginia line........	4–30–1784
Gillaspy, William.......	100....	3868....	3 years soldier Virginia line........	5–10–1785
Gilleham, Clem.........	200....	1117....	During war soldier in Virginia line...	6–24–1783
Gilliam, John...........	2,666⅔...	4526....	During war lieutenant Virginia line...	6–30–1791
Gillison, Capt John	4,000....	588....	3 years captain Virginia line........	5–16–1783
Gillon, Hugh...........	200....	3007....	3 years soldier Virginia line........	4–22–1784
Gilmore, Robert........	100....	2967....	3 years soldier Virginia line........	4–20–1784
Gimbo, William.........	200....	2150....	3 years sergeant Virginia line.......	12–17–1783
Ginomon, Henry........	100....	975....	3 years soldier Virginia line........	6–20–1783
Gist, Nathaniel.........	6,666⅔...	147....	3 years colonel Virginia Cont. line....	2–25–1783
Gist, Thomas...........	100....	4250....	3 years soldier Virginia line........	1–12–1787
Given, William.........	100....	4524....	3 years soldier Virginia line........	5– 5–1791
Glascock, Robert........	100....	4370....	During war soldier Virginia line.....	1–23–1788
Glascock, Thomas.......	2,666⅔...	2938....	3 years lieutenant Virginia line......	4–17–1784
Glason, Patrick.........	200....	2100....	During war soldier Virginia line.....	12–11–1783
Glass, Hugh............	100....	936....	3 years soldier Virginia line........	6–20–1783
Glass, Isaac............	100....	884....	3 years soldier Virginia line........	6–20–1783
Glenn, Bernard.........	2,666⅔...	4462....	Services in Crocketts regiment......	8–10–1789
Gloucaster, James.......	200....	1175....	During war soldier Virginia line.....	6–25–1783
Goatley, John...........	233⅓...	3368....	7 years soldier Virginia line........	7–31–1784
Godwin, Sherod........	100....	1903....	3 years soldier Virginia line........	11–17–1783
Goff, Philip............	200....	1444....	During war musician Virginia line....	7–30–1783
Goff, Samuel...........	200....	654....	During war soldier Virginia line.....	5–27–1783
Gold, James............	100....	3922....	3 years soldier Virginia line........	6–21–1785
Gold, Michael..........	233⅓...	1900....	7 years Virginia line...............	11–17–1783
Goldman, Daniel........	200....	370....	During war soldier state line........	4–19–1783
Golson, William........	400....	3104....	During war sergeant Virginia line....	5–27–1784
Goodall, John..........	200....	1418....	3 years sergeant Virginia line.......	7–22–1783
Goodin, Benjamin.......	200....	2885....	3 years sergeant Virginia line.......	4– 5–1784
Goodman, Thomas......	200....	4542....	During war soldier Virginia line.....	11–11–1791
Goodrum, Thomas......	200....	1930....	3 years corporal Virginia line.......	11–22–1783
Goodwin, Dinwiddie.....	2,666⅔...	3530....	3 years subaltern Virginia line.......	11–20–1784
Gordan, Alben.........	200....	129....	3 years sergeant of Virginia cavalry...	2–15–1783
Gordon, Arthur........	2,666⅔...	2752....	3 years lieutenant Virginia line......	3–11–1784
Gordon, John..........	100....	4188....	3 years soldier Virginia line........	7–18–1786
Gordon, Reuben........	2,666⅔...	2262....	3 years lieutenant Virginia line......	1–21–1784
Gore, Jacob............	400....	4142....	During war sergeant Virginia line....	4– 6–1786
Gossett, John...........	200....	1071....	During war soldier Virginia line.....	6–24–1783
Goulding, John.........	100....	1905....	3 years Virginia line...............	10–23–1783
Gowdon, William.......	100....	2806....	3 years soldier Virginia line........	3–22–1784
Gowen, Bryant.........	200....	1048....	During war soldier Virginia line.....	6–24–1783
Grady, Jonathan........	100....	4077....	3 years soldier Virginia line........	1–14–1786
Grafton, John..........	100....	1491....	3 years soldier Virginia line........	8– 4–1783
Graham, Arthur........	400....	349....	During war sergeant state line.......	4–16–1783
Graham, Arther........	100....	2064....	3 years soldier Virginia line........	12– 9–1783
Graham, Walter........	4,000....	690....	3 years Capt. Lieut. Virginia line.....	5–30–1783
Granger, William.......	200....	428....	During war soldier Virginia line.....	4–26–1783
Grant, Daniel..........	100....	1362....	3 years soldier Virginia line........	7–12–1783
Grant, Daniel..........	100....	1853....	3 years gunner mate Virginia line....	11– 4–1783
Grant, John............	100....	1903....	3 years soldier Virginia line........	10–22–1783
Grant, William.........	100....	1757....	3 years soldier Virginia line........	9–12–1783
Grass, Frederick........	100....	4345....	3 years soldier Virginia line........	11–30–1787
Gratton, John..........	2,666⅔...	1495....	3 years lieutenant Virginia line......	8 –4–1783
Graves, Francis.........	100....	2412....	3 years soldier Virginia line........	2– 5–1784
Graves, Jeremiah.......	100....	3645....	3 years soldier Virginia line........	12–30–1784
Graves, John...........	200....	3107....	During war soldier Virginia line.....	5–28–1784
Graves, William........	2,666⅔...	119....	3 years cornsk of cavalry...........	2– 8–1783
Graves, William........	100....	565....	3 years soldier state line............	5– 9–1783
Graves, William........	100....	2590....	3 years artificer Virginia line........	2–23–1784
Graves, William........	200....	3571....	During war soldier Virginia line.....	12–14–1784
Gray, Benjamin.........	100....	971....	3 years soldier Virginia line........	6–20–1783
Gray, Daniel...........	200....	1869....	During war soldier Virginia line.....	11– 6–1783
Gray, David...........	200....	2083....	3 years sergeant Virginia line.......	12–10–1783
Gray, David...........	100....	4297....	3 years soldier Virginia line........	6–14–1787
Gray, Francis..........	2,666⅔...	1925....	3 years lieutenant Virginia line......	10–28–1783
Gray, George..........	100....	2174....	3.years soldier Virginia line........	12–20–1783
Gray, George..........	4,000....	242....	3 years captain dragoons Cont. line...	4– 1–1783
Gray, James...........	400....	1741....	During war sergeant Virginia line....	9–11–1783
Gray, James...........	4,000....	2631....	3 years captain Virginia line........	2–25–1784
Gray, Robert...........	100....	2717....	3 years soldier Virginia line........	3– 5–1784
Gray, Thomas..........	200....	3110....	During war soldier Virginia line.....	5–29–1784
Gray, William..........	1,666⅔...	243....	3 years lieutenant Virginia line......	4– 1–1783
Gray, Wilson...........	100....	4615....	3 years private Virginia line........	5–27–1793
Grayson, William........	6,666⅔...	1005....	3 years colonel Virginia line........	6–23–1783
Green, Gabriel.........	2,666⅔...	1939....	3 years lieutenant Virginia line......	10–31–1783
Green, John............	7,777⅔...	107....	7 years colonel Virginia line........	2– 1–1783
Green, John............	100....	916....	3 years soldier Virginia line........	6–20–1783
Green, John............	200....	1600....	During war soldier Virginia line.....	8–20–1783

Name	Acres	Warrant	Service	Date
Green, Lieut John	2,666⅔	108	— years lieutenant	2– 1–1783
Green, Jesse	100	700	3 years soldier Virginia line	5–31–1783
Green, Moses	100	3425	3 years soldier Virginia line	8–28–1784
Green, Robert	2,666⅔	323	3 years lieutenant Virginia Cont. line	4–12–1783
Green, Samuel B	6,666⅔	3451	3 years ensign Virginia line	9–25–1784
Green, Thomas	100	3635	3 years soldier Virginia line	12–29–1784
Green, William	200	1472	During war soldier Virginia line	8– 1–1783
Green, William	100	2077	3 years gunner Virginia line	12–10–1783
Green, William	1,400	4422	3 years gunner Virginia navy	7–17–1788
Green, William	1,666⅔	4423	3 years gunner Virginia navy	7–17–1788
Greer, Charles	2,000	1164	3 years surgeon Virginia line	6–24–1783
Greer, Charles	1,000	1165	3 years surgeon Virginia line	6–24–1783
Greer, Charles	1,000	1166	3 years surgeon Virginia line	6–24–1783
Greer, Charles	2,000	1167	3 years surgeon Virginia line	6–24–1783
Gregory, John	2,666⅔	4594	During war lieutenant Virginia line	11–19–1792
Gregory, Obediah	200	2461	3 years sergeant Virginia line	2–11–1784
Gregory, Walter	200	1704	3 years sergeant Virginia line	9– 1–1783
Gregory, William	100	1437	3 years soldier Virginia line	7–28–1783
Gregory, William	100	1703	3 years soldier Virginia line	9– 1–1783
Gresham, John	100	772	3 years private Virginia line	6– 9–1783
Gressitt, Thomas	100	2743	3 years soldier Virginia line	3– 9–1784
Grey, Sabrad	100	4362	3 years soldier Virginia line	1–12–1788
Grey, William	100	1872	3 years soldier Virginia line	10–15–1783
Griffin, James	200	3923	During war soldier Virginia line	6–21–1785
Griffin, Peter	200	3102	During war soldier Virginia line	5–26–1784
Griffin, Reuben	100	1314	3 years soldier Virginia line	6–30–1783
Griffin, Robert	100	1725	3 years soldier Virginia line	9– 4–1783
Griffin, Thomas Jr	100	2209	3 years soldier Virginia line	12–23–1783
Griffin, Thompson	100	2004	3 years soldier Virginia line	12– 2–1783
Griffith, David	6,000	377	3 years regimental surgeon	4–19–1783
Griffith, David	400	4390	During war corporal Virginia line	3–12–1788
Griffith, Revd David	6,666⅔	352	3 years brigade chaplain Virginia line	4–17–1783
Griffith, Michael	200	2907	During war soldier Virginia line	4– 8–1784
Grigg, Abner	100	1753	3 years soldier Virginia line	9–11–1783
Grig, George	233⅓	1231	7 years soldier Virginia line	6–27–1783
Grigg, Lewis	100	1752	3 years soldier Virginia line	9–11–1783
Grigsby, Moses	100	3520	3 years soldier Virginia line	11–12–1784
Grindson, Benjamin	200	4042	During war private Virginia line	12–15–1785
Grinstead, James	100	1388	3 years soldier Virginia line	7–17–1783
Grinter, John	200	3078	3 years sergeant Virginia line	5–14–1784
Grissell, John	100	1662	3 years soldier Virginia line	8–25–1783
Grissel, Joel	200	2018	3 years sergeant Virginia line	12– 5–1783
Grove, Anthony	100	963	3 years soldier Virginia line	6–20–1783
Groves, Thomas	200	1288	During war drummer Virginia line	6–28–1783
Grubbs, Hensley	200	2343	During war soldier Virginia line	1–31–1784
Grunsley, James	100	1755	3 years soldier Virginia line	10–13–1783
Grymes, George	200	1589	3 years sergeant Virginia line	8–20–1783
Grymes, William	200	1368	3 years corporal Virginia line	7–12–1783
Grymes, William	4,000	3990	3 years captain Virginia line	11– 2–1785
Guilder, Daniel	100	4307	3 years soldier Virginia line	9–22–1787
Guille, John	100	1182	3 years soldier Virginia line	6–25–1783
Guilliams, William	200	2119	During war soldier Virginia line	12–13–1783
Gully, Richard	100	4302	3 years soldier Virginia line	7–27–1787
Gunn, James	4,666⅔	4618	7 years captain Virginia line	7–17–1793
Gunnell, John	200	3966	During war soldier Virginia line	8–26–1783
Gunnell, Joseph	200	545	During war soldier state line	5– 5–1783
Gunner, James	100	3768	3 years soldier Virginia line	3– 5–1785
Gunnett, William	200	3486	During war soldier Virginia line	10–26–1784
Gunter, Charles	100	2166	3 years soldier Virginia line	12–20–1783
Guthery, George	2,666⅔	1892	3 years lieutenant Virginia line	10–18–1783
Guthrie, James	200	706	3 years sergeant Virginia line	5–31–1783
Guthrie, John	100	287	3 years fifer Virginia line	4– 4–1783
Guthrie, John	100	705	3 years soldier Virginia line	5–31–1783
Guthrey, John	200	1140	During war soldier Virginia line	6–24–1783
Gwinn, John	200	4438	During war soldier Virginia line	10–22–1788
Hacker, John	100	3325	3 years soldier Virginia line	7–15–1784
Hackett, James	200	1272	During war soldier Virginia line	6–28–1783
Hackett, John	233⅓	1170	7 years soldier Virginia line	6–24–1783
Hackley, John	200	596	3 years lieutenant Virginia line	5–20–1783
Hackney, William	100	3213	3 years soldier Virginia line	6–26–1784
Hackworth, William	200	4192	3 years corporal Virginia line	8– 5–1786
Hadley, Isaac	200	407	During war soldier Virginia line	4–25–1783
Hagard, Baker	200	2793	During war soldier Virginia line	3–19–1784
Hagerly, John	100	4048	3 years soldier Virginia line	12–20–1785
Hagerly, Nicholas	400	1040	During war corporal Virginia line	6–24–1783
Hagerly, Patrick	400	1354	During war sergeant Virginia line	7–11–1783
Hagin, Barney	200	2878	During war sergeant Virginia line	4– 5–1784
Hagin, John	100	4237	3 years soldier Virginia line	12–16–1786
Haidyman, John	2,666⅔	123	Lieutenant state line	2–12–1783
Haild, Caleb	100	2823	3 years soldier Virginia line	3–26–1784
Hailey, Daniel	200	2346	During war soldier Virginia line	1–31–1784

Name	Acres	Warrant	Service	Date
Haines, George..........	400	1254	3 years sergeant Virginia line........	6–27–1783
Halbert, William........	200	2598	7 years soldier Virginia line.........	2–23–1784
Halcomb, John..........	4,000	827	3 years captain Virginia line.........	6–14–1783
Haldrop, Thomas........	100	2351	3 years soldier Virginia line.........	1–31–1784
Haldrop, Thomas........	100	2384	3 years fifer Virginia line..........	2– 3–1784
Haley, Daniel...........	100	3094	3 years soldier Virginia line..........	5–22–1784
Haley, George...........	200	2961	During war soldier Virginia line.....	4–19–1784
Haley, Martin..........	4,000	3169	3 years captain Virginia line.........	6–17–1784
Haley, Peter...........	100	3372	3 years sailor Virginia navy.........	8– 3–1784
Haley, Peter...........	100	2973	3 years soldier Virginia line.........	4–20–1784
Haley, Thomas..........	200	1091	During war soldier Virginia line.....	6–24–1783
Haley, William.........	233½	1885	7 years soldier Virginia line.........	11–11–1783
Haley, William.........	100	2976	3 years soldier Virginia line.........	4–20–1784
Halfpenny, Isaac.......	200	1135	During war soldier Virginia line.....	6–24–1783
Halfpenny, John........	200	906	During war soldier Virginia line.....	6–20–1783
Halks, James...........	100	4070	3 years soldier Virginia line.........	1–10–1786
Hall, George...........	100	4184	3 years sailor Virginia navy.........	7– 5–1786
Hall, John.............	100	38	3 years soldier state artillery........	12–11–1782
Hall, John.............	200	3037	3 years corporal Virginia line.........	5– 3–1784
Hall, John.............	533	2365	During war sergeant Virginia line....	2– 2–1784
Hall, Robert...........	2,666⅔	4311	3 years master Virginia navy........	10– 6–1787
Hall, Thomas..........	200	942	3 years sergeant Virginia line........	6–20–1783
Hall, William..........	100	109	3 years soldier state regiment........	2– 2–1783
Halloby, Thomas.......	400	844	During war surgeon Virginia line.....	6–16–1783
Haly, William.........	200	1571	During war soldier Virginia line.....	8–14–1783
Ham, William..........	100	1503	3 years seaman Virginia navy........	8– 5–1783
Hamam, John..........	100	3424	3 years soldier Virginia line.........	8–28–1784
Hambrick, David.......	200	2613	During war corporal Virginia line....	2–24–1784
Hames, Peter..........	100	958	3 years soldier Virginia line.........	6–20–1783
Hamilton, James........	2,666⅔	687	3 years lieutenant Virginia line......	5–30–1783
Hamilton, John.........	100	2887	3 years soldier Virginia line.........	4– 5–1784
Hammilton, John........	2,666⅔	4090	3 years lieutenant Virginia navy.....	1–23–1786
Hamilton, John.........	100	4549	3 years soldier Virginia line.........	11–18–1791
Hamilton, Robert.......	400	4200	During war sergeant Virginia line....	8–28–1785
Hamilton, Thomas......	4,000	4388	3 years captain Virginia line.........	3– 4–1788
Hammond, John........	100	2622	3 years soldier Virginia line.........	2–24–1784
Hammontree, John......	100	3269	3 years sailor Virginia navy.........	7– 1–1784
Hampton, John.........	200	4164	During war soldier Virginia line.....	6– 1–1786
Hampton, Thomas......	100	1842	3 years soldier Virginia line.........	10–10–1783
Hampton, William......	100	267	3 years soldier state line............	4– 3–1783
Hancock, Bennett.......	200	2456	During war soldier Virginia line.....	2–11–1784
Hancock, Henry........	100	2073	3 years soldier Virginia line.........	12–10–1783
Haney, Holland........	2,666⅔	2804	3 years lieutenant Virginia line......	3–22–1784
Hannah, Robert........	100	1873	3 years soldier Virginia line.........	11–11–1783
Hanson, John...........	100	4204	3 years soldier Virginia line.........	8–30–1786
Hanson, Thomas........	100	3076	3 years soldier Virginia line.........	5–13–1784
Hansford, William......	200	1080	During war soldier Virginia line.....	6–24–1783
Harcam, Rodham.......	2,666⅔	2098	3 years midshipman Virginia navy...	12–10–1783
Harcum, Lot..........	2,666⅔	4399	3 years midshipman Virginia navy...	5– 1–1788
Hardaway, Joseph.......	200	640	3 years soldier Virginia cavalry......	5–26–1783
Harden, Junes.........	100	720	3 years soldier Virginia line.........	6– 3–1783
Harden, John...........	100	1316	During war soldier Virginia line......	7– 1–1783
Hardy, John............	100	3777	3 years soldier Virginia line.........	3–12–1785
Hardy, John............	200	3794	During war soldier Virginia line......	4– 2–1785
Hardyman, John........	200	581	3 years sergeant state line...........	5–15–1783
Harlen, George.........	100	4273	3 years soldier Virginia line.........	4– 7–1787
Harney, Michael........	200	1051	During war sergeant Virginia line....	6–24–1783
Harper, David..........	200	3452	3 years sergeant Virginia line........	9–30–1784
Harper, James..........	2,666⅔	316	3 years lieutenant Virginia state line..	4–12–1783
Harper, John...........	200	716	3 years corporal Virginia line.........	6– 2–1783
Harrison, Charles.......	6,666⅔	2360	3 years colonel Virginia line.........	2– 2–1784
Harrell, James.........	200	2766	During war soldier Virginia line.....	3–16–1784
Harris, David..........	100	4167	3 years soldier Virginia line.........	6– 5–1786
Harris, Edward.........	400	1328	During war drum major Virginia line.	7– 5–1783
Harris, James..........	100	2527	3 years soldier Virginia line.........	2–19–1784
Harris, James..........	200	3370	During war soldier Virginia line......	8– 2–1784
Harriss, John..........	100	1841	3 years soldier Virginia line.........	10– 9–1783
Harriss, John..........	2,666⅔	2252	End war lieutenant Virginia line.....	1–21–1784
Harris, John...........	5,333⅓	2800	3 years captain Virginia navy........	3–20–1784
Haris, John............	100	4506	3 years soldier Virginia line..........	11–25–1790
Harris, John...........	100	4570	3 years soldier Virginia line.........	2–21–1792
Harris, Jordon.........	2,666⅔	2402	End war lieutenant Virginia line......	2– 4–1784
Harris, Richard.........	200	4364	3 years sergeant Virginia line........	1–14–1788
Harris, Robert.........	100	2565	3 years soldier Virginia line.........	2–20–1784
Harris, Thomas........	100	2318	3 years soldier Virginia line.........	8–11–1783
Harris, Walter.........	100	1546	3 years soldier Virginia line.........	3–26–1784
Harris, William........	400	1404	During war drum major Virginia line.	7–21–1783
Harriss, William.......	100	1902	3 years soldier Virginia line.........	10–22–1783
Harrison, James........	2,666⅔	2829	3 years lieutenant Virginia line......	3–26–1784
Harrison, John..........	1,333⅓	236	3 years lieutenant Virginia Cont. line.	4– 1–1783
Harrison, John..........	1,333⅓	237	3 years lieutenant Virginia Cont. line.	4– 1–1783

Name	Acres	Warrant	Service	Date
Harrison, John..........	100	3125	3 years soldier Virginia line.........	6- 5-1784
Harrison, John..........	100	3639	3 years soldier Virginia line.........	12-30-1784
Harrison, John Peyton....	4,000	171	3 years captain Virginia Cont. line....	3-10-1783
Harrison, Joseph........	200	1351	3 years sergeant Virginia line........	7-10-1783
Harrison, Philip.........	400	4589	During war sergeant Virginia line....	10-19-1792
Harrison, Richard.......	2,666⅔	3031	3 years lieutenant Virginia line......	4-29-1784
Harrison, Richard.......	100	3264	3 years soldier Virginia line.........	6-30-1784
Harrison, Robert........	200	4420	During war soldier Virginia line......	7-17-1788
Harrison, Valentine......	4,000	1580	3 years captain Virginia line........	8-18-1783
Harrison, William Butler..	2,666⅔	1774	During war cornet Virginia line......	9-19-1783
Harrison, Alias Starkes, Wm................	100	1901	3 years drummer Virginia line.......	10-21-1783
Harrup, Arthur.........	400	2072	During war sergeant Virginia line.....	12-10-1783
Hart, James............	100	582	3 years soldier Virginia line.........	5-15-1783
Hart, Leonard...........	200	487	During war soldier state line........	4-30-1783
Hart, Robert............	400	1665	During war drum major Virginia line.	8-25-1783
Hart, Robert............	200	1668	3 years drum major Virginia line....	8-26-1783
Hart, Thomas...........	100	2517	3 years soldier Virginia line.........	2-19-1784
Hart, William...........	100	3825	3 years soldier Virginia artillery.....	3-23-1785
Harves, Samuel.........	7,000	821	7 years lieutenant-colonel Virginia line.	6-14-1783
Harvey, Edward.........	100	3827	3 years soldier Virginia line.........	4-27-1785
Harvey, Rhodins........	200	552	During war soldier state line........	5- 6-1783
Harvey, Richard........	100	3430	3 years soldier Virginia line.........	8-31-1784
Harwood, Littleberry....	200	595	3 years sergeant Virginia line.......	5-19-1783
Hasly, Clem	100	4304	3 years soldier Virginia line.........	8-15-1787
Hasty, John............	100	3096	3 years soldier Virginia line.........	5-24-1784
Hatton, Samuel.........	100	3627	3 years soldier Virginia line.........	12-29-1784
Hatcher, William........	400	3135	During war corporal Virginia line....	•6- 8-1784
Hatcher, William........	400	4320	During war corporal Virginia line....	10-23-1787
Hatton, William........	200	1604	During war soldier Virginia line......	8-20-1783
Hawkins, Benjamin......	200	3419	During war soldier Virginia line......	8-27-1784
Hawkins, Benjamin......	100	3655	3 years soldier Virginia line.........	12-31-1784
Hawkins, James........	100	1925	3 years soldier Virginia line.........	11-21-1783
Hawkins, John..........	2,666⅔	2540	3 years lieutenant Virginia line......	2-19-1784
Hawkins, John..........	1,333⅓	3829	3 years captain Virginia line........	4-28-1785
Hawkins, Joseph........	100	2998	3 years soldier Virginia line.........	4-21-1784
Hawkins, Moses........	4,000	3326	3 years captain Virginia line........	7-17-1784
Hawley, Rawleigh.......	200	1827	During war soldier Virginia line......	10- 6-1783
Hay, Joseph............	6,000	4596	3 years surgeon Virginia line........	11-27-1792
Hay, Morning...........	100	2731	3 years soldier Virginia line.........	3- 6-1784
Hayes, John............	200	1802	During war soldier Virginia line......	9-30-1783
Hayes, Joseph..........	200	451	During war soldier state line........	4-28-1783
Hayes, Thomas.........	2,666⅔	1417	3 years lieutenant Virginia line......	7-22-1783
Haynes, Gabriel.........	200	2082	3 years sergeant Virginia line.......	12-10-1783
Haynes, Griffith.........	200	2807	During war soldier Virginia line......	3-23-1784
Haynes, William........	200	1608	During war soldier Virginia line......	8-20-1783
Haynice, William........	100	3651	3 years soldier Virginia line.........	12-31-1784
Hays, John.............	5,333⅓	204	3 years major Virginia line..........	3-27-1783
Hays, John.............	200	3690	3 years sergeant Virginia line.......	1-20-1785
Hays, John M	100	3960	3 years soldier Virginia line.........	8-12-1785
Hays, William..........	200	4057	During war soldier Virginia line......	12-31-1785
Hayword, John Hall.....	200	524	During war soldier state line........	5- 2-1783
Hazlewood, Richard.....	100	2369	3 years soldier Virginia line.........	2- 2-1784
Hazlewood, William......	400	1932	During war sergeant Virginia line....	11-22-1783
Heaby, James...........	200	2519	3 years sergeant Virginia line.......	2-19-1784
Head, Benjamin.........	100	2691	3 years soldier Virginia line.........	3- 3-1784
Headen, Anthony........	200	890	During war soldier Virginia line.....	6-20-1783
Heaken, William........	100	271	3 years soldier state line............	4- 3-1783
Hearn, Daniel..........	200	1933	3 years sergeant Virginia line.......	10-29-1783
Hebron, John...........	200	338	During war soldier Virginia line......	4-15-1783
Heirs, Henry...........	100	3721	3 years soldier Virginia line.........	1-28-1785
Helm, Leonard.........	200	3838	During war soldier Virginia line......	4-29-1785
Helms, Meredith........	100	1720	3 years seaman Virginia navy.......	9- 2-1783
Henderson, David.......	2,666⅔	1851	3 years midshipman Virginia navy....	11- 4-1783
Henderson, John........	100	3755	3 years soldier Virginia line.........	2-17-1785
Henderson, Sampson.....	100	4199	3 years soldier Virginia line.........	8-26-1786
Henly, Henry...........	200	3363	3 years sergeant Virginia line.......	7-28-1784
Hendrake, Moses........	100	2714	3 years soldier Virginia line.........	3- 5-1784
Hendren, William........	400	2912	During war sergeant Virginia line....	4-10-1784
Hendrick, Benjamin......	100	4300	3 years soldier Virginia line.........	7- 3-1787
Hendrick, Elijah.........	200	3	3 years sergeant Virginia Cont. line...	8- 2-1782
Hendrin, Ephram........	200	361	During war soldier Virginia line......	4-18-1783
Hendron, Robert........	100	3880	3 years soldier Virginia line.........	5-23-1785
Hennage, George........	100	3596	3 years soldier Virginia line.........	12-21-1784
Henry, Christopher......	200	548	During war soldier state line........	5- 5-1783
Henry, James...........	100	2177	3 years soldier Virginia line.........	12-20-1783
Henshaw, William.......	200	1871	During war soldier Virginia line......	11- 7-1783
Hensley, William........	100	3469	3 years soldier Virginia line.........	10-18-1784
Henson, Reuben........	100	4288	3 years soldier Virginia line.........	5-25-1787
Henson, Shadrack.......	200	4068	During war soldier Virginia line......	1- 6-1786
Henthorn, Philip........	200	1060	During war soldier Virginia line......	6-24-1783

Name	Acres	Warrant	Service	Date
Hepperling, John	200	4289	During war soldier Virginia line	5–31–1787
Herbert, Thomas	4,000	3316	3 years captain Virginia navy	7– 5–1784
Herbert, William	200	1053	During war soldier Virginia line	6–24–1783
Heth, Henry	4,000	1894	3 years captain Virginia line	10–20–1783
Heth, John	1,000	1821	3 years lieutenant Virginia line	10– 4–1783
Heth, John	1,000	1822	3 years lieutenant Virginia line	10– 4–1783
Heth, William	1,000	2161	7 years colonel Virginia line	12–20–1783
Heth, William	6,777	2162	7 years colonel Virginia line	12–20–1783
Hewett, Thomas	200	1709	During war soldier Virginia line	9– 2–1783
Hicks, William	100	941	3 years soldier Virginia line	6–20–1783
Hicks, William	100	4435	3 years soldier Virginia line	10–20–1788
Hifferlin, John	100	3595	3 years soldier Virginia line	12–21–1784
Higgins, John	100	2475	3 years soldier Virginia line	2–11–1783
Higgins, Peter	2,666⅔	771	3 years lieutenant Virginia line	6– 9–1783
Higgins, Robert	4,000	1693	3 years captain Virginia line	8–30–1783
Higden, Charles	100	4212	3 years sailor Virginia navy	10– 4–1786
Higden, John	100	759	3 years sailor Virginia navy	6– 6–1783
Higginbotham, William	400	4606	During war sergeant Virginia line	3– 9–1793
Highland, Robert	200	402	During war drummer Virginia line	4–25–1783
Highland, William	200	356	During war soldier state line	4–17–1783
Hight, George	100	3299	3 years soldier Virginia line	7– 1–1784
Hill, Thomas	5,333⅓	76	3 years major Virginia Cont. army	12–27–1782
Hill, Abraham	100	4030	3 years private Virginia line	12– 9–1785
Hill, Amos	200	362	— soldier in state line	4–18–1783
Hill, Baylor	4,000	96	3 years captain light dragoons	1–21–1782
Hill, Caleb	100	4582	3 years soldier Virginia line	6–21–1792
Hill, George	2,666⅔	2608	During war subaltern Virginia line	2–24–1784
Hill, Gideon●	100	2459	3 years soldier Virginia line	2–11–1784
Hill, Henry	100	1907	3 years soldier Virginia line	11–18–1783
Hill, James	100	2925	3 years sailor Virginia navy	4–13–1784
Hill, James	100	4049	3 years private Virginia line	12–21–1785
Hill, John	100	1538	3 years soldier Virginia line	8– 9–1783
Hill, John	200	4448	During war soldier Virginia line	1–29–1789
Hill, Spencer	100	3882	3 years soldier Virginia line	5–25–1785
Hill, Thomas	200	1645	During war soldier Virginia line	8–23–1783
Hillard, Joseph	200	1647	During war soldier Virginia line	8–23–1783
Hiller, John	100	3500	3 years soldier Virginia line	11– 4–1784
Hines, James	200	817	3 years corporal Virginia line	6–14–1783
Hines, James	100	4571	3 years soldier Virginia line	
Hines, John	200	1043	During war fifer Virginia line	6–24–1783
Hines, John	100	2589	3 years soldier Virginia line	2–23–1784
Hinley, Matthew	200	1079	During war soldier Virginia line	6–24–1783
Hinton, William	100	2428	3 years sailor Virginia navy	2– 9–1784
Hipkenstall, James	200	3759	During war soldier Virginia line	2–24–1785
Hite, Abraham	2,000	300	3 years captain Virginia Cont. line	4– 7–1783
Hite, Abraham	2,000	301	3 years captain Virginia Cont. line	4– 7–1783
Hite, Isaac	2,666⅔	3123	3 years lieutenant Virginia line	6– 5–1784
Hite, James	200	539	3 years sergeant state line	5– 2–1783
Hite, Julius	400	3047	During war corporal Virginia line	5– 9–1783
Hix, Edward	100	1540	3 years soldier Virginia line	8– 9–1783
Hix, James	100	3262	3 years soldier Virginia line	6–30–1784
Hix, William	100	652	3 years soldier Virginia line	5–27–1783
Hobbs, Frederick	233⅓	1275	7 years soldier Virginia line	6–28–1783
Hobbs, Thomas	200	358	During war soldier state line	4–17–1783
Hobday, William	100	1777	3 years soldier Virginia line	9–20–1783
Hockaday, Phillip	2,666⅔	2000	3 years lieutenant Virginia line	11–29–1783
Hodge, James	200	1470	3 years sergeant Virginia line	8– 1–1783
Hodges, Williamson	233⅓	1277	7 years soldier Virginia line	6–28–1783
Hodgins, Joseph	200	490	During war soldier state line	4–30–1783
Hodgings, Samuel	200	2190	During war soldier Virginia line	12–22–1783
Hogan, Francis	100	3244	3 years soldier Virginia line	6–29–1784
Hogan, Nicholas	200	4588	During war private Virginia line	10–17–1792
Hogg, Samuel	4,000	73	3 years captain Virginia Cont. line	12–24–1782
Hogins, Isham	200	2186	3 years sergeant Virginia line	12–22–1783
Hogland, Evert	200	1913	3 years corporal Virginia line	10–25–1783
Holback, Eddy	100	3381	3 years soldier Virginia line	8– 5–1784
Holbrook, Jesse	100	3409	3 years soldier Virginia line	8–25–1784
Holderley, William	400	4100	During war sergeant Virginia line	1–30–1786
Holl, Thomas	4,000	633	3 years captain Virginia line	5–24–1783
Holland, Drury	100	3461	3 years soldier Virginia line	10–13–1784
Holland, George	2,166⅔	2374	3 years lieutenant Virginia line	2– 3–1784
Holland, George	50	2373	3 years lieutenant Virginia line	2– 3–1784
Holliday, Henry	200	4547	3 years drummer Virginia line	11–14–1791
Holliday, James	100	2192	3 years soldier Virginia line	12–22–1783
Holloway, George	200	3357	During war soldier Virginia line	7–23–1784
Holloway, Thomas	200	3695	3 years sergeant Virginia line	1–20–1785
Holloway, Thomas	200	3695	3 years sergeant Virginia line	1–20–1785
Hollyday, William	100	4546	3 years fifer Virginia line	11–14–1791
Holman, Tandy	200	4436	During war soldier Virginia line	10–22–1788
Holmes, Esqr Benjamin	400	8	3 years captain Virginia Cont. line	9–17–1782
Holmes, Bartlet	200	4412	During war soldier Virginia line	7–17–1788

Name	Acres	Warrant	Service	Date
Holmes, Christian	5,333⅓	2744	3 years major Virginia line	3– 9–1784
Holmes, David	3,000	214	3 years surgeon Virginia Cont. line	4– 1–1783
Holmes, David	3,000	215	3 years surgeon Virginia Cont. line	4–1–1783
Holmes, Isaac	2,666⅔	1750	3 years lieutenant Virginia line	9–11–1783
Holmes, Lewis	100	1678	3 years soldier Virginia line	8–27–1783
Holt, James	2,666⅔	1797	3 years lieutenant Virginia line	9–27–1783
Holt, John Hunter	4,000	34	3 years captain Virginia state line	12– 5–1782
Holt, Samuel	100	4457	3 years soldier Virginia line	5–14–1789
Honey, Elias	200	2110	During war soldier Virginia line	12–12–1783
Hood, John	100	1008	3 years soldier Virginia cavalry	6–23–1783
Hood, Thomas	400	1891	During war sergeant Virginia line	10–81–1783
Hood, William	100	2756	3 years soldier Virginia line	3–11–1784
Hoof, James	400	4141	During war corporal Virginia line	4– 6–1786
Hoofer, John	200	1776	During war soldier Virginia line	9–19–1783
Hooffer, Samuel	100	3558	3 years soldier Virginia line	12– 7–1784
Hoffler, William	4,000	112	3 years captain state line	2– 5–1783
Hoofman, Joseph	100	1885	3 years soldier Virginia line	10–16–1783
Hoofman, Reuben	100	1886	3 years soldier Virginia line	10–16–1783
Hooks, William	100	3744	3 years soldier Virginia line	2– 7–1785
Hoomes, Thomas Claiborn	2,666⅔	12	3 years lieutenant Virginia Cont. line	11– 4–1782
Hooper, Walter	200	2102	During war soldier Virginia line	12–12–1783
Hopewell, Thomas	100	3226	3 years soldier Virginia line	6–28–1784
Hopkins, David	5,333⅓	4583	During war major Virginia line	7– 6–1792
Hopkins, Patrick	100	1875	3 years private Virginia navy	11– 7–1783
Hopkins, Samuel	7,000	688	7 years lieutenant-colonel Virginia line	5–30–1783
Hopkins, Thomas	200	3208	During war soldier Virginia line	6–24–1784
Hopkinstock, Christopher	200	1643	During war soldier Virginia line	8–23–1783
Hopper, John	100	2474	3 years soldier Virginia line	2–11–1784
Hopper, John	400	3653	During war corporal Virginia line	12–31–1784
Hopper, John	400	3828	During war captain Virginia line	4–27–1785
Hord, Capt Thomas	4,666⅔	600	7 years captain Virginia line	5–20–1783
Horn, Ralph	100	2834	3 years soldier Virginia line	3–27–1784
Horsley, James	200	4026	During war soldier Virginia line	12– 5–1785
Horton, Samuel	200	4620	During war private Virginia line	8–12–1793
Hosfield, Thomas	400	1038	During war sergeant Virginia line	6–24–1783
Hoskins, Joseph	100	3677	3 years soldier Virginia line	1– 5–1785
Hourager, Patrick	100	2751	3 years soldier Virginia line	3–11–1784
Howard, Charles	200	4125	During war soldier Virginia line	3–10–1786
Howard, James	200	4268	During war soldier Virginia line	4– 5–1787
Howard, John	100	1812	3 years soldier Virginia line	10– 1–1783
Howard, Peter	200	2880	During war soldier Virginia line	4– 5–1784
Howard, Robert	100	997	3 years soldier Virginia line	6–21–1783
Howell, Abner	100	2908	3 years soldier Virginia line	4– 8–1784
Howell, David	100	2992	3 years soldier Virginia line	4–21–1784
Howell, Phillison	400	355	During war corporal state line	4–17–1783
Howell, Vincent	100	2525	3 years soldier Virginia line	2–19–1783
Howell, Vincent	2,666⅔	3622	3 years lieutenant Virginia line	12–27–1784
Hoye, Alexander	200	4185	During war soldier Virginia line	7– 4–1786
Hubbard, Charles	100	3460	3 years sailor Virginia navy	10–13–1784
Hubbard, Elias	100	2333	3 years soldier Virginia line	1–31–1784
Hubbard, Eppa	200	2812	3 years sergeant Virginia line	3–24–1784
Hubbard, James	200	2582	During war soldier Virginia line	2–21–1784
Hubbard, John	2,666⅔	4386	3 years midshipman Virginia navy	2– 6–1788
Hubbard, William	100	4472	3 years sailor Virginia navy	10–22–1789
Hubbert, Isaac	100	3983	3 years soldier Virginia line	10–18–1785
Huddleston, John	200	508	During war soldier state line	5– 1–1783
Hudgins, Moses	100	593	3 years soldier Virginia line	5–17–1783
Hudgins, Samuel	100	3215	3 years soldier Virginia line	6–26–1784
Hudnall, Thomas	200	3489	During war soldier Virginia line	10–29–1784
Hudson, John	4,000	1378	3 years captain Virginia line	7–15–1783
Hudson, John	200	1517	During war soldier Virginia line	8– 7–1783
Hudson, John	100	2148	3 years soldier Virginia line	12–18–1783
Hudson, Rush	400	1926	During war corporal Virginia line	10–28–1783
Huey, John	100	2062	3 years soldier Virginia line	12– 9–1783
Huffman, Lud Philip	2,666⅔	177	3 years lieutenant Virginia Cont. line	3–13–1783
Hughs, Benjamin	100	1914	3 years soldier Virginia line	10–25–1783
Hughes, Henry	2,666⅔	3487	End of war lieutenant Virginia line	10–27–1784
Hughes, George	400	3568	During war sergeant Virginia line	12– 9–1784
Hughes, James	400	1740	During war sergeant Virginia line	9–10–1783
Hughes, Jasper	2,666⅔	2742	3 years cornet Virginia line	3– 9–1784
Hughes, Jacob	200	4025	3 years sergeant Virginia line	12– 5–1785
Hughes, Jesse	100	1760	3 years soldier Virginia line	9–13–1783
Hughes, John	200	3784	During war soldier Virginia line	3–22–1785
Hughes, John	4,666⅔	2741	7 years captain Virginia line	3– 9–1784
Hughes, Joseph	100	1898	3 years soldier Virginia line	11–14–1783
Hughes, Nathan	100	394	3 years soldier Virginia Cont. line	4–24–1783
Hughes, Pratt	3,110⅓	760	7 years lieutenant Virginia line	6– 6–1783
Hughes, Reuben	100	2811	3 years soldier Virginia line	3–24–1784
Hughes, Thomas	100	3502	3 years soldier Virginia line	11– 4–1784
Hughlate, John	2,666⅔	4428	3 years midshipman Virginia navy	8– 2–1788
Hull, Bucham	200	4059	During war soldier Virginia line	12–31–1785

Name	Acres	Warrant	Service	Date
Hull, David...............	100	1738	3 years soldier Virginia line.........	9–10–1783
Hull, Hopewell...........	100	4040	3 years private Virginia line..:......	12–15–1785
Hull, John...............	400	1095	During war sergeant Virginia line.....	6–24–1783
Hull, Thomas............	100	4039	3 years private Virginia line.........	12–15–1785
Hulling, James...........	200	1090	During war soldier Virginia line.....	6–24–1783
Huls, James..............	100	1754	3 years soldier Virginia line.........	9–12–1783
Hulse, William...........	200	1917	3 years sergeant Virginia line........	10–25–1783
Humphlet, William.......	100	1959	3 years seaman Virginia navy........	11–22–1783
Humphrey, John..........	100	2029	3 years soldier Virginia line.........	12– 6–1783
Humphreys, Reuben.....	100	186	3 years soldier cavalry..............	3–20–1783
Humphrey**s**, Samuel......	100	2005	3 years seaman Virginia navy........	12– 2–1783
Humphries, John.........	2,666⅔	2106	3 years lieutenant Virginia line......	12–12–1783
Humphries, John.........	100	2356	3 years soldier Virginia line.........	1–31–1784
Humphries, Ralph........	100	3072	3 years soldier Virginia line.........	5–11–1784
Humphries, Robert.......	100	3059	3 years soldier Virginia line.........	5– 8–1784
Humphries, Thomas......	200	3153	3 years sergeant Virginia line........	6–12–1784
Hundley, Joshua.........	100	1723	3 years soldier Virginia line.........	9– 3–1783
Hunny, Calis............	100	874	3 years soldier Virginia line.........	6–19–1783
Hunt, James.............	100	835	3 years soldier Virginia line.........	6–16–1783
Hunt, Munacan..........	100	3893	3 years soldier Virginia line.........	6–15–1785
Hunt, Samuel............	233⅓	2241	7 years soldier Virginia line.........	1–12–1784
Hunt, Thomas...........	200	3521	During war soldier Virginia line.....	11–12–1784
Hunt, William...........	200	1597	During war soldier Virginia line.....	8–20–1783
Hunter, William.........	100	3772	3 years soldier Virginia line.........	3– 9–1785
Hupp, Philip............	100	2897	3 years soldier Virginia line.........	4– 6–1784
Hurt, James.............	777⅔	4576	3 years captain Virginia line.........	5–22–1792
Hurt, John..............	7,000	2247	7 years chaplain Virginia line.......	1–15–1784
Hurt, West..............	100	1184	3 years soldier Virginia line.........	6–25–1783
Huse, William...........	200	2068	3 years gunner Virginia navy........	12–10–1783
Hutcheson, Charles......	200	2893	3 years sergeant Virginia line........	4– 5–1784
Hutcheson, Thomas......	200	1920	3 years sergeant Virginia line........	10–25–1783
Hutchings, Charles......	200	1381	During war soldier Virginia line.....	7–17–1783
Hutchinson, James.......	200	3496	During war soldier Virginia line.....	11– 3–1784
Hutchinson, John........	100	4281	3 years soldier Virginia line.........	4– 9–1787
Hutchinson, Thomas.....	200	3248	3 years corporal Virginia line........	6–29–1789
Hutchison, Joseph.......	200	4456	3 years sergeant Virginia line........	5–14–1784
Hutson, William.........	100	1191	3 years soldier Virginia line.........	6–26–1783
Hutt, Read..............	100	1434	3 years soldier Virginia line.........	7–28–1783
Hutt, Read..............	200	1435	During war soldier Virginia line.....	7–28–1783
Hutts, Jacob............	200	1427	During war soldier Virginia line.....	7–25–1783
Hutts, Leonard..........	200	1426	During war soldier Virginia line.....	7–25–1783
Hynes, James............	200	1664	During war soldier Virginia line.....	8–25–1783
Inloe, Thomas...........	100	4571	3 years soldier Virginia line.........	4–28–1792
Irby, William...........	100	4292	3 years soldier Virginia line.........	6–14–1787
Ireson, George..........	100	3011	3 years soldier Virginia line.........	4–24–1784
Ironmonger, Robert......	200	869	3 years fife major Virginia line......	6–19–1783
Irvin, John..............	100	4407	3 years soldier Virginia line.........	6–20–1788
Irving, William..........	200	2352	3 years sergeant Virginia line........	1–31–1784
Isaacs, John.............	200	4293	During war soldier Virginia line.....	6–14–1787
Isbele, Daniel........-..	100	3230	3 years soldier Virginia line.........	6–29–1784
Isbell, Thomas..........	100	3928	3 years soldier Virginia line.........	8– 1–1785
Isby, Hardyman.........	200	1395	3 years sergeant Virginia line........	7–19–1783
Isdell, Thomas..........	100	2494	3 years soldier Virginia line.........	2–14–1784
Jackson, Edward........	100	4237	3 years soldier Virginia line.........	12–13–1786
Jackson, Hezekiah.......	100	4246	3 years soldier Virginia line.........	12–30–1786
Jackson, Isaac..........	200	2045	During war soldier Virginia line.....	12– 9–1783
Jackson, James..........	400	3498	During war sergeant Virginia line.....	11– 4–1784
Jackson, John...........	200	2080	During war soldier Virginia line.....	12–10–1783
Jackson, John...........	200	3252	3 years sergeant Virginia line........	6–30–1784
Jackson, Michael........	100	2596	3 years soldier Virginia line.........	2–23–1784
Jackson, Nathaniel......	200	3681	During war soldier Virginia line.....	1–11–1785
Jackson, Samuel.........	100	2173	3 years soldier Virginia line.........	12–20–1783
Jackson, Thomas........	200	1126	During war soldier Virginia line.....	6–24–1783
Jackson, William........	200	2313	During war soldier Virginia line.....	1–29–1784
Jackson, William........	100	2593	3 years soldier Virginia line.........	2–23–1784
Jackson, William........	100	4029	3 years private Virginia line.........	12– 9–1785
Jaco, William....,......	100	1867	3 years soldier Virginia line.........	10–14–1783
Jacobs, Benjamin........	100	4024	3 years soldier Virginia line.........	12– 5–1785
Jacobs, John............	200	3617	During war soldier Virginia line.....	12–23–1783
Jacobs, Roley...........	100	923	3 years soldier Virginia line.........	6–20–1783
Jacobs, Samuel..........	100	3173	3 years soldier Virginia line.........	6–19–1784
Jacobs, William.........	100	935	3 years soldier Virginia line.........	6–20–1783
James, Elisha...........	100	1318	3 years soldier Virginia line.........	7– 2–1783
James, Michael.........	2,666⅔	3375	3 years lieutenant Virginia navy.....	8– 3–1784
James, Peter............	100	1327	3 years soldier Virginia line.........	7– 4–1783
James, William..........	100	3576	3 years soldier Virginia line.........	12–15–1784
Jameson, John..........	6,000	192	3 years lieutenant & colonel cavalry..	3–20–1783
Jameson, John..........	1,000	3174	7 years lieut col. Virginia line........	6–19–1784
Jarrell, Solomon........	100	2303	3 years soldier Virginia line.........	1–28–1784
Jeffcoat, John...........	100	4053	3 years soldier Virginia line.........	12–21–1785
Jeffers, Thomas.........	200	416	3 years sergeant state line...........	4–26–1783

Name	Acres	Warrant	Service	Date
Jeffries, Elisha	100	2032	3 years soldier Virginia line	12- 6-1783
Jeffries, Isaac	2,666⅔	4598	During war ensign Virginia line	12-12-1792
Jeffries, James	100	3570	3 years soldier Virginia line	12-14-1784
Jeffries, William	200	4002	During war soldier Virginia line	11-19-1785
Jenkins, Abraham	100	4349	3 years soldier Virginia line	12- 5-1787
Jenkins, Isaac	100	4350	3 years soldier Virginia line	12- 5-1787
Jenkins, Job	100	3953	3 years soldier Virginia line	8-12-1785
Jenkins, John	200	3903	During war soldier Virginia line	6-21-1785
Jenkins, Richard	200	1815	3 years sergeant Virginia line	10- 2-1783
Jenkins, Richard	100	1950	3 years soldier Virginia line	11-22-1783
Jenkins, William	200	919	3 years sergeant Virginia line	6-20-1783
Jenkins, William	100	3703	3 years soldier Virginia line	1-20-1785
Jenkins, William	200	4450	During war soldier Virginia line	2-26-1789
Jennings, John	2,666⅔	1877	3 years sailing master Virginia navy	10-15-1783
Jennings, Solomon	200	2152	3 years sergeant Virginia line	12-19-1783
Jennings, Thomas	100	1948	3 years sailor Virginia navy	11-22-1783
Jennings, William	100	1949	3 years sailor Virginia navy	11-22-1783
Jerow, Jacob	100	1853	3 years soldier Virginia line	10-13-1783
Jesse, Turner	200	2467	3 years sergeant Virginia line	2-11-1784
Jett, John	100	680	3 years seaman Virginia navy	5-29-1783
Johns, James	100	4568	3 years soldier Virginia line	2- 1-1792
Johnson, Banjamin	200	4613	During war private Virginia line	5-27-1793
Johnson, Edward	100	3329	3 years soldier Virginia line	7-19-1784
Johnson, Edward	100	4290	3 years soldier Virginia line	6- 5-1787
Johnson, Ellis	100	4476	3 years soldier Virginia line	10-13-1789
Johnson, James	100	4160	3 years soldier Virginia line	5-26-1786
Johnson, John	100	2922	3 years soldier Virginia line	4-12-1784
Johnson, Joseph	200	499	During war soldier state line	5- 1-1783
Johnson, Philip	200	3479	3 years sergeant Virginia line	10-23-1784
Johnson, Richard	200	2125	3 years corporal Virginia line	12-15-1783
Johnson, Stephen	200	2135	During war soldier Virginia line	12-15-1783
Johnson, William	100	2178	3 years sailor Virginia navy	12-20-1783
Johnson, William	4,666⅔	2199	7 years captain Virginia line	12-23-1783
Johnson, William	200	3080	3 years non-com. officer Virginia line	5-17-1784
Johnson, William	100	3662	3 years soldier Virginia line	12-31-1784
Johnston, Cornelius	100	3767	3 years soldier Virginia line	3- 5-1785
Johnston, Edward	200	658	3 years soldier Virginia line	5-27-1783
Johnston, George	6,000	4189	3 years lieutenant Virginia line	7-20-1786
Johnston, Gideon	4,000	669	3 years captain Virginia line	5-29-1783
Johnston, Jacob	100	4612	3 years private Virginia line	5-27-1793
Johnston, James	200	1102	During war soldier Virginia line	6-24-1783
Johnston, James	200	3782	During war soldier Virginia line	3-19-1785
Johnston, John	100	973	3 years soldier Virginia line	6-20-1783
Johnston, John B	4,000	2117	3 years captain Virginia line	12-13-1783
Johnston, Moses	100	956	3 years soldier Virginia line	6-20-1783
Johnston, Peter	2,666⅔	2586	End of war lieutenant Virginia line	2-23-1784
Johnston, Richard	100	3716	3 years soldier Virginia line	1-21-1785
Johnston, Silas	100	3818	3 years soldier Virginia line	4-21-1785
Johnston, Thomas	200	1905	During war soldier Virginia line	11-18-1783
Johnston, Thomas	100	3433	3 years soldier Virginia line	9- 2-1784
Johnston, William	2,000	1825	3 years captain Virginia line	10- 6-1783
Johnston, William	2,000	1826	3 years captain Virginia line	10- 6-1783
Joins, Levin	3,000	3014	3 years lieutenant Virginia line	4-24-1784
Joins, Levin	1,000	3015	3 years lieutenant Virginia line	4-24-1784
Joins, Leven	1,000	3016	3 years lieutenant Virginia line	4-24-1784
Joins, Leven	1,000	3017	3 years lieutenant Virginia line	4-24-1784
Joines, John	400	3340	During war sergeant Virginia line	7-19-1784
Jolliffe, John	2,666⅔	825	3 years lieutenant Virginia line	6-14-1783
Jomden, Michael	200	525	During war soldier state line	5- 2-1783
Jones, Albridgton	2,666⅔	2126	3 years lieutenant Virginia line	12-15-1783
Jones, Alexander	200	766	3 years soldier Virginia line	6- 7-1783
Jones, Ambrose	100	3003	3 years soldier Virginia line	4-22-1784
Jones, Benjamin	100	4470	3 years soldier Virginia line	10-22-1789
Jones, Cadwallader	2,000	2576	3 years captain Virginia line	2-21-1784
Jones, Cadwallader	1,000	2577	3 years captain Virginia line	2-21-1784
Jones, Cadwallader	1,000	2578	3 years captain Virginia line	2-21-1784
Jones, Charles	444	2721	7 years lieutenant Virginia line	3- 6-1784
Jones, Charles	2,666⅔	1451	3 years lieutenant Virginia line	7-31-1783
Jones, Charles	200	4557	3 years sergeant Virginia line	12- 3-1791
Jones, Churchill	4,000	2311	3 years captain Virginia line	1-29-1784
Jones, Edward	200	1230	During war soldier Virginia line	6-27-1783
Jones, Elisha	100	3439	3 years soldier Virginia line	9-11-1784
Jones, Gabriel	4,000	2920	3 years captain Virginia line	4-12-1784
Jones, George	200	2755	During war soldier Virginia line	3-11-1784
Jones, Godfrey	100	2081	3 years soldier Virginia line	12-10-1783
Jones, James	200	2754	During war soldier Virginia line	3-11-1784
Jones, James	100	4543	3 years bombardier Virginia line	11-11-1791
Jones, James	100	4562	3 years soldier Virginia line	12-22-1791
Jones, Jessie	100	1233	3 years soldier Virginia line	6-27-1783
Jones, Joel	200	3365	During war soldier Virginia line	7-29-1784
Jones, John	200	1360	During war soldier Virginia line	7-12-1783

Name	Acres	Warrant	Service	Date
Jones, John..............	200	1686	During war soldier Virginia line......	8–27–1783
Jones, John..............	200	2408	During war soldier Virginia line.....	2– 5–1784
Jones, John..............	100	3848	3 years soldier Virginia line.........	5– 5–1785
Jones, John..............	100	4179	3 years soldier Virginia line.........	6–22–1786
Jones, Lewis.............	2,666⅔	1200	3 years lieutenant Virginia line......	6–26–1783
Jones, Lewis.............	2,666⅔	1201	3 years masters mate Virginia line....	6–26–1783
Jones, Peter.............	200	1706	3 years corporal Virginia line.........	9– 2–1783
Jones, Peter.............	4,000	1889	3 years captain Virginia line.........	10–18–1783
Jones, Peter.............	100	4012	3 years soldier Virginia line.........	12– 2–1785
Jones, Richard..........	400	1609	During war sergeant Virginia line.....	8–21–1783
Jones, Richard..........	100	2258	3 years soldier Virginia line.........	1–21–1784
Jones, Richard..........	200	2269	End war soldier Virginia line.........	1–21–1784
Jones, Richard..........	100	3524	3 years soldier Virginia line.........	11–16–1784
Jones, Richard..........	100	4563	3 years soldier Virginia line.........	12–22–1791
Jones, Robert...........	200	1732	3 years sergeant Virginia line.........	9– 8–1783
Jones, Samuel...........	4,000	60	3 years captain Virginia Cont. line....	12–19–1782
Jones, Samuel...........	200	1895	During war corporal Virginia line.....	11–12–1783
Jones, Samuel...........	200	4118	During war soldier Virginia line......	3– 7–1786
Jones, Solomon..........	200	2111	During war soldier Virginia line.....	12–13–1783
Jones, Strother..........	4,000	88	3 years captain in Cont. Virginia line.	1– 3–1783
Jones, Thomas..........	200	1134	During war soldier Virginia line......	6–24–1783
Jones, Thomas..........	100	2264	3 years soldier Virginia line.........	1–21–1784
Jones, Thomas..........	100	3036	3 years soldier Virginia line.........	5– 3–1784
Jones, Thomas..........	200	3421	During war soldier Virginia line......	8–28–1784
Jones, Thomas..........	100	4014	3 years soldier Virginia line.........	12– 2–1785
Jones, William...........	200	390	During war soldier Virginia line......	4–24–1783
Jones, William...........	200	1359	During war soldier Virginia line......	7–12–1783
Jones, William...........	400	1842	During war corporal Virginia line.....	10–31–1783
Jones, William...........	200	2500	3 years sergeant Virginia line.........	2–16–1784
Jones, William...........	400	3373	During war sergeant Virginia line.....	8– 3–1784
Jones, William...........	100	3687	3 years soldier Virginia line.........	1–11–1785
Jones, Zackariah.........	100	1178	3 years soldier Virginia line.........	6–25–1783
Jordain, John............	100	1867	3 years soldier Virginia line.........	11– 6–1783
Jordan, James...........	100	4168	3 years soldier Virginia line.........	6– 9–1786
Jordan, John............	4,666⅔	2509	7 years captain Virginia line.........	2–18–1784
Jouett, Mathew..........	4,000	463	3 years captain Virginia line.........	4–28–1783
Jouitt, Robert............	2,666⅔	2675	3 years lieutenant Virginia line.......	3– 3–1784
Joy, Richard.............	200	2160	During war soldier Virginia line......	12–19–1783
Junes, James............	6,666⅔	2214	3 years colonel Virginia line.........	12–27–1783
Junial, Anthony..........	100	3964	3 years soldier Virginia line.........	8–13–1785
Kairns, John.............	400	1262	During war corporal Virginia line.....	6–27–1783
Kanard, James...........	100	2615	3 years soldier Virginia line.........	2–24–1784
Karr, James..............	200	1146	During war soldier Virginia line......	6–24–1783
Kautzman, John..........	2,666⅔	3054	3 years lieutenant Virginia navy......	5– 7–1784
Kays, Robert.............	200	556	3 years lieutenant Virginia Cont. line.	5– 7–1783
Kean, Thomas............	200	1274	7 years soldier Virginia line.........	6–28–1783
Kearns, John.............	100	3590	3 years soldier Virginia line.........	12–21–1784
Keen, John...............	200	3534	During war soldier Virginia line......	11–23–1784
Keep, James.............	200	1298	During war soldier Virginia line......	6–30–1783
Keeth, Isham.............	2,666⅔	3320	Services as lieutenant Virginia line...	7– 9–1784
Keeton, Wm Edmund.....	200	3644	3 years soldier Virginia line.........	12–30–1784
Keith, Daniel.............	200	2122	During war soldier Virginia line......	12–13–1783
Kellar, Abraham..........	4,000	3321	3 years captain Virginia line.........	7–12–1784
Kelly, Andrew............	200	2388	3 years corporal Virginia line........	2– 3–1784
Kelly, Benjamin..........	100	578	3 years soldier Virginia line.........	5–14–1783
Kelly, Benjamin..........	200	379	During war soldier Virginia line......	4–22–1783
Kelly, Gordon............	100	4343	3 years soldier Virginia line.........	11–28–1787
Kelly, John..............	100	280	3 years soldier Virginia line.........	4– 3–1783
Kelly, John..............	100	922	3 years soldier Virginia line.........	6–20–1783
Kelly, Jesse..............	200	1915	During war soldier Virginia line......	11–20–1783
Kelly, Thaddily..........	4,000	170	3 years captain Virginia state line.....	3–10–1783
Kelly, Timothy..........	100	3725	3 years soldier Virginia line..........	1–31–1785
Kelly, William...........	200	3511	During war soldier Virginia line......	11– 8–1784
Kemp, James............	2,666⅔	2933	3 years ensign Virginia line..........	4–15–1784
Kemp, James........,....	100	4391	3 years soldier Virginia line..........	3–12–1788
Kemp, Peter.............	4,000	191	3 years captain artillery.............	3–20–1783
Kemp, William...........	200	3392	During war soldier Virginia line......	8–13–1784
Kenard, Joshua..........	100	2614	3 years soldier Virginia line.........	2–24–1784
Kendall, George.........	200	528	During war soldier state line..........	5– 2–1783
Kendall, Gustus.........	4,666⅔	2926	7 years captain Virginia line.........	4–13–1784
Kendall, Jesse...........	100	4211	3 years soldier Virginia line.........	10– 4–1786
Kendrick, Daniel.........	100	1188	3 years soldier Virginia line.........	6–26–1783
Kennady, John...........	200	3087	During war soldier Virginia line......	5–22–1784
Kennady, Andrew........	100	4365	3 years soldier Virginia line.........	1–17–1788
Kennady, Moses.........	200	421	During war soldier Virginia line......	4–26–1783
Kennedy, James.........	2,666⅔	66	3 years lieutenant Garrison regiment..	12–20–1782
Kennedy, William........	100	1894	3 years soldier Virginia line.........	11–12–1783
Kenner, Howson.........	2,666⅔	3783	3 years midshipman Virginia navy.....	3–21–1785
Kenner, Rodham........	100	3043	3 years soldier Virginia line.........	5– 4–1784
Kenner, Rosham........	100	3780	3 years soldier Virginia line.........	3–17–1785
Kennon, John...........	1,333⅓	3133	3 years captain Virginia line.........	6– 7–1784

Name	Acres	Warrant	Service	Date
Kenny, Joseph	100	2143	3 years soldier Virginia line	12–16–1783
Kent, Jesse	2,666⅔	4194	3 years lieutenant Virginia navy	8– 9–1786
Kent, Smith	200	1910	3 years sergeant Virginia line	10–24–1783
Kent, Thomas	100	4232	3 years sailor Virginia navy	11–16–1786
Kent, William	100	4234	3 years sailor Virginia navy	11–16–1786
Kenton, Mark	233⅓	1866	7 years soldier Virginia line	11– 6–1783
Kents, Alexander	100	2990	3 years soldier Virginia line	4–21–1784
Kerford, William	200	986	3 years sergeant Virginia line	6–20–1783
Kerney, John	1,000	1161	3 years captain Virginia line	6–24–1783
Kerney, John	1,500	1162	3 years captain Virginia line	6–24–1783
Kerney, John	1,500	1163	3 years captain Virginia line	6–24–1783
Kersey, William	100	3445	3 years soldier Virginia line	9–20–1784
Kertiller, Abraham	100	3152	3 years soldier Virginia line	6–11–1784
Key, George	100	3382	3 years soldier Virginia line	8– 5–1784
Keysar, William	100	3074	3 years soldier Virginia line	5–12–1784
Kibble, William	200	2477	3 years sergeant Virginia line	2–11–1784
Kidd, Benjamin	100	1270	3 years soldier Virginia line	6–28–1783
Kilty, John	4,000	4609	During war captain Virginia line	4–11–1793
Kimble, Robert	100	1856	3 years soldier Virginia line	10–13–1783
King, Elisha	2,666⅔	1911	3 years lieutenant Virginia line	11–19–1783
King, Charles	200	4336	3 years sergeant Virginia line	11–13–1787
King, Francis	100	268	3 years soldier state line	4– 3–1783
King, Francis	200	1929	During war soldier Virginia line	10–28–1783
King, James	200	3204	3 years sergeant Virginia line	6–24–1784
King, John	100	169	3 years soldier Virginia Cont. line	3–10–1783
King, John	100	2145	3 years soldier Virginia line	12–17–1783
King, John	200	3387	During war soldier Virginia line	8–10–1784
King, Miles	2,666⅔	2700	3 years surgeon Virginia line	3– 4–1784
King, Nicholas	200	3330	During war soldier Virginia line	7–19–1784
King, Zackariah	100	2512	3 years soldier Virginia line	2–18–1784
King, William	100	2769	3 years soldier Virginia line	3–17–1783
Kinbey, Benjamin	4,000	2711	3 years captain Virginia line	3– 5–1784
Kingore, William	100	949	3 years soldier Virginia line	6–20–1784
Kinney, Richard	233⅓	1830	During war sergeant Virginia line	10– 7–1784
Kirby, John	200	190	3 years drummer Virginia Cont. line	3–20–1783
Kirk, Robert	2,666⅔	1383	3 years lieutenant Virginia line	7–17–1783
Kirkpatrick, Abraham	4,666⅔	2052	7 years captain Virginia line	12– 9–1783
Kirkpatrick, James	200	1636	During war soldier Virginia line	8–23–1783
Klung, Henry	200	1287	During war soldier Virginia line	6–28–1783
Knight, Andrew	100	2154	3 years soldier Virginia line	12–19–1783
Knight, James	100	928	3 years soldier Virginia line	6–20–1783
Knight, James	200	3564	3 years sergeant Virginia line	12– 9–1784
Knight, John	2,000	216	3 years surgeon Virginia Cont. line	4– 1–1783
Knight, John	2,000	217	3 years surgeon Virginia Cont. line	4– 1–1783
Knight, John	100	1424	3 years soldier Virginia line	7–25–1783
Knight, John	100	1425	3 years soldier Virginia line	7–25–1783
Knight, William	100	3606	3 years soldier Virginia line	12–22–1784
Knox, George	100	4348	3 years soldier Virginia line	12– 5–1787
Knox, James	5,333⅓	2025	3 years major Virginia line	12– 6–1783
Knox, Thomas	100	2860	3 years soldier Virginia line	4– 2–1784
Kollins, Daniel	100	4214	3 years soldier Virginia line	10– 4–1786
Konip, Peter	100	2727	3 years soldier Virginia line	3– 6–1784
Konts, Jacob	233⅓	1278	During war soldier Virginia line	6–28–1783
Kurns, John	200	3722	During war soldier Virginia line	1–28–1785
Lacy, Henry R.	100	2503	3 years soldier Virginia line	2–17–1784
Lahaw, David	100	972	Services soldier Virginia line	6–20–1783
Lahaw, Jeremiah	100	961	3 years soldier Virginia line	6–20–1783
Lalimes, Henry	200	4103	3 years soldier Virginia line	2– 1–1786
Lamb, Joseph	100	2392	End of war soldier Virginia line	2– 3–1784
Lamber, Charles	200	4034	During war soldier Virginia line	12–10–1785
Lambert, John	400	454	During war sergeant state line	4–28–1783
Lamkin, John	100	4340	3 years soldier Virginia line	11–28–1787
Lamme, Nathan	4,000	4083	3 years captain Virginia line	1–17–1786
Land, Lewis	100	3823	3 years soldier Virginia line	4–23–1785
Landrum, Thomas	100	656	3 years soldier Virginia line	5–27–1783
Landwick, William	200	2694	3 years corporal Virginia line	3– 3–1784
Lane, James	400	1094	Sergeant during war Virginia line	6–24–1783
Lane, William	100	3761	3 years soldier Virginia line	2–26–1785
Lane, Zackariah	100	1942	3 years soldier Virginia line	11–22–1783
Langfitt, Francis	100	1906	3 years soldier Virginia line	10–23–1783
Langfitt, Philip	100	1909	3 years soldier Virginia line	10–24–1783
Langford, Enelid	100	634	3 years soldier Virginia line	5–24–1783
Langham, Elias	2,666⅔	1400	3 years lieutenant Virginia line	7–21–1783
Langsdon, Charles	200	4007	During war soldier Virginia line	11–24–1785
Langsdon, Daniel	200	4001	During war soldier Virginia line	11–19–1785
Langsdon, William	200	4006	During war soldier Virginia line	11–24–1785
Langston, William	100	4147	3 years soldier Virginia line	4–24–1786
Lank, John	100	2063	3 years soldier Virginia line	12– 9–1783
Lapsley, John	2,666⅔	389	3 years lieutenant Virginia Cont. line	4–23–1783
Largent, James	100	3604	3 years soldier Virginia line	12–21–1784

Name	Acres	Warrant	Service	Date
Larkin, Edward	200	4261	During war soldier Virginia line	3–24–1787
Larty, John	4,000	2282	3 years captain Virginia line	1–24–1784
Lattimore, Matthew	200	4603	During war private Virginia line	12–21–1792
Laveall, James	200	1063	During war soldier Virginia line	6–24–1783
Lawe, John	100	1541	3 years soldier Virginia line	8– 9–1783
Lawless, Austin	100	1669	3 years soldier Virginia line	8–26–1783
Lawless, Austin	100	4252	3 years soldier Virginia line	1–13–1787
Lawrence, Thomas	200	617	3 years sergeant Virginia line	5–21–1783
Laws, John	100	3532	3 years soldier Virginia line	11–22–1784
Lawson, Andrew	100	1011	3 years soldier Virginia line	6–23–1783
Lawson, Benjamin	2,666⅔	761	3 years lieutenant Virginia line	6– 6–1783
Lawson, Benjamin	100	2760	3 years soldier Virginia line	3–12–1784
Lawson, Claiborne	4,000	2655	3 years captain Virginia line	3– 1–1784
Lawson, Henry	100	3708	3 years soldier Virginia line	1–20–1785
Lawson, John Sr	100	3068	3 years soldier Virginia line	5–10–1784
Lawson, Robert	10,000	1921	3 years brigadier general Virginia line	11–21–1783
Layne, John	200	1285	During war soldier Virginia line	6–28–1783
Layne, Josiah	100	2496	3 years soldier Virginia line	2–14–1784
Layton, Reuben	100	2971	3 years soldier Virginia line	4–20–1784
League, James	200	1588	During war soldier Virginia line	8–20–1783
Lear, John	200	2362	During war soldier Virginia line	2– 2–1784
Lear, George	200	3546	During war soldier Virginia line	11–29–1784
Learwood, Josiah	100	1551	3 years soldier Virginia line	8–11–1783
Leath, Peter	100	3984	3 years soldier Virginia line	10–19–1785
Lee, Bart	200	4587	During war private Virginia line	10–12–1792
Lee, Edward	200	439	3 years soldier Virginia line	4–26–1783
Lee, Henry	7,777⅔	1937	7 years lieutenant colonel Virginia line	10–31–1783
Lee, James	100	1603	3 years soldier Virginia line	8–20–1783
Lee, James	100	3675	3 years soldier Virginia line	1– 5–1785
Lee, Jesse	100	3294	3 years soldier Virginia line	7– 1–1784
Lee, John	100	3091	3 years soldier Virginia line	5–22–1784
Lee, John	200	4465	3 years corporal Virginia line	10– 5–1789
Lee, Major John	5,333⅓	474	3 years major Virginia line	4–29–1783
Lee, Peter	100	4502	3 years soldier Virginia line	11– 9–1790
Lee, Randolph	100	1897	3 years soldier Virginia line	11–14–1783
Lee, Richard	200	1908	3 years corporal Virginia line	10–23–1783
Lee, Richard	200	1911	During war soldier Virginia line	10–25–1783
Lee, Richard Francis	4,000	3175	3 years captain Virginia line	6–21–1784
Lee, Simmons	100	3290	3 years soldier Virginia line	7– 1–1784
Leech, George	100	2476	3 years soldier Virginia line	2–11–1784
Lefeey, Shadrack	100	3929	3 years soldier Virginia line	8– 1–1785
Leftwick, John	200	3112	3 years sergeant Virginia line	5–29–1784
Legg, John	100	647	3 years soldier Virginia line	5–27–1783
Legget, Owen	200	514	During war soldier state line	5– 1–1783
Leigh, John	200	138	3 years sergeant Virginia line	2–20–1783
Leigh, John	2,466⅔	2555	3 years lieutenant Virginia line	2–20–1784
Leitch, Andrew	5,333⅓	3394	3 years major Virginia line	8–14–1784
Leitch, James	400	1786	During war corporal Virginia line	9–24–1783
Leith, George	200	4247	3 years sergeant Virginia line	1– 1–1787
Leman, Dedrick	100	2041	3 years soldier Virginia line	12– 9–1783
Lemasters, James	100	2854	3 years soldier Virginia line	4– 1–1784
Lemmon, John	200	3385	During war soldier Virginia line	8– 6–1784
Lemmon, Samuel	200	1116	During war soldier Virginia line	6–24–1783
Lenwick, Samuel	200	2460	3 years corporal Virginia line	2–11–1784
Leonard, Robert	233⅓	1901	During war soldier Virginia line	11–17–1783
Leonard, William	100	1951	3 years sailor Virginia navy	11–22–1783
Lepling, Joseph	400	324	During war corporal cavalry	4–12–1783
Leptwich, Joel	100	1781	3 years soldier Virginia line	9–22–1783
LeRockett, Michael	100	4409	3 years soldier Virginia line	7– 1–1788
Letrell, James	400	3840	During war sergeant Virginia line	4–29–1785
Letrell, Joseph	200	3839	During war soldier Virginia line	4–29–1785
Levele, Henry	200	3522	During war soldier Virginia line	11–13–1784
Levingston, Justice	2,000	1408	3 years surgeon Virginia navy	7–22–1783
Levingston, Justice	2,000	1409	3 years surgeon Virginia navy	7–22–1783
Levingston, Justice	1,000	1410	3 years surgeon Virginia navy	7–22–1783
Levingston, Justice	1,000	1411	3 years surgeon Virginia navy	7–22–1783
Lewis, Addison	4,000	396	– years captain Virginia cavalry	4–25–1783
Lewis, Ambrose	100	1847	3 years soldier Virginia line	11– 1–1783
Lewis, Andrew	2,666⅔	728	3 years lieutenant Virginia line	6– 3–1783
Lewis, Daniel	200	4301	During war soldier Virginia line	7–10–1787
Lewis, George	4,000	367	3 years captain Virginia cavalry	4–19–1783
Lewis, James	200	3009	During war soldier Virginia line	4–23–1784
Lewis, John	200	1286	During war soldier Virginia line	6–28–1783
Lewis, John	100	2164	3 years soldier Virginia line	12–20–1783
Lewis, John	100	2735	3 years soldier Virginia line	3– 6–1784
Lewis, Joseph	200	3035	During war soldier Virginia line	5– 3–1784
Lewis, Matthew	100	1946	3 years seaman Virginia navy	11–22–1783
Lewis, Stephen	2,666⅔	2898	3 years lieutenant Virginia line	4– 6–1784
Lewis, Thomas	1,333⅓	4190	3 years lieutenant Virginia line	7–28–1786
Lewis, Thomas	1,333⅓	4191	3 years lieutenant Virginia line	7–28–1786
Lewis, William	6,222	72	7 years major Virginia Cont. line	12–24–1782

Name	Acres	Warrant	Service	Date
Lewis, William	200	2002	During war soldier Virginia line	12– 1–1783
Lewis, Zackariah	200	2371	3 years sergeant Virginia line	2– 3–1784
Lightburn, Richard	2,666⅔	1202	3 years lieutenant Virginia line	6–26–1783
Lightfoot, Philip	200	876	3 years corporal Virginia line	6–19–1783
Lilly, Thomas	5,333⅓	3019	3 years captain Virginia line	4–26–1784
Limay, John	100	4098	3 years soldier Virginia line	1–27–1786
Lina, Arthur	4,000	345	3 years captain Virginia Cont. line	4–15–1783
Lincoln, Michael	100	65	3 years soldier Virginia regiment	12–20–1782
Lindsay, William	4,000	1199	3 years captain Virginia line	6–26–1783
Lindsey, David	100	2867	3 years soldier Virginia line	4– 2–1784
Linsey, Edward	100	3466	3 years soldier Virginia line	10–16–1784
Lindsey, Hezekiah	100	1028	3 years soldier Virginia line	6–23–1783
Lindsey, Peter	200	2037	During war soldier Virginia line	12– 6–1783
Link, John	100	609	3 years soldier Virginia line	5–21–1783
Lintner, Edward	100	3559	3 years soldier Virginia line	12– 7–1784
Linton, John	2,666⅔	2305	3 years lieutenant Virginia line	1–28–1784
Linton, John	444	2411	Lieutenant Virginia line	2– 5–1784
Lipscomb, Archibald	100	2116	2 years soldier Virginia line	12–13–1783
Lipscomb, Benjamin	100	2965	3 years soldier Virginia line	4–19–1784
Lipscomb, Bernard	400	80	3 years captain of artillery	12–31–1782
Lipscomb, Henry	200	1234	During war fifer Virginia line	6–27–1783
Lipscomb, James	200	4452	3 years sergeant Virginia line	3– 7–1789
Lipscomb, John	200	683	3 years captain Virginia line	5–30–1783
Lipscomb, Maj	200	4089	3 years sergeant Virginia line	1–23–1786
Lipscomb, Mourning	100	1465	3 years soldier Virginia line	8– 1–1783
Lipscomb, Reuben	4,000	81	— years captain Cont. line	12–31–1782
Lipscomb, Thomas	100	1466	3 years soldier Virginia line	8– 1–1783
Lipscomb, Yancy	4,000	82	3 years captain artillery of Virginia	12–31–1782
Litchfield, Francis	100	4335	3 years soldier Virginia line	11–13–1787
Little, Moses	100	2057	3 years soldier Virginia line	12– 9–1783
Littlepage, John	200	3987	During war soldier Virginia line	10–26–1785
Lixton, William	100	2692	3 years soldier Virginia line	3– 3–1784
Loaden, William	200	1525	During war soldier Virginia line	8– 7–1783
Lock, William	200	320	During war soldier cavalry	4–12–1783
Lockart, John	200	1045	During war soldier Virginia line	6–24–1783
Locke, John	400	3557	3 years corporal Virginia line	12– 6–1784
Lockett, Benjamin	100	3390	3 years soldier Virginia line	8–11–1784
Lockett, Benjamin	100	4015	During war soldier Virginia line	12– 2–1785
Lockett, Jacob	100	2801	3 years soldier Virginia line	3–22–1784
Lockhart, James	100	2144	3 years soldier Virginia line	12–16–1783
Lockhart, William	200	3588	During war soldier Virginia line	12–20–1784
Lockley, Daniel	100	4367	3 years soldier Virginia line	1–17–1788
Locks, Joseph	100	395	3 years soldier Virginia line	4–24–1783
Loden, Benjamin	200	3233	During war soldier Virginia line	6–29–1784
Loden, Jesse	200	372	During war soldier state line	4–19–1783
London, William	100	1221	3 years soldier Virginia line	6–26–1783
Long, Armstead	200	4602	3 years sergeant Virginia line	12–21–1792
Long, Daniel	100	3129	3 years soldier Virginia line	6– 5–1784
Long, Evans	200	2521	3 years sergeant Virginia line	2–19–1784
Long, Gabriel	4,000	2202	3 years captain Virginia line	12–23–1783
Long, Levi	200	4229	During war soldier Virginia line	11–15–1786
Long, Nicholas	200	2522	3 years sergeant Virginia line	2–19–1784
Long, Reuben	100	4225	3 years soldier Virginia line	11– 1–1786
Long, Reuben	2,666⅔	1570	3 years lieutenant Virginia line	8–14–1783
Long, Richard	200	3255	3 years corporal Virginia line	6–30–1784
Long, William	4,000	731	3 years captain Virginia line	6– 3–1783
Longwith, Burress	2,666⅔	2818	3 years lieutenant Virginia line	3–25–1784
Longwith, John	100	2487	3 years seaman Virginia navy	2–13–1784
Lord, Roberson	200	746	During war soldier Virginia line	6– 5–1783
Lorde, John	400	521	During war sergeant state line	5– 1–1783
Loudon, Adam	200	2863	3 years soldier Virginia line	4– 2–1784
Love, John	400	420	During war sergeant Virginia line	4–26–1783
Lovel, Richard	200	3327	During war soldier Virginia line	7–19–1784
Lovel, Robert	2,666⅔	4477	3 years lieutenant Virginia line	11–19–1789
Lovely, William L	4,000	288	3 years captain Virginia Cont. regmt.	4– 4–1783
Low, James	200	1124	During war soldier Virginia line	6–24–1783
Lowe, John	200	2042	During war soldier Virginia line	12– 9–1783
Lowe, Thomas	200	1542	3 years sergeant Virginia line	8– 9–1783
Lowry, William	100	3285	3 years sailor Virginia navy	7– 1–1784
Loyal, John	100	3686	3 years soldier Virginia line	1–11–1785
Loyd, George	200	1964	3 years sergeant Virginia line	11–25–1783
Loyd, George	100	4397	3 years soldier Virginia line	4– 3–1788
Loyd, James	100	4393	3 years soldier Virginia line	3–25–1788
Loyd, Morris	2,666⅔	4401	3 years gunners mate Virginia navy	6– 1–1788
Loyd, Thomas	100	2690	3 years soldier Virginia line	3– 3–1784
Loyd, William	100	2533	3 years soldier Virginia line	2–19–1784
Lucas, Humphrey	200	3965	During war soldier Virginia line	8–17–1785
Lucas, James	5,333⅓	2553	3 years major Virginia line	2–20–1784
Lucas, Nathaniel	4,000	3263	Services captain	6–30–1784
Lucas, Samuel	400	513	During war fife major	5– 1–1783
Lucas, Samuel	100	2055	3 years soldier Virginia line	12– 9–1783

Name	Acres	Warrant	Service	Date
Lucas, Thomas	200	551	During war soldier state line	5- 6-1783
Lucas, William	100	2910	3 years soldier Virginia line	4- 8-1784
Ludeman, J William	2,666⅔	818	3 years lieutenant Virginia line	6-14-1783
Lunciford, Elias	100	2488	3 years sailor Virginia navy	2-13-1784
Lunsford, Moses	200	4538	During war soldier Virginia line	11-10-1791
Lunsford, William	2,666⅔	3288	3 years cornet Virginia line	7- 1-1784
Luster, William	100	3930	3 years soldier Virginia line	8- 1-1785
Lyle, Charles	100	1219	3 years soldier Virginia line	6-26-1783
Lyles, Elijah	100	2777	3 years soldier Virginia line	3-18-1784
Lynch, James	200	1397	During war soldier Virginia line	7-19-1783
Lynch, Patrick	100	786	3 years soldier Virginia line	6-11-1783
Lynch, Timothy	200	477	During war soldier state line	4-30-1783
Lyne, John	100	3937	3 years soldier Virginia line	8- 2-1785
Lyne, Nabas	100	2385	3 years soldier Virginia line	2- 3-1784
Lynes, John	100	4213	3 years soldier Virginia line	10- 4-1786
Lyner, Philip	100	4244	3 years soldier Virginia line	12-26-1786
Lyon, James	100	2837	3 years soldier Virginia line	3-27-1784
Lyon, Thomas	400	408	During war sergeant Virginia line	4-25-1783
Lyon, Thomas	100	4455	3 years soldier Virginia line	5-14-1789
Lyon, William	100	2438	3 years soldier Virginia line	2- 9-1784
McAdams, Alexander	100	3871	3 years soldier Virginia line	5-10-1785
McAdam, John	2,666⅔	3286	3 years lieutenant Virginia line	7- 1-1784
McAdam, Joseph	2,666⅔	2628	3 years surgeon Virginia line	2-26-1784
McCale, Michael	200	2864	3 years soldier Virginia line	4- 2-1784
McCall, Samuel	200	719	3 years sergeant Virginia line	6- 3-1783
McCallister, John	200	4360	3 years sergeant Virginia line	1- 7-1788
McCannon, Christopher	100	2977	3 years soldier Virginia line	4-20-1784
McCannon, Christopher	100	4591	3 years private Virginia line	11- 1-1792
McCant, James	200	2185	During war soldier Virginia line	12-22-1783
McCargo, Stephen	200	3020	During war soldier Virginia line	4-26-1784
McCarkle, Samuel	100	3302	3 years soldier Virginia line	7- 2-1784
McCartee, James	100	3512	3 years soldier Virginia line	11- 8-1784
McCartney, Peter	200	1078	During war soldier Virginia line	6-24-1783
McCartney, Peter	200	1845	During war soldier state line	10-31-1783
McCarty, Charles	200	380	During war soldier state line	4-22-1783
McCarty, Richard	4,000	3000	3 years captain Virginia line	4-22-1784
McCarty, Timothy	200	4186	During war drummer Virginia line	7-11-1786
McCawly, John	200	3581	During war soldier Virginia line	12-16-1784
McClain, Thomas	100	1350	3 years soldier Virginia line	7-10-1783
McClain, Thomas	100	4097	3 years soldier Virginia line	1-25-1786
McClanachan, Elijah	100	264	3 years soldier state line	4- 3-1783
McClanahan, Elijah	200	1804	During war soldier Virginia line	9-30-1783
McClanahan, Alexander	6,666⅔	3289	Services colonel Virginia line	7- 1-1784
McClean, Laughlin	200	1084	During war soldier Virginia line	6-24-1783
McCline, William	200	3098	During war soldier Virginia line	5-24-1784
McCloud, Archibald	233⅓	3443	7 years soldier Virginia line	9-16-1784
McClurg, James	6,000	1900	3 years director of hospital Virginia	10-21-1783
McClurg, Walter	6,000	2972	3 years surgeon Virginia line	4-20-1784
McComeskry, Moses	100	2866	3 years soldier Virginia line	4- 2-1784
McConn, James	100	2770	3 years soldier Virginia line	3-18-1784
McConner, Christopher	400	2047	During war sergeant Virginia line	12- 9-1783
McCord, Samuel	200	1144	During war soldier Virginia line	6-24-1783
McCorkle, Andrew	100	3303	3 years soldier Virginia line	7- 2-1784
McCormack, Adam	200	1621	During war soldier Virginia line	8-22-1783
McCormack, William	200	4378	During war soldier Virginia line	1-23-1788
McCormick, James	100	4313	3 years soldier Virginia line	10-16-1787
McCoy, William	200	3348	During war soldier Virginia line	7-22-1784
McCraw, Francis	200	4113	During war soldier Virginia line	3- 4-1786
McCraw, John	100	2108	3 years soldier Virginia line	12-12-1783
McCue, Henry	100	1189	3 years soldier Virginia line	6-26-1783
McCune, Patrick	100	1301	3 years soldier Virginia line	6-30-1783
McCune, Peter	200	2882	3 years sergeant Virginia line	4- 5-1784
McDade, James	100	4406	3 years soldier Virginia line	6-12-1788
McDaniel, Andrew	100	4136	3 years soldier Virginia line	3-24-1786
McDanold, Terence	100	665	3 years soldier Virginia line	5-28-1783
McDermot, Francis	200	4092	During war soldier Virginia line	1-23-1786
McDeus, Daniel	100	263	3 years soldier state line	4- 3-1783
McDonald, Anger	100	3816	3 years soldier Virginia line	4-21-1785
McDonald, Benjamin	200	2043	During war soldier Virginia line	12- 9-1783
McDonald, Benjamin	100	3844	3 years soldier Virginia line	5- 2-1785
McDonald, Edward	200	1085	Soldier during war Virginia line	6-24-1783
McDonald, Reuben	100	3124	3 years soldier Virginia line	6- 5-1784
McDonnan, James	100	604	3 years private Virginia line	5-20-1783
McDorman, David	200	3906	During war soldier Virginia line	6-21-1785
McDorman, David	200	4527	During war soldier Virginia line	7- 7-1791
McDougle, John	100	276	3 years drummer Virginia line	4- 3-1783
McDowell, John	2,666⅔	728	3 years lieutenant Virginia line	6-14-1783
McDowell, John	200	2300	During war soldier Virginia line	1-26-1784
McDowell, John	233⅓	2872	During war soldier Virginia line	4- 5-1784
McDowell, Matthew	100	862	3 years soldier Virginia line	6-18-1783
McElroy, William	100	3705	3 years soldier Virginia line	1-20-1785

Name	Acres	Warrant	Service	Date
McElwin, Moses	200	1098	During war drummer Virginia line	6-24-1783
McFeely, John	100	3942	3 years soldier Virginia line	8- 9-1785
McGann, James	200	1884	During war soldier Virginia line	11-11-1783
McGannon, Darby	200	3369	3 years sergeant Virginia line	7-31-1784
McGill, Dan	200	2879	During war soldier Virginia line	4- 5-1784
McGinnes, Ambrose	100	4056	3 years soldier Virginia line	12-26-1785
McGouem, James	200	4227	During war soldier Virginia line	11-13-1786
McGowan, William	200	4392	3 years soldier Virginia line	3-14-1788
McGraw, James	100	3718	3 years soldier Virginia line	1-24-1785
McGraw, James	100	4269	3 years soldier Virginia line	4- 6-1787
McGraw, James	100	4418	3 years soldier Virginia line	7-17-1788
McGuire, Andrew	233½	1490	During war soldier Virginia line	8- 4-1783
McGuire, William	2,666⅔	2499	During war lieutenant Virginia line	2-14-1784
McGuy, Bennett	200	1283	During war soldier Virginia line	6-28-1783
McHene, John	100	272	3 years soldier state line	4- 3-1783
McIlhany, James	100	3515	3 years soldier Virginia line	11- 9-1784
McIlhenay, John	4,000	661	3 years captain Virginia line	5-27-1783
McIntire, William	200	2006	3 years sergeant Virginia line	12- 2-1783
McIntosh, Alexander	200	1059	During war soldier Virginia line	6-24-1783
McIntosh, William	100	1365	3 years soldier Virginia line	7-12-1783
McIntosh, William	233½	1412	During war soldier Virginia line	7-22-1783
McKannon, Christopher	400	4572	During war sergeant Virginia line	5-11-1792
McKay, Eneas	200	1066	During war soldier Virginia line	6-24-1783
McKee, Richard	200	3492	During war soldier Virginia line	11- 1-1784
McKenney, Daniel	100	1996	3 years soldier Virginia line	11-29-1783
McKenney, John	100	1019	3 years soldier Virginia line	6-23-1783
McKennon, Martin	400	4196	During war sergeant Virginia line	8-14-1786
McKinley, Alexander	100	3519	3 years soldier Virginia line	11-11-1784
McKinley, Charles	100	3693	3 years soldier Virginia line	1-20-1785
McKinley, Charles	100	3693	3 years soldier Virginia line	1-20-1785
McKinley, John	233½	1439	7 years soldier Virginia line	7-28-1783
McKinney, James	100	3869	3 years soldier Virginia line	5-10-1785
McKinney, Dennis	100	3607	3 years soldier Virginia line	12-22-1784
McKinsey, Alexander	400	3220	During war sergeant Virginia line	6-26-1784
McKnight, Benjamin	100	2859	3 years soldier Virginia line	4- 2-1784
McKnight, William	100	977	3 years soldier Virginia line	6-20-1783
McLardy, Alexander	200	1183	3 years corporal Virginia line	6-25-1783
McLocklin, John	100	4461	3 years soldier Virginia line	6-24-1789
McMahan, Andrew	400	3728	During war sergeant Virginia line	2- 2-1785
McMahan, Andrew	100	3791	3 years soldier Virginia line	4- 1-1785
McMahan, Roger	100	2001	3 years soldier Virginia line	11-29-1783
McManay, John	100	4303	3 years soldier Virginia line	8-11-1787
McMasters, Michael	100	1242	3 years soldier Virginia line	6-27-1783
McMeans, William	100	1026	3 years soldier Virginia line	6-23-1783
McMechen, William	6,000	1893	3 years surgeon Virginia line	10-20-1783
McMeehen, Robert	100	1972	3 years soldier Virginia line	11-26-1783
McMeekin, Joseph	200	714	3 years drum major Virginia line	6- 2-1783
McMullin, James	100	3697	3 years soldier Virginia line	1-20-1785
McNamara, Timothy	200	1646	3 years soldier Virginia line	8-23-1783
McNeal, David	100	2393	3 years soldier Virginia line	2- 3-1784
McNeal, Peter	100	3197	3 years soldier Virginia line	6-23-1784
McNolly, Michael	100	920	3 years soldier Virginia line	6-20-1783
McNutton, Daniel	100	4110	3 years soldier Virginia line	2-21-1786
McQuillin, Robert	200	1844	During war soldier Virginia line	10-10-1783
McSwain, Edward	200	1559	3 years sergeant Virginia line	8-12-1783
McTear, Frizzle	200	2035	3 years sergeant Virginia line	12- 6-1783
McTear, William	200	2034	3 years sergeant Virginia line	12- 6-1783
McValley, James	200	519	During war soldier state line	5- 1-1783
McWilliams, John	100	2993	3 years soldier Virginia line	4-21-1784
McWilliams, Joshua	2,666⅔	1334	3 years midshipman Virginia navy	7- 5-1783
Mabin, James	4,000	196	3 years captain Virginia line	3-25-1783
Mabon, James	666⅔	2324	—captain Virginia line	1-31-1784
MacCrel, James	200	657	During war soldier Virginia line	5-27-1784
Macklin, James	100	1352	3 years soldier Virginia line	7-10-1783
Maclin, William	100	3730	During war soldier Virginia line	2- 3-1785
Macomber, John	400	1295	During war corporal Virginia line	6-28-1783
Maconiber, Zenos	100	4317	3 years soldier Virginia line	10-23-1787
Madden, Thomas	100	2951	3 years soldier Virginia line	4-17-1784
Madder, Martin	200	3696	During war soldier Virginia line	1-20-1785
Maddox, Claiborne	200	4166	3 years sergeant Virginia line	6- 5-1786
Maddox, John	200	2281	During war soldier Virginia line	1-24-1784
Maddox, John	100	4389	3 years soldier Virginia line	3-12-1788
Maddox, Notley	200	1460	During war soldier Virginia line	8- 1-1783
Maddox, William	100	3958	3 years soldier Virginia line	8-12-1785
Maden, Robert	200	2136	During war soldier Virginia line	12-16-1783
Maderson, John	100	646	3 years soldier Virginia line	5-26-1783
Madison, William	100	1535	3 years soldier Virginia line	8- 9-1783
Madison, William	100	3005	3 years soldier Virginia line	4-22-1784
Madrid, Elisha	100	4045	3 years private Virginia line	12-17-1785
Magill, Charles	2,000	1887	3 years major Virginia line	11-12-1783
Magill, Charles	1,000	1888	3 years major Virginia line	11-12-1783

Name	Acres	Warrant	Service	Date
Magill, Charles	1,000	1889	3 years major Virginia line	11–12–1783
Magill, Charles	1,000	1890	3 years major Virginia line	11–12–1783
Magill, Charles	333⅓	1891	3 years major Virginia line	11–12–1783
Mahanes, Tapley	100	1522	3 years soldier Virginia line	8– 7–1783
Mahoney, Florence	100	4220	3 years soldier Virginia line	10–23–1786
Mahoney, James	200	1869	During war soldier Virginia line	10–15–1783
Mahoney, Joseph	200	896	During war soldier Virginia line	6–20–1783
Maine, Phillip	100	4094	3 years soldier Virginia line	1–23–1786
Maines, Francis	200	1082	During war soldier Virginia line	6–24–1783
Mains, Thomas	2,666⅔	3580	3 years quarter master Virginia navy	12–15–1784
Major, Ironmonger	100	1480	3 years soldier Virginia line	8– 2–1783
Major, James	200	3833	During war soldier Virginia line	4–29–1785
Major, John	100	3830	3 years soldier Virginia line	4–28–1785
Maley, James	100	2824	3 years soldier Virginia line	3–26–1784
Malloharns, Thomas	100	3932	3 years soldier Virginia line	8– 1–1785
Malone, John	100	3913	3 years soldier Virginia line	6–21–1785
Mallory, John	200	1006	3 years sergeant Virginia line	6–23–1783
Mallory, John	100	2698	3 years soldier Virginia line	3– 3–1784
Mallory, Philip	4,000	79	3 years captain Virginia Cont. line	12–31–1782
Mallott, Stephen	100	2310	3 years soldier Virginia line	1–29–1784
Mann, Claiborne	200	3583	During war soldier Virginia line	12–16–1784
Mann, David	2,666⅔	314	3 years lieutenant garrison regiment	4–11–1783
Manning, Jesse	200	594	During war soldier state line	5–17–1783
Manning, Samuel	200	418	During war soldier Virginia line	4–26–1783
Manry, Abraham	2,666⅔	89	3 years lieutenant Virginia Cont. line	1– 3–1783
Mansfield, George	200	3878	During war soldier Virginia line	5–20–1785
Mansfield, Thomas	100	256	3 years soldier state line	4– 3–1783
Mansfield, Thomas	200	437	During war soldier state line	4–26–1783
March, William	2,666⅔	4369	3 years midshipman Virginia navy	1–23–1788
Mardis, William	100	940	3 years soldier Virginia line	6–20–1783
Mark, John	400	7	3 years captain Virginia Cont. line	9– 3–1782
Markham, James	4,000	2215	7 years captain Virginia navy	12–27–1783
Markham, James	2,222	2216	7 years captain Virginia navy	12–27–1783
Marks, Isaiah	4,000	1695	3 years captain Virginia navy	8–30–1783
Marks, John	100	3217	3 years sailor Virginia navy	6–26–1784
Marrow, Robert	4,000	638	3 years captain Virginia line	5–26–1783
Mars, Barbabas	100	742	3 years soldier Virginia line	6– 5–1783
Marshall, Benjamin	200	3488	3 years master arms Virginia navy	10–28–1784
Marshall, David	100	1576	3 years soldier Virginia line	8–18–1783
Marshall, James Markham	2,666⅔	2380	During war lieutenant Virginia line	2– 3–1784
Marshall, John	400	30	3 years captain in army	11–30–1782
Marshall, John	200	2220	3 years boatsman Virginia navy	1– 5–1784
Marshall, Henry	400	893	During war sergeant Virginia line	6–20–1783
Marshall, Henry	200	894	3 years sergeant Virginia line	6–20–1783
Marshall, Humphrey	4,000	62	3 years captain in state artillery	12–19–1782
Marshall, Richard	466⅔	1987	During war corporal Virginia line	11–28–1783
Marshall, Richard	200	3616	During war soldier Virginia line	12–23–1784
Marshall, Thomas	4,000	61	3 years captain state artillery	12–19–1782
Marshall, Thomas	400	1338	During war sergeant Virginia line	7– 8–1783
Marshall, Thomas	6,666⅔	1349	3 years colonel Virginia line	7–10–1783
Marters, Richard	400	1331	3 years captain Virginia line	7– 5–1783
Martin, Alexander	200	409	During war drummer Virginia line	4–25–1783
Martin, James	400	459	During war corporal state line	4–28–1783
Martin, John	200	647	During war soldier Virginia line	5–28–1783
Martin, John	100	822	3 years soldier Virginia line	6–14–1783
Martin, John	200	1873	During war soldier Virginia line	10–15–1783
Martin, John	200	2480	3 years sergeant Virginia line	2–12–1784
Martin, John	100	4175	3 years soldier Virginia line	6–20–1786
Martin, Patrick	200	2299	During war soldier Virginia line	1–26–1784
Martin, Patrick	100	2768	3 years soldier Virginia line	3–17–1784
Martin, Thomas	200	3618	During war soldier Virginia line	12–23–1784
Martin, Thomas	1,000	2328	3 years lieutenant Virginia line	1–31–1784
Martin, Thomas	1,666⅔	2329	3 years lieutenant Virginia line	1–31–1784
Martin, Thomas	444⅓	3200	7 years lieutenant Virginia line	6–23–1784
Martin, William	200	1307	During war soldier Virginia line	6–30–1783
Martin, William	200	1151	3 years soldier Virginia line	6–24–1783
Mash, Thomas	100	2440	3 years soldier Virginia line	2– 9–1784
Mason, Daniel	100	2466	3 years soldier Virginia line	2–11–1784
Mason, John	200	3168	During war soldier Virginia line	6–17–1784
Mason, Thomas	200	1883	During war soldier Virginia line	10–16–1783
Mason, William	200	4622	During war private Virginia line	9–16–1793
Massenburg, Nicholas	2,666⅔	4601	During war lieutenant Virginia line	12–20–1792
Massey, Dade	100	3184	3 years soldier Virginia line	6–22–1784
Massey, John	100	4245	3 years soldier Virginia line	12–27–1786
Massey, Taliaferro	100	3183	3 years soldier Virginia line	6–22–1784
Massey, Theodorick	200	344	During war soldier state line	4–15–1783
Massey, Thomas	2,333⅓	1174	3 years major Virginia line	6–25–1783
Masston, John	200	506	3 years lieutenant state line	5– 1–1783
Masten, Josiah	200	3109	During war soldier Virginia line	5–29–1784
Matingly, John	100	643	3 years soldier Virginia line	5–26–1783
Matthews, Benjamin	100	2131	5 years soldier Virginia line	12–15–1783

Name	Acres	Warrant	Service	Date
Matthews, George	7,777⅔	1934	7 years colonel Virginia line	11–22–1783
Matthews, Thomas	6,000	3210	3 years lieutenant Virginia line	6–25–1784
Matthews, William	200	1833	3 years corporal Virginia line	10– 7–1783
Matthias, Griffith	100	3814	3 years soldier Virginia line	4–21–1785
Maughan, George	100	1991	3 years seaman Virginia navy	11–28–1783
Maupin, Gabriel	400	3773	3 years captain Virginia line	3–10–1785
May, Thomas	400	3614	During war corporal Virginia line	12–23–1784
May, William	200	3082	During war soldier Virginia line	5–20–1784
Mayfield, Henry	200	2308	During war soldier Virginia line	1–28–1784
Mayfield, John	200	2307	During war soldier Virginia line	1–28–1784
Mayfield, Micajah	100	3333	3 years soldier Virginia line	7–19–1784
Maynard, Nathaniel	200	2479	3 years corporal Virginia line	2–12–1784
Maynor, Henry	100	3806	3 years soldier Virginia line	4–14–1785
Mazaret, John	3,000	3611	3 years major Virginia navy	12–23–1784
Mazaret, John	2,333⅓	3612	3 years major Virginia line	12–23–1784
Meacham, William	200	3166	3 years sergeant Virginia line	6–17–1784
Mead, Everard	5,333⅓	2560	3 years major Virginia line	2–20–1784
Mead, John	100	934	3 years soldier Virginia line	6–20–1783
Mead, Mahlon	100	2195	3 years soldier Virginia line	12–22–1783
Mead, Richard Kidder	6,000	877	3 years lieutenant colonel Virginia line	6–19–1783
Mead, William	2,666⅔	3842	3 years ensign Virginia line	4–29–1785
Meanly, Robert	100	861	3 years soldier Virginia line	6–18–1783
Means, John	200	2947	3 years corporal Virginia line	4–17–1784
Meats, Samuel	100	2244	3 years seaman Virginia navy	1–12–1784
Meed, John	400	2449	During war sergeant Virginia line	2–10–1784
Meehie, George	200	3199	3 years sergeant Virginia line	6–23–1784
Melcher, John	100	2862	3 years soldier Virginia line	4– 2–1784
Melton, Hardy	100	1724	3 years soldier Virginia line	9– 3–1783
Melton, Isham	100	1927	3 years soldier Virginia line	11–22–1783
Melton, John	100	1928	3 years soldier Virginia line	11–22–1783
Mercer, Hugh	10,000	1159	3 years brigadier general Virginia line	6–24–1783
Mercer, Isaac	1,333⅓	4209	3 years lieutenant Virginia navy	9–27–1786
Mercer, Isaac	1,333⅓	4210	3 years lieutenant Virginia navy	9–27–1786
Mercer, John F	4,000	2219	3 years captain Virginia line	1– 5–1784
Meredith, William	4,000	2319	3 years captain Virginia line	1–30–1784
Meriwether, James	2,666⅔	2468	3 years lieutenant Virginia line	2–11–1784
Meriwether, David	2,666⅔	652	3 years captain Virginia line	5–28–1783
Meriwether, James	2,666⅔	1382	During war lieutenant Virginia line	7–17–1783
Meriwether, James	2,666⅔	2326	3 years lieutenant Virginia line	1–31–1784
Merewether, Thomas	5,333⅓	22	— year major Virginia line	11–25–1782
Merriss, John	200	365	During war soldier state line	4–18–1783
Merrit, Major	200	4624	During war private Virginia line	9–19–1793
Merritt, Samuel	100	1663	3 years soldier Virginia line	6–25–1784
Merritt, Archelans	100	1185	3 years soldier Virginia line	8–25–1783
Merryman, Francis	100	900	3 years soldier Virginia line	6–25–1783
Messaw, Joseph	200	488	During war soldier state line	6–20–1783
Metcalf, Walter	100	4183		4–30–1783
Metcalfe, Gordon	200	4044	3 years quarter master Virginia navy	7– 5–1786
Michael, Conrod	100	4205	3 years soldier Virginia line	12–17–1785
Micham, John	100	3836	3 years soldier Virginia line	8–31–1786
Middlebrook, John	200	3356	During war soldier Virginia line	4–29–1785
Middleton, John	100	3886	During war soldier Virginia line	7–23–1784
Middleton, Russell	6,000	2274	3 years surgeon Virginia line	6– 1–1785
Miles, John	100	1195	3 years soldier Virginia line	1–23–1784
Miles, James	100	429	3 years soldier Virginia line	6–26–1783
Miles, Michael	400	3393	During war sergeant Virginia line	4–26–1783
Miles, Wm	100	1187	3 years soldier Virginia line	8–14–1784
Miller, David	3,110⅔	310	7 years lieutenant Virginia Cont. line	6–26–1783
Miller, Francis	200	3359	During war soldier Virginia line	4– 9–1783
Miller, James	200	317	During war soldier cavalry	7–24–1784
Miller, Javan	3,110⅔	1623	7 years lieutenant Virginia line	4–12–1783
Miller, John	200	1759	During war soldier Virginia line	8–23–1783
Miller, Lodewick	100	2941	3 years soldier Virginia line	9–13–1783
Miller, Robert	100	2465	3 years soldier Virginia line	4–17–1784
Miller, Thomas	2,666⅔	3105	3 years lieutenant Virginia line	2–11–1784
Miller, William	4,000	151	3 years Capt and Lieut Virginia line	5–27–1784
Miller, William	100	4277	3 years soldier Virginia line	2–27–1783
Miller, William Laugh	100	3311	3 years soldier Virginia line	4– 7–1787
Milligan, John	100	4120	3 years soldier Virginia line	7– 2–1784
Milligan, John	200	4119	During war soldier Virginia line	3– 7–1786
Millisons, William	100	4464	3 years soldier Virginia line	3– 7–1786
Millivons, Henry	100	3317	3 years soldier Virginia line	9–18–1789
Millon, Thomas	100	2625	3 years soldier Virginia line	7– 6–1784
Mills, Anthony	200	4518	3 years sergeant Virginia line	2–24–1784
Mills, John	1,300	230	3 years lieutenant Virginia Cont. line	2–24–1791
Mills, John	1,366⅔	231	3 years lieutenant Virginia Cont. line	4– 1–1783
Mills, John	100	749	3 years soldier Virginia line	4– 1–1783
Mills, Moses	100	4174	3 years soldier Virginia line	6– 5–1783
Mills, Nicholas	100	637	3 years soldier Virginia line	6–19–1786
Milton, Charles	100	3453	3 years soldier Virginia line	5–26–1783
Minnes, Holman	4,000	2271	3 years captain Virginia line	10– 2–1784
				1–22–1784

Name	Acres	Warrant	Service	Date
Minnes, John	200	1229	During war soldier Virginia line	6-26-1783
Minnis, Francis	4,666⅔	769	7 years captain Virginia line	6- 7-1783
Minnis, Calohill	4,666⅔	2272	7 years captain Virginia line	1-22-1784
Minton, Barker	200	3899	During war soldier Virginia line	6-21-1785
Mintor, John	200	2906	3 years soldier Virginia line	4- 7-1784
Miskel, John	200	4286	3 years sergeant Virginia line	5-24-1787
Miskel, Jonathan	200	4287	3 years sergeant Virginia line	5-24-1787
Mitchell, David	100	1837	3 years soldier Virginia line	10- 7-1783
Mitchell, George	200	2203	3 years sergeant Virginia line	12-23-1783
Mitchell, James	400	495	During war corporal state line	4-30-1783
Mitchell, James	100	4251	3 years soldier Virginia line	1-12-1787
Mitchell, John	400	2142	During war sergeant Virginia line	12-16-1783
Mitchell, John	100	4187	3 years soldier Virginia line	7-12-1786
Mitchell, Mark	100	1192	3 years soldier Virginia line	6-26-1783
Mitchell, Reaps	400	1204	3 years sergeant Virginia line	6-26-1783
Mitchell, Thomas	100	999	3 years soldier Virginia line	6-21-1783
Mitchell, Thomas	100	4382	3 years sailor Virginia navy	1-29-1788
Mitchell, William	200	849	3 years corporal Virginia line	6-17-1783
Moffett, William	100	3700	3 years soldier Virginia line	1-20-1785
Molton, James	100	2114	3 years soldier Virginia line	12-13-1783
Monk, Joseph	200	1676	3 years sergeant Virginia line	8-27-1783
Monroe, George	6,000	1619	3 years surgeon Virginia line	8-22-1783
Monroe, James	5,333⅓	2368	3 years major Virginia line	2- 2-1784
Monroe, John	100	4400	3 years soldier Virginia line	5- 9-1788
Monroe, William	100	3148	3 years soldier Virginia line	6-11-1784
Montague, Richard	2,666⅔	1432	3 years lieutenant Virginia line	7-27-1783
Montgomery, James	2,666⅔	2677	3 years lieutenant Virginia line	3- 3-1784
Montgomery, John	6,000	2685	3 years lieutenant Virginia line	3- 3-1784
Moody, Edward	4,666⅔	37	7 years captain state artillery	12-10-1783
Moody, James	2,000	1557	3 years captain Virginia line	8-12-1783
Moody, James	2,000	1558	3 years captain Virginia line	8-12-1783
Moody, William	200	1897	During war soldier Virginia line	10-21-1783
Moody, William	100	3608	3 years soldier Virginia line	12-22-1784
Moody, William	200	3737	During war soldier Virginia line	2- 7-1785
Mooney, Isaac	100	2224	3 years soldier Virginia line	1- 7-1784
Moore, Alexander	2,000	141	3 years midshipman of navy	2-21-1783
Moor, Alexander	200	3920	During war soldier Virginia line	6-21-1785
Moorehead, Charles	400	2871	During war sergeant Virginia line	4- 5-1784
Moore, Cleon	4,000	3243	Services captain Virginia line	6-29-1784
Moore, Henly	200	4446	3 years sergeant Virginia line	12-26-1788
Moore, James	100	4018	3 years soldier Virginia line	12- 3-1785
Moore, John	2,666⅔	1854	3 years master Virginia navy	11- 4-1783
Moore, John	100	1981	3 years soldier Virginia line	11-28-1783
Moore, John	400	3386	During war sergeant Virginia line	8- 6-1784
Moore, John	100	3610	3 years soldier Virginia line	12-22-1784
Moore, Lewis	200	427	During war soldier Virginia line	4-26-1783
Moore, Michael	100	2086	3 years soldier Virginia line	12-10-1783
Moore, Michael	200	4133	During war soldier Virginia line	3-18-1786
Moore, Nicholas	200	2030	During war soldier Virginia line	12- 6-1783
Moore, Nicholas	200	3750	During war soldier Virginia line	2- 9-1785
Moore, Peter	2,666⅔	2485	Service Crockette regiment	2-13-1784
Moore, Peter	200	3106	During war soldier Virginia line	5-28-1784
Moore, Ralph	400	1671	During war corporal Virginia line	8-26-1783
Moore, Richard	200	3719	3 years corporal Virginia line	1-24-1785
Moore, Thomas	100	114	3 years soldier state line	2- 8-1783
Moore, Thomas	200	1087	During war soldier Virginia line	6-24-1783
Moore, William	400	530	During war sergeant state line	5- 2-1783
Moore, William	100	1366	3 years soldier Virginia line	7-12-1783
Moore, William	2,666⅔	1820	3 years lieutenant Virginia line	10- 4-1783
Moore, William	100	2315	3 years soldier Virginia line	1-29-1784
Moore, William Daniel	100	4016	3 years soldier Virginia line	12- 2-1785
Morgan, Andrew	200	1745	3 years sergeant Virginia line	9-11-1783
Morgan, Charles	200	1127	During war soldier Virginia line	6-24-1783
Morgan, Daniel	5,000	19	7 years Brig. Gen. Comr. war	11-24-1782
Morgan, Daniel	6,666⅔	20	7 years Brig. Gen. Comr. war	11-24-1782
Morgan, David	200	1289	During war soldier Virginia line	6-28-1783
Morgan, John	200	29	— years soldier Virginia Cont. line	11-30-1782
Morgan, John	200	1969	3 years sergeant Virginia line	11-26-1783
Morgan, John	2,666⅔	3874	3 years ensign Virginia line	5-10-1785
Morgan, Jonas	200	4270	During war soldier Virginia line	4- 7-1787
Morgan, Simon	4,666⅔	2629	7 years captain Virginia line	2-25-1784
Morgan, Spencer	2,666⅔	2845	3 years ensign Virginia line	3-30-1784
Morgan, William	233⅓	1555	During war soldier Virginia line	8-12-1783
Morgan, Brig-Gen	11,666⅔	1000	7 years Brig. Gen. Virginia line	6-21-1783
Morris, John	100	1906	3 years soldier Virginia line	11-18-1783
Morris, Moses	100	2935	3 years soldier Virginia line	4-16-1784
Morris, Samuel	100	4621	3 years private Virginia line	9-13-1793
Morrison, Hugh	200	1817	3 years sergeant Virginia line	10- 3-1783
Morrison, John	200	1139	During war soldier Virginia line	6-24-1783
Morrison, William	200	3256	3 years sergeant Virginia line	6-30-1784
Morriss, Gilson	100	3139	3 years soldier Virginia line	6- 9-1784

Name	Acres	Warrant	Service	Date
Morriss, Isaac............	200	2217	During war soldier Virginia line......	1- 3-1784
Morriss, John............	200	734	During war soldier Virginia line......	6- 4-1783
Morriss, Reuben..........	100	3137	3 years soldier Virginia line..........	6- 9-1784
Morriss, Robert..........	100	788	3 years soldier Virginia line..........	6-12-1783
Morrough, George........	100	3619	3 years soldier Virginia line..........	12-23-1784
Morton, Hezekiah........	4,000	660	5 years captain Virginia line........	5-27-1783
Morton, James...........	2,666⅔	74	3 years lieutenant Virginia Cont. line.	12-26-1782
Morxwell, William........	200	411	During war soldier Virginia line....	4-25-1783
Mosby, William..........	200	2107	During war soldier Virginia line.....	12-12-1783
Mosely, Benjamin........	2,666⅔	1468	3 years lieutenant Virginia artillery.....	8- 1-1783
Mosely, Benjamin........	2,666⅔	75	3 years lieutenant Virginia line......	12-26-1782
Mosely, William.........	5,333⅔	115	3 years major Cont. line..............	2- 8-1783
Moses, John.............	200	415	During war soldier Virginia line......	4-26-1783
Moss, Henry.............	4,000	614	3 years captain Virginia line.........	5-21-1783
Moss, Henry.............	100	777	3 years soldier Virginia line..........	6-10-1783
Moss, Julius.............	100	4374	3 years soldier Virginia line..........	1-23-1788
Moth, Thomas...........	100	3573	3 years soldier Virginia line.........	12-15-1784
Mothershead, Nathaniel...	200	1922	3 years sergeant Virginia line........	10-27-1783
Moulden, Thomas........	200	210	3 years corporal state line...........	3-31-1783
Moughan, Matthias......	100	3577	3 years soldier Virginia line.........	12-15-1784
Mount, Mathew..........	100	2986	3 years soldier Virginia line..........	6-21-1784
Mountjoy, William......	4,000	3222	Services captain Virginia line........	6-28-1784
Moxly, Rodham..........	2,666⅔	2957	3 years subaltern Virginia line.......	4-17-1784
Moxley, George..........	400	2934	During war corporal Virginia line.....	4-15-1784
Muhlenberg, Peter.......	11,666⅔	176	7 years Brig. Genl. Virginia Cont. line	3-13-1783
Muir, Francis...........	4,000	1474	3 years Capt. Lieut. Virginia line.....	8- 1-1783
Muir, John..............	2,666⅔	2745	3 years midshipman Virginia navy....	3-10-1784
Mulins, Anthony.........	200	1616	During war soldier Virginia line......	8-21-1783
Mullin, John............	200	3415	3 years sergeant Virginia line........	8-27-1784
Mullin, John............	400	3416	During war sergeant Virginia line....	8-27-1784
Mullins, David..........	100	2827	3 years soldier Virginia line..........	3-26-1784
Mumpower, Nicholas.....	100	2464	3 years soldier Virginia line..........	2-11-1784
Munden, Edward.........	200	754	7 years soldier Virginia line..........	6- 6-1783
Munden, Thomas.........	100	2716	3 years soldier Virginia line..........	3- 5-1784
Murden, Peter...........	200	1371	During war soldier Virginia line......	7-12-1783
Murdock, Joseph.........	100	974	3 years soldier Virginia line..........	6-20-1783
Murfrey, John...........	100	2074	3 years soldier Virginia line..........	12-10-1783
Murlat, Abraham........	200	3850	During war soldier Virginia line.....	5- 6-1785
Murphey, Charles........	100	1971	3 years soldier Virginia line.........	11-26-1783
Murphey, John...........	100	1015	3 years soldier Virginia line..........	6-23-1783
Murphey, John...........	100	3431	3 years soldier Virginia line.........	8-31-1784
Murphey, Leander.......	100	2842	3 years soldier Virginia line.........	3-29-1784
Murphey, Martin........	400	1441	During war sergeant Virginia line....	7-30-1783
Murphey, Michael........	200	1152	3 years soldier Virginia line.........	6-24-1783
Murphey, Owen..........	100	1017	3 years soldier Virginia line.........	6-23-1783
Murphey, Patrick........	233⅓	1279	7 years soldier Virginia line.........	6-28-1783
Murphey, Samuel........	100	3164	3 years soldier Virginia line.........	6-16-1784
Murphy, Michael........	200	1737	During war soldier Virginia line......	9-10-1783
Murrah, George.........	100	1402	3 years soldier Virginia line.........	7-21-1783
Murray, Daniel..........	200	2275	During war soldier Virginia line......	1-23-1784
Murray, Francis.........	200	452	During war soldier state line.........	4-28-1783
Murray, George.........	100	1251	3 years soldier Virginia line.........	6-27-1783
Murray, James..........	200	2276	During war soldier Virginia line.....	1-23-1784
Murray, Ralph..........	100	1690	3 years soldier Virginia line.........	8-30-1783
Murray, Richard........	100	1756	3 years soldier Virginia line.........	9-12-1783
Murrick, John...........	200	4351	During war soldier Virginia line.....	12-19-1787
Murry, William.........	100	1217	3 years soldier Virginia line.........	6-26-1783
Murry, Duncan..........	200	627	During war in Virginia Cont. line....	5-23-1783
Muse, George...........	200	1311	3 years sergeant Virginia line........	6-30-1783
Muse, Jesse.............	2,666⅔	4226	3 years lieutenant Virginia navy......	11- 5-1786
Musgrove, William......	100	969	3 years soldier Virginia line.........	6-20-1783
Musgrove, William......	200	988	3 years captain Virginia line.........	6-20-1783
Mush, Robert...........	200	1514	During war soldier Virginia line......	8- 6-1783
Muter, George...........	6,666⅔	41	3 years colonel state garrison regmt..	12-12-1782
Myer, Christopher........	2,666⅔	4442	3 years lieutenant Virginia line......	11- 1-1788
Nance, Frederick........	200	3008	3 years sergeant Virginia line........	4-22-1784
Nance, Robert..........	4,000	850	3 years captain Virginia line.........	6-17-1783
Nance, Zackariah........	100	3114	3 years soldier Virginia line.........	5-29-1784
Nann, Henry............	200	1067	During war soldier Virginia line......	6-24-1783
Napper, Moses..........	100	2594	3 years soldier Virginia line.........	2-23-1784
Napier, James...........	400	375	During war sergeant state line.......	4-19-1783
Narvale, Aquilla........	200	584	3 years sergeant Virginia line........	5-15-1783
Nash, Thomas...........	200	4551	During war soldier Virginia line.....	11-24-1791
Nash, William...........	100	3934	3 years soldier Virginia line.........	8- 1-1785
Neal, Charles...........	200	2673	3 years sergeant Virginia line........	3- 2-1784
Neal, Nicholas..........	466⅔	1519	During war sergeant Virginia line....	8- 7-1783
Neal, William...........	100	3121	3 years soldier Virginia line.........	6- 4-1784
Nealls, Thomas..........	100	3308	3 years soldier Virginia line.........	7- 2-1784
Needham, Isaac..........	200	2442	During war soldier Virginia line.....	2- 9-1784
Nelmo, Charles..........	200	2656	3 years sergeant Virginia line........	3- 1-1784
Nelson, George..........	200	3785	3 years sergeant Virginia line........	3-25-1785

Name	Acres	Warrant	Service	Date
Nelson, John	5,333⅓	1790	3 years major Virginia line	9–25–1783
Nelson, John	4,000	2236	3 years captain Virginia line	1–12–1784
Nelson, Roger	1,000	2843	During war lieutenant Virginia line	3–29–1784
Nelson, Roger	1,666⅔	2844	During war lieutenant Virginia line	3–29–1784
Nelson, William	6,000	2213	3 years lieutenant Virginia line	12–27–1783
Nevill, John	7,777⅔	937	7 years colonel Virginia line	6–20–1783
Nevill, Presley	7,000	18	3 years Lieut. Col. Virginia Cont. line	11–24–1782
New, Jesse	100	433	3 years soldier Virginia Cont. line	4–26–1783
Newby, John	100	1479	3 years soldier Virginia line	8– 2–1783
Newby, Leroy	200	3586	3 years sergeant Virginia line	12–17–1784
Newby, Thomas	100	757	3 years soldier Virginia line	6– 6–1783
Newcombs, Thomas	200	4310	3 years corporal Virginia line	10– 6–1787
Newell, John	200	1735	3 years sergeant Virginia line	9– 8–1783
Newland, John	200	4150	During war soldier Virginia line	4–29–1786
Newman, George	100	4050	3 years private Virginia line	12–21–1785
Newman, Joseph	200	2747	During war soldier Virginia line	3–10–1784
Newman, Joseph Sr	100	4481	3 years soldier Virginia line	11–25–1789
Newman, Owen	466⅔	1924	7 years sergeant Virginia line	11–21–1783
Newman, Thomas	400	401	During war sergeant Virginia line	4–25–1783
Newman, Thomas	100	2398	3 years soldier Virginia line	2– 3–1784
Newton, Thomas	100	3307	3 years soldier Virginia line	7– 2–1784
Nichols, Charles	100	2911	3 years soldier Virginia line	4– 9–1784
Nichols, John	100	1592	3 years soldier Virginia line	8–20–1783
Nichols, John	200	2403	End war soldier Virginia line	2– 4–1784
Nicholson, Jesse	100	4134	3 years soldier Virginia line	3–22–1786
Nicholson, William	200	388	During war soldier state line	4–23–1783
Nickens, Edward	100	2427	3 years sailor Virginia navy	2– 9–1784
Nickens, Nathaniel	100	4468	3 years soldier Virginia line	10–22–1789
Nickens, Richard	100	1477	3 years seaman Virginia navy	8– 2–1783
Nickens, William	100	337	During war drummer state line	4–15–1783
Nickers, John	200	436	During war soldier state line	4–26–1783
Nicking, James	100	1716	3 years soldier Virginia line	9– 2–1783
Nightingale, Matthew	200	3273	3 years boatswain Virginia navy	7– 1–1784
Nincom, Solomon	200	1461	During war soldier Virginia line	8–11–1783
Nixon, Andrew	4,000	368	3 years captain Virginia cavalry	4–19–1783
Noel, Achilles	200	2350	3 years sergeant Virginia line	1–31–1784
Noell, Richard	200	2340	3 years corporal Virginia line	1–31–1784
Nolan, Pierce	2,666⅔	1835	3 years lieutenant Virginia line	10– 7–1783
Norman, William	100	1990	3 years seaman Virginia navy	11–28–1783
Norris, Baxaleel	200	4522	During war private Virginia line	4–23–1791
Norwood, Joseph	100	864	3 years soldier Virginia line	6–18–1783
Nowell, Henry Holcraft	200	796	3 years sergeant Virginia line	6–12–1783
Nowell, Lipscomb	2,666⅔	315	3 years lieutenant Virginia Cont. line	4–11–1783
Nowlin, Matthew	200	3904	During war soldier Virginia line	6–21–1785
Nunally, David	100	4148	3 years soldier Virginia line	4–24–1786
Nunally, Joseph	100	2635	3 years soldier Virginia line	2–25–1784
Nunnally, Obadiah	100	2605	3 years soldier Virginia line	2–24–1784
Nunnally, Obediah	400	2636	During war sergeant Virginia line	2–25–1784
Nunnamaker, John	100	3793	3 years soldier Virginia line	4– 1–1785
Nunnemaker, Lewis	100	2159	3 years soldier Virginia line	12–19–1783
Nutt, Thomas	100	3275	3 years sailor Virginia navy	7– 1–1784
Nuttal, Juerson	2,666⅔	1708	3 years midshipman Virginia navy	9– 2–1783
Oakley, George	200	2469	3 years sergeant Virginia line	2–11–1784
Oakman, William	100	4153	3 years soldier Virginia line	5– 6–1786
Obannon, Thomas	200	4291	During war soldier Virginia line	6– 9–1787
Obrian, James	100	4219	3 years soldier Virginia line	10–16–1786
O'Conner, Timothy	100	3371	3 years soldier Virginia line	8– 2–1784
Odell, Reuben	100	3837	3 years soldier Virginia line	4–29–1785
Ogan, Thomas	200	3956	During war soldier Virginia line	8–12–1785
Ogden, Mathew	200	1626	During war soldier Virginia line	8–22–1783
Ogilsby, Robert	100	4208	3 years soldier Virginia line	8–31–1786
Ogle, Thomas	200	4514	3 years sergeant Virginia line	12–21–1790
Oldham, Capt Conway	4,000	14	3 years captain Virginia Cont. line	11–11–1782
Olephant, Benjamin	100	4038	3 years private Virginia line	12–15–1785
Olfer, Thomas	200	2581	3 years soldier Virginia line	2–21–1784
Olive, John	200	502	During war soldier state line	5– 1–1783
Oliver, Moses	200	3952	During war soldier Virginia line	8–12–1785
Oliver, William	4,000	693	3 years Capt. Lieut. state artillery	5–30–1783
Oliver, William	100	3216	3 years soldier Virginia line	6–26–1784
Oliver, William	100	3026	3 years soldier Virginia line	4–27–1784
Omenate, John	400	1611	During war sergeant Virginia line	8–21–1783
Oneal, Farrel	4,000	1387	3 years captain Virginia line	7–17–1783
Oneal, Ferdinand	200	2314	During war soldier Virginia line	1–29–1784
Oneal, John	100	1799	3 years soldier Virginia line	9–29–1783
Oneal, William	100	981	3 years soldier Virginia line	6–20–1783
Oram, Henry	100	250	3 years soldier Virginia regiment	4– 3–1783
Orr, Samuel	200	1787	During war soldier Virginia line	9–24–1783
Osburn, Elijah	200	1608	During war soldier Virginia line	6–24–1783
Osburn, Samuel	400	1403	During war corporal Virginia line	7–21–1783
Oust, George	200	1109	During war soldier Virginia line	6–24–1783
Oush, James	200	1099	During war soldier Virginia line	6–24–1783
Overlin, William				

Name	Acres	Warrant	Service	Date
Overton, John	4,000	153	3 years captain Virginia regiment	2–28–1783
Overton, Thomas	2,666⅔	44	3 years lieutenant Virginia Cont. line	12–13–1782
Overton, Thomas	1,333⅓	1908	3 years lieutenant Virginia line	11–19–1783
Overstreet, Benone	200	3013	3 years sergeant Virginia line	4–24–1784
Overstreet, John	100	3890	3 years soldier Virginia line	6–15–1785
Owen, Vincent	100	2980	3 years soldier Virginia line	4–20–1784
Owens, Charles	200	566	3 years soldier state line	5– 9–1783
Owens, Christopher	200	3154	3 years sergeant Virginia line	6–12–1784
Owens, Ephram	200	3643	3 years corporal Virginia line	12–20–1784
Owens, Evans	100	3811	3 years soldier Virginia line	4–18–1785
Owl, Robert	200	1544	During war soldier Virginia line	8–11–1783
Pace, William	200	1895	During war soldier Virginia line	10–20–1783
Packett, Richard	100	1726	3 years soldier Virginia line	9– 4–1783
Page, Carter	4,000	3209	Service captain Virginia line	6–24–1784
Pair, George	200	608	During the war soldier Virginia line	5–21–1783
Pair, George	200	3963	During war soldier Virginia line	8–13–1785
Pailer, James	200	1118	During war soldier Virginia line	6–24–1783
Palmer, Charles	100	3801	3 years soldier Virginia line	4–12–1785
Palmer, David	400	423	During war corporal Virginia line	4–26–1783
Palmer, Thomas	100	574	3 years private Virginia line	5–14–1783
Palmer, William	200	293	3 years corporal Virginia line	4– 5–1783
Pamy, Moses	200	3462	3 years sergeant Virginia line	10–13–1784
Papp, Venit	100	921	3 years soldier Virginia line	6–20–1783
Parish, Henry	200	4109	3 years sergeant Virginia line	2– 7–1786
Parish, Peter	200	2078	3 years sergeant Virginia line	12–10–1783
Parish, William	200	2820	3 years sergeant Virginia line	3–26–1784
Parker, Alexander	5,333⅓	1892	8 years captain Virginia line	11–12–1783
Parker, Jeremiah	200	1548	3 years sergeant Virginia line	8–11–1783
Parker, John	200	4560	During war soldier Virginia line	12–15–1791
Parker, Joseph	200	1810	3 years corporal Virginia line	9–30–1783
Parker, Josiah	6,666⅔	1920	3 years colonel Virginia line	11–21–1783
Parker, Nicholas	2,666⅔	858	3 years lieutenant Virginia line	6–18–1783
Parker, Richard	6,666⅔	735	3 years colonel Virginia line	6– 4–1783
Parker, Robert	200	780	3 years captain Virginia line	6–10–1783
Parker, Thomas	4,000	732	3 years captain Virginia line	6– 3–1783
Parker, Thomas	666⅔	3130	7 years captain Virginia line	4–28–1784
Parker, Thomas	4,000	3029	7 years captain Virginia line	4–28–1784
Parker, Thomas	100	4170	3 years soldier Virginia line	6–13–1786
Parker, Warren	400	1784	During war sergeant Virginia line	9–24–1783
Parker, Watts	200	1852	3 years sergeant Virginia line	11– 4–1783
Parker, William Haswar	2,666⅔	1013	3 years lieutenant Virginia line	6–23–1783
Parker, Wyatt	100	800	3 years soldier Virginia line	6–13–1783
Parks, Henry	200	531	During war soldier state line	5– 2–1783
Parrett, James	100	3428	3 years soldier Virginia line	8–28–1784
Parsons, George	100	1975	3 years soldier Virginia line	11–26–1783
Parsons, Thomas	100	1018	3 years soldier Virginia line	6–23–1783
Parsons, William	4,000	2321	3 years captain Virginia line	1–30–1784
Parsons, William	100	2587	3 years soldier Virginia line	2–23–1784
Parton, David	100	2891	3 years soldier Virginia line	4– 5–1784
Paskill, George	200	3995	During war soldier Virginia line	11–15–1785
Pasley, Joel	100	1934	3 years soldier Virginia line	11–22–1784
Pastens, Bluett	100	1943	3 years seaman Virginia navy	11–22–1783
Pate, Matthew	100	768	3 years soldier Virginia line	6– 7–1783
Patillo, James	200	1858	3 years sergeant Virginia line	10–14–1783
Patman, William	200	1346	3 years sergeant Virginia line	7–10–1783
Patterson, Israel	200	1515	During war soldier Virginia line	8– 7–1783
Patterson, John	400	664	During war sergeant Virginia line	5–28–1783
Patterson, Thomas	4,000	2739	Service Virginia line	3– 8–1784
Patterson, Tilman	400	2251	During war sergeant Virginia line	1–16–1784
Patton, Alexander	100	2627	3 years soldier Virginia line	2–24–1784
Patton, William	100	3819	3 years soldier Virginia line	4–22–1785
Paul, Edward	200	1061	During war soldier Virginia line	6–24–1783
Payne, Charles	100	3594	3 years soldier Virginia line	12–21–1784
Payne, Jacob	200	2079	3 years sergeant Virginia line	12–10–1783
Payne, John	200	2151	During war soldier Virginia line	12–19–1783
Payne, Joseph	1,000	1654	3 years lieutenant Virginia line	8–23–1783
Payne, Joseph	1,000	1655	3 years lieutenant Virginia line	8–23–1783
Payne, Joseph	666⅔	1656	3 years lieutenant Virginia line	8–23–1783
Payne, Josiah	2,666⅔	2674	End of war lieutenant Virginia line	3– 3–1784
Payne, Tarlton	4,666⅔	699	7 years captain Virginia line	5–31–1783
Payne, Thomas	4,000	55	3 years captain Virginia Cont. line	12–17–1782
Payne, William	4,000	3810	3 years captain Virginia line	4–18–1785
Paythress, Francis	400	4256	During war sergeant Virginia line	2– 5–1787
Paythress, William	4,000	1878	3 years captain Virginia line	11– 8–1783
Payton, William	100	2567	3 years soldier Virginia line	2–20–1784
Peace, Samuel	200	603	3 years sergeant Virginia line	5–20–1783
Pearman, Harrison	200	1658	During war soldier Virginia line	8–23–1783
Pearman, Thomas	200	2595	End of war soldier Virginia line	2–23–1784
Pearson, Thomas	2,666⅔	904	3 years lieutenant Virginia line	6–20–1783
Peay, Elias	200	3947	3 years soldier Virginia line	8–10–1785
Peay, Thomas	200	3946	3 years corporal Virginia line	8–10–1785

Name	Acres	Warrant	Service	Date
Pediford, Edward	100	2233	3 years soldier Virginia line	1–12–1784
Pee, William	100	1374	3 years soldier Virginia line	7–15–1783
Pelham, Charles	6,222	279	7 years major Virginia Cont. line	4– 3–1783
Pemberton, Thomas	4,000	398	— years captain Virginia Cont. line	4–25–1783
Pendleton, James	4,666⅔	113	7 years captain artillery Virginia line	2– 7–1783
Pendleton, Nathaniel	4,666⅔	1391	7 years captain Virginia line	7–18–1783
Penn, John	100	1742	3 years sailor Virginia navy	9–11–1783
Penn, William	2,666⅔	4055	3 years lieutenant Virginia line	12–26–1785
Pennry, Robert	100	3912	3 years soldier Virginia line	6–21–1785
Penny, John	100	479	3 years soldier state line	4–30–1783
Perault, Michael	4,000	2689	3 years captain Virginia line	3– 3–1784
Perkins, Archeland	2,666⅔	2383	During war lieutenant Virginia line	2– 3–1784
Perkins, Joseph	200	1312	During war soldier Virginia line	6–30–1783
Perkinton, William	200	1245	3 years sergeant Virginia line	6–27–1783
Perpeson, James	200	3440	During war soldier Virginia line	9–15–1784
Perrin, John	100	3664	3 years soldier Virginia line	1– 1–1785
Perry, Henry	100	1462	3 years soldier Virginia line	8– 1–1783
Perry, Hildry	400	430	During war sergeant Virginia line	4–26–1783
Perry, John	2,666⅔	1617	3 years cornet Virginia line	8–21–1783
Perry, William	100	1306	3 years soldier Virginia line	6–30–1783
Perry, William	100	715	3 years drummer Virginia line	6– 2–1783
Perryman, Benono	100	1554	3 years fifer Virginia line	8–11–1783
Perryman, Daniel	100	1868	3 years soldier Virginia line	10–15–1783
Perryman, Phillip	100	840	3 years soldier Virginia line	6–16–1783
Peters, James	100	3468	3 years soldier Virginia line	1–17–1788
Peters, Samuel	2,000	4592	During war lieutenant Virginia line	11– 9–1792
Peters, Thomas	100	1353	3 years soldier Virginia line	7–11–1783
Peterson, Conrod	100	3253	3 years soldier Virginia line	6–30–1784
Petrie, Alexander	200	2225	3 years sergeant Virginia line	1– 8–1784
Pettiford, Drury	100	3537	3 years soldier Virginia line	11–24–1784
Pettiford, Elias	100	3536	3 years soldier Virginia line	11–24–1784
Pettus, John	1,000	2424	3 years captain Virginia line	2– 7–1784
Pettus, John	1,000	2425	3 years captain Virginia line	2– 7–1784
Pettus, John	2,000	2426	3 years captain Virginia line	2– 7–1784
Petty, William	100	4162	3 years soldier Virginia line	5–27–1786
Pew, David	200	3228	3 years soldier Virginia line	6–28–1784
Peyton, Charles	100	3646	3 years soldier Virginia line	12–31–1784
Peyton, Dave	2,666⅔	3235	3 years lieutenant Virginia line	6–29–1784
Peyton, Francis	100	1828	3 years soldier Virginia line	10– 7–1783
Peyton, George	2,666⅔	3437	3 years ensign Virginia line	9–11–1784
Peyton, Robert	2,666⅔	3438	3 years lieutenant Virginia line	9–11–1784
Peyton, Henry	4,333⅓	3234	3 years major Virginia line	6–29–1784
Peyton, James	100	2297	3 years soldier Virginia line	1–26–1784
Peyton, John	4,000	56	3 years captain Virginia Cont. line	12–17–1782
Peyton, Valentine	4,000	1296	3 years captain Virginia line	6–28–1783
Phelps, George	200	1055	During war soldier Virginia line	6–24–1783
Philips, Jacob	100	4204	3 years soldier Virginia line	8–31–1786
Philips, John	100	2796	3 years soldier Virginia line	3–19–1784
Philips, John	100	3660	3 years soldier Virginia line	12–31–1784
Phillips, Benjamin	200	455	During war soldier state line	4–28–1783
Phillips, John	200	1107	During war soldier Virginia line	6–24–1783
Phillips, John	200	3143	3 years corporal Virginia line	6–10–1784
Phillips, John	100	4032	3 years private Virginia line	12–24–1785
Phillips, Larkin	100	283	3 years soldier Virginia line	4– 3–1783
Phillips, Newton	100	3040	3 years soldier Virginia line	5– 4–1784
Phillips, Samuel	2,666⅔	15	3 years ensign Virginia Cont. line	11–11–1782
Phipps, George	200	424	During war soldier Virginia line	4–26–1784
Picken, Spencer M	100	3268	3 years sailor Virginia navy	7– 1–1784
Picket, John	100	1896	3 years soldier Virginia line	10–20–1783
Pickett, Francis	400	481	During war drummer state line	4–30–1783
Pickett, George	200	491	During war drummer state line	4–30–1783
Pickrel, Samuel	100	1369	3 years drummer Virginia line	7–12–1783
Pierce, Thomas	100	2179	3 years sailor Virginia navy	12–20–1783
Pierce, William	4,666⅔	2443	7 years captain Virginia line	2– 9–1784
Piggett, Abraham	100	1956	3 years soldier Virginia line	11–22–1783
Pigue, William	400	3335	During war sergeant Virginia line	7–19–1783
Pile, Benjamin	200	3919	During war soldier Virginia line	6–21–1785
Pile, Richard	400	3916	During war soldier Virginia line	6–21–1785
Pile, Richard	200	2088	3 years sergeant Virginia line	12–10–1783
Piles, William	100	4323	3 years soldier Virginia line	10–26–1787
Pilkinton, Drury	100	4347	3 years soldier Virginia line	12–21–1787
Pilman, Buckner	200	3337	3 years sergeant Virginia line	7–19–1784
Pinchback, Thomas	200	2508	3 years sergeant Virginia line	2–17–1784
Pinkstone, Shadrack	100	3997	3 years soldier Virginia line	11–19–1785
Pinter, William	2,666⅔	197	3 years lieutenant Virginia Cont. line	3–25–1783
Pinyear, Thomas	100	842	3 years soldier Virginia line	6–16–1783
Piper, William	200	1455	3 years sergeant Virginia line	7–31–1783
Pitman, George	200	1995	3 years sergeant Virginia line	11–29–1783
Pitman, Isaac	200	1874	3 years sergeant Virginia line	11– 7–1783

Name	Acres	Warrant	Service	Date
Pitts, Bradley	100	3402	3 years soldier Virginia line	8–18–1784
Pitts, David	100	3401	3 years soldier Virginia line	8–18–1784
Plummer, Armistend	100	1639	3 years soldier Virginia line	8–23–1783
Plummer, William	200	1699	3 years sergeant Virginia line	8–30–1783
Plunket, Reuben	200	1851	3 years corporal Virginia line	10–13–1783
Plunkett, Thomas	200	3053	During war soldier Virginia line	5– 7–1784
Poe, Thomas	100	1222	3 years soldier Virginia line	6–26–1783
Pollard, Absalôm	200	3297	3 years corporal Virginia line	7– 1–1784
Pollard, Braxton	400	497	During war corporal state line	4–30–1783
Pollock, Thomas	100	984	3 years soldier Virginia line	6–20–1783
Pomberton, Reuben	200	4600	During war private Virginia line	12–18–1792
Pool, Baxter	100	1927	3 years soldier Virginia line	10–28–1783
Pool, Edward	200	2169	3 years corporal Virginia line	12–20–1783
Pool, Peter	100	3678	3 years soldier Virginia line	1– 8–1785
Pool, Robert	100	675	3 years soldier Virginia line	5–29–1783
Pope, Fortunatus	200	1747	3 years sergeant Virginia line	9–11–1783
Pope, William	100	3724	3 years soldier Virginia line	1–31–1785
Poplar, Hack	100	1873	3 years seaman Virginia navy	11– 7–1783
Porter, Calvert	200	384	3 years sergeant Virginia Cont. line	4–23–1783
Porter, Daniel	400	374	During war sergeant state line	4–19–1783
Porter, Elisha	100	1032	3 years soldier Virginia line	6–23–1783
Porter, Thomas	200	2895	3 years sergeant Virginia line	4– 6–1784
Porter, William	200	448	During war soldier state line	4–28–1783
Porter, William	2,666⅔	670	3 years lieutenant Virginia line	5–29–1783
Porter, William	2,666⅔	2894	3 years subaltern Virginia line	4– 6–1784
Porterfield, Col Charles	6,000	58	3 years lieutenant colonel	12–18–1782
Porterfield, Robert	4,000	57	3 years captain comrs war	12–18–1782
Posey, Thomas	7,000	240	7 years lieutenant colonel Virginia line	4– 1–1783
Posey, Zephamiah	100	2962	3 years soldier Virginia line	4–19–1784
Potter alias Potts Nathaniel	100	4314	3 years soldier Virginia line	10–23–1787
Potts, David	100	2939	3 years soldier Virginia line	4–17–1784
Potts, John	100	2104	3 years soldier Virginia line	12–12–1783
Potts, Jonathan	100	2942	3 years soldier Virginia line	4–17–1784
Pough, Michael	100	3552	3 years soldier Virginia line	12– 6–1784
Poulson, John	6,222	792	7 years major Virginia line	6–12–1783
Pound, William	200	1934	3 years corporal Virginia line	10–30–1783
Powell, Adron	200	779	3 years sergeant Virginia artillery	6–10–1783
Powell, Benjamin	200	4062	During war soldier Virginia line	12–31–1785
Powell, Charles	200	1687	3 years sergeant Virginia line	8–30–1783
Powell, John	200	442	During war soldier state line	10–26–1783
Powell, John	400	3147	During war sergeant Virginia line	6–10–1784
Powell, Levin	2,000	3396	3 years lieutenant colonel Virginia line	8–17–1784
Powell, Levin	2,000	3397	3 years lieutenant colonel Virginia line	8–17–1784
Powell, Levin	2,000	3398	3 years lieutenant colonel Virginia line	8–17–1784
Powell, Levin	200	3629	During war soldier Virginia line	12–29–1784
Powell, Leven	6,000	3429	Service lieutenant colonel Virginia line	8–30–1784
Powell, Peyton	1,666⅔	1415	3 years lieutenant Virginia line	7–22–1783
Powell, Peyton	1,000	1416	3 years lieutenant Virginia line	7–22–1783
Powell, Richard	100	3975	3 years soldier Virginia line	9–16–1785
Powell, Robert	4,000	903	3 years captain Virginia line	6–20–1783
Powell, Thomas	2,266⅔	679	Service lieutenant Virginia line	5–29–1783
Power, Robert	3,110⅓	1775	7 years cornet Virginia line	9–19–1783
Powers, John	100	3877	3 years soldier Virginia line	5–16–1785
Powers, William	100	2205	3 years soldier Virginia line	12–23–1783
Powers, William	200	2564	During war soldier Virginia line	2–20–1784
Powle, William	100	989	3 years sergeant Virginia line	6–21–1783
Pratt, John	100	3896	3 years soldier Virginia line	6–21–1785
Prayle, John	100	4379	3 years sailor Virginia navy	1–23–1788
Preston, Nathan	100	3892	3 years soldier Virginia line	6–15–1785
Price, Burdett	200	3663	During war soldier Virginia line	1– 1–1785
Price, David	400	1642	During war sergeant Virginia line	8–23–1783
Price, Ebenezer	2,666⅔	4298	3 years quartermaster Virginia line	6–25–1787
Price, George	100	3306	3 years soldier Virginia line	7– 2–1784
Price, Isaac	100	2987	3 years soldier Virginia line	4–21–1784
Price, Thomas	100	3203	3 years soldier Virginia line	6–24–1784
Pride, William	2,666⅔	1500	3 years lieutenant Virginia line	8– 5–1783
Pritchard, James	200	1789	During war soldier Virginia line	9–24–1783
Pritchard, James	200	3982	During war soldier Virginia line	10–18–1785
Pritchard, Thomas	100	3760	3 years soldier Virginia line	2–25–1785
Prithett, John	200	386	3 years sergeant Virginia Cont. line	4–23–1783
Pritchett, Peter	200	3057	3 years sergeant Virginia line	5– 7–1784
Proctor, John	200	1370	3 years sergeant Virginia line	7–12–1783
Pruder, Henry	200	3970	3 years sergeant Virginia line	9–12–1785
Pryor, John	4,000	126	3 years captain Cont. line Virginia	2–13–1783
Puckett, Josiah	200	3752	During war soldier Virginia line	2–11–1785
Puckett, Womack	100	4	3 years soldier Virginia Cont. line	8–27–1782
Pugh, Lewis	200	1250	During war soldier Virginia line	6–27–1783
Pugh, Willis	2,666⅔	13	3 years ensign Virginia regiment	11– 9–1782
Pulham, John	100	1196	3 years soldier Virginia line	6–26–1783
Puller, John	100	3815	3 years soldier Virginia line	4–21–1785

Name	Acres	Warrant	Service	Date
Pullin, George	100	2612	3 years soldier Virginia line	2–24–1784
Pully, William	100	3241	3 years soldier Virginia line	6–29–1784
Punch, Patrick	200	4411	During war soldier Virginia line	7–17–1788
Punsley, William	200	547	3 years sergeant state line	5– 5–1783
Punter, Henry	200	332	3 years sergeant Virginia artillery	4–14–1783
Purcell, John	200	1598	During war soldier Virginia line	8–20–1783
Purcell, Robert	100	2182	3 years soldier Virginia line	12–20–1783
Pursley, Lawrennee	100	2944	3 years soldier Virginia line	*4–17–1784
Purvis, James	4,000	3563	Captain Virginia line	12– 8–1784
Purvis, William	100	1973	3 years soldier Virginia line	11–26–1783
Puryear, Jesse	100	1710	3 years soldier Virginia line	9– 2–1783
Putten, Henry	100	3883	3 years soldier Virginia line	5–25–1785
Putton, William	200	1749	3 years sergeant Virginia line	9–11–1783
Pyatt, Benjamin	200	3866	3 years sergeant Virginia line	5–10–1785
Quall, John	100	3480	3 years soldier Virginia line	10–25–1784
Quarles, Abner	200	1294	During war soldier Virginia line	6–28–1783
Quarles, Henry	4,000	651	3 years captain Virginia line	5–28–1783
Quarles, James	4,000	84	3 years captain Virginia line	12–31–1782
Quarles, James	1,333⅓	150	Service major & captain Virginia line..	2–26–1783
Quarles, John	4,000	2666	3 years captain Virginia line	3– 2–1784
Quarles, John	2,666⅔	2900	3 years lieutenant Virginia line	4– 6–1784
Quarles, Moses	200	3902	During war soldier Virginia line	6–21–1785
Quarles, Nathaniel	200	378	3 years sergeant Virginia line	4–21–1783
Quarles, Robert	2,666⅔	2381	During war lieutenant Virginia line..	2– 3–1784
Quarles, Thomas	2,666⅔	799	3 years lieutenant Virginia line	6–13–1783
Quarles, William	2,000	2569	During war lieutenant Virginia line..	2–21–1784
Quarles, William	666⅔	2570	During war lieutenant Virginia line..	2–21–1784
Quin, Patrick	200	1136	During war soldier Virginia line	7–28–1783
Quinley, William	200	2651	3 years sergeant Virginia line	2–28–1784
Quirk, Thomas	1,000	1342	3 years major Virginia line	7– 9–1783
Quirk, Thomas	1,000	1343	3 years major Virginia line	7– 9–1783
Quirk, Thomas	3,333⅓	1344	3 years major Virginia line	7– 9–1783
Radford, William	400	4439	During war sergeant Virginia line	10–25–1788
Ragor, Bartholomew	100	978	3 years soldier Virginia line	6–20–1783
Ragsdale, Drury	4,000	397	— years captain in Cont. line	4–25–1783
Rains, John	100	1454	3 years soldier Virginia line	7–31–1783
Rains, Henry	100	3632	3 years soldier Virginia line	12–29–1784
Rains, Robert	200	3746	During war soldier Virginia line	2– 7–1785
Ralph, Ephram	2,666⅔	4096	3 years lieutenant Virginia line	1–25–1786
Ramble, Samuel	200	1553	During war soldier Virginia line	8–11–1783
Ramsey, Francis	200	1886	During war soldier Virginia line	11–12–1783
Ramsey, James	200	4556	During war soldier Virginia line	12– 3–1791
Ramsey, James	100	4154	3 years soldier Virginia line	5– 6–1786
Randolph, Adam	200	446	During war soldier Virginia line	4–26–1783
Randolph, Henry	200	3888	3 years corporal Virginia line	6– 9–1785
Randolph, John	100	1761	3 years soldier Virginia line	9–13–1783
Randolph, John Wm	2,666⅔	3069	3 years lieutenant Virginia line	5–11–1784
Randolph, Robert	4,000	811	3 years captain Virginia line	6– 4–1784
Ranger, Joseph	100	733	3 years sailor Virginia navy	6– 4–1784
Ranger, Joseph	100	4221	3 years sailor Virginia navy	10–24–1786
Rankin, Robert	200	1485	3 years sergeant Virginia line	8– 2–1783
Rankin, William	100	1483	3 years soldier Virginia line	8– 2–1783
Rankins, Benjamin	100	2472	3 years soldier Virginia line	2–11–1784
Rankins, James	100	3694	3 years soldier Virginia line	1–20–1785
Rankins, James	100	3694	3 years soldier Virginia line	1–20–1785
Rankins, Robert	2,666⅔	165	3 years lieutenant Virginia Cont. line	3– 8–1783
Ranadall, Thomas	4,000	167	3 years captain Virginia line	3– 9–1783
Ransome, Robert	100	1640	3 years soldier Virginia line	8–23–1783
Raphite, Jean	100	2663	3 years soldier Virginia line	3– 1–1784
Ratchelor, Peter	200	2532	During war soldier Virginia line	2–19–1784
Rath, Frederick	200	3324	During war soldier Virginia line	7–15–1784
Ravens, Michael	200	1073	During war soldier Virginia line	6–24–1783
Ravenscraft, Francis	100	4404	3 years soldier Virginia line	6–11–1788
Ravenscraft, Thomas	100	782	3 years soldier Virginia line	6–10–1783
Rawlings, Moses	200	3648	During war soldier Virginia line	12–31–1784
Ray, Daniel	100	943	3 years soldier Virginia line	6–20–1783
Ray, David	100	3296	3 years soldier Virginia line	7– 1–1784
Ray, Thomas	100	3659	3 years soldier Virginia line	12–31–1784
Read, Alexander	466⅔	2899	During war sergeant Virginia line	4– 6–1784
Read, Clement	2,666⅔	68	— years lieutenant of cavalry	12–23–1782
Read, Col. Isaac	6,666⅔	46	3 years colonel in army	12–14–1782
Read, William	200	1419	3 years corporal Virginia line	7–22–1783
Reade, Edmond	4,000	54	3 years captain in state cavalry	12–16–1782
Reagen, Daniel	200	2478	3 years sergeant Virginia line	2–11–1784
Reardon, George	200	304	3 years sergeant state line	4– 8–1783
Reasden, George	400	489	During war sergeant state line	4–30–1783
Reasons, William	100	2529	3 years soldier Virginia line	2–19–1784
Reatley, James	200	2103	During war soldier Virginia line	12–12–1783
Reaves, James	100	2490	3 years sailor Virginia navy	2–13–1784
Reddick, Jason	4,000	3140	3 years captain Virginia line	6–10–1784
Reddick, Willis	4,000	3141	3 years captain Virginia line	6–10–1784

Name	Acres	Warrant	Service	Date
Reddy, Demus	200	33	3 years sergeant Virginia Cont. line	12- 3-1782
Redman, Solomon	100	4236	3 years soldier Virginia line	12-13-1786
Redwood, John	100	2632	3 years soldier Virginia line	2-25-1784
Reid, Capt Nathan	4,000	601	3 years captain Virginia line	5-20-1783
Resner, John	200	3858	During war soldier Virginia line	5- 6-1785
Reynolds, Aaron	200	3261	3 years corporal Virginia line	6-30-1784
Reynolds, Bernard	200	376	During war soldier Virginia state line	4-19-1783
Reynolds, James	200	1058	During war soldier Virginia line	6-24-1783
Reynolds, William	200	2290	3 years sergeant Virginia line	1-26-1784
Reynolds, William	2,666⅔	4264	3 years lieutenant Virginia line	3-25-1787
Reynor, John	200	371	During war soldier state line	4-19-1783
Rhea, Mathew	2,666⅔	1452	3 years lieutenant Virginia line	7-31-1783
Rhoads, William	466⅔	1524	During war corporal Virginia line	8- 7-1783
Rhoads, William	100	1575	3 years soldier Virginia line	8-16-1783
Rhodes, Elijah	100	3052	3 years soldier Virginia line	5- 7-1784
Rhodes, John	200	460	During war soldier Virginia line	4-28-1783
Rice, Basdill	100	2778	3 years soldier Virginia line	3-18-1784
Rice, George	4,000	856	3 years captain Virginia line	6-17-1783
Rice, George	400	1458	During war corporal Virginia line	8- 1-1783
Rice, Isaac	100	4380	3 years soldier Virginia line	1-29-1788
Rice, Nathanial	2,666⅔	90	Lieutenant Virginia artillery	1- 3-1783
Rice, William	200	1501	3 years sergeant Virginia line	8- 5-1783
Rice, William	100	2621	3 years soldier Virginia line	2-24-1784
Rich, William	100	1511	3 years soldier Virginia line	8- 6-1783
Richard, Thomas	100	3702	3 years soldier Virginia line	1-20-1785
Richards, Boswell	100	4123	3 years soldier Virginia line	3-10-1786
Richards, Clement	100	4177	3 years soldier Virginia line	6-20-1786
Richards, John	200	2572	3 years stewart Virginia navy	2-21-1784
Richards, Thomas	200	1529	During war sergeant Virginia line	8- 8-1783
Richards, Thomas	200	823	3 years sergeant Virginia line	6-14-1783
Richardson, Daniel	2,666⅔	3457	3 years lieutenant Virginia navy	10- 7-1784
Richardson, Mourning	100	3779	3 years soldier Virginia line	3-15-1785
Richardson, Richard	200	2027	During war soldier Virginia line	12- 6-1783
Richardson, Robert	100	2234	3 years soldier Virginia line	1-12-1784
Richardson, William	100	2448	3 years soldier Virginia line	2-10-1784
Richee, James	100	2802	3 years soldier Virginia line	3-22-1784
Richeson, Holt	6,000	2507	3 years lieutenant Virginia line	2-17-1784
Richeson, James	400	695	3 years sergeant Virginia line	5-31-1783
Richeson, John	200	1155	During war soldier Virginia line	6-24-1783
Richeson, Robert	100	2414	3 years soldier Virginia line	2- 5-1784
Richeson, Walker	2,666⅔	1624	3 years lieutenant Virginia line	8-22-1783
Richman, William	6,666⅔	2245	3 years colonel Virginia line	1-13-1784
Ricketts, William	100	274	3 years soldier state line	4- 3-1783
Rider, Adam	100	2857	3 years soldier Virginia line	4- 1-1784
Ridden, Robert	100	255	3 years soldier state line	4- 3-1782
Ridley, Alexander	100	2463	3 years soldier Virginia line	2-11-1784
Ridley, John	200	1345	3 years sergeant Virginia line	7-10-1783
Ridley, Thomas	5,333⅓	2127	3 years major Virginia line	12-15-1783
Riggin, William	100	4425	3 years soldier Virginia line	7-17-1788
Riggs, Jacob	200	4063	During war soldier Virginia line	12-31-1785
Riley, Daniel	200	2896	During war private Virginia line	4- 6-1784
Riley, John	200	1101	During war soldier Virginia line	6-24-1783
Ringo, Burtus	200	331	During war soldier cavalry	4-14-1783
Rinker, Jesse	100	3499	3 years soldier Virginia line	11- 4-1784
Rinkin, Edward	200	2959	3 years sergeant Virginia line	3-17-1784
Ritchie, Abraham	100	3698	3 years soldier Virginia line	1-20-1785
Ritchie, William	100	3706	3 years soldier Virginia line	1-20-1785
Ritcher, John	200	3350	3 years soldier Virginia line	7-22-1784
Roach, John	200	2471	3 years corporal Virginia line	2-11-1784
Roach, Richard	200	1054	During war soldier Virginia line	6-24-1783
Roach, William	466⅔	1260	7 years soldier Virginia line	6-27-1783
Roane, Christopher	4,000	92	Captain artillery legion commander	1- 3-1783
Roane, Christopher	666⅔	1808	7 years captain Virginia line	9-30-1783
Roberts, Ambrose	100	1291	3 years soldier Virginia line	6-28-1783
Roberts, Anthony	200	458	During war soldier state line	4-28-1783
Roberts, Elisha	200	3908	During war soldier Virginia line	6-21-1785
Roberts, George	200	4028	3 years sergeant Virginia line	12- 9-1784
Roberts, Daniel	100	3188	3 years soldier Virginia line	6-23-1784
Roberts, Gerrard	200	677	3 years sergeant Virginia line	5-29-1783
Roberts, John	6,000	105	3 years sergeant Virginia Cont. line	1-30-1783
Roberts, John	100	1591	3 years soldier Virginia line	8-20-1783
Roberts, John	100	3151	3 years soldier Virginia line	6-11-1784
Roberts, John	400	3738	During war sergeant Virginia line	2- 7-1785
Roberts, Joseph	200	2658	During war soldier Virginia line	3- 1-1784
Roberts, Obedience	200	1613	During war soldier Virginia line	8-21-1783
Roberts, Thomas	200	2927	3 years sergeant Virginia line	4-13-1784
Roberts, William	100	2639	3 years soldier Virginia line	2-26-1784
Roberts, William	100	3699	3 years soldier Virginia line	1-20-1785
Roberts, William	100	4198	3 years sailor Virginia navy	8-26-1786
Robertson, Benjamin	200	4046	3 years sergeant Virginia line	12-19-1785
Robertson, Daniel	200	1801	During war soldier Virginia line	9-30-1783

Name	Acres	Warrant	Service	Date
Robertson, George	100	636	3 years soldier Virginia line	5–24–1783
Robertson, George	100	2266	3 years soldier Virginia line	1–21–1784
Robertson, Hugh	200	1497	3 years sergeant Virginia line	8– 5–1783
Robertson, James	100	2825	3 years soldier Virginia line	3–26–1784
Robertson, John	200	1108	During war soldier Virginia line	6–24–1783
Robertson, John	100	3756	3 years soldier Virginia line	2–18–1785
Robertson, Mordecai	100	2059	3 years soldier Virginia line	12– 9–1783
Robertson, William	2,666⅔	414	3 years lieutenant Virginia Cont. line	4–26–1783
Robertson, Wm	200	710	3 years soldier Virginia line	5–31–1783
Robinett, Joseph	233⅓	1879	During war soldier Virginia line	10–15–1783
Robins, John	2,666⅔	1847	3 years lieutenant Virginia line	10–11–1783
Robins, John	266⅔	3490	3 years midshipman Virginia navy	10–29–1784
Robins, William	100	3100	3 years soldier Virginia line	5–26–1784
Robinson, Andrew	100	4137	3 years soldier Virginia line	3–24–1786
Robinson, Charles	200	1131	During war soldier Virginia line	6–24–1783
Robinson, Cole	200	709	3 years sergeant Virginia line	5–31–1783
Robins Cole	2,666⅔	4513	3 years ensign Virginia line	12– 9–1790
Robinson, Green	200	1862	During war soldier Virginia line	10–14–1783
Robinson, James	200	2231	3 years corporal Virginia line	1–12–1784
Robinson, John	2,666⅔	2158	3 years lieutenant Virginia line	12–19–1783
Robinson, Maxemillion	100	2954	3 years soldier Virginia line	4–17–1784
Robinson, Mordecai	200	1849	During war soldier Virginia line	10–11–1783
Robinson, William	400	2028	During war sergeant Virginia line	12– 6–1783
Robson, Green	100	1211	3 years soldier Virginia line	6–26–1783
Rock, John	200	1844	During war soldier Virginia line	10–31–1783
Rock, John	200	3467	During war soldier Virginia line	10–18–1784
Rock, William	200	2720	During war soldier Virginia line	3– 6–1784
Rodden, John	200	1507	During war soldier Virginia line	8– 6–1783
Roe, William	100	2520	3 years soldier Virginia line	2–19–1784
Roe, William	2,666⅔	4180	3 years surgeon Virginia navy	6–22–1786
Rogers, Bernard	200	2531	3 years sergeant Virginia line	2–19–1784
Rogers, Bowling	200	4114	During war soldier Virginia line	3– 4–1786
Rogers, John	3,000	148	3 years captain Virginia line	2–26–1783
Rogers, John	1,000	149	3 years captain Virginia line	2–26–1783
Rogers, John	200	2339	During war soldier Virginia line	1–31–1784
Rogers, William	4,000	859	3 years lieutenant Virginia line	6–18–1783
Rokins, Bartlet	100	2997	3 years soldier Virginia line	4–21–1784
Roney, John	3,110⅔	2242	7 years lieutenant Virginia line	1–12–1784
Rooke, John	200	1105	During war soldier Virginia line	6–24–1783
Root, Tucker	200	1304	3 years sergeant Virginia line	6–30–1783
Roots, John	3,000	3753	———	2–14–1785
Rose, Alexander	2,000	3993	3 years captain Virginia line	11–11–1785
Rose, Alexander	2,000	3994	3 years captain Virginia line	11–11–1785
Rose, Archibald	400	1816	During war sergeant Virginia line	10– 2–1783
Rose, George	200	354	During war soldier Virginia line	4–17–1783
Rose, Isaac	200	2945	3 years corporal Virginia line	4–17–1784
Rose, Jesse	100	1865	3 years soldier Virginia line	11– 6–1783
Rose, Robert	7,000	1850	7 years surgeon Virginia line	11– 1–1783
Rose, William	100	1864	3 years soldier Virginia line	11– 6–1783
Ross, Elijah	100	3861	3 years soldier Virginia line	5– 7–1785
Ross, James	100	4101	3 years soldier Virginia line	1–30–1786
Ross, John	200	625	3 years soldier Virginia line	5–23–1783
Ross, Valentine	200	1632	During war soldier Virginia line	8–22–1783
Rossei, John	100	2701	3 years soldier Virginia line	3– 4–1784
Rosson, William	100	4005	3 years soldier Virginia line	11–23–1785
Routen, Richard	200	1010	3 years corporal Virginia line	6–23–1783
Roux, Anthony Lee	200	2597	During war soldier Virginia line	2–23–1784
Row, James	200	2762	3 years corporal Virginia line	3–15–1784
Rowe, John	200	435	During war soldier state line	4–26–1783
Rowe, William	100	3985	3 years soldier Virginia line	10–21–1785
Rowman, John	100	2604	3 years soldier Virginia line	2–24–1784
Rowsel, Thomas	100	2732	3 years soldier Virginia line	3– 6–1784
Roy, Beverly	4,000	154	3 years captain Virginia line	3– 3–1783
Royal, Grief	100	847	3 years soldier Virginia line	6–17–1783
Royale, Francis	100	873	3 years soldier Virginia line	6–19–1783
Royster, John	200	1848	3 years sergeant Virginia line	10–11–1783
Rucker, Angus	4,000	98	3 years captain Virginia infantry	1–21–1783
Rucker, Jacob	200	1114	During war soldier Virginia line	6–24–1783
Ruckey, Elliott	2,666⅔	136	3 years lieutenant Virginia state line	2–20–1783
Rudd, Benjamin	100	2176	3 years sailor Virginia navy	12–20–1783
Rudder, Epaphudelus	2,666⅔	128	3 years lieutenant Virginia cavalry	2–13–1783
Rumage, David	100	979	3 years soldier Virginia line	6–20–1783
Ruport, George	200	3338	During war soldier Virginia line	7–19–1784
Russell, Albert	2,666⅔	342	3 years lieutenant Virginia Cont. line	4–15–1783
Russell, Andrew	2,666⅔	3630	3 years major Virginia line	12–29–1784
Russell, Andrew	2,666⅔	3631	3 years major Virginia line	12–29–1784
Russell, Charles	2,666⅔	249	3 years lieutenant state line	4– 2–1783
Russell, Charles	400	1985	3 years corporal Virginia line	11–28–1783
Russell, Ephram	200	3427	During war soldier Virginia line	8–28–1784
Russell, James	200	1009	3 years sergeant Virginia line	6–23–1783
Russell, John	2,666⅔	278	3 years lieutenant Virginia state line	4– 3–1783

Name	Acres	Warrant	Service	Date
Russell, John	100	1947	3 years soldier Virginia line	11–22–1783
Russell, Nicholas	100	1916	3 years soldier Virginia line	10–25–1783
Russell, Thomas	200	466	During war soldier state line	4–29–1783
Russell, Thomas	100	3911	3 years soldier Virginia line	6–21–1785
Russell, Vincent	100	3954	3 years soldier Virginia line	8–12–1785
Russell, William	100	762	3 years soldier Virginia line	6– 6–1783
Russell, William	6,666⅔	2023	3 years colonel Virginia line	12– 6–1783
Russell, William	100	4111	3 years soldier Virginia line	2–22–1786
Rust, Benjamin	2,666⅔	1431	3 years lieutenant Virginia line	7–27–1783
Rust, George	200	3482	During war soldier Virginia line	10–25–1784
Rust, Vincent	200	3481	During war soldier Virginia line	10–25–1784
Rutherford, Julius	100	3667	3 years soldier Virginia line	1– 3–1785
Rutter, Adain	200	1707	During war soldier Virginia line	9– 2–1783
Ryan, George	100	2974	3 years soldier Virginia line	4–20–1784
Ryalls, James	200	4516	During war soldier Virginia line	2– 1–1791
Rycroft, Thomas	100	824	3 years soldier Virginia line	6–14–1783
Rydman, John	2,666⅔	819	3 years gunner Virginia navy	6–14–1783
Ryland, John	400	2358	During war corporal Virginia line	1–31–1784
Saduskie, Jonathan	100	3551	3 years soldier Virginia line	12– 6–1784
Sallards, Eliphalet	100	2979	3 years soldier Virginia line	4–20–1784
Salmon, George	400	1562	During war sergeant Virginia line	8–12–1783
Salusbury, Newman	200	2277	During war soldier Virginia line	1–23–1784
Sammons, John	100	2076	3 years soldier Virginia line	12–10–1783
Sample, James	200	1281	During war soldier Virginia line	6–28–1783
Samson, John	200	2680	During war soldier Virginia line	3– 3–1784
Samuel, Gray	200	3605	3 years sergeant Virginia line	12–22–1784
Sandefer, Samuel	100	1941	3 years soldier Virginia line	11–22–1783
Sanderford, Samuel	200	500	During war soldier state line	5– 1–1783
Sanders, David	200	4608	During war private Virginia line	3–23–1793
Sanders, John	200	3150	During war soldier Virginia line	6–11–1784
Sanders, Joseph	2,666⅔	1718	3 years lieutenant Virginia line	9– 2–1783
Sanders, Presley	200	1717	3 years sergeant Virginia line	9– 2–1783
Sanders, Thomas	200	4607	During war private Virginia line	3–23–1793
Sanderson, Samuel	100	3347	3 years soldier Virginia line	7–22–1784
Sandford, Thomas	100	3682	During war soldier Virginia line	1–11–1785
Sanford, John	200	523	During war soldier state line	5– 2–1783
Sansum, Phillip	4,000	63	3 years captain Virginia Cont. Reg	12–20–1782
Satterwhite, John	400	1513	During war sergeant Virginia line	8– 6–1783
Satterwhite, William	200	4215	3 years sergeant Virginia line	10– 4–1786
Saulee, William	100	2132	3 years soldier Virginia line	12–15–1783
Saunders, Coley	4,666⅔	175	Services as captain state navy	3–12–1783
Saunders, Richard	2,666⅔	1813	3 years midshipman Virginia navy	10– 1–1783
Saunders, William	666⅔	4178	3 years captain Virginia line	6–21–1786
Saunders, Capt Wm	4,000	605	3 years captain Virginia line	5–20–1783
Savage, George	100	4181	3 years soldier Virginia line	6–29–1786
Savage, Joseph	2,666⅔	2628	3 years surgeon Virginia line	2–25–1784
Savage, Nathanial	2,666⅔	118	3 years lieutenant cavalry state line	2– 8–1783
Savey, John	200	2423	During war soldier Virginia line	2– 6–1784
Saxton, John	100	3666	3 years soldier Virginia line	1– 3–1785
Sayers, Robert	1,000	3623	Services as captain Virginia line	12–27–1784
Sayers, Robert	1,000	3624	Services captain Virginia line	12–27–1784
Sayers, Robert	1,000	3625	Services captain Virginia line	12–27–1784
Sayers, Robert	1,000	3626	Services captain Virginia line	12–27–1784
Saymore, William	100	2773	3 years soldier Virginia line	3–18–1784
Scantlin, William	200	4510	3 years sergeant Virginia line	12– 7–1790
Scarbrough, John	2,666⅔	3414	3 years lieutenant Virginia line	8–26–1784
Scars, Thomas	100	1980	3 years soldier Virginia line	11–24–1783
Scott, Charles	11,666⅔	815	7 years Brig. Genl. Virginia line	6–14–1783
Scott, Charles	1,666⅔	2012	8 years Brig. Genl. Virginia line	12– 5–1783
Scott, Charles	2,666⅔	2444	During war cornet Virginia line	2–10–1784
Scott, Drury	200	2363	During war soldier Virginia line	2– 2–1784
Scott, George	100	3535	3 years soldier Virginia line	11–24–1784
Scott, Isaac	100	4480	3 years soldier Virginia line	11–21–1789
Scott, James	200	511	During war soldier state line	5– 1–1783
Scott, James	100	1945	3 years soldier Virginia line	11–22–1783
Scott, John	200	1635	During war soldier Virginia line	8–23–1783
Scott, John	4,000	1884	3 years captain lieutenant Virginia line	10–16–1783
Scott, John	100	2548	3 years soldier Virginia line	2–20–1784
Scott, John	2,666⅔	2609	During war subaltern Virginia line	2–24–1784
Scott, John	2,666⅔	3187	3 years subaltern Virginia line	6–23–1784
Scott, John	100	3218	3 years sailor Virginia navy	6–26–1784
Scott, Joseph	4,000	1887	3 years captain Virginia line	10–17–1783
Scott, Joseph	100	2549	3 years soldier Virginia line	2–20–1784
Scott, Joseph Sr	4,666⅔	51	7 years captain Virginia Cont. Reg	12–14–1782
Scott, Littleberry	200	3006	During war soldier Virginia line	4–22–1784
Scott, Mathew	200	3101	3 years sergeant Virginia line	5–26–1784
Scott, Robert	200	1778	3 years corporal Virginia line	9–20–1783
Scott, Stephen	200	4604	During war private Virginia line	1–25–1793
Scott, Walter	2,666⅔	1798	3 years lieutenant Virginia line	9–29–1783
Scott, William	400	567	3 years sergeant Virginia state line	5– 9–1783
Scott, William	233½	1315	During war drummer Virginia line	7– 1–1783

Name	Acres	Warrant	Service	Date
Scott, William...........	100	2087	3 years soldier Virginia line.........	12–10–1783
Sculley, James..........	200	4564	During war soldier Virginia line......	1–21–1792
Seagres, John..........	6,000	4500	3 years Lieut. & Col. Virginia line....	9– 4–1790
Sears, Joseph............	200	4066	During war soldier Virginia line.....	1– 6–1786
Sears, Thomas..........	2,666⅔	2418	During war lieutenant Virginia line...	2– 6–1784
Seay, James............	100	2776	3 years soldier Virginia line........	3–18–1784
Seay, Rueben............	100	2254	3 years soldier Virginia line.........	1–21–1784
Sebastain, Benjamin......	233⅓	2835	3 years soldier Virginia line........	3–27–1784
Sebry, William..........	200	2722	During war soldier Virginia line.....	3– 6–1784
Seburn, Jacob...........	200	4013	During war soldier Virginia line.....	12– 2–1785
Seldon, Samuel..........	2,666⅔	2291	3 years lieutenant Virginia line.....	1–26–1784
Self, Larkin.............	200	2506	During war soldier Virginia line.....	2–17–1784
Sell, George.............	200	1265	During war soldier Virginia line.....	6–27–1783
Sellers, Michael.........	200	3745	During war soldier Virginia line.....	2– 7–1785
Selman, Joseph..........	100	4202	3 years soldier Virginia line........	8–29–1786
Settle, Benjamin.........	200	2915	3 years corporal Virginia line........	4–12–1784
Settle, Strother.........	2,666⅔	2858	End war lieutenant Virginia line......	4– 2–1784
Sewell, Thomas..........	200	4051	3 years sergeant Virginia line........	12–21–1785
Shackelford, Alexander....	100	3525	3 years soldier Virginia line........	11–20–1784
Shackelford, Henry......	100	2208	3 years soldier Virginia line.........	12–23–1783
Shackelford, Mag........	100	2207	3 years soldier Virginia line.........	12–23–1783
Shackelford, William.....	2,666⅔	2930	3 years lieutenant Virginia line......	4–13–1784
Shacklett, Edward.......	100	4041	3 years private Virginia line.........	12–15–1785
Shanks, James..........	100	2865	3 years soldier Virginia line........	4– 2–1784
Shannon, Patrick........	200	1025	3 years sergeant Virginia line........	6–23–1783
Sharp, Josiah...........	100	4459	3 years soldier Virginia line........	5–25–1789
Sharpless, John..........	6,000	4487	3 years surgeon Virginia navy.......	1– 2–1790
Sharrow, Richard.......	200	1074	During war soldier Virginia line.....	6–24–1783
Shauer, George..........	100	3936	3 years soldier Virginia line........	8– 2–1785
Shaver, Frederick........	200	4625	During war private Virginia line.....	9–13–1793
Shaver, George.........	100	3864	3 years soldier Virginia line........	5–10–1785
Shaver, John............	100	3865	3 years soldier Virginia line........	5–10–1785
Shaw, Matthew..........	200	4130	During war soldier Virginia line.....	3–18–1786
Shaw, William..........	100	3867	3 years soldier Virginia line........	5–10–1785
Shay, Demus............	200	1516	During war soldier Virginia line.....	8– 7–1783
Shea, John..............	200	1115	During war soldier Virginia line.....	6–24–1783
Shearman, Martin.......	2,666⅔	1722	3 years midshipman Virginia navy....	9– 2–1783
Shearman, Robert.......	200	623	3 years fife major Virginia navy.....	5–23–1783
Sheeney, Mathias........	200	3707	3 years sergeant Virginia line........	1–20–1785
Sheffield, Peter..........	200	522	During war soldier state line.........	5– 1–1783
Sheffield, Thomas........	100	3379	3 years soldier Virginia line........	8– 5–1784
Sheldon, Peter F	200	3980	During war fifer Virginia line	10–15–1785
Sheldon, Alias Chilton, Thomas..............	533⅓	1896	5 years major Virginia line	11–12–1783
Shelton, Clough.........	4,000	111	3 years captain Virginia Cont. line....	2– 3–1783
Shelton, Clough.........	666⅔	2446	7 years captain Virginia line........	2–10–1784
Shelton, David..........	100	1736	3 years soldier Virginia line........	9–10–1783
Sheiton, Thomas........	200	509	During war soldier state line........	5– 1–1783
Shepherd, Abraham......	4,000	290	3 years captain Virginia Cont. line...	4– 5–1783
Shepherd, David........	100	2330	3 years soldier Virginia line........	1–31–1784
Shepherd, David........	100	3410	3 years soldier Virginia line........	8–25–1784
Shepherd, James........	200	2409	3 years sergeant Virginia line........	2– 5–1784
Shibler, Frederick.......	100	4093	3 years soldier Virginia line........	1–23–1786
Shield, John.............	4,000	3041	3 years captain Virginia line........	5– 4–1784
Shields, James..........	100	1240	3 years soldier Virginia line........	6–27–1783
Shires, Nicholas.........	200	2344	During war soldier Virginia line.....	1–31–1784
Shirley, James..........	100	3046	3 years soldier Virginia line........	5– 5–1784
Shores, Thomas..........	100	1023	3 years soldier Virginia line........	6–23–1783
Shoup, William..........	400	3601	During war sergeant Virginia line....	12–21–1784
Shouse, Samuel..........	100	3553	3 years soldier Virginia line........	12– 6–1784
Shurles, Benjamin.......	100	865	3 years soldier Virginia line........	6–18–1783
Sickner, John Simon.....	200	4132	During war soldier Virginia line.....	3–18–1786
Simmons, Bryan........	100	1002	3 years soldier Virginia line........	6–21–1783
Simmons, George........	100	569	3 years soldier state line...........	5–12–1783
Simmons, James.........	200	1253	During war soldier Virginia line.....	6–27–1783
Simmons, James.........	100	4325	3 years soldier Virginia line........	11– 3–1787
Simmons, Joshua........	400	1235	During war fifer Virginia line.......	6–27–1783
Simmons, William.......	233⅓	1280	7 years soldier Virginia line........	6–28–1783
Simms, Charles..........	6,000	351	3 years Lieut. Col. Virginia line.....	4–17–1783
Simms, Edward.........	200	403	3 years sergeant Virginia line........	4–25–1783
Simms, Isaac...........	200	1247	During war soldier Virginia line.....	6–27–1783
Simpkins, Garret........	100	3674	3 years soldier Virginia line........	1– 5–1785
Simpkins, James........	100	3673	3 years soldier Virginia line........	1– 5–1785
Simpkins, William.......	100	4359	3 years soldier Virginia line........	1– 4–1788
Simpson, Daniel.........	200	3976	3 years corporal Virginia line........	9–16–1785
Simpson, George........	100	4558	3 years soldier Virginia line........	12– 8–1791
Simpson, Jeremiah......	200	2889	3 years sergeant Virginia line........	4– 5–1784
Simpson, John..........	100	1689	3 years soldier Virginia line........	8–30–1783
Simpson, Spencer........	100	2188	3 years soldier Virginia line........	12–22–1783
Sims, Thomas...........	200	2828	3 years sergeant Virginia line........	3–26–1784
Singleton, Anthony.......	4,000	2120	3 years captain Virginia line........	12–13–1783

Name	Acres	Warrant	Service	Date
Singleton, Anthony	666⅔	4585	7 years captain Virginia line	9-15-1792
Singleton, Frederick	200	4253	During war soldier Virginia line	1-27-1787
Sinah, John	100	3561	3 years soldier Virginia line	12- 8-1784
Singleton, Joshua	2,666⅔	572	— years lieutenant state navy	5-12-1783
Singleton, Joshua	200	1865	3 years sergeant Virginia line	10-14-1783
Skinner, Alexander	6,000	736	3 years surgeon, Virginia Cont. line	6- 4-1783
Skinner, Alexander	1,000	3176	7 years regimental Virginia line	6-21-1784
Skinner, Henry	200	1142	During war soldier Virginia line	6-24-1783
Skinner, Richard	100	1319	3 years soldier Virginia line	7- 2-1783
Slate, James	400	1508	During war corporal Virginia line	8- 6-1783
Slate, John	200	2112	3 years corporal Virginia line	12-13-1783
Slaughter, Augustine	3,000	3541	Surgeon Virginia line	11-24-1784
Slaughter, Augustine	3,000	3542	Surgeon Virginia line	11-24-1784
Slaughter, Francis Lighfoot	200	3131	During war soldier Virginia line	6- 5-1784
Slaughter, George	1,833⅓	3540	Services major Virginia line	11-24-1784
Slaughter, George	2,500	3538	Services major Virginia line	11-24-1784
Slaughter, George	1,000	3539	Services major Virginia line	11-24-1784
Slaughter, Lawrence	2,666⅔	246	3 years lieutenant state line	4- 1-1783
Slaughter, John	100	644	3 years soldier Virginia line	5-26-1783
Slaughter, John	2,666⅔	2498	3 years sublatern Virginia line	2-14-1784
Slaughter, John	100	4387	3 years soldier Virginia line	2-11-1788
Slaughter, Nathanial	100	2228	3 years soldier Virginia line	1-12-1784
Slaughter, Phil	4,000	69	3 years captain Virginia Cont. line	12-23-1782
Slaughter, William	2,666⅔	212	3 years lieutenant Virginia state line	3-31-1783
Slaughter, William	666⅔	3075	7 years lieutenant Virginia line	5-12-1784
Slaven, Cornelius	100	1902	3 years soldier Virginia line	11-17-1783
Slayden, Daniel	100	45	3 years 4th regiment light dragoons	12-13-1782
Sledd, Seaton	100	2928	3 years soldier Virginia line	4-13-1784
Sledd, Seaton	300	3807	During war sergeant Virginia line	4-13-1785
Small, Henry	100	2085	3 years soldier Virginia line	12-10-1783
Smart, Richard	2,666⅔	752	3 years masters mate Virginia line	6- 5-1783
Smaw, John	200	573	3 years sergeant Virginia Cont. line	5-13-1783
Smith, Aaron	200	185	— services for war as soldier	3-19-1783
Smith, Andrew	100	2623	3 years soldier Virginia line	2-24-1784
Smith, Ballard	2,666⅔	200	3 years lieutenant Virginia line	3-26-1783
Smith, Charles	100	4217	3 years soldier Virginia line	10-13-1786
Smith, Elijah	100	1421	3 years soldier Virginia line	7-22-1783
Smith, Francis	2,666⅔	70	3 years lieutenant Virginia army	12-24-1782
Smith, Francis	100	992	3 years fifer Virginia line	6-21-1783
Smith, Francis	100	3064	3 years soldier Virginia line	5-10-1784
Smith, George	100	930	3 years soldier Virginia line	6-20-1783
Smith, Granvill	2,666⅔	2932	3 years ensign Virginia line	4-15-1784
Smith, Gregory	6,666⅔	124	3 years colonel state line	2-13-1783
Smith, Isaac	100	2786	3 years soldier Virginia line	3-18-1784
Smith, Isaac	200	2791	3 years sergeant Virginia line	3-19-1784
Smith, Isaac	100	4440	3 years soldier Virginia line	10-27-1788
Smith, Jacob	100	1453	3 years soldier Virginia line	7-31-1783
Smith, James	200	1086	During war soldier Virginia line	6-24-1783
Smith, James	200	1648	During war soldier Virginia line	8-23-1783
Smith, James	100	3787	3 years soldier Virginia line	3-25-1785
Smith, James	200	4067	3 years corporal Virginia line	1- 6-1786
Smith, James	400	4525	During war sergeant Virginia line	5-31-1791
Smith, James	100	4567	3 years soldier Virginia line	1-31-1792
Smith, John	100	954	3 years soldier Virginia line	6-20-1783
Smith, John	200	1041	During war drummer Virginia line	6-24-1783
Smith, John	200	1489	During war soldier Virginia line	8- 4-1783
Smith, John	100	1729	3 years soldier Virginia line	9- 8-1783
Smith, John	100	2771	3 years soldier Virginia line	3-18-1784
Smith, John	100	2919	3 years soldier Virginia line	4-12-1784
Smith, John	100	3304	3 years soldier Virginia line	7- 2-1784
Smith, John	200	3856	3 years sergeant Virginia line	5- 6-1785
Smith, John	100	4272	3 years soldier Virginia line	4- 7-1787
Smith, Jonathan	2,666⅔	127	3 years lieutenant Virginia line	2-13-1783
Smith, Joseph	100	3146	3 years soldier Virginia line	6-10-1784
Smith, Larkin	4,000	619	3 years captain Virginia line	5-22-1783
Smith, Major	100	4203	3 years soldier Virginia line	8-30-1786
Smith, Michael	200	767	3 years sergeant Virginia line	6- 7-1783
Smith, Michael	200	1075	During war soldier Virginia line	6-24-1783
Smith, Minor	100	3517	3 years soldier Virginia line	11-11-1784
Smith, Nathan	2,666⅔	2960	End of war sergeant mate Virginia line	4-19-1784
Smith, Obadiah	2,666⅔	685	3 years lieutenant Virginia line	5-30-1783
Smith, Richard	200	3668	During war soldier Virginia line	1- 4-1785
Smith, Richard	100	4218	3 years soldier Virginia line	10-13-1786
Smith, Samuel	200	1062	During war soldier Virginia line	6-24-1783
Smith, Stephen	100	1793	3 years soldier Virginia line	9-25-1783
Smith, Stephen	200	4295	During war soldier Virginia line	6- 1-1787
Smith, Thomas	100	1999	3 years soldier Virginia line	11-29-1783
Smith, Thomas	400	4117	During war drum major Virginia line	3- 7-1786
Smith, Underwood	100	543	3 years soldier state line	5- 3-1783
Smith, Weedan	100	3634	3 years soldier Virginia line	12-29-1784
Smith, William	200	413	During war soldier Virginia line	4-25-1783

Name	Acres	Warrant	Service	Date
Smith, William	200	1057	During war soldier Virginia line	6–24–1783
Smith, William	200	1430	3 years sergeant Virginia line	7–27–1783
Smith, William	200	1770	During war drummer Virginia line	9–17–1783
Smith, William	2,666⅔	1843	3 years lieutenant Virginia line	10–10–1783
Smith, William	100	3182	3 years soldier Virginia line	6–22–1784
Smith, William	200	3328	During war soldier Virginia line	7–19–1784
Smith, William	100	3507	3 years boatswain Virginia navy	11– 8–1784
Smith, William	200	3831	3 years sergeant Virginia line	4–28–1785
Smith, William	100	4207	3 years soldier Virginia line	8–31–1786
Smith, William	2,666⅔	1843	3 years lieutenant Virginia line	11–23–1787
Smith, William S.	2,666⅔	146	3 years lieutenant Virginia Cont. line	2–24–1783
Smither, Benjamin	200	3996	During war soldier Virginia line	11–15–1785
Smither, Benjamin	100	4054	3 years soldier Virginia line	12–22–1785
Smithers, Stephen	466⅔	1628	7 years sergeant Virginia line	8–22–1783
Smithy, Benjamin	100	1266	3 years soldier Virginia line	6–27–1783
Smithy, Robert	100	2544	3 years soldier Virginia line	2–19–1784
Smock, Jacob	200	1022	3 years sergeant Virginia line	6–23–1783
Smothers, William	200	2734	During war soldier Virginia line	3– 6–1784
Snead, Holman	100	1363	3 years soldier Virginia line	7–12–1783
Snead, Smith	6,223	1159	7 years major Virginia line	6–24–1783
Sneed, John	100	2510	3 years soldier Virginia line	2–18–1784
Sneed, Thomas	100	2838	3 years soldier Virginia line	3–27–1784
Snuggs, George	100	3436	3 years soldier Virginia line	9–10–1784
Soles, William	100	2206	3 years soldier Virginia line	12–23–1783
Sollers, William	100	950	3 years soldier Virginia line	6–20–1783
Solloman, George	100	998	3 years soldier Virginia line	6–21–1783
Solomons, Henry	100	3155	3 years soldier Virginia line	6–12–1784
Somers, William	200	1782	3 years corporal Virginia line	9–23–1783
Sommers, Simon	4,000	3585	3 years adjutant Virginia line	12–17–1784
Son, Anthony	400	1323	During war sergeant Virginia cavalry	7– 3–1783
Sorrell, James	100	2066	3 years soldier Virginia line	12– 9–1783
Sorrell, Richard	100	3095	3 years soldier Virginia line	5–24–1784
Southall, Stephen	2,666⅔	2270	End war lieutenant Virginia line	1–22–1784
Southerland, William	233⅓	3045	7 years soldier Virginia line	5– 4–1784
Southworth, Thomas	200	1293	During war soldier Virginia line	6–28–1783
Spalding, Charles	100	3813	3 years soldier Virginia line	4–21–1785
Span, James	100	1528	3 years soldier Virginia line	8– 8–1783
Span, Richard	100	1527	3 years soldier Virginia line	8– 8–1783
Spang, David	100	3938	3 years soldier Virginia line	8– 2–1785
Sparks, James	200	908	During war soldier Virginia line	6–20–1783
Spearman, James	200	2600	3 years sergeant Virginia line	2–23–1784
Spencer, Abraham	200	1879	During war private Virginia navy	11– 8–1779
Spencer, Benjamin	200	4201	During war soldier Virginia line	8 –28–1786
Spencer, Beverly	100	2334	3 years soldier Virginia line	1–31–1784
Spencer, Henry	100	878	3 years soldier Virginia line	6–19–1783
Spencer, John	2,666⅔	2813	3 years lieutenant Virginia line	3–24–1784
Spencer, John	100	4454	3 years soldier Virginia line	4– 6–1789
Spencer, Moses	100	3817	3 years soldier Virginia line	4–21–1785
Spencer, William	2,666⅔	2451	During war lieutenant Virginia line	2–11–1784
Spencer, William	100	4158	3 years soldier Virginia line	5–22–1786
Spencer, William	200	4372	During war soldier Virginia line	1–23–1788
Spiller, William	4,000	95	3 years captain artillery state line	1–21–1783
Spinner, Richard	100	3435	3 years soldier Virginia line	9–10–1784
Spitter, Benjamin	4,000	3765	3 years captain Virginia line	2–28–1785
Spitzfathem, John	200	3751	3 years sergeant Virginia line	2– 9–1785
Splann, Thomas	100	1333	3 years soldier Virginia line	7– 5–1783
Spotswood, John, Capt	4,000	597	3 years captain Virginia line	5–20–1783
Spratley, Richard	200	535	3 years corporal state line	5– 2–1783
Sprig, Nathan	100	4354	3 years soldier Virginia line	12–20–1787
Springer, Jacob	1,000	228	3 years lieutenant Virginia Cont. line	4– 1–1783
Springer, Jacob	1,366⅔	229	3 years lieutenant Virginia Cont. line	4– 1–1783
Springer, Uriah	2,000	222	3 years captain Virginia Cont. line	4– 1–1783
Springer, Uriah	2,000	223	3 years captain Virginia Cont. line	4– 1–1783
Spruce, John	100	1176	3 years soldier Virginia line	6–25–1783
Spur, John	200	4449	3 years sergeant Virginia line	2–26–1789
Stacey, John	100	1714	3 years soldier Virginia line	9– 2–1783
Stacey, Simon	100	2036	3 years soldier Virginia line	12– 6–1783
Stacy, Stephen	100	2707	3 years soldier Virginia line	3– 4–1784
Stackpole, James	200	1136	During war soldier Virginia line	5–24–1783
Staekhouse, John	100	3504	3 years soldier Virginia line	11– 4–1784
Stakely, Charles	444	1569	Lieutenant Virginia line services	8–14–1783
Stakes, Silvanus	100	2643	3 years soldier Virginia line	2–26–1784
Stanback, Littleberry	100	3291	3 years sailor Virginia navy	7– 1–1784
Standley, Moses	100	3186	3 years soldier Virginia line	6–22–1784
Stanley, William	100	2015	3 years soldier Virginia line	12– 5–1783
Stape, Thomas	200	2306	During war soldier Virginia line	1–28–1784
Staples, Jos.	200	3658	3 years soldier Virginia line	12–31–1784
Staves, William	200	419	During war soldier Virginia line	4–26–1783
Stark, Richard	2,666⅔	137	3 years lieutenant Virginia line	2–20–1783
Starks, Burwell	2,666⅔	2433	3 years lieutenant Virginia line	2– 9–1784
Steed, John	4,000	826	3 years captain Virginia line	6–14–1783

Name	Acres	Warrant	Service	Date
Steel, John..............	200....	602....	3 years lieutenant Virginia line......	5–20–1783
Steel, William...........	1,000...	1672....	3 years lieutenant Virginia line......	8–26–1783
Steel, William...........	1,666⅔..	1673....	3 years lieutenant Virginia line......	8–26–1783
Stencham, Henry........	400....	1401....	During war corporal Virginia line....	7–21–1783
Stephard, Edward.......	200....	1141....	During war soldier Virginia line......	6–24–1783
Stephens, John..........	100....	3620....	3 years soldier Virginia line.........12–23–1784
Stephens, John..........	200....	4515....	During war soldier Virginia line.....	2– 1–1791
Stephens, Richard.......	100....	2413....	3 years soldier Virginia line.........	2– 5–1784
Stephens, Thomas.......	400....	1405....	7 years corporal Virginia line.......	7–21–1783
Stephenson, David......	6,222..	347....	7 years major Virginia Cont. line....	4–16–1783
Stevens, Edward........	5,000...	1917....	3 years brigadier general Virginia line.11–21–1783
Stevens, Edward........	3,000...	1918....	3 years brigadier general Virginia line.11–21–1783
Stevens, Edward........	2,000...	1919....	3 years brigadier general Virginia line.11–21–1783
Stevens, Edward........	200....	3349....	3 years sergeant Virginia line........	7–22–1784
Stevens, James.........	100....	2676....	3 years soldier Virginia line.........	3– 3–1784
Stevens, John..........	200....	1839....	3 years sergeant Virginia line........10– 9–1783
Stevens, John..........	100....	2750....	3 years soldier Virginia line.........	3–10–1784
Stevens, John..........	100....	2805....	3 years soldier Virginia line.........	3–22–1784
Stevens, Joseph........	200....	4479....	3 years sergeant Virginia line........11–21–1789
Stevens, Peter..........	200....	3388....	3 years sergeant Virginia line........	8–10–1784
Stevens, Warrington.....	100....	3628....	3 years soldier Virginia line.........12–29–1784
Stevens, William.......	2,666⅔..	1791....	3 years lieutenant Virginia line......	9–25–1783
Stevenson, Hugh........	6,666⅔..	2988....	3 years colonel Virginia line........	4–21–1784
Stevenson, William......	2,666⅔..	4140....	3 years lieutenant Virginia line......	4– 5–1786
Stern, Charles..........	200....	1566....	3 years sergeant Virginia line........	8–13–1783
Stern, David...........	400....	4584....	During war sergeant Virginia line....	7–11–1792
Stewart, Benjamin.......	233⅓...	1854....	7 years soldier Virginia line.........10–13–1783
Stewart, Edward........	100....	3366....	3 years soldier Virginia line.........	7–29–1784
Stewart, Marks.........	100....	3778....	3 years soldier Virginia line.........	3–12–1785
Stewart, Patrick........	100....	1510....	3 years soldier Virginia line.........	8– 6–1783
Stewart, Philip.........	2,666⅔..	2338....	During war lieutenant Virginia line...	1–31–1784
Stewart, Solomon.......	100....	252....	3 years soldier state line............	4– 3–1783
Stewart, Robert........	100....	4163....	3 years soldier Virginia line.........	5–29–1786
Stewart, William.......	100....	39....	3 years soldier state artillery........12–11–1782
Steuben, Maj-Genl......	15,000..	104....	Military service by special act.......	1–30–1783
Stillwell, Joseph........	100....	4275....	3 years soldier Virginia line.........	4– 7–1787
Stith, John.............	5,000...	26....	3 years captain Virginia Cont. line...11–30–1782
Stith, John.............	4,000...	1852....	3 years captain Virginia line.........10–13–1783
StLeger, William........	100....	1715....	3 years soldier Virginia line.........	9– 2–1783
Stockdell, John.........	100....	2850....	3 years soldier Virginia line.........	3–31–1784
Stokely, Charles........	2,666⅔..	793....	3 years lieutenant Virginia Cont. line. 6–12–1783
Stokes, Christopher......	200....	2123....	3 years sergeant Virginia line........12–15–1783
Stokes, John...........	4,666⅔..	1396....	7 years captain Virginia line.........	7–19–1783
Stokes, John...........	100....	3547....	3 years soldier Virginia line.........11–30–1784
Stokes, Robert.........	200....	907....	During war soldier Virginia line......	6–20–1783
Stoakes, Zackariah.......	100....	3323....	3 years soldier Virginia line.........	7–14–1784
Stoll, William..........	2,666⅔..	2870....	3 years lieutenant Virginia navy.....	4– 3–1784
Stone, William.........	100....	2016....	3 years soldier Virginia line.........12– 5–1783
Stonnett, alias Stoner, Richard..............	200....	4161....	During war soldier Virginia line......	5–27–1786
Story, John.............	100....	3649....	3 years soldier Virginia line.........12–31–1784
Stotherd, Thomas.......	100....	914....	3 years soldier Virginia line.........	6–20–1783
Stowark, Henry.........	200....	4548....	During war soldier Virginia line......11–15–1791
Strange, William........	100....	2617....	3 years soldier Virginia line.........	2–24–1784
Stratton, Seth..........	200....	3834....	During war soldier Virginia line......	4–29–1785
Straughan, John........	100....	1206....	3 years soldier Virginia line.........	6–26–1783
Straughan, Presley.......	100....	1923....	3 years soldier Virginia line.........10–27–1783
Street, John............	100....	2956....	3 years soldier Virginia line.........	4–17–1784
Stribling, Segismond.....	4,666⅔..	996....	7 years captain Virginia line.........	6–21–1783
Stringfellow, David......	400....	3044....	During war sergeant Virginia line....	5– 4–1784
Stringfellow, Henry......	200....	3613....	During war soldier Virginia line......12–23–1784
Strong, William........	200....	3935....	3 years corporal Virginia line........	8– 1–1785
Strother, William.......	400....	2534....	During war sergeant Virginia line....	2–19–1785
Stuart, James..........	200....	4623....	During war private Virginia line......	9–18–1793
Stuart, John...........	100....	4000....	3 years soldier Virginia line.........11–19–1785
Stubblefield, Beverly.....	4,000...	1203....	3 years captain Virginia line.........	6–26–1783
Stubblefield, George.....	2,166⅔..	1171....	3 years ensign Virginia Cont. line....	6–25–1783
Stubbs, Allen..........	200....	2810....	During war soldier Virginia line......	3–23–1784
Stubbs, Allen..........	100....	3407....	3 years soldier Virginia line.........	8–23–1784
Stubbs, Francis.........	100....	616....	3 years soldier Virginia line.........	5–21–1783
Stubling, William........	400....	3478....	During war sergeant Virginia line....10–22–1784
Stump, Michael........	100....	933....	3 years soldier Virginia line.........	6–20–1783
Stur, Thomas..........	100....	1459....	3 years sailor Virginia navy.........	8– 1–1783
Sturdivan, John.........	200....	3389....	During war soldier Virginia line......	8–11–1784
Sublett, Benjamin.......	200....	899....	3 years sergeant Virginia line........	6–20–1783
Suddeth, William.......	200....	3495....	3 years corporal Virginia line........11– 3–1784
Suddeth, William.......	100....	2746....	3 years soldier Virginia line.........	3–10–1784
Suddoth, John..........	100....	3073....	3 years soldier Virginia line.........	5–11–1784
Sullins, William........	200....	3959....	During war soldier Virginia line......	8–12–1785
Sullivan, Craven........	100....	3259....	3 years soldier Virginia line.........	6–30–1784
Sullivan, Frederick.......	100....	3355....	3 years soldier Virginia line.........	7–23–1784

Name	Acres	Warrant	Service	Date
Sullivan, John	200	1364	3 years corporal Virginia line	7–12–1783
Sulser, Matthew	100	3650	3 years soldier Virginia line	12–31–1784
Summers, James	200	422	During war soldier Virginia line	4–26–1783
Summerson, Gavin	2,666⅔	1579	3 years midshipman Virginia navy	8–18–1783
Summerson, George	200	1907	During war soldier Virginia line	10–23–1783
Sunkins, Reuben	200	3998	During war soldier Virginia line	6–21–1785
Susong, Andrew	100	3851	3 years soldier Virginia line	5– 6–1785
Sutton, Benjamin	200	2524	3 years corporal Virginia line	2–19–1784
Sutton, Martin	100	4324	3 years soldier Virginia line	11– 1–1787
Sutton, Rowland	100	2526	3 years soldier Virginia line	2–19–1784
Swan, John	4,666⅔	3039	7 years captain Virginia line	5– 3–1784
Swart, James	200	1593	During war soldier Virginia line	8–20–1783
Swearingen, Joseph	4,000	341	3 years captain Virginia Cont. line	4–15–1783
Swearingen, Joseph	666⅔	4478	7 years captain Virginia line	11–19–1789
Sweeny, Thomas	200	4616	During war private Virginia line	6–20–1793
Swillivant, James	100	2659	3 years soldier Virginia line	3– 1–1784
Swope, John	1,000	86	3 years surgeon in navy of Virginia	1– 2–1783
Swope, John	5,000	87	3 years surgeon in navy of Virginia	1– 2–1783
Sydnor, Fortunatus	200	3085	During war soldier Virginia line	5–21–1784
Sykes, George	100	704	3 years soldier Virginia line	5–31–1783
Tabb, Augustine	4,000	313	3 years captain Virginia state line	4–11–1783
Talley, John Jr	200	3798	During war soldier Virginia line	4– 6–1785
Talley, John Sr	200	3797	During war soldier Virginia line	4– 6–1785
Talley, Thomas	100	4415	3 years soldier Virginia line	7–17–1788
Taliaferro, Nicholas	2,666⅔	854	3 years lieutenant Virginia line	6–17–1783
Taliaferro, William	6,000	1963	3 years lieutenant colonel Virginia line	11–25–1783
Talliaferro, Capt Ben	4,666⅔	559	7 years captain Virginia Cont. line	5– 8–1783
Tallom, Peter	100	2795	3 years soldier Virginia line	3–19–1784
Tennehill, Josiah	1,333.½	234	3 years lieutenant Virginia Cont. line	4– 5–1783
Tannehill, Josiah	1,333.½	235	3 years lieutenant Virginia Cont. line	4– 1–1783
Tannehill, Thomas	400	1037	During war sergeant Virginia line	6–24–1783
Tanner, John	100	4447	3 years soldier Virginia line	1– 9–1789
Tanner, William	100	2903	3 years soldier Virginia line	4– 7–1784
Tapley, Thomas	200	1630	During war soldier Virginia line	8–22–1783
Tapp, Vincent	200	1322	3 years sergeant Virginia line	7– 3–1783
Tapscott, Ezekiel	100	3319	3 years sailor Virginia navy	7– 6–1784
Tapscott, John	100	3318	3 years sailor Virginia navy	7– 6–1784
Tapscott, John	200	4574	3 years sergeant Virginia line	5– 5–1792
Tasker, James	100	2189	3 years soldier Virginia line	12–22–1783
Tate, Adam	200	438	During war fifer state line	4–26–1783
Tate, James	100	3939	3 years soldier Virginia line	8– 2–1785
Tate, Robert	100	3688	3 years soldier Virginia line	1–11–1785
Tate, Robert	100	4383	3 years sailor Virginia navy	1–29–1788
Tatum, Zackariah	2,666⅔	2648	3 years subaltern Virginia line	2–28–1784
Taylor, Archibald	200	1602	During war soldier Virginia line	8–20–1783
Taylor, Benjamin	2,666⅔	1012	3 years midshipman Virginia navy	6–23–1783
Taylor, Bartholomew	200	333	During war soldier cavalry	4–14–1783
Taylor, Charles	100	2056	3 years soldier Virginia line	12– 9–1783
Taylor, Ferguson	100	1496	3 years fifer in Virginia line	8– 5–1783
Taylor, Francis	5,333⅓	1937	3 years major Virginia line	11–22–1783
Taylor, Humphrey	100	668	3 years soldier Virginia line	5–29–1783
Taylor, Isaac	466⅔	1276	7 years sergeant Virginia line	6–28–1783
Taylor, Isaac	4,000	2686	3 years captain Virginia line	3– 3–1784
Taylor, James	200	1499	3 years sergeant Virginia line	8– 5–1783
Taylor, James	100	2341	3 years soldier Virginia line	1–31–1784
Taylor, James	200	2422	3 years sergeant Virginia line	2– 6–1784
Taylor, James	200	2877	During war soldier Virginia line	4– 5–1784
Taylor, James	100	4052	3 years drum major Virginia line	12–21–1785
Taylor, James	200	4626	During war private Virginia line	10–26–1793
Taylor, John	100	4047	3 years soldier Virginia line	12–20–1785
Taylor, Major	200	336	During war soldier cavalry	4–14–1783
Taylor, Reuben	4,000	1936	3 years captain Virginia line	11–22–1783
Taylor, Richard	5,333⅓	133	3 years captain in navy	2–19–1783
Taylor, Richard	6,000	1734	3 years lieutenant colonel Virginia line	9– 8–1783
Taylor, Robert	200	3364	3 years sergeant Virginia line	7–29–1784
Taylor, Robert	100	3854	3 years soldier Virginia line	5– 6–1785
Taylor, Samuel	100	334	3 years soldier Virginia Cont. line	4–14–1783
Taylor, Thornton	2,666⅔	3446	3 years lieutenant Virginia line	9–20–1784
Taylor, William	5,333⅓	132	3 years major Virginia line	2–19–1783
Taylor, William	200	3636	3 years sergeant Virginia line	12–29–1784
Taylor, William	200	4074	3 years soldier Virginia line	1–14–1786
Teagle, Severn	4,000	4578	3 years captain Virginia line	6– 4–1792
Tear, Hammer	100	1859	3 years soldier Virginia line	11– 6–1783
Telkins, John	100	1932	3 years soldier Virginia line	10–29–1783
Temple, Alexander	100	3824	3 years sailor Virginia navy	4–23–1785
Temple, Benjamin	6,000	2417	3 years lieutenant Virginia line	2– 6–1784
Temple, John	100	3298	3 years soldier Virginia line	7– 1–1784
Terrant, Manlove	400	3584	During war sergeant Virginia line	12–16–1784
Terrell, Edward	200	1974	3 years sergeant Virginia line	11–26–1783
Terrell, William	400	1394	During war corporal Virginia line	7–19–1783
Terry, James	100	3961	3 years soldier Virginia line	8–12–1785

Name	Acres	Warrant	Service	Date
Terry, Nathanial	4,666⅔	2601	7 years captain Virginia line	2–23–1784
Terry, Stephen	200	203	3 years corporal state line	3–26–1783
Tharp, Elkana	400	2280	7 years sergeant Virginia line	1–24–1784
Thayers, William	466⅔	1637	During war sergeant major Virginia line	8–23–1783
Theel, Levi	100	3342	3 years soldier Virginia line	7–19–1784
Thomas, Amos	200	540	During war soldier state line	5– 3–1783
Thomas, Daniel	200	1256	During war soldier Virginia line	6–27–1783
Thomas, Elisha	100	3463	3 years soldier Virginia line	10–15–1784
Thomas, Henry	100	2892	3 years soldier Virginia line	4– 5–1784
Thomas, Jacob	100	2765	3 years soldier Virginia line	3–16–1784
Thomas, John	4,000	4071	3 years captain Virginia navy	1–13–1786
Thomas, Joseph	100	3177	3 years soldier Virginia line	6–21–1784
Thomas, Joseph	100	3464	3 years soldier Virginia line	10–15–1784
Thomas, Lewis	4,000	2753	6 years captain Virginia line	3–11–1784
Thomas, Massey	100	2539	3 years soldier Virginia line	2–19–1784
Thomas, William	400	526	During war corporal state line	5– 2–1783
Thomas, William	200	541	During war soldier state line	5– 3–1783
Thomas, William	100	2058	3 years soldier Virginia line	12– 9–1783
Thomas, William	100	2940	3 years soldier Virginia line	4–17–1784
Thompson, Clanders	400	1422	During war corporal Virginia line	7–23–1783
Thompson, Daniel	100	662	3 years soldier Virginia line	5–28–1783
Thompson, George	2,666⅔	2481	3 years lieutenant Virginia line	2–12–1784
Thompson, George	100	3931	3 years soldier Virginia line	8– 1–1785
Thompson, Henry	100	2788	3 years soldier Virginia line	3–18–1784
Thompson, James	100	939	3 years soldier Virginia line	6–20–1783
Thompson, John	200	2611	3 years sergeant Virginia line	2–24–1784
Thompson, John	100	2816	3 years soldier Virginia line	3–24–1784
Thompson, John	400	4169	During war corporal Virginia line	6–12–1786
Thompson, Littlebony	100	266	3 years soldier state line	4– 3–1783
Thompson, Patrick	200	2094	3 years sergeant Virginia line	12–10–1783
Thompson, Robert	200	1284	During war soldier Virginia line	6–28–1783
Thompson, Royal	100	2439	3 years soldier Virginia line	2– 9–1784
Thompson, Smith	100	3004	3 years soldier Virginia line	4–22–1784
Thompson, Thomas	100	1237	3 years soldier Virginia line	6–27–1783
Thompson, William	4,000	36	3 years captain regiment artillery	12–10–1782
Thompson, William	200	3332	3 years corporal Virginia line	7–19–1784
Thorn, Richard	200	3509	During war soldier Virginia line	11– 8–1784
Thornburn, John	200	1321	During war soldier Virginia line	7– 2–1783
Thornhill, Thomas	200	3254	During war soldier Virginia line	6–30–1784
Thornton, Pat	200	1122	During war soldier Virginia line	6–24–1783
Thornton, Presley	4,000	846	3 years captain Virginia line	6–17–1783
Thornton, William	200	2026	During war soldier Virginia line	12– 6–1783
Thweatt, Thomas	4,000	205	3 years captain Virginia line	3–27–1783
Thrall, John	2,666⅔	4195	3 years lieutenant Virginia line	8– 9–1786
Throckmorton, Albion	100	3206	During war subaltern Virginia line	6–24–1784
Throckmorton, Albion Jr.	1,666⅔	3207	During war subaltern Virginia line	6–24–1784
Thurstien, William	100	4011	3 years soldier Virginia line	12– 2–1785
Tibbs, Thomas	400	1330	3 years captain Virginia line	7– 5–1783
Tiller, William	200	3134	3 years corporal Virginia line	6– 8–1784
Tillery, John	200	1448	During war soldier Virginia line	7–31–1783
Timberlake, Joseph	233⅓	1205	7 years soldier Virginia line	6–26–1783
Times, Peter	200	4131	During war soldier Virginia line	3–18–1786
Timmons, John	200	3448	3 years sergeant Virginia line	9–23–1784
Tinsley, Johnathan	200	1634	During war soldier Virginia line	8–22–1783
Tinsley, Samuel	2,666⅔	2017	3 years cornet Virginia line	12– 5–1783
Tipton, Abraham	4,000	4458	3 years captain Virginia line	5–18–1789
Todd, Robert	4,000	2580	3 years captain Virginia line	2–21–1784
Toler, William	200	1180	3 years corporal Virginia artillery	6–25–1783
Tolin, Elias	200	925	3 years sergeant Virginia line	6–20–1783
Tomlin, John	100	964	3 years soldier Virginia line	6–20–1783
Tomlin, William	200	2484	3 years sergeant Virginia line	2–13–1784
Tomlinson, Herbert	100	3239	3 years soldier Virginia line	6–29–1784
Tomlinson, Joseph	100	3240	3 years soldier Virginia line	6–29–1784
Tomlinson, Littleberry	100	3238	3 years soldier Virginia line	6–29–1784
Tompkins, Christopher	2,666⅔	2497	3 years subaltern Virginia line	2–14–1784
Tompkins, Christopher	2,666⅔	4544	3 years lieutenant Virginia navy	11–14–1791
Tompkins, Daniel	1,000	2667	3 years lieutenant Virginia line	3– 2–1784
Tompkins, Daniel	1,666⅔	2668	3 years lieutenant Virginia line	3– 2–1784
Tompkins, Henry	2,666⅔	405	3 years ensign Cont. line	4–25–1783
Tompkins, Robert	2,666⅔	404	3 years lieutenant Cont. line	4–25–1783
Tompkins, Robert	4,000	4545	3 years captain Virginia navy	11–14–1791
Tony, Vincent	100	2396	3 years soldier Virginia line	2– 3–1784
Toney, Archibald	100	3992	3 years soldier Virginia line	11– 9–1785
Toney, Reuben	100	3991	3 years soldier Virginia line	11– 9–1785
Tonnell, George	200	3422	During war soldier Virginia line	8–28–1784
Toot, James	200	3914	During war soldier Virginia line	6–21–1785
Tornham, Thomas	100	3257	3 years soldier Virginia line	6–30–1784
Towers, John	200	648	During war soldier Virginia line	5–28–1783
Towers, John	100	100	3 years soldier Virginia line	1–23–1783
Towels, Oliver	6,000	855	3 years lieutenant colonel Virginia line	6–17–1783
Towns, John	2,666⅔	1986	3 years lieutenant Virginia line	11–28–1783

Name	Acres	Warrant	Service	Date
Townsend, Ewel	200	3579	3 years corporal Virginia line	12–15–1784
Townsend, George	100	254	3 years soldier state line	4– 3–1783
Townsend, John	200	3796	During war soldier Virginia line	4– 6–1785
Townsend, William	200	1389	During war soldier Virginia line	7–17–1783
Trabue, John	2,666⅔	2515	During war lieutenant Virginia line	2–18–1784
Trabue, William	200	2729	3 years sergeant Virginia line	3– 6–1784
Travis, Edward	5,333⅓	2653	3 years captain Virginia line	2–28–1784
Travis, Miles	100	4149	3 years soldier Virginia line	4–26–1786
Treach, Dawson	100	667	3 years soldier Virginia line	5–29–1783
Treach, John	100	666	3 years soldier Virginia line	5–28–1783
Treacle, William	100	676	3 years soldier Virginia line	5–29–1783
Treacle, William	100	2353	3 years soldier Virginia line	1–31–1784
Treekle, John	100	592	3 years soldier Virginia line	5–17–1783
Trent, Thomas	200	2370	3 years sergeant Virginia line	2– 3–1784
Trezvant, John	6,000	2377	During war surgeon Virginia line	2– 3–1784
Trice, Dabney	100	3565	3 years soldier Virginia line	12– 9–1784
Trice, William	100	3566	3 years soldier Virginia line	12– 9–1784
Tripps, Adam	200	3018	3 years sergeant Virginia line	4–26–1784
Triplett, Daniel	200	467	3 years sergeant state line	4–29–1783
Triplett, George	2,666⅔	245	3 years lieutenant Virginia line	4– 1–1783
Triplett, Nathaniel	400	2050	During war sergeant Virginia line	12– 9–1783
Triplett, Roger	1,000	4528	3 years lieutenant Virginia line	7–21–1790
Triplett, Roger	1,000	4529	3 years lieutenant Virginia line	7–21–1791
Triplett, Roger	666⅔	4530	3 years lieutenant Virginia line	7–21–1791
Triplett, William	200	737	3 years soldier Virginia line	6– 4–1783
Triplett, William	2,666⅔	4099	3 years lieutenant Virginia line	1–28–1786
Trotter, John	200	2875	During war soldier Virginia line	4– 5–1784
Trout, Lawrence	4,000	649	3 years captain Virginia line	5–28–1783
Tucker, James	200	1552	3 years sergeant Virginia line	8–11–1783
Tucker, Michael	200	2981	3 years sergeant Virginia line	4–21–1784
Tucker, Robert	100	4429	3 years soldier Virginia line	8– 4–1788
Tucker, William	100	615	3 years soldier Virginia line	5–21–1783
Tuggle, Henry	100	2399	3 years soldier Virginia line	2– 3–1784
Tuggles, Joshua	100	2147	3 years soldier Virginia line	12–18–1783
Tugler, William	200	1870	During war soldier Virginia line	11– 7–1783
Tune, William	200	2128	3 years sergeant Virginia line	12–15–1783
Tunstall, Edward	200	59	3 years sergeant state artillery	12–19–1782
Tunstall, Henry	200	2774	3 years sergeant Virginia line	3–18–1784
Tunstall, Thomas Jr	200	1876	3 years sergeant Virginia line	10–15–1783
Tupman, John	2,666⅔	213	3 years master state navy	4– 1–1784
Turk, James	100	1235	3 years soldier Virginia line	6–27–1783
Turk, Robert	100	1242	3 years soldier Virginia line	6–27–1783
Turlington, Jacob	100	4334	3 years soldier Virginia line	11–13–1787
Turner, Francis	100	1763	3 years soldier Virginia line	9–13–1783
Turner, George	100	4555	3 years soldier Virginia line	11–29–1791
Turner, G	100	4417	3 years soldier Virginia line	7–17–1788
Turner, John	2,666⅔	2407	During war lieutenant Virginia line	2– 5–1784
Turner, John	200	4102	3 years sergeant Virginia line	1–31–1786
Turner, Johan	100	4483	3 years soldier Virginia line	12– 4–1789
Turner, Richard	200	3450	During war soldier Virginia line	9–25–1784
Turner, Thomas	100	4484	3 years soldier Virginia line	12– 4–1789
Turner, William	100	1443	3 years soldier Virginia line	7–30–1783
Turner, William	100	4421	3 years soldier Virginia line	7–17–1788
Turpin, Obediah	200	2958	3 years sergeant Virginia line	4–17–1784
Turvey, William	200	2019	During war soldier Virginia line	12– 5–1783
Tutt, Charles	2,666⅔	369	— years lieutenant Virginia Cont. line	4–19–1783
Tyler, Benjamin	200	3884	During war soldier Virginia line	5–26–1785
Tyler, John	2,666⅔	3301	3 years lieutenant Virginia line	7– 1–1784
Tyler, William	100	1859	3 years soldier Virginia line	10–14–1783
Tyler, William	200	2783	During war soldier Virginia line	3–18–1784
Tyree, John	100	3654	3 years soldier Virginia line	12–31–1784
Tyree, William	100	312	3 years soldier Virginia Cont. line	4–11–1783
Tyser, Cornelius	100	364	3 years soldier state line	4–18–1783
Underwood, Gideon	200	590	3 years corporal Virginia line	5–17–1783
Upshaw, James	4,000	3276	Services as captain Virginia line	7– 1–1784
Upshaw, Thomas	4,000	340	3 years captain state line	4–15–1783
Usher, William	100	1367	3 years soldier Virginia line	7–12–1783
Utterback, Benjamin	100	1913	3 years soldier Virginia line	11–20–1783
Vaden, Bradock	200	3506	During war soldier Virginia line	11– 5–1784
Vaden, John	200	790	3 years corporal Virginia line	6–12–1783
Valentine, Edward	4,000	2761	3 years captain Virginia line	3–15–1784
Valentine, Isham	100	3600	3 years soldier Virginia line	12–21–1784
Valentine, Jacob	4,000	179	3 years captain Virginia state line	3–14–1783
Valentine, Joseph	100	4590	3 years private Virginia line	10–30–1792
Vandewall, Markes	2,666⅔	139	3 years lieutenant Virginia Cont. line	2–21–1783
Vanmeter, Joseph	2,666⅔	744	3 years ensign Virginia line	6– 5–1783
Vance, Joseph	100	938	3 years soldier Virginia line	6–20–1783
Vance, William	4,000	3554	3 years captain Virginia line	12– 6–1784
Vasser, Daniel	200	2603	3 years sergeant Virginia line	2–24–1784
Vasser, Isham	200	2390	3 years corporal Virginia line	2– 3–1784
Vaughan, Claiborn	2,666⅔	2556	3 years surgeon Virginia line	2–20–1784

Name	Acres	Warrant	Service	Date
Vaughan, James.........	200	4228	3 years sergeant Virginia line.........	11–15–1786
Vaughan, John...........	2,666⅔	2568	3 years lieutenant Virginia line......	2–21–1784
Vaughan, John...........	200	4541	3 years sergeant Virginia line.......	11–10–1791
Vaughan, Patrick........	100	3855	3 years soldier Virginia line.........	5– 6–1785
Vaughan, Richard.......	100	1856	3 years soldier Virginia line.......	11– 5–1783
Vaughan, Sherwood......	200	4124	3 years sergeant Virginia line.......	3–10–1786
Vaughan, Thomas.......	100	2301	3 years soldier Virginia line........	1–27–1784
Vawler, Beverly.........	100	3792	3 years soldier Virginia line........	4– 1–1785
Vawler, William.........	2,666⅔	97	3 years lieutenant Virginia line......	1–21–1783
Vawter, Benjamin.......	100	739	3 years soldier Virginia line........	6– 4–1783
Veal, Solomon...........	200	917	3 years sergeant Virginia line.......	6–20–1783
Verat, Joel.............	100	2634	3 years soldier Virginia line........	2–25–1784
Vernan, Thomas.........	100	2916	3 years soldier Virginia line........	4–12–1784
Veroney, Joseph.........	200	2780	During war soldier Virginia line.....	3–18–1784
Vest, George...........	100	3362	3 years soldier Virginia line........	7–27–1785
Vincent, John...........	200	4466	3 years corporal Virginia line.......	10– 5–1789
Vickers, William........	200	3193	During war soldier Virginia line.....	6–23–1784
Vickers, William........	100	3361	3 years soldier Virginia line........	7–27–1784
Violet, John...........	200	1104	During war soldier Virginia line.....	6–24–1783
Vogluson, Armand.......	4,000	21	3 years captain state cavalry........	11–25–1782
Vowles, Charles........	2,666⅔	161	3 years lieutenant state line........	3– 7–1783
Vowles, Henry..........	4,000	162	3 years captain artillery...........	3– 7–1783
Vowles, Walter.........	4,666⅔	163	Services as captain state line.......	3– 7–1783
Waddy, Thomas.........	200	4058	During war soldier Virginia line.....	12–31–1785
Waddy, Shapleigh.......	2,666⅔	3281	3 years midshipman Virginia navy....	7– 1–1784
Wade, Acro............	200	2872	During war soldier Virginia line.....	3– 2–1784
Wade, David...........	100	269	3 years soldier state line...........	4– 3–1783
Wade, Moses...........	100	795	3 years soldier Virginia line.........	6–12–1783
Wafield, George.........	100	952	3 years soldier Virginia line........	6–20–1783
Waggoner, Andrew.......	6,222	1003	7 years major Virginia line..........	6–21–1783
Waggoner, William......	200	3454	3 years sergeant Virginia line.......	10– 2–1784
Wail, Wilmore..........	100	4356	3 years soldier Virginia line........	12–28–1787
Walch, David...........	200	4491	3 years matross Virginia line........	3–24–1790
Walden, Elijah..........	100	2923	3 years soldier Virginia line........	4–12–1784
Walden, George.........	200	1271	3 years sergeant Virginia line.......	6–28–1783
Walden, John...........	200	1268	3 years corporal Virginia line.......	6–28–1783
Walden, Spencer........	100	4375	3 years soldier Virginia line........	1–23–1788
Walden, Zackariah......	100	282	3 years soldier Virginia line........	4– 3–1783
Walker, David..........	2,666⅔	1890	3 years lieutenant Virginia line......	10–18–1783
Walker, Edward........	200	1123	During war soldier Virginia line.....	6–24–1783
Walker, Henry..........	100	1875	3 years soldier Virginia line........	10–15–1783
Walker, Jacob..........	4,000	814	3 years captain Virginia line........	6–14–1783
Walker, James..........	100	3267	3 years sailor Virginia navy........	7– 1–1784
Walker, Jeremiah.......	100	1938	3 years soldier Virginia line........	10–31–1783
Walker, Jeremiah.......	200	2695	During war soldier Virginia line.....	3– 3–1784
Walker, John...........	200	1845	During war soldier Virginia line.....	10–10–1783
Walker, John...........	100	1878	3 years soldier Virginia line........	10–15–1783
Walker, John...........	100	4328	3 years soldier Virginia line........	11– 3–1787
Walker, John...........	200	4595	During war private Virginia line.....	11–26–1792
Walker, Levin..........	2,666⅔	2376	3 years lieutenant Virginia line......	2– 3–1784
Walker, Levin..........	2,666⅔	2849	3 years lieutenant Virginia line......	3–30–1784
Walker, Thomas........	100	4091	3 years soldier Virginia line........	1–23–1786
Walker, William........	100	385	3 years Virginia Cont. line.........	4–23–1783
Walkerholt, Jacob.......	100	2886	3 years soldier Virginia line........	4– 5–1784
Wallace, Adam.........	4,000	3195	3 years captain Virginia line........	6–23–1784
Wallace, Andrew.......	4,000	3196	3 years captain Virginia line........	6–23–1784
Wallace, Edward.......	100	4262	3 years soldier Virginia line........	3–25–1787
Wallace, Edmund.......	200	3071	During war soldier Virginia line.....	5–11–1784
Wallace, Gustanus B.....	7,000	102	7 years lieutenant colonel Virginia line	1–30–1784
Wallace, James.........	100	1531	3 years soldier Virginia line.........	8– 8–1783
Wallace, James.........	2,666⅔	3194	3 years ensign Virginia line.........	6–23–1784
Wallace, Dr James......	6,000	1004	3 years surgeon Virginia line........	6–23–1783
Wallace, Nathaniel......	100	770	3 years soldier Virginia line........	6– 7–1783
Wallace, Thomas.......	200	4605	During war private Virginia line.....	1–25–1793
Wallace, Thomas.......	2,666⅔	4501	3 years lieutenant Virginia line......	10–22–1790
Wallace, William B......	2,666⅔	702	7 years lieutenant Virginia line......	5–31–1783
Waller, Daniel..........	100	3159	3 years soldier Virginia line........	6–15–1784
Waller, Edward........	2,500	3804	3 years major Virginia line..........	4–12–1785
Waller, Edward........	2,666⅔	3805	3 years major Virginia line..........	4–12–1785
Waller, John...........	200	1567	3 years sergeant Virginia line.......	8–13–1783
Waller, John...........	200	4408	3 years sergeant Virginia line.......	6–27–1788
Waller, William........	100	983	3 years soldier Virginia line........	6–20–1783
Waller, William........	200	447	During war soldier Virginia line.....	4–28–1783
Wallerson, Robert.......	200	2165	3 years corporal Virginia line.......	12–20–1783
Walls, George..........	7,110⅔	3315	8 years major Virginia line..........	7– 3–1784
Walter, William........	200	2579	During war soldier Virginia line.....	2–21–1784
Walton, Tilman........	200	2748	3 years sergeant Virginia line.......	3–10–1784
Ward, George..........	100	1692	3 years soldier Virginia line........	8–30–1783
Ward, Lawrence........	100	3313	3 years soldier Virginia line........	7– 2–1784
Ward, William.........	100	4085	3 years soldier Virginia line........	1–19–1786
Ware, Moses...........	400	1097	During war sergeant Virginia line.....	6–24–1783

Name	Acres	Warrant	Service	Date
Ware, William	100	1357	3 years soldier Virginia line	7–12–1783
Warick, William	200	839	3 years sergeant Virginia line	6–16–1783
Waring, Henry	2,666⅔	4182	3 years lieutenant Virginia line	6–29–1786
Warman, Capt Thomas	2,000	620	3 years captain Virginia line	5–22–1783
Warman, Capt Thomas	1,000	621	3 years captain Virginia line	5–22–1783
Warman, Capt Thomas	1,000	622	3 years captain Virginia line	5–22–1783
Warneck, Frederick	5,000	829	3 years lieutenant colonel Virginia line.	6–14–1783
Warneck, Frederick	200	830	3 years lieutenant colonel Virginia line.	6–14–1783
Warneck, Frederick	200	831	3 years lieutenant colonel Virginia line.	6–14–1783
Warneck, Frederick	200	832	3 years lieutenant colonel Virginia line.	6–14–1783
Warneck, Frederick	200	833	3 years lieutenant colonel Virginia line.	6–14–1783
Warneck, Frederick	200	834	3 years lieutenant colonel Virginia line.	6–14–1783
Warner, John	200	891	During war musician Virginia line	6–20–1783
Warner, John	100	892	During war musician Virginia line	6–20–1783
Warner, John	200	3406	3 years sergeant Virginia line	8–23–1784
Warren, Drury	100	4430	3 years soldier Virginia line	8– 4–1788
Warren, Gabriel	100	3786	3 years soldier Virginia line	3–25–1785
Warren, John	200	1463	During war soldier Virginia line	8– 1–1783
Warren, John	100	4566	3 years soldier Virginia line	1–31–1792
Wash, Benjamin	100	2502	3 years soldier Virginia line	2–16–1784
Wash, Thomas	200	2501	3 years soldier Virginia line	2–16–1784
Washington, George	2,666⅔	135	3 years lieutenant Virginia line	2–20–1783
Washington, William	7,000	2265	7 years lieutenant colonel Virginia line	1–21–1784
Waterfield, John	200	3897	During war soldier Virginia line	6–21–1785
Waterfield, Peter	100	2134	3 years soldier Virginia line	12–15–1783
Waters, James	400	1848	During war sergeant Virginia line	11– 1–1783
Waters, James	100	2170	3 years sailor Virginia navy	12–20–1783
Waters, Richard	666⅔	2222	— captain Virginia line	1– 7–1784
Waters, Thomas	200	1899	During war soldier Virginia line	11–15–1783
Watkins, David	100	4453	3 years soldier Virginia line	4– 8–1789
Watkins, Jesse	100	3949	3 years soldier Virginia line	8–10–1785
Watkins, John	200	2757	3 years sergeant Virginia line	3–12–1784
Watkins, Robert	200	3309	3 years sergeant Virginia line	7– 2–1784
Watkins, Samuel	200	3339	During war soldier Virginia line	7–19–1784
Watkins, William	200	517	During war soldier Virginia state line	5– 1–1783
Watson, James	100	3704	3 years soldier Virginia line	1–20–1785
Watson, William	400	449	During war captain Virginia line	4–28–1783
Watts, Gideon	200	2008	During war soldier Virginia line	12– 3–1783
Watts, John	4,666⅔	1936	7 years captain Virginia line	10–31–1783
Watts, Martin	200	2781	During war soldier Virginia line	3–18–1784
Watts, Reuben	100	3647	3 years soldier Virginia line	12–31–1784
Watts, Samuel	200	4022	3 years corporal Virginia line	12– 5–1785
Watts, William	100	3820	3 years soldier Virginia line	4–22–1785
Wayland, Joshua	100	3116	3 years soldier Virginia line	5–30–1784
Wayne, Benjamin	100	4509	3 years soldier Virginia line	12– 7–1790
Weaver, John	200	392	During war soldier Virginia line	4–24–1783
Weaver, John	200	2404	During war soldier Virginia line	2– 4–1784
Webb, James	100	1512	3 years sailor Virginia navy	8– 6–1783
Webb, John	6,000	116	3 years lieutenant Virginia regiment	2– 8–1783
Webb, Joseph	100	3955	3 years sailor Virginia navy	8–12–1785
Webb, Isaac	200	2246	3 years lieutenant Virginia line	1–13–1784
Webb, Richard	200	399	During war soldier Virginia line	4–25–1783
Webb, Thomas	100	1743	3 years soldier Virginia line	9–11–1783
Webber, Philip	200	2662	3 years sergeant Virginia line	3– 1–1784
Webster, Richard	100	4318	3 years soldier Virginia line	10–23–1787
Wedgbar, William	200	1449	During war soldier Virginia line	7–31–1783
Weeden, Augustine	200	1300	3 years sergeant Virginia line	6–30–1783
Weedon, George	10,000	91	3 years Brig. Genl. Virginia Cont. line.	1– 3–1783
Weedon, Brig Genl George.	1,666⅔	798	7 years military service	6–13–1783
Welch, Benjamin	100	2759	3 years soldier Virginia line	3–12–1784
Welch, Dominick	200	2787	During war soldier Virginia line	3–18–1784
Welch, Isaac	100	2657	3 years soldier Virginia line	3– 1–1784
Welch, John	200	3736	3 years sergeant Virginia line	2– 7–1785
Welch, Jonathan	200	1149	During war soldier Virginia line	6–24–1783
Welch, Lang	200	577	During war soldier Virginia state line	5–14–1783
Welch, Nathaniel	4,000	443	3 years captain Virginia line	4–26–1783
Welch, Patrick	200	2364	3 years sergeant Virginia line	2– 2–1784
Welch, Robert	200	1526	During war soldier Virginia line	8– 8–1783
Welch, Sylvester	100	2758	3 years soldier Virginia line	3–12–1784
Weldy, William	200	3353	During war soldier Virginia line	7–22–1784
Wells, James	100	1997	3 years soldier Virginia line	11–29–1783
West, Beriah	200	4139	3 years corporal Virginia line	4– 5–1786
West, Charles	5,333⅓	3242	Services as major	6–29–1784
West, Randolph	100	3163	3 years soldier Virginia line	6–16–1784
West, Thomas	100	3145	3 years soldier Virginia line	6–10–1784
West, William	100	2491	3 years sailor Virginia navy	2–13–1784
Westcott, Wright	4,000	311	3 years captain state navy	4–11–1783
Westmoreland, Jesse	100	2814	3 years soldier Virginia line	3–24–1784
Westmoreland, Joseph	100	2815	3 years soldier Virginia line	3–24–1784
Wetherale, John	100	3130	3 years soldier Virginia line	6– 5–1784
Whale, John	200	441	During war soldier Virginia line	4–26–1783

Name	Acres	Warrant	Service	Date
Whaling, John	200	3569	3 years soldier Virginia line	12–13–1784
Whealer, John	100	3656	3 years soldier Virginia line	12–31–1784
Wheattey, William	200	3917	During war soldier Virginia line	6–21–1785
Wheeler, James	100	3657	3 years soldier Virginia line	12–31–1784
Wheller, John	200	440	During war soldier state line	4–26–1783
Wherley, Mathew	100	2963	3 years soldier Virginia line	4–19–1784
Wheely, John	100	639	3 years soldier Virginia line	5–26–1783
Whistler, Sawney	200	3081	During war soldier Virginia line	5–17–1784
Whitaker, James	200	496	During war soldier state line	4–30–1783
Whitaker, Thomas	100	3769	3 years soldier Virginia line	3– 5–1785
Whitaker, William	2,666⅔	2121	3 years lieutenant Virginia line	12–13–1783
White, Anthony W	6,666⅔	4254	3 years lieutenant colonel Virginia line	1–29–1787
White, Benjamin	100	4146	3 years soldier Virginia line	4–19–1786
White, Edward	100	1803	3 years soldier Virginia line	9–30–1783
White, George	100	2841	3 years soldier Virginia line	3–29–1784
White, James	200	725	3 years soldier Virginia line	6– 3–1783
White, James	100	726	3 years soldier Virginia line	6– 3–1783
White, James	100	3022	3 years soldier Virginia line	4–26–1784
White, James	100	3232	3 years soldier Virginia line	6–29–1784
White, James	400	4355	During war corporal Virginia line	12–22–1787
White, Jesse	100	4033	3 years soldier Virginia line	12–10–1785
White, John	2,666⅔	651	Services lieutenant Virginia cavalry	5–27–1783
White, John	2,666⅔	1376	3 years lieutenant Virginia line	7–15–1783
White, John	444	2248	—lieutenant Virginia line	1–15–1784
White, John	100	3058	3 years sailor Virginia navy	5– 7–1784
White, Randolph	100	4536	3 years soldier Virginia line	11–10–1791
White, Richard	200	1258	During war soldier Virginia line	6–27–1783
White, Robert	4,000	303	Lieutenant Virginia Cont. line	4– 8–1783
White, Robert	100	3108	3 years soldier Virginia line	5–28–1784
White, Tarpley	4,000	1375	3 years captain Virginia line	7–15–1783
White, Thomas	2,666⅔	2320	3 years lieutenant Virginia line	1–30–1784
White, Thomas	100	2470	3 years soldier Virginia line	2–11–1784
White, William	2,666⅔	99	3 years lieutenant infantry	1–21–1783
White, William	4,000	174	3 years captain Virginia Cont. line	3–11–1783
White, William	4,000	1572	3 years captain Virginia line	8–15–1783
White, William	666⅔	2504	7 years captain Virginia line	2–17–1784
White, William	100	2890	3 years soldier Virginia line	4– 5–1784
White, William	100	2913	3 years soldier Virginia line	4–10–1784
White, William	100	3711	3 years soldier Virginia line	1–20–1785
Whitehead, John	100	2345	3 years sailor Virginia navy	1–31–1784
Whitetors, Levi	200	1961	3 years soldier Virginia line	11–24–1784
Whitfield, Edward	100	3024	3 years soldier Virginia line	4–27–1784
Whitfield, Haynes	100	1954	3 years sailor Virginia navy	11–22–1783
Whiting, Francis	2,666⅔	131	3 years lieutenant cavalry	2–19–1783
Whiting, Henry	4,000	2349	3 years captain Virginia line	1–31–1784
Whitley, Abraham	100	3360	3 years soldier Virginia line	7–26–1784
Whitlow, Francis	100	134	3 years soldier Virginia line	2–19–1783
Whitlow, Michael	200	2650	During war soldier Virginia line	2–28–1784
Whitmore, William	400	512	During war soldier state line	5– 1–1783
Whitmore, William	100	3592	3 years soldier Virginia line	12–21–1784
Whirley, Peter	100	3661	3 years soldier Virginia line	12–31–1784
Whitsoll, Jacob	100	3875	3 years soldier Virginia line	5–10–1785
Whitson, Anthony	100	3354	3 years soldier Virginia line	7–22–1784
Whitt, Shadrack	200	4599	During war private Virginia line	12–13–1792
Whitton, Daniel	200	3345	During war soldier Virginia line	7–19–1784
Widdows, Robert	100	3312	3 years soldier Virginia line	7– 2–1784
Wigley, Job	100	3314	3 years soldier Virginia line	7– 3–1784
Wilday, George	400	462	During war corporal Virginia line	4–28–1783
Wilder, James	100	2429	3 years sailor Virginia navy	2– 9–1784
Wilder, George	100	2489	3 years sailor Virginia navy	2–13–1784
Wilhiby, Jesse	100	2528	3 years soldier Virginia line	2–19–1784
Wilkerson, Benjamin	100	3548	3 years soldier Virginia line	11–30–1784
Wilkerson, Barnabas	200	2710	3 years sergeant Virginia line	3– 5–1784
Wilkerson, David	200	2640	During war soldier Virginia line	2–26–1784
Wilkerson, Drury	100	2664	3 years soldier Virginia line	3– 1–1784
Wilkerson, Thomas	100	2709	3 years soldier Virginia line	3– 5–1784
Wilkins, Thomas	200	1457	During war drummer Virginia line	8– 1–1783
Wilkins, Thomas	200	3894	During war soldier Virginia line	6–16–1785
Wilkinson, John	200	4035	During war soldier Virginia line	12–12–1785
Wilks, Burrell	200	2075	3 years sergeant Virginia line	12–10–1783
Williams, Alexander	100	2994	3 years soldier Virginia line	4–21–1784
Williams, Charles	100	2704	3 years soldier Virginia line	3– 4–1784
Williams, Christopher	200	445	During war soldier Virginia line	4–26–1783
Williams, Daniel	100	3236	3 years soldier Virginia line	6–29–1784
Williams, Daniel	200	4361	During war soldier Virginia line	1–10–1788
Williams, David	2,666⅔	860	3 years lieutenant Virginia line	6–18–1783
Williams, Edward	2,666⅔	743	3 years ensign Virginia line	6– 5–1783
Williams, George	200	882	During war soldier Virginia line	6–20–1783
Williams, Henry	100	1581	3 years soldier Virginia line	8–18–1783
Williams, Capt James	4,666⅔	598	7 years captain Virginia line	5–20–1783
Williams, Jarrett	2,666⅔	2682	3 years lieutenant Virginia line	3– 3–1784

Name	Acres	Warrant	Service	Date
Williams, John	4,000	155	3 years captain artillery Virginia line	3– 3–1783
Williams, John	200	343	During war soldier state line	4–15–1783
Williams, John	400	887	During war sergeant Virginia line	6–20–1783
Williams, John	200	888	3 years sergeant Virginia line	6–20–1783
Williams, John	400	1036	Service as sergeant Virginia line	6–24–1783
Williams, John	200	2405	During war soldier Virginia line	2– 4–1784
Williams, John	200	3470	During war soldier Virginia line	10–18–1784
Williams, John	4,000	4561	3 years captain Virginia line	12–22–1791
Williams, Lawrence Lot	100	473	3 years soldier state line	4–29–1783
Williams, Moses	100	3283	3 years sailor Virginia navy	7– 1–1784
Williams, Philemon	200	366	During war soldier state line	4–19–1783
Williams, Rice	100	2204	3 years soldier Virginia line	12–23–1783
Williams, Thomas	100	260	3 years soldier state line	4– 3–1783
Williams, Thomas	100	3672	3 years soldier Virginia line	1– 5–1785
Williams, William	100	262	3 years soldier state line	4– 3–1783
Williams, William	200	1282	During war soldier Virginia line	6–28–1783
Williams, Zebediah	100	259	3 years soldier state line	4– 3–1783
Williamson	100	2718	3 years soldier Virginia line	3– 5–1784
Willis, Henry	4,000	1033	3 years captain Virginia line	6–23–1783
Willis, James	100	4366	3 years sailor Virginia navy	1–17–1788
Willis, John	200	393	During war soldier Virginia line	4–24–1783
Willis, John	6,222	753	7 years major Virginia line	6– 6–1783
Willis, William	200	1456	During war soldier Virginia line	7–31–1783
Willis, William	200	4259	3 years sergeant Virginia line	2–21–1787
Willoughby, William	100	2401	3 years soldier Virginia line	2– 3–1784
Wills, George	200	4395	During war soldier Virginia line	3–31–1788
Wills, Nathaniel	200	4593	During war private Virginia line	11– 9–1792
Willson, Thomas	2,666⅔	4537	3 years lieutenant Virginia line	11–10–1791
Wilmington, John	200	2775	3 years soldier Virginia line	3–18–1784
Wilson, Henry	100	4619	3 years private Virginia line	8– 5–1793
Wilson, Isaac	200	2287	3 years sergeant Virginia line	1–26–1784
Wilson, James	100	1241	3 years soldier Virginia line	6–27–1783
Wilson, James	200	2830	3 years sergeant Virginia line	3–26–1784
Wilson, James	200	3907	During war soldier Virginia line	6–21–1785
Wilson, James	100	4128	3 years soldier Virginia line	3–18–1786
Wilson, John	2,666⅔	4309	3 years lieutenant Virginia line	10– 1–1787
Wilson, John	100	2140	3 years soldier Virginia line	12–16–1783
Wilson, John Madvy	100	3300	3 years soldier Virginia line	7– 1–1784
Wilson, Peter	100	2917	3 years soldier Virginia line	4–12–1784
Wilson, Stacey	400	1261	During war sergeant Virginia line	6–27–1783
Wilson, Whitfield	200	4088	During war soldier Virginia line	1–21–1786
Wilson, Willis	2,666⅔	2	3 years lieutenant Virginia Cont. line	8–15–1782
Wilson, Willis	5,333⅓	2869	3 years captain Virginia navy	4– 3–1784
Wily, George, Jr	6,000	117	3 years lieutenant Virginia regiment	2– 8–1783
Wimbish, John	200	2808	3 years sergeant Virginia line	3–23–1784
Winder, Jesse	200	1721	3 years sergeant Virginia line	9– 2–1783
Wingall, Martin	100	2950	3 years soldier Virginia line	4–17–1784
Winlock, Joseph	1,333⅓	238	3 years lieutenant Virginia Cont. line	4– 1–1783
Winlock, Joseph	1,333⅓	239	3 years lieutenant Virginia Cont. line	4– 1–1783
Winn, Harrison	200	4236	During war soldier Virginia line	12–16–1786
Winphrey, John	100	1684	3 years soldier Virginia line	8–29–1783
Winslow, Benjamin	2,666⅔	425	3 years ensign Virginia Cont. line	4–26–1783
Winston, Capt John	4,000	610	3 years captain Virginia line	5–21–1783
Winston, Robert	100	4586	3 years private Virginia line	10– 2–1792
Winston, William	2,666⅔	1677	3 years lieutenant Virginia line	8–27–1783
Winter, George	100	642	3 years soldier Virginia line	5–26–1783
Winters, Stephen	200	1138	During war soldier Virginia line	6–24–1783
Wise, Samuel	100	2486	3 years soldier Virginia line	2–13–1784
Wofler, Thomas	100	2943	3 years soldier Virginia line	4–17–1784
Wolf, Andrew	200	3734	During war soldier Virginia line	2– 7–1785
Wolf, George	100	2523	3 years soldier Virginia line	2–19–1784
Wolfinburger, Philip	200	3689	During war soldier Virginia line	1–11–1785
Wollard, John	100	2434	3 years soldier Virginia line	2– 9–1784
Womack, Ephram	200	2250	3 years corporal Virginia line	1–16–1784
Wood, Benjamin	200	4573	During war soldier Virginia line	5– 5–1792
Wood, Edward	200	326	During war soldier Virginia line	4–12–1783
Wood, Edward	100	4248	3 years soldier Virginia line	1– 5–1787
Wood, James	1,000	297	3 years colonel Virginia line	4– 7–1783
Wood, James	1,000	298	3 years colonel Virginia Cont. line	4– 7–1783
Wood, James	4,666⅔	299	3 years colonel Virginia Cont. line	4– 7–1783
Wood, James	200	1625	During war soldier Virginia line	8–22–1783
Wood, James	1,111	3889	3 years colonel Virginia line	9–26–1783
Wood, Jesse	100	1795	3 years soldier Virginia line	12–12–1783
Wood, John	200	2109	3 years sergeant Virginia line	3– 6–1784
Wood, John	100	2725	3 years soldier Virginia line	6–30–1784
Wood, John	100	3258	3 years soldier Virginia line	11– 3–1787
Wood, John	100	4326	3 years soldier Virginia line	5–12–1786
Wood, John L	100	4157	3 years soldier Virginia line	6–24–1783
Wood, Joseph	200	1150	During war soldier Virginia line	8–22–1783
Wood, Nicholas	200	1633	During war soldier Virginia line	4–30–1783
Wood, Phillip	200	492	During war soldier state line	4–30–1783

Name	Acres	Warrant	Service	Date
Wood, Robert	200	431	During war soldier state line	4–26–1783
Wood, Thomas	400	1035	3 years sergeant major Virginia line	6–24–1783
Wood, William	400	1638	During war corporal Virginia line	8–23–1783
Wood, William	100	4278	3 years soldier Virginia line	4– 7–1787
Woodcock, John	100	360	3 years soldier Virginia Cont. line	4–18–1783
Woodford, William	10,000	1606	3 years brig. gen. Virginia line	8–20–1783
Woodman, John	200	1125	During war soldier Virginia line	6–24–1783
Woods, Alexander	200	4495	7 years soldier Virginia line	5–27–1790
Woods, William	200	1120	During war soldier Virginia line	6–24–1783
Woodson, Abselom	100	2387	3 years soldier Virginia line	2– 3–1784
Woodson, Frederick	4,000	470	3 years captain state line	4–29–1783
Woodson, Hughes	4,000	1751	3 years captain Virginia line	9–11–1783
Woodson, Robert	4,000	180	7 years captain Virginia Cont. line	3–15–1783
Woodson, Robert	666⅔	181	7 years captain Virginia Cont. line	3–15–1783
Woodson, Tarlton	5,333⅓	1928	3 years major Virginia line	10–28–1783
Woodward, Charles	100	251	3 years soldier state line	4– 3–1783
Woolfork, Francis	200	1679	3 years sergeant Virginia line	8–27–1783
Woolfork, William	200	2316	3 years sergeant Virginia line	1–29–1784
Woolridge, Joseph	100	4552	3 years soldier Virginia line	11–26–1791
Woosley, Aaron	200	2671	During war soldier Virginia line	3– 2–1784
Woosley, Moses	100	2455	3 years ——————	2–11–1784
Woosley, Thomas	200	2670	During war soldier Virginia line	3– 2–1784
Wootten, Thomas	200	2361	During war soldier Virginia line	2– 2–1784
Word, Hugh	200	3733	During war soldier Virginia line	2– 7–1785
Worsham, John	2,666⅔	2647	3 years lieutenant Virginia line	2–27–1784
Worsham, Richard	1,000	183	3 years lieutenant Virginia Cont. line	3–18–1783
Worsham, Richard	1,666⅔	184	3 years lieutenant Virginia Cont. line	3–18–1783
Worsham, William	2,666⅔	3533	3 years lieutenant Virginia line	11–23–1783
Worth, William	100	758	3 years sailor Virginia navy	6– 6–1783
Woster, William	400	2726	During war soldier Virginia line	3– 6–1784
Wren, Alexander	100	1933	3 years soldier Virginia line	11–22–1783
Wren, Robert	100	4100	3 years soldier Virginia line	1–28–1786
Wren, Travis	100	3358	3 years soldier Virginia line	7–24–1784
Wright, James	4,666⅔	2740	7 years captain Virginia line	3– 9–1784
Wright, James	100	2873	3 years soldier Virginia line	4– 5–1784
Wright, Jarrott	200	4306	3 years corporal Virginia line	8–20–1787
Wright, John	100	2090	3 years soldier Virginia line	12–10–1783
Wright, Moses	100	2936	3 years soldier Virginia line	4–16–1784
Wright, Patrick	4,000	42	3 years captain state artillery	12–12–1782
Wright, Paul	100	2454	3 years soldier Virginia line	2–11–1784
Wright, Richard	100	1336	3 years soldier Virginia line	7– 5–1783
Wright, Robert	100	776	3 years soldier Virginia line	6–10–1783
Wright, Thomas	100	1016	3 years soldier Virginia line	6–23–1783
Wright, Thomas	200	3808	During war soldier Virginia line	4–16–1785
Wyatt, Benjamin	200	607	3 years private Virginia line	5–21–1783
Wyatt, Carey	4,000	120	3 years captain state artillery	2– 8–1783
Wyatt, Edward	100	4426	3 years soldier Virginia line	7–17–1788
Wyatt, George	200	2728	3 years sergeant Virginia line	3– 6–1784
Wyatt, John	100	684	3 years soldier Virginia line	5–30–1783
Wyatt, Pitman	100	3067	3 years soldier Virginia line	5–10–1784
Wyatt, William	100	756	3 years soldier Virginia line	6– 6–1783
Wyne, Benjamin	200	2040	During war soldier Virginia line	12– 9–1783
Yager, John	200	3967	During war soldier Virginia line	9–12–1785
Yancey, Absalom	100	3978	3 years soldier Virginia line	10– 5–1785
Yancey, James	200	4023	3 years corporal Virginia line	12– 5–1785
Yancey, Robert	1,000	201	3 years captain light dragoons	3–26–1783
Yancey, Robert	3,000	202	3 years captain light dragoons	3–26–1782
Yancey, Robert	666⅔	3132	7 years captain Virginia line	6– 5–1784
Yancy, Layton	2,666⅔	2921	3 years subaltern Virginia line	4–12–1784
Yancy, Lewis	100	3127	3 years soldier Virginia line	6– 5–1784
Yancy, Ludwell	100	3070	3 years soldier Virginia line	5–11–1784
Yarbrough, Charles	2,666⅔	1730	3 years lieutenant Virginia line	9– 8–1783
Yarrington, Oliver	100	763	3 years Virginia artillery	6– 6–1783
Yates, George	1,000	4321	3 years surgeons mate Virginia navy	10–20–1787
Yates, George	666⅔	4322	3 years surgeons mate Virginia navy	10–26–1787
Yates, John	2,666⅔	4084	3 years lieutenant Virginia line	1–18–1786
Yearly, Samuel	200	3957	3 years sergeant Virginia line	8–12–1785
Yeger, Henry	100	2554	3 years soldier Virginia line	2–20–1784
Young, Duncan	200	3170	During war soldier Virginia line	6–17–1784
Young, Frederick	200	275	3 years sergeant Virginia line	4– 3–1783
Young, Captain Henry	4,000	612	3 years captain Virginia line	5–21–1783
Young, John	200	1052	During war soldier Virginia line	6–24–1783
Young, Nathan	200	1020	3 years soldier Virginia line	6–23–1783
Young, Robert	100	2876	3 years soldier Virginia line	4– 5–1784
Young, Samuel	100	2115	3 years soldier Virginia line	12–13–1783
Young, Thomas	4,000	4385	3 years captain Procketts regiment	2– 4–1788
Young, William	200	2630	3 years soldier Virginia line	2–25–1784
Yours, William	200	164	3 years corporal Virginia Cont. line	3– 8–1783
Yowell, Samuel	100	1977	3 years soldier Virginia line	11–26–1783
Zimmerman, John	100	3945	3 years soldier Virginia line	8–10–1785
Zimmerman, William	200	1539	3 years sergeant Virginia line	8– 9–1783

VI

MILITARY ENTRIES

(1784-1797)

Entree	Acres	Book	Page	Entry Date	Watercourse	Notes
Alexander, Jesse	400	1	219	8- 1-1791	Russell Cr	Surveyed
Allen, Jno	1,000	1	287	4-30-1792	Upper Beaver Cr	Surveyed
Allen, Jno	1,000	1	288	4-30-1792	Big Barren R	Surveyed
Allen & Montgomery	1,200	1	115	8-13-1784	Cumberland R	Withdrawn
Allen & Montgomery	1,200	1	176	4-14-1786	Barren R	Surveyed
Allison, Jno	1,200	1	11	8- 3-1784	Mississippi R	
Allison, Jno	1,200	1	37	8- 6-1784	None	Withdrawn
Allison, Jno	1,200	1	74	8-10-1784	None	
Allison, Jno	1,200	1	94	8-11-1784	Clarks R	
Allison, Jno	1,200	1	97	8-12-1784	Red Stone Cr	
Allison, Jno	1,200	1	129	8-14-1784	None	
Anderson, David	600	1	24	8- 4-1784	Cumberland R	Withdrawn
Anderson, David	600	1	45	8- 6-1784	Tennessee R	
Anderson, David	600	1	49	8- 6-1784	Mayfield Cr	Withdrawn
Anderson, David	866⅔	1	60	8- 7-1784	Tennessee R	Withdrawn
Anderson, David	866⅔	1	75	8-10-1784	Tennessee R	Withdrawn
Anderson, David	600	1	95	8-11-1784	Ohio R	
Anderson, David	600	1	102	8-12-1784	None	
Anderson, David	600	1	103	8-12-1784	Mississippi R	
Anderson, David	866⅔	1	131	9-28-1784	Tennessee R	Surveyed
Anderson, David	866⅔	1	131	9-28-1784	Tennessee R	Surveyed
Anderson, David	1,500	1	148	10- 2-1785	Russell Cr	Surveyed
Anderson, David	2,000	1	150	10- 3-1785	Glenns Cr	Surveyed
Anderson, David	4,000	1	170	1-11-1786	Russell Cr	Withdrawn
Anderson, David	3,200	1	184	10- 1-1786	Glenns Cr	Surveyed
Anderson, David	928	1	202	3- 8-1788	Russell Cr	Surveyed.
Anderson, Richard	1,000	1	89	8-11-1784	Harlans Cr	
Anderson, Richard	900	1	79	8-10-1784	Cumberland R	Surveyed
Anderson, Richard	1,000	1	35	8- 5-1784	Tennessee R	
Anderson, Richard	1,000	1	25	8- 4-1784	Skeggs Cr	Surveyed
Anderson, Richard	900	1	6	8- 2-1784	Mississippi R	
Anderson, Richard	1,110⅔	1	3	8- 2-1784	Mississippi R	
Anderson & Fousher	1,000	1	70	8-10-1784	S Fk Clarks Cr	
Andrews, Robt	400	1	54	8- 7-1784	W Fk Crocus Cr	Surveyed
Andrews, Robt	1,000	1	64	8- 7-1784	N Fk W Fk Red R.	Withdrawn
Andrews, Robt	500	1	283	4-28-1792	Green R	Surveyed
Andrews, Robt	500	1	283	4-28-1792	Green R	Amended
Andrews, Robt	500	1	284	4-28-1792	Green R	Surveyed
Andrews, Robt	1,000	1	289	4-30-1792	Big Barren R	Withdrawn
Armistead, Wm	1,000	1	40	8- 6-1784	Fk Big Barren R	Surveyed
Armstead, Wm	1,000	1	84	8-11-1784	None	
Armstead, Wm	1,000	1	88	8-11-1784	None	
Armstead, Wm	1,000	1	105	8-12-1784	Skeggs Cr	
Ashey, David	100	1	180	7-10-1786	Whipporwill Cr	Withdrawn
Askey, Zachariah	200	1	171	3- 8-1786	N Fk Red R	Withdrawn
Askey, Zachariah	100	1	294	4-30-1792	Far Fk Red R	
Askey, Zachariah	100	1	294	4-30-1792	S Pilot Knob	
Askey, Zachariah	50	1	294	4-30-1792	Spring Cr	Surveyed
Askey, Zachariah	50	1	294	4-30-1792	Far Fk Red R	
Austin, Jno W	400	1	30	8- 5-1784	Russell Cr	
Ayers, Saml	200	1	181	7-11-1786	Green R	Surveyed
Bailey, Jno	1,000	1	10	8- 3-1784	S Fk Clarks Cr	
Bailey, Jno	1,000	1	22	8- 4-1784	Big Barren R	Surveyed
Bailey, Jno	1,000	1	98	8-12-1784	Cumberland R	
Bailey, Jno	1,000	1	100	8-12-1784	Cumberland R	Withdrawn
Bailey, Jno	1,000	1	239	9-16-1791	Skeggs Cr	Withdrawn
Bailey, Jno	1,000	1	251	2-25-1792	Little Barren R	Withdrawn
Bailey, Jno	1,000	1	264	4-27-1792	Caney Cr	Surveyed
Ballard, Wm	666½	1	160	12-13-1785	Fk Skeggs Cr	Surveyed
Ballard, Wm	666½	1	162	12-13-1785	Big Barren R	Withdrawn
Ballard, Wm	666½	1	162	12-13-1785	Skeggs Cr	Surveyed
Ballard, Wm	666⅔	1	163	12-13-1785	Big Barren R	Surveyed
Ballard, Wm	666⅔	1	200	2-24-1788	E Fk Drakes Cr	Surveyed
Ballendin, Thos & Wm.	300	1	293	4-30-1792	None	Surveyed
Banks & Roberts	1,000	1	141	5-18-1785	Clarks R	Withdrawn
Banks & Roberts	1,000	1	141	5-18-1785	Clarks R	Withdrawn
Banks & Roberts	3,000	1	148	8-13-1785	Russell Cr	Withdrawn
Banks & Roberts	4,000	1	148	8-13-1785	Wolf Cr	Withdrawn
Banks & Roberts	850	1	168	1-11-1786	Russell Cr	Surveyed
Banks & Roberts	4,510¾	1	169	1-11-1786	Russell Cr	Withdrawn

Entree	Acres	Book	Page	Entry Date	Watercourse	Notes
Banks & Roberts	100	1	182	9-29-1786	Red R	Surveyed
Banks & Roberts	300	1	182	9-29-1786	M Fk Red R	
Banks & Roberts	100	1	182	9-29-1786	Red R	Surveyed
Banks & Roberts	1,000	1	184	10- 1-1786	Wolf Cr	
Banks & Roberts	7,110⅔	1	184	10- 1-1786	Wolf & Russell Crs.	Surveyed
Banks & Roberts	1,531	1	184	10- 1-1786	Russell Cr	Surveyed
Banks & Roberts	2,666⅔	1	184	10- 1-1786	Sulphur Fk	Surveyed
Banks & Roberts	1,500	1	185	10- 1-1786	Fk Cumberland R	Surveyed
Banks & Roberts	300	1	185	1- 9-1787	Red R	Withdrawn
Banks & Roberts	1,152¼	1	224	8- 2-1791	Russell Cr	Withdrawn
Banks & Roberts	300	1	235	9- 1-1791	Russell Cr	Withdrawn
Banks & Roberts	1,152⅔	1	242	12- 9-1791	Cumberland R	Surveyed
Banks & Roberts	472⅔	1	242	12- 9-1791	Crocus Cr	Withdrawn
Banks & Roberts	472⅓	1	295	5- 1-1792	Marrowbone Cr	Surveyed
Barnett, Andrew	750	1	154	12- 7-1785	Buck Cr	
Barnett, Wm & Andrew	300	1	218	8- 1-1791	Green R	
Barnett, Wm & Andrew	250	1	218	8- 1-1791	Little Barren R	Withdrawn
Barnett, Wm & Andrew	50	1	218	8- 1-1791	Little Barren R	
Barnett, Wm & Andrew	150	1	220	8- 2-1791	Bear Wallow Grove.	Withdrawn
Barnett, Wm & Andrew	100	1	228	8- 2-1791	Russell Cr	
Barnett, Wm & Andrew	50	1	233	8-23-1791	Bear Wallow	
Barren, Jas	2,000	1	100	8-12-1784	Mayfield Cr	
Barren, Richard	1,333⅓	1	50	8- 6-1784	W Fk Fishing Cr	
Barren, Richard	2,000	1	106	8-12-1784	Skeggs Cr	
Barrett, Jno	200	1	38	8- 6-1784	Russell Cr	Surveyed
Barron, James	2,000	1	3	8- 2-1784	Cumberland R	
Barron, Jas	2,000	1	102	8-12-1784	None	
Barron, Jas	1,777⅔	1	90	8-11-1784	Harlans Cr	
Barron, Richard	2,000	1	86	8-11-1784	Harlins Cr	
Bartlett, Jno	200	1	186	2- 1-1787	Pitman Cr	
Baytop, Jno	1,000	1	31	8- 5-1784	Skeggs Cr	Surveyed
Baytop, Jno	1,666⅔	1	76	8-10-1784	Hunting Cr	
Beale, Jno	1,000	1	12	8- 3-1784	Adtown Columbia	
Bella, Jno	400	1	161	12-13-1785	Skeggs Cr	Surveyed
Bently, Thos	500	1	54	8- 7-1784	W Fk Crocus Cr	Surveyed
Berry, Benj	1,000	1	123	8-14-1784	——— R	
Berry, Benj	1,000	1	123	8-14-1784	——— R	
Berry, Benj	1,000	1	124	8-14-1784	——— R	
Berry, Benj	1,000	1	124	8-14-1784	None	
Biddle, Clement	1,600	1	5	8- 2-1784	5 Mile E Fk Jefferson	
Biddle, Clement	1,000	1	33	8- 5-1784	Tennessee R	
Biddle, Clement	1,000	1	59	8- 7-1784	Delaware Cr	
Biddle, Clement	1,000	1	85	8-11-1784	Hunting Cr	
Biddle, Clement	1,000	1	86	8-11-1784	Hunting Cr	
Biddle, Clement	1,000	1	87	8-11-1784	Hunting Cr	
Biddle, Clement	1,000	1	93	8-11-1784	Clarks R	
Biddle, Clement	1,000	1	98	8-12-1784	Mayfield Cr	
Bivens, Jno A	500	1	193	12-27-1787	Cumberland R	Surveyed
Blackwell, Jno	2,000	1	44	8- 6-1784	E Fk Crocus Cr	Surveyed
Blackwell, Jno	2,000	1	95	8-11-1784	W Fk Clark R	Withdrawn
Blackwell, Jno	2,000	1	221	8- 2-1791	E Fk Barren R	Surveyed
Blakely, Jno	200	1	77	8-10-1784	Flat Lick Br	Surveyed
Bohannon, Ambrose	800	1	114	8-13-1784	Mississippi R	Withdrawn
Bohannon, Ambrose	800	1	114	8-13-1784	Mississippi	Withdrawn
Bohannon, Ambrose	1,066⅔	1	116	8-13-1784	Cumberland R	Withdrawn
Bohannon, Ambrose	1,000	1	177	4-15-1786	Big Barren R	Surveyed
Bohannon, Ambrose	1,000	1	178	5-10-1786	Little R	Surveyed
Bohannon, Ambrose	666⅔	1	197	1-15-1788	Big Barren R	Surveyed
Boswell, Michen	1,000	1	34	8- 5-1784	Cumberland R	Surveyed
Boswell, Mechan	1,000	1	63	8- 7-1784	S Fk Big Barren R.	Surveyed
Boswell, Mechan	1,000	1	83	8-11-1784	Little R	
Boswell, Mechan	1,000	1	86	8-11-1784	Green R	Surveyed
Boush, Chas.	1,300	1	176	4-14-1786	Cumberland R	Withdrawn
Boush, Chas.	700	1	233	8- 4-1791	None	Withdrawn
Boush, Chas	1,000	1	234	8-23-1791	Cumberland Trace	Withdrawn
Boush, Chas	150	1	234	8-30-1791	Green R	Withdrawn
Boush, Chas	200	1	234	8-30-1791	Green R	Withdrawn
Boush, Goodrich	2,000	1	280	4-28-1792	Peter Cr	Surveyed
Boush, Goodrich	1,000	1	280	4-28-1792	N Fk Red R	Surveyed
Boush, Goodrich	500	1	281	4-28-1792	Drakes Cr	Surveyed
Boush, Goodrich	1,000	1	281	4-28-1792	Indian Cr	Surveyed
Boush, Goodrich	833⅓	1	281	4-28-1792	Spring Fk Red R	Surveyed
Bowls, Thos	200	1	77	8-10-1784	Flat Lick Br	Surveyed
Bradford, David	1,700	1	188	3-28-1787	E Fk Little Barren R	Surveyed
Bradford, David	300	1	190	3-28-1787	E Fk Drakes Cr	Withdrawn
Bradford, David	450	1	197	2- 6-1788	Drakes Cr	Surveyed
Bradford, David	2,000	1	211	8- 1-1791	Drakes Cr	
Bradford, Jno	100	1	181	9- 9-1786	Fk Green R	Surveyed
Bradford, Jno	100	1	295	4-30-1792	Skeggs Cr	

Entree	Acres	Book	Page	Entry Date	Watercourse	Notes
Bradford, Samuel K...	900	1	113	8–13–1784	Big Barren R	....
Bradley, James	1,000	1	8	8– 3–1784	Cumberland R	....
Bradley, Jas	1,000	1	20	8– 4–1784	Cane Cr	Surveyed
Bradley, Jas	1,000	1	31	8– 5–1784	Delaware Cr	....
Bradley, Jas	1,000	1	72	8–10–1784	None	....
Brashear, Richard	1,000	1	12	8– 3–1782	Mouth Obyan Cr	....
Brashear, Richard	1,000	1	38	8– 6–1784	Virginia & Carolina Line	....
Brashear, Richard	1,000	1	79	8–10–1784	Cumberland R	Surveyed
Brashear, Richard	1,000	1	102	8–12–1784	Mayfield Cr	....
Brent, Wm	2,000	1	16	8– 4–1784	None	....
Brent, Wm	2,666⅔	1	102	8–12–1784	Island Cr	....
Brent, Wm	2,000	1	108	8–12–1784	None	....
Broadus, Wm	1,000	1	65	8– 7–1784	N Fk W Fk Red R	Surveyed
Brodhed, Daniel Jr	1,000	1	151	12– 6–1785	Green R	Surveyed
Brodhed, Daniel Jr	1,000	1	151	12– 6–1785	Green R	Surveyed
Brodhed, Daniel Jr	1,000	1	152	12– 7–1785	None	Surveyed
Brodhed, Daniel Jr	1,000	1	152	12– 7–1785	None	Surveyed
Brodhead, Daniel Jr	750	1	154	12– 7–1785	Buck Cr	Surveyed
Brodie, Lodawick	1,200	1	14	8– 3–1784	Big Eddy Cr	....
Brodie, L	1,200	1	58	8– 7–1784	S Fk Big Barren R	Surveyed
Brodie, Lodawick	1,200	1	66	8– 7–1784	Pitman Cr	....
Broadie, Lodawick	1,200	1	80	8–10–1784	Cumberland R	Surveyed
Brodie, Ludawick	1,200	1	81	8–10–1784	Cumberland R	Surveyed
Brook, Walter	2,166⅔	1	42	8– 6–1784	Tennessee R	....
Brook, Walter	1,500	1	55	8– 7–1784	Pitman Cr	Surveyed
Brook, Walter	1,500	1	99	8–12–1784	Mayfield Cr	....
Brook, Walter	1,500	1	101	8–12–1784	Mayfield Cr	....
Brough, Thos	400	1	134	1–21–1785	Big Barren R	Surveyed
Brough, Thos	400	1	139	3–31–1785	Big Barren R	Surveyed
Broush, Robt	2,000	1	281	4–28–1792	Big Barren R	Surveyed
Broush, Robt	1,333⅓	1	281	4–28–1792	Indian Cr	Surveyed
Broush, Robt	2,200	1	282	4–28–1792	Drakes Cr	Surveyed
Broush, Robt	666⅔	1	282	4–28–1792	E Fk Little Barren R	Surveyed
Brown, Winsor	1,000	1	14	8– 3–1784	N Fk Clark Cr	....
Brown, Winsor	1,000	1	16	8– 3–1784	Fk Willow Cr	....
Brown, Windsor	1,000	1	70	8–10–1784	Hunting Cr	....
Brown, Winsor	1,666⅔	1	80	8–10–1784	Cumberland R	Amended
Brown, Winsor	1,666⅔	1	147	8–13–1785	Cumberland R	Surveyed
Bryan, Morgan	700	1	170	1–21–1786	Main Beaver Cr	Withdrawn
Bryan, Morgan	100	1	170	1–11–1786	Cumberland R	Withdrawn
Bryan, Morgan	700	1	182	9–11–1786	Cumberland R	Withdrawn
Bryan, Morgan	400	1	193	12– 6–1787	Cumberland R	Surveyed
Bryan, Morgan	300	1	193	12– 6–1787	Cumberland R	Withdrawn
Bryan, Morgan	300	1	203	5–12–1788	Green R	Surveyed
Bryan & Todd	100	1	208	8– 8–1788	Russell Cr	....
Buckner, Philip	100	1	236	9– 8–1791	Crocus Cr	Surveyed
Buford, Abraham	1,666⅔	1	52	8– 6–1784	Big Barren R	....
Buford, Abraham	1,000	1	100	8–12–1784	Cumberland R	....
Bullock, Rice	366⅔	1	164	12–13–1785	Skeggs Cr	Surveyed
Butler, Wm	100	1	279	4–28–1792	W Fk Wolf Cr	....
Callender, Eleazer	2,666⅔	1	46	8– 6–1784	None	Withdrawn
Callender, Eleazer	2,666⅔	1	73	8–10–1784	Pitmans Cr	Withdrawn
Callender, Eleazer	2,000	1	176	4–14–1786	Big Barren R	....
Callender, Eleazer	2,200	1	178	5–10–1786	Cumberland R	Surveyed
Callender, Eleazer	1,133⅓	1	179	5–10–1786	Big Barren R	Withdrawn
Callender, Eleazer	1,133⅓	1	288	4–30–1792	Big Barren R	....
Calloway, Jno	1,000	1	134	1–21–1785	Pitman Cr	Surveyed
Calvert, Joseph	666⅔	1	24	8– 4–1784	Glens Cr	Surveyed
Calvert, Joseph	1,000	1	32	8– 5–1784	Columbia	Withdrawn
Calvert, Joseph	1,666⅔	1	129	8–16–1784	Wolf Cr	Amended
Calvert, Joseph	1,666⅔	1	149	10– 3–1785	None	Surveyed
Calvert, Joseph	500	1	234	8–23–1791	Green R	....
Calvert, Joseph	1,000	1	241	11–30–1791	Caney Fk	....
Calvert, Joseph	100	1	254	4– 9–1792	Green R	Withdrawn
Calvert, Joseph	300	1	254	4– 9–1792	Whipporwill Cr	....
Calvert, Joseph	100	1	278	4–28–1792	Caney Fk	....
Campbell, Wm	1,000	1	8	8– 3–1784	S Fk Consolas Cr	....
Campbell, Wm	1,000	1	25	8– 4–1784	Little R	Withdrawn
Campbell, Wm	1,000	1	46	8– 6–1784	Tennessee R	Withdrawn
Campbell, Wm	1,000	1	73	8–10–1784	None	Withdrawn
Campbell, Wm	1,000	1	220	8– 2–1791	Big Barren R	Surveyed
Campbell, Wm	1,000	1	220	8– 2–1791	Peter Cr	Amended
Campbell, Wm	1,000	1	220	8– 2–1791	Peter Cr	Surveyed
Campbell, Wm	1,000	1	220	8– 2–1791	Peter Cr	Surveyed
Campbell, Wm	1,000	1	285	4–28–1792	Cooks Cr	Surveyed
Campbell, Wm	1,000	1	286	4–28–1792	Peter Cr	Surveyed
Carr, Peter	1,500	1	216	8– 1–1791	Big Barren R	Amended
Carr, Peter	1,000	1	216	8– 1–1791	Sulphur Lick	....
Carr, Peter	1,000	1	216	8– 1–1791	Cumberland R	Withdrawn
Carr, Peter	1,166⅔	1	217	8– 1–1791	Cumberland R	Withdrawn

Entree	Acres	Book	Page	Entry Date	Watercourse	Notes
Carr, Peter	1,500	1	249	2–25–1792	Peter Cr	Surveyed
Carr, Peter	1,166⅔	1	256	4–24–1792	Glovers Cr	Withdrawn
Carr, Peter	1,000	1	257	4–25–1792	Glovers Cr	Surveyed
Carrington, Edward	1,000	1	47	8– 6–1784	Mississippi R	Amended
Carrington, Edward	1,133⅓	1	70	8– 9–1784	Mississippi R	
Carrington, Edward	1,000	1	129	8–16–1784	Cumberland R	
Carrington, Edward	1,000	1	136	2–16–1785	——— R	Surveyed
Carrington, Joseph	1,000	1	2	8– 2–1784	Mississippi	
Carrington, Joseph	1,000	1	19	8– 4–1784	Cumberland R	Withdrawn
Carrington, Joseph	666⅔	1	50	8– 6–1784	——— Cr	Withdrawn
Carrington, Joseph	666⅔	1	137	2–16–1785	Cumberland R	Surveyed
Carrington, Mayo	4,000	1	1	8– 2–1784	Mississippi	
Carrington, Mayo	1,000	1	13	8– 3–1784	Big Eddy Cr	Surveyed
Carrington, Mayo	1,666⅔	1	28	8– 5–1784	Cumberland R	Surveyed
Carrington, Mayo	1,000	1	29	8– 5–1784	Obyan Cr	
Carrington, Mayo	1,000	1	59	8– 7–1784	Mississippi R	
Carrington, Mayo	766⅔	1	81	8–10–1784	Mississippi R	
Carrington, Mayo	1,000	1	98	8–12–1784	Cumberland R	Amended
Carrington, Mayo	1,000	1	148	8–13–1785	Big Eddy	Surveyed
Carter, Chas	100	1	124	8–14–1784	Green R	Suryeyed
Carter, Thos	1,200	1	8	8– 3–1784	None	
Carter, Thos	1,200	1	18	8– 4–1784	Red Stone Cr	Withdrawn
Carter, Thos	1,200	1	21	8– 4–1784	Russells Cr	Surveyed
Carter, Thos	1,200	1	54	8– 7–1784	W Fk Fishing Cr	
Carter, Thos	1,200	1	89	8–11–1784	Harlans Cr	
Carter, Thos	200	1	260	4–26–1792	Nolin Cr	Surveyed
Carter, Thos	1,000	1	260	4–26–1792	Big Barren R	Surveyed
Cary, Samuel	1,333⅓	1	253	3–12–1792	Green R	Withdrawn
Cary, Samuel	1,333	1	253	3–12–1792	Green R	Withdrawn
Cary, Samuel	666⅓	4	271	4–28–1792	Green R	Surveyed
Cary, Samuel	666	1	272	4–28–1792	Fks S Fk Russell Cr	Surveyed
Cary, Samuel	1,334	1	272	4–28–1792	S Fk Green R	
Catlett, Peter	210	1	238	9–10–1791	E Fk Little Barren R	
Chamberlain, Geo	1,000	1	20	8– 4–1784	Cane Cr	Surveyed
Chamberlain, Geo	1,000	1	20	8– 4–1784	Cane Cr	Surveyed
Chamberlain, Geo	1,000	1	21	8– 4–1784	Cane Cr	
Chamberlain, Geo	1,000	1	53	8– 7–1784	Fishing Cr	
Chaplin, Abraham	1,333⅓	1	44	8– 6–1784	Skeggs Cr	Withdrawn
Chaplain, Abraham	666⅔	1	71	8–10–1784	Skeggs Cr	Withdrawn
Chaplin, Abraham	2,000	1	75	8–10–1784	Big Barren R	Withdrawn
Chapline, Abraham	666⅔	1	133	1– 7–1785	Skeggs Cr	Surveyed
Chaplin, Abraham	336⅔	1	137	3–18–1785	Skeggs Cr	Withdrawn
Chaplin, Abraham	336⅔	1	153	12– 7–1785	Beaver Cr	Withdrawn
Chaplin, Abraham	183	1	153	12– 7–1785	Big Barren R	Surveyed
Chaplin, Abraham	174	1	165	12–13–1785	Blue Spring	Surveyed
Chaplin, Abraham	66⅔	1	165	12–13–1785	Blue Spring	Surveyed
Chaplin, Abraham	1,160	1	168	12–19–1785	Beaver Cr	Withdrawn
Chapline, Abraham	1,166⅔	1	177	5– 1–1786	Beaver Cr	Surveyed
Chapline, Abraham	200	1	190	3–28–1787	Little Barren R	Surveyed
Chapline, Abraham	820	1	191	3–29–1787	E Fk Drakes Cr	Withdrawn
Chapline, Abraham	153⅔	1	200	2–24–1788	E Fk Drakes Cr	Surveyed
Chaplin, Chas	1,333⅓	1	132	1– 7–1785	Skeggs Cr	Surveyed
Chapman, Joseph	2,000	1	93	8–11–1784	Clarks R	
Chapman, Joseph	2,000	1	103	8–12–1784	Mulberry Field	
Chism, Jno	100	1	77	8–10–1784	Flat Lick Br	Surveyed
Chism, Jno	200	1	153	12– 7–1785	Fk Red R	Surveyed
Christie, Jas	800	1	144	7– 4–1785	None	Withdrawn
Christie, Jas	400	1	144	7– 4–1785	Cumberland R	Surveyed
Christie, Jas	400	1	144	7– 4–1785	Pitmans Cr	Surveyed
Christie & Coleman	800	1	116	8–13–1784	Cumberland R	Withdrawn
Clark, Daniel	900	1	10	8– 3–1784	None	
Clark, Daniel	866⅔	1	26	8– 4–1784	Ohio R	
Clark, Daniel	900	1	51	8– 6–1784	Ohio R	Withdrawn
Clark, Daniel	900	1	72	8–10–1784	Ohio R	
Clark, Daniel	900	1	85	8–11–1784	Hunting Cr	
Clark, Daniel	900	1	93	8–11–1784	Clarks R	
Clark, Daniel	866⅔	1	101	8–12–1784	Fk Mayfield Cr	
Clark, Daniel	600	1	119	8–14–1784	Clarks R	
Clark, Geo	1,500	1	97	8–12–1784	Cumberland R	Surveyed
Clark, Geo R	1,500	1	16	8– 4–1784	Main Red R	Withdrawn
Clark, Geo R	2,000	1	27	8– 5–1784	Cumberland R	Withdrawn
Clark, Geo Rogers	1,500	1	47	8– 6–1784	W Fk Russell Cr	Withdrawn
Clark, Geo Rogers	1,500	1	49	8– 6–1784	Br Mayfield Cr	Withdrawn
Clark, Geo R	2,000	1	104	8–12–1784	Green R	Withdrawn
Clark, Geo R	1,500	1	130	9–10–1784	Tennessee R	Withdrawn
Clark, Geo R	1,500	1	139	3–31–1785	None	Withdrawn
Clark, Geo R	257	1	140	3–31–1785	Main Red R	Surveyed
Clark, Geo R	420	1	140	3–31–1785	Red R	Surveyed
Clark, Geo R	1,500	1	141	4–10–1785	Clarks R	
Clark, Geo R	1,000	1	230	8– 2–1791	S Fk Little Barren R	Surveyed

Entree	Acres	Book	Page	Entry Date	Watercourse	Notes
Clark, Geo R	500	1	250	2-25-1792	Peter Cr	Surveyed
Clark, Geo R	1,000	1	250	2-25-1792	Peter Cr	Withdrawn
Clark, Geo R	500	1	251	2-25-1792	Boyds Cr	Withdrawn
Clark, Geo R	2,000	1	256	4-24-1792	Little Barren R	Surveyed
Clark, Geo R	1,000	1	268	4-28-1792	S Fk Glovers Cr	Surveyed
Clark, Richard	1,000	1	12	8- 3-1784	Fk Green R	Surveyed
Clark, Richard	1,000	1	60	8- 7-1784	Green R	Surveyed
Clark, Richard	666⅔	1	62	8- 7-1784	Tennessee R	Surveyed
Clark, Thos	100	1	236	9- 8-1791	Fk Red R	Surveyed
Clark, Wm	666⅔	1	14	8- 3-1784	Mayfield Cr	
Clark, Wm	1,000	1	42	8- 6-1784	Russell Cr	Surveyed
Clark, Wm	1,000	1	36	8- 5-1784	None	Withdrawn
Clark, Wm	1,000	1	229	8- 2-1791	S Fk Little Barren R	Surveyed
Clark, Wm	50	1	253	2-25-1792	Little Barren R	Withdrawn
Clark, Wm	50	1	257	4-25-1792	S Fk Little Barren	
Cleverins, Benj	1,000	1	5	8- 2-1784	Mississippi R	
Cleverins, Benj	1,000	1	7	8- 2-1784	Mississippi R	
Cleverins, Benj	1,000	1	9	8- 3-1784	Clay Lick Cr	Surveyed
Cleverins, Benj	1,000	1	74	8-10-1784	N Fk Big Barren R	Surveyed
Clay, Thos	1,000	1	18	8- 4-1784	Cumberland R	Withdrawn
Clay, Thos	1,000	1	37	8- 6-1787	Tennessee R	
Clay, Thos	1,000	1	67	8- 9-1784	None	
Clay, Thos	1,000	1	81	8-10-1784	Cumberland R	Surveyed
Clay, Thos	1,000	1	110	8-12-1784	Goose Pond	
Coleman, James	1,333⅓	1	13	8- 3-1784	Cumberland R	Surveyed
Coleman, Jas	1,333⅓	1	44	8- 6-1784	Crocus Cr	Surveyed
Coleman & Christie	200	1	116	8-13-1784	Cumberland R	
Cook, Jno	100	1	32	8- 5-1784	Russell Cr	Surveyed
Cottrel, Wm	1,366⅔	1	96	8-11-1784	None	
Couch, Samuel	1,066⅔	1	127	8-14-1784	Little Barren R	Withdrawn
Couch, Samuel	1,100	1	127	8-14-1784	—— R	Withdrawn
Couch, Samuel	1,000	1	127	8-14-1784	Beaver Cr	Withdrawn
Couch, Samuel	1,066⅔	1	155	12-13-1785	Little Barren R	Withdrawn
Couch, Samuel	1,000	1	157	12-13-1785	Skeggs Cr	Surveyed
Couch, Samuel	1,000	1	165	12-13-1785	Skeggs Cr	Surveyed
Couch, Samuel	805	1	185	11- 5-1786	Cumberland R	Surveyed
Couch, Samuel	285	1	209	10- 6-1788	Greasy Cr	Surveyed
Cowne, Augustine	1,000	1	8	8- 3-1784	Mouth Island Cr	
Cowne, Augustine	1,666⅔	1	91	8-11-1784	None	
Cowne, Robt	1,000	1	29	8- 5-1784	Little Rock Lick Cr	Surveyed
Cowne, Robt	1,000	1	39	8- 6-1784	Russell Cr	
Cowne, Robt	1,000	1	41	8- 6-1784	None	Surveyed
Cowne, Robt	1,000	1	100	8-12-1784	Mayfield Cr	
Craddock, Robt	590	1	190	3-28-1787	Main Fk Little Barren R	Surveyed
Craddock, Robt	210	1	238	9-10-1791	E Fk Little Barren R	
Craig, Adam	1,000	1	6	8- 2-1784	Mayfield Cr	
Craig, Adam	1,000	1	20	8- 4-1784	Skinn House Cr	Surveyed
Craig, Adam	666⅔	1	25	8- 4-1784	Cumberland R	Surveyed
Craig, Adam	1,000	1	25	8- 4-1784	Cumberland R	Surveyed
Craig, Adam	1,000	1	33	8- 5-1784	Cumberland R	
Craig, Adam	1,100	1	35	8- 5-1784	E Fk Little R	
Craig, Adam	1,000	1	37	8- 6-1784	Cumberland R	
Craig, Adam	666⅔	1	38	8- 6-1784	Cumberland R	Surveyed
Craig, Adam	1,000	1	48	8- 6-1784	W Fk Little R	Surveyed
Craig, Adam	1,000	1	66	8- 7-1784	W Fk Red R	Surveyed
Craig, Adam	1,000	1	108	8-12-1784	Stewarts Skinn House	Surveyed
Craig, Adam	1,000	1	109	8-12-1784	—— R	Surveyed
Craig, Andrew	1,000	1	268	4-28-1792	S Fk Glovers Cr	Surveyed
Craig, Andrew	1,000	1	269	4-28-1792	Glovers Cr	Surveyed
Craig, Andrew	3,000	1	269	4-28-1792	Glovers Cr	
Craig, Andrew	1,000	1	270	4-28-1792	Skeggs Cr	
Craig, Andrew	3,300	1	275	4-28-1792	Clay Lick Fk	Surveyed
Craig, Jno	1,000	1	128	8-14-1784	Russell Cr	Surveyed
Craig, Tolexero	1,000	1	127	8-14-1784	Russell Cr	Surveyed
Crockett, Joseph	1,666⅔	1	30	8- 5-1784	Cumberland R	Withdrawn
Crockett, Joseph	1,000	1	30	8- 5-1784	Cumberland R	Withdrawn
Crockett, Joseph	1,000	1	49	8- 6-1784	None	Withdrawn
Crockett, Joseph	2,000	1	99	8-12-1784	Little R	Withdrawn
Crockett, Joseph	1,000	1	109	8-12-1784	—— Cr	
Crockett, Joseph	2,000	1	138	3-31-1785	W Fk Red R	Surveyed
Crockett, Joseph	1,000	1	138	3-31-1785	W Fk Red R	Surveyed
Crockett, Joseph	2,666⅔	1	172	3- 8-1786	Cumberland R	Surveyed
Crockett, Joseph	583⅓	1	172	3- 8-1786	Green R	Surveyed
Croghan, Wm	4,000	1	1	8- 2-1784	Mississippi	
Croghan, Wm	1,366⅔	1	2	8- 2-1784	Ohio R	
Croghan, Wm	1,000	1	4	8- 2-1784	Mayfield Cr	
Croghan, Wm	1,666⅔	1	24	8- 4-1784	Br Skeggs Cr	Surveyed

Entree	Acres	Book	Page	Entry Date	Watercourse	Notes
Croghan, Wm	1,300	1	34	8– 5–1784	Green R	Surveyed
Croghan, Wm	1,000	1	34	8– 5–1784	Cumberland R	Surveyed
Croghan, Wm	1,000	1	37	8– 6–1784	Cumberland R	
Croghan, Wm	1,366⅔	1	65	8– 7–1784	Br Mayfield Cr	
Croghan, Wm	1,100	1	79	8–10–1784	Ohio R	Withdrawn
Croghan, Wm	1,300	1	81	8–10–1784	Mississippi R	Withdrawn
Croghan, Wm	100	1	122	8–14–1784	Cumberland Island	Withdrawn
Croghan, Wm	2,666⅔	1	131	9–28–1784	Cumberland R	Withdrawn
Croghan, Wm	1,000	1	132	9–28–1784	Green R	Withdrawn
Croghan, Wm	2,633⅓	1	134	1–21–1785	Ohio R	Surveyed
Croghan, Wm	1,000	1	134	1–21–1785	Cumberland R	Withdrawn
Croghan, Wm	400	1	134	1–21–1785	Cumberland R	Surveyed
Croghan, Wm	1,000	1	134	1–21–1785	Tennessee R	Withdrawn
Croghan, Wm	1,000	1	135	1–21–1785	Cumberland R	Surveyed
Croghan, Wm	1,450	1	135	1–21–1785	Cumberland R	Surveyed
Croghan, Wm	1,366⅔	1	137	3–18–1785	Ohio R	Surveyed
Croghan, Wm	1,000	1	138	4– 7–1785	Clarks R	Withdrawn
Croghan, Wm	400	1	143	6–17–1785	Cumberland R	Withdrawn
Croghan, Wm	200	1	143	6–17–1785	Cumberland R	Withdrawn
Croghan, Wm	500	1	143	6–22–1785	Tennessee R	Withdrawn
Croghan, Wm	340	1	143	6–22–1785	Big Barren R	Surveyed
Croghan, Wm	450	1	144	7–21–1785	Big Barren R	Surveyed
Croghan, Wm	150	1	146	8–13–1785	Tennessee R	Withdrawn
Croghan, Wm	666⅔	1	147	8–13–1785	Cumberland R	Surveyed
Croghan, Wm	1,000	1	147	8–13–1785	Fk Big Eddy Cr	Withdrawn
Croghan, Wm	500	1	152	12– 7–1785	Clarks R	Withdrawn
Croghan, Wm	650	1	153	12– 7–1785	Big Barren R	Surveyed
Croghan, Wm	930	1	155	12–13–1785	Little Barren R	Withdrawn
Croghan, Wm	1,140	1	158	12–13–1785	Tennessee R	Surveyed
Croghan, Wm	600	1	166	12–13–1785	Little Barren R	Surveyed
Croghan, Wm	1,620	1	167	12–13–1785	Cumberland R	Surveyed
Croghan, Wm	100	1	175	4–14–1786	Green R	Surveyed
Croghan, Wm	100	1	180	7– 2–1786	None	Surveyed
Croghan, Wm	1,000	1	183	10– 1–1786	Russell Cr	Surveyed
Croghan, Wm	1,000	1	183	10– 1–1786	Russell Cr	Surveyed
Croghan, Wm	250	1	197	2– 6–1788	Little Barren R	Surveyed
Croghan, Wm	500	1	203	5–18–1788	Green R	Surveyed
Croghan, Wm	300	1	208	9– 6–1788	Big Barren R	Surveyed
Croghan, Wm	200	1	208	9– 6–1788	Big Barren R	Surveyed
Croghan, Wm	1,000	1	209	10– 6–1788	Big Barren R	Surveyed
Croghan, Wm	600	1	209	10– 6–1788	Little Barren R	Surveyed
Croghan, Wm	600	1	235	9– 8–1791	Cumberland R	Withdrawn
Croghan, Wm	400	1	235	9– 8–1791	Cumberland R	Withdrawn
Croghan, Wm	500	1	238	9–12–1791	Cumberland R	Withdrawn
Crump, Abner	1,000	1	17	8– 4–1784	Mississippi	
Crump, Abner	1,500	1	30	8– 5–1784	W Fk Red R	Withdrawn
Crump, Abner	500	1	43	8– 6–1784	Beaver Cr	Withdrawn
Crump, Abner	1,000	1	52	8– 7–1784	Cumberland R	Withdrawn
Crump, Abner	1,000	1	123	8–14–1784	Cumberland R	Withdrawn
Crump, Abner	1,000	1	133	1– 7–1785	Skeggs Cr	Surveyed
Crump, Abner	500	1	135	1–31–1785	Sinks of Beaver Cr	Surveyed
Crump, Abner	1,000	1	141	5–12–1785	Cumberland R	Surveyed
Crump, Abner	1,500	1	271	4–28–1792	Peter Cr	
Currie, James	1,000	1	4	8– 2–1784	Mississippi	
Currie, Jas	1,000	1	20	8– 4–1784	Town Cr	
Currie, Jas	1,000	1	38	8– 6–1784	Mouth Town Cr	
Currie, Jas	866⅔	1	60	8– 7–1784	Delaware Cr	
Currie, Jas	600	1	63	8– 7–1784	Green R	Surveyed
Currie, Jas	1,000	1	72	8–10–1784	Ohio R	
Currie, Jas	900	1	78	8–10–1784	Consolos Cr	
Currie, Jas	1,000	1	96	8–11–1784	None	
Currie, Jas	900	1	102	8–12–1784	——— Cr	
Dabney, Chas	1,000	1	15	8– 3–1784	None	
Dabney, Chas	1,000	1	21	8– 4–1784	Cumberland R	Withdrawn
Dabney, Chas	1,000	1	33	8– 5–1784	Green R	Surveyed
Dabney, Chas	1,000	1	39	8– 6–1784	Russell Cr	Surveyed
Dabney, Chas	2,666⅔	1	66	8– 7–1784	S W Fk Big Barren R	Amended
Dabney, Chas	1,000	1	80	8–10–1784	Little R	Withdrawn
Dabney, Chas	2,666⅔	1	130	8–29–1784	S Fk Big Barren R	Withdrawn
Dabney, Chas	2,666⅔	1	133	1– 7–1785	Big Barren R	Withdrawn
Dabney, Chas	1,000	1	137	2–22–1785	Cumberland R	Withdrawn
Dabney, Chas	1,000	1	137	2–22–1785	Cumberland R	Withdrawn
Dabney, Chas	1,000	1	150	10– 3–1785	None	Surveyed
Dabney, Chas	666⅔	1	158	12–13–1785	Big Barren R	Surveyed
Dabney, Chas	2,000	1	158	12–13–1785	Boyds Cr	Surveyed
Dabney, Chas	480	1	164	12–13–1785	Big Barren R	Surveyed
Davies, Jno R	600	1	111	8–12–1784	Little Barren R	Surveyed
Davies, Jno R	1,000	1	112	8–13–1784	Mississippi	
Davis, Jno	200	1	30	8– 5–1784	Russell Cr	
Deklanman, Christ C	1,280	1	177	5– 1–1786	Tennessee R	Surveyed

Entree	Acres	Book	Page	Entry Date	Watercourse	Notes
Deklanman, Christ C..	870	1	177	5- 1-1786	Straight Cr	Surveyed
Deklanman, Christ C..	1,850	1	178	5-10-1786	Big Barren R	Surveyed
Deklanman, Christ C..	1,333⅓	1	201	2-24-1788	Cumberland R	Withdrawn
Deklanman, Christ C..	1,333⅓	1	201	2-24-1788	Cumberland R	Surveyed
Delapartie, Joseph	100	1	228	8- 2-1791	Crocus Cr	....
Demombreen, Timothy	500	1	295	9-23-1792	Green R	Withdrawn
Demombreen, Timothy	600	1	295	9-23-1792	Green R	Withdrawn
Demombreen, Timothy	400	1	296	9-23-1792	Green R	Withdrawn
Demombreen, Timothy	250	1	296	9-29-1792	Green R	Withdrawn
Demombreen, Timothy	250	1	296	9-23-1792	Green R	Withdrawn
Demombreen, Timothy	100	1	296	9-23-1792	Green R	Withdrawn
Demombreen, Timothy	200	1	296	9-23-1792	Green R	Withdrawn
Demombreen, Timothy	150	1	296	9-23-1792	Grove & Spring	Withdrawn
Demombreen, Timothy	100	1	296	9-23-1792	Cumberland Trace	Withdrawn
Demombreen, Timothy	116⅔	1	297	9-23-1792	None	Withdrawn
Demombrough, Timothy	1,777⅔	1	297	12- 2-1796	Little R	Surveyed
Demombrough, Timothy	422⅔	1	297	12- 2-1796	Little R	Withdrawn
Demombrough, Timothy	466⅔	1	297	12- 2-1796	Little R	Surveyed
Demombreen, Timothy	422⅔	1	298	7- 7-1797	Skinframe Cr	Surveyed
Demombreen, Timothy	422	1	298	8- 8-1797	Little R	Surveyed
Deoaly, David	100	1	292	4-30-1792	Little Barren R	Withdrawn
Deshouse, Edward	200	1	292	4-30-1792	E Fk Crocus Cr	Surveyed
Dick, Alexander	2,000	1	5	8- 2-1784	Ohio R	....
Dick, Alexander	2,000	1	26	8- 4-1784	Russell Cr	Withdrawn
Dick, Alexander	500	1	31	8- 5-1784	Glenns Cr	Surveyed
Dick, Alexander	500	1	32	8- 5-1784	Russell Cr	Surveyed
Dick, Alexander	1,333⅓	1	51	8- 6-1784	Fk Crocus Cr	Surveyed
Dick, Alexander	2,000	1	150	10- 3-1785	——— Cr	Surveyed
Dick & Lewis	2,666⅔	1	39	8- 6-1784	Cumberland R	Surveyed
Dick & Lewis	3,110⅔	1	71	8-10-1784	Wolf Cr	Surveyed
Dick & Lewis	3,110⅔	1	149	10- 3-1785	None	Surveyed
Dickerson, James Jr	200	1	250	2-25-1792	Skeggs Cr	Surveyed
Dixon, Anthony T	2,000	1	122	8-14-1784	——— R	Withdrawn
Dixon, Anthony T	1,000	1	122	8-14-1784	Mississippi R	Withdrawn
Dixon, Anthony T	1,000	1	122	8-14-1784	——— R	Withdrawn
Dixon, Anthony T	1,000	1	123	8-14-1784	——— R	Withdrawn
Dixon, Anthony T	2,000	1	267	4-27-1792	Big Barren R	Surveyed
Dixon, Anthony T	1,000	1	267	4-27-1792	Peter Cr	Surveyed
Dixon, Anthony T	1,000	1	268	4-28-1792	Peter Cr	Surveyed
Dixon, Anthony T	1,000	1	268	4-28-1792	Fk Peter Cr	Surveyed
Downey, Michael	1,000	1	77	8-10-1784	Flat Lick Br	Surveyed
Downing, Jno	2,066⅔	1	146	8-13-1785	Tennessee R	Surveyed
Downing, Jno	1,000	1	149	10- 3-1785	Beaver Cr	Withdrawn
Downing, Jno	200	1	185	11- 5-1786	Russell Cr	Surveyed
Downing, Jno	1,000	1	191	3-29-1787	Skeggs Cr	Surveyed
Dowse, Edward	900	1	2	8- 2-1784	Green R	....
Dowse, Edward	400	1	32	8- 5-1784	Russell Cr	Surveyed
Dowse, Edward	866⅔	1	61	8- 7-1784	Pittman Cr	Surveyed
Dowse, Edward	1,000	1	92	8-11-1784	Mayfield Cr	....
Dowse, Edward	900	1	110	8-12-1784	Cumberland R	....
Dowse, Edward	1,000	1	119	8-14-1784	Big Barren R	....
Dowse, Edward	1,000	1	119	8-14-1784	Big Barren R	Withdrawn
Dowse, Edward	1,000	1	119	8-14-1784	Big Barren R	Withdrawn
Dowse, Edward	1,000	1	119	8-14-1784	Cumberland R	Surveyed
Dowse, Edward	1,000	1	120	8-14-1784	Cumberland R	....
Dowse, Edward	1,000	1	120	8-14-1784	Cumberland R	....
Dowse, Edward	666⅔	1	120	8-14-1784	Cumberland R	Withdrawn
Dowse, Edward	450	1	155	12-13-1785	Beaver Cr	Surveyed
Dowse, Edward	1,360	1	168	1-19-1785	Skeggs Cr	Surveyed
Dudley, Harry	1,000	1	58	8- 7-1784	Russell Cr	Surveyed
Dudley, Henry	1,000	1	103	8-12-1784	None	....
Dudley, Henry	1,000	1	36	8- 5-1784	——— R	....
Dunkard, Wm	1,000	1	74	8-10-1784	None	....
Edloe, Jno	1,000	1	111	8-12-1784	Little Barren R	Surveyed
Edloe, Jno	1,116⅔	1	292	4-30-1792	Big Barren R	....
Edloe, Jno	1,550	1	292	4-30-1792	Cumberland R	....
Edmond, Elias	1,000	1	117	8-13-1784	Big Barren R	Withdrawn
Edmond, Elias	1,000	1	117	8-13-1784	N Fk Big Barren R	Withdrawn
Edmond, Elias	2,000	1	196	12-27-1787	Cumberland R	Surveyed
Edmonds, Elias	2,000	1	117	8-13-1784	Cumberland R	Withdrawn
Edmonds, Elias	4,000	1	203	5-12-1788	Goose Cr	Withdrawn
Edmunson, Benj	1,000	1	212	8- 1-1791	S Fk Little Barren R	Withdrawn
Edmunson, Benj	1,000	1	212	8- 1-1791	——— Cr	Withdrawn
Edmunson, Benj	666⅔	1	212	8- 1-1791	S Fk Little Barren R	Withdrawn
Edmunson, Benj	1,000	1	232	8- 3-1791	None	Withdrawn
Edmunson, Benj	1,666⅔	1	232	8- 3-1791	None	Withdrawn
Edmunson, Benj	830	1	239	9-16-1791	Clay Lick Fk	Surveyed
Edmunson, Benj	900	1	239	9-16-1791	Cumberland R	Surveyed
Edmunson, Benj	936⅔	1	239	9-16-1791	Cumberland R	Withdrawn
Edmunson, Benj	705	1	260	4-26-1792	Cumberland R	Surveyed

Entree	Acres	Book	Page	Entry Date	Watercourse	Notes
Edmunson, Benj	231¾	1	288	4–30–1792	Big Barren R	Surveyed
Elliott, Alexander	666⅔	1	210	8– 1–1791	Cabin Cr	Amended
Elliott, Alexander	1,000	1	210	8– 1–1791	Cumberland R	Withdrawn
Elliott, Alexander	500	1	211	8– 1–1791	Cumberland R	Withdrawn
Elliott, Alexander	500	1	211	8– 1–1791	Russell Cr	Withdrawn
Elliott, Jno	2,000	1	211	8– 1–1791	Fk Russell Cr	Withdrawn
Elliott, Geo	2,000	1	211	8– 1–1791	Butler Lick Fk	Withdrawn
Elliott, Geo	800	1	242	12– 9–1791	Cumberland R	Surveyed
Elliott, Geo	1,200	1	242	12– 9–1791	Cumberland R	Surveyed
Elliott, Geo	900	1	246	2– 9–1792	Butlers Fk	Withdrawn
Elliott, Geo	300	1	246	2– 9–1792	Big Fk Russell Cr	Surveyed
Elliott, Geo	100	1	246	2– 9–1792	Big Fk Russell Cr	Surveyed
Elliott, Geo	200	1	246	2– 9–1792	Butlers Fk	
Elliott, Geo	100	1	246	2– 9–1792	Big Fk Russell Cr	
Elliott, Alexander	1,000	1	264	4–27–1794	Big Barren R	Surveyed
Elliott, Alexander	500	1	264	4–27–1792	Cumberland R	Surveyed
Elliott, Alexander	558	1	265	4–27–1792	Cabin Cr	
Elliott, Alexander	108⅔	1	276	4–28–1792	Montgomery Fk	Surveyed
Ellis, Jas	100	1	21	8– 4–1784	Fishing Cr	
Elms, Wm	200	1	259	4–26–1792	Big Barren R	Surveyed
Elzey, Wm	500	1	193	12–27–1787	Cumberland R	Surveyed
Elzey, Wm	1,000	1	277	4–28–1792	Cumberland R	Surveyed
Elzey, Wm	500	1	277	4–28–1792	W Fk Wolf Cr	Surveyed
Elzey, Wm	500	1	277	4–28–1792	Cumberland R	Surveyed
Elzey, Wm	500	1	277	4–28–1792	S Fk Cumberland R	
Elzey, Wm	1,000	1	277	4–28–1792	E Fk Wolf Cr	Surveyed
Elzey, Wm	500	1	278	4–28–1792	Wolf Cr	Surveyed
Epple, Andrew	1,000	1	23	8– 4–1784	W Fk Red R	Surveyed
Eskridge, Geo	1,953¾	1	194	12–27–1787	Cumberland R	Surveyed
Eskridge, Geo	713	1	194	12–27–1787	Cumberland R	Surveyed
Evans, Philip	1,125	1	255	4–24–1792	Glovers Cr	Surveyed
Evans, Philip	1,000	1	269	4–28–1792	Glovers Cr	Surveyed
Evans, Philip	1,000	1	285	4–28–1792	Clay Lick Fk	Surveyed
Evans & Saunders	350	1	292	4–30–1792	Big Barren R	Surveyed
Ewell, Chas	2,000	1	82	8–11–1784	Cumberland R	Withdrawn
Ewell, Chas	2,000	1	91	8–11–1784	None	
Ewell, Chas	1,000	1	142	6– 7–1785	Consalas Cr	
Ewell, Chas	1,000	1	200	2–24–1788	Cumberland R	
Ewell, Thos	2,000	1	42	8– 6–1784	Buck Cr	Surveyed
Ewell, Thos	2,000	1	75	8–10–1784	N Fk Big Barren R	Surveyed
Ewell & Trevis	500	1	142	6– 7–1785	S Fk Consalas Cr	
Ferguson, Robt	666⅔	1	151	12– 6–1785	Russell Cr	Surveyed
Ferguson, Robt	2,000	1	151	12– 6–1785	Knob Lick Cr	Surveyed
Fleet, Jno	666⅔	1	9	8– 3–1784	Cumberland R	Surveyed
Fleet, Jno	1,000	1	78	8–10–1784	Consales Cr	Withdrawn
Fleet, Jno	1,000	1	107	8–12–1784	———— R	Withdrawn
Fleet, Jno	920	1	185	11– 5–1786	Little Barren R	Surveyed
Flowaree, Daniel	700	1	112	8–13–1784	Pitman Cr	Surveyed
Flynn, Geo	1,000	1	147	8–13–1785	Fk Big Eddy Cr	Withdrawn
Fonshu & Anderson	1,000	1	70	8–10–1784	S Fk Clarks Cr	
Foster, Peter	100	1	101	8–12–1784	None	
Frogett, Wm	200	1	101	8–12–1784	None	Withdrawn
Frogett, Wm	200	1	222	8– 2–1791	Big Barren R	Surveyed
Gallego & Therice	1,200	1	112	8–13–1784	W Fk Red R	Withdrawn
Gallego & Therice	1,200	1	289	4–30–1792	Big Barren R	Surveyed
Galleton, Albert	800	1	111	8–12–1784	None	
Galleton, Albert	1,000	1	111	8–12–1784	Little Barren R	Surveyed
Galleton, Albert	422	1	112	8–13–1784	Mississippi R	Withdrawn
Galleton, Albert	933⅔	1	115	8–13–1784	Big Barren R	Surveyed
Galleton, Albert	422	1	201	2–24–1788	Cumberland R	
Garey, Jno	200	1	101	8–12–1784	None	
Garnett, Thos	733⅓	1	217	8– 1–1791	Skeggs Cr	Surveyed
Garnett, Thos	733⅓	1	248	2–29–1792	None	Surveyed
Garratt, Mark	1,000	1	116	8–13–1784	Big Barren R	Surveyed
George, Robt	1,000	1	15	8– 3–1784	Red Stone Cr	
George, Robt	1,000	1	45	8– 6–1784	Beaver Cr	Surveyed
George, Robt	1,000	1	75	8–10–1784	Consales Cr	
George, Robt	1,000	1	76	8–10–1784	———— Cr	
George, Robt	716	1	223	8– 2–1791	Skeggs Cr	Amended
George, Robt	716	1	247	2–25–1792	Skeggs Cr	Surveyed
Geralt, Jno	1,000	1	24	8– 4–1784	Mississippi	Withdrawn
Geralt, Jno	1,000	1	25	8– 4–1784	Continental Line	Withdrawn
Gerand, Honore	600	1	112	8–13–1784	Little Barren R	Surveyed
Gerand, Honore	700	1	202	2–24–1788	Cumberland R	Surveyed
Gerault, Jno	1,000	1	6	8–12–1784	Town Land	
Gerault, Jno	1,000	1	68	8– 9–1784	Mississippi	
Gerault, Jno	1,000	1	111	8–12–1784	Clarks R	
Gerault, Jno	1,000	1	135	1–31–1785	Sinks Beaver Cr	Surveyed
Gerrard, Honore	666⅔	1	4	8– 2–1784	Cumberland R	
Gerrard, Honore	700	1	113	8–13–1784	Big Barren R	Withdrawn
Gerrard, Honore	700	1	113	8–13–1784	Big Barren R	Surveyed

Entree	Acres	Book	Page	Entry Date	Watercourse	Notes
Gibbs, Churchel	1,000	1	167	12-13-1785	Green R	
Gibbs, Churchel	1,000	1	167	12-13-1785	Big Barren	Amended
Gibbs, Churchel	666⅔	1	167	12-13-1785	Big Barren R	Surveyed
Gibbs, Churchel	1,000	1	247	2-25-1792	Skeggs Cr	Surveyed
Gibson, Geo	2,666⅔	1	11	8- 3-1784	Mississippi R	
Gibson, Geo	1,000	1	22	8- 4-1784	Cumberland R	
Gibson, Geo	1,000	1	62	8- 7-1784	S Fk Big Barren R	Surveyed
Gibson, Geo	1,000	1	99	8-12-1784	Mayfield Cr	
Gibson, Geo	1,000	1	103	8-12-1784	Ohio R	
Givins, Jno	400	1	214	8- 1-1791	Big Barren R	Withdrawn
Givins, Jno	400	1	229	8- 2-1791	Little Barren R	Surveyed
Givins, Jno	50	1	268	4-28-1792	Little Barren R	Surveyed
Gore, Michael	100	1	136	1-31-1785	None	Surveyed
Graham, Walter	2,000	1	14	8- 3-1784	Big Eddy Cr	Surveyed
Graham, Walter	2,000	1	71	8-10-1784	——— Cr	Withdrawn
Graham, Walter	2,000	1	200	2-24-1788	Cumberland R	Surveyed
Graham, Walter	1,000	1	286	4-28-1792	Peter Cr	Surveyed
Graves, Wm	2,666⅔	1	124	8-14-1784	Cumberland R	
Graves, Francis	2,000	1	191	3-29-1787	E Fk Little Barren	Surveyed
Graves, Francis	666⅔	1	191	3-29-1787	Skeggs Cr	Withdrawn
Graves, Francis	100	1	290	4-30-1792	Warport Lick	Surveyed
Graves & Montgomery	566⅔	1	290	4-30-1792	——— R	Surveyed
Greenhow, Jno	1,000	1	259	4-26-1792	Green R	Surveyed
Greenhow, Jno	666⅔	1	259	4-26-1792	Green R	Surveyed
Grier, Chas	1,000	1	12	8- 3-1784	Willow Cr	Withdrawn
Grier, Chas	1,000	1	95	8-11-1784	W Fk Clark R	Withdrawn
Grier, Chas	1,714	1	160	12-13-1785	Big Barren R	Surveyed
Grier, Chas	2,286	1	161	12-13-1785	Boyd Cr	Surveyed
Griffin, Samuel	1,200	1	74	8-10-1784	S Fk Clark R	
Griffin, Thos	100	1	101	8-12-1784	None	
Griffin, Wm	3,000	1	63	8- 7-1784	Tennessee R	
Griffin, Wm	2,333⅓	1	87	8-11-1784	Tennessee R	Surveyed
Hambleton, Patsy	2,000	1	212	8- 1-1791	E Fk Little Barren	Surveyed
Hambleton, Patsy	666⅔	1	212	8- 1-1791	Skeggs Cr	Surveyed
Hanson, Richard	1,000	1	94	8-11-1784	Clarks R	
Hanvood, Littleberry	200	1	10	8- 3-1784	Russells Cr	Surveyed
Harper, Jas	900	1	30	8- 5-1784	Tennessee R	
Harper, Jas	866⅔	1	78	8-10-1784	Consales Cr	Withdrawn
Harper, Jas	900	1	108	8-12-1784	Tennessee R	Surveyed
Harper, Jas	366⅔	1	248	2-29-1792	Skeggs	Surveyed
Harper, Jas	500	1	253	2-25-1792	Rays Spring Br	Withdrawn
Harper & Hudson	560	1	277	4-28-1792	N Fk Skeggs Cr	Surveyed
Harris, Wm	1,000	1	134	1-21-1785	Pitman Cr	Surveyed
Harrison, Benj	1,000	1	198	2-24-1788	Cumberland R	Withdrawn
Harrison, Benj	2,000	1	198	2-24-1788	Big Barren R	
Harrison, Benj	1,000	1	198	2-24-1788	S Fk Little Barren R	Surveyed
Harrison, Benj	1,000	1	237	9-10-1791	S Fk Little Barren R	Surveyed
Harrison, Benj	1,000	1	265	4-27-1792	Skeggs Cr	Withdrawn
Harrison, Benj	1,000	1	278	4-28-1792	Indian Cr	
Harrison, Richard	666⅔	1	5	8- 2-1784	Green R	
Harrison, Richard	1,000	1	96	8-11-1784	None	
Harvey, Robt	1,000	1	134	1-21-1785	Pitman Cr	Surveyed
Harvie, Jno	1,000	1	7	8- 2-1784	Mississippi R	
Harvie, Jno	2,466⅔	1	204	6-10-1788	Grassy Cr	Surveyed
Harvie, Jno	200	1	227	8- 2-1791	Bear Wallow Grove	Surveyed
Hawkins, Jno	1,000	1	128	8-14-1784	Russell Cr	Surveyed
Henderson, Wm	100	1	173	4-14-1786	Cumberland R	Withdrawn
Henderson, Wm	100	1	181	7-11-1786	Green R	Surveyed
Henderson, Wm	100	1	196	12-27-1787	Pitman Cr	Surveyed
Hendricks, Wm	1,000	1	135	1-31-1785	Sinks of Beaver Cr	Surveyed
Henricks, Byrd	100	1	136	1-31-1785	None	Surveyed
Hickman, Wm	900	1	73	8-10-1784	Ohio R	100 acres withdrawn
Hoffler, Wm	1,000	1	10	8- 3-1784	Cumberland R	Withdrawn
Hoffler, Wm	1,000	1	78	8-10-1784	Consales Cr	
Hoffler, Wm	1,000	1	82	8-11-1784	Cumberland R	Withdrawn
Hoffler, Wm	1,000	1	92	8-11-1784	None	
Hoffler, Wm	900	1	207	7-19-1788	Wolf Cr	Surveyed
Hoffler, Wm	200	1	207	7-19-1788	Russell Cr	Surveyed
Hoffler, Wm	562	1	207	7-19-1788	Cumberland R	Surveyed
Hoffler, Wm	200	1	207	7-19-1788	Russell Cr	Surveyed
Hoffler, Wm	138	1	221	8- 2-1791	W Fk Crocus Cr	Surveyed
Hogdon & Pickering	1,000	1	73	8-10-1784	Ohio R	
Hogdon & Pickering	1,000	1	268	4-28-1792	S Fk Glovers Cr	Surveyed
Hogdon & Pickering	1,000	1	269	4-28-1792	Glovers Cr	Surveyed
Hogdon & Pickering	3,000	1	269	4-28-1792	Glovers Cr	
Hogdon & Pickering	3,300	1	275	4-28-1792	Clay Lick Fk	Surveyed
Hogdon & Pickering	1,000	1	270	4-28-1792	Skeggs Cr	
Hogg, Richard	1,200	1	37	8- 6-1784	Delaware Cr	
Hollinsworth, Levi	300	1	156	12-13-1785	Sinks of Beaver Cr	Surveyed
Holmes, Isaac	1,000	1	18	8- 4-1784	Ohio	

Entree	Acres	Book	Page	Entry Date	Watercourse	Notes
Holmes, Isaac	666⅔	1	88	8-11-1784	Harlans Cr	
Holmes, Isaac	1,000	1	80	8-10-1784	Cumberland R	Surveyed
Holt, Jno	1,000	1	94	8-11-1784	Clark R	
Holt, Jno H	1,000	1	23	8- 4-1784	Buck & Pitman Cr	Surveyed
Holt, Jno H	1,000	1	77	8-10-1784	Big Barren R	Surveyed
Holt, Jno H	1,000	1	87	8-11-1784	Harlans Cr	
Holt, Jno H	1,000	1	9	8- 3-1784	Cumberland R	
Hudson, Jno	1,000	1	32	8- 5-1784	N E Fk Russell Cr	Surveyed
Hudson, Jno	1,000	1	58	8- 7-1784	Skeggs Cr	Surveyed
Hudson, Jno	1,000	1	76	8-10-1784	N Fk Big Barren R	Withdrawn
Hudson, Jno	1,000	1	229	8- 2-1791	S Fk Little Barren R	Surveyed
Hudson, Jno	60	1	253	2-25-1792	Rays Spring Br	Withdrawn
Hudson & Harper	560	1	277	4-28-1792	N Fk Skeggs Cr	Surveyed
Hunter, Moses	1,000	1	48	8- 6-1784	Tennessee R	
Hunter, Moses	1,000	1	74	8-10-1784	N Fk Clark R	
Hunter, Moses	1,000	1	106	8-12-1784	None	
Ingraham, Duncan	1,000	1	268	4-28-1792	S Fk Glovers Cr	Surveyed
Ingraham, Duncan	1,000	1	269	4-28-1792	Glovers Cr	Surveyed
Ingraham, Duncan	3,000	1	269	4-28-1792	Glovers Cr	
Ingraham, Duncan	1,000	1	270	4-28-1792	Skeggs Cr	
Ingraham, Duncan	3,300	1	275	4-28-1792	Clay Lick Fk	Surveyed
Isaac, Cohen & Mordia.	500	1	111	8-12-1784	Little Barren R	Surveyed
Jackson, David	400	1	180	7- 2-1786	Little Barren R	
James, Geo	50	1	142	6- 7-1785	Flat Lick Cr	
James, Geo	100	1	142	6- 7-1785	Cumberland R	
Johnston, Wm	1,000	1	127	8-14-1784	Russell Cr	Surveyed
Johnston, Wm	100	1	294	4-30-1792	Red R	Surveyed
Johnston, Zachariah	666⅔	1	15	8- 3-1784	N E Fk Russells Cr	Surveyed
Johnston, Zachariah	1,000	1	17	8- 4-1784	Cumberland R	Surveyed
Johnston, Zachariah	1,000	1	21	8- 4-1784	Skinn House Cr	Surveyed
Johnston, Zachariah	1,100	1	35	8- 5-1784	E Fk Little R	
Jones, Alexander	200	1	50	8- 6-1784	Cumberland R	Surveyed
Jones, Robt	1,000	1	208	10- 6-1788	Grassy Cr	Surveyed
Jones, Robt	1,250	1	224	8- 2-1791	Crocus Cr	Surveyed
Jones, Robt	450	1	224	8- 2-1791	Clay Lick Cr	Surveyed
Jones, Robt	500	1	233	8- 4-1791	Russell Cr	Surveyed
Jones, Robt	800	1	233	8- 4-1791	Clay Lick Fk	Withdrawn
Jones, Robt	800	1	235	9- 1-1791	Clay Lick Fk	Withdrawn
Jones, Robt	800	1	239	9-16-1791	Clay Lick Fk	Withdrawn
Jones, Robt	500	1	243	12-11-1791	Cumberland R	Withdrawn
Jones, Robt	300	1	243	12-11-1791	Russell Cr	Surveyed
Jones, Robt	450	1	262	4-27-1792	Russell Cr	Surveyed
Jones, Robt	50	1	266	4-27-1792	Crocus Cr	Surveyed
Jones, Stephen	1,333⅓	1	258	4-25-1792	Big Barren R	Surveyed
Karney, Jno	1,500	1	89	8-11-1784	Harlans Cr	Withdrawn
Karney, Jno	1,500	1	101	8-12-1784	Mayfield Cr	Withdrawn
Karney, Jno	1,050	1	252	2-25-1792	Fk Big Barren	Withdrawn
Karney, Jno	1,050	1	265	4-27-1792	Caney Fk	
Keene, Lawrence	1,100	1	18	8- 4-1784	None	
Keller, Mary	570	1	224	8- 2-1791	Crocus Cr	Surveyed
Keller, Mary	800	1	225	8- 2-1791	Crocus	Surveyed
Keller, Mary	1,315	1	225	8- 2-1791	Clay Lick Cr	Withdrawn
Keller, Mary	1,315	1	225	8- 2-1791	Dry Fk	Withdrawn
Keller, Mary	460	1	232	8- 3-1791	—— Cr	Amended
Keller, Mary	200	1	232	8- 3-1791	Little Barren R	Surveyed
Keller, Mary	460	1	235	9- 1-1791	Clay Lick Fk	Surveyed
Keller, Mary	1,315	1	235	9- 1-1791	S Fk Little Barren R	Withdrawn
Keller, Mary	680	1	239	9-16-1791	S Fk Little Barren R	Withdrawn
Keller, Mary	1,300	1	239	9-16-1791	Cumberland R	Withdrawn
Keller, Mary	1,300	1	243	12-11-1791	Cumberland R	Withdrawn
Keller, Mary	1,430	1	261	4-26-1792	Cumberland R	Surveyed
Keller, Mary	413	1	261	4-26-1792	Cumberland R	Surveyed
Keller, Mary	400	1	261	4-26-1792	Buffalo Cr	Surveyed
Keller, Mary	352	1	261	4-26-1792	Green R	Surveyed
Keller, Mary	300	1	261	4-26-1792	Sinking Br	Surveyed
Keller, Mary	680	1	263	4-27-1792	Cumberland R	
Kelly, Thaddy	1,060	1	4	8- 2-1784	Cumberland R	
Kelly, Thaddy	1,000	1	89	8-11-1784	None	
Kelly, Thaddy	1,000	1	102	8-12-1784	Ohio R	
Kelly, Thaddy	1,000	1	107	8-12-1784	—— R	Surveyed
Kelly, Thaddy	1,000	1	125	8-14-1784	Cumberland R	Surveyed
Kemp, James	2,666⅔	1	8	8- 3-1784	Mouth Island Cr	
Kennedy, James	1,000	1	55	8- 7-1784	Pitman Cr	Surveyed
Kemp, Peter	1,000	1	58	8- 7-1784	Tennessee R	
Kemp, Peter	1,000	1	107	8-12-1784	Tennessee R	Surveyed
Kemp, Capt Peter	666⅔	1	48	8- 6-1784	Fk Buck Cr	Surveyed
Kennedy, James	1,000	1	55	8- 7-1784	Crocus Cr	
Kennedy, James	1,000	1	55	8-14-1784	Ohio R	Withdrawn
Kercheval, Jno	800	1	129	8-14-1784	Cumberland R	Surveyed
Kerchevel, Jno	800	1	293	4-30-1792	Cumberland R	Surveyed
Kerney, Jas	500	1	186	3-28-1787	Little Barren R	Surveyed
Kerney, Jno	1,950	1	159	12-13-1785	Boyds Cr	Surveyed

Entree	Acres	Book	Page	Entry Date	Watercourse	Notes
Kerney, Jno	1,050	1	179	7- 2-1786	S Fk Skeggs Cr	Withdrawn
Knox, David	323	1	183	10- 1-1786	Glenn Cr	Surveyed
Lafong, Nicholas	200	1	38	8- 6-1784	Russell Cr	Surveyed
Lamm, Samuel	600	1	191	3-29-1787	Sinking Cr	Surveyed
Lamm, Samuel	500	1	252	2-25-1792	Big Barren R	Withdrawn
Lamm, Samuel	100	1	267	4-27-1792	Boyds Cr	Surveyed
Lamm, Wm	884	1	187	3-28-1787	Little Barren R	Withdrawn
Lamm, Wm	1,000	1	187	3-28-1787	E Fk Little Barren R	Surveyed
Lamm, Wm	500	1	187	3-28-1787	E Fk Little Barren R	Surveyed
Lamm, Wm	500	1	187	3-28-1787	Big Barren R	Withdrawn
Lamm, Wm	782¾	1	188	3-28-1787	Big Barren	Withdrawn
Lamm, Wm	297¼	1	188	3-28-1787	Big Barren	Withdrawn
Lamm, Wm	920	1	197	2- 6-1788	Little Barren	Surveyed
Lamm, Wm	500	1	205	6-10-1788	S Fk Little Barren	Surveyed
Lamm, Wm	500	1	237	9-10-1791	S Fk Little Barren R	Withdrawn
Lamm, Wm	1,080	1	265	4-27-1792	Skeggs Cr	Surveyed
Larty, Jno	4,000	1	17	8- 4-1784	Harlan Cr	Withdrawn
Larty, Jno	1,500	1	205	6-10-1788	E Fk Little Barren R	Surveyed
Larty, Jno	2,500	1	205	6-10-1788	Little Barren R	680 acres surveyed 1,820 acres withdrawn
Leaper, Jno	100	1	227	8- 2-1791	N C & Va Line	
Lee, Jno	1,000	1	5	8- 2-1784	Cane Cr	
Lee, Jno	1,000	1	9	8- 3-1784	Far Fk Red R	Surveyed
Lee, Jno	1,000	1	11	8- 3-1784	Willow Cr	
Lee, Jno	1,000	1	41	8- 6-1784	Russell Cr	Surveyed
Lee, Jno	1,333½	1	108	8-12-1784	Big Barren R	Surveyed
Lee, Richard B	200	1	293	4-30-1792	Skeggs Cr	
Lewis & Dick	2,666⅔	3	422	8- 6-1784	Cumberland R	Surveyed
Lewis & Dick	3,110⅔	1	71	8-10-1784	Wolf Cr	Surveyed
Lewis & Dick	3,110⅔	1	149	10- 3-1785	None	Surveyed
Lipscomb, Bernard	1,000	1	29	8- 5-1784	Russell Cr	Surveyed
Lipscomb, Bernard	1,000	1	49	8- 6-1784	Russell Cr	Surveyed
Lipscomb, Bernard	1,000	1	56	8- 7-1784	Russell Cr	Surveyed
Lipscomb, Bernard	1,000	1	64	8- 7-1784	Pitman Cr	Surveyed
Lipscomb, Yancy	1,000	1	9	8- 3-1784	Cumberland R	Surveyed
Lipscomb, Yancy	1,000	1	44	8- 6-1784	Fk Pitman Cr	Surveyed
Lipscomb, Yancy	1,000	1	58	8- 7-1784	S Fk Big Barren R	Surveyed
Lipscomb, Yancy	1,000	1	107	8-12-1784	Tennessee R	Surveyed
Livingston, Justice	1,000	1	7	8- 2-1784	S Fk Mayfield Cr	
Livingston, Justice	1,000	1	32	8- 5-1784	Russell Cr	Surveyed
Long, Wm	1,522	1	262	4-27-1792	Russell Cr	Surveyed
Long, Wm	400	1	262	4-27-1792	Russell Cr	
Long, Wm	430	1	262	4-27-1792	Russell Cr	
Long, Wm	1,648	1	262	4-27-1792	Greasy Cr	
Loyde, Morris	1,500	1	210	8- 1-1791	Cumberland R	Surveyed
Loyde, Morris	666⅔	1	210	8- 1-1791	E Fk Crocus Cr	Withdrawn
Loyde, Morris	500	1	210	8- 1-1791	Crocus Cr	Withdrawn
Loyde, Morris	400	1	266	4-27-1792	E Fk Crocus Cr	Surveyed
Loyde, Morris	666⅔	1	266	4-27-1792	Big Barren R	Surveyed
Loyde, Morris	300	1	266	4-27-1792	Green R	Surveyed
Loyde, Morris	300	1	266	4-27-1792	Green R	Surveyed
Lurtye, Jno	1,820	1	227	8- 2-1791	Skeggs Cr	Withdrawn
Lurtye, Jno	1,820	1	230	8- 2-1791	Skeggs Cr	Surveyed
Lyne, Jno	300	1	132	10-21-1784	Br Green R	Surveyed
Lynch, Chas	400	1	138	4- 7-1785	Fk Little Barren R	Surveyed
McClurg, Barb V	3,000	1	128	8-14-1784	None	Surveyed
McClurg, Barb V	3,000	1	128	8-14-1784	Tennessee R	Surveyed
McClurg, Jas	1,000	1	85	8-11-1784	Green R	Surveyed
McClurg, Jas	4,325	1	189	3-28-1787	Big Barren R	Surveyed
McClurg, Jas	1,675	1	189	3-28-1787	Fk Big Barren R	Withdrawn
McClurg, Jas	1,675	1	228	8- 2-1791	Lick Island	Surveyed
McClung & Price	500	1	71	8-10-1784	Big Barren R	
McDermot, Francis	333⅓	1	197	2- 6-1788	Cumberland R	Withdrawn
McDermot, Francis	200	1	274	4-28-1792	Green R	
McDermot & Todd	200	1	208	8- 8-1788	Green R	Withdrawn
McDonald, James	300	1	258	4-25-1792	Old Trace	Surveyed
McDougall, Jno	200	1	204	6-10-1788	N Fk Big Barren R	Surveyed
McDougall, Jno	200	1	230	8- 2-1791	Little Barren R	Surveyed
McElhaney, Jno	2,000	1	125	8-14-1784	Straight Cr	Surveyed
McElhaney, Jno	2,000	1	125	8-14-1784	Cumberland R	Withdrawn
McElhaney, Jno	1,000	1	201	2-24-1788	Cumberland R	Withdrawn
McElhaney, Jno	1,000	1	201	2-24-1788	Cumberland R	Withdrawn
McElhaney, Jno	1,333½	1	264	4-27-1792	Cumberland R	Surveyed
McKee, Wm	1,000	1	273	4-28-1792	Sulphur Fk	
McKee, Wm	1,666⅔	1	273	4-28-1792	Flatt Cr	
McKenny, Stephen	110	1	279	4-28-1792	S Fk Little Barren R	Surveyed
McPherson, Jno	300	1	182	9-30-1786	Spring Cr	Withdrawn
McPherson, Jno	700	1	182	9-30-1786	Whipporwill Cr	Withdrawn
McPherson, Jno	1,000	1	231	8- 3-1791	None	Withdrawn

Entree	Acres	Book	Page	Entry Date	Watercourse	Notes
McPherson, Jno	200	1	231	8- 3-1791	Whipporwill Cr	Surveyed
McPherson, Jno	200	1	231	8- 3-1791	Whipporwill Cr	
McPherson, Jno	100	1	231	8- 3-1791	Sinking Cr	Withdrawn
McPherson, Jno	50	1	231	8- 3-1791	Whipporwill Cr	Surveyed
McPherson, Jno	100	1	231	8- 3-1791	Whipporwill Cr	Surveyed
McPherson, Jno	100	1	231	8- 3-1791	Whipporwill Cr	
McPherson, Jno	100	1	231	8- 3-1791	Whipporwill Cr	
McPherson, Jno	100	1	232	8- 3-1791	Salt Peter Cave	Surveyed
McPherson, Jno	50	1	232	8- 3-1791	Whipporwill Cr	Surveyed
McPherson, Jno	50	1	295	4-30-1792	Whipporwill Cr	
McRoberts, Alexander.	600	1	38	8- 6-1784	Russell Cr	Surveyed
Mallory, Jno	100	1	30	8- 5-1784	Russell Cr	
Mansfield, Thos	200	1	30	8- 5-1784	Russell Cr	
Markham, James	1,000	1	6	8- 2-1784	Mulberry Field	
Markham, Jas	2,000	1	75	8-10-1784	N Fk Big Barren	Surveyed
Markham, Jos	1,000	1	87	8-11-1784	None	
Markham, Jas	1,000	1	93	8-11-1784	None	
Marshall, Humphrey	1,000	1	118	8-13-1784	Harlans Cr	Surveyed
Marshall, Humphrey	1,000	1	118	8-13-1784	Tennessee R	Surveyed
Marshall, Humphrey	1,000	1	118	8-13-1784	Big Barren R	Surveyed
Marshall, Humphrey	1,000	1	119	8-14-1784	——— R	Surveyed
Marshall, James M	1,000	1	3	8- 2-1784	Cumberland R	
Marshall, James M	1,666⅔	1	78	8-10-1784	Blue Spring Cr	
Marshall, Thos	1,000	1	3	8- 2-1784	Cumberland R	
Marshall, Thos	2,000	1	43	8- 6-1784	Green R	Surveyed
Marshall, Thos	1,000	1	45	8- 6-1784	Cumberland R	
Marshall, Thos	1,666⅔	1	87	8-11-1784	Cumberland R	
Marshall, Thos	1,000	1	107	8-12-1784	Blue Spring Cr	Surveyed
Marshall, Thos	1,000	1	145	8-13-1785	Russell Cr	Surveyed
Marshall, Thos Jr	1,000	1	146	8-13-1785	None	Amended
Marshall, Thos Jr	1,000	1	172	3- 8-1786	Russell Cr	Surveyed
Marshall, Thos Jr	2,000	1	181	7-11-1786	Camp Cr	Surveyed
Marshall, Thos Jr	1,000	1	125	8-14-1784	Russell Cr	
Martin, James	600	1	202	2-24-1788	Russell Cr	Surveyed
Martin & Roberts	200	1	121	8-14-1784	Red Stone Cr	
Mason, Stephen T	1,000	1	121	8-14-1784	Red Stone & Willow Crs	
Mason, Stephen T	1,000	1	122	8-14-1784	Red Stone & Willow Crs	
Masston, Jno	1,000	1	19	8- 4-1784	Red Stone Cr	Surveyed
Masston, Jno	1,000	1	26	8- 4-1784	Pitman Cr	Surveyed
Masston, Jno	666⅔	1	53	8- 7-1784	Crocus Cr	Surveyed
Matthews, Thos	1,348	1	194	12-27-1787	Cumberland R	Surveyed
Matthews, Thos	1,561	1	195	12-27-1787	Cumberland R	Surveyed
Matthews, Thos	500	1	195	12-27-1787	Cumberland R	Surveyed
Matthews, Thos	750	1	195	12-27-1787	Cumberland R	Surveyed
Matthews, Thos	921	1	195	12-27-1787	Cumberland R	
Matthews, Thos	884	1	195	12-27-1787	Cumberland R	Surveyed
Mazarett, Jno	333⅓	1	257	4-25-1792	Big Barren R	Surveyed
Mazarett & Roam	300	1	275	4-28-1792	Skeggs Cr	Surveyed
Mazaset, Jno	333⅓	1	204	6-10-1788	Big Barren R	Withdrawn
Mazaset, Jno	1,750	1	227	8- 2-1791	E Fk Little Barren	Surveyed
Mazaset, Jno	333⅓	1	241	9-26-1791	Skeggs Cr	Withdrawn
Meats, Samuel	100	1	101	8-12-1784	None	
Meriwether, James	1,300	1	15	8- 3-1784	None	
Meriwether, James	1,366⅔	1	16	8- 3-1784	None	
Meriwether, James	1,000	1	19	8- 4-1784	Ft Jefferson	
Meriwether, James	1,666⅔	1	73	8-10-1784	None	
Miller, Chas	500	1	216	8- 1-1791	Russell Cr	Surveyed
Montgomery, Jas	1,000	1	29	8- 5-1784	Tennessee R	Amended
Montgomery, Jas	1,000	1	63	8- 7-1784	——— Cr	Withdrawn
Montgomery, Jas	666⅔	1	86	8-11-1784	Big Barren R	Withdrawn
Montgomery, Jas	1,000	1	139	3-31-1785	W Fk Red R	Withdrawn
Montgomery, Jas	1,000	1	140	3-31-1785	Ohio R	Withdrawn
Montgomery, Jas	150	1	236	9-10-1791	Bay Spring	Withdrawn
Montgomery, Jas	150	1	236	9-10-1791	Big Barren R	Surveyed
Montgomery, Jas	100	1	237	9-10-1791	Big Barren R	Surveyed
Montgomery, Jas	500	1	240	9-26-1791	Skeggs Cr	
Montgomery, Jas	100	1	240	9-26-1791	Big Barren R	Surveyed
Montgomery, Jas	500	1	241	11-30-1791	Big Barren R	Surveyed
Montgomery, Jas	200	1	251	2-25-1792	Sinking Cr	Surveyed
Montgomery, Jas	300	1	252	2-25-1792	Big Barren R	Surveyed
Montgomery, Jas	150	1	286	4-28-1792	Rays Spring Br	Surveyed
Montgomery, Jno	1,200	1	22	8- 4-1784	N Fk Red R	Withdrawn
Montgomery, Jno	4,000	1	1	8- 2-1784	Mississippi R	
Montgomery, Jno	1,200	1	12	8- 3-1784	Whipporwill Cr	Withdrawn
Montgomery, Jno	1,200	1	14	8- 3-1784	Red R	Withdrawn
Montgomery, Jno	1,200	1	32	8- 5-1784	W Fk Red R	Withdrawn
Montgomery, Jno	1,200	1	61	8- 7-1784	N Fk W Fk Red R	Withdrawn
Montgomery, Jno	1,200	1	116	8-13-1784	Spring Cr	Withdrawn

Entree	Acres	Book	Page	Entry Date	Watercourse	Notes
Montgomery, Jno	6,000	1	139	3-31-1785	None	Withdrawn
Montgomery, Jno	542	1	139	3-31-1785	Whipporwill Cr	Surveyed
Montgomery, Jno	1,120	1	139	3-31-1785	W Fk Red R	Surveyed
Montgomery, Jno	795	1	139	3-31-1785	W Fk Red R	Surveyed
Montgomery, Jno	156	1	140	3-31-1785	Far Fk Red R	Surveyed
Montgomery, Jno	369	1	140	3-31-1785	N Fk W Fk Red R	Withdrawn
Montgomery, Jno	43	1	173	4-14-1786	Red R	Surveyed
Montgomery, Jno	100	1	173	4-14-1786	Whipporwill Cr	Surveyed
Montgomery, Jno	57	1	173	4-14-1786	Red R	Surveyed
Montgomery, Jno	200	1	192	5- 1-1787	W Fk Red R	Surveyed
Montgomery, Jno	200	1	192	5- 1-1787	Walnut Bottom	Surveyed
Montgomery, Jno	50	1	204	6-10-1788	Red R	Surveyed
Montgomery, Jno	100	1	204	6-10-1788	W Fk Red R	Surveyed
Montgomery, Jno	2,727	1	241	10- 2-1791	Little W Fk Red R	Surveyed
Montgomery, Wm	200	1	21	8- 4-1784	Fishing Cr	Withdrawn
Montgomery, Wm	100	1	142	5-31-1785	Indian Cr	Surveyed
Montgomery, Wm	200	1	145	8-13-1785	Green R	Withdrawn
Montgomery, Wm	100	1	219	8- 1-1791	Green R	Surveyed
Montgomery, Wm	200	1	219	8- 1-1791	Green R	Surveyed
Montgomery & Allen	1,200	1	115	8-13-1784	Cumberland R	Withdrawn
Montgomery & Allen	1,200	1	176	4-14-1786	Barren R	Surveyed
Montgomery & Graves	666⅔	1	290	4-30-1792	——— R	Surveyed
Moody, Elizabeth	1,000	1	8	8- 3-1784	Ohio R	
Moody, Elizabeth	1,666⅔	1	18	8- 4-1784	Mouth Red Stone Cr	
Moody, Elizabeth	1,000	1	22	8- 4-1784	None	Surveyed
Moody, Elizabeth	1,000	1	24	8- 4-1784	Big Barren R	Withdrawn
Moody, Elizabeth	1,000	1	279	4-28-1792	Indian Cr	
Moody, James	2,000	1	53	8- 7-1784	Cumberland R	Withdrawn
Moody, Jas	2,000	1	91	8-11-1784	Richland Cr	Withdrawn
Moody, Jas	1,000	1	183	10- 1-1786	Russell Cr	Surveyed
Moody, Jas	1,000	1	183	10- 1-1786	Russell Cr	Surveyed
Moody, Jas	1,000	1	193	12-27-1787	Fishing Cr	Surveyed
Moody, Jas	1,000	1	194	12-27-1787	Cumberland R	Surveyed
Moore, Peter	1,333⅓	1	25	8- 4-1784	Russells Cr	Surveyed
Moore, Peter	1,333⅓	1	60	8- 7-1784	Big Barren R	Surveyed
Moore, Wm	100	1	77	8-10-1784	Flat Lick Br	Surveyed
Morgan, Ralph	200	1	224	8- 2-1791	Skeggs Cr	Withdrawn
Morgan & Shipp	400	1	270	4-28-1792	N Fk Skeggs Cr	
Morrison, Isaac	100	1	258	4-25-1792	Sinking Fk	
Moseley, Thos	100	1	192	5- 1-1787	Red R	Withdrawn
Moseley, Thos	100	1	234	9- 1-1791	Whipporwill Cr	
Motley, Joel	200	1	189	3-28-1787	Little Barren R	
Muhlenberg, Peter	1,000	1	50	8- 6-1784	Sulphur Lick Cr	Amended
Muhlenberg, Peter	1,000	1	149	10- 3-1785	None	Surveyed
Muse, Jeremiah	2,666⅔	1	293	4-30-1792	Big Barren R	Surveyed
Muse, Lawrence	800	1	7	8- 2-1784	Buffalo R	
Muter, Geo	1,666⅔	1	5	8- 2-1784	Mississippi R	
Muter, Geo	1,500	1	33	8- 5-1784	Tennessee R	Withdrawn
Muter, Geo	1,500	1	56	8- 7-1784	Tennessee R	Withdrawn
Muter, Geo	1,500	1	68	8- 9-1784	None	Withdrawn
Muter, Geo	1,000	1	97	8-12-1784	None	
Muter, Geo	1,000	1	104	8-12-1784	Green R	Surveyed
Muter, Geo	1,500	1	129	8-14-1784	Tennessee R	
Muter, Geo	1,500	1	158	12-13-1785	Skeggs Cr	Surveyed
Nall, Wm	200	1	273	4-28-1792	Russell Cr	Surveyed
Nelson, Jno	1,000	1	1	8- 2-1784	Mouth Town Cr	
Nelson, Jno	1,000	1	8	8- 3-1784	Ohio R	
Nelson, Jno	1,000	1	84	8-11-1784	Ohio R	
Nelson, Jno	1,333⅓	1	85	8-11-1784	Big Barren R	Surveyed
Nelson, Jno	1,000	1	97	8-12-1784	Fk Jefferson	
Nicholson, Wm	1,000	1	28	8- 5-1784	Fk Pitman Cr	Surveyed
North, Jno	1,000	1	56	8- 7-1784	Fk Big Barren R	Surveyed
Norton, Geo F	1,000	1	117	8-13-1784	Cumberland R	
Norton, Geo F	1,000	1	118	8-13-1784	Cumberland R	
Norton, Geo F	1,000	1	118	8-13-1784	Cumberland R	
O'Bannon, Jno	400	1	112	8-13-1784	Pitman Cr	Withdrawn
O'Bannon, Jno	400	1	278	4-28-1792	Clay Lick Fk	Surveyed
Oliver, Wm	2,000	1	213	8- 1-1791	S Fk Little Barren R	Withdrawn
Oliver, Wm	2,000	1	232	8- 3-1791	———Cr	Withdrawn
Oliver, Wm	2,000	1	235	9- 1-1791	None	Withdrawn
Oliver, Wm	1,000	1	240	9-17-1791	Cumberland R	Withdrawn
Oliver, Wm	1,000	1	240	9-17-1791	Cumberland R	Withdrawn
Oliver, Wm	1,776	1	260	4-26-1792	Cumberland R	Surveyed
Oliver, Wm	224	1	279	4-28-1792	Little Barren R	Surveyed
Ozburn, Richard	200	1	236	9-10-1791	Nolands Cr	Withdrawn
Ozburn, Richard	200	1	288	4-30-1792	Green R	Surveyed
Parker, Jno	277	1	181	7-11-1786	Green R	Surveyed
Parker, Wm	666⅔	1	28	8- 5-1784	Fishing Cr	Surveyed
Parker, Wm H	1,000	1	47	8- 6-1784	Little Barren R	
Parker, Wm H	1,000	1	83	8-11-1784	Little R	
Payne, Wm	4,800	1	171	3- 8-1786	E Fk Drakes Cr	Surveyed

Entree	Acres	Book	Page	Entry Date	Watercourse	Notes
Pearl, Wm............	300....	1...237....		9-10-1791....	N Fk Skeggs Cr....	Withdrawn
Pearl, Wm............	300....	1...251....		2-25-1792....	Cumberland Trace..	....
Pearson, Matthew.....	633⅓..	1...225....		8- 2-1791....	Skeggs Cr.........	Amended
Pearson, Matthew.....	1,000..	1...225....		8- 2-1791....	Green R..........	Amended
Pearson, Matthew.....	1,000..	1...226....		8- 2-1791....	Sulphur Lick......	Amended
Pearson, Matthew.....	1,000..	1...226....		8- 2-1791....	Sinkhole Sp........	Withdrawn
Pearson, Matthew.....	1,000..	1...229....		8- 2-1791....	Green R..........	Surveyed
Pearson, Matthew.....	1,800..	1...229....		8- 2-1791....	Fk Big Barren R...	Surveyed
Pearson & Read......	1,000..	1...285....		4-28-1792....	Sulphur Lick......	
Pearson & Read......	1,000..	1...285....		4-28-1792....	Fk Clay Lick......	Surveyed
Pearson & Read......	633⅓..	1...285....		4-28-1792....	None.............	Surveyed
Pennock, Wm........	1,000..	1... 22....		8- 4-1784....	Red Stone Cr......	....
Pennock, Wm........	1,666⅔..	1... 23....		8- 4-1784....	Red Stone Cr......	....
Pennock, Wm........	1,000..	1... 33....		8- 5-1784....	Tennessee R.......	....
Pennock, Wm........	900....	1... 56....		8- 7-1784....	Tennessee R.......	....
Pennock, Wm........	1,000..	1... 90....		8-11-1784....	Ohio R...........	....
Perault, Michael......	1,000..	1... 60....		8- 7-1784....	S Fk Big Barren R.	Surveyed
Perault, Michael......	1,000..	1... 82....		8-11-1784....	Cumberland R.....	Surveyed
Perault, Michael......	1,000..	1...100....		8-12-1784....	Mayfield Cr.......	
Perault, Michael......	1,000..	1...106....		8-12-1784....	———— R...........	Withdrawn
Perkins, Philimon.....	666⅔..	1...196....		12-27-1787....	Green R..........	
Perkman, Jno........	1,000..	1... 40....		8- 6-1784....	Tennessee R.......	Withdrawn
Perkman, Jno........	500....	1...289....		4-30-1792....	Green R..........	Surveyed
Perkman, Jno........	500....	1...289....		4-30-1792....	Cumberland R.....	Surveyed
Perkman, Jno........	500....	1...290....		4-30-1792....	Cumberland R.....	Withdrawn
Pickering & Hogdon...	1,000..	1... 73....		8-10-1784....	Ohio R...........	
Pickering & Hogdon...	1,000..	1...268....		4-28-1792....	S Fk Glovers Cr....	Surveyed
Pickering & Hogdon...	1,000..	1...269....		4-28-1792....	Glovers Cr........	Surveyed
Pickering & Hogdon...	3,000..	1...269....		4-28-1792....	Glovers Cr........	....
Pickering & Hogdon...	1,000..	1...270....		4-28-1792....	Skeggs Cr.........	
Pickering & Hogdon...	3,300..	1...275....		4-28-1792....	Clay Lick Fk......	Surveyed
Plum, Wm Executor...	2,000..	1...282....		4-28-1792....	Fk Little Barren R.	Surveyed
Plum, Wm Executor...	1,000..	1...282....		4-28-1792....	N Fk Glovers Cr...	
Plum, Wm Executor...	1,000..	1...282....		4-28-1792....	None.............	Surveyed
Plum, Wm Executor...	700....	1...283....		4-28-1792....	Little Barren R....	Surveyed
Plum, Wm Executor...	633⅓..	1...283....		4-28-1792....	Skeggs Cr.........	Surveyed
Porterfield, Robt.....	1,200..	1... 27....		8- 5-1784....	Ohio R...........	Amended
Porterfield, Robt.....	1,333⅓..	1... 57....		8- 7-1784....	None.............	Amended
Porterfield, Robt.....	1,200..	1... 59....		8- 7-1784....	None.............	Amended
Porterfield, Robt.....	1,200..	1... 59....		8- 7-1784....	———— R...........	Withdrawn
Porterfield, Robt.....	1,333⅓..	1... 67....		8- 9-1784....	Ohio.............	Amended
Porterfield, Robt.....	1,200..	1... 67....		8- 9-1784....	Delaware Cr.......	....
Porterfield, Robt.....	1,200..	1... 68....		8- 9-1784....	Delaware Cr.......	....
Porterfield, Robt.....	1,200..	1... 76....		8-10-1784....	Hunting Cr........	....
Porterfield, Robt.....	1,333⅓..	1... 79....		8-10-1784....	Cumberland R.....	Amended
Porterfield, Robt.....	1,200..	1...105....		8-12-1784....	None.............	
Porterfield, Robt.....	1,333⅓..	1...147....		8-13-1785....	———— R...........	Surveyed
Powell, Aaron........	200....	1... 21....		8- 4-1784....	Fishing Cr........	
Price, Abraham.......	400....	1...144....		7-21-1785....	Cumberland R.....	Surveyed
Price, Jno W.........	600....	1...288....		4-30-1792....	Green R..........	Surveyed
Price, Pugh..........	1,333⅓..	1... 77....		8-10-1784....	N Fk Big Barren R	Surveyed
Price, Pugh..........	1,333⅓..	1...115....		8-13-1784....	Cumberland R.....	Withdrawn
Price, Pugh..........	———	1...222....		8- 2-1791....	Russell Cr........	Surveyed
Price & McClung.....	600....	1... 71....		8-10-1784....	Big Barren R......	Withdrawn
Pryor, Jno...........	666⅔..	1...219....		8- 1-1791....	Skeggs Cr.........	Withdrawn
Pryor, Jno...........	1,000..	1...220....		8- 2-1791....	Beaver Cr.........	Withdrawn
Pryor, Jno...........	500....	1...238....		9-10-1791....	Skeggs Cr.........	Surveyed
Pryor, Jno...........	500....	1...238....		9-10-1791....	E Fk Little Barren R	Withdrawn
Pryor, Jno...........	2,166⅔..	1...257....		4-25-1792....	Beaver Cr.........	....
Purcell, Robt........	100....	1...101....		8-12-1784....	None.............	....
Pursley, Lawrence....	100....	1...193....		12-27-1787....	Cumberland R.....	Surveyed
Quarles, Henry.......	1,000..	1... 15....		8- 3-1784....	Green R..........	Surveyed
Quarles, Henry.......	1,000..	1... 20....		8- 4-1784....	Green R..........	Surveyed
Quarles, Henry.......	1,000..	1... 72....		8-10-1784....	S Fk Big Barren R	....
Quarles, Henry.......	1,000..	1... 85....		8-11-1784....	W Fk Consales Cr..	
Quarles, James.......	1,000..	1... 13....		8- 3-1784....	Cumberland R.....	Surveyed
Quarles, Jas.........	1,000..	1... 62....		8- 7-1784....	S Fk Big Barren R..	Surveyed
Quarles, Jas.........	1,000..	1... 64....		8- 7-1784....	Pitman Cr.........	Surveyed
Quarles, Jas.........	1,333⅓..	1... 71....		8-10-1784....	Hunting Cr........	
Quarles, Jas.........	1,000..	1... 91....		8-11-1784....	Tennessee R.......	....
Read, Edmund.......	1,000..	1... 7....		8- 2-1784....	Mulberryfield.....	
Read, Edmund.......	1,000..	1... 10....		8- 3-1784....	Fk Willow Cr......	....
Read, Edmund.......	1,000..	1... 30....		8- 5-1784....	Tennessee R.......	....
Read, Edmund.......	1,000..	1... 87....		8-11-1784....	Harlans Cr........	....
Read, Geo...........	1,000..	1...225....		8- 2-1791....	Green R..........	Amended
Read, Geo...........	633⅓..	1...225....		8- 2-1791....	Skeggs Cr.........	Amended
Read, Geo...........	1,000..	1...226....		8- 2-1791....	Sulphur Lick......	Amended
Read, Geo...........	1,000..	1...226....		8- 2-1791....	Sinkhole Sp	Withdrawn
Read, Geo...........	1,000..	1...229....		8- 2-1791....	Green R..........	Surveyed
Read, Geo...........	1,800..	1...229....		8- 2-1791....	Fk Big Barren R...	Surveyed
Read, Jno...........	1,333⅓..	1... 14....		8- 3-1784....	Cumberland R.....	Surveyed

Entree	Acres	Book	Page	Entry Date	Watercourse	Notes
Read, Jno	1,333¾	1	57	8- 7-1784	S Fk Big Barren R.	....
Read & Pearson	1,000	1	285	4-28-1792	Sulphur Lick	Surveyed
Read & Pearson	1,000	1	285	4-28-1792	Fk Clay Lick	Surveyed
Read & Pearson	633⅓	1	285	4-28-1792	None	Surveyed
Renick, Henry	500	1	218	8- 1-1791	Fk of Cr	Withdrawn
Renick, Henry	200	1	218	8- 1-1791	Russell Cr	Surveyed
Renick, Henry	100	1	244	2- 9-1792	Crocus Cr	Surveyed
Renick, Henry	200	1	245	2- 9-1792	Russell Cr	Surveyed
Renick, Henry	200	1	245	2- 9-1792	Russell Cr	Surveyed
Renick, Henry	212	1	245	2- 9-1792	Butlers Fk.	Surveyed
Renick, Henry	121½	1	273	4-28-1792	Russell Cr	Surveyed
Reynolds, Wm	1,000	1	54	8- 7-1784	Crocus Cr	Surveyed
Reynolds, Wm	1,300	1	71	8-10-1784	Skeggs Cr	Surveyed
Reynolds & Wright	500	1	86	8-11-1784	Green R.	Surveyed
Reynolds, Wm	1,333⅓	1	198	2-24-1788	S Fk Little Barren R	Surveyed
Reynolds, Wm	1,000	1	198	2-24-1788	Cumberland R.	Surveyed
Reynolds, Wm	1,000	1	199	2-24-1788	Cumberland R.	Surveyed
Reynolds, Wm	1,666⅔	1	199	2-24-1788	Cumberland R.	Surveyed
Reynolds, Wm	1,000	1	199	2-24-1788	Cumberland R.	Surveyed
Reynolds, Wm	666⅔	1	199	2-24-1788	Cumberland R.	Withdrawn
Reynolds, Wm	2,000	1	199	2-24-1788	Drakes Cr	Surveyed
Reynolds, Wm	1,333	1	200	2-24-1788	E Fk Little Barren R	Withdrawn
Reynolds, Wm	2,000	1	202	5-12-1788	S Fk Little Barren R	Surveyed
Reynolds, Wm	866⅔	1	202	5-12-1788	S Fk Little Barren R	Surveyed
Reynolds, Wm	1,000	1	213	8- 1-1791	Smoking Sp Br	Surveyed
Reynolds, Wm	1,000	1	213	8- 1-1791	Cumberland R.	Withdrawn
Reynolds, Wm	766⅔	1	213	8- 1-1791	——— R.	Withdrawn
Reynolds, Wm	700	1	214	8- 1-1791	Cumberland R.	Withdrawn
Reynolds, Thos	1,500	1	217	8- 1-1791	Big Barren R	Withdrawn
Reynolds, Wm	2,000	1	217	8- 1-1791	Skeggs Cr	Surveyed
Reynolds, Thos	1,366⅔	1	217	8- 1-1791	Skeggs Cr	Withdrawn
Reynolds, Wm	666⅔	1	218	8- 1-1791	——— Cr	Withdrawn
Reynolds, Wm	1,270	1	230	8- 2-1791	S Fk Little Barren R	Surveyed
Reynolds, Wm	2,000	1	237	9-10-1791	Little Barren R.	Surveyed
Reynolds, Wm	1,333⅓	1	237	9-10-1791	S Fk Little Barren..	Surveyed
Reynolds, Wm	1,270	1	238	9-10-1791	Drakes Cr	....
Reynolds, Thos & Wm	2,033⅓	1	252	2-25-1792	Fk Big Barren R.	Withdrawn
Reynolds, Wm	600	1	263	4-27-1792	Cumberland R.	Surveyed
Reynolds, Wm	2,466⅔	1	263	4-27-1792	Skeggs Cr	Surveyed
Reynolds, Thos & Wm	2,033⅓	1	264	4-27-1792	Caney Fk.	Surveyed
Reynolds, Wm	1,333⅓	4	270	4-28-1792	E Fk Little Barren R	Surveyed
Reynolds, Thos	1,500	1	285	4-28-1792	Big Barren R.	Surveyed
Reynolds, Wm	1,100	1	294	4-30-1792	Russell Cr	Surveyed
Rhodes, Jno	250	1	155	12-13-1785	Far Fk Red R.	Surveyed
Rice, Geo	1,200	1	77	8-10-1784	None	Withdrawn
Rice, Geo	33⅓	1	258	4-25-1792	Old Trace	Surveyed
Rice, Geo	1,200	1	293	4-30-1792	Cumberland R.	Surveyed
Richards, Jno	200	1	77	8-10-1784	Flat Lick Br.	Surveyed
Richardson, Daniel	2,666⅔	1	206	7-19-1788	S Fk Little Barren R	Withdrawn
Richardson, Daniel	1,480	1	230	8- 2-1791	S Fk Little Barren R	Surveyed
Richardson, Daniel	500	1	284	4-28-1792	E Fk Little Barren R	....
Richardson, Daniel	686⅔	1	284	4-28-1792	E Fk Little Barren R	....
Ridley, Jno	200	1	77	8-10-1784	Flat Lick Br.	Surveyed
Roan, Christopher	1,000	1	15	8-23-1784	Town Columbia	....
Roan, Christopher	1,000	1	18	8- 4-1784	Ohio R.	Surveyed
Roan, Christopher	1,000	1	34	8- 5-1784	Beaver Cr	Withdrawn
Roan, Christopher	1,000	1	60	8- 7-1784	None	....•......
Roan, Christopher	666⅔	1	61	8- 7-1784	Ohio R.	Surveyed
Roan, Christopher	1,000	1	133	1- 7-1785	Skeggs Cr	Surveyed
Roan, Christopher	200	1	217	8- 1-1791	S Fk Little Barren R	Withdrawn
Roan & Mazarett	100	1	275	4-28-1792	Skeggs Cr	Surveyed
Roberts, Wm	100	1	170	1-26-1786	Salt Peter Cave	Surveyed
Roberts, Wm	100	1	171	1-26-1786	Middle Fk Red R.	Withdrawn
Roberts, Wm	200	1	171	1-26-1786	None	Surveyed
Roberts, Wm	100	1	174	4-14-1786	Whipporwill Cr	Withdrawn
Roberts, Wm	400	1	174	4-14-1786	Red R.	Surveyed
Roberts, Wm	70	1	175	4-14-1786	Red R.	Withdrawn
Roberts, Wm	100	1	175	4-14-1786	Red R.	Surveyed
Roberts, Wm	30	1	175	4-14-1786	Red R.	....
Roberts, Wm	100	1	175	4-14-1786	Red R.	Withdrawn
Roberts, Wm	100	1	192	5- 1-1787	Maulding Fk Red R	Surveyed
Roberts, Wm	100	1	192	5- 1-1787	E Sinking Fk.	Withdrawn
Roberts, Wm	200	1	203	6-10-1788	Mauldings Fk Red R	Surveyed
Roberts, Wm	500	1	215	8- 1-1791	Petits & Butlers Fk.	Withdrawn
Roberts, Wm	500	1	215	8- 1-1791	Butlers Fk.	Withdrawn
Roberts, Wm	366⅔	1	215	8- 1-1791	Russell Cr	Withdrawn
Roberts, Wm	300	1	215	8- 1-1791	Maulding Fk Red R	Surveyed
Roberts, Wm	500	1	216	8- 1-1791	Russell Cr	Surveyed
Roberts, Wm	300	1	226	8- 2-1791	Big Fk Russell Cr..	Withdrawn
Roberts, Wm	400	1	233	8- 4-1791	Sinking Cr	....

Entree	Acres	Book	Page	Entry Date	Watercourse	Notes
Roberts, Wm	470	1	234	9- 1-1791	Sinking Fk Russell Cr	Surveyed
Roberts, Wm	240	1	243	12-11-1791	Russell Cr	Surveyed
Roberts, Wm	926⅔	1	243	12-11-1791	Russell Cr	Surveyed
Roberts, Wm	100	1	247	2-25-1792	Russell Cr	Surveyed
Roberts, Wm	50	1	261	4-26-1792	Maulding Fk Red R	Surveyed
Roberts, Wm	50	1	274	4-28-1792	Red R	Surveyed
Roberts, Wm	50	1	274	4-28-1792	N Fk W Fk Red R	Surveyed
Roberts, Wm	90	1	274	4-28-1792	N Fk W Fk Red R	Surveyed
Roberts, Wm	2,000	1	274	4-28-1792	Rains Lick Cr	Surveyed
Roberts & Banks	1,000	1	141	5-18-1785	Clarks R	Withdrawn
Roberts & Banks	1,000	1	141	5-18-1785	Clarks R	Withdrawn
Roberts & Banks	3,000	1	148	8-13-1785	Russell Cr	Withdrawn
Roberts & Banks	4,000	1	148	8-13-1785	Wolf Cr	Withdrawn
Roberts & Banks	1,150	1	168	1-11-1786	Russell Cr	Withdrawn
Roberts & Banks	100	1	182	9-29-1786	Red R	Surveyed
Roberts & Banks	300	1	182	9-29-1786	Middle Fk Red R	....
Roberts & Banks	100	1	182	9-29-1786	Red R	Surveyed
Roberts & Banks	1,000	1	184	10- 1-1786	Wolf Cr	....
Roberts & Banks	7,110⅔	1	184	10- 1-1786	Wolf & Russell Cr	Surveyed
Roberts & Banks	1,531	1	184	10- 1-1786	Russell Cr	Surveyed
Roberts & Banks	2,666⅔	1	184	10- 1-1786	Sulphur Fk	Surveyed
Roberts & Banks	1,500	1	185	10- 1-1786	Fk Cumberland R	Surveyed
Roberts & Banks	1,152½	1	224	8- 2-1791	Russell Cr	Withdrawn
Roberts & Banks	1,152½	1	242	12- 9-1791	Cumberland R	Surveyed
Roberts & Banks	472½	1	242	12- 9-1791	Crocus Cr	Withdrawn
Roberts & Banks	472½	1	295	5- 1-1792	Marrowbone Cr	Surveyed
Roberts & Martin	200	1	202	2-24-1788	Russell Cr	Surveyed
Rochester, Wm	100	1	165	12-13-1785	Boyds Cr	Surveyed
Rogers, Edmund	450	1	155	12-13-1785	Beaver Cr	Surveyed
Rogers, Edmund	500	1	216	8- 1-1791	Skeggs Cr	Withdrawn
Rogers, Edmund	1,000	1	256	4-24-1792	Clay Lick Fk	Surveyed
Rogers, Edmund	500	1	284	4-28-1792	Skeggs Cr	Surveyed
Rogers, Geo	200	1	124	8-14-1784	Mississippi R	Withdrawn
Rogers, Geo	200	1	222	8- 2-1791	Skeggs Cr	Withdrawn
Rogers, Geo	200	1	249	2-25-1792	Skeggs Cr	Surveyed
Rogers, Jno	4,000	1	1	8- 2-1784	Mississippi R	....
Rogers, Jno	1,000	1	11	8- 3-1784	Fk Tennessee R	Surveyed
Rogers, Jno	1,000	1	51	8- 6-1784	None	....
Rogers, Jno	1,000	1	53	8- 7-1784	Tennessee R	Surveyed
Rogers, Jno	1,000	1	109	8-12-1784	Lilly Cr	Withdrawn
Rogers, Jno	960	1	141	4-25-1785	Tennessee R	Withdrawn
Rogers, Jno	40	1	144	7- 6-1785	Island Ohio R	....
Rogers, Jno	600	1	146	8-13-1785	Cumberland R	....
Ross, David	400	1	120	8-14-1784	None	....
Ross, David & Co	1,000	1	113	8-13-1784	Mississippi R	....
Rowland, Jno	200	1	258	4-25-1792	Peter Cr	....
Rucker, Angus	1,000	1	27	8- 5-1784	Obyan Cr	....
Rucker, Angus	1,000	1	43	8- 6-1784	Cumberland R	Surveyed
Rucker, Angus	1,000	1	93	8-11-1784	Clarks R	....
Rucker, Angus	1,000	1	101	8-12-1784	None	....
Rucker, Elliott	1,000	1	10	8- 3-1784	Willow Cr	Withdrawn
Rucker, Elliott	1,000	1	69	8- 9-1784	E Fk Consales Cr	....
Rucker, Elliott	666⅔	1	77	8-10-1784	None	Withdrawn
Rucker, Elliott	1,000	1	221	8- 2-1791	Russell Cr	Surveyed
Rucker, Elliott	1,000	1	221	8- 2-1791	Russell Cr	Surveyed
Rucker, Elliott	666⅔	1	221	8- 2-1791	Petits Fk	....
Russell, Chas	1,333⅓	1	2	8- 2-1784	Mouth Town Cr	....
Russell, Chas	1,333⅓	1	93	8-11-1784	—— R	....
Rust, Benj	1,000	1	103	8-12-1784	None	....
Rust, Benj	1,666⅔	1	105	8-12-1784	Big Barren R	Surveyed
Saunders, Jno	1,000	1	19	8- 4-1784	Cane Cr	Surveyed
Saunders, Jno	1,000	1	46	8- 6-1784	Little Barren R	....
Saunders, Jno	1,000	1	92	8-11-1784	None	....
Saunders, Jno	1,666⅔	1	110	8-12-1784	Little Barren R	Surveyed
Saunders, Joseph	666⅔	1	43	8- 6-1784	Rock Lick Cr	Surveyed
Saunders, Joseph	1,000	1	49	8- 6-1784	Cumberland R	Surveyed
Saunders, Joseph	1,000	1	84	8-11-1784	Ohio R	....
Saunders, Joseph	500	1	210	10- 7-1788	Russell Cr	Surveyed
Saunders, Joseph	666⅔	1	223	8- 2-1791	Big Barren R	Surveyed
Saunders, Joseph	500	1	223	8- 2-1791	Peter Cr	Surveyed
Saunders, Joseph	500	1	223	8- 1-1791	Peter Cr	Surveyed
Saunders, Wm	1,000	1	23	8- 4-1784	Buck Cr	Surveyed
Saunders, Wm	1,000	1	40	8- 6-1784	Flat Lick Cr	....
Saunders, Wm	1,000	1	83	8-11-1784	Little R	....
Saunders, Wm	1,000	1	106	8-12-1784	—— R	....
Saunders & Evans	350	1	292	4-30-1792	Big Barren R	Surveyed
Savage, Nathaniel	900	1	53	8- 7-1784	Crocus Cr	Surveyed
Savage, Nathaniel	900	1	57	8- 7-1784	S Fk Big Barren R	Surveyed
Savage, Nathaniel L	866⅔	1	8	8- 3-1784	None	....
Shaffer, David	2,000	1	92	8-11-1784	—— Cr	Surveyed

Entree	Acres	Book	Page	Entry Date	Watercourse	Notes
Sharman, Martin	666⅔	1	7	8- 3-1787	N Fk Mayfield Cr	....
Sharman, Martin	1,000	1	33	8- 5-1784	Skeggs Cr	Surveyed
Sharman, Martin	1,000	1	95	8-11-1784	W Fk Clarks R	....
Shaw, Thos	1,000	1	11	8- 3-1784	Mississippi R	....
Shepherd, David	1,000	1	179	7- 2-1786	S Fk Little Barren R	Withdrawn
Shepherd, David	1,000	1	190	3-28-1787	E Fk Drakes Cr	Surveyed
Shepherd, Jas	200	1	101	8-12-1784	None	....
Shepherd, Jno M	600	1	63	8- 7-1784	Green R	Withdrawn
Shepherd, Jno M	1,000	1	76	8-10-1784	Beaver Cr	Withdrawn
Shepherd, Jno M	1,000	1	136	1-31-1785	Sinks of Beaver Cr	Surveyed
Shepherd, Jno M	600	1	136	1-31-1785	Sinks of Beaver Cr	Surveyed
Shepherd, Jno M	600	1	156	12-13-1785	Skeggs Cr	Surveyed
Shields, Jno	1,000	1	126	8-14-1784	Russell Cr	Withdrawn
Shields, Jno	3,000	1	130	8-17-1784	Tennessee R	Withdrawn
Shields, Jno	500	1	222	8- 2-1791	Peter Cr	....
Shields, Jno	1,000	1	286	4-30-1792	Peter Cr	Surveyed
Shields, Jno	1,000	1	286	4-30-1792	Peter Cr	Surveyed
Shields, Jno	1,000	1	287	4-30-1792	Peter Cr	Surveyed
Shields, Jno	500	1	287	4-30-1792	Peter Cr	Surveyed
Shinner, Coms	300	1	152	12- 7-1785	None	Surveyed
Shipp & Morgan	400	1	270	4-28-1792	N Fk Skeggs Cr	....
Slaughter, Geo	1,500	1	149	10- 3-1785	W Fk Glenns Cr	Surveyed
Slaughter, Geo	666⅔	1	160	12-13-1785	Skeggs Cr	Surveyed
Slaughter, Geo	2,000	1	161	12-13-1785	Skeggs Cr	Withdrawn
Slaughter, Geo	1,000	1	163	12-13-1785	Skeggs Cr	Surveyed
Smith, Geo	1,500	1	27	8- 4-1784	Buck & Pitman Cr	Surveyed
Smith, Geo	1,000	1	39	8- 6-1784	None	....
Smith, Geo	1,000	1	69	8- 9-1784	Hunting Cr	....
Smith, Geo	1,666⅔	1	96	8-11-1784	Willow Cr	....
Smith, Gregory	1,500	1	92	8-11-1784	None	....
Smith, Wm	200	1	154	12- 7-1785	Far Fk Red R	Surveyed
Snell, Chas	116⅔	1	166	12-13-1785	Rock Lick Br	Surveyed
Scott, Jno	2,663	1	159	12-13-1785	Skeggs Cr	Surveyed
Scott, Jno	1,250	1	189	3-28-1787	Little Barren	Surveyed
Scott, Jno	87	1	253	2-25-1792	Spring Lick	Surveyed
Scott, Walter	1,000	1	16	8- 3-1784	None	....
Scott, Walter	1,000	1	38	8- 6-1784	Russell Cr	Surveyed
Scott, Walter	666⅔	1	62	8- 7-1784	S Fk Big Barren R	Surveyed
Spencer, Wm	1,000	1	19	8- 4-1784	Mayfield Cr	....
Spencer, Wm	666⅔	1	41	8- 6-1784	Mayfield Cr	....
Spencer, Wm	1,000	1	109	8-12-1784	None	....
Spengler & Stover	3,110⅔	1	297	9-23-1792	Fk Big Barren R	....
Spiller, Wm	1,000	1	15	8- 3-1784	Br Cane Cr	Surveyed
Spiller, Wm	1,000	1	27	8- 5-1784	Little Barren R	Surveyed
Spiller, Wm	1,000	1	82	8-11-1784	Little R	Withdrawn
Spiller, Wm	1,000	1	88	8-11-1784	None	....
Spiller, Wm	333	1	290	4-30-1792	Cumberland R	Surveyed
Spiller, Wm	667	1	291	4-30-1792	E Fk Beaver Cr	Surveyed
Stephens, James	100	1	203	5-12-1788	Cumberland R	....
Strode, Jno	700	1	186	2- 1-1787	Cumberland R	Surveyed
Strode, Jno	300	1	186	2- 1-1787	None	Surveyed
Strode, Jno	166⅔	1	276	4-28-1792	Russell Cr	Surveyed
Strode, Jno	200	1	276	4-28-1792	Russell Cr	Surveyed
Strode, Jno	300	1	276	4-28-1792	Russell Cr	Surveyed
Strong, Walter E	1,100	1	53	8- 6-1784	Cumberland R	Surveyed
Strong, Walter E	1,100	1	105	8-12-1784	Mayfield Cr	....
Strong, Walter E	200	1	166	12-13-1785	Skeggs Cr	Surveyed
Strong, Walter E	600	1	176	4-14-1786	Little Barren R	Surveyed
Strong, Walter E	600	1	176	4-14-1786	Skeggs Cr	Surveyed
Stover & Spengler	3,110⅔	1	297	9-23-1792	Fk Big Barren R	....
Stewart, Jno	1,333½	1	58	8- 7-1784	Green R	Surveyed
Stewart, Jno	2,000	1	84	8-11-1784	Tennessee R	Surveyed
Summers, Jas	200	1	123	8-14-1784	Pitman Cr	....
Swearingen, Benone	2,947	1	157	12-13-1785	Skeggs Cr	Surveyed
Swearingen, Benone	103	1	179	7- 2-1786	Big Barren R	Withdrawn
Swearingen, Benone	2,000	1	206	7-19-1788	Little Barren R	Surveyed
Swearingen, Benone	1,066⅔	1	206	7-19-1788	Little Barren R	Surveyed
Swearingen, Benone	2,000	1	228	8- 2-1791	N Fk Skeggs Cr	Surveyed
Swearingen, Benone	881	1	263	4-27-1792	N Fk Skeggs Cr	Surveyed
Tabb, Augustine	1,000	1	13	8- 3-1784	Cumberland R	Surveyed
Tabb, Augustine	1,000	1	83	8-11-1784	Little R	....
Tabb, Augustine	1,000	1	90	8-11-1784	None	....
Tabb, Augustine	1,000	1	99	8-12-1784	Mayfield Cr	....
Tardevain, Peter	600	1	156	12-13-1785	Beaver Cr	Surveyed
Tardevain, Peter	200	1	264	4-27-1792	Caney Fk	Surveyed
Taylor, Benj	1,000	1	61	8- 2-1784	1st Fk Red R	....
Taylor, Benj	1,000	1	102	8-12-1784	Far Fk Red R	Surveyed
Taylor, Benj	666⅔	1	110	8-12-1784	Far Fk Red R	Surveyed
Taylor, Jas	100	1	101	8-12-1784	None	....
Taylor, Richard	1,000	1	9	8- 3-1784	Mouth Straight Cr	Surveyed

Entree	Acres	Book	Page	Entry Date	Watercourse	Notes
Taylor, Richard	1,000	1	19	8- 4-1784	None	
Taylor, Richard	1,000	1	36	8- 5-1784	None	
Taylor, Richard	1,000	1	50	8- 6-1784	None	
Taylor, Richard	1,333⅓	1	110	8-12-1784	None	
Taylor, Richard	1,333⅓	1	146	8-13-1785	Cumberland R	Surveyed
Taylor, Richard	1,000	1	255	4-24-1792	Glovers Cr	Surveyed
Terrell, Oliver	1,000	1	134	1-21-1785	Pitman Cr	Surveyed
Therice & Gallego	1,200	1	112	8-13-1784	W Fk Red R	Withdrawn
Therice & Gallego	1,200	1	289	4-30-1792	Big Barren R	Surveyed
Thompson, Jno	100	1	241	10- 2-1791	Green R	
Thompson, Jno	100	1	241	10- 2-1791	Beaver Cr	Surveyed
Thompson, Wm	1,000	1	12	8- 3-1784	Cumberland R	Amended
Thompson, Wm	1,000	1	48	8- 6-1784	Big Barren R	Surveyed
Thompson, Wm	1,000	1	54	8- 7-1784	Crocus Cr	Surveyed
Thompson, Wm	1,000	1	103	8-12-1784	None	
Thompson, Wm	1,000	1	147	8-13-1785	Cumberland R	Surveyed
Thorns, Alexander	2,000	1	259	4-26-1792	Big Barren R	Surveyed
Throckmorton Richard	2,166⅔	1	291	4-30-1792	Cumberland R	Surveyed
Throckmorton, Richard	500	1	291	4-30-1792	Cumberland R	Surveyed
Tinsley, Samuel	1,000	1	17	8- 4-1784	Green R	Surveyed
Tinsley, Samuel	666⅔	1	40	8- 6-1784	Little Barren R	
Tinsley, Samuel	1,000	1	90	8-11-1784	Harlans Cr	
Tipton, Samuel	2,666⅔	1	218	8- 1-1791	Crocus Cr	Withdrawn
Tipton, Samuel	400	1	272	4-28-1792	Short Cr	Surveyed
Tipton, Samuel	400	1	272	4-28-1792	Russell Cr	Surveyed
Tipton, Samuel	200	1	272	4-28-1792	Cumberland R	
Todd, Robt	1,000	1	3	8- 2-1784	Mississippi R	
Todd, Robt	1,000	1	59	8- 7-1784	Main Crocus Cr	Withdrawn
Todd, Robt	1,000	1	65	8- 7-1784	Main Crocus Cr	Withdrawn
Todd, Robt	1,000	1	70	8- 9-1784	Cumberland R	Withdrawn
Todd, Robt	350	1	143	6-17-1785	Big Barren R	Withdrawn
Todd, Robt	1,333⅓	1	145	8-13-1785	Russell Cr	Surveyed
Todd, Robt	1,533⅓	1	145	8-13-1785	Russell Cr	Withdrawn
Todd, Robt	200	1	145	8-13-1785	Green R	Surveyed
Todd, Robt	500	1	152	12- 7-1785	Green R	Surveyed
Todd, Robt	200	1	152	12- 7-1785	Green R	Surveyed
Todd, Robt	920	1	153	12- 7-1785	Green R	Withdrawn
Todd, Robt	1,000	1	154	12- 7-1785	Big Barren R	Surveyed
Todd, Robt	700	1	175	4-14-1791	Mauscars Trace	Surveyed
Todd, Robt	200	1	180	7-10-1786	Green R	Surveyed
Todd, Robt	300	1	180	7-10-1786	Green R	Surveyed
Todd, Robt	543	1	180	7-10-1786	Green R	Surveyed
Todd, Robt	1,000	1	183	10- 1-1786	Russell Cr	Surveyed
Todd, Robt	920	1	188	3-28-1787	Little Barren R	Surveyed
Todd, Robt	300	1	196	12-27-1787	Cumberland R	Withdrawn
Todd, Robt	333⅓	1	197	2- 6-1788	Cumberland R	Withdrawn
Todd, Robt	200	1	254	3-12-1792	Green R	
Todd, Robt	500	1	271	4-28-1792	S Fk Russell Cr	Surveyed
Todd, Robt	500	1	271	4-28-1792	Russell Cr	Surveyed
Todd, Robt	1,000	1	271	4-28-1792	S Fk Green R	Surveyed
Todd, Robt	400	1	272	4-28-1792	Russell Cr	Surveyed
Todd, Robt	100	1	273	4-28-1792	Green R	Surveyed
Todd, Robt	100	1	273	4-28-1792	Green R	Surveyed
Todd, Capt Robt	80	1	150	12- 5-1785	Green R	Surveyed
Todd, Capt Robt	920	1	150	12- 5-1785	Green R	Withdrawn
Todd, Robt Jr	200	1	145	8-13-1785	Green R	Surveyed
Todd, Robt Jr	1,000	1	150	12- 5-1785	Green R	Surveyed
Todd, Robt Jr	100	1	151	12- 6-1785	Knob Lick Fk	Surveyed
Todd & Bryan	633	1	208	8- 8-1788	Russell Cr	
Todd & McDermot	300	1	208	8- 8-1788	Green R	Withdrawn
Thompkins, Christopher	2,666⅔	1	283	4-28-1792	Indian Cr	Surveyed
Tompkins, Jas	1,666⅔	1	26	8- 4-1784	Fk Buck Cr	Surveyed
Tompkins, Robt	4,000	1	280	4-28-1792	Peter Cr	
Tompkins, Robt	1,333⅓	1	280	4-28-1792	Big Barren R	Withdrawn
Tompkins, Robt	1,333⅓	1	290	4-30-1792	Big Barren	Surveyed
Tribble, Andrew	200	1	203	5-12-1788	Cumberland R	Surveyed
Trenis & Ewell	500	1	142	6- 7-1785	S Fk Consales Cr	
Tupman, Jno	1,000	1	1	8- 2-1787	Mississippi	
Tupman, Jno	666⅔	1	36	8- 5-1784	Russell Cr	
Tupman, Jno	1,000	1	38	8- 6-1784	Russell Cr	Surveyed
Turner, Jno	1,666⅔	1	76	8-10-1784	N Fk Big Barren R	Surveyed
Turner, Jno	1,000	1	77	8-10-1784	Pitman Cr	Surveyed
Turpin, Philip	1,000	1	196	12-27-1787	Pitman Cr	Surveyed
Turpin, Philip	2,000	1	222	8- 2-1791	Cumberland R	
Tyson, Cornileus	250	1	155	12-13-1785	Fk Red R	Surveyed
Upshaw, Thos	4,000	1	39	8- 6-1784	Tennessee R	Surveyed
Vaughan, Jno	666⅔	1	18	8- 4-1784	Green R	Surveyed

Entree	Acres	Book	Page	Entry Date	Watercourse	Notes
Vaughan, Jno	1,000	1	69	8- 9-1784	S Fk Clarks Cr	....
Vaughan, Jno	1,000	1	106	8-12-1784	Tennessee R	....
Vogluson, Armand	3,300	1	291	4-30-1792	Cumberland R	Surveyed
Vogluson, Armand	700	1	292	4-30-1792	Big Barren R	Surveyed
Voss, Edward	1,000	1	61	8- 7-1784	Carolina Line	....
Voss, Edward	666⅔	1	111	8-12-1784	Little Barren R	Surveyed
Voss, Edward	1,000	1	115	8-13-1784	Cumberland R	Surveyed
Vowls, Henry	2,000	1	9	8- 3-1784	Cumberland R	Surveyed
Vowls, Henry	2,666⅔	1	23	8- 4-1784	Russells Cr	Surveyed
Vowls, Henry	2,000	1	31	8- 5-1784	Big Barren R	Surveyed
Vowls, Henry	2,000	1	72	8-10-1784	None	Surveyed
Vawter, Benj	400	1	219	8- 1-1791	Russell Cr	Surveyed
Walker, Levin	1,000	1	21	8- 4-1784	None	Surveyed
Walker, Levin	1,666⅔	1	94	8-11-1784	Clarks R	Surveyed
Wallace, Jno	200	1	278	4-28-1792	Clay Lick Fk	Surveyed
Wallace, Wm	200	1	28	8- 5-1784	Flat Lick Br	Withdrawn
Wallace, Wm	1,000	1	134	1-21-1785	Pitman Cr	Surveyed
Wallis, Wm	115	1	163	12-13-1785	Skeggs Cr	Surveyed
Wallace, Edward	640	1	163	12-13-1785	None	Withdrawn
Wallace, Wm	285	1	223	8- 2-1791	Skeggs Cr	Withdrawn
Wallace, Wm	285	1	247	2-25-1792	Skeggs Cr	Surveyed
Wallace & Warren	200	1	213	8- 1-1791	S Fk Little Barren R	Withdrawn
Walls, Geo	1,000	1	13	8- 3-1784	Mississippi	Withdrawn
Walls, Geo	1,000	1	27	8- 4-1784	Little Barren R	Withdrawn
Walls, Geo	1,000	1	90	8-11-1784	Harlans Cr	Withdrawn
Walls, Geo	1,333⅓	1	92	8-11-1784	None	Withdrawn
Walls, Geo	1,000	1	94	8-11-1784	Clarks R	Withdrawn
Walters, Conrad	2,666⅔	1	214	8- 1-1791	Beaver Cr	Withdrawn
Walter, Conrad	333⅓	1	244	12-29-1791	Green R	Withdrawn
Walter, Conrad	1,333⅓	1	244	12-29-1791	Sink Hole Sp	Surveyed
Walters, Conrad	333⅓	1	256	4-24-1792	Sinking Cr	Surveyed
Walters, Richard J	200	1	276	4-28-1792	Rains Lick Cr	Surveyed
Walton, Matthew	1,300	1	219	8- 1-1791	Fishing & Buck Cr	Surveyed
Walton, Matthew	1,122⅔	1	219	8- 1-1791	None	Surveyed
Walton, Matthew	444	1	219	8- 1-1791	None	Surveyed
Warnick, Frederick	1,000	1	23	8- 4-1784	Pitmans Cr	Surveyed
Warwick, Fred	1,000	1	64	8- 7-1784	Little Barren R	Surveyed
Warrick, Fred	1,000	1	69	8- 9-1784	S Fk Clarks Cr	....
Warnick, Fred	1,000	1	82	8-11-1784	Pitman Cr	Surveyed
Warnick, Fred	1,000	1	84	8-11-1784	Clarks R	....
Warnick, Wm	400	1	219	8- 1-1791	Russell Cr	Surveyed
Warren, Thos	200	1	278	4-28-1792	Clay Lick Fk	Surveyed
Warren & Wallace	200	1	213	8- 1-1791	S Fk Little Barren R	Withdrawn
Webber, Philip & Co	1,200	1	114	8-13-1784	Big Barren R	Surveyed
Welch, Nathaniel	1,000	1	17	8- 4-1784	Flat Lick Br	Surveyed
Welch, Nathaniel	1,000	1	40	8- 6-1784	Russell Cr	Surveyed
Welch, Nathaniel	1,000	1	72	8-10-1784	Pitman Cr	Surveyed
Welch, Nathaniel	1,000	1	88	8-11-1784	W Fk Pitman Cr	Surveyed
Westcalt, Wright	1,000	1	14	8- 3-1784	Cumberland R	Surveyed
Westcalt, Wright	1,000	1	28	8- 5-1784	Big Barren R	....
Westcott, Wright	1,000	1	52	8- 6-1784	Crocus Cr	Surveyed
Westcott, Wright	1,000	1	55	8- 7-1784	W Fk Little Barren R	....
White, Thos	666⅔	1	63	8- 7-1784	Pitman Cr	....
White, Thos	1,000	1	83	8-11-1784	Little R	Surveyed
White, Thos	1,000	1	89	8-11-1784	Harlans Cr	Surveyed
White, Wm	1,000	1	22	8- 4-1784	Russells Cr	Surveyed
White, Wm	1,000	1	34	8- 5-1784	——— Cr	Withdrawn
White, Wm	666⅔	1	88	8-11-1784	Harlans Cr	Withdrawn
White, Wm	600	1	209	10- 6-1788	Green R	Surveyed
White, Wm	600	1	209	10- 6-1788	Little Barren R	Withdrawn
White, Wm	800	1	221	8- 2-1791	Big Barren R	Surveyed
White, Wm	40	1	233	8-23-1791	Green R	Surveyed
White, Wm	640	1	287	4-30-1792	Green R	Surveyed
Williams, Jarrett	666⅔	1	31	8- 5-1784	Fk Drakes Cr	Withdrawn
Williams, Jarrett	1,000	1	46	8- 6-1784	Beaver Cr	Withdrawn
Williams, Jarrett	1,000	1	54	8- 7-1784	Crocus Cr	Surveyed
Williams, Jarrett	666⅔	1	139	3-31-1785	Drakes Cr	Withdrawn
Williams, Jarrett	360	1	162	12-13-1785	Big Barren R	Surveyed
Williams, Jarrett	640	1	162	12-13-1785	Big Barren R	Withdrawn
Williams, Jarrett	520	1	164	12-13-1785	Big Barren R	Surveyed
Williams, Jarrett	120	1	166	12-13-1785	Skeggs Cr	Withdrawn
Williams, Jarrett	120	1	206	7-19-1788	Skeggs Cr	Withdrawn
Williams, Jarrett	120	1	251	2-25-1792	Little Barren R	Surveyed
Williams, Edward	100	1	181	8-16-1786	Green R	Surveyed
Williams, Jno	1,000	1	2	8- 2-1784	None	....
Williams, Jno	1,000	1	26	8- 4-1784	Russell Cr	Surveyed
Williams, Jno	1,000	1	39	8- 6-1784	Skeggs Cr	Withdrawn
Williams, Jno	1,000	1	75	8-10-1784	None	....

Entree	Acres	Book	Page	Entry Date	Watercourse	Notes
Williams, Jno	500	1	157	12-13-1785	Skeggs Cr	Surveyed
Williams, Jno	500	1	205	6-10-1788	S Fk Little Barren R	Withdrawn
Williams, Jno	350	1	267	4-27-1792	Beaver Cr	Surveyed
Williams, Jno	150	1	267	4-27-1792	Little Barren R	....
Wilson, Joseph	1,200	1	114	8-12-1784	Big Barren R	Surveyed
Wilson, Thos	400	1	248	2-29-1792	Skeggs Cr	Withdrawn
Wilson, Thos	200	1	248	2-29-1792	Sinking Cr	Withdrawn
Wilson, Thos	400	1	249	2-25-1792	Skeggs Cr	Surveyed
Wilson, Thos	100	1	249	2-25-1792	Beaver Cr	Withdrawn
Wilson, Thos	200	1	249	2-25-1792	Big Barren R	Withdrawn
Wilson, Thos	200	1	250	2-25-1792	Skeggs Cr	Withdrawn
Wilson, Thos	666⅔	1	250	2-25-1792	Peter Cr	Withdrawn
Wilson, Thos	460	1	255	4-24-1792	S Fk Little Barren R	Surveyed
Wilson, Thos	1,206⅔	1	255	4-24-1792	Glen Cr	Surveyed
Wilson, Thos	200	1	256	4-24-1792	Clay Lick Fk	Surveyed
Wilson, Thos	1,750	1	275	4-28-1792	Clay Lick Fk	Surveyed
Wilson, Thos	200	1	284	4-28-1792	Skeggs Cr	Surveyed
Wilson, Willis	2,000	1	125	8-14-1784	None	Withdrawn
Wilson, Willis	1,000	1	125	8-14-1784	None	....
Wilson, Willis	1,000	1	126	8-14-1784	None	....
Wilson, Willis	1,000	1	126	8-14-1784	None	....
Wilson, Willis	1,000	1	126	8-14-1784	Beaver Cr	Surveyed
Wilson, Willis	333⅓	1	126	8-14-1784	None	....
Wilson, Willis	1,420	1	138	3-31-1785	Skeggs Cr	Surveyed
Woodson, Frederick	1,000	1	4	8-2-1784	Town Cr	....
Woodson, Frederick	1,000	1	104	8-12-1784	None	....
Woodson, Frederick	1,000	1	104	8-12-1784	Little Barren R	Surveyed
Woodson, Frederick	1,000	1	110	8-12-1784	Consolas Cr	....
Wright, Matthew	1,000	1	26	8-4-1784	Red Stone Cr	....
Wright, Matthew	1,000	1	31	8-5-1784	Red Stone Cr	....
Wright, Matthew	1,000	1	35	8-5-1784	Tennessee R	....
Wright, Matthew	1,000	1	55	8-7-1784	Tennessee R	....
Wright, Matthew	1,000	1	56	8-7-1784	Tennessee R	....
Wright, Matthew	500	1	57	8-7-1784	Cumberland R	....
Wright, Matthew	1,000	1	61	8-7-1784	E Fk Jefferson	....
Wright, Matthew	1,000	1	65	8-7-1784	Consolas Cr	Withdrawn
Wright, Matthew	1,000	1	79	8-10-1784	Consolas Cr	....
Wright, Matthew	1,000	1	80	8-10-1784	Consolas Cr	....
Wright, Matthew	1,000	1	81	8-10-1784	Mayfield Cr	....
Wright, Matthew	500	1	97	8-12-1784	Mayfield Cr	....
Wright, Matthew	1,000	1	99	8-12-1784	None	....
Wright, Matthew	500	1	105	8-12-1784	Buck Cr	Surveyed
Wright, Matthew	1,166⅔	1	109	8-12-1784	—— R	....
Wright, Matthew	1,000	1	120	8-14-1784	Big Barren R	....
Wright, Matthew	1,000	1	121	8-14-1784	S & N Fks Clarks R	....
Wright, Matthew	1,000	1	121	8-14-1784	S & N Fks Clarks R	....
Wright, Patrick	1,000	1	12	8-3-1784	Cane Cr	....
Wright, Patrick	1,000	1	13	8-3-1784	Cumberland R	....
Wright, Patrick	1,000	1	16	8-4-1784	None	....
Wright, Patrick	1,000	1	22	8-4-1784	Cumberland R	....
Wright, Patrick	100	1	130	8-17-1784	None	....
Wright & Reynolds	600	1	86	8-11-1784	Green R	Surveyed
Wyatt, Cary	1,000	1	6	8-2-1784	Green R	....
Wyatt, Cary	1,000	1	45	8-6-1784	Crocus Cr	Surveyed
Wyatt, Cary	1,000	1	91	8-11-1784	None	....
Wyatt, Cary	1,000	1	104	8-12-1784	Big Barren R	Surveyed
Young, Jas	200	1	226	8-2-1784	E Fk Crocus Cr	Surveyed
Young, Thos	1,800	1	206	7-19-1788	Cumberland R	Surveyed
Young, Thos	500	1	206	7-19-1788	Green R	Surveyed
Young, Thos	500	1	207	7-19-1788	Russell Cr	Surveyed
Young, Thos	500	1	207	7-19-1788	Russell Cr	Surveyed
Young, Thos	700	1	228	8-2-1791	Big Fk Russell Cr	Surveyed

VII

COURT OF APPEALS DEEDS-GRANTEES

(1783-1909)

(Only one deed recorded after 1846)

Grantee	Residence	Deed Date	Acres	Book	Page	Watercourse
Abbott, Wm & Daniel	Frederick	10–14–1806	———	L	106	Ohio R
Abercromley, Jas	Philadelphia	8–14–1809	14,000	N	126	Buffaloe Rd
Adair, Wm J	Green	12–13–1816	19,000	R	83	Green R
Addison, Lloyd D	———	1–24–1835	Lot	Z	486	Louisville
Adkins, Jno	Gallatin	3–19–1816	200	Q	385	None
Admirer, Jas	Henry	5– 5–1818	1,000	S	121	Mill Cr
Adams, Richard	Richmond	5–12–1802	1,000	G	156	Green R
Adams, Samuel G	Richmond	1–28–1799	50,000	D	348	Green R
Adams, Samuel G	Richmond	3– 7–1808	1,000	R	458	Cypress Cr
Adams, Reynolds & Co	Louisville	10–13–1830	Lots	Z	21	Frankfort
Ailes, Amos	———	9– 7–1790	300	B-2	208	McConnells & Lecomts R
Akers, Peter	Owen	8–20–1832	18	Z	404	Eagle Cr
Allen, Alie	———	12–15–1815	500	R	18	Dry Fk Big Eddy C
Allen, David H	Frederick	6– 1–1823	609	W	364	Shawnee Run
Alby, Jno	Nelson	3– 5–1792	300	B-2	417	Cartwrights Cr
Ales, Wm	Lewis	9– 6–1809	500	N	36	Big Barren R
Ales, Wm	Lewis	8–19–1809	500	N	40	Big Barren R
Ales, Wm	Lewis	8–24–1809	500	N	44	Big Barren R
Ales, Wm	Lewis	7–26–1811	500	O	107	Big Barren R
Alexander, Chas	Woodford	8–15–1841	12½	27	346	Bulls Run
Alexander, Chas	Woodford	2——1845	41	27	471	S Elkhorn
Alexander, Jno	———	5– 6–1818	100	S	125	Ohio R
Alexander, Jno	———	12–10–1822	105	V	434	Ohio R
Alexander, Richard B	London	3–14–1800	9,000	E	145	Dremmins Lick Cr
Alexander, Robt	Woodford	3–25–1796	4,184	E	117	Nohim
Alexander, Robt	Woodford	12–27–1805	2,000	K	156	M Elkhorn
Alexander, Robt	Woodford	9– 3–1808	188½	M	429	N Fk Glens Cr
Alexander, Robt	———	10–24–1809	7,500	N	258	Mouth Big Miami
Alexander, Robt	———	10–24–1809	7,500	O	142	Mouth Big Miami
Alexander, Thos C	Stafford	9– 3–1805	1,100	K	222	Panther Cr
Alexander, Wm	Scott	3– 7–1799	———	D	130	S Fk Elkhorn
Allen, Jas V	Franklin	3–18–1818	Lot	S	75	Frankfort
Allen, Jno	Woodford	6–10–1791	200	B-2	345	S Fk Beargrass Cr
Allen, Jno	Frankfort	7–20–1807	147	L	115	Gesses Cr
Allen, Jno	Shelby	11– 7–1810	500	O	75	Clear Cr
Allen, Jno	Woodford	11– 1–1813	15	P	323	Clear Cr
Allen, Jno	Richmond	8–24–1815	866⅔	R	169	Tennessee R
Allen, Jno	Richmond	8–24–1815	866⅔	R	172	Br Tennessee R
Allen, Jno, heirs	Shelby	7– 6–1814	221½	P	489	Sulphur Lick Fk
Allen, Joseph	Breckinridge	10–11–1821	15,331	V	147	Brush Cr
Allen, Washington	Shelby	6– 2–1804	873	H	191	Brashears Cr
Allen, Washington & Co	Shelby	5–26–1803	643	G	334	Harrisons Cr
Allen, Wilson	Richmond	7–30–1806	2,000	L	12	Big Bone Lick
Allen, Wm	Fayette	3–18–1791	1,240	B-2	258	Deer Cr
Allen & Ellis	Richmond	5–18–1812	1,600	O	452	Michauz Br
Allison, David	Philadelphia	3–10–1796	70,000	Q	166	Big Sandy R
Allison, Henry	Franklin	12–25–1823	59½	W	164	Beech Cr
Alsap, Sarah Ann	Spalsylvania	11–25–1830	1,094⅔	Z	48	Tennessee & Ohio R Little Ohio & Drakes Cr
Alsbury, Thos	Christian	4–24–1821	390	V	149	None
Alvey, Robt	Union	4– 2–1814	———	P	411	None
Alvey, Robt	Union	4– 2–1814	———	P	555	None
Amsindon, Otis	Philadelphia	4– 3–1815	Lots	R	393	Philadelphia
Anderson, Amos	Frankfort	10–26–1801	Lots	F	104	Frankfort
Anderson, Chas	Frankfort	4–10–1805	———	J	303	Station Camp & Big Benson
Anderson, Colbert	Burkley	1–23–1805	2,131	J	356	Ohio R
Anderson, Cuthbert S	Frankfort	4–23–1821	2,750	U	536	None
Anderson, Cuthbert S	Frankfort	9– 3–1822	———	W	88	Tennessee R
Anderson, Daniel	Petersburg	4–19–1799	1,000	E	111	Sandy R
Anderson, Daniel	Petersburg	4–19–1799	1,000	E	115	Sandy R
Anderson, Henry	Campbell	7– 3–1805	122	J	344	Dry Cr
Anderson, James	Madison	1–23–1816	150	Q	452	Silver Cr
Anderson, J Wm P	Mercer	3– 1–1796	———	A-2	263	Little Mt Cr
Anderson, Patrick	Hanover	3——1812	2,419½	O	493	Tennessee R

Grantee	Residence	Deed Date	Acres	Book	Page	Watercourse
Anderson, Patrick	Hanover	10- 2-1812	1,000	P	200	Cumberland R
Anderson, Presley	Fayette	11-10-1789	250	B-2	132	Lower Howards Cr
Anderson, Reubin	Woodford	9- 1-1794	Lot	E	65	Frankfort
Anderson, Richard C	Jefferson	6- 4-1801	400	E	410	N Fk W Fk Red R
Anderson, Col Richard C	Kentucky	3-16-1808	11,200	N	207	W Fk Little R & Cumberland R
Anderson, Wm	—— ——	2-12-1788	——-——	A	356	Robinson Cr
Andrews, Robt, Trustee	Williamsburg	4-28-1800	Lots	E	133	Bardstown
Apperson, Richard	Franklin	12-27-1805	2,500	K	165	M Elkhorn & Big Bone Cr
Apperson, Richard	Franklin	3-20-1818	——	S	109	Flkhorn Cr
Apperson, Rob S	Fayette	4- 9-1828	158	X	398	Elkhorn
Archer, Jno	Jefferson	7-15-1802	90	F	468	Harrods Cr
Archer, S C & R T	Amelia	10-23-1818	1,000	U	85	—— Cr
Armistead, Jno B	—— ——	4-21-1819	4,500	U	33	None
Armistead, Robt L	Henry	3-18-1819	150	S	504	Ky R
Armistead, Robt L	Henry	3-15-1819	500	S	502	None
Armstrong, Ellis	Essex	5- 1-1812	117½	O	366	None
Arnold, Jno	Franklin	8-10-1812	386½	P	341	Bensons Cr
Arnold, Jonathan	Providence	5-17-1796	50,612½	D	88	Red R
Arnett, Thos	Nicholas	10- 7-1824	95	X	63	None
Arnold, Thos	Owen	5-24-1827	154	X	296	Eagle Cr
Arnold, Thos	Bourbon	7-25-1833	2,574½	Z	384	Green R & N E Fk Panther Cr
Ashby, Mauzey Q	Madison	6-30-1821	3,797	U	458	Elk Cr
Ashby, Mauzey Q	Madison	11-12-1822	3,797	V	369	Elk Cr
Ashby, Mauzey G	Madison	3-30-1824	60	W	232	Green R
Ashby, Mauzey Q	Madison	3-22-1825	165	W	10	Green R
Ashton, Lawrence	Fanquier	7-11-1829	——	Y	363	Drakes Cr
Ashton, Lawrence	Fanquier	8-12-1829	——	Y	379	None
Ashton, Lawrence	Kentucky	11-26-1828	——	Y	380	None
Atkins, Edward	—— ——	11- 5-1818	——	T	23	None
Atkinson, Saml C	Philadelphia	7- 6-1844	1,280	28	51	M Ky Pinchon
Atkinson, Saml C	Philadelphia	5- 8-1839	4,320	28	62	Tennessee R
Austin, Chapman	Hanover	9-24-1786	1,000	A	249	Simpsons Cr
Austin, Jno Sr	Hanover	10-10-1797	477	N	103	Chickahomany Swamp
Bacchus, Gordon H	—— ——	10-——-1811	1,000	P	110	Tennessee R
Bacon, Chas P	Franklin	3-25-1831	Lots	Z	106	Frankfort
Bacon, Chas P	Franklin	11-22-1831	160	Z	164	Mississippi R
Bacon, Chas P	Franklin	6-18-1832	96	Z	200	Franklin Co
Bacon, Chas P	Franklin	3-22-1833	Lots	Z	357	Frankfort
Bacon, Elizabeth	Franklin	4-15-1822	146	V	218	None
Bacon, Jno	—— ——	3-21-1812	170	O	338	Ky R
Bacon, Jno C	Owen	10-21-1823	2,942	W	204	Cumberland R
Bacon, Lyddall	Franklin	11-22-1827	158	X	323	Elkhorn
Bacon, Lyddall	Franklin	2-13-1828	158	X	381	Elkhorn
Bacon, Lyddall	Franklin	8-21-1828	158	X	452	Elkhorn
Bacon, Lyddall	Franklin	10-14-1828	——	X	481	None
Bacon, Langston	Franklin	12-10-1830	85	Z	65	None
Bacon, Wm R	Franklin	11- 2-1841	Lot	27	274	Frankfort
Bacon, Wm R	—— ——	12-31-1845	Lot	28	43	Frankfort
Bailey, Saml	Fairfax	—— —— 1807	1,250	N	32	Wolf Cr
Bailey, Wm	Pennsylvania	11- 7-1789	200	B	143	Chaplins Fk
Baird, Jno	Petersburg	2- 7-1815	2,000	Q	532	Ohio R
Baker, Absolum	Lincoln	3-13-1792	100	B-2	None
Baker, Betsy Allen & Jno	Franklin	5-25-1830	40	Y	482	M Elkhorn
Baker, Dudly Willis &. Nancy	Franklin	5-25-1830	40	Y	482	M Elkhorn
Baker, Frederick	Mercer	5-12-1790	Lot	B-2	124	Danville
Baker, Isaac	Winchester	4-14-1808	966⅔	N	73	Highland Cr
Baker, James	Jessamine	3-10-1800	200	E	104	Savin Cr
Baker, James	Jessamine	9-24-1800	468¾	E	329	Savin Cr
Baker, Thomas	Franklin	7-23-1799	911	D	304	W Fk Sinking Cr
Baker, Wm	Baltimore	6- 3-1801	——	F	7	None
Ball, Thos	Lincoln	6-15-1790	260	B-2	148	Hanging Fk
Baldock, Levi	—— ——	4-23-1806	3,000	K	515	None
Ballinger, Jno	Clark	9- 1-1827	90	X	390	Grassy Cr Butler Co
Ballinger, Col Jno	Kentucky	12-17-1805	5,000	J	466	Cumberland R
Ballinger, Richard	Mercer	9- 6-1788	——	A	437	White Oak Cr
Baltzell, Thos L & Geo Jr	—— ——	1- 1-1823	Lot	X	435	Frankfort
Banart, Jno	—— ——	11-18-1819	Lots	T	289	Port Williams
Banister, Jno M	Petersburg	— —1818	1,328	T	91	Big Barren R
Banister, Jno M	Petersburg	8-10-1818	——	T	94	None
Bank of Kentucky	Kentucky	10-——-1816	205¼	R	306	Hickman 4 mile & Howards Cr
Bank of Kentucky	Kentucky	10-——-1816	Lots	R	306	Winchester
Bank of Kentucky	Kentucky	12-15-1821	Lots	V	159	Columbus, Ohio

Grantee	Residence	Deed Date	Acres	Book	Page	Watercourse
Bank of Kentucky	Kentucky	10–31–1822	Lots	W	68	Frankfort
Bank of Kentucky	Kentucky	10–31–1822	14	W	74	Ky R
Bank of Kentucky	Kentucky	10–31–1822	Lot	W	77	Frankfort
Bank of Kentucky	Kentucky	10–31–1822	263¾	W	79	Hammond Cr
Bank of Kentucky	Kentucky	12–21–1827	4,450	X	339	Ohio & Cypress Cr
Bank of Kentucky	Kentucky	10–22–1830	Lot	Z	28	Frankfort
Bank of Kentucky	Kentucky	10–29–1830	Lot	Z	29	Mt Sterling
Bank of Kentucky	Kentucky	7– 5–1831	14	Z	97	Glenn Willis place
Bank of Kentucky	Kentucky	6–22–1832	280	Z	210	Big Bone Lick Cr
Bank North America	Philadelphia	3– 5–1795	615,180	28	341	In Kentucky
Bank of Pennsylvania	Philadelphia	9–29–1803	54	G	430	None
Bank of Pennsylvania	Philadelphia	3– 5–1795	615,180	28	341	In Kentucky
Bank of U S	————	9–11–1820	Lots	U	59	Georgetown
Bank of U S	————	10–19–1820	109	U	67	Howards & Boones Cr
Bank of U S	Scott	10– 1–1821	Lot	V	227	Georgetown
Bank of U S	Scott	11–19–1821	540	V	228	M Eagle Cr
Bank of U S	Scott	11–14–1821	300	V	230	Ohio R
Bank of U S	Scott	10– 2–1821	Lot	V	232	Georgetown
Bank of U S	Scott	12–19–1821	2,852	V	235	Ohio R, Woolford & Gun Powder Cr
Bank of U S	Scott	5——1822	2,000	V	297	Benson Cr
Bank of U S	Scott	12–25–1821	Lot	V	298	Georgetown
Bank of U S	Scott	10– 1–1821	Lots	V	300	Georgetown
Bank of U S	Scott	12–25–1821	Lot	V	344	Georgetown
Bank of U S	Scott	11–16–1821	20	V	346	Royal Sp Br
Bank of U S	Scott	10– 1–1821	150	V	348	S Elkton
Bank of U S	Scott	10– 1–1821	Lots	V	348	Georgetown
Bank of U S	Scott	9–25–1822	Lots	V	357	Louisville
Bank of U S	Scott	9–26–1821	1,891	V	358	Ohio R
Bank of U S	Scott	9–26–1821	Lots	V	358	Louisville
Bank of U S	Kentucky	10–11–1824	5,000	X	61	Ohio R & Woolpers Cr
Bank of U S	Kentucky	11–24–1826	239	Y	244	S Beargrass Cr
Bank of U S	Kentucky	11– 8–1826	15	Y	249	In Fleming Co
Bank of U S	Kentucky	2– 2–1827	600	Y	266	Camp Fk Green R
Bank of U S	Kentucky	5–10–1830	225	Y	456	Floyds Fk
Bank of U S	Kentucky	5–19–1830	Lot	Y	499	Barbourville
Bank of U S	Kentucky	5–19–1830	——	Y	499	Little Richland Cr
Bank of U S	Kentucky	6–28–1830	——	Y	501	Br Sycamore Fk
Bank of U S	Philadelphia	11– 1–1833	Lots	Z	365	Lexington
Bank of U S	Philadelphia	4–21–1834	Lots	Z	431	Richmond, Va
Bank of U S	Philadelphia	3– 5–1795	615,180	28	341	Kentucky
Bank of Virginia	Virginia	4–21–1834	Lots	Z	431	Richmond, Va
Banks, Cuthbert	Fayette	4– 9–1801	2,000	E	402	Floyds Fk
Banks, Cuthbert	Fayette	7–22–1801	500	E	405	Br Licking
Banks, Cuthbert	Fayette	7–22–1801	30,000	F	125	Green R
Banks, Cuthbert	Fayette	10–13–1801	307	F	166	S Fk Elkhorn
Banks, Henry	Virginia	5– 7–1795	——	A-2	346	None
Banks, Henry	Virginia	5– 5–1795	——	A-2	347	None
Banks, Henry	Virginia	5– 5–1795	——	A-2	349	None
Banks, Henry	Richmond	7–13–1796	3,110	A-2	412	Salt R
Banks, Henry	Richmond	5–27–1818	1,000	S	146	Barren R
Banks, Henry	Virginia	4–16–1814	——	S	228	Ohio R
Banks, Henry	Richmond	10–16–1819	Lots	T	124	——
Banks, Henry	Richmond	11–20–1821	1,000	V	120	None
Banta, Henry & Peter	Mercer	5– 4–1797	3,000	A-2	698	None
Barbee, Joshua	Mercer	6–22–1790	Lot	B-2	183	Danville
Barbee, Joshua	Mercer	4– 4–1804	600	H	251	None
Barbee, Thos	Lincoln	3– 1–1785	Negro	A	30	None
Barbee, Thos	Mercer	11– 7–1786	Lot	A	233	None
Barbee, Thos	Mercer	9–20–1787	½	A	368	None
Barbee, Thos	Mercer	6–27–1788	Lot	A	429	None
Barbee, Thos	Mercer	9–29–1790	Lot	B-2	192	Danville
Barbee, Thos	Mercer	10– 1–1790	150	B-2	200	None
Barbee & Warren	Danville	2–27–1795	842	A-2	425	S Fk Licking
Barbour, Jas	Orange	7–26–1802	——	G	154	None
Barbour, James	Orange	5–10–1805	——	J	243	None
Barbour, Jas	Orange	8– 1–1805	——	J	261	None
Barbour, Jas	Orange	3–26–1809	——	N	422	None
Barbour, Jas	Estill	3–13–1818	540	S	65	Ky R
Barbour, Jas	————	1——1814	2,660	T	352	Biggerstaff Cr & Muddy R
Barbour, Jas	Kentucky	10– 4–1822	1,400	V	454	None
Barbour, Jas	————	10– 5–1839	2,000	27	84	Ohio R
Barbour, Richard	Orange	——1800	3,000	E	239	—— R
Barbour, Thos	Mercer	9–18–1789	4	B-2	75	Danville
Barbour, Thos T	Louisville	10–24–1823	2,000	W	300	None
Barclay, Jno	————	3– 5–1795	431,043	D	312	Many Water Courses
Barclay, Jno	Philadelphia	3– 5–1795	615,180	28	341	In Kentucky
Barclay, Joshua G	Louisville	1– 1–1818	Lot	S	303	Louisville

Grantee	Residence	Deed Date	Acres	Book	Page	Watercourse
Barclay, Joshua G	————	10- 3-1831	400	Z	159	Gilmores Cr
Barker, Wm	Henry	5- 5-1818	1,000	S	121	Mill Cr
Barker, Wm	Fanquier	4-25-1806	4,000	W	380	None
Barlow, Henry, Jr	Woodford	3-19-1790	300	B-2	134	Boones Mill Cr
Barnett, Andrew	Green	12- 6-1802	————	G	374	Big Bensons Cr
Barnett, Andrew	Green	10- 8-1811	2,000	O	136	Buck Cr
Barnett, Andrew	Green	2- 8-1831	1,500	Z	116	Russell Cr
Barnett, Alexander	Ohio	12-26-1804	8,000	H	494	Slate Cr
Barnett, James	Madison	2-25-1806	250	L	72	M Fk Ky R
Barnett, Schuyler	Lincoln	12-28-1821	590	V	168	Silver Cr
Barney, Joshua	Baltimore	8- 7-1786	50,000	G	146	Otter Cr
Barney, Joshua	Baltimore	1- 6-1812	56,000	R	208	Rowling Cr & Green R
Barret, Jno	Richmond	6-13-1791	25,993	B-2	359	Salt Lick Cr
Barrett, Jno	Henrico	1- 4-1790	12,140	N	491	Ohio & Licking
Barrett, Wm	Richmond	12-13-1824	3,000	Y	148	Poages, N Fk Trade Water & Goose Cr
Barry, Armstead M	Fayette	2- 1-1839	————	27	40	None
Barry, Catherine	————	5- 6-1812	————	O	512	None
Barry, Catherine A	Washington City	2-21-1831	————	27	107	None
Barry, James	Baltimore	6- 1-1797	1,250	D	236	Otter Cr
Barry, James	Baltimore	7-22-1799	1,250	D	240	Otter Cr
Barry, James	Baltimore	6- 1-1797	8,000	D	244	N Fk Sandy R
Barry, James	Baltimore	6- 1-1797	10,000	D	252	S Fk Ky R
Barry, James	Baltimore	11-12-1799	5,000	F	11	Straight Cr
Barry, James	Baltimore	11-12-1799	5,000	F	26	Laurel R
Barry, James	Baltimore	11-12-1799	10,000	F	30	Straight Cr
Barry, James	Baltimore	11-12-1799	10,000	F	34	Cumberland R
Barry, Wm T	Fayette	7-17-1817	237	R	592	None
Barry, W T	Lexington	5-17-1817	Slaves	R	596	None
Barry, W T	Lexington	3-28-1818	Slaves	S	133	None
Bartlett, Harry	Sposylvania	9-28-1786	500	A	304	None
Bartlett, Jas	————	12- 8-1817	7,750	R	606	None
Basey, Taylor	Shelby	12- 5-1821	393	V	139	None
Bastrop, Philip H N L	Frederick	8-30-1799	7,270	D	460	Little Benson & S Fk Elkhorn
Bastrop, Philip H N T	Frederick	11- 6-1799	823½	D	465	N Fk Elkhorn
Bastrop, P H N T	Frederick	1-11-1800	9,850	D	497	N & S Fk Elkhorn & Clear Cr
Baswell, Bushead & Thos E	Fayette	11-20-1818	114	T	6	None
Batchelor, Jno	Dublin	12- 4-1802	7,932½	G	343	Ky Ohio & Salt R
Bate, James	Jefferson	3- 8-1816	————	Q	376	None
Bate, Jas S	Jefferson	4-25-1814	————	P	513	None
Bate, James S	Jefferson	6- 7-1814	6,891	P	451	Goose, Dix & Ohio R Skeggs Cr
Bates, Jno C	Franklin	9-26-1845	2,500	28	35	Elkhorn & Cedar Cr
Bates, Jno C	Franklin	5- 4-1846	63	28	83	Elkhorn
Bates, Jno C	Franklin	11-22-1845	1,920	28	113	Cedar Cr
Batts, Alexander L	Richmond	3-23-1831	————	27	61	None
Batts, Alexander L, Trustee	Richmond	5-14-1834	————	27	79	None
Batts, Thos H	Fredericksburg	11-16-1839	2,500	27	96	M Elkhorn
Baylor, Walker	Bourbon	11-14-1815	————	Q	241	None
Baylor, Walker & Geo W	Bourbon	8-29-1816	773½	R	126	Stoners Fk & Green R
Baynham, Wm	————	10-25-1813	1,000	P	249	Cabin Cr
Bays, Samuel	Philadelphia	11-12-1801	————	O	232	None
Bays & McCallmoret	Philadelphia	10-29-1798	————	D	389	Ohio R
Beachamp, Caston	Shelby	10-17-1815	666⅔	Q	206	None
Beale, Thos	Macae, China	2- 4-1818	9,812	S	298	Salt Lick Cr
Beall, Andrew	Lincoln	9-10-1785	Lot	A	165	None
Beall, Benj	Mercer	6-16-1788	Lot	A	419	None
Beall, Benj	Campbell	11-19-1800	2,000	E	179	Licking
Beall, Benj	Campbell	11-21-1801	250	F	155	Coopers Run
Beall, Benj	Campbell	11-13-1802	3,000	G	65	Raven Cr
Beall, Benj Adair	Campbell	11-13-1802	400	G	43	Harrods Cr
Beall, Norbond B	Jefferson	10-28-1819	8,178	T	336	Rolling Fk & Buffaloe Cr & Glens Cr
Beall, Norbond B	Jefferson	10-28-1819	Lots	T	336	Bardstown
Beall, Noland B	Jefferson	12-28-1813	Lot	P	355	Louisville
Beall, Walter	Nelson	9-21-1788	520	A	351	Dix R & Hanging Fk
Beall, Walter	Nelson	9-21-1787	500	B-2	87	Slate Cr
Beall, Walter	Nelson	9-21-1787	2,400	B-2	88	Fks Otter Cr
Beall, Walter	Nelson	9-21-1787	7,500	B-2	89	Floyds Fk
Beall, Walter	Nelson	9-21-1787	5,825	B-2	91	Cartwrights Cr
Beall, Walter	Nelson	1-28-1790	555	B-2	111	Ky R
Beall, Walter	Nelson	5-24-1791	5,434	B-2	318	Big Slate Cr
Beall, Walter	Nelson	5- 2-1801	600	E	378	Ky R

Grantee	Residence	Deed Date	Acres	Book	Page	Watercourse
Beall, Walter	Bardstown	8–21–1800	Lots	K	375	Bardstown
Beall, Walter	Nelson	5– 6–1808	1,000	M	16	Br Big Benson Cr
Beard, Joseph	————	4–21–1826	5,746½	X	206	Ky & Big Barren Rs etc
Beard, Joseph	————	4–21–1826	5,746½	X	206	Ky & Big Barren Rs etc
Beard, Joseph	————	4–21–1826	6,479¾	Y	134	Salt, Big Barren, Cumb Rs etc
Beard, Wm & Sarah, heirs	————	4–21–1826	5,746½	X	206	Ky & Big Barren Rs etc
Beats, Frederick	Philadelphia	10–25–1819	————	T	184	None
Beatty, Cornelius	Lexington	10–29–1798	1,000	D	378	Russells Cr
Beaty, Chas C	Morrisville	10–29–1830	1,021	Z	23	Nolinn
Beaty, Chas C	Obington	2– 1–1831	10,000	Z	94	S Fk Sandy R
Beauchamp, Joshua	Shelby	4–25–1814	16,380	P	428	Salt R & Crooked Cr
Beauchamp, Joshua	————	10–10–1814	308	P	534	Salt R
Beauchamp, Joshua	————	11–29–1814	106	P	566	None
Beauchamp, Joshua	————	11– 7–1815	553	Q	223	Wolf Br
Beauchamp, Joshua	Shelby	4– 3–1816	200	Q	432	Chaplins Fk & Salt R
Beauford, Wm	Woodford	5–30–1817	1,000	R	338	Little R
Beck, Henry A	Philadelphia	7–28–1807	1,000	O	356	None
Beadford, Jno & Benj F	Bourbon	12–13–1833	666⅔	Z	378	S Fk Tradewater
Bedford, Littleberry	Bourbon	8–27–1821	400	U	537	Highland Cr
Bedford, Thos	Maclinnburgh	10– 3–1796	400	A-2	644	Highland Cr
Bedinger, Daniel	Berkley	1– 2–1799	1,000	D	168	Grapefield
Beebee, Saml	New York	9–19–1807	35,456	Q	535	None
Bell, Jno	————	6–20–1786	Lot	A	172	None
Bell, Jno	Mercer	9–10–1790	25	B-2	197	Hanging Fk
Bell, Wm, Jr	Philadelphia	5–31–1819	1,916⅔	U	413	Ohio R
Benbridge, Henry, Jr	Philadelphia	8–14–1798	10,000	C	307	N Fk Ky R
Bennett, Edward	Washington	10–22–1814	————	Q	60	None
Bennett, Edward	Washington	10–22–1814	————	Q	62	None
Bennett, Thos	————	11– 5–1818	————	T	23	None
Bernard, D P & Robt	————	9– 7–1840	200	27	151	E Fk Floyds Fk
Bernard, Dudly P & Robt	————	8–12–1841	114½	27	262	E Br Floyds Fk
Berry, Benj	Frederick	5– 9–1796	1,000	C	34	Clay Lick Cr
Berry, Benj	Fayette	11–30–1805	1,000	K	151	Highland Cr
Berry, Benj	Fayette	4– 9–1814	————	P	395	Shannon R
Berry, Benj, Jr	Frederick	3–10–1796	1,000	C	30	Poges Cr
Berry, George	Franklin	3– 8–1815	80	Q	22	S Fk Benson Cr
Berry, Geo C	Scott	1– 5–1818	1,000	R	603	None
Berry, Henry K & A M	Fayette	6–11–1829	366½	Z	63	Deer Cr
Berry, Henry K & A M	Fayette	6–11–1829	500	Z	64	Clay Lick Cr
Berry, Joseph	Bath	5–30–1827	7½	X	238	None
Berry, Lawrence	King George	9–21–1807	6,222	M	70	Green, Muddy Pond Rs
Berry, Reuben	Jessamine	6–11–1829	366½	Z	63	Deer Cr
Berry, Reuben	Jessamine	6–11–1829	500	Z	64	Clay Lick Cr
Berry, Jack	————	10–19–1824	400	X	58	None
Berryman, Jos S	————	8– 9–1830	————	Y	506	S Elkhorn
Berryman, Jos S	————	8– 9–1830	192	Y	507	S Elkhorn
Berryman, Thos A	Owen	1–10–1844	————	27	386	Cumberland R
Berryman, Thos	Owen	4– 1–1824	1,052	W	354	Long Lick Run
Berryman, Thos A	Owen	11–22–1844	4,762	27	464	M Livingston & Trigg Crs
Best, Josiah E	Harrison	4– 7–1818	580	S	86	None
Best, Thomas & Saml	England	7–21–1801	20,698	H	518	Killicanick Cr
Bett, Osburn	————	9– 1–1824	————	X	51	None
Beverly, Carter	Culpepper	2–23–1808	800	N	105	Big Barren R
Beverly, Robt Jr	Culpepper	1–22–1795	2,000	Z	45	Ohio R
Bibb, Edward B	————	3– 1–1820	6,550	T	420	None
Bibb, Geo M	————	8– 1–1802	11,483⁷⁄₁₂	G	58	Licking
Bibb, Geo M & Richard	————	3– 1–1820	6,550	T	420	None
Bibb, Jno B	Logan	1– 6–1819	1,800	S	409	Hardins Cr
Bibb, Richard	Prince Edward	9–19–1797	5,850	C	92	Fk Hardins Cr
Bibb, Richard	Prince Edward	8–25–1797	————	C	95	None
Bibb, Richard	Prince Edward	9–19–1797	————	C	113	None
Bibb, Richard	Fayette	7–30–1798	200	D	148	Ky R
Bibb, Richard	Bullitt	7–19–1800	————	E	161	None
Bibb, Richard	Bullitt	11–20–1800	500	E	168	Ohio R & Crooked Cr
Bibb, Richard	Bullitt	11–25–1801	918	F	131	Otter Cr & Ky R
Bibb, Richard	Bullitt	11–23–1803	1,126	H	47	Limestone Cr
Bibb, Richard	Bullitt	12– 8–1804	5,350	J	406	Bartons Fk Big Clifty

Grantee	Residence	Deed Date	Acres	Book	Page	Watercourse
Bibb, Richard	———	3–6–1806	346	K	185	None
Bibb, Richard	———	3–6–1806	346	K	187	None
Bibb, Richard	Kentucky	5–5–1807	8,255½	L	192	Rolling Fk
Bibb, Richard, Jr	Bullitt	11–21–1803	5,850	H	36	Salt R
Bibb, Richard, Sr	———	8–25–1818	15,347	S	219	Green R & Rough Cr
Bibb & Sneed	———	6–16–1808	Negro	M	308	None
Bickham, Geo	Philadelphia	7–16–1808	7,870	M	263	Elkhorn
Biggs, Jno	Lincoln	3–3–1789	110	A	484	Hanging Fk
Bishop, David	New Jersey	5–15–1807	86,035	W	165	None
Black, Jean	Scott	6–26–1798	500	D	17	Log Cr
Black, Robt	Fayette	3–14–1792	106	B-2	470	Curds Road
Blackburn, Churchill J	Woodford	2–26–1842	8,114	27	273	Bealls Run
Blackburn, Edward M	Woodford	———1825	45	X	156	None
Blackmore, David	Jefferson	10–30–1818	Lots	S	270	Millton
Blackmore, Geo	Frederick	10–2–1797	1,333⅓	C	222	Highland Cr
Blackmore, James	Frederick	3–1–1802	200	H	69	E Fk Floyds Fk
Blackmore, James	Frederick	4–2–1801	200	H	74	E Fk Floyds Fk
Blackmore, James	Frederick	3–1–1802	100	H	79	E Fk Floyds Fk
Blackwell, Wm	Washington	12–16–1830	6,000	Z	151	Clay Lick Deer, Bio Buck, & Rough Crs
Blair, Anna Henry	———	9–8–1829	100	Y	395	Plum Cr
Blair, Francis P	Franklin	3–2–1820	Lots	T	394	Frankfort
Blair, F P	Franklin	10–22–1830	———	Z	29	Big Benson Cr
Blakemore, Eliza N	Fredrick	6–7–1826	333⅔	X	357	Highland Cr
Blakemore, Geo N	Frederick	6–7–1826	418⅓	X	360	Tradewater
Blakemore, Jno M	Frederick	6–7–1826	418⅓	X	358	Tradewater
Blakemore, Lewis	Oldham	2–23–1827	120	X	285	Rough Cr
Blakemore, Preston	Fayette	2–23–1827	480	X	288	Rough Cr
Blakemore, Thos	Frederick	6–7–1826	417⅓	X	355	Tradewater
Blakie, Mills & Co	Philadelphia	8–1–1817	Lots	S	289	Lexington
Blanton, Carter	———	12–14–1811	Slaves	O	206	None
Blanton, Carter	Franklin	11——1820	600	U	192	Eagle Cr
Blanton, Harrison	Franklin	12–11–1819	———	T	268	Ky R
Blanton, Harrison	———	3–31–1821	172	U	433	None
Blanton, Harrison	Franklin	1–12–1834	106	Z	490	Elkhorn
Blanton, Harrison	Franklin	10–29–1846	217	28	79	In Woodford Co
Blanton, Jas	Franklin	1–13–1804	Lot	H	152	Frankfort
Blanton, Jno	Shelby	1–16–1805	5,812	J	161	Plum Cr
Blanton, Jno	Shelby	1–10–1806	50,000	K	240	S Brs Salt R
Blanton, Jno	Shelby	12–9–1806	47,897	K	517	Salt R
Blanton, Jno dec'd	Woodford	7–16–1816	583	R	320	Cedar Cr
Blanton, O M Wm C & Read H	Mississippi	9–13–1839	Lot	27	75	Frankfort
Blanton, Wm	Gallatin	1–2–1815	39	P	617	Dry Run
Blanton, Wm	Gallatin	1–6–1819	1,537	S	376	Eagle Cr
Blanton, Wm	Kentucky	5–14–1819	Lot	T	128	Frankfort
Blanton, Wm W	———	10–9–1809	Slaves	M	443	None
Blanton, Willis	Franklin	10——1820	———	U	42	Dry Run
Blanton, Willis	Franklin	12–17–1821	2,000	V	157	Dry Run
Blanton, Willis	Franklin	4–15–1822	146	V	218	None
Blanton, Willis	Franklin	2–25–1822	———	V	226	Dry Run
Blanton, Willis & & Richard	Franklin	10–30–1817	583	R	446	Cedar Cr
Bledsoe, Jesse	———	12–31–1808	Lot	M	332	Lexington
Bledsoe, Jesse	Fayette	9–12–1810	1,000	N	308	Fks Ky R
Bledsoe, Jesse	Paris	11–25–1820	600	U	173	Eagle Cr
Bledsoe, Joseph	Gallatin	10–3–1802	260	G	161	Bank Lick Cr
Bledsoe, Wm	———	11–18–1801	681¾	F	123	Lynn Camp Cr
Bledsoe, Wm M	———	12–2–1800	1,237	E	186	Clear Fk Rough Cr
Bledsoe, Wm M	Garrard	2——1809	6,203	M	311	M Fk Ky R
Bledsoe, Wm M	Garrard	1–7–1815	———	P	583	Gilberts Cr
Blighs, Saml	Philadelphia	10–23–1809	113.482	N	161	Ohio R
Blieghs, Saml	Philadelphia	10–25–1809	31,778	N	166	Little Sandy & E Fk Dix R
Blieghs, Saml	Philadelphia	11–13–1809	37,827½	N	171	Ohio R
Blieghs, Saml	Philadelphia	12–27–1809	5,277	N	176	Ohio R
Blight, Saml	Philadelphia	8–6–1813	———	P	278	None
Blight, Saml	Philadelphia	10–29–1813	———	P	288	None
Blight, Saml	Philadelphia	11–30–1813	1,000	P	291	Hogback Grove
Blight, Saml	Philadelphia	12–22–1809	500	P	299	None
Blight, Saml	Philadelphia	12–29–1809	2,000	P	302	Ohio R
Blight, Saml	Philadelphia	12–29–1809	2,000	P	305	Ohio R
Blight, Saml, Wife	Philadelphia	5–15–1813	Lots	P	268	Philadelphia
Blight, Dr Saml	Philadelphia	1–27–1815	———	Q	23	Hill Grove
Blight, Dr Saml	Philadelphia	1–27–1815	640	Q	24	Elk Grove
Blight, Dr Saml	Philadelphia	8–26–1815	———	Q	245	None
Blithe, Saml	Franklin	4–29–1807	183,388½	O	470	Big Sandy R
Bliss, Geo	Springfield	3–25–1796	64,184	A-2	521	Nolinn
Bloomfield, Isabella	New York	8–16–1842	9,188	27	308	Chaplins Fk
Boan, Nehemiah	Breckinridge	6–2–1821	———	V	288	Rolling Fk & Ohio

Grantee	Residence	Deed Date	Acres	Book	Page	Watercourse
Board of Internal Improvements	Franklin	10-31-1845	1	28	34	Fks Elkhorn
Board of Internal Improvements	Franklin	1- 3-1846	¼	28	44	Buck Run
Bodley, Thos	Fayette	7-20-1798	400	D	131	Ky R
Bodley, Thos	Fayette	11-27-1800	3,000	E	175	——R
Bodley, Thos	Fayette	12-13-1799	1,000	E	289	Cedar & Auter Crs
Bodley, Thos	Fayette	4- 9-1801	2,000	E	402	Floyds Fk
Bodley, Thos	Fayette	7-22-1801	500	E	405	Br Licking
Bodley, Thos	Fayette	7-22-1801	30,000	F	125	Green R
Bodley, Thos	Kentucky	12-10-1802	45,000	G	99	Beech Fk
Bodley, Thos	Fayette	12-11-1802	15,000	G	106	N Fk Sandy R
Bodley, Thos	Fayette	7-23-1804	6,052	H	472	Johnsons Fk
Bodley, Thos	Fayette	9- 9-1806	11,517½	L	29	N Fk & main Licking
Bodley, Thos	Fayette	11-30-1808	26,000	M	278	Cane Run
Bodley, Thos	Fayette	5-25-1810	246,900¼	N	224	Ohio R
Bodley, Thos	Fayette	9-12-1810	1,000	N	308	Fks Ky R
Bodley, Thos	Fayette	7-21-1813	206	P	321	Little Ky R
Bodley, Thos	Lexington	10-25-1817	Lots	R	564	Frankfort
Bodley, Thos	——	10-20-1819	186	X	128	Glens Cr
Bodley, Thos, Trustee	——	3-26-1814	2,000	Q	100	Yellow Cr
Boggs, James	Philadelphia	11-18-1797	4,000	C	232	Fk Deer Cr
Boggs, James	Philadelphia	10- 3-1810	2,000	N	297	Deer Cr
Boggs, Jos	New York	6- 6-1832	4,000	Z	201	Deer Cr
Boggs, Jno M	Fayette	10-13-1801	307	F	166	S Fk Elkhorn
Boggs, Jno M	Lexington	3-10-1804	6,000	H	369	Ohio R Lawrence Cr
Boissean, Benj Jr	Dinwiddie	11-12-1806	1,000	L	33	Green R
Bolton, Curtis	New York	12-19-1842	21,288	27	332	Hardin&Grayson Co
Bond, Robt	Owen	10- 7-1823	64	W	198	None
Booker, David	Jefferson	6-28-1811	47½	O	323	Floyds Fk
Booker, Paul J	Washington	12-21-1823	——	W	223	None
Booker, Saml	Washington	12-18-1823	——	W	221	None
Boone, Joseph	Washington	1-10-1824	35	W	169	Shepherds Run
Booth, James	Dinwiddie	4-15-1816	4,000	R	199	None
Booth, Wm	Dinwiddie	4-15-1816	4,000	R	197	None
Bordley, Jno	Baltimore	1- 4-1800	14,500	E	32	Ky R
Borrough, Sidney H & Wife	Providence	8- 3-1813	Lots	R	402	Philadelphia
Boswell, Geo	——	11-12-1818	1,000	S	323	Brashears Cr
Boswell, Geo	Fayette	10-10-1826	500	Y	248	Cumberland R
Boulden, Thos S	Richmond	6-23-1821	——	V	20	Ky R
Bouldin, Thos T	——	12- 2-1818	1,000	T	155	Ohio R
Bouldin, Thos T	Richmond	6-23-1821	——	V	45	None
Bouldin, Thos T	——	3-28-1818	——	W	328	None
Bouldin, Thos T, Executor	——	11- 5-1818	——	T	23	None
Bouldin, Thos T, Executor	——	11-30-1820	300	U	194	Eagle Cr
Bouldin, Thos T, Executor	Richmond	6-18-1821	——	V	41	None
Boust, Wilson	Jefferson	7- 8-1801	822½	E	365	N Fk Red R
Bousnan, Abraham	Fayette	6-18-1789	400	B-2	60	None
Bower, Gustaves	Scott	6-23-1821	225½	V	96	Eagle Cr
Bower, Wm	Dorcester	7-20-1801	20,698	H	514	Killiconick Cr
Bowers, Saml	Mason	6- 7-1838	——	27	9	Little R
Bowlware, Richie	Franklin	12-28-1809	Negro	N	116	None
Bowlware, Richard	Franklin	9——1814	——	U	393	Elkhorn Cr
Bowls, Walter	Scott	2-27-1823	50	W	23	None
Bowman, Joseph	Fayette	2-22-1825	200	X	122	Shannons Run
Boyce, Robt	——	5-27-1807	175	L	59	Dix R
Boyer, Alfred Z	Franklin	7-14-1843	Lot	27	353	Frankfort
Bozarth, Jonathan	Christian	7- 4-1809	1,000	N	282	Benson Cr
Bradford, Daniel	Scott	5-28-1822	1,000	W	341	W Fk Drakes Cr
Bradford, Fielding	——	11- 7-1809	2,270	N	86	None
Bradford, Jno	Davidson	4-12-1814	2,270	P	502	Licking
Bradford, Wm	Muhlenberg	5- 7-1812	1,200	O	374	None
Bradford, Wm	——	1-21-1815	105½	Q	1	Little N Elkhorn
Bradley, Daniel	——	6-16-1821	153½	U	506	None
Bradley, Jno	Franklin	1- 5-1837	125	27	34	N Elkhorn
Bradley, Robt	Fayette	8-15-1797	3,150	D	511	Main Fk Licking
Bramlett, Martin	Scott	8-28-1818	2,118	S	221	Eagle Cr
Brand, Jno	Fayette	12-11-1822	256	V	407	Hickman Cr
Brand, Jno	Fayette	2-21-1831	98	Z	100	Grays Run
Branham, Beverly	Scott	10——1834	13	Z	468	Elkhorn
Branham, Geo C	Owen	6-17-1842	175	27	290	Severns & Cedar Cr
Brashears, Brazen	Gallatin	8-21-1813	80	P	243	Ohio R
Bratton, Jos & Wife	Montgomery	5-10-1805	680	J	42	Ohio R
Bratton, Robt	——	8-18-1808	——	M	333	None
Breathitt, Jno	Logan	1-17-1833	1,000	Z	256	Drakes Cr
Breathitt, Susanna M	Warren	3- 6-1829	901	Y	398	Tennessee R
Breckenridge, Alice D	Jefferson	3- 7-1817	2,500	R	186	Big Bone Mud Lick Cr

Grantee	Residence	Deed Date	Acres	Book	Page	Watercourse
Breckenridge, Cabel	Fayette	12–24–1810	—	N	398	None
Breckenridge, James	Batecourt	10– 8–1805	2,000	K	34	Ohio R
Breckenridge, Jas	Batecourt	9–16–1808	1,000	M	187	Elkhorn
Breckenridge, Jas	Batecourt	10–29–1798	—	D	389	Ohio R
Breckenridge, Jas	Fayette	10– 9–1840	446	27	155	Fayette Co
Breckenridge, Jas D	Jefferson	5–13–1814	1,000	P	507	Ohio R
Breckenridge, Jas D	Jefferson	6– 9–1814	11,300	P	508	Green R Rough Cr
Breckenridge, Jas D	Jefferson	1–20–1818	Lots	S	185	Portland
Breckenridge, Jos D	Louisville	11–11–1823	1,000	W	201	Ohio R
Breckenridge, Jos D	Jefferson	9–15–1828	—	X	464	None
Breckenridge, Jos D	Jefferson	4–11–1843	Lot	27	342	Louisville
Breckenridge, Jno	Fayette	4–14–1797	5,500	A-2	673	Harrods Cr
Breckenridge, Jno	Kentucky	3– 7–1802	6,000	F	491	Ohio R
Breckenridge, Jno	Fayette	7–28–1802	1,250	G	197	Slate Cr
Breckenridge, Jno	Fayette	9–21–1804	13,500	H	454	Ohio R & Patton Cr
Breckenridge, Jno	Fayette	10– 9–1840	446	27	155	Fayette Co
Breckenridge, Jno	Fayette	10–14–1818	—	S	416	None
Breckenridge, Jno C	Lexington	10– 9–1840	446	27	155	Fayette Co
Breckenridge, Joseph C	Fayette	10– 9–1840	446	27	155	Fayette Co
Breckenridge, Robt	Montgomery	6–22–1807	150	L	77	Pleasant Run
Breckenridge, Robt	Jefferson	12–24–1810	—	N	398	None
Breckenridge, Robt J.	Fayette	10– 9–1840	500	27	155	Fayette Co
Breckenridge, Wm L	Fayette	10– 9–1840	500	27	155	Fayette Co
Brenham, Robt	—	2– 9–1809	466⅔	M	341	Enlows Lick
Brent, Richard	Prince William	8–30–1800	900	E	292	Ohio R
Brent, Richard	—	12– 6–1813	—	P	511	None
Brenton, Mary	Jefferson	9– 5–1791	200	B-2	401	Fox Run
Brents, Jos	Green	3–10–1823	250	V	458	Cypress Cr
Brents, Joshua	Hart	7– 9–1831	245	Z	161	Little Barren R
Brents, Saml	Green	12–14–1803	1,000	H	83	Cumberland R
Brents, Saml	Green	3–10–1823	325	V	459	Cypress Cr
Brents, Saml	Green	6– 7–1828	500	X	460	Mississippi R
Brents, Saml	Green	10– 8–1832	500	Z	239	Mississippi R
Bridges, Jno L	Mercer	4–29–1803	Lot	G	293	Danville
Bridges, Jno S	Mercer	12–10–1804	400	H	451	Beech Fk
Bridgewater, Jonathan	Frankfort	10–26–1801	Lots	F	106	Frankfort
Briscoe, Jeremiah	—	6–25–1790	Negroes	B-2	188	None
Briscoe, Parmenos	—	3–14–1789	—	A	519	None
Bristow, Jas	Shelby	4– 1–1818	—	T	129	None
Bristow, Jas	Shelbyville	12–27–1819	4,500	V	52	Skaggs Cr & Ky R
Bristow, Jas	Shelby	6– 2–1821	—	V	288	Rolling Fk & Ohio R
Broadders, Jno	Jessamine	3–10–1800	200	E	105	Savin Cr
Brodhead, Daniel	Jefferson	3– 5–1792	668	B-2	419	Beech Fk
Broadhead, Daniel, Jr	Goochland	8–12–1797	—	F	489	None
Broadhead, Daniel, Jr	—	9– 8–1788	9,800	P	413	Old Ft Jefferson
Brodhead, Lucas	Franklin	6–17–1829	200	Y	382	Clear Cr
Brooke, Judith	Woodford	7– 4–1800	697	H	485	Ky R
Brooking, Thos A	Fayette	10–12–1818	250	S	336	None
Brooks, Elisha	—	5– 3–1815	100	Q	51	None
Brooks, Francis W	Fanquier	3—1823	250	W	217	Ky R
Brooks, Joseph	Jefferson	10–13–1791	1,400	B-2	391	Floyds Fk
Brooks, Joseph	Jefferson	10–22–1790	1,400	B-2	405	Floyds Fk
Brooks, Wm	Hardin	12– 7–1815	90	Q	262	Green R
Brosnam	Frankfort	8– 7–1819	Lot	T	69	Frankfort
Brothers, Henry	Frederick	6–23–1789	2,000	B-2	38	Slate Cr
Brough, Courtney	Elizabeth City	7–10–1823	7,144⅓	W	95	Cumberland R Russell & Drakes Cr
Brough, Robert	Norfolk	4–15–1801	811	E	358	Green R
Brough, Robt	Norfolk	9–19–1801	4,000	F	39	Green & Cumberland Rs
Brown, Collier	Woodford	11–12–1824	50	X	35	Big Benson Cr
Brown, Daniel	Mercer	7–31–1790	200	B-2	271	Cartwrights Cr
Brown, Daniel	Green	10–21–1815	200	Q	270	None
Brown, Daniel	Scott	10–25–1818	100	S	67	None
Brown, Dawson	Kentucky	5–25–1815	21¼	Q	117	None
Brown, Frederick	Madison	2–12–1792	138	B-2	447	Sugar Cr
Brown, Geo	Logan	10–26–1800	1,000	N	55	Cumberland R
Brown, Geo	Franklin	4– 6–1819	188	V	188	Dry Run
Brown, Hezakiah	Franklin	5–13–1799	1,000	D	371	Ky R
Brown, Hezakiah	Franklin	10–20–1815	125	Q	277	Ky R
Brown, James	Richmond	5–11–1795	8,123	A-2	328	S Fk Little Barren & Skeggs Cr
Brown, James	Mercer	5– 5–1791	1,000	B-2	395	Green R
Brown, James	Richmond	6–17–1812	8,800	O	449	W Fk Little & Cumberland R
Brown, James	Richmond	12–14–1812	Lots	P	185	Washington City
Brown, James	Richmond	9–14–1821	2,500	R	51	N Fk Tradewater Br
Brown, Jas	Richmond	1–12–1814	5,320	R	257	S E Fk Skeggs Big Barren & Green R
Brown, Jas	Richmond	9– 6–1816	4,788	R	263	Fk Barren & Green R
Brown, Jas	Nelson	6– 2–1821	—	V	288	Rolling Fk & Ohio R

Grantee	Residence	Deed Date	Acres	Book	Page	Watercourse
Brown, Senator James	Louisiana	9–13–1822	519	V	315	None
Brown, Jas D		11–23–1831		Z	450	None
Brown, Jas D	Franklin	12– 4–1839	50	27	92	S Elkhorn
Brown, Jas D	Franklin	12– 2–1839	50	27	110	S Elkhorn
Brown, Jas D	Franklin	6–11–1840	50	27	120	S Elkhorn
Brown, Jas D	Franklin	4–20–1840	116	27	120	S Elkhorn
Brown, Jas D	Franklin	6–13–1840	50	27	122	S Elkhorn
Brown, Jas D	Franklin	5–14–1841	50	27	200	Elkhorn
Brown, Jos D	Franklin	8–18–1841	50	27	218	Elkhorn
Brown, Jos D	Franklin	12–22–1843		27	393	S Elkhorn
Brown, Jos D	Franklin	10–27–1845		28	33	S Fk Elkhorn
Brown, Jno	Mercer	3–23–1787	400	A	296	Irish Station
Brown, Jno	Mercer	3–19–1789	Lot	A	527	None
Brown, Jno		11–17–1796	30	A-2	562	None
Brown, Jno	Campbell	3–22–1797	500	A-2	646	Lick Cr
Brown, Jno	Frankfort	4–25–1797	1,000	A-2	679	Beech Fk
Brown, Jno	Philadelphia	9–29–1789	500	B-2	78	Salt R
Brown, Jno	Mercer	5– 5–1791	1,000	B-2	393	Green R
Brown, Jno	Kentucky	3–27–1797	41,778	D	31	Little Sandy & Blane Cr
Brown, Jno	Frankfort	11– 9–1801	1,075	F	101	Lecompts Run
Brown, Jno	Richmond	3–29–1803	1,168	G	438	Clear Cr
Brown, Jno	Richmond	1–19–1803	745	G	441	Clover Cr
Brown, Jno		4–11–1804	560	H	417	None
Brown, Jno	Richmond	2–12–1805	2,000	J	249	Big Mud Cr
Brown, Jno	Mercer	10–13–1791	2,400	M	327	Indian Camp Cr
Brown, Jno	Essex	5– 1–1812	125	O	367	Haskins Cr
Brown, Jno	Calvert	2–20–1815	366	Q	67	Livingston Cr
Brown, Jno	Frankfort	11–16–1815	314	Q	242	None
Brown, Jno	Frankfort	3–15–1828	277	X	393	None
Brown, Jno	Franklin	7–15–1830	1,025	Y	502	Ky R
Brown, Senator Jno	Franklin	11–16–1829	6,500	Y	504	Frazier Cr
Brown, Senator Jno		3– 9–1800	8,520	E	195	N & S Fk Elkhorn
Brown, Jno P W	Nashville	1– 6–1844		27	421	Ohio R & Mill Cr
Brown, Jonathan	Hardin	7–13–1810	1,000	N	281	Benson Cr
Brown, Joseph	Franklin	3–19–1833	Lot	Z	298	Frankfort
Brown, Mary	Frankfort	6–13–1805	150	J	125	S Fk Elkhorn
Brown, Mason	Franklin	4– 9–1829	Lots	Y	408	Frankfort
Brown, Mason	Franklin	6– 6–1833	266	Z	356	Ohio R
Brown, Mason	Franklin	2– 4–1835	Lot	Z	487	Frankfort
Brown, Mason	Kentucky	3– 1–1839	552	27	13	Barren Co
Brown, Mason & Orlander	Franklin	5– 7–1842	200	27	287	R
Brown, Mason & Orlander	Franklin	5– 7–1842	200	27	292	Ky R
Brown, Michael & Jno M	Philadelphia	11–18–1809	13,571½	S	201	N Fk Ky R
Brown, Orlands	Franklin	4– 9–1839	Lot	27	20	Frankfort
Brown, Orlands	Franklin	1– 6–1844	167	27	421	Ohio R
Brown, Preston W	Franklin	11– 3–1822	688	V	353	Ohio R
Brown, Scott	Franklin	6–28–1805	28	J	193	Cedar Cr
Brown, Scott	Franklin	5–11–1810	Lot	N	254	Frankfort
Brown, Saml	Nelson	6– 2–1821		V	288	Rolling Fk & Ohio R
Brown, Wm	Harrison	11–19–1816	400	R	123	Sugar Cr
Brown, Wm	Harrison	10–13–1824	276½	W	494	Coopers Run
Browning, Chas		10– 2–1815	100	Q	198	Shepherds Cr
Browning, Elijah G	Clark	3–23–1818	Lots	S	191	Winchester
Bruce, Henry C		9–21–1811	450	O	171	Ky R
Brumfield, Jas		6–25–1796	Negroes	B-2	180	None
Bryan, Guy	Philadelphia	11–13–1805		N	156	None
Bryan, Jno	New Jersey	12–31–1796	40,857	Q	499	Ohio R
Bryan, Mary	Alexandria	2–10–1837		27	457	Ky
Bryan, Mary	Alexandria	12–26–1836		27	458	Kentucky
Bryan, Nicholas	Woodford	4–14–1829	75	Y	336	S Elkhorn
Bryan, Thos	Frankfort	1–12–1808	50	L	291	None
Bryan, Thos	Franklin	3–16–1818	Lot	S	101	Frankfort
Bryant, Thos	Franklin	12–16–1814	202½	Q	249	Ohio Mouth Salt R
Bryant, Thos Y	Lexington	10–31–1799	170	F	519	Salt R
Buck, Chas	Indiana	8–25–1829		Y	381	Elkhorn
Buck, Peter C		7– 5–1813	100	P	339	Ky R
Buck, Peter C	Franklin	9–12–1826	1,000	Y	213	Green & Pond R
Buck, Thos	Frederick	9–27–1788		A	479	W Fk Grassy Lick
Buck, Thos	Frederick	9–26–1788		A	499	W Fk Grassy Lick
Buck, Wm C	Union	3–23–1835	800	Z	504	Deer Cr
Buck, Wm E	Jefferson	4–27–1839	800	27	32	Deer Cr
Buckannan, Wm	Stafford	6–25–1816	800	R	318	Ohio R
Buckman, Jas A	Baltimore	6–14–1803	5,000	H	52	Saxtons Cr
Buckner, Aylett H	Hart	8–23–1822	224	V	295	None
Buckner, Jno	Carolina	10–26–1812	328	O	480	None
Buckner, Jno C	Scott	10–29–1816	224	R	65	Elkhorn

Grantee	Residence	Deed Date	Acres	Book	Page	Watercourse
Buckner, Jno W	Hickman	2–23–1833	1,000	Z	260	Hickman Co
Buckner, Nicholas	Frankfort	7–15–1802	400	F	465	Floyds Fk
Buckner, Nicholas	Louisville	11– 5–1805	14,272	J	373	Buck & Benson Cr Ky & Green R
Buckner, Nicholas	Jefferson	4–14–1817	100	R	266	Floyds Fk
Buckner, Philip	Jefferson	4–25–1791	8,000	B-2	411	Ohio R
Buckner, Philip	Bracken	11– 4–1800	400	E	227	—— Br
Buckner, Philip	Hardin	1–27–1813	776	P	58	Bacon Cr
Budd, Joseph	Philadelphia	11–28–1800	1,150	F	48	None
Buford, Daniel	Mercer	5–11–1810	Lot	N	252	Frankfort
Buford, Vegrand	Woodford	4–13–1829	153	Y	337	S Elkhorn
Buford, Wm	Lincoln	9–27–1796	533½	A-2	611	Little Muddy Cr
Bull, Ezekiel	Shannon Hill	9–30–1805	2,000	M	203	None
Bullitt, Cuthbert	Jefferson	12–22–1819	722	U	3	Deer Cr
Bullitt, Wm C	Louisville	10– 2–1818	——	S	262	None
Bullock, David	Louisa	10–15–1795	2,000	B	200	Little Muddy Cr
Bullock, David	Louisa	11–25–1799	637	E	229	N Fk Tradewater
Bullock, David R	——	10– 1–1811	637	P	446	N Fk Tradewater
Bullock, Leonard H	North Carolina	1– 6–1775	——	C	60	Ohio Cumberland & Green R
Bullock, Lewis	Mason	10–26–1802	236	G	340	Br Green R
Bullock, Walter	Green	12–14–1803	1,000	H	83	Cumberland R
Bullock, Wingfield	Shelby	3– 8–1805	10,000	J	149	None
Bunce, Matthew	New York City	7–10–1800	4,000	E	52	Hinches Run
Bunton, Andrew	Washington	6–16–1786	500	A	104	Sinking Cr
Bunton, Jno	Franklin	11–30–1819	50½	T	170	Salt R
Bunton, Jno	Franklin	1–24–1824	115	W	339	None
Bunton, Jno	Franklin	9–16–1824	2	X	84	Salt R
Bunton, Thos	Washington	6– 7–1824	125	W	340	Salt R
Burdett, Jno	Rockcastle	2–10–1814	——	P	379	Dix & Rockcastle
Burdit, Jno	Garrard	2– 9–1806	400	P	334	None
Burditt, Enoch		10–21–1816	100	R	160	None
Burk, Saml	Jessamine	6–26–1819	1,000	T	106	Caney Fk Peter Cr
Burnes, Joseph & Chas	Tennessee	12–14–1815	2,000	Q	280	Salt R
Burneston, Isaac	Baltimore	6– 3–1801	——	F	7	None
Burrough, Elizabeth	Philadelphia	8–18–1815	Lots	R	404	Philadelphia
Burrows, Nathan	Fayette	1–27–1808	1,000	L	293	Eagle Cr
Burrows, Wm W	Philadelphia	11– 8–1797	——	D	211	Eagle Cr
Busey, Jno	Franklin	11–30–1819	81½	T	168	Salt R
Bustard, Jno	Kentucky	12– 4–1822	200	X	125	Drakes Cr
Byers, Jeremiah	Lincoln	3–22–1792	250	B-2	463	None
Byers, Jeremiah	Lincoln	3–22–1792	100	B-2	465	Dix R
Byrne, James	Dinwiddie	7– 8–1799	10,000	D	299	Big Sandy R
Cabell, Wm	Amherst	3– 1–1792	1,000	B-2	474	Chaplin Fk
Cahill, Robt H	——	4–27–1824	30,000	W	346	Licking & Sulbergreed Cr
Caldwell, Adam	Franklin	7–20–1799	Lot	D	305	Frankfort
Caldwell, Adam	Franklin	7–12–1800	——	E	313	Elkhorn
Caldwell, David	Logan	2–13–1797	1,200	B	178	Cedar Cr
Caldwell, Elias B	Washington City	7– 3–1811	——	Q	522	None
Caldwell, Elias B	Washington	7– 3–1811	——	Q	527	None
Caldwell, Elias B	Washington	7– 3–1811	64,659	X	368	Ohio & Ky R & Mobile Bay
Caldwell, Elias B	Washington	7– 3–1811	——	X	374	None
Caldwell, Geo	Mercer	11–17–1791	230	B-2	509	Clarks Run
Caldwell, Philip	Franklin	12– 2–1800	200	G	316	Little Caney Cr
Caldwell, Susan H	——	2–11–1819	1,443	S	470	Panther Cr
Caldwell, Saml K	Bourbon	8–28–1816	773½	R	126	Stoners Fk & Green R
Caldwell, Wm	Bourbon	6 – 1790	200	B-2	145	Br Stoners Fk
Caldwell, Wm	Adair	8–18–1813	528½	W	195	Lost Cr
Calhoun, James Jr	Baltimore	10– 2–1810	2,500	N	425	None
Calhouse, Jas	Baltimore	6–14–1803	5,000	H	52	Saxtons Cr
Call, Daniel		7–15–1824	1,200	W	477	None
Calloway, Jas	Amherst	3– 6–1788	1,000	A	339	Silver Cr
Calloway, Jas	Bourbon	10– 6–1802	1,000	F	515	Hustons Fk
Calloway, Jno	Bedford	9–15–1791	400	B-2	456	Hustons Fk
Calloway, Jno	Campbell	10– 7–1802	300	F	517	Hustons Fk
Callums, Geo	Breckinridge	10–24–1818	100	S	404	Blackfords Cr
Calmes, Geo	Hampshire	1–27–1816	950	Q	420	Silver Cr
Calmers, Marquis	Woodford	2–26–1806	500	L	73	M Fk Ky R
Calmers, Marquis	Woodford	2–24–1806	328½	L	75	—— R
Calvert, Presley	Scott	6–10–1818	75	S	183	Lecompts Run
Camac, Turner	Philadelphia	10– 4–1811	22,000	P	612	Floyds Fk Eagle & Rough Cr
Camfield, Abiel	Augusta	7–24–1821	100	V	242	Ky R
Camp, Robt	Philadelphia	11– 4–1800	20,300	E	130	Red R & Rough Cr
Campbell, Benj P	Christian	9–13–1811	750	O	197	Spring Cr
Campbell, Chas	——	10–12–1819	1,193	T	181	Rolling Fk
Campbell, David H	Claibourne	3–14–1816	5,990	O	387	None
Campbell, Jno	Jefferson	1– 2–1788	55	A	425	Beargrass Cr
Campbell, Jno	Fayette	10–14–1797	70	B	206	18-Mile Island

Grantee	Residence	Deed Date	Acres	Book	Page	Watercourse
Campbell, Jno	Fayette	2– 9–1798	Lot	B	325	None
Campbell, Jno	Pittsburg	2– 6–1776	2,000	B-2	1	Ohio R
Campbell, Jno	Augusta	2-25–1775	2,000	B-2	11	Ohio R
Campbell, Jno	Jefferson	11–21–1788	2,000	B-2	15	Ohio R
Campbell, Jno	Jefferson	11–21–1788	Lots	B-2	18	Louisville
Campbell, Jno	Jefferson	11–21–1788	1,000	B-2	20	Ohio R
Campbell, Jno	Jefferson	6– 9–1789	900	B-2	33	Salt R
Campbell, Jno		6– 9–1789	900	B-2	516	None
Campbell, Jno	Fayette	11–10–1798	7	D	66	None
Campbell, Jno & Wife	Franklin	12–23–1829	Lot	Y	510	Frankfort
Campbell, Josias	Mercer	7– 8–1801	600	E	391	Licking
Campbell, Robt	Richmond	9– 9–1796		A-2	532	None
Campbell, Robt	Richmond	8–19–1796	7,000	A-2	572	Ohio R
Campbell, Robt		7– 6–1795	1,000	A-2	613	None
Campbell, Robt	Richmond	8–24–1795	1,000	A-2	615	R
Campbell, Robt		9–30–1796	2,433	A-2	628	Little Ky
Campbell, Robt	Richmond	5–15–1797	1,000	B	286	Tradewater
Campbell, Robert	Richmond	5–15–1797	1,500	B	290	Goose Cr
Campbell, Robt	Richmond	5–15–1797		B	295	Tradewater
Campbell, Robt	Richmond	8–18–1797	7,100	B	318	Ohio R
Campbell, Robt	Richmond	4–10–1797	10,869	C	18	Ohio R
Campbell, Robt	Richmond	10–22–1798	1,000	D	125	Cox & Willsons Crs
Campbell, Robt	Richmond	8– 4–1810	8,000	N	289	Laurel R
Campbell, Robt	Woodford	9–11–1825	120	Y	23	None
Campbell, R		1– 1–1814	3,000	P	330	Consoles Cr
Campbell, Saml	Scott	1–30–1817	75	R	247	Lecompts Fk Elkhorn
Campbell & Hicks	Richmond	9–30–1796	1,018½	A-2	631	Hinkston Fk
Campbell & Hicks	Richmond	7–18–1797	600	B	175	S Fk Licking
Camper, Wm	Fayette	3–24–1792	200	B-2	460	W Fk Buck Lick Cr
Campfield, Abraham	Woodford	4–12–1805	15,000	K	317	Green R
Cantrell, Caleb	Hart	7– 9–1831	365	Z	160	Little Barren R
Capron, Henry	Philadelphia	8–10–1796	1,000	D	323	Big Benson Cr
Capron, Henry	Philadelphia	8–10–1796	1,000	D	325	Big Benson Cr
Cariner, Jonathan	Kentucky	3–20–1818		S	104	Elkhorn Cr
Carnan, Chas	Baltimore	11–21–1805	1,000	K	488	None
Carne, Wm	Alexandria	2– 3–1802	1,000	J	274	S Fk Licking
Carneal, Sarah		5–31–1821	Slaves	U	490	None
Carneal, Thos	Fayette	2–25–1796	2,500	C	261	N Fk Tradewater
Carneal, Thos	Fayette	7–12–1798	200	C	294	Hardins Road
Carneal, Thos	Fayette	5–29–1799	666⅔	D	154	Ohio R
Carneal, Thos	Kentucky	5–27–1799	8,750	D	156	Salt R
Carneal, Thos	Campbell	9– 9–1790	384	D	376	Leestown Bottom
Carneal, Thos	Boone	7– 7–1801	21,645	E	408	Ohio & Green R
Carneal, Thos		12–14–1801	1,000	F	171	Mill Cr
Carneal, Thos	Boone	8– 1–1805	22,950	J	282	Panther Doe Run & Ohio R
Carneal, Thos	Kentucky	7–11–1805	500	J	289	Big Bone Cr
Carneal, Thos	Boone	10– 1–1805	492	K	162	Elkhorn
Carneal, Thos	Frankfort	1–15–1808	2,250	L	278	Big Bone Lick
Carneal, Thos	Kentucky	11–15–1809	4,800	N	117	None
Carneal, Thos	Kentucky	12–16–1809	2,174	N	256	Ohio R
Carneal, Thos		9–28–1810		N	271	None
Carneal, Thos	Kentucky	10–10–1810	950	O	314	Ohio R
Carneal, Thos	Fayette	7–30–1797	2,000	P	520	Big Bend Green R
Carneal, Thos D	Campbell	3– 7–1817	2,500	R	186	Big Bone & Mud Lick Cr
Carneal, Thos	Boone	9–20–1799	15,000	R	295	None
Carneal, Thos D	Franklin	9–16–1807	5,222	L	264	Rock Lick & Caney Cr
Carneal, Thos D	Campbell	12–19–1821	2,437½	V	214	Br Big Bone Lick Cr
Carneal, Thos D	Campbell	12–11–1823	750	W	180	Big Bone Cr
Carneal, Thos D	Campbell	12–11–1823	1,770	W	182	Ohio R & Big Bone Cr
Carneal, Thos D	Campbell	10– 5–1829	Lot	Y	498	Louisville
Carneal, Thos D Adair	Franklin	2–15–1817		R	285	None
Carpenter, Saml		2– 5–1833	2,300	Z	271	Rough Cr
Carrall, Chas H	Livingston	12– 1–1831	7,200	Z	235	Russells, Grave & Rough Cr
Carrell, Jno	Philadelphia	1– 8–1807	15,196	L	284	Tygerts Cr & Fks Sandy
Carrico, Levi		4–18–1833		Z	278	None
Carrington, Richard A		2–16–1836		28	9	Ky
Carrington, Sarah	Halifax	3–18–1820	1,500	Z	122	Beaver & Russell Cr
Carrington, Sarah	Halifax	3–18–1820	2,000	Z	126	Beaver, Russell Cr & Little Barren R
Carson, Alexander		5– 6–1807	708	L	20	None
Carter, Alfred S	Tanquier	8–20–1827		X	290	None
Carter, Chas	Culpepper	12–17–1802	2,666⅔	H	178	N Fk W Fk Red R & Br Green R
Carter, Thos Jr & Jesse		12– 2–1829		Y	413	None

Grantee	Residence	Deed Date	Acres	Book	Page	Watercourse
Cary, Joseph	Alexandria	12- 5-1795	1,250	D	233	Otter Cr
Cary, Joseph	Alexandria	11-21-1797	25,334⅔	D	248	S Fk Ky R
Cary, Thos	Gloucester	3-18-1815		T	149	None
Casedy, Samuel	Jefferson	1- 7-1833	Lots	Z	317	Louisville
Casey, Peter	Mercer	7-10-1798	1,500	C	263	N Fk Tradewater
Casey, Peter	Mercer	3-20-1803	2,000	G	353	Lost Cr
Casey, Peter	Mercer	11-30-1805	1,000	K	151	Highland Cr
Cassity, Michael, heirs	Fleming	11-10-1809	Slaves	N	114	None
Castleman, David	Frederick	2- 4-1811	10,000	O	24	Little Sandy R
Castleman, Jno	Franklin	1-10-1825	213	X	294	Eagle Cr
Castleman, David	Frederick	3-10-1829	981	Y	346	Ohio R & Otter Cr
Castleman, David	Fayette	1-19-1839	——	27	17	None
Castleman, David	Fayette	1-11-1839	——	27	18	None
Castleman, David	Fayette	1-11-1839	——	27	19	None
Castleman, David	Fayette	6-27-1839	——	27	52	None
Castleman, David	Fayette	8-12-1839	——	27	77	None
Castleman, David	Fayette	12-18-1839	——	27	94	None
Castleman, David	Fayette	1-21-1840	——	27	102	None
Castleman, David	Fayette	1-11-1840	——	27	131	None
Castleman, David & Wife	Fayette	10- 9-1840	446	27	155	Fayette Co
Castleman, David	Fayette	8-21-1840	——	27	175	None
Castleman, David	Fayette	12-29-1840	——	27	176	None
Castleman, David	Fayette	9-23-1840	——	27	177	None
Castlemna, David	Fayette	10-10-1840	——	27	188	None
Castleman, David	Fayette	7-20-1841	——	27	220	None
Castleman, David	Fayette	8-21-1843	——	27	378	None
Castleman, David	Fayette	8-26-1843	——	27	379	None
Castleman, David	Fayette	10-16-1843	——	27	389	None
Castleman, David	Fayette	12-20-1843	——	27	391	None
Castleman, David	Fayette	1-15-1845	——	27	467	None
Castleman, David	Fayette	4-23-1845	——	28	15	None
Castleman, David	Fayette	11-10-1845	——	28	77	None
Cates, O G	Franklin	1- 1-1840	1,000	27	100	Obyon Cr
Cates, O G	Franklin	10- 1-1839	1,000	27	146	Obion Cr
Cates, O G	Franklin	2- 4-1841	1,000	27	197	Tennessee R
Cates, Owen G	Franklin	12-27-1841	1,000	27	281	Hickman Co
Cates, Owen G	Frankfort	9-28-1843	500	27	387	Fk Clarks R
Catlett, Peter	Boone	4-24-1826	1,000	Y	221	Green & Pond R
Cave, Richard	Woodford	7-10-1802	600	G	163	Clear Cr
Certner, Daniel	Fayette	4- 9-1801	2,000	E	402	Floyds Fk
Certner, Daniel	Fayette	7-22-1801	500	E	405	Br Licking
Chaffer, H Jr & Jno	Windsore	1-20-1797	40,000	G	265	Br Big Sandy R
Challis, Jno W & Jas M	New Jersey	8- 1-1828	——	X	423	Salt R
Chambers, David	——	1-26-1802	4,875	F	363	Rd to Ohio Falls
Chambers, Wm	Mason	2- 5-1812	255	O	305	Locust Cr
Chambers, Wm	Jefferson	11- 8-1817	104	R	568	None
Chamberlain, Lewis W	Richmond	2-14-1823	1,724	Y	68	None
Chamberlane, Wm B	Richard	2-14-1823	1,724	Y	68	None
Champney, Thos	Stamford Street	6-12-1798	12,000	E	211	Ky R
Chandllee, Goldsmith	Frederick	3-10-1803	500	G	418	Poages Cr
Chandler, Robt, heirs	Culpepper	6- 9-1821	——	U	531	None
Chapman, Jno S	Henry	3-15-1819	500	S	502	None
Chapman, Jno S	Henry	3-18-1819	150	S	504	Ky R
Chapman, Jno S	Frankfort	3-13-1823	250	W	162	Martins Br
Chapman, Jno S	Frankfort	4-23-1824	11,550½	X	53	Ky R
Chase, Saml	Maryland	3-26-1786	2,000	A	106	Green R
Chase, Saml	Maryland	3-27-1786	3,000	A	109	Green R
Cheatham, Jas	Henderson	9-21-1816	250	R	388	None
Cherry, Moses	Scott	4- 5-1796	300	A-2	529	Brashears Cr
Cherry, Moses	Woodford	2-29-1791	300	B-2	363	Clear Cr
Chevis, Henry T	Kentucky	4- 1-1821	——	V	4	None
Chew, Robt S	Fredericksburg	2-23-1824	500	W	304	Paraquet Cr
Child, Henry	Baltimore	12- 7-1826	2,483	X	465	Elk Cr
Chiles, Jno	Mercer	9-10-1794	10,300	A-2	284	Ky R & Bensons Cr Slate Cr & Hinkston Fk
Chiles, Walter	Shelby	11-22-1802	3,000	G	191	Salt R
Chiles, Wm	Montgomery	3-21-1811	1,000	N	442	Hinkston Fk
Chiles, Wm	Montgomery	1- 8-1817	——	R	441	None
Chiles, Wm	Montgomery	3- 2-1846	2,500	28	74	Mill Cr
Chinn, Christopher, heirs	——	8-22-1798	500	F	95	None
Chinn, Rawleigh	Fayette	10-30-1787	——	A	434	Br Coxes Cr
Chinn, Richard H	Lexington	12- 7-1822	600	W	17	Highland Cr
Chisham, Geo & Benj	Scott	2-25-1823	50	V	439	Fks Elkhorn
Chisham, Richard	Nelson	10- 5-1790	400	B-2	204	Sinking Cr
Christ, Henry	Bullitt	11-25-1802	2,000	G	67	Cedar Cr

Grantee	Residence	Deed Date	Acres	Book	Page	Watercourse
Christian, Jonathan Jr & Wife	Virginia	3- 1-1810	1,366⅔	O	1	None
Church, Robt W	Franklin	6-20-1840	109	27	130	M Elkhorn
Church, Thos	Franklin	9-24-1816	60	R	81	None
Church, Wm S	Franklin	8-29-1841	68	27	234	Elkhorn
Claiborne, Herbert A	Richmond	2-14-1823	1,724	Y	68	None
Clark, Benj O	Fayette	11-23-1827	756	X	399	Peters Cr
Clark, Benj O	Fayette	11-23-1827	200	X	400	Wolf R
Clark, Ebenezer	———	6-19-1806	1,275	K	336	None
Clark, Chester	Manchester	1-19-1808	1,650	M	62	Big Bone Lick
Clark, Francis	Mercer	1-10-1799	500	E	298	None
Clark, Geo	Henrico	1-18-1808	1,000	M	86	Deer Cr
Clark, Geo	Hanover	4-19-1809	1,000	M	420	Tradewater
Clark, Geo	Hanover	3-16-1808	11,200	N	207	W Fk Little R & Cumberland R
Clark, Geo	Fayette	5-30-1812	———	O	445	———
Clark, Geo	Fayette	11- 6-1816	800	R	57	Snells Cr
Clark, Geo	———	12- 1-1818	1,250	S	387	None
Clark, Geo	Kentucky	3-28-1820	———	T	304	Tradewater
Clark, Geo	Fayette	1-22-1821	800	U	279	Peter Cr
Clark, George	Kentucky	10-28-1824	28,500	X	40	Big Barren W Fk Little & Cumb R
Clark, Geo W	Louisville	10- 2-1817	1,293½	S	325	Little Ky R
Clark, Isaac	Jefferson	7- 6-1832	———	Z	251	None
Clark, James	Campbell	6- 4-1794	1,000	M	181	Green R
Clark, Jonathan	Jefferson	3-31-1804	200	H	423	Br Cumberland R
Clark, Genl Jonathan	Kentucky	3-16-1808	11,200	N	207	W Fk Little R & Cumberland R
Clark, Nicholas	Jefferson	10-12-1801	———	F	77	Green R
Clark, Nicholas	Jefferson	2-15-1804	8,000	H	331	Miami R
Clark, Nicholas	Frankfort	4-10-1805	———	J	303	Station Camp & Big Benson
Clark, Rebtin	Madison	8-26-1802	470	H	16	M Licking
Clark, Robt Jr	Bedford	3- 8-1788	216	A	362	E Fk Coxes Cr
Clark, Robt Jr	Bedford	3- 8-1788	600	A	364	Coxes Cr
Clark, Robt Jr	Bedford	3- 8-1788	596	A	366	E Fk Coxes Cr
Clark, Saml	Stanton	5-31-1808	5,250	N	67	Little Bullskin Cr
Clark, Wm	Jefferson	7-28-1803	73,962	H	61	Ohio R
Clark, Wm	Louisville	10- 2-1817	3,500	S	329	Crab Orchard Fk
Clark, Wm	Louisville	10-10-1818	422	S	333	None
Clark, Wm	Fayette	7- 6-1832	———	Z	251	None
Clark, Wm Jr	Madison	8-26-1802	470	H	24	M Licking
Clay, Brutus J	Bourbon	3-30-1830	1,207½	Y	486	None
Clay, Brutus J	Bourbon	11-10-1831	8,847½	Z	198	Bank Lick Cr
Clay, Brutus J	Bourbon	3-19-1845	———	28	3	None
Clay, Green	Madison	9-13-1797	5,218	C	77	Bank Lick Cr
Clay, Green	Madison	9-13-1797	6,016½	C	80	Bank Lick Cr
Clay, Green	Madison	4-28-1803	3,500	G	370	Licking
Clay, Green	Madison	11-28-1804	666⅔	H	397	Little Barren R
Clay, Green	Madison	1-15-1799	———	N	210	None
Clay, Green	Madison	10-28-1811	9,507	O	285	Silver Muddy & Station Camp Cr
Clay, Green	Madison	1-17-1814	5,000	P	325	Ohio R
Clay, Green	Madison	4- 6-1801	6,170½	Q	348	Sinking Valley & Cumberland R
Clay, Green, heirs	Madison	4-13-1831	———	Z	169	None
Clay, Green, heirs	Madison	5-27-1833	11,000	Z	296	Tennessee & Clarks
Clay, Henry	Kentucky	5- 1-1802	8,000	F	463	——— Cr
Clay, Henry	———	12-16-1804	250	H	482	Licking
Clay, Henry	Lexington	9-13-1806	32,500	L	53	Ky R & Bank Lick
Clay, Henry	———	10-24-1809	7,500	N	258	Mouth Big Miami
Clay, Henry	———	11- 1-1810	2,000	N	293	Ohio R
Clay, Henry	———	11- 1-1810	2,000	N	295	Ohio R
Clay, Henry	———	6-10-1811	1,000	O	83	Tennessee R
Clay, Henry	———	10-24-1809	7,500	O	142	Mouth Big Miami
Clay, Henry	Fayette	10- 1-1811	1,700	O	170	None
Clay, Henry	Kentucky	9-29-1821	750	V	81	None
Clay, Henry	Fayette	12-19-1829	75	Z	7	Ky R
Clay, Henry, Executor	———	6-27-1831	1,500	Z	144	Highland Cr
Clay, Jno	Bourbon	3- 3-1846	140	28	78	M Woodford Cr
Clay, Junius B	Fayette	1-18-1821	469	U	180	Bank Lick Cr
Clay, Matthew	Pittsylvania	12- 5-1795	1,000	A-2	539	Cumberland R
Clay, Porter	———	11- 8-1808	———	M	423	Red R Iron Works
Clay, Saml H	Bourbon	12-23-1840	400	27	183	Panther Cr
Clay, Sidney P	Fayette	1-18-1821	469	U	180	Bank Lick Cr
Clay, Sidney P	Bourbon	3-30-1830	1,207½	Y	486	None
Clay, Sidney P & Brutus J	Bourbon	7- 4-1828	19,244½	X	497	Licking Red Ky R & Strodes Cr
Clayton, Thos	Philadelphia	5- 5-1797	1,000	C	83	Br Little Rockcastle
Cleany, Eliza	———	11-28-1806	1,000	K	481	None
Cleany, Joseph	———	11-28-1806	14,000	K	479	None

Grantee	Residence	Deed Date	Acres	Book	Page	Watercourse
Clements, Isham	———.	4–19–1815	75	Q	43	Brashears Cr
Cleveland, Levi	Campbell	7– 3–1805	57	J	348	Dry Cr
Cloud, Cabbie	Fayette	11– 5–1819	600	T	183	Middle Valley Cr
Cluke, Livia	Montgomery	2– 4–1829	225,000	Y	401	None
Cobbs, Jno	Georgia	3– 9–1789	1,000	B-2	35	Elkhorn Cr
Cobuni, James	Jefferson	2– 6–1790	1,000	B-2	352	Brashears Cr
Cobuni, James	———.	8–26–1791	300	B-2	356	Mulberry Cr
Cocke, Bowler	Henrico	5–18–1795	7,750	A-2	268	Buck Cr & Dix
Cocke, Bowler	Henrico	7–20–1795	4,000	A-2	498	N Fk Tradewater
Cocke, Jno	———.	10–10–1813	1,800	P	293	N Fk Rough Cr
Cocke, Jno H	Virginia	3– 5–1790	6,000	B-2	178	N Fk Licking
Cocke, Sterling	Hawkins	6– 1–1802	4,000	S	550	S Fk Licking
Cocke, Wm	Nelson	4– 3–1811	3,833½	N	465	Ohio & Little Ky
Cockran, Alex	Philadelphia	7–16–1808	7,870	M	263	Elkhorn
Cockran, Jno	Mercer	3–12–1789	¼	A	518	None
Cockran, Jno	Mercer	3–19–1789	1	B-2	23	Danville
Cockran, Jno	Mercer	10– 5–1789	½	B-2	94	Danville
Cockran, Wm	Philadelphia	12– 6–1799	407	F	448	Ohio R
Coghill, Jos	———.	5–18–1820	562	T	334	None
Cohen, Robt	———.	11–12–1818	1,000	S	323	Brashears Cr
Cohoon, Thos	New York	10– 7–1805	537	J	318	Clay Lick Cr
Cohurn, Jno	———.	11–10–1786	Lot	A	232	None
Coleman, Chapman	Frankfort	5–11–1820	Lot	U	435	Frankfort
Coleman, Chapman	Frankfort	1–15–1823	Lot	V	440	Frankfort
Coleman, Edwards S	Franklin	2–14–1814	Lots	P	462	Frankfort
Coleman, Francis	Spatsylvania	9– 1–1800	10,250	E	260	Tripletts Cr
Coleman, Jas	Lexington	12–11–1805	1,000	J	444	None
Coleman, Jas	Lexington	12–11–1805	30,000	J	447	Nolinn & Green R
Coleman, James	Lexington	12–11–1805	10,000	J	451	Salt R
Coleman, Jas	Fayette	1–16–1808	2,120	L	279	Caney & N Fk Rough Crs
Coleman, Jas	Lexington	2– 9–1814	Lot	P	391	Frankfort
Coleman, Jas	Harrison	9–30–1815	666⅔	Q	196	Rough Cr
Coleman, Jas	———.	12–20–1815	400	Q	272	S Fk Licking
Coleman, Jas	Lexington	3–29–1803	1,000	G	256	Licking
Coleman, Jas Addnir	Fayette	9–21–1811	492	O	166	Elkhorn
Coleman, Colonel Jas, heirs	Fairfax	8–21–1820	———	W	258	None
Coleman, Jas Jr	Franklin	1–17–1801	200	E	420	N Fk Tradewater
Coleman, Jas Jr	London	12–23–1805	1,000	K	182	Ky R
Coleman, Jas & Co	———.	11–25–1808	8,571	M	213	None
Coleman, Jno	Bullitt	10–21–1823	110	W	147	None
Coleman, Meredith	———.	5– 1–1822	Slaves	V	401	None
Collins, Benj	Bullitt	10–21–1823	264	W	144	None
Collins, Jno	Woodford	8–19–1802	133½	F	473	Butlers Fk
Collins, Joel	———.	11–30–1798	400	D	114	N Fk Ky R
Collins, Thos	Stafford	4–15–1802	167	F	238	Logans Cr
Colston, Edward	Berkley	5– 9–1812	1,000	O	477	Ohio R
Colston, Rawleigh	Fredrick	3–30–1798	20,000	C	332	None
Colston, Rawleigh	Fredrick	3–30–1798	9,000	C	337	Huston Fk
Colston, Rawleigh	Berkley	9–19–1801	1,332½	F	402	Br Green R
Colston, Rawleigh	Virginia	7–10–1801	9,000	F	405	None
Colston, Rawleigh	Berkley	6–26–1802	3,000	G	170	Big Barren & Cumberland R
Colston, Rawleigh	Virginia	7– 9–1802	1,000	G	173	Ohio R
Colston, Rawleigh	Berkley	6–19–1802	3,000	G	177	Drakes Cr
Colston, Rawleigh	Berkley	2–11–1811	1,333½	O	473	Hunters Cr
Colurse, Jno	Philadelphia	10– 5–1791	10,000	K	53	Salt R
Combs, Jas M	Washington	8–16–1842	9,188	27	308	Chaplins Fk
Combs, Leslie	Fayette	10–19–1830	210	Z	160	Boones Cr
Combs, Leslie	Fayette	6–25–1844	300	28	41	Breckinridge Co
Commonwealth of Ky	Kentucky	2–25–1833	Railroad	Z	261	None
Compton, Henry T	Prince George	3–29–1802	1,500	F	204	Fks Licking
Coningham, David H	Philadelphia	2– 1–1827	15,375	Y	264	Tygerts Cr
Conn, Hezakial	Fredrick	5– 2–1816	1,000	R	42	Ohio R
Conn, Natley	Bourbon	12–18–1795	1,000	E	278	Ohio R
Conner, Rice	Frankfort	6– 8–1805	Lot	J	176	Frankfort
Conover, Lewis H	———.	5–19–1819	2,000	T	102	None
Conpar, Robt	Fredericksburg	3–20–1804	11,000	H	608	Kennekamie Cr
Contee, Thos	———.	6–28–1805	4,833	K	546	Cow Cr & Red R
Conyugham, David H	Philadelphia	3–18–1800	5,000	E	80	Main Licking
Conyugham, David H	Philadelphia	6– 3–1801	———	F	85	None
Cook, Dawson	King & Queen	9– 1–1796	1,000	N	246	Tennessee R
Cook, James	Shelby	5– 6–1822	160	V	225	Crooked Cr
Cook, Jno	Berkley	2–10–1798	1,000	C	242	Green R
Coorod, Valentine	———.	10– 2–1815	23½	Q	227	None
Cope, Iseral	Baltimore	3–25–1800	800	E	349	Green R
Cope, Iseral	Baltimore	7–26–1799	800	T	157	Green R
Cope, Jasper	Philadelphia	6– 1–1818	800	T	160	Green R
Copland, Chas	Richmond	5– 3–1796	1,000	B	4	Tradewater
Copland, Chas	Richmond	12– 1–1796	1,400	B	39	N Fk Tradewater

Grantee	Residence	Deed Date	Acres	Book	Page	Watercourse
Copland, Chas	Richmond	3–29–1797	400	B	44	Pitmans
Copland, Chas	Richmond	4– 5–1799	333⅓	D	437	Big Barren R
Copland, Chas	Richmond	4– 5–1799	1,750	D	440	Little Barren R
Copeland, Chas	Richmond	5–18–1812	1,600	O	452	Michaux Br
Coppage, Bartholomew	Harrison	5–15–1830	34¾	Y	464	Br Cedar Cr
Corbin, Wm & Jno	Mercer	10–15–1790	Lot	B-2	249	Danville
Cornegys, Cornelius	——	3– 1–1827	Lot	Y	273	Mt Sterling
Cornegys, Cornelius	——	3– 1–1827	600	Y	275	Owingsville Rd
Corp, Saml	New York	5–31–1799	260,178	R	232	Ohio R
Cortmill, Jno & Andrew	Bath	11–13–1815	1,500	R	27	Slate & Rockcastle
Coryell, W D	Mason	7– 9–1832	50	Z	229	Franklin Co
Cosby, Fortunatus	Kentucky	12–21–1807	734½	M	54	Rough Cr
Cosby, Fortunatus	——	11– 1–1810	2,000	N	293	Ohio R
Cosby, Fortunatus	——	11– 1–1810	2,000	N	295	Ohio R
Cosby, Overton, Executor	——	12–18–1802	1,500	H	258	Ohio R
Cotton, Geo T	Woodford	7– 6–1815	20	Q	178	Glens Cr
Cotton, G T	Woodford	7–24–1816	500	R	245	None
Courtnay, Isabella	——	10–10–1802	350	G	136	Elkhorn Cr
Covington, Elijah M	Warren	12–11–1804	200	H	462	Drakes Cr
Covington, Elijah M	Warren	12–11–1804	200	H	464	Drakes Cr
Covington, Elijah M	Warren	12– 2–1805	200	J	420	Drakes Cr
Covington, Elijah M	Warren	1–15–1810	100	N	98	Drakes Cr
Cowan, Jared	——	5– 8–1789	400	B-2	24	None
Cowden, Jas Jr	——	7–31–1806	5,000	K	421	None
Cowne, Thos W	Culpepper	6–22–1820	3,550	T	449	Pitman & Russell Cr
Cox, Austin P	Frankfort	6– 8–1821	1,000	U	441	Clifty & Poplar Camp
Cox, Austin P	Frankfort	11– 3–1821	152	V	126	Big Beaver Cr
Cox, Austin P	Franklin	2– 7–1840	——	27	103	None
Cox, Austin P	Franklin	4–30–1840	Lot	27	124	Frankfort
Cox, Austin P	Franklin	6–22–1840	1,800	27	125	Ky R & Big Benson Cr
Cox, Austin P	Franklin	4–22–1842	Lots	27	286	Frankfort
Cox, Austin P	Franklin	12–13–1843	——	27	449	Big Benson Cr
Cox, Benj S	Lexington	6– 9–1796	3,000	A-2	504	Beech Fk
Cox, Catherine	New York	9–19–1818	21,000	S	447	Chaplins Fk
Cox, Daniel W	Philadelphia	10–17–1816	22,000	R	390	None
Cox, Edward	Chesterfield	4–29–1824	——	X	158	None
Cox, Isaac B	New York	11– 3–1816	21,000	S	444	Chaplins Fk
Cox, Isaac B	New York	9–22–1818	3,500	S	451	Chaplins Fk
Cox, Jas & Matilda	Woodford	2——1845	57	27	469	S Elkhorn
Cox, Jno	Powhatan	7– 2–1810	1,000	N	230	N Fk Clay Lick Cr
Cox, Jno	Powhatan	3–13–1811	626½	N	441	Clay Lick Cr
Cox, Jno F	New York	9–22–1818	3,500	S	455	Chaplins Fk
Cox, Lazarus	Scott	11–29–1800	160	E	235	Ky R
Cox, Lazarus	Scott	11–29–1800	160	E	236	Ky R
Cox, Saml	Pendleton	11–25–1816	200	R	356	Eagle & Little Sugar
Cox, Saml	Grant	3–13–1830	80	Y	450	M Gallatin Co
Cox, Tarlton	Amelia	12– 1–1802	666⅔	G	365	Little Barren R
Craddock, Paschal D	Green	6–23–1820	200	U	23	Green R
Craddock, Paschal D	Green	6–27–1820	200	U	25	Green R
Craddock, Paschal D	Green	6–27–1820	200	U	27	Green R
Craddock, Paschal D	Green	11– 6–1820	200	U	388	Green R
Craddock, Paschal D	Jefferson	5– 1–1835	1,226⅔	27	50	Green Co
Craddock, Robt	——	9– 4–1787	Lot	A	369	Town Sp
Craddock, Robt	Mercer	5–17–1792	5½	B-2	492	Danville
Craddock, Robt	Danville	10–29–1798	1,000	D	378	Russells Cr
Craig, Adam	Richmond	12–23–1790	1,200	A-2	379	None
Craig, Adam	Richmond	3– 5–1800	4,000	E	109	None
Craig, Adam Executor	Williamsburg	4–13–1798	3,600	D	76	Cumberland R
Craig, Benj	Gallatin	10– 8–1804	143	H	447	Mill Cr
Craig, Elijah	Fayette	6–22–1789	1,000	B-2	29	Elkhorn Cr
Craig, Elijah	Woodford	12–31–1790	1,340	B-2	293	—— Cr
Craig, Elijah	Woodford	4–26–1791	250	B-2	304	N Fk Clear Cr
Craig, Elijah	Woodford	4–26–1791	——	B-2	308	None
Craig, Elijah	Scott	1–20–1817	500	R	415	W Fk Drakes Cr
Craig, Elijah & Jno	Fayette	9– 1–1786	3,111	A	474	None
Craig, Joel	——	3–22–1806	6,666⅔	K	277	Ohio & Licking
Craig, Joel	Scott	1–10–1809	——	M	293	Ohio R
Craig, Jno Hawkins	Woodford	11–17–1796	1,296½	C	26	Little Sandy R
Craig, Jno Hawkins	Woodford	11–17–1796	7,838	C	28	Little Sandy R
Craig, Jno H	Woodford	1–16–1796	1,359½	C	315	Little Sandy R
Craig, Jno Jr	Morgan	7–16–1808	360	M	60	Clear & Jessamine
Craig, Joseph	Fayette	10–15–1808	550	M	210	S Fk Elkhorn
Craig, Levi, Lewis	——	11–18–1819	Lots	T	289	Port Williams
Craig, Lewis	Mason	9– 9–1796	7,023	A-2	542	Brashears Cr
Craig, Lewis & Silas	Gallatin	6– 9–1817	Lot	R	304	Frankfort
Craig, Nancy	Gallatin	5–17–1814	Lots	T	292	Port Williams
Craig, Nancy	——	11–18–1819	Lots	T	289	Port Williams

Grantee	Residence	Deed Date	Acres	Book	Page	Watercourse
Craig, Robert	Manchester	11- 7-1794	1,000	A-2	61	Ohio R
Craig, Stewart & Silas	——	11-18-1819	Lots	T	289	Port Williams
Craig, W M	Shelby	4-30-1810	11,200	N	267	Little R & Kettle Cr
Craik, James	Alexandria	8- 1-1795	568	A-2	307	Green R
Craine, Jno	Fanquier	9-16-1802	1,000	G	20	None
Cravens, Jno	Fayette	11-25-1834	176¾	Z	467	Fayette Co
Crawford, Robt	Baltimore	6- 9-1788	5,000	A	383	Ohio R
Creath, Jacob	Kentucky	8- 7-1815	1,000	Q	530	Ohio R
Creath, Jacob	Kentucky	3-20-1818	—	S	104	Elkhorn Cr
Creed, Elijah	Shelby	8-23-1806	—	K	550	Cypress Cr
Creighton, Wm Jr	Chillicothe	9-22-1822	2,350	V	65	Licking
Crenshaw, Spotswood D	——	2-22-1827	2,950	Z	344	Mississippi R
Crist, Henry	Bullitt	9-15-1800	1,500	D	549	Salt R
Crist, Henry	——	12-15-1802	547	G	102	Salt R
Crist, Henry	Bullitt	12-10-1805	200	J	432	Road to Long Lick
Crist, Henry	Fayette	11- 8-1806	1,000	K	476	Salt R
Crittenden, Thos T	Fayette	10-21-1815	16	R	601	Cane Run
Crittenden, Ann Maria	——	10-25-1819	513	T	217	None
Crockett, Andrew	Wythe, Va	11- 9-1804	1,670	H	471	Salt R
Croghan, Geo	Parish of St John	11-30-1820	8,875	Z	303	Ohio R & Locust Cr
Croghan, Serena Eliza	New Orleans	8- 2-1824	2,250	W	372	W Fk Red R
Croghan, Wm	Jefferson	12- 5-1798	1,530	D	173	E Fk Marrowbone
Croghan, Wm	Jefferson	11-21-1799	444	D	481	Cumberland R
Croghan, Wm	Jefferson	6-19-1801	1,254	F	79	Little Barren R
Croghan, Wm	Jefferson	5-26-1801	4,220	F	182	Mississippi R
Croghan, Wm	Jefferson	4-26-1802	2,000	G	182	None
Croghan, Wm	Jefferson	2-15-1804	8,000	H	331	Miami R
Croghan, Wm	Jefferson	1- 2-1810	Lot	N	111	Beargrass Cr
Croghan, Wm	Jefferson	10- 9-1809	316	N	187	S Fk Little R
Croghan, Wm	Jefferson	5- 4-1812	1,900	O	372	Little Barren R
Croghan, Wm	Jefferson	9- 5-1812	1,000	P	118	None
Croghan, Wm	Jefferson	10-12-1814	1,082	Q	63	Skeggs Cr
Croghan, Wm	Jefferson	8-24-1814	1,082	Q	65	Skeggs Cr
Croghan, Wm	Jefferson	6- 6-1817	500	S	1	Crocus Cr
Croghan, Wm	Jefferson	6- 1-1824	4,000	W	362	Cumberland R
Croghan, Wm Jr	Jefferson	8-28-1817	1,000	S	66	Marrowbone Cr
Crook, Jno	Madison	4-30-1812	2,000	O	360	Goose Cr
Crook, Michael	——	11-23-1818	150	S	343	None
Croudson, Saml	Shannondoah	7-12-1799	1,250	D	366	None
Crow, Elizabeth & Linsey	——	8-18-1808	—	M	333	None
Crowder, Starling	Jessamine	7-24-1816	—	Q	518	Ky R
Crowder, Starling	——	7-24-1816	80	Q	520	Ky R
Cruger, Bertram P	New York City	1-25-1809	56,000	M	306	Eagle Cr
Cruger, Martha	New York	8-16-1842	9,188	27	308	Chaplins Fk
Crump, Goodrich, heirs	Powhatan	4-28-1803	3,500	G	367	Licking
Crump, Jas O	Tuskaloosa	12- 9-1819	33,642	T	235	Ky R
Crutcher, Bartlett & Thos	——	1-13-1846	153	28	45	S Elkhorn
Crutcher, Henry	Georgia	1-12-1811	1,767	N	412	Eagle Cr & S Fk Licking
Crutcher, Henry	Franklin	11-20-1834	494	Z	480	Sulphur Lick Cr
Crutcher, Henry	Franklin	1-13-1846	24	28	46	S Elkhorn
Crutcher, Jno	Jessamine	11-25-1816	215	R	251	Ky R
Crutcher, Lewis	Woodford	3-22-1820	199¾	T	369	None
Crutcher, Robt R	Jessamine	6-18-1817	200	R	310	Ky R
Cummings, Alexander	Chilicothe	10- 5-1814	—	S	271	None
Cummings, Chas	Washington	11-12-1802	400	G	29	Green R
Cummings, Chas	Washington	11-13-1802	496½	G	36	M Fk Licking
Cummings, Robt E	Washington	6-14-1811	496½	P	261	M Fk Licking
Cumpson, Thos	Philadelphia	6- 3-1801	—	F	85	None
Cumpton, Meredith	Green	12-23-1799	240	D	496	Pitman Cr
Cumpton, Thos	Philadelphia	2-12-1802	—	P	605	None
Cundiff, Richard	Adair	12-29-1819	200	T	242	Russell Cr
Cunningham, Geo	Franklin	11-11-1844	Lot	27	439	Frankfort
Cunningham, Geo	Franklin	8- 5-1844	Lot	27	450	Frankfort
Cunningham, Geo	Franklin	12-26-1844	—	27	452	Armstrong Fk
Cunningham, J F	Norfolk	6-16-1817	500	R	371	None
Curd, Edmund	Shelby	9-30-1799	321	E	6	Sandy Cr
Curd, Edmund	Shelby	9-30-1799	429	E	7	Sandy Cr
Curd, Jas	Fayette	5-18-1789	350	B-2	69	Guesses Fk
Curd, Jno	Goochland	10-16-1797	6,000	B	247	Big Bone Lick
Curd, Joseph	Mercer	9-19-1814	800	Q	54	Ohio R
Curd, Pleasant	Buckingham	7-10-1811	200	O	457	Big Barren R
Currie, Jas	Richmond	9-16-1799	9,000	D	445	Cabin Cr
Currie, Dr James	Richmond	8-24-1803	2,000	G	435	None
Currie, James	——	10-30-1824	—	W	399	Fk Big Bone Lick
Currier, Andrew	Philadelphia	10-17-1816	22,000	R	390	None
Curtright, Daniel	Bourbon	10-16-1822	150	V	461	Green Cr
Dabney, Chas, Jr	Louisa	8- 2-1813	700	P	197	Rough Cr
Dabney, Chas, Jr	Louisa	9- 3-1822	—	W	88	Tennessee R

Grantee	Residence	Deed Date	Acres	Book	Page	Watercourse
Dale, Jno	Hatton Garden	6–12–1898	12,000	E	211	Ky R
Daley, Lawrence	Fayette	2——1827	253	Y	270	6 Mile Cr
Dallam, Elizabeth M	Fayette	4–12–1834	Lot	Z	420	Lexington
Dallam, Richard	Logan	2– 6–1808	760	L	299	Fk Red R
Dallam, Wm S	Lexington	8——1823	666⅔	W	116	S Fk Ky R
Dallam, Wm S	Fayette	3– 2–1824	300	W	278	Little Fk Eagle Cr
Dandridge, Wm	New Kent	2–27–1796	1,000	A-2	398	Big Cr of Ky R
Daniel, Henry	Montgomery	8–13–1821	1,000	V	66	Highland Cr
Daniel, Henry	Montgomery	5– 4–1821	——	V	387	None
Daniel, Martin	Jefferson	3–17–1791	112	B-2	252	None
Daniel, Martin	Jefferson	10– 6–1791	208	B-2	365	Hanging Fk
Daniel, Martin	Jefferson	10– 7–1791	1,000	B-2	368	Beech Fk
Daniel, Robt	Jefferson	9–24–1786	940	A	258	Beargrass Cr
Daniel, Thos	——	12–14–1811	Slaves	O	206	None
Daniel, Wm	Frankfort	2– 8–1810	Lot	P	83	Frankfort
Dant, Thos	Washington	4–21–1812	128	P	42	N Br Ky R
Darby, Adam	Fredericksburg	8– 1–1798	650	D	151	Green R
Darby, Patrick H	Meade	7–29–1828	Lots	X	434	Brandenburg
Darby, Patrick H	Meade	7–29–1828	113,482	X	434	Otter Cr & Nolinn
Darby, Patrick H	Meade	10– 1–1828	244,482	X	482	Nolinn
Dardis, James	Baltimore	6–14–1803	5,000	H	52	Saxtons Cr
Dardis, James	Knoxville	3–18–1815	2,500	S	496	None
David & Moorman	Breckinridge	6– 2–1821	——	V	288	Rolling Fk & Ohio
Davis, Allen Jr	Alexandria	7–27–1802	500	G	168	None
Davis, Charity	Jefferson	11– 1–1827	200	X	412	None
Davis, Edward	Mercer	3– 7–1791	1,000	B-2	246	Beech Fk
Davis, Henry	Woodford	4–27–1820	21	W	124	Elkhorn
Davis, Henry, heirs	Woodford	10– 2–1829	10½	Y	404	S Elkhorn
Davis, Hancock W & Jno H	Woodford	11——1834	118	Z	493	S Fk Elkhorn
Davis, H W S & J H	Woodford	2– 7–1832	118	Z	184	S Elkhorn
Davis, Ishmahel	Franklin	1–31–1820	Lot	T	440	Frankfort
Davis, James	Lincoln	5– 5–1788	——	A	493	None
Davis, Jno	Gallatin	5–18–1809	72	M	395	None
Davis, Jno, heirs	——	5– 6–1818	154	S	123	None
Davis, Joseph	Lincoln	6–21–1786	Lot	A	236	None
Davis, Joseph	Mercer	6–20–1787	800	A	327	Licking
Davis, Presley	Shelby	9– 6–1833	Slaves	Z	343	None
Davis, Thos	Oldham	11–20–1827	50	X	413	None
Davis, Thos B	Pittsburg	12–30–1815	2,244	Q	341	Boones & Indian Cr
Davis, Thos W, heirs	——	6–12–1831	315	Z	68	None
Davis, W	Kentucky	2– 4–1829	315	Y	333	Lex & Frankfort Rd
Davis, Wm	Woodford	2–27–1809	77	M	335	None
Davidson, Hezakiah	——	11–27–1834	——	Z	510	Hart Co
Davidson, Jas	Washington	1–20–1812	564	O	309	Tavern Spg Bt
Davidson, James	Washington	5–28–1812	556	O	461	Laurel R
Davidson, Jas W	Simpson	11–20–1824	——	X	148	None
Davidson, Genl John	Annapolis	12–17–1805	416½	K	402	None
Davidson, Joseph	Philadelphia	5– 5–1798	——	D	520	None
Davison, Joseph	Woodford	10– 6–1803	500	H	236	Clear Cr
Davidson, Wm	Frederick	10– 4–1810	1,250	O	10	Ohio R
Dawkin, Jno	Henry	5– 5–1818	1,000	S	121	Mill Cr
Dawson, Jno	Hardin	12–27–1815	300	Q	296	Bacon Cr
Dawson, Thos	Hardin	1–27–1813	200	P	68	None
Dawson, Thos	Hardin	1–10–1819	306½	S	491	Green R & Bacon cr
Dawson, Robt D	New Madrid	10–12–1819	Lots	T	121	——
Dean, James	North Carolina	9–17–1791	650	B-2	430	Bear Cr
Dean, Joseph	Philadelphia	3– 6–1786	13,666⅔	D	193	N Fk 3 Fks Ky R
Dean, Thos	Washington	10– 8–1811	2,000	O	136	Buck Cr
Dearing, Walker	——	3–25–1808	Lots	L	353	Frankfort
Dehoof, Frederick	——	11–11–1815	88	Q	231	—— Cr
De Graffenreid, Robt	Virginia	6–11–1800	1,478½	E	88	Eagle Cr
De Grassey, Chas	Philadelphia	11–15–1785	8,270	O	427	Salt R
De Lormerie, Louis Philipp Gallot	Larisin France	2–16–1787	5,277	A-2	596	Ohio R
De Lormerie, Louis Philipp Gallot	Paris France	2– 2–1799	5,227	D	334	Ohio R
Demere, Saml	Lincoln	7–25–1786	1,000	A	196	Big Cr
Denemaurs, Victor D	New York City	1–25–1809	56,000	M	306	Eagle Cr
Denemaurs, Victor D	New York City	5–25–1802	56,000	L	138	None
Denman, Saml	Philadelphia	12– 2–1806	1,000	M	3	Green R
Denman, Saml	Philadelphia	7–16–1808	7,870	M	263	Elkhorn
de Valconlon, Jno S	Richmond	9–15–1786	10,000	N	1	None
Dewitt, Wm	Lincoln	10– 9–1790	Stock	B-2	220	None
Dewitt, Wm	Lincoln	9–13–1790	Lot	B-2	221	None
Dickinson, Daniel H	Franklin	6–10–1844	Lot	27	415	Frankfort
Dickinson, Martin, heirs	——	7– 6–1819	500	T	16	Grassy Lick Cr
Dillard, Geo	Sussex	4–30–1798	1,000	D	268	Big Barren R
Dinsmore, Jas	Louisiana	8–20–1839	431	27	71	Indian Fk Eagle Cr
Dobson, Robt	Lincoln	9– 6–1788	400	A	488	Rough Cr

Grantee	Residence	Deed Date	Acres	Book	Page	Watercourse
Dodge, David	————	7–11–1818	193½	S	364	4 Mile lower Howard & Hickman Cr
Dodge, Joseph	Belvedere	4–19–1808	Working machine	L	376	None
Doran, Patrick	Mercer	10– 2–1789	Negros	B-2	85	None
Dorsey, Chas Jr	Gallatin	4– 3–1811	7,666½	N	462	Ohio & Little Ky
Dorsey, Greenberry	Mercer	3–25–1791	Lot	B-2	261	Danville
Dorsey, Greenberry	————	6–28–1791	Lot	B-2	369	Danville
Dorsey, Greenberry	Philadelphia	9–13–1791	Lot	B-2	404	Danville
Dorsey, Greenberry	Mercer	10–29–1791	Lots	B-2	415	Danville
Dorsey, Jno	Maryland	3–26–1786	2,000	A	106	Green R
Dorsey, Jno	Maryland	3–27–1786	3,000	A	109	Green R
Dorsey, Jno	Maryland	3–27–1786	12,000	A	111	Green R
Dorsey, Mary Jane	Baltimore	10–13–1834	1,791½	Z	473	Pond Fk Salt R
Dougherty, Jas	Fayette	9–——1816	262	R	167	Br Green R
Dougherty, Moses	Fayette	12– 2–1789	913	B-2	255	Hickman Cr
Dougherty, Thos	Franklin	11–25–1828	————	X	489	None
Dougherty, Wm	Mason	8–21–1839	87	27	53	N Elkhorn
Dougherty, Wm	Franklin	7– 1–1841	45	27	212	Wranglin Run
Douglass, Adam	Winchester	12– 1–1806	1,000	L	1	Green R
Douglas, Geo Jr	New York	7–30–1798	260,178	R	225	Ohio R
Douglas, Geo Jr	New York	5–31–1799	260,178	R	232	Ohio R
Douglass, Richard H & Wm	Baltimore	1–12–1820	Lots	T	254	New Albany, Ind
Dowdall, James	————	11– 5–1806	900	K	457	None
Downing, Jno	Lincoln	6–19–1790	106	B-2	160	Clear Cr
Dowing, Jno	————	3– 4–1794	1,000	N	100	—
Downs, Benj	Fayette	3–13–1821	300	V	124	Short Cr
Drake, Abraham	Bourbon	7–15–1788	1,400	A	441	Lees Cr
Drake, Saml Sr	Franklin	5–24–1819	Lots	S	519	Port Williams
Drake, Saml Sr	Franklin	5–24–1819	90,793½	S	519	Ky Red & Sandy R
Drummond, Wm	Fredericksburg	3–18–1803	3,000	L	163	Cumberland R
Dubbs, Martin	Philadelphia	6–12–1806	6,000	L	329	None
Dubs, Martha	Philadelphia	4–23–1796	6,000	A-2	453	None
Duckham, Thos	Lawrence	8–23–1839	89,000	27	88	Red R & Licking
Dudley, Benj W	Lexington	9– 7–1819	800	T	151	None
Dudley, Jeptha	Franklin	7–15–1818	120	S	187	None
Dudley, Jeptha	————	4– 4–1823	Lot	W	83	Frankfort
Dudley, Jeptha	Franklin	11–30–1841	195	27	298	Ky R
Dudley, Joseph	Franklin	7– 2–1832	Lot	Z	241	Frankfort
Duffield, Abraham	Manor	11–12–1789	3,000	E	98	Fks Licking
Duffield, Thos	Gallatin	10– 1–1806	200	L	79	None
Duke, Jno B	Bourbon	9– 3–1830	500	Z	30	Soo M Cr & Big Barren R
Duke, Jno B	Bourbon	10–19–1830	Lot	Z	31	Mt Sterling
Duke, Richard & Jas	Albemarle	3–11–1816	2,266½	R	301	Bigger Staff & Mud
Dulton, Thos	Prince George	3–31–1806	5,000	M	171	Rolling Fk
Duncan, Elizabeth	————	8–27–1828	125	X	454	Eagle Cr
Duncan, Joseph	Bourbon	6–23–1789	500	B-2	83	Doctors Fk
Dunlap, Ann	Philadelphia	5–15–1813	Lots	P	268	Philadelphia
Dunlap, Charlotte	Philadelphia	5–15–1813	Lots	P	268	Philadelphia
Dunlap, Jas	————	4– 5–1786	½	A	150	None
Dunlap, James	Montgomery	3– 8–1798	51,500	C	177	Nolinn
Dunlap, Jno	Alexandria	12– 4–1802	7,932½	G	343	Ky Ohio & Salt R
Dunlap, Jno	Alexandria	11–25–1805	500	J	435	Buffaloe Cr
Dunlap, Jno	Philadelphia	8– 6–1813	Lots	P	275	Philadelphia
Dunlap, Jno	Mercer	9–17–1802	Lot	R	578	Danville
Dunlap, Jno Jr	Philadelphia	10– 5–1812	Lot	P	39	Frankfort
Dunlap, Jno, dec'd heirs	Philadelphia	5–15–1813	Lots	P	269	Philadelphia
Dunn, Samuel	Lincoln	6–17–1786	800	A	127	Rolling Fk
Dunnell, Jacob	Philadelphia	9–18–1819	1,519½	T	331	Bear Fk Green R
Dunwoody, Jno	Philadelphia	2– 7–1801	8,212½	G	406	None
Dunwoody, Mary A & Selina	Philadelphia	1–18–1820	12,616	X	394	Rough, Panther, Otter Cr & Salt R
During, Walker	Kentucky	5–14–1819	Lot	T	128	Frankfort
Durrell, James	————	7– 3–1809	Slaves	N	450	None
Duval, Anne	————	11–10–1794	2,500	A-2	69	Main Licking
Duval, Ann	Richmond	11–10–1794	778	A-2	78	Caney & Rough Cr
Duval, Burr H	————	7–11–1807	2,000	L	111	Ohio R
Duval, Claiborne Jr	Virginia	3– 1–1810	1,366½	O	1	None
Duval, Jno	Scott	11–29–1824	500	X	31	Elm Lick & Caney Fk Cedar Cr
Duval, Lott, & Wife	Franklin	5–10–1826	111	Y	161	———— Cr
Duval, Lucy	————	11–10–1794	2,500	A-2	67	None
Duval, Lucy & Anne	————	11–10–1794	2,400	A-2	73	Green R
Duval, M	Mason	4– 9–1802	915	F	533	Br Rough, Clover & Mill Cr
Duval, Philip	Buckingham	7– 1–1813	1,200	P	160	Russell Cr
Duval, Samuel P	————	2– 1–1796	400	A-2	392	Cedar Cr

Grantee	Residence	Deed Date	Acres	Book	Page	Watercourse
Duval, Wm	———	11–22–1794	1,878	A-2	63	None
Duval, Wm	———	1794	1,437½	A-2	65	Chaplins Fk
Duval, Wm	Richmond	11–22–1794	105½	A-2	71	N Fk & Johnsons
Duval, Wm	Richmond	11– 7–1794	8,593	A-2	80	Green R
Duval, Wm	Richmond	5– 7–1795	389	A-2	82	Ky R
Duval, Wm	Richmond	7–28–1794	———	A-2	84	Ohio R
Duval, Wm	Richmond	7–28–1795	20,000	A-2	258	Craigs Cr
Duval, Wm	Richmond	3– 2–1799	12,000	D	361	Fk Licking
Duval, Wm	Richmond	5–19–1800	1,800	E	271	Rough Cr
Duval, Wm	Richmond	5–25–1800	12,000	E	274	Licking
Duval, Wm	———	9– 5–1801	754	F	43	Clover Cr
Duval, Wm	Richmond	11– 4–1801	600	F	360	Russell Cr
Duval, Wm	Richmond	2–27–1804	20,440	H	123	Licking
Duval, Wm	Richmond	4–14–1804	10,000	H	359	None
Duval, Wm	Richmond	12–31–1799	2,000	L	108	Ohio R
Duval, Wm	Henrico	1– 4–1790	12,140	N	491	Ohio & Licking
Duval, Wm	Buckingham	9– 8–1820	6,923	U	70	Rough Cr
Duval, Wm	Virginia	10–22–1827	50,050	X	312	Cumberland & Sandy R, & Tygarts Cr
Duval, Wm N & Jno	Richmond	11–12–1794	11,650	A-2	75	Green R
Duval, Wm P Jr	Nelson	18–1807	600	L	113	None
Duval, Wm P & Wife	———	9–21–1825	1,512	Y	258	Rock Lick Island Ohio R & Indian Camp Cr
Dwight, Jonathan	Springfield	3–25–1796	64,184	A-2	521	Nolinn
Dyer, Wm	Nelson	9–25–1786	300	A	244	Rolling Fk
Ealy, Henry	Scott	1–24–1810	360	N	109	Ohio R
Ealy, James	———	11–15–1805	1,000	K	496	None
Ealy, James	———	11–15–1805	7,000	K	498	None
Earheart, Martin	Washington	9–18–1796	750	D	1	Salt R
Early, Joel	Culpepper	6– 2–1789	2,000	B-2	27	Little Ky R
Early, Joel	Culpepper	6– 1–1789	1,000	B-2	32	Cabin Cr
Early, Whitfield	Boone	10– 6–1812	———	R	222	None
Earnest, Matthew	Allegana	9–23–1796	6,900	A-2	635	Green R
Easterday, Lewis	Gallatin	5–18–1811	560	O	22	Ky R
Easterday, Lewis	Gallatin	12–11–1823	888	W	199	None
Eastham, James	Pulaski	1–16–1801	500	F	245	Pitman Cr
Eastland, Thos	———	11– 9–1810	220	N	310	Mill & Distillery
Eckford, Henry	New York	9–24–1822	8,875	Z	306	Ohio R Locust & Indian Cr
Edmonson, Jno	Washington	6–15–1813	568	P	247	Sulphur Lick Cr
Edmonson, Joseph, heirs	Culpepper	6– 9–1821	———	U	531	None
Edrington, Benj	Franklin	9–14–1813	———	P	396	Elkhorn Cr
Edrington, Henry L	Livingston	1–19–1822	150	V	224	Eagle Cr
Edwards, Elisha B	Nelson	9–26–1811	422	O	164	Mill Cr
Edwards, Harden	Franklin	4–18–1801	———	E	327	None
Edwards, Harden	Woodford	11–10–1801	350	F	107	Town Fk
Edwards, Harden	Franklin	5–18–1802	3,530	F	400	Harbour & Cabin Cr
Edwards, Harden	Frankfort	5–25–1802	50	F	440	S Fk Elkhorn
Edwards, Harden	Frankfort	6– 1–1802	50	F	442	——— Cr
Edwards, Harden & Wife	Franklin	11– 7–1799	———	D	453	None
Edwards, James	Mercer	9–23–1788	Lot	A	465	None
Edwards, Jno	Bourbon	1–24–1787	1,000	A	264	Coopers Run
Edwards, Ninian	Logan	12– 3–1802	Lots	G	77	Frankfort
Eggleston, Richard	Amelia	2–26–1796	300	D	373	Green R
Eidson, Jno	Franklin	12–24–1804	150	O	312	None
Elder, Robt	Scott	3– 7–1799	———	D	130	S Fk Elkhorn
Elgin, Samuel	———	6– 6–1808	300	M	10	None
Eliason, Ebenezer	Georgetown	3–11–1814	1,325	P	537	Big Reedy Cr
Ellicott, Thos	Maryland	10–17–1827	1,896	X	362	None
Ellicott, Thos	Baltimore	11–14–1829	30,821	Y	425	Slate, Stepstone, Flat, Licking & Miller Cr
Ellington, Joseph & Wife	Franklin	5–10–1826	111	Y	161	——— Cr
Elliott, Alexander	Adair	12–20–1804	318	K	520	Beaver Cr
Elliott, Thos	King William	4–15–1802	2,000	G	72	Br E Fk Little Barren R
Elliott, Thos	Baltimore	11–26–1821	119,289½	V	174	Licking, Shelby & Green R
Elliott, Thos	Baltimore	6– 2–1827	1,900	X	249	Slate Cr
Ellis, Chas	Richmond	8–24–1815	866⅔	R	169	Tennessee R
Ellis, Chas	Richmond	8–24–1815	866⅔	R	172	Br Tennessee R
Ellis, Jonah	Richmond	5–11–1818	1,508⅔	S	148	Rough, Brush & Richland Cr
Ellis & Allen	Richmond	5–18–1812	1,600	O	452	Michaux
Elliston, Jno	Gallatin	5–21–1810	300	N	265	None
Elliston, Jno	———	12–14–1811	Slaves	O	206	None

Grantee	Residence	Deed Date	Acres	Book	Page	Watercourse
Elston, David	Henry	5–16–1822	————	V	217	Mill Cr
Elmendorf, Lucas	Ulster	4–18–1803	8,000	G	279	None
Emmons, Wm	————	3–12–1810	Mortg	N	145	None
Endicott, Joseph	————	7– 5–1813	100	P	339	Ky R
English, Robt & Joseph	Franklin	3–22–1802	255	F	200	Little Ky & Corn Cr
Enlow, Isham	Hardin	10–16–1805	800	K	24	Nolinn
Epes, Mary P	————	2– 2–1847	Lots	28	125	Owensboro
Epes, Polly	Petersburg	11–28–1811	20,000	O	213	Hinkston Fk
Epes, Polly	Petersburg	2–19–1812	692	O	319	Island in Ohio R
Epes, Polly	————	6– 8–1813	50,000	P	367	Vanons Water Courses
Epes, Polly	Petersburg	8– 9–1819	1,500	T	55	Ashes Cr
Etting, Reuben	Baltimore	10–23–1795	8,800	A-2	684	Ohio R
Eubank, Thos T	Campbell	3–23–1829	406½	Y	323	Panther Cr
Euing, Pitman	Bath	3————1833	250	Z	368	Mill Cr
Evans, Jno	Campbell	6–10–1798	400	C	248	Crooked Cr
Evans, Jno	Philadelphia	4–12–1802	Lot	F	478	Frankfort
Evans, Jno	Philadelphia	7–15–1812	Lot	O	502	Frankfort
Evans, Jno Jr	Jefferson	1–30–1817	Lot	R	457	Middleton
Eve, George	————	12–12–1811	2,000	O	219	Little N Fk Elkhorn
Eve, William	Culpepper	3– 8–1803	313	G	425	S Fk Licking
Eve, Wm	Culpepper	3–17–1804	1,000	H	580	Clay Lick Cr
Ewers, Wm	Adair	12–29–1819	200	T	242	Russell Cr.
Ewing, Baker	Lincoln	9–13–1785	5½	A	55	None
Ewing, Baker	Lincoln	9–19–1787	200	A	331	Bowmans Cr
Ewing, Baker	Lincoln	10–23–1788	500	A	512	Rough Cr
Ewing, Baker	Lincoln	9–22–1791	1,000	B-2	476	Hingston Fk
Ewing, Baker	Franklin	3–20–1799	1,000	D	218	Fk Station Camp Cr
Ewing, Baker	Franklin	11–28–1803	600	K	352	Main Licking
Ewing, Jno	Hardin	8–10–1804	200	H	376	Bear Cr
Ewing, Young	Christian	12–13–1802	450	G	112	Little R
Ewing, Young	Christian	11– 4–1809	190	N	63	W Fk Red R
Ezrey, Jno	Nelson	1–30–1787	235	A	299	Long Lick Cr
Fackler, Jacob	Richmond	6–16–1807	444	L	156	Cumberland R
Fallon, Jno O	St Louis	6–10–1824	746	W	291	Little Ky R
Farish, Edmund	Barren	12–23–1833	876⅔	Z	402	Little Barren, Tenn & Ohio Rs
Farish, Geo R	Cumberland	12–23–1833	876⅔	Z	402	Little Barren, Tenn & Ohio Rs
Farley, Daniel	Gallatin	4– 8–1825	23	X	133	Ohio R
Farmers Bank	Virginia	4– 3–1824	Lots	Y	123	Richmond
Farmers Bank	Virginia	4– 3–1824	647	Y	123	Poages Cr
Farmers Bank	Virginia	4–21–1834	Lots	Z	431	Richmond, Va
Farrar, Ann C	St Louis	6–10–1824	746	W	291	Little Ky R
Farrow, Catherine & Susannah	Montgomery	2– 4–1829	225,000	Y	401	None
Farrow, Barnard G	St Louis	2– 9–1820	5,647¾	T	341	Rough Cr Floyds Fk & Ohio R
Farrow, Isaac	Montgomery	2–12–1805	1,271	H	546	Slate & Flatt Crs
Farrow, Kenaz	Montgomery	10–14–1829	2,000	Y	447	Bourbon Co
Farthing, Landy	James City	11– 9–1803	517	H	19	Green R
Fatterd, Jno O	St Louis	2– 9–1820	5,647¾	T	341	Rough Cr Floyds Fk & Ohio R
Feland, James	Lincoln	3– 2–1789	150	A	486	Hanging Fk
Fentress, Jno	Albemarle	9– 7–1804	20,300	J	154	Red R, M Fk Rough
Fenwick, Jas W	Jefferson	10–17–1833	156	Z	412	Elkhorn
Fenwick, Joseph	Philadelphia	6– 9–1796	3,000	A-2	504	Beech Fk
Fenwick, Robt	Woodford	10– 8–1791	158	B-2	489	Jeffersons Cr
Fenwick, Wm	————	6–23–1797	60,000	B	229	Big Sandy R
Fenwick, Wm	Frankfort	12–13–1805	57	K	71	Stewarts Cr
Field, Geo W	Pennsylvania	2– 5–1800	Lot	N	212	Frankfort
Field, Jno & Jno	Philadelphia	8– 7–1797	Lots	D	12	Frankfort
Fields, Benj	Mercer	9–30–1790	Lots	B-2	262	Danville
Fields, Benj	Mercer	9————1790	Lots	B-2	264	Danville
Fields, Jno	Philadelphia	10–16–1795	1,524	A-2	620	Meeting & Rough
Fields, Willis	Woodford	5–11–1813	8,000	P	343	Ky R & Hustons Fk
Fields, Willis	Woodford	2–26–1814	1,500	P	433	Ky R
Finley, Jno	Franklin	3– 6–1815	Slaves	Q	56	None
Finley, Jas C	Washington	11–23–1811	200	O	203	Stewarts Cr
Finley, Samuel	Mercer	8–19–1790	500	B-2	205	Flat Cr
Finnie, Jno	Woodford	12–22–1795	————	N	228	None
Fishback, Elizabeth R & Chas	————	5–13–1830	1,524	Y	483	Drennons Lick Cr
Fishback, Harriet S	————	5–13–1830	1,524	Y	483	Drennons Lick Cr
Fishback, Henry & Wm H	————	5–13–1830	1,524	Y	483	Drennons Lick Cr
Fishback, Isaac F	————	5–13–1830	1,524	Y	483	Drennons Lick Cr
Fishback, James	Barren	7– 8–1806	200	K	358	Skaggs Cr
Fishback, Jno	Jessamine	10–21–1815	7,000	Q	266	Panther
Fishback, Rebecca V	Hardin	6–22–1815	4,150	Q	199	6 Mi & Drennons Cr
Fisher, Adam	Mercer	3– 5–1829	2,704	Y	390	Panther & Rough Cr
Fisher, Benj	Mercer	4–22–1802	100	F	467	Beaver Cr

Grantee	Residence	Deed Date	Acres	Book	Page	Watercourse
Fisher, James	Richmond	5–12–1802	1,000	G	156	Green R
Fisher, Maddox	Ohio State	5– 2–1818	—	S	128	Little N Fk Elkhorn
Fisher, Mary B	——	2–11–1819	1,443	S	470	Panther Cr
Fisher, Stephen	Mercer	——1791	17	B-2	371	Dix R
Fisher & Macumirdo	Richmond	1–21–1802	3,000	K	450	Deer Cr
Fitzgerald, Daniel	Woodford	12–16–1811	45	P	527	Glens Cr
Fitzhugh, Dennis	Louisville	2– 9–1820	5,647¾	T	341	Rough Cr Floyds Fk & Ohio R
Fitzhugh, Philip	Maryland	11– 7–1801	4,466	F	475	Miller Cr
Flahavan, Thos	Philadelphia	5–10–1793	17,823	A-2	616	Ky R
Fleming, Leonard J	——	3– 4–1790	1,000	B-2	112	Goose Cr
Fleming, Leonard J	Woodford	12–22–1831	200	Z	171	S Elkhorn
Fleming, Wm	Nelson	3– 9–1785	1,000	A	5	Indian Camp Cr
Fleming, Wm	Fleming	4–16–1806	233	K	413	Indian Cr
Fletcher, Thos	Montgomery	5–11–1807	570	L	31	Flatt Cr
Fletcher, Thos	Bath	5–18–1819	4,539	S	510	Tygrets Cr
Flournoy, David, Jno J & Matthew	——	10–14–1806	1,000	K	477	N Elkhorn
Floyd, Geo R C	Jefferson	7–15–1812	1,010	O	433	Ohio R &·Goose Cr
Floyd, Geo R C	Louisville	7–28–1812	—	O	533	None
Floyd, Geo R C	New Orleans	3– 1–1813	—	P	258	None
Floyd, Geo R C	Jefferson	9–15–1815	1,010	Q	210	Ohio R & Goose Cr
Floyd, Jno		11– 7–1809	550	N	123	None
Floyd, Jno	Montgomery	10–11–1821	1,000	V	82	Ohio R
Floyd, Jno	Montgomery	10–11–1821	600	V	83	None
Floyd, Jno	Philadelphia	11–28–1817	—	W	3	None
Floyd, Dr Jno	Montgomery	7–15–1812	980	O	431	Ohio R
Flynn, Thos	Franklin	6–12–1845	25	27	479	nr Frankfort
Forbes, James	Essex	12–11–1793	10,400¾	E	206	Bald Eagle Township
Forbes, Jonathan	——	11–20–1806	1,250	K	499	None
Forbes, Jonathan	——	11–20–1806	1,170	K	501	None
Forbes, Jno Jr	Richmond	3– 1–1830	—	Z	13	None
Forbes, Wm	Westmoreland	4– 2–1796	—	B	299	Goose Cr
Forbes, Wm	Westmoreland	4– 2–1796	2,000	B	303	Tradewater
Forbes, William	Philadelphia	9–30–1786	4,400	K	460	Beech Fk
Forbis, Mary	Green	7–12–1803	700	G	372	Russell & Caney Cr
Forbis, Mary	Philadelphia	6– 3–1802	4,400	G	402	Beech Fk
Ford, Jno Edward	Charles	6–29–1799	800	J	113	Green R
Ford, Standish	Philadelphia	4– 1–1805	67,647	Y	204	Ky & Green Rs
Foreman, Thos		4–19–1820	—	T	434	Elk Cr
Forrest, Sarah	Philadelphia	5–15–1813	Lots	P	268	Philadelphia
Forrest, Uriah	Montgomery	3– 8–1798	51,500	C	177	Nolinn
Forrest, Uriah	Montgomery	3– 9–1798	50,000	C	191	Sextons Cr
Foster, Evans	——	9– 3–1828	135	X	475	None
Foster, Nathaniel	——	9–24–1824	—	X	69	S Fk Benson Cr
Fountain, Aaron	Jefferson	——1810	200	O	315	Little Barren R
Fountain, Jno	Prince Edward	6–20–1789	5,300	B-2	100	None
Foushee, Frances	Hafarm	12– 1–1796	5,000	B	108	Highland Cr
Foushee, Frances	Stafford	12– 1–1796	7,333⅓	B	333	Highland Cr
Fowler, Abraham	New York	8–12–1793	225,000	A-2	209	N & M Fks Ky R
Fowler, Jno	Lexington	2–25–1796	204	A-2	91	Silver Cr
Fowler, Jno	Lexington	10–25–1795	6,000	A-2	127	Bank Lick Cr
Fowler, Jno	Lexington	2–25–1796	5,900	A-2	136	Silver & Goose Crs
Fowler, Jno	Fayette	8–24–1795	1,784	A-2	139	None
Fowler, Jno	Fayette	7–24–1795	1,939	A-2	142	None
Fowler, Jno	Fayette	1–10–1796	—	A-2	145	None
Fowler, Jno	Fayette	8–26–1796	1,000	A-2	429	Russell Cr
Fowler, Jno	Kentucky	8–16–1796	4,530	B	327	Blue Lick Rd
Fowler, Jno	Fayette	4–23–1799	861	D	143	Hingston Fk
Fowler, Jno	Fayette	12– 5–1796	1,000	G	143	Salt R
Fowler, Jno	Fayette	11–14–1804	22,050	J	74	None
Fowler, Jno	Fayette	12–11–1804	22,054½	J	77	Licking & Eagle Cr
Fowler, Jno	Fayette	8–22–1805	341	L	303	S Fk Licking
Fowler, Jno	Lexington	2–25–1796	5,900	M	50	Silver, Muddy & Station Camp Crs
Fowler, Jno	——	12–23–1808	13,333⅓	M	244	Main Licking & Flat Cr
Fowler, Jno	Fayette	12–27–1808	1,000	M	251	Fleming Cr
Fowler, Jno	Lexington	8–14–1809	14,000	N	124	Buffaloe Rd
Fowler, Jno	Lexington	9–16–1808	6,000	N	146	Bank Lick Cr
Fowler, Jno	Fayette	1– 9–1811	5,000	N	437	Salt Lick Cr
Fowler, Jno	Lexington	3–29–1795	26,597½	N	495	Crossings 3 Crs
Fowler, Jno	Fayette	5–11–1812	20,440	O	526	Large Cr
Fowler, Jno	Fayette	12– 1–1813	300	P	338	Mud Lick Fk
Fowler, Jno, Atty	Fayette	3–26–1814	2,000	Q	100	Yellow Cr
Fowler, Jno, Atty	Fayette	11– 8–1799	353	D	416	Tates Cr
Fowler, Theodosius	New York	2–19–1796	100,000	A-2	188	N & M Fk Ky R
Fowler, Theodosius	New York	2–18–1796	100,000	A-2	192	N & M Fk Ky R
Fowler, Theodosius	New York	2– 6–1795	54,156	A-2	213	N & M Fk Ky R
Fowler, Theodosius	New York	3–21–1795	15,554	A-2	217	N & M Fk Ky R

Grantee	Residence	Deed Date	Acres	Book	Page	Watercourse
Fowlke, Thos	Baltimore	7–26–1799	800	T	157	Green R
Fox, Jno	Richmond	2–28–1811	1,000	O	126	Br Green R
Fox, Jno & Chas	Richmond	12– 1–1819	1,000	T	231	Muddy R
Fox, Richard	Woodford	3– 6–1804	378½	H	413	Glenns Cr
Fox, Saml & Wife	———	———1820	Lot	U	184	Louisville
Franklin, Henry	New York City	2– 4–1809	10,000	N	93	Ky R
Frazier, Alexander	Warren	12–21–1840	978½	27	169	Little Barren R & Glovers Cr
Frazier, Eliphalet	———	11–17–1807	790	M	108	None
Frazier, Eliphabet	———	11–18–1807	1,000	M	110	None
Frazier, Elizabeth M	———	1– 1–1845	Lot	27	477	Lexington
Frazier, Elizabeth M	———	J– 1–1845	200	27	477	Logan Co
French, Dr Geo	Fredericksburg	12– 9–1802	1,000	G	221	Paroquet Cr
French, Henry	Mercer	6–15–1787	400	A	323	Salt R
French, Richard	Clark	12– 8–1818	———	T	8	None
French, Wm	Gallatin	11–14–1815	518	Q	286	Ohio R
French, Wm	Franklin	2– 4–1829	225,000	Y	401	None
Fresh, Frances	Lincoln	10–13–1789	200	B-2	125	Slate Cr
Fries, Jno	Philadelphia	11–13–1805	———	N	156	None
Froman, Jacob	Mercer	11–10–1789	200	B-2	114	Ky R
Froman, Jacob	Mercer	8–16–1790	2,355	B-2	226	Salt R
Froman, Jacob	Woodford	12–12–1807	1,670	L	221	Salt R
Froman, Jacob	Woodford	2– 9–1809	———	M	309	Shawnee Run
Fry, Joshua	Mercer	4– 2–1802	4,300	F	221	——— R
Fry, Joshua	Danville	10– 8–1810	700	N	475	Ohio R
Fry, Wm	Jessamine	7– 1–1817	1,754½	S	20	Crocus Cr
Fuller, Benj	Philadelphia	2–21–1787	1,400	A	411	None
Fuller, Benj	Philadelphia	5– 1–1787	1,000	A	415	None
Fuller, Benj	Philadelphia	8–25–1786	———	A-2	108	Ohio R
Fuller, Benj	Philadelphia	6–17–1784	10,000	27	376	None
Fullerton, R A	Philadelphia	7–31–1813	Lots	R	397	Philadelphia
Funk, Peter	Jessamine	8–20–1819	900	T	17	Big Barren R
Fuqua, Wm	———	12– 6–1811	2,500	O	222	None
Furnish, Jas	Gallatin	8– 6–1818	230	S	235	Ohio R
Furnish, Thos	———	12–10–1822	100	V	433	Ohio R
Gadde, Wm	Hardin	1–27–1813	150	P	62	Bacon Cr
Gaines, Jas M	———	1–25–1828	12,000	X	367	Gaines Tavern
Gaines, Jas M	Boone	7–19–1827	6,074	X	479	None
Gale, Geo W	Franklin	9– 2–1816	Slaves	R	45	None
Gale, James	Franklin	3–18–1818	Lot	S	75	Frankfort
Gale, Jno	Gallatin	1– 6–1819	1,112	S	374	Eagle Cr
Gale, Robt F	Woodford	7–18–1814	30	P	524	Glenns Cr
Gale, Thos	Hanover	8–31–1811	30	O	92	None
Galey, Wm	Shelby	3– 4–1815	50	Q	19	None
Galy, James	Shelby	10– 6–1810	150½	N	317	None
Galles, Severe	———	12– 6–1799	666⅔	D	443	N Fk Mayfield Cr
Gallandet, Peter W	Philadelphia	6– 4–1796	578½	E	78	None
Gamble, Jno G	Richmond	3–26–1825	2,647	Y	116	Poages Cr Tradewater Beaver Dam N Fk Tradewater
Gamble, Robt	Richmond	11– 4–1795	1,000	W	307	Beaver Cr & N Fk Tradewater
Gano, Lydia G	Franklin	12– 5–1804	400	H	443	Ky R
Garnett, Benj	———	11–12–1818	1,000	S	323	Brashears Cr
Garnett, Fleming H	Shelby	1–16–1845	637	27	456	Crooked Cr
Garrett, Jas M C	Spencer	4– 4–1832	20	Z	184	Buck Cr
Garrett, Jno	Scott	12–18–1804	166¼	H	498	Twin Cr
Garrett, Wm	———	12– 3–1798	125	D	109	None
Gary, Ann	Washington	5– 6–1816	811	R	1	None
Gary, Everard	Georgetown	10– 9–1804	717	H	588	Caney Bear & Reedy Crs
Gary, Everard	Georgetown	5– 3–1805	10,000	K	60	Caney Bear & Reedy Crs
Gary, Everard	Georgetown	5– 2–1805	7,500	K	66	Caney Bear & Reedy Crs
Gary, Everard	Georgetown	6–10–1812	1,875	O	463	Caney Bear & Reedy Crs
Gary, Thos E	Dinwiddie	11–12–1806	1,000	L	33	Green R
Garriatt, Ambron	Jefferson	7–15–1802	150	F	469	Harrods Cr
Garriche, Jno Peter	Washington	6–10–1823	575	W	45	Cypress Cr
Gates, Jacob	Boston	8–19–1820	2,000	T	494	Hatens Cr
Gatewood, Robt	Lexington	7–24–1813	1,000	P	281	Cumberland R
Gerard, Stephen	Philadelphia	5–11–1787	4,775	A-2	49	None
Gettings, James	Baltimore	7– 3–1825	16,000	A-2	382	——— Cr
Gibbs, Benj	Washington	3– 4–1812	1,926	O	388	Green R & Nolinn
Gibbs, Zachariah	Madison	8–26–1802	470	H	7	M Licking
Gibson, Patrick	———	8–23–1819	Lots	U	269	Richmond, Va
Gill, Leo	Shelby	1–29–1829	1,750	Y	319	Salt R
Gill, Thos	Shelby	4–21–1808	257	L	378	Benson & Beech Cr
Gilles, Sarah	Franklin	6– 7–1824	125	W	340	Salt R

Grantee	Residence	Deed Date	Acres	Book	Page	Watercourse
Gillispie, Richard	Franklin	8– 3–1841	Lot...27		219	Frankfort
Gillispie, Richard	Franklin	9–16–1844	Lots...27		440	Frankfort
Gillispie, David	Mercer	5– 8–1790	251	B-2	291	None
Gillispie, David	Mercer	5–10–1791	Lots	B-2	396	Danville
Gilman, Mary	Newton	5–20–1812	30,420	P	205	None
Gilman, Mary	Newton	7–16–1814	———	Q	473	None
Gilman, Mary	Newton	8–20–1814	———	Q	477	None
Gilman, Mary, heirs	———	10–12–1833	2,106½	Z	360	Hardin Co
Gilman, Mary, heirs	Fayette	4–14–1842	2,109	27	327	Middle & Valley Cr
Gilmore, Saml	Lincoln	6– 2–1787	250	A	312	None
Gilpin, Joshua & Thos	Philadelphia	3–12–1806	20,313½	K	537	Green R
Gish, Geo	Bothcourt	10–24–1809	100	M	446	Glade Cr
Gist, Thos N	Hopkins	12–28–1832	500	27	99	Poages Cr
Glass, Robt	Nelson	8–26–1791	300	B-2	354	Brashears Cr
Glassell, Andrew	Madison	5– 3–1798	———	C	239	Deer Cr
Glassell, Wm	Fredericksburg	10– 5–1796	———	C	236	Deer Cr
Glentworth, Jos	Philadelphia	11–18–1807	6,174	S	380	Cumberland R & Br Pond Cr
Goings, Sanford	Franklin	3–20–1844	Lot...27		414	Frankfort
Goings, Sanford	Franklin	12–28–1844	Lot...27		451	Frankfort
Gooch, Thos	Green	10– 6–1830	39	Z	25	Little Barren R
Goodall, Parke	Richmond	1– 1–1801	1,000	E	392	Coxes & Wilsons
Goode, Edward	Chesterfield	4–18–1834	114	Z	446	nr Frankfort
Goodloe, Vivian	Woodford	4–27–1790	500	B-2	214	Br S Fk Elkhorn
Goodman, Jno	Frankfort	9–13–1805	Lots	J	292	Frankfort
Goodwin, Jno	New York	7–30–1798	260,178	R	225	Ohio R
Goodwin, Thos	Philadelphia	6–22–1796	1,807	A-2	506	Beech Cr
Goodwin, Wm	Baltimore	5– 9–1793	23,200	N	21	Ky & Ohio Rs
Gordon, Alexander	Alexandria	1– 9–1796	3,600	B	18	Stinking Cr
Gordon, Archibald	Mercer	3–30–1808	117	M	161	Ky R
Gordon, Bazel	Stafford	6–16–1828	1,065	Z	57	Licking
Gordon, Catherine, J M & Mary	———	10–30–1824	———	W	399	Fk Big Bone Lick Cr
Gordon, Ellis, Wm & Lillian T	———	10–30–1824	———	W	399	Fk Big Bone Lick Cr
Gordon, Isabella, M & Jas C	———	10–30–1824	———	W	399	Fk Big Bone Lick Cr
Gordon, Janetta M & Robt M	———	10–30–1824	———	W	399	Fk Big Bone Lick Cr
Gordon, William	———	9–11–1804	1,000	P	556	Ohio R
Gordon, Wm	Mercer	8–13–1806	217	K	415	Todds Ferry Rd
Gore, Andrew	Baltimore	2– 5–1800	250	D	508	N Fk Licking
Goreham, Wm A	Franklin	8– 5–1830	160	Z	26	N qr Sec 15—T 58 R R 20 W
Gorin, Henry	Warren	12–11–1802	10,500	G	96	Ohio & Sandy Rs
Goss, Jno	Albermarle	5–13–1805	1,100	J	236	None
Gott, Jno	Kentucky	3– 7–1804	1,500	H	267	None
Gott, Richard Jr	Montgomery	3– 7–1804	1,500	H	267	None
Gower, Stanly P	New Kent	4–23–1814	———	P	410	None
Grady, Wm L	Woodford	8–25–1827	210	X	274	Glenns Cr
Grady, Wm L	Woodford	8–25–1827	Slaves	X	277	None
Graff, Jno	———	9–20–1806	2,000	K	541	None
Grafton, James	Shelby	1–29–1806	216	K	137	Bullskin Cr
Graham, David	Frankfort	7– 5–1818	Lot...S		238	Frankfort
Graham, David	Frankfort	7–16–1819	———	T	52	None
Graham, David	Frankfort	7–16–1819	Lot...T		64	Frankfort
Graham, David	Frankfort	6–16–1819	Lots...T		68	Frankfort
Graham, Geo & Jno	Virginia	7–26–1800	3,000	E	153	Rolling Fk
Graham, Geo & Wife	Fairfax	4–20–1804	745	J	1	Quick Run
Graham, Jno	———	5–31–1792	2,500	P	97	Tennessee & Ohio R
Graham, Jno	———	7–17–1812	———	Q	392	None
Graham, Jno	Frankfort	7–17–1812	338	Q	395	Elkhorn
Graham, Saml	Mercer	11–15–1810	100	N	315	Shawnee Run
Graham, Wm	———	10–15–1815	3,689¾	Q	208	Cumberland R
Grainger, Wm, heirs	Baltimore	12– 7–1826	2,483	X	465	Elk Cr
Grainger, Wm	Baltimore	8– 8–1798	6,134¼	C	311	Main Licking
Granger, Gideon	Washington	1– 1–1812	64,184	O	515	Nolin & Bacon Crs
Granger, Gideon Jr	Suffied	3–25–1796	64,184	A-2	521	Nolin
Grant, Jno	Bourbon	11– 3–1788	500	A	446	Fleming Cr
Grant, Jno, heirs	Fayette	3———1826	10,000	Y	138	M Licking & Grassy Crs
Grant, Thedoria S	Newbrunswick	10–28–1824	———	X	32	None
Grant, Rev Thos	Ainwell	5–16–1807	86,035	W	171	None
Grant, Thos R & Thos B	Newbrunswick	10–28–1824	———	X	32	None
Gratz, Benj	Fayette	9– 1–1837	7,823	27	28	Ky R
Gratz, Hyman	Pennsylvania	6–28–1828	1,140	X	470	Mammouth Cave & Green R
Gratz, Hyman	Philadelphia	7–18–1820	200	Y	436	Big Barren R
Gratz, Michael	Philadelphia	10– 3–1793	9,198	A-2	56	None
Gratz, Michael	Philadelphia	2–14–1795	10,000	A-2	515	Sandy R

Grantee	Residence	Deed Date	Acres	Book	Page	Watercourse
Gratz, Michael	Philadelphia	11–15–1794	10,000	A-2	517	Big Sandy R
Gratz, Michael	Philadelphia	10– 3–1795	8,800	A-2	681	Ohio R
Gratz, Michael	Philadelphia	10– 1–1794	5,000	H	326	M Licking
Gratz, Simon	Philadelphia	8– 2–1802	2,000	G	320	Fox Run
Gratz, Simon	Philadelphia	9–16–1829	598	Y	457	Green R
Gratz, Simon, Joseph & Jacob	Philadelphia	10–28–1819	—	T	189	None
Graves, Elizabeth R	Boone	12– 9–1808	425	M	262	Cypress Cr
Graves, Francis	Richmond	3–17–1795	1,200	A-2	276	—Cr
Graves, Jno D	Franklin	2– 9–1839	25	27	26	S Elkhorn
Gray, French S	—	2–28–1835	1	Z	491	Morganfield
Gray, Jas	Richmond	4–13–1825	1,237	Y	73	Chaplins Fk
Gray, Jno	—	10–30–1805	400	K	523	None
Gray, Robert	Philadelphia	1– 1–1798	4,000	C	284	Salt R
Gray, Vincent	Alexandria	3–12–1798	3,000	E	413	None
Gray, Wm	Petersburg	5–25–1797	10,000	B	141	Goose Cr
Grayson, Alfred W	Mason	3–18–1803	61,564	N	435	Little Sandy R
Grayson, Benj	—	8–21–1800	Lot	R	269	Bardstown
Grayson, Benj	—	8–21–1800	Lot	R	270	Bardstown
Grayson, F W S	Bullitt	3–11–1814	—	P	544	None
Grayson, F W S	Bullitt	12–24–1810	—	N	398	None
Grayson, F W S	Jefferson	6–29–1819	1,483	T	98	Salt Lick Cr
Grayson, Letitia P	Fayette	10– 9–1840	685	27	155	In Fayette Co
Grayson, Peter A	Nelson	5–26–1817	1,200	R	424	James R
Grayson, Robt H	Mason	9–30–1808	41½	M	221	Salt Lick Cr
Grayson, Thos	Franklin	10– 1–1838	135	27	30	N Elkhorn
Grayson, Wm	Fairfax	11–16–1796	500	D	256	None
Green, Caleb S	Huntsboro	5–16–1829	16,380	Z	266	Salt R
Green, Duff	Baltimore	7–11–1840	2,552,304¾	27	204	Va & Ky
Green, Jno	—	11–28–1806	14,000	K	479	None
Green, Jno W	Fredricksburg	3–17–1804	1,000	H	566	Clay Lick Cr
Green, Jonathan H	Fayette	6–28–1839	10,000	27	45	In Fayette & Jefferson Cos
Green, Richard A	James City	11–21–1814	—	S	176	None
Green, Saml S	Delaware	11– 8–1836	—	27	42	None
Green, Thos	Richmond	3– 4–1833	—	Z	309	None
Green, Thos	—	5–29–1834	32,000	Z	442	None
Green, Wm	Lincoln	9–24–1785	—	A	23	None
Green, Wm	Woodford	11– 9–1805	1,778⅔	K	86	Cumberland R
Green, Wm & Wife	Kentucky	8–26–1800	9,800	F	352	Eagle Cr & Red R
Green, Willis	Lincoln	3–15–1785	Lot Danville	A	13	None
Green, Willis	Nelson	6–10–1785	575	A	27	E Fk Cox Cr
Green, Willis	Lincoln	5–24–1791	5,434	B-2	318	Big Slate Cr
Green, Zachariah	Nelson	5– 2–1827	104	X	226	Salt R
Green, Zachariah	Nelson	5–10–1827	8,270	X	236	Salt R
Greenfield, Miss Mary	—	11–23–1799	156	F	4	Mill Road
Greenvell, Bennett	Scott	1– 1–1829	107	Y	297	S Elkhorn
Greenham, Daniel	Bourbon	7–21–1801	20,698	H	518	Killicanick Cr
Greenhan, Geo	Richmond	8–29–1799	3,500	E	28	Locust Cr
Greenhow, Saml	Fredricksburg	5–17–1769	—	A-2	400	Floyds Fk Rockcastle N Fk Elkhorn Miller Licking & Hardins Crs
Greenhow, Saml	Richmond	6–17–1796	666⅔	A-2	535	Little Barren R
Greenhow, Saml	Fredricksburg	5–17–1796	—	D	102	Floyds Fk Sandy R Rockcastle N Fk Elkhorn Millers Cr & Green R
Greenhow, Saml	Richmond	10–17–1799	Lots	D	535	Richmond
Greenhow, Saml	Richmond	10–17–1799	17,937¾	D	535	None
Greenlaw, Saml	Richmond	10–17–1799	112,134¼	D	538	Ganley R Little Kenhawa R & & Lewis Cr
Greenlaw, Saml	Richmond	4–16–1799	9,937	D	543	Lick Fk Richland & Goose Crs
Greenhaw, Saml	Richmond	4–16–1799	7,000	D	546	Goose Cr
Greenup, Christopher	—	9–13–1785	1	A	48	None
Greenup, Christopher	Mercer	9–28–1786	Lot	A	241	None
Greenup, Christopher	—	3–23–1787	½	A	298	None
Greenup, Christopher	Mercer	6–17–1790	Lot	B-2	163	Danville
Greenup, Christopher	Mercer	9–29–1790	Lot	B-2	192	Danville
Greenup, Christopher	Mercer	5–24–1791	5,434	B-2	318	Big Slate Cr
Greenup, Christopher	Mercer	6–28–1788	Negro	B-2	386	None
Greenup, Christopher	Mercer	10– 8–1791	Lot	B-2	398	Danville
Gregory, Abraham	Woodford	3–29–1814	161½	P	389	None
Gregory, Alexander F	Charlestown	6–29–1825	500	X	151	Beargrass & Goose
Greer, George	Franklin	4–19–1811	2,000	O	215	Cumberland R
Griffin, Saml	James City	10–10–1796	1,000	A-2	671	Tradewater
Griffin, Spencer	Mason	1– 7–1822	1,000	V	155	Clifty & Poplar Camp

Grantee	Residence	Deed Date	Acres	Book	Page	Watercourse
Griffith, Remus	Daviess	9– 5–1817	————	R	570	None
Griffith, Wm R	Daviess	2–00–1825	500	X	174	N Panther Cr
Griffith, Wm R	Daviess	12–28–1825	500	Y	226	Green R
Griffith, Wm R	Daviess	5–15–1828	5,000	Y	300	N Fk Panther Cr
Griffith, Wm R	Kentucky	1–14–1834	1,600	Z	389	Ohio R
Griffith, Wm R	Daviess	2–15–1841	20	27	190	Daviess Co
Griner, P	Shelby	7–29–1833	1,500	Z	320	Beech Fk
Griner, P	Shelby	7–29–1833	750	Z	321	Licking
Griner, P	Shelby	7–29–1833	100	Z	322	Licking
Griner, P	Shelby	7–29–1833	100	Z	323	Salt R
Griner, P	Shelby	7–29–1833	1,000	Z	324	Brush Cr
Griner, P	Shelby	7–29–1833	1,100	Z	325	In Shelby Co
Griner, P	Shelby	7–29–1833	1,000	Z	327	Licking
Griner, P	Shelby	7–29–1833	1,971¾	Z	328	Blue Lick Fk Licking
Griner, P	Shelby	7–29–1833	941	Z	329	Indian Lick Cr
Gritton, Jno	Lincoln	10– 1–1784	200	A	80	Harrods Run
Groverman, Wm	Frederick	10–12–1795	6,000	A-2	419	Ohio R
Groves, Jno & Co	Richmond	6–16–1790	6,000	B-2	166	Big Sandy R
Grubbs, Higgason	Madison	1–21–1807	4,400	L	296	Otter & Muddy Cr
Grubbs, Higgason	————	1– 1–1807	300	L	301	None
Guthrey, Benj & Alex Jr	Woodford	10–26–1802	500	G	187	Wolf Cr
Guthrey, Elizabeth	Baltimore	4–18–1812	————	P	8	None
Guthrie, James	Jefferson	12–18–1844	Lot	27	448	Louisville
Guthrie, Jas	Jefferson	2– 3–1847	Lot	28	124	Louisville
Guthry, James	Jefferson	2– 8–1816	1,000	R	215	Cedar Cr
Gwatheney, Temple	Richmond	8–10–1820	————	W	351	Beaver Fk N Fk Tradewater
Gwin, Geo W	Franklin	11–28–1830	Lot	Z	66	Frankfort
Gwin, Geo W	Franklin	6– 4–1842	Lot	27	306	Frankfort
Hackett, Eliza A	Shelby	9–22–1832	492½	Z	230	Little Ky R & Sulphur Cr
Hackley, Clarrisa	Nicholas	10– 7–1824	95	X	63	None
Hackley, Edward	Fredericksburg	6– 2–1796	1,000	E	322	Cabin Cr
Hackley, Lot	————	9–23–1802	————	F	488	None
Hackley, Richard S	Fredericksburg	10– 1–1795	9,302	A-2	293	Lynn Camp & Robertson Cr
Hackley, Richard S	Fredericksburg	10– 1–1795	10,240	A-2	297	Richland Cr & Laurel R
Hackley, Richard S	Fredericksburg	4– 3–1796	1,200	A-2	375	Little Ky R
Hackley, Richard S	Fredericksburg	4– 3–1796	800	A-2	377	Little Ky R
Hackley, Richard S	Fredericksburg	5–17–1796	————	A-2	400	Floyds Fk Rockcastle & Elkhorn Cr
Hackley, Richard S	Fredericksburg	5– 5–1796	2,000	A-2	694	W Fk Glenns Cr
Hackley, Richard S	Fredericksburg	10–10–1797	2,000	B	221	N Fk Tradewater
Hackley, Richard S	Fredericksburg	5–17–1796	————	D	102	Floyds Fk Sandy R & Rockcastle Cr
Hackley, Richard S	Fredericksburg	6– 3–1799	10,023	D	446	Richland, Collins Fk & Stricking
Hackley, Richard S	Fredericksburg	10– 1–1795	36,000	A-2	290	Richland Cr
Haden, James	Franklin	8–16–1805	237¼	K	251	Drennons Lick
Haden, Jas	Henry	8–16–1805	16	K	254	Drennons Lick
Haggerty, Jno	————	5–17–1824	50	W	271	None
Haggin, Jas	Woodford	10–23–1827	3,300	X	295	Cedar Cr
Haggin, Jas	Franklin	11–20–1827	————	X	345	Eagle Cr
Haggin, Jas	Kentucky	4– 9–1828	5,000	X	397	Chappin Fk
Haggin, Jas	Franklin	10– 6–1829	50	Y	398	None
Haggin, Jas	Franklin	4– 7–1831	50	Z	114	Cedar Cr
Haggin, Jas	Franklin	2–11–1831	14,911½	Z	158	Ky R
Haggin, Jas	Franklin	1–10–1835	————	Z	505	Cedar Cr
Haggin, Jas	Franklin	6– 3–1835	————	Z	515	Cedar Cr
Haggins, Francis H	Bourbon	11–18–1826	1,000	Y	227	State of Ohio
Hale, Joseph	Lincoln	6–23–1785	200	A	30	Chaplains Fk
Hall, Henry	Maryland	3–30–1800	1,000	R	451	Big Benson Cr
Hall, Jno	Philadelphia	10–12–1797	4,000	C	228	Fk Deer Cr
Hall, Robt R & Wife	Shelby	5–29–1827	200	X	364	Ky R
Hall, Simeon	Philadelphia	9–17–1816	————	W	6	None
Hall, Thos	————	2–20–1812	150	O	320	None
Hall, Thos	Franklin	1–22–1806	1,000	U	72	Eagle Cr
Hall, Thos	Franklin	5–17–1827	125	X	253	Glenns & Elkhorn
Hall, Wm	Franklin	1–18–1844	————	27	409	S Benson Cr
Hall, Wm W	Virginia	6–19–1827	390¾	X	257	Mill Cr
Hallock, Ratchel	Bourbon	10–28–1826	120	X	252	**None**
Hamilton, Betty T	Henry	9–22–1832	492½	Z	230	Little Ky R & Sulphur Cr
Hamilton, Jas	————	8– 4–1817	200	R	368	Rolling Fk
Hamilton, Margaret	Baltimore	4–18–1812	————	P	8	None
Hamilton, N T & Harriett T	Henry	9–22–1832	492½	Z	230	Little Ky R & Sulphur Cr
Hamilton, Sally T	Virginia	9–22–1832	492½	Z	230	Little Ky R & Sulphur Cr

Grantee	Residence	Deed Date	Acres	Book	Page	Watercourse
Hamman, Frederick	Baltimore	6–19–1813	8,965	P	253	None
Hammond, Nathan	Am-Arundel	11– 2–1793	3,067	A-2	287	None
Hammonds, Joel	Petersburg	7– 3–1809	Slaves	N	450	None
Hampden, Sidney & Wife	Providence	5–15–1813	Lots	P	268	Philadelphia
Hampton, Jno	Virginia	11–24–1809	97	N	61	Caskade
Hampton, Jno	Franklin	2– 1–1824	Horse	X	80	None
Hampton, Preston	Pendleton	9– 2–1812	200	O	466	None
Hampton, Preston	Gallatin	10–23–1824	28	X	37	M Elkhorn
Hampton, Preston	Grant	6–20–1830	100	Y	488	None
Hampton, Preston	Grant	6–20–1830	200	Y	489	None
Hampton, Thos	Logan	5–17–1802	907	G	4	Little Muddy Cr
Hancock, Mrs Eliza C, heirs	——	7– 1–1838	——	28	115	None
Hancock, Monroe B	Franklin	5–30–1826	113	Y	152	S Fk Big Benson Cr
Hancock, Thos G	Franklin	11–20–1834	494	Z	480	Sulphur Lick Cr
Handley, Geo	Daviess	9– 5–1817	——	R	570	None
Handley, Jno	Ohio	4–10–1806	4,000	K	262	Rock Lick & Long Lick Crs
Handley, Jno	Ohio	4–10–1806	700	K	265	Rough Cr
Handley, Jno	Kentucky	11–21–1814	900	P	560	Dry Fk Big Eddy
Hanks, Wm	Hardin	12–20–1814	500	P	571	None
Hanks, Thos	Gallatin	6–15–1822	90	V	254	None
Hanna, Jno	Frankfort	9–11–1809	Lot	N	393	Frankfort
Hanna, Jno H	Frankfort	4–29–1813	Lot	P	314	Frankfort
Hanna, Jno H	Frankfort	3– 2–1814	Lots	P	404	Frankfort
Hanna, Jno H	——	4–12–1819	Lot	T	380	Lexington
Hanna, Jno H	Frankfort	4–17–1820	Lots	T	391	Columbus, Ohio
Hanna, Jno H	Franklin	1–15–1820	Lots	T	393	Frankfort
Hanna, Jno H	——	6– 3–1823	Lots	W	52	Frankfort
Hanna, Jno H	Franklin	3–19–1833	Lots	Z	293	Frankfort
Hanna, Jno H	Franklin	9–24–1834	230	Z	456	Ohio R
Hanna, Jno H	Kentucky	2–26–1835	Lot	Z	492	Frankfort
Hanna, Jno H	Franklin	3–10–1835	Lot	Z	507	Frankfort
Hanna, Jno H	Franklin	11–30–1839	Lots	27	90	Frankfort
Hanna, Jno H	Franklin	9–16–1844	Lot	27	432	Frankfort
Hansborough, Wm	——	4– 9–1818	85	S	100	Elk Cr
Hardesty, Henry	Bourbon	9–18–1798	62	D	10	None
Hardin, Ben	Nelson	4– 8–1835	——	Z	497	Nelson Co
Hardin, Ben	Nelson	12–22–1838	32,400	27	3	Mead Co
Hardin, Benj	Nelson	10–11–1821	15,331	V	147	Brush Cr
Hardin, Elizabeth	Franklin	3–28–1828	50	X	392	Frankfort & Versailles Road
Hardin, Elizabeth	Franklin	10–23–1826	1,048	Z	489	Spencer Co
Hardin, Elizabeth & Jno J	Franklin	9– 8–1829	——	Y	419	Ky R & Cedar Cr
Hardin, Enos	——	6–17–1811	426	O	46	Ky R
Hardin, Enos	Franklin	10– 9–1804	300	P	407	Ky R
Hardin, Innis	Franklin	10– 9–1804	500	P	408	Ky R
Hardin, Jno J	Franklin	7– 2–1832	Lot	Z	240	Louisville
Hardin, Martin D	Frankfort	10–16–1819	Lots	T	141	Frankfort
Hardin, Martin D	Frankfort	11– 7–1810	166⅔	O	72	Clear Cr
Hardin, M D, heirs	Franklin	9– 8–1829	——	Y	419	Ky R & Cedar Cr
Hardin, Martin D, heirs	Franklin	2–20–1830	206	Y	445	Fks Elkhorn
Hardin, Mark	Shelby	2– 5–1820	Lot	T	237	Danville
Hardin, Wm	Breckinridge	5– 7–1808	3,500	L	380	Sinking Cr
Harding, Vachel M D	Baltimore	4– 3–1826	2,200	X	204	Benson Cr
Hardman, Edward	Frankfort	6–17–1815	39	Q	133	Georgetown Road
Hardwick, Wm H	Buckingham	5– 1–1817	388½	T	144	Ohio R
Hardy, Arnold	Scott	6–16–1821	153½	U	509	Cane Run
Hare, Andrew	Jefferson	5–17–1786	½	A	136	None
Hare, Andrew	Mercer	6–29–1790	Lot	B-2	185	Danville
Harper, Michael	Woodford	7– 9–1821	3	U	518	None
Harrington, Wm	Logan	5–17–1802	907	G	4	Little Muddy Cr
Harris, Benj	Albemarle	8–20–1800	1,200	E	248	Big Barren R & Hay Fk
Harris, Edward	Franklin	4–24–1824	700	X	77	Salt R
Harris, Hannah	——	6–13–1797	1,400	B	102	Trough Spring
Harris, Hannah	——	8–19–1803	500	H	449	Glenns Cr
Harris, Hannah	Woodford	2–10–1804	Dowery	L	290	None
Harris, Jno	Woodford	2–10–1804	527½	L	288	Trough Spring Fk Glenns Cr
Harris, Jordan	Powhatan	12– 6–1804	2,000	J	60	M Licking
Harris, Nolty E	Woodford	3–10–1840	176	27	108	Glenns Cr
Harris, Nathaniel	Nelson	6– 5–1786	700	A	90	Cedar Cr
Harris, Wm S	Franklin	11– 8–1831	87½	Z	256	Elkhorn
Harris, Wm S	Franklin	1– 1–1829	158	27	7	M Elkhorn
Harris, Wm S	Franklin	2–26–1839	Lots	27	14	Frankfort
Harris, Wm S	Franklin	2– 8–1840	——	27	105	None
Harrison, Burr	Nelson	5–23–1815	——	27	214	Rolling Fk

Grantee	Residence	Deed Date	Acres	Book	Page	Watercourse
Harrison, Chas L	————	5–27–1824	———	W	293	None
Harrison, Geo E & Wm B	Prince George	2–23–1829	———	Y	341	None
Harrison, Hezakiah	Fayette	5–21–1805	900	X	332	Dry & Gunpowder Cr
Harrison, Jno	Louisville	5– 9–1803	Lots	T	206	Smithland
Harrison, Jno	Louisville	10–24–1812	Lots	W	381	Louisville
Harrison, Jno	Louisville	6–17–1803	1,791¾	W	385	Town Cr
Harrison, Joseph	Philadelphia	3–31–1800	11,500	E	25	Br Ohio R
Harrison, Richard	New York	2–19–1796	130,000	A-2	196	N & M Fk Ky R
Harrison, Richard	New York	1–18–1796	130,000	A-2	200	N & M Fk Ky R
Harrison, Richard	New York	3–21–1795	33,700	A-2	204	N & M Fk Ky R
Harrison, Richard	New York	3– 7–1796	30,000	A-2	224	None
Harrison, Richard	Alexandria	6–28–1801	1,628	F	136	Br Licking
Harrison, Richard	Alexandria	9– 9–1806	5,830	L	150	M Fk Licking & Glade Cr
Harrison, Robt C	Cumberland	1–11–1805	411	J	119	None
Harrison, Robt C	Fayette	12–19–1808	1,500	M	232	Cumberland R
Harrod, Jas & Ann	Mercer	6– 9–1789	700	B-2	72	Ohio R
Harrod, Jno	Franklin	6–13–1842	785	27	297	Ky R
Harrow, Jno	Mason	11–16–1799	500	D	422	———— Cr
Hart, Archibald	Baltimore	11–16–1839	2,500	27	96	M Elkhorn
Hart, Archibald	Baltimore	1– 1–1844	2,500	27	395	In Franklin Co
Hart, David	North Carolina	1– 6–1775	———	C	60	Ohio Cumberland & Green Rs
Hart, Jno	————	10– 5–1839	Lot	27	79	Frankfort
Hart, Jno & Chamless	Philadelphia	10–11–1786	5,000	O	422	N Fk Ky R
Hart, Nathaniel & Jno	Mercer	10–13–1796	Lot	A-2	528	Frankfort
Hart, Thomas	Fayette	4– 1–1796	8,000	A-2	557	Foxes Cr
Hart, Thos	Mercer	8–27–1788	200	B-2	56	None
Hart, Thos Jr	Fayette	4– 8–1800	984	E	70	Salt R
Hart, Thos Jr	Lexington	9–13–1806	32,500	L	53	Ky R & Bank Lick
Hart, Thos Sr	Fayette	7–20–1798	Lots	D	135	Russellville
Hart, Thos Sr	Fayette	7–20–1798	550	D	136	None
Hart, Thos Sr	Fayette	10–17–1804	125	H	475	Mud Lick
Hart, Thos & Nathaniel	North Carolina	1– 6–1775	———	C	60	Ohio, Cumberland & Green R
Hart, Wm	New Jersey	7–31–1819	Hogs	T	65	Elkhorn Cr
Hartel, Peter H B	New York	2–18–1820	205	W	239	None
Hartman, Lewis	New York	5– 7–1820	1,000	Z	173	Harrison Co
Harvie, Jno	Henrico	11– 8–1803	1,000	H	32	Limestone Cr
Harvie, Jno	Franklin	5–14–1829	Lot	Y	354	Browns Ferry
Harvie, Jno	Franklin	2– 1–1830	250	Y	438	Big Benson Cr
Harvie, Jno	Franklin	9–21–1830	250	Z	16	None
Harvie, Jno	Kentucky	5– 6–1833	130	Z	334	Green Co
Harvie, Jno, heirs	————	11–18–1817	3,372	R	572	None
Hascall, David A	Essex	11–30–1813	1,000	P	286	Hogback Grove
Hawes, Isaac	Jefferson	5–30–1817	200	S	7	None
Hawes, Richard	Jefferson	9–17–1819	18,000	T	239	Ohio R
Hawes, Richard	————	11–12–1834	———	Z	477	None
Hawes, Richard Jr	Fayette	3– 1–1823	373	W	119	None
Haws, Thos	Gallatin	1–30–1811	200	O	106	Ohio R
Hawkins, Isham K	Franklin	6– 4–1835	67	Z	518	S Benson Cr
Hawkins, Jno	Bath	4–25–1812	277	O	358	Flat Cr
Hawkins, Jno	Christian	9–29–1822	1,350	V	378	Canoe Cr & Little Ky R
Hawkins, Jas, heirs	————	7–11–1818	4,051¾	S	158	None
Hawkins, Jas, heirs	Louisa	2–22–1822	1,400	V	206	Ohio R
Hawkins, J W	Franklin	11–30–1818	Lot	S	400	Frankfort
Hawkins, Littleberry	Fayette	4–29–1809	Lot	M	442	Cynthiana
Hawkins, Thos W & Jas W	————	6–10–1819	Lot	T	71	Versailles
Hawkins, Wm	Franklin	2–21–1817	———	R	152	Big Bensons Cr
Hawkins, Wm	Woodford	1– 1–1818	Lot	S	17	Versailles
Hawkins, Wm	Franklin	6– 1–1821	35	U	482	None
Hawthorn, Jas	Frankfort	12–12–1801	180	F	348	Stewarts Cr
Hawthorn, Jas	Mercer	5–24–1791	Lot	B-2	316	Danville
Haxall, Philip & Henry	————	11– 5–1818	———	T	23	None
Hay, Wm	Richmond	4– 3–1795	2,000	A-2	86	Green R
Hay, Wm Jr	Frederick	6–20–1818	500	S	284	W Fk Crocus Cr
Haydon, James	Franklin	9–18–1805	100	K	116	———— Br
Hays, Chas	Green	7–16–1802	1,000	F	471	Tradewater
Hays, Chas	Adair	11– 7–1803	1,000	H	274	Tradewater
Hays, Thos	Nelson	1–21–1809	300	M	301	Coxes Cr
Hays, Wm	Fayette	8–26–1805	920	K	284	Salt R
Hearn, Andrew	Franklin	3– 5–1839	43	27	16	Franklin Co
Hearne, Wm	Bourbon	5–15–1830	37½	Y	462	Silas Cr
Hecks, Jno	Richmond	8–19–1796	7,000	A-2	572	Ohio R
Helm, Chas	Hardin	1–10–1806	50,000	K	240	S Brs Salt R
Helm, Chas	Hardin	12– 9–1806	47,897	K	517	Salt R

Grantee	Residence	Deed Date	Acres	Book	Page	Watercourse
Helm, Chas	——	5-26-1806	6,348	M	193	Ky R & Big Benson Cr
Helm, Chas	Hardin	2- 9-1809	5,274	M	338	Ohio R
Helm, Geo	Hardin	10-16-1805	880	K	15	Nolin
Helm, Jno	Washington	10-20-1804	425	K	216	Clover Cr
Helm, Jno D	Bedford	2-27-1810	Lot	N	133	Liberty
Helm, Thos	Woodford	6-28-1811	615	O	71	Cumberland R
Hencock, Tine	Woodford	10-30-1799	200	D	482	Gun Powder & Middle Cr
Henderson, Alexander	Dumfries	6- 9-1804	6,500	H	615	None
Henderson, Alexander	——	12- 6-1813	——	P	511	None
Henderson, David	Fredericksburg	3-17-1804	1,000	H	566	Clay Lick Cr
Henderson, James	Kentucky	11- 2-1801	10,000	F	234	None
Henderson, Joseph	Madison	11-18-1819	116	T	244	Br Muddy Cr
Henderson, Jos L	Scott	4-20-1801	34,200	F	119	Yellowhams, Panther & Licking
Henderson, J L	Shelby	4-18-1803	550	G	272	Plum Cr
Henry, Jno	Richmond	9-16-1796	4,000	A-2	493	N Fk Tradewater
Henderson, Town of	Christian	8- 9-1797	214 Lots	C	53	Ohio R
Henderson, Richard & Co	North Carolina	1- 6-1775	——	C	60	Ohio, Cumberland & Green
Henderson, Richard & Co	——	8- 9-1797	50,000	D	286	Green R
Henderson, Wm	Campbell	9-18-1795	400	A-2	300	Licking
Hendon, Elisha	Franklin	10- 6-1829	100	Z	179	Big Benson Cr
Hendon, Joseph	Scott	5- 3-1825	350	X	188	Canoe Cr
Hendon, Joseph	Scott	1-23-1807	——	K	553	None
Hendricks, Byrd	Amherst	7-20-1795	500	D	489	Chaplins Fk Glenns Lick
Hendrin, Patrick	——	11- 5-1818	——	T.!	23	None
Hendrow, Patrick	Charles City	10-11-1811	2,400	O	156	Ohio & Br Muddy R
Henley, Leonard	Williamsburg	1- 1-1815	850	Q	236	Russells Fk
Henley, Ozbourne	Mason	9-12-1808	2,500	M	325	None
Henning, Alexander	Virginia	3-23-1808	272	L	348	Lost Cr
Henning, Robt	Fredericksburg	1——1803	3,500	J	204	Skaggs and Big Bone Lick Cr
Henning, Robt	Fredericksburg	10-31-1806	1,000	O	184	Deer Cr
Henry, Alexander	Philadelphia	11-18-1797	4,000	C	232	Fk Deer Cr
Henry, Bellfield	Green	10-21-1815	250	Q	461	Pitmans Cr
Henry, Eliza	Maryland	8-14-1822	1,000	V	291	Salt R
Henry, Wm	——	10-14-1806	1,000	K	477	N Elkhorn
Henshaw, Jno	Orange	2-19-1811	1,330	O	178	None
Hensley, Benj	Franklin	3-22-1833	Lot	Z	293	Frankfort
Heran, David	Shelby	5-30-1826	——	Y	166	None
Heron, James	Richmond	5- 7-1799	1,000	D	225	W Fk Pitman Cr
Heron, Jas	Richmond	5- 7-1799	1,200	D	227	S Fk Skaggs Cr
Herndon, Elisha	Franklin	11-21-1831	Slaves	Z	180	None
Herndon, Jno M	Fredericksburg	11-16-1839	2,500	27	96	M Elkhorn
Herren, David	Shelby	12- 8-1825	——	Y	101	None
Hertick, Joseph	Mercer	6-14-1800	650	E	45	3 Fks Cumberland R
Hertick, Joseph	Mercer	6-17-1800	5,000	E	46	3 Fks Cumberland R
Hesler, Jacob	Franklin	3- 2-1819	300	S	475	Br Eagle Cr
Hesler, Jacob	Owen	8- 9-1819	150	T	61	Indian Gap
Heth, William	Henrico	9-12-1798	1,000	E	1	Ohio R
Hewitt, Jno	——	10-11-1823	1,000	W	263	Pouges Cr
Hickman, Jno L	Kentucky	12- 1-1821	70	V	133	None
Hicks, Jno	Richmond	9- 9-1796	——	A-2	532	None
Hicks, Jno	——	9-30-1796	2,433	A-2	628	Little Ky
Hicks, Jno	Richmond	8-18-1797	7,100	B	318	Ohio R
Hicks, Jno	Richmond	4-10-1801	10,869	C	18	Ohio R
Hicks, Jno Jr	Franklin	9- 1-1823	400	W	100	Trammels Fk
Hicks & Campbell	Richmond	9-30-1796	1,018½	A-2	631	Hinkston Fk
Hicks & Campbell	Richmond	7-18-1797	600	B	175	S Fk Licking
Higginbotham, Jesse	Richmond	5-18-1812	1,600	O	452	Michaux Br
Higginbotham, Jesse	Richmond	5-11-1818	1,508⅔	S	148	Rough, Brush & Richland Cr
Higgins, Durrett	Cumberland	1- 2-1811	1,118	O	194	None
Higgins, Wm	Fayette	1- 2-1811	1,118	O	194	None
High Dutch Lutheran Church	Mercer	9——1791	1	B-2	279	None
High Dutch Lutheran Church	Mercer	6- 6-1791	1	B-2	281	None
Hildrith, Jno	Bourbon	10-16-1822	150	V	461	Green Cr
Hill, Atkinson	——	12-20-1802	Lots	G	120	Bardstown
Hill, H B & Co	Jefferson	8-16-1841	320	27	223	Graves & Hickman Crs
Hill, Richard	Kentucky	2-14-1821	500	U	450	M Licking
Hill, Richard	Kentucky	2-14-1821	2,500	U	453	S Fk Rolling Fk
Hillegar, Michael	Philadelphia	3-14-1798	57,000	D	185	None
Hinch, Samuel	——	6- 9-1789	500	B-2	414	Green R

Grantee	Residence	Deed Date	Acres	Book	Page	Watercourse
Hinde, Thos S.	Ross	3–27–1815	——	S	275	None
Hinde, Thos S.	Ross	9– 1–1815	——	S	281	None
Hines, James	Lincoln	3– 5–1792	300	B-2	422	Beech Fk
Hines, Mary	Nelson	9–21–1825	2,268	Y	261	Little Reedy, Rock Lick & Indian Camp Cr
Hines, Wm R.	Bardstown	5– 7–1806	4,000	K	344	None
Hines, Wm R.	Bardstown	12–13–1813	450	P	328	Blackfords Cr
Hines, Wm R.	——	10–13–1814	975	P	550	Salt R
Hines, Wm R.	——	7–10–1824	650	W	358	Ohio R Clover Cr
Hite, Abraham	Hardy	4– 2–1787	1,000	A	325	Highland Cr
Hite, Abraham	Jefferson	6– 1–1802	2,474	F	434	Green R, N Fk, S Fk Licking & Ohio R
Hite, Abraham	Jefferson	6– 1–1802	1,000	F	436	Buffaloe Cr
Hite, Abraham	Jefferson	11–10–1802	1,400	G	62	Salt R
Hite, A & Joseph & Jacob	Jefferson	6–22–1815	4,150	Q	199	6 Mi & Drennons Cr
Hite, Abraham & Joseph & Jacob	Jefferson	5–13–1830	1,524	Y	483	Drennons Lick Cr
Hite, Isaac	Jefferson	10–22–1791	2,000	B-2	407	Ohio R
Hite, Isaac	Jefferson	10–31–1791	——	B-2	466	None
Hite, Isaac	Jefferson	9–13–1785	1	A	53	None
Hix, Jesse	Chesterfield	4–29–1824	——	X	158	None
Hoagland, Okey	Gallatin	2– 7–1829	135	Y	321	Ohio R
Hobson, Jas	Cumberland	10–14–1834	1,000	Z	464	Muddy R
Hockersmith, Henry	Franklin	10– 1–1838	75	27	12	N Elkhorn
Hodges, Albert G	Franklin	4– 9–1839	Lot	27	20	Frankfort
Hodges, Robt	Hardin	10–16–1805	960	K	27	Nolinn
Hodgson, William	Alexandria	12–29–1798	745	E	86	Quick Run
Hoffman, Josiah Ogden	New York	2–19–1796	130,000	A-2	196	N & M Fk Ky R
Hoffman, Josiah Ogden	New York	1–18–1796	130,000	A-2	200	N & M Fk Ky R
Hoffman, Josiah O.	New York	3–21–1795	33,700	A-2	204	N & M Fk Ky R
Hoffman, Josiah	New York	3– 7–1796	30,000	A-2	224	None
Hogg, James	North Carolina	1– 6–1775	——	C	60	Ohio, Cumberland & Green R
Hoke, Adam		10– 2–1815	Lots	Q	228	Jefferson
Holbrook, Darius B	Alexandria	7–16–1838	2552304¾	27	201	Varnons Water Course
Holder, Jno	Clark	5–23–1804	305	H	227	Indian Cr
Holder, Jno	Clark	5–23–1804	248	H	229	Indian Cr
Holliday, Thos & Lewis	——	1– 4–1844	30	27	381	Lower Blue Licks
Hollingsworth, Henry	Philadelphia	3– 9–1825	42,197	X	144	None
Hollingsworth, Isaac	Frederick	10– 4–1810	1,250	O	10	Ohio R
Hollingsworth, Jesse	Baltimore	6–22–1786	400	A	143	M Br Clear Cr
Hollingsworth, Jesse	Baltimore	6–22–1786	400	A	522	M Br Clear Cr
Hollingsworth, Jno	Woodford	4– 9–1800	2,000	E	3	Buck Cr
Hollingsworth, Jno	——	7– 7–1796	1,920	A-2	364	Slate Cr
Hollingsworth, Levi	Philadelphia	11– 5–1795	3,015¼	A-2	166	Tennessee R
Hollingsworth, Levi	Philadelphia	11– 5–1795	4,015¼	A-2	168	Ohio R
Hollingsworth, Levi	Philadelphia	2–27–1795	1,000	A-2	388	Guyandot & Sandy
Hollingsworth, Levi	Philadelphia	7–29–1794	42,629	C	46	Green R
Hollingsworth, Levi		10–17–1814	45,000	P	598	Beech Fk
Hollingsworth, Rachel	Woodford	2– 1–1806	——	Y	113	None
Hollingsworth, Robt	Frederick	10– 2–1797	800	C	225	Highland Cr
Holloway, Chas	Franklin	11–23–1798	22½	D	81	Elkhorn
Holmes, Andrew	Lexington	4– 1–1795	6,365	W	390	Br Indian Camp Cr
Holmes, Andrew	Lexington	4– 1–1795	600	W	392	Buffaloe Cr
Holmes, Andrew	Lexington	4—1795	3,000	W	394	Bear Cr
Holmes, Andrew	Lexington	4– 1–1795	2,500	W	395	Rough Cr
Holmes, Jno, Trustee	Maryland	9–21–1804	13,500	H	454	Ohio R & Patton Cr
Holmes, Robt	Fayette	2–16–1807	Lot	L	129	Louisville
Holton, Elijah	Mason	4–25–1811	1,570	N	509	M Fk Licking
Hood, Jno	Philadelphia	3–31–1800	11,500	E	25	Br Ohio R
Hood, Jno		11–11–1807	30,000	L	175	None
Hood, Jno	Philadelphia	11–11–1807	30,000	L	177	Buffaloe Lick
Hood, Robt T	Alexandria	6–28–1800	1,628	F	136	Br Licking
Hood, Theodotia	Bath	2– 4–1829	225,000	Y	401	None
Hooe, Robt Townsend	Alexandria	8– 1–1792	42,400	A-2	176	Hardins Cr
Hooe, Robt T	Alexandria	8– 5–1792	60,000	A-2	179	None
Hooe, Robt T	Alexandria	8– 2–1792	42,400	A-2	182	Hardins Cr
Hooe, Robt T	Alexandria	9– 9–1806	5,830	L	150	M Fk Licking & Glade Cr
Hooke, Horace	Windsore	1–20–1797	40,000	G	265	Br Big Sandy R
Hooker, Jno	Springfield	3–25–1796	64,184	A-2	521	Nolinn
Hopencleaver, Mary	Philadelphia	2–20–1801	——	E	417	Ohio R
Hopkins, Agness, Executrix	Washington	3–20–1789	526	B-2	277	Caseys Cr
Hopkins, Jno	——	1–26–1802	4,875	F	363	Road to Ohio Falls
Hopkins, Jno	Richmond	10–13–1801	1,000	F	366	——
Hopkins, Jno	Richmond	2–25–1801	138	F	524	W Fk Crocus Cr
Hopkins, Jno	Alexandria	6– 7–1809	3,500	N	13	Tennessee & Ohio R

Grantee	Residence	Deed Date	Acres	Book	Page	Watercourse
Hopkins, Jno	Alexandria	2– 1–1813	18,000	P	150	Peters, Snells & Russell Cr
Hopkins, Mary & Elizabeth A	Cumberland	7– 1–1817	1,754½	S	20	Crocus Cr
Hord, F P	Jessamine	10–21–1815	7,000	Q	266	Panther Cr
Hord, James	Lincoln	4–18–1786	600	A	235	Dix R
Hord, James	Mercer	9–19–1787	400	A	329	Brashears Cr
Horine, Geo	Lincoln	7–20–1791	400	B-2	428	Slate Cr
Horine, Geo	Mercer	8–24–1805	500	K	281	None
Horine, Michael	Lincoln	3–20–1790	530	B-2	139	Dix R
Hotchkiss, Samuel	Burlington	3–10–1815	537	Q	95	Clay Lick Cr
Houston, Robt	Tennessee	1–29–1803	5,500	G	413	Powell R
Houston, Robt	Knox	12– 3–1805	5,375	K	9	Big Valley
Howard, Benj	Fayette	12– 4–1801	1,015	F	152	Pond R
Howard, Benj & Wife	————	5– 6–1812		O	512	None
Howard, Joshua	Frederick	9– 3–1807	3,530	M	158	Ohio R
Howe, Jno W	Green	10– 4–1819	250	T	104	Sandy R
Howell, Daniel S	————	2– 5–1833	2,300	Z	271	Rough Cr
Hudson, Rauleigh	Woodford	5–25–1815	150	Q	116	None
Hugg, Jacob	Baltimore	9–14–1797		C	287	Br M Fk Licking
Hughes, Abijah	Franklin	1–19–1829	100	Y	315	Cedar Cr
Hughes, Abijah	Franklin	7–20–1833	106	Z	318	Cedar Cr
Hughes, Daniel	————	7–16–1799	6,750	D	393	Green R
Hughes, Col Daniel	Washington	8– 1–1790	21,615	D	394	Ohio & Green R
Hughes, Felix	Green	9–15–1802	500	F	480	Foxes Cr
Hughes, James	Lexington	6–20–1800	1,000	E	49	Glovers Cr
Hughes, James	Fayette	7–12–1804	500	H	420	Glovers Cr
Hughes, James	Fayette	7–23–1804	6,052	H	472	Johnsons Fk
Hughes, Jas	————	7–24–1806	213,866	K	363	Br Sandy R
Hughes, Jas	Frankfort	6–24–1812	7,720	O	528	Little Sandy
Hughes, James	Frankfort	11–19–1814	912½	P	592	Blue Spring Grove
Hughes, Jas	Frankfort	9–28–1815	33,261¾	Q	411	Johnsons Fk & N Fk Licking
Hughes, James	Fayette	2–25–1807	9,922	Q	511	N Fk Licking
Hughes, Jas, dec'd	Louisiana	10– 3–1821	15,000	V	184	Lawrence Cr
Hughes, Jno	Lincoln	3–11–1789	464	A	515	Hanging Fk
Hughes, Lucinda	Nicholas	10– 7–1824	95	X	63	None
Hughes, Susana	————	10–10–1802	350	G	136	Elkhorn Cr
Hughes, Thos	Franklin	10– 8–1808	500	Q	508	Ky R
Hughes, Thos & A S	Bourbon	8–29–1816	773½	R	126	Stoners Fk & Green R
Hughes, Thos R	Bourbon	12– 9–1826	Lot	Y	229	Paris, Ky
Hulett, Jas	Franklin	12– 5–1846	37	28	111	None
Hume, Jno	Madison	8–26–1802	470	H	29	M Licking
Humphrey, Alexander	Augusta	12–18–1795	8,476	A-2	447	Brush Cr
Humphrey, Chas	————	11–10–1808	5,000	M	243	None
Humphrey, Chas	Fayette	11–30–1808	26,000	M	278	Cane Run
Humphrey, David C	————	7–24–1832	704½	Z	228	S Fk Elkhorn
Humphrey, David C	Woodford	8–21–1846	143	28	102	Dry Run
Humphrey, Joshua	Fayette	2–26–1820	3,000	U	36	Otter Cr
Humphrey, Joshua	Fayette	2–26–1822	123	V	190	Otter Cr
Humphrey, Mary	Franklin	9–19–1834	Lot	Z	470	Frankfort
Hunt, David	Jefferson	10–16–1827	930	X	298	Boones Cr
Hunt, David	Jefferson	10–29–1827	691	X	305	Boone Cr
Hunt, Jno	Fayette	2–27–1796	1,000	A-2	143	Mill Cr
Hunt, Jno	Fayette	12– 6–1796	2,000	A-2	592	Bullskin Cr
Hunt, Jno	Franklin	9–18–1798	87	D	8	Elkhorn & Licking
Hunt, Jno O	Fayette	4–10–1819	803	S	516	None
Hunt, Jno W	Fayette	2–16–1799	500	D	140	Caseys Cr
Hunter, Jno	Lincoln	2–22–1785	Lot— Danville	A	16	None
Hunt, Jno W	Lexington	10–19–1819	2,637	T	203	Red R
Hunt, Jno W	Fayette	9–21–1821	Lot	V	54	Portland
Hunt, Jno W	Fayette	6– 3–1823	Lots	W	44	Frankfort
Hunt, Jno W	Fayette	4–10–1828	1	X	445	Cave Spring
Hunt, Jonathan	Franklin	3– 9–1818	100	S	73	None
Hunt, Jonathan	Franklin	3–10–1818	Lot	S	74	Frankfort
Hunt, Levi	Fayette	9–18–1798	28	D	7	None
Hunt, Abijah & Jno W	————	6–15–1796		A-2	318	None
Hunt, Abijah & Jno W	Lexington	7–10–1796	258	A-2	410	Johnsons Fk
Hunt, Abijah & Jno W	Fayette	6–12–1798	1,000	C	251	Br Cumberland R
Hunt, Abijah & Jno W	Fayette	6–12–1798	500	C	253	Little Barren R
Hunt, Abijah & Jno W	Fayette	11–24–1798	389	D	141	Fk Caseys Cr
Hunt, Abijah & Jno W	Lexington	10–17–1804	2,000	K	417	Buck Cr
Hunt, Abijah & Jno W	Fayette	3–27–1797	1,000	Q	163	Green R
Hunt, Abijah & Jno W	Fayette	8–19–1815	1,000	Q	165	None
Hunt, Abijah & Jesse	Hamilton	9– 5–1800	100	E	320	Ashes Cr
Hunt, Ralph W	Warren	1–28–1824	15,000	W	237	Rolling Fk
Hunter, Mary	————	6–13–1797	1,400	B	102	Trough Spring
Hunter, Mary	————	8–19–1803	500	H	449	Glenns Cr
Hunter, Mary	Woodford	3–25–1807		L	43	Blackfords Fk

Grantee	Residence	Deed Date	Acres	Book	Page	Watercourse
Hunter, Mary	Woodford	2- 4-1814	Lot	P	335	Versailles
Hunter, S M & C	——	12-25-1815	9,910	Q	294	Clear & Sunfish Cr Ky & Green R
Hunter, Wm	Frankfort	3-14-1812	Lot	O	350	Frankfort
Hunter, Wm	Frankfort	6-17-1815	39	Q	133	Georgetown Rd
Hunter, Wm	Franklin	2-29-1820	103	T	366	None
Hunter, Wm	Franklin	2-29-1820	100	T	367	None
Hunter, Wm	Franklin	9-26-1819	199¾	T	371	None
Hunton, Chas B	Albermarle	11-21-1800	6,250	E	376	Big Sandy R
Hunton, Thos	Albermarle	3-29-1804	2,000	K	199	Lick Cr
Hurst, Jno	Scott	8-16-1806	——	K	380	Cylas Cr
Hurst, Jno	Scott	11-28-1811	600	O	327	Ohio R
Hurst, Jno	Scott	11-28-1811	418	O	329	Ohio R
Hurst, Jas	Jefferson	6- 8-1824	300	W	368	Shawnee Run
Huston, Jno	Daviess	1- 5-1835	4,000	Z	481	Cypress Cr
Huston, Joseph	Breckinridge	11-18-1803	1,000	H	34	Limestone Cr
Huston, Nathan, heirs	——	11-12-1806	3,770	L	217	Dix R Rough & Richland Cr
Huston, Wm	Hardin	1-27-1813	150	P	60	Bacon Cr
Huttsell, Mathias C	Nicholas	3- 6-1821	Contract	V	87	None
Ingle, Joseph	Campbell	6——1798	400	C	246	Crooked Cr
Ingrain, Jeremiah & Wife	——	4-27-1816	1,500	R	124	Goose Cr
Ingram, Sally & Jeremiah	Adair	12- 8-1808	739	M	259	Lost Cr
Innis, Ann	Franklin	3-20-1818	——	S	109	Elkhorn Cr
Innis, Elizabeth E	Fayette	5-25-1825	60	Y	16	None
Innis, Elizabeth Admtrx	Williamsburg	7-21-1801	7,750	E	389	None
Innis, Harry	Lincoln	9- 9-1785	1	A	33	None
Innis, Harry	——	9-13-1785	1	A	48	None
Innis, Harry	Mercer	11-24-1786	Lot	A	243	None
Innis, Harry	Mercer	7- 7-1788	Lots	A	472	None
Innis, Harry	Franklin	11-26-1796	1,470	A-2	580	Ohio R
Innis, Harry	Franklin	10-27-1796	4,351	A-2	585	Ohio R
Innis, Harry	Mercer	5-24-1793	200	A-2	602	None
Innis, Harry	Mercer	5-24-1793	1,047	A-2	605	Rolling Fk
Innis, Harry	Mercer	8-23-1787	1,400	B-2	95	Lees Cr
Innis, Harry	Mercer	5- 6-1791	200	B-2	290	Br Wilson Cr
Innis, Harry	Woodford	9-22-1793	Lot	C	250	Frankfort
Innis, Harry Ag	Frankfort	12-19-1800	Slaves	E	245	None
Innis, Harry	——	1-20-1800	Slaves	E	258	None
Innis, Harry	——	4- 1-1801	Slaves	E	304	None
Innis, Harry	Frankfort	1-13-1806	Slaves	K	234	None
Innis, Harry	Frankfort	3-13-1805	——	L	81	None
Innis, Harry	Franklin	8-15-1814	1,200	P	504	Glens Cr
Innis, Harry	Frankfort	6-13-1798	Lots	Q	234	Frankfort
Innis, Harry	Franklin	11-19-1834	1,000	Z	472	Station Camp Cr
Innis, Hugh	Franklin	6- 9-1803	60	H	11	Elkhorn
Innis, James	Richmond	3- 1-1797	4,000	C	214	Deer Cr
Innis, James	Fayette	1-26-1811	190½	O	112	Elkhorn
Innis, Robt	Franklin	6- 9-1803	60	H	249	None
Inskeep, Jno	Philadelphia	2-12-1802	——	P	605	None
Instorn, Jno	Franklin	7- 3-1802	Lot	F	443	Frankfort
Instorn, Jno	Franklin	6-28-1802	50	F	444	S Fk Elkhorn
Instorn, Jno	Franklin	6-28-1802	3½	F	447	Elkhorn Cr
Instorn, Jno	Frankfort	4-28-1802	50	F	505	—— Cr
Ireland, Edward	Baltimore	8-25-1796	390,000	A-2	320	Ohio R
Irish, Wm B	Allegheny	12- 8-1801	20,200	P	148	Sandy R
Irvin, Saml	——	4-19-1786	½	A	117	None
Irvin, Saml	——	9- 4-1787	Lot	A	369	Town Spring
Irvin, Saml	Mercer	1-26-1788	Lot	A	444	None
Irvin, Thos	Alexandria	4- 4-1804	500	J	427	Buffaloe Cr
Irvin, Thos	——	3-22-1810	3,039	N	391	Beaver Cr
Irvin, Wm & Jno	Fayette	1-23-1816	Lot	Q	435	Louisville
Irwin, Capt James	Cumberland	3-27-1798	687½	C	117	Little Kanawha R
Irwin, Jno	Tennessee	7- 1-1797	6,000	B	103	None
Irwin, Thos	Alexandria	3-19-1802	500	G	206	Buffaloe Cr
Irwin, Thos	Alexandria	12- 4-1802	7,932½	G	343	Ky Ohio & Salt R
Jackson, Henry	Boston	6-21-1796	20,781	C	278	N Fk Ky R
Jackson, Jno	Woodford	8- 2-1802	355	G	10	Clear Cr
Jackson, Saml	Philadelphia	3-11-1796	70,000	A-2	366	Big Sandy
Jacoby, Jacob	——	9- 1-1826	223	X	218	None
Jacoby, Jacob	——	9- 1-1826	66	X	221	None
James, Joseph	Philadelphia	7-29-1786	15,000	E	15	S Br Nolinn R
Jamey, Jno & Thos	Alexandria	1- 3-1809	2,000	N	480	Bays Cr
Jameson, Jno	Culpepper	11- 1-1796	2,250	B	55	Muddy Cr
Jameson, Jno	Culpepper	1-11-1802	4,000	F	368	Big Mud Cr
Jameson, Jno	Virginia	6-19-1827	625	X	259	None
January, Jas	N W Territory	8- 2-1802	667	F	543	Cherry Fk Bush Cr
January, Jas	N W Territory	10-20-1802	689	F	544	Eagle Cr

Grantee	Residence	Deed Date	Acres	Book	Page	Watercourse
Jarrett, Abraham	Hartford	2- 6-1809	6,160	M	406	Drennons Lick Cr
Jenkins, Wm	Franklin	4- 1-1824	400	X	81	Hammonds & Big Benson Cr
Jennings, Jonathan	Gallatin	1-29-1805	48	H	559	Ky R
Jerome, Wm J	Paris France	11-22-1819	910,954	U	90	N Fk Ky & Big Sandy R
Jerrell, Will	Shelby	5-25-1815	214	Q	120	Elk Cr
Jesup, Lucy Ann, heirs	————	7- 1-1838	————	28	115	None
Jesup, Genl Thos P, heirs	U S Army	7- 1-1838	————	28	115	None
Jett, Richard C	Daviess	2-19-1840	410	27	112	Panther Cr
Jewell, Wm	Franklin	11-30-1819	79¾	T	166	Salt R
Johns, Acquilla	St Marys	6- 4-1811	2,000	P	382	None
Johnson, Benj B	————	9-13-1844	73	27	446	Benson Cr
Johnson, Chapman	Stanton	8-14-1809	800	N	107	Big Barren R
Johnson, Chapman	Richmond	4-30-1830	10,000	Z	147	Rough Cr
Johnson, Cave	Campbell	12-24-1796	400	B	258	Ohio R
Johnson, Cave	Boone	11- 4-1806	450	K	456	Hingston & Stoners Fk
Johnson, Cave	Kentucky	7-31-1812	1,692	P	155	Ohio R
Johnson, Cave	Boone	11- 8-1822	550	V	354	Ohio R
Johnson, Cave	Kentucky	2-15-1823	2,000	V	456	Sinking Cr
Johnson, Cave	Boone	3-24-1833	1,310	Z	350	Ohio R
Johnson, Cave Jr	Boone	6- 6-1829	20	Y	350	Ohio R
Johnson, Edward P	Franklin	3-19-1833	Lots	Z	293	Frankfort
Johnson, Edward P	Franklin	3-19-1833	Lot	Z	297	Frankfort
Johnson, Edward P	————	10-30-1839	Lot	27	87	Frankfort
Johnson, Edward P	Fayette		Lot	27	434	Frankfort
Johnson, Edward P	Fayette	8-26-1845	Lots	28	25	Frankfort
Johnson, Elijah	Fayette	6- 3-1800	1,033½	E	9	Deer Cr
Johnson, Geo	Scott	3-17-1801	10,346½	F	190	Stoners Fk Mill Sta Camp & S Fk Licking
Johnson, Geo N	Richmond	5- 1-1840	12,600	27	142	Rough Cr & N Fk Sandy R
Johnson, Jos	————	6——1818	285	U	522	Dry Fk Craigs Cr
Johnson, Jos	Scott	12——1821	1,702	V	339	Ohio R
Johnson, Jos	Scott	12-17-1821	150	V	342	Woolper Cr
Johnson, Jas	Scott	11-13-1822	403	V	356	Skinhouse Fk
Johnson, Jno	Augusta	8- 3-1802	1,000	H	3	Skinhouse Fk
Johnson, Jno S	Scott	10- 9-1824	4000	X	59	Ohio R & Woolpers
Johnson, Jno T	Scott	2- 8-1820	300	U	520	Ohio R Cr
Johnson, Jno Yarbrough	————	7-12-1802	Contract	G	47	None
Johnson, Joel	————	6——1818	285	U	522	Ohio R
Johnson, Richard	Woodford	2-16-1827	253	Y	269	6 Mile Cr
Johnson, Richard M	Scott	2-27-1819	32¾	U	195	N Elkhorn
Johnson, Richard M	Scott	11- 3-1823	————	W	127	N Elkhorn
Johnson, Richard M	Scott	8-31-1831	150	Z	157	Beaver & Myers Br
Johnson, Richard M	Scott	9- 3-1831	203	Z	157	Beaver & Myers Br
Johnson, Richard M	Scott	6-17-1831	1,110	Z	269	Ohio R
Johnson, Richard M	Scott	5-19-1835	15	Z	510	N Elkhorn
Johnson, Robt	Scott	9-20-1796	600	A-2	445	None
Johnson, Robt	Scott	12-28-1796	1,000	B	256	Ohio R
Johnson, Robt	Woodford	4-26-1791	250	B-2	304	N Fk Clear Cr
Johnson, Robt	Woodford	4-26-1791	————	B-2	308	None
Johnson, Robt	Scott	8- 6-1800	700	E	423	Fern Cr
Johnson, Robt	Scott	3-25-1793	4,500	F	54	Ohio R
Johnson, Robt	Scott	2-14-1800	1,000	F	380	Ohio R
Johnson, Robt	Scott	5- 5-1802	————	G	150	None
Johnson, Robt	Scott	11-19-1803	400	H	50	Cane & S Fk Elkhorn
Johnson, Robt	Scott	5-23-1805	3,470	K	105	Stoners Fk
Johnson, Robt	Scott	1-24-1810	240	N	110	N Fk Elkhorn
Johnson, Robt	Scott	6-15-1810	6,000	N	329	Little N Elkhorn
Johnson, Robt	————	12-12-1811	2,000	O	219	Little N Fk Elkhorn
Johnson, Robt	Scott	8-13-1811	5,000	S	542	Ky R
Johnson, Robt, heirs	Boone	7-31-1817	5,000	S	545	Ky R
Johnson, Wm, heirs	————	6——1818	285	U	522	Dry Fk Craigs Cr
Johnson, Zachariah	Rockbridge	3-13-1801	6,100	P	170	Mayfield & Skin house Cr
Johnston, Andrew	Quincy	10-24-1843	————	27	459	M Clay Cr
Johnston, Jas	Monojalia	3- 7-1787	500	A	469	Cartwright Cr
Johnston, Jas	Scott	1- 9-1808	100	M	30	M Elkhorn
Johnston, Jno	Rockbridge	3-13-1801	6,100	P	170	Mayfield & Skin-house Cr
Johnston, Jno	————	4- 5-1815	————	Q	42	Whiskey Path
Johnston, Robt	————	2- 9-1808	14,720	M	206	Ohio R
Johnston, Wm	North Carolina	1- 6-1775	————	C	60	Ohio, Cumberland & Green Rs
Jones, Mrs Ann	Franklin	2-28-1832	7,500	27	178	Little Sandy R

Grantee	Residence	Deed Date	Acres	Book	Page	Watercourse
Jones, Armstead	Woodford	9–22–1829	10½	Y	403	S Elkhorn
Jones, Fielding	Franklin	7–29–1842	——	27	312	N Elkhorn
Jones, Isral	Frederick	3–12–1800	1,000	E	267	Cumberland R
Jones, James	Carlone	10–26–1813	——	P	252	None
Jones, Jno	Scott	12–9–1801	544	F	454	Big Barren R
Jones, Jno	Scott	12–9–1801	400	F	457	Big Barren R
Jones, Jno	Scott	12–9–1801	450	F	458	Big Barren R
Jones, Jno	Brunswick	9–20–1794	1,666⅔	N	184	Ky R
Jones, Jno	Essex	5–1–1812	Mill	O	364	Hoskins Cr
Jones, Jno	Scott	12–23–1812	450	P	88	Big Barren R
Jones, Jno Francis	Philadelphia	7–16–1796	1,000	A-2	500	Beech Fk
Jones, Joseph	Gallatin	1–16–1804	1,406½	H	147	Twin & Eagle Crs
Jones, Joseph	——	7–3–1809	Slaves	N	450	None
Jones, Joseph	——	6–8–1813	50,000	P	367	Various water courses
Jones, Joshua	Frederick	12–8–1804	200	J	23	Big Barren R
Jones, Kennon	Dinwiddie	1–17–1803	1,000	K	331	Eagle Cr
Jones, Leonard	Hart	3–18–1841	Lots	27	224	Columbus
Jones, Levi	Henderson	6–12–1821	1,000	V	256	Cumberland R
Jones, Lewis	——	6–11–1845	Lot	28	12	Midway
Jones, Lowry	Shelby	7–2–1817	600	R	341	Rough Cr
Jones, Lowry	Shelby	10–23–1817	800	R	436	Drennons Lick Cr
Jones, Robt K	——	11–5–1818	——	T	23	None
Jones, Robt K	——	11–5–1818	——	T	39	None
Jones, Robt K	Petersburg	6–23–1821	——	V	20	Ky R
Jones, Samuel	Philadelphia	11–28–1797	1,000	D	145	Ohio R
Jones, Saml	Cumberland	6–27–1803	1,066⅔	J	197	Cumberland R
Jones, Dr Saml	Dublin	9–4–1809	56,741	M	449	Ohio R
Jones, Thos	Petersburg	7–3–1809	Slaves	N	450	None
Jones, Thos	Essex	10–9–1810	1,000	S	531	Fk Panther Cr
Jones, Thos	Kentucky	12–1–1818	——	S	535	E Fk Panther Cr
Jones, Thos Jr	Bourbon	8–19–1805	180	K	248	Hustons Fk
Jones, Thomas Sr	Bourbon	12–10–1799	25	E	55	Hustons Fk
Jones, Thos Sr	Bourbon	11–18–1800	4,600	E	237	None
Jones, Walter	Washington	—— 1819	4,266⅔	T	283	Deer Cr & N Fk Tradewater
Jones, Wm	Warren	3–3–1800	400	F	424	Big Barren R
Jones, Wm	McCracken	4–28–1840	2,000	27	163	In Gallatin Co
Jones, Wm	Mason	11–22–1843	10,000	27	369	None
Jordan, Jno Jr	Fayette	10–13–1801	307	F	166	S Fk Elkhorn
Jordan, Jno Jr	Lexington	5–2–1804	Lot	H	506	Louisville
Jordan, Jno Jr	Kentucky	9–10–1799	116	H	592	N Fk Elkhorn
Jordan, Jno Jr	——	11–25–1808	8,571	M	213	None
Jouitt, Jno	Kentucky	1–26–1802	4,875	F	438	Road to Ohio Falls
Joyes, Patrick	Jefferson	8–20–1786	192	V	385	Leestown Bottom
Joyse, Patrick	Jefferson	6–15–1790	400	B-2	177	E Fk Ashes Cr
Julian, Chas H	Franklin	12–31–1846	——	28	110	Franklin Co
Kain, Maurice	Wilkes	3–22–1806	2,100	L	6	None
Karns, Thos	Henrico	4–29–1824	——	X	158	None
Kean, Oliver	Fayette	10–11–1834	42,656	Z	462	Mason Co
Kean, J C	——	6–11–1843	Lot	28	11	Midway
Keasinger, Soloman	Nelson	8–10–1791	207½	B-2	511	Little Barren R
Keener, Christian	Baltimore	3–21–1792	——	B-2	452	Flat & Gars Crs
Kennon, Adam C	——	4–21–1831	2	Z	119	Shelbyville Road
Kennon, Adam C	——	7–14–1831	1½	Z	156	Shelbyville Pike
Kennon, Adam C	Franklin	2–5–1839	Slaves	27	23	None
Keer, James	Mercer	3–21–1792	221	B-2	437	None
Keller, Abraham	Bourbon	5–4–1812	730	O	370	Br Crocus Cr
Kennady, James	Campbell	11–19–1800	2,000	E	179	Licking
Kendley, James	——	12–26–1811	46	P	138	None
Kennady, Jos Admr	Campbell	11–13–1802	400	G	43	Harrods Cr
Kenton, Simon	Franklin	11–26–1804	200	H	434	Buck Cr
Kenton, Simon	Franklin	12–24–1804	664	H	500	Evans Mill Cr
Kenton, Simon Jr	Franklin	3–29–1805	3,040	J	57	Little Sandy
Kennady, Thos	Madison	6–2–1788	200	A	391	Paint Lick & Drakes Crs
Kennady, Thos	Madison	6–2–1788	200	A	394	Paint Lick
Kennady, Thos	Campbell	12–9–1801	200	F	196	Ohio R
Kennady, Thos	Campbell	1–10–1809	Ferry	M	295	Licking & Ohio
Kennady, Wm	Lincoln	6–22–1786	130	A	132	None
Kennady, Wm	Campbell	12–1–1798	105	D	95	Cane Run
Kennady, Wm	Mercer	2–10–1796	681½	H	477	Brushy Fk
Kenneth, D H	Bourbon	9–18–1830	Lots	Z	11	Millersburg
Kerby, Green	Madison	10–29–1828	1,000	Y	299	Willis Cr
Kercheval, Jno	Mason	1–9–1802	20,000	F	207	Licking
Kercheval, Jno	——	12–10–1805	200	J	461	Salt Lick Cr
Kerr, Peter	Montgomery	1–31–1814	100	P	588	Elkhorn
Kerr, Robt & Wife	Richmond	3–24–1832	333⅓	Z	330	Green Co
Kerr, Robt & Wife	Richmond	3–24–1832	5,000	Z	332	Montgomery Co
Kerr, Wm	Scott	5–30–1815	333⅓	Q	59	Big Barren R
Kerr, Wm	Barren	8–23–1816	584	R	22	Big Barren R

Grantee	Residence	Deed Date	Acres	Book	Page	Watercourse
Kester, Jno	Shelby	5–26–1815	35	Q	121	Elk Cr
Kincaid, Jas	———	3–10–1796	3,300	A-2	170	Todds Cr
King, James Jr	Sullivan	9–26–1814	1,600	P	516	Beaver Cr
King, Jno	———	11–15–1805	1,000	K	496	None
King, Jno	———	11–15–1805	7,000	K	498	None
Kinmon, Saml	———	7–1–1817	218	T	75	Eagle Cr
Kinney, Jacob	Staunton	10–5–1801	———	O	228	Ohio R
Kinney, Jno	New Jersey	3–26–1805	332	J	295	Drennons Lick Cr
Kinney, Jno	New Jersey	3–26–1805	500	J	299	Drennons Lick Cr
Kinney, Jno	New Jersey	2–6–1806	906	K	207	Rolling Fk
Kenney, Jno	Morris	12–25–1805	228¾	K	213	Rough Cr
Kinney, Jno	Morristown	4–19–1806	700	K	287	Wilsons Cr & Rolling Fk
Kintz, Daniel	Georgetown	5–18–1818	4,000	X	108	Ohio R
Kintz, Daniel	Georgetown	5–18–1818	685	X	109	Green R
Kintz, Daniel	Georgetown	5–18–1818	1,100	X	111	Rough Cr
Kintz, Daniel	Georgetown	5–18–1818	1,000	X	113	Russell Cr
Kintz, Daniel	Georgetown	5–18–1818	900	X	115	W Fk Pond R
Kintz, Daniel	Georgetown	5–18–1818	800	X	117	Big Barren R
Kintz, Daniel	Georgetown	5–18–1818	1,000	X	119	Grave Cr
Kitley, Wm	———	6–15–1807	750	L	130	Cow Cr & Red R
Knapp, David	Sheffield	4–18–1808	1,000	L	371	Cumberland R
Knox, Hugh	Henderson	6–30–1814	———	Q	372	None
Knox, Hugh	Henderson	7–18–1815	———	Q	374	None
Knox, Hugh	Union	7–18–1815	———	Q	379	None
Knox, Jos	Shelby	11–4–1812	5,000	P	14	Big Benson Cr
Knox, Wm A	Fredericksburg	7–10–1814	2,000	R	312	N Fk Tradewater
Kurtz, Daniel	Washington, D C	1–20–1826	1,325	Y	97	Big Reedy Fk & Green R
Lacassagne & Moore	Jefferson	12–4–1788	½	B-2	49	Louisville
Lackey, Gabriel	Lincoln	2–17–1818	300	S	302	Licking
Lake, Francis	Louisiana	9–1840	———	27	107	New Orleans
Lamme, Saml	Mercer	3–5–1787	400	A	260	S Fk Licking
Lancaster, Jno	Washington	6–11–1802	400	F	417	Hardins Cr
Lancaster, Jno	Washington	9–23–1812	500	O	490	Rough Cr
Lancaster, Jno	Washington	9–1–1813	500	P	210	Hardins Cr
Lancaster, Ralphead	Nelson	12–18–1805	57	K	74	Stewarts Cr
Landrum, James	Culpepper	3–25–1811	1,469	O	406	Rough Cr
Lane, Wm N	Clark	6–1–1804	205¼	H	262	Limestone Cr
Lang, Thos Jr	Wakefield	6–3–1796	19,000	G	15	Green R & Bacon C
Langford, Stephen	Lincoln	5–30–1791	400	B-2	282	Little Clifty Cr
Langford, Stephen	Rockcastle	4–30–1812	2,000	O	360	Goose Cr
Langlin, Wm	Lewis	4–16–1807	79	L	16	Ohio R
Langlin, Wm	Lewis	8–10–1812	79	O	441	Ohio R
Langster, Thos	———	4–30–1811	1,000	B-2	374	Ash Cr
Lanman, Geo	Philadelphia	2–18–1795	11,858½	A-2	115	Eagle Cr
Lanman, Geo	Philadelphia	2–18–1795	15,000	A-2	121	Rolling Fk
Lanman, Geo	Philadelphia	2–18–1795	11,415	A-2	124	Ohio R
Lanman, Geo	Philadelphia	12–1–1796	283,413	A-2	702	Licking S Fk Ky R
Lanman, Geo	Philadelphia	12–1–1796	118,626	C	1	Lick Cr Mill Cr & Green R
Lanman, Frederick	———	8–5–1799	1,000	D	309	Big Barren R
Lanman, Geo	Philadelphia	4–1–1795	6,365	W	390	Indian Camp Cr
Lanman, Geo	Philadelphia	4–1–1795	600	W	392	Buffaloe Cr
Lanman, Geo	Lexington	4—1795	3,000	W	394	Bear Cr
Lanman, Geo	Philadelphia	4–1–1795	2,500	W	395	Rough Cr
Lansdale, Wm & Wife	———	1820	Lot	U	184	Louisville
Lapsley, Jno	Philadelphia	4–21–1807	———	L	49	None
La Rue, Jabey	Hardin	2–7–1807	1,000	M	320	Benson Cr
La Rue, Jabey	Hardin	8–9–1808	6,250	M	323	Cedar Cr
La Rue, Jacob	Hardin	8–6–1801	———	E	400	Nolinn
La Rue, Jacob	———	3–10–1820	1,096	T	264	None
La Rue, James	Fredericks	10–16–1805	818	K	18	Nolinn
La Rue, James	Hardin	6–4–1803	200	K	29	Ky R
La Rue, Jas	Hardin	7–13–1821	Lot	U	476	Elizabeth
La Rue, Wm	Hardin	10–16–1805	352	K	21	Nolinn
Laswell, Jno	Rockcastle	3–24–1815	100	Q	37	Clear Cr
Latham, Thos	Fauquir	1–13–1812	5,312½	O	437	Hingston Fk
Latham, Thos	Fauquir	7–30–1812	1,767	O	459	Eagle Cr
Latta, Matthew	Woodford	8–14–1813	500	P	191	Glenns Cr
Law, Thomas	Columbia	11–10–1803	4,000	H	27	Green R
Lawless, Benj	Warren	5–4–1807	450	L	18	Big Barren R
Lawless, Benj	Scott	1–13–1813	450	P	90	Big Barren R
Lawrence, Elizabeth Eliza & Nancy	Warren	10–10–1815	2,500	S	150	None
Lawrence, Leaven & Co	Louisville	11–4–1805	9,682	J	380	Beech & Benson Cr Ky & Green R
Lawrence, Saml	Mercer	6–1–1792	Lots	B-2	502	Danville
Lawrence, Walcott	Pittsfield	5–16–1814	537	P	495	Clay Lick Cr
Lawson, Thos	Norfolk	4–20–1806	355	K	443	Salt R
Lawson, Thos	Norfolk	4–20–1806	1,043	K	446	Salt R

Grantee	Residence	Deed Date	Acres	Book	Page	Watercourse
Lawson, Thos & Wife	Norfolk	3–20–1807	942	L	99	Salt R
Lay, Geo	Jefferson	3–10–1823	1,000	W	266	Poages Cr
Layson, Robt	Bourbon	9–16–1788	326	B-2	41	Stoners Fk
Leacraft, Geo	Franklin	4–19–1802	10,000	F	243	Red R
Leake, Elisha	Goochland	8–12–1795	1,000	F	156	Blackfords Cr
Lear, Conrad	————	7–31–1806	390	K	386	None
Lear, Conrad	————	7–31–1806	90	K	388	None
Lear, Conrad	————	7–31–1806	200	K	389	None
Lear, Conrad	————	8–16–1806	1,000	K	454	None
Leathers, Jno	Campbell	11–18–1806	500	K	512	Dry Cr
Leavy, Wm	Lexington	4———1814	263	R	275	None
Lee, Charles	Alexandria	7–23–1804		H	504	None
Lee, Daniel	————	4–23–1813		P	129	Ohio R & Otter Cr
Lee, Edmund J	Alexandria	1– 1–1806	4,675	L	267	Big Barren & Gasper R
Lee, Edmund J	Alexandria	6–23–1810		N	488	None
Lee, Francis L	Alexandria	1– 3–1804		H	512	None
Lee, Francis Lightfoot	————	11–19–1810	3,400	N	477	Green R & M Licking
Lee, Geo K	Virginia	6– 4–1818	12,500	W	11	None
Lee, Henry	Mason	4–10–1790	4,000	B-2	150	Cedar Cr
Lee, Jno	Orange	8–24–1790	600	A-2	443	Bank Lick Cr
Lee, Major Jno	Fredericksburg	5– 5–1796	2,000	A-2	694	W Fk Glenns Cr
Lee, Jno M	————	12– 9–1805	750	J	455	None
Lee, Jno M	————	12– 9–1805	999	K	45	None
Lee, Jno M	————	12– 9–1805	400	K	47	None
Lee, Jno M	————	12– 9–1805	1,089	K	50	None
Lee, Lewis W	Logan	————1826	295	Y	189	Blackfords Cr
Lee, Richard H	Lincoln	10–22–1803	249	H	313	Baileys Run
Lee, William	Green	7–19–1803	935	G	383	Big Barren R
Leftwich, Robt	Logan	12–11–1816	24	R	91	None
Leigh, Benj W	Petersburg	7– 3–1809	Slaves	N	450	None
Leigh, Henry & Wife	Washington	12–14–1829	308¾	Z	175	Hardins & Rolling Fk
Leiper, Thos	Philadelphia	7–31–1817	5,078¼	T	483	Cases Cr
Leitz, Jno	————	8– 5–1799	1,000	D	309	Big Barren R
Letcher, Stephen	Mercer	11– 1–1799		D	516	W Fk Shot Pouch Cr
Levy, Aaron	Northumberland	5–30–1786	5,000	D	258	Large Cr
Levy, Aaron	Northumberland	6–16–1786	2,500	D	261	None
Lewis, Alexander	Charlston	9–25–1803	1,015	H	45	Otter Cr
Lewis, Andrew	Botecourt	1–11–1812	875	O	386	None
Lewis, Benj	Richmond	6–24–1819		T	109	None
Lewis, Coleman	Fairfax	10–23–1807	500	L	204	Hardins Cr
Lewis, Daniel	Nelson	11– 4–1806	2,000	K	494	Ohio R
Lewis, Gabriel	Fredericksburg	2–13–1800	2,500	E	269	Ky R
Lewis, Gabriel	Kentucky	7–20–1801	556	E	411	Eddy Cr
Lewis, Gabriel	Fayette	12– 1–1801	1,000	F	395	Poages Cr
Lewis, Gabriel	Lexington	3–13–1804	1,000	H	183	Caseys Cr
Lewis, Geo	Spottsylvania	9–25–1793	7,000	A-2	624	Deer Cr
Lewis, Geo	Bourbon	6–23–1789	300	B-2	120	———— R
Lewis, Geo	Bourbon	6–23–1789	400	B-2	122	Ohio R
Lewis, Geo	Bourbon	3–12–1790	500	B-2	123	Upper Blue Lick
Lewis, Geo	Bourbon	6–20–1789	400	B-2	333	Ohio R
Lewis, Jno	Fredericksburg	7–23–1808	Lot	M	297	Fredericksburg
Lewis, Jno	Breckinridge	12– 7–1809	1,750	N	65	Harrods Cr
Lewis, Jno	Breckinridge	4– 2–1811	1,630	O	208	Hogback Grove
Lewis, Jno B	Bath	4–28–1820	666⅔	T	302	None
Lewis, Joniah Jr	Wilkes Barre	10–30–1846		28	131	In Ky
Lewis, Joseph Jr	London	1–30–1846	41,185½	N	300	Rolling Fk & Wilsons Cr Big Sandy R
Lewis, Lawrence	Fairfax	4———1804	1,000	H	181	Panther Cr
Lewis, Meriwether	Albermarle	7–13–1797	799½	C	16	Red R
Lewis, Nicholas	Mercer	3–25–1791	Lot	B-2	260	Danville
Lewis, Nicholas	Fayette	12– 6–1796	300	A-2	581	S Fk Bensons Cr
Lewis, Thos & Wife	Chesterfield	8–16–1802	2,080	G	31	Rolling Fk
Lewis, Thos & Wife	Dinwiddie	4–18–1805	1,000	K	80	Rolling Fk
Lewis, Thos & Wife	Dinwiddie	3– 5–1807	32,696	L	183	Rough Panther & Caney Cr
Lewis, Thos & Wife	Dinwiddie	5– 5–1807	8,255½	L	192	Rolling Fk Battle Rough & Coxes Cr
Lewis, Thos & Wife	————	5– 5–1807		S	244	None
Lewis, Robt	Stafford	2–15–1808	1,000	N	48	None
Lewis, Robt	Stafford	2–15–1808	1,000	N	52	None
Lewis, Saml	Franklin	1– 3–1809	1,000	N	16	None
Lewis, Saml	Franklin	1–11–1812	875	O	386	None
Lewis, Saml	Franklin	11–20–1815	Lots	Q	247	Frankfort
Lewis, Sharp D	Wilkes-Barre	10–30–1846		28	131	Ky
Lewis, Stephen D	Fayette	12–12–1815	6,617	Q	358	Bank Lick Cr
Lewis, Stephen D	Fayette	12–12–1815	2,130	Q	361	None
Lewis, Stephen, Trustee	Fayette	1–18–1821	469	U	180	Bank Lick Cr
Lewis, Thomas	————	4– 1–1797	15,000	B	182	Little Ky R
Lewis, Thos	Petersburg	8–24–1809	2,625	N	121	Beech Cr

Grantee	Residence	Deed Date	Acres	Book	Page	Watercourse
Lewis, Thos	Dinwiddie	5–30–1811	22	O	301	Greers Cr
Lewis, Thos	Petersburg	8– 1–1811	20,000	O	524	Hinkston Fk
Lewis, Thos	Virginia	5– 7–1808	——	P	12	None
Lewis, Thos	——	5–12–1813	881	P	125	Coxes Cr
Lewis, Thos	Petersburg	6–10–1814	233⅓	Q	110	Doe Run
Lewis, Thos	Dinwiddie	11–20–1807	1,666⅔	R	121	Hickman & Jessamine Cr
Lewis, Thos	Petersburg	1– 6–1817	166⅞	R	345	Doe Run
Lewis, Thos	——	7– 8–1817	250	R	347	Sugar Cr
Lewis, Thos	Petersburg	7–14–1817	250	R	349	Sugar Cr
Lewis, Thos	——	5–23–1818	1,000	S	143	Hardins Cr
Lewis, Thos	Virginia	8–15–1818	1,500	S	209	Ohio R
Lewis, Thos	Virginia	7– 4–1818	1,089	S	396	Jessamine & Hickman Cr
Lewis, Warner W	Spottsylvania	5–10–1802	1,000	F	401	Poages Cr
Lewis, Warren W	Spottsylvania	7– 7–1802	2,500	F	429	Ky R
Lewis, Warren W	Kentucky	12–26–1808	1,500	M	329	Highland Cr
Lewis, Warren W	——	7–11–1810	778	N	307	Deer Cr
Lewis, Warren W	Fredericksburg	9–24–1811	1,000	O	186	M Fk, N F, W Fk, Red R
Lewis, Warren W	Frederick	10– 2–1811	——	O	189	Br Red R
Lewis, Wm	Fayette	3– 5–1790	374	B-2	195	Jessamine Cr
Lewis, Wm, heirs	Philadelphia	2–21–1812	4,000	O	504	W Fk Pitmans Cr
Lexington & Ohio R R Co	Kentucky	12–21–1833	Lot	Z	387	Frankfort
Lexington & Ohio R R Co	Kentucky	12–21–1833	Lots	Z	388	Frankfort
Lexington & Ohio R R Co	Kentucky	5– 5–1836	Lots	27	436	Lexington
Leyhurne, Jno	Lexington	6–10–1801	4,566⅔	F	109	Ohio, Cumberland & Little Rs
Libby, Richard	Alexandria	2– 3–1802	5,000	J	274	S Fk Licking
Licard, Stephen	Philadelphia	5–25–1798	6,680	G	300	Chaplins Fk
Lighthouse, Richard	Scott	9–26–1819	——	T	133	None
Lillard, Jno	Lincoln	7–18–1786	1,400	A	180	None
Linder, Nathaniel	——	11– 8–1816	237½	R	60	Valley Cr
Lindsay, Landy	Versailles	1– 1–1818	Lot	S	19	Versailles
Lindsay, Elisha	Franklin	7–18–1798	50	C	323	None
Lindsay, Thos N	Franklin	8–12–1839	Lots	27	73	Frankfort
Linthicum, T. P	——	2– 5–1833	2,300	Z	271	Rough Cr
Linton, Jno	——	12– 6–1813	——	P	511	None
Linville, Jno	Baltimore	9–18–1798	1,000	D	5	Salt R
Lipscomb, Daniel	Green	2– 5–1834	2,000	Z	405	Skeggs Cr
Lipscomb, Daniel	Green, Ala	7– 3–1834	2,000	Z	500	S Fk Skeggs Cr
Lipscomb, Daniel Jr	King William	6–12–1821	428⁴⁷⁄₇	V	73	Tennessee R
Lipscomb, Daniel Jr	King William	7–27–1821	3,000	V	76	Skaggs Cr
Lipscomb, Daniel Jr	King William	5–10–1821	2,000	V	79	None
Lipscomb, Wm	Louisa	11–14–1786	400	A	190	Muddy Cr
Lipscomb, Wm	Louisa	11–14–1786	——	A	192	Muddy Cr
Lipscomb, Wm	Louisa	11–14–1786	500	A	194	Muddy Cr
Little Alexander	Franklin	3–21–1809	——	M	356	None
Little, Wm	Hamilton	2–20–1813	800	P	241	Cumberland R
Little, Wm	——	1–31–1815	——	P	609	None
Livers, Wm	Nelson	12– 1–1806	200	K	504	Main Coxes Cr
Livingston, Jno	Fayette	3– 6–1792	100	B-2	472	Ky R
Livingston, Jno N Jr	New York	6–18–1840	——	28	57	None
Lloyd, Francis	Franklin	4–22–1844	Lot	27	401	Frankfort
Locker, Geo L	——	7–31–1806	200	K	391	None
Locker, Geo L	——	7–31–1806	1,000	K	393	None
Lockhart, Triplett	Owen	1–17–1822	200	V	221	Eagle Cr
Lockhart, Triplett	Owen	12–12–1821	200	V	223	Eagle Cr
Lockwood, Wm	New York	8–16–1823	690	W	106	Cumberland R
Loftus, Geo	Christian	2– 3–1824	666	W	410	Red R
Loftus, Geo	Christian	2– 3–1824	200	W	411	Crooked Cr
Loftus, Geo	Christian	1–29–1824	1,000	W	417	Rough Cr
Loftus, Geo	Christian	1–18–1824	547	W	419	Cumberland R
Loftus, Geo	Christian	2–28–1824	833⅓	W	421	Panther Cr
Loftus, Geo	Christian	2– 6–1824	2,000	W	423	E Fk Little Barren R
Loftus, Geo	Christian	1– 4–1824	1,000	W	425	Clear Cr
Loftus, Geo	Christian	1– 4–1824	1,090	W	427	Cumberland R
Loftus, Geo	Christian	1–18–1824	415	W	429	Ohio R
Loftus, Geo	Christian	1– 4–1824	1,000	W	430	N Fk Tradewater
Loftus, Geo	Christian	1–15–1824	200	W	432	Muddy R
Loftus, Geo	Christian	1– 4–1824	500	W	434	Coffields Fk Deer Cr
Loftus, Geo	Christian	2–16–1824	400	W	436	Deer Cr
Loftus, Geo	Christian	1– 4–1824	300	W	438	Little R
Loftus, Geo	Christian	1–28–1824	400	W	439	Little R
Loftus, Geo	Christian	2– 2–1824	557	W	441	Cumberland R
Loftus, Geo	Christian	2–16–1824	100	W	443	Fk Buck Cr
Loftus, Geo	Christian	2– 3–1824	666⅔	W	445	None

Grantee	Residence	Deed Date	Acres	Book	Page	Watercourse
Loftus, Geo	Christian	1– 4–1824	666⅔	W	447	Cypress Cr
Loftus, Geo	Christian	1–28–1824	560	W	451	Rough Cr
Loftus, Geo	Christian	1– 4–1824	400	W	453	Deer Cr
Loftus, Geo	Christian	1–22–1824	250	W	455	Clifty Cr
Loftus, Geo	Christian	2– 6–1824	200	W	456	None
Loftus, Geo	Christian	1–24–1824	1,000	W	459	N Fk Tradewater
Loftus, Geo	Christian	2– 7–1824	30	W	461	Flyns Fk
Loftus, Geo	Christian	1–18–1824	200	W	480	Panther Cr
Loftus, Geo	Christian	2– 8–1824	666	W	482	Cumberland R
Loftus, Geo	Christian	1–22–1824	360	W	484	Camp Cr
Loftus, Geo	Christian	1–29–1824	400	W	486	None
Loftus, Geo	Christian	2– 3–1824	1,450	W	488	Cumberland R
Loftus, Geo	Christian	1– 4–1824	900	W	490	Tradewater
Loftus, Geo	Christian	1–31–1824	1,000	W	492	Deer Cr
Loftus, Geo	Christian	2– 3–1824	1,000	W	495	Cumberland R
Loftus, Geo	Christian	1–10–1824	1,000	W	498	Tradewater
Loftus, Geo	Christian	2– 7–1824	1,100	W	500	Pond R
Loftus, Geo	Christian	2–25–1824	400	W	509	Beaver Fk Highland Cr
Loftus, Geo	Christian	1–29–1824	500	W	512	Cumberland R
Loftus, Geo	Christian	1–25–1824	610	X	1	None
Loftus, Geo	Christian	1–10–1824	610	X	3	None
Loftus, Geo	Christian	1–15–1824	666	X	5	Cumberland R
Logan, Benj	Lincoln	9– 5–1786	——	A	168	Green R
Logan, Benj	Lincoln	8–26–1786	400	A	170	Green R
Logan, Benj	Lincoln	12– 6–1785	——	A	174	Hickman Cr
Logan, Benj	Lincoln	9–23–1789	1,600	B-2	155	Indian Camp Cr
Logan, Benj	Shelby	4–14–1801	4,500	H	141	Indian Camp Cr
Logan, Benj	Shelby	7–10–1797	9,412	H	153	Mississippi
Logan, Benj	Shelby	1–30–1817	29,000	R	134	None
Logan, Jno, heirs	——	1–14–1812	394½	O	299	Elk Fk Red R
Logan, Jno, heirs	——	9–20–1813	500	P	430	N Fk Licking
Logan, Wm	Lincoln	2– 4–1807	400	L	134	Gren R
Logan, Wm	Shelby	3–15–1813	1,000	P	153	Ky R
Logan, Wm	——	7–22–1814	150	T	73	None
Logan, Wm	Shelby	5– 9–1820	1,000	U	63	Ohio R
Logsdon, Jno	Hardin	1–27–1813	450	P	56	Racoon Cr
Loinheart, Harman Jos	Philadelphia	7– 9–1791	368,000	A-2	7	Sandy R & Green R
Long, Anderson	Warren	9– 5–1808	——	M	156	Jones Big Spring
Lomax, Joseph T	Richmond	2–14–1823	1,724	Y	68	None
Long, Chas		12–25–1815	9,910	Q	294	Clear & Sunfish Crs Ky & Green R
Long, Gabriel	Culpepper	8–21–1800	100	E	254	Poages Cr
Long, Gabriel	Culpepper	4–28–1800	100	E	256	None
Long, Nimrod	Culpepper	3–22–1799	1,000	D	160	None
Long, Nimrod	Culpepper	3–19–1799	——	D	162	None
Long, Richard	Franklin	6–15–1839	11	27	72	Franklin Co
Long, Stephen H	U S Army	6–10–1819	200	U	190	Clarks Run
Long, Thos	Franklin	9– 2–1816	Slaves	R	45	None
Long, Wm B	Woodford	3–17–1815	20	Q	29	Glens Cr
Love, Jno	Mercer	6–25–1790	700	B-2	223	Hingston Fk
Love, Jno	Woodford	6– 9–1791	300	B-2	329	Shawnee Run
Love, Matthew	Jefferson	1–21–1820	276	T	364	Shiveleys Mill Cr
Love, Saml	London	4– 6–1798	4,110	C	343	Lynn Camp Cr
Love, Thomas	Franklin	11– 8–1803	5,000	H	21	Green R
Lovelace, Zadock	Nelson	2–16–1805	200	H	550	Wilsons Cr
Lovett, Wm	New York	8——1812	56,000	Z	286	None
Lowe, Jas R M	Prince George	2–17–1831	——	Z	112	None
Lowe, Floyd Mc C	Prince George	2–17–1831	——	Z	116	None
Lowe, Nicholas	New York	8–26–1786	30,000	T	322	Nolinn & Green R
Lowery, Robt	Washington	6–15–1813	568	P	247	Sulphur Lick Cr
Lucas, Thos	Amherst	11– 3–1787	400	A	332	Robinson Cr
Luke, Jno L, Eliza A Ann M	Mason	5–24–1823	——	W	89	S Elkhorn & Sinking Cr
Luke, Wm H W Monta J & Francis E L	Mason	5–24–1823	——	W	89	S Elkhorn & Sinking Cr
Luttrell, Jno	North Carolina	1– 6–1775	——	C	60	Ohio, Cumberland & Green R
Lyle, James	Chesterfield	12–10–1808	Slave	M	237	None
Lyman, Thos & Jno W	Philadelphia	9–18–1819	1,519½	T	331	Bear Fk Green R
Lynch, Chas	Shelby	7– 8–1801	14,546	E	369	Gess & Benson Crs
Lynch, Chas	Shelby	7–21–1801	2,000	E	387	Little Ky R
Lynch, Chas	Shelby	11–10–1803	5,992	H	216	Jepthas, Benson & Buck Crs
Lynch, Chas	Shelby	11–10–1803	2,106	H	219	—— Cr
Lynch, Chas	Shelby	4–13–1804	2,000	H	242	Mulberry Cr
Lynch, Chas	Shelby	5– 7–1800	7,023	K	110	Road from Boones Station

Grantee	Residence	Deed Date	Acres	Book	Page	Watercourse
Lynch, Chas	——	11- 9-1805	11,520	K	126	N & S Fk Elkhorn Ky R Clear & Green Crs
Lynch, Wm	——	3-13-1816	202¾	R	24	Ohio R
Lyon, Dr James	Eastern Shore	10-31-1811	1,333⅓	O	210	Cypress Cr
McAfee	——	12-17-1827	Lots	X	329	Owensboro
McAfee	——	12-17-1827	417	X	329	Ohio R
McAlister, Hannah	Baltimore	9-18-1798	1,000	D	2	Salt R
McAllister, Jno	Lincoln	7-27-1815	666¾	Q	149	Glenns Cr
McBride, Lapsley	Franklin	7-10-1811	479	O	94	Cumberland R
McBride, Lewis	Anderson	9- 6-1828	114	X	459	Benson Cr
McCall, Geo C	Philadelphia	4-28-1832	10,781	Z	376	N Fk Ky R
McCalla, Andrew	Lincoln	3- 7-1785	Lot Danville	A	7	None
McCalla, Andrew	Lincoln	3- 7-1785	Lot Danville	A	10	None
McCalla, Andrew	Lincoln	9-13-1785	——	A	60	None
McCalla, Jno M	Fayette	1-30-1828	Lots	X	478	Greensburg
McCallmont & Boys	Philadelphia	10-29-1798	——	D	389	Ohio R
McCarrall, Jno	Christian	6-19-1827	2,375	X	254	Caney Fk Tradewater
McCarty, Jas	Hardin	6- 2-1821	——	V	288	Rolling Fk & Ohio R
McCaull, Jno	Culpepper	1-17-1795	1,050	A-2	636	Hingston Fk
McCaull, Neil	Richmond	6-16-1807	444	L	156	Cumberland R
McCaw, Jas Drew	Richmond	3- 2-1830	——	Z	15	None
McCaw, Sarah	Richmond	3- 5-1801	5,133⅓	E	361	Skeggs Cr
McClanahan, Wm	Bourbon	8-29-1816	773⅓	R	126	Stoners Fk & Green R
McClane, Niel	Kentucky	3-26-1821	1,000	U	333	Drakes Cr
McClane, Niel	Kentucky	3-26-1821	1,800	U	336	Floyds Fk
McClane, Niel	Kentucky	3-26-1821	2,000	U	339	Big Bone Cr
McClane, Niel	Kentucky	3-26-1821	1,000	U	341	Ohio R
McClane, Niel	Kentucky	3-26-1821	500	U	344	None
McClane, Niel	Kentucky	3-26-1821	400	U	347	Caney Fk
McClane, Niel	Kentucky	3-26-1821	200	U	351	Cumberland R
McClellan, David	Nelson	5- 7-1800	500	E	219	Big Slate Cr
McClellan, David	Nelson	5- 7-1800	5,158	E	223	Ohio R
McClenahan, Robt	Chester	8-10-1805	4,000	J	326	None
McClenahan, Robt	Chester	5-15-1799	4,000	Q	160	Salt R
McClure, Andrew	——	10- 4-1791	700	B-2	358	Bucks Cr
McClure, Alexander	Woodford	9-12-1817	——	R	430	Ky R
McColgan, Jno	Green	4-24-1797	200	B	279	Sinking Cr
McConathy, Jas	Gallatin	1-31-1823	200	V	437	Ohio R
McCormick, Chas	Frederick	2- 4-1811	10,000	O	24	Little Sandy R
McCormick, Chas	Frederick	3-10-1829	981	Y	346	Ohio R & Otter Cr
McCormick, Daniel	Lincoln	3-10-1787	Negro	A	278	None
McCormick, Ralph & Jno	——	9-13-1828	136	X	462	Hinkston Fk
McCormick, Walter	——	11- 7-1827	201½	X	317	None
McCosky, Jno	Franklin	11- 2-1812	200	P	27	Armstrongs Br
McCracken, Jno	Bracken	12- 6-1817	100	R	594	Ohio R
McCracken, Otha	Franklin	3-31-1830	170	Y	446	Elkhorn
McCracken, Ovid, heirs	Meade	5-11-1842	1,533	27	283	Otter Cr
McCraw, Samuel	Richmond	4-10-1797	10,869	C	18	Ohio R
McCraw, Samuel	Richmond	10-17-1799	112,134¼	D	538	Gauley R Little Kenhowa R & Lewis Cr
McCraw, Samuel	Richmond	4-19-1809	9,700	N	285	Big Laurel R
McCurdy, Isaac	Woodford	4-27-1820	21	W	124	Elkhorn
McDonald, Alexander	Baltimore	6-19-1813	8,965	P	253	None
McDonald, Angus	Frederick	6-13-1803	1,000	K	171	Ohio R
McDonald, Jas	Frederick	1- 8-1819	8,212½	S	419	Ohio R Little Otter Cr & Br Ky R
McDonald, Jas	——	8-28-1819	5,500	T	162	Rough & Panther Cr
McDonald, Jno	Franklin	12-12-1819	97	T	266	Big Br
McDowell, Ephram	Mercer	7-26-1813	Lot	P	209	Danville
McDowell, Ephram	Mercer	3-18-1816	400	Q	382	None
McDowell, Ephram & Wife	Mercer	5- 9-1814	476	P	476	Harrods Run
McDowell, Geo	Scott	1- 4-1830	50	Y	440	Cedar Cr
McDowell, Jas	Rockbridge	3-24-1809	734	M	384	Crocus Cr
McDowell, Jesse	——	10-12-1819	1,193	T	181	Rolling Fk
McDowell, Jesse	——	2- 5-1833	2,300	Z	271	Rough Cr
McDowell, Jno	Kentucky	10- 3-1791	500	B-2	426	Houstons Fk
McDowell, Joseph	Mercer	3-21-1816	6	R	184	Wilsons Cr
McDowell, Samuel	Lincoln	6-24-1786	400	A	113	None
McDowell, Samuel Jr	Mercer	9- 3-1788	400	B-2	97	Shawnee Run
McFawl, David	Bedford	6- 7-1785	300	A	18	Little Cove
McElroy, Jas	Washington	1- 7-1817	1,500	R	132	Pleasant Run
McGee, Rachel A & Mary M	Louisville	5-22-1816	Lot	W	235	Louisville

Grantee	Residence	Deed Date	Acres	Book	Page	Watercourse
McGee, H P & Eliza M.	Louisville	5–22–1816	Lot	W	235	Louisville
McGehee, Samuel	——	10– 4–1803	350	H	59	None
McGill, Archibald	Winchester	8–28–1806	962	L	82	Yellow Bank of Ohio R
McGinnis, Edmund	Cable	2–23–1809	2,100	M	317	Ohio R
McGinnis, Wm	Mercer	3–23–1808	150	L	350	Chaplins Fk
McGinniss, Sarah W	New York	7–31–1827	Lot	X	403	Maysville
McGowan, Elizabeth	——	4–21–1826	5,746¾	X	206	Ky R Bullskin Bear Grass Cr & Big Barren R
McGowan, Elizabeth	——	4–21–1826	6,479¾	Y	134	Salt, Big Barren & Cumberland Rs
McGuire, Jno	N Carolina	2–25–1803	1,000	Z	186	N Fk Elkhorn
McGuire, Wm	Frederick	10–13–1806	962	L	104	Ohio R
McIntire & Yates	New York	4–13–1833	562	Z	277	Cumberland & Little Barren
McIver, Jno	Alexandria	4–20–1804	745	J	1	Quick Run
McIver, Jno	Alexandria	7–17–1802	800	J	11	None
McIver, Jno	Alexandria	7– 9–1803	14,936½	J	91	18 Mi Cr Hardins & Cartwrights Cr
McIver, Jno	Alexandria	5–20–1807	13,588	M	1	Green R & Bear Cr
McIver, Jno	Alexandria	6– 1–1803	——	M	37	None
McIver, Jno	Alexandria	11–21–1808	3,000	N	78	Green R
McIver, Jno	Alexandria	11– 4–1809	4,700	N	142	Green R
McKean, Samuel	Baltimore	12–29–1809	2,000	O	346	Beaver Cr
McKee, Benj	Anderson	5– 3–1844	——	27	410	None
McKee, James		9– 3–1828	168	X	473	Ohio R
McKee Robt	Woodford	12–17–1796	500	A-2	471	Ky R
McKee, Wm R	Kentucky	12–30–1843	Lot	27	385	Midway
McKee & Swigert	Franklin	10– 8–1844	Lot	27	435	Midway
McKenney, Ben F	St Louis	5–15–1841	204	27	251	St Louis Co Mo
McKenney, Jno	Bourbon	10– 7–1795	3,000	A-2	692	Eagle Cr
McKenney, Jno	Bourbon	12–20–1802	400	G	122	Rolling Fk
McKenney, Thos L	Georgetown	11– 4–1816	1,325	R	176	Big Rudy Cr
McKenney, Wm	Lincoln	9–10–1785	Lot	A	166	None
McKenzie, Daniel	Kentucky	9–21–1807	2,950	L	124	Panther Cr
McKim, Jno Jr	Baltimore	7–11–1805	Mill	K	299	Fks Elkhorn
McKimm, Wm	——	6– 4–1792	400	B-2	499	Rolling Fk
McKinley, Jno	Lincoln	9–12–1806	1,000	K	395	Ohio R
McKnight, Virgil	Shelby	4–15–1824	190	W	449	None
McLean, Alvey	Muhlenburg	12–31–1804	——	H	564	Pond R
McLin, Alexander	Franklin	8– 9–1819	Lot	T	374	Frankfort
McMeekin, Chas	Hamilton	7– 7–1846	10,000	28	93	Big Sandy R & Claim Cr
McNair, Dunning	Aleganey	11– 1–1806	——	N	239	None
McNair, Dunning	Allega4ny	8–13–1806	——	N	240	None
McNeil, Hector	Petersburg	6– 8–1808	——	M	117	None
McNeil, Hector		7– 3–1809	Slaves	N	450	None
McPherson, Jno	Frederick	3– 9–1798	50,000	C	191	Sextons Cr
McPherson, Jno	——	1– 4–1808	200	M	12	None
McVicker, Jno	——	3–20–1807	1,000	L	9	None
McVicker, Jno	——	3–20–1807	700	L	10	—— Br
Macey, Leander & Jefferson	Franklin	7– 5–1832	390	Z	206	Ky R
Macklin, Alex W	Franklin	1–27–1841	100	27	182	N Elkhorn
Macklin, Alexander W	Franklin	8– 1–1842	——	27	323	Rope Walk
Macklin, Alexander W	Franklin	12– 2–1842	40	27	398	M & S Elkhorn
Macklin, Alexander W	Franklin	5– 3–1844	50	27	406	M Elkhorn
Macklin, Alexander W	Franklin	2—–1845	24	27	468	S Elkhorn
Macklin, Alexander W	Franklin	7–10–1845	13	28	18	Ky R
Macklin, Jno	Franklin	7–29–1842	——	27	307	N Elkhorn
Maclin, Patrick	Scotland Power Attorney	9–22–1785	——	A	19-21	None
Maclin, Peter	Mason	7–22–1803	7,019	G	376	Townsends Run Ohio R & Mill Cr
Macmurdo & Fisher	Richmond	1–21–1802	3,000	K	450	Deer Cr
Macy, Alexander	Franklin	11–20–1815	Lots	Q	247	Frankfort
Macey, Alexander	Franklin	11– 7–1817	Lots	R	566	Frankfort
Maddox, David	Scott	3– 5–1806	200	K	178	Eagle Cr
Maddox, Jas	——	11– 1–1827	53	X	306	Eagle Cr
Maddox, Notley	——	5–13–1805	400	K	25	Cow Cr & Red R
Maddox, Ralph	Lincoln	10–14–1789	200	B-2	127	Slate Cr
Maddox, Sherwood	Gallatin	12– 1–1807	200	L	338	Eagle Cr
Maddox, Sherwood	——	11– 1–1827	241	X	309	Eagle Cr
Madison, Jos	Prince Edward	4–24–1834	Lots	Z	431	Richmond Va
Madison, Geo	Franklin	11–26–1804	200	H	434	Buck Cr
Madison, Geo	Franklin	12–11–1804	200	H	462	Drakes Cr
Madison, Geo	Franklin	12–11–1804	200	H	464	Drakes Cr
Madison, Geo	Franklin	12–27–1805	2,000	K	156	M Elkhorn
Madison, Geo	Frankfort	3–14–1812	Lot	O	350	Frankfort
Magill, Chas	Frederick	10–12–1795	6,000	A-2	419	Ohio R

Grantee	Residence	Deed Date	Acres	Book	Page	Watercourse
Magill, Jas	Kentucky	2–26–1834	150	Z	413	Dry Run
Magill, Jas	Kentucky	6——1839	150	28	23	None
Major, Jno	Franklin	3–19–1814	Corn Cr	P	392	None
Major, Jno S	Franklin	9–17–1827	——	X	284	None
Major, Lewis R	Franklin	4– 2–1814	——	P	403	S Elkhorn
Major, Saml J M	Frankfort	11–18–1826	1,000	Y	227	State of Ohio
Major, Saml J M	Franklin	12– 7–1829	56	Y	420	Big Benson Cr
Mallory, Frances	Virginia	7– 8–1844	4,577⅔	27	416	Russell & Drakes Cr
Mandaville, Jonathan	Alexandria	3–29–1798	1,000	D	402	Chaplins Fk
Mandaville, Jonathan	Alexandria	3–29–1798	1,000	D	405	Bayse Cr
Mann, Judith H	Chesterfield	3– 7–1834	114	Z	443	near Frankfort
Mansfield, Jno	Mercer	3–22–1791	Lot	B-2	250	Danville
Marable, Benj	Halifax	9–26–1808	1,000	P	36	Little Barren R
Marie, Jno	Philadelphia	6–29–1786	5,000	O	415	N Fk Ky R
Markley, Jno A	Franklin	7–28–1819	——	T	126	None
Markley, Jno A	Franklin	10–15–1821	25	Y	219	None
Marquedent, Chas	Philadelphia	4–23–1796	6,000	A-2	453	None
Marshall, Chas & Wife	Franklin	5–10–1826	111	Y	161	—— Cr
Marshall, Francis	Nashville	12–23–1833	876⅔	Z	402	Little Barren, Tenn & Ohio R
Marshall, Humphrey	Fayette	9–23–1786	248	A	283	S Fk Elkhorn
Marshall, Humphrey	Fayette	9–23–1786	172	A	285	S Fk Elkhorn
Marshall, Humphrey	Fayette	9–23–1786	90	A	287	S Fk Elkhorn
Marshall, Humphrey	Woodford	3–20–1790	½	B-2	136	Louisville
Marshall, Humphrey	Woodford	1–20–1798	145.937½	C	326	Rough Cr, Ohio, Big Sandy, Licking
Marshall, Humphrey	Woodford	1–15–1799	34,000	D	213	Eagle Cr
Marshall, Humphrey	Kentucky	5– 5–1800	2,352	E	61	Twins Cr
Marshall, Humphrey	——	8–19–1800	——	E	215	Ohio R
Marshall, Humphrey	——	11– 8–1801	75,000	F	383	Rough Cr
Marshall, Humphrey	Woodford	10–14–1801	793½	F	385	Br Muddy Cr
Marshall, Humphrey	——	4–30–1802	5,189	F	387	Dry Cr & Gun Pdr
Marshall, Humphrey	Woodford	8–19–1800	——	F	511	Ohio R
Marshall, Humphrey	——	11–23–1802	3,939	G	49	Licking
Marshall, Humphrey	Kentucky	1–29–1803	4,584	G	262	Ohio R
Marshall, Humphrey	Frankfort	11–19–1803	12,311	H	65	Hingston Fk
Marshall, Humphrey	——	11–20–1804	1,778⅔	H	415	Cumberland R
Marshall, Humphrey	——	11–28–1804	1,515	H	479	Twins Cr
Marshall, Humphrey	Woodford	10–12–1801	1,000	M	229	Rougs Run
Marshall, Humphrey	Franklin	7– 5–1810	1,500	N	260	Woolperts Cr
Marshall, Humphrey & Wife	——	11– 8–1808	14,724	M	240	Ohio R & Licking
Marshall, Jno	——	11–30–1801	1,000	F	159	White Oak Cr
Marshall, Lewis & Geo	Richmond	10– 3–1793	9,198	A-2	56	None
Marshall, Saml	Bourbon	9–13–1806	200	L	346	Hustons Fk
Marshall, Saml R & Wife	Philadelphia	12–25–1797	6,680	G	304	Chaplins Fk
Marshall, Thos	——	11–28–1804	1,515	H	479	Twins Cr
Marshall, Thos	Lewis	2–18–1840	——	27	106	Twins Cr
Marshall, Thos, heirs	Franklin	5–10–1826	111	Y	161	—— Cr
Martin, Jno L	Frankfort	7– 7–1802	——	F	461	Elkhorn
Martin, Jno L	——	11–13–1824	1,000	W	413	Eagle Cr
Martin, Elias	Fanquir	6–16–1828	1,065	Z	57	Licking
Martin, Russell	Kentucky	12–17–1802	137	G	325	Hammonds Cr
Martin, Wm	——	8– 8–1797	237	C	125	Beech Fk
Martin, Wm R	Anderson	9–28–1827	55	X	286	Benson Cr
Marx, Asher	Manchester	7–29–1802	1,326	G	23	Green R
Mason, Geo	Lexington	6–21–1794	——	W	245	None
Mason, Geo, heirs	Gunston	6–21–1794	——	W	245	None
Mason, Jno	Georgetown	8–30–1800	900	E	292	Ohio R
Mason, Jno T	Washington	5–22–1817	6,000	R	580	Greensburg Rd
Mason, Jno T	Washington	5–23–1817	2,000	R	584	Pottingers Cr
Mason, Jno T Jr	Bath	5– 1–1822	800	V	327	None
Mason, Mary	London	5–22–1817	6,000	R	580	Greensburg Rd
Mason, Mary	London	5–23–1817	2,000	R	584	Pottingers Cr
Mason, Mary & Jno T	London	5–23–1817	5,000	R	588	Green R
Mason, Stephen T	London	2–22–1799	6,844	D	473	Pitman Skeggs & N Fk Tradewater
Mason, Stephen T	London	2–22–1799	13,766⅔	D	476	Little Miami, Paint & Crocus Crs
Mason, Stephen T	London	2–22–1799	——	D	477	None
Mason, Thos	Jefferson	6–28–1811	47½	O	321	Floyds Fk
Massie, Henry	State Ohio	2——1805	666⅔	H	585	Ohio R
Masterson, Jno	Kentucky	1–15–1825	500	V	406	Ohio R
Masterson, Richard	Gallatin	11– 6–1804	2,500	H	460	Two Branches
Mather, Richard	New York City	4–26–1800	4,000	E	22	S Br Nolinn
Mather, Richard	Kentucky	3–10–1803	500	G	390	Ohio R
Maund, Jno Jas	Westmoreland	12–21–1796	7,333⅓	B	329	None
Maury, Abram	Fluvania	1– 6–1796	900	A-2	565	Green R
Maury, Abram	Fluvania	11–12–1795	5,625	A-2	567	Green R
Maury, Abram	Fluvania	2–26–1796	562½	A-2	569	Green R

Grantee	Residence	Deed Date	Acres	Book	Page	Watercourse
Maury, Maud R	New York	4–21–1834	Lots	Z	431	Richmond Va
Maxwell, Jno	Fayette	——1787	250	A	321	None
Maxwell, Wm M	———	7– 9–1824	100	W	463	None
Maxwell, Wm M	———	7– 9–1824	218	W	466	None
Maxwell, Wm M	———	7– 9–1824	905	W	470	None
Maxwell, Wm M	———	7– 9–1824	500	W	473	S Fk Sandy R
May, Geo	Nelson	6–23–1789	515	B-2	62	Knob Cr
May, Geo	Denwiddie	8–25–1797	——	C	95	None
May, George	Denwiddie	9–13–1799	8,800	D	450	Little Rudy Cr
May, Jno L	———	6– 8–1813	50,000	P	367	Various Water Courses
May, Joseph	Suffolk	6–28–1796	7,813	D	84	Sandy R
May, Wm	Nelson	1–21–1809	300	M	303	Green R
May, Wm	Nelson	9–10–1810	2,800	N	283	Clear Fk Rough Cr
May, Wm	Nelson	2– 8–1812	500	O	306	Mill Cr
May, Wm	Nelson	2–28–1813	500	P	93	None
Mayes, Daniel	Christian	7– 6–1821	Lot	U	511	Versailles
Mayes, Daniel	Franklin	9–12–1826	1,000	Y	213	Green & Pond R
Mayfield, City Plat	Graves	3–27–1824	Lots	Y	268	Mayfield
Maylan, Jno	Philadelphia	8–14–1795	20,781	C	274	N Fk Ky R
Mayo, Philip	Richmond	6–21–1823	40,000	W	402	None
Mayo, Robt A	———	4–27–1824	30,000	W	346	Licking & Sulbergreed Cr
Mays, Geo	Bath	1–19–1819	666⅔	T	300	None
Mays, Wm	Fayette	11– 8–1799	353	D	416	Tates Cr
May, Wm	Nelson	4–29–1817	2,800	R	297	None
Meade, David	Kentucky	7–14–1800	6,000	F	210	Salt R
Means, Robt	Richmond	5–27–1795	1,200	A-2	272	Cr
Means, Robt	———	3– 7–1795	100	A-2	277	Bryants Lick
Means, Robt	Richmond	8– 3–1797	1,000	B	204	Cumberland R
Means, Robt	Richmond	12–15–1801	200	F	355	Flat Lick Cr
Means, Robt	Richmond	4–29–1801	333⅓	F	357	Big Barren R
Means, Robt	Richmond	1–19–1802	730	F	359	Cumberland R
Medde, David	Virginia	11–16–1795	2,000	A-2	525	Ohio R
Meeker, Saml	Philadelphia	12– 6–1799	407	F	448	Ohio R
Meeker, Saml & Wm P.	Philadelphia	7–16–1808	7,870	M	263	Elkhorn
Meeker, Wm	Philadelphia	12– 2–1806	1,000	L	3	Green R
Melton, Alexander & Wife	———	3–15–1803	2,000	H	112	Ohio R
Menifee, Wm	Virginia	1– 1–1814	——	P	364	None
Mercer, Chas F	London	6– 1–1815	2,333⅓	S	310	Ky & Green R & Crocus Cr
Mercer, Chas F	Virginia	11– 9–1821	——	V	123	Crocus & Greasy Crs
Merchie, Jno	Chesterfield	12– 1–1812	1,050	P	1	Crews Cr
Meredith, Jonathan	Baltimore	6– 2–1827	1,900	X	249	Slate Cr
Meredith, Jonathan	Maryland	10–17–1827	1,896	X	362	None
Meredith, Jonathan	Baltimore	11–14–1829	30,821	Y	425	Slate, Licking Crs
Meredith, Jonathan	Baltimore	11–26–1831	119,289½	V	174	Licking, Shelby & Green R
Meredith, Saml	Fayette	6–14–1796	Lot	A-2	584	Frankfort
Meredith & Spencer	Baltimore	11–16–1839	2,500	27	96	M Elkhorn
Meredith & Spencer	Baltimore	1– 1–1844	2,500	27	395	M Franklin Co
Meriwether, David W.	Jefferson	6–22–1788	36	A	430	E Fk Coxes Cr
Meriwether, Richard	———	5– 1–1809	273½	M	425	None
Meriwether, Richard & Patty	———	2–24–1786	1,000	A	84	——
Meriwether, Wm Sr.	Jefferson	6–16–1812	333⅔	P	16	Rough Cr
Merry, Prettyman	Buckenham	11–17–1806	250	L	148	N Fk Barren R
Michie, Geo	———	3– 4–1794	1,000	N	100	M Ky
Michie, Jno	Louisa	8–20–1798	164	N	96	Rolling Fk
Michie, Jno	———	3– 4–1794	1,000	N	100	M Ky
Middleton, Thos J	Woodford	2– 6–1841	55½	27	186	S Elkhorn
Middleton, Thos J	———	2–12–1845	62	27	463	S Elkhorn
Mifflin, Saml	Philadelphia	4–21–1807	——	L	49	None
Milam, Jno	Franklin	4–18–1821	50	U	378	S Elkhorn
Milam, Jno	Franklin	6–15–1821	78	U	504	None
Miles, Jos M & Walker.	Trimble	5– 9–1839	5,000	27	22	Little Ky R
Millegan, Jennett	Woodford	6–26–1798	500	D	17	Lees Cr
Miller, Andrew	Franklin	7–22–1814	Lot	P	491	Frankfort
Miller, Francis	———	7–15–1819	223¾	T	77	None
Miller, Jacob	Spencer	2– 9–1831	136½	Z	98	Salt R & Big Beech Cr
Miller, Jno	Botetaust	12– 1–1796	4,000	C	122	None
Miller, Jno	———	9–19–1797	——	D	107	None
Miller, Jno Andrew	Westmoreland	5–13–1789	200	B-2	173	Elkhorn
Miller, Jno C	Kentucky	1–15–1823	500	V	406	Ohio R
Miller, Lewis Colon	———	5– 2–1843	Lot	27	345	Frankfort
Miller, Maurice L	Mercer	3–23–1817	10,200	R	189	Cedar, Fern & Floyds Fk
Miller, Maurice L	Danville	8– 1–1818	——	S	339	None
Miller, Robt	Shelby	9– 8–1806	75	K	384	Guesses Cr

Grantee	Residence	Deed Date	Acres	Book	Page	Watercourse
Mills, Benj	Paris	10- 8-1822	113½	V	319	None
Mills, Benj	Franklin	9- 1-1830	3,708	Z	9	Sinking Sp, Meade Co
Mills, Jno	Botetaust	10-26-1799	1,500	F	390	Big Benson & Ky R
Mills, Peter	———	11-17-1807	3,000	L	230	None
Mills, Peter	———	11-20-1807	10,460	L	232	None
Mills, Peter	———	11-17-1807	5,000	L	234	None
Mills, Peter	———	11-17-1807	21,079	L	236	None
Mills, Peter	———	11-18-1807	1,260	L	238	None
Mills, Peter	———	11-17-1807	3,807	L	240	None
Mills, Peter	———	11-17-1807	3,954	L	242	None
Mills, Peter	———	11-17-1807	4,950	L	244	None
Mills, Peter	———	11-17-1807	1,000	L	246	None
Mills, Peter	———	11-17-1807	3,500	L	248	None
Mills, Peter	———	11-17-1807	2,040	L	250	None
Mills, Peter	———	11-20-1807	1,800	L	252	None
Mills, Peter	———	11-20-1807	2,000	L	254	None
Mills, Peter	———	11-17-1807	5,000	L	256	None
Mills, Peter	———	11-17-1807	700	L	258	None
Mills, Peter	———	11-17-1807	400	L	260	None
Mills, Peter	———	11-17-1807	614	L	262	None
Mills, Robt P	Franklin	8-20-1839	84	27	54	N Elkhorn
Mills, Robt P	Franklin	3-11-1839	———	27	123	N Elkhorn
Mills, Dr Wm	Louisa	3-17-1801	500	F	162	N Fk Licking
Mills, Dr Wm Jr	Louisa	3-17-1801	299	F	176	Flat Cr
Milton, Ebin	Frederick	3-27-1829	23	Y	357	Shannons Run
Milton, Jno	Fayette	3-12-1829	104	Y	360	Shannons Run
Minor, Dabney	Albemarle	4- 1-1809	200	N	412	Cumberland R
Minter, Joseph	———	9-21-1799	470	D	527	Wolperts Cr
Mitchell, Abram S	Franklin	10- 1-1846	Lot	28	112	Frankfort
Mitchell, Alexander, Jr	Franklin	9- 7-1816	700	R	111	Clear Cr
Mitchell, Alexander J Jr	Franklin	12- 8-1842	Lots	27	326	Frankfort
Mitchell, Daniel	Scott	8-28-1818	2,118	S	221	Eagle Cr
Mitchell, Jno A	Franklin	10-10-1811	Lots	O	191	Frankfort
Mitchell, Jno A	Frankfort	3-20-1812	Lot	O	381	Frankfort
Mitchell, Jno A	Franklin	5-11-1813	Lot	P	152	Frankfort
Mitchell, Lucy	Gallatin	6-11-1822	112	V	350	None
Mitchell, Saml, heirs	Franklin	2-23-1815	45	Q	27	None
Mitchell, Thos H	Virginia	6- 4-1818	12,500	W	11	None
Mitchell, Wm	———	2-16-1797	200	H	481	S Fk Elkhorn
Moale, Saml Trustee	———	11-18-1803	4,916	H	135	M Island Cr
Mondiville, Jonathan	Alexander	11-21-1805	99	K	1	Bays Cr
Monks, Jas A & Joseph	———	10- 1-1839	466	27	76	Hurricane Cr
Montague, E & N	Franklin	3-21-1803	Lot	G	204	Frankfort
Montague, Wm	Woodford	12-30-1843	Lot	27	384	Midway
Montgomery, Jno	———	5- 6-1818	104	S	126	Ohio R
Montgomery, Robt	Lincoln	10- 7-1790	372	B-2	212	Dix R
Montgomery, Robt, heirs	Garrard	11- 7-1807	1,400	L	206	Tygerts Cr
Montgomery, Robt Sr	Lincoln	3-13-1788	200	A	376	Jessamine Cr
Montgomery, Saml L	Washington	9-13-1819	1,200	T	139	Lost Cr
Montgomery, Thos	Lincoln	3-13-1788	652	A	377	Jessamine Cr
Montgomery, Thos	———	12-14-1818	760	S	406	Caseys Cr
Montgomery, Thos	Lincoln	10-23-1818	730	S	408	Green R & Caseys Cr
Montgomery, Wm	Lincoln	6-19-1790	106	B-2	157	Clear Cr
Montgomery, Wm	Lincoln	11-26-1798	350	D	82	Caseys Cr
Monroe, Jas	President U S	10-16-1821	10,000	W	407	Licking R
Monroe, Thos B	Franklin	5-16-1829	100	Y	364	Glens Cr
Monroe, Thos B	Franklin	5-16-1829	616	Y	365	None
Monroe, Thos B	Franklin	9-27-1841	50	27	225	Chaplins Fk
Moore, Archibald	Richmond	6-18-1807	444	L	156	Cumberland R
Moore, David	Deerfield	4-28-1786	900	L	22	None
Moore, G	———	1-12-1846	Lot	28	49	Midway
Moore, Jas, heirs	Fayette	12- 5-1815	200	Q	403	Rough Cr
Moore, Rev Jas, heirs	Fayette	12- 5-1815	200	Q	346	Rough Cr
Moore, Jos B	Mississippi	10-10-1823	2,910	W	283	Green R
Moore, Jos F	Shelby	6-10-1830	900	27	76	Cumberland R
Moore, Jno L	Albemarle	12- 4-1807	1,240	M	440	Green R
Moore, Joseph	Frankfort	10-25-1803	326	H	101	Baileys Run
Moore, Peter	Fayette	2-20-1808	333½	L	386	None
Moore, Peter	Bourbon	6- 1-1824	88	W	282	Coopers Run
Moore, Robt	Petersburg	5-21-1798	1,785	D	41	Ohio & Tennessee Rs
Moore, Robt	Petersburg	5-21-1798	1,000	D	44	Ohio R
Moore, Robt K	Philadelphia	9-15-1791	13,195	B-2	442	Youngers & Brashears Crs
Moore, Wm	Kentucky	7- 4-1805	300	J	259	Little N Elkhorn
Moore, Wm	Fayette	5-31-1811	400	O	121	None
Moore & Lacassaugne	Jefferson	12- 4-1788	½	B-2	49	Louisville

Grantee	Residence	Deed Date	Acres	Book	Page	Watercourse
Moorehouse, Abraham	Ouachita	9–13–1800	—	E	264	None
Mooreman, David	Breckinridge	6– 2–1821	—	V	288	Rolling Fk & Ohio R
Moorehead, Chas	Kentucky	3– 1–1839	552	27	13	M Barren Co
Moorehead, Chas S	Franklin	9– 6–1839	Lots	27	74	Frankfort
Moran, Jno	Prince George	5–13–1805	100	K	53	Cow Cr & Red R
Morehead, Chas S	Franklin	9–26–1845	25	28	26	Dry Run
Moreland, Jno	Oldham	2– 1–1831	120	Z	96	Ohio R
Moreman, Jos C	Campbell	12–10–1807	443	L	227	Hustons Fk
Moreman, Jos C	Campbell	12–10–1807	443	M	179	Hustons Fk
Moreman, Jesse	Hardin	3–29–1816	42,000	Q	455	Salt & Laurel Rs
Morgan, Benj R	Philadelphia	4– 1–1805	22,000	O	235	Floyds Fk
Morgan, Chas	—	11–23–1802	793	G	53	Big Mud and Nowlands Crs
Morgan, Chas	Muhlenberg	10–25–1803	400	H	1	Chapins Fk
Morgan, Chas	Muhlenberg	10– 4–1806	1,169	L	60	Licking
Morgan, Chas	Muhlenberg	10–31–1806	200	L	63	Nolin
Morgan, Daniel	—	12–22–1800	2,000	M	218	Tradewater & Ohio R
Morgan, Daniel	Mason	1– 7–1819	2,090	S	378	Rolling Fk
Morgan, Ephram	—	3– 5–1796	27,018	E	233	Sandy R
Morgan, Jas & Wm	Fauquier	4–26–1802	2,000	F	540	Cumberland R
Morgan, James & Wm Sr	—	4– 1–1796	2,947	A-2	587	Skeggs Cr
Morgan, Jno B	Bath	11–13–1815	1,950	R	27	Slate & Rockcastle Crs
Morgan, Jno B	Bath	11–13–1815	1,000	R	30	Slate Cr
Morgan, Joseph	Mercer	5–17–1833	384	Z	290	Salt R
Morgan, Van	Clark	11–13–1818	—	S	524	Contract
Morgan, Willis	Muhlenberg	11–21–1805	2,000	J	393	Clear Cr
Morgan, Willis	Muhlenberg	11–21–1805	1,000	J	398	Big Cr
Morgan, Willis	Muhlenberg	9–12–1806	1,000	K	395	Ohio R
Morgan, Willis	—	10–30–1805	400	K	523	None
Morgan, Willis	Muhlenburg	8–30–1809	1,000	N	151	Poages Cr
Morgan, Willis	Muhlenburg	2–12–1810	2,500	N	153	Pond R
Morgan, Willis	Muhlenberg	3–21–1811	666⅔	N	459	Eddy Cr
Mority, David	Northampton	11–25–1803	3,000	H	305	None
Morris, David	Bourbon	7–15–1788	1,400	A	441	Lees Cr
Morris, Jno	Franklin	12–27–1805	2,000	K	156	M Elkhorn
Morris, Jno	Franklin	9– 3–1805	450	K	195	Elkhorn
Morris, Jno	Franklin	7–29–1815	56	Q	343	Cane Run
Morris, Jno	Franklin	7– 1–1815	Lots	Q	389	Frankfort & Lexington
Morris, Jno	Frankfort	1–31–1816	338	Q	401	Elkhorn
Morris, Jno	Franklin	1–14–1817	1,100	R	249	Panther Cr
Morris, Jno	Franklin	4–12–1819	Lot	T	380	Lexington
Morris, Jno	Franklin	10– 4–1819	680	T	382	Johnsons Fk
Morris, Jno	Franklin	10– 3–1820	1,000	U	58	Cypress Cr
Morris, Mary Ann	—	1–24–1842	4¼	27	268	Armstrong Br
Morris, Richard	Louisa	11– 2–1808	1,000	M	247	Ohio R
Morris, Robt	Philadelphia	11–10–1795	5,000	A-2	235	Rough Cr
Morris, Robt	Philadelphia	3–18–1796	70,935	A-2	340	N Fk Licking & Ohio
Morris, Robt	Lynchburg	1–29–1818	6,500	S	206	None
Morris, Turner	Fayette	6–16–1798	400	C	305	Crooked Cr
Morris, Wm Sr	Hanover	2–27–1804	1,260	H	239	None
Morrison, James	Fayette	4– 9–1801	2,000	E	402	Floyds Fk
Morrison, Jas	Fayette	7–22–1801	500	E	405	Br Licking
Morrison, Jas	Fayette	7–22–1801	30,000	F	125	Green R
Morrison, Jas	Fayette	3–24–1801	1,000	G	252	W Fk Bear Cr
Morrison, James	—	1–14–1806	6,845½	K	397	Elkhorn
Morrison, Jas	Fayette	4–19–1806	27,000	K	405	Green R
Morrison, Jas	Lexington	9– 4–1806	1,050	N	182	Muddy R, Cypress & Thompson Crs
Morrison, Jas	Lexington	11–17–1810	Lot	N	404	Frankfort
Morrison, Jas	Kentucky	11– 5–1811	300	O	362	Ohio R
Morrison, Jas	Lexington	5– 6–1814	600	P	521	Ohio R
Morrison, Jas	Lexington	10–25–1808	300	P	533	Ohio R
Morrison, Jas	Kentucky	5–17–1817	Slaves	R	596	None
Morrison, Jas	Lexington	3–28–1818	Slaves	S	133	None
Morrison, Jas	Fayette	3–18–1808	600	S	136	———— R
Morrison, Jas	Fayette	12– 9–1819	600	T	179	None
Morrison, James	—	4– 1–1820	—	T	459	None
Morrison, Jas	Lexington	7– 5–1819	5,000	V	140	Licking
Morrison, Jas	Lexington	9–13–1822	400	V	320	None
Morrison, Jas	Fayette	12–17–1829	75	Z	7	Ky R
Morrison, Jas, heirs	—	6–27–1831	1,500	Z	144	Highland Cr
Morrison, J J	Kentucky	1–31–1824	300	X	7	Tates Cr
Morrison, J J	Kentucky	1–22–1824	100	X	9	Tates Cr
Morrison, J J	Kentucky	1–22–1824	1,000	X	12	Paint Lick
Morrison, J J	Christian	1–22–1824	1,000	X	14	Green R
Morrison, J J	Christian	1–23–1824	400	X	16	None

Grantee	Residence	Deed Date	Acres	Book	Page	Watercourse
Morrison, Robt	Fleming	11– 5–1802	1,000	F	186	Longfall Cr
Morton, Geo W	Fayette	10–31–1825	Lot	Y	25	Lexington
Morton, Geo W	Fayette	8– 3–1830	300	Z	46	N Fk Tradewater
Morton, Geo W	Fayette	1–26–1832	Lots	Z	223	Frankfort
Morton, Geo W	Fayette	4–12–1833	7¾	Z	279	Cane Run
Morton, Geo W	Fayette	3–22–1833	30	Z	280	Cane Run
Morton, Jno H	————	10– 7–1816	————	R	69	None
Morton, Jno H	Fayette	7–19–1816	Slaves	R	72	Red R, Iron Works
Morton, Richard L	Kentucky	3– 1–1828	120	X	389	Waltons Cr
Morton, Thos	Montgomery	2–24–1804	3,000	H	401	Ohio R
Morton, Wm	Fayette	7–30–1796	400	A-2	373	Green R
Morton, Wm	Fayette	4– 9–1801	2,000	E	402	Floyds Fk
Morton, Wm	Fayette	7–22–1801	500	E	405	Br Licking
Morton, Wm	Fayette	7–22–1801	30,000	F	125	Green R
Morton, Wm & Co	Lexington	7–24–1800	2,000	E	90	Green R
Mosby, Benj	Richmond	4– 2–1807	983	L	89	Salt R
Mosby, Benj	Richmond	4– 2–1807	415	L	92	Salt R
Mosby, Benj	Richmond	1–20–1808	194,493	M	124	Various waters
Mosby, Benj	Augusta	10– 2–1808	2,000	M	269	Big Bone Lick
Mosby, Benj	————	11–24–1808	6,000	M	271	Big Bone Lick
Mosby, Benj	Augusta	8–14–1809	800	N	107	Big Barren R
Mosby, Jno G	Henrico	5– 5–1826	————	27	56	Henrico Co & Curles Neck
Mosby, Jno G	Henrico	5–14–1834	1,325	27	64	Virginia
Mosby, Jno G, heirs	Richmond	7– 1–1845	————	28	6	None
Mosby, Littleberry H	Powhatan	5– 5–1826	————	27	56	Henrico Co & Curles Neck
Mosby, Littleberry H	Powhatan	5–14–1834	1,325	27	64	Virginia
Mosby, Mrs Mary W, heirs	Richmond	7– 1–1845	————	28	6	None
Mosby, Wade	Powhatan	3–17–1798	13,833	D	29	None
Mosby, Wade	Powhatan	11–15–1796	————	Q	547	None
Mosby, Wade	Powhatan	11–15–1796	————	Z	430	None
Mosby, Wade	Henrico	5– 5–1826	————	27	56	Henrico Co & Curles Neck
Mosby, Wade	Henrico	5–14–1834	1,325	27	64	Virginia
Mosby, Wm W & Edward C	Henrico	5–14–1834	1,325	27	64	Virginia
Mosby, Wm W & Edward C	Henrico	5– 5–1826	————	27	56	Henrico Co & Curles Neck
Moseley, Jacob	Scott	8– 4–1812	43	O	440	Little N Elkhorn
Moses, Wm S	New York	8————1812	56,000	Z	286	None
Mott, Wm	Philadelphia	6– 7–1797	50,000	B	209	Mill Cr
Mowatt, Jno Jr	New York City	12– 6–1809	10,000	N	134	Ky R
Moylan, Maria, heirs	————	5– 8–1846	60,000	28	87	Kinniconick & Tripletts Cr
Moylan, Jasper, heirs	————	5– 8–1846	60,000	28	87	Kinniconick & Tripletts Cr
Moylan, Col Jno, heirs	————	5– 8–1846	60,000	28	87	Kinniconick & Tripletts Cr
Moylan, Stephen, heirs	————	5– 8–1846	60,000	28	87	Kinniconick & Tripletts Cr
Muhlenberg, Peter	Philadelphia	4–30–1806	1,000	K	410	Crocus Cr
Muhlenberg, Peter	————	9–20–1806	2,000	K	541	None
Mulligan, Wm	Henry	1–10–1824	————	W	170	Little Ky R
Mulligan, Wm	Henry	1–10–1824	100	X	168	Little Ky R
Munford, Richard J	Hart	3– 1–1828	165	X	388	Lynn Camp Cr
Mure, Walker	Westmoreland	7–21–1801	————	F	485	Green R
Murray, Francis	Newton	9–29–1803	54	G	430	None
Murray, Jas G	Frankfort	7–25–1805	Lot	J	388	Frankfort
Murray, Jno, heirs	Baltimore	3–21–1792	600	B-2	449	Bottingers Cr
Murray, Wm	Lincoln	9–20–1785	220	A	68	None
Musgrove, Henry	Bullitt	10–21–1823	116	W	146	None
Muter, Geo	Lincoln	9–13–1785	1½	A	51	None
Muter, Geo	Woodford	6–13–1799	————	D	400	None
Myers, Benj	Lincoln	10–31–1821	2,437½	V	215	Br Big Bone Cr
Myers, Jacob	Lincoln	3– 8–1788	1,000	A	354	S Fk, lh Fk Otter Cr
Myers, Jacob	Lincoln	3–17–1788	40	A	379	Dix R
Myers, Jacob	Lincoln	10–21–1788	116	A	516	Hanging Fk
Myers, Jacob	Lincoln	9–21–1790	Still house	B-2	410	None
Myers, Jacob	Goochland	7–30–1806	2,000	L	12	Big Bone Lick
Myers, Jacob	Lincoln	8–17–1791	1,000	N	180	Br Licking
Myers, Jno	Bullitt	1–21–1814	————	P	547	None
Myers, Lewis	Lincoln	3– 3–1788	1,000	A	360	Fks Bacon Cr
Myers, Lewis	Lincoln	6– 5–1788	556½	A	432	None
Myers, Saml	————	2–15–1799	5,700	D	222	Sandy R
Nagle, Maurice	Mercer	11– 1–1786	Lot	A	247	None
Nagel, Maurice	Mercer	9– 1–1788	400	B-2	435	Bald Hill Cr
Naylor, Nicholas	Green	11–23–1801	34	F	133	Pettits Fk
Naylor, Nicholas	Green	11–23–1801	414	F	134	Pettits Fk

Grantee	Residence	Deed Date	Acres	Book	Page	Watercourse
O'Hara, Kean	Franklin	6– 2–1803	2	G	332	Frankfort
O'Hara, Kean	Franklin	12–26–1834	10¾	Z	473	Elkhorn
O'Hara, Kean	Franklin	3–11–1835	10¾	Z	494	S Elkhorn
Oliver, Benj	Hanover	12–20–1786	1,000	A	253	Red R
Oliver, Benj	Hanover	12–20–1786	1,000	H	356	Red R
Oliver, Jno	Baltimore	1– 6–1812	65,000	O	331	Rolling Fk Green R & Fish Cr
Oliver, Jno	Franklin	10–13–1829	34¾	Y	406	Elkhorn
Oliver, Rice W	Franklin	1–11–1839	11½	27	25	Elkhorn
Oliver, Robt	————	11–20–1833	15,000	Z	372	None
Oldham, Colo Wm, Heirs	Kentucky	7–16–1812	3,000	P	47	None
Omealy, Michael	Baltimore	11– 8–1804	15,000	H	363	Eagle Cr
Omealy, M Trustee	Maryland	9–21–1804	13,500	H	454	Ohio R & Patton Cr
Omealy, Michael	————	11–18–1801	100,000	F	128	Eagle Cr
O'Neal, Wm	Gallatin	5–17–1814	Lots	T	292	Port Williams
Orr, John D	Louisiana	10– 3–1821	15,000	V	184	Lawrence Cr
Orr, Benj G	Westmoreland	2–17–1795	15,000	A-2	118	Rolling Fk
Orr, Benj G	Philadelphia	8–20–1796	82,235	B	149	Big Sandy R
Osborne, Abner	Nottaway	11–15–1803	1,000	J	352	Ohio R
Otkies, Henry	Lincoln	7– 2–1788	500	A	504	Beech Fk
Overton, Dandridge	Shelby	2–21–1817	811	T	135	None
Overton, Jas Jr	Lincoln	11–26–1785	1,000	A	95	Shawnee Run
Overton, Walter	————	12–21–1807	1,250	M	53	Rough Cr
Ousings, Jno C	Baltimore	6–23–1786	500	A	120	Wilsons Cr
Owen, David	Livingston	12–29–1822	2,000	V	431	None
Owens, Thos	Pike	1–28–1829	————	Y	316	None
Owings, Jno Cocky	Baltimore	6–23–1786	1,500	A	124	Sinking Cr
Owings, Jno Cocky	Baltimore	1–24–1787	1,000	A	262	Coopers Run
Owings, Jno Cocky	Baltimore	7–11–1796	3,120	A-2	350	Slate Cr
Owings, Jno Cocky	Baltimore	9–13–1789	583	B-2	80	Main Fk Licking
Owings, Jno Cocky	Baltimore	9–24–1789	400	B-2	81	Foxes Run
Owings, Jno Cocky	Baltimore	12–23–1789	2,000	B-2	109	Flat Lick Cr
Owings, Jno Cocky	Baltimore	5–24–1791	5,434	B-2	318	Big Slate Cr
Owings, Jno Cocky	Mercer	4–23–1792	Lot	B-2	497	Lexington
Owings, Jno Cocky	Baltimore	9–20–1801	500	F	144	Stewarts Cr &——R
Owings, Jno Cocky	Maryland	4–13–1809	1,000	N	139	M Elkhorn
Owings, Langhome & Co	Merchants	2–22–1812	Mill	O	394	Main Licking
Owings, Mary N	Bath	5– 7–1835	2,787½	Z	506	Licking
Owings, Thos D	Bath	2–12–1811	45,000	N	500	Various waters
Owings, Thos D	Bath	2– 4–1819	500	S	431	Roes Run
Owings, Thos D	Bath	2– 4–1819	2,500	S	433	Bullskin Cr
Owings, Thos D	Bath	11–22–1833	400	27	304	Slate Cr
Owsley, Thos	Madison	2–12–1792	223	B-2	444	Sugar Cr
Paca, Francis	Fayette	4–12–1834	Lot	Z	420	Lexington
Page, Chas C	King William	10– 2–1812	1,000	P	200	Cumberland R
Page, Chas C & Jno	King William	3————1812	2,419½	O	493	Tennessee R
Page, Jno	Hanover	10– 2–1812	1,000	P	200	Cumberland R
Page, Matthew	Frederick	12– 2–1797	2,766⅔	C	291	Ohio R
Page, Matthew	Frederick	11–29–1799	3,000	E	123	Paint Lick & Sugar Crs
Page, Matthew	Frederick	11–29–1799	2,766⅔	E	126	Ohio R
Page, Thos S	Franklin	7–16–1834	1,248	Z	457	Allen Co
Page, Thos S	Franklin	3–26–1839	100	27	132	Ky R
Page, Thos S	Franklin	4–25–1839	Lots	27	191	Frankfort
Page, Thos S	Franklin	5–24–1841	2	27	193	Frankfort
Page, Thos S, Atty	————	5–29–1834	32,000	Z	442	None
Palmer, Legrand	Hardin	6–11–1818	242	S	151	Bacon Cr
Palmer, Philip	Mason	11–22–1843	10,000	27	369	None
Parent, Jno	Franklin	4–18–1806	100	K	290	N Fk Bensons Cr
Parham, Joseph & Wife	Philadelphia	5–15–1813	Lots	P	268	Philadelphia
Parker, Jno	Fayette	2–22–1825	91	X	99	Shannons Run
Parker, Jno	————	10–20–1819	185	X	128	Glenns Cr
Parker, Jno	Fayette	7– 1–1828	7	Y	375	Shannons Run
Parker, Jno & Robert	Fayette	7–20–1798	400	D	131	Ky R
Prrker, Joseph	Philadelphia	12–13–1798	7,500	D	292	Bank Lick Cr
Parker, Mary	Fayette	7– 7–1829	————	Y	435	Ohio R
Parker, Robt	————	10–20–1819	186	X	128	Glenns Cr
Parker, Stafford H	Caroine	3–25–1821	————	V	2	None
Parrish, Humphrey	Goochland	9–24–1811	385	O	324	None
Paschall, Thos	Philadelphia	3–10–1789	13,666⅔	D	195	N Fk 3 Fks Ky R
Pattie, Jno	Mercer	6– 4–1802	241	F	425	None
Pattie, Jno	Franklin	6–30–1807	Negro	L	116	None
Pattie, Jno	Franklin	6–30–1807	Negro	L	118	None
Pattie, Jno	Franklin	3–19–1833	Lot	Z	294	Frankfort
Patterson, Chas	Franklin	5–27–1799	477	D	457	Russell Cr
Patterson, Jno & Jas	————	3–13–1816	202⅔	R	24	Ohio R
Patterson, Mary	————	3–14——	————	27	129	N Elkhorn
Patterson, Peter	Frankfort	3– 5–1818	1,000	S	62	Hingston Fk
Patterson, Peter	Frankfort	1–12–1822	————	V	517	Drennons Lick Cr

Grantee	Residence	Deed Date	Acres	Book	Page	Watercourse
Patterson, Robt	Franklin	5–13–1797	995	B	268	Big Barren R
Patterson, Robt	Fayette	8–19–1803	500	H	489	Glenns Cr
Patterson, Robt, heirs	Franklin	11–10–1805	5,000	K	219	Eagle Cr
Patterson, Samuel	Fayette	11–30–1831	4	Z	167	Cane Run
Patton, Robt	Fredericksburg	10– 1–1795	36,000	A-2	290	Richland Cr
Patton, Robt	Fredericksburg	10– 1–1795	9,302	A-2	293	Lynn Camp & Robertson Cr
Patton, Robt	Fredericksburg	10– 1–1795	10,240	A-2	297	Richland Cr & Laurel R
Patton, Robt	Fredericksburg	5–17–1796	——	A-2	400	Floyds Fk Rock-castle, N Fk Elk-horn, Miller Cr
Patton, Robt	Fredericksburg	4– 3–1796	1,200	A-2	375	Little Ky R
Patton, Robt	Fredericksburg	4– 3–1796	800	A-2	377	Little Ky
Patton, Robt	Fredericksburg	5– 5–1796	2,000	A-2	694	W Fk Glenns Cr
Patton, Robt	Fredericksburg	5–17–1796	——	D	102	Floyds Fk, Sandy R, Rockcastle & Green R
Patton, Robt	Fredericksburg	6– 2–1796	1,000	E	322	Cabin Cr
Patton, Robt	Spotsylvania	4– 8–1799	1,000	E	342	Tradewater
Patton, Robt	Fredericksburg	5– 4–1805	3,720	J	218	Skaggs & Big Bone Lick
Patton, Robt Jr & Jno M	Fredericksburg	12–27–1822	21,787½	V	463	Cabin Cr & Ky R
Patton, Robt Jr & Jno M	Fredericksburg	4–18–1812	20,006⅔	V	328	Cabin & Glenns Cr
Patrick, Jno	Augusta	2–10–1801	1,500	G	90	Fks Elkhorn Ky R & Lawrence Cr
Paul, Jno	Rockbridge	6–26–1823	——	W	127	Shoemakers Cr
Paxton, Joseph	Lincoln	12–23–1828	640	X	494	Benson Cr
Payne, Daniel Mc	Fayette	3– 2–1824	300	W	278	Little Fk Eagle Cr
Payne, Daniel Mc	——	9– 4–1824	666⅔	W	361	Tradewater
Payne, Daniel Mc	Davies	2–12–1829	——	Y	325	Ohio R
Payne, Edward C	Fayette	9–22–1824	Lots	W	379	Lexington
Payne, Edward C	Fayette	10– 1–1828	3,000	X	496	Harrods Cr
Payne, Edward C & Daniel M	Fayette	7–18–1828	5,000	X	418	Harrods Cr
Payne, Jas B	Davies	2–12–1829	382	Y	325	Fk Springer Cr
Payne, Jas B	Fayette	7–13–1829	349	Y	367	Fks Br
Payne, Jno	Scott	5–23–1805	3,470	K	105	2 Mi Cr & Stoners Fk, Green & Hunt-ing Cr & Flatt Cr
Payne, Jno	Scott	11–17–1821	450	V	309	Wren
Payne, Jno Jr	Scott	5– 2–1823	8,000	W	21	Woolpers Cr
Payne, Jno & Wife	——	6—— 1818	285	U	522	Ohio R
Payne, Jno B	Daviess	2–12–1829	349	Y	325	Rocky Br
Payne, J M & J B	Kentucky	11– 3–1813	1,000	P	400	Ohio R & Doe Run
Payne, Thos J	Daviess	2–12–1829	349	Y	325	—— Br
Payton, Joseph	Woodford	7– 8–1817	48	S	170	Gilberts Cr
Peak, Presley & Spencer	Scott	10–14–1811	110	O	201	Ohio R
Pearce, Ann	Jefferson	12– 1–1831	1,000	Z	253	Green R
Pearce, Jas A & Wife	Louisville	10– 2–1817	1,000	V	70	Green R
Peast, Francis	Virginia	4–28–1808	1,034	M	26	None
Peast, LeRoy G	Woodford	4– 1–1801	811	E	351	Green R
Peast, LeRoy G	Virginia	4–28–1808	864	M	26	None
Peast, Sarah G	Virginia	4–28–1808	936	M	26	None
Peck, Jno	Middlesex	9– 2–1803	3,593½	P	30	Ohio R
Peck, Jno	Boston	7–20–1811	16,513	R	96	Slate, Millers, Eagle, & Ohio R
Peck, Jno	Lexington	12– 8–1824	42,629	X	18	Green R
Peck, Jno	Fayette	2–11–1833	Lots	Z	455	Frankfort
Peck, Jno & Wife	——	9–29–1834	6,098½	Z	499	Licking
Peck, Jno	——	10–12–1933	2,106½	Z	360	Hardin Co
Peck, Jno & Eliza	Fayette	4–14–1842	2,109	27	327	M & Valley Cr
Pemberton, Jno	Franklin	2–14–1804	82	J	54	M Elkhorn
Pemberton, Thos	Goochland	5–10–1800	4,000	E	395	Deer Cr
Pendleton, Edmund	Culpepper	8–27–1805	500	K	259	Little Sandy
Pendleton, Edmund	Culpepper	8–27–1805	880	K	271	6 Mi of Salt Works
Pendleton, Edmund	Culpepper	8–27–1805	500	K	274	Little Sandy
Pendleton, Jno T	——	2– 9–1819	Lots	S	464	Frankfort
Pendleton, Jno T	Franklin	3– 2–1820	Lots	T	394	Frankfort
Pendleton, Wm G	Richmond	5–14–1834	1,325	27	64	Virginia
Penn, Geo	Franklin	11–16–1833	190	Z	371	Elkhorn
Pennebaker, Wm	——	9–11–1804	2,158	H	320	Ohio R
Pennell, Joseph	Virginia	3– 1–1810	1,366¾	O	1	None
Pepper, Elijah	Woodford	10– 8–1824	185	X	49	N Fk Glenns Cr
Pepper, Jesse	Mason	12–12–1806	3,040	K	510	None
Perciful, Jas	——	1–14–1828	12,500	X	350	Poplar Camp
Perciful, Samuel	Grayson	2–21–1819	2,395	S	473	Nolin & M Cr
Perciful, Samuel	——	2– 5–1814	2,395	P	528	M Cr

Grantee	Residence	Deed Date	Acres	Book	Page	Watercourse
Perkins, Benj	Garrard	9–12–1799	563	D	506	Sandy Cr
Perkins, Benj	Mercer	9–12–1799	500	D	514	Reeds Cr
Perkins, Benj	Mercer	1– 6–1797	500	H	561	Pattingers Cr
Perkins, Benj	Mercer	1– 6–1797	500	C	39	Pattingers Cr
Perkins, Geo	Goochland	12–29–1807	1,400	Z	267	Hardins & Big Bone Cr
Perkins, Joseph	Louisa	10–16–1797	6,000	B	247	Big Bone Lick
Perkins, Joseph	Louisa	11– 1–1799	400	E	381	Hardins Cr
Perkins, Joseph Jr	Amhurst	12–29–1807	1,400	Z	267	Hardins & Big Bone Cr
Perkins, Robt	Louisa	12–29–1807	1,400	Z	267	Hardins & Big Bone Cr
Perkins, Thos	Lincoln	9– 9–1785	3	A	35	None
Perry, Jno	Jessamine	7–19–1842	320	27	296	Hickman & Graves Crs
Perry, Randolph	Shelby	3–29–1810	Lot	N	219	Frankfort
Perry, Roderick	Woodford	10– 5–1804	207	J	179	N Fk Glenns Cr
Perry, Rederick & Sanford	Woodford	9– 2–1819	10	T	297	Glenns Cr
Pershouse	———	3– 1–1827	Lot	Y	273	Mt Sterling
Pershouse, Jno	———	3– 1–1827	600	Y	275	Owingsville Road
Peter, Robt Jr	Georgetown	3–24–1806	12,000	K	381	Ohio R
Peters, Belvard J	Bath	9–29–1834	6,098¾	Z	498	Licking
Pettit, Rodham	Franklin	6– 9–1823	136	W	337	Salt R
Petty, Rodman	Franklin	11–30–1819	78½	T	172	Salt R
Pew, Gilbert	———	6–14–1804	2	H	270	None
Peyton, Jno	Winchester	4–18–1801	400	F	192	Quicks Run
Pfister, Mary Von P	New York	8–16–1842	9,188	27	308	Chopkins Fk
Phelpo, Wm J	Franklin	11–18–1833	1,000	Z	364	Richland & Robertson Cr
Phillips, Isaac	Tennessee	5–31–1791	200	B-2	284	Little Clifty Cr
Phillips, Jno	Philadelphia	9– 9–1794	2,000	A-2	456	Highland & Muddy Crs
Phillips, Jno	Philadelphia	9–10–1794	2,000	A-2	460	Muddy R
Phillips, Jno	Philadelphia	9– 9–1794	2,000	A-2	464	Cypress Cr
Phillips, Jno	Philadelphia	9– 9–1794	2,000	A-2	468	Muddy R
Phillips, Jno	Philadelphia	9– 9–1794	768¾	A-2	472	Walnut Bottom & Goose Cr
Phillips, Jno	Baltimore	9–18–1798	1,000	D	4	Salt R
Phillips, Jno	Philadelphia	3– 1–1787	19,000	G	6	Green R & Bacon Cr
Phillips, Jno	Philadelphia	8–15–1794	22,943¾	G	225	M Fk Licking
Phillips, Jno	Philadelphia	12–17–1788	8,000	G	231	None
Phillips, Jno	Philadelphia	8–15–1794	1,000	G	238	Hingston Fk
Phillips, Jno	Philadelphia	11–20–1794	4,924	G	258	Rough Cr
Phillips, Jno	Philadelphia	11–19–1796	31,520	H	125	Big Sandy R
Phillips, Jno	Philadelphia	2–19–1794	4,400	K	463	Beech Fk
Phillibert, McLouis	Paris France	11–22–1819	910,954	U	90	N Fk Ky & Big Sandy R
Phillips, Philip, Heirs	Tennessee	3– 3–1819	35,940	V	112	Welches Bear Little Clifty & Dog Cr
Phillips, Ralph	New Jersey	7–13–1803	3,000	G	395	Salt R
Phillips, Ralph	New Jersey	12–27–1804	200	H	509	Buck Cr
Phillips, Ralph	Henderson	3–29–1814	360	P	385	Salt R
Phillips, Ralph	Henderson	3–29–1814	760	P	387	Salt R
Phillips, Ralph	New Jersey	7–31–1819	Hogs	T	65	Elkhorn Cr
Phillips, Ralph	New Jersey	10– 3–1819	Mill	T	246	Fks Elkhorn
Phillips, Ralph	Hunterdon	10–28–1820	16,380	U	155	Salt R
Phillips, Ralph	Hunterdon	6– 4–182–	213	U	439	Beech Cr
Phillips, Wm	Philadelphia	6–26–1809	1,000	P	311	Licking
Phillips, Wm	Philadelphia	3– 9–1825	4,924	X	142	None
Pickett, Chas G & Robt	Virginia	3– 6–1802	23,875	G	1	Eagle Cr
Pickett, Geo	Richmond	1– 5–1797	1,000	A-2	669	Tradewater
Pickett, Geo	Richmond	7– 3–1797	4,000	B	265	Goose Cr
Pickett, Geo	Henrico	8–25–1796	———	B	340	Ohio & Cypress Cr
Pickett, Geo	Richmond	1–27–1798	7,333⅓	D	229	Highland Cr
Pickett, Geo	Richmond	7–12–1799	2,000	E	47	E Fk Crocus Cr
Pickett, Geo	Richmond	2–27–1802	9,446⅔	F	373	Sinking Fk Little R
Pickett, Geo	Richmond	3–16–1809	5,500	M	369	Cypress Cr
Pickett, Geo	Richmond	12–20–1808	1,400	M	388	Little Miami & Scioto R
Pickett, Geo	Richmond	4–19–1809	500	M	426	Scioto & Miami R
Pickett, Geo	Richmond	2–28–1811	1,000	O	126	Br Green R
Pickering, Jno Jr	Boston	11–28–1838	6,633	27	164	Little Barren R Glovers & Deer Cr
Pickering, Octavius	Boston	5–30–1833	6,633	Z	421	Little Barren R & Glovers Cr
Pickering, Octavius	———	8–21–1831	1,000	Z	451	Little Barren R
Pickering, Octavius	———	8–21–1834	1,533	Z	452	Little Barren R
Pickering, Octavius	———	8–21–1834	1,000	Z	453	Glovers Cr
Pickering, Octavius	Boston	11–13–1838	6,633	27	166	Little Barren R Glovers & Deer Cr

Grantee	Residence	Deed Date	Acres	Book	Page	Watercourse
Pickering, Octavius	———	3-31-1842	1,100	27	334	None
Pickering, Timothy	———	8-21-1834	1,000	Z	453	Glovers Cr
Pickering, Timothy	———	8-21-1834	1,533	Z	452	Little Barren R
Pickering, Timothy heirs	———	8-21-1834	1,000	Z	451	Little Barren R
Picquet, Claude	Paris	12- 6-1809	10,781	N	321	N Fk Ky R
Pierson, Thornton P	Franklin	3-25-1845	Lot	28	47	Frankfort
Pierson, Thornton P	Franklin	9-11-1846	Lot	28	106	Frankfort
Pike, Henry	Spencer	2- 9-1831	136½	Z	99	Salt R
Pindell, Richard Trustee	Fayette	9-13-1841	Slaves	27	229	None
Pinkerton, Lewis L	———	6-17-1845	Lot	28	845	Midway
Pitman, Jos & Wife	———	12- 4-1815	3,353¾	Q	369	None
Pitman, Wm	Adair	3-22-1833	250	Z	359	Br Eagle Cr
Pitman, Williamson	Adair	11-10-1830	275	Z	42	Pendleton Co
Pittinger, Abraham	Shelby	5-26-1815	181	Q	122	Elk Cr
Platt, Nathaniel & Wife	———	11-19-1817	Lot	S	39	Lexington
Pleasant, Isreal & Jno P	Baltimore	6- 6-1805	29,376	L	180	Green R mouth Nolinn
Pleasant, Jas Jr & Arch	Goochland	5- 7-1798	2,827½	D	386	Licking
Pleasant, Jno P	Baltimore	8- 6-1812	1,050	P	162	Fk Blackfords Cr
Pleasant, Jno P	Baltimore	5-17-1797	2,000	K	339	Cumberland R
Pleasant, Thos	Goochland	3-15-1804	2,827½	J	143	Licking
Pleasant, Thos, Exec	Goochland	5- 7-1798	2,827½	D	386	Licking
Plerurger, Bertram	New York City	8-24-1805	56,000	L	136	None
Plique, G	Island St Domingo	8- 8-1787	10,000	H	382	S Fk Sandy R
Plique, G	Philadelphia	9-14-1784	1,000	H	386	None
Plique, G	Philadelphia	9-10-1784	2,000	H	391	None
Plummer, Mary	Port Williams	7-25-1818	Lot	S	362	Port Williams
Poage, Robt	Mason	9-16-1796	250	A-2	431	Shawnee & Ky R
Pogue, Edwin P, heirs	Mason	12-19-1844	19¾	27	445	Mason Co
Pogue, Robt	Mason	11-14-1805	2,000	J	402	Ohio R
Pogue, Robt	———	7-24-1806	213,866	K	363	Br Sandy R
Poindexter, James	Louisa	4-30-1801	259	F	65	Green R
Poindexter, Jno Jr	Louisa	2- 4-1801	259	F	62	Green R
Poindexter, Peter	Scott	———1824	56	X	38	M Elkhorn
Pollard, Elizabeth B, heirs	———	3-16-1814	Slaves	R	20	None
Pollard, Joseph Jr	Jefferson	3-18-1814	1,000	P	441	Ohio R & Doe Run
Pollard, Robt	Richmond	3-23-1796	2,000	A-2	476	Muddy R
Pollard, Robt	Richmond	3-23-1796	2,000	A-2	479	Cypress Cr
Pollard, Robt	Richmond	3-23-1796	2,000	A-2	483	Muddy R
Pollard, Robt	Richmond	3-23-1796	2,000	A-2	486	Highland Cr & Muddy R
Pollard, Robt	Richmond	3-23-1796	3,166⅔	A-2	489	Walnut Bottom & Grove Cr
Pollard, Robt	Richmond	5-19-1797	1,000	B	125	——— R
Pollard, Robt	Richmond	7- 3-1797	4,000	B	265	Goose Cr
Pollard, Robt	Richmond	9-20-1796	1,000	C	207	Ohio R
Pollard, Robt	Richmond	10-11-1798	1,000	D	38	Harlins Cr
Pollard, Robt	Richmond	12-26-1797	24,000	D	70	Chaplins Fk
Pollard, Robt	Richmond	10-23-1797	2,000	D	363	Ohio R
Pollard, Robt	Richmond	7-12-1799	2,000	E	47	E Fk Crocus Cr
Pollard, Robt	Richmond	2-27-1802	———	F	371	Goose Cr
Pollard, Robt	Richmond	3-16-1809	6,453⅔	M	375	Muddy R & Highland Cr
Pollard, Robt	Richmond	3-16-1809	1,000	M	380	W Fk Sciota R
Pollard, Robt	Richmond	4-15-1809	732	M	416	None
Pollard, Robt	Richmond	7-13-1811	2,000	O	443	Red R
Pollard, Robt	———	1- 1-1814	3,000	P	330	Consolas Cr
Pollard, Robt	Virginia	10-22-1827	50,050	X	312	Cumberland & Sandy R Tygerts Cr
Pollard, Thos	Todd	7-15-1825	407	X	199	Renfrows Pond & Spring Cr
Pollock, Jno	Fayette	4- 8-1818	80	S	254	None
Pope, Henry	Lincoln	6-19-1786	313	A	292	Hanging Fk
Pope, Henry	Lincoln	12-19-1787	450	A	337	State Cr
Pope, Geo	Lincoln	6-19-1786	237	A	294	Hanging Fk
Pope, Geo Sr	Lincoln	12-19-1787	250	A	335	State Cr
Pope, Wm	Jefferson	12-28-1813	Lot	P	355	Louisville
Porter, Jno P	Woodford	10-30-1830	21⅓	Z	32	S Elkhorn
Porter, Jno P	Woodford	11- 3-1830	21⅓	Z	33	S Elkhorn
Porter, Letitia P	Fayette	10- 9-1840	2,597	27	155	E Fk Little Miami R
Porter, Wm	Franklin	12-19-1797	200	B	297	Drennons Lick Cr
Porter, Wm	Franklin	12-12-1816	Lot	R	157	Covington
Porter, Wm	———	4- 8-1818	Lot	S	96	Frankfort
Porter, Wm Sr	Franklin	9-18-1818	Lot	S	370	Port Williams
Porter, Wm Jr & Wm Sr	Franklin	4-15-1822	146	V	218	None
Posey, Thos	Franklin	11- 8-1800	350	E	240	Elkhorn

Grantee	Residence	Deed Date	Acres	Book	Page	Watercourse
Posey, Thomas	Franklin	1–13–1802	28,000	F	408	Green R
Posey, Thos	Spotsylvania	12–15–1797	1,286	F	410	None
Posey, Thos	Spotsylvania	12–16–1797	800	F	412	N Fk Tradewater
Posey, Genl Thos	——	11– 2–1802	2,250	G	134	None
Postlethwait, Saml & Co	Lexington	7–24–1800	2,000	E	90	Green R
Pottinger, Saml Jr	Nelson	6– 2–1821	——	V	288	Rolling Fk & Ohio
Powell, Lewis	Lowdonn	4– 6–1791	2,054	B-2	338	Floyds Fk & Simpson Cr
Poyles, Geo W	Bullitt	6– 7–1843	1,000	27	348	Ballard Cr
Prather, Thos	——	9–22–1804	535	H	367	Ohio R
Prentis, James	Petersburg	6–23–1821	——	V	20	Ky R
Prentis, James	Petersburg	6–23–1821	——	V	45	None
Prentis, Wm	Washington City	9–11–1805	5,415½	J	267	Cedar Cr
Prentis, Wm	Petersburg	4–13–1818	2,000	T	88	Ohio R
Prentis, Wm	Petersburg	8– 1–1818	——	T	426	None
Preston, Jno	Montgomery	4–10–1797	5,500	A-2	674	Harrods Cr
Preston, Jno & Wife	——	2–25–1800	1,000	E	191	Skaggs Cr
Preston, Letitia	Fayette	4–12–1834	Lot	Z	420	Lexington
Preston, Robt	——	2–24–1816	200	Q	356	Bays Fk
Preston, Wm	Jefferson	4–10–1819	1,000	S	512	Green R
Prewitt, Jos W	Franklin	7–23–1819	100	U	80	None
Prewit, Joseph	——	5–23–1814	114	P	475	Fks Wolf Run
Price, Benj & Wife	London	3– 2–1814	Lots	P	404	Frankfort
Price, Christopher M	St. Louis	8– 3–1826	——	Y	215	None
Price, Henry	Culpepper	3–21–1801	500	E	367	N E Fk Clover Cr
Price, Jno	Franklin	11–22–1805	55	K	132	Fks Elkhorn
Price, Jno	Franklin	3– 6–1806	2,000	K	226	N & S Fk Elkhorn
Price, Jno	Franklin	9–10–1805	63	K	237	Fks Elkhorn
Price, Jno Trustee	Williamsburg	4–28–1800	Lots	E	133	Bardstown
Price, Jno R	Fayette	2– 2–1819	Slaves	T	100	None
Price, Saml	Fayette	7–20–1798	Lots	D	135	Russellville
Price, Saml	Fayette	7–20–1798	550	D	136	None
Price, Wm	Richmond	4–15–1796	600	A-2	394	Russell Cr
Price, Wm	Richmond	3– 8–1796	1,878	A-2	396	None
Price, Wm	Richmond	4–12–1797	4,000	B	281	Deer Cr
Price, Wm	Jefferson	3–24–1790	100	B-2	240	Beaver Cr
Price, Wm	Richmond	9– 5–1804	333	H	351	Green R
Price, Wm	——	7–11–1807	2,000	L	111	Ohio R
Price, Wm	Richmond	11– 2–1807	2,666⅔	M	74	Goose & Highland Crs
Pringle, Jas	——	2–12–1823	37	W	71	None
Pringle, Jas	——	2–12–1823	37	W	73	None
Pulliam, Chas S	Hardin	1–27–1813	272	P	67	None
Pullman, Moody	Woodford	5–22–1810	Negro	N	235	None
Purny, Jno Sr	Frankfort	4–12–1820	Lots	T	389	Frankfort
Purviance, Henry	——	11–16–1803	114,911	H	205	Ohio & Salt Rs
Purviance, Henry	Kentucky	11–17–1803	113,911	H	232	Ohio R & Elk R
Purviance, Henry	Lexington	6–23–1810	5,753	N	220	Ohio R
Purviance, Robt	——	10–10–1802	350	G	136	Elkhorn Cr
Purviance, Saml & Robt	Baltimore	1–25–1787	1,000	A	257	Mill Cr
Purviance, Saml & Robt	Baltimore	9–27–1786	1,500	A	314	Pleasant Run
Purviance, Saml & Robt	Baltimore	9–27–1786	4,000	A	317	Licking
Quarles, Tunstal	Woodford	5– 9–1803	1,000	G	411	Pitman Cr
Quarrier, Alexander	Richmond	6– 9–1795	7,200	A-2	265	Stinking Cr
Quarrier, Alexander	Richmond	11– 5–1795	11,000	A-2	274	None
Quarrier, Alexander	Richmond	11–19–1795	1,200	A-2	279	Bet Junctions & N Fk Licking
Quinn, Benj	Scott	11– 8–1799	140	D	455	Tates Cr
Quinn, Jno J	Franklin	6——1845	Lot	27	478	Frankfort
Quisenberry, Jno	Orange	12–22–1788	300	A	495	Howards Cr
Quisenberry, Jno	Clark	9– 6–1808	——	M	154	Longs Big Spring
Radford, Wm	Richmond	6–27–1796	1,420	A-2	496	Skeggs Cr
Radford, Wm	Richmond	12–10–1797	700	B	343	Big Barren R
Radford, Wm	Richmond	3–13–1797	1,000	C	119	None
Radford, Wm	Richmond	5–22–1799	1,200	D	344	Big Barren R
Radford, Wm	Richmond	2–13–1799	1,000	D	534	Ohio R
Radford, Wm	Richmond	1–14–1800	700	E	66	Big Barren R
Railey, Randolph	Woodford	8–20–1827	3,250	X	280	Grassy Cr
Railey, Randolph Jr	Woodford	6–18–1823	5,097⅜	W	66	Bullitts Lick
Railey, Randolph Jr	Woodford	11–22–1825	1,180	Y	224	Licking & Bank Lick
Rainsberry, Jno	Frederick	10–20–1790	1,000	B-2	268	Salt R
Ralston, Robt	Philadelphia	4– 1–1790	——	Q	46	None
Ramsay, Jno	New York	7–30–1798	260,178	R	225	Ohio R
Ramsay, Jno, heirs	New York	11– 3–1816	21,000	S	444	Chaplins Fk
Ramsey, Elizabeth	New York	8–16–1842	9,188	27	308	Chaplins Fk
Ramsey, Saml G & Wife	Knox	5–10–1805	668	J	30	Dunbars Run

Grantee	Residence	Deed Date	Acres	Book	Page	Watercourse
Ramy, Henry	————	1-23-1828	42,283	X	366	None
Ranch, Christopher	Philadelphia	12-28-1787	1,000	O	353	None
Randolph, Chas C & Wife	Stafford	12-26-1825	1,200	Y	94	Pattons Cr
Randolph, Thos	————	8- 8-1797	263	C	129	Beech Fk
Rankin, Adam	Mercer	1-13-1791	Lot	B-2	254	Danville
Rankin, Adam	————	11- 8-1798	108	D	68	None
Rankin, Adam	————	2-17-1799	408	D	133	Ohio & Green R
Rankin, Adam	Lexington	10-31-1816	920	V	259	Indian Cr
Rapier, Richard J	————	10- 7-1816	500	R	303	Beech Fk
Raquet, Anna	Philadelphia	10-24-1821	28,270	V	448	Salt & N Fk Ky R
Raquet, Claudius Paul	Philadelphia	5-29-1789	8,270	V	451	Salt R
Raquet, Claudius P	Philadelphia	5- 3-1786	56,000	Z	283	None
Raquet, Paul, heirs	————	7-31-1818	————	S	226	None
Ratliff, Benj	Bourbon	3-16-1791	1,000	B-2	348	M Fk Stoners Fk
Ratliff, Francis	Kentucky	6- 8-1805	Lot	J	173	Frankfort
Ratcliff, Francis	Franklin	————1804	Lot	N	270	Frankfort
Rawl, Wm, Trustee	Philadelphia	11-21-1821	5,400	V	127	None
Ray, James	Essex	7- 1-1813	1,000	P	157	Cabin Cr
Ray, Jno	Illinois	1-28-1831	60	Z	77	Salt R
Ray, Nicholas	Washington	11-23-1811	737	O	204	Rolling Fk
Rayman, Jno	Bullitt	8- 1-1828	————	X	421	Salt R
Read, Jno	Philadelphia	4- 1-1805	67,647	Y	204	Floyds Fk & Ky R
Reader, Martha	————	12- 8-1829	98½	Z	255	Cane Run
Reading, Geo	Bourbon	11-29-1791	549	B-2	483	S Fk Big Benson Cr
Reading, Geo	Harrison	1-23-1805	181½	K	221	None
Reading, Geo	Harrison	2- 9-1809	215	M	337	S Fk Big Benson Cr
Reading, Geo Jr	Bourbon	11-29-1791	203	B-2	481	Rolling Fk
Reading, Geo Jr	Bourbon	11-29-1791	814	B-2	486	S Fk Big Benson Cr
Reading, Geo Jr	Harrison	7-20-1798	759	D	112	None
Reading, Jno M	Franklin	10-13-1804	383	J	67	S Fk Big Benson Cr
Reed, Amos	Monongolia	12- 7-1814	————	S	278	None
Reed, Andrew	Rockridge	11-30-1791	200	B-2	507	Green R
Reed, Jacob	————	10-26-1815	259	Q	462	None
Reed, Jno	Bourbon	2-16-1791	1,000	B-2	348	M Fk Stoners Fk
Reed, Jno	Madison	10-12-1791	300	B-2	387	Harts Fk
Reed, Nathaniel	————	5-12-1787	2,000	Q	239	Gesses Cr
Reed, Wm	Philadelphia	11-20-1819	10,000	T	193	Salt R
Reese, Jacob	Philadelphia	7-16-1808	7,870	M	263	Elkhorn
Reese, Wm B & Wife	Knoxville	1- 6-1844	167	27	421	Ohio R & Mill Cr
Reeston, Thos	Philadelphia	11-19-1796	31,520	H	125	Big Sandy R
Reinholdt, Geo	Philadelphia	10-16-1800	3,000	H	301	None
Reinholdt, Geo	Philadelphia	12-19-1798	3,000	H	310	None
Reinholdt, Geo	Philadelphia	11-24-1803	22,000	H	314	None
Reinicker, Geo	Baltimore	10-10-1843	2,000	27	366	Fayette Co
Renkin, Jas	Washington	11- 7-1807	————	L	388	Salt R
Renner, Daniel	Georgetown	3-11-1814	1,100	P	541	Big Caney Cr
Renney, Chesley	Stanton	5-31-1808	5,250	N	67	Little Bullskin Cr
Resspass, Thos	Fayette	12-12-1796	1,000	B	261	———— Cr
Resspass, Thos	Fayette	10-13-1803	600	H	92	Gasper R
Reynolds, Andrew	Richmond	5-11-1795	8,123	A-2	328	S Fk Little Barren & Skeggs Crs
Reynolds, Edward	Hardin	1-27-1813	400	P	72	None
Reynolds, Francis	Franklin	10-27-1828	Lot	Y	405	Frankfort
Reynolds, Jedediah	St Louis	10-24-1843	————	27	459	Clay Co
Reynolds, Wm	Henrico	11-27-1792	1,250	A-2	311	Rolling Fk
Reynolds, Wm	Henrico	11-27-1792	1,437½	A-2	313	Chaplins Fk
Rhea, Jno	Tennessee	1-29-1803	5,500	G	413	Powell R
Rice, Benj	Campbell	10- 3-1802	260	G	161	Bank Lick Cr
Rice, Edmund Jr & Jas	Jefferson	3-21-1817	762½	R	357	Cumberland R
Rice, Jno	————	8-12-1816	————	R	161	None
Rice, Saml	Hardin	7-17-1799	400	D	358	Long Br
Richard, Isaac	Woodford	3-22-1820	199½	T	369	None
Richard, Jno	————	8-23-1819	Lots	U	269	Richmond, Va
Richard, Jno	Richmond	6-21-1823	40,000	W	402	None
Richards, Edward & Wife	Norfolk	12-20-1816	2,500	R	599	Goose Cr
Richards, Geo B	Bath	10- 3-1826	1,000	Y	317	Deer Cr
Richards, Wm	Culpepper	5- 1-1803	1,765	G	285	Otter Cr
Richards, Wm	Stafford	5- 2-1808	1,000	M	41	Deer Cr
Richardson, Jas	Franklin	11- 5-1841	Lot	27	269	Frankfort
Richardson, Jno C	Fayette	5-31-1811	258½	O	116	N Fk Elkhorn
Richardson, Jno D	Frankfort	9- 8-1803	Lot	H	99	Frankfort
Richardson, Robt D	Newport	3- 4-1816	2,600	Q	444	Lick Cr & Beech Fk
Richardson, Wm H	Fayette	9-29-1822	1,350	V	378	Canoe Cr & Little Ky R
Richeson, Francis W	King William	10- 8-1804	————	O	148	None
Richeson, Jno B	Kentucky	11-15-1809	4,800	N	117	None
Richeson, Jno B	King William	8-20-1811	————	O	150	None
Richeson, Jno B	King William	10-11-1811	3,600	O	153	Clover Lick & Ohio R

Grantee	Residence	Deed Date	Acres	Book	Page	Watercourse
Ricketts, Caleb H	Fairfax	3–17–1806	4,110⅔	K	347	Lynn Camp & Wolf Cr
Ricketts, Caleb H	Fairfax	3–17–1806	2,110⅔	K	483	Main Br Wolf Cr
Ricketts, Jno T	Fairfax	5– 2–1797	4,110⅔	B	23	Br Green R
Ricketts, Jno T	Alexandria	4– 5–1798	2,055	B	347	Main Fk W Fk Wolf Cr
Ricketts, Jno Thos	Alexandria	5–19–1797	4,110	B	8	Lynn Camp Cr
Rickord, Michael	Fanquier	8–11–1826	———	Y	254	None
Riddle, Jas	Campbell	10–24–1821	7,000	V	121	Rough Cr
Riddle, Joseph	Alexandria	1– 3–1809	2,000	N	480	Bays Cr
Riddle, Wm	Scott	8–28–1818	2,118	S	221	Eagle Cr
Ridge, Wm S	Hamilton	6–11–1832	23	Z	224	S Elkhorn
Ridgeley, Chas	Baltimore	6–23–1786	800	A	147	Small Br
Ridgeley, Frederick	Fayette	4– 9–1801	2,000	E	402	Floyds Fk
Ridgeley, Frederick	Fayette	7–22–1801	500	E	405	Br Licking
Ridgeley, Frederick	Fayette	7–22–1801	30,000	F	125	Green R
Ridgeley, Frederick	Lexington	8–18–1811	15,625	O	146	M Licking
Ridgeley, Frederick		9–10–1811	16,000	O	160	Ky R
Ridgeley, Nicholas G	Baltimore	6–19–1813	8,965	P	253	None
Ridgly, Wm Short	Lexington	1–22–1828	65	X	353	S Fk Elkhorn
Riggs, Jno H	Montgomery	11– 9–1839	295	27	136	Grassy Lick Cr
Riggs, Jno H	Montgomery	11–19–1839	290	27	138	Grassy Lick Cr
Robards, Jesse	Mercer	10– 9–1800	200	E	151	Harrods Run
Robards, Jesse	Mercer	11–20–1800	500	E	263	Harrods Run
Robert, Peter Dominick	Fayette	6–29–1803	2,000	G	447	Welches Cr
Robert, Peter & Jno Baptist & Wife	Lexington	12–15–1821	5,002	V	270	Indian, Halls Crs & N Fk Ky R
Roberts, Peter Dominick	Philadelphia	8– 9–1793	12,566½	A-2	93	Caney Cr
Roberts, Elizabeth		3– 1–1820	6,550	T	420	None
Roberts, J G F & H B		11– 9–1839	835	27	83	Ky R & Stoney Cr
Roberts, Nathan	Madison	3–24–1815	900	Q	36	Clear Cr
Roberts, Thos Quick	Fayette	8–31–1804	885	J	64	Ky R
Roberts, Thos Q	Franklin	9– 3–1805	711	J	391	W Fk Sinking
Roberts, Wm	Shelby	5– 7–1801	———	E	328	Bensons Cr
Roberts, Wm	Shelby	6– 4–1799	500	K	113	Carrington R
Roberts, Wm	Shelby	11–20–1827	170	X	411	None
Roberts, Wm	Shelby	7–24–1828	386	X	420	Floyds Fk
Robertson, Alexander	Mercer	1–15–1788	1,000	A	459	S Fk Elkhorn
Robertson, Alexander	Lincoln	2–27–1784	1,000	B	226	Ohio R
Robertson, Ann	Philadelphia	2– 8–1788	1,080	G	398	None
Robertson, Wm	Richmond	5–22–1797	3,000	D	435	Green R
Robertson, Wyndham	Richmond	5– 5–1826	———	27	56	Henrico Co & Curles Neck
Robertson, Wyndham	Richmond	5–14–1834	1,325	27	64	In Virginia
Robins, Moses	Franklin	6– 3–1800	1,333½	E	8	Deer Cr
Robinson, Elizabeth		8–16–1841	66⅔	27	222	Shelby Co
Robinson, Jno	Montgomery	1–15–1799	400	D	301	Rolling Fk
Robinson, Jno	Cumberland	10– 1–1800	1,000	E	94	Cumberland R
Robinson, Lyles R	Jefferson	12–31–1813	2,000	P	497	Clay Lick
Robinson, Stephen	Amharst	9–24–1796	600	A-2	608	Bank Lick Cr
Robinson, Wm	Lincoln	11– 1–1790	400	B-2	288	Ball & Hill Cr
Rodgers, Andrew	Bourbon	1–26–1804	958½	H	454	Wallace & Phillip Cr
Rogers, Edmund		7– 7–1803	250	P	559	S Fk Little Barren R
Rogers, Edmond	Kentucky	10–28–1824	28,500	X	40	Big Barren, W Fk Little & Cumb R
Rolling, Geo	Hardin	8–10–1804	205	H	378	Clifty & Bear Crs
Ronalds, Andrew	Richmond	7–29–1795	5,320	A-2	335	Big Barren & Green
Rootes, Edmund W	Richmond	7–30–1806	2,000	L	12	Big Bone Lick
Rose, Alexander F	Virginia	2–25–1811	2,000	O	400	Buck Cr
Rose, Alexander F	Fredericksburg	9–10–1814	1,500	Q	466	Gasper R
Rose, Duncan, Executor		4– 1–1797	15,000	B	182	Little Ky R
Rose, Jno	Westmoreland	5– 8–1794	1,500	S	88	Gasper R
Ross, Andrew & Wife	Gallatin	11– 5–1810	80	N	309	Ohio R
Ross, David	Virginia	9–26–1794	939	B	129	N Fk Elkhorn
Ross, David	Bedford	12–22–1780	1,000	B	132	Big Bone Cr
Ross, David		1– 7–1793	1,400	J	48	Lawrence & Lee Crs
Ross, David	Fiuvanna	4– 9–1789	———	J	228	None
Ross, David	Richmond	1– 3–1807	1,000	L	360	None
Ross, David, decd		11– 5–1818	———	T	23	None
Ross, David, heirs	Richmond	6–18–1821	———	V	41	None
Ross, James		10–28–1842	192	27	322	Leestown Bottom
Roundtree, Dudly	Hardin	1–23–1811	80	N	428	Green R
Roundtree, Dudly Jr	Hardin	1–23–1811	130	N	429	Green R
Roundtree, Dudly	Hardin	1–27–1813	1,750	P	64	None
Roundtree, Dudly	Hardin	1–28–1813	490	P	73	Green R
Roundtree, Dudly	Hart	11– 6–1824	44	W	408	None
Rowan, Jno	Franklin	1– 9–1806	158	K	144	Jeffersons Cr

Grantee	Residence	Deed Date	Acres	Book	Page	Watercourse
Rowan, Jno	Kentucky	9– 9–1825	847½	X	191	Little Miami & Sciota R
Rowlings, Jas	————	4–21–1834	Lots	Z	431	Richmond, Va
Rowzee, Phileman	Kentucky	10– 4–1805	116	J	315	N Fk Elkhorn
Royall, Mary G	Powhatan	5– 5–1826	————	27	56	Henrico Co & Curles Neck
Royall, Mary G	Powhatan	5–14–1834	1,325	27	64	In Virginia
Royster, David	Hanover	6– 8–1799	485	D	452	Tradewater
Royster, Ann & Wm & Elliott	Caroline	5–24–1809	350	M	430	Floyds Fk
Rucks, Jas & Wife	Jackson	1– 6–1844	167	27	421	Ohio R
Rucker, Elliott	Madison	11– 7–1805	1,000	K	119	Butlers Fk
Rucker, LeGrand F	Shelby	11– 1–1820	302	U	431	Drennons Lick Cr
Rumsey, Edward	Batetourt	6– 9–1800	200	E	317	Small Br
Runnals, Richard	Madison	9–22–1787	940	A	342	Br Harrods Cr
Runnals, Richard	Madison	9–22–1787	400	A	344	Paint Lick
Runnals, Richard	Madison	9–22–1787	230	A	346	None
Runnals, Richard	Madison	9–22–1787	660	A	348	Rolling Fk
Rupe, Nicholas		9– 2–1814	————	P	530	Big Benson Cr
Rupe, Nicholas	Franklin	9–10–1814	116	Q	75	Big Benson Cr
Russell, James	Berkley	1– 9–1804	1,100	J	416	Cumberland R
Russell, Mary Owen	Fayette	3–11–1806	200	K	327	Pond Cr
Russell, Geo	Fayette	12– 3–1802	2,000	G	79	Rough Cr
Russell, Geo	Fayette	12– 3–1802	3,000	G	82	Nolinn Cr
Rutherford, Robt	Berkely	10– 1–1796	1,000	A-2	648	Grapefield
Rutherford, Robt	Berkely	10– 1–1796	2,000	A-2	651	Hammond Cr
Rutherford, Robt	Berkely	10– 1–1796	300	A-2	653	Ohio R
Rutherford, Thos	Richmond	1–25–1798	3,300	C	197	Cumberland R
Rutherford, Thos	Richmond	3–10–1798	2,000	C	200	N Fk Tradewater
Rutherford, Thos	————	12–20–1797	1,000	C	204	Tradewater
Rutherford, Thos	Henrico	2–22–1799	1,000	D	342	N Fk Tradewater
Rutherford, Thos	Richmond	3–15–1800	1,000	E	68	Marble Cr
Rutherford, Van	Berkley	12–13–1799	1,000	E	289	Cedar & Anter Crs
Rutting, Thos	Baltimore	10–23–1795	8,800	A-2	684	Ohio R
Sackett, Saml	New York	1–28–1797	63,791	Q	538	Ohio R
Sale Saml	Spottsylvania	5–30–1798	500	C	217	———— R
Salter, Robt, heirs		9–21–1798	————	D	52	Ohio & Green R
Samuel, Chas P	Franklin	8–30–1830	————	Z	8	Versailles Road
Samuel, Chas P	Franklin	1–11–1839	5½	27	26	M Elkhorn
Samuel, Churchill	Franklin	5–27–1839	Lots	27	46	Frankfort
Samuel, Jno	Orange	2–25–1791	200	B-2	433	Rolling Fk
Samuel, Larkin	Franklin	11– 5–1841	Lot	27	269	Frankfort
Samuel, Larkin	Kentucky	7–19–1845	Lot	28	20	Frankfort
Samuel, Robt		8– 4–1817	553	R	366	Wilners Cr
Samuel, Riley G	Franklin	3– 7–1837	222	27	364	N Fk Elkhorn
Samuel, S R	Franklin	7–16–1819	Lot	T	78	Frankfort
Sanders, Lemuel & wife	Franklin	3– 1–1842	3	27	324	M Elkhorn
Sanders, Lewis Jr	Franklin	3–31–1835	————	Z	502	M Eagle Cr
Sanders, Lewis Jr	Mississippi	9–23–1839	10,000	27	81	Ky R
Sanders, Lewis Jr	Mississippi	9–26–1839	3,400	27	82	Eagle Cr
Sanders, Lewis Jr	Franklin	8–10–1839	Lot	27	192	Frankfort
Sanders, Sally, heirs	————	6– 5–1816	6,000	R	3	None
Sandidge, Jno		9–16–1810	200	O	124	Cumberland R
Sappington, Jno	Montgomery	9–23–1828	————	X	469	None
Sappington, Jno	Montgomery	9– 1–1826	————	Y	197	None
Satterwhite, Waldr	Franklin	7–23–1819	100	U	80	None
Saunders, Alexander	New York	5–18–1811	1,000	O	29	Eagle Cr
Saunders, Nathaniel	Gallatin	12– 7–1819	339	T	378	Eagle Cr
Savary, Jno	Fayette	6–29–1795	36,700	A-2	1	Green R
Savary, Jno	Washington	8–14–1795	90,000	A-2	26	Cumberland R
Savary, Jno	Washington	2– 9–1796	4½	A-2	105	Clover Lick Cr
Savary, Jno de Valconlon	Richmond	9–15–1786	10,000	N	1	None
Savary, Jno	Washington	8–18–1797	5,222⅔	N	10	Little Barren & Cumberland R
Savary, Jno	Bourbon	7–20–1814	250	P	602	None
Savary, Jno, dec'd	————	7–31–1818	————	S	226	None
Sayre, Leonard	Philadelphia	12–————1795	3,000	E	101	Fk Licking
Scanland, Jas	Culpepper	6– 9–1821	————	U	531	None
Scantland, Jno	————	10–28–1840	100	27	150	S Benson Cr
Scearce, Henry	Shelby	11–27–1813	100	P	481	Tick Cr
Scearce, James	Shelby	11–27–1813	100	P	484	Tick Cr
Scearce, Nathan	Shelby	11–27–1813	100	P	482	Tick & Guests Cr
Schooling, Jos	————	4–30–1833	96	Z	291	Pleasant Run
Scott, Ann, Guardian	Stafford	11–10–1798	2,500	D	97	Main Elkhorn
Scott, Geo, Elisha, Levi & Elijah	Bourbon	4–14–1798	2,433	D	54	Little Ky R
Scott, Jas	Washington	10– 8–1811	2,000	O	136	Buck Cr
Scott, Jesse	Chesterfield	4–29–1824	————	X	158	None
Scott, Jno	————	12–14–1811	Slaves	O	206	None

Grantee	Residence	Deed Date	Acres	Book	Page	Watercourse
Scott, Jno	Gallatin	12–30–1819	5,000	U	83	Twin Cr
Scott, Jno	Jessamine	12–17–1823	1,596¼	W	226	Little Hickman Cr
Scott, Jno	Gallatin	1–24–1828	106	X	365	Eagle Stevens & Indian Cr
Scott, Jno		1–23–1828	42,283	X	366	None
Scott, Jno	Fredericksburg	11– 9–1829	1,000	Z	484	Deer Fk Green R
Scott, Jno F	——	7– 1–1831	1,162	Z	145	Ohio R
Scott, Joel	Franklin	11–26–1827	Lot	X	325	Frankfort
Scott, Joel	Woodford	1–25–1841	——	27	275	In Woodford Co
Scott, Robt G	Williamsburg	2–16–1816	1,850	S	43	Fks Sandy R
Scott, Robt W	Franklin	5–24–1832	Lot	Z	209	Frankfort
Scott, Robt W	Franklin	1–18–1834	115½	Z	408	Dry Run
Scott, Robt W	Franklin	1–18–1834	205¾	Z	409	Dry Run
Scott, Robt W	Franklin	12– 7–1844	167	27	462	Ohio R & Mill Cr
Scott, Robt W	Kentucky	6——1839	205¾	28	23	Locust Hill
Scott, Robt W & Wife	Franklin	1– 6–1844	167	27	421	Ohio R
Searcy, Bartlett	Fayette	8–13–1787	1,400	Q	180	Ky R
Searcy, Jno	Gallatin	2– 4–1810	200	N	233	None
Searcy, Jno	Gallatin	5–10–1815	160	Q	175	Eagle Cr
Searcy, Wm	Fayette	1–25–1830	263¼	Y	429	Near Lexington
Sebastain, Benj	Jefferson	7– 2–1796	1,000	A-2	451	Cumberland R
Sebree, Uriel	Boone	1–13–1816	681¼	Q	351	Ohio R
Sebree, Uriel	Boone	6–18–1817	526	R	419	In Woolperts Cr
Sebree, Wm D	Franklin	3– 7–1842	15	27	272	N Elkhorn
Seddon, Thos	Stafford	3–26–1823	1,095	W	61	Cane Run Mill & Drennons Lick Cr
Seddon, Thos	Fredericksburg	8– 3–1826	1,750	X	239	None
Sellars, Nathan	Bourbon	11–15–1786	——	A	230	Hinkston Fk
Semple, Jno W	——	1– 2–1814	1,000	P	331	Harlins Cr
Shadburn, Wm	Nelson	3–26–1814	383	P	448	Big Barren R
Shackleford, Geo	Madison	1–19–1827	333⅓	Y	263	Tygarts Cr
Shalherst, Elizabeth	Philadelphia	2–20–1802	——	E	417	Ohio R
Shanks, James	——	11–19–1807	751	L	215	None
Sharp, Leander J	Frankfort	4–11–1824	——	W	254	Big Barren R
Sharp, Maxwell	Christian	9– 4–1824	900	W	503	Tradewater
Sharp, Maxwell	Christian	9– 4–1824	2,500	W	506	Deer Cr & Tradewater
Sharpless, Jesse	Philadelphia	8– 2–1803	500	G	388	S Brs Nolinn
Shaw, Gabriel	New York City	2– 6–1809	5,000	M	397	Collins Fk & Br Little Richland Cr
Shaw, Wm S	New York City	12– 7–1808	8,571	M	256	Ky R
Sheill, Ann	Lincoln	5– 9–1786	294	A	99	Hanging Fk
Shelby, Isaac	Lincoln	1–15–1790	800	B-2	146	Hickman Cr
Shelby, Isaac	Lincoln	10–25–1800	560	F	146	None
Shelby, Isaac	Frankfort	7– 8–1814	350	P	479	Cumberland R
Shelby, Isaac	Franklin	2–21–1815	226	Q	13	Hays Fk Silver Cr
Shelby, Isaac	Lincoln	7–26–1819	Lot	T	48	Frankfort
Shelby, Isaac	Lincoln	7–27–1819	Slaves	U	477	None
Shelby, James	——	7– 1–1815	500	Q	93	Green Fk Licking
Shelby, Jno J	Kentucky	9–19–1783	1,000	A	3	Br
Shelby, E & M	Fayette	10–13–1783	2,000	A	1	Elkhorn
Shepherd, Adam	Bullitt	4–18–1812	——	P	8	None
Shepherd, Joseph	Henico	10– 3–1788	2,000	C	212	Salt Lick Cr
Shepherd, Philip	Richmond	4–12–1797	4,000	B	281	Deer Cr
Shepherd, Susanna	Baltimore	4–18–1812	——	P	8	None
Sherwood, Robt	Kentucky	5–25–1799	1,000	D	164	None
Shilman, Jno	Breckinridge	6– 2–1821	——	V	288	Rolling Fk & Ohio R
Shipp, Colly	Owen	5–28–1827	175	X	235	Cedar Cr
Shipp, Elizabeth	Woodford	11–16–1831	5	Z	163	Dry Cr
Shore, Thomas	Chesterfield	3–30–1795	——	N	446	None
Short, Jno C	Cincinnati	1– 5–1815	——	P	622	None
Short, Jno C	Ohio	5–23–1822	3,046	V	253	Licking
Short, Chas W	Fayette	12–31–1833	88	Z	382	S Fk Elkhorn
Short, Peyton	——	6–14–1797	3,000	D	216	Ohio R
Short, Peyton	Woodford	11– 6–1799	1,500	D	421	Ohio R
Short, Peyton	Woodford	11–28–1801	16,000	F	160	Ky R
Short, Peyton	Woodford	5– 1–1802	——	F	507	—— Cr
Short, Peyton	Woodford	12–21–1803	615	H	254	Cumberland R
Short, Peyton	Stafford	5–23–1804	1,000	J	27	Pond R
Short, Peyton	Woodford	2–10–1806	400	N	317	None
Short, Peyton	Estill	11– 3–1815	314	Q	235	None
Short, Peyton	Estill	11–17–1815	550	Q	243	Little R
Short, Peyton	Franklin	1– 8–1818	32,025	S	49	Slate Cr Licking & Ky R
Short, Wm	——	11– 9–1810	220	N	312	Mill & Distillery
Short, Wm	Philadelphia	10–14–1826	10,955¾	Y	281	Little Cumberland R Pond, Dry Casey Cr & S Elkhorn
Shortridge, Eli	Montgomery	1–17–1821	460	U	167	Elk Cr & Ohio R
Shrader, Jas W	Oldham	7–19–1840	895	27	161	Blackfords & Panther Cr

Grantee	Residence	Deed Date	Acres	Book	Page	Watercourse
Shrader, Jas W & Jno W	Oldham	12-21-1838	894	27	4	In Daviess Co
Shreader, Jacob	——	8- 8-1809	734	N	12	Rough Cr
Shreave, Leven L	——	8-28-1819	5,500	T	162	Rough & Panther Cr
Shyrock, Gideon	Fayette	12- 4-1832	75	Z	243	Shelbyville Pike
Shyrock, Gideon	Fayette	12- 6-1832	1,310	Z	244	Donelsons Fk
Shuff, Isaac	Scott	5-15-1830	——	Y	464	Silas & Cherry Run
Shyrin, Mrs Ann	Frankfort	11- 1-1801	Lot	H	598	Frankfort
Siesnan, Luke	Baltimore	11-12-1824	11,113	X	22	Ky R
Silvers, Jno	Nelson	6-23-1789	200	B-2	64	Skeggs Cr
Silvertooth, Geo	Mercer	9-22-1788	560	B-2	330	Chaplins Fk
Simms, Jesse	Alexandria	1- 3-1800	13,982	E	138	Rolling Fk & Little Ky
Simon, Joseph	Lancaster	6- 1-1786	2,000	A-2	406	Fox Run
Simond, Lewis	New York	7- 1-1812	1,793	P	536	None
Simpson, Joseph	Shelby	6- 2-1804	400	H	189	Brashears Cr
Sinclair, Robt	Scott	5-18-1801	200	E	380	Floyds Fk
Singleton, Anthony	Richmond	6-20-1795	10,000	A-2	548	N Fk Sandy R
Sisle, Jno Jr	Philadelphia	11-13-1805	——	N	156	None
Skinner, Mary	Nelson	5- 2-1827	400	X	232	Salt R
Skinner, Richard	Kentucky	9-30-1814	400	P	523	Br Salt R
Skipwith, Henry	Cumberland	9-10-1790	400	B-2	202	Skeggs Cr
Skipwith, Henry	——	5-22-1802	500	F	413	Goose Cr
Skipwith, Henry	Williamsburg	7-12-1809	1,000	M	439	Cumberland R
Skipworth, Henry	——	1-10-1798	4,354	D	61	Ohio R
Shipworth, Peyton	Cumberland	8-28-1790	2,450	B-2	231	Licking
Skyson, Jno	Philadelphia	3-13-1805	Lot	H	599	Frankfort
Slade, Chas	Alexandria	2- 3-1802	5,000	J	274	S Fk Licking
Slater, Wm Trustee	Maryland	9-21-1804	13,500	H	454	Ohio R & Patton Cr
Slaughter, Augustus	Mercer	7- 2-1812	570	O	409	Panther Cr
Slaughter, Gabriel	Mercer	5-13-1800	721½	E	201	Panther Cr
Slaughter, Gabriel	Frankfort	11-22-1819	290	T	207	Shawnee Run
Slaughter, Geo	Jefferson	9-13-1785	1	A	58	None
Slaughter, Geo Jr	——	9- 8-1801	10,000	F	231	None
Slaughter, Lucy B	——	3- 1-1820	6,550	T	420	None
Slaughter, Philip	Culpepper	3-27-1801	1,000	E	340	Tradewater
Smedes, Geo M	Fayette	5- 1-1828	122	X	448	Shannons Run
Smelsher, Peter	Bourbon	8-23-1791	600	B-2	379	Fleming Cr
Smiley, James	——	9-22-1804	535	H	367	Ohio R
Smiley, James	Bardstown	5- 4-1811	400	O	55	Cox Cr
Smiley, Jas	Bardstown	5- 4-1811	Lots	O	55	Bardstown
Smith, Augustine J	Alexandria	11-19-1796	30,000	D	19	Drennons Lick Cr
Smith, Augustine J	Alexandria	4-27-1796	30,000	A-2	655	Rolling & Chaplins Fks
Smith, Augustine L	Alexandria	5-18-1795	3,000	A-2	172	Clover Cr
Smith, A & J	Augusta	10- 2-1808	2,000	M	269	Big Bone Lick
Smith, A & J	Augusta	12-16-1808	——	M	274	None
Smith, Benj	Shelby	12- 1-1820	228¾	U	391	Rough Cr
Smith, Bird	——	8-28-1819	5,500	T	162	Rough & Panther Cr
Smith, Geo	Powhatan	3-18-1800	1,128¾	E	62	Cumberland R
Smith, Geo	Franklin	9-21-1810	626½	N	274	Clay Lick Cr
Smith, Geo S, heirs	——	11- 5-1824	400	X	139	Hingston Fk
Smith, Hubbard B	Grant	3-14-1822	Lot	V	377	Lexington
Smith, Jas	Hardin	6- 3-1816	238½	Q	489	Mill Cr
Smith, Jas	Hardin	6- 3-1816	146	Q	492	Mill Cr
Smith, James Jr	Philadelphia	6- 1-1807	——	L	127	Brush Cr
Smith, Jos H	Henry	5- 5-1818	1,000	S	121	Mill Cr
Smith, Nellie	Kentucky	8-26-1800	9,800	F	352	Eagle Cr & Red R
Smith, Jno	Bourbon	12- 3-1796	5,000	B	1	Main Licking
Smith, Jno	Woodford	5-26-1809	1,500	M	432	Br Dix R
Smith, Jno	——	1826	450	Y	232	None
Smith, Jno S	Baltimore	10-28-1818	6,000	S	367	Muddy R
Smith, Jno Speed	Madison	12-22-1815	10,498	Q	364	Cedar & N Fk Rockcastle
Smith, Jno Speed & wife	Madison	9-28-1815	1,900	Q	194	Salt Lick & Lees Cr
Smith, Joseph	——	2-12-1788	——	A	356	Robinson Cr
Smith, Joseph	Leesburg	3-13-1799	400	D	208	Cumberland R
Smith, Peter F	Chesterfield	4-29-1824	——	X	158	None
Smith, Richard	Richmond	9- 9-1794	20,781	C	270	N Fk Ky R
Smith, Richard	——	5-31-1792	2,500	P	97	Tennessee & Ohio R
Smith, Robt	Philadelphia	8-22-1786	12,231	E	38	Salt R
Smith, Robt	Philadelphia	11-19-1814	768	P	595	Blue Sp Grove
Smith, Saml	Baltimore	3-10-1803	3,200	G	244	Green R & W Fk Bear Cr
Smith, Saml	Baltimore	3-10-1803	6,000	G	248	Muddy R
Smith, Saml	Baltimore	6-14-1803	5,000	H	52	Saxtons Cr
Smith, Saml	Baltimore	9-15-1806	93,813¾	K	426	Stinking, Shelby & Main Licking

Grantee	Residence	Deed Date	Acres	Book	Page	Watercourse
Smith, Saml decd	Baltimore	11-14-1829	30,821	Y	425	Slate, Stepstone, Flat, Licking & Miller Crs
Smith, Saml & Robt	Baltimore	3- 6-1796	8,000	A-2	131	Shebly Cr
Smith, Saml & Robt	Baltimore	3- 8-1796	6,200	A-2	134	Small Br
Smith, Saml & Robt	Baltimore	3-11-1796	25,291½	A-2	151	None
Smith, Saml & Robt	Baltimore	4-12-1796	27,500	A-2	227	M Fk Ky R
Smith, Saml & Robt	Baltimore	3- 8-1796	5,000	A-2	238	Main Licking
Smith, Saml & Robt	Baltimore	3- 8-1796	7,118½	A-2	239	Main Licking
Smith, Saml & Robt	Baltimore	3- 8-1796	3,000	A-2	241	Main Licking
Smith, Saml & Robt	Baltimore	——1796	11,400	A-2	243	Green R
Smith, Thos	Madison	11——1821	100	V	107	Greasy Cr
Smith, Thos S	Jessamine	11- 8-1809	1,060	N	213	S Fk Benson Cr
Smith, Wm	Fredericksburg	3-19-1803	500	J	17	None
Smither, Robt	Powhatan	11-10-1805	5,000	K	219	Eagle Cr
Smither, Robt	Franklin	8-17-1807	390	L	119	——— Br
Smither, Robt Jr	Franklin	6- 6-1800	800	H	421	Twin Cr
Sneed, Archibald	Franklin	12-30-1798	Lot	D	111	Frankfort
Sneed, Achilles	———	2-20-1801	9	E	307	Dix R
Sneed, Achilles	Franklin	5-18-1801	700½	E	330	Brush Cr
Sneed, Achilles	Franklin	5-18-1801	200	E	332	3 Fks Cumberland R
Sneed, Achilles	Franklin	8-21-1800	Lot	F	2	Frankfort
Sneed, Achilles	Franklin	9-20-1802	170	F	522	Salt R
Sneed, Achilles	Frankfort	2-21-1803	666⅔	G	164	Ohio R
Sneed, Achilles	Frankfort	6- 2-1803	15,599¼	G	337	Eagle & Elkhorn
Sneed, Achilles	Frankfort	3- 5-1803	745⅓	H	211	Muddy Cr & N Fk Rockcastle
Sneed, Achilles	Frankfort	11-28-1804	1,861	H	623	Cabin Cr
Sneed, Achilles	Frankfort	9-11-1805	5,415½	J	264	Cedar Cr
Sneed, Achilles	Franklin	12-27-1805	2,000	K	156	M Elkhorn
Sneed, Achilles	———	7-10-1806	500	K	419	Cedar Cr
Sneed, Achilles	Frankfort	6- 3-1807	1,760	L	56	Big Benson Cr
Sneed, Achilles	Franklin	8-17-1807	390	L	119	——— Br
Sneed, Achilles	Frankfort	1-25-1804	3,791	L	355	Eagle Cedar & Elkhorn Crs
Sneed, Achilles	Frankfort	9-10-1807	———	M	21	Ky & Tennessee R
Sneed, Achillis	Frankfort	1-18-1808	1,000	M	86	Deer Cr
Sneed, Achillis	———	1-18-1808	5,312½	M	89	Hingston Fk
Sneed, Achilles	Franklin	1-16-1808	1,000	M	91	Paroquet Cr
Sneed, Achilles	Franklin	5-31-1806	2,474	M	93	Green R
Sneed, Achillis	Franklin	9-23-1807	627	M	96	Ky R
Sneed, Achillis	Frankfort	11-28-1804	1,861	M	98	Cabin Cr
Sneed, Achilles	Franklin	5-21-1808	1,000	M	101	Robinsons Cr
Sneed, Achilles	———	5-26-1806	6,348	M	193	Ky R & Big Barren Cr
Sneed, Achilles	———	4- 5-1807	692½	M	198	Ky R
Sneed, Achilles	———	2- 8-1809	Negro	M	314	None
Sneed, Achillis	Frankfort	12-23-1808	780	M	343	Green & Dix R
Sneed, Achillis	Frankfort	6-19-1809	4,172	M	410	N Fk Rockcastle & Copper Cr, Muddy & Sta Camp Cr Paint Lick & Silver Cr
Sneed, Achillis	———	5- 5-1807	Slaves	N	88	None
Sneed, Achillis	Frankfort	8-24-1809	5,263	N	202	N Fk Rockcastle & Muddy Paint Lick Cr
Sneed, Achillis	Frankfort	2-19-1810	4,475	N	203	Rockcastle, Copper & Muddy Cr
Sneed, Achillis	Frankfort	11-30-1808	5,562	N	204	None
Sneed, Achillis	Frankfort	11- 8-1809	———	N	232	Whites Cr
Sneed, Achillis	———	3-17-1810	281	N	245	Utterbacks
Sneed, Achillis	Frankfort	10- 2-1810	600	N	433	Br N Fk Tradewater
Sneed, Achillis	Franklin	7-13-1811	1,140	O	96	Paint Lick & Silver
Sneed, Achillis	Frankfort	10-31-1811	1,333⅓	O	210	Cypress Cr
Sneed, Achillis	Franklin	4-19-1811	2,000	O	215	Cumberland R
Sneed, Achillis	Franklin	2- 7-1812	500	O	317	Ky R
Sneed, Achillis	Frankfort	3——1812	500	O	343	Big Benson Cr
Sneed, Achillis	Frankfort	5-14-1812	15,000	O	383	Bacon Cr
Sneed, Achillis	Franklin	6-14-1811	386½	O	391	S Fk Benson Cr
Sneed, Achillis	Frankfort	6-17-1812	5,900	P	2	M S Elkhorn
Sneed, Achillis	Franklin	5-19-1812	10	P	20	Ky R
Sneed, Achillis	Franklin	10- 1-1812	———	P	25	Ky R
Sneed, Achillis	Franklin	11-28-1812	200	P	28	Armstrong Br
Sneed, Achillis	Frankfort	5-13-1812	1,500	P	44	None
Sneed, Achillis	Frankfort	5- 7-1813	1,525	P	122	Sandy R
Sneed, Achillis	Franklin	1-28-1812	5,312½	P	284	None
Sneed, Achillis	Franklin	8-10-1812	386½	P	341	Bensons Cr
Sneed, Achillis	Frankfort	3- 9-1813	Lots	P	464	Frankfort
Sneed, Achiilis	Franklin	5——1814	Lots	P	531	Frankfort
Sneed, Achillis	Franklin	7-12-1814	1,000	P	582	Gilberts Cr

Grantee	Residence	Deed Date	Acres	Book	Page	Watercourse
Sneed, Achillis	Franklin	12–27–1814	——	P	596	Silver Paint Lick Muddy & Drowning Crs
Sneed, Achillis	Franklin	11–11–1814	——	Q	6	Ky R
Sneed, Achillis	Franklin	3–25–1815	Slaves	Q	32	None
Sneed, Achillis	Frankfort	7– 8–1815	332½	Q	144	Ky R
Sneed, Achillis	Franklin	9–16–1815	Lot	Q	192	Frankfort
Sneed, Achillis	Franklin	10– 7–1815	600	Q	204	Gleen R
Sneed, Achillis	Franklin	10–18–1815	1,000	Q	260	Glenns Cr
Sneed, Achillis	Franklin	10–20–1815	106	Q	274	Benson & Ky
Sneed, Achillis	Franklin	12– 4–1815	——	Q	337	Rockhouse Br & Ky R
Sneed, Achillis	Frankfort	12– 4–1815	——	Q	425	Ky R Clear & Howards Cr
Sneed, Landon	Shelby	9–10–1814	500	Q	428	N Fk Big Benson Cr
Sneed, Achillis	Franklin	2–15–1816	Lot	Q	525	Frankfort
Sneed, Achillis	Franklin	5–10–1817	1,060	R	291	Ky R & Big Benson
Sneed, Wm	Franklin	5–28–1817	102	R	337	Cedar Cr
Sneed, Achillis	Franklin	1–31–1817	92	R	416	Whites Br
Sneed, Achillis	——	5–21–1818	199¾	S	180	None
Sneed, Achillis	——	5–21–1818	Lot	S	180	Frankfort
Sneed, Achillis	Franklin	7–13–1818	120	S	187	None
Sneed, Achillis	Franklin	9–22–1818	4,000	S	256	Sandy R
Sneed, Achillis	——	2– 9–1819	Lots	S	464	Frankfort
Sneed, Achillis	Frankfort	10——1819	175	T	275	None
Sneed, Achillis	Frankfort	7–23–1819	Lot	T	384	Portland
Sneed, Achillis	Frankfort	7–23–1819	Lots	T	384	Frankfort
Sneed, Achillis	Frankfort	7–23–1819	Lots	T	384	Lexington
Sneed, Achillis	Frankfort	8– 2–1819	4,000	U	77	None
Sneed, Achillis	Frankfort	2–25–1819	Lots	U	176	Frankfort
Sneed, Achillis	Frankfort	7–19–1816	10	U	470	None
Sneed, Achillis	Frankfort	4–10–1821	1,000	V	9	Glenn Cr
Sneed, Achillis	Franklin	8–26–1822	4,720	W	108	Crooked Cr
Sneed, Achillis	Franklin	3–13–1823	12,148	W	113	—— Cr
Sneed, Achillis	Franklin	10– 9–1823	——	W	126	Cumberland R
Sneed, Achillis	Franklin	2–13–1822	Ferry	X	71	Ky R
Sneed, Achillis	Frankfort	9– 1–1823	——	X	73	None
Sneed, Achillis	Franklin	9– 1–1823	280	X	74	Skeggs Cr
Sneed, Achillis	Franklin	6–19–1824	Slaves	X	75	None
Sneed, Achillis, heirs	Franklin	3–24–1832	75,000	Z	181	In Hardin Co
Sneed, Lewis & Wm C	Franklin	7–14–1843	Lot	27	354	Frankfort
Sneed, Landon	Franklin	9–25–1804	100	H	502	Bensons Cr
Sneed, Saml	Gallatin	5–10–1815	346	Q	173	Eagle Cr
Sneed, Saml C	——	12–14–1811	Slaves	O	206	None
Sneed, Thos	Mercer	9–17–1800	54½	E	107	Ky R
Sneed, Thos	——	2–20–1801	18	E	309	Ky R
Sneed & Bibb	——	6–16–1808	Negro	M	308	None
Snelling, Wm	Bourbon	9–13–1806	73	L	344	Hustons Fk
Snyder, Simon	Northumberland	1–28–1799	2,500	D	264	None
Society of Shakers	Mercer	7–14–1816	1,400	R	333	—— R
South, Jno G	Franklin	1– 9–1827	5,000	Y	243	N Fk Ky R
South, J W	Breathitt	10–17–1842	——	27	343	N Fk Ky R
Southall, James Executor	Williamsburg	4–13–1798	3,600	D	76	Cumberland R
Southard, Ivyson	Owen	11– 9–1822	100	V	368	Dickeys Fk Eagle Cr
Southcomb, Thos	Fredericksburg	5– 5–1798	1,500	D	382	Goose Cr
Southcomb, Thos	——	5–25–1798	3,500	J	82	Goose Cr & Tradewater R
Southgate, Jno	King & Queen	5– 1–1812	108	O	369	None
Sowder, Allen & wife	Prince William	1–11–1802	2,100	F	240	None
Spalding, Wm	Union	2–26–1831	150	Z	119	Salt R
Speed, Jos	Lincoln	5–24–1785	——	A	73	Salt R
Speed, James	Lincoln	7–25–1785	1,400	A	76	Salt R
Speed, Jos	Lincoln	10– 1–1784	200	A	78	Harrods Run
Speed, James	Lincoln	11–10–1786	450	A	97	None
Speed, James	Lincoln	7–25–1785	1,400	A	159	None
Speed, James	Lincoln	7–18–1786	1,400	A	180	None
Speed, James	Lincoln	11–15–1784	43½	A	245	Harrods & Dry Cr
Speed, James	Mercer	6– 9–1789	700	B-2	73	Ohio R
Speed, James	——	7– 9–1789	700	B-2	129	Ohio R
Speed, Susan M	Powhatan	5– 5–1826	——	27	56	Henrico Co & Curley Neck
Speed, Susan M	Powhatan	5–14–1834	1,325	27	64	Virginia
Speed, Thos	Kentucky	3–21–1789	Lot	B-2	22	Danville
Speed, Thos	Bullitt	8– 8–1798	1,863½	C	317	Station Camp Cr
Speed, Thos	Nelson	8–26–1817	28,556	R	561	Stoners Hingston Fk Licking & Salt R
Spencer, Thos & wife	Culpepper	6– 9–1821	——	U	531	None
Spilman, Jas	Mercer	6– 2–1792	Lots	B-2	504	Danville
Spotswood, Alexander	Spottsylvania	——1795	3,000	A-2	160	Rough Cr
Spottswood, Alexander	Spottsylvania	10–17–1798	2,666⅔	D	48	—— Cr

Grantee	Residence	Deed Date	Acres	Book	Page	Watercourse
Spotswood, Geo W & Wm L M		9–22–1823	2,666⅔	X	340	Highland Cr
Sprigg, Thos	Frederick	11– 4–1800	304	E	121	None
Springer, Isaac	Nelson	10– 3–1791	200	B-2	351	Popes Cr
Sproule, Chas	Frankfort	6–17–1815	39	Q	133	Georgetown Road
Spurr, Barabara		1–24–1842	4¼	27	268	Armstrongs Br
Stafford, Henry	Kentucky	5–27–1790	600	B-2	513	Elkhorn Cr
Stainton, Andrew	Prince Edward	9–11–1799		F	117	None
Stamper, Gabriel		4– 4–1823	31	W	85	Cave Spring Br
Stapp, Elijah, heirs	Scott	9–24–1821	Horse	V	63	None
Stapp, Gholson	Garrard	12– 5–1798	1,000	D	93	Br Cumberland R
Starling, Lyne	Ohio	3–23–1827	Lots	X	229	Henderson
Starling, Lyne	Ohio	3–23–1827	2,807	X	229	None
Starling, Lyne	Ohio	3–23–1827	Slaves	X	229	None
Starling, Wm	Frankfort	11–23–1819	630	T	178	Muddy Cr
Starling, Wm Jr	Frankfort	3–28–1818	400	S	242	None
Starling, Wm Jr	Frankfort	5–12–1818	200	S	243	None
Starling, Wm Jr	Frankfort	7–31–1819	Lot	T	53	Frankfort
Starling, Wm Jr	Frankfort	5–16–1821		U	479	Ky R
State Commonwealth	Kentucky	7–20–1841	6½	27	216	Ky R
State Commonwealth	Kentucky	10–23–1841	3½	27	232	Ky R
State Commonwealth	Kentucky	10–23–1841		27	233	Ky R
State Commonwealth	Kentucky	6– 2–1841		27	288	None
Stedman, Saml & Wife		7–12–1834	50	Z	448	Elkhorn
Steele, Adam	Shelby	5– 7–1801		E	328	Bensons Cr
Steele, Adam	Shelby	11–21–1805	1,000	J	398	Big Cr
Steele, Adam & Richard	Shelbyville	4– 5–1802	1,320	F	225	Otter Cr Muddy
Steele, Adam & Richard	Shelbyville	4– 5–1802	1,333⅓	F	227	Big Barren R
Steele, Adam & Richard	Shelbyville	4– 5–1802	1,000	F	229	Highland Cr R
Steele, Adam & Richard	Shelbyville	9– 4–1815	Lot	Q	398	Shelbyville
Steele, James	Hartford	4–10–1806	4,000	L	166	Green R & Nolinn
Steel, James	Maryland	4–19–1798	1,000	O	139	E Br Nolinn
Steele, Saml	Woodford	12–26–1804	200	H	510	Buck Cr
Steele, Saml	Shelby	2–22–1810	3,000	N	141	Salt R & Buck Cr
Steele, Richard Sr	Fayette	10– 5–1804	1,000	N	243	Town Fk Elkhorn
Steele, Richard Jr	Jefferson	12–12–1811	2,000	O	219	Little N Fk Elkhorn
Steele, Wm & Co		12–22–1821	1,025	W	233	Ky R
Stegar, Jno	Gallatin	10–16–1815	160	Q	216	Eagle Cr
Stephens, Jacob	Lincoln	6–17–1789	350	B-2	54	Harris Cr
Stephen, Gen Edward, heirs	Culpepper	6– 9–1821		U	531	None
Stephens, Richard	Nelson	8–15–1796	3,110	A-2	414	Salt R
Stern, Chas	Pendleton	2– 1–1813	333⅓	P	77	Licking
Stern, Geo, heirs		11–12–1818	1,000	S	323	Brashears Cr
Stevens, Benj	Philadelphia	10–16–1797	6,680	G	308	Choplins Fk
Stevenson, Isaac	Woodford	7–25–1814	110	P	590	N Fk Glens Cr
Stevenson, Susan	Kentucky	1–25–1839	Lot	27	10	Carrolton
Stewart, Philip	Maryland	4–23–1813	1,000	P	120	Parragone Cr
Stewart, Robt	New York City	7–27–1815	666⅔	Q	154	Glens Cr
Stewart, Robt	New York City	7–26–1804	2,000	L	36	W Fk Glenns Cr
Sthreskley, Thos	Fayette	11–21–1798	666⅔	E	36	Ohio R
Sthreskley, Thos	Fayette	3– 3–1800	1,000	E	301	Floyds Fk
Sthreskley, Wm	Woodford	11–21–1798	666⅔	E	36	Ohio R
Still, Bartlett	Richmond	4– 8–1802	1,000	F	431	Ohio R
Still, Bartlett	Richmond	8–25–1803	1,000	H	353	Ohio R
Stith, Benj		2– 1–1815	1,059	Q	40	Green R
Stith, Benj		11–25–1817	15,000	R	576	None
Stith, Benj	Hardin	5– 6–1818	75,000	S	140	Rough Cr
Stivers, Richard	Garrard	7–20–1822	461	V	462	Benson Cr
Stout, Amos	Franklin	12–15–1819	Lot	U	188	Frankfort
Stout, Amos	Woodford	11–26–1827	Lot	X	326	Frankfort
Stout, Benj	Fayette	12–14–1790	187⅓	B-2	236	Foxes Run
Stout, Elijah Jr	Shelby	9– 5–1823	367	Z	105	None
Stout, Reubin	Kentucky	5–25–1799	1,000	D	164	None
Stout, Wm	Fayette	12–14–1790	187⅓	B-2	233	Foxes Run
Stoval, Hezakiah	Hardin	5–30–1815	135	Q	125	Mill Cr
Stoval, Hezakiah	Hardin	6– 3–1816	165	Q	495	Mill Cr
Stras, Geo Frederick	Henrico	4– 9–1796	1,000	A-2	662	Deer Cr
Stras, Geo Frederick	Henrico	4– 9–1796	2,000	A-2	666	Deer Cr
Stribling, Francis & Jno	Frederick	10– 5–1796	6,000	D	63	Ohio R
Strode, Jno	Culpepper	3–13–1790	1,000	B-2	141	Muddy R
Strode, Thos	Culpepper	1–31–1810	981	O	482	Ohio R & Otter Cr
Strode, Thos	Culpeper	11– 3–1817	12,500	W	9	None
Strong, Walter	Mercer	9–25–1790	Cattle	B-2	229	None
Strong, Walter Edward	Mercer	5–17–1788	Lots	A	398	None
Strong, Walter E	Mercer	6–10–1788	Lots	A	404	None
Strong, Walter E	Mercer	7– 1–1788	Lot	A	462	None
Strong, Walter E	Mercer	12–22–1795	1,000	A-2	344	E Fk Little Barren
Strong, Walter E	Mercer	11–14–1795	5,896½	A-2	416	Salt R
Strong, Walter E	Mercer	9–14–1791	8,000	B-2	424	Cedar Cr

Grantee	Residence	Deed Date	Acres	Book	Page	Watercourse
Strother, Wm	Woodford	11–30–1798	——	D	86	Hog Run
Stuart, Lewis	Greenbrier	10–12–1814	100	P	553	Little Ky R
Stubblefield, Geo	Frederick	3–16–1791	3,030	B-2	244	Foxes Cr
Stubbs, Robt	Mercer	6–16–1790	——	B-2	152	N Fk Elkhorn
Sugget, Jno	Scott	8–20–1811	700	O	283	Mud Lick Fk
Sullivan, Jas & Lewis	Woodford	3– 2–1818	410	Y	217	Rough Cr
Sullivan, Jos & Lewis	Woodford	1– 8–1819	160	Y	219	Rough Cr
Sullivan, Lewis	Kentucky	10–18–1826	333	Y	212	Br Green R
Sullivan, Owen	Fanquire	9–16–1802	1,000	G	20	None
Summers, Benj	Bullitt	4–19–1805	500	J	134	Cedar Cr
Summers, Jno	Madison	3–16–1791	110	B-2	241	Sugar Cr
Surrency, David	Bath	11–13–1815	1,500	R	27	Slate & Rockcastle
Sutton, David	——	4– 1–1808	150	M	32	None
Swan, David C	Hardin	11–22–1819	910,954	U	90	N Fk Ky & Big Sandy R
Swan, David Cooper	Jefferson	8–13–1842	21,288	27	329	Hardin & Grayson Co
Swan, James	Massachusetts	8– 3–1795	32,104	A-2	248	Red R
Swan, Jas	Dorchester	7–28–1795	20,000	A-2	258	Craigs Cr
Swan, James	Dorchester	3– 9–1796	43,058½	A-2	355	Big Sandy
Swan, James	Dorchester	9–23–1796	8,000	B	63	Buck House Cr
Swan, Jas	Dorchester	9–23–1796	107,681	B	71	N Fk Ky R
Swan, James	Dorchester	5–16–1797	——	B	217	None
Swan, Jas	Boston	1–16–1797	26,500	C	42	Killicanick Cr
Swan, James	Dorchester	6–21–1796	20,781	C	278	N Fk Ky R
Swan, James	Dorchester	2– 5–1799	64,100	D	429	Killcamick & Tygert Crs
Swan, Jno	Powhatan	7– 3–1805	600	J	341	Dry Cr
Swan, Jas	Dorchester	8–11–1795	44,378	P	212	None
Swan, James	Boston	11–22–1819	1,840,000	V	468	Various
Swearingen, Elmira V	Fayette	9–13–1841	Slaves	27	229	None
Swearingen, Henry T	Jefferson	11–20–1816		R	108	None
Swearingen, Thos Van	——	5–11–1810	1,000	N	194	Muddy Cr
Swearingen, Thos V	——	5–11–1807	1,200	N	196	Little Muddy Cr
Swearingen, Thos V	——	5–11–1810	1,147	N	198	Muddy Cr
Sweeney, Thos	Fayette	3– 7–1821	1,100	U	299	None
Sweeney, Thos	Fayette	3– 7–1821	7,000	U	302	None
Sweeney, Thos	Fayette	3– 6–1821	1,000	U	304	None
Sweeney, Thos	Fayette	3– 6–1821	2,000	U	307	None
Sweeney, Thos	Fayette	3– 6–1821	1,500	U	309	None
Sweeney, Thos	Fayette	3– 7–1821	1,800	U	312	None
Sweeney, Thos	Fayette	3– 6–1821	325	U	314	None
Swift, Jonathan	Alexandria	9– 5–1809	4,700	N	81	Green R
Swigert, Jacob	Franklin	5–10–1824	74	W	360	Eagle Cr
Swigert, Jacob	Franklin	3– 1–1831	2,787½	Z	100	Licking
Swigert, Jacob	Franklin	1– 7–1831	179	Z	117	S Benson Cr
Swigert, Jacob	Kentucky	12–27–1831	88½	Z	207	S Benson Cr
Swigert, Jacob	Franklin	6– 7–1833	300	Z	299	Lower Twin Cr
Swigert, Jacob	Franklin	7–24–1833	75	Z	319	Ky R
Swigert, Jacob	Franklin	9–12–1833	67	Z	352	S Benson Cr
Swigert, Jacob	Franklin	11–25–1833	Lot	Z	374	Frankfort
Swigert, Jacob	Franklin	3–10–1835	Lot	Z	507	Frankfort
Swigert, Jacob	Franklin	11– 1–1838	Lots	27	6	Frankfort
Swigert, Jacob	Franklin	12– 1–1838	Lots	27	29	Frankfort
Swigert, Jacob	Franklin	11–12–1839	Lots	27	87	Frankfort
Swigert, Jacob	Franklin	1–20–1841	Lots	27	181	Frankfort
Swigert, Jacob	Franklin	6– 1–1841	Lots	27	276	Frankfort
Swigert, Jacob	Franklin	3– 4–1841	Lots	27	280	Frankfort
Swigert, Jacob	Franklin	3–30–1841	13	27	344	nr Louisville
Swigert, Jacob	Franklin	6–21–1843	Lot	27	356	Frankfort
Swigert, Jacob	Franklin	7–10–1843	Lot	27	358	Frankfort
Swigert, Jacob	Franklin	2– 2–1844	Lot	27	394	Frankfort
Swigert, Jacob	Franklin	10–14–1844	43	27	441	N Elkhorn
Swigert, Jacob	Franklin	7–12–1844	300	28	42	Breckinridge Co
Swigert, Jacob	Franklin	1–19–1846	Lot	28	50	Frankfort
Swigert, Jacob	Franklin	2–18–1846	95	28	59	Ky R
Swigert, Jacob	Franklin	2–18–1846	Lots	28	59	Frankfort
Swigert, Jacob	Franklin	2–11–1843	Lot	28	69	Frankfort
Swigert, Jacob	Franklin	3–31–1843	Lot	28	72	Frankfort
Swigert, Jacob & Philip	Franklin	4–24–1833	50	Z	282	Ky R
Swigert, Jacob & Philip	Franklin	10–30–1839	Lots	27	90	Frankfort
Swigert, Jacob & Philip	Franklin	10– 6–1838	4	27	113	Ky R
Swigert, Jacob & Philip	Franklin	12–14–1840	Lot	27	180	Frankfort
Swigert, J & P	Franklin	3–25–1844	2	27	412	Ky R
Swigert, Jacob & Philip	Franklin	5–30–1844	68	27	429	Benson Cr
Swigert, J & P	Franklin	9–16–1844	Lots	27	444	Louisville
Swigert, J & P	Franklin	9–27–1845	3	28	32	Ky R
Swigert, Jno	Gallatin	5– 8–1820	74	T	412	Eagle Cr
Swigert, Philip	Franklin	1–17–1818	Lots	Z	260	Frankfort
Swigert, Philip	Franklin	3– 8–1833	Lot	Z	281	Frankfort
Swigert, Philip	Franklin	3–30–1834	114	Z	410	S Benson Cr

Grantee	Residence	Deed Date	Acres	Book	Page	Watercourse
Swigert, Philip	Franklin	6– 5–1834	114	Z	447	near Frankfort
Swigert, Philip	Kentucky	2– 4–1835	Lot	Z	487	Frankfort
Swigert, Philip	Kentucky	2– 4–1835	Lot	Z	488	Frankfort
Swigert, Philip	Kentucky	3– 1–1839	552	27	13	Barren Co
Swigert, Philip	Franklin	4–15–1839	Lots	27	33	Frankfort
Swigert, Philip	Franklin	7–21–1840	Lot	27	144	Frankfort
Swigert, Philip	Kentucky	12–30–1843	Lot	27	385	Midway
Swigert, Philip	Franklin	9–18–1844	——	27	430	Franklin Co
Swigert, Philip	Franklin	9–17–1844	Lot	27	433	Frankfort
Swigert, Philip	Franklin	9–16–1844	Lots	27	442	Frankfort
Swigert, Philip	Franklin	12–29–1845	Lot	28	54	Frankfort
Swigert, Philip Atty	——	5–29–1834	32,000	Z	442	None
Swigert, Philip & Jacob	Franklin	1– 4–1839	Lot	27	8	Frankfort
Swigert, Philip & Jacob	Franklin	11–30–1839	Lots	27	90	Frankfort
Swigert, P & J	Franklin	10– 2–1843	Lots	27	371	Frankfort
Swigert, P & J	Franklin	10– 3–1843	25	27	373	Franklin Co
Swigert, Philip & Jacob	Franklin	2–26–1844	Lot	27	411	Frankfort
Swigert, P & J	Franklin	2–——–1845	24	27	468	S Elkhorn
Swigert & McKee	Franklin	10– 8–1844	Lot	27	435	Midway
Swope, Geo	Shelby	6–11–1817	284	R	340	None
Swope, Jacob	Staunton	6–10–1801	4,566⅔	F	109	Ohio Cumberland & Little R
Swope, Jacob	Lincoln	4–21–1826	2,437	Y	129	2nd Cr below Big Bone
Tabele, Jno & Wm	New York City	11– 8–1803	1,000	H	119	Ohio R
Talbot, Isham	Frankfort	6– 2–1803	15,599¼	G	337	Eagle & Elkhorn
Talbot, Isham	Frankfort	1–25–1804	3,791	L	355	Eagle Cedar & Elkhorn Crs
Talbot, Isham	Frankfort	5– 9–1808	750	M	163	Ohio R
Talbot, Isham	Frankfort	6–30–1807	1,200	M	361	Caseys Cr
Talbot, Isham	Franklin	3–30–1810	——	N	251	Caseys Cr
Talbot, Isham	Franklin	4– 8–1811	500	N	458	Br Glens Cr
Talbot, Isham	Franklin	4–29–1811	750	N	460	Br Chaplins Fk
Talbott, Isham	Franklin	11–12–1816	300	R	119	Little R
Talbot, Isham	Franklin	12–——–1819	130	T	413	Hanging Fk
Talbott, Isham	Frankfort	——–1821	366⅔	U	502	6 Mile Cr
Talbott, Isham	Frankfort	——–1821	100	U	503	Clear & 6 Mile Cr
Talbott, Isham	Franklin	12–29–1827	2,000	X	346	Green R
Talbott, Isham	Franklin	2–13–1828	102	X	380	Cedar Cr
Talbott, Isham	Franklin	11– 4–1833	3,000	Z	367	Breckinridge Co
Talbot, Isham, Trustee	——	2– 5–1814	Lot	P	358	Frankfort
Talbot, Jas S	Lincoln	9–13–1790	Lot	B-2	221	None
Talbot, Silas	New York City	1– 9–1796	3,528	F	415	Beech Fk
Talbot, Silas	New York City	5– 9–1798	3,018	G	128	Beech Fk
Talbot, D'Movil	Bourbon	10–18–1820	1,352	U	6	Crews Cr & Licking
Talbott, Thos & Matthew	Wilkes Geo	8–13–1804	2,100	H	286	None
Taleafarro, Chas C	Carolina	6– 1–1815	2,500	S	310	Beech Fk
Tardivean, Peter	Lincoln	9–10–1785	½	A	161	None
Tardivean, Peter	Lincoln	9–10–1785	½	A	162	None
Tardivean, Peter	Lincoln	9–10–1785	⅓	A	163	None
Tardivean, Peter	Mercer	10–23–1788	600	A	507	Rough Cr
Tardivean, Peter	Falls Ohio	2– 8–1790	500	B-2	439	14 Mile Cr
Tardivin, Bros	Mercer	5–24–1788	Lots	A	400	None
Tarrison, Bartholomew	Philadelphia	8–21–1786	23,300	A-2	19	Nolinn
Tatesman, Mathias	Lincoln	3–12–1790	100	B-2	138	Dix R
Tatour, Nicholas S	Garrard	5–28–1815	350	Q	300	Lick Br
Taylor, Ben	Scott	11–14–1815	518	Q	286	Ohio R
Taylor, Ben	Georgetown	12–——–1815	450	R	5	N & S Fk Elkhorn
Taylor, Ben	Scott	12–13–1815	1,700	R	37	Elkhorn
Taylor, Ben	Woodford	2– 1–1823	95¼	W	19	Ohio R
Taylor, Ben	Woodford	11– 3–1823	100	W	343	N Elkhorn
Taylor, Ben	Woodford	11– 8–1829	100	Y	407	Elkhorn
Taylor, Ben	Woodford	6– 6–1829	60	Y	424	Frankfort Lex Rd
Taylor, Benj	Franklin	11–20–1815	Lots	Q	247	Frankfort
Taylor, Benj	Scott	12–23–1815	1,000	R	34	N Elkhorn
Taylor, Benj	Franklin	11–13–1816	224	R	67	Elkhorn
Taylor, Edmund	Carolina	8–12–1816	1,433⅓	T	359	None
Taylor, Edmund, heirs	——	5–17–1806	——	K	320	None
Taylor, Edmund H	——	10– 8–1805	100	J	423	Rough Cr
Taylor, Edmund H	Frankfort	7–20–1820	2,000	T	444	Beaver Cr
Taylor, Edmund H	Franklin	7–18–1820	400	T	442	Green R
Taylor, Edmund H	Frankfort	8–20–1821	857¼	V	18	Cedar Cr
Taylor, Edmund H	Frankfort	8–21–1821	1,000	V	17	Ohio R
Taylor, Edmund H	Frankfort	11–20–1821	400	V	128	Red R
Taylor, Edmund H	Franklin	8–15–1830	Ferry	Y	509	Ky R Big Benson Cr
Taylor, Edmund H	Franklin	1–14–1832	1,000	Z	178	Mississippi R
Taylor, Edmund H	Kentucky	2–26–1835	Lot	Z	492	Frankfort
Taylor, Edmund H	Franklin	1– 1–1840	1,000	27	100	Obyon Cr
Taylor, E H	Franklin	10– 1–1839	1,000	27	146	Obion Cr

Grantee	Residence	Deed Date	Acres	Book	Page	Watercourse
Taylor, Edmund H	Franklin	10- 3-1843	246	27	374	Ky R
Taylor, Francis	Orange	7-20-1814	2,000	P	525	Blackfords Cr
Taylor, Geo C	Hickman	2-23-1823	1,000	Z	260	Hickman Cr
Taylor, Geo G	Clark	10-23-1804	500	K	31	Panther Cr
Taylor, Geo G	Clark	5-30-1796	200	K	279	Ohio R
Taylor, Geo G	——	11-19-1822	———	V	436	None
Taylor, Griffin	Frederick	12- 2-1809	650	N	262	None
Taylor, Griffin	Frederick	2- 4-1811	———	O	37	Green R
Taylor, Hubbard	Orange	1-19-1786	479	A	272	—— Br
Taylor, Hubbard	Orange	10- 6-1786	1,281½	A	275	Green R
Taylor, Hubbard	Clark	9- 4-1800	1,428	H	144	—— Cr
Taylor, Hubbard	——	11- 5-1806	666⅔	K	529	Floyds Fk
Taylor, Hubbard	Clark	11-——-1806	5	K	536	Br Hancock Cr
Taylor, Hubbard	Clark	6- 2-1807	9,000	L	209	E Fk Dix R
Taylor, Hubbard	Clark	8-31-1807	500	M	208	Floyds Fk
Taylor, Hubbard	Clark	3-25-1801	1,000	N	498	Floyds Fk
Taylor, Hubbard	Kentucky	4-20-1811	5,659	O	86	Fk Big Benson Cr
Taylor, Hubbard	Kentucky	12-31-1810	666⅔	O	280	Floyds Fk
Taylor, Hubbard	Clark	7- 6-1812	190¾	O	410	Panther Cr
Taylor, Hubbard	Orange	7-20-1814	1,000	P	525	Blackfords Cr
Taylor, Hubbard	Clark	10-20-1795	500	Q	44	W Fk Skeggs Cr
Taylor, Hubbard	Kentucky	2-14-1814	3,593½	Q	80	Salt R
Taylor, Hubbard	Kentucky	2-14-1814	1,083⅓	Q	84	—— R
Taylor, Hubbard	Kentucky	2-14-1814	6,706	Q	89	Rough Cr
Taylor, Hubbard	Clark	11-11-1816	693½	R	288	Rough Cr
Taylor, Hubbard	Clark	12-26-1817	5,000	S	46	None
Taylor, Hubbard	Clark	9-17-1823	1,882	W	373	W Fk Floyds Fk
Taylor, Hubbard, Jr	Clark	3-23-1818	Lots	S	191	Winchester
Taylor, Hubbard, Jr	Bourbon	7-27-1832	5,941	Z	216	Green R & Panther Cr
Taylor, Hubbard, Sr	Clark	12- 5-1820	50	U	186	Panther Cr
Taylor, Hubbard, Sr	Clark	9-19-1815	11,382¾	Q	188	Green & Salt R
Taylor, Hubbard, Sr	Clark	7- 6-1829	160	Y	374	Harrods Cr
Taylor, Hubbard, M H & Alice Ann	Clark	7-27-1832	3,453	Z	213	Pitsman & Rough Crs
Taylor, James	Campbell	12-21-1803	845	H	94	M Licking
Taylor, Jos	Campbell	5-13-1805	11½	N	93	None
Taylor, Jos	Newport	1-10-1816	1,000	Q	419	Tradewater
Taylor, James	Campbell	7-28-1814	1,293	Q	463	Cedar Cr
Taylor, Jas	Campbell	2-19-1817	1,000	S	78	Deer Cr
Taylor, Jas	——	2- 9-1819	Lots	S	464	Frankfort
Taylor, Jas	Campbell	11-25-1819	25,000	V	233	Welches Cr
Taylor, James	Campbell	4-26-1803	2,000	V	239	Rough Cr
Taylor, Jas	Campbell	5-30-1822	1,000	V	391	Tradewater
Taylor, Jas	Campbell	5-30-1822	5,000	V	393	Ohio R
Taylor, Jas	Campbell	5-30-1822	1,000	V	395	Tradewater
Taylor, Jas	Campbell	5-28-1823	3,327	W	56	Welches Cr & Licking
Taylor, Jas	Campbell	6- 2-1823	Lot	W	58	Frankfort
Taylor, Jas	Franklin	1- 1-1831	10,000	Z	93	S Fk Sandy R
Taylor, Jas	Campbell	11-22-1811	500	28	36	Pogues Cr
Taylor, Jas W	Franklin	6-21-1833	1,000	Z	302	Mississippi
Taylor, Jas & Edmund	Campbell	6-28-1805	5,823⅓	K	308	Green R, Mill Cr & Floyds Fk
Taylor, Jno	Orange	4-15-1799	350	D	412	Little Ky R
Taylor, Jno	Boone	8-13-1801	2,000	F	71	Otter Cr
Taylor, Jno	Gallatin	8-16-1803	1,000	H	245	Ohio R & "Mount Bird"
Taylor, Jno	Gallatin	8- 5-1807	600	L	220	Ohio R
Taylor, Jno	Gallatin	12- 4-1810	518	O	337	Ohio R
Taylor, Jno	Gallatin	6- 8-1814	500	O	459	Long Falls Cr
Taylor, Jno	Franklin	12-30-1814	237	Q	2	Fks Elkhorn
Taylor, Jno	Gallatin	11-13-1814	———	Q	97	None
Taylor, Jno	Franklin	5-21-1819	1,670	T	213	Br Ohio R
Taylee, Jno	Mt Airy	4-10-1797	19,542	B	49	Lynn Camp & Robertson Crs
Taylor, Jno P	Clark	7-27-1832	5,916	Z	218	Blackford, Panther Crs & Green R
Taylor, Joseph	Franklin	5-20-1817	501	R	343	Ohio R
Taylor, Joseph	Franklin	7-10-1818	120	S	556	None
Taylor, Joseph	Franklin	7-28-1819	———	T	62	None
Taylor, Joseph	Franklin	11- 1-1819	17¹⁰⁄₁₀	U	264	None
Taylor, Joseph	Gallatin	12-24-1823	800	W	134	Ohio R
Taylor, Mary Ann	Clark	8-21-1833	2,574⅓	Z	385	Green R & N E Fk Panther Cr
Taylor, Mary & Wm	——	10-12-1807	———	N	472	None
Taylor, Philip	Frankfort	2- 8-1813	Lot	P	84	Frankfort
Taylor, Philip W	——	11-10-1814	158	P	557	Brashears Cr
Taylor, Reuben T	Caroline	6-28-1805	5,823⅓	K	308	Green R, Mill Cr & Floyds Fk

Grantee	Residence	Deed Date	Acres	Book	Page	Watercourse
Taylor, Richard	Caroline	1–19–1786	1,000	A	270	Rough Cr
Taylor, Richard	Woodford	9–28–1805	126	K	322	Bealls Run
Taylor, Richard	Frankfort	10– 1–1808	41½	M	224	Salt Lick Cr
Taylor, Richard	Frankfort	5–30–1811	22	O	301	Greens Cr
Taylor, Richard	Woodford	1– 2–1815	118	P	616	Elkhorn
Taylor, Richard, Jr	Jefferson	9– 7–1804	4,450	J	182	Floyds Fk, Elkhorn & Rough Cr
Taylor, Richard, Jr	Jefferson	10–11–1806	1,000	M	239	Ohio R
Taylor, Richard, Jr	Franklin	8–29–1811		O	376	None
Taylor, Richard, Jr	Frankfort	7– 8–1815	318	Q	141	Big Benson Cr
Taylor, Robt J	Alexandria	12– 4–1802	7,932½	G	343	Ky, Ohio & Salt R
Taylor, Robt J	Alexandria	6– 8–1812	11,000	O	403	Kennekanic Cr
Taylor, Roger	Clark	8–10–1811	600	O	104	Floyds Fk
Taylor, Saml	Franklin	1– 3–1809	54¾	M	352	Shawnee Run
Taylor, Saml	Mercer	11– 4–1796	413	N	149	Beech Fk
Taylor, Saml	——	5– 6–1807	Lot	N	496	Frankfort
Taylor, Saml	Manchester	6–21–1823	40,000	W	402	None
Taylor, Saml	Mercer	10– 2–1798	768	D	25	None
Taylor, Saml, Trustee	Chesterfield	4–29–1824	——	X	158	None
Taylor, Thos	——	1–26–1802	4,875	F	363	Ohio Falls
Taylor, Thomas M	Bourbon	7–27–1832	3,505½	Z	214	Blackford, Panther Crs & Green R
Taylor, Thos M & Jno P	Clark	10–24–1829	Slaves	Y	421	None
Taylor, Thurston M	Clark	4– 5–1810	388	27	217	Beargrass & Rough Crs
Taylor, Thurston M	——	9–22–1810	——	N	467	None
Taylor, Wm	Jefferson	11–19–1799	500	D	478	Ohio R
Taylor, Wm	Shelby	5–10–1805	668	J	37	Ohio R
Taylor, Wm		7– 8–1806	400	K	337	Ohio R
Taylor, Wm	Shelby	12–27–1809	500	N	120	E Br Floyds Fk
Taylor, Wm	Shelby	8– 9–1813	Cont	P	198	None
Taylor, Wm	Shelby	1–24–1815	9,000	P	625	Pattons, Little Ky & 18 Mile Cr
Taylor, Wm	Shelby	9–24–1815	750	Q	221	Panther Cr & Floyds Fk
Taylor, Wm	Shelby	8–20–1817	11,000	S	60	Bullskin Cr
Taylor, Wm	Jefferson	7–25–1820	400	T	473	Floyds Fk
Taylor, Wm	Jefferson	7–18–1820	400	T	475	Floyds Fk
Taylor, Wm	Jefferson	7–18–1820	4,000	T	477	Floyds Fk
Taylor, Wm	Jefferson	6– 1–1820	400	U	11	Floyds Fk
Taylor, Wm	Norfolk	11– 7–1820	100	U	49	None
Taylor, Wm	Norfolk	12– 5–1820	400	U	50	Panther Cr
Taylor, Wm	Norfolk	12– 5–1820	450	U	52	Panther Cr
Taylor, Wm	Norfolk	12–20–1820	5,740	U	54	Ohio R & Clear Cr
Taylor, Wm	Norfolk	12–20–1820	500	U	266	Ohio R
Taylor, Wm	Norfolk	2–10–1821	14,911½	U	282	Ohio R & Clover Cr
Taylor, Wm	Norfolk	2–22–1821	5,740	U	357	Ohio R & E Fk Clover Cr
Taylor, Wm	Norfolk	4– 3–1821	100	U	359	Floyds Fk
Taylor, Wm	Norfolk	—10–1821	50	U	483	None
Taylor, Wm, Jr	——	10–29–1810	3,400	O	33	Little Sandy
Taylor, Wm Penn	Caroline	7–18–1816	1,433½	T	355	None
Taylor, Wm F	Cambletown	9–17–1805	4,400	K	466	Buck Fk
Tebb, Alice	Harrison	7–27–1832	3,380½	Z	220	Panther, Blackford Crs & Green R
Technor, Jacob	——	5–25–1814	50	P	473	Wolf Run
Telford, Isaac	New York	5–31–1799	260,178	R	232	Ohio R
Telford, Isaac & wife	Staunton	9–26–1822	2,650	W	97	Dix & Green R
Telford, Jno	Fayette	12–11–1822	256	V	407	Hickman Cr
Temple, Elenor E	Logan	7– 6–1832	——	Z	251	None
Temple, Benj	Warren	12–20–1805	Lots	K	453	Frankfort
Temple, Benj	Warren	1–24–1814	500	Q	16	Todd Fk Little Miami
Tennent, Geo W	Caroline	10–30–1799	1,210	F	46	None
Terrell, Jno H	McCracken	2–19–1839	10,018	27	114	Ohio R
Terrill, Richard	Jefferson	5–12–1796	123	A-2	281	Ohio R
Terrison, Bartholomew	Philadelphia	9–10–1784	30,000	A-2	33	None
Terrison, Bartholomew	Philadelphia	9–14–1784	31,370	A-2	38	None
Terrison, Bartholomew	Philadelphia	9–16–1784	14,000	A-2	44	None
Tevis, Saml	Shelby	11–16–1830	2,200	Z	41	Gists Cr
Thatcher, Jno P	Kentucky	12– 8–1825	2,666⅔	Y	90	Pond R
Thatcher, Jno P	Kentucky	7– 2–1831	800	Z	155	Crab Orchard & English
Thatcher, Jno B	Franklin	9–22–1831	15,000	Z	233	Salt R
Theobald, Tho S	Franklin	3–25–1844	2	27	412	Ky R
Theobald, Swigert & Co	Franklin	10–21–1844	——	27	438	Ky R
Thomas, Ann	Franklin	10–19–1830	——	Z	27	None
Thomas, Mrs Ann	Franklin	1–15–1831	148	Z	67	Benson Cr
Thomas Caleb	Charles	5–13–1805	100	K	543	None
Thomas, Edmund	Frankfort	9–15–1800	1,500	D	549	Salt R

Grantee	Residence	Deed Date	Acres	Book	Page	Watercourse
Thomas, Edmund	Frankfort	6–14–1800	650	E	45	3 Fks Cumberland
Thomas, Edmund	Frankfort	6–17–1800	5,000	E	46	3 Fks Cumberland
Thomas, Edmund	Franklin	11– 5–1800	1,000	E	311	Cumberland R
Thomas, Edmund	Frankfort	5–12–1800	683	F	165	None
Thomas, Edmund	Franklin	3–17–1801	10,346½	F	190	Stoners Fk Mill Sta Camp & S Fk Licking
Thomas, Edmund	Franklin	7–21–1802	400	G	114	Green R
Thomas, Jack	Grayson	10–11–1821	15,331	V	147	Brush Cr
Thomas, Jack	Grayson	11–12–1827	66,831	X	328	Nolinn & Lynn Camp Cr
Thomas, Jno & Jas	————	12– 8–1829	98¾	Z	255	Cane Run
Thomas, Joseph	Mercer	11–24–1806	48	K	521	Ky R
Thomas, Philman	Fayette	2–25–1790	1,000	B-2	296	None
Thomas, Philman	Fayette	2–25–1791	2,566	B-2	298	Hickman Cr
Thomas, Philman	Fayette	2–25–1791	1,500	B-2	300	None
Thomas, Philman	Fayette	2–25–1791	2,000	B-2	302	W Fk Lick Cr
Thomas, Philman	Mason	1–28–1803	11,250	K	89	Hingston Fk
Thomas, Robt	Henry	5– 5–1818	1,000	S	121	Mill Cr
Thomas, Robinson	Essex	9– 1–1801	10,000	G	358	Ohio R
Thomasson, Saml	Scott	6–——–1821	666	U	498	S Elkhorn Cr
Thomasson, Saml	Scott	6–13–1821	78	U	500	S Elkhorn
Thompson, Arch	Lincoln	7–18–1786	1,000	A	281	Salt R
Thompson, Henry	Baltimore	12– 7–1826	2,483	X	465	Elk Cr
Thompson, H, Trustee	Richard	9–21–1804	13,500	H	454	Ohio R & Patton Cr
Thompson, Jno	Jefferson	3–——–1799	300	D	307	Russell Cr
Thompson, Jonah	Alexandria	10–25–1820	336	U	321	S Fk Bensons Cr
Thompson, Nathaniel	Woodford	11–18–1806	73	K	506	Ohio R
Thompson, Reger	Franklin	12–10–1805	100	K	124	S Fk Big Benson Cr
Thompson, Robt J	Franklin	9–30–1826	Lot	Y	198	Croghansville Ohio
Thompson, Thos	Pittsgrove	5–29–1800	150	W	59	Ky R
Thompson, Waddy	Greenup	7–26–1806	100	K	361	Ohio R
Thompson, Wm L	Jefferson	8– 9–1819	360	T	57	None
Thompson, Wm M	Culpepper	9–11–1818	666⅔	S	484	Gasper R
Thompson, Wm R	Frankfort	11– 2–1822	Lot	V	337	Frankfort
Thornburg, Joseph	Baltimore	10–16–1795	1,524	A-2	620	Meeting & Rough Cr
Thornton, Margaret	————	6–11–1845	Lots	28	2	Midway
Thornton, Margaret	Woodford	1–12–1846	Lot	28	49	Midway
Thornton, Philip	Spotsylvania	1–12–1813	2,000	P	141	N Fk Tradewater
Thornton, Philip	Spotsylvania	1–12–1813	2,000	P	277	N Fk Tradewater
Thorp, David	Hardin	1–27–1813	250	P	53	Bacon Cr
Thorp, Jno	Hardin	1–27–1813	120	P	70	None
Threlkeld, Wm	Scott	3–23–1811	274	Q	39	Twin Cr
Throckmorton, Saml	Franklin	7– 2–1802	131½	F	453	Elkhorn
Throckmorton, Thos	Prince, William	4–18–1801	400	F	192	Quirks Run
Thruston, Alfred	Jefferson	9–10–1840	158	27	152	E Fk Floyds Fk
Thruston, Alfred	Jefferson	8– 8–1840	464½	27	153	Shelby Co
Thruston, Chas M	Louisville	8–16–1817	9,000	R	411	S M Fk Rough Cr
Thruston, Chas M	Jefferson	9–18–1840	158¼	27	260	E Br Floyds Fk
Thruston, Chas M	Jefferson	8–12–1841	234	27	261	E Br Floyds Fk
Thruston, Chas M	Jefferson	8–14–1841	100	27	264	E Br Floyds Fk
Thruston, Chas M	Jefferson	10–13–1841	334	27	265	E Br Floyds Fk
Thruston, Maria	Shelby	1–——–1841	9,113	27	194	Walnut Bottom
Thursby, Edward	Philadelphia	7–16–1808	7,870	M	263	Elkhorn
Thurston, Buckner	Fayette	3– 2–1796	1,793	A-2	148	None
Thurston, Buckner	Fayette	11– 5–1798	204¾	D	74	Beargrass Cr
Thurston, Jno Buckner & Chas	Frederick	10–12–1787	————	L	223	W Allegheny Mts
Tibbs, Daniel	Jefferson	3– 2–1809	750	P	80	Harrods Cr & Floyds Fk
Tibbs, Daniel	Jefferson	3– 2–1809	750	P	165	Harrods & Floyds Fk
Tibbs, Jos	Mason	11–22–1843	10,000	27	369	None
Tierman, Luke	Baltimore	7– 3–1827	7,508	X	266	M Licking Mill & Slate Cr
Tierman, Luke	Baltimore	3– 1–1827	5,000	Y	277	Slate & State Cr
Tiffany, Duvall & Co	Baltimore	11–16–1839	2,500	27	96	M Elkhorn
Tiffany, Duvall & Co	Baltimore	1– 1–1844	2,500	27	395	Franklin Co
Tilford, David	Mercer	2– 8–1790	260	B-2	116	Ky R
Tilford, Jeremiah	Mercer	11– 9–1786	265¾	A	184	Tilfords Spring Br
Tilford, Jno	————	8–28–1819	5,500	T	162	Rough & Panther Cr
Tiller, Saml	Philadelphia	11–10–1841	1,360	27	294	Tennessee R
Tiller, Saml	Philadelphia	5– 8–1839	4,320	28	62	W Tennessee R
Timberlake, David	Frederick	10–10–1798	500	D	503	Fox Cr
Tipping, Ebenezer	————	10– 2–1804	Slaves	H	446	None
Tipping, Ebenezer	Franklin	10– 8–1804	Negro	H	496	None
Todd, Chas S	Franklin	7–29–1815	56	Q	343	Cane Run
Todd, Chas S	————	7– 1–1815	Lots	Q	389	Frankfort & Lex
Todd, Chas S	Franklin	5–15–1819	200	S	548	Ky R
Todd, Chas S	Franklin	9–17–1819	Lot	T	392	Versailles
Todd, Chas S	Franklin	5– 1–1819	382	T	395	Sinking Fk Little R
Todd, Chas S & Wife	————	5–12–1819	800	S	500	Hays Fk Silver Cr

Grantee	Residence	Deed Date	Acres	Book	Page	Watercourse
Todd, Chas S & Wife	Frankfort	1–14–1819	Lots	U	515	Frankfort
Todd, Elizabeth L	Woodford	8–21–1846	143	28	102	Dry Run
Todd, Geo & Chas S	———	7–27–1819	———	T	80	None
Todd, James	Philadelphia	6– 7–1797	50,000	B	209	Mill Cr
Todd, Jno	Montgomery	6–22–1807	140	L	76	Pleasant Run
Todd, Jno H	Frankfort	7–23–1819	Lot	T	97	Frankfort
Todd, Jno H & Thos	Franklin	8– 4–1819	Lots	T	397	Columbus Ohio
Todd, Jno H & Thos	Franklin	8– 4–1819	1,102	T	397	Hays Fk Silver Cr Ky R & Sinking Fk Little R
Todd, Jno H & Thos	Frankfort	6– 5–1821	Lots	U	513	Columbus Ohio
Todd, John H & Thos	Franklin	8– 4–1819	Lots	T	397	New Castle
Todd, Levi L & Wife	Montgomery	6–30–1821	———	U	456	None
Todd, Mrs Lucy P	Franklin	6– 2–1827	Lot	X	251	Frankfort
Todd, Robt S	Louisville	8– 5–1816	1,962½	R	16	Rock Lick Cr
Todd, Robt S	Fayette	10– 8–1846	38	28	108	Dry Run
Todd, Saml	Kentucky	2–14–1831	3,422	Z	120	Ky R
Todd, Thos	Mercer	9–25–1788	½	A	467	None
Todd, Thos	Lincoln	6–25–1789	344	B-2	67	Hanging Fk
Todd, Thos	Franklin	9–20–1802	700	F	503	Chaplin, Fk
Todd, Thos	Frankfort	3– 3–1803	Slaves	G	189	None
Todd, Thos	Franklin	8–21–1801	1,200	H	405	Silver Cr
Todd, Thos	Woodford	2–11–1804	527½	H	409	Trough Spring Fk
Todd, Thomas	Woodford	1–22–1806	Lot	K	225	Frankfort
Todd, Thos	Woodford	4–10–1805	15,000	K	314	Green R
Todd, Thos	Woodford	3–23–1807	———	L	45	Blackfords Fk
Todd, Thomas	Woodford	3–13–1805	———	L	81	None
Todd, Thos	Woodford	11–16–1807	Slaves	L	334	None
Todd, Thos	Woodford	12–15–1809	1,198	N	118	Paint Lick & Back
Todd, Thos	Franklin	8–15–1814	Lot	P	503	Frankfort
Todd, Thos	Franklin	8–15–1814	1,200	P	504	Glens Cr
Todd, Thos	Woodford	1–31–1814	83	P	587	Elkhorn & Glens Cr
Todd, Thos	Franklin	6– 3–1817	278	S	47	None
Todd, Thos	Franklin	6——1818	Lots	T	211	Frankfort
Todd, Thos	———	12–28–1819	Lots	T	388	Frankfort
Todd, Thos	Franklin	4–18–1820	Slaves	U	1	None
Todd, Thos	Frankfort	5–31–1821	Slaves	U	489	None
Todd, Thos	Frankfort	1–10–1822	Lots	V	166	Frankfort
Todd, Thos	Franklin	4–18–1820	Slaves	V	220	None
Todd, Thos	Gallatin	10–25–1823	148	W	186	None
Todd, Wm & Robt	Fayette	4–14–1813	750	P	195	Pitman Cr & Cumberland R
Tomlinson, Nathaniel	———	3–20–1802	500	F	381	None
Tompkins, H & J	Fayette	11–15–1802	1,500	G	362	Harrisons Cr
Tonlinn, Harry	Frankfort	4–10–1804	1,990	H	194	Slate Cr
Tonlinn, Harry	Franklin	11– 7–1804	53	H	429	None
Tonlinn, Harry	———	10– 2–1804	Slaves	H	446	None
Tonlinn, Harry	Franklin	2– 6–1805	4,213	H	552	Middle & Valley Cr
Towles, Henry	Bourbon	12–13–1833	666⅔	Z	378	S Fk Tradewater
Towles, Wm	Owen	6–17–1842	140	27	291	Severn & Cedar Cr
Tracy, Wm G & Uriah	———	11–19–1817	Lot	S	39	Lexington
Travis, Jno	Philadelphia	5– 5–1798	———	D	520	None
Trigg, Elizabeth	Bedford	3–10–1790	932	B-2	111	Hingston Fk
Trigg, Harrit T	———	7– 1–1837	———	27	111	Franklin Co
Trimble, Jas	Baltimore	4–19–1806	2,200	K	470	Bensons Cr
Triplett, Jno R	———	7– 1–1831	1,162	Z	146	Ohio R
Triplett, Jno R	———	4–21–1834	Lots	Z	431	Richmond, Va
Triplett, Frederick	Shelby	3– 4–1815	50	O	20	None
Triplett, Robt	Franklin	3–13–1823	12,148	W	113	——— Cr
Triplett, Robt	Frankfort	2– 3–1825	1,950	X	92	Yellow Banks in Daviess Co
Triplett, Robt	Franklin	9– 1–1825	1,000	X	170	Ohio R
Triplett, Robt	Franklin	1–26–1827	———	X	209	None
Triplett, Robt	Franklin	4–21–1826	1,233	Y	167	None
Triplett, Robt	Kentucky	4–21–1826	666⅔	Y	169	Tennessee R & Consols Cr
Triplett, Robt	Kentucky	5–18–1826	1,000	Y	171	Ohio R
Triplett, Robt	Kentucky	2– 8–1826	750	Y	174	Ohio R
Triplett, Robt	Kentucky	6–15–1832	———	Z	203	None
Triplett, Robt	Kentucky	1–14–1834	1,600	Z	389	Ohio R
Triplett, Thos	Franklin	10–21–1824	Lot	X	65	Frankfort
Triplett, Thos	Franklin	1–26–1828	Slaves	X	367	None
Triplett, Thos	Franklin	2–13–1826	521	Y	133	None
Triplett, Thos	Franklin	12–26–1829	———	Y	440	Elkhorn
Triplett, Thos	Franklin	12–26–1829	———	Y	461	Elkhorn
Trotter, Joseph	Scott	9–21–1813	272	P	519	Lost Cr
Trout, Daniel	Shenandoah	12– 3–1810	532	O	336	Ohio R
Troxcel, Jno	———	11–25–1803	———	H	57	None
Trustees Benson Creek Church	Franklin	2–26–1810	Lot	P	244	Burging Lot
Trustees, M E Church	Franklin	1– 1–1844	Lot	27	413	Frankfort

Grantee	Residence	Deed Date	Acres	Book	Page	Watercourse
Trustees, Concorde	Mercer	9–21–1789	2	B-2	76	Danville
Trustees, Danville	Lincoln	9–14–1785	———	A	64	None
Trustees Dist. No. 19	Franklin	11– 9–1841	¼	27	249	N & Main Elkhorn
Trustees, Frankfort	Franklin	3– 7–1803	Lot	G	210	Frankfort
Trustee, Frankfort	Franklin	4– 2–1838	Lot	28	94	Frankfort
Trustees, Frankfort Cemetery	Franklin	4–24–1845	12	28	14	Ky R
Trustees, Town of Jefferson	Jefferson	10– 2–1815	57¼	Q	226	None
Trustees, Transylvania U	Kentucky	11–27–1832	75	Z	242	Shelbyville Pike
Tryon, Clifford	New York	9–16–1816	———	W	6	None
Tucker, Jno	Richmond	7– 4–1798	640	D	101	None
Tunstall, Mildred	Frankfort	12– 1–1818	Lot	S	522	Frankfort
Tunstall, Mildred	Frankfort	7– 6–1821	Lots	U	487	Frankfort
Tunstall, Thos	Frankfort	3–13–1805	———	L	306	None
Turner, Henry S	Jefferson	6–30–1807	1,000	L	160	Br Pages Cr
Turner, Henry S	Jefferson	9– 1–1813	———	U	46	None
Turner, Jas	Hartford	7– 6–1812	250	O	500	Green R Nohim & Little Caney
Turner, Robt & Geo	Richmond	3–10–1807	415	L	95	Salt R
Turner, Thos Jr	Montgomery	3– 9–1798	50,000	C	191	Sextons Cr
Turpin, Geo	Woodford	3– 1–1819	———	X	66	None
Turpin, Geo	———	6–11–1833	2,000	Z	356	Laurel Co
Turpin, Philip	Chesterfield	5– 2–1802	1,400	F	451	Station Camp Cr
Tutt, James	Spotsylvania	10– 2–1802	750	G	159	W Fk Red R
Tyler, Chas	Montgomery	11–14–1845	1,920	28	60	Cedar Cr
Ubery, Peter	Lincoln	9– 5–1791	300	B-2	389	Slate Cr
Underwood, Francis	Louisa	10–16–1797	6,000	B	247	Big Bone Lick
Underwood, Geo	Hanover	10–16–1797	6,000	B	247	Big Bone Lick
Underwood, Geo	Hanover	9–12–1799	720	D	513	Sandy Cr
Underwood, Geo	Hanover	10–20–1799	1,000	K	78	Sandy
Underwood, Joseph R	Kentucky	10–28–1824	28,500	X	40	Big Barren, W Fk Little & Cumberland R
Underwood, J R	Warren	9–23–1829	Lots	Y	396	Columbus, Ky
Underwood, J R	Warren	5–23–1831	1,000	Z	130	Bayo Cr
Underwood, J R	Warren	4–16–1840	9,050	27	140	Ohio & Cumberland
Underwood, J R	Warren	9– 5–1842	5,050	27	313	Locust & Indian Cr
Underwood, Thos	Virginia	1– 9–1807	4,000	M	200	None
Upson, Renselar	Bristol	6–14–1841	320	27	253	Tennessee R
Useleton, Jno	Woodford	7–27–1813	81½	P	169	Glenns Cr
Utman, Joseph	Lincoln	4–15–1791	200	B-2	286	Boones Mill Cr
Utterback, Benj	Franklin	2– 7–1817	206¾	R	283	Stone Lick Br
Vallandingham, Richard	———	5–27–1812	564	X	82	Twins Cr
Vance, Samuel	Louisville	1– 5–1818	666⅔	S	168	Green R
Vance, Samuel	Jefferson	———1820	606⅔	U	169	None
Vandyke, Peter Sr	———	—15–1815	248	Q	232	None
Vanmeter, Jacob	———	12–30–1806	18,608	K	525	None
Vanmeter, Jacob	———	1–27–1808	4,550	L	292	Sinking Cr
Vanpelt, Samuel	Carroll	10– 5–1842	Lot	27	325	Carrollton
Vanuxem, James	Philadelphia	7– 9–1791	36,000	A-2	7	Sandy R & Green
Vanuxem, James	Philadelphia	5–16–1798	36,700	D	328	Sandy R & M Cr
Vanuxem, Jas	Philadelphia	4– 1–1790	———	Q	46	None
Vanuxem, Jas	———	6–27–1818	6,700	S	224	Middle & Valley Cr
Vanuxem, Jas	Morrisville	10–29–1830	1,021	Z	23	Nohim
Vanuxem, Jas, heirs	Philadelphia	2–15–1828	10,850	X	383	Rolling Fk, Middle & Valley Cr
Vanuxem, Jas, heirs	Philadelphia	11–23–1829	15,000	Y	416	S Fk Sandy & Cumberland R
Vaughan, Edmund	Franklin	3– 3–1846	140	28	78	Woodford Co
Vaughan, Jno	Philadelphia	6–21–1796	20,781	C	278	N Fk Ky R
Vaughan, Shadrack	Goochland	11– 5–1799	2,500	D	417	Sandy R
Vaughter, Wm	———	7–29–1808	125	M	104	None
Vawter, Wm	Woodford	11– 6–1804	———	H	437	Twin Cr
Vawter, Wm	Woodford	11–28–1804	1,000	H	487	Butlers Fk
Vawter, Wm	Woodford	7– 3–1805	580	J	339	Dry Cr
Veech, Jas	Shelby	1–19–1830	20	V	439	Beech Cr
Veness, Jno	Franklin	7–19–1796	———	A-2	371	Big Benson Cr
Vennable, Samuel W	Prince Edward	3– 1–1792	1,000	B-2	474	Chaplin Fk
Vertner, Daniel	Fayette	7–22–1801	30,000	F	125	Green R
Vest, Jno J	Franklin	3–19–1833	Lot	Z	292	Frankfort
Vigus, Jobz	Fayette	11–18–1805	Lot	J	384	Frankfort
Vincent, Eli	———	4– 1–1813	364	P	116	Ky R
Vineyard, Society	Lexington District	5–20–1801	———	E	73	For Vineyard
Voorhies, Peter G	Franklin	2–14–1804	10	H	426	Elkhorn Cr
Voorhies, Peter G	Franklin	10– 3–1815	600	Q	470	Sinking Br
Voorhies, Peter G	Franklin	10– 3–1815	———	Q	480	None
Voorhies, Peter G	Franklin	10–28–1819	200	T	137	M Elkhorn

Grantee	Residence	Deed Date	Acres	Book	Page	Watercourse
Voss, Nicholas	Richmond	5–10–1794	1,000	A-2	640	Sulphur Lick
Voss, Nicholas	Richmond	5–15–1794	666⅔	A-2	642	Little Barren R
Vowels, Zachariah	Falmouth	1–—–1803	3,500	J	204	Skeggs & Big Bone Lick Cr
Waddington, Joshua	New York	6–20–1818	Lot	S	166	Frankfort
Wadlington, Jno	Philadelphia	6– 3–1801	———	F	85	None
Waggener, Edmund M	U S A	1–12–1831	Plough	Z	425	Patent Bar Shear Plough
Waggoner, Alexander	Adair	7–27–1815	666⅔	Q	149	Glenn Cr
Waggoner, Jno	Mercer	7–10–1798	1,000	C	265	N Fk Tradewater
Waggoner, Jno	Adair	9–22–1808	400	M	363	E Br Little Ky
Waggoner, Nancy & Herbert	Adair	12– 8–1808	528½	M	261	Lost Cr
Wagnon, Jno P	Lexington	4– 2–1808	134	M	358	Dix R
Walden, Jno	Fanquir	6–16–1828	1,065	Z	57	Licking
Walden, Zephaniah	Woodford	12– 5–1816	11¼	R	79	Buck Cr
Walford, Jno	Adair	11– 9–1821	1,333⅓	V	98	Crocus & Greasy Cr
Walker, Alexander	Scott	3– 7–1799	———	D	130	S Fk Elkhorn
Walker, Benj	New York	12–30–1795	30,000	A-2	221	None
Walker, David Jr		5– 5–1818	———	S	161	None
Walker, Jno	Henrico	5–28–1790	10,000	A-2	513	Sandy R
Walker, Jno C	Kentucky	12—–1818	———	S	508	Sovern Cr
Walker, Merry	Madison	9–26–1805	2,000	J	329	N Fk Licking
Walker, Merry	Madison	9–26–1805	3,000	J	334	Raven Cr
Walker, Merry	Madison	6–29–1807	2,000	L	67	N Fk Licking
Walker, Mary A	Shelby	1—–1841	1,444	27	194	Mayfield Cr
Walker, Wm, heirs	Woodford	1–17–1800	146¾	D	526	Butler Fk
Wallace, Caleb	Lincoln	3–22–1786	Negro	A	93	None
Wallace, Cobb	Woodford	4–23–1804	8,098	H	225	None
Wallace, Cobb	Woodford	5–17–1806	100	K	334	Rough Cr
Wallace, Cobb	———	9–28–1807	300	L	142	S Elkhorn
Wallace, Cobb	Kentucky	9–28–1807	100	L	145	Rough Cr
Wallace, Cobb	———	9–28–1807	230⅓	L	147	N Fk Lost Cr
Wallace, Cobb	———	2–25–1786	300	L	170	S Fk Elkhorn
Wallace, Cobb	Woodford	2–12–1810	2,998	N	216	Tradewater
Wallace, Cobb	Woodford	9– 1–1810	3,000	N	385	Rough Cr
Wallace, Cobb	Woodford	9– 1–1810	233⅓	N	388	Lost Cr
Wallace, Cobb	Lincoln	1–12–1811	1,380	N	410	Elkhorn
Wallace, Cobb	Woodford	4–26–1811	666⅔	O	40	Eddy Cr
Wallace, Cobb	———	10– 8–1796	400	O	42	Barnetts Cr
Wallace, Cobb	Woodford	9– 1–1810	233⅓	P	318	Lost Cr
Wallace, Christian & Henry	———	7–22–1814	150	T	73	None
Wallace, Fanny	———	9–22–1810	———	N	469	None
Wallace, Jno	Clark	8–25–1808	189½	M	152	Floyds Fk
Wallace, Jno	Clark	4– 5–1810	44	N	215	Ohio R
Wallace, Jno	Clark	10–16–1810	Lots	N	306	Louisville
Wallace, Jno	Woodford	4–24–1812	———	O	379	None
Wallace, Jno	———	9–12–1806	1,611	Y	178	Ohio R
Wallace, Lucinda & Mary D	Stafford	5–11–1799	6,000	D	486	Ohio R
Wallace, Mary D & Lucinda	———	9–12–1806	1,554	Y	178	Ohio R
Wallace, Mary, heirs	———	5–21–1833	2,000	Z	291	Deer Cr
Wallace, Michael	———	9–12–1806	1,200	Y	178	Ohio R
Wallace, Robt	Fayette	7–11–1796	1,000	A-2	433	Skeggs Cr
Wallace, Saml, executor	Woodford	12–14–1829	1,524	Y	490	Bullskin Cr & Flat Lick
Wallace, Thos	Lexington	3–13–1799	Lots	D	138	Louisville
Wallace, Thos	———	9–12–1806	1,384	Y	178	Ohio R
Wallace, Wm B	Stafford	6–21–1816	800	R	315	Ohio R
Wallace, Wm B	Franklin	3–26–1823	1,095	W	61	Cane Run, Mill & Drennons Lick Cr
Wallace, Wm B	Franklin	7–24–1823	———	W	189	None
Wallace, Wm B	———	9–12–1806	1,496	Y	178	Ohio R
Waller, Wm	Fayette	10–25–1796	200	A-2	550	Br Buck Cr
Waller, Wm S	Franklin	12–24–1804	664	H	500	Evens Mill Cr
Walton, Matthew	Washington	8– 8–1795	14,686¼	A-2	185	Rolling Fk & Big Sandy R
Walton, Matthew	Washington	11–18–1796	100	A-2	544	Br S Fk Nolinn
Walton, Matthew	Washington	11–26–1796	1,002	A-2	601	Beech Fk
Walton, Matthew	Washington	2–11–1797	———	A-2	610	Beech Fk
Walton, Matthew	———	12–27–1789	2,000	B-2	187	Stones Fk
Walton, Matthew	Washington	12–19–1798	1,212	D	99	Sinking Cr
Walton, Matthew	Washington	9–10–1799	687	D	410	Br Rough Cr
Walton, Matthew	Scott	12–18–1800	148	E	244	None
Walton, Matthew	Washington	11–17–1802	1,230	G	76	Beech Fk
Walton, Matthew	Kentucky	12–10–1802	45,000	G	99	Beech Fk
Walton, Matthew	Washington	11–30–1815	890	Q	288	Beech & Black Fks
Walton, Genl Matthew	Washington	9– 7–1799	3,435	D	408	Green R
Walton, Genl Matthew	Washington	11–25–1801	10,000	F	142	Chaplins Fk

Grantee	Residence	Deed Date	Acres	Book	Page	Watercourse
Walsh, Jacob Jr	Baltimore	4–26–1800	10,023	E	82	Richland, Stinking & Goose Crs
Walsh, Robt & Wife	———	———1820	Lot	U	184	Louisville
Wants, Stephen	Baltimore	9–22–1801	———	F	52	None
Wants, Stephen & Co	Baltimore	7–12–1798	1,000	C	296	N Fk Elkhorn
Ward, David L	Jefferson	12–15–1815	70,000	Q	422	Little Sandy R
Ward, David L	Jefferson	8–28–1816	6,713½	R	85	Salt Lick Cr & Little Sandy R
Ward, David L	Jefferson	12– 8–1819	70,000	T	210	Little Sandy Salt Works
Ward, Jno Sr	———	3– 2–1805	274	K	135	Clay Lick Fk
Ward, Jno Sr	———	3– 2–1805	274	K	140	Clay Lick Fk
Ward, Sally, heirs	———	6——1818	285	U	522	Dry Fk Craigs Cr
Ward, Susannah T	Franklin	4–25–1825	Lot	X	131	Frankfort
Warder, Jno	Philadelphia	8–12–1797	6,000	E	42	Rolling Fk
Warden, Jesse	Kentucky	3– 1–1828	87½	X	389	Waltons Cr
Ware, James	Christian	10——1819	Lot	T	361	Frankfort
Ware, Saml	Franklin	4–19–1821	117	Z	342	Franklin Co
Ware, Saml	———	2–26–1834	126	Z	415	Dry Run
Ware, Saml	Kentucky	6——1839	126	28	23	None
Warfield, Chas	Frederick	2– 2–1808	600	M	65	Big Barren R
Warfield, Chas	Frederick	1–27–1808	100	M	77	Big Barren R
Warfield, Chas	Bedford	5–12–1808	100	M	80	Big Barren R
Warfield, Chas	Frederick	2–19–1808	300	M	83	Big Barren R
Warfield, Chas	Frederick	4–24–1809	100	M	434	Big Barren R
Warfield, Chas A	Frederick	4–15–1809	100	M	436	Big Barren R
Warfield, Elisha	Fayette	12–11–1822	256	V	407	Hickman Cr
Warfield, Rachel	Frankfort	6– 5–1821	102½	V	51	Benson Cr
Warfield, Walter	Jefferson	7– 9–1796	1,000	A-2	437	Elkhorn
Warfield, Walter	Jefferson	2– 8–1796	916	A-2	552	Cumberland R
Warfield, Walter	Fayette	2–10–1800	1,000	D	524	Sulphur Lick Fk
Warfield, Walter	———	6– 6–1808	37,837	M	14	———
Warfield, Walter	Lexington	6– 6–1810	1,500	P	567	Big Barren R
Warfield, Walker	Lexington	8–24–1822	1,000	W	99	None
Warfield, Walter	Fayette	6–18–1825	———	X	193	Swifts Camp Cr
Warfield, Dr Walter	Lexington	9–22–1807	27,500	L	126	Ky R
Warford, Jno	Jefferson	9– 3–1790	600	B-2	199	Brashears Cr
Waring, Jno Upshaw	Fayette	11–26–1813	100	P	487	Ky R
Waring, Jno U	Fayette	12–13–1814	584	P	575	Puncheon Camp Cr
Waring, Jno U	Fayette	12–13–1814	1,085	P	577	Pond Cr
Waring, Jno U	Fayette	12–13–1814	1,333⅓	P	578	Big Barren R
Waring, Jno U	Fayette	12–13–1814	1,000	P	580	Ohio R
Waring Jno U	Fayette	1– 1–1815	666⅔	P	584	Russell Cr
Waring, Jno U	Fayette	12–21–1815	2,000	Q	283	Hingston Fk
Waring, Jno U	Fayette	6–13–1815	1,000	Q	416	Tradewater
Waring, Jno U	Fayette	12–23–1815	2,470	R	53	Benson Cr
Warning, Jno U	Fayette	3–18–1817	951	R	272	Hingston Fk
Warning, Jno U	Fayette	1–21–1818	1,000	S	8	Twin Cr
Waring, Jno U	Fayette	1– 1–1818	5½	S	119	None
Waring, Jno U	Fayette	10–22–1818	500	S	265	Sulphur Lick Fk
Waring, Jno U	Warren	6–21–1819	100	T	11	Pitman Cr
Waring, Jno U	Kentucky	6–21–1819	800	T	13	Cumberland R
Waring, Jno U	Fayette	10–18–1818	Lot	T	66	Versailles
Waring, Jno U	Fayette	10–13–1818	200	T	220	Shawnee Run
Waring, Jno U	Fayette	8–26–1814	100	T	403	Ky R
Waring, Jno U	———	11–17–1820	40	U	443	None
Waring, Jno U	Fayette	5– 9–1818	———	Y	195	None
Waring, Jno U	———	5–18–1829	———	Y	372	Ky R
Waring, Jno U	Union	9–25–1829	333	Y	388	Cumberland R
Waring, Jno U	Union	7–23–1833	———	Z	393	None
Waring, Jno U	Union	9–28–1833	———	Z	395	None
Waring, Jno U	Union	9–28–1833	———	Z	398	None
Waring, Jno U	Union	6–11–1834	50	Z	440	Ohio R
Waring, Jno U	Kentucky	3–10–1834	———	Z	513	None
Waring, Jno U	Union	6– 1–1835	1,000	Z	514	Tennessee R
Waring, Jno U	Union	1–18–1842	1,000	27	256	Tradewater
Waring, Robt Payne	Virginia	4–21–1834	666⅔	Z	469	Tradewater
Warner, Jacob	———	6–18–1804	175	H	281	Slate Cr
Warren, Jno	Mercer	9–10–1791	5,000	B-2	478	Brashears Cr
Warren, Thos B	Franklin	12– 8–1804	300	H	439	Little N Elkhorn
Warren, Thos B	Franklin	2–12–1805	28,399	H	549	Ohio R, Licking & Big Benson Cr
Warren, Thos B	———	1–18–1808	5,312½	M	89	Hingston Fk
Warren, Thos B	Fayette	5–31–1811	190¼	O	118	None
Warren, Wm	Lincoln	10–23–1788	300	A	509	Rough Cr
Warren, Wm	Lincoln	10–23–1788	300	A	510	Rough L Cr
Warren, Wm	———	12– 8–1808	224	M	365	None
Warren & Barbee	Danville	2–27–1795	842	A-2	425	S Fk Licking
Warring, Jno Upshaw	Fayette	12– 9–1814	1,000	P	569	Tradewater
Wash, Lucy	Cumberland	12–23–1833	876⅔	Z	402	Little Barren, Tennessee & Ohio R

Grantee	Residence	Deed Date	Acres	Book	Page	Watercourse
Washington, George	Mt Vernon	11– 5–1798	5,000	D	484	Rough L Cr
Washington, Jno	Logan	9– 4–1805	Lots & slaves	K	121	Lexington
Washington, Lund	Washington City	11–16–1796	500	D	256	None
Watkins, Francis, heirs.———	———	5–29–1823	1,000	W	40	! Rough Cr
Watkins, Isaac	Shelby	12–19–1817	———	S	53	None
Watkins, Isaac	Shelby	2– 2–1818	———	S	56	None
Watkins, Jno	Franklin	3– 4–1811	Negro	N	444	None
Watkins, Jno	Franklin	5–28–1812	Horses	O	397	None
Watkins, Joseph & Robt	Goochland	12– 9–1796	1,000	B	136	Parroquette Cr
Watkins, Thos	Ponstation	8–26–1800	1,000	E	113	N Fk Clay Lick Cr
Watkins, Thos B	Goochland	12–10–1804	1,000	J	271	None
Watson, James	Alexandria	5–18–1795	3,000	A-2	172	Clover Cr
Watson, James	Alexandria	4–27–1796	30,000	A-2	655	Rolling & Chaplains Fks
Watson, James	Alexandria	11–19–1796	30,000	D	19	Drennons Lick Cr
Watson, Jno	Franklin	4–14–1846	143	28	101	Franklin Co
Watson, Joab	Warren	10–30–1807	50	T	209	None
Watson, Josiah	Alexandria	10–16–1788	2,743	T	174	Buck Fk
Wattie, Jas, Trustee	———	8– 1–1817	Lots	S	289	Lexington
Watts, Edmond	Frankfort	5–20–1811	160	O	224	Big Benson Cr
Watts, Jno	Bedford	4–17–1800	500	E	10	Goose Cr
Wayman, Edmund	Shelby	2–21–1817	811	T	135	None
Weakley, Stephen	Shelby	11–27–1813	215	P	347	Gists Fk
Weakley, Thos	Shelby	11–27–1813	100	P	485	Guests Fk
Weaver, Jacob	Fanquier	3——1823	250	W	217	Ky R
Weaver, Jacob	Fanquier	6–16–1828	1,065	Z	57	Licking
Weaver, Jacob	Fanquier	4–16–1829	1,065	Z	60	Licking
Weaver, Samuel	Fanquier	6–16–1828	1,065	Z	57	Licking
Webb, Augustus	Fayette	3–15–1790	50	B-2	130	Lower Howards Cr
Webb, Leo	Clark	3–23–1818	Lots	S	191	Winchester
Webb. Isaac	———	4–28–1792	200	A-2	302	None
Webb. Isaac	———	4–28–1792	200	H	105	None
Webber, Richard W	Cumberland	10–18–1816	———	R	335	None
Weeks, Selathiel	Prince George	12–21–1796	600	F	60	Caseys Cr
Weir, Geo	Richmond	6–20–1795	10,000	A-2	548	N Fk Sandy R
Weir, Henry & Jas Jr	Lexington	9– 6–1820	238	U	19	S Elkhorn
Weisiger, Daniel	Franklin	12–27–1805	2,000	K	156	M Elkhorn
Weisiger, Daniel	Franklin	11–15–1804	898	P	349	Ky R
Weisiger, Daniel	———	4–27–1824	30,000	W	346	Licking & — Cr Lulbergrud
Weisiger, Daniel	Chesterfield	4–29–1824	———	X	158	None
Weisiger, Joseph	Mercer	12–10–1830	711	Z	51	Town Fk Salt R
Weisiger, Samuel P	Frankfort	2– 8–1831	Lots	Z	164	Frankfort
Weisiger, Samuel P	Franklin	12–28–1831	Lot	Z	172	Frankfort
Weisiger, Samuel P & Lucy	Franklin	3– 5–1835	100	Z	495	Ky R
Weisiger, Samuel P & wife	Franklin	8–12–1839	Lots	27	73	Frankfort
Welch, Geo	Fayette	10–11–1790	178	B-2	217	Dix R
Welch, James	Greenbrier	5–10–1800	200	E	319	Small Br
Welch, James	Greenbrier	1–18–1800	14,166¼	F	92	Little Sandy
Welch, Jno	Spotsylvania	5–18–1802	3,530	P	398	None
Welch, Silvester	Franklin	9–26–1845	49	28	28	Dry Run
Welch, Wm	Shelby	8–19–1839	180	27	55	Franklin Co
Wellford, Jno S & Wm	Fredericksburg	8– 4–1813	———	S	526	Barnetts Cr
Wellford, Jno S & Wm	Fredericksburg	8– 4–1818	———	S	528	Panther Cr
Wells, Francis	———	2–14–1814	Negro	P	532	None
Welsh, Benj	Ross	10–22–1814	———	Q	60	None
Welsh, Benj	Ross	10–22–1814	———	Q	62	None
Welsh, Benj	Ross	1–25–1816	———	Q	485	None
Wenzel, Jno C	Fayette	10–22–1825	20,000	X	177	Sandy R
Wenzel, Jno C	Fayette	10–22–1825	10,000	X	179	N Fk Ky R
Wenzel Jno C	Fayette	10–22–1825	10,000	X	180	N Fk Ky R
Wenzel, Jno C	Fayette	10–22–1825	5,000	X	182	Rockhouse Cr Bourboun Co
Wenzel, Jno C	Fayette	10–22–1825	15,000	X	184	None
Wenzel, Jno C	Fayette	10–22–1825	10,000	X	186	N Fk Ky R
Wenzel, Jno C	Fayette	10–22–1825	20,000	Y	2	Sandy R
Wenzel, Jno C	Fayette	10–22–1825	10,000	Y	4	N Fk Ky R
Wenzel, Jno C	Fayette	10–22–1825	10,000	Y	5	N Fk Ky R
Wenzel, Jno C	Fayette	10–22–1825	5,000	Y	6	Rockhouse Cr
Wenzel, Jno C	Fayette	10–22–1825	15,000	Y	7	Buckhorn Cr
Wenzel, Jno C	Fayette	10–22–1825	10,000	Y	9	N Fk Ky R
Wescott, Geo	Philadelphia	5–17–1799	37,855¾	E	56	Cumberland & Laurel R
Wescott, Henry	Philadelphia	10– 3–1800	23,250	E	171	Big Sandy R
West, Francis	Philadelphia	10– 5–1808	44,172	M	345	Halls Cr
West, Francis	Philadelphia	4–25–1827	3,000	X	224	Lick Cr
Wescott, Geo	Philadelphia	5– 5–1798	———	D	520	None

Grantee	Residence	Deed Date	Acres	Book	Page	Watercourse
West, James	Baltimore	1- 2-1800	9,728	M	184	E Fk Lewis Cr
West, James	Baltimore	7-16-1808	7,870	M	263	Elkhorn
West, Lynn	Georgetown	7-26-1817	333½	S	59	Big Barren R
West, Lynn	Scott	5- 2-1832	456	Z	211	Green R
West, Thomas	Kentucky	3-21-1797	1,115	B	108	Middle Fk Sugar Cr
West, Thos	Kentucky	3-21-1797	500	B	121	None
West, Thomas	Franklin	5——1799	Lot	D	206	Frankfort
West, Wm	Lexington	1-10-1803	Slaves	G	132	None
Whitaker, Wm W	———	8-16-1806	1,500	L	362	None
Whitaker, Wm W	———	8-16-1806	489	L	364	None
Whitaker, Wm W	———	8-16-1806	500	L	367	None
White, Ambrose	Frankfort	2——1814	60	L	486	M Elkhorn
White, Chas	Philadelphia	8-21-1787	250	B-2	273	None
White, Jno	Woodford	9- 3-1796	1,500	A-2	424	Little Ky
White, Jno	Richmond	10-17-1799	112,134¼	D	538	Ganley R, Little Kenhowa R & Lewis Cr
White, Josiah	Philadelphia	6-22-1805	1,000	M	112	Clay Lick Cr
White, Mildred B	Owen	1-18-1842	362	27	258	2-mi Chrn
White, Robt	Franklin	8- 8-1801	150	F	202	Spring of Dix R
White, Robt	———	7-28-1802	1,000	G	427	Cumberland R
White, Thos	Bourbon	9-23-1799	378½	E	2	M Fk Licking
White, Zachariah	Frankfort	4-12-1820	Lots	T	389	Frankfort
Whitehead, Isabella	Franklin	8-24-1833	Lot	Z	337	Frankfort
Whitehead, Richard	Micklenburg	9-20-1794	1,666⅔	N	184	Ky R
Whitesides, Wm	Philadelphia	4-13-1821	6,000	U	418	None
Whiting, Robt	———	9- 7-1840	200	27	151	E Fk Floyds Fk
Whiting, Robt	———	8-12-1841	114½	27	262	E Br Floyds Fk
Whittington, Isaac	Woodford	8-25-1827	210	X	274	Glenns Cr
Whittington Isaac	Woodford	8-25-1827	Slaves	X	277	None
Whittington, Littleton	Woodford	2- 7-1817	400	R	281	Ky R & Glenns Cr
Wickham, Jno	Richmond	2- 4-1809	1,000	M	413	Highland Cr
Wickham, Jno	———	5-17-1824	2,666⅔	W	269	Cumberland R
Wickliffe, Chas A	Nelson	4- 1-1823	1,600	W	24	Cypress Cr
Wickliffe, Chas A	Nelson	4- 1-1823	500	W	26	Rolling Fk
Wickliffe, Chas A	Nelson	4- 1-1823	4,000	W	27	Robinson Cr
Wickliffe, Chas A	Nelson	4- 1-1823	1,000	W	30	Beech Fk
Wickliffe, Chas A	Nelson	4- 1-1823	1,800	W	32	Sinking Cr
Wickliffe, Chas A	Nelson	4- 1-1823	1,410	W	34	Tradewater
Wickliffe, Chas A	Nelson	4- 1-1823	1,000	W	36	Tradewater
Wickliffe, Chas A	Nelson	4- 1-1823	1,000	W	38	Tradewater
Wickliffe, Chas A	Nelson	6-18-1823	Lots	W	112	Bardstown
Wickliffe, Nathaniel & Wife	Nelson	4-30-1829	Slaves	Y	353	None
Wickliffe, Robt	Lexington	6-13-1817	Lot	R	352	Lexington
Wickliffe, Robt	———	3-30-1816	———	R	359	None
Wickliffe, Robt	———	5——1816	———	R	361	None
Wickliffe, Robt	Lexington	10-23-1817	968	R	438	Tripletts Cr
Wickliffe, Robt	Lexington	4-14-1818	———	S	118	None
Wickliffe, Robt	Lexington	9- 3-1818	———	S	314	None
Wickliffe, Robt	Fayette	4-10-1819	803	S	516	None
Wickliffe, Robt	———	5-12-1820	———	T	312	None
Wickliffe, Robt	Lexington	4-15-1820	1,000	V	67	Ohio R
Wickliffe, Robt	Lexington	9- 2-1822	885	V	321	None
Wickliffe, R	Fayette	10-22-1823	452	W	174	None
Wickliffe, Robt	Fayette	12-11-1823	1,332	W	185	Big Bone Cr
Wickliffe, Robt	Fayette	10-25-1828	800	X	488	None
Wickliffe, Robt	Franklin	2-19-1835	Lot	Z	502	Frankfort
Wickliffe, Robt	———	5-29-1835	———	Z	512	Elkhorn & Hickman Cr
Wickliffe, Robt	Fayette	7-25-1836	Land	28	337	In Kentucky
Wiggington, Jno	Culpepper	1-14-1799	1,000	D	165	Frammels Cr
Wiggs, Richard	———	2-26-1834	150	Z	413	Dry Run
Wiggs, Richard	Kentucky	6——1839	150	28	23	None
Wiggs, Wheeler	———	1-12-1846	Lot	28	49	Midway
Wight, Andrew & Jas	Frankfort	12- 2-1815	Lot	Q	430	Frankfort
Wight, Hezakiah L	Richmond	3- 1-1824	2,000	W	326	Deer Cr
Wight, Jas	Frankfort	1-10-1817	Lot	R	150	Frankfort
Wight, Jas	———	10-21-1800	200	U	40	Br Eagles Cr
Wight, Jas	Franklin	7-27-1830	160	Z	26	N E Qr, Sec 6, T 53, N N 21, W
Wilcocks, Jno	Philadelphia	8-22-1786	10,000	T	317	Salt R
Wilcocks, Jno	Philadelphia	8-26-1786	10,000	T	326½	Nolinn & Green R
Wilcocks, Richard H	Philadelphia	3-26-1810	10,000	O	131	Salt R
Wilcocks, Richard H	Philadelphia	3-26-1810	30,000	O	133	Nolinn & Green R
Wilcox, Saml	Philadelphia	6- 6-1788	4,000	Z	38	Salt R
Wilcox, Jno	Shelby	8-10-1815	500	Q	219	Panther Cr
Wilder, Jno	———	7- 3-1809	Slaves	N	450	None
Wilder, Jno	Petersburg	5- 9-1807	———	S	68	None
Wilder, Jno	Petersburg	5- 8-1817	6,000	T	82	Richland Cr
Wilder, Joseph G	Petersburg	7- 3-1809	Slaves	N	450	None

Grantee	Residence	Deed Date	Acres	Book	Page	Watercourse
Wiley, Henry	Shelby	2–23–1815	91	Q	26	Benson & Beech Cr
Wilkerson, Geo	New Kent	12– 5–1798	600	D	356	M Fk Licking
Wilkins, Chas	Kentucky	1–18–1800	1,000	D	529	Deer Cr
Wilkins, Chas	——	9– 7–1799	300	D	375	Green R
Wilkins, Chas	Woodford	6– 9–1800	130	E	12	None
Wilkins, Chas	Bardstown	5– 4–1811	Lots	O	55	Bardstown
Wilkins, Chas	Lexington	5– 4–1811	400	O	55	Cox Cr
Wilkins, Jas H	Simpson	7– 1–1845		28	54	Simpson Co
Wilkins, Jno & Chas	Pittsburg	9–23–1796	6,900	A-2	635	Green R
Wilkins, Jno, heirs	——	4– 3–1824	6,900	W	284	None
Wilkins, Jno, heirs	——	9–23–1828	6,900	Y	391	Green R
Wilkinson, James	Fayette	8– 1–1786	2,148	A	289	Salt Spring
Wilkinson, Jas	Fayette	10–16–1788		A	457	S Fk Elkhorn
Wilkinson, James	N W of Ohio R	10–18–1796	4,000	A-2	531	Ohio R
Wilkinson, Jos	Fayette	2–26–1790	243½	R	154	Br Ky R
Wilkinson, Jno	——	2–14–1812	400	O	468	Pond R
Willett, Richard	Hardin	10–15–1816	441	R	40	Ohio R
Williams, Ayelor	——	1–31–1834		Z	402	In Bullitt
Williams, Chas Henry	Baltimore	3– 9–1797	8,800	A-2	687	Ohio R
Williams, Edward G	Baltimore	5– 3–1796	2,519	A-2	245	—— Cr
Williams, Eleanor F	New York	8–16–1842	9,188	27	308	Chaplins Fk
Williams, Elie	Maryland	9– 8–1796	2,000	A-2	427	Beaver Cr
Williams, Elie	Maryland	9–17–1796	1,000	A-2	439	Russell Cr
Williams, Elie	Maryland	9–16–1796	1,000	A-2	441	Graves Cr
Williams, Elie	Maryland	11–10–1797	400	D	128	Ohio R
Williams, Elie	Maryland	8– 7–1797	6,000	G	88	Muddy R
Williams, Elie	Hagerstown	3– 8–1797	1,400	G	312	Green R
Williams, Elie	Washington City	7– 3–1811		Q	522	None
Williams, Eli	Washington	7– 3–1811		Q	527	None
Williams, Elie	Washington	7– 3–1811	64,659	X	368	Ohio R & Mobile Bay
Williams, Elie	Washington	7– 3–1811		X	374	None
Williams, Henry Lee	Baltimore	5– 3–1796	2,519	A-2	245	—— Cr
Williams, Jas	Richmond	9– 4–1827		X	320	None
Williams, Jno	Woodford	2–26–1789	440	B-2	266	S Fk Elkhorn
Williams, Jno	North Carolina	1– 6–1775	——	C	60	Ohio, Cumberland & Green Rs
Williams, Jno C	Scott	10– 3–1827	330	X	287	Cedar Cr
Williams, Jno C	Culpepper	4–30–1800	500	E	344	Benson Cr
Williams, Jno D	Berton	6– 6–1803	——	H	173	None
Williams, Jno Davis	Boston	4–11–1804	30,059	H	156	Slate & Boyds Crs
Williams, Jonathan	Philadelphia	3–25–1796	4,184	E	117	Nolinn
Williams, Otto Holland	Baltimore	5– 3–1796	2,519	A-2	245	—— Cr
Williams, Peter	Hampshire	7–26–1800	666⅔	E	287	Fishing Cr
Williams, Philip	Shenandoah	7–20–1804	4,166½	H	466	None
Williams, Thos	Alexandria	12– 5–1795	1,250	D	233	Otter Cr
Williams, Thos	Alexandria	11–21–1797	25,334¾	D	248	S Fk Ky R
Williams, Thos	Alexandria	11–12–1799	5,000	F	11	Straight Cr
Williamson, Thos	Richmond	11– 4–1801	600	F	360	Russell Cr
Williams, Wm C	——	1–20–1808	194,493	M	124	Various Waters
Williams, Wm C	Richmond	2–28–1811	1,000	O	126	Br Green R
Williams, Wm Elie	Baltimore	5– 3–1796	2,519	A-2	245	—— Cr
Williams, Zephemiah	Franklin	7–14–1843	Lot	27	353	Frankfort
Willing, Thos	——	3– 5–1795	431,043	D	312	Many water courses
Willing, Thos	Philadelphia	3– 5–1795	615,180	28	341	In Kentucky
Willis, Edmund	Adair	12– 8–1808	680	M	254	Cypress Cr
Willis, Jno & Ed & Wm & Robt	——	4–27–1816	1,500	R	124	Goose Cr
Willis, Jonathan	Philadelphia	6– 7–1788	1,500	Y	476	Salt R
Willis, Jonathan Jr	Philadelphia	12– 9–1822	2,850	Y	478	Salt R
Willis, Jonathan Jr	Philadelphia	6– 6–1788	4,000	Z	38	Salt R
Willis, Robt	Adair	12– 8–1808	641	M	253	Cypress Cr
Willis, Seth	Philadelphia	3– 4–1786	13,666⅔	D	190	N Fk Three Fks Ky R
Willis, Wm Jr	Adair	12– 8–1808	442	M.:	257	Cypress Cr
Wills, Peachy	Williamsburg	4–19–1805	——	J	138	Cedar Cr
Wilmins, Jno & Jos	Woodford	5– 5–1810	11	N	186	Glens Cr
Wilson, Benj	Philadelphia	3–13–1805	Lot	H	599	Frankfort
Wilson, Geo	Woodford	6– 9–1791	717	B-2	327	Hingston Fk
Wilson, Geo	Bourbon	8–18–1809	2,179	N	18	Little Ky
Wilson, Henry	Mercer	1–13–1791	700	B-2	336	—— Br
Wilson, Henry	Bourbon	11–15–1797	800	D	146	Ky R
Wilson, James	Mason	9–19–1799	247¼	D	532	None
Wilson, Jeremiah	Woodford	5–25–1815	11¼	Q	118	None
Wilson, Jno	Scott	8–20–1818	36	S	213	Ohio R
Wilson, Joshua	——	9–29–1810	688	N	276	Cumberland R
Wilson, Margaret	——	8–21–1807	224	L	120	Jessamine & Curds Ferry
Wilson, Richard	Jefferson	8–20–1818	——	S	211	Ohio R
Wilson, Spicer	Madison	8–26–1802	470	H	13	M Licking
Wilson, Spicer	Madison	8–26–1802	1,000	H	42	Kinkades Cr

Grantee	Residence	Deed Date	Acres	Book	Page	Watercourse
Wilson, Thos	Richmond	2– 4–1801	10,000	E	337	Licking
Wilson, Thos	Grant	6–15–1822	150	V	351	Eagle Cr
Wilson, Thos	———	11– 9–1787	200	A	334	Br Rowling Fk
Wilson, Thos, Atty	———	12———1802	1,500	H	258	Beargrass & Goose Crs & Ohio R
Wilson, Wm	———	8– 6–1817	800	R	369	Green R & Halstein
Winchester, Stephen	Fredericksburg	5– 4–1805	3,720	J	218	Skaggs and Big Bone Lick
Winchester, Stephen	———	7–10–1806	3,530	K	377	Harbone & Cabin Crs
Wing, Chas Fox	Muhlenburg	12–31–1804	——	H	564	Pond R
Wing, Chas Fox	Muhlenburg	1–29–1808	500	L	274	Pond Cr
Wing, Chas Fox	Muhlenburg	1–29–1808	100	L	275	Pond Cr
Wing, Chas Fox	Muhlenburg	1–29–1808	100	L	276	Alstons Cr
Wing, Chas Fox	———	11–29–1809	Lot	N	201	Frankfort
Wingate, Isaac	Franklin	2– 9–1839	2	27	27	S Elkhorn
Winlock, Joseph	———	11– 8–1805	1,400	K	7	None
Winslow, Henry	Gallatin	5– 2–1818	Lot	S	402	Port Williams
Winslow, Wm	Gallatin	7–23–1814	5	P	620	Port Williams
Winslow, Wm	Port Williams	7–25–1818	Lot	S	362	Port Williams
Winston, Saml	Newport	2–15–1845	2,450	27	472	Miss. R, Town, Consola, Highland & Goose Cr
Winter, Joseph	New York City	4–16–1810	707	N	279	Ky R
Withers, Benj	Hardin	5– 1–1817	——	R	432	None
Withers, Jno & Jas	Virginia	3– 6–1826	Lots	Y	106	Port Williams
Withers, Jno & Jas	Virginia	3– 6–1826	4,004	Y	106	None
Wood, Geo Trustee	———	8– 1–1817	Lots	S	289	Lexington
Wood, Thos	Ohio	2– 1–1819	100	T	287	Fk Muddy Cr
Woods, Archibald Sr	Madison	5– 8–1802	2,000	G	116	Big Bone Lick & Bank Lick Cr
Woods, Jno	Franklin	7–23–1819	100	U	80	None
Woods, Wm	Woodford	5–14–1821	171	U	493	N Fk Glens Cr
Woods, Wm	Woodford	2–10–1832	97	Z	177	Glens Cr
Woodson, Richard K	Woodford	12–16–1839	Lot	27	93	Frankfort
Woodson, Richard K	Franklin	11–30–1841	450	27	302	Ky R
Woodson, Richard K	Franklin	12–18–1841	450	27	303	Ky R
Woodworth, Jno	———	3– 5–1796	27,018	E	233	Sandy R
Wooldridge, Edward	———	9– 4–1806	1,000	K	508	None
Wooldridge, Josiah	Woodford	7–19–1804	300	K	329	Russell Cr
Wooldridge, Jno W	Franklin	8–20–1812	31,985	O	534	None
Wooldridge, Jno W	Christian	1– 9–1833	Lots	Z	250	Port Williams
Wooldridge, Powhatan	Christian	1–13–1824	18,500	W	225	None
Wooldridge, Thos	Franklin	8–16–1805	262	K	256	Drennons Lick
Woolfolk, Jno H	Woodford	10– 6–1810	413	O	6	M Elkhorn
Woolfolk, Robt Jr	Carolina	4–16–1796	310	H	110	Br Ky R
Woolfolk, Thos	———	5–27–1812	564	X	82	Twins Cr
Woolfolk, Thos H	Woodford	10–20–1833	6,747	27	361	Eagle, Muddy & Long Fall Crs
Woolfork, Lowyel	Woodford	12–10–1803	Slaves	H	90	None
Woolfork, Lowyel	Woodford	10–20–1808	100	M	402	N Fk Elkhorn
Worley, Francis	Philadelphia	9–24–1819	1,500	T	404	Eagle Cr
Worthington, Jno T & Chas	Baltimore	8– 1–1807	1,000	L	211	Big Barren R
Worthington, Robt	———	12–31–1802	713½	G	421	Br Salt R
Worthington, Thos C	Frederick	1– 7–1811	4,833	O	3	None
Worthington, Wm G D	Baltimore	1– 7–1811	2,416½	O	100	None
Worthington, Walter T	Maryland	7–18–1800	1,000	E	64	Big Barren R
Wright, Edwin	———	1–23–1847	4	28	120	Franklin Co
Wright, James	Franklin	4———1820	100	T	308	Twins Cr
Wright, Matthew	Frederick	10–12–1795	6,000	A-2	419	Ohio R
Wynkoop, Abraham	Philadelphia	11– 5–1836	——	27	43	None
Wynkoop, Benj	Philadelphia	8– 7–1788	5,000	A-2	15	Sandy R
Wynkoop, Benj	Philadelphia	6–26–1784	15,000	G	213	None
Wynkoop, Benj	Philadelphia	7– 8–1786	10,000	27	44	Fayette & Jeff Co
Wynkoop, Henry	Philadelphia	9–14–1784	3,000	H	289	None
Wynkoop, Henry	Philadelphia	9–14–1784	3,000	H	295	None
Yager, Elijah	Franklin	3–31–1810	100	N	236	S Fk Big Benson Cr
Yancy, Philip	Owen	1–16–1840	426	27	101	Large Twin Cr
Yates & McIntire	New York	4–13–1833	562	Z	277	Cumberland & Little Barren R
Yeatman, Thos H	Ohio	12–23–1829	Lot	Y	510	Frankfort
Yeiser, Elizabeth	Baltimore	2–15–1798	23,000	C	267	Br M Fk Licking
Yeiser, Englehard	Baltimore	3–30–1798	69,000	D	56	Main Licking
Yeiser, Englehard	Baltimore	11–18–1799	92,000	E	31	Licking
Yoder, Jacob	———	12– 3–1816	2,000	R	75	None
Yoder, Jacob	———	12– 3–1816	1,000	R	77	None
Young, Jno	———	10–18–1827	295	X	291	Blackfords Cr
Young, Jno Jr	Philadelphia	7–30–1786	5,000	D	175	Br Ky R
Young, Jno D	Fayette	5–21–1805	900	X	332	Dry & Gunpowder C

Grantee	Residence	Deed Date	Acres	Book	Page	Watercourse
Young, Milton	Union	8–24–1844	400½	27	427	Chaplins & Salt R
Young, Robt	Alexandria	5–10–1801	1,187	E	325	Johnsons Fk
Young, Saml	Philadelphia	9–27–1787	10,000	E	95	N Fk 3 Fks Ky R
Young, Sarah	Frankfort	8–19–1812	Lot	P	40	Frankfort
Young, Thos	Lexington	4–20–1789	1,000	B-2	57	Foxes Run
Young, Willis	Bourbon	8–29–1816	773½	R	126	Stoners Fk & Green
Younger, Jno	Franklin	1–13–1804	Lot	H	150	Frankfort
Younger, Jno	Kentucky	5–14–1819	Lot	T	128	Frankfort
Zachary, Wm	Bourbon	1–16–1800	500	F	393	None
Zimmerman, Geo	Mercer	6–20–1790	700	B-2	190	Hingston Fk

VIII

COURT OF APPEALS DEEDS-GRANTORS

(1783–1909)

(Only one deed recorded after 1846)

Grantor	Residence	Deed Date	Acres	Book	Page	Watercourse
Abercromlie, Jas	Philadelphia	9–16–1784	14,000	A-2	44	None
Abercronley, Jas	Philadelphia	8–14–1809	14,000	N	124	Buffaloe Rd
Abercrombie, Rev Jos	Philadelphia	8–15–1794	1,000	G	238	Hingston Fk
Able, Robt	Nelson	2– 5–1833	2,300	Z	271	Rough Cr
Adair, Ann, Catherin & Jno A		11–27–1834	——	Z	510	Hart Co
Adair, Jno	Mercer	11– 2–1789	——	B-2	165	None
Adair, Jno	Mercer	——1796	11,400	A-2	243	Green R
Adair, Jno	Register Land Office	6– 2–1804	400	H	189	Brashears Cr
Adair, Jno	Register Land Office	6– 2–1804	873	H	191	Brashears Cr
Adair, Jno	Register Land Office	4–10–1804	1,990	H	194	Slate Cr
Adair, Jno	Register Land Office	5–23–1804	305	H	227	Indian Cr
Adair, Jno	Register Land Office	5–23–1804	248	H	229	Indian Cr
Adair, Jno	Register Land Office	11– 8–1804	15,000	H	363	Eagle Cr
Adair, Jno	Register Land Office	11–26–1804	200	H	434	Buck Cr
Adair, Jno	Register Land Office	12– 5–1804	400	H	443	Ky R
Adair, Jno	Register Land Office	12–10–1804	400	H	451	Beech Fk
Adair, Jno	Register Land Office	12–11–1804	200	H	462	Drakes Cr
Adair, Jno	Register Land Office	12–11–1804	200	H	464	Drakes Cr
Adair, Jno	Register Land Office	11–28–1804	1,000	H	487	Butlers Fk
Adair, Jno	Register Land Office	12–26–1804	8,000	H	494	Slate Cr
Adair, Jno	Register Land Office	12–24–1804	664	H	500	Evens Mill Cr
Adair, Jno	Register Land Office	2–12–1805	1,271	H	546	Slate & Flatt Crs
Adair, Jno	Register Land Office	2– 6–1805	4,213	H	552	Middle & Valley Cr
Adair, Jno	Register Land Office	11–28–1804	1,861	H	623	Cabin Cr
Adair, Jno	Register Land Office	3–29–1805	3,040	J	57	Little Sandy
Adair, Jno	Register Land Office	1–16–1805	5,812	J	161	Plum Cr
Adair, Jno	Register Land Office	9–11–1805	5,415½	J	264	Cedar Cr
Adair, Jno	Register Land Office	3–26–1805	332	J	295	Drennons Lick Cr
Adair, Jno	Register Land Office	3–26–1805	500	J	299	Drennons Lick Cr
Adair, Jno	Register Land Office	10–23–1805	630	J	311	Paint Lick
Adair, Jno	Danville	11– 9–1805	11,520	K	126	N & S Fk Elkhorn, Ky R, Clear & Greers Crs
Adair, Jno	Register Land Office	4–10–1805	15,000	K	314	Green R
Adair, Jno	Mercer	1–29–1808	500	L	274	Pond Cr
Adair, Jno	Mercer	1–29–1808	100	L	275	Pond Cr
Adair, Jno	Mercer	1–29–1808	100	L	276	Alstons Cr
Adair, Jno	Register Land Office	11–28–1804	1,861	M	98	Cabin Cr
Adair, Jno & Wife	Mercer	12– 2–1800	200	G	316	Little Caney Cr
Adair, Jno & Wife	Franklin	8–10–1804	200	H	376	Bear Cr
Adair, Jno & Wife	Franklin	8–10–1804	205	H	378	Clifty & Bear Cr
Adair, Wm Mary & A M	——	11–27–1834	——	Z	510	Hart Co
Adam, Geo	Frankfort	11–21–1821	5,400	V	127	None
Adams, Geo	Mississippi	2–23–1833	1,000	Z	260	Hickman Co
Adams, Geo	Mississippi	6–21–1833	1,000	Z	302	Mississippi R
Adams, Jno	Gallatin	5– 8–1820	74	T	412	Eagle Cr
Adams, Reynolds & Co	Louisville	3–25–1831	Lots	Z	106	Frankfort
Adams, Richard		3– 7–1802	6,000	F	491	Ohio R
Adams, Richard Jr		4–13–1798	3,600	D	76	Cumberland R
Adams, Saml G	Virginia	3–30–1800	1,000	R	451	Big Benson Cr
Adams, Saml G	Richmond	10– 3–1820	1,000	U	58	Cypress C
Adkins, Elijah	Pike	1–26–1828	Slaves	X	367	None
Alcocke, Robt	Albermarle	9–12–1808	2,500	M	325	None
Alcock, Thos & Wife	Carolina	8–12–1795	1,000	F	156	Blackfords Cr
Alderman, Joel	Pittsgrove	5–29–1800	150	W	59	Ky R
Aldridge, Jno P & Wife	Jefferson	8–24–1822	1,000	W	99	None
Alexander, Jno K	Woodford	8–15–1841	12½	27	346	Bulls Run
Alexander, Hugh & Wife	Scott	3– 7–1799	——	D	130	S Fk Elkhorn
Alexander, Robt		7–15–1812	Lot	O	502	Frankfort
Alexander, Robt	Woodford	2–15–1828	10,850	X	383	Rolling Fk Middle & Valley Cr
Alexander, Robt	Woodford	11–23–1829	15,000	Y	416	S Fk Sandy & Cumberland R
Alexander, Robt	Woodford	10–29–1830	1,021	Z	23	Nolinn
Alexander, Robt Trustee	Kentucky	6–28–1811	615	O	71	Cumberland R
Alexander, Robt Trustee	Franklin	4–25–1825	Lot	X	131	Frankfort
Alexander, Robt Trustee	——	7– 1–1837	——	27	111	Franklin Co

Grantor	Residence	Deed Date	Acres	Book	Page	Watercourse
Alexander, Thos C & Wife	Henrico	1–14–1817	1,100	R	249	Panther Cr
Alexander, Wm	Augusta	5– 3–1796	1,000	B	4	Tradewater
Alexander, Wm	Franklin	1– 1–1812	64,184	O	515	Nolinn & Bacons Cr
Alfrey, Moses B	Hart	3–18–1841	Lots	27	224	Columbus
Allen, David H & Wife	Frederick	6– 8–1824	300	W	368	Shawnee Run
Allen, David H Wife	Frederick	2–22–1825	91	X	99	Shannons Run
Allen, David H & Wife	Frederick	2–22–1825	200	X	122	Shannons Run
Allen, David H & Wife	Frederick	5– 1–1828	122	X	448	Shannons Run
Allens, David H & Wife	Frederick	3–27–1829	23	Y	357	Shannons Run
Allen, David H Wife	Frederick	3–12–1829	104	Y	360	Shannons Run
Allen, David H & Wife	Frederick	7– 1–1828	7	Y	375	Shannons Run
Allen, James	Augusta	3–18–1791	1,240	B-2	258	Deer Cr
Allen, Jas & Thos	Fredericksburg	8– 6–1812	1,050	P	162	Fk Blackfords Cr
Allen, Jno, heirs	Shelby	10–25–1819	513	T	217	None
Allen, Jos & Wife	Breckinridge	11–12–1827	66,831	X	328	Nolinn & Lynn Camp Cr
Allen, Thos	————	6–24–1786	9	A	153	None
Allen, Thos	————	3–31–1797	Lots	C	135	Henderson
Allen, Thos	————	3–31–1797	Lots	C	143	Henderson
Allen, Thos Surveyor	Christian	8– 9–1797	264	C	53	Ohio R
Allen, Wilson	Richmond	10– 2–1808	2,000	M	269	Big Bone Lick
Allen, Wilson & Wife	Carolina	9–19–1815	11,382¾	Q	188	Green & Salt R
Allen, Wilson & Wife	Carolina	12–26–1817	5,000	S	46	None
Allison, David	Philadelphia	3–11–1796	70,000	A-2	366	Big Sandy
Allison, David	Philadelphia	12– 1–1796	283,413	A-2	702	Licking, S Fk Ky R
Allison, David	Philadelphia	8–20–1796	82,235	B	149	Big Sandy R
Allison, David	Philadelphia	12– 1–1796	118,626	C	1	Lick Cr, Mill Cr & Green R
Allison, David	Philadelphia	3–27–1797	41,778	D	31	Little Sandy & Blanes Cr
Allison, Saml	Philadelphia	7–16–1838	2,552,304¼	27	201	Va & Ky
Alsap, Benj & Wife	Warren	3– 6–1829	901	Y	398	Tennessee R
Alsbury, Thos	Christian	11–12–1816	300	R	119	Little R
Alvey, Robt	Union	4–25–1814	—	P	513	None
Ambrose, Jacob	Bardstown	5– 7–1806	4,000	K	344	None
Ammidan, Otis & Wife	Philadelphia	8–18–1815	Lots	R	404	Philadelphia
Anderson, Andrew	Woodford	11–26–1813	100	P	487	Ky R
Anderson, Andrew & Wife	Woodford	8–26–1814	100	T	403	Ky R
Anderson, Amos	Franklin	1–13–1804	Lot	H	150	Frankfort
Anderson, Amos	Franklin	1–13–1804	Lot	H	152	Frankfort
Anderson, C S Atty	————	2–12–1823	37	W	71	None
Anderson, C S Co	————	2–12–1823	37	W	73	None
Anderson, Francis	Louisa	2– 4–1801	259	F	62	Green R
Anderson, Richard C	Kentucky	11–12–1795	5,625	A-2	567	Green R
Anderson, Richard C	Jefferson	6– 4–1799	500	K	113	Carringtons R
Anderson, Richard C	Jefferson	4–30–1810	11,200	N	267	W Fk Little R & Kettle Cr
Anderson, Robt	Virginia	7–14–1800	6,000	F	210	Salt R
Anderson, Robt & Wife	Bedford	5–27–1799	477	D	457	Russell Cr
Anderson, Sally	Shelby	5–14–1819	Lot	T	128	Frankfort
Anderson, Wm	Fayette	3– 1–1796	—	A-2	263	Little Mt Cr
Andrews, Robt		3– 7–1802	6,000	F	491	Ohio R
Andrews, Robt, heirs	Williamsburg	4–20–1806	355	K	443	Salt R
Andrews, Robt, heirs	Williamsburg	4–20–1806	1,043	K	446	Salt R
Andrews, Robt Trustee	————	12–31–1799	2,000	L	108	Ohio R
Anthony, Jos & Michael	Philadelphia	10–29–1813	—	P	288	None
Anthony, Thos	Philadelphia	10–29–1813	—	P	288	None
Apperson, Edm R Atty	Newkent	11–22–1827	158	X	323	Elkhorn
Apperson, Jno C & Wife	————	10–14–1828	—	X	481	None
Apperson, Matilda H	————	10–14–1828	—	X	481	None
Apperson, Richard	Franklin	10– 1–1805	492	K	162	Elkhorn
Appison, Richard	Franklin	3– 7–1817	2,500	R	186	Big Bone & Mud Lick Cr
Apperson, Richard	Franklin	8–25–1817	492	S	33	Elkhorn
Apperson, Richard	Madison	4– 9–1828	158	X	398	Elkhorn
Apperson, Rich Decd	Franklin	9– 4–1827	—	X	320	None
Apperson, Richard Executor	Franklin	3–20–1818	—	S	104	Elkhorn Cr
Apperson, Rich, heirs	————	10–14–1828	—	X	481	None
Anchor, Abraham & Wife	King William	6–12–1821	428 4/7	V	73	Tennessee R
Archer, Richard	Amelia	2–26–1796	562½	A-2	569	Green R
Archer, Rich T Atty	Amelia	10–14–1834	1,000	Z	464	Muddy R
Archer, Stephen	Scott	4– 5–1796	300	A-2	529	Brashears Cr
Archer, Stephen	Woodford	2–29–1791	300	B-2	363	Clear Cr
Armstead, Jno A	Virginia	11–25–1820	600	U	173	Eagle Cr
Armstead, Jno B	Henry	3–15–1819	500	S	502	None
Armstead, Jno B	Henry	3–18–1819	150	S	504	Ky R

Grantor	Residence	Deed Date	Acres	Book	Page	Watercourse
Armstead, Wm & Wife	Elizabeth City	4–30–1798	1,000	D	268	Big Barren R
Armstrong, Chas M	U S Navy	8–16–1842	9,188	27	308	Chaplins Fk
Armstrong, James	———	3–12–1810	Mortg.	N	145	None
Armstrong, Robt	Franklin	2–26–1810	Lot	P	244	Burying Lot
Arnett, Samuel	Nicholas	10– 7–1824	95	X	63	None
Arnold, Jas	Lincoln	9–20–1785	220	A	68	None
Arnold, James	Franklin	6–28–1805	28	J	193	Cedar Cr
Arnold, Jno Jr	Franklin	2– 7–1817	400	R	281	Ky R & Glenns Cr
Arnold, Jno Jr & Wife	Franklin	2– 7–1817	206¾	R	283	Stone Lick Br
Arnold, Stephen	Franklin	2– 9–1809	215.{	M	337	S Fk Big Benson Cr
Arnold, Thos	Bourbon	8–21–1833	2,574½	Z	385	Green R & N E Fk Panther Cr
Ashby, Nathaneil, heirs	Fayette	1–17–1821	460	U	167	Elk Cr & Ohio R
Ashby, Jno G	Madison	11–12–1822	3,797	V	369	Elk Cr
Ashby, Jno G	Madison	3–30–1824	60	W	232	Green R
Ashby, Jno G	Madison	3–22–1825	165	Y	10	Green R
Atkinson, Henry & Wife	Woodford	9– 2–1819	10	T	297	Glenns Cr
Atkinson, Richard, Atty	———	12– 7–1819	339	T	378	Eagle Cr
Atchison, Samuel A, Atty	Warren	12–21–1840	978½	27	169	Little Barren R Clay Lick Fk & Glovers
Atkinson, Samuel C	Philadelphia	11–10–1841	1,360	27	294	Tennessee R
Austergus, James	Jefferson	6–10–1791	200	B-2	345	S Fk Beargrass Cr
Austin, Chapman	Hanover	12–20–1786	1,000	A	253	Red R
Austin, Chapman	———	2– 1–1796	400	A-2	392	Cedar Cr
Austin, Chapman	Hanover	12–20–1786	1,000	H	356	Red R
Austin, Daniel, heirs	New York	1–25–1839	Lot	27	10	Carrollton
Austin, Horace	Manchester	9–16–1796	1,000	A-2	441	Grace Cr
Austin, Stephen	Philadelphia	8– 7–1788	5,000	A-2	15	Sandy R
Ayers, E M & W N	Woodford	2–19–1839	10,018	27	114	Ohio R
Ayers, Mary	Gallatin	12–14–1811	Slaves	O	206	None
Ayers, Nathan & Wife	Woodford	1–25–1841	———	27	275	Woodford Cr
Ayers, Nathan & Wife	Woodford	2–19–1839	10,018	27	114	Ohio R
Ayeres, Walter, heirs	Woodford	2–19–1839	10,018	27	114	Ohio R
Bacchus, Gordon H	Richmond	6– 4–1812	2,000	O	446	Tennessee R
Bacon, Benedict	Frankfort	8–24–1809	5,263	N	202	N Fk Rockcastle Muddy & Paint Lick Cr
Bacon, Chas P	Franklin	5–10–1826	111	Y	161	——— Cr
Bacon, Chas P	Franklin	10–13–1830	Lots	Z	21	Frankfort
Bacon, Edmond	Franklin	3– 5–1803	745½	H	211	Muddy Cr & N Fk Rockcastle
Bacon, Edmund & Wife	Frankfort	2–19–1810	4,473	N	203	Rockcastle Copper & Muddy Cr
Bacon, Elizabeth	Franklin	4–19–1821	117	Z	342	Franklin Co
Bacon, Jno C & Wife	Franklin	4–23–1814	———	P	410	None
Bacon, Jno C & Wife	Franklin	12–27–1814	———	P	596	Silver Paint Lick Muddy & Drowning Crs
Bacon, Jno, heirs	Franklin	5–10–1826	111	Y	161	——— Cr
Bacon, Longston & Wife	Frankfort	2–19–1810	4,473	N	203	Rockcastle Copper & Muddy Cr
Bacon, Langston & Wife & Edmund & Wife	Frankfort	6–19–1809	4,172	M	410	N Fk Rockcastle Copper Muddy & Station Camp Cr
Bacon, Lyddall Jr & Wife	Frankfort	6–19–1809	4,172,	M	410	N Fk Rockcastle Copper Muddy & Station Camp Cr
Bacon, Lyddall Jr & Wife	Frankfort	2–19–1810	4,473	N	203	Rockcastle Copper & Muddy Cr
Bacon, Lydall & Wife	Franklin	12–10–1830	85	Z	65	None
Bacon, Lydall & Wife	Franklin	8– 3–1841	Lot	27	219	Frankfort
Bacon, Lyddall Sr	Franklin	11– 2–1841	Lot	27	274	Frankfort
Bacon, Lyddall & Benedict	Frankfort	11–30–1808	5,562	N	204	None
Baggat, Geo	———	9–10–1840	158	27	152	E Fk Floyds Fk
Baggat, Geo	Virginia	8– 8–1840	464½	27	153	Shelby Co
Baggat, Geo	Fredericksburg	10–13–1841	334	27	265	E Br Floyds Fk
Baggat, Geo & Wife	———	9– 7–1840	200	27	151	E Fk Floyds Fk
Bailey, Jno & Wife	Lincoln	2– 6–1808	760	L	299	Fks Red R
Bainbridge, E T	Jefferson	7–19–1842	320	27	296	Hickman & Graves Cos

Grantor	Residence	Deed Date	Acres	Book	Page	Watercourse
Bainbridge & Way, Trustees	Jefferson	8-16-1841	320	27	223	Graves & Hickman Cos
Baird, David & Wife	Pennsylvania	4-25-1797	1,000	A-2	679	Buck Fk
Baird, Jno	Petersburg	4-13-1818	2,000	T	88	Ohio R
Baird, Richard	Franklin	5- 4-1797	3,000	A-2	698	None
Baker, Henry, heirs	Winchester	4-14-1808	966⅔	N	73	Highland Cr
Baker, Henry W & Jno	Winchester	4-14-1808	966⅔	N	73	Highland Cr
Baker, Jno	Franklin	5-25-1830	40	Y	482	M Elkhorn
Baker, Joseph B, Adm'r	Nansemond	12-14-1812	Lots	P	185	Washington City
Baker, Joseph B, Adm'r	——	9-14-1812	2,500	R	51	Br N Fk Tradewater
Baker, Joshua	Jefferson	11-16-1799	500	D	422	—— Cr
Baker, Robt	Franklin	7-23-1799	911	D	304	W Fk Sinking Cr
Baker, Thos	Franklin	9- 3-1805	711	J	391	W Fk Sinking Cr
Baker, Wm	Baltimore	2- 2-1808	600	M	65	Big Barren R
Ball, Burgess & Wife	London	5- 8-1794	1,500	S	88	Gasper R
Ball, Edward P	Mason	9-19-1814	800	Q	54	Ohio R
Ball, Jeham & Wife	——	6-27-1820	200	U	25	Green R
Ballard, Wm	Stafford	12-22-1795	——	N	228	None
Baltzell, Geo & Wife	——	1- 1-1823	Lot	V	435	Frankfort
Banister, Jno M	Petersburg	3- 5-1807	32,696	L	183	Rough Panther & Caney Cr
Banister, Jno M	Sussex	6-23-1821	——	V	45	None
Banister, Jno, heirs	——	6-23-1821	——	V	20	Ky R
Banister, Theodorick B	Petersburg	3- 5-1807	32,696	L	183	Rough Panther & Caney Cr
Banister, Theodorick & Jno M	Petersburg	6- 8-1808	——	M	117	None
Bank of Kentucky	Kentucky	9-18-1830	Lots	Z	11	Millersburg
Bank of Kentucky	Kentucky	10-22-1830	——	Z	29	Big Benson Cr
Bank of Kentucky	Kentucky	12-28-1831	Lot	Z	172	Frankfort
Bank of Kentucky	Kentucky	2- 4-1835	Lot	Z	487	Frankfort
Bank of Kentucky	Kentucky	2- 4-1835	Lot	Z	488	Frankfort
Bank of Kentucky	Kentucky	2-26-1835	Lot	Z	492	Frankfort
Bank of Kentucky	Kentucky	4- 8-1835	——	Z	497	Nelson Co
Bank of Kentucky	Kentucky	11- 1-1838	Lots	27	6	Frankfort
Bank of Kentucky	Kentucky	3- 1-1839	552	27	13	Barren Co
Bank of Kentucky	Kentucky	11- 9-1839	835	27	83	Ky R & Stony Cr
Bank of Kentucky	Kentucky	10-30-1839	Lot	27	87	Frankfort
Bank of Kentucky	Kentucky	10- 6-1838	4	27	113	Ky R
Bank of U S	Philadelphia	2- 8-1831	Lots	27	164	Frankfort
Bank of U S	Philadelphia	6-17-1831	1,110	Z	269	Ohio R
Bank of U S	Philadelphia	11-25-1834	176¼	Z	467	Fayette Co
Bank of U S	Philadelphia	3-31-1835	——	Z	502	M Eagle Cr
Bank of U S	Philadelphia	5- 5-1836	Lots	27	436	Lexington
Bank of U S	Philadelphia	7-25-1836	Land	28	337	Kentucky
Banks, Cuthbert	——	11- 6-1805	2,000	J	370	Floyds Fk
Banks, Cuthbert	Montgomery	11-20-1821	1,000	V	120	None
Banks, Cuthbert, Atty	Lexington	10-29-1798	1,000	D	378	Russells Cr
Banks, Henry	Richmond	8- 2-1792	42,400	A-2	182	Hardins Cr
Banks, Henry	Richmond	8-15-1796	3,110	A-2	414	Salt R
Banks, Henry	Richmond	12- 6-1796	2,000	A-2	592	Bullskin Cr
Banks, Henry	Richmond	2-16-1787	5,277	A-2	596	Ohio R
Banks, Henry	Richmond	2- 2-1909	5,227	D	334	Ohio R
Banks, Henry	Richmond	12- 1-1813	300	P	338	Mud Lick Fk
Banks, Henry	Richmond	10- —1819	175	T	275	None
Banks, Henry	Richmond	12-29-1822	2,000	V	431	None
Banks, Henry	Virginia	10-23-1827	3,300	X	295	Cedar Cr
Banks, Henry	Richmond	11-20-1827	——	X	345	Cedar Cr
Banks, Henry	Richmond	1-14-1828	12,500	X	350	Poplar Camp
Banks, Henry	Virginia	4- 9-1828	5,000	X	397	Chaplins Fk
Banks, Henry	Richmond	11-20-1827	170	X	411	None
Banks, Henry	Richmond	11- 1-1827	200	X	412	None
Banks, Henry	Richmond	11-20-1827	50	X	413	None
Banks, Henry	Richmond	7-24-1828	386	X	420	Floyds Fk
Banks, Henry	Richmond	7- 2-1831	800	Z	155	Craborchard & English Cr
Banks, Henry & Wife	Richmond	4-10-1797	10,869	C	18	Ohio R
Banta, Abraham	Lincoln	7-25-1786	1,000	A	196	Big Cr
Barbayne, Jno Benardus	So Carolina	2- 5-1799	64,100	D	429	Kill Carmick & Tyger Crs
Barbee, Jno	Lincoln	3- 6-1785	Negro	A	30	None
Barbee, Joshua	Mercer	8- 1-1806	4,287	K	423	Green R
Barbee, Joshua, Atty	Mercer	12- 1-1821	70	V	133	None
Barber, David	Louisville	12-13-1798	7,500	D	292	Bank Lick Cr
Barbour, Ambrose	Kentucky	10-10-1810	950	O	314	Ohio R
Barbour, James	Culpepper	5-24-1785	——	A	73	Salt R
Barbour, Jas	Virginia	2-15-1823	2,000	V	456	Sinking Cr

Grantor	Residence	Deed Date	Acres	Book	Page	Watercourse
Barbour, Jas	Orange	2— —1825	500	X	174	N Panther Cr
Barbour, Jas	Washington	5–15–1828	5,000	Y	300	N Fk Panther Cr
Barbour, Jas	Virginia	12–26–1836	———	27	458	Kentucky
Barbour, James & Wife	Orange	5– 5–1802	———	G	150	None
Barbour, Jas & Wife	Orange	5–13–1805	1,100	J	236	None
Barbour, Jas & Wife	Orange	8– 1–1805	22,950	J	282	Panther Doe Run & Ohio R
Barbour, Jas & Wife	Orange	3–11–1816	2,266¾	R	301	Bigger Staff & Mud
Barbour, Jas & Wife	———	9– 1–1826	223	X	218	None
Barbour, Philip	Richmond	8– 1–1792	42,400	A-2	176	Hardins Cr
Barbour, Philip	Richmond	8– 5–1792	60,000	A-2	179	None
Barbour, Philip	Culpepper	8– 7–1786	50,000	G	146	Otter Cr
Barbour, Philip & Wife	Orange	5–10–1805	———	J	243	None
Barbour, Philip P & Wife	Orange	3–26–1809	———	N	422	None
Barbour, Philip C S	Orange	1–24–1815	9,000	P	625	Pattons Little Ky & 18 mi Cr
Barbour, Philip S C	Bourbon	2–26–1820	3,000	U	36	Otter Cr
Barbour, Philip C S	Jefferson	9– 1–1830	3,708	Z	9	Sinking Sp Meade Co
Barbour, Philip P	Virginia	2–10–1837	———	27	457	Kentucky
Barbour, Richard	Orange	11–27–1800	3,000	E	175	——— R
Barbour, Thos	Orange	8–16–1796	4,530	B	327	Blue Lick Road
Barbour, Thos	Orange	12– 4–1807	1,240	M	440	Green R
Barbour, Thos	Orange	10– 4–1822	1,400	V	454	None
Barbour, Thos & Wife	Orange	———1800	3,000	E	239	——— R
Barbour, Thos & Wife	Jefferson	11– 8–1822	550	V	354	Ohio R
Barbour, Thomas Jr	Madison	10–30–1799	1,210	F	46	None
Bard, Richard, heirs	———	10–26–1799	1,500	F	390	Big Benson & Ky R
Barnes, Philip & Wife	Great Barrington	6–14–1841	320	27	253	Tennessee R
Barnesback, Geo	Jefferson	8–23–1806	———	K	550	Cypress Cr
Barnett, James, Atty	———	2–24–1806	328¾	L	75	——— R
Barnett, Jas & Wife	Madison	2–16–1799	500	D	140	Caseys Cr
Barnett, Jas & Wife	Madison	11–24–1798	389	D	141	Fk Caseys Cr
Barnett, Joseph	Nelson	9– 6–1788	400	A	488	Rough Cr
Barnett, Joseph	Nelson	10–23–1788	600	A	507	Rough Cr
Barnett, Joseph	Nelson	10–23–1788	300	A	509	Rough Cr
Barnett, Joseph	Nelson	10–23–1788	300	A	510	Rough Cr
Barnett, Joseph	Nelson	10–23–1788	500	A	512	Rough Cr
Barnett, Joseph	Nelson	5– 5–1791	1,000	B-2	395	Green R
Barnett, Jas, Atty	———	2–26–1806	500	L	73	M Fk Ky R
Barnett, Joseph & Wife	Nelson	5– 5–1791	1,000	B-2	393	Green R
Barnett, Nathan, Atty	———	10–22–1803	249	H	103	Baileys Run
Barnett, Thos	———	3– 4–1794	———	N	100	
Barnett, Wm	Madison	10–29–1828	1,000	V	299	Willis Cr
Barney, Harret & Adell	———	11–20–1833	15,000	Z	372	None
Barney, Joshua	Baltimore	1– 6–1812	65,000	O	331	Rowling Fk, Green R & Fish Cr
Barrett, Alexander M	Louisa	12–13–1824	3,000	Y	148	N Fk Tradewater & Goose Cr
Barrett, Chas	Virginia	5–25–1815	150	Q	116	None
Barrett, Chas	Virginia	5–25–1815	21¼	Q	117	None
Barrett, Chas	Virginia	5–25–1815	11¼	Q	118	None
Barrett, Chas & Wife	Louisa	12–13–1824	3,000	Y	148	N F Tradewater & Goose Cr
Barrett, Mary	Louisa	12–13–1824	3,000	Y	148	N Fk Tradewater & Goose Cr
Barrett, Peter S	Louisa	12–13–1824	3,000	Y	148	N Fk Tradewater & Goose Cr
Bartlett, Anthony	Henry	12–15–1809	1,198	N	118	Paint Lick & Back Cr
Bartlett, Geo W	Mercer	10–21–1815	200	Q	270	None
Barton, Seth	Spotsylvania	7–11–1810	778	N	307	Deer Cr
Barton, Seth & Wife	Spotsylvania	7–23–1808	Lot	M	297	Fredericksburg
Bass, Thos H & Richard & Edward	Virginia	3– 7–1834	114	Z	443	Frankfort
Bastrop, Philip Henry, N Tot	Frederick	11– 7–1799	———	D	453	None
Bastrop, P H, N T	Frederick	3– 9–1800	8,520	E	195	N & S Fk Elkhorn
Bastrop, P H, N T	Ovachita	9–13–1800	———	E	264	None
Bates, Thomas	Goochland	3–15–1804	2,827½	J	143	Licking
Bates, Thos L	Goochland	5– 7–1798	2,827½	D	386	Licking
Battle, Hay	Carolina	11–19–1800	2,000	E	179	Licking
Bayler, Walker	Fayette	9– 4–1805	Lots & slaves	K	121	Lexington
Baylor, Jno W	Bourbon	8–29–1816	773½	R	126	Stoners Fk & Green R
Beale, Thos	Maco, China	10– 1–1839	1,000	27	146	Obion Cr
Beall, Asa	Franklin	1–11–1800	9,850	D	497	N & S Fks Elkhorn & Clear Crs

Grantor	Residence	Deed Date	Acres	Book	Page	Watercourse
Beall, Asa, Atty	——	7–10–1806	3,530	K	377	Harbour & Cabin Crs
Beall, Benj	Mercer	10–13–1796	Lot	A-2	528	Frankfort
Beall, Benj	Campbell	11–18–1800	4,600	E	237	None
Beall, Benj	Campbell	11–13–1802	496½	G	36	M Fk Licking
Beall, Benj	Campbell	10–25–1803	400	H	1	Chaplins Fk
Beall, Benj & Wife	Campbell	6–13–1799	——	D	400	None
Beall, Norborn B, Atty	Kentucky	7–11–1805	500	J	289	Big Bone Cr
Beall, Nathan & Azra	Kentucky	11– 4–1800	304	E	121	None
Beall, Richard, Atty	Mercer	5–24–1791	Lot	B-2	316	Danville
Beall, Saml T	Nelson	10–28–1819	Lots	T	336	Bardstown
Beall, Saml T	Nelson	10–28–1819	8,178	T	336	Rolling Fk Buffalo & Glens Crs
Beall, Walter	Bardstown	7–28–1802	1,250	G	197	Slate Cr
Beall, Walter Sr	Nelson	4–28–1800	Lots	E	133	Bardstown
Beard, Joseph	Pulaski	11–21–1799	444	D	481	Cumberland R
Beard, Joseph & Wife	——	1–31–1815	——	P	609	None
Beard, William	Woodford	8–24–1795	1,784	A-2	139	None
Beard, Wm	Woodford	7–24–1795	1,939	A-2	142	None
Beates, Fredrick	Philadelphia	10–28–1819	——	T	189	None
Beaty, Adam & Wife	Mason	5–11–1813	Lot	P	152	Frankfort
Beaty, Chas C, Atty	Abington	1– 1–1831	10,000	Z	93	S Fk Sandy R
Bedford, Thos J	Bourbon	12–13–1833	666⅔	Z	378	S Fk Tradewater
Bedford, Thos, heirs	Bourbon	8–27–1821	400	U	537	Highland Cr
Beeler, Jordan P	Jefferson	8–14–1841	100	27	264	E Br Floyds Fk
Bell, Joseph	Augusta	4– 1–1818	——	T	129	None
Bell, Joseph	Philadelphia	5–31–1819	1,916½	U	413	Ohio R
Bell, Jno	——	3–23–1787	½	A	298	None
Bell, Jno	Mercer	9–10–1790	400	B-2	202	Skeggs Cr
Bell, Saml, by Trustees	——	4–28–1800	Lots	E	133	Bardstown
Bell, Saml T	——	10–12–1819	1,193	T	181	Rolling Fk
Bell, Thomas	Charlottsville	11– 4–1795	1,000	W	307	Beaver Cr & N Fk Tradewater
Bell, Thomas & Wife	Woolford	7–26–1806	100	K	361	Ohio R
Bell, Thos, heirs	Kentucky	10–29–1846	217	28	79	Woodford Co
Bell, Wm	Philadelphia	11–10–1795	5,000	A-2	235	Rough Cr
Bell, Wm	Philadelphia	3–18–1796	70,937	A-2	340	N Fk Licking & Ohio R
Bell, William & Wife	Augusta	5–10–1800	200	E	319	Small Br
Bell, Wm & Wife	Barren	11–25–1816	215	R	251	Ky R
Bell, Wm, heirs	Philadelphia	5–31–1819	1,916½	U	413	Ohio R
Bener, Wm	Paris	7–26–1817	333½	S	59	Big Barren R
Bennett, Benj	Franklin	7–19–1796	——	A-2	371	Big Benson Cr
Bennett, Bartlet	Virginia	3–22–1797	500	A-2	646	Lick Cr
Bennett, Bartlett	Orange	3– 8–1803	313	Q	425	S Fk Licking
Bennett, Ed & Wife	Washington	1–25–1816	——	Q	485	None
Bennett, Elisha & Wife	Baltimore	5–12–1808	100	M	80	Big Barren R
Bennett, Elisha & Wife	Maryland	8–19–1809	500	N	40	Big Barren R
Bennett, H & Wife	Campbell	1–29–1818	6,500	S	206	None
Bennett, Susanna	Jefferson	10–22–1814	——	Q	60	None
Bennett, Van & Thos	Jefferson	10–22–1814	——	Q	62	None
Benoist, Sarah	Mercer	11– 2–1789	——	B-2	165	None
Bernard, Dudly P	Virginia	8– 8–1840	464½	27	153	Shelby Co
Bernard, Jno & Richard	Virginia	12–31–1796	40,857	Q	499	Ohio R
Berkley, Nelson	Richmond	10–13–1801	1,000	F	366	—— Cr
Berry, Alice	Campbell	9–17–1823	1,882	W	373	W Fk Floyds Fk
Berry, Benj & Jno	Fayette	3–10–1803	500	G	418	Poages Cr
Berry, Benj & Wife	Fayette	6–11–1829	366⅓	Z	63	Deer Cr
Berry, Benj & Wife	Fayette	6–11–1829	500	Z	64	Clay Lick Cr
Berry, Francis	——	4–27–1801	184	L	46	Ky R
Berry, Henry	Franklin	2–14–1814	Negro	P	532	None
Berry, Henry	Franklin	3– 8–1815	80	Q	22	S Fk Benson Cr
Berryman, Jas S	Franklin	3–10–1834	——	Z	513	None
Beswick, Christopher	Kentucky	11–12–1789	3,000	E	98	Fk Licking
Betts, Mormaduke	Scott	9– 8–1829	——	Y	419	Ky R & Cedar Cr
Beverly, Carter	Stanton	8–14–1809	800	N	107	Big Barren Cr
Bibb, Richard	Bullitt	8– 1–1802	11,483⁷⁄₁₂	G	58	Licking
Bibb, Richard	Kentucky	5– 5–1807	——	S	244	None
Bibb, Richard	Logan	3– 1–1820	6,550	T	420	None
Bibb, Richard & Wife	Bullitt	5– 1–1803	1,765	G	285	Otter Cr
Bibb, Richard Sr	Bullitt	11–21–1803	5,850	H	36	Salt R
Billingslea, Wm	Maryland	4–19–1798	1,000	O	139	E Br Nolinn
Binns, Jno Alexander & Wife	London	3–13–1799	400	D	208	Cumberland R
Bishop, David	Ainwell	5–16–1807	86,035	W	171	None
Blackden, Saml	Massachusetts	2–16–1787	5,277	A-2	596	Ohio R
Blackden, Saml & Wife	Fishtails	5–16–1797	——	B	217	None
Blackburn, C J & Wife	Woodford	1–18–1842	362	27	258	2 Mile Cr
Blackburn, E M, Atty	——	11–22–1843	10,000	27	369	None

Grantor	Residence	Deed Date	Acres	Book	Page	Watercourse
Blackburn, E M, Atty	Woodford	12–19–1844	19$\frac{3}{4}$	27	445	Mason Co
Blackburn, Wm B Jr & Wife	———	8– 9–1830	———	Y	506	S Elkhorn
Blackford, Jno	Washington	11–20–1816	———	R	108	None
Blackwell, Jno	Fauquier	4–28–1800	100	E	256	None
Blaine, Jas	Green	2– 9–1809	———	M	309	Shawnee Run
Blair, Archibald	Richmond	4–15–1796	600	A-2	394	Russell Cr
Blair, Archibald	———	4–13–1798	3,600	D	76	Cumberland R
Blair, David & Jas, Attorneys	Fredericksburg	2–13–1799	1,000	D	534	Ohio R
Blair, F P & Wife	Franklin	10–22–1830	Lot	Z	28	Frankfort
Blair, James	———	12–16–1804	250	H	482	Licking
Blair, Thos P	Franklin	12–15–1821	Lots	V	159	Columbus Ohio
Blake, Joseph	Boston	6– 6–1803	———	H	173	None
Blakemore, Geo	Frederick	6– 7–1826	417$\frac{1}{3}$	X	355	Tradewater
Blakemore, Geo	Frederick	6– 7–1826	333$\frac{2}{3}$	X	357	Highland Cr
Blakemore, Geo	Frederick	6– 7–1826	418$\frac{1}{3}$	X	358	Tradewater
Blakemore, Geo	Frederick	6– 7–1826	418$\frac{1}{3}$	X	360	Tradewater
Blakemore, Jno	Oldham	2–23–1827	120	X	285	Rough Cr
Blakemore, Jno	Oldham	2–23–1827	480	X	288	Rough Cr
Blancett, Rodham	Prince William	11–16–1796	500	D	256	None
Blanchard, Jno	Warren	3– 1–1823	373	W	119	None
Blanton, Carter	Franklin	11–30–1820	300	U	194	Eagle Cr
Blanton, Harrison	Frankfort	12– 2–1815	Lot	Q	430	Frankfort
Blanton, Harrison	Franklin	9– 6–1839	Lots	27	74	Frankfort
Blanton, Harrison	Franklin	3–25–1844	2	27	412	Ky R
Blanton, Harrison	Franklin	10–21–1844	———	27	438	Ky R
Blanton, Harrison	Franklin	3– 3–1846	140	28	78	Woodford Co
Blanton, Harrison Com'r	Frankfort	10–31–1822	Lots	W	68	Frankfort
Blanton, Harrison Com'r	———	10–31–1822	263$\frac{3}{4}$	W	79	Hammonds Cr
Blanton, Harrison Com'r	———	4– 4–1823	Lot	W	83	Frankfort
Blanton, Harrison & Wife	Franklin	10–21–1824	Lot	X	65	Frankfort
Blanton, Harrison & Wife	Franklin	6– 6–1833	266	Z	356	Ohio R
Blanton, James & Wife	———	3–25–1808	Lots	L	353	Frankfort
Blanton, James & Wife	Lexington	2–25–1822	———	V	226	Dry Run
Blanton, Richard, dec'd	Franklin	6–19–1824	Slaves	X	75	None
Blanton, Richard & Wife	Frankfort	10——1820	———	U	42	Dry Run
Blanton, Wm & Wife	Gallatin	6– 2–1803	2	G	332	Frankfort
Blanton, Wm & Wife	Gallatin	7–19–1816	10	U	470	None
Blanton, Wm & Wife	Franklin	8–30–1830	———	Z	8	Versailles Rd
Blanton, Willis	Franklin	6–19–1824	Slaves	X	75	None
Blanton, Willis	Franklin	5–10–1826	111	Y	161	———Cr
Blanton, Willis & Wife	Franklin	4–19–1821	117	Z	342	Franklin Co
Bledsoe, Aaron	Orange	12–22–1788	300	A	495	Howards Cr
Bledsoe, Moses	———	12–31–1808	Lot	M	332	Lexington
Bledsoe, Wm	Gallatin	10–21–1815	250	Q	461	Pitmans Cr
Bledsoe, Wm M & Moses, Attorneys	———	5–12–1800	683	F	165	None
Blewitt, Garland J Com'r	Warren	3– 6–1829	901	Y	398	Tennessee R
Blight, Saml	Philadelphia	11–30–1813	1,000	P	286	Hogback Grove
Bliss, George	Springfield	3–25–1796	4,184	E	117	Nolinn
Bliss, James	Fayette	4–29–1809	Lot	M	442	Cynthiana
Board of Internal Improvement	Kentucky	10– 8–1844	Lot	27	435	Midway
Board of Internal Improvements	———	12–30–1843	Lot	27	384	Midway
Board of Internal Improvements	———	12–30–1843	Lot	27	385	Midway
Boardly, Margaret	Baltimore	1–10–1824	35	W	169	Shepherds Run
Boardly, Margaret	———	5–17–1824	50	W	271	None
Bodley, Harry J, Comr	Fayette	6–27–1831	1,500	Z	144	Highland Cr
Bodley, Jno & Wife	Fayette	11– 1–1813	15	P	323	Clear Cr
Bodley, Thos	———	11– 6–1805	2,000	J	370	Floyds Fk
Bodley, Thos	Lexington	11–19–1814	912$\frac{1}{2}$	P	592	Blue Spring Grove
Bodley, Thos	Fayette	12–30–1815	2,244	Q	341	Boones & Indian Cr
Bodley, Thos	Lexington	7–29–1815	56	Q	343	Cane Run
Bodley, Thos	Lexington	9–28–1815	33,261$\frac{2}{3}$	Q	411	Johnsons Fk & N Fk Licking
Bodley, Thos & Wife	Fayette	11– 7–1817	Lots	R	566	Frankfort
Bodley, Thos	———	4–12–1819	Lot	T	380	Lexington
Bodley, Thos	Fayette	10–18–1820	1,352	N	6	Crews Cr & Licking
Bodley, Thos & Wife	Lexington	1–21–1807	4,400	L	296	Otter & Muddy Cr
Bodley, Thos & Wife	———	1– 1–1807	300	L	301	None
Bodley, Thos & Wife	Lexington	6–23–1810	5,753	N	220	Ohio R
Bodley, Thos & Wife	Lexington	6–24–1812	7,720	O	528	Little Sandy

Grantor	Residence	Deed Date	Acres	Book	Page	Watercourse
Bodley, Thos & Wife	Fayette	10– 4–1819	680	T	382	Johnsons Fk
Bodley, Thos, Attorney	———	11– 6–1805	2,000	J	370	Floyds Fk
Bodley, Thos, Executor	Fayette	11–15–1804	898	P	349	Ky R
Bohannan, Wm T & Richard A	———.	8– 9–1830	——	Y	506	S Elkhorn
Boles, Walter	Scott	2–25–1823	50	V	439	Fk Elkhorn
Bolware, Ramsey & Wife	Woodford	10–15–1821	25	V	219	None
Bond, Phenias, Att'y	Philadelphia	1–20–1808	194,493	M	124	Various waters
Booker, Edward M & Wife	Jefferson	5–30–1826	——	Y	166	None
Booker, Lewis & Wife	Gloucester	9– 1–1796	1,000	N	246	Tennessee R
Booker, Paul J & Wife	Washington	12–18–1823	——	W	221	None
Booker, Saml & Wife	Washington	12–21–1823	——	W	223	None
Booker, Richardson, heirs	Amelia	6–23–1820	200	U	23	Green R
Booker, Richardson, heirs	Amelia	6–27–1820	200	U	25	Green R
Booker, Wm & Wife	Wilkes	11– 6–1820	200	U	388	Green R
Boone, Squire & Wife	Jefferson	9– 5–1791	200	B-2	401	Fox Run
Booth, James & Wife	Dinwiddie	4–15–1816	4,000	R	197	None
Booth, Wm	Dinwiddie	4–15–1816	4,000	R	199	——
Booth, Wm A & Wife	Shannandoah	3–22–1799	1,000	D	160	None
Boothe, Jas & Wife	Virginia	12–30–1819	5,000	U	83	Twin Cr
Boothe, Jno	Washington	12–31–1813	2,000	P	497	Clay Lick
Boothe, Jno	Maryland	9–23–1839	10,000	27	81	Ky R
Borrough, Sidney H	Providence	4– 3–1815	Lots	R	393	Philadelphia
Borrough, Sidney H & Wife	Providence	7–31–1813	Lots	R	397	Philadelphia
Boswell, Joseph & Wife	Fayette	5–30–1817	1,000	R	338	Little R
Boswell, Thos E	Fayette	9–18–1844	———	27	430	Franklin Co
Botts, Alexander L	New York	7– 1–1845	———	28	6	None
Botts, Thos H	Fredericksburg	1– 1–1844	2,500	27	395	Franklin Co
Bouldin, Thos T	Virginia	6–11–1822	112	V	350	None
Bouldin, Thos T	Virginia	6–15–1822	150	V	351	Eagle Cr
Bouldin, Thos T	Virginia	10–21–1823	264	W	144	None
Bouldin, Thos T	Virginia	10–21–1823	116	W	146	None
Bouldin, Thos T	Virginia	10–21–1823	110	W	147	None
Bouldin, Thos T	Virginia	10– 7–1823	64	W	198	None
Bouldin, Thos T	Virginia	11– 1–1827	241	X	309	Eagle Cr
Bouldin, Thos T	———	12–17–1827	Lots	X	329	Owensboro
Bouldin, Thos T	———	12–17–1827	417	X	329	Ohio R
Bouldin, Thos T	———	1–25–1828	42,283	X	366	None
Bouldin, Thos T	Virginia	8–27–1828	125	X	454	Eagle Cr
Bouldin, Thos T	Virginia	9– 3–1828	168	X	473	Ohio R
Bouldin, Thos T	Virginia	9– 3–1828	135	X	475	None
Bouldin, Thos T	Virginia	——1826	295	Y	189	Blackfords Cr
Bouldin, Thos T	Washington City	6–15–1832	———	Z	203	None
Bouldin, Thos T, Executor	Virginia	11– 5–1818	———.	T	39	None
Bouldin, Thos T, Executor	Virginia	11——1820	600	U	192	Eagle Cr
Bouldin, Thos T, Trustee	Virginia	6–15–1822	90	V	254	None
Bouldin, Thos T, Trustee	Virginia	10–18–1827	295	X	291	Blacksfords Cr
Bouldin, Thos T, Trustee	Virginia	11– 1–1827	53	X	306	Eagle Cr
Bouldin, Thos T, Trustee	———	5–18–1826	1,000	Y	171	Ohio R
Bouldin, Thos T, Trustee	Virginia	2– 8–1826	750	Y	174	Ohio R
Bouldin, Thos T, Trustee	———.	1–31–1834	———	Z	402	Bullitt Co
Bower, Wm	Dorcester	7–21–1801	20,698	H	518	Killicanick Cr
Bowin, Wm & Wife	Franklin	6– 1–1804	205½	H	262	Limestone Cr
Bowles, Thos & Wife	Hanover	12–15–1801	200	F	355	Flat Lick Cr
Bowlware, Ramsey	Franklin	12–28–1809	Negro	N	116	None
Bowlware, Richard	Franklin	3–19–1814	Corn Cr	P	392	None
Bowlware, Richard	Franklin	9–14–1813	——	P	396	Elkhorn Cr
Bowlware, Richard & Wife	Franklin	4– 2–1814	——	P	403	S Elkhorn
Bowman, Abraham	Fayette	6–15–1790	260	B-2	148	Hanging Fk
Bowman, Abraham, Attorney	Fayette	8–18–1809	2,179	N	18	Little Ky
Bowman, Benj	Virginia	12– 1–1821	70	V	133	None
Bowman, Jacob	South Carolina	6–18–1789	400	B-2	60	None
Bowne, Matthew Franklin	Alexandria	8– 3–1795	32,104	A-2	248	Red R M Fk Clear Cr Ky R Green R & Nolinn

Grantor	Residence	Deed Date	Acres	Book	Page	Watercourse
Boyd, Geo & Wife	Washington	5–28–1812	556	O	461	Laurel R
Boyd, Saml	New York	2–19–1796	100,000	A-2	188	N & M Fk Ky R
Boyd, Saml	New York	2–18–1796	100,000	A-2	192	N & M Fk Ky R
Boyle, Jno Jr	Garrard	11——1821	100	V	107	Greasy Cr
Boyle, Jno, Executor	Kentucky	10–18–1826	333	Y	212	Br Green R
Boys, Saml	Philadelphia	2–12–1802	——	P	605	None
Bozarth, Jonathan	Christian	7–13–1810	1,000	N	281	Benson Cr
Bradford, Fielding	Scott	4–12–1814	2,270	P	502	Licking
Bradford, Wm	Muhlenburg	9– 4–1806	1,050	N	182	Muddy R Cypress Isaac & Thompsons Cr
Brand, Jno	Lexington	6–17–1815	39	Q	133	Georgetown Rd
Brandenburg, David & Wife	Clark	2–26–1822	123	V	190	Otter Cr
Brashear Alfred & Wife	Louisiana	4–11–1843	Lot	27	342	Louisville
Brashear, Walter	Bardstown	5– 4–1811	400	O	55	Cox Cr
Brashears, Walter	Bardstown	5– 4–1811	Lots	O	55	Bardstown
Bratton, Jas & Wife	Montgomery	5–10–1805	668	J	30	Dunbars Run
Bray, Jno Attorney	New Brunswick	9– 1–1801	10,000	G	358	Ohio R
Brechmer, Jacob	Nelson	6– 9–1796	3,000	A-2	504	Beech Fk
Brechmer, Jacob	Nelson	6–22–1796	1,807	A-2	506	Beech Cr
Brechmer, Jacob	Nelson	5– 5–1797	1,000	C	83	Br Little Rockcastle
Brechmer, Jacob	Nelson	8–12–1797	——	F	489	None
Breckenridge, Alexander & Wife, Executor	Jefferson	3– 9–1789	1,000	B-2	35	Elkhorn Cr
Breckenridge, Henry B.	Louisville	7–28–1812	——	O	533	None
Breckenridge, Jane	——	11– 7–1809	550	N	123	None
Breckenridge, Jas	——	10– 5–1801	——	O	228	Ohio R
Breckenridge, Jas & Wife	Batecourt	3– 7–1808	1,000	R	458	Cypress Cr
Breckenridge, Jno	Fayette	7–15–1802	90	F	468	Harrods Cr
Breckenridge, Jno	Fayette	7–15–1802	150	F	469	Harrods Cr
Breckenridge, Jno & Wife	Fayette	5– 2–1801	600	E	378	Ky R
Breckenridge, Jno, heirs	Fayette	10– 9–1840	——	27	155	Fayette Co
Breckenridge, Joseph C	Frankfort	12– 7–1822	600	W	17	Highland Cr
Breckenridge, Joseph C, heirs	——	6–27–1831	1,500	Z	144	Highland Cr
Breckenridge, J D & Wife	Kentucky	7–31–1812	1,692	P	155	Ohio R
Breckenridge, Preston	Fayette	5– 2–1818	——	S	128	Little N Fk Elkhorn
Breckenridge, Robt	Natchez	3– 1–1813	——	P	258	None
Breckenridge, Robt	Jefferson	12– 7–1822	600	W	17	Highland Cr
Breckenridge, Robt & Henry	Jefferson	5–13–1814	1,000	P	507	Ohio R
Breckenridge, Wm T	——	2–28–1835	1	Z	491	Morganfield
Breckenridge, Wm & Wife	Fayette	8——1823	666⅔	W	116	S Fk Ky R
Breen, Jno	——	1–24–1835	Lot	Z	504	Louisville
Brents, Samuel	——	11–20–1804	1,778⅓	H	415	Cumberland R
Brents, Samuel	Green	6–10–1823	575	W	45	Cypress Cr
Brents, Samuel & Wife	Green	2– 8–1831	1,500	Z	116	Russell Cr
Bridges, James	So Carolina	11–14–1786	400	A	190	Muddy Cr
Bridges, James	So Carolina	11–14–1786	——	A	192	Muddy Cr
Bridges, James	So Carolina	11–14–1786	500	A	194	Muddy Cr
Bridges, Sarah, heirs	King & Queen	9–28–1833	——	Z	398	None
Bridges, Wm M	Augusta	9–28–1833	——	Z	398	None
Bridgewater, Jonathan	Amherst	11– 4–1801	600	F	360	Russell Cr
Bridgewater, Jonathan	Shelbyville	9–13–1805	Lots	J	292	Frankfort
Briggs, Gray, Guardian	——	1–10–1798	4,354	D	61	Ohio R
Brightman, Walter & Wife	Franklin	12– 6–1802	——	G	374	Big Bensons Cr
Briscoe, Garrard	Virginia	10– 8–1791	158	B-2	489	Jeffersons Cr
Briscoe, Jno	Kentucky	7–20–1798	400	D	131	Ky R
Briscoe, Jno	Jefferson	9–12–1817	——	R	430	Ky R
Briscoe, Parmenas	Mercer	10– 2–1789	Negroes	B-2	85	None
Briscoe, Parmenas	——	6–25–1790	Negroes	B-2	180	None
Briscoe, Parmenas	Mercer	6–28–1788	Negro	B-2	386	None
Briscoe, Parmenas	——	3–21–1792	Negroes	B-2	454	None
Briscoe, Parmenas, Atty	Virginia	10– 8–1791	158	B-2	489	Jeffersons Cr
Brite, Albertus	Fayette	12–19–1797	200	B	277	Drennons Lick Cr
Brite, Albertus	Fayette	5–18–1789	350	B-2	69	Guesses Fk
Brite, Albertus & Wife	Fayette	9– 8–1806	75	K	384	Guesses Cr
Broadhead, Daniel	Philadelphia	5–17–1799	37,855¾	E	56	Cumberland & Laurel R
Broadhead, Daniel Jr.	Jefferson	9–30–1786	4,400	K	460	Beech Fk
Broadhead, Daniel Jr.	——	3– 4–1794	——	N	100	——
Broker, Richard & Wife	——	6–27–1820	200	U	29	Green R

Grantor	Residence	Deed Date	Acres	Book	Page	Watercourse
Brooke, Francis & Wife	Fredericksburg	7–20–1801	556	E	411	Eddy Cr
Brooke, Geo	King & Queen	9– 9–1796	———	A-2	532	None
Brook, George, Atty	Powhatan	11–10–1805	5,000	K	219	Eagle Cr
Brook, Thos A	Montgomery	1–20–1812	564	O	309	Tavern Sp Br
Brooking, Thos A & Wife & Thos V&Wife	———	11–17–1820	40	U	443	None
Brooking, Thos V & Wife	Chesterfield	10–12–1818	250	S	336	None
Brooks, Joseph	Jefferson	7–12–1798	200	C	294	Hardins Road
Broom, Jas M	Delaware	5–15–1819	200	S	548	Ky R
Broom, Jas M	Philadelphia	11–25–1820	600	U	173	Eagle Cr
Brough, Courtney	Virginia	7– 8–1844	4,577⅜	27	416	Russell & Drakes Cr
Brough, Robt	Norfolk	7–10–1823	7,144½	W	95	Cumberland R Russell & Drakes Cr
Brough, Robt & Wife	Norfolk	4– 1–1801	811	E	351	Green R
Brown, Daniel E & Wife	Franklin	4– 6–1819	188	V	188	Dry Run
Brown, Elijah	Philadelphia	6–17–1784	10,000	27	376	None
Brown, Geo	Fayette	10–12–1814	1,082	Q	63	Skeggs Cr
Brown, Geo	———	11–23–1831		Z	450	None
Brown, Geo & Wife	Henderson	1– 7–1831	179	Z	117	S Benson Cr
Brown, Hezakiah	Franklin	10– 8–1804	Negro	H	496	None
Brown, Hezakiah & Wife	Franklin	10–20–1815	106	Q	274	Benson & Ky
Brown, James	Richmond	10–28–1824	28,500	X	40	Big Barren W Fk Little & Cumberland R
Brown, Jas Jr & Wife	Richmond	8– 3–1826	1,750	X	239	None
Brown, Jno	Franklin	10–14–1797	70	B	206	18-mile Island
Brown, Jno	———	5– 8–1789	400	B-2	24	None
Brown, Jno	Kentucky	11–10–1797	400	D	128	Ohio R
Brown, Jno	Campbell	6– 4–1796	578¾	E	78	None
Brown, Jno	Bardstown	8–21–1800	Lots	K	375	Bardstown
Brown, Jno	Frankfort	2– 1–1813	333⅓	P	77	Licking
Brown, Jno	———	8–21–1800	Lot	R	269	Bardstown
Brown, Jno	———	8–21–1800	Lot	R	270	Bardstown
Brown, Jno	Boone	7–31–1817	5,078¾	T	483	Cases Cr
Brown, Jno	Franklin	4–10–1828	1	X	445	Cave Spg
Brown, Jno	Franklin	4– 9–1829	Lots	Y	408	Frankfort
Brown, Jno, Senator	Franklin	6– 3–1800	1,333½	E	8	Deer Cr
Brown, Jno & Wife	Frankfort	9–20–1801	500	F	144	Stewarts Cr & ——— R
Brown, Jno & Wife	Franklin	10–25–1800	560	F	146	None
Brown, Jno & Wife	Franklin	12–13–1802	450	G	112	Little R
Brown, Jno & Wife	Frankfort	12– 2–1809	650	N	262	None
Brown, Jno & Wife	Franklin	11–17–1815	550	Q	243	Little R
Brown, Jno & Wife	Frankfort	4–——1814	263	R	275	None
Brown, Jno & Wife	Franklin	1–21–1820	276	T	364	Shiveleys Mill Cr
Brown, Jno & Wife	Frankfort	1–25–1830	263½	Y	429	Lexington
Brown, Jno & Wife	Illinois	1–18–1844		27	409	S Benson
Brown, Jno B & Wife	———	4–18–1833	———	Z	278	None
Brown, Jno P W	———	6–21–1843	Lot	27	356	Frankfort
Brown, Mason	Franklin	5–14–1829	Lot	Y	354	Browns Ferry
Brown, Mason & Wife	Franklin	4– 2–1838	Lot	28	94	Frankfort
Brown, Matthew F & Wife	Alexandria	8–11–1795	44,378	P	212	None
Brown, Nicholas & Wife	Providence	7–31–1827	Lot	X	403	Maysville
Brown, Orlander & Wife	Franklin	4– 2–1838	Lot	28	94	Frankfort
Brown, Orlander & Mason	Franklin	6–21–1843	Lot	27	356	Frankfort
Brown, Dr Preston W, heirs	———	1– 6–1844	836½	27	421	Ohio R
Brown, Robt & Jno S	New York	10–17–1842		27	343	N Fk Ky R
Brown, Thos, heirs	———	11–13–1815	1,500	R	27	Slate & Rockcastle
Brown, Wm	Boone	11–13–1815	1,000	R	30	Slate Cr
Brown, Wm C	Gallatin	12–29–1840	———	27	176	None
Browning, Elijah G	Clark	7–18–1820	4,000	T	477	Floyds Fk
Brownlee, Wm	Green	11– 7–1803	1,000	H	274	Tradewater
Bruster, Jas	Lincoln	6–17–1786	800	A	127	Rolling Fk
Bryan, Geo & Wife	Bourbon	5– 2–1818	Lot	S	402	Port Williams
Bryan, Guy	Philadelphia	10–23–1809	113,482	N	161	Ohio R
Bryan, Guy	Philadelphia	10–25–1809	31,778	N	166	Little Sandy & E Fk Dix R
Bryan, Jno & Wife	Somerset	7– 3–1797	4,000	B	265	Goose Cr
Bryan, Jno & Wife	Somerset, N J	7–12–1799	2,000	E	47	E Fk Crocus Cr
Bryan, Jno & Wife	Somerset	1–28–1797	63,791	Q	538	Ohio R
Bryant, Thos Y	Franklin	9–20–1802	170	F	522	Salt R
Buck, Anthony	Fredericksburg	8– 6–1812	1,050	P	162	Fk Blackfords Cr
Buck, Chas	———	2–21–1815	226	Q	13	Hays Fk Silver Cr

Grantor	Residence	Deed Date	Acres	Book	Page	Watercourse
Buck, Chas	Franklin	12–21–1827	4,450	X	339	Ohio R & Cypress Cr
Buck, Chas, 3rd	Union	3–23–1835	800	Z	504	Deer Cr
Buckley, Jeremiah	Woodford	5–19–1812	10	P	20	Ky R
Buckner, Jno C & Wife	Scott	11–13–1816	224	R	67	Elkhorn
Buckner, Robt & Wife	Oldham	12– 8–1825	—	Y	101	None
Buckner, Wm	Kentucky	10–16–1795	1,524	A-2	620	Meeting & Rough
Buford, Abraham	Mercer	11– 7–1789	200	B-2	143	Chaplins Fk
Buford, Abraham	Scott	7– 8–1814	350	P	479	Cumberland R
Bugler, Jno	Mercer	10–13–1796	Lot	A-2	528	Frankfort
Bukey, Rudolphus	—	— 1820	Lot	U	184	Louisville
Bullitt, Alexander Scott	Jefferson	9– 1–1786	3,111	A	474	None
Bullitt, Cuthbert & Wife	—	4–30–1791	1,000	B-2	374	Ash Cr
Bullitt, Thos & Wife	Jefferson	12–22–1819	722	U	3	Deer Cr
Bullock, David	Louisa	10–26–1802	236	G	340	Br Green R
Bullock, David	—	10– 1–1811	637	P	446	N Fk Tradewater
Bullock, David	Richmond	3–16–1814	Slaves	R	20	None
Bullock, Len H	Tenant in common	1– 6–1775	—	D	272	Ohio & Green R
Bullock, Lewis, Atty	Mason	10– 1–1811	637	P	446	N Fk Tradewater
Bullock, Thos, Atty	Woodford	1–10–1825	213	X	294	Eagle Cr
Bullock, Walter	—	11–20–1804	1,778¾	H	415	Cumberland R
Bullock & Ficklin	Philadelphia	9– 4–1815	Lots	Q	398	Shelbyville
Bundanlegnose, Louis Phililost	Paris, France	11–22–1819	1,840,000	V	468	Various Water Courses
Bunner, Andrew, heirs	Philadelphia	10–28–1820	16,380	U	155	Salt R
Bunner, Chas F	New York City	4–25–1814	16,380	P	428	Salt R & Croocked Cr
Bunner, Chas F	New York	11–30–1819	79¾	T	166	Salt R
Bunner, Chas F	New York	11–30–1819	81½	T	168	Salt R
Bunner, Chas F	New York	11–30–1819	50½	T	170	Salt R
Bunner, Chas F	New York	11–30–1819	78¼	T	172	Salt R
Bunner, Chas F	New York	10–28–1820	16,380	U	155	Salt R
Bunner, Sarah	Philadelphia	4–25–1814	16,380	P	428	Salt R & Crooked Cr
Bunner, Sarah	Philadelphia	10–28–1820	16,380	U	155	Salt R
Burchfield, Robt & Wife	Henry	8–19–1802	133¼	F	473	Butlers Fk
Burditt, Wm	—	10–21–1816	100	R	160	None
Burneston, Isaac	Baltimore	2– 2–1808	600	M	65	Big Barren R
Burnett, Jos & Wife	Logan	8–24–1814	1,082	Q	65	Skeggs Cr
Burrough, Elizabeth	Philadelphia	8–26–1815	—	Q	245	None
Burrows, Nathan	Fayette	10–13–1801	307	F	166	S Fk Elkhorn
Burrows, Wm W & Wife	Philadelphia	1–15–1799	34,000	D	213	Eagle Cr
Burton, Robt	Granville	8–13–1787	1,400	Q	180	Ky R
Burwell, Nathaniel	Virginia	7–14–1800	6,000	F	210	Salt R
Burwell, Nathaniel	—	3– 7–1802	6,000	F	491	Ohio R
Burwell, N, Trustee	—	12–31–1799	2,000	L	108	Ohio R
Bush, Chas, Atty	—	5–12–1800	683	F	165	None
Bush, Jno & Wife	Boone	3–20–1799	1,000	D	218	Fk Station Camp Cr
Bush, Philip, heirs	Casey	12–29–1827	2,000	X	346	Green R
Bustard, Jno	Tennessee	12– 4–1822	200	X	125	Drakes Cr
Butler, Anthony	Mississippi	9–13–1822	400	V	320	None
Butler, Geo & Wife	Franklin	1–24–1842	4¾	27	268	Armstrongs Br
Butler, Jno	Franklin	4–10–1805	—	J	303	Station Camp & Big Benson
Butler, Percival, Comr	Gallatin	9–13–1811	750	O	197	Spring Cr
Buyers, Jno	Northumberland	4–10–1806	700	K	265	Rough Cr
Buyers, Jno, Administrator	Northumberland	4–10–1806	4,000	K	262	Rock Lick & Long Lick Crs
Byrd, Thos & Wife	Fredrick	5– 9–1796	1,000	C	34	Clay Lick Cr
Byrd, Thos T, Trustee	Fredrick	11–29–1799	3,000	E	123	Paint Lick & Sugar Crs
Byrd, Thos T, Trustee	Fredrick	11–29–1799	2,766⅔	E	126	Ohio R
Byrd, Wm Jr, Atty	Lexington	6– 7–1814	6,891	P	451	Goose, Dix, Ohio R & Skeggs Cr
Cabill, Wm Jr & Wife	Amhurst	7–20–1795	500	D	489	Chaplins Fk & Glens Lick
Cabell, W H & Wife	Richmond	3–26–1825	2,647	Y	116	Poages Cr & N Fk Tradewater
Caldwell, Adam	Franklin	4–18–1801	—	E	327	None
Caldwell, Adam, Atty	Frankfort	8–10–1805	4,000	J	326	None
Caldwell, Adam & Wife	Frankfort	2– 9–1814	Lot	P	391	Frankfort
Caldwell, Jno	Livingston	11–21–1801	250	F	155	Coopers Run
Caldwell, Philip	Franklin	5–31–1806	2,474	M	93	Green R
Caldwell, Robt	Mercer	4–23–1799	861	D	143	Hingston Fk

Grantor	Residence	Deed Date	Acres	Book	Page	Watercourse
Calhoon, Geo	Nelson	9- 1-1788	400	B-2	435	Bald Hill Cr
Calhoon, Geo	Henry	4- 3-1816	200	Q	432	Chaplins Fk & Salt R
Calhoun, Jos Jr	Baltimore	3-18-1815	2,500	S	496	None
Call, Daniel	Richmond	7- 9-1824	218	W	466	None
Call, Daniel	Richmond	7- 9-1824	905	W	470	None
Call, Daniel	Richmond	7- 9-1824	500	W	473	S Fk Sandy R
Call, Daniel, Comr.	Richmond	11- 5-1818		T	23	None
Call, Daniel, Executor	Richmond	7- 9-1824	100	W	463	None
Call, Daniel, Executor	Richmond	3-24-1832	333⅓	Z	330	Green Co
Call, Daniel, Executor	Richmond	3-24-1832	5,000	Z	332	Montgomery Co
Call, Wm	Prince George	5- 9-1807		S	68	None
Calloway, Flanders	Montgomery	11- 5-1824	400	X	139	Hingston Fk
Calloway, James	Bedford	11-17-1796	1,296¼	C	26	Little Sandy R
Calloway, Jas	Bourbon	10- 7-1802	300	F	517	Hustons Fk
Calloway, Jno	Campbell	12-10-1807	443	L	227	Hustons Fk
Calloway, Jno	Campbell	9-13-1806	73	L	344	Hustons Fk
Calloway, Jno	Campbell	9-13-1806	200	L	346	Hustons Fk
Calloway, Jno		12-10-1807	443	M	179	Hustons Fk
Calloway, Jno	Campbell	3-24-1815	900	Q	36	Clear Cr
Calloway, Jno	Campbell	3-24-1815	100	Q	37	Clear Cr
Calloway, Jno, Decd	Montgomery	11- 5-1824	400	X	139	Hingston Fk
Calloway, Micajah	Amhurst	9-15-1791	400	B-2	456	Hustons Fk
Calmes, Spencer N		12- 1-1818	1,250	S	387	None
Calmes, Marquis		8-21-1800	Lot	F	2	Frankfort
Calmes, Marquis	Woodford	2-25-1806	250	L	72	M Fk Ky R
Calmes, Marquis	Woodford	1-27-1816	950	Q	420	Silver Cr
Cammick, Christopher & Wife	Franklin	5——1799	Lot	D	206	Frankfort
Camp, Jane D	New Jersey	7-18-1825	5,000	X	418	Harrods Cr
Camp, Robt	Culpepper	9- 7-1804	20,300	J	154	Red R & Middle Fk Rough Cr
Campbell, Ahill, heirs	Richmond	3-26-1839	100	27	132	Ky R
Campbell, Allen	Scott	1-30-1817	75	R	247	Lecompts Fk Elkhorn
Campbell, Archibald	Fanquir	4-24-1826	1,000	Y	221	Green & Pond Rs
Campbell, Chas	Lincoln	2-12-1792	223	B-2	444	Sugar Cr
Campbell, Chas	Lincoln	2-12-1792	138	B-2	447	Sugar Cr
Campbell, Chas L & Wife	Louisville	3-14-1816	5,990	Q	387	None
Campbell, Geo	Philadelphia	9-22-1832	15,000	Z	233	Salt R
Campbell, Geo, Atty	Philadelphia	10-24-1821	28,270	V	448	Salt & N Fk Ky R
Campbell, Jno	Muhlenburg	11-29-1809	Lot	N	201	Frankfort
Campbell, Jno	Jefferson	4-26-1790	243½	R	154	Br Ky R
Campbell, Jno, Decd	Fayette	4-21-1826	5,746½	X	206	Ky R, Bullskin Cr & Big Barren R
Campbell, Jno, heirs	Fayette	7- 8-1801	14,546	E	369	Gesses & Benson Crs
Campbell, Jno, heirs	Fayette	4-21-1826	6,479⅔	Y	134	Bullskin & Cumberland R
Campbell, Michael	Davidson	9- 5-1809	4,700	N	81	Green R
Campbell, Robt	Richmond	6-16-1807	444	L	156	Cumberland R
Campbell, Robt	Richmond	4-19-1809	9,700	N	285	Big Laurel R
Campbell, Robt & Wife	Richmond	5-19-1797	1,000	B	125	—— R
Campbell, Robt & Wife	Richmond	5- 5-1798	1,500	D	382	Goose Cr
Campbell, Robt & Wife	Richmond	1- 1-1801	1,000	E	392	Coxes & Wilsons Crs
Campbell, Robt & Wife		5-25-1798	3,500	J	82	Goose Cr & Tradewater R
Campbell, Saml & Wife	Jennings	6-10-1818	75	S	183	Lecompts Run
Campbell, Wm	Kentucky	12——1818		S	508	Sovern Cr
Cannon, Jno	Prince William	1-11-1802	2,100	F	240	None
Cardwell, Wm J	Franklin	11-11-1844	Lot	27	439	Frankfort
Cariner, Jonathan	Kentucky	3-20-1818		S	109	Elkhorn Cr
Carman, Joseph, heirs	Kentucky	2- 7-1807	1,000	M	320	Benson Cr
Carman, Joshua	Shelby	9- 2-1814		P	530	Big Benson Cr
Carnan, Jno	Cecil	5-10-1793	17,823	A-2	616	Ky R
Carnan, Jno	Maryland	9-27-1787	10,000	E	95	N Fk 3 Fks Ky R
Carnan, Jno	Baltimore	8-23-1839	89,000	27	88	Red R & Licking
Carneal, Sarah	Frankfort	5-31-1821	Slaves	U	489	None
Carneal, Thos	Kentucky	9-26-1794	939	B	129	N Fk Elkhorn
Carneal, Thos	Fayette	5-13-1797	995	B	268	Big Barren R
Carneal, Thos	Shelby	7-10-1798	1,500	C	263	N Fk Tradewater
Carneal, Thos	Shelby	7-10-1798	1,000	C	265	N Fk Tradewater
Carneal, Thos	Campbell	9-13-1799	8,800	D	450	Little Reedy Cr
Carneal, Thos	Boone	8-13-1801	2,000	F	71	Otter Cr
Carneal, Thos	Frankfort	5-17-1802	907	G	4	Little Muddy Cr
Carneal, Thos	Boone	6-29-1803	2,000	G	447	Welches Cr
Carneal, Thos	Boone	10-13-1803	600	H	92	Gasper R
Carneal, Thos	Boone	8- 1-1805		J	261	None
Carneal, Thos	Boone	12-27-1805	2,000	K	156	M Elkhorn
Carneal, Thos	Boone	12-27-1805	2,500	K	165	M Elkhorn & Big Bone Cr

Grantor	Residence	Deed Date	Acres	Book	Page	Watercourse
Carneal, Thos	———	12– 1–1806	200	K	504	Main Coxes Cr
Carneal, Thos	Franklin	9–16–1807	5,222	L	264	Rock Lick & Caney Cr
Carneal, Thos	Franklin	11–16–1807	Slaves	L	334	None
Carneal, Thos	Frankfort	12–27–1809	500	N	120	E Br Floyds Fk
Carneal, Thos	Frankfort	9–10–1810	2,800	N	283	Clear Fk Rough Cr
Carneal, Thos	Boone	5–21–1805	900	X	332	Dry & Gunpowder Crs
Carneal, Thos & Wife	Franklin	2–20–1808	333½	L	386	None
Carneal, Thos & Wife	Franklin	1–21–1809	300	M	301	Coxes Cr
Carneal, Thos & Wife	Oakley	1–21–1809	300	M	303	Green R
Carneal, Thos & Wife	Franklin	8–24–1809	2,625	N	121	Beech Cr
Carneal, Thos & Wife	Franklin	10– 8–1810	700	N	475	Ohio R
Carneal, Thos & Wife	Franklin	12– 3–1810	532	O	336	Ohio R
Carneal, Thos & Wife	Franklin	12– 4–1810	518	O	337	Ohio R
Carneal, Thos, Atty	Kentucky	12– 4–1801	1,015	F	152	Pond R
Carneal, Thos, Atty	———	12– 1–1807	200	L	338	Eagle Cr
Carneal, Thos, Atty	———	5– 7–1808	3,500	L	380	Sinking Cr
Carneal, Thos, heirs	Fayette	10–11–1811	3,600	O	153	Clover Lick & Ohio R
Carneal, Thos, heirs	Kentucky	7–31–1812	1,692	P	155	Ohio R
Carneal, Thos, heirs	Frankfort	10–12–1811	492	P	467	Elkhorn
Carneal, Thos Davis	Franklin	1–16–1808	2,120	L	279	Caney & Fks N Fk Rough Cr
Carneal, Thos D	Jefferson	12–28–1813	Lot	P	355	Louisville
Carneal, Thos D	———	5–31–1821	Slaves	U	490	None
Carneal, Thos D	Campbell	10– 9–1823	———	W	126	Cumberland R
Carneal, Thos D	Campbell	12–11–1823	1,332	W	185	Big Bone R
Carneal, Thos D & Wife	Covington	8– 5–1816	1,962½	R	16	Rock Lick Cr
Carr, Garland	Albemarle	2–22–1799	1,000	D	342	N Fk Tradewater
Carr, Garland	Albemarle	11–25–1799	637	E	229	N Fk Tradewater
Carr, Peter	Albemarle	6– 6–1810	1,500	P	567	Big Barren R
Carr, Peter & Wife	Albemarle	2–10–1800	1,000	D	524	Sulphur Lick Fk
Carrington, Edw, heirs	Richmond	12– 4–1815	3,353¾	Q	369	None
Carrington, Mayo	Cumberland	1– 6–1796	900	A-2	565	Green R
Carrington, Mayo	Cumberland	6–27–1803	1,066⅔	J	197	Cumberland R
Carrington, Paul	Charlotte	3– 1–1792	1,000	B-2	474	Chaplin Fk
Carrington, Wm E	Cumberland	1–14–1821	1,000	Z	178	Mississippi R
Carroll, Daniel	Duddington	12– 1–1831	7,200	Z	235	Russell Garve & Rough Cr
Carter, Chas	Frederick	10– 2–1811	———	O	189	Br Red R
Carter, Jane	Franklin	12– 2–1829	———	Y	413	None
Carter, Chas & Wife	Culpepper	9–11–1818	666⅔	S	484	Gasper R
Carter, Robt	Greenup	8–20–1827	———	X	290	—
Carter, Wm C & Wife	Albermarle	9–11–1799	———	F	117	None
Cary, Joseph	Alexandria	6– 1–1797	1,250	D	236	Otter Cr
Cary, Joseph	Alexandria	6– 1–1797	8,000	D	244	N Fk Sandy R
Cary, Joseph	Alexandria	6– 1–1797	10,000	D	252	S Fk Ky R
Cary, Joseph	Alexandria	11–12–1799	5,000	F	11	Straight Cr
Cary, Joseph	Alexandria	11–12–1799	5,000	F	26	Laurel R
Cary, Joseph	Alexandria	11–12–1799	10,000	F	30	Straight Cr
Cary, Joseph	Alexandria	11–12–1799	10,000	F	34	Cumberland R
Casey, Peter	Mercer	6–30–1807	1,200	M	361	Caseys Cr
Casey, Peter	Henderson	3–30–1810	———	N	251	Caseys Cr
Casey, Peter & Wife	Mercer	3–16–1791	1,000	B-2	348	M Fk, Stones Fk
Casey, Peter & Wife	Mercer	11–10–1802	1,400	G	62	Salt R
Cassell, Henry	Baltimore	3–21–1792	600	B-2	449	Battinger Cr
Cassell, Hiram & Wife	Union	6– 7–1838	———	27	9	Little R
Cassity, Michael	Fleming	11–10–1809	Slaves	N	114	None
Castleman, David	Fayette	2– 2–1844	Lot	27	394	Frankfort
Castleman, Elbridge	Boone	10–16–1843	———	27	389	None
Cathers, Edward & Wife	Woodford	11–10–1789	200	B-2	114	Ky R
Catlett, David & Wife	Frederick	4– 2–1801	200	H	74	E Fk, Floyds Fk
Catlett, Gramson	Montgomery	4–24–1821	390	V	149	None
Catlett, Lawrence & Wife	Carolin	1–12–1813	2,000	P	141	N Fk Tradewater
Catlett, Lawrence & Wife	Carolin	1–12–1813	2,000	27	277	N Fk Tradewater
Catlett, Peter	Boone	9–12–1826	1,000	Y	213	Green & Pond R
Catlett, Robt & Wife	Frederick	3– 1–1802	100	H	79	E Fk Floyds Fk
Catlett, Robt & Wife	Frederick	3– 1–1802	200	H	69	E Fk Floyds Fk
Catlett, Thos & Wife	Caroline	1–12–1813	2,000	P	141	N Fk Tradewater
Catlett, Saml & Wife	Carolin	1–12–1813	2,000	P	141	N Fk Tradewater
Catlett, Saml & Thos	Caroline	1–12–1813	2,000	27	277	N Fk Tradewater
Challis, Jas M & Wife	Monmouth	8– 1–1828	———	X	421	Salt R
Challis, Jno W & Wife	Salem	8– 1–1828	———	X	421	Salt R
Chamberlain, Wm B	Henrico	4–13–1825	1,237	Y	73	Chaplins Fk
Chamberlain, Will B, Attorney	Henrico	12–11–1823	750	W	180	Big Bone Cr

Grantor	Residence	Deed Date	Acres	Book	Page	Watercourse
Chamberlain, Will B, Attorney	Henrico	12–11–1823	1,770	W	182	Ohio R & Big Bone
Chambers, B S & Wife	Scott	10– 2–1821	Lot	V	232	Georgetown
Chaplin, Abraham	Mercer	6–23–1789	200	B-2	64	Skeggs Cr
Chaplin, Abraham	Mercer	3–24–1790	100	B-2	240	Beaver Cr
Chapman, Jno L & Wife	Meade	10– 1–1828	244,482	X	482	Nolinn
Chapman, Jno S, Atty	Delaware	5–15–1819	200	S	548	Ky R
Chenault, Stephen	——	7–10–1824	650	W	358	Ohio R & Clover Cr
Cherokee Tribe of Indians	——	1– 6–1775	——	D	272	Ohio & Green R
Cherokee Tribe of Indiana	——	1– 6–1775	——	C	60	Ohio, Cumberland & Green Rs
Cherry, Wm	Jefferson	12–31–1802	713½	G	421	Br Salt R
Childress, Jno	Knox	12– 3–1805	5,375	K	9	Big Valley
Childress, Sarah	——	6–23–1820	200	U	23	Green R
Chiles, Thos C	Shelby	3——1833	250	Z	368	Mill Cr
Chiles, Wm	Franklin	3——1833	250	Z	368	Mill Cr
Chiles, Wm	Montgomery	3——1833	250	Z	368	Mill Cr
Chinn, Richard H & Wife	Fayette	10–31–1825	I ot	Y	25	Lexington
Chinoweth, Richard	Jefferson	9–22–1793	Lot	C	250	Frankfort
Chisham, Geo & Benj	Scott	2–27–1823	50	W	23	None
Christain, Gideon	——	10–14–1828	——	X	481	None
Christain, Gilbert & Wife	Franklin	4–18–1806	100	K	290	N Fk Bensons Cr
Christian, Jonathan	Buckingham	5– 1–1817	388⅓	T	144	Ohio R
Christian, Wm	Montgomery	9–19–1783	1,000	A	3	Br
Christian, Wm & Wife	Montgomery	12–22–1780	1,000	B	132	Big Bone Cr
Christie, Thos	Hanover	12– 1–1796	1,400	B	39	N Fk Tradewater
Christie, Wm & Wife	——	10– 8–1805	100	J	423	Rough Cr
Christie, Wm & Wife	St Louis	6– 1–1820	400	U	11	Floyds Fk
Church, Robt W	Franklin	8–29–1841	68	27	234	Elkhorn
Church, Wm	Franklin	10–13–1829	34¾	Y	406	Elkhorn
Church, Wm	Franklin	3–31–1830	170	Y	446	Elkhorn
Church, Wm S	Franklin	6–20–1840	109	27	130	M Elkhorn
Churchill, Armstead & Wife	Jefferson	4–10–1790	4,000	B-2	150	Cedar Cr
Churchill, Jno, Atty	Hardin	10– 4–1806	1,169	L	60	Licking
Churchill, Sarah, heirs	Nelson	9–21–1825	1,512	Y	258	Rock Lick, Island Ohio R & Indian Camp Cr
Churchill, Wm	Hardin	10– 4–1806	1,169	L	60	Licking
Churchman, Jno	Augusta	12–27–1841	1,000	27	281	Hickman Co
Claiborne, Herbert A	Richmond	4–13–1825	1,237	Y	73	Chaplins Fk
Claiborne, Richard	Monongolia	2– 2–1799	5,227	D	334	Ohio R
Clark, Cary L, Atty	——	3–10–1803	500	G	390	Ohio R
Clark, Christopher	Georgia	6–14–1794	1,000	M	181	Green R
Clark, Geo, Atty	Lexington	10–11–1798	1,000	D	38	Harlins Cr
Clark, Geo, Atty	——	12– 6–1799	666⅔	D	443	N Fk Mayfield Cr
Clark, Geo & Wife	Hanover	4–15–1809	732	M	416	None
Clark, Geo & Wife	Fayette	11–23–1827	756	X	399	Peters Cr
Clark, Geo & Wife	Fayette	11–23–1827	200	X	400	Wolf R
Clark, Geo W	Fayette	7– 6–1832	——	Z	251	None
Clark, Geo W	Fayette	12– 1–1831	1,000	Z	253	Green R
Clark, Geo & Jonathan	Fayette	4–30–1810	11,200	N	267	W Fk Little R & Kettle Cr
Clark, Geo Rogers	Jefferson	10–27–1796	4,351	A-2	585	Ohio R
Clark, Geo R	Jefferson	5–26–1801	4,220	F	182	Clover Lick & Mississippi R
Clark, Geo R	Jefferson	7–28–1803	73,962	H	61	Ohio R
Clark, Geo R	——	9– 8–1788	9,800	P	413	Old Ft Jefferson
Clark, Jas A & Wife	——	8– 9–1830	——	Y	506	S Elkhorn
Clark, Jas N & Wife	——	8– 9–1830	192	Y	507	S Elkhorn
Clark, Jno	Richmond	11– 7–1794	1,000	A-2	61	Ohio R
Clark, Jno	Hamilton	9–10–1799	116	N	592	N Fk Elkhorn
Clark, Jno & Wife	Green	10– 8–1832	500	Z	239	Mississippi R
Clark, Jno H	Louisville	10–10–1818	422	S	333	None
Clark, Jno H & Isaac	Jefferson	10– 2–1817	1,000	V	70	Green R
Clark, Jno H, Isaac & Geo W	——	10– 2–1817	3,500	S	329	Crab Orchard Fk
Clark, Jno H, Isaac & Wm	——	10– 2–1817	1,293½	S	325	Little Ky R
Clark, Matthew	Franklin	3–15–1803	2,000	H	112	Ohio R
Clark, Matthew	Franklin	2–16–1805	200	H	550	Wilsons Cr
Clark, Matthew Jr, heirs	Franklin	2– 5–1839	Slaves	27	23	None
Clark, Matthew Sr, heirs	Franklin	2– 5–1839	Slaves	27	23	None
Clark, Robt & Wife	Clark	9–18–1819	1,519½	T	331	Bear Fk, Green R

Grantor	Residence	Deed Date	Acres	Book	Page	Watercourse
Clark, Robt Jr	Bedford	3– 8–1788	1,000	A	354	S Fk Otter Cr
Clark, Robt Jr & Wife	Clark	12–10–1800	2,600	E	203	Rough Cr
Clark, Robt Jr & Wife	Clark	12–10–1800	2,600	E	252	Rough Cr
Clark, Robt Jr, heirs	————	3–22–1810	3,039	N	391	Beaver Cr
Clark, Wm	Madison	8–26–1802	1,000	H	42	Kinkades Cr
Clark, Wm & Wife	Madison	8–26–1802	470	H	7	M Licking
Clark, Wm & Wife	Madison	8–26–1802	470	H	13	M Licking
Clark, Wm & Wife	Madison	8–26–1802	470	H	16	M Licking
Clark, Wm & Wife	Madison	8–26–1802	470	H	24	M Licking
Clark, Wm & Wife	Madison	8–26–1802	470	H	29	M Licking
Clark, Wm & Wife	Trigg	6– 1–1835	1,000	Z	514	Tennessee R
Clark, Wm & Geo W	Jefferson	10– 2–1817	1,000	V	70	Green R
Clay, Brutus J	Bourbon	3–30–1830	1,207½	Y	486	None
Clay, Elizabeth	Franklin	1–18–1834	115½	Z	408	Dry Run
Clay, Elizabeth	Franklin	1–18–1834	205¾	Z	409	Dry Run
Clay, Elizabeth	————	2–26–1824	150	Z	413	Dry Run
Clay, Elizabeth	————	2–26–1834	126	Z	415	Dry Run
Clay, Green & Wife	Madison	9–28–1815	1,900	Q	194	Salt Lick & Lees Cr
Clay, Green & Wife	Madison	12–12–1815	6,617	Q	358	Bank Lick Cr
Clay, Green & Wife	Madison	12–12–1815	2,130	Q	361	None
Clay, Green & Wife	Madison	12–22–1815	10,498	Q	364	Cedar & N Fk Rockcastle
Clay, Green & Wife	Madison	7– 4–1828	19,244½	X	497	Licking Red Ky R & Strodes Cr
Clay, Henry	Lexington	9–22–1807	27,500	L	126	Ky R
Clay, Henry	Lexington	9–16–1808	6,000	N	146	Bank Lick Cr
Clay, Henry	————	9–29–1810	688	N	276	Cumberland R
Clay, Henry	————	6– 8–1813	50,000	P	367	Various Waters
Clay, Henry	————	10– 7–1816		R	69	None
Clay, Henry	Fayette	4–10–1819	803	S	516	None
Clay, Henry	Kentucky	7– 2–1832	Lot	Z	241	Frankfort
Clay, Henry	Kentucky	11–27–1832	75	Z	242	Shelbyville Pike
Clay, Henry, Trustee	Kentucky	6–28–1811	615	O	71	Cumberland R
Clay, Henry, Executor	Kentucky	7–14–1831	1½	Z	156	Shelbyville Pike
Clay, Henry, Executor	Kentucky	11–12–1834	————	Z	477	None
Clay, Henry, Executor	Kentucky	5–15–1841	204	27	251	St Louis Co Mo
Clay, Matthew	Pittsylvania	5– 2–1802	1,400	F	451	Station Camp Cr
Clay, Sally	Madison	4–13–1831		Z	169	None
Clay, Sidney P	Bourbon	3–30–1830	1,207½	Y	486	None
Clay, Sidney P & Wife	Bourbon	11–10–1831	8,847½	Z	198	Bank Lick Cr
Clayborne, Richard	Richmond	2–16–1787	5,277	A-2	596	Ohio R
Clements, Mace	Essex	11–26–1828	Contract	Y	380	————
Clements, Mace	Essex	1–22–1795	2,000	Z	45	Ohio R
Clements, Mace	Essex	7–23–1833	————	Z	390	None
Clements, Smith	Fredericksburg	7–11–1829	————	Y	363	Drakes Cr
Cleverins, Holt	York	3– 5–1800	4,000	E	109	None
Cliffton, Jno	Philadelphia	4– 1–1805	22,000	O	235	Floyds Fk
Cliffton, Jno Jr	Philadelphia	4– 1–1805	67,647	Y	204	Floyds Fk, Sandy, Rockcastle, N Fk Elkhorn Crs, Ky & Green R
Cloud, Joseph & Wife	Philadelphia	5– 2–1805	7,500	K	66	Caney, Bear & Reedy Cr
Cloud, Ohmer	Georgetown	10– 9–1804	717	H	588	Caney, Bear & Reedy Crs
Cobb, Jno	Jefferson	11–15–1802	1,500	G	362	Harrisons Cr
Cobbs, Jno	Georgia	6–22–1789	1,000	B-2	29	Elkhorn
Cobuni, James & Wife	Mercer	8–26–1791	300	B-2	354	Brashears Cr
Cochran, Jno & Wife	Newcastle	3–30–1798	69,000	D	56	Main Licking
Cochran, Wm	Baltimore	6–10–1801	4,566⅔	F	109	Ohio, Cumberland & Little R
Cocke, Bowler	Henrico	9–16–1796	4,000	A-2	493	N Fk Tradewater
Cocke, Collin & Wife	Prince George	12– 9–1796	4,000	B	136	Parroquette Cr
Cocke, Stephen, heirs	Virginia	10–14–1834	1,000	Z	441	Muddy R
Cocke, Thos	————	10– 7–1795	3,000	A-2	692	Eagle Cr
Cocke, Wm	Hawkins	6– 1–1802	4,000	S	550	S Fk Licking & Grays Cr
Cohen, Jacob J	————	11–10–1794	2,500	A-2	67	None
Cohen, Jacob J	Richmond	11–10–1794	2,500	A-2	69	Main Licking
Cohen, Jacob J	Richmond	8–24–1803	2,000	G	435	None
Cohoon, Samuel	Pittsfield	3–10–1815	537	Q	95	Clay Lick Cr
Cohoon, Thos	Pittsfield	5–16–1814	537	P	495	Clay Lick Cr
Coin, Solomon & Wife	Lincoln	9– 7–1790	300	B-2	208	McConnells & Lecounts Runs
Coleman, Chapman	U S Marshall	11–11–1823	1,000	W	201	Ohio R
Coleman, Chapman	U S Marshall	10–24–1823	2,000	W	300	None
Coleman, Chapman	U S Marshall	11–12–1824	11,113	X	22	Ky R
Coleman, Chapman	U S Marshall	4–23–1824	11,550½	X	53	Ky R
Coleman, Chapman	U S Marshall	3–23–1827	Slaves	X	229	None
Coleman, Chapman	U S Marshall	3–23–1827	Lots	X	229	Henderson

Grantor	Residence	Deed Date	Acres	Book	Page	Watercourse
Coleman, Chapman	U S Marshall	3-23-1827	2,807	X	229	None
Coleman, Chapman	U S Marshall	6- 2-1827	1,900	X	249	Slate Cr
Coleman, Chapman	U S Marshall	6-19-1827	2,375	X	254	Caney Fk Tradewater
Coleman, Chapman	U S Marshall	6-19-1827	390¾	X	257	Mill Cr
Coleman, Chapman	U S Marshall	6-19-1827	625	X	259	None
Coleman, Chapman	U S Marshall	7- 3-1827	7,508	X	266	M Licking, Mill & Slate Cr
Coleman, Chapman	U S Marshall	10-22-1827	50,050	X	312	Cumberland & Sandy R, Tygarts Cr
Coleman, Chapman	U S Marshall	10-17-1827	1,896	X	362	None
Coleman, Chapman	U S Marshall	10-25-1828	800	X	488	None
Coleman, Chapman	U S Marshall	12-23-1828	640	X	494	Benson Cr
Coleman, Chapman	U S Marshall	2-13-1826	521	Y	133	None
Coleman, Chapman	U S Marshall	12- 9-1826	Lot	Y	229	Paris, Ky
Coleman, Chapman	U S Marshall	11-24-1826	239	Y	244	S Beargrass Cr
Coleman, Chapman	U S Marshall	11- 8-1826	15	Y	249	Fleming Co
Coleman, Chapman	U S Marshall	2- 2-1827	600	Y	266	Camp Fk Green R
Coleman, Chapman	U S Marshall	3- 1-1827	Lot	Y	273	Mt Sterling
Coleman, Chapman	U S Marshall	3- 1-1827	600	Y	275	Owingsville Road
Coleman, Chapman	U S Marshall	3- 1-1827	5,000	Y	277	Slate & State Cr
Coleman, Chapman	U S Marshall	10-14-1826	10,955¾	Y	281	Little Cumberland R, Pond, Dry, CaseysCrs&S Elkhorn
Coleman, Chapman	U S Marshall	5-27-1829	11,445½	Y	343	Land Sp
Coleman, Chapman	U S Marshall	6- 6-1829	20	Y	350	Ohio R
Coleman, Chapman	U S Marshall	11-14-1829	30,821	Y	425	Slate,Stepstone,Flat, Licking & Mill Cr
Coleman, Chapman	U S Marshall	12-15-1829	5,100	Y	453	None
Coleman, Chapman	U S Marshall	5-10-1830	225	Y	456	Floyds Fk
Coleman, Chapman	U S Marshall	5-19-1830	Lot	Y	499	Barbourville
Coleman, Chapman	U S Marshall	5-19-1830	———	Y	499	Little Richland Cr
Coleman, Chapman	U S Marshall	9-20-1830	9,124	Z	11	Floyds Fk
Coleman, Chapman	U S Marshall	11-16-1830	2,200	Z	41	Gists Cr
Coleman, Chapman	U S Marshall	3- 1-1831	2,787½	Z	100	Licking
Coleman, Chapman	U S Marshall	9- 5-1823	367	Z	105	None
Coleman, Edward S & Wife	Frankfort	3- 9-1813	Lots	P	464	Frankfort
Coleman, Edward S & Wife	Frankfort	2-25-1819	Lots	U	176	Frankfort
Coleman, Julius	Pendleton	3-29-1803	1,000	G	256	Licking
Coleman, Jas	Lexington	4-30-1806	1,000	K	410	Crocus Cr
Coleman, Jas	Harrison	6- 1-1821	35	U	482	None
Coleman, Jas & Wife	Harrison	1-17-1801	200	E	420	N Fk Tradewater
Coleman, Jas & Wife	Fayette	3-26-1810	10,000	O	131	Salt R
Coleman, Jas & Wife	Fayette	3-26-1810	30,000	O	133	Nolinn & Green R
Coleman, Jas & Wife	Kentucky	7-31-1812	1,692	P	155	Ohio R
Coleman, Jas & Wife	Woodford	2-14-1814	Lots	P	462	Frankfort
Coleman, Samuel & Wife	Henrico	11-12-1806	1,000	L	33	Green R
Coleman, Whitehead & Wife	Essex	5-17-1797	2,000	K	339	Cumberland R
Coleman, Wm & Wife	Montgomery	12-13-1815	1,700	R	37	Elkhorn
Collett, Jno & Wife	———	2-14-1812	400	O	468	Pond R
Collins, Betsy	Louisville	8-19-1815	1,000	Q	165	None
Collins, Betsy	Louisville	1- 8-1819	8,212½	S	419	Ohio R, Little Otter Cr & Br Ky R
Collins, Joseph Sr	Woodford	11-30-1798	400	D	114	N Fk Ky R
Colquhoun, Jas, Atty	———	12- 1-1807	200	L	338	Eagle Cr
Colquhoun, J, Atty	———	5- 7-1808	3,500	L	380	Sinking Cr
Colquhoun, Jno	Kentucky	7- 1-1797	6,000	B	103	None
Colquhoun, Walter, Atty	Falmouth	4-18-1801	400	F	192	Quirks Run
Colston, Rawleigh	Berkley	5- 9-1812	1,000	O	477	Ohio R
Colt, Roswell	Baltimore	5-11-1842	1,533	27	283	Otter Cr
Combs, Leslie	Fayette	7-12-1844	300	28	42	Breckinridge Co
Combs, Wm R & Wife	———	3-31-1821	172	U	433	None
Conally, Jno	———	4-15-1820	1,000	V	67	Ohio R
Connally, Jno	Fort Pitt	2- 6-1776	2,000	B-2	1	Ohio R
Connolly, Jno	Lieut Col British Army	11-21-1788	2,000	B-2	15	Ohio R
Connolly, Jno	Lieut Col British Army	11-21-1788	Lots	B-2	18	Louisville
Connolly, Jno	Lieut Col British Army	11-21-1788	1,000	B-2	20	Ohio R
Connolly, Jno	———	11- 1-1810	2,000	N	293	Ohio R
Connolly, Jno & Wife	Augusta	2-25-1775	2,000	B-2	11	Ohio R
Conner, Rice	Frankfort	11-18-1805	Lot	J	384	Frankfort
Conover, Peter	Illinois	1-10-1825	213	X	294	Eagle Cr
Conover, Wm	Gallatin	1-10-1825	213	X	294	Eagle Cr

Grantor	Residence	Deed Date	Acres	Book	Page	Watercourse
Contee, Alexander, Trustee	———	5–13–1805	100	K	531	Cow Cr & Red R
Contee, Alexander, Trustee	———	5–13–1805	100	K	543	None
Contee, Alexander, Trustee	———	6–28–1805	4,833	K	546	Cow Cr & Red R
Contee, Alexander, Trustee	———	5–13–1805	400	L	25	Cow Cr & Red R
Contee, Alexander, Trustee	———	6–15–1807	750	L	130	Cow Cr & Red R
Contee, Thos	Prince George	1– 7–1811	4,833	O	3	None
Contee, Thos	Prince George	1– 7–1811	2,416½	O	100	None
Conway, Collett	Orange	6– 2–1807	9,000	L	209	E Fk Dix R
Conway, Collett	Orange	5–26–1809	1,500	M	432	Br Dix R
Cook, Valentine, heirs	Kentucky	5–28–1815	350	Q	300	Lick Br
Cook, Jas P	Virginia	10–14–1834	1,000	Z	464	Muddy R
Cooke, Jno	Woodford	1–10–1803	Slaves	G	132	None
Cope, Iseral	Baltimore	6– 1–1818	800	T	160	Green R
Copelan, Jacob & Wife	Lincoln	10– 7–1790	372	B-2	212	Dix R
Copland, Chas	Richmond	4–29–1801	333⅓	F	357	Big Barren R
Copland, Chas	Richmond	4–30–1830	10,000	Z	147	Rough Cr
Copland, Jacob & Wife	Kentucky	6– 4–1792	400	B-2	499	Rolling Fk
Corben, Jefferson & Wife	Decatur	11–25–1828	———	X	489	None
Corbin, Robt & Wife	Mercer	3–21–1789	Lot	B-2	22	Danville
Cordell, Jno	Frederick	4–28–1792	200	A-2	302	None
Cordell, Jno & Wife	Frederick	4–28–1792	200	H	105	None
Corp, Samuel, Atty	———	9–19–1807	35,456	Q	535	None
Cosley, Fortmoters & Wife	———	8– 8–1809	734	N	12	Rough Cr
Couch, Samuel	Goochland	11– 5–1795	11,000	A-2	274	None
Couper, Robt	Fredericksburg	6– 8–1812	11,000	O	403	Kennekamie Cr
Coutts, Reubin	Henrico	8–29–1799	3,500	E	28	Locust Cr
Cowan, Jas, Atty	Lexington	1–22–1828	65	X	353	S Fk Elkhorn
Cowan, Jared	Mercer	10– 3–1791	200	B-2	351	Popes Cr
Cowan, Jarrard	Mercer	10– 1–1790	150	B-2	200	None
Cowan, Jno	Lincoln	6–22–1786	130	A-2	132	None
Cowland, Wm	Middle Sex	6–12–1798	12,000	E	211	Ky R
Cowne, Robt	Culpepper	6–22–1820	3,550	T	449	Pitman & Russell Cr
Cox, Austin P	Frankfort	1– 7–1822	1,000	V	155	Clifty & Poplar Cr
Cox, Austin P, Atty	———	1– 5–1835	4,000	Z	481	Cypress Cr
Cox, Austin P, Atty	Kentucky	3– 5–1839	43	27	16	Franklin Co
Cox, Austin P	———	1–10–1844	———	27	386	Cumberland R
Cox, Austin P	Franklin	1– 1–1844	Lot	27	413	Frankfort
Cox, Austin P	Franklin	1–16–1845	637	27	456	Crooked Cr
Cox, Austin P & Wife	Franklin	2– 8–1840	———	27	105	None
Cox, Austin P & Wife	Franklin	10– 3–1843	25	27	373	Franklin Co
Cox, Austin P & Wife	Franklin	10– 3–1843	246	27	374	Ky R
Cox, Catherine	New York	9–22–1818	3,500	S	451	Chaplins Fk
Cox, Catherine	New York	9–22–1818	3,500	S	455	Chaplins Fk
Cox, Daniel W	Philadelphia	4–13–1821	6,000	U	418	None
Cox, Isaac	New York	11– 3–1816	21,000	S	444	Chaplins Fk
Cox, Isaac & Wife	Nelson	5–22–1816	Lot	W	235	Louisville
Cox, Isaac, heirs	———	8–16–1790	2,355	B-2	226	Salt R
Cox, Isaac B & Jno F & Wife	New York	9–19–1818	21,000	S	447	Chaplins Fk
Cox, Jno	Powhatan	9–21–1810	626½	N	274	Clay Lick Cr
Cox, Richard, Atty	Jefferson	11–28–1804	666⅔	H	397	Little Barren R
Cox, Samuel	Boone	10– 6–1810	413	O	6	M Elkhorn
Cox, Samuel	Pendleton	9– 2–1812	200	O	466	None
Cox, Talton	Powhatan	11–28–1804	666⅔	H	397	Little Barren R
Coyle, Cornelius	Fayette	10–18–1820	1,352	U	6	Crews Cr & Licking
Craddock, Robt	Mercer	8– 1–1806	4,287	K	423	Green R
Craddock, Robt	Warren	10–10–1815	2,500	S	150	None
Craddock, Robt	Warren	11–19–1834	1,000	Z	472	Station Camp Cr
Craig, Adam	Richmond	3–13–1801	6,100	P	170	Mayfield & Skin House Cr
Craig, Adam & Wife	Richmond	3–16–1808	11,200	N	207	W Fk Little R Cumberland R
Craig, Elijah	Scott	6–26–1798	500	D	17	Lees Cr
Craig, Elijah, Trustee	———	7–10–1802	600	G	163	Clear Cr
Craig, Elijah, Trustee	———	8–19–1803	500	H	449	Glenns Cr
Craig, Elijah, Trustee	———	2–16–1797	200	H	481	S Fk Elkhorn
Craig, Elijah, Trustee	———	8–19–1803	500	H	489	Glenns Cr
Craig, Elijah Sr	Scott	10–12–1801	1,000	M	229	Rougs Run
Craig, Elijah & J H	———	3–21–1812	170	O	338	Ky R
Craig, Jno	Fayette	6–22–1786	400	A	522	M Br Clear Cr
Craig, Jno	Woodford	6– 2–1789	2,0C0	B-2	27	Little Ky R
Craig, Jno	Boone	2–27–1804	20,440	H	123	Licking
Craig, Jno	Fayette	1–12–1811	1,380	N	410	Elkhorn
Craig, Jno & Wife	Woodford	6–16–1790	6,000	B-2	166	Big Sandy R
Craig, Jno & Wife	Woodford	4–26–1791	250	B-2	304	N Fk Clear Cr

Grantor	Residence	Deed Date	Acres	Book	Page	Watercourse
Craig, Jno & Wife	Woodford	4–26–1791	——	B-2	308	None
Craig, Jno & Wife	Boone	10– 6–1803	500	H	236	Clear C
Craig, Jno & Wife	Mason	10– 3–1815	600	Q	470	Sinking Br
Craig, Jno Sr	Boone	3– 6–1804	378¼	H	413	Glenns Cr
Craig, Jno Sr	Boone	10–12–1801	1,000	M	229	Rougs Run
Craig, Jno H	Campbell	12–28–1796	1,000	B	256	Ohio
Craig, Jno H	Campbell	12–24–1796	400	B	258	Ohio R
Craig, Jno H	Boone	8–15–1814	Lot	P	503	Frankfort
Craig, Jno H	Boone	8–15–1814	1,200	P	504	Glenns Cr
Craig, Jno H & Wife	Boone	9–10–1805	63	K	237	Fks Elkhorn
Craig, Jno & Jno H Jr	Fayette	3–31–1800	11,500	E	25	Br Ohio R
Craig, Jno & Elyot	Scott	5–28–1822	1,000	W	341	W Fk Drakes Cr
Craig, Joel & Wife	Scott	1–10–1809	Ferry	M	295	Junction Licking & Ohio
Craig, Joseph	Franklin	8– 7–1797	Lots	D	12	Frankfort
Craig, Joseph	Fayette	11– 5–1800	1,000	E	311	Cumberland R
Craig, Joseph	Franklin	3–21–1803	Lot	G	204	Frankfort
Craig, Joseph	Franklin	9– 7–1816	700	R	111	Clear Cr
Craig, Joseph	Franklin	6– 9–1817	Lot	R	304	Frankfort
Craig, Joseph, Atty	Franklin	9–19–1799	247½	D	532	None
Craig & Johnson, Trustees	Scott	2–14–1800	1,000	F	380	Ohio R
Craig & Johnson, Trustees	Scott	3–20–1802	500	F	381	None
Craig, Lewis	Fayette	11–10–1786	450	A	97	None
Craig, Lewis	Fayette	7–25–1785	1,400	A	159	None
Craig, Lewis	Fayette	7–18–1786	1,400	A	180	None
Craig, Lewis	Fayette	7–18–1786	1,000	A	281	Salt R
Craig, Lewis	Fayette	6– 1–1789	1,000	B-2	32	Cabin Cr
Craig, Lewis	Mason	11– 7–1804	53	H	429	None
Craig, Lewis	Mason	11– 6–1804	——	H	437	Twin Cr
Craig, Lewis	Mason	5– 7–1800	7,023	K	110	Road from Boones Station
Craig, Lewis	Bracken	1– 9–1808	100	M	30	M N Fk Elkhorn
Craig, Lewis Sr	Mason	7–16–1808	360	M	60	Clear & Jessamine
Craig, Lewis & Wife	Mason	7–18–1798	50	C	323	None
Craig, Lewis & Wife	Mason	10–15–1808	550	M	210	S Fk Elkhorn
Craig, Nancy Sr	——	2–20–1830	206	Y	445	Fks Elkhorn
Craig, Toliver Jr	Scott	1–20–1817	500	R	415	W Fk Drakes Cr
Craig, Wm M	Richmond	6–17–1812	8,800	O	449	W Fk Little & Cumberland R
Craig, Wm & Wife	Scott	7–20–1841	——	27	220	None
Craig, Whitfield	Bracken	10– 3–1815	600	Q	470	Sinking Br
Craik, Jas & Wife	Alexandria	5–20–1807	13,588	M	1	Green R & Bear Cr
Craik, James & Wife	Alexandria	11–21–1808	3,000	N	78	Green R
Crawford, James, Atty	Philadelphia	9–14–1784	3,000	H	295	None
Crawford, Jas, Atty	Philadelphia	9–14–1784	1,000	H	386	None
Crawford, Jno	Amherst	11– 3–1787	400	A	332	Robinson Cr
Creath, Jacob	Kentucky	3–20–1818	——	S	109	Elkhorn Cr
Creath, Jacob & Wife	Bourbon	4– 8–1818	80	S	254	None
Crenshaw, Spotswood D	Richmond	2–15–1845	2,450	27	472	Mississippi R Town Consola Highland & Goose Cr
Crist, Henry	——	12– 1–1806	200	K	504	Main Coxes Cr
Crist, Henry	Bullitt	3–29–1816	42,000	Q	455	Salt & Laurel R
Crittenden, Henry, Com'r	Shelby	10–23–1826	1,048	Z	489	Spencer Co
Crittenden, Jno, heirs	——	10–16–1821	10,000	W	407	Licking R
Crittenden, Jno, heirs	Fayette	3——1826	10,000	Y	138	M Licking & Grassy
Crittenden, Thos T	Franklin	7–27–1830	160	Z	26	N E qr Sec 6 T 53 N R 21 W
Crittenden, Thos T	Franklin	8– 5–1830	160	Z	26	N qr sec 15 T 58 N R 20 W
Crockett, Andrew	Wyth	12–12–1807	1,670	L	221	Salt R
Crockett, Anthony & Wife	Franklin	2– 9–1809	215	M	337	S Fk Big Benson Cr
Crockett, Joseph	Kentucky Clerk	12–11–1805	1,000	J	444	None
Crockett, Joseph	Kentucky Clerk	12– 9–1805	750	J	455	None
Crockett, Joseph	U S Marshall	11– 8–1805	1,400	K	7	None
Crockett, Joseph	U S Marshall	12– 9–1805	999	K	45	None
Crockett, Joseph	U S Marshall	12– 9–1805	400	K	47	None
Crockett, Joseph	U S Marshall	12– 9–1805	1,089	K	50	None
Crockett, Joseph	U S Marshall	3– 6–1806	346	K	185	None
Crockett, Joseph	U S Marshall	3– 6–1806	346	K	187	None
Crockett, Joseph	U S Marshall	7–24–1806	213,866	K	363	Brs Sandy R
Crockett, Joseph	U S Marshall	7–31–1806	390	K	386	None
Crockett, Joseph	U S Marshall	7–31–1806	90	K	388	None
Crockett, Joseph	U S Marshall	7–31–1806	200	K	389	None
Crockett, Joseph	U S Marshall	7–31–1806	200	K	391	None
Crockett, Joseph	U S Marshall	7–31–1806	1,000	K	393	None

Grantor	Residence	Deed Date	Acres	Book	Page	Watercourse
Crockett, Joseph	U S Marshall	7–31–1806	5,000	K	421	None
Crockett, Joseph	U S Marshall	8–16–1806	1,000	K	454	None
Crockett, Joseph	U S Marshall	11– 5–1806	900	K	457	None
Crockett, Joseph	U S Marshall	11–28–1806	14,000	K	479	None
Crockett, Joseph	U S Marshall	11–28–1806	1,000	K	481	None
Crockett, Joseph	U S Marshall	11–15–1805	1,000	K	496	None
Crockett, Joseph	U S Marshall	11–15–1805	7,000	K	498	None
Crockett, Joseph	U S Marshall	11–20–1806	1,250	K	499	None
Crockett, Joseph	U S Marshall	11–20–1806	1,170	K	501	None
Crockett, Joseph	U S Marshall	11–20–1806	1,000	K	503	None
Crockett, Joseph	U S Marshall	9– 4–1806	1,000	K	508	None
Crockett, Joseph	U S Marshall	4–23–1806	3,000	K	515	None
Crockett, Joseph	U S Marshall	10–30–1805	400	K	523	None
Crockett, Joseph	U S Marshall	12–30–1806	18,608	K	525	None
Crockett, Joseph	U S Marshall	9–20–1806	2,000	K	541	None
Crockett, Joseph	U S Marshall	5– 6–1807	708	L	20	None
Crockett, Joseph	U S Marshall	11–11–1807	30,000	L	175	None
Crockett, Joseph	U S Marshall	11–19–1807	751	L	215	None
Crockett, Joseph	U S Marshall	11–17–1807	3,000	L	230	None
Crockett, Joseph	U S Marshall	11–20–1807	10,460	L	232	None
Crockett, Joseph	U S Marshall	11–17–1807	5,000	L	234	None
Crockett, Joseph	U S Marshall	11–17–1807	21,079	L	236	None
Crockett, Joseph	U S Marshall	11–18–1807	1,260	L	238	None
Crockett, Joseph	U S Marshall	11–17–1807	3,807	L	240	None
Crockett, Joseph	U S Marshall	11–17–1807	3,954	L	242	None
Crockett, Joseph	U S Marshall	11–17–1807	4,950	L	244	None
Crockett, Joseph	U S Marshall	11–17–1807	1,000	L	246	None
Crockett, Joseph	U S Marshall	11–17–1807	3,500	L	248	None
Crockett, Joseph	U S Marshall	11–17–1807	2,040	L	250	None
Crockett, Joseph	U S Marshall	11–20–1807	1,800	L	252	None
Crockett, Joseph	U S Marshall	11–20–1807	2,000	L	254	None
Crockett, Joseph	U S Marshall	11–16–1807	5,000	L	256	None
Crockett, Joseph	U S Marshall	11–17–1807	700	L	258	None
Crockett, Joseph	U S Marshall	11–17–1807	400	L	260	None
Crockett, Joseph	U S Marshall	11–17–1807	614	L	262	None
Crockett, Joseph	U S Marshall	8–16–1806	1,500	L	362	None
Crockett, Joseph	U S Marshall	8–16–1806	489	L	364	None
Crockett, Joseph	U S Marshall	8–16–1806	500	L	367	None
Crockett, Joseph	U S Marshall	6– 6–1808	300	M	1	None
Crockett, Joseph	U S Marshall	1– 4–1808	200	M	12	None
Crockett, Joseph	U S Marshall	6– 6–1808	37,837	M	14	None
Crockett, Joseph	U S Marshall	4– 1–1808	150	M	32	None
Crockett, Joseph	U S Marshall	7–29–1808	125	M	104	None
Crockett, Joseph	U S Marshall	11–17–1807	790	M	108	None
Crockett, Joseph	U S Marshall	11–18–1807	1,000	M	110	None
Crockett, Joseph	U S Marshall	11–25–1808	8,571	M	213	None
Crockett, Joseph	U S Marshall	11–10–1808	5,000	M	243	None
Crockett, Joseph	U S Marshall	12– 8–1808	224	M	365	None
Crockett, Joseph	U S Marshall	5– 1–1809	273½	M	425	None
Crockett, Joseph	U S Marshall	11– 7–1809	2,270	N	86	None
Crockett, Robt	U S Marshall	12– 6–1811	2,500	O	222	None
Crockett, Robt	U S Marshall	3–23–1817	10,200	R	189	Cedar Fern & Floyds Fk
Crockett, Robt	U S Marshall	7–14–1817	250	R	349	Sugar Cr
Crockett, Robt	U S Marshall	11–19–1817	Lot	S	39	Lexington
Crockett, Robt & Wife	Jessamine	10–19–1819	2,637	T	203	Red R
Crockett, Robt & Wife	Bath	5– 1–1822	800	V	327	None
Croghan, Geo	New Orleans	6– 1–1824	4,000	W	362	Cumberland R
Croghan, Geo	U S Army	10– 6–1830	39	Z	25	Elks Lick Little Barren R
Croghan, Geo	Washington	4–16–1840	9,050	27	140	Ohio & Cumberland Rs
Croghan, Geo	U S Army	6–18–1840		28	57	None
Croghan, Geo & Wife		7– 9–1831	365	Z	160	Little Barren R
Croghan, Geo & Wife		7– 9–1831	245	Z	161	Little Barren R
Croghan, Geo & Wife	Louisiana	9–24–1822	8,875	Z	306	Ohio R Locust & Indian Cr
Croghan, Col Geo	U S Army	4–13–1833	562	Z	277	Cumberland & Little Barren Rs
Croghan, Jno G & W	Kentucky	7– 1–1838		28	115	None
Croghan, Lucy	Jefferson	8– 2–1824	2,250	W	372	W Fk Red R
Croghan, Wm	Jefferson	6– 9–1788	5,000	A	383	Ohio R
Croghan, Wm	Jefferson	7– 8–1801	833⅓	E	365	N Fk Red R
Croghan, Wm	Jefferson	10–12–1801		F	77	Green R
Croghan, Wm	Jefferson	11–19–1801	244	G	56	W Fk Red R
Croghan, Wm	Jefferson	5– 4–1812	730	O	370	Br Crocus Cr
Croghan, Wm	Jefferson	5– 9–1803	Lots	T	206	Smithland
Croghan, Wm	Jefferson	11–30–1820	8,875	Z	303	Ohio R & Locust Cr
Croghan, Wm	Pittsburg	1– 1–1840	1,000	27	100	Obyon Cr
Croghan, Wm & Wife	Jefferson	10– 2–1802	750	G	159	W Fk Red R
Croghan, Wm, Atty		1– 1–1814	3,000	P	330	Consolos Cr

Grantor	Residence	Deed Date	Acres	Book	Page	Watercourse
Croghan, Wm, Atty...	———...	1– 2–1814	1,000	P	331	Harlins Cr
Croudsore, Saml	Shenandoah	7–20–1804	4,166½	H	466	None
Crow, Joel	Cumberland	3– 4–1812	1,926	O	388	Green R & Nolinn
Crow, Jno & Wife	Mercer	9–21–1789	2	B-2	76	Danville
Crow, Jno & Wife	Mercer	———1791	17	B-2	371	Dix R
Crow, Wm	Lincoln	4–12–1796	27,500	A-2	227	M Fk Ky R
Crowder, Wm	Amelia	9–10–1799	687	D	410	Br Rough Cr
Croxton, Saml	Prince Edward	9–28–1833	——	Z	395	None
Cruger, Bertram J	New York	8———1812	56,000	Z	286	None
Crump, H H	Cumberland	12– 9–1819	33,642	T	235	Rockcastle & S Fk Ky R
Crutcher, Henry	Georgia	9–10–1791	5,000	B-2	478	Brashears Cr
Crutcher, Henry	Georgia	7–30–1812	1,767	O	459	Eagle Cr
Crutcher, Henry, Atty.	Frankfort	2– 8–1809	Negro	M	314	None
Crutcher, James	Jessamine	12–13–1799	1,000	E	289	Cedar & Auter Crs
Crutcher, Jas & Wife	Hardin	10–30–1817	583	R	446	Cedar Cr
Crutcher, Jas, Atty	Hardin	2–13–1828	102	X	380	Cedar Cr
Crutcher, Jas & wife	Hardin	7–16–1816	583	R	320	Cedar Cr
Crutcher, Jno	Franklin	2– 1–1824	Horse	X	80	None
Crutcher, Jno & Wife	Franklin	6–18–1817	200	R	310	Ky R
Crutchfield, Robt	Spotsylvania	3–18–1803	3,000	L	163	Cumberland R
Cummings, Alexander & Wife	Ross	3–27–1815	——	S	275	None
Cummings, Chas	Washington	2– 4–1807	400	L	134	Green R
Cummings, Chas	Washington	6–14–1811	496½	P	261	M Fk Licking
Cummings, Jas & Robt, Attys	Washington	11–13–1802	400	G	43	Harrods Cr
Cunningham, Geo	Franklin	1–23–1847	4	28	120	Franklin Co
Cunningham, Fountain & Wm	Henderson	5–14–1841	50	27	200	Elkhorn
Cunningham, Wm & Co	Falmouth	4–18–1801	400	F	192	Quirks Run
Curd, James	———...	10– 4–1803	350	H	59	None
Curd, Jno	Virginia	1– 9–1807	4,000	M	200	None
Curd, Jno & Price, heirs	———.	7–20–1822	461	V	462	Benson Cr
Curd, Joseph	Buckingham	7–10–1811	200	O	457	Big Barren R
Curd, Richard A. Atty.	Fayette	10–29–1827	691	X	305	Boone Cr
Curd, Woodford	———.	7–20–1822	461	V	462	Benson Cr
Curle, Richmond J	Richmond	8– 3–1826	——	Y	215	None
Currie, Andrew	Philadelphia	4–13–1821	6,000	U	418	None
Currie, Jas	Richmond	9–23–1796	107,681	B	71	N Fk Ky R
Currie, Jas & Wife	———.	3–28–1820	——	T	304	Tradewater
Currie, Jas & Wife	———	8–23–1819	Lots	U	269	Richmond, Va
Curry, Dr James	Richmond	9– 9–1794	20,781	C	270	N Fk Ky R
Dabney, Chas	Hanover	7–29–1795	5,320	A-2	335	Big Barren & Green R
Dabney, Chas	Hanover	12– 5–1815	200	Q	346	Rough Cr
Dabney, Chas	Hanover	12– 5–1815	200	Q	403	Rough Cr
Dabney, Chas Sr	Hanover	9– 3–1822	——	W	88	Tennessee R
Dabney, Geo, Sheriff.	King William	5–10–1821	2,000	V	79	None
Dabney, Richard	Richmond	10———1811	1,000	P	110	Tennessee R
Daingerfield, Jno, Atty.	Essex	7–21–1802	400	G	114	Green R
Dale, Thos & Wife	Spencer	6–17–1829	200	Y	382	Clear Cr
Daley, Lawrence & Wife	Fayette	2–16–1827	253	Y	269	6 Mile Cr
Dallam, Wm S.	Fayette	9———1816	262	R	167	Br Green R
Dallam, Wm S.	Logan	1– 1–1845	Lot	27	477	Lexington
Dallam, Wm S.	Logan	1– 1–1845	200	27	477	Logan Co
Danar, Robt	Jefferson	9–13–1785	1	A	53	None
Dandridge, Jno, Exr.	New Kent	11–17–1796	7,838	C	28	Little Sandy R
Dangerfield, Jno	———.	3– 7–1802	6,000	F	491	Ohio R
Dangerfield, Wm	Kentucky	7–16–1802	1,000	F	471	Tradewater
Daniel, Martin	Jefferson	3– 7–1785	Lot	Danville A	7	None
Daniel, Martin	Jefferson	3– 7–1785	Lot	Danville A	10	None
Daniel, Martin	Jefferson	3–15–1785	Lot	Danville A	13	None
Daniel, Martin	Jefferson	2–22–1785	Lot	Danville A	16	None
Daniel, Martin	———.	11–10–1786	Lot	A	232	None
Daniel, Martin	Jefferson	11– 1–1786	Lot	A	247	None
Daniel, Martin	Jefferson	6–10–1788	Lots	A	404	None
Daniel, Martin	Jefferson	6–16–1788	Lot	A	419	None
Daniel, Martin, Atty.	Jefferson	9–18–1789	4	B-2	75	Danville
Daniel, Martin, Atty.	Jefferson	9–23–1789	1,600	B-2	155	Indian Camp Cr
Daniel, Martin, Atty.	Jefferson	6–22–1790	Lot	B-2	183	Danville
Daniel, Martin, Atty.	Jefferson	3–16–1791	110	B-2	241	Sugar Cr
Daniel, Martin, Atty.	Jefferson	10–15–1790	Lot	B-2	249	Danville
Daniel, Martin, Atty.	Jefferson	3–22–1791	Lot	B-2	250	Danville

Grantor	Residence	Deed Date	Acres	Book	Page	Watercourse
Daniel, Robt	Lincoln	3– 9–1785	1,000	A	5	Indian Camp Cr
Daniel, Robt	Jefferson	9– 9–1785	1	A	33	None
Daniel, Robt	Jefferson	9– 9–1785	3	A	35	None
Daniel, Robt	Jefferson	9–13–1785	1	A	48	None
Daniel, Robt	Jefferson	9–13–1785	1½	A	51	None
Daniel, Robt	Jefferson	9–13–1785	5½	A	55	None
Daniel, Robt	Jefferson	9–13–1785	1	A	58	None
Daniel, Robt	Lincoln	9–13–1785	———	A	60	None
Daniel, Robt	Jefferson	9–14–1785	———	A	64	None
Daniel, Robt	Jefferson	4– 5–1786	½	A	150	None
Daniel, Robt	Jefferson	9–10–1785	½	A	161	None
Daniel, Robt	Jefferson	9–10–1785	½	A	162	None
Daniel, Robt	Jefferson	9–10–1785	⅓	A	163	None
Daniel, Robt	Jefferson	9–10–1785	Lot	A	165	None
Daniel, Robt	Jefferson	9–10–1785	Lot	A	166	None
Daniel, Robt	Jefferson	6–20–1786	Lot	A	172	None
Daniel, Robt	Jefferson	11– 7–1786	Lot	A	233	None
Daniel, Robt	Jefferson	11–24–1786	Lot	A	243	None
Daniel, Robt	Jefferson	5–24–1788	Lots	A	400	None
Daniel, Robt	Jefferson	1– 2–1788	55	A	425	Beargrass Cr
Daniel, Robt	Jefferson	1–26–1788	Lot	A	444	None
Daniel, Robt	Jefferson	7– 1–1788	Lot	A	462	None
Daniel, Robt	———	9–23–1788	Lot	A	465	None
Daniel, Robt	Nelson	7– 7–1788	Lots	A	472	None
Daniel, Robt	Jefferson	10– 5–1789	½	B-2	94	Danville
Daniel, Robt	Jefferson	9–23–1789	1,600	B-2	155	Indian Camp Cr
Daniel, Robt	Mercer	5–10–1791	Lots	B-2	396	Danville
Daniel, Robt	Fayette	10– 8–1791	Lot	B-2	398	Danville
Daniel, Robt	Fayette	6– 1–1792	Lots	B-2	502	Danville
Daniel, Robt	Fayette	6– 2–1792	Lots	B-2	504	Danville
Daniel, Saml	Adams	2–20–1813	800	P	241	Cumberland R
Darby, Daniel	Philadelphia	9–14–1784	3,000	H	295	None
Darby, Daniel	Philadelphia	9–14–1784	1,000	H	386	None
Darby, Jno	Richmond	2–25–1807	9,922	Q	511	N Fk Licking
Dardis, James	Knoxville	10– 2–1810	2,500	N	425	None
Davidson, Jas H & Wife	Simpson	11–20–1824	———	X	148	None
Davidson, Wm	Frederick	5– 2–1816	1,000	R	42	Ohio R
Daviess, Joseph H, Ex	———	6–18–1804	175	H	281	Slate Cr
Daviess, Joseph H	———	12–14–1802	200	G	104	Panther Cr
Davis, Allen	Amherst	7–27–1802	500	G	168	None
Davis, Catherine	Nelson	5– 1–1817	———	R	432	None
Davis, David	New York	12–29–1809	2,000	P	302	Ohio R
Davis, Jas, Atty	———	1– 8–1817	———	R	441	None
Davis, Jas E, Com'r	Fayette	7–11–1818	4,051⅔	S	158	None
Davis, Joseph H	Franklin	4–29–1803	Lot	G	293	Danville
Davis, Joseph H	Kentucky	12–27–1831	88½	Z	207	S Benson Cr
Davis, Joseph H	Franklin	2——1845	24	27	468	S Elkhorn
Davis, Joseph H	Franklin	2——1845	57	27	469	S Elkhorn
Davis, Joseph H & Wife	Franklin	8– 5–1844	Lot	27	450	Frankfort
Davis, Joseph H & Wife	Franklin	12–28–1844	Lot	27	451	Frankfort
Davis, Joseph H & Wife	Franklin	2——1845	41	27	471	S Elkhorn
Davis, Mary C	Hamilton	2– 4–1841	1,000	27	197	Tennessee R
Davis, Phileman	Orange	2–25–1791	200	B-2	433	Rolling Fk
Davis, Saml	———	2– 4–1841	1,000	27	197	Tennessee R
Davis, Sanford	Woodford	11——1834	118	Z	493	S Fk Elkhorn
Davis, Thos	Lincoln	12——1819	130	T	413	Hanging Fk
Davis, Thos	Virginia	12–27–1831	88½	Z	207	S Benson Cr
Davis, Wm & Wife	Woodford	7–22–1814	Lot	P	491	Frankfort
Dawes, Thos Jr	Boston	6– 6–1803	———	H	173	None
Dawson, Jno Sr & Wife	Fayette	9– 1–1827	90	X	390	Grassy Cr, Butler Co
Dawson, Robt D	New Madrid	10–16–1819	Lots	T	124	———
Dean, Joseph Atty	Philadelphia	3– 4–1786	13,666⅔	D	190	N Fk, Three Fks, Ky
Dean, Jno & Wife	Carroll	10–23–1841	3½	27	232	Ky R
Deaver, Richard	———	7–27–1819	———	T	80	None
Deering, Walker & Wife	Frankfort	2– 8–1810	Lot	P	83	Frankfort
Deering, Walker & Wife	Frankfort	2– 8–1813	Lot	P	84	Frankfort
De Grafey, Chas	Philadelphia	5–29–1789	8,270	V	451	Salt R
DeGraffenaid, Frances	Cumberland	8–28–1817	1,000	S	66	Marrowbone Cr
De Graffenried, Robt	Luninburg	8–25–1800	3,000	M	165	None
De Lormore, Pierce, L P G	Philadelphia	12–27–1809	5,277	N	176	Ohio R
Demint, Wm & Wife	Carroll	10–23–1841	———	27	233	Ky R
Denemaurs, Peter S D & Wife	New York City	5–25–1802	56,000	L	138	None
Denemaurs, V D	New York City	8–24–1805	56,000	L	136	None
Dennis, Saml	Mercer	3– 5–1787	400	A	260	S Fk Licking
Dennison, Jas	Bourbon	10–16–1822	150	V	461	Green Cr
Denny, Jas W	Louisville	9–25–1822	Lots	V	357	Louisville
Denny, Richard	Richmond	7–29–1802	1,326	G	23	Green R
Denton, Thos & Wife	Mercer	6– 9–1789	900	B-2	33	Salt R

Grantor	Residence	Deed Date	Acres	Book	Page	Watercourse
Denton, Thos & Wife	Mercer	9-29-1789	500	B-2	78	Salt R
Denton, Thos & Wife	Mercer	10- 5-1790	400	B-2	204	Sinking Cr
Denton, Thos & Wife	Mercer	6- 9-1789	500	B-2	414	Green R
Denton, Thos & Wife	———	6- 9-1789	900	B-2	516	None
Deweese, Farnor & Wife	Fayette	3-25-1845	Lot	28	47	Frankfort
Dewhurst, Jno	New York City	4-26-1800	4,000	E	22	S Br Nolinn
Dewitt, Walter	Lincoln	10-11-1790	178	B-2	217	Dix R
Dewitt, Walter	Lincoln	9-13-1790	Lots	B-2	221	None
De Wolf, Jas	Rhode Island	11-30-1831	4	Z	167	Cane Run
Deyerle, Peter	Montgomery	8-18-1809	2,179	N	18	Little Ky
Dickerson, Elizabeth B	Jefferson	8-24-1822	1,000	W	99	None
Dickinson, Elizabeth B	———	9- 8-1829	100	Y	395	Plum Cr
Dickerson, Richard	Jefferson	8- 5-1799	1,000	D	309	Big Barren R
Dickinson, Richard	Jefferson	7- 9-1796	1,000	A-2	437	Elkhorn
Dickerson, Richard, Atty	Jefferson	11-15-1802	1,500	G	362	Harrisons Cr
Directors Pub. Bldg	Frankfort	2- 5-1800	Lot	N	212	Frankfort
Directors Pub. Bldg	Frankfort	5- 6-1807	Lot	N	496	Frankfort
Directors Pub. Bldg	Frankfort	5——1814	Lots	P	531	Frankfort
Divine, Roger	Franklin	8-25-1817	2,992	S	29	Big Bone Cr
Dix, Alexander	———	9- 3-1818	———	S	314	None
Dix, Jno	Mason	9- 9-1806	11,517½	L	29	N Fk, Main Licking
Dixon, Richard	Middleham	7-21-1801	20,698	H	518	Killicainick Cr
Dobbins, Jno	North Carolina	2-23-1803	1,000	Z	186	N Fk Elkhorn
Dodge, David	Clark	5-17-1817	Slaves	R	596	None
Dodge, David	Winchester	3-28-1818	Slaves	S	133	None
Dodge, David & Wife	Clark	10-—1816	Lots	R	306	Winchester
Dodge, David & Wife	Clark	10——1816	205¼	R	306	Hickman, 4 Mile & lower Howards Cr
Dodge, David & Wife	Clark	8- 1-1817	Lot	S	289	Lexington
Dodge, Joseph	Belvedere	4-18-1808	1,000	L	371	Cumberland R
Doom, Wm H	Marion, Mo	10- 8-1846	38	28	108	Dry Run
Donnell, Jno	Faundownship	2- 8-1788	1,080	G	398	None
Donnelly, Thos	Richmond	4- 9-1789	———	J	228	None
Doran, Patrick	Mercer	6-23-1789	500	B-2	83	Doctors Fk
Dorsey, Alexander	Baltimore	10-13-1834	1,791¾	Z	473	Pond Fk, Salt R
Dorsey, Greenberry	Mercer	10-13-1796	Lot	A-2	528	Frankfort
Dougherty, Bernard	Franklin	7- 1-1841	45	27	212	Wranglin Run
Doughtery, Bernard & Wife	Franklin	8-21-1839	87	27	53	N Elkhorn
Doughtery, Bernard & Wife	Franklin	8-20-1839	84	27	54	N Elkhorn
Doughtery, Henry	Lincoln	12-22-1795	1,000	A-2	344	E Fk Little Barren
Doughtery, Jas	Fayette	7-17-1817	237	R	592	None
Doughtery, Jas & Wife	Scott	4-27-1820	21	W	124	Elkhorn
Doughtery, Jno	Lincoln	6-19-1786	313	A	292	Hanging Fk
Doughtery, Jno	Lincoln	6-19-1786	237	A	294	Hanging Fk
Doughtery, Jno	Jefferson	10- 8-1804	143	H	447	Mill Cr
Doughtery, Jno & Wife	Lincoln	3-20-1790	530	B-2	139	Dix R
Doughtery, Michael	Henry	6- 6-1815	250	Q	126	Little Ky R
Doughtery, Robt	Fayette	6-17-1789	350	B-2	54	Harris Cr
Doughtery, Wm	Mason	8-20-1839	84	27	54	N Elkhorn
Douglas, Adam	Frederick	12- 2-1806	1,000	L	3	Green R
Douthit, Hiram & Wife	Madison	1-11-1839	———	27	19	None
Douthit, Jno & Wife	Decatur	8-12-1839	———	27	77	None
Douthit, Lewis & Wife	Montgomery	1-11-1839	———	27	18	None
Douthit, P	Frankfort	1-19-1846	Lot	28	50	Frankfort
Douthit, Piersaul & Wife	Franklin	6-27-1839	———	27	52	None
Downing, James & Wife	Lincoln	6-19-1790	106	B-2	160	Clear Cr
Downing, Jno & Wife	Lincoln	6-19-1790	106	B-2	157	Clear Cr
Dowse, Edward	Dedham	2-22-1799	6,844	D	473	Pitman, Skeggs & N Fk Tradewater
Dowse, Edward	Dedham	2-22-1799	13,766⅔	D	476	Little Miami, Paint & Crocus Crs
Dowse, Edward	Dedham	2-22-1799	———	D	477	None
Doyle, David	Richmond	10——1811	1,000	P	110	Tennessee R
Dozier, Zachoriah & Wife	Clark	9-23-1812	500	O	490	Rough Cr
Dromgoole, James	Logan	7-20-1798	550	D	136	None
Dryden, Wm	Lincoln	10-12-1791	300	B-2	387	Harts Fk
Dryden, Wm & Wife	Lincoln	3-24-1792	200	B-2	460	W Fk Buck Lick Cr
Duckham, Saml	Lawrence	2-11-1831	14,911½	Z	158	Ky R
Duckham, Thos	Franklin	5-24-1819	90,793½	S	519	Ky, Red & Sandy R
Duckham, Thos	Franklin	5-24-1819	Lots	S	519	Port Williams
Duckham, Thos	Franklin	7-28-1819	———	T	62	None
Duckham, Thos	Frankfort	7-31-1819	Hogs	T	65	Elkhorn Cr
Duckham, Thos	Franklin	7-28-1819	———	T	126	None
Duckham, Thos	Lawrence	2-11-1831	14,911½	Z	158	Ky R
Dudley, Benj W	Fayette	9- 1-1837	7,823	27	28	Ky R

Grantor	Residence	Deed Date	Acres	Book	Page	Watercourse
Dudley, Benj W, Executor	Fayette	6–28–1828	1,140	X	470	Mammouth Cave & Green R
Dudley, Jeptha	Franklin	7– 2–1832	Lot	Z	240	Louisville
Dudley, Jeptha & Wife	Franklin	12–18–1841	450	27	303	Ky R
Dudley, Peter, Comr	Franklin	4– 4–1823	31	W	85	Cave Spring Br
Dudley, Peter	Franklin	1– 4–1839	Lot	27	8	Frankfort
Duely, Peter	Batetourt	6–20–1790	700	B-2	190	Hingston Fk
Duely, Peter & Wife	Batetourt	6–25–1790	700	B-2	223	Hingston Fk
Duffield, Abraham	Manor	12——1795	3,000	E	101	Fk Licking
Duffold, Jno & Wife	——	3–28–1818	——	W	328	None
Dufour, Jno James	Lexington District	5–20–1801	——	E	73	For Vineyard
Duke, Jno P & Wife	Bourbon	10–29–1830	Lot	Z	29	Mt Sterling
Dulton, Thos & Wife	Norfolk	6–16–1817	500	R	371	None
Duncan, Lewis	Winchester	9–24–1819	1,500	T	404	Eagle Cr
Dunlap, Ann & Charlotte	Philadelphia	8– 6–1813	Lots	P	275	Philadelphia
Dunlap, Jno	Philadelphia	5–15–1813	Lots	P	268	Philadelphia
Dunlap, Jno	Philadelphia	8– 6–1813	——	P	278	None
Dunn, Saml	Mercer	9–25–1786	300	A	244	Rolling Fk
Dunscomb, Andrew & Wife	——	3–13–1797	1,000	C	119	None
Dunwoody, Jno	——	5–16–1822	——	V	217	Mill Cr
Dupey, Jno	Henry	3–21–1811	1,000	N	442	Hinkston Fk
Dupey, Jno	Henry	4–25–1812	277	O	358	Flat Cr
Duvall, Benj	Richmond	2–14–1823	1,724	Y	68	None
Duval, Chas & Wife	Jefferson	6– 5–1821	102½	V	51	Benson Cr
Duval, Daniel	Henrico	5–28–1790	10,000	A-2	513	Sandy R
Duval, Humphrey B	Dinwiddie	11– 2–1807	2,666⅔	M	74	Goose & Highland Cr
Duvall, Jno H & Wife	Baltimore	9–26–1845	2,500	28	35	Elkhorn & Cedar Cr
Duval, Jno P	Mason	4– 9–1802	915	F	533	Br Rough, Clover & Mill Cr
Duval, Philip & Wm	Buchingham	3–13–1823	12,148	W	113	—— Cr
Duval, Saml P	Frankfort	12–19–1800	Slaves	E	245	None
Duval, Saml P	——	1–20–1800	Slaves	E	258	None
Duval, Saml P	Ohio	5–19–1800	1,800	E	271	Rough Cr
Duval, Saml P	Kentucky	5–25–1800	12,000	E	274	Licking
Duval, Saml P	Frankfort	4– 1–1801	Slaves	E	304	None
Duval, Saml P, Atty	Kentucky	2– 4–1801	10,000	E	337	Licking
Duval, Saml S	Kentucky	10–22–1798	1,000	D	125	Cox & Willsons Crs
Duval, Wm	Richmond	10– 3–1793	9,198	A-2	56	None
Duval, Wm	Richmond	11–10–1794	2,400	A-2	73	Green R
Duval, Wm	Richmond	11–12–1794	11,650	A-2	75	Green R
Duval, Wm	Richmond	11–10–1794	778	A-2	78	Caney & Rough Cr
Duval, Wm	Richmond	3– 8–1796	1,878	A-2	396	None
Duval, Wm	Richmond	2–27–1796	1,000	A-2	398	Big Cr of Ky R
Duval, Wm	Richmond	10– 3–1795	8,800	A-2	681	Ohio R
Duval, Wm	Henrico	12–26–1797	24,000	D	70	Chaplins Fk
Duval, Wm	Richmond	8–24–1803	2,000	G	435	None
Duval, Wm	Richmond	1–19–1803	745	G	441	Clover Cr
Duval, Wm	Richmond	1——1803	3,500	J	204	Skeggs & Big Bone Lick Cr
Duval, Wm	Richmond	12– 8–1804	5,350	J	406	Bartons Fk Big Clifty
Duval, Wm	Virginia	——18–1807	600	L	113	None
Duval, Wm	Buckingham	3– 1–1810	1,366⅔	O	1	None
Duval, Wm, Atty	Richmond	10– 1–1794	5,000	H	326	M Licking
Duval, Wm Sr	Virginia	7–11–1807	2,000	L	111	Ohio R
Dwight, Jonathan	Springfield	3–25–1796	4,184	E	117	Nolinn
Dyer, Saml & Wife	Calloway	6– 1–1824	88	W	282	Coopers Run
Ealy, Henry & Wife	Scott	1–24–1810	240	N	110	N Fk Elkhorn
Early, Joel & Wife	Culpepper	12–31–1790	1,340	B-2	293	—— Cr
Early, Joel & Wife	Culpepper	2–25–1790	1,000	B-2	296	None
Early, Joel & Wife	Culpepper	2–25–1791	2,566	B-2	298	Hickman Cr
Early, Joel & Wife	Culpepper	2–25–1791	1,500	B-2	300	None
Early, Joel & Wife	Culpepper	2–25–1791	2,000	B-2	302	W Fk Lick Cr
Early, Joseph, heirs	Madison	5–11–1813	8,000	P	343	Ky R & Hustons Fk
Eastin, Myra	Louisanna	4– 3–1821	100	U	359	Floyds Fk
Eastin, Wm	Tennessee	12– 4–1822	200	X	125	Drakes Cr
Eastland, Jno A	Bardstown	12–13–1813	450	P	328	Blackfords Cr
Easton, Reubin & Wife	Jefferson	9– 7–1804	4,450	J	182	Floyds Fk, Elkhorn & Rough Cr
Edrington, Benj & Wife	Franklin	9——1814	——	U	393	Elkhorn Cr
Edrington, Benj & Wife	Franklin	5–17–1827	125	X	253	Glens & Elkhorn
Edrington, Benj & Wife	Woodford	10–27–1845	——	28	33	S Fk Elkhorn
Edrington, Joseph	——	5–21–1818	Lot	S	180	Frankfort
Edrington, Joseph	——	5–21–1818	199¼	S	180	None
Edrington, Joseph	Franklin	2–29–1820	103	T	366	None
Edrington, Joseph & Benj	Franklin	2–29–1820	100	T	367	None
Edwards, Haden	Franklin	7–12–1800	——	E	315	Elkhorn
Edwards, Haden	Franklin	5–18–1802	3,530	F	398	None

Grantor	Residence	Deed Date	Acres	Book	Page	Watercourse
Edwards, Haden	Franklin	7– 3–1802	Lot	F	443	Frankfort
Edwards, Haden	Franklin	6–28–1802	50	F	444	S Fk Elkhorn
Edwards, Haden	————	7–10–1806	3,530	K	377	Harbour & Cabin Cr
Edwards, Haden & Wife	Franklin	7–12–1798	1,000	C	296	N Fk Elkhorn
Edwards, Haden & Wife	Franklin	11– 6–1799	823½	D	465	N Fk Elkhorn
Edwards, Haden & Wife	Kentucky	11– 4–1800	304	6	121	None
Edwards, Haden & Wife	Woodford	11–28–1801	16,000	F	160	Ky R
Edward, Haden & Wife	Franklin	12– 3–1802	Lots	G	77	Frankfort
Edwards, Jno	Bourbon	1–24–1787	1,000	A	262	Coopers Run
Edwards, Jno	Bourbon	3–19–1790	300	B-2	134	Boones Mill Cr
Edwards, Jno & Wife	Bourbon	9– 7–1790	300	B-2	208	McConnell & Lecomts Runs
Edwards, Thos	Boston	6– 6–1803	————	H	173	None
Eggliston, Mary Ann	Christian	2–13–1828	158	X	381	Elkhorn
Eggliston, Richard	Amelia	9– 7–1799	300	D	375	Green R
Eichellergen, Martin	Baltimore	2– 6–1809	5,000	M	397	Collins Fk & Br Little Richland Cr
Eidson, Jno & Wife	————	2–20–1812	150	O	320	None
Elley, Henry & Wife	Scott	1–30–1811	200	O	106	Ohio R
Elley, Henry & Wife	Scott	11– 5–1810	80	N	309	Ohio R
Elley, Henry Sr	Scott	8–21–1813	80	P	243	Ohio R
Ellington, Hezakiah	Cumberland	3–21–1817	762½	R	357	Cumberland R
Elliott, Jos & Wife	Scott	10——1828	100	X	468	N Elkhorn
Elliott, Thos & Wife	King William	3–29–1804	2,000	K	199	Lick Cr
Ellis, Benj	Kentucky	7–19–1845	Lot	28	20	Frankfort
Ellis, David	Gallatin	9–23–1840	————	27	177	None
Ellis, Wm C	Cecil	9–14–1797	————	C	287	Br M Fk Licking
Ellis, Wm C	Cecil	11–18–1799	92,000	E	31	Licking
Elliston, Jno & Wife	Gallatin	3–23–1811	274	Q	39	Twin Cr
Elmendorf, Lucas	Ulster	4–18–1803	550	G	272	Plum Cr
Elmendorf, Lucas	Ulster	12– 8–1829	98½	Z	255	Cane Run
Elzey, Wm	Loudon	11–21–1797	25,334⅔	D	248	S Fk Ky R
Elzey, Wm	Loudon	1– 9–1804	1,160	J	416	Cumberland R
Elzey, Wm & Wife	Loudon	———1807	1,250	N	32	Wolf Cr
Elzey, Wm & Wife	Loudon	4–30–1830	10,000	Z	147	Rough Cr
Elzey, Wm Jr	Loudon	8– 8–1795	14,686½	A-2	185	Rolling Fk Station Camp Cr & Big Sandy R
Embree, Geo, heirs	New York	10–17–1842	————	27	343	N Fk Ky R
Embree, Lawrence E	New York	10–17–1842	————	27	343	N Fk Ky R
English, Elisha	Franklin	3–22–1802	255	F	200	Little Ky & Corn Cr
Epes, Daniel	Petersburg	7– 3–1809	Slaves	N	450	None
Epes, Daniel & Wife	Petersburg	2–28–1813	500	P	93	None
Epes, Daniel & Wife	————	4– 1–1813	364	P	116	Ky R
Epes, Daniel & Wife	————	5–12–1813	881	P	125	Coxes Cr
Epes, Daniel & Wife	————	10–10–1813	1,800	P	293	N Fk Rough Cr
Epes, Daniel & Wife	————	7– 6–1814	221½	P	489	Sulphur Lick Fk
Epes, Daniel & Wife	————	5– 6–1818	154	S	123	None
Epes, Daniel & Wife	————	5– 6–1818	100	S	125	Ohio R
Epes, Daniel & Wife	————	5– 6–1818	140	S	126	Ohio R
Epes, Daniel & Wife	Virginia	8– 1–1818	————	S	339	None
Epes, Daniel & Wife	————	1– 6–1819	1,112	S	374	Eagle Cr
Epes, Daniel & Wife	————	1– 6–1819	1,537	S	376	Eagle Cr
Epes, Daniel & Wife	————	7– 4–1818	1,089	S	396	Jessamine & Hickman Cr
Epes, Daniel & Wife	————	8– 9–1819	360	T	57	None
Epes, Daniel & Wife	————	7– 1–1817	218	T	75	Eagle Cr
Epes, Daniel & Wife	————	5–21–1819	1,670	T	213	Br Ohio R
Epes, Daniel & Wife	————	3–10–1820	1,096	T	264	None
Epes, Daniel & Wife	Petersburg	8– 1–1818	————	T	426	None
Epes, Daniel & Wife	Virginia	9– 8–1820	6,923	U	70	Rough Cr
Epes, Daniel & Wife	————	6–15–1822	90	V	254	None
Epes, Daniel & Wife	————	6–11–1822	112	V	350	None
Epes, Daniel & Wife	————	6–15–1822	150	V	351	Eagle Cr
Epes, Mary P	————	2– 3–1825	1,950	X	92	Yellow Banks in Daviess Co
Epes, Mary P	————	12–17–1827	Lots	X	329	Owensboro
Epes, Mary P	————	12–17–1827	417	X	329	Ohio R
Epes, Polly	————	12–10–1822	100	V	433	Ohio R
Epes, Polly	————	12–10–1822	105	V	434	Ohio R
Epes, Polly	————	10–21–1823	264	W	144	None
Epes, Polly	————	10–21–1823	116	W	146	None
Epes, Polly	————	10–21–1823	110	W	147	None
Epes, Polly	————	10–25–1823	148	W	186	None
Ernest, Matthew, heirs	————	9–23–1828	6,900	Y	391	Green R

Grantor	Residence	Deed Date	Acres	Book	Page	Watercourse
Ernest, Wm H, executor	Fayette	6–28–1828	1,140	X	470	Mammoth Cave & Green R
Erskine, Jno	Mifflin	5– 6–1814	600	P	521	Ohio R
Estill, Benj & Wife	Madison	10–28–1811	9,507	O	285	Silver Muddy & Station Camp Cr
Estill, Jas & Jonathan & Wives	Madison	10–28–1811	9,507	O	285	Silver Muddy & Station Camp Cr
Estill, Wallace & Wife	Madison	10–28–1811	9,507	O	285	Silver Muddy & Station Camp Cr
Etting, Reuben	Baltimore	3– 9–1797	8,800	A-2	687	Ohio R
Eubank, Jas	Clark	3–23–1829	406½	Y	323	Panther Cr
Eubanks, Lucy, dec'd	Clark	9–17–1823	1,882	W	373	W Fk Floyds Fk
Evans, Henry P & Wife	——	6–27–1820	200	U	29	Green R
Evans, Nathaniel	Fayette	3– 2–1789	150	A	486	Hanging Fk
Evans, Nathaniel	Fayette	3– 3–1789	110	A	484	Hanging Fk
Evans, Saml	Montgomery	8–10–1796	1,000	D	325	Big Benson Cr
Evans, Saml	Montgomery	8–10–1796	1,000	D	323	Big Benson Cr
Evans, Saml & Wife	Montgomery	5– 3–1805	10,000	K	60	Caney Bear & Reedy Crs
Evans, Thos R & Wife	——	10– 8–1804	—	O	148	None
Eve, Wm & Wife	Culpepper	3–17–1804	1,000	H	566	Clay Lick Cr
Eve, William & Wife	Culpepper	3–20–1804	11,000	H	608	Kannekanic Cr
Everhart, Martin, heirs	Washington	12–14–1829	308¾	2	175	Hardins & Rolling Fk
Ewell, Thos	Prince William	10–11–1821	15,331	V	147	Brush Cr
Ewers, Wm	Amherst	11– 4–1801	600	F	360	Russell Cr
Ewing, Baker	Gallatin	2–10–1806	400	N	313	None
Ewing, Baker	Gallatin	2– 9–1806	400	P	334	None
Ewing, Baker & Wife	Lincoln	6–15–1790	400	B-2	177	E Fk Ashes Cr
Ewing, Baker & Wife	Lincoln	5–17–1792	5½	B-2	492	Danville
Ewing, Baker Attorney	——	9–10–1791	5,000	B-2	478	Brashears Cr
Ewing, Thos & Wife	Philadelphia	9– 4–1809	56,741	M	449	Ohio R
Ewing, Robt	Logan	2–00–1809	6,203	M	311	M Fk Ky R
Ewing, Young	Lincoln	5–30–1791	400	B-2	282	Little Clifty Cr
Fairfax, Ferdenando & Wife	Shannon Hill	9–30–1805	2,000	M	203	None
Fairfax, Geo Wm, heirs	Fluvana	10–26–1812	20,000	P	147	Eagle Cr
Fountleroy, Robt & Wife	Richmond	9– 1–1813	—	U	46	None
Farmer, Gracy	——	6–23–1820	200	U	23	Green R
Farish, Jno & Wife	Warren	3– 6–1829	901	Y	398	Tennessee R
Farish, Hazelwood	——	9– 1–1824	—	X	51	None
Farris, Jno	Lincoln	2–13–1797	1,200	B	178	Cedar Cr
Farris, Marshall & Wife	——	6–27–1820	200	U	25	Green R
Fendall, Philip R	Alexandria	1–30–1804	41,185¾	N	300	RollingFk & Wilsons Cr & Big Sandy R
Fentress, Jno	Muhlenburg	6– 9–1814	11,600	P	508	Green R Rough Cr
Fenwick, Robt	Franklin	1– 9–1806	158	K	144	Jeffersons Cr
Fenwick, Wm	Henrico	6–21–1823	40,000	W	402	None
Fenwick, Robt & Wife	Frankfort	12–13–1805	57	K	71	Stewarts Cr
Fenwick, Wm & Wife	Frankfort	12–18–1805	57	K	74	Stewarts Cr
Ferguson, Robt	Fayette	5–11–1812	20,440	O	526	Large Cr
Ficklin & Bullock	Philadelphia	9– 4–1815	Lots	Q	398	Shelbyville
Fields, Benj	Mercer	10–11–1796	4,813	A-2	527	Slate Cr
Fields, Jno & Wife	Bourbon	2–26–1814	1,500	P	433	Ky R
Fields, Jno & Wife & Jno Jr	Philadelphia	4–12–1802	Lot	F	478	Frankfort
Fields, Wm & Wife	Mercer	3–21–1792	221	B-2	437	None
Figgins, Daniel, heirs	Ohio	4–28–1840	2,000	21	163	Gallatin Co
Fink, Mark	Madison	3– 5–1829	2,704	Y	390	Panther & Rough Cr
Fishback, Jas & Wife	——	9– 8–1829	100	Y	395	Plum Cr
Fishback, Jacob & Wife	Clark	8–19–1800	—	E	215	Ohio R
Fishback, Jacob & Wife	Clark	8–19–1800	—	F	511	Ohio R
Fisher, Elijah	Fayette	10–22–1823	452	W	174	None
Fisher, Stephen	Lincoln	6–24–1786	400	A	113	None
Fisher, Stephen & Wife	Mercer	6– 6–1791	1	B-2	281	None
Fisk, Martin	——	7–18–1820	400	T	475	Floyds Fk
Fitzhugh, Harrison	Fairfax	7–29–1842	—	27	312	N Elkhorn
Fitzhugh, Harrison & Wife	Fairfax	7–29–1842	—	27	307	N Elkhorn
Fitzhugh, Perigrin	Ontario	6– 4–1811	2,000	P	382	None
Fitzhugh, Wm	Washington	4–17–1800	500	E	10	Goose Cr
Fitzhugh, Wm	Washington	2–20–1815	366	Q	67	Livingston Cr
Fitzhugh, Wm Jr	——	5–22–1802	500	F	413	Goose Cr
Fitzhugh, Wm, executor	Washington	3–24–1806	12,000	K	381	Ohio R
Fitzhugh, Wm, executor	Washington	2–24–1804	3,000	H	401	Ohio R
Flanagan, Chas	Madison	8–28–1819	5,500	T	162	Rough & Panther Cr
Fleming, James	Alleghany	11– 1–1806	—	N	239	None
Fleming, Jas & Wife	Fayette	3–13–1821	300	V	124	Short Cr

Grantor	Residence	Deed Date	Acres	Book	Page	Watercourse
Fleming, Jno & Wife	Fayette	8–27–1788	200	B-2	56	None
Fleming, Robt	Alleghany	8–13–1806		N	240	None
Fleming, Wm	Chesterfield	5–18–1795	7,750	A-2	268	Buck Cr & Dix R
Fleming, Wm	Baltimore	3– 4–1790	1,000	B-2	112	Goose Cr
Fleming, Wm	Baltimore	3–10–1790	932	B-2	118	Hingston Fk
Fleming, Wm	Chesterfield	5–18–1812	1,600	O	452	Michaux Br
Fleming, Wm	Virginia	12–31–1796	40,857	Q	499	Ohio R
Fletcher, Thos	Bath	10–18–1820	1,352	U	6	Crews Cr & Licking
Fload, Noah & Wife	Woodford	2–19–1839	10,018	27	114	Ohio R
Flournoy, Francis, Com'r	Fayette	3——1826	10,000	Y	138	M Licking & Grassy Cr
Flournoy, Jordan	Powhatan	11–22–1798	666⅔	E	36	Ohio R
Flournoy, Jordan & Wife	Powhatan	5–13–1805	11½	N	59	None
Flournoy, Lawrence, heirs	——	9– 1–1826	——	Y	197	None
Flournoy, Roy B & Rowland	——	9–23–1828	——	X	469	None
Flournoy, Solomon, Lawrence & Jones		9–23–1828	——	X	469	None
Flower, Thos	Bourbon	3–24–1801	1,000	G	252	W Fk Bear Cr
Flowers, Thos	Warren	10–30–1807	50	T	209	None
Floyd, Geo R. C.	Jefferson	7–15–1812	980	O	431	Ohio R
Floyd, Geo R C	Jefferson	10–11–1821	1,000	V	82	Ohio R
Floyd, Geo R C	Jefferson	10–11–1821	600	V	83	None
Floyd, Jno	Jefferson	3– 9–1789	1,000	B-2	35	Elkhorn Cr
Floyd, Dr Jno	Montgomery	7–15–1812	1,010	O	433	Ohio R & N Fk Goose Cr
Floyd, Dr Jno & Wife	Montgomery	9–15–1815	1,010	Q	210	Ohio R N Fk Goose & Beargrass Cr
Folsom, Ebenezer	Georgia	12–17–1802	137	G	325	Hammonds Cr
Forbes, David, heirs	——	5– 4–1821	——	V	387	None
Forbes, Jno Jr	Richmond	3– 2–1830	——	Z	15	None
Forbes, Hugh, heirs	——	5– 4–1821	——	V	387	None
Forbes, Mary, administratrix	Germantown	9–17–1805	4,400	K	466	Beech Fk
Forbes, William	Philadelphia	2–19–1794	4,400	K	463	Beech Fk
Forbes, Wm & Wife	Westmoreland	5–15–1797	1,000	B	286	Tradewater
Forbes, Wm & Wife	Westmoreland	5–15–1797	1,500	B	290	Goose Cr
Forbes, Wm & Wife	Westmoreland	5–15–1797	——	B	295	Tradewater
Ford, Ben B	Hanover	8– 2–1813	700	P	197	Rough Cr
Ford, Chas	Mercer	8– 1–1806	4,287	K	423	Green R
Ford, Jno E	Charles	7–26–1799	800	T	157	Green R
Ford, Saml	Amelia	3– 2–1799	12,000	D	361	Fk Licking
Ford, Standish & Wife	Philadelphia	6–19–1801	1,254	F	79	Clay Lick & Little Barren R
Ford, Standish & Wife	——	1– 4–1806	6,845½	K	397	Elkhorn
Fore, Jno Attorney	Chesterfield	11–22–1798	666⅔	E	36	Ohio R
Foreman, David	——	9–11–1804	2,158	H	320	Ohio R
Foreman, David	——	9–11–1804	1,000	H	556	Ohio R
Forrest, Sarah	Philadelphia	8– 6–1813	Lots	P	275	Philadelphia
Forrest, Uriah	Washington	6–14–1803	5,000	H	52	Saxtons Cr
Foster, Jno M	Register Land Office	12– 9–1814	1,000	P	569	Tradewater
Foster, Jno M	Register Land Office	12–13–1814	584	P	575	Puncheon Camp Cr
Foster, Jno M	Register Land Office	12–13–1814	1,085	P	577	Pond Cr
Foster, Jno M	Register Land Office	12–13–1814	1,333⅓	P	578	Big Barren R
Foster, Jno M	Register Land Office	12–13–1814	1,000	P	580	Ohio R
Foster, Jno M	Register Land Office	7–12–1814	1,000	P	582	Gilberts Cr
Foster, Jno M	Register Land Office	10– 7–1815	600	Q	204	Green R
Foster, Jno M	Register Land Office	12– 7–1815	90	Q	262	Green R
Foster, Jno M	Register Land Office	12–20–1815	400	Q	272	S Fk Licking
Foster, Jno M	Register Land Office	12–14–1815	2,000	Q	280	Salt R
Foster, Jno M	Register Land Office	12–21–1815	2,000	Q	283	Hingston Fk
Foster, Jno M	Register Land Office	12–23–1815	2,470	R	53	Benson Cr
Foster, Jno M	Register Land Office	11– 6–1816	800	R	57	Snells Cr
Foster, Jno M	Register Land Office	12– 3–1816	2,000	R	75	None
Foster, Jno M	Register Land Office	12– 3–1816	1,000	R	77	None
Foster, Jno M	Register Land Office	12–13–1816	19,000	R	83	Green R
Foster, Jno M	Register Land Office	1– 7–1817	1,500	R	132	Pleasant Run
Foster, Jno M	Register Land Office	4–14–1817	100	R	266	Floyds Fk
Foster, Jno M	Register Land Office	3–18–1817	951	R	272	Hingston Fk
Foster, Jno M	Register Land Office	7– 2–1817	600	R	341	Rough Cr
Foster, Jno M	Register Land Office	10–23–1817	800	R	436	Drennons Lick Cr
Foster, Jno M	Register Land Office	10–23–1817	968	R	438	Tripletts Cr
Foster, Jno M	Register Land Office	1– 5–1818	1,000	R	603	None
Foster, Jno M	Register Land Office	1–21–1818	1,000	S	8	Twin Cr
Foster, Jno M	Register Land Office	3– 5–1818	1,000	S	62	Hingston Fk
Foster, Jno M	Register Land Office	8–28–1818	2,118	S	221	Eagle Cr
Foster, Jno M	Register Land Office	9–22–1818	4,000	S	256	Sandy R
Foster, Jno M	Register Land Office	10–22–1818	500	S	265	Sulphur Lick Fk

Grantor	Residence	Deed Date	Acres	Book	Page	Watercourse
Foster, Jno M	Register Land Office	6–20–1818	500	S	284	W Fk Crocus Cr
Foster, Jno M	Register Land Office	1– 7–1819	2,090	S	378	Rolling Fk
Foster, Jno M	Register Land Office	1– 6–1819	1,800	S	409	Hardins Cr
Foster, Jno M	Register Land Office	2– 4–1819	500	S	431	Roes Run
Foster, Jno M	Register Land Office	2– 4–1819	2,500	S	433	Bullskin Cr
Foster, Jno M	Register Land Office	10– 4–1819	250	T	104	Sandy R
Foster, Jno M	Register Land Office	12– 9–1819	600	T	179	None
Foster, Jno M	Register Land Office	12–29–1819	200	T	242	Russell Cr
Foster, Jno M	Register Land Office	7–18–1820	400	T	442	Green R
Foster, Jno M	Register Land Office	7–20–1820	2,000	T	444	Beaver Cr
Foster, Jno M	Register Land Office	8– 2–1819	4,000	U	77	None
Foster, Jno M	Register Land Office	8–20–1821	857½	V	18	Cedar Cr
Foster, Jno M	Register Land Office	8–21–1821	1,000	V	17	Ohio R
Foster, Jno M	Register Land Office	6–23–1821	225½	V	96	Eagle Cr
Foster, Jno M	Register Land Office	11–20–1821	400	V	128	Red R
Foster, Jno M	Register Land Office	12–28–1821	590	V	168	Silver Cr
Foster, Jno M	Register Land Office	6–18–1823	5,097¾	W	66	Bullitts Lick
Foster, Jno M	Register Land Office	10–22–1825	20,000	Y	2	Sandy R
Foster, Jno M	Register Land Office	10–22–1825	10,000	Y	4	N Fk Ky R
Foster, Jno M	Register Land Office	10–22–1825	10,000	Y	5	N Fk Ky R
Foster, Jno M	Register Land Office	10–22–1825	5,000	Y	6	Rockhouse Cr
Foster, Jno M	Register Land Office	10–22–1825	15,000	Y	7	Buckhorn Cr
Foster, Jno M	Register Land Office	10–22–1825	10,000	Y	9	N Fk Ky R
Foster, Jno M	Register Land Office	4–21–1826	2,437	Y	129	2nd Cr below Big Bone
Foster, Jno M	Register Land Office	3– 2–1818	410	Y	217	Rough Cr
Foster, Jno M	Register Land Office	1– 8–1819	160	Y	219	Rough Cr
Foster, Jno M	Register Land Office	1–19–1827	333⅓	Y	263	Tygerts Cr
Foster, Jno M	Register Land Office	9–25–1829	333	Y	388	Cumberland R
Foster, Jno M	Register Land Office	7–18–1820	200	Y	436	Big Barren R
Foster, Jno M	Register Land Office	7–15–1830	1,205	Y	502	Ky R
Foster, Jno M	Register Land Office	12–10–1830	711	Z	51	Town Fk Salt R
Foster, Jno M	Register Land Office	7–29–1833	1,500	Z	320	Beech Fk
Foster, Jno M	Register Land Office	7–29–1833	750	Z	321	Licking
Foster, Jno M	Register Land Office	7–29–1833	100	Z	322	Licking
Foster, Jno M	Register Land Office	7–29–1833	100	Z	323	Salt R
Foster, Jno M	Register Land Office	7–29–1833	1,000	Z	324	Brush Cr
Foster, Jno M	Register Land Office	7–29–1833	1,100	Z	325	Shelby Co
Foster, Jno M	Register Land Office	7–29–1833	1,000	Z	327	Licking
Foster, Jno M	Register Land Office	7–29–1833	1,971¾	Z	328	Blue Lick Fk Licking
Foster, Jno M	Register Land Office	7–29–1833	941	Z	329	Indian Lick Cr
Foster, Jno M	Register Land Office	3–30–1834	114	Z	410	S Benson Cr
Foster, Jno M	Register Land Office	8–21–1834	1,000	Z	451	Little Barren R
Foster, Jno M	Register Land Office	8–21–1834	1,533	Z	452	Little Barren R
Foster, Jno M	Register Land Office	8–21–1834	1,000	Z	453	Glovers Cr
Foster, Jno M	Register Land Office	10–11–1834	42,656	Z	462	Mason Co
Foster, Jno M	Register Land Office	2–28–1832	7,500	27	178	Little Sandy R
Foster, Jno M	Register Land Office	5–17–1824	2,666⅔	W	269	Cumberland R
Foster, Jno M	Register Land Office	12– 8–1824	42,629	X	18	Green R
Foster, Jno M	Register Land Office	10–22–1825	20,000	X	177	Sandy R
Foster, Jno M	Register Land Office	10–22–1825	10,000	X	179	N Fk Ky R
Foster, Jno M	Register Land Office	10–22–1825	10,000	X	180	N Fk Ky R
Foster, Jno M	Register Land Office	10–22–1825	5,000	X	182	Rockhouse Cr Bourbon Co
Foster, Jno M	Register Land Office	10–22–1825	15,000	X	184	None
Foster, Jno M	Register Land Office	10–22–1825	10,000	X	186	N Fk Ky R
Foulke, Thos	Baltimore	3–25–1800	800	E	349	Green R
Fountain, Jas	Georgia	6–20–1789	5,300	B-2	100	None
Fountain, Wm & Wife	Hanover	12– 1–1801	1,000	F	395	Poages Cr
Foushee, Francis	Stafford	12–21–1796	7,333⅓	B	329	None
Foushee, Francis	Stafford	6–28–1796	7,813	D	84	Sandy R
Fowler, Abraham	New York	3–21–1795	33,700	A-2	204	N & M Fk Ky R
Fowler, Abraham	New York	2– 6–1795	54,156	A-2	213	N & M Fk Ky R
Fowler, Abraham	New York	3–21–1795	15,554	A-2	217	N & M Fk Ky R
Fowler, Jno	Fayette	9–17–1796	1,000	A-2	439	Russell Cr
Fowler, Jno	————	9–21–1790 Stillhouse		B-2	410	None
Fowler, Jno	Fayette	10–29–1800	1,040	E	425	None
Fowler, Jno	Fayette	11– 8–1806	1,000	K	476	Salt R
Fowler, Jno	Lexington	8–14–1809	14,000	N	126	Buffaloe Road
Fowler, Jno	Fayette	9–12–1810	1,000	N	308	Fks Ky R
Fowler, Jno	Fayette	6–26–1809	1,000	P	311	Licking
Fowler, Jno	Fayette	5–18–1819	4,539	S	510	Tygerts Cr
Fowler, Jno	Lexington	4–25–1827	3,000	X	224	Lick Cr
Fowler, Jno	Lexington	2– 1–1827	15,375	Y	264	Tygerts Cr
Fowler, Jno, Atty	Fayette	11– 8–1799	140	D	455	Tates Cr
Fowler, Jno & Wife	Fayette	3–10–1796	1,000	C	30	Poges Cr
Fowler, Jno & Wife	Fayette	11–10–1798	7	D	66	None
Fowler, Jno & Wife	Fayette	11–10–1798	2,500	D	97	Main Elkhorn
Fowler, Jno & Wife	Fayette	11–28–1800	1,150	F	48	None
Fowler, Jno & Wife	————	1–27–1808	4,550	L	292	Sinking Cr

Grantor	Residence	Deed Date	Acres	Book	Page	Watercourse
Fowler, Jno & Wife	Fayette	8–20–1811	700	O	283	Mud Lick Fk
Fowler, Jno & Wife	Fayette	2– 5–1812	255	O	305	Locust Cr
Fowler, Jno & Wife	Fayette	12– 1–1812	1,050	P	1	Creus Cr
Fowler, Jno & Wife	Fayette	7–28–1814	1,293	Q	463	Cedar Cr
Fowler, Jno & Wife	Fayette	10–18–1820	1,352	U	6	Creus Cr & Licking
Fowler, Theodosius	New York	2–19–1796	130,000	A-2	196	N & M Fk Ky R
Fowler, Theodosius	New York	1–18–1796	130,000	A-2	200	N & M Fk Ky R
Fox, Stephen	N Carolina	5– 3–1825	350	X	188	Canoe Cr
Frankfort City	Franklin	2–28–1805	Plat	M	212	Ky R
Franklin A & Wife & Jno & Wife	New York City	2– 4–1809	10,000	N	93	Ky R
Franklin, Henry & Wife	New York City	12– 6–1809	10,000	N	134	Ky R
Franklin, Thos	Philadelphia	8–12–1793	225,000	A-2	209	N & M Fk Ky R
Franklin, Thos	Philadelphia	12–30–1795	30,000	A-2	221	None
Franklin, Thos	——	2– 4–1829	225,000	Y	401	None
Frawner, Geo & Wife	Franklin	2–26–1842	8¼	27	273	Bealls Run
Frazier, Oliver & Wife	Fayette		Lots	27	434	Frankfort
Frazier, Wm, Comr	Daviess	2–12–1829	1,080	Y	325	Ohio R
Frazier, Wm, Comr	Fayette	7– 7–1829	——	Y	435	Ohio R
French, Francis B	Franklin	9–11–1846	Lot	28	106	Frankfort
French, Henry	Mercer	10–20–1790	1,000	B-2	268	Salt R
French, Jos, Atty	Montgomery	2– 4–1829	225,000	Y	401	None
French, Jno A	Spotsylvania	2–23–1824	500	W	304	Paraquet Cr
French, Richard	Clark	11–19–1822	——	V	436	None
French, Wm & Wife	Dinwiddie	11– 2–1807	2,666⅔	M	74	Goose & Highland Crs
Fries, Jno	Philadelphia	10–23–1809	113,482	N	161	Ohio R
Fries, Jno	Philadelphia	10–25–1809	31,778	N	166	Little Sandy & E Fk Dix R
Froman, Jacob Sr	Woodford	11– 9–1804	1,670	H	471	Salt R
Fry, Joshua	Garrard	11– 3–1822	688	V	353	Ohio R
Fulber, Wm & Wife	Henry	10–10–1840	——	27	188	None
Fulberton, R A	Philadelphia	8– 3–1813	Lots	R	402	Philadelphia
Fuqua, Moses	Mason	12– 6–1799	407	F	448	Ohio R
Gains, Benj, Atty	Mason	6–16–1790	——	B-2	152	N Fk Elkhorn
Gallagher, Chas Jr	Jefferson	9– 6–1833	Slaves	Z	343	None
Gallatin, Albert	Fayette	8–18–1797	5,222⅔	N	10	Little Barren & Cumberland R
Galligo, Joseph & Wife	Richmond	5–22–1799	1,200	D	344	Big Barren R
Galt, Jno M	——	3– 7–1802	6,000	F	491	Ohio R
Galt, Wm C & Wife	Jefferson	9–17–1819	18,000	T	239	Ohio R
Gamble, Elizabeth	Monongalia	12– 7–1814	——	S	278	None
Gamble, Elizabeth	——	9– 1–1815	——	S	281	None
Gamble, Jno & Wife	Richmond	8–10–1820	——	W	351	Beaver Fk N Fk Tradewater
Gamble, Jno G & Wife	Richmond	4– 3–1824	Lots	Y	123	Richmond
Gamble, Jno G & Wife	Richmond	4– 3–1824	647	Y	123	Poages Cr
Gamble, Robt	Richmond	3–26–1825	2,647	Y	116	Poages Cr & N Fk Tradewater
Gamble, Robt, heirs	Richmond	3–26–1825	2,647	Y	116	Poages Cr & N Fk Tradewater
Gano, Daniel	Frankfort	5–17–1796	50,612½	D	88	Red R
Gano, Daniel	Franklin	6– 9–1800	130	E	12	None
Gano, Daniel	Franklin	4–19–1802	10,000	F	243	Red R
Gano, Daniel	Franklin	1–22–1806	Lot	K	225	Frankfort
Gano, Lydia & Isaac	Franklin	12– 5–1804	100	H	411	Ky R
Garland, Jno	Hanover	11– 7–1794	8,593	A-2	80	Green R
Garland, Jno	Hanover	4– 3–1795	2,000	A-2	86	Green R
Garland, Jno	——	7– 6–1795	1,000	A-2	613	None
Garner, Thos	Franklin	6–17–1815	39	U	133	Georgetown Road
Garnett, Benj & Wife	Shelby	2–15–1816	Lot	Q	525	Frankfort
Garnett, James, Atty	——	5– 5–1796	2,000	A-2	694	W Fk Glenns Cr
Garnett, Thos S & Wife	——	10– 5–1839	2,000	27	84	Ohio R
Garrard, Daniel	Franklin	10–12–1833	2,106½	Z	360	Hardin Co
Garrard, Jos	Kentucky	3–10–1835	Lot	Z	507	Frankfort
Garrard, Jno M	Kentucky	11– 4–1833	3,000	Z	367	Breckinridge Co
Garrell, Thos	——	2–12–1788	——	A	356	Robinson Cr
Garrett, Ashton & Wife	Montgomery	10–25–1817	Lots	R	564	Frankfort
Garrett, Ashton & Wife	Montgomery	8–13–1821	1,000	V	66	Highland Cr
Garrett, Jos M C	Spencer	1–19–1830	20	Y	439	Beech Cr
Gary, Ann	Washington	2–21–1817	811	T	135	None
Gary, Everard & Wife	Georgetown	3–11–1814	1,325	P	537	Big Reedy Cr
Gary, Everard & Wife	Georgetown	3–11–1814	1,100	P	541	S Br Big Caney Cr
Gaskins, Thos	Northumberland	4– 2–1796	——	B	299	Goose Cr
Gaskins, Thos	Northumberland	4– 2–1796	2,000	B	303	Tradewater
Gatewood, Andrew	Fayette	3–16–1791	3,030	B-2	244	Foxes Cr
Gayle, Geo	Henderson	6– 4–1842	Lot	27	306	Frankfort
Gayle, Robt D	Woodford	8–31–1811	30	O	92	None
Gibbons, Jos & Wife	Chesterfield	4–29–1796	10,000	B	236	None
Gibbs, Robt M	Baltimore	5–11–1842	1,533	27	283	Otter Cr

Grantor	Residence	Deed Date	Acres	Book	Page	Watercourse
Gibson, Patrick	Richmond	12–15–1821	5,002	V	2 0	Indian Cr & N Fk Ky R
Gilchrist, Archibald	———	12– 2–1818	1,000	T	155	Ohio R
Giles, Wm B & Wife	Amelia	12–21–1803	615	H	254	Cumberland R
Gill, Absolom B & Wife	Louisville	8–16–1817	9,000	R	411	S M Fk Rough Cr
Gill, Wm, heirs	———	2–24–1816	200	Q	356	Bays Fk
Gillespie, Jos E	Mercer	3–18–1816	400	Q	382	None
Gilpin, Geo	———	7– 9–1803	14,936¼	J	91	18 Mile Cr, Hardins & Cartwrights Crs
Gilpin, Geo, Comr	Alexandria	6– 1–1803	———	M	37	None
Gilpin, Iseral & Wife	Bourbon	12–10–1799	25	E	55	Hustons Fk
Gist, Nathaniel, heirs	Kentucky	9– 9–1825	847⅓	X	191	Little Miami & Scioto R
Gist, Thos N & Wife	Clark	10–10–1826	500	Y	248	Cumberland R
Givens, Saml & Wife	Mercer	2–26–1789	440	B-2	266	S Fk Elkhorn
Glass, Robt	———	8–26–1791	300	B-2	356	Mulberry Cr
Glassell, Wm & Wife	Fredricksburg	5– 3–1798	———	C	239	Deer Cr
Glenn, Hugh G	Van Buren	8–26–1843	———	27	379	None
Glenn, Wm	Woodford	9—8–1805	126	K	322	Bealls Run
Glenn, Wm & Wife	Woodford	10–18–1815	1,000	Q	260	Glens Cr
Goar, Adam	Elbert	4–22–1802	100	F	467	Beaver Cr
Goings, Sanford & Wife	Franklin	6———1845	Lot	27	478	Frankfort
Gooch, Thos & Wife	Shelby	5–21–1810	300	N	265	None
Good, Robt	Prince Edward	11–18–1796	100	A-2	544	Br S Fk Nolinn
Goode, Edward	Chesterfield	6– 5–1834	114	Z	447	nr Frankfort
Goodlett, Adam	Scott	11–30–1798	———	D	86	Hog Run
Goodlett, Adam	Scott	12– 1–1798	105	D	95	Cane Run
Goodman, Jno	Frankfort	4–29–1813	Lot	P	314	Frankfort
Goodrich, Jos Jr	Franklin	5–28–1812	Horses	O	397	None
Goodwynn, Boswell	Petersburghin	6– 9–1795	7,200	A-2	265	Stinking Cr
Gordon, Wm	———	9–11–1804	2,158	H	320	Ohio R
Gordon, Wm	———	9–11–1804	1,000	H	556	Ohio R
Gordon, James, heirs	———	9–21–1811	450	O	171	Ky R
Gore, Joseph & Wife	Franklin	11– 1–1819	17¹⁄₁₀	U	264	None
Gore, Wm & Wife	Franklin	1– 2–1815	118	P	616	Elkhorn
Gore, Wm & Wife	Franklin	1– 2–1815	39	P	617	Dry Run
Gorsin, Franklin & Wife	Warren	3– 6–1829	901	Y	398	Tennessee R
Gown, Stanly P	Spencer	4– 1–1824	1,052	W	354	Long Lick Run
Graham, Christopher & Wife	Nelson	10–17–1815	666⅔	Q	206	None
Graham, Christopher & Wife	Nelson	10–15–1815	3,689⅔	Q	208	Cumberland R
Graham, Daniel	Nashville	8–13–1842	21,288	27	329	Hardin & Grayson Cos
Graham, David	———	2–12–1823	37	W	71	None
Graham, David & Wife	Frankfort	12– 1–1818	Lot	S	522	Frankfort
Graham, Francis & Wife	Franklin	10–24–1809	100	M	446	Glade Cr
Graham, Francis, heirs	Franklin	7–17–1812	———	Q	392	None
Graham, Geo	Prince William	12–29–1798	745	E	86	Quick Run
Graham, Geo	Washington	5– 9–1820	1,000	U	63	Ohio R
Graham, Geo W	Frankfort	10–16–1819	Lots	T	141	Frankfort
Graham, Geo & Jno	Virginia	12– 6–1813	———	P	511	None
Graham, Jno	Richmond	6– 7–1809	3,500	N	13	Tennessee R Ohio R
Graham, Jno	Frankfort	1–31–1816	338	Q	401	Elkhorn Cr
Graham, Richard, Decd	Virginia	12– 6–1813	———	P	511	None
Graham, Walter	Prince William	4–26–1802	2,000	F	540	Cumberland R
Graham, Wm & Wife	Franklin	6–13–1842	785	27	297	Ky R
Granger, Gideon Jr	Hartford	3–25–1796	4,184	E	117	Nolinn
Grant, Thos & Wife	New Jersey	5–15–1807	86,035	W	165	None
Grant, Mary C	Trenton	10–28–1824	———	X	32	None
Gratten, Jno	Rockingham	9– 1–1813	500	P	210	Hardins Cr
Gratz, Benj & Wife	Fayette	12–28–1832	500	27	99	Poages Cr
Gratz, Barnard, Atty	Philadelphia	7–28–1795	20,000	A-2	258	Craigs Cr
Gratz, Hyman	Philadelphia	9–16–1829	598	Y	457	Green R
Gratz, Michael	Philadelphia	7–28–1795	20,000	A-2	258	Craigs Cr
Gratz, Michael & Wife	Philadelphia	10–23–1795	8,800	A-2	684	Ohio R
Gratz, Michael, heirs	Philadelphia	10–25–1819	———	T	184	None
Graves, Francis	Richmond	5–27–1795	1,200	A-2	272	——— Cr
Graves, Francis	———	3– 7–1795	100	A-2	277	Bryants Lick
Graves, Jno, Atty	Richmond	6–20–1795	10,000	A-2	548	N Fk Sandy R
Graves, Jno D	Franklin	2– 9–1839	2	27	27	S Elkhorn
Graves, Mary	Richmond	2–11–1811	1,333⅓	O	473	Hunters Cr
Grayson, Alfred W, Atty	———	10– 1–1808	41½	M	224	Salt Lick Cr
Grayson, Alfred W & Wife	Fayette	12–24–1810	———	N	398	None
Grayson, Benj	———	4–19–1786	½	A	117	None
Grayson, Benj	Fayette	6–21–1786	Lot	A	236	None
Grayson, Benj	———	9– 4–1787	Lot	A	369	Town Sp

Grantor	Residence	Deed Date	Acres	Book	Page	Watercourse
Grayson, Benj........	Nelson...........	9–15–1828...	——...	X...	464..	None
Grayson, Benj & Wife .	Mercer...........	6–23–1789...	2,000...	B-2..	38..	Slate Cr
Grayson, Frederick W S	Jefferson.........	12– 7–1822...	600...	W...	17..	Highland Cr
Grayson, Frederick W S, heirs	——.	6–27–1831...	1500...	Z....	144..	Highland Cr
Grayson, Geo W.....	Mason..........	3–18–1803...	61,564...	N...	435..	Little Sandy R
Grayson, Geo W & Wife	Fauquier.........	8–27–1805...	500...	K...	259..	Little Sandy
Grayson, Geo W & Wife	Fauquier.........	8–27–1805...	880...	K...	271..	6 Mile of Salt Works
Grayson, Geo W & Wife	Fauquier.........	8–27–1805...	500...	K...	274..	Little Sandy
Grayson, Harrison & Wife.............	Jefferson........	8–28–1816...	6,713½..	R ...	85..	Beargrass & Salt Lick Cr, Little Sand R
Grayson, Latitia P.....	——.	10–14–1818...	——...	S....	416..	None
Grayson, Robt......	Mason..........	10– 1–1808...	41½..	M...	224..	Salt Lick Cr
Grayson, Robt H.....	Jefferson........	5–26–1817...	1,200...	R ...	424..	James R
Grayson, Robt H & Wife.............	Greenup.........	12–15–1815...	70,000...	Q...	422..	Little Sandy R
Grayson, Robt H & Wife.............	Jefferson........	6–29–1819...	1,483...	T ..	98..	Salt Lick Cr
Grayson, Robt H & Wife.............	Jefferson........	12– 8–1819...	70,000...	T...	210..	Little Sandy Salt Works
Gray, Geo & Wife.....	Culpepper........	9–20–1796...	1,000...	C...	207..	Ohio R
Gray, Geo & Wife.....	Culpepper........	10–23–1797...	2,000...	D...	363..	Ohio R
Gray, Joseph.........	Franklin.........	1–19–1846...	Lot...	28...	50..	Frankfort
Gray, Robt..........	Redding.........	8–10–1805...	4,000...	J...	326..	None
Gray, Robt..........	Mifflin..........	10–25–1808...	300...	P...	533..	Ohio
Gray, Wm..........	——.	5– 6–1814...	600...	P...	521..	Ohio R
Gregory, Wm & Wife..	Nelson..........	12–19–1817...	——...	S...	53..	None
Gresham, Job........	Lincoln.........	9–20–1813...	500...	P...	430..	N Fk Licking
Greathouse, Jno G...	Illinois.........	2– 5–1839...	Slaves...	27...	23..	None
Green, Duff & Wife...	——.	9– 1–1826...	223...	X...	218..	None
Green, Jno..........	Philadelphia......	12–17–1788...	8,000...	G...	231..	None
Green, Jno..........	Campbell.........	9– 1–1826...	223...	X...	218..	None
Green, Jno, heirs.....	Lincoln.........	9– 1–1826...	66...	X...	221..	None
Green, Jno & Wife....	Lincoln.........	9– 1–1826...	223...	X...	218..	None
Green, Jno W.......	Fredericksburg....	6–22–1805...	1,000...	M...	112..	Clay Lick Cr
Green, Jno W.......	Fredericksburg....	11– 3–1817...	12,500...	W...	9..	None
Green, Moses, Executor	Culpepper........	7–12–1799...	1,250...	D...	366..	None
Green, Nancy W, Martha E & Lewis W	——.	9– 1–1826...	223...	X...	218..	None
Green, Saml S........	Fayette..........	6–28–1839...	10,000...	27...	45..	Fayette & Jefferson Co
Green, Saml S........	Delaware.........	7– 7–1846...	10,000...	28...	93..	Big Sandy R & Claim Cr
Green, Thos.........	Richmond........	1– 5–1835...	4,000...	Z...	481..	Cypress Cr
Green, Thos.........	——.	12–22–1838...	32,400...	27...	3..	Meade Co
Green, Wm.........	Mercer..........	3–13–1790...	1,000...	B-2..	141..	Muddy R
Green, Wm.........	Wayne..........	9– 1–1826...	223...	X...	218..	None
Green, Willis........	Fayette..........	9–24–1785...	——...	A...	23..	None
Green, Willis........	Lincoln.........	9–27–1786...	1,500...	A...	314..	Pleasant Run
Green, Willis........	Lincoln.........	9–27–1786...	4,000...	A...	317..	Licking
Green, Willis & Wife..	Lincoln.........	6–17–1790...	Lot...	B-2..	163..	Danville
Green, Willis & Wife..	Lincoln.........	7–31–1790...	200...	B-2..	271..	Cartwright Cr
Greenhone, Saml & Wife	——.	9–19–1797...	——...	D...	107..	None
Greenleaf, Jas Atty...	Amsterdam......	3– 5–1795..	615,180...	28...	341..	Kentucky
Greenleaf, James.....	Philadelphia.....	3– 5–1795..	431,043...	D...	312..	Many water courses
Greenough, Wm......	Pittsburg........	7–29–1786...	15,000...	E ...	15..	S Br Nolinn R
Greenup, Christopher.	Mercer..........	1–25–1787...	1,000...	A...	257..	Mill Cr
Greenup, Christopher..	——.	9–21–1790	Stillhouse...	B-2..	410..	None
Greenup, Christopher.	Franklin........	10–17–1804...	125...	H...	475..	Mud Lick
Greenup, Christopher.	Danville.........	11– 9–1805...	11,520...	K...	126..	N & S Fk Elkhorn, Ky R, Clear & Greer Cr
Greenup, Christopher.	Frankfort... ...	6–22–1807...	150...	L...	77..	Pleasant Run
Greenup, Christopher.	——.	3–21–1812...	170...	O...	338..	Ky R
Greenup, Christopher.	Franklin........	10– 1–1812...	——...	P...	25..	Ky R
Greenup, Christopher.	Frankfort.......	7– 1–1813...	1,200...	P...	160..	Russells Cr
Greenup, Christopher.	Franklin........	4– 7–1818...	580...	S...	86..	None
Greenup, Christopher Attorney..........	Mercer.........	10–22–1791...	2,000...	B-2..	407..	Ohio R
Greenup, Christopher Decd.............	Kentucky......	6–11–1834...	50...	Z....	440..	Ohio R
Greenup, Christopher, heirs.............	Kentucky	8–15–1830...	Ferry...	Y....	509..	Ky R & Big Benson Cr
Greenup, Christopher & Wife.............	Mercer..........	6–29–1790...	Lot...	B-2..	185..	Danville

Grantor	Residence	Deed Date	Acres	Book	Page	Watercourse
Greenup, Christopher & Wife	Mercer	5–10–1791	Lots	B-2	396	Danville
Greenup, Christopher & Wife	Mercer	3–14–1792	106	B-2	470	Curds Rd
Greenup, Christopher & Wife	Mason	3– 6–1792	100	B-2	472	Ky R
Greenup, Christopher & Wife	Frankfort	6–22–1807	140	L	76	Pleasant Run
Greenup, Christopher & Wife	——	8–21–1807	224	L	120	Jessamine & Curds Ferry
Greenup & Trigg Com'r.	——	6– 8–1813	50,000	P	367	Various water courses
Greer, Geo	Baltimore	6–19–1813	8,965	P	253	None
Greer, Geo & Wife	Frankfort	1– 2–1810	Lot	N	111	Beargrass Cr
Griffin, Cyrus, heirs	——	1– 1–1829	107	Y	297	S Elkhorn
Griffin, Cyrus, heirs	Kentucky	4–14–1829	75	Y	336	S Elkhorn
Griffin, Cyrus, heirs	Kentucky	4–13–1829	153	Y	337	S Elkhorn
Griffin, Cyrus, heirs	Virginia	6– 6–1829	60	Y	424	Frankfort & Lex Rd
Griffin, Saml	James City	1– 5–1797	1,000	A-2	669	Tradewater
Griffin, Spencer	Prince Edward	1– 9–1796	3,600	B	18	Stinking Cr
Griffin, Thos L	——	5–12–1820	——	T	312	None
Griffith, C & Sarah	Alexandria	2– 6–1809	6,160	M	406	Drennons Lick Cr
Griffiith, David, heirs	——	6–22–1815	4,150	Q	199	6 Mile & Drennons Lick Cr
Griffith, Cornelius & Wife	Alexandria	12——1815	450	R	5	N & S Fk Elkhorn
Griffith, Iseral T	Virginia	9–22–1832	492½	Z	230	Little Ky R & Sulphur Cr
Grigsby, Nathaniel	Nelson	4– 3–1816	200	Q	432	Chaplins Fk & Salt
Griman, Daniel, Atty	Fredericksburg	2–13–1799	1,000	D	534	Ohio R
Grimes, Carl	Clark	12–23–1840	400	27	183	Panther Cr
Grimes, Chas	Richmond	11–19–1795	1,200	A-2	279	Bet Junctions & N Fk Licking
Grimes, Chas & Wife	Glouster	9–19–1801	1,332½	F	402	Br Green R
Grimes, Chas W	Fayette	12–23–1840	400	27	183	Panther Cr
Grimes, Jno	Montgomery	7–23–1814	5	P	620	Port Williams
Grover, Jno	Baltimore	6–23–1797	60,000	B	229	Big Sandy R
Grovesman, Wm & Wife	Fredericks	10– 5–1796	6,000	D	63	Ohio R
Grover, Thos	Shelby	6– 8–1821	1,000	U	441	Clifty & Poplar Camp
Grubbs, Higgason	Madison	2–28–1811	1,000	O	126	Br Green R
Grubbs, Higgason	Madison	2–28–1811	1,000	P	50	Br Green R
Guatheney, Robt	Richmond	4–30–1830	10,000	Z	147	Rough Cr
Guerant, Chas	Richmond	2–22–1827	2,950	Z	344	Miss R, Town, Highland & Goose Crs
Guerant, Peter	Buckingham	12– 6–1804	2,000	J	60	M Licking
Gum, Shepherd	Nelson	9–17–1791	650	B-2	430	Bear Cr
Guthry, Alexander Sr	Cumberland	10–26–1802	500	G	187	Wolf Cr
Guthry, Elizabeth	——	11–29–1814	106	P	566	None
Gurthy, Elizabeth	Baltimore	5–25–1814	50	P	473	Wolf Run
Guthry, Elizabeth	Baltimore	5–23–1814	114½	P	475	Fks Wolf Run
Guthry, Elizabeth	——	4–19–1815	75	Q	43	Brashears Cr
Guthry, Elizabeth	——	5– 3–1815	100	Q	51	None
Guthry, Elizabeth	Baltimore	5–25–1815	214	Q	120	Elk Cr
Guthry, Elizabeth	Baltimore	5–26–1815	35	Q	121	Elk Cr
Guthry, Elizabeth	Baltimore	5–26–1815	181	Q	122	Elk Cr
Guthry, Elizabeth	——	10– 2–1815	100	Q	198	Shepherds Cr
Guthry, Elizabeth	——	2– 8–1816	1,000	R	215	Cedar Cr
Guthry, Elizabeth	Baltimore	11– 8–1817	104	R	568	None
Guthry, Elizabeth	——	4– 9–1818	85	S	100	Elk Cr
Guthry, Elizabeth	Baltimore	5– 5–1818	1,000	S	121	Mill Cr
Guthry, Elizabeth	——	11–23–1818	150	S	343	None
Guthry, Elizabeth	——	4–19–1820	——	T	434	Elk Cr
Guthry, Elizabeth	Baltimore	12– 5–1821	393	V	139	None
Hackley, Goodrich L	Hardin	9–23–1802	——	F	488	None
Hackley, Richard S & Wife	Fredericksburg	4–10–1797	19,542	B	49	Lynn Camp & Robertson Crs
Hackley, Richard S & Wife	Spottsylvania	3–10–1798	2,000	C	200	N Fk Tradewater
Hackley, Richard S & Wife	——	9–19–1797	——	D	107	None
Hackley, Richard S & Wife	Fredericksburg	4–16–1799	93,937	D	543	Lick Fk Richland Goose Crs
Hackley, Richard S & Wife	Fredericksburg	4–16–1799	7,000	D	546	Goose Cr

Grantor	Residence	Deed Date	Acres	Book	Page	Watercourse
Hackley, Richard S & Wife	Fredericksburg	4–26–1800	10,023	E	82	Richland & Stinking Crs Goose Cr
Hackley, Richard S.	New York City	7–26–1804	2,000	L	36	W Fk Glenns Cr
Haden, Wm	Gallatin	1–12–1808	50	L	291	None
Haggin, Jas	Franklin	1– 4–1830	50	Y	440	Cedar Cr
Haggin, Jas	Franklin	11–16–1833	190	Z	371	Elkhorn
Haggin, J Attorney	———	7–11–1818	193½	S	364	4 Mile, Lower Howard & Hickman Cr
Haggin, Jas & Wife	Franklin	3–22–1833	30	Z	280	Cane Run
Haines, Mary	New Jersey	7– 6–1844	1,280	28	51	N Ky Punchon
Haines, Michael & Wife	Mercer	2– 5–1800	250	D	508	N Fk Licking
Hall, Elisha	Frederick	2– 7–1801	8,212½	G	406	None
Hall, Jno & Wife	Philadelphia	11–18–1797	4,000	C	232	Fk Deer Cr
Hall, Robt R.	Shelby	5– 7–1842	200	27	287	——— R
Hall, Simeon	Philadelphia	11–28–1817	———	W	3	None
Hall, Thos	Franklin	12– 6–1817	100	R	594	Ohio R
Hallock, Benj H	Bourbon	10–28–1826	120	X	252	None
Hamilton, Jas T	Alexandria	8– 3–1795	32,104	A-2	248	Red R M Fk Clear Cr Ky R Green R & Nolinn
Hamilton, Jas T & Wife	Alexandria	8–11–1795	44,378	P	212	None
Hamilton, Margaret	Baltimore	5–25–1814	50	P	473	Wolf Run
Hamilton, Margaret	Baltimore	5–23–1814	114½	P	475	Fk Wolf Run
Hamilton, Margaret	———	11–29–1814	106	P	566	None
Hamilton, Margaret	———	4–19–1815	75	Q	43	Brashears Cr
Hamilton, Margaret	———	5– 3–1815	100	Q	51	None
Hamilton, Margaret	Baltimore	5–25–1815	214	Q	120	Elk Cr
Hamilton, Margaret	Baltimore	5–26–1815	35	Q	121	Elk Cr
Hamilton, Margaret	Baltimore	5–26–1815	181	Q	122	Elk Cr
Hamilton, Margaret	———	10– 2–1815	100	Q	198	Shepherds Cr
Hamilton, Margaret	———	2– 8–1816	1,000	R	215	Cedar Cr
Hamilton, Margaret	Baltimore	11– 8–1817	104	R	568	None
Hamilton, Margaret	———	4– 9–1818	85	S	100	Elk Cr
Hamilton, Margaret	Baltimore	5– 5–1818	1,000	S	121	Mill Cr
Hamilton, Margaret	———	11–23–1818	150	S	343	None
Hamilton, Margaret	———	4–19–1820	———	T	434	Elk Cr
Hamilton, Margaret	Baltimore	12– 5–1821	393	V	139	None
Hamilton, Margaret	Baltimore	1–10–1824	35	W	169	Shepherds Run
Hamilton, Margaret	———	5–17–1824	50	W	271	None
Hammelin, Jno A Dec'd	Washington	10–17–1814	45,000	P	598	Beech Fk
Hammon, Joel	———	5– 8–1817	6,000	T	82	Richland Cr
Hampton, Henry W & Wife	Gallatin	10–23–1824	28	X	37	M Elkhorn
Hampton, Jos & Wife	———	11–24–1809	97	N	61	Caskade
Hampton, Preston & Wife	Owen	1824	56	X	38	M Elkhorn
Hampton, Wm & Wife	Franklin	1824	56	X	38	M Elkhorn
Handley, Jno	Green River	12–15–1815	500	R	18	Dry Fk Big Eddy C
Hann, Jno & Wife	Garrard	7–14–1816	1,400	R	333	——— R
Hanna, Jas	Bucks	6–29–1797	1,400	88	97	Glenns Cr
Hanna, Jno	Harrodsburg	3–20–1812	Lot	O	381	Frankfort
Hanna, Jno	Frankfort	1–14–1819	Lots	U	515	Frankfort
Hanna, Jno H	Frankfort	10– 5–1812	Lot	P	39	Frankfort
Hanna, Jno H	Frankfort	7– 1–1815	Lots	Q	389	Frankfort & Lexington
Hanna, Jno H	———	2– 9–1819	Lots	S	464	Frankfort
Hanna, Jno H	Franklin	9–17–1819	Lot	T	392	Versailles
Hanna, Jno H	Franklin	9–21–1821	Lot	V	54	Portland
Hanna, Jno H	Franklin	6– 3–1823	Lots	W	44	Frankfort
Hanna, Jno H	Franklin	11–12–1839	Lot	27	87	Frankfort
Hanna, Jno H	Franklin	4–25–1839	Lots	27	191	Frankfort
Hanna, Jno H	Franklin	9–16–1844	Lots	27	442	Frankfort
Hanna, Jno H Atty	Franklin	1–29–1829	1,750	Y	319	Salt R
Hanna, Jno H Atty	Franklin	5–27–1839	Lots	27	46	Frankfort
Hanna, Jno H Comr	———	2–24–1816	200	Q	356	Bays Fk
Hanna, Jno H Comr	Franklin	5–13–1830	1,524	Y	483	Drennons Lick Cr
Hanna, Jno H Comr	Franklin	11– 1–1833	Lots	Z	365	Lexington
Hanna, Jno H Comr	Franklin	11–20–1833	15,000	Z	372	None
Hanna, Jno H Comr	Kentucky	11–25–1834	176¾	Z	467	Fayette Co
Hanna, Jno H & Wife	Frankfort	5–11–1820	Lot	U	435	Frankfort
Hanna, Jno H & Wife	Franklin	12–23–1829	Lot	Y	510	Frankfort
Hanna, Jno H & Wife	Franklin	9–16–1844	Lots	27	444	Louisville
Hanna, Mary	———	3–13–1805	———	L	306	None
Hansford, Alexander	Fauquier	10–31–1806	1,000	O	184	Deer Cr
Haptonstall, Abraham	Woodford	10–23–1804	500	K	31	Panther Cr
Haptonstall, Abraham	———	8–10–1815	500	Q	219	Panther Cr
Hardenburg, Jacob R.	New Brunswick	3–10–1803	500	G	390	Ohio R
Hardesty, Henry	Fayette	7– 5–1832	390	26	206	Ky R
Hardin, Jno J	Morgan	7– 2–1832	Lot	Z	241	Frankfort

Grantor	Residence	Deed Date	Acres	Book	Page	Watercourse
Hardin, Jno J	Kentucky	3–19–1833	Lot	Z	292	Frankfort
Hardin, Jno J	Kentucky	3–22–1833	Lot	Z	293	Frankfort
Hardin, Jno J	Kentucky	3–19–1833	Lots	Z	293	Frankfort
Hardin, Jno J	Kentucky	3–19–1833	Lot	Z	294	Frankfort
Hardin, Jno J	Kentucky	3–19–1833	Lot	Z	298	Frankfort
Hardin, Jno J	Kentucky	8–24–1833	Lot	Z	337	Frankfort
Hardin, Jno J	Kentucky	3–22–1833	Lots	Z	357	Frankfort
Hardin, Jno J	Illinois	1–18–1834	115½	Z	408	Dry Run
Hardin, Jno J	Illinois	1–18–1834	205¾	Z	409	Dry Run
Hardin, Jno J	Illinois	2–26–1834	150	Z	413	Dry Run
Hardin, Jno J	Illinois	2–26–1834	126	Z	415	Dry Run
Hardin, Jno J & Wife	Illinois	2–9–1831	136½	Z	98	Salt R, Big Beech Cr
Hardin, Jno J & Wife	Illinois	2–9–1831	136½	Z	99	Salt R
Hardin, Jno J, Executor	————	4–30–1833	96	Z	291	Pleasant Run
Hardin, Jno J, Executor	Kentucky	3–19–1833	Lot	Z	297	Frankfort
Hardin, Mark	Register Land Office	11–21–1805	2,000	J	393	Clear Cr
Hardin, Mark	Register Land Office	11–21–1805	1,000	J	398	Big Cr
Hardin, Mark	Register Land Office	11–14–1805	2,000	J	402	Ohio R
Hardin, Mark	Register Land Office	12–2–1805	200	J	420	Drakes Cr
Hardin, Mark	Register Land Office	12–11–1805	30,000	J	447	Nolinn & Green R
Hardin, Mark	Register Land Office	12–11–1805	10,000	J	451	Salt R
Hardin, Mark	Register Land Office	2–6–1806	906	K	207	Rolling Fk
Hardin, Mark	Register Land Office	1–10–1806	50,000	K	240	S Brs Salt R
Hardin, Mark	Register Land Office	4–19–1806	700	K	287	Wilsons Cr & Rolling Fk
Hardin, Mark	Register Land Office	9–12–1806	1,000	K	395	Ohio R
Hardin, Mark	Register Land Office	4–16–1806	233	K	413	Indian Cr
Hardin, Mark	Register Land Office	12–9–1806	47,897	K	517	Salt R
Hardin, Mark	Register Land Office	9–21–1807	2,950	L	124	Panther Cr
Hardin, Mark	Register Land Office	1–27–1808	1,000	L	293	Eagle Cr
Hardin, Mark	Register Land Office	1–18–1808	1,000	M	86	Deer Cr
Hardin, Mark	Register Land Office	1–18–1808	5,312½	M	89	Hingston Fk
Hardin, Mark	Register Land Office	1–16–1808	1,000	M	91	Paraquet Cr
Hardin, Mark	Register Land Office	9–23–1807	627	M	96	Ky R
Hardin, Mark	Register Land Office	5–21–1808	1,000	M	101	Robinsons Cr
Hardin, Mark	Register Land Office	12–19–1808	1,500	M	232	Cumberland R
Hardin, Mark	Register Land Office	12–23–1808	13,333⅓	M	244	Main Licking & Flat Cr
Hardin, Mark	Register Land Office	12–27–1808	1,000	M	251	Flemings Cr
Hardin, Mark	Register Land Office	1–25–1809	56,000	M	306	Eagle Cr
Hardin, Mark	Register Land Office	2–9–1809	5,274	M	338	Ohio R
Hardin, Mark	Register Land Office	12–23–1808	780	M	343	Green & Dix R
Hardin, Mark	Register Land Office	1–15–1810	100	N	98	Drakes Cr
Hardin, Mark	Register Land Office	5–11–1810	1,000	N	194	Muddy Cr
Hardin, Mark	Register Land Office	5–11–1807	1,200	N	196	Little Muddy Cr
Hardin, Mark	Register Land Office	5–11–1810	1,147	N	198	Muddy Cr
Hardin, Mark	Register Land Office	11–15–1810	100	N	315	Shawnee Run
Hardin, Mark	Register Land Office	1–23–1811	80	N	428	Green R
Hardin, Mark	Register Land Office	1–23–1811	130	N	429	Green R
Hardin, Mark	Register Land Office	2–5–1811	300	N	431	Licking
Hardin, Mark	Register Land Office	10–8–1811	2,000	O	136	Buck Cr
Hardin, Mark	Register Land Office	10–31–1811	1,333⅓	O	210	Cypress Cr
Hardin, Mark	Register Land Office	12–12–1811	2,000	O	219	Little N Fk Elkhorn
Hardin, Mark	Register Land Office	4–30–1812	2,000	O	360	Goose Cr
Hardin, Mark	Register Land Office	5–14–1812	15,000	O	383	Bacon Cr
Hardin, Mark	Register Land Office	1–28–1813	490	P	73	Green R
Hardin, Mark	Register Land Office	5–7–1813	1,525	P	122	Sandy R
Hardin, Mark	Register Land Office	1–22–1806	1,000	U	72	Eagle Cr
Hardin, Mark & Wife	Henry	1–19–1839	————	27	17	None
Hardin, Martin	Register Land Office	4–19–1811	2,000	O	215	Cumberland R
Hardin, Martin D, Executor	————	10–25–1819	513	T	217	None
Hardin, Martin D, heirs	————	3–19–1833	Lots	Z	293	Frankfort
Hardin, M D	Morgan	7–2–1832	Lot	Z	241	Frankfort
Hardin, M D, heirs	Kentucky	3–19–1833	Lot	Z	298	Frankfort
Hardin, M D, heirs	Kentucky	6–00–1839	482	28	23	Kentucky
Hardin, M D & Wife	Franklin	6–18–1823	Lots	W	112	Bardstown
Hardin, Sarah E	————	2–26–1834	150	Z	413	Dry Run
Hardin, Sarah E	————	2–26–1834	121	Z	415	Dry Run
Hardy, Arnold	Scott	6–16–1821	153½	U	506	None
Hardy, Casper & Wife	Ralls, Mo	2–7–1832	118	Z	184	S Elkhorn
Hare, Andrew	Lexington	3–13–1799	Lots	D	138	Louisville
Hare, Andrew & Wife	Lexington	10–31–1799	170	F	519	Salt R
Harper, Thos & Wife	Philadelphia	5–2–1827	104	X	226	Salt R
Harper, Thos & Wife	Philadelphia	5–2–1827	400	X	232	Salt R
Harper, Thos & Wife	Philadelphia	5–10–1827	8,270	X	236	Salt R
Harper, Thos & Wife	Philadelphia	1–9–1827	5,000	Y	243	N Fk Ky R
Harper, Thos & Wife	Philadelphia	9–22–1832	15,000	Z	233	Salt R
Harris, Daniel H & Jno F	Franklin	1–1–1839	158	27	7	M Elkhorn
Harris, Edward & Wife	Franklin	9–16–1824	2	X	84	Salt R

Grantor	Residence	Deed Date	Acres	Book	Page	Watercourse
Harris, Frederick	Louisa	2–14–1831	3,422.	.Z	120	Ky R
Harris, Fredrick	Louisa	11–18–1833	1,000.	.Z	364	Richland & Robertson Crs
Harris, Hannah	Newton	9–22–1788	560.	.B-2	330	Chaplins Fk
Harris, Hannah	Woodford	3–27–1798	687½.	.C	117	Little Kanawha R
Harris, Hannah	Woodford	9–20–1802	700.	.F	503	Chaplins Fk
Harris, Hannah	Kentucky	9–29–1803	54.	.G	430	None
Harris, Hannah	Woodford	2–10–1804	527½.	.L	288	Trough Spring Fk Glens Cr
Harris, Hannah	Woodford	11–23–1811	200.	.O	203	Stewarts Cr
Harris, Hannah	——	7–15–1819	223¾.	.T	77	None
Harris, Jno	Powhatan	11–26–1796	1,470.	.A-2	580	Ohio R
Harris, Jno	——	6–29–1797	1,400.	.B	97	Glens Cr
Harris, Jno	——	6–13–1797	1,400.	.B	102	Trough Spring
Harris, Jno	Woodford	2–11–1804	527½.	.H	409	Trough Spring Fk
Harris, Jno	Powhatan	12–11–1804	22,054¼.	.J	77	Licking & Eagle Cr
Harris, Jno	Woodford	2–10–1804	Dowery.	.L	290	None
Harris, Jno	Powhatan	3–29–1795	26,597½.	.N	495	Crossing 3 Crs
Harris, Jno	Woodford	6– 3–1817	278.	.S	47	None
Harris, Jno, heirs	——	9–29–1803	54.	.G	430	None
Harris, Jno & Wife	Poweban	12– 3–1796	5,000.	.B	1	Main Licking
Harris, Jordan	Powhatan	11–14–1804	22,050.	.J	74	None
Harris, Nancy S & Betsey	Almelia	10–18–1816	——	.R	335	None
Harris, Rachel & Hannah	——	3–13–1805	——	.L	306	None
Harris, Randolph	Woodford	3–10–1800	200.	.E	104	Savin Cr
Harris, Randolph	Woodford	3–10–1800	200.	.E	105	Savin Cr
Harris, Saml	Chesterfield	11–22–1798	666⅔.	.E	36	Ohio R
Harris, Thos & Wife	——	5–30–1833	6,633.	.Z	421	Little Barren R & Glovers Cr
Harris, Wm	Amhurst	11–26–1798	350.	.D	82	Caseys Cr
Harris, Wm S	——	1–16–1845	637.	.27	456	Crooked Cr
Harris, Wm S & Wife	Franklin	2– 7–1840	——	.27	103	None
Harris, Wm S & Wife	——	1–10–1844	——	.27	386	Cumberland R
Harrison, Benj, Dec'd	Prince George	2–23–1829	——	.Y	341	None
Harrison, Burr, Atty	——	10–13–1814	975.	.P	550	Salt R
Harrison, Elizabeth, heirs	Nelson	9–21–1825	1,512.	.Y	258	Rock Lick & Ohio R
Harrison, Jno Peyton	Famquire	10–30–1787	——	.A	434	Br Coxes Cr
Harrison, Philip B	Jefferson	9–10–1807	2,000.	.M	21	Ky & Tennessee Rs
Harrison, Richard, heirs	——	9–28–1843	500.	.27	387	Fk Clarks R
Harrison, Robt	Harrison	9–23–1799	378½.	.E	2	M Fk Licking
Harrison, Valentine & Wife	Londoun	10–16–1788	2,743.	.T	174	Beech Fk
Harrison, Valentine, heirs	Virginia	11–12–1818	1,000.	.S	323	Brashears Cr
Harrison, Wm L H	Petersburg	2– 7–1815	2,000.	.Q	532	Ohio R
Harrison, Wm Henry & Wife	Hamilton	1– 5–1815	——	.P	622	None
Harrod, Jas	Mercer	6–15–1787	400.	.A	323	Salt R
Harrod, James	Mercer	2– 6–1790	1,000.	.B-2	352	Brashears Cr
Harrod, James & Wife	——	7– 9–1789	700.	.B-2	129	Ohio R
Harrod, Wm	Washington	2– 8–1790	500.	.B-2	439	14 Mile Cr
Harry, Mary	Hardin	2–23–1809	2,100.	.M	317	Ohio R
Hart, Archibald & Wife	Baltimore	9–26–1845	2,500.	.28	35	Elkhorn & Cedar Cr
Hart, Jno & Wife	Philadelphia	8–26–1786	30,000.	.T	322	Nolinn & Green R
Hart, Jno & Wife	Philadelphia	8–26–1786	10,000.	.T	326½	Nolinn & Green R
Hart, Thomas	Lexington	9–22–1807	27,500.	.L	126	Ky R
Hart, Col Thomas	Lexington	9–21–1798	——	.D	52	Ohio & Green R
Hart, Col Thos	Lexington	8– 1–1790	21,615.	.D	394	Ohio & Green R
Hart, Thos, Executor	——	7–16–1799	6,750.	.D	393	Green R
Hart, Thos, Jr	Lexington	9–16–1808	6,000.	.N	146	Bank Lick Cr
Hart, Thos & Nathaniel Tenants in & David	Common	1– 6–1775	——	.D	272	Ohio & Greens R
Harvey, Robt & Wife	Botetourt	3–29–1797	400.	.B	44	Pitmans Cr
Harvie, Edwin J & Wife	Richmond	8–13–1811	5,000.	.S	542	Ky R
Harvie, Jaquelin	Henrico	7–31–1817	5,000.	.S	545	Ky R
Harvie, Jacquetine B	Richmond	4–21–1826	1,233.	.Y	167	None
Harvie, J B & Wife	Richmond	5– 6–1833	130.	.Z	334	Green Co
Harvie, Jno	Virginia	5–13–1797	995.	.B	268	Big Barren R
Harvie, Jno	Henrico	11–18–1803	1,000.	.H	34	Limestone Cr
Harvie, Jno	Richmond	1– 4–1790	12,140.	.N	491	Ohio & Licking
Harvie, Jno & Wife	Henrico	9–20–1799	15,000.	.R	295	None
Harvie, Jno & Wife	Henrico	2–20–1801	——	.E	417	Ohio R
Harvie, Jno B & Lewis	Powhatan	5– 1–1835	1,226⅔.	.27	50	Green Co
Hasbrook, Abram, heirs	Jefferson	2–11–1843	Lot.	.28	69	Frankfort

Grantor	Residence	Deed Date	Acres	Book	Page	Watercourse
Hasbrook, Abram, heirs	Jefferson	3–31–1843	Lot	28	72	Frankfort
Hatton, Demey	Franklin	10–26–1801	Lots	F	104	Frankfort
Hatton, Demey	Frankfort	10–26–1801	Lots	F	106	Frankfort
Hatton, Robt	Franklin	11–20–1815	Lots	Q	247	Frankfort
Hawes, Thos	Gallatin	5–30–1817	200	S	7	None
Hawkins, Francis G	Owen	12–18–1839	——	27	94	None
Hawkins, Harrison & Wife	Owen	10– 3–1827	330	X	287	Cedar Cr
Hawthorn, James	Danville	9–13–1791	Lot	B-2	404	Danville
Hawkins, James	——	5– 5–1818	——	S	161	None
Hawkins, Jas, heirs	Logan	2–22–1822	1,400	V	206	Ohio R
Hawkins, Jas W	——	11–13–1824	1,000	W	413	Eagle Cr
Hawkins, Jas W & Wife	Franklin	3– 2–1824	300	W	278	Littles Fk Eagle Cr
Hawkins, Jno & Wife	Scott	5–18–1811	1,000	O	29	Eagle Cr
Hawkins, Jno T & Wife	Franklin	11–20–1807	1,666½	R	121	Hickman & Jessamine Crs
Hawkins, Martin	Richmond	9–24–1786	1,000	A	249	Simpsons Cr
Hawkins, Martin & Wife	——	12–14–1801	1,000	F	171	Mill Cr
Hawkins, Martin L	Barren	3– 6–1826	Lots	Y	106	Port Williams
Hawkins, Martin L	Barren	3– 6–1826	4,004	Y	106	None
Hawkins, Thos W	Bourbon	9–29–1822	1,350	V	378	Canoe Cr & Little Ky R
Hawkins, Wm Sr & Wife	Franklin	5–28–1817	102	R	337	Cedar Cr
Haxall, Wm, Executor	Petersburg	2–23–1829	——	Y	341	None
Hay, George	Richmond	3– 4–1815	50	Q	19	None
Hay, Geo	Richmond	3– 4–1815	50	Q	20	None
Hay, Jno	Philadelphia	7–16–1796	1,000	A-2	500	Beech Fk
Hays, Geo C	Adair	3–10–1823	250	V	458	Cypress Cr
Hays, Wm	Fayette	3– 6–1788	1,000	A	339	Silver Cr
Hays, Wm, heirs	——	1– 8–1817	——	R	441	None
Hayt, Geo Jr	Louisville	8–16–1823	690	W	106	Cumberland R
Head, Jno A	Franklin	2–15–1841	20	27	190	Daviss Co
Head, Wm	Daviess	5–19–1835	15	Z	510	N Elkhorn
Hedges, Elias	Morris, N J	8–16–1805	237½	K	251	Drennons Lick
Hedges, Elias	Morris	8–16–1805	262	K	256	Drennons Lick
Hellegas, Michael	Philadelphia	9–17–1802	Lot	R	578	Danville
Helm, Chas	Hardin	2– 9–1809	466⅔	M	341	Enlows Lick
Helm, Chas	Hardin	3–25–1815	Slaves	Q	32	None
Helm, Chas & Wife	——	4– 5–1807	6,921½	M	198	Ky R
Helm, Geo & Wife	Hardin	2–23–1809	2,100	M	317	Ohio R
Helm, Thos & Wife	Woodford	1– 1–1818	5½	S	119	None
Hempstone, Christian T	Montgomery	11– 9–1839	295	27	136	Grassy Lick Cr
Henderson, Alexander Jr	Alexandria	6– 9–1804	6,500	H	615	None
Henderson, David	Fredericksburg	6–22–1805	1,000	M	112	Clay Lick Cr
Henderson, Jas L	Shelby	3– 8–1805	10,000	J	149	None
Henderson, J L & Wife	Shelby	4–18–1803	8,000	G	279	None
Henderson, Richard	Tenants in Common	1– 6–1775	——	D	272	Ohio & Green R
Henderson, Richard & Co	——	3–31–1797	Lots	C	143	Henderson
Henderson, Richard & Co	——	3–31–1797	Lots	C	135	Henderson
Henderson, Robt	Madison	3– 8–1796	5,000	A-2	238	Main Licking
Henderson, Robt	Madison	3– 8–1796	7,118½	A-2	239	Main Licking
Henderson, Robt	Madison	3– 8–1796	3,000	A-2	241	Main Licking
Hendon, Jas & Wife	Franklin	11–21–1831	Slaves	Z	180	None
Hendon, Jno W	Fredericksburg	1– 1–1844	2,500	27	395	Franklin Co
Hendrin, Patrick, Atty	——	12– 7–1819	339	T	378	Eagle Cr
Henly, Leonard	Williamsburg	2–16–1816	1,850	S	43	Fk Sandy R
Henning, Robt	Fredericksburg	5– 4–1805	3,720	J	218	Skeggs & Big Bone Lick
Henning, Robt & Wife	Fredericksburg	5– 2–1808	1,000	M	41	Deer Cr
Henry, Alexander & Wife	Philadelphia	6– 6–1832	4,000	Z	201	Deer Cr
Henry, Alexander & Wife	Philadelphia	10– 3–1810	2,000	N	297	Deer Cr
Henry, Wm	Scott	12–19–1798	1,212	D	99	Sinking Cr
Hensley, Benj & Wife	Indiana	3– 4–1841	Lots	27	280	Frankfort
Herndon, Benj & Polly	Fayette	1–23–1807	——	K	553	None
Herndon, Edward	Spottsylvania	9– 9–1796	7,023	A-2	542	Brashears Cr
Herndon, Edward	Spottsylvania	9– 3–1796	1,500	A-2	424	Little Ky
Herndon, Jno C	Franklin	1–11–1839	11½	27	25	Elkhorn
Herndon, Jno C	Franklin	3–11–1839	——	27	123	N Elkhorn
Herndon, Joseph & Wife	Logan	10– 1–1838	75	27	12	N Elkhorn
Herndon, Joseph & Wife	Logan	10– 1–1838	135	27	30	N Elkhorn

Grantor	Residence	Deed Date	Acres	Book	Page	Watercourse
Herring, Alexander	Rockingham	9–21–1813	272	P	519	Lost Cr
Hersey, Benj	Georgetown	11– 4–1816	1,325	R	176	Big Reedy Cr
Herson, James	Richmond	12– 5–1795	1,000	A-2	539	Cumberland R
Heth, Berl	———	3– 4–1833	———	Z	309	None
Heth, Jno & Wife	———	3– 4–1833	———	Z	309	None
Hickman, Benj F	Franklin	12–16–1839	Lot	27	93	Frankfort
Hickman, Benj F	Franklin	12– 2–1839	50	27	110	S Elkhorn
Hickman, Edwin A	Franklin	6–13–1840	50	27	122	S Elkhorn
Hickman, Ezra	Jackson	12–22–1843	———	27	393	S Elkhorn
Hickman, Jas R	Shelby	8–18–1841	50	27	218	Elkhorn
Hickman, J L & Wife	Frankfort	7–16–1819	Lot	T	64	Frankfort
Hickman, Jas L & Wife	Franklin	7–16–1819	Lot	T	78	Frankfort
Hickman, Paschall	Franklin	6–17–1812	5,900	P	2	M S Elkhorn
Hickman, Paschal, heirs	Virginia	6–11–1832	23	Z	224	S Elkhorn
Hickman, Thos, heirs	———	12– 4–1839	50	27	92	S Fk Elkhorn
Hickman, Wm & Wife	Franklin	6–11–1840	50	27	120	S Elkhorn
Hicks, Harris	Woodford	9–24–1800	468¾	E	329	Savin Cr
Hicks, Jno	Richmond	9– 1–1823	———	X	73	None
Hicks, Jno Jr	Frankfort	9– 1–1823	280	X	74	Skeggs Cr
Hieronyemer, Henry	Clark	4– 2–1808	134	M	358	Dix R
Hill, H B & Co	Jefferson	7–19–1842	320	27	296	Hickman & Graves County
Hillegas, Michael	Philadelphia	10–16–1800	3,000	H	301	None
Hillegas, Michael, heirs	Philadelphia	10–29–1813	———	P	288	None
Hillegas, Saml, heirs	Philadelphia	10–29–1813	———	P	288	None
Hinde, Thos S & Wife	Chilecothe	10– 5–1814	———	S	271	None
Hines, Abner	———	10–13–1814	975	P	550	Salt R
Hines, Abner	Nelson	5–23–1815	———	27	214	Rolling Fk
Hines, Andrew, heirs	Bardstown	3– 3–1819	35,940	V	112	Welcher, Bear, Little Clifty & Dog Cr
Hines, Andrew, heirs	Nelson	9–21–1825	1,512	Y	258	Rock Lick, Ohio R & Indian Camp Cr
Hines, Wm R	Bardstown	3– 3–1819	35,940	V	112	Welcher, Bear, Little Clifty & Dog Crs
Hinton, Hugh C & Wife	Franklin	2–10–1832	97	Z	177	Glens Cr
Hinton, Thos Jr	Woodford	10– 5–1804	207	J	179	N Fk Glens Cr
Hite, Geo & Wife	Berkley	2–10–1798	1,000	C	242	Big Bend Green R
Hite, Isaac	Jefferson	9–20–1787	½	A	368	None
Hite, Isaac & Wife	Jefferson	9—–1790	Lots	B-2	264	Danville
Hite, Isaac & Wife	Jefferson	4– 6–1791	2,054	B-2	338	Br Floyds Fk & Simpson Cr
Hite, Isaac & Wife	Frederick	4–30–1800	500	E	344	Benson Cr
Hoagland, O Key	Gallatin	1–31–1823	200	V	437	Ohio R
Hockersmith, Henry	Franklin	11– 9–1841	¼	27	249	N & Main Elkhorn
Hodgdon, Alexander L	Philadelphia	5–30–1833	6,633	Z	421	Little Barren R & Glovers Cr
Hodgdon, Saml, heirs	Philadelphia	5–30–1833	6,633	Z	421	Little Barren R & Glovers Cr
Hodgen, Robt & Wife	———	5–26–1806	6,348	M	193	Ky R & Big Benson
Hodges, Wm	Franklin	12–25–1823	59½	W	164	Beech Cr
Hodgin, Robt	Hardin	2–23–1809	2,100	M	317	Ohio R
Hodgson, Wm & Wife	Alexandria	4–20–1804	745	J	1	Quick Run
Hoff, Hannah	New Jersey	7–18–1828	5,000	X	418	Harrods Cr
Hoffler, Wm	Norfolk	2–25–1801	138	F	524	W Fk Crocus Cr
Hoffman, Isaac	Shanondoah	3–21–1811	666⅔	N	459	Eddy Cr
Hoffman, Peter & Wife	Shanondoah	8–30–1809	1,000	N	151	Poages Cr
Hogan, Elizabeth & Vitella	Charles	6–29–1799	800	J	113	Green R
Hogan, Henry & Henrietta	Charles	6–29–1799	800	J	113	Green R
Hog, James	———	5–13–1830	1,524	Y	483	Drennons Lick Cr
Hogg, James	Tenants in common	1– 6–1775	———	D	272	Ohio & Green R
Hogg, Jas	———	7–16–1799	6,750	D	393	Green R
Hoggins, Solomon	Bourbon	11–18–1826	1,000	Y	227	State of Ohio
Hogland, Cornelius	Fayette	2– 1–1823	95¼	W	19	Ohio R
Hogland, Solomon S & Wife	Fayette	2– 1–1823	95¼	W	19	Ohio R
Holbrook, Darius B	Illinois	7–11–1840	2,552,304¾	27	204	Va & Ky
Holder, Jno	Fayette	10–22–1790	1,400	B-2	405	Floyds Fk
Holder, Jno	———	3–16–1792	1,000	B-2	431	None
Holeman, Edward Jr	Woodford	7– 5–1813	100	P	339	Ky R
Hollenger, Henry	Fredericksburg	8–12–1829	———	Y	379	None
Hollenger, Smith	Fredericksburg	7–11–1829	———	Y	363	Drakes Cr
Hollingsworth, Isaac	Fredericks	5– 2–1816	1,000	R	42	Ohio R
Hollingsworth, Jesse	Baltimore	10–17–1804	2,000	K	417	Buck Cr
Hollingsworth, Jesse	Baltimore	2– 1–1806	———	Y	113	None
Hollingsworth, Jno	Fayette	7–11–1796	3,120	A-2	350	Slate Cr
Hollingsworth, Levi	Philadelphia	11–19–1796	31,520	H	125	Big Sandy R
Hollingsworth, Levi	Philadelphia	4–25–1814	16,380	P	428	Salt R & Crooked
Hollingsworth, Levi	Philadelphia	11–30–1819	79¾	T	166	Salt R
Hollingsworth, Levi	Philadelphia	11–30–1819	81½	T	168	Salt R

Grantor	Residence	Deed Date	Acres	Book	Page	Watercourse
Hollingsworth, Levi	Philadelphia	11–30–1819	50½	T	170	Salt R
Hollingsworth, Levi	Philadelphia	11–30–1819	78¼	T	172	Salt R
Hollingsworth, Levi & Wife	Philadelphia	10–28–1820	16,380	U	155	Salt R
Hollingsworth, Rachel	Pittsburg	10–31–1821	2,437½	V	215	Br Big Bone Cr
Holloway, Geo & Wife	Jessamine	7–24–1816	500	R	245	None
Holmes, Andrew	Fayette	1–10–1796	———	A-2	145	None
Holmes, Andrew	Lexington	3– 2–1796	1,793	A-2	148	None
Holmes, Andrew	Lexington	6–13–1798	Lots	Q	234	Frankfort
Holmes, Andrew, Com'r	Shelby	6–22–1815	4,150	Q	199	6 Mile & Drennons Lick Cr
Holmes, Hugh	Philadelphia	5– 6–1814	600	P	521	Ohio R
Holmes, Wm	Montgomery	10–25–1817	Lots	R	564	Frankfort
Hoogland, Mary	Gallatin	7–18–1828	5,000	X	418	Harrods Cr
Hooker, Jno	Springfield	3–25–1796	4,184	E	117	Nolinn
Hoomes, Benj	King & Queen	1– 3–1807	1,000	L	360	None
Hoomes, Jno & Wife	Carolina	4–16–1796	310	H	110	Br Ky R
Hoomes, Jno, heirs	Carolina	4–20–1811	5,659	O	86	Fk Big Benson Cr
Hoomes, Jno, heirs	Virginia	2–14–1814	3,593½	Q	80	Salt R
Hoomes, Jno, heirs	Virginia	2–14–1814	1,083⅓	Q	84	——— R
Hoomes, Jno, heirs	Virginia	2–14–1814	6,706	Q	89	Rough Cr
Hoomes, Jno, heirs	Carolina	7– 8–1817	48	S	170	Gilberts Cr
Hopkins, Arthur	Cumberland	7– 1–1817	1,754½	S	20	Crocus Cr
Hopkins, Jno	Alexandria	6–30–1807	1,000	L	160	Br Poages Cr
Hopkins, Jno	Alexandria	12–20–1808	1,400	M	388	Little Miami & Scioto R
Hopkins, Jno	Alexandria	2–23–1808	800	N	105	Big Barren R
Hopkins, Jno	Frederick	———1819	4,266⅔	T	283	Deer Cr & N Fk Tradewater
Hopkins, Saml	Christian	8– 9–1797	264 Lots	C	53	Ohio R
Hopkins, Saml	Henderson	10– 1–1811	1,700	O	170	None
Hopkins, Saml	———	10– 7–1816	———	R	69	None
Hopkins, Saml, Agent	———	3–31–1797	Lots	C	135	Henderson
Hopkins, Saml, Agent	———	3–31–1797	Lots	C	143	Henderson
Hopkins, Saml, executor	———	7–16–1799	6,750	D	393	Green R
Hopkins, Wm & Wife	Woodford	12– 3–1798	125	D	109	None
Hord, Geo T	Carolina	7– 2–1812	570	O	409	Panther Cr
Hord, Geo T & Richard	Virginia	7– 6–1812	190¾	O	410	Panther Cr
Hord, Jno	Carolina	5–13–1800	721½	E	201	Panther Cr
Hord, Willis & Wife	Jefferson	10– 7–1805	537	J	318	Clay Lick Cr
Horine, Geo	Mercer	4– 8–1811	500	N	458	Br Glenns Cr
Horine, Jacob	Jefferson	8–24–1805	500	K	281	None
Hoscall, David A	Essex	11–30–1813	1,000	P	291	Hogback Grove
Houre, Geo	New York	12–29–1809	2,000	P	305	Ohio R
Houree, Michael & Wife	Lincoln	3–12–1790	100	B-2	138	Dix R
Houston, Franklin R & Wife	———	5– 4–1821	———	V	387	None
Howard, Benj	Kentucky	9–25–1803	1,015	H	45	Otter Cr
Howell, Jno	Ohio	12–25–1805	228¾	K	213	Rough Cr
Howle, Jacqueline & Wife	———	10–14–1828	———	X	481	None
Hubble, Margaret	Scott	7– 9–1832	50	Z	229	Franklin Co
Hugg, Jacob & Wife	Baltimore	2–15–1798	23,000	C	267	M Fk Licking
Hughes, Andrew S, Atty	Nicholas	3– 9–1825	4,924	X	142	None
Hughes, Andrew S, Atty	Nicholas	3– 9–1825	42,197	X	144	None
Hughes, James	Lincoln	1–10–1799	500	E	298	None
Hughes, James	———	10–14–1806	1,000	K	477	N Elkhorn
Hughes, Jas & Wife	Fayette	1– 8–1807	15,196	L	28	Tygerts Cr & Fk Sandy
Hughes, Jas & Wife	Fayette	11–30–1808	26,000	M	278	Cane Run
Hughes, Jas & Wife	Frankfort	11–19–1814	768	P	595	Blue Sp Grove
Hughes, Jno	Jefferson	10– 9–1809	316	N	187	S Fk Little R
Hughes, Thos & Wife	Frankfort	3——1812	500	O	343	Big Benson Cr
Hughes, Wm	Lincoln	9–25–1790	Cattle	B-2	229	None
Humphry, Chas	———	10– 3–1821	15,000	V	184	Lawrence Cr
Humphry, Joshua	Richmond	12– 6–1785	———	A	174	Hickman Cr
Humphrey, Thos	Culpepper	11– 3–1817	12,500	W	9	None
Humphreys, Chas	Lexington	9–28–1815	33,261⅔	Q	411	Johnsons Fk & N Fk Licking
Humphreys, Chas	Lexington	11–19–1814	912½	P	592	Blue Sp Grove
Humphreys, David & Wife	———	5–30–1798	500	C	217	——— R
Hunt, Abijah	Cincinnati	12– 5–1798	1,000	D	93	Br Cumberland R
Hunt, Jno W	Lexington	12– 5–1798	1,000	D	93	Br Cumberland R
Hunt, Jno W	Fayette	12–11–1822	256	V	407	Hickman Cr
Hunt, Jno W & Wife	Fayette	6– 2–1823	Lot	W	58	Frankfort
Hunt, Jno Jr	Fleming	8–19–1805	180	K	248	Hustons Fk
Hunt, Jonathan	Frankfort	12– 2–1815	Lot	Q	430	Frankfort
Hunt, Saml	New Jersey	1–28–1831	60	Z	77	Salt R
Hunter, Chas S	Woodford	3–25–1807	———	L	43	Blackfords Fk
Hunter, Chas S	Anderson	5– 3–1844	———	27	410	None
Hunter, Chas & Wife	Woodford	3–23–1807	———	L	45	Blackfords Fk

Grantor	Residence	Deed Date	Acres	Book	Page	Watercourse
Hunter, Jas & Mary	Philadelphia	9–22–1788	560	B-2	330	Chaplins Fk
Hunter, Mary	Woodford	9–28–1805	126	K	322	Bealls Run
Hunter, Mary	Bucks	6–29–1797	1,400	B	97	Glens Cr
Hunter, Mary	Woodford	9–26–1811	422	O	164	Mill Cr
Hunter, Mary	Woodford	11–23–1811	200	O	203	Stewarts Cr
Hunter, Mary	Woodford	11–23–1811	737	O	204	Rolling Fk
Hunter, Mary	Kentucky	12–16–1811	45	P	527	Glens Cr
Hunter, Mary	Woodford	12–25–1815	9,910	Q	294	Clear & Sunfish Crs Ky & Green R
Hunter, Mary	———	7–15–1819	223¾	T	77	None
Hunter, Wm	Franklin	6–20–1818	Lot	S	166	Frankfort
Hunter, Wm & Wife	Franklin	3–22–1820	199¾	T	369	None
Hunter, Wm & Wife	Washington	4–24–1845	12	28	14	Ky R
Hunter, Wm & Wife	Frankfort	9– 7–1819	800	T	151	None
Hunton, Thos & Wife	Albermerle	4– 1–1809	200	N	412	Cumberland R
Hunton, Wm Jr	Fanquire	11–21–1800	6,250	E	376	Big Sandy R
Huston, Joseph	Breckenridge	11– 8–1803	1,000	H	32	Limestone Cr
Huston, Robt	———	11–25–1834	176¾	Z	467	Fayette Co
Huston, Thabes	Lincoln	5–11–1818	1,508⅔	S	148	Rough Brush & Richland Cr
Hutton, Jas & Wife	Frankfort	5–20–1811	160	O	224	Big Benson Cr
Hyson, Rebecca	New Castle	3–30–1798	69,000	D	56	Main Licking
Imlay, Gilbert	Virginia	8– 1–1786	2,148	A	289	Salt Spring
Imlay, Gilbert	———	12–27–1789	2,000	B-2	187	Stoners Fk
Imlay, Gilbert	———	11–19–1810	3,400	N	477	Green R & M Licking
Inlish, Thos	Hawkins	5–27–1790	600	B-2	513	Elkhorn Cr
Innis, Ann, Executrix	Franklin	3–20–1818	———	S	104	Elkhorn Cr
Innis, Elizabeth, Administratrix	Williamsburg	7–21–1801	2,000	E	387	Little Ky R
Innis, Harry	Mercer	7–15–1788	1,400	A	441	Lees Cr
Innis, Harry	Franklin	10–18–1796	4,000	A-2	531	Ohio R
Innis, Harry	Mercer	9–––1791	1	B-2	279	None
Innis, Harry	Mercer	5– 8–1790	251	B-2	291	None
Innis, Harry	Franklin	1–16–1796	1,359¼	C	315	Little Sandy R
Innis, Harry	Franklin	11– 8–1800	350	E	240	Elkhorn
Innis, Harry	Frankfort	9–28–1805	126	K	322	Bealls Run
Innis, Harry	Frankfort	9–26–1811	422	O	164	Mill Cr
Innis, Harry	Franklin	11–23–1811	200	O	203	Stewarts Cr
Innis, Harry	Frankfort	11–23–1811	737	O	204	Rolling Fk
Innis, Harry	Frankfort	12–26–1811	46	P	138	None
Innis, Harry	Kentucky	12–16–1811	45	P	527	Glens Cr
Innis, Harry	Franklin	7–25–1814	110	P	590	N Fk Glens Cr
Innis, Harry, Administrator	Franklin	1–29–1805	48	H	559	Ky R
Innis, Harry, Atty	Franklin	11– 5–1795	4,015¾	A-2	166	Tennessee R
Innis, Harry, Atty	Franklin	11– 5–1795	4,015¾	A-2	168	Ohio R
Innis, Harry, Atty	Franklin	3– 4–1815	50	Q	19	None
Innis, Harry, Atty	Franklin	3– 4–1815	50	Q	20	None
Innis, Harry & Wife	Frankfort	7–17–1812	338	Q	395	Elkhorn
Innis, Harry & Wife	Mercer	9–29–1790	Lot	B-2	192	Danville
Innis, Harry & Wife	Mercer	9–30–1790	Lots	B-2	262	Danville
Innis, Harry & Wife	Frankfort	9– 3–1805	450	K	195	Elkhorn
Innis, Harry & Wife	Frankfort	9– 3–1805	1,100	K	222	Panther Cr
Innis, Harry & Wife	Franklin	1–21–1807	4,400	L	296	Otter & Muddy Cr
Innis, Harry & Wife	———	1– 1–1807	300	L	301	None
Innis, Harry & Wife	———	3–13–1805	———	L	306	None
Innis, Harry & Wife	Franklin	7–26–1813	Lot	P	209	Danville
Innis, Hugh	Franklin	6– 9–1803	60	H	249	None
Innis, Hugh	Franklin	1–26–1811	190¼	O	112	Elkhorn
Innis, Hugh & Wife	Franklin	12– 8–1804	300	H	439	Little N Elkhorn
Innis, Hugh & Wife	Franklin	7– 4–1805	300	J	259	Little N Elkhorn
Innis, Hugh & Wife	Franklin	5–31–1811	258⅔	O	116	N Fk Elkhorn
Innis, Hugh & Wife	Franklin	5–31–1811	190¼	O	118	None
Innis, Hugh & Wife	Franklin	5–31–1811	400	O	121	None
Innis, Hugh & Wife	Frankfort	2–––1814	60	U	486	M Elkhorn
Innis, Jas & Wife	Henrico	4–12–1797	4,000	B	281	Deer Cr
Innis, Robt Executor	Franklin	5–25–1825	60	Y	16	None
Instone, Jno	Frankfort	5–25–1802	50	F	440	S Fk Elkhorn
Instone, Jno	Frankfort	6– 1–1802	50	F	442	——— Cr
Instone, Jno	Frankfort	5– 1–1802	50	F	507	——— Cr
Instone, Jno	Frankfort	11– 1–1801	Lot	H	598	Frankfort
Instone, Jno	Frankfort	3– 6–1815	Slaves	Q	56	None
Instone, Jno & Wife	Frankfort	3–13–1805	Lot	H	599	Frankfort
Instone, Jno & Wife	Frankfort	7–11–1805	Mill	K	299	Fks Elkhorn
Ireland, Edward	Baltimore	2–21–1787	1,400	A	411	None
Irvin, Thos	Alexandria	11–25–1805	500	J	435	Buffaloe Cr
Irwin, Jno M C	Woodford	1–20–1818	Lots	S	185	Portland
Irwin, Saml	Frankfort	9– 8–1796	2,000	A-2	427	Beaver Cr
Irwins, Wm & Stephen	Fayette	1–20–1818	Lots	S	185	Portland
Isaacs, Isaiah	Richmond	10– 1–1794	5,000	H	326	M Licking

Grantor	Residence	Deed Date	Acres	Book	Page	Watercourse
Iselstine, Jno	Pauleshook	8–14–1798	10,000	C	307	N Fk Ky R
Jackson, Bolton & Wife	Baltimore	10– 5–1829	Lot	Y	498	Louisville
Jackson, Jno & Wife	Woodford	8– 2–1802	667	F	543	Cherry Fk Bush Cr
Jackson, Jno & Wife	Woodford	10–20–1802	689	F	544	Eagle Cr
Jackson, Wm	Franklin	2–12–1805	28,399	H	549	Ohio R, Licking & Big Benson Cr
James, Abraham	Mercer	11– 9–1786	265¾	A	184	Tilfords Sp Br
James, Geo	Culpepper	11–27–1792	1,250	A-2	311	Rolling Fk
James, Geo	Culpepper	11–27–1792	1,437½	A-2	313	Chaplins Fk
James, Geo	Virginia	6– 4–1792	400	B-2	499	Rolling Fk
James, Jno	Pulaski	12– 2–1800	1,237	E	186	Clear Fk Rough Cr
James, Wm & Wife	Matthews	9– 1–1796	1,000	N	246	Tennessee R
Jameson, Jno & Wife	Culpepper	2–12–1805	2,000	J	249	Big Mud Cr
January, Jas & Wife	Adams	8– 2–1802	355	G	10	Clear Cr
Jefferson, Thos	———	2–16–1787	5,277	A-2	596	Ohio R
Jeffries, Ambrose	Frankfort	9– 8–1803	Lot	H	99	Frankfort
Jeffries, Ambrose	Frankfort	6– 8–1805	Lot	J	173	Frankfort
Jeffries, Ambrose	Frankfort	6– 8–1805	Lot	J	176	Frankfort
Jenks, Joseph	Columbia	3–17–1798	13,833	D	29	None
Jennings, Daniel	Montgomery	10–12–1819	Lots	T	121	———
Jennings, Jonathan & Wife	———	11–27–1806	48	K	521	Ky R
Jerome, C G J	Paris, France	11–22–1819	1,840,000	V	468	Various water courses
Johnson, Andrew	Platt, Mo	4–23–1845	———	28	15	None
Johnson, Ann	Rockridge	8– 3–1802	1,000	H	3	Skinhouse Fk
Johnson, Benj	Orange	3–25–1793	4,500	F	54	Ohio R
Johnson, Benj	Scott	10– 1–1821	Lots	V	300	Georgetown
Johnson, Cane	Boone	11–13–1822	403	V	356	Ohio R
Johnson, Benj & Wife	Boone	12–17–1821	150	V	342	Woolper Cr
Johnson, Benj B	Franklin	5–30–1844	68	27	429	Benson Cr
Johnson, Cane	Boone	4–25–1811	1,570	N	509	M Fk Licking
Johnson, Cane	Boone	12–16–1814	202½	Q	249	Ohio & Salt R
Johnson, Cane	Boone	10–15–1816	441	R	40	Ohio R
Johnson, Cane	Boone	12——1821	1,702	V	339	Ohio R
Johnson, Cane & Wife	Boone	10–14–1811	110	O	201	Ohio R
Johnson, Chapman	Richmond	5– 1–1840	12,600	27	142	Rough Cr & N Fk Sandy R
Johnson, Chas	———	10–16–1819	4,333⅓	T	222	N Fk Tradewater & Highland Cr
Johnson, Edward P	Fayette	11–30–1839	Lots	27	90	Frankfort
Johnson, Edward P	Fayette	11–30–1839	Lots	27	90	Frankfort
Johnson, Edward P	Fayette	7–21–1840	Lot	27	144	Frankfort
Johnson, Edward P	Fayette	9–16–1844	Lot	27	432	Frankfort
Johnson, Edward P	Fayette	9–17–1844	Lot	27	433	Frankfort
Johnson, Edward P & Wife	Scott	12–25–1821	Lot	V	344	Georgetown
Johnson, Elizabeth	Annearundel	9– 6–1809	500	N	36	Big Barren R
Johnson, Geo	Kentucky	5–11–1802	8,000	F	463	——— Cr
Johnson, Henry	Scott	9–11–1820	Lots	U	59	Georgetown
Johnson, Jas	Scott	12–19–1821	2,852	V	235	Ohio R, Woolpher & Gunpowder Cr
Johnson, James & Wife	Franklin	11–12–1824	50	X	35	Big Benson Cr
Johnson, Jas C	Louisville	1– 8–1819	8,212½	S	419	Ohio R, Little Otter Cr & Br Ky R
Johnson, Jas C	Louisville	9–26–1821	1,891	V	358	Ohio R
Johnson, Jas C	Louisville	9–26–1821	Lots	V	358	Louisville
Johnson, Joel	Scott	2– 8–1820	300	U	520	Ohio R
Johnson, Jno & Joel	Scott	10–29–1816	224	R	65	Elkhorn
Johnson, Jno S	Scott	10–11–1824	5,000	X	61	Ohio R & Woolpers
Johnson, Jno T, Atty	Scott	1–18–1821	469	U	180	Bank Lick Cr
Johnson, Jno T & Wife	Scott	11–14–1821	300	V	230	Ohio R
Johnson, Jno T & Wife	Scott	10– 1–1821	150	V	348	S Elkhorn
Johnson, Jno T & Wife	Scott	10– 1–1821	Lots	V	348	Georgetown
Johnson, Jno & Zachariah Executors	———	7–28–1802	1,000	G	427	Cumberland R
Johnson, Richard	Woodford	2——1827	253	Y	270	6 Mile Cr
Johnson, Richard M	Scott	10– 1–1821	Lot	V	227	Georgetown
Johnson, Richard M	Scott	11– 8–1829	100	Y	407	Elkhorn
Johnson, Richard M	Scott	3–24–1833	1,310	Z	350	Ohio R
Johnson, Richard M & Jas	Scott	11–17–1821	450	V	309	None
Johnson, Robt	Fayette	6–22–1786	400	A	522	Middle Br Clear Cr
Johnson, Robt	Scott	8– 6–1801	———	E	400	Nolinn
Johnson, Robt	———	8–21–1800	Lot	F	2	Frankfort
Johnson, Robt	Scott	11–13–1802	3,000	G	65	Raven Cr
Johnson, Robt	Scott	10– 3–1802	260	G	161	Bank Lick Cr
Johnson, Robt	Scott	8–16–1803	1,000	H	245	Ohio R & Mount Bird
Johnson, Robt	Scott	7– 3–1805	580	J	339	Dry Cr
Johnson, Robt	Scott	7– 3–1805	600	J	341	Dry Cr

Grantor	Residence	Deed Date	Acres	Book	Page	Watercourse
Johnson, Robt	Scott	7- 3-1805	122	J	344	Dry Cr
Johnson, Robt	Scott	7- 3-1805	57	J	348	Dry Cr
Johnson, Robt	Scott	11-18-1806	500	K	512	Dry Cr
Johnson, Robt	Scott	11-17-1806	250	L	148	N Fk Big Barren R
Johnson, Robt	Scott	7- 5-1810	1,500	N	260	Woolperts Cr
Johnson, Robt	Scott	1- 2-1811	1,118	O	194	None
Johnson, Robt & Wife	Scott	6-26-1798	500	D	17	Lees Cr
Johnson, Robt & Wife	Scott	10- 1-1800	1,000	E	94	Cumberland R
Johnson, Robt & Wife	Scott	7-10-1802	600	G	163	Clear Cr
Johnson, Robt & Wife	Scott	5-11-1807	570	L	31	Flatt Cr
Johnson, Robt & Wife	———	11- 8-1808	14,724	M	240	Ohio R & Licking
Johnson, Robt & Wife	Scott	1-24-1810	360	N	109	Ohio R
Johnson, Robt & Wife	———	9-28-1810		———	271	None
Johnson, Robt, heirs	Scott	1-18-1821	469	U	180	Bank Lick Cr
Johnson, Robt, heirs	———	6——1818	285	U	522	Ohio R
Johnson, Robt, heirs	———	6——1818	285	U	522	Dry Fk Craigs Cr
Johnson, Robt, heirs	———	6——1818	285	U	522	Ohio R
Johnson, Robt, heirs	Scott	5——1822	2,000	V	297	Benson Cr
Johnson, Robt, Trustee	———	8-19-1803	500	H	449	Glenns Cr
Johnson, Robt, Trustee	Scott	2-16-1797	200	H	481	S Fk Elkhorn
Johnson, Robt, Trustee	Scott	8-19-1803	500	H	489	Glens Cr
Johnson, Robt, Trustee	———	3-17-1810	281	N	245	Utterbacks
Johnson, Robt, Trustee	———	6-15-1810	6,000	N	329	Little N Elkhorn & Stoney Fk
Johnson, Robt M	Scott	11- 3-1823	100	W	343	N Elkhorn
Johnson, Thos	Fayette	9-23-1786	248	A	283	S Fk Elkhorn
Johnson, Thos	Fayette	9-23-1786	172	A	285	S Fk Elkhorn
Johnson, Thos	Fayette	9-23-1786	90	A	287	S Fk Elkhorn
Johnson, Thos	Mercer	6-20-1787	800	A	327	Licking
Johnson, Thos	———	4-27-1790	500	B-2	214	Br S Fk Elkhorn
Johnson, Thos & Wife	Campbell	7-12-1802	Contract	G	47	
Johnson, Wm	Orange	7-26-1802		G	154	None
Johnson, Wm, heirs	Louisville	8-19-1815	1,000	Q	165	None
Johnson, Wm S, heirs	———	7-10-1843	Lot	27	358	Frankfort
Johnson & Craig, Trustees	Scott	2-14-1800	1,000	F	380	Ohio R
Johnson & Craig, Trustees	Scott	3-20-1802	500	F	381	None
Johnston, Benj Jr, Atty	Louisville	10-24-1812	Lots	W	381	Louisville
Johnston, Benj, heirs	St Louis	10-24-1812	Lots	W	381	Louisville
Johnston, Chas & Wife	Campbell	3-16-1809	5,500	M	369	Cypress Cr
Johnston, Chas & Wife	Campbell	3-16-1809	6,453¾	M	375	Muddy R & Highland Cr
Johnston, Chas & Wife	Campbell	3-16-1809	1,000	M	380	W Fk Sciota R
Johnston, Elizabeth	Ammeremdale	2- 2-1808	600	M	65	Big Barren R
Johnston, Gabriel J & Ben W	———	5-27-1824		———	293	None
Johnston, Geo Washington	Knox	6-17-1803	1,791⅔	W	385	Town Cr
Johnston, Robt	Scott	10-12-1801	1,000	M	229	Rough Run
Johnston, Robt & Wife	Franklin	1- 9-1796	3,528	F	415	Beech Fk
Johnston, Robt & Wife	Scott	1-15-1808	2,250	L	278	Big Bone Lick
Johnston, Wm	Tenant in common	1- 6-1775		D	272	Ohio & Green R
Johnston, Wm & Wife	Jefferson	3-27-1797	1,000	Q	163	Green R
Johnston, Wm Jr	Carolina	12- 5-1798	600	D	356	M Fk Licking
Johnston, Thos J	———	5-27-1824		———	293	None
Jones, Gabriel, heirs	Mercer	5- 6-1791	200	B-2	290	Br Wilson Cr
Jones, Hamberry & Wife	Franklin	3- 9-1818	100	S	73	None
Jones, Jno	Scott	5- 4-1807	450	L	18	Big Barren R
Jones, Jno	Jefferson	——1810	200	O	315	Little Barren R
Jones, Jno & Wife	Scott	9- 5-1808		M	156	Jones Big Sp
Jones, Jno & Wife	Scott	1-13-1813	450	P	90	Big Barren R
Jones, Joshua & Wife	Frederick	2-19-1808	300	M	83	Big Barren R
Jones, Joshua & Wife	Frederick	8-24-1809	500	N	44	Big Barren R
Jones, Kennon, heirs	———	6-23-1821		V	20	Ky R
Jones, Leonard	Union	6-12-1821	1,000	V	256	Cumberland R
Jones, Leonard	———	11-16-1829	6,500	Y	504	Fraziers Cr
Jones, Lowry	Shelby	1-12-1822		V	517	Drennons Lick Cr
Jones, Lowry	Shelby	5-29-1827	200	X	364	Ky R
Jones, Richard & Wife	Fayette	9- 5-1800	100	E	320	Ashes Cr
Jones, Robt E	Virginia	12- 7-1819	339	T	378	Eagle Cr
Jones, Robt K	———	6-15-1822	150	V	351	Eagle Cr
Jones, Robt K	———	10-21-1823	264	W	144	None
Jones, Robt K	———	10-21-1823	116	W	146	None
Jones, Robt K	———	10-21-1823	110	W	147	None
Jones, Robt K	———	10- 7-1823	64	W	198	None
Jones, Robt K	Virginia	11- 1-1827	241	X	309	Eagle Cr
Jones, Dr Samuel	Philadelphia	11-13-1809	37,827⅓	N	171	Ohio R
Jones, Stephen	Frederick	4- 5-1802	1,320	F	225	Otter Cr Muddy R
Jones, Stephen	Frederick	4- 5-1802	1,333⅓	F	227	Big Barren R

Grantor	Residence	Deed Date	Acres	Book	Page	Watercourse
Jones, Stephen	Frederick	4- 5-1802	1,000	F	229	Highland Cr
Jones, Thos	——	5- 8-1817	6,000	T	82	Richland Cr
Jones, Walter Jr	Alexandria	7-26-1800	3,000	E	153	Rolling Fk
Jones, William	Bourbon	10-25-1795	6,000	A-2	127	Bank Lick Cr
Jones, Wm	Warren	12- 9-1801	544	F	454	Big Barren R
Jones, Wm	Warren	12- 9-1801	400	F	457	Big Barren R
Jones, Wm	Warren	12- 9-1801	450	F	458	Big Barren R
Jones, Wm	Bourbon	12-23-1812	450	P	88	Big Barren R
Jones, Wm, heirs	Garrard	11——1821	100	V	107	Greasy Cr
Jordan, Jno Jr	Lexington	9-13-1806	32,500	L	53	Ky R & Bank Lick
Jordan, Jno Jr	Fayette	12- 7-1808	8,571	M	256	Ky R
Jordan, Jno Jr	Lexington	7-16-1808	7,870	M	263	Elkhorn
Jordan, Jno Jr	Lexington	10- 5-1808	44,172	M	345	Halls Cr
Jordan, Jno Jr & Wife	Fayette	10- 4-1805	116	J	315	N Fk Elkhorn
Jordan, Jno Jr & Wife	Fayette	2-16-1807	Lot	L	129	Louisville
Jordan, Jno Jr & Wife	Lexington	1- 2-1800	9,728	M	184	E Fk Lewis Cr
Jouit, Jno	Kentucky	1-26-1802	4,875	F	363	Rd to Ohio Falls
Joyes, Patrick	Louisville	5-12-1796	123	A-2	281	Island Ohio R
Joyes, Patrick	——	11-17-1796	30	A-2	562	None
Joyes, Patrick	Jefferson	3-20-1790	½	B-2	136	Louisville
Joyes, Patrick, heirs	——	10-28-1842	192	27	322	Leestown Bottom
Kates, Jno & Wife	Philadelphia	11-18-1809	13,571½	S	201	N Fk Ky R
Keen, Oliver & Wife	Fayette	3-19-1845	——	28	3	None
Keene, Ellen & H E & Jas B & Lenox R	——	3-31-1842	1,100	27	334	None
Keene, Jno & Wife	London	12-23-1815	1,000	R	34	N Elkhorn
Keighler, Wm H & Wife	Baltimore	9-26-1845	2,500	28	35	Elkhorn & Cedar Cr
Keihn, Peter	Philadelphia	3-12-1806	20,313½	K	537	Green R
Keller, Abraham	Bourbon	5- 4-1812	1,900	O	372	Little Barren R
Kelley, Edward & Mary Ann	Loudown	6-20-1830	100	Y	488	None
Kelly, Edward & Mary Ann	Loudown	6-20-1830	200	Y	489	None
Kelley, Joseph, heirs	London	11-25-1816	200	R	356	Eagle & Little Sugar Cr
Kelley, Mary A & Edw	London	3-13-1830	80	Y	450	Gallatin Co
Kemp, Hannah	Richmond	4-21-1826	666⅔	Y	169	Tennessee R & Consols Cr
Kemp, Peter, heirs	Richmond	4-21-1826	666⅔	Y	169	Tennessee R & Consols Cr
Kemper, Nathan M	Gallatin	9-23-1840	——	27	177	None
Kemper, Thos J & Wife	Harrison	12- 1-1819	1,000	T	231	Muddy R
Kendall, Amos & Wife	——	7-12-1834	50	Z	448	Elkhorn
Kennady, Archibald	Green	2- 9-1796	4½	A-2	105	Clover Lick Cr
Kennady, James	Campbell	11-18-1800	4,600	E	237	None
Kennady, James	Campbell	11-13-1802	496½	G	36	M Fk Licking
Kennady, Thos & Wife	Campbell	1-10-1809	——	M	293	Ohio R
Kennady, Wm	Campbell	11-13-1802	496½	G	36	M Fk Licking
Kenner, Rodman	Virginia	9-30-1815	666⅔	Q	196	Rough Cr
Kent, Jas	New York	2-19-1796	100,000	A-2	188	N & M Fk Ky R
Kent, James	New York	2-18-1796	100,000	A-2	192	N & M Fk Ky R
Kenton, Simon	——	6-19-1806	1,275	K	336	None
Kenton, Simon & Wife	Champaign	11- 7-1807	1,400	L	206	Tygerts Cr
Kenton, Simon Jr	Frankfort	12-12-1806	3,040	K	510	None
Kerchival, Jno	——	11-21-1805	99	K	1	Bays Cr
Kerchival, Jno & Wife	Mason	7-22-1799	1,250	D	240	Otter Cr
Kerchival, Jno & Wife	Frederick	12- 5-1795	1,250	D	233	Otter Cr
Kerr, David	Scott	5-30-1815	333⅓	Q	59	Big Barren R
Keywood, Stephen	Tennessee	1-29-1803	5,500	G	413	Powell R
Kiger, Geo W & Wife	——	10-29-1810	3,400	O	33	Little Sandy
Kiger, Geo & Wife	Kentucky	8-12-1816	——	R	161	None
Kincaid, James	Madison	3-11-1796	25,291½	A-2	151	None
Kincaid, Jos	Madison	4- 6-1801	6,170½	Q	348	Sinking Valley & Cumberland R
Kincannon, Andrew	N Carolina	12-26-1829	——	Y	440	Elkhorn
Kincannon, Andrew	N Carolina	12-26-1829	——	Y	461	Elkhorn
Kincannon, Andrew, heirs	North Carolina	1-12-1834	106	Z	490	Elkhorn
Kincheloe, Lewis W	Nelson	8-24-1844	400¼	27	427	Chaplins & Salt R
Kinney, Geo W, Atty	Shelby	12- 1-1820	228¾	U	391	Rough Cr
Kinney, Geo W, Atty	Shelby	11- 1-1820	302	U	431	Drennons Lick Cr
Kinney, Jacob	Staunton	11-12-1801	——	O	232	None
Kinney, Jno	Morris	8-16-1805	16	K	254	Drennons Lick
Kinney, Jno	Morris	12- 1-1820	228¾	U	391	Rough Cr
Kinney, Jno	Morris	11- 1-1820	302	U	431	Drennons Lick Cr
Kinney, Jno, Atty	Morris N J	8-16-1805	237½	K	251	Drennons Lick
Kinney, Jno, Atty	Morris	8-16-1805	262	K	256	Drennons Lick
Kirkham, Henry	Champaign	12-14-1810	——	N	380	Sinks of Beaver Cr
Kirkham, Saml	Fayette	9- 6-1788	——	A	437	White Oak Cr
Knapp, David	Sheffield	4-19-1808	Washing machine	L	376	None

Grantor	Residence	Deed Date	Acres	Book	Page	Watercourse
Knight, Jno	Fayette	11–29–1788	Contract	A	478	———
Knox, Hugh	Henderson	11–30–1805	1,000	K	151	Highland Cr
Knox, Hugh	Union	3– 8–1816	———	Q	376	None
Kobler, Jno & Wife	Madison	10– 6–1812	———	R	222	None
Kuhl, Henry & Wife	Philadelphia	10–29–1813	———	P	288	None
Lacassagne, Michael	Jefferson	7–30–1797	2,000	P	520	Big Ben & Green R
Lafon, Nicholas	Franklin	8–26–1796	1,000	A-2	429	Russell Cr
Lafon, Nicholas & Wife	Scott	3– 7–1803	Lot	G	210	Frankfort
Lake, Saml	Kentucky	—— 9–1840	———	27	107	In New Orleans
Lamox, Mary	Essex	6– 2–1796	1,000	E	322	Cabin Cr
Lambert, Wm & Wife	———	3– 4–1833	———	Z	309	None
Lane, Hordage	Montgomery	11–23–1799	156	F	4	Mill Rd
Lane, Jas B	London	12–23–1815	1,000	R	34	N Elkhorn
Lane, Mildred T	Clark	12–21–1838	894	27	4	In Daviess Co
Lane, Mildred T	Clark	7–19–1840	895	27	161	Blackfords & Panther Cr
Lane, Saml	Washington	2–27–1819	32⅔	U	195	N Elkhorn
Lane, Wm N	Clark	3–23–1818	Lots	S	191	Winchester
Lane, Wm N	Clark	7–18–1820	4,000	T	477	Floyds Fk
Langford, Stephen	Lincoln	5–31–1791	200	B-2	284	Little Clifty Cr
Langham, Elias, Atty	Chillicothe	3–20–1803	2,000	G	353	Lost Cr
Langhead, David & Wife	Fayette	10– 9–1804	300	P	407	Ky R
Langhead, David & Wife	Fayette	10– 9–1804	500	P	408	Ky R
Larowe, Isaac	London	12–12–1796	1,000	B	261	——— Cr
Larue, Isaac	Hardin	6– 4–1803	200	K	29	Ky R
Larue, Isaac & Wife	———	2–20–1801	9	E	307	Dix R
Larue, Isaac & Wife	———	2–20–1801	18	E	309	Ky R
Larue, Isaac, heirs	———	5–26–1806	6,348	M	193	Ky R & Big Benson
Larue, Isaac Sr	Hardin	2–23–1809	2,100	M	317	Ohio R
Larue, Jacob, Atty	Hardin	5– 7–1801	———	E	328	Benson Cr
Larue, Jacob & Wife	Hardin	8– 6–1800	700	E	423	Fern Cr
Larue, Jacob & Peter	Hardin	2–23–1809	2,100	M	317	Ohio R
Larue, Jahez	Hardin	7– 4–1809	1,000	N	282	Benson Cr
Larue, Jno, heirs	———	5–26–1806	6,348	M	193	Ky R & Big Benson
Larue, Jno, heirs	Hardin	8– 9–1808	6,250	M	323	Cedar Cr
Latham, Robt	Culpepper	4– 4–1804	600	H	251	None
Lawson, Thos & Wife	Norfolk	3–10–1807	415	L	95	Salt R
Lawrence, David	———	8–16–1841	66⅔	27	222	Shelby Co
Lawrence, M Elizabeth	———	2– 4–1841	1,000	27	197	Tennessee R
Lawrence, James	Mercer	9–25–1788	½	A	467	None
Lawrence, Jas & Wife	Mercer	1–13–1791	Lot	B-2	254	Danville
Lawrence, Jno B	New York	10–17–1842	———	27	343	N Fk Ky R
Lawrence, Nathaniel	New York	5–31–1799	260,178	R	232	Ohio R
Lawrence, Saml	Mercer	11– 9–1787	200	A	334	Br Rowling Fk
Lay, George & Wife	———	10–11–1823	1,000	W	263	Poages Cr
Lea, Zachas, Atty	———	3–15–1828	277	X	393	None
Leavy, Jno	Clark	7–25–1818	Lot	S	362	Port Williams
Lee, Chas & Wife	Alexandria	1– 3–1804	———	H	512	None
Lee, Daniel	Frederick	10– 4–1810	1,250	O	10	Ohio R
Lee, Daniel	Frederick	3–10–1829	981	Y	346	Ohio R & Otter Cr
Lee, Francis L	Alexandria	7–23–1804	———	H	504	None
Lee, Francis L	Virginia	6–23–1810	———	N	488	None
Lee, Henry	Westmoreland	——1795	3,000	A-2	160	Rough Cr
Lee, Henry	Virginia	5– 7–1795	———	A-2	346	None
Lee, Henry	Mason	9–14–1791	8,000	B-2	424	Cedar Cr
Lee, Henry	Westmoreland	11– 5–1798	5,000	D	484	Rough Cr
Lee, Henry	———	7–10–1806	500	K	419	Cedar Cr
Lee, Henry	Mason	1–10–1835	———	Z	505	Cedar Cr
Lee, Henry, Atty	Virginia	5– 5–1795	———	A-2	347	None
Lee, Henry, Atty	Virginia	5– 5–1795	———	A-2	349	None
Lee, Henry, Atty	———	11–19–1810	3,400	N	477	Green R, M Licking
Lee, Henry, Executor	Westmoreland	12–23–1790	1,200	A-2	379	None
Lee, Henry & Wife	Stratford	1– 1–1806	4,675	L	267	Big Barren & Gasper R
Lee, Jno, Atty	———	9–24–1796	600	A-2	608	Bank Lick Cr
Lee, Jno, Atty	Woodford	8–26–1800	9,800	F	352	Eagle Cr & Red R
Lee, Jno & Wife	Woodford	8–26–1800	9,800	F	352	Eagle Cr & Red R
Lee, Mary	Woodford	7– 5–1831	14	Z	97	Glenn Willis Place
Lee, Mary	Franklin	5–17–1833	384	Z	290	Salt R
Lee, Wm P & Wife	Jefferson	4–10–1819	1,000	S	512	Green R
Lee, Wm A, Comr	———	1–17–1814	5,000	P	325	Ohio R
Lee, Willis A	Franklin	8–31–1804	885	J	64	Ky R
Lee, Willis & Wife	Franklin	4– 8–1800	984	E	70	Salt R
Leeper, Hugh	Tennessee	2–17–1818	300	S	302	Licking
Leigh, Benj W	———	5– 8–1817	6,000	T	10	Richland Cr
Lemmon, Robt	Somerset	4–18–1812	———	P	8	None
Letcher, Benj & Wife	Garrard	7–14–1816	1,400	R	333	——— R
Letcher, Stephen G	Mercer	11– 1–1799	400	E	381	Hardins Cr
Levy, Aaron	Philadelphia	1–28–1799	2,500	D	264	None

Grantor	Residence	Deed Date	Acres	Book	Page	Watercourse
Lewis, Andrew & Wife & Wm & Wife	Botetourt	9-16-1808	1,000	M	187	Elkhorn
Lewis, Ann, heirs	———	5-10-1815	346	Q	173	Eagle Cr
Lewis, Ann, heirs	———	5-10-1815	160	Q	175	Eagle Cr
Lewis, Ann, heirs	———	11-30-1815	890	Q	288	Beech & Black Fks
Lewis, Ann, heirs	———	5-23-1818	1,000	S	143	Hardins Cr
Lewis, Ann, heirs	———	8-15-1818	1,500	S	209	Ohio R
Lewis, Ann, heirs	———	8-25-1818	15,347	S	219	Green R & Rough Cr
Lewis, Ann, heirs	———	8- 6-1818	230	S	235	Ohio R
Lewis, Ann, heirs	———	10-25-1818	100	S	267	None
Lewis, Ann, heirs	———	6-23-1821	———	V	20	Ky R
Lewis, Amzi	Winchester	9-24-1819	1,500	T	404	Eagle Cr
Lewis, Chas	Goochland	7- 4-1798	640	D	101	None
Lewis, Gabriel	Fayette	5-10-1802	1,000	F	401	Poages Cr
Lewis, Gabriel	Fayette	7- 7-1802	2,500	F	429	Ky R
Lewis, Gabriel, Atty	———	3- 3-1800	1,000	E	301	Floyds Fk
Lewis, Gabriel, Atty	Kentucky	7- 7-1801	21,645	E	408	Ohio & Green R
Lewis, Geo	Mason	3- 9-1796	43,058¾	A-2	355	Big Sandy
Lewis, George	Jefferson	8-12-1797	6,000	E	42	Rolling Fk
Lewis, Geo	King George	3-13-1804	1,000	H	183	Caseys Cr
Lewis, Geo	Virginia	5-15-1819	200	S	548	Ky R
Lewis, Geo	Virginia	11-25-1820	600	U	173	Eagle Cr
Lewis, Geo & Wife	Spottsylvania	4- 9-1796	1,000	A-2	662	Deer Cr
Lewis, Geo & Wife	Spottsylvania	4- 9-1796	2,000	A-2	666	Deer Cr
Lewis, Geo & Wife	Fredericksburg	10-12-1797	4,000	C	228	Fk Deer Cr
Lewis, Geo & Wife	Fredericksburg	10- 5-1796	———	C	236	Deer Cr
Lewis, Howell	Culpepper	4——1804	1,000	H	181	Panther Cr
Lewis, Jno	Spottsylvania	10- 1-1795	36,000	A-2	290	Richland Cr
Lewis, Jno	Spottsylvania	10- 1-1795	9,302	A-2	293	Lynn Camp & Robertson Crs
Lewis, Jno	Spottsylvania	10- 1-1795	10,240	A-2	297	Richland Cr & Laurel R
Lewis, Jno	Fredericksburg	5-17-1796	———	A-2	400	Floyds Fk, Rockcastle, N Fk Elkhorn, Millers, Licking & Hardins Crs
Lewis, Jno	Fredericksburg	2-13-1800	2,500	E	269	Ky R
Lewis, Jno	Fredericksburg	3- 3-1800	1,000	E	301	Floyds Fk
Lewis, Jno	Fredericksburg	1-13-1802	28,000	F	408	Green R
Lewis, Jno	Fredericksburg	12-26-1808	1,500	M	329	Highland Cr
Lewis, Jno	Franklin	1- 3-1846	¼	28	44	Buck Run
Lewis, Jno, Atty	Breckinridge	11-25-1802	2,000	G	67	Cedar Cr
Lewis, Jno, Atty	———	5- 7-1808	3,500	L	380	Sinking Cr
Lewis, Jno & Wife	Fredericksburg	5-17-1796	———	D	102	Floyds Fk, Sandy R, Rockcastle, Elkhorn, Millers Cr & Green R
Lewis, Joseph & Wife	Bardstown	5-22-1817	600	R	580	Greensburg Rd
Lewis, Joseph & Wife	Nelson	4- 1-1795	6,365	W	390	Br Indian Camp Cr
Lewis, Joseph & Wife	Nelson	4- 1-1795	600	W	392	Buffaloe Cr
Lewis, Joseph & Wife	Nelson	4——1795	3,000	W	394	Bear Cr
Lewis, Joseph & Wife	Nelson	4- 1-1795	2,500	W	395	Rough Cr
Lewis, Josiah	Lackawanna	10-30-1846	———	28	131	In Ky
Lewis, Josiah & Wife	———	9-13-1828	136	X	462	Hinkston Fk
Lewis, Josiah & Francis	———	11- 7-1827	201¼	X	317	None
Lewis, Nicholas	Fayette	1- 6-1797	500	C	39	Pottingers Cr
Lewis, Nicholas	Jessamine	9-12-1799	563	D	506	Sandy Cr
Lewis, Nicholas	Jessamine	9-12-1799	720	D	513	Sandy Cr
Lewis, Nicholas	Jessamine	9-12-1799	500	D	514	Reeds Cr
Lewis, Nicholas	Fayette	12- 5-1796	1,000	G	143	Salt R
Lewis, Nicholas	Fayette	1- 6-1797	500	H	561	Pottingers Cr
Lewis, Nicholas & Wife	Mercer	3-25-1791	Lot	B-2	261	Danville
Lewis, Nicholas & Wife	Mercer	3-13-1792	100	B-2	468	None
Lewis, Nicholas & Wife	Jessamine	4- 9-1800	2,000	E	3	Buck Cr
Lewis, Saml & Wife	Woodford	7- 9-1821	3	U	518	None
Lewis, Stephen D	Clark	11-10-1831	8,847½	Z	198	Bank Lick Cr
Lewis, Thos	Dinwiddie	11- 4-1806	2,000	K	494	Ohio R
Lewis, Thos	Petersburg	4- 3-1811	7,666½	N	462	Ohio & Little Ky
Lewis, Thos	Petersburg	4- 3-1811	3,833¼	N	465	Ohio & Little Ky
Lewis, Thos	Petersburg	4- 2-1811	1,630	O	208	Hogback Grove
Lewis, Thos & Wife	Chesterfield	8-25-1797	———	C	95	None
Lewis, Thos & Wife	———	1-10-1798	4,354	D	61	Ohio R
Lewis, Thos & Wife	Chesterfield	5-27-1799	8,750	D	156	Salt R
Lewis, Thos & Wife	Chesterfield	1-15-1799	400	D	301	Rolling Fk
Lewis, Thos & Wife	Chesterfield	11- 6-1799	1,500	D	421	Ohio R
Lewis, Thos & Wife	Chesterfield	11-20-1800	500	E	168	Ohio R & Crooked Cr
Lewis, Thos & Wife	———	11- 4-1800	400	E	227	——— Br
Lewis, Thos & Wife	Chesterfield	11-25-1801	918	F	131	Otter Cr & Ky R
Lewis, Thos & Wife	Chesterfield	9-15-1802	500	F	480	Foxes Cr
Lewis, Thos & Wife	Chesterfield	11-25-1802	2,000	G	67	Cedar Cr

Grantor	Residence	Deed Date	Acres	Book	Page	Watercourse
Lewis, Thos & Wife	Chesterfield	11–23–1803	1,126	H	47	Limestone Cr
Lewis, Thos & Wife	Virginia	11–19–1803	400	H	50	Cane & S Fk Elkhorn
Lewis, Thos & Wife	Chesterfield	12–10–1805	200	J	432	Rd to Long Lick
Lewis, Thos & Wife	Chesterfield	12–10–1805	200	J	461	Salt Lick Cr
Lewis, Thos & Wife	Virginia	1–28–1803	11,250	K	89	Hingston Fk
Lewis, Thos & Wife	Virginia	10–23–1807	500	L	204	Hardins Cr
Lewis, Thos & Wife	Virginia	5– 6–1808	1,000	M	16	Br Big Benson Cr
Lewis, Thos & Wife	Chesterfield	9–30–1808	41½	M	221	Salt Lick Cr
Lewis, Thos & Wife	Petersburg	5–18–1809	72	M	395	None
Lewis, Thos & Wife	Chesterfield	12–16–1809	2,174⅓	N	256	Ohio R
Lewis, Wm	Philadelphia	5–19–1819	2,000	T	102	None
Lewis, Wm & Wife	Baltimore	1– 3–1809	1,000	N	16	None
Lewis, Wm, heirs	———	11– 7–1827	201¼	X	317	None
Lewis, Wm, heirs	———	9–13–1828	136	X	462	Hinkston Fk
Lexington & Ohio R R	Kentucky	2–25–1833	Railroad	Z	261	None
Lexington & Ohio R R	Kentucky	6– 2–1842	———	27	288	None
Lipscomb, Bernard & Wife	King William	3– 1–1797	4,000	C	214	Deer Cr
Lipscomb, Bernard & Wife	King William	5–10–1800	4,000	E	395	Deer Cr
Lipscomb, Bernard & Wife	King William	5– 9–1803	1,000	G	411	Pitmans Cr
Lipscomb, Hudson P & Jas	Campbell	7–27–1821	3,000	V	76	Skeggs Cr
Lipscomb, Jno P & Wife	Green, Ala	7– 3–1834	2,000	Z	500	S Fk Skeggs Cr
Lipscomb, Yancey & Wife	King William	3———1812	2,419½	O	493	Tennesse R
Lipscomb, Yancy & Wife	King William	10– 2–1812	1,000	P	200	Cumberland R
Lipscomb, Yancy, heirs	Campbell	7–27–1821	3,000	V	76	Skeggs Cr
List, Geo	———	5–27–1807	175	L	59	Dix R
Lithgow, Alexander	Prince William	7–17–1802	800	J	11	None
Little, Thos	Mercer	11– 2–1812	200	P	27	Armstrongs Br
Little, Wm	Louisville	1–23–1816	Lot	Q	435	Louisville
Little, Wm & Wife	Cincinnati	1– 1–1818	Lot	S	303	Louisville
Little, Wm, Guardian	Louisville	11–21–1814	900	P	560	Dry Fk Big Eddy
Littlepage, Jno C	Hanover	9– 9–1806	5,830	L	150	M Fk Licking & Glade Cr
Littlepage, Jno C	Hanover	11– 2–1808	1,000	M	247	Ohio R
Lloyd, Morris	Augusta	3–24–1809	734	M	384	Crocus Cr
Lloyd, Morris	Staunton	1–19–1819	666⅔	T	300	None
Lockhart, Triplett & Wife	Owen	1–19–1822	150	V	224	Eagle Cr
Loftus, Geo	Christian	4–11–1824	———	W	254	Big Barren R
Loftus, Geo	Christian	9– 4–1824	900	W	503	Tradewater
Loftus, Geo	Christian	9– 4–1824	2,500	W	506	Deer Cr & Tradewater
Logan, Benj	Lincoln	11–17–1791	230	B-2	509	Clarks Run
Logan, Benj	Shelby	11–12–1802	400	G	29	Green R
Logan, Jno	Franklin	7–30–1796	400	A-2	373	Green R
Logan, Jno & Wife	Franklin	4–15–1802	167	F	238	Logans Cr
Logan, Nathaniel	Lincoln	6– 2–1787	250	A	312	None
Logan, Nathaniel	Lincoln	———1787	250	A	321	None
Logan, Wm, Atty	———	2–17–1818	300	S	302	Licking
Logan, Wm, Executor	———	10–25–1819	513	T	217	None
Logwood, Wm	Chesterfield	7–20–1798	759	D	112	None
Long, Anderson & Wife	Warren	9– 6–1808	———	M	154	Longs Big Sp
Long, Jno Jr	Woodford	9–11–1809	Lot	N	393	Frankfort
Long, Joseph	Paulsbrook	8–14–1798	10,000	C	307	N Fk Ky R
Long, Nimrod	Culpepper	5–25–1799	1,000	D	164	None
Long, Nimrod	Franklin	9– 2–1816	Slaves	R	45	None
Long, Nimrod & Wife	Culpepper	3–21–1801	500	E	367	N E Fk Clover Cr
Long, Wm B & Wife	Woodford	7– 6–1815	20	Q	178	Glenns Cr
Long, Zachariah B	Woodford	5– 9–1818	———	Y	195	None
Loofbowrow, Thos V	Frankfort	10–16–1819	Lots	T	141	Frankfort
Louis, Wm B & Wife	Louisa	12–13–1824	3,000	V	148	Poages, N Fk Trade-water & Goose Cr
Love, Chas J	Fairfax	3–17–1806	4,110⅔	K	347	Lynn Camp & Wolf Crs
Love, Geo, Atty	———	11–12–1818	1,000	S	323	Brashears Cr
Love, James	Frankfort	6–16–1808	Negro	M	308	None
Love, James	Knox	4–19–1809	9,700	N	285	Big Laurel R
Love, Jas	Hardin	4–26–1803	2,000	V	239	Rough Cr
Love, Jas & Wife	Kentucky	5– 7–1808	———	P	12	None
Love, Jno & Wife	Woodford	6– 9–1791	717	B-2	327	Hingston Fk
Love, Thomas	Franklin	11–10–1803	4,000	H	27	Green R
Love, Wm	Shelbyville	12–27–1819	4,500	V	52	Skeggs Cr & Ky R
Love, Wm, Com'r	Nelson	9–21–1825	1,512	Y	258	Rock Lick, Island Ohio R & Indian Camp Cr

Grantor	Residence	Deed Date	Acres	Book	Page	Watercourse
Love, Wm, Com'r	Nelson	9–21–1825	2,268	Y	261	Little Reedy, Rocklick & Indian Camp Cr
Lowe, Jas R M & Wife	Prince George	2–17–1831	——	Z	110	None
Lowe, Lloyd Mc C	Prince George	2–17–1831	——	Z	112	None
Luggett, David & Wife	Scott	7–20–1841	——	27	220	None
Luke, Eliza G	Fairfax	1–11–1812	875	O	386	None
Lumpkins, Philip	Georgia	9–20–1813	500	P	430	N Fk Licking
Luthell, J	Tennant in common	1– 6–1775	——	D	272	Ohio & Green R
Lynch, Chas	Shelby	6–12–1798	1,000	C	251	Br Cumberland R
Lynch, Chas	Shelby	6–12–1798	500	C	253	Little Barren R
Lynch, Chas	Shelby	7–10–1798	1,500	C	263	N Fk Tradewater
Lynch, Chas	Shelby	7–10–1798	1,000	C	265	N Fk Tradewater
Lynch, Chas	Shelby	7–21–1801	7,750	E	389	None
Lynch, Chas	Shelby	4–23–1804	8,098	H	225	None
Lynch, Chas	Shelby	2–27–1804	1,260	H	239	None
Lynch, Chas	Kentucky	10–20–1799	1,000	K	78	Sandy
Lynch, Chas	——	3– 6–1806	2,000	K	226	N & S Fk Elkhorn
Lynch, Chas	Shelby	8–20–1817	11,000	S	60	Bullskin Cr
Lynch, Chas & Wife	Shelby	11–22–1805	55	K	132	Fk of Elkhorn
Lyne, Edmund	Bourbon	9–22–1787	940	A	342	Br Harrods Cr
Lyne, Edmund	Bourbon	9–22–1787	400	A	344	Paint Lick
Lyne, Edmund	Bourbon	9–22–1787	230	A	346	None
Lyne, Edmund	Bourbon	9–22–1787	660	A	348	Rolling Fk
Lyon, Thomas	Philadelphia	6–26–1784	15,000	G	213	None
McAlister, James	Franklin	9–18–1798	750	D	1	Salt R
McAlister, James	Franklin	9–18–1798	1,000	D	2	Salt R
McAlister, Jas	Franklin	9–18–1798	1,000	D	4	Salt R
McAlister, James	Franklin	9–18–1798	1,000	D	5	Salt R
McAllister, Jno	Lincoln	7–27–1815	666⅔	Q	154	Glens Cr
McAnuelly, Jno	Lincoln	7–19–1804	300	K	329	Russell Cr
McBride, Lapsley & Wife	Franklin	7–13–1811	1,140	O	96	Paint Lick & Silver Cr
McBride, Wm & Wife	Franklin	10– 9–1800	200	E	151	Harrods Run
McBride, Wm & Wife	Mercer	7–10–1811	479	O	94	Cumberland R
McCalla, Wm & Wife	Philadelphia	1–30–1828	Lots	X	478	Greensburg
McCalla, Andrew	Mercer	9–28–1786	Lot	A	241	None
McCalla, Andrew	Lexington	2– 5–1820	Lot	T	237	Danville
McCalla, Jno M	U S Marshall	10–19–1830	210	32	102	Boones & —— R
McCalla, Jno M	Revenue collector	5– 2–1832	456	Z	211	Green R
McCalla, Jno M	U S Marshall	2–26–1839	Lots	27	14	Frankfort
McCalla, Jno M	Tax collector	9–26–1839	3,400	27	82	Eagle Cr
McCalla, Jno M	Tax collector	8–23–1839	89,000	27	88	Red R & Licking
McCallmont, Geo	Philadelphia	10– 5–1801	——	O	228	Ohio R
McCalmont, Geo	Philadelphia	2–12–1802	——	P	605	None
McCampbell, Jno	Franklin	9–25–1804	100	H	502	Bensons Cr
McCampbell, Jno	Knox	10– 6–1829	100	Z	179	Big Benson Cr
McCaw, Jas Drew&Wife	Richmond	3– 1–1830	——	Z	13	None
McCaw, Sarah Harris	Richmond	3– 1–1830	——	Z	13	None
McClarty, Jno	Kentucky	6–25–1844	300	28	41	Breckinridge Co
McClelland, Alexander	Alleghany	11–28–1811	600	O	327	Ohio R
McClelland, Alexander	Alleghany	11–28–1811	418	O	329	Ohio R
McClelland, David	Nelson	10–23–1805	630	J	311	Paint Lick
McClenahan, Robt	Chester	1– 1–1798	4,000	C	284	Salt R
McClenahan, Robt & Wife	Augusta	5–31–1808	5,250	N	67	Little Bullskin Cr
McClung, Jno A & Alexander	Mason	10–20–1833	6,747	Z	361	Eagle, Muddy & Longfall Crs
McConel, Niel	——	8–25–1803	1,000	H	353	Ohio R
McConn, Jno	Mercer	3–29–1814	760	P	387	Salt R
McConnell, Jas, heirs	Fayette	2–10–1801	1,500	G	90	Fk Elkhorn, Ky R & Lawrence Cr
McConnico, Christopher	Petersburg	3–30–1795	——	N	446	None
McCorkle, James	Montgomery	2–27–1784	1,000	B	226	Ohio R
McCormack, Wm	Kentucky	8–12–1816	——	R	161	None
McCoskey, Jno	Franklin	11–28–1812	200	P	28	Armstrongs Br
McCracken, Seneca, heirs	Franklin	11– 8–1831	87½	Z	256	Elkhorn
McCracken, Virgil & Ovid & Cyrus	Woodford	8–16–1806	——	K	380	Cylas Cr
McCraw, Saml	Richmond	8–18–1797	7,100	B	318	Ohio R
McCraw, Saml	Richmond	8– 4–1810	8,000	N	289	Laurel R
McCreery, Wm	Baltimore	6–10–1801	4,566⅔	F	109	Ohio & Cumberland Rs
McCuddy, Isaac B & Wife	Woodford	9–22–1829	10½	Y	403	S Elkhorn
McCuddy, Isaac B & Wife	Woodford	10– 2–1829	10½	Y	404	S Elkhorn
McDonald, Aaron	Madison	12–12–1819	97	T	266	Big Br
McDonald, Angus & Wife	Winchester	8–28–1806	962	L	82	Yellow Banks of Ohio R

Grantor	Residence	Deed Date	Acres	Book	Page	Watercourse
McDonald, Daniel & Wife	Culpepper	12–18–1795	1,000	E	278	Ohio R
McDonald, James	Freerick	6– 6–1817	500	S	1	Crocus Cr
McDonald, Jas	Fredderick	1–18–1820	12,616	X	394	Rough, Panther, Otter Cr & Salt R
McDonald, Jas & Wife	Fredericks	3–29–1798	1,000	D	402	Chaplins Fk
McDonald, Jas & Wife	Fredericks	3–29–1798	1,000	D	405	Bayse Cr
McDowell, Debrah	Frankfort	9–26–1819	——	T	133	None
McDowell, Geo & Wife	Owen	4– 7–1831	50	Z	114	Cedar Cr
McDowell, James	Rockbridge	10– 3–1791	500	B-2	426	Houstons Fk
McDowell, Saml & Wife	Warren	11–23–1819	630	T	178	Muddy Cr
McDowell, Saml & Wife	Warren	11–22–1819	290	T	207	Shawnee Run
McFawl, Joseph	Lincoln	6– 7–1785	300	A	18	Little Cove
McGee, Jno, heirs	Mercer	3–29–1814	360	P	385	Salt R
McGehee, Saml	Fayette	5–18–1789	350	B-2	69	Guesses Fk
McGehee, Saml	——	11–25–1803	——	H	57	None
McGougal, Jas	Staunton	1–19–1819	666⅔	T	300	None
McGowen, Chas & Wife	——	1–31–1815	——	P	609	None
McGuire, Wm & Wife	Frederick	10–14–1806	——	L	106	Ohio R
McIntire, Jacob	Bath	10–14–1829	2,000	Y	447	Bourbon Co
McIver, Jno	Rutherford	8–13–1842	21,288	27	329	Hardin & Grayson Co
McIver, Jno, Atty	——	11–25–1805	500	J	435	Buffaloe Cr
McIver, Jno, Atty	Alexandria	12–17–1805	5,000	J	466	Cumberland Cr
McIver, Jno, Atty	——	6– 8–1812	11,000	O	403	Kennekanic Cr
McIver, Jno, heirs	Washington	8–13–1842	21,288	27	329	Hardin & Grayson Co
McKee, Saml & Wife	Garrard	7–14–1816	1,400	R	333	—— R
McKee, Wm	Lincoln	12–17–1796	500	A-2	674	Ky R
McKee, Wm	Fayette	6–17–1845	Lot	28	13	Midway
McKee, Wm R	Fayette	6–11–1845	Lots	28	2	Midway
McKee, Wm R	Fayette	6–11–1845	Lot	28	11	Midway
McKee, Wm R	Fayette	6–11–1845	Lot	28	11	Midway
McKee, Wm R	Fayette	6–11–1845	Lot	28	12	Midway
McKee, Wm R	Fayette	1–12–1846	Lot	28	49	Midway
McKee, Wm R	Fayette	1–12–1846	Lot	28	49	Midway
McKendrick, Alex	Franklin	11–11–1844	Lot	27	439	Frankfort
McKenney, Jno Jr & Wife	Woodford	8–20–1827	3,250	X	280	Grassy Cr
McKenney, Thos L	Washington, D C	1–20–1826	1,325	Y	97	Big Reedy Fk Green R
McKim, Jno Jr & Wife	Baltimore	10– 3–1819	Mill	T	246	Fks Elkhorn
McLardy, Alexander	——	11–18–1801	681¾	F	123	Lynn Camp Cr
McMunn, Alexander	Shelby	11– 7–1810	166⅔	O	72	Clear Cr
McMunn, Alexander	Shelby	11– 7–1810	500	O	75	Clear Cr
McMurdo, C J Jr & Wife	——	3– 4–1833	——	Z	309	None
McMurty, Joseph & Wife	Greenup	9– 3–1830	500	Z	30	Sovern Cr & Big Barren R
McNeil, Daniel	Hardy	4– 2–1787	1,000	A	325	Highland Cr
McNeil, Hector	Petersburg	2–21–1819	2,395	S	473	Nolinn & Middle Cr
McNutt, Joseph	Washington	10– 5–1804	1,000	N	243	Town Fk Elkhorn
McPherson, Jno	Washington	6–14–1803	5,000	H	52	Saxtons Cr
McPherson, Wm	Philadelphia	6–20–1795	10,000	A-2	548	N Fk Sandy R
McRea, Richard	Petersburg	7– 3–1809	Slaves	N	450	None
McVay, Langston	Lincoln	11– 4–1809	190	N	63	W Fk Red R
Mackir, Jno	Lincoln	9–22–1785	Power Atty	A	19–21	None
Mackir, Jno, Atty	Mason	7–22–1803	7,019	G	376	Townsend Run & Ohio R & Mill Cr
Macklin, Alexander W	Franklin	3– 1–1842	3	27	324	M Elkhorn
Macklin, Alexander W	Franklin	1–13–1846	153	28	45	S Elkhorn
Macklin, Alexander W	Franklin	1–13–1846	24	28	46	S Elkhorn
Madison, Gabriel	Fayette	10–13–1791	2,400	M	327	Indian Camp Cr
Madison, Geo	——	3–20–1807	1,000	L	9	None
Madison, Geo	——	3–20–1807	700	L	10	—— Br
Madison, Geo	Franklin	1–14–1812	394½	O	299	Elk Fk Red R
Madison, Geo	——	7–15–1812	Lot	O	502	Frankofrt
Madison, Geo & Wife	Franklin	7–18–1800	1,000	E	64	Big Barren R
Madison, Geo & Wife	Franklin	3– 1–1800	400	F	424	Big Barren R
Madison, Jno	Frankfort	3–28–1818	400	S	242	None
Maddox, Jno & Wife	——	10– 8–1804	——	O	148	None
Madison, Patrick H	Warren	5–23–1831	1,000	Z	130	Bayo Cr
Magill, Archibald	Frederick	10–13–1806	962	L	104	Ohio R
Magill, Chas	Winchester	1– 5–1818	666⅔	S	168	Green R
Magill, Jas & Wife	Woodford	9–26–1845	25	28	26	Dry Run
Magill, Jas & Wife	Woodford	9–26–1845	49	28	28	Dry Run
Magruder, Betsy D & Henry W	Campbell	9– 1–1826	223	X	218	None

Grantor	Residence	Deed Date	Acres	Book	Page	Watercourse
Major, Littleton	Anderson	9-17-1827	———	X	284	None
Major, Saml J M Com'r	Frankfort	10-31-1822	Lots	W	68	Frankfort
Major, Saml J M Com'r	———	10-31-1822	14	W	74	Ky R
Major, Saml J M Com'r	———	10-31-1822	Lot	W	77	Frankfort
Major, Saml J M Com'r	———	10-31-1822	263¾	W	79	Hammond Cr
Major, Saml J M Com'r	———	4- 4-1823	Lot	W	83	Frankfort
Major, Saml J M & Wife	———	8- 9-1830	192	Y	507	S Elkhorn
Major, Widen & Wife	Franklin	5-30-1826	113	Y	152	S Fk Big Benson Cr
Mallory, Chas K & Wife	———	1———1814	2,660	T	352	Biggerstaff Cr & Muddy R
Malone, Jas & Wife	Cooper	5- 7-1842	200	27	292	Ky R
Malone, Jno & Wife	Woodford	10-18-1818	Lot	T	66	Versailles
Manderville, Jonathan & Wife	Alexandria	1- 3-1809	2,000	N	480	Bayo Cr
Mann, Judith	Chesterfield	4-18-1834	114	Z	446	Near Frankfort
Mansfield, Jno & Wife	Mercer	10-29-1791	Lots	B-2	415	Danville
Manson, Peter, heirs	Dinwiddie	8-16-1802	2,080	G	31	Rolling Fk
Marable, Geo	Halifax	9-26-1808	1,000	P	36	Little Barren R
Marble, Peter F	Harrison	2-22-1812	Mill	O	394	Main Licking
Marie, Jno	Philadelphia	9-14-1784	3,000	H	295	None
Marie, Jno	Philadelphia	10-11-1786	5,000	O	422	N Fk Ky R
Marie. Jno, Atty	Philadelphia	9-14-1784	1,000	H	386	None
Markham, Jas	Fanquier	4-25-1806	4,000	W	380	None
Markley, Jno A	Frankfort	10-12-1819	———	X	66	None
Marks, Solomon	Philadelphia	10- 3-1800	23,250	E	171	Big Sandy R
Marriatt, Jas H & Wife	Ann Arundel	10-12-1819	Lots	T	121	———
Mariatt, Joshua & Wife	Baltimore	10-12-1819	Lots	T	121	———
Marshall, Alexander K & Wife	Mason	5-24-1823	———	W	89	S Elkhorn & Sinking Cr
Marshall, Chas	———	11-15-1794	10,000	A-2	517	Big Sandy R
Marshall, Chas	Warren	4-19-1799	1,000	E	111	Sandy R
Marshall, Chas	Virginia	12-31-1796	40,857	Q	499	Ohio R
Marshall, Chas & Wife	Fanquier	3-29-1803	1,168	G	438	Clear Cr
Marshall, Chas & Wm	———	11-22-1794	1,878	A-2	63	None
Marshall, Chas & Wm	———	11-22-1794	105½	A-2	71	N Fk & Johnsons Fk
Marshall, Humphry	Woodford	6-28-1791	Lot	B-2	369	Danville
Marshall, Humphry	———	11-30-1801	1,000	F	159	White Oak Cr
Marshall, Humphry	———	11-28-1804	1,515	H	479	Twins Cr
Marshall, Humphry	———	3-22-1806	6,666¾	K	277	Ohio & Licking
Marshall, Humphry	———	2- 1-1815	1,059	Q	40	Green R
Marshall, Humphry	Franklin	5- 6-1818	75,000	S	140	Rough Cr
Marshall, Humphry	Franklin	4———1820	100	T	308	Twins Cr
Marshall, Humphry	———	10- 8-1822	113½	V	319	None
Marshall, Humphry	Franklin	10-30-1824	———	W	399	Fk Big Bone Lick C
Marshall, Humphry, Trustee	———	11- 6-1801	75,000	F	382	Rough Cr
Marshall, Humphry & Wife	———	9-21-1799	470	D	527	Walperts Cr
Marshall, Humphry & Wife	———	11-23-1802	793	G	53	Big Mud & Now-lands Crs
Marshall, Humphry & Wife	Frankfort	12-14-1803	1,000	H	83	Cumberland R
Marshall, Humphry & Wife	Franklin	11- 9-1805	1,778¾	K	86	Cumberland R
Marshall, Humphry & Wife	Frankfort	2- 4-1814	Lot	P	335	Versailles
Marshall, Humphry & Wife	Fayette	8-20-1786	192	V	385	Leestown Bottom
Marshall, Humphry & Wife	———	5-27-1812	564	X	82	Twins Cr
Marshall, H & T A	———	10-21-1800	200	U	40	Br Eagle Cr
Marshall, Jas	Woodford	3- 5-1790	6,000	B-2	178	N Fk Licking
Marshall, James	Woodford	8-28-1790	2,450	B-2	231	Licking
Marshall, Jno J	Cincinnati	5-24-1827	154	X	296	Eagle Cr
Marshall, Jno J	Franklin	6-22-1832	280	Z	210	Big Bone Lick
Marshall, Jno J	Franklin	2-23-1833	1,000	Z	260	Hickman Co
Marshall, Jno J	Franklin	6- 7-1833	300	Z	299	Lower Twin C
Marshall, Jno J	Franklin	6-21-1833	1,000	Z	302	Mississippi R
Marshall, J J	Cincinnati	8-20-1832	18	Z	404	Eagle Cr
Marshall, J J Com'r	Franklin	7-19-1827	6,074	X	479	None
Marshall, Louis & Wife	Frankfort	7-23-1804	6,052	H	472	Johnsons Fk
Marshall, Markham	Lincoln	6-15-1790	260	B-2	148	Hanging Fk

Grantor	Residence	Deed Date	Acres	Book	Page	Watercourse
Marshall, Saml R & Wife	Philadelphia	5-25-1798	6,680	G	300	Chaplins Fk
Marshall, Stephen & Wife	Warren	8-26-1805	920	K	284	Salt R
Marshall, Thos	——	11-28-1804	1,515	H	479	Twins Cr
Marshall, Thos	Mason	7- 4-1800	697	H	485	Ky R
Marshall, Thos	Richmond	11——1806	5	K	536	Br Hancock Cr
Marshall, Thos A	——	11-25-1817	15,000	R	576	None
Marshall, Thos A	Fayette	3-20-1844	Lot	27	414	Frankfort
Marshall, Wm	Richmond	5- 7-1795	389	A-2	82	Ky R
Marshall, Wm	——	4-13-1798	3,600	D	76	Cumberland R
Marshall, Wm	Granville	4-19-1799	1,000	E	115	Sandy R
Marshall, Wm, Atty	Virginia	12-31-1796	40,857	Q	499	Ohio R
Martin, Henry Jr & Wife	——	1- 7-1793	1,400	J	48	Lawrence & Lee Crs
Martin, Jno	Lincoln	3-10-1787	Negro	A	278	None
Martin, Jno	Lincoln	10-16-1788	——	A	457	S Fk Elkhorn
Martin, Jno	Lincoln	3-17-1801	10,346⅓	F	190	Stoners Fk, Mill, Station Camp & S Fk Licking
Martin, Jno & Wife	Lincoln	9-16-1788	326	B-2	41	Stoners Fk
Martin, Jno & Wife	Lincoln	9-13-1789	583	B-2	80	Main Fk Licking
Martin, Jno & Wife	Lincoln	10- 6-1791	208	B-2	365	Hanging Fk
Martin, Jno L	Fayette	12-23-1805	1,000	K	182	Ky R
Martin, Jno L & Wife	Franklin	7- 2-1802	131½	F	453	Elkhorn
Martin, Jordan & Wife	Virginia	3- 7-1834	114	Z	443	Frankfort
Martin, Saml & Wife	Woodford	10- 1-1806	200	L	79	None
Martin, Thos	Scott	2-19-1840	410	27	112	Panther Cr
Marx, Asher & Wife	New York	9-19-1818	21,000	S	447	Chaplins Fk
Marx, Asher & Geo	Manchester	7-29-1802	1,326	G	23	Green R
Mason, George	Caroline	5-13-1799	1,000	D	371	Ky R
Mason, Geo	Lexington	6-21-1794	——	W	245	None
Mason, Geo, heirs	Gunster Hall	6-21-1794	——	W	245	None
Mason, Jno T	U S Marshall	3- 7-1821	1,100	U	299	None
Mason, Jno T	U S Marshall	3- 7-1821	7,000	U	302	None
Mason, Jno T	U S Marshall	3- 6-1821	1,000	U	304	None
Mason, Jno T	U S Marshall	3- 6-1821	2,000	U	307	None
Mason, Jno T	U S Marshall	3- 6-1821	1,500	U	309	None
Mason, Jno T	U S Marshall	3- 7-1821	1,800	U	312	None
Mason, Jno T	U S Marshall	3- 6-1821	325	U	314	None
Mason, Jno T	Fayette	9- 2-1822	885	V	321	None
Mason, Jno T & Wife	Michigan	2-21-1831	——	Z	107	None
Mason, Mary & Jno T	——	5- 6-1812	——	O	512	None
Mason, Peter, Atty	Fayette	5-13-1799	1,000	D	371	Ky R
Mason, Richard	Philadelphia	8-21-1787	250	B-2	273	None
Mason, Richard B	Virginia	4-14-1818	——	S	118	None
Mason, Stephen T & Wife	London	2- 1-1839	——	27	40	None
Mason, S T, heirs	——	10-11-1815	10,146	R	142	Cedar Cr, Green R & Rolling Fk
Massie, Jno M	Claiborne	8-16-1841	320	27	223	Graves & Hickman Cos
Massie, Wm & Wife	Scott	4-18-1821	50	U	378	S Elkhorn
Massie, Wm & Wife	Scott	6-13-1821	78	U	500	S Elkhorn
Massie, Wm & Wife	Scott	6-16-1821	153½	U	509	Cane Run
Masterson, Milly & Lucy	Virginia	12-30-1819	5,000	U	83	Twin Cr
Mather, Richard	New York City	7-10-1800	4,000	E	52	Hinches Run
Matthews, Geo & Chas.	Mississippi Territory	9-21-1807	6,222	M	70	Green & Pond Rs Rock Cr
Matthew, Richard, Atty	Augusta	6- 7-1797	50,000	B	209	Mill Cr
Matthews, Thos	Norfolk	6- 7-1797	50,000	B	209	Mill Cr
Maupin, Gabriel Jr & Wife	Williamsburg	1-14-1799	1,000	D	165	Trammes Cr
Maury, Abraham	Fluvanna	9-23-1796	6,900	A-2	635	Green R
Maury, Abraham	Davidson	7- 8-1799	10,000	D	299	Big Sandy R
Maury, Abraham	Fluvanna	2-26-1796	300	D	373	Green R
Maury, Abraham & Wife	Orange	12-16-1797	800	F	412	N Fk Tradewater
Maury, Fontain	——	9-22-1823	2,666⅔	X	340	Highland Cr
Maury, Fontain & Wife	Fredricksburg	10-10-1797	2,000	B	221	N Fk Tradewater
Maury, Fontain & Wife	Fredricks	10-17-1798	2,666⅔	D	48	—— Cr
Maury, Wm Sr & Jr	Lexington	4-20-1789	1,000	B-2	57	Foxes Run
Maxwell, Wm M	——	7-15-1824	1,200	W	477	None
May, Banister & Co	——	10- 7-1795	3,000	A-2	692	Eagle Cr
May, Banister & Co	——	4- 1-1797	15,000	B	182	Little Ky R
May, Banister & Co	——	5- 7-1808	3,500	L	380	Sinking Cr
May, Banister & Co	——	6-23-1821	——	V	20	Ky R
May, Banister & Co	——	12-11-1823	888	W	199	None

Grantor	Residence	Deed Date	Acres	Book	Page	Watercourse
May, Banister & Co...	————	1-23-1828	42,283	X	366	None
May, Banister & Co...	————	————1826	295	Y	189	Blackfords Cr
May, Banister & Co...	————	6-15-1832	————	Z	203	None
May, Banister & Co...	————.	1-31-1834	————	Z	402	Bullitt Co
May, Benj H	Petersburg	————1818	1,328	T	91	Big Barren R
May, Geo	Dinwiddie	6-23-1789	400	B-2	122	Ohio R
May, Geo	Dinwiddie	11-20-1794	18,125	C	169	Nolinn
May, Geo	Dinwiddie	11-21-1794	47,056¾	D	199	Big Sandy R
May, George	Dinwiddie	11-20-1794	4,924	G	258	Rough Cr
May, George	Dinwiddie	5- 5-1807	8,255½	L	192	Rolling Fk, Battle Rough & Coxes Cr
May, George	Dinwiddie	5- 5-1807	————	S	244	None
May, Geo & Wife	Dinwiddie	6-20-1789	400	B-2	333	Ohio R
May, Geo & Wife	Dinwiddie	9-19-1797	5,850	C	92	Fks Hardins Cr
May, Geo & Wife	Dinwiddie	9-19-1797	————	C	113	None
May, Geo & Wife	Dinwiddie	11-15-1797	800	D	146	Ky R
May, Geo & Wife	Dinwiddie	9- 7-1799	3,435	D	408	Green R
May, George & Wife	Dinwiddie	7-19-1800	————	E	161	None
May, Geo & Wife	Dinwiddie	9-20-1794	1,666⅔	N	184	Ky R
May, Jno	Dinwiddie	6-22-1786	400	A	143	M Br Clear Cr
May, Jno	————	8- 9-1819	360	T	57	None
May, Jno, heirs	————	5-10-1815	160	Q	175	Eagle Cr
May, Jno, heirs	————	11-30-1815	890	Q	288	Beech & Black Fk
May, Jno, heirs	————	7- 8-1817	250	R	347	Sugar Cr
May, Jno, heirs	————	5-23-1818	1,000	S	143	Hardins Cr
May, Jno, heirs	————	8-15-1818	1,500	S	209	Ohio R
May, Jno, heirs	————	8-25-1818	15,347	S	219	Green R & Rough Cr
May, Jno, heirs	————	8- 6-1818	230	S	235	Ohio R
May, Jno, heirs	————	10-25-1818	100	S	267	None
May, Jno, heirs	————	5-10-1815	346	Q	173	Eagle Cr
May, Jno, heirs	————	6-23-1821	————	V	20	Ky R
May, Jno, heirs	————	10-25-1823	148	W	186	None
May, Jno F & Wife	Petersburg	8-10-1818	————.	T	94	None
May, Jno L	————	11-28-1811	20,000	O	213	Hinkston Fk
May, Jno L	Dinwiddie	2- 8-1812	500	O	306	Mill Cr
May, Jno L...	Dinwiddie	2-19-1812	692	O	319	Island in Ohio R
May, Jno L	Petersburg	2-28-1813	500	P	93	None
May, Jno L	————	4- 1-1813	364	P	116	Ky R
May, Jno L	————	5-12-1813	881	P	125	Coxes Cr
May, Jno L	————	10-10-1813	1,800	P	293	N Fk Rough Cr
May, Jno L	————	5- 6-1818	154	S	123	None
May, Jno L	————	5- 6-1818	104	S	126	Ohio R
May, Jno L	————	1- 6-1819	1,112	S	374	Eagle Cr
May, Jno L	————	1- 6-1819	1,537	S	376	Eagle Cr
May, Jno L	————	7- 4-1818	1,089	S	396	Jessamine & Hickman Cr
May, Jno L	Virginia	8- 9-1819	1,500	T	55	Ashes Cr
May, Jno L	————	7- 1-1817	218	T	75	Eagle Cr
May, Jno L	————	5-21-1819	1,670	T	213	Br Ohio R
May, Jno L	————	3-10-1820	1,096	T	264	None
May, Jno L	Virginia	9- 8-1820	6,923	U	70	Rough Cr
May, Jno L	————	6-15-1822	90	V	254	None
May, Jno L	————	6-11-1822	112	V	350	None
May, Jno L	————	6-15-1822	150	V	351	Eagle Cr
May, Jno L	————	12-10-1822	100	V	433	Ohio R
May, Jno L	————	12-10-1822	105	V	434	Ohio R
May, Jno L	————	10-21-1823	264	W	144	None
May, Jno L	————	10-21-1823	116	W	146	None
May, Jno L	————	10-21-1823	110	W	147	None
May, Jno L	————	10-25-1823	148	W	186	None
May, Jno L	————	2- 3-1825	1,950	X	92	Yellow Banks in Daviess Co
May, Jno L	————	12-17-1827	Lots	X	329	Owensboro
May, Jno L	————	12-17-1827	417	X	329	Ohio R
May, Jno L	————	2- 8-1826	750	Y	174	Ohio R
May, Jno L, Atty	————	7- 6-1814	221½	P	489	Sulphur Lick Fk
May, Wm	Nelson	8-23-1787	1,400	B-2	95	Lees Cr
May, Wm & Wife	Nelson	10-13-1791	2,400	M	327	Indian Camp Cr
Mayes, Daniel & Wife	Christian	5- 1-1819	382	T	395	Sinking Fk Little R
Maylan, Jno	Philadelphia	1-16-1797	26,500	C	42	Killicanick Cr
Maylan, Jno	Pennsylvania	11- 8-1797	————	D	211	Eagle Cr
Maylan, Jno	Philadelphia	6-21-1796	20,781	C	278	N Fk Ky R
Maynard, Stith	Lynchburg	3-26-1814	2,000	Q	100	Yellow Cr
Mayo, Jno, heirs	Richmond	4-27-1824	30,000	W	346	Licking & Sulbergreed Cr
Mayo, Wm	Fayette	11- 8-1799	140	D	455	Tates Cr
Mayo, Wm	Henrico	5-27-1833	11,000	Z	296	Tenn & Clark R
Mays, Geo	Bath	4-28-1820	666⅔	T	302	None
Mays, Moses & Wife	Simpson	7- 1-1845	————	28	54	Simpson Co
Meade, David	Jessamine	9-22-1821	2,350	V	65	Licking
Means, Robt	————	8- 3-1795	10,000	A-2	325	N Fk Ky R

Grantor	Residence	Deed Date	Acres	Book	Page	Watercourse
Means, Robt	Richmond	5- 7-1799	1,000	D	225	W Fk Pitmans Cr
Means, Robt	Richmond	5- 7-1799	1,200	D	227	S Fk Skeggs Cr
Means, Robt, heirs	————	7- 9-1824	100	W	463	None
Means, Robt, heirs	————	7- 9-1824	218	W	466	None
Means, Robt, heirs	————	7- 9-1824	905	W	470	None
Means, Robt, heirs	————	7- 9-1824	500	W	473	S Fk Sandy R
Means, Robt, heirs	Richmond	3-24-1832	333⅓	Z	330	In Green Co
Means, Robt, heirs	Richmond	3-24-1832	5,000	Z	332	Montgomery Co
Meary, Jonas	Scott	10- 6-1829	50	Y	398	None
Mercantile Ins Co	New York	9- 5-1842	5,050	27	313	Locust & Indian Cr
Mercer, Chas F	London	6- 1-1815	2,500	S	310	Beech Fk
Mercer, Chas F	————	9- 3-1818	————	S	314	None
Mercer, Chas F	————	5-18-1820	562	T	334	None
Mercer, Chas F	Virginia	11- 9-1821	1,333⅓	V	98	Crocus & Greasy Cr
Mercer, Chas F	Virginia	1-10-1824	————	W	170	Little Ky R
Mercer, Chas F	Virginia	1-10-1824	100	X	168	Little Ky R
Mercer, Chas F	————	5- 9-1839	5,000	27	22	Little Ky R
Mercer, Genl Hugh, heirs	Fredericksburg	2-19-1811	1,330	A-2	178	None
Mercer, James	Spottsylvania	9-25-1793	7,000	A-2	624	Deer Cr
Mercer, Jno Fenton	————	5- 5-1796	2,000	A-2	694	W Fk Glenns Cr
Mercer, Jno Fenton	London	5- 2-1797	4,110⅔	B	23	Br Green R
Mercer, Jno F	Maryland	7- 9-1802	1,000	G	173	Ohio R
Mercer, Jno Francis	Maryland	6-19-1802	3,000	G	177	Drakes Cr
Meredith, Maria M	Baltimore	9-26-1845	2,500	28	35	Elkhorn & Cedar Cr
Meredith, Saml	Trenton	2- 1-1813	333⅓	P	77	Licking
Meredith, Thos	Baltimore	9-26-1845	2,500	28	35	Elkhorn & Cedar Cr
Meriwether, Frances	Spottsylvania	11-26-1785	1,000	A	95	Shawnee Run
Meriwether, Nicholas	Jefferson	2-24-1786	1,000	A	84	None
Meriwether, Nicholas	Jefferson	9-23-1789	1,600	B-2	155	Indian Camp Cr
Meriwether, Nicholas	Shelby	4-14-1801	4,500	H	141	Indian Camp Cr
Meriwether, Nicholas & Wife	Shelby	12-21-1803	845	H	94	M Licking
Meriwether, Pricilla	Oldham	1-17-1833	1,000	Z	256	Drakes Cr
Meriwether, Valentine & Wife	Jefferson	6-16-1812	333⅔	P	16	Rough Cr
Meriwether, Wm N & Jas	Shelby	12- 8-1825	————	Y	101	None
Merriman, H E & Geo	Bristol	6-14-1841	320	27	253	Tennessee R
Merrimee, Lewis	Bullitt	3-26-1814	383	P	448	Big Barren R
Merry, Calvin	Christian	10- 2-1804	Slaves	H	446	None
Merry, Prityman	Orange	9-28-1786	500	A	304	None
Merry, Prettyman	Buckingham	11- 4-1806	450	K	456	Hingstons & Stoners Fks
Michie, George	————	8-20-1798	164	N	96	Rolling Fk
Mfflin, Saml	Philadelphia	4-15-1820	1,000	V	67	Ohio R
Milam, Jefferson	Scott	6-——-1821	666	U	498	S Elkhorn
Milam, Jno & Wife	Franklin	6-——-1821	666	U	498	S Elkhorn Cr
Miles, Chas	Jefferson	1-20-1841	Lots	27	181	Frankfort
Miles, Tarlton	Crittenden	5- 4-1846	63	28	83	Elkhorn
Millegan, Wm & Wife	Woodford	12- 3-1798	125	D	109	None
Miller, Anderson & Wife	————	2- 5-1814	Lot	P	358	Frankfort
Miller, Anderson & Wife	Frankfort	4- 9-1814	————	P	395	Shannons Run
Miller, Anderson & Wife	Jefferson	———-1820	606⅔	U	169	None
Miller, Ann	Philadelphia	7-16-1796	1,000	A-2	500	Beech Fk
Miller, Hannah	Lincoln	5- 5-1788	————	A	493	None
Miller, Jno	Batetourt	2-15-1799	5,700	D	222	Sandy R
Miller, Dr Jno	Alabama	2- 4-1829	225,000	Y	401	None
Miller, Jno & Wife	Batetourt	12-10-1797	700	B	343	Big Barren R
Miller, Jno & Wife	Batetourt	1-25-1798	3,300	C	197	Cumberland R
Miller, Jno & Wife	Batetourt	1-28-1799	50,000	D	348	Green R
Miller, Jno & Wife	Batetourt	10-29-1798	————	D	389	Ohio R
Miller, Jno & Wife	Batetourt	1-14-1800	700	E	66	Big Barren R
Miller, Jno & Wife	Batetourt	11- 7-1801	4,466	F	475	Miller Cr
Miller, Jno & Wife	Montgomery	4-16-1814	————	S	228	Ohio R
Miller, Jno & Thos	Powhatan	9-19-1799	247¾	D	532	None
Miller, Joseph J	Philadelphia	5- 5-1798	————	D	520	None
Miller, Maurice L	————	2- 3-1825	1,950	X	92	Yellow Banks in Daviess Co
Miller, Maurice L	Henry	1-26-1827	————	X	209	None
Miller, Robt	Franklin	8- 9-1819	Lot	T	374	Frankfort
Miller, Robt & Wife	Madison	10-28-1811	9,507	O	285	Silver Muddy & Station Camp Cr
Miller, Wm	————	1-26-1836	————	28	9	In Ky
Mills, Benj, Atty	Bourbon	2-26-1820	3,000	U	36	Otter Cr
Mills, Jno	Wayne	2- 7-1812	500	O	317	Ky R
Mills, Nicholas & Wife	Chesterfield	9- 6-1816	4,788	R	263	Fk Barren & Green R
Mills, Robt P	Franklin	3-14-———	————	27	129	N Elkhorn
Milton, Alexander & Wife	Frederick	6-13-1803	1,000	K	171	Ohio R

Grantor	Residence	Deed Date	Acres	Book	Page	Watercourse
Ming, George	Amherst	10-25-1803	326	H	101	Baileys Run
Ming, George	Amherst	10-22-1803	249	H	103	Baileys Run
Minor, Dabney & Wife	——	9-16-1810	200	O	124	Cumberland R
Minor, Elizabeth	Spottsylvania	9-17-1823	1,882	W	373	W Fk Floyds Fk
Minor, Garrett	Louisa	7-11-1796	1,000	A-2	433	Skeggs Cr
Mitchell, Alexander J.	Fayette	——	Lots	27	434	Frankfort
Mitchell, Alexander J.	Fayette	8-26-1845	Lots	28	25	Frankfort
Mitchell, Jno	——	12-15-1802	547	G	102	Salt R
Mitchell, Jno A & Wife	Frankfort	6-16-1819	Lots	T	68	Frankfort
Mitchell, Jno A & Wife	Franklin	1-31-1820	Lot	T	440	Frankfort
Mitchell, Margaret	Franklin	12- 8-1842	Lots	27	326	Frankfort
Mitchell, Ohmer	New Kent	9- 4-1827	——	X	320	None
Mitchell, Robt	——	4-13-1798	3,600	D	76	Cumberland R
Mitchell, Robt	Mercer	7- 8-1801	600	E	391	Licking
Mitchell, Robt & Wife	Mercer	1-26-1804	958½	H	454	Wallace & Phillips
Mitchell, Saml	Bourbon	11-19-1816	400	R	123	Sugar Cr
Moale, Saml, Trustee	Baltimore	11-17-1803	113,911	H	232	M Island Cr, Ohio, Pocatillico Cr & Elk R
Monday, Jno	Fanquier	9-16-1802	1,000	G	20	None
Monroe, Jas	——	2- 9-1808	14,720	M	206	Ohio R
Monroe, Jas	Washington City	11-13-1814	——	Q	97	None
Monroe, Jas	Washington City	7- 5-1819	5,000	V	140	Licking
Monroe, Jas & Wife	Virginia	1-29-1803	4,584	G	262	Ohio R
Monroe, Victor Guardian	——	11-27-1834	——	Z	510	In Hart Co
Montague, Thos & Wife	——	6-27-1820	200	U	29	Green R
Montgomery, Jno	Lincoln	12-14-1818	760	S	406	Caseys Cr
Montgomery, Robt	Wayne	10-23-1818	730	S	408	Green R & Caseys Cr
Montgomery, Thos, Comr	Lincoln	11-12-1806	3,770	L	217	Dix R, Rough & Richland Cr
Montgomery, Wm & Wife	Lincoln	3-20-1789	526	B-2	277	Caseys Cr
Moody, James	Lexington	7-24-1800	2,000	E	90	Green R
Moore, Elizabeth Executor	Jefferson	——1810	200	O	315	Little Barren R
Moore, Hector W & N H	Jefferson	——1810	200	O	315	Little Barren R
Moore, Colo Jas F K.	Jefferson	——1810	200	O	315	Little Barren R
Moore, Jno	Caldwell	2-21-1815	226	Q	13	Hays Fk Silver Cr
Moore, Jno & Wife	Caldwell	10-10-1823	2,910	W	283	Green R
Moore, Peter & Wife	Fayette	9- 9-1790	384	D	376	Leestown Bottom
Moore, Saml, heirs	Fayette	3-23-1808	150	L	350	Chaplins Fk
Moore, Wm & Wife	Washington	6-15-1813	568	P	247	Sulphur Lick Cr
Moorhouse, Abraham	Danville	9-22-1801	——	F	52	None
Morehead, Chas S	Franklin	6- 1-1841	Lots	27	276	Frankfort
Morehead, Chas S & Wife	Franklin	9-13-1839	Lot	27	75	Frankfort
Morgan, Benj R	Philadelphia	10- 4-1811	22,000	P	612	Floyds Fk, Eagle & Rough Cr
Morgan, Chas	Muhlenburg	6- 2-1803	15,599½	G	337	Eagle & Elkhorn
Morgan, Chas	Muhlenburg	11-19-1803	12,311	H	65	Hingston Fk
Morgan, Chas	Muhlenburg	11-28-1803	600	K	352	Main Licking
Morgan, Chas	Muhlenburg	7- 6-1819	500	T	16	Grassy Lick Cr
Morgan, Chas & Wife	Campbell	8-19-1800	——	E	215	Ohio R
Morgan, Chas & Wife	Campbell	8-19-1800	——	F	511	Ohio R
Morgan, Chas & Wife	——	11-23-1802	3,939	G	49	Licking
Morgan, Chas, heirs	Muhlenburg	6- 3-1835	——	Z	515	Cedar Cr
Morgan, Jno.	Muhlenburg	6- 3-1835	——	Z	515	Cedar Cr
Morgan, Simon	——	11-22-1794	1,878	A-2	63	None
Morgan, Simon	——	11-22-1794	105½	A-2	71	N Fk & Johnsons Fk
Morgan, Simon & Wife	Fanquier	8-25-1796	——	B	340	Ohio & Cypress Cr
Morgan, Willis	Muhlenburg	2-12-1810	2,998	N	216	Tradewater
Morgan, Willis & Wife	Muhlenburg	4-26-1811	666⅔	O	40	Eddy Cr
Moritz, David & Wife	Northampton	11-24-1803	22,000	H	314	None
Morris, Jno	Franklin	9-10-1814	116	Q	75	Big Benson Cr
Morris, Jno	Franklin	9-10-1814	500	Q	428	N Fk Big Benson Cr
Morris, Jno	Tennessee	6-27-1820	200	U	25	Green R
Morris, Jno, Atty	Franklin	12- 5-1815	200	Q	346	Rough Cr
Morris, Jno, Atty	Frankfort	12- 5-1815	200	Q	403	Rough Cr
Morris, Robt	Philadelphia	11-16-1795	2,000	A-2	525	Ohio R
Morris, Robt & Wife	Philadelphia	1-20-1798	145,932½	C	326	Rough Cr, Ohio, Big Sandy & Licking
Morris, Robt & Wife	Philadelphia	3-30-1798	20,000	C	332	None
Morris, Robt & Wife	Philadelphia	3-30-1798	9,000	C	337	Huston Fk
Morris, Robt & Wife	Philadelphia	3- 5-1795	431,043	D	312	Many water courses
Morris, Robt & Wife	Philadelphia	7-10-1801	9,000	F	405	None
Morris, Robt & Wife	Philadelphia	3- 5-1795	615,180	28	341	In Kentucky
Morris, Wm	Hanover	4-13-1804	2,000	H	242	Mulberry Cr
Morris, Wm, Atty	Hanover	9-10-1814	500	Q	428	N Fk Big Benson Cr

Grantor	Residence	Deed Date	Acres	Book	Page	Watercourse
Morrison, James	Fayette	4–10–1806	4,000	L	166	Green R & Nolinn
Morrison, Jas	Kentucky	7– 2–1832	Lot	Z	241	Frankfort
Morrison, Jas	Kentucky	11–27–1832	75	Z	242	Shelbyville Pike
Morrison, Jas, Atty	Lexington	4–30–1806	1,000	K	410	Crocus Cr
Morrison, Jas, Atty	Fayette	4–10–1806	4,000	L	166	Green R & Nolinn
Morrison, James, Ex	————	6–18–1804	175	H	281	Slate Cr
Morrison, James	————	11– 6–1805	2,000	J	370	Floyds Fk
Morrison, Jas, Decd	————	11–12–1834	———	Z	477	None
Morrison, Jas, heirs	Kentucky	5–15–1841	204	27	251	In St Louis Co Mo
Morrison, Jas & Wife	Lexington	6–12–1806	6,000	L	329	None
Morrison, Jas & Wife	Fayette	5– 7–1812	1,200	O	374	None
Mortimer, Jno	Spottsylvania	12–26–1825	1,200	Y	94	Pattons Cr
Morton, Geo W	Fayette	2–11–1833	Lots	Z	455	Frankfort
Morton, Jno & Wife	Lincoln	6———1790	200	B-2	145	Br Stoners Fk
Morton, Jno H	2nd Dist Kentucky	6–21–1819	800	T	13	Cumberland R
Morton, Jno H	2nd Dist Kentucky	6–26–1819	1,000	T	106	Caney Fk Peter Cr
Morton, Jno H	2nd Dist Kentucky	1–22–1821	800	U	279	Peter Cr
Morton, Jno H	2nd Dist Collector	3–26–1821	1,000	U	333	Drakes Cr
Morton, Jno H	2nd Dist Collector	3–26–1821	1,800	U	336	Floyds Fk
Morton, Jno H	2nd Dist Collector	3–26–1821	2,000	U	339	Big Bone Cr
Morton, Jno H	2nd Dist Collector	3–26–1821	1,000	U	341	Ohio R
Morton, Jno H	2nd Dist Collector	3–26–1821	500	U	344	None
Morton, Jno H	2nd Dist Collector	3–26–1821	400	U	347	Caney Fk
Morton, Jno H	2nd Dist Collector	3–26–1821	200	U	351	Cumberland R
Morton, Jno H	2nd Dist Collector	2–14–1821	500	U	450	M Licking
Morton, Jno H	2nd Dist Collector	2–14–1821	2,500	U	453	S Fk Rolling Fk
Morton, Jno H	2nd Dist Collector	11–25–1819	25,000	V	233	Welches Cr
Morton, Jno H	2nd Dist Collector	5–30–1822	1,000	V	391	Tradewater
Morton, Jno H	2nd Dist Collector	5–30–1822	5,000	V	393	Ohio R
Morton, Jno H	2nd Dist Collector	5–30–1822	1,000	V	395	Tradewater
Morton, Jno H	2nd Dist Collector	4– 1–1823	1,600	W	24	Cypress Cr
Morton, Jno H	2nd Dist Collector	4– 1–1823	500	W	26	Rolling Fk
Morton, Jno H	2nd Dist Collector	4– 1–1823	4,000	W	27	Robinson Cr
Morton, Jno H	2nd Dist Collector	4– 1–1823	1,000	W	30	Beech Fk
Morton, Jno H	2nd Dist Collector	4– 1–1823	1,800	W	32	Sinking Cr
Morton, Jno H	2nd Dist Collector	4– 1–1823	1,410	W	34	Tradewater
Morton, Jno H	2nd Dist Collector	4– 1–1823	1,000	W	36	Tradewater
Morton, Jno H	2nd Dist Collector	4– 1–1823	1,000	W	38	Tradewater
Morton, Jno H	2nd Dist Collector	5–28–1823	3,327	W	56	Welches Cr & Licking
Morton, Jno H	2nd Dist Collector	12–18–1823	1,040	W	193	None
Morton, Jno H	2nd Dist Collector	2– 3–1824	666	W	410	Red R
Morton, Jno H	2nd Dist Collector	2– 3–1824	200	W	411	Crooked Cr
Morton, Jno H	2nd Dist Collector	1–29–1824	1,000	W	417	Rough Cr
Morton, Jno H	2nd Dist Collector	1–18–1824	547	W	419	Cumberland R
Morton, Jno H	2nd Dist Collector	2–28–1824	833⅓	W	421	Panther Cr
Morton, Jno H	2nd Dist Collector	2– 6–1824	2,000	W	423	E Fk Little Barren
Morton, Jno H	2nd Dist Collector	1– 4–1824	1,000	W	425	Clear Cr
Morton, Jno H	2nd Dist Collector	1– 4–1824	1,090	W	427	Cumberland R
Morton, Jno H	2nd Dist Collector	1–18–1824	415	W	429	Ohio R
Morton, Jno H	2nd Dist Collector	1– 4–1824	1,000	W	430	N Fk Tradewater
Morton, Jno H	2nd Dist Collector	1–15–1824	200	W	432	Muddy R
Morton, Jno H	2nd Dist Collector	1– 4–1824	500	W	434	Coffields Fk Deer C
Morton, Jno H	2nd Dist Collector	2–16–1824	400	W	436	Deer Cr
Morton, Jno H	2nd Dist Collector	1– 4–1824	300	W	438	Little R
Morton, Jno H	2nd Dist Collector	1–28–1824	400	W	439	Little R
Morton, Jno H	2nd Dist Collector	2– 2–1824	557	W	441	Cumberland R
Morton, Jno H	2nd Dist Collector	2–16–1824	100	W	443	Fk Buck Cr
Morton, Jno H	2nd Dist Collector	2– 3–1824	666⅔	W	445	None
Morton, Jno H	2nd Dist Collector	1– 4–1824	666⅔	W	447	Cypress Cr
Morton, Jno H	2nd Dist Collector	1–28–1824	560	W	451	Rough Cr
Morton, Jno H	2nd Dist Collector	1– 4–1824	400	W	453	Deer Cr
Morton, Jno H	2nd Dist Collector	1–22–1824	250	W	455	Clifty Cr
Morton, Jno H	2nd Dist Collector	2– 6–1824	200	W	456	None
Morton, Jno H	2nd Dist Collector	1–24–1824	1,000	W	459	N Fk Tradewater
Morton, Jno H	2nd Dist Collector	2– 7–1824	30	W	461	Flyns Fk
Morton, Jno H	2nd Dist Collector	1–18–1824	200	W	480	Panther Cr
Morton, Jno H	2nd Dist Collector	2– 8–1824	666	W	482	Cumberland R
Morton, Jno H	2nd Dist Collector	1–22–1824	360	W	484	Camp Cr
Morton, Jno H	2nd Dist Collector	1–29–1824	400	W	486	None
Morton, Jno H	2nd Dist Collector	2– 3–1824	1,450	W	488	Cumberland R
Morton, Jno H	2nd Dist Collector	1– 4–1824	900	W	490	Tradewater
Morton, Jno H	2nd Dist Collector	1–31–1824	1,000	W	492	Deer Cr
Morton, Jno H	2nd Dist Collector	2– 3–1824	1,000	W	495	Cumberland R
Morton, Jno H	2nd Dist Collector	1–10–1824	1,000	W	498	Tradewater
Morton, Jno H	2nd Dist Collector	2– 7–1824	1,100	W	500	Pond R
Morton, Jno H	2nd Dist Collector	2–25–1824	400	W	509	Beaver Fk Highland Cr
Morton, Jno H	2nd Dist Collector	1–29–1824	500	W	512	Cumberland R
Morton, Jno H	2nd Dist Collector	1–25–1824	610	X	1	None
Morton, Jno H	2nd Dist Collector	1–10–1824	610	X	3	None

Grantor	Residence	Deed Date	Acres	Book	Page	Watercourse
Morton, Jno H	2nd Dist Collector	1-15-1824	666	X	5	Cumberland R
Morton, Jno H	2nd Dist Collector	1-31-1824	300	X	7	Tates Cr
Morton, Jno H	2nd Dist Collector	1-22-1824	100	X	9	Tates Cr
Morton, Jno H	2nd Dist Collector	1-22-1824	1,000	X	12	Paint Lick
Morton, Jno H	2nd Dist Collector	1-22-1824	1,000	X	14	Green R
Morton, Jno H	2nd Dist Collector	1-23-1824	400	X	16	None
Morton, Jno H	2nd Dist Collector	12- 8-1825	2,666⅔	Y	90	Pond R
Morton, Jno M	2nd Dist Kentucky	6-21-1819	100	T	11	Pitman Cr
Morton, Thomas	Montgomery	3- 7-1804	1,500	H	267	None
Morton, Wm	————	11- 6-1805	2,000	J	370	Floyds Fk
Morton, Wm, Com'r	Fayette	5-25-1810	246,900¼	N	224	Ohio R
Mosby, Benj	Augusta	2- 4-1809	1,000	M	413	Highland Cr
Mosby, Benj	————	2- 5-1814	2,395	P	528	Middle Cr
Mosby, Benj, Trustee	————	5-18-1811	560	O	22	Ky R
Mosby, Benj & Wife	Augusta	12-16-1808	—	M	274	None
Mosby, Benj, heirs	Boone	12-11-1823	750	W	180	Big Bone Cr
Mosby, Ben, heirs	Boone	12-11-1823	1,770	W	182	Ohio R & Big Bone
Mosby, Littleberry Jr	Powhatan	11-15-1796	—	Z	430	None
Mosby, Littleberry Jr & Wife	Powhatan	11-15-1796	—	Q	547	None
Mosby, Mary W	Richmond	3-23-1831	—	27	61	None
Mosby, Robt	————	8-21-1800	Lot	F	2	Frankfort
Mosby, Robt	Mercer	11- 4-1796	413	N	149	Beech Fk
Mosby, Wade	Powhatan	11-28-1797	1,000	D	145	Ohio R
Mosby, Wade & Wife	Virginia	9-29-1821	750	V	81	None
Mosby, Wade & Wife	Powhatan	5- 5-1826	—	27	56	Hennrico Co & Curles Neck
Mosby, Wade & Wife	Powhatan	5-14-1834	1,325	27	64	In Virginia
Mosby, Wade Sr	Powhatan	5-14-1834	—	27	79	None
Mosby, Wade Sr & Wife	Powhatan	9-13-1822	519	V	315	None
Mosby, Wm W	Powhatan	3-23-1831	—	27	61	None
Moseby, Littleberry	Powhatan	4- 1-1796	8,000	A-2	557	Foxes Cr
Moseby, Littleberry Jr	Powhatan	2-27-1796	1,000	A-2	143	Mud Cr
Mound, Jno Jas & Wife	Westmoreland	1-27-1798	7,333⅓	D	229	Highland Cr
Mountjoy, Edw & Wife	Franklin	4- 1-1824	400	X	81	Hammonds & Big Benson Cr
Moxley, Saml	Franklin	9- 2-1812	200	O	466	None
Moxley, Saml, heirs	Franklin	7-10-1818	120	S	556	None
Moylan, Jno, heirs	————	1-16-1840	426	27	101	Large Twin Cr
Moylan, Jno, heirs	————	2-18-1840	—	27	106	Twins Cr
Muhlenberg, Peter	Philadelphia	3-20-1803	2,000	G	353	Lost Cr
Muir, Frances	————	6-13-1815	1,000	Q	416	Tradewater
Munday, Edward	Lincoln	3-22-1786	Negro	A	93	None
Munsell, Luke	Franklin	5-18-1829	—	Y	372	Ky R
Munsell, Luke & Wife	Marion	6-22-1840	1,800	27	125	Ky R & Big Benson
Munsell, Luke & Wife	————	1-10-1844	—	27	386	Cumberland R
Munsell, L & Wife	Marion	4-30-1840	Lot	27	124	Frankfort
Munsell, L & Wife	————	1-16-1845	637	27	456	Crooked Cr
Murray, Wm	Philadelphia	6- 1-1786	2,000	A-2	406	Fox Run
Murray, Wm, Atty	Fayette	12-14-1790	187½	B-2	233	Foxes Run
Murray, Wm, Atty	Fayette	12-14-1790	187½	B-2	236	Foxes Run
Muse, Geo, Dec'd	Nelson	12-19-1817	—	S	53	None
Muse, Jeremiah	Westmoreland	7-21-1801	—	F	485	Green R
Muter, Geo	Woodford	3-25-1791	Lot	B-2	260	Danville
Muter, Thos & Wife	————	3- 7-1802	6,000	F	491	Ohio R
Myers, Benj	Lincoln	12-19-1821	2,437½	V	214	Br Big Bone Lick Cr
Myers, Jacob	Lincoln	6-10-1785	575	A	27	E Fk Cox Cr
Myers, Jacob	Lincoln	6-16-1786	500	A	104	Sinking Cr
Myers, Jacob	Lincoln	3-26-1786	2,000	A	106	Green R
Myers, Jacob	Lincoln	3-27-1786	3,000	A	109	Green R
Myers, Jacob	Lincoln	3-27-1786	12,000	A	111	Green R
Myers, Jacob	Lincoln	6-23-1786	500	A	120	Wilsons Cr
Myers, Jacob	Lincoln	6-23-1786	1,500	A	124	Sinking Cr
Myers, Jacob	Lincoln	6-23-1786	800	A	147	Small Br
Myers, Jacob	Lincoln	9- 5-1786	—	A	168	Green R
Myers, Jacob	Lincoln	8-26-1786	400	A	170	Green R
Myers, Jacob	Lincoln	1-30-1787	235	A	299	Long Lick Cr
Myers, Jacob	Lincoln	12-19-1787	250	A	335	Slate Cr
Myers, Jacob	Lincoln	12-19-1787	450	A	337	Slate Cr
Myers, Jacob	Lincoln	9-21-1787	520	A	351	Dix R & Hanging Fk
Myers, Jacob	Lincoln	12-21-1787	500	A	358	Slate Cr
Myers, Jacob	Lincoln	3- 3-1788	1,000	A	360	Fks Bacon Cr
Myers, Jacob	Lincoln	3- 8-1788	216	A	362	E Fk Coxes Cr
Myers, Jacob	Lincoln	3- 8-1788	600	A	364	Coxes Cr
Myers, Jacob	Lincoln	3- 8-1788	596	A	366	E Fk Coxes Cr
Myers, Jacob	Lincoln	3-13-1788	200	A	376	Jessamine Cr
Myers, Jacob	Lincoln	3-13-1788	652	A	377	Jessamine Cr
Myers, Jacob	Lincoln	6-22-1788	36	A	430	E Fk Coxes Cr
Myers, Jacob	Lincoln	6- 5-1788	556½	A	432	None
Myers, Jacob	Lincoln	7- 2-1788	500	A	504	Beech Fk

Grantor	Residence	Deed Date	Acres	Book	Page	Watercourse
Myers, Jacob	Lincoln	3-11-1789	464	A	515	Hanging Fk
Myers, Jacob	Clark	9-10-1794	10,300	A-2	284	Ky R & Bensons Cr Slate Cr & Hinkston Fk
Myers, Jacob	——	7- 7-1796	1,920	A-2	364	Slate Cr
Myers, Jacob	Clark	11-14-1795	5,896¼	A-2	416	Salt R
Myers, Jacob	Lincoln	4-24-1797	200	B	279	Sinking Cr
Myers, Jacob	Lincoln	12- 4-1788	½	B-2	49	Louisville
Myers, Jacob	Lincoln	6-23-1789	515	B-2	62	Knob Cr
Myers, Jacob	Lincoln	9-24-1789	400	B-2	81	Foxes Run
Myers, Jacob	Lincoln	9-21-1787	500	B-2	87	Slate Cr
Myers, Jacob	Lincoln	9-21-1787	2,400	B-2	88	Fks Otter Cr
Myers, Jacob	Lincoln	9-21-1787	7,500	B-2	89	Floyds Fk
Myers, Jacob	Lincoln	9-21-1787	5,825	B-2	91	Cartwrights Cr
Myers, Jacob	Lincoln	12-23-1789	2,000	B-2	109	Flat Lick Cr
Myers, Jacob	Lincoln	1-28-1790	555	B-2	111	Ky R
Myers, Jacob	Lincoln	3-12-1790	500	B-2	123	Upper Blue Lick
Myers, Jacob	Lincoln	10-13-1789	200	B-2	125	Slate Cr
Myers, Jacob	Lincoln	10-14-1789	200	B-2	127	Slate Cr
Myers, Jacob	Lincoln	9- 3-1790	600	B-2	199	Brashears Cr
Myers, Jacob	Lincoln	8-19-1790	500	B-2	205	Flat Cr
Myers, Jacob	Lincoln	4-15-1791	200	B-2	286	Boones Mill Cr
Myers, Jacob	Lincoln	5-24-1791	5,434	B-2	318	Big Slate Cr
Myers, Jacob	Lincoln	8-23-1791	600	B-2	379	Flemings Cr
Myers, Jacob	Lincoln	9- 5-1791	300	B-2	389	Slate Cr
Myers, Jacob	Lincoln	7-20-1791	400	B-2	428	Slate Cr
Myers, Jacob	Bullitt	9-15-1800	1,500	D	549	Salt R
Myers, Jacob	Bullitt	6-14-1800	650	E	45	3Fks Cumberland R
Myers, Jacob	Bullitt	6-17-1800	5,000	E	46	3 Fks Cumberland R
Myers, Jacob	Bullitt	8- 8-1801	150	F	202	Sp of Dix R
Myers, Jacob	Bullitt	7-10-1797	9,412	H	153	Mississippi R
Myers, Jacob	Lincoln	5- 9-1793	23,200	N	21	Ky R Twin Slate Lick Cr & Ohio R
Myers, Jacob & Wife	——	3-28-1818		W	328	None
Myers, J, heirs	——	1-21-1814		——	547	None
Myers, Jno & Wife	Bullitt	3-11-1814		——	544	None
Myers, Lewis	Lincoln	5-17-1786		A	136	None
Myers, Lewis	Grant	5-16-1829	616	Y	365	None
Myers, Solomon	Harrison	8-11-1826		Y	254	None
Nagle, Maurice	Mercer	6-27-1788	Lot	A	429	None
Nagle, Maurice	——	3-19-1789	Lot	A	527	None
Nagle, Maurice	Mercer	11- 1-1790	400	B-2	288	Balled Hill Cr
Napier, Benj W Sheriff	Casey	12-29-1827	2,000	X	346	Green R
Naylor, Benj & Wife	Adair	3-22-1833	250	Z	359	Br Eagle Cr
Nesbitt, Robt & Wife	Richmond	1-26-1802	4,875	F	438	Rd to Ohio Falls
Netherland, Benj	——	6- 8-1813	50,000	P	367	Various water courses
Netherland, Benj & Wife	Jessamine	9- 4-1800	1,428	H	144	—— Cr
Nevill, Presley	Pittsburg	3- 8-1797	1,400	G	312	Green R
New, Anthony Jr, Atty	——	10-25-1813	1,000	P	249	Cabin Cr
Nicholas, Geo	Mercer	5- 3-1796	2,519	A-2	245	—— Cr
Nicholas, Geo	Lexington	8- 7-1797	6,000	G	88	Muddy R
Nicholas, Jas Bruce	Fairfax	4- 5-1798	2,055	B	347	Main Fk W Fk Wolf Cr
Nicholas, Jas B & Wife	Fairfax	4- 6-1798	4,110	C	343	Lynn Camp Cr
Nicholas, Jas Bruce & Jno Thos	Alexandria	5-19-1797	4,110	B	8	Lynn Camp Cr
Nicholas, Wilson C	——	4- 1-1820		T	459	None
Nicholson, Agnes	Richmond	4-30-1830	10,000	Z	147	Rough Cr
Nicholson, Geo, heirs	Virginia	4-30-1830	10,000	Z	147	Rough Cr
Nicholson, Jno	Philadelphia	3-12-1798	3,000	E	413	None
Nicholson, Jno & Wife	Philadelphia	3- 8-1798	51,500	C	177	Nolinn
Nicholson, Jno & Wife	Philadelphia	3- 9-1798	50,000	C	191	Sextons Cr
Nicholson, Jno & Wife	Philadelphia	3-14-1798	57,000	D	185	None
Nicholson, Jno & Wife	Philadelphia	3- 5-1795	431,043	D	312	Many water courses
Nicholson, Jno & Wife	Philadelphia	3- 5-1795	615,180	28	341	In Kentucky
Nicholson, Robt & Wife	Petersburg	3-31-1806	5,000	M	171	Rolling Fk
Nicholson, Saml	Franklin	4-29-1807	183,388⅓	O	470	Big Sandy R
Noel, Robt S & Wife	Essex	7-23-1833		Z	393	None
Noel, Silas M	Franklin	9-21-1811	491	O	166	Elkhorn
Noel, Silas M	Franklin	1-30-1817	Lot	R	457	Middleton
Noel, Silas M	Kentucky	3-20-1818		S	109	Elkhorn Cr
Noel, Silas M & Wife	Franklin	5- 1-1812	Mill	O	364	Hoskins Cr
Noel, Silas M & Wife	Franklin	5- 1-1812	117½	O	366	None
Noel, Silas M & Wife	Franklin	5- 1-1812	125	O	367	Hoskins Cr
Noel, Silas M & Wife	Franklin	5- 1-1812	108	O	369	None
Noel, Wm & Wife	Washington	5-11-1810	Lot	N	252	Frankfort
Noel, Wm & Wife	Washington	5-11-1810	Lot	N	254	Frankfort

Grantor	Residence	Deed Date	Acres	Book	Page	Watercourse
Norton, Daniel	Norfolk	9- 9-1794	2,000	A-2	456	Highland & Muddy Crs
Norton, Daniel	Norfolk	9-10-1794	2,000	A-2	460	Muddy R
Norton, Daniel	Norfolk	9- 9-1794	2,000	A-2	464	Cypress Cr
Norton, Daniel	Norfolk	9- 9-1794	2,000	A-2	468	Muddy R
Norton, Daniel	Norfolk	9- 9-1794	768⅔	A-2	472	Walnut Bottom & Grove Cr
Norton, Geo	Fayette	2-20-1819	Slaves	T	100	None
Norton, Geo F	Fredericks	12- 1-1796	5,000	B	108	Highland Cr
Norton, Geo F	Fredericks	12- 1-1796	7,333½	B	333	Highland Cr
Norton, Jno H	Winchester	10-12-1795	6,000	A-2	419	Ohio R
Nourse, Chas & Wife	Bardstown	5-22-1817	6,000	R	580	Greensburg Rd
Nourse, Chas & Wife	Nelson	5-23-1817	2,000	R	584	Pottingers Cr
Nourse, Chas & Wife	Nelson	5-23-1817	5,000	R	588	Green R
Nourse, James	Mercer	9-19-1787	200	A	331	Bowmans Cr
Nourse, Jas	———	10- 8-1796	400	O	42	Barnetts Cr
Norvell, Thos	Hanover	3-10-1804	6,000	H	369	Ohio R & Lawrence Cr
Norvell, Thos	Richmond	6- 1-1807	———	L	127	Brush Cr
Norwell, Lipscomb & Wife	Lincoln	3-22-1792	250	B-2	463	None
Norwell, Lipscomb & Wife	Lincoln	3-22-1792	100	B-2	465	Dix R
Norwell, Thos	Richmond	4- 8-1802	1,000	F	431	Ohio R
Norwell, Thos	Richmond	1-17-1803	1,000	K	331	Eagle Cr
Norwood, Frederick & Wife	Henry	1- 9-1833	Lots	Z	250	Port Williams
Numan, Obediah	———	9- 5-1801	754	F	43	Clover Cr
O'Bannon, Elija	Jessamine	7-24-1816	500	R	245	None
O'Bannon, Jno & Wife	———	11- 8-1801	75,000	F	383	Rough Cr
O'Fallon, Jno	St Louis	6-10-1819	200	U	190	Clarks Run
O'Farrel, Jno & Wife	Berkley	1-18-1800	14,166½	F	92	Little Sandy
Offutt, Hugh	Scott	9-11-1820	Lots	U	59	Georgetown
Offutt, Lobert	Scott	10-11-1824	5,000	X	61	Ohio R & Woolpers C
Offutt, Thos B	Montgomery	6-10-1812	1,875	O	463	Caney Bear & Reedy
Ogden, Masterson	Shelby	1821	366½	U	502	6 Mile Cr
Ogden, Masterson	Shelby	1821	100	U	503	Clear & 6 Mile Crs
O'Hara, Kean	Woodford	8-11-1838	Lots	27	271	Lebanon
O'Hara, Kean & Wife	Franklin	2- 6-1841	55½	27	186	S Elkhorn
O'Hara, Kean & Wife	Franklin	4-22-1844	Lot	27	401	Frankfort
O'Hara, Kean & Wife	Franklin	2-12-1845	62	27	463	S Elkhorn
Old, Wm & Wife	Powhatan	5- 1-1835	1,226⅔	27	50	In Green Co
Oldham, Jno P & Wife	Jefferson	6- 2-1821	———	V	288	Rolling Fk & Ohio R
Oldham, Richard & Wife	Campbell	6- 2-1821	———	V	288	Rolling Fk & Ohio R
Oliver, Chas	Baltimore	5-11-1842	1,533	27	283	Otter Cr
Oliver, Jno	Baltimore	1- 6-1812	56,000	R	208	Rowling Cr & Green R
Oliver, Rice W & Wife	Franklin	1-11-1839	5½	27	26	M Elkhorn
Oliver, Robt Atty	Baltimore	1- 6-1812	56,000	R	208	Rowling Cr & Green R
Oliver, Robt, heirs	Baltimore	5-11-1842	1,533	27	283	Otter Cr
O'Neal, Wm Trustee	———	11-18-1819	Lots	T	289	Port Williams
Orr, Alexander D	Mason	8-30-1800	900	E	292	Ohio R
Orr, Benj G	Westmoreland	2-18-1795	11,858½	A-2	115	Eagle Cr
Orr, Benj G	Westmoreland	2-18-1795	15,000	A-2	121	Rolling Fk
Orr, Benj G	Westmoreland	2-18-1795	11,415	A-2	124	Ohio R
Orr, Benj G	Philadelphia	3-10-1796	70,000	Q	166	Big Sandy R
Outteridge, Edward	Washington	4-21-1812	128	P	42	N Br Ky R
Owings, Conquest W & Wife	Mason	4-12-1833	7¾	Z	279	Cane Run
Owings, Geo	Montgomery	4-13-1809	1,000	N	139	M Elkhorn
Owings, Jno Cocky	Baltimore	1-24-1787	1,000	A	264	Coopers Run
Owings, Jno Cocky	Baltimore	11- 9-1801	1,075	F	101	Lecompts Run
Owings, Jno Cocky	Baltimore	12-20-1802	Lot	G	130	Bardstown
Owings, Jno Cocky	Bardstown	8-21-1800	Lots	K	375	Bardstown
Owings, Jno C	Baltimore	2-12-1811	45,000	N	500	Various waters
Owings, Jno Cocky	———	8-21-1800	Lot	R	269	Bardstown
Owings, Jno Cocky	———	8-21-1800	Lot	R	270	Bardstown
Owings, Thos D	Bath	7-19-1816	Slaves	R	72	Red R Iron Works
Owings, Thos Dye Atty	Baltimore	11- 9-1801	1,075	F	101	Lecompts Run
Owings, Thos D Atty	———	8-21-1800	Lot	R	269	Bardstown
Owings, Thos D Atty	———	8-21-1800	Lot	R	270	Bardstown
Owsley, Wm	Garrard	11-00-1821	100	V	107	Greasy Cr
Owsley, Wm	———	5-29-1835	———	Z	512	Elkhorn & Hickman Crs
Owsley, Wm, Executor	Kentucky	10-18-1826	333	Y	212	Br Green R
Overton, Jno	Louisa	2- 8-1796	916	A-2	552	Cumberland R
Overton, Jno	Louisa	5-12-1787	2,000	Q	239	Gesses Cr
Overton, Thos	Louisa	10-15-1795	2,000	B	200	Little Muddy Cr

Grantor	Residence	Deed Date	Acres	Book	Page	Watercourse
Page, Thos S	Frankfort	11- 3-1821	152	V	126	Big Beaver Cr
Page, Thos S	Franklin	3- 4-1841	Lots	27	280	Frankfort
Page, Thos S & Wife	——	7-12-1834	50	Z	448	Elkhorn
Palmer, Chas & Wife	——	10- 8-1804	——	O	148	None
Panebaker, Peter	Nelson	5- 7-1800	500	E	219	Big Slate Cr
Panebaker, Peter	Nelson	5- 7-1800	5,158	E	223	Ohio R
Parberry, Jas	Virginia	2-13-1797	1,200	B	178	Cedar Cr
Parberry, Jas, heirs	——	3-30-1816	——	R	359	None
Parberry, Jas, heirs	——	5—1816	——	R	361	None
Parker, Alexander Comr	Fayette	5-25-1810	246.900¼	N	224	Ohio R
Parker, Jno, Executor	Fayette	11-15-1804	898	P	349	Ky R
Parker, Jno Todd & Wife	Woodford	10-27-1828	Lot	Y	405	Frankfort
Parker, Josiah Decd	——	9-14-1812	2,500	R	51	Br N Fk Tradewater
Parker, Stafford H	Carolina	4- 1-1821	——	V	4	None
Parker, Robt, heirs	Fayette	11-15-1804	898	P	349	Ky R
Parker, Robt, heirs	——	10-20-1819	557	X	128	Glenns Cr
Parker, Wm H	Westmoreland	7-26-1800	666⅔	E	287	Fishing Cr
Parkman, Saml & Wife	Boston	7-16-1814	——	Q	473	None
Parkman, Saml & Wife	Boston	7-20-1811	16,513	R	96	Slate Millers Eagle Cr & Ohio R
Parsons, Joseph	Whitley	4-23-1821	2,750	U	536	None
Pate, Lewis & Wife	Union	4- 2-1814	——	P	411	None
Pate, Lewis & Wife	Union	4- 2-1814	——	P	555	None
Pate, Lewis & Wife	Union	7-18-1815	——	P	379	None
Patrick, Jno	Green	1-17-1800	146¾	D	526	Butlers Fk
Patterson, Chas	Franklin	11-23-1801	34	F	133	Pettets Fk
Patterson, Chas	Franklin	11-23-1801	414	F	134	Pettets Fk
Patterson, Chas & Wife	Franklin	7-19-1803	935	G	383	Big Barren R
Patterson, David	Chesterfield	1- 9-1811	5,000	N	437	Salt Lick Cr
Patterson, Jno	Fayette	5- 9-1786	294	A	99	Hanging Fk
Patterson, Robt Atty	Fayette	11-28-1811	600	O	327	Ohio R
Patterson, Robt & Wife	Montgomery	1-31-1814	100	P	588	Elkhorn
Patterson, Robt & Wife	Montgomery	1-31-1814	83	P	587	Elkhorn & Glenns Crs
Pattie, Wm H F & P R	Franklin	9-16-1844	Lots	27	440	Frankfort
Patton, Robt	Fredericksburg	4-10-1797	19,542	B	49	Lynn Camp & Robertson Crs
Patton, Robt	Fredericksburg	7- 8-1806	200	K	358	Skeggs Cr
Patton, Robt	Fredericksburg	4-18-1821	20,006⅔	V	328	Cabin & Glenns Crs
Patton, Robt	Culpepper	12-27-1822	21,787½	V	463	Cabin Cr & Ky R
Patton, Robt, Com'r	Richmond	12- 9-1802	1,000	G	221	Paraquet Cr
Patton, Robt & Wife	——	9-19-1797	——	D	107	None
Patton, Robt & Wife	Fredericksburg	6- 3-1799	10,023	D	446	Richland Collins Fk & Stinking
Patton, Robt & Wife	Fredericksburg	4-16-1799	9,937	D	543	Lick Fk Richland & Goose Cr
Patton, Robt & Wife	Fredericksburg	4-16-1799	7,000	D	546	Goose Cr
Patton, Robt & Wife	Fredericksburg	3-27-1801	1,000	E	340	Tradewater
Patton, Robt & Wife	Fredericksburg	9-22-1808	400	M	363	E Br Little Ky
Patty, Jno & Wife	Franklin	3-19-1816	200	Q	385	None
Paul, Andrew	Rockridge	6-26-1823	——	W	127	Shoemakers Cr
Paul, Jno	Jefferson	6- 8-1814	500	P	459	Long Falls Cr
Paul, Peter Sr	Grant	3-14-1822	Lot	V	377	Lexington
Pawling, Henry	Lincoln	3- 7-1791	1,000	B-2	246	Beech Fk
Payne, Daniel M C	Fayette	9-22-1824	Lots	W	379	Lexington
Payne, Daniel M C	Fayette	10- 1-1828	3,000	X	496	Harrods Cr
Payne, Elizabeth, heirs	——	7- 7-1829	——	Y	435	Ohio R
Payne, Jesse B & Wife	Henry	3-18-1814	1,000	P	441	Ohio R & Doe Run
Payne, Jno & Wife	Scott	11-19-1821	540	V	228	M Eagle Cr
Payne, Jno & Wife	Scott	11-16-1821	20	V	346	Royal Sp Br
Payne, Jno & Wife	Scott	10- 9-1824	4,000	X	59	Ohio R & Woolpers Cr
Payne, Smith	Goochland	8-21-1801	1,200	H	405	Silver Cr
Payne, Thos J	Fayette	7-13-1829	349	Y	367	Fk Branch
Payne, Wm & Wife	Franklin	9-16-1844	Lots	27	440	Frankfort
Pearce, James & Wife	Frederick	2-19-1808	300	M	83	Big Barren R
Pearce, James & Wife	Frederick	8-24-1809	500	N	44	Big Barren R
Pearce, Jos A & Wife	——	10- 2-1817	3,500	S	329	Craborchard Fk
Pearie, Thos	Nelson	3- 7-1787	500	A	469	Cartwright Cr
Pearson, Edmund B, Atty	Fayette	11-18-1833	1,000	Z	364	Richland & Robertson Cr
Pearson, Thos	Jefferson	7- 2-1796	1,000	A-2	451	Cumberland R
Peart, LeRoy G	Woodford	4-15-1801	811	E	358	Green R
Peart, LeRoy G	Woodford	9-19-1801	4,000	F	39	Green & Cumberland R & Delaware Cr
Peart, Griffin, heirs	Virginia	4-28-1808	864	M	26	None

Grantor	Residence	Deed Date	Acres	Book	Page	Watercourse
Peart, Griffin, heirs	Virginia	4-28-1808	936	M	26	None
Peart, Griffin, heirs	Virginia	4-28-1808	1,034	M	26	None
Peck, Jno	Newton	5-20-1812	30,420	P	205	None
Peck, Jno	Fayette	11- 5-1819	600	T	183	Middle Valley Cr
Peck, Jno	Fayette	8-31-1831	150	Z	157	Beaver & Myers Br
Peck, Jno	Fayette	1-26-1832	Lots	Z	223	Frankfort
Peebles, Thos	Fayette	5-30-1815	135	Q	125	Mill Cr
Pegram, Baker	——	8-16-1802	2,080	G	31	Rolling Fk
Peirce, Jno	—·—	3- 7-1802	6,000	F	491	Ohio R
Peirce, Jno, Trustee	——	12-31-1799	2,000	L	108	Ohio R
Peirsol, Wm & Lydia, heirs	——	7-24-1832	704½	Z	228	S Fk Elkhorn
Pemberton, Bennett	Franklin	6-28-1802	3⅓	F	447	Elkhorn Cr
Pemberton, Bennett	Franklin	2-14-1804	10	H	426	Elkhorn Cr
Pemberton, Bennett	Franklin	2-14-1804	82	J	54	M Elkhorn
Pemberton, Thos	Goochland	7-20-1795	4,000	A-2	498	N Fk Tradewater
Pendergrass, Jesse	Gallatin	11-29-1800	160	E	189	Ky R
Pendergrass, Jesse & Wife	Gallatin	11-29-1800	160	E	236	Ky R
Pendergrasp, Jesse & Wife	Jefferson	6- 4-1802	241	F	425	None
Pendleton, Geo M & Wife	King & Queen	2- 5-1834	2,000	Z	405	Skeggs Cr
Pendleton, Jno S	Franklin	12-15-1821	Lots	V	159	Columbus Ohio
Pendleton, Jno T	——	6- 3-1823	Lots	W	52	Frankfort
Pendleton, Wm G	Richmond	5- 5-1826	——	27	56	Henrico Co & Curles Neck
Pennebaker, Wm & Peter	——	9-11-1804	2,158	H	320	Ohio R
Pennabaker, Wm & Peter	——	9-11-1804	1,000	H	556	Ohio R
Penny, L S, heirs	——	5- 1-1822	Slaves	V	401	None
Penny, Sally	——	5- 1-1822	Slaves	V	401	None
Penticost, Dorsey	Jefferson	2-27-1795	1,000	A-2	388	Guyandot & Sandy
Percifull, Jos & Wife	Meade	7-29-1828	Lots	X	434	Brandenburg
Percifull, Jos & Wife	Meade	7-29-1828	113.482	X	434	Otter Cr & Nolinn
Perkins, Joseph	Louisa	11- 1-1799	——	D	516	W Fk Shot Pouch Cr
Perkins, Joseph	Virginia	1- 9-1807	4,000	M	200	None
Perkins, Joseph R Sr	Louisa	12-29-1807	1,400	Z	267	Hardins&BigBoneCr
Perkins, Mary & Elisha Davis		3- 6-1821	Contract	V	87	......
Perry, Jno, heirs	Frankfort	7-19-1816	10	U	470	None
Perry, Robt	Woodford	3-29-1810	Lot	N	219	Frankfort
Perry, Robt & Wife	Woodford	9- 3-1808	188½	M	429	N Fk Glenns Cr
Peters, Belvard J & Wife	Bath	9-29-1834	6,098¾	Z	499	Licking
Pettit, Franklin D	Franklin	8-10-1839	Lot	27	192	Frankfort
Pew, Gilbert	Frankfort	7-25-1805	Lot	J	388	Frankfort
Pew, Jno	Augusta	7-24-1821	100	V	242	Ky R
Peyton, Francis	——	7- 9-1803	14,936¼	J	91	18 Mile Cr Hardins & Cartwright Crs
Peyton, Francis, Com'r	Alexandria	6- 1-1803	——	M	37	None
Peyton, Jno	Winchester	10- 1-1796	2,000	A-2	651	Hammond Cr
Peyton, Jno & Wife	Winchester	10- 1-1796	1,000	A-2	648	Grapefield
Peyton, Jno & Wife	Winchester	10- 1-1796	300	A-2	653	Ohio R
Phillips, Jno	Philadelphia	3-23-1796	2,000	A-2	476	Muddy R
Phillips, Jno	Philadelphia	3-23-1796	2,000	A-2	479	Cypress Cr
Phillips, Jno	Philadelphia	3-23-1796	2,000	A-2	483	Muddy R
Phillips, Jno	Philadelphia	3-23-1796	2,000	A-2	486	Highland Cr & Muddy R
Phillips, Jno	Philadelphia	3-23-1796	3,166⅔	A-2	489	Walnut Bottom & Grove Cr
Phillips, Jno	Philadelphia	6- 3-1802	4,400	G	402	Beech Fk
Phillips, Jno & Wife	Philadelphia	1-18-1800	1,000	D	529	Deer Cr
Phillips, Jno & Wife	Philadelphia	6- 3-1796	19,000	G	15	Green R & Bacon Cr
Phillips, Jno	Philadelphia	5- 3-1786	56,000	Z	283	None
Phillips, Colo Joseph	Maidenhead	10-16-1797	6,680	G	308	Chaplins Fk
Phillips, Lewis W R	New Jersey	1-29-1829	1,750	Y	319	Salt R
Phillips, Lieut W R	Hunterdon	5-16-1829	16,380	Z	266	Salt R
Phillips, Phillip	Davidson	9- 5-1809	4,700	N	81	Green R
Phillips, Ralph	New Jersey	12-26-1804	200	H	510	Buck Cr
Phillips, Ralph	New Jersey	2-22-1810	3,000	N	141	Salt R & Beech Cr
Phillips, Ralph	Maidenhead	9-10-1810	2,800	N	283	Clear Fk Rough Cr
Phillips, Ralph	Hunterdon	4-29-1817	2,800	R	297	None
Phillips, Ralph	Maidenhead	5- 6-1822	160	V	225	Crooked Cr
Phillips, Ralph	Hunterdon	8-14-1822	1,000	V	291	Salt R
Phillips, Ralph	Hunterdon	8-26-1822	4,720	W	108	Crooked Cr
Phillips, Ralph	Maidenhead	1-28-1824	15,000	W	237	Rolling Fk
Phillips, Ralph	Hunterdon	6- 9-1823	136	W	337	Salt R
Phillips, Ralph	Hunterdon	1-24-1824	115	W	339	None
Phillips, Ralph	Hunterdon	6- 7-1824	125	W	340	Salt R
Phillips, Ralph	Hunterdon	4-24-1824	700	X	77	Salt R

Grantor	Residence	Deed Date	Acres	Book	Page	Watercourse
Phillips, Robt, & Wife	Jessamine	12-23-1799	240	D	496	Pitman Cr
Phillips, Wm	Franklin	1-15-1823	500	V	406	Ohio R
Pickering, Jno Jr	Boston	11-13-1838	6,633	27	166	Little Barren R Glovers & Deer C r
Pickering, Octavius	Boston	12-21-1840	978½	27	169	Little Barren R,Clay Lick Fk & Glovers Cr
Pickering, Timothy, heirs	Essex	11-28-1838	6,633	27	164	Little Barren R Glovers & Deer Crs
Pickett, Geo	Richmond	10- 3-1793	9,198	A-2	56	None
Pickett, Geo	Richmond	7-28-1794	———	A-2	84	Ohio R
Pickett, Geo & Wife	Richmond	2-27-1802	———	F	371	Goose Cr
Pickett, Geo & Wife	Virginia	3- 6-1802	23,875	G	1	Eagle Cr
Pickett, Geo & Wife	Richmond	3-16-1809	6,453⅔	M	375	Muddy R & Highland Cr
Pickett, Geo & Wife	Richmond	3-16-1809	1,000	M	380	W Fk Scioto R
Pickett, Geo & Wife	Richmond	4-15-1809	732	M	416	None
Pickett, Geo & Wife	Richmond	4-19-1809	1,000	M	420	Tradewater
Pickett, Geo & Wife	Richmond	2-28-1811	1,000	P	50	Br Green R
Pickett, Geo & Wife	Richmond	2- 4-1818	9,812	S	298	Salt Lick Cr
Pickett, Geo Jr	Richmond	3-28-1820	———	T	304	Tradewater
Pickett, Geo Jr	Richmond	2- 1-1813	18,000	P	150	Peter Snell & Russell Cr
Pickett, Geo, Trustee	Henrico	2-22-1827	2,950	Z	344	Mississippi R Town Highland & Goose Crs
Pickett, Geo, Dec'd	———	12-22-1838	32,400	27	3	Meade Co
Pickett, Geo, heirs ,	Richmond	3- 4-1833	———	Z	309	None
Pickett, Geo, heirs	———	1- 5-1835	4,000	Z	481	Cypress Cr
Pickett, Geo C	Franklin	9- 1-1825	1,000	X	170	Ohio R
Pickett, Geo C & Robt	———	3- 4-1833	———	Z	309	None
Pickett, Margaret	Richmond	3- 4-1833	———	Z	309	None
Pickett, Thos	Winchester	2-10-1821	14,911½	U	282	Ohio R & Clover Cr
Pierce, Jos A	———	10- 2-1817	1,293½	S	325	Little Ky R
Pierce, Jno	Virginia	7-14-1800	6,000	F	210	Salt R
Pierce, Jno, Executor	Kentucky	7-11-1805	500	J	289	Big Bone Cr
Pierce, Wm L	Georgia	11-22-1811	500	28	86	Pogues Cr
Piggott, Abner & Wife	York	11-21-1814	———	S	176	None
Pinnell, Joseph	Buckingham	3-13-1816	202⅔	R	24	Ohio R
Pitts, Joseph	Franklin	6-30-1807	Negro	L	116	None
Pitts, Joseph	Franklin	6-30-1807	Negro	L	118	None
Pleasant, Saml	Philadelphia	6- 6-1805	29,376	L	180	Green R at Mouth Nolinn
Pleasant, Archibald & Wife	Goochland	3-15-1804	2,827½	J	143	Licking
Plume, Wm, Executor	Norfolk	3- 5-1801	5,133⅓	E	361	Skeggs Cr
Poage, Elijah	Fayette	9- 1-1813	500	P	210	Hardins Cr
Poindexter, Jno Jr	Louisa	4-30-1801	259	F	65	Green R
Pollard, Joseph Jr	Henry	1-27-1815	———	Q	23	Hill Grove
Pollard, Joseph Jr	Henry	1-27-1815	640	Q	24	Elk Grove
Pollard, Robt	Richmond	5-30-1812	2,000	O	445	Red R
Pollard, Robt	———	1- 2-1814	1,000	P	331	Harlins Cr
Pollard, Robt	Todd	7-15-1825	407	X	199	Renfros Pond & Spring Cr
Pollard, Robt	Richmond	7-16-1834	1,248	Z	457	Allen Co
Pollard, Robt & Wife	Richmond	2-27-1802	9,446⅔	F	373	Sinking Fk Little R
Pollard, Robt & Wife	Richmond	3-16-1809	5,500	M	369	Cypress Cr
Pollard, Robt & Wife	Richmond	4-19-1809	1,000	M	420	Tradewater
Pollard, Robt & Wife	Richmond	4-19-1809	500	M	426	Scioto & Miami R
Pollard, Robt & Geo	———	4-21-1834	Lots	Z	431	Richmond Va
Pollard, Wm	Philadelphia	3- 1-1787	19,000	G	6	Green R, Bacon Cr
Pope, Jno	———	10-14-1806	1,000	K	477	N Elkhorn
Pope, Jno	Lexington	10- 8-1808	500	Q	508	Ky R
Pope, Jno	Frankfort	7- 5-1818	Lot	S	238	Frankfort
Pope, Jno	Washington	3- 1-1828	120	X	389	Waltons Cr
Pope, Jno	———	9- 8-1829	100	Y	395	Plum Cr
Pope, Jno	Arkansas	2- 1-1830	250	Y	438	Big Benson Cr
Pope, Jno	Arkansas	8-15-1830	Ferry	Y	509	Ky R & Big Benson
Pope, Jno	Kentucky	6-11-1834	50	Z	440	Ohio R
Pope, Jno, Atty	———	3-11-1806	200	K	327	Pond Cr
Pope, Jno, Atty	Washington	5-16-1822	———	V	217	Mill Cr
Pope, Jno & Wife	Fayette	10-10-1811	Lots	O	191	Frankfort
Pope, Jno & Wife	Washington	3- 1-1828	165	X	388	Lynn Camp Cr
Pope, Jno & Wife	Washington	3- 1-1828	87½	X	389	Waltons Cr
Pope, Jno & Wife	Arkansas	12- 7-1829	56	Y	420	Big Benson Cr
Pope, Wm	———	10-16-1797	6,000	B	247	Big Bone Lick
Pope, Wm	———	3- 9-1789	1,000	B-2	35	Elkhorn
Porter, Jeremiah	Oldham	11- 3-1830	21½	Z	33	S Elkhorn
Porter, Nathaniel & Wife	Port Williams	10-00-1819	Lot	T	361	Frankfort

Grantor	Residence	Deed Date	Acres	Book	Page	Watercourse
Porter, Richard	Henry	10-30-1830	21⅓	Z	32	S Elkhorn
Porter, Wm & Wife	Franklin	10——1819	Lot	F	361	Frankfort
Porter, Wm & Wife	Franklin	4-19-1821	117	Z	342	Franklin Co
Porter, Wm Jr & Wife	Gallatin	4-19-1821	117	Z	342	Franklin Co
Posey, Thos & Wife	Franklin	10-10-1802	350	G	136	Elkhorn Cr
Powell, Burr, Atty	Loudoun	6- 1-1802	1,000	F	436	Buffaloe Cr
Powell, Burr, Atty	——	6- 1-1802	2,474	F	434	Green R N Fk S Fk Licking & Ohio R
Powell, Leven	Loudoun	10-22-1791	2,000	B-2	407	Ohio R
Powell, Leven & Wife	——	10-31-1791	———	B-2	466	None
Powell, Owen	Franklin	8-16-1806	———	K	380	Cylos Cr
Powell, Wm	Woodford	11- 5-1802	1,000	F	186	Longfall Cr
Prather, Basil	Monongalia	3-23-1787	400	A	296	Irish Station
Prather, Basil	——	9- 5-1801	754	F	43	Clover Cr
Prather, Thos	Lincoln	11-15-1784	43½	A	245	Harrods & Dry Cr
Prentis, Jas	——	6-11-1822	112	V	350	None
Prentis, Jas	——	6-15-1822	150	V	351	Eagle Cr
Prentis, Jas	——	10-21-1823	264	W	144	None
Prentis, Jas	——	10-21-1823	116	W	146	None
Prentis, Jas	——	10-21-1823	110	W	147	None
Prentis, Jas	——	10- 7-1823	64	W	198	None
Prentis, Jas	Virginia	11- 1-1827	241	X	309	Eagle Cr
Prentis, Jas	——	12-17-1827	Lots	X	329	Owensboro
Prentis, Jas	——	12-17-1827	417	X	329	Ohio R
Prentis, Jas	——	1-23-1828	42,283	X	366	None
Prentis, Jas	Virginia	8-27-1828	125	X	454	Eagle Cr
Prentis, Jas	Virginia	9- 3-1828	168	X	473	Ohio R
Prentis, Jas	Virginia	9- 3-1828	135	X	475	None
Prentis, Jas, Trustee	——	6-15-1822	90	V	254	None
Prentis, Jas, Trustee	Virginia	10-18-1827	295	X	291	Blackfords Cr
Prentis, Jas, Trustee	Virginia	11- 1-1827	53	X	306	Eagle Cr
Prentis, Jas, Trustee	——	5-18-1826	1,000	Y	171	Ohio R
Prentis, Jas, Trustee	——	2- 8-1826	750	Y	174	Ohio R
Prentis, Jas, Trustee	Virginia	——1826	295	Y	189	Blackfords Cr
Prentis, Jas, Trustee	———	1-31-1834	———	Z	402	Bullitt Co
Prentis, Wm	Petersburg	6-23-1821	———	V	45	None
Preston, Francis & Wife	Washington	10- 2-1818	———	S	262	None
Preston, Jno	Montgomery	4-14-1797	5,500	A-2	673	Harrods Cr
Preston, Jno & Wife	——	12- 4-1815	3,353⅓	Q	369	None
Preston, Wm, by Executor	——	6- 9-1789	700	B-2	72	Ohio R
Preston, Wm, by Executor	——	6- 9-1789	700	B-2	73	Ohio R
Price, Robt	King William	8-19-1796	7,000	A-2	572	Ohio R
Price, Robt, Executor	King & Queen	9- 9-1796	———	A-2	532	None
Price, Saml	Bourbon	10-13-1791	1,400	B-2	391	Floyds Fk
Price, Saml & Wife	Franklin	9-18-1798	87	D	8	Elkhorn & Licking
Price, Saml & Wife	Franklin	9-18-1798	62	D	10	None
Price, Saml & Wife	Franklin	9-18-1798	28	D	7	None
Price, Thos	——	12-20-1797	1,000	C	204	Tradewater
Price, Thos	Hanover	2-22-1799	1,000	D	342	N Fk Tradewater
Price, Thos	Hanover	11-25-1799	637	E	229	N Fk Tradewater
Price, Thos	Russell	1- 1-1815	850	Q	236	Russell Fk
Price, Wm, Atty	Richmond	10-22-1798	1,000	D	125	Cox & Williams Crs
Proctor, Thos, heirs	Pennsylvania	3-15-1828	277	X	393	None
Pryor, Jno	———	7-20-1822	461	V	462	Benson Cr
Pryors, C A, Mary, Jno & Elizabeth	——	1- 4-1844	30	27	381	Lower Blue Lick
Pullam, Nathan	Garrard	5-22-1810	Negro	N	235	None
Pulliam, Benj	Franklin	10-28-1819	200	T	137	N Elkhorn
Pulliam, Benj & Wife	Franklin	3-10-1818	Lot	S	74	Frankfort
Pulliam, Benj & Wife & Ballard	Franklin	3- 9-1818	100	S	73	None
Pulliam, Wm & Wife	Franklin	3-16-1818	Lot	S	101	Frankfort
Purviance, Henry	——	11- 2-1802	2,250	G	134	None
Purviance, Henry, Atty	——	11- 8-1798	108	D	68	None
Purivance, Henry, Atty	——	2-17-1799	408	D	123	Ohio & Green R
Purviance, Henry, Atty	——	8- 9-1797	50,000	D	286	Green R
Purviance, Henry & Wife	——	11-18-1803	4,916	H	135	Middle Island Cr
Purviance, Jno	Philadelphia	3- 4-1786	13,666⅔	D	190	N Fk 3 Fks Ky R
Purviance, Robt	——	2-17-1799	408	D	133	Ohio & Green R
Purviance, Saml, heirs	——	11- 2-1802	2,250	G	134	None
Purviance, Saml, heirs	——	11-16-1803	114.911	H	205	Ohio & Salt R
Quarles, Benj & Wife	——	10- 8-1804	———	O	148	None
Quarrier, Alexander & Wife	Kanawha	12-22-1823	1,025	W	233	Ky R
Quinn, Benj	Scott	11- 8-1799	353	D	416	Tates Cr
Quirk, Thos	Franklin	11-10-1801	350	F	107	Town Fk
Radford, Wm & Wife	Richmond	2-25-1800	1,000	E	191	Skeggs Cr

Grantor	Residence	Deed Date	Acres	Book	Page	Watercourse
Radford, Wm & Wife	Richmond	8-20-1800	1,200	E	248	Big Barren R & Bays Fk
Raffity, Malcum	Madison	5- 8-1802	2,000	G	116	Big Bone Lick & Bank Lick Cr
Ragsdale, Drury	————	12-22-1800	2,000	M	218	Tradewater&Ohio R
Ragsdale, Drury & Wife	King William	3- 1-1797	4,000	C	214	Deer Cr
Ralston, Robt	Philadelphia	3-10-1789	13,666⅔	D	195	N Fk 3 Fk Ky R
Ramsay, Jno	New York	11- 3-1816	21,000	S	444	Chaplins Fk
Ramsey, Enos & Wife	Franklin	3-28-1828	50	X	392	Frankfort & Versailles Rd
Ramsey, Saml G & Wife	Knox	5-10-1805	668	J	37	Ohio R
Ramsey, Saml G & Wife	Knox	5-10-1805	680	J	42	Ohio R
Ranch, Margaret	Reading	7-28-1807	1,000	O	356	None
Randall, Thos B	Baltimore	1- 4-1800	14,500	E	32	Ky R
Randolph, Peyton & Wife	————	12- 8-1817	7,750	R	606	None
Ranald, Wm & Wife	Montgomery	8-18-1808	———	M	333	None
Ranscin, Elizabeth C	Washington	11-14-1845	1,920	28	60	Cedar Cr
Raquet, Claudius Paul	Philadelphia	8-21-1786	23,300	A-2	19	Nolinn
Raquet, Claudius P, heirs	————	10-10-1814	308	P	534	Salt R
Raquet, Claudius & Wife	Philadelphia	9-22-1832	15,000	Z	233	Salt R
Raquet, Condy	Philadelphia	10-24-1821	28,270	V	448	Salt & N Fk Ky R
Raquet, Paul, heirs	Pennsylvania	9-30-1814	400	P	523	Br Salt R
Raquet, Paul, heirs	Philadelphia	6-27-1818	6,700	S	224	Middle & Valley Cr
Rash, Nicholas & Wife	Philadelphia	12-28-1787	1,000	O	353	None
Rawle, Wm	————	11- 7-1827	201½	X	317	None
Rawle, Wm	————	9-13-1828	136	X	462	Hinkstons Fk
Rawlings, Richard	Maryland	12-17-1805	416½	K	402	None
Ray, James	Washington City	9- 1-1801	10,000	G	358	Ohio R
Rayman, Jno	Bullitt	8- 1-1828	———	X	423	Salt R
Read, Isaac	Philadelphia	11-28-1817	———	W	3	None
Read, Isaac & Wife	Philadelphia	9-16-1816	———	W	6	None
Read, Jonathan, heirs	Washington	12-18-1823	———	W	221	None
Reading, Geo	Harrison	12- 6-1796	300	A-2	581	S Fk Benson Cr
Reading, Geo	Harrison	12-10-1805	100	K	124	S Fk Big Benson Cr
Reading, Jno M	Franklin	1-23-1805	181½	K	221	None
Reading, Jno M & Wife	Franklin	5-10-1817	1,060	R	291	Ky R & Big Benson Cr
Reading, Saml	————	6- 3-1807	1,760	L	56	Big Benson Cr
Reading, Saml	Franklin	12-11-1816	24	R	91	None
Reading, Saml	Franklin	1-31-1817	92	R	416	Whites Br
Rector, Chas	Frederick	9-27-1788	———	A	479	W Fk Grassy Lick
Rector, Chas	Frederick	9-26-1788	———	A	499	W Fk Grassy Lick
Reed, Amos	Monongalia	9- 1-1815	———	S	281	None
Reed, Jno, Com'r	Washington	10-17-1814	45,000	P	598	Beech Fk
Reed, Jno & Wife	Philadelphia	6-19-1801	1,254	F	79	Clay Lick & Little Barren R
Reed, Jno & Wife	————	1- 4-1806	6,845½	K	397	Elkhorn
Reed, Jno & Wife	Philadelphia	11-18-1807	6,174	S	380	Cumberland R & Br Pond Cr
Reed, Geo & Wife	Union	6-30-1814	———	Q	372	None
Reed, Geo & Wife	Union	7-18-1815	———	Q	374	None
Rees, Thos F	Henry	9-18-1805	100	K	116	——— Br
Reese, Wm	————	6-21-1843	Lot	27	356	Frankfort
Reinholdt, Geo	Philadelphia	11-25-1803	3,000	H	305	None
Reinholdt, Geo	Philadelphia	10-17-1816	22,000	R	390	None
Reinholdt, Geo, Atty	Philadelphia	4-13-1821	6,000	U	418	None
Reinicker, Henry & Edward	Baltimore	10-10-1843	2,000	27	366	Fayette Co
Renick, Henry	Barren	9- 5-1812	1,000	P	118	None
Renkin, David & Wife	Washington	11- 7-1807	———	L	388	Salt R
Rentfro, James	Lincoln	11-23-1798	22½	D	81	Elkhorn
Respass, Thos	Bourbon	10- 2-1810	600	N	433	Br N Fk Tradewater
Reynolds, Ann	Adams	10-24-1843	———	27	459	Clay Co
Reynolds, Chas F	Franklin	4-22-1842	Lots	27	286	Frankfort
Reynolds, James	Philadelphia	7-30-1786	5,000	D	175	Br Ky R
Reynolds, Jas	Philadelphia	9-15-1786	10,000	N	1	None
Reynolds, Jas	Philadelphia	6-29-1786	5,000	O	415	N Fk Ky R
Reynolds, Wm	————	————1794	1,437½	A-2	65	Chaplins Fk
Reynolds, Wm	Henrico	5-11-1795	8,123	A-2	328	S Fk Little Barren & Skeggs Cr
Reyburn, Mary	Frankfort	6-13-1817	Lot	R	352	Lexington
Rice, Edmund, heirs	Frederick	8-12-1816	———	R	161	None
Rice, Elizabeth	Kentucky	8-12-1816	———	R	161	None
Rice, Geo	Frederick	10- 2-1797	1,333⅓	C	222	Highland Cr
Rice, Geo	Fredericks	10- 2-1797	800	C	225	Highland Cr
Rice, George & Wife	Frederick	2- 4-1811	10,000	O	24	Little Sandy R
Rice, Geo & Wife	Frederick	2- 4-1811	———	O	37	Green R
Rice, Jno	Mercer	1- 3-1809	54¾	M	352	Shawnee Run
Richard, Jno	Richmond	3-28-1820	———	T	304	Tradewater

Grantor	Residence	Deed Date	Acres	Book	Page	Watercourse
Richards, Geo B & Wife	Bath	11- 9-1829	1,000	Z	484	Deer Fk Green R
Richards, Gregory B & Geo	Norfolk	12-20-1816	2,500	R	599	Goose Cr
Richards, Humphrey	Petersburg	5-25-1797	10,000	B	141	Goose Cr
Richards, Wm	Culpepper	1-31-1810	981	O	482	Ohio R & Otter Cr
Richards, Wm, heirs	Culpepper	11- 3-1817	12,500	W	9	None
Richards, Wm, heirs	Bath	10- 3-1826	1,000	Y	317	Deer Cr
Richardson, F R & Nathaniel	Franklin	9-12-1833	67	Z	352	S Benson Cr
Richardson, Jno C, Com'r	Kentucky	11-25-1834	176¾	Z	467	Fayette Co
Richardson, Jno D & Wife	Frankfort	8-19-1812	Lot	P	40	Frankfort
Richardson, Marquis	Franklin	3- 4-1811	Negro	N	444	None
Richardson, Marquis & Wife	Clark	10-19-1820	109	N	67	Howards & Boones Cr
Richardson, Nathaniel	Franklin	8-17-1807	390	L	119	—— Br
Richardson, Nathaniel	Franklin	——1826	450	Y	232	None
Richardson, Preston	Marion	11-22-1831	160	Z	164	Mississippi R
Richeson, Elizabeth H	King William	8-20-1811	——	O	150	None
Richeson, Francis W & Wife	Virginia	11-15-1809	4,800	N	117	None
Richeson, Jno B	King William	10-11-1811	2,400	O	156	Ohio & Br Muddy R
Richmond, Ezra	Franklin	12-14-1840	Lot	27	180	Frankfort
Richmond, Ezra & Wife	Marion	7-10-1845	13	28	18	Ky R
Ricketts, Jno T	Alexandria	5-19-1797	4,110⅔	B	30	Green R
Ricketts, Jno Thos	Fairfax	4- 5-1798	4,110⅔	C	348	Lynn Camp Cr
Ricketts, Jno T & Wife	Fairfax	3-17-1806	3,110⅔	K	483	Main Br Wolf Cr
Riddick, Thos F	St Louis	10-26-1809	1,000	N	55	Cumberland R
Ridgeley, Frederick	——	11- 6-1805	2,000	J	370	Floyds Fk
Ridgeley, Frederick	Lexington	11- 3-1815	314	Q	235	None
Ridgeley, Frederick	Lexington	1- 8-1818	32,025	S	49	Slate Cr, Licking & Ky Rs
Ridgeley, Frederick Atty	——	10-24-1809	7,500	N	258	Mo Big Miami
Ridgeley, Frederick & Wife	Fayette	3-18-1808	600	S	136	—— R
Ridgeley, Richard	——	11- 2-1793	3,067	A-2	287	None
Ridgeley, Wm S	Cincinnati	12-31-1833	88	Z	382	S Fk Elkhorn
Roach, Rush	Kentucky	8-12-1816	——	R	161	None
Roam, Jas & Wm	Virginia	4- 5-1799	333⅓	D	437	Big Barren R
Roam, James & Wm	Virginia	4- 5-1799	1,750	D	440	Little Barren R
Roam, Dr Jno	Dinwiddie	2- 4-1841	1,000	27	197	Tennessee R
Roane, Christopher	——	2- 4-1841	1,000	27	197	Tennessee R
Roane, James & Wife	Charles City	5-21-1798	1,785	D	41	Ohio & Tennessee R
Roane, James & Wife	Charles City	5-21-1798	1,000	D	44	Ohio R
Roberson, Abner	Richmond	3-20-1807	942	L	99	Salt R
Roberts, Benj & Wife	Jefferson	8-17-1791	1,000	N	180	Br Licking
Roberts, Benson	Harrison	2-21-1831	98	Z	100	Grays Run
Roberts, Jas & Wife	——	6-14-1804	2	H	270	None
Roberts, Jno	——	3-17-1795	1,200	A-2	276	—— Cr
Roberts, Dr Jno	Franklin	12-20-1805	Lots	K	453	Frankfort
Roberts, Jno & Wife	Franklin	1-24-1814	500	Q	16	Todds Fk Little Miami
Roberts, Wm	Shelby	6- 4-1801	400	E	410	N Fk W Fk Red R
Roberts, Wm	Shelby	12-20-1804	318	K	520	Beaver Cr
Robertson, Abner	Virginia	4- 2-1807	983	L	89	Salt R
Robertson, Alexander	Mercer	9-24-1786	940	A	258	Beargrass Cr
Robertson, Alexander & Wife	Mercer	9-24-1786	940	A	258	Beargrass Cr
Robertson, Jas	Mercer	11- 4-1796	413	N	149	Beech Fk
Robertson, Jas	Garrard	7-14-1816	1,400	R	333	—— R
Robertson, Jas	Reg Land Office	1-18-1842	1,000	27	256	Tradewater
Robertson, Geo & Wife	Garrard	7-14-1816	1,400	R	333	—— R
Robertson, Wm A	Illinois	2- 5-1839	Slaves	27	23	None
Robins, Moses	Fayette	6- 3-1800	1,033½	E	9	Deer Cr
Robins, Moses	Shelby	11- 9-1803	517	H	19	Green R
Robinson, Chas B & Wife	Stafford	6-21-1816	800	R	315	Ohio R
Robinson, Chas B & Wife	Stafford	6-25-1816	800	R	318	Ohio R
Robinson, Henry & Wife	Spotsylvania	3-19-1803	500	J	17	None
Robinson, Jno	——	8-24-1790	600	A-2	443	Bank Lick Cr
Robinson, Jno	Amhurst	9-20-1796	600	A-2	445	None
Robinson, Jno	Amhurst	9-24-1796	600	A-2	608	Bank Lick Cr
Robinson, Jno	Franklin	2-26-1810	Lot	P	244	Banging Lot
Robson, Jno S	Frankfort	10-16-1819	Lots	T	141	Frankfort
Rogers, Edmund	Barren	11-25-1830	1,094¼	Z	48	Tennessee R, Bayo. Little Obin. Drake Cr & Ohio R
Rogers, Edmund	Barren	12-23-1833	876¾	Z	402	Little Barren Tennessee & Ohio Rs

Grantor	Residence	Deed Date	Acres	Book	Page	Watercourse
Rogers, Geo Dec'd	——	12-23-1833	876⅔	Z	402	Little Barren, Tennessee & Ohio Rs
Rogers, Jno	——	5-31-1792	2,500	P	97	Tennessee & Ohio R
Rogers, Saml	Boston	6- 6-1803	——	H	173	None
Rogers, Thos	Warren	9-23-1829	Lots	Y	396	Columbus Ky
Rogers, Thos	Warren	11-25-1830	1,094¾	Z	48	Tennessee & Ohio Rs Little Obin & Drake Cr
Rogers, Thos	Warren	12-23-1833	876⅔	Z	402	Little Barren Tennessee & Ohio R
Rollings, Nancy	Palmyra	2- 2-1818	——	S	56	None
Ronald, Andrew, heirs	Richmond	1-12-1814	5,320	R	257	S E Fk Skeggs Cr, Big Barren & Green R,
Rooter, Edmund W	Richmond	10- 2-1808	2,000	M	269	Big Bone Lick
Rose, Jno, heirs	Westmoreland	9-10-1814	1,500	Q	466	Gasper R
Ross, David	Richmond	9-23-1796	8,000	B	63	Rock House Cr
Ross, David	Richmond	9-23-1796	107,681	B	71	N Fk Ky R
Ross, David	Richmond	9- 9-1794	20,781	C	270	N Fk Ky R
Ross, David	Cumberland	9-16-1799	9,000	D	445	Cabin Cr
Ross, David	Cumberland	10-20-1804	425	K	216	Clover Cr
Ross, David	Cumberland	7-30-1806	2,000	L	12	Big Bone Lick
Ross, David	Richmond	3- 5-1807	32,696	L	183	Rough Panther & Caney Crs
Ross, David	——	12- 1-1807	200	L	338	Eagle Cr
Ross, David	——	5- 7-1808	3,500	L	380	Sinking Cr
Ross, David	Richmond	1-20-1808	194,493	M	124	Various Waters
Ross, David	Richmond	1- 1-1808	200	S	114	None
Ross, Davids Adm'r	——	6-14-1797	3,000	D	216	Ohio R
Ross, Davids Dec'd	Buckingham	6-24-1819	——	T	109	None
Ross, Davids Dec'd	——	11——1820	600	U	192	Eagle Cr
Ross,Davids Dec'd, heirs	——	11- 5-1818	——	T	39	None
Ross, David, heirs	——	6-23-1821	——	V	20	Ky R
Ross, David, heirs	——	6-15-1832	——	Z	203	None
Ross, David & Fredrick A	——	3-28-1818	——	W	328	None
Rowan, Jno & Wife	Frankfort	12-12-1801	180	F	348	Stewarts Cr
Rowan, Jno & Wife	King & Queen	4-15-1802	2,000	G	72	Br E Fk Little Barren
Roy, James & Wife	——	10-25-1813	1,000	P	249	Cabin Cr
Roy, Ralph L	Essex	4- 3-1796	1,200	A-2	375	Little Ky R
Roy, Ralph L	Essex	4- 3-1796	800	A-2	377	Little Ky
Roy, William Atty	Essex	6- 2-1796	1,000	E	322	Cabin Cr
Royster, Conquest & Wife	Gloucester	9- 1-1796	1,000	N	246	Tennessee R
Royster. Thos	——	10-16-1797	6,000	B	247	Big Bone Lick
Royster, Thos B & Wife	Matthews	9- 1-1796	1,000	N	246	Tennessee R
Rucker, Angus & Wife	Madison	7-24-1813	1,000	P	281	Cumberland R
Rucker, Elliott & Wife	Woodford	1- 1-1815	666⅔	P	584	Russels Cr
Rucker, Ephram & Wife	Anderson	9-28-1827	55	X	286	Benson Cr
Rucks, Jas	——	6-21-1843	Lot	27	356	Frankfort
Rucks, Jas & Wife	Jackson	12- 7-1844	167	27	462	Ohio R & Mill Cr
Rupe, Nicholas & Wife	Franklin	12- 5-1846	37	28	111	None
Ruter, Thos	Baltimore	3- 9-1797	8,800	A-2	687	Ohio R
Rutherford, Robt & Wife	Berkley	1- 2-1799	1,000	D	168	Grapefield
Ryland, Jno	Maclenburgh	10- 3-1796	400	A-2	644	Highland Cr
Sackett, Saml	New York	9-19-1807	35,456	Q	535	None
Sackett, Saml	New York	7-30-1798	260,178	R	225	Ohio R
Sacry, Robt & Wife	Franklin	3- 7-1842	15	27	272	N Elkhorn
Sadler, Thos	Charlotte	2-10-1796	681¼	H	477	Brushy Fk
Sale, Robt	Gallatin	8-22-1805	341	L	303	S Fk Licking
Sallee, Rana S	Mercer	5-16-1829	100	Y	364	Glenns Cr
Salter, Wm D	New Jersey	8-16-1842	9,188	27	308	Chaplins Fk
Samuel, Churchill	Franklin	3- 4-1841	Lots	27	280	Frankfort
Samuel, Chas P	Franklin	3-11-1839	——	27	123	N Elkhorn
Samuel, Chas P & Wife	Franklin	1-11-1839	11½	27	25	Elkhorn
Samuel, Chas P & Wife	Franklin	11-16-1831	5	Z	163	Dry Cr
Samuel, Jno T	Franklin	1-21-1840	——	27	102	None
Samuel, Juliet M	Franklin	6-12-1845	25	27	479	Near Frankfort
Samuel, Larkin	——	2-12-1823	37	W	73	None
Samuel, Larkin & Wife	Frankfort	7-16-1819	——	T	52	None
Samuel, Riley G	Franklin	8-19-1839	180	27	55	Franklin Co
Samuel, Wm, heirs	——	4-14-1846	143	28	101	Franklin Co
Sanders, Jno & Wife	Franklin	7-18-1798	50	C	323	None
Sanders, Jno & Wife	Gallatin	1-24-1828	106	X	365	Eagle Stevens & Indian Cr
Sanders, Joseph	Brunswick	8- 3-1797	1,000	B	204	Cumberland R
Sanders, Lemuel	Franklin	12- 2-1842	40	27	398	M & S Elkhorn
Sanders, Lemuel	Franklin	10-31-1845	1	28	34	Fks Elkhorn
Sanders, Lewis Jr	Natchez	8-20-1839	431	27	71	Indian Fk Eagle Cr
Sanders, Lewis & Wife	Fayette	10-21-1815	16	R	601	Cane Run
Sanders, L U	Gallatin	8- 9-1819	150	T	61	Indian Gap

Grantor	Residence	Deed Date	Acres	Book	Page	Watercourse
Sanders, Nathaniel Sr.	Gallatin	6- 5-1816	6,000	R	3	None
Sanders, Nathaniel & Wife	Gallatin	1-25-1815	40	Q	4	Fk Elkhorn
Saunders, Jno	Gallatin	11- 7-1804	53	H	429	None
Satterwhite, Walker	Franklin	7-23-1819	100	U	80	None
Savage, Wm	Henrico	1-19-1802	730	F	359	Cumberland R
Savary, Jno	Bourbon	5-16-1798	36,700	D	328	Sandy R & Middle Cr
Savary, Jno	Millersburg	7- 1-1812	1,793	P	536	None
Sawyer, Robt	Pulaski	8-25-1829	———	Y	381	Elkhorn
Say, Benj	Philadelphia	8-14-1795	90,000	A-2	26	Cumberland R
Schwizer, Jno G	Paris	12- 6-1809	10,781	N	321	N Fk Ky R
Scott, Chas & Wife	———	5-30-1798	500	C	217	——— R
Scott, Ezekiel F	Missouri	10——1834	13	Z	468	Elkhorn
Scott, Joel	Frankfort	11-26-1827	Lot	X	326	Frankfort
Scott, Jno	Amelia	10-23-1818	1,000	U	85	——— Cr
Scott, Jno	Gallatin	1-17-1822	200	V	221	Eagle Cr
Scott, Jno	Gallatin	12-12-1821	200	V	223	Eagle Cr
Scott, Jno & Wife	Gallatin	2- 4-1810	200	N	233	None
Scott, Jno & Wife	Gallatin	1——1813	100	P	193	Eagle Cr
Scott, Jno & Wife	Gallatin	10-16-1815	160	Q	216	Eagle Cr
Scott, Jno & Wife	Gallatin	3-19-1816	200	Q	385	None
Scott, Jno & Wife	Gallatin	10-16-1815	360	Q	497	Eagle Cr
Scott, Jno & Wife	Gallatin	10-16-1815	360	R	202	Eagle Cr
Scott, Jno & Wife	Gallatin	10-16-1815	350	R	204	Eagle Cr
Scrogin, Joseph & Wife	Gallatin	10-13-1818	200	T	220	Shawnee River
Scott, Matthew T & Wife	Fayette	3-25-1845	Lot	28	47	Frankfort
Scott, Thos Com'r	Clark	3-22-1810	3,039	N	391	Beaver Cr
Scott, Thos C	Falmouth	11-16-1839	2,500	27	96	M Elkhorn
Scott, Thos C & Wife	Stafford	1- 1-1844	2,500	27	395	Franklin Co
Scott, Robt W	———	6-21-1843	Lot	27	356	Frankfort
Scott, Robt W	———	6-21-1843	Lot	27	356	Frankfort
Scott, Robt W & Wife	Franklin	11-25-1833	Lot	Z	374	Frankfort
Scott, Wm & Wife	Powhatan	8-24-1815	$866\frac{2}{3}$	R	169	Tennessee R
Scott, Wm & Wife	Powhatan	8-24-1815	$866\frac{2}{3}$	R	172	Br Tennessee R
Searcy, Bartlett, heirs	Fayette	12- 4-1815	———	Q	337	Rockhouse Br & Ky R
Searcy, Bartlett, heirs	Fayette	12- 4-1815	———	Q	425	Ky R Clear & Howards Cr
Searcy, Edmund, heirs	Shelby	1——1841	$10,586\frac{2}{3}$	27	194	Mayfield Cr & Walnut Bottom
Seay, Austin	———	6-27-1820	200	U	29	Green R
Seay, Austin Atty	———	6-27-1820	200	U	25	Green R
Selby, Benj	Adair	3-10-1823	325	V	459	Cypress Cr
Selby, Benj Auditor	Kentucky	6- 2-1842	———	27	288	None
Sergeant, Joseph G	Kentucky	6-25-1844	300	28	41	Breckinridge Co
Settles, Nancy, heirs	———	10- 8-1832	500	Z	239	Mississippi R
Settles, Sally	Green	10- 8-1832	500	Z	239	Mississippi R
Shannon, Elias & Wife	Henry	3-11-1833	$10\frac{3}{4}$	Z	494	S Elkhorn
Shannon, Jas	Woodford	12-26-1834	$10\frac{3}{8}$	Z	473	Elkhorn
Shannon, Jas & Wife	Louisville	3-18-1818	Lot	S	75	Frankfort
Shannon, Saml & Wife	Shelby	5-23-1805	3,470	K	105	2 Mile, Stony, Green Hunting & Flatt Crs
Shannon, Wm & Wife	Philadelphia	11-13-1805	———	N	156	None
Shaw, Thos	Adair	5-12-1818	200	S	243	None
Shaw, Wm C & Wife	Baltimore	9-26-1845	2,500	28	35	Elkhorn & Cedar Cr
Sharp, Francis R	Anderson	7-20-1841	$6\frac{1}{2}$	27	316	Ky R
Sherman, Martin	Lancaster	12- 6-1799	$666\frac{2}{3}$	D	443	N Fk Mayfield Cr
Sheffey, Hugh W	Augusta	12-27-1841	1,000	27	281	Hickman Co
Shelby, Evan	Lincoln	12- 1-1838	Lots	27	29	Frankfort
Shelby, Evan Sr	Fayette	10-13-1783	2,000	A	1	Elkhorn
Shelby, Isaac	———	4-11-1804	560	H	417	None
Shelby, Isaac	———	2-13-1815	660	P	627	Dix R
Shelby, Isaac	———	7- 1-1815	500	Q	93	Green Fk Licking
Shelby, Isaac	———	8- 1-1815	300	Q	177	Green R
Shelby, Isaac	Lincoln	5-12-1819	800	S	500	Hays Fk Silver Cr
Shelby, Isaac Executor	Lincoln	9-26-1814	1,600	P	516	Beaver Cr
Shelby, Isaac & Wife	Frankfort	5- 9-1814	476	P	476	Harrods Run
Shelby, Isaac & Wife	Lincoln	1-10-1822	Lot	V	166	Frankfort
Shelby, Isaac & Wife	Lincoln	11-28-1830	Lot	Z	66	Frankfort
Shelby, Jno Jr & Jno Sr	Sullivan	12- 2-1789	913	B-2	255	Hickman Cr
Shelby, Moses	N Carolina	1-15-1790	800	B-2	146	Hickman Cr
Shelton, Jno	Goochland	11-15-1804	898	P	349	Ky R
Shelton, Saml	Mercer	3-17-1788	40	A	379	Dix R
Shepherd, Jno M & Wife	Richmond	3-15-1800	1,000	E	68	Marble Cr
Shepherd, Peter, heirs	———	11-10-1814	158	P	557	Brashears Cr
Shepherd, Peter, heirs	———	11- 7-1815	553	Q	223	Wolf Br
Shepherd, Peter, heirs	———	10- 2-1815	$57\frac{1}{4}$	Q	226	None
Shepherd, Peter, heirs	———	10- 2-1815	$23\frac{1}{2}$	Q	227	None
Shepherd, Peter, heirs	———	10- 2-1815	Lots	Q	228	Jefferson
Shepherd, Peter, heirs	———	11-11-1815	88	Q	231	——— Cr
Shepherd, Peter, heirs	———	—-15-1815	248	Q	232	None

Grantor	Residence	Deed Date	Acres	Book	Page	Watercourse
Shepherd, Peter, heirs	———	10-26-1815	259	Q	462	None
Shepherd, Peter, heirs	———	6- 3-1816	238½	Q	489	Mill Cr
Shepherd, Peter, heirs	———	6- 3-1816	146	Q	492	Mill Cr
Shepherd, Peter, heirs	———	6- 3-1816	165	Q	495	Mill Cr
Shepherd, Peter, heirs	———	11- 8-1816	237½	R	60	Valley Cr
Shepherd, Peter, heirs	———	10- 7-1816	500	R	303	Beech Fk
Shepherd, Peter, heirs	Baltimore	6-11-1817	284	R	340	None
Shepherd, Peter, heirs	———	8- 4-1817	553	R	366	Wilsons Cr
Shepherd, Peter, heirs	———	8- 4-1817	200	R	368	Rolling Fk
Shepherd, Peter, heirs	———	12- 7-1826	2,483	X	465	Elk Cr
Shepherd, Susan	Baltimore	5-25-1814	50	P	473	Wolf Run
Shepherd, Susan	Baltimore	5-23-1814	114½	P	475	Fk Wolf Run
Shepherd, Susan	———	11-29-1814	106	P	566	None
Shepherd, Susan	———	4-19-1815	75	Q	43	Brashears Cr
Shepherd, Susan	———	5- 3-1815	100	Q	51	None
Shepherd, Susan	Baltimore	5-25-1815	214	Q	120	Elk Cr
Shepherd, Susan	Baltimore	5-26-1815	35	Q	121	Elk Cr
Shepherd, Susan	Baltimore	5-26-1815	181	Q	122	Elk Cr
Shepherd, Susan	———	10- 2-1815	100	Q	198	Shepherds Cr
Shepherd, Susan	———	2- 8-1816	1,000	R	215	Cedar Cr
Shepherd, Susan	Baltimore	11- 8-1817	104	R	568	None
Shepherd, Susan	———	4- 9-1818	85	S	100	Elk Cr
Shepherd, Susan	Baltimore	5- 5-1818	1,000	S	121	Mill Cr
Shepherd, Susan	———	11-23-1818	150	S	343	None
Shepherd, Susan	———	4-19-1820	———	T	434	Elk Cr
Shepherd, Susan	Baltimore	12- 5-1821	393	V	139	None
Shepherd, Susan	Baltimore	1-10-1824	35	W	169	Shepherds Run
Shepherd, Susan	———	5-17-1824	50	W	271	None
Shepwith, Henry	Cumberland	9-10-1790	25	B-2	197	Hanging Fk
Sheriff, Bath Co	Bath	9-29-1834	6,098¾	Z	498	Licking
Sheriff, Franklin Co	Franklin	2-13-1822	Ferry	X	71	Ky R
Sheriff, Franklin Co	Franklin	5-18-1829	———	Y	372	Ky R
Sheriff, Franklin Co	Franklin	6-18-1832	96	Z	200	Franklin Co
Sheriff, Franklin Co	Franklin	3- 8-1833	Lot	Z	281	Frankfort
Sheriff, Franklin Co	Franklin	11-20-1834	494	Z	480	Sulphur Lick Cr
Sheriff, Franklin Co	Franklin	1-27-1841	100	27	182	N Elkhorn
Sheriff, Franklin Co	Franklin	11-30-1841	195	27	298	Ky R
Sheriff, Franklin Co	Franklin	11-30-1841	450	27	302	Ky R
Sheriff, Franklin Co	Franklin	10- 2-1843	Lots	27	371	Frankfort
Sheriff, Jefferson Co	Jefferson	3-30-1843	13	27	344	Near Louisville
Sheriff, Livingston Co	Livingston	5-13-1812	1,500	P	44	None
Sheriff, Union Co	Union	4-21-1834	666⅔	Z	469	Tradewater
Sherman, Rowland	Louisville	8-16-1823	690	W	106	Cumberland R
Shields, Patrick	Lincoln	2- 8-1790	260	B-2	116	Ky R
Shiell, Ann, Executrix	Lincoln	6-25-1789	344	B-2	67	Hanging Fk
Shipp, Colby & Wife	Scott	8- 8-1798	6,134¼	C	311	Main Licking
Shore, Thomas, heirs	———	2-25-1796	5,900	A-2	136	Silver & Goose Crs
Shore, Thomas, heirs	———	2-25-1796	5,900	M	50	Silver, Muddy & Station Camp Cr
Shore, Thos, dec'd	———	11- 5-1818	———	T	23	None
Short, Chas W & Wife	Jefferson	4-20-1840	116	27	120	S Elkhorn
Short, Peyton	Woodford	4- 2-1802	4,300	F	221	——— R
Short, Peyton	Woodford	4-28-1802	50	F	505	——— Cr
Short, Peyton	Woodford	4-26-1802	2,000	G	182	None
Short, Peyton	Woodford	2-15-1804	8,000	H	331	Miami R
Short, Peyton	Woodford	9-21-1804	13,500	H	454	Ohio R & Patton Cr
Short, Peyton	Woodford	12-31-1804	———	H	564	Pond R
Short, Peyton	Lexington	7-12-1809	1,000	M	439	Cumberland R
Short, Peyton	———	10-24-1809	7,500	N	258	Mouth Big Miami
Short, Peyton	———	11- 9-1810	220	N	310	Mill & Distillery
Short, Peyton	———	11- 9-1810	220	N	312	Mill & Distillery
Short, Peyton	Lexington	6-28-1811	615	O	71	Cumberland R
Short, Peyton	———	10-24-1809	7,500	O	142	Mouth Big Miami
Short, Peyton	West Florida	8-18-1811	15,625	O	146	M Licking
Short, Peyton	———	9-10-1811	16,000	O	160	Ky R
Short, Peyton	Estill	11-16-1815	314	Q	242	None
Short, Peyton	Franklin	3-13-1818	540	S	65	Ky R
Short, Peyton	Christian	5-23-1822	3,046	V	253	Licking
Short, Peyton, Atty	———	10-17-1798	2,666⅔	D	48	——— Cr
Short, Peyton & Wife	———	9-22-1804	535	H	367	Ohio R
Short, Wm	Philadelphia	1-22-1828	65	X	353	S Fk Elkhorn
Shortridge, Eli	Montgomery	6-30-1821	———	U	456	None
Shrieve, Thos T	Greenup	12-17-1823	1,596¾	W	226	Little Hickman Cr
Shryock, Gidion & Wife	Fayette	7-24-1833	75	Z	319	Ky R
Shryock, Gideon & Wife	Kentucky	4-12-1834	Lot	Z	420	Lexington
Siddon, Thos	Fredericksburg	7-24-1823	———	W	189	None
Siemer, Paul	Philadelphia	12-19-1798	3,000	H	310	None
Simmons, Joseph	Lancaster	8- 2-1802	2,000	G	320	Fox Run
Simmons, Jno B, Atty	———	10-10-1814	308	P	534	Salt R
Simms, Jesse	Alexandria	3-14-1800	9,000	E	145	Drennons Lick Cr
Simms, Jesse	Alexandria	7-26-1800	3,000	E	153	Rolling Fk

Grantor	Residence	Deed Date	Acres	Book	Page	Watercourse
Simpson, David	Amherst	6- 2-1788	200	A	391	Paint Lick & Drakes
Simpson, David	Amherst	6- 2-1788	200	A	394	Paint Lick
Simpson, Jas, Com'r	Clark	3-22-1810	8,039	N	391	Beaver Cr
Simpson, Patrick	Vincemis Knox	12- 5-1798	1,530	D	173	E Fk Marrowbone C
Simpson, Robt & Wife	Mercer	3-29-1814	360	P	385	Salt R
Sinclair, Wm P, heirs	Scott	3- 7-1837	222	27	364	N Fk Elkhorn
Sisle, Jno	Philadelphia	10-23-1809	113,482	N	161	Ohio R
Sisle, Jno	Philadelphia	10-25-1809	31,778	N	166	Little Sandy & E Fk Dix R
Skiles, Wm H & Wife	Warren	3- 6-1829	901	Y	398	Tennessee R
Skillem, Geo, heirs	——	7- 8-1817	250	R	347	Sugar Cr
Skipwith, Henry	Williamsburg	6- 7-1814	6,891	P	451	Goose, Dix & Ohio R
Skirvin, Robt L	Gallatin	12-29-1840	——	27	176	None
Slaughter, Augustine	Norfolk	11- 1-1796	2,250	B	55	Muddy Cr
Slaughter, Augustine	Norfolk	1-11-1802	4,000	F	368	Big Mud Cr
Slaughter, Gabriel	Frankfort	2-11-1819	1,443	S	470	Panther Cr
Slaughter, Geo	Jefferson	10-21-1798	116	A	516	Hanging Fk
Slaughter, Geo	Jefferson	3-12-1789	½	A	518	None
Slaughter, Geo & Wife	Spotsylvania	11- 2-1801	10,000	F	234	None
Slaughter, Lawrence & Wife	Spottsylvania	1-17-1795	1,050	A-2	636	Hingston Fk
Slaughter, Lawrence & Wife	Susanna	9- 8-1801	10,000	F	231	None
Slaughter, Philip	Culpepper	12-17-1802	2,666⅔	H	178	Red R & Br Green R
Slaughter, Philip & Wife	Culpepper	3-17-1804	1,000	H	580	Clay Lick Cr
Slaughter, Philip & Wife	Culpepper	2-15-1808	1,000	N	48	None
Slaughter, Philip & Wife	Culpepper	2-15-1808	1,000	N	52	None
Sledge, Louisa	Hamilton	2- 4-1841	1,000	27	197	Tennessee R
Smart, Jas P & Wife		9-24-1824	——	X	69	S Fk Benson Cr
Smith, Asa	Washington	12-22-1809	500	P	299	None
Smith, Augustus J & Wife	Fairfax	1- 3-1800	13,982	E	138	Rolling Fk & Little Ky
Smith, Beverly & Wife	Manchester	4-29-1824	——	X	158	None
Smith, Billy & Jno	Louisa & Hanover	4-10-1797	5,500	A-2	674	Harrods Cr
Smith, Chas	Fayette	7-25-1785	1,400	A	76	Salt R
Smith, Chas Sr & John	Harrison	4-10-1821	1,000	V	9	Glen Cr
Smith, Clement	Fayette	6-10-1830	900	27	76	Cumberland R
Smith, David & Wife	McCracken	5- 8-1839	4,320	28	62	W Tennessee R
Smith, Edwin B & Wife	Bath	5-12-1802	1,000	G	156	Green R
Smith, Elman D	Jefferson	9- 1-1826	223	X	218	None
Smith, Francis	Franklin	10-25-1796	200	A-2	550	Br Buck Cr
Smith, Geo	Lincoln	10- 1-1784	200	A	78	Harrods Cr
Smith, Geo	Lincoln	10- 1-1784	200	A	80	Harrods Run
Smith, Geo	Powhatan	11-29-1791	203	B-2	481	Rolling Fk
Smith, Geo	Powhatan	11-29-1791	549	B-2	483	S Fk Big Benson Cr
Smith, Geo	Powhatan	11-29-1791	814	B-2	486	S Fk Big Benson Cr
Smith, Geo	Franklin	3-13-1811	626½	N	441	Clay Lick Cr
Smith, Geo & Wife	Franklin	2-10-1814	——	P	379	Dix & Rock Castle
Smith, Geo & Wife	Franklin	12-30-1814	237	Q	2	Fks Elkhorn
Smith, Geo W	Richmond	1——1803	3,500	J	204	Skaggs & Big Bone Lick Cr
Smith, Hugh & Wife	Mercer	3-29-1814	360	P	385	Salt R
Smith, Jas	Mercer	11- 3-1788	500	A	446	Fleming Cr
Smith, James Jr	Philadelphia	7-13-1811	2,000	O	443	Red R
Smith, Jas & Wife	Mercer	3-29-1814	360	P	385	Salt R
Smith, Jno	Fayette	9-24-1785	——	A	25	None
Smith, Jno	Batetourt	6-23-1789	300	B-2	120	—— R
Smith, Jno A W	Virginia	5-15-1819	200	S	548	Ky R
Smith, Jno A W	Virginia	11-25-1820	600	U	173	Eagle Cr
Smith, Jno A W	Fanquier	3-26-1823	1,095	W	61	Cane Run Mill & Drennons Lick Cr
Smith, Jno A W	Fanquier	3-13-1823	250	W	162	Martins Br
Smith, Jno A W	Fanquier	3——1823	250	W	217	Ky R
Smith, Jno A W &Wife	Fanquier	7-24-1823	——	W	189	None
Smith, Larkin	King & Queen	10-10-1796	1,000	A-2	671	Trade Water
Smith, Larkin	King & Queen	9-12-1798	1,000	E	1	Ohio R
Smith, Nicholas, Atty	Henry	4- 5-1802	1,320	F	225	Otter Cr Muddy R
Smith, Nicholas, Atty	Henry	4- 5-1802	1,333⅓	F	227	Big Barren R
Smith, Nicholas, Atty	Henry	4- 5-1802	1,000	F	229	Highland Cr
Smith, Peter	Hamilton	5-23-1804	1,000	J	27	Pond R
Smith, Richard	Richmond	8-14-1795	20,781	C	274	N Fk Ky R
Smith, Richard	Middlesex	7-20-1801	20,698	H	514	Killicanick Cr
Smith, Richard	Middlesex	7-21-1801	20,698	H	518	Killicanick Cr
Smith, Robt	Philadelphia	8-25-1786	——	A-2	108	Ohio R
Smith, Robt	Philadelphia	8-25-1796	390,000	A-2	320	Ohio R
Smith, Robt & Wife	Baltimore	9-15-1806	93,813¾	K	426	Stinking, Shelby & Main Licking
Smith, Robt & Wife	Philadelphia	2-21-1812	4,000	O	504	W Fk Pitmans Cr
Smith, Saml	Baltimore	10-28-1818	6,000	S	367	Muddy R
Smith, Saml	——	4- 1-1820	——	T	459	None

Grantor	Residence	Deed Date	Acres	Book	Page	Watercourse
Smith, Saml & Wife	Baltimore	11-26-1821	119,289½	V	174	Licking, Shelby & Green R
Smith, Sarah	———	3-13-1805	———	L	306	None
Smith, Sarah	Woodford	11-16-1807	Slaves	L	334	None
Smith, Thos	Warren	10-13-1804	383	J	67	S Fk Big Benson Cr
Smith, Thos	Warren	11- 8-1809	1,060	N	213	S Fk Big Benson Cr
Smith, Thos J	Jessamine	11- 8-1809	———	N	232	Whites Cr
Smith, Thos P, Atty	Bourbon	4-10-1821	1,000	V	9	Glen Cr
Smith, Thos P, Com'r	Bourbon	8-27-1821	400	U	537	Highland Cr
Smith, Thos R	Green	10- 8-1832	500	Z	239	Mississippi R
Smith, Thos S	Jessamine	10-13-1804	383	J	67	S Fk Big Benson Cr
Smith, Wm	———	11- 8-1808	———	M	423	Red River Iron Works
Smith, Wm R & Wife	Philadelphia	10-29-1813	———	P	288	None
Smith, Wm S & Wife	Powhatan	8-26-1800	1,000	E	113	N Fk Clay Lick Cr
Smith, Willis R	Bourbon	7- 6-1829	160	Y	374	Harrods Cr
Smither, Robt Jr	Franklin	1-16-1804	1,406½	H	147	Twin & Eagle Crs
Smither, Robt Jr	Franklin	12-18-1804	166¼	H	498	Twin Cr
Smither, Robt Sr	Franklin	6- 6-1800	800	H	421	Twin Cr
Smither, Sally	Franklin	5- 3-1844	50	27	406	M Elkhorn
Sneed, Achillis	Franklin	3-17-1815	20	Q	29	Glens Cr
Sneed, Achillis	Franklin	10-20-1815	125	Q	277	Ky R
Sneed, Achillis	Franklin	7-24-1816	———	Q	518	Ky R
Sneed, Achillis	Frankfort	12- 5-1816	11¼	R	79	Buck Cr
Sneed, Achillis	Franklin	9- 7-1816	700	R	111	Clear Cr
Sneed, Achillis	Franklin	2-21-1817	———	R	152	Big Benson Cr
Sneed, Achillis	Frankfort	11- 5-1816	400	R	196	Dry Ridge Road
Sneed, Achillis	Franklin	6-11-1818	242	S	151	Bacon Cr
Sneed, Achillis	Frankfort	1-10-1819	306½	S	491	Green R & Bacon Cr
Sneed, Achillis	Franklin	11-20-1818	114	T	6	None
Sneed, Achillis	Franklin	11-18-1819	116	T	244	Br Muddy Cr
Sneed, Achillis	Frankfort	2- 1-1819	100	T	287	Fks Muddy Cr
Sneed, Achillis	Franklin	12-15-1819	Lot	U	188	Frankfort
Sneed, Achillis	Frankfort	7-13-1821	Lot	U	476	Elizabeth
Sneed, Achillis	Frankfort	1-17-1822	200	V	221	Eagle Cr
Sneed, Achillis	Frankfort	12-12-1821	200	V	223	Eagle Cr
Sneed, Achillis	Frankfort	8-23-1822	224	V	295	None
Sneed, Achillis	Franklin	11- 9-1822	100	V	368	Dickeys Fk Eagle Cr
Sneed, Achillis	———	6- 3-1823	Lots	W	52	Frankfort
Sneed, Achillis	Franklin	9- 1-1823	400	W	100	Trammels Fk
Sneed, Achillis	Frankfort	11- 6-1824	44	W	408	None
Sneed, Achillis	Frankfort	11-29-1824	500	X	31	Caney Fk Cedar Cr
Sneed, Achillis, heirs	Franklin	7-19-1827	6,074	X	479	None
Sneed, Achillis, heirs	Franklin	3- 5-1839	43	27	16	In Franklin Co
Sneed, Achillis, Atty	———	11- 1-1810	2,000	N	295	Ohio R
Sneed, Achillis, Atty	Frankfort	4-25-1814	16,380	P	428	Salt R & Crooked Cr
Sneed, Achillis, Atty	Frankfort	7-27-1815	666⅔	Q	149	Glens Cr
Sneed, Achillis, Com'r	———	11- 1-1810	2,000	N	293	Ohio R
Sneed, Achillis, Com'r	Franklin	4-29-1811	750	N	460	Br Chaplins Fk
Sneed, Achillis, Com'r	Franklin	7- 8-1817	250	R	347	Sugar Cr
Sneed, Acnilles, Trustee	Frankfort	9-26-1819	199¾	T	371	None
Sneed, Achillis & Wife	Franklin	2——1805	666⅔	H	585	Ohio R
Sneed, Achillis & Wife	Frankfort	9-11-1805	5,415½	J	267	Cedar Cr
Sneed, Achillis & Wife	Frankfort	5- 5-1810	11	N	186	Glens Cr
Sneed, Achillis & Wife	Frankfort	1-12-1811	1,767	N	412	Eagle Cr & S Fk Licking
Sneed, Achillis & Wife	———	6-17-1811	426	O	46	Ky R
Sneed, Achillis & Wife	Franklin	1-13-1812	5,312½	O	437	Hingston Fk
Sneed, Achillis & Wife	Franklin	1-27-1813	250	P	53	Bacon Cr
Sneed, Achillis & Wife	Franklin	1-27-1813	450	P	56	Bacon Cr
Sneed, Achillis & Wife	Franklin	1-27-1813	776	P	58	Bacon Cr
Sneed, Achillis & Wife	Frankfort	1-27-1813	150	P	60	Bacon Cr
Sneed, Achillis & Wife	Franklin	1-27-1813	150	P	62	Bacon Cr
Sneed, Achillis & Wife	Franklin	1-27-1813	1,750	P	64	None
Sneed, Achillis & Wife	Franklin	1-27-1813	272	P	67	None
Sneed, Achillis & Wife	Franklin	1-27-1813	200	P	68	None
Sneed, Achillis & Wife	Frankfort	1-27-1813	120	P	70	None
Sneed, Achillis & Wife	Franklin	1-27-1813	400	P	72	None
Sneed, Achillis & Wife	Franklin	4-23-1813	1,000	P	120	Parrogone Cr
Sneed, Achillis & Wife	Franklin	7- 1-1813	1,000	P	157	Cabin Cr
Sneed, Achillis & Wife	Franklin	7-27-1813	81½	P	169	Glens Cr
Sneed, Achillis & Wife	Franklin	8-14-1813	500	P	191	Glens Cr
Sneed, Achillis & Wife	Frankfort	7-18-1814	30	P	524	Glens Cr
Sneed, Achillis & Wife	Franklin	12-20-1814	500	P	571	None
Sneed, Achillis & Wife	Franklin	1- 7-1815	———	P	583	Gilberts Cr
Sneed, Achillis & Wife	Franklin	2-23-1815	91	Q	26	Benson & Beech Cr
Sneed, Achillis & Wife	Franklin	2-23-1815	45	Q	27	None
Sneed, Achillis & Wife	Frankfort	7- 8-1815	318	Q	141	Ky R Big Benson
Sneed, Achillis & Wife	Franklin	12-27-1815	300	Q	296	Bacon Cr
Sneed, Achillis & Wife	Franklin	1-23-1816	150	Q	452	Silver Cr
Sneed, Achillis & Wife	Franklin	10- 3-1815	———	Q	480	None

Grantor	Residence	Deed Date	Acres	Book	Page	Watercourse
Sneed, Achillis & Wife	Franklin	10-16-1815	360	Q	497	Eagle Cr
Sneed, Achillis & Wife	Frankfort	10-16-1815	360	R	202	Eagle Cr
Sneed, Achillis & Wife	Frankfort	10-16-1815	350	R	204	Eagle Cr
Sneed, Eliza	Franklin	5-18-1829	———	Y	372	Ky R
Sned, Jedediah	Hanover	3- 1-1824	2,000	W	326	Deer Cr
Sneed, Jno	Tennessee	2-13-1828	102	X	380	Cedar Cr
Sneed, Laudon & Wife	Franklin	3-21-1809	———	M	356	None
Sneed, Saml C & Wife	Gallatin	3- 5-1806	200	K	178	Eagle Cr
Sneed, Sarah	Mercer	5- 5-1807	Slaves	N	88	None
Southall, Geo & Peyton	———	3- 7-1802	6,000	F	491	Ohio R
Southard, Daniel R	———	11-20-1833	15,000	Z	372	None
Southerland, Wm	Orkney N Britain	2-13-1799	1,000	D	534	Ohio R
Southgate, Orville	———	1-10-1844	———	27	386	Cumberland R
Southgate, Orville	———	1-16-1845	637	27	456	Crooked Cr
Spalding, Ignatius A & Wife	Union	2-26-1831	150	Z	119	Salt R
Spears, Paul	Bourbon	11-15-1786	———	A	230	Hinkston Fk
Speed, James		3-14-1789	———	A	519	None
Speed, James	Mercer	3-15-1790	50	B-2	130	Lower Howards Cr
Speed, James	Mercer	11-10-1789	250	B-2	132	Lower Howards Cr
Speed, James	Mercer	8- 8-1798	1,863½	C	317	Station Camp Cr
Speed, James & Wife	Mercer	3-11-1806	200	K	327	Pond Cr
Speed, Jno & Wife	Jefferson	8-26-1817	28,556	R	561	Licking & Salt R
Spencer, Edward	Baltimore	9-26-1845	2,500	28	35	Elkhorn & Cedar Cr
Spilman, Jas	Green	2-27-1795	842	A-2	425	S Fk Licking
Spotwood, Jno & Wife	Orange	4- 8-1799	1,000	E	342	Tradewater
Sprigg, Joseph	Washington	7-16-1812	3,000	P	47	None
Springer, Chas	Frankfort	3-14-1812	Lot	O	350	Frankfort
Spurr, Barbara	Fayette	12-26-1844	———	27	452	Armstrong Fk
Stafford, Wm	Fayette	9-19-1787	400	A	329	Brashears Cr
Stafford, Wm	Fayette	3- 8-1796	6,200	A-2	134	Small Br
Stafford, Wm	Fayette	5-18-1789	350	B-2	69	Guesses Fk
Stafford, Wm	Shelby	8-13-1804	2,100	H	286	None
Stainton, Andrew	Prince Edward	4-20-1801	34,200	F	119	Yellowbanks, Panther & Licking
Stanford, Wm	Shelby	3———1833	250	Z	368	Mill Cr
Stapp, Achillis	Scott	9-24-1821	Horse	V	63	None
Stapp, Elijah & Wife	Adair	11-10-1830	275	Z	42	Pendleton Co
Starting, Wm	Logan	2-23-1833	1,000	Z	260	Hickman Co
Starting, Wm	Logan	6-21-1833	1,000	Z	302	Mississippi R
Starling, Wm & Wife	Franklin	3-21-1816	6	R	184	Wilsons Cr
Starling, Wm Jr & Wife	Frankfort	8- 7-1819	Lot	T	69	Frankfort
Starling, Wm Sr	Springfield	5-16-1821	———	U	479	Ky R
State Com'lth	Kentucky	12-30-1843	Lot	27	384	Midway
State Com'lth	Kentucky	10- 8-1844	Lot	27	435	Midway
State of Kentucky	Kentucky	12-30-1843	Lot	27	385	Midway
St. Clair, Alexander	Stanton	3-15-1813	1,000	P	153	Ky R
St. Clair, Alexander	Augusta	12-18-1795	8,476½	A-2	447	Brush Cr
Steele, James	Maryland	4-19-1806	27,000	K	405	Green R
Steele, James	Hartford	7- 6-1812	250	O	500	Green R
Steele, Saml	Woodford	12-27-1804	200	H	509	Buck Cr
Steele, Wm	Woodford	7-17-1799	400	D	358	Long Br
Steele, Wm, Atty	Woodford	10- 6-1802	1,000	F	515	Hustons Fk
Steene, Jno	Mercer	2- 9-1798	Lot	B	325	None
Stello, Amy Ann	Providence	7-31-1827	Lot	X	403	Maysville
Sterrett, Jno & Wife	Scott	12-18-1800	148	E	244	None
Stephens, Benj & Jas W	Philadelphia	2-17-1795	15,000	A-2	118	Rolling
Stephens, Polly	Culpepper	6- 9-1821	———	U	531	None
Stephens, Richard	Nelson	7-13-1796	3,110	A-2	412	Salt R
Stephens, Richard	———	4- 1-1797	15,000	B	182	Little Ky R
Stephens, Richard	Nelson	12- 7-1809	1,750	N	65	Harrods Cr
Stevens, Benj	Philadelphia	12-25-1797	6,680	G	304	Chaplins Fk
Stevens, Richard	Breckinridge	10-14-1801	793½	F	385	Br Muddy Cr
Stevenson, Job	Scott	12-25-1821	Lot	V	298	Georgetown
Stevenson, Saml	Hardin	3-25-1815	Slaves	Q	32	None
Stevenson, Susan	Franklin	10- 5-1842	Lot	27	325	Carrollton
Stevenson, Susannah T	Franklin	8- 1-1842	———	27	323	Rope Walk
Stevenson, T B	Franklin	1-19-1846	Lot	28	50	Frankfort
Stewart, Ayers	Logan	7-20-1798	Lots	Z	135	Russellville
Stewart, James	Washington	11-30-1791	200	B-2	507	Green R
Stewart, James	Philadelphia	1-25-1804	3,791	L	355	Eagle Cedar & Elkrn
Stewart, Jas H	Lexington	8- 2-1803	500	G	388	S Br Nolinn
Stewart, Jas H	Bourbon	11-11-1807	30,000	L	177	Buffaloe Lick
Stewart, Jno	Culpepper	9-24-1811	1,000	O	186	M Fk N Fk Red R
Stewart, Jno & Wife	Oglethorp	10-16-1827	930	X	298	Boones Cr
Stewart, Jno & Wife	Oglethorp	10-29-1827	691	X	305	Boone Cr
Stewart, Robt	New York City	7-27-1815	666⅔	Q	149	Glens Cr
Stewart, Wm, Dec'd	Woodford	11-23-1811	200	O	203	Stewarts Cr
Sthreshly, Thos, heirs	———	8- 9-1830	———	Y	506	S Elkhorn
Sthreshly, Thos, heirs	———	8- 9-1830	192	Y	507	S Elkhorn
Sthreshlys, Thos & Wife	Fayette	5-29-1799	666⅔	D	154	Ohio R
Sthreshlys, Wm & Wife	Fayette	5-29-1799	666⅔	D	154	Ohio R

Grantor	Residence	Deed Date	Acres	Book	Page	Watercourse
Still, Bartlett	Richmond	11- 8-1803	1,000	H	119	Ohio R
Stockdell, Jno & Wife	Henrico	10- 3-1788	2,000	C	212	Salt Lick Cr
Stogdill, Jno & Wife	Richmond	6-13-1791	25,993	B-2	359	Salt Lick Cr
Stom, Bryant & Wife	Nelson	3- 2-1819	200	S	475	Br Eagle Cr
Stom, Wm S & Wife	Fredricksburg	9- 1-1800	10,250	E	260	Tripletts Cr
Storm, Thos	New York	10-28-1820	16,380	U	155	Salt R
Story, David	Buck	12- 9-1822	2,850	Y	478	Salt R
Story, Jno	New York City	5- 9-1788	3,018	G	128	Beech Fk
Story, Jno Jr	Philadelphia	6- 7-1788	1,500	Y	476	Salt R
Story, Jno Jr	Philadelphia	6- 6-1788	4,000	Z	38	Salt R
Story, Jno Jr, heirs	Philadelphia	12- 9-1822	2,850	Y	478	Salt R
Stout, Amos & Wife	Woodford	11-26-1827	Lot	X	325	Frankfort
Stras, Geo F	Richmond	1-21-1802	3,000	K	450	Deer Cr
Stras, Martha,Executrix	Henrico	2-19-1817	1,000	S	78	Deer Cr
Stringer, Richard	Ann-Arundel	11- 2-1793	3,067	A-2	287	None
Strode, Jno	Culpepper	3——1799	300	D	307	Russell Cr
Strode, Thos & Wife	Louisville	4-23-1813	——	P	129	Ohio R & Otter Cr
Strode, Thos & Wife	Virginia	6- 4-1818	12,500	W	11	None
Strong, Walter E	Mercer	5-12-1790	Lot	B-2	124	Danville
Strong, Walter E	Mercer	8-10-1791	207½	B-2	511	Little Barren R
Strother, French & Wife	Culpepper	9-30-1796	2,433	A-2	628	Little Ky R
Strother, French & Wife	Culpepper	9-30-1796	1,018½	A-2	631	Hinkston Fk
Strother, Joseph, heirs	Kentucky	1- 1-1814	——	P	364	None
Stuart, Jno	Greenbrier	10-12-1814	100	P	553	Little Ky R
Stubblefield, Geo	Frederick	10-10-1798	500	D	503	Fox Cr
Stubbs, Thos R	Green	10- 8-1832	500	Z	239	Mississippi R
Sturgas, Daniel	Georgia	9-22-1791	1,000	B-2	476	Hingston Fk
Sturges, Jonah, Atty	New York	8-16-1825	690	W	106	Cumberland R
Sublett, Benj	Powhatan	3-18-1800	1,128¾	E	62	Cumberland R
Suggett, David & Wife	Scott	7-20-1841	——	27	220	None
Suggett, Jas M	Scott	11-10-1845	——	28	77	None
Sullivan, Jas	Jefferson	1-15-1788	1,000	A	459	S Fk Elkhorn
Summers, Benj	Bullitt	4-19-1805	——	J	138	Cedar Cr
Surghuor, Jas & Wife	——	11-12-1818	1,000	S	323	Brashears Cr
Sutton, David & Wife	Mercer	9-16-1815	Lot	Q	192	Frankfort
Sutton, Jno Jr	Scott	8- 5-1807	600	L	220	Ohio R
Swan, David Cooper	Jefferson	12-19-1842	21,288	27	332	In Hardin & Grayson Co
Swan, David Cawper	Hardin	11-22-1819	1,840,000	V	468	Various watercourses
Swan, Jas	Boston	11-22-1819	910,954	U	90	N Fk Ky & Big Sandy R
Swan, Jno	Powhatan	7-17-1799	400	D	358	Long Br
Swan, Jno	Powhatan	10- 6-1802	1,000	F	515	Hustons Fk
Swan, Jno	Scott	10-20-1808	100	M	402	N Fk Elkhorn
Swearingen, Benonia & Wife	Maryland	4- 1-1796	2,947	A-2	587	Skeggs Cr
Swearingen, Thos V	Fayette	9-13-1841	Slaves	27	229	None
Sweeny, Thos	New York	2-18-1820	205	W	239	None
Sweeny, Thos	New York	5- 7-1820	1,000	Z	173	In Harrison Co
Swift, Jonathan	Alexandria	8- 1-1795	568	A-2	307	Green R
Swift, Jonathan	Alexandria	11- 4-1809	4,700	N	142	Green R
Swigert, Jacob	Franklin	5-18-1829	——	Y	372	Ky R
Swigert, Jacob	Fayette	12-21-1833	Lot	Z	387	Frankfort
Swigert, Jacob	Franklin	5- 7-1835	2,787½	Z	506	Licking
Swigert, Jacob	Franklin	6- 4-1835	67	Z	518	S Benson Cr
Swigert, J	Franklin	4- 9-1839	Lot	27	20	Frankfort
Swigert, Jacob	Franklin	10-28-1840	100	27	150	S Benson Cr
Swigert, Jacob	Franklin	12-31-1845	Lot	28	43	Frankfort
Swigert, Jacob & Philip	Franklin	9-13-1844	73	27	446	Benson Cr
Swigert, Jacob & Philip	Franklin	12-18-1844	Lot	27	448	Louisville
Swigert, J & P	Franklin	1-13-1846	153	28	45	S Elkhorn
Swigert, J & P	Franklin	1-13-1846	24	28	46	S Elkhorn
Swigert, J & P	Franklin	12-31-1846	——	28	110	In Franklin Co
Swigert, P & J	Franklin	10- 1-1846	Lot	28	112	Frankfort
Swigert, J & P	Franklin	2- 3-1847	Lot	28	124	Louisville
Swigert, Jno	Owen	5-10-1824	74	W	360	Eagle Cr
Swigert, Philip	Franklin	10- 5-1839	Lot	27	79	Frankfort
Swigert, Philip & Jacob	Franklin	12-13-1843	——	27	449	Big Benson Cr
Swigert, Philip	Fayette	6-11-1845	Lots	28	2	Midway
Swigert, Philip	Franklin	6-11-1845	Lot	28	11	Midway
Swigert, Philip	Franklin	6-11-1845	Lot	28	11	Midway
Swigert, Philip	Franklin	6-11-1845	Lot	28	12	Midway
Swigert, Philip	Franklin	6-17-1845	Lot	28	13	Midway
Swigert, Philip	Franklin	1-12-1846	Lot	28	49	Midway
Swigert, Philip	Franklin	1-12-1846	Lot	28	49	Midway
Swigert, Philip	Franklin	2-18-1846	Lots	28	59	Frankfort
Swigert, Philip	Franklin	2-18-1846	95	28	59	Ky R
Swigert, Philip, Atty	Franklin	9-26-1845	2,500	28	35	Elkhorn & Cedar Cr
Swigert, Philip, Com'r	Franklin	4-14-1846	143	28	101	In Franklin Co
Swigert, Philip & Wife	Franklin	5- 2-1843	Lot	27	345	Frankfort
Swope, Benedict	Lincoln	3-21-1792	——	B-2	452	Flat & Goss Cr
Swope, Jacob, Atty	Lincoln	3-21-1792	600	B-2	449	Bottingers Cr

Grantor	Residence	Deed Date	Acres	Book	Page	Watercourse
Tabb, Edmund B	Gloucester	3-18-1815	———	T	149	None
Talbott, Isham	Shelby	9-13-1797	6,016½	C	80	Bank Lick Cr
Talbott, Isham	Franklin	———1821	12	U	495	6 Mile Cr
Talbott, Isham	Franklin	———1821	354	U	496	6 Mile Cr
Talbott, Isham	Frankfort	5-28-1827	175	X	235	Cedar Cr
Talbott, Isham	Franklin	1-19-1829	100	Y	315	Cedar Cr
Talbott, Isham	Franklin	7-20-1833	106	Z	318	Cedar Cr
Talbott, James	Shelby	9-13-1797	5,218	C	77	Bank Lick Cr
Talbott, Thos & Wife	Welkes	3-22-1806	2,100	L	6	None
Taliaferro, Ann	Campbell	9-17-1823	1,882	W	373	W Fk Floyds Fk
Taliaferro, Benj F & Wife	———	10-5-1839	2,000	27	84	Ohio R
Taliaferro, Chas	———.	5-5-1796	2,000	A-2	694	W Fk Glenns Cr
Taliferro, Charles C	Caroline	5-2-1797	4,110⅞	B	23	Br Green R
Taliaferro, Chas C	Caroline	6-1-1815	2,333⅓	S	310	Ky & Green, Crocus
Taliaferro, Chas C	———	8-3-1818	———	S	314	None
Taliaferro, Chas C	Virginia	1-10-1824	100	X	168	Little Ky R
Tandy, David C	Fayette	1-15-1845	———	27	467	None
Tandy, Lewis C	Shelby	1-11-1840	———	27	131	None
Tandy, Moses	Harrison	6-15-1796	———	A-2	318	None
Tanner, Wm & Wife	Franklin	9-27-1841	50	27	225	Chaplins Cr
Tardivean, Bartholomew	Illinois	8-9-1793	12,566½	A-2	93	Caney Cr
Tardivean, Brothers	Jefferson	9-15-1791	13,195	B-2	442	Youngers & Brashears Crs
Tardivean, Peter	Mercer	5-17-1788	Lots	A	398	None
Tardivean, Peter	Mercer	8-9-1793	12,566½	A-2	93	Caney Cr
Tardivean, Peter	Mercer	5-24-1793	200	A-2	602	None
Tardivean, Peter	Mercer	5-24-1793	1,047	A-2	605	Rolling Fk
Tardivean, Peter	Mercer	3-19-1789	1	B-2	23	Danville
Tardivean, Peter	Mercer	10-7-1791	1,000	B-2	368	Beech Fk
Tardivean, Peter	Mercer	5-17-1792	5½	B-2	492	Danville
Tardivean, Peter	Mercer	4-23-1792	Lot	B-2	497	Lexington
Tarlton, Alfred	Jefferson	10-17-1833	156	Z	412	Elkhorn
Tatham, Chas, Atty	Richmond	4-14-1798	2,433	D	54	Little Ky R
Tatham, Chas, Atty	Lexington	10-29-1798	1,000	D	378	Russells Cr
Taylor, Benj & Wife	Woodford	1-31-1823	200	V	437	Ohio R
Taylor, Benj & Wife	Woodford	11-3-1823	———	W	127	N Elkhorn
Taylor, Ben & Wife	Woodford	4-8-1825	23	X	133	Ohio R
Taylor, Benj & Wife	Woodford	———1825	45	X	156	None
Taylor, Benj & Wife	Franklin	9-11-1825	120	Y	23	None
Taylor, Edmund	———.	2-25-1786	300	L	170	S Fk Elkhorn
Taylor, Edmund H	Jefferson	5-30-1796	200	K	279	Ohio R
Taylor, Edmund H	Clark	2-27-1809	77	M	335	None
Taylor, Edmund H	Franklin	1-15-1831	148	Z	67	Benson Cr
Taylor, Ed H	Franklin	4-9-1839	Lot	27	20	Frankfort
Taylor, Edmund H	Franklin	6-7-1843	1,000	27	348	In Ballard Co
Taylor, E H, Atty	Franklin	4-11-1843	Lot	27	342	Louisville
Taylor, Edmund & Wife	Caroline	7-18-1816	1,433⅓	T	355	None
Taylor, Edmund H & Wife	Jefferson	5-17-1806	100	K	334	Rough Cr
Taylor, Francis	Orange	7-20-1814	1,000	P	525	Blackfords Cr
Taylor, Francis S	Norfolk	10-16-1810	Lots	N	306	Louisville
Taylor, Geo & Wife	Clark	7-21-1813	206	P	321	Little Ky R
Taylor, Geo G	Clark	11-19-1799	500	D	478	Ohio R
Taylor, Geo G	———.	9-28-1807	300	L	142	S Elkhorn
Taylor, Geo G	Kentucky	9-28-1807	100	L	145	Rough Cr
Taylor, Geo G	———	9-28-1807	230⅓	L	147	N Fk Lost Cr
Taylor, Geo G	Clark	3-23-1818	Lots	S	191	Winchester
Taylor, Geo G	Clark	7-18-1820	4,000	T	477	Floyds Fk
Taylor, Geo G	Franklin	12-5-1820	400	U	50	Panther Cr
Taylor, Geo G	Franklin	12-20-1820	5,740	U	54	Ohio R & Clover C·
Taylor, Geo G	Frankfort	12-5-1820	50	U	186	Panther Cr
Taylor, Geo G, Atty	———.	7-18-1820	400	T	475	Floyds Fk
Taylor, Geo G & Wife	Clark	10-16-1805	880	K	15	Nolinn
Taylor, Geo G & Wife	Clark	10-16-1805	818	K	18	Nolinn
Taylor, Geo G & Wife	Clark	10-16-1805	352	K	21	Nolinn
Taylor, Geo G & Wife	Clark	10-16-1805	800	K	24	Nolinn
Taylor, Geo G & Wife	Clark	10-16-1805	960	K	27	Nolinn
Taylor, Geo G & Wife	———.	5-17-1806	———	K	320	None
Taylor, Geo G & Wife	Clark	9-1-1810	3,000	N	385	Rough Cr
Taylor, Geo G & Wife	Clark	9-1-1810	233⅓	N	388	Lost Cr
Taylor, Geo G & Wife	———	9-22-1810	———	N	467	None
Taylor, Geo G & Wife	———	9-22-1810	———	N	469	None
Taylor, Geo G & Wife	———	10-12-1807	———	N	472	None
Taylor, Geo G & Wife	Clark	9-1-1810	233⅓	P	318	Lost Cr
Taylor, Geo G & Wife	Clark	12-8-1818	———	T	8	None
Taylor, Griffin, Decd	Fredrick	3-27-1829	32	Y	357	Shannons Run
Taylor, Griffin, Decd	Fredrick	3-12-1829	104	Y	360	Shannons Run
Taylor, Griffin, heirs	Fredrick	7-1-1828	7	Y	375	Shannons Run
Taylor, Hancock	Jefferson	4-27-1839	800	27	32	Deer Cr
Taylor, Hubbard	Orange	7-20-1814	2,000	P	525	———
Taylor, Hubbard	Clark	1-30-1817	29,000	R	134	None

Grantor	Residence	Deed Date	Acres	Book	Page	Watercourse
Taylor, Hubbard	Clark	10-24-1818	100	S	404	Blackfords Cr
Taylor, Hubbard	————	12- 5-1820	450	U	52	Panther Cr
Taylor, Hubbard	Clark	3-23-1829	406½	Y	323	Panther Cr
Taylor, Hubbard & Wife	Clark	11-20-1800	500	E	263	Harrods Run
Taylor, Hubbard & Wife	Clark	5-24-1809	350	M	430	Floyds Fk
Taylor, Hubbard & Wife	Clark	3- 2-1809	750	P	80	Harrods Cr & Floyds Fk
Taylor, Hubbard & Wife	Clark	3- 2-1809	750	P	165	Harrods & Floyds Fk
Taylor, Hubbard Sr	Clark	10-21-1815	7,000	Q	266	Panther Cr
Taylor, Hubbard Sr	Clark	——10-1821	50	U	483	None
Taylor, Hubbard Sr	Clark	10-24-1829	Slaves	Y	421	None
Taylor, Hubbard Sr	Clark	7-25-1833	2,574½	Z	384	Green R & Panther
Taylor, Hubbard Sr & Wife	Clark	11- 4-1812	5,000	P	14	Big Benson Cr
Taylor, Hubbard Sr & Wife	Clark	7-27-1832	3,453	Z	213	Pitman & Rough Cr
Taylor, Hubbard Sr & Wife	Clark	7-27-1832	3,505½	Z	214	Blackford, Panther & Green R
Taylor, Hubbard Sr & Wife	Clark	7-27-1832	5,941	Z	216	Green R & Panther
Taylor, Hubbard Sr & Wife	Clark	7-27-1832	5,916.	Z	218	Blackford & Panther Cr & Green R
Taylor, Hubbard Sr & Wife	Clark	7-27-1832	3,380½	Z	220	Panther, Blackford Crs & Green R
Taylor, Hubbard Jr	Clark	7-18-1820	4,000	T	477	Floyds Fk
Taylor, Hubard Jr. Atty.	Clark	9-19-1815	11,382¾	U	188	Green & Salt R
Taylor, James	Caroline	6-28-1805	5823⅓	K	308	Green R, Mill Cr & Floyds Fk
Taylor, James	Caroline	8-31-1807	500	M	208	Floyds Fk
Taylor, James	Caroline	3-25-1801	1,000	N	498	Floyds Fk
Taylor, Jas	————	6- 3-1823	Lots	W	52	Frankfort
Taylor, Jas	Campbell	11-22-1825	1,180	Y	224	Licking & Bank Lick
Taylor, Jas	Frankfort	2- 1-1831	10,000	Z	94	S Fk Sandy R
Taylor, Jas Agt	————	7- 7-1803	250	P	559	S Fk Little Barren R
Taylor, Jas Jr, Atty	————	3-25-1801	1,000	N	498	Floyds Fk
Taylor, Jesse	Alexandria	5-18-1795	3,000	A-2	172	Clover Cr
Taylor, Jesse	Alexandria	4-27-1796	30,000	A-2	655	Rolling & Chaplain
Taylor, Jesse & Wife	Alexandria	11-19-1796	30,000	D	19	Drennons Lick Cr
Taylor, Jno	Mason	11-17-1802	1,230	G	70	Beech Fk
Taylor, Jno	Orange	8- 9-1813	Contract	P	198	————
Taylor, Jno	Caroline	11- 3-1813	1,000	P	400	Ohio R & Doe Run
Taylor, Jno	Franklin	11-14-1815	518	Q	286	Ohio R
Taylor, Jno	Franklin	5-20-1817	501	R	343	Ohio R
Taylor, Jno	Franklin	6-18-1817	526	R	419	Woolperts Cr
Taylor, Jno	Franklin	2- 1-1831	120	Z	96	Ohio R
Taylor, Jno & Wife	Mercer	12-30-1798	Lot	D	111	Frankfort
Taylor, Jno & Wife	Franklin	1-13-1816	681¼	Q	351	Ohio R
Taylor, Jno & Wife	Franklin	12-24-1823	800	W	134	Ohio R
Taylor, Jno B & Wife	Fredrick	6- 1-1823	609	W	364	Shawnee Run
Taylor, Jno B & Wife	Fredrick	4-15-1824	190	W	449	None
Taylor, Jno B & Wife	Fredrick	5- 1-1828	122	X	448	Shannons Run
Taylor, Jno B & Wife	Fredrick	3-27-1829	23	Y	357	Shannons Run
Taylor, Jno B & Wife	Fredrick	3-12-1829	104	Y	360	Shannons Run
Taylor, Jno B & Wife	Fredrick	7- 1-1828	7	Y	375	Shannons Run
Taylor, Joseph & Wife	Franklin	8-20-1818		S	211	Ohio R
Taylor, Joseph & Wife	Franklin	8-20-1818	36	S	213	Ohio R
Taylor, Joseph & Wife	Franklin	10-30-1818	Lots	S	270	Millton
Taylor, Joseph & Wife	Franklin	2- 7-1829	135	Y	321	Ohio R
Taylor, Mary W	Fredrick	6- 1-1823	609	W	364	Shawnee Run
Taylor, Philip	Frankfort	4- 8-1818	Lot	S	96	Frankfort
Taylor, Richard	Jefferson	7-12-1804	500	H	420	Glovers Cr
Taylor, Richard	Franklin	12-11-1819		T	268	Ky R
Taylor, Richard	Woodford	12-17-1821	2,000	V	157	Dry Run
Taylor, Richard	Fayette	4-21-1826	6,479⅔	Y	134	Bullskin Cr & Cumberland R
Taylor, Richard Executor	Jefferson	4-21-1826	5,746⅓	X	206	Ky R, Bullskin, Beargrass & Big Barren R
Taylor, Richard & Wife	Jefferson	6-28-1811	47½	O	321	Floyds Fk
Taylor, Richard & Wife	Jefferson	6-28-1811	47½	O	323	Floyds Fk
Taylor, Richard Sr	Jefferson	10-11-1806	1,000	M	239	Ohio R
Taylor, Richard Sr	Frankfort	8-10-1811	600	O	104	Floyds Fk
Taylor, Richard Jr	Franklin	11- 7-1820	100	U	49	None
Taylor, Richard Jr	Franklin	2-22-1821	5,740	U	357	Ohio R & Clover Cr
Taylor, Richard Jr	Hickman	1-15-1831	148	Z	67	Benson Cr
Taylor, Richard Jr, Atty	————	4- 5-1810	44	N	215	Ohio R
Taylor, Richard Jr & Wife	Frankfort	4-24-1812	————	O	379	None

Grantor	Residence	Deed Date	Acres	Book	Page	Watercourse
Taylor, Richard Jr & Wife	Frankfort	7- 8-1815	332½	Q	144	Ky R
Taylor, Richard Jr & Wife	Franklin	7-25-1820	400	T	473	Floyds Fk
Taylor, Wm	Point Coop	4- 5-1810	44	N	215	Ohio R
Taylor, Wm, Executor	Shelby	8-10-1815	500	Q	219	Panther Cr
Taylor, Wm & Wife	Jefferson	4-25-1791	8,000	B-2	411	Ohio R
Taylor, Thruston M & Wife	Clark	8-25-1808	189½	M	152	Floyds Fk
Taylor, Wm P	Caroline	8-12-1816	1,433½	T	359	None
Telcoferro, Chas C	Virginia	1-10-1824	———	W	170	Little Ky R
Telfair. Jane & Anne E	Staunton	9-26-1822	2,650	W	97	Dix & Green R
Telford, Jeremiah	Lincoln	6- 5-1786	700	A	90	Cedar Cr
Temple, Benj, heirs		11- 5-1806	666⅔	K	529	Floyds Fk
Temple, Benj, heirs	King William	12-31-1810	666⅔	O	280	Floyds Fk
Temple, Benj & Wife	———	10- 2-1817	1,293½	S	325	Little Ky R
Temple, Benj & Wife	———	10- 2-1817	3,500	S	329	Craborchard Fk
Temple, Benj & Wife	Jefferson	10- 2-1817	1,000	V	70	Green R
Tenason, B	Philadelphia	8- 8-1787	10,000	H	382	S Fk Sandy R
Teneman, Thos & Wife	Mason	10- 3-1815	600	Q	470	Sinking Br
Tenaant, Jno	Caroline	10- 6-1786	1,281½	A	275	Green R
Tennent, Helen C & Chas B	Caroline	3-25-1821	———	V	2	None
Terrasson, Bartholomew	Philadelphia	5-11-1787	4,775	A-2	49	None
Terrasson, Bartholomew	Philadelphia	4- 1-1790	———	Q	46	None
Terrell, Jno D	———	3- 2-1805	274	K	135	Clay Lick Fk
Terrell, Jno D	———	3- 2-1805	274	K	140	Clay Lick Fk
Terrell, Richard	Jefferson	7-10-1796	258	A-2	41	Johnsons Fk
Terrell, Richard Atty	———	2-10-1800	1,000	D	524	Sulphur Lick Fk
Tevis, Saml, Comr	Shelby	10-23-1826	1,048	Z	489	In Spencer Co
Thatcher, Jno P, Atty	———	1- 9-1827	5,000	Y	243	N Fk Ky R
Theobald, Thos S	Franklin	1-19-1846	Lot	28	50	Frankfort
Theobald, Thos S & Wife	Franklin	9-27-1845	3	28	32	Ky R
Thomas, Amos & Wife	Pike Mo	8-21-1840	———	27	175	None
Thomas, Benj P, Atty	———	7-24-1816	80	Q	520	Ky R
Thomas, Edward	Register Land Office	5-10-1801	1,187	E	325	Johnsons Fk
Thomas, Edmund	Register Land Office	5-18-1801	700½	E	330	Brush Cr
Thomas, Edmund	Register Land Office	5-18-1801	200	E	332	3 Fks Cumberland R
Thomas, Edmund	Register Land Office	4- 9-1801	2,000	E	402	Floyds Fk
Thomas, Edmund	Register Land Office	7-22-1801	500	E	405	Br Licking
Thomas, Edmund	Register Land Office	7-22-1801	30,000	F	125	Green R
Thomas, Edmund	Register Land Office	11-18-1801	100,000	F	128	Eagle Cr
Thomas, Edmund	Register Land Office	11-25-1801	10,000	F	142	Chaplins Fk
Thomas, Edmund	Register Land Office	12- 8-1801	20,200	F	148	Sandy R
Thomas, Edmund	Register Land Office	3-17-1801	500	F	162	N Fk Licking
Thomas, Edmund	Register Land Office	1-17-1802	1,000	F	172	Clay Lick
Thomas, Edmund	Register Land Office	3-17-1801	299	F	176	Flat Cr
Thomas, Edmund	Register Land Office	1-12-1802	1,000	F	180	Ohio R
Thomas, Edmund	Register Land Office	1- 9-1802	20,000	F	207	Licking
Thomas, Edmund	Register Land Office	6-11-1802	400	F	417	Hardins Cr
Thomas, Edmund	Register Land Office	7-15-1802	400	F	465	Floyds Fk
Thomas, Edmund	Register Land Office	12- 3-1802	2,000	G	79	Rough Cr
Thomas, Edmund	Register Land Office	12- 3-1802	3,000	G	82	Nolinn Cr
Thomas, Edmund	Register Land Office	12-11-1802	10,500	G	96	Ohio & Sandy R
Thomas, Edmund	Register Land Office	12-10-1802	45,000	G	99	Beech Fk
Thomas, Edmund	Register Land Office	12-11-1802	15,000	G	106	N Fk Sandy R
Thomas, Edmund	Register Land Office	12-15-1802	2,000	G	109	Ky R
Thomas, Edmund	Register Land Office	12-20-1802	400	G	122	Rolling Fk
Thomas, Edmund	Register Land Office	2-21-1803	666⅔	G	164	Ohio R
Thomas, Edmund	Register Land Office	3-11-1803	2,000	G	184	Licking
Thomas, Edmund	Register Land Office	11-22-1802	3,000	G	191	Salt R
Thomas, Edmund	Register Land Office	3-18-1803	1,000	G	194	Licking
Thomas, Edmund	Register Land Office	6- 1-1803	9,500	G	329	Ohio R
Thomas, Edmund	Register Land Office	5-26-1803	643	G	334	Harrisons Cr
Thomas, Edmund	Register Land Office	11- 8-1803	5,000	H	21	Green R
Thomas, Edmund & Wife	Franklin	3-12-1800	1,000	E	267	Cumberland R
Thomas, Jno P	Franklin	7-13-1818	120	S	187	None
Thomas, Jno & Wife	Owen	12-20-1843	———	27	391	None
Thomas, Landon & Wife	Franklin	3- 2-1846	2,500	28	74	Mill Cr
Thomas, Phileman	Kentucky	8- 1-1811	20,000	O	524	Hinkston Fk
Thomas, Philman	Kentucky	5- 9-1808	750	M	163	Ohio R
Thomas, Philman	———	7-24-1816	80	Q	520	Ky R
Thomas, Philman	Gallatin	11-18-1817	3,372	R	572	None
Thomas, Richard S	———	12- 8-1804	200	J	23	Big Barren R
Thomasson, Saml	Scott	6-15-1821	78	U	504	None
Thompson, Anthony, heirs	———	7- 3-1805	122	J	344	Dry Cr
Thompson, Anthony, heirs	———	7- 3-1805	57	J	348	Dry Cr

Grantor	Residence	Deed Date	Acres	Book	Page	Watercourse
Thompson, Anthony, heirs	Kentucky	11-18-1806	500	K	512	Dry Cr
Thompson, Chas	———	12-20-1797	1,000	C	204	Tradewater
Thompson, Geo	———	3-10-1796	3,300	A-2	170	Todds Cr
Thompson, Henry	Woodford	11-18-1806	73	K	506	Ohio R
Thompson, James & Wife	Lincoln	5-12-1791	400	B-2	381	Dix R
Thompson, Jno W	Baltimore	12- 7-1826	2,483	X	465	Elk Cr
Thompson, Jonah	———	7- 9-1803	14,936¼	J	91	18 Mile Cr, Hardins & Cartwrights Cr
Thompson, Jonah Comr	Alexandria	6- 1-1803	———	M	37	None
Thompson, Lawrence	Madison	1-15-1799	———	N	210	None
Thompson, Lawrence & Wife	Madison	8-22-1798	500	F	95	None
Thompson, Richard	Philadelphia	5-30-1786	5,000	D	258	Large Cr
Thompson, Richard	Philadelphia	6-16-1786	2,500	D	261	None
Thomspon, Richard	Philadelphia	4-28-1786	900	L	22	None
Thompson, Roger & Wife	Franklin	3-31-1810	100	N	236	S Fk Big Benson Cr
Thompson, Wm	Madison	9-21-1816	250	R	388	None
Thompson, Wm R	Mercer	9-30-1826	Lot	Y	198	Croghansville Ohio
Thornberry, Drusilla	Jefferson	11-13-1818	Contract	S	524	None
Thornton, Arthur W	Carlisle	2-25-1811	2,000	O	400	Buck Cr
Thornton, Jno & Wife	Culpepper	12-15-1797	1,286	F	410	None
Thornton, Polly	Carolina	9-17-1823	1,882	W	373	W Fk Floyds Fk
Thornton, Philip & Wife	Carolina	7-10-1814	2,000	R	312	N Fk Tradewater
Thosburn, Joseph	———	7-18-1820	400	T	475	Floyds Fk
Throckmorton, Saml	Franklin	7- 7-1802	———	F	461	Elkhorn
Thruston, Ann Clark	Louisville	2- 9-1820	5,647¾	T	341	Rough Cr, Floyds Fk & Ohio R
Thruston, Alfred	Jefferson	9-18-1840	158¼	27	260	E Br Floyds Fk
Thruston, Alfred	Jefferson	8-12-1841	234	27	261	E Br Floyds Fk
Thruston, Alfred	Jefferson	8-12-1841	229	27	262	E Br Floyds Fk
Thruston, Buckner	Dist Columbia	12-28-1825	500	Y	226	Green R
Thruston, Chas W	Louisville	6-10-1824	746	W	291	Little Ky R
Thruston, Chas M & Wife	Louisville	5- 2-1823	8,000	W	21	Woolpers Cr
Thruston, Chas M	Frederick	10-12-1787	———	L	223	W of Allegheny Mt
Thurston, Chas M & Wife	Frederick	12- 1-1796	5,000	B	108	Highland Cr
Thurston, Chas M & Wife	Frederick	12- 1-1796	7,333⅓	B	333	Highland Cr
Tidball, Joseph	Frederick	11- 5-1811	300	O	362	Ohio R
Tiffany, Duvall & Co	Baltimore	9-26-1845	2,500	28	35	Elkhorn & Cedar Cr
Tiffany, Laura & Ann C	Baltimore	9-26-1845	2,500	28	35	Elkhorn & Cedar Cr
Tiffany, Ormond C & Comport	Baltimore	9-26-1845	2,500	28	35	Elkhorn & Cedar Cr
Tilford, Isaac	———	9-19-1807	35,456	Q	535	None
Tinsley, Saml	Virginia	12- 1-1802	666⅔	G	365	Little Barren R
Tinsley, Wm & Wife	Shelby	10-26-1812	328	O	480	None
Tinsley, Wm & Wife	Shelby	10-26-1813	———	P	252	None
Todd, Charles	Kentucky	11-12-1789	3,000	E	98	Fks Licking
Todd, Chas & Wife	Carolina	11-11-1816	693¼	R	288	Rough Cr
Todd, Chas & Wife	Frankfort	6- 5-1821	Lots	U	513	Columbus Ohio
Todd, Chas S	Frankfort	9-14-1819	Lot	T	147	Frankfort
Todd, Chas S	Franklin	3- 2-1820	Lots	T	394	Frankfort
Todd, Chas S	Frankfort	4-18-1820	Slaves	V	220	None
Todd, Chas S	Franklin	———1826	450	Y	232	None
Todd, Chas S	Shelby	3-22-1833	Lots	Z	357	Frankfort
Todd, Chas S & Wife	Franklin	11-30-1818	Lot	S	400	Frankfort
Todd, Chas S & Wife	Franklin	7-26-1819	Lot	T	48	Frankfort
Todd, Chas S & Wife	Frankfort	7-23-1819	Lot	T	97	Frankfort
Todd, Chas S & Wife	———	7-23-1819	Lots	T	384	Lexington
Todd, Chas S & Wife	Frankfort	4-12-1820	Lots	T	389	Frankfort
Todd, Chas S & Wife	Frankfort	4-17-1820	Lots	T	391	Columbus Ohio
Todd, Chas S & Wife	Franklin	1-15-1820	Lots	T	393	Frankfort
Todd, Chas S & Wife	Franklin	8- 4-1819	1,102	T	397	Hays Fk Silver Cr, Ky R & Sinking Fk Little R
Todd, Chas S & Wife	Franklin	8- 4-1819	Lots	T	397	Columbus Ohio
Todd, Chas S & Wife	Franklin	8- 4-1819	Lots	T	397	New Castle
Todd, Chas S & Wife	Franklin	1-31-1820	Lot	T	440	Frankfort
Todd, Chas S & Wife	Franklin	4-18-1820	Slaves	U	1	None
Todd, Levi S & Wife	Montgomery	1-17-1821	460	U	167	Elk Cr & Ohio R
Todd, Chas S & Wife	Franklin	7-27-1819	Slaves	U	477	None
Todd, Chas S & Wife	Frankfort	7- 6-1821	Lots	U	487	Frankfort
Todd, Chas S & Wife	Franklin	7- 6-1821	Lot	U	511	Versailles
Todd, Chas S & Wife	Franklin	12-15-1821	Lots	V	159	Columbus Ohio
Todd, Chas S & Wife	Shelby	9-24-1834	230	Z	456	Ohio R
Todd, Chas S & Wife	Shelby	12- 1-1838	Lots	27	29	Frankfort

Grantor	Residence	Deed Date	Acres	Book	Page	Watercourse
Todd, Jno F & Wife	Warren	3- 6-1829	901	Y	398	Tennessee R
Todd, Jno H	———	12-28-1819	Lots	T	388	Frankfort
Todd, Jno H & Wife	———	7-23-1819	Lots	T	384	Lexington
Todd, Jno H & Chas S	———	7-23-1819	Lot	T	384	Portland
Todd, Jno H & Chas S	———	7-23-1819	Lots	T	384	Frankfort
Todd, Jno H & Thos	Franklin	12-15-1821	Lots	V	159	Columbus Ohio
Todd, Levi L & Wife	Montgomery	6-30-1821	3,797	U	458	Elk Cr
Todd, Lucy P		4-21-1831	2	Z	119	Shelbyville Rd
Todd, Lucy P	Frankfort	4-24-1833	50	Z	282	Ky R
Todd, Lucy P	Franklin	3- 5-1835	100	Z	495	Ky R
Todd, Robt, Executor	Fayette	11-15-1804	898	P	349	Ky R
Todd, Saml & Wife	———	10- 3-1831	400	Z	159	Gilmores Cr
Todd, Saml & Wife	Franklin	1- 7-1833	Lots	Z	317	Louisville
Todd, Saml & Wife	Kentucky	1-24-1835	Lot	Z	486	Louisville
Todd, Thos	Woodford	4-12-1805	15,000	K	317	Green R
Todd, Thos	Woodford	9-28-1805	126	K	322	Bealls Run
Todd, Thos	Woodford	9-26-1811	422	O	164	Mill Cr
Todd, Thos	Woodford	11-23-1811	737	O	204	Rolling Fk
Todd, Thos	Kentucky	12-16-1811	45	P	527	Glens Cr
Todd, Thos	Franklin	7-25-1814	110	P	590	N Fk Glens Cr
Todd, Thos	Franklin	7-22-1814	150	T	73	None
Todd, Thos, Atty	Woodford	12-10-1807	443	L	227	Hustons Fk
Todd, Thos, Atty	———	9-13-1806	73	L	344	Hustons Fk
Todd, Thos, Atty	———	12-10-1807	443	M	179	Hustons Fk
Todd, Thos, Trustee	Franklin	2-15-1817	———	R	285	None
Todd, Thos, Trustee	———	7-15-1819	223¾	T	77	None
Todd, Thos, Decd	Woodford	11-23-1811	200	O	203	Stewarts Cr
Todd, Judge Thos, heirs	Franklin	5-27-1839	Lots	27	46	Frankfort
Todd, Thos & Wife	Franklin	1-16-1801	500	F	245	Pitman Cr
Todd, Thos & Wife	Franklin	1-16-1800	500	F	393	None
Todd, Thos & Wife	Franklin	6- 9-1803	60	H	11	Elkhorn
Todd, Thos & Wife	———	3-13-1805	———	L	306	None
Todd, Thos & Wife	Franklin	9-24-1816	50	R	81	None
Todd, Thos & Wife	Franklin	5-14-1821	171	U	493	N Fk Glens Cr
Todd, Thos & Wife	Franklin	10- 8-1824	185	X	49	N Fk Glens Cr
Toodd, Wm	Woodford	3- 3-1803	Slaves	G	189	None
Tolinn, Harry & Wife	Frankfort	12-24-1804	150	O	312	None
Torbitt, Chas A	Henry	1- 9-1833	Lots	Z	250	Port Williams
Toulinn, Harry, heirs	Alabama	10-12-1833	2,106½	Z	360	Hardin Co
Toulinn, Harry, heirs	Franklin	4-14-1842	2,109	27	327	Middle & Valley Cr
Toulinn, Harry & Wife	Frankfort	4-11-1804	30,059	H	156	Slate & Boyds Cr
Toulinn, Harry & Wife	Franklin	9- 2-1803	3,593½	P	30	Ohio R
Toulinn, Jno B	Mobile	4-14-1842	2,109	27	327	Middle & Valley Cr
Trenor, James	Battetourt	11-26-1796	1,002	A-2	601	Beech Fk
Trigg, Saml & Wife	Montgomery	9- 3-1788	400	B-2	97	Shawnee Run
Trigg, Wm	Franklin	10- 2-1798	768	D	25	None
Trigg, Wm	Franklin	8-31-1804	885	J	64	Ky R
Trigg, Wm	Franklin	8-13-1806	217	K	415	Todds Terry Rd
Trigg, Wm	———	10-14-1806	1,000	K	477	N Elkhorn
Trigg, Wm	Franklin	3-30-1808	117	M	161	Ky R
Trigg, Wm	Franklin	8- 4-1812	43	O	440	Little N Elkhorn
Trigg, Wm	Frankfort	11- 2-1822	Lot	V	337	Frankfort
Trigg, Wm, heirs	Franklin	9-16-1796	250	A-2	431	Shawnee & Ky R
Trigg, Wm & Wife	Franklin	11-27-1813	100	P	481	Tick Cr
Trigg, Wm & Wife	Franklin	11-27-1813	100	P	482	Tick & Guests Cr
Trigg, Wm & Wife	Frankfort	11-27-1813	100	P	484	Tick Cr
Trigg, Wm & Wife	Franklin	11-27-1813	100	P	485	Guests Fk
Trigg, Wm & Wife	Franklin	12-22-1831	200	Z	171	S Elkhorn
Trigg, Wm & Wife	Franklin	11-27-1813	215	P	347	Gists Fk
Trigg, Wm & Susannah	Franklin	4-25-1825	Lot	X	131	Frankfort
Trigg, Wm & Susan	———	7- 1-1837		27	111	Franklin Co
Trigg & Greenup, Comrs.	———	6- 8-1813	50,000	P	367	Various Watercourses
Trimble, Jno	Baltimore	4- 3-1826	2,200	X	204	Benson Cr
Trimble, Jno & Wife	Fayette	4-19-1806	2,200	K	470	Bensons Cr
Triplett, Robt	Franklin	12-17-1827	Lots	X	329	Owensboro
Triplett, Robt	———	1-25-1828	12,000	X	367	Gaines Tavern
Triplett, Robt	Kentucky	9- 3-1828	135	X	475	None
Triplett, Robt	Kentucky	5-29-1834	32,000	Z	442	None
Triplett, Robt	Kentucky	5- 8-1846	60,000	28	87	Kinniconick & Tripletts Cr
Triplett, Robt	Kentucky	2- 2-1847	Lots	28	125	Owensboro
Triplett, Robt, Atty	Frankfort	12-11-1823	888	W	199	None
Triplett, Robt, Atty	Franklin	10-18-1827	295	X	291	Blackfords Cr
Triplett, Robt, Atty	Frankfort	11- 1-1827	53	X	306	Eagle Cr
Triplett, Robt, Atty	Franklin	12-17-1827	417	X	329	Ohio R
Triplett, Robt, Atty	Franklin	8-27-1828	125	X	454	Eagle Cr
Triplett, Robt, Atty	Kentucky	9- 3-1828	168	X	473	Ohio R
Triplett, Robt, Atty	Franklin	———1826	295	Y	189	Blackfords Cr
Triplett, Robt, Atty	Fayette	11-30-1831	4	Z	167	Cane Run
Triplett, Robt & Wife	Virginia	7- 1-1831	1,162	Z	145	Ohio R
Triplett, Robt & Wife	Richmond	7- 1-1831	1,162	Z	146	Ohio R

Grantor	Residence	Deed Date	Acres	Book	Page	Watercourse
Triplett, Rogers	Scott	6-20-1800	1,000	E	49	Glovers Cr
Triplett, Thos	Franklin	6-18-1825	——	X	193	Swifts Camp Cr
Triplett, Thos	Franklin	1-28-1829	——	Y	316	None
Triplett, Thos	Franklin	6-28-1830	——	Y	501	Br Sycamore Fk
Triplett, Thos	Franklin	9-21-1830	250	Z	16	None
Triplett, Thos	Franklin	9- 3-1831	203	Z	157	Beaver & Myers Br
Triplett, Thos, Atty.	Kentucky	6-11-1834	50	Z	440	Ohio R
Trotter, Joseph	Scott	3-23-1808	272	L	348	Lost Cr
Trotter, Joseph	——	10- 4-1791	700	B-2	358	Bucks Cr
Trotter, Joseph & Wife	Augusta	3- 5-1792	668	B-2	419	Buck Fk
Trotter, Joseph & Wife	Augusta	3- 5-1792	300	B-2	422	Buck Fk
Trotter, Joseph & Wm	Franklin	9-13-1819	1,200	T	139	Lost Cr
Troup, Robt	New York	2-19-1796	100,000	A-2	188	N & M Fk Ky R
Troup, Robt	New York	2-18-1796	100,000	A-2	192	N & M Fk Ky R
Trustees, Covington	Kenton	12-12-1816	Lot	R	157	Covington
Trustees, Frankfort	Kentucky	7-20-1799	Lot	D	305	Frankfort
Trustees, Frankfort	Franklin	1804	Lot	N	270	Frankfort
Trustees, Frankfort	Franklin	1-17-1818	Lots	Z	260	Frankfort
Trustees, Frankfort	Franklin	9-19-1834	Lot	Z	470	Frankfort
Trustees, Frankfort	Franklin	3-18-1839	Ordinance	27	35	None
Trustees, Frankfort	Franklin	11- 5-1841	Lot	27	269	Frankfort
Trustees, Henderson Seminary	Henderson	1-21-1815	105½	O	1	Little N Elkhorn
Trustees, Mayfield	Graves	3-27-1824	Lots	Y	268	Mayfield
Trustees, Newport Academy	Newport	7- 7-1803	250	P	559	S Fk Little Barren
Trustees, Owen Sem	Owen	10-21-1823	2,942	W	204	Cumberland R
Trustees, Owen Co Seminary	Owen	11-22-1844	4,762	27	464	Livingston & Trigg
Trustees, Port Williams	Port Williams	5-17-1814	Lots	T	292	Port Williams
Trustees, Transylvania University	Kentucky	12- 4-1832	75	Z	243	Shelbyville Pike
Trustees, Transylvania University	Kentucky	12- 6-1832	1,310	Z	244	Donelson Fk
Trustees, Washington Academy	Washington	12-16-1830	6,000	Z	151	Clay Lick & Deer Cr
Tryson, Cliford	New York	11-28-1817	——	W	3	None
Tubman, Richard & Wife	Augusta	10-19-1830	——	Z	27	None
Tuck, Bennet & Wife	King William	4-15-1802	2,000	G	72	Br Little Barren R
Tucker, Geo	Richmond	1——1803	3,500	J	204	Skaggs & Big Bone Lick Crs
Tunman, Edward & Wife	Kentucky	3-29-1802	1,500	F	204	Fks Licking
Tunstall, Henry	Franklin	10- 9-1809	Slaves	M	443	None
Tunstall, Thos	Frankfort	1-13-1806	Slaves	K	234	None
Tunstall, Thos	Franklin	3-13-1805	——	L	81	None
Tunstall, Thos	Franklin	12-10-1808	Slaves	M	237	None
Tupman, Jno, heirs	——	10- 8-1832	500	Z	239	Mississippi R
Tupman, Jno	Adair	6- 7-1828	500	X	460	Mississippi R
Tupman, Wm	——	10- 8-1832	500	Z	239	Mississippi R
Turnbull, Robt	Prince George	5-22-1797	3,000	D	435	Green R
Turnbull, Robt	Prince George	12-21-1796	600	F	60	Caseys Cr
Turner, Henry Smith	Jefferson	3-10-1823	1,000	W	266	Ponges Cr
Turner, Robt & Geo	Virginia	4- 2-1807	983	L	89	Salt R
Turner, Robt & Geo	Richmond	4- 2-1807	415	L	92	Salt R
Turner, Robt & Geo	Richmond	3-20-1807	942	L	99	Salt R
Turner, Thos	Washington	6-14-1803	5,000	H	52	Saxtons Cr
Turpin, Philip	Chesterfield	4-14-1813	750	P	195	Pitman Cr & Cumberland R
Turpin, Thos	Powhatan	4-28-1803	3,500	G	367	Licking
Turpin, Thos	Powhatan	4-28-1803	3,500	G	370	Licking
Turpin, Thos	Powhatan	11-10-1805	5,000	K	219	Eagle Cr
Tyler, Chas & Wife	Montgomery	11-22-1845	1,920	28	113	Cedar Cr
Underwood, Jas & Geo	Goochland	9-24-1811	385	O	324	None
Underwood, Geo	Hanover	11- 5-1799	2,500	D	417	Sandy R
Underwood, Geo	Hanover	9-30-1799	321	E	6	Sandy Cr
Underwood, Geo	Hanover	9-30-1799	429	E	7	Sandy Cr
Underwood, Geo	Hanover	11- 6-1804	2,500	H	460	Two Branches
Underwood, Geo	Hanover	1-11-1805	411	J	119	None
Underwood, Geo	Goochland	4-18-1805	1,000	K	80	Rolling Fk
Underwood, Geo & Francis	Virginia	1- 9-1807	4,000	M	200	None
Underwood, J R Atty	Warren	10- 6-1830	39	Z	25	Elk Lick & Little Barren R
Underwood, J R Atty	Warren	7- 9-1831	365	Z	160	Little Barren R
Underwood, J R Atty	Warren	7- 9-1831	245	Z	161	Little Barren R
Underwood, Joseph R & Wife	Warren	3- 6-1829	901	Y	398	Tennessee R
Underwood, Thos	Richmond	10-16-1797	6,000	B	247	Big Bone Lick
Underwood, Thos	Hanover	1-11-1805	411	J	119	None

Grantor	Residence	Deed Date	Acres	Book	Page	Watercourse
Underwood, Thos Jr & Wife	Richmond	9– 5–1804	333	H	351	Green R
Underwood, Warner L & Wife	Warren	3– 6–1829	901	Y	398	Tennessee R
Utterback, Benj	Franklin	2– 7–1817	400	R	281	Ky R & Glens Cr
Vance, Benj	Warren	8– 3–1830	300	Z	46	N Fk Tradewater
Vandurson, Saml A & Abraham	Frankfort	7–31–1819	Lot	T	53	Frankfort
Vanmeter, Isaac & Joseph	Hardy	1– 6–1817	166¾	R	345	Doe Run
Vanmeter, Isaac & Joseph	Hardy	6–10–1814	233⅓	Q	110	Doe Run
Vanpelt, Saml & Wife	———	10– 1–1839	466	27	76	Hurricane Cr
Vanuxem, Jas	Philadelphia	6–29–1795	36,700	A-2	1	Green R
Vanuxem, Jas	———	7–31–1818	———	S	226	None
Vanuxem, Jas, heirs	Philadelphia	1– 1–1831	10,000	Z	93	S Fk Sandy R
Vaughan, Edmund	Powhatan	10–30–1799	200	D	482	Gun Powder & Middle Cr
Vaughan, Edmund	Franklin	12–29–1845	Lot	28	54	Frankfort
Vaughan, Edmund & Wife	Franklin	4–16–1807	79	L	16	Ohio R
Vaughan, Edmund & Wife	Franklin	8–10–1812	79	O	441	Ohio R
Vaughan, Edmund & Wife	———	3–31–1821	172	U	433	None
Vaughan, Jas	Amelia	7–13–1797	799½	C	16	Red R
Vaughan, Jno	Philadelphia	4–28–1832	10,781	Z	376	N Fk Ky R
Vawter, Wm	Woodford	11– 7–1805	1,000	K	119	Butlers Fk
Vawter, Wm	Woodford	5–30–1811	22	O	301	Greers Cr
Vawter, Wm, Atty	———	11– 4–1800	400	E	227	—— Br
Vawter, Wm, Atty	———	1–28–1803	11,250	K	89	Hingston Fk
Vawter, Wm, Atty	Woodford	3– 6–1806	2,000	K	226	N & S Fk Elkhorn
Vawter, Will, Atty	———	5– 9–1808	750	M	163	Ohio R
Veech, Jas	Shelby	4– 4–1832	20	Z	184	Buck Cr
Veitch, Richard & Wife	Alexandria	10–23–1820	336	U	321	S Fk Benson Cr
Vertner, Daniel	———	11– 6–1805	2,000	J	370	Floyds Fk
Vest, Jno J & Wife	Franklin	8–12–1839	Lots	27	73	Frankfort
Vogleson, Armand	Norfolk	12– 1–1796	4,000	C	122	None
Voorhies, Peter G	Franklin	8–25–1817	2,992	S	29	Big Bone Cr
Voorhies, Peter G & Wife	Franklin	6– 4–1821	213	U	439	Beech Cr
Vories, Jno	———	5–27–1807	175	L	59	Dix R
Voss, Edward	Culpepper	5–10–1794	1,000	A-2	640	Sulphur Lick
Voss, Edward	Culpepper	5–15–1794	666⅔	A-2	642	Little Barren R
Voss, Nicholas	Fredricksburg	6–17–1796	666⅔	A-2	525	Little Barren R
Vowels, Zachariah	Falmouth	5– 4–1805	3,720	J	218	Skaggs & Big Bone Lick
Waddy, Wm	Louisa	3– 5–1796	27,018	E	233	Sandy R
Wade, Jas	Montgomery	10–31–1806	200	L	63	Nolinn
Waggoner, Alexander	Adair	7–27–1815	666⅔	Q	154	Glens Cr
Waggoner, Andrew & Wife	Berkley	1–23–1805	2,131	J	356	Ohio R
Waggoner, Herbert G & Wife	Adair	8–18–1813	528½	W	195	Lost Cr
Waggoner, Oliver G	Hart	5–24–1841	2	27	193	Nr Frankfort
Waggoner, Oliver G, Comr	———	11–18–1817	3,372	R	572	None
Waggoner, Oliver G, Comr	———	12– 8–1817	7,750	R	606	None
Waite, Obed	Barkly	10– 4–1810	1,250	O	10	Ohio R
Waites, David & Wife	Franklin	10–13–1824	276½	W	494	Coopers Run
Walden, Ambron, heirs	———	11–22–1843	10,000	27	369	None
Walden, Ambron, heirs	Virginia	12–19–1844	19¾	27	445	In Mason Co
Walden, Geo & Wife	Carolina	3–31–1804	200	H	423	Br Cumberland R
Walker, Benj	New York	3– 7–1796	30,000	A-2	224	None
Walker, Geo	———	6– 8–1813	50,000	P	367	Various Watercourses
Walker, Joel	Mason	9– 9–1806	11,517½	L	29	N Fk & Main Licking
Walker, Jno	Richmond	2–14–1795	10,000	A-2	515	Sandy R
Walker, Mary L	———	6–12–1831	315	Z	68	None
Walker, Martin & Wife	———	5–12–1820	———	T	312	None
Walker, Martin & Wife	Philadelphia	2– 4–1829	315	Y	333	Lexington & Frankfort Road
Walker, Martin & Wife	Fayette	5–30–1827	7½	X	238	None
Walker, Merry	Virginia	4–30–1802	5,189	F	387	Dry Cr & Gun Powder
Walker, Robt, Comr	Richmond	12– 9–1802	1,000	G	221	Paroquit Cr
Walker, Thos C	Baltimore	11–21–1805	1,000	K	488	None
Walker, Wm	Fayette	6–29–1807	2,000	L	67	N Fk Licking
Walker, Wm Sr	Madison	9–26–1805	2,000	J	329	N Fk Licking
Walker, Wm Sr	Madison	9–26–1805	3,000	J	334	Raven Cr

Grantor	Residence	Deed Date	Acres	Book	Page	Watercourse
Walker, Wm Sr & Jr	Madison	6——1798	400	C	246	Crooked Cr
Walker, Wm Sr & Jr	Madison	6-10-1798	400	C	248	Crooked Cr
Walker, Wm Sr & Jr	Madison	6-16-1798	400	C	305	Crooked Cr
Wallace, Caleb	Woodford	2-11-1797	——	A-2	610	Beech Fk
Wallace, Caleb	Woodford	6-13-1805	150	J	125	S Fk Elkhorn
Wallace, Caleb	——	7- 8-1806	400	K	337	Ohio R
Wallace, Caleb	——	10-14-1806	1,000	K	477	N Elkhorn
Wallace, Caleb	Woodford	4-21-1808	257	L	378	Benson & Beech Crs
Wallace, Caleb & Wife	Woodford	8- 8-1797	237	C	125	Beech Fk
Wallace, Caleb & Wife	Woodford	8- 8-1797	263	C	129	Beech Fk
Wallace, Caleb & Wife	Woodford	11-10-1803	5,992	H	216	Jepthas, Benson & Beech Crs
Wallace, Caleb & Wife	Woodford	11-10-1803	2,106	H	219	—— Cr
Wallace, Caleb & Wife	Woodford	10- 8-1805	2,000	K	34	Ohio R
Wallace, Caleb & Wife	Woodford	2-12-1810	2,500	N	153	Pond R
Wallace, Gustavus B	Charlestown	5-11-1799	6,000	D	486	Ohio R
Wallace, Jno & Wife	Clark	8-29-1811	——	O	376	None
Wallace, Jno & Wife	Henry	12-20-1810	500	U	266	Ohio R
Wallace, Jno & Wife	Clark	4- 5-1810	388	27	217	Beargrass & Rough
Wallace, Mary	Woodford	7-22-1814	150	T	73	None
Wallace, Thos, Comir	Fayette	5-25-1810	246,900½	N	224	Ohio R
Waller, Wm L & Wife	Franklin	6——1818	Lots	T	211	Frankfort
Walsh, Jacob Jr	Baltimore	2- 6-1809	5,000	M	397	Collins Fk & Br Little Richland Cr
Walters, K & Wife	Hardin	2-23-1809	2,100	M	317	Ohio R
Walton, Matthew	Washington	6-11-1800	1,478½	E	88	Eagle Cr
Walton, Matthew	Washington	11- 4-1800	20,300	E	130	Red R & Rough Cr
Wante, Stephen & Co	Baltimore	8-30-1799	7,270	D	460	Little Benson & S Fk Elkhorn
Ward, Chas & Wife	——	10-14-1828	——	X	481	None
Warder, Jeremiah	Philadelphia	3-10-1789	13,666⅔	D	195	N Fk 3 Fks Ky R
Ware, James Jr & Wife	Frederick	11- 5-1798	204½	D	74	Beargrass Cr
Ware, Robt	Caroline	1-19-1786	1,000	A	270	Rough Cr
Ware, Robt	Caroline	1-19-1786	479	A	272	—— Br
Ware, Robt	Edgefield	10-20-1795	500	Q	44	W Fk Skeggs Cr
Ware, Samuel	Franklin	4-15-1822	146	V	218	None
Ware, Wm, heirs	Franklin	6-11-1833	2,000	Z	356	In Laurel Co
Warfield, Alexander	Frederick	1-27-1808	100	M	77	Big Barren R
Warfield, Alexander	Frederick	4-24-1809	100	M	434	Big Barren R
Warfield, Alexander & Wife	Frederick	8-24-1809	500	N	44	Big Barren R
Warfield, Chas	Baltimore	8-20-1819	900	T	17	Big Barren R
Warfield, Chas H & Wm C	——	9- 8-1829	100	Y	395	Plum Cr
Warfield, David	Baltimore	2- 2-1808	600	M	65	Big Barren R
Warfield, David	Baltimore	9- 6-1809	500	N	36	Big Barren R
Warfield, Elijah	——	12- 8-1804	200	J	23	Big Barren R
Warfield, Elijah	Baltimore	7-26-1811	500	O	107	Big Barren R
Warfield, Lott	Frederick	6- 3-1801	——	F	7	None
Warfield, Lott	Dorchester	4-15-1809	100	M	436	Big Barren R
Warfield, Lott & Chas	Dorchester	8-19-1809	500	N	40	Big Barren R
Warfield, Walter, Atty	Lexington	6- 7-1814	6,891	P	451	Goose, Dix & Ohio R, Skeggs Cr
Waring, Jno U	Fayette	11-11-1814	——	Q	6	Ky R
Waring, Jno U	Fayette	1-10-1816	1,000	Q	419	Tradewater
Waring, Jno U	Fayette	8- 7-1815	1,000	Q	530	Ohio R
Waring, Jno U	Fayette	8-23-1816	584	R	22	Big Barren R
Waring, Jno U & Wife	Fayette	1- 1-1818	Lot	S	17	Versailles
Waring, Jno U & Wife	Fayette	1- 1-1818	Lot	S	19	Versailles
Waring, Jno U & Wife	Fayette	6-10-1819	Lot	T	71	Versailles
Warnick, Frederick	Kentucky	7-13-1803	3,000	G	395	Salt R
Warnstaff, Chas	——	11- 1-1810	2,000	N	295	Ohio R
Warren, Thos B	Kentucky	1-12-1811	1,767	N	412	Eagle Cr & S Fk Licking
Warren, Thos B	Fayette	1-28-1812	5,312½	P	284	None
Washington, Jno	Logan	11-14-1815	——	Q	241	None
Washington, Lund & Wife	Prince William	6-28-1800	1,628	F	136	Br Licking
Waters, Jno, Atty	Montgomery	11-21-1814	900	P	560	Dry Fk Big Eddy
Waters, Jno, Atty	Shelby	10-12-1819	Lots	T	121	——
Waters, Richard J	Louisville	11-21-1814	900	P	560	Dry Fk Big Eddy
Waters, Richard J, heirs	Maryland	10-12-1819	Lots	T	121	——
Waters, Thos J & Wife	Prince George	10-12-1819	Lots	T	121	——
Watkins, Edward Jr & Wife	Powhatan	7-18-1797	600	B	175	S Fk Licking
Watkins, Jno	Carolina	4-18-1786	600	A	235	Dix R
Watkins, Jno	Virginia	3-21-1797	1,115	B	108	Middle Fk Sugar Cr
Watkins, Jno	Virginia	3-21-1797	500	B	121	None
Watkins, Jno	——	2-16-1836	——	28	9	In Ky
Watkins, Joseph	——	10-16-1797	6,000	B	247	Big Bone Lick
Watkins, Joseph	Goochland	6- 8-1799	485	D	452	Tradewater

Grantor	Residence	Deed Date	Acres	Book	Page	Watercourse
Watkins, Joseph, heirs	Virginia	5-15-1830	37½	Y	462	Silas Cr
Watkins, Joseph, heirs	Virginia	5-15-1830	34¾	Y	464	Br Cedar Cr
Watkins, Joseph, heirs.	Virginia	5-15-1830	——	Y	464	Silas & Cherry Run
Watkins, Mary, Died	——	2-16-1836	——	28	9	Ky
Watkins, Robt	Chesterfield	12-10-1804	1,000	J	271	None
Watkins, Robt	Chesterfield	11-15-1803	1,000	J	352	Ohio R
Watkins, Thos & Wife	Powhatan	7- 2-1810	1,000	N	230	N Fk Clay Lick Cr
Watson, Jas	Washington	4-21-1819	4,500	U	33	None
Watson, Jno	Franklin	2-26-1844	Lot	27	411	Frankfort
Watson, Jno	Franklin	8-21-1846	143	28	102	Dry Run
Watson, Joseph	Philadelphia	5-31-1819	1,916⅔	U	413	Ohio R
Watson, Josiah	Alexandria	6- 1-1803	——	M	37	None
Watson, Josiah & Wife	Alexandria	12- 4-1802	7,932½	G	343	Ky Ohio & Salt R
Watson, Josiah & Wife	Alexandria	2- 3-1802	5,000	J	274	S Fk Licking
Wattie, James	Fayette	7-11-1818	193½	S	364	4-Mile Howard & Hickman Cr
Way, Chas M	Jefferson	7-19-1842	320	27	296	In Hickman & Graves Co
Way & Bainbridge, Trustees	Jefferson	8-16-1841	320	27	223	Graves & Hickman
Wayland, Lewis	Augusta	6-17-1842	175	27	290	Severn & Cedar Cr
Wayland, Lewis	Augusta	6-17-1824	140	27	291	Severn & Cedar Cr
Weaver, Joseph	Fanquier	6-16-1828	1,065	Z	57	Licking
Weaver, Saml	Fanquier	4-16-1829	1,065	Z	60	Licking
Webb, Conrad, Executor	——	11- 5-1818	——	T	23	None
Webb, Geo	Clark	7-18-1820	4,000	T	477	Floyds Fk
Webber, Geo A	Kentucky	7-13-1803	3,000	G	395	Salt R
Weir, James	Lexington	9- 6-1820	238	U	19	S Elkhorn
Weisinger, Daniel	——	8-21-1800	Lot	F	2	Frankfort
Weisinger, Daniel	Franklin	8-25-1817	2,992	S	29	Big Bone Cr
Weisinger, Daniel	Frankfort	10-24-1821	7,000	V	121	Rough Cr
Weisinger, Daniel	Franklin	5-10-1826	111	Y	161	—— Cr
Weisinger, Daniel & Wife	Frankfort	1-15-1823	Lot	V	440	Frankfort
Weisinger, Daniel & Wife	Franklin	6- 2-1827	Lot	X	251	Frankfort
Weisinger, Daniel & Wife	Franklin	9- 6-1828	114	X	459	Benson Cr
Weisinger, Lucy	Franklin	6-10-1844	Lot	27	415	Frankfort
Weinsiger, Saml P	Franklin	12-19-1829	75	Z	7	Ky R
Weisinger, Saml P	Franklin	12-21-1833	Lots	Z	388	Frankfort
Welch, George	Fayette	10- 9-1790	Stock	B-2	220	None
Welch, Geo S	St. Louis	6-15-1839	11	27	72	In Franklin Co
Welch, James	Greenbrier	10-17-1799	Lots	D	535	Richmond
Welch, James	Greenbrier	10-17-1799	17,937¾	D	535	None
Welch, James	Greenbrier	10-17-1799	112,134¾	D	538	Gauley R, Little Kenhawa R & Lewis Cr
Welch, James	Greenbrier	6- 9-1800	200	E	317	Small Br
Welch, James	Bullitt	12- 9-1801	200	F	196	Ohio R
Welch, Jno	Spottsylvania	5-18-1802	3,530	F	400	Hardins & Cabin C
Welch, Wm & Wife	Shelby	10-14-1844	43	27	441	N Elkhorn
Wellford, Robt P	Fredericksburg	10- 9-1810	1,000	S	531	N Fk Panther Cr
Wellford, Robt & Wife	Fredericksburg	8- 4-1813	——	S	526	Barnetts Cr
Wellford, Robt & Wife	Fredericksburg	8- 4-1818	——	S	528	Panther Cr
Wellford, Robt & Wife	Fredericksburg	12- 1-1818	——	S	535	E Fk Panther Cr
Wells, Haden & Wife	Shelby	7-20-1807	147	L	115	Gesses Cr
Wescott, Geo	Philadelphia	10- 5-1791	10,000	K	53	Salt R
Wescott, Geo	Philadelphia	4-23-1796	6,000	A-2	453	None
West, Francis	Philadelphia	6- 3-1801	——	F	85	None
West, Francis	Philadelphia	4-21-1807	—•—	L	49	None
West, Francis & Wife	Philadelphia	3-18-1800	5,000	E	80	Main Licking
West, Thos	Carolina	7-14-1843	Lot	27	353	Frankfort
West, Thos	Carolina	7-14-1843	Lot	27	354	Frankfort
West, Wm	Franklin	8-16-1806	——	K	380	Cylos Cr
Westerfield, Windelin	Island St Domingo	1-12-1820	Lots	T	254	New Albany Ind
Wharton, Jno	Philadelphia	3-10-1789	13,666⅔	D	195	N Fk 3 Fks Ky R
Wheeler, Geo & Wife	Fredericksburg	8- 1-1798	650	D	151	Green R
Wheelock, Simon & Wife	Madison	9- 5-1817	——	R	570	None
Whitaker, Jas S	Shelby	3——1833	250	Z	368	Mill Cr
Whiting, Robt	Virginia	8- 8-1840	464½	27	153	Shelby Co
Whiting, Ruggles	Boston	8-19-1820	2,000	T	494	Hatties Cr
Whitledge, Thos	Bourbon	5-18-1801	200	E	380	Floyds Fk
White, Ambrose & Wife	Franklin	2-27-1810	Lot	N	133	Liberty
White, Philip & Wife	Franklin	10-10-1797	477	N	103	Chickahomeny Swamp
White, Robt Jr	Winchester	12- 1-1806	1,000	L	1	Green R
White, Wm	Hanover	10-10-1797	477	N	103	Chickahomeny Swamp
White, U	Montgomery	5- 6-1816	811	R	1	None
Whitson, Chas, Atty	Tennessee	9-21-1816	250	R	388	None

Grantor	Residence	Deed Date	Acres	Book	Page	Watercourse
Wickliffe, Chas A, Atty———.		10–11–1815	10,146	R	142	Cedar Cr, Green R & Rolling Fk
Wickliffe, Morgan P, heirs	———.	7– 7–1829	———.	Y	435	Ohio R
Wickliffe, Nathaniel & Wife	Nelson	12–14–1829	1,524	Y	490	Bullskin Cr & Flat Lick
Wickliffe, Robt	Lexington	9–18–1818	Lot	S	370	Port Williams
Wickliffe, Robt	————	5–18–1820	562	T	334	None
Wickliffe, Robt	Lexington	11– 9–1821	1,333⅓	V	98	Crocus & Greasy Cr
Wickliffe, R	————	5–29–1823	1,000	W	40	Rough Cr
Wickliffe, Robt	————.	10–19–1824	400	X	58	None
Wickliffe, R	Fayette	4–30–1829	Slaves	Y	353	None
Wickliffe, Robt	Fayette	5–21–1833	2,000	Z	291	Deer Cr
Wickliffe, Robt	Kentucky	1–14–1834	1,600	Z	389	Ohio R
Wickliffe, Robt	Franklin	2–19–1835	Lot	Z	502	Frankfort
Wickliffe, Robt	Fayette	5–11–1842	1,533	27	283	Otter Cr
Wickliffe, Robt	Fayette	11–22–1833	400	27	304	Slate Cr
Wickliffe, Robt, Atty	Kentucky	5–25–1814	50	P	473	Wolf Run
Wickliffe, Robt, Atty	Kentucky	5–23–1814	114½	P	475	Fks Wolf Run
Wickliffe, Robt, Atty	————.	11–29–1814	106	P	566	None
Wickliffe, Robt, Atty	Kentucky	5–25–1815	150	Q	116	None
Wickliffe, Robt	Kentucky	5–25–1815	21¼	Q	117	None
Wickliffe, Robt, Atty	Kentucky	5–25–1815	11¼	Q	118	None
Wickliffe, Robt, Atty	Kentucky	11– 7–1815	553	Q	223	Wolf Br
Wickliffe, Robt, Atty	Kentucky	10– 2–1815	57¼	Q	226	None
Wickliffe, Robt, Atty	Lexington	8– 4–1817	553	R	366	Wilsons Cr
Wickliffe, Robt, Atty	Lexington	8– 4–1817	200	R	368	Rolling Fk
Wickliffe, Robt, Atty	Fayette	5–15–1830	37½	Y	462	Silas Cr
Wickliffe, Robt, Atty	Fayette	5–15–1830	34¼	Y	464	Br Cedar Cr
Wickliffe, Robt, Atty	Fayette	5–15–1830	———.	Y	464	Silas & Cherry Run
Wickliffe, R, Atty	————	6–12–1831	315	Z	68	None
Wickliffe, R, Atty	Fayette	5– 9–1839	5,000	27	22	Little Ky R
Wickliffe, Robt & Wife	Lexington	5–27–1818	1,000	S	146	Barren R
Wiggs, Richard & Wife	Woodford	9–26–1845	25	28	26	Dry Run
Wiggs, Richard & Wife	Woodford	9–26–1845	49	28	28	Dry Run
Wight, Andrew & Wife	Frankfort	1–10–1817	Lot	R	150	Frankfort
Wight, Andrew & Wife	Wayne, Mo	5–24–1832	Lot	Z	209	Frankfort
Wilcocks, Richard H	Philadelphia	11–20–1819	10,000	T	193	Salt R
Wilcox, Jno	Shelby	9–24–1815	750	Q	221	Panther Cr & Floyd
Wilder, Jno	Petersburg	6–23–1821	———.	V	45	None
Wilder, Joseph G	————.	5– 8–1817	6,000	T	82	Richland Cr
Wilhite, Louis, Atty	Lincoln	3– 5–1829	2,704	Y	390	Panther & Rough Cr
Wilkerson, Robt	Franklin	8–25–1817	2,992	S	29	Big Bone Cr
Wilkins, Chas	————.	4– 3–1824	6,900	W	284	None
Wilkins, Chas, Atty	————	10–24–1809	7,500	N	258	Mouth Big Miami
Wilkins, Chas, Atty	————	11– 9–1810	220	N	310	Mill & Distillery
Wilkins, Chas, Atty	————	11– 9–1810	220	N	312	Mill & Distillery
Wilkins, Chas, heirs	Fayette	6–28–1828	1,140	X	470	Mammoth Cave & Green R
Wilkinson, Jas	N W Ohio R	6–14–1796	Lot	A-2	584	Frankfort
Wilkinson, Jas	Washington	11–17–1810	Lots	N	404	Frankfort
Wilkinson, Jas	Washington City	7– 3–1811	———.	Q	522	None
Wilkinson, Jas	Washington	7– 3–1811	———.	Q	527	None
Wilkinson, Jas	Washington	7– 3–1811	64,659	X	368	Ohio & Ky R & Mobile Bay
Wilkinson, Jas	Washington	7– 3–1811	———.	X	374	None
Wilkinson, Jas & Wife	Hamilton	9– 1–1794	Lot	E	65	Frankfort
Wilkinson, Jas P & Saml & Nancy & Lucy	Virginia	8–21–1828	158	X	452	Elkhorn
Wilkinson, Lyddall, Atty	Kentucky	2–13–1828	158	X	381	Elkhorn
Wilkinson, Peggy & Patsy C	————.	10–14–1828	———.	X	481	None
Williams, Alice G	Richmond	6–18–1821	———.	V	41	None
Williams, Chas & Wife	Berkly	12——1815	450	R	5	N & S Fk Elkhorn
Williams, David	Mercer	3–16–1791	1,000	B-2	348	M Fk Stoners Fk
Williams, Eli	Washington	3–10–1803	3,200	G	244	Green R & Bear Cr
Williams, Eli	Washington	3–10–1803	6,000	G	248	Muddy R
Williams, Eli	Washington	12–29–1809	2,000	O	346	Beaver Cr
Williams, Eli	Georgetown	5–18–1818	4,000	X	108	Ohio R
Williams, Eli	Georgetown	5–18–1818	685	X	109	Green R
Williams, Eli	Georgetown	5–18–1818	1,100	X	111	Rough Cr
Williams, Eli	Georgetown	5–18–1818	1,000	X	113	Russell Cr
Williams, Eli	Georgetown	5–18–1818	900	X	115	W Fk Pond R
Williams, Eli	Georgetown	5–18–1818	800	X	117	Big Barren R
Williams, Eli	Georgetown	5–18–1818	1,000	X	119	Grave Cr
Williams, Eliza	Alexandria	12——1815	450	R	5	N & S Fk Elkhorn
Williams, Isaac H & Wife	Monnongalia	3–19–1799	———.	D	162	None
Williams, James	Anapolis	5– 5–1800	2,352	E	61	Twins Cr
Williams, Jas	Richmond	11–22–1827	158	X	323	Elkhorn

Grantor	Residence	Deed Date	Acres	Book	Page	Watercourse
Williams, Jas, Executor	Richmond	12- 9-1802	1,000	G	221	Paraquet Cr
Williams, Jno	Monongahala	3- 5-1790	374	B-2	195	Jessamine Cr
Williams, Jno	Tenant in common	1- 6-1775	——	D	272	Ohio & Green R
Williams, Jno	Monongahala	7-22-1803	7,019	G	376	Townsend Run, Ohio R & Mill Cr
Williams, Jno	Montgomery	10-19-1830	Lot	Z	31	Mt Sterling
William, Major Jno	Monongalia	12-——1802	1,500	H	258	Beargrass & Goose Cr & Ohio R
Williams, Major Jno	Culpepper	6-29-1825	500	X	151	Beargrass & Goose C
Williams, Jonathan, Atty	Philadelphia	3-25-1796	64,184	A-2	521	Nolinn
Williams, Jno C	Culpepper	3-19-1799	——	D	162	None
Williams, Jno G	Richmond	6-18-1821	——	V	41	None
Williams, Jno R	Prince Edward	3-18-1820	1,500	Z	122	Beaver & Russell Cr
Williams, Jno R	Prince Edward	3-18-1820	2,000	Z	126	Beaver & Russell Cr & Little Barren R
Williams, Josiah & Wife	Woodford	3-29-1814	161½	P	389	None
Williams, Mary	Bath	11-19-1839	290	27	138	Grassy Lick Cr
Williams, Milly Jane	Calloway	8-21-1843	——	27	378	None
Williams, Thos	Alexandria	11-12-1799	5,000	F	26	Laurel R
Williams, Thos	Alexandria	11-12-1799	10,000	F	30	Straight Cr
Williams, Thos	Alexandria	11-12-1799	10,000	F	34	Cumberland R
Williams, Thos & Wife	Alexandria	6- 1-1797	1,250	D	236	Otter Cr
Williams, Thos & Wife	Alexandria	6- 1-1797	8,000	D	244	N Fk Sandy R
Williams, Thos & Wife	Alexandria	6- 1-1797	10,000	D	252	S Fk Ky R
Williams, Wm C	Richmond	11-24-1808	6,000	M	271	Big Bone Lick
Williams, Wm C	Richmond	2- 4-1809	1,000	M	413	Highland Cr
Williams, Wm C	——	10-16-1819	4,333½	T	222	Tradewater & Highland Cr
Williams, Wm C, heirs	Richmond	6-18-1821	——	V	41	None
Williams, Wm J	Nicholas	3- 9-1825	4,924	X	142	None
Williams, Wm J	Nicholas	3- 9-1825	42,197	X	144	None
Willing, Chas	Philadelphia	9-10-1784	30,000	A-2	33	None
Willing, Chas	Philadelphia	9-10-1784	2,000	H	391	None
Willis, Joseph	Lincoln	6-23-1785	200	A	30	Chaplains Fk
Willis, Joshua & Wife	Madison	4-15-1799	350	D	412	Little Ky R
Willis, Nathaniel & Wife	Ross	3- 4-1816	2,600	Q	444	Lick Cr & Beech Fk
Willis, Seth	Philadelphia	3- 6-1786	13,666⅔	D	193	N Fk 3 Fks Ky R
Willis, Wm	Adair	12- 8-1808	680	M	254	Cypress Cr
Willis, Wm	Adair	12- 8-1808	528½	M	261	Lost Cr
Willis, Wm	Boone	4-27-1816	1,500	R	124	Goose Cr
Willis, Wm Sr	Adair	12- 8-1808	641	M	253	Cypress Cr
Willis, Wm Sr	Adair	12- 8-1808	442	M	257	Cypress Cr
Willis, Wm Sr	Adair	12- 8-1808	739	M	259	Lost Cr
Willis, Wm Sr	Adair	12- 9-1808	425	M	262	Cypress Cr
Wills, Peachy	Williamsburg	4-19-1805	500	J	134	Cedar Cr
Wills, Peachy	Williamsburg	1-29-1806	216	K	137	Bullskin Cr
Wills, Peachy	Virginia	10- 6-1810	150½	N	317	None
Wilson, Alexander	Franklin	8-10-1812	386½	P	341	Bensons Cr
Wilson, Alexander	Franklin	6-14-1811	386½	O	391	S Fk Benson Cr
Wilson, Alexander	Franklin	——1826	450	Y	232	None
Wilson, Geo	——	12-15-1802	547	G	102	Salt R
Wilson, Geo	Louisville	5- 2-1804	Lot	H	506	Louisville
Wilson, Geo	Louisville	11- 5-1805	14,272	J	373	Beech & Benson Cr Ky & Green R
Wilson, Geo	Louisville	11- 4-1805	9,682	J	380	Beech & Benson Cr Ky & Green R
Wilson, Geo & Wife	Woodford	6- 9-1791	300	B-2	329	Shawnee Run
Wilson, Henry, Atty	——	10- 4-1791	700	B-2	358	Bucks Fk
Wilson, Henry, Atty	Bourbon	3- 5-1792	668	B-2	419	Beech Fk
Wilson, Henry, Atty	Bourbon	3- 5-1792	300	B-2	422	Beech Fk
Wilson, Henry & Wife	Bourbon	7-30-1798	200	D	148	Ky R
Wilson, Henry Jr & Wife	Mercer	5-13-1789	200	B-2	173	Elkhorn
Wilson, Henry Sr & Wife	Bourbon	3- 5-1792	300	B-2	417	Cartwrights Cr
Wilson, James	Kahnawa	7-20-1814	250	P	602	None
Wilson, Jas W & Wife	Warren	3- 6-1829	901	Y	398	Tennessee R
Wilson, Jno	Philadelphia	7- 3-1795	16,000	A-2	382	—— Cr
Wilson, Jno & Wife	Clark	9-27-1796	533½	A-2	611	Little Muddy Cr
Wilson, Joshua & Wife	Kentucky	8-12-1816	——	R	161	None
Wilson, Robt	——	8- 6-1817	800	R	369	Green R & Holstein
Wilson, Thos	Richmond	4-14-1804	10,000	H	359	None
Wilson, Wm & Wife	Augusta	10-31-1816	920	V	259	Indian Cr
Wilson, Willis	Norfolk	6-27-1796	1,420	A-2	496	Skeggs Cr
Wilson, Willis & Wife	Cumberland	6-15-1797	666⅔	D	219	Anderson Cr
Winchester, Stephen	Fredericksburg	7- 8-1806	200	K	358	Skeggs Cr
Winchester, Stephen	Fredericksburg	1-19-1808	1,650	M	62	Big Bone Lick
Winchester, Stephen	Spottsylvania	9- 3-1807	3,530	M	158	Ohio R
Wingate, Cyrus, Atty	Owen	10-21-1823	2,942	W	204	Cumberland R
Wingate, Isaac	Franklin	1- 5-1837	125	27	34	N Elkhorn
Wingate, Isaac & Wife	Franklin	2- 9-1839	25	27	26	S Elkhorn
Winlock, Joseph	Jefferson	11-29-1788	Contract	A	478	Floyds Fk

Grantor	Residence	Deed Date	Acres	Book	Page	Watercourse
Winn, Jas & Wife	Jefferson	3-17-1791	112	B-2	252	None
Winn, Thos & Wife	Woodford	8-25-1827	210	X	274	Glens Cr
Winn, Thos	Woodford	8-25-1827	Slaves	X	277	None
Winslow, Wm & Wife	Spottsylvania	8-15-1797	3,150	D	511	Main Fk Licking
Winston, Caswell & Chriswell B	Louisa	12-13-1824	3,000	Y	148	Poages, N Fk Tradewater & Goose Cr
Winston, Isaac	Culpepper	3-25-1811	1,469	O	406	Rough Cr
Winston, Isaac & Wife	Culpepper	12-21-1807	1,250	M	53	Rough Cr
Winston, Isaac & Wife	Culpepper	12-21-1807	734½	M	54	Rough Cr
Winston, Jno	——	12-20-1797	1,000	C	204	Tradewater
Winston, Overton & Eliza	Louisa	12-13-1824	3,000	Y	148	Poages, N Fk Tradewater & Goose Cr
Winston, Wm	——	12-20-1797	1,000	C	204	Tradewater
Winter, Elisha & Wife	——	4-16-1810	707	N	279	Ky R
Winthrop, Thos L	Boston	8-20-1814	——	Q	477	None
Wirt, Wm & Wife	Richmond	3-26-1825	2,647	Y	116	Poages Cr, Tradewater, Beaver Dam
Wirst, Wynkoop & Wife	Philadelphia	5- 2-1827	104	X	226	Salt R
Wirst, Wynkoop & Wife	Philadelphia	5- 2-1827	400	X	232	Salt R
Wirts, Wynkoop & Wife	Philadelphia	5-10-1827	8,270	X	236	Salt R
Wirts, Wenicoop & Wife	Philadelphia	1- 9-1827	5,000	Y	243	N Fk Ky R
Wirts, Wynkoop & Wife	Philadelphia	9-22-1832	15,000	Z	233	Salt R
Wise, Saml & Wife	Culpepper	8-21-1800	100	E	254	Poages Cr
Wolcott, Alexander	Hartford	1-20-1797	40,000	G	265	Br Big Sandy R
Wolfolk, Lowell, Atty	——	11-26-1799	350	D	82	Caseys Cr
Wolford, Jno	Adair	11- 9-1821		V	123	Crocus & Greasy Cr
Wood, Geo	Fayette	7-11-1818	193½	S	364	4-Mile lower Howard & Hickman Cr
Woodford Jno T & Wife	Caroline	2-25-1796	2,500	C	261	N Fk Tradewater
Woods, Andrew & Wife	Mercer	3-29-1814	770	P	387	Salt R
Woods, Saml Jr & Wife	Mercer	9-17-1800	54½	E	107	Ky R
Woodson, Frederick	Powhatan	8-24-1795	1,000	A-2	615	—— R
Woodson, Frederick	——	1- 1-1814	3,000	P	330	Consolas Cr
Woodson, Frederick	——	1- 2-1814	1,000	P	331	Harlins Cr
Woodson, Richard K	Woodford	3-10-1840	176	27	108	Glens Cr
Woodson, Richard K	Woodford	12- 2-1839	50	27	110	S Elkhorn
Wooldridge, Jno W	——	6-10-1811	1,000	O	83	Tennessee R
Wooldridge, J W	Christian	1-13-1824	18,500	W	225	None
Wooldridge, Jno W. heirs	Christian	4-15-1839	Lots	27	33	Frankfort
Wooldridge, Powhatan	Woodford	8-20-1812	31,985	O	534	None
Woolfolk, Richard, Atty	Nelson	11-19-1800	2,000	E	179	Licking
Woolfolk, Richard	Jessamine	12-10-1803	Slaves	H	90	None
Worthen, Elias & Wife	Fairfax	8-21-1820	——	W	258	None
Worthington, Walter	Anne Arundel	8- 1-1807	1,000	L	211	Big Barren R
Wren, Jno	Fairfax	3-19-1802	500	G	206	Buffaloe Cr
Wren, Jno	Fairfax	4- 4-1804	500	J	427	Buffaloe Cr
Wren, Jno	Fairfax	11-25-1805	500	J	435	Buffaloe Cr
Wright, Matthew	Frederick	12- 2-1797	2,766⅔	C	291	Ohio R
Wright, Matthew W	Frederick	6-26-1802	3,000	G	170	Big Barren & Cumberland R
Wynkoop, Abraham	Philadelphia	11- 8-1836	——	27	42	None
Wynkoop, Ann W	Philadelphia	11- 5-1836	——	27	43	None
Wynkoop, Ben	Philadelphia	5- 1-1787	1,000	A	415	None
Wynkoop, Benj	Philadelphia	7- 9-1791	36,000	A-2	7	Sandy R & Green R
Wynkoop, Benj	Philadelphia	8-22-1786	12,231	E	38	Salt R
Wynkoop, Benj	Philadelphia	5-15-1799	4,000	Q	160	Salt R
Wynkoop, Benj	Philadelphia	8-22-1786	10,000	T	317	Salt R
Wynkoop, Benj & Wife	Philadelphia	4-15-1793	50,000	C	188	Ky R
Wyatt, Jacob	Frankfort	2-25-1796	204	A-2	91	Silver Cr
Yancy, Robt	Louisa	9-18-1795	400	A-2	300	Licking
Yarbrough, Jno	Nicholas	9-14-1824	666⅔	W	361	Tradewater
Yates, Benj P, Adm'r	——	6-13-1815	1,000	Q	416	Tradewater
Yeater, Richard	Green	7-12-1803	700	G	372	Russell & Caney Cr
Young, Bryan R & Wife	Hardin	3-24-1832	75,000	Z	181	Hardin Co
Young, Chas & Wife	Philadelphia	11-15-1785	8,270	O	427	Salt R
Young, Jno	Philadelphia	9-14-1784	31,370	A-2	38	None
Young, Jno	Philadelphia	9-14-1784	3,000	H	289	None
Young, Jno	Philadelphia	5- 3-1786	56,000	Z	283	None
Young, Jno	Philadelphia	7- 8-1786	10,000	27	44	Fayette-Jefferson Co
Young, Jno & Wife	Philadelphia	7-29-1794	42,629	C	46	Green R
Young, Jno Jr	Philadelphia	4-28-1789	5,000	D	182	Br Ky R
Young, Jno Jr	Philadelphia	8-15-1794	22,943¾	G	225	M Fk Licking
Young, Levin	——	11- 1-1833	Lots	Z	365	Lexington
Young, Richard	Woodford	3- 6-1796	8,000	A-2	131	Shelby Cr
Young, Richard, Atty	——	7-20-1798	400	D	131	Ky R
Young, Robt & Wife	Alexandria	1-30-1804	41,185¾	N	300	Rolling Fk & Wilsons Cr Big Sandy
Young, Saml & Wife	Philadelphia	12-11-1793	10,400¼	E	206	Bald Eagle Towns
Young, Sarah	——	4- 5-1815	——	Q	42	Whisky Path
Zimmerman, Geo	Mercer	1-13-1791	700	B-2	336	—— Br

IX

COURT OF APPEALS DEEDS—WILLS

(1769-1850)

Testator	Residence	Date	Book	Page	Notes
Adams, Richard	Richmond	1-30-1800	Y	84	Will
Alexander, Richard B	Prince William	9-18-1821	Y	192	Will
Allison, Jno	Wilkes	4-14-1803	T	249	Will
Archer, R	Amelia	7-23-1796	U	365	Will
Arnett, Wm	Mercer	4- 8-1806	A	307	Deed
Ashby, Lewis	Frederick	5-20-1806	U	428	Will
Balch, Hezakiah J	Jefferson	7-16-1816	W	224	Will
Banta, Jacob	———	6-11-1787	J	31	Inv.
Beall, Samuel	James City	———	L	108	Deed
Bell, Jno	Augusta	2-11-1797	V	293	Will
Bell, Saml	Augusta	9-23-1782	V	292	Will
Bell, Thomas	Albemarle	5- 9-1797	V	374	Will
Brown, Benj	Hanover	2-11-1781	V	388	Will
Bullock, Wm	Granville	7-16-1794	V	92	Will
Bunner, Andrew	Philadelphia	6-20-1791	P	417	
Burke, Thos	Essex	5-23-1794	V	171	Will
Calloway, Richard	———	12-21-1772	J	9	Will
Camp, Rebecca	James City	7-12-1816	S	174	Will
Clements, Mace	Essex	10- 1-1806	Y	141	Will
Clymer, Geo	Philadelphia	1- 5-1813	V	108	Will
Cole, Wm	Essex	12- 8-1783	V	285	Will
Coleman, James	Fairfax	1-27-1817	Y	11	Will
Coleman, James	Fairfax	1-27-1812	S	458	Will
Colston, Rawleigh	Berkley	9-26-1818	Y	56	Will
Connelly, Jno	St. Johns	7- 1-1811	U	380	Will
Craig, Adam	Richmond	3-16-1808	W	241	Will
Craig, Adam	Richmond	3-16-1808	P	181	Will
Dick, Alexander	Fredericksburg	1-29-1815	V	366	Will
Dobbins, Jno	N Carolina	2———1801	U	401	Will
Dunlap, Jno	Philadelphia	10- 1-1807	P	265	Will
Earley, Joseph	Culpepper	2-12-1780	R	216	Will
Feagin, Edward	Fanquier	7- 8-1780	V	404	Will
Fields, Ezekiel	———	3- 4-1783	J	12	Inv.
Flournoy, Thos	Powhatan	3-14-1794	P	95	Deed
Fox, Mary	Mecklenburg	10- 9-1795	Y	208	Will
Fuller, Benj	Philadelphia	12-26-1797	W	249	Will
Gore, Jno	Culpepper	11-14-1812	V	172	Will
Graham, Jno	Richmond	7———1820	V	55	Will
Hale, Wm	Fanquier	2- 7-1818	V	208	Will
Harrison, Richard	Pickering	1-14-1800	M	23	Will
Harrison, Wm	Petersburg	5-29-1812	U	290	Will
Harvie, Jno	Henrico	11-26-1806	S	537	Will
Harvie, Jno	Henrico	11-26-1806	U	424	Will
Heron, James	Richmond	9-21-1800	V	102	Will
Hite, Isaac, Sr	Frederick	———	D	161	Deed
Humphreys, Benj	Jefferson	11- 1-1827	X	347	Deed
Innis, James	Williamsburg	3-20-1798	E	385	Deed
Johnston, Robt	Franklin	11-12-1808	W	129	Will
Jones, Benj	Putman	2- 3-1844	28	158	Will
Joynes, Levin	Accomack	12-15-1793	H	337	Will
Lane, Wm	Fairfax	2-11-1808	28	326	Will
Lee, Arthur	Lansdown	10-25-1792	V	323	Will
Levington, Justice	King William	4———1785	F	529	Will
Lewis, Wm	Philadelphia	8- 7-1819	W	255	Will
Lightfoal, Mildred	Charles City	3- 2-1798	A	25	Will
Luttrell, Jno	Orange	3-20-1775	U	326	Will
McDermed, Francis	Fayette	5-16-1792	B-2	506	Will
McNew, Jeremiah	———	3-14-1788	J	37	Inv.
Marks, Josiah	London	8- 8-1785	K	147	Will
Mason, George	Fairfax	4- 7-1795	W	135	Will
Means, Robt	Richmond	4-12-1808	V	261	Will
Mercer, James	Fredericksburg	5-23-1791	V	361	Will
Miller, Abram	Augusta	5- 8-1769	J	14	Will
Miller, Jno	Lincoln	7- 1-1785	J	28	Will
Minor, Garrett	Louisa	1-19-1798	T	488	Will
Mitchell, Joseph	Ohio Co., Va	8- 5-1789	K	149	Will
Moore, Robt K	Richmond	4-20-1786	Y	1	Will
Morgan, Chas	Alleghany	5- 6-1800	V	244	Will
Morgan, Wm., Sr	Lincoln	4-29-1797	M	62	Deed
Murphy, Geo	Memphis	2-24-1851	28	163	Will
Noel, Rice	Essex	4- 5-1798	V	417	Will

Testator	Residence	Date	Book	Page	Notes
Oliver, Robt	Baltimore	1–30–1834	28	143	Will
Overall, Jno	Kentucky	12–16–1816	V	153	Will
Parker, Josiah	Isle of Wight	3– 8–1810	P	188	Will
Parker, Josiah	Isle of Wight	3– 8–1810	R	48	Will
Parker, Nathaniel Sr	Sumner	2–25–1811	Z	369	Will
Perkins, Thos	————	6–13–1788	T	38	Inv.
Phillips, Philip	Davidson	2– 3–1797	V	194	Will
Pickett, George Sr	Richmond	2–24–1821	V	423	Will
Poythress, Wm	Pr. George	9– 2–1794	V	416	Will
Preston, Wm	Montgomery	3–29–1777	W	149	Will
Protzman, John	Washington	6–29–1804	U	296	Will
Raquet, Claudius Paul	Burgundy, France	7–19–1791	Y	21	Will
Rawlings, Francis	Anne Arundel	7–21–1793	W	40	Will
Ritchy, Robt	Charlotte	1–21–1774	J	34	Will
Ronald, Andrew	Richmond	7–10–1798	R	253	Will
Rose, Jno	Westmoreland	3–18–1802	S	90	Will
Ross, David	Richmond	4–24–1817	S	389	Will
Searcy, Wm	Maryland	2–22–1815	V	141	Will
Skinner, Alexander	Richmond	11–12–1788	P	114	Will
Smith, Leny	Green Co., Ind	2–14–1826	Y	128	Will
Smith, Solomon	Burke	11–28–1802	V	85	Will
Smith, Solomon	Burke	11–28–1802	V	304	Will
Sneed, Col. Smith	Northampton	7–20–1803	H	279	Will
Stark, Bolling	Richmond	11–20–1787	V	370	Will
Stewart, Chas	Bucks Co., Pa	5–12–1787	B	97	Deed
Stokes, Basil	————	3– 6–1787	J	88	Inv.
Swearingen, Thos	Berkley	6–21–1811	V	257	Will
Taylor, Edmund	Frederick	9–13–1783	Y	145	Will
Taylor, James	Caroline	11–12–1811	Q	76	Will
Tebbs, Willoughby	Dumfries	10–22–1803	Q	7	Deed
Tennent, Jno	Caroline	7–28–1790	V	382	Will
Thomas, Westly	Warrick	6–28–1815	Y	137	Will
Travis, Champion	Williamsburg	8–15–1810	U	372	Will
Trigg, Stephen	————	9–20–1780	J	1	Will
Tucker, Enoch	————	11–30–1786	J	40	Inv.
Walden, Jno	Caroline	8–29–1793	V	409	Will
Wallace, James	Jacksonborough	12–10–1790	Y	179	Will
Watkins, Joseph	Goochland	3–16–1804	U	405	Will
Watkins, Mayo C	Goochland	11–21–1812	U	410	Will
Weedon, George	Fredericksburg	11–26–1793	V	419	Will
Wellford, Jno S	Fredericksburg	12– 9–1841	28	133	Will
Wellford, Robt	Fredericksburg	5–22–1822	28	137	Will
Wellford, Wm	Fredericksburg	1– 1–1817	28	140	Will
Wickliffe, Robt	Kentucky	6–17–1850	28	161	Will
Wood, Jno Scott	Davidson	5–25–1812	V	381	Will
Worke, Bolling	Richmond	11–20–1787	V	370	Will

X

COURT OF APPEALS DEEDS—ATTORNEYS

(1781-1853)

Grantees in Power of Attorney

Grantee	Residence	Deed Date	Book	Page	Notes
Adams, Saml G	———	6–20–1799	D	353	Contract
Allen, Jno	Philadelphia	4–18–1820	T	414	Contract
Alexander, Robt	Frankfort	8– 1–1818	S	229	Contract
Alexander, Robt	Woodford	1–23–1828	X	414	Contract
Anderson, Cuthbert S	Frankfort	5–19–1819	T	402	Contract
Anderson, Cuthbert S	Frankfort	1–22–1819	T	405	Contract
Anderson, Cuthbert S	Frankfort	8– 7–1820	T	471	Contract
Anderson, Cuthbert S	Franklin	2–10–1820	T	480	Contract
Anderson, Cuthbert S	Franklin	7–10–1820	T	486	Contract
Anderson, Cuthbert S	———	6– 3–1819	U	75	Contract
Anderson, Cuthbert S	Kentucky	3–15–1821	U	354	Contract
Anderson, Cuthbert S	Kentucky	3–15–1821	U	355	Contract
Anderson, Cuthbert S	Franklin	10–19–1821	V	88	Contract
Anderson, Cuthbert S	Frankfort	7–28–1823	W	55	Contract
Anderson, Cuthbert S	Franklin	8–27–1823	W	101	Contract
Anderson, Cuthbert S	Franklin	8–24–1823	W	103	Contract
Anderson, Cuthbert S	Frankfort	8–27–1823	W	104	Contract
Anderson, Dr Jno	Bedford	5–10–1802	F	351	Contract
Apperson, Edmond R	New Kent	9–29–1827	X	322	Contract
Apperson, Richard	Montgomery	4——1837	27	21	Contract
Apperson, Richard	Montgomery	1–26–1842	27	267	Contract
Archer, Richard T	Amelia	4– 7–1820	T	438	Contract
Archer, Richard T	Amelia	3–28–1823	W	1	Contract
Archer, Stephen C	Amelia	9–27–1821	V	106	Contract
Armstead, Jno	Fanquier	11–22–1815	Q	291	Contract
Ashley, Elizabeth	Kentucky	2–26–1853	28	331	Contract
Ashton, Lawrence	Kentucky	10–14–1826	X	242	Contract
Ashton, Lawrence	Kentucky	10– 2–1826	X	243	Contract
Ashton, Lawrence	Virginia	11–23–1825	Y	144	Contract
Atchison, Saml A	Warren	5–11–1839	27	167	Contract
Atkinson, Richard	———	11——1818	T	46	Contract
Bacon, Jno C	Owen	4–10–1820	W	203	Contract
Ballenger, Col Jno	Kentucky	12–17–1805	J	466	Contract
Banks, Cuthbert	Lexington	8– 9–1802	H	38	Contract
Banks, Henry	Richmond	7–22–1817	S	3	Contract
Barbee, Joshua	Kentucky	5– 9–1804	H	467	Contract
Barbee, Joshua	Mercer	6–16–1815	V	132	Contract
Barber, David	Kentucky	4–27–1798	D	201	Contract
Barber, David	Kentucky	8– 2–1800	E	128	Contract
Barber, David	Kentucky	8–13–1802	F	481	Contract
Barbour, James	Orange	8– 7–1802	J	279	Contract
Barnett, Alexander Jr	Ohio	1–22–1819	T	3	Contract
Barnett, Jas	Madison	12– 3–1805	L	70	Contract
Barnett, Nathan	Amherst	——1802	G	450	Contract
Barry, W T	Lexington	5–25–1810	P	535	Contract
Barry, Wm T	Lexington	5– 7–1816	Q	543	Contract
Barry, Wm T	Lexington	12– 9–1816	R	294	Contract
Beatty, Dr Chas C	Montgomery	2– 2–1828	X	424	Contract
Beatty, Dr Chas C	Montgomery	6–11–1828	X	426	Contract
Beatty, Dr Chas C	Montgomery	5–24–1828	X	428	Contract
Beatty, Dr Chas C	Montgomery	5–24–1828	X	430	Contract
Beatty, Dr Chas C	Montgomery	12–27–1827	X	432	Contract
Beauchamp, Jeroboam	Washington	11–24–1814	P	573	Contract
Beazley, Joseph	Caroline	11–13–1806	K	473	Contract
Bell, Thompson	Greenup	1– 6–1813	P	87	Contract
Bell, Thompson	Greenup	8– 8–1820	T	458	Contract
Berry, Jno	Fayette	1–31–1803	G	416	Contract
Berry, Taylor	St. Louis	10– 6–1819	T	112	Contract
Blackburn, Edward	Woodford	2–24–1834	Z	476	Contract
Blair, David & Jas	Frederick	8–11–1798	N	55½	Contract
Blair, David & Jas	Fredericksburg	8–11–1798	N	189	Contract
Blanton, Carter	Franklin	4– 8–1803	G	269	Contract
Blanton, Thos	Frankfort	2–18–1807	K	551	Contract
Blanton, Willis	Frankfort	7– 6–1821	U	468	Contract
Bodly, Thos	Lexington	1–22–1801	E	312	Contract
Bodly, Thos	Lexington	10– 6–1800	E	313	Contract
Bodly, Thos	Kentucky	12–10–1803	J	187	Contract
Bond, Wm	———	3–24–1821	U	485	Contract
Bonta, Henry	Madison	8–20–1818	S	216	Contract

Grantee	Residence	Deed Date	Book	Page	Notes
Bonta, Henry	Madison	8-18-1818	S	214	Contract
Booker, Paul J	Washington	11-29-1832	Z	263	Contract
Booker, Paul J	Washington	11-13-1832	Z	264	Contract
Bowman, Abraham	Fayette	3-16-1809	N	17	Contract
Branch Bank	Bowling Green	7-11-1826	Y	165	Contract
Branch Bank	Falmouth	12-17-1821	V	152	Contract
Branch Bank	Glasgow	4-19-1822	V	192	Contract
Branch Bank	Harrodsburg	8-21-1821	V	11	Contract
Branch Bank	Hartford	8-21-1821	V	12	Contract
Branch Bank	Lexington	5- 9-1821	U	398	Contract
Branch Bank	Lexington	8-21-1821	V	14	Contract
Branch Bank	Louisville	3-23-1821	U	395	Contract
Branch Bank	Prinston	8-21-1821	V	12	Contract
Branch Bank	Louisville	8-21-1821	V	13	Contract
Branch Bank	Richmond	2-28-1822	V	185	Contract
Bray, Jno	New Brunswick	1-18-1799	G	355	Contract
Breckenridge, Joseph C	Lexington	1- 1-1815	Q	50	Contract
Breckenridge, J C	Frankfort	5-14-1823	W	53	Contract
Breckenridge, Robt	Jefferson	7-15-1802	F	470	Contract
Breckenridge, Robt	Jefferson	2-16-1808	P	313	Contract
Breckenridge, Wm L	Fayette	12-21-1827	X	435	Contract
Breckenridge, Wm L	Fayette	8-19-1828	X	437	Contract
Briscoe, Thos	————	4-10-1817	R	428	Contract
Bristow, Jas	Shelbyville	6- 5-1819	T	131	Contract
Broadhead, Lucas	Kingston	11-17-1819	T	375	Contract
Broadnax, Henry	Kentucky	10- 9-1798	D	340	Contract
Brodhead, Lucas	Franklin	7- 2-1829	Y	393	Contract
Brough, Robt	Norfolk	7- 1-1817	R	374	Contract
Brough, Robt	Norfolk	7- 1-1817	R	376	Contract
Brooking, Thos A	————	12-19-1818	U	445	Contract
Brown, Jas	Washington	10-22-1804	H	347	Contract
Brown, Jno	Frankfort	11-27-1804	H	380	Contract
Brown, Jno	Frankfort	12-29-1812	P	76	Contract
Brown, Jno	Frankfort	9-21-1822	V	443	Contract
Brown, Jno B & Wife	————	4-18-1833	Z	279	Contract
Brown, Mason	Franklin	5-23-1833	Z	316	Contract
Browning, Jas	Kentucky	4- 8-1814	P	493	Contract
Bruce, Jno	Kentucky	7-29-1819	U	317	Contract
Bryan, Thos	Franklin	7-30-1807	S	259	Contract
Bryan, Thos	Franklin	10-11-1819	T	215	Contract
Buckner, Wm	Green	12- 1-1798	D	494	Contract
Bullock, Saml R	Fayette	7-17-1845	28	5	Contract
Bunley & Triplett	Frankfort	4- 6-1827	X	227	Contract
Bunley & Triplett	Franklin	5-24-1827	X	269	Contract
Bunley & Triplett	Franklin	12- 3-1827	X	351	Contract
Bureau, Jno P R	Ohio	8- 7-1843	27	363	Contract
Buster, Claudins	Russell	10-28-1830	Z	341	Contract
Cabot, Saml	Boston	6-17-1837	27	145	Contract
Caldwell, Adam	Frankfort	5-14-1805	J	323	Contract
Campbell, Aaron	Logan	1-28-1822	X	103	Contract
Carneal, Thos	Kentucky	12- 6-1800	F	150	Contract
Cary, Thos G	Boston	6-17-1837	27	145	Contract
Cates, O G	Franklin	5-19-1840	27	337	Contract
Cates, O G	Frankfort	10-15-1845	28	75	Contract
Cates, O G	Franklin	———— 1846	28	120	Contract
Chamberlain, Will B	Henrico	11-25-1823	W	175	Contract
Chambers, Will B	Scott	8-29-1826	Y	256	Contract
Chapman, Jno S	New York	12- 8-1819	T	177	Contract
Chinn, Christopher	Mercer	5-30-1845	28	1	Contract
Christman, Joseph	Jessamine	1-18-1823	W	118	Contract
Claiborne, Richard	Richmond	1-25-1786	N	401	Contract
Clark, Geo	Lexington	3-24-1798	D	39	Contract
Clark, Geo	Kentucky	12-27-1798	D	442	Contract
Clark, Geo	Lexington	5-30-1801	E	429	Contract
Clark, Geo	Kentucky	7- 7-1801	F	73	Contract
Clark, Geo	Kentucky	5- 5-1800	F	75	Contract
Clark, Geo	Fayette	7- 3-1812	P	139	Contract
Clark, Geo	Lexington	1———— 1816	Q	488	Contract
Clark, Geo	Lexington	2-25-1818	S	132	Contract
Clark, Geo	Lexington	11- 4-1815	S	481	Contract
Clark, Geo	Kentucky	2-29-1820	T	273	Contract
Clark, Geo	Lexington	7-31-1820	U	15	Contract
Clark, Wm	St. Louis	1-20-1820	T	279	Contract
Clay, Elizabeth	Kentucky	3- 4-1831	27	270	Contract
Clay, Henry	Kentucky	10-16-1806	K	491	Contract
Clay, Henry	Kentucky	4- 1-1811	O	61	Contract
Clay, Henry	Kentucky	4- 1-1811	O	65	Contract
Coleman, Jas	Fayette	10-15-1811	O	174	Contract
Coleman, James	Harrison	11-13-1799	G	125	Contract
Coleman, Jos	Harrison	6- 2-1821	V	167	Contract
Colston, Edward	Berkley	5- 7-1811	O	48	Contract
Colston, Edward	Berkley	5- 7-1811	O	52	Contract

Grantee	Residence	Deed Date	Book	Page	Notes
Colston, Edward	Berkley	7-13-1812	O	479	Contract
Colston, Edward	——	10-17-1829	Y	410	Contract
Colston, Rauleigh	Berkley	11- 2-1814	P	554	Contract
Combs, Leslie	Fayette	12-24-1818	S	424	Contract
Combs, Leslie	Lexington	2- 1-1819	T	50	Contract
Combs, Leslie	Lexington	2-23-1819	T	200	Contract
Combs, Leslie	Lexington	1-19-1820	T	418	Contract
Combs, Leslie	Fayette	4-24-1820	U	319	Contract
Combs, Leslie	Lexington	10-29-1827	X	318	Contract
Combs, Leslie	Lexington	1-28-1828	X	385	Contract
Combs, Leslie	Lexington	2-16-1828	X	386	Contract
Combs, Leslie	Fayette	12-30-1829	Y	441	Contract
Combs, Leslie	Fayette	7- 3-1830	Y	504	Contract
Combs, Leslie	Fayette	11-29-1845	28	64	Contract
Combs, Leslie	Fayette	6-18-1845	28	66	Contract
Cone, Joseph	Alexandria	4-28-1821	U	447	Contract
Conover, Lewis H	——	8- 2-1820	U	2	Contract
Conway, Wm B	Hardin	2-16-1834	Z	407	Contract
Conyngham, David	New Orleans	10- 1-1840	27	418	Contract
Corbin, Richard R	Mississippi	5- 9-1845	27	475	Contract
Coupland, Wm R	Cumberland	8-25-1819	U	44	Contract
Cowan, Jas	Lexington	1-13-1819	V	135	Contract
Cowan, Jas	Lexington	6- 4-1821	V	137	Contract
Cowan, Jas	Lexington	9- 3-1822	V	326	Contract
Cowan, Jas	Lexington	12- 8-1827	X	352	Contract
Cowan, Jno	Shelby	12- 5-1833	Z	416	Contract
Cox, Austin P	Franklin	8-11-1834	Z	458	Contract
Cox, Austin P	Franklin	8- 9-1834	Z	460	Contract
Cox, Austin P	Franklin	6-16-1835	Z	517	Contract
Cox, Austin P	Franklin	11-15-1838	27	2	Contract
Cox, Austin P	Frankfort	2-11-1840	27	104	Contract
Cox, Austin P	Franklin	6-22-1840	27	126	Contract
Cox, Isaac B	——	5- 4-1815	S	436	Contract
Cox, Isaac B	New York	10-26-1816	S	439	Contract
Cox, Isaac B	New York	9-21-1816	S	441	Contract
Cox, Nathaniel	Kentucky	10-15-1804	H	334	Contract
Cox, Richard	Powhatan	10-30-1798	H	399	Contract
Craig, Wm	——	4-15-1839	27	69	Contract
Craig, Wm	Illinois	1-29-1840	27	116	Contract
Crawford, Alexander	Frankfort	10-25-1810	O	77	Contract
Crump, Chas C	——	5-11-1826	Y	155	Contract
Crump, Chas C	——	5-12-1826	Y	153	Contract
Crutcher, Henry	Georgia	8- 8-1808	M	312	Contract
Crutcher, Jas	Hardin	10-27-1827	X	379	Contract
Crutcher, Wm	——	5- 4-1799	D	205	Contract
Cummings, Jas & Robt	Washington	10-19-1802	G	40	Contract
Cummings, Robt E	Washington	1- 8-1807	N	383	Contract
Cunningham, Jno	Jessamine	10- 6-1825	X	190	Contract
Curd, Richard A	Fayette	10-16-1827	X	301	Contract
Curry, Jno Wm	Paris	9- 5-1818	S	428	Contract
Curtz, Tho Jr	Lycoming	11-25-1822	Y	286	Contract
Dade, Lawrence S	Orange	3- 9-1833	Z	295	Contract
Daniel, Henry	Montgomery	12- 9-1823	W	188	Contract
Daniels, Robertson	Jefferson	8-22-1832	Z	226	Contract
Daviess, Samuel	Mercer	10-26-1819	27	48	Contract
Davis, Jas	Clark	11- 2-1816	R	115	Contract
Davis, Jno	Gallatin	12-15-1813	P	298	Contract
Dawson, Robt D	Montgomery	5-29-1812	O	412	Contract
Day, Edward	Baltimore	10-15-1811	O	345	Contract
Dennis, Jesse	Frankfort	3-10-1820	U	507	Contract
Denny, Wm H	Pittsburg	7-20-1832	Z	465	Contract
Dickenson, Richard	Kentucky	5- 8-1800	F	15	Contract
Dodge, Joseph	Belvedere	11- 2-1807	L	374	Contract
Donaldson, Robt	Frederick	12- 8-1801	F	188	Contract
Donnell, Jno R	York	5-20-1822	V	305	Contract
Donnell, Jno R	York	4- 5-1822	V	306	Contract
Drake, Jno T	Cincinnati	5-24-1824	W	303	Contract
Drake, Jno T	Cincinnati	11- 5-1821	W	397	Contract
Drake, Jno T	Cincinnati	2-23-1825	X	137	Contract
Duckham, Thos	Frankfort	8-12-1819	V	1	Contract
Dudley, Thos P	——	5-24-1824	W	274	Contract
Duncan, Daniel	Paris	7-12-1821	U	473	Contract
Duncan, Lewis	Clark	5- 5-1828	X	441	Contract
Duval, Wm	——	7-28-1794	H	323	Contract
Duval, Wm	——	9- 3-1822	V	446	Contract
Duval, Wm Pope	——	12-13-1820	U	362	Contract
Early, Whitefield	Boone	10- 3-1812	R	219	Contract
Early, Whitefield	Boone	11-13-1812	R	224	Contract
Eastin, Wm B	Parish St. Martin	7-10-1826	Y	210	Contract
Edwards, Achillis	Bourbon	1- 5-1824	W	231	Contract
Ellesbeck, Joseph	Kentucky	9-25-1816	R	181	Contract
Epperson, Edmund	New Kent	11-25-1802	G	76	Contract

Grantee	Residence	Deed Date	Book	Page	Notes
Fenwick, Wm	Richmond	7- 9-1800	E	183	Contract
Ficklin, Joseph	Logan	5- 7-1806	K	304	Contract
Ficklin, Joseph	Logan	5-31-1806	K	325	Contract
Finley, Jno	Washington	1- 2-1815	Q	31	Contract
Fitzhugh, Dennis	Louisville	3-24-1817	T	278	Contract
Fleming, Wm P	Flemingsburg	8-19-1817	S	11	Contract
Fleming, Wm P	Kentucky	6-24-1831	Z	187	Contract
Fleming, Wm P	Kentucky	11-18-1831	Z	192	Contract
Fleming, Wm P	Kentucky	9- 2-1831	Z	193	Contract
Fleming, Wm P	Kentucky	8- 2-1831	Z	195	Contract
Fore, Jno	Chesterfield	9- 3-1798	D	171	Contract
Fowler, Jno	Woodford	9- 7-1798	E	427	Contract
Gaitshill, Joseph	Wapping	11- 4-1805	J	363	Contract
Gay, Benj P	Clark	8-31-1820	V	130	Contract
Gilchrist, Chas, C P	Henderson	4-21-1817	R	409	Contract
Gipson, Jas	Kentucky	4- 8-1814	P	493	Contract
Gist, Rezin H	Kentucky	4- 1-1811	O	61	Contract
Gist, Rezin H	Clark	3-14-1811	O	63	Contract
Gist, Rezin H	Kentucky	4- 1-1811	O	65	Contract
Glass, Robt	Shelby	6- 7-1814	P	563	Contract
Goodwin, Caleb V	Baltimore	9-12-1809	N	29	Contract
Graham, Jno	Washington	10-15-1800	E	159	Contract
Graham, Jno	———	10-17-1800	E	205	Contract
Green, Geo Mason	Culpepper	7- 3-1845	28	81	Contract
Greenup, Christopher	Kentucky	2-10-1808	L	370	Contract
Griffin, Thos L	———	5-12-182–	T	315	Contract
Griffith, Wm R	Kentucky	5-16-1832	Z	478	Contract
Grinnan, Daniel	Frederick	8-11-1798	N	55½	Contract
Grinnan, Daniel	Fredericksburg	8-11-1798	N	189	Contract
Hackaday, Isaac	St. Charles	8-15-1815	Q	326	Contract
Hamilton, Joseph D	———	5-22-1824	W	272	Contract
Hampton, David	Clark	5- 7-1827	Y	340	Contract
Hanna, Jno H	Franklin	11- 7-1829	Y	412	Contract
Hanna, Jno H	Franklin	4-21-1829	Z	101	Contract
Hanna, Jno H	Franklin	3-16-1831	Z	131	Contract
Hanna, Jno H	Franklin	3- 5-1831	Z	132	Contract
Hanna, Jno H	Franklin	9-16-1829	Z	152	Contract
Hanna, Jno H	Franklin	11-19-1832	Z	318	Contract
Hanna, Jno H	Franklin	7-27-1833	Z	336	Contract
Hanna, Jno H	Franklin	9-24-1834	Z	457	Contract
Hanna, Jno H	Frankfort	5-21-1807	L	48	Contract
Hanna, Jno H	Franklin	11- 5-1827	X	316	Contract
Hanna, Jno H	Franklin	9- 3-1828	X	459	Contract
Hanna, Jno H	Franklin	6-26-1839	27	47	Contract
Hanna, Jno H	Franklin	6- 4-1840	27	139	Contract
Hanna, Jno H	Franklin	7- 3-1845	28	107	Contract
Hardin, Mark	Kentucky	3-18-1818	S	103	Contract
Harris, Jas	Tennessee	5-30-1845	28	98	Contract
Harrison, Philip B	Jefferson	7-18-1807	L	122	Contract
Hart, Nathaniel	Franklin	10- 6-1806	M	57	Contract
Hart, Nathaniel, Executor	———	4-22-1813	Q	483	Contract
Hart, Wm D	Albemarle	10- 4-1845	28	37	Contract
Hart, Wm D	Albemarle	11-13-1845	28	39	Contract
Hawkins, J H	———	5- 1-1810	R	454	Contract
Hellam, Gabriel "Free man of color"	St Louis	4- 6-1835	Z	496	Contract
Henderson, Leonard	———	1——1797	D	277	Contract
Hendrin, Patrick	———	11——1818	T	46	Contract
Henry, Alexander Jr	London	3-31-1806	K	231	Contract
Herndon, Elisha	Franklin	5-22-1816	R	62	Contract
Heron, Jno E	Richmond	10-12-1830	Z	50	Contract
Hiatt, Joseph	———	5-15-1813	T	416	Contract
Hickman, Benj	Frankfort	10-18-1817	T	435	Contract
Hoagland, Moses T	Gallatin	10-18-1824	X	417	Contract
Hoomes, Richard H	Carolina	11-12-1842	27	359	Contract
Hopkins, Jacob B	Henderson	4-21-1817	R	409	Contract
Howard, Beall	———	6-21-1805	K	268	Contract
Howell, Wm W	Philadelphia	8-16-1821	V	144	Contract
Hughes, Jas	Franklin	11- 6-1816	R	82	Contract
Hunt, Seth	Washington	9-28-1811	P	217	Contract
Hunter, Wm	Frankfort	9- 5-1801	F	98	Contract
Hunter, Wm	Frankfort	6-20-1818	S	162	Contract
Hunter, Wm S	———	5-18-1804	H	187	Contract
Innis, Harry	Kentucky	5- 9-1800	E	385	Contract
Innis, Harry	Frankfort	6- 8-1803	J	166	Contract
Innis, Harry	Franklin	5-19-1810	O	111	Contract
Innis, Harry	Frankfort	9-26-1811	O	163	Contract
Innis, Harry	Franklin	3- 3-1812	Q	17	Contract
Innis, Harry	Mercer	6-27-1788	Q	52	Contract
Innis, Harry	Kentucky	5- 7-1790	R	382	Contract
January, Ephram	Jessamine	9-28-1802	G	12	Contract
Jeffreys, Ambrose	Franklin	9- 4-1801	F	1	Contract

Grantee	Residence	Deed Date	Book	Page	Notes
Jenkins, Edmund B	Columbia	12-10-1794	L	342	Contract
Johnson, Geo W	Shelby	8-24-1844	27	453	Contract
Johnson, Jas	Northampton	6-25-1804	H	342	Contract
Johnson, Jno T & Richard M	——	6-27-1821	U	526	Contract
Johnson, Robt	Scott	8-23-1798	D	28	Contract
Jones, Leslie Grove	Lieut-Cols	3-11-1816	R	9	Contract
Jones, Thos	Fleming	5-28-1819	T	1	Contract
Keen, Jno T	Muhlenberg	2- 7-1827	X	211	Contract
Kelley, Edward	London	10-22-1824	V	448	Contract
Kelley, Wm	Kentucky	4- 1-1811	O	61	Contract
Kincannon, Geo		3- 4-1829	Y	355	Contract
Kinney, Geo W	Morris	11-16-1818	S	477	Contract
Kinney, Jno	New Jersey	7-12-1804	K	142	Contract
Kinney, Jno	Morris	2- 2-1804	K	209	Contract
Kirk, Thos	Lawrence	11-23-1843	27	368	Contract
Lale, Wm	Carolina	9- 4-1801	F	1	Contract
Langham, Elias	Chillicothe	1-20-1803	G	350	Contract
Langham, Maurice	Bourbon	12-15-1810	N	382	Contract
LaRue, Jacob	Kentucky	4-20-1798	P	85	Contract
Lewis, Daniel	——	6-23-1828	X	463	Contract
Lewis, Gabriel	Fredericksburg	10- 3-1795	E	303	Contract
Lewis, Jno Jr	——	1- 6-1808	M	106	Contract
Lewis, Thos	Petersburg	8-10-1819	T	60	Contract
Lewis, Vincent	Nelson	3-13-1820	T	437	Contract
Lee, Henry Jr	Westmoreland	11-10-1786	Q	449	Contract
Lee, Zachariah Proctor	Lycoming	12- 4-1822	Y	291	Contract
Lee, Zachariah Proctor	Lycoming	5- 1-1827	Y	293	Contract
Lindsey, Thos N	Frankfort	11- 3-1840	27	185	Contract
Linn, Lewis F	——	4- 1-1815	W	279	Contract
Linton, Jno	Pikeville	9- 8-1829	Y	385	Contract
Linton, Nathan	Ohio	2- 5-1808	M	46	Contract
Little, Wm	Shelby	11-16-1816	R	276	Contract
Logan, James	Kentucky	1-24-1806	K	244	Contract
Logan, Wm	Lincoln	8-31-1803	S	300	Contract
Logan, Wm	Shelby	7-14-1821	V	187	Contract
Long, Nimrod	Shennandoah	2-15-1813	P	316	Contract
Love, George	Fauquier	10-13-1818	V	248	Contract
Love, James	Ohio	6-14-1808	M	45	Contract
Love, Thos	Franklin	5-26-1807	L	65	Contract
Love, Wm	Grayson	——1818	S	154	Contract
McCall, Geo C	Philadelphia	12-20-1833	Z	379	Contract
McCall, Geo C	Philadelphia	11-14-1840	27	169	Contract
McClure, Jno A	Anderson	1- 9-1839	27	5	Contract
McConnell, Adam	Woodford	6- 9-1801	F	213	Contract
McCurdy, Jno F	——	8- 5-1824	W	355	Contract
McDowell, Joseph	Mercer	9-28-1822	V	441	Contract
McIver, Jno	——	4- 4-1804	J	427	Contract
McIver, Jno	Alexandria	5-28-1807	M	7	Contract
McIver, Jno	——	9-14-1810	N	489	Contract
McIver, Jno	Fairfax	9-25-1810	N	493	Contract
McIver, Jno	Alexandria	10-22-1804	O	67	Contract
McIver, Jno	Alexandria	6-25-1807	O	69	Contract
McKinley, Jas	Russell	12-21-1831	Z	305	Contract
McKinn, Jr	Baltimore	3-16-1805	K	294	Contract
McKnight, Andrew, Executor	——	4-22-1813	Q	483	Contract
Madison, Geo	Frankfort	4- 6-1803	G	217	Contract
Major, J M	Frankfort	5-19-1827	X	234	Contract
Manifee, Wm	Culpepper	11-15-1813	P	359	Contract
Manifee, Wm	Culpepper	11-20-1813	P	361	Contract
Manifee, Wm	Culpepper	11-24-1813	P	363	Contract
Marshall, Alexander K	Mason	3-12-1822	V	308	Contract
Mason, Chas	Fayette	6-11-1807	M	235	Contract
Mason, Jno T	Kentucky	4-22-1815	S	189	Contract
Mason, Jno T Jr	Lexington	5- 7-1816	Q	543	Contract
Mason, Jno T Jr	Lexington	12- 9-1816	R	294	Contract
Mason, Peter	Fayette	2-12-1810	O	80	Contract
Matthews, Chas L	——	12-24-1805	M	68	Contract
May, Jno Langly	Virginia	10-22-1812	O	508	Contract
Meade, David	——	7- 4-1798	D	50	Contract
Mercer, Chas F	Leesburg	6-27-1811	S	306	Contract
Mereweather, Valentine	Shelby	10-23-1811	O	176	Contract
Mereweather, Thos	Richmond	1- 1-1786	W	47	Contract
Mereweather, Thos	Richmond	8-22-1786	W	50	Contract
Merryman, Nicholas R	Baltimore	1- 3-1825	X	87	Contract
Miller, Jno	Lycoming	1-15-1823	Y	289	Contract
Mills, Benj	Paris	8- 1-1809	V	169	Contract
Mills, Peter	Charlestown	9-21-1807	R	242	Contract
Milton, Eben & Jno	Kentucky	4- 5-1830	Z	43	Contract
Mitchell, Jas P	Mercer	2-16-1826	Y	104	Contract
Moore, Coldwallader C	New York	3-29-1833	Z	299	Contract
Moore, Jas B	Caldwell	2- 9-1821	V	64	Contract
Morgan, Jno	Muhlenberg	8-25-1817	S	14	Contract

Grantee	Residence	Deed Date	Book	Page	Notes
Morgan, Willis	Muhlenberg	1- 8-1812	P	515	Contract
Morris, Jno	Hanover	6- 6-1801	E	334	Contract
Morris, Jno	Kentucky	——1801	F	216	Contract
Morris, Jno	Kentucky	3-24-1802	F	389	Contract
Morris, Jno	Kentucky	5-25-1801	H	116	Contract
Morris, Jno	Franklin	12-21-1810	N	457	Contract
Morris, Jno	Franklin	3- 5-1817	R	448	Contract
Morris, Thos W	Philadelphia	10- 7-1816	S	232	Contract
Morrison, Jas	Kentucky	5-22-1816	R	31	Contract
Morrison, Jas	Lexington	4-18-1817	R	455	Contract
Morrison, Jas	——	4- 1-1820	T	459	Contract
Morrison, Jas	——	5- 1-1810	R	454	Contract
Mosley, H L	——	12-28-1821	V	212	Contract
Mosly, Wade Jr	Powhatan	6-19-1816	Q	550	Contract
Munford, Jno D	Richmond	9- 6-1833	Z	352	Contract
Mure, Major Walker	Westmoreland	7-21-1801	F	483	Contract
Muter, Geo	Woodford	7- 9-1800	E	183	Contract
Neeley, James	Rutherford	——1818	S	154	Contract
New, Anthony Jr	Middlesex	8-31-1813	P	250	Contract
Nicholas, Saml S	Franklin	1- 9-1821	Z	154	Contract
Nixon, Jno	Philadelphia	9-10-1799	D	346	Contract
Noel, Silas M	——	3-20-1818	V	19	Contract
Norris, Wm	London, Great Britain	3-18-1806	K	204	Contract
Ochwig, Adam	Tennessee	5-30-1845	28	98	Contract
Oliver, Robt	Baltimore	10-12-1815	R	206	Contract
Owing, Thos Dye	Kentucky	5- 9-1804	H	467	Contract
Owing, Thos D	Montgomery	3-16-1805	K	294	Contract
Owing, Thos D	Kentucky	10-16-1806	K	491	Contract
Owing, Thos D	Kentucky	3-18-1808	M	367	Contract
Owsley, Wm	Frankfort	5- 7-1841	27	211	Contract
Page, Thos S	Franklin	3-28-1832	Z	227	Contract
Page, Thos S	Franklin	7- 9-1833	Z	459	Contract
Page, Thos S	Franklin	7-11-1834	Z	461	Contract
Palmer, Jno	Shelby	11-17-1837	27	91	Contract
Parish, James	Madison	6- 3-1820	T	453	Contract
Patterson, Jas	Scott	5- 2-1840	27	118	Contract
Patterson, Robt	Lexington	12-24-1800	E	284	Contract
Patterson, Col Robt	Lexington	6- 9-1801	F	213	Contract
Payne, Col Deval	Mason	9- 5-1801	F	98	....
Pearson, Edmund B	Fayette	11-12-1827	Z	363	Contract
Peast, Francis	Woodford	7-13-1801	F	56	Contract
Peast, Francis	Woodford	7- 3-1802	F	501	Contract
Peast, Thos	Woodford	8-23-1809	N	20	Contract
Peck, Jno	Fayette	12-29-1830	Z	53	Contract
Pumberton, Bennett	Franklin	2-13-1799	H	273	Contract
Pendleton, Jno T	Frankfort	4-18-1820	T	295	Contract
Perkins, Thos H	Boston	6-17-1837	27	145	Contract
Phelps, Robt M	Washington	1-17-1833	27	316	Contract
Phillips, Jno	Davidson	6- 1-1816	R	14	Contract
Phillips, Lewis W R	Franklin	10-11-1827	X	315	Contract
Phillips, Ralph	New Jersey	10-26-1821	V	204	Contract
Pope, Jno	Frankfort	11-24-1819	T	199	Contract
Pope, Jno	Frankfort	11-24-1819	T	201	Contract
Pope, Warren	——	11-26-1814	P	565	Contract
Powell, Burr	London	9-13-1790	F	428	Contract
Prather, Thos	Kentucky	3-23-1821	U	395	Contract
Prentis, Wm	Kentucky	10-17-1828	X	485	Contract
Prentis, Wm	Kentucky	10-18-1828	X	486	Contract
Prentis, Wm	Kentucky	3- 2-1829	Y	328	....
Price, Wm	Richmond	4- 9-1803	G	218	Contract
Primrose, Wm	Franklin	5-30-1840	27	134	Contract
Pryor, Thos M	Tennessee	5-30-1845	28	98	Contract
Purviance, Henry	Washington	5-22-1796	D	279	Contract
Purviance, Henry	Washington	1- 8-1796	D	281	Contract
Purviance, Henry	Washington	1-31-1796	D	283	Contract
Purviance, Henry	Washington	1- 8-1796	D	284	Contract
Purviance, Henry	Baltimore	6-29-1797	D	288	Contract
Purviance, Henry	Washington	1- 1-1796	D	290	Contract
Purviance, Henry	Kentucky	7- 5-1800	E	92	Contract
Purviance, Henry	——	11-29-1800	E	187	Contract
Radel, Augustin	Philadelphia	5-12-1786	Z	284	Contract
Raquet, Jas	Bucks	3- 6-1806	K	192	Contract
Read, Francis S	Lincoln	5- 7-1806	K	304	Contract
Read, Geo	Clark	4-10-1828	X	402	Contract
Read, Isaac	Philadelphia	10- 7-1817	W	4	Contract
Read, James Jr	Greenbrier	11- 9-1818	X	85	Contract
Redd, Mordicae	Kentucky	10- 2-1798	G	297	Contract
Reinholdt, Geo	Philadelphia	6-19-1818	S	199	Contract
Ricard, Michael	——	7- 3-1829	Y	387	Contract
Richardson, Jno C Jr	Fayette	5-20-1828	Y	309	Contract
Richardson, Saml Q	Franklin	8-18-1830	Z	2	Contract
Ridgeley, Frederick	Lexington	10-16-1809	M	444	Contract

Grantee	Residence	Date Date	Book	Page	Notes
Robert, Lewis J D	———	3-22-1810	Y	228	Contract
Roberts, Jno	Logan	6-10-1830	Z	114	Contract
Rogers, Thos & Edmund	Caroline	10-13-1810	P	105	Contract
Routt, Wm	Fleming	2- 5-1814	P	337	Contract
Routt, Wm	Campbell	2-24-1817	R	180	Contract
Routt, Wm	Campbell	8- 8-1817	S	138	Contract
Routt, Wm	Campbell	12-27-1821	V	156	Contract
Rucker, Jno	Woodford	8-26-1806	N	89	Contract
Ruthford, Jas	Rockenham	8-15-1804	H	288	Contract
Samuel, Larkin	Franklin	1-29-1820	T	411	Contract
Samuel, & Tilford	Franklin	8- 3-1846	28	95	Contract
Scott, Gustavis H	Fairfax	5-23-1821	V	6	Contract
Scott, Jno	Gallatin	8-17-1814	P	564	Contract
Scott, Jno	Gallatin	3-19-1816	Q	434	Contract
Scott, Jno	Gallatin	11- 4-1816	R	56	Contract
Scott, Jno	Gallatin	5- 2-1820	T	299	Contract
Scott, Jno M	Franklin	5-26-1807	L	65	Contract
Scott, Jno M	Frankfort	1-12-1810	O	82	Contract
Scott, Matthew S	Lexington	10-24-1817	R	443	Contract
Scott, Moses	Boone	10- 2-1822	V	318	Contract
Scott, Moses	Boone	11- 6-1824	X	79	Contract
Scott, Robt	Fayette	5-20-1828	Y	309	Contract
Shaw, Jno	Henry	10-11-1826	Y	253	Contract
Shepherd, Thos	Bourbon	12-29-1830	Z	53	Contract
Shepherd, Thos W	Bourbon	12-29-1830	Z	52	Contract
Sheppey, Hugh W	Augusta	11- 7-1840	27	173	Contract
Short, Peyton	———	7- 4-1798	D	50	Contract
Shy, Saml	Fayette	11-29-1845	28	64	Contract
Shy, Saml	Fayette	6-18-1845	28	66	Contract
Slaughter, Philip	Culpepper	4- 3-1801	E	347	Contract
Smith, Abraham	———	5-24-1824	W	276	Contract
Smith, Joseph	Augusta	12-16-1808	M	277	Contract
Smith, Joseph	Franklin	9- 3-1828	X	459	Contract
Smith, Nicholas	Henry	3- 3-1802	F	222	Contract
Smith, R E	Louisville	6-10-1824	W	333	Contract
Smith, Thos R	———	2-23-1821	V	9	Contract
Smith, Willis R	Clark	6-12-1815	Q	182	Contract
Smith, Willis R	Clark	6-15-1815	Q	183	Contract
Smith, Wm	Clark	7-26-1820	U	370	Contract
Sneed, Achilles	Frankfort	9- 5-1801	F	98	Contract
Sneed, Achilles	Frankfort	1-20-1804	H	276	Contract
Sneed, Achilles	Frankfort	8-18-1804	H	491	Contract
Snead, Achilles	Frankfort	3- 7-1807	L	41	Contract
Sneed, Achilles	Frankfort	5- 1-1806	L	326	Contract
Sneed, Achilles	Frankfort	2- 8-1809	M	316	Contract
Sneed, Achilles	Frankfort	6- 8-1811	O	79	Contract
Sneed, Achilles	Frankfort	6-13-1812	P	419	Contract
Sneed, Achilles	Frankfort	6-15-1812	P	422	Contract
Sneed, Achilles	Frankfort	6-16-1812	P	426	Contract
Sneed, Achilles	Frankfort	10-24-1812	P	604	Contract
Sneed, Achilles	Frankfort	4-18-1820	T	295	Contract
Sneed, Achilles	Frankfort	4-14-1819	T	430	Contract
Sneed, Achilles	Frankfort	4-14-1819	U	288	Contract
Sneed, Achilles	Frankfort	4-24-1811	U	480	Contract
Sneed, Achilles	Frankfort	10-27-1821	V	251	Contract
Sneed, Achilles	Franklin	8-17-1822	W	114	Contract
Sneed, Achilles	Frankfort	2-27-1824	W	260	Contract
Snelson, Nathaniel	Petersburg	6- 9-1808	M	121	Contract
Somerville, Jas	Fredericksburg	8-19-1796	M	215	Contract
South, Jno G	Franklin	6- 5-1827	X	271	Contract
South, Jno G	Frankfort	12- 1-1827	X	348	Contract
South, Saml & Weldon & Wm	Kentucky	6-18-1821	Z	508	Contract
Southall, Peyton	York	8- 1-1808	27	1	Contract
Spencer, Wm	Butler	5- 5-1828	X	422	Contract
St. Clair, Andrew	Augusta	5-29-1801	O	226	Contract
Stephens, Daniel J	Breckinridge	5-10-1821	U	437	Contract
Stephens, Richard	Kentucky	1- 6-1799	D	418	Contract
Sterrett, Thos	Raphoe	11-22-1817	S	345	Contract
Sterrett, Thos	Lancaster	9-11-1818	S	353	Contract
Sterrett, Thos	Raphoe	9-16-1818	S	357	Contract
Sturges, Josiah	New York	10-12-1820	W	104	Contract
Sudduth, Wm	Kentucky	4- 1-1811	O	65	Contract
Swan, James	Dorchester	6-30-1798	D	423	Contract
Swigert, Jacob	Kentucky	3- 4-1831	27	270	Contract
Swigert, Nathaniel	Cincinnati	3- 8-1841	27	189	Contract
Swigert, Philip	Franklin	7- 9-1833	Z	459	Contract
Swigert, Philip	Franklin	7-11-1834	Z	461	Contract
Swigert, Philip	Franklin	5- 8-1844	27	407	Contract
Tatham, Chas	Richmond	1-14-1797	S	98	Contract
Taylor, Edmund H	Jefferson	8-18-1810	N	277	Contract
Taylor, Edmund H	Franklin	5-23-1835	Z	516	Contract
Taylor, Edmund H	Franklin	12-28-1841	27	341	Contract

Grantee	Residence	Deed Date	Book	Page	Notes
Taylor, Edmund H	Frankfort	6- 7-1843	27	349	Contract
Taylor, Hubbard	——	7- 4-1798	D	50	Contract
Taylor, Hubbard	Kentucky	10- 9-1798	D	340	Contract
Taylor, Hubbard	Kentucky	7-16-1801	G	140	Contract
Taylor, Hubbard	Kentucky	10- 2-1798	G	297	Contract
Taylor, Hubbard	Kentucky	5- 4-1805	J	224	Contract
Taylor, Hubbard	Clark	9-18-1807	M	48	Contract
Taylor, Hubbard Jr	Clark	6-12-1815	Q	182	Contract
Taylor, Hubbard Jr	Clark	6-15-1815	Q	183	Contract
Taylor, Hubbard Jr	Clark	6-15-1815	Q	185	Contract
Taylor, Hubbard Sr & Jr & Jas	Kentucky	4-10-1815	Q	269	Contract
Taylor, Jas	Campbell	11-16-1799	F	154	Contract
Taylor, Jas	Campbell	10-15-1813	Q	11	Contract
Taylor, James	Newport	9-10-1814	S	80	Contract
Taylor, Jas	Campbell	2- 2-1820	U	285	Contract
Taylor, Jno	Prince William	5-14-1820	V	145	Contract
Taylor, Jno E	Frankfort	9-12-1826	Y	194	Contract
Taylor, Jno W	Shelby	4- 3-1826	X	247	Contract
Taylor, Richard Jr	Hickman	11- 6-1824	W	400	Contract
Taylor, Wm	Kentucky	——1801	F	216	Contract
Taylor, Wm	Shelby	3- 1-1806	K	246	Contract
Taylor, Wm	Shelby	10- 3-1817	R	450	Contract
Taylor, Wm	Shelby	2——1818	S	64	Contract
Taylor, Wm	Oldham	——1828	X	491	Contract
Temple, Benj	Kentucky	5-19-1806	K	527	Contract
Tevis, Saml	Shelbyville	12- 7-1819	T	347	Contract
Tevis, Saml	Shelbyville	12- 9-1819	T	349	Contract
Thatcher, Jno P	Frankfort	7- 7-1828	X	416	Contract
Thomas, Benj F	Mt Sterling	12-12-1831	Z	170	Contract
Thomas, Benj P	Baton Rouge	9- 8-1814	Q	514	Contract
Thomas, Benj P	Mason	11-22-1816	R	117	Contract
Thomas, Jack	Grayson	12-25-1826	X	264	Contract
Thompson, Francis	London England	12- 9-1806	K	514	Contract
Thompson, Henry	Baltimore	7-19-1803	X	484	Contract
Thornton, Anthony Jr	Carolina	4-25-1801	E	336	Contract
Thornton, Anthony Jr	Carolina	10- 1-1798	E	383	Contract
Thornton, Henry P	Bourbon	9- 5-1814	R	32	Contract
Tilford & Samuel	Franklin	8- 3-1846	28	95	Contract
Todd, Chas S	Franklin	5- 2-1816	Q	505	Contract
Todd, L L	——	1-17-1821	U	76	Contract
Todd, Saml	Franklin	4-26-1844	27	405	Contract
Todd, Thos	Frankfort	9- 5-1801	F	98	Contract
Todd, Thos	Kentucky	5- 7-1790	R	382	Contract
Todd, Thos	Frankfort	4-18-1820	T	295	Contract
Todd, Wm H	Kentucky	7-19-1842	27	310	Contract
Todd, Wm H	Kentucky	6——1842	27	311	Contract
Trabue, Danl, Stephen & Edw	Kentucky	10- 1-1803	J	70	Contract
Trigg, Stephen	Lincoln	12-10-1781	D	203	Contract
Triplett, Robt	Kentucky	11-27-1818	S	392	Contract
Triplett, Robt	——	11-10-1819	T	153	Contract
Triplett, Robt	Kentucky	6-29-1821	V	32	Contract
Triplett, Robt	Kentucky	6-23-1821	V	36	Contract
Triplett, Robt	Kentucky	8-12-1822	V	301	Contract
Triplett, Robt	Kentucky	8-23-1822	V	310	Contract
Triplett, Robt	Kentucky	12-19-1821	V	397	Contract
Triplett, Robt	Kentucky	3- 8-1823	W	120	Contract
Triplett, Robt	Kentucky	3——1823	W	122	Contract
Triplett, Robt	Kentucky	12——1822	W	123	Contract
Triplett, Robt	Frankfort	12- 6-1823	W	197	Contract
Triplett, Robt	Frankfort	4-22-1824	W	309	Contract
Triplett, Robt	Frankfort	4- 1-1824	W	311	Contract
Triplett, Robt	Frankfort	6- 4-1824	W	313	Contract
Triplett, Robt	Frankfort	3-25-1824	W	314	Contract
Triplett, Robt	Frankfort	4- 9-1824	W	316	Contract
Triplett, Robt	Frankfort	5-25-1824	W	317	Contract
Triplett, Robt	Frankfort	3-28-1823	W	318	Contract
Triplett, Robt	Frankfort	1-14-1824	W	322	Contract
Triplett, Robt	Frankfort	3-20-1824	W	324	Contract
Triplett, Robt	Frankfort	4-27-1824	W	325	Contract
Triplett, Robt	——	5-13-1824	W	350	Contract
Triplett, Robt	Frankfort	6-30-1824	W	356	Contract
Triplett, Robt	Frankfort	1-19-1825	X	89	Contract
Triplett, Robt	Kentucky	3-31-1825	X	102	Contract
Triplett, Robt	Frankfort	4-20-1825	X	106	Contract
Triplett, Robt	Kentucky	5-21-1828	X	405	Contract
Triplett, Robt	Kentucky	5-28-1828	X	406	Contract
Triplett, Robt	Kentucky	9- 1-1828	X	444	Contract
Triplett, Robt	Franklin	4-26-1828	X	457	Contract
Triplett, Robt	Franklin	8-12-1828	X	458	Contract
Triplett, Robt	Kentucky	8-19-1828	V	338	Contract
Triplett, Robt	Daviess	6-30-1832	Z	204	Contract
Triplett & Bunley	Frankfort	4- 6-1827	X	227	Contract

Grantee	Residence	Deed Date	Book	Page	Notes
Triplett & Bunley	Franklin	5-24-1827	X	269	Contract
Triplett & Bunley	Franklin	12- 3-1827	X	351	Contract
Triplett & Bunly	Franklin	2- 6-1828	X	407	Contract
Triplett & Bunly	Franklin	1-14-1828	X	409	Contract
Triplett & Bunly	Franklin	1826	X	410	Contract
Triplett & Bunly	Frankfort	4-21-1826	Y	156	Contract
Trueman, Henry B	Mead	3- 8-1826	X	203	Contract
Trustees Centre College	Kentucky	9- 9-1826	Y	199	Contract
Tunstall, Wm	Pittsylvania	10- 8-1811	N	510	Contract
Twyman, James	Scott	10- 4-1802	G	85	Contract
Underwood, Joseph R	Warren	6- 2-1826	X	260	Contract
Underwood, Joseph R	Warren	1-22-1827	X	262	Contract
Underwood, Joseph R	Warren	4-10-1827	X	263	Contract
Underwood, Joseph R	Warren	7-13-1827	X	272	Contract
Underwood, Joseph R	Warren	1-22-1828	Y	305	Contract
Underwood, Joseph R	Warren	8-29-1828	Y	306	Contract
Underwood, Joseph R	Warren	7-17-1828	Y	308	Contract
Underwood, Joseph R	Warren	12-15-1829	Y	451	Contract
Underwood, J R	Warren	9-10-1832	Z	232	Contract
Underwood, J R	Warren	7- 6-1832	Z	273	Contract
Underwood, J R	Warren	3-30-1832	Z	274	Contract
Underwood, J R	Warren	6-13-1832	Z	276	Contract
Underwood, J R	Warren	3= 1-1841	27	236	Contract
Underwood, J R	Warren	4- 2-1838	27	242	Contract
Underwood, J R	Warren	9- 8-1841	27	244	Contract
Underwood, J R	Warren	2-26-1841	27	246	Contract
Underwood, J R	Warren	12- 6-1838	27	247	Contract
Underwood, J R	Warren	3-15-1841	27	248	Contract
Underwood, J R	Warren	2- 2-1843	27	402	Contract
Underwood, J R	Warren	9- 1-1842	27	403	Contract
Underwood, J R	Warren	11- 4-1844	28	3	Contract
Underwood, J R	Warren	6-17-1845	28	55	Contract
Underwood, J R	Warren	8-22-1845	28	56	Contract
Underwood, J R	Warren	9-15-1846	28	104	Contract
Underwood, J R	Warren	8-18-1846	28	115	Contract
Underwood, J R	Warren	11- 7-1846	28	117	Contract
Underwood, J R	Warren	11-30-1846	28	118	Contract
Upshaw, Edwin	King & Queen	8-17-1821	V	88	Contract
Vawter, Wm	Kentucky	1- 6-1799	D	418	Contract
Vawter, Wm	Woodford	1-20-1806	O	91	Contract
Voorhies, Peter G	Frankfort	2- 8-1809	M	316	Contract
Walker, David	Allen	7-10-1820	T	439	Contract
Walker, Martin	Philadelphia	4- 8-1820	T	310	Contract
Walker, Martin & Wife		5-12-1820	T	315	Contract
Wallace, Thos	Lexington	9-14-1801	F	9	Contract
Walsh, Robt Jr	Baltimore	5-31-1815	R	380	Contract
Warfield, Dr Walter	Lexington	5-11-1812	P	442	Contract
Waring, Jno U		9-14-1821	V	99	Contract
Ward, Geo W	Culpepper	11-26-1818	S	372	Contract
Ward, Robt J		10-10-1845	28	31	Contract
Waters, Jno	Montgomery	6-15-1810	O	14	Contract
Waters, Jno	Montgomery	1-27-1814	P	435	Contract
Waters, Jno	Montgomery	1-21-1814	P	437	Contract
Waters, Jno	Montgomery	1-14-1814	P	439	Contract
Waters, Jno	Montgomery	3-11-1817	T	113	Contract
Waters, Jno	Montgomery	2-18-1817	T	116	Contract
Waters, Jno	Montgomery	3-18-1817	T	119	Contract
Waters, Wm	Franklin	5-18-1811	O	20	Contract
Weaver, Saml	Fanquier	10-25-1830	Z	55	Contract
Weisiger, Daniel	Frankfort	5-16-1816	R	200	Contract
Weisiger, Daniel	Chesterfield	6-20-1825	X	163	Contract
Weisiger, Daniel	Chesterfield	7- 9-1825	X	165	Contract
Weisiger, Daniel Sr	Franklin	1-15-1825	Y	140	Contract
Wenzel, Jno C	Fayette	3-10-1825	Y	108	Contract
West, Wm	Franklin	8- 7-1820	27	352	Contract
Wickliffe, Chas A	Bardstown	1-18-1815	P	624	Contract
Wickliffe, Robt	Kentucky	12-19-1811	P	471	Contract
Wickliffe, Robt		11-12-1814	P	558	Contract
Wickliffe, Robt	Franklin	7-22-1814	Q	112	Contract
Wickliffe, Robt	Kentucky	7-20-1814	Q	114	Contract
Wickliffe, Robt	Lexington	11-15-1815	Q	405	Contract
Wickliffe, Robt	Lexington	7-21-1815	Q	408	Contract
Wickliffe, Robt	Lexington	3-26-1816	R	300	Contract
Wickliffe, Robt	Lexington	5——1816	R	363	Contract
Wickliffe, Robt	Lexington	4-20-1816	R	365	Contract
Wickliffe, Robt	Lexington	4-18-1817	R	455	Contract
Wickliffe, Robt	Lexington	4-14-1818	S	117	Contract
Wickliffe, Robt	Lexington	5- 6-1818	S	239	Contract
Wickliffe, Robt	Fayette	2-14-1817	S	260	Contract
Wickliffe, Robt	Lexington	10- 8-1818	S	317	Contract
Wickliffe, Robt	Fayette	9- 4-1818	S	321	Contract
Wickliffe, Robt	———	11-27-1818	S	399	Contract

Grantee	Residence	Deed Date	Book	Page	Notes
Wickliffe, Robt	Lexington	11–21–1818	S	412	Contract
Wickliffe, Robt	Lexington	6–22–1819	T	421	Contract
Wickliffe, Robt	Lexington	11– 4–1819	U	21	Contract
Wickliffe, Robt	Kentucky	5– 6–1820	U	261	Contract
Wickliffe, Robt	Lexington	4– 3–1822	V	312	Contract
Wickliffe, Robt	Lexington	1– 1–1822	V	313	Contract
Wickliffe, Robt	Lexington	10– 1–1822	V	444	Contract
Wickliffe, Robt	Kentucky	——–1825	W	335	Contract
Wickliffe, Robt	Lexington	4– 7–1828	X	401	Contract
Wickliffe, Robt	Fayette	2– 7–1829	Y	330	Contract
Wickliffe, Robt	Fayette	2– 4–1829	Y	332	Contract
Wickliffe, Robt	Fayette	8– 1–1821	Y	351	Contract
Wickliffe, R	Fayette	4–15–1831	Z	122	Contract
Wickliffe, Robt	Fayette	6– 9–1831	Z	138	Contract
Wickliffe, Robt	Fayette	10–11–1832	Z	288	Contract
Wickliffe, Robt	Fayette	3– 4–1833	Z	289	Contract
Wickliffe, Robt	Fayette	5–17–1834	Z	425	Contract
Wickliffe, Robt, Atty	Lexington	5–12–1820	T	314	Contract
Wickliffe, Robt, Atty	Lexington	2– 1–1816	Q	354	Contract
Wight, James	Franklin	12– 6–1819	T	417	Contract
Wight, Jas	Franklin	12– 6–1819	T	419	Contract
Wight, Jas	Shelby	1– 5–1839	27	11	Contract
White, Whitfield	Franklin	12– 4–1820	U	88	Contract
White, Wm Pinkney	Baltimore	3– 3–1846	28	84	Contract
Whitesides, Thos C	Bedford	5–30–1845	28	98	Contract
Whitledge, Thos	Harrison	9–13–1826	X	214	Contract
Whitson, Chas	Tennessee	4– 6–1813	R	387	Contract
Wilkes, Chas	New York	4–25–1817	S	129	Contract
Wilkins, Chas	Lexington	10–16–1809	M	444	Contract
Wilkins, Chas	Lexington	7– 7–1807	N	420	Contract
Wilkins, Chas	Lexington	10–24–1817	R	443	Contract
Wilkinson, Jas P	New Kent	8–13–1827	X	453	Contract
Willing, Thos M	Philadelphia	10– 7–1816	S	232	Contract
Wilson, Alexander	Cumberland	8–10–1816	R	113	Contract
Wilson, Jas	———	8–31–1806	K	373	Contract
Winn, Minor	Harrison	7–31–1823	V	202	Contract
Winston, Saml	———	7–28–1845	28	21	Contract
Woolfolk, Richard Jr	Fayette	10–27–1795	K	306	Contract
Wright, Unjah	Henry	6–22–1825	X	215	Contract
Wylie, Andrew Jr	———	9–23–1845	28	29	Contract
Yager, Elisha	Franklin	5–28–1808	L	391	Contract
Young, Ambrose	Fayette	3–13–1809	N	319	Contract

Grantors in Power of Attorney

Grantor	Residence	Deed Date	Book	Page	Notes
Adams, Richard	Richmond	6-20-1799	D	353	Contract
Alcock, Thos	Stafford	3-13-1809	N	319	Contract
Alexander, Robt	Woodford	7- 7-1828	X	416	Contract
Alexander, Robt, Dec'd	Kentucky	8- 7-1843	27	363	Contract
Alexander, Robt S C A	Airdrie, Scotland	8- 7-1843	27	363	Contract
Alexander, Wm	Augusta	3-12-1796	A-2	519	Contract
Allen, Isham	Henrico	11- 5-1823	W	175	Contract
Allen, Jno	———	8- 2-1820	U	2	Contract
Allen, Sophia	Caroline	10-15-1845	28	75	Contract
Allen, Thos	Mercer	11- 7-1786	A	266	Contract
Allison, Rebecca, heirs	———	———1846	28	120	Contract
Allison, Robt M & Wm C	Wilkes	2-10-1820	T	480	Contract
Allison, Wm C	Wilkes	11- 6-1824	W	400	Contract
Anderson, Richard	———	11-17-1787	A	341	Contract
Anderson, Wm P	Tennessee	12- 9-1823	W	188	Contract
Apperson, Jno C & Wife	New Kent	5-24-1827	X	269	Contract
Apperson, Lyddall, heirs	New Kent	5-24-1827	X	269	Contract
Arbuckle, Jno	Lincoln	6- 3-1785	A	239	Contract
Archer, Abraham	———	8-23-1798	D	28	Contract
Archer, Judith E & Mary C	Amelia	3-28-1823	W	1	Contract
Archer, Richard T	Amelia	9-27-1821	V	106	Contract
Archer, Richard T	Amelia	7-28-1823	W	55	Contract
Archer, Richard T	Amelia	12- 6-1823	W	197	Contract
Archer, R T & S C	Amelia	7-10-1820	T	486	Contract
Archer, Stephen C	Amelia	4- 7-1820	T	438	Contract
Archer, Stephen C & Richard T	Amelia	10-19-1821	V	88	Contract
Archer, Stephen & Richard T	Amelia	3-25-1824	W	314	Contract
Armstrong, Chas M	U S Navy	6-———1842	27	311	Contract
Ashley, Jno	Philadelphia	2-23-1825	X	137	Contract
Atchley, Isaac & Wife	Tennessee	7-26-1820	U	370	Contract
Bacon, Edmund	Franklin	11-25-1802	G	76	Contract
Bacon, Job & Wife	York	4- 5-1822	V	306	Contract
Bailey, Wm	Lynchburg	5- 7-1841	27	211	Contract
Banister, Jno M	Petersburg	4-14-1819	T	430	Contract
Banister, Jno M	Sussex	3-———1823	W	122	Contract
Banister, Theoderick B	Amelia	8-10-1816	R	113	Contract
Bank of Kentucky	Kentucky	10-24-1817	R	443	Contract
Bank of Kentucky	Kentucky	3-23-1821	U	395	Contract
Bank of Kentucky	Kentucky	5- 9-1821	U	398	Contract
Bank of Kentucky	Kentucky	7-12-1821	U	473	Contract
Bank of Kentucky	Kentucky	8-21-1821	V	11	Contract
Bank of Kentucky	Kentucky	8-21-1821	V	12	Contract
Bank of Kentucky	Kentucky	8-21-1821	V	12	Conrtact
Bank of Kentucky	Kentucky	8-21-1821	V	13	Contract
Bank of Kentucky	Kentucky	8-21-1821	V	14	Contract
Bank of Kentucky	Kentucky	12-17-1821	V	152	Contract
Bank of Kentucky	Kentucky	2-28-1822	V	185	Contract
Bank of Kentucky	Kentucky	4-19-1822	V	192	Contract
Bank of Kentucky	Kentucky	10- 2-1822	V	318	Contract
Bank of Kentucky	Kentucky	5-22-1824	W	272	Contract
Bank of Kentucky	Kentucky	5-24-1824	W	274	Contract
Bank of Kentucky	Kentucky	5-24-1824	W	276	Contract
Bank of Kentucky	Kentucky	7-11-1826	Y	165	Contract
Bank of U S	Philadelphia	10-11-1832	Z	288	Contract
Banks, Henry	Richmond	11-10-1795	A-2	282	Contract
Banks, Henry	Richmond	1-25-1786	N	401	Contract
Banks, Henry	Richmond	6- 2-1821	V	167	Contract
Banks, Henry	Richmond	11- 6-1824	X	79	Contract
Banks, Henry	Richmond	9- 8-1829	Y	385	Contract
Banks, Henry	Richmond	8-18-1830	Z	2	Contract
Banks, Henry	Richmond	12-12-1831	Z	170	Contract
Banks, Wm Cuthbert	———	11-10-1795	A-2	282	Contract
Barbee, Thos	Lincoln	6-20-1786	A	131	Contract
Barbour, Jas & Wife	———	6-27-1821	U	526	Contract
Barbour, Philip C S	Orange	8- 1-1809	V	169	Contract
Barbour, Thos	Orange	8- 7-1802	J	279	Contract
Barnett, Ambrose	Fanquier	12- 3-1805	L	70	Contract
Barrett, Chas	Louisa	7-20-1814	Q	114	Contract
Barrett, Jno	Louisa	6-30-1824	W	356	Contract
Bartlett, Martha	———	4-11-1796	A-2	449	Contract
Bartlett, Robt & Wife	New Madrid	4-21-1817	R	409	Contract
Batts, Alexander L	———	4-15-1839	27	69	Contract
Beale, Thos	Maco, China	6-17-1837	27	145	Contract
Beall, Andrew	———	6-20-1786	A	157	Contract
Beall, Walter	Montgomery	3-20-1787	A	506	Contract
Beall, Walter	Nelson	5-24-1791	B-2	323	Contract
Beauchamp, Jno & Wife	Pike	8-22-1832	Z	226	Contract

Grantor	Residence	Deed Date	Book	Page	Notes
Beddle, Thos & Wife	Philadelphia	1–23–1828	X	414	Contract
Bedinger, Capt Henry	Berkely	6–16–1790	B-2	154	Contract
Bedinger, Henry & Wife	Berkely	8–19–1817	S	11	Contract
Beebee, Saml	New York	9–21–1807	R	242	Contract
Bell, Jno	St. Louis	8– 8–1820	T	458	Contract
Bennett, Thos	————	11——1818	T	46	Contract
Berry, Benj	Fayette	1–31–1803	G	416	Contract
Berry, Lawrence	————	9–10–1814	S	80	Contract
Bibb, Geo	Kentucky	9–19–1797	C	220	Contract
Bibb, Richard	Prince Edward	9– 1–1796	C	89	Contract
Bilbo, Archibald, heirs	Mercer	2–16–1826	Y	104	Contract
Bilbo, Wm	Mercer	2–16–1826	Y	104	Contract
Binns, Chas	Londun	9–12–1789	B-2	71	Contract
Bird, Chas W	————	11–21–1794	A-2	99	Contract
Blair, Alexander	Great Britain	3–11–1816	R	9	Contract
Blair, Francis P	Franklin	8–27–1823	W	101	Contract
Blair, Jno G & Wife	Richmond	10–12–1830	Z	50	Contract
Blanchard, Jno	Warren	1–18–1823	W	118	Contract
Bonar, Andrew	Great Britain	3–11–1816	R	9	Contract
Booth, Jas	Dinwiddie	5–16–1816	R	200	Contract
Booth, Jas & Wife	Georgia	1–15–1825	Y	140	Contract
Bordleg, Margaretta	————	10– 1–1822	V	444	Contract
Bouldin, Thos T	————	11——1818	T	46	Contract
Bouldin, Thos T	————	11–10–1819	T	153	Contract
Boulden, Thos T	Richmond	6–29–1821	V	32	Contract
Bouldin, Thos T	Richmond	6–23–1821	V	36	Contract
Bouldin, Thos T, Executor	Richmond	11–27–1818	S	392	Contract
Boush, Wilson	Norfolk	9–10–1794	B	253	Contract
Boush, Wilson	Norfolk	7– 1–1817	R	374	Contract
Bowman, Benj	Shenandoah	6–16–1815	V	132	Contract
Bowman, Jacob	So Carolina	3–13–1788	A	490	Contract
Bowman, Jacob	So Carolina	6–15–1789	B-2	61	Contract
Bowne, Matthew F	Alexandria	7–29–1795	A-2	509	Contract
Brashear, Alfred & Wife	Point Coupee	12–28–1841	27	341	Contract
Brashear, Walter & Wife	St. Mary	5–20–1828	Y	309	Contract
Breckenridge, Jas D	————	7– 3–1829	Y	387	Contract
Breckenridge, Jno	Fayette	7–15–1802	F	470	Contract
Breckenridge, Jno	Montgomery	10– 6–1806	M	57	Contract
Breckenridge, Jno, heirs	————	12–21–1827	X	435	Contract
Breckenridge, Jno, heirs	————	8–19–1828	X	437	Contract
Breckenridge, Jno (preacher)	Baltimore	12–21–1827	X	435	Contract
Bridges, Sarah	Essex	8–17–1821	V	88	Contract
Briscoe, Jno Sr	Jefferson	4–10–1817	R	428	Contract
Briscoe, Parmenor	————	6–25–1790	B-2	184	Contract
Brodhead, Daniel	————	10–18–1783	A	226	Contract
Brooking, Thos V	Chesterfield	12–19–1818	U	445	Contract
Brooks, Mary C, heirs	Virginia	8–22–1845	28	56	Contract
Brooks, Walter, heirs	U S Navy	2–22–1843	27	402	Contract
Brooks, Walter, heirs	U S Navy	9– 1–1842	27	403	Contract
Brooks, Walter D, heirs	Virginia	6–17–1845	28	55	Contract
Brooks, Commodore Walter, heirs	Virginia	8–22–1845	28	56	Contract
Brooks, Commodore Walter, heirs	Virginia	6–17–1845	28	55	Contract
Brothers, Henry	Maryland	6– 6–1787	A	308	Contract
Brough, Courtney	Virginia	5–23–1835	Z	516	Contract
Brough, Robt	Norfolk	9–10–1794	B	271	Contract
Brough, Robt	Norfolk	7–13–1801	F	56	Contract
Brough, Robt	Norfolk	8–23–1809	N	20	Contract
Brown, James	Richmond	3–24–1798	D	39	Contract
Brown, Jas	Richmond	7– 3–1812	P	139	Contract
Brown, Jas	Louisiana	9–21–1822	V	443	Contract
Brown, Jas	Richmond	9–10–1832	Z	232	Contract
Brown, Jas	Louisiana	5–23–1833	Z	316	Contract
Brown, Jno	Montgomery	10– 6–1806	M	57	Contract
Brown, Yeoman J	Concord	11– 2–1807	L	374	Contract
Bruce, Alexander, heirs	Fanquier	7–29–1819	U	317	Contract
Bruce, Jno	Fanquier	4–24–1820	U	319	Contract
Bruster, James	Lincoln	6– 3–1785	A	239	Contract
Bryan, Daniel & Wife	Alexandria	9–23–1845	28	29	Contract
Bryan, Guy	Philadelphia	1–28–1828	X	385	Contract
Bryan, Guy, heirs	Philadelphia	12–30–1829	Y	441	Contract
Bryan, Morgan H	Frankfort	10–22–1804	H	347	Contract
Bryan, Saml & Wife	Monroe	1– 5–1839	27	11	Contract
Bryant, Jno	Lincoln	7–14–1788	A	513	Contract
Buchannon, Jas	Bourbon	3– 7–1788	A	374	Contract
Buckner, Jno	Caroline	9–19–1797	B	123	Contract
Bunner, Chas F	New York City	6–13–1812	P	419	Contract
Bunner, Sarah Executrix	Philadelphia	6–15–1812	P	422	Contract
Burton, Robt	Granville	11– 7–1786	A	266	Contract
Burton, Robt Atty	————	8–19–1797	B	310 ••	Contract
Burton, Wm & Wife	Henrico	11–25–1823	W	175	Contract

Grantor	Residence	Deed Date	Book	Page	Notes
Butler, Percival	Fayette	11- 9-1785	A	83	Contract
Cabell, Louden	Virginia	8-25-1819	U	44	Contract
Cabell, Robt H	——	5-13-1824	W	350	Contract
Caldwell, Elias B Trustee	——	5-22-1816	R	31	Contract
Callender, Jno	Boston	1- 1-1815	Q	50	Contract
Campbell, Ferdinand & Wife	Williamsburg	1- 1-1822	V	313	Contract
Campbell, Jno	Jefferson	6- 3-1789	B-2	26	Contract
Campbell, Michael	Davidson	6- 1-1816	R	14	Contract
Campbell, Robt	Richmond	1-14-1797	S	98	Contract
Carneal, Thos D	Campbell	8-18-1817	S	138	Contract
Carneal, Thos D	Kentucky	5-16-1832	Z	478	Contract
Carneal, Thos D & Wife	Fayette	10-15-1811	O	174	Contract
Carneggs, Cornilius	Philadelphia	4- 7-1828	X	401	Contract
Carrico, Levi	——	4-18-1833	Z	279	Contract
Caster, Chas L	Spotsylvania	6-21-1805	K	268	Contract
Cassle, Henry	Frederick	10-24-1787	B-2	47	Contract
Castleman, David	Frederick	4- 5-1830	Z	43	Contract
Cave, Catherine R	Alexandria	4-28-1821	U	447	Contract
Challis, Jno W & Wife	Salem	5- 5-1828	X	422	Contract
Challis, Jas M & Wife	Monmouth	5- 5-1828	X	422	Contract
Chambers, Daniel	Lincoln	6-17-1789	B-2	46	Contract
Chew, Joseph	Montreal	3-25-1796	A-2	599	Contract
Child, Henry	——	7-19-1803	X	484	Contract
Chilton, Chas	Fanquire	6-14-1788	A	410	Contract
Christian, Gideon	New Kent	2- 6-1828	X	407	Contract
Clark, Geo	Kentucky	12-24-1796	C	210	Contract
Clark, Wm	St. Louis	3-24-1817	T	278	Contract
Clarkson, Mildred, heirs	——	6-24-1831	Z	187	Contract
Clay, Green	——	6-18-1786	A	129	Contract
Clay, Henry	——	11-25-1812	P	550	Contract
Clerk, Jno	Great Britain	3-11-1816	R	9	Contract
Clopton, Wm E	New Kent	5-11-1826	Y	155	Contract
Clopton, Wm E & Wife	——	4- 6-1827	X	227	Contract
Clymer, Geo	Philadelphia	12-20-1833	Z	379	Contract
Clymer, Geo, heirs	Philadelphia	4-22-1815	S	189	Contract
Clymer, Geo, heirs	Pennsylvania	5-30-1840	27	134	Contract
Cobb, Jno A & Henry W	Georgia	10-26-1819	27	48	Contract
Cobbs, Jno	Richmond	11-13-1787	B-2	44	Contract
Cobbs, Jno	Richmond	12- 9-1788	B-2	106	Contract
Cocke, Chas	Albemarle	3-28-1823	W	1	Contract
Cocke, Jas P & Jane S	Amelia	3-28-1823	W	1	Contract
Colston, Edward	Berkly	11- 2-1814	P	554	Contract
Colston, Edward Atty	Berkly	7-10-1820	T	439	Contract
Colston, Elizabeth	Richmond	10-17-1829	Y	410	Contract
Colston, Rawleigh	Richmond	2- 5-1785	B	246	Contract
Colston, Rawleigh	Berkley	5- 7-1811	O	48	Contract
Colston, Rawleigh	Berkley	5- 7-1811	O	52	Contract
Colston, Rawleigh & Wife	Berkley	7-13-1812	O	479	Contract
Cone, Joseph Atty	Alexandria	7- 6-1821	U	468	Contract
Conrad, Matthew	Philadelphia	9- 3-1822	V	326	Contract
Conyngham, David & Wife	Philadelphia	1-13-1819	V	135	Contract
Conyngham, David & Wife	Philadelphia	6- 4-1821	V	137	Contract
Conyngham, David H, heirs	Philadelphia	10- 1-1840	27	418	Contract
Cook, Dawson	King & Queen	1-22-1819	T	405	Contract
Copher, Thos & Wife	Howard	8-31-1820	V	130	Contract
Corbin, Rebecca A, heirs	——	4 ——-1837	27	21	Contract
Couper, Robt	——	9-14-1810	N	489	Contract
Courtenay, Henry & Wife	Baltimore	7- 5-1800	E	92	Contract
Cowan, Jas	Fayette	12- 5-1833	Z	416	Contract
Cowan, Jas, heirs	——	12- 5-1833	Z	416	Contract
Cowan, Mary, Henry J & Wm C	Mercer	12- 5-1833	Z	416	Contract
Cox, Austin P	Franklin	6- 4-1845	28	17	Contract
Cox, Daniel W	Philadelphia	6-19-1818	S	199	Contract
Cox, Jno F	New York	5- 4-1815	S	436	Contract
Cox, Jno F & Wife	New York	9-21-1816	S	441	Contract
Cox, Talton	Powhatan	10-30-1798	H	399	Contract
Craig, Betsy D	Campbell	12-27-1821	V	156	Contract
Craig, Wm	Illinois	5- 2-1840	27	118	Contract
Craik, Jas	Alexandria	5-28-1807	M	7	Contract
Crawford, Alexander	Frankfort	6- 8-1811	O	79	Contract
Creach, Jacob	——	3-20-1818	V	19	Contract
Crittenden, Jno J	Frankfort	4- 6-1835	Z	496	Contract
Crittenden, Jno J	Kentucky	2-26-1853	28	331	Marriage Contract
Croghan, Geo	Philadelphia	11- 4-1844	28	3	Contract
Croghan, Geo & Wife	U S Army	6- 2-1826	X	260	Contract
Croghan, Jno'Wm & Chas	Jefferson	4-10-1827	X	263	Contract
Croghan, Mary Angelico	Washington	3-15-1841	27	248	Contract
Croghan, Serena E	Philadelphia	11- 7-1846	28	117	Contract
Crow, Wm	Lincoln	7-24-1788	A	439	Contract
Crump, Sally W	New Kent	5-11-1826	Y	155	Contract
Crutcher, Henry	Franklin	11-13-1806	K	473	Contract

Grantor	Residence	Deed Date	Book	Page	Notes
Crutcher, Henry	Georgia	2- 8-1809	M	316	Contract
Cull, Henry	Quebec	2-20-1795	B	91	Contract
Cummings, Chas	Washington	10-19-1802	G	40	Contract
Cummings, Chas	Washington	1- 8-1807	N	383	Contract
Cummings, Robt E	Washington	12-15-1810	N	382	Contract
Cunningham, Jas	Spotsylvania	12- 4-1820	U	88	Contract
Curcier, Andrew	Philadelphia	6-19-1818	S	199	Contract
Curril, Jas	Virginia	3-15-1821	U	354	Contract
Curtz, Thos	Lycoming	5- 1-1827	V	293	Contract
Dabney, Geo & Chas	Hanover	11-13-1797	B	307	Contract
Dabney, Geo & Chas	Hanover	5-25-1801	H	116	Contract
Dabney, Wm Jr	Kentucky	11-13-1797	B	307	Contract
Dale, Thos & Wife	Spencer	7- 2-1829	Y	393	Contract
Dallam, Richard B & Wife	St Louis	6-10-1830	Z	114	Contract
Daniel, Jno	Caroline	12-25-1796	A-2	690	Contract
Daniel, Robt	————	5-18-1786	A	229	Contract
Daniel, Robt Admr Walker David, decd	————	5-15-1786	A	206	Contract
Daniel, Thos	Georgia	4- 6-1789	B-2	103	Contract
Daniel, Walker	————	12-10-1782	A	211	Contract
Daniel, Walker	————	10-18-1783	A	226	Contract
Dandridge, Wm, heirs	Virginia	3-28-1823	W	318	Contract
Dardis, Jas	Tennessee	8- 3-1846	28	95	Contract
Dardis, Jas	Tennessee	5-30-1845	28	98	Contract
Davis, David Guardian	Norfolk	9-10-1794	B	273	Contract
Davidson, Fanny	Norfolk	8-29-1828	Y	306	Contract
Davis, Isaac	————	11-12-1814	P	558	Contract
Davis, Saml, heirs	————	11- 7-1840	27	173	Contract
Dawson, Martha	Norfolk	7- 3-1802	F	501	Contract
De Cevereaux, St. John Consul France New York		7-31-1787	A-2	595	Agreement
Decker, Michael	Washington	5-28-1808	L	391	Contract
Demett, Abraham & Wife	Preble	8-20-1818	S	216	Contract
DeRedorn, Sigismond E C	Paris France	3-10-1825	Y	108	Contract
Desha, Joseph	Mason	11- 6-1816	R	82	Contract
Deyerle, Peter	Montgomery	3-16-1809	N	17	Contract
Dickenson, Jas G & Wife	Virginia	10- 4-1845	28	37	Contract
Dix, Alexander	————	6-27-1811	S	306	Contract
Doggett, Ann Wm & Chas T	N Carolina	8-29-1826	Y	256	Contract
Doggett, Geo R L Coleman & Jas	N Carolina	8-29-1826	Y	256	Contract
Donington, David & Wife	Virginia	3-28-1823	W	318	Contract
Donnel, Moria M	York	4- 5-1822	V	306	Contract
Donnel, Isabelle	York	4- 5-1822	V	306	Contract
Donnell, Jno, heirs	Pennsylvania	5-20-1822	V	305	Contract
Doran, Patrick	Mercer	6-25-1790	B-2	184	Contract
Doswell, James	Hanover	3-24-1802	F	389	Contract
Dougherty, Robt, heirs	Washington	5-19-1819	T	402	Contract
Downing, Jno	Louisa	12-24-1796	C	210	Contract
Downing, Hunt	Chester	2-23-1819	T	200	Contract
Downing, Hunt	Pennsylvania	11-24-1819	T	201	Contract
Dowse, Edward	Richmond	2- 5-1785	B	246	Contract
Doyle, David Admr	Richmond	10-13-1810	P	105	Contract
Drake, Saml Sr	Frankfort	8-12-1819	V	1	Contract
Dryden, David	Green	5-15-1813	T	416	Contract
Duncan, Jas & Wife	Lincoln	5- 5-1828	X	441	Contract
Dunwoody, Jno, heirs	Philadelphia	11-24-1819	T	199	Contract
Duvall, Jno H & Wife	Baltimore	5- 8-1844	27	407	Contract
Duval, Philip	————	9- 3-1822	V	446	Contract
Duval, Wm	Buckingham	12-13-1820	U	362	Contract
Duval, Wm	Buckingham	1-19-1825	X	89	Contract
Dyer, Saml & Wife	Albemarle	2-14-1817	S	260	Contract
Dyer, Wm	Lincoln	6- 3-1785	A	239	Contract
Early, Paschal Wm & Joseph	Madison	10- 3-1812	R	219	Contract
Eastin, Miss Myra	Parish Lafayette	7-10-1826	Y	210	Contract
Edwards, Benj F & Wife	Madison	11-29-1832	Z	263	Contract
Eggleson, Wm T	Amelia	3-28-1823	W	1	Contract
Ella, Jno Jr	Philadelphia	2-23-1825	X	137	Contract
Ellicatt, Thos	Baltimore	8- 1-1821	Y	351	Contract
Elliatt, Evan T & N H	Maryland	12- 1-1827	X	348	Contract
Elliatt, Geo Jr	Maryland	12- 1-1827	X	348	Contract
Elliatt, & Co	Maryland	12- 1-1827	X	348	Contract
Elmondor, Lucas	Kingston	11-17-1819	T	375	Contract
Epes, Daniel & Wife	————	8-17-1814	P	564	Contract
Epes, Daniel & Wife	————	11-22-1816	R	117	Contract
Epes, Daniel & Wife	Petersburg	8-10-1819	T	60	Contract
Epes, Polly & Daniel	Petersburg	10-22-1812	O	508	Contract
Ewell, Thos & Wife	Washington	5-14-1820	V	145	Contract
Farish, Hazlewood & Wife	Fredericksburg	7-22-1817	S	3	Contract
Farrar, Bernard	Frankfort	5-21-1807	L	48	Contract
Fenwick, Joseph	Louisiana	10- 4-1802	G	85	Contract
Field, Daniel, heirs	Fauquier	6-22-1825	X	215	Contract
Fisher, Stephen	————	6-24-1786	A	148	Contract

Grantor	Residence	Deed Date	Book	Page	Notes
Fitch, Jabez G	Vergennis	2-10-1795	B	91	Contract
Flournoy, Jordon	Powhatan	9- 3-1798	D	171	Contract
Fontain, Jas	Richmond	12- 9-1788	B-2	106	Contract
Ford, Standish	Louisville	12-21-1831	Z	305	Contract
Ford, Srandish	Jefferson	10-28-1830	Z	341	Contract
Foster, Elizabeth	Essex	11-23-1825	Y	144	Contract
Fowler, Jno	Lexington	6-15-1796	A-2	327	Contract
Fowler, Jno	Lexington	3- 7-1798	C	132	Contract
Fowler, Jno	Fayette	11-16-1799	F	154	Contract
Fowler, Jno	Fayette	11-13-1799	G	125	Contract
Fowler, Jno	Fayette	2- 5-1814	P	337	Contract
Fowler, Jno	Fayette	2-24-1817	R	180	Contract
Fox, Saml & Wife	————	11-15-1815	Q	405	Contract
Fox, Saml & Wife	————	7-21-1815	Q	408	Contract
Fox, Saml & Wife	————	11-21-1818	S	412	Contract
Fristone, Thos & Wife	Stafford	6- 7-1814	P	563	Contract
Fulton, Jno G & Wife	Virginia	10- 4-1845	28	37	Contract
Gaitshill, Henry & Wife	Clark	11- 4-1805	J	363	Contract
Galt, Wm	Richmond	1——1810	Q	488	Contract
Gelston, Hugh	Maryland	6-10-1824	W	333	Contract
Girard, Stephen	Philadelphia	4-20-1825	X	106	Contract
Gist, Henry C	Franklin	8-24-1823	W	103	Contract
Gist, Henry C	Franklin	8-27-1823	W	104	Contract
Gist, Independent	Frederick	4- 1-1811	O	65	Contract
Gist, Joshua	Frederick	4- 1-1811	O	61	Contract
Gist, Thomas	Baltimore	3-14-1811	O	63	Contract
Givens, Jno & Wife	Virginia	10- 4-1845	28	37	Contract
Goldman, Edward	Louisiana	3- 8-1826	X	203	Contract
Goodwin, Wm	Baltimore	9-12-1809	N	29	Contract
Gordon, Jas Fae	Great Britain	3-11-1816	R	9	Contract
Gordon, Janetta	Richmond	3-15-1821	U	355	Contract
Gordon, Mrs Jannetta, heirs	Virginia	5-30-1845	28	1	Contract
Gordon, Robt	Richmond	3-15-1821	U	355	Contract
Gordon, Robt & Wife	Richmond	7-31-1820	U	15	Contract
Gould, Jas	Maryland	6-10-1824	W	333	Contract
Graham, Geo & Jno	————	9- 5-1801	F	98	Contract
Grasscross, Margaret & Alexander	Pennsylvania	12-24-1800	E	284	Contract
Graves, Jno	Richmond	3- 4-1789	A-2	546	Contract
Gray, Henretta Maria Hill	Virginia	4- 9-1824	W	316	Contract
Gray, Mary A & Ann M	Virginia	4- 9-1824	W	316	Contract
Gray, Robt	Redding	5-14-1805	J	323	Contract
Grayson, Benj	Kentucky	6- 6-1787	A	308	Contract
Grayson, Fred W S, decd	————	7- 3-1829	Y	387	Contract
Greenup, Christopher	Lincoln	6-23-1786	A	142	Contract
Greenup, Christopher	————	6-20-1786	A	157	Contract
Greenup, Christopher	Danville	9-12-1789	B-2	71	Contract
Greenup, Christopher	Mercer	5-24-1791	B-2	323	Contract
Green, Caleb	Hunterdon	7-27-1833	Z	336	Contract
Green, Jno	Campbell	12-27-1821	V	156	Contract
Green, Thos	Richmond	7- 9-1833	Z	459	Contract
Green, Thos	Richmond	7-11-1834	Z	461	Contract
Green, Thos	Richmond	7- 3-1845	28	81	Contract
Green, Willis	————	12-10-1782	A	211	Contract
Green, Willis	Lincoln	11- 5-1788	A	502	Contract
Green, Willis	Lincoln	5-24-1791	B-2	323	Contract
Green, Willis	————	11-29-1800	E	187	Contract
Greer, Geo	Frankfort	4-24-1811	U	480	Contract
Griffin, Dr Jno T	Goochland	4- 8-1820	T	310	Contract
Griffin, Saml S & Wife	Williamsburg	————1828	X	491	Contract
Griffin, Thomas L	Goochland	4- 8-1820	T	310	Contract
Griffin, Thos L	————	5-12-1820	T	314	Contract
Guthry, Elizabeth	Baltimore	12-19-1811	P	471	Contract
Guthry, Elizabeth	Baltimore	3-26-1816	R	300	Contract
Gwathmy, Temple	Richmond	4-22-1824	W	309	Contract
Hall, Simeon	Philadelphia	10- 7-1817	W	4	Contract
Hamilton, Jas T	Alexandria	7-29-1795	A-2	509	Contract
Hamilton, Margaret	Baltimore	12-19-1811	P	471	Contract
Hamilton, Margaret	Baltimore	3-26-1816	R	300	Contract
Hancock, Geo & Wife	Montgomery	7-13-1827	X	272	Contract
Hancock, Simon	Franklin	4-11-1796	A-2	449	Contract
Hanna, Jno H	Franklin	10- 6-1819	T	112	Contract
Hanna, Jno H	Franklin	10-10-1845	28	31	Contract
Hardin, Jno J	————	3- 4-1831	27	270	Contract
Hardin, Mark	Frankfort	1- 8-1812	P	515	Contract
Hardin, Martin D	————	3- 4-1831	27	270	Contract
Harper, Jno, heirs	Alexandria	6- 3-1819	U	75	Contract
Harper, Thos & Wife	Philadelphia	10-27-1821	V	251	Contract
Harris, Frederick	Louisa	11-12-1827	Z	363	Contract
Harris, Hannah	Newton	5-27-1789	B-2	65	Contract
Harris, Hannah	Woodford	9-14-1801	F	9	Contract
Harris, Hannah	Newtown	5- 7-1790	R	382	Contract

Grantor	Residence	Deed Date	Book	Page	Notes
Harris, Jno Sr	Powhatan	1–15–1794	A-2	147	Contract
Harris, Jordon	Powhatan	1–15–1794	A-2	147	Contract
Harris, Joshua & Wife	Howard	4–10–1828	X	402	Contract
Harris, Wm M	Richmond	4–21–1826	Y	156	Contract
Harris, Wm S & Wife	Frankfort	2–11–1840	27	104	Contract
Harrison, Geo E & Wm B	Prince George	7–17–1828	Y	308	Contract
Harrison, Valentine, heirs	Frederick	10–13–1818	V	248	Contract
Harrison, Wm Henry	Vincennes	7– 7–1807	N	420	Contract
Harrod, James	Mercer	11– 5–1788	A	502	Contract
Hart, Jno	———	11–25–1812	P	550	Contract
Hart, Thomas	Lexington	6–29–1797	D	288	Contract
Harvie, Jno	Henrico	8– 9–1802	H	38	Contract
Harvin, Jno	Bank of Ky	3–23–1821	U	395	Contract
Haxall, P & Henry	———	11——1818	T	46	Contract
Haxall, Wm	Petersburg	3– 8–1823	W	120	Contract
Hay, George	Richmond	3– 3–1812	Q	17	Contract
Hay, Wm	Frederick	11– 4–1815	S	481	Contract
Hays, heirs	St. Charles	11– 2–1816	R	115	Contract
Hayt, Geo Jr	Louisville	10–12–1820	W	104	Contract
Heald, Thos	Concord	11– 2–1807	L	374	Contract
Hedges, Elias	New Jersey	7–12–1804	K	142	Contract
Henderson, Archibald	Salisbury	1——1797	D	277	Contract
Henderson, Richard & Co	———	8–19–1797	B	310	Contract
Hendren, Patrick	Charles City	12– 8–1819	T	177	Contract
Hengerford, J W	Westmoreland	2–26–1841	27	246	Contract
Henry, Patrick	Virginia	6–20–1786	A	131	Contract
Herndon, Edward	Spotsylvania	3– 1–1796	A-2	422	Contract
Herndon, Edward	Spotsylvania	3– 1–1796	A-2	422	Contract
Hickey, Catherine A	Fayette	7–17–1845	28	5	Contract
Hickman, Wm & Wife	Illinois	1–29–1840	27	116	Contract
Hicks, Jno	Richmond	1–14–1797	S	98	Contract
Hicks, Jno	Hanover	8–17–1822	W	114	Contract
Higgins, Jas R & Wife	Washington	5–28–1819	T	1	Contract
Hight, Jno & Wife	Monroe	2–16–1826	Y	104	Contract
Hines, Mary	Nelson	2–16–1834	Z	407	Contract
Hite, Abraham	Hardy	11–13–1786	A	188	Contract
Hite, Absolom Jr	Jefferson	6–15–1789	B-2	61	Contract
Hite, Isaac	Jefferson	11–13–1786	A	188	Contract
Hite, Isaac	———	12–10–1782	A	211	Contract
Hite, Isaac	———	5–18–1786	A	229	Contract
Hite, Isaac Admr Walker Daniel Decd	———	5–15–1786	A	206	Contract
Hite, Isaac & Co	———	11–15–1786	A	198	Contract
Hix, Jesse	Chesterfield	6–20–1825	X	163	Contract
Hollingsworth, Jesse	Baltimore	6–23–1786	A	134	Contract
Hollingsworth, Levi	Philadelphia	10– 6–1800	E	313	Contract
Hollingsworth, Levi	Philadelphia	5– 1–1806	L	326	Contract
Hollingsworth, Levi	Philadelphia	6–16–1812	P	426	Contract
Hollingsworth, Levi	Philadelphia	9–25–1816	R	181	Contract
Holmes, Thompson & Wife	Virginia	3–30–1832	Z	274	Contract
Holt, Wm	Williamsburg	6–24–1786	A	153	Contract
Hoomes, Jno	Caroline	10– 9–1798	D	340	Contract
Hoomes, Jno, heirs	Caroline	6–12–1815	Q	182	Contract
Hoomes, Jno, heirs	Caroline	6–15–1815	Q	183	Contract
Hoomes, Jno, heirs	Caroline	6–15–1815	Q	185	Contract
Hoomes, heirs	Spotsylvania	11–12–1842	27	359	Contract
Hord, Jno	Caroline	12–25–1796	A-2	690	Contract
Howles, Jaquline & Wife	New Kent	5–24–1827	X	269	Contract
Hughes, Robt & Wife	Washington	1– 8–1796	D	284	Contract
Humphreys, Henry & Wife	Fayette	12– 5–1833	Z	416	Contract
Hunsaker, Jno & Wife	Johnston	8–25–1817	S	14	Contract
Hunsaker, Saml & Wife	Johnston	8–25–1817	S	14	Contract
Hunt, Saml	New Jersey	9–16–1829	Z	152	Contract
Hunter, Jas & Mary	Philadelphia	5–27–1789	B-2	65	Contract
Hunter, Jas & Mary	Philadelphia	5– 7–1790	R	382	Contract
Hunter, Mary	Woodford	5–18–1804	H	187	Contract
Hunter, Mary	Woodford	9–26–1811	O	163	Contract
Hunter, Wm & Wife	Frankfort	5–10–1802	F	351	Contract
Imlay, Gilbert	———	6–12–1786	A	102	Contract
Imlay, Gilbert	Jefferson	11–10–1786	Q	449	Contract
Innis, Ann	———	10– 3–1817	R	450	Contract
Innis, Ann	Franklin	2——1818	S	64	Contract
Innis, Ann	Franklin	1–26–1842	27	267	Contract
Innis, Elizabeth	Williamsburg	5– 9–1800	E	385	Contract
Innis, Harry	Lincoln	12–27–1786	B-2	50	Contract
Innis, Harry	Mercer	5–27–1789	B-2	65	Contract
Innis, Harry & Wife	———	9–10–1799	D	346	Contract
Innis, Harry	Kentucky	10–15–1804	H	334	Contract
Innis, Harry	Kentucky	3– 6–1806	K	192	Contract
Innis, Harry	Frankiln	5–19–1810	O	111	Contract
Innis, Harry Executor	———	8–31–1806	K	373	Contract
Instone, Jno	Frankfort	3–16–1805	K	294	Contract

Grantor	Residence	Deed Date	Book	Page	Notes
Irvin, Thos	Alexandria	4- 4-1804	J	427	Contract
Isaac, Isaiah	——	7-28-1794	H	323	Contract
Jackson, Batton	Baltimore	10-25-1810	O	77	Contract
Jackson, Wm H	Georgia	10-26-1819	27	48	Contract
James, Geo	Culpepper	8-16-1785	A	38	Contract
James, Geo	Culpepper	8-16-1785	A	44	Receipt
James, Geo	Culpepper	6-11-1788	A	406	Contract
James, Geo	Culpepper	6-27-1788	Q	52	Contract
Jameson, Jno	Culpepper	5-19-1827	X	234	Contract
January, Jos & Wife	Adams	9-28-1802	G	12	Contract
Jefferson, Thos Ambassador	Gate Charllot	7-31-1787	A-2	595	Agreement
Jenkins, Jas	Columbia	12-10-1794	L	342	Contract
Jennings, Daniel	Montgomery	3-18-1817	T	119	Contract
Jesup, Thos L & Wife	Louisville	1-22-1827	X	262	Contract
Jesup, Thos S & Wife	Washington	1-22-1828	Y	305	Contract
Jesup, Thos S & Lucy Ann	Washington	8-18-1846	28	115	Contract
Johnson, Benj, heirs	——	6-27-1821	U	526	Contract
Johnson, Jas	Jefferson	7-24-1788	A	439	Contract
Johnson, Letha, heirs	——	6-24-1831	Z	187	Contract
Johnson, Robt	Woodford	6- 9-1791	B-2	346	Contract
Johnson, Robt, heirs	——	6-27-1821	U	526	Contract
Johnson, Wm	——	6-27-1821	U	256	Contract
Johnston, Chas P & E P	Virginia	8- 2-1831	Z	195	Contract
Johnston, Wm	Caroline	4-25-1801	E	336	Contract
Jones, Iseral & Wife	Weakley	10-11-1826	Y	253	Contract
Jones, Gabriel, heirs	Mercer	9-28-1822	V	441	Contract
Jones, Joseph	——	7- 9-1785	A	87	Contract
Jones, Joseph	Dinwiddie	11- 1-1786	A	302	Contract
Jones, Joseph	Prince George	3-20-1787	A	506	Contract
Jones, Joseph	Dinwiddie	4-24-1798	C	260	Contract
Jones, Robt K	——	11——1818	T	46	Contract
Jones, Robt K	Petersburg	6-23-1821	V	36	Contract
Jones, Stephen	Frederick	3- 3-1802	F	222	Contract
Jones, Saml	Franklin	9-28-1822	V	441	Contract
Jordan, Peter	Mercer	2-13-1799	H	273	Contract
Keighler, W H & Wife	Baltimore	5- 8-1844	27	407	Contract
Kelley, Jno W	Philadelphia	9- 3-1822	V	326	Contract
Kelley, Mary A	London	10-22-1824	Y	448	Contract
Kemp, Hannah	Richmond	6- 4-1824	W	313	Contract
Kennady, Wm	Lincoln	6-20-1786	A	131	Contract
Kentucky Land Co	Kentucky	4-27-1798	D	201	Contract
Kenworthy, Wm	Maryland	12- 1-1827	X	348	Contract
Kernsor, Jonathan	——	3-20-1821	V	19	Contract
Kincannon, Andrew	N Carolina	11- 7-1829	Y	412	Contract
Kincannon, Andrew, heirs	N Carolina	3- 5-1831	Z	132	Contract
Kincannon, Andrew Sr	N Carolina	3- 4-1829	Y	355	Contract
Kincannon, Andrew & Geo	Wythe Va	3-16-1831	Z	131	Contract
Kinney, Jno	Morris	11-16-1818	S	477	Contract
Knox, James	——	9- 4-1786	A	255	Contract
Knox, James	Lincoln	12- 1-1798	D	494	Contract
Knox, James	Shelby	7-14-1821	V	187	Contract
Knox, Wm A	Fredericksburg	10-14-1826	X	242	Contract
Lafon, Nicholas & Wife	Woodford	9-14-1821	V	99	Contract
Lansdale, Eliza C	Baltimore	5-31-1815	R	380	Contract
Lansdale, Wm & Wife	——	11-21-1818	S	412	Contract
Lansdale, Wm & Wife	——	11-15-1815	Q	405	Contract
Lansdale, Wm M	——	2- 1-1816	Q	354	Contract
LaRue, Peter	Hampshire	4-20-1798	P	85	Contract
Lansdale, Wm & Wife	——	7-21-1815	Q	408	Contract
Lee, Edmund	Alexandria	6-25-1807	O	69	Contract
Lee, Edmund J	Alexandria	9-26-1810	N	493	Contract
Lee, Henry	Westmoreland	3-26-1795	A-2	163	Contract
Leeper, Hugh	Lincoln	8-31-1803	S	300	Contract
Lee, Jno Geo Wm & Jacob	Bourbon	9- 5-1814	R	32	Contract
Lee, Richard Evers	Virginia	5- 2-1798	C	319	Contract
Leigh, Benj W	——	9-15-1846	28	104	Contract
Leigh, B W Executor	——	3- 1-1841	27	236	Contract
Lemon, Jno J & Wife	Illinois	1-29-1840	27	116	Contract
Levering, Aaron & Wife	Baltimore	-28-1821	U	447	Contract
Lewis, Daniel	Nelson	3-13-1820	T	437	Contract
Lewis, Geo	Mason	12-31-1795	A-2	354	Contract
Lewis, Jno	Fredericksburg	10- 3-1795	E	303	Contract
Lewis, Jno Jr	Kentucky	4-27-1798	C	256	Contract
Lewis, Sarah	Conway	4- 3-1826	X	247	Contract
Lewis, Thos	Chesterfield	4-24-1798	C	260	Contract
Lewis, Thos	Petersburg	12-15-1813	P	298	Contract
Lewis, Thos	Petersburg	11- 4-1816	R	56	Contract
Lewis, Thos	Petersburg	6-18-1817	R	344	Contract
Lewis, Thos, heirs	Virginia	5-10-1821	U	437	Contract
Lewis, Thos, heirs	——	6-23-1828	X	463	Contract
Lewis, Thos & Wife	Chesterfield	4-27-1798	C	256	Contract
Lewis, Thos & Wife	Chesterfield	1- 6-1808	M	106	Contract

Grantor	Residence	Deed Date	Book	Page	Notes
Lewis, Thos & Wife Executors	Chesterfield	1- 6-1799	D	418	Contract
Lewis, Vincent	Nelson	5- 2-1820	T	299	Contract
Lewis, Vincent	————	6-23-1828	X	463	Contract
Lewis, Vincent & David	Nelson	5-10-1821	U	437	Contract
Lewis, Wm	Kentucky	11-13-1786	A	186	Contract
Lewis, Wm, heirs	————	4-18-1820	T	414	Contract
Lewis, Wm, heirs	Luzern	4- 3-1822	V	312	Contract
Lexington Branch Bank	Lexington	10-24-1817	R	443	Contract
Lightfoot, Philip	Port Royal	3- 5-1817	R	448	Contract
Livingston, Jno R Jr	New York	11- 7-1846	28	117	Contract
Love, Thomas	Frankfort	4- 6-1803	G	217	Contract
Lumsden, Geo	Louisa	3-14-1796	A-2	415	Contract
Lyles, James	Kentucky	9- 1-1828	X	444	Contract
Lyle, James	Chesterfield	9- 3-1828	X	459	Contract
McArthur, Jno & Wife	Louisville	4- 1-1815	W	279	Contract
McCallmont, Geo	Philadelphia	5-29-1801	O	226	Contract
McCaughan, Sophia W	Baltimore	4-28-1821	U	447	Contract
McCaw, Jas D	Richmond	12- 6-1838	27	247	Contract
McClellan, Jno	Pensylvania	12-24-1800	E	284	Contract
McClellan, Robt	Westmoreland	6- 9-1801	F	213	Contract
McClure, Saml	Knox	1-12-1810	O	82	Contract
McClurg, Jas	Virginia	2-29-1820	T	273	Contract
McClurg, Dr Jas, heirs	Richmond	3-31-1825	X	102	Contract
McClurg, Jas, Decd	Richmond	3- 1-1841	27	236	Contract
McClurg, Jas, heirs	————	9-15-1846	28	104	Contract
McCormick, Chas	Frederick	4- 5-1830	Z	43	Contract
McCracken, Martha	————	4-22-1813	Q	483	Contract
McCully, Geo	Ft Pit Penn	11- 9-1785	A	83	Contract
McDonald, Alexander	Baltimore	4-21-1829	Z	101	Contract
McDonald, James	Frederick	12- 8-1801	F	188	Contract
McDonald, Jas	Virginia	12-24-1818	S	424	Contract
McDonald, Jas	Frederick	2- 1-1819	T	50	Contract
McDonald, Jas	Frederick	1-19-1820	T	418	Contract
McDowell, Abraham J	Franklin	3-18-1818	S	103	Contract
McDowell, Saml	————	6-24-1786	A	148	Contract
McIntyre, Archibald	New York	11-30-1846	28	118	Contract
McIver, Jno	Alexandria	12-17-1805	J	466	Contract
McKim, Jno Jr	Baltimore	7-22-1814	Q	112	Contract
McKinley, Jno	Lincoln	5- 7-1806	K	304	Contract
McKenney, Wm	Indiana	11-17-1837	27	91	Contract
McLain, W & Wife	————	7-28-1845	28	21	Contract
McNeel, Hector	Petersburg	10-24-1812	P	604	Contract
McNeill, Hector	Petersburg	6- 9-1808	M	121	Contract
McPherson, Jno	Frederick	5-23-1821	V	6	Contract
McPherson, Wm	Philadelphia	3- 4-1789	A-2	546	Contract
McRea, Jas M, heirs	————	—1846	28	120	Contract
Macher, Jno	Lincoln	3-20-1786	A	477	Contract
Madison, Col Gabriel	Mercer	2- 7-1787	A	301	Contract
Madison, Geo Ex	————	6-14-1808	M	45	Contract
Madison, James	Orange	3-25-1796	A-2	599	Contract
Maitland, Robt	New York	4-26-1828	X	457	Contract
Mallory, Francis	Virginia	5- 9-1845	27	475	Contract
Mancrieff, Jas	Great Britain	3-11-1816	R	9	Contract
Marriatt, Joshua & Wife	Baltimore	1-21-1814	P	437	Contract
Marriatt, Joshua & Wife	Baltimore	3-11-1817	T	113	Contract
Marriatt, Joshua & Wife	Maryland	1-27-1814	P	435	Contract
Marriatt, Jas H & Wife	Maryland	2-18-1817	T	116	Contract
Marshall, Humphry	Frankfort	1-20-1820	T	279	Contract
Marshall, Jas	Fayette	9-12-1785	A	62	Contract
Marshall, Jas M	————	6-12-1786	A	102	Contract
Marshall, Jno	Franklin	3-12-1822	V	308	Contract
Marshall, Thos Jr	Fayette	6-14-1788	A	410	Contract
Marshall, Wm Jr	————	9-12-1785	A	62	Contract
Martin, Hugh	Pennsylvania	12-24-1800	E	284	Contract
Martin, Jno L Ex	————	6-14-1808	M	45	Contract
Martin, Nancy, heirs	Howard Mo	5- 7-1827	Y	340	Contract
Marx, Asher & Wife	New York	5- 4-1815	S	436	Contract
Mason, Armstead T	Londoun	5- 7-1816	Q	543	Contract
Mason, Geo	Caroline	6-11-1807	M	235	Contract
Mason, Geo	Caroline	2-12-1810	O	80	Contract
Mason, Jno T	Washington	12- 9-1816	R	294	Contract
Mason, Mary	Londoun	5- 7-1816	Q	543	Contract
Mason, Richard B	Virginia	4-14-1818	S	117	Contract
Mason, S T, heirs	Londoun	5- 7-1816	Q	543	Contract
Masterson, Lucy	Dinwiddie	5-16-1816	R	200	Contract
Matthews, Geo, Sr	Mississippi Ter	12-24-1805	M	68	Contract
Matthews, Richard	Augusta	3-25-1796	B	215	Contract
Matthews, Thos	Norfolk	3-25-1796	B	215	Contract
Maury, Abraham	Williamson	5-25-1810	P	535	Contract
Maury, Fontain	Fredericks	7- 4-1798	D	50	Contract
Maux, Richard H	New Kent	5-11-1826	Y	155	Contract
Maux, Wm & Wife	King William	5-12-1826	Y	153	Contract

Grantor	Residence	Deed Date	Book	Page	Notes
May, Banister & Co	— — —	12-19-1821	V	397	Contract
May, Benj H & Wife	Petersburg	12-15-1829	Y	451	Contract
May, Geo	— — —	11-15-1786	A	198	Contract
May, Geo	— — —	5-15-1786	A	206	Contract
May, Geo	— — —	12-10-1782	A	211	Contract
May, Geo	— — —	5-18-1786	A	229	Contract
May, Geo	Dinwiddie	9- 1-1796	C	89	Contract
May, George	Amherst	—— -1802	G	450	Contract
May, Jno	— — —	7- 9-1785	A	87	Contract
May, Jno	Virginia	6-23-1786	A	139	Contract
May, Jno	— — —	6-24-1786	A	148	Contract
May, Jno	— — —	11-—-1786	A	188	Contract
May, Jno	— — —	11-15-1786	A	231	Contract
May, Jno	Kentucky	11- 1-1786	A	302	Contract
May, Jno	Fayette	12-27-1786	B-2	50	Contract
May, Jno	— — —	8-17-1814	P	564	Contract
May, Jno L	— — —	11-22-1816	R	117	Contract
May, Jno L	Franklin	6-30-1832	Z	204	Contract
Maylan, Jno	Philadelphia	6-30-1798	D	423	Contract
Mayland, Jno	Philadelphia	12-27-1786	B-2	50	Contract
Mayo, Abegail	Richmond	4-27-1824	W	325	Contract
Mayo, Robt A	— — —	5-13-1824	W	350	Contract
Mayo, Wm	Henrico	9- 7-1798	E	427	Contract
Mayo, Wm	Henrico	3- 9-1833	Z	295	Contract
Mayo, Wm, Jr	Henrico	5-30-1801	E	429	Contract
Meanley, Wm R	New Kent	2- 6-1828	X	407	Contract
Mercer, Chas F	Londoun	10- 8-1818	S	317	Contract
Mercer, Chas F	— — —	9- 4-1818	S	321	Contract
Mercer, Hugh & Wife	Fredericksburg	—— -1828	X	491	Contract
Meredith, Jonathan	Baltimore	8- 1-1821	Y	351	Contract
Meredith, Saml, heirs	Wayne	5-30-1840	27	134	Contract
Meredith, Thos	Baltimore	5- 8-1844	27	407	Contract
Merewether, Jas	Augusta	8-22-1786	W	50	Contract
Meridith, Saml	Trenton	12-29-1812	P	76	Contract
Merryman, Jno	Baltimore	1- 3-1825	X	87	Contract
Meyne, Jno F A & Wife	— — —	10- 7-1816	S	232	Contract
Miller, Jno	Lycoming	5- 1-1827	Y	293	Contract
Miller, Henry, heirs	Augusta	9- 5-1818	S	428	Contract
Miller, Patrick, heirs	Dalswington	3-11-1816	R	9	Contract
Millford, Robt	Pendleton S C	5-22-1816	R	62	Contract
Minor, Garrett	Louisa	3-18-1796	A-2	435	Contract
Mooer, Gabrielta & Jno	Hamilton	9-28-1822	V	441	Contract
Moore, Jno	Caldwell	2- 9-1821	V	64	Contract
Moore, Wm W & Wife	Baltimore	6-13-1832	Z	276	Contract
Morgan, David	Floyd	2-16-1808	P	313	Contract
Morgan Willis	Muhlenberg	5- 7-1806	K	304	Contract
Morgan Willis	Muhlenberg	5-31-1806	K	325	Contract
Morris, Jno Atty	— — —	10- 3-1817	R	450	Contract
Morris, Rice & Wife	Virginia	11-13-1845	28	39	Contract
Morris, Richard	Louisa	11-17-1787	A	341	Contract
Morris, Robt	Philadelphia	11-21-1794	A-2	99	Contract
Morris, Wm Sr	Hanover	12-21-1810	N	457	Contract
Morrison, Moses B	Frankfort	12-12-1831	Z	170	Contract
Morrow, James & Wife	State Ohio	4- 8-1814	P	493	Contract
Morton, Jno	Amherst	8-26-1806	N	89	Contract
Mosby, Benj	Augusta	12-16-1808	M	277	Contract
Mosby, Jno G	Henrico	1-14-1824	W	322	Contract
Mosby, Jno G	Richmond	4-15-1839	27	69	Contract
Mosby, Lydia O	— — —	7-28-1845	28	21	Contract
Mosby Mary R	— — —	7-28-1845	28	21	Contract
Mosby, Virginia	— — —	7-28-1845	28	21	Contract
Mosby, Wade	Powhatan	6-19-1816	Q	550	Contract
Mosby, Wade	Powhatan	12-28-1821	V	212	Contract
Mosby, W W	— — —	4-15-1839	27	69	Contract
Moses, Moses L	New York	3-29-1833	Z	299	Contract
Muhlenburg, Peter	Philadelphia	1-20-1803	G	350	Contract
Muir, Francis	Dinwiddie	7- 9-1800	E	183	Contract
Munsell, Luke & Wife	Marion	6-22-1840	27	126	Contract
Munsell, L & Eliza T	Indianapolis	11-15-1838	27	2	Contract
Muse, Jeremiah	Westmoreland	7-21-1801	F	483	Contract
Muter, Geo	Kentucky	8-24-1787	A	452	Contract
Muter, Geo	Kentucky	6-27-1787	A	448	Contract
Muter, Geo	Woodford	5- 2-1798	C	319	Contract
Muter, Geo	Woodford	7-20-1798	C	321	Contract
Myers, Elijah & Wife	St. Charles	1-22-1819	T	3	Contract
Myers, Jacob	Lincoln	6-23-1786	A	142	Contract
Myers, Jacob	Kentucky	6- 6-1787	A	308	Contract
Myers, Jacob	Lincoln	5-24-1791	B-2	323	Contract
Nelson, Alexander	Augusta	7- 3-1830	Y	504	Contract
Netherland, B	— — —	7- 9-1785	A	87	Contract
Newberry, Henty	Franklin	12- 6-1819	T	419	Contract
Newton, Wm C	Alexandria	11-22-1815	Q	291	Contract

Grantor	Residence	Deed Date	Book	Page	Notes
Nicholas, Wilson C	Albemarle	5- 1-1810	R	454	Contract
Nicholas, Wilson C	Virginia	4-18-1817	R	455	Contract
Nicholas, Wilson C	————	4- 1-1820	T	459	Contract
Nisbet, Isabella	Richmond	4- 1-1824	W	311	Contract
Nivell, Col Prestly	Charters Creek	6- 3-1789	B-2	26	Contract
Noland, Wm & Wife	Washington	4- 2-1838	27	242	Contract
North, Ann Jane & Wm N	Philadelphia	2- 7-1829	Y	330	Contract
North, Sophia R & Elizabeth F P	Philadelphia	2- 7-1829	Y	330	Contract
Norris, James	Woodford	3-18-1806	K	204	Contract
Norris, James	Franklin	3-31-1806	K	231	Contract
Norris, James	Franklin	12- 9-1806	K	514	Contract
Nourse, Jas	Nelson	8-16-1785	A	38	Contract
Nourse, James	Nelson	8-16-1785	A	44	Contract
Nourse, Jas	Nelson	6-11-1788	A	406	Contract
Nowland, Jno M	Franklin	1-29-1820	T	411	Contract
Oliver, Jno	Baltimore	10-12-1815	R	206	Contract
Oliver, Robt	Baltimore	6- 9-1831	Z	138	Contract
Orr, Alexander D	Mason	12-31-1795	A-2	354	Contract
Orr, Benj Grason	Alexandria	7-29-1795	A-2	509	Contract
Overton, Jas	————	11-17-1787	A	341	Contract
Overton, James	Louisa	9-19-1790	B-2	458	Contract
Overton, Waller & Jno	————	9-19-1790	B-2	458	Contract
Owings, Jno Cocky	Kentucky	6-23-1786	A	134	Contract
Owings, Jno Cocky	Lincoln	6-23-1786	A	139	Contract
Owings, Jno Cocky	Baltimore	6-17-1789	B-2	46	Contract
Owings, Jno Cocky	Baltimore	5-24-1791	B-2	323	Contract
Owings, Jno Cocky	Baltimore	5- 9-1804	H	467	Contract
Owings, Jno Cocky	Baltimore	10-16-1806	K	491	Contract
Owings, Jno C	Baltimore	3-18-1808	M	367	Contract
Page, Thos S	Franklin	8-11-1834	Z	458	Contract
Page, Thos S	Franklin	8- 9-1834	Z	460	Contract
Parberry, Jos, heirs	————	5- —1816	R	363	Contract
Parberry, Jos, heirs	————	4-20-1816	R	365	Contract
Parberry, Wm	————	11-27-1818	S	399	Contract
Parker, Geo Guardian	————	1-20-1804	H	276	Contract
Parsons, Wm	Prince George	9-19-1797	C	220	Contract
Pattie, Jno	————	3-19-1816	Q	434	Contract
Patton, Robt	Fredericksburg	4- 3-1801	E	347	Contract
Patton, Robt	Fredericksburg	5- 4-1805	J	224	Contract
Peart, Sarah G	Philadelphia	2-10-1808	L	370	Contract
Pendleton, Nathaniel	New York City	5- 8-1800	E	15	Contract
Perkins, Enoch	Plimoth	8-24-1787	A	452	Contract
Perkins, Enoch	Bridgewater	5- 6-1796	A-2	315	Contract
Perkins, Thos	Bridgewater	4- 5-1784	A	456	Contract Marriage
Perrin, Geo H	South Carolina	1- 5-1824	W	231	Contract
Pettus, Wm	Spottsylvania	3-14-1796	A-2	415	Contract
Peyton, Mary	————	6-27-1811	S	306	Contract
Phillips, Lewis W R	New Jersey	11- 5-1827	X	316	Contract
Phillips, Philip, heirs	————	— -1818	S	154	Contract
Phillip, Wm	Philadelphia	1-22-1801	E	312	Contract
Phillips, Wm	Philadelphia	9-25-1816	R	181	Contract
Phipps, Wm	Philadelphia	5- 1-1806	L	326	Contract
Pickering, Octavius	Boston	5-11-1839	27	167	Contract
Pickett, Geo	Richmond	5- 5-1800	F	75	Contract
Pickett, Geo Decd	————	7- 9-1833	Z	459	Contract
Pickett, Geo, heirs	————	1-19-1825	X	89	Contract
Pickett, Geo Jr	Virginia	3-15-1821	U	354	Contract
Pickett, Geo C	Richmond	8-12-1822	V	301	Contract
Pickett, Geo C	Richmond	12 — 1822	W	123	Contract
Pickett, Geo C Executor	————	8-12-1828	X	458	Contract
Pickett, Geo C & Robt	————	7- 9-1833	Z	459	Contract
Pickett, Martin, heirs	————	6-24-1831	Z	187	Contract
Pickett, Wm	Caroline	10- 1-1798	E	383	Contract
Pierce, Humphrey	Baltimore	4-21-1829	Z	101	Contract
Pollard, Robt	Richmond	7- 7-1801	F	73	Contract
Pollard, Robt	Richmond	8-23-1822	V	310	Contract
Pollard, Robt	Richmond	5-25-1824	W	317	Contract
Pollard, Robt	————	1-19-1825	X	89	Contract
Pope, Wm	Jefferson	6-24-1786	A	153	Contract
Porter, Jno A	Orange	12-25-1826	X	264	Contract
Porter, Peter B & Wife	Erie	5-14-1823	W	53	Contract
Porter, Peter B & Wife	Black Rock	8-19-1828	X	437	Contract
Potter, Jno	Natches	2-10-1791	B-2	384	Contract
Potts, Amy	————	11-— 1786	A	188	Contract
Powell, Leven	London	9-13-1790	F	428	Contract
Poyles, Geo W	Bullitt	6- 7-1843	27	349	Contract
Prather, Basil	————	2- 7-1787	A	301	Contract
Prentis, Jas	Petersburg	6-29-1821	V	32	Contract
Prentis, Jos	Petersburg	6-23-1821	V	36	Contract
Prentis, Wm	Petersburg	4-14-1819	T	430	Contract

Grantor	Residence	Deed Date	Book	Page	Notes
Prentis, Wm	Williamsburg	1- 1-1786	W	47	Contract
Prentis, Wm	Kentucky	12-29-1830	Z	52	Contract
Premtis, Wm	Kentucky	12-29-1830	Z	53	Contract
Preston, Jno & Francis	Montgomery	10- 6-1806	M	57	Contract
Price, Jno M	Philadelphia	5-24-1824	W	303	Contract
Price, Hannah	Frankfort	9-14-1821	V	99	Contract
Price, Wenfrey E	Jessamine	10- 6-1825	X	190	Contract
Proctor, Francis, heirs	Lycoming	11-25-1822	Y	286	Contract
Proctor, Genl Thos, heirs	Philadelphia	11-25-1822	Y	286	Contract
Proctor, Genl Thos, heirs	Philadelphia	1 -15-1823	Y	289	Contract
Proctor, Genl Thos, heirs	Philadelphia	12- 4-1822	Y	291	Contract
Proctor, Genl Thos, heirs	Philadelphia	5- 1-1827	Y	293	Contract
Purviance, Elizabeth J	Baltimore	1- 8-1796	D	281	Contract
Purviance, Jno H	Baltimore	5-22-1796	D	279	Contract
Purviance, Letitia	Baltimore	1-31-1796	D	283	Contract
Purviance, Margaret W	Lexington	11-26-1814	P	565	Contract
Purviance, Robt	Baltimore	1- 1-1796	D	290	Contract
Purviance, Robt & Saml	————	8-19-1797	B	310	Contract
Quigley, Jno	Virginia	9- 8-1841	27	244	Contract
Ragnet, Clandins P	Philadelphia	5-12-1786	Z	284	Contract
Ragnet, Elizabeth & Anna	Philadelphia	10-27-1821	V	251	Contract
Ragnet, Lydia, heirs	Philadelphia	11-14-1840	27	169	Contract
Ramsay, Elizabeth	New York	10-26-1816	S	439	Contract
Ramsey, David, heirs	South Carolina	6-22-1819	T	421	Contract
Ramsey, Dr David, heirs	————	3- 4-1833	Z	289	Contract
Ramsey, Jno, heirs	New York	1- 9-1839	27	5	Contract
Ray, James	Washington City	1-18-1799	G	355	Contract
Read, Alexander	Shelby	11- 9-1818	X	85	Contract
Richards, Jane	Philadelphia	1-15-1823	Y	289	Contract
Richard, Jno	Virginia	3-15-1821	U	354	Contract
Richards, Mary Gregory & Geo	Virginia	3-20-1824	W	324	Contract
Richardson, Robt D	Campbell	5- 2-1816	Q	505	Contract
Roam, Dr Jno, heirs	Dinwiddie	11- 7-1840	27	173	Contract
Robert, Peter J & Henry J J	Fayette	3-22-1810	Y	228	Contract
Roberts, Dr Jno	Frankfort	7- 5-1808	M	46	Contract
Robinson, Wm	————	9-10-1814	S	80	Contract
Ronald, Andrew	Richmond	3-24-1798	D	39	Contract
Rose, Jno, decd	————	9-10-1814	S	80	Contract
Rose, Margaret Executrix	————	9-10-1814	S	80	Contract
Rose, Dr Robt	Surgeon in army	9-10-1814	S	80	Contract
Ross, David	Cumberland	12- 6-1800	F	150	Contract
Ross, David, decd	————	11-10-1819	T	153	Contract
Ross, Frederick A	Kentucky	8-19-1828	Y	338	Contract
Ross, Capt Philip	Charters Creek	6- 3-1789	B-2	26	Contract
Rowlan, Joseph G	Delaware	7- 6-1832	Z	273	Contract
Roy, Jas & Wife	————	8-31-1813	P	250	Contract
Rucker, Juliana	Boone	11-13-1812	R	224	Contract
Russell, Claud	Great Britian	3-11-1816	R	9	Contract
Rutherford, Jno	Franklin	8-15-1804	H	288	Contract
Salter, Wm D & Wife	New Jersey	7-19-1842	27	310	Contract
Salisberry, Jno	Galloway	5- 6-1818	S	239	Contract
Say, Dr Benj, heirs	————	6- 5-1827	X	271	Contract
Scott, Genl Chas	————	11-17-1787	A	341	Contract
Scott, Jesse & Wife	Charlottsville	6- 5-1819	T	131	Contract
Scott, Jno	————	3-24-1821	U	485	Contract
Seddon, Thos	Fredericksburg	10- 2-1826	X	243	Contract
Shannan, Wm	Philadelphia	8- 2-1800	E	128	Contract
Shannon, Wm	Philadelphia	8-13-1802	F	481	Contract
Shaw, Wm C	Baltimore	5- 8-1844	27	407	Contract
Shearman, Martin	Lancaster	12-27-1798	D	442	Contract
Shearman, Rowland	Louisville	10-12-1820	W	104	Contract
Shelton, Jno	Goochland	12-10-1803	J	187	Contract
Shepherd, Elizabeth W	Salem	5- 5-1828	X	422	Contract
Shepherd, Jno M	Richmond	6-15-1796	A-2	327	Contract
Shepherd, Jno M	Henrico	3- 7-1798	C	132	Contract
Shepherd, Peter, heirs	————	3- 2-1829	Y	328	Contract
Shepherd, Peter, heirs	————	12-29-1830	Z	52	Contract
Shepherd, Susan	Baltimore	12-19-1811	P	471	Contract
Shepherd, Susan	Baltimore	3-26-1816	R	300	Contract
Shields, Ann Executrix	Lincoln	12-27-1786	B-2	50	Contract
Shirley, Ann D	Norfolk	7- 1-1817	R	376	Contract
Shivers, Thos & Wife	Winchester	11-24-1813	P	363	Contract
Shore, Thos, heirs	Philadelphia	6-18-1845	28	66	Contract
Short, Jno C	Cincinnati	1-18-1815	P	624	Contract
Short, Peyton	————	10-16-1809	M	444	Contract
Short, Wm	Philadelphia	12- 8-1827	X	352	Contract
Shortridge, E	————	1-17-1821	U	516	Contract
Sicard, Stephen	Philadelphia	1- 2-1815	Q	31	Contract
Simms, Jesse	Alexandria	10-15-1800	E	159	Contract
Simms, Jesse	————	10-17-1800	E	205	Contract
Simms, Jesse	Alexandria	9- 5-1801	F	98	Contract
Simond, Lewis	Paris France	4-25-1817	S	129	Contract

Grantor	Residence	Deed Date	Book	Page	Notes
Singleton, Richard	Richmond	9- 6-1833	Z	352	Contract
Skilbern, Wm	———	11-15-1786	A	231	Contract
Skipwith, Henry	Williamsburg	5-11-1812	P	442	Contract
Slaughter, Augusta	Georgia	9- 2-1831	Z	193	Contract
Slaughter, Arthur	Alabama	11-18-1831	Z	192	Contract
Slaughter, Jno H	Kentucky	8- 7-1843	27	363	Contract
Smith, Abraham	Augusta	12-16-1808	M	277	Contract
Smith, Chas & Jno	———	2-23-1821	V	9	Contract
Smith, Edward W	Chesterfield	7- 9-1825	X	165	Contract
Smith, Geo	Powhatan	7-14-1788	A	513	Contract
Smith, Jno	———	6-25-1804	H	342	Contract
Smith, Jno J	Philadelphia	8-16-1821	V	144	Contract
Smith, Jno Spear	Baltimore	1- 9-1821	Z	154	Contract
Smith, Nathan & Wife	Philadelphia	5-24-1828	X	428	Contract
Smith, Peter F	Chesterfield	6-20-1825	X	163	Contract
Smith, Saml	———	4- 1-1820	T	459	Contract
Smoot, Wm	Culpepper	11-26-1818	S	372	Contract
Sneed, Achillis	Franklin	6- 6-1801	E	334	Contract
Sneed, Achillis	Franklin	5-26-1807	L	65	Contract
Sneed, Achillis	Frankfort	1- 6-1813	P	87	Contract
Sneed, Achillis	Franklin	7-30-1807	S	259	Contract
Sneed, Achillis	Frankfort	3-10-1820	U	507	Contract
Sneed, Benj, heirs	Kentucky	9- 4-1801	F	1	Contract
Sneed, Benj, heirs	———	4- 8-1803	G	269	Contract
Sneed, Elizabeth	Stafford	8- 8-1808	M	312	Contract
Sneed, Jno	Davidson	10-27-1827	X	379	Contract
Sneed, Mary, heirs	———	5- 4-1799	D	205	Contract
Sneed, Saml K & Wife	New Albany	11-13-1832	Z	264	Contract
Snoddy, Abner & Wife	Bourbon	9- 5-1814	R	32	Contract
South, Jno heirs	Kentucky	6-18-1821	Z	508	Contract
Southall, Geo	Cumberland	8- 1-1808	27	1	Contract
Spencer, Edward	Baltimore	5- 8-1844	27	407	Contract
Spilman, Nathaniel	Lincoln	6-17-1789	A	498	Contract
Spilman, Thos	Culpepper	6-17-1789	A	498	Contract
Spotswood, Alexander	Spotsylvania	3-26-1795	A-2	163	Contract
Sprigg, Michal C	Hampshire	12- 9-1819	T	349	Contract
Sprigg, Osborn, heirs	Hampshire	12- 7-1819	T	347	Contract
St Clair, Alexander	Augusta	9- 4-1786	A	255	Contract
Stephens, Jacob	———	6-20-1786	A	157	Contract
Stephens, Richard	Kentucky	4-27-1798	C	256	Contract
Stephens, Richard, heirs	Hanover	11-16-1816	R	276	Contract
Sterrett, David, Thos & Robt	———	11-22-1817	S	345	Contract
Sterrett, Robt	———	9-11-1818	S	353	Contract
Stevens, Jno	Orange	5- 6-1820	U	261	Contract
Stevenson, Wm W	Little Rock	8-24-1844	27	453	Contract
Stewart, Jno & Wife	Oglesthorp	10-16-1827	X	301	Contract
Stewart, Robt	New York City	3- 7-1807	L	41	Contract
Stewart, Wm & Wife	Woodford	4- 9-1803	G	218	Contract
Stones, Miriam	———	4——1837	27	21	Contract
Story, Jno, heirs	Philadelphia	1-17-1833	27	316	Contract
Strother, Joseph	Shennondoah	11-20-1813	P	361	Contract
Strother, Wm	Madison	11-15-1813	P	359	Contract
Stuart, David	Fairfax	10-23-1811	O	176	Contract
Stubbs, Robt	Mercer	6-16-1790	B-2	154	Contract
Sutherland, Wm	95 Regiment	8-19-1796	M	215	Contract
Sutherland, Wm	95 Regiment	8-11-1798	N	55½	Contract
Sutherland, Wm	95 Regiment	8-11-1798	N	189	Contract
Swan, Jas	Boston	9-28-1811	P	217	Contract
Swearingen, Hannah V & Virginia	Virginia	9- 8-1841	27	244	Contract
Swearingen, Thos V & Ellen E	Virginia	9- 8-1841	27	244	Contract
Swigert, Jacob	Kentucky	8- 7-1843	27	363	Contract
Swigert, Jacob	Franklin	6- 4-1845	28	17	Contract
Swigert, Philip	Franklin	8- 9-1834	Z	460	Contract
Swigert, Philip	Franklin	6- 4-1845	28	17	Contract
Swope, Jacob	Lincoln	10-12-1787	B-2	47	Contract
Symms, Wm J	Andovering	6-27-1787	A	448	Contract
Talbott, Christopher & Wife	St Charles	8-15-1815	Q	326	Contract
Talbott, Christopher & Wife	Clark	6- 3-1820	T	453	Contract
Taliaferro, Chas C	———	6-27-1811	S	306	Contract
Taliaferro, Chas C	———	9- 4-1818	S	321	Contract
Tanner, Jno	———	6-18-1786	A	129	Contract
Tardevean, Peter	Lincoln	6-20-1786	A	131	Contract
Taylor, Cornelius C	Dinwiddie	1-14-1828	X	409	Contract
Taylor, Edmund H	Franklin	6-16-1835	Z	517	Contract
Taylor, Edmund H	Franklin	6- 4-1845	28	17	Contract
Taylor, Hubbard	Clark	12- 1-1798	D	494	Contract
Taylor, Jas Executor	Kentucky	10-27-1795	K	306	Contract
Taylor, Jas & Edmund	Campbell	3- 1-1806	K	246	Contract
Taylor, Jas W	Frankfort	12-12-1831	Z	170	Contract
Taylor, Jane	Petersburg	5-21-1828	X	405	Contract
Taylor, Lewis M	Frankfort	9-12-1826	Y	194	Contract

Grantor	Residence	Deed Date	Book	Page	Notes
Taylor, Lucy H	Richmond	9- 6-1833	Z	352	Contract
Taylor, Reubin	Caroline	3- 1-1806	K	246	Contract
Taylor, Reuben T	Caroline	9-18-1807	M	48	Contract
Taylor, Reuben T	Caroline	4-10-1815	Q	269	Contract
Taylor, Saml	Mason	11-13-1787	B-2	44	Contract
Taylor, Saml	Cumberland	12-10-1781	D	203	Contract
Taylor, Thos & Wife	Allegamy	6- 9-1801	F	213	Contract
Teitsort, Abraham & Wife	Butler	8-18-1818	S	214	Contract
Temple, Col Benj, heirs	King William	5-19-1806	K	527	Contract
Tennet, Jno, heirs	Caroline	5-19-1840	27	337	Contract
Terrell, Richard	Jefferson	3-18-1796	A-2	435	Contract
Terrell, Richard	Kentucky	5-14-1788	B-2	400	Contract
Terrell, Richard	Lexington	9-10-1794	B	253	Contract
Terrell, Richard	Lexington	9-10-1794	B	271	Contract
Terrell, Richard	Lexington	9-10-1794	B	273	Contract
Terrell, Samuel	Lincoln	5-14-1788	B-2	400	Contract
Tharp, Eliza L	Virginia	10- 4-1845	28	37	Contract
Thomas, Philman	Mason	1-20-1806	O	91	Contract
Thomas, Philman	Batton Rouge	9- 8-1814	Q	514	Contract
Thompson, Henry	Baltimore	10-17-1828	X	485	Contract
Thompson, Jno	Baltimore	12-29-1830	Z	52	Contract
Thompson, Jno W	Maryland	10-18-1828	X	486	Contract
Thompson, Jno W	Baltimore	3- 2-1829	Y	328	Contract
Thompson, Mary	Allegheny	4- 2-1838	27	242	Contract
Thompson, Sarah Ann	Lycoming	12- 4-1822	Y	291	Contract
Thompson, Wm	Montgomery	3- 7-1788	A	374	Contract
Thompson, Wm	N Carolina	4- 6-1813	R	387	Contract
Thompson, Wm	Lycoming	12- 4-1822	Y	291	Contract
Thornton, Benj T	Bourbon	9- 5-1814	R	32	Contract
Thornton, Jno Jr	Hanover	1801	F	216	Contract
Thruston, Buckner	Washington City	10-29-1827	X	318	Contract
Thruston, Chas M	Roane	8-18-1810	N	277	Contract
Tibbs, Willoughby, heirs		10-15-1813	Q	11	Contract
Tiffany, Comfort & Wife	Baltimore	5- 8-1844	27	407	Contract
Tiffany, Duvall & Co	Baltimore	5- 8-1844	27	407	Contract
Tiffany, Osmond C & Wife	Baltimore	5- 8-1844	27	407	Contract
Tilghman, Elizabeth C	Baltimore	3- 3-1846	28	84	Contract
Tilghman, Richard C	Baltimore	3- 3-1846	28	84	Contract
Tiller, Saml & Wife	Philadelphia	11-29-1845	28	64	Contract
Tinsley, Wm & Wife	Frankfort	9-19-1797	B	123	Contract
Todd, Chas S	Frankfort	4-18-1820	T	295	Contract
Todd, C S	Shelby	9-24-1834	Z	457	Contract
Todd, Lucy P	Jefferson	6-26-1839	27	47	Contract
Todd, Lucy P	Jefferson	6- 4-1840	27	139	Contract
Todd, Lucy P	Jefferson	11- 3-1840	27	185	Contract
Todd, Mary	Woodford	10- 8-1811	N	510	Contract
Todd, Thos	Mercer	5-27-1789	B-2	65	Contract
Todd, Thos	Kentucky	10-15-1804	H	334	Contract
Todd, Thos	Kentucky	3- 6-1806	K	192	Contract
Todd, Thos Executor		8-31-1806	K	373	Contract
Todd, Wm	Farrington	4-26-1844	27	405	Contract
Tompkins, Giles	Wilkes	4- 6-1789	B-2	103	Contract
Tompkins, Giles	Wilkes	4- 2-1789	B-2	104	Contract
Tompkins, Humphry	Wilkes	4- 2-1789	B-2	104	Contract
Trabue, Jane E	Charlotte	10- 1-1803	J	70	Contract
Trent, Joseph	Richmond	8- 7-1820	T	471	Contract
Triplitt, Robt	Frankfort	8- 5-1824	W	355	Contract
Trustees, Owen Seminary	Owen	4-10-1820	W	203	Contract
Trustees, Presbyterian Church	Kentucky	9- 9-1826	Y	199	Contract
Tryon, Clifford	New York	10- 7-1817	W	4	Contract
Tulley, Jas Executor	Jefferson	7-18-1807	L	122	Contract
Tucker, Travis	Norfolk	7-20-1798	C	321	Contract
Turner, Caleb H	Muhlenburg	2- 7-1827	X	211	Contract
Turner, Henry L	Jefferson	2- 2-1820	U	285	Contract
Tutt, James	Spotsylvania	10- 2-1798	G	297	Contract
Tuttle, Moses, heirs	New Jersey	10-18-1824	X	417	Contract
Underwood, Eliza	Illinois	1-29-1840	27	116	Contract
Underwood, Thos		11-13-1786	A	186	Contract
Upshaw, Jno, heirs	Essex	9-14-1821	V	99	Contract
Utterback, Reuben	Bourbon	9- 5-1814	R	32	Contract
Van Nest, Abraham	Hunterdon	2- 2-1804	K	209	Contract
Vanuxem, Edward H & Jas	Ohio	6-11-1828	X	426	Contract
Vanuxem, Jas	Philadelphia	11-24-1814	P	573	Contract
Vanuxem, Jas	Philadelphia	8- 1-1818	S	229	Contract
Vanuxem, Lardner	Philadelphia	12-27-1827	X	432	Contract
Vanuxem, Louis C & Wife	Philadelphia	2- 2-1828	X	424	Contract
Vaughan, Edward	Powhatan	6- 9-1791	B-2	346	Contract
Vaughan, Wm		2-18-1807	K	551	Contract
Vawters, Wm	Kentucky	4-27-1798	C	256	Contract
Venable, Jas & Joseph M	Shelby	12- 5-1833	Z	416	Contract
Von Pfister, Alexander	New York	10-26-1816	S	439	Contract
Waddington, Joshua	New York	6-20-1818	S	162	Contract

Grantor	Residence	Deed Date	Book	Page	Notes
Wagner, Cornelius, heirs	————	4——1837	27	21	Contract
Walden, Ambrose	Fanquier	2-24-1834	Z	476	Contract
Walker, Maria L	Philadelphia	4-15-1831	Z	122	Contract
Walker, Martin & Wife	————	5-12-1820	T	314	Contract
Walker, Martin & Wife	Philadelphia	2- 4-1829	Y	332	Contract
Wallace, Jno	Shelby	11-27-1804	H	380	Contract
Walsh, Robt Guardian	Philadelphia	5-17-1834	Z	425	Contract
Walsh, Robt Jr & Wife	————	11-15-1815	Q	405	Contract
Walsh, Robt Jr & Wife	————	7-21-1815	Q	408	Contract
Walsh, Robt Jr & Wife	————	11-21-1818	S	412	Contract
Ward, Chas & Wife	Albemarle	12- 3-1827	X	351	Contract
Ware, James	Frankfort	10-18-1817	T	435	Contract
Waring, Frances G, heirs	Essex	8-17-1821	V	88	Contract
Warner, Joseph	Philadelphia	11- 5-1821	W	397	Contract
Wash, Thos	Louisa	3-14-1796	A-2	415	Contract
Waters, Jno	Montgomery	5-18-1811	O	20	Contract
Waters, Jno	Montgomery	5-29-1812	O	412	Contract
Waters, Mary	Prince George	1-14-1814	P	439	Contract
Waters, Richard J, heirs	Anne Armdle	6-15-1810	O	14	Contract
Waters, Richard J, heirs	Montgomery	5-29-1812	O	412	Contract
Watkins, Joseph	Goochland	11- 4-1819	U	21	Contract
Watkins, Joseph, heirs	Goochland	————1825	W	335	Contract
Watkins, Jno D	New Kent	5-28-1828	X	406	Contract
Watts, Robt & Jno	New York City	7-16-1801	G	140	Contract
Weaver, Jacob	Fanquier	10-25-1830	Z	55	Contract
Webb, Augustine	Orange	10-11-1819	T	215	Contract
Webb, Foster L & Wife	Mercer	2-16-1826	Y	104	Contract
Weisiger, Daniel	————	5-13-1824	W	350	Contract
Weisiger, Joseph	Kentucky	8- 7-1843	27	363	Contract
Weisiger, Saml P	Franklin	11-19-1832	Z	318	Contract
West, Thos	Caroline	8- 7-1820	27	352	Contract
Wester, Jno & Chas J	Philadelphia	5-24-1824	W	303	Contract
Wheeler, Peter	Concord	11- 2-1807	L	374	Contract
Whilledge, Lyna	Pike Mo.	9-13-1826	X	214	Contract
White, Mary S	Baltimore	3- 3-1846	28	84	Contract
Whitman, Ezekial	Bridgewater	5- 6-1796	A-2	315	Contract
Whittemore, Wm	West Cambridge	3- 8-1841	27	189	Contract
Whitton, Wm & Wife	Bedford	1-28-1822	X	103	Contract
Wickliffe, Robt	Lexington	5-12-1820	T	315	Contract
Wickliffe, Robt	Fayette	11-23-1843	27	368	Contract
Wickham, Jno	Richmond	3-31-1825	X	102	Contract
Wickham, Jno, decd	————	3- 1-1841	27	236	Contract
Wickham, Jno, heirs	————	9-15-1846	28	104	Contract
Wight, Andrew	Franklin	12- 6-1819	T	417	Contract
Wilcox, Saml	Philadelphia	10-11-1821	X	315	Contract
Wilcox, Saml	Philadelphia	7- 3-1845	28	107	Contract
Wilder, Jno	Petersburg	4-14-1819	T	430	Contract
Wilder, Jno	Petersburg	4-14-1819	U	288	Contract
Wilkes, Chas	New York	2-25-1818	S	132	Contract
Wilkins, Gen Jno, heirs	Pittsburg	7-20-1832	Z	465	Contract
Wilkinson, Elizabeth	Kentucky	————1826	X	410	Contract
Wilkinson, Jas	————	6-12-1786	A	102	Contract
Wilkinson, James	Fayette	12-27-1786	B-2	50	Contract
Wilkinson, Peggie	————	4- 6-1827	X	227	Contract
Wilkinson, Saml	Isle of Wight	8-13-1827	X	453	Contract
Williams, Eli	Georgetown	10-15-1811	O	345	Contract
Williams, Eli Trustee	————	5-22-1816	R	31	Contract
Williams, Eliza	Virginia	11-13-1845	28	39	Contract
Williams, Henry J	Philadelphia	1-23-1828	X	414	Contract
Williams, H L & E G	Baltimore	3- 3-1846	28	84	Contract
Williams, Jas	Richmond	9-29-1827	X	322	Contract
Williams, Jno	Shanando	3-20-1786	A	477	Contract
Williams, Jno Sr	Culpepper	2-15-1813	P	316	Contract
Williams, Jonathan	Mt Pleasant	3-12-1796	A-2	519	Contract
Williams, Mary S Wm S & O H	Baltimore	3- 3-1846	28	84	Contract
Williams, Otho H	Baltimore	3- 3-1846	28	84	Contract
Williams, Susan & Anne	Baltimore	3-28-1832	Z	227	Contract
Williams, Wm Eli, heirs	Baltimore	3- 3-1846	28	84	Contract
Williamson, Benj T	King William	5-12-1826	Y	153	Contract
Willing, Elizabeth Hannah	Philadelphia	6- 4-1788	A-2	101	Contract
Willing, Thomas	Philadelphia	6- 4-1788	A-2	101	Contract
Willis, Jonathan	Philadelphia	10-26-1821	V	204	Contract
Willis, Jonathan	Philadelphia	2-16-1828	X	386	Contract
Wills, Peachy	Williamsburg	6- 8-1803	J	166	Contract
Wilson, Geo & Wife	Allegany	6- 9-1801	F	213	Contract
Wilson, Wm	Alexandria	10-22-1804	O	67	Contract
Wilson, Zacheus	Pennsylvania	12-24-1800	E	284	Contract
Winchester, Stephen	Fredericksburg	5- 4-1805	J	224	Contract
Winchester, Stephen	Spotsylvania	6-21-1805	K	268	Contract
Winn, Minor, heirs	Fanquier	7-31-1823	Y	202	Contract
Winston, Wm & Wife	Henrico	11-25-1823	W	175	Contract

Grantor	Residence	Deed Date	Book	Page	Notes
Wirty, Wynkoop & Wife	Philadelphia	2-27-1824	W	260	Contract
Wolf, Geo	Natches	2-10-1791	B-2	384	Contract
Woods, Adam, heirs	Erie	11-22-1817	S	345	Contract
Woods, David	Leacock	11-22-1817	S	345	Contract
Woods, Esther Thos S & Maria A	Leacock	9-16-1818	S	357	Contract
Wren, Jno	Fairfax	4- 4-1804	J	427	Contract
Wright, Geo Kelly	Norfolk	8-18-1804	H	491	Contract
Wright, Matthew	Richmond	2- 5-1785	B	246	Contract
Wurtes, Chas S & Wife	Philadelphia	5-24-1828	X	430	Contract
Yates, Henry	New York	11-30-1846	28	118	Contract
Yeiser, Englihard, heirs	Virginia	11-13-1845	28	39	Contract
Young, Jno & Chas	Philadelphia	5-12-1786	Z	284	Contract
Yuill, Thos	Halifax	1-24-1806	K	244	Contract